The Pocket Oxford Dictionary

of Current English

First edited by
F. G. and H. W. Fowler

REVISED EIGHTH EDITION

Edited by
DELLA THOMPSON

DELHI
OXFORD UNIVERSITY PRESS
CALCUTTA CHENNAI MUMBAI

Oxford University Press, Great Clarendon Street, Oxford OX2 6DP

Oxford   New York
Athens   Auckland   Bangkok   Calcutta
Cape Town   Chennai   Dar es Salaam   Delhi
Florence   Hong Kong   Istanbul   Karachi
Kuala Lumpur   Madrid   Melbourne   Mexico City
Mumbai   Nairobi   Paris   Singapore
Taipei   Tokyo   Toronto

and associates in
Berlin   Ibadan

ISBN 0 19 564070 5

First edition 1924
Second edition 1934
Third edition 1939
Fourth edition 1942
Fifth edition 1969
Sixth edition 1978
Seventh edition 1984
Eighth edition 1992
This revised edition 1996
This edition first printed in India 1996
Seventh impression 1997

Reprinted by arrangement with Oxford University Press, Oxford for sale in
India, Bangladesh, Nepal, Bhutan, Sri Lanka and Myanmar only
and not for export therefrom.

Printed in India
at Rekha Printers Pvt. Ltd., New Delhi 110020
and published by Manzar Khan, Oxford University Press
YMCA Library Building, Jai Singh Road, New Delhi 110001

Contents

Editorial Staff

Managing Editor — Dr Della Thompson

General Editors — Mr Andrew Hodgson
Mr Chris Stewart

Science Editor — Dr Alexandra Clayton

Freelance Editors — Mrs Barbara Burge
Mrs Anna Howes
Ms Louise Jones

Critical Readers — Dr I. Grafe
Mr M. W. Grose

Keyboarding Manager — Mrs Anne Whear

Keyboarding Assistants — Mrs Pam Marjara
Mrs Kay Pepler
Miss Doreen Stanbury

Proofreaders and General Contributors — Mrs Deirdre Arnold
Mr Keith Harrison
Mr Richard Lindsay
Ms Elizabeth McIlvanney
Dr Bernadette Paton
Ms Lucy Reford
Dr Anne St John-Hall
Ms Joanna Thompson
Mr F. Roland Whear

This edition owes much in its content and style to the eighth edition of the *Concise Oxford Dictionary* edited by Dr Robert Allen, who also revised the etymologies for this dictionary.

Preface to the Eighth Edition

The eighth edition of the *Pocket Oxford Dictionary* takes even further the aims of the seventh edition towards making information easier to find and easier to understand. This is evident firstly in the continuation of the policy of denesting, i.e. the listing of words in a single alphabetical sequence of main entries with fewer items 'nested' at the end of entries. For example, in this edition, compound nouns written as two words (e.g. *German measles*) as well as some phrases (e.g. *long in the tooth*) are now main entries, while phrasal verbs and idioms remain listed under their first or main element (e.g. *look up to, look smart*). This makes words easier to find and reduces very long entries to a more manageable length.

Secondly, this edition no longer contains lists of undefined entries as were previously found for words with prefixes such as *over-*, *re-*, and *un-*. Instead, each is now treated as a main entry.

Thirdly, the use of sense numbers within each part of speech section (noun, verb, adjective, etc.) makes it easier to distinguish senses which in previous editions were divided only by semi-colons.

Another major enhancement in this edition is in the presentation of etymologies. The formulaic approach of earlier editions has been replaced by a more straightforward explanation, emphasizing the language of origin of each word and spelling out the names of languages in full.

The amount of information given in the dictionary about the forms of nouns, adjectives, and verbs has been greatly increased. Many more difficult plural forms of nouns are specified (e.g. for *callus*, *larynx*, and *racoon*), the treatment of verb conjugations is fuller (see, for example, *cry*, *dye*, and *veto*), and more comparative and superlative forms of adjectives (e.g. for *dry, noble*, and *unwieldy*, are provided.

More prominence has been given in this edition to guidance on disputed and controversial usage, and special usage notes have been introduced to this end. These are based on the current norms of standard English, i.e. the form of written and spoken English most generally accepted as a normal basis of communication in everyday life in the United Kingdom. Similarly, words that may cause great offence have been marked with the label *offens.* (offensive), in order to warn the reader of the likely effect of their use. Their inclusion in the dictionary does not in any way imply that their use is generally acceptable.

Since the seventh edition of the *Pocket*, published in 1984, the world has changed in many, sometimes astonishing, ways. The dictionary has kept pace with these events by introducing new vocabulary and updating old definitions. The political upheavals in eastern Europe, including the breakup of the Soviet Union, have necessitated changes to many entries (e.g. *communism, Ukrainian,* and *Deutschmark*), while the move towards greater economic union in western Europe has led to the introduction of several new words, e.g. *ecu, EMU,* and *ERM*. The prominence of the Middle East in current affairs has resulted in the familiarization in English of words such as *fatwa, intifada, jihad,* and *mujahidin.*

The gathering of evidence for new words and usages has been greatly enhanced by access to the Oxford Corpus, a growing database containing (at the time of publication) over 25 million words of text from books, magazines, and newspapers as well as from memos and conversations. This has allowed the editors to verify the relative importance of new words and make even more informed decisions as to what to include in the dictionary, as well as to check which senses of a word are the most common.

Another aspect of computer technology that has greatly contributed to the dictionary's production has been the access online to the larger Oxford dictionaries (the *Concise Oxford Dictionary,* the *New Shorter Oxford English Dictionary,* and the twenty-volume *Oxford English Dictionary*). The *Pocket* too has now been compiled for the first time online. This has greatly aided processes such as cross-reference checking and has allowed updating throughout the text right up to the time of printing.

January 1992

D. J. T.

Guide to the Use of the Dictionary

1. Headword

1.1 The headword is printed in bold type, or in bold italic type if the word is not naturalized in English and is usually found in italics in printed matter.

1.2 Variant spellings are given before the definition (e.g. **cabby** n. (also **cabbie**)); in all such cases the form given as the headword is the preferred form. When the variant form is alphabetically remote from the main form it is given at its proper place in the dictionary (e.g. **caiman** var. of CAYMAN).

1.3 Words that are different but spelt the same way (homographs) are distinguished by superior figures (e.g. **bat**[1] and **bat**[2]).

1.4 Words that are normally spelt with a capital initial are given in this form as the headword; when they are in some senses spelt with a small initial and in others with a capital initial this is indicated by repetition of the full word in the appropriate form within the entry (as at **carboniferous**).

1.5 Variant American spellings are indicated by the designation US (e.g. **favour**. . . US **favor**).

2. Pronunciation

Guidance on pronunciation follows the system of the International Phonetic Alphabet (IPA). Only the pronunciation standard in southern England is given. A key to the symbols used appears on page xiv.

3. Part-of-speech label

3.1 This is given for all main entries and derivatives.

3.2 Different parts of speech of a single word are listed separately.

3.3 Verbs, whether transitive, intransitive, or both, are given the simple designation v. The designation *absol.* (absolute) denotes use with an implied object (as at **abdicate**).

4. Inflexion

4.1 *Plurals of Nouns*:
Nouns that form their plural regularly by adding *-s* (or *-es* when

they end in -*s*, -*x*, -*z*, -*sh*, or soft -*ch*), receive no comment. Plural forms of those ending in -*o* (preceded by any letter other than another *o*) are always given. Other irregular forms are also given, except when the word is a compound of obvious formation (e.g. **footman**, **schoolchild**).

4.2 *Forms of Verbs*:

4.2.1 The following regular forms receive no comment:
(i) third person singular present forms adding -*s* to the stem (or -*es* to stems ending in -*s, -x, -z, -sh*, or soft -*ch*).
(ii) past tenses and past participles adding -*ed* to the stem.

4.2.2 A doubled consonant in verbal inflexions (e.g. *rubbed, rubbing, sinned, sinning*) is shown in the form (-**bb**-, -**nn**-, etc.). Where practice differs in American usage this is noted (as at **cavil**).

4.3 *Comparative and Superlative of Adjectives and Adverbs*: The following regular forms receive no comment:

4.3.1 Words of one syllable adding -*er* and -*est* (e.g. *greater, greatest*).

4.3.2 Words of one syllable ending in silent *e*, which drop the *e* and add -*er* and -*est* (e.g. *braver, bravest*).

5. Definition

5.1 Definitions are listed in order of comparative familiarity and importance, with the most current and important senses first.

5.2 They are separated by a number, or by a letter when the two senses are more closely related.

5.3 Round brackets enclose letters or words that are optional (as at **crash** *v.* where '(cause to) make a loud smashing noise' can mean either 'make a loud smashing noise' or 'cause to make a loud smashing noise'), and indicate typical objects of transitive verbs (such as '*milk*' and '*the skin*' in two senses of **cream** *v.*).

6. Subject and Usage labels

6.1 These are used to clarify the particular context in which a word or phrase is normally used.

6.2 Words and phrases more common in informal spoken English than in formal written English are labelled *colloq.* (colloquial) or *slang* as appropriate.

6.3 Some subject labels are used to indicate the particular relevance of a term or subject with which it is associated (e.g. *Mus.*, *Law*, *Physics*). They are not used when this is sufficiently clear from the definition itself.

6.4 Two categories of deprecated usage are indicated by special markings: *coarse slang* indicates a word that, although widely found, is still unacceptable to many people; *offens.* (offensive) indicates a use that is regarded as offensive by members of a particular ethnic, religious, or other group.

6.5 Usage notes found at the end of entries give guidance on the current norms of standard English. Some of the rules given may legitimately be broken in less formal English, and especially in conversation.

7. Phrases

Phrases are listed in alphabetical order after the treatment of the main word. The words *a, the, one,* and *person* do not count for purposes of alphabetical order.

8. Compounds

8.1 Compound terms forming one word (e.g. **bathroom, jellyfish**) are listed as main entries, as are those consisting of two or more words (e.g. **chain reaction**) or joined by a hyphen (e.g. **chain-gang**).

8.2 When a hyphened compound in bold type is divided at the end of a line the hyphen is repeated at the beginning of the next line to show that it is a permanent feature of the spelling and not just an end-of-line hyphen.

9. Derivatives

9.1 Words formed by adding a suffix to another word are in many cases listed at the end of the entry for the main word (e.g. **chalkiness** and **chalky** at **chalk**). In this position they are not defined since they can be understood from the sense of the main word and that given at the suffix concerned; when further definition is called for they are given main entries in their own right (e.g. **changeable**).

9.2 For reasons of space words formed by certain suffixes are not always included except when some special feature of spelling or

pronunciation or meaning is involved. These suffixes are -ABLE, -ER[1] (in the sense '. . .that does'), -ER[2] and -EST (see also 4.3), -ISH, -LESS, -LIKE, -LY[2], and -NESS.

10. Etymology

10.1   This is given in square brackets [ ] at the end of the entry. In the space available it can only give the direct line of derivation in outline. Forms in other languages are not given if they are exactly or nearly the same as the English form.

10.2   'Old English' is used for words that are known to have been used before AD 1150.

10.3   'Anglo-French' denotes the variety of French current in England in the Middle Ages after the Norman Conquest.

10.4   'Latin' denotes classical and Late Latin up to about AD 600; 'medieval Latin' that of the period about 600–1500; 'Anglo-Latin' denotes Latin as used in medieval England.

10.5   Where the origin of a word cannot be reliably ascertained, the form 'origin uncertain' or 'origin unknown' is used.

10.6   Names of the rarer languages that have contributed to English (such as Balti at **polo**, and Cree at **wapiti**) are given in full without explanation; they may be found explained in larger dictionaries or in encyclopedias.

10.7   An etymology is not given when it is identical in essentials with that of a neighbouring entry, when the word is an abbreviation or compound of obvious formation (such as **bathroom**), or when the derivation is clear from the definition (as at **burgundy**).

11. Prefixes and Suffixes

11.1   A large selection of these is given in the main body of the text; prefixes are given in the form **ex-**, **re-**, etc., and suffixes in the form **-ion**, **-ness**, etc. These entries should be consulted to explain the many derivatives given at the end of entries (see 9.1).

11.2   Prefixes and suffixes are not normally given a pronunciation since this can change considerably when they form part of a word.

12. Cross-Reference

12.1   Cross-reference to main entries is indicated by small capitals (e.g. **calk** US var. of CAULK; **put a person wise** see WISE).

12.2   Cross-reference in italics to a defined phrase or compound refers to the entry for the first word unless another is specified.

12.3   A homograph (see 1.3) is indicated by a superior figure (e.g. **calves** *pl.* of CALF[1], CALF[2]).

Note on Proprietary Status

This dictionary includes some words which are, or are asserted to be, proprietary names or trade marks. Their inclusion does not imply that they have acquired for legal purposes a non-proprietary or general significance, nor is any other judgement implied concerning their legal status. In cases where the editor has some evidence that a word is used as a proprietary name or trade mark this is indicated by the designation *propr.*, but no judgement concerning the legal status of such words is made or implied thereby.

Abbreviations used in the Dictionary

Abbreviations in general use (such as etc., i.e.) are explained in the Dictionary itself.

abbr.	abbreviation	Eccl.	Ecclesiastical
absol.	absolute(ly)	Econ.	Economics
adj.	adjective	Electr.	Electricity
adv.	adverb	ellipt.	elliptical(ly)
Aeron.	Aeronautics	emphat.	emphatic
Anat.	Anatomy	esp.	especially
Anglo-Ind.	Anglo-Indian	euphem.	euphemism
Antiq.	Antiquity	Exod.	Exodus
Archaeol.	Archaeology		
Archit.	Architecture	fem.	feminine
assim.	assimilated	foll.	followed
Astrol.	Astrology		
Astron.	Astronomy	Gen.	Genesis
Astronaut.	Astronautics	Geol.	Geology
attrib.	attributive(ly)	Geom.	Geometry
attrib. adj.	attributive adjective	Gk	Greek
		Gram.	Grammar
Austral.	Australian		
aux.	auxiliary	Hist.	History
		hist.	with historical reference
Bibl.	Biblical		
Biochem.	Biochemistry		
Biol.	Biology	imper.	imperative
Bot.	Botany	Ind.	of the subcontinent comprising India, Pakistan, and Bangladesh
Chem.	Chemistry		
Cinematog.	Cinematography		
collect.	collective(ly)		
colloq.	colloquial(ly)	infin.	infinitive
comb.	combination; combining	int.	interjection
		interrog.	interrogative
compar.	comparative	interrog. adj.	interrogative adjective
compl.	complement		
conj.	conjunction	interrog. adv.	interrogative adverb
contr.	contraction		
		interrog. pron.	interrogative pronoun
demons. adj.	demonstrative adjective	Ir.	Irish
demons. pron.	demonstrative pronoun	iron.	ironical
derog.	derogatory	joc.	jocular
dial.	dialect	Judg.	Judges

Lev.	Leviticus	predic. adj.	predicative adjective
masc.	masculine	prep.	preposition
Math.	Mathematics	pres.	present
Matt.	Matthew	pres. part.	present participle
Mcch.	Mechanics	pron.	pronoun
Med.	Medicine	pronunc.	pronunciation
Meteorol.	Meteorology	propr.	proprietary term
Mil.	Military	Psychol.	Psychology
Mineral.	Mineralogy		
Mus.	Music	RC Ch.	Roman Catholic Church
Mythol.	Mythology	ref.	reference
n.	noun	refl.	reflexive
Naut.	Nautical	rel. adj.	relative adjective
neg.	negative	rel. adv.	relative adverb
N.Engl.	Northern English	rel. pron.	relative pronoun
n.pl.	noun plural	Relig.	Religion
NZ	New Zealand	Rev.	Revelation
		rhet.	rhetorical
obj.	objective (case)	Rom.	Roman
offens.	offensive		
opp.	as opposed to	S.Afr.	South African
orig.	originally	Sc.	Scottish
		Sci.	Science
Parl.	Parliament(ary)	sing.	singular
part.	participle	Stock Exch.	Stock Exchange
past part.	past participle	superl.	superlative
Pharm.	Pharmacy; Pharmacology	symb.	symbol
Philos.	Philosophy	Theatr.	Theatre
Phonet.	Phonetics	Theol.	Theology
Photog.	Photography		
phr.	phrase	US	American, in American use
Physiol.	Physiology		
pl.	plural	usu.	usually
poet.	poetical		
Polit.	Politics	v.	verb
poss.	possessive (case)	var.	variant(s)
poss. pron.	possessive pronoun	v.aux.	auxiliary verb
		v.refl.	reflexive verb
prec.	preceded		
predic.	predicative(ly)	Zool.	Zoology

Pronunciation Symbols

Consonants

b	*b*ut	n	*n*o	ʃ	*sh*e
d	*d*og	p	*p*en	ʒ	vi*s*ion
f	*f*ew	r	*r*ed	θ	*th*in
g	*g*et	s	*s*it	ð	*th*is
h	*h*e	t	*t*op	ŋ	ri*ng*
j	*y*es	v	*v*oice	x	lo*ch*
k	*c*at	w	*w*e	tʃ	*ch*ip
l	*l*eg	z	*z*oo	dʒ	*j*ar
m	*m*an				

Vowels

æ	c*a*t	ʌ	r*u*n	əʊ	n*o*
ɑ:	*ar*m	ʊ	p*u*t	eə	h*air*
e	b*e*d	u:	t*oo*	ɪə	n*ear*
ɜ:	h*er*	ə	*a*go	ɔɪ	b*oy*
ɪ	s*i*t	aɪ	m*y*	ʊə	p*oor*
i:	s*ee*	aʊ	h*ow*	aɪə	f*ire*
ɒ	h*o*t	eɪ	d*ay*	aʊə	s*our*
ɔ:	s*aw*				

(ə) signifies the indeterminate sound as in gard*e*n, carn*a*l, and rhyth*m*.

(r) at the end of a word indicates an r that is sounded when a word beginning with a vowel follows, as in *clutter up* and *an acre of land*.

The mark ˜ indicates a nasalized sound, as in the following sounds that are not natural in English:

  æ̃ (t*im*bre)
  ɑ̃ (él*an*)
  ɔ̃ (b*on* voyage)

The main or primary stress of a word is shown by   preceding the relevant syllable; any secondary stress in words or phrases of three or more syllables is shown by   preceding the relevant syllable.

A

A¹ /eɪ/ n. (pl. **As** or **A's**) **1** (also **a**) first letter of the alphabet. **2** Mus. sixth note of the diatonic scale of C major. **3** first hypothetical person or example. **4** highest category (of roads, marks, etc.). **5** (usu. **a**) Algebra first known quantity. □ **A1** /eɪ 'wʌn/ colloq. first-rate, excellent. **from A to B** from one place to another. **from A to Z** from beginning to end.

A² abbr. (also **A.**) **1** ampere(s). **2** answer.

a¹ /ə, eɪ/ adj. (also **an** /æn, ən/ before a vowel sound) (called the indefinite article) **1** one, some, any. **2** one like (a Judas). **3** one single (not a chance). **4** the same (all of a size). **5** per (twice a year; seven a side). [Old English ān onc]

a² /ə/ prep. (usu. as prefix) **1** to, towards (ashore; aside). **2** (with verb in pres. part. or infin.) doing or being (a-hunting; abuzz). **3** on (afire). **4** in (nowadays). [Old English an, on, ON]

Å abbr. ångström(s).

a- prefix (also **an-** before a vowel sound) not, without (amoral). [Greek]

AA abbr. **1** Automobile Association. **2** Alcoholics Anonymous. **3** anti-aircraft.

aardvark /'ɑːdvɑːk/ n. mammal with a tubular snout and a long tongue, feeding on termites. [Afrikaans]

ab- prefix off, away, from (abduct). [Latin]

aback /ə'bæk/ adv. □ **take aback** surprise, disconcert. [Old English: related to A²]

abacus /'æbəkəs/ n. (pl. **-cuses**) **1** frame with wires along which beads are slid for calculating. **2** Archit. flat slab on top of a capital. [Latin from Greek from Hebrew]

abaft /ə'bɑːft/ Naut. —adv. in the stern half of a ship. —prep. nearer the stern than. [from A², -baft: see AFT]

abandon /ə'bænd(ə)n/ —v. **1** give up. **2** forsake, desert. **3** (often foll. by to; often refl.) yield to a passion, another's control, etc. —n. freedom from inhibitions. □ **abandonment** n. [French: related to AD-, BAN]

abandoned adj. **1** deserted, forsaken. **2** unrestrained, profligate.

abase /ə'beɪs/ v. (**-sing**) (also refl.) humiliate, degrade. □ **abasement** n. [French: related to BASE²]

abashed /ə'bæʃt/ predic. adj. embarrassed, disconcerted. [French es- EX-¹, bair astound]

abate /ə'beɪt/ v. (**-ting**) make or become less strong etc.; diminish. □ **abatement** n. [French abatre from Latin batt(u)o beat]

abattoir /'æbə,twɑː(r)/ n. slaughterhouse. [French abatre fell, as ABATE]

abbacy /'æbəsɪ/ n. (pl. **-ies**) office or jurisdiction of an abbot or abbess. [Latin: related to ABBOT]

abbé /'æbeɪ/ n. (in France) abbot or priest. [French from Latin: related to ABBOT]

abbess /'æbɪs/ n. head of a community of nuns.

abbey /'æbɪ/ n. (pl. **-s**) **1** building(s) occupied by a community of monks or nuns. **2** the community itself. **3** building that was once an abbey.

abbot /'æbət/ n. head of a community of monks. [Old English from Latin abbas]

abbreviate /ə'briːvɪ,eɪt/ v. (**-ting**) shorten, esp. represent (a word etc.) by a part of it. □ **abbreviation** /-'eɪʃ(ə)n/ n. [Latin: related to BRIEF]

ABC /,eɪbiː'siː/ n. **1** the alphabet. **2** rudiments of a subject. **3** alphabetical guide.

abdicate /'æbdɪ,keɪt/ v. (**-ting**) **1** (usu. absol.) give up or renounce (the throne). **2** renounce (a duty, right, etc.). □ **abdication** /-'keɪʃ(ə)n/ n. [Latin dico declare]

abdomen /'æbdəmən/ n. **1** the belly, including the stomach, bowels, etc. **2** the hinder part of an insect etc. □ **abdominal** /æb'dɒmɪn(ə)l/ adj. [Latin]

abduct /əb'dʌkt/ v. carry off or kidnap illegally. □ **abduction** n. **abductor** n. [Latin duco lead]

abeam /ə'biːm/ adv. at right angles to a ship's or an aircraft's length.

Aberdeen Angus /,æbədiːn 'æŋgəs/ n. animal of a Scottish breed of hornless black cattle. [Aberdeen in Scotland]

Aberdonian /,æbə'dəʊnɪən/ —adj. of Aberdeen. —n. native or citizen of Aberdeen. [medieval Latin]

aberrant /ə'berənt/ adj. deviating from what is normal or accepted. [Latin: related to ERR]

aberration /,æbə'reɪʃ(ə)n/ n. **1** aberrant behaviour; moral or mental lapse. **2** Biol. deviation from a normal type. **3** distortion of an image because of a defect in a lens or mirror. **4** Astron. apparent displacement of a celestial body.

abet /ə'bet/ v. (-tt-) (usu. in **aid and abet**) encourage or assist (an offender or offence). [French: related to AD-, BAIT]

abeyance /ə'beɪəns/ n. (usu. prec. by in, into) temporary disuse. [French: related to AD-, beer gape]

abhor /əb'hɔː(r)/ v. (-rr-) detest; regard with disgust. [Latin: related to HORROR]

abhorrence /əb'hɒrəns/ n. disgust; detestation.

abhorrent /əb'hɒrənt/ adj. (often foll. by to) disgusting or hateful.

abide /ə'baɪd/ v. (-ding; past **abided** or rarely **abode** /ə'bəʊd/) 1 (usu. in neg.) tolerate, endure (can't abide him). 2 (foll. by by) a act in accordance with (abide by the rules). b keep (a promise). 3 archaic remain, continue. [Old English a- intensive prefix, BIDE]

abiding adj. enduring, permanent.

ability /ə'bɪlɪtɪ/ n. (pl. -ies) 1 (often foll. by to + infin.) capacity or power. 2 cleverness, talent. [French: related to ABLE]

-ability suffix forming nouns of quality from, or corresponding to, adjectives in -able.

ab initio /ˌæb ɪ'nɪʃɪəʊ/ adv. from the beginning. [Latin]

abject /'æbdʒekt/ adj. miserable, wretched; degraded; despicable. □ **abjection** /æb'dʒekʃ(ə)n/ n. [Latin jacio -ject- throw]

abjure /əb'dʒʊə(r)/ v. (-ring) renounce on oath (an opinion, cause, etc.). □ **abjuration** /ˌæbdʒʊ'reɪʃ(ə)n/ n. [Latin juro swear]

ablative /'æblətɪv/ Gram. –n. case (in Latin) of nouns and pronouns indicating an agent, instrument, or location. –adj. of or in the ablative. [Latin ablatus taken away]

ablaze /ə'bleɪz/ predic. adj. & adv. 1 on fire. 2 glittering, glowing. 3 greatly excited.

able /'eɪb(ə)l/ adj. (**abler**, **ablest**) 1 (often foll. by to + infin.; used esp. in is able, will be able, etc., replacing tenses of can) having the capacity or power (not able to come). 2 talented, clever. □ **ably** adv. [Latin habilis]

-able suffix forming adjectives meaning: 1 that may or must be (eatable; payable). 2 that can be made the subject of (dutiable; objectionable). 3 relevant to or in accordance with (fashionable; seasonable). [Latin -abilis]

able-bodied adj. fit, healthy.

able-bodied seaman n. ordinary trained seaman.

ablution /ə'bluːʃ(ə)n/ n. (usu. in pl.) 1 ceremonial washing of the hands, sacred vessels, etc. 2 colloq. a ordinary bodily washing. b place for this. [Latin ablutio from luo lut- wash]

-ably suffix forming adverbs corresponding to adjectives in -able.

ABM abbr. anti-ballistic missile.

abnegate /'æbnɪˌgeɪt/ v. (-ting) give up or renounce (a pleasure or right etc.). [Latin nego deny]

abnegation /ˌæbnɪ'geɪʃ(ə)n/ n. denial; renunciation of a doctrine.

abnormal /æb'nɔːm(ə)l/ adj. deviating from the norm; exceptional. □ **abnormality** /-'mælɪtɪ/ n. (pl. -ies). **abnormally** adv. [French: related to ANOMALOUS]

Abo /'æbəʊ/ (also **abo**) Austral. slang usu. offens. –n. (pl. -s) Aboriginal. –adj. Aboriginal. [abbreviation]

aboard /ə'bɔːd/ adv. & prep. on or into (a ship, aircraft, etc.). [from A²]

abode¹ /ə'bəʊd/ n. dwelling-place. [related to ABIDE]

abode² see ABIDE.

abolish /ə'bɒlɪʃ/ v. put an end to (esp. a custom or institution). [Latin aboleo destroy]

abolition /ˌæbə'lɪʃ(ə)n/ n. abolishing or being abolished. □ **abolitionist** n.

A-bomb /'eɪbɒm/ n. = ATOMIC BOMB. [A for ATOMIC]

abominable /ə'bɒmɪnəb(ə)l/ adj. 1 detestable, loathsome. 2 colloq. very unpleasant (abominable weather). □ **abominably** adv. [Latin abominor deprecate]

Abominable Snowman n. supposed manlike or bearlike Himalayan animal; yeti.

abominate /ə'bɒmɪˌneɪt/ v. (-ting) detest, loathe. □ **abomination** /-'neɪʃ(ə)n/ n. [Latin: related to ABOMINABLE]

aboriginal /ˌæbə'rɪdʒɪn(ə)l/ –adj. 1 indigenous, inhabiting a land from the earliest times, esp. before the arrival of colonists. 2 (usu. **Aboriginal**) of Australian Aborigines. –n. 1 aboriginal inhabitant. 2 (usu. **Aboriginal**) aboriginal inhabitant of Australia. [Latin: related to ORIGIN]

aborigine /ˌæbə'rɪdʒɪnɪ/ n. (usu. in pl.) 1 aboriginal inhabitant. 2 (usu. **Aborigine**) aboriginal inhabitant of Australia.

■ **Usage** When referring to the people, Aboriginal is preferred for the singular form and Aborigines for the plural, although Aboriginals is also acceptable.

abort /ə'bɔːt/ v. 1 miscarry. 2 a effect abortion of (a foetus). b effect abortion in (a mother). 3 end or cause (a project etc.) to end before completion. [Latin orior be born]

abortion /ə'bɔːʃ(ə)n/ *n.* **1** natural or (esp.) induced expulsion of a foetus from the womb before it is able to survive independently. **2** stunted or deformed creature or thing. **3** failed project or action □ **abortionist** *n.*

abortive /ə'bɔːtɪv/ *adj.* fruitless, unsuccessful.

abound /ə'baʊnd/ *v.* **1** be plentiful. **2** (foll. by *in*, *with*) be rich; teem. [Latin *unda* wave]

about /ə'baʊt/ –*prep.* **1 a** on the subject of (*a book about birds*). **b** relating to (*glad about it*). **c** in relation to (*symmetry about a plane*). **2** at a time near to (*about six*). **3 a** in, round (*walked about the town; a scarf about her neck*). **b** all round from a centre (*look about you*). **4** at points in (*strewn about the house*). **5** carried with (*no money about me*). **6** occupied with (*about her business*). –*adv.* **1 a** approximately (*about ten miles*). **b** *colloq.* in an understatement (*just about had enough*). **2** nearby (*a lot of flu about*). **3** in every direction (*look about*). **4** on the move; in action (*out and about*). **5** in rotation or succession (*turn and turn about*). □ **be about** (or **all about**) *colloq.* have as its essential nature (*life is all about having fun*). **be about to** be on the point of (*was about to laugh*). [Old English]

about-face *n. & int.* = ABOUT-TURN, ABOUT TURN.

about-turn –*n.* **1** turn made so as to face the opposite direction. **2** change of opinion or policy etc. –*int.* (**about turn**) *Mil.* command to make an about-turn.

above /ə'bʌv/ –*prep.* **1** over; on the top of; higher than; over the surface of (*head above water; above the din*). **2** more than (*above twenty people*). **3 a** higher in rank, importance, etc., than. **4 a** too great or good for (*not above cheating*). **b** beyond the reach of (*above my understanding; above suspicion*). –*adv.* **1** at or to a higher point; overhead (*the floor above; the sky above*). **2** earlier on a page or in a book (*as noted above*). –*adj.* preceding (*the above argument*). –*n.* (prec. by *the*) preceding text (*the above shows*). □ **above all** most of all, more than anything else. **above oneself** conceited, arrogant. [Old English: related to A²]

above-board *adj. & adv.* without concealment; open or openly.

abracadabra /ˌæbrəkə'dæbrə/ –*int.* supposedly magic word used in conjuring. –*n.* spell or charm. [Latin from Greek]

abrade /ə'breɪd/ *v.* (**-ding**) scrape or wear away (skin, rock, etc.) by rubbing. [Latin *rado* scrape]

abrasion /ə'breɪʒ(ə)n/ *n.* **1** scraping or wearing away (of skin, rock, etc.). **2** resulting damaged area.

abrasive /ə'breɪsɪv/ –*adj.* **1 a** tending to rub or graze. **b** capable of polishing by rubbing or grinding. **2** harsh or hurtful in manner. –*n.* abrasive substance.

abreast /ə'brest/ *adv.* **1** side by side and facing the same way. **2** (foll. by *of*) up to date.

abridge /ə'brɪdʒ/ *v.* (**-ging**) shorten (a book, film, etc.). □ **abridgement** *n.* [Latin: related to ABBREVIATE]

abroad /ə'brɔːd/ *adv.* **1** in or to a foreign country or countries. **2** widely (*scatter abroad*). **3** in circulation (*rumour abroad*).

abrogate /'æbrəˌgeɪt/ *v.* (**-ting**) repeal, abolish (a law etc.). □ **abrogation** /-'geɪʃ(ə)n/ *n.* [Latin *rogo* propose a law]

abrupt /ə'brʌpt/ *adj.* **1** sudden, hasty (*abrupt end*). **2** (of manner etc.) curt. **3** steep, precipitous. □ **abruptly** *adv.* **abruptness** *n.* [Latin: related to RUPTURE]

abscess /'æbsɪs/ *n.* (*pl.* **abscesses**) swelling containing pus. [Latin: related to AB-, CEDE]

abscissa /əb'sɪsə/ *n.* (*pl.* **abscissae** /-siː/ or -s) *Math.* (in a system of coordinates) shortest distance from a point to the vertical or *y*-axis. [Latin *abscindo* cut off]

abscond /əb'skɒnd/ *v.* depart hurriedly and furtively, esp. to avoid arrest; escape. [Latin *abscondo* secrete]

abseil /'æbseɪl/ –*v.* descend by using a doubled rope coiled round the body and fixed at a higher point. –*n.* descent made by abseiling. [German *ab* down, *Seil* rope]

absence /'æbs(ə)ns/ *n.* **1** being away. **2** time of this. **3** (foll. by *of*) lack of. □ **absence of mind** inattentiveness. [Latin *absentia*]

absent –*adj.* /'æbs(ə)nt/ **1** not present. **2** not existing; lacking. **3** inattentive. –*v.refl.* /æb'sent/ go, or stay, away. □ **absently** *adv.* (in sense 3 of *adj.*).

absentee /ˌæbsən'tiː/ *n.* person not present.

absenteeism /ˌæbsən'tiːɪz(ə)m/ *n.* absenting oneself from work or school etc., esp. frequently or illicitly.

absentee landlord *n.* one who lets a property while living elsewhere.

absent-minded *adj.* forgetful or inattentive. □ **absent-mindedly** *adv.* **absent-mindedness** *n.*

absinth /'æbsɪnθ/ *n.* **1** wormwood. **2** (usu. **absinthe**) aniseed-flavoured liqueur based on this. [French from Latin]

absolute /'æbsə,lu:t/ —*adj.* **1** complete, utter (*absolute bliss*). **2** unconditional (*absolute authority*). **3** despotic (*absolute monarch*). **4** not relative or comparative (*absolute standard*). **5** *Gram.* **a** (of a construction) syntactically independent of the rest of the sentence, as in *dinner being over, we left the table*. **b** (of an adjective or transitive verb) without an expressed noun or object (e.g. *the deaf, guns kill*). **6** (of a legal decree etc.) final. —*n. Philos.* (prec. by *the*) that which can exist independently of anything else. [Latin: related to ABSOLVE]

absolutely *adv.* **1** completely, utterly. **2** in an absolute sense (*God exists absolutely*). **3** /-'lu:tlɪ/ *colloq.* (used in reply) quite so; yes.

absolute majority *n.* majority over all rivals combined.

absolute pitch *n.* ability to recognize or sound any given note.

absolute temperature *n.* one measured from absolute zero.

absolute zero *n.* theoretical lowest possible temperature calculated as –273.15° C (or 0° K).

absolution /,æbsə'lu:ʃ(ə)n/ *n.* formal forgiveness of sins.

absolutism /'æbsəlu:,tɪz(ə)m/ *n.* principle or practice of absolute government. □ **absolutist** *n.*

absolve /əb'zɒlv/ *v.* (-**ving**) (often foll. by *from, of*) set or pronounce free from blame or obligation etc. [Latin: related to SOLVE]

absorb /əb'sɔ:b/ *v.* **1** incorporate as part of itself or oneself. **2** take in, suck up (liquid, heat, knowledge, etc.). **3** reduce the effect or intensity of; deal easily with (an impact, sound, difficulty, etc.). **4** consume (resources etc.). **5** (often as **absorbing** *adj.*) engross the attention of. [Latin *sorbeo* suck in]

absorbent —*adj.* tending to absorb. —*n.* absorbent substance or organ.

absorption /əb'sɔ:pʃ(ə)n/ *n.* **1** absorbing or being absorbed. **2** mental engrossment. □ **absorptive** *adj.*

abstain /əb'steɪn/ *v.* **1** (usu. foll. by *from*) refrain from indulging (*abstained from smoking*). **2** decline to vote. [Latin *teneo tent-* hold]

abstemious /əb'sti:mɪəs/ *adj.* moderate or ascetic, esp. in eating and drinking. □ **abstemiously** *adv.* [Latin: related to AB-, *temetum* strong drink]

abstention /əb'stenʃ(ə)n/ *n.* abstaining, esp. from voting. [Latin: related to ABSTAIN]

abstinence /'æbstɪnəns/ *n.* abstaining, esp. from food or alcohol. □ **abstinent** *adj.* [French: related to ABSTAIN]

abstract —*adj.* /'æbstrækt/ **1 a** of or existing in thought or theory rather than matter or practice; not concrete. **b** (of a word, esp. a noun) denoting a quality, condition, etc., not a concrete object. **2** (of art) achieving its effect by form and colour rather than by realism. —*v.* /əb'strækt/ **1** (often foll. by *from*) extract, remove. **2** summarize. —*n.* /'æbstrækt/ **1** summary. **2** abstract work of art. **3** abstraction or abstract term. [Latin: related to TRACT[1]]

abstracted /əb'stræktɪd/ *adj.* inattentive, distracted. □ **abstractedly** *adv.*

abstraction /əb'strækʃ(ə)n/ *n.* **1** abstracting or taking away. **2** abstract or visionary idea. **3** abstract qualities (esp. in art). **4** absent-mindedness.

abstruse /əb'stru:s/ *adj.* hard to understand, profound. [Latin *abstrudo -trus- conceal*]

absurd /əb'sɜ:d/ *adj.* wildly illogical or inappropriate; ridiculous. □ **absurdity** *n.* (*pl.* -**ies**). **absurdly** *adv.* [Latin: related to SURD]

ABTA /'æbtə/ *abbr.* Association of British Travel Agents.

abundance /ə'bʌnd(ə)ns/ *n.* **1** plenty; more than enough; a lot. **2** wealth. [Latin: related to ABOUND]

abundant *adj.* **1** plentiful. **2** (foll. by *in*) rich (*abundant in fruit*). □ **abundantly** *adv.*

abuse —*v.* /ə'bju:z/ (-**sing**) **1** use improperly, misuse. **2** insult verbally. **3** maltreat. —*n.* /ə'bju:s/ **1** misuse. **2** insulting language. **3** unjust or corrupt practice. **4** maltreatment (*child abuse*). □ **abuser** /ə'bju:zə(r)/ *n.* [Latin: related to USE]

abusive /ə'bju:sɪv/ *adj.* insulting, offensive. □ **abusively** *adv.*

abut /ə'bʌt/ *v.* (-**tt-**) **1** (foll. by *on*) (of land) border on. **2** (foll. by *on, against*) (of a building) touch or lean upon (another). [Anglo-Latin *butta* strip of land: related to BUTT[1]]

abutment *n.* lateral supporting structure of a bridge, arch, etc.

abuzz /ə'bʌz/ *adv.* & *adj.* in a state of excitement or activity.

abysmal /ə'bɪzm(ə)l/ *adj.* **1** *colloq.* extremely bad (*abysmal food*). **2** profound, utter (*abysmal ignorance*). □ **abysmally** *adv.* [Latin: related to ABYSS]

abyss /ə'bɪs/ *n.* **1** deep chasm. **2** immeasurable depth (*abyss of despair*). [Latin from Greek, = bottomless]

AC *abbr.* **1** (also **ac**) alternating current. **2** aircraftman.

Ac *symb.* actinium.

a/c *abbr.* account. [*account current*]

-ac *suffix* forming adjectives often (or only) used as nouns (*cardiac; maniac*). [Latin *-acus*, Greek *-akos*]

acacia /ə'keɪʃə/ *n.* tree with yellow or white flowers, esp. one yielding gum arabic. [Latin from Greek]

academia /ækə'diːmɪə/ *n.* the academic world; scholastic life.

academic /ækə'demɪk/ *—adj.* 1 scholarly, of learning. 2 of no practical relevance; theoretical. *—n.* teacher or scholar in a university etc. □ **academically** *adv.*

academician /ə,kædə'mɪʃ(ə)n/ *n.* member of an Academy. [French *académicien*].

academy /ə'kædəmɪ/ *n.* (*pl.* -ies) 1 place of specialized training (*military academy*). 2 (usu. **Academy**) society or institution of distinguished scholars, artists, scientists, etc. (*Royal Academy*). 3 *Scot.* secondary school. [Greek *akadēmeia* the place in Athens where Plato taught]

acanthus /ə'kænθəs/ *n.* (*pl.* -thuses) 1 herbaceous plant with spiny leaves. 2 *Archit.* representation of its leaf. [Latin from Greek]

a cappella /ˌɑː kə'pelə, ˌæ-/ *adj.* & *adv.* (of choral music) unaccompanied. [Italian, = in church style]

ACAS /'eɪkæs/ *abbr.* Advisory, Conciliation, and Arbitration Service.

accede /ək'siːd/ *v.* (-**ding**) (foll. by *to*) 1 take office, esp. as monarch. 2 assent or agree. [Latin: related to CEDE]

accelerate /ək'seləˌreɪt/ *v.* (-**ting**) move or cause to move or happen more quickly. □ **acceleration** /-'reɪʃ(ə)n/ *n.* [Latin: related to CELERITY]

accelerator *n.* 1 device for increasing speed, esp. the pedal controlling the speed of a vehicle's engine. 2 *Physics* apparatus for imparting high speeds to charged particles.

accent *—n.* /'æks(ə)nt/ 1 particular (esp. local or national) mode of pronunciation. 2 distinctive feature or emphasis (*accent on speed*). 3 prominence given to a syllable by stress or pitch. 4 mark on a letter or word to indicate pitch, stress, or vowel quality. *—v.* /æk'sent/ 1 emphasize (a word or syllable etc.). 2 write or print accents on (words etc.). 3 accentuate. [Latin *cantus* song]

accentuate /ək'sentʃʊˌeɪt/ *v.* (-**ting**) emphasize, make prominent. □ **accentuation** /-'eɪʃ(ə)n/ *n.* [medieval Latin: related to ACCENT]

accept /ək'sept/ *v.* 1 (also *absol.*) willingly receive (a thing offered). 2 (also *absol.*) answer affirmatively (an offer etc.). 3 regard favourably; treat as welcome (*felt accepted*). 4 believe, receive (an opinion, explanation, etc.) as adequate or valid. 5 take as suitable (*does accept cheques*). 6 undertake (an office or duty). [Latin *capio* take]

acceptable *adj.* 1 worth accepting, welcome. 2 tolerable. □ **acceptability** /-'bɪlɪtɪ/ *n.* **acceptably** *adv.* [French: related to ACCEPT]

acceptance *n.* 1 willingness to accept. 2 affirmative answer to an invitation etc. 3 approval, belief (*found wide acceptance*).

access /'ækses/ *—n.* 1 way of approach or entry (*shop with rear access*). 2 a right or opportunity to reach or use or visit; admittance (*access to secret files, to the prisoner*). b accessibility. 3 *archaic* outburst (*an access of anger*). *—v.* 1 *Computing* gain access to (data etc.). 2 accession. [French: related to ACCEDE]

accessible /ək'sesɪb(ə)l/ *adj.* (often foll. by *to*) 1 reachable or obtainable; readily available. 2 easy to understand. □ **accessibility** /-'bɪlɪtɪ/ *n.*

accession /ək'seʃ(ə)n/ *—n.* 1 taking office, esp. as monarch. 2 thing added. *—v.* record the addition of (a new item) to a library etc.

accessory /ək'sesərɪ/ *n.* (*pl.* -ies) 1 additional or extra thing. 2 (usu. in *pl.*) small attachment, fitting, or subsidiary item of dress (e.g. shoes, gloves). 3 (often foll. by *to*) person who abets or is privy to an (esp. illegal) act. [medieval Latin: related to ACCEDE]

access road *n.* road giving access only to the properties along it.

access time *n. Computing* time taken to retrieve data from storage.

accident /'æksɪd(ə)nt/ *n.* 1 unfortunate esp. harmful event, caused unintentionally. 2 event that is unexpected or without apparent cause. □ **by accident** unintentionally. [Latin *cado* fall]

accidental /ˌæksɪ'dent(ə)l/ *—adj.* happening by chance or accident. *—n. Mus.* sign indicating a note's momentary departure from the key signature. □ **accidentally** *adv.*

accident-prone *adj.* clumsy.

acclaim /ə'kleɪm/ *—v.* 1 welcome or applaud enthusiastically. 2 hail as (*acclaimed him king*). *—n.* applause, welcome, public praise. [Latin *acclamo*: related to CLAIM]

acclamation /ˌæklə'meɪʃ(ə)n/ *n.* 1 loud and eager assent. 2 (usu. in *pl.*) shouting in a person's honour.

acclimatize /ə'klaɪməˌtaɪz/ *v.* (also **-ise**) (-**zing** or **-sing**) adapt to a new climate or conditions. □ **acclimatization** /-'zeɪʃ(ə)n/ *n.* [French *acclimater*: related to CLIMATE]

accolade /'ækə,leɪd/ n. **1** praise given. **2** touch made with a sword at the conferring of a knighthood. [Latin *collum* neck]

accommodate /ə'kɒmə,deɪt/ v. (**-ting**) **1** provide lodging or room for (*flat accommodates two*). **2** adapt, harmonize, reconcile (*must accommodate himself to new ideas*). **3 a** do favour to, oblige (a person). **b** (foll. by *with*) supply (a person) with. [Latin: related to COMMODE]

accommodating adj. obliging, compliant.

accommodation /ə,kɒmə'deɪʃ(ə)n/ n. **1** lodgings. **2** adjustment, adaptation. **3** convenient arrangement; settlement, compromise.

accommodation address n. postal address used by a person unable or unwilling to give a permanent address.

accompaniment /ə'kʌmpənɪmənt/ n. **1** instrumental or orchestral support for a solo instrument, voice, or group. **2** accompanying thing. □ **accompanist** n. (in sense 1).

accompany /ə'kʌmpənɪ/ v. (**-ies, -ied**) **1** go with; escort. **2** (usu. in *passive*; foll. by *with, by*) be done or found with; supplement. **3** *Mus.* partner with accompaniment. [French: related to COMPANION]

accomplice /ə'kʌmplɪs/ n. partner in a crime etc. [Latin: related to COMPLEX]

accomplish /ə'kʌmplɪʃ/ v. succeed in doing; achieve, complete. [Latin: related to COMPLETE]

accomplished adj. clever, skilled.

accomplishment n. **1** completion (of a task etc.). **2** acquired, esp. social, skill. **3** thing achieved.

accord /ə'kɔːd/ –v. **1** (often foll. by *with*) be consistent or in harmony. **2** grant (permission, a request, etc.); give (a welcome etc.). –n. **1** agreement, consent. **2** *Mus. & Art* etc. harmony. □ **of one's own accord** on one's own initiative; voluntarily. **with one accord** unanimously. [Latin *cor cord-* heart]

accordance n. □ **in accordance with** in conformity to. □ **accordant** adj.

according adv. **1** (foll. by *to*) **a** as stated by (*according to Mary*). **b** in proportion to (*lives according to his means*). **2** (foll. by *as* + clause) in a manner or to a degree that varies as (*pays according as he is able*).

accordingly adv. **1** as circumstances suggest or require (*please act accordingly*). **2** consequently (*accordingly, he left the room*).

accordion /ə'kɔːdɪən/ n. musical reed instrument with concertina-like bellows, keys, and buttons. □ **accordionist** n. [Italian *accordare* to tune]

accost /ə'kɒst/ v. **1** approach and address (a person), esp. boldly. **2** (of a prostitute) solicit. [Latin *costa* rib]

account /ə'kaʊnt/ –n. **1** narration, description (*an account of his trip*). **2** arrangement at a bank etc. for depositing and withdrawing money, credit, etc. (*open an account*). **3** record or statement of financial transactions with the balance (*kept detailed accounts*). –v. consider as (*account him wise, a fool*). □ **account for 1** serve as or provide an explanation for (*that accounts for his mood*). **2** answer for (money etc. entrusted, one's conduct, etc.). **3** kill, destroy, defeat. **4** make up a specified amount of (*rent accounts for 50% of expenditure*). **by all accounts** in everyone's opinion. **call to account** require an explanation from. **give a good (or bad) account of oneself** impress (or fail to impress); be successful (or unsuccessful). **keep account of** keep a record of; follow closely. **of no account** unimportant. **of some account** important. **on account 1** (of goods) to be paid for later. **2** (of money) in part payment. **on one's account** on one's behalf (*not on my account*). **on account of** because of. **on no account** under no circumstances. **take account of** (or **take into account**) consider (*took their age into account*). **turn to account** (or **good account**) turn to one's advantage. [French: related to COUNT[1]]

accountable adj. **1** responsible; required to account for one's conduct. **2** explicable, understandable. □ **accountability** /-'bɪlɪtɪ/ n.

accountant n. professional keeper or verifier of accounts. □ **accountancy** n.

accounting n.

accoutrements /ə'kuːtrəmənts/ n.pl. (*US* **accouterments** /-təmənts/) **1** equipment, trappings. **2** soldier's equipment excluding weapons and clothes. [French]

accredit /ə'kredɪt/ v. (**-t-**) **1** (foll. by *to*) attribute (a saying etc.) to (a person). **2** (foll. by *with*) credit (a person) with (a saying etc.). **3** (usu. foll. by *to* or *at*) send (an ambassador etc.) with credentials. **4** gain influence for or make credible (an adviser, a statement, etc.). [French: related to CREDIT]

accredited adj. **1** officially recognized. **2** generally accepted.

accretion /ə'kriːʃ(ə)n/ n. **1** growth or increase by accumulation, addition, or organic enlargement. **2** the resulting whole. **3 a** matter so added. **b** adhesion of this to the core matter. [Latin *cresco cret-* grow]

accrue /əˈkruː/ v. (-ues, -ued, -uing) (often foll. by to) come as a natural increase or advantage, esp. financial. [Latin: related to ACCRETION]

accumulate /əˈkjuːmjʊˌleɪt/ v. (-ting) 1 acquire an increasing number or quantity of; amass, collect. 2 grow numerous; increase. [Latin: related to CUMULUS]

accumulation /əˌkjuːmjʊˈleɪʃ(ə)n/ n. 1 accumulating or being accumulated. 2 accumulated mass. 3 growth of capital by continued interest. □ **accumulative** /əˈkjuːmjʊlətɪv/ adj.

accumulator n. 1 rechargeable electric cell. 2 bet placed on a sequence of events, with the winnings and stake from each placed on the next.

accuracy /ˈækjʊrəsɪ/ n. exactness or careful precision. [Latin cura care]

accurate /ˈækjʊrət/ adj. careful, precise; conforming exactly with the truth or a standard. □ **accurately** adv.

accursed /əˈkɜːsɪd/ adj. 1 under a curse. 2 colloq. detestable, annoying. [Old English a- intensive prefix, CURSE]

accusation /ˌækjuːˈzeɪʃ(ə)n/ n. accusing or being accused. [French: related to ACCUSE]

accusative /əˈkjuːzətɪv/ Gram. –n. case expressing the object of an action. –adj. of or in this case.

accusatory /əˈkjuːzətərɪ/ adj. of or implying accusation.

accuse /əˈkjuːz/ v. (-sing) (often foll. by of) charge with a fault or crime; blame. [Latin accusare: related to CAUSE]

accustom /əˈkʌstəm/ v. (foll. by to) make used to (accustomed him to hardship). [French: related to CUSTOM]

accustomed adj. 1 (usu. foll. by to) used to a thing. 2 customary, usual.

ace –n. 1 playing-card etc. with a single spot and generally signifying 'one'. 2 a person who excels in some activity. b pilot who has shot down many enemy aircraft. 3 (in tennis) unreturnable stroke (esp. a service). –adj. slang excellent. □ **within an ace of** on the verge of. [Latin as unity]

acellular /eɪˈseljʊlə(r)/ adj. having no cells; not consisting of cells.

-aceous suffix forming adjectives in the sense 'of the nature of', esp. in the natural sciences (herbaceous). [Latin -aceus]

acerbic /əˈsɜːbɪk/ adj. harsh and sharp, esp. in speech or manner. □ **acerbity** n. (pl. -ies). [Latin acerbus sour]

acetaldehyde /ˌæsɪˈtældɪˌhaɪd/ n. colourless volatile liquid aldehyde. [from ACETIC, ALDEHYDE]

acetate /ˈæsɪˌteɪt/ n. 1 salt or ester of acetic acid, esp. the cellulose ester. 2 fabric made from this.

acetic /əˈsiːtɪk/ adj. of or like vinegar. [Latin acetum vinegar]

acetic acid n. clear liquid acid giving vinegar its characteristic taste.

acetone /ˈæsɪˌtəʊn/ n. colourless volatile liquid that dissolves organic compounds, esp. paints, varnishes, etc.

acetylene /əˈsetɪˌliːn/ n. hydrocarbon gas burning with a bright flame, used esp. in welding.

ache /eɪk/ –n. 1 continuous dull pain. 2 mental distress. –v. (-ching) suffer from or be the source of an ache. [Old English]

achieve /əˈtʃiːv/ v. (-ving) 1 reach or attain, esp. by effort (achieved victory; achieved notoriety). 2 accomplish (a feat or task). [French achever: related to CHIEF]

achievement n. 1 something achieved. 2 act of achieving.

Achilles' heel /əˈkɪliːz/ n. person's weak or vulnerable point. [Achilles, Greek hero in the Iliad]

Achilles' tendon n. tendon connecting the heel with the calf muscles.

achromatic /ˌækrəʊˈmætɪk/ adj. Optics 1 transmitting light without separation into constituent colours (achromatic lens). 2 without colour. □ **achromatically** adv. [French: related to A-, CHROME]

achy /ˈeɪkɪ/ adj. (-ier, -iest) full of or suffering from aches.

acid /ˈæsɪd/ –n. 1 a any of a class of substances that liberate hydrogen ions in water, are usu. sour and corrosive, turn litmus red, and have a pH of less than 7. b any compound or atom donating protons. 2 any sour substance. 3 slang the drug LSD. –adj. 1 sour. 2 biting, sharp (an acid wit). 3 Chem. having the essential properties of an acid. □ **acidic** /əˈsɪdɪk/ adj. **acidify** /əˈsɪdɪˌfaɪ/ v. (-ies, -ied). **acidity** /əˈsɪdɪtɪ/ n. **acidly** adv. [Latin aceo sour]

acid house n. a type of synthesized music with a simple repetitive beat, often associated with hallucinogenic drugs.

acid rain n. acid, esp. from industrial waste gases, falling with rain.

acid test n. severe or conclusive test.

acidulous /əˈsɪdjʊləs/ adj. somewhat acid.

ack-ack /æˈkæk/ colloq. –adj. anti-aircraft. –n. anti-aircraft gun etc. [formerly signallers' term for AA]

acknowledge /əkˈnɒlɪdʒ/ v. (-ging) 1 recognize; accept the truth of (acknowledged its failure). 2 confirm the receipt of (a letter etc.). 3 a show that one has noticed (acknowledged my arrival with

a grunt). **b** express appreciation of (a service etc.). **4** recognize the validity of, own (*the acknowledged king*). [from AD-, KNOWLEDGE]

acknowledgement *n.* **1** act of acknowledging. **2 a** thing given or done in gratitude. **b** letter confirming receipt of something. **3** (usu. in *pl.*) author's statement of gratitude, prefacing a book.

acme /'ækmɪ/ *n.* highest point (of achievement etc.). [Greek]

acne /'æknɪ/ *n.* skin condition with red pimples. [Latin]

acolyte /'ækə,laɪt/ *n.* **1** person assisting a priest. **2** assistant; beginner. [Greek *akolouthos* follower]

aconite /'ækə,naɪt/ *n.* **1** any of various poisonous plants, esp. monkshood. **2** drug from these. [Greek *akoniton*]

acorn /'eɪkɔːn/ *n.* fruit of the oak, with a smooth nut in a cuplike base. [Old English]

acoustic /ə'kuːstɪk/ *adj.* **1** of sound or the sense of hearing. **2** (of a musical instrument etc.) without electrical amplification (*acoustic guitar*). □ **acoustically** *adv.* [Greek *akouō* hear]

acoustics *n.pl.* **1** properties or qualities (of a room etc.) in transmitting sound. **2** (usu. as *sing.*) science of sound.

acquaint /ə'kweɪnt/ *v.* (usu. foll. by *with*) make aware of or familiar with (*acquaint me with the facts*). □ **be acquainted with** have personal knowledge of; know slightly. [Latin: related to AD-, COGNIZANCE]

acquaintance *n.* **1** being acquainted. **2** person one knows slightly. □ **acquaintanceship** *n.*

acquiesce /,ækwɪ'es/ *v.* (-cing) **1** agree, esp. by default. **2** (foll. by *in*) accept (an arrangement etc.). □ **acquiescence** *n.* **acquiescent** *adj.* [Latin: related to AD-, QUIET]

acquire /ə'kwaɪə(r)/ *v.* (-ring) gain for oneself; come into possession of. [Latin: related to AD-, *quaero quisit-* seek]

acquired immune deficiency syndrome see AIDS.

acquired taste *n.* **1** liking developed by experience. **2** object of this.

acquirement *n.* thing acquired, esp. a mental attainment.

acquisition /,ækwɪ'zɪʃ(ə)n/ *n.* **1** thing acquired, esp. when useful. **2** acquiring or being acquired. [Latin: related to ACQUIRE]

acquisitive /ə'kwɪzɪtɪv/ *adj.* keen to acquire things.

acquit /ə'kwɪt/ *v.* (-tt-) **1** (often foll. by *of*) declare not guilty. **2** *refl.* **a** behave or perform in a specified way (*acquitted herself well*). **b** (foll. by *of*) discharge (a

duty or responsibility). □ **acquittal** *n.* [Latin: related to AD-, QUIT]

acre /'eɪkə(r)/ *n.* measure of land, 4,840 sq. yds., 0.405 ha. [Old English]

acreage /'eɪkərɪdʒ/ *n.* a number of acres; extent of land.

acrid /'ækrɪd/ *adj.* (-er, -est) bitterly pungent. □ **acridity** /ə'krɪdɪtɪ/ *n.* [Latin *acer* keen, pungent]

acrimonious /,ækrɪ'məʊnɪəs/ *adj.* bitter in manner or temper. □ **acrimony** /'ækrɪmənɪ/ *n.*

acrobat /'ækrə,bæt/ *n.* entertainer performing gymnastic feats. □ **acrobatic** /,ækrə'bætɪk/ *adj.* **acrobatically** /,ækrə'bætɪkəlɪ/ *adv.* [Greek *akrobatēs* from *akron* summit, *bainō* walk]

acrobatics /,ækrə'bætɪks/ *n.pl.* **1** acrobatic feats. **2** (as *sing.*) art of performing these.

acronym /'ækrənɪm/ *n.* word formed from the initial letters of other words (e.g. *laser*, *Nato*). [Greek *akron* end, *onoma* name]

acropolis /ə'krɒpəlɪs/ *n.* citadel of an ancient Greek city. [Greek *akron* summit, *polis* city]

across /ə'krɒs/ *–prep.* **1** to or on the other side of (*across the river*). **2** from one side to another side of (*spread across the floor*). **3** at or forming an angle with (*a stripe across the flag*). *–adv.* **1** to or on the other side (*ran across*). **2** from one side to another (*stretched across*). □ **across the board** applying to all. [French *à, en, croix*: related to CROSS]

acrostic /ə'krɒstɪk/ *n.* poem etc. in which certain letters (usu. the first and last in each line) form a word or words. [Greek *akron* end, *stikhos* row]

acrylic /ə'krɪlɪk/ *–adj.* of synthetic material made from acrylic acid. *–n.* acrylic fibre or fabric. [Latin *acer* pungent, *oleo* to smell]

acrylic acid *n.* a pungent liquid organic acid.

act *–n.* **1** something done; a deed. **2** process of doing (*caught in the act*). **3** item of entertainment. **4** pretence (*all an act*). **5** main division of a play etc. **6 a** decree of a legislative body. **b** document attesting a legal transaction. *–v.* **1** behave (*acted wisely*). **2** perform an action or function; take action (*act as referee*; *brakes failed to act*; *he acted quickly*). **3** (also foll. by *on*) have an effect (*alcohol acts on the brain*). **4 a** perform a part in a play, film, etc. **b** pretend. **5 a** play the part of (*acted Othello*; *acts the fool*). **b** perform (a play etc.). **c** portray (an incident) by actions. □ **act for** be the (esp. legal) representative of. **act of God** natural event, e.g. an earthquake. **act**

up *colloq.* misbehave; give trouble (*car is acting up*). **get one's act together** *slang.* become properly organized; prepare. **put on an act** *colloq.* make a pretence. [Latin *ago act-* do]

acting –*n.* art or occupation of an actor. –*attrib. adj.* serving temporarily or as a substitute (*acting manager*).

actinism /ˈæktɪˌnɪz(ə)m/ *n.* property of short-wave radiation that produces chemical changes, as in photography. [Greek *aktis* ray]

actinium /ækˈtɪnɪəm/ *n. Chem.* radioactive metallic element found in pitchblende. [as ACTINISM]

action /ˈækʃ(ə)n/ *n.* **1** process of doing or acting (*demanded action*). **2** forcefulness or energy. **3** exertion of energy or influence (*action of acid on metal*). **4** deed, act (*not aware of his actions*). **5** (**the action**) **a** series of events in a story, play, etc. **b** *slang* exciting activity (*missed the action*). **6** battle, fighting (*killed in action*). **7 a** mechanism of an instrument. **b** style of movement of an animal or human. **8** lawsuit. □ **out of action** not working. [Latin: related to ACT]

actionable *adj.* giving cause for legal action.

action-packed *adj.* full of action or excitement.

action point *n.* proposal for action.

action replay *n.* playback of part of a television broadcast, esp. a sporting event, often in slow motion.

action stations *n.pl.* positions taken up by troops etc. ready for battle.

activate /ˈæktɪˌveɪt/ *v.* (**-ting**) **1** make active. **2** *Chem.* cause reaction in. **3** make radioactive.

active /ˈæktɪv/ –*adj.* **1** marked by action; energetic; diligent (*an active life*). **2** working, operative (*active volcano*). **3** not merely passive or inert; positive (*active support; active ingredients*). **4** radioactive. **5** *Gram.* designating the form of a verb whose subject performs the action (e.g. *saw* in *he saw a film*). –*n. Gram.* active form or voice of a verb. □ **actively** *adv.* [Latin: related to ACT]

active service *n.* military service in wartime.

activism *n.* policy of vigorous action, esp. for a political cause. □ **activist** *n.*

activity /ækˈtɪvɪtɪ/ *n.* (*pl.* **-ies**) **1** being active; busy or energetic action. **2** (often in *pl.*) occupation or pursuit (*outdoor activities*). **3** – RADIOACTIVITY.

actor *n.* person who acts in a play, film, etc. [Latin: related to ACT]

actress *n.* female actor.

actual /ˈæktʃʊəl/ *adj.* (usu. *attrib.*) **1** existing in fact; real. **2** current. [Latin: related to ACT]

actuality /ˌæktʃʊˈælɪtɪ/ *n.* (*pl.* **-ies**) **1** reality. **2** (in *pl.*) existing conditions.

actually /ˈæktʃʊəlɪ/ *adv.* **1** as a fact, really (*not actually very rich*). **2** strange as it may seem (*he actually refused!*).

actuary /ˈæktʃʊərɪ/ *n.* (*pl.* **-ies**) statistician, esp. one calculating insurance risks and premiums. □ **actuarial** /-ˈeərɪəl/ *adj.* [Latin *actuarius* bookkeeper]

actuate /ˈæktʃʊˌeɪt/ *v.* (**-ting**) **1** cause (a machine etc.) to move or function. **2** cause (a person) to act. [Latin]

acuity /əˈkjuːɪtɪ/ *n.* sharpness, acuteness. [medieval Latin: related to ACUTE]

acumen /ˈækjʊmən/ *n.* keen insight or discernment. [Latin, = ACUTE thing]

acupuncture /ˈækjuːˌpʌŋktʃə(r)/ *n.* medical treatment using needles in parts of the body. □ **acupuncturist** *n.* [Latin *acu* with needle]

acute /əˈkjuːt/ –*adj.* (**acuter, acutest**) **1** serious, severe (*acute hardship*). **2** (of senses etc.) keen, penetrating. **3** shrewd. **4** (of a disease) coming quickly to a crisis. **5** (of an angle) less than 90°. **6** (of a sound) high, shrill. –*n.* = ACUTE ACCENT. □ **acutely** *adv.* [Latin *acutus* pointed]

acute accent *n.* diacritical mark (´) placed over certain letters in French etc., esp. to show pronunciation.

-acy *suffix* forming nouns of state or quality (*accuracy; piracy*), or an instance of it (*conspiracy; fallacy*). [French *-acie*, Latin *-acia*, *-atia*, Greek *-ateia*]

AD *abbr.* of the Christian era. [ANNO DOMINI]

ad *n. colloq.* advertisement. [abbreviation]

ad- *prefix* (altered or assimilated before some letters) implying motion or direction to, reduction or change into, addition, adherence, increase, or intensification. [Latin]

adage /ˈædɪdʒ/ *n.* traditional maxim, proverb. [French from Latin]

adagio /əˈdɑːʒɪəʊ/ *Mus.* –*adv.* & *adj.* in slow time. –*n.* (*pl.* **-s**) such a movement or passage. [Italian]

Adam /ˈædəm/ *n.* the first man. □ **not know a person from Adam** be unable to recognize a person. [Hebrew, = man]

adamant /ˈædəmənt/ *adj.* stubbornly resolute; unyielding. □ **adamantly** *adv.* [Greek *adamas adamant-* untameable]

Adam's apple *n.* projection of cartilage at the front of the neck.

adapt /əˈdæpt/ *v.* **1 a** (foll. by *to*) fit, adjust (one thing to another). **b** (foll. by

to, for) make suitable for a purpose. **c** modify (esp. a text for broadcasting etc.). **2** (also *refl.*, usu. foll. by *to*) adjust to new conditions. □ **adaptable** *adj.* **adaptation** /,ædæp'teɪʃ(ə)n/ *n.* [Latin: related to AD-, APT]

adaptor *n.* **1** device for making equipment compatible. **2** device for connecting several electrical plugs to one socket.

add *v.* **1** join (one thing to another) as an increase or supplement. **2** put together (numbers) to find their total. **3** say further. □ **add in** include. **add up 1** find the total of. **2** (foll. by *to*) amount to. **3** *colloq.* make sense. [Latin *addo*]

addendum /ə'dendəm/ *n.* (*pl.* **-da**) **1** thing to be added. **2** material added at the end of a book.

adder *n.* small venomous snake, esp. the common viper. [Old English, originally *nadder*]

addict /'ædɪkt/ *n.* **1** person addicted, esp. to a drug. **2** *colloq.* devotee (*film addict*). [Latin: related to AD-, *dico* say]

addicted /ə'dɪktɪd/ *adj.* **1** (usu. foll. by *to*) dependent on a drug etc. as a habit. **2** devoted to an interest. □ **addiction** /ə'dɪkʃ(ə)n/ *n.*

addictive *adj.* causing addiction.

addition /ə'dɪʃ(ə)n/ *n.* **1** adding. **2** person or thing added. □ **in addition** (often foll. by *to*) also, as well (as). [Latin: related to ADD]

additional *adj.* added, extra, supplementary. □ **additionally** *adv.*

additive /'ædɪtɪv/ *n.* substance added to improve another, esp. to colour, flavour, or preserve food. [Latin: related to ADD]

addle /'æd(ə)l/ *v.* (**-ling**) **1** muddle, confuse. **2** (usu. as **addled** *adj.*) (of an egg) become rotten. [Old English, = filth]

address /ə'dres/ *—n.* **1 a** place where a person lives or an organization is situated. **b** particulars of this, esp. for postal purposes. **c** *Computing* location of an item of stored information. **2** discourse to an audience. *—v.* **1** write postal directions on (an envelope etc.). **2** direct (remarks etc.). **3** speak or write to, esp. formally. **4** direct one's attention to. **5** *Golf* take aim at (the ball). □ **address oneself to 1** speak or write to. **2** attend to. [French: related to AD-, DIRECT]

addressee /,ædre'siː/ *n.* person to whom a letter etc. is addressed.

adduce /ə'djuːs/ *v.* (**-cing**) cite as an instance or as proof or evidence. □ **adducible** *adj.* [Latin: related to AD-, *duco* lead]

adenoids /'ædɪ,nɔɪdz/ *n.pl.* area of enlarged lymphatic tissue between the nose and the throat, often hindering

breathing in the young. □ **adenoidal** /-'nɔɪd(ə)l/ *adj.* [Greek *adēn* gland]

adept /'ædept/ *—adj.* (foll. by *at, in*) skilful. *—n.* adept person. [Latin *adipiscor adept-* attain]

adequate /'ædɪkwət/ *adj.* sufficient, satisfactory. □ **adequacy** *n.* **adequately** *adv.* [Latin: related to AD-, EQUATE]

à deux /ɑː 'dɜː/ *adv. & adj.* for or between two. [French]

adhere /əd'hɪə(r)/ *v.* (**-ring**) **1** (usu. foll. by *to*) stick fast to a substance etc. **2** (foll. by *to*) behave according to (a rule, undertaking, etc.). **3** (foll. by *to*) give allegiance. [Latin *haereo* stick]

adherent *—n.* supporter. *—adj.* sticking, adhering. □ **adherence** *n.*

adhesion /əd'hiːʒ(ə)n/ *n.* **1** adhering. **2** unnatural union of body tissues due to inflammation.

adhesive /əd'hiːsɪv/ *—adj.* sticky, causing adhesion. *—n.* adhesive substance. □ **adhesiveness** *n.*

ad hoc /æd 'hɒk/ *adv. & adj.* for one particular occasion or use. [Latin]

adieu /ə'djuː/ *int.* goodbye. [French, = to God]

ad infinitum /æd ,ɪnfɪ'naɪtəm/ *adv.* without limit; for ever. [Latin]

adipose /'ædɪ,pəʊz/ *adj.* of fat; fatty (*adipose tissue*). □ **adiposity** /-'pɒsɪti/ *n.* [Latin *adeps* fat]

adjacent /ə'dʒeɪs(ə)nt/ *adj.* (often foll. by *to*) lying near; adjoining. □ **adjacency** *n.* [Latin *jaceo* lie]

adjective /'ædʒɪktɪv/ *n.* word used to describe or modify a noun or pronoun. □ **adjectival** /,ædʒɪk'taɪv(ə)l/ *adj.* [Latin *jaceo* lie]

adjoin /ə'dʒɔɪn/ *v.* be next to and joined with. [Latin *jungo* join]

adjourn /ə'dʒɜːn/ *v.* **1** put off, postpone; break off (a meeting etc.) temporarily. **2** (of a meeting) break and disperse or (foll. by *to*) transfer to another place (*adjourned to the pub*). □ **adjournment** *n.* [Latin: related to AD-, *diurnum* day]

adjudge /ə'dʒʌdʒ/ *v.* (**-ging**) **1** pronounce judgement on (a matter). **2** pronounce or award judicially. □ **adjudgement** *n.* (also **adjudgment**). [Latin *judex* judge]

adjudicate /ə'dʒuːdɪ,keɪt/ *v.* (**-ting**) **1** act as judge in a competition, court, etc. **2** adjudge. □ **adjudication** /-'keɪʃ(ə)n/ *n.* **adjudicative** *adj.* **adjudicator** *n.*

adjunct /'ædʒʌŋkt/ *n.* **1** (foll. by *to, of*) subordinate or incidental thing. **2** *Gram.* word or phrase used to explain or amplify the predicate, subject, etc. [Latin: related to ADJOIN]

adjure /ə'dʒʊə(r)/ v. (-ring) (usu. foll. by to + infin.) beg or command. □ **adjuration** /ˌædʒʊə'reɪʃ(ə)n/ n. [Latin adjuro put to oath: related to JURY]

adjust /ə'dʒʌst/ v. 1 order or position; regulate; arrange. 2 (usu. foll. by to) become or make suited; adapt. 3 harmonize (discrepancies). 4 assess (loss or damages). □ **adjustable** adj. **adjustment** n. [Latin juxta near]

adjutant /'ædʒʊt(ə)nt/ n. 1 a army officer assisting a superior in administrative duties. b assistant. 2 (in full **adjutant bird**) giant Indian stork. [Latin: related to AD-, juvo jut- help]

ad lib /æd 'lɪb/ —v. (-bb-) improvise. —adj. improvised. —adv. as one pleases, to any desired extent. [abbreviation of Latin ad libitum according to pleasure]

admin /'ædmɪn/ n. colloq. administration. [abbreviation]

administer /əd'mɪnɪstə(r)/ v. 1 manage (business affairs etc.). 2 a deliver or dispense, esp. formally (a punishment, sacrament, etc.). b (usu. foll. by to) direct the taking of (an oath). [Latin: related to AD-, MINISTER]

administrate /əd'mɪnɪˌstreɪt/ v. (-ting) administer (esp. business affairs); act as an administrator.

administration /əd,mɪnɪ'streɪʃ(ə)n/ n. 1 administering, esp. public affairs. 2 government in power.

administrative /əd'mɪnɪstrətɪv/ adj. of the management of affairs.

administrator /əd'mɪnɪ,streɪtə(r)/ n. manager of a business, public affairs, or a person's estate.

admirable /'ædmərəb(ə)l/ adj. deserving admiration; excellent. □ **admirably** adv. [Latin: related to ADMIRE]

admiral /'ædmər(ə)l/ n. 1 a commander-in-chief of a navy. b high-ranking naval officer, commander. 2 any of various butterflies. [Arabic: related to AMIR]

Admiralty n. (pl. -ies) (in full **Admiralty Board**) hist. committee superintending the Royal Navy.

admiration /ˌædmə'reɪʃ(ə)n/ n. 1 respect; warm approval or pleasure. 2 object of this.

admire /əd'maɪə(r)/ v. (-ring) 1 regard with approval, respect, or satisfaction. 2 express admiration of. □ **admirer** n. **admiring** adj. **admiringly** adv. [Latin: related to AD-, miror wonder at]

admissible /əd'mɪsɪb(ə)l/ adj. 1 (of an idea etc.) worth accepting or considering. 2 Law allowable as evidence. [Latin: related to ADMIT]

admission /əd'mɪʃ(ə)n/ n. 1 acknowledgement (admission of error). 2 a process or right of entering. b charge for this (admission is £5).

admit /əd'mɪt/ v. (-tt-) 1 (often foll. by to be, or that + clause) acknowledge; recognize as true. 2 (foll. by to) confess to (a deed, fault, etc.). 3 allow (a person) entrance, access, etc. 4 take (a patient) into hospital. 5 (of an enclosed space) accommodate. 6 (foll. by of) allow as possible. [Latin mitto miss- send]

admittance n. admitting or being admitted, usu. to a place.

admittedly adv. as must be admitted.

admixture /æd'mɪkstʃə(r)/ n. 1 thing added, esp. a minor ingredient. 2 adding of this.

admonish /əd'mɒnɪʃ/ v. 1 reprove. 2 urge, advise. 3 (foll. by of) warn. □ **admonishment** n. **admonition** /ˌædmə'nɪʃ(ə)n/ n. **admonitory** adj. [Latin moneo warn]

ad nauseam /æd 'nɔːzɪˌæm/ adv. excessively; disgustingly. [Latin, = to sickness]

ado /ə'duː/ n. fuss, busy activity; trouble. [from AT, DO[1]: originally in much ado = much to do]

adobe /ə'dəʊbɪ/ n. 1 sun-dried brick. 2 clay for making these. [Spanish]

adolescent /ˌædə'les(ə)nt/ —adj. between childhood and adulthood. —n. adolescent person. □ **adolescence** n. [Latin adolesco grow up]

Adonis /ə'dəʊnɪs/ n. handsome young man. [Latin, name of a youth loved by Venus]

adopt /ə'dɒpt/ v. 1 legally take (a person) into a relationship, esp. another's child as one's own. 2 choose (a course of action etc.). 3 take over (another's idea etc.). 4 choose as a candidate for office. 5 accept responsibility for the maintenance of (a road etc.). 6 accept or approve (a report, accounts, etc.). □ **adoption** n. [Latin: related to AD-, OPT]

adoptive adj. because of adoption (adoptive son). [Latin: related to ADOPT]

adorable /ə'dɔːrəb(ə)l/ adj. 1 deserving adoration. 2 colloq. delightful, charming.

adore /ə'dɔː(r)/ v. (-ring) 1 love intensely. 2 worship as divine. 3 colloq. like very much. □ **adoration** /ˌædə'reɪʃ(ə)n/ n. **adorer** n. [Latin adoro worship]

adorn /ə'dɔːn/ v. add beauty to; decorate. □ **adornment** n. [Latin: related to AD-, orno decorate]

adrenal /ə'driːn(ə)l/ —adj. 1 at or near the kidneys. 2 of the adrenal glands. —n. (in full **adrenal gland**) either of two ductless glands above the kidneys, secreting adrenalin. [from AD-, RENAL]

adrenalin /ə'drenəlɪn/ n. (also **adrenaline**) 1 stimulative hormone secreted by the adrenal glands. 2 this extracted or synthesized for medicinal use.

adrift /ə'drɪft/ adv. & predic.adj. 1 drifting. 2 powerless; aimless. 3 colloq. a unfastened. b out of order, wrong (plans went adrift).

adroit /ə'drɔɪt/ adj. dexterous, skilful. [French à droit according to right]

adsorb /əd'sɔːb/ v. (usu. of a solid) hold (molecules of a gas or liquid etc.) to its surface, forming a thin film. □ **adsorbent** adj. & n. **adsorption** n. [from AD-, ABSORB]

adulation /ˌædjʊ'leɪʃ(ə)n/ n. obsequious flattery. [Latin adulor fawn on]

adult /'ædʌlt/-adj. 1 mature, grown-up. 2 (attrib.) of or for adults (adult education). -n. adult person. □ **adulthood** n. [Latin adolesco adultus grow up]

adulterate /ə'dʌltə,reɪt/ v. (-ting) debase (esp. foods) by adding other substances. □ **adulterant** adj. & n. **adulteration** /-'reɪʃ(ə)n/ n. [Latin adultero corrupt]

adulterer /ə'dʌltərə(r)/ n. (fem. **adulteress**) person who commits adultery.

adultery n. voluntary sexual intercourse between a married person and a person other than his or her spouse. □ **adulterous** adj.

adumbrate /'ædʌm,breɪt/ v. (-ting) 1 indicate faintly or in outline. 2 foreshadow. 3 overshadow. □ **adumbration** /-'breɪʃ(ə)n/ n. [Latin: related to AD-, umbra shade]

advance /əd'vɑːns/ -v. (-cing) 1 move or put forward; progress. 2 pay or lend (money) beforehand. 3 promote (a person, cause, etc.). 4 present (a suggestion etc.). 5 (as **advanced** adj.) a well ahead. b socially progressive. -n. 1 going forward; progress. 2 prepayment; loan. 3 (in pl.) amorous approaches. 4 rise in price. -attrib. adj. done or supplied beforehand (advance warning). □ **advance on** approach threateningly. **in advance** ahead in place or time. [Latin: related to AB-, ante before]

advanced level n. high level of GCE examination.

advancement n. promotion of a person, cause, or plan.

advantage /əd'vɑːntɪdʒ/ -n. 1 beneficial feature. 2 benefit, profit. 3 (often foll. by over) superiority. 4 (in tennis) the next point after deuce. -v. (-ging) benefit, favour. □ **take advantage of** 1 make good use of. 2 exploit, esp. unfairly. 3 euphem. seduce. □ **advantageous** /ˌædvən'teɪdʒəs/ adj. [French: related to ADVANCE]

Advent /'ædvent/ n. 1 season before Christmas. 2 coming of Christ. 3 (**advent**) important arrival. [Latin adventus from venio come]

Adventist n. member of a Christian sect believing in the imminent second coming of Christ.

adventitious /ˌædven'tɪʃəs/ adj. 1 accidental, casual. 2 added from outside. 3 Biol. formed accidentally or under unusual conditions. [Latin: related to ADVENT]

adventure /əd'ventʃə(r)/ -n. 1 unusual and exciting experience. 2 enterprise (spirit of adventure). -v. (-ring) dare, venture; engage in adventure. [Latin: related to ADVENT]

adventure playground n. playground with climbing-frames, building blocks, etc.

adventurer n. (fem. **adventuress**) 1 person who seeks adventure, esp. for personal gain or enjoyment. 2 financial speculator.

adventurous adj. venturesome, enterprising.

adverb /'ædvɜːb/ n. word indicating manner, degree, circumstance, etc., used to modify an adjective, verb, or other adverb (e.g. gently, quite, then). □ **adverbial** /əd'vɜːbɪəl/ adj. [Latin: related to AD-, verbum word, VERB]

adversary /'ædvəsərɪ/ n. (pl. -ies) enemy, opponent.

adverse /'ædvɜːs/ adj. unfavourable; harmful. □ **adversely** adv. [Latin: related to AD-, verto vers- turn]

adversity /əd'vɜːsɪtɪ/ n. misfortune, distress.

advert /'ædvɜːt/ n. colloq. advertisement. [abbreviation]

advertise /'ædvə,taɪz/ v. (-sing) 1 promote (goods or services) publicly to increase sales. 2 make generally known. 3 (often foll. by for) seek by a notice in a newspaper etc. to buy, employ, sell, etc. [French avertir: related to ADVERSE]

advertisement /əd'vɜːtɪsmənt/ n. 1 public announcement, esp. of goods etc. for sale or wanted, vacancies, etc. 2 advertising. [French avertissement: related to ADVERSE]

advice /əd'vaɪs/ n. 1 recommendation on how to act. 2 information given; news. 3 formal notice of a transaction.

advisable /əd'vaɪzəb(ə)l/ adj. to be recommended, expedient. □ **advisability** /-'bɪlɪtɪ/ n.

advise /əd'vaɪz/ v. (-sing) 1 (also absol.) give advice to. 2 recommend (advised me to rest). 3 (usu. foll. by of, or that + clause) inform. [Latin: related to AD-, video vis- see]

advisedly /əd'vaɪzɪdlɪ/ adv. after due consideration; deliberately.

adviser n. (also **advisor**) person who advises, esp. officially.

■ **Usage** The variant *advisor* is fairly common, but is considered incorrect by many people.

advisory *adj.* giving advice (*advisory body*).

advocaat /ˌædvəˈkɑːt/ *n.* liqueur of eggs, sugar, and brandy. [Dutch, = AD-VOCATE]

advocacy /ˈædvəkəsɪ/ *n.* support or argument for a cause, policy, etc.

advocate −*n.* /ˈædvəkət/ **1** (foll. by *of*) person who supports or speaks in favour. **2** person who pleads for another, esp. in a lawcourt. −*v.* /ˈædvəˌkeɪt/ (-**ting**) recommend by argument. [Latin: related to AD-, *voco* call]

adze /ædz/ *n.* (also *US* **adz**) tool like an axe, with an arched blade at right angles to the handle. [Old English]

aegis /ˈiːdʒɪs/ *n.* protection; support. [Greek *aigis* shield of Zeus or Athene]

aeolian harp /iːˈəʊlɪən/ *n.* stringed instrument or toy sounding when the wind passes through it. [Latin *Aeolus* wind-god, from Greek]

aeon /ˈiːɒn/ *n.* (also **eon**) **1** long or indefinite period. **2** an age. [Latin from Greek]

aerate /ˈeəreɪt/ *v.* (-**ting**) **1** charge (a liquid) with carbon dioxide. **2** expose to air. □ **aeration** /-ˈreɪʃ(ə)n/ *n.* [Latin *aer* AIR]

aerial /ˈeərɪəl/ −*n.* device for transmitting or receiving radio waves. −*adj.* **1** by or from the air; involving aircraft (*aerial attack*). **2** existing in the air. **3** of or like air. [Greek: related to AIR]

aero- *comb. form* air; aircraft. [Greek *aero-* from *aēr* air]

aerobatics /ˌeərəˈbætɪks/ *n.pl.* **1** spectacular flying of aircraft, esp. to entertain. **2** (as *sing.*) performance of these. [from AERO-, after ACROBATICS]

aerobics /eəˈrəʊbɪks/ *n.pl.* vigorous exercises designed to increase oxygen intake. □ **aerobic** *adj.* [from AERO-, Greek *bios* life]

aerodrome /ˈeərəˌdrəʊm/ *n.* small airport or airfield. [from AERO-, Greek *dromos* course]

aerodynamics /ˌeərəʊdaɪˈnæmɪks/ *n.pl.* (usu. treated as *sing.*) dynamics of solid bodies moving through air. □ **aerodynamic** *adj.*

aerofoil /ˈeərəˌfɔɪl/ *n.* structure with curved surfaces (e.g. a wing, fin, or tailplane) designed to give lift in flight.

aeronautics /ˌeərəʊˈnɔːtɪks/ *n.pl.* (usu. treated as *sing.*) science or practice of motion in the air. □ **aeronautic** *adj.* **aeronautical** *adj.* [from AERO-, NAUTICAL]

aeroplane /ˈeərəˌpleɪn/ *n.* powered heavier-than-air flying vehicle with fixed wings. [French: related to AERO-, PLANE¹]

aerosol /ˈeərəˌsɒl/ *n.* **1** pressurized container releasing a substance as a fine spray. **2** system of minute particles suspended in gas (e.g. fog or smoke). [from AERO-, SOL]

aerospace /ˈeərəʊˌspeɪs/ *n.* **1** earth's atmosphere and outer space. **2** aviation in this.

aesthete /ˈiːsθiːt/ *n.* person who has or professes a special appreciation of beauty. [Greek *aisthanomai* perceive]

aesthetic /iːsˈθetɪk/ −*adj.* **1** of or sensitive to beauty. **2** artistic, tasteful. −*n.* (in *pl.*) philosophy of beauty, esp. in art. □ **aesthetically** *adv.* **aestheticism** /-ˌsɪz(ə)m/ *n.*

aetiology /ˌiːtɪˈɒlədʒɪ/ *n.* (*US* **etiology**) study of causation or of the causes of disease. □ **aetiological** /-əˈlɒdʒɪk(ə)l/ *adj.* [Greek *aitia* cause]

AF *abbr.* audio frequency.

afar /əˈfɑː(r)/ *adv.* at or to a distance.

affable /ˈæfəb(ə)l/ *adj.* **1** friendly. **2** courteous. □ **affability** /-ˈbɪlɪtɪ/ *n.* **affably** *adv.* [Latin *affabilis*]

affair /əˈfeə(r)/ *n.* **1** matter, concern, or thing to be attended to (*that is my affair*). **2 a** celebrated or notorious happening. **b** *colloq.* thing or event (*puzzling affair*). **3** = LOVE AFFAIR. **4** (in *pl.*) public or private business. [French *à faire* to do]

affect /əˈfekt/ *v.* **1 a** produce an effect on. **b** (of disease etc.) attack. **2** move emotionally. **3** pretend (*affected ignorance*). **4** pose as or use for effect (*affects the aesthete*; *affects fancy hats*). □ **affecting** *adj.* **affectingly** *adv.* [Latin *afficio affect-* influence]

■ **Usage** *Affect* should not be confused with *effect*, meaning 'to bring about'. Note also that *effect* is used as a noun as well as a verb.

affectation /ˌæfekˈteɪʃ(ə)n/ *n.* **1** artificial manner. **2** (foll. by *of*) studied display. **3** pretence.

affected /əˈfektɪd/ *adj.* **1** pretended, artificial. **2** full of affectation.

affection /əˈfekʃ(ə)n/ *n.* **1** goodwill, fond feeling. **2** disease; diseased condition.

affectionate /əˈfekʃənət/ *adj.* loving, fond. □ **affectionately** *adv.*

affidavit /ˌæfɪˈdeɪvɪt/ *n.* written statement confirmed by oath. [Latin, = has stated on oath]

affiliate /əˈfɪlɪˌeɪt/ −*v.* (-**ting**) (foll. by *to*, *with*) attach, adopt, or connect as a member or branch. −*n.* affiliated person etc. [Latin: related to FILIAL]

affiliation /ə,fɪlɪ'eɪʃ(ə)n/ *n.* affiliating or being affiliated.

affiliation order *n.* legal order against the supposed father of an illegitimate child for support.

affinity /ə'fɪnɪtɪ/ *n.* (*pl.* -**ies**) **1** liking or attraction; feeling of kinship. **2** relationship, esp. by marriage. **3** similarity of structure or character suggesting a relationship. **4** *Chem.* the tendency of certain substances to combine with others. [Latin *finis* border]

affirm /ə'fɜːm/ *v.* **1** assert, state as a fact. **2** *Law* make a solemn declaration in place of an oath. □ **affirmation** /,æfə'meɪʃ(ə)n/ *n.* [Latin: related to FIRM[1]]

affirmative /ə'fɜːmətɪv/ —*adj.* affirming; expressing approval. —*n.* affirmative statement or word etc.

affix —*v.* /ə'fɪks/ **1** attach, fasten. **2** add in writing. —*n.* /'æfɪks/ **1** addition. **2** *Gram.* prefix or suffix. [Latin: related to FIX]

afflict /ə'flɪkt/ *v.* distress physically or mentally. [Latin *fligo flict-* strike down]

affliction /ə'flɪkʃ(ə)n/ *n.* **1** distress, suffering. **2** cause of this.

affluent /'æfluənt/ *adj.* wealthy, rich. □ **affluence** *n.* [Latin: related to FLUENT]

afford /ə'fɔːd/ *v.* **1** (prec. by *can* or *be able to*) **a** have enough money, time, etc., for; be able to spare. **b** be in a position (*can't afford to be critical*). **2** provide (*affords a view of the sea*). [Old English *ge-* prefix implying completeness, FORTH]

afforest /ə'fɒrɪst/ *v.* **1** convert into forest. **2** plant with trees. □ **afforestation** /-'steɪʃ(ə)n/ *n.* [Latin: related to FOREST]

affray /ə'freɪ/ *n.* breach of the peace by fighting or rioting in public. [Anglo-French = 'remove from peace']

affront /ə'frʌnt/ —*n.* open insult. —*v.* insult openly; offend, embarrass. [Latin: related to FRONT]

Afghan /'æfɡæn/ —*n.* **1 a** native or national of Afghanistan. **b** person of Afghan descent. **2** official language of Afghanistan. —*adj.* of Afghanistan. [Pashto]

Afghan hound *n.* tall hunting dog with long silky hair.

aficionado /ə,fɪsjə'nɑːdəʊ/ *n.* (*pl.* -**s**) devotee of a sport or pastime. [Spanish]

afield /ə'fiːld/ *adv.* to or at a distance (esp. *far afield*). [Old English: related to A[2]]

aflame /ə'fleɪm/ *adv.* & *predic.adj.* **1** in flames. **2** very excited.

afloat /ə'fləʊt/ *adv.* & *predic.adj.* **1** floating. **2** at sea. **3** out of debt or difficulty. **4** current. [Old English: related to A[2]]

afoot /ə'fʊt/ *adv.* & *predic.adj.* in operation; progressing.

afore /ə'fɔː(r)/ *prep.* & *adv.* *archaic* before; previously; in front (of). [Old English: related to A[2]]

afore- *comb. form* before, previously (*aforementioned*; *aforesaid*).

aforethought *adj.* premeditated (following a noun: *malice aforethought*).

afraid /ə'freɪd/ *predic. adj.* alarmed, frightened. □ **be afraid** *colloq.* politely regret (*I'm afraid we're late*). [originally past part. of AFFRAY]

afresh /ə'freʃ/ *adv.* anew; with a fresh beginning. [earlier *of fresh*]

African /'æfrɪkən/ —*n.* **1** native (esp. dark-skinned) of Africa. **2** person of African descent. —*adj.* of Africa. [Latin]

African elephant *n.* the elephant of Africa, larger than that of India.

African violet *n.* house-plant with velvety leaves and blue, purple, or pink flowers.

Afrikaans /,æfrɪ'kɑːns/ *n.* language derived from Dutch, used in S. Africa. [Dutch, = 'African']

Afrikaner /,æfrɪ'kɑːnə(r)/ *n.* Afrikaans-speaking White person in S. Africa, esp. of Dutch descent.

Afro /'æfrəʊ/ —*adj.* (of hair) tightly-curled and bushy. —*n.* (*pl.* -**s**) Afro hairstyle.

Afro- *comb. form* African.

Afro-American /,æfrəʊə'merɪkən/ —*adj.* of American Blacks or their culture. —*n.* American Black.

Afro-Caribbean /,æfrəʊ,kærɪ'biːən/ —*n.* Caribbean person of African descent. —*adj.* of Afro-Caribbeans.

aft /ɑːft/ *adv.* *Naut.* & *Aeron.* at or towards the stern or tail. [earlier *baft*]

after /'ɑːftə(r)/ —*prep.* **1** following in time; later than (*after a week*). **2** in view of, in spite of (*after what you did what do you expect?*; *after all my efforts I still lost*). **3** behind (*shut the door after you*). **4** in pursuit or quest of (*run after them*). **5** about, concerning (*asked after her*). **6** in allusion to (*named after the prince*). **7** in imitation of (*a painting after Rubens*). **8** next in importance to (*best one after mine*). —*conj.* later than (*left after they arrived*). —*adv.* **1** later (*soon after*). **2** behind (*followed on after*). —*adj.* **1** later, following (*in after years*). **2** *Naut.* nearer the stern (*after cabins*). □ **after all** in spite of everything (*after all, what does it matter?*). **after one's own heart** to one's taste. [Old English]

afterbirth *n.* placenta etc. discharged from the womb after childbirth.

after-care *n.* attention after leaving hospital etc.

after-effect *n.* delayed effect following an accident, trauma, etc.

afterglow *n.* glow remaining after its source has disappeared.

afterlife *n.* life after death.

aftermath /'ɑ:ftə,mæθ/ *n.* **1** consequences, esp. unpleasant (*aftermath of war*). **2** new grass growing after mowing. [from AFTER, *math* mowing]

afternoon /,ɑ:ftə'nu:n/ *n.* time from noon or lunch time to evening.

afterpains *n.pl.* pains caused by contraction of the womb after childbirth.

afters *n.pl. colloq.* = DESSERT 1.

aftershave *n.* lotion used after shaving.

aftertaste *n.* taste after eating or drinking.

afterthought *n.* thing thought of or added later.

afterwards /'ɑ:ftəwədz/ *adv.* (*US* **afterward**) later, subsequently. [Old English: related to AFTER, -WARD]

Ag *symb.* silver. [Latin *argentum*]

again /ə'gen/ *adv.* **1** another time; once more. **2** as previously (*home again; well again*). **3** in addition (*as much again*). **4** further, besides (*again, what about you?*). **5** on the other hand (*I might, and again I might not*). □ **again and again** repeatedly. [Old English]

against /ə'genst/ *prep.* **1** in opposition to (*fight against crime*). **2** into collision or in contact with (*lean against the wall*). **3** to the disadvantage of (*my age is against me*). **4** in contrast to (*against a dark background*). **5** in anticipation of (*against his coming; against the cold*). **6** as a compensating factor to (*income against expenditure*). **7** in return for (*issued against payment of the fee*). □ **against the grain** see GRAIN. **against time** see TIME. [from AGAIN, with inflectional -*s*]

agape /ə'geɪp/ *predic. adj.* gaping, openmouthed. [from A²]

agaric /'ægərɪk/ *n.* fungus with a cap and stalk, e.g. the common mushroom. [Greek *agarikon*]

agate /'ægət/ *n.* hard usu. streaked chalcedony. [Greek *akhatēs*]

agave /ə'geɪvɪ/ *n.* plant with rosettes of narrow spiny leaves and flowers on tall stem. [*Agave*, name of a woman in Greek mythology]

age – *n.* **1** length of time that a person or thing has existed. **2 a** *colloq.* (often in *pl.*) a long time (*waited for ages*). **b** distinct historical period (*Bronze Age*). **3** old age. – *v.* (**ageing**) **1** show or cause to show signs of advancing age. **2** grow old. **3** mature. □ **come of age** reach adult status (esp. *Law* at 18, formerly 21). [Latin *aetas*]

-age *suffix* forming nouns denoting: **1** action (*breakage*). **2** condition (*bondage*). **3** aggregate or number (*coverage; acreage*). **4** cost (*postage*). **5** result (*wreckage*). **6** place or abode (*anchorage; orphanage*). [Latin -*aticus*]

aged *adj.* **1** /eɪdʒd/ (*predic.*) of the age of (*aged 3*). **2** /'eɪdʒɪd/ old.

ageism *n.* prejudice or discrimination on grounds of age. □ **ageist** *adj. & n.*

ageless *adj.* **1** never growing or appearing old. **2** eternal.

agelong *adj.* existing for a very long time.

agency /'eɪdʒənsɪ/ *n.* (*pl.* -**ies**) **1** business or premises of an agent. **2** action; intervention (*free agency; by the agency of God*). [Latin: related to ACT]

agenda /ə'dʒendə/ *n.* (*pl.* -**s**) **1** list of items to be considered at a meeting. **2** things to be done.

agent /'eɪdʒ(ə)nt/ *n.* **1 a** person who acts for another in business etc. **b** spy. **2** person or thing that exerts power or produces an effect.

agent provocateur /,ɑ:ʒɑ̃ prə,vɒkə'tɜ:(r)/ *n.* (*pl.* **agents provocateurs** pronunc. same) person used to tempt suspected offenders to self-incriminating action. [French, = provocative agent]

age of consent *n.* age at which consent to sexual intercourse is valid in law.

age-old *adj.* very long-standing.

agglomerate – *v.* (-**ting**) /ə'glɒmə,reɪt/ collect into a mass. – *n.* /ə'glɒmərət/ mass, esp. of fused volcanic fragments. – *adj.* /ə'glɒmərət/ collected into a mass. □ **agglomeration** /-'reɪʃ(ə)n/ *n.* [Latin *glomus -meris* ball]

agglutinate /ə'glu:tɪ,neɪt/ *v.* (-**ting**) stick as with glue. □ **agglutination** /-'neɪʃ(ə)n/ *n.* **agglutinative** /-nətɪv/ *adj.* [Latin: related to GLUTEN]

aggrandize /ə'grændaɪz/ *v.* (also -**ise**) (-**zing** or -**sing**) **1** increase the power, rank or wealth of. **2** make seem greater. □ **aggrandizement** /-dɪzmənt/ *n.* [French: related to GRAND]

aggravate /'ægrə,veɪt/ *v.* (-**ting**) **1** make worse or more serious. **2** annoy. □ **aggravation** /-'veɪʃ(ə)n/ *n.* [Latin *gravis* heavy]

■ **Usage** The use of *aggravate* in sense 2 is regarded by some people as incorrect, but it is common in informal use.

aggregate – *n.* /'ægrɪgət/ **1** sum total, amount assembled. **2** crushed stone etc. used in making concrete. **3** rock formed of a mass of different particles or minerals. – *adj.* /'ægrɪgət/ combined, collective, total. – *v.* /'ægrɪ,geɪt/ (-**ting**) **1** collect, combine into one mass. **2** *colloq.*

amount to. **3** unite. □ **in the aggregate** as a whole. □ **aggregation** /-'geɪʃ(ə)n/ n. **aggregative** /'ægrɪ,geɪtɪv/ adj. [Latin grex greg- flock]

aggression /ə'greʃ(ə)n/ n. **1** unprovoked attacking or attack. **2** hostile or destructive behaviour. [Latin gradior gress- walk]

aggressive /ə'gresɪv/ adj. **1** given to aggression; hostile. **2** forceful, self-assertive. □ **aggressively** adv.

aggressor n. person or party that attacks without provocation.

aggrieved /ə'griːvd/ adj. having a grievance. [French: related to GRIEF]

aggro /'ægrəʊ/ n. slang **1** aggressive hostility. **2** trouble, difficulty. [abbreviation of aggravation or aggression]

aghast /ə'gɑːst/ predic. adj. filled with dismay or consternation. [past part. of obsolete (a)gast frighten]

agile /'ædʒaɪl/ adj. quick-moving, nimble, active. □ **agility** /ə'dʒɪlɪtɪ/ n. [Latin agilis: related to ACT]

agitate /'ædʒɪ,teɪt/ v. (-**ting**) **1** disturb or excite (a person or feelings). **2** (often foll. by for, against) campaign, esp. politically (agitated for tax reform). **3** shake briskly. □ **agitation** /-'teɪʃ(ə)n/ n. **agitator** n. [Latin agito: related to ACT]

aglow /ə'gləʊ/ predic. adj. glowing.

AGM abbr. annual general meeting.

agnail /'ægneɪl/ n. piece of torn skin at the root of a fingernail; resulting soreness. [Old English, = tight (metal) nail, hard excrescence in flesh]

agnostic /æg'nɒstɪk/ –n. person who believes that the existence of God is not provable. –adj. of agnosticism. □ **agnosticism** /-,sɪz(ə)m/ n. [from A-, GNOSTIC]

ago /ə'gəʊ/ adv. (prec. by duration) earlier, in the past. [originally agone= gone by]

agog /ə'gɒg/ predic. adj. eager, expectant. [French gogue fun]

agonize /'ægə,naɪz/ v. (also -**ise**) (-**zing** or -**sing**) **1** undergo (esp. mental) anguish; suffer or cause to suffer agony. **2** (as **agonized** adj.) expressing agony (an agonized look).

agony /'ægənɪ/ n. (pl. -**ies**) **1** extreme mental or physical suffering. **2** severe struggle. [Greek agōn struggle]

agony aunt n. colloq. person (esp. a woman) who answers letters in an agony column.

agony column n. colloq. **1** column in a magazine etc. offering personal advice to correspondents. **2** = PERSONAL COLUMN.

agoraphobia /,ægərə'fəʊbɪə/ n. abnormal fear of open spaces or public places.

□ **agoraphobic** adj. & n. [Greek agora market-place]

agrarian /ə'greərɪən/ –adj. **1** of the land or its cultivation. **2** of landed property. –n. advocate of the redistribution of land. [Latin ager field]

agree /ə'griː/ v. (-**ees**, -**eed**, -**eeing**) **1** hold the same opinion (I agree with you). **2** consent (agreed to go). **3** (often foll. by with) **a** become or be in harmony. **b** suit (fish didn't agree with him). **c** Gram. have the same number, gender, case, or person as. **4** reach agreement about (agreed a price). **5** (foll. by on) decide mutually on (agreed on a compromise). □ **be agreed** be of one opinion. [Latin: related to AD-, gratus pleasing]

agreeable adj. **1** pleasing, pleasant. **2** willing to agree. □ **agreeably** adv.

agreement n. **1** act or state of agreeing. **2** arrangement or contract.

agriculture /'ægrɪ,kʌltʃə(r)/ n. cultivation of the soil and rearing of animals. □ **agricultural** /-'kʌltʃər(ə)l/ adj. **agriculturalist** /-'kʌltʃərəlɪst/ n. [Latin ager field]

agrimony /'ægrɪmənɪ/ n. (pl. -**ies**) perennial plant with small yellow flowers. [Greek argemōnē poppy]

agronomy /ə'grɒnəmɪ/ n. science of soil management and crop production. □ **agronomist** n. [Greek agros land]

aground /ə'graʊnd/ predic. adj. & adv. on or on to the bottom of shallow water (run aground).

ague /'eɪgjuː/ n. **1** hist. malarial fever. **2** shivering fit. [Latin: related to ACUTE]

AH abbr. in the year of the Hegira (AD 622); of the Muslim era. [Latin anno Hegirae]

ah /ɑː/ int. expressing surprise, pleasure, realization, etc. [French a]

aha /ɑː'hɑː/ int. expressing surprise, triumph, mockery, etc. [from AH, HA¹]

ahead /ə'hed/ adv. **1** further forward in space or time. **2** in the lead (ahead on points).

ahem /ə'həm/ int. used to attract attention, gain time, etc. [from HEM²]

ahoy /ə'hɔɪ/ int. Naut. call used in hailing. [from AH, HOY]

AI abbr. **1** artificial insemination. **2** artificial intelligence.

AID abbr. artificial insemination by donor.

aid –n. **1** help. **2** person or thing that helps. –v. **1** help. **2** promote (sleep will aid recovery). □ **in aid of 1** in support of. **2** colloq. for the purpose of (what's it all in aid of?). [Latin: related to AD-, juvo help]

aide /eɪd/ n. **1** aide-de-camp. **2** esp. US assistant. [French]

aide-de-camp /,eɪd də 'kɑ̃/ n. (pl. **aides--de-camp** pronunc. same) officer assisting a senior officer. [French]

Aids n. (also **AIDS**) acquired immune deficiency syndrome, an often fatal viral syndrome marked by severe loss of resistance to infection. [abbreviation]

ail v. **1** archaic (only in 3rd person interrog. or indefinite constructions) trouble or afflict (what ails him?). **2** (usu. **be ailing**) be ill. [Old English]

aileron /'eɪləˌrɒn/ n. hinged flap on an aeroplane wing. [French aile wing]

ailing adj. **1** ill. **2** in poor condition.

ailment n. minor illness or disorder.

aim –v. **1** intend or try; attempt (aim at winning; aim to win). **2** (usu. foll. by at) direct or point (a weapon, remark, etc.). **3** take aim. –n. **1** purpose or object. **2** the directing of a weapon etc. at an object. □ **take aim** direct a weapon etc. at a target. [Latin aestimare reckon]

aimless adj. without aim or purpose. □ **aimlessly** adv.

ain't /eɪnt/ contr. colloq. **1** am, is, or are not. **2** have or has not.

■ **Usage** The use of ain't is usually regarded as unacceptable in spoken and written English.

air /eə(r)/ –n. **1** mixture mainly of oxygen and nitrogen surrounding the earth. **2** earth's atmosphere; open space in it; this as a place for flying aircraft. **3** a distinctive impression or manner (air of mystery) b (esp. in pl.) pretentiousness (gave himself airs). **4** tune. **5** light wind. –v. **1** expose (clothes, a room, etc.) to fresh air or warmth to remove damp. **2** express and discuss publicly (an opinion, question, grievance, etc.). □ **by air** by or in an aircraft. **in the air 1** (of opinions etc.) prevalent. **2** (of plans etc.) uncertain. **on** (or **off**) **the air** being (or not being) broadcast. [Greek aēr]

airbase n. base for military aircraft.

air-bed n. inflatable mattress.

airborne adj. **1** transported by air. **2** (of aircraft) in the air after taking off.

air-brick n. perforated brick used for ventilation.

Airbus n. propr. short-haul passenger aircraft

Air Chief Marshal n. RAF officer of high rank, above Air Marshal.

Air Commodore n. RAF officer next above Group Captain.

air-conditioning n. **1** system for regulating the humidity, ventilation, and temperature in a building. **2** apparatus for this. □ **air-conditioned** adj.

aircraft n. (pl. same) machine capable of flight, esp. an aeroplane or helicopter.

aircraft-carrier n. warship carrying and used as a base for aircraft.

aircraftman n. lowest rank in the RAF.

aircraftwoman n. lowest rank in the WRAF.

aircrew n. crew of an aircraft.

air-cushion n. **1** inflatable cushion. **2** layer of air supporting a hovercraft etc.

Airedale /'eədeɪl/ n. large terrier of a rough-coated breed. [Airedale in Yorkshire]

airer n. stand for airing or drying clothes etc.

airfield n. area with runway(s) for aircraft.

air force n. branch of the armed forces fighting in the air.

airgun n. gun using compressed air to fire pellets.

airhead n. slang stupid or foolish person.

air hostess n. stewardess in a passenger aircraft.

airless adj. stuffy; still, calm.

air letter n. sheet of light paper forming a letter for sending by airmail.

airlift –n. emergency transport of supplies etc. by air. –v. transport thus.

airline n. public air transport system or company.

airliner n. large passenger aircraft.

airlock n. **1** stoppage of the flow by an air bubble in a pump or pipe. **2** compartment permitting movement between areas at different air pressures.

airmail n. **1** system of transporting mail by air. **2** mail carried by air.

airman n. pilot or member of an aircraft crew, esp. in an air force.

Air Marshal n. RAF officer of high rank, above Air Vice-Marshal.

airplane n. US = AEROPLANE.

air pocket n. apparent vacuum causing an aircraft to drop suddenly.

airport n. airfield with facilities for passengers and goods.

air raid n. attack by aircraft on ground targets.

air rifle n. rifle using compressed air to fire pellets.

airs and graces n.pl. affected manner.

airscrew n. aircraft propeller.

airship n. power-driven aircraft lighter than air.

airsick adj. nauseous from air travel.

airspace n. air above a country and subject to its jurisdiction.

air speed n. aircraft's speed relative to the air.

airstrip n. strip of ground for the take-off and landing of aircraft.

air terminal n. building with transport to and from an airport.

airtight adj. impermeable to air.

air traffic controller n. official who controls air traffic by radio.

Air Vice-Marshal n. RAF officer of high rank, just below Air Marshal.

airwaves n.pl. colloq. radio waves used in broadcasting.

airway n. recognized route of aircraft.

airwoman n. woman pilot or member of an aircraft crew, esp. in an air force.

airworthy adj. (of an aircraft) fit to fly.

airy adj. (-ier, -iest) 1 well-ventilated, breezy. 2 flippant, superficial. 3 light as air. 4 ethereal. □ **airily** adv.

airy-fairy adj. colloq. unrealistic, impractical.

aisle /aɪl/ n. 1 the part of a church on either side of the nave, divided from it by pillars. 2 passage between rows of pews, seats, etc. [Latin ala wing]

aitch /eɪtʃ/ n. the letter H. [French ache]

aitchbone n. 1 rump bone of an animal. 2 cut of beef over this. [originally nache-bone from Latin natis buttock]

ajar /ə'dʒɑː(r)/ adv. & predic.adj. (of a door) slightly open. [from A², obsolete char from Old English cerr a turn]

Akela /ɑː'keɪlə/ n. adult leader of Cub Scouts. [name of the leader of the wolf-pack in Kipling's Jungle Book]

akimbo /ə'kɪmbəʊ/ adv. (of the arms) with hands on the hips and elbows turned outwards. [originally in kene-bowe, probably from Old Norse]

akin /ə'kɪn/ predic. adj. 1 related by blood. 2 similar.

Al symb. aluminium.

-al suffix 1 (also **-ial**) forming adjectives meaning 'relating to, of the kind of' (central; tidal; dictatorial). 2 forming nouns, esp. of verbal action (removal). [Latin -alis]

à la /'æ lɑː/ prep. in the manner of (à la russe). [French from À LA MODE]

alabaster /'ælə,bɑː:stə(r)/ —n. translucent usu. white form of gypsum, used for carving etc. —adj. 1 of alabaster. 2 white or smooth. [Greek alabastros]

à la carte /,æ lɑː 'kɑː:t/ adv. & adj. with individually priced dishes. [French]

alacrity /ə'lækrɪtɪ/ n. briskness; cheerful readiness. [Latin alacer brisk]

à la mode /,æ lɑː 'məʊd/ adv. & adj. in fashion; fashionable. [French]

alarm /ə'lɑː:m/ —n. 1 warning of danger etc. 2 **a** warning sound or device. **b** = ALARM CLOCK. 3 apprehension (filled with alarm). —v. 1 frighten or disturb. 2 warn. □ **alarming** adj. **alarmingly** adv. [Italian all'arme! to arms]

alarm clock n. clock that rings at a set time.

alarmist n. person stirring up alarm.

alas /ə'læs/ int. expressing grief, pity, or concern. [French: related to AH, Latin lassus weary]

alb n. long white vestment worn by Christian priests. [Latin albus white]

albatross /'ælbə,trɒs/ n. 1 **a** long-winged, stout-bodied bird related to the petrel. **b** encumbrance. 2 Golf score of three strokes under par at any hole. [alteration of alcatras, from Spanish and Portuguese alcatraz from Arabic, = the jug]

albeit /ɔː'biːɪt/ conj. literary though. [all be it]

albino /æl'biːnəʊ/ n. (pl. **-s**) 1 person or animal lacking pigment in the skin and hair (which are white), and the eyes (usu. pink). 2 plant lacking normal colouring. □ **albinism** /'ælbɪ,nɪz(ə)m/ n. [Spanish and Portuguese: related to ALB]

album /'ælbəm/ n. 1 book for photographs, stamps, etc. 2 **a** long-playing gramophone record. **b** set of these. [Latin, = blank tablet, from albus white]

albumen /'ælbjʊmɪn/ n. 1 egg-white. 2 substance found between the skin and germ of many seeds, usu. the edible part. [Latin: related to ALBUM]

albumin /'ælbjʊmɪn/ n. water-soluble protein found in egg-white, milk, blood, etc. □ **albuminous** /æl'bjuːmɪnəs/ adj.

alchemy /'ælkəmɪ/ n. medieval chemistry, esp. seeking to turn base metals into gold. □ **alchemist** n. [Arabic]

alcohol /'ælkə,hɒl/ n. 1 (in full **ethyl alcohol**) colourless volatile inflammable liquid, esp. as the intoxicant in wine, beer, spirits, etc., and as a solvent, fuel, etc. 2 liquor containing this. 3 Chem. any of many organic compounds containing one or more hydroxyl groups attached to carbon atoms. [Arabic: related to KOHL]

alcoholic /,ælkə'hɒlɪk/ —adj. of, like, containing, or caused by alcohol. —n. person suffering from alcoholism.

alcoholism /'ælkəhɒ,lɪz(ə)m/ n. condition resulting from addiction to alcohol.

alcove /'ælkəʊv/ n. recess, esp. in the wall of a room. [Arabic, = the vault]

aldehyde /'ældɪ,haɪd/ n. Chem. any of a class of compounds formed by the oxidation of alcohols. [from ALCOHOL, DE-, HYDROGEN]

al dente /æl 'dentɪ, -teɪ/ adj. (of pasta etc.) cooked so as to be still firm when bitten. [Italian, = 'to the tooth']

alder /'ɔːldə(r)/ n. tree related to the birch. [Old English]

alderman /'ɔ:ldəmən/ n. esp. hist. co-opted member of an English county or borough council, next in dignity to the mayor. [Old English aldor chief, MAN]

ale n. beer. [Old English]

aleatory /'eɪliətəri/ adj. depending on chance. [Latin alea DIE[2]]

alehouse n. hist. tavern.

alembic /ə'lembɪk/ n. 1 hist. apparatus formerly used in distilling. 2 means of refining or extracting. [Greek ambix, -ikos cap of a still]

alert /ə'lɜ:t/ —adj. 1 watchful, vigilant. 2 nimble, attentive. —n. 1 warning call or alarm. 2 state or period of special vigilance. —v. (often foll. by to) warn. [French alerte from Italian all'erta to the watch-tower]

A level n. = ADVANCED LEVEL.

Alexander technique /ˌælɪg'zɑːn-də(r)/ n. technique for controlling posture as an aid to well-being. [Alexander, name of a physiotherapist]

alexandrine /ˌælɪg'zændraɪn/ —adj. (of a line of verse) having six iambic feet. —n. alexandrine line. [French Alexandre, title of a romance using this metre]

alfalfa /æl'fælfə/ n. clover-like plant used for fodder. [Arabic, = a green fodder]

alfresco /æl'freskəu/ adv. & adj. in the open air. [Italian]

alga /'ælgə/ n. (pl. algae /-dʒi:/) (usu. in pl.) non-flowering stemless water-plant, esp. seaweed and plankton. [Latin]

algebra /'ældʒɪbrə/ n. branch of mathematics that uses letters etc. to represent numbers and quantities. □ **algebraic** /-'breɪk/ adj. [ultimately from Arabic al-jabr, = reunion of broken parts]

Algol /'ælgɒl/ n. high-level computer programming language. [from ALGO-(RITHM), L(ANGUAGE)]

algorithm /'ælgərɪð(ə)m/ n. process or set of rules used for calculation etc., esp. with a computer. □ **algorithmic** /-'rɪðmɪk/ adj. [Persian, name of a 9th-c. mathematician al-Kuwārizmī]

alias /'eɪliəs/ —adv. also named or known as. —n. assumed name. [Latin, = at another time]

alibi /'ælɪˌbaɪ/ n. (pl. -s) 1 claim or proof that one was elsewhere when a crime etc. was committed. 2 informal excuse. [Latin, = elsewhere]

■ **Usage** The use of alibi in sense 2 is considered incorrect by some people.

alien /'eɪliən/ —adj. 1 (often foll. by to) unfamiliar; unacceptable or repugnant. 2 foreign. 3 of beings from other worlds. —n. 1 foreign-born resident who is not

naturalized. 2 being from another world. [Latin alius other]

alienable adj. Law able to be transferred to new ownership.

alienate v. (-ting) 1 estrange, make hostile. 2 transfer ownership of. □ **alienation** /-'neɪʃ(ə)n/ n.

alight[1] /ə'laɪt/ predic. adj. 1 on fire. 2 lit up; excited. [on a light (= lighted) fire]

alight[2] /ə'laɪt/ v. 1 (often foll. by from) descend from a vehicle. 2 come to earth, settle. [Old English]

align /ə'laɪn/ v. 1 put or bring into line. 2 (usu. foll. by with) ally (oneself etc.) with (a cause, party, etc.). □ **alignment** n. [French à ligne into line]

alike /ə'laɪk/ —adj. (usu. predic.) similar, like. —adv. in a similar way.

alimentary /ˌælɪ'mentəri/ adj. of or providing food or nourishment. [Latin alo nourish]

alimentary canal n. passage along which food passes during digestion.

alimony /'ælɪmənɪ/ n. money payable to a spouse or former spouse after separation or divorce.

■ **Usage** In UK usage this term has been replaced by maintenance.

aliphatic /ˌælɪ'fætɪk/ adj. Chem. of organic compounds in which carbon atoms form open chains, not aromatic rings. [Greek aleiphar -phat- fat]

aliquot /'ælɪˌkwɒt/ —adj. (of a part or portion) contained by the whole an integral number of times (4 is an aliquot part of 12). —n. 1 aliquot part. 2 (in general use) any known fraction of a whole; sample. [Latin, = several]

alive /ə'laɪv/ adj. (usu. predic.) 1 living. 2 lively, active. 3 (foll. by to) aware of; alert. 4 (foll. by with) swarming or teeming with. [Old English: related to A[2], LIFE]

alkali /'ælkəˌlaɪ/ n. (pl. -s) 1 **a** any of a class of substances that liberate hydroxide ions in water, usu. form caustic or corrosive solutions, turn litmus blue, and have a pH of more than 7, e.g. caustic soda. **b** similar but weaker substance, e.g. sodium carbonate. 2 Chem. any substance that reacts with or neutralizes hydrogen ions. □ **alkaline** adj.

alkalinity /-'lɪnɪtɪ/ n. [Arabic, = the calcined ashes]

alkaloid /'ælkəˌlɔɪd/ n. nitrogenous organic compound of plant origin, e.g. morphine, quinine.

alkane /'ælkeɪn/ n. Chem. saturated aliphatic hydrocarbon having the general formula C_nH_{2n+2}, including methane and ethane.

alkene /'ælki:n/ n. Chem. unsaturated aliphatic hydrocarbon containing a

double bond and having the general formula C_nH_{2n}, including ethylene.

alkyne /ˈælkaɪn/ n. Chem. unsaturated aliphatic hydrocarbon containing a triple bond and having the general formula C_nH_{2n-2}, including acetylene.

all /ɔːl/ —adj. 1 whole amount, quantity, or extent of (all day; all his life; take it all). 2 any whatever (beyond all doubt). 3 greatest possible (with all speed). —n. 1 all concerned; everything (all were present; all is lost). 2 (foll. by of) a the whole of (take all of it). b every one of (all of us). c colloq. as much as (all of six feet). d colloq. in a state of (all of a dither). 3 one's whole strength or resources (prec. by my, your, etc.). 4 (in games) each (two goals all). —adv. 1 a entirely, quite (dressed all in black). b as an intensifier (stop all this grumbling). 2 colloq. very (went all shy). 3 (foll. by the + compar.) to that, or the utmost, extent (if they go, all the better; that makes it all the worse). □ all along from the beginning. all and sundry everyone. all but very nearly. all for colloq. strongly in favour of. all found with board and lodging provided free. all in colloq. exhausted. all in all everything considered. all manner of every kind of. all of a sudden suddenly. all one (or the same) (usu. foll. by to) a matter of indifference. all out using all one's strength (also (with hyphen) attrib.: all-out effort). all over 1 completely finished. 2 in or on all parts of (mud all over the carpet). 3 colloq. typically (you all over). 4 slang effusively attentive to (a person). all right (predic.) 1 satisfactory; safe and sound; in good condition. 2 satisfactorily (it worked out all right). 3 a expressing consent. b as an intensifier (that's the one all right). all round 1 in all respects. 2 for each person. all the same nevertheless. all there colloq. mentally alert or normal. all the time throughout (despite some contrary expectation etc.). all together all at once; all in one place or in a group (came all together) (cf. ALTOGETHER). all up with hopeless for (a person). at all (with neg. or interrog.) in any way; to any extent (did not swim at all; did you like it at all?). in all in total; altogether. [Old English]

■ **Usage** Note the differences in meaning between all together and altogether: see note at altogether.

Allah /ˈælə/ n. the Muslim and Arab name of God. [Arabic]

allay /əˈleɪ/ v. 1 diminish (fear, suspicion, etc.). 2 alleviate (pain etc.). [Old English a- intensive prefix, LAY[1]]

all-clear n. signal that danger etc. is over.

all comers n.pl. anyone who applies, takes up a challenge, etc.

allegation /ˌælɪˈɡeɪʃ(ə)n/ n. 1 assertion, esp. unproved. 2 alleging. [Latin allego adduce]

allege /əˈledʒ/ v. (-ging) 1 declare, esp. without proof. 2 advance as an argument or excuse. [Latin lis lit- lawsuit]

allegedly /əˈledʒɪdlɪ/ adv. as is alleged.

allegiance /əˈliːdʒ(ə)ns/ n. 1 loyalty (to a person or cause etc.). 2 the duty of a subject. [French: related to LIEGE]

allegory /ˈælɪɡərɪ/ n. (pl. -ies) story whose moral is represented symbolically. □ **allegorical** /ˌælɪˈɡɒrɪk(ə)l/ adj.

allegorize /ˈælɪɡəˌraɪz/ v. (also -ise) (-zing or -sing). [Greek allēgoria other speaking]

allegretto /ˌælɪˈɡretəʊ/ Mus. —adv. & adj. in a fairly brisk tempo. —n. (pl. -s) such a passage or movement. [Italian, diminutive of ALLEGRO]

allegro /əˈleɡrəʊ/ Mus. —adv. & adj. in a brisk tempo. —n. (pl. -s) such a passage or movement. [Italian, = lively]

alleluia /ˌælɪˈluːjə/ (also **hallelujah** /ˌhæl-/) —int. God be praised. —n. song or shout of praise to God. [Hebrew]

Allen key /ˈælən/ n. propr. spanner designed to turn an Allen screw. [Allen, name of the US manufacturer]

Allen screw /ˈælən/ n. propr. screw with a hexagonal socket in the head.

allergic /əˈlɜːdʒɪk/ adj. 1 (foll. by to) a having an allergy to. b colloq. having a strong dislike for. 2 caused by an allergy.

allergy /ˈælədʒɪ/ n. (pl. -ies) 1 adverse reaction to certain substances, esp. particular foods, pollen, fur, or dust. 2 colloq. antipathy. [Greek allos other]

alleviate /əˈliːvɪˌeɪt/ v. (-ting) make (pain etc.) less severe. □ **alleviation** /-ˈeɪʃ(ə)n/ n. [Latin levo raise]

alley /ˈælɪ/ n. (pl. -s) 1 narrow street or passageway. 2 enclosure for skittles, bowling, etc. 3 walk or lane in a park etc. [French aller go]

alliance /əˈlaɪəns/ n. 1 union or agreement to cooperate, esp. of States by treaty or families by marriage. 2 (**Alliance**) political coalition party. 3 relationship; friendship. [French: related to ALLY]

allied /ˈælaɪd/ adj. 1 (also **Allied**) associated in an alliance. 2 connected or related.

alligator /ˈælɪˌɡeɪtə(r)/ n. large reptile of the crocodile family with a head broader and shorter than a crocodile's. [Spanish el lagarto the lizard]

all-in attrib. adj. inclusive of all.

all-in wrestling n. wrestling with few or no restrictions.

alliteration /əˌlɪtəˈreɪʃ(ə)n/ n. repetition of the same letter or sound at the beginning of adjacent or closely connected words (e.g. *cool, calm, and collected*). □ **alliterate** /əˈlɪtəˌreɪt/ v. (-ting). **alliterative** /əˈlɪtərətɪv/ adj. [Latin: related to LETTER]

allocate /ˈæləˌkeɪt/ v. (-ting) (usu. foll. by *to*) assign or devote to (a purpose, person, or place). □ **allocation** /-ˈkeɪʃ(ə)n/ n. [Latin: related to LOCAL]

allot /əˈlɒt/ v. (-tt-) apportion or distribute to (a person), esp. as a share or task (*they were allotted equal sums*). [French *a* to, LOT]

allotment n. **1** small piece of land rented by a local authority for cultivation. **2** share. **3** allotting.

allotropy /əˈlɒtrəpɪ/ n. existence of two or more different physical forms of a chemical element. □ **allotropic** /ˌæləˈtrɒpɪk/ adj. [Greek *allos* different, *tropos* manner]

allow /əˈlaʊ/ v. **1** (often foll. by *to* + infin.) permit. **2** assign a limited amount etc. (*was allowed £500*). **3** (usu. foll. by *for*) provide or set aside for a purpose; add or deduct in consideration (*allow £50 for expenses*; *allow for wastage*). [originally = commend, from French: related to AD-, Latin *laudo* praise, *loco* place]

allowance n. **1** amount or sum allowed, esp. regularly for a stated purpose. **2** amount allowed in reckoning. **3** deduction or discount. □ **make allowances** (often foll. by *for*) **1** consider (mitigating circumstances). **2** make excuses for (a person, bad behaviour, etc.).

alloy /ˈælɔɪ/ –n. **1** mixture of two or more metals. **2** inferior metal mixed esp. with gold or silver. –v. **1** mix (metals). **2** debase by admixture. **3** moderate (*pleasure alloyed with pain*). [French: related to ALLY]

all-purpose attrib. adj. having many uses.

all-right attrib. adj. colloq. acceptable (*an all-right guy*).

all-round attrib. adj. (of a person) versatile.

all-rounder n. versatile person.

All Saints' Day n. 1 Nov., Christian festival in honour of saints.

All Souls' Day n. 2 Nov., Roman Catholic festival with prayers for the souls of the dead.

allspice n. **1** aromatic spice obtained from the berry of the pimento plant. **2** the berry.

all-time attrib. adj. (of a record etc.) unsurpassed.

allude /əˈluːd/ v. (-ding) (foll. by *to*) refer to, esp. indirectly or briefly. [Latin: related to AD-, *ludo* play]

allure /əˈljʊə(r)/ –v. (-ring) attract, charm, or entice. –n. attractiveness, personal charm, fascination. □ **allurement** n. [French: related to AD-, LURE]

allusion /əˈluːʒ(ə)n/ n. (often foll. by *to*) passing or indirect reference. □ **allusive** /əˈluːsɪv/ adj. [Latin: related to ALLUDE]

alluvial /əˈluːvɪəl/ –adj. of alluvium. –n. alluvium, esp. containing a precious metal.

alluvium /əˈluːvɪəm/ n. (pl. **-via**) deposit of usu. fine fertile soil left behind by a flood, esp. in a river valley. [Latin *luo* wash]

ally /ˈælaɪ/ –n. (pl. **-ies**) State, person, etc., formally cooperating or united with another, esp. (also **Ally**) in war. –v. also /əˈlaɪ/ (-ies, -ied) (often *refl.* and foll. by *with*) combine in alliance. [Latin *alligo* bind]

Alma Mater /ˌælmə ˈmɑːtə(r)/ n. one's university, school, or college. [Latin, = bounteous mother]

almanac /ˈɔːlmənæk/ n. (also **almanack**) calendar, usu. with astronomical data. [medieval Latin from Greek]

almighty /ɔːlˈmaɪtɪ/ adj. **1** having complete power. **2** (**the Almighty**) God. **3** slang very great (*almighty crash*). [Old English: related to ALL, MIGHTY]

almond /ˈɑːmənd/ n. **1** nutlike kernel of a fruit allied to the peach and plum. **2** tree bearing this. [Greek *amugdalē*]

almoner /ˈɑːmənə(r)/ n. social worker attached to a hospital. [French: related to ALMS]

■ **Usage** The usual term now is *medical social worker*.

almost /ˈɔːlməʊst/ adv. all but; very nearly. [Old English: related to ALL, MOST]

alms /ɑːmz/ n.pl. hist. donation of money or food to the poor. [Greek *eleēmosunē* pity]

almshouse n. hist. charitable institution for the poor.

aloe /ˈæləʊ/ n. **1** plant of the lily family with toothed fleshy leaves. **2** (in pl.) (in full **bitter aloes**) strong laxative from aloe juice. [Old English from Greek]

aloft /əˈlɒft/ predic. adj. & adv. **1** high up, overhead. **2** upwards. [Old Norse *á lopti* in air]

alone /əˈləʊn/ –predic. adj. **1** without the presence or help of others. **2** lonely (*felt alone*). –adv. only, exclusively. [earlier *al one*: related to ALL, ONE]

along /əˈlɒŋ/ –prep. beside or through (part of) the length of. –adv. **1** onward,

into a more advanced state (*come along*; *getting along nicely*). **2** with oneself or others (*bring a book along*). **3** beside or through part or the whole length of a thing. □ **along with** in addition to; together with. [Old English, originally adj. = facing against]

alongside /əlɒŋ'saɪd/ —*adv.* at or to the side. —*prep.* close to the side of.

aloof /ə'luːf/ —*adj.* distant, unsympathetic. —*adv.* away, apart (*he kept aloof*). [originally *Naut.*, from A² + LUFF]

aloud /ə'laʊd/ *adv.* audibly.

alp *n.* **1 a** high mountain. **b (the Alps)** high range of mountains in Switzerland and adjoining countries. **2** pasture land on a Swiss mountainside. [originally *alps*, from Greek *alpeis*]

alpaca /æl'pækə/ *n.* **1** shaggy S. American mammal related to the llama. **2** its wool; fabric made from this. [Spanish from Quechua]

alpha /'ælfə/ *n.* **1** first letter of the Greek alphabet (A, α). **2** first-class mark for a piece of work etc. □ **alpha and omega** beginning and end. [Latin from Greek]

alphabet /'ælfə,bet/ *n.* **1** set of letters used in writing a language. **2** symbols or signs for these. □ **alphabetical** /-'betɪk(ə)l/ *adj.* [Greek ALPHA, BETA]

alphanumeric /,ælfənju:'merɪk/ *adj.* containing both letters and numbers.

alpha particle *n.* helium nucleus emitted by a radioactive substance.

alpine /'ælpaɪn/ —*adj.* of mountainous regions or (**Alpine**) the Alps. —*n.* **1** plant growing in mountainous regions. **2** = ROCK-PLANT. [Latin: related to ALP]

already /ɔːl'redɪ/ *adv.* **1** before the time in question (*I knew that already*). **2** as early or as soon as this (*is back already*). [from ALL, READY]

alright /ɔːl'raɪt/ *adv.* = *all right* (see ALL).

■ **Usage** Although widely used, *alright* is still non-standard and is considered incorrect by many people.

Alsatian /æl'seɪʃ(ə)n/ *n.* large dog of a breed of wolfhound (also called GERMAN SHEPHERD). [Latin *Alsatia* Alsace]

also /'ɔːlsəʊ/ *adv.* in addition, besides. [Old English: related to ALL, SO¹]

also-ran *n.* **1** loser in a race. **2** undistinguished person.

altar /'ɔːltə(r)/ *n.* **1** table or flat block for sacrifice or offering to a deity. **2** Communion table. [Latin *altus* high]

altarpiece *n.* painting etc. above or behind an altar.

alter /'ɔːltə(r)/ *v.* make or become different; change. □ **alteration** /-'reɪʃ(ə)n/ *n.* [Latin *alter* other]

altercate /'ɔːltə,keɪt/ *v.* (**-ting**) (often foll. by *with*) dispute, wrangle. □ **altercation** /-'keɪʃ(ə)n/ *n.* [Latin]

alter ego /,ɔːltər 'iːgəʊ/ *n.* (*pl.* **-s**) **1** one's hidden or second self. **2** intimate friend. [Latin, = other self]

alternate —*v.* /'ɔːltə,neɪt/ (**-ting**) **1** (often foll. by *with*) occur or cause to occur by turns. **2** (foll. by *between*) go repeatedly from one to another (*alternated between hope and fear*). —*adj.* /ɔːl'tɜːnət/ **1** (with noun in *pl.*) every other (*on alternate days*). **2** (of things of two kinds) alternating (*alternate joy and misery*). □ **alternately** /-'tɜːnətlɪ/ *adv.* **alternation** /-'neɪʃ(ə)n/ *n.* [Latin *alterno* do by turns: related to ALTER]

■ **Usage** See note at *alternative*.

alternate angles *n.pl.* two angles formed alternately on two sides of a line.

alternating current *n.* electric current reversing its direction at regular intervals.

alternative /ɔːl'tɜːnətɪv/ —*adj.* **1** available as another choice (*alternative route*). **2** unconventional (*alternative medicine*). —*n.* **1** any of two or more possibilities. **2** choice (*had no alternative but to go*). □ **alternatively** *adv.*

■ **Usage** The adjective *alternative* should not be confused with *alternate*, as in 'there will be a dance on alternate Saturdays'.

alternator /'ɔːltə,neɪtə(r)/ *n.* dynamo that generates an alternating current.

although /ɔːl'ðəʊ/ *conj.* = THOUGH. [from ALL, THOUGH]

altimeter /'æltɪ,miːtə(r)/ *n.* instrument indicating altitude reached.

altitude /'æltɪ,tjuːd/ *n.* height, esp. of an object above sea level or above the horizon. [Latin *altus* high]

alto /'æltəʊ/ *n.* (*pl.* **-s**) **1** = CONTRALTO. **2 a** highest adult male singing-voice, above tenor. **b** singer with this voice. **3** instrument pitched second- or third-highest in its family. [Italian *alto* (*canto*) high (singing)]

altogether /,ɔːltə'geðə(r)/ *adv.* **1** totally, completely. **2** on the whole. **3** in total. □ **in the altogether** *colloq.* naked. [from ALL, TOGETHER]

■ **Usage** Note that *altogether* means 'in total', whereas *all together* means 'all at once' or 'all in one place'. The phrases *six rooms altogether* (in total) and *six rooms all together* (in one place) illustrate the difference.

altruism /'æltruː,ɪz(ə)m/ *n.* unselfishness as a principle of action. □ **altruis**

n. **altruistic** /ˌæltruː'ɪstɪk/ *adj.* [Italian *altrui* somebody else]

alum /'æləm/ *n.* double sulphate of aluminium and potassium. [Latin *alumen -min-*]

alumina /ə'luːmɪnə/ *n.* aluminium oxide occurring naturally as corundum and emery.

aluminium /ˌæljʊ'mɪnɪəm/ *n.* (*US* **aluminum** /ə'luːmɪnəm/) silvery light and malleable metallic element resistant to tarnishing by air.

aluminize /ə'luːmɪˌnaɪz/ *v.* (also **-ise**) (**-zing** or **-sing**) coat with aluminium.

alumnus /ə'lʌmnəs/ *n.* (*pl.* **alumni** /-naɪ/; *fem.* **alumna**, *pl.* **alumnae** /-niː/) former pupil or student. [Latin, = nursling, pupil]

always /'ɔːlweɪz/ *adv.* **1** at all times; on all occasions. **2** whatever the circumstances. **3** repeatedly, often. [from ALL, WAY]

alyssum /'ælɪsəm/ *n.* plant with small usu. yellow or white flowers. [Greek, = curing madness]

Alzheimer's disease /'ælts,haɪməz/ *n.* brain disorder causing senility. [*Alzheimer*, name of a neurologist]

AM *abbr.* amplitude modulation.

Am *symb.* americium.

am *1st person sing. present* of BE.

a.m. *abbr.* before noon. [Latin *ante meridiem*]

amalgam /ə'mælgəm/ *n.* **1** mixture or blend. **2** alloy of mercury and another metal, used esp. in dentistry. [Greek *malagma* an emollient]

amalgamate /ə'mælgəˌmeɪt/ *v.* (**-ting**) **1** mix, unite. **2** (of metals) alloy with mercury. □ **amalgamation** /-'meɪʃ(ə)n/ *n.* [medieval Latin: related to AMALGAM]

amanuensis /əˌmænjuː'ensɪs/ *n.* (*pl.* **-enses** /-siːz/) literary assistant, esp. writing from dictation. [Latin *a manu* 'at hand']

amaranth /'æməˌrænθ/ *n.* **1** plant with small green, red, or purple tinted flowers. **2** imaginary unfading flower. **3** purple colour. □ **amaranthine** /-'rænθaɪn/ *adj.* [Greek *amarantos* unfading]

amaryllis /ˌæmə'rɪlɪs/ *n.* bulbous plant with lily-like flowers. [Greek, a girl's name]

amass /ə'mæs/ *v.* heap together; accumulate. [French: related to AD-, MASS¹]

amateur /'æmətə(r)/ *n.* person who engages in a pursuit as a pastime rather than a profession, or performs with limited skill. □ **amateurish** *adj.* **amateurism** *n.* [Latin *amator* lover: related to AMATORY]

amatory /'æmətərɪ/ *adj.* of sexual love. [Latin *amo* love]

amaze /ə'meɪz/ *v.* (**-zing**) surprise greatly, fill with wonder. □ **amazement** *n.* **amazing** *adj.* [earlier *amase* from Old English *āmasod*]

Amazon /'æməz(ə)n/ *n.* **1** female warrior of a mythical race in the Black Sea area. **2** (**amazon**) large, strong, or athletic woman. □ **Amazonian** /-'zəʊnɪən/ *adj.* [Latin from Greek]

ambassador /æm'bæsədə(r)/ *n.* **1** diplomat sent to live abroad to represent his or her country's interests. **2** promoter (*ambassador of peace*). □ **ambassadorial** /-'dɔːrɪəl/ *adj.* [Latin *ambactus* servant]

amber –*n.* **1 a** yellow translucent fossilized resin used in jewellery. **b** colour of this. **2** yellow traffic-light meaning caution. –*adj.* of or like amber. [French from Arabic]

ambergris /'æmbəgrɪs/ *n.* waxlike secretion of the sperm whale, found floating in tropical seas and used in perfumes. [French, = grey amber]

ambidextrous /ˌæmbɪ'dekstrəs/ *adj.* able to use either hand equally well. [Latin *ambi-* on both sides, DEXTER]

ambience /'æmbɪəns/ *n.* surroundings or atmosphere. [Latin *ambio* go round]

ambient *adj.* surrounding.

ambiguous /æm'bɪgjʊəs/ *adj.* **1** having an obscure or double meaning. **2** difficult to classify. □ **ambiguity** /-'gjuːɪtɪ/ *n.* (*pl.* **-ies**). [Latin *ambi-* both ways, *ago* drive]

ambit /'æmbɪt/ *n.* scope, extent, or bounds. [Latin: related to AMBIENCE]

ambition /æm'bɪʃ(ə)n/ *n.* **1** determination to succeed. **2** object of this. [Latin, = canvassing: related to AMBIENCE]

ambitious *adj.* **1** full of ambition or high aims. **2** (foll. by *of*, or *to* + infin.) strongly determined.

ambivalence /æm'bɪvələns/ *n.* coexistence of opposing feelings. □ **ambivalent** *adj.* [Latin *ambo* both, EQUIVALENCE]

amble /'æmb(ə)l/ –*v.* (**-ling**) move at an easy pace. –*n.* such a pace. [Latin *ambulo* walk]

ambrosia /æm'brəʊzɪə/ *n.* **1** (in classical mythology) the food of the gods. **2** sublimely delicious food etc. [Greek, = elixir of life]

ambulance /'æmbjʊləns/ *n.* **1** vehicle equipped for conveying patients to hospital. **2** mobile hospital serving an army. [Latin: related to AMBLE]

ambulatory /'æmbjʊlətərɪ/ –*adj.* **1** of or for walking. **2** movable. –*n.* (*pl.* **-ies**)

arcade or cloister. [Latin: related to AMBLE]

ambuscade /ˌæmbəˈskeɪd/ n. & v. (-**ding**) = AMBUSH.

ambush /ˈæmbʊʃ/ —n. **1** surprise attack by persons hiding. **2** hiding-place for this. —v. attack from an ambush; waylay. [French: related to IN-[1], BUSH[1]]

ameliorate /əˈmiːlɪəˌreɪt/ v. (-**ting**) make or become better. □ **amelioration** /əˌmiːlɪəˈreɪʃ(ə)n/ n. **ameliorative** adj. [from AD-, Latin melior better]

amen /ɑːˈmen/ int. (esp. at the end of a prayer etc.) so be it. [Church Latin from Hebrew, = certainly]

amenable /əˈmiːnəb(ə)l/ adj. **1** responsive, docile. **2** (often foll. by to) answerable to law etc. [French: related to AD-, Latin mino drive animals]

amend /əˈmend/ v. **1** make minor alterations in to improve. **2** correct an error in (a document etc.). [Latin: related to EMEND]

■ **Usage** Amend is often confused with emend, a more technical word used in the context of textual correction.

amendment n. minor alteration or addition in a document, resolution, etc.

amends n. □ **make amends** (often foll. by for) compensate (for).

amenity /əˈmiːnɪtɪ/ n. (pl. -**ies**) **1** pleasant or useful feature or facility. **2** pleasantness (of a place etc.). [Latin amoenus pleasant]

American /əˈmerɪkən/ —adj. of America, esp. the United States. —n. **1** native, citizen, or inhabitant of America, esp. the US. **2** English as used in the US. □ **Americanize** v. (also **-ise**) (**-zing** or **-sing**). [name of navigator Amerigo Vespucci]

American dream n. ideal of democracy and prosperity.

American football n. football evolved from Rugby.

American Indian see INDIAN.

Americanism n. word etc. of US origin or usage.

americium /ˌæməˈrɪsɪəm/ n. artificial radioactive metallic element. [America, where first made]

Amerind /ˈæmərɪnd/ adj. & n. (also **Amerindian** /-ˈrɪndɪən/) = AMERICAN INDIAN (see INDIAN).

amethyst /ˈæməθɪst/ n. semiprecious stone of a violet or purple variety of quartz. [Greek, = preventing drunkenness]

Amharic /æmˈhærɪk/ —n. official and commercial language of Ethiopia. —adj. of this language. [Amhara, region of Ethiopia]

amiable /ˈeɪmɪəb(ə)l/ adj. (esp. of a person) friendly and pleasant, likeable. □ **amiably** adv. [Latin: related to AMICABLE]

amicable /ˈæmɪkəb(ə)l/ adj. (esp. of an arrangement, relations, etc.) friendly. □ **amicably** adv. [Latin amicus friend]

amid /əˈmɪd/ prep. in the middle of, among. [Old English: related to ON, MID]

amidships adv. in or into the middle of a ship. [from AMID, alternative form midships]

amidst var. of AMID.

amine /ˈeɪmiːn/ n. compound formed from ammonia by replacement of one or more hydrogen atoms by an organic radical or radicals.

amino acid /əˈmiːnəʊ/ n. Biochem. any of a group of nitrogenous organic acids occurring naturally in plant and animal tissues and forming the basic constituents of proteins. [from AMINE, ACID]

amir var. of EMIR.

amiss /əˈmɪs/ —predic. adj. wrong, out of order. —adv. wrong(ly), inappropriately (everything went amiss). □ **take amiss** be offended by. [Old Norse à mis so as to miss]

amity /ˈæmɪtɪ/ n. friendship. [Latin amicus friend]

ammeter /ˈæmɪtə(r)/ n. instrument for measuring electric current in amperes. [from AMPERE, -METER]

ammo /ˈæməʊ/ n. slang ammunition. [abbreviation]

ammonia /əˈməʊnɪə/ n. **1** pungent strongly alkaline gas. **2** (in general use) solution of ammonia in water. [as SAL AMMONIAC]

ammonite /ˈæməˌnaɪt/ n. coil-shaped fossil shell. [Latin, = horn of Jupiter Ammon]

ammunition /ˌæmjʊˈnɪʃ(ə)n/ n. **1** supply of bullets, shells, grenades, etc. **2** information usable in an argument. [French la MUNITION taken as l'ammu-]

amnesia /æmˈniːzɪə/ n. loss of memory. □ **amnesiac** /-zɪˌæk/ n. [Latin from Greek]

amnesty /ˈæmnɪstɪ/ —n. (pl. -**ies**) general pardon, esp. for political offences. —v. (-**ies**, -**ied**) grant an amnesty to. [Greek amnēstia oblivion]

amniocentesis /ˌæmnɪəʊsenˈtiːsɪs/ n. (pl. -**teses** /-siːz/) sampling of amniotic fluid to detect foetal abnormality. [from AMNION, Greek kentēsis pricking]

amnion /ˈæmnɪən/ n. (pl. amnia) innermost membrane enclosing an embryo. □ **amniotic** /-ˈɒtɪk/ adj. [Greek, = caul]

amoeba /əˈmiːbə/ n. (pl. -**s**) microscopic aquatic amorphous one-celled organism. □ **amoebic** adj. [Greek, = change]

amok /ə'mɒk/ *adv.* □ **run amok** (or **amuck**) run wild. [Malay]

among /ə'mʌŋ/ *prep.* (also **amongst**) **1** surrounded by, with (*lived among the trees*; *be among friends*). **2** included in (*among us were dissidents*). **3** in the category of (*among his best works*). **4 a** between; shared by (*divide it among you*). **b** from the joint resources of (*among us we can manage it*). **5** with one another (*talked among themselves*). [Old English, = in a crowd]

amoral /eɪ'mɒr(ə)l/ *adj.* **1** beyond morality. **2** without moral principles.

amorous /'æmərəs/ *adj.* of, showing, or feeling sexual love. [Latin *amor* love]

amorphous /ə'mɔ:fəs/ *adj.* **1** of no definite shape. **2** vague. **3** *Mineral. & Chem.* non-crystalline. [Greek *a-* not, *morphē* form]

amortize /ə'mɔ:taɪz/ *v.* (also **-ise**) (**-zing** or **-sing**) gradually extinguish (a debt) by regular instalments. [Latin *ad mortem* to death]

amount /ə'maʊnt/ — *n.* quantity, esp. a total in number, size, value, extent, etc. — *v.* (foll. by *to*) be equivalent to in number, significance, etc. [Latin *ad montem* upward]

amour /ə'mʊə(r)/ *n.* (esp. secret) love affair. [French, = love]

amour propre /æ,mʊə 'prɒpr/ *n.* self-respect. [French]

amp[1] *n.* ampere. [abbreviation]

amp[2] *n. colloq.* amplifier. [abbreviation]

ampelopsis /,æmpɪ'lɒpsɪs/ *n.* (*pl.* same) climbing plant related to the vine. [Greek *ampelos* vine, *opsis* appearance]

amperage /'æmpərɪdʒ/ *n.* strength of an electric current in amperes.

ampere /'æmpeə(r)/ *n.* SI base unit of electric current. [*Ampère*, name of a physicist]

ampersand /'æmpə,sænd/ *n.* the sign '&' (= *and*). [corruption of *and* PER SE *and*]

amphetamine /æm'fetə,mi:n/ *n.* synthetic drug used esp. as a stimulant. [abbreviation of chemical name]

amphibian /æm'fɪbɪən/ — *adj.* of a class of vertebrates (e.g. frogs) with an aquatic larval stage followed by a terrestrial adult stage. — *n.* **1** vertebrate of this class. **2** vehicle able to operate both on land and in water. [Greek *amphi-* both, *bios* life]

amphibious *adj.* **1** living or operating on land and in water. **2** involving military forces landed from the sea.

amphitheatre /'æmfɪ,θɪətə(r)/ *n.* esp. circular unroofed building with tiers of seats surrounding a central space. [Greek *amphi-* round]

amphora /'æmfərə/ *n.* (*pl.* **-phorae** /-,ri:/) narrow-necked Greek or Roman vessel with two handles. [Greek *amphoreus*]

ample /'æmp(ə)l/ *adj.* (**ampler**, **amplest**) **1 a** plentiful, abundant, extensive. **b** *euphem.* large, stout. **2** more than enough. □ **amply** *adv.* [Latin *amplus*]

amplifier /'æmplɪ,faɪə(r)/ *n.* electronic device for increasing the strength of electrical signals, esp. for conversion into sound.

amplify /'æmplɪ,faɪ/ *v.* (**-ies**, **-ied**) **1** increase the strength of (sound, electrical signals, etc.). **2** add detail to, expand (a story etc.). □ **amplification** /-fɪ'keɪʃ(ə)n/ *n.* [Latin: related to AMPLE]

amplitude /'æmplɪ,tju:d/ *n.* **1** maximum departure from average of an oscillation, alternating current, etc. **2** spaciousness; abundance. [Latin: related to AMPLE]

amplitude modulation *n.* modulation of a wave by variation of its amplitude.

ampoule /'æmpu:l/ *n.* small sealed capsule holding a solution for injection. [French: related to AMPULLA]

ampulla /æm'pʊlə/ *n.* (*pl.* **-pullae** /-li:/) **1** Roman globular flask with two handles. **2** ecclesiastical vessel. [Latin]

amputate /'æmpju,teɪt/ *v.* (**-ting**) cut off surgically (a limb etc.). □ **amputation** /-'teɪʃ(ə)n/ *n.* **amputee** /-'ti:/ *n.* [Latin *amb-* about, *puto* prune]

amuck var. of AMOK.

amulet /'æmjʊlɪt/ *n.* charm worn against evil. [Latin]

amuse /ə'mju:z/ *v.* (**-sing**) **1** cause to laugh or smile. **2** interest or occupy. □ **amusing** *adj.* [French *a* cause to, *muser* stare]

amusement *n.* **1** thing that amuses. **2** being amused. **3** mechanical device (e.g. a roundabout) for entertainment at a fairground etc.

amusement arcade *n.* indoor area with slot-machines.

an see A[1].

an- see A-.

-an *suffix* (also **-ian**) forming adjectives and nouns, esp. from names of places, systems, classes, etc. (*Mexican*; *Anglican*; *crustacean*). [French *-ain*, Latin *-anus*]

Anabaptist /,ænə'bæptɪst/ *n.* member of a religious group believing in baptism only of adults. [Greek *ana* again]

anabolic steroid /,ænə'bɒlɪk/ *n.* synthetic steroid hormone used to increase muscle size.

anabolism /ə'næbə,lɪz(ə)m/ *n.* synthesis of complex molecules in living organisms from simpler ones together

with the storage of energy. [Greek *anabolē* ascent]

anachronism /ə'nækrə,nɪz(ə)m/ *n.* **1 a** attribution of a custom, event, etc., to the wrong period. **b** thing thus attributed. **2** out-of-date person or thing. □ **anachronistic** /-'nɪstɪk/ *adj.* [Greek *ana-* against, *khronos* time]

anaconda /,ænə'kɒndə/ *n.* large nonpoisonous snake killing its prey by constriction. [Sinhalese]

anaemia /ə'niːmɪə/ *n.* (*US* **anemia**) deficiency of red blood cells or their haemoglobin, causing pallor and weariness. [Greek, = want of blood]

anaemic /ə'niːmɪk/ *adj.* (*US* **anemic**) **1** of or suffering from anaemia. **2** pale, listless.

anaesthesia /,ænɪs'θiːzɪə/ *n.* (*US* **anes-**) absence of sensation, esp. artificially induced before surgery. [Greek]

anaesthetic /,ænɪs'θetɪk/ (*US* **anes-**) —*n.* substance producing anaesthesia. —*adj.* producing anaesthesia.

anaesthetist /ə'niːsθətɪst/ *n.* (*US* **anes-**) specialist in the administration of anaesthetics.

anaesthetize /ə'niːsθə,taɪz/ *v.* (*US* **anes-**) (also **-ise**) (**-zing** or **-sing**) administer an anaesthetic to.

anagram /'ænə,græm/ *n.* word or phrase formed by transposing the letters of another. [Greek *ana* again, *gramma* letter]

anal /'eɪn(ə)l/ *adj.* of the anus.

analgesia /,ænəl'dʒiːzɪə/ *n.* absence or relief of pain. [Greek]

analgesic —*adj.* relieving pain. —*n.* analgesic drug.

analog *US* var. of ANALOGUE.

analogize /ə'nælə,dʒaɪz/ *v.* (also **-ise**) (**-zing** or **-sing**) use, or represent or explain by, analogy.

analogous /ə'næləgəs/ *adj.* (usu. foll. by *to*) partially similar or parallel. [Greek *analogos* proportionate]

analogue /'ænə,lɒg/ *n.* (*US* **analog**) **1** analogous thing. **2** (*attrib.*) (usu. **analog**) (of a computer etc.) using physical variables, e.g. voltage, to represent numbers (cf. DIGITAL).

analogy /ə'nælədʒɪ/ *n.* (*pl.* **-ies**) **1** correspondence; partial similarity. **2** arguing or reasoning from parallel cases. □ **analogical** /,ænə'lɒdʒɪk(ə)l/ *adj.* [Greek *analogia* proportion]

analyse /'ænə,laɪz/ *v.* (*US* **analyze**) (**-sing** or **-zing**) **1** examine in detail; ascertain the constituents of (a substance, sentence, etc.). **2** psychoanalyse.

analysis /ə'nælɪsɪs/ *n.* (*pl.* **-lyses** /-,siːz/) **1 a** detailed examination of elements or structure. **b** statement of the result of this. **2** *Chem.* determination of the constituent parts of a mixture or compound. **3** psychoanalysis. [Greek *ana* up, *luō* loose]

analyst /'ænəlɪst/ *n.* **1** person skilled in (esp. chemical or computer) analysis. **2** psychoanalyst.

analytical /,ænə'lɪtɪk(ə)l/ *adj.* (also **analytic**) of or using analysis.

analyze *US* var. of ANALYSE.

anapaest /'ænə,piːst/ *n.* metrical foot consisting of two short syllables followed by one long syllable (∪∪–). [Greek *anapaistos* reversed (dactyl)]

anarchism /'ænə,kɪz(ə)m/ *n.* political theory that all government and laws should be abolished. [French: related to ANARCHY]

anarchist /'ænəkɪst/ *n.* advocate of anarchism. □ **anarchistic** /-'kɪstɪk/ *adj.*

anarchy /'ænəkɪ/ *n.* disorder, esp. political. □ **anarchic** /ə'nɑːkɪk/ *adj.* [Greek *an-* without, *arkhē* rule]

anathema /ə'næθəmə/ *n.* (*pl.* **-s**) **1** detested thing (*is anathema to me*). **2** ecclesiastical curse. [Greek, = thing devoted (i.e. to evil)]

anathematize *v.* (also **-ise**) (**-zing** or **-sing**) curse.

anatomy /ə'nætəmɪ/ *n.* (*pl.* **-ies**) **1** science of animal or plant structure. **2** such a structure. **3** analysis. □ **anatomical** /,ænə'tɒmɪk(ə)l/ *adj.* **anatomist** *n.* [Greek *ana-* up, *temnō* cut]

anatto var. of ANNATTO.

ANC *abbr.* African National Congress.

-ance *suffix* forming nouns expressing: **1** quality or state or an instance of one (*arrogance*; *resemblance*). **2** action (*assistance*). [French *-ance*, Latin *-antia*]

ancestor /'ænsestə(r)/ *n.* **1** person, animal, or plant from which another has descended or evolved. **2** prototype or forerunner. [Latin *ante-* before, *cedo* go]

ancestral /æn'sestr(ə)l/ *adj.* belonging to or inherited from one's ancestors.

ancestry /'ænsestrɪ/ *n.* (*pl.* **-ies**) **1** family descent, lineage. **2** ancestors collectively.

anchor /'æŋkə(r)/ —*n.* **1** heavy metal weight used to moor a ship or a balloon. **2** stabilizing thing. —*v.* **1** secure with an anchor. **2** fix firmly. **3** cast anchor. **4** be moored by an anchor. [Greek *agkura*]

anchorage *n.* **1** place for anchoring. **2** anchoring or lying at anchor.

anchorite /'æŋkə,raɪt/ *n.* hermit; religious recluse. [Greek *anakhōreō* retire]

anchorman *n.* coordinator, esp. as compère in a broadcast.

anchovy /'æntʃəvɪ/ *n.* (*pl.* **-ies**) small strong-flavoured fish of the herring family. [Spanish and Portuguese *anchova*]

ancien régime /ɑ̃,sjæ reˈʒiːm/ n. (pl. **anciens régimes** pronunc. same) **1** political and social system of pre-Revolutionary (before 1787) France. **2** any superseded regime. [French, = old rule]

ancient /ˈeɪnʃ(ə)nt/ adj. **1** of long ago, esp. before the fall of the Roman Empire in the West. **2** having lived or existed long. □ **the ancients** people of ancient times, esp. the Greeks and Romans. [Latin *ante* before]

ancillary /ænˈsɪlərɪ/ —adj. **1** (esp. of health workers) providing essential support. **2** (often foll. by *to*) subordinate, subservient. —n. (pl. **-ies**) **1** ancillary worker. **2** auxiliary or accessory. [Latin *ancilla* handmaid]

-ancy suffix forming nouns denoting a quality (*constancy*) or state (*infancy*). [Latin *-antia*]

and /ænd, ənd/ conj. **1 a** connecting words, clauses, or sentences, to be taken jointly (*you and I*). **b** implying progression (*better and better*). **c** implying causation (*she hit him and he cried*). **d** implying great duration (*cried and cried*). **e** implying a great number (*miles and miles*). **f** implying addition (*two and two*). **g** implying variety (*there are books and books*). **2** colloq. to (*try and come*). **3** in relation to (*Britain and the EC*). □ **and/or** either or both of two stated alternatives. [Old English]

andante /ænˈdæntɪ/ *Mus.* —adv. & adj. in a moderately slow tempo. —n. such a passage or movement. [Italian, = going]

andiron /ˈænd,aɪən/ n. metal stand (usu. one of a pair) for supporting logs in a fireplace. [French *andier*]

androgynous /ænˈdrɒdʒɪnəs/ adj. **1** hermaphrodite. **2** *Bot.* with stamens and pistils in the same flower. [Greek *anēr andr-* man, *gunē* woman]

android /ˈændrɔɪd/ n. robot with a human appearance. [Greek *anēr andr-* man, -OID]

anecdote /ˈænɪk,dəʊt/ n. short, esp. true, account or story. □ **anecdotal** /-ˈdəʊt(ə)l/ adj. [Greek *anekdota* things unpublished]

anemia US var. of ANÆMIA.
anemic US var. of ANÆMIC.

anemometer /,ænɪˈmɒmɪtə(r)/ n. instrument for measuring wind force. [Greek *anemos* wind]

anemone /əˈnemənɪ/ n. plant of the buttercup family, with vividly-coloured flowers. [Greek, = wind-flower]

aneroid /ˈænə,rɔɪd/ —adj. (of a barometer) measuring air-pressure by its action on the lid of a box containing a vacuum. —n. aneroid barometer. [Greek *a-* not, *nēros* water]

anesthesia etc. US var. of ANAESTHESIA etc.

aneurysm /ˈænjʊ,rɪz(ə)m/ n. (also **aneurism**) excessive localized enlargement of an artery. [Greek *aneurunō* widen]

anew /əˈnjuː/ adv. **1** again. **2** in a different way. [earlier *of newe*]

angel /ˈeɪndʒ(ə)l/ n. **1 a** attendant or messenger of God. **b** representation of this in human form with wings. **2** virtuous or obliging person. **3** *slang* financial backer of a play etc. [Greek *aggelos* messenger]

angel cake n. light sponge cake.
angel-fish n. fish with winglike fins.
angelic /ænˈdʒelɪk/ adj. of or like an angel. □ **angelically** adv.

angelica /ænˈdʒelɪkə/ n. aromatic plant or its candied stalks. [medieval Latin, = angelic (herb)]

angelus /ˈændʒɪləs/ n. **1** Roman Catholic prayers commemorating the Incarnation, said at morning, noon, and sunset. **2** bell announcing this. [Latin *Angelus domini* (= the angel of the Lord), opening words]

anger /ˈæŋgə(r)/ —n. extreme or passionate displeasure. —v. make angry. [Old Norse *angr* grief]

angina /ænˈdʒaɪnə/ n. (in full **angina pectoris** /ˈpektərɪs/) chest pain brought on by exertion, caused by an inadequate blood supply to the heart. [Greek *agkhonē* strangling]

angiosperm /ˈændʒɪə,spɜːm/ n. plant producing flowers and reproducing by seeds enclosed within a carpel, including herbaceous plants, grasses, and most trees. [Greek *aggeion* vessel]

Angle /ˈæŋg(ə)l/ n. (usu. in pl.) member of a N. German tribe that settled in E. Britain in the 5th c. [Latin *Anglus*, from the name *Angul* in Germany]

angle[1] /ˈæŋg(ə)l/ —n. **1** space between two meeting lines or surfaces, esp. as measured in degrees. **2** corner. **3** point of view. —v. (**-ling**) **1** move or place obliquely. **2** present (information) in a biased way. [Latin *angulus*]

angle[2] /ˈæŋg(ə)l/ v. (**-ling**) **1** fish with hook and line. **2** (foll. by *for*) seek an objective indirectly (*angled for a loan*). □ **angler** n. [Old English]

Anglican /ˈæŋglɪkən/ —adj. of the Church of England. —n. member of the Anglican Church. □ **Anglicanism** n. [Latin *Anglicanus*: related to ANGLE]

Anglicism /ˈæŋglɪ,sɪz(ə)m/ n. peculiarly English word or custom. [Latin *Anglicus*: related to ANGLE]

Anglicize /ˈæŋglɪ,saɪz/ v. (also **-ise**) (**-zing** or **-sing**) make English in character etc.

Anglo- *comb. form* 1 English. 2 of English origin. 3 English or British and. [Latin: related to ANGLE]

Anglo-Catholic /ˌæŋɡləʊˈkæθəlɪk/ —*adj.* of a High Church Anglican wing emphasizing its Catholic tradition. —*n.* member of this group.

Anglo-French /ˌæŋɡləʊˈfrentʃ/ —*adj.* English (or British) and French. —*n.* French language as developed in England after the Norman Conquest.

Anglo-Indian /ˌæŋɡləʊˈɪndɪən/ —*adj.* 1 of England and India. 2 of British descent but Indian residence. —*n.* Anglo-Indian person.

Anglo-Norman /ˌæŋɡləʊˈnɔːmən/ —*adj.* English and Norman. —*n.* Norman dialect used in England after the Norman Conquest.

Anglophile /ˈæŋɡləʊˌfaɪl/ *n.* person who greatly admires England or the English.

Anglo-Saxon /ˌæŋɡləʊˈsæks(ə)n/ —*adj.* 1 of the English Saxons before the Norman Conquest. 2 of English descent. —*n.* 1 Anglo-Saxon person. 2 Old English. 3 *colloq.* plain (esp. crude) English.

angora /æŋˈɡɔːrə/ *n.* 1 fabric or wool from the hair of the angora goat or rabbit. 2 long-haired variety of cat, goat, or rabbit. [*Angora* (= Ankara) in Turkey]

angostura /ˌæŋɡəˈstjʊərə/ *n.* aromatic bitter bark used as a flavouring. [*Angostura* (= Ciudad Bolívar) in Venezuela]

angry /ˈæŋɡrɪ/ *adj.* (-**ier**, -**iest**) 1 feeling, showing, or suggesting anger (*angry sky*). 2 (of a wound etc.) inflamed, painful. □ **angrily** *adv.*

angst /æŋst/ *n.* anxiety, neurotic fear; guilt, remorse. [German]

angstrom /ˈæŋstrəm/ *n.* unit of length equal to 10⁻¹⁰ metre. [*Ångström*, name of a physicist]

anguish /ˈæŋɡwɪʃ/ *n.* 1 severe mental suffering. 2 pain, agony. □ **anguished** *adj.* [Latin *angustia* tightness]

angular /ˈæŋɡjʊlə(r)/ *adj.* 1 having sharp corners or (of a person) features. 2 forming an angle. 3 measured by angle (*angular distance*). □ **angularity** /-ˈlærɪtɪ/ *n.* [Latin: related to ANGLE¹]

anhydrous /ænˈhaɪdrəs/ *adj. Chem.* without water, esp. water of crystallization. [Greek *an-* without, *hudōr* water]

aniline /ˈænɪˌliːn/ *n.* colourless oily liquid used in making dyes, drugs, and plastics. [German *Anil* indigo, former source]

animadvert /ˌænɪmædˈvɜːt/ *v.* (foll. by *on*) *literary* criticize, censure. □ **animadversion** *n.* [Latin *animus* mind, ADVERSE]

animal /ˈænɪm(ə)l/ —*n.* 1 living organism, esp. other than man, which feeds and usu. has sense-organs and a nervous system and can move quickly. 2 brutish person. —*adj.* 1 of or like an animal. 2 bestial; carnal. [Latin *animalis* having breath]

animalism *n.* 1 nature and activity of animals. 2 belief that humans are mere animals.

animality /ˌænɪˈmælɪtɪ/ *n.* 1 the animal world. 2 animal behaviour.

animalize /ˈænɪməˌlaɪz/ *v.* (also -**ise**) (-**zing** or -**sing**) make (a person) bestial, sensualize.

animate —*adj.* /ˈænɪmət/ 1 having life. 2 lively. —*v.* /ˈænɪˌmeɪt/ (-**ting**) 1 enliven. 2 give life to. [Latin *anima* breath]

animated /ˈænɪˌmeɪtɪd/ *adj.* 1 lively, vigorous. 2 having life. 3 (of a film etc.) using animation.

animation /ˌænɪˈmeɪʃ(ə)n/ *n.* 1 vivacity, ardour. 2 being alive. 3 technique of producing a moving picture from a sequence of drawings or puppet poses etc.

animism /ˈænɪˌmɪz(ə)m/ *n.* belief that inanimate and natural phenomena have souls. □ **animist** *n.* **animistic** /-ˈmɪstɪk/ *adj.*

animosity /ˌænɪˈmɒsɪtɪ/ *n.* (*pl.* -**ies**) spirit or feeling of hostility. [Latin: related to ANIMUS]

animus /ˈænɪməs/ *n.* animosity, ill feeling. [Latin, = spirit, mind]

anion /ˈænˌaɪən/ *n.* negatively charged ion. □ **anionic** /-ˈɒnɪk/ *adj.* [Greek *ana* up, ION]

anise /ˈænɪs/ *n.* plant with aromatic seeds. [Greek *anison*]

aniseed /ˈænɪˌsiːd/ *n.* seed of the anise, used for flavouring.

ankle /ˈæŋk(ə)l/ *n.* 1 joint connecting the foot with the leg. 2 this part of the leg. [Old Norse]

anklet /ˈæŋklɪt/ *n.* ornament or fetter worn round the ankle.

ankylosis /ˌæŋkɪˈləʊsɪs/ *n.* stiffening of a joint by fusion of the bones. [Greek *agkulos* crooked]

annals /ˈæn(ə)lz/ *n.pl.* 1 narrative of events year by year. 2 historical records. □ **annalist** *n.* [Latin *annus* year]

annatto /əˈnætəʊ/ *n.* (also **anatto**) orange-red dye from the pulp of a tropical fruit, used for colouring foods. [Carib name of the fruit-tree]

anneal /əˈniːl/ *v.* heat (metal or glass) and cool slowly, esp. to toughen it. [Old English *ælan* bake]

annelid /ˈænəlɪd/ *n.* segmented worm, e.g. the earthworm. [Latin *anulus* ring]

annex /æˈneks/ *v.* 1 (often foll. by *to*) add as a subordinate part. 2 incorporate

(territory) into one's own. **3** add as a condition or consequence. **4** *colloq.* take without right. □ **annexation** /-'seɪʃ(ə)n/ *n.* [Latin *necto* bind]

annexe /'æneks/ *n.* **1** separate or added building. **2** addition to a document.

annihilate /ə'naɪəˌleɪt/ *v.* (**-ting**) completely destroy or defeat. □ **annihilation** /-'leɪʃ(ə)n/ *n.* [Latin *nihil* nothing]

anniversary /ˌænɪ'vɜːsərɪ/ *n.* (*pl.* **-ies**) **1** date of an event in a previous year. **2** celebration of this. [Latin *annus* year, *verto vers-* turn]

Anno Domini /ˌænəʊ 'dɒmɪˌnaɪ/ *adv.* years after Christ's birth. [Latin, = in the year of the Lord]

annotate /'ænəˌteɪt/ *v.* (**-ting**) add explanatory notes to. □ **annotation** /-'teɪʃ(ə)n/ *n.* [Latin *nota* mark]

announce /ə'naʊns/ *v.* (**-cing**) **1** make publicly known. **2** make known the arrival or imminence of (a guest, dinner, etc.). **3** be a sign of. □ **announcement** *n.* [Latin *nuntius* messenger]

announcer *n.* person who announces, esp. in broadcasting.

annoy /ə'nɔɪ/ *v.* **1** (often in *passive*) anger or distress slightly (*am annoyed with you*). **2** molest, harass. □ **annoyance** *n.* [Latin *in odio* hateful]

annual /'ænjʊəl/ *—adj.* **1** reckoned by the year. **2** occurring yearly. **3** living or lasting (only) a year. *—n.* **1** book etc. published yearly. **2** plant that lives only a year. □ **annually** *adv.* [Latin *annus* year]

annualized *adj.* (of rates of interest etc.) calculated on an annual basis, as a projection from figures obtained for a shorter period.

annuity /ə'njuːɪtɪ/ *n.* (*pl.* **-ies**) **1** yearly grant or allowance. **2** investment yielding a fixed annual sum.

annul /ə'nʌl/ *v.* (**-ll-**) **1** declare invalid. **2** cancel, abolish. □ **annulment** *n.* [Latin *nullus* none]

annular /'ænjʊlə(r)/ *adj.* ring-shaped. [Latin *anulus* ring]

annular eclipse *n.* solar eclipse in which a ring of light remains visible.

annulate /'ænjʊlət/ *adj.* marked with or formed of rings.

annunciation /əˌnʌnsɪ'eɪʃ(ə)n/ *n.* **1** announcement, esp. (**Annunciation**) that made by the angel Gabriel to Mary. **2** festival of this. [Latin: related to AN-NOUNCE]

anode /'ænəʊd/ *n.* positive electrode in an electrolytic cell etc. [Greek *anodos* way up]

anodize /'ænəˌdaɪz/ *v.* (also **-ise**) (**-zing** or **-sing**) coat (metal) with a protective layer by electrolysis.

anodyne /'ænəˌdaɪn/ *—adj.* **1** pain-relieving. **2** mentally soothing. *—n.* anodyne drug etc. [Greek *an-* without, *odunē* pain]

anoint /ə'nɔɪnt/ *v.* **1** apply oil or ointment to, esp. ritually. **2** (usu. foll. by *with*) smear. [Latin *inungo* anoint]

anomalous /ə'nɒmələs/ *adj.* irregular, deviant, abnormal. [Greek *an-* not, *homalos* even]

anomaly /ə'nɒm*əlɪ/ *n.* (*pl.* **-ies**) anomalous thing; irregularity.

anon /ə'nɒn/ *adv.* *archaic* soon, shortly. [Old English *on ān* into one]

anon. /ə'nɒn/ *abbr.* anonymous.

anonymous /ə'nɒnɪməs/ *adj.* **1** of unknown name or authorship. **2** without character; featureless. □ **anonymity** /ˌænə'nɪmɪtɪ/ *n.* [Greek *an-* without, *onoma* name]

anorak /'ænəˌræk/ *n.* waterproof usu. hooded jacket. [Eskimo]

anorexia /ˌænə'reksɪə/ *n.* lack of appetite, esp. (in full **anorexia nervosa** /nɜː'vəʊsə/) an obsessive desire to lose weight by refusing to eat. □ **anorexic** *adj. & n.* [Greek *an-* without, *orexis* appetite]

another /ə'nʌðə(r)/ *—adj.* **1** an additional; one more (*another cake*). **2** person like (*another Hitler*). **3** a different (*another matter*). **4** some other (*another man's work*). *—pron.* additional, other, or different person or thing. [earlier *an other*]

answer /'ɑːnsə(r)/ *—n.* **1** something said or done in reaction to a question, statement, or circumstance. **2** solution to a problem. *—v.* **1** make an answer or response (to) (*answer the door*). **2** suit (a purpose or need). **3** (foll. by *to, for*) be responsible (*you will answer to me for your conduct*). **4** (foll. by *to*) correspond, esp. to a description. □ **answer back** answer insolently. [Old English, = swear against (a charge)]

answerable *adj.* **1** (usu. foll. by *to, for*) responsible (*answerable to them for any accident*). **2** that can be answered.

answering machine *n.* tape recorder which answers telephone calls and takes messages.

answerphone *n.* = ANSWERING MACHINE.

ant *n.* small usu. wingless insect living in complex social colonies and proverbial for industry. [Old English]

-ant *suffix* **1** forming adjectives denoting attribution of an action (*repentant*) or state (*arrogant*). **2** forming agent nouns (*assistant*). [Latin *-ant-*, present participial stem of verbs]

antacid /ænt'æsɪd/ *—adj.* preventing or correcting acidity. *—n.* antacid agent.

antagonism /æn'tægə,nɪz(ə)m/ n. active hostility. [French: related to AGONY]

antagonist n. opponent or adversary. □ **antagonistic** /-'nɪstɪk/ adj.

antagonize /æn'tægə,naɪz/ v. (also -ise) (-zing or -sing) make hostile; provoke.

Antarctic /ænt'ɑ:ktɪk/ —adj. of the south polar regions. —n. this region. [Latin: related to ARCTIC]

Antarctic Circle n. parallel of latitude 66° 32′ S., forming an imaginary line round the Antarctic region.

ante /'æntɪ/ —n. **1** stake put up by a player in poker etc. before receiving cards. **2** amount payable in advance. —v. (-tes, -ted) **1** put up as an ante. **2** US a bet, stake. b (foll. by up) pay.

ante- prefix before, preceding. [Latin, = before]

anteater n. any of various mammals feeding on ants and termites.

antecedent /,æntɪ'si:d(ə)nt/ —n. **1** preceding thing or circumstance. **2** Gram. word or phrase etc. to which another word (esp. a relative pronoun) refers. **3** (in pl.) person's past history or ancestors. —adj. previous. [Latin cedo go]

antechamber /'æntɪ,tʃeɪmbə(r)/ n. ante-room.

antedate /,æntɪ'deɪt/ v. (-ting) **1** precede in time. **2** assign an earlier than actual date to.

antediluvian /,æntɪdɪ'lu:vɪən/ adj. **1** of the time before the Flood. **2** colloq. very old or out of date. [from ANTE-, Latin diluvium deluge]

antelope /'æntɪ,ləʊp/ n. (pl. same or -s) swift-moving deerlike ruminant, e.g. the gazelle and gnu. [Greek antholops]

antenatal /,æntɪ'neɪt(ə)l/ adj. **1** before birth. **2** of pregnancy.

antenna /æn'tenə/ n. **1** (pl. -tennae /-ni:/) each of a pair of feelers on the heads of insects, crustaceans, etc. **2** (pl. -s) = AERIAL n. [Latin, = sail-yard]

antepenultimate /,æntɪpɪ'nʌltɪmət/ adj. last but two.

ante-post /,æntɪ'pəʊst/ adj. (of betting) done at odds determined at the time of betting, in advance of the event concerned. [from ANTE-, POST¹]

anterior /æn'tɪərɪə(r)/ adj. **1** nearer the front. **2** (often foll. by to) prior. [Latin from ante before]

ante-room /'æntɪ,ru:m/ n. small room leading to a main one.

anthem /'ænθəm/ n. **1** elaborate choral composition usu. based on a passage of scripture. **2** solemn hymn of praise etc., esp. = NATIONAL ANTHEM. [Latin: related to ANTIPHON]

anther /'ænθə(r)/ n. part of a stamen containing pollen. [Greek anthos flower]

anthill n. moundlike nest built by ants or termites.

anthology /æn'θɒlədʒɪ/ n. (pl -ies) collection of poems, essays, stories, etc. □ **anthologist** n. [Greek anthos flower, -logia collection]

anthracite /'ænθrə,saɪt/ n. hard type of coal burning with little flame and smoke. [Greek: related to ANTHRAX]

anthrax /'ænθræks/ n. disease of sheep and cattle transmissible to humans. [Greek, = coal, carbuncle]

anthropocentric /,ænθrəpəʊ'sentrɪk/ adj. regarding mankind as the centre of existence. [Greek anthrōpos man]

anthropoid /'ænθrə,pɔɪd/ —adj. human in form. —n. anthropoid ape.

anthropology /,ænθrə'pɒlədʒɪ/ n. study of mankind, esp. its societies and customs. □ **anthropological** /-pə'lɒdʒɪk(ə)l/ adj. **anthropologist** n.

anthropomorphism /,ænθrəpə 'mɔ:fɪz(ə)m/ n. attribution of human characteristics to a god, animal, or thing. □ **anthropomorphic** adj. [Greek morphē form]

anthropomorphous /,ænθrəpə 'mɔ:fəs/ adj. human in form.

anti /'æntɪ/ —prep. opposed to. —n. (pl. -s) person opposed to a policy etc.

anti- prefix **1** opposed to (anticlerical). **2** preventing (antifreeze). **3** opposite of (anticlimax). **4** unconventional (antihero). [Greek]

anti-abortion /,æntɪə'bɔ:ʃ(ə)n/ adj. opposing abortion. □ **anti-abortionist** n.

anti-aircraft /,æntɪ'eəkrɑ:ft/ adj. (of a gun or missile) used to attack enemy aircraft.

antibiotic /,æntɪbaɪ'ɒtɪk/ —n. substance (e.g. penicillin) that can inhibit or destroy susceptible micro-organisms. —adj. functioning as an antibiotic. [Greek bios life]

antibody /'æntɪ,bɒdɪ/ n. (pl. -ies) a blood protein produced in response to and then counteracting antigens. [translation of German Antikörper]

antic /'æntɪk/ n. (usu. in pl.) foolish behaviour or action. [Italian antico ANTIQUE]

Antichrist /'æntɪ,kraɪst/ n. enemy of Christ. □ **antichristian** /-'krɪstʃ(ə)n/ adj.

anticipate /æn'tɪsɪ,peɪt/ v. (-ting) **1** deal with or use before the proper time. **2** expect, foresee (did not anticipate a problem). **3** forestall (a person or thing). **4** look forward to. □ **anticipation** /-'peɪʃ(ə)n/ n. **anticipatory** adj. [Latin anti- before, capio take]

anticlerical /ˌæntɪˈklerɪk(ə)l/ *adj.* opposed to clerical influence, esp. in politics.

anticlimax /ˌæntɪˈklaɪmæks/ *n.* disappointingly trivial conclusion to something significant.

anticlockwise /ˌæntɪˈklɒkwaɪz/ *adj. & adv.* moving in a curve opposite in direction to the hands of a clock.

anticyclone /ˌæntɪˈsaɪkləʊn/ *n.* system of winds rotating outwards from an area of high pressure, producing fine weather.

antidepressant /ˌæntɪdɪˈpres(ə)nt/ —*n.* drug etc. that alleviates depression. —*adj.* alleviating depression.

antidote /ˈæntɪˌdəʊt/ *n.* **1** medicine etc. used to counteract poison. **2** anything counteracting something unpleasant. [Greek *antidotos* given against]

antifreeze /ˈæntɪˌfriːz/ *n.* substance added to water to lower its freezing-point, esp. in a vehicle's radiator.

antigen /ˈæntɪdʒ(ə)n/ *n.* foreign substance (e.g. toxin) which causes the body to produce antibodies. [Greek *-genēs* of a kind]

anti-hero /ˈæntɪˌhɪərəʊ/ *n.* (*pl.* **-es**) central character in a story, lacking conventional heroic qualities.

antihistamine /ˌæntɪˈhɪstəˌmiːn/ *n.* drug that counteracts the effects of histamine, used esp. in treating allergies.

antiknock /ˌæntɪˈnɒk/ *n.* substance added to motor fuel to prevent premature combustion.

anti-lock /ˈæntɪˌlɒk/ *attrib. adj.* (of brakes) set up so as to prevent locking and skidding when applied suddenly.

antilog /ˈæntɪˌlɒg/ *n. colloq.* = ANTI-LOGARITHM. [abbreviation]

antilogarithm /ˌæntɪˈlɒgəˌrɪð(ə)m/ *n.* number to which a logarithm belongs.

antimacassar /ˌæntɪməˈkæsə(r)/ *n.* detachable protective cloth for the back of a chair etc.

antimatter /ˈæntɪˌmætə(r)/ *n.* matter composed solely of antiparticles.

antimony /ˈæntɪmənɪ/ *n.* brittle silvery metallic element used esp. in alloys. [medieval Latin]

antinomian /ˌæntɪˈnəʊmɪən/ —*adj.* believing that Christians need not obey the moral law. —*n.* (**Antinomian**) *hist.* person believing this. [Greek *nomos* law]

antinomy /ænˈtɪnəmɪ/ *n.* (*pl.* **-ies**) contradiction between two reasonable beliefs or conclusions.

antinovel /ˈæntɪˌnɒv(ə)l/ *n.* novel avoiding the conventions of the form.

anti-nuclear /ˌæntɪˈnjuːklɪə(r)/ *adj.* opposed to the development of nuclear weapons or power.

antiparticle /ˈæntɪˌpɑːtɪk(ə)l/ *n.* elementary particle with the same mass but opposite charge etc. to another particle.

antipathy /ænˈtɪpəθɪ/ *n.* (*pl.* **-ies**) (often foll. by *to, for, between*) strong aversion or dislike. □ **antipathetic** /-ˈθetɪk/ *adj.* [Greek: related to PATHETIC]

antiperspirant /ˌæntɪˈpɜːspərənt/ *n.* substance preventing or reducing perspiration.

antiphon /ˈæntɪf(ə)n/ *n.* **1** hymn sung alternately by two groups. **2** versicle or phrase from this. □ **antiphonal** /-ˈtɪfən(ə)l/ *adj.* [Greek *phōnē* sound]

antipodes /ænˈtɪpəˌdiːz/ *n.pl.* places diametrically opposite to one another on the earth, esp. (also **Antipodes**) Australasia in relation to Europe. □ **antipodean** /-ˈdiːən/ *adj. & n.* [Greek, = having the feet opposite]

antipope /ˈæntɪˌpəʊp/ *n.* pope set up in opposition to one chosen by canon law.

antipyretic /ˌæntɪpaɪəˈretɪk/ —*adj.* preventing or reducing fever. —*n.* antipyretic drug.

antiquarian /ˌæntɪˈkweərɪən/ —*adj.* of or dealing in antiques or rare books. —*n.* antiquary. □ **antiquarianism** *n.*

antiquary /ˈæntɪkwərɪ/ *n.* (*pl.* **-ies**) student or collector of antiques etc. [Latin: related to ANTIQUE]

antiquated /ˈæntɪˌkweɪtɪd/ *adj.* old-fashioned.

antique /ænˈtiːk/ —*n.* old object, esp. a piece of furniture, of high value. —*adj.* **1** of or from an early date. **2** old-fashioned. [Latin *antiquus*]

antiquity /ænˈtɪkwətɪ/ *n.* (*pl.* **-ies**) **1** ancient times, esp. before the Middle Ages. **2** great age. **3** (usu. in *pl.*) relics from ancient times. [Latin: related to ANTIQUE]

antirrhinum /ˌæntɪˈraɪnəm/ *n.* plant with two-lipped flowers, esp. the snapdragon. [Greek, = snout]

anti-Semite /ˌæntɪˈsiːmaɪt/ *n.* person who is prejudiced against Jews. □ **anti-Semitic** /-sɪˈmɪtɪk/ *adj.* **anti-Semitism** /-ˈsemɪˌtɪz(ə)m/ *n.*

antiseptic /ˌæntɪˈseptɪk/ —*adj.* **1** counteracting sepsis, esp. by destroying germs. **2** sterile, uncontaminated. **3** lacking character. —*n.* antiseptic agent.

antiserum /ˈæntɪˌsɪərəm/ *n.* serum with a high antibody content.

antisocial /ˌæntɪˈsəʊʃ(ə)l/ *adj.* **1** opposed or harmful to society. **2** not sociable.

■ **Usage** *Antisocial* is sometimes used mistakenly instead of *unsocial* in the phrase *unsocial hours*. This should be avoided.

antistatic /ˌæntɪˈstætɪk/ *adj.* counteracting the effects of static electricity.

anti-tank /ˌæntɪˈtæŋk/ *attrib. adj.* used against tanks.

antitetanus /ˌæntɪˈtetənəs/ *adj.* effective against tetanus.

antithesis /ænˈtɪθəsɪs/ *n.* (*pl.* **-theses** /-ˌsiːz/) **1** (foll. by *of*, *to*) direct opposite. **2** contrast. **3** rhetorical use of strongly contrasted words. □ **antithetical** /-ˈθetɪk(ə)l/ *adj.* [Greek *antitithēmi* set against]

antitoxin /ˌæntɪˈtɒksɪn/ *n.* antibody counteracting a toxin. □ **antitoxic** *adj.*

antitrades /ˈæntɪˌtreɪdz/ *n.pl.* winds blowing in the opposite direction to (and usu. above) trade winds.

antiviral /ˌæntɪˈvaɪər(ə)l/ *adj.* effective against viruses.

antler /ˈæntlə/ *n.* branched horn of a stag or other deer. □ **antlered** *adj.* [French]

antonym /ˈæntənɪm/ *n.* word opposite in meaning to another. [Greek *onoma* name]

antrum /ˈæntrəm/ *n.* (*pl.* **antra**) natural cavity in the body, esp. in a bone. [Greek, = cave]

anus /ˈeɪnəs/ *n.* (*pl.* **anuses**) excretory opening at the end of the alimentary canal. [Latin]

anvil /ˈænvɪl/ *n.* iron block on which metals are worked. [Old English]

anxiety /æŋˈzaɪətɪ/ *n.* (*pl.* **-ies**) **1** being anxious. **2** worry or concern. **3** eagerness, troubled desire. [Latin *anxietas* from *ango* choke]

anxious /ˈæŋkʃəs/ *adj.* **1** mentally troubled. **2** causing or marked by anxiety (*anxious moment*). **3** eager, uneasily wanting (*anxious to please*). □ **anxiously** *adv.* [Latin *anxius*]

any /ˈenɪ/ *—adj.* **1 a** one, no matter which, of several (*cannot find any answer*). **b** some, no matter how much or many or of what sort (*if any books arrive*; *have you any sugar?*). **2** a minimal amount of (*hardly any difference*). **3** whichever is chosen (*any fool knows*). **4** an appreciable or significant (*did not stay for any length of time*; *has any amount of money*). *—pron.* **1** any one (*did not know any of t'hem*). **2** any number or amount (*are any of them yours?*). *—adv.* (usu. with *neg.* or *interrog.*) at all (*is that any good?*). [Old English *ænig*: related to ONE, -Y[1]]

anybody *n.* & *pron.* **1** any person. **2** person of importance (*is he anybody?*).

anyhow *adv.* **1** anyway. **2** in a disorderly manner or state (*does his work anyhow*).

anyone *pron.* anybody.

■ **Usage** *Anyone* is written as two words to emphasize a numerical sense, as in *any one of us can do it.*

anything *pron.* any thing; thing of any sort. □ **anything but** not at all.

anyway *adv.* **1** in any way or manner. **2** at any rate. **3** to resume (*anyway, as I was saying*).

anywhere *—adv.* in or to any place. *—pron.* any place (*anywhere will do*).

AOB *abbr.* any other business.

aorta /eɪˈɔːtə/ *n.* (*pl.* **-s**) main artery, giving rise to the arterial network carrying oxygenated blood to the body from the heart. □ **aortic** *adj.* [Greek *aeirō* raise]

apace /əˈpeɪs/ *adv. literary* swiftly. [French *à pas*]

Apache /əˈpætʃɪ/ *n.* member of a N. American Indian tribe. [Mexican Spanish]

apart /əˈpɑːt/ *adv.* **1** separately, not together (*keep your feet apart*). **2** into pieces (*came apart*). **3** to or on one side. **4** to or at a distance. □ **apart from 1** excepting, not considering. **2** in addition to (*apart from roses we grow irises*). [French *à part* to one side]

apartheid /əˈpɑːteɪt/ *n.* (esp. in S. Africa) racial segregation or discrimination. [Afrikaans]

apartment /əˈpɑːtmənt/ *n.* **1** (in *pl.*) suite of rooms. **2** single room. **3** *US* flat. [Italian *a parte*, apart]

apathy /ˈæpəθɪ/ *n.* lack of interest; indifference. □ **apathetic** /-ˈθetɪk/ *adj.* [Greek *a-* without, PATHOS]

ape *—n.* **1** tailless monkey-like primate, e.g. the gorilla, chimpanzee, orangutan, or gibbon. **2** imitator. *—v.* (**-ping**) imitate, mimic. [Old English]

apeman *n.* extinct primate held to be the forerunner of present-day man.

aperient /əˈpɪərɪənt/ *—adj.* laxative. *—n.* laxative medicine. [Latin *aperio* open]

aperitif /əˌperɪˈtiːf/ *n.* alcoholic drink taken before a meal. [Latin *aperio* open]

aperture /ˈæpəˌtʃə(r)/ *n.* opening or gap, esp. a variable opening in a camera for admitting light. [Latin *aperio* open]

Apex /ˈeɪpeks/ *n.* (also **APEX**) (often *attrib.*) system of reduced fares for scheduled flights. [*Advance Purchase Excursion*]

apex /ˈeɪpeks/ *n.* (*pl.* **-es**) **1** highest point. **2** tip or pointed end. [Latin]

aphasia /əˈfeɪzɪə/ *n.* loss of verbal understanding or expression, owing to

brain damage. [Greek *aphatos* speechless]

aphelion /ə'fi:lɪən/ *n.* (*pl.* **-lia**) point in a celestial body's orbit where it is furthest from the sun. [Greek *aph'hēliou* from the sun]

aphid /'eɪfɪd/ *n.* small insect infesting and damaging plants, e.g. the greenfly.

aphis /'eɪfɪs/ *n.* (*pl.* **aphides** /-,di:z/) aphid. [invented by Linnaeus: perhaps a misreading of Greek *koris* bug]

aphorism /'æfə,rɪz(ə)m/ *n.* short pithy maxim. □ **aphoristic** /-'rɪstɪk/ *adj.* [Greek *aphorismos* definition]

aphrodisiac /,æfrə'dɪzɪ,æk/ *–adj.* arousing sexual desire. –*n.* aphrodisiac substance. [Greek *Aphroditē* goddess of love]

apiary /'eɪpɪərɪ/ *n.* (*pl.* **-ies**) place where bees are kept. □ **apiarist** *n.* [Latin *apis* bee]

apical /'eɪpɪk(ə)l/ *adj.* of, at, or forming an apex.

apiculture /'eɪpɪ,kʌltʃə(r)/ *n.* beekeeping. □ **apiculturist** /-'kʌltʃərɪst/ *n.* [Latin *apis* bee, CULTURE]

apiece /ə'pi:s/ *adv.* for each one; severally (*five pounds apiece*). [or. ʒinally *a piece*]

apish /'eɪpɪʃ/ *adj.* 1 of or like an ape. 2 foolishly imitating.

aplomb /ə'plɒm/ *n.* skilful self-assurance. [French, = straight as a plummet]

apocalypse /ə'pɒkəlɪps/ *n.* 1 violent or destructive event. 2 (**the Apocalypse**) Revelation, the last book of the New Testament. 3 revelation, esp. about the end of the world. □ **apocalyptic** /-'lɪptɪk/ *adj.* [Greek *apokaluptō* reveal]

Apocrypha /ə'pɒkrɪfə/ *n.pl.* 1 books included in the Septuagint and Vulgate versions of the Old Testament but not in the Hebrew Bible. 2 (**apocrypha**) writings etc. not considered genuine. [Greek *apokruptō* hide away]

apocryphal *adj.* of doubtful authenticity.

apogee /'æpə,dʒi:/ *n.* 1 highest point; climax. 2 point in a celestial body's orbit where it is furthest from the earth. [Greek *apogeion*]

apolitical /,eɪpə'lɪtɪk(ə)l/ *adj.* not interested in or concerned with politics.

apologetic /ə,pɒlə'dʒetɪk/ *–adj.* 1 showing or expressing regret. 2 of apologetics. –*n.* (usu. in *pl.*) reasoned defence, esp. of Christianity. □ **apologetically** *adv.*

apologia /,æpə'ləʊdʒɪə/ *n.* formal defence of opinions or conduct. [Greek: see APOLOGY]

apologist /ə'pɒlədʒɪst/ *n.* person who defends something by argument.

apologize /ə'pɒlə,dʒaɪz/ *v.* (also **-ise**) (**-zing** or **-sing**) make an apology, express regret.

apology /ə'pɒlədʒɪ/ *n.* (*pl.* **-ies**) 1 statement of regret for an offence or failure. 2 explanation or defence. 3 (foll. by *for*) poor specimen of. [Greek *apologia* from *apologeomai* speak in defence]

apophthegm /'æpə,θem/ *n.* = APHORISM. [Latin from Greek]

apoplectic /,æpə'plektɪk/ *adj.* 1 of or causing apoplexy. 2 *colloq.* enraged.

apoplexy /'æpə,pleksɪ/ *n.* sudden paralysis caused by blockage or rupture of a brain artery; stroke. [Greek *applēssō* disable by stroke]

apostasy /ə'pɒstəsɪ/ *n.* (*pl.* **-ies**) renunciation of a belief or faith, abandoning of principles, etc. [Greek, = defection]

apostate /ə'pɒsteɪt/ *n.* person who renounces a former belief etc. □ **apostatize** *v.* (also **-ise**) (**-zing** or **-sing**).

a posteriori /,eɪ pɒ,sterɪ'ɔːraɪ/ *–adj.* (of reasoning) proceeding from effects to causes; inductive. *–adv.* inductively. [Latin, = from what comes after]

apostle /ə'pɒs(ə)l/ *n.* 1 (**Apostle**) any of the twelve men sent out by Christ to preach the gospel. 2 leader, esp. of a new movement. [Greek *apostolos* messenger]

apostolate /ə'pɒstələt/ *n.* 1 position or authority of an Apostle. 2 leadership in reform.

apostolic /,æpə'stɒlɪk/ *adj.* 1 of the Apostles or their teaching. 2 of the Pope.

apostolic succession *n.* supposed uninterrupted transmission of spiritual authority from the Apostles through popes and bishops.

apostrophe /ə'pɒstrəfɪ/ *n.* 1 punctuation mark (') indicating: **a** omission of letters or numbers (e.g. *can't*; *May '92*). **b** possessive case (e.g. *Harry's book*; *boys' coats*). 2 exclamatory passage addressed to (an often absent) person or thing. □ **apostrophize** *v.* (also **-ise**) (**-zing** or **-sing**) (in sense 2). [Greek, = turning away]

apothecaries' measure *n.* (also **apothecaries' weight**) units formerly used in pharmacy.

apothecary /ə'pɒθəkərɪ/ *n.* (*pl.* **-ies**) *archaic* dispensing chemist. [Greek *apothēkē* storehouse]

apotheosis /ə,pɒθɪ'əʊsɪs/ *n.* (*pl.* **-theoses** /-si:z/) 1 elevation to divine status, deification. 2 glorification of a thing; sublime example (*apotheosis of chivalry*). [Greek *theos* god]

appal /ə'pɔːl/ *v.* (**-ll-**) 1 greatly dismay or horrify. 2 (as **appalling** *adj.*) *colloq.* very bad, shocking. [French *apalir* grow pale: related to PALE[1]]

apparatus /ˌæpəˈreɪtəs/ n. 1 equipment for a particular function, esp. scientific or technical. 2 political or other complex organization. [Latin *paro* prepare]

apparel /əˈpær(ə)l/ n. *formal* clothing, dress. □ **apparelled** adj. [Romanic, = make fit, from Latin *par* equal]

apparent /əˈpærənt/ adj. 1 readily visible; obvious. 2 seeming. □ **apparently** adv. [Latin: related to APPEAR]

apparition /ˌæpəˈrɪʃ(ə)n/ n. remarkable or unexpected thing that appears; ghost or phantom.

appeal /əˈpiːl/ —v. 1 request earnestly or formally; plead. 2 (usu. foll. by *to*) attract, be of interest. 3 (foll. by *to*) resort to for support. 4 *Law* a (often foll. by *to*) apply (to a higher court) for reconsideration of a legal decision. b refer (a case) to a higher court. 5 *Cricket* call on the umpire to declare whether a batsman is out. —n. 1 act of appealing. 2 request for public support, esp. financial. 3 *Law* referral of a case to a higher court. 4 attractiveness. [Latin *appello* address]

appear /əˈpɪə(r)/ v. 1 become or be visible. 2 seem (*appeared unwell*). 3 present oneself publicly or formally. 4 be published. [Latin *appareo*]

appearance /əˈpɪərəns/ n. 1 act of appearing. 2 outward form as perceived (*appearance of prosperity*). 3 semblance. □ **keep up appearances** maintain an impression or pretence of virtue, affluence, etc. **make** (or **put in**) **an appearance** be present, esp. briefly.

appease /əˈpiːz/ v. (**-sing**) 1 make calm or quiet, esp. conciliate (a potential aggressor) by making concessions. 2 satisfy (an appetite, scruples). □ **appeasement** n. [French *à* to, *pais* PEACE]

appellant /əˈpelənt/ n. person who appeals to a higher court. [Latin *appello* address]

appellate /əˈpelət/ attrib. adj. (esp. of a court) concerned with appeals.

appellation /ˌæpəˈleɪʃ(ə)n/ n. *formal* name or title; nomenclature.

appellative /əˈpelətɪv/ adj. 1 naming. 2 *Gram.* (of a noun) designating a class, common.

append /əˈpend/ v. (usu. foll. by *to*) attach, affix, add, esp. to a written document. [Latin *appendo* hang]

appendage /əˈpendɪdʒ/ n. thing attached; addition.

appendectomy /ˌæpenˈdektəmɪ/ n. (also **appendicectomy** /-dɪˈsektəmɪ/) (pl. **-ies**) surgical removal of the appendix. [from APPENDIX, -ECTOMY]

appendicitis /əˌpendɪˈsaɪtɪs/ n. inflammation of the appendix.

appendix /əˈpendɪks/ n. (pl. **-dices** /-ˌsiːz/) 1 tissue forming a tube-shaped sac attached to the large intestine. 2 addition to a book etc. [Latin: related to APPEND]

appertain /ˌæpəˈteɪn/ v. (foll. by *to*) relate, belong, or be appropriate. [Latin: related to PERTAIN]

appetite /ˈæpɪˌtaɪt/ n. 1 natural craving, esp. for food or sexual activity. 2 (usu. foll. by *for*) inclination or desire. [Latin *peto* seek]

appetizer /ˈæpɪˌtaɪzə(r)/ n. (also **-iser**) small amount, esp. of food or drink, to stimulate the appetite.

appetizing adj. (also **-ising**) stimulating the appetite, esp. for food; tasty.

applaud /əˈplɔːd/ v. 1 express strong approval, esp. by clapping. 2 commend, approve (a person or action). [Latin *applaudo* clap hands]

applause /əˈplɔːz/ n. 1 approval shown by clapping the hands. 2 warm approval.

apple /ˈæp(ə)l/ n. 1 roundish firm fruit with crisp flesh. 2 tree bearing this. □ **apple of one's eye** cherished person or thing. [Old English]

apple-pie bed n. bed made (as a joke) with sheets folded so as to prevent a person lying flat.

apple-pie order n. extreme neatness.

appliance /əˈplaɪəns/ n. device etc. for a specific task. [related to APPLY]

applicable /ˈæplɪkəb(ə)l/ adj. (often foll. by *to*) that may be applied; relevant; appropriate. □ **applicability** /-ˈbɪlɪtɪ/ n. [medieval Latin: related to APPLY]

applicant /ˈæplɪkənt/ n. person who applies for something, esp. a job.

application /ˌæplɪˈkeɪʃ(ə)n/ n. 1 formal request. 2 act of applying. 3 substance applied. 4 a relevance. b use (*has many applications*). 5 diligence.

applicator /ˈæplɪˌkeɪtə(r)/ n. device for applying ointment etc.

applied /əˈplaɪd/ adj. practical, not merely theoretical (*applied science*).

appliqué /əˈpliːkeɪ/ —n. cutting out of fabric patterns and attaching them to another fabric. —v. (**-qués, -quéd, -quéing**) decorate with appliqué. [French, = applied]

apply /əˈplaɪ/ v. (**-ies, -ied**) 1 (often foll. by *for*, *to*, or *to* + infin.) formally request. 2 be relevant. 3 a make use of; employ (*apply the rules*; *apply common sense*). b operate (*apply the brakes*). 4 (often foll. by *to*) put or spread on. 5 *refl.* (often foll. by *to*) devote oneself. [Latin *applico* fasten to]

appoint /əˈpɔɪnt/ v. 1 assign a job or office to. 2 (often foll. by *for*) fix (a time, place, etc.). 3 (as **appointed** adj.)

equipped, furnished (*well-appointed*).
□ **appointee** /-'ti:/ *n.* [French *à point* to a point]

appointment *n.* **1** appointing or being appointed. **2** arrangement for meeting or consultation. **3 a** post or office open to applicants. **b** person appointed. **4** (usu. in *pl.*) furniture, fittings; equipment.

apportion /ə'pɔ:ʃ(ə)n/ *v.* (often foll. by *to*) share out; assign as a share. □ **apportionment** *n.* [medieval Latin: related to PORTION]

apposite /'æpəzɪt/ *adj.* (often foll. by *to*) apt, appropriate; well expressed. [Latin *appono* apply]

apposition /æpə'zɪʃ(ə)n/ *n.* juxtaposition, esp. *Gram.* of elements sharing a syntactic function (e.g. *William the Conqueror; my friend Sue*).

appraisal /ə'preɪz(ə)l/ *n.* appraising or being appraised.

appraise /ə'preɪz/ *v.* (-sing) **1** estimate the value or quality of. **2** set a price on (esp. officially). [earlier *apprize*, assimilated to PRAISE]

appreciable /ə'pri:ʃəb(ə)l/ *adj.* significant, considerable. [French: related to APPRECIATE]

appreciate /ə'pri:ʃɪ,eɪt/ *v.* (-ting) **1 a** esteem highly; value. **b** be grateful for. **2** understand, recognize (*appreciate the danger*). **3** rise or raise in value. □ **appreciative** /-ʃətɪv/ *adj.* **appreciatory** /-ʃətərɪ/ *adj.* [Latin *pretium* price]

appreciation /ə,pri:ʃɪ'eɪʃ(ə)n/ *n.* **1** favourable or grateful recognition. **2** sensitive estimation or judgement. **3** rise in value. [French: related to APPRECIATE]

apprehend /,æprɪ'hend/ *v.* **1** seize, arrest. **2** understand, perceive. [Latin *prehendo* grasp]

apprehension /,æprɪ'henʃ(ə)n/ *n.* **1** uneasiness, dread. **2** understanding. **3** arrest, capture.

apprehensive /,æprɪ'hensɪv/ *adj.* uneasily fearful. □ **apprehensively** *adv.*

apprentice /ə'prentɪs/ —*n.* **1** person learning a trade by working in it for an agreed period at low wages. **2** novice. —*v.* (-cing) (usu. foll. by *to*) engage as an apprentice (*apprenticed to a builder*). □ **apprenticeship** *n.* [French *apprendre* learn]

apprise /ə'praɪz/ *v.* (-sing) *formal* inform. [French *appris(e)* learnt, taught]

appro /'æprəʊ/ *n. colloq.* □ **on appro** = *on approval* (see APPROVAL). [abbreviation]

approach /ə'prəʊtʃ/ —*v.* **1** come near or nearer (to) in space or time. **2** tentatively propose to. **3** be similar or approximate to (*approaching 5 million*). **4** set

about (a task etc.). —*n.* **1** act or means of approaching. **2** approximation. **3** technique (*try a new approach*). **4** *Golf* stroke from the fairway to the green. **5** *Aeron.* part of a flight before landing. [Latin *prope* near]

approachable *adj.* **1** friendly, easy to talk to. **2** able to be approached.

approbation /,æprə'beɪʃ(ə)n/ *n.* approval, consent. [Latin *probo* test]

appropriate —*adj.* /ə'prəʊprɪət/ suitable, proper. —*v.* /ə'prəʊprɪ,eɪt/ (-ting) **1** take, esp. without authority. **2** devote (money etc.) to special purposes. □ **appropriately** *adv.* **appropriation** /-'eɪʃ(ə)n/ *n.* [Latin *proprius* own]

approval /ə'pru:v(ə)l/ *n.* **1** approving. **2** consent; favourable opinion. □ **on approval** (of goods supplied) returnable if not satisfactory.

approve /ə'pru:v/ *v.* (-ving) **1** confirm; sanction. **2** (often foll. by *of*) regard with favour. [Latin *probo* test]

approx. *abbr.* approximate(ly).

approximate —*adj.* /ə'prɒksɪmət/ fairly correct, near to the actual (*approximate price*). —*v.* /ə'prɒksɪ,meɪt/ (-ting) (often foll. by *to*) bring or come near (esp. in quality, number, etc.). □ **approximately** *adv.* **approximation** /-'meɪʃ(ə)n/ *n.* [Latin *proximus* nearest]

appurtenance /ə'pɜ:tɪnəns/ *n.* (usu. in *pl.*) belonging; accessory. [Latin *pertineo* belong to]

APR *abbr.* annual or annualized percentage rate (esp. of interest on loans or credit).

Apr. *abbr.* April.

après-ski /,æpreɪ'ski:/ —*n.* social activities following a day's skiing. —*attrib. adj.* (of clothes, drinks, etc.) suitable for these. [French]

apricot /'eɪprɪ,kɒt/ —*n.* **1 a** small juicy soft orange-yellow peachlike fruit. **b** tree bearing it. **2** its colour. —*adj.* orange-yellow. [Portuguese and Spanish from Arabic, ultimately from Latin *praecox* early-ripe]

April /'eɪprə(ə)l/ *n.* fourth month of the year. [Latin]

April Fool *n.* person successfully tricked on 1 April.

a priori /,eɪ praɪ'ɔ:raɪ/ —*adj.* **1** (of reasoning) from causes to effects; deductive. **2** (of concepts etc.) logically independent of experience; not derived from experience. **3** assumed without investigation (*an a priori conjecture*). —*adv.* **1** deductively. **2** as far as one knows. [Latin, = from what is before]

apron /'eɪprən/ *n.* **1** garment for covering and protecting the front of the clothes. **2** *Theatr.* part of a stage in front of the curtain. **3** area on an airfield for

manoeuvring or loading. □ **tied to a person's apron-strings** dominated by or dependent on that person (usu. a woman). [originally *napron*, from French *nape* table-cloth]

apropos /ˌæprə'pəʊ/ —*adj.* **1** appropriate. **2** *colloq.* (often foll. by *of*) in respect of. —*adv.* **1** appropriately. **2** (*absol.*) incidentally. [French *à propos*]

apse /æps/ *n.* large arched or domed recess, esp. at the end of a church. [related to APSIS]

apsis /'æpsɪs/ *n.* (*pl.* **apsides** /-ˌdiːz/) either of two points on the orbit of a planet etc. nearest to or furthest from the body round which it moves. [Greek (*h*)*apsis* arch, vault]

apt *adj.* **1** appropriate, suitable. **2** tending (*apt to break down*). **3** clever; quick to learn. [Latin *aptus* fitted]

aptitude /'æptɪˌtjuːd/ *n.* **1** natural talent. **2** ability or fitness, esp. specified. [French: related to APT]

aqua /'ækwə/ *n.* the colour aquamarine. [abbreviation]

aqua fortis /ˌækwə 'fɔːtɪs/ *n.* nitric acid. [Latin, = strong water]

aqualung /'ækwəˌlʌŋ/ *n.* portable breathing-apparatus for divers. [Latin *aqua* water]

aquamarine /ˌækwəmə'riːn/ —*n.* **1** bluish-green beryl. **2** its colour. —*adj.* bluish-green. [Latin *aqua marina* sea water]

aquaplane /'ækwəˌpleɪn/ —*n.* board for riding on water, pulled by a speedboat. —*v.* (**-ning**) **1** ride on this. **2** (of a vehicle) glide uncontrollably on a wet surface. [Latin *aqua* water, PLANE¹]

aqua regia /ˌækwə 'riːdʒɪə/ *n.* highly corrosive mixture of acids, attacking many substances unaffected by other reagents. [Latin, = royal water]

aquarelle /ˌækwə'rel/ *n.* painting in thin usu. transparent water-colours. [French from Italian]

aquarium /ə'kweərɪəm/ *n.* (*pl.* **-s**) tank of water for keeping and showing fish etc. [Latin *aquarius* of water]

Aquarius /ə'kweərɪəs/ *n.* (*pl.* **-es**) **1** constellation and eleventh sign of the zodiac (the Water-carrier). **2** person born when the sun is in this sign. [Latin: related to AQUARIUM]

aquatic /ə'kwætɪk/ —*adj.* **1** growing or living in water. **2** (of a sport) played in or on water. —*n.* **1** aquatic plant or animal. **2** (in *pl.*) aquatic sports. [Latin *aqua* water]

aquatint /'ækwətɪnt/ *n.* etched print resembling a water-colour. [Italian *acqua tinta* coloured water]

aqua vitae /ˌækwə 'viːtaɪ/ *n.* strong alcoholic spirit, esp. brandy. [Latin, = water of life]

aqueduct /'ækwɪˌdʌkt/ *n.* water channel, esp. a bridge on columns across a valley. [Latin *aquae ductus* conduit]

aqueous /'eɪkwɪəs/ *adj.* of or like water. [Latin *aqua* water]

aqueous humour *n.* clear fluid in the eye between the lens and the cornea.

aquilegia /ˌækwɪ'liːdʒə/ *n.* (usu. blue-flowered) columbine. [Latin]

aquiline /'ækwɪˌlaɪn/ *adj.* **1** of or like an eagle. **2** (of a nose) curved. [Latin *aquila* eagle]

Ar *symb.* argon.

-ar *suffix* forming adjectives (*angular*; *linear*). [Latin *-aris*]

Arab /'ærəb/ —*n.* **1** member of a Semitic people originating in Saudi Arabia and neighbouring countries, now widespread throughout the Middle East. **2** horse of a breed orig. native to Arabia. —*adj.* of Arabia or the Arabs (esp. with ethnic reference). [Arabic *araps*]

arabesque /ˌærə'besk/ *n.* **1** *Ballet* posture with one leg extended horizontally backwards and arms outstretched. **2** design of intertwined leaves, scrolls, etc. **3** *Mus.* florid piece. [French from Italian from *arabo* Arab]

Arabian /ə'reɪbɪən/ —*adj.* of or relating to Arabia (esp. in geographical contexts) (*Arabian desert*). —*n.* native of Arabia.

■ **Usage** In the sense 'native of Arabia', the usual term is now *Arab*.

Arabic /'ærəbɪk/ —*n.* Semitic language of the Arabs. —*adj.* of the Arabs (esp. their language or literature).

arabic numeral *n.* any of the numerals 0-9.

arable /'ærəb(ə)l/ *adj.* (of land) suitable for crop production. [Latin *aro* to plough]

arachnid /ə'ræknɪd/ *n.* arthropod of a class comprising spiders, scorpions, etc. [Greek *arakhnē* spider]

arak var. of ARRACK.

Araldite /'ærəlˌdaɪt/ *n. propr.* epoxy resin for mending china etc. [origin unknown]

Aramaic /ˌærə'meɪɪk/ —*n.* branch of the Semitic family of languages, esp. the language of Syria used as a lingua franca in the Near East from the sixth century BC. —*adj.* of or in Aramaic. [Greek *Aramaios* of Aram (Hebrew name of Syria)]

arbiter /'ɑːbɪtə(r)/ *n.* **1** arbitrator in a dispute. **2** person influential in a specific field (*arbiter of taste*). [Latin from *arbitror* to judge]

arbitrary /'ɑːbɪtrərɪ/ adj. **1** random. **2** capricious; despotic. □ **arbitrarily** adv.

arbitrate /'ɑːbɪˌtreɪt/ v. (**-ting**) decide by arbitration.

arbitration /ˌɑːbɪ'treɪʃ(ə)n/ n. settlement of a dispute by an impartial third party.

arbitrator n. person appointed to arbitrate.

arbor[1] /'ɑːbə(r)/ n. axle or spindle. [Latin, = tree]

arbor[2] US var. of ARBOUR.

arboreal /ɑː'bɔːrɪəl/ adj. of or living in trees. [Latin arbor tree]

arborescent /ˌɑːbə'res(ə)nt/ adj. tree-like in growth or form.

arboretum /ˌɑːbə'riːtəm/ n. (pl. **-ta**) place cultivating and displaying rare trees.

arboriculture /'ɑːbərɪˌkʌltʃə(r)/ n. cultivation of trees and shrubs. [Latin arbor tree, after agriculture]

arbor vitae /ˌɑːbə 'viːtaɪ/ n. any of various evergreen conifers. [Latin, = tree of life]

arbour /'ɑːbə(r)/ n. (US **arbor**) shady garden alcove enclosed by trees etc. [Latin herba herb: assimilated to Latin arbor tree]

arbutus /ɑː'bjuːtəs/ n. tree or shrub with clusters of flowers and strawberry-like berries. [Latin]

arc – n. **1** part of the circumference of a circle or other curve. **2** Electr. luminous discharge between two electrodes. – v. (**arced**; **arcing** /'ɑːkɪŋ/) form an arc; move in a curve. [Latin arcus bow]

arcade /ɑː'keɪd/ n. **1** covered walk, esp. lined with shops. **2** series of arches supporting or set along a wall. [Romanic: related to ARC]

Arcadian /ɑː'keɪdɪən/ – n. idealized country dweller. – adj. poetically rural. [Greek Arkadia in the Peloponnese]

arcane /ɑː'keɪn/ adj. mysterious, secret. [Latin arceo shut up]

arch[1] – n. **1** curved structure as an opening, as a support for a bridge, floor, etc., or as an ornament. **2** any arch-shaped curve. – v. **1** provide with or form into an arch. **2** span like an arch. **3** form an arch. [Latin arcus arc]

arch[2] adj. self-consciously or affectedly playful. □ **archly** adv. [from ARCH-, originally in arch rogue etc.]

arch- comb. form **1** chief, superior (archbishop). **2** pre-eminent, esp. unfavourably (arch-enemy). [Greek arkhos chief]

Archaean /ɑː'kiːən/ (US **Archean**) – adj. of the earliest geological era. – n. this time. [Greek arkhaios ancient]

archaeology /ˌɑːkɪ'ɒlədʒɪ/ n. (US **archeology**) study of ancient cultures, esp. by the excavation and analysis of physical remains. □ **archaeological** /-'lɒdʒɪk(ə)l/ adj. **archaeologist** n. [Greek arkhaiologia ancient history]

archaeopteryx /ˌɑːkɪ'ɒptərɪks/ n. fossil bird with teeth, feathers, and a reptilian tail. [Greek arkhaios ancient, pterux wing]

archaic /ɑː'keɪɪk/ adj. **1 a** antiquated. **b** (of a word etc.) no longer in ordinary use. **2** of an early period of culture. □ **archaically** adv. [Greek arkhē beginning]

archaism /'ɑːkeɪˌɪz(ə)m/ n. **1** use of the archaic esp. in language or art. **2** archaic word or expression. □ **archaistic** /-'ɪstɪk/ adj.

archangel /'ɑːkˌeɪndʒ(ə)l/ n. angel of the highest rank.

archbishop /ɑːtʃ'bɪʃəp/ n. chief bishop of a province.

archbishopric n. office or diocese of an archbishop.

archdeacon /ɑːtʃ'diːkən/ n. church dignitary next below a bishop. □ **archdeaconry** n. (pl. **-ies**).

archdiocese /ɑːtʃ'daɪəsɪs/ n. diocese of an archbishop. □ **archdiocesan** /-daɪ'ɒsɪs(ə)n/ adj.

archduke /ɑːtʃ'djuːk/ n. hist. chief duke (esp. as the title of a son of the Emperor of Austria). □ **archduchy** /-'dʌtʃɪ/ n. (pl. **-ies**). [medieval Latin archidux]

Archean US var. of ARCHAEAN.

arch-enemy /ɑːtʃ'enəmɪ/ n. (pl. **-ies**) **1** chief enemy. **2** the Devil.

archeology US var. of ARCHAEOLOGY.

archer n. **1** person who shoots with a bow and arrows. **2** (**the Archer**) zodiacal sign or constellation Sagittarius. [Latin arcus bow]

archery n. shooting with a bow and arrows, esp. as a sport.

archetype /'ɑːkɪˌtaɪp/ n. **1** original model; prototype. **2** typical specimen. □ **archetypal** /-'taɪp(ə)l/ adj. [Greek tupon stamp]

archidiaconal /ˌɑːkɪdaɪ'ækən(ə)l/ adj. of an archdeacon. [medieval Latin]

archiepiscopal /ˌɑːkɪɪ'pɪskəp(ə)l/ adj. of an archbishop. [Church Latin from Greek]

archimandrite /ˌɑːkɪ'mændraɪt/ n. **1** superior of a large monastery in the Orthodox Church. **2** honorary title of a monastic priest. [Greek arkhi- chief, mandritēs monk]

archipelago /ˌɑːkɪ'peləˌgəʊ/ n. (pl. **-s**) **1** group of islands. **2** sea with many islands. [Greek arkhi- chief, pelagos sea]

architect /'ɑːkɪˌtekt/ n. **1** designer of buildings etc., supervising their construction. **2** (foll. by of) person who

brings about a specified thing (*architect of peace*). [Greek *arkhi-* chief, *tektōn* builder]

architectonic /ˌɑːkɪtek'tɒnɪk/ *adj.* **1** of architecture. **2** of the systematization of knowledge.

architecture /'ɑːkɪˌtektʃə(r)/ *n.* **1** design and construction of buildings. **2** style of a building. **3** buildings etc. collectively. □ **architectural** /-'tek tʃər(ə)l/ *adj.*

architrave /'ɑːkɪˌtreɪv/ *n.* **1** (in classical architecture) main beam resting across the tops of columns. **2** moulded frame around a doorway or window. [Italian *archi-* ARCH-, Latin *trabs* beam]

archive /'ɑːkaɪv/ —*n.* (usu. in *pl.*) **1** collection of documents or records. **2** store for these. —*v.* (-ving) **1** place or store in an archive. **2** *Computing* transfer (data) to a less frequently used file. [Greek *arkheia* public records]

archivist /'ɑːkɪvɪst/ *n.* keeper of archives.

archway *n.* arched entrance or passage.

arc lamp *n.* (also **arc light**) light using an electric arc.

Arctic /'ɑːktɪk/ —*adj.* **1** of the north polar regions. **2** (**arctic**) *colloq.* very cold. —*n.* Arctic regions. [Greek *arktos* Great Bear]

Arctic Circle *n.* parallel of latitude 66° 33' N, forming an imaginary line round the Arctic region.

arc welding *n.* use of an electric arc to melt metals to be welded.

ardent /'ɑːd(ə)nt/ *adj.* **1** eager, fervent, passionate. **2** burning. □ **ardently** *adv.* [Latin *ardeo* burn]

ardour /'ɑːdə(r)/ *n.* (*US* ardor) zeal, enthusiasm, passion.

arduous /'ɑːdjuːəs/ *adj.* hard to accomplish; laborious, strenuous. [Latin, = steep]

are[1] *2nd sing. present & 1st, 2nd, 3rd pl. present* of BE.

are[2] /ɑː(r)/ *n.* metric unit of measure, 100 square metres. [Latin: related to AREA]

area /'eərɪə/ *n.* **1** extent or measure of a surface (*over a large area*). **2** region (*southern area*). **3** space for a specific purpose (*dining area*). **4** scope or range. **5** space in front of the basement of a building. [Latin, = vacant space]

arena /ə'riːnə/ *n.* **1** central part of an amphitheatre etc. **2** scene of conflict; sphere of action. [Latin, = sand]

aren't /ɑːnt/ *contr.* **1** are not. **2** (in *interrog.*) am not (*aren't I coming too?*).

areola /æ'riːələ/ *n.* (*pl.* **-lae** /-liː/) circular pigmented area, esp. a near a nipple. □ **areolar** *adj.* [Latin diminutive of AREA]

arête /æ'reɪt/ *n.* sharp mountain ridge. [French from Latin *arista* spine]

argent /'ɑːdʒ(ə)nt/ *n.* & *adj. Heraldry* silver; silvery-white. [Latin *argentum*]

argon /'ɑːgɒn/ *n.* inert gaseous element. [Greek *argos* idle]

argosy /'ɑːgəsɪ/ *n.* (*pl.* **-ies**) *poet.* large merchant ship. [Italian *Ragusea nave* ship of Ragusa (in Dalmatia)]

argot /'ɑːgəʊ/ *n.* jargon of a group or class. [French]

argue /'ɑːgjuː/ *v.* (-ues, -ued, -uing) **1** (often foll. by *with, about,* etc.) exchange views forcefully or contentiously. **2** (often foll. by *that*) maintain by reasoning; indicate. **3** (foll. by *for, against*) reason. **4** treat (a matter) by reasoning. **5** (foll. by *into, out of*) persuade. □ **argue the toss** *colloq.* dispute a choice already made. □ **arguable** *adj.* **arguably** *adv.* [Latin *arguo* make clear, prove]

argument /'ɑːgjʊmənt/ *n.* **1** (esp. contentious) exchange of views; dispute. **2** (often foll. by *for, against*) reason given; reasoning process. **3** summary of a book etc.

argumentation /ˌɑːgjʊmen'teɪʃ(ə)n/ *n.* methodical reasoning; arguing.

argumentative /ˌɑːgjʊ'mentətɪv/ *adj.* given to arguing.

Argus /'ɑːgəs/ *n.* watchful guardian. [Greek *Argos* mythical giant with 100 eyes]

argy-bargy /ˌɑːdʒɪ'bɑːdʒɪ/ *n.* (*pl.* **-ies**) *joc.* dispute, wrangle. [originally Scots]

aria /'ɑːrɪə/ *n.* long accompanied solo song in an opera etc. [Italian]

arid /'ærɪd/ *adj.* **1** dry, parched. **2** uninteresting. □ **aridity** /ə'rɪdɪtɪ/ *n.* [Latin *areo* be dry]

Aries /'eəriːz/ *n.* (*pl.* same) **1** constellation and first sign of the zodiac (the Ram). **2** person born when the sun is in this sign. [Latin, = ram]

aright /ə'raɪt/ *adv.* rightly.

arise /ə'raɪz/ *v.* (-sing; *past* arose; *past part.* arisen /ə'rɪz(ə)n/) **1** originate. **2** (usu. foll. by *from, out of*) result. **3** come to one's notice; emerge. **4** rise, esp. from the dead or from kneeling. [Old English *a-* intensive prefix]

aristocracy /ˌærɪ'stɒkrəsɪ/ *n.* (*pl.* **-ies**) **1** ruling class or élite; nobility. **2 a** government by an élite. **b** State so governed. **3** (often foll. by *of*) best representatives. [Greek *aristokratia* rule by the best]

aristocrat /'ærɪstəˌkræt/ *n.* member of the aristocracy.

aristocratic /ˌærɪstə'krætɪk/ *adj.* **1** of or like the aristocracy. **2 a** distinguished. **b** grand, stylish.

Aristotelian /ˌærɪstə'tiːlɪən/ —*n.* disciple or student of Aristotle. —*adj.* of

Aristotle or his ideas. [Greek *Aristotelēs* (4th c. BC), name of a Greek philosopher]

arithmetic –*n.* /əˈrɪθmətɪk/ **1** science of numbers. **2** use of numbers; computation. –*adj.* /ˌærɪθˈmetɪk/ (also **arithmetical**) of arithmetic. [Greek *arithmos* number]

arithmetic mean *n.* = AVERAGE 2.

arithmetic progression *n.* sequence of numbers with constant intervals (e.g. 9, 7, 5, 3, etc.).

ark *n.* ship in which Noah escaped the Flood with his family and animals. [Old English from Latin *arca*]

Ark of the Covenant *n.* chest or cupboard containing the tables of Jewish Law.

arm[1] *n.* **1** upper limb of the human body from shoulder to hand. **2** forelimb or tentacle of an animal. **3 a** sleeve of a garment. **b** arm support of a chair etc. **c** thing branching from a main stem (*an arm of the sea*). **d** control, means of reaching (*arm of the law*). □ **arm in arm** with arms linked. **at arm's length** at a distance. **with open arms** cordially. □ **armful** *n.* (*pl.* -s). [Old English]

arm[2] –*n.* **1** (usu. in *pl.*) weapon. **2** (in *pl.*) military profession. **3** branch of the military (e.g. infantry, cavalry). **4** (in *pl.*) heraldic devices (*coat of arms*). –*v.* **1** supply, or equip oneself, with weapons etc., esp. in preparation for war. **2** make (a bomb etc.) ready. □ **take up arms** go to war. **under arms** equipped for war. **up in arms** (usu. foll. by *against*, *about*) actively resisting, highly indignant. [Latin *arma* arms]

armada /ɑːˈmɑːdə/ *n.* fleet of warships, esp. (**Armada**) that sent by Spain against England in 1588. [Spanish from Romanic]

armadillo /ˌɑːməˈdɪləʊ/ *n.* (*pl.* -s) S. American mammal with a plated body and large claws. [Spanish *armado* armed man]

Armageddon /ˌɑːməˈged(ə)n/ *n.* huge battle or struggle, esp. marking the end of the world. [Rev. 16:16]

armament /ˈɑːməmənt/ *n.* **1** (often in *pl.*) military equipment. **2** equipping for war. **3** force equipped. [Latin: related to ARM[2]]

armature /ˈɑːmətʃə(r)/ *n.* **1** rotating coil or coils of a dynamo or electric motor. **2** iron bar placed across the poles of a horseshoe magnet to preserve its power. **3** metal framework on which a sculpture is moulded. [Latin *armatura*, = armour]

armband *n.* band worn around the upper arm to hold up a shirtsleeve, or as identification, or to aid swimming.

armchair *n.* **1** chair with arm supports. **2** (*attrib.*) theoretical rather than active (*armchair critic*).

armhole *n.* each of two holes for arms in a garment.

armistice /ˈɑːmɪstɪs/ *n.* truce, esp. permanent. [Latin *arma* arms, *sisto* make stand]

Armistice Day *n.* anniversary of the armistice of 11 Nov. 1918.

armlet *n.* ornamental band worn round the arm.

armor etc. *US* var. of ARMOUR etc.

armorial /ɑːˈmɔːrɪəl/ *adj.* of heraldry or coats of arms. [related to ARMOUR]

armour /ˈɑːmə(r)/ –*n.* **1** protective usu. metal covering formerly worn in fighting. **2 a** (in full **armour-plate**) protective metal covering for an armed vehicle, ship, etc. **b** armed vehicles collectively. **3** protective covering or shell of an animal or plant. **4** heraldic devices. –*v.* (usu. as **armoured** *adj.*) provide with protective covering, and often guns (*armoured car*; *armoured train*). [Latin *armatura*: related to ARM[2]]

armourer *n.* **1** maker of arms or armour. **2** official in charge of arms.

armoury *n.* (*pl.* -ies) arsenal.

armpit *n.* hollow under the arm at the shoulder.

armrest *n.* = ARM[1] 3b.

arms race *n.* competitive accumulation of weapons by nations.

arm-wrestling *n.* trial of strength in which each party tries to force the other's arm down

army *n.* (*pl.* -ies) **1** organized armed land force. **2** (prec. by *the*) the military profession. **3** (often foll. by *of*) very large number (*army of locusts*). **4** organized civilian body (*Salvation Army*). [French: related to ARM[2]]

arnica /ˈɑːnɪkə/ *n.* **1** plant of the daisy family with yellow flowers. **2** medicine prepared from this. [origin unknown]

aroma /əˈrəʊmə/ *n.* **1** esp. pleasing smell, often of food. **2** subtle pervasive quality. [Greek, = spice]

aromatherapy *n.* use of plant extracts and oils in massage. □ **aromatherapist** *n.*

aromatic /ˌærəˈmætɪk/ –*adj.* **1** fragrant, spicy. **2** of organic compounds having an unsaturated ring, esp. containing a benzene ring. –*n.* aromatic substance. [Latin: related to AROMA]

arose *past* of ARISE.

around /əˈraʊnd/ –*adv.* **1** on every side; all round; round about. **2** *colloq.* **a** in existence; available. **b** near at hand. **3** here and there (*shop around*). –*prep.* **1** on or along the circuit of. **2** on every side of. **3** here and there in or near (*chairs*

around the room). **4 a** round (*church around the corner).* **b** at a time near to (*came around four o'clock).* □ **have been around** *colloq.* be widely experienced.

arouse /əˈraʊz/ v. (**-sing**) **1** induce (esp. an emotion). **2** awake from sleep. **3** stir into activity. **4** stimulate sexually. □ **arousal** n. [*a-* intensive prefix]

arpeggio /ɑːˈpedʒɪəʊ/ n. (pl. **-s**) *Mus.* notes of a chord played in succession. [Italian *arpa* harp]

arrack /ˈærək/ n. (also **arak**) alcoholic spirit, esp. made from coco sap or rice. [Arabic]

arraign /əˈreɪn/ v. **1** indict, accuse. **2** find fault with; call into question (an action or statement). □ **arraignment** n. [Latin *ratio* reason]

arrange /əˈreɪndʒ/ v. (**-ging**) **1** put into order; classify. **2** plan or provide for; take measures (*arranged a meeting*; *arrange to see him*; *arranged for a taxi*). **3** agree (*arranged it with her*). **4** *Mus.* adapt (a composition) for a particular manner of performance. [French: related to RANGE]

arrangement n. **1** arranging or being arranged. **2** manner of this. **3** something arranged. **4** (in pl.) plans, measures (*made my own arrangements*). **5** *Mus.* composition adapted for performance in a particular way.

arrant /ˈærənt/ adj. *literary* downright, utter (*arrant liar*). [var. of ERRANT, originally in *arrant* (= outlawed, roving) *thief* etc.]

arras /ˈærəs/ n. *hist.* rich tapestry or wall-hanging. [*Arras* in France]

array /əˈreɪ/ —n. **1** imposing or well-ordered series or display. **2** ordered arrangement, esp. of troops (*battle array*). —v. **1** deck, adorn. **2** set in order; marshal (forces). [Latin *ad-*, READY]

arrears /əˈrɪəz/ n.pl. amount (esp. of work, rent, etc.) still outstanding or uncompleted. □ **in arrears** behind, esp. in payment. [medieval Latin *adretro* behindhand]

arrest /əˈrest/ —v. **1** lawfully seize (a suspect etc.). **2** stop or check the progress of. **3** attract (a person's attention). —n. **1** arresting or being arrested. **2** stoppage (*cardiac arrest*). [Latin *resto* remain]

arrester n. device for slowing an aircraft after landing.

arrière-pensée /ˌærjerpɑ̃ˈseɪ/ n. **1** secret motive. **2** mental reservation. [French]

arris /ˈærɪs/ n. *Archit.* sharp edge at the junction of two surfaces. [French *areste*, = ARÊTE]

arrival /əˈraɪv(ə)l/ n. **1** arriving; appearance on the scene. **2** person or thing that has arrived.

arrive /əˈraɪv/ v. (**-ving**) **1** (often foll. by *at, in*) reach a destination. **2** (foll. by *at*) reach (a conclusion etc.). **3** *colloq.* become successful. **4** *colloq.* (of a child) be born. **5** (of a time) come. [Latin *ripa* shore]

arriviste /ˌæriːˈviːst/ n. ambitious or ruthless person. [French: related to ARRIVE]

arrogant /ˈærəgənt/ adj. aggressively assertive or presumptuous. □ **arrogance** n. **arrogantly** adv. [related to ARROGATE]

arrogate /ˈærəˌgeɪt/ v. (**-ting**) **1** (often foll. by *to* oneself) claim (power etc.) without right. **2** (often foll. by *to*) attribute unjustly (to a person). □ **arrogation** /-ˈgeɪʃ(ə)n/ n. [Latin *rogo* ask]

arrow /ˈærəʊ/ n. **1** pointed slender missile shot from a bow. **2** representation of this, esp. indicating direction. [Old English]

arrowhead n. **1** pointed tip of an arrow. **2** water-plant with arrow-shaped leaves.

arrowroot n. **1** nutritious starch. **2** plant yielding this.

arse /ɑːs/ n. (US **ass** /æs/) *coarse slang* buttocks. [Old English]

arsehole n. (US **asshole**) *coarse slang* **1** anus. **2** *offens.* contemptible person.

arsenal /ˈɑːsən(ə)l/ n. **1** store, esp. of weapons. **2** place for the storage and manufacture of weapons and ammunition. [Arabic, = workshop]

arsenic —n. /ˈɑːsənɪk/ **1** non-scientific name for arsenic trioxide, a highly poisonous white powder used in weedkillers etc. **2** *Chem.* brittle semi-metallic element. —adj. /ɑːˈsenɪk/ of or containing arsenic. [French, ultimately from Persian *zar* gold]

arson /ˈɑːs(ə)n/ n. crime of deliberately setting fire to property. □ **arsonist** n. [Latin *ardeo ars-* burn]

art n. **1 a** human creative skill or its application. **b** work showing this. **2 a** (in pl.; prec. by *the*) branches of creative activity concerned with the production of imaginative designs, sounds, or ideas, e.g. painting, music, writing. **b** any one of these. **3** creative activity resulting in visual representation (*good at music but not art*). **4** human skill as opposed to nature (*art and nature combined*). **5** (often foll. by *of*) **a** skill, knack. **b** cunning; trick, stratagem. **6** (in pl.; usu. prec. by *the*) supposedly creative subjects (esp. languages, literature, and history) as opposed to scientific, technical, or vocational subjects. [Latin *ars art-*]

art deco /ɑ:t 'dekəʊ/ n. decorative art style of 1910–30, with geometric motifs and strong colours.

artefact /'ɑ:tɪˌfækt/ n. (also **artifact**) man-made object, esp. a tool or vessel as an archaeological item. [Latin *arte* by art, *facio* make]

arterial /ɑ:'tɪərɪəl/ adj. **1** of or like an artery. **2** (esp. of a road) main, important. [French: related to ARTERY]

arteriosclerosis /ɑ:ˌtɪərɪəʊsklɪə'rəʊsɪs/ n. loss of elasticity and thickening of artery walls, esp. in old age. [from ARTERY, SCLEROSIS]

artery /'ɑ:tərɪ/ n. (pl. **-ies**) **1** any of the blood-vessels carrying blood from the heart. **2** main road or railway line. [Greek, probably from *airō* raise]

artesian well /ɑ:'ti:zɪən/ n. well in which water rises to the surface by natural pressure through a vertically drilled hole. [*Artois*, old French province]

artful adj. crafty, deceitful. □ **artfully** adv.

arthritis /ɑ:'θraɪtɪs/ n. inflammation of a joint or joints. □ **arthritic** /-'θrɪtɪk/ adj. & n. [Greek *arthron* joint]

arthropod /'ɑ:θrəˌpɒd/ n. invertebrate with a segmented body and jointed limbs, e.g. an insect, spider, or crustacean. [Greek *arthron* joint, *pous* podfoot]

artichoke /'ɑ:tɪˌtʃəʊk/ n. **1** plant allied to the thistle. **2** (in full **globe artichoke**) its partly edible flower-head (see also JERUSALEM ARTICHOKE). [Italian from Arabic]

article /'ɑ:tɪk(ə)l/ —n. **1** item or thing. **2** non-fictional journalistic essay. **3** clause or item in an agreement or contract. **4** definite or indefinite article. —v. (**-ling**) employ under contract as a trainee. [Latin *articulus* from *artus* joint]

articled clerk n. trainee solicitor.

articular /ɑ:'tɪkjʊlə(r)/ adj. of a joint or joints. [Latin: related to ARTICLE]

articulate —adj. /ɑ:'tɪkjʊlət/ **1** fluent and clear in speech. **2** (of sound or speech) having clearly distinguishable parts. **3** having joints. —v. /ɑ:'tɪkjʊˌleɪt/ (**-ting**) **1 a** pronounce distinctly. **b** speak or express clearly. **2** (usu. in *passive*) connect by joints. **3** mark with apparent joints. **4** (often foll. by *with*) form a joint. □ **articulately** adv.

articulated lorry n. one with sections connected by a flexible joint.

articulation /ɑ:ˌtɪkjʊ'leɪʃ(ə)n/ n. **1 a** speaking or being spoken. **b** articulate utterance; speech. **2 a** act or mode of jointing. **b** joint. [Latin: related to ARTICULATE]

artifact var. of ARTEFACT.

artifice /'ɑ:tɪfɪs/ n. **1** trick or clever device. **2** cunning. **3** skill, ingenuity. [Latin *ars art-* and, *facio* make]

artificer /ɑ:'tɪfɪsə(r)/ n. **1** craftsman. **2** skilled military mechanic.

artificial /ˌɑ:tɪ'fɪʃ(ə)l/ adj. **1** not natural (*artificial lake*). **2** imitating nature (*artificial flowers*). **3** affected, insincere. □ **artificiality** /-ʃɪ'ælɪtɪ/ n. **artificially** adv. [Latin: related to ARTIFICE]

artificial insemination n. non-sexual injection of semen into the uterus.

artificial intelligence n. use of computers for tasks normally regarded as needing human intelligence.

artificial respiration n. manual or mechanical stimulation of breathing.

artillery /ɑ:'tɪlərɪ/ n. (pl. **-ies**) **1** heavy guns used in land warfare. **2** branch of the army using these. □ **artilleryman** n. [French *artiller* equip]

artisan /ˌɑ:tɪ'zæn/ n. skilled manual worker or craftsman. [Latin *artio* instruct in the arts]

artist /'ɑ:tɪst/ n. **1** practitioner of any of the arts, esp. painting. **2** artiste. **3** person using skill or taste. □ **artistry** n. [French *artiste* from Italian]

artiste /ɑ:'ti:st/ n. professional performer, esp. a singer or dancer.

artistic /ɑ:'tɪstɪk/ adj. **1** having natural skill in art. **2** skilfully or tastefully done. **3** of art or artists. □ **artistically** adv.

artless adj. **1** guileless, ingenuous. **2** natural. **3** clumsy. □ **artlessly** adv.

art nouveau /ˌɑ: nu:'vəʊ/ n. art style of the late 19th century, with flowing lines.

artwork n. **1** illustrative material in printed matter. **2** works of art collectively (*exhibition of children's artwork*).

arty adj. (**-ier**, **-iest**) colloq. pretentiously or affectedly artistic.

arum /'eərəm/ n. plant with arrow-shaped leaves. [Greek *aron*]

-ary suffix forming adjectives (*contrary*; *primary*). [French *-aire*, Latin *-ari(u)s*]

Aryan /'eərɪən/ —n. **1** speaker of any of the languages of the Indo-European family. **2** *improperly* (in Nazi ideology) non-Jewish Caucasian. —adj. of Aryans. [Sanskrit]

As symb. arsenic.

as[1] /æz, əz/ —adv. & conj. (adv. as antecedent in main sentence; conj. in relative clause expressed or implied) to the extent to which … is or does etc. (*am as tall as he*; *am as tall as he is*; (colloq.) *am as tall as him*; *as recently as last week*). —conj. (with relative clause expressed or implied) **1** (with antecedent *so*) expressing result or purpose (*came early so as to meet us*). **2** (with antecedent adverb omitted) although

(*good as it is* = although it is good). **3** (without antecedent adverb) **a** in the manner in which (*do as you like*; *rose as one man*). **b** in the capacity or form of (*I speak as your friend*; *Olivier as Hamlet*). **c** while (*arrived as I was eating*). **d** since, seeing that (*as you are here, we can talk*). **e** for instance (*cathedral cities, as York*). *—rel. pron.* (with verb of relative clause expressed or implied) **1** that, who, which (*I had the same trouble as you*; *he is a writer, as is his wife*; *such countries as France*). **2** (with a sentence as antecedent) a fact that (*he lost, as you know*). □ **as for** with regard to (*as for you, I think you are wrong*). **as from** on and after (a specified date). **as if** (or **though**) as would be the case if (*acts as if he were in charge*). **as it were** in a way; to some extent (*he is, as it were, infatuated*). **as long as** see LONG[1]. **as much** see MUCH. **as of 1** = *as from*. **2** as at (a specified time). **as per** see PER. **as regards** see REGARD. **as soon as** see SOON. **as such** see SUCH. **as though** see *as if*. **as to** with regard to. **as well 1** in addition. **2** advisable, desirable, reasonably. **as well as** in addition to. **as yet** until now or up to a particular time (*have received no news as yet*). [Old English, = ALSO]

as[2] /æs/ n. (*pl.* **asses**) Roman copper coin. [Latin]

asafoetida /ˌæsəˈfetɪdə/ n. (*US* **asafetida**) resinous pungent plant gum used in cooking and formerly in medicine. [Persian *azā* mastic: related to FETID]

a.s.a.p. *abbr.* as soon as possible.

asbestos /æsˈbestɒs/ n. **1** fibrous silicate mineral. **2** this as a heat-resistant or insulating material. [Greek, = unquenchable]

ascend /əˈsend/ v. **1** move or slope upwards, rise. **2** climb; go up. □ **ascend the throne** become king or queen. [Latin *scando* climb]

ascendancy n. (often foll. by *over*) dominant power or control.

ascendant *—adj.* **1** rising. **2** *Astron.* rising towards the zenith. **3** *Astrol.* just above the eastern horizon. **4** predominant. *—n. Astrol.* ascendant point of the sun's apparent path. □ **in the ascendant** gaining or having power or authority.

ascension /əˈsenʃ(ə)n/ n. **1** ascent. **2** (**Ascension**) ascent of Christ into heaven.

ascent /əˈsent/ n. **1** ascending, rising, or progressing. **2** upward slope or path etc.

ascertain /ˌæsəˈteɪn/ v. find out for certain. □ **ascertainment** n. [French: related to CERTAIN]

ascetic /əˈsetɪk/ *—adj.* severely abstinent; self-denying. *—n.* ascetic, esp. religious, person. □ **asceticism** /-tɪˌsɪz(ə)m/ n. [Greek *askeō* exercise]

ASCII /ˈæskɪ/ *abbr. Computing* American Standard Code for Information Interchange.

ascorbic acid /əˈskɔːbɪk/ n. vitamin C, which prevents scurvy. [from A-, SCORBUTIC]

ascribe /əˈskraɪb/ v. (**-bing**) (usu. foll. by *to*) **1** attribute (*ascribes his health to exercise*). **2** regard as belonging. □ **ascription** /əˈskrɪpʃ(ə)n/ n. [Latin *scribo* write]

asepsis /eɪˈsepsɪs/ n. **1** absence of sepsis or harmful micro-organisms. **2** method of achieving asepsis in surgery. □ **aseptic** *adj.*

asexual /eɪˈseksjʊəl/ *adj.* **1** without sex, sexual organs, or sexuality. **2** (of reproduction) not involving the fusion of gametes. □ **asexually** *adv.*

ash[1] n. **1** (often in *pl.*) powdery residue left after burning. **2** (*pl.*) human remains after cremation. **3** (**the Ashes**) *Cricket* trophy competed for by Australia and England. [Old English]

ash[2] n. **1** tree with silver-grey bark. **2** its hard, pale wood. [Old English]

ashamed /əˈʃeɪmd/ *adj.* (usu. *predic.*) **1** embarrassed by shame (*ashamed of myself*). **2** (foll. by *to* + infin.) hesitant, reluctant out of shame (*am ashamed to say*). [Old English *a*- intensive prefix]

ashcan n. *US* dustbin.

ashen *adj.* like ashes, esp. grey or pale.

Ashkenazi /ˌæʃkəˈnɑːzɪ/ n. (*pl.* **-zim**) East European Jew. [Hebrew]

ashlar /ˈæʃlə(r)/ n. **1** large square-cut stone used in building; masonry made of these. **2** thin slabs of masonry used for facing walls. [Latin *axis* board]

ashore /əˈʃɔː(r)/ *adv.* towards or on the shore or land.

ashram /ˈæʃrəm/ n. place of religious retreat for Hindus. [Sanskrit]

ashtray n. small receptacle for cigarette ash, stubs, etc.

ashy *adj.* (**-ier**, **-iest**) **1** = ASHEN. **2** covered with ashes.

Asian /ˈeɪʃ(ə)n/ *—n.* **1** native of Asia. **2** person of Asian descent. *—adj.* of Asia. [Latin from Greek]

Asiatic /ˌeɪʃɪˈætɪk/ *—n. offens.* Asian. *—adj.* Asian. [Latin from Greek]

aside /əˈsaɪd/ *—adv.* to or on one side; away, apart. *—n.* words spoken aside, esp. confidentially to the audience by an actor.

asinine /ˈæsɪˌnaɪn/ *adj.* like an ass, esp. stupid or stubborn. □ **asininity** /-ˈnɪnɪtɪ/ n. [Latin *asinus* ass]

ask /ɑːsk/ v. **1** call for an answer to or about (*ask her about it; ask him his name*). **2** seek to obtain from someone (*ask a favour of*). **3** (usu. foll. by *out, in,* or *over,* or *to* (a function etc.)) invite (*must ask them over; asked her to dinner*). **4** (foll. by *for*) seek to obtain, meet, or be directed to (*ask for help; asking for you; ask for the bar*). □ **ask after** inquire about (esp. a person). **ask for it** *slang* invite trouble. [Old English]

askance /əˈskæns/ adv. sideways or squinting. □ **look askance at** regard suspiciously. [origin unknown]

askew /əˈskjuː/ −adv. awry, crookedly. −predic. adj. oblique; awry.

aslant /əˈslɑːnt/ −adv. obliquely or at a slant. −prep. obliquely across.

asleep /əˈsliːp/ predic. adj. & adv. **1 a** in or into a state of sleep. **b** inactive, inattentive. **2** (of a limb etc.) numb. **3** *euphem.* dead.

asp n. small venomous snake of North Africa or Southern Europe. [Greek *aspis*]

asparagus /əˈspærəgəs/ n. **1** plant of the lily family. **2** edible shoots of this. [Latin from Greek]

aspect /ˈæspekt/ n. **1** viewpoint, feature, etc. to be considered (*one aspect of the problem*). **2** appearance or look (*cheerful aspect*). **3** side of a building or location facing a particular direction (*southern aspect*). [Latin *adspicio* look at]

aspen /ˈæspən/ n. poplar with very tremulous leaves. [Old English: originally adj.]

asperity /əˈsperɪtɪ/ n. (pl. -ies) **1** sharpness of temper or tone. **2** roughness; rough excrescence. [Latin *asper* rough]

aspersion /əˈspɜːʃ(ə)n/ n. □ **cast aspersions on** attack the reputation of. [Latin *aspergo* besprinkle]

asphalt /ˈæsfælt/ −n. **1** dark bituminous pitch. **2** mixture of this with sand, gravel, etc., for surfacing roads etc. −v. surface with asphalt. [Latin from Greek]

asphodel /ˈæsfədel/ n. **1** plant of the lily family. **2** *poet.* immortal flower growing in Elysium. [Latin from Greek]

asphyxia /æsˈfɪksɪə/ n. lack of oxygen in the blood, causing unconsciousness or death; suffocation. □ **asphyxiant** adj. & n. [Greek *a-* not, *sphuxis* pulse]

asphyxiate /æsˈfɪksɪeɪt/ v. (-ting) suffocate. □ **asphyxiation** /-ˈeɪʃ(ə)n/ n.

aspic /ˈæspɪk/ n. savoury jelly used esp. to contain game, eggs, etc. [French, = ASP, suggested by the colours of the jelly]

aspidistra /ˌæspɪˈdɪstrə/ n. house-plant with broad tapering leaves. [Greek *aspis* shield]

aspirant /ˈæspɪrənt/ −adj. aspiring. −n. person who aspires. [Latin: related to ASPIRE]

aspirate /ˈæspərət/ −adj. pronounced with an exhalation of breath; blended with the sound of *h*. −n. sound of *h*; consonant pronounced in this way. −v. /-ˌreɪt/ (-ting) **1** pronounce with breath or with initial *h*. **2** draw (fluid) by suction from a cavity etc.

aspiration /ˌæspɪˈreɪʃ(ə)n/ n. **1** ambition or desire. **2** drawing breath or *Phonet.* aspirating.

aspirator /ˈæspɪˌreɪtə(r)/ n. apparatus for aspirating fluid. [Latin: related to ASPIRE]

aspire /əˈspaɪə(r)/ v. (-ring) (usu. foll. by *to* or *after,* or *to* + infin.) have ambition or a strong desire. [Latin *aspiro* breathe upon]

aspirin /ˈæsprɪn/ n. (pl. same or -s) **1** white powder, acetylsalicylic acid, used to reduce pain and fever. **2** tablet of this. [German]

ass[1] n. **1 a** four-legged long-eared mammal related to the horse. **b** donkey. **2** stupid person. [Old English from Latin]

ass[2] *US* var. of ARSE.

assagai var. of ASSEGAI.

assail /əˈseɪl/ v. **1** attack physically or verbally. **2** tackle (a task) resolutely. □ **assailant** n. [Latin *salio* leap]

assassin /əˈsæsɪn/ n. killer, esp. of a political or religious leader. [Arabic, = hashish-eater]

assassinate /əˈsæsɪneɪt/ v. (-ting) kill for political or religious motives. □ **assassination** /-ˈneɪʃ(ə)n/ n.

assault /əˈsɔːlt/ −n. **1** violent physical or verbal attack. **2** *Law* threat or display of violence against a person. −v. make an assault on. □ **assault and battery** *Law* threatening act resulting in physical harm to a person. [Latin: related to ASSAIL]

assay /əˈseɪ/ −n. testing of a metal or ore to determine its ingredients and quality. −v. make an assay of (a metal or ore). [French, var. of *essai* ESSAY]

assegai /ˈæsɪˌgaɪ/ n. (also **assagai**) light iron-tipped S. African spear. [Arabic, = the spear]

assemblage /əˈsemblɪdʒ/ n. **1** assembling. **2** assembled group.

assemble /əˈsemb(ə)l/ v. (-ling) **1** gather together; collect. **2** esp. *Mech.* fit together (components, a whole). [Latin *ad* to, *simul* together]

assembler /əˈsemblə(r)/ n. **1** person who assembles a machine etc. **2** *Computing* **a** program for converting

instructions written in low-level symbolic code into machine code. **b** the low-level symbolic code itself.

assembly /ə'semblɪ/ n. (pl. -ies) 1 assembling. 2 assembled group, esp. as a deliberative body. 3 assembling of components.

assembly line n. machinery arranged so that a product can be progressively assembled.

assent /ə'sent/ —v. (usu. foll. by to) 1 express agreement. 2 consent. —n. consent or approval, esp. official. □ **assenter** n. [Latin sentio think]

assert /ə'sɜːt/ v. 1 declare, state clearly. 2 refl. insist on one's rights. 3 enforce a claim to (assert one's rights). [Latin assero -sert-]

assertion /ə'sɜːʃ(ə)n/ n. declaration, forthright statement.

assertive /ə'sɜːtɪv/ adj. tending to assert oneself; forthright, positive. □ **assertively** adv. **assertiveness** n.

assess /ə'ses/ v. 1 estimate the size or quality of. 2 estimate the value of (property etc.) for taxation. □ **assessment** n. [Latin assideo -sess- sit by]

assessor n. 1 person who assesses (esp. for tax or insurance). 2 legal adviser on technical questions.

asset /'æset/ n. 1 useful or valuable person or thing. 2 (usu. in pl.) property and possessions, esp. that can be set against debts etc. [French asez from Latin ad satis to enough]

asset-stripping n. the taking over of a company and selling off of its assets to make a profit.

asseverate /ə'sevə,reɪt/ v. (-ting) declare solemnly. □ **asseveration** /-'reɪʃ(ə)n/ n. [Latin severus serious]

asshole US var. of ARSEHOLE.

assiduous /ə'sɪdjʊəs/ adj. 1 persevering, hard-working. 2 attending closely. □ **assiduity** /,æsɪ'djuːɪtɪ/ n. **assiduously** adv. [Latin: related to ASSESS]

assign /ə'saɪn/ —v. 1 (usu. foll. by to) **a** allot as a share or responsibility. **b** appoint to a position, task, etc. 2 fix (a time, place, etc.). 3 (foll. by to) ascribe to (a reason, date, etc.) (assigned the manuscript to 1832). 4 (foll. by to) Law transfer formally (esp. property) to (another). —n. assignee. □ **assigner** n. **assignor** n. Law. [Latin assigno mark out]

assignation /,æsɪg'neɪʃ(ə)n/ n. 1 appointment to meet, esp. by lovers in secret. 2 assigning or being assigned.

assignee /,æsaɪ'niː/ n. Law person to whom a right or property is assigned.

assignment /ə'saɪnmənt/ n. 1 task or mission. 2 assigning or being assigned. 3 legal transfer.

assimilate /ə'sɪmɪ,leɪt/ v. (-ting) 1 absorb or be absorbed, either physically or mentally. 2 (usu. foll. by to, with) make like; cause to resemble. □ **assimilable** adj. **assimilation** /-'leɪʃ(ə)n/ n. **assimilative** /-lətɪv/ adj. **assimilator** n. [Latin similis like]

assist /ə'sɪst/ v. (often foll. by in + verbal noun) help. □ **assistance** n. [Latin assisto stand by]

assistant n. 1 (often attrib.) person who helps, esp. as a subordinate. 2 = SHOP ASSISTANT.

assizes /ə'saɪzɪz/ n.pl. hist. court periodically administering the civil and criminal law. [French: related to ASSESS]

■ **Usage** In 1972 the civil jurisdiction of assizes in England and Wales was transferred to the High Court and the criminal jurisdiction to the Crown Court.

Assoc. abbr. Association.

associate —v. /ə'səʊʃɪ,eɪt/ (-ting) 1 connect mentally (associate holly with Christmas). 2 join or combine, esp. for a common purpose. 3 refl. declare oneself or be in agreement. 4 (usu. foll. by with) meet frequently or deal. —n. /ə'səʊʃɪət/ 1 partner, colleague. 2 friend, companion. 3 subordinate member of a society etc. —adj. /ə'səʊʃɪət/ 1 joined or allied. 2 of lower status (associate member). □ **associative** /-ʃɪətɪv/ adj. [Latin socius allied]

association /ə,səʊsɪ'eɪʃ(ə)n/ n. 1 group organized for a joint purpose; society. 2 associating or being associated. 3 companionship. 4 mental connection of ideas. [medieval Latin: related to ASSOCIATE]

Association Football n. football played with a round ball which may not be handled except by the goalkeepers.

assonance /'æsənəns/ n. partial resemblance of sound between two syllables e.g. sonnet, porridge, and killed, cold, culled. □ **assonant** adj. [Latin sonus sound]

assort /ə'sɔːt/ v. 1 classify or arrange in sorts. 2 (usu. foll. by with) suit or harmonize with. [French: related to SORT]

assorted adj. 1 of various sorts, mixed. 2 classified. 3 matched (ill-assorted pair).

assortment n. diverse group or mixture.

assuage /ə'sweɪdʒ/ v. (-ging) 1 calm or soothe. 2 appease (an appetite). □ **assuagement** n. [Latin suavis sweet]

assume /ə'sjuːm/ v. (-ming) 1 (usu. foll. by that) take to be true. 2 simulate (ignorance etc.). 3 undertake (an office

etc.). **4** take or put on (an aspect, attribute, etc.) (*assumed immense importance*). [Latin *sumo* take]

assuming *adj.* arrogant, presumptuous.

assumption /ə'sʌmpʃ(ə)n/ *n.* **1** assuming. **2** thing assumed. **3** (**Assumption**) reception of the Virgin Mary bodily into heaven.

assurance /ə'ʃʊərəns/ *n.* **1** emphatic declaration; guarantee. **2** insurance, esp. life insurance. **3** certainty. **4** self-confidence; assertiveness.

assure /ə'ʃʊə(r)/ *v.* (**-ring**) **1** (often foll. by *of*) **a** convince. **b** tell (a person) confidently (*assured him all was well*). **2** ensure; guarantee (a result etc.). **3** insure (esp. a life). **4** (as **assured** *adj.*) **a** guaranteed. **b** self-confident. [Latin *securus* safe]

assuredly /ə'ʃʊərɪdlɪ/ *adv.* certainly.

AST *abbr.* Atlantic Standard Time.

astatine /'æstə,tiːn/ *n.* radioactive element, the heaviest of the halogens. [Greek *astatos* unstable]

aster *n.* plant with bright daisy-like flowers. [Greek, = star]

asterisk /'æstərɪsk/ *–n.* symbol (*) used to mark words or to indicate omission etc. *–v.* mark with an asterisk. [Greek, = little star]

astern /ə'stɜːn/ *adv.* (often foll. by *of*) **1** in or to the rear of a ship or aircraft. **2** backwards.

asteroid /'æstə,rɔɪd/ *n.* **1** any of the minor planets orbiting the sun, mainly between the orbits of Mars and Jupiter. **2** starfish. [Greek; related to ASTER]

asthma /'æsmə/ *n.* respiratory condition marked by wheezing. [Greek *azō* breathe hard]

asthmatic /æs'mætɪk/ *–adj.* of or suffering from asthma. *–n.* asthmatic person.

astigmatism /ə'stɪgmə,tɪz(ə)m/ *n.* eye or lens defect resulting in distorted images. □ **astigmatic** /,æstɪg'mætɪk/ *adj.* [from A-, STIGMA]

astir /ə'stɜː(r)/ *predic. adj. & adv.* **1** in motion. **2** out of bed.

astonish /ə'stɒnɪʃ/ *v.* surprise greatly, amaze. □ **astonishment** *n.* [Latin *ex-* forth, *tono* thunder]

astound /ə'staʊnd/ *v.* astonish greatly.

astraddle /ə'stræd(ə)l/ *adv.* astride.

astrakhan /,æstrə'kæn/ *n.* **1** dark curly fleece of young Astrakhan lambs. **2** cloth imitating this. [*Astrakhan* in Russia]

astral /'æstr(ə)l/ *adj* of the stars; starry. [Latin *astrum* star]

astray /ə'streɪ/ *adv. & predic.adj.* out of the right way, erring. □ **go astray** be

missing. [Latin *extra* away, *vagor* wander]

astride /ə'straɪd/ *–adv.* **1** (often foll. by *of*) with a leg on each side. **2** with legs apart. *–prep.* astride of; extending across.

astringent /ə'strɪndʒ(ə)nt/ *–adj.* **1** checking bleeding by contracting body tissues. **2** severe, austere. *–n.* astringent substance. □ **astringency** *n.* [Latin *astringo* draw tight]

astrolabe /'æstrə,leɪb/ *n.* instrument formerly used to measure the altitude of stars etc. [Greek, = star-taking]

astrology /ə'strɒlədʒɪ/ *n.* study of supposed planetary influence on human affairs. □ **astrologer** *n.* **astrological** /,æstrə'lɒdʒɪk(ə)l/ *adj.* **astrologist** *n.* [Greek *astron* star]

astronaut /'æstrə,nɔːt/ *n.* crew member of a spacecraft. [Greek *astron* star, *nautēs* sailor]

astronautics /,æstrə'nɔːtɪks/ *n.pl.* (treated as *sing.*) science of space travel. □ **astronautical** *adj.*

astronomical /,æstrə'nɒmɪk(ə)l/ *adj.* (also **astronomic**) **1** of astronomy. **2** vast, gigantic. □ **astronomically** *adv.*

astronomy /ə'strɒnəmɪ/ *n.* the scientific study of celestial bodies. □ **astronomer** *n.* [Greek *astron* star, *nemō* arrange]

astrophysics /,æstrəʊ'fɪzɪks/ *n.pl.* (treated as *sing.*) the study of the physics and chemistry of celestial bodies. □ **astrophysical** *adj.* **astrophysicist** /-sɪst/ *n.* [Greek *astron* star]

astute /ə'stjuːt/ *adj.* shrewd. □ **astutely** *adv.* **astuteness** *n.* [Latin *astus* craft]

asunder /ə'sʌndə(r)/ *adv. literary* apart.

asylum /ə'saɪləm/ *n.* **1** sanctuary; protection, esp. for fugitives from the law (*seek asylum*). **2** *hist.* institution for the mentally ill or destitute. [Greek *a-* not, *sulon* right of seizure]

asymmetry /æ'sɪmɪtrɪ/ *n.* lack of symmetry. □ **asymmetric** /-'metrɪk/ *adj.* **asymmetrical** /-'metrɪk(ə)l/ *adj.* [Greek]

At *symb.* astatine.

at /æt, ət/ *prep.* **1** expressing position (*wait at the corner; at school*). **2** expressing a point in time (*at dawn*). **3** expressing a point in a scale (*at his best*). **4** expressing engagement in an activity etc. (*at war*). **5** expressing a value or rate (*sell at £10 each*). **6 a** with or with reference to (*annoyed at losing; came at a run*). **b** by means of (*starts at a touch*). **7** expressing motion or aim towards (*aim at the target; laughed at us*). □ **at all** see ALL. **at hand** see HAND. **at home** see HOME. **at it** engaged in an activity; working hard. **at once** see

ONCE. **at that 1** moreover (*a good one at that*). **2** then (*at that he left*). **at times** see TIME. [Old English]

atavism /'ætə,vɪz(ə)m/ *n.* **1** reappearance of a remote ancestral characteristic, throwback. **2** reversion to an earlier type. □ **atavistic** /-'vɪstɪk/ *adj.* [Latin *atavus* ancestor]

ataxia /ə'tæksɪə/ *n. Med.* imperfect control of bodily movements. [Greek *a-* without, *taxis* order]

ate past of EAT.

-ate[1] *suffix* forming nouns denoting status, function, or office (*doctorate*; *consulate*). [Latin]

-ate[2] *suffix* forming adjectives with the sense 'having, full of' (*foliate*; *passionate*). [Latin participial ending *-atus*]

atelier /ə'telɪ,eɪ/ *n.* workshop or artist's studio. [French]

atheism /'eɪθɪ,ɪz(ə)m/ *n.* belief that there is no God. □ **atheist** *n.* **atheistic** /-'ɪstɪk/ *adj.* [Greek *a-* not, *theos* god]

atherosclerosis /,æθərəʊsklə'rəʊsɪs/ *n.* degeneration of the arteries caused by a build-up of fatty deposits. [Greek *athērē* groats]

athirst /ə'θɜːst/ *predic. adj. poet.* **1** (usu. foll. by *for*) eager. **2** thirsty.

athlete /'æθliːt/ *n.* person who engages in athletics, exercise, etc. [Greek *athlon* prize]

athlete's foot *n.* fungal foot condition.

athletic /æθ'letɪk/ *adj.* **1** of athletes or athletics. **2** physically strong or agile. □ **athletically** *adv.* **athleticism** /-,sɪz(ə)m/ *n.* [Latin: related to ATHLETE]

athletics *n.pl.* (usu. treated as *sing.*) physical exercises, esp. track and field events.

at-home *n.* social reception in a person's home.

-ation *suffix* **1** forming nouns denoting an action or an instance of it (*flirtation*; *hesitation*). **2** forming nouns denoting a result or product of action (*plantation*; *starvation*). [Latin *-atio*]

Atlantic /ət'læntɪk/ *adj.* of or adjoining the ocean between Europe and Africa to the east and America to the west. [Greek: related to ATLAS]

atlas /'ætləs/ *n.* book of maps or charts. [Greek *Atlas*, the Titan who held up the universe]

atmosphere /'ætməsfɪə(r)/ *n.* **1 a** gases enveloping the earth, any other planet, etc. **b** air in a room etc., esp. if fetid. **2** pervading tone or mood of a place, situation, or work of art. **3** unit of pressure equal to mean atmospheric pressure at sea level, 101,325 pascals. □ **atmospheric** /-'ferɪk/ *adj.* [Greek *atmos* vapour, SPHERE]

atmospherics /,ætməs'ferɪks/ *n.pl.* **1** electrical atmospheric disturbance, esp. caused by lightning. **2** interference with telecommunications caused by this.

atoll /'ætɒl/ *n.* ring-shaped coral reef enclosing a lagoon. [Maldive]

atom /'ætəm/ *n.* **1 a** smallest particle of a chemical element that can take part in a chemical reaction. **b** this as a source of nuclear energy. **2** minute portion or thing (*atom of pity*). [Greek *atomos* indivisible]

atom bomb *n.* bomb in which energy is released by nuclear fission.

atomic /ə'tɒmɪk/ *adj.* **1** of or using atomic energy or atomic bombs. **2** of atoms.

atomic bomb *n.* = ATOM BOMB.

atomic energy *n.* nuclear energy.

atomic mass *n.* mass of an atom measured in atomic mass units.

atomic mass unit *n.* unit of mass used to express atomic and molecular weights, equal to one-twelfth of the mass of an atom of carbon-12.

atomic number *n.* number of protons in the nucleus of an atom.

atomic theory *n.* theory that all matter consists of atoms.

atomic weight *n.* = RELATIVE ATOMIC MASS.

atomize /,ætə'maɪz/ *v.* (also **-ise**) (**-zing** or **-sing**) reduce to atoms or fine particles.

atomizer *n.* (also **-iser**) = AEROSOL 1.

atonal /eɪ'təʊn(ə)l/ *adj. Mus.* not written in any key or mode. □ **atonality** /-'nælɪtɪ/ *n.*

atone /ə'təʊn/ *v.* (**-ning**) (usu. foll. by *for*) make amends (for a wrong). [from ATONEMENT]

atonement *n.* **1** atoning. **2** (**the Atonement**) expiation by Christ of mankind's sins. [*at one* + -MENT]

atrium /'eɪtrɪəm/ *n.* (*pl.* **-s** or **atria**) **1 a** central court of an ancient Roman house. **b** (usu. skylit) central court rising through several storeys. **2** each of the two upper cavities of the heart. [Latin]

atrocious /ə'trəʊʃəs/ *adj.* **1** very bad or unpleasant (*atrocious manners*). **2** wicked (*atrocious cruelty*). □ **atrociously** *adv.* [Latin *atrox* cruel]

atrocity /ə'trɒsɪtɪ/ *n.* (*pl.* **-ies**) **1** wicked or cruel act. **2** extreme wickedness. [Latin: related to ATROCIOUS]

atrophy /'ætrəfɪ/ *—n.* wasting away, esp. through disuse; emaciation. *—v.* (**-ies**, **-ied**) suffer atrophy or cause atrophy in. [Greek *a-* without, *trophē* food]

atropine /'ætrə,piːn/ *n.* poisonous alkaloid in deadly nightshade. [Greek *Atropos*, the Fate who cut the thread of life]

attach /ə'tætʃ/ v. 1 fasten, affix, join. 2 (in *passive*; foll. by *to*) be very fond of. 3 attribute or be attributable; assign (*can't attach a name to it*; *no blame attaches to us*). 4 accompany; form part of (*no conditions are attached*). 5 *refl.* (usu. foll. by *to*) take part in; join (*attached himself to the team*). 6 seize by legal authority. [French from Germanic]

attaché /ə'tæʃeɪ/ n. specialist member of an ambassador's staff.

attaché case n. small rectangular document case.

attachment n. 1 thing attached, esp. for a purpose. 2 affection, devotion. 3 attaching or being attached. 4 legal seizure. 5 temporary position in an organization.

attack /ə'tæk/ v. 1 try to hurt or defeat using force. 2 criticize adversely. 3 act harmfully upon (*rust attacks metal*). 4 vigorously apply oneself to. 5 *Sport* try to gain ground or score (against). —n. 1 act of attacking. 2 offensive operation. 3 sudden onset of an illness. □ **attacker** n. [French from Italian]

attain /ə'teɪn/ v. 1 reach, gain, accomplish (a goal etc.). 2 (foll. by *to*) arrive at by effort or development. [Latin *attingo* reach]

attainment n. 1 (often in *pl.*) accomplishment or achievement. 2 attaining.

attar /'ætə:(r)/ n. perfume made from rose-petals. [Persian]

attempt /ə'tempt/ —v. 1 (often foll. by *to* + infin.) try to do or achieve (*attempted to explain*). 2 try to conquer (a mountain etc.). —n. (often foll. by *at*, *on*, or *to* + infin.) attempting; endeavour (*attempt at winning*; *attempt on his life*). [Latin *tempto* try]

attend /ə'tend/ v. 1 **a** be present (at) (*attended the meeting*). **b** go regularly to (*attends church*). 2 escort. 3 **a** (often foll. by *to*) turn or apply one's mind. **b** (foll. by *to*) deal with (*attend to the matter*). [Latin *tendo* stretch]

attendance n. 1 attending or being present. 2 number present (*high attendance*).

attendant —n. person escorting or providing a service (*cloakroom attendant*). —adj. 1 accompanying (*attendant costs*). 2 (often foll. by *on*) waiting (*attendant on the queen*).

attendee /ˌæten'di:/ n. person who attends (a meeting etc.).

attention /ə'tenʃ(ə)n/ n. 1 act or faculty of applying one's mind; notice (*attention wandered*; *attract his attention*). 2 consideration, care. 3 (in *pl.*) **a** courtesies. **b** sexual advances. 4 erect esp. military attitude of readiness.

attentive /ə'tentɪv/ adj. 1 concentrating; paying attention. 2 assiduously polite. □ **attentively** adv. **attentiveness** n.

attenuate /ə'tenjʊˌeɪt/ v. (-ting) 1 make thin. 2 reduce in force, value, etc. □ **attenuation** /-'eɪʃ(ə)n/ n. [Latin *tenuis* thin]

attest /ə'test/ v. 1 certify the validity of. 2 (foll. by *to*) bear witness to. □ **attestation** /ˌæte'steɪʃ(ə)n/ n. [Latin *testis* witness]

Attic /'ætɪk/ —adj. of ancient Athens or Attica, or the form of Greek used there. —n. Greek as used by the ancient Athenians. [Greek *Attikos*]

attic /'ætɪk/ n. space or room at the top of a house, usu. under the roof. [from ATTIC, with ref. to an architectural feature]

attire /ə'taɪə(r)/ *formal* —n. clothes, esp. formal. —v. (-ring) (usu. as **attired** adj.) dress, esp. formally. [French *à tire* in order]

attitude /'ætɪˌtjuːd/ n. 1 opinion or way of thinking; behaviour reflecting this (*don't like his attitude*). 2 bodily posture; pose. 3 position of an aircraft etc. relative to given points. [Latin *aptus* fitted]

attitudinize /ˌætɪ'tjuːdɪˌnaɪz/ v. (also **-ise**) (-zing or -sing) adopt (esp. affected) attitudes; pose.

attorney /ə'tɜːnɪ/ n. (pl. **-s**) 1 lawyer etc. appointed to act for another in business or legal matters. 2 *US* qualified lawyer. [French *atorner* assign]

Attorney-General n. (pl. **Attorneys-General**) chief legal officer in some countries.

attract /ə'trækt/ v. 1 (also *absol.*) (of a magnet etc.) draw to itself or oneself. 2 arouse interest or admiration in. [Latin *traho* draw]

attraction /ə'trækʃ(ə)n/ n. 1 **a** attracting or being attracted. **b** attractive quality (*can't see the attraction in it*). **c** person or thing that attracts. 2 *Physics* tendency of bodies to attract each other.

attractive /ə'træktɪv/ adj. 1 attracting (esp. interest or admiration). 2 aesthetically pleasing; good-looking. □ **attractively** adv.

attribute —v. /ə'trɪbjuːt/ (-ting) (usu. foll. by *to*) regard as belonging to, written or said by, etc. (*a poem attributed to Milton*). 2 ascribe to (a cause) (*delays attributed to snow*). —n. /'ætrɪˌbjuːt/ 1 esp. characteristic quality ascribed to a person or thing. 2 object symbolizing or appropriate to a person, office, or status. □ **attributable** /ə'trɪbjʊtəb(ə)l/ adj. **attribution** /ˌætrɪ'bjuːʃ(ə)n/ n. [Latin *tribuo* allot]

attributive /ə'trɪbjʊtɪv/ *adj. Gram.* (of an adjective or noun) preceding the word described, as *old* in *the old dog*.

attrition /ə'trɪʃ(ə)n/ *n.* **1** gradual wearing down (*war of attrition*). **2** abrasion, friction. [Latin *tero trit-* rub]

attune /ə'tjuːn/ *v.* (-**ning**) **1** (usu. foll. by *to*) adjust to a situation etc. **2** *Mus.* tune. [related to TUNE]

atypical /eɪ'tɪpɪk(ə)l/ *adj.* not typical. □ **atypically** *adv.*

Au *symb.* gold. [Latin *aurum*]

aubergine /'əʊbə,ʒiːn/ *n.* plant with white or purple egg-shaped fruit used as a vegetable; eggplant. [French, ultimately from Sanskrit]

aubrietia /ɔː'briːʃə/ *n.* (also **aubretia**) dwarf perennial rock-plant with purple or pink flowers. [*Aubriet*, name of an artist]

auburn /'ɔːbən/ *adj.* reddish-brown (usu. of hair). [originally = yellowish white: from Latin *albus* white]

auction /'ɔːkʃ(ə)n/ −*n.* sale in which articles are sold to the highest bidder. −*v.* sell by auction. [Latin *augeo auct-* increase]

auction bridge *n.* game in which players bid for the right to name trumps.

auctioneer /,ɔːkʃə'nɪə(r)/ *n.* person who conducts auctions, esp. for a living.

audacious /ɔː'deɪʃəs/ *adj.* **1** daring, bold. **2** impudent. □ **audacity** /ɔː'dæsɪtɪ/ *n.* [Latin *audax* bold]

audible /'ɔːdɪb(ə)l/ *adj.* able to be heard. □ **audibility** /-'bɪlɪtɪ/ *n.* **audibly** *adv.* [Latin *audio* hear]

audience /'ɔːdɪəns/ *n.* **1 a** assembled listeners or spectators, esp. at a play, concert, etc. **b** people addressed by a film, book, etc. **2** formal interview with a superior. [Latin: related to AUDIBLE]

audio /'ɔːdɪəʊ/ *n.* (usu. *attrib.*) sound or its reproduction. [Latin *audio* hear]

audio- *comb. form* hearing or sound.

audio frequency *n.* frequency able to be perceived by the human ear.

audiotape *n.* (also **audio tape**) **1 a** magnetic tape for recording sound. **b** a length of this. **2** a sound recording on tape.

audio typist *n.* person who types from a tape-recording.

audiovisual /,ɔːdɪəʊ'vɪzʊəl/ *adj.* (of teaching methods etc.) using both sight and sound.

audit /'ɔːdɪt/ −*n.* official scrutiny of accounts. −*v.* (-**t**-) conduct an audit of.

audition /ɔː'dɪʃ(ə)n/ −*n.* test of a performer's suitability or ability. −*v.* assess or be assessed at an audition. [Latin *audio* hear]

auditor *n.* person who audits accounts. [French from Latin]

auditorium /,ɔːdɪ'tɔːrɪəm/ *n.* (*pl.* **-s**) part of a theatre etc. for the audience. [Latin]

auditory /'ɔːdɪtərɪ/ *adj.* of hearing.

au fait /əʊ 'feɪ/ *predic. adj.* (usu. foll. by *with*) conversant (*au fait with the rules*). [French]

Aug. *abbr.* August.

Augean /ɔː'dʒiːən/ *adj.* filthy. [Greek *Augeas*, a mythical king: his filthy stables were cleaned by Hercules diverting a river through them]

auger /'ɔːgə(r)/ *n.* tool with a screw point for boring in wood. [Old English]

aught /ɔːt/ *n. archaic* anything. [Old English]

augment /ɔːg'ment/ *v.* make or become greater; increase. □ **augmentation** /-'teɪʃ(ə)n/ *n.* [Latin: related to AUCTION]

augmentative /ɔːg'mentətɪv/ *adj.* augmenting.

au gratin /əʊ 'grætæ̃/ *adj.* cooked with a crust of breadcrumbs or melted cheese. [French]

augur /'ɔːgə(r)/ −*v.* portend, serve as an omen (*augur well* or *ill*). −*n. hist.* Roman religious official interpreting natural phenomena in order to pronounce on proposed actions. [Latin]

augury /'ɔːgjərɪ/ *n.* (*pl.* **-ies**) **1** omen. **2** interpretation of omens.

August /'ɔːgəst/ *n.* eighth month of the year. [Latin *Augustus*, first Roman emperor]

august /ɔː'gʌst/ *adj.* venerable, imposing. [Latin]

Augustan /ɔː'gʌst(ə)n/ *adj.* **1** of the reign of Augustus, esp. as a flourishing literary period. **2** (of literature) refined and classical in style. [Latin: see AUGUST]

auk /ɔːk/ *n.* black and white sea bird with short wings, e.g. the guillemot, puffin, etc. [Old Norse]

auld lang syne /,ɔːld læŋ 'saɪn/ *n.* times long past. [Scots, = old long since]

aunt /ɑːnt/ *n.* **1** sister of one's father or mother. **2** uncle's wife. **3** *colloq.* (form of address by a child to) parent's female friend. [Latin *amita*]

auntie /'ɑːntɪ/ *n.* (also **aunty**) (*pl.* **-ies**) *colloq.* = AUNT.

Aunt Sally *n.* **1** game in which sticks or balls are thrown at a wooden dummy. **2** target of general abuse.

au pair /əʊ 'peə(r)/ *n.* young foreigner, esp. a woman, helping with housework etc. in exchange for board and lodging. [French]

aura /'ɔːrə/ *n.* (*pl.* **-s**) **1** distinctive atmosphere. **2** subtle emanation. [Greek, = breeze]

aural /'ɔːr(ə)l/ *adj.* of the ear or hearing. □ **aurally** *adv.* [Latin *auris* ear]

aureate /'ɔːrɪət/ *adj. literary* **1** golden. **2** resplendent. [Latin *aurum* gold]

aureole /'ɔːrɪˌəʊl/ *n.* (also **aureola** /ɔː'riːələ/) **1** halo or circle of light, esp. in a religious painting. **2** corona round the sun or moon. [Latin, = golden (crown)]

au revoir /ˌəʊ rəˈvwɑː(r)/ *int. & n.* goodbye (until we meet again). [French]

auricle /'ɔːrɪk(ə)l/ *n.* **1** each atrium of the heart. **2** external ear of animals. □ **auricular** /-'rɪk-/ *adj.* [related to AURICULA]

auricula /ɔː'rɪkjʊlə/ *n.* (*pl.* **-s**) primula with ear-shaped leaves. [Latin, diminutive of *auris* ear]

auriferous /ɔː'rɪfərəs/ *adj.* yielding gold. [Latin *aurifer* from *aurum* gold]

aurochs /'ɔːrɒks/ *n.* (*pl.* same) extinct wild ox. [German]

aurora /ɔː'rɔːrə/ *n.* (*pl.* **-s** or **aurorae** /-riː/) luminous phenomenon, usu. of streamers of light in the night sky above the northern (**aurora borealis** /ˌbɒrɪ'eɪlɪs/) or southern (**aurora australis** /ɔː'streɪlɪs/) magnetic pole. [Latin, = dawn, goddess of dawn]

auscultation /ˌɔːskəl'teɪʃ(ə)n/ *n.* listening, esp. to sounds from the heart, lungs, etc., for purposes of diagnosis. [Latin *ausculto* listen]

auspice /'ɔːspɪs/ *n.* **1** (in *pl.*) patronage (esp. *under the auspices of*). **2** omen, premonition. [originally 'observation of bird-flight': Latin *avis* bird]

auspicious /ɔː'spɪʃəs/ *adj.* promising well; favourable.

Aussie /'ɒzɪ/ *slang* **—n. 1** Australian. **2** Australia. **—adj.** Australian. [abbreviation]

austere /ɒ'stɪə(r)/ *adj.* (**-terer, -terest**) **1** severely simple. **2** morally strict. **3** stern, grim. [Greek *austēros*]

austerity /ɒ'sterɪtɪ/ *n.* (*pl.* **-ies**) being austere; hardship.

austral /'ɔːstr(ə)l/ *adj.* **1** southern. **2** (**Austral**) of Australia or Australasia. [Latin *auster* south]

Australasian /ˌɒstrə'leɪʒ(ə)n/ *adj.* of Australasia, including Australia and the islands of the SW Pacific.

Australian /ɒ'streɪlɪən/ **—n. 1** native or national of Australia. **2** person of Australian descent. **—adj.** of Australia.

autarchy /'ɔːtɑːkɪ/ *n.* absolute rule; despotism. [Greek *autos* self, *arkhē* rule]

autarky /'ɔːtɑːkɪ/ *n.* self-sufficiency, esp. economic. [Greek *autos* self, *arkeō* suffice]

authentic /ɔː'θentɪk/ *adj.* **1** of undisputed origin; genuine. **2** reliable, trustworthy. □ **authentically** *adv.* **authenticity** /-'tɪsɪtɪ/ *n.* [Greek *authentikos*]

authenticate /ɔː'θentɪˌkeɪt/ *v.* (**-ting**) establish as true, genuine, or valid. □ **authentication** /-'keɪʃ(ə)n/ *n.*

author /'ɔːθə(r)/ *n.* (*fem.* **authoress** /'ɔːθrɪs/) **1** writer, esp. of books. **2** originator of an idea, event, etc. [Latin *auctor*]

authoritarian /ɔːˌθɒrɪ'teərɪən/ **—adj.** favouring or enforcing strict obedience to authority. **—n.** authoritarian person.

authoritative /ɔː'θɒrɪtətɪv/ *adj.* **1** reliable, esp. having authority. **2** official.

authority /ɔː'θɒrɪtɪ/ *n.* (*pl.* **-ies**) **1 a** power or right to enforce obedience. **b** (often foll. by *for*, or *to* + infin.) delegated power. **2** (esp. in *pl.*) body having authority. **3** influence based on recognized knowledge or expertise. **4** expert. [Latin *auctoritas*]

authorize /'ɔːθəˌraɪz/ *v.* (also **-ise**) (**-zing** or **-sing**) **1** officially approve, sanction. **2** (foll. by *to* + infin.) give authority to (a person to do a thing). □ **authorization** /-'zeɪʃ(ə)n/ *n.*

Authorized Version *n.* English translation of the Bible made in 1611.

authorship *n.* **1** origin of a book etc. **2** profession of an author.

autism /'ɔːtɪz(ə)m/ *n.* condition characterized by self-absorption and social withdrawal. □ **autistic** /ɔː'tɪstɪk/ *adj.* [related to AUTO-]

auto /'ɔːtəʊ/ *n.* (*pl.* **-s**) *US colloq.* car. [abbreviation of AUTOMOBILE]

auto- *comb. form* **1** self. **2** one's own. **3** of or by oneself or itself. [Greek *autos*]

autobahn /'ɔːtəʊˌbɑːn/ *n.* (*pl.* **-s**) German, Austrian, or Swiss motorway. [German]

autobiography /ˌɔːtəʊbaɪ'ɒgrəfɪ/ *n.* (*pl.* **-ies**) **1** written account of one's own life. **2** this as a literary genre. □ **autobiographer** *n.* **autobiographical** /-ˌbaɪə'græfɪk(ə)l/ *adj.*

autoclave /'ɔːtəˌkleɪv/ *n.* sterilizer using high-pressure steam. [Latin *clavus* nail or *clavis* key]

autocracy /ɔː'tɒkrəsɪ/ *n.* (*pl.* **-ies**) **1** rule by an autocrat. **2** dictatorship. [Greek *kratos* power]

autocrat /'ɔːtəˌkræt/ *n.* **1** absolute ruler. **2** dictatorial person. □ **autocratic** /-'krætɪk/ *adj.* **autocratically** /-'krætɪkəlɪ/ *adv.*

autocross /'ɔːtəʊˌkrɒs/ *n.* motor racing across country or on unmade roads.

Autocue /'ɔːtəʊˌkjuː/ *n. propr.* screen etc. from which a speaker reads a television script.

auto-da-fé /ˌɔːtəʊdɑː'feɪ/ *n.* (*pl.* **autos-da-fé** /ˌɔːtəʊz-/) *hist.* **1** ceremonial judgement of heretics by the Spanish Inquisition. **2** public burning of heretics. [Portuguese, = act of the faith]

autograph /'ɔːtəˌɡrɑːf/ —*n.* signature, esp. that of a celebrity. —*v.* sign or write on in one's own hand. [Greek *graphō* write]

autoimmune /ˌɔːtəʊɪˈmjuːn/ *adj.* (of a disease) caused by antibodies produced against substances naturally present in the body.

automat /'ɔːtəˌmæt/ *n.* US **1** slot-machine. **2** cafeteria dispensing food and drink from slot-machines. [French: related to AUTOMATON]

automate /'ɔːtəˌmeɪt/ *v.* (**-ting**) convert to or operate by automation.

automatic /ˌɔːtəˈmætɪk/ —*adj.* **1** working by itself, without direct human intervention. **2 a** done spontaneously (*automatic reaction*). **b** following inevitably (*automatic penalty*). **3** (of a fire arm) able to be loaded and fired continuously. **4** (of a vehicle or its transmission) using gears that change automatically. —*n.* **1** automatic machine, firearm, or tool. **2** vehicle with automatic transmission. □ **automatically** *adv.* [related to AUTOMATON]

automatic pilot *n.* device for keeping an aircraft or ship on a set course.

automation /ˌɔːtəˈmeɪʃ(ə)n/ *n.* **1** use of automatic equipment in place of manual labour. **2** production of goods etc. by this.

automatism /ɔːˈtɒməˌtɪz(ə)m/ *n.* **1** involuntary action. **2** unthinking routine. [French: related to AUTOMATON]

automaton /ɔːˈtɒmət(ə)n/ *n.* (*pl.* **-mata** or **-s**) **1** machine controlled automatically; robot. **2** person acting like a robot. [Greek, = acting of itself]

automobile /'ɔːtəməˌbiːl/ *n.* US motor car. [French]

automotive /ˌɔːtəˈməʊtɪv/ *adj.* of motor vehicles.

autonomous /ɔːˈtɒnəməs/ *adj.* **1** having self-government. **2** acting or free to act independently. [Greek *nomos* law]

autonomy *n.* **1** self-government. **2** personal freedom.

autopilot *n.* = AUTOMATIC PILOT.

autopsy /'ɔːtɒpsɪ/ *n.* (*pl.* **-ies**) post-mortem. [Greek *autoptēs* eye-witness]

autoroute /'ɔːtəʊˌruːt/ *n.* French motorway. [French]

autostrada /'ɔːtəʊˌstrɑːdə/ *n.* (*pl.* **-s** or **-strade** /-deɪ/) Italian motorway. [Italian]

auto-suggestion /ˌɔːtəʊsəˈdʒestʃ(ə)n/ *n.* hypnotic or subconscious suggestion made to oneself.

autumn /'ɔːtəm/ *n.* **1** (often *attrib.*) season between summer and winter. **2** time of incipient decline. □ **autumnal** /ɔːˈtʌmn(ə)l/ *adj.* [Latin *autumnus*]

autumn equinox *n.* (also **autumnal equinox**) equinox about 22 Sept.

auxiliary /ɔːgˈzɪljərɪ/ —*adj.* **1** subsidiary, additional. **2** giving help. —*n.* (*pl.* **-ies**) **1** auxiliary person or thing. **2** (in *pl.*) foreign or allied troops in the service of a nation at war. **3** verb used to form tenses or moods of other verbs (e.g. *have* in *I have seen*). [Latin *auxilium* help]

auxin /'ɔːksɪn/ *n.* plant hormone that regulates growth.

AV *abbr.* Authorized Version.

avail /əˈveɪl/ —*v.* **1** help; be of use. **2** *refl.* (foll. by *of*) make use of, profit by. —*n.* use, profit (*of no avail*). [Latin *valeo* be strong]

available *adj.* **1** at one's disposal, obtainable. **2 a** (of a person) free, not committed. **b** able to be contacted. □ **availability** /-ˈbɪlɪtɪ/ *n.*

avalanche /'ævəˌlɑːntʃ/ *n.* **1** rapidly sliding mass of snow and ice on a mountain. **2** sudden abundance (*avalanche of work*). [French]

avant-garde /ˌævãˈɡɑːd/ —*n.* pioneers or (esp. artistic) innovators. —*adj.* new; pioneering. [French, = vanguard]

avarice /'ævərɪs/ *n.* extreme greed for wealth. □ **avaricious** /-ˈrɪʃəs/ *adj.* [Latin *avarus* greedy]

avatar /'ævəˌtɑː(r)/ *n.* (in Hindu mythology) descent of a deity etc. to earth in bodily form. [Sanskrit, = descent]

Ave /'ɑːveɪ/ *n.* (in full **Ave Maria**) prayer to the Virgin Mary (Luke 1:28). [Latin]

Ave. *abbr.* Avenue.

avenge /əˈvendʒ/ *v.* (**-ging**) **1** inflict retribution on behalf of. **2** take vengeance for (an injury). □ **be avenged** avenge oneself. [Latin *vindico*]

avenue /'ævəˌnjuː/ *n.* **1 a** broad esp. tree-lined road or street. **b** tree-lined path etc. **2** approach (*explored every avenue*). [French *avenir* come to]

aver /əˈvɜː(r)/ *v.* (**-rr-**) *formal* assert, affirm. □ **averment** *n.* [Latin *verus* true]

average /'ævərɪdʒ/ —*n.* **1** usual amount, extent, or rate. **2** amount obtained by adding two or more numbers and dividing by how many there are. **3** (with ref. to speed etc.) ratio obtained by subtracting the inital from the final value of each element of the ratio (*average of 50 miles per hour*). **4** *Law* damage to or loss of a ship or cargo. —*adj.* **1 a** usual, ordinary. **b** mediocre. **2** constituting an average (*the average age is 72*). —*v.* (**-ging**) **1** amount on average to. **2** do on average. **3** estimate the average of. □ **average out** (**at**) result in an average (of). **law of averages** principle †hat if one of two

extremes occurs the other will also. **on** (or **on an**) **average** as an average rate or estimate. [Arabic, = damaged goods]

averse /ə'vɜːs/ *predic. adj.* (usu. foll. by *to*) opposed, disinclined. [Latin *verto vers-* turn]

aversion /ə'vɜːʃ(ə)n/ *n.* 1 (usu. foll. by *to, for*) dislike or unwillingness. 2 object of this.

avert /ə'vɜːt/ *v.* (often foll. by *from*) 1 turn away (one's eyes or thoughts). 2 prevent or ward off (esp. danger).

Avesta /ə'vestə/ *n.* (usu. prec. by *the*) sacred writings of Zoroastrianism (cf. ZEND). [Persian]

aviary /'eɪvɪərɪ/ *n.* (*pl.* **-ies**) large cage or building for keeping birds. [Latin *avis* bird]

aviation /ˌeɪvɪ'eɪʃ(ə)n/ *n.* science or practice of flying aircraft. [Latin: related to AVIARY]

aviator /'eɪvɪˌeɪtə(r)/ *n.* person who flies aircraft.

avid /'ævɪd/ *adj.* eager, greedy. □ **avidity** /ə'vɪdɪtɪ/ *n.* **avidly** *adv.* [Latin *aveo* crave]

avionics /ˌeɪvɪ'ɒnɪks/ *n.pl.* (usu. treated as *sing.*) electronics as applied to aviation. [from AVIATION, ELECTRONICS]

avocado /ˌævə'kɑːdəʊ/ *n.* (*pl.* **-s**) 1 (in full **avocado pear**) dark green edible pear-shaped fruit with yellowish-green creamy flesh. 2 tree bearing it. [Spanish from Aztec]

avocet /'ævəˌset/ *n.* long-legged wading bird with an upward curved bill. [French from Italian]

avoid /ə'vɔɪd/ *v.* 1 keep away or refrain from. 2 escape; evade. 3 *Law* quash, annul. □ **avoidable** *adj.* **avoidance** *n.* [French]

avoirdupois /ˌævədə'pɔɪz/ *n.* (in full **avoirdupois weight**) system of weights based on a pound of 16 ounces or 7,000 grains. [French, = goods of weight]

avow /ə'vaʊ/ *v. formal* declare, confess. □ **avowal** *n.* **avowedly** /ə'vaʊɪdlɪ/ *adv.* [Latin *voco* call]

avuncular /ə'vʌŋkjʊlə(r)/ *adj.* like or of an uncle, esp. in manner. [Latin *avunculus* uncle]

await /ə'weɪt/ *v.* 1 wait for. 2 be in store for. [French: related to WAIT]

awake /ə'weɪk/ *–v.* (**-king**; *past* **awoke**; *past part.* **awoken**) 1 cease to sleep or arouse from sleep. 2 (often foll. by *to*) become or make alert, aware, or active. *–predic. adj.* 1 not asleep. 2 (often foll. by *to*) alert, aware. [Old English: related to A²]

awaken *v.* = AWAKE *v.*

■ **Usage** *Awake* and *awaken* are interchangeable but *awaken* is much rarer than *awake* as an intransitive verb.

award /ə'wɔːd/ *–v.* give or order to be given as a payment or prize. *–n.* 1 thing or amount awarded. 2 judicial decision. [French]

aware /ə'weə(r)/ *predic. adj.* 1 (often foll. by *of* or *that*) conscious; having knowledge. 2 well-informed. □ **awareness** *n.* [Old English]

■ **Usage** *Aware* is also found used attributively in sense 2, as in 'a very *aware* person', but this should be avoided in formal contexts.

awash /ə'wɒʃ/ *predic. adj.* 1 level with the surface of, and just covered by, water. 2 (foll. by *with*) overflowing, abounding.

away /ə'weɪ/ *–adv.* 1 to or at a distance from the place, person, or thing in question (*go, give, look, away*; *5 miles away*). 2 into non-existence (*explain, fade, away*). 3 constantly, persistently (*work away*). 4 without delay (*ask away*). *–attrib. adj. Sport* not played on one's own ground (*away match*). *–n. Sport* away match or win. [Old English: related to A², WAY]

awe /ɔː/ *–n.* reverential fear or wonder. *–v.* (**awing**) inspire with awe. [Old Norse]

aweigh /ə'weɪ/ *predic. adj.* (of an anchor) clear of the bottom.

awe-inspiring *adj.* awesome; magnificent.

awesome /'ɔːsəm/ *adj.* inspiring awe; dreaded.

awful /'ɔːfʊl/ *adj.* 1 *colloq.* very bad or unpleasant (*has awful writing*; *awful weather*). 2 (*attrib.*) as an intensifier (*awful lot of money*). 3 *poet.* inspiring awe.

awfully *adv.* 1 badly; unpleasantly (*played awfully*). 2 *colloq.* very (*awfully pleased*).

awhile /ə'waɪl/ *adv.* for a short time. [*a while*]

awkward /'ɔːkwəd/ *adj.* 1 difficult to use or deal with. 2 clumsy, ungainly. 3 **a** embarrassed. **b** embarrassing. [obsolete *awk* perverse]

awl *n.* small tool for piercing holes, esp. in leather. [Old English]

awn *n.* bristly head of a sheath of barley and other grasses. [Old Norse]

awning *n.* sheet of canvas etc. stretched on a frame as a shelter against the sun or rain. [origin uncertain]

awoke *past* of AWAKE.

awoken *past part.* of AWAKE.

AWOL /'eɪwɒl/ *abbr. colloq.* absent without leave.

awry /ə'raɪ/ —*adv.* 1 crookedly, askew. 2 amiss, wrong. —*predic. adj.* crooked; unsound.

axe /æks/ (*US* **ax**) —*n.* 1 chopping-tool with a handle and heavy blade. 2 (**the axe**) dismissal (of employees); abandonment of a project etc. —*v.* (**axing**) cut (esp. costs or staff) drastically; abandon (a project). □ **an axe to grind** private ends to serve. [Old English]

axial /'æksɪəl/ *adj.* of, forming, or placed round an axis.

axil /'æksɪl/ *n.* upper angle between a leaf and stem. [Latin *axilla* armpit]

axiom /'æksɪəm/ *n.* 1 established or accepted principle. 2 self-evident truth. □ **axiomatic** /-'mætɪk/ *adj.* [Greek *axios* worthy]

axis /'æksɪs/ *n.* (*pl.* **axes** /-siːz/) 1 a imaginary line about which a body rotates. b line which divides a regular figure symmetrically. 2 fixed reference line for the measurement of coordinates etc. 3 (**the Axis**) alliance of Germany, Italy, and later Japan, in the war of 1939–45. [Latin, = axle]

axle /'æks(ə)l/ *n.* spindle on which a wheel is fixed or turns. [Old Norse]

axolotl /'æksə,lɒt(ə)l/ *n.* newtlike salamander, which in natural conditions retains its larval form of life. [Nahuatl, = water-servant]

ayatollah /,aɪə'tɒlə/ *n.* Shiite religious leader in Iran. [Persian from Arabic, = token of God]

aye /aɪ/ —*adv. archaic* or *dial.* yes. —*n.* affirmative answer or vote. [probably from *I*, expressing assent]

azalea /ə'zeɪlɪə/ *n.* a kind of rhododendron. [Greek *azaleos* dry]

azimuth /'æzɪməθ/ *n.* angular distance from a north or south point of the horizon to the intersection with the horizon of a vertical circle passing through a given celestial body. □ **azimuthal** /-'mʌθ(ə)l/ *adj.* [French from Arabic]

AZT *abbr.* drug intended for use against the Aids virus. [from the chemical name]

Aztec /'æztek/ —*n.* 1 member of the native Mexican people overthrown by the Spanish in 1519. 2 language of this people. —*adj.* of the Aztecs or their language. [Nahuatl, = men of the north]

azure /'æʒə(r)/ —*n.* 1 deep sky-blue colour. 2 *poet.* clear sky. —*adj.* deep sky-blue. [Arabic]

B

B¹ /biː/ *n.* (*pl.* **Bs** or **B's**) **1** (also **b**) second letter of the alphabet. **2** *Mus.* seventh note of the diatonic scale of C major. **3** second hypothetical person or example. **4** second highest category (of roads, academic marks, etc.). **5** (usu. **b**) *Algebra* second known quantity.

B² *symb.* boron.

B³ *abbr.* (also **B.**) black (pencil-lead).

b. *abbr.* **1** born. **2** *Cricket* **a** bowled by. **b** bye.

BA *abbr.* **1** Bachelor of Arts. **2** British Airways.

Ba *symb.* barium.

baa /baː/ —*v.* (**baas**, **baaed** or **baa'd**) bleat. —*n.* sheep's cry. [imitative]

babble /'bæb(ə)l/ —*v.* (**-ling**) **1 a** talk, chatter, or say incoherently or excessively. **b** (of a stream etc.) murmur. **2** repeat or divulge foolishly. —*n.* **1** babbling. **2** murmur of voices, water, etc. [imitative]

babe *n.* **1** *literary* baby. **2** innocent or helpless person. **3** *US slang* young woman. [as BABY]

babel /'beɪb(ə)l/ *n.* **1** confused noise, esp. of voices. **2** scene of confusion. [Hebrew, = Babylon (Gen. 11)]

baboon /bə'buːn/ *n.* large long-nosed African and Arabian monkey. [French or medieval Latin]

baby /'beɪbɪ/ —*n.* (*pl.* **-ies**) **1** very young child. **2** childish person. **3** youngest member of a family etc. **4** (often *attrib.*) **a** very young animal. **b** small specimen. **5** *slang* sweetheart. **6** one's special concern etc. —*v.* (**-ies**, **-ied**) treat like a baby; pamper. □ **babyhood** *n.* **babyish** *adj.* [imitative of child's *ba ba*]

baby boom *n.* *colloq.* temporary increase in the birthrate.

Baby Buggy *n.* *propr.* a kind of child's pushchair.

baby carriage *n.* *US* pram.

baby grand *n.* small grand piano.

Babygro *n.* (*pl.* **-s**) *propr.* stretchy all-in-one baby suit.

babysit *v.* (**-tt-**; *past* and *past part.* **-sat**) look after a child while its parents are out. □ **babysitter** *n.*

baccalaureate /ˌbækə'lɔːrɪət/ *n.* final secondary school examination in France and many international schools. [medieval Latin *baccalaureus* bachelor]

baccarat /'bækə.raː/ *n.* gambling card-game. [French]

bacchanal /'bækən(ə)l/ —*n.* **1** drunken revelry or reveller. **2** priest or follower of Bacchus. —*adj.* **1** of or like Bacchus. **2** drunkenly riotous. [Latin *Bacchus* from Greek, god of wine]

Bacchanalia /ˌbækə'neɪlɪə/ *n.pl.* **1** Roman festival of Bacchus. **2** (**bacchanalia**) drunken revelry.

bacchant /'bækənt/ —*n.* (*fem.* **bacchante** /bə'kæntɪ/) **1** priest or follower of Bacchus. **2** drunken reveller. —*adj.* **1** of or like Bacchus or his rites. **2** drunkenly riotous, roistering.

Bacchic /'bækɪk/ *adj.* = BACCHANAL *adj.*

baccy /'bækɪ/ *n.* (*pl.* **-ies**) *colloq.* tobacco. [abbreviation]

bachelor /'bætʃələ(r)/ *n.* **1** unmarried man. **2** person with a university first degree. □ **bachelorhood** *n.* [related to BACCALAUREATE]

bachelor girl *n.* independent young single woman.

bacillus /bə'sɪləs/ *n.* (*pl.* **bacilli** /-laɪ/) rod-shaped bacterium, esp. one causing disease. □ **bacillary** *adj.* [Latin, diminutive of *baculus* stick]

back —*n.* **1 a** rear surface of the human body from shoulder to hip. **b** upper surface of an animal's body. **c** spine (*broke his back*). **d** keel of a ship. **2** backlike surface (*back of the head, chair, shirt*). **3** reverse or more distant part (*back of the room; sat in the back; write it on the back*). **4** defensive player in football etc. —*adv.* **1** to the rear (*go back a bit; looked back*). **2** in or into a previous state, place, or time (*came back; put it back; back in June*). **3** at a distance (*stand back*). **4** in return (*pay back*). **5** in check (*hold him back*). —*v.* **1 a** give moral or financial support to. **b** bet on (a horse etc.). **2** (often foll. by *up*) move backwards. **3 a** put or serve as a back, background, or support to. **b** *Mus.* accompany. **4** lie at the back of (*beach backed by cliffs*). **5** (of the wind) move anticlockwise. —*adj.* **1** situated to the rear; remote, subsidiary (*back teeth*). **2** past; not current (*back pay; back issue*). **3** reversed (*back flow*). □ **back and forth** to and fro. **back down** withdraw from confrontation. **the back of beyond** very remote place. **back off** **1** draw back, retreat. **2** = *back down*. **back on to** have its back adjoining (*backs on to a*

field). **back out** (often foll. by *of*) withdraw from a commitment. **back-pedal** reverse one's action or opinion. **back to back** with backs adjacent and facing each other (*stood back to back*). **back up 1** give (esp. moral) support to. **2** *Computing* make a backup of (data, a disk, etc.). **get** (or **put**) **a person's back up** annoy a person. **get off a person's back** stop troubling a person. **turn one's back on** abandon; ignore. □ **backer** *n.* (in sense 1 of *v.*). **backless** *adj.* [Old English]

backache *n.* ache in the back.

back-bencher *n.* MP not holding a senior office.

backbiting *n.* malicious talk.

back-boiler *n.* boiler behind a domestic fire.

backbone *n.* **1** spine. **2** chief support. **3** firmness of character.

back-breaking *adj.* (esp. of manual work) extremely hard.

back-burner *n.* **on the back-burner** receiving little attention.

backchat *n. colloq.* verbal insolence.

backcloth *n.* **1** painted cloth at the back of a stage. **2** background to a scene or situation.

backcomb *v.* comb (the hair) towards the scalp to give it fullness.

back-crawl *n.* = BACKSTROKE.

backdate *v.* (-**ting**) **1** make retrospectively valid. **2** put an earlier date to than the actual one.

back door *n.* secret or ingenious means.

backdrop *n.* = BACKCLOTH.

backfire *v.* (-**ring**) **1** (of an engine or vehicle) ignite or explode too early in the cylinder or exhaust. **2** (of a plan etc.) rebound adversely on its originator.

back-formation *n.* **1** formation of a word from its seeming derivative (e.g. *laze* from *lazy*). **2** word so formed.

backgammon *n.* board-game with pieces moved according to throws of the dice. [from BACK + obsolete form of GAME[1]]

background *n.* **1** part of a scene or picture furthest from the observer. **2** (often *attrib.*) inconspicuous position (*kept in the background*; *background music*). **3** person's education, social circumstances, etc. **4** explanatory or contributory information or events.

backhand –*attrib. adj.* (of a stroke) made with the hand across one's body. –*n.* such a stroke.

backhanded /bæk'hændɪd/ *adj.* **1** made with the back of the hand. **2** indirect; ambiguous (*backhanded compliment*).

backhander *n.* **1 a** backhand stroke. **b** backhanded blow. **2** *slang* bribe.

backing *n.* **1 a** support, esp. financial or moral. **b** material used for a thing's back or support. **2** musical accompaniment, esp. to a pop singer.

backing track *n.* recorded musical accompaniment.

backlash *n.* **1** violent, usu. hostile, reaction. **2** sudden recoil in a mechanism.

backlist *n.* publisher's list of books still in print.

backlog *n.* arrears of work.

back number *n.* **1** out-of-date issue of a periodical. **2** *slang* out-of-date person or thing.

backpack –*n.* rucksack. –*v.* travel or hike with this. □ **backpacker** *n.*

back passage *n. colloq.* rectum.

backrest *n.* support for the back.

back room *n.* (often, with hyphen, *attrib.*) place where secret work is done.

back seat *n.* less prominent or important position.

back-seat driver *n.* person eager to advise without taking responsibility.

backside *n. colloq.* buttocks.

back slang *n.* slang using words spelt backwards (e.g. *yob*).

backslide *v.* (-**ding**; *past* -**slid**; *past part.* -**slid** or -**slidden**) return to bad habits etc.

backspace *v.* (-**cing**) move a typewriter carriage etc. back one or more spaces.

backspin *n.* backward spin making a ball bounce erratically.

backstage *adv.* & *adj.* behind the scenes.

backstairs –*n.pl.* rear or side stairs of a building. –*attrib. adj.* (also **backstair**) underhand; secret.

backstitch *n.* sewing with each stitch starting behind the end of the previous one.

back-stop *n.* **1** *Cricket* etc. **a** position directly behind the wicket-keeper. **b** fielder in this position. **2** last resort.

backstreet –*n.* side-street, alley. –*attrib. adj.* illicit; illegal (*backstreet abortion*).

backstroke *n.* swimming stroke done on the back.

back-to-back *adj.* (of houses) with a party wall at the rear.

back to front *adj.* **1** with back and front reversed. **2** in disorder.

back-to-nature *attrib. adj.* seeking a simpler way of life.

backtrack *v.* **1** retrace one's steps. **2** reverse one's policy or opinion.

backup *n.* (often *attrib.*) **1** support; reserve (*back-up team*). **2** *Computing* **a** making of spare copies of data for safety. **b** copy so made.

backward /'bækwəd/ –adv. = BACK-WARDS. –adj. **1** towards the rear or starting-point (backward look). **2** reversed (backward roll). **3** slow to develop or progress. **4** hesitant, shy.

backwards adv. **1** away from one's front (lean backwards). **2 a** with the back foremost (walk backwards). **b** in reverse of the usual way (count backwards). **3 a** into a worse state. **b** into the past. **c** (of motion) back towards the starting-point (roll backwards). □ **backwards and forwards** to and fro. **bend** (or **fall** or **lean**) **over backwards** colloq. make every effort, esp. to be fair or helpful.

backwash n. **1** receding waves made by a ship etc. **2** repercussions.

backwater n. **1** peaceful, secluded, or dull place. **2** stagnant water fed from a stream.

backwoods n.pl. **1** remote uncleared forest land. **2** remote region. □ **backwoodsman** n.

backyard n. yard behind a house etc.

bacon /'beɪkən/ n. cured meat from the back or sides of a pig. [French from Germanic]

bacteriology /ˌbæktɪərɪ'ɒlədʒɪ/ n. the study of bacteria.

bacterium /bæk'tɪərɪəm/ n. (pl. **-ria**) unicellular micro-organism lacking an organized nucleus, esp. of a kind causing disease. □ **bacterial** adj. [Greek, = little stick]

■ **Usage** A common mistake is the use of the plural form bacteria as the singular. This should be avoided.

bad –adj. (**worse, worst**) **1** inadequate, defective (bad work, light). **2** unpleasant (bad weather). **3** harmful (is bad for you). **4** (of food) decayed. **5** colloq. ill, injured (feeling bad today; a bad leg). **6** colloq. regretful, guilty (feels bad about it). **7** serious, severe (a bad headache, mistake). **8 a** morally unacceptable (bad man; bad language). **b** naughty. **9** not valid (a bad cheque). **10** (**badder, baddest**) esp. US slang excellent. –n. ill fortune; ruin. –adv. US colloq. badly. □ **not** (or **not so**) **bad** colloq. fairly good. **too bad** colloq. regrettable. [Old English]

bad blood n. ill feeling.

bad books see BOOK.

bad breath n. unpleasant-smelling breath.

bad debt n. debt that is not recoverable.

baddy n. (pl. **-ies**) colloq. villain in a story, film, etc.

bade see BID.

bad egg see EGG[1].

bad faith n. intent to deceive.

badge n. **1** small flat emblem worn to signify office, membership, etc., or as decoration. **2** thing that reveals a condition or quality. [origin unknown]

badger –n. nocturnal burrowing mammal with a black and white striped head. –v. pester, harass. [origin uncertain]

badinage /'bædɪˌnɑːʒ/ n. playful ridicule. [French]

bad lot n. person of bad character.

badly adv. (**worse, worst**) **1** in a bad manner. **2** colloq. very much (wants it badly). **3** severely (badly defeated).

badminton /'bædmɪnt(ə)n/ n. game with rackets and a shuttlecock. [Badminton in S. England]

bad-mouth v. esp. US slang abuse verbally, put down.

bad news n. colloq. unpleasant or troublesome person or thing.

bad-tempered adj. irritable.

baffle /'bæf(ə)l/ –v. (**-ling**) **1** perplex. **2** frustrate, hinder. –n. device that checks flow esp. of fluid or sound waves. □ **bafflement** n. [origin uncertain]

BAFTA /'bæftə/ abbr. British Association of Film and Television Arts.

bag –n. **1** soft open-topped receptacle. **2 a** piece of luggage. **b** woman's handbag. **3** (in pl.; usu. foll. by of) colloq. large amount (bags of time). **4** slang derog. woman. **5** animal's sac. **6** amount of game shot by one person. **7** (usu. in pl.) baggy skin under the eyes. **8** slang particular interest (folk music is not my bag). –v. (**-gg-**) **1** colloq. **a** secure (bagged the best seat). **b** (often in phr. **bags I**) colloq. claim as being the first (bags I go next). **2** put in a bag. **3** (cause to) hang loosely; bulge. □ **in the bag** colloq. achieved, secured. □ **bagful** n. (pl. **-s**). [origin unknown]

bagatelle /ˌbægə'tel/ n. **1** game in which small balls are struck into holes on a board. **2** mere trifle. **3** short piece of esp. piano music. [French from Italian]

bagel /'beɪg(ə)l/ n. ring-shaped bread roll. [Yiddish]

baggage /'bægɪdʒ/ n. **1** luggage. **2** portable army equipment. **3** joc. or derog. girl or woman. **4** mental encumbrances. [French]

baggy adj. (**-ier, -iest**) hanging loosely. □ **baggily** adv. **bagginess** n.

bagpipe n. (usu. in pl.) musical instrument consisting of a windbag connected to reeded pipes.

baguette /bæ'get/ n. long thin French loaf. [French]

bah int. expressing contempt or disbelief. [French]

Baha'i /bə'haɪ/ n. (pl. -s) member of a monotheistic religion emphasizing religious unity and world peace. [Persian *bahá* splendour]

bail¹ – n. 1 money etc. pledged against the temporary release of an untried prisoner. 2 person(s) giving this. – v. (usu. foll. by *out*) 1 release or secure the release of (a prisoner) on payment of bail. 2 release from a difficulty; rescue. □ **on bail** released after payment of bail. [Latin *bajulus* carrier]

bail² n. 1 *Cricket* either of two cross-pieces bridging the stumps. 2 bar holding the paper against a typewriter platen. 3 bar separating horses in an open stable. [French]

bail³ v. (also **bale**) 1 (usu. foll. by *out*) scoop water out of (a boat etc.). 2 scoop (water etc.) out. □ **bail out** var. of *bale out* 1 (see BALE¹). [French]

bailey /'beɪlɪ/ n. (pl. -s) 1 outer wall of a castle. 2 court enclosed by it. [French: related to BAIL²]

Bailey bridge /'beɪlɪ/ n. prefabricated military bridge for rapid assembly. [Sir D. *Bailey*, name of its designer]

bailiff /'beɪlɪf/ n. 1 sheriff's officer who executes writs and carries out distraints. 2 landlord's agent or steward. [French: related to BAIL¹]

bailiwick /'beɪlɪwɪk/ n. 1 *Law* district of a bailiff. 2 *joc.* person's particular interest. [as BAILIFF, obsolete *wick* district]

bain-marie /ˌbænmə'riː/ n. (pl. **bains-marie** pronunc. same) pan of hot water holding a pan containing sauce etc. for slow heating. [French, translation of medieval Latin *balneum Mariae* bath of Maria (a supposed alchemist)]

bairn n. *Scot.* & *N.Engl.* child. [Old English: related to BEAR¹]

bait – n. 1 food used to entice prey. 2 allurement. – v. 1 harass, torment, or annoy (a person or chained animal). 2 put bait on (a hook, trap, etc.). [Old Norse]

baize n. usu. green woollen felted material, used for coverings. [French pl. *baies* chestnut-coloured]

bake v. (-king) 1 cook or become cooked by dry heat, esp. in an oven. 2 *colloq.* (usu. as **be baking**) (of weather, a person, etc.) be very hot. 3 harden by heat. [Old English]

baked beans n.pl. baked haricot beans, usu. tinned in tomato sauce.

Bakelite /'beɪkəˌlaɪt/ n. *propr.* plastic made from formaldehyde and phenol, used formerly for buttons, plates, etc. [German from *Baekeland*, name of its inventor]

baker n. person who bakes and sells bread, cakes, etc., esp. for a living.

Baker day n. *colloq.* day set aside for in-service training of teachers. [*Baker*, name of the Education Secretary responsible for introducing them]

baker's dozen n. thirteen.

bakery n. (pl. -ies) place where bread and cakes are made or sold.

Bakewell tart /'beɪkwel/ n. open pastry case lined with jam and filled with almond paste. [*Bakewell* in Derbyshire]

baking-powder n. mixture of sodium bicarbonate, cream of tartar, etc., as a raising agent.

baking-soda n. sodium bicarbonate.

baklava /'bækləvə/ n. rich sweetmeat of flaky pastry, honey, and nuts. [Turkish]

baksheesh /'bækʃiː.ʃ/ n. gratuity, tip. [Persian]

Balaclava /ˌbælə'klɑːvə/ n. (in full **Balaclava helmet**) usu. woollen covering for the whole head and neck, except for the face. [*Balaclava* in the Crimea, the site of a battle in 1854]

balalaika /ˌbælə'laɪkə/ n. guitar-like stringed instrument with a triangular body. [Russian]

balance /'bæləns/ – n. 1 **a** even distribution of weight or amount. **b** stability of body or mind. 2 apparatus for weighing, esp. one with a central pivot, beam, and two scales. 3 **a** counteracting weight or force. **b** (in full **balance-wheel**) regulating device in a clock etc. 4 decisive weight or amount (*balance of opinion*). 5 **a** agreement or difference between credits and debits in an account. **b** amount still owing or outstanding (*will pay the balance*). **c** amount left over. 6 **a** *Art* harmony and proportion. **b** *Mus.* relative volume of sources of sound. 7 (**the Balance**) zodiacal sign or constellation Libra. – v. (-cing) 1 bring into, keep, or be in equilibrium (*balanced a book on her head; balanced on one leg*). 2 (often foll. by *with*, *against*) offset or compare (one thing) with another (*balance the pros and cons*). 3 counteract, equal, or neutralize the weight or importance of. 4 (usu. as **balanced** *adj.*) make well-proportioned and harmonious (*balanced diet; balanced opinion*). 5 **a** compare and esp. equalize the debits and credits of (an account). **b** (of an account) have credits and debits equal. □ **in the balance** uncertain; at a critical stage. **on balance** all things considered. [Latin *bilanx* scales]

balance of payments n. difference in value between payments into and out of a country.

balance of power n. 1 situation of roughly equal power among the chief

States of the world. **2** power held by a small group when larger groups are of equal strength.

balance of trade n. difference in value between imports and exports.

balance sheet n. statement giving the balance of an account

balcony /'bælkəni/ n. (pl. **-ies**) **1** usu. balustraded platform on the outside of a building with access from an upper floor. **2** upper tier of seats in a theatre etc. □ **balconied** adj. [Italian]

bald /bɔːld/ adj. **1** lacking some or all hair on the scalp. **2** lacking the usual hair, feathers, leaves, etc. **3** colloq. with a worn surface (bald tyre). **4** plain, direct (bald statement, style). □ **balding** adj. (in senses 1–3). **baldly** adv. (in sense 4). **baldness** n. [Old English]

balderdash /'bɔːldədæʃ/ n. nonsense. [origin unknown]

bale[1] −n. tightly bound bundle of merchandise or hay. −v. (**-ling**) make up into bales. □ **bale out 1** (also **bail out**) (of an airman) make an emergency parachute descent. **2** var. of BAIL[1] v. 2. [Dutch: related to BALL[1]]

bale[2] var. of BAIL[3].

baleen /bə'liːn/ n. whalebone. [Latin balaena whale]

baleful /'beɪlfʊl/ adj. **1** menacing in look, manner, etc. **2** malignant, destructive. □ **balefully** adv. [archaic bale evil]

balk var. of BAULK.

Balkan /'bɔːlkən/ adj. **1** of the region of SE Europe bounded by the Adriatic, Aegean, and Black Sea. **2** of its peoples or countries. [Turkish]

ball[1] /bɔːl/ −n. **1** sphere, esp. for use in a game. **2 a** ball-shaped object; material in the shape of a ball (ball of snow, wool). **b** rounded part of the body (ball of the foot). **3** cannon-ball. **4** single delivery or pass of a ball in cricket, baseball, football, etc. **5** (in pl.) coarse slang **a** testicles. **b** (usu. as int.) nonsense. **c** = BALLS-UP. **d** courage, 'guts'. −v. form into a ball. □ **balls up** coarse slang bungle; make a mess of. **on the ball** colloq. alert. [Old Norse]

ball[2] /bɔːl/ n. **1** formal social gathering for dancing. **2** slang enjoyable time (esp. have a ball). [Greek ballō throw]

ballad /'bæləd/ n. **1** poem or song narrating a popular story. **2** slow sentimental song. [Provençal: related to BALL[2]]

balladry n. ballad poetry.

ball-and-socket joint n. joint in which a rounded end lies in a concave socket.

ballast /'bæləst/ −n. **1** heavy material stabilizing a ship, the car of a balloon, etc. **2** coarse stone etc. as the bed of a railway track or road. **3** mixture of coarse and fine aggregate for making concrete. −v. provide with ballast. [Low German or Scandinavian]

ball-bearing n. **1** bearing in which the two halves are separated by a ring of small balls. **2** one of these balls.

ballboy n. (fem. **ballgirl**) (in tennis) boy or girl who retrieves balls.

ballcock n. floating ball on a hinged arm controlling the water level in a cistern.

ballerina /ˌbælə'riːnə/ n. female ballet-dancer. [Italian: related to BALL[2]]

ballet /'bæleɪ/ n. **1** dramatic or representational style of dancing to music. **2** particular piece or performance of ballet. □ **balletic** /bə'letɪk/ adj. [French: related to BALL[2]]

ballet-dancer n. dancer of ballet.

ball game n. **1 a** game played with a ball. **b** US baseball game. **2** esp. US colloq. affair; matter (a whole new ball game).

ballista /bə'lɪstə/ n. (pl. **-stae** /-stiː/) (in ancient warfare) catapult for hurling large stones etc. [Latin from Greek ballō throw]

ballistic /bə'lɪstɪk/ adj. of projectiles.

ballistic missile n. missile that is powered and guided but falls by gravity.

ballistics n.pl. (usu. treated as sing.) science of projectiles and firearms.

ballocking var. of BOLLOCKING.

ballocks var. of BOLLOCKS.

balloon /bə'luːn/ −n. **1** small inflatable rubber toy or decoration. **2** large usu. round inflatable flying bag, often carrying a basket for passengers. **3** colloq. balloon shape enclosing dialogue etc. in a comic strip or cartoon. −v. **1** (cause to) swell out like a balloon. **2** travel by balloon. □ **balloonist** n. [French or Italian, = large ball]

ballot /'bælət/ −n. **1** occasion or system of voting, in writing and usu. secret. **2** total of such votes. **3** paper etc. used in voting. −v. (**-t-**) **1** (usu. foll. by for) **a** hold a ballot; give a vote. **b** draw lots for precedence etc. **2** take a ballot of (balloted the members). [Italian ballotta: related to BALLOON]

ballot-box n. sealed box for completed ballot-papers.

ballot-paper n. = BALLOT n. 3.

ballpark n. US **1** baseball ground. **2** colloq. sphere of activity, etc. **3** (attrib.) colloq. approximate. □ **in the right ballpark** colloq. approximately correct.

ball-point n. (in full **ball-point pen**) pen with a tiny ball as its writing point.

ballroom n. large room for dancing.

ballroom dancing n. formal social dancing.

balls-up *n. coarse slang* bungle, mess.

bally /'bælɪ/ *adj. & adv. slang* mild form of *bloody* (see BLOODY *adj.* 3). [alteration of BLOODY]

ballyhoo /ˌbælɪ'huː/ *n.* **1** loud noise or fuss. **2** noisy publicity. [origin unknown]

balm /bɑːm/ *n.* **1** aromatic ointment. **2** fragrant oil or resin exuded from certain trees and plants. **3** thing that heals or soothes. **4** aromatic herb. [Latin: related to BALSAM]

balmy /'bɑːmɪ/ *adj.* (**-ier, -iest**) **1** mild and fragrant; soothing. **2** *slang* = BARMY. □ **balmily** *adv.* **balminess** *n.*

baloney var. of BOLONEY.

balsa /'bɔːlsə/ *n.* **1** (in full **balsa-wood**) tough lightweight wood used for making models etc. **2** tropical American tree yielding it. [Spanish, = raft]

balsam /'bɔːlsəm/ *n.* **1** resin exuded from various trees and shrubs. **2** ointment, esp. containing oil or turpentine. **3** tree or shrub yielding balsam. **4** any of several flowering plants. □ **balsamic** /-'sæmɪk/ *adj.* [Latin *balsamum*]

baluster /'bæləstə(r)/ *n.* short post or pillar supporting a rail. [Greek *balaustion* wild-pomegranate flower]

■ **Usage** *Baluster* is often confused with *banister*. A baluster is usually part of a balustrade whereas a banister supports a stair handrail.

balustrade /ˌbælə'streɪd/ *n.* railing supported by balusters, esp. on a balcony.

bamboo /bæm'buː/ *n.* **1** tropical giant woody grass. **2** its stem, used for canes, furniture, etc. [Dutch from Malay]

bamboo-shoot *n.* young shoot of bamboo, eaten as a vegetable.

bamboozle /bæm'buːz(ə)l/ *v.* (**-ling**) *colloq.* cheat; mystify. □ **bamboozlement** *n.* [origin unknown]

ban –*v.* (**-nn-**) forbid, prohibit, esp. formally. –*n.* formal prohibition (*ban on smoking*). [Old English, = summon]

banal /bə'nɑːl/ *adj.* trite, commonplace. □ **banality** /-'nælɪtɪ/ *n.* (*pl.* **-ies**). **banally** *adv.* [French, related to BAN: originally = compulsory, hence = common]

banana /bə'nɑːnə/ *n.* **1** long curved soft fruit with a yellow skin. **2** treelike plant bearing it. □ **go bananas** *slang* go mad. [Portuguese or Spanish, from an African name]

banana republic *n. derog.* small State, esp. in Central America, dependent on foreign capital.

band –*n.* **1** flat, thin strip or loop of paper, metal, cloth, etc., put round something esp. to hold or decorate it. **2 a** strip of material on a garment. **b** stripe. **3** group

of esp. non-classical musicians. **4** organized group of criminals etc. **5** range of frequencies, wavelengths, or values. **6** belt connecting wheels or pulleys. –*v.* **1** (usu. foll. by *together*) unite. **2** put a band on. **3** mark with stripes. [Old Norse (related to BIND) and French]

bandage /'bændɪdʒ/ –*n.* strip of material used to bind a wound etc. –*v.* (**-ging**) bind with a bandage. [French: related to BAND]

bandanna /bæn'dænə/ *n.* large patterned handkerchief or neckerchief. [Portuguese from Hindi]

b. & b. *abbr.* bed and breakfast.

bandbox *n.* hatbox.

bandeau /'bændəʊ/ *n.* (*pl.* **-x** /-dəʊz/) narrow headband. [French]

banderole /ˌbændə'rəʊl/ *n.* **1** long narrow flag with a cleft end. **2** ribbon-like inscribed scroll. [Italian: related to BANNER]

bandicoot /'bændɪˌkuːt/ *n.* **1** catlike Australian marsupial. **2** (in full **bandicoot rat**) destructive rat in India. [Telugu, = pig-rat]

bandit /'bændɪt/ *n.* robber or outlaw, esp. one attacking travellers etc. □ **banditry** *n.* [Italian]

bandmaster *n.* conductor of a band.

bandog /'bændɒg/ *n.* fighting-dog bred for its strength and ferocity. [from BAND, DOG]

bandolier /ˌbændə'lɪə(r)/ *n.* (also **bandoleer**) shoulder belt with loops or pockets for cartridges. [Dutch or French]

band-saw *n.* mechanical saw with a blade formed by an endless toothed band.

bandsman *n.* player in a band.

bandstand *n.* outdoor platform for musicians.

bandwagon *n.* □ **climb** (or **jump**) **on the bandwagon** join a popular or successful cause etc.

bandwidth *n.* range of frequencies within a given band.

bandy[1] *adj.* (**-ier, -iest**) **1** (of the legs) curved so as to be wide apart at the knees. **2** (also **bandy-legged**) having bandy legs. [perhaps from obsolete *bandy* curved stick]

bandy[2] *v.* (**-ies, -ied**) **1** (often foll. by *about*) **a** pass (a story, rumour, etc.) to and fro. **b** discuss disparagingly (*bandied her name about*). **2** (often foll. by *with*) exchange (blows, insults, etc.). [perhaps from French]

bane *n.* **1** cause of ruin or trouble. **2** *poet.* ruin. **3** *archaic* (except in *comb.*) poison (*ratsbane*). □ **baneful** *adj.* [Old English]

bang —n. **1** loud short sound. **2** sharp blow. **3** *coarse slang* act of sexual intercourse. **4** *US* fringe cut straight across the forehead. —v. **1** strike or noisily (*banged the door shut*). **2** (cause to) make a bang. **3** *coarse slang* have sexual intercourse (with). —adv. **1** with a bang. **2** *colloq.* exactly (*bang in the middle*). □ **bang on** *colloq.* exactly right. **go bang 1** shut noisily. **2** explode. **3** (as **bang goes** etc.) *colloq.* be suddenly lost (*bang go my hopes*). [imitative]

banger n. **1** *slang* sausage. **2** *slang* noisy old car. **3** firework designed to go bang.

bangle /'bæŋg(ə)l/ n. rigid bracelet or anklet. [Hindi *bangri*]

banian var. of BANYAN.

banish /'bænɪʃ/ v. **1** condemn to exile. **2** dismiss (esp. from one's mind). □ **banishment** n. [Germanic: related to BAN]

banister /'bænɪstə(r)/ n. (also **bannister**) (usu. in *pl.*) uprights and handrail beside a staircase. [corruption of BALUSTER]

■ **Usage** See note at *baluster*.

banjo /'bændʒəʊ/ n. (pl. **-s** or **-es**) guitar-like stringed instrument with a circular body. □ **banjoist** n. [US southern corruption of *bandore* from Greek *pandoura* lute]

bank¹ —n. **1** sloping ground beside a river. **2** raised area, esp. in the sea; slope. **3** mass of cloud, fog, snow, etc. —v. **1** (often foll. by *up*) heap or rise into banks. **2** pack (a fire) tightly for slow burning. **3 a** (of a vehicle, aircraft, etc.) round a curve with one side higher than the other. **b** cause to do this. [Old Norse: related to BENCH]

bank² —n. **1** establishment for depositing, withdrawing, and borrowing money. **2** kitty in some gambling games. **3** storage place (*blood bank*). —v. **1** deposit (money etc.) in a bank. **2** (often foll. by *at, with*) keep money (at a bank). □ **bank on** *colloq.* rely on (*I'm banking on you*). [French *banque* or Italian *banca*: related to BANK¹]

bank³ n. row of similar [...] lights, switches, oars [...] from Germanic: rel[...] when

bankable adj. [...]ing a bank.

bank ca[...]er money.

CHEQU[...]

ba[...]

bankrupt /'bæŋkrʌpt/ —adj. **1** legally declared insolvent. **2** (often foll. by *of*) exhausted or drained (of emotion etc.). —n. insolvent person, esp. one whose assets are used to repay creditors. —v. make bankrupt. □ **bankruptcy** n. (pl. -ies). [Italian *banca rotta* broken bench: related to BANK²]

banksia /'bæŋksɪə/ n. Australian evergreen flowering shrub. [*Banks*, name of a naturalist]

banner n. **1** large sign bearing a slogan or design, esp. in a demonstration or procession; flag. **2** slogan, esp. political. [Latin *bandum* standard]

banner headline n. large, esp. front-page, newspaper headline.

bannister var. of BANISTER.

bannock /'bænək/ n. *Scot.* & *N.Engl.* round flat loaf, usu. unleavened. [Old English]

banns n.pl. notice announcing an intended marriage, read out in a parish church. [pl. of BAN]

banquet /'bæŋkwɪt/ —n. sumptuous, esp. formal, feast or dinner. —v. (-t-) attend, or entertain with, a banquet; feast. [French diminutive of *banc* bench]

banquette /bæŋ'ket/ n. upholstered bench, esp. in a restaurant or bar. [French from Italian]

banshee /'bænʃiː/ n. *Ir.* & *Scot.* wailing female spirit warning of death in a house. [Irish, = fairy woman]

bantam /'bæntəm/ n. **1** a kind of small domestic fowl. **2** small but aggressive person. [apparently from *Bāntān* in Java]

bantamweight n. **1** weight in ce[...]ain sports between flyweight and [...] kg. [...] weight, in amateur box[...]ing. —v. **2** sportsman of this w[...]ter. [origin

banter —n. good-[...]. same or -s) **1 1** tease. **2** [...]r of a large group of unkno[...]uages [...]ern African Blacks. **2** [...]ese peoples or languages spoken by them. [...]stan [...] people]

Ba[...] [...] offens. = HOMELAND 2.

[...]yan /'bænjən/ n. (also **banian**) Indian fig tree with self-rooting branches. [Portuguese from Sanskrit, = trader]

ntu:'stɑːn/ n. *S.Af[...]*

baobab /'beɪəʊˌbæb/ n. African tree with a massive trunk and large pulpy fruit. [probably African dial.]

bap n. soft flattish bread roll. [origin unknown

baptism /'bæptɪz(ə)m/ n. symbolic admission to the Christian Church, with water and usu. name-giving. □ **baptismal** /-'tɪzm(ə)l/ adj. [Greek baptizō baptize]

baptism of fire n. 1 initiation into battle. 2 painful initiation into an activity.

baptist n. 1 person who baptizes, esp. John the Baptist. 2 (**Baptist**) Christian advocating baptism by total immersion.

baptistery /'bæptɪstərɪ/ n. (pl. -ies) 1 a part of a church used for baptism. b hist. separate building used for baptism. 2 (in a Baptist chapel) receptacle used for immersion.

baptize /bæp'taɪz/ v. (also -ise) (-zing or -sing) 1 administer baptism to. 2 give a name or nickname to.

bar[1] —n. 1 long piece of rigid material, esp. used to confine or obstruct. 2 a something of similar form (bar of soap; bar of chocolate). b band of colour or light. c heating element of an electric fire. d metal strip below the clasp of a medal, awarded as an extra distinction. e Heraldry narrow horizontal stripe across a shield. 3 a counter for serving alcohol etc. on. b room or building containing it. c small shop or stall serving refreshments (snack bar). d counter for a special service (heel bar). 4 a barrier. b restriction (colour bar; bar to promotion). 5 prisoner's enclosure in a lawcourt. 6 any of the sections into which a piece of music is divided by vertical lines. 7 (**the Bar**) Law a barristers collectively. b profession of barrister. —v. (-rr-) 1 a fasten with a bar or ba__. b (usu. foll. by in, out) shut or keep in or out. 2 obstruct, prevent. 3 (usu. foll. ___) prohibit, exclude. 4 mark with the ___. —prep. except. □ **be called to ___** admitted as barrister. **be-___ ___** ___ison. [French]

bar[2] n. ___ one atmospl___ unit of pressure, 10⁵ newto___

barathea /__ ___ ___/ [origin unknow___

barb —n. 1 secon___ projection from a___ etc. 2 hurtful remark ___ at the mouth of some fis___ barb. 2 (as **barbed** adj.) ___cing etc.) deliberately hurtful. ___ beard]

barbarian /bɑː'beərɪən/ —n. ___tured or brutish person. 2 mem___ primitive tribe etc. —adj. 1 rough ___ uncultured. 2 uncivilized. [Greek ___ baros foreign]

barbaric /bɑː'bærɪk/ adj. 1 uncul___ brutal, cruel. 2 primitive.

barbarism /'bɑːbə,rɪz(ə)m/ n. 1 barbaric state or act. 2 non-standard word or expression.

barbarity /bɑː'bærɪtɪ/ n. (pl. -ies) 1 savage cruelty. 2 brutal act.

barbarous /'bɑːbərəs/ adj. = BARBARIC 1.

barbecue /'bɑːbɪ,kjuː/ —n. 1 a meal cooked over charcoal etc. out of doors. b party for this. 2 grill etc. used for this. —v. (-ues, -ued, -uing) cook on a barbecue. [Spanish from Haitian]

barbed wire n. wire with interwoven sharp spikes, used in fences and bar-riers.

barbel /'bɑːb(ə)l/ n. 1 freshwater fish with barbs. 2 = BARB n. 3. [Latin: related to BARB]

barbell n. iron bar with removable weights at each end, used for weightlift-ing.

barber n. person who cuts men's hair etc. by profession. [medieval Latin barba beard]

barberry /'bɑːbərɪ/ n. (pl. -ies) 1 shrub with yellow flowers and red berries. 2 its berry. [French berberis]

barber-shop n. colloq. close harmony singing for four male voices.

barber's pole n. pole with spiral red and white stripes as a barber's sign.

barbican /'bɑːbɪkən/ n. outer defence, esp. a double tower above a gate or drawbridge. [French]

barbie /'bɑːbɪ/ n. Austral. slang barbe-cue. [abbreviation]

bar billiards n.pl. form of billiards with holes in the table.

barbiturate /bɑː'bɪtjʊrət/ n. soporific or sedative drug from barbituric acid. [German, from the name Barbara]

barbituric acid /,bɑːbɪ'tjʊərɪk/ n. organic acid from which barbiturates are derived.

Barbour /'bɑːbə(r)/ n. propr. type of green waxed jacket. [Barbour, name of a draper]

barcarole /,bɑːkə'rəʊl/ n. 1 gondoliers' song. 2 music imitating this. [Italian barca boat]

bar-code n. machine-readable striped code on packaging etc.

bard n. 1 poet. poet. 2 a hist. Celtic ___ instrel. b prizewinner at an Eisted-d___ □ **bardic** adj. [Celtic]

___ adj. 1 unclothed or uncovered. 2 ___furnished; empty. 3 plain, ___ e bare truth; bare facts). ___ just sufficient (a bare ___sities). —v. (-ring) ___his teeth; bared

___ a saddle.

barefoot *adj.* & *adv.* (also **barefooted** /-'fʊtɪd/) wearing nothing on the feet.

bareheaded /beə'hedɪd/ *adj.* & *adv.* wearing nothing on the head.

barely *adv.* 1 scarcely (*barely escaped*). 2 scantily (*barely furnished*).

bargain /'bɑːgɪn/ —*n.* 1 **a** agreement on the terms of a sale etc. **b** this from the buyer's viewpoint (*a bad bargain*). 2 cheap thing. —*v.* (often foll. by *with*, *for*) discuss the terms of a sale etc. (*bargained with me*; *bargain for the table*). □ **bargain for** (or *colloq.* **on**) be prepared for; expect. **bargain on** rely on. **into the bargain** moreover. [French from Germanic]

barge —*n.* 1 long flat-bottomed cargo boat on a canal or river. 2 long ornamental pleasure boat. —*v.* (**-ging**) 1 (foll. by *in*, *into*) **a** intrude rudely or awkwardly (*barged in on him*). **b** collide with (*barged into her*). 2 (often foll. by *around*) move clumsily about. [French: related to BARQUE]

bargeboard *n.* board fixed to the gable-end of a roof to hide the ends of the roof timbers. [perhaps from medieval Latin *bargus* gallows]

bargee /bɑː'dʒiː/ *n.* person sailing a barge.

bargepole *n.* □ **would not touch with a bargepole** refuse to be associated or concerned with.

baritone /'bærɪˌtəʊn/ *n.* 1 **a** second-lowest adult male singing voice. **b** singer with this voice. 2 instrument pitched second-lowest in its family. [Greek *barus* heavy, *tonos* tone]

barium /'beərɪəm/ *n.* white soft metallic element. [from BARYTA]

barium meal *n.* mixture swallowed to reveal the abdomen in X-rays.

bark[1] —*n.* 1 sharp explosive cry of a dog, fox, etc. 2 sound like this. —*v.* 1 (of a dog etc.) give a bark. 2 speak or utter sharply or brusquely. 3 *colloq.* cough harshly. □ **bark up the wrong tree** make false assumptions. [Old English]

bark[2] —*n.* 1 tough outer skin of tree-trunks, branches, etc. —*v.* 1 graze (one's shin etc.). 2 strip bark from. [Scandinavian]

barker *n.* tout at an auction, sideshow, etc. [from BARK[1]]

barley /'bɑːlɪ/ *n.* 1 cereal used as food and in spirits. 2 (also **barleycorn**) its grain. [Old English]

barley sugar *n.* sweet made from sugar, usu. in twisted sticks.

barley water *n.* drink made from a boiled barley mixture.

barm *n.* froth on fermenting malt liquor. [Old English]

barmaid *n.* woman serving in a pub etc.

barman *n.* man serving in a pub etc.

bar mitzvah /bɑː 'mɪtsvə/ *n.* 1 religious initiation ceremony of a Jewish boy at 13. 2 boy undergoing this. [Hebrew, = son of the commandment]

barmy /'bɑːmɪ/ *adj.* (**-ier**, **-iest**) *slang* crazy, stupid. [from BARM: earlier, = frothy]

barn *n.* large farm building for storing grain etc. [Old English, = barley house]

barnacle /'bɑːnək(ə)l/ *n.* 1 marine crustacean clinging to rocks, ships' bottoms, etc. 2 tenacious attendant or follower. [French or medieval Latin]

barnacle goose *n.* Arctic goose.

barn dance *n.* 1 informal gathering for country dancing. 2 a kind of country dance.

barney /'bɑːnɪ/ *n.* (*pl.* **-s**) *colloq.* noisy quarrel. [perhaps dial.]

barn-owl *n.* a kind of owl frequenting barns.

barnstorm *v.* tour rural areas as an actor or political campaigner. □ **barnstormer** *n.*

barnyard *n.* area around a barn.

barograph /'bærəˌgrɑːf/ *n.* barometer equipped to record its readings. [Greek *baros* weight]

barometer /bə'rɒmɪtə(r)/ *n.* 1 instrument measuring atmospheric pressure, used in meteorology. 2 anything which reflects change. □ **barometric** /ˌbærə'metrɪk/ *adj.* [related to BAROGRAPH]

baron /'bærən/ *n.* 1 member of the lowest order of the British or foreign nobility. 2 powerful businessman, entrepreneur, etc. 3 *hist.* person holding lands from the sovereign. □ **baronial** /bə'rəʊnɪəl/ *adj.* [medieval Latin, = man]

baroness /'bærənɪs/ *n.* 1 woman holding the rank of baron. 2 baron's wife or widow.

baronet /'bærənɪt/ *n.* member of the lowest hereditary titled British order. □ **baronetcy** *n.* (*pl.* **-ies**).

baron of beef *n.* double sirloin.

barony /'bærənɪ/ *n.* (*pl.* **-ies**) domain or rank of a baron.

baroque /bə'rɒk/ —*adj.* 1 highly ornate and extravagant in style, esp. of European art etc. of the 17th and 18th c. 2 of this period. —*n.* baroque style or art. [Portuguese, originally = misshapen pearl]

bar person *n.* barmaid or barman.

barque /bɑːk/ *n.* 1 sailing-ship with the rear mast fore-and-aft rigged and other masts square-rigged. 2 *poet.* boat. [Provençal from Latin *barca*]

barrack[1] /'bærək/ —*n.* (usu. in *pl.*, often treated as *sing.*) 1 housing for soldiers. 2

barrack

BASIC

large bleak building. −*v*. lodge (soldiers etc.) in barracks. [Italian or Spanish]

barrack² /'bærək/ *v*. 1 shout or jeer at (players, a speaker, etc.). 2 (foll. by *for*) cheer for, encourage (a team etc.). [perhaps from Australian slang *borak* banter]

barracouta /ˌbærə'kuːtə/ *n*. (*pl*. same or -**s**) long slender fish of southern oceans. [var. of BARRACUDA]

barracuda /ˌbærə'kuːdə/ *n*. (*pl*. same or -**s**) large tropical marine fish. [Spanish]

barrage /'bærɑːʒ/ *n*. 1 concentrated artillery bombardment. 2 rapid succession of questions or criticisms. 3 artificial barrier in a river etc. [French *barrer* BAR¹]

barrage balloon *n*. large anchored balloon used as a defence against low-flying aircraft.

barratry /'bærətrɪ/ *n*. fraud or gross negligence by a ship's master or crew. [French *barat* deceit]

barre /bɑː(r)/ *n*. horizontal bar at waist level, used in dance exercises. [French]

barré /'bæreɪ/ *n*. method of playing a chord on the guitar etc. with a finger laid across the strings at a particular fret. [French *barrer* bar]

barrel /'bær(ə)l/ −*n*. 1 cylindrical usu. convex container. 2 its contents. 3 measure of capacity (30 to 40 gallons). 4 cylindrical tube forming part of an object, e.g. a gun or a pen. −*v*. (-**ll**-; *US* -**l**-) put into a barrel or barrels. □ **over a barrel** *colloq*. helpless, at a person's mercy. [French]

barrel-organ *n*. mechanical musical instrument with a rotating pin-studded cylinder.

barren /'bærən/ *adj*. (-**er**, -**est**) 1 **a** unable to bear young. **b** (of land, a tree, etc.) unproductive. 2 unprofitable, dull. □ **barrenness** *n*. [French]

barricade /ˌbærɪ'keɪd/ −*n*. barrier, esp. improvised. −*v*. (-**ding**) block or defend with this. [French *barrique* cask]

barrier /'bærɪə(r)/ *n*. 1 fence etc. that bars advance or access. 2 obstacle (*class barriers*). [Romanic: related to BAR¹]

barrier cream *n*. protective skin cream.

barrier reef *n*. coral reef separated from the shore by a channel.

barring /'bɑːrɪŋ/ *prep*. except, not including.

barrister /'bærɪstə(r)/ *n*. advocate entitled to practise in the higher courts. [from BAR¹: cf. MINISTER]

barrow¹ /'bærəʊ/ *n*. 1 two-wheeled handcart. 2 = WHEELBARROW. [Old English: related to BEAR¹]

barrow² /'bærəʊ/ *n*. ancient grave-mound. [Old English]

bar sinister *n*. = BEND SINISTER.

bartender *n*. person serving in a pub etc.

barter −*v*. 1 trade in goods without using money. 2 exchange (goods). −*n*. trade by bartering. [perhaps from French]

baryon /'bærɪˌɒn/ *n*. heavy elementary particle (i.e. a nucleon or a hyperon). [Greek *barus* heavy]

baryta /bə'raɪtə/ *n*. barium oxide or hydroxide. [from BARYTES]

barytes /bə'raɪtiːz/ *n*. mineral form of barium sulphate. [Greek *barus* heavy]

basal /'beɪs(ə)l/ *adj*. of, at, or forming a base.

basalt /'bæsɔːlt/ *n*. a dark volcanic rock. □ **basaltic** /bə'sɔːltɪk/ *adj*. [Latin *basaltes* from Greek]

base¹ −*n*. 1 **a** part supporting from beneath or serving as a foundation. **b** notional support or foundation (*power base*). 2 principle or starting-point. 3 esp. *Mil*. headquarters. 4 main or important ingredient. 5 number in terms of which other numbers or logarithms are expressed. 6 substance capable of combining with an acid to form a salt. 7 *Baseball* etc. each of the four stations on a pitch. −*v*. (-**sing**) 1 (usu. foll. by *on*, *upon*) found or establish (a theory, hope, etc.). 2 station (*troops based in Malta*). [Greek *basis* stepping]

base² *adj*. 1 cowardly, despicable. 2 menial. 3 alloyed (*base coin*). 4 (of a metal) low in value. [Latin *bassus*]

baseball *n*. 1 game played esp. in the US with a circuit of four bases which batsmen must complete. 2 ball used in this.

baseless *adj*. unfounded, groundless.

baseline *n*. 1 line used as a base or starting-point. 2 line marking each end of a tennis-court.

basement /'beɪsmənt/ *n*. floor of a building below ground level.

base rate *n*. interest rate set by the Bank of England, used as the basis for other banks' rates.

bases *pl*. of BASE¹, BASIS.

bash −*v*. 1 **a** strike bluntly or heavily. **b** (often foll. by *up*) *colloq*. attack violently. **c** (often foll. by *down*, *in*, etc.) damage or break by striking forcibly. 2 (foll. by *into*) collide with. −*n*. 1 heavy blow. 2 *slang* attempt. [imitative]

bashful /'bæʃfʊl/ *adj*. shy, diffident. □ **bashfully** *adv*. [as ABASHED]

BASIC /'beɪsɪk/ *n*. computer programming language using familiar English words. [*B*eginner's *A*ll-purpose *S*ymbolic *I*nstruction *C*ode]

basic /'beɪsɪk/ —*adj.* **1** serving as a base; fundamental. **2 a** simplest or lowest in level (*basic pay, needs*). **b** vulgar (*basic humour*). —*n.* (usu. in *pl.*) fundamental facts or principles. □ **basically** *adv.*

basic slag *n.* fertilizer containing phosphates formed as a by-product in steel manufacture.

basil /'bæz(ə)l/ *n.* aromatic herb used as flavouring. [Greek *basilikos* royal]

basilica /bə'zɪlɪkə/ *n.* **1** ancient Roman hall with an apse and colonnades, used as a lawcourt etc. **2** similar building as a Christian church. [Greek *basilikē (stoa)* royal (portico)]

basilisk /'bæzɪlɪsk/ *n.* **1** mythical reptile with lethal breath and glance. **2** small American crested lizard. [Greek, diminutive of *basileus* king]

basin /'beɪs(ə)n/ *n.* **1** round open vessel for holding liquids or preparing food in. **2** = WASH-BASIN. **3** hollow depression. **4** sheltered mooring area. **5** round valley. **6** area drained by a river. □ **basinful** *n.* (*pl.* -s). [medieval Latin *ba(s)cinus*]

basis /'beɪsɪs/ *n.* (*pl.* **bases** /-siːz/) **1** foundation or support. **2** main principle or ingredient (*on a friendly basis*). **3** starting-point for a discussion etc. [Greek: related to BASE¹]

bask /bɑːsk/ *v.* **1** relax in warmth and light. **2** (foll. by *in*) revel in (*basking in glory*). [Old Norse: related to BATHE]

basket /'bɑːskɪt/ *n.* **1** container made of interwoven cane, reed, wire, etc. **2** amount held by this. **3** the goal in basketball, or a goal scored. **4** *Econ.* group or range (of currencies). [French]

basketball *n.* **1** game in which goals are scored by putting the ball through high nets. **2** ball used in this.

basketry *n.* **1** art of weaving cane etc. **2** work so produced.

basket weave *n.* weave like wickerwork.

basketwork *n.* = BASKETRY.

basking shark *n.* large shark which lies near the surface of the sea.

Basque /bæsk/ —*n.* **1** member of a people of the Western Pyrenees. **2** their language. —*adj.* of the Basques or their language. [Latin *Vasco*]

bas-relief /'bæsrɪ,liːf/ *n.* sculpture or carving with figures projecting slightly from the background. [French and Italian]

bass¹ /beɪs/ —*n.* **1 a** lowest adult male singing voice. **b** singer with this voice. **2** instrument pitched lowest in its family. **3** *colloq.* bass guitar or double-bass. **4** low-frequency output of a radio, record-player, etc. —*adj.* **1** lowest in musical pitch. **2** deep-sounding. □ **bassist** *n.* (in

sense 3). [from BASE² altered after Italian *basso*]

bass² /bæs/ *n.* (*pl.* same or -es) **1** common perch. **2** other spiny-finned fish of the perch family. [Old English]

bass clef *n.* clef placing F below middle C on the second highest line of the staff.

basset /'bæsɪt/ *n.* (in full **basset-hound**) sturdy hunting-dog with a long body and short legs. [French diminutive of *bas* low]

bass guitar *n.* electric guitar tuned as a double-bass.

bassinet /,bæsɪ'net/ *n.* child's wicker cradle, usu. hooded. [French diminutive of *bassin* BASIN]

basso /'bæsəʊ/ *n.* (*pl.* -s) singer with a bass voice. [Italian, = BASS¹]

bassoon /bə'suːn/ *n.* bass instrument of the oboe family. □ **bassoonist** *n.* [Italian: related to BASS¹]

bast /bæst/ *n.* fibre from the inner bark of a tree (esp. the lime). [Old English]

bastard /'bɑːstəd/ often *offens.* —*n.* **1** person born of an unmarried mother. **2** *slang* **a** unpleasant or despicable person. **b** person of a specified kind (*poor, lucky, bastard*). **3** *slang* difficult or awkward thing. —*attrib. adj.* **1** illegitimate by birth. **2** unauthorized, counterfeit, hybrid. □ **bastardy** *n.* (in sense 1 of *n.*). [French from medieval Latin]

bastardize *v.* (also -ise) (-zing or -sing) **1** corrupt, debase. **2** declare (a person) illegitimate.

baste¹ /beɪst/ *v.* (-ting) **1** moisten (meat) with fat etc. during cooking. **2** beat, thrash. [origin unknown]

baste² /beɪst/ *v.* (-ting) sew with large loose stitches, tack. [French from Germanic]

bastinado /,bæstɪ'neɪdəʊ/ —*n.* beating with a stick on the soles of the feet. —*v.* (-es, -ed) punish in this way. [Spanish *baston* stick]

bastion /'bæstɪən/ *n.* **1** projecting part of a fortification. **2** thing regarded as protecting (*bastion of freedom*). [Italian *bastire* build]

bat¹ —*n.* **1** implement with a handle, used for hitting balls in games. **2** turn with this. **3** batsman. —*v.* (-tt-) **1** hit with or as with a bat. **2** take a turn at batting. □ **off one's own bat** unprompted, unaided. [Old English from French]

bat² *n.* mouselike nocturnal flying mammal. [Scandinavian]

bat³ *v.* (-tt-) □ **not** (or **never**) **bat an eyelid** *colloq.* show no reaction or emotion. [var. of obsolete *bate* flutter]

batch —*n.* **1** group of things or persons considered or dealt with together; instalment. **2** loaves produced at one baking. **3** *Computing* group of records

processed as one unit. −*v.* arrange or deal with in batches. [related to BAKE]

bated /'beɪtɪd/ *adj.* □ **with bated breath** very anxiously. [as ABATE]

bath /bɑ:θ/ −*n.* (*pl.* -s /bɑ:ðz/) **1 a** (usu. plumbed-in) container for sitting in and washing the body. **b** its contents. **2** act of washing in it (*have a bath*). **3** (usu. in *pl.*) public building with baths or a swimming-pool. **4 a** vessel containing liquid for immersing something, e.g. a film for developing. **b** its contents. −*v.* **1** wash (esp. a baby) in a bath. **2** take a bath. [Old English]

Bath bun /bɑ:θ/ *n.* round spiced bun with currants, often iced. [*Bath* in S. England]

Bath chair /bɑ:θ/ *n.* wheelchair for invalids.

bath cube *n.* cube of soluble substance for scenting or softening bath-water.

bathe /beɪð/ −*v.* (-**thing**) **1** immerse oneself in water, esp. to swim or wash oneself. **2** immerse in, wash, or treat with liquid. **3** (of sunlight etc.) envelop. −*n.* swim. [Old English]

bathhouse *n.* public building with baths.

bathing-costume *n.* (also **bathing-suit**) garment worn for swimming.

bathos /'beɪθɒs/ *n.* lapse in mood from the sublime to the absurd or trivial; anticlimax. □ **bathetic** /bə'θetɪk/ *adj.* **bathotic** /bə'θɒtɪk/ *adj.* [Greek, = depth]

bathrobe *n.* esp. *US* dressing-gown, esp. of towelling.

bathroom *n.* **1** room with a bath, wash-basin, etc. **2** *US* room with a lavatory.

bath salts *n.pl.* soluble powder or crystals for scenting or softening bath-water.

bathyscaphe /'bæθɪ,skæf/ *n.* manned vessel for deep-sea diving. [Greek *bathus* deep, *skaphos* ship]

bathysphere /'bæθɪ,sfɪə(r)/ *n.* vessel for deep-sea observation. [Greek *bathus* deep, SPHERE]

batik /bə'ti:k/ *n.* **1** method of dyeing textiles by applying wax to parts to be left uncoloured. **2** cloth so treated. [Javanese, = painted]

batiste /bæ'ti:st/ *n.* fine linen or cotton cloth. [French from *Baptiste*, name of the first maker]

batman /'bætmən/ *n.* army officer's servant. [*bat* pack-saddle, from French]

baton /'bæt(ə)n/ *n.* **1** thin stick for conducting an orchestra etc. **2** short stick passed on in a relay race. **3** stick carried by a drum major. **4** staff of office. [French from Latin]

baton round *n.* rubber or plastic bullet.

batrachian /bə'treɪkɪən/ −*n.* amphibian that discards its gills and tail, esp. a frog or toad. −*adj.* of batrachians. [Greek *batrakhos* frog]

bats *predic. adj. slang* crazy. [originally pl. of BAT²]

batsman *n.* person who bats, esp. in cricket.

battalion /bə'tæljən/ *n.* **1** army unit usu. of 300–1000 men. **2** large group with a common aim. [Italian *battaglia* BATTLE]

batten¹ /'bæt(ə)n/ −*n.* **1 a** long flat strip of squared timber. **b** horizontal strip of wood to which laths, tiles, etc., are fastened. **2** strip for securing tarpaulin over a ship's hatchway. −*v.* strengthen or (often foll. by *down*) fasten with battens. [French: related to BATTER]

batten² /'bæt(ə)n/ *v.* (foll. by *on*) thrive at the expense of (another). [Old Norse]

Battenberg /'bæt(ə)n,bɜ:g/ *n.* oblong sponge cake, usu. of two colours and covered with marzipan. [*Battenberg* in Germany]

batter¹ *v.* **1 a** strike hard and repeatedly. **b** (often foll. by *against*, *at*, etc.) pound insistently (*batter at the door*). **2** (often in *passive*) **a** subject to long-term violence (*battered baby*, *wife*). **b** criticize severely. □ **batterer** *n.* [French *battre* beat: related to BATTLE]

batter² *n.* mixture of flour, egg, and milk or water, used for pancakes etc. [French: related to BATTER¹]

battered *adj.* coated in batter and deep-fried.

battering-ram *n. hist.* beam used in breaching fortifications.

battery /'bætərɪ/ *n.* (*pl.* -**ies**) **1** usu. portable container of an electrically charged cell or cells as a source of current. **2** (often *attrib.*) series of cages for the intensive breeding and rearing of poultry or cattle. **3** set of similar units of equipment; series, sequence. **4** emplacement for heavy guns. **5** *Law* unlawful physical violence against a person. [Latin: related to BATTLE]

battle /'bæt(ə)l/ −*n.* **1** prolonged fight between armed forces. **2** difficult struggle; contest (*battle for supremacy*; *battle of wits*). −*v.* (-**ling**) engage in battle; fight. □ **half the battle** key to the success of an undertaking. [Latin *battuo* beat]

battleaxe *n.* **1** large axe used in ancient warfare. **2** *colloq.* formidable older woman.

battlebus *n. colloq.* bus used by a politician during an election campaign as a mobile centre of operations.

battle-cruiser *n. hist.* warship of higher speed and lighter armour than a battleship.

battle-cry *n.* cry or slogan used in a battle or contest.

battledore /'bæt(ə)l,dɔː(r)/ *n. hist.* 1 (in full **battledore and shuttlecock**) game played with a shuttlecock and rackets. 2 racket used in this. [perhaps from Provençal *batedor* beater]

battledress *n.* everyday uniform of a soldier.

battlefield *n.* (also **battleground**) scene of a battle.

battlement /'bæt(ə)lmənt/ *n.* (usu. in *pl.*) recessed parapet along the top of a wall, as part of a fortification. [French *batailler* fortify]

battle royal *n.* 1 battle of many combatants; free fight. 2 heated argument.

battleship *n.* heavily armoured warship.

batty /'bætɪ/ *adj.* (-ier, -iest) *slang* crazy. [from BAT²]

batwing *attrib. adj.* (esp. of a sleeve) shaped like a bat's wing.

bauble /'bɔːb(ə)l/ *n.* showy worthless trinket or toy. [French *ba(u)bel* toy]

baulk /bɔːlk, bɔːk/ (also **balk**) *— v.* 1 (often foll. by *at*) jib, hesitate. 2 a thwart, hinder. **b** disappoint. 3 miss, let slip (a chance etc.). *— n.* 1 hindrance; stumbling-block. 2 roughly-squared timber beam. [Old English]

bauxite /'bɔːksaɪt/ *n.* claylike mineral, the chief source of aluminium. [French from *Les Baux* in S. France]

bawdy /'bɔːdɪ/ *— adj.* (-ier, -iest) humorously indecent. *n.* such talk or writing. [*bawd* brothel-keeper from French *baudetrot*]

bawdy-house *n.* brothel.

bawl /bɔːl/ *v.* 1 speak or shout noisily. 2 weep loudly. □ **bawl out** *colloq.* reprimand angrily. [imitative]

bay¹ *n.* broad curving inlet of the sea. [Spanish *bahia*]

bay² *n.* 1 laurel with deep green leaves. 2 (in *pl.*) bay wreath, for a victor or poet. [Latin *baca* berry]

bay³ *n.* 1 recess; alcove in a wall. 2 compartment (*bomb bay*). 3 area specially allocated (*loading bay*). [French *baer* gape]

bay⁴ *— adj.* (esp. of a horse) dark reddish-brown. *— n.* bay horse. [Latin *badius*]

bay⁵ *— v.* bark or howl loudly and plaintively. *— n.* sound of this, esp. of hounds in close pursuit. □ **at bay** cornered, unable to escape. **keep at bay** hold off (a pursuer). [French *bayer* to bark]

bayberry *n.* (*pl.* -ies) fragrant N. American tree.

bay-leaf *n.* leaf of the bay-tree, used for flavouring.

bayonet /'beɪə,net/ *— n.* 1 stabbing blade attachable to the muzzle of a rifle. 2 electrical fitting pushed into a socket and twisted. *— v.* (-t-) stab with bayonet. [French, perhaps from *Bayonne* in SW France]

bay rum *n.* perfume distilled orig. from bayberry leaves in rum.

bay window *n.* window projecting outwards from a wall.

bazaar /bə'zɑː(r)/ *n.* 1 oriental market. 2 fund-raising sale of goods, esp. for charity. [Persian]

bazooka /bə'zuːkə/ *n.* anti-tank rocket-launcher. [origin unknown]

BB *abbr.* double-black (pencil-lead).

BBC *abbr.* British Broadcasting Corporation.

BC *abbr.* British Columbia.

BC *abbr.* before Christ.

BCG *abbr.* Bacillus Calmette-Guérin, an anti-tuberculosis vaccine.

BD *abbr.* Bachelor of Divinity.

bdellium /'delɪəm/ *n.* 1 tree yielding resin. 2 this used in perfumes. [Latin from Greek]

Be *symb.* beryllium.

be /biː, bɪ/ *v.* (*sing. present* **am**; **are** /ɑː(r)/; **is** /ɪz/; *past* **was** /wɒz/; **were** /wɜː(r)/; *pres. part.* **being**; *past part.* **been**) 1 exist, live (*I think, therefore I am*; *there is no God*). 2 a occur; take place (*dinner is at eight*). b occupy a position (*he is in the garden*). 3 remain, continue (*let it be*). 4 linking subject and predicate, expressing: a identity (*she is the person*). b condition (*he is ill today*). c state or quality (*he is kind*; *they are my friends*). d opinion (*I am against hanging*). e total (*two and two are four*). f cost or significance (*it is £5 to enter*; *it is nothing to me*). 5 *v.aux.* a with a past participle to form the passive (*it was done*; *it is said*). b with a present participle to form continuous tenses (*we are coming*; *it is being cleaned*). c with an infinitive to express duty or commitment, intention, possibility, destiny, or hypothesis (*I am to tell you*; *we are to wait here*; *he is to come at four*; *it was not to be found*; *they were never to meet again*; *if I were to die*). □ **be at** occupy oneself with (*what is he at?*; *mice have been at the food*). **be off** *colloq.* go away; leave. **-to-be** of the future (in *comb.*: *bride-to-be*). [Old English]

be- *prefix* forming verbs: 1 (from transitive verbs) a all over; all round (*beset*). b thoroughly, excessively (*begrudge*). 2 (from intransitive verbs) expressing transitive action (*bemoan*; *bestride*). 3

(from adjectives and nouns) expressing transitive action (*becalm*). **4** (from nouns) **a** affect with (*befog*). **b** treat as (*befriend*). **c** (forming adjectives in -ed) having (*bejewelled*). [Old English, = BY]

beach –*n.* pebbly or sandy shore esp. of the sea. –*v.* run or haul (a boat etc.) on to a beach. [origin unknown]

beachcomber *n.* person who searches beaches for articles of value.

beachhead *n.* fortified position set up on a beach by landing forces.

beacon /'biːkən/ *n.* **1** fire or light set up high as a warning etc. **2** visible warning or guiding device (e.g. a lighthouse, navigation buoy, etc.). **3** radio transmitter whose signal helps fix the position of a ship or aircraft. **4** = BELISHA BEACON. [Old English]

bead –*n.* **1 a** small usu. rounded piece of glass, stone, etc., for threading to make necklaces etc., or sewing on to fabric, etc. **b** (in *pl.*) bead necklace; rosary. **2** drop of liquid. **3** small knob in the foresight of a gun. **4** inner edge of a pneumatic tyre gripping the rim of the wheel. –*v.* adorn with or as with beads. □ **draw a bead on** take aim at. [Old English, = prayer]

beading *n.* **1** moulding or carving like a series of beads. **2** bead of a tyre.

beadle /'biːd(ə)l/ *n.* **1** ceremonial officer of a church, college, etc. **2** *Scot.* church officer serving the minister. **3** *hist.* minor parish disciplinary officer. [French from Germanic]

beady *adj.* (**-ier, -iest**) (esp. of the eyes) small, round, and bright.

beady-eyed *adj.* **1** with beady eyes. **2** observant.

beagle /'biːg(ə)l/ *n.* small short-haired hound used for hunting hares. [French]

beak[1] *n.* **1 a** bird's horny projecting jaws. **b** similar jaw of a turtle etc. **2** *slang* hooked nose. **3** *hist.* pointed prow of a warship. **4** spout. [French from Celtic]

beak[2] *n. slang* **1** magistrate. **2** schoolmaster. [probably thieves' cant]

beaker *n.* **1** tall cup or tumbler. **2** lipped glass vessel for scientific experiments. [Old Norse]

be-all and end-all *n. colloq.* (often foll. by *of*) whole being, essence.

beam –*n.* **1** long sturdy piece of squared timber or metal used in house-building etc. **2** ray or shaft of light or radiation. **3** bright look or smile. **4** series of radio or radar signals as a guide to a ship or aircraft. **5** crossbar of a balance. **6 a** ship's breadth. **b** width of a person's hips. **7** (in *pl.*) horizontal cross-timbers of a ship. –*v.* **1** emit or direct (light, approval, etc.). **2 a** shine. **b** look or smile

radiantly. □ **off** (or **off the**) **beam** *colloq.* mistaken. **on the beam** *colloq.* on the right track. [Old English, = tree]

bean *n.* **1 a** climber with edible seeds in long pods. **b** seed or pod of this. **2** similar seed of coffee etc. □ **full of beans** *colloq.* lively, exuberant. **not a bean** *slang* no money. [Old English]

beanbag *n.* **1** small bag filled with dried beans and used as a ball. **2** large bag filled usu. with polystyrene pieces and used as a chair.

beanfeast *n.* **1** *colloq.* celebration. **2** workers' annual dinner.

beano /'biːnəʊ/ *n.* (*pl.* **-s**) *slang* celebration, party.

beanpole *n.* **1** support for bean plants. **2** *colloq.* tall thin person.

bean sprout *n.* sprout of a bean seed as food.

beanstalk *n.* stem of a bean plant.

bear[1] /beə(r)/ *v.* (*past* **bore**; *past part.* **borne** or **born**) **1** carry, bring, or take (esp. visibly) (*bear gifts*). **2** show; have, esp. characteristically (*bear marks of violence*; *bears no relation to the case*; *bore no name*). **3 a** produce, yield (fruit etc.). **b** give birth to (*has borne a son*; *was born last week*). **4 a** sustain (a weight, responsibility, cost, etc.). **b** endure (an ordeal, difficulty, etc.). **5** (usu. with *neg.* or *interrog.*) **a** tolerate (*can't bear him*). **b** admit of (*does not bear thinking about*). **6** carry mentally (*bear a grudge*). **7** veer in a given direction (*bear left*). **8** bring or provide (something needed) (*bear him company*). □ **bear down** press downwards. **bear down on** approach inexorably. **bear on** (or **upon**) be relevant to. **bear out** support or confirm as evidence. **bear up** not despair. **bear with** tolerate patiently. **bear witness** testify. [Old English]

bear[2] /beə(r)/ *n.* **1** any of several large heavy mammals with thick fur. **2** rough or uncouth person. **3** person who sells shares hoping to repurchase them more cheaply. □ **the Great Bear**, **the Little Bear** constellations near the North Pole. [Old English]

bearable *adj.* endurable.

beard –*n.* **1** facial hair on the chin etc. **2** similar tuft etc. on an animal. –*v.* oppose; defy. □ **bearded** *adj.* **beardless** *adj.* [Old English]

bearer *n.* **1** person or thing that bears, carries, or brings. **2** person who presents a cheque etc.

beargarden *n.* rowdy scene.

bear-hug *n.* tight embrace.

bearing *n.* **1** bodily attitude; general manner. **2** (foll. by *on, upon*) relevance to (*has no bearing on it*). **3** endurability

(*beyond bearing*). **4** part of a machine supporting a rotating part. **5 a** direction or position relative to a fixed point. **b** (in *pl.*) knowledge of one's relative position. **6** *Heraldry* device or charge.

Béarnaise sauce /ˌbeɪəˈneɪz/ *n.* rich thick sauce with egg-yolks. [French]

bearskin *n.* **1** skin of a bear, esp. as a wrap etc. **2** tall furry hat worn by some regiments.

beast *n.* **1** animal, esp. a wild mammal. **2 a** brutal person. **b** *colloq.* objectionable person or thing. **3** (prec. by *the*) the animal nature in man. [Latin *bestia*]

beastly –*adj.* (-ier, -iest) **1** *colloq.* objectionable, unpleasant. **2** like a beast; brutal. –*adv.* *colloq.* very, extremely.

beast of prey *n.* animal which hunts animals for food.

beat –*v.* (*past* **beat**; *past part.* **beaten**) **1 a** strike persistently and violently. **b** strike (a carpet, drum, etc.) repeatedly. **2** (foll. by *against*, *at*, *on*, etc.) pound or knock repeatedly. **3 a** overcome; surpass. **b** be too hard for; perplex. **4** (often foll. by *up*) whisk (eggs etc.) vigorously. **5** (often foll. by *out*) shape (metal etc.) by blows. **6** (of the heart etc.) pulsate rhythmically. **7** (often foll. by *out*) **a** indicate (a tempo etc.) by tapping etc. **b** sound (a signal etc.) by striking a drum etc. (*beat a tattoo*). **8** move or cause (wings) to move up and down. **9** make (a path etc.) by trampling. **10** strike (bushes etc.) to rouse game. –*n.* **1 a** main accent in music or verse. **b** rhythm indicated by a conductor (*watch the beat*). **c** (in popular music) strong rhythm. **2 a** stroke or blow or measured sequence of strokes. **b** throbbing movement or sound. **3 a** police officer's route or area. **b** person's habitual round. –*predic. adj.* *slang* exhausted, tired out. □ **beat about the bush** not come to the point. **beat the bounds** mark parish boundaries by striking certain points with rods. **beat down 1** cause (a seller) to lower the price by bargaining. **2** strike to the ground (*beat the door down*). **3** (of the sun, rain, etc.) shine or fall relentlessly. **beat it** *slang* go away. **beat off** drive back (an attack etc.). **beat a person to it** arrive or do something before another person. **beat up** beat, esp. with punches and kicks. □ **beatable** *adj.* [Old English]

beater *n.* **1** implement for beating (esp. eggs). **2** person who rouses game at a shoot.

beatific /ˌbiːəˈtɪfɪk/ *adj.* **1** *colloq.* blissful (*beatific smile*). **2** making blessed. [Latin *beatus* blessed]

beatify /biːˈætɪˌfaɪ/ *v.* (-ies, -ied) **1** *RC Ch.* declare (a person) to be 'blessed',

often as a step towards canonization. **2** make happy. □ **beatification** /-fɪˈkeɪʃ(ə)n/ *n.*

beatitude /biːˈætɪˌtjuːd/ *n.* **1** perfect bliss or happiness. **2** (in *pl.*) blessings in Matt. 5:3–11.

beatnik /ˈbiːtnɪk/ *n.* member of a movement of socially unconventional young people in the 1950s.

beat-up *adj. colloq.* dilapidated.

beau /bəʊ/ *n.* (*pl.* **-x** /bəʊz/) **1** esp. *US* admirer; boyfriend. **2** fop; dandy. [Latin *bellus* pretty]

Beaufort scale /ˈbəʊfət/ *n.* scale of wind speed ranging from 0 (calm) to 12 (hurricane). [Sir F. *Beaufort*, name of an admiral]

Beaujolais /ˈbəʊʒəˌleɪ/ *n.* red or white wine from the Beaujolais district of France.

Beaujolais Nouveau /nuːˈvəʊ/ *n.* Beaujolais wine sold in the first year of a vintage.

beauteous /ˈbjuːtɪəs/ *adj. poet.* beautiful.

beautician /bjuːˈtɪʃ(ə)n/ *n.* specialist in beauty treatment.

beautiful /ˈbjuːtɪˌfʊl/ *adj.* **1** having beauty, pleasing to the eye, ear, or mind etc. (*beautiful voice*). **2** pleasant, enjoyable (*had a beautiful time*). **3** excellent (*beautiful specimen*). □ **beautifully** *adv.*

beautify /ˈbjuːtɪˌfaɪ/ *v.* (-ies, -ied) make beautiful; adorn. □ **beautification** /-fɪˈkeɪʃ(ə)n/ *n.*

beauty /ˈbjuːtɪ/ *n.* (*pl.* -ies) **1** combination of shape, colour, sound, etc., that pleases the senses. **2** *colloq.* **a** excellent specimen (*what a beauty!*). **b** attractive feature; advantage (*that's the beauty of it!*). **3** beautiful woman. [Latin *bellus* pretty]

beauty parlour *n.* (also **beauty salon**) establishment for cosmetic treatment.

beauty queen *n.* woman judged most beautiful in a contest.

beauty spot *n.* **1** place of scenic beauty. **2** small facial mark considered to enhance the appearance.

beaux *pl.* of BEAU.

beaver[1] –*n.* **1 a** amphibious broadtailed rodent which cuts down trees with its teeth and dams rivers. **b** its fur. **c** hat of this. **2** (**Beaver**) boy aged six or seven affiliated to the Scouts. –*v. colloq.* (usu. foll. by *away*) work hard. [Old English]

beaver[2] *n. hist.* lower face-guard of a helmet. [French, = bib]

beaver lamb *n.* lamb's wool made to look like beaver fur.

bebop /'bi:bɒp/ n. type of 1940s jazz with complex harmony and rhythms. [imitative]

becalm /bɪ'kɑːm/ v. (usu. in *passive*) deprive (a ship) of wind.

became *past* of BECOME.

because /bɪ'kɒz/ *conj.* for the reason that; since. □ **because of** on account of; by reason of. [from BY, CAUSE]

béchamel /'beʃə,mel/ n. a kind of thick white sauce. [Marquis de *Béchamel*, name of a courtier]

beck¹ n. *N.Engl.* brook; mountain stream. [Old Norse]

beck² n. □ **at a person's beck and call** subject to a person's constant orders. [from BECKON]

beckon /'bekən/ v. 1 (often foll. by *to*) summon by gesture. 2 entice. [Old English]

become /bɪ'kʌm/ v. (**-ming**; *past* **became**; *past part.* **become**) 1 begin to be (*became king, famous*). 2 (often as **becoming** adj.) a look well on; suit (*blue becomes him*). b befit (*it ill becomes you to complain*; *becoming modesty*). □ **become of** happen to (*what became of her?*). [Old English: related to BE-]

becquerel /'bekə,rel/ n. SI unit of radioactivity. [*Becquerel*, name of a physicist]

bed –n. 1 piece of furniture for sleeping on. 2 any place used for sleep or rest. 3 garden plot, esp. for flowers. 4 a bottom of the sea, a river, etc. b foundations of a road or railway. 5 stratum, layer. –v. (**-dd-**) 1 (usu. foll. by *down*) put or go to bed. 2 *colloq.* have sexual intercourse with. 3 (usu. foll. by *out*) plant in a garden bed. 4 cover up or fix firmly. 5 arrange as a layer. □ **bed of roses** life of ease. **go to bed** 1 retire to sleep. 2 (often foll. by *with*) have sexual intercourse. [Old English]

B.Ed. *abbr.* Bachelor of Education.

bed and board n. lodging and food.

bed and breakfast n. 1 room and breakfast in a hotel etc. 2 establishment providing this.

bedaub /bɪ'dɔːb/ v. smear or daub.

bedazzle /bɪ'dæz(ə)l/ v. (**-ling**) 1 dazzle. 2 confuse.

bedbug n. wingless parasite infesting beds etc.

bedclothes n.pl. sheets, blankets, etc., for a bed.

bedding n. 1 mattress and bedclothes. 2 litter for animals. 3 geological strata.

bedding plant n. plant suitable for a garden bed.

bedeck /bɪ'dek/ v. adorn.

bedevil /bɪ'dev(ə)l/ v. (**-ll-**; US **-l-**) 1 trouble, vex. 2 confound, confuse. 3 torment, abuse. □ **bedevilment** n.

bedew /bɪ'dju:/ v. cover or sprinkle (as) with dew.

bedfellow n. 1 person who shares a bed. 2 associate.

bedizen /bɪ'daɪz(ə)n/ v. *poet.* deck out gaudily. [from BE-, obsolete *dizen* deck out]

bedjacket n. jacket worn when sitting up in bed.

bedlam /'bedləm/ n. uproar and confusion. [St Mary of *Bethlehem*, name of a hospital in London]

bedlinen n. sheets and pillowcases.

Bedlington terrier /'bedlɪŋt(ə)n/ n. terrier with a narrow head, long legs, and curly grey hair. [*Bedlington* in Northumberland]

Bedouin /'beduːɪn/ n. (also **Beduin**) (*pl.* same) 1 nomadic desert Arab. 2 wandering person. [Arabic, = dwellers in the desert]

bedpan n. portable toilet for use in bed.

bedpost n. each of four upright supports of a bed.

bedraggled /bɪ'dræg(ə)ld/ adj. dishevelled, untidy.

bedrest n. recuperation in bed.

bedridden adj. confined to bed by infirmity.

bedrock n. 1 solid rock underlying alluvial deposits etc. 2 basic principles.

bedroom n. room for sleeping in.

bedside n. space beside esp. a patient's bed. □ **bedside manner** (esp. doctor's) way with patients.

bedsit n. (also **bedsitter, bedsitting room**) combined bedroom and sitting-room with cooking facilities.

bedsock n. warm sock worn in bed.

bedsore n. sore developed by lying in bed.

bedspread n. cover for a bed.

bedstead n. framework of a bed.

bedstraw n. small herbaceous plant.

bedtime n. (often *attrib.*) usual time for going to bed (*bedtime drink*).

Beduin var. of BEDOUIN.

bedwetting n. involuntary urination when asleep in bed.

bee n. 1 four-winged stinging insect, collecting nectar and pollen and producing wax and honey. 2 (usu. **busy bee**) busy person. 3 esp. *US* meeting for work or amusement. □ **a bee in one's bonnet** obsession. [Old English]

Beeb n. (prec. by *the*) *colloq.* BBC. [abbreviation]

beech n. 1 large smooth grey tree with glossy leaves. 2 its hard wood. [Old English]

beechmast n. (*pl.* same) fruit of the beech.

beef –n. 1 flesh of the ox, bull, or cow for eating. 2 *colloq.* male muscle. 3 (*pl.*

beeves or *US* **-s**) ox etc. bred for beef. **4** (*pl.* **-s**) *slang* complaint. *—v. slang* complain. □ **beef up** *slang* strengthen, reinforce. [Latin *bos bovis* ox]

beefburger *n.* = HAMBURGER.

beefcake *n.* esp. *US slang* male muscle.

beefeater *n.* **1** warder at the Tower of London. **2** Yeoman of the Guard.

beefsteak *n.* thick slice of beef for grilling or frying.

beef tea *n.* stewed beef extract for invalids.

beef tomato *n.* large tomato.

beefy *adj.* (**-ier, -iest**) **1** like beef. **2** solid, muscular. □ **beefiness** *n.*

beehive *n.* **1** artificial shelter for a colony of bees. **2** busy place.

bee-keeper *n.* keeper of bees. □ **bee-keeping** *n.*

beeline *n.* □ **make a beeline for** go directly to.

Beelzebub /biːˈelzɪˌbʌb/ *n.* the Devil. [Hebrew, = lord of the flies]

been *past part.* of BE.

beep *—n.* sound of a (esp. motor-car) horn. *—v.* emit a beep. [imitative]

beer *n.* **1** alcoholic drink made from fermented malt etc., flavoured with hops. **2** glass of this. □ **beer and skittles** amusement. [Old English]

beer-cellar *n.* cellar for storing, or selling and drinking, beer.

beer garden *n.* (also **beer hall**) garden (or large room) where beer is sold and drunk.

beer-mat *n.* small mat for a beer-glass.

beery *adj.* (**-ier, -iest**) **1** affected by beer-drinking. **2** like beer.

beeswax *—n.* **1** wax secreted by bees to make honeycombs. **2** this used to polish wood. *—v.* polish with beeswax.

beeswing *n.* filmy second crust on old port.

beet *n.* plant with an edible root (see BEETROOT, SUGAR BEET). [Old English]

beetle[1] /ˈbiːt(ə)l/ *—n.* insect, esp. black, with hard protective outer wings. *—v.* (**-ling**) *colloq.* (foll. by *about, off, etc.*) hurry, scurry. [Old English: related to BITE]

beetle[2] /ˈbiːt(ə)l/ *—adj.* projecting, shaggy, scowling (*beetle brows*). *—v.* (usu. as **beetling** *adj.*) (of brows, cliffs, etc.) project, overhang. [origin unknown]

beetle[3] /ˈbiːt(ə)l/ *n.* heavy tool for ramming, crushing, etc. [Old English: related to BEAT]

beetle-browed *adj.* with shaggy, projecting, or scowling eyebrows.

beetroot *n.* beet with an edible dark-red root.

beeves *pl.* of BEEF.

befall /bɪˈfɔːl/ *v.* (*past* **befell**; *past part.* **befallen**) *poet.* happen; happen to. [Old English: related to BE-]

befit /bɪˈfɪt/ *v.* (**-tt-**) be appropriate for; be incumbent on.

befog /bɪˈfɒg/ *v.* (**-gg-**) **1** confuse, obscure. **2** envelop in fog.

before /bɪˈfɔː(r)/ *—conj.* **1** earlier than the time when (*see me before you go*). **2** rather than that (*would die before he stole*). *—prep.* **1** earlier than (*before noon*). **2 a** in front of, ahead of (*before her in the queue*). **b** in the face of (*recoil before the attack*). **c** awaiting (*the future before them*). **3** rather than (*death before dishonour*). **4 a** in the presence of (*appear before the judge*). **b** for the attention of (*put before the committee*). *—adv.* **1** previously; already (*happened long before; done it before*). **2** ahead (*go before*). **3** on the front (*hit before and behind*). [Old English: related to BY, FORE]

Before Christ *adv.* (of a date) reckoned backwards from the birth of Christ.

beforehand *adv.* in advance, in readiness.

befriend /bɪˈfrend/ *v.* act as a friend to; help.

befuddle /bɪˈfʌd(ə)l/ *v.* (**-ling**) **1** make drunk. **2** confuse.

beg *v.* (**-gg-**) **1 a** (usu. foll. by *for*) ask for (food, money, etc.). **b** live by begging. **2** ask earnestly, humbly, or formally (for) (*begged for mercy; beg your indulgence; beg leave*). **3** (of a dog etc.) sit up with the front paws raised expectantly. **4** (foll. by *to* + infin.) take leave (*I beg to differ*). □ **beg off 1** ask to be excused from something. **2** get (a person) excused a penalty etc. **beg pardon** see PARDON. **beg the question** assume the truth of a proposition needing proof. **go begging** be unwanted or refused. [related to BID]

■ **Usage** The expression *beg the question* is often used incorrectly to mean (1) to avoid giving a straight answer, or (2) to invite the obvious question (that . . .). These uses should be avoided.

began *past* of BEGIN.

beget /bɪˈget/ *v.* (**-tt-**; *past* **begot**; *archaic* **begat**; *past part.* **begotten**) *literary* **1** father, procreate. **2** cause (*anger begets violence*). [Old English: related to BE-]

beggar /ˈbegə(r)/ *—n.* **1** person who lives by begging. **2** *colloq.* person (*cheeky beggar*). *—v.* **1** make poor. **2** be too extraordinary for (*beggar description*). □ **beggarly** *adj.*

begin /bɪˈgɪn/ *v.* (**-nn-**; *past* **began**; *past part.* **begun**) **1** perform the first part of; start (*begin work; begin crying; begin to understand*). **2** come into being (*war*

began in 1939; Wales begins here). **3** (usu. foll. by *to* + infin.) start at a certain time *(soon began to feel ill).* **4** be begun *(meeting began at 7).* **5 a** start speaking *('No,' he began).* **b** take the first step, be the first *(shall I begin?).* **6** (usu. with *neg.*) *colloq.* show any likelihood *(can't begin to compete).* [Old English]

beginner *n.* trainee, learner. □ **beginner's luck** supposed good luck of a beginner.

beginning *n.* **1** time or place at which anything begins. **2** source or origin. **3** first part.

begone /bɪˈgɒn/ *int. poet.* go away at once! [*be gone*]

begonia /bɪˈgəʊnɪə/ *n.* garden plant with bright flowers and leaves. [*Bégon,* name of a patron of science]

begot *past* of BEGET.

begotten *past part.* of BEGET.

begrudge /bɪˈgrʌdʒ/ *v.* (**-ging**) **1** resent; be dissatisfied at. **2** envy (a person) the possession of. □ **begrudgingly** *adv.*

beguile /bɪˈgaɪl/ *v.* (**-ling**) **1** charm; amuse. **2** wilfully divert, seduce. **3** (usu. foll. by *of, out of,* or *into* + verbal noun) delude; cheat. □ **beguilement** *n.* **beguiling** *adj.*

beguine /bɪˈgiːn/ *n.* popular dance of W. Indian origin. [French *béguin* infatuation]

begum /ˈbeɪgəm/ *n.* in India or Pakistan: **1** Muslim woman of high rank. **2** (**Begum**) title of a married Muslim woman. [Turkish *bigam* princess]

begun *past part.* of BEGIN.

behalf /bɪˈhɑːf/ *n.* □ **on behalf of** (or **on a person's behalf**) in the interests of; as representative of. [earlier *bihalve* on the part of]

behave /bɪˈheɪv/ *v.* (**-ving**) **1** act or react (in a specified way) *(behaved well).* **2** (often *refl.*) conduct oneself properly *(behave yourself!).* **3** (of a machine etc.) work well (or in a specified way). [from BE-, HAVE]

behaviour /bɪˈheɪvjə(r)/ *n.* (*US* **behavior**) way of behaving or acting. □ **behavioural** *adj.*

behavioural science *n.* (*US* **behavioral**) the study of human behaviour.

behaviourism *n.* (*US* **behaviorism**) *Psychol.* theory that human behaviour is determined by conditioned response to stimuli, and that psychological disorders are best treated by altering behaviour. □ **behaviourist** *n.*

behead /bɪˈhed/ *v.* cut the head off (a person), esp. as execution. [Old English: related to BE-]

beheld *past* and *past part.* of BEHOLD.

behemoth /bɪˈhiːmɒθ/ *n.* huge creature or thing. [Hebrew (Job 40:15)]

behest /bɪˈhest/ *n. literary* command; request. [Old English]

behind /bɪˈhaɪnd/ –*prep.* **1 a** in or to the rear of. **b** on the far side of *(behind the bush).* **c** hidden or implied by *(something behind that remark).* **2 a** in the past in relation to *(trouble is behind me now).* **b** late regarding *(behind schedule).* **3** inferior to; weaker than *(behind the others in maths).* **4 a** in support of *(she's behind us).* **b** responsible for *(the man behind the project).* **5** in the tracks of; following. –*adv.* **1 a** in or to the rear; further back *(the street behind; glance behind).* **b** on the further side *(wall with a field behind).* **2** remaining after others' departure *(stay behind).* **3** (usu. foll. by *with*) **a** in arrears. **b** late in finishing a task etc. *(getting behind).* **4** in a weak position; backward *(behind in Latin).* **5** following *(dog running behind).* –*n. colloq.* buttocks. □ **behind the scenes** see SCENE. **behind time** late. **behind the times** old-fashioned, antiquated. [Old English]

behindhand *adv. & predic. adj.* **1** (usu. foll. by *with, in*) late; in arrears. **2** out of date.

behold /bɪˈhəʊld/ *v.* (*past & past part.* **beheld**) (esp. in *imper.*) *literary* see, observe. [Old English: related to BE-]

beholden *predic. adj.* (usu. foll. by *to*) under obligation.

behove /bɪˈhəʊv/ *v.* (**-ving**) *formal* **1** be incumbent on. **2** befit *(it ill behoves him to protest).* [Old English: related to BE, HEAVE]

beige /beɪʒ/ –*n.* pale sandy fawn colour. –*adj.* of this colour. [French]

being /ˈbiːɪŋ/ *n.* **1** existence. **2** nature or essence (of a person etc.) *(his whole being revolted).* **3** person or creature.

bejewelled /bɪˈdʒuːəld/ *adj.* (*US* **bejeweled**) adorned with jewels.

bel *n.* unit of relative power level, esp. of sound, corresponding to an intensity ratio of 10 to 1 (cf. DECIBEL). [*Bell,* name of the inventor of the telephone]

belabour /bɪˈleɪbə(r)/ *v.* (*US* **belabor**) **1** attack physically or verbally. **2** labour (a subject).

belated /bɪˈleɪtɪd/ *adj.* late or too late. □ **belatedly** *adv.*

belay /bɪˈleɪ/ –*v.* secure (a rope) by winding it round a peg etc. –*n.* act of belaying. [Dutch *beleggen*]

bel canto /bel ˈkæntəʊ/ *n.* lyrical richtoned style of operatic singing. [Italian, = fine song]

belch –*v.* **1** emit wind noisily through the mouth. **2** (of a chimney, gun, etc.)

send (smoke etc.) out or up. —*n.* act of belching. [Old English]

beleaguer /bɪˈliːɡə(r)/ *v.* **1** besiege. **2** vex; harass. [Dutch *leger* camp]

belfry /ˈbelfrɪ/ *n.* (*pl.* -**ies**) **1** bell tower. **2** space for bells in a church tower. [Germanic, probably = peace-protector]

Belial /ˈbiːlɪəl/ *n.* the Devil. [Hebrew, = worthless]

belie /bɪˈlaɪ/ *v.* (**belying**) **1** give a false impression of (*its appearance belies its age*). **2** fail to fulfil or justify. [Old English: related to BE-]

belief /bɪˈliːf/ *n.* **1** firm opinion; acceptance (*that is my belief*). **2** religious conviction (*belief in the after life; has no belief*). **3** (usu. foll. by *in*) trust or confidence. [related to BELIEVE]

believe /bɪˈliːv/ *v.* (**-ving**) **1** accept as true or as conveying the truth (*I believe it; don't believe him*). **2** think, suppose. **3** (foll. by *in*) **a** have faith in the existence of (*believes in God*). **b** have confidence in (*believes in homoeopathy*). **c** have trust in as a policy (*believes in telling the truth*). **4** have (esp. religious) faith. □ **believable** *adj.* **believer** *n.* [Old English]

Belisha beacon /bəˈliːʃə/ *n.* flashing orange ball on a striped post, marking some pedestrian crossings. [Hore-*Belisha*, who introduced it]

belittle /bɪˈlɪt(ə)l/ *v.* (**-ling**) disparage, make appear insignificant. □ **belittlement** *n.*

bell¹ —*n.* **1** hollow esp. cup-shaped usu. metal object sounding a note when struck. **2** such a sound, esp. as a signal. **3** thing resembling a bell, esp. in sound or shape. —*v.* provide with a bell. □ **give a person a bell** *colloq.* telephone a person. [Old English]

bell² —*n.* cry of a stag. —*v.* make this cry. [Old English]

belladonna /ˌbeləˈdɒnə/ *n.* **1** deadly nightshade. **2** drug from this. [Italian, = fair lady]

bell-bottom *n.* **1** marked flare below the knee (of a trouser-leg). **2** (in *pl.*) trousers with these. □ **bell-bottomed** *adj.*

bellboy *n.* esp. US page in a hotel or club.

belle /bel/ *n.* beautiful or most beautiful woman. [French, feminine of BEAU]

belles-lettres /bel ˈletr/ *n.pl.* (also treated as *sing.*) literary writings or studies. [French, = fine letters]

bellicose /ˈbelɪkəʊs/ *adj.* eager to fight; warlike. [Latin *bellum* war]

belligerence /bɪˈlɪdʒərəns/ *n.* **1** aggressive behaviour. **2** status of a belligerent.

belligerent —*adj.* **1** engaged in war or conflict. **2** pugnacious. —*n.* belligerent nation or person. [Latin *belligero* wage war]

bell-jar *n.* bell-shaped glass cover or container for use in a laboratory.

bellow /ˈbeləʊ/ —*v.* **1** emit a deep loud roar. **2** utter loudly. —*n.* loud roar. [origin uncertain]

bellows *n.pl.* (also treated as *sing.*) **1** device for driving air into or through something. **2** expandable part, e.g. of a camera. [related to BELLY]

bell-pull *n.* handle etc. sounding a bell when pulled.

bell-push *n.* button operating an electric bell.

bell-ringer *n.* ringer of church bells or handbells. □ **bell-ringing** *n.*

bell-wether *n.* **1** leading sheep of a flock. **2** ringleader.

belly /ˈbelɪ/ —*n.* (*pl.* -**ies**) **1** trunk below the chest, containing the stomach and bowels. **2** stomach. **3** front of the body from waist to groin. **4** underside of an animal. **5** cavity or bulging part. —*v.* (**-ies, -ied**) (often foll. by *out*) swell; bulge. [Old English, = bag]

bellyache —*n.* *colloq.* stomach pain. —*v.* (**-ching**) *slang* complain noisily or persistently.

belly button *n.* *colloq.* navel.

belly-dance *n.* oriental dance performed by a woman, with voluptuous belly movements. □ **belly-dancer** *n.* **belly-dancing** *n.*

bellyflop *n.* *colloq.* dive with the belly landing flat on the water.

bellyful *n.* (*pl.* -**s**) **1** enough to eat. **2** *colloq.* more than one can tolerate.

belly-laugh *n.* loud unrestrained laugh.

belong /bɪˈlɒŋ/ *v.* **1** (foll. by *to*) **a** be the property of. **b** be correctly assigned to. **c** be a member of. **2** fit socially (*just doesn't belong*). **3** (foll. by *in, under*) be correctly placed or classified. [from BE-, obsolete *long* belong]

belongings *n.pl.* possessions or luggage.

Belorussian var. of BYELORUSSIAN.

beloved /bɪˈlʌvɪd/ —*adj.* much loved. —*n.* much loved person.

below /bɪˈləʊ/ —*prep.* **1** lower in position, amount, status, etc., than. **2** beneath the surface of (*head below water*). **3** unworthy of. —*adv.* **1** at or to a lower point or level. **2** downstream. **3** further forward on a page or in a book (*as noted below*). [be- BY, LOW¹]

belt —*n.* **1** strip of leather etc. worn esp. round the waist. **2** circular band in machinery; conveyor belt. **3** distinct strip of colour etc. **4** region or extent

(*cotton belt*). **5** *slang* heavy blow. *−v.* **1** put a belt round; fasten with a belt. **2** *slang* hit hard. **3** *slang* rush, hurry. □ **below the belt** unfair(ly). **belt out** *slang* sing or play (music) loudly or vigorously. **belt up 1** *slang* be quiet. **2** *colloq.* put on a seat belt. **tighten one's belt** economize. **under one's belt** securely acquired. [Old English]

beluga /bɪˈluːgə/ *n.* (*pl.* same or **-s**) **1 a** large kind of sturgeon. **b** caviare from it. **2** white whale. [Russian]

belvedere /ˈbɛlvɪˌdɪə(r)/ *n.* raised summer-house or gallery for viewing scenery. [Italian, = beautiful view]

BEM *abbr.* British Empire Medal.

bemoan /bɪˈməʊn/ *v.* lament; complain about.

bemuse /bɪˈmjuːz/ *v.* (**-sing**) puzzle, bewilder. [from BE-, MUSE[1]]

bench *n.* **1** long seat of wood or stone. **2** strong work-table. **3** (prec. by *the*) **a** judge's seat. **b** lawcourt. **c** judges and magistrates collectively. [Old English]

bencher *n.* senior member of an Inn of Court.

benchmark *n.* **1** surveyor's mark cut in a wall etc. as a reference point in measuring altitudes. **2** standard or point of reference.

bend[1] *−v.* (*past* and *past part.* **bent** except in *bended knee*) **1 a** force or adapt (something straight) into a curve or angle. **b** (of an object) be so altered. **2** (often foll. by *down*, *over*, etc.) curve, incline, or stoop (*road bends*; *bent down to pick it up*; *bent her head*). **3** interpret or modify (a rule) to suit oneself. **4** turn (one's steps, eyes, or energies) in a new direction. **5** be flexible, submit, or force to submit. *−n.* **1** curve; departure from a straight course. **2** bent part. **3** (in *pl.*; prec. by *the*) *colloq.* decompression sickness. □ **bend over backwards** see BACKWARDS. **round the bend** *colloq.* crazy, insane. □ **bendy** *adj.* (**-ier, -iest**). [Old English]

bend[2] *n.* **1** any of various knots. **2** *Heraldry* diagonal stripe from top right to bottom left of a shield (from its wearer's position). [Old English: related to BIND]

bender *n.* *slang* wild drinking-spree. [from BEND[1]]

bend sinister *n.* *Heraldry* diagonal stripe from top left to bottom right of a shield, as a sign of bastardy.

beneath /bɪˈniːθ/ *−prep.* **1** unworthy of (*beneath him to reply*). **2** below, under. *−adv.* below, underneath. [Old English: related to BE-, NETHER]

Benedictine /ˌbɛnɪˈdɪktɪn/ *−n.* **1** monk or nun of an order following the rule of St Benedict. **2** /-ˌtiːn/ *propr.* liqueur orig.

made by Benedictines. *−adj.* of St Benedict or the Benedictines. [Latin *Benedictus* Benedict]

benediction /ˌbɛnɪˈdɪkʃ(ə)n/ *n.* blessing, esp. at the end of a religious service or as a special Roman Catholic service. □ **benedictory** *adj.* [Latin *benedico* bless]

benefaction /ˌbɛnɪˈfæk∫(ə)n/ *n.* **1** donation, gift. **2** giving or doing good. [Latin: related to BENEFIT]

benefactor /ˈbɛnɪˌfæktə(r)/ *n.* (*fem.* **benefactress**) person giving (esp. financial) support.

benefice /ˈbɛnɪfɪs/ *n.* a living from a church office.

beneficent /bɪˈnɛfɪs(ə)nt/ *adj.* doing good; generous, kind. □ **beneficence** *n.*

beneficial /ˌbɛnɪˈfɪʃ(ə)l/ *adj.* advantageous; having benefits. □ **beneficially** *adv.*

beneficiary /ˌbɛnɪˈfɪʃərɪ/ *n.* (*pl.* **-ies**) **1** person who benefits, esp. from a will. **2** holder of a benefice.

benefit /ˈbɛnɪfɪt/ *−n.* **1** favourable or helpful factor etc. **2** (often in *pl.*) insurance or social security payment (*sickness benefit*). **3** public performance or game in aid of a charitable cause etc. *−v.* (**-t-**; *US* **-tt-**) **1** help; bring advantage to. **2** (often foll. by *from*, *by*) receive benefit. □ **the benefit of the doubt** concession that a person is innocent, correct, etc., although doubt exists. [Latin *benefactum* from *bene* well, *facio* do]

benevolent /bɪˈnɛvələnt/ *adj.* **1** wellwishing; actively friendly and helpful. **2** charitable (*benevolent fund*). □ **benevolence** *n.* [French from Latin *bene volens* well wishing]

Bengali /bɛŋˈgɔːlɪ/ *−n.* (*pl.* **-s**) **1** native of Bengal. **2** language of Bengal. *−adj.* of Bengal, its people, or language. [*Bengal*, former Indian province]

benighted /bɪˈnaɪtɪd/ *adj.* intellectually or morally ignorant.

benign /bɪˈnaɪn/ *adj.* **1** gentle, mild, kindly. **2** fortunate, salutary. **3** (of a tumour etc.) not malignant. □ **benignly** *adv.* [Latin *benignus*]

benignant /bɪˈnɪgnənt/ *adj.* **1** kindly, esp. to inferiors. **2** salutary, beneficial. □ **benignancy** *n.*

benignity /bɪˈnɪgnɪtɪ/ *n.* (*pl.* **-ies**) kindliness.

bent[1] *past* and *past part.* of BEND[1] *v.* *−adj.* **1** curved, angular. **2** *slang* dishonest, illicit. **3** *slang* sexually deviant. **4** (foll. by *on*) set on doing or having. *−n.* **1** inclination or bias. **2** (foll. by *for*) talent.

bent[2] *n.* **1** reedy grass with stiff stems. **2** stiff flower stalk of a grass. [Old English]

bentwood *n.* wood artificially shaped for making furniture.

benumb /bɪˈnʌm/ *v.* 1 make numb; deaden. 2 paralyse (the mind or feelings).

benzene /ˈbenziːn/ *n.* colourless liquid found in coal tar and used as a volatile solvent etc. [as BENZOIN]

benzine /ˈbenziːn/ *n.* mixture of liquid hydrocarbons obtained from petroleum.

benzoin /ˈbenzəʊɪn/ *n.* fragrant gum resin from an E. Asian tree. □ **benzoic** /-ˈzəʊɪk/ *adj.* [ultimately from Arabic *lubān jāwī* incense of Java]

benzol /ˈbenzɒl/ *n.* benzene, esp. unrefined.

bequeath /bɪˈkwiːð/ *v.* 1 leave to a person in a will. 2 hand down to posterity. [from BE-: related to QUOTH]

bequest /bɪˈkwest/ *n.* 1 bequeathing; bestowal by will. 2 thing bequeathed. [from BE-, obsolete *quiste* saying]

berate /bɪˈreɪt/ *v.* (-**ting**) scold, rebuke.

Berber /ˈbɜːbə(r)/ −*n.* 1 member of the indigenous mainly Muslim Caucasian peoples of N. Africa. 2 language of these peoples. −*adj.* of the Berbers or their language. [Arabic]

berceuse /beəˈsɜːz/ *n.* (*pl.* -**s** pronunc. same) 1 lullaby. 2 instrumental piece in this style. [French]

bereave /bɪˈriːv/ *v.* (-**ving**) (esp. as **bereaved** *adj.*) (often foll. by *of*) deprive of a relation, friend, etc., esp. by death. □ **bereavement** *n.* [Old English, from *reave* deprive of]

bereft /bɪˈreft/ *adj.* (foll. by *of*) deprived (*bereft of hope*). [past part. of BEREAVE]

beret /ˈbereɪ/ *n.* round flattish brimless cap of felt etc. [French: related to BIRETTA]

berg *n.* = ICEBERG. [abbreviation]

bergamot[1] /ˈbɜːgəmɒt/ *n.* 1 perfume from the fruit of a dwarf orange tree. 2 aromatic herb. [*Bergamo* in Italy]

bergamot[2] /ˈbɜːgəmɒt/ *n.* variety of fine pear. [Turkish, = prince's pear]

beriberi /ˌberɪˈberɪ/ *n.* nervous disease caused by a deficiency of vitamin B_1. [Sinhalese]

berk *n.* (also **burk**) *slang* stupid person. [*Berkshire Hunt*, rhyming slang for *cunt*]

berkelium /bɜːˈkiːlɪəm/ *n.* artificial radioactive metallic element. [*Berkeley* in US, where first made]

Bermuda shorts /bəˈmjuːdə/ *n.pl.* (also **Bermudas**) close-fitting knee-length shorts. [*Bermuda* in the W. Atlantic]

berry *n.* (*pl.* -**ies**) 1 any small roundish juicy stoneless fruit. 2 *Bot.* fruit with its

seeds enclosed in pulp (e.g. a banana or tomato). [Old English]

berserk /bəˈzɜːk/ *adj.* (esp. in **go berserk**) wild, frenzied; in a rage. [originally = Norse warrior: Icelandic, = bear-coat]

berth −*n.* 1 bunk on a ship, train, etc. 2 place for a ship to moor or be at anchor. 3 adequate room for a ship. 4 *colloq.* job. −*v.* 1 moor (a ship); be moored. 2 provide a sleeping place for. □ **give a wide berth** to stay away from. [probably from a special use of BEAR[1]]

beryl /ˈberɪl/ *n.* 1 transparent precious stone, esp. pale green. 2 mineral species including this, emerald, and aquamarine. [Greek *bērullos*]

beryllium /bəˈrɪlɪəm/ *n.* hard white metallic element.

beseech /bɪˈsiːtʃ/ *v.* (*past* and *past part.* **besought** /-ˈsɔːt/ or **beseeched**) 1 (foll. by *for*, or *to* + infin.) entreat. 2 ask earnestly for. [from BE-, SEEK]

beset /bɪˈset/ *v.* (-**tt**-; *past* and *past part.* **beset**) 1 attack or harass persistently (*beset by worries*). 2 surround (a person etc.). [Old English: related to BE-]

beside /bɪˈsaɪd/ *prep.* 1 at the side of; near. 2 compared with. 3 irrelevant to (*beside the point*). □ **beside oneself** frantic with worry etc. [Old English: related to BY, SIDE]

besides −*prep.* in addition to; apart from. −*adv.* also; moreover.

besiege /bɪˈsiːdʒ/ *v.* (-**ging**) 1 lay siege to. 2 crowd round eagerly. 3 harass with requests.

besmirch /bɪˈsmɜːtʃ/ *v.* 1 soil, discolour. 2 dishonour.

besom /ˈbiːz(ə)m/ *n.* broom of twigs. [Old English]

besotted /bɪˈsɒtɪd/ *adj.* 1 infatuated. 2 intoxicated, stupefied.

besought *past* and *past part.* of BESEECH.

bespangle /bɪˈspæŋg(ə)l/ *v.* (-**ling**) adorn with spangles.

bespatter /bɪˈspætə(r)/ *v.* 1 spatter all over. 2 slander, defame.

bespeak /bɪˈspiːk/ *v.* (*past* **bespoke**; *past part.* **bespoken** or as *adj.* **bespoke**) 1 engage in advance. 2 order (goods). 3 suggest; be evidence of.

bespectacled /bɪˈspektək(ə)ld/ *adj.* wearing spectacles.

bespoke *past* and *past part.* of BESPEAK. *adj.* 1 made to order. 2 making goods to order.

bespoken *past part.* of BESPEAK.

best −*adj.* (*superl.* of GOOD) of the most excellent or desirable kind. −*adv.* (*superl.* of WELL[1]). 1 in the best manner. 2 to the greatest degree. 3 most usefully (*is best ignored*). −*n.* 1 that which is best

(*the best is yet to come*). **2** chief merit or advantage (*brings out the best in him*). **3** (foll. by *of*) winning majority of (games played etc.) (*the best of five*). **4** one's best clothes. −*v. colloq.* defeat, outwit, outbid, etc. □ **at best** on the most optimistic view. **best bib and tucker** one's best clothes. **the best part of** most of. **do one's best** do all one can. **get the best of** defeat, outwit. **had best** would find it wisest to. **make the best of** derive what limited advantage one can from. [Old English]

bestial /'bestɪəl/ *adj.* **1** brutish, cruel. **2** of or like a beast. [Latin: related to BEAST]

bestiality /,bestɪ'ælɪtɪ/ *n.* **1** bestial behaviour. **2** sexual intercourse between a person and an animal.

bestiary /'bestɪərɪ/ *n.* (*pl.* **-ies**) medieval treatise on beasts. [medieval Latin: related to BEAST]

bestir /bɪ'stɜː(r)/ *v.refl.* (**-rr-**) exert or rouse oneself.

best man *n.* bridegroom's chief attendant.

bestow /bɪ'stəʊ/ *v.* (foll. by *on*, *upon*) confer (a gift, right, etc.). □ **bestowal** *n.* [Old English *stow* a place]

bestrew /bɪ'struː/ *v.* (*past part.* **bestrewed** or **bestrewn**) **1** (usu. foll. by *with*) strew (a surface). **2** lie scattered over.

bestride /bɪ'straɪd/ *v.* (**-ding**; *past* **-strode**; *past part.* **-stridden**) **1** sit astride on. **2** stand astride over.

best seller *n.* **1** book etc. sold in large numbers. **2** author of such a book.

bet −*v.* (**-tt-**; *past* and *past part.* **bet** or **betted**) **1** risk a sum of money on the result of a race, contest, etc. (*I don't bet on horses*). **2** risk (a sum) thus, or risk (a sum) against (a person) (*bet £10 on a horse; he bet me £10 I'd lose*). **3** *colloq.* feel sure. −*n.* **1** act of betting (*make a bet*). **2** money etc. staked (*put a bet on*). **3** *colloq.* opinion (*that's my bet*). **4** *colloq.* choice or possibility (*she's our best bet*). □ **you bet** *colloq.* you may be sure. [origin uncertain]

beta /'biːtə/ *n.* **1** second letter of the Greek alphabet (*B*, *β*). **2** second-class mark for a piece of work etc. [Latin from Greek]

beta-blocker *n.* drug preventing unwanted stimulation of the heart, used to treat angina and high blood pressure.

betake /bɪ'teɪk/ *v.refl.* (**-king**; *past* **betook**; *past part.* **betaken**) (foll. by *to*) go to (a place or person).

beta particle *n.* fast-moving electron emitted by the radioactive decay of substances.

betatron /'biːtə,trɒn/ *n.* apparatus for accelerating electrons in a circular path. [from BETA, ELECTRON]

betel /'biːt(ə)l/ *n.* leaf chewed in the East with the betel-nut. [Portuguese from Malayalam]

betel-nut *n.* seed of a tropical palm.

bête noire /bert 'nwɑː(r)/ *n.* (*pl.* *bêtes noires* pronunc. same) person or thing one hates or fears. [French, literally = 'black beast']

bethink /bɪ'θɪŋk/ *v.refl.* (*past* and *past part.* **bethought**) *formal* **1** reflect; stop to think. **2** be reminded by reflection. [Old English: related to BE-]

betide /bɪ'taɪd/ *v.* □ **woe betide a person** used as a warning (*woe betide us if we fail*). [from BE-, *tide* befall]

betimes /bɪ'taɪmz/ *adv. literary* early, in good time. [related to BY]

betoken /bɪ'təʊkən/ *v.* be a sign of; indicate. [Old English: related to BE-]

betony /'betənɪ/ *n.* (*pl.* **-ies**) purple-flowered plant. [French from Latin]

betook *past of* BETAKE.

betray /bɪ'treɪ/ *v.* **1** be disloyal or treacherous to (a friend, one's country, a person's trust, etc.). **2** reveal involuntarily or treacherously; be evidence of. **3** lead astray. □ **betrayal** *n.* [from BE-, obsolete *tray* from Latin *trado* hand over]

betroth /bɪ'trəʊð/ *v.* (usu. as **betrothed** *adj.*) engage to marry. □ **betrothal** *n.* [from BE-, TRUTH]

better −*adj.* (*compar.* of GOOD). **1** of a more excellent or desirable kind. **2** partly or fully recovered from illness (*feeling better*). −*adv.* (*compar.* of WELL[1]). **1** in a better manner. **2** to a greater degree. **3** more usefully (*is better forgotten*). −*n.* **1** better thing etc. (*the better of the two*). **2** (in *pl.*) one's superiors. −*v.* **1** improve on; surpass. **2** improve. **3** *refl.* improve one's position etc. □ **the better part of** most of. **get the better of** defeat, outwit. **had better** would find it prudent to. [Old English]

better half *n. colloq.* one's spouse.

betterment *n.* improvement.

better off *adj.* **1** in a better situation. **2** having more money.

betting *n.* **1** gambling by risking money on an unpredictable outcome. **2** odds offered on this. □ **what's the betting?** *colloq.* it is likely or to be expected (*what's the betting he'll be late?*).

betting-shop *n.* bookmaker's shop or office.

between /bɪ'twiːn/ −*prep.* **1 a** at a point in the area bounded by two or more other points in space, time, etc. (*between London and Dover*; *between now and Friday*). **b** along the extent of such an

area (*no shops between here and the centre*; *numbers between 10 and 20*). **2** separating (*difference between right and wrong*). **3 a** shared by (*£5 between us*). **b** by joint action (*agreement between us*). **4** to and from (*runs between London and Oxford*). **5** taking one of (*choose between them*). –*adv.* (also **in between**) at a point or in the area bounded by two or more other points (*not fat or thin but in between*). □ **between ourselves** (or **you and me**) in confidence. [Old English: related to BY, TWO]

betwixt /bɪˈtwɪkst/ *adv.* □ **betwixt and between** *colloq.* neither one thing nor the other. [Old English]

bevel /ˈbev(ə)l/ –*n.* **1** slope from the horizontal or vertical in carpentry etc.; sloping surface or edge. **2** tool for marking angles. –*v.* (**-ll-**; *US* **-l-**) **1** reduce (a square edge) to a sloping edge. **2** slope at an angle. [French]

bevel gear *n.* gear working another at an angle to it.

beverage /ˈbevərɪdʒ/ *n. formal* drink. [Latin *bibo* drink]

bevy /ˈbevɪ/ *n* (*pl.* **-ies**) company (of quails, larks, women, etc.). [origin unknown]

bewail /bɪˈweɪl/ *v.* lament; wail over.

beware /bɪˈweə(r)/ *v.* (only in *imper.* or *infin.*; often foll. by *of*) be cautious (of) (*beware of the dog*; *beware the Ides of March*). [from BE, *ware* cautious]

bewilder /bɪˈwɪldə(r)/ *v.* perplex, confuse. □ **bewildering** *adj.* **bewilderment** *n.* [from BE-, obsolete *wilder* lose one's way]

bewitch /bɪˈwɪtʃ/ *v.* **1** enchant. **2** cast a spell on.

beyond /bɪˈjɒnd/ –*prep.* **1** at or to the further side of. **2** outside the scope or understanding of (*beyond repair*; *it is beyond me*). **3** more than. –*adv.* **1** at or to the further side. **2** further on. –*n.* (prec. by *the*) the unknown after death. [Old English: related to BY, YON]

bezel /ˈbez(ə)l/ *n.* **1** sloped edge of a chisel. **2** oblique faces of a cut gem. **3** groove holding a watch-glass or gem. [French]

bezique /bɪˈziːk/ *n.* card-game for two. [French]

b.f. *abbr.* **1** *colloq.* bloody fool. **2** brought forward.

bhang /bæŋ/ *n.* Indian hemp used as a narcotic. [Portuguese from Sanskrit]

b.h.p. *abbr.* brake horsepower.

Bi *symb.* bismuth.

bi- *comb. form* forming nouns, adjectives, and verbs, meaning: **1** division into two (*biplane*; *bisect*). **2 a** occurring twice in every one or once in every two

(*bi-weekly*). **b** lasting for two (*biennial*). **3** *Chem.* substance having a double proportion of what is indicated by the simple word (*bicarbonate*). **4** *Bot.* & *Zool.* having divided parts which are themselves similarly divided (*bipinnate*). [Latin]

biannual /baɪˈænjʊəl/ *adj.* occurring etc. twice a year.

bias /ˈbaɪəs/ –*n.* **1** (often foll. by *towards*, *against*) predisposition or prejudice. **2** *Statistics* distortion of a statistical result due to a neglected factor. **3** edge cut obliquely across the weave of a fabric. **4** *Sport* **a** irregular shape given to a bowl. **b** oblique course this causes it to run. –*v.* (**-s-** or **-ss-**) **1** (esp. as **biased** *adj.*) influence (usu. unfairly); prejudice. **2** give a bias to. □ **on the bias** obliquely, diagonally. [French]

bias binding *n.* strip of fabric cut obliquely and used to bind edges.

biathlon /baɪˈæθlən/ *n.* athletic contest in skiing and shooting or cycling and running. [from BI-, after PENTATHLON]

bib *n.* **1** piece of cloth etc. fastened round a child's neck while eating. **2** top front part of an apron, dungarees, etc. [origin uncertain]

bib-cock *n.* tap with a bent nozzle. [perhaps from BIB]

Bible /ˈbaɪb(ə)l/ *n.* **1 a** (prec. by *the*) Christian scriptures of Old and New Testaments. **b** (**bible**) copy of these. **2** (**bible**) *colloq.* authoritative book. □ **biblical** /ˈbɪblɪk(ə)l/ *adj.* [Greek *biblia* books]

Bible-bashing *n.* (also **Bible-thumping**) *slang* aggressive fundamentalist preaching. □ **Bible-basher** *n.* (also **-thumper**).

bibliography /ˌbɪblɪˈɒɡrəfɪ/ *n.* (*pl.* **-ies**) **1** list of books on a specific subject, by a particular author, etc.; book containing this. **2** the study of books, their authorship, editions, etc. □ **bibliographer** *n.* **bibliographical** /-əˈɡræfɪk(ə)l/ *adj.* [Greek: related to BIBLE]

bibliophile /ˈbɪblɪəˌfaɪl/ *n.* lover or collector of books.

bibulous /ˈbɪbjʊləs/ *adj.* tending to drink alcohol. [Latin *bibo* drink]

bicameral /baɪˈkæmər(ə)l/ *adj.* (of a legislative body) having two chambers. [from BI-, Latin *camera* chamber]

bicarb /ˈbaɪkɑːb/ *n. colloq.* = BICARBONATE 2. [abbreviation]

bicarbonate /baɪˈkɑːbənɪt/ *n.* **1** any acid salt of carbonic acid. **2** (in full **bicarbonate of soda**) sodium bicarbonate used as an antacid or in baking-powder.

bicentenary /ˌbaɪsen'tiːnəri/ n. (pl. -ies) **1** two-hundredth anniversary. **2** celebration of this.

bicentennial /ˌbaɪsen'teniəl/ esp. US —n. bicentenary. —adj. occurring every two hundred years.

biceps /'baɪseps/ n. (pl. same) muscle with two heads or attachments, esp. that bending the elbow. [Latin caput head]

bicker v. argue pettily. [origin unknown]

bicuspid /baɪ'kʌspɪd/ —adj. having two cusps. —n. the premolar tooth in humans. [from BI-, CUSP]

bicycle /'baɪsɪk(ə)l/ —n. pedal-driven two-wheeled vehicle. —v. (-ling) ride a bicycle. [Greek kuklos wheel]

bid —v. (-dd-; past bid, archaic bade /beɪd, bæd/; past part. bid, archaic bidden) **1** (past and past part. bid) **a** (esp. at an auction) make an offer (of) (bid for the vase; bid £20). **b** offer a service for a stated price. **2** literary command; invite (bid the soldiers shoot; bade her start). **3** literary utter (a greeting or farewell) to (I bade him welcome). **4** (past and past part. bid) Cards state before play how many tricks one intends to make. —n. **1** act of bidding. **2** amount bid. **3** colloq. attempt; effort (bid for power). □ **bidder** n. [Old English]

biddable adj. obedient.

bidding n. **1** command, request, or invitation. **2** bids at an auction or in a card-game.

biddy n. (pl. -ies) slang woman (esp. old biddy). [a form of the name Bridget]

bide v. (-ding) □ **bide one's time** wait for a good opportunity. [Old English]

bidet /'biːdeɪ/ n. low basin for sitting on to wash the genital area. [French, = pony]

biennial /baɪ'eniəl/ —adj. lasting, or recurring every, two years. —n. plant that grows from seed one year and flowers and dies the following. [Latin annus year]

bier n. movable frame on which a coffin or corpse rests. [Old English]

biff slang —n. sharp blow. —v. strike (a person). [imitative]

bifid /'baɪfɪd/ adj. divided by a deep cleft into two parts. [Latin findo cleave]

bifocal /baɪ'fəʊk(ə)l/ —adj. having two focuses, esp. of a lens with a part for distant and a part for near vision. —n. (in pl.) bifocal spectacles.

bifurcate /'baɪfə,keɪt/ —v. (-ting) fork. —adj. forked; branched. □ **bifurcation** /-'keɪʃ(ə)n/ n. [Latin furca fork]

big —adj. (**bigger, biggest**) **1 a** of considerable size, amount, intensity, etc. **b** of a large or the largest size (big toe). **2** important (my big day). **3** adult, elder

(big sister). **4** colloq. **a** boastful (big words). **b** often iron. generous (big of him). **c** ambitious (big ideas). **5** (usu. foll. by with) advanced in pregnancy (big with child). —adv. colloq. impressively or grandly (think big). □ **in a big way** colloq. with great enthusiasm, display, etc. □ **biggish** adj. [origin unknown]

bigamy /'bɪgəmi/ n. (pl. -ies) crime of marrying while still married to another person. □ **bigamist** n. **bigamous** adj. [Greek gamos marriage]

Big Apple n. US slang New York City.

big bang theory n. theory that the universe began with the explosion of dense matter.

Big Brother n. supposedly benevolent watchful dictator.

big end n. (in a vehicle) end of the connecting-rod, encircling the crank-pin.

big-head n. colloq. conceited person. □ **big-headed** adj.

big-hearted adj. generous.

bight /baɪt/ n. **1** bay, inlet, etc. **2** loop of rope. [Old English]

big money n. large amounts of money.

big noise n. (also **big shot**) colloq. = BIGWIG.

bigot /'bɪgət/ n. obstinate believer who is intolerant of others. □ **bigoted** adj. **bigotry** n. [French]

big stick n. colloq. display of force.

big time n. (prec. by the) slang success, esp. in show business. □ **big-timer** n.

big top n. main tent in a circus.

big wheel n. Ferris wheel.

bigwig n. colloq. important person.

bijou /'biːʒuː/ —n. (pl. -x pronunc. same) jewel; trinket. —attrib. adj. (**bijou**) small and elegant. [French]

bike colloq. —n. bicycle or motor cycle. —v. (-king) ride a bike. □ **biker** n. [abbreviation]

bikini /br'kiːnɪ/ n. (pl. -s) two-piece swimsuit for women. [Bikini, Pacific atoll]

bilateral /baɪ'lætər(ə)l/ adj. **1** of, on, or with two sides. **2** affecting or between two parties, countries, etc. □ **bilaterally** adv.

bilberry /'bɪlbəri/ n. (pl. -ies) **1** hardy N. European shrub of heaths and mountains. **2** its small dark-blue edible berry. [Scandinavian]

bile n. **1** bitter digestive fluid secreted by the liver. **2** bad temper; peevish anger. [Latin bilis]

bilge /bɪldʒ/ n. **1 a** the almost flat part of a ship's bottom. **b** (in full **bilge-water**) filthy water that collects there. **2** slang nonsense. [probably var. of BULGE]

bilharzia /bɪlˈhɑːtsɪə/ n. chronic tropical disease caused by a parasitic flatworm. [*Bilharz*, name of a physician]

biliary /ˈbɪlɪərɪ/ adj. of the bile. [French: related to BILE]

bilingual /barˈlɪŋgw(ə)l/ —adj. 1 able to speak two languages. 2 spoken or written in two languages. —n. bilingual person. □ **bilingualism** n. [Latin *lingua* tongue]

bilious /ˈbɪlɪəs/ adj. 1 affected by a disorder of the bile. 2 bad-tempered. [Latin: related to BILE]

bilk v. slang 1 cheat. 2 elude. 3 avoid paying (a creditor or debt). [origin uncertain]

Bill n. = OLD BILL. [diminutive of *William*]

bill[1] —n. 1 statement of charges for goods or services. 2 draft of a proposed law. 3 poster, placard. 4 programme of entertainment. 5 *US* banknote. —v. 1 send a statement of charges to. 2 put in the programme; announce. 3 (foll. by *as*) advertise as. [medieval Latin *bulla* seal]

bill[2] —n. 1 bird's beak. 2 narrow promontory. —v. (of doves etc.) stroke bills. □ **bill and coo** exchange caresses. [Old English]

bill[3] n. 1 *hist.* weapon with a hooked blade. 2 = BILLHOOK. [Old English]

billabong /ˈbɪləˌbɒŋ/ n. (in Australia) backwater of a river. [Aboriginal]

billboard n. large outdoor advertising hoarding.

billet[1] /ˈbɪlɪt/ —n. 1 **a** place where troops etc. are lodged. **b** order to provide this. 2 *colloq.* job. —v. (-t-) (usu. foll. by *on*, *in*, *at*) quarter (soldiers etc.). [Anglo-French diminutive of BILL[1]]

billet[2] /ˈbɪlɪt/ n. 1 thick piece of firewood. 2 small metal bar. [French diminutive of *bille* tree-trunk]

billet-doux /ˌbɪliˈduː/ n. (pl. **billets-doux** /-ˈduːz/) often *joc.* love-letter. [French, = sweet note]

billhook n. pruning tool with a hooked blade.

billiards /ˈbɪljədz/ n. 1 game played on a table, with three balls struck with cues. 2 (**billiard**) (in *comb.*) used in billiards (*billiard-ball*). [French: related to BILLET[2]]

billion /ˈbɪljən/ adj. & n. (pl. same or (in sense 3) -s) 1 a thousand million (10⁹). 2 (now less often) a million million (10¹²). 3 (in pl.) *colloq.* a very large number (*billions of years*). □ **billionth** adj. & n. [French]

billionaire /ˌbɪljəˈneə(r)/ n. person who has over a billion pounds, dollars, etc. [after MILLIONAIRE]

bill of exchange n. written order to pay a sum of money on a given date to the drawer or to a named payee.

bill of fare n. menu.

bill of lading n. detailed list of a ship's cargo.

billow /ˈbɪləʊ/ —n. 1 wave. 2 any large mass. —v. rise, fill, or surge in billows. □ **billowy** adj. [Old Norse]

billposter n. (also **billsticker**) person who pastes up advertisements on hoardings.

billy[1] /ˈbɪlɪ/ n. (pl. -ies) (in full **billycan**) *Austral.* tin or enamel outdoor cooking-pot. [perhaps from Aboriginal *billa* water]

billy[2] /ˈbɪlɪ/ n. (pl. -ies) (in full **billy-goat**) male goat. [from the name *Billy*]

bimbo /ˈbɪmbəʊ/ n. (pl. -s or -es) *slang* usu. *derog.* attractive but unintelligent young woman. [Italian, = little child]

bimetallic /ˌbaɪmɪˈtælɪk/ adj. using or made of two metals. [French]

bin n. large receptacle for rubbish or storage. [Old English]

binary /ˈbaɪnərɪ/ —adj. 1 of two parts, dual. 2 of the binary system. —n. (pl. -ies) 1 something having two parts. 2 binary number. [Latin *bini* two together]

binary star n. system of two stars orbiting each other.

binary system n. system using the digits 0 and 1 to code information, esp. in computing.

binaural /baɪˈnɔːr(ə)l/ adj. 1 of or used with both ears. 2 (of sound) recorded using two microphones and usu. transmitted separately to the two ears. [from BI-, AURAL]

bind /baɪnd/ —v. (*past* and *past part.* **bound**) 1 tie or fasten tightly. 2 restrain forcibly. 3 (cause to) cohere. 4 compel; impose a duty on. 5 **a** edge with braid etc. **b** fasten (the pages of a book) in a cover. 6 constipate. 7 ratify (a bargain, agreement, etc.). 8 (often foll. by *up*) bandage. —n. *colloq.* nuisance; restriction. □ **bind over** *Law* order (a person) to do something, esp. keep the peace. [Old English]

binder n. 1 cover for loose papers etc. 2 substance that binds things together. 3 *hist.* reaping-machine that binds grain into sheaves. 4 bookbinder.

bindery n. (pl. -ies) bookbinder's workshop.

binding —n. thing that binds, esp. the covers, glue, etc., of a book. —adj. obligatory.

bindweed n. 1 convolvulus. 2 honeysuckle or other climber.

bine n. 1 twisting stem of a climbing plant, esp. the hop. 2 flexible shoot. [dial. form of BIND]

bin end n. one of the last bottles from a bin of wine, usu. sold at a reduced price.

binge /bɪndʒ/ slang –n. bout of excessive eating, drinking, etc.; spree. –v. (-ging) indulge in a binge. [probably dial., = soak]

bingo /'bɪŋgəʊ/ n. gambling game in which each player has a card with numbers to be marked off as they are called. [origin uncertain]

bin-liner n. bag for lining a rubbish bin.

binman n. colloq. dustman.

binnacle /'bɪnək(ə)l/ n. case for a ship's compass. [Latin habitaculum dwelling]

binocular /baɪ'nɒkjʊlə(r)/ adj. for both eyes. [Latin bini two together, oculus eye]

binoculars /bɪ'nɒkjʊləz/ n.pl. instrument with a lens for each eye, for viewing distant objects.

binomial /baɪ'nəʊmɪəl/ –n. algebraic expression of the sum or the difference of two terms. –adj. of two terms. [Greek nomos part]

binomial theorem n. formula for finding any power of a binomial.

bint n. slang, usu. offens. girl or woman. [Arabic]

bio- comb. form 1 life (biography). 2 biological; of living things. [Greek bios life]

biochemistry /,baɪəʊ'kemɪstrɪ/ n. the study of the chemistry of living organisms. □ **biochemical** adj. **biochemist** n.

biodegradable /,baɪəʊdɪ'greɪdəb(ə)l/ adj. capable of being decomposed by bacteria or other living organisms.

bioengineering /,baɪəʊ,endʒɪ'nɪərɪŋ/ n. 1 the application of engineering techniques to biological processes. 2 the use of artificial tissues, organs, etc. to replace parts of the body, e.g. artificial limbs, pacemakers, etc.

biogenesis /,baɪəʊ'dʒenɪsɪs/ n. 1 hypothesis that a living organism arises only from a similar living organism. 2 synthesis of substances by living organisms.

biography /baɪ'ɒgrəfɪ/ n. (pl. -ies) 1 account of a person's life, written usu. by another. 2 these as a literary genre. □ **biographer** n. **biographical** /,baɪə'græfɪk(ə)l/ adj. [French: related to BIO-]

biological /,baɪə'lɒdʒɪk(ə)l/ adj. of biology or living organisms. □ **biologically** adv.

biological clock n. innate mechanism controlling an organism's rhythmic physiological activities.

biological warfare n. use of toxins or micro-organisms against an enemy.

biology /baɪ'ɒlədʒɪ/ n. the study of living organisms. □ **biologist** n. [German: related to BIO-]

bionic /baɪ'ɒnɪk/ adj. having electronically operated body parts or the resulting superhuman powers. [from BIO- after ELECTRONIC]

bionics n.pl. (treated as sing.) the study of mechanical systems that function like living organisms.

biophysics /,baɪəʊ'fɪzɪks/ n.pl. (treated as sing.) science of the application of the laws of physics to biological phenomena. □ **biophysical** adj. **biophysicist** n.

biopsy /'baɪɒpsɪ/ n. (pl. -ies) examination of severed tissue for diagnosis. [Greek bios life, opsis sight]

biorhythm /'baɪəʊ,rɪð(ə)m/ n. any recurring biological cycle thought to affect one's physical or mental state.

biosphere /'baɪəʊ,sfɪə(r)/ n. regions of the earth's crust and atmosphere occupied by living things. [German: related to BIO-]

biosynthesis /,baɪəʊ'sɪnθɪsɪs/ n. production of organic molecules by living organisms. □ **biosynthetic** /-'θetɪk/ adj.

biotechnology /,baɪəʊtek'nɒlədʒɪ/ n. branch of technology exploiting biological processes, esp. using micro-organisms, in industry, medicine, etc.

biotin /'baɪətɪn/ n. vitamin of the B complex, found in egg-yolk, liver, and yeast. [Greek bios life]

bipartisan /,baɪpɑː'tɪzæn/ adj. of or involving two parties.

bipartite /baɪ'pɑːtaɪt/ adj. 1 of two parts. 2 shared by or involving two parties. [Latin bipartio divide in two]

biped /'baɪped/ –n. two-footed animal. –adj. two-footed. □ **bipedal** /-'piːd(ə)l/ adj. [Latin bipes -edis]

biplane /'baɪpleɪn/ n. aeroplane with two sets of wings, one above the other.

bipolar /baɪ'pəʊlə(r)/ adj. having two poles or extremities.

birch –n. 1 tree with pale hard wood and thin peeling bark, bearing catkins. 2 bundle of birch twigs used for flogging. –v. beat with a birch. [Old English]

bird n. 1 two-legged feathered winged vertebrate, egg-laying and usu. able to fly. 2 slang young woman. 3 slang person. 4 slang prison; prison sentence. □ **a bird in the hand** something secured or certain. **the birds and the bees** euphem. sexual activity and reproduction. **birds of a feather** similar

people. **for the birds** *colloq.* trivial, uninteresting. **get the bird** *slang* be rejected, esp. by an audience. [Old English]

bird-bath *n.* basin with water for birds to bathe in.

birdbrain *n. colloq.* stupid or flighty person. □ **birdbrained** *adj.*

birdcage *n.* cage for birds.

birdie *n.* 1 *colloq.* little bird. 2 *Golf* hole played in one under par.

birdlime *n.* sticky substance spread to trap birds.

bird-nesting *n.* hunting for birds' eggs.

bird of paradise *n.* bird, the male of which has brilliant plumage.

bird of passage *n.* 1 migrant. 2 habitual traveller.

bird of prey *n.* bird which hunts animals for food.

birdseed *n.* blend of seeds for caged birds.

bird's-eye view *n.* detached view from above.

birdsong *n.* musical cry of birds.

bird table *n.* platform on which food for birds is placed.

bird-watcher *n.* person who observes wild birds as a hobby. □ **bird-watching** *n.*

biretta /bɪˈretə/ *n.* square usu. black cap worn by Roman Catholic priests. [Latin *birrus* cape]

Biro /ˈbaɪrəʊ/ *n.* (*pl.* **-s**) *propr.* a kind of ball-point pen. [*Biró,* name of its inventor]

birth *n.* 1 emergence of a baby or young from its mother's body. 2 beginning (*birth of civilization*). 3 **a** ancestry (*of noble birth*). **b** high or noble birth; inherited position. □ **give birth to** 1 produce (young). 2 be the cause of. [Old Norse]

birth certificate *n.* official document detailing a person's birth.

birth control *n.* contraception.

birthday *n.* 1 day on which one was born. 2 anniversary of this.

birthing pool *n.* large bath for giving birth in.

birthmark *n.* unusual coloured mark on one's body at or from birth.

birthplace *n.* place where one was born.

birth rate *n.* number of live births per thousand of population per year.

birthright *n.* inherited, esp. property, rights.

birthstone *n.* gem popularly associated with the month of one's birth.

biscuit /ˈbɪskɪt/ *n.* 1 flat thin unleavened cake, usu. crisp and sweet. 2 fired unglazed pottery. 3 light brown colour. [Latin *bis* twice, *coquo* cook]

bisect /baɪˈsekt/ *v.* divide into two (strictly, equal) parts. □ **bisection** *n.*

bisector *n.* [from BI-, Latin *seco sect-* cut]

bisexual /baɪˈsekʃʊəl/ *–adj.* 1 feeling or involving sexual attraction to people of both sexes. 2 hermaphrodite. *–n.* bisexual person. □ **bisexuality** /-ˈælɪtɪ/ *n.*

bishop /ˈbɪʃəp/ *n.* 1 senior clergyman in charge of a diocese. 2 mitre-shaped chess piece. [Greek *episkopos* overseer]

bishopric /ˈbɪʃəprɪk/ *n.* office or diocese of a bishop.

bismuth /ˈbɪzməθ/ *n.* 1 reddish-white metallic element used in alloys etc. 2 compound of it used medicinally. [German]

bison /ˈbaɪs(ə)n/ *n.* (*pl.* same) wild hump-backed ox of Europe or N. America. [Latin from Germanic]

bisque[1] /bɪsk/ *n.* rich soup, esp. of lobster. [French]

bisque[2] /bɪsk/ *n.* advantage of one free point or stroke in certain games. [French]

bisque[3] /bɪsk/ *n.* = BISCUIT 2.

bistre /ˈbɪstə(r)/ *n.* (*US* **bister**) brownish pigment from wood soot. [French]

bistro /ˈbiːstrəʊ/ *n.* (*pl.* **-s**) small informal restaurant. [French]

bit[1] *n.* 1 small piece or quantity. 2 (prec. by *a*) fair amount (*sold quite a bit*). 3 often *colloq.* short or small time, distance, or amount (*wait a bit; move up a bit; a bit tired; a bit of an idiot*). □ **bit by bit** gradually. **do one's bit** *colloq.* make a useful contribution. [Old English]

bit[2] *past* of BITE.

bit[3] *n.* 1 metal mouthpiece of a bridle. 2 tool or piece for boring or drilling. 3 cutting or gripping part of a plane, pincers, etc. [Old English]

bit[4] *n. Computing* unit of information expressed as a choice between two possibilities. [*binary digit*]

bitch *–n.* 1 female dog or other canine animal. 2 *slang offens.* spiteful woman. 3 *slang* unpleasant or difficult thing. *–v.* 1 speak scathingly or spitefully. 2 complain. [Old English]

bitchy *adj.* (**-ier**, **-iest**) *slang* spiteful. □ **bitchily** *adv.* **bitchiness** *n.*

bite *–v.* (**-ting**; *past* **bit**; *past part.* **bitten**) 1 cut or puncture with the teeth. 2 (foll. by *off, away,* etc.) detach thus. 3 (of an insect etc.) sting. 4 (of a wheel etc.) grip, penetrate. 5 accept bait or an inducement. 6 be harsh in effect, esp. intentionally. 7 (in *passive*) **a** swindle. **b** (foll. by *by, with,* etc.) be infected by (enthusiasm etc.). 8 *colloq.* worry, perturb. 9 cause smarting pain (*biting wind*). 10 be sharp or effective (*biting wit*). 11 (foll. by *at*) snap at. *–n.* 1 act of

biting. **2** wound etc. made by biting. **3 a** mouthful of food. **b** snack. **4** taking of bait by a fish. **5** pungency (esp. of flavour). **6** incisiveness, sharpness. **7** position of the teeth when the jaws are closed. □ **bite the dust** *slang* die. **bite a person's head off** *colloq.* respond angrily. **bite one's lip** repress emotion etc. [Old English]

bit on the side *n. slang* sexual relationship involving infidelity.

bit part *n.* minor role.

bitter —*adj.* **1** having a sharp pungent taste; not sweet. **2** causing, showing, or feeling mental pain or resentment (*bitter memories*). **3 a** harsh; virulent (*bitter animosity*). **b** piercingly cold. —*n.* **1** beer flavoured with hops and tasting slightly bitter. **2** (in *pl.*) liquor flavoured esp. with wormwood, used in cocktails. □ **to the bitter end** to the very end in spite of difficulties. □ **bitterly** *adv.* **bitterness** *n.* [Old English]

bittern /'bɪt(ə)n/ *n.* wading bird of the heron family. [French *butor* from Latin *butio*]

bitter-sweet —*adj.* sweet with a bitter aftertaste. —*n.* **1** such sweetness. **2** = WOODY NIGHTSHADE.

bitty *adj.* (**-ier, -iest**) made up of bits; scrappy.

bitumen /'bɪtjʊmɪn/ *n.* tarlike mixture of hydrocarbons derived from petroleum. [Latin]

bituminous /bɪ'tju:mɪnəs/ *adj.* of or like bitumen.

bituminous coal *n.* coal burning with a smoky flame.

bivalve /'baɪvælv/ —*n.* aquatic mollusc with a hinged double shell, e.g. the oyster and mussel. —*adj.* with such a shell.

bivouac /'bɪvʊ,æk/ —*n.* temporary open encampment without tents. —*v.* (**-ck-**) make, or camp in, a bivouac. [French, probably from German]

biz *n. colloq.* business. [abbreviation]

bizarre /bɪ'zɑː(r)/ *adj.* strange; eccentric; grotesque. [French]

Bk *symb.* berkelium.

BL *abbr.* British Library.

blab *v.* (**-bb-**) **1** talk foolishly or indiscreetly. **2** reveal (a secret etc.); confess. [imitative]

blabber —*n.* (also **blabbermouth**) person who blabs. —*v.* (often foll. by *on*) talk foolishly or inconsequentially.

black —*adj.* **1** reflecting no light, colourless from lack of light (like coal or soot); completely dark. **2** (**Black**) of the human group with dark-coloured skin, esp. African. **3** (of the sky etc.) heavily overcast. **4** angry; gloomy (*black look, mood*). **5** implying disgrace etc. (*in his*

black books). **6** wicked, sinister, deadly. **7** portending trouble (*things look black*). **8** comic but sinister (*black comedy*). **9** (of tea or coffee) without milk. **10** (of industrial labour or its products) boycotted, esp. by a trade union, in a strike etc. —*n.* **1** black colour or pigment. **2** black clothes or material (*dressed in black*). **3 a** (in a game) black piece, ball, etc. **b** player of this. **4** credit side of an account (*in the black*). **5** (**Black**) member of a dark-skinned race, esp. an African. —*v.* **1** make black (*blacked his boots*). **2** declare (goods etc.) 'black'. □ **black out 1** effect a blackout on. **2** undergo a blackout. [Old English]

black and blue *adj.* bruised.

black and white —*n.* writing or printing (*in black and white*). —*adj.* **1** (of a film etc.) monochrome. **2** consisting of extremes only, oversimplified.

black art *n.* = BLACK MAGIC.

blackball *v.* reject (a candidate) in a ballot.

black beetle *n.* the common cockroach.

black belt *n.* **1** highest grade of proficiency in judo, karate, etc. **2** holder of this grade, entitled to wear a black belt.

blackberry *n.* (*pl.* **-ies**) black fleshy edible fruit of the bramble.

blackbird *n.* common thrush of which the male is black with an orange beak.

blackboard *n.* board with a smooth dark surface for writing on with chalk.

black box *n.* flight-recorder.

blackcap *n.* small warbler, the male of which has a black-topped head.

Black Country *n.* (prec. by *the*) industrial area of the Midlands.

blackcurrant *n.* **1** cultivated flowering shrub. **2** its small dark edible berry.

Black Death *n.* (prec. by *the*) 14th-c. plague in Europe.

black economy *n.* unofficial and untaxed trade.

blacken *v.* **1** make or become black or dark. **2** defame, slander.

black eye *n.* bruised skin around the eye.

black flag *n.* flag of piracy.

blackfly *n.* **1** dark coloured thrips or aphid. **2** these collectively.

Black Forest gateau *n.* chocolate sponge with cherries and whipped cream.

Black Friar *n.* Dominican friar.

blackguard /'blæɡɑːd/ *n.* villain, scoundrel. □ **blackguardly** *adj.* [originally = menial]

blackhead *n.* black-topped pimple on the skin.

black hole n. region of space from which matter and radiation cannot escape.

black ice n. thin hard transparent ice on a road etc.

blacking n. black polish, esp. for shoes.

blackjack n. = PONTOON¹.

blacklead n. graphite.

blackleg —n. derog. person refusing to join a strike etc. —v. ('gg-') act as a blackleg.

blacklist —n. list of people in disfavour etc. —v. put on a blacklist.

blackmail —n. 1 a extortion of payment in return for silence. b payment so extorted. 2 use of threats or moral pressure. —v. 1 (try to) extort money etc. from by blackmail. 2 threaten, coerce. □ **blackmailer** n. [obsolete *mail* rent]

Black Maria /ma'raɪə/ n. slang police van.

black mark n. mark of discredit.

black market n. illicit trade in rationed, prohibited, or scarce commodities. □ **black marketeer** n.

Black Mass n. travesty of the Mass, in worship of Satan.

blackout n. 1 temporary loss of consciousness or memory. 2 loss of electric power, radio reception, etc. 3 compulsory darkness as a precaution against air raids. 4 temporary suppression of news. 5 sudden darkening of a theatre stage.

black pepper n. pepper made by grinding the whole dried pepper berry including the outer husk.

Black Power n. movement for Black rights and political power.

black pudding n. sausage of pork, dried pig's blood, suet, etc.

Black Rod n. principal usher of the House of Lords.

black sheep n. colloq. member of a family, group, etc. regarded as a disgrace or failure.

blackshirt n. hist. member of a Fascist organization.

blacksmith n. smith who works in iron.

black spot n. 1 place of danger or trouble. 2 plant disease producing black spots.

black tea n. tea that is fully fermented before drying.

blackthorn n. thorny shrub bearing white blossom and sloes.

black tie n. 1 black bow-tie worn with a dinner jacket. 2 colloq. man's formal evening dress.

black velvet n. mixture of stout and champagne.

Black Watch n. (prec. by *the*) Royal Highland Regiment.

black widow n. venomous spider of which the female devours the male.

bladder n. 1 a sac in some animals, esp. that holding urine. b this adapted for various uses. 2 inflated blister in seaweed etc. [Old English]

bladderwrack n. brown seaweed with air bladders.

blade n. 1 cutting part of a knife etc. 2 flattened part of an oar, propeller, etc. 3 a flat narrow leaf of grass etc. b broad thin part of a leaf. 4 flat bone, e.g. in the shoulder. [Old English]

blame —v. (-ming) 1 assign fault or responsibility to. 2 (foll. by on) fix responsibility for (an error etc.) on (*blamed it on his brother*). —n. 1 responsibility for an error etc. 2 blaming or attributing of responsibility (*got all the blame*). □ **be to blame** be responsible; deserve censure. □ **blameable** adj. **blameless** adj. **blameworthy** adj.

blanch /blɑːntʃ/ v. 1 make or become white or pale. 2 a peel (almonds etc.) by scalding. b immerse (vegetables etc.) briefly in boiling water. 3 whiten (a plant) by depriving it of light. [French: related to BLANK]

blancmange /blə'mɒndʒ/ n. sweet opaque jelly of flavoured cornflour and milk. [French, = white food]

bland adj. 1 a mild, not irritating. b tasteless; insipid. 2 gentle in manner; suave. □ **blandly** adv. **blandness** n. [Latin *blandus* smooth]

blandish /'blændɪʃ/ v. flatter; coax. □ **blandishment** n. (usu. in pl.). [Latin: related to BLAND]

blank —adj. 1 a (of paper) not written or printed on. b (of a document) with spaces left for a signature or details. 2 a empty (*blank space*). b unrelieved (*blank wall*). 3 a without interest, result, or expression (*blank face*). b having (temporarily) no knowledge etc. (*mind went blank*). 4 complete (*a blank refusal; blank despair*). —n. 1 a unfilled space, esp. in a document. b document having blank spaces. 2 (in full **blank cartridge**) cartridge containing gunpowder but no bullet. 3 dash where a word or letter is (usu. foll. by *off, out*) screen, obscure. □ **draw a blank** get no response; fail. □ **blankly** adv. **blankness** n. [French *blanc* white, from Germanic]

blank cheque n. 1 cheque left for the payee to fill in. 2 colloq. unlimited freedom of action.

blanket /'blæŋkɪt/ —n. 1 large esp. woollen sheet used as a bed-covering etc. 2

blanket bath *n.* body wash given to a bedridden patient.

blanket stitch *n.* stitch used to finish the edges of a blanket etc.

blank verse *n.* unrhymed verse, esp. iambic pentameters.

blare —*v.* (-ring) 1 sound or utter loudly. 2 make the sound of a trumpet. —*n.* blaring sound. [Low German or Dutch, imitative]

blarney /'blɑːnɪ/ —*n.* cajoling talk; flattery. —*v.* (-eys, -eyed) flatter, cajole. [*Blarney*, castle near Cork]

blasé /'blɑːzeɪ/ *adj.* bored or indifferent through over-familiarity. [French]

blaspheme /blæs'fiːm/ *v.* (-ming) 1 use religious names irreverently; treat a religious or sacred subject irreverently. 2 talk irreverently about; use blasphemy against. [Greek *blasphēmeō*]

blasphemy /'blæsfəmɪ/ *n.* (*pl.* -ies) 1 irreverent talk or treatment of a religious or sacred thing. 2 instance of this. □ **blasphemous** *adj.*

blast /blɑːst/ —*n.* 1 strong gust of air. 2 a destructive wave of air from this. b explosion. 3 loud note from a wind instrument, car horn, etc. 4 *colloq.* severe reprimand. —*v.* 1 blow up with explosives. 2 wither, blight (*blasted oak*; *blasted her hopes*). 3 (cause to) make a loud noise. —*int.* expressing annoyance. □ **at full blast** *colloq.* at maximum volume, speed, etc. **blast off** take off from a launching site. [Old English]

blasted *colloq.* —*attrib. adj.* damned; annoying. —*adv.* damned; extremely.

blast-furnace *n.* smelting furnace into which hot air is driven.

blast-off *n.* launching of a rocket etc.

blatant /'bleɪt(ə)nt/ *adj.* 1 flagrant, unashamed. 2 loudly obtrusive. □ **blatantly** *adv.* [coined by Spenser]

blather /'blæðə(r)/ —*n.* (also **blether**) foolish talk. —*v.* talk foolishly. [Old Norse]

blaze[1] —*n.* 1 bright flame or fire. 2 violent outburst (of passion etc.). 3 brilliant display (*blaze of scarlet, of glory*). —*v.* (-zing) 1 burn or shine brightly or fiercely. 2 be consumed with anger, excitement, etc. □ **blaze away** (often foll. by *at*) 1 shoot continuously. 2 work vigorously. [Old English, = torch]

blaze[2] —*n.* 1 white mark on an animal's face. 2 mark cut on a tree, esp. to show a route. —*v.* (-zing) mark (a tree or a path) with blazes. □ **blaze a trail** show the way for others. [origin uncertain]

blazer *n.* jacket without matching trousers, esp. lightweight and often part of a uniform. [from BLAZE[1]]

blazon /'bleɪz(ə)n/ —*v.* 1 proclaim (esp. *blazon abroad*). 2 *Heraldry* describe or paint (arms). —*n.* *Heraldry* shield or coat of arms. □ **blazonment** *n.* **blazonry** *n.* [French, originally = shield]

bleach —*v.* whiten in sunlight or by a chemical process. —*n.* bleaching substance or process. [Old English]

bleak *adj.* 1 exposed, windswept. 2 dreary, grim. [Old Norse]

bleary /'blɪərɪ/ *adj.* (-ier, -iest) 1 dim; blurred. 2 indistinct. [Low German]

bleary-eyed *adj.* having dim sight.

bleat —*v.* 1 (of a sheep, goat, or calf) make a wavering cry. 2 (often foll. by *out*) speak or say plaintively. —*n.* bleating cry. [Old English]

bleed —*v.* (*past and past part.* **bled**) 1 emit blood. 2 draw blood from surgically. 3 *colloq.* extort money from. 4 (often foll. by *for*) suffer wounds or violent death. 5 a emit sap. b (of dye) come out in water. 6 empty (a system) of excess air or fluid. —*n.* act of bleeding. □ **one's heart bleeds** usu. *iron.* one is very sorrowful. [Old English]

bleeder *n.* *coarse slang* unpleasant or contemptible person.

bleeding *adj.* & *adv.* *coarse slang* expressing annoyance or antipathy.

bleep —*n.* intermittent high-pitched electronic sound. —*v.* 1 make a bleep. 2 summon with a bleeper. [imitative]

bleeper *n.* small electronic device bleeping to contact the carrier.

blemish /'blemɪʃ/ —*n.* flaw, defect, or stain. —*v.* spoil, mark, or stain. [French]

blench *v.* flinch, quail. [Old English]

blend —*v.* 1 mix together as required. 2 become one. 3 (often foll. by *with, in*) mingle; mix thoroughly. 4 (esp. of colours) merge imperceptibly; harmonize. —*n.* mixture. [Old Norse]

blender *n.* machine for liquidizing, chopping, or puréeing food.

blenny /'blenɪ/ *n.* (*pl.* -ies) small spiny-finned scaleless marine fish. [Greek *blennos* mucus]

bless *v.* (*past and past part.* **blessed**, *poet.* **blest**) 1 ask God to look favourably on, esp. by making the sign of the cross over. 2 consecrate (food etc.). 3 glorify (God). 4 attribute one's good luck to (stars etc.); thank. 5 (usu. in *passive*) make happy or successful (*blessed with children*). □ **bless me** (or **my soul**) exclamation of surprise etc. **bless you!** exclamation of endearment, gratitude, etc., or to a person who has just sneezed. [Old English]

blessed /'blesɪd, blest/ adj. (also poet. blest) 1 holy. 2 in paradise. cursed. □ nuisance). 3 RC Ch. beatified. □ **bles-sedness** n.

blether var. of BLATHER.

blew past of BLOW.

blight /blaɪt/ n. 1 plant disease caused by insects etc. 2 such an insect etc. 3 harmful or destructive force. 4 ugly urban area. —v. 1 affect with blight. 2 harm, destroy. 3 spoil. [origin unknown]

blighter n. colloq. contemptible or annoying person.

Blighty /'blaɪtɪ/ n. Mil. slang England; home. [Hindustani]

blimey /'blaɪmɪ/ int. coarse slang expression of surprise, contempt, etc. [(God) blind me!]

blimp n. 1 (also (Colonel) Blimp) reactionary person. 2 small non-rigid airship. 3 soundproof cover for a cinecamera. [origin uncertain]

blind /blaɪnd/ —adj. 1 lacking the power of sight. 2 a without adequate foresight, discernment, or information (blind effort). b (often foll. by to) unwilling or unable to appreciate a factor etc. (blind to argument). 3 not governed by purpose or reason (blind forces). 4 reckless (blind hitting). 5 a concealed (blind ditch). b closed at one end. 6 (of flying) using instruments only. 7 Cookery (of a flan case etc.) baked without a filling. —v. 1 deprive of sight. 2 rob of judgement; deceive; overawe. 3 slang go recklessly. —n. 1 screen for a window; awning. 2 thing used to hide the truth. 3 obstruction to sight or light. —adv. blindly. □ **blindly** adv. **blindness** n. [Old English]

blind alley n. 1 alley closed at one end. 2 futile course.

blind date n. colloq. date between two people who have not previously met.

blind drunk adj. colloq. extremely drunk.

blindfold —v. cover the eyes of (a person) with a tied cloth etc. —n. cloth etc. so used. —adj. & adv. 1 with eyes covered. 2 without due care. [originally blindfelled = struck blind]

blind man's buff n. game in which a blindfold player tries to catch others.

blind spot n. 1 point on the retina insensitive to light. 2 area where vision or understanding is lacking.

blindworm n. = SLOW-WORM.

blink —v. 1 shut and open the eyes quickly. 2 (often foll. by back) prevent (tears) by blinking. 3 shine unsteadily, flicker. —n. 1 act of blinking. 2 momentary gleam or glimpse. □ **blink at** 1 look at while blinking. 2 ignore, shirk. **on the blink** slang not working properly; out of order. [Dutch, var. of BLENCH]

blinker —n. 1 (usu. in pl.) each of two screens on a bridle preventing lateral vision. 2 device that blinks. —v. 1 obscure with blinkers 2 (as blinkered adj.) having narrow and prejudiced views.

blinking adj. & adv. slang expressing annoyance etc.

blip —n. 1 minor deviation or error. 2 quick popping sound. 3 small image on a radar screen. —v. (-pp-) make a blip. [imitative]

bliss n. 1 perfect or 2 being in heaven. □ **blissful** adj. **blissfully** adv. [Old English]

blister —n. 1 small bubble on the skin filled with watery fluid and caused by heat or friction. 2 similar swelling on plastic, wood, etc. —v. 1 come up in blisters. 2 raise a blister on. 3 attack sharply. [origin uncertain]

blithe /blaɪð/ adj. 1 cheerful, happy. 2 careless, casual. □ **blithely** adv. [Old English]

blithering /'blɪðərɪŋ/ attrib. adj. colloq. hopeless; contemptible (esp. in blithering idiot). [blithe, var. of BLATHER]

Blitt. abbr. Bachelor of Letters. [Latin Baccalaureus Litterarum]

blitz /blɪts/ colloq. —n. 1 a intensive or sudden (esp. aerial) attack. b intensive period of work etc. (must have a blitz on this room). 2 (the Blitz) German air raids on London in 1940. —v. inflict a blitz on. [abbreviation of BLITZKRIEG]

blitzkrieg /'blɪtskriːg/ n. intense military campaign intended to bring about a swift victory. (German, = lightning war)

blizzard /'blɪzəd/ n. severe snowstorm. [origin unknown]

bloat v. 1 inflate, swell. 2 (as bloated adj.) inflated with pride, wealth, or food. 3 cure (a herring) by salting and smoking lightly. [Old Norse]

bloater n. bloated herring.

blob n. small drop or spot. [imitative]

bloc n. group of governments etc. sharing a common purpose. [French: related to BLOCK]

block —n. 1 solid piece of hard material, esp. stone or wood. 2 this as a base for chopping etc., as a stand, or for mounting a horse from. 3 a large building, esp. when subdivided. b group of buildings between streets. 4 obstruction. 5 two or more pulleys mounted in a case. 6 piece of wood or metal engraved for printing. 7 slang head. 8 (often attrib.) number of,

things as a unit, e.g. shares, theatre seats (*block booking*). **9** sheets of paper glued along one edge. —*v.* **1 a** (often foll. by *up*) obstruct. **b** impede. **2** restrict the use of. **3** *Cricket* stop (a ball) with a bat defensively. □ **block in 1** sketch roughly; plan. **2** confine. **block out 1** shut out (light, noise, a memory, view, etc.). **2** sketch roughly; plan. **block up** confine; enclose. [Low German or Dutch]

blockade /blɒˈkeɪd/ —*n.* surrounding or blocking of a place by an enemy to prevent entry and exit. —*v.* (-**ding**) subject to a blockade.

blockage *n.* obstruction.

block and tackle *n.* system of pulleys and ropes, esp. for lifting.

blockbuster *n. slang* **1** thing of great power, esp. a very successful film, book, etc. **2** highly destructive bomb.

block capitals *n.pl.* (also **block letters**) letters printed without serifs, or written with each letter separate and in capitals.

blockhead *n.* stupid person.

blockhouse *n.* **1** reinforced concrete shelter. **2** *hist.* small fort of timber.

block vote *n.* vote proportional in power to the number of people a delegate represents.

bloke *n. slang* man, fellow. [Shelta]

blond (of a woman usu. **blonde**) —*adj.* (of a person, hair, or complexion) light-coloured, fair. —*n.* blond person. [Latin *blondus* yellow]

blood /blʌd/ —*n.* **1** usu. red fluid circulating in the arteries and veins of animals. **2** bloodshed, esp. killing. **3** passion, temperament. **4** race, descent, parentage (*of the same blood*). **5** relationship; relations (*blood is thicker than water*). **6** dandy. —*v.* **1** give (a hound) a first taste of blood. **2** initiate (a person). □ **in one's blood** inherent in one's character. [Old English]

blood bank *n.* store of blood for transfusion.

blood bath *n.* massacre.

blood count *n.* number of corpuscles in a specific amount of blood.

blood-curdling *adj.* horrifying.

blood donor *n.* person giving blood for transfusion.

blood group *n.* any of the types of human blood.

blood-heat *n.* normal human temperature, about 37 °C or 98.4 °F.

bloodhound *n.* large keen-scented dog used in tracking.

bloodless *adj.* **1** without blood or bloodshed. **2** unemotional. **3** pale. **4** feeble.

blood-letting *n.* surgical removal of blood.

blood-money *n.* **1** money paid as compensation for a death. **2** money paid to a killer.

blood orange *n.* red-fleshed orange.

blood-poisoning *n.* diseased condition caused by micro-organisms in the blood.

blood pressure *n.* pressure of the blood in the arteries etc., measured for diagnosis.

blood relation *n.* (also **blood relative**) relative by birth.

bloodshed *n.* killing.

bloodshot *adj.* (of an eyeball) inflamed.

blood sport *n.* sport involving the killing or wounding of animals.

bloodstain *n.* stain caused by blood. □ **bloodstained** *adj.*

bloodstream *n.* blood in circulation.

bloodsucker *n.* **1** leech. **2** extortioner. □ **bloodsucking** *adj.*

blood sugar *n.* amount of glucose in the blood.

blood test *n.* examination of blood, esp. for diagnosis.

bloodthirsty *adj.* (-**ier**, -**iest**) eager for bloodshed.

blood-vessel *n.* vein, artery, or capillary carrying blood.

bloody —*adj.* (-**ier**, -**iest**) **1** of, like, running with, or smeared with blood. **2 a** involving bloodshed. **b** bloodthirsty, cruel. **3** *coarse slang* expressing annoyance or antipathy, or as an intensifier (*bloody fool; a bloody sight better*). **4** red. —*adv. coarse slang* as an intensifier (*bloody awful*). —*v.* (-**ies**, -**ied**) stain with blood.

Bloody Mary *n.* mixture of vodka and tomato juice.

bloody-minded *adj. colloq.* deliberately uncooperative.

bloom —*n.* **1 a** flower, esp. cultivated. **b** state of flowering (*in bloom*). **2** one's prime (*in full bloom*). **3 a** healthy glow of the complexion. **b** fine powder on fresh fruit and leaves. —*v.* **1** bear flowers; be in flower. **2** be in one's prime; flourish. [Old Norse]

bloomer [1] *n. slang* blunder. **2** plant that produces in a specified way.

bloomer [2] *n.* long loaf with diagonal marks. [origin uncertain]

bloomers *n.pl.* **1** women's long loose knickers. **2** *hist.* women's loose knee-length trousers. [Mrs A. *Bloomer*, name of the originator]

blooming —*adj.* **1** flourishing; healthy. **2** *slang* an intensifier (*blooming miracle*). —*adv. slang* an intensifier (*blooming difficult*).

blossom /ˈblɒsəm/ n. **1** flower or mass of flowers, esp. of a fruit-tree. **2** promising stage (*blossom of youth*). —v. **1** open into flower. **2** mature, thrive. [Old English]

blot n. **1** spot or stain of ink etc. **2** disgraceful act or quality. **3** blemish. —v. (**-tt-**) **1** make a blot on, stain. **2** dry with blotting-paper. □ **blot out 1** obliterate. **2** obscure (a view, sound, etc.). [probably Scandinavian]

blotch n. **1** discoloured or inflamed patch on the skin. **2** irregular patch of colour. —v. cover with blotches. □ **blotchy** adj. (**-ier**, **-iest**). [obsolete *plotch*, BLOT]

blotting-paper n. absorbent paper for drying wet ink.

blotto /ˈblɒtəʊ/ adj. slang very drunk. [origin uncertain]

blouse /blaʊz/ n. **1** woman's garment like a shirt. **2** upper part of a military uniform. —v. (**-sing**) make (a bodice etc.) full like a blouse. [French]

blouson /ˈbluːzɒn/ n. short blouse-shaped jacket. [French]

blow¹ /bləʊ/ v. (past **blew**; past part. **blown**) **1** direct a current of air (at) esp. from the mouth. **2** drive or be driven by blowing (*blew the door open*). **3** (esp. of the wind) move rapidly. **4** expel by breathing (*blew smoke*). **5** sound or be sounded by blowing. **6** (past part. **blowed**) (esp. in imper.) curse, confound (*I'm blowed if I know; blow it!*). **7** clear (the nose) by blowing. **8** puff, pant. **9** slang depart suddenly (from). **10** shatter etc. by an explosion. **11** make or shape (glass or a bubble) by blowing. **12** a melt from overloading (*the fuse has blown*). **b** break or burst suddenly. **13** (of a whale) eject air and water. **14** break into with explosives. **15** slang **a** squander (*blew £20*). **b** bungle (an opportunity etc.). **c** reveal (a secret etc.). —n. **1** act of blowing. **2 a** gust of wind or air. **b** exposure to fresh air. □ **be blowed if one will** collog. be unwilling to. **blow a gasket** slang lose one's temper. **blow hot and cold** collog. vacillate. **blow in 1** break inwards by an explosion. **2** collog. arrive unexpectedly. **blow a person's mind** slang cause to have hallucinations etc. **blow off 1** escape or allow (steam etc.) to escape forcibly. **2** slang break wind noisily. **blow out 1** extinguish by blowing. **2** send outwards by an explosion. **blow over (of trouble etc.) fade away. blow one's top** collog. explode in rage. **blow up 1** explode. **2** collog. rebuke strongly (a person etc.). **3** inflate (a tyre etc.). **4** collog. **a** enlarge (a photograph).

b exaggerate. **5** collog. arise, happen. **6** collog. lose one's temper. [Old English]

blow² /bləʊ/ n. **1** hard stroke with a hand or weapon. **2** sudden shock or misfortune. [origin unknown]

blow-by-blow attrib. adj. (of a narrative etc.) detailed.

blow-dry —v. arrange (the hair) while drying it. —n. act of doing this.

blower n. **1** device for blowing. **2** collog. telephone.

blowfly n. bluebottle.

blow-hole n. **1** nostril of a whale. **2** hole (esp. in ice) for breathing or fishing through. **3** vent for air, smoke, etc.

blow-job n. coarse slang instance of fellatio or cunnilingus.

blowlamp n. device with a very hot flame for burning off paint, plumbing, etc.

blown past part. of BLOW¹.

blow-out n. collog. **1** burst tyre. **2** melted fuse. **3** huge meal.

blowpipe n. **1** tube for blowing air through, esp. to intensify a flame or to blow glass. **2** tube for propelling poisoned darts etc. by blowing.

blowtorch n. US = BLOWLAMP.

blow-up n. collog. enlargement (of a photograph etc.). **2** explosion.

blowzy /ˈblaʊzɪ/ adj. (**-ier**, **-iest**) **1** coarse-looking; red-faced. **2** slovenly. [obsolete *blowze* beggar's wench]

blub v. (**-bb-**) slang sob. [shortening of BLUBBER]

blubber —n. whale fat. —v. **1** sob loudly. **2** sob out (words). —adj. swollen, thick. [probably imitative]

bludgeon /ˈblʌdʒ(ə)n/ —n. heavy club. —v. **1** beat with this. **2** coerce. [origin unknown]

blue /bluː/ —adj. (**bluer, bluest**) **1** having the colour of a clear sky. **2** sad, depressed. **3** pornographic (*a blue film*). **4** politically conservative. —n. **1** blue colour or pigment. **2** blue clothes or material (*dressed in blue*). **3** person who represents a university in a sport, esp. Oxford or Cambridge. **4** Conservative party supporter. —v. (**blues, blued**, **bluing** or **blueing**) **1** make blue. **2** slang squander. □ **once in a blue moon** very rarely. **out of the blue** unexpectedly. [French from Germanic]

blue baby n. baby with a blue complexion due to a congenital heart defect.

bluebell n. woodland plant with bell-shaped blue flowers.

blueberry n. (pl. **-ies**) small blue-black edible fruit of various plants.

blue blood n. noble birth.

Blue Book n. report issued by Parliament or the Privy Council.

bluebottle n. large buzzing fly; blowfly.

blue cheese n. cheese with veins of blue mould.

blue-collar attrib. adj. (of a worker or work) manual; industrial.

blue-eyed boy n. colloq. favourite.

blue funk n. colloq. terror or panic.

bluegrass n. a kind of instrumental country-and-western music.

blue-pencil v. censor or cut (a manuscript, film, etc.).

Blue Peter n. blue flag with a white square flown by a ship about to leave port.

blueprint n. 1 photographic print of plans in white on a blue background. 2 detailed plan.

blue rinse n. bluish dye for grey hair.

blues n.pl. 1 (prec. by the) bout of depression. 2 a (prec. by the, often treated as sing.) melancholic music of Black American origin, usu. in a twelve-bar sequence. b (pl. same) (as sing.) piece of such music (played a blues).

bluestocking n. usu. derog. intellectual or literary woman. [18th-c. Blue Stocking Society]

blue tit n. common tit with a blue crest.

blue whale n. rorqual, the largest known living mammal.

bluff¹ —v. pretend strength, confidence, etc. —n. act of bluffing. □ **call a person's bluff** challenge a person to prove a claim. [Dutch bluffen brag]

bluff² —adj. 1 blunt, frank, hearty. 2 vertical or steep and broad in front. —n. steep cliff or headland. [origin unknown]

bluish /ˈbluːɪʃ/ adj. fairly blue.

blunder —n. serious or foolish mistake. —v. 1 make a blunder. 2 move clumsily; stumble. [probably Scandinavian]

blunderbuss /ˈblʌndəbʌs/ n. hist. short large-bored gun. [Dutch donderbus thunder gun]

blunt —adj. 1 not sharp or pointed. 2 direct, outspoken. —v. make blunt or less sharp. □ **bluntly** adv. (in sense 2 of adj.). **bluntness** n. [probably Scandinavian]

blur —v. (-rr-) make or become unclear or less distinct; smear. —n. blurred object, sound, memory, etc. [perhaps related to BLEARY]

blurb n. promotional description, esp. of a book. [coined by G. Burgess 1907]

blurt v. (usu. foll. by out) utter abruptly, thoughtlessly, or tactlessly. [imitative]

blush —v. 1 a become pink in the face from embarrassment or shame. b (of the face) redden thus. 2 feel embarrassed or ashamed. 3 redden. —n. 1 act of blushing. 2 pink tinge. [Old English]

blusher n. rouge.

bluster —v. 1 behave pompously or boisterously. 2 (of the wind etc.) blow fiercely. —n. bombastic talk; empty threats. □ **blustery** adj. [imitative]

BM abbr. 1 British Museum. 2 Bachelor of Medicine.

BMA abbr. British Medical Association.

B.Mus. abbr. Bachelor of Music.

BMX /ˌbiːemˈeks/ n. 1 organized bicycle-racing on a dirt-track. 2 bicycle used for this. [abbreviation of bicycle moto-cross]

BO abbr. colloq. body odour.

boa /ˈbəʊə/ n. 1 large snake which kills by crushing and suffocating. 2 long stole of feathers or fur. [Latin]

boa constrictor n. species of boa.

boar n. 1 male wild pig. 2 uncastrated male pig. [Old English]

board —n. 1 a flat thin piece of sawn timber, usu. long and narrow. b material resembling this, of compressed fibres. c thick slab of wood etc. d thick stiff card used in bookbinding. 2 provision of regular meals, usu. with accommodation, for payment. 3 directors of a company; official administrative body. 4 (in pl.) stage of a theatre. 5 side of a ship. —v. 1 go on board (a ship, train, etc.). 2 receive, or provide with, meals and usu. lodging. 3 (usu. foll. by up) cover with boards; seal or close. □ **go by the board** be neglected or discarded. **on board** on or on to a ship, aircraft, oil rig, etc. **take on board** consider; take notice of; accept. [Old English]

boarder n. 1 person who boards, esp. at a boarding-school. 2 person who boards a ship, esp. an enemy.

board-game n. game played on a board.

boarding-house n. unlicensed establishment providing board and lodging, esp. to holiday-makers.

boarding-school n. school in which pupils live in term-time.

boardroom n. room in which a board of directors etc. meets regularly.

boast —v. 1 declare one's virtues, wealth, etc. with excessive pride. 2 own or have with pride (hotel boasts a ball-room). —n. 1 act of boasting. 2 thing one is proud of. [Anglo-French]

boastful adj. given to boasting. □ **boastfully** adv.

boat —n. 1 small vessel propelled on water by an engine, oars, or sails. 2 any ship. 3 long low jug for sauce etc. —v. go in a boat, esp. for pleasure. □ **in the same boat** having the same problems. [Old English]

boater n. flat-topped straw hat with a brim.

boat-hook *n.* long hooked pole for moving boats.

boat-house *n.* waterside shed for housing boats.

boating *n.* rowing or sailing as recreation.

boatman *n.* person who hires out boats or provides transport by boat.

boat people *n.pl.* refugees travelling by sea.

boatswain /ˈbəʊs(ə)n/ *n.* (also **bosun**, **bo'sun**) ship's officer in charge of equipment and crew.

boat-train *n.* train scheduled to meet or go on a boat.

bob¹ –*v.* (**-bb-**) **1** move quickly up and down. **2** (usu. foll. by *back, up*) bounce or emerge buoyantly or suddenly. **3** cut (the hair) in a bob. **4** curtsy. —*n.* **1** jerking or bouncing movement, esp. upward. **2** hairstyle with the hair hanging evenly above the shoulders. **3** weight on a pendulum etc. **4** horse's docked tail. **5** curtsy. [imitative]

bob² *n.* (*pl.* same) *hist. slang* shilling (now = 5 pence). [origin unknown]

bob³ *n.* □ **bob's your uncle** *slang* expression of completion or success. [pet form of *Robert*]

bobbin /ˈbɒbɪn/ *n.* spool or reel for thread etc. [French]

bobble /ˈbɒb(ə)l/ *n.* small woolly ball on a hat etc. [diminutive of BOB¹]

bobby *n.* (*pl.* **-ies**) *colloq.* police officer. [*Sir Robert* Peel, 19th-c. statesman]

bob-sled *n. US* = BOB-SLEIGH.

bob-sleigh –*n.* mechanically-steered and -braked racing sledge. –*v.* race in a bob-sleigh.

bobtail *n.* **1** docked tail. **2** horse or dog with this.

Boche /bɒʃ/ *n. slang derog.* German, esp. a soldier. [French]

bod *n. colloq.* person. [shortening of BODY]

bode *v.* (**-ding**) be a sign of, portend. □ **bode well** (or **ill**) be a good (or bad) sign. [Old English]

bodega /bəʊˈdɜːɡə/ *n.* cellar or shop selling wine. [Spanish]

bodge var. of BOTCH.

bodice /ˈbɒdɪs/ *n.* **1** part of a woman's dress above the waist. **2** woman's vest-like undergarment. [originally *pair of bodies*]

bodily /ˈbɒdɪlɪ/ —*adj.* of the body. —*adv.* **1** as a whole body (*threw them bodily*). **2** in the flesh, in person.

bodkin /ˈbɒdkɪn/ *n.* blunt thick needle for drawing tape etc. through a hem. [origin uncertain]

body /ˈbɒdɪ/ *n.* (*pl.* **-ies**) **1** whole physical structure, including the bones, flesh, and organs, of a person or an animal,

whether dead or alive. **2** = TRUNK 2. **3** main or central part; bulk or majority (*body of opinion*). **4 a** group regarded as a unit. **b** (usu. foll. by *of*) collection (*body of facts*). **5** quantity (*body of water*). **6** piece of matter (*heavenly body*). **7** *colloq.* person. **8** full or substantial quality of flavour, tone, etc. □ **in a body** all together. [Old English]

body-blow *n.* severe setback.

body-building *n.* exercises to enlarge and strengthen the muscles.

bodyguard *n.* person or group escorting and protecting another.

body language *n.* communication through gestures and poses.

body odour *n.* smell of the human body, esp. when unpleasant.

body politic *n.* nation or State as a corporate body.

body shop *n.* workshop where body-work is repaired.

body stocking *n.* woman's undergarment covering the torso.

bodysuit *n.* close-fitting all-in-one garment for women, worn esp. for sport.

bodywork *n.* outer shell of a vehicle.

Boer /bɔː(r)/ —*n.* South African of Dutch descent. —*adj.* of the Boers. [Dutch, = farmer]

boffin /ˈbɒfɪn/ *n. colloq.* research scientist. [origin unknown]

bog –*n.* **1 a** wet spongy ground. **b** stretch of this. **2** *slang* lavatory. –*v.* (**-gg-**) (foll. by *down*; usu. in *passive*) impede (*bogged down by snow*). □ **boggy** *adj.* (**-ier, -iest**). [Irish or Gaelic *bogach*]

bogey¹ /ˈbəʊɡɪ/ *n.* (*pl.* **-eys**) *Golf* **1** score of one stroke more than par at any hole. **2** (formerly) par. [perhaps from *Bogey*, as an imaginary player]

bogey² /ˈbəʊɡɪ/ *n.* (also **bogy**) (*pl.* **-eys** or **-ies**) **1** evil or mischievous spirit; devil. **2** awkward thing. **3** *slang* piece of dried nasal mucus. [originally (*Old*) *Bogey* the Devil]

bogeyman *n.* (also **bogyman**) frightening person etc.

boggle /ˈbɒɡ(ə)l/ *v.* (**-ling**) *colloq.* be startled or baffled (esp. *the mind boggles*). [probably dial. *boggle* BOGEY²]

bogie /ˈbəʊɡɪ/ *n.* wheeled undercarriage below a locomotive etc. [origin unknown]

bogus /ˈbəʊɡəs/ *adj.* sham, spurious. [origin unknown]

bogy var. of BOGEY².

bogyman var. of BOGEYMAN.

Bohemian /bəʊˈhiːmɪən/ —*n.* **1** native of Bohemia, a Czech. **2** (also **bohemian**) socially unconventional person, esp. an artist or writer. —*adj.* **1** of Bohemia or its people. **2** (also **bohemian**) socially

unconventional. □ **bohemianism** n. [*Bohemia*, part of Czechoslovakia]

boil[1] —v. **1 a** (of a liquid) start to bubble up and turn into vapour on reaching a certain temperature. **b** (of a vessel) contain boiling liquid (*kettle is boiling*). **2 a** bring to boiling-point. **b** cook in boiling liquid. **c** subject to boiling water, e.g. to clean. **3 a** move or seethe like boiling water. **b** be very angry. —n. act or process of boiling; boiling-point (*on the boil*; *bring to the boil*). □ **boil down 1** reduce in volume by boiling. **2** reduce to essentials. **3** (foll. by *to*) amount to. **boil over 1** spill over in boiling. **2** lose one's temper. [Latin *bullio* to bubble]

boil[2] n. inflamed pus-filled swelling under the skin. [Old English]

boiler n. **1** apparatus for heating a hot-water supply. **2** tank for heating water or turning it to steam. **3** tub for boiling laundry etc. **4** fowl etc. for boiling.

boiler-room n. room with a boiler and other heating equipment, esp. in a basement.

boiler suit n. protective outer garment of trousers and jacket in one.

boiling adj. colloq. very hot.

boiling-point n. **1** temperature at which a liquid begins to boil. **2** great excitement.

boisterous /ˈbɔɪstərəs/ adj. **1** noisily exuberant, rough. **2** (of the sea etc.) stormy. [origin unknown]

bold /bəʊld/ adj. **1** confidently assertive, adventurous, brave. **2** impudent. **3** vivid (*bold colours*). □ **make** (or **be**) **so bold as** to presume to; venture to. □ **boldly** adv. **boldness** n. [Old English]

bole n. trunk of a tree. [Old Norse]

bolero n. (pl. -s) **1** /bəˈleərəʊ/ Spanish dance, or the music for it, in triple time. **2** /ˈbɒlərəʊ/ woman's short open jacket. [Spanish]

boll /bəʊl/ n. round seed-vessel of cotton, flax, etc. [Dutch]

bollard /ˈbɒlɑːd/ n. **1** short post in the road, esp. on a traffic island. **2** short post on a quay or ship for securing a rope. [perhaps related to BOLE]

bollocking /ˈbɒləkɪŋ/ n. (also **ballocking**) coarse slang severe reprimand.

bollocks /ˈbɒləks/ n. (also **ballocks**) coarse slang **1** (usu. as int.) nonsense. **2** testicles. [Old English: related to BALL[1]]

boloney /bəˈləʊnɪ/ n. (also **baloney**) slang nonsense. [origin uncertain]

Bolshevik /ˈbɒlʃɪvɪk/ —n. **1** hist. member of the radical faction of the Russian Social Democratic Party becoming the Communist Party in 1918. **2** Russian Communist. **3** any revolutionary socialist. —adj. **1** of the Bolsheviks. **2** Communist. □ **Bolshevism** n. **Bolshevist** n. [Russian, = member of the majority]

Bolshie /ˈbɒlʃɪ/ (also **Bolshy**) slang —adj. (usu. **bolshie**) **1** uncooperative; bad-tempered. **2** left-wing. —n. (pl. **-ies**) Bolshevik. [abbreviation]

bolster /ˈbəʊlstə(r)/ —n. long cylindrical pillow. —v. (usu. foll. by up) encourage, support, prop up. [Old English]

bolt[1] /bəʊlt/ —n. **1** sliding bar and socket used to fasten a door etc. **2** large metal pin with a thread, usu. used with a nut, to hold things together. **3** discharge of lightning. **4** act of bolting. —v. **1** fasten with a bolt. **2** (foll. by in, out) keep (a person etc.) in or out by bolting a door. **3** (of a horse) suddenly gallop out of control. **5** gulp down (food) unchewed. **6** (of a plant) run to seed. —adv. (usu. in **bolt upright**) rigidly, stiffly. □ **bolt from the blue** complete surprise. [Old English]

bolt[2] /bəʊlt/ v. (also **boult**) sift (flour etc.). [French]

bolt-hole n. means of escape.

bomb /bɒm/ —n. **1** container filled with explosive, incendiary material, etc., designed to explode and cause damage. **2** (prec. by the) the atomic or hydrogen bomb. **3** slang large sum of money (cost a bomb). —v. **1** attack with bombs; drop bombs on. **2** (usu. foll. by along, off) colloq. go very quickly. □ **like a bomb** colloq. **1** very successfully. **2** very fast. [Greek bombos hum]

bombard /bɒmˈbɑːd/ v. **1** attack with heavy guns or bombs etc. **2** (often foll. by with) question or abuse persistently. **3** Physics direct a stream of high-speed particles at. □ **bombardment** n. [Latin: related to BOMB]

bombardier /ˌbɒmbəˈdɪə(r)/ n. **1** non-commissioned officer in the artillery. **2** US crew member in an aircraft who aims and releases bombs.

bombast /ˈbɒmbæst/ n. pompous language; hyperbole. □ **bombastic** /-ˈbæstɪk/ adj. [earlier bombace cotton wool]

Bombay duck /bɒmˈbeɪ/ n. dried fish as a relish, esp. with curry. [corruption of bombil, native name of fish]

bombazine /ˈbɒmbəziːn/ n. twilled worsted dress-material. [Greek bombux silk]

bomber /ˈbɒmə(r)/ n. **1** aircraft equipped to drop bombs. **2** person using bombs, esp. illegally.

bomber jacket n. jacket gathered at the waist and cuffs.

bombshell n. 1 overwhelming surprise or disappointment. 2 artillery bomb. 3 slang very attractive woman.

bomb-site n. area where bombs have caused destruction.

bona fide /ˌbəʊnə ˈfaɪdɪ/ —adj. genuine; sincere. —adv. genuinely; sincerely. [Latin]

bonanza /bəˈnænzə/ n. 1 source of wealth or prosperity. 2 large output (esp. of a mine). [Spanish, = fair weather]

bon-bon n. sweet. [French]

bond —n. 1 thing or force that unites or restrains. 2 (usu. in pl.) restraint etc. 3 Commerce certificate issued by a government or a company promising to repay borrowed money at a fixed rate of interest. 4 adhesiveness. 5 Law deed binding a person to make payment to another. 6 Chem. linkage between atoms in a molecule. —v. 1 hold or tie together. 2 connect or reinforce with a bond. 3 place (goods) in bond. □ **in bond** stored by Customs until duty is paid. [var. of BAND]

bondage n. 1 slavery. 2 subjection to constraint etc. 3 sexual practices involving constraint. [Anglo-Latin: related to BONDSMAN]

bonded adj. 1 stored in or for storing in bond (bonded whisky, warehouse). 2 (of a debt) secured by bonds.

bond paper n. high-quality writing paper.

bondsman n. serf, slave. [Old English bonda husbandman]

bone —n. 1 any piece of hard tissue making up the skeleton in vertebrates. 2 (in pl.) a skeleton, esp. as remains. b body. 3 material of bones or similar material, e.g. ivory. 4 thing made of bone. 5 (in pl.) essentials (the bones of an agreement). 6 strip of stiffening in a corset etc. —v. (-ning) 1 remove the bones from. 2 stiffen with bone etc. □ **bone up** (often foll. by on) colloq. study intensively. **have a bone to pick** (usu. foll. by with) have cause for dispute (with a person). **make no bones about** 1 be frank about. 2 not hesitate or scruple. □ **boneless** adj. [Old English]

bone china n. fine china made of clay mixed with bone ash.

bone-dry adj. completely dry.

bone-idle adj. utterly idle.

bone-marrow n. = MARROW 2.

bone-meal n. crushed bones, esp. as a fertilizer.

bone of contention n. source of dispute.

boneshaker n. decrepit or uncomfortable old vehicle.

bonfire n. large open-air fire, esp. for burning rubbish. [from BONE (because bones were once used), FIRE]

bongo /ˈbɒŋgəʊ/ n. (pl. -s or -es) either of a pair of small drums usu. held between the knees and played with the fingers. [American Spanish]

bonhomie /ˈbɒnɒˈmiː/ n. good-natured friendliness. [French]

bonk —v. 1 bang, bump. 2 coarse slang have sexual intercourse (with). —n. instance of bonking (bonk on the head). [imitative]

bonkers /ˈbɒŋkəz/ predic. adj. slang crazy. [origin unknown]

bon mot /bɒ̃ ˈməʊ/ n. (pl. bons mots /-məʊz/) witty saying. [French]

bonnet /ˈbɒnɪt/ n. 1 a hat tied under the chin, worn esp. by babies. b Scotsman's floppy beret. 2 hinged cover over a vehicle's engine. [French]

bonny /ˈbɒnɪ/ adj. (-ier, -iest) esp. Scot. & N.Engl. 1 a physically attractive. b healthy-looking. 2 good, pleasant. [perhaps from French bon good]

bonsai /ˈbɒnsaɪ/ n. (pl. same) 1 dwarfed tree or shrub. 2 art of growing these. [Japanese]

bonus /ˈbəʊnəs/ n. extra benefit or payment. [Latin, = good]

bon vivant /bɒ̃ viːˈvɑ̃/ n. (pl. bon or bons vivants pronunc. same) person fond of good food and drink. [French]

bon voyage /bɒ̃ vwaˈjɑːʒ/ int. expression of good wishes to a departing traveller. [French]

bony /ˈbəʊnɪ/ adj. (-ier, -iest) 1 thin with prominent bones. 2 having many bones. 3 of or like bone. □ **boniness** n.

boo —int. 1 expression of disapproval etc. 2 sound intended to surprise. —n. utterance of boo, esp. to a performer etc. —v. (boos, booed) 1 utter boos at by booing. 2 jeer at by booing. [imitative]

boob colloq. —n. 1 silly mistake. 2 foolish person. —v. make a silly mistake. [shortening of BOOBY]

boob[2] n. slang woman's breast. [origin uncertain]

booby n. (pl. -ies) stupid or childish person. [Spanish bobo]

booby prize n. prize given for coming last.

booby trap n. 1 practical joke in the form of a trap. 2 disguised explosive device triggered by the unknowing victim.

boodle /ˈbuːd(ə)l/ n. slang money, esp. gained or used dishonestly. [Dutch boedel possessions]

boogie /ˈbuːgɪ/ v. (-ies, -ied, -ieing) slang dance to pop music.

boogie-woogie /ˈbuːgɪˈwuːgɪ/ n. style of playing blues or jazz on the piano. [origin unknown]

book /buk/ —n. 1 a written or printed work with pages bound along one side. b work intended for publication. 2 bound blank sheets for notes, records, etc. 3 bound set of tickets, stamps, matches, etc. 4 (in pl.) set of records or accounts. 5 main division of a large literary work. 6 telephone directory. 7 colloq. magazine. 8 libretto, script, etc. 9 record of bets. —v. 1 a (also absol.) reserve (a seat etc.) in advance. b engage (an entertainer etc.). 2 a take the personal details of (an offender or rulebreaker). b enter in a book or list. □ **book in** register at a hotel etc. **book up** 1 buy tickets in advance. 2 (as **booked up**) with all places reserved. **bring to book** call to account. **go by the book** proceed by the rules. **in a person's good** (or **bad**) **books** in (or out of) favour with a person. [Old English]

bookbinder n. person who binds books for a living. □ **bookbinding** n.

bookcase n. cabinet of shelves for books.

book club n. society in which selected books are available cheaply.

book end n. prop used to keep books upright.

bookie /ˈbukɪ/ n. colloq. = BOOKMAKER. [abbreviation]

booking n. reservation or engagement.

booking-hall n. (also **booking-office**) ticket office at a railway station etc.

bookish adj. 1 studious; fond of reading. 2 having knowledge mainly from books.

bookkeeper n. person who keeps accounts, esp. for a living. □ **bookkeeping** n.

booklet /ˈbuklɪt/ n. small book usu. with a paper cover.

bookmaker n. professional taker of bets. □ **bookmaking** n.

bookmark n. thing used to mark a reader's place.

book-plate n. decorative personalized label stuck in a book.

bookseller n. dealer in books.

bookshop n. shop selling books.

bookstall n. stand selling books, newspapers, etc.

book token n. voucher exchangeable for books.

bookworm n. 1 colloq. devoted reader. 2 larva feeding on the paper and glue in books.

Boolean /ˈbuːlɪən/ adj. denoting a system of algebraic notation to represent logical propositions. [Boole, name of a mathematician]

Boolean logic n. use of 'and', 'or', and 'not' in retrieving information from a database.

boom[1] —n. deep resonant sound. —v. make or speak with a boom. [imitative]

boom[2] —n. period of economic prosperity or activity. —v. be suddenly prosperous. [perhaps from BOOM[1]]

boom[3] n. 1 pivoted spar to which a sail is attached. 2 long pole carrying a microphone, camera, etc. 3 barrier across a harbour etc. [Dutch, = BEAM]

boomerang /ˈbuːməˌræŋ/ —n. 1 flat V-shaped hardwood missile used esp. by Australian Aboriginals, able to return to its thrower. 2 plan that recoils on its originator. —v. (of a plan etc.) backfire. [Aboriginal]

boon[1] n. advantage; blessing. [Old Norse]

boon[2] adj. intimate, favourite (usu. boon companion). [French bon from Latin bonus good]

boor n. ill-mannered person. □ **boorish** adj. [Low German or Dutch]

boost colloq. —v. 1 promote or encourage. 2 increase, assist. 3 push from below. —n. act or result of boosting. [origin unknown]

booster n. 1 device for increasing power or voltage. 2 auxiliary engine or rocket for initial speed. 3 dose, injection, etc. renewing the effect of an earlier one.

boot[1] —n. 1 outer foot-covering reaching above the ankle. 2 luggage compartment of a car. 3 colloq. a firm kick. b (prec. by the) dismissal (got the boot). —v. 1 kick. 2 (often foll. by out) eject forcefully. 3 (usu. foll. by up) make (a computer) ready. □ **put the boot in** 1 kick brutally. 2 harm a person. [Old Norse]

boot[2] n. □ **to boot** as well, in addition. [Old English]

bootblack n. US person who polishes boots and shoes.

bootee /buːˈtiː/ n. baby's soft shoe.

booth /buːð/ n. 1 small temporary structure used esp. as a market stall. 2 enclosure for telephoning, voting, etc. 3 cubicle in a restaurant etc. [Old Norse]

bootleg —adj. (esp. of alcohol) smuggled, illicit. —v. (-**gg**-) illicitly make or deal in (alcohol etc.). □ **bootlegger** n.

bootlicker n. colloq. toady.

boots n. hotel servant who cleans shoes etc.

bootstrap n. loop used to pull a boot on. □ **pull oneself up by one's bootstraps** better oneself.

booty /ˈbuːtɪ/ n. 1 loot, spoil. 2 colloq. prize or gain. [German]

booze colloq. —n. alcoholic drink. —v. (-zing) drink alcohol, esp. to excess. □ BOOZE¹]

boozer n. colloq. 1 habitual drinker. 2 public house.

booze-up n. colloq. a spell of drinking bout

bop¹ n. colloq. 1 a social occasion for this. 2 to pop music. b dance, esp. to pop music. □ BEBOP. —v. (-pp-) (abbreviation)

bop² colloq. —v. (-pp-) hit or punch, esp. lightly. —n. esp. light blow or hit. [imitative]

boracic /bəˈræsɪk/ adj. of borax.

boracic acid n. = BORIC ACID.

borage /ˈbɒrɪdʒ/ n. plant with leaves used as flavouring. [French ultimately from Arabic]

borax /ˈbɔːræks/ n. salt used in making glass and china, and as an antiseptic. [French ultimately from Persian]

Bordeaux /bɔːˈdəʊ/ n. (pl. same /-dəʊz/) wine (esp. red) from the Bordeaux district in SW France.

border —n. 1 edge or boundary, or the part near it. 2 a line or region separating two countries. b (**the Border**) boundary between Scotland and England (usu. **the Borders**), or N. Ireland and the Irish Republic. 3 esp. ornamental strip round an edge. 4 long narrow flower-bed (herbaceous border). —v. 1 be a border to. 2 provide with a border. 3 (usu. foll. by on, upon) a adjoin; come close to being. b resemble. [French from Germanic: related to BOARD]

borderer n. person living near a border.

borderland n. 1 district near a border. 2 condition between two extremes. 3 area for debate.

borderline —n. 1 line dividing two conditions. 2 line marking a boundary. —adj. 1 on the borderline. 2 barely acceptable.

Border collie n. sheepdog of the North Country.

Border terrier n. small rough-haired terrier.

bore¹ —v. (**-ring**) 1 make (a hole), esp. with a revolving tool. 2 make a hole in, hollow out. —n. 1 hollow of a firearm barrel or of a cylinder in an internal-combustion engine. 2 diameter of this. 3 deep hole made esp. to find water. [Old English]

bore² —n. tiresome or dull person or thing. —v. (**-ring**) weary by tedious talk or dullness. □ **bored** adj. **boring** adj. [origin unknown]

bore³ n. high tidal wave in an estuary. [Scandinavian]

bore⁴ past of BEAR¹.

boredom n. state of being bored. [from BORE²]

boric acid /ˈbɔːrɪk/ n. acid derived from borax, used as an antiseptic.

born adj. 1 existing as a result of birth. 2 a (usu. foll. by to + infin.) destined (born lucky; born to be king). 3 (in comb.) of a certain status by birth (French-born; well-born). [past part. of BEAR¹]

born-again attrib. adj. converted (esp. to fundamentalist Christianity).

borne /bɔːn/ past part. of BEAR¹. —adj. (in comb.) carried by (airborne).

boron /ˈbɔːrɒn/ n. non-metallic crystalline element. [from BORAX, after carbon]

borough /ˈbʌrə/ n. 1 a town represented in the House of Commons. b town or district granted the status of a borough. 2 hist. town with a municipal corporation conferred by a royal charter. [Old English]

borrow /ˈbɒrəʊ/ v. 1 a acquire temporarily, promising or intending to return. b obtain money thus. 2 use (another's idea, invention, etc.); plagiarize. □ **borrower** n. [Old English]

Borstal /ˈbɔːstəl/ n. hist. residential institution for youth custody. [Borstal in Kent]

■ **Usage** This term has now been replaced by detention centre and youth custody centre.

bortsch /bɔːtʃ/ n. Russian soup of beetroot, cabbage, etc. [Russian]

borzoi /ˈbɔːzɔɪ/ n. large silky-coated dog. [Russian, = swift]

bosh n. & int. slang nonsense. [Turkish, = empty]

bosom /ˈbʊzəm/ n. 1 a person's (esp. woman's) breast. b colloq. each of a woman's breasts. c enclosure formed by the breast and arms. 2 emotional centre (bosom of one's family). [Old English]

bosom friend n. intimate friend.

boss¹ colloq. —n. employer, manager, or supervisor. —v. (usu. foll. by about, around) give orders to; order about. [Dutch baas]

boss² n. 1 round knob, stud, etc., esp. on the centre of a shield. 2 Archit. ornamental carving etc. at the junction of the ribs in a vault. [French]

bossa nova /ˌbɒsə ˈnəʊvə/ n. 1 dance like the samba. 2 music for this. [Portuguese, = new flair]

boss-eyed adj. colloq. 1 cross-eyed; blind in one eye. 2 crooked. [boss = bad shot, origin unknown]

bossy adj. (-ier, -iest) colloq. domineering. □ **bossiness** n.

bosun (also **bo'sun**) var. of BOATSWAIN.

botany /'bɒtəni/ n. the study of plants. □ **botanic** /bə'tænɪk/ adj. **botanical** /bə'tænɪk(ə)l/ adj. **botanist** n. [Greek botanē plant]

botch (also **bodge**) —v. **1** bungle; do badly. **2** patch clumsily. —n. bungled or spoilt work. [origin unknown]

both /bəʊθ/ —adj. & pron. the two, not only one (both boys; both the boys; both of the boys; I like both). —adv. with equal truth in two cases (is both hot and dry). [Old Norse]

bother /'bɒðə(r)/ —v. **1** trouble; worry, disturb. **2** (often foll. by about, with, or to + infin.) take the time or trouble (didn't bother to tell me; shan't bother with dessert). —n. **1 a** person or thing that worry. —int. expressing irritation. [Irish bodhraim deafen]

botheration /bɒðə'reɪʃ(ə)n/ n. & int. colloq. = BOTHER n, int.

bothersome /'bɒðəsəm/ adj. causing bother.

bottle /'bɒt(ə)l/ —n. **1** container, esp. glass or plastic, for storing liquid. **2** amount filling it. **3** baby's feeding-bottle. **4** = HOT-WATER BOTTLE. **5** metal cylinder for liquefied gas. **6** slang courage. —v. (-ling) **1** put into, or preserve in, bottles or jars. **2** (foll. by up) conceal or restrain (esp. a feeling). □ **hit the bottle** slang drink heavily. [medieval Latin: related to BUTT[4]]

bottle bank n. place for depositing bottles for recycling.

bottle-feed v. feed (a baby) from a bottle as opposed to the breast.

bottle green adj. & n. (as adj. often hyphenated) dark green.

bottleneck n. **1** narrow congested area, esp. on a road. **2** impeding thing.

bottlenose dolphin n. dolphin with a bottle-shaped snout.

bottle party n. party to which guests bring bottles of drink.

bottom /'bɒtəm/ —n. **1 a** lowest point or part. **b** base. **c** underneath part. **d** furthest or inmost part. **2** colloq. **a** buttocks. **b** seat of a chair etc. **3 a** less honourable end of a table, class, etc. **b** person occupying this (he's bottom of the class). **4** ground below water. **5** basis or origin. **6** essential character. —adj. lowest, last. —v. **1** put a bottom to (a chair etc.). **2** find the extent of. **3** touch the bottom or lowest point (of). □ **at bottom** basically. **be at the bottom of** have caused. **bottom out** reach the lowest level. **get to the bottom of** fully investigate and explain. [Old English]

bottom drawer n. linen etc. stored by a woman for marriage.

bottomless adj. **1** without a bottom. **2** inexhaustible.

bottom line n. colloq. underlying truth; ultimate, esp. financial, criterion.

botulism /'bɒtjʊ,lɪz(ə)m/ n. poisoning caused by a bacillus in badly preserved food. [Latin botulus sausage]

bouclé /'buːkleɪ/ n. **1** looped or curled yarn (esp. wool). **2** fabric made of this. [French; = curled]

boudoir /'buːdwɑː(r)/ n. woman's private room. [French bouder sulk]

bouffant /'buːfɑ̃/ adj. (of a dress, hair, etc.) puffed out. [French]

bougainvillaea /ˌbuːɡən'vɪlɪə/ n. tropical plant with large coloured bracts. [Bougainville, name of a navigator]

bough /baʊ/ n. main branch of a tree. [Old English]

bought past and past part. of BUY.

bouillon /'buːjɒn/ n. clear broth. [French bouillir to boil]

boulder /'bəʊldə(r)/ n. large smooth rock. [Scandinavian]

boule /buːl/ n. (also **boules** pronunc. same) French form of bowls played on rough ground. [French]

boulevard /'buːlə,vɑːd/ n. **1** broad tree-lined avenue. **2** esp. US broad main road. [French from German]

boult var. of BOLT[2].

bounce —v. (-cing) (cause to) rebound. **2** slang (of a cheque) be returned by a bank when there are no funds to meet it. **3** (foll. by about, up, in, out, etc.) jump, move, or rush boisterously. —n. **1 a** rebound. **b** power of rebounding. **2** colloq. **a** swagger, self-confidence. **b** liveliness. □ **bounce back** recover well after a setback. □ **bouncy** adj. (-ier, -iest). [imitative]

bouncer n. **1** slang doorman ejecting troublemakers from a dancehall, club, etc. **2** = BUMPER 3.

bouncing adj. (esp. of a baby) big and healthy.

bound[1] —v. **1** spring, leap. **2** (of a ball etc.) bounce. —n. **1** springy leap. **2** bounce. [French bondir from Latin bombus hum]

bound[2] —n. (usu. in pl.) **1** limitation; restriction. **2** border, boundary. —v. **1** limit. **2** be the boundary of. □ **out of bounds** outside a permitted area. [French from medieval Latin]

bound[3] adj. **1** (usu. foll. by for) starting or having started (bound for stardom). **2** (in comb.) in a specified direction (northbound). [Old Norse; = ready]

bound[4] past and past part. of BIND. □ **bound to** certain to (he's bound to come). **bound up with** closely associated with.

boundary /ˈbaʊndərɪ/ n. (pl. -ies) 1 line marking the limits of an area etc. 2 Cricket hit crossing the limits of the field, scoring 4 or 6 runs. [related to BOUND²]

bounden duty /ˈbaʊnd(ə)n/ n. formal solemn responsibility. [archaic past part. of BIND]

bounder n. colloq. cad.

boundless adj. unlimited.

bounteous /ˈbaʊntɪəs/ adj. poet. = BOUNTIFUL. [French: related to BOUNTY]

bountiful /ˈbaʊntɪfʊl/ adj. 1 generous. 2 ample.

bounty /ˈbaʊntɪ/ n. (pl. -ies) 1 generosity. 2 reward, esp. from the State. 3 gift. [French from Latin bonus good]

bouquet /buːˈkeɪ/ n. 1 bunch of flowers, esp. professionally arranged. 2 scent of wine etc. 3 compliment. [French bois wood]

bouquet garni /ˌbuːkeɪ ˈgɑːnɪ/ n. (pl. **bouquets garnis** /ˌbuːkeɪz ˈgɑːnɪ/) bunch or bag of herbs for seasoning. [French]

bourbon /ˈbɜːbən/ n. US whisky from maize and rye. [Bourbon County, Kentucky]

bourgeois /ˈbʊəʒwɑː/ often derog. —adj. 1 a conventionally middle-class. b materialistic. 2 capitalist. —n. (pl. same) bourgeois person. [French]

bourgeoisie /ˌbʊəʒwɑːˈziː/ n. 1 capitalist class. 2 middle class. [French]

bourn /bɔːn/ n. small stream. [var. of BURN²]

bourse /bʊəs/ n. 1 (Bourse) Paris Stock Exchange. 2 money-market. [French; related to PURSE]

bout n. 1 (often foll. by of) a spell (of work or activity). b attack (bout of flu). 2 wrestling- or boxing-match. [obsolete bought bending]

boutique /buːˈtiːk/ n. small shop selling esp. fashionable clothes. [French]

bouzouki /buːˈzuːkɪ/ n. (pl. -s) Greek form of mandolin. [modern Greek]

bovine /ˈbəʊvaɪn/ adj. 1 of cattle. 2 stupid, dull. [Latin bos ox]

bovine spongiform encephalopathy see BSE.

bow¹ /bəʊ/ —n. 1 a slip-knot with a double loop. b ribbon etc. so tied. 2 curved piece of wood etc. with a string stretched across its ends, for shooting arrows. 3 rod with horsehair stretched along its length, for playing the violin etc. 4 shallow curve or bend; thing of this form. —v. (also absol.) use a bow on (a violin etc.). [Old English]

bow² /baʊ/ —v. 1 incline the head or body, esp. in greeting or acknowledgement. 2 submit (bowed to the inevitable). 3 cause (the head etc.) to incline. —n. act of bowing. □ **bow and scrape** toady. **bow down** 1 bend or kneel esp. in submission or reverence. 2 make stoop; crush (bowed down by care). **bow out** 1 exit (esp. formally). 2 withdraw; retire. □ **take a bow** acknowledge applause. [Old English]

bow³ /baʊ/ n. 1 (often in pl.) front end of a boat. 2 rower nearest this. [Low German or Dutch: related to BOUGH]

bowdlerize /ˈbaʊdləraɪz/ v. (also -ise) (-zing or -sing) expurgate (a book etc.) □ **bowdlerization** /-ˈzeɪʃ(ə)n/ n. [Bowdler, name of an expurgator of Shakespeare]

bowel /ˈbaʊəl/ n. 1 (often in pl.) INTESTINE. 2 (in pl.) innermost parts. [Latin botulus sausage]

bower /ˈbaʊə(r)/ n. 1 arbour; summer-house. 2 poet. inner room. [Old English, = dwelling]

bowerbird n. Australasian bird, the male of which constructs elaborate runs.

bowie /ˈbəʊɪ/ n. (in full **bowie knife**) a kind of long hunting-knife. [Bowie, name of an American soldier]

bowl¹ /bəʊl/ n. 1 a usu. round deep basin for food or liquid. b contents of a bowl. 2 hollow part of a tobacco-pipe, spoon, etc. [Old English]

bowl² /bəʊl/ —n. 1 hard heavy ball, made with a bias to run in a curve. 2 (in pl.; usu. treated as sing.) game played with these on grass. 3 spell or turn of bowling in cricket. —v. 1 a roll (a ball etc.). b play bowls. 2 (also absol.) Cricket etc. a deliver (a ball, over, etc.). b (often foll. by out) dismiss (a batsman) by knocking down the wicket with a ball. 3 (often foll. by along) go along rapidly. □ **bowl out** Cricket etc. dismiss (a batsman or a side). **bowl over** 1 knock down. 2 colloq. impress greatly; overwhelm. [Latin bulla bubble]

bow-legs n.pl. bandy legs. □ **bow-legged** adj.

bowler¹ n. 1 Cricket etc. player who bowls. 2 bowls-player.

bowler² n. (in full **bowler hat**) man's hard round felt hat. [Bowler, name of a hatter]

bowline /ˈbəʊlɪn/ n. 1 rope from a ship's bow keeping the sail taut against the wind. 2 knot forming a non-slipping loop at the end of a rope.

bowling n. the game of skittles, tenpin bowling, or bowls.

bowling-alley n. 1 long enclosure for skittles or tenpin bowling. 2 building with these.

bowling-green n. lawn for playing bowls.

bowman n. archer.

bowsprit /ˈbəusprɪt/ n. spar running forward from a ship's bow.

bowstring n. string of an archer's bow.

bow-tie n. necktie in the form of a bow.

bow-window n. curved bay window.

bow-wow —int. /bauˈwau/ imitation of a dog's bark. —n. /ˈbauwau/ colloq. dog. [imitative]

box¹ —n. 1 container, usu. flat-sided and firm. 2 amount contained in a box. 3 compartment, e.g. in a theatre or law-court. 4 receptacle or kiosk for a special purpose (often in comb.: money box; telephone box). 5 facility at a newspaper office for receiving replies to an advertisement. 6 (prec. by the) colloq. television. 7 enclosed area or space. 8 area of print enclosed by a border. 9 light shield for the genitals in cricket etc. 10 (prec. by the) Football colloq. penalty area. —v. 1 put in or provide with a box. 2 (foll. by in, up) confine. [Latin buxis: related to BOX³]

box² —v. 1 a take part in boxing. b fight (an opponent) at boxing. 2 slap (esp. a person's ears). —n. hard slap, esp. on the ears. [origin unknown]

box³ n. 1 small evergreen tree with dark green leaves. 2 its fine hard wood. [Latin buxus, Greek puxos]

Box and Cox n. two people sharing accommodation etc. in shifts. [names of characters in a play (1847)]

box camera n. simple box-shaped camera.

boxer n. 1 person who boxes, esp. as a sport. 2 medium-size short-haired dog with a pugilike face.

boxer shorts n.pl. men's loose under-pants like shorts.

box girder n. hollow girder square in cross-section.

boxing n. fighting with the fists, esp. as a sport.

Boxing Day n. first weekday after Christmas. [from BOX¹, from the custom of giving Christmas-boxes]

boxing glove n. each of a pair of heavily padded gloves worn in boxing.

box junction n. road area marked with a yellow grid, which a vehicle should enter only if its exit is clear.

box number n. number for replies to a private advertisement in a newspaper.

box office n. ticket-office at a theatre etc.

box pleat n. arrangement of parallel pleats folding in alternate directions.

boxroom n. small room for storing boxes, cases, etc.

box spring n. each of a set of vertical springs in a frame, e.g. in a mattress.

boxwood n. = BOX³ 2.

boxy adj. (-ier, -iest) cramped.

boy —n. 1 male child, son. 2 young man. 3 male servant etc. —int. expressing pleasure, surprise, etc. □ **boyhood** n. **boyish** adj. [origin uncertain]

boycott /ˈbɔɪkɒt/ —v. 1 refuse to have social or commercial relations with (a person, country, etc.). 2 refuse to handle (goods). —n. such a refusal. [Capt. Boycott, so treated from 1880]

boyfriend n. person's regular male companion or lover.

boyo /ˈbɔɪəu/ n. (pl. -s) Welsh & Ir. colloq. (esp. as a form of address) boy, mate.

boy scout n. = SCOUT n. 4.

BP abbr. 1 boiling-point. 2 blood pressure. 3 before the present (era). 4 British Petroleum. 5 British Pharmacopoeia.

Bq abbr. becquerel.

BR abbr. British Rail.

Br symb. bromine.

bra /brɑː/ n. undergarment worn by women to support the breasts. [abbreviation]

brace —n. 1 device that clamps or fastens tightly. 2 timber etc. strengthening a framework. 3 (in pl.) straps supporting trousers from the shoulders. 4 wire device for straightening the teeth. 5 (pl. same) pair (esp. of game). 6 rope for trimming a sail. 7 connecting mark { or } in printing. —v. (-cing) 1 make steady by supporting. 2 fasten tightly to make firm. 3 (esp. as **bracing** adj.) invigorate, refresh. 4 (often refl.) prepare for a difficulty, shock, etc. [Latin bracchia arms]

brace and bit n. revolving tool for boring, with a D-shaped central handle.

bracelet /ˈbreɪslɪt/ n. 1 ornamental band or chain worn on the wrist or arm. 2 slang handcuff.

brachiosaurus /ˌbrækɪəˈsɔːrəs, ˌbræk-/ n. (pl. -ruses) plant-eating dinosaur with forelegs longer than its hind legs. [Latin from Greek brakhión arm, sauros lizard]

bracken /ˈbrækən/ n. 1 large coarse fern. 2 mass of these. [Old Norse]

bracket /ˈbrækɪt/ —n. 1 (esp. angled) support projecting from a vertical surface. 2 shelf fixed to a wall with this. 3 each of a pair of marks () [] {} enclosing words or figures. 4 group or classification (income bracket). —v. (-t-) 1 enclose in brackets. 2 group or classify together. [Latin bracae breeches]

brackish /ˈbrækɪʃ/ adj. (of water etc.) slightly salty. [Low German or Dutch]

bract n. leaf-like and often brightly coloured part of a plant, growing before the flower. [Latin bractea thin sheet]

brad n. thin flat nail with a head on only one side. [Old Norse]

bradawl /ˈbrædɔːl/ n. small pointed tool for boring holes by hand.

brae /breɪ/ n. Scot. hillside. [Old Norse]

brag —v. (-gg-) talk boastfully. —n. 1 card-game like poker. 2 boastful statement or talk. [origin unknown]

braggart /ˈbrægət/ —n. boastful person. —adj. boastful.

Brahma /ˈbrɑːmə/ n. 1 Hindu Creator. 2 supreme divine Hindu reality. [Sanskrit, = creator]

Brahman /ˈbrɑːmən/ n. (pl. -s) 1 (also **Brahmin**) member of the highest or priestly Hindu caste. 2 = BRAHMA. □ **Brahmanic** /-ˈmænɪk/ adj. **Brahmanism** n.

braid —n. 1 woven band as edging or trimming. 2 US plait of hair. —v. 1 US plait 2 trim with braid. □ **braiding** n. [Old English]

Braille /breɪl/ —n. system of writing and printing for the blind, with patterns of raised dots. —v. (-ling) print or transcribe in Braille. [Braille, name of its inventor]

brain —n. 1 organ of soft nervous tissue in the skull of vertebrates, the centre of sensation and of intellectual and nervous activity. 2 a colloq. intelligent person. b (often in pl.) intelligence. 3 (usu. in pl.; prec. by the) colloq. cleverest person in a group, mastermind. 4 electronic device functioning like a brain. —v. 1 dash out the brains of. 2 colloq. strike hard on the head. □ **on the brain** colloq. obsessively in one's thoughts. [Old English]

brainchild n. colloq. person's clever idea or invention.

brain death n. irreversible brain damage causing the end of independent respiration, regarded as indicative of death. □ **brain-dead** adj.

brain drain n. colloq. loss of skilled personnel by emigration.

brainless adj. foolish.

brainpower n. mental ability or intelligence.

brainstorm n. 1 sudden mental disturbance. 2 colloq. mental lapse. 3 US brainwave. 4 pooling of spontaneous ideas about a problem etc. □ **brainstorming** n. (in sense 4).

brains trust n. group of experts answering questions, usu. publicly and impromptu.

brainwash v. implant ideas or esp. ideology into (a person) by repetition etc. □ **brainwashing** n.

brainwave n. 1 (usu. in pl.) electrical impulse in the brain. 2 colloq. sudden bright idea.

brainy adj. (-ier, -iest) intellectually clever.

braise /breɪz/ v. (-sing) stew slowly with a little liquid in a closed container. [French braise live coals]

brake[1] —n. 1 (often in pl.) device for stopping or slowing a wheel, vehicle, etc. 2 thing that impedes. —v. (-king) 1 apply a brake. 2 slow or stop with a brake. [probably obsolete brake = curb]

brake[2] n. large estate car. [var. of BREAK]

brake[3] —n. 1 toothed instrument for crushing flax and hemp. 2 (in full brake-harrow) heavy harrow. —v. (-king) crush (flax or hemp). [Low German or Dutch: related to BREAK]

brake[4] n. thicket or clump of brushwood. [Old English]

brake drum n. cylinder attached to a wheel, on which the brake shoes press to brake.

brake horsepower n. power of an engine measured by the force needed to brake it.

brake lining n. strip of fabric increasing the friction of a brake shoe.

brake shoe n. long curved block which presses on a brake drum to brake.

bramble /ˈbræmb(ə)l/ n. wild thorny shrub, esp. the blackberry. □ **brambly** adj. [Old English]

brambling /ˈbræmblɪŋ/ n. the speckled finch. [German: related to BRAMBLE]

bran n. grain husks separated from flour. [French]

branch /brɑːntʃ/ —n. 1 limb of a tree or bough. 2 lateral extension or subdivision, esp. of a river, road, or railway. 3 subdivision of a family, knowledge, etc. 4 local office etc. of a large business. —v. (often foll. by off) 1 diverge. 2 divide into branches. □ **branch out** extend one's field of interest. [Latin branca paw]

brand —n. 1 a particular make of goods. b identifying trade mark, label, etc. 2 (usu. foll. by of) characteristic kind (brand of humour). 3 identifying mark burned esp. on livestock. 4 iron used for this. 5 piece of burning or charred wood. 6 stigma; mark of disgrace. 7 poet. torch. —v. 1 mark with a hot iron. 2 stigmatize (branded him a liar). 3 impress unforgettably. 4 assign a trademark etc. to. [Old English]

brandish /ˈbrændɪʃ/ v. wave or flourish as a threat or display. [French from Germanic]

brand-new adj. completely new.

brandy /ˈbrændɪ/ n. (pl. -ies) strong alcoholic spirit distilled from wine or fermented fruit juice. [Dutch brandewijn]

brandy butter n. mixture of brandy, butter and sugar.

brandy-snap n. crisp rolled ginger-bread wafer usu. filled with cream.

bran-tub n. lucky dip with prizes hidden in bran.

brash adj. vulgarly self-assertive; impudent. □ **brashly** adv. **brashness** n. [dial.]

brass /brɑːs/ —n. 1 yellow alloy of copper and zinc. 2 brass objects collectively. 3 brass wind instruments. 4 slang money. 5 brass memorial tablet. 6 colloq. effrontery. —adj. made of brass. □ **brassed off** slang fed up. [Old English]

brass band n. band of brass instruments.

brasserie /ˈbræsəri/ n. restaurant, orig. one serving beer with food. [French brasser brew]

brassica /ˈbræsɪkə/ n. plant of the cabbage family. [Latin, = cabbage]

brassière /ˈbræzɪə(r)/ n. = BRA. [French]

brass monkey n. coarse slang used in various phrases to indicate extreme cold.

brass-rubbing n. 1 practice of taking impressions by rubbing heelball etc. over paper laid on engraved brasses. 2 impression obtained by this.

brass tacks n.pl. slang essential details.

brassy /ˈbrɑːsɪ/ adj. (-ier, -iest) 1 of or like brass. 2 impudent. 3 vulgarly showy. 4 loud and blaring.

brat n. usu. derog. child, esp. an ill-behaved one. [origin unknown]

bravado /brəˈvɑːdəʊ/ n. show of boldness. [Spanish]

brave —adj. 1 able or ready to face and endure danger, disgrace, or pain. 2 formal splendid, spectacular. —n. American Indian warrior. —v. (-ving) face bravely or defiantly. □ **bravely** adv. **braveness** n. **bravery** n. [ultimately Latin barbarus barbarian]

bravo /brɑːˈvəʊ/ —int. expressing approval. —n. (pl. -s) cry of 'bravo'. [French from Italian]

bravura /brəˈvjʊərə/ n. 1 brilliance of execution. 2 (often attrib.) passage of (esp. vocal) music requiring brilliant technique. [Italian]

brawl —n. noisy quarrel or fight. —v. 1 engage in a brawl. 2 (of a stream) run noisily. [Provençal]

brawn n. 1 muscular strength. 2 muscle; lean flesh. 3 jellied meat made from a pig's head. □ **brawny** adj. (-ier, -iest) [French from Germanic]

bray —n. 1 cry of a donkey. 2 harsh sound like this. —v. 1 make a bray. 2 utter harshly. [French braire]

braze v. (-zing) solder with an alloy of brass and zinc. [French braser]

brazen /ˈbreɪz(ə)n/ —adj. 1 shameless; insolent. 2 of or like brass. 3 harsh in sound. —v. (foll. by out) face or undergo defiantly (brazen it out). □ **brazenly** adv. [Old English]

brazier¹ /ˈbreɪzɪə(r)/ n. metal pan or stand holding burning coals etc. [French; related to BRAISE]

brazier² /ˈbreɪzɪə(r)/ n. worker in brass. [probably from BRASS]

Brazil /brəˈzɪl/ n. 1 tall S. American tree. 2 (in full **Brazil nut**) its large three-sided nut. [Brazil in S. America]

breach —n. 1 (often foll. by of) breaking or non-observation of a law, contract, etc. 2 breaking of relations; quarrel. 3 opening, gap. —v. 1 break through; make a gap in. 2 break (a law, contract, etc.). □ **step into the breach** help in a crisis, esp. as a replacement. [Germanic: related to BREAK]

breach of promise n. breaking of a promise, esp. to marry.

breach of the peace n. crime of causing a public disturbance.

bread /bred/ —n. 1 baked dough of flour and water, usu. leavened with yeast. 2 necessary food. 3 slang money. —v. coat with breadcrumbs for cooking. [Old English]

bread and butter —n. one's livelihood. —attrib. adj. (**bread-and-butter**) done or produced for a basic living.

breadboard n. 1 board for cutting bread on. 2 board for making an experimental model of an electric circuit.

breadcrumb n. small fragment of bread, esp. (in pl.) for use in cooking.

breadfruit n. 1 fruit which resembles new bread when roasted. 2 tropical evergreen tree bearing it.

breadline n. subsistence level (esp. on the breadline).

bread sauce n. white sauce thickened with breadcrumbs.

breadth /bredθ/ n. 1 distance or measurement from side to side of a thing. 2 freedom from prejudice or intolerance. [Old English: related to BROAD]

breadwinner n. person who works to support a family.

break /breɪk/ —v. (past **broke**; past part. **broken** /ˈbrəʊk(ə)n/) 1 a separate into pieces under a blow or strain; shatter. b make or become inoperative. c break a bone in or dislocate (part of the body). 2 a interrupt (broke our journey). b have an interval (broke for tea). 3 fail to keep (a law, promise, etc.). 4 a make or become subdued or weak; (cause to) yield; destroy. b weaken the effect of (a fall, blow, etc.). c = break in 3c. 5 surpass (a record). 6 (foll. by with) end a friendship with (a person etc.). 7 be no

longer subject to (a habit), **b** (foll. by *of*) free (a person) from a habit (*broke them of their addiction*). **8** reveal or be revealed (*broke the news; story broke*). **9 a** (of fine weather) change suddenly. **b** (of waves) curl over and foam. **c** (of the day) dawn. **d** (of clouds) move apart. **e** (of a storm) begin violently. **10** *Electr.* disconnect (a circuit). **11 a** (of a boy's voice) change with emotion. **b** (*of a voice*) change at puberty. **12 a** (often foll. by *up*) divide (a set etc.). **b** change (a banknote etc.) for coins. **13** ruin (especially (see also BROKE *adj.*) financially (see also BROKE *adj.*). **14** penetrate (e.g. a safe) by force. **15** decipher (a code). **16** make (a way, path, etc.) by force. **17** burst forth (*sun broke through*). **18 a** (of troops) disperse in confusion. **b** rupture (ranks). **19 a** (usu. foll. by *free, loose, out, etc.*) escape by a sudden effort. **b** escape or emerge from (prison, bounds, cover, etc.). **20** *Tennis* etc. win a game against (an opponent's service). **21** (of boxers etc.) come out of a clinch. **22** *Billiards* etc. disperse the balls at the start of a game. —*n.* **1 a** act or instance of breaking. **b** point of breaking; gap. **2** interval, interruption, pause. **3** sudden dash (esp. to escape). **4** *colloq.* piece of luck; fair chance. **5** *Cricket* deflection of a bowled ball on bouncing. **6** *Billiards* etc. a series of points scored during one turn. **b** opening shot dispersing the balls. □ **break away** make or become free or separate. **break the back of** do the hardest or greatest part of. **break down 1 a** fail mechanically; cease to function. **b** (of human relationships etc.) fail, collapse. **c** fail in (esp. mental) health. **d** collapse in tears or emotion. **2 a** demolish, destroy. **b** suppress (resistance). **c** force to yield. **3** analyse into components. **break even** make neither profit nor loss. **break a person's heart** see HEART. **break the ice** begin to overcome formality or shyness. **break in 1** enter by force, esp. with criminal intent. **2** interrupt. **3 a** accustom to a habit etc. **b** wear etc. until comfortable. **c** tame (an animal); accustom (a horse) to a saddle etc. **break in on** disturb; interrupt. **break into 1** enter forcibly. **2 a** burst forth with (a song, laughter, etc.). **b** change pace for (a faster one) (*broke into a gallop*). **3** interrupt. **break off 1** detach by breaking. **2** bring to an end. **3** cease talking etc. **break open** open forcibly. **break out 1** escape by force, esp. from prison. **2** begin suddenly. **3** (foll. by *in*) become covered in (a rash etc.). **4** exclaim. **break up 1** break into small pieces. **2** disperse; disband. **3** end the school term. **4** (cause to) terminate a relationship;

disband. **break wind** release gas from the anus. [Old English]

breakable —*adj.* easily broken. —*n.* (esp. in *pl.*) breakable thing.

breakage *n.* **1 a** broken thing. **b** damage caused by breaking. **2** act or instance of breaking.

breakaway *n.* (often *attrib.*) breaking away; secession (*breakaway group*).

break-dancing *n.* acrobatic style of street-dancing.

breakdown *n.* **1 a** mechanical failure. **b** loss of (esp. mental) health. **2** collapse (*breakdown of communication*). **3** analysis (of statistics etc.).

breaker *n.* **1** heavy breaking wave. **2** person or thing that breaks something.

breakfast /ˈbrekfəst/ —*n.* first meal of the day. —*v.* have breakfast.

break-in *n.* illegal forced entry, esp. with criminal intent.

breaking and entering *n.* (formerly) the illegal entering of a building with intent to commit a felony.

breaking-point *n.* point of greatest strain.

breakneck *attrib. adj.* (of speed) dangerously fast.

break-out *n.* forcible escape.

breakthrough *n.* **1** major advance or discovery. **2** act of breaking through an obstacle etc.

breakup *n.* **1** disintegration or collapse. **2** dispersal.

breakwater *n.* barrier breaking the force of waves.

bream *n.* (*pl.* same) **1** yellowish arch-backed freshwater fish. **2** (in full sea **bream**) similar marine fish. [French from German]

breast /brest/ —*n.* **1 a** either of two milk-secreting organs on a woman's chest. **b** corresponding part of a man's body. **2 a** chest. **b** corresponding part of an animal. **3** part of a garment that covers the breast. **4** breast as a source of nourishment or emotion. —*v.* **1** contend with. **2** reach the top of (a hill). □ **make a clean breast of** confess fully. [Old English]

breastbone *n.* thin flat vertical bone in the chest between the ribs.

breast-feed *v.* feed (a baby) from the breast.

breastplate *n.* armour covering the breast.

breast-stroke *n.* swimming stroke made by extending both arms forward and sweeping them back.

breastwork *n.* low temporary defence or parapet.

breath /breθ/ *n.* **1 a** air drawn into or expelled from the lungs. **b** one respiration of air. **c** breath as perceived by

the senses. **2** a slight movement of air. **b** whiff (of perfume etc.). **3** whisper; murmur (esp. of scandal). □ **catch one's breath 1** cease breathing momentarily in surprise etc. **2** rest to restore normal breathing. **hold one's breath** cease gasping for air, esp. after exercise. **take one's breath away** surprise, delight, etc. **under one's breath** in a whisper. [Old English]

Breathalyser /ˈbreθəˌlaɪzə(r)/ n. (also **-lyzer**) *propr.* instrument for measuring alcohol levels in the breath exhaled into it. □ **breathalyse** v. (also **-lyze**) (**-sing** or **-zing**). [from BREATH, ANALYSE]

breathe /briːð/ v. (**-thing**) **1** draw air into and expel it from the lungs. **2** be or seem alive. **3 a** utter or sound (esp. quietly). **b** express (*breathed defiance*). **4** pause. **5** send out or take in (as if with the breath (*breathed new life into them*; *breathed whisky*). **6** (of wine etc.) be exposed to the air. □ **breathe again** (or **freely**) feel relief.

breather /ˈbriːðə(r)/ n. **1** *colloq.* brief pause for rest. **2** brief period in the fresh air.

breathing-space n. time to recover; pause.

breathless *adj.* **1** panting, out of breath. **2** holding the breath. **3** still, windless. □ **breathlessly** *adv.*

breathtaking *adj.* astounding; aweinspiring. □ **breathtakingly** *adv.*

breath test n. test with a Breathalyser.

bred past and past part. of BREED.

breech n. back part of a rifle or gun barrel. [Old English]

breech birth n. (also **breech delivery**) delivery of a baby with the buttocks or feet foremost.

breeches /ˈbrɪtʃɪz/ n.pl. short trousers esp. fastened below the knee.

breeches buoy n. lifebuoy with canvas breeches for the user's legs.

breed –v. (past and past part. **bred**) **1** (of animals) produce young. **2** propagate; raise (animals). **3** yield; result in. **4** arise; spread. **5** bring up; train. **6** create (fissile material) by nuclear reaction. –n. **1** stock of similar animals or plants within a species, usu. developed by deliberate selection. **2** race; lineage. **3** sort, kind. □ **breeder** n. [Old English]

breeder reactor n. nuclear reactor creating surplus fissile material.

breeding n. **1** raising of offspring; propagation. **2** social behaviour; ancestry.

breeze[1] –n. **1** gentle wind. **2** *colloq.* quarrel. **3** esp. *US colloq.* easy task. –v.

(**-zing**) (foll. by *in*, *out*, *along*, etc.) *colloq.* saunter casually. [probably Spanish and Portuguese *briza*]

breeze[2] n. small cinders. [French: related to BRAISE]

breeze-block n. lightweight building block, esp. of breeze mixed with sand and cement.

breezy *adj.* (**-ier**, **-iest**) **1** slightly windy. **2** *colloq.* cheerful, light-hearted, casual.

Bren n. (in full **Bren gun**) lightweight quick-firing machine-gun. [*Brno* in Czechoslovakia, *Enfield* in England]

brent n. (in full **brent-goose**) small migratory goose. [origin unknown]

brethren see BROTHER.

Breton /ˈbret(ə)n/ –n. **1** native of Brittany. **2** Celtic language of Brittany. –*adj.* of Brittany, its people, or language. [French, = BRITON]

breve n. **1** *Mus.* note twice the length of a semibreve. **2** mark (˘) indicating a short or unstressed vowel. [var. of BRIEF]

breviary /ˈbriːvɪərɪ/ n. (*pl.* **-ies**) book containing the Roman Catholic daily office. [Latin: related to BRIEF]

brevity /ˈbrevɪtɪ/ n. **1** economy of expression; conciseness. **2** shortness (of time etc.). [Anglo-French: related to BRIEF]

brew /bruː/ –v. **1** make (beer etc.) by infusion, boiling, and fermentation. **b** make (tea etc.) by infusion. **2** undergo these processes. **3** gather force; threaten (*storm is brewing*). **4** concoct (a plan etc.). –n. **1** liquid or amount brewed; concoction. **2** process of brewing. □ **brew up** make tea. □ **brewer** n. [Old English]

brewery /ˈbruːərɪ/ n. (*pl.* **-ies**) factory for brewing beer etc.

brew-up n. instance of making tea.

briar[1] var. of BRIER[1].

briar[2] var. of BRIER[2].

bribe –v. (**-bing**) (often foll. by *to* + infin.) persuade to act improperly in one's favour by a gift of money etc. –n. money or services offered in bribing. □ **bribery** n. [French *briber* beg]

bric-à-brac /ˈbrɪkəbræk/ n. (also **bric-a-brac**) cheap ornaments, trinkets, etc. [French]

brick –n. **1** a small usu. rectangular block of fired or sun-dried clay used in building. **b** material of this. **2** child's toy block. **3** brick-shaped thing. **4** *slang* generous or loyal person. –v. (foll. by *in*, *up*) close or block with brickwork. –*adj.* **1** built of brick (*brick wall*). **2** (also **brick-red**) dull red. [Low German or Dutch]

brickbat n. **1** piece of brick, esp. as a missile. **2** insult.

brickie n. *slang* bricklayer.

bricklayer n. person who builds with bricks, esp. for a living. □ **bricklaying** n.

brickwork n. building or work in brick.

brickyard n. place where bricks are made.

bridal /ˈbraɪd(ə)l/ adj. of a bride or wedding. [Old English]

bride n. woman on her wedding day and during the period just before and after it. [Old English]

bridegroom n. man on his wedding day and during the period just before it. [Old English]

bridesmaid n. girl or unmarried woman attending a bride at her wedding.

bridge[1] —n. **1 a** a structure providing a way across a river, road, railway, etc. **b** thing joining or connecting. **2** operational superstructure on a ship. **3** upper bony part of the nose. **4** piece of wood on a violin etc. over which the strings are stretched. **5** = BRIDGEWORK. —v. (**-ging**) **1** be or make a bridge over. **2** reduce (a gap, deficiency, etc.). [Old English]

bridge[2] n. card-game derived from whist. [origin unknown]

bridgehead n. fortified position held on the enemy's side of a river etc.

bridging loan n. loan to cover the interval between buying a house etc. and selling another.

bridle /ˈbraɪd(ə)l/ —n. **1** headgear for controlling a horse, including reins and bit. **2** restraining thing. —v. (**-ling**) **1** put a bridle on. **2** curb, restrain. **3** (often foll. by *up*) express anger, offence, etc., esp. by throwing up the head and drawing in the chin. [Old English]

bridle-path n. (also **bridle-way**) rough path for riders or walkers.

Brie /briː/ n. a kind of soft cheese. [*Brie* in N. France]

brief —adj. **1** of short duration. **2** concise; abrupt, brusque. **3** scanty (*brief skirt*). —n. **1** (in pl.) short pants. **2 a** summary of a case drawn up for counsel. **b** piece of work for a barrister. **3** instructions for a task **4** papal letter on discipline. —v. **1** instruct (a barrister) by brief. **2** inform or instruct in advance. □ **hold a brief for** argue in favour of, **in brief** to sum up. □ **briefly** adv. **briefness** n. [Latin *brevis* short]

briefcase n. flat document case.

brier[1] /ˈbraɪə(r)/ n. (also **briar**) wild rose or other prickly bush. [Old English]

brier[2] /ˈbraɪə(r)/ n. (also **briar**) **1** white heath of S. Europe. **2** tobacco pipe made from its root. [French *bruyère*]

Brig. *abbr.* Brigadier.

brig[1] n. two-masted square-rigged ship. [abbreviation of BRIGANTINE]

brig[2] n. *Scot. & N.Engl.* bridge. [var. of BRIDGE[1]]

brigade /brɪˈɡeɪd/ n. **1** military unit, usu. three battalions, as part of a division. **2** group organized for a special purpose. [Italian *briga* strife]

brigadier /brɪɡəˈdɪə(r)/ n. **1** officer commanding a brigade. **2** staff officer of similar standing.

brigand /ˈbrɪɡənd/ n. member of a robber band; bandit. □ **brigandage** n. [Italian *brigante*: related to BRIGADE]

brigantine /ˈbrɪɡəntiːn/ n. two-masted ship with a square-rigged foremast and a fore-and-aft rigged mainmast. [French or Italian: related to BRIGAND]

bright /braɪt/ —adj. **1** emitting or reflecting much light; shining. **2** intense, vivid. **3** clever. **4** cheerful. —adv. esp. *poet.* brightly. □ **brightly** adv. **brightness** n. [Old English]

brighten v. make or become brighter.

Bright's disease /braɪts/ n. kidney disease. [*Bright*, name of a physician]

brill[1] n. (pl. same) European flat-fish. [origin unknown]

brill[2] adj. *colloq.* = BRILLIANT adj. 4. [abbreviation]

brilliant /ˈbrɪljənt/ —adj. **1** very bright; sparkling. **2** *colloq.* outstandingly talented. **3** showy. **4** *colloq.* excellent. —n. diamond of the finest cut with many facets. □ **brilliance** n. **brilliantly** adv. [French *briller* shine, from Italian]

brilliantine /ˈbrɪljəntiːn/ n. dressing for making the hair glossy. [French: related to BRILLIANT]

brim —n. **1** edge or lip of a vessel. **2** projecting edge of a hat. —v. (**-mm-**) fill or be full to the brim. □ **brim over** overflow. [origin unknown]

brim-full adj. (also **brimful**) filled to the brim.

brimstone n. *archaic* sulphur. [from BURN[1] STONE]

brindled /ˈbrɪnd(ə)ld/ adj. (esp. of domestic animals) brown or tawny with streaks of another colour.- [Scandinavian]

brine n. **1** water saturated or strongly impregnated with salt. **2** sea water. [Old English]

bring v. (*past* and *past part.* **brought** /brɔːt/) **1** come carrying; lead, accompany; convey. **2** cause or result in (*war brings misery*). **3** be sold for; produce as income. **4 a** prefer (a charge), **b** initiate (legal action). **5** cause to become or to

reach a state (*brings me alive*; *cannot bring myself to agree*). **6** adduce (evidence, an argument, etc.). □ **bring about** cause to happen. **bring back** call to mind. **bring down 1** cause to fall. **2** lower (a price). **bring forth 1** give birth to. **2** cause. **bring forward 1** move to an earlier time. **2** transfer from the previous page or account. **3** draw attention to. **bring home to** cause to realize fully. **bring the house down** receive rapturous applause. **bring in 1** introduce. **2** yield as income or profit. **bring off** achieve successfully. **bring on** cause to happen, appear, or make progress. **bring out 1** emphasize; make evident. **2** publish. **bring over** convert to one's own side. **bring round 1** restore to consciousness. **2** persuade. **bring through** aid (a person) through adversity, esp. illness. **bring to** restore to consciousness (*brought him to*). **bring up 1** rear (a child). **2** vomit. **3** call attention to. **4** (*absol.*) stop suddenly. [Old English]

bring-and-buy sale *n.* charity sale at which people bring items for sale and buy those brought by others.

brink *n.* **1** extreme edge of land before a precipice, river, etc. **2** furthest point before danger, discovery, etc. □ **on the brink of** about to experience or suffer; in imminent danger of. [Old Norse]

brinkmanship *n.* pursuit (esp. habitual) of danger etc. to the brink of catastrophe.

briny —*adj.* (-ier, -iest) of brine or the sea; salty. —*n.* (prec. by *the*) *slang* the sea.

briquette /brɪˈket/ *n.* block of compressed coal-dust as fuel. [French diminutive: related to BRICK]

brisk —*adj.* **1** quick, lively, keen (*brisk pace, trade*). **2** enlivening (*brisk wind*). —*v.* (often foll. by *up*) make or grow brisk. □ **briskly** *adv.* **briskness** *n.* [probably French BRUSQUE]

brisket /ˈbrɪskɪt/ *n.* animal's breast, esp. as a joint of meat. [French]

brisling /ˈbrɪzlɪŋ/ *n.* small herring or sprat. [Norwegian and Danish]

bristle /ˈbrɪs(ə)l/ —*n.* short stiff hair, esp. one on an animal's back, used in brushes. —*v.* (-ling) **1 a** (of hair) stand upright. **b** make (hair) do this. **2** show irritation. **3** (usu. foll. by *with*) be covered or abundant (in). □ **bristly** *adj.* (-ier, -iest). [Old English]

Brit *n. colloq.* British person. [abbreviation]

Britannia /brɪˈtænjə/ *n.* personification of Britain, esp. as a helmeted woman with shield and trident. [Latin]

Britannia metal *n.* silvery alloy of tin, antimony, and copper.

Britannic /brɪˈtænɪk/ *adj.* (esp. in His or Her Britannic Majesty) of Britain.

Briticism /ˈbrɪtɪsɪz(ə)m/ *n.* idiom used only in Britain. [after *Gallicism*]

British /ˈbrɪtɪʃ/ *adj.* of Great Britain, the British Commonwealth, or their people. —*n.* (prec. by *the*; treated as *pl.*) the British people. [Old English]

British English *n.* English as used in Great Britain.

British Legion *n.* = ROYAL BRITISH LEGION.

British summer time *n.* = SUMMER TIME.

British thermal unit *n.* amount of heat needed to raise 1 lb of water through one degree Fahrenheit, equivalent to 1.055×10^3 joules.

Briton /ˈbrɪt(ə)n/ *n.* **1** inhabitant of S. Britain before the Roman conquest. **2** native or inhabitant of Great Britain. [Latin *Britto-onis*]

brittle /ˈbrɪt(ə)l/ *adj.* hard and fragile; apt to break. □ **brittlely** *adv.* (also **brittly**). [Old English]

brittle-bone disease *n.* = OSTEOPOROSIS.

broach —*v.* **1** raise for discussion. **2** pierce (a cask) to draw liquor. **3** open and start using. —*n.* **1** bit for boring. **2** roasting-spit. [Latin *broccus* projecting]

broad /brɔːd/ —*adj.* **1** large in extent from one side to the other; wide. **2** in breadth (*two metres broad*). **3** extensive (*broad acres*). **4** full and clear (*broad daylight*). **5** explicit (*broad hint*). **6** general (*broad intentions, facts*). **7** tolerant, liberal (*broad view*). **8** coarse (*broad humour*). **9** markedly regional (*broad Scots*). —*n.* **1** broad part (*broad of the back*). **2** US *slang* woman. **3** (**the Broads**) large areas of water in E. Anglia, formed where rivers widen. □ **broadly** *adv.* **broadness** *n.* [Old English]

broad bean *n.* **1** bean with large edible flat seeds. **2** one such seed.

broadcast —*v.* (*past* and *past part.* **broadcast**) **1** transmit by radio or television. **2** take part in such a transmission. **3** scatter (seed etc.). **4** disseminate (information) widely. —*n.* radio or television programme or transmission. □ **broadcaster** *n.* **broadcasting** *n.*

broadcloth *n.* fine cloth of wool, cotton, or silk.

broaden *v.* make or become broader.

broad gauge *n.* railway track with a wider than standard gauge.

broad-leaved *adj.* (of a tree) deciduous and hard-timbered.

broadloom *adj.* (esp. of carpet) woven in broad widths.

broad-minded *adj.* tolerant, liberal.

broadsheet *n.* 1 large-sized newspaper. 2 large sheet of paper printed on one side only.

broadside *n.* 1 vigorous verbal attack. 2 simultaneous firing of all guns from one side of a ship. 3 side of a ship above the water between the bow and quarter. □ **broadside on** sideways on.

broadsword *n.* broad-bladed sword, for cutting rather than thrusting.

brocade /brə'keɪd/ —*n.* rich fabric woven with a raised pattern. —*v.* (-**ding**) weave in this way. [Italian *broccato* twisted thread]

broccoli /'brɒkəlɪ/ *n.* brassica with greenish flower-heads. [Italian]

brochure /'brəʊʃə(r)/ *n.* pamphlet or booklet, esp. with descriptive information. [French *brocher* stitch]

broderie anglaise /ˌbrəʊdərɪ ɑ̃'gleɪz/ *n.* open embroidery on white linen etc. [French, = English embroidery]

brogue[1] /brəʊg/ *n.* 1 strong outdoor shoe with ornamental perforations. 2 rough shoe of untanned leather. [Gaelic and Irish *brōg* from Old Norse]

brogue[2] /brəʊg/ *n.* marked accent, esp. Irish. [perhaps related to BROGUE[1]]

broil[1] *v.* esp. *US* 1 grill (meat). 2 make or become very hot, esp. from the sun. [French *bruler* burn]

broil[2] *n.* young chicken for broiling or roasting.

broke *past* of BREAK. *predic. adj. colloq.* having no money.

broken *past part.* of BREAK. —*adj.* 1 having been broken. 2 reduced to despair; beaten. 3 (of language) badly spoken, esp. by a foreigner. 4 interrupted (*broken sleep*).

broken-down *adj.* 1 worn out by age, use, etc. 2 not functioning.

broken-hearted *adj.* overwhelmed with grief.

broken home *n.* family disrupted by divorce or separation.

broker *n.* 1 agent; middleman. 2 member of the Stock Exchange dealing in stocks and shares. 3 official appointed to sell or appraise distrained goods. □ **broking** *n.* [Anglo-French]

■ **Usage** In sense 2, brokers have officially been called *broker-dealers* in the UK since Oct. 1986, and entitled to act as agents and principals in share dealings.

brokerage *n.* broker's fee or commission.

brolly /'brɒlɪ/ *n.* (*pl.* -**ies**) *colloq.* umbrella. [abbreviation]

---

bromide /'brəʊmaɪd/ *n.* 1 any binary compound of bromine. 2 trite remark. 3 reproduction or proof on paper coated with silver bromide emulsion. [Greek *brōmos* stink]

bromine /'brəʊmiːn/ *n.* poisonous liquid element with a choking smell. [Greek *brōmos* stink]

bronchi *pl.* of BRONCHUS.

bronchial /'brɒŋkɪəl/ *adj.* of the bronchi (see BRONCHUS) or of the smaller tubes into which they divide.

bronchitis /brɒŋ'kaɪtɪs/ *n.* inflammation of the mucous membrane in the bronchial tubes.

bronchus /'brɒŋkəs/ *n.* (*pl.* -**chi** /-kaɪ/) either of the two main divisions of the windpipe. [Latin from Greek]

bronco /'brɒŋkəʊ/ *n.* (*pl.* -**s**) wild or half-tamed horse of the western US. [Spanish, = rough]

brontosaurus /ˌbrɒntə'sɔːrəs/ *n.* (*pl.* -**ruses**) large plant-eating dinosaur with a long whiplike tail. [Greek *thunder*, *sauros* lizard]

bronze —*n.* 1 alloy of copper and tin. 2 its brownish colour. 3 thing of bronze, esp. a sculpture. —*adj.* made of or coloured like bronze. —*v.* (-**zing**) make or become brown; tan. [French from Italian]

Bronze Age *n.* Archaeol. period when weapons and tools were usu. made of bronze.

bronze medal *n.* medal, usu. awarded as third prize.

brooch /brəʊtʃ/ *n.* ornamental hinged pin. [French *broche*: related to BROACH]

brood —*n.* 1 young of esp. a bird born or hatched at one time. 2 *colloq.* children of a family. —*v.* 1 worry or ponder (esp. resentfully). 2 (of a bird) sit on eggs to hatch them. [Old English]

broody *adj.* (-**ier**, -**iest**) 1 (of a hen) wanting to brood. 2 sullenly thoughtful. 3 *colloq.* (of a woman) wanting pregnancy.

brook[1] /brʊk/ *n.* small stream. [Old English]

brook[2] /brʊk/ *v.* (usu. with *neg.*) *literary* tolerate, allow. [Old English]

broom *n.* 1 long-handled brush for sweeping. 2 shrub with bright yellow flowers. [Old English]

broomstick *n.* handle of a broom.

Bros. *abbr.* Brothers (esp. in the name of a firm).

broth *n.* thin soup of meat or fish stock. [Old English]

brothel /'brɒθ(ə)l/ *n.* premises for prostitution. [originally = worthless fellow, from Old English]

brother /'brʌðə(r)/ *n.* 1 man or boy in relation to his siblings. 2 close male friend or associate. 3 (*pl.* also **brethren**) a member of a male religious

order, esp. a monk. **b** fellow Christian etc. **4** fellow human being. □ **brotherly** *adj.* [Old English]

brother german see GERMAN.

brotherhood *n.* **1** relationship between brothers. **2** association of people with a common interest. **3** community of feeling between human beings.

brother-in-law *n.* (*pl.* **brothers-in-law**) **1** one's wife's or husband's brother. **2** one's sister's or sister-in-law's husband.

brought *past* and *past part.* of BRING.

brouhaha /ˈbruːhɑːhɑː/ *n.* commotion; sensation. [French]

brow /brau/ *n.* **1** forehead. **2** eyebrow. **3** summit of a hill etc. **4** edge of a cliff etc. [Old English]

browbeat *v.* (*past* **-beat**; *past part.* **-beaten**) intimidate, bully.

brown /braun/ —*adj.* **1** having the colour of dark wood or rich soil. **2** dark-skinned or suntanned **3** (of bread) made from wholemeal or wheatmeal flour. —*n.* **1** brown colour or pigment. **2** brown clothes or material. —*v.* make or become brown. □ **browned off** *colloq.* fed up, disheartened. □ **brownish** *adj.* [Old English]

brown bear *n.* large N. American brown bear.

brown coal *n.* = LIGNITE.

Brownie *n.* **1** (in full **Brownie Guide**) junior Guide. **2** (**brownie**) small square of chocolate cake with nuts. **3** (**brownie**) benevolent elf.

Brownie point *n. colloq.* notional mark awarded for good conduct etc.

browning *n.* additive to colour gravy.

brown owl *n.* **1** any of various owls, esp. the tawny owl. **2** (**Brown Owl**) adult leader of Brownie Guides.

brown rice *n.* unpolished rice.

brown sugar *n.* unrefined or partially refined sugar.

browse /brauz/ —*v.* (**-sing**) **1** read desultorily or look over goods for sale. **2** (often foll. by *on*) feed on leaves, twigs, etc. —*n.* **1** twigs, shoots, etc. as fodder. **2** act of browsing. [French *brost* bud]

brucellosis /bruːsɪˈləʊsɪs/ *n.* bacterial disease, esp. of cattle. [Sir D. *Bruce*, name of a physician]

bruise /bruːz/ —*v.* —*n.* **1** discoloration of the skin caused esp. by a blow. **2** similar damage on a fruit etc. —*v.* (**-sing**) **1 a** inflict a bruise on. **b** hurt mentally. **2** be susceptible to bruising. [originally = crush, from Old English]

bruiser *n. colloq.* **1** large tough-looking person. **2** professional boxer.

bruit /bruːt/ *v.* (often foll. by *abroad, about*) spread (a report or rumour). [French, = noise]

brunch *n.* combined breakfast and lunch. [portmanteau word]

brunette /bruːˈnet/ *n.* woman with dark brown hair. [French diminutive]

brunt *n.* chief impact of an attack, task, etc. (esp. *bear the brunt of*). [origin unknown]

brush —*n.* **1** implement with bristles, hair, wire, etc. set into a block, for cleaning, painting, arranging the hair, etc. **2** act of brushing. **3** (usu. foll. by *with*) short esp. unpleasant encounter. **4** fox's bushy tail. **5** piece of carbon or metal as an electrical contact esp. with a moving part. **6** = BRUSHWOOD 2. —*v.* **1** sweep, scrub, treat, or tidy with a brush. **2** remove or apply with a brush. **3** graze in passing. □ **brush aside** dismiss curtly or lightly. **brush off** dismiss abruptly. **brush up 1** clean up or smarten. **2** revise (a subject). [French]

brush-off *n.* abrupt dismissal.

brush-up *n.* act of brushing up.

brushwood *n.* **1** undergrowth, thicket. **2** cut or broken twigs etc.

brushwork *n.* **1** use of the brush in painting. **2** painter's style in this.

brusque /brusk/ *adj.* abrupt or offhand. □ **brusquely** *adv.* **brusqueness** *n.* [Italian *brusco* sour]

Brussels sprout /ˈbrasəlz/ *n.* **1** brassica with small cabbage-like buds on a stem. **2** such a bud. [*Brussels* in Belgium]

brutal /ˈbruːt(ə)l/ *adj.* **1** savagely cruel. **2** harsh, merciless. □ **brutality** /-ˈtælɪtɪ/ *n.* (*pl.* **-ies**). **brutally** *adv.* [French: related to BRUTE]

brutalize /ˈbruːtə‚laɪz/ *v.* (also **-ise**) (**-zing** or **-sing**) **1** make brutal. **2** treat brutally.

brute /bruːt/ —*n.* **1 a** brutal or violent person. **b** *colloq.* unpleasant person or difficult thing. **2** animal. —*attrib. adj.* **1** unthinking (*brute force*). **2** cruel; stupid; sensual. □ **brutish** *adj.* **brutishly** *adv.* **brutishness** *n.* [Latin *brutus* stupid]

bryony /ˈbraɪənɪ/ *n.* (*pl.* **-ies**) climbing plant with red berries. [Latin from Greek]

BS *abbr.* **1** Bachelor of Surgery. **2** British Standard(s).

B.Sc. *abbr.* Bachelor of Science.

BSE *abbr.* bovine spongiform encephalopathy, a usu. fatal cattle disease.

BSI *abbr.* British Standards Institution.

BST *abbr.* **1** British Summer Time. **2** bovine somatotrophin, a growth hormone added to cattle-feed to boost milk production.

BT *abbr.* British Telecom.

Bt. *abbr.* Baronet.

B.th.u. *abbr.* (also **B.t.u.,** **BTU,** **B.Th.U.**) British thermal unit(s).

bubble /ˈbʌb(ə)l/ —*n.* **1 a** a thin sphere of liquid enclosing air etc. **b** air-filled cavity in a liquid or solidified liquid. **2** transparent domed canopy. **3** visionary or unrealistic project. —*v.* (**-ling**) **1** rise in or send up bubbles. **2** make the sound of boiling. □ **bubble over** (often foll. by *with*) be exuberant. [imitative]

bubble and squeak *n.* cooked cabbage etc. fried with cooked potatoes.

bubble bath *n.* foaming preparation for adding to bath water.

bubble car *n.* small domed car.

bubble gum *n.* chewing-gum that can be blown into bubbles.

bubbly —*adj.* (**-ier, -iest**) **1** having or like bubbles. **2** exuberant. —*n. colloq.* champagne.

bubo /ˈbjuːbəʊ/ *n.* (*pl.* **-es**) inflamed swelling in the armpit or groin. [Greek *boubōn* groin]

bubonic plague /bjuːˈbɒnɪk/ *n.* contagious disease with buboes.

buccaneer /bʌkəˈnɪə/ *n.* **1** pirate. **2** unscrupulous adventurer. □ **buccaneering** *n. & adj.* [French]

buck¹ —*n.* **1** male deer, hare, rabbit, etc. **2** *archaic* dandy. **3** (*attrib.*) *slang* male. —*v.* **1** (of a horse) jump upwards with its back arched. **2** (usu. foll. by *off*) throw (a rider) in this way. **3** (usu. foll. by *up*) *colloq.* **a** cheer up. **b** hurry up. make an effort. [Old English]

buck² *n. US slang* dollar. [origin unknown]

buck³ *n. slang* (in poker) article placed before the next dealer. □ **pass the buck** *colloq.* shift responsibility (to another). [origin unknown]

bucket /ˈbʌkɪt/ —*n.* **1 a** a round open container with a handle, for carrying or drawing water etc. **b** amount contained in this. **2** (in *pl.*) *colloq.* large quantities. esp. of rain or tears. **3** scoop in a wheel, dredger, etc. —*v.* (**-t-**) *colloq.* **1** (often foll. by *down*) (esp. of rain) pour heavily. **2** (often foll. by *along*) move or drive fast or bumpily. [Anglo-French]

bucket seat *n.* seat with a rounded back for one person, esp. in a car.

bucket-shop *n.* **1** unregistered broking agency. **2** *colloq.* travel agency specializing in cheap air tickets.

buckle /ˈbʌk(ə)l/ —*n.* clasp with a hinged pin for securing a belt, strap, etc. —*v.* (**-ling**) **1** (often foll. by *up, on,* etc.) fasten with a buckle. **2** (often foll. by *up*) (cause to) crumple under pressure. □ **buckle down** make a determined effort. [Latin *buccula* cheek-strap]

buckler *n. hist.* small round shield. [French]

buckram /ˈbʌkrəm/ *n.* coarse linen etc. stiffened with paste etc. [French *boquerant*]

Buck's Fizz *n.* cocktail of champagne and orange juice. [*Buck's Club* in London]

buckshee /bʌkˈʃiː/ *adj. & adv. slang* free of charge. [corruption of BAKSHEESH]

buckshot *n.* coarse lead shot.

buckskin *n.* **1** leather from a buck's skin. **2** thick smooth cotton or woollen cloth.

buckthorn *n.* thorny shrub with berries formerly used as a purgative.

buck-tooth *n.* upper projecting tooth.

buckwheat *n.* seed of a plant related to rhubarb, used to make flour, or as an alternative to rice. [Dutch = beech-wheat]

bucolic /bjuːˈkɒlɪk/ —*adj.* of shepherds; rustic; pastoral. —*n.* (usu. in *pl.*) pastoral poem or poetry. [Greek *boukolos* herdsman]

bud —*n.* **1 a** knoblike shoot from which a stem, leaf, or flower develops. **b** flower or leaf not fully open. **2** asexual outgrowth from an organism separating to form a new individual. —*v.* (**-dd-**) **1** form buds. **2** begin to grow or develop (*budding artist*). **3** graft a bud of (a plant) on to another. [origin unknown]

Buddha /ˈbʊdə/ *n.* **1** title of the Indian philosopher Gautama (5th c. BC) and his successors. **2** sculpture etc. of Buddha. [Sanskrit, = enlightened]

Buddhism /ˈbʊdɪz(ə)m/ *n.* Asian religion or philosophy founded by Gautama Buddha. □ **Buddhist** *n. & adj.*

buddleia /ˈbʌdlɪə/ *n.* shrub with fragrant flowers attractive to butterflies. [*Buddle,* name of a botanist]

buddy /ˈbʌdɪ/ *n.* (*pl.* **-ies**) esp. *US colloq.* friend or mate. [perhaps from BROTHER]

budge *v.* (**-ging**) (usu. with *neg.*) **1** move slightly. **2** (cause to) change an opinion. □ **budge up** (or **over**) make room for another person by moving. [French *bouger*]

budgerigar /ˈbʌdʒərɪgɑː(r)/ *n.* small parrot, often kept as a cage-bird. [Aboriginal]

budget /ˈbʌdʒɪt/ —*n.* **1** amount of money needed or available. **2 a** (**the Budget**) Government's annual estimate or plan of revenue and expenditure. **b** similar estimate by a company etc. **3** (*attrib.*) inexpensive. —*v.* (**-t-**) (often foll. by *for*) allow or arrange for in a budget. □ **budgetary** *adj.* [Latin *bulga* bag]

budgie /ˈbʌdʒɪ/ *n. colloq.* = BUDGERIGAR. [abbreviation]

buff —*adj.* of a yellowish beige colour (*buff envelope*). —*n.* **1** this colour. **2** (in *comb.*) *colloq.* enthusiast (*railway buff*). **3** velvety dull-yellow ox-leather. —*v.* **1**

buffalo /'bʌfələʊ/ n. (pl. same or -es) 1 wild ox of Africa or Asia. 2 N. American bison. [Greek *boubalos* ox]

buff n. 1 thing that deadens impact, esp. a device on a train or at the end of a track. 2 substance that maintains the constant acidity of a solution. 3 *Computing* temporary memory area or queue for data. [imitative]

buffer² n. *slang* silly or incompetent old man. [perhaps from BUFFER¹]

Buffer State n. small State between two larger ones, regarded as reducing friction.

buffet¹ /'bʊfeɪ/ n. 1 room or counter where refreshments are sold. 2 self-service meal of several dishes set out at once. 3 also /bʌfɪt/ sideboard or recessed cupboard. [French, = stool]

buffet² /'bʌfɪt/ —v. (-t-) 1 strike repeatedly. 2 contend with (waves etc.). —n. 1 blow, esp. of the hand. 2 shock. [French diminutive of *bufe* blow]

buffet car n. railway coach serving refreshments.

buffoon /bə'fuːn/ n. clownish or stupid person. □ **buffoonery** n. [Latin *buffo* clown]

bug —n. 1 a any of various insects with mouthparts modified for piercing and sucking. b esp. *US* small insect. 2 *slang* virus; infection. 3 *slang* concealed microphone. 4 *slang* error in a computer program or system etc. 5 *slang* obsession, enthusiasm, etc. —v. (-gg-) 1 *slang* conceal a microphone in. 2 *slang* annoy. [origin unknown]

bugbear /'bʌgbeə/ n. 1 cause of annoyance. 2 object of baseless fear. [*bug* = bogey]

bugger *coarse slang* —n. 1 a unpleasant or awkward person or thing. b person of a specified kind (*clever bugger!*). 2 person who commits buggery. —v. 1 as an exclamation of annoyance (*bugger it!*). b (often foll. by *up*) a ruin; spoil. b exhaust. 3 commit buggery with. —int. expressing annoyance. □ **bugger-all** nothing. **bugger about** (or **around**) (often foll. by *with*) mess about. **bugger off** (often in *imper.*) go away. [Latin *Bulgarus* Bulgarian heretic]

buggery n. 1 anal intercourse. 2 = BESTIALITY 2.

buggy /'bʌgɪ/ n. (pl. -ies) 1 small, sturdy, esp. open, motor vehicle. 2 lightweight push-chair. 3 light, horse-drawn vehicle for one or two people. [origin unknown]

bugle /'bjuːg(ə)l/ —n. brass military instrument like a small trumpet. —v.

(-ling) 1 sound a bugle. 2 sound (a call etc.) on a bugle. □ **bugler** n. [Latin *bucculus* young bull]

bugloss /'bjuːglɒs/ n. plant with bright blue tubular flowers, related to borage. [French *buglosse* from Greek, = ox-tongued]

build /bɪld/ —v. (*past* and *past part.* **built** /bɪlt/) 1 construct or cause to be constructed. 2 a (often foll. by *up*) establish or develop (*built the business up*). b (often foll. by *on*) base (hopes, theories, etc.). 3 (as **built** *adj.*) of specified build (*sturdily built*). —n. 1 physical proportions (*slim build*). 2 style of construction; make. □ **build in** incorporate. **build on** add (an extension etc.). **build up** 1 increase in size or strength. 2 praise; boost. 3 gradually become established. [Old English]

builder n. person who builds, esp. a building contractor.

building n. 1 permanent fixed structure e.g. a house, factory, or stable. 2 constructing of these.

building society n. public finance company paying interest to investors and lending capital for mortgages etc.

build-up n. 1 favourable advance publicity. 2 gradual approach to a climax. 3 accumulation or increase.

built *past* and *past part.* of BUILD.

built-in *adj.* integral.

built-up *adj.* 1 (of a locality) densely developed. 2 increased in height etc. by addition. 3 made of prefabricated parts.

bulb n. 1 a globular base of the stem of some plants, sending roots downwards and leaves upwards. b plant grown from this, e.g. a daffodil. 2 = LIGHT-BULB. 3 object or part shaped like a bulb. [Latin *bulbus* from Greek, = onion]

bulbous *adj.* bulb-shaped; fat or bulging.

bulge —n. 1 irregular swelling. 2 *colloq.* temporary increase (*baby bulge*). —v. (-ging) swell outwards. □ **bulgy** *adj.* [Latin *bulga* bag]

bulimia /bjuː'lɪmɪə/ n. (in full **bulimia nervosa**) disorder in which overeating alternates with self-induced vomiting, fasting, etc. [Greek *bous* ox, *limos* hunger]

bulk —n. 1 a size; magnitude (esp. large). b large mass, body, etc. c large quantity. 2 (treated as *pl.* & usu. prec. by *the*) greater part or number (*the bulk of the applicants are women*). 3 roughage. —v. 1 seem (in size or importance) (*bulks large*). 2 make (a book etc.) thicker etc. □ **in bulk** in large quantities. [Old Norse]

bulk buying n. buying in quantity at a discount.

bulkhead n. upright partition in a ship, aircraft, etc.

bulky adj. (-ier, -iest) awkwardly large. □ **bulkiness** n.

bull¹ /bʊl/ n. 1 a uncastrated male bovine animal. b male of the whale, elephant, etc. 2 (**the Bull**) zodiacal sign or constellation Taurus. 3 bull's-eye of a target. 4 person who buys shares hoping to sell them at a profit. □ **take the bull by the horns** face danger or a challenge boldly. □ **bullish** adj. [Old Norse]

bull² /bʊl/ n. papal edict. [Latin bulla seal]

bull³ /bʊl/ n. 1 slang a nonsense. b unnecessary routine tasks. [origin unknown] 2 absurdly illogical statement. [origin unknown]

bulldog n. 1 short-haired heavy-jowled sturdy dog. 2 tenacious and courageous person.

bulldog clip n. strong sprung clip for papers.

bulldoze v. (-zing) 1 clear with a bulldozer. 2 colloq. a intimidate. b make (one's way) forcibly.

bulldozer n. powerful tractor with a broad vertical blade at the front for clearing ground.

bullet /ˈbʊlɪt/ n. small pointed missile fired from a rifle, revolver, etc. [French diminutive of boule ball]

bulletin /ˈbʊlɪtɪn/ n. 1 short official news report. 2 society's regular list of information etc. [Italian diminutive: related to BULL²]

bulletproof adj. designed to protect from bullets.

bullfight n. public baiting, and usu. killing, of bulls. □ **bullfighter** n. **bullfighting** n.

bullfinch n. pink and black finch.

bullfrog n. large N. American frog with a booming croak.

bull-headed adj. obstinate, blundering.

bullion /ˈbʊljən/ n. gold or silver in bulk before coining, or valued by weight. [French: related to BOIL¹]

bullock /ˈbʊlək/ n. castrated male of domestic cattle. [Old English diminutive of BULL¹]

bullring n. arena for bullfights.

bull's-eye n. 1 centre of a target. 2 hard minty sweet. 3 hemispherical ship's window. 4 small circular window. 5 a hemispherical lens. b lantern with this. 6 boss of glass in a blown glass sheet.

bullshit coarse slang –n. (often as int.) nonsense; pretended knowledge. –v. (-tt-) talk nonsense or as if one has specialist knowledge (to). □ **bullshitter** n. [from BULL³]

bull-terrier n. cross between a bulldog and a terrier.

bully¹ /ˈbʊlɪ/ –n. (pl. -ies) person coercing others by fear. –v. (-ies, -ied) persecute or oppress by force or threats. –int. (foll. by for) often iron. expressing approval (bully for you). [Dutch]

bully² /ˈbʊlɪ/ (in full **bully off**) –n. (pl. -ies) start of play in hockey in which two opponents strike each other's sticks three times and then go for the ball. –v. (-ies, -ied) start play in this way. [origin unknown]

bully³ /ˈbʊlɪ/ n. (in full **bully beef**) corned beef. [French: related to BOIL¹]

bulrush /ˈbʊlrʌʃ/ n. 1 a kind of tall rush. 2 Bibl. papyrus. [perhaps from BULL¹ = coarse + RUSH²]

bulwark /ˈbʊlwək/ n. 1 defensive wall, esp. of earth. 2 protecting person or thing. 3 (usu. in pl.) ship's side above deck. [Low German or Dutch]

bum¹ n. slang buttocks. [origin uncertain]

bum² US slang –n. loafer or tramp; dissolute person. –v. (-mm-) 1 (often foll. by around) loaf or wander around. 2 cadge. –attrib. adj. of poor quality. [German Bummler loafer]

bum-bag n. slang small pouch worn on a belt round the waist or hips.

bumble /ˈbʌmb(ə)l/ v. (-ling) 1 (foll. by on) speak in a rambling way. 2 (often as **bumbling** adj.) be inept; blunder. [from BOOM¹]

bumble-bee n. large bee with a loud hum.

bumf n. colloq. usu. derog. papers, documents. [abbreviation of bum-fodder = toilet-paper]

bump –n. 1 dull-sounding blow or collision. 2 swelling or dent so caused. 3 uneven patch on a road etc. 4 prominence on the skull thought to indicate a mental faculty. –v. 1 a hit or come against with a bump. b (often foll. by against, into) collide. 2 (often foll. by against, on) hurt or damage by striking (bumped my head, the car). 3 (usu. foll. by along) move along with jolts. –adv. with a bump; suddenly; violently. □ **bump into** colloq. meet by chance. **bump off** slang murder. **bump up** colloq. increase (prices etc.). □ **bumpy** adj. (-ier, -iest). [imitative]

bumper n. 1 horizontal bar at the front or back of a motor vehicle, reducing damage in a collision. 2 (usu. attrib.) unusually large or fine example (bumper crop). 3 Cricket ball rising high after pitching. 4 brim-full glass.

bumper car n. = DODGEM.

bumpkin /ˈbʌmpkɪn/ n. rustic or socially inept person. [Dutch]

bumptious /'bʌmpʃəs/ adj. offensively self-assertive or conceited. [from BUMP, after *fractious*]

bun n. 1 small sweet bread roll or cake, often with dried fruit. 2 hair coiled and pinned to the head. [origin unknown]

bunch —n. 1 things gathered together. 2 collection; lot (*best of the bunch*). 3 *colloq.* group; gang. —v. 1 make into a bunch; gather into close folds. 2 form into a group or crowd. [origin unknown]

bundle /'bʌnd(ə)l/ —n. 1 things tied or fastened together. 2 set of nerves etc. 3 *slang* large amount of money. —v. (-ling) 1 (usu. foll. by *up*) tie or make into a bundle. 2 (usu. foll. by *out*, *off*, *away*, etc.) send away hurriedly. □ **be a bundle of nerves** (or *fun* etc.) be extremely nervous (or amusing etc.). **go a bundle on** *slang* admire; like. [Low German or Dutch]

bun fight n. *slang* tea party.

bung —n. stopper, esp. for a cask. —v. 1 stop with a bung. 2 *slang* throw. □ **bunged up** blocked up. [Dutch]

bungalow /'bʌŋgələʊ/ n. one-storeyed house. [Gujarati, = of Bengal]

bungee /'bʌndʒi/ n. (in full **bungee cord, rope**) elasticated cord or rope used for securing baggage or in bungee jumping.

bungee jumping n. sport of jumping from a height while secured by a bungee from the ankles or a harness.

bungle /'bʌŋg(ə)l/ —v. (-ling) 1 mismanage or fail at (a task). 2 work badly or clumsily. —n. bungled attempt or work. [imitative]

bunion /'bʌnjən/ n. swelling on the foot, esp. on the big toe. [French]

bunk[1] n. shelflike bed against a wall, esp. in a ship. [origin unknown]

bunk[2] *slang* —v. (often foll. by *off*) play truant (from). —n. (in **do a bunk**) leave or abscond hurriedly. [origin unknown]

bunk[3] n. *slang* nonsense, humbug. [shortening of BUNKUM]

bunk-bed n. each of two or more tiered beds forming a unit.

bunker n. 1 container for fuel. 2 reinforced underground shelter. 3 sandy hollow in a golf-course. [origin unknown]

bunkum /'bʌŋkəm/ n. nonsense, humbug. [*Buncombe* in US]

bunny /'bʌni/ n. (pl. -ies) 1 child's name for a rabbit. 2 (in full **bunny girl**) club hostess, waitress, etc., wearing rabbit ears and tail. [dial. *bun* rabbit]

Bunsen burner /'bʌns(ə)n/ n. small adjustable gas burner used in a laboratory. [*Bunsen*, name of a chemist]

bunting[1] /'bʌntɪŋ/ n. small bird related to the finches. [origin unknown]

bunting[2] /'bʌntɪŋ/ n. 1 flags and other decorations. 2 loosely-woven fabric for these. [origin unknown]

buoy /bɔɪ/ —n. 1 anchored float as a navigation mark etc. 2 lifebuoy. —v. 1 (usu. foll. by *up*) **a** keep afloat. **b** encourage, uplift. 2 (often foll. by *out*) mark with a buoy. [Dutch, perhaps from Latin *boia* collar]

buoyant /'bɔɪənt/ adj. 1 able or apt to keep afloat. 2 resilient; exuberant. □ **buoyancy** n. [French or Spanish: related to BUOY]

BUPA /'buːpə/ abbr. British United Provident Association, a private health insurance organization.

bur n. 1 **a** prickly clinging seed-case or flower-head. **b** any plant having these. 2 clinging person. 3 var. of BURR n. 2. [Scandinavian]

burble /'bɜːb(ə)l/ v. 1 talk ramblingly. 2 make a bubbling sound. [imitative]

burbot /'bɜːbət/ n. (pl. same) eel-like freshwater fish. [French]

burden /'bɜːd(ə)n/ —n. 1 load, esp. a heavy one. 2 oppressive duty, expense, emotion, etc. 3 bearing of loads (*beast of burden*). 4 **a** refrain of a song. **b** chief theme of a speech, book, etc. —v. load with a burden; oppress. □ **burdensome** adj. [Old English: related to BIRTH]

burden of proof n. obligation to prove one's case.

burdock /'bɜːdɒk/ n. plant with prickly flowers and docklike leaves. [from BUR, DOCK[1]]

bureau /'bjʊərəʊ/ n. (pl. -x or -s /-z/) 1 **a** desk with drawers and usu. an angled hinged top. **b** US chest of drawers. 2 **a** office or department for specific business. **b** government department. [French, originally = baize]

bureaucracy /bjʊə'rɒkrəsi/ n. (pl. -ies) 1 **a** government by central administration. **b** State etc. so governed. 2 government officials, esp. regarded as oppressive and inflexible. 3 conduct typical of these.

bureaucrat /'bjʊərəkræt/ n. 1 official in a bureaucracy. 2 inflexible administrator. □ **bureaucratic** /-'krætɪk/ adj. **bureaucratically** /-'krætɪkəli/ adv.

burette /bjʊə'ret/ n. (US **buret**) graduated glass tube with an end-tap for measuring liquid in chemical analysis. [French]

burgeon /'bɜːdʒ(ə)n/ v. *literary* grow rapidly; flourish. [Latin *burra* wool]

burger /'bɜːgə(r)/ n. *colloq.* hamburger. [abbreviation]

burgher /'bɜːgə(r)/ n. citizen of a Continental town. [German or Dutch]

burglar /ˈbɜːglə(r)/ *n.* person who commits burglary. [Anglo-French]

burglary *n.* (*pl.* -ies) 1 illegal entry with intent to commit theft, do bodily harm, or do damage. 2 instance of this.

■ **Usage** Before 1968 in English law, burglary was a crime under statute and common law; since 1968 it has been a statutory crime only; cf. HOUSEBREAKING.

burgle /ˈbɜːg(ə)l/ *v.* (-ling) commit burglary (on).

burgomaster /ˈbɜːgəmɑːstə(r)/ *n.* mayor of a Dutch or Flemish town. [Dutch]

burgundy /ˈbɜːgəndɪ/ *n.* (*pl.* -ies) 1 (also Burgundy) a red or white wine from Burgundy in E. France. b *hist.* similar wine from elsewhere. 2 dark red colour of this.

burial /ˈberɪəl/ *n.* 1 a burying of a corpse. b funeral. 2 *Archaeol.* grave or its remains.

burin /ˈbjʊərɪn/ *n.* 1 tool for engraving copper or wood. 2 *Archaeol.* chisel-pointed flint tool. [French]

burk var. of BERK.

burlesque /bɜːˈlesk/ —*n.* 1 a comic imitation, parody. b this as a genre. 2 *US* variety show, esp. with striptease. —*v.* (-ques, -qued, -quing) parody. [Italian *burla* mockery]

burly /ˈbɜːlɪ/ *adj.* (-ier, -iest) large and sturdy. [Old English]

burn¹ —*v.* (*past and past part.* burnt or burned) 1 (cause to) be consumed or destroyed by fire. 2 blaze or glow with fire. 3 (cause to) be injured or damaged by fire, heat, radiation, acid, etc. 4 use or be used as fuel, etc. 5 char in cooking. 6 produce (a hole, mark, etc.) by fire or heat. 7 a heat (clay, chalk, etc.). b harden (bricks) by fire. 8 colour, tan, or parch with heat or light. 9 (be) put to death by fire. 10 cauterize, brand. 11 make, be, or feel hot, esp. painfully. 12 (often foll. by *with*) (cause to) feel great emotion or passion (*burn with shame*). 13 *slang* drive fast. —*n.* mark or injury caused by burning. □ **burn one's boats** (or **bridges**) commit oneself irrevocably. **burn the candle at both ends** work etc. excessively. **burn down** be or destroyed or destroy by burning. **burn one's fingers** suffer for meddling or rashness. **burn the midnight oil** read or work late. **burn out 1** be reduced to nothing by burning. 2 (cause to) fail by burning. 3 (usu. *refl.*) suffer exhaustion. **burn up 1** get rid of by fire. 2 begin to blaze. [Old English]

burn² *n. Scot.* brook. [Old English]

burner *n.* part of a gas cooker, lamp, etc. that emits the flame.

burning *adj.* 1 ardent, intense. 2 hotly discussed, vital, urgent.

burning-glass *n.* lens for concentrating the sun's rays to produce a flame.

burnish /ˈbɜːnɪʃ/ *v.* polish by rubbing. [French *brunir* from *brun* brown]

burnous /bɜːˈnuːs/ *n.* Arab or Moorish hooded cloak. [Arabic from Greek]

burn-out *n.* exhaustion. □ **burnt-out** *adj.*

burnt see BURN¹.

burnt ochre *n.* (also **burnt sienna** or **burnt umber**) pigment darkened by burning.

burnt offering *n.* offering burnt on an altar as a sacrifice.

burp *colloq.* —*v.* 1 belch. 2 make (a baby) belch. —*n.* belch. [imitative]

burr —*n.* 1 a whirring sound. b rough sounding of the letter *r*. 2 (also **bur**) a rough edge on metal or paper. b surgeon's or dentist's small drill. 3 var. of BUR 1, 2. —*v.* make a burr. [imitative]

burrow /ˈbʌrəʊ/ —*n.* hole or tunnel dug by a rabbit etc. as a dwelling or shelter. —*v.* 1 make a burrow. 2 make (a hole, etc.) by digging. 3 (foll. by *into*) investigate, search. [apparently var. of BOROUGH]

bursar /ˈbɜːsə(r)/ *n.* treasurer, esp. of a college. 2 holder of a bursary. [medieval Latin *bursarius* from *bursa* purse]

bursary *n.* (*pl.* -ies) grant, esp. a scholarship. [medieval Latin: related to BURSAR]

burst —*v.* (*past and past part.* burst) 1 (cause to) break violently apart, open forcibly from within. 2 a (usu. foll. by *in*, *out*) make one's way suddenly or by force. b break away from or through (*river burst its banks*). 3 be full to overflowing. 4 appear or come suddenly (*burst into flame*). 5 foll. by *into*) suddenly begin to shed tears) or utter. 6 seem about to burst from effort, excitement, etc. —*n.* 1 act of bursting. 2 sudden issue or outbreak (*burst of flame*, *burst of applause*). 3 sudden effort, spurt. □ **burst out 1** suddenly begin (*burst out laughing*). 2 exclaim. [Old English]

burton /ˈbɜːt(ə)n/ *n.* □ **go for a burton** *slang* be lost, destroyed, or killed. [origin uncertain]

bury /ˈberɪ/ *v.* (-ies, -ied) 1 place (a corpse) in the earth, a tomb, or the sea. 2 lose by death (*buried two sons*). 3 a put or hide under ground. b cover up; conceal. 4 consign to obscurity; forget. 5 (*refl.* or *passive*) involve deeply (*buried in a book*). □ **bury the hatchet** cease to quarrel. [Old English]

bus —*n.* (*pl.* **buses** or *US* **busses**) **1** large esp. public passenger vehicle, usu. travelling a fixed route. **2** *colloq.* car, aeroplane, etc. —*v.* (**buses** or **busses**, **bused**, **bussing**) **1** go by bus. **2** *US* transport by bus, esp. to aid racial integration. [abbreviation of OMNIBUS]

busby /ˈbʌzbi/ *n.* (*pl.* **-ies**) tall fur hat worn by hussars etc. [origin unknown]

bush[1] /bʊʃ/ *n.* **1** shrub or clump of shrubs. **2** thing like a bush, esp. a clump of hair. **3** (esp. in Australia and Africa) uncultivated area, woodland or forest. [Old English and Old Norse]

bush[2] /bʊʃ/ —*n.* **1** metal lining for a hole enclosing a revolving shaft etc. **2** sleeve giving electrical insulation. —*v.* fit with a bush. [Dutch *busse* box]

bush-baby *n.* (*pl.* **-ies**) small African lemur.

bushed *adj. colloq.* tired out.

bushel /ˈbʊʃ(ə)l/ *n.* measure of capacity for corn, fruit, etc. (8 gallons or 36.4 litres). [French]

bushfire *n.* forest or scrub fire often spreading widely.

bushman *n.* **1** traveller or dweller in the Australian bush. **2** (**Bushman**) member or language of a S.African aboriginal people.

bush telegraph *n.* rapid spreading of information, rumour, etc.

bushy *adj.* (**-ier**, **-iest**) **1** growing thickly like a bush. **2** having many bushes.

business /ˈbɪznɪs/ *n.* **1** one's regular occupation or profession. **2** one's own concern. **3** task or duty. **4** serious work or activity. **5** (difficult or unpleasant) matter or affair. **6** thing(s) needing attention or discussion. **7** buying and selling; trade. **8** commercial firm. □ **mind one's own business** not meddle. [Old English: related to BUSY]

businesslike *adj.* efficient, systematic.

businessman *n.* (*fem.* **businesswoman**) man or woman engaged in trade or commerce.

business park *n.* area designed for commerce and light industry.

business person *n.* businessman or businesswoman.

busk *v.* perform esp. music in the street etc. for tips. □ **busker** *n.* [obsolete *busk* peddle]

bus lane *n.* part of a road mainly for use by buses.

busman *n.* bus driver.

busman's holiday *n.* holiday spent in an activity similar to one's regular work.

bus shelter *n.* shelter beside a bus-stop.

bus station *n.* centre where buses depart and arrive.

bus-stop *n.* **1** regular stopping-place of a bus. **2** sign marking this.

bust[1] *n.* **1** human chest, esp. of a woman; bosom. **2** sculpture of a person's head, shoulders, and chest. □ **busty** *adj.* (**-ier**, **-iest**). [French from Italian]

bust[2] —*v.* (*past* and *past part.* **busted** or **bust**) *colloq.* **1** break, burst. **2** a raid, search, & arrest. —*adj.* (also **busted**) **1** broken, burst. **2** bankrupt. □ **bust up 1** collapse. **2** (esp. of a married couple) separate. [var. of BURST]

bustard /ˈbʌstəd/ *n.* large land bird that can run very fast. [Latin *avis tarda* slow bird ('slow' unexplained)]

buster *n.* esp. *US slang* mate; fellow. [from BUST[1]]

bustier /ˈbʌstɪˌeɪ/ *n.* strapless close-fitting bodice. [French]

bustle[1] /ˈbʌs(ə)l/ —*v.* (**-ling**) **1** (often foll. by *about*) (cause to) move busily and energetically. **2** (as **bustling** *adj.*) active, lively. —*n.* excited or energetic activity. [perhaps from obsolete *busk* prepare]

bustle[2] /ˈbʌs(ə)l/ *n. hist.* padding worn under a skirt to puff it out behind. [origin unknown]

bust-up *n.* **1** quarrel. **2** collapse.

busy /ˈbɪzi/ —*adj.* (**-ier**, **-iest**) **1** occupied or engaged in work etc. **2** full of activity; fussy (*busy evening, street; busy design*). **3** esp. *US* (of a telephone line) engaged. —*v.* (**-ies**, **-ied**) (often *refl.*) keep busy; occupy. □ **busily** *adv.* [Old English]

busybody *n.* (*pl.* **-ies**) meddlesome person.

busy Lizzie *n.* plant with abundant esp. red, pink, or white flowers.

but /bʌt, bət/ —*conj.* **1 a** nevertheless, however (*tried but failed*). **b** on the other hand; on the contrary (*I am old but you are young*). **2** except, otherwise than (*cannot choose but do it; what could we do but run?*). **3** without the result that (*it never rains but it pours*). —*prep.* except; apart from; other than (*all cried but me; nothing but trouble*). —*adv.* **1** only; no more than; only just (*we can but try; is but a child; had but arrived*). **2** in emphatic repetition; definitely (*would see nobody, but nobody*). —*rel. pron.* who not; that not (*not a man but feels pity*). —*n.* objection (*ifs and buts*). □ **but for** without the help or hindrance etc. of (*but for you I'd be rich*). **but one** (or two etc.) excluding one (or two) from the number (*next door but one; last but one*). **but then** however (*I won, but then I am older*). [Old English]

butane /'bju:teɪn/ n. gaseous alkane hydrocarbon, used in liquefied form as fuel. [from BUTYL]

butch /butʃ/ adj. slang masculine; tough-looking. [origin uncertain]

butcher /'butʃ(ə)r/ —n. 1 a person who deals in meat. b slaughterer. 2 brutal murderer. —v. 1 slaughter or cut up (an animal) for food. 2 kill wantonly or cruelly. 3 colloq. ruin through incompetence. [French from BUCK']

butchery n. (pl. -ies) 1 needless or cruel slaughter (of people). 2 butcher's trade.

butler n. principal manservant of a household. [French bouteille bottle]

butt¹ —v. 1 push or strike with the head or horns. 2 (cause to) meet edge to edge. □ **butt in** interrupt, meddle. [French from Germanic]

butt² n. (often foll. by of) object of ridicule etc. 2 a mound behind a target. b (in pl.) shooting-range. [French but goal]

butt³ —n. 1 thicker end, esp. of a tool or weapon. 2 stub of a cigarette etc. 3 esp. US slang buttocks. [Dutch]

butt⁴ n. cask. [Latin buttis]

butter —n. 1 solidified churned cream, used as a spread and in cooking. 2 substance of similar texture (peanut butter). —v. spread, cook, or serve with butter. □ **butter up** colloq. flatter. [Greek bouturon]

butter-bean n. 1 flat, dried, white lima bean. 2 yellow-podded bean.

butter-cream n. mixture of butter, icing sugar, etc., as a filling etc. for a cake.

buttercup n. wild plant with yellow cup-shaped flowers.

butterfat n. essential fats of pure butter.

butter-fingers n. colloq. person prone to drop things.

butterfly n. (pl. -flies) 1 insect with four usu. brightly coloured wings. 2 (in pl.) colloq. nervous sensation in the stomach.

butterfly nut n. a kind of wing-nut.

butterfly stroke n. stroke in swimming, with arms raised and lifted forwards together.

butter-icing n. = BUTTER-CREAM.

buttermilk n. liquid left after churning butter.

butter muslin n. thin loosely-woven cloth, orig. for wrapping butter.

butterscotch n. brittle toffee made from butter, brown sugar, etc.

buttery¹ /'bʌtəri/ n. (pl. -ies) food store, esp. in a college; snack-bar etc. [related to BUTT⁴]

buttery² adj. like or containing butter.

buttock /'bʌtək/ n. 1 each of the two fleshy protuberances at the rear of the human trunk. 2 corresponding part of an animal. [butt ridge]

button /'bʌt(ə)n/ —n. 1 small disc etc. sewn to a garment as a fastener or worn as an ornament. 2 small round knob etc. pressed to operate electronic equipment. —v. = button up 1 fasten with buttons. 2 colloq. complete satisfactorily. 3 colloq. be silent. [French from Germanic]

buttonhole —n. 1 slit in cloth for a button. 2 flower etc. worn in a lapel buttonhole. —v. (-ling) colloq. accost and detain (a reluctant listener).

button mushroom n. young unopened mushroom. [French from Germanic]

buttress /'bʌtrɪs/ —n. 1 projecting support built against a wall. 2 source of help or support. —v. (often foll. by up) 1 support with a buttress. 2 support by argument etc. (buttressed by facts; [related to BUTT']

butty /'bʌtɪ/ n. (pl. -ies) N.Engl. sandwich. [from BUTTER]

butyl /'bju:taɪl/ n. the univalent alkyl radical C_4H_9. [Latin butyrum BUTTER]

buxom /'bʌksəm/ adj. (esp. of a woman) plump and rosy, busty. [earlier = pliant; related to BOW²]

buy /baɪ/ —v. (buys, buying; past and past part. bought /bɔːt/) 1 a obtain for money etc. b serve to obtain (money can't buy happiness; the best that money can buy). 2 procure by bribery etc. b bribe. 3 get by sacrifice etc. 4 slang believe in, accept. 5 be a buyer for a store etc. —n. colloq. purchase. □ **buy in** buy a stock of. **buy into** buy a share in (an enterprise). **buy off** pay to get rid of. **buy oneself out** obtain one's release (esp. from the armed services) by payment. **buy out** pay (a person) for owner-ship, an interest, etc **buy up** 1 buy as much as possible of. 2 absorb (a firm etc.) by purchase. [Old English]

buyer n. 1 person employed to purchase stock for a large store etc. 2 purchaser, customer.

buyer's market n. (also buyers' market) trading conditions favourable to buyers.

buyout n. purchase of a controlling share in a company etc.

buzz —n. 1 hum of a bee etc. 2 sound of a buzzer. 3 a low murmur as of conversation. b stir; hurried activity (buzz of excitement). 4 slang telephone call. 5 slang thrill. —v. 1 hum. 2 a summon with a buzzer. b slang telephone. 3 a (often foll. by about) move busily. b (of a place) appear busy or full of excitement. □ **buzz off** slang go or hurry away. [imitative]

buzzard /ˈbʌzəd/ n. large bird of the hawk family. [Latin *buteo* falcon]

buzzer n. electrical buzzing device as a signal.

buzz-word n. *colloq.* fashionable technical or specialist word; catchword.

by /baɪ/ —*prep.* 1 near, beside (*sit by me; path by the river*). 2 through the agency or means of (*by proxy; poem by Donne; by bus; by cheating; divide by two; killed by robbers*). 3 not later than (*by next week*). 4 a past, beyond (*drove by the church*). b through; via (*went by Paris*). 5 during (*by day; by daylight*). 6 to the extent of (*missed by a foot; better by far*). 7 according to; using as a standard or unit (*judge by appearances; paid by the hour*). 8 with the succession of (*worse by the minute; day by day*). 9 concerning; in respect of (*did our duty by them; Smith by name*). 10 used in mild oaths (*by God*). 11 expressing dimensions of an area etc. (*three feet by two*). 12 avoiding, ignoring (*passed us by*). 13 inclining to (*north by north-west*). —*adv.* 1 near (*sat by*). 2 aside; in reserve (*put £5 by*). 3 past (*marched by*). —*n.* (*pl.* **byes**) = BYE¹. □ **by and by** before long; eventually. **by and large** on the whole. **by the by** (or **bye**) incidentally. **by oneself** 1 a unaided. b unprompted. 2 alone. [Old English]

by- *prefix* subordinate, incidental (*by-effect; byroad*).

bye¹ /baɪ/ n. 1 *Cricket* run scored from a ball that passes the batsman without being hit. 2 status of an unpaired competitor in a sport, who proceeds to the next round by default. [from BY as a noun]

bye² /baɪ/ *int.* (also **bye-bye**) *colloq.* = GOODBYE. [abbreviation]

by-election n. election to fill a vacancy arising between general elections.

Byelorussian /ˌbjelə'rʌʃ(ə)n/ (also **Belorussian** /ˌbelə-/) —*n.* native or language of Byelorussia in eastern Europe.

—*adj.* of Byelorussia, its people, or language. [Russian from *belyĭ* white, *Russiya* Russia]

bygone —*adj.* past, antiquated. —*n.* (in phr. **let bygones be bygones**) forgive and forget past quarrels.

by-law n. regulation made by a local authority or corporation. [obsolete *by* town]

byline n. 1 line naming the writer of a newspaper article etc. 2 secondary line of work. 3 goal-line or touch-line.

bypass —n. 1 main road passing round a town or its centre. 2 a secondary channel or pipe etc. used in emergencies. b alternative passage for the circulation of blood through the heart. —*v.* avoid, go round (a town, difficulty, etc.).

byplay n. secondary action, esp. in a play.

by-product n. 1 incidental product made in the manufacture of something else. 2 secondary result.

byre /ˈbaɪə(r)/ n. cowshed. [Old English]

byroad n. minor road.

byssinosis /ˌbɪsɪ'nəʊsɪs/ n. lung disease caused by textile fibre dust. [Greek *bussinos* made of linen]

bystander n. person present but not taking part; onlooker.

byte /baɪt/ n. *Computing* group of eight binary digits, often representing one character. [origin uncertain]

byway n. 1 byroad or secluded path. 2 minor activity.

byword n. 1 person or thing as a notable example (*is a byword for luxury*). 2 familiar saying.

Byzantine /bɪ'zæntaɪn, baɪ-/ —*adj.* 1 of Byzantium or the E. Roman Empire. 2 of its highly decorated style of architecture. 3 (of a political situation etc.) complex, inflexible, or underhand. —*n.* citizen of Byzantium or the E. Roman Empire. □ **Byzantinism** n. **Byzantinist** n. [Latin *Byzantium*, now Istanbul]

C¹ /siː/ n. (pl. **Cs** or **C's**) **1** (also **c**) third letter of the alphabet. **2** *Mus.* first note of the diatonic scale of C major. **3** third hypothetical person or example. **4** third highest category etc. **5** *Algebra* (usu. **c**) third known quantity. **6** (as a Roman numeral) 100. **7** (also ©) copyright.

C² *symb.* carbon.

C³ abbr. (also **C.**) **1** century. **2** coulomb(s). **2** cent(s).

c. abbr. **1** century. **2** cent(s).

ca. abbr. circa.

CA abbr. Civil Aviation Authority.

cab n. **1** taxi. **2** driver's compartment in a lorry, train, or crane etc. [abbreviation of CABRIOLET]

cabal /kə'bæl/ n. **1** secret intrigue. **2** political clique. [French from Latin]

cabaret /'kæbə,reɪ/ n. entertainment in a nightclub or restaurant. [French, = tavern]

cabbage /'kæbɪdʒ/ n. **1** vegetable with a round head and green or purple leaves. **2** = VEGETABLE 2. [French *caboche* head]

cabbage white n. butterfly whose caterpillars feed on cabbage leaves.

cabby n. (also **cabbie**) (pl. **-ies**) *colloq.* taxi-driver.

caber /'keɪbə(r)/ n. trimmed tree-trunk tossed as a sport in the Scottish Highlands. [Gaelic]

cabin /'kæbɪn/ n. **1** small shelter or house, esp. of wood. **2** room or compartment in an aircraft or ship for passengers or crew. **3** driver's cab. [French from Latin]

cabin-boy n. boy steward on a ship.

cabin cruiser n. large motor boat with accommodation.

cabinet /'kæbɪnɪt/ n. **1 a** cupboard or case for storing or displaying things. **b** casing of a radio, television, etc. **2** (**Cabinet**) committee of senior ministers in a government. [diminutive of CABIN]

cabinet-maker n. skilled joiner.

cable /'keɪb(ə)l/ –n. **1** encased group of insulated wires for transmitting electricity etc. **2** thick rope of wire or hemp. **3** cablegram. **4** (in full **cable stitch**) knitting stitch resembling twisted rope. –v. (**-ling**) transmit (a message) or inform (a person) by cablegram. [Latin *caplum* halter, from Arabic]

cable-car n. small cabin suspended on a looped cable, for carrying passengers up and down a mountain etc.

cablegram n. telegraph message sent by undersea cable.

cable television n. television transmission by cable to subscribers.

cabman n. driver of a cab.

caboodle /kə'buːd(ə)l/ n. □ **the whole caboodle** *slang* the whole lot. [origin uncertain]

caboose /kə'buːs/ n. **1** kitchen on a ship's deck. **2** *US* guard's van on a train [Dutch]

cabriole /'kæbrɪ,əʊl/ n. a kind of esp. 18th-c. curved table or chair leg. [French: related to CAPRIOLE]

cabriolet /ˌkæbrɪəʊ'leɪ/ n. **1** car with a folding top. **2** light two-wheeled one-horse carriage with a hood. [French; related to CAPRIOLE]

cacao /kə'kaʊ/ n. (pl. **-s**) **1** seed from which cocoa and chocolate are made. **2** tree bearing these. [Spanish from Nahuatl]

cache /kæʃ/ –n. **1** hiding-place for treasure, stores, guns, etc. **2** things so hidden. –v. (**-ching**) put in a cache. [French *cacher* hide]

cachet /'kæʃeɪ/ n. **1** prestige. **2** distinguishing mark or seal. **3** flat capsule of medicine. [French *cacher* press]

cachou /'kæʃuː/ n. lozenge to sweeten the breath. [Portuguese *cachu* from Malay *kāchu*]

cack-handed /kæk'hændɪd/ adj. *colloq.* **1** clumsy. **2** left-handed. [dial. *cack* excrement]

cackle /'kæk(ə)l/ –n. **1** clucking of a hen etc. **2** raucous laugh. **3** noisy chatter. –v. (**-ling**) **1** emit a cackle. **2** chatter noisily. [imitative]

cacophony /kə'kɒfənɪ/ n. (pl. **-ies**) harsh discordant sound. □ **cacophonous** adj. [Greek *kakos* bad, *phōnē* sound]

cactus /'kæktəs/ n. (pl. **-ti** /-taɪ/ or **cactuses**) plant with a thick fleshy stem and usu. spines but no leaves. [Latin from Greek]

CAD abbr. computer aided design.

cad n. man who behaves dishonourably. □ **caddish** adj. [abbreviation of CADDIE]

cadaver /kə'dævə(r)/ n. esp. *Med.* corpse. [Latin *cado* fall]

cadaverous /kə'dævərəs/ adj. corpse-like; very pale and thin.

caddie /ˈkædɪ/ (also **caddy**) —n. (pl. **-ies**) person who carries a golfer's clubs during play. —v. (**-ies, -ied, caddying**) act as a caddie. [French CADET]

caddis-fly /ˈkædɪs/ n. small nocturnal insect living near water. [origin unknown]

caddis-worm /ˈkædɪs/ n. (also **caddis**) larva of the caddis-fly. [origin unknown]

caddy[1] /ˈkædɪ/ n. (pl. **-ies**) small container for tea. [Malay]

caddy[2] var. of CADDIE.

cadence /ˈkeɪd(ə)ns/ n. **1** rhythm; the measure or beat of a sound or movement. **2** fall in pitch of the voice. **3** tonal inflection. **4** close of a musical phrase. [Latin *cado* fall]

cadenza /kəˈdenzə/ n. virtuoso passage for a soloist. [Italian: related to CADENCE]

cadet /kəˈdet/ n. young trainee for the armed services or police force. □ **cadetship** n. [French, ultimately from Latin *caput* head]

cadge v. (**-ging**) colloq. get or seek by begging. [origin unknown]

cadi /ˈkɑːdɪ/ n. (pl. **-s**) judge in a Muslim country. [Arabic]

cadmium /ˈkædmɪəm/ n. soft bluish-white metallic element. [Greek *kadmia* Cadmean (earth)]

cadre /ˈkɑːdə(r)/ n. **1** basic unit, esp. of servicemen. **2** group of esp. Communist activists. [French from Latin *quadrus* square]

caecum /ˈsiːkəm/ n. (US **cecum**) (pl. **-ca**) blind-ended pouch at the junction of the small and large intestines. [Latin *caecus* blind]

Caenozoic var. of CENOZOIC.

Caerphilly /keəˈfɪlɪ/ n. a kind of mild white cheese. [*Caerphilly* in Wales]

Caesar /ˈsiːzə(r)/ n. **1** title of Roman emperors. **2** autocrat. [Latin (C. Julius) *Caesar*]

Caesarean /sɪˈzeərɪən/ (US **Cesarean, Cesarian**) —adj. (of birth) effected by Caesarean section. —n. Caesarean section. [from CAESAR: Julius Caesar was supposedly born this way]

Caesarean section n. delivery of a child by cutting through the mother's abdomen.

caesium /ˈsiːzɪəm/ n. (US **cesium**) soft silver-white element. [Latin *caesius* blue-grey]

caesura /sɪˈzjuərə/ n. (pl. **-s**) pause in a line of verse. □ **caesural** adj. [Latin *caedo* cut]

café /ˈkæfeɪ/ n. small coffee-house or restaurant. [French]

cafeteria /kæfɪˈtɪərɪə/ n. self-service restaurant. [American Spanish, = coffee-shop]

caffeine /ˈkæfiːn/ n. alkaloid stimulant in tea-leaves and coffee beans. [French *café* coffee]

caftan /ˈkæftæn/ n. (also **kaftan**) **1** long tunic worn by men in the Near East. **2** long loose dress or shirt. [Turkish]

cage —n. **1** structure of bars or wires, esp. for confining animals or birds. **2** similar open framework, esp. a lift in mine etc. —v. (**-ging**) place or keep in a cage. [Latin *cavea*]

cagey /ˈkeɪdʒɪ/ adj. (also **cagy**) (**-ier, -iest**) colloq. cautious and non-committal. □ **cagily** adv. **caginess** n. [origin unknown]

cagoule /kəˈguːl/ n. thin hooded windproof jacket. [French]

cahoots /kəˈhuːts/ n.pl. □ **in cahoots** slang in collusion. [origin uncertain]

caiman var. of CAYMAN.

Cain n. □ **raise Cain** colloq. = *raise the roof*. [Cain, eldest son of Adam (Gen. 4)]

Cainozoic var. of CENOZOIC.

cairn n. **1** mound of stones as a monument or landmark. **2** (in full **cairn terrier**) small shaggy short-legged terrier. [Gaelic]

cairngorm /ˈkeəngɔːm/ n. semiprecious form of quartz. [*Cairngorms*, in Scotland]

caisson /ˈkeɪs(ə)n/ n. watertight chamber for underwater construction work. [Italian *cassone*]

cajole /kəˈdʒəʊl/ v. (**-ling**) persuade by flattery, deceit, etc. □ **cajolery** n. [French]

cake —n. **1** mixture of flour, butter, eggs, sugar, etc. baked in the oven and often iced and decorated. **2** other food in a flat round shape (*fish cake*). **3** flattish compact mass (*cake of soap*). —v. (**-king**) **1** form into a compact mass. **2** (usu. foll. by *with*) cover (with a hard or sticky mass). □ **have one's cake and eat it** colloq. enjoy both of two mutually exclusive alternatives. **a piece of cake** colloq. something easily achieved. **sell** (or **go**) **like hot cakes** colloq. be sold (or go) quickly; be popular. [Old Norse]

cakewalk n. **1** obsolete American Black dance. **2** colloq. easy task. **3** fairground entertainment consisting of a promenade moved by machinery.

Cal abbr. large calorie(s).

cal abbr. small calorie(s).

calabash /ˈkæləbæʃ/ n. **1** gourd-bearing tree of tropical America. **2** such a gourd, used as a vessel for water, etc. [French from Spanish]

calabrese /ˌkæləˈbriːs/ n. variety of broccoli. [Italian, = Calabrian]

calamine /ˈkæləmaɪn/ n. powdered form of zinc carbonate and ferric oxide used as a skin lotion. [French from Latin]

calamity /kəˈlæmɪtɪ/ n. (pl. -ies) disaster; great misfortune. □ **calamitous** adj. [French from Latin]

calcareous /kælˈkeərɪəs/ adj. of or containing calcium carbonate. [related to CALX]

calceolaria /ˌkælsɪəˈleərɪə/ n. plant with slipper-shaped flowers. [Latin calceus shoe]

calces pl. of CALX.

calciferol /kælˈsɪfərɒl/ n. vitamin (D₂) promoting calcium deposition in the bones. [related to CALX]

calciferous /kælˈsɪfərəs/ adj. yielding calcium salts, esp. calcium carbonate.

calcify /ˈkælsɪfaɪ/ v. (-ies, -ied) 1 harden by the depositing of calcium salts. 2 convert or be converted to calcium carbonate. □ **calcification** /-fɪˈkeɪʃ(ə)n/ n.

calcine /ˈkælsaɪn/ v. (-ning) decompose or be decomposed by strong heat. □ **calcination** /-ˈneɪʃ(ə)n/ n. [French or medieval Latin: related to CALX]

calcite /ˈkælsaɪt/ n. natural crystalline calcium carbonate. [Latin: related to CALX]

calcium /ˈkælsɪəm/ n. soft grey metallic element occurring in limestone, marble, chalk, etc. [related to CALX]

calcium carbide n. greyish solid used in the production of acetylene.

calcium carbonate n. white insoluble solid occurring as chalk, marble, etc.

calcium hydroxide n. white crystalline powder used in the manufacture of mortar.

calcium oxide n. white crystalline solid from which many calcium compounds are manufactured.

calculate /ˈkælkjʊleɪt/ v. (-ting) 1 ascertain or forecast esp. by mathematics or reckoning. 2 plan deliberately. 3 (foll. by on) rely on; reckon on. □ **calculable** adj. [Latin: related to CALCULUS]

calculated adj. 1 (of an action) done deliberately or with foreknowledge. 2 (foll. by to + infin.) designed or suitable; intended.

calculating adj. scheming, mercenary.

calculation /ˌkælkjʊˈleɪʃ(ə)n/ n. act, process, or result of calculating. [Latin: related to CALCULUS]

calculator n. device (esp. a small electronic one) for making mathematical calculations.

calculus /ˈkælkjʊləs/ n. (pl. -luses or -li /-ˌlaɪ/) 1 particular method of mathematical calculation or reasoning. 2 stone

or mineral mass in the body. [Latin, = small stone (used on an abacus)]

caldron var. of CAULDRON.

Caledonian /ˌkælɪˈdəʊnɪən/ literary —adj. of Scotland. —n. Scotsman. [Latin Caledonia N. Britain]

calendar /ˈkælɪndə(r)/ n. 1 system fixing the year's beginning, length, and subdivision. 2 chart etc. showing such subdivisions. 3 timetable of dates, events, etc. —v. enter in a calendar; register (documents). [Latin: related to CALENDS]

calendar year n. period from 1 Jan. to 31 Dec. inclusive.

calender /ˈkælɪndə(r)/ —n. machine in which cloth, paper, etc. is rolled to glaze or smooth it. —v. press in a calender. [French]

calends /ˈkælendz/ n.pl. (also **kalends**) first of the month in the ancient Roman calendar. [Latin Kalendae]

calendula /kæˈlendjʊlə/ n. plant with large yellow or orange flowers, esp. the marigold. [Latin diminutive of Kalendae]

calf¹ /kɑːf/ n. (pl. **calves** /kɑːvz/) 1 young cow or bull. 2 young of other animals, e.g. the elephant, deer, and whale. 3 calfskin. [Old English]

calf² /kɑːf/ n. (pl. **calves**) fleshy hind part of the human leg below the knee. [Old Norse]

calf-love n. romantic adolescent love.

calfskin n. calf-leather.

calibrate /ˈkælɪbreɪt/ v. (-ting) 1 mark (a gauge) with a scale of readings. 2 correlate the readings of (an instrument or system of measurement) with a standard. 3 determine the calibre of (a gun). □ **calibration** /-ˈbreɪʃ(ə)n/ n.

calibre /ˈkælɪbə(r)/ n. (US **caliber**) 1 a internal diameter of a gun or tube. b diameter of a bullet, shell. 2 strength or quality of character; ability, importance. [French from Italian from Arabic]

calices pl. of CALIX.

calico /ˈkælɪkəʊ/ —n. (pl. -es or US -s) 1 cotton cloth, esp. plain white or unbleached. 2 US printed cotton fabric. —adj. 1 of calico. 2 US multicoloured. [Calicut in India]

californium /ˌkælɪˈfɔːnɪəm/ n. artificial radioactive metallic element. [California in US, where first made]

caliper var. of CALLIPER.

caliph /ˈkeɪlɪf/ n. esp. hist. chief Muslim civil and religious ruler. □ **caliphate** n. [Arabic, = successor (of Muhammad)]

calisthenics var. of CALLISTHENICS.

calix var. of CALYX.

calk US var. of CAULK.

call /kɔːl/ *v.* **1 a** (often foll. by *out*) cry, shout; speak loudly. **b** (of a bird etc.) emit its characteristic sound. **2** communicate with by telephone or radio. **3** summon. **4** (often foll. by *at, in, on*) pay a brief visit. **5** order to take place (*called a meeting*); describe as. **7** regard as (*call that silly*). **8** rouse from sleep. **9** (foll. by *for*) demand. **10** (foll. by *on, upon*) appeal to (*called on us to be quiet*). **11** name (a suit) in bidding at cards. **12** guess the outcome of tossing a coin etc. —*n.* **1** shout, cry. **2** a characteristic cry of a bird etc. **b** instrument for imitating it. **3** brief visit. **4 a** act of telephoning. **b** telephone conversation. **5 a** invitation, summons. **b** vocation. **6** need, occasion (*no call for rudeness*). **7** demand (*a call on one's time*). **8** signal on a bugle etc. **9** option of buying stock at a fixed price at a given date. **10** *Cards* a player's right or turn to make a bid. **b** bid made. □ **call in 1** withdraw from circulation. **2** seek the advice or services of. **call off 1** cancel (an arrangement). **2** order (an attacker or pursuer) to desist. **call out 1** summon to action. **2** order (workers) to strike. **call the shots** (or **tune**) *colloq.* be in control; take the initiative. **call up 1** telephone. **2** recall. **3** summon to military service. **on call** ready or available if required. [Old English from Old Norse]

call-box *n.* telephone box.

caller *n.* person who calls, esp. one who pays a visit or makes a telephone call.

call-girl *n.* prostitute accepting appointments by telephone.

calligraphy /kəˈlɪɡrəfɪ/ *n.* **1** handwriting, esp. when fine. **2** art of this. □ **calligrapher** *n.* **calligraphic** /-ˈɡræfɪk/ *adj.* **calligraphist** *n.* [Greek *kallos* beauty]

calling *n.* **1** profession or occupation. **2** vocation.

calliper /ˈkælɪpə(r)/ *n.* (also **caliper**) **1** (in *pl.*) compasses for measuring diameters. **2** metal splint to support the leg. [var. of CALIBRE]

callisthenics /ˌkælɪsˈθenɪks/ *n.pl.* (also **calisthenics**) exercises for fitness and grace. □ **callisthenic** *adj.* [Greek *kallos* beauty, *sthenos* strength]

callosity /kəˈlɒsɪtɪ/ *n.* (*pl.* **-ies**) area of hard thick skin. [Latin: related to CALLOUS]

callous /ˈkæləs/ *adj.* **1** unfeeling, insensitive. **2** (also **calloused**) (of skin) hardened. □ **callously** *adv.* **callousness** *n.* [Latin: related to CALLUS]

callow /ˈkæləʊ/ *adj.* inexperienced, immature. [Old English, = bald]

call-up *n.* summons to do military service.

callus /ˈkæləs/ *n.* (*pl.* **calluses**) **1** area of hard thick skin or tissue. **2** hard tissue formed round bone ends after a fracture. [Latin]

calm /kɑːm/ —*adj.* **1** tranquil, quiet, windless. **2** serene; not agitated. —*n.* calm condition or period. —*v.* (often foll. by *down*) make or become calm. □ **calmly** *adv.* **calmness** *n.* [Greek *kauma* heat]

calomel /ˈkæləmel/ *n.* compound of mercury used as a cathartic. [Greek *kalos* beautiful, *melas* black]

Calor gas /ˈkælə/ *n. propr.* liquefied butane gas stored under pressure in containers for domestic use. [Latin *calor* heat]

calorie /ˈkælərɪ/ *n.* (*pl.* **-ies**) unit of quantity of heat, the amount needed to raise the temperature of one gram (**small calorie**) or one kilogram (**large calorie**) of water by 1 °C. [Latin *calor* heat]

calorific /ˌkæləˈrɪfɪk/ *adj.* producing heat.

calorimeter /ˌkælɪˈrɪmɪtə(r)/ *n.* instrument for measuring quantity of heat.

calumniate /kəˈlʌmnɪeɪt/ *v.* (**-ting**) slander. [Latin]

calumny /ˈkæləmnɪ/ *n.* (*pl.* **-ies**) slander; malicious representation. □ **calumnious** /kəˈlʌmnɪəs/ *adj.* [Latin]

calvados /ˈkælvə,dɒs/ *n.* apple brandy. [*Calvados* in France]

calve /kɑːv/ *v.* (**-ving**) give birth to a calf. [Old English: related to CALF[^1]]

calves *pl.* of CALF[^1], CALF[^2].

Calvinism /ˈkælvɪˌnɪz(ə)m/ *n.* theology of Calvin or his followers, stressing predestination and divine grace. □ **Calvinist** *n.* & *adj.* **Calvinistic** /-ˈnɪstɪk/ *adj.* [*Calvin*, name of a theologian]

calx *n.* (*pl.* **calces** /ˈkælsiːz/) powdery substance formed when an ore or mineral has been heated. [Latin *calx* = lime]

calypso /kəˈlɪpsəʊ/ *n.* (*pl.* **-s**) W. Indian song with improvised usu. topical words and a syncopated rhythm. [origin unknown]

calyx /ˈkeɪlɪks/ *n.* (*pl.* **calyces** /-siːz/ or **-es**) (also **calix**) **1** sepals forming the protective case of a flower in bud. **2** cuplike cavity or structure. [Greek, = husk]

cam *n.* projection on a wheel etc., shaped to convert circular into reciprocal or variable motion. [Dutch *kam* comb]

camaraderie /ˌkæməˈrɑːdərɪ/ *n.* friendly comradeship. [French]

camber —n. convex surface of a road, deck, etc. —v. build with a camber. [Latin camurus curved]

Cambrian /ˈkæmbriən/ —adj. 1 Welsh. 2 Geol. of the first period in the Palaeozoic era. —n. this period. [Welsh related to CYMRIC]

cambric /ˈkeɪmbrɪk/ n. fine linen or cotton fabric. [Cambrai in France]

Cambridge blue /ˈkeɪmbrɪdʒ/ adj. & n. (as adj. often hyphenated) pale blue. [Cambridge in England]

camcorder /ˈkæmkɔːdə(r)/ n. combined video camera and sound recorder. [from CAMERA, RECORDER]

came past of COME.

camel /ˈkæml/ n. 1 long-legged ruminant with one hump (Arabian camel) or two humps (Bactrian camel). 2 fawn colour. [Greek]

camel-hair n. fine soft hair used in artists' brushes or for fabric.

camellia /kəˈmiːlɪə/ n. evergreen shrub with shiny leaves and showy flowers. [Camellus, name of a botanist]

Camembert /ˈkæməmbeə(r)/ n. a kind of soft creamy French cheese. [Camembert in France]

cameo /ˈkæmɪəʊ/ n. (pl. -s) 1 small piece of hard stone carved in relief with a background of a different colour. 2 a short descriptive literary sketch or acted scene. b small character part in a play or film, usu. brief and played by a distinguished actor. [French and medieval Latin]

camera /ˈkæmərə/ n. 1 apparatus for taking photographs or moving film. 2 equipment for converting images into electrical signals. □ in camera Law in private. [Latin: related to CHAMBER]

cameraman n. person who operates a camera professionally, esp. in film-making or television.

camiknickers /ˈkæmɪnɪkəz/ n.pl. women's knickers and vest combined. [from CAMISOLE, KNICKERS]

camisole /ˈkæmɪsəʊl/ n. women's light-weight vest. [Italian or Spanish: related to CHEMISE]

camomile /ˈkæməmaɪl/ n. (also **chamomile**) aromatic plant with daisy-like flowers used esp. to make tea. [Greek, = earth-apple]

camouflage /ˈkæməflɑːʒ/ —n. 1 a disguising of soldiers, tanks, etc. so that they blend into the background. b such a disguise. 2 the natural blending colouring of an animal. 3 misleading or evasive behaviour etc. —v. (-ging) hide by camouflage. [French camoufler disguise]

---

camp[1] —n. 1 place where troops are lodged or trained. 2 temporary accommodation of huts, tents, etc. for, detainees, holiday-makers, etc. 3 ancient fortified site. 4 party supporters etc. regarded collectively. —v. set up or spend time in a camp. [Latin campus level ground]

camp[2] colloq. —adj. 1 affected, effeminate, theatrically exaggerated. 2 homosexual. —n. camp manner or style. —v. behave or do in a camp way. □ camp it up overact; behave affectedly. □ campy adj. [origin uncertain]

campaign /kæmˈpeɪn/ —n. 1 organized course of action, esp. to gain publicity. 2 military operations towards a particular objective. —v. take part in a campaign. □ campaigner n. [Latin: related to CAMP[1]]

campanile /kæmpəˈniːlɪ/ n. bell-tower (usu. free-standing), esp. in Italy. [Italian campana 'bell': from Latin]

campanology /kæmpəˈnɒlədʒɪ/ n. 1 the study of bells. 2 bell-ringing. □ campanologist n. [Latin campana bell]

campanula /kæmˈpænjʊlə/ n. plant with bell-shaped usu. blue, purple, or white flowers. [diminutive: related to CAMPANOLOGY]

camp-bed n. portable folding bed.

camper n. 1 person who camps. 2 large motor vehicle with beds etc.

camp-follower n. 1 civilian worker in a military camp. 2 disciple or adherent.

camphor /ˈkæmfə(r)/ n. pungent white crystalline substance used in making celluloid, medicine, and mothballs. [French ultimately from Sanskrit]

camphorate v. (-ting) impregnate or treat with camphor.

campion /ˈkæmpɪən/ n. wild plant with usu. pink or white notched flowers. [origin uncertain]

campsite n. place for camping.

campus /ˈkæmpəs/ n. (pl. -es) 1 grounds of a university or college. 2 esp. US a university. [Latin, = field]

CAMRA /ˈkæmrə/ abbr. Campaign for Real Ale.

camshaft n. shaft with one or more cams.

---

can[1] /kæn, kən/ v.aux. (3rd sing. present can; past could /kʊd/) 1 a be able to; know how to. b be potentially capable of (these storms can last for hours). 2 be permitted to. [Old English, = know]

can[2] —n. 1 metal vessel for liquid. 2 sealed tin container for the preservation of food or drink. 3 (in pl.) slang headphones. 4 (prec. by the) US slang prison. b US lavatory. —v. (-nn-

Canada goose *n.* preserve in a can. □ **in the can** *colloq.* completed, ready. [Old English]

Canada goose /'kænədə/ *n.* wild N. American goose with a brownish-grey body and white neck and breast.

canaille /kæ'nɑːɪ/ *n.* rabble; populace. [French from Italian]

canal /kə'næl/ *n.* **1** artificial inland waterway. **2** tubular duct in a plant or animal. [Latin *canalis*]

canalize /'kænəlaɪz/ *v.* (also *-ise*) (*-zing* or *-sing*) **1** provide with or convert into a canal or canals. **2** channel. □ **canalization** /-'zeɪʃ(ə)n/ *n.* [French: related to CANAL]

canapé /'kænəpeɪ/ *n.* small piece of bread or pastry with a savoury topping. [French]

canard /'kænɑːd/ *n.* unfounded rumour or story. [French, = duck]

canary /kə'neərɪ/ *n.* (*pl.* *-ies*) small songbird with yellow feathers. [*Canary* Islands]

canasta /kə'næstə/ *n.* card-game using two packs and resembling rummy. [Spanish, = basket]

cancan /'kænkæn/ *n.* lively stage-dance with high kicking. [French]

cancel /'kæns(ə)l/ *v.* (*-ll-*; *US* *-l-*) **1** revoke or discontinue (an arrangement etc.). **2** delete (writing etc.). **3** mark (a ticket, stamp, etc.) to invalidate it. **4** annul; make void. **5** (often foll. by *out*) neutralize or counterbalance. **6** *Math.* strike out (an equal factor) on each side of an equation etc. □ **cancellation** /-'leɪʃ(ə)n/ *n.* [Latin: related to CHANCEL]

cancer /'kænsə(r)/ *n.* **1 a** malignant tumour of body cells. **b** disease caused by this. **2** evil influence or corruption. **3** (**Cancer**) **a** constellation and fourth sign of the zodiac (the Crab). **b** person born when the sun is in this sign. □ **cancerous** *adj.* [Latin, = crab]

cancroid *adj.* [Latin, = crab]

candela /kæn'diːlə/ *n.* SI unit of luminous intensity. [Latin, = candle]

candelabrum /kændɪ'lɑːbrəm/ *n.* (also *-bra*) (*pl.* *-bra*, *US* *-brums*, *-bras*) large branched candlestick or lampholder. [Latin: related to CANDELA]

■ **Usage** The form *candelabra* is, strictly speaking, the plural. However, *candelabra* (singular) and *candelabras* (plural) are often found in informal use.

candid /'kændɪd/ *adj.* **1** frank; open. **2** (of a photograph) taken informally, usu. without subject's knowledge. □ **candidly** *adv.* **candidness** *n.* [Latin *candidus* white]

candida /'kændɪdə/ *n.* fungus causing thrush. [Latin *candidus*: related to CANDID]

candidate /'kændɪdət/ *n.* **1** person nominated for or seeking office, an award, etc. **2** person or thing likely to gain some distinction or position. **3** person entered for an examination. □ **candidacy** *n.* **candidature** *n.* [Latin, = white-robed]

candle /'kænd(ə)l/ *n.* cylinder or block of wax or tallow with a central wick which gives light when burning. □ **cannot hold a candle to** is much inferior to. **not worth the candle** not justifying cost or trouble. [Latin *candela*]

candlelight *n.* light from candles. □ **candlelit** *adj.*

Candlemas /'kænd(ə)l,mæs/ *n.* feast of the Purification of the Virgin Mary (2 Feb.). [Old English: related to MASS²]

candlepower *n.* unit of luminous intensity.

candlestick *n.* holder for one or more candles.

candlewick *n.* **1** thick soft cotton yarn. **2** tufted material from this.

candour /'kændə(r)/ *n.* (*US* **candor**) frankness; openness. [Latin *candor*]

C. & W. *abbr.* country-and-western (music).

candy /'kændɪ/ *-n.* (*pl.* *-ies*) **1** (in full **sugar-candy**) sugar crystallized by repeated boiling and slow evaporation. **2** *US* sweets; a sweet. *-v.* (*-ies*, *-ied*) (usu. as **candied** *adj.*) preserve (fruit etc.) in candy. [French from Arabic]

candyfloss *n.* fluffy mass of spun sugar round a stick.

candystripe *n.* alternate stripes of white and a colour. □ **candystriped** *adj.*

candytuft /'kændɪtʌft/ *n.* plant with white, pink, or purple flowers in tufts. [*Candia* Crete, TUFT]

cane *-n.* **1 a** hollow jointed stem of giant reeds or grasses. **b** solid stem of slender palms. **2** = SUGAR CANE. **3** cane used for wickerwork etc. **4** cane used as a walking-stick, plant support, or for punishment, etc. *-v.* (*-ning*) **1** beat with a cane. **2** weave cane into (a chair etc.). [Greek *kanna* reed]

cane-sugar *n.* sugar from sugar-cane.

canine /'keɪnaɪn/ *-adj.* of a dog or dogs. *-n.* **1** dog. **2** (in full **canine tooth**) pointed tooth between incisors and premolars. [Latin *canis* dog]

canister /'kænɪstə(r)/ *n.* **1** small container for tea etc. **2** cylinder of shot, tearing charge, etc., exploding on impact. [Greek *kanastron* wicker basket]

canker *-n.* **1** destructive disease of trees and plants. **2** ulcerous ear disease of animals. **3** corrupting influence. *-v.* **1** infect with canker. **2** corrupt. **3** (as **cankered** *adj.*) soured, malignant. □

cankerous adj. [Latin: related to CANKER]

canna /ˈkænə/ n. tropical plant with bright flowers and ornamental leaves. [Latin: related to CANE]

cannabis /ˈkænəbɪs/ n. 1 hemp plant. 2 parts of it used as a narcotic. [Latin from Greek]

canned adj. 1 pre-recorded (canned music). 2 sold in a can (canned beer). 3 slang drunk.

cannelloni /ˌkænəˈləʊnɪ/ n.pl. tubes of pasta stuffed with a savoury mixture. [Italian]

cannery /ˈkænərɪ/ n. (pl. -ies) canning factory.

cannibal /ˈkænɪb(ə)l/ n. person or animal that eats its own species. □ **cannibalism** n. **cannibalistic** /-ˈbɪlstɪk/ adj. [Spanish from Carib]

cannibalize /ˈkænɪbəlaɪz/ v. (also -ise) (-zing or -sing) use (a machine etc.) as a source of spare parts. □ **cannibalization** /-ˈzeɪʃ(ə)n/ n. [related to CANNIBAL]

cannon /ˈkænən/ n. 1 hist. (pl. usu. same) large heavy esp mounted gun. 2 Billiards hitting of two balls successively by the player's ball. —v. (usu. foll. by against, into) collide. [Italian: related to CANE]

cannonade /ˌkænəˈneɪd/ —n. period of continuous heavy gunfire. —v. (-ding) bombard with a cannonade. [Italian: related to CANNON]

cannon-ball n. hist. large ball fired by a cannon.

cannon-fodder n. soldiers regarded as expendable.

cannot /ˈkænɒt/ v.aux can not.

canny /ˈkænɪ/ adj. (-ier, -iest) 1 shrewd, worldly-wise; thrifty. 2 Scot. & N.Engl. pleasant, agreeable. □ **cannily** adv. **canniness** n. [from CAN¹]

canoe /kəˈnuː/ —n. small narrow boat with pointed ends, usu. paddled. —v. (-noes, -noed, -noeing) travel in a canoe. □ **canoeist** n. [Spanish and Haitian]

canon /ˈkænən/ n. 1 a general law, rule, principle, or criterion. b church decree or law. 2 (fem. canoness) member of a cathedral chapter. 3 body of (esp. sacred) writings accepted as genuine. 4 the part of the Roman Catholic Mass containing the words of consecration. 5 Mus. piece with different parts taking up the same theme successively. [Greek kanōn rule]

cañon var. of CANYON.

canonical /kəˈnɒnɪk(ə)l/ —adj. (also canonic) 1 a according to canon law. b included in the canon of Scripture. 2 authoritative, accepted. 3 of a cathedral chapter or a member of it. —n. (in pl.)

canonical dress of clergy. [medieval Latin: related to CANON]

canonist /ˈkænənɪst/ n. expert in canon law.

canonize /ˈkænənaɪz/ v. (also -ise) (-zing or -sing) 1 a declare officially to be a saint, usu. with a ceremony. b regard as a saint. 2 admit to the canon of Scripture. 3 sanction by Church authority. □ **canonization** /-ˈzeɪʃ(ə)n/ n. [medieval Latin: related to CANON]

canon law n. ecclesiastical law.

canoodle /kəˈnuːd(ə)l/ v. (-ling) colloq. kiss and cuddle. [origin unknown]

canopy /ˈkænəpɪ/ —n. (pl. -ies) 1 a covering suspended over a throne, bed, etc. b overhanging shelter. 2 Archit. rooflike projection over a niche etc. 3 expanding part of a parachute. —v. (-ies, -ied) supply or be a canopy to. [Greek, = mosquito-net]

canst archaic 2nd person sing. of CAN¹.

cant¹ —n. 1 insincere pious or moral talk. 2 language peculiar to a class, profession, etc.; jargon. —v. use cant. [probably from Latin: related to CHANT]

cant² —n. 1 slanting surface, bevel. 2 oblique push or jerk. 3 tilted position. —v. push or pitch out of level; tilt. [Low German or Dutch, = edge]

can't /kɑːnt/ contr. can not.

Cantab. /ˈkæntæb/ abbr. of Cambridge University. [Latin Cantabrigiensis]

cantabile /kænˈtɑːbɪleɪ/ Mus. —adv. & adj. in smooth flowing style. —n. cantabile passage or movement. [Italian, = singable]

Cantabrigian /ˌkæntəˈbrɪdʒən/ —adj. of Cambridge or its university. —n. person from Cambridge or its university. [Cantabrigia, Latinized name of Cambridge]

cantaloup /ˈkæntəluːp/ n. (also cantaloupe) small round ribbed melon. [Cantaluppi near Rome, where it was first grown in Europe]

cantankerous /kænˈtæŋkərəs/ adj. bad-tempered, quarrelsome. □ **cantankerously** adv. **cantankerousness** n. [origin uncertain]

cantata /kænˈtɑːtə/ n. Mus. composition with vocal solos and usu. choral and orchestral accompaniment. [Italian: related to CHANT]

canteen /kænˈtiːn/ n. 1 a restaurant for employees in an office, factory, etc. b shop for provisions in a barracks or camp. 2 case of cutlery. 3 soldier's or camper's water-flask. [Italian, = cellar]

canter /ˈkæntə/ —n. horse's pace between a trot and a gallop. —v. go or make go at a canter. [Canterbury gallop of medieval pilgrims]

canticle /ˈkæntɪk(ə)l/ n. song or chant with a biblical text. [Latin *canticum* CHANT]

cantilever /ˈkæntɪˌliːvə(r)/ n. 1 bracket or beam etc. projecting from a wall to support a balcony etc. 2 beam or girder fixed at one end only. □ **cantilevered** adj. [origin unknown]

canto /ˈkæntəʊ/ n. (pl. -s) division of a long poem. [Latin *cantus*: related to CHANT]

canton —n. /ˈkæntən/ subdivision of a country, esp. of Switzerland. —v. /kænˈtuːn/ put (troops) into quarters. [French, = corner: related to CANT²]

cantonment /kænˈtuːnmənt/ n. 1 lodging assigned to troops. 2 *hist.* permanent military station in India. [French: related to CANTON]

cantor /ˈkæntɔː(r)/ n. 1 church choir leader. 2 precentor in a synagogue. [Latin, = singer]

canvas /ˈkænvəs/ —n. 1 strong coarse cloth used for sails and tents etc. and for oil-painting. 2 a painting on canvas, esp. in oils. —v. (-ss-; US -s-) cover with canvas. □ **under canvas** 1 in tents. 2 with sails spread. [Latin: related to CANNABIS]

canvass /ˈkænvəs/ —v. 1 solicit votes, esp. from a constituency electorate. 2 a ascertain the opinions of. b seek custom from. 3 propose (an idea or plan etc.). —n. canvassing, esp. of electors. □ **canvasser** n. [originally = toss in sheet, from CANVAS]

canyon /ˈkænjən/ n. (also cañon) deep gorge. [Spanish *cañón* tube]

CAP abbr. Common Agricultural Policy (of the EC).

cap —n. 1 a soft brimless hat, usu. with a peak. b head-covering worn in a particular profession. c cap as a sign of membership of a sports team. d mortarboard. 2 a cover like a cap (*kneecap*). b top for a bottle, jar, pen, camera lens, etc. 3 = PERCUSSION CAP. 4 = DUTCH CAP. 5 dental crown. —v. (-pp-) 1 a put a cap on. b cover the top or end of. c set a limit to. 2 award a sports cap to. 3 form the top of. 4 surpass, excel. □ **cap in hand** humbly. **if the cap fits** (or a remark) if it applies to you, so be it. **to cap it all** after everything else. [Latin *cappa*]

capability /ˌkeɪpəˈbɪlɪtɪ/ n. (pl. -ies) 1 ability, power. 2 undeveloped or unused faculty.

capable /ˈkeɪpəb(ə)l/ adj. 1 competent, able, gifted. 2 (foll. by *of*) a having the ability, fitness, etc. for. b admitting of (explanation, improvement, etc.). □ **capably** adv. [Latin *capio* hold]

capacious /kəˈpeɪʃəs/ adj. roomy. □ **capaciousness** n. [Latin *capax*: related to CAPABLE]

capacitance /kəˈpæsɪt(ə)ns/ n. 1 ability to store electric charge. 2 ratio of change in the electric charge in a system to the corresponding change in its potential.

capacitor /kəˈpæsɪtə(r)/ n. device able to store electric charge.

capacity /kəˈpæsɪtɪ/ n. (pl. -ies) 1 a power to contain, receive, experience, or produce (*capacity for heat, pain,* etc.). b maximum amount that can be contained or produced etc. c (*attrib.*) fully occupying the available space etc. (*capacity crowd*). 2 mental power. 3 position or function. 4 legal competence. □ **to capacity** fully. [Latin: related to CAPACIOUS]

caparison /kəˈpærɪs(ə)n/ *literary* —n. 1 (usu. in pl.) horse's trappings. 2 equipment, finery. —v. adorn. [Spanish, = saddle-cloth]

cape¹ n. 1 sleeveless cloak. 2 this worn over or as part of a longer cloak or coat. [Latin *cappa* CAP]

cape² n. 1 headland, promontory. 2 (**the Cape**) the Cape of Good Hope. [Latin *caput* head]

caper¹ —v. jump or run playfully. —n. 1 playful leap. 2 a prank. b *slang* illicit activity. □ **cut a caper** frolic. [abbreviation of CAPRIOLE]

caper² n. 1 bramble-like shrub. 2 (in pl.) its pickled buds used esp. in a sauce. [Greek *kapparis*]

capercaillie /ˌkæpəˈkeɪljɪ/ n. (also **capercailzie** /-lzɪ/) large European grouse. [Gaelic, = horse of the forest]

capillarity /ˌkæpɪˈlærɪtɪ/ n. the rise or depression of a liquid in a narrow tube. [French: related to CAPILLARY]

capillary /kəˈpɪlərɪ/ —attrib. adj. 1 of or like a hair, esp. (of a tube) of very small diameter. 2 of the branching blood-vessels connecting arteries and veins. —n. (pl. -ies) 1 capillary tube. 2 capillary blood vessel. [Latin *capillus* hair]

capillary action n. = CAPILLARITY.

capital /ˈkæpɪt(ə)l/ —n. 1 a chief town or city of a country or region. 2 a money etc. with which a company starts in business. b accumulated wealth. 3 capitalists collectively. 4 capital letter. 5 head of a column or pillar. —adj. 1 a principal, most important. b *colloq.* excellent. 2 a involving punishment by death. b (of an error etc.) vitally harmful, fatal. 3 (of letters of the alphabet) large in size, used to begin sentences and names etc. □ **make capital out of**

use to one's advantage. [Latin *caput -itis* head]

capital gain *n.* profit from the sale of investments or property.

capital goods *n.pl.* machinery, plant, etc.

capitalism *n.* economic and political system dependent on private capital and profit-making.

capitalist *n.* 1 person investing or possessing capital. 2 advocate of capitalism. —*adj.* of or favouring capitalism. □ **capitalistic** /-'lɪstɪk/ *adj.*

capitalize *v.* (also -**ise**) (-**zing** or -**sing**) 1 (foll. by *on*) use to one's advantage. 2 convert into or provide with capital. 3 a write (a letter of the alphabet) as a capital. b begin (a word) with a capital letter. □ **capitalization** /-'zeɪʃ(ə)n/ *n.* [French: related to CAPITAL]

capital levy *n.* tax on wealth or property.

capital sum *n.* lump sum, esp. payable to an insured person.

capital transfer tax *n. hist.* tax levied on the transfer of capital by gift or bequest etc.

■ *Usage* This tax was replaced in 1986 by *inheritance tax.*

capitation /kæpɪ'teɪʃ(ə)n/ *n.* tax or fee paid per person. [Latin: related to CAP-ITAL]

capitular /kə'pɪtjʊlə(r)/ *adj.* of a cathedral chapter. [Latin *capitulum* CHAPTER]

capitulate /kə'pɪtjʊleɪt/ *v.* (-**ting**) surrender. □ **capitulation** /-'leɪʃ(ə)n/ *n.* [medieval Latin, = put under headings]

capo /'kæpəʊ/ *n.* (*pl.* -**s**) device fitted across the strings of a guitar etc. to raise their pitch equally. [Italian *capo tasto* head stop]

capon /'keɪpən/ *n.* castrated cock fattened for eating. [Latin *capo*]

cappuccino /kæpʊ'tʃiːnəʊ/ *n.* (*pl.* -**s**) frothy milky coffee. [Italian, = Capuchin]

caprice /kə'priːs/ *n.* 1 a whim. b tendency to this. 2 lively or fanciful work of art, music, etc. [Italian *capriccio* sudden start]

capricious /kə'prɪʃəs/ *adj.* subject to whims; unpredictable. □ **capriciously** *adv.* **capriciousness** *n.*

Capricorn /'kæprɪkɔːn/ *n.* 1 constellation and tenth sign of the zodiac (the Goat). 2 person born when the sun is in this sign. [Latin *caper -pri* goat, *cornu* horn]

capriole /'kæprɪəʊl/ —*n.* leap, caper, esp. of a trained horse. —*v.* (-**ling**) perform this. [Italian: related to CAPRI-CORN]

capsicum /'kæpsɪkəm/ *n.* 1 plant with edible fruits, esp. any of several varieties of pepper. 2 red, green, or yellow fruit of these. [Latin *capsa* case]

capsize /kæp'saɪz/ *v.* (-**zing**) (of a boat etc.) be overturned; overturn. [Spanish *capuzar* sink]

capstan /'kæpst(ə)n/ *n.* 1 thick revolving cylinder for winding a cable etc. 2 revolving spindle carrying the spool on a tape recorder. [Provençal]

capstan lathe *n.* lathe with a revolving tool-holder.

capsule /'kæpsjuːl/ *n.* 1 small edible soluble case enclosing medicine. 2 detachable compartment of a spacecraft or nose of a rocket. 3 enclosing membrane in the body. 4 dry fruit that releases its seeds when ripe. 5 (*attrib.*) concise; condensed. □ **capsular** *adj.* **capsulize** *v.* (also -**ise**) (-**zing** or -**sing**) put (information etc.) in compact form. [Latin *capsa* case]

Capt. *abbr.* Captain.

caption /'kæpʃ(ə)n/ —*n.* 1 wording appended to an illustration, cartoon, etc. 2 wording on a cinema or television screen. 3 heading of a chapter, article, etc. —*v.* provide with a caption. [Latin *capio* take]

captious /'kæpʃəs/ *adj.* fault-finding. [Latin: related to CAPTION]

captivate /'kæptɪveɪt/ *v.* (-**ting**) fascinate; charm. □ **captivation** /-'veɪʃ(ə)n/ *n.* [Latin: related to CAPTIVE]

captive /'kæptɪv/ —*n.* confined or imprisoned person or animal. —*adj.* 1 taken prisoner; restrained. 2 unable to escape (*captive audience*). □ **captivity** /-'tɪvɪtɪ/ *n.* [Latin *capio capt-* take]

captor /'kæptə(r)/ *n.* person who captures. [Latin: related to CAPTIVE]

capture /'kæptʃə(r)/ —*v.* (-**ring**) 1 take prisoner; seize. b obtain by force or trickery. 2 portray; record on film etc. 3 absorb (a subatomic particle). 4 record (data) for use in a computer. —*n.* 1 act of capturing. 2 thing or person captured. [Latin: related to CAPTIVE]

Capuchin /'kæpjʊtʃɪn/ *n.* 1 Franciscan friar. 2 (**capuchin**) a monkey with cowl-like head hair. b pigeon with a cowl-like head and neck. [Italian *cappuccio* cowl]

capybara /kæpɪ'bɑːrə/ *n.* large semi-aquatic S. American rodent. [Tupi]

car *n.* 1 (in full **motor car**) motor vehicle for a driver and small number of passengers. 2 (in *comb.*) road vehicle or

caracul var. of KARAKUL.

carafe /kəˈræf/ n. glass container for water or wine. [French from Arabic]

caramel /ˈkærəˌmel/ n. **1 a** burnt sugar or syrup as a flavouring or colouring. **b** a kind of soft toffee. **2** light-brown colour. □ **caramelize** /-məˌlaɪz/ v. (also **-ise**) (**-zing** or **-sing**). [French from Spanish]

carapace /ˈkærəˌpeɪs/ n. upper shell of a tortoise or crustacean. [French from Spanish]

carat /ˈkærət/ n. **1** unit of weight for precious stones (200 mg). **2** measure of purity of gold (pure gold = 24 carats). [French ultimately from Greek *kerus horn*]

caravan /ˈkærəˌvæn/ n. **1** vehicle equipped for living in and usu. towed by a car. **2** people travelling together, esp. across a desert. □ v. (**-nn-**) travel or live in a caravan. □ **caravanner** n. [French from Persian]

caravanserai /ˌkærəˈvænsəˌraɪ/ n. Eastern inn with a central court. [Persian, = caravan place]

caravel /ˈkærəˌvel/ n. (also **carvel** /ˈkɑːv(ə)l/) *hist.* small light fast ship. [Greek *karabos*, literally 'horned beetle']

caraway /ˈkærəˌweɪ/ n. plant with tiny white flowers. [Spanish from Arabic]

caraway seed n. fruit of the caraway as flavouring and a source of oil.

carb n. *colloq.* carburettor. [abbreviation]

carbide /ˈkɑːbaɪd/ n. **1** binary compound of carbon. **2** = CALCIUM CARBIDE.

carbine /ˈkɑːbaɪn/ n. short rifle orig. for cavalry use. [French]

carbohydrate /ˌkɑːbəˈhaɪdreɪt/ n. energy-producing organic compound of carbon, hydrogen, and oxygen (e.g. starch, sugar).

carbolic /kɑːˈbɒlɪk/ n. (in full **carbolic acid**) phenol. [from CARBON]

carbolic soap n. soap containing carbolic.

car bomb n. terrorist bomb placed in or under a parked car.

carbon /ˈkɑːbən/ n. **1** non-metallic element occurring naturally as diamond, graphite, and charcoal, and in all organic compounds. **2 a** = CARBON COPY. **b** = CARBON PAPER. **3** rod of carbon in an arc lamp. [Latin *carbo* charcoal]

carbonaceous /ˌkɑːbəˈneɪʃəs/ adj. **1** consisting of or containing carbon. **2** of or like coal or charcoal.

carbonate /ˈkɑːbəˌneɪt/ —n. *Chem.* salt of carbonic acid. —v. (**-ting**) fill with carbon dioxide. [French: related to CARBON]

carbon copy n. **1** copy made with carbon paper. **2** exact copy.

carbon dating n. determination of the age of an organic object from the ratio of isotopes, which changes as carbon-14 decays.

carbon dioxide n. gas occurring naturally in the atmosphere and formed by respiration.

carbon fibre n. thin strong crystalline filament of carbon used as a strengthening material.

carbon-14 n. radioisotope of mass 14, used in carbon dating.

carbonic /kɑːˈbɒnɪk/ adj. containing carbon.

carbonic acid n. weak acid formed from carbon dioxide in water.

carboniferous /ˌkɑːbəˈnɪfərəs/ —adj. **1** producing coal. **2** (**Carboniferous**) of the fifth period in the Palaeozoic era, with extensive formation of coal. —n. (**Carboniferous**) this period.

carbonize /ˈkɑːbəˌnaɪz/ v. (also **-ise**) (**-zing** or **-sing**) **1** convert into carbon. **2** reduce to charcoal or coke. **3** coat with carbon. □ **carbonization** /-ˈzeɪʃ(ə)n/ n.

carbon monoxide n. toxic gas formed by the incomplete burning of carbon.

carbon paper n. thin carbon-coated paper used for making copies.

carbon tetrachloride n. colourless liquid used as a solvent.

carbon-12 n. stable isotope of carbon, used as a standard.

car-boot sale n. sale of goods from (tables stocked from) the boots of cars.

carborundum /ˌkɑːbəˈrʌndəm/ n. compound of carbon and silicon used esp. as an abrasive. [from CARBON, CORUNDUM]

carboy /ˈkɑːbɔɪ/ n. large globular glass bottle usu. in a frame. [Persian]

carbuncle /ˈkɑːbʌŋk(ə)l/ n. **1** severe skin abscess. **2** bright-red gem. [Latin: related to CARBON]

carburettor /ˌkɑːbəˈretə(r)/ n. (*US* **carburetor**) apparatus in an internal-combustion engine for mixing petrol and air to make an explosive mixture.

carcass /ˈkɑːkəs/ n. (also **carcase**) **1** dead body of an animal, esp. as meat. **2** bones of a cooked bird. **3** *colloq.* human body; corpse. **4** framework. **5** worthless remains. [French]

carcinogen /kɑːˈsɪnədʒ(ə)n/ n. substance producing cancer. □ **carcinogenic** /-ˈdʒenɪk/ adj. [related to CARCINOMA]

carcinoma /ˌkɑːsɪˈnəʊmə/ n. (pl. -s or -mata) cancerous tumour. [Greek karkinos crab]

card[1] n. 1 thick stiff paper or thin paste-board. 2 a piece of this for writing or printing on, esp. to send greetings, to identify a person, or to record informa-tion. b small rectangular piece of plastic used for identity etc. 3 a = PLAYING-CARD. b (in pl.) card-playing. 4 (in pl.) colloq. tax and national insurance docu-ments etc., held by an employer. 5 pro-gramme of events at a race-meeting etc. 6 colloq. odd or amusing person. □ card up one's sleeve plan or secret weapon in reserve. get one's cards colloq. be dismissed from one's employment. on the cards possible or likely. put (or lay) one's cards on the table reveal one's resources, intentions, etc. [Greek khartēs papyrus-leaf]

card[2] n. wire brush etc. for raising a nap on cloth etc. —v. brush or comb with a card. [Latin caro card (v.)]

cardamom /ˈkɑːdəməm/ n. seeds of an aromatic SE Asian plant used as a spice. [Latin from Greek]

cardboard n. pasteboard or stiff paper, esp. for making boxes.

cardboard city n. area where home-less people make shelters from card-board boxes etc.

card-carrying adj. registered as a member (esp. of a political party or trade union).

card-game n. game using playing-cards.

cardiac /ˈkɑːdɪˌæk/ adj. of the heart. [Greek kardia heart]

cardigan /ˈkɑːdɪgən/ n. knitted jacket. [Earl of Cardigan]

cardinal /ˈkɑːdɪn(ə)l/ —adj. 1 chief, fun-damental. 2 deep scarlet. —n. 1 (as a title Cardinal) leading Roman Catholic dig-nitary, one of the college electing the Pope. 2 small scarlet American song-bird. [Latin cardo din- hinge]

cardinal number n. number denoting quantity (1, 2, 3, etc.), as opposed to an ordinal number.

cardinal points n.pl. four main points of the compass (N., S., E., W.).

cardinal virtues n.pl. justice, pru-dence, temperance, and fortitude.

card index n. index with a card for each entry.

cardiogram /ˈkɑːdɪəʊˌgræm/ n. record of heart movements. [Greek kardia heart]

cardiograph /ˈkɑːdɪəʊˌgrɑːf/ n. instru-ment recording heart movements. □ **cardiographer** /-ˈɒgrəf(r)/ n. **cardio-graphy** /-ˈɒgrəfi/ n.

cardiology /ˌkɑːdɪˈɒlədʒɪ/ n. branch of medicine concerned with the heart. □ **cardiologist** n.

cardiovascular /ˌkɑːdɪəʊˈvæskjʊlə(r)/ adj. of the heart and blood-vessels.

cardoon /kɑːˈduːn/ n. thistle-like plant with leaves used as a vegetable. [French from Latin]

cardphone n. public telephone oper-ated by a machine-readable card instead of money.

card-sharp n. (also **card-sharper**) swindler at card-games.

card-table n. (esp. folding) table for card-playing.

card vote n. = BLOCK VOTE.

care —n. 1 worry, anxiety. 2 cause of this. 3 serious attention; caution. 4 a protection, looking after, charge. b = CHILD CARE. 5 thing to be done or seen to. —v. (-ring) 1 (usu. foll. by about, for, whether) feel concern or interest. 2 (usu. foll. by for) like, be fond of (don't care for jazz). 3 (foll. by to + infin.) wish or be willing (would you care to try?). □ **care for** provide for, look after, care of at the address of. **in care** (of a child) in local authority care. **not care a damn** etc. (see DAMN) etc. take **no care a damn** have, etc. take **not care a damn** etc. = not give a damn. **take care** 1 be careful. 2 (foll. by to + infin.) not fail or neglect. **take care of** 1 look after. 2 deal with, dispose of. [Old Eng-lish; = sorrow]

■ **Usage** Sense 3 of careen is influenced by the verb career.

career /kəˈrɪə(r)/ —n. 1 one's profes-sional etc. progress through life. 2 pro-fession or occupation, esp. as offering advancement. 3 (attrib.) a pursuing or wishing to pursue a career (career woman). b working permanently in a specified profession (career diplomat). 4 swift course (in full career). —v. 1 move or swerve about wildly. 2 go swiftly. [Latin: related □ CAR]

careen /kəˈriːn/ v. 1 turn (a ship) on one side for repair etc. 2 tilt, lean over. 3 swerve about. [Latin carina keel]

careerist n. person predominantly con-cerned with personal advancement.

carefree adj. light-hearted; joyous.

careful adj. 1 painstaking, thorough. 2 cautious. 3 taking care; not neglecting (careful to remind them). □ **carefully** adv. **carefulness** n.

careless adj. 1 lacking care or atten-tion. 2 unthinking, insensitive. 3 light-hearted. 4 (foll. by of) not concerned about. □ **carelessly** adv. **carelessness** n.

carer n. person who cares for a sick or elderly person, esp. a relative at home.

caress /kə'res/ —v. touch or stroke gently or lovingly. —n. loving or gentle touch. [Latin *carus* dear]

caret /'kærət/ n. mark (∧, ∧) indicating a proposed insertion in printing or writing. [Latin, = is lacking]

caretaker n. 1 person employed to look after a house, building, etc. 2 (*attrib.*) exercising temporary authority (*caretaker government*).

careworn adj. showing the effects of prolonged worry.

cargo /'kɑːgəʊ/ n. (pl. **-es** or **-s**) goods carried on a ship or aircraft. [Spanish: related to CHARGE]

Carib /'kærɪb/ —n. 1 aboriginal inhabitant of the southern W. Indies or adjacent coasts. 2 their language. —adj. of the Caribs. [Spanish from Haitian]

Caribbean /ˌkærə'biːən/ adj. of the Caribs or the W. Indies generally.

caribou /'kærɪˌbuː/ n. (pl. same) N. American reindeer. [French from American Indian]

caricature /'kærɪkətʃʊə(r)/ —n. 1 grotesque usu. comically exaggerated representation of a person. 2 ridiculously poor imitation or version. —v. (-ring) make or give a caricature of. □ **caricaturist** n. [Italian *caricare* exaggerate]

caries /'keəriːz/ n. (pl. same) decay of a tooth or bone. [Latin]

carillon /kə'rɪljən/ n. 1 set of bells sounded either from a keyboard or mechanically. 2 tune played on bells. [French]

caring adj. 1 kind, humane. 2 (*attrib.*) concerned with looking after people (*caring professions*).

carioca /ˌkærɪ'əʊkə/ n. 1 Brazilian dance like the samba. 2 music for this. [Portuguese]

Carmelite /'kɑːməˌlaɪt/ —n. 1 friar of the order of Our Lady of Carmel. 2 nun of a similar order. —adj. of the Carmelites. [Mt. *Carmel* in Palestine, where the order was founded]

carminative /'kɑːmɪnətɪv/ —adj. relieving flatulence. —n. carminative drug. [Latin *carmino* heal by CHARM]

carmine /'kɑːmɪn/ —adj. of vivid crimson colour. —n. 1 this colour. 2 carmine pigment made from cochineal. [probably from Latin *carmesinum* CRIMSON]

carnage /'kɑːnɪdʒ/ n. great slaughter, esp. in battle. [Latin: related to CARNAL]

carnal /'kɑːn(ə)l/ adj. 1 of the body or flesh; worldly. 2 sensual, sexual. □ **carnality** /-'nælɪtɪ/ n. [Latin *caro carn-* flesh]

carnation /kɑː'neɪʃ(ə)n/ —n. 1 clove-scented pink. 2 rosy-pink colour. —adj. rosy-pink. [Italian: related to CARNAL because of the flesh-colour]

carnelian var. of CORNELIAN.

carnet /'kɑːneɪ/ n. permit to drive across a frontier, use a camp-site, etc. [French, = notebook]

carnival /'kɑːnɪv(ə)l/ n. 1 a annual festivities including a parade through the streets in fancy dress. b festival preceding Lent. 2 merrymaking. 3 US funfair or circus. [Latin *carnem levo* put away meat]

carnivore /'kɑːnɪˌvɔː(r)/ n. carnivorous animal or plant, esp. a mammal of the order including cats, dogs, and bears.

carnivorous /kɑː'nɪvərəs/ adj. (of an animal or plant) feeding on flesh. [Latin: related to CARNAL, *voro* devour]

carob /'kærəb/ n. seed pod of a Mediterranean tree used as a chocolate substitute. [Arabic *karrūba*]

carol /'kær(ə)l/ —n. joyous song, esp. a Christmas hymn. —v. (-ll-; US -l-) 1 sing carols. 2 sing joyfully. [French]

Carolingian /ˌkærə'lɪndʒɪən/ adj. of the Frankish dynasty founded by Charlemagne. —n. member of this dynasty. [Latin *Carolus* Charles]

carotene /'kærəˌtiːn/ n. orange-coloured pigment found in carrots, tomatoes, etc., acting as a source of vitamin A. [Latin: related to CARROT]

carotid /kə'rɒtɪd/ —n. each of the two main arteries carrying blood to the head and neck. —adj. of these arteries. [Latin from Greek]

carouse /kə'raʊz/ —v. (-sing) have a lively drinking-party. —n. such a party. □ **carousal** n. **carouser** n. [German *gar aus* (drink) right out]

carousel /ˌkærə'sel/ n. 1 US merry-go-round. 2 rotating luggage delivery system at an airport etc. [French from Italian]

carp¹ n. (pl. same) freshwater fish often bred for food. [Provençal or Latin]

carp² v. find fault; complain pettily. □ **carper** n. [Old Norse, = brag]

carpal /'kɑːp(ə)l/ —adj. of the bones in the wrist. —n. wrist-bone. [from CARPUS]

car park n. area for parking cars.

carpel /'kɑːp(ə)l/ n. female reproductive organ of a flower. [Greek *karpos* fruit]

carpenter /'kɑːpɪntə(r)/ —n. person skilled in woodwork. —v. 1 make or construct in wood. 2 construct; fit together. □ **carpentry** n. [Latin *carpentum* wagon]

carpet /'kɑːpɪt/ —n. 1 a thick fabric for covering floor or stairs. b piece of this. 2 thing resembling this etc. (*carpet of snow*). —v. (-t-) 1 cover with or as with carpet. 2 colloq. reprimand. □ **on the carpet** colloq. 1 being reprimanded. 2

under consideration. **sweep under the carpet** conceal (a problem or difficulty). [Latin *carpo* pluck]

carpet-bag *n.* travelling-bag, orig. made of carpet-like material.

carpet-bagger *n. colloq.* 1 esp. *US* political candidate etc. without local connections. 2 unscrupulous opportunist.

carpeting *n.* 1 material for carpets. 2 carpets collectively.

carpet slipper *n.* soft slipper.

carpet-sweeper *n.* household implement for sweeping carpets.

car phone *n.* radio-telephone for use in a car etc.

carport *n.* roofed open-sided shelter for a car.

carpus /ˈkɑːpəs/ *n. (pl. -pi /-paɪ/)* small bones forming the wrist in humans and similar parts in other mammals. [Latin from Greek]

carrageen /ˈkærəgiːn/ *n. (also carragheen)* edible red seaweed. [origin uncertain]

carrel /ˈkær(ə)l/ *n.* small cubicle for a reader in a library. [French from medieval Latin]

carriage /ˈkærɪdʒ/ *n.* 1 railway passenger vehicle. 2 wheeled horse-drawn passenger vehicle. 3 a conveying of goods. b cost of this. 4 carrying part of a machine (e.g. a typewriter). 5 gun-carriage. 6 bearing, deportment. [French: related to CARRY]

carriageway *n.* the part of a road intended for vehicles.

carrier /ˈkærɪə(r)/ *n.* 1 person or thing that carries. 2 transport or freight company. 3 = CARRIER BAG. 4 framework on a bicycle for luggage or a passenger. 5 person or animal that may transmit disease etc. without suffering from it. 6 = AIRCRAFT-CARRIER.

carrier bag *n.* plastic or paper bag with handles.

carrier pigeon *n.* pigeon trained to carry messages.

carrier wave *n.* high-frequency electromagnetic wave modulated in amplitude or frequency to convey a signal.

carrion /ˈkærɪən/ *n.* 1 dead putrefying flesh. 2 something vile or filthy. [Latin *caro* flesh]

carrot /ˈkærət/ *n.* 1 a plant with a tapering orange-coloured root. b this as a vegetable. 2 incentive. □ **carroty** *adj.*

carry /ˈkærɪ/ *v.* (**-ies, -ied**) 1 support or hold up, esp. while moving. 2 convey with one or have on one's person. 3 conduct or transmit (*pipe carries water*). 4 (often foll. by *to*) take a (process etc.) to a specified point; continue; prolong (*carry into effect*; *carry a joke too far*). 5 involve, imply (*carries 6% interest*). 6 *Math.* transfer (a figure) to a column of higher value. 7 hold in a specified way (*carry oneself erect*). 8 a (of a newspaper etc.) publish. b (of a radio or television station) broadcast. 9 keep a regular stock of. 10 a (of sound) be audible at a distance. b (of a missile or gun etc.) travel or propel to a specified distance. 11 a win victory or acceptance for (a proposal etc.). b win acceptance from (*carried the audience with her*). c win, capture (a prize, fortress, etc.). 12 a endure the weight of; support. b be the driving force in (*you carry the department*). 13 be pregnant with. *—n.* (*pl. -ies*) 1 act of carrying. 2 *Golf* distance a ball travels before reaching the ground. □ **carry away 1** remove. **2** inspire. **3** deprive of self-control (*got carried away*). **carry the can** *colloq.* bear the responsibility or blame. **carry the day** be victorious or successful. **carry forward** transfer to a new page or account. **carry it off** do well under difficulties. **carry off 1** take away, esp. by force. **2** win (a prize). **3** (esp. of a disease) kill. **carry on 1** continue. **2** engage in (conversation or business). **3** *colloq.* behave strangely or excitedly. **4** (often foll. by *with*) *colloq.* flirt or have a love affair. **carry out** put (an idea etc.) into practice. **carry over 1** = *carry forward*. **2** postpone. **carry through 1** complete successfully. **2** bring safely out of difficulties. **carry weight** be influential or important. [Anglo-French: related to CAR]

carry-cot *n.* portable cot for a baby.

carryings-on *n.pl.* = CARRY-ON.

carry-on *n. slang* 1 fuss, excitement 2 questionable behaviour. 3 flirtation or love affair.

carry-out *attrib. adj. & n. esp. Scot. & US* = TAKE-AWAY.

carsick *adj.* nauseous from car travel. □ **carsickness** *n.*

cart *—n.* 1 open usu. horse-drawn vehicle for carrying loads. 2 light vehicle for pulling by hand. *—v.* 1 convey in a cart 2 *slang* carry or convey with effort. □ **put the cart before the horse** reverse the proper order or procedure. [Old English and Old Norse]

carte blanche /kɑːt ˈblɑ̃ʃ/ *n.* full discretionary power. [French, = blank paper]

cartel /kɑːˈtel/ *n.* union of suppliers etc. to control prices. [Italian diminutive: related to CARD]

Cartesian /kɑːˈtiːzɪən/ *adj.* of Descartes or his philosophy. —*n.* follower of Descartes. [Latin *Cartesius* Descartes]

Cartesian coordinates *n.pl.* system for locating a point by reference to its distance from axes intersecting at right angles.

cart-horse *n.* thickset horse.

Carthusian /kɑːˈθjuːzɪən/ —*n.* monk of a contemplative order founded by St Bruno. —*adj.* of this order. [Latin: related to CHARTREUSE]

cartilage /ˈkɑːtɪlɪdʒ/ *n.* firm flexible connective tissue, mainly replaced by bone in adulthood. □ **cartilaginous** /ˌkɑːtɪˈlædʒɪnəs/ *adj.* [French from Latin]

cartography /kɑːˈtɒɡrəfɪ/ *n.* map-drawing. □ **cartographer** *n.* **cartographic** /-təˈɡræfɪk/ *adj.* [French *carte* map]

carton /ˈkɑːt(ə)n/ *n.* light esp. cardboard box or container. [French: related to CARTOON]

cartoon /kɑːˈtuːn/ *n.* **1** humorous, esp. topical, drawing in a newspaper etc. **2** sequence of drawings telling a story. **3** animated sequence of these on film. **4** full-size preliminary design for a tapestry etc. □ **cartoonist** *n.* [Italian: related to CARD¹]

cartouche /kɑːˈtuːʃ/ *n.* **1** scroll-like ornamentation. **2** oval ring enclosing the name and title of a pharaoh. [French: related to CARTOON]

cartridge /ˈkɑːtrɪdʒ/ *n.* **1** case containing an explosive charge or bullet for firearms or blasting. **2** sealed container of film etc. **3** component carrying the stylus on a record-player. **4** ink-container for insertion in a pen. [French: related to CARTOON]

cartridge-belt *n.* belt with pockets or loops for cartridges.

cartridge paper *n.* thick paper for drawing etc.

cartwheel *n.* **1** wheel of a cart. **2** circular sideways handspring with arms and legs extended.

cart-wright *n.* maker of carts.

carve *v.* (-**ving**) **1** produce or shape by cutting. **2 a** cut patterns etc. in. **b** (foll. by *into*) form a pattern etc. from (*carved it into a bust*). **3** (*absol.*) cut (meat etc.) into slices. □ **carve out 1** take from a larger whole. **2** establish (a career etc.) purposefully. **carve up 1** subdivide. **2** drive aggressively into the path of (another vehicle). [Old English]

carvel var. of CARAVEL.

carvel-built *adj.* (of a boat) made with planks flush, not overlapping.

carver *n.* **1** person who carves. **2** carving knife. **3** chair with arms, for a person carving:

carvery *n.* (*pl.* -**ies**) buffet or restaurant with joints displayed for carving.

carve-up *n.* *slang* sharing-out, esp. of spoils.

carving *n.* carved object, esp. as a work of art.

carving knife *n.* knife for carving meat.

Casanova /ˌkæsəˈnəʊvə/ *n.* notorious womanizer. [Italian adventurer]

cascade /kæˈskeɪd/ —*n.* **1** small waterfall, esp. one of series. **2** thing falling or arranged like a cascade. —*v.* (-**ding**) fall in or like a cascade. [Latin: related to CASE¹]

cascara /kæˈskɑːrə/ *n.* bark of a Californian buckthorn, used as a laxative. [Spanish]

case¹ *n.* **1** instance of something occurring. **2** hypothetical or actual situation. **3** a person's illness, circumstances, etc., as regarded by a doctor, social worker, etc. **b** such a person. **4** matter under esp. police investigation. **5** suit at law. **6 a** sum of the arguments on one side, esp. in a lawsuit. **b** set of arguments (*have a good case*). **c** valid set of arguments (*have no case*). **7** *Gram.* relation of a word to other words in a sentence. **b** form expressing this. **8** *colloq.* comical person. □ **in any case** whatever the truth is; whatever may happen. **in case 1** in the event that; if. **2** lest; in provision against a possibility (*took it in case*). **in case of** in the event of. **is** (or **is not**) **the case** is (or is not) so. [Latin *casus* from *cado* fall]

case² —*n.* **1** container or enclosing covering. **2** this with its contents. **3** protective outer covering. **4** item of luggage, esp. a suitcase. —*v.* (-**sing**) **1** enclose in a case. **2** (foll. by *with*) surround. **3** *slang* reconnoitre (a house etc.) before burgling it. [Latin *capsa* box]

case-harden *v.* **1** harden the surface of (esp. iron by carbonizing). **2** make callous.

case history *n.* record of a person's life or medical history for use in professional treatment.

casein /ˈkeɪsɪn/ *n.* the main protein in milk and cheese. [Latin *caseus* cheese]

case-law *n.* law as established by the outcome of former cases.

casemate /ˈkeɪsmeɪt/ *n.* **1** embrasured room in a fortress wall. **2** armoured enclosure for guns on a warship. [French and Italian]

casement /ˈkeɪsmənt/ *n.* window or part of a window hinged to open like a door. [Anglo-Latin: related to CASE²]

casework *n.* social work concerned with studying a person's family and background. □ **caseworker** *n.*

cash /kæʃ/ *n.* 1 money in coins or notes. 2 (also cash down) full payment at the time of purchase. 3 *colloq.* wealth. —*v.* give or obtain cash for (a note, cheque, etc.). □ **cash in** 1 obtain cash for. 2 *colloq.* (usu. foll. by *on*) profit (from). **take advantage (of). cash up** count and check the day's takings. [Latin: related to CASE²]

cash and carry *n.* system (esp. in wholesaling) of cash payment for goods taken away by the purchaser. 2 store where this operates.

cash-book *n.* book for recording receipts and cash payments.

cashcard *n.* plastic card for withdrawing money from a cash dispenser.

cash crop *n.* crop produced for sale.

cash desk *n.* counter etc. where payment is made in a shop.

cash dispenser *n.* automatic machine for the withdrawal of cash, esp. with a cashcard.

cashew /ˈkæʃuː/ *n.* 1 evergreen tree bearing kidney-shaped nuts. 2 this edible nut. [Portuguese from Tupi]

cash flow *n.* movement of money into and out of a business.

cashier¹ /kæˈʃɪə(r)/ *n.* person dealing with cash transactions in a shop, bank, etc.

cashier² /ˌkæˈʃɪə(r)/ *v.* dismiss from service, esp. with disgrace. [French: related to QUASH]

cashmere /ˈkæʃmɪə(r)/ *n.* 1 fine soft wool, esp. that of a Kashmir goat. 2 material made from this. [*Kashmir* in Asia]

cash on delivery *n.* payment for goods when they are delivered.

cashpoint *n.* = CASH DISPENSER.

cash register *n.* till recording sales, totalling receipts, etc.

casing /ˈkeɪsɪŋ/ *n.* protective or enclosing cover or material.

casino /kəˈsiːnəʊ/ *n.* (*pl.* -s) public room or building for gambling. [Italian diminutive of *casa* house]

cask /kɑːsk/ *n.* 1 barrel, esp. for alcohol. 2 its contents. [French *casque* or Spanish *casco* helmet]

casket /ˈkɑːskɪt/ *n.* 1 small often ornamental box for jewels etc. 2 US coffin. [Latin: related to CASE²]

cassata /kəˈsɑːtə/ *n.* ice-cream containing fruit and nuts. [Italian]

cassava /kəˈsɑːvə/ *n.* 1 plant with starchy roots. 2 starch or flour from these, used e.g. in tapioca. [Taino]

casserole /ˈkæsərəʊl/ —*n.* 1 covered dish for cooking food in the oven. 2 food cooked in this. —*v.* (-ling) cook in a casserole. [Greek *kua-thion* little cup]

cassette /kæˈset/ *n.* sealed case containing magnetic tape, film etc. ready for insertion in a tape recorder, camera, etc. [French: diminutive: related to CASE²]

cassia /ˈkæsɪə/ *n.* 1 tree from the leaves of which senna is extracted. 2 cinnamon-like bark of this used as a spice. [Greek *kasia* from Hebrew]

cassis /kæˈsiːs/ *n.* blackcurrant flavouring for drinks etc. [French]

cassock /ˈkæsək/ *n.* long usu. black or red clerical garment. □ **cassocked** *adj.* [French from Italian]

cassoulet /ˈkæsʊleɪ/ *n.* ragout of meat and beans. [French]

cassowary /ˈkæsəwɛərɪ/ *n.* (*pl.* -ies) large flightless Australasian bird. [Malay]

cast /kɑːst/ —*v.* (*past and past part.* cast) 1 throw, esp. deliberately or forcefully. 2 (often foll. by *on*, *over*) a direct or cause (one's eyes, a glance, light, a shadow, a spell, etc.) to fall. b express (doubts, aspersions etc.). 3 throw out (a fishing-line etc.). 4 let down (an anchor etc.). 5 a throw off, get rid of. b shed or lose (horns, skin, a horseshoe, etc.). 6 =register (a vote). 7 a shape (molten metal etc.) in a mould. b make thus. 8 a (usu. foll. by *as*) assign (an actor) to a role. b allocate roles in a play (etc.). 9 (foll. by *in*, *into*) arrange (facts etc.) in a specified form. 10 reckon, add up (accounts or figures). 11 calculate (a horoscope). —*n.* 1 throwing of a missile, dice, line, net, etc. 2 a object made in a mould. b moulded mass of solidified material, esp. plaster for a broken limb. 3 actors in a play etc. 4 form, type, or quality. 5 tinge or shade of colour. 6 slight squint. 7 worm-cast. □ **cast about** (or around) search. **cast aside** abandon. **cast down** deject. **cast loose** detach (oneself). **cast lots** see LOT. **cast off** 1 abandon. 2 finish a piece of knitting. 3 set a ship free from a quay etc. **cast on** make the first row of a piece of knitting. **cast up** 1 deposit on the shore. 2 add up (figures etc.). [Old Norse]

castanet /ˌkæstəˈnet/ *n.* (usu. in *pl.*) each of a pair of hand-held pieces of wood etc., clicked together as an accompaniment, esp. by Spanish dancers. [Latin: related to CHESTNUT]

castaway /ˈkɑːstəweɪ/ —*n.* shipwrecked person. —*adj.* shipwrecked.

caste /kɑːst/ *n.* 1 any of the Hindu hereditary classes whose members have no social contact with other

classes. 2 exclusive social class or system of classes. □ **lose caste** descend in social order. [Spanish and Portuguese; related to CHASTE]

casteism /'ka:stɪz(ə)m/ n. caste system.

castellated /'kastəleɪtɪd/ adj. 1 having battlements. 2 castle-like. □ **castellation** /-'leɪʃ(ə)n/ n. [medieval Latin: related to CASTLE]

caster var. of CASTOR.

castigate /'kastɪgeɪt/ v. (-ting) rebuke or punish severely. □ **castigation** /-'geɪʃ(ə)n/ n. **castigator** n. [Latin castus pure]

casting /'ka:stɪŋ/ n. cast, esp. of molten metal.

casting vote n. deciding vote when the votes on two sides are equal. [from an obsolete sense of cast, = turn the scale]

cast iron n. hard alloy of iron, carbon, and silicon cast in a mould.

cast-iron adj. 1 of cast iron. 2 very strong; rigid; unchallengeable.

castle /'ka:s(ə)l/ —n. 1 large fortified building with towers and battlements. 2 Chess = ROOK². —v. (-ling) Chess move a rook next to the king and the king to the other side of the rook. □ **castles in the air** day-dream; impractical scheme. [Latin castellum]

cast-off —adj. abandoned, discarded. —n. cast-off thing, esp. a garment.

castor /'ka:stə(r)/ n. (also **caster**) 1 small swivelled wheel on the leg or underside of a piece of furniture. 2 small perforated container for sprinkling sugar, flour, etc. [from CAST]

castor² /'ka:stə(r)/ n. oil from the seeds of a tropical plant, used as a purgative and lubricant. [origin uncertain]

castor sugar n. finely granulated white sugar.

castrate /ka'streɪt/ v. (-ting) 1 remove the testicles of; geld. 2 deprive of vigour. □ **castration** n. [Latin castro]

castrato /kæ'strɑːtəʊ/ n. (pl. -ti /-tɪ/) hist. castrated male soprano or alto singer. [Italian: related to CASTRATE]

casual /'kaʒʊəl/ —adj. 1 accidental; chance. 2 not regular or permanent (casual work). 3 a unconcerned b careless; unthinking. 4 (of clothes) informal. —n. 1 casual worker. 2 (usu. in pl.) casual clothes or shoes. □ **casually** adv. **casualness** n. [French and Latin: related to CASE²]

casualty /'kaʒʊəltɪ/ n. (pl. -ies) 1 person killed or injured in a war or accident. 2 thing lost or destroyed. 3 = CASUALTY DEPARTMENT. 4 accident, mishap. [medieval Latin: related to CASUAL]

casualty department n. part of a hospital where casualties are dealt with.

casuist /'kazjʊɪst/ n. 1 person who uses clever but false reasoning in matters of conscience etc. 2 sophist, quibbler. □ **casuistic** /-'ɪstɪk/ adj. **casuistry** n. [Latin: related to CASE²]

cat n. 1 small soft-furred four-legged domesticated animal. 2 wild animal of the same family, e.g. lion, tiger. 3 colloq. malicious or spiteful woman. 4 = CAT-O'-NINE-TAILS. □ **the cat's whiskers** colloq. excellent person or thing. **let the cat out of the bag** reveal a secret. **like a cat on hot bricks** very agitated. **put (or set) the cat among the pigeons** cause trouble. **rain cats and dogs** rain hard. [Latin cattus]

cata- prefix 1 down. 2 wrongly. [Greek]

catabolism /kə'tabə,lɪz(ə)m/ n. breakdown of complex molecules in living organisms to release energy; destructive metabolism. □ **catabolic** /,katə'bɒlɪk/ adj. [Greek katabolē throwing down]

catachresis /,katə'kriːsɪs/ n. (pl. -chreses /-siːz/) incorrect use of words. □ **catachrestic** /-'kriːstɪk/ adj. [Greek khraomai use]

cataclysm /'katə,klɪz(ə)m/ n. 1 a violent upheaval or disaster. b great change. 2 great flood. □ **cataclysmic** /-'klɪzmɪk/ adj. [Greek kluzō wash]

catacomb /'katə,kuːm/ n. (often in pl.) underground cemetery, esp. Roman. [French from Latin]

catafalque /'katəfælk/ n. decorated bier, used esp. in State funerals or for lying in state. [French from Italian]

Catalan /'katə,lan/ —n. native or language of Catalonia in Spain. —adj. of Catalonia. [French from Spanish]

catalepsy /'katə,lepsɪ/ n. trance or seizure with unconsciousness and rigidity of the body. □ **cataleptic** /-'leptɪk/ adj. & n. [Greek lēpsis seizure]

catalogue /'katə,lɒg/ (US catalog) —n. 1 complete alphabetical or otherwise ordered list of items, often with a description of each. 2 extensive list (catalogue of disasters). —v. (-logues, -logued, -loguing; US -logs, -loged, -loging) 1 make a catalogue of. 2 enter in a catalogue. [Greek legō choose]

catalpa /kə'talpə/ n. tree with long pods and showy flowers. [N. American Indian]

catalyse /'katə,laɪz/ v. (US -yze) (-sing or -zing) produce (a reaction) by catalysis.

catalysis /kə'talɪsɪs/ n. (pl. -lyses /-siːz/) acceleration of a chemical reaction by a catalyst. [Greek luō set free]

catalyst /ˈkatəlist/ n. **1** substance that does not itself change, but speeds up a chemical reaction. **2** person or thing that precipitates change.

catalytic /katəˈlitik/ adj. of or involving catalysis.

catalytic converter n. device incorporated in a vehicle's exhaust system, with a catalyst for converting pollutant gases into harmless products.

catamaran /katəməˈran/ n. **1** boat with parallel twin hulls. **2** raft of yoked logs or boats. [Tamil]

catamite /ˈkatəmaɪt/ n. passive partner (esp. a boy) in homosexual practices. [Latin, = Ganymede]

cat-and-dog adj. (of a relationship etc.) quarrelsome.

catapult /ˈkatəpʌlt/ —n. **1** forked stick etc. with elastic for shooting stones. **2** Mil. hist. machine for hurling large stones etc. **3** device for launching a glider etc. —v. **1 a** hurl from or launch with a catapult. **b** fling forcibly. **2** leap or be hurled forcibly. [Latin from Greek]

cataract /ˈkatərakt/ n. **1 a** large waterfall. **b** downpour; rush of water. **2** eye condition in which the lens becomes progressively opaque. [Greek kataraktēs = down-rushing]

catarrh /kəˈtɑː(r)/ n. **1** inflammation of the mucous membrane of the nose, air-passages, etc. **2** mucus caused by this. □ **catarrhal** adj. [Greek rheō flow]

catastrophe /kəˈtastrəfi/ n. **1** great and usu. sudden disaster. **2** denouement of a drama. □ **catastrophic** /-ˈstrɒfik/ adj. **catastrophically** /-ˈstrɒfikəli/ adv. [Greek strephō turn]

catatonia /katəˈtəʊnɪə/ n. **1** schizophrenia with intervals of catalepsy and sometimes violence. **2** catalepsy. □ **catatonic** /-ˈtɒnik/ adj. & n. [Greek: related to CATA-, TONE]

cat burglar n. burglar who enters by climbing to an upper storey.

catcall —n. shrill whistle of disapproval. —v. make a catcall.

catch —v. (past and past part. caught /kɔːt/) **1** capture in a trap, one's hands, etc. **2** detect or surprise (esp. a guilty person). **3 a** intercept and hold (a moving thing). **b** Cricket dismiss (a batsman) by catching the ball before it reaches the ground. **4 a** contract (a disease) from an infected person. **b** acquire (a quality etc.) from another. **5** reach in time and board (a train, bus, etc.). **b** be in time to see etc. (a person or thing about to leave or finish). **6** apprehend with the senses or mind (esp. a thing occurring quickly or briefly). **7** (of an artist etc.) reproduce faithfully. **8 a** (cause to) become fixed,

entangled, or checked. **b** (often foll. by on) hit, deal a blow to (caught his elbow on the table). **9** draw the attention of; captivate (caught his eye, caught her fancy). **10** begin to burn. **11** reach or overtake (a person etc. ahead). **12** (foll. by at) try to grasp. —n. **1 a** act of catching. **b** Cricket chance or act of catching the ball. **2 a** amount of a thing caught, esp. of fish **b** thing or person caught or worth catching, esp. in marriage. **3 a** question, trick, etc., intended to deceive, incriminate, etc. **b** unexpected or hidden difficulty or disadvantage. **4** device for fastening a door or window etc. **5** Mus. round, esp. with words arranged to produce a humorous effect. □ **catch fire** see FIRE. **catch hold of** grasp, seize. **catch it** slang be punished. **catch on** colloq. **1** become popular. **2** understand what is meant. **catch out 1** detect in a mistake etc. **2** take unawares. **3** = sense 3b of v. **catch up 1 a** (often foll. by with) reach a person etc. ahead (often foll. by with, on) make up arrears. **b** (often foll. by with, on) make up arrears. **2** pick up hurriedly. **3** (often in passive) **a** involve; entangle (caught up in crime). **b** fasten up (hair caught up in a ribbon). [Latin capio try to catch]

catch-all n. (often attrib.) thing designed to be all-inclusive.

catch-as-catch-can n. wrestling with few holds barred.

catching adj. (of a disease, practice, etc.) infectious.

catchline n. short line of type, esp. at the head of copy or as a running headline.

catchment n. collection of rainfall.

catchment area n. **1** area served by a school, hospital, etc. **2** area from which rainfall flows into a river etc.

catchpenny attrib. adj. intended merely to sell quickly; superficially attractive.

catch-phrase n. phrase in frequent use.

catch-22 n. (often attrib.) colloq. unresolvable situation containing conflicting or mutually dependent conditions.

catchweight —adj. unrestricted as regards weight. —n. unrestricted weight category in sports.

catchword n. **1** phrase, word, or slogan in frequent current use. **2** word so placed as to draw attention.

catchy adj. (-ier, -iest) (of a tune) easy to remember; attractive.

cat door var. of CAT FLAP.

catechism /ˈkatəkız(ə)m/ n. **1 a** principles of a religion in the form of questions and answers. **b** book containing

this. **2** series of questions. [Church Latin: related to CATECHIZE]

catechist /'kætɪkɪst/ *n.* religious teacher, esp. one using a catechism.

catechize /'kætɪ,kaɪz/ *v.* (also **-ise**) (**-zing** or **-sing**) instruct by using a catechism. [Greek *katēkheō* cause to hear]

catechumen /,kætɪ'kju:mən/ *n.* Christian convert under instruction before baptism. [Church Latin *catechumenus*]

categorical /,kætɪ'gɒrɪk(ə)l/ *adj.* unconditional, absolute; explicit. □ **categorically** *adv.* [related to CATEGORY]

categorize /'kætɪgə,raɪz/ *v.* (also **-ise**) (**-zing** or **-sing**) place in a category. □ **categorization** /-'zeɪʃ(ə)n/ *n.*

category /'kætɪgərɪ/ *n.* (*pl.* **-ies**) class or division (of things, ideas, etc.). [Greek, = statement]

cater /'keɪtə(r)/ *v.* **1** supply food. **2** (foll. by *for*) provide what is needed or desired (*caters for all tastes*). **3** (foll. by *to*) pander to (esp. low tastes). [Anglo-French *acatour* buyer, from Latin *capto*: related to CATCH]

caterer *n.* professional supplier of food for social events.

caterpillar /'kætə,pɪlə(r)/ *n.* **1** larva of a butterfly or moth. **2** (Caterpillar *propr.*) (in full **Caterpillar track** or **tread**) *propr.* steel band passing round the wheels of a tractor etc. for travel on rough ground. **b** vehicle with these. [Anglo-French, = hairy cat]

caterwaul /'kætə,wɔ:l/ *v.* make the shrill howl of a cat. —*n.* this noise. [from CAT, *-waul* imitative]

catfish *n.* (*pl.* same) freshwater fish with whisker-like barbels round the mouth.

cat flap *n.* (also **cat door**) small swinging flap in an outer door, for a cat to pass in and out.

catgut *n.* material used for the strings of musical instruments and surgical sutures, made of intestines of the sheep, horse, etc. (but not cat).

catharsis /kə'θɑːsɪs/ *n.* (*pl.* **catharses** /-siːz/) **1** emotional release in drama or art. **2** *Psychol.* freeing and elimination of repressed emotion. **3** emptying of the bowels. [Greek *katharos* clean]

cathartic /kə'θɑːtɪk/ —*adj.* **1** effecting catharsis. **2** laxative. —*n.* laxative.

cathedral /kə'θiːdr(ə)l/ *n.* principal church of a diocese. [Greek *kathedra* seat]

Catherine wheel /'kæθərɪn/ *n.* flat coiled firework spinning when lit. [St *Catherine*, who was martyred on a spiked wheel]

catheter /'kæθɪtə(r)/ *n.* tube inserted into a body cavity for introducing or

removing fluid. [Greek *kathiēmi* send down]

cathode /'kæθəʊd/ *n. Electr.* **1** negative electrode in an electrolytic cell. **2** positive terminal of a battery etc. [Greek *kathodos* way down]

cathode ray *n.* beam of electrons from the cathode of a vacuum tube.

cathode-ray tube *n.* vacuum tube in which cathode rays produce a luminous image on a fluorescent screen.

catholic /'kæθlɪk/ —*adj.* **1** all-embracing; of wide sympathies or interests. **2** of interest or use to all; universal. **3** (**Catholic**) **a** Roman Catholic. **b** including all Christians, or all of the Western Church. —*n.* (**Catholic**) Roman Catholic. □ **Catholicism** /kə'θɒlɪ,sɪz(ə)m/ *n.* **catholicity** /,kæθə'lɪsɪtɪ/ *n.* [Greek *holos* whole]

cation /'kæt,aɪən/ *n.* positively charged ion. □ **cationic** /-'ɒnɪk/ *adj.* [from CATA-, ION]

catkin *n.* small spike of usu. hanging flowers on a willow, hazel, etc. [Dutch, = kitten]

catlick *n. colloq.* perfunctory wash.

catmint *n.* pungent plant attractive to cats.

catnap —*n.* short sleep. —*v.* (**-pp-**) have a catnap.

catnip *n.* = CATMINT. [from CAT, dial. *nip* catmint]

cat-o'-nine-tails *n. hist.* whip with nine knotted lashes.

cat's cradle *n.* child's game of forming patterns from a loop of string.

Cat's-eye *n. propr.* reflector stud set into a road.

cat's-eye *n.* precious stone.

cat's-paw *n.* **1** person used as a tool by another. **2** slight breeze.

catsuit *n.* close-fitting garment with trouser legs, covering the whole body.

catsup *US* var. of KETCHUP.

cattery *n.* (*pl.* **-ies**) place where cats are boarded or bred.

cattle /'kæt(ə)l/ *n.pl.* large ruminant animals with horns and cloven hoofs, esp. bred for milk or meat. [Anglo-French *catel*: related to CAPITAL]

cattle-grid *n.* grid over a ditch, allowing people and vehicles but not livestock to pass over.

catty *adj.* (**-ier, -iest**) spiteful. □ **cattily** *adv.* **cattiness** *n.*

catwalk *n.* narrow footway or platform.

Caucasian /kɔː'keɪʒ(ə)n/ —*adj.* **1** of the White or light-skinned race. **2** of the Caucasus. —*n.* Caucasian person. [*Caucasus* in Georgia]

Caucasoid /'kɔːkə,sɔɪd/ *adj.* of Caucasians.

caucus /ˈkɔːkəs/ n. (pl. **-es**) **1** US meeting of party members, esp. in the Senate etc., to decide policy. **2** often derog. **a** meeting of a group within a larger organization or party. **b** such a group. [perhaps from Algonquian]

caudal /ˈkɔːd(ə)l/ adj. **1** of or like a tail. **2** of the posterior part of the body. [Latin cauda tail]

caudate /ˈkɔːdeɪt/ adj. tailed.

caught past and past part. of CATCH.

caul /kɔːl/ n. **1** membrane enclosing a foetus. **2** part of this occasionally found on a child's head at birth. [French]

cauldron /ˈkɔːldrən/ n. (also **caldron**) large deep vessel used for boiling. [Latin caldarium hot bath]

cauliflower /ˈkɒlɪflaʊə(r)/ n. cabbage with a large white flower-head. [French chou fleuri flowered cabbage]

cauliflower ear n. ear thickened by repeated blows.

caulk /kɔːk/ v. (also **calk**) **1** stop up (the seams of a boat etc.). **2** make (esp. a boat) watertight. [Latin calco tread]

causal /ˈkɔːz(ə)l/ adj. **1** of or forming a cause. **2** relating to cause and effect. □ **causally** adv.

causality /kɔːˈzælɪtɪ/ n. **1** relation of cause and effect. **2** principle that everything has a cause.

causation /kɔːˈzeɪʃ(ə)n/ n. **1** act of causing. **2** = CAUSALITY.

causative /ˈkɔːzətɪv/ adj. acting as or expressing a cause.

cause /kɔːz/ —n. **1 a** thing that produces an effect. **b** person or thing that occasions or produces something. **c** reason or motive. **2** adequate reason (show cause). **3** principle, belief, or purpose. **4 a** matter to be settled at law. **b** case offered at law (plead a cause). —v. (-sing) te the cause of, produce, make happen. [Latin causa]

cause célèbre /ˌkɔːz seˈlebr/ n. (pl. **causes célèbres** pronunc. same) lawsuit that attracts much interest. [French]

causerie /ˈkəʊzərɪ/ n. (pl. **-s** pronunc. same) informal article or talk. [French]

causeway /ˈkɔːzweɪ/ n. **1** raised road across low ground or water. **2** raised path or a road. [Anglo-French caucée from Latin CALX]

caustic /ˈkɔːstɪk/ —adj. **1** corrosive; burning. **2** sarcastic, biting. —n. caustic substance. □ **caustically** adv. **causticity** /-ˈtɪstɪ/ n. [Greek kaiō burn]

caustic soda n. sodium hydroxide.

cauterize /ˈkɔːtəraɪz/ v. (also **-ise**) (-zing or -sing) burn (tissue), esp. to stop bleeding. [French: related to CAUTERY]

caution /ˈkɔːʃ(ə)n/ —n. **1** attention to safety, prudence, carefulness. **2 a** Law warning, esp. a formal one. **b** warning and reprimand. **3** colloq. amusing or surprising person or thing. —v. **1** warn or admonish. **2** issue a caution to. [Latin caveo take heed]

cautionary adj. giving or serving as a warning.

cautious adj. having or showing caution. □ **cautiously** adv. **cautiousness** n.

cavalcade /ˌkævəlˈkeɪd/ n. procession or assembly of riders, vehicles, etc. [Italian related to CHEVALIER]

cavalier /ˌkævəˈlɪə(r)/ —n. **1** hist. (Cavalier) supporter of Charles I in the Civil War. **2** courtly gentleman. **3** archaic horseman. —adj. offhand, supercilious, curt. [related to CAVALCADE]

cavalry /ˈkævəlrɪ/ n. (pl. **-ies**) (usu. treated as pl.) soldiers on horseback or in armoured vehicles. [related to CAVALCADE]

cave —n. large hollow in the side of a cliff, hill, etc., or underground. —v. (-ving) explore caves. □ **cave in 1** (cause to) subside or collapse. **2** yield, give up. [Latin cavus hollow]

caveat /ˈkæviæt/ n. **1** warning, proviso. **2** Law process in court to suspend proceedings. [Latin, = let him beware]

caveat emptor /ˈemptɔː(r)/ n. principle that the buyer alone is responsible if dissatisfied. [Latin, = let the buyer beware]

caveman n. **1** prehistoric person living in caves. **2** crude person.

cavern /ˈkæv(ə)n/ n. cave, esp. a large or dark one. □ **cavernous** adj. [Latin caverna: related to CAVE]

caviare /ˈkævɪɑː(r)/ n. (US **caviar**) pickled roe of sturgeon or other large fish. [Italian from Turkish]

cavil /ˈkævɪl/ —v. (-ll-, US -l-) (usu. foll. by at, about) make petty objections; carp. —n. trivial objection. [Latin cavilor]

cavity /ˈkævɪtɪ/ n. (pl. **-ies**) **1** hollow within a solid body. **2** decayed part of a tooth. [Latin related to CAVE]

cavity wall n. double wall with a space between.

cavort /kəˈvɔːt/ v. caper excitedly. [origin uncertain]

cavy /ˈkeɪvɪ/ n. (pl. **-ies**) small S. American rodent, esp. the guinea pig. [from Galibi]

caw —n. harsh cry of a rook, crow, etc. —v. utter this cry. [imitative]

cayenne /keɪˈen/ n. (in full **cayenne pepper**) powdered red pepper. [Tupi]

cayman /ˈkeɪmən/ n. (also **caiman**) (pl. **-s**) S. American alligator-like reptile. [Spanish and Portuguese from Carib]

CB *abbr.* **1** citizens' band. **2** Companion of the Order of the Bath.

CBE *abbr.* Commander of the Order of the British Empire.

CBI *abbr.* Confederation of British Industry.

cc *abbr.* (also **c.c.**) **1** cubic centimetre(s). **2** copy or copies (to).

Cd *symb.* cadmium.

cd *abbr.* candela.

CD-ROM /ˌsiːdiːˈrɒm/ *abbr.* compact disc read-only memory (for the retrieval of text or data on a VDU screen).

CDT *abbr.* craft, design, and technology.

CD-video /ˌsiːdiːˈvɪdɪəʊ/ *n.* (*pl.* **-s**) **1** system of simultaneously reproducing high-quality sound and video pictures from a compact disc. **2** such a compact disc.

Ce *symb.* cerium.

cease *formal* — *v.* (**-sing**) stop; bring or come to an end. — *n.* (in *without cease*) unending. [Latin *cesso*]

cease-fire *n.* **1** period of truce. **2** order to stop firing.

ceaseless *adj.* without end. □ **ceaselessly** *adv.*

cecum *US* var. of CAECUM.

cedar /ˈsiːdə(r)/ *n.* **1** spreading evergreen conifer. **2** its hard fragrant wood. [Greek *kedros*]

cede *v.* (**-ding**) *formal* give up one's rights to or possession of. [Latin *cedo cess-* yield]

cedilla /sɪˈdɪlə/ *n.* **1** mark written under *c*, esp. in French, to show its sibilant (as in *façade*). **2** similar mark under *s* in Turkish etc. [Spanish diminutive of *zeda* Z]

Ceefax /ˈsiːfæks/ *n. propr.* teletext service provided by the BBC. [representing a pronunciation of *seeing* + *facsimile*]

ceilidh /ˈkeɪlɪ/ *n.* informal gathering for music, dancing, etc. [Gaelic]

ceiling /ˈsiːlɪŋ/ *n.* **1** upper interior surface of a room or other compartment. **2** upper limit. **3** maximum altitude a given aircraft can reach. [origin uncertain]

celandine /ˈselənˌdaɪn/ *n.* yellow-flowered plant. [Greek *khelidōn* a swallow]

celebrant /ˈselɪbrənt/ *n.* person who performs a rite, esp. the priest at the Eucharist.

celebrate /ˈselɪˌbreɪt/ *v.* (**-ting**) **1** mark with or engage in festivities. **2** perform (a rite or ceremony). **3** praise publicly. □ **celebration** /-ˈbreɪʃ(ə)n/ *n.* **celebrator** *n.* **celebratory** /-ˈbreɪtərɪ/ *adj.* [Latin *celeber* renowned]

celebrity /sɪˈlebrɪtɪ/ *n.* (*pl.* **-ies**) **1** well-known person. **2** fame. [Latin: related to CELEBRATE]

celeriac /sɪˈlerɪˌæk/ *n.* variety of celery. [from CELERY]

celerity /sɪˈlerɪtɪ/ *n. archaic* or *literary* swiftness. [Latin *celer* swift]

celery /ˈselərɪ/ *n.* plant with crisp long whitish leaf-stalks used as a vegetable. [Greek *selinon* parsley]

celesta /sɪˈlestə/ *n.* small keyboard instrument with steel plates struck to give a bell-like sound. [French: related to CELESTIAL]

celestial /sɪˈlestɪəl/ *adj.* **1** of the sky or heavenly bodies. **2** heavenly; divinely good; sublime. [Latin *caelum* sky]

celestial equator *n.* the great circle of the sky in the plane perpendicular to the earth's axis.

celestial sphere *n.* imaginary sphere, of any radius, of which the observer is the centre and in which celestial bodies are represented as lying.

celibate /ˈselɪbət/ — *adj.* **1** unmarried or committed to sexual abstention, esp. for religious reasons. **2** having no sexual relations. — *n.* celibate person. □ **celibacy** *n.* [Latin *caelebs* unmarried]

cell *n.* **1** small room, esp. in a prison or monastery. **2** small compartment, e.g. in a honeycomb. **3** small, active, esp. subversive, political group. **4** **a** smallest structural and functional unit of living matter, consisting of cytoplasm and a nucleus enclosed in a membrane. **b** enclosed cavity in an organism etc. **5** vessel containing electrodes for current-generation or electrolysis. [Latin *cella*]

cellar /ˈselə(r)/ — *n.* **1** storage room below ground level in a house. **2** stock of wine in a cellar. — *v.* store in a cellar. [Latin *cellarium*: related to CELL]

cello /ˈtʃeləʊ/ *n.* (*pl.* **-s**) bass instrument of the violin family, held between the legs of the seated player. □ **cellist** *n.* [abbreviation of VIOLONCELLO]

Cellophane /ˈseləˌfeɪn/ *n. propr.* thin transparent viscose wrapping material. [from CELLULOSE: cf. DIAPHANOUS]

cellphone *n.* small portable radio-telephone.

cellular /ˈseljʊlə(r)/ *adj.* consisting of cells, of open texture; porous. □ **cellularity** /-ˈlærɪtɪ/ *n.* [French: related to CELL]

cellular radio *n.* system of mobile radio-telephone transmission with an area divided into 'cells', each served by a small transmitter.

cellulite /ˈseljʊˌlaɪt/ *n.* lumpy fat, esp. on the hips and thighs of women.

celluloid /ˈseljʊˌlɔɪd/ *n.* **1** plastic made from camphor and cellulose nitrate. **2** cinema film.

cellulose /ˈseljʊləʊs/ *n.* **1** carbohydrate forming plant-cell walls, used in textile fibres. **2** (in general use) paint or lacquer consisting of esp. cellulose acetate or nitrate in solution. [Latin: related to CELL]

Celsius /ˈselsɪəs/ *adj.* of a scale of temperature on which water freezes at 0° and boils at 100°. [name of an astronomer]

■ **Usage** See note at *centigrade*.

Celt /kelt/ *n.* (also **Kelt**) member of an ethnic group, including the inhabitants of Ireland, Wales, Scotland, Cornwall, and Brittany. [Latin from Greek]

Celtic /ˈkeltɪk/ —*adj.* of the Celts. —*n.* group of Celtic languages, including Gaelic and Irish, Welsh, Cornish, and Breton.

cement /sɪˈment/ —*n.* **1** powdery substance of calcined lime and clay, mixed with water to form mortar or used in concrete. **2** similar substance. **3** uniting factor or principle. **4** substance used in filling teeth, doing hip replacements, etc. —*v.* **1 a** unite with or as with cement. **b** establish or strengthen (a friendship etc.). **2** apply cement to. **3** line or cover with cement. □ **cementation** /ˌsiːmenˈteɪʃ(ə)n/ *n.* [Latin *caedo* cut]

cemetery /ˈsemɪtrɪ/ *n.* (*pl.* **-ies**) burial ground, esp. one not in a churchyard. [Greek *koimaō* put to sleep]

cenobite *US* var. of CŒNOBITE.

cenotaph /ˈsenəˌtɑːf/ *n.* tomblike monument to a person whose body is elsewhere. [Greek *kenos* empty, *taphos* tomb]

Cenozoic /ˌsiːnəˈzəʊɪk/ (also **Cainozoic** /ˌkaɪnə-/, **Caenozoic** /ˌsiːn-/) —*adj.* of the most recent geological era marked by the evolution and development of mammals etc. —*n.* this era. [Greek *kainos* new, *zōion* animal]

censer /ˈsensə(r)/ *n.* vessel for burning incense. [Anglo-French: related to INCENSE[1]]

censor /ˈsensə(r)/ —*n.* official authorized to suppress or expurgate books, films, news, etc., on grounds of obscenity, threat to security, etc. —*v.* **1** act as a censor of. **2** make deletions or changes in. □ **censorial** /-ˈsɔːrɪəl/ *adj.* **censorship** *n.* [Latin *censeo* assess]

■ **Usage** As a verb, *censor* is often confused with *censure*.

censorious /senˈsɔːrɪəs/ *adj.* severely critical. □ **censoriously** *adv.*

censure /ˈsenʃə(r)/ —*v.* (**-ring**) criticize harshly; reprove. —*n.* hostile criticism; disapproval. [Latin: related to CENSOR]

■ **Usage** As a verb, *censure* is often confused with *censor*.

census /ˈsensəs/ *n.* (*pl.* **-suses**) official count of population etc. [Latin: related to CENSOR]

cent *n.* **1** a one-hundredth of a dollar or other decimal currency unit. **b** coin of this value. **2** *colloq.* very small amount. [Latin *centum* 100]

centaur /ˈsentɔː(r)/ *n.* creature in Greek mythology with the upper half of a man and the lower half of a horse. [Latin from Greek]

centenarian /ˌsentɪˈneərɪən/ —*n.* person a hundred or more years old. —*adj.* a hundred or more years old.

centenary /senˈtiːnərɪ/ —*n.* (*pl.* **-ies**) **1** hundredth anniversary. **2** celebration of this. —*adj.* **1** of a centenary. **2** occurring every hundred years. [Latin *centeni* 100 each]

centennial /senˈtenɪəl/ —*adj.* **1** lasting for a hundred years. **2** occurring every hundred years. —*n.* *US* **=** CENTENARY *n.* [Latin *centum* 100 + ANNUAL]

center *US* var. of CENTRE.

centerboard *US* var. of CENTREBOARD.

centerfold *US* var. of CENTREFOLD.

centesimal /senˈtesɪm(ə)l/ *adj.* reckoning or reckoned by hundredths. [Latin *centum* 100]

centi- *comb. form* **1** one-hundredth. **2** hundred. [Latin *centum* 100]

centigrade /ˈsentɪˌgreɪd/ *adj.* **1** = CELSIUS. **2** having a scale of a hundred degrees. [Latin *gradus* step]

■ **Usage** In sense 1 *Celsius* is usually preferred in technical contexts.

centigram /ˈsentɪˌgræm/ *n.* (also **centigramme**) metric unit of mass, equal to 0.01 gram.

centilitre /ˈsentɪˌliːtə(r)/ *n.* (*US* **centiliter**) 0.01 litre.

centime /ˈsɒntiːm/ *n.* **1** one-hundredth of a franc. **2** coin of this value. [Latin *centum* 100]

centimetre /ˈsentɪˌmiːtə(r)/ *n.* (*US* **centimeter**) 0.01 metre.

centipede /ˈsentɪˌpiːd/ *n.* arthropod with a segmented wormlike body and many legs. [Latin *pes ped-* foot]

central /ˈsentr(ə)l/ *adj.* **1** of, at, or forming the centre. **2** from the centre. **3** chief, essential, most important. □ **centrally** /ˈtreɪltɪ/ *adv.* **centrality** /-ˈtrælɪtɪ/ *n.*

central bank *n.* national bank issuing currency etc.

central heating *n.* method of heating a building by pipes, radiators, etc., fed from a central source.

centralism *n.* system that centralizes (esp. administration). □ **centralist** *n.*

centralize v. (also **-ise**) (**-zing** or **-sing**) **1** concentrate (esp. administration) at a single centre. **2** subject (a State) to this system. □ **centralization** /-'zeɪʃ(ə)n/ n.

central processor n. (also **central processing unit**) principal operating part of a computer.

centre /'sentə(r)/ (*US* **center**) —n. **1** middle point or axis of rotation. **3 a** place or buildings forming a central point or a main area for an activity (*shopping centre; town centre*). **b** (with a preceding word) equipment for a number of connected functions (*music centre*). **4** point of concentration or dispersion; nucleus, source. **5** political party or group holding moderate opinions. **6** filling in chocolate etc. **7** *Sport* **a** middle player in a line in some field games. **b** kick or hit from the side to the centre of a pitch. **8** (*attrib.*) of or at the centre. —v. (**-ring**) **1** (foll. by *in, on, round*) have as its main centre. **2** place in the centre. **3** (foll. by *in* etc.) concentrate. [Greek *kentron* sharp point]

■ **Usage** The use of the verb in sense 1 with *round* is common and used by good writers, but is still considered incorrect by some people.

centre back n. *Sport* middle player or position in a half-back line.

centreboard n. (*US* **centerboard**) board lowered through a boat's keel to prevent leeway.

centrefold n. (*US* **centerfold**) centre spread of a magazine etc., esp. with nude photographs.

centre forward n. *Sport* middle player or position in a forward line.

centre half n. = CENTRE BACK.

centre of gravity n. (also **centre of mass**) point at which the weight of a body may be considered to act.

centre-piece n. **1** ornament for the middle of a table. **2** principal item.

centre spread n. two facing middle pages of a newspaper etc.

centric adj. **1** at or near the centre. **2** from a centre. □ **centrical** adj. **centrically** adv.

centrifugal /sentrɪ'fju:g(ə)l/ adj. moving or tending to move from a centre. □ **centrifugally** adv. [from CENTRE, Latin *fugio* flee]

centrifugal force n. apparent force that acts outwards on a body moving about a centre.

centrifuge /'sentrɪfju:dʒ/ n. rapidly rotating machine designed to separate liquids from solids etc.

centripetal /sen'trɪpɪt(ə)l/ adj. moving or tending to move towards a centre. □ **centripetally** adv. [Latin *peto* seek]

centripetal force n. force acting on a body causing it to move towards a centre.

centrist n. *Polit.* often *derog.* person holding moderate political opinions. □ **centrism** n.

centurion /sen'tjuərɪən/ n. commander of a century in the ancient Roman army. [Latin: related to CENTURY]

century /'sentʃərɪ/ n. (*pl.* **-ies**) **1 a** 100 years. **b** any century reckoned from the birth of Christ (*twentieth century* = 1901–2000; *fifth century* BC = 500–401 BC). **2** score etc. of 100 esp. by one batsman in cricket. **3** company in the ancient Roman army, orig. of 100 men. [Latin *centuria*: related to CENT]

■ **Usage** Strictly speaking, since the first century ran from the year 1–100, the first year of a given century should be that ending in 01. However, in popular use this has been moved back a year, and so the twenty-first century will commonly be regarded as running from 2000–2099.

cephalic /sə'fælɪk/ adj. of or in the head. [Greek *kephalē* head]

cephalopod /'sefələ,pɒd/ n. mollusc with a distinct tentacled head, e.g. the octopus. [from CEPHALIC, Greek *pous pod-* foot]

ceramic /sɪ'ræmɪk/ —adj. **1** made of (esp.) baked clay. **2** of ceramics. —n. ceramic article or product. [Greek *keramos* pottery]

ceramics n.pl. **1** ceramic products collectively. **2** (usu. treated as *sing.*) art of making ceramic articles.

cereal /'sɪərɪəl/ —n. **1 a** wheat, maize, rye, etc. producing food. **b** grass, maize, rye, etc. producing this. **2** breakfast food made from a cereal. —adj. of edible grain. [Latin *Ceres* goddess of agriculture]

cerebellum /,serɪ'beləm/ n. (*pl.* **-s** or **-bella**) part of the brain at the back of the skull. [Latin diminutive of CEREBRUM]

cerebral /'serɪbr(ə)l/ adj. **1** of the brain. **2** intellectual; unemotional. [related to CEREBRUM]

cerebral palsy n. paralysis resulting from brain damage before or at birth, involving spasm of the muscles and involuntary movements.

cerebrospinal /,serɪbrəʊ'spaɪn(ə)l/ adj. of the brain and spine.

cerebrum /'serɪbrəm/ n. (*pl.* **-bra**) principal part of the brain in vertebrates, at the front of the skull. [Latin]

ceremonial /ˌserɪˈməʊnɪəl/ —*adj.* of or of or characterized by ceremony; formal. □ **ceremonially** *adv.*

ceremonious /ˌserɪˈməʊnɪəs/ *adj.* fond of or characterized by ceremony; formal. □ **ceremoniously** *adv.*

ceremony /ˈserɪmənɪ/ *n.* (*pl.* **-ies**) 1 formal procedure, esp. at a public event or anniversary. 2 formalites, esp. ritualistic. 3 excessively polite behaviour. □ **stand on ceremony** insist on formality. [Latin *caerimonia* worship]

cerise /səˈriːz/ *n.* light clear red. [French: related to CHERRY]

cerium *n.* silvery metallic element of the lanthanide series. [*Ceres*, name of an asteroid]

CERN /sɜːn/ *abbr.* European Organization for Nuclear Research. [French *Conseil Européen pour la Recherche Nucléaire*, former title]

cert *n.* (esp. **dead cert**) *slang* a certainty. [abbreviation]

cert. *abbr.* 1 certificate. 2 certified.

certain /ˈsɜːt(ə)n/ —*adj.* 1 a confident, convinced. b indisputable (*it is certain that he is guilty*). 2 (often foll. by *to* + infin.) sure; destined (*it is certain to rain; certain to win*). 3 unerring, reliable. 4 that need not be specified or may not be known to the reader or nearer (*of a certain age; a certain John Smith*). 5 some but not much (*a certain reluctance*). —*pron.* (as *pl.*) some but not all (*certain of them knew*). □ **for certain** without doubt. [Latin *certus*]

certainly *adv.* 1 undoubtedly. 2 (in answer) yes; by all means.

certainty *n.* (*pl.* **-ies**) 1 a undoubted fact. b indubitable prospect. 2 absolute conviction. 3 reliable thing or person.

Cert. Ed. *abbr.* Certificate in Education.

certifiable /ˈsɜːtɪfaɪəb(ə)l/ *adj.* 1 able or needing to be certified. 2 *colloq.* insane.

certificate —*n.* /səˈtɪfɪkət/ formal document attesting a fact, esp. birth, marriage, or death, a medical condition, or a qualification. —*v.* /-keɪt/ (**-ting**) (esp. as **certificated** *adj.*) provide with, license, or attest by a certificate. □ **certification** /ˌsɜːtɪfɪˈkeɪʃ(ə)n/ *n.* [Latin: related to CERTIFY]

Certificate of Secondary Education *n.* *hist.* secondary-school leaving examination in England, Wales, and Northern Ireland.

■ **Usage** This examination was replaced in 1988 by the *General Certificate of Secondary Education* (GCSE).

certified cheque *n.* cheque guaranteed by a bank.

certify /ˈsɜːtɪfaɪ/ *v.* (**-ies, -ied**) 1 attest; attest to, esp. formally 2 declare by certificate. 3 officially declare insane. [Latin *certus*]

certitude /ˈsɜːtɪtjuːd/ *n.* feeling of certainty. [Latin: related to CERTAIN]

cerulean /səˈruːlɪən/ *adj.* & *n.* *literary* deep sky-blue. [Latin *caeruleus*]

cervical /ˈsɜːvɪk(ə)l, səˈvaɪk(ə)l/ *adj.* of the neck or the cervix (*cervical vertebrae*). [related to CERVIX]

cervical screening *n.* mass routine examination for cervical cancer.

cervical smear *n.* specimen from the neck of the womb for examination.

cervix /ˈsɜːvɪks/ *n.* (*pl.* **cervices** /-siːz/) 1 necklike structure esp. the neck of the womb. 2 the neck. [Latin]

Cesarean (also **Cesarian**) US var. of CAESAREAN.

cesium US var. of CAESIUM.

cessation /seˈseɪʃ(ə)n/ *n.* ceasing or pause. [Latin: related to CEASE]

cession /ˈseʃ(ə)n/ *n.* 1 ceding. 2 territory etc. ceded. [Latin: related to CEDE]

cesspit /ˈsespɪt/ *n.* (also **cesspool**) covered pit for the temporary storage of liquid waste or sewage. [origin uncertain]

cetacean /sɪˈteɪʃ(ə)n/ —*n.* marine mammal, e.g. the whale. —*adj.* of cetaceans. [Greek *kētos* whale]

cetane /ˈsiːteɪn/ *n.* liquid hydrocarbon used in standardizing ratings of diesel fuel. [from SPERMACETI]

Cf *symb.* californium.

cf. *abbr.* compare. [Latin *confer*]

CFC *abbr.* chlorofluorocarbon, a usu. gaseous compound of carbon, hydrogen, chlorine, and fluorine, used in refrigerants, aerosol propellants, etc., and thought to harm the ozone layer.

CFE *abbr.* College of Further Education.

cg *abbr.* centigram (s).

CH *abbr.* Companion of Honour.

Chablis /ˈʃæbliː/ *n.* (*pl.* same /-liːz/) very dry white wine from Chablis in E. France. [*Chablis* in E. France]

cha-cha /ˈtʃɑːtʃɑː/ *n.* (also **cha-cha-cha** /ˈtʃɑːtʃɑːtʃɑː/) 1 Latin-American dance. 2 music for this. [American Spanish]

chaconne /ʃəˈkɒn/ *n.* 1 musical variations over a ground bass. 2 dance performed to this. [French from Spanish]

chafe —*v.* (**-fing**) 1 make or become sore or damaged by rubbing. 2 make or become annoyed fret. 3 rub (esp. the skin to restore warmth or sensation). —*n.* sore caused by rubbing. [Latin *calefacio* make warm]

chaff /tʃɑːf/ —*n.* 1 separated husks of corn etc. 2 chopped hay or straw. 3 light-

hearted teasing. **4** worthless things. *—v.* tease, banter. [Old English]

chaffinch /'tʃæfɪntʃ/ *n.* a common European finch. [Old English: related to CHAFF, FINCH]

chafing-dish *n.* vessel in which food is cooked or kept warm at table.

chagrin /'ʃæɡrɪn/ *—n.* acute annoyance or disappointment. *—v.* affect with chagrin. [French]

chain *—n.* **1 a** connected flexible series of esp. metal links. **b** thing resembling this. **2** (in *pl.*) fetters; restraining force. **3** sequence, series, or set. **4** group of associated hotels, shops, etc. **5** badge of office in the form of a chain worn round the neck. **6** unit of length (66 ft). *—v.* (often foll. by *up*) secure or confine with a chain. [Latin *catena*]

chain-gang *n. hist.* team of convicts chained together to work out of doors.

chain-mail *n.* armour made of interlaced rings.

chain reaction *n.* **1** chemical or nuclear reaction forming products which initiate further reactions. **2** series of events, each caused by the previous one.

chain-saw *n.* motor-driven saw with teeth on an endless chain.

chain-smoke *v.* smoke continually, esp. by lighting the next cigarette etc. from the previous one. □ **chain-smoker** *n.*

chain store *n.* one of a series of similar shops owned by one firm.

chair *—n.* **1** seat for one person usu. with a back. **2** professorship. **3 a** chairperson. **b** seat or office of a chairperson. **4** *US* = ELECTRIC CHAIR. *—v.* **1** preside over (a meeting). **2** carry (a person) aloft in triumph. □ **take the chair** preside over a meeting. [Greek *kathedra*]

chair-lift *n.* series of chairs on a looped cable, for carrying passengers up and down a mountain etc.

chairman *n.* (*fem.* also **chairwoman**) **1** person chosen to preside over a meeting. **2** permanent president of a committee, board of directors, etc.

chairperson *n.* chairman or chairwoman.

chaise /ʃeɪz/ *n. esp. hist.* horse-drawn usu. open carriage for one or two persons. [French]

chaise longue /ʃeɪz 'lɒŋ/ *n.* (*pl. chaise longues* or *chaises longues* pronunc. same) sofa with only one arm rest. [French = long chair]

chalcedony /kæl'sedənɪ/ *n.* (*pl.* -ies) type of quartz with many varieties, e.g. onyx. [Latin from Greek]

chalet /'ʃæleɪ/ *n.* **1** Swiss mountain hut or cottage with overhanging eaves. **2**

house in a similar style. **3** small cabin in a holiday camp etc. [Swiss French]

chalice /'tʃælɪs/ *n.* **1** goblet. **2** Eucharistic cup. [Latin CALIX]

chalk /tʃɔːk/ *—n.* **1** white soft limestone. **2 a** similar substance, sometimes coloured, for writing or drawing. **b** piece of this. *—v.* **1** rub, mark, draw, or write with chalk. **2** (foll. by *up*) **a** write or record with chalk. **b** register or gain (success etc.). □ **by a long chalk** by far. □ **chalky** *adj.* (-ier, -iest). **chalkiness** *n.* [Latin CALX]

challenge /'tʃælɪndʒ/ *—n.* **1** summons to take part in a contest etc. or to prove or justify something. **2** demanding or difficult task. **3** objection made to a jury member. **4** call to respond. *—v.* (**-ging**) **1** issue a challenge to. **2** dispute, deny. **3** (as **challenging** *adj.*) stimulating; difficult. **4** object to (a jury member, evidence, etc.). □ **challenger** *n.* [Latin *calumnia* calumny]

chalybeate /kə'lɪbiət/ *adj.* (of water etc.) impregnated with iron salts. [Latin *chalybs* steel, from Greek]

chamber /'tʃeɪmbə(r)/ *n.* **1 a** hall used by a legislative or judicial body. **b** body that meets in it, esp. any of the houses of a parliament. **2** (in *pl.*) **a** rooms used by a barrister or barristers, esp. in Inns of Court. **b** judge's room for hearing cases not needing to be taken in court. **3** *archaic* room, esp. a bedroom. **4** *Mus.* (*attrib.*) of or for a small group of instruments. **5** cavity or compartment in the body, machinery, etc. (esp. the part of a gun-bore that contains the charge). [Greek *kamara* vault]

chamberlain /'tʃeɪmbəlɪn/ *n.* **1** officer managing a royal or noble household. **2** treasurer of a corporation etc. [Germanic: related to CHAMBER]

chambermaid *n.* woman who cleans hotel bedrooms.

Chamber of Commerce *n.* association to promote local commercial interests.

chamber-pot *n.* receptacle for urine etc., used in the bedroom.

chameleon /kə'miːlɪən/ *n.* **1** small lizard able to change colour for camouflage. **2** variable or inconstant person. [Greek, = ground-lion]

chamfer /'tʃæmfə(r)/ *—v.* bevel symmetrically (a right-angled edge or corner). *—n.* bevelled surface at an edge or corner. [French *chant* edge, *fraint* broken]

chamois *n.* (*pl.* same /-wɑːz/) **1** /'ʃæmwɑː/ agile European and Asian mountain antelope. **2** /'ʃæmɪ/ (in full **chamois leather**) a soft leather from

sheep, goats, deer, etc. **b** piece of this. [French]

chamomile var. of CAMOMILE.

champ¹ —*v.* munch or chew noisily. —*n.* chewing noise. □ **champ at the bit** be restlessly impatient. [imitative]

champ² *n. slang* champion. [abbreviation]

champagne /ʃæmˈpeɪn/ *n.* **1 a** white sparkling wine from Champagne. **b** similar wine from elsewhere. **2** pale cream colour. [*Champagne*, former province in E. France]

■ **Usage** The use of this word in sense **1b** is, strictly speaking, incorrect.

champers /ˈʃæmpəz/ *n. slang* champagne.

champion /ˈtʃæmpɪən/ —*n.* **1** (often *attrib.*) person or thing that has defeated or surpassed all rivals. **2** person who fights or argues for a cause or another person. —*v.* support the cause of, defend. —*adj., colloq. splendid.* —*adv. colloq. splendidly.* [medieval Latin *campio* fighter]

championship *n.* **1** (often in *pl.*) contest to decide the champion in a sport etc. **2** position of champion.

chance /tʃɑːns/ —*n.* **1** possibility. **2** (often in *pl.*) probability. **3** unplanned occurrence. **4** opportunity. **5** fortune; luck. **6** (often **Chance**) course of events regarded as a power; fate. —*attrib. adj.* fortuitous, accidental. —*v.* (-**cing**) **1** *colloq.* happen (*I chanced to find it*). **2** *colloq.* risk (*I'll chance it*). □ **by any chance** perhaps. **by chance** fortuitously. **chance one's arm** try though unlikely to succeed. **chance on** (or **upon**) happen to find, meet, etc. **game of chance** one decided by luck, not skill. **on the off chance** just in case (the unlikely occurs). **stand a chance** have a prospect of success etc. **take a chance** (or **chances**) risk failure; behave riskily. **take a** (or one's) **chance on** (or **with**) risk the consequences of. [Latin *cado* fall]

chancel /ˈtʃɑːns(ə)l/ *n.* part of a church near the altar. [Latin *cancelli* grating]

chancellery /ˈtʃɑːnsələri/ *n.* (*pl.* -**ies**) **1** chancellor's department, staff, or residence. **2** *US* office attached to an embassy or consulate.

chancellor /ˈtʃɑːnsələ(r)/ *n.* **1** State or legal official. **2** head of government in some European countries. **3** nonresident honorary head of a university. [Latin *cancellarius* secretary]

Chancellor of the Exchequer *n.* UK finance minister.

chancery /ˈtʃɑːnsəri/ *n.* (*pl.* -**ies**) **1** (**Chancery**) Lord Chancellor's division of the High Court of Justice. **2** records

office. **3** chancellery [contraction of CHANCELLERY]

chancy /ˈtʃɑːnsɪ/ *adj.* (-**ier**, -**iest**) uncertain; risky. □ **chancily** *adv.*

chandelier /ˌʃændəˈlɪə(r)/ *n.* ornamental branched hanging support for lights. [French: related to CANDLE]

chandler /ˈtʃɑːndlə(r)/ *n.* dealer in candles, oil, soap, paint, etc. [French: related to CANDLE]

change /tʃeɪndʒ/ —*n.* **1 a** making or becoming different. **b** alteration or modification. **2 a** money exchanged for money in larger units or a different currency. **b** money returned as the balance of that given in payment. **3** new experience; variety (*need a change*). **4** substitution of one thing for another (*change of scene*). **5** (in full **change of life**) *colloq.* menopause. **6** (usu. in *pl.*) one of the different orders in which bells can be rung. —*v.* (-**ging**) **1** undergo, show, or subject to change; make or become different. **2 a** take or use another instead of. **b** go from one to another (*change one's socks; changed trains*). **b** (usu. foll. by *with*) give up or get rid of in exchange (*changed the car for a van*). **3** give or get money in exchange for. **4** put fresh clothes or coverings on. **5** (often foll. by *with*) give and receive, exchange. **6** change trains etc. **7** (of the moon) arrive at a fresh phase. □ **change down** engage a lower gear. **change gear** engage a different gear. **change hands** **1** pass to a different owner. **2** substitute one hand for the other. **change one's mind** adopt a different opinion or plan. **change over** change from one system or situation to another. **change one's tune 1** voice a different opinion from before. **2** become more respectful. **change up** engage a higher gear. **get no change out of** *slang* **1** get no information or help from. **2** fail to outwit (in business etc.). □ **changeful** *adj.* **changeless** *adj.* [Latin *cambio* barter]

changeable *adj.* **1** inconstant. **2** that can change or be changed.

change-over *n.* change from one system to another.

change of clothes *n.* second outfit in reserve.

change of heart *n.* conversion to a different view.

changeling *n.* child believed to be substituted for another.

channel /ˈtʃæn(ə)l/ —*n.* **1 a** piece of water wider than a strait, joining esp. two seas. **b** (**the Channel**) the English Channel. **2** medium of communication; agency. **3** band of frequencies used in radio and television transmission, esp.

by a particular station. **4** course in which anything moves. **5 a** hollow bed of water. **b** navigable part of a waterway. **6** passage for liquid. **7** lengthwise strip on recording tape etc. —v. (**-ll-**; *US* **-l-**) **1** guide, direct. **2** form channel(s) in. [Latin: related to CANAL]

chant /tʃɑːnt/ —n. **1** spoken singsong phrase. **2 a** simple tune used for singing unmetrical words, e.g. psalms. **b** song, esp. monotonous or repetitive. —v. **1** talk or repeat monotonously. **2** sing or intone (a psalm etc.). [Latin *canto* from *cano* sing]

chanter n. melody-pipe of bagpipes.

chanticleer /ˌtʃæntɪˈklɪə(r)/ n. name given to a domestic cock in stories. [French: related to CHANT, CLEAR]

chantry /ˈtʃɑːntrɪ/ n. (pl. **-ies**) **1** priests, chapel, etc., so endowed. [French: related to CHANT]

chaos /ˈkeɪɒs/ n. **1** utter confusion. **2** formless matter supposed to have existed before the creation of the universe. □ **chaotic** /keɪˈɒtɪk/ adj. **chaotically** /-ˈɒtɪkəlɪ/ adv. [Latin from Greek]

chap¹ n. colloq. man, boy, fellow. [abbreviation of CHAPMAN]

chap² —v. (**-pp-**) **1** (esp. of the skin) develop cracks or soreness. **2** (of the wind, cold, etc.) cause to chap. —n. (usu. in pl.) crack in the skin etc. [origin uncertain]

chaparral /ˌʃæpəˈræl/ n. US dense tangled brushwood. [Spanish]

chapatti /tʃəˈpɑːtɪ/ n. (also **chapati**, **chupatty**) (pl. **chapat(t)is** or **chupatties**) flat thin cake of unleavened bread. [Hindi]

chapel /ˈtʃæp(ə)l/ n. **1 a** place for private Christian worship in a Cathedral or large church, with its own altar. **b** this attached to a private house etc. **2 a** place of worship for Nonconformists. **b** chapel service. **3** members or branch of a printers' trade union at a place of work. [medieval Latin *cappa* cloak: the first chapel was a sanctuary in which St Martin's cloak (*cappella*) was preserved]

chaperon /ˈʃæpərəʊn/ —n. person, esp. an older woman, ensuring propriety by accompanying a young unmarried woman on social occasions. —v. act as chaperon to. □ **chaperonage** /-rənɪdʒ/ n. [French from *chape* cope: related to CAPE¹]

chaplain /ˈtʃæplɪn/ n. member of the clergy attached to a private chapel, institution, ship, regiment, etc. □ **chaplaincy** n. (pl. **-ies**). [Latin: related to CHAPEL]

chaplet /ˈtʃæplɪt/ n. **1** garland or circlet for the head. **2** short string of beads; rosary. [Latin: related to CAP]

chapman /ˈtʃæpmən/ n. hist. pedlar. [Old English: related to CHEAP, MAN]

chappie n. colloq. = CHAP.

chapter n. **1** main division of a book. **2** period of time (in a person's life etc.). **3 a** canons of a cathedral or members of a religious community. **b** meeting of these. [Latin diminutive of *caput* head]

chapter and verse n. exact reference or details.

chapter of accidents n. series of misfortunes.

char¹ v. (**-rr-**) **1** make or become black by burning; scorch. **2** burn to charcoal. [from CHARCOAL]

char² colloq. —n. = CHARWOMAN. —v. (**-rr-**) work as a charwoman. [Old English, = turn]

char³ n. slang tea. [Chinese *cha*]

char⁴ n. (pl. same) a kind of small trout. [origin unknown]

charabanc /ˈʃærəˌbæŋ/ n. hist. early form of motor coach. [French *char à bancs* seated carriage]

character /ˈkærɪktə(r)/ n. **1** collective qualities or characteristics that distinguish a person or thing. **2 a** moral strength. **b** reputation. **c** good reputation. **3 a** person in a novel, play, etc. **b** part played by an actor; role. **4** colloq. person, esp. an eccentric one. **5** printed or written letter, symbol, etc. **6** written description of a person's qualities. **7** characteristic (esp. of a biological species). □ **in** (or **out of**) **character** consistent (or inconsistent) with a person's character. □ **characterless** adj. [Greek *kharaktēr*]

characteristic /ˌkærɪktəˈrɪstɪk/ —adj. typical, distinctive. —n. characteristic feature or quality. □ **characteristically** adv.

characterize /ˈkærɪktəˌraɪz/ v. (also **-ise**) (**-zing** or **-sing**) **1 a** describe the character of. **b** (foll. by *as*) describe as. **2** be characteristic of. **3** impart character to. □ **characterization** /-ˈzeɪʃ(ə)n/ n.

charade /ʃəˈrɑːd/ n. **1** (usu. in pl., treated as sing.) game of guessing a word from acted clues. **2** absurd pretence. [Provençal *charra* chatter]

charcoal /ˈtʃɑːkəʊl/ n. **1** a form of carbon consisting of black residue from partially burnt wood etc. **b** piece of this for drawing. **c** a drawing in charcoal. **2** (in full **charcoal grey**) dark grey. [origin unknown]

charge —v. (**-ging**) **1 a** ask (an amount) as a price. **b** ask (a person) for an amount as a price. **2 a** (foll. by *to*, *up to*) debit the cost to (a person or account).

b debit (a person or account). **3 a** (often foll. by *with*) accuse (of an offence). **b** (foll. by *that* + clause) make an accusation that. **4** (often foll. by *with*) instruct or urge. **5** (foll. by *to* + infin.) entrust with. **6** make a rushing attack (on). **7** (often foll. by *up*) give an electric charge to. **b** store energy in (a battery). **8** (often foll. by *with*) load or fill (a vessel, gun, etc.) to the full or proper extent. **9** (usu. as **charged** *adj.*) **a** (foll. by *with*) saturated with. **b** (usu. foll. by *by* or *with*) pervaded with strong feelings etc. □ −*n.* **1 a** price asked for services or goods. **b** financial liability or commitment. **2** accusation. **3 a** task, duty, commission. **b** care, custody. **c** person or thing entrusted. **4 a** impetuous rush or attack, esp. in battle. **b** signal for this. **5** appropriate amount of material to be put into a receptacle, mechanism, etc. at one time, esp. of explosive for a gun. **6 a** property of matter causing electrical phenomena. **b** quantity of this carried by the body. **c** energy stored chemically for conversion into electricity. **7** exhortation; direction, orders. **8** heraldic device or bearing. □ **in charge** having command. □ **take charge** (often foll. by *of*) assume control. □ **chargeable** *adj.* [Latin *carrus* CAR]

charge-capping *n.* imposition of an upper limit on the community charge leviable by a local authority.

charge card *n.* = CREDIT CARD.

chargé d'affaires /ˌʃɑːʒeɪ dæˈfeə(r)/ *n.* (*pl.* **chargés** pronunc. same) **1** ambassador's deputy. **2** envoy to a minor country. [French]

charger *n.* **1** cavalry horse. **2** apparatus for charging a battery.

chariot /ˈtʃærɪət/ *n. hist.* two-wheeled vehicle drawn by horses, used in ancient warfare and racing. [French: related to CAR]

charioteer /ˌtʃærɪəˈtɪə(r)/ *n.* chariot-driver.

charisma /kəˈrɪzmə/ *n.* **1** power to inspire or attract others; exceptional charm. **2** divinely conferred power or talent. □ **charismatic** /ˌkærɪzˈmætɪk/ *adj.* [Greek *kharis* grace]

charitable /ˈtʃærɪtəb(ə)l/ *adj.* **1** generous in giving to those in need. **2** of or relating to a charity or charities. **3** generous in judging others. □ **charitably** *adv.*

charity /ˈtʃærɪtɪ/ *n.* (*pl.* **-ies**) **1** giving voluntarily to those in need. **2** organization set up to help those in need or for the common good. **3 a** kindness, benevolence. **b** tolerance in judging others. **c** love of fellow men. [Latin *caritas* from *carus* dear]

charlady *n.* = CHARWOMAN.

charlatan /ˈʃɑːlət(ə)n/ *n.* person falsely claiming knowledge or skill. □ **charlatanism** *n.* [Italian, = babbler]

charleston /ˈtʃɑːlstən/ *n.* (also **Charleston**) lively dance of the 1920s with side-kicks from the knee. [*Charleston* in S. Carolina]

charlotte /ˈʃɑːlət/ *n.* pudding of stewed fruit covered with bread etc. [French]

charm −*n.* **1** power or quality of delighting, arousing admiration, or influencing; fascination, attractiveness. **2** trinket on a bracelet etc. **3** object, act, or word(s) supposedly having magic power. −*v.* **1** delight, captivate. **2** influence or protect as if by magic (a *charmed life*). **3** obtain or gain by charm (*charmed his way into the BBC*). □ **charmer** *n.* [Latin *carmen* song]

charming *adj.* delightful. □ **charmingly** *adv.*

charnel-house /ˈtʃɑːn(ə)lhaus/ *n.* repository of corpses or bones. [Latin: related to CARNAL]

chart −*n.* **1 a** geographical map or plan, esp. for navigation. **2** sheet of information in the form of a table, graph, or diagram. **3** (usu. in *pl.*) *colloq.* listing of the currently best-selling pop records. −*v.* make a chart of, map. [Latin *charta*: related to CARD]

charter −*n.* **1 a** document granting rights, issued esp. by a sovereign or legislature. **b** written constitution or description of an organization's functions etc. **2** contract to hire an aircraft, ship, etc., for a special purpose. −*v.* **1** grant a charter to. **2** hire (an aircraft, ship, etc.). [Latin *chartula*: related to CHART]

chartered *attrib. adj.* (of an accountant, engineer, librarian, etc.) qualified member of a professional body that has a royal charter.

charter flight *n.* flight by chartered aircraft.

Chartism *n. hist.* UK Parliamentary reform movement of 1837–48. □ **Chartist** *n.* [from CHARTER: name taken from 'People's Charter']

chartreuse /ʃɑːˈtrɜːz/ *n.* pale green or yellow brandy-based liqueur. [*Chartreuse*, monastery in S. France]

charwoman *n.* woman employed as a cleaner in a house.

chary /ˈtʃeərɪ/ *adj.* (**-ier, -iest**) **1** cautious, wary. **2** sparing; ungenerous. [Old English: related to CARE]

Charybdis see SCYLLA AND CHARYBDIS.

chase −*v.* (**-sing**) **1** run after; pursue. **2** (foll. by *from, out of,* etc.) force to run away or flee. **3 a** (foll. by *after*) hurry in pursuit of. **b** (foll. by *round* etc.) *colloq.*

act or move about hurriedly. **4** (usu. foll. by *up*) *colloq.* pursue (a thing overdue). **5** *colloq.* **a** try to attain. **b** court persistently. □ —*n.* **1** pursuit. **2** unenclosed hunting-land. **3** (prec. by *the*) hunting, esp. as a sport. [Latin *capto*: related to CATCH]

chase² *v.* (-**sing**) emboss or engrave (metal). [French: related to CASE²]

chaser *n.* **1** horse for steeplechasing. **2** *colloq.* drink taken after another of a different kind.

chasm /'kæz(ə)m/ *n.* **1** deep cleft or opening in the earth, rock, etc. **2** wide difference of feeling, interests, etc. [Latin from Greek]

chassis /'ʃæsɪ/ *n.* (*pl.* same /-sɪz/) **1** base-frame of a motor vehicle, carriage, etc. **2** frame to carry radio etc. components. [Latin: related to CASE²]

chaste /tʃeɪst/ *adj.* **1** abstaining from extramarital, or from all, sexual intercourse. **2** pure, virtuous. **3** simple, unadorned. □ **chastely** *adv.* **chasteness** *n.* [Latin *castus*]

chasten /'tʃeɪs(ə)n/ *v.* **1** (esp. as **chastening**, **chastened** *adjs.*) subdue, restrain. **2** discipline, punish.

chastise /tʃæs'taɪz/ *v.* (-**sing**) **1** rebuke severely. **2** punish, esp. by beating. □ **chastisement** *n.*

chastity /'tʃæstɪtɪ/ *n.* being chaste.

chasuble /'tʃæzjub(ə)l/ *n.* loose sleeveless usu. ornate outer vestment worn by a celebrant at Mass or the Eucharist. [Latin *casubla*]

chat —*v.* (-**tt**-) talk in a light familiar way. —*n.* **1** pleasant informal talk. **2** any of various songbirds. □ **chat up** *colloq.* chat to, esp. flirtatiously or with an ulterior motive. [shortening of CHATTER]

château /'ʃætəʊ/ *n.* (*pl.* -**x** /-təʊz/) large French country house or castle. [French: related to CASTLE]

chatelaine /'ʃætəleɪn/ *n.* **1** mistress of a large house. **2** *hist.* set of short chains attached to a woman's belt, for carrying keys etc. [medieval Latin *castellanus*: related to CASTLE]

chatline *n.* telephone service which sets up a conference call among youngsters.

chat show *n.* television or radio broadcast in which celebrities are interviewed informally.

chattel /'tʃæt(ə)l/ *n.* (usu. in *pl.*) movable possession. [French: related to CATTLE]

chatter —*v.* **1** talk quickly, incessantly, trivially, or irrelevantly. **2** (of a bird monkey, etc.) emit short quick sounds. **3** (of teeth) click repeatedly together. —*n.* chattering talk or sounds. [imitative]

chatterbox *n.* talkative person.

chatty *adj.* (-**ier**, -**iest**) **1** fond of chatting. **2** resembling chat. □ **chattily** *adv.* **chattiness** *n.*

chauffeur /'ʃəʊfə(r)/ —*n.* (*fem.* **chauffeuse** /-'fɜːz/) person employed to drive a car. —*v.* drive (a car or person) as a chauffeur. [French, = stoker]

chauvinism /'ʃəʊvɪnɪz(ə)m/ *n.* **1** exaggerated or aggressive patriotism. **2** excessive or prejudiced support or loyalty for one's cause or group. [*Chauvin*, name of a character in a French play 1831]

chauvinist *n.* **1** person exhibiting chauvinism. **2** (in full **male chauvinist**) man who shows prejudice against women. □ **chauvinistic** /-'nɪstɪk/ *adj.* **chauvinistically** /-'nɪstɪkəlɪ/ *adv.*

cheap —*adj.* **1** low in price; worth more than its cost. **2** charging low prices; offering good value. **3** of poor quality; inferior. **4** costing little effort and hence of little worth. —*adv.* cheaply. □ **on the cheap** cheaply. □ **cheaply** *adv.* **cheapness** *n.* [Old English, = price, bargain]

cheapen *v.* make or become cheap; depreciate, degrade.

cheapjack —*n.* seller of inferior or shoddy goods at low prices. —*adj.* inferior, shoddy.

cheapskate *n.* esp. *US colloq.* stingy person.

cheat —*v.* **1 a** (often foll. by *into*, *out of*) deceive or trick. **b** (foll. by *of*) deprive of. **2** gain an unfair advantage by deception or breaking rules. —*n.* **1** person who cheats. **2** trick, deception. □ **cheat on** *colloq.* be sexually unfaithful to. [from ESCHEAT]

check —*v.* **1 a** examine the accuracy or quality of. **b** make sure, verify. **2 a** stop or slow the motion of; curb. **b** *colloq.* rebuke. **3** *Chess* directly threaten (the opposing king). **4** *US* agree on comparison. **5** *US* mark with a tick etc. **6** *US* deposit (luggage etc.). —*n.* **1** means or act of testing or ensuring accuracy, quality, etc. **2 a** stopping or slowing of motion. **b** rebuff or rebuke. **c** person or thing that restrains. **3 a** pattern of small squares. **b** fabric so patterned. **c** (*attrib.*) so patterned. **4** (*also as int.*) *Chess* exposure of a king to direct attack. **5** *US* restaurant bill. **6** *US* = CHEQUE. **7** *US* token of identification for left luggage etc. **8** *US Cards* counter used in games. **9** temporary loss of the scent in hunting. □ **check in** **1** arrive or register at a hotel, airport, etc. **2** record one's arrival at (a hotel etc.). **check off** mark on a list etc. as having been examined. **check on** examine, verify, keep watch on. **check out** **1** (often foll. by *of*) leave a hotel etc. with due formalities. **2** esp. *US*

investigate. **check up** make sure, verify. **check up on** = *check on*. [Persian.
= king]

checked /tʃekd/ *adj.* having a check pattern.

checker[1] *n.* person etc. that examines,
esp. in a factory etc.

checker[2] *n.* 1 var. of CHEQUER. 2 *US* **a** (in
pl., usu. treated as *sing.*) draughts. **b**
piece used in this game.

check-in *n.* act or place of checking in.

checkmate —*n.* (also as *int.*) *Chess*
check from which a king cannot escape.
—*v.* (**-ting**) **1** *Chess* put into checkmate. **2**
frustrate. [French: related to CHECK]

checkout *n.* 1 act of checking out. 2 pay-
desk in a supermarket etc.

checkpoint *n.* place, esp. a barrier or
entrance, where documents, vehicles,
etc. are inspected.

check-up *n.* thorough (esp. medical)
examination.

Cheddar /tʃedə(r)/ *n.* a kind of firm
smooth cheese. [*Cheddar* in Somerset]

cheek —*n.* 1 **a** side of the face below the
eye. **b** side-wall of the mouth. 2 **a** impertinence; cool confidence. **b** impertinent
speech. 3 *slang* buttock. —*v.* be impertinent to. □ **cheek by jowl** close
together; intimate. [Old English]

cheek-bone *n.* bone below the eye.

cheeky *adj.* (**-ier**, **-iest**) impertinent. □
cheekily *adv.* **cheekiness** *n.*

cheep —*n.* weak shrill cry of a young
bird. —*v.* make such a cry. [imitative]

cheer —*n.* 1 shout of encouragement or
applause. 2 mood, disposition (*full of
good cheer*). 3 (in *pl.*; as *int.*) *colloq.* **a**
expressing good wishes on parting or
before drinking. **b** expressing gratitude.
—*v.* 1 **a** applaud with shouts. **b** (usu. foll.
by *on*) urge with shouts. 2 shout for joy.
3 gladden; comfort. □ **cheer up** make or
become less depressed. [Latin *cara* face,
from Greek]

cheerful *adj.* 1 in good spirits, noticeably happy. 2 bright, pleasant. □ **cheerfully** *adv.* **cheerfulness** *n.*

cheerio /tʃɪərɪˈəʊ/ *int. colloq.* expressing
good wishes on parting.

cheer-leader *n.* person who leads
cheers of applause etc.

cheerless *adj.* gloomy, dreary.

cheery *adj.* (**-ier**, **-iest**) cheerful. □
cheerily *adv.* **cheeriness** *n.*

cheese /tʃiːz/ *n.* 1 food made from
curds of milk. **b** cake of this with rind. 2
conserve with the consistency of soft
cheese. □ **cheesy** *adj.* [Latin *caseus*]

cheeseburger *n.* hamburger with
cheese in or on it.

cheesecake *n.* 1 tart filled with sweetened curds etc. 2 *slang* portrayal of

---

women in a sexually stimulating manner.

cheesecloth *n.* thin loosely-woven
cloth.

cheesed /tʃiːzd/ *adj. slang* (often foll. by
off) bored, fed up. [origin unknown]

cheese-paring *adj.* stingy.

cheese plant *n.* climbing plant with
holes in its leaves.

cheetah /tʃiːtə/ *n.* swift-running spotted leopard-like feline. [Hindi]

chef /ʃef/ *n.* (usu. male) cook, esp. the
chief cook in a restaurant. [French]

Chelsea bun /tʃelsɪ/ *n.* currant bun in
the form of a flat spiral. [*Chelsea* in
London]

Chelsea pensioner *n.* inmate of the
Chelsea Royal Hospital for old or disabled soldiers.

chemical /ˈkemɪk(ə)l/ —*adj.* of, made
by, or employing chemistry or chemicals. —*n.* substance obtained or used in
chemistry. □ **chemically** *adv.* [related to
ALCHEMY]

chemical engineering *n.* creation
and operation of industrial chemical
plants.

chemical warfare *n.* warfare using
poison gas and other chemicals.

chemise /ʃəˈmiːz/ *n. hist.* woman's
loose-fitting undergarment or dress.
[Latin *camisia* shirt]

chemist /ˈkemɪst/ *n.* 1 dealer in medicinal drugs etc. 2 expert in chemistry.
[French: related to ALCHEMY]

chemistry /ˈkemɪstrɪ/ *n.* (*pl.* **-ies**) 1
branch of science dealing with the elements and the compounds they form
and the reactions they undergo. 2 chemical composition and properties of a
substance. 3 *colloq.* sexual attraction.

chemotherapy /ˌkiːməʊˈθerəpɪ/ *n.*
treatment of disease, esp. cancer, by
chemical substances.

chenille /ʃəˈniːl/ *n.* 1 tufty velvety cord
or yarn. 2 fabric of this. [French,
= caterpillar, from Latin *canicula* little
dog]

cheque /tʃek/ *n.* 1 written order to a
bank to pay the stated sum from the
drawer's account. 2 printed form on
which this is written. [from CHECK]

cheque card *n.* card issued by a bank to
guarantee the honouring of cheques up
to a stated amount.

cheque-book *n.* book of forms for writing cheques.

chequer /ˈtʃekə(r)/ —*n.* 1 (often in *pl.*)
pattern of squares often alternately coloured. 2 var. of CHECKER[2] 2. —*v.* 1 mark
with chequers. 2 variegate; break the
uniformity of. 3 (as **chequered** *adj.*)
with varied fortunes (*chequered
career*). [from EXCHEQUER]

cherish /'tʃerɪʃ/ *v.* 1 protect or tend lovingly. 2 hold dear, cling to (hopes, feelings, etc.). [French *cher* dear, from Latin *carus*]

cheroot /ʃə'ruːt/ *n.* cigar with both ends open. [French from Tamil]

cherry /'tʃerɪ/ —*n.* (*pl.* -ies) 1 a small soft round stone-fruit. b tree bearing this. c its wood. 2 light red colour. —*adj.* of light red colour. [Greek *kerasos*]

cherub /'tʃerəb/ *n.* 1 (*pl.* -im) angelic being of the second order of the celestial hierarchy. 2 a representation of a winged child or its head. b beautiful or innocent child. □ **cherubic** /tʃɪ'ruːbɪk/ *adj.* [ultimately from Hebrew]

chervil /'tʃɜːvɪl/ *n.* herb used for flavouring. [Greek *khairephullon*]

Cheshire /'tʃeʃə(r)/ *n.* a kind of firm crumbly cheese. □ **like a Cheshire cat** with a broad fixed grin. [*Cheshire* in England]

chess *n.* game for two with 16 men each, played on a chessboard. [French: related to CHECK]

chessboard *n.* chequered board of 64 squares on which chess and draughts are played.

chessman *n.* any of the 32 pieces and pawns with which chess is played.

chest *n.* 1 large strong box. 2 a part of the body enclosed by the ribs. b front surface of the body from the neck to the bottom of the ribs. 3 small cabinet for medicines etc. □ **get a thing off one's chest** *colloq.* disclose a secret etc. to relieve one's anxiety about it. [Latin *cista*]

chest of drawers *n.* piece of furniture consisting of a set of drawers in a frame.

chesty *adj.* (-ier, -iest) *colloq.* inclined to or symptomatic of chest disease. □ **chestily** *adv.* **chestiness** *n.*

chestnut /'tʃesnʌt/ —*n.* 1 a glossy hard brown edible nut. b tree bearing it. 2 = HORSE CHESTNUT. 3 wood of any chestnut. 4 horse of a reddish-brown colour. 5 *colloq.* stale joke etc. 6 reddish-brown. —*adj.* reddish-brown. [Greek *kastanea* nut]

chesterfield /'tʃestəfiːld/ *n.* sofa with arms and back of the same height and curved outwards at the top. [Earl of *Chesterfield*]

cheval-glass /ʃə'væl/ *n.* tall mirror swung on an upright frame. [Latin *caballus* horse]

chevalier /ʃevə'lɪə(r)/ *n.* member of certain orders of knighthood, or of the French Legion of Honour etc. [medieval Latin *cabalarius* horseman]

chevron /'ʃevrən/ *n.* V-shaped line or stripe. [Latin *caper* goat]

chew —*v.* work (food etc.) between the teeth. —*n.* 1 act of chewing. 2 chewy sweet. □ **chew on** 1 work continuously between the teeth. 2 think about. **chew over 1** think about. 2 talk over. **2** think about. [Old English]

chewing-gum *n.* flavoured gum for chewing.

chewy *adj.* (-ier, -iest) 1 needing much chewing. 2 suitable for chewing. □ **chewiness** *n.*

chez /ʃeɪ/ *prep.* at the home of. [French *casa* cottage]

chi /kaɪ/ *n.* twenty-second letter of the Greek alphabet (X, χ). [Greek]

Chianti /kɪ'æntɪ/ *n.* (*pl.* -s) red wine from the Chianti area in Italy.

chiaroscuro /kɪˌɑːrə'skʊərəʊ/ *n.* 1 treatment of light and shade in drawing and painting. 2 use of contrast in literature etc. [Italian, = clear dark]

chic /ʃiːk/ —*adj.* (chic-er, chic-est) stylish, elegant. —*n.* stylishness, elegance. [French]

chicane /ʃɪ'keɪn/ —*n.* 1 artificial barrier or obstacle on a motor racecourse. 2 chicanery. —*v.* (-ning) *archaic* 1 use chicanery. 2 (usu. foll. by *into*, *out of*, etc.) cheat (a person). [French]

chicanery /ʃɪ'keɪnərɪ/ *n.* (*pl.* -ies) 1 clever but misleading talk. 2 trickery, deception. [French]

chick *n.* 1 young bird. 2 *slang* young woman. [Old English: related to CHICKEN]

chicken /'tʃɪkɪn/ —*n.* 1 a domestic fowl. b its flesh as food. 2 young bird of a domestic fowl. 3 youthful person (*is no chicken*). —*adj.* *colloq.* cowardly. —*v.* (foll. by *out*) *colloq.* withdraw through cowardice. [Old English]

chicken-feed *n.* 1 food for poultry. 2 *colloq.* trivial amount, esp. of money.

chickenpox *n.* infectious disease, esp. of children, with a rash of small blisters.

chicken-wire *n.* light wire netting with a hexagonal mesh.

chick-pea *n.* yellow pea-like seed used as a vegetable. [Latin *cicer*]

chickweed *n.* small weed with tiny white flowers.

chicle /'tʃɪk(ə)l/ *n.* milky juice of a tropical tree, used in chewing-gum. [Spanish from Nahuatl]

chicory /'tʃɪkərɪ/ *n.* (*pl.* -ies) 1 plant with leaves used in salads. 2 its root, roasted and ground and used with or instead of coffee. 3 esp. *US* = ENDIVE. [Greek *kikhorion*]

chide *v.* (*past* **chided** or **chid**; *past part.* **chided** or **chidden**) *archaic* scold, rebuke. [Old English]

chief —*n.* 1 a leader or ruler. b head of a tribe, clan, etc. 2 head of a department;

Chief Constable highest official. —*adj.* **1** first in position, importance, influence, etc. **2** prominent, leading. [Latin *caput* head]

chiefly *adv.* above all; mainly but not exclusively.

Chief of Staff *n.* senior staff officer of a service or command.

chieftain /'tʃiːftən/ *n.* leader of a tribe, clan, etc. □ **chieftaincy** *n.* (*pl.* -ies). [Latin: related to CHIEF]

chiffchaff /'tʃɪftʃæf/ *n.* small European warbler. [imitative]

chiffon /'ʃɪfɒn/ *n.* light diaphanous fabric of silk, nylon, etc. [French *chiffe* rag]

chignon /'ʃiːnjɔ̃/ *n.* coil of hair at the back of a woman's head. [French]

chihuahua /tʃɪˈwɑːwɑ/ *n.* dog of a very small smooth-haired breed. [*Chihuahua* in Mexico]

chilblain /'tʃɪlbleɪn/ *n.* painful itching swelling on a hand, foot, etc., caused by exposure to cold. [from CHILL, *blain* inflamed sore, blister]

child /tʃaɪld/ *n.* (*pl.* **children** /'tʃɪldrən/) **1 a** young human being below the age of puberty. **b** unborn or newborn human being. **2** one's son or daughter. **3** (foll. by *of*) descendant; follower, or product of. **4** childish person. □ **childless** *adj.* [Old English]

child abuse *n.* maltreatment of a child, esp. by physical violence or sexual interference.

child benefit *n.* regular payment by the State to the parents of a child up to a certain age.

childbirth *n.* giving birth to a child.

child care *n.* the care of children, esp. by a local authority.

childhood *n.* state or period of being a child.

childish *adj.* **1** of, like, or proper to a child. **2** immature, silly. □ **childishly** *adv.* **childishness** *n.*

childlike *adj.* having the good qualities of a child, such as innocence, frankness, etc.

child-minder *n.* person looking after children for payment.

child's play *n.* easy task.

chili var. of CHILLI.

chill —*n.* **1 a** unpleasant cold sensation; lowered body temperature. **b** feverish cold. **2** unpleasant coldness (of air, water, etc.). **3** depressing influence. **4** coldness of manner. —*v.* **1** make or become cold or (food or drink) by cooling. **2** depress; horrify. **3** preserve (food or drink) by cooling. —*adj. literary* chilly. [Old English]

chilli con carne /kɒn 'kɑːnɪ/ *n.* dish of chilli-flavoured mince and beans.

chilly *adj.* (-**ier**, -**iest**) **1** somewhat cold. **2** sensitive to the cold **3** unfriendly; unemotional.

Chiltern Hundreds /'tʃɪltə(ə)n/ *n.pl.* Crown manor, whose administration is a nominal office for which an MP applies as a way of resigning from the House of Commons. [*Chiltern* Hills in S. England]

chime —*n.* **1** set of attuned bells. **2** sounds made by this. —*v.* (-**ming**) **1** (of bells) ring. **2** show (the time) by chiming. **3** (usu. foll. by *together, with*) be in agreement. □ **chime in 1** interject a remark. **2** join in harmoniously. **3** (foll. by *with*) agree with. [Old English]

chimera /kaɪˈmɪərə/ *n.* **1** (in Greek mythology) monster with a lion's head, goat's body, and serpent's tail. **2** bogey. **3** wild or fantastic conception. □ **chimerical** /-ˈmerɪk(ə)l/ *adj.* [Latin from Greek]

chimney /'tʃɪmnɪ/ *n.* (*pl.* -**s**) **1** channel conducting smoke etc. up and away from a fire, engine, etc. **2** part of this above a roof. **3** glass tube protecting the flame of a lamp. **4** narrow vertical crack in a rock-face. [Latin *caminus* oven, from Greek]

chimney-breast *n.* projecting wall surrounding a chimney.

chimney-pot *n.* earthenware or metal pipe at the top of a chimney.

chimney-stack *n.* number of chimneys grouped in one structure.

chimney-sweep *n.* person who removes soot from inside chimneys.

chimp *n. colloq.* = CHIMPANZEE. [abbreviation]

chimpanzee /ˌtʃɪmpænˈziː/ *n.* small African manlike ape. [French from Kongo]

chin *n.* front of the lower jaw. □ **keep one's chin up** *colloq.* remain cheerful. **take on the chin** suffer a severe blow from; endure courageously. [Old English]

china /'tʃaɪnə/ —*n.* **1** fine white or translucent ceramic ware, porcelain, etc. **2** things made of this. —*adj.* made of china. [*China* in Asia]

china clay *n.* kaolin.

Chinaman /'tʃaɪnəmən/ *n.* **1** *archaic* or *derog.* (now usu. *offens.*) native of China. **2** *Cricket* ball bowled by a left-handed bowler that spins from off to leg.

chinchilla /tʃɪnˈtʃɪlə/ *n.* **1 a** small S. American rodent. **b** its soft grey fur. **2** breed of cat or rabbit. [Spanish *chinche* bug]

chine —n. **1 a** backbone. **b** joint of meat containing all or part of this. **2** ridge. —v. (**-ning**) cut (meat) through the backbone. [Latin *spina* SPINE]

Chinese /tʃaɪˈniːz/ —adj. of China. —n. **1** Chinese language. **2** (pl. same) **a** native or national of China. **b** person of Chinese descent.

Chinese lantern n. **1** collapsible paper lantern. **2** plant with an orange-red papery calyx.

Chinese leaf n. lettuce-like cabbage.

Chink n. slang offens. a Chinese. [abbreviation]

chink[1] n. narrow opening; slit. [related to *chine* narrow ravine]

chink[2] —v. (cause to) make a sound like glasses or coins striking together. —n. this sound. [imitative]

chinless adj. colloq. weak or feeble in character.

chinless wonder n. ineffectual esp. upper-class person.

chinoiserie /ʃɪnˈwaːzəri/ n. **1** imitation of Chinese motifs in painting and in decorating furniture. **2** object(s) in this style. [French]

chintz /tʃɪnts/ n. printed multicoloured usu. glazed cotton fabric. [Hindi from Sanskrit]

chintzy adj. (**-ier**, **-iest**) **1** like chintz. **2** gaudy, cheap. **3** characteristic of decor associated with chintz soft furnishings.

chin-wag slang —n. talk or chat. —v. (**-gg-**) chat.

chip —n. **1** small piece removed by chopping etc. **2** place or mark where a piece has been broken off. **3 a** strip of potato, usu. deep-fried. **b** US potato crisp. **4** counter used in some games to represent money. **5** = MICROCHIP. —v. (**-pp-**) **1** (often foll. by off, away) cut or break (a piece) from a hard material. **2** (often foll. by at, away at) cut pieces off (a hard material) to alter its shape etc. **3** be apt to break at the edge. **4** (usu. as **chipped** adj.) make (potatoes) into chips. □ **chip in** colloq. **1** interrupt. **2** contribute (money etc.). **a chip off the old block** child resembling its parent, esp. in character. **a chip on one's shoulder** colloq. inclination to feel resentful or aggrieved. **when the chips are down** colloq. when it comes to the point. [Old English]

chipboard n. board made from compressed wood chips.

chipmunk /ˈtʃɪpmʌŋk/ n. striped N. American ground squirrel. [Algonquian]

chipolata /tʃɪpəˈlɑːtə/ n. small thin sausage. [French from Italian]

Chippendale /ˈtʃɪpəndeɪl/ adj. (of furniture) of an elegantly ornate 18th-c. style. [name of a cabinet-maker]

chiro- comb. form hand. [Greek kheir]

chiromancy /ˈkaɪərəʊˌmænsɪ/ n. palmistry. [Greek mantis seer]

chiropody /kɪˈrɒpədɪ/ n. treatment of the feet and their ailments. □ **chiropodist** n. [Greek pous podos foot]

chiropractic /ˌkaɪərəʊˈpræktɪk/ n. treatment of disease by manipulation of esp. the spinal column. □ **chiropractor** /ˈkaɪərəʊ-/ n. [Greek prattō do]

chirp —v. **1** (of small birds, grasshoppers, etc.) utter a short sharp note. **2** speak or utter merrily. —n. chirping sound. [imitative]

chirpy adj. colloq. (**-ier**, **-iest**) cheerful, lively. □ **chirpily** adv. **chirpiness** n.

chirrup /ˈtʃɪrəp/ —v. (**-p-**) chirp, esp. repeatedly. —n. chirruping sound. [imitative]

chisel /ˈtʃɪz(ə)l/ —n. hand tool with a squared bevelled blade for shaping wood, stone, or metal. —v. **1** (-ll-; US -l-) cut or shape with a chisel. **2** (as **chiselled** adj.) (of facial features) clear-cut, fine. **3** slang cheat. [Latin caedo cut]

chit[1] n. **1** derog. or joc. young small woman (esp. a chit of a girl). **2** young child. [originally = whelp, cub]

chit[2] n. **1** note of requisition, of a sum owed, etc. **2** note or memorandum. [Hindi from Sanskrit]

chit-chat n. colloq. light conversation; gossip. [reduplication of CHAT]

chivalrous /ˈʃɪvəlrəs/ adj. **1** gallant, honourable. **2** of or showing chivalry. □ **chivalrously** adv. [Latin: related to CHEVALIER]

chivalry /ˈʃɪvəlrɪ/ n. **1** medieval knightly system with its religious, moral, and social code. **2** honour, courtesy, and readiness to help the weak. □ **chivalric** adj.

chive n. small plant with long onion-flavoured leaves. [Latin cepa onion]

chivvy /ˈtʃɪvɪ/ v. (**-ies**, **-ied**) urge persistently, nag. [probably from ballad of *Chevy Chase*]

chloral /ˈklɔːr(ə)l/ n. **1** colourless liquid aldehyde used in making DDT. **2** (in full **chloral hydrate**) Pharm. crystalline solid made from this and used as a sedative. [French: related to CHLORINE, ALCOHOL]

chloride /ˈklɔːraɪd/ n. **1** compound of chlorine and another element or group. **2** bleaching agent containing this.

chlorinate /ˈklɔːrɪneɪt/ v. (**-ting**) impregnate or treat with chlorine. □ **chlorination** /-ˈneɪʃ(ə)n/ n.

chlorine /'klɔːriːn/ n. poisonous gaseous element used for purifying water etc. [Greek khlōros green]

chloroform /'klɒrəfɔːm/ —n. colourless volatile liquid formerly used as a general anaesthetic. —v. render unconscious with this. [from CHLORINE, FORMIC ACID]

chlorophyll /'klɒrəfɪl/ n. green pigment found in most plants. [Greek khlōros green, phullon leaf]

chock —n. block or wedge to check the motion of a wheel etc. —v. make fast with chocks. [French]

chock-a-block predic. adj. (often foll. by with) crammed together or full.

chock-full predic. adj. (often foll. by of) crammed full.

chocolate /'tʃɒklət/ —n. 1 a food preparation in the form of a paste or solid block made from ground cacao seeds and usu. sweetened. b sweet made of or coated with this. c drink containing this. 2 deep brown. —adj. 1 made from chocolate. 2 deep brown. [Aztec chocolatl]

choice —n. 1 a act of choosing. b thing or person chosen. 2 range from which to choose. 3 power or opportunity to choose. —adj. of superior quality. [German: related to CHOOSE]

choir /'kwaɪə(r)/ n. 1 regular group of singers, esp. in a church. 2 part of a cathedral or large church between the altar and nave. [Latin: related to CHORUS]

choirboy n. (fem. choirgirl) boy singer in a church choir.

choke —v. 1 (king) 1 stop the breathing of (a person or animal), esp. by constricting the windpipe or (of gas, smoke, etc.) by being unbreathable. 2 suffer a stoppage of breath. 3 make or become speechless from emotion. 4 retard the growth of or kill (esp. plants) by depriving of light etc. 5 (often foll. by back) suppress (feelings) with difficulty. 6 block or clog (a passage, tube, etc.). 7 (as choked adj.) colloq. disgusted, disappointed. —n. 1 valve in a carburettor controlling the intake of air. 2 device for smoothing the variations of an alternating current. □ choke up block in a church choir. [Old English]

choker n. close-fitting necklace.

cholecalciferol /,kɒlɪkæl'sɪfərɒl/ n. a vitamin (D₃) produced by the action of sunlight on a steroid in the skin. [from CHOLER, CALCIFEROL]

choler /'kɒlə(r)/ n. 1 hist. one of the four humours, bile. 2 poet. or archaic anger, irascibility. [Greek kholē bile]

cholera /'kɒlərə/ n. infectious often fatal bacterial disease of the small intestine. [related to CHOLER]

cholesterol /kə'lestərɒl/ n. sterol found in most body tissues, including the blood where high concentrations promote arteriosclerosis. [from CHOLER, Greek stereos stiff]

choose v. = CHAMP² [imitative]

choose v. (past chose /tʃəʊz/; past part. chosen) 1 select out of a greater number. 2 (usu. foll. by between, from) take or select one or another. 3 (usu. foll. by to + infin.) decide, be determined. 4 select as (was chosen leader). □ nothing (or little) to choose between them they are very similar. [Old English]

choosy /'tʃuːzɪ/ adj. (-ier, -iest) colloq. fastidious. □ choosiness n.

chop¹ —v. (-pp-) 1 (usu. foll. by off, down, etc.) cut or fell by the blow of an axe etc. 2 (often foll. by up) cut into small pieces. 3 strike (esp. a ball) with a short heavy edgewise blow. —n. 1 cutting blow. 2 thick slice of meat, esp. pork or lamb, usu. including a rib. 3 short chopping stroke in cricket etc. 4 (prec. by the) killing or being killed. [related to CHAP²]

chop² n. (usu. in pl.) jaw. [origin unknown]

chop³ v. (-pp-) □ chop and change vacillate; change direction frequently. □ chop logic argue pedantically. [perhaps related to CHAP¹]

chopper n. 1 a short axe with a large blade. b butcher's cleaver. 2 colloq. helicopter. 3 colloq. type of bicycle or motorcycle with high handlebars.

choppy adj. (-ier, -iest) (of the sea etc.) fairly rough. □ choppily adv. choppiness n. [from CHOP¹]

chopstick n. each of a pair of sticks held in one hand as eating utensils by the Chinese, Japanese, etc. [pidgin English from Chinese, = nimble ones]

chopsuey /tʃɒp'suːɪ/ n. (pl. -s) Chinese-style dish of meat fried with vegetables and rice. [Chinese, = mixed bits]

choral /'kɔːr(ə)l/ adj. of, for, or sung by a choir or CHORUS. [medieval Latin: related to CHORUS]

chorale /kɒ'rɑːl/ n. 1 simple stately hymn tune; harmonized form of this. 2 esp. US choir. [German: related to CHORAL]

chord¹ /kɔːd/ n. group of notes sounded together. [originally cord from ACCORD]

chord² /kɔːd/ n. 1 straight line joining the ends of an arc or curve. 2 *poet.* string of a harp etc. □ **strike a chord** elicit sympathy. [var. of CORD]

chordate /ˈkɔːdeɪt/ —n. animal having a cartilaginous skeletal rod at some stage of its development. —*adj.* of chordates. [Latin *chorda* CHORD² after *Vertebrata* etc.]

chore n. tedious or routine task, esp. domestic. [from CHAR²]

choreograph /ˈkɒrɪəɡrɑːf/ v. compose choreography for (a ballet etc.). □ **chor-eographer** /-ˈtɒɡrəfə(r)/ n.

choreography /ˌkɒrɪˈɒɡrəfɪ/ n. design or arrangement of a ballet etc. □ **cho-reographic** /-əˈɡræfɪk/ adj. [Greek *khoreia* dance]

chorister /ˈkɒrɪstə(r)/ n. member of a choir, esp. a choirboy. [French: related to CHOIR]

chortle /ˈtʃɔːt(ə)l/ —n. gleeful chuckle. —v. (-ling) utter or express with a chortle. [probably from CHUCKLE, SNORT]

chorus /ˈkɔːrəs/ —n. (*pl.* -es) 1 group of singers; choir. 2 music composed for a choir. 3 refrain or main part of a song. 4 simultaneous utterance. 5 group of singers and dancers performing together. 6 *Gk Antiq.* a group of per-formers who comment on the action in a Greek play. b character speaking the prologue in a play. —v. (-s-) speak or utter simultan-eously. [Latin from Greek]

chose past of CHOOSE.

chosen past part. of CHOOSE.

chough /tʃʌf/ n. bird with glossy blue-black plumage and red legs. [imitative]

choux pastry /ʃuː/ n. very light pastry enriched with eggs. [French]

chow n. 1 *slang* food. 2 dog of a Chinese breed with long woolly hair. [Chinese *chow-chow*]

chow mein /tʃaʊ ˈmeɪn/ n. Chinese-style dish of fried noodles with shredded meat or shrimps etc. and vegetables. [Chinese *chao mian* fried flour]

Christ /kraɪst/ —n. 1 title, also now treated as a name, given to Jesus. 2 Messiah as prophesied in the Old Testa-ment. —*int. slang* expressing surprise, anger, etc. [Greek, = anointed]

christen /ˈkrɪs(ə)n/ v. 1 baptize as a sign of admission to the Christian Church. 2 give a name to. 3 *colloq.* use for the first time. □ **christening** n. [Latin: related to CHRISTIAN]

Christendom /ˈkrɪsəndəm/ n. Chris-tians worldwide.

Christian /ˈkrɪstʃ(ə)n/ —adj. 1 of Christ's teaching or religion. 2 believing in or fol-lowing the religion of Christ. 3 showing the associated qualities. 4 *colloq.* kind. —n. adherent of Christianity. [Latin *Christianus* of CHRIST]

Christian era n. era reckoned from Christ's birth.

Christianity /ˌkrɪstɪˈænɪtɪ/ n. 1 Chris-tian religion. 2 being a Christian; Chris-tian quality or character.

Christian name n. forename, esp. as given at baptism.

Christian Science n. Christian sect believing in the power of healing by prayer alone. □ **Christian Scientist** n.

Christmas /ˈkrɪsməs/ n. 1 (also Christ-mas Day) annual festival of Christ's birth, celebrated on 25 Dec. 2 period around this. □ **Christmassy** adj. [Old English: related to CHRIST, MASS²]

Christmas-box n. present or gratuity given at Christmas.

Christmas Eve n. 24 Dec.

Christmas pudding n. rich boiled pudding of flour, suet, dried fruit, etc.

Christmas rose n. white-flowered winter-blooming hellebore.

Christmas tree n. evergreen tree or imitation of this set up and decorated at Christmas.

chromatic /krəˈmætɪk/ adj. 1 of colour; in colours. 2 *Mus.* a of or having notes not belonging to a particular diatonic scale. b (of a scale) ascending or des-cending by semitones. □ **chromat-ically** adv. [Greek *khrōma*-colour]

chromatin /ˈkrəʊmətɪn/ n. chromo-some material in a cell nucleus which stains with basic dyes. [Greek: related to CHROME]

chromatography /ˌkrəʊməˈtɒɡrəfɪ/ n. separation of the components of a mix-ture by slow passage through or over material which adsorbs them differ-ently. [Greek: related to CHROME]

chrome /krəʊm/ n. 1 chromium, esp. as plating. 2 (in full **chrome yellow**) yel-low pigment got from a certain com-pound of chromium. [Greek *khrōma* colour]

chromite /ˈkrəʊmaɪt/ n. mineral of chromium and iron oxides.

chromium /ˈkrəʊmɪəm/ n. metallic ele-ment used as a shiny decorative or protective coating.

chromium plate n. protective coating of chromium.

chromosome /ˈkrəʊməsəʊm/ n. threadlike structure, usu. found in the cell nucleus of animals and plants, carrying genes. [Greek: related to CHROME, *sōma* body]

chronic /ˈkrɒnɪk/ adj. 1 (esp. of an illness) long-lasting. 2 having a chronic complaint. 3 *colloq.* very bad; intense, severe. 4 *colloq.* habitual, inveterate (*a*

chronic, liar). □ **chronically** *adv.* [Greek *khronos* time]

■ **Usage** The use of *chronic* in sense 3 is very informal, and its use in sense 4 is considered incorrect by some people.

chronicle /ˈkronɪk(ə)l/ —*n.* register of events in order of occurrence. —*v.* (-ling) record (events) thus. [Greek *khronika*: related to CHRONIC]

chronological /kronəˈlɒdʒɪk(ə)l/ *adj.* 1 according to order of occurrence. 2 of chronology. □ **chronologically** *adv.*

chronology /krəˈnɒlədʒɪ/ *n.* (*pl.* -ies) 1 science of determining dates. 2 a arrangement of determining dates etc. in order of occurrence. b table or document displaying this. [Greek *khronos* time, -LOGY]

chronometer /krəˈnɒmɪtə(r)/ *n.* time-measuring instrument, esp. one used in navigation. [from CHRONOLOGY, -METER]

chrysalis /ˈkrɪsəlɪs/ *n.* (*pl.* -lises) 1 pupa of a butterfly or moth. 2 case enclosing it. [Greek *khrusos* gold]

chrysanthemum /krɪˈsænθəməm/ *n.* garden plant of the daisy family blooming in autumn. [Greek, = gold flower]

chrysoberyl /ˈkrɪsəberɪl/ *n.* yellowish-green gem. [Greek *khrusos* gold, BERYL]

chrysolite /ˈkrɪsəlaɪt/ *n.* precious variety of olivine. [Greek *khrusos* gold, *lithos* stone]

chrysoprase /ˈkrɪsəpreɪz/ *n.* apple-green variety of chalcedony. [Greek *khrusos* gold, *prason* leek]

chub *n.* (*pl.* same) thick-bodied river fish. [origin unknown]

Chubb *n.* (in full **Chubb lock**) *propr.* lock with a device for fixing the bolt immovably should someone try to pick it. [*Chubb*, name of a locksmith]

chubby *adj.* (-ier, -iest) plump and rounded. [from CHUB]

chuck¹ —*v.* 1 *colloq.* fling or throw carelessly or casually. 2 (often foll. by *in*, *up*) *colloq.* give up; reject. 3 touch playfully, esp. under the chin. —*n.* 1 playful touch under the chin. 2 toss. □ **the chuck** *slang* dismissal; rejection. **chuck out** *colloq.* 1 expel (a person) from a gathering etc. 2 get rid of, discard. [perhaps from French *chuquer* knock]

chuck² —*n.* 1 cut of beef from neck to ribs. 2 device for holding a workpiece or bit. —*v.* fix to a chuck. [var. of CHOCK]

chuckle /ˈtʃʌk(ə)l/ —*v.* (-ling) laugh quietly or inwardly. —*n.* quiet or suppressed laugh. [chuck CLUCK]

chuff *v.* (of an engine etc.) work with a regular sharp puffing sound. [imitative]

chuffed *adj.* *slang* delighted. [*chuff*]

chug —*v.* (**-gg-**) 1 emit a regular muffled explosive sound, as of an engine running slowly. 2 move with this sound. —*n.* chugging sound. [imitative]

chukka boot *n.* ankle-high leather boot.

chukker *n.* (also **chukka**) period of play in polo. [Sanskrit *cakra* wheel]

chum *n.* *colloq.* close friend. □ **chum up** (**-mm-**) (often foll. by *with*) become a close friend (of). □ **chummy** *adj.* (-ier, -iest) **chummily** *adv.* **chumminess** *n.* [abbreviation of *chamber-fellow*]

chump *n.* 1 *colloq.* foolish person. 2 thick end of a loin of lamb or mutton (*chump chop*). 3 short thick block of wood. □ **off one's chump** *slang* crazy. [blend of CHUNK, LUMP]

chunk *n.* 1 thick piece cut or broken off. 2 substantial amount [var. of CHUCK²]

chunky *adj.* (-ier, -iest) 1 containing or resembling chunks; thick, substantial. 2 small and sturdy. □ **chunkiness** *n.*

chunter *v.* *colloq.* mutter, grumble. [probably imitative]

chupatty var. of CHAPATTI.

church *n.* 1 building for public Christian worship. 2 public worship (*met after church*). 3 (**Church**) a body of all Christians. b clergy or clerical profession. c organized Christian society (*the early Church*). [Greek *kuriakon* Lord's (house)]

churchgoer *n.* person attending church regularly.

churchman *n.* member of the clergy or of a Church.

Church of England *n.* English Protestant Church.

churchwarden *n.* either of two elected lay representatives of an Anglican parish.

churchyard *n.* enclosed ground around a church used for burials.

churl *n.* 1 ill-bred person. 2 *archaic* peasant. [Old English, = man]

churlish *adj.* surly, mean. □ **churlishly** *adv.* **churlishness** *n.* [from CHURL]

churn —*n.* 1 large milk-can. 2 butter-making machine. —*v.* 1 agitate (milk or cream) in a churn. 2 produce (butter) in a churn. 3 (usu. foll. by *up*) upset, agitate. □ **churn out** produce in large quantities. [Old English]

chute¹ /ʃuːt/ *n.* sloping channel or slide for sending things to a lower level. [Latin *cado* fall]

chute² /ʃuːt/ *n.* *colloq.* parachute. [abbreviation]

chutney /ˈtʃʌtnɪ/ *n.* (*pl.* -s) pungent condiment of fruits, vinegar, spices, etc. [Hindi]

chutzpah /ˈxʊtspə/ *n. slang* shameless audacity. [Yiddish]

chyle /kaɪl/ *n.* milky fluid of food materials formed in the intestine after digestion. [Greek *khulos* juice]

chyme /kaɪm/ *n.* acid pulp formed from partly-digested food. [Greek *khumos* juice]

CIA *abbr.* (in the US) Central Intelligence Agency.

ciao /tʃaʊ/ *int. colloq.* 1 goodbye. 2 hello. [Italian]

cicada /sɪˈkɑːdə/ *n.* large transparent-winged insect making a rhythmic chirping sound. [Latin]

cicatrice /ˈsɪkətrɪs/ *n.* scar left by a wound. [Latin]

cicely /ˈsɪsəlɪ/ *n.* (*pl.* **-ies**) flowering plant related to parsley and chervil. [Greek *seselis*]

cicerone /ˌtʃɪtʃəˈrəʊnɪ/ *n.* (*pl.* **-roni** pronunc. same) person who guides sightseers. [Latin *Cicero*, name of a Roman statesman]

CID *abbr.* Criminal Investigation Department.

-cide *suffix* 1 person or substance that kills (*regicide*; *insecticide*). 2 killing of (*infanticide*). [Latin *caedo* kill]

cider *n.* drink of fermented apple juice. [Hebrew, = strong drink]

cigar /sɪˈgɑː(r)/ *n.* tight roll of tobacco leaves for smoking. [French or Spanish]

cigarette /ˌsɪgəˈret/ *n.* finely-cut tobacco rolled in paper for smoking. [French diminutive]

cilium /ˈsɪliəm/ *n.* (*pl.* **cilia**) 1 minute hairlike structure on the surface of many animal cells. 2 eyelash. □ **ciliary** *adj.* **ciliate** *adj.* [Latin, = eyelash]

cinch *n. colloq.* 1 sure thing; certainty. 2 easy task. [Spanish *cincha* saddle-girth]

cinchona /sɪŋˈkəʊnə/ *n.* 1 **a** S. American evergreen tree or shrub. **b** its bark, containing quinine. 2 drug from this. [Countess of *Chinchon*]

cincture /ˈsɪŋktʃə(r)/ *n. literary* girdle, belt, or border. [Latin *cingo* gird]

cinder *n.* 1 residue of coal or wood etc. after burning. 2 (in *pl.*) ashes. [Old English *sinder* = slag]

Cinderella /ˌsɪndəˈrelə/ *n.* person or thing of unrecognized or disregarded merit or beauty. [name of a girl in a fairy tale]

cine- *comb. form* cinematographic (*cine-camera*). [abbreviation]

cinema /ˈsɪnəmə/ *n.* 1 theatre where films are shown. 2 **a** films collectively. **b** art or industry of producing films. □ **cinematic** /-ˈmætɪk/ *adj.* related to KINEMATIC

cinematography /ˌsɪnɪməˈtɒɡrəfɪ/ *n.* art of making films. □ **cinematographer** *n.* **cinematographic** /-ˌmætəˈɡræfɪk/ *adj.*

cineraria /ˌsɪnəˈreərɪə/ *n.* composite plant with bright flowers and ash-coloured down on its leaves. [Latin *cinis -ner-* ashes]

cinnabar /ˈsɪnəbɑː(r)/ *n.* 1 bright red mercuric sulphide. 2 vermilion. 3 moth with reddish-marked wings. [Latin from Greek]

cinnamon /ˈsɪnəmən/ *n.* 1 aromatic spice from the bark of an SE Asian tree. 2 this tree. 3 yellowish-brown. [Greek *kinnamon*]

cinque /sɪŋk/ *n.* the five on dice. [Latin *quinque* five]

cinquefoil /ˈsɪŋkfɔɪl/ *n.* 1 plant with compound leaves of five leaflets. 2 *Archit.* five-cusped ornament in a circle or arch. [Latin: related to CINQUE, *folium* leaf]

Cinque Ports *n.pl.* group of (orig. five) ports in SE England with ancient privileges. [Latin *quinque portus* five ports]

cipher /ˈsaɪfə(r)/ (also **cypher**) —*n.* 1 **a** secret or disguised writing. **b** thing so written. **c** key to it. 2 arithmetical symbol (0) used to occupy a vacant place in decimal etc. numeration. 3 person or thing of no importance. —*v.* write in cipher. [Arabic *ṣifr*]

circa /ˈsɜːkə/ *prep.* (preceding a date) about. [Latin]

circadian /sɜːˈkeɪdiən/ *adj. Physiol.* occurring about once per day. [from CIRCA, Latin *dies* day]

circle /ˈsɜːk(ə)l/ —*n.* 1 **a** round plane figure whose circumference is everywhere equidistant from its centre. 2 circular or roundish enclosure or structure. 3 curved upper tier of seats in a theatre etc. 4 circular route. 5 persons grouped round a centre of interest. 6 set or restricted group (*literary circles*). —*v.* (**-ling**) 1 (often foll. by *round*, *about*) move in a circle. 2 **a** revolve round. **b** form a circle round. □ **come full circle** return to the starting-point. [Latin diminutive: related to CIRCUS]

circlet /ˈsɜːklɪt/ *n.* 1 small circle. 2 circular band, esp. as an ornament.

circuit /ˈsɜːkɪt/ *n.* 1 line or course enclosing an area; the distance round. 2 **a** path of an electric current. **b** apparatus through which a current passes. 3 **a** judge's itinerary through a district to hold courts. **b** such a district. **c** lawyers following a circuit. 4 chain of theatres, cinemas, etc. under a single management. 5 motor-racing track. 6 itinerary or specific sphere of operation (*election circuit*; *cabaret circuit*). 7 sequence of

sporting events or athletic exercises.
[Latin: related to CIRCUM, *eo it-* go]

circuit-breaker *n.* automatic device for interrupting an electric circuit.

circuitous /sə'kju:itəs/ *adj.* 1 indirect. 2 going a long way round.

circuitry /'sə:kitri/ *n.* (*pl.* -ies) 1 system of electric circuits. 2 equipment forming this.

circular /'sə:kjulə(r)/ —*adj.* 1 a having the form of a circle. b moving (roughly) in a circle, finishing at the starting-point (*circular walk*). 2 (of reasoning) using for its conclusion the point it is trying to prove as evidence for its conclusion, hence invalid 3 (of a letter etc.) distributed to a number of people. —*n.* circular letter, leaflet, etc. □ **circularity** /-'læriti/ *n.* [Latin: related to CIRCLE]

circularize *v.* (also **-ise**) (-zing or -sing) distribute circulars to.

circular saw *n.* power saw with a rapidly rotating toothed disc.

circulate /'sə:kjuleit/ *v.* (-ting) 1 be in circulation. spread. 2 a put into circulation. b send circulars to. 3 move about among guests etc. [Latin: related to CIRCLE]

circulation /sə:kju'leiʃ(ə)n/ *n.* 1 movement to and fro, or from and back to a starting-point, esp. that of the blood from and to the heart. 2 a transmission or distribution. b number of copies sold. □ **in** (or **out of**) **circulation** active (or not active) socially.

circulatory /sə:kju'leitəri/ *adj.* of circulation, esp. of the blood.

circum- *comb. form* round, about. [Latin]

circumcise /'sə:kəmsaiz/ *v.* (-sing) cut off the foreskin or clitoris of. □ **circumcision** /-'siʒ(ə)n/ *n.* [Latin *caedo* cut]

circumference /sə'kʌmfərəns/ *n.* 1 enclosing boundary, esp. of a circle. 2 distance round. □ **circumferential** /-'ren(ʃ)əl/ *adj.* [Latin *fero* carry]

circumflex /'sə:kəm,fleks/ *n.* (in full **circumflex accent**) mark (^) placed over a vowel to show contraction, length, etc. [Latin: related to FLEX']

circumlocution /ˌsə:kəmlə'kju:ʃ(ə)n/ *n.* 1 a roundabout expression. b evasive talk. 2 verbosity. □ **circumlocutory** /-'lɒkjʊtəri/ *adj.*

circumnavigate /ˌsə:kəm'nævɪ,geɪt/ *v.* (-ting) sail round (esp. the world). □ **circumnavigation** /-'geɪʃ(ə)n/ *n.*

circumscribe /'sə:kəm,skraɪb/ *v.* (-bing) 1 (of a line etc.) enclose or outline. 2 lay down the limits of, confine, restrict. 3 *Geom.* draw (a figure) round another, touching it. □ **circumscription** /-'skrɪp(ʃ)ən/ *n.* [Latin *scribo* write]

circumspect /'sə:kəm,spekt/ *adj.* cautious; taking everything into account. □ **circumspection** /-'spek(ʃ)ən/ *n.* **circumspectly** *adv.* [Latin *specio spect-* look]

circumstance /'sə:kəmst(ə)ns/ *n.* 1 fact, occurrence, or condition, esp. (in *pl.*) connected with or influencing an event. (bad) luck (*victim of circumstance(s)*). 2 (in *pl.*) one's financial or material condition. 3 ceremony, fuss. □ **in** (or **under**) **the circumstances** (or **under**) **no circumstances** not at all; never. □ **circumstanced** *adj.* [Latin *sto* stand]

circumstantial /ˌsə:kəm'stæn(ʃ)əl/ *adj.* 1 giving full details (*circumstantial account*). 2 (of evidence etc.) indicating a conclusion by inference from known facts but hard to explain otherwise. □ **circumstantiality** /-ʃi'ælɪti/ *n.*

circumvent /ˌsə:kəm'vent/ *v.* 1 evade, find a way round. 2 baffle, outwit. □ **circumvention** *n.* [Latin *venio veni-* come]

circus /'sə:kəs/ *n.* (*pl.* -es) 1 travelling show of performing acrobats, clowns, animals, etc. 2 *colloq.* a scene of lively action. b group of people in a common activity, esp. spor-. 3 open space in a town, where several streets converge. 4 *Rom. Antiq.* arena for sports and games. [Latin, = ring]

cirrhosis /sɪ'rəʊsɪs/ *n.* chronic liver disease, as a result of alcoholism etc. [Greek *kirrhos* tawny]

cirrus /'sɪrəs/ *n.* (*pl.* **cirri** /-raɪ/) 1 white wispy cloud at high altitude. 2 tendril or appendage of a plant or animal. [Latin, = curl]

cisalpine /sɪs'ælpaɪn/ *adj.* on the south side of the Alps. [Latin *cis-* on this side of]

cissy var. of SISSY.

Cistercian /sɪ'stɜ:ʃ(ə)n/ —*n.* monk or nun of the order founded as a stricter branch of the Benedictines. —*adj.* of the Cistercians. [French *Cîteaux* in France]

cistern /'sɪst(ə)n/ *n.* 1 tank for storing water. 2 underground reservoir. [Latin *cista* box, from Greek]

cistus /'sɪstəs/ *n.* shrub with large white or red flowers. [Latin from Greek]

citadel /'sɪtəd(ə)l/ *n.* fortress, usu. on high ground, protecting or dominating a city. [French *citadelle*]

citation /saɪ'teɪʃ(ə)n/ *n.* 1 citing; passage cited. 2 *Mil.* mention in dispatches. 3 description of the reasons for an award.

cite *v.* (-ting) 1 mention as an example etc. 2 quote (a book etc.). in support. 3 *Mil.* mention in dispatches. 4 summon

to appear in court. [Latin *cieo* set in motion]

citizen /ˈsɪtɪz(ə)n/ *n.* **1** member of a State, either native or naturalized. **2** inhabitant of a city. **3** *US* civilian. □ **citizenry** *n.* **citizenship** *n.* [Anglo-French: related to CITY]

citizen's band *n.* system of local inter-communication by individuals on special radio frequencies.

citrate /ˈsɪtreɪt/ *n.* a salt of citric acid.

citric /ˈsɪtrɪk/ *adj.* derived from citrus fruit.

citric acid *n.* sharp-tasting acid in citrus fruits.

citron /ˈsɪtrən/ *n.* **1** tree with large lemon-like fruits. **2** this fruit. [French from Latin CITRUS]

citronella /ˌsɪtrəˈnelə/ *n.* **1** a fragrant oil. **2** grass from S. Asia yielding it.

citrus /ˈsɪtrəs/ *n.* (*pl.* **-es**) **1** tree of a group including the lemon, orange, and grapefruit. **2** (in full **citrus fruit**) fruit of such a tree. [Latin]

city /ˈsɪtɪ/ *n.* (*pl.* **-ies**) **1** large town, strictly one created by charter and usu. containing a cathedral. **2** (**the City**) **a** part of London governed by the Lord Mayor and Corporation. **b** business part of this. **c** commercial circles. [Latin *civitas*: related to CIVIC]

city-state *n.* esp. *hist.* city that with its surrounding territory forms an independent State.

civet /ˈsɪvɪt/ *n.* **1** (in full **civet-cat**) cat-like animal of Central Africa. **2** strong musky perfume obtained from it. [French ultimately from Arabic]

civic /ˈsɪvɪk/ *adj.* **1** of a city. **2** of citizens or citizenship. □ **civically** *adv.* [Latin *civis* citizen]

civic centre *n.* **1** area where municipal offices etc. are situated. **2** the offices themselves.

civics *n.pl.* (usu. treated as *sing.*) the study of the rights and duties of citizenship.

civil /ˈsɪv(ə)l/ *adj.* **1** of or belonging to citizens. **2** of ordinary citizens; non-military. **3** polite, obliging, not rude. **4** *Law* concerning private rights and not criminal offences. **5** (of the length of a day, year, etc.) fixed by custom or law, not natural or astronomical. □ **civilly** *adv.* [Latin *civilis*: related to CIVIC]

civil defence *n.* organizing of civilians for protection during wartime attacks.

civil disobedience *n.* refusal to comply with certain laws as a peaceful protest.

civil engineer *n.* one who designs or maintains roads, bridges, dams, etc.

civilian /sɪˈvɪlɪən/ —*n.* person not in the armed services or police force. —*adj.* of or for civilians.

civility /sɪˈvɪlɪtɪ/ *n.* (*pl.* **-ies**) **1** politeness. **2** act of politeness. [Latin: related to CIVIL]

civilization /ˌsɪvɪlaɪˈzeɪʃ(ə)n/ *n.* (also **-isation**) **1** advanced stage or system of social development. **2** peoples of the world that are regarded as having this. **3** a people or nation (esp. of the past) regarded as an element of social evolution (*Inca civilization*).

civilize /ˈsɪvɪlaɪz/ *v.* (also **-ise**) (**-zing** or **-sing**) **1** bring out of a barbarous or primitive stage of society. **2** enlighten; refine and educate. [French: related to CIVIL]

civil liberty *n.* (often in *pl.*) freedom of action subject to the law.

civil list *n.* annual allowance voted by Parliament for the royal family's household expenses.

civil marriage *n.* one solemnized without religious ceremony.

civil rights *n.pl.* rights of citizens to freedom and equality.

civil servant *n.* member of the civil service.

civil service *n.* branches of State administration, excluding military and judicial branches and elected politicians.

civil war *n.* war between citizens of the same country.

civvies *n.pl.* *slang* civilian clothes. [abbreviation]

Civvy Street *n.* *slang* civilian life. [abbreviation]

Cl *symb.* chlorine.

cl *abbr.* centilitre(s).

clack —*v.* **1** make a sharp sound as of boards struck together. **2** chatter. —*n.* clacking noise or talk. [imitative]

clad *adj.* **1** clothed. **2** provided with cladding. [past part. of CLOTHE]

cladding *n.* covering or coating on a structure or material etc.

cladistics /kləˈdɪstɪks/ *n.pl.* (usu. treated as *sing.*) *Biol.* method of classifying animals and plants on the basis of shared characteristics. [Greek *klados* branch]

claim —*v.* **1** state, declare, assert. **2** demand as one's due or property. **3** represent oneself as having or achieving (*claim victory*). **4** (foll. by + infin.) profess. **5** have as an achievement or consequence (*fire claimed two victims*). **6** (of a thing) deserve (attention etc.). —*n.* **1** demand or request for a thing considered one's due (*lay claim to; put in a claim*). **2** (foll. by *to, on*) right or title to a

thing. **3** assertion. **4** thing claimed. [Latin *clamo* call out]

claimant *n.* person making a claim, esp. in a lawsuit, or claiming State benefit.

clairvoyance /kleə'vɔɪəns/ *n.* supposed faculty of perceiving the future or things beyond normal sensory perception. □ **clairvoyant** *n. & adj.* [French: related to CLEAR, *voir* see]

clam *n.* edible bivalve mollusc. —*v.* (-mm-) (foll. by *up*) *colloq* refuse to talk. [related to CLAMP[1]]

clammy /'klæmɪ/ *adj.* (-ier, -iest) unpleasantly damp and sticky. □ **clamminess** *n.* [from *clam* to daub]

clamour /'klæmə(r)/ (*US* clamor) —*n.* **1** loud or vehement shouting or noise. **2** protest, demand. —*v.* **1** make a clamour. **2** utter with a clamour. □ **clamorous** *adj.* [Latin: related to CLAIM]

clamp[1] —*n.* **1** device, esp. a brace or band of iron etc., for strengthening or holding things together. **2** device for immobilizing an illegally parked vehicle. —*v.* **1** strengthen or fasten with a clamp; fix firmly. **2** immobilize (a vehicle) with a clamp. □ **clamp down** (usu. foll. by *on*) become stricter (about); suppress. [Low German or Dutch]

clamp[2] *n.* potatoes etc. stored under straw or earth. [Dutch: related to CLUMP]

clamp-down *n.* sudden policy of suppression.

clan *n.* **1** group of people with a common ancestor, esp. in the Scottish Highlands. **2** large family as a social group. **3** group with a strong common interest. [Gaelic]

clandestine /klæn'destɪn, 'klæn-/ *adj.* surreptitious, secret. [Latin]

clang —*n.* loud resonant metallic sound. —*v.* (cause to) make a clang. [imitative: cf. Latin *clango* resound]

clanger *n. slang* mistake, blunder.

clangour /'klæŋgə(r)/ *n.* (*US* clangor) prolonged clanging. □ **clangorous** *adj.*

clank —*n.* sound as of metal on metal. —*v.* (cause to) make a clank. [imitative]

clannish *adj.* often *derog.* (of a family or group) associating closely with each other; inward-looking.

clansman *n.* (*fem.* clanswoman) member of or fellow-member of a clan.

clap —*v.* (-pp-) **1 a** strike the palms of one's hands together, esp. repeatedly as applause. **b** strike (the hands) together in this way. **2** applaud thus. **3** put or place quickly or with determination (*clapped him in prison; clap a tax on*

whisky). **4** (foll. by *on*) give a friendly slap (*clapped him on the back*). —*n.* **1** act of clapping, esp. as applause. **2** explosive sound, esp. of thunder. **3** slap, pat. □ **clap eyes on** *colloq* see. [Old English]

clap[2] *n. coarse slang* venereal disease, esp. gonorrhoea. [French]

clapped out *adj. slang* worn out; exhausted.

clapper *n.* tongue or striker of a bell. □ **like the clappers** *slang* very fast or hard.

clapperboard *n.* device in film-making of hinged boards struck together to synchronize the starting of picture and sound machinery.

claptrap *n.* insincere or pretentious talk, nonsense.

claque /klæk/ *n.* group of people hired to applaud. [French]

claret /'klærət/ *n.* **1** red wine, esp. from Bordeaux. **2** purplish-red. [French: related to CLARIFY]

clarify /'klærɪfaɪ/ *v.* (-ies, -ied) **1** make or become clearer. **2 a** free (liquid etc.) from impurities. **b** make transparent. □ **clarification** /-fɪ'keɪʃ(ə)n/ *n.* [Latin: related to CLEAR]

clarinet /klærɪ'net/ *n.* woodwind instrument with a single reed. □ **clarinettist** *n.* (*US* clarinetist). [French diminutive of *clarine*, a kind of bell]

clarion /'klærɪən/ *n.* **1** clear rousing sound. **2** *hist.* shrill war-trumpet. [Latin: related to CLEAR]

clarity /'klærɪtɪ/ *n.* clearness.

clash —*n.* **1** a loud jarring sound as of metal objects struck together. **b** collision. **2 a** conflict. **b** discord of colours etc. —*v.* **1** (cause to) make a clashing sound. **2 a** collide. **b** coincide awkwardly. **3** (often foll. by *with*) **a** come into conflict or be at variance. **b** (of colours) be discordant. [imitative]

clasp /klɑːsp/ —*n.* **1** device with interlocking parts for fastening. **2 a** embrace. **b** grasp, handshake. **3** bar on a medal-ribbon. —*v.* **1** fasten with or as with a clasp. **2 a** grasp, hold closely. **b** embrace. [Old English]

clasp-knife *n.* folding knife, usu. with a catch to hold the blade open.

class /klɑːs/ —*n.* **1** any set of persons or things grouped together, or graded by quality. **4 a** division or order of society (*upper class*). **2** distinction, high quality. **4 a** group of students taught together. **b** occasion when they meet. **c** their course of instruction. **5** division of candidates by merit in an examination. **6** *Biol.* next grouping of organisms below a division or phylum. —*v.* assign to a class or

class-conscious

category. □ **in a class of** (or **on**) **its** (or **one's**) **own** unequalled. □ **classless** *adj.* [Latin *classis* assembly]

class-conscious *adj.* aware of social divisions or one's place in them. □ **class-consciousness** *n.*

classic /ˈklæsik/ —*adj.* **1** first-class; of lasting value and importance. **2** very typical (*a classic case*). **3 a** of ancient Greek and Latin literature, art, etc. **b** (of style) simple, harmonious. **4** famous because long-established. —*n.* **1** classic writer, artist, work, or example. **2** (in *pl.*) ancient Greek and Latin. [Latin *classicus*; related to CLASS]

classical *adj.* **1 a** of ancient Greek or Roman literature or art. **b** (of a language) having the form used by ancient standard authors. **2** (of music) serious or conventional, or of the period from c.1750–1800. **3** restrained in style. □ **classicality** /-ˈkælɪtɪ/ *n.* **classically** *adv.*

classicism /ˈklæsɪˌsɪz(ə)m/ *n.* **1** following of a classic style. **2** classical scholarship. **3** ancient Greek or Latin idiom. □ **classicist** *n.*

classify /ˈklæsɪˌfaɪ/ *v.* (**-ies, -ied**) **1 a** arrange in classes or categories. **b** assign to a class or category. **2** designate as officially secret or not for general disclosure. □ **classifiable** *adj.* **classification** /-fɪˈkeɪʃ(ə)n/ *n.* **classificatory** /-ˈkeɪtəri/ *adj.* [French; related to CLASS]

classmate *n.* person in the same class at school.

classroom *n.* room where a class of students is taught.

classy *adj.* (**-ier, -iest**) *colloq.* superior, stylish. □ **classily** *adv.* **classiness** *n.*

clatter —*n.* sound as of hard objects struck together. —*v.* (cause to) make a clatter. [Old English]

clause /klɔːz/ *n.* **1** *Gram.* part of a sentence, including a subject and predicate. **2** single statement in a treaty, law, contract, etc. □ **clausal** *adj.* [Latin *clausula*: related to CLOSE]

Clause 28 *n.* clause in the Local Government Bill (and later Act) banning local authorities from promoting homosexuality.

claustrophobia /ˌklɔːstrəˈfəʊbɪə/ *n.* abnormal fear of confined places. □ **claustrophobic** *adj.* [Latin *claustrum* CLOISTER, -PHOBIA]

clavichord /ˈklævɪˌkɔːd/ *n.* small keyboard instrument with a very soft tone. [medieval Latin: related to CLAVICLE]

clavicle /ˈklævɪk(ə)l/ *n.* collar-bone. [Latin *clavis* key]

claw —*n.* **1 a** pointed nail on an animal's foot. **b** foot armed with claws. **2** pincers of a shellfish. **3** device for grappling,

holding, etc. —*v.* scratch, maul, or pull with claws or fingernails. [Old English]

claw back *v.* regain laboriously or gradually.

claw-hammer *n.* hammer with one side of the head forked for extracting nails.

clay *n.* **1** stiff sticky earth, used for making bricks, pottery, etc. **2** *poet.* substance of the human body. □ **clayey** *adj.* [Old English]

claymore /ˈkleɪmɔː(r)/ *n. hist.* Scottish two-edged broadsword. [Gaelic, = great sword]

clay pigeon *n.* breakable disc thrown up from a trap as a target for shooting.

clean —*adj.* **1** free from dirt or impurities, unsoiled. **2** clear; unused; pristine (*clean air; clean page*). **3** not obscene or indecent. **4** attentive to personal hygiene and cleanliness. **5** complete, clear-cut. **6** showing no record of crime, disease, etc. **7** fair (*a clean fight*). **8** streamlined; well-formed. **9** adroit, skilful. **10** (of a nuclear weapon) producing relatively little fallout. —*adv.* **1** completely, outright, simply. **2** in a clean manner. —*v.* make or become clean. —*n.* act or process of cleaning. □ **clean out 1** clean thoroughly. **2** *slang* empty or deprive (esp. of money). **clean up 1 a** clear away (a mess). **b** (also *absol.*) put (things) tidy. **c** make (oneself) clean. **2** restore order or morality to. **3** *slang* acquire as or make a profit. **come clean** *colloq.* confess fully. **make a clean breast of** see BREAST. [Old English]

clean bill of health *n.* declaration that there is no disease or defect.

clean-cut *adj.* **1** sharply outlined or defined. **2** (of a person) clean and tidy.

cleaner *n.* **1** person employed to clean rooms etc. **2** establishment for cleaning clothes etc. **3** device or substance for cleaning. □ **take a person to the cleaners** *slang* **1** defraud or rob a person. **2** criticize severely.

cleanly[1] *adv.* in a clean way.

cleanly[2] /ˈklɛnlɪ/ *adj.* (**-ier, -iest**) habitually clean; with clean habits. □ **cleanliness** *n.*

cleanse /klɛnz/ *v.* (**-sing**) make clean or pure. □ **cleanser** *n.*

clean-shaven *adj.* without beard or moustache.

clean sheet *n.* (also **clean slate**) freedom from commitments or imputations; removal of these from one's record.

clean-up *n.* act of cleaning up.

clear —*adj.* **1** free from dirt or contamination. **2** (of weather, the sky, etc.) not dull. **3** transparent. **4 a** easily perceived; distinct; evident (*a clear voice; it is clear that*). **b** easily understood. **5** discerning

readily and accurately (*clear mind*). **6** confident, convinced. **7** (of a conscience) free from guilt. **8** (of a road etc.) unobstructed. **9 a** net, without deduction. **b** complete (*three clear days*). **10** (often foll. by *of*) free, unhampered; unencumbered.—*adv.* **1** clearly. **2** completely (*got clear away*). **3** apart, out of contact (*keep clear*).—*v.* **1** make or become clear. **2** (often foll. by *of*) make or become free from obstruction etc. **3** (often foll. by *of*) show (a person) to be innocent. **4** approve (a person etc.) for a special duty, access, etc. **5** pass over or by, safely or without touching. **6** make (an amount of money) as a net gain or to balance expenses. **7** pass (a cheque) through a clearing-house. **8** pass through (customs etc.) **9** disappear (*mist cleared*). □ **clear the air** remove suspicion, tension, etc. **clear away 1** remove (esp. dishes etc.). **2** disappear. **clear the decks** prepare for action. **clear off** *colloq.* go away. **clear out 1** empty, tidy by emptying. **2** remove. **3** *colloq.* go away. **clear up 1** tidy up. **2** solve. **3** (of weather) become fine. **4** disappear (*cold has cleared up*). **clear a thing with** get approval or authorization for it from (a person). **in the clear** free from suspicion or difficulty. □ **clearly** *adv.* **clearness** *n.* [Latin *clarus*]

clearance *n.* **1** removal of obstructions etc. **2** space allowed for the passing of two objects or parts in machinery etc. **3** special authorization. **4 a** clearing by customs. **b** certificate showing this. **5** clearing of cheques. **6** clearing out.

clear-cut *adj.* sharply defined.

clear-headed *adj.* thinking clearly, sensible.

clearing *n.* open area in a forest.

clearing bank *n.* bank which is a member of a clearing-house.

clearing-house *n.* **1** bankers' establishment where cheques and bills are exchanged, only the balances being paid in cash. **2** agency for collecting and distributing information etc.

clear-out *n.* tidying by emptying and sorting.

clear-sighted *adj.* seeing, thinking, or understanding clearly.

clear-up *n.* **1** tidying up. **2** (usu. *attrib.*) solving of crimes (*clear-up rates*).

clearway *n.* main road (other than a motorway) on which vehicles may not normally stop.

cleat *n.* **1** piece of metal, wood, etc., bolted on for fastening ropes to, or to strengthen woodwork etc. **2** projecting piece on a spar, gangway, etc. to prevent slipping. [Old English]

cleavage /ˈkliːvɪdʒ/ *n.* **1** hollow between a woman's breasts. **2** division, splitting. **3** line along which rocks, crystals, etc. split.

cleave¹ *v.* (*-ving; past* **clove** or **cleft** or **cleaved;** *past part.* **cloven** or **cleft** or **cleaved**) *literary* **1** chop or break apart; split, esp. along the grain or line of cleavage. **2** make one's way through (air or water). [Old English]

cleave² *v.* (*-ving*) (foll. by *to*) *literary* stick fast; adhere. [Old English]

cleaver *n.* butcher's heavy chopping tool.

clef *n. Mus.* symbol indicating the pitch of notes on a staff. [Latin *clavis* key]

cleft¹ *adj.* split, partly divided. [past part. of CLEAVE¹]

cleft² *n.* split, fissure. [Old English: related to CLEAVE¹]

cleft palate *n.* congenital split in the roof of the mouth.

clematis /ˈklemətɪs/ *n.* climbing plant with white, pink, or purple flowers. [Greek]

clement /ˈklemənt/ *adj.* **1** (of weather) mild. **2** merciful. □ **clemency** *n.* [Latin *clemens*]

clementine /ˈkleməntiːn/ *n.* small tangerine-like citrus fruit. [French]

clench —*v.* **1** close (the teeth, fingers, etc.) tightly. **2** grasp firmly. —*n.* clenching action; clenched state. [Old English]

clerestory /ˈklɪəstɔːrɪ/ *n.* (*pl.* **-ies**) upper row of windows in a cathedral or large church, above the level of the aisle roofs. [*clear storey*]

clergy /ˈklɜːdʒɪ/ *n.* (*pl.* **-ies**) (usu. treated as *pl.*) those ordained for religious duties. [French (related to CLERIC) and Church Latin]

clergyman *n.* member of the clergy.

cleric /ˈklerɪk/ *n.* member of the clergy. [Greek *klērikos* from *klēros* lot, heritage]

clerical *adj.* **1** of clergy or clergymen. **2** of or done by clerks.

clerical collar *n.* stiff upright white collar fastening at the back.

clerihew /ˈklerɪhjuː/ *n.* short comic biographical verse in two rhyming couplets. [E. *Clerihew* Bentley, name of its inventor]

clerk /klɑːk/ *n.* **1** person employed to keep records, accounts, etc. **2** secretary or agent of a local council, court, etc. **3** lay officer of a church.—*v.* work as clerk. [Old English and French: related to CLERIC]

clever /ˈklevə(r)/ *adj.* (**-er**, **-est**) **1** skilful, talented; quick to understand and learn. **2** adroit, dexterous. **3** ingenious. □ **cleverly** *adv.* **cleverness** *n.* [Old English]

cliché /ˈkliːʃeɪ/ n. 1 hackneyed phrase or opinion. 2 metal casting of a stereotype or electrotype. □ **cliché'd** adj. (also **cliché'd**). [French]

click –n. slight sharp sound. –v. 1 (cause to) make a click. 2 colloq. a become clear or understood. b be popular. c (foll. by with) strike up a rapport. [imitative]

client /ˈklaɪənt/ n. 1 person using the services of a lawyer, architect, or other professional person. 2 customer. [Latin cliens]

clientele /ˌkliːɒnˈtel/ n. 1 clients collectively. 2 customers. [French and Latin: related to CLIENT]

cliff n. steep rock-face, esp. on a coast. [Old English]

cliff-hanger n. story etc. with a strong element of suspense.

climacteric /klaɪˈmæktərɪk/ n. period of life when fertility and sexual activity are in decline. [Greek: related to CLIMAX]

climate /ˈklaɪmɪt/ n. 1 prevailing weather conditions of an area. 2 region with particular weather conditions. 3 prevailing trend of opinion or feeling. □ **climatic** /-ˈmætɪk/ adj. **climatically** /-ˈmætɪkəlɪ/ adv. [Greek klima]

climax /ˈklaɪmæks/ –n. 1 event or point of greatest intensity or interest; culmination. 2 orgasm. –v. colloq. reach or bring to a climax. □ **climactic** /-ˈmæktɪk/ adj. [Greek, = ladder]

climb /klaɪm/ –v. 1 (often foll. by up) ascend, mount, go or come up. 2 grow up a wall etc. by clinging or twining. 3 progress, esp. in social rank. –n. 1 ascent by climbing. 2 hill etc. climbed or to be climbed. □ **climb down** 1 descend, esp. using hands. 2 withdraw from a stance taken up in an argument etc. □ **climber** n. [Old English]

climb-down n. withdrawal from a stance taken up.

climbing-frame n. structure of joined bars etc. for children to climb on.

clime n. literary 1 region. 2 climate. [Latin: related to CLIMATE]

clinch –v. 1 confirm or settle (an argument, bargain, etc.) conclusively. 2 (of boxers etc.) become too closely engaged. 3 secure (a nail or rivet) by driving the point sideways when through. –n. 1 a clinching action. b clinched state. 2 colloq. embrace. [var. of CLENCH]

clincher n. colloq. point or remark that settles an argument etc.

cling v. (past and past part. **clung**) 1 (often foll. by to) adhere. 2 (foll. by to) be unwilling to give up; be emotionally dependent on (a habit, idea, friend, etc.). 3 (often foll. by to) maintain grasp; keep

hold; resist separation. □ **clingy** adj. (-ier, -iest). [Old English]

cling film n. thin transparent plastic covering for food.

clinic /ˈklɪnɪk/ n. 1 private or specialized hospital. 2 place or occasion for giving medical treatment or specialist advice. 3 gathering at a hospital bedside for medical teaching. [Greek klinē bed]

clinical adj. 1 of or for the treatment of patients. 2 dispassionate, coolly detached. 3 (of a room, building, etc.) bare, functional. □ **clinically** adv. [Greek: related to CLINIC]

clinical death n. death judged by professional observation of a person's condition.

clink[1] –n. sharp ringing sound. –v. (cause to) make a clink. [Dutch: imitative]

clink[2] n. slang prison. [origin unknown]

clinker n. 1 mass of slag or lava. 2 stony residue from burnt coal. [Dutch: related to CLINK[1]]

clinker-built adj. (of a boat) having external planks overlapping downwards and secured with clinched nails. [clink, Northern English var. of CLINCH]

clip[1] –n. 1 device for holding things together or for attaching something. 2 piece of jewellery fastened by a clip. 3 set of attached cartridges for a firearm. –v. (-pp-) fix with a clip. [Old English]

clip[2] –v. (-pp-) 1 cut (hair, wool, etc.) short with shears or scissors. 2 trim or remove the hair or wool of 3 colloq. hit smartly. 4 a omit (a letter etc.) from a word. b omit letters or syllables of (words uttered). 5 punch a hole in (a ticket) to show it has been used. 6 cut from a newspaper etc. 7 slang swindle, rob. –n. 1 act of clipping. 2 colloq. smart blow. 3 sequence from a motion picture. 4 yield of wool etc. 5 colloq. speed, esp. rapid. [Old Norse]

clipboard n. small board with a spring clip for holding papers etc.

clip-joint n. slang club etc. charging exorbitant prices.

clip-on adj. attached by a clip.

clipper n. 1 (usu. in pl.) instrument for clipping hair etc. 2 hist. fast sailing-ship.

clipping n. piece clipped, esp. from a newspaper.

clique /kliːk/ n. small exclusive group of people. □ **cliquey** adj. (**cliquier**, **cliquiest**) **cliquish** adj. [French]

clitoris /ˈklɪtərɪs/ n. small erectile part of the female genitals at the upper end of the vulva. □ **clitoral** adj. [Greek]

Cllr. abbr. Councillor.

cloak —v. **1** outdoor usu. long and sleeveless over-garment. **2** covering. □ conceal, disguise. □ **under the cloak of** using as pretext. [ultimately from medieval Latin *clocca* bell]

cloak-and-dagger adj. involving intrigue and espionage.

cloakroom n. **1** room where outdoor clothes or luggage may be left. **2** *euphem.* lavatory.

clobber¹ v. *slang* **1** hit, beat up **2** defeat. **3** criticize severely. [origin unknown]

clobber² n. *slang* clothing, belongings. [origin unknown]

cloche /klɒʃ/ n. **1** small translucent cover for protecting outdoor plants. **2** (in full **cloche hat**) woman's close-fitting bell-shaped hat. [French, = bell, medieval Latin *clocca*]

clock¹ —n. **1** instrument for measuring and showing time. **2 a** measuring device resembling this. **b** *colloq.* speedometer, taximeter, or stopwatch. **3** *slang* person's face. **4** seed-head of the dandelion. —v. **1** *colloq.* **a** (often foll. by *up*) attain or register (a stated time, distance, or speed). **b** time (a race) with a stopwatch. **2** *slang* hit at work. □ **clock in** (or **on**) register one's arrival at work. **clock off** (or **out**) register one's departure from work. **round the clock** all day and (usu.) night. [medieval Latin *clocca* bell]

clock² n. ornamental pattern on the side of a stocking or sock near the ankle. [origin unknown]

clockwise adj. & adv. in a curve corresponding in direction to that of the hands of a clock.

clockwork n. **1** mechanism like that of a clock, with a spring and gears. **2** (attrib.) driven by clockwork. □ **like clockwork** smoothly, regularly, automatically.

clod n. lump of earth, clay, etc. [var. of clot]

cloddish adj. loutish, foolish, clumsy.

clodhopper n. (usu. in *pl.*) *colloq.* large heavy shoe.

clog —n. shoe with a thick wooden sole. —v. (**-gg-**) **1** (often foll. by *up*) obstruct or become obstructed; choke. **2** impede. [origin unknown]

cloister n. **1** covered walk round a quadrangle, esp. in a college or ecclesiastical building. **2** monastic life or seclusion. —v. seclude. □ **cloistered** adj. **cloistral** adj. [Latin *claustrum*: related to close¹]

clomp var. of clump v. 2

clone —n. **1 a** group of organisms produced asexually from one stock or an ancestor. **b** one such organism. **2** *colloq.* person or thing regarded as identical to another. —v. (**-ning**) propagate as a clone. □ **clonal** adj. [Greek *klōn* twig]

clonk —n. abrupt heavy sound of impact. —v. **1** make this sound. [imitative]

close¹ /kləʊs/ —adj. **1** (often foll. by *to*) situated at a short distance or interval. **2 a** having a strong or immediate relation or connection (*close friend*). **b** in intimate friendship or association. **c** corresponding almost exactly (*close resemblance*). **3** in or almost in contact (*close combat*). **4** dense, compact, with no or only slight intervals. **5** (of a contest etc.) in which competitors are almost equal. **6** leaving no gaps or weaknesses, rigorous (*close reasoning*). **7** concentrated, searching. **8** (of air etc.) stuffy, humid. **9** closed, shut. **10** limited to certain persons etc. (*close corporation*). **11** hidden, secret; secretive. **12** niggardly. —n. **1** street closed at one end. **2** precinct of a cathedral. □ **at close quarters** very close together. □ **closely** adv. **closeness** n. [Latin *clausus* from *claudo* shut]

close² /kləʊz/ —v. (**-sing**) **1 a** shut. **b** block up. **2** bring or come to an end. **3** end the day's business. **4** bring or come closer or into contact. **5** make (an electric circuit etc.) continuous. —n. conclusion, end. □ **close down** (of a shop etc.) discontinue business. **close in 1** enclose. **2** come nearer. **3** (of days) get successively shorter. **close up 1** (often foll. by *to*) move closer. **2** shut. **3** block up. **4** (of an aperture) grow smaller. [Latin: related to close¹]

closed book n. subject one does not understand.

closed-circuit adj. (of television) transmitted by wires to a restricted set of receivers.

closed shop n. business etc. where employees must belong to a specified trade union.

close harmony n. harmony in which the notes of a chord are close together.

close-knit adj. tightly interlocked; closely united in friendship.

close season n. season when the killing of game etc. is illegal.

close shave n. also **close thing**.

closet /klɒzɪt/ —n. **1** small room. **2** cupboard. **3** = WATER-CLOSET. **4** (attrib.) secret (*closet homosexual*). —v. (**-t-**) shut away, esp. in private conference or study. [French diminutive: related to CLOSE¹]

close-up n. photograph etc. taken at close range.

closure /ˈkləʊʒə(r)/ n. **1** closing. **2** closed state. **3** procedure for ending a debate and taking a vote. [Latin: related to CLOSE²]

clot —n. **1** thick mass of coagulated liquid etc., esp. of blood. **2** colloq. foolish person. —v. (-**tt**-) form into clots. [Old English]

cloth n. **1** woven or felted material. **2** piece of this, esp. for a particular purpose; tablecloth, dishcloth, etc. **3** fabric for clothes. **4 a** status, esp. of the clergy, as shown by clothes. **b** (prec. by *the*) the clergy. [Old English]

clothe /kləʊð/ v. (-**thing**; past and past part. **clothed** or formal **clad**) **1** put clothes on; provide with clothes. **2** cover as with clothes. [Old English]

clothes /kləʊðz/ n.pl. **1** garments worn to cover the body and limbs. **2** bedclothes. [Old English]

clothes-horse n. frame for airing washed clothes.

clothes-line n. rope etc. on which clothes are hung to dry.

clothes-peg n. clip etc. for securing clothes to a clothes-line.

clothier /ˈkləʊðɪə(r)/ n. seller of men's clothes.

clothing /ˈkləʊðɪŋ/ n. clothes collectively.

clotted cream n. thick cream obtained by slow scalding.

cloud —n. **1** visible mass of condensed watery vapour floating high above the ground. **2** mass of smoke or dust. **3** (foll. by *of*) mass of insects etc. moving together. **4** state of gloom, trouble, or suspicion. —v. **1** cover or darken with clouds or gloom or trouble. **2** (often foll. by *over*, *up*) become overcast or gloomy. **3** make unclear. □ **on cloud nine** colloq. extremely happy. **under a cloud** out of favour, under suspicion. **with one's head in the clouds** day-dreaming. □ **cloudless** adj. [Old English]

cloud chamber n. device containing vapour for tracking the paths of charged particles, X-rays, and gamma rays.

cloud-cuckoo-land n. fanciful or ideal place. [translation of Greek *Nephelokokkugia* in Aristophanes' *Birds*]

cloudy adj. (-**ier**, -**iest**) **1** (of the sky, weather) covered with clouds, overcast. **2** not transparent; unclear. □ **cloudily** adv. **cloudiness** n.

clout —n. **1** heavy blow. **2** colloq. influence, power of effective action. **3** dial. piece of cloth or clothing. —v. hit hard. [Old English]

clove¹ n. dried bud of a tropical plant used as a spice. [Latin *clavus* nail (from its shape)]

clove² n. small segment of a compound bulb, esp. of garlic. [Old English: related to CLEAVE¹]

clove³ past of CLEAVE¹.

clove hitch n. knot by which a rope is secured to a spar etc. [clove, old past part. of CLEAVE¹]

cloven /ˈkləʊv(ə)n/ adj. split, partly divided. [past part. of CLEAVE¹]

cloven hoof n. (also **cloven foot**) divided hoof, esp. of oxen, sheep, or goats, or of the Devil.

clover n. trefoil fodder plant. □ **in clover** in ease and luxury. [Old English]

clown —n. **1** comic entertainer, esp. in a circus. **2** foolish or playful person. —v. (often foll. by *about*, *around*) behave like a clown (origin uncertain]

cloy v. satiate or sicken with sweetness, richness, etc. [obsolete ENCLAVE from Anglo-French: related to ENCLAVE]

club —n. **1** heavy stick with a thick end, esp. as a weapon. **2** stick with a head used in golf. **3** association of persons meeting periodically for a shared activity. **4** organization or premises offering members social amenities, meals, temporary residence, etc. **5 a** playing-card of the suit denoted by a black trefoil. **b** (in pl.) this suit. **6** commercial organization offering subscribers special deals (book club). —v. (-**bb**-) **1** beat with or as with a club. **2** (foll. by together, with) combine; raise a sum of money for a purpose. [Old Norse]

clubbable adj. sociable; fit for club membership.

club class n. class of fare on an aircraft etc. designed for business travellers.

club-foot n. congenitally deformed foot.

clubhouse n. premises of a (usu. sporting) club.

clubland n. area where there are many nightclubs.

club-root n. disease of cabbages etc. with swelling at the base of the stem.

club sandwich n. sandwich with two layers of filling between three slices of toast or bread.

cluck —n. guttural cry like that of a hen. —v. emit cluck(s). [imitative]

clue /kluː/ —n. **1** fact or idea that serves as a guide, or suggests a line of inquiry, in a problem or investigation. **2** piece of evidence etc. in the detection of a crime. **3** verbal formula as a hint to what is to be inserted in a crossword. —v. (**clues**, **clued**, **cluing** or **clueing**) provide a clue to. □ **clue in** (or **up**) slang inform.

not have a clue be ignorant or incompetent. [var. of Old English *clew*]

clueless *adj. colloq.* ignorant, stupid.

clump –*n.* (foll. by *of*) cluster or mass, esp. of trees. –*v.* **1 a** form a clump. **b** heap or plant together. **2** walk with a heavy tread. [Low German or Dutch]

clumsy /ˈklʌmzi/ *adj.* (-ier, -iest) **1** awkward in movement or shape; ungainly. **2** difficult to handle or use. **3** tactless. □ **clumsily** *adv.* **clumsiness** *n.* [obsolete *clumse* be numb with cold]

clung *past* and *past part.* of CLING.

clunk –*n.* dull sound as of thick pieces of metal meeting. –*v.* make such a sound. [imitative]

cluster –*n.* close group or bunch of similar people or things growing or occurring together. –*v.* **1** bring into, come into, or be in cluster(s). **2** (foll. by *round, around*) gather. [Old English]

clutch¹ –*v.* **1** seize eagerly; grasp tightly. **2** (foll. by *at*) try desperately to seize. –*n.* **1** tight grasp. **2** (in *pl.*) grasping hands; cruel or relentless grasp or control. **3 a** (in a vehicle) device for connecting and disconnecting the engine and the transmission. **b** pedal operating this. [Old English]

clutch² *n.* **1** set of eggs for hatching. **2** brood of chickens. [Old Norse, = hatch]

clutch bag *n.* slim flat handbag without handles.

clutter –*n.* **1** crowded and untidy collection of things. **2** untidy state. –*v.* (often foll. by *up, with*) crowd untidily, fill with clutter. [related to CLOT]

Cm *symb.* curium.

cm *abbr.* centimetre(s)

CMG *abbr.* Companion (of the Order) of St Michael and St George.

CND *abbr.* Campaign for Nuclear Disarmament.

CO *abbr.* Commanding Officer.

Co *symb.* cobalt.

CO *abbr.* **1** company. **2** county.

Co. *abbr.* **1** company. **2** county.

co- *prefix* added to: **1** nouns, with the sense 'joint, mutual, common' (*co-author; coequality*). **2** adjectives and adverbs, with the sense 'jointly, mutually' (*coequal*). **3** verbs, with the sense 'together with another or others' (*cooperate*). [var. of COM-]

c/o *abbr.* care of.

coach –*n.* **1** single-decker bus, usu. comfortably equipped for long journeys. **2** railway carriage. **3** closed horse-drawn carriage. **4 a** instructor or trainer in a sport. **b** private tutor. –*v.* train or teach as a coach. [French from Magyar]

coachload *n.* group of tourists etc. taken by coach.

coachman *n.* driver of a horse-drawn carriage.

coachwork *n.* bodywork of a road or rail vehicle.

coagulate /kəʊˈæɡjʊleɪt/ *v.* (-ting) change from a fluid to a semisolid. **2** clot, curdle. □ **coagulant** *n.* **coagulation** /-ˈleɪʃ(ə)n/ *n.* [Latin *coagulum* rennet]

coal *n.* **1** hard black matter, found underground and used as a fuel. **2** piece of this, esp. one that is burning. □ **coals to Newcastle** something brought to a place where it is already plentiful. haul (or call) over the coals reprimand. [Old English]

coalesce /kəʊəˈles/ *v.* (-cing) come together and form a whole. □ **coalescence** *n.* **coalescent** *adj.* [Latin *alo* nourish]

coalface *n.* exposed working surface of coal in a mine.

coalfield *n.* extensive area yielding coal.

coal gas *n.* mixed gases formerly extracted from coal and used for lighting and heating.

coalition /kəʊəˈlɪʃ(ə)n/ *n.* **1** temporary alliance, esp. of political parties. **2** fusion into one whole. [medieval Latin: related to COALESCE]

coalman *n.* man who carries or delivers coal.

coalmine *n.* mine in which coal is dug. □ **coalminer** *n.*

coal-scuttle *n.* container for coal for a domestic fire.

coal tar *n.* thick black oily liquid distilled from coal and used as a source of benzene.

coal-tit *n.* small greyish bird with a black head.

coaming /ˈkəʊmɪŋ/ *n.* raised border round a ship's hatches etc. to keep out water. [origin unknown]

coarse *adj.* **1** rough or loose in texture; made of large particles. **2** lacking refinement; crude; obscene. □ **coarsely** *adv.* **coarseness** *n.* [origin unknown]

coarse fish *n.* freshwater fish other than salmon and trout.

coarsen *v.* make or become coarse.

coast –*n.* border of land near the sea; seashore. –*v.* **1** ride or move, usu. downhill, without the use of power. **2** make progress without much effort. **3** sail along the coast. □ **the coast is clear** there is no danger of being observed or caught. □ **coastal** *adj.* [Latin *costa* side]

coaster *n.* **1** ship that travels along the coast. **2** small tray or mat for a bottle or glass.

coastguard *n.* **1** member of a group of people employed to keep watch on

coasts to save life, prevent smuggling, etc. **2** such a group.

coastline n. line of the seashore, esp. with regard to its shape.

coat —n. **1** outer garment with sleeves, usu. extending below the hips; overcoat or jacket. **2** animal's fur or hair. **3** covering of paint etc. laid on a surface at one time. —v. **1** (usu. foll. by *with, in*) cover with a coat or layer. **2** (of paint etc.) form a covering to. [French from Germanic]

coat-hanger see HANGER 2.

coating n. **1** layer of paint etc. **2** material for coats.

coat of arms n. heraldic bearings or shield of a person, family, or corporation.

coat of mail n. jacket covered with mail.

coat-tail n. each of the flaps formed by the back of a tailcoat.

coax v. **1** persuade gradually or by flattery. **2** (foll. by *out of*) obtain (a thing from a person) thus. **3** manipulate (a thing) carefully or slowly. [obsolete *cokes* a fool]

coaxial /kəʊˈæksɪəl/ adj. **1** having a common axis. **2** *Electr.* (of a cable or line) transmitting by means of two concentric conductors separated by an insulator.

cob n. **1** roundish lump. **2** domed loaf. **3** = CORN-COB. **4** large hazelnut. **5** sturdy riding-horse with short legs. **6** male swan. [origin unknown]

cobalt /ˈkəʊbɔːlt/ n. **1** silvery-white metallic element. **2 a** pigment made from this. **b** its deep-blue colour. [German, probably = *kobold* demon in mines]

cobber n. *Austral. & NZ colloq.* companion, friend. [origin uncertain]

cobble[1] /ˈkɒb(ə)l/ —n. (in full **cobblestone**) small rounded stone used for paving. —v. (**-ling**) pave with cobbles. [from COB]

cobble[2] /ˈkɒb(ə)l/ v. (**-ling**) **1** mend or patch up (esp. shoes). **2** (often foll. by *together*) join or assemble roughly. [from COBBLER]

cobbler n. **1** person who mends shoes professionally. **2** stewed fruit topped with scones. **3** (in *pl.*) *slang* nonsense. [origin unknown]

COBOL /ˈkəʊbɒl/ n. computer language for use in commerce. [common business oriented language]

cobra /ˈkəʊbrə/ n. venomous hooded snake of Africa and Asia. [Latin *colubra* snake]

cobweb n. **1** fine network spun by a spider from liquid it secretes. **2** thread of

this. □ **cobwebby** adj. [obsolete *coppe* spider]

coca /ˈkəʊkə/ n. **1** S. American shrub. **2** its dried leaves, chewed as a stimulant. [Spanish from Quechua]

cocaine /kəʊˈkeɪn/ n. drug from coca, used as a local anaesthetic and as a stimulant.

coccyx /ˈkɒksɪks/ n. (*pl.* **coccyges** /-ˌdʒiːz/) small triangular bone at the base of the spinal column. [Greek, = cuckoo (from shape of its bill)]

cochineal /ˌkɒtʃɪˈniːl/ n. **1** scarlet dye used esp. for colouring food. **2** insects whose dried bodies yield this. [Latin *coccinus* scarlet, from Greek]

cock[1] —n. **1** male bird, esp. of the domestic fowl. **2** *slang* (as a form of address) friend; fellow. **3** *coarse slang* penis. **4** *slang* nonsense. **5 a** firing lever in a gun, raised to be released by the trigger. **b** cocked position of this. **6** tap or valve controlling flow. —v. **1** raise or make upright or erect. **2** turn or move (the eye or ear) attentively or knowingly. **3** set aslant; turn up the brim of (a hat). **4** raise the cock of (a gun). □ **at half cock** only partly ready. **cock a snook** see SNOOK. **cock up** *slang* bungle; make a mess of. [Old English and French]

cock[2] n. conical heap of hay or straw. [perhaps from Scandinavian]

cockade /kɒˈkeɪd/ n. rosette etc. worn in the hat as a badge. [French: related to COCK[1]]

cock-a-doodle-doo n. cock's crow.

cock-a-hoop adj. exultant.

cock-a-leekie n. Scottish soup of boiling fowl and leeks.

cock-and-bull story n. absurd or incredible account.

cockatoo /ˌkɒkəˈtuː/ n. crested parrot. [Dutch from Malay]

cockchafer /ˈkɒktʃeɪfə(r)/ n. large pale-brown beetle. [from COCK[1]]

cock crow n. dawn.

cocker n. (in full **cocker spaniel**) small spaniel with a silky coat. [related to COCK[1]]

cockerel /ˈkɒkər(ə)l/ n. young cock. [diminutive of COCK[1]]

cock-eyed adj. *colloq.* **1** crooked, askew. **2** absurd, not practical. [from COCK[1]]

cock-fight n. fight between cocks as sport.

cockle /ˈkɒk(ə)l/ n. **1 a** edible bivalve shellfish. **b** its shell. **2** (in full **cockle-shell**) small shallow boat. **3** pucker or wrinkle in paper, glass, etc. □ **warm the cockles of one's heart** make one contented. [French *coquille* from Greek: related to CONCH]

cockney /'kɒknɪ/ —n. (pl. -s) 1 native of London, esp. of the East End. 2 dialect or accent used there. —adj. of cockneys or their dialect. [cokeney 'cock's egg']

cockpit n. 1 a compartment for the pilot (and crew) of an aircraft or spacecraft. b driver's seat in a racing car. c space for the helmsman in some yachts. 2 arena of war or other conflict. 3 place for cock-fights.

cockroach /'kɒkrəʊtʃ/ n. flat dark-brown beetle-like insect infesting kitchens, bathrooms, etc. [Spanish cucaracha]

cockscomb /'kɒkskəʊm/ n. crest of a cock.

cocksure /kɒk'ʃɔː(r)/ adj. arrogantly confident. [from cock]

cocktail /'kɒkteɪl/ n. 1 drink made of various spirits, fruit juices, etc. 2 appetizer containing shellfish or fruit. 3 any hybrid mixture. [origin unknown]

cocktail dress n. short evening dress worn at a party.

cocktail stick n. small pointed stick for serving an olive, cherry, etc.

cocky adj. (-ier, -iest) colloq. conceited, arrogant. □ cockily adv. cockiness n. [from cock]

coco /'kəʊkəʊ/ n. (pl. -s) coconut palm. [Portuguese and Spanish, = grimace]

cocoa /'kəʊkəʊ/ n. 1 powder made from crushed cacao seeds, often with other ingredients. 2 drink made from this. [altered from cacao]

cocoa bean n. cacao seed.

cocoa butter n. fatty substance obtained from the cocoa bean.

coconut /'kəʊkənʌt/ n. large brown seed of the coco, with a hard shell and edible white lining enclosing milky juice.

coconut matting n. matting made of fibre from coconut husks.

coconut shy n. fairground sideshow where balls are thrown to dislodge coconuts.

cocoon /kə'kuːn/ —n. 1 silky case spun by insect larvae for protection as pupae. 2 protective covering. —v. wrap or coat in a cocoon. [Provençal coca shell]

cocotte /kə'kɒt/ n. small fireproof dish for cooking and serving an individual portion. [French]

COD abbr. cash (US collect) on delivery.

cod¹ n. (pl. same) large sea fish. [origin unknown]

cod² slang —n. 1 parody. 2 hoax. —v. (-dd-) 1 parody. 2 hoax. [origin unknown]

cod³ n. slang nonsense. [abbreviation of CODSWALLOP]

coda /'kəʊdə/ n. 1 Mus. final additional passage of a piece or movement. 2 concluding section of a ballet. [Latin cauda tail]

coddle /'kɒd(ə)l/ v. (-ling) 1 treat as an invalid; protect attentively; pamper. 2 cook (an egg) in water below boiling point. □ coddler n. [a dialect form of caudle invalids' gruel]

code —n. 1 system of words, letters, symbols, etc., used to represent others for secrecy or brevity. 2 system of pre-arranged signals used to ensure secrecy in transmitting messages. 3 Computing piece of program text. 4 systematic set of laws etc. 5 prevailing standard of moral behaviour. —v. (-ding) put into code. [Latin codex]

codeine /'kəʊdiːn/ n. alkaloid derived from morphine, used to relieve pain. [Greek kōdeia poppy-head]

codependency /kəʊdɪ'pendənsɪ/ n. addiction to a supportive role in a relationship. □ codependent adj. & n.

codex /'kəʊdeks/ n. (pl. codices /-dɪsiːz/) 1 ancient manuscript text in book form. 2 collection of descriptions of drugs etc. [Latin, = tablet, book]

codfish n. (pl. same) = COD¹.

codger /'kɒdʒə(r)/ n. (usu. in old codger) colloq. person, esp. a strange one. [origin uncertain]

codicil /'kɒdɪsɪl/ n. addition to a will. [Latin diminutive of codex]

codify /'kəʊdɪfaɪ/ v. (-ies, -ied) arrange (laws etc.) systematically into a code. □ codification /-fɪ'keɪʃ(ə)n/ n. codifier n.

codling /'kɒdlɪŋ/ n. (also codlin) 1 a kind of cooking apple. 2 moth whose larva feeds on apples. [Anglo-French quer de lion lion-heart]

codling² n. small codfish.

cod-liver oil n. oil from cod livers, rich in vitamins D and A.

codpiece n. hist. bag or flap at the front of a man's breeches. [cod scrotum]

codswallop /'kɒdzwɒləp/ n. slang nonsense. [origin unknown]

coed /kəʊ'ed/ colloq. —n. 1 school for both sexes. 2 esp. US female pupil of a coed school. —adj. coeducational.

coeducation /ˌkəʊedjʊ'keɪʃ(ə)n/ n. education of pupils of both sexes together. □ coeducational adj. [abbreviation]

coefficient /ˌkəʊɪ'fɪʃ(ə)nt/ n. 1 Math. quantity placed before and multiplying an algebraic expression. 2 Physics multiplier or factor by which a property is measured (coefficient of expansion). [related to CO-, EFFICIENT]

coelacanth /'siːləkænθ/ n. large sea fish formerly thought to be extinct. [Greek koilos hollow, akantha spine]

158

coelenterate /si:'lentə,reit/ *n.* marine animal with a simple tube-shaped or cup-shaped body, e.g. jellyfish, corals, and sea anemones. [Greek *koilos* hollow, *enteron* intestine]

coeliac disease /'si:lɪ,æk/ *n.* disease of the small intestine, brought on by contact with dietary gluten. [Latin *coeliacus* from Greek *koilia* belly]

coenobite /'si:nə,baɪt/ *n.* (*US* **cenobite**) member of a monastic community. [Greek *koinos bios* common life]

coequal /kəʊ'i:kw(ə)l/ *adj.* & *n. archaic or literary* equal.

coerce /kəʊ'ɜ:s/ *v.* (-**cing**) persuade or restrain by force. □ **coercible** *adj.* **coercion** /-'ɜ:ʃ(ə)n/ *n.* **coercive** *adj.* [Latin *coerceo* restrain]

coeval /kəʊ'i:v(ə)l/ *formal* —*adj.* of the same age; existing at the same time; contemporary. —*n.* coeval person or thing. □ **coevally** *adv.* [Latin *aevum* age]

coexist /,kəʊɪɡ'zɪst/ *v.* (often foll. by *with*) exist together. **2** (esp. of nations) exist in mutual tolerance of each other's ideologies etc. □ **coexistence** *n.* **coexistent** *adj.*

coextensive /,kəʊɪk'stensɪv/ *adj.* extending over the same space or time.

C. of E. *abbr.* Church of England.

coffee /'kɒfɪ/ *n.* **1 a** drink made from roasted and ground beanlike seeds of a tropical shrub. **b** cup of this. **2 a** the shrub. **b** its seeds. **3** pale brown. [Turkish from Arabic]

coffee bar *n.* bar or café serving coffee and light refreshments from a counter.

coffee-mill *n.* small machine for grinding roasted coffee beans.

coffee morning *n.* morning gathering, esp. for charity, at which coffee is served.

coffee shop *n.* small informal restaurant, esp. in a hotel or department store.

coffee-table *n.* small low table.

coffee-table book *n.* large lavishly illustrated book.

coffer *n.* **1** large strong box for valuables. **2** (in *pl.*) treasury, funds. **3** sunken panel in a ceiling etc. [Latin *cophinus* basket]

coffer-dam *n.* watertight enclosure pumped dry to permit work below the waterline, e.g. building bridges etc. or repairing a ship.

coffin /'kɒfɪn/ *n.* box in which a corpse is buried or cremated. [Latin: related to COFFER]

cog *n.* **1** each of a series of projections on the edge of a wheel or bar transferring motion by engaging with another series. **2** unimportant member of an organization etc. [probably Scandinavian]

cogent /'kəʊdʒ(ə)nt/ *adj.* (of an argument etc.) convincing, compelling. □ **cogency** *n.* **cogently** *adv.* [Latin *cogo* drive]

cogitate /'kɒdʒɪ,teɪt/ *v.* (-**ting**) ponder, meditate. □ **cogitation** /-'teɪʃ(ə)n/ *n.* **cogitative** /-tətɪv/ *adj.* [Latin *cogito*]

cognac /'kɒnjæk/ *n.* high-quality brandy, properly that distilled in Cognac in W. France.

cognate /'kɒɡneɪt/ —*adj.* **1** related to or descended from a common ancestor. **2** (of a word) having the same linguistic family or derivation. —*n.* **1** relative. **2** cognate word. [Latin *cognatus*]

cognate object *n. Gram.* object related in origin and sense to its verb (as in *live a good life*).

cognition /kɒɡ'nɪʃ(ə)n/ *n.* **1** knowing, perceiving, or conceiving as an act or faculty distinct from emotion and volition. **2** result of this. □ **cognitional** *adj.* **cognitive** /'kɒɡ-/ *adj.* [Latin *cognitio*: related to COGNIZANCE]

cognizance /'kɒɡnɪz(ə)ns/ *n. formal* **1** knowledge or awareness; perception. **2** sphere of observation or concern. **3** *Heraldry* distinctive device or mark. [Latin *cognosco* get to know]

cognizant *adj.* (foll. by *of*) *formal* having knowledge or being aware of.

cognomen /kɒɡ'nəʊmen/ *n.* **1** nickname. **2** ancient Roman's third or fourth name designating a branch of a family, as in Marcus Tullius *Cicero*, or as an epithet, as in P. Cornelius Scipio *Africanus*. [Latin]

cognoscente /,kɒnjə'ʃenti/ *n.* (*pl.* -**ti** /-ti/) connoisseur. [Italian]

cog-wheel *n.* wheel with cogs.

cohabit /kəʊ'hæbɪt/ *v.* (-**t-**) (esp. of an unmarried couple) live together as husband and wife. □ **cohabitation** /-'teɪʃ(ə)n/ *n.* **cohabitee** /-'ti:/ *n.* [Latin *habito* dwell]

cohere /kəʊ'hɪə/ *v.* (-**ring**) **1** (of parts or a whole) stick together; remain united. **2** (of reasoning etc.) be logical or consistent. [Latin *haereo haes-* stick]

coherent *adj.* **1** intelligible and articulate. **2** (of an argument etc.) consistent; easily followed. **3** cohering. **4** *Physics* (of waves) having a constant phase relationship. □ **coherence** *n.* **coherently** *adv.*

cohesion /kəʊ'hi:ʒ(ə)n/ *n.* **1 a** sticking together. **b** tendency to cohere. **2** *Chem.* force with which molecules cohere. □ **cohesive** *adj.*

cohort /'kəʊhɔ:t/ *n.* **1** ancient Roman military unit, one-tenth of a legion. **2** band of warriors. **3 a** persons banded together. **b** group of persons with a

coif common statistical characteristic. [Latin]

coif /kɔɪf/ n. hist. close-fitting cap, carbonated drink usu. flavoured with helmet. [Latin]

coif /kwɑːf/ v. (usu. as **coiffed** adj.) dress or arrange (the hair). [French coiffer]

coiffeur /kwɑːˈfɜː(r)/ n. (fem. **coiffeuse** /-ˈfɜːz/) hairdresser. [French]

coiffure /kwɑːˈfjʊə(r)/ n. hairstyle. [French]

coil −v. 1 arrange or be arranged in spirals or concentric rings. 2 move sinuously. −n. 1 coiled arrangement. 2 coiled length of rope etc. 3 single turn of something coiled. 4 flexible loop as a contraceptive device in the womb. 5 coiled wire for the passage of an electric current and acting as an inductor. [Latin: related to COLLECT[1]]

coin −n. 1 stamped disc of metal as official money. 2 (collect.) metal money. −v. 1 make (coins) by stamping. 2 make (metal) into coins. 3 invent (esp. a new word or phrase). □ **coin money** make much money quickly. [Latin cuneus wedge]

coinage n. 1 coining. 2 a coins. b system of coins in use. 3 invention, esp. of a word.

coin-box n. 1 telephone operated by inserting coins. 2 receptacle for these.

coincide /kəʊɪnˈsaɪd/ v. (-ding) 1 occur at the same time. 2 occupy the same portion of space. 3 (often foll. by with) agree or be identical. [Latin: related to INCIDENT]

coincidence /kəʊˈɪnsɪd(ə)ns/ n. 1 coinciding. 2 remarkable concurrence of events etc. apparently by chance. □ **coincidental** /kəʊˌɪnsɪˈdent(ə)l/ adj. in the nature of or resulting from a coincidence. **coincidentally** adv.

coir /ˈkɔɪə(r)/ n. coconut fibre used for ropes, matting, etc. [Malayalam kāyar cord]

coition /kəʊˈɪʃ(ə)n/ n. = COITUS. [Latin: coitio from eo go]

coitus /ˈkəʊɪtəs/ n. sexual intercourse. □ **coital** adj. [Latin: related to COITION]

coitus interruptus /ˌɪntəˈrʌptəs/ n. sexual intercourse with withdrawal of the penis before ejaculation.

coke[1] −n. solid substance left after gases have been extracted from coal. −v. (-king) convert (coal) into coke. [dial. colk core]

coke[2] n. slang cocaine. [abbreviation]

Col. abbr. Colonel.

col n. depression in a chain of mountains. [Latin collum neck]

col- abbr. column.

col- see COM-.

cola /ˈkəʊlə/ n. (also **kola**) 1 W. African tree bearing seeds containing caffeine. 2 carbonated drink usu. flavoured with these. [West African]

colander /ˈkʌləndə(r)/ n. perforated vessel used to strain off liquid in cookery. [Latin colo strain]

cold /kəʊld/ −adj. 1 of or at a low temperature. 2 not heated; cooled after heat. 3 feeling cold. 4 lacking ardour, friendliness, or affection. 5 a depressing, uninteresting. b (of colour) suggestive of cold. 6 a dead. b colloq. unconscious. 7 (of a scent in hunting) grown faint. 8 (in games) far from finding what is sought. −n. 1 a prevalence of low temperature. b cold weather or environment. 2 infection of the nose or throat with sneezing, catarrh, etc. −adv. unrehearsed. □ **in cold blood** without emotion, deliberately. **out in the cold** ignored, neglected. **throw (or pour) cold water on** be discouraging about. □ **coldly** adv. **coldness** n. [Old English]

cold-blooded adj. 1 having a body temperature varying with that of the environment. 2 callous; deliberately cruel. □ **cold-bloodedly** adv. **cold-bloodedness** n.

cold call −n. marketing call on a person who has previously not shown interest in the product. −v. visit or telephone (a person) in this way.

cold chisel n. chisel for cutting metal, stone, or brick.

cold comfort n. poor consolation.

cold cream n. ointment for cleansing and softening the skin.

cold feet n.pl. colloq. loss of nerve.

cold frame n. unheated glass-topped frame for growing small plants.

cold fusion n. nuclear fusion at room temperature, esp. as a possible energy source.

cold-hearted adj. lacking sympathy or kindness. □ **cold-heartedly** adv. **cold-heartedness** n.

cold shoulder −n. (prec. by the) intentional unfriendliness. −v. (**cold-shoulder**) be deliberately unfriendly towards.

cold sore n. inflammation and blisters in and around the mouth, caused by a virus infection.

cold storage n. 1 storage in a refrigerator. 2 temporary putting aside (of an idea etc.). postponement.

cold sweat n. sweating induced by fear or illness.

cold table n. selection of dishes of cold food.

cold turkey n. slang abrupt withdrawal from addictive drugs.

cold war *n.* hostility between nations without actual fighting.

cole *n.* (usu. in *comb.*) cabbage. [Latin *caulis*]

coleopteron /ˌkɒlɪˈɒptərɒn/ *n.* insect with front wings serving as sheaths, e.g. the beetle and weevil. □ **coleopterous** *adj.* [Greek *koleon* sheath, *pteron* wing]

coleslaw /ˈkəʊlslɔː/ *n.* dressed salad of sliced raw cabbage etc. [from COLE, Dutch *sla* salad]

coleus /ˈkəʊlɪəs/ *n.* plant with variegated leaves. [Greek *koleon* sheath]

coley /ˈkəʊlɪ/ *n.* (*pl.* -s) any of several fish used as food, e.g. the rock-salmon. [origin uncertain]

colic /ˈkɒlɪk/ *n.* severe spasmodic abdominal pain. □ **colicky** *adj.* [Latin: related to COLON²]

colitis /kəˈlaɪtɪs/ *n.* inflammation of the lining of the colon.

collaborate /kəˈlæbəˌreɪt/ *v.* (-ting) (often foll. by *with*) 1 work together. 2 cooperate with an enemy. □ **collaboration** /-ˈreɪʃ(ə)n/ *n.* **collaborative** /-rətɪv/ *adj.* **collaborator** *n.* [Latin: related to LABOUR]

collage /ˈkɒlɑːʒ/ *n.* form or work of art in which various materials are fixed to a backing. [French, = gluing]

collagen /ˈkɒlədʒ(ə)n/ *n.* protein found in animal connective tissue, yielding gelatin on boiling. [Greek *kolla* glue]

collapse /kəˈlæps/ —*n.* 1 falling down or in of a structure; folding up; giving way. 2 sudden failure of a plan etc. 3 physical or mental breakdown; exhaustion. —*v.* (-sing) 1 (cause to) undergo collapse. 2 *colloq.* lie or sit down and relax, esp. after prolonged effort. 3 fold up. □ **collapsible** *adj.* [Latin *labor laps-* slip]

collar /ˈkɒlə(r)/ —*n.* 1 neckband, upright or turned over. 2 band of leather etc. round an animal's neck. 3 band or ring or pipe in machinery. 4 piece of meat rolled up and tied. —*v.* 1 capture, seize. 2 *colloq.* accost. 3 *slang* appropriate. [Latin *collum* neck]

collar-bone *n.* bone joining the breast-bone and shoulder-blade.

collate /kəˈleɪt/ *v.* (-ting) 1 assemble and arrange systematically. 2 compare (texts, statements, etc.). □ **collator** *n.* [Latin: related to CONFER]

collateral /kəˈlætər(ə)l/ —*n.* 1 security pledged as a guarantee for the repayment of a loan. 2 person having the same ancestor as another but by a different line. —*adj.* 1 descended from the same ancestor but by a different line. 2 side by side; parallel. 3 **a** additional but subordinate. **b** contributory. **c** connected but aside from the main subject, course, etc.

□ **collaterally** *adv.* [Latin: related to LATERAL]

collation /kəˈleɪʃ(ə)n/ *n.* 1 collating. 2 thing collated. 3 light meal. [Latin: related to CONFER]

colleague /ˈkɒliːg/ *n.* fellow worker, esp. in a profession or business. [Latin *collega*]

collect¹ /kəˈlekt/ —*v.* 1 bring or come together; assemble, accumulate. 2 systematically seek and acquire, esp. as hobby. 3 obtain (contributions etc.) from a number of people. 4 call for; fetch. 5 **a** *refl.* regain control of oneself. **b** concentrate (one's thoughts etc.). **c** (as **collected** *adj.*) not perturbed or distracted. —*adj.* & *adv.* *US* (of a telephone call, parcel, etc.) to be paid for by the receiver. [Latin *lego lect-* pick]

collect² /ˈkɒlekt/ *n.* short prayer of the Anglican or Roman Catholic Church. [Latin *collecta*]

collectable /kəˈlektəb(ə)l/ (also **collectible**) —*adj.* worth collecting. —*n.* item sought by collectors.

collection /kəˈlekʃ(ə)n/ *n.* 1 collecting or being collected. 2 things collected, esp. systematically. 3 money collected, esp. at a meeting or church service.

collective /kəˈlektɪv/ —*adj.* of, by, or relating to a group or society as a whole; joint; shared. —*n.* 1 cooperative enterprise; its members. 2 = COLLECTIVE NOUN. □ **collectively** *adv.*

collective bargaining *n.* negotiation of wages etc. by an organized body of employees.

collective farm *n.* jointly-operated esp. State-owned amalgamation of several smallholdings.

collective noun *n.* singular noun denoting a collection or number of individuals (e.g. *assembly, family, troop*).

collective ownership *n.* ownership of land etc., by all for the benefit of all.

collectivism *n.* theory and practice of collective ownership of land and the means of production. □ **collectivist** *n.* & *adj.*

collectivize *v.* (also **-ise**) (-zing or -sing) organize on the basis of collective ownership. □ **collectivization** /-ˈzeɪʃ(ə)n/ *n.*

collector *n.* 1 person who collects things of interest. 2 person who collects money etc. due.

collector's item *n.* (also **collector's piece**) thing of interest to collectors.

colleen /kɒˈliːn/ *n.* *Ir.* girl. [Irish *cailín*]

college /ˈkɒlɪdʒ/ *n.* 1 establishment for further, higher, or professional education. 2 college premises (*lived in college*). 3 students and teachers in a college. 4 school. 5 organized body of

persons with shared functions and privileges. [Latin: related to COLLEAGUE]

collegiate /kə'liːdʒiət/ *adj.* **1** of, or constituted as, a college; corporate. **2** (of a university) consisting of different colleges.

collegiate church *n.* church endowed for a chapter of canons but without a bishop's see.

collide /kə'laɪd/ *v.* (**-ding**) (often foll. by *with*) come into collision or conflict. [Latin *collido -lis-* clash]

collie /'kɒlɪ/ *n.* sheepdog of an orig. Scottish breed. [perhaps from *coaly* COAL]

collier /'kɒlɪə(r)/ *n.* **1** coalminer. **2 a** coal-ship. **b** member of its crew. [from COAL]

colliery /'kɒljərɪ/ *n.* (*pl.* **-ies**) coalmine and its buildings.

collision /kə'lɪʒ(ə)n/ *n.* **1** violent impact of a moving body with another or with a fixed object. **2** clashing of interests etc. [Latin: related to COLLIDE]

collocate /'kɒləkeɪt/ *v.* (**-ting**) juxtapose (a word etc.) with another. □ **collocation** /-'keɪʃ(ə)n/ *n.* [Latin: related to LOCUS]

colloid /'kɒlɔɪd/ *n.* **1** substance consisting of ultramicroscopic particles. **2** mixture of such particles dispersed in another substance. □ **colloidal** /kə'lɔɪd(ə)l/ *adj.* [Greek *kolla* glue]

colloquial /kə'ləʊkwɪəl/ *adj.* of ordinary or familiar conversation, informal. □ **colloquially** *adv.* [Latin: related to COLLOQUY]

colloquialism *n.* **1** colloquial word or phrase. **2** use of these.

colloquium /kə'ləʊkwɪəm/ *n.* (*pl.* **-s** or **-quia**) academic conference or seminar. [Latin: related to COLLOQUY]

colloquy /'kɒləkwɪ/ *n.* (*pl.* **-quies**) literary conversation, talk. [Latin *loquor* speak]

collude /kə'luːd/ *v.* (**-ding**) conspire together. □ **collusion** *n.* **collusive** *adj.* [Latin *ludo lus-* play]

collywobbles /'kɒlɪwɒb(ə)lz/ *n.pl. colloq.* **1** rumbling or pain in the stomach. **2** apprehensive feeling. [from COLIC, WOBBLE]

cologne /kə'ləʊn/ *n.* eau-de-Cologne or similar toilet water. [abbreviation]

colon¹ /'kəʊlən/ *n.* punctuation mark(:), used esp. to mark illustration or antithesis. [Greek, = clause]

colon² /'kəʊlən/ *n.* lower and greater part of the large intestine. [Latin from Greek]

colonel /'kɜːn(ə)l/ *n.* army officer in command of a regiment, ranking next below brigadier. □ **colonelcy** *n.* (*pl.* **-ies**). [Italian *colonnello*: related to COLUMN]

colonial /kə'ləʊnɪəl/ *-adj.* **1** of a colony or colonies. **2** of colonialism. *-n.* inhabitant of a colony.

colonialism *n.* **1** policy of acquiring or maintaining colonies. **2** *derog.* exploitation of colonies. □ **colonialist** *n. & adj.*

colonist /'kɒlənɪst/ *n.* settler in or inhabitant of a colony.

colonize /'kɒlənaɪz/ *v.* (also **-ise**) (**-zing**) **1** establish a colony in. **2** join a colony. □ **colonization** /-'zeɪʃ(ə)n/ *n.*

colonnade /ˌkɒlə'neɪd/ *n.* row of columns, esp supporting an entablature or roof. □ **colonnaded** *adj.* [French: related to COLUMN]

colony /'kɒlənɪ/ *n.* (*pl.* **-ies**) **1 a** settlement or settlers in a new country, fully or partly subject to the mother country. **b** their territory. **2 a** people of one nationality, occupation, etc., esp. forming a community in a city. **b** separate or segregated group *'nudist colony'*. **3** group of animals, plants, etc., living close together. [Latin *colonia* farm]

colophon /'kɒlə(ə)n/ *n.* **1** publisher's imprint, esp. on the title-page. **2** tailpiece in a manuscript or book, giving the writer's or printer's name, date, etc. [Greek, = summit]

color etc. *US var. of* COLOUR etc.

Colorado beetle /ˌkɒlə'rɑːdəʊ/ *n.* yellow and black beetle, with larva destructive to the potato plant. [*Colorado* in US]

coloration /ˌkʌlə'reɪʃ(ə)n/ *n.* (also **colouration**) **1** appearance as regards colour. **2** act or mode of colouring. [Latin: related to COLOUR]

coloratura /ˌkɒlərə'tʊərə/ *n.* **1** elaborate ornamentation of a vocal melody. **2** soprano skilled in this. [Italian: related to COLOUR]

colossal /kə'lɒs(ə)l/ *adj.* **1** huge. **2** *colloq.* splendid. □ **colossally** *adv.* [related to COLOSSUS]

colossus /kə'lɒsəs/ *n.* (*pl.* **-ssi** /-saɪ/ or **-ssuses**) **1** statue much bigger than life size. **2** gigantic or remarkable person etc. **3** imperial power personified. [Latin from Greek]

colostomy /kə'lɒstəmɪ/ *n.* (*pl.* **-ies**) operation on the colon to make an opening in the abdominal wall to provide an artificial anus. [from COLON²]

colour /'kʌlə(r)/ (US **color**) *-n.* **1** sensation produced on the eye by rays of light when resolved as by a prism into different wavelengths. **2** one, or any mixture, of the constituents into which light can be separated as in a spectrum or rainbow, sometimes including (loosely) black and white. **3** colouring substance, esp. paint. **4** use of all colours in photography etc. **5 a** pigmentation of the skin,

esp. when dark. **b** this as ground for discrimination. **6** ruddiness of complexion. **7** (in *pl.*) appearance or aspect (*saw them in their true colours*). **8** (in *pl.*) **a** coloured ribbon or uniform etc. worn to signify membership of a school, club, team, etc. **b** flag of a regiment or ship. **9** quality, mood, or variety in music, literature, etc. **10** show of reason; pretext (*lend colour to*; *under colour of*). –*v.* **1** apply colour to, esp. by painting, dyeing, etc. **2** influence. **3** misrepresent, exaggerate. **4** take on colour; blush. □ **show one's true colours** reveal one's true character or intentions. [Latin *color*]

colouration var. of COLORATION.

colour bar *n.* racial discrimination against non-White people.

colour-blind *adj.* unable to distinguish certain colours. □ **colour-blindness** *n.*

colour code –*n.* use of colours as a means of identification. –*v.* (**colour-code**) identify by means of a colour code.

coloured (*US* **colored**) –*adj.* **1** having colour. **2** (**Coloured**) **a** wholly or partly of non-White descent. **b** *S.Afr.* of mixed White and non-White descent. –*n.* **1** (**Coloured**) **a** Coloured person. **b** *S.Afr.* person of mixed descent speaking Afrikaans or English as his or her mother tongue. **2** (in *pl.*) coloured clothing etc. for washing.

colourful *adj.* (*US* **color-**) **1** full of colour; bright. **2** full of interest; vivid. □ **colourfully** *adv.*

colouring *n.* (*US* **color-**) **1** appearance as regards colour, esp. facial complexion. **2** use or application of colour. **3** substance giving colour.

colourless *adj.* (*US* **color-**) **1** without colour. **2** lacking character or interest.

colour scheme *n.* arrangement of colours, esp. in interior design.

colour-sergeant *n.* senior sergeant of an infantry company.

colour supplement *n.* magazine with colour printing, as a supplement to a newspaper.

colposcopy /kɒl'pɒskəpɪ/ *n.* examination of the vagina and neck of the womb. □ **colposcope** /'kɒlpə,skəʊp/ *n.* [Greek *kolpos* womb]

colt /kəʊlt/ *n.* **1** young male horse. **2** *Sport* inexperienced player. □ **coltish** *adj.* [Old English]

colter *US* var. of COULTER.

coltsfoot *n.* (*pl.* **-s**) wild plant with large leaves and yellow flowers.

columbine /'kɒləm,baɪn/ *n.* garden plant with purple-blue flowers like a cluster of doves. [Latin *columba* dove]

column /'kɒləm/ *n.* **1** pillar, usu. of circular section and with a base and capital. **2** column-shaped object. **3** vertical cylindrical mass of liquid or vapour. **4** vertical division of a printed page. **5** part of a newspaper etc. regularly devoted to a particular subject. **6** vertical row of figures in accounts etc. **7** narrow-fronted arrangement of troops or armoured vehicles in successive lines. □ **columnar** /kə'lʌmnə(r)/ *adj.* **columned** *adj.* [French and Latin]

columnist /'kɒləmnɪst/ *n.* journalist contributing regularly to a newspaper etc.

com- *prefix* (also **co-**, **col-**, **con-**, **cor-**) with, together, jointly, altogether. [Latin *com-*, *cum* with]

■ **Usage** *Com-* is used before *b*, *m*, *p*, and occasionally before vowels and *f*; *co-* esp. before vowels, *h*, and *gn*; *col-* before *l*, *cor-* before *r*, and *con-* before other consonants.

---

coma /'kəʊmə/ *n.* (*pl.* **-s**) prolonged deep unconsciousness. [Latin from Greek]

comatose /'kəʊmə,təʊs/ *adj.* **1** in a coma. **2** drowsy, sleepy.

comb /kəʊm/ –*n.* **1 a** toothed strip of rigid material for tidying the hair. **b** similar curved decorative strip worn in the hair. **2** thing like a comb, esp. a device for tidying and straightening wool etc. **3** red fleshy crest of a fowl, esp. a cock. **4** honeycomb. –*v.* **1** draw a comb through (the hair). **2** dress (wool etc.) with a comb. **3** *colloq.* search (a place) thoroughly. □ **comb out 1** arrange (the hair) loosely by combing. **2** remove with a comb. **3** search out and get rid of. [Old English]

combat /'kɒmbæt/ –*n.* fight, struggle, contest. –*v.* (**-t-**) **1** engage in combat (with). **2** oppose; strive against. [Latin: related to BATTLE]

combatant /'kɒmbət(ə)nt/ –*n.* person engaged in fighting. –*adj.* **1** fighting. **2** for fighting.

combative /'kɒmbətɪv/ *adj.* pugnacious.

combe var. of COOMB.

combination /,kɒmbɪ'neɪʃ(ə)n/ *n.* **1** combining or being combined. **2** combined set of things or people. **3** sequence of numbers or letters used to open a combination lock. **4** motor cycle with a side-car attached. **5** (in *pl.*) single undergarment for the body and legs. [Latin: related to COMBINE]

combination lock *n.* lock that can be opened only by a specific sequence of movements.

combine –*v.* /kəm'baɪn/ (**-ning**) **1** join together; unite for a common purpose. **2**

combine harvester n. machine that reaps and threshes in one operation.

combings /ˈkəumɪŋz/ n.pl. hairs combed off.

combining form n. linguistic element used in combination with another to form a word (e.g. *Anglo-* = English).

combo /ˈkɒmbəu/ n. (pl. -s) *slang* small jazz or dance band. [abbreviation of COMBINATION]

combustible /kəmˈbʌstɪb(ə)l/ —adj. capable of or used for burning. —n. combustible substance. □ **combustibility** /-ˈbɪlɪtɪ/ n. [Latin *comburo -bust-* burn up]

combustion /kəmˈbʌstʃ(ə)n/ n. 1 burning. 2 development of light and heat from the chemical combination of a substance with oxygen.

come /kʌm/ —v. (-ming; past came; past part. come) 1 move, be brought towards, or reach a specified situation or result (came to no harm). 3 reach or extend to a specified point. 4 traverse or accomplish (with compl.: *have come a long way*). 5 occur, happen; (of time) arrive in due course (*how did you come to break your leg?; the day soon came*). 6 take or occupy a specified position in space or time (*Nero came after Claudius*). 7 become perceptible or known (*it will come to me*). 8 be available (*comes in three sizes*). 9 become (*come loose*). 10 (foll. by *from, of*) a be descended from. b be the result of (*that comes of complaining*). 11 colloq. play the part of, behave like (*don't come the bully with me*). 12 slang have an orgasm. 13 (in subjunctive) colloq. when a specified time is reached (*come next month*). 14 (as int.) expressing mild protest or encouragement (*come, it cannot be that bad*). —n. slang semen ejaculated. □ **come about** happen. **come across** 1 meet or find by chance. 2 be effective or understood; give a specified impression. **come again** colloq. 1 make a further effort. 2 (as imper.) what did you say? **come along** 1 make progress. 2 (as imper.) hurry up. **come apart** disintegrate. **come at** 1 attack. 2 reach, get access to. **come away** 1 become detached. 2 (foll. by *with*) be left with (an impression etc.). **come back** 1 return. 2 recur to one's memory. 3 (often foll. by *in*) become fashionable or popular again. **come between** 1 interfere with the relationship of. 2 separate.

come by 1 call on a visit. 2 obtain. **come clean** see CLEAN. **come down** 1 lose position or wealth. 2 be handed down by tradition. 3 be reduced. 4 (foll. by *against, in favour of*) reach a decision. 5 (foll. by *to*) amount basically. 6 (foll. by *on*) criticize harshly; rebuke, punish. 7 (foll. by *with*) begin to suffer from (a disease). **come forward** 1 come to collect. 2 offer oneself for a task, post, etc. **come in** 1 enter. 2 take a specified position in a race etc. (*came in third*). 3 become fashionable or seasonable. 4 (with compl.) prove to be (useful etc.) (*came in handy*). 5 have a part to play (*where do I come in?*). 6 be received (*news has just come in*). 7 begin speaking, interrupt. 8 return to base (*come in, number 9*). **come into** 1 enter. 2 receive, esp. as an heir. **come of age** see AGE. **come off 1** (of an action) succeed, occur. 2 fare (badly, well, etc.). 3 be detached or detachable (from). **come off it** colloq. expression of disbelief, disapproval, etc. **come on 1** advance. 2 make progress. 3 begin (*came on to rain*). 4 appear on a stage, field of play, etc. 5 (as imper.) expressing encouragement or disbelief. 6 = *come upon*. **come out 1** emerge; become known. 2 b openly declare that one is a homosexual. 4 go on strike. 5 (of a photograph or thing photographed) be produced satisfactorily and clearly. 6 attain a specified result in an examination etc. 7 (of a stain etc.) be removed. 8 make one's debut in society etc. 9 (foll. by *in*) become covered with (*came out in spots*). 10 be solved. 11 (foll. by *with*) declare openly; disclose. **come over 1 a** come from some distance to visit etc. **b** come nearer. 2 change sides or one's opinion. 3 a (of a feeling etc.) overtake or affect (a person). b colloq. feel suddenly (*came over faint*). 4 appear or sound in a specified way. **come round 1** pay an informal visit. 2 recover consciousness. 3 be converted to another person's opinion. 4 (of a date) recur. **come through 1** recover consciousness. 2 amount to. **come to one's senses** see SENSE. **come up 1** arise, present itself, be mentioned or discussed. 2 attain position or wealth. 3 (often foll. by *to*) approach. 4 (foll. by *to*) match (a standard etc.). 5 (foll. by *with*) produce (an idea etc.). 6 (of a plant etc.) spring up out of the ground. 7 become brighter (e.g. with polishing). **come up against** be faced with or opposed by. **come upon**

comeback 1 meet or find by chance. 2 attack by surprise. [Old English]

comeback *n.* 1 return to a previous (esp. successful) state. 2 *slang* retaliation or retort.

Comecon /ˈkɒmɪˌkɒn/ *n.* economic association of Socialist countries in E. Europe. [abbreviation of *Council for Mutual Economic Assistance*]

comedian /kəˈmiːdɪən/ *n.* 1 humorous entertainer. 2 comedy actor. 3 *slang* buffoon. [French]

comedienne /kəˌmiːdɪˈen/ *n.* female comedian. [French feminine]

comedown *n.* 1 loss of status. 2 disappointment.

comedy /ˈkɒmədɪ/ *n.* (*pl.* **-ies**) **1 a** play, film, etc., of amusing character, usu. with a happy ending. **b** such works as a dramatic genre. 2 humour; amusing aspects. □ **comedic** /kəˈmiːdɪk/ *adj.* [Greek: related to COMIC]

comedy of manners *n.* satirical play portraying the social behaviour of the upper classes.

come-hither *attrib. adj. colloq.* flirtatious, inviting.

comely /ˈkʌmlɪ/ *adj.* (**-ier**, **-iest**) *literary* handsome, good-looking. □ **comeliness** *n.* [Old English]

come-on *n. slang* enticement.

comer /ˈkʌmə(r)/ *n.* person who comes as an applicant etc. (*offered it to the first comer*).

comestibles /kəˈmestɪb(ə)lz/ *n.pl. formal or joc.* food. [French from Latin]

comet /ˈkɒmɪt/ *n.* hazy object moving in a path about the sun, usu. with a nucleus of ice surrounded by gas and with a tail pointing away from the sun. [Greek *komētēs*]

comeuppance /kʌmˈʌpəns/ *n. colloq.* deserved punishment. [*come up*, -ANCE]

comfit /ˈkʌmfɪt/ *n. archaic* sweet consisting of a nut etc. in sugar. [Latin: related to CONFECTION]

comfort /ˈkʌmfət/ —*n.* **1 a** state of physical well-being. **b** (usu. in *pl.*) things that make life easy or pleasant. 2 relief of suffering or grief, consolation. 3 person or thing giving consolation. —*v.* soothe in grief, console. [Latin *fortis* strong]

comfortable *adj.* 1 giving ease. 2 free from discomfort; at ease. 3 having an easy conscience. **4 a** having an adequate standard of living; free from financial worry. **b** sufficient (*comfortable income*). **5 a** with a wide margin (*comfortable win*). **b** appreciable (*comfortable margin*). □ **comfortably** *adv.*

comforter *n.* 1 person who comforts. 2 baby's dummy. 3 *archaic* woollen scarf.

comfortless *adj.* 1 dreary, cheerless. 2 without comfort.

comfort station *n. US euphem.* public lavatory.

comfrey /ˈkʌmfrɪ/ *n.* (*pl.* **-s**) tall bell-flowered plant growing in damp, shady places. [French from Latin]

comfy /ˈkʌmfɪ/ *adj.* (**-ier**, **-iest**) *colloq.* comfortable. [abbreviation]

comic /ˈkɒmɪk/ —*adj.* 1 of or like comedy. 2 funny. —*n.* 1 comedian. 2 periodical in the form of comic strips. □ **comical** *adj.* comically *adv.* [Greek *kōmos* revel]

comic strip *n.* sequence of drawings telling a story.

coming /ˈkʌmɪŋ/ —*attrib. adj.* 1 approaching, next (*the coming week*). 2 of potential importance (*coming man*). —*n.* arrival.

comity /ˈkɒmɪtɪ/ *n.* (*pl.* **-ies**) *formal* 1 courtesy, friendship. **2 a** association of nations etc. **b** (in full **comity of nations**) mutual recognition by nations of the laws and customs of others. [Latin *comis* courteous]

comma /ˈkɒmə/ *n.* punctuation mark (,) indicating a pause or break between parts of a sentence etc. [Greek, = clause]

command /kəˈmɑːnd/ —*v.* 1 (often foll. by *to* + infin., or *that* + clause) give a formal order or instruction to. 2 (also *absol.*) have authority or control over. 3 have at one's disposal or within reach (a skill, resources, etc.). 4 deserve and get (sympathy, respect, etc.). 5 dominate (a strategic position) from a superior height; look down over. —*n.* 1 order, instruction. 2 mastery, control, possession. 3 exercise or tenure of authority, esp. naval or military. **4 a** body of troops etc. **b** district under a commander. [Latin: related to MANDATE]

commandant /ˈkɒmənˌdænt/ *n.* commanding officer, esp. of a military academy. [French or Italian or Spanish: related to COMMAND]

commandeer /ˌkɒmənˈdɪə(r)/ *v.* 1 seize (esp. goods) for military use. 2 take arbitrary possession of. [Afrikaans *kommanderen*]

commander /kəˈmɑːndə(r)/ *n.* 1 person who commands, esp. a naval officer next below captain. 2 (in full **knight commander**) member of a higher class in some orders of knighthood.

commander-in-chief *n.* (*pl.* **commanders-in-chief**) supreme commander, esp. of a nation's forces.

commanding *adj.* 1 exalted, impressive. 2 (of a position) giving a wide view. 3 (of an advantage etc.) substantial (*commanding lead*).

commandment *n.* divine command.

command module n. control compartment in a spacecraft.

commando /kə'mɑːndəʊ/ n. (pl. -s) 1 unit of shock troops. 2 member of this. [Portuguese: related to COMMAND]

Command Paper n. paper laid before Parliament by royal command or film performance given at royal request.

commemorate /kə'meməreɪt/ v. (-ting) 1 preserve in memory by a celebration or ceremony. 2 be a memorial of. □ **commemorative** /-rətɪv/ adj. [Latin: related to MEMORY]

commence /kə'mens/ v. (-cing) formal begin. [Latin: related to COM, INITIATE]

commencement n. formal beginning.

commend /kə'mend/ v. 1 praise. 2 entrust, commit. 3 recommend. □ **commendation** /ˌkɒmen'deɪʃ(ə)n/ n. [Latin: related to MANDATE]

commendable adj. praiseworthy. □ **commendably** adv.

commensurable /kə'menʃərəb(ə)l/ adj. 1 (often foll. by with, to) measurable by the same standard. 2 (foll. by to) proportionate to. 3 Math. (of numbers) in a ratio equal to the ratio of integers. □ **commensurability** /-'bɪlɪtɪ/ n. [Latin: related to MEASURE]

commensurate /kə'menʃərət/ adj. 1 (usu. foll. by with) coextensive. 2 (often foll. by to, with) proportionate. [Latin]

comment /'kɒment/ n. 1 brief critical or explanatory remark or note; opinion. 2 commenting; criticism (aroused much comment; his art is a comment on society). —v. (often foll. by on or that) make (esp. critical) remarks. □ **no comment** colloq. I decline to answer your question. [Latin]

commentary /'kɒmənt(ə)rɪ/ n. (pl. -ies) 1 descriptive spoken esp. broadcast account of an event or performance as it happens. 2 set of explanatory notes on a text etc. [Latin]

commentate /'kɒmənteɪt/ v. (-ting) act as a commentator.

commentator n. 1 person who provides a commentary. 2 person who comments on current events. [Latin]

commerce /'kɒmɜːs/ n. financial transactions, esp. buying and selling; trading. [Latin: related to MERCER]

commercial /kə'mɜːʃ(ə)l/ —adj. 1 of or engaged in commerce. 2 having financial profit as its primary aim. 3 (of chemicals) for industrial use. —n. television or radio advertisement. □ **commercially** adv.

commercial broadcasting n. broadcasting financed by advertising.

commercialism n. 1 commercial practices. 2 emphasis on financial profit.

commercialize v. (also -ise) (-zing or -sing) 1 exploit or spoil for profit. 2 make commercial. □ **commercialization** /-'zeɪʃ(ə)n/ n.

commercial traveller n. firm's representative visiting shops etc. to get orders.

Commie /'kɒmɪ/ n. slang derog. Communist. [abbreviation]

commination /ˌkɒmɪ'neɪʃ(ə)n/ n. literary threatening of divine vengeance. □ **comminatory** /'kɒmɪnətərɪ/ adj. [Latin: related to MENACE]

commingle /kə'mɪŋg(ə)l/ v. (-ling) literary mingle together.

comminute /'kɒmɪnjuːt/ v. (-ting) 1 reduce to small fragments. 2 divide (property) into small portions. □ **comminution** /-'njuːʃ(ə)n/ n. [Latin: related to MINUTE²]

comminuted fracture n. fracture producing multiple bone splinters.

commiserate /kə'mɪzəreɪt/ v. (-ting) (usu. foll. by with) express or feel sympathy. □ **commiseration** /-'reɪʃ(ə)n/ n. [Latin: related to MISER]

commissar /'kɒmɪsɑː(r)/ n. hist. 1 official of the Soviet Communist Party responsible for political education and organization. 2 head of a government department in the USSR. [Latin: related to COMMIT]

commissariat /ˌkɒmɪ'seərɪət/ n. 1 esp. Mil. a department for the supply of food etc. b food supplied. 2 hist. government department of the USSR. [related to COMMISSARY]

commissary /'kɒmɪsərɪ/ n. (pl. -ies) 1 deputy, delegate. 2 US Mil. store for supplies of food etc. [Latin: related to COMMIT]

commission /kə'mɪʃ(ə)n/ —n. 1 a authority to perform a task etc. b person(s) entrusted with such authority. c task given to such person(s). 2 order for something to be produced specially. 3 a warrant conferring the rank of officer in the armed forces. b person's rank so conferred. 4 pay or percentage paid to an agent. 5 act of committing (a crime etc.). —v. 1 empower by commission. 2 a give (an artist etc.) a commission for a piece of work. b order (a work) to be written etc. 3 a give (an officer) command of a ship. b prepare (a machine etc.) into operation. □ **in (or out of) commission** ready (or not ready) for service. [Latin: related to COMMIT]

commission-agent n. bookmaker.

commissionaire /kə‚mɪʃə'neə(r)/ n. uniformed door-attendant. [French: related to COMMISSIONER]

commissioner n. **1** person appointed by a commission to perform a specific task, e.g. the head of the London police etc. **2** member of a government commission. **3** representative of government in a district, department, etc. [medieval Latin: related to COMMISSION]

Commissioner for Oaths n. solicitor authorized to administer an oath in an affidavit etc.

commit /kə'mɪt/ v. (-tt-) **1** do or make (a crime, blunder, etc.). **2** (usu. foll. by to) entrust or consign for safe keeping or treatment. **3** send (a person) to prison. **4** pledge or bind (esp. oneself) to a certain course or policy. **5** (as **committed** adj.) (often foll. by to) a dedicated. **b** obliged. □ **commit to memory** memorize. **commit to paper** write down. [Latin committo -miss-]

commitment n. **1** engagement or obligation. **2** committing or being committed. **3** dedication; committing oneself.

committal n. act of committing, esp. to prison.

committee /kə'mɪtɪ/ n. **1** body of persons appointed for a special function by (and usu. out of) a larger body. **2** (Committee) House of Commons sitting as a committee. [from COMMIT, -EE]

committee stage n. third of five stages of a bill's progress through Parliament.

commode /kə'məʊd/ n. **1** chamber-pot in a chair with a cover. **2** chest of drawers. [Latin commodus convenient]

commodious /kə'məʊdɪəs/ adj. roomy. [Latin commodus convenient]

commodity /kə'mɒdɪtɪ/ n. (pl. -ies) article of trade, esp. a raw material or product as opposed to a service. [Latin: related to COMMODE]

commodore /'kɒmə‚dɔː(r)/ n. **1** naval officer above captain and below rear-admiral. **2** commander of a squadron or other division of a fleet. **3** president of a yacht-club. [French: related to COMMANDER]

common /'kɒmən/ —adj. (-er, -est) **1 a** occurring often. **b** ordinary; without special rank or position. **2 a** shared by, coming from, more than one (common knowledge). **b** belonging to the whole community; public. **3** derog. low-class; vulgar; inferior. **4** of the most familiar type (common cold). **5** Math. belonging to two or more quantities (common denominator). **6** Gram. (of gender) referring to individuals of either sex. —n. **1** piece of open public land. **2** slang = COMMON SENSE. □ **in common 1** in joint use; shared. **2** of joint interest. **in**

common with in the same way as. [Latin communis]

commonality /‚kɒmə'nælɪtɪ/ n. (pl. -ies) **1** sharing of an attribute. **2** common occurrence. **3** = COMMONALTY. [var. of COMMONALTY]

commonalty /'kɒmənəltɪ/ n. (pl. -ies) **1** the common people. **2** the general body (esp. of mankind). [medieval Latin: related to COMMON]

commoner n. **1** one of the common people (below the rank of peer). **2** university student without a scholarship. [medieval Latin: related to COMMON]

common ground n. point or argument accepted by both sides in a dispute.

common law n. unwritten law based on custom and precedent.

common-law husband n. (also **common-law wife**) partner recognized by common law without formal marriage.

commonly adv. usually, frequently; ordinarily.

Common Market n. European Community.

common noun n. Gram. name denoting a class of objects or a concept, not a particular individual.

common or garden adj. colloq. ordinary.

commonplace —adj. lacking originality, trite; ordinary. —n. **1** event, topic, etc. that is ordinary or usual. **2** trite remark. [translation of Latin locus communis]

common-room n. room for the social use of students or teachers at a college etc.

commons n.pl. **1** (**the Commons**) = House of Commons. **2** the common people.

common sense n. sound practical sense.

commonsensical /‚kɒmən'sensɪk(ə)l/ adj. having or marked by common sense.

common time n. Mus. four crotchets in a bar.

commonwealth n. **1** independent State or community, esp. a democratic republic. **2** (**the Commonwealth**) **a** association of the UK with States that were previously part of the British Empire. **b** republican government of Britain 1649–60. **3** federation of States.

commotion /kə'məʊʃ(ə)n/ n. confused and noisy disturbance, uproar. [Latin: related to COM-]

communal /'kɒmjʊn(ə)l/ adj. **1** shared between members of a group or community; for common use. **2** (of conflict etc.) between esp. ethnic or religious

communities. □ **communally** *adv.*
[Latin: related to COMMUNE[1]]

commune[2] /kəˈmjuːn/ *v.* (**-ning**) (usu. foll. by *with*) 1 speak intimately. 2 feel in close touch (with nature etc.). [French: related to COMMON]

commune[1] /ˈkɒmjuːn/ *n.* 1 group of people sharing accommodation, goods, etc. 2 small district of local government in France etc. [medieval Latin: related to COMMON]

communicable /kəˈmjuːnɪkəb(ə)l/ *adj.* (esp. of a disease) able to be passed on. [Latin: related to COMMUNICATE]

communicant /kəˈmjuːnɪkənt/ *n.* 1 person who receives Holy Communion. 2 person who imparts information. [related to COMMUNICATE]

communicate /kəˈmjuːnɪkeɪt/ *v.* (**-ting**) 1 impart, transmit (news, heat, motion, feelings, disease, ideas, etc.). 2 succeed in conveying information. 3 (often foll. by *with*) relate socially; have dealings. 4 (in *pl.*) science and practice of transmitting information. □ **communicator** *n.* **communicatory** *adj.* [Latin: related to COMMON]

communication /kəˌmjuːnɪˈkeɪʃ(ə)n/ *n.* 1 **a** communicating or being communicated. **b** information etc. communicated. **c** letter, message, etc. 2 connection or means of access. 3 social dealings. 4 (in *pl.*) science and practice of transmitting information.

communication cord *n.* cord or chain pulled to stop a train in an emergency.

communication(s) satellite *n.* artificial satellite used to relay telephone circuits or broadcast programmes.

communicative /kəˈmjuːnɪkətɪv/ *adj.* ready to talk and impart information.

communion /kəˈmjuːnɪən/ *n.* 1 sharing, esp. of thoughts etc.; fellowship. 2 participation; sharing in common (*communion of interests*). 3 (**Communion**, **Holy Communion**) Eucharist. 4 (*the Methodist communion* etc.) body or group within the Christian faith. [Latin: related to COMMON]

communiqué /kəˈmjuːnɪkeɪ/ *n.* official communication, esp. a news report. [French, = communicated]

communism /ˈkɒmjʊnɪz(ə)m/ *n.* 1 **a** social system in which most property is publicly owned and each person works for the common benefit. **b** political theory advocating this. 2 (usu. **Communism**) the form of socialist society established in Cuba, China, etc., and previously, the USSR. [French: related to COMMON]

communist /ˈkɒmjʊnɪst/ *n.* 1 person advocating communism. 2 (usu. **Communist**) supporter of Communism or member of a Communist Party. —*adj.* 1 of or relating to communism. 2 (usu. **Communist**) of Communists or a Communist Party. □ **communistic** /-ˈnɪstɪk/ *adj.*

Communist Party *n.* political party advocating communism or Communism.

community /kəˈmjuːnɪtɪ/ *n.* (*pl.* **-ies**) 1 body of people living in one place, district, or country. 2 body of people having religion, ethnic origin, profession, etc., in common. 3 fellowship (*community of interests*). 4 commune. 5 joint ownership or liability. [Latin: related to COMMON]

community centre *n.* place providing social facilities for a neighbourhood.

community charge *n.* tax levied locally on every adult.

■ **Usage** The *community charge*, or *poll tax*, replaced household rates in 1989-90 and is itself to be replaced by a *council tax* in 1993.

community home *n.* place providing young offenders and other juveniles.

community service *n.* unpaid work in the community, esp. by an offender.

community singing *n.* singing by a large group, esp. of old popular songs or hymns.

community spirit *n.* feeling of belonging to a community, expressed in mutual support etc.

commute /kəˈmjuːt/ *v.* (**-ting**) 1 travel some distance to and from work. 2 (usu. foll. by *to*) change (a punishment) to one less severe. 3 (often foll. by *into*, *for*) change (one kind of payment or obligation) for another. 4 exchange. □ **commutable** *adj.* **commutation** /ˌkɒmjuːˈteɪʃ(ə)n/ *n.* Latin *muto* change]

commuter *n.* person who commutes to and from work.

compact[1] —*adj.* /kəmˈpækt/ 1 closely or neatly packed together. 2 small and economically designed. 3 concise. 4 (of a person) small but well-proportioned. —*v.* /kəmˈpækt/ make compact. —*n.* /ˈkɒmpækt/ (in full **powder compact**) small flat case for face-powder. □ **compactly** *adv.* **compactness** *n.* [Latin *pango fasten*]

compact[2] /ˈkɒmpækt/ *n.* agreement, contract. [Latin: related to PACT]

compact disc /kɒmˈpækt/ *n.* disc on which information or sound is recorded digitally and reproduced by reflection of laser light.

companion /kəmˈpænjən/ n. **1 a** person who accompanies or associates with another. **b** (foll. by *in, of*) partner, sharer. **c** person employed to live with and assist another. **2** handbook or reference book. **3** thing that matches another. **4** (**Companion**) member of some orders of knighthood. [Latin *panis* bread]

companionable *adj.* sociable, friendly. □ **companionably** *adv.*

companionship n. friendship; being together.

companion-way n. staircase from a ship's deck to the saloon or cabins.

company /ˈkʌmpəni/ n. (pl. **-ies**) **1 a** number of people assembled. **b** guest(s). **2** person's associates in this. **3 a** commercial business. **b** partners in this. **4** actors etc. working together. **5** subdivision of an infantry battalion. **6** body of people combined for a common purpose (*the ship's company*). **7** being with another or others. □ **in company with** together with. **keep a person company** remain with a person to be sociable. **part company** (often foll. by *with*) cease to associate; separate; disagree. [French: related to COMPANION]

comparable /ˈkɒmpərəb(ə)l/ *adj.* (often foll. by *with, to*) able or fit to be compared. □ **comparability** /-ˈbɪlɪtɪ/ n. **comparably** *adv.* [Latin: related to COMPARE]

■ **Usage** Use of *comparable* with *to* and *with* corresponds to the senses of *compare: to* is more common.

comparative /kəmˈpærətɪv/ —*adj.* **1** perceptible or estimated by comparison; relative (*in comparative comfort*). **2** of or involving comparison (*a comparative study*). **3** *Gram.* (of an adjective or adverb) expressing a higher degree of a quality (e.g. *braver, more quickly*). —n. *Gram.* comparative expression or word. □ **comparatively** *adv.* [Latin: related to COMPARE]

compare /kəmˈpeə(r)/ —v. (**-ring**) **1** (usu. foll. by *to*) express similarities in; liken. **2** (often foll. by *to, with*) estimate the similarity of. **3** (often foll. by *with*) bear comparison. **4** *Gram.* form comparative and superlative degrees of (an adjective or adverb). —n. *literary* comparison (*beyond compare*). □ **compare notes** exchange ideas or opinions. [Latin *compar* equal]

■ **Usage** In current use, *to* and *with* are generally interchangeable, but *with* often implies a greater element of formal analysis.

comparison /kəmˈpærɪs(ə)n/ n. **1** comparing. **2** illustration or example of similarity. **3** capacity for being likened (*there's no comparison*). **4** (in full **degrees of comparison**) *Gram.* positive, comparative, and superlative forms of adjectives and adverbs. □ **bear** (or **stand**) **comparison** (often foll. by *with*) be able to be compared favourably. **beyond comparison 1** totally different in quality. **2** greatly superior; excellent. [Latin: related to PAIR]

compartment /kəmˈpɑːtmənt/ n. **1** space within a larger space, separated by partitions. **2** watertight division of a ship. **3** area of activity etc. kept apart from others in a person's mind. [Latin: related to PART]

compartmental /ˌkɒmpɑːtˈment(ə)l/ *adj.* of or divided into compartments or categories.

compartmentalize v. (also **-ise**) (**-zing** or **-sing**) divide into compartments or categories.

compass /ˈkʌmpəs/ n. **1** instrument showing the direction of magnetic north and bearings from it. **2** (usu. in *pl.*) instrument for taking measurements and describing circles, with two arms connected at one end by a hinge. **3** circumference or boundary. **4** area, extent; scope; range. [Latin *passus* pace]

compassion /kəmˈpæʃ(ə)n/ n. pity inclining one to help or be merciful. [Church Latin: related to PASSION]

compassionate /kəmˈpæʃənət/ *adj.* showing compassion, sympathetic. □ **compassionately** *adv.*

compassionate leave n. leave granted on grounds of bereavement etc.

compatible /kəmˈpætəb(ə)l/ *adj.* **1 a** able to coexist; well-suited. **b** (often foll. by *with*) consistent. **2** (of equipment etc.) able to be used in combination. □ **compatibility** /-ˈbɪlɪtɪ/ n. [medieval Latin: related to PASSION]

compatriot /kəmˈpætrɪət/ n. fellow-countryman. [Latin *compatriota*]

compel /kəmˈpel/ v. (**-ll-**) **1** force, constrain. **2** arouse irresistibly (*compels admiration*). **3** (as **compelling** *adj.*) rousing strong interest, conviction, or admiration. □ **compellingly** *adv.* [Latin *pello puls-* drive]

compendious /kəmˈpendɪəs/ *adj.* comprehensive but brief. [Latin: related to COMPENDIUM]

compendium /kəmˈpendɪəm/ n. (pl. **-s** or **-dia**) **1** concise summary or abridgement. **2** collection of table-games etc. [Latin]

compensate /ˈkɒmpenˌseɪt/ v. (**-ting**) **1 a** (often foll. by *for*) recompense (a person). **b** recompense (loss, damage,

etc.). 2 (usu. foll. by *for* a thing) make amends. 3 counterbalance. 4 offset distress or frustration by development in another direction. □ **compensatory** /-'seitəri/ *adj*. [Latin: related to PENSE]

compensation /ˌkɒmpenˈseɪʃ(ə)n/ *n*. 1 compensating or being compensated. 2 money etc. given as recompense.

compère /ˈkɒmpeə(r)/ —*n*. person who introduces a variety show etc. —*v.* (-**ring**.) act as compère (to). [French, = godfather]

compete /kəmˈpiːt/ *v.* (-**ting**) 1 take part in a contest etc. 2 (often foll. by *with, against* a person, *for* a thing, strive. [Latin *peto* seek]

competence /ˈkɒmpɪt(ə)ns/ *n.* (also **competency**) 1 ability; being competent. 2 income large enough to live on. 3 legal capacity.

competent *adj.* 1 adequately qualified or capable. 2 effective. □ **competently** *adv.* [Latin: related to COMPETE]

competition /ˌkɒmpɪˈtɪʃ(ə)n/ *n.* 1 (often foll. by *for*) competing. 2 event in which people compete. 3 the other people or trade competing. [Latin related to COMPETE]

competitive /kəmˈpetɪtɪv/ *adj.* 1 of or involving competition. 2 (of prices etc.) comparing favourably with those of rivals. 3 having a strong urge to win. □ **competitiveness** *n.*

competitor /kəmˈpetɪtə(r)/ *n.* person who competes; rival, esp. in business.

compile /kəmˈpaɪl/ *v.* (-**ling**) 1 a collect and arrange (material) into a list, book, etc. **b** produce (a book etc.) thus. 2 *Computing* translate (a programming language) into machine code. □ **compilation** /ˌkɒmpɪˈleɪʃ(ə)n/ *n.* [Latin *compilo* plunder]

compiler *n.* 1 person who compiles. 2 *Computing* program for translating a programming language into machine code.

complacent /kəmˈpleɪs(ə)nt/ *adj.* smugly self-satisfied or contented. □ **complacence** *n.* **complacency** *n.* **complacently** *adv.* [Latin *placeo* please]

complain /kəmˈpleɪn/ *v.* 1 express dissatisfaction. 2 (foll. by *of*) **a** say that one is suffering from (an ailment). **b** state a grievance concerning. 3 creak under strain. [Latin *plango lamen-*]

complainant *n.* plaintiff in certain lawsuits.

complaint *n.* 1 complaining. 2 grievance, cause of dissatisfaction. 3 ailment. 4 formal accusation.

■ **Usage** *Complacent* is often confused with *complaisant*.

complaisant /kəmˈpleɪz(ə)nt/ *adj. formal* 1 deferential. 2 willing to please; acquiescent. □ **complaisance** *n.* [French: related to COMPLACENT]

■ **Usage** *Complaisant* is often confused with *complacent*.

complement —*n.* /ˈkɒmplɪmənt/ 1 thing that completes; counterpart. 2 full number needed. 3 the words(s) added to a verb to complete the predicate of a sentence. 4 amount by which an angle is less than 90°. —*v.* /ˈkɒmplɪˌment/ 1 complete. 2 form a complement to. [Latin *compleo* fill up]

complementary /ˌkɒmplɪˈmentəri/ *adj.* 1 completing, forming a complement. 2 (of two or more things) complementing each other. □ **complementary medicine** *n.* alternative medicine.

complete /kəmˈpliːt/ —*adj.* 1 having all its parts; entire. 2 finished. 3 total, in every way. —*v.* (-**ting**) 1 finish. 2 make complete. 3 fill in (a form etc.). 4 conclude the sale or purchase of property. □ **complete with** having (as an important feature) (*comes complete with instructions*). □ **completely** *adv.* **completeness** *n.* **completion** *n.* [Latin: related to COMPLEMENT]

complex /ˈkɒmpleks/ —*n.* 1 building, series of rooms, etc. made up of related parts (*shopping complex*). 2 *Psychol.* group of usu. repressed feelings or thoughts which cause abnormal behaviour or mental states. 3 preoccupation; feeling of inadequacy. —*adj.* 1 complicated. 2 consisting of related parts; composite. □ **complexity** /kəmˈpleksɪtɪ/ *n.* (*pl.* -**ies**). [Latin *complexus*]

complexion /kəmˈplekʃ(ə)n/ *n.* 1 natural colour, texture, and appearance of the skin, esp. of the face. 2 aspect, character (*puts a different complexion on the matter*). [Latin: related to COMPLEX]

compliance /kəmˈplaɪəns/ *n.* 1 obedience to a request, command, etc. 2 capacity to yield. □ **in compliance with** according to.

compliant *adj.* obedient; yielding. □ **compliantly** *adv.*

complicate /ˈkɒmplɪˌkeɪt/ *v.* (-**ting**) 1 make difficult or complex. 2 (as **complicated** *adj.*) complex; intricate. [Latin *plico* to fold]

complication /ˌkɒmplɪˈkeɪʃ(ə)n/ *n.* 1 **a** involved or confused condition or state. **b** complicating circumstance; difficulty. 2 (often in *pl.*) disease or condition aggravating or arising out of a previous one. [Latin: related to COMPLICATE]

complicity /kəm'plɪsɪtɪ/ n. partnership in wrongdoing. [French: related to COMPLEX]

compliment –n. /'kɒmplɪmənt/ **1 a** polite expression of praise. **b** act implying praise. **2** (in pl.) **a** formal greetings accompanying a present etc. **b** praise. –v. /'kɒmplɪment/ (often foll. by on) congratulate; praise. [Latin: related to COMPLEMENT]

complimentary /kɒmplɪ'mentərɪ/ adj. **1** expressing a compliment. **2** given free of charge.

compline /'kɒmplɪn/ n. **1** last of the canonical hours of prayer. **2** service during this. [Latin: related to COMPLY]

comply /kəm'plaɪ/ v. (-ies, -ied) (often foll. by with) act in accordance (with a request or command). [Latin compleo fill up]

component /kəm'pəʊnənt/ –n. part of a larger whole. –adj. being part of a larger whole. [Latin: related to COMPOUND¹]

comport /kəm'pɔːt/ v.refl. literary conduct oneself; behave. □ **comport with** suit, befit. □ **comportment** n. [Latin porto carry]

compose /kəm'pəʊz/ v. (-sing) **1** create in music or writing. **2** constitute; make up. **3** arrange artistically, neatly, or for a specified purpose. **4 a** (often refl.) calm; settle. **b** (as **composed** adj.) calm, self-possessed. **5** Printing **a** set up (type). **b** arrange (an article etc.) in type. □ **composed of** made up of, consisting of. □ **composedly** /-zɪdlɪ/ adv. [French: related to POSE]

composer n. person who composes (esp. music).

composite /'kɒmpəzɪt/ –adj. **1** made up of parts. **2** of mixed Ionic and Corinthian style. **3** (of a plant) having a head of many flowers forming one bloom. –n. composite thing or plant. [Latin: related to COMPOSE]

composition /kɒmpə'zɪʃ(ə)n/ n. **1 a** act or method of putting together; composing. **b** thing composed, esp. music. **2** constitution of a substance. **3** school essay. **4** arrangement of the parts of a picture etc. **5** compound artificial substance. □ **compositional** adj.

compositor /kəm'pɒzɪtə(r)/ n. person who sets up type for printing. [Latin: related to COMPOSE]

compos mentis /kɒmpɒs 'mentɪs/ adj. sane. [Latin]

compost /'kɒmpɒst/ –n. **1** mixture of decayed organic matter. **2** loam soil with fertilizer for growing plants. –v. **1** treat with compost. **2** make into compost. [Latin: related to COMPOSE]

composure /kəm'pəʊʒə(r)/ n. tranquil manner. [from COMPOSE]

compote /'kɒmpəʊt/ n. fruit preserved or cooked in syrup. [French: related to COMPOSE]

compound¹ /'kɒmpaʊnd/ –n. **1** mixture of two or more things. **2** word made up of two or more existing words. **3** substance formed from two or more elements chemically united in fixed proportions. –adj. **1** made up of two or more ingredients or parts. **2** combined; collective. –v. /kəm'paʊnd/ **1** mix or combine (ingredients or elements). **3** increase or complicate (difficulties etc.). **3** make up (a composite whole). **4** settle (a matter) by mutual agreement. **5** Law condone or conceal (a liability or offence) for personal gain. **6** (usu. foll. by with) Law come to terms with a person. [Latin compono -pos- put together]

compound² /'kɒmpaʊnd/ n. **1** enclosure or fenced-in space. **2** enclosure, esp. in India, China, etc., in which a factory or house stands. [Malay kampong]

compound fracture n. fracture complicated by a wound.

compound interest n. interest payable on capital and its accumulated interest.

comprehend /kɒmprɪ'hend/ v. **1** grasp mentally; understand. **2** include. [Latin comprehendo seize]

comprehensible adj. that can be understood. [Latin: related to COMPREHEND]

comprehension n. **1 a** understanding. **b** text set as a test of understanding. **2** inclusion.

comprehensive –adj. **1** including all or nearly all, inclusive. **2** (of motor insurance) providing protection against most risks. –n. (in full **comprehensive school**) secondary school for children of all abilities. □ **comprehensively** adv. **comprehensiveness** n.

compress –v. /kəm'pres/ **1** squeeze together. **2** bring into a smaller space or shorter time. –n. /'kɒmpres/ pad of lint etc. pressed on to part of the body to relieve inflammation, stop bleeding, etc. □ **compressible** /kəm'presɪb(ə)l/ adj. [Latin: related to PRESS¹]

compression /kəm'preʃ(ə)n/ n. **1** compressing. **2** reduction in volume of the fuel mixture in an internal-combustion engine before ignition.

compressor /kəm'presə(r)/ n. machine for compressing air or other gases.

comprise /kəm'praɪz/ v. (-sing) **1** include. **2** consist of. **3** make up, compose. [French: related to COMPREHEND]

■ **Usage** See note at comprise.

■ **Usage** The use of this word in sense 3 is considered incorrect and *compose* is generally preferred.

compromise /ˈkɒmprəmaɪz/ —n. 1 settlement of a dispute by mutual concession. 2 (often foll. by *between*) intermediate state between conflicting opinions, actions, etc. —v. (-**sing**) 1 settle a dispute by mutual concession. 2 modify one's opinions, demands, etc. b bring into disrepute or danger by indiscretion. [Latin: related to PROMISE]

comptroller /kənˈtrəʊlə(r)/ n. controller (used in the title of some financial officers). [var. of CONTROLLER]

compulsion /kəmˈpʌlʃ(ə)n/ n. 1 compelling or being compelled. 2 irresistible urge. [Latin: related to COMPEL]

compulsive /kəmˈpʌlsɪv/ adj. 1 compelling. 2 resulting or acting (as if) from compulsion. 3 irresistible (*compulsive gambler*). □ **compulsively** adv. □ **compulsiveness** n. [medieval Latin: related to COMPEL]

compulsory /kəmˈpʌlsərɪ/ adj. 1 required by law or a rule. 2 essential. □ **compulsorily** adv.

□ **compulsory purchase** n. enforced sale of land or property to a local authority etc.

compunction /kəmˈpʌŋkʃ(ə)n/ n. 1 pricking of conscience. 2 slight regret; scruple. [Church Latin: related to POINT]

compute /kəmˈpjuːt/ v. (-**ting**) 1 reckon or calculate. 2 use a computer. □ **computation** /ˌkɒmpjuːˈteɪʃ(ə)n/ n. [Latin *puto* reckon]

computer n. electronic device for storing and processing data, making calculations, or controlling machinery.

computer science n. the study of the principles and use of computers.

computerize v. (also -**ise**) (-**zing** or -**sing**) 1 equip with a computer. 2 store, perform, or produce by computer. □ **computerization** /-ˈzeɪʃ(ə)n/ n.

computer-literate adj. able to use computers.

computer virus n. self-replicating code maliciously introduced into a computer program and intended to corrupt the system or destroy data.

comrade /ˈkɒmreɪd/ n. 1 associate or companion in some activity. 2 fellow socialist or Communist. □ **comradely** adj. **comradeship** n. [Spanish: related to CHAMBER]

con[1] *slang* —n. confidence trick. —v. (-**nn**-) swindle; deceive. [abbreviation]

con[2] —prep. & adv. against (cf. PRO[2]). [Latin *contra* against]

con[3] n. *slang* convict. [abbreviation]

con[4] v. (US **conn**) (-**nn**-) direct the steering of (a ship). [originally *cond* from French: related to *conquer*]

con- see COM-.

concatenation /kɒnˌkætɪˈneɪʃ(ə)n/ n. series of linked things or events. [Latin *catena* chain]

concave /ˈkɒnkeɪv/ adj. curved like the interior of a circle or sphere. □ **concavity** /-ˈkævɪtɪ/ n. [Latin: related to CAVE]

conceal /kənˈsiːl/ v. 1 keep secret 2 hide. □ **concealment** n. [Latin *celo* hide]

concede /kənˈsiːd/ v. 1 admit to be true. 2 admit defeat in. 3 grant (a right, privilege, etc.). [Latin: related to CEDE]

conceit /kənˈsiːt/ n. 1 personal vanity; pride. 2 *literary* a far-fetched comparison. b fanciful notion. [from CONCEIVE]

conceited adj. vain. □ **conceitedly** adv.

conceivable /kənˈsiːvəb(ə)l/ adj. capable of being grasped or imagined. □ **conceivably** adv.

conceive /kənˈsiːv/ v. (-**ving**) 1 become pregnant (with). 2 a (often foll. by *of*) imagine, think. b (usu. in *passive*) formulate (a belief, plan, etc.). [Latin *concipio*]

concentrate /ˈkɒnsəntreɪt/ —v. (-**ting**) 1 (often foll. by *on*) focus one's attention or thought. 2 bring together to one point. 3 increase the strength of (a liquid etc.) by removing water etc. 4 (as **concentrated** adj.) intense, strong. —n. concentrated substance. [Latin: related to CENTRE]

concentration /ˌkɒnsənˈtreɪʃ(ə)n/ n. 1 concentrating or being concentrated. 2 mental attention. 3 something concentrated. 4 weight of a substance in a given amount of material.

concentration camp n. camp where political prisoners etc. are detained.

concentric /kənˈsentrɪk/ adj. having a common centre. □ **concentrically** adv. [French or medieval Latin: related to CENTRE]

concept /ˈkɒnsept/ n. general notion; abstract idea. [Latin: related to CONCEIVE]

conception /kənˈsepʃ(ə)n/ n. 1 conceiving or being conceived. 2 idea, plan. 3 understanding (*has no conception*). □ **conceptional** adj. [French from Latin: related to CONCEPT]

conceptual /kənˈseptjʊəl/ adj. of mental conceptions or concepts. □ **conceptually** adv.

conceptualize *v.* (also **-ise**) (**-zing** or **-sing**) form a concept or idea of. □ **conceptualization** /-'zeɪʃ(ə)n/ *n.*

concern /kən'sɜːn/ *—v.* **1 a** be relevant or important to. **b** relate to; be about. **2** (*refl.*; often foll. by *with, about, in*) interest or involve oneself. **3** worry, affect. *—n.* **1** worry, anxiety. **2 a** a matter of interest or importance to one. **b** interest, connection (*has a concern in politics*). **3** business, firm. **4** *colloq.* complicated thing, contrivance. [Latin *cerno* sift]

concerned *adj.* **1** involved, interested. **2** troubled, anxious. □ **be concerned** (often foll. by *in*) take part. □ **concernedly** /-ɪdlɪ/ *adv.* **concernedness** /-ɪdnɪs/ *n.*

concerning *prep.* about, regarding.

concert /'kɒnsət/ *n.* **1** musical performance of usu. several separate compositions. **2** agreement. **3** combination of voices or sounds. [Italian: related to CONCERTO]

concerted /kən'sɜːtɪd/ *adj.* **1** jointly arranged or planned. **2** *Mus.* arranged in parts for voices or instruments.

concertina /ˌkɒnsə'tiːnə/ *—n.* musical instrument like an accordion but smaller. *—v.* (**-nas, -naed** /-nad/ or **-na'd, -naing**) compress or collapse in folds like those of a concertina.

concerto /kən'tʃeətəʊ/ *n.* (*pl.* **-s** or **-ti** /-tɪ/) composition for solo instrument(s) and orchestra. [Italian]

concert pitch *n.* pitch internationally agreed whereby A above middle C = 440 Hz.

concession /kən'seʃ(ə)n/ *n.* **1 a** conceding. **b** thing conceded. **2** reduction in price for a certain category of persons. **3 a** right to use land etc. **b** right to sell goods in a particular territory. □ **concessionary** *adj.* [Latin: related to CONCEDE]

concessive /kən'sesɪv/ *adj. Gram.* (of a preposition or conjunction) introducing a phrase or clause which contrasts with the main clause (e.g. *in spite of, although*). [Latin: related to CONCEDE]

conch /kɒntʃ/ *n.* **1** thick heavy spiral shell of various marine gastropod molluscs. **2** any such gastropod. [Latin *concha*]

conchology /kɒŋ'kɒlədʒɪ/ *n.* the study of shells. [from CONCH]

concierge /ˌkɔ̃sɪ'eəʒ/ *n.* (esp. in France) door-keeper or porter of a block of flats etc. [French]

conciliate /kən'sɪlɪˌeɪt/ *v.* (**-ting**) **1** make calm and amenable; pacify; gain

the goodwill of. **2** reconcile. □ **conciliation** /-'eɪʃ(ə)n/ *n.* **conciliator** *n.* **conciliatory** /-'sɪlɪətərɪ/ *adj.* [Latin: related to COUNCIL]

concise /kən'saɪs/ *adj.* brief but comprehensive in expression. □ **concisely** *adv.* **conciseness** *n.* **concision** /-'sɪʒ(ə)n/ *n.* [Latin *caedo* cut]

conclave /'kɒŋkleɪv/ *n.* **1** private meeting. **2** *RC Ch.* **a** assembly of cardinals for the election of a pope. **b** meeting-place for this. [Latin *clavis* key]

conclude /kən'kluːd/ *v.* (**-ding**) **1** bring or come to an end. **2** (often foll. by *from* or *that*) infer. **3** settle (a treaty etc.). [Latin *concludo*: related to CLOSE¹]

conclusion /kən'kluːʒ(ə)n/ *n.* **1** ending, end. **2** judgement reached by reasoning. **3** summing-up. **4** settling (of peace etc.). **5** *Logic* proposition reached from given premisses. □ **in conclusion** lastly, to conclude. [Latin: related to CONCLUDE]

conclusive /kən'kluːsɪv/ *adj.* decisive, convincing. □ **conclusively** *adv.* [Latin: related to CONCLUDE]

concoct /kən'kɒkt/ *v.* **1** make by mixing ingredients. **2** invent (a story, lie, etc.). □ **concoction** /-'kɒkʃ(ə)n/ *n.* [Latin *coquo coct-* cook]

concomitant /kən'kɒmɪt(ə)nt/ *—adj.* (often foll. by *with*) accompanying, occurring together. *—n.* accompanying thing. □ **concomitance** *n.* [Latin *comes comit-* companion]

concord /'kɒŋkɔːd/ *n.* agreement, harmony. □ **concordant** /kən'kɔːd(ə)nt/ *adj.* [Latin *cor cord-* heart]

concordance /kən'kɔːd(ə)ns/ *n.* **1** agreement. **2** alphabetical index of words used in a book or by an author. [medieval Latin: related to CONCORD]

concordat /kən'kɔːdæt/ *n.* agreement. esp. between the Church and a State. [Latin: related to CONCORD]

concourse /'kɒŋkɔːs/ *n.* **1** crowd, gathering. **2** large open area in a railway station etc. [Latin: related to CONCUR]

concrete /'kɒŋkriːt/ *—adj.* **1 a** existing in a material form; real. **b** specific, definite (*concrete evidence; a concrete proposal*). **2** *Gram.* (of a noun) denoting a material object as opposed to a quality, state, etc. *—n.* (often *attrib.*) mixture of gravel, sand, cement, and water, used for building. *—v.* (**-ting**) cover with or embed in concrete. [Latin *cresco cret-* grow]

concretion /kən'kriːʃ(ə)n/ *n.* **1** hard solid mass. **2** forming of this by coalescence. [Latin: related to CONCRETE]

concubine /'kɒŋkjuˌbaɪn/ *n.* **1** *literary* or *joc.* mistress. **2** (among polygamous peoples) secondary wife. □ **concubinage** /kən'kjuːbɪnɪdʒ/ *n.* [Latin *cubo* lie]

concupiscence /kən'kjupɪs(ə)ns/ n. *formal* lust. □ **concupiscent** *adj*. [Latin *cupio* desire]

concur /kən'kɜː(r)/ v. (**-rr-**) **1** (often foll. by *with*) have the same opinion. **2** coincide. [Latin *curro* run]

concurrent /kən'kʌrənt/ *adj*. **1** (often foll. by *with*) existing or in operation at the same time or together. **2** (of three or more lines) meeting at or tending towards one point. **3** agreeing, harmonious. □ **concurrence** n. **concurrently** *adv*.

concuss /kən'kʌs/ v. subject to concussion. [Latin *quatio* shake]

concussion /kən'kʌʃ(ə)n/ n. **1** temporary unconsciousness or incapacity due to a blow to the head, a fall, etc. **2** violent shaking.

condemn /kən'dem/ v. **1** express utter disapproval of. **2 a** find guilty; convict. **b** (usu. foll. by *to*) sentence to (a punishment). **3** pronounce (a building etc.) unfit for use. **4** (usu. foll. by *to*) doom or assign (to something un pleasant). □ **condemnation** /ˌkɒndem'neɪʃ(ə)n/ n. **condemnatory** /-'demnətəri/ *adj*. [Latin: related to DAMN]

condensation /ˌkɒnden'seɪʃ(ə)n/ n. **1** condensing or being condensed. **2** condensed liquid (esp. water on a cold surface). **3** abridgement. [Latin: related to CONDENSE]

condense /kən'dens/ v. (**-sing**) **1** make denser or more concentrated. **2** express in fewer words. **3** reduce or be reduced from a gas or vapour to a liquid. [Latin: related to DENSE]

condensed milk n. milk thickened by evaporation and sweetened.

condenser n. **1** apparatus or vessel for condensing vapour. **2** *Electr*. = CAPACITOR. **3** lens or system of lenses for concentrating light.

condescend /ˌkɒndɪ'send/ v. **1** be gracious enough (to do a thing) esp. while showing one's sense of dignity or superiority (*condescended to attend*). **2** (foll. by *to*) pretend to be on equal terms with (an inferior) **3** (as **condescending** *adj*.) patronizing. □ **condescendingly** *adv*. **condescension** /-'senʃ(ə)n/ n. [Latin: related to DESCEND]

condign /kən'daɪn/ *adj*. (of a punishment etc.) severe and well-deserved. [Latin *dignus* worthy]

condiment /'kɒndɪmənt/ n. seasoning or relish for food. [Latin *condio* pickle]

condition /kən'dɪʃ(ə)n/ —n. **1** stipulation; thing upon the fulfilment of which something else depends. **2 a** state of being or fitness cf a person or thing. **b** ailment, abnormality (*heart condition*). **3** (in *pl*.) circumstances, esp. those

affecting the functioning or existence of something (*good working conditions*). —v. **1 a** bring into a good or desired state. **b** make fit (dogs or horses). **2** teach or accustom. **3 a** impose conditions on. **b** be essential to. □ **in** (or **out of**) **condition** in good (or bad) condition. **on condition that** with the stipulation that. [Latin *dico* say]

conditional *adj*. **1** (often foll. by *on*) dependent; not absolute; containing a condition. **2** *Gram*. (of a clause, mood, etc.) expressing a condition. □ **conditionally** *adv*. [Latin: related to CONDITION]

conditioned reflex n. reflex response to a non-natural stimulus, established by training.

conditioner n. agent that conditions, esp. the hair.

condole /kən'dəʊl/ v. (**-ling**) (foll. by *with*) express sympathy with (a person over a loss etc. [Latin *condoleo* grieve with another)

■ **Usage** *Condole* is often confused with *console*.

condolence n. (often in *pl*.) expression of sympathy.

condom /'kɒndəm/ n. contraceptive sheath worn by men. [origin unknown]

condominium /ˌkɒndə'mɪnɪəm/ n. **1** joint rule or sovereignty. **2** *US* building containing individually owned flats. [Latin *dominium* lordship]

condone /kən'dəʊn/ v. (**-ning**) forgive or overlook (an offence or wrongdoing). [Latin *dono* give]

condor /'kɒndɔː(r)/ n. large S. American vulture. [Spanish from Quechua]

conduce /kən'djuːs/ v. (**-cing**) (foll. by *to*) contribute to (a result). [Latin: related to CONDUCT]

conducive *adj*. (often foll. by *to*) contributing or helping (towards something).

conduct —n. /'kɒndʌkt/ **1** behaviour. **2** activity or manner of directing or managing (a business, war, etc.). —v. /kən'dʌkt/ **1** lead or guide. **2** direct or manage (a business etc.). **3** (also *absol*.) be the conductor of (an orchestra etc.). **4** transmit (heat, electricity, etc.) by conduction. **5** *refl*. behave. [Latin *duco duct-* lead]

conductance /kən'dʌkt(ə)ns/ n. power of a specified material to conduct electricity.

conduction /kən'dʌkʃ(ə)n/ n. transmission of heat, electricity, etc. through a substance. [Latin: related to CONDUCT]

conductive /kən'dʌktɪv/ *adj*. transmitting (esp. heat, electricity, etc.). □ **conductivity** /ˌkɒndʌk'tɪvɪtɪ/ n.

conductor *n.* **1** person who directs an orchestra etc. **2** (*fem.* **conductress**) person who collects fares in a bus etc. **3** thing that conducts heat or electricity. [Latin: related to CONDUCT]

conduit /'kondɪt, -djuɪt/ *n.* **1** channel or pipe conveying liquids. **2** tube or trough protecting insulated electric wires. [medieval Latin: related to CONDUCT]

cone *n.* **1** solid figure with a circular (or other curved) plane base, tapering to a point. **2** thing of similar shape. **3** dry fruit of a conifer. **4** ice-cream cornet. [Latin from Greek]

coney var. of CONY.

confab /'konfæb/ *colloq.* —*n.* = CONFABU-LATION (see CONFABULATE). —*v.* (**-bb-**) = CONFABULATE. [abbreviation]

confabulate /kən'fæbjʊˌleɪt/ *v.* (**-ting**) converse, chat. □ **confabulation** /-ˈleɪʃ(ə)n/ *n.* [Latin: related to FABLE]

confection /kənˈfekʃ(ə)n/ *n.* dish or delicacy made with sweet ingredients. [Latin *conficio* prepare]

confectioner *n.* maker or retailer of confectionery.

confectionery *n.* confections, esp. sweets.

confederacy /kənˈfedərəsɪ/ *n.* (*pl.* **-ies**) league or alliance, esp. of confederate States. [French: related to CONFEDER-ATE]

confederate /kənˈfedərət/ —*adj.* esp. *Polit.* allied. —*n.* **1** ally, esp. (in a bad sense) accomplice. **2** (**Confederate**) supporter of the Confederate States. —*v.* /-ˌreɪt/ (**-ting**) (often foll. by *with*) bring or come into alliance. [Latin: related to FEDERAL]

Confederate States *n.pl.* States which seceded from the US in 1860-1.

confederation /kənˌfedəˈreɪʃ(ə)n/ *n.* **1** union or alliance, esp. of States. **2** confederating or being confederated.

confer /kənˈfɜː(r)/ *v.* (**-rr-**) **1** (often foll. by *on, upon*) grant or bestow. **2** (often foll. by *with*) converse, consult. □ **conferrable** *adj.* [Latin *confero collat-bring together]

conference /ˈkɒnfərəns/ *n.* **1** consultation. **2** meeting for discussion. [French or medieval Latin: related to CONFER]

conferment /kənˈfɜːmənt/ *n.* conferring of a degree, honour, etc.

confess /kənˈfes/ *v.* **1 a** (also *absol.*) acknowledge or admit (a fault, crime, etc.). **b** (foll. by *to*) admit to. **2** admit reluctantly. **3 a** (also *absol.*) declare (one's sins) to a priest. **b** (of a priest) hear the confession of. [Latin *confiteor fess-*]

confessedly /kənˈfesɪdlɪ/ *adv.* by one's own or general admission.

confession /kənˈfeʃ(ə)n/ *n.* **1 a** act of confessing. **b** thing confessed. **2** (in full **confession of faith**) declaration of one's beliefs or principles.

confessional —*n.* enclosed stall in a church in which the priest hears confessions. —*adj.* of confession.

confessor *n.* priest who hears confessions and gives spiritual counsel.

confetti /kənˈfetɪ/ *n.* small bits of coloured paper thrown by wedding guests at the bride and groom. [Italian]

confidant /ˈkɒnfɪˌdænt/ *n.* (*fem.* **confidante** *pronunc.* same) person trusted with knowledge of one's private affairs. [related to CONFIDE]

confide /kənˈfaɪd/ *v.* (**-ding**) **1** (foll. by *in*) talk confidentially to. **2** (usu. foll. by *to*) tell (a secret etc.) in confidence. **3** (foll. by *to*) entrust (an object of care, a task, etc.) to. [Latin *confido* trust]

confidence /ˈkɒnfɪd(ə)ns/ *n.* **1** firm trust. **2 a** feeling of reliance or certainty. **b** sense of self-reliance; boldness. **3** something told as a secret. □ **in confidence** as a secret. □ **in a person's confidence** trusted with a person's secrets. **take into one's confidence** confide in.

confidence trick *n.* swindle in which the victim is persuaded to trust the swindler. □ **confidence trickster** *n.*

confident *adj.* feeling or showing confidence; bold. □ **confidently** *adv.* [Italian: related to CONFIDE]

confidential /ˌkɒnfɪˈdenʃ(ə)l/ *adj.* **1** spoken or written in confidence. **2** entrusted with secrets (*confidential secretary*). **3** confiding. □ **confidentiality** /-ʃɪˈælɪtɪ/ *n.* **confidentially** *adv.*

configuration /kənˌfɪɡjʊˈreɪʃ(ə)n/ *n.* **1** arrangement in a particular form. **2** form or figure resulting from this. **3** *Computing* hardware and its arrangement of connections etc. □ **configure** *v.* (**-ring**). [Latin: related to FIGURE]

confine —*v.* /kənˈfaɪn/ (**-ning**) **1** keep or restrict (within certain limits). **2** imprison. —*n.* /ˈkɒnfaɪn/ (usu. in *pl.*) limit, boundary. [Latin *finis* limit]

confinement *n.* **1** confining or being confined. **2** time of childbirth.

confirm /kənˈfɜːm/ *v.* **1** provide support for the truth or correctness of. **2** (foll. by *in*) encourage (a person) in (an opinion etc.). **3** establish more firmly (power, possession, etc.). **4** make formally valid. **5** administer the religious rite of confirmation to. [Latin: related to FIRM[1]]

confirmation /ˌkɒnfəˈmeɪʃ(ə)n/ *n.* **1** confirming or being confirmed. **2** rite confirming a baptized person as a member of the Christian Church.

confirmed *adj.* firmly settled in some habit or condition (*confirmed bachelor*).

confiscate /'kɒnfɪskeɪt/ *v.* (-ting) take or seize by authority. □ **confiscation** /-'skeɪʃ(ə)n/ *n.* [Latin: related to FISCAL]

conflagration /ˌkɒnfləˈgreɪʃ(ə)n/ *n.* great and destructive fire. [Latin: related to FLAGRANT]

conflate /kənˈfleɪt/ *v.* (-ting) blend or fuse together (esp. two variant texts into one). □ **conflation** /-ˈfleɪʃ(ə)n/ *n.* [Latin *flo flat-* blow]

conflict —*n.* /ˈkɒnflɪkt/ **1 a** fight, struggle. **b** state of opposition. **2** (often foll. by *of*) clashing of opposed interests etc. —*v.* /kənˈflɪkt/ clash; be incompatible. [Latin *fligo flict-* strike]

confluence /ˈkɒnfluəns/ *n.* **1** place where two rivers meet. **2 a** coming together. **b** crowd of people. [Latin *fluo* flow]

confluent /ˈkɒnfluənt/ *adj.* flowing together, uniting. —*n.* stream joining another.

conform /kənˈfɔːm/ *v.* **1** comply with rules or general custom. **2** (foll. by *to, with*) comply with; be in accordance with. **3** (often foll. by *to*) be or make suitable. [Latin: related to FORM]

conformable *adj.* **1** (often foll. by *to*) similar. **2** (often foll. by *with*) consistent. **3** (often foll. by *to*) adaptable. □ **conformably** *adv.*

conformation /ˌkɒnfɔːˈmeɪʃ(ə)n/ *n.* way a thing is formed; shape.

conformist /kənˈfɔːmɪst/ —*n.* person who conforms to an established practice. —*adj.* conforming, conventional. □ **conformism** *n.*

conformity *n.* **1** accordance with established practice. **2** agreement, suitability.

confound /kənˈfaʊnd/ *v.* **1** perplex, baffle. **2** confuse (in one's mind). **3** *archaic* defeat, overthrow. —*int.* expressing annoyance (*confound you!*). [Latin *confundo fus-* mix up]

confounded *adj.* *colloq.* damned.

confront /kənˈfrʌnt/ *v.* **1 a** face in hostility or defiance. **b** face up to and deal with. **2** (of a difficulty etc.) present itself to. **3** (foll. by *with*) bring (a person) face to face with (an accusation etc.). **4** meet or stand facing. □ **confrontation** /ˌkɒnfrʌnˈteɪʃ(ə)n/ *n.* **confrontational** /ˌkɒnfrʌnˈteɪʃən(ə)l/ *adj.* [French from medieval Latin]

Confucian /kənˈfjuːʃ(ə)n/ *adj.* of Confucius or his philosophy. □ **Confucianism** *n.* [*Confucius*, name of a Chinese philosopher]

confuse /kənˈfjuːz/ *v.* (-sing) **1** perplex, bewilder. **2** mix up in the mind; mistake (one for another). **3** make indistinct

(*confuse the issue*). **4** (often as **confused** *adj.*) throw into disorder. □ **confusedly** /-zɪdlɪ/ *adv.* **confusing** *adj.* [related to CONFOUND]

confusion *n.* confusing or being confused.

conga /ˈkɒŋgə/ —*n.* **1** Latin-American dance, with a line of dancers one behind the other. **2** tall narrow drum beaten with the hands. —*v.* (**congas, congaed** or **conga'd, congaing** /-gəɪŋ/) perform the conga. [Spanish *conga* (feminine) = of the Congo]

congeal /kənˈdʒiːl/ *v.* **1** make or become semi-solid by cooling. **2** (of blood etc.) coagulate. □ **congelation** /ˌkɒndʒɪˈleɪʃ(ə)n/ *n.* [French from Latin *gelo* freeze]

congenial /kənˈdʒiːnɪəl/ *adj.* **1** (often foll. by *with, to*) pleasant because likeminded. **2** (often foll. by *to*) suited or agreeable. □ **congeniality** /-ˈælɪtɪ/ *n.* **congenially** *adv.* [from COM, GENIAL]

congenital /kənˈdʒenɪt(ə)l/ *adj.* **1** (esp. of disease) existing from birth. **2** as such from birth (*congenital liar*). □ **congenitally** *adv.* [Latin: related to COM]

conger /ˈkɒŋgə/ *n.* (in full **conger eel**) large marine eel. [Greek *goggros*]

congeries /kənˈdʒɪəriːz/ *n.* (*pl.* same) disorderly collection; mass, heap. [Latin *congero* heap together]

■ **Usage** The form *congery*, formed under the misapprehension that *congeries* is plural only, is incorrect.

congest /kənˈdʒest/ *v.* (esp. as **congested** *adj.*) affect with congestion. [Latin *congero -gest-* heap together]

congestion /kənˈdʒestʃ(ə)n/ *n.* abnormal accumulation or obstruction, esp. of traffic etc. or of blood or mucus in part of the body.

conglomerate /kənˈglɒmərət/ —*adj.* gathered into a rounded mass. —*n.* **1** heterogeneous mass. **2** group or corporation of merged firms. —*v.* /kənˈglɒməreɪt/ (-ting) collect into a coherent mass. □ **conglomeration** /kənˌglɒməˈreɪʃ(ə)n/ *n.* [Latin *glomus -eris* ball]

congratulate /kənˈgrætjʊleɪt/ *v.* (-ting) (often foll. by *on*) **1** express pleasure at the happiness, good fortune, or excellence of (a person). **2** *refl.* think oneself fortunate or clever. □ **congratulatory** /-lətərɪ/ *adj.* [Latin *gratus* pleasing]

congratulation /kənˌgrætʃʊˈleɪʃ(ə)n/ *n.* **1** congratulating. **2** (usu. in *pl.*) expression of this.

congregate /ˈkɒŋgrɪgeɪt/ *v.* (-**ting**) collect or gather into a crowd. [Latin *grex greg-* flock]

congregation /ˌkɒŋgrɪˈgeɪʃ(ə)n/ *n.* **1** gathering of people, esp. for religious worship. **2** body of persons regularly attending a particular church etc. [Latin: related to CONGREGATE]

congregational *adj.* **1** of a congregation. **2** (**Congregational**) of or adhering to Congregationalism.

Congregationalism *n.* system whereby individual churches are largely self-governing. □ **Congregationalist** *n.*

congress /ˈkɒŋgres/ *n.* **1** formal meeting of delegates for discussion. **2** (**Congress**) national legislative body, esp. of the US. □ **congressional** /kənˈgreʃən(ə)l/ *adj.* [Latin *gradior gress-* walk]

congressman *n.* (*fem.* **congresswoman**) member of the US Congress.

congruent /ˈkɒŋgruənt/ *adj.* **1** (often foll. by *with*) suitable, agreeing. **2** *Geom.* (of figures) coinciding exactly when superimposed. □ **congruence** *n.* **congruency** *n.* [Latin *congruo* agree]

congruous /ˈkɒŋgruəs/ *adj.* suitable, agreeing; fitting. □ **congruity** /kənˈgruːɪtɪ/ *n.* [Latin: related to CONGRUENT]

conic /ˈkɒnɪk/ *adj.* of a cone. [Greek: related to CONE]

conical *adj.* cone-shaped.

conifer /ˈkɒnɪfə(r)/ *n.* tree usu. bearing cones. □ **coniferous** /kəˈnɪfərəs/ *adj.* [Latin: related to CONE]

conjectural /kənˈdʒektʃər(ə)l/ *adj.* based on conjecture.

conjecture /kənˈdʒektʃə(r)/ —*n.* **1** formation of an opinion on incomplete information; guessing. **2** guess. —*v.* (-**ring**) guess. [Latin *conjectura* from *jacio* throw]

conjoin /kənˈdʒɔɪn/ *v. formal* join, combine.

conjoint /kənˈdʒɔɪnt/ *adj. formal* associated, conjoined.

conjugal /ˈkɒndʒʊg(ə)l/ *adj.* of marriage or the relationship of husband and wife. [Latin *conjux conjug-* consort]

conjugate —*v.* /ˈkɒndʒʊgeɪt/ (-**ting**) **1** *Gram.* list the different forms of (a verb). **2 a** unite. **b** become fused. —*adj.* /ˈkɒndʒʊgət/ **1** joined together, paired. **2** fused. [Latin *jugum* yoke]

conjugation /ˌkɒndʒʊˈgeɪʃ(ə)n/ *n.* *Gram.* system of verbal inflection.

conjunct /kənˈdʒʌŋkt/ *adj.* joined together; combined; associated. [Latin from *jungo* joined]

conjunction /kənˈdʒʌŋkʃ(ə)n/ *n.* **1** joining; connection. **2** *Gram.* word used to connect clauses or sentences or words in the same clause (e.g. *and*, *but*, *if*). **3** combination (of events or circumstances). **4** apparent proximity to each other of two bodies in the solar system.

conjunctiva /ˌkɒndʒʌŋkˈtaɪvə/ *n.* (*pl.* -**s**) mucous membrane covering the front of the eye and the lining inside the eyelids.

conjunctive /kənˈdʒʌŋktɪv/ *adj.* **1** serving to join. **2** *Gram.* of the nature of a conjunction.

conjunctivitis /kənˌdʒʌŋktɪˈvaɪtɪs/ *n.* inflammation of the conjunctiva.

conjure /ˈkʌndʒə(r)/ *v.* (-**ring**) **1** perform tricks which are seemingly magical, esp. by movements of the hands. **2** summon (a spirit or demon) to appear. **3** /kənˈdʒʊə(r)/ *formal* appeal solemnly to. □ **conjure up 1** produce as if by magic. **2** evoke. [Latin *juro* swear]

conjuror *n.* (also **conjurer**) performer of conjuring tricks.

conk[1] *v.* (usu. foll. by *out*) *colloq.* **1** (of a machine etc.) break down. **2** (of a person) become exhausted and give up; fall asleep; faint; die. [origin unknown]

conk[2] *slang* —*n.* **1** nose or head. **2** punch on the nose or head. —*v.* hit on the nose or head. [perhaps = CONCH]

conker *n.* **1** fruit of the horse chestnut. **2** (in *pl.*) children's game played with conkers on strings. [dial. *conker* snail-shell]

con man *n.* confidence trickster.

conn *US* var. of CON[4].

connect /kəˈnekt/ *v.* **1** (often foll. by *to*, *with*) join (two things, or one thing with another). **2** be joined or joinable. **3** (often foll. by *with*) associate mentally or practically. **4** (foll. by *with*) (of a train etc.) be timed to arrive with another, so passengers can transfer. **5** put into communication by telephone. **6 a** (usu. in *passive*; foll. by *with*) associate with others in relationships etc. **b** be meaningful or relevant. **7** *colloq.* hit or strike effectively. [Latin *necto nex-* bind]

connecting-rod *n.* rod between the piston and crankpin etc. in an internal combustion engine.

connection /kəˈnekʃ(ə)n/ *n.* (also **connexion**) **1** connecting or being connected. **2** point at which two things are connected. **3** link, esp. by telephone. **4** connecting train etc. **5** (often in *pl.*) relative or associate, esp. one with influence. **6** relation of ideas. □ **in connection with** with reference to.

connective *adj.* connecting, esp. of body tissue connecting, separating, etc., organs etc.

connector *n.* thing that connects. [Latin *necto* knit]

conning tower *n.* 1 superstructure of a submarine containing the periscope. 2 armoured wheel-house of a warship. [from CON¹]

connive /kə'naɪv/ *v.* (**-ving**) 1 (foll. by *at*) disregard or tacitly consent to (a wrongdoing). 2 (usu. foll. by *with*) conspire. □ **connivance** *n.* [Latin *conniveo* shut the eyes]

connoisseur /ˌkɒnə'sɜː(r)/ *n.* (often foll. by *of, in*) expert judge in matters of taste. [French *connaître* know]

connote /kə'nəʊt/ *v.* (**-ting**) 1 (of a word etc.) imply in addition to the literal or primary meaning. 2 mean, signify. □ **connotation** /ˌkɒnə'teɪʃ(ə)n/ *n.* □ **connotative** /'kɒnəteɪtɪv/ *adj.* [medieval Latin: related to NOTE]

connubial /kə'njuːbɪəl/ *adj.* of marriage or the relationship of husband and wife. [Latin *nubo* marry]

conquer /'kɒŋkə(r)/ *v.* 1 a overcome and control militarily. b be victorious. 2 overcome by effort. □ **conqueror** *n.* [Latin *conquiro* win]

conquest /'kɒŋkwest/ *n.* 1 conquering or being conquered. 2 a conquered territory. b something won. 3 person whose affection has been won.

consanguineous /ˌkɒnsæŋ'gwɪnɪəs/ *adj.* descended from the same ancestor; akin. □ **consanguinity** *n.* [Latin *sanguis* blood]

conscience /'kɒnʃ(ə)ns/ *n* moral sense of right and wrong, esp. as affecting behaviour. □ **in all conscience** *colloq.* by any reasonable standard. **on one's conscience** causing one feelings of guilt. **prisoner of conscience** person imprisoned by the State for his or her political or religious views. [Latin: related to SCIENCE]

conscience money *n.* sum paid to relieve one's conscience, esp. regarding a payment previously evaded.

conscience-stricken *adj.* (also **conscience-struck**) made uneasy by a bad conscience.

conscientious /ˌkɒnʃɪ'enʃəs/ *adj.* diligent and scrupulous. □ **conscientiously** *adv.* **conscientiousness** *n.* [medieval Latin: related to CONSCIENCE]

conscientious objector *n.* person who for reasons of conscience objects to military service etc.

conscious /'kɒnʃəs/ *—adj.* 1 awake and aware of one's surroundings and identity. 2 (usu. foll. by *of* or *that*) aware, knowing. 3 (of actions, emotions, etc.) realized or recognized by the doer; intentional. 4 (in comb.) aware of, concerned with (*fashion-conscious*). *—n.* (prec. by *the*) the conscious mind. □

consciously *adv.* **consciousness** *n.* [Latin *scio* know]

conscript *—v.* /kən'skrɪpt/ summon for compulsory State (esp. military) service. *—n.* /'kɒnskrɪpt/ conscripted person. □ **conscription** /kən'skrɪpʃ(ə)n/ *n.* [Latin *scribo* write]

consecrate /'kɒnsɪkreɪt/ *v.* (**-ting**) 1 make or declare sacred; dedicate formally to religious or divine purpose. 2 (foll. by *to*) devote to (a purpose). □ **consecration** /-'kreɪʃ(ə)n/ *n.* [Latin: related to SACRED]

consecutive /kən'sekjʊtɪv/ *adj.* 1 a following continuously. b in an unbroken or logical order. 2 *Gram.* expressing a consequence. □ **consecutively** *adv.* [Latin *sequor secut-* follow]

consensus /kən'sensəs/ *n.* (often foll. by *of*, often *attrib.*) general agreement or opinion. [Latin: related to CONSENT]

consent /kən'sent/ *—v.* (often foll. by *to*) express willingness, give permission, agree. *—n.* voluntary agreement, permission. [Latin *sentio* feel]

consequence /'kɒnsɪkwəns/ *n.* 1 result or effect of what has gone before. 2 importance. □ **in consequence** as a result. **take the consequences** accept the results of one's choice or action. [Latin: related to CONSEQUENT]

consequent /'kɒnsɪkwənt/ *adj.* 1 (often foll. by *on*, *upon*) following as a result or consequence. 2 logically consistent. [Latin: related to CONSEQUENCE]

consequential /ˌkɒnsɪ'kwenʃ(ə)l/ *adj.* 1 consequent; resulting indirectly. 2 important.

consequently *adv. & conj.* as a result; therefore.

conservancy /kən'sɜːvənsɪ/ *n.* (*pl.* **-ies**) 1 body controlling a port, river, etc. or preserving the environment. 2 official environmental conservation. [Latin: related to CONSERVE]

conservation /ˌkɒnsə'veɪʃ(ə)n/ *n.* preservation, esp. of the natural environment. [Latin: related to CONSERVE]

conservationist *n.* supporter of environmental conservation.

conservation of energy *n.* principle that the total quantity of energy in any system that is not subject to external action remains constant.

conservative /kən'sɜːvətɪv/ *—adj.* 1 a averse to rapid change. b (of views, taste, etc.) moderate, avoiding extremes. 2 (of an estimate etc.) purposely low. 3 (usu. **Conservative**) of the Conservative Party. 4 tending to conserve. *—n.* 1 conservative person. 2 (usu. **Conservative**) supporter or member of the Conservative Party. □ **conservatism** *n.* [Latin: related to CONSERVE]

Conservative Party *n.* political party promoting free enterprise and private ownership.

conservatoire /kən'sɜːvə,twɑː(r)/ *n.* (usu. European) school of music or other arts. [French from Italian]

conservatory /kən'sɜːvətəri/ *n.* (*pl.* -**ies**) **1** greenhouse for tender plants, esp. attached to a house. **2** esp. *US* = CONSERVATOIRE. [Latin and Italian: related to CONSERVE]

conserve —*v.* /kən'sɜːv/ (-**ving**) keep from harm or damage, esp. for later use. —*n.* /'kɒnsɜːv/ fresh fruit jam. [Latin *servo* keep]

consider /kən'sɪdə(r)/ *v.* **1** contemplate mentally, esp. in order to reach a conclusion. **2** examine the merits of. **3** look attentively at. **4** take into account; show consideration or regard for. **5** (foll. by *that*) have the opinion. **6** regard as. **7** (as **considered** *adj.*) formed after careful thought (*a considered opinion*). □ **all things considered** taking everything into account. [French from Latin]

considerable *adj.* **1** much; a lot of (*considerable pain*). **2** notable, important. □ **considerably** *adv.*

considerate /kən'sɪdərət/ *adj.* thoughtful towards others; careful not to cause hurt or inconvenience. □ **considerately** *adv.* [Latin: related to CONSIDER]

consideration /kən,sɪdə'reɪʃ(ə)n/ *n.* **1** careful thought. **2** thoughtfulness for others; being considerate. **3** fact or thing taken into account. **4** compensation; payment or reward. □ **in consideration of** in return for; on account of. **take into consideration** make allowance for. **under consideration** being considered.

considering —*prep. & conj.* in view of; taking into consideration. —*adv. colloq.* taking everything into account (*not so bad, considering*).

consign /kən'saɪn/ *v.* (often foll. by *to*) **1** hand over; deliver. **2** assign; commit. **3** transmit or send (goods). □ **consignee** /,kɒnsaɪ'niː/ *n.* **consignor** /,kɒnsaɪ'nɔː/ *n.* [Latin: related to SIGN]

consignment *n.* **1** consigning or being consigned. **2** goods consigned.

consist /kən'sɪst/ *v.* **1** (foll. by *of*) be composed; have as ingredients. **2** (foll. by *in, of*) have its essential features as specified. [Latin *sisto* stop]

consistency /kən'sɪstənsi/ *n.* (*pl.* -**ies**) **1** degree of density, firmness, or viscosity, esp. of thick liquids. **2** being consistent. [Latin: related to CONSIST]

consistent *adj.* **1** (usu. foll. by *with*) compatible or in harmony. **2** (of a person) constant to the same principles. □ **consistently** *adv.* [Latin: related to CONSIST]

consistory /kən'sɪstəri/ *n.* (*pl.* -**ies**) *RC Ch.* council of cardinals (with or without the pope). [Latin: related to CONSIST]

consolation /,kɒnsə'leɪʃ(ə)n/ *n.* **1** consoling or being consoled. **2** consoling thing or person. □ **consolatory** /kən'splətəri/ *adj.*

consolation prize *n.* prize given to a competitor who just fails to win a main prize.

console¹ /kən'səʊl/ *v.* (-**ling**) comfort, esp. in grief or disappointment. [Latin: related to SOLACE]

■ **Usage** *Console* is often confused with *condole*, which is different in that it is always followed by *with*.

console² /'kɒnsəʊl/ *n.* **1** panel for switches, controls, etc. **2** cabinet for a television etc. **3** cabinet with the keyboards and stops of an organ. **4** bracket supporting a shelf etc. [French]

consolidate /kən'sɒlɪdeɪt/ *v.* (-**ting**) **1** make or become strong or secure. **2** combine (territories, companies, debts, etc.) into one whole. □ **consolidation** /-'deɪʃ(ə)n/ *n.* **consolidator** *n.* [Latin: related to SOLID]

consommé /kən'sɒmeɪ/ *n.* clear soup from meat stock. [French]

consonance /'kɒnsənəns/ *n.* agreement, harmony. [Latin *sono* sound⁻]

consonant —*n.* **1** speech sound in which the breath is at least partly obstructed, and which forms a syllable by combining with a vowel. **2** letter(s) representing this. —*adj.* (foll. by *with, to*) consistent; in agreement or harmony. □ **consonantal** /-'nænt(ə)l/ *adj.*

consort¹ —*n.* /'kɒnsɔːt/ wife or husband, esp. of royalty. —*v.* /kən'sɔːt/ **1** (usu. foll. by *with, together*) keep company. **2** harmonize. [Latin: related to SORT]

consort² /'kɒnsɔːt/ *n. Mus.* small group of players, singers, or instruments. [var. of CONCERT]

consortium /kən'sɔːtɪəm/ *n.* (*pl.* -**tia** or -**s**) association, esp. of several business companies. [Latin: related to CONSORT¹]

conspicuous /kən'spɪkjʊəs/ *adj.* **1** clearly visible; attracting notice. **2** noteworthy. □ **conspicuously** *adv.* [Latin *specio* look]

conspiracy /kən'spɪrəsi/ *n.* (*pl.* -**ies**) **1** secret plan to commit a crime; plot. **2** conspiring. [Latin: related to CONSPIRE]

conspiracy of silence *n.* agreement to say nothing.

conspirator /kən'spɪrətə(r)/ *n.* person who takes part in a conspiracy. □ **conspiratorial** /-'tɔːrɪəl/ *adj.*

conspire /kən'spaɪə(r)/ v. 1 combine secretly for an unlawful or harmful together. **2** (of events) seem to be working together. [Latin *spiro* breathe]

constable /'kʌnstəb(ə)l/ n. 1 (also **po-lice constable**) police officer of the lowest rank. **2** governor of a royal castle. [Latin *comes stabuli* count of the stable]

constabulary /kən'stæbjʊlərɪ/ n. (pl. -**ies**) police force. [medieval Latin: related to CONSTABLE]

constancy /'kʌnstənsɪ/ n. being unchanging and dependable; faithfulness. [Latin: related to CONSTANT]

constant —adj. 1 continuous (*constant attention*). 2 occurring frequently (*constant complaints*). 3 unchanging, faithful, dependable. —n. 1 anything that does not vary. 2 *Math. & Physics* quantity or number that remains the same. □ **constantly** adv. [Latin *sto stand*]

constellation /ˌkʌnstə'leɪʃ(ə)n/ n. 1 group of fixed stars. 2 group of associated persons etc. [Latin *stella* star]

consternation /ˌkʌnstə'neɪʃ(ə)n/ n. anxiety, dismay. [Latin *sterno* throw down]

constipate /'kʌnstɪpeɪt/ v. (-**ing**) (esp. as **constipated** adj.) affect with constipation. [Latin *stipo* cram]

constipation /ˌkʌnstɪ'peɪʃ(ə)n/ n. difficulty in emptying the bowels.

constituency /kən'stɪtjʊənsɪ/ n. (pl. -**ies**) 1 body of voters who elect a representative. 2 area so represented.

constituent /kən'stɪtjʊənt/ —adj. 1 composing or helping to make a whole. 2 able to make or change a constitution (*constituent assembly*). 3 electing. —n. 1 member of a constituency. 2 component part. [Latin: related to CONSTITUTE]

constitute /'kʌnstɪtjuːt/ v. (-**ting**) 1 be the components or essence of; compose. 2 **a** amount to (*this constitutes a warning*). **b** formally establish (*constitutes a precedent*). 3 give legal or constitutional form to. [Latin *constituo* establish]

constitution /ˌkʌnstɪ'tjuːʃ(ə)n/ n. 1 act or method of constituting; composition. 2 body of fundamental principles by which a State or other body is governed. 3 person's inherent state of health, strength, etc. [Latin: related to CONSTITUTE]

constitutional —adj. 1 of or in line with the constitution. 2 inherent (*constitutional weakness*). —n. walk taken regularly as healthy exercise. □ **constitutionality** /-'nælɪtɪ/ n. **constitutionally** adv.

constitutive /'kʌnstɪtjuːtɪv/ adj. 1 able to form or appoint. 2 component. 3 essential.

constrain /kən'streɪn/ v. 1 compel. 2 **a** confine forcibly; imprison. **b** restrict severely. 3 (as **constrained** adj.) forced, embarrassed. [Latin *str ngo strict-* tie]

constraint /kən'streɪnt/ n. 1 constraining or being constrained. 2 restriction. 3 self-control.

constrict /kən'strɪkt/ v. make narrow or tight; compress. □ **constriction** n. **constrictive** adj. [Latin: related to CONSTRAIN]

constrictor n. 1 snake that kills by compressing. 2 muscle that contracts an organ or part of the body.

construct —v. /kən'strʌkt/ 1 make by fitting parts together; build, form. delineate (a figure). —n. /'kʌnstrʌkt/ thing constructed, esp. by the mind. □ **constructor** /kən'strʌktə(r)/ n. [Latin *struo struct-* build]

construction /kən'strʌkʃ(ə)n/ n. 1 constructing or being constructed. 2 thing constructed. 3 interpretation or explanation. 4 syntactical arrangement of words. □ **constructional** adj.

constructive /kən'strʌktɪv/ adj. 1 **a** tending to form a basis for ideas. **b** helpful, positive. 2 derived by inference. □ **constructively** adv.

construe /kən'struː/ v. (-**strues**, -**strued**, -**struing**) 1 interpret. 2 (often foll. by *with*) combine (words) grammatically. 3 analyse the syntax of (a sentence). 4 translate literally. [Latin: related to CONSTRUCT]

consubstantial /ˌkʌnsəb'stænʃ(ə)l/ adj. *Theol.* of one substance. [Church Latin: related to SUBSTANCE]

consubstantiation /ˌkʌnsəbstænʃɪ'eɪʃ(ə)n/ n. *Theo.* presence of Christ's body and blood together with the bread and wine in the Eucharist.

consul /'kɒns(ə)l/ n. 1 official appointed by a State to protect its citizens and interests in a foreign city. 2 *hist.* either of two chief magistrates in ancient Rome. □ **consular** /-sjʊlə(r)/ adj. **consulship** n. [Latin]

consulate /'kʌnsjʊlət/ n. 1 official building of a consul. 2 position of consul.

consult /kən'sʌlt/ v. 1 seek information or advice from 2 (often foll. by *with*) refer to a person for advice etc. 3 take into account (feelings, interests, etc.). □ **consultative** adj. [Latin *consulo consult-* take counsel]

consultancy n. (pl. -**ies**) practice or position of a consultant.

consultant n. 1 person providing professional advice etc. 2 senior medical specialist in a hospital.

consultation /ˌkɒnsəlˈteɪʃ(ə)n/ *n.* **1** meeting arranged to consult. **2** act or process of consulting.

consume /kənˈsjuːm/ *v.* (**-ming**) **1** eat or drink. **2** destroy. **3** preoccupy, possess (*consumed with rage*). **4** use up. □ **consumable** *adj. & n.* [Latin *consumo -sumpt-*]

consumer *n.* **1** person who consumes, esp. one who uses a product. **2** purchaser of goods or services.

consumer durable *n.* durable household product (e.g. a radio or washing machine).

consumer goods *n.pl.* goods for consumers, not for producing other goods.

consumerism *n.* **1** protection of consumers' interests. **2** (often *derog.*) continual increase in the consumption of goods. □ **consumerist** *adj.*

consummate –*v.* /ˈkɒnsəˌmeɪt/ (**-ting**) **1** complete; make perfect. **2** complete (a marriage) by sexual intercourse. –*adj.* /kənˈsʌmɪt/ complete, perfect; fully skilled. □ **consummation** /-ˈmeɪʃ(ə)n/ *n.* [Latin *summus* utmost]

consumption /kənˈsʌmpʃ(ə)n/ *n.* **1** consuming or being consumed. **2** amount consumed. **3** use by a particular group (*a film unsuitable for children's consumption*). **4** *archaic* tuberculosis of the lungs. **5** purchase and use of goods etc. [related to CONSUME]

consumptive /kənˈsʌmptɪv/ *archaic* –*adj.* suffering or tending to suffer from consumption. –*n.* consumptive person. [medieval Latin: related to CONSUMPTION]

cont. *abbr.* **1** contents. **2** continued.

contact /ˈkɒntækt/ –*n.* **1** state or condition of touching, meeting, or communicating. **2** person who is or may be communicated with for information, assistance, etc. **3** connection for the passage of an electric current. **4** person likely to carry a contagious disease through being near an infected person. –*v.* **1** get in touch with (a person). **2** begin correspondence or personal dealings with. [Latin *tango tact-* touch]

contact lens *n.* small lens placed directly on the eyeball to correct vision.

contact print *n.* photographic print made by placing a negative directly on to printing paper and exposing it to light.

contagion /kənˈteɪdʒ(ə)n/ *n.* **1 a** spreading of disease by bodily contact. **b** contagious disease. **2** moral corruption. [related to CONTACT]

contagious /kənˈteɪdʒəs/ *adj.* **1 a** (of a person) likely to transmit a disease by contact. **b** (of a disease) transmitted in

this way. **2** (of emotions etc.) likely to spread (*contagious enthusiasm*).

contain /kənˈteɪn/ *v.* **1** hold or be capable of holding within itself; include or comprise. **2** (of measures) be equal to (*a gallon contains eight pints*). **3** prevent from moving or extending. **4** control or restrain (feelings etc.). **5** (of a number) be divisible by (a factor) without a remainder. [Latin *teneo* hold]

container *n.* **1** box, jar, etc., for holding things. **2** large metal box for transporting goods.

containerize *v.* (also **-ise**) (**-zing** or **-sing**) pack in or transport by container. □ **containerization** /-ˈzeɪʃ(ə)n/ *n.*

containment *n.* action or policy of preventing the expansion of a hostile country or influence.

contaminate /kənˈtæmɪˌneɪt/ *v.* (**-ting**) **1** pollute, esp. with radioactivity. **2** infect. □ **contaminant** *n.* **contamination** /-ˈneɪʃ(ə)n/ *n.* **contaminator** *n.* [Latin *tamen-* related to *tango* touch]

contemplate /ˈkɒntəmˌpleɪt/ *v.* (**-ting**) **1** survey visually or mentally. **2** regard (an event) as possible. **3** intend (*he is not contemplating retiring*). **4** meditate. □ **contemplation** /-ˈpleɪʃ(ə)n/ *n.* [Latin]

contemplative /kənˈtɛmplətɪv/ –*adj.* of or given to (esp. religious) contemplation; thoughtful. –*n.* person devoted to religious contemplation. [Latin: related to CONTEMPLATE]

contemporaneous /kənˌtɛmpəˈreɪnɪəs/ *adj.* (usu. foll. by *with*) existing or occurring at the same time. □ **contemporaneity** /-ˈniːɪtɪ/ *n.* [Latin: related to COM-, *tempus* time]

contemporary /kənˈtɛmpərərɪ/ –*adj.* **1** living or occurring at the same time. **2** of approximately the same age. **3** modern in style or design. –*n.* (*pl.* **-ies**) contemporary person or thing. [medieval Latin: related to CONTEMPORANEOUS]

contempt /kənˈtɛmpt/ *n.* **1** feeling that a person or thing deserves scorn or extreme reproach. **2** condition of being held in contempt. **3** (in full **contempt of court**) disobedience to or disrespect for a court of law. [Latin *temno tempt-* despise]

contemptible *adj.* deserving contempt. □ **contemptibly** *adv.*

contemptuous *adj.* (often foll. by *of*) feeling or showing contempt. □ **contemptuously** *adv.*

contend /kənˈtɛnd/ *v.* **1** (usu. foll. by *with*) fight, argue. **2** compete. **3** assert, maintain. □ **contender** *n.* [Latin: related to TEND[1]]

content[1] /kənˈtɛnt/ –*predic. adj.* **1** satisfied; adequately happy. **2** (foll. by *to* + infin.) willing. –*v.* make content;

content

satisfy. —*n.* contented state; satisfaction. □ to **one's heart's content** as much as one wishes. [Latin: related to CONTAIN]

content[2] /'kɒntent/ *n.* 1 (usu. in *pl.*) what is contained, esp. in a vessel, book, or house. 2 amount (of a constituent) contained (*high fat content*). 3 substance (of a speech etc.) as distinct from form. 4 capacity or volume. [medieval Latin: related to CONTAIN]

contented /kən'tentɪd/ *adj.* happy, satisfied. □ **contentedly** *adv.* **contentedness** *n.*

contention /kən'tenʃ(ə)n/ *n.* 1 dispute or argument; rivalry. 2 point contended for in an argument. [Latin: related to CONTEND]

contentious /kən'tenʃəs/ *adj.* 1 quarrelsome. 2 likely to cause an argument. □ **contentiously** *adv.* **contentiousness** *n.*

contentment *n.* satisfied state; tranquil happiness.

contest —*n.* /'kɒntest/ 1 contending; strife. 2 a competition. —*v.* /kən'test/ 1 dispute (a decision etc.). 2 contend or compete for; compete in (an election). [Latin *testis* witness]

contestant /kən'test(ə)nt/ *n.* person taking part in a contest.

context /'kɒntekst/ *n.* 1 parts that surround a word or passage and clarify its meaning. 2 relevant circumstances. □ **in** (or **out of**) **context** with (or without) the surrounding words or circumstances. □ **contextual** /kən'tekstjʊəl/ *adj.* **contextualize** /kən'tekstjʊəlaɪz/ *v.* (also **-ise**) (**-zing** or **-sing**). [Latin: related to TEXT]

contiguous /kən'tɪgjʊəs/ *adj.* (usu. foll. by *with, to*) touching; in contact. □ **contiguity** /ˌkɒntɪ'gjuːɪti/ *n.* [Latin: related to CONTACT]

continent[1] /'kɒntɪnənt/ *n.* 1 any of the main continuous expanses of land (Europe, Asia, Africa, N. and S. America, Australia, Antarctica. 2 (**the Continent**) mainland of Europe as distinct from the British Isles. [Latin: related to CONTAIN]

continent[2] /'kɒntɪnənt/ *adj.* 1 able to control one's bowels and bladder. 2 exercising self-restraint, esp. sexually. □ **continence** *n.* [Latin: related to CONTAIN]

continental /ˌkɒntɪ'nent(ə)l/ *adj.* 1 of or characteristic of a continent. 2 (**Continental**) of or characteristic of mainland Europe.

continental breakfast *n.* light breakfast of coffee, rolls, etc.

continental quilt *n.* duvet.

continental shelf *n.* area of shallow seabed bordering a continent.

contingency /kən'tɪndʒənsɪ/ *n.* (*pl.* **-ies**) 1 event that may or may not occur. 2 something dependent on another uncertain event. [Latin: related to CONTINGENT]

contingent —*adj.* 1 (usu. foll. by *on, upon*) conditional, dependent (on **a** uncertain event or circumstance). 2 **a** fortuitous. **b** fortuitous. —*n.* 1 body (of troops, ships, etc.) forming part of a larger group. 2 group of people sharing an interest, origin, etc. (*the Oxford contingent*). [Latin: related to CONTACT]

continual /kən'tɪnjʊəl/ *adj.* constantly or frequently recurring; always happening. □ **continually** *adv.* [French: related to CONTINUE]

■ **Usage** *Continual* is often confused with *continuous. Continual* is used of something that happens very frequently (e.g. *there were continual interruptions*), while *continuous* is used of something that happens without a pause (e.g. *continuous rain all day*).

continuance /kən'tɪnjʊəns/ *n.* 1 continuing in existence or operation. 2 duration.

continuation /kənˌtɪnjʊ'eɪʃ(ə)n/ *n.* 1 continuing or being continued. 2 part that continues something else.

continue /kən'tɪnjuː/ *v.* (**-ues, -ued, -uing**) 1 maintain, not stop (an action etc.) (*continued to read, reading*). 2 (also *absol.*) resume or prolong (a narrative, journey, etc.). 3 be a sequel to. 4 remain, stay (*will continue as manager; weather continued fine*). [Latin: related to CONTAIN]

continuo /kən'tɪnjʊəʊ/ *n.* (*pl.* **-s**) *Mus.* accompaniment providing a bass line played usu. on a keyboard instrument. [Italian]

continuous /kən'tɪnjʊəs/ *adj.* uninterrupted, connected throughout in space or time. □ **continuously** *adv.* [Latin: related to CONTAIN]

■ **Usage** See note at *continual.*

continuous assessment *n.* evaluation of a pupil's progress throughout a course of study.

continuum /kən'tɪnjʊəm/ *n.* (*pl.* **-nua**) thing having a continuous structure. [Latin: related to CONTINUOUS]

contort /kən'tɔːt/ *v.* twist or force out of its normal shape. □ **contortion** *n.* [Latin *torqueo tort-* twist]

contortionist /kənˈtɔːʃənɪst/ n. entertainer who adopts contorted postures.

contour /ˈkɒntʊə(r)/ —n. 1 outline. 2 (in full **contour line**) line on a map joining points of equal altitude. —v. mark with contour lines. [Italian *contornare* draw in outline]

contra /ˈkɒntrə/ n. (pl. -s) member of a counter-revolutionary force in Nicaragua. [abbreviation of Spanish *contra-revolucionario* counter-revolutionary]

contra- *comb. form* against, opposite. [Latin]

contraband /ˈkɒntrəˌbænd/ —n. 1 smuggled goods. 2 smuggling; illegal trade. —adj. forbidden to be imported or exported. [Spanish from Italian]

contraception /ˌkɒntrəˈsɛpʃ(ə)n/ n. prevention of pregnancy; use of contraceptives. [from CONTRA-, CONCEPTION]

contraceptive /ˌkɒntrəˈsɛptɪv/ —adj. preventing pregnancy. —n. contraceptive device or drug.

contract —n. /ˈkɒntrækt/ 1 written or spoken agreement, esp. one enforceable by law. 2 document recording this. —v. /kənˈtrækt/ 1 make or become smaller. 2 a (usu. foll. by *out*) arrange (work) to be done by contract. 3 become affected by (a disease). 4 enter into (marriage). 5 incur (a debt etc.). 6 draw together (the muscles, brow, etc.), or be drawn together. □ **contract in** (or **out**) choose to enter (or not to enter) a scheme or commitment. [Latin *contractus*: related to TRACT[1]]

contractable adj. (of a disease) that can be contracted.

contract bridge n. bridge in which only tricks bid and won count towards the game.

contractile adj. that can be shrunk or drawn together.

contractile /kənˈtræktaɪl/ adj. capable of or producing contraction. □ **contractility** /ˌkɒntrækˈtɪlɪtɪ/ n.

contraction /kənˈtrækʃ(ə)n/ n. 1 contracting or being contracted. 2 *Med.* shortening of the uterine muscles during childbirth. 3 shrinking, diminution. 4 shortened form of a word or words (e.g. *he's*).

contractor /kənˈtræktə(r)/ n. person who makes a contract, esp. to conduct building operations.

contractual /kənˈtræktjʊəl/ adj. of or in the nature of a contract. □ **contractually** adv.

contradict /ˌkɒntrəˈdɪkt/ v. 1 deny (a statement). 2 deny a statement made by (a person). 3 be in opposition to or in conflict with. □ **contradiction** n. **contradictory** adj. [Latin *dico dict-* say]

contradistinction /ˌkɒntrədɪˈstɪŋkʃ(ə)n/ n. distinction made by contrasting.

contraflow /ˈkɒntrəˌfləʊ/ n. transfer of traffic from its usual half of the road to the other half by borrowing one or more of the other half's lanes.

contralto /kənˈtræltəʊ/ n. (pl. -s) 1 lowest female singing-voice. 2 singer with this voice. [Italian: related to CONTRA-, ALTO]

contraption /kənˈtræpʃ(ə)n/ n. machine or device, esp. a strange or cumbersome one. [origin unknown]

contrapuntal /ˌkɒntrəˈpʌnt(ə)l/ adj. *Mus.* of or in counterpoint. □ **contrapuntally** adv. [Italian]

contrariwise /kənˈtreərɪˌwaɪz/ adv. 1 on the other hand. 2 in the opposite way. 3 perversely.

contrary /ˈkɒntrərɪ/ —adj. 1 (usu. foll. by *to*) opposed in nature or tendency. 2 /kənˈtreərɪ/ perverse, self-willed. 3 (of a wind) unfavourable, impeding. 4 opposite in position or direction. —n. (prec. by *the*) the opposite. —adv. (foll. by *to*) in opposition or contrast (*contrary to expectations*). □ **on the contrary** expressing denial of what has just been implied or stated. **to the contrary** to the opposite effect. □ **contrariness** /kənˈtreərɪnəs/ n. [Latin: related to CONTRA-]

contrast —n. /ˈkɒntrɑːst/ 1 a juxtaposition or comparison showing differences. b difference so revealed. 2 (often foll. by *to*) thing or person having different qualities. 3 degree of difference between the tones in a television picture or photograph. —v. /kənˈtrɑːst/ (often foll. by *with*) 1 set together so as to reveal a contrast. 2 have or show a contrast. [Italian from Latin *sto* stand]

contravene /ˌkɒntrəˈviːn/ v. (-ning) 1 infringe (a law etc.). 2 (of things) conflict with. □ **contravention** /-ˈvɛnʃ(ə)n/ n. [Latin *venio* come]

contretemps /ˈkɒntrəˌtɒ̃/ n. (pl. same /-ˌtɒ̃z/) 1 unfortunate occurrence. 2 unexpected mishap. [French]

contribute /kənˈtrɪbjuːt, ˈkɒntrɪˌbjuːt/ v. (-ting) (often foll. by *to*) 1 give (time, money, etc.) towards a common purpose. 2 help to bring about a result etc. 3 (also *absol.*) supply (an article etc.) for publication with others. □ **contributor** n. [Latin: related to TRIBUTE]

■ **Usage** The second pronunciation, stressed on the first syllable, is considered incorrect by some people.

contribution /ˌkɒntrɪˈbjuːʃ(ə)n/ n. 1 act of contributing. 2 thing contributed.

contributory /kənˈtrɪbjutəri/ *adj.* **1** that contributes. **2** using contributions.

contrite /ˈkɒntraɪt/ *adj.* penitent, feeling great guilt. □ **contritely** *adv.* **contrition** /kənˈtrɪʃ(ə)n/ *n.* [Latin: related to TO TRITE]

contrivance /kənˈtraɪv(ə)ns/ *n.* **1** something contrived, esp. a plan or mechanical device. **2** act of contriving.

contrive /kənˈtraɪv/ *v.* (**-ving**) **1** devise; plan or make resourcefully or with skill. **2** (often foll. by *to* + infin.) manage. [French from Latin]

contrived *adj.* artificial, forced.

control /kənˈtrəʊl/ —*n.* **1** power of directing. **2** means of restraining, esp. self-restraint. **3** means of restraint. **4** (usu. in *pl.*) means of regulating. **5** (usu. in *pl.*) switches and other devices by which a machine is controlled. **6** place where something is controlled or verified. **7** standard of comparison for checking the results of an experiment. —*v.* (**-ll-**) **1** have control of, regulate. **2** hold in check. **3** check, verify. □ **in control** (often foll. by *of*) directing an activity. **out of control** no longer manageable. **under control** being controlled; in order. □ **controllable** *adj.* [medieval Latin, = keep copy of accounts: related to CONTRA-, ROLL]

control tower *n.* tall building at an airport etc. from which air traffic is controlled.

controller *n.* **1** person or thing that controls. **2** person in charge of expenditure.

controversial /ˌkɒntrəˈvɜːʃ(ə)l/ *adj.* causing or subject to controversy. [Latin: related to CONTROVERT]

controversy /ˈkɒntrəvɜːsɪ, kənˈtrɒvəsɪ/ *n.* (*pl.* **-ies**) prolonged argument or dispute. [Latin: related to CONTROVERT]

■ **Usage** The second pronunciation, stressed on the second syllable, is considered incorrect by some people.

controvert /ˈkɒntrəvɜːt/ *v.* dispute, deny. [Latin *verto vers-* turn]

contumacious /ˌkɒntjuːˈmeɪʃəs/ *adj.* stubbornly or wilfully disobedient. □ **contumacy** /ˈkɒntjʊməsɪ/ *n.* (*pl.* **-ies**) [Latin *tumeo* swell]

contumely /ˈkɒntjuːmlɪ/ *n.* **1** insolent language or treatment. **2** disgrace. [Latin: related to CONTUMACIOUS]

contuse /kənˈtjuːz/ *v.* (**-sing**) bruise. □ **contusion** *n.* [Latin *tundo tus-* thump]

conundrum /kəˈnʌndrəm/ *n.* **1** riddle, esp. one with a pun in its answer. **2** hard question. [origin unknown]

conurbation /ˌkɒnɜːˈbeɪʃ(ə)n/ *n.* extended urban area, esp. consisting of

several towns and merging suburbs. [Latin *urbs* city]

convalesce /ˌkɒnvəˈles/ *v.* (**-cing**) recover health after illness. [Latin *valeo* be well]

convalescent —*adj.* recovering from an illness. —*n.* convalescent person. □ **convalescence** *n.*

convection /kənˈvekʃ(ə)n/ *n.* heat transfer by upward movement of a heated and less dense medium. [Latin *veho vect-* carry]

convector /kənˈvektə(r)/ *n.* heating appliance that circulates warm air by convection.

convene /kənˈviːn/ *v.* (**-ning**) **1** summon or arrange (a meeting etc.). **2** assemble. [Latin *venio vent-* come]

convener *n.* (also **convenor**) **1** person who convenes a meeting. **2** senior trade union official at a workplace.

convenience /kənˈviːnɪəns/ *n.* **1** state of being convenient; suitability. **2** useful thing. **3** advantage. **4** lavatory, esp. a public one. □ **at one's convenience** at a time or place that suits one. [Latin: related to CONVENE]

convenience food *n.* food requiring little preparation.

convenient *adj.* **1 a** serving one's comfort or interests. **b** suitable. **c** free of trouble or difficulty. **2** available for or occurring at a suitable time or place. **3** well situated (*convenient for the shops*). □ **conveniently** *adv.*

convent /ˈkɒnv(ə)nt/ *n.* **1** religious community, esp. of nuns, under vows. **2** premises occupied by this. [Latin: related to CONVENE]

conventicle /kənˈventɪk(ə)l/ *n.* esp. *hist.* secret or unlawful religious meeting, esp. of dissenters. [Latin: related to CONVENE]

convention /kənˈvenʃ(ə)n/ *n.* **1 a** general agreement on social behaviour etc. by implicit majority consent. **b** custom or customary practice. **2** conference of people with a common interest. **3** formal agreement, esp. between States. [Latin: related to CONVENE]

conventional *adj.* **1** depending on or according with convention. **2** (of a person) bound by social conventions. **3** usual; agreed significance. **4** not spontaneous or sincere or original. **5** (of weapons etc.) non-nuclear. □ **conventionalism** *n.* **conventionality** /ˈnælɪtɪ/ *n.* (*pl.* **-ies**) **conventionally** *adv.*

converge /kənˈvɜːdʒ/ *v.* (**-ging**) **1** come together or towards the same point. **2** (foll. by *on, upon*) approach from different directions. □ **convergence** *n.* **convergent** *adj.* [Latin *vergo* incline]

conversant /kən'vɜːs(ə)nt/ *adj.* (foll. by *with*) well acquainted with. [French: related to CONVERSE¹]

conversation /ˌkɒnvə'seɪʃ(ə)n/ *n.* **1** informal spoken communication. **2** instance of this. [Latin: related to CONVERSE¹]

conversational *adj.* **1** of or in conversation. **2** colloquial. □ **conversationally** *adv.*

conversationalist *n.* person good at or fond of conversation.

converse¹ /kən'vɜːs/ *v.* (-**sing**) (often foll. by *with*) talk. [Latin: related to CONVERT]

converse² /'kɒnvɜːs/ *adj.* opposite, contrary, reversed. —*n.* something, esp. a statement or proposition, that is opposite or reversed. □ **conversely** *adv.* [Latin: related to CONVERT]

conversion /kən'vɜːʃ(ə)n/ *n.* **1** converting or being converted. **2** converted building or part of this. [Latin: related to CONVERT]

convert —*v.* /kən'vɜːt/ **1** (usu. foll. by *into*) change in form or function. **2** cause (a person) to change belief etc. **3** change (moneys etc.) into others of a different kind. **4** make structural alterations in (a building) for a new purpose. **5** (also *absol.*) *Rugby* score extra points from (a try) by a successful kick at the goal. —*n.* /'kɒnvɜːt/ (often foll. by *to*) person converted to a different belief etc. [Latin *verto vers-* turn]

convertible /kən'vɜːtɪb(ə)l/ —*adj.* able to be converted. —*n.* car with a folding or detachable roof. □ **convertibility** /-'bɪlɪtɪ/ *n.* [Latin: related to CONVERT]

convex /'kɒnveks/ *adj.* curved like the exterior of a circle or sphere. □ **convexity** /-'veksɪtɪ/ *n.* [Latin]

convey /kən'veɪ/ *v.* **1** transport or carry (goods, passengers, etc.). **2** communicate (an idea, meaning, etc.). **3** transmit (sound etc.). **4** *Law* transfer the title to (a property). [Latin *via* way]

conveyance *n.* **1** conveying or being conveyed. **2** means of transport; vehicle. **3** *Law* **a** transfer of property. **b** document effecting this. □ **conveyancer** *n.* (in sense 3). □ **conveyancing** *n.* (in sense 3).

conveyor *n.* (also **conveyer**) person or thing that conveys.

conveyor belt *n.* endless moving belt for conveying articles, esp. in a factory.

convict —*v.* /kən'vɪkt/ **1** (often foll. by *of*) prove to be guilty (of a crime etc.). **2** declare guilty by a legal process. —*n.* /'kɒnvɪkt/ chiefly *hist.* person serving a prison sentence. [Latin *vinco vict-* conquer]

conviction /kən'vɪkʃ(ə)n/ *n.* **1** convicting or being convicted. **2 a** being convinced. **b** firm belief. [Latin: related to CONVICT]

convince /kən'vɪns/ *v.* (-**cing**) firmly persuade. □ **convincible** *adj.* **convincing** *adj.* **convincingly** *adv.* [Latin: related to CONVICT]

convivial /kən'vɪvɪəl/ *adj.* fond of good company; sociable and lively. □ **conviviality** /-'ælɪtɪ/ *n.* [Latin *vivo* live]

convocation /ˌkɒnvə'keɪʃ(ə)n/ *n.* **1** convoking or being convoked. **2** large formal gathering. [Latin: related to CONVOKE]

convoke /kən'vəʊk/ *v.* (-**king**) *formal* call together; summon to assemble. [Latin *voco* call]

convoluted /'kɒnvə,luːtɪd/ *adj.* **1** coiled, twisted. **2** complex. [Latin *volvo volut-* roll]

convolution /ˌkɒnvə'luːʃ(ə)n/ *n.* **1** coiling. **2** coil or twist. **3** complexity. **4** sinuous fold in the surface of the brain.

convolvulus /kən'vɒlvjʊləs/ *n.* (*pl.* -**luses**) twining plant, esp. bindweed. [Latin]

convoy /'kɒnvɔɪ/ —*n.* group of ships, vehicles, etc., travelling together or under escort. —*v.* escort, esp. with armed force. □ **in convoy** as a group. [French: related to CONVEY]

convulse /kən'vʌls/ *v.* (-**sing**) **1** (usu. in *passive*) affect with convulsions. **2** cause to laugh uncontrollably. □ **convulsive** *adj.* **convulsively** *adv.* [Latin *vello vuls-* pull]

convulsion /kən'vʌlʃ(ə)n/ *n.* **1** (usu. in *pl.*) violent irregular motion of the limbs or body caused by involuntary contraction of muscles. **2** violent disturbance. **3** (in *pl.*) uncontrollable laughter.

cony /'kəʊnɪ/ *n.* (also **coney**) rabbit fur. [Latin *cuniculus*]

coo —*n.* soft murmuring sound as of a dove. —*v.* (**coos, cooed**) **1** emit a coo. **2** talk or say in a soft or amorous voice. —*int. slang* expressing surprise or disbelief. [imitative]

cooee /'kuːiː/ *n.* & *int. colloq.* call used to attract attention. [imitative]

cook /kʊk/ —*v.* **1** prepare (food) by heating it. **2** (of food) undergo cooking. **3** *colloq.* falsify (accounts etc.). **4** (as **be cooking**) *colloq.* be happening or about to happen. —*n.* person who cooks, esp. professionally or in a specified way (*a good cook*). □ **cook up** *colloq.* concoct (a story, excuse, etc.). [Latin *coquus*]

cookbook *n.* *US* cookery book.

cook-chill *attrib. adj.* (of food, meals, etc.) sold in pre-cooked and refrigerated form.

cooker *n.* 1 appliance or vessel for cooking food. 2 fruit (esp. an apple) suitable for cooking.

cookery *n.* art or practice of cooking.

cookery book *n.* book containing recipes.

cookie /'kuki/ *n. US* 1 sweet biscuit. 2 *colloq.* person (*a tough cookie*). [Dutch *koekje*]

cool —*adj.* 1 of or at a fairly low temperature, fairly cold. 2 suggesting or achieving coolness. 3 calm, unexcited. 4 lacking enthusiasm. 5 unfriendly (*a cool reception*). 6 calmly audacious. 7 (*prec. by a*) *colloq.* at least (*cost a cool thousand*). 8 *slang* esp. *US* marvellous. —*n.* 1 coolness. 2 cool air or place 3 *slang* calmness, composure. —*v.* (often foll. by *down, off*) make or become cool. □ **cool it** *slang* relax, calm down. □ **coolly** /'ku:lli/ *adv.* **coolness** *n.* [Old English]

coolant *n.* cooling agent, esp. fluid.

cool-bag *n.* (also **cool-box**) insulated container for keeping food cool.

cooler *n.* 1 vessel in which a thing is cooled. 2 *US* refrigerator. 3 *slang* prison cell.

coolie /'ku:li/ *n.* unskilled native labourer in Eastern countries. [perhaps from *Kuli*, tribe in India]

cooling-off period *n.* interval to allow for a change of mind.

cooling tower *n.* tall structure for cooling hot water before reuse, esp. in industry.

coomb /ku:m/ *n.* (also **combe**) 1 valley on the side of a hill. 2 short valley running up from the coast. [Old English]

coon *n.* 1 *US* racoon. 2 *slang offens.* Black. [abbreviation]

coop —*n.* cage for keeping poultry. —*v.* (often foll. by *up, in*) confine (a person). [Latin *cupa* cask]

co-op /'kəʊp/ *n. colloq.* cooperative society or shop. [abbreviation]

cooper *n.* maker or repairer of casks, barrels, etc. [Low German or Dutch; related to coop]

cooperate /kəʊ'ɒpəreɪt/ *v.* (also **co-operate**) (**-ting**) 1 (often foll. by *with*) work or act together. 2 be helpful and do as one is asked. □ **cooperation** /-'reɪ(ə)n/ *n.* [related to co-]

cooperative /kəʊ'ɒpərətɪv/ (also **co-operative**) —*adj.* 1 willing to cooperate. 2 of or characterized by cooperation. 3 (of a business) owned and run jointly by its members, with profits shared. —*n.* cooperative farm, society, or business.

co-opt /kəʊ'ɒpt/ *v.* appoint to membership of a body by invitation of the existing members. □ **co-option** *n.* **co-optive** *adj.* [Latin *coopto* from *opto* choose]

coordinate (also **co-ordinate**) —*v.* /kəʊ'ɔ:dɪneɪt/ (**-ting**) 1 cause (parts, movements, etc.) to function together efficiently. 2 work or act together effectively. —*n.* /kəʊ'ɔ:dɪnət/ equal in rank or importance. —*n.* /kəʊ'ɔ:dɪnət/ 1 *Math.* each of a system of values used to fix the position of a point, line, or plane. 2 (in *pl.*) matching items of clothing. □ **coordination** /-'neɪʃ(ə)n/ *n.* **coordinator** /-'neɪtə(r)/ *n.* [Latin *ordino*: related to ORDER]

coot *n.* 1 black aquatic bird with a white horny plate on its forehead. 2 *colloq.* stupid person. [probably Low German]

cop *slang* —*n.* 1 police officer. 2 capture or arrest (*it's a fair cop*). —*v.* (**-pp-**) 1 catch or arrest (an offender). 2 receive, suffer. 3 take, seize. □ **cop it** get into trouble; be punished. **cop out** 1 withdraw; give up 2 go back on a promise or undertaking. **not much cop** of little value or use. [French *caper* seize]

copal /'kəʊp(ə)l/ *n.* resin of a tropical tree, used for varnish. [Spanish from Aztec]

copartner /kəʊ'pɑ:tnə(r)/ *n.* partner or associate. □ **copartnership** *n.*

cope[1] *v.* (**-ping**) (often foll. by *with*) deal effectively or contend; manage. [French: related to coup]

cope[2] —*n.* priest's long cloaklike vestment. —*v.* (**-ping**) cover with a cope or coping. [Latin *cappa* CAP]

copeck /'kəʊpek/ *n.* (also **kopeck, kopek**) Russian coin worth one-hundredth of a rouble. [Russian *kopeika*]

Copernican system /kə'pɜ:nɪkən/ *n.* theory that the planets (including the earth) move round the sun. [*Copernicus*, name of an astronomer]

copier /'kɒpɪə(r)/ *n.* machine that copies (esp. documents).

copilot /'kəʊpaɪlət/ *n.* second pilot in an aircraft.

coping *n.* top (usu. sloping) course of masonry in a wall. [from cope[2]]

coping saw *n.* D-shaped saw for cutting curves in wood. [from cope[2]]

coping-stone *n.* stone used in coping.

copious /'kəʊpɪəs/ *adj.* 1 abundant. 2 producing much. □ **copiously** *adv.* [Latin *copia* plenty]

cop-out *n.* cowardly evasion.

copper[1] —*n.* 1 malleable red-brown metallic element. 2 bronze coin. 3 large metal vessel for boiling esp. laundry. —*adj.* made of or coloured like copper. —*v.* cover with copper. [Latin *cuprum*]

copper[2] *n. slang* police officer. [from

copper beech *n.* variety of beech with copper-coloured leaves.

copper-bottomed *adj.* **1** having a bottom sheathed with copper. **2** genuine or reliable.

copperhead *n.* venomous N. American or Australian snake.

copperplate *n.* **1 a** polished copper plate for engraving or etching. **b** print made from this. **2** ornate style of handwriting.

coppice /ˈkɒpɪs/ *n.* area of undergrowth and small trees. [medieval Latin: related to COUP]

copra /ˈkɒprə/ *n.* dried coconut-kernels. [Portuguese from Malayalam]

copse *n.* = COPPICE. [shortened form]

Copt *n.* **1** native Egyptian in the Hellenistic and Roman periods. **2** native Christian of the independent Egyptian Church. [French from Arabic]

Coptic —*n.* language of the Copts. —*adj.* of the Copts.

copula /ˈkɒpjʊlə/ *n.* (*pl.* **-s**) connecting word, esp. part of the verb *be* connecting subject and predicate. [Latin]

copulate /ˈkɒpjʊleɪt/ *v.* (**-ting**) (often foll. by *with*) (esp. of animals) have sexual intercourse. □ **copulation** /-ˈleɪʃ(ə)n/ *n.*

copy /ˈkɒpɪ/ —*n.* (*pl.* **-ies**) **1** thing made to imitate another. **2** single specimen of a publication or issue. **3** material to be printed, esp. regarded as good etc. reading matter (*the crisis will make exciting copy*). —*v.* (**-ies, -ied**) **1** make a copy of. **2** imitate, do the same as. [Latin *copia* transcript]

copybook *n.* **1** book containing models of handwriting for learners to imitate. **2** (*attrib.*) **a** exemplary. **b** tritely conventional.

copycat *n. colloq.* person who copies another, esp. slavishly.

copyist *n.* person who makes (esp. written) copies.

copyright —*n.* exclusive legal right to print, publish, perform, film, or record material. —*adj.* protected by copyright. —*v.* secure copyright for (material).

copy-typist *n.* typist who types from documents rather than dictation.

copywriter *n.* person who writes or prepares advertising copy for publication.

coq au vin /ˌkɒk əʊ ˈvæ̃/ *n.* casserole of chicken pieces in wine. [French]

coquetry /ˈkɒkɪtrɪ/ *n.* woman who flirts.

coquette /kɒˈket/ *n.* woman who flirts. □ **coquettish** *adj.* [French diminutive: related to COCK¹]

cor *int. slang* expressing surprise etc. [corruption of *God*]

cor- *see* COM-.

coracle /ˈkɒrək(ə)l/ *n.* small boat of wickerwork covered with watertight material. [Welsh]

coral /ˈkɒr(ə)l/ —*n.* hard red, pink, or white calcareous substance secreted by marine polyps for support and habitation. —*adj.* **1** red or pink, like coral. **2** made of coral. [Greek *korallion*]

coral island *n.* (also **coral reef**) island (or reef) formed by the growth of coral.

coralline /ˈkɒrəlaɪn/ —*n.* seaweed with a hard jointed stem. —*adj.* of or like coral. [French and Italian: related to CORAL]

cor anglais /kɔːr ˈɒŋgleɪ/ *n.* (*pl.* **cors anglais** /kɔːz/) alto woodwind instrument of the oboe family. [French]

corbel /ˈkɔːb(ə)l/ *n.* projection of stone, timber, etc., jutting out from a wall to support a weight. □ **corbelle¹** *adj.*

cord —*n.* **1 a** flexible material like thick string, made from twisted strands. **b** piece of this. **2** similar structure in the body. **3 a** ribbed fabric. **b** corduroy. **b** (in *pl.*) corduroy trousers. **4** electric flex. —*v.* **1** fasten or bind with cord. **2** (as **corded** *adj.*) (of cloth) ribbed. [Greek *khordē* string]

cordial /ˈkɔːdɪəl/ —*adj.* **1** heartfelt. **2** friendly. —*n.* fruit-flavoured drink. □ **cordiality** /-ˈælɪtɪ/ *n.* **cordially** *adv.* [Latin *cor cord-* heart]

cordite /ˈkɔːdaɪt/ *n.* smokeless explosive. [from CORD, because of its appearance]

cordless *adj.* (of a hand-held electrical device) usable without a power cable because working from an internal source of energy or battery.

cordon /ˈkɔːd(ə)n/ —*n.* **1** line or circle of police, soldiers, guards, etc., esp. preventing access. **2** ornamental cord or braid. **3** fruit-tree trained to grow as a single stem. —*v.* (often foll. by *off*) enclose or separate with a cordon of police etc. [Italian and French: related to CORD]

cordon bleu /ˌkɔːdɒ̃ ˈblɜː/ *Cookery* —*adj.* of the highest class. —*n.* cook of this class. [French]

cordon sanitaire /ˌkɔːdɒ̃ ˌsænɪˈteə(r)/ *n.* **1** guarded line between infected and uninfected districts. **2** measure designed to prevent the spread of undesirable influences.

corduroy /ˈkɔːdərɔɪ/ *n.* **1** thick cotton fabric with velvety ribs. **2** (in *pl.*) corduroy trousers. [*cord* = ribbed fabric]

core —*n.* **1** horny central part of certain fruits, containing the seeds. **2** central or most important part of anything (also *attrib.: core curriculum*). **3** inner central region of the earth. **4** part of a

nuclear reactor containing fissile material. **5** *hist.* structural unit in a computer, storing one bit of data (see bit*). **6** inner strand of an electric cable. **7** piece of soft iron forming the centre of an electromagnet or induction coil. —*v.* (-ring) remove the core from. [origin unknown]

co-respondent /ˈkəʊrɪˈspɒnd(ə)nt/ *n.* person cited in a divorce case as having committed adultery with the respondent.

corgi /ˈkɔːgɪ/ *n.* (*pl.* **-s**) dog of a short-legged breed with a foxlike head. [Welsh]

coriander /ˌkɒrɪˈændə(r)/ *n.* **1** aromatic plant. **2** its seeds used for flavouring. [Greek *koriannon*]

Corinthian /kəˈrɪnθɪən/ *adj.* **1** of ancient Corinth in southern Greece. **2** *Archit.* of the order characterized by ornate decoration and acanthus leaves. [Latin from Greek]

cork —*n.* **1** buoyant light-brown bark of a S. European oak. **2** bottle-stopper of cork etc. **3** float of cork. **4** (*attrib.*) made of cork. —*v.* (often foll. by *up*) **1** stop or confine. **2** restrain (feelings etc.). [Spanish *alcorque*]

corked *adj.* **1** stopped with a cork. **2** (of wine) spoilt by a decayed cork.

corker *n. slang* excellent person or thing.

corkscrew —*n.* **1** spiral device for extracting corks from bottles. **2** (often *attrib.*) thing with a spiral shape. —*v.* move spirally; twist.

corm *n.* underground swollen stem base of some plants. [Greek *kormos* lopped tree-trunk]

cormorant /ˈkɔːmərənt/ *n.* diving sea bird with black plumage. [Latin *corvus marinus* sea-raven]

corn¹ *n.* **1 a** cereal before or after harvesting, esp. the chief crop of a region. **b** grain or seed of a cereal plant. **2** *colloq.* something corny or trite. [Old English]

corn² *n.* small tender area of horny skin, esp. on the toe. [Latin *cornu* horn]

corn-cob *n.* cylindrical centre of a maize ear on which the grains grow.

corncrake *n.* rail inhabiting grassland and nesting on the ground.

corn dolly *n.* figure of plaited straw.

cornea /ˈkɔːnɪə/ *n.* transparent circular part of the front of the eyeball. □ **corneal** *adj.* [medieval Latin: related to CORN²]

corned *adj.* (esp. of beef) preserved in salt or brine. [from CORN¹]

cornelian /kɔːˈniːliən/ *n.* (also **carnelian** /kɑːˈ/) dull red variety of chalcedony. [French]

corner —*n.* **1** place where converging sides or edges meet. **2** projecting angle, esp. where two streets meet. **3** internal space or recess formed by the meeting of two sides, esp. of a room. **4** difficult position, esp. one with no escape. **5** secluded place. **6** region or quarter, esp. a remote one. **7** action or result of buying or controlling the whole stock of a commodity. **8** *Boxing & Wrestling* corner of the ring where a contestant rests between rounds. **9** *Football & Hockey* free kick or hit from the corner of a pitch. —*v.* **1** force into a difficult or inescapable position. **2** establish a corner in (a commodity). **3** (esp. of or in a vehicle) go round a corner. [Latin: related to CORN²]

cornerstone *n.* **1 a** stone in the projecting angle of a wall. **b** foundation-stone. **2** indispensable part or basis.

cornet /ˈkɔːnɪt/ *n.* **1** brass instrument resembling a trumpet but shorter and wider. **2** conical wafer for holding ice-cream. □ **cornettist** /kɔːˈnetɪst/ *n.* (also **cornetist**). [Latin *cornu*: related to CORN²]

cornflake *n.* **1** (in *pl.*) breakfast cereal of toasted maize flakes. **2** flake of this cereal.

cornflour *n.* fine-ground flour, esp. of maize or rice.

cornflower *n.* plant with deep-blue flowers originally growing among corn.

cornice /ˈkɔːnɪs/ *n.* ornamental moulding, esp. round a room just below the ceiling or as the topmost part of an entablature. [French from Italian]

Cornish /ˈkɔːnɪʃ/ —*adj.* of Cornwall. —*n.* Celtic language of Cornwall.

Cornish pasty *n.* pastry envelope containing meat and vegetables.

corn on the cob *n.* maize cooked and eaten from the corn-cob.

cornucopia /ˌkɔːnjʊˈkəʊpɪə/ *n.* **1** horn overflowing with flowers, fruit, and corn, as a symbol of plenty. **2** abundant supply. [Latin: related to CORN², COPI-OUS]

corny *adj.* (-ier, -iest) *colloq.* **1** banal. **2** feebly humorous. **3** sentimental. □ **cornily** *adv.* **corniness** *n.* [from CORN¹]

corolla /kəˈrɒlə/ *n.* whorl of petals forming the inner envelope of a flower. [Latin diminutive of CORONA]

corollary /kəˈrɒlərɪ/ *n.* (*pl.* **-ies**) **1** proposition that follows from one already proved. **2** (often foll. by *of*) natural consequence. [Latin, = gratuity: related to COROLLA]

corona /kəˈrəʊnə/ n. (pl. **-nae** /-niː/) **1 a** halo round the sun or moon. **b** gaseous envelope of the sun, seen as an area of light around the moon during a total solar eclipse. **2** *Anat.* crownlike structure. **3** crownlike outgrowth from the inner side of a corolla. **4** glow around an electric conductor. □ **coronal** *adj.* [Latin, = crown]

coronary /ˈkɒrənərɪ/ —*adj.* *Anat.* resembling or encircling like a crown. —*n.* (pl. **-ies**) = CORONARY THROMBOSIS. [Latin: related to CORONA]

coronary artery n. artery supplying blood to the heart.

coronary thrombosis n. blockage caused by a blood clot in a coronary artery.

coronation /ˌkɒrəˈneɪʃ(ə)n/ n. ceremony of crowning a sovereign or consort. [medieval Latin: related to CORONA]

coroner /ˈkɒrənə(r)/ n. official holding inquests on deaths thought to be violent or accidental [Anglo-French: related to CROWN]

coronet /ˈkɒrənɪt/ n. **1** small crown. **2** circlet of precious materials, esp. as a headdress. [French diminutive: related to CROWN]

corpora pl. of CORPUS.

corporal[1] /ˈkɔːpər(ə)l/ n. non-commissioned army or air-force officer ranking next below sergeant. [French from Italian]

corporal[2] /ˈkɔːpər(ə)l/ adj. of the human body. □ **corporality** /-ˈrælɪtɪ/ n. [Latin *corpus* body]

corporal punishment n. physical punishment.

corporate /ˈkɔːpərət/ adj. **1** forming a corporation. **2** of, belonging to, or united in a group. [Latin: related to CORPORAL[2]]

corporation /ˌkɔːpəˈreɪʃ(ə)n/ n. **1** group of people authorized to act as an individual, esp. in business. **2** municipal authorities of a borough, town, or city. **3** *joc.* large stomach.

corporeal /kɔːˈpɔːrɪəl/ adj. bodily, physical, material. □ **corporeality** /-ˈælɪtɪ/ n. **corporeally** adv. [Latin: related to CORPORAL[2]]

corps /kɔː(r)/ n. (pl. **corps** /kɔːz/) **1 a** body of troops with special duties (*intelligence corps*). **b** main subdivision of an army in the field. **2** body of people engaged in a special activity (*diplomatic corps*). [French: related to CORPSE]

corps de ballet /ˌkɔː də ˈbæleɪ/ n. group of ensemble dancers in a ballet. [French]

corpse n. dead body. [Latin: related to CORPUS]

corpulent /ˈkɔːpjʊlənt/ adj. physically bulky; fat. □ **corpulence** n. [Latin: related to CORPUS]

corpus /ˈkɔːpəs/ n. (pl. **-pora**) body or collection of writings, texts, etc. [Latin, = body]

corpuscle /ˈkɔːpʌs(ə)l/ n. minute body or cell in an organism, esp. (in pl.) the red or white cells in the blood of vertebrates. □ **corpuscular** /-ˈpʌskjʊlə(r)/ adj. [Latin diminutive of CORPUS]

corral /kəˈrɑːl/ —n. **1** *US* pen for cattle, horses, etc. **2** enclosure for capturing wild animals. —v. (**-ll-**) put or keep in a corral. [Spanish and Portuguese: related to KRAAL]

correct /kəˈrekt/ —adj. **1** true, accurate. **2** proper, in accordance with taste or a standard. —v. **1** set right; amend. **2** mark errors in. **3** substitute a right thing for (a wrong one). **4 a** admonish (a person). **b** punish (a person or fault). **5** counteract (a harmful quality). **6** adjust (an instrument etc.). □ **correctly** adv. **correctness** n. **corrector** n. [Latin *rego rect-* guide]

correction /kəˈrekʃ(ə)n/ n. **1** correcting or being corrected. **2** thing substituted for what is wrong. **3** *archaic* punishment. □ **correctional** adj. [Latin: related to CORRECT]

correctitude /kəˈrektɪtjuːd/ n. consciously correct behaviour. [from CORRECT, RECTITUDE]

corrective /kəˈrektɪv/ —adj. serving to correct or counteract something harmful. —n. corrective measure or thing. [Latin: related to CORRECT]

correlate /ˈkɒrəleɪt/ —v. (**-ting**) (usu. foll. by *with, to*) have or bring into a mutual relation or dependence. —n. correlative. **2** (of words) corresponding to each other and used together (as *neither* and *nor*). —n. correlative word or thing. □ **correlation** /-ˈleɪʃ(ə)n/ n. [medieval Latin *correlatio*]

correlative /kəˈrelətɪv/ —adj. **1** (often foll. by *with, to*) having a mutual relation. **2** (of words) corresponding to each other and used together (as *neither* and *nor*). —n. correlative word or thing. [Latin: related to CORRELATE]

correspond /ˌkɒrɪˈspɒnd/ v. **1 a** (usu. foll. by *to*) be similar or equivalent. **b** (usu. foll. by *with, to*) be in agreement, not contradict. **2** (usu. foll. by *with*) exchange letters. □ **correspondingly** adv. [French from medieval Latin]

correspondence n. **1** agreement or similarity. **2 a** exchange of letters. **b** letters.

correspondence course *n.* course of study conducted by post.

correspondent *n.* 1 person who writes letters. 2 person employed to write or report for a newspaper or for broadcasting etc.

corridor /ˈkɒrɪdɔː(r)/ *n.* 1 passage giving access into rooms. 2 passage in a train giving access into compartments. 3 strip of territory of one State passing through that of another. 4 route which an aircraft must follow, esp. over a foreign country. [French from Italian]

corridors of power *n. pl.* places where covert influence is said to be exerted in government.

corrigendum /ˌkɒrɪˈgendəm/ *n. (pl.* **-da**) error to be corrected. [Latin]

corrigible /ˈkɒrɪdʒɪb(ə)l/ *adj.* 1 able to be corrected. 2 submissive. □ **corrigibly** *adv.* medieval Latin: related to CORRIGENDUM]

corroborate /kəˈrɒbəreɪt/ *v.* **(-ting)** confirm or give support to (a statement or belief etc.). □ **corroboration** /-ˈreɪʃ(ə)n/ *n.* **corroborative** /-rətɪv/ *adj.* **corroborator** *n.* [Latin *robur* strength]

corrode /kəˈrəʊd/ *v.* **(-ding) 1 a** wear away, esp. by chemical action. **b** decay. **2** destroy gradually. [Latin *rodo ros-* gnaw]

corrosion /kəˈrəʊʒ(ə)n/ *n.* 1 corroding or being corroded. 2 corroded area.

corrosive /kəˈrəʊsɪv/ *adj. & n.*

corrugate /ˈkɒrʊgeɪt/ *v.* **(-ting)** (esp. as **corrugated** *adj.*) form into alternate ridges and grooves, esp. to strengthen. □ **corrugation** /-ˈgeɪʃ(ə)n/ *n.* [Latin *ruga* wrinkle]

corrupt /kəˈrʌpt/ *adj.* 1 dishonest, esp. using bribery. 2 immoral, wicked. 3 (of a text etc.) made unreliable by errors or alterations. —*v.* make or become corrupt. □ **corruptible** *adj.* **corruptibility** /-ˈbɪlɪ/ *n.* **corruption** *n.* **corruptive** *adj.* **corruptly** *adv.* **corruptness** *n.* [Latin *rumpo rupt-* break]

corsage /kɔːˈsɑːʒ/ *n.* small bouquet worn by women. [French: related to CORSE]

corsair /ˈkɔːseə(r)/ *n.* 1 pirate ship. 2 pirate. [French: related to COURSE]

corselet /ˈkɔːslɪt/ *n.* combined corset and bra. [French *corslet* armour covering trunk]

corset /ˈkɔːsɪt/ *n.* closely-fitting undergarment worn to shape the body or to support it after injury. □ **corsetry** *n.* [French diminutive: related to CORSE]

cortège /kɔːˈteʒ/ *n.* procession, esp. for a funeral. [French]

cortex /ˈkɔːteks/ *n. (pl.* **-tices** /-tɪsiːz/) outer part of an organ, esp. of the brain or kidneys. □ **cortical** /-tɪk(ə)l/ *adj.* [Latin, = bark]

cortisone /ˈkɔːtɪzəʊn/ *n.* hormone used esp. in treating inflammation and allergy. [abbreviation of chemical name]

corundum /kəˈrʌndəm/ *n.* extremely hard crystallized alumina, used esp. as an abrasive. [Tamil from Sanskrit]

coruscate /ˈkɒrəskeɪt/ *v.* **(-ting)** sparkle. □ **coruscation** /-ˈskeɪʃ(ə)n/ *n.* [Latin]

corvette /kɔːˈvet/ *n.* 1 small naval escort-vessel. 2 hist. warship with one tier of guns. [French from Dutch]

corymb /ˈkɒrɪmb/ *n.* flat-topped cluster of flowers with the outer flower-stalks proportionally longer. [Latin from Greek]

cos[1] *n.* lettuce with crisp narrow leaves. [*Kos*, Greek island]

cos[2] /kɒz/ *abbr.* cosine.

cos[3] /kɒz/ *conj. & adv.* because. [abbreviation]

cosec /ˈkəʊsek/ *abbr.* cosecant.

cosecant /kəʊˈsiːkənt/ *n. Math.* ratio of the hypotenuse (in a right-angled triangle) to the side opposite an acute angle.

cosh[1] *colloq.* —*n.* heavy blunt weapon. —*v.* hit with a cosh. [origin unknown]

cosh[2] /kɒʃ, kɒsˈeɪtʃ/ *abbr.* hyperbolic cosine.

co-signatory /kəʊˈsɪgnətərɪ/ *n. (pl.* **-ies**) person or State signing a treaty etc. jointly with others.

cosine /ˈkəʊsaɪn/ *n.* ratio of the side adjacent to an acute angle (in a right-angled triangle) to the hypotenuse.

cosmetic /kɒzˈmetɪk/ —*adj.* 1 beautifying, enhancing. 2 superficially improving or beneficial. 3 (of surgery or a prosthesis) imitating, restoring, or enhancing normal appearance. —*n.* cosmetic preparation, esp. for the face. □ **cosmetically** *adv.* [Greek, = order]

cosmic /ˈkɒzmɪk/ *adj.* 1 of the cosmos or its scale; universal (*of cosmic significance*). 2 of or for space travel.

cosmic rays *n. pl.* high-energy radiations from space etc.

cosmogony /kɒzˈmɒgənɪ/ *n. (pl.* **-ies)** origin of the universe. 2 theory about this. [Greek *-gonia* -begetting]

cosmology /kɒzˈmɒlədʒɪ/ *n.* science or theory of the universe. □ **cosmological** /-məˈlɒdʒɪk(ə)l/ *adj.* **cosmologist** *n.* [from COSMOS, -LOGY]

cosmonaut /ˈkɒzmənɔːt/ *n.* Soviet astronaut. [from COSMOS, Greek *nautēs* sailor]

cosmopolitan /ˌkʌzmə'pɒlɪt(ə)n/ —*adj.* **1** of, from, or knowing many parts of the world. **2** free from national limitations or prejudices. —*n.* cosmopolitan person. □ **cosmopolitanism** *n.* [Greek *politēs* citizen]

cosmos /'kɒzmɒs/ *n.* the universe as a well-ordered whole. [Greek]

Cossack /'kɒsæk/ *n.* member of a people of southern Russia. [Turki *quzzāq*]

cosset /'kɒsɪt/ *v.* (-t-) pamper. [dialect *cosset* = pet lamb, probably from Old English, = cottager]

cost —*v.* (*past* and *past part.* **cost**) **1** be obtainable for (a sum of money); have as a price. **2** involve as a loss or sacrifice (*it cost him his life*). **3** (*past* and *past part.* **costed**) fix or estimate the cost of. —*n.* **1** what a thing costs; price. **2** loss or sacrifice. **3** (in *pl.*) legal expenses. □ **at all costs** (or **at any cost**) whatever the cost or risk may be. [Latin *consto* stand at a price]

costal /'kɒst(ə)l/ *adj.* of the ribs. [Latin *costa* rib]

cost-effective *adj.* effective in relation to its cost.

costermonger /'kɒstə,mʌŋgə(r)/ *n.* person who sells produce from a barrow. [*costard* large apple: related to COSTAL]

costing *n.* estimation of cost(s).

costive /'kɒstɪv/ *adj.* constipated. [Latin: related to CONSTIPATE]

costly *adj.* (-ier, -iest) costing much; expensive. □ **costliness** *n.*

cost of living *n.* level of prices esp. of basic necessities.

cost price *n.* price paid for a thing by one who later sells it.

costume /'kɒstjuːm/ —*n.* **1** style of dress, esp. of a particular place or time. **2** set of clothes. **3** clothing for a particular activity (*swimming-costume*). **4** actor's clothes for a part. —*v.* (-ming) provide with a costume. [Latin: related to CUSTOM]

costume jewellery *n.* artificial jewellery.

costumier /kɒ'stjuːmɪə(r)/ *n.* person who makes or deals in costumes. [French: related to COSTUME]

cosy /'kəʊzɪ/ (*US* **cozy**) —*adj.* (-ier, -iest) comfortable and warm; snug. —*n.* (*pl.* -ies) cover to keep a teapot etc. hot. □ **cosily** *adv.* **cosiness** *n.* [origin unknown]

cot¹ *n.* **1** small bed with high sides for a baby. **2** small light bed. [Hindi]

cot² *n.* **1** small shelter; cote. **2** *poet.* cottage. [Old English]

cot³ *abbr.* cotangent.

cotangent /kəʊ'tænʤ(ə)nt/ *n.* ratio of the side adjacent to an acute angle (in a right-angled triangle) to the opposite side.

cot-death *n.* unexplained death of a sleeping baby.

cote *n.* shelter for animals or birds. [Old English]

coterie /'kəʊtərɪ/ *n.* exclusive group of people sharing interests. [French]

cotoneaster /kə,təʊnɪ'æstə(r)/ *n.* shrub bearing usu. bright red berries. [Latin *cotoneum* QUINCE]

cottage /'kɒtɪʤ/ *n.* small simple house, esp. in the country. [Anglo-French: related to cot³]

cottage cheese *n.* soft white lumpy cheese made from skimmed milk curds.

cottage industry *n.* business activity carried on at home.

cottage pie *n.* dish of minced meat topped with mashed potato.

cottager *n.* person who lives in a cottage.

cotter *n.* **1** bolt or wedge for securing parts of machinery etc. **2** (in full **cotter pin**) split pin that can be opened after passing through a hole. [origin unknown]

cotton /'kɒt(ə)n/ *n.* **1** soft white fibrous substance covering the seeds of certain plants. **2** such a plant. **3** thread or cloth from this. □ **cotton on** (often foll. by *to*) *colloq.* begin to understand. [French from Arabic]

cotton wool *n.* fluffy wadding of a kind orig. made from raw cotton.

cotyledon /,kɒtɪ'liːd(ə)n/ *n.* embryonic leaf in seed-bearing plants. [Greek *kotulē* cup]

couch¹ —*n.* **1** upholstered piece of furniture for several people; sofa. **2** long padded seat with a headrest at one end. —*v.* **1** (foll. by *in*) express in (certain terms). **2** *archaic* (of an animal) lie, esp. in its lair. [Latin *colloco* lay in place]

couch² /kaʊʧ, kuːʧ/ *n.* (in full **couch grass**) a grass with long creeping roots. [var. of QUITCH]

couchette /kuː'ʃet/ *n.* **1** railway carriage with seats convertible into sleeping-berths. **2** berth in this. [French, = little bed]

couch potato *n.* *US slang* person who likes lazing at home.

cougar /'kuːgə(r)/ *n.* *US* puma. [French from Guarani]

cough /kɒf/ —*v.* **1** expel air etc. from the lungs with a sudden sharp sound. **2** (of an engine etc.) make a similar sound. **3** *slang* confess. —*n.* **1** act of coughing. **2** condition of respiratory organs causing coughing. □ **cough up 1** eject with coughs. **2** *slang* bring out or give (money or information) reluctantly. [imitative, related to Dutch *kuchen*]

cough mixture n. liquid medicine to relieve a cough.

could past of CAN¹. v. colloq. feel inclined to (*I could murder him*).

couldn't /ˈkʊd(ə)nt/ contr. could not.

coulomb /ˈkuːlɒm/ n. SI unit of electric charge. [*Coulomb*, name of a physicist]

coulter /ˈkəʊltə(r)/ n. (US **colter**) vertical blade in front of a ploughshare. [Latin *culter* knife]

council /ˈkaʊns(ə)l/ n. 1 a advisory, deliberative, or administrative body. b meeting of such a body. 2 a local administrative body of a parish, district, town, etc. b (*attrib.*) provided by a local council (*council flat*). [Latin *concilium*]

councillor n. member of a (esp. local) council.

council tax n. proposed new local tax based on the value of a property and the number of people living in it, to replace the community charge.

counsel /ˈkaʊns(ə)l/ —n. 1 advice, esp. formally given. 2 consultation for advice. 3 (*pl.* same) legal adviser, esp. a barrister; body of these. —v. (**-ll-**; US **-l-**) 1 advise (a person). 2 give esp. professional advice to (a person) on personal problems. 3 recommend (a course of action). □ **keep one's own counsel** not confide in others. **take counsel** (usu. foll. by *with*) consult. □ **counselling** n. [Latin *consilium*]

counsellor n. (US **counselor**) 1 adviser. 2 person giving professional guidance on personal problems. 3 US barrister.

counsel of perfection n. ideal but impracticable advice.

count¹ —v. 1 determine the total number of, esp. by assigning successive numbers. 2 repeat numbers in ascending order. 3 (often foll. by *in*) include or be included in one's reckoning or plan. 4 consider or regard to be (*lucky etc.*). 5 (often foll. by *for*) have value; matter (*my opinion counts for little*). —n. 1 a counting or being counted. b total of a reckoning. 2 *Law* each charge in an indictment. □ **count against** be reckoned to the disadvantage of. **count one's blessings** be grateful for what one has. **count on** (or *upon*) rely on; expect. **count out 1** count while taking from a stock. 2 complete a count of ten seconds over (a fallen boxer etc.). 3 *colloq.* exclude, disregard. 4 *Polit.* adjourn (the House of Commons) when fewer than 40 members are present. **count up** find the sum of. **keep count** take note of or how many there have been etc. **lose count** forget the number etc. counted. **out for the**

count 1 defeated. 2 unconscious; asleep. [Latin: related to COMPUTE]

count² n. foreign noble corresponding to an earl. [Latin *comes* companion]

countable *adj.* 1 that can be counted. 2 *Gram.* (of a noun) that can form a plural or be used with the indefinite article.

countdown n. 1 act of counting backwards to zero, esp. at the launching of a rocket etc. 2 period immediately before an event.

countenance /ˈkaʊntɪnəns/ —n. 1 the face or facial expression. 2 composure. 3 moral support. —v. (**-cing**) support, approve. [French: related to CONTAIN]

counter¹ n. 1 long flat-topped fitment in a shop etc., across which business is conducted. 2 a small disc for playing or scoring in board-games etc. b token representing a coin. 3 apparatus for counting. □ **under the counter** surreptitiously, esp. illegally. [related to COUNT¹]

counter² —v. 1 a oppose, contradict. b meet by countermove. 2 *Boxing* give a return blow while parrying. —*adv.* in the opposite direction or manner. —*adj.* opposite. —n. parry; countermove. [related to COUNTER³]

counter- *comb. form* denoting: 1 retaliation, opposition, or rivalry (*counter-threat*). 2 opposite direction (*counter-clockwise*). 3 correspondence (*counterpart*; *countersign*). [Latin *contra* against]

counteract /kaʊntəˈrækt/ v. hinder or neutralize by contrary action. □ **counteraction** n. **counteractive** *adj.*

counter-attack —n. attack in reply to a preceding attack. —v. attack in reply.

counterbalance —n. weight or influence balancing another. —v. (**-cing**) act as a counterbalance to.

counter-clockwise /ˌkaʊntəˈklɒkwaɪz/ *adv.* & *adj.* US = ANTI-CLOCKWISE.

counter-espionage /ˌkaʊntərˈespɪənɑːʒ/ n. action taken against enemy spying.

counterfeit /ˈkaʊntəfɪt/ —*adj.* made in imitation; not genuine; forged. —n. a forgery or imitation. —v. imitate fraudulently; forge. [French]

counterfoil n. part of a cheque, receipt, etc. retained by the payer as a record.

counter-intelligence /ˌkaʊntərɪnˈtelɪdʒ(ə)ns/ n. = COUNTER-ESPIONAGE.

countermand /ˌkaʊntəˈmɑːnd/ —v. 1 revoke (a command). 2 recall by a contrary order. —n. order revoking a previous one. [Latin: related to MANDATE]

countermeasure n. action taken to counteract a danger, threat, etc.

countermove n. move or action in opposition to another.

counterpane /ˈkaʊntəˌpeɪn/ n. bedspread. [medieval Latin *culcita puncta* quilted mattress]

counterpart n. 1 person or thing like another or forming the complement or equivalent to another. 2 duplicate.

counterpoint /ˈkaʊntəˌpɔɪnt/ n. 1 a art or practice of combining melodies according to fixed rules. b melody combined with another. 2 contrasting argument, plot, literary theme, etc. [medieval Latin *contrapunctum* marked opposite]

counterpoise /ˈkaʊntəˌpɔɪz/ —n. 1 counterbalance. 2 state of equilibrium. —v. (-sing) counterbalance. [Latin *pensum* weight]

counter-productive /ˈdʌktɪv/ adj. having the opposite of the desired effect.

counter-revolution /ˌkaʊntəˌrevə ˈluːʃ(ə)n/ n. revolution opposing a former one or reversing its results.

countersign —v. add a signature to (a document already signed by another). —n. 1 password spoken to a person on guard. 2 mark used for identification etc. [Latin: related to SIGN]

countersink v. (*past* and *past part.* -sunk) 1 shape (the rim of a hole) so that a screw or bolt can be inserted flush with the surface. 2 sink (a screw etc.) in such a hole.

counter-tenor n. 1 male alto singing-voice. 2 singer with this voice. [Italian: related to CONTRA-]

countervail /ˈkaʊntəˌveɪl/ v. *literary* (often foll. by *against*) oppose, usu. successfully. [Latin *valeo* have worth]

counterweight n. counterbalancing weight.

countess /ˈkaʊntɪs/ n. 1 wife or widow of a count or earl. 2 woman holding the rank of count or earl. [Latin *comitissa*: related to COUNT²]

countless adj. too many to be counted.

countrified /ˈkʌntrɪˌfaɪd/ adj. rustic in manner or appearance.

country /ˈkʌntrɪ/ n. (pl. -ies) 1 territory of a nation; State. 2 (often *attrib.*) rural districts as opposed to towns or the capital. 3 land of a person's birth or citizenship. 4 region with regard to its aspect, associations, etc. (*mountainous country*; *Hardy country*). 5 national population, esp. as voters. [medieval Latin *contrata* (terra) (land) lying opposite]

country-and-western n. type of folk music originated by Whites in the southern US.

country club n. sporting and social club in a rural setting.

country dance n. traditional dance, esp. English, usu. with couples facing each other in lines.

countryman n. (*fem.* **countrywoman**) 1 person living in a rural area. 2 (also **fellow-countryman**) person of one's own country.

country music n. = COUNTRY-AND-WESTERN.

countryside n. rural areas.

country-wide adj. & adv. extending throughout a nation.

county /ˈkaʊntɪ/ —n. (pl. -ies) 1 territorial division in some countries, forming the chief unit of local administration. 2 US political and administrative division of a State. —adj. of or like the gentry. [Latin *comitatus*: related to COUNT²]

county council n. elected governing body of an administrative county.

county court n. judicial court for civil cases.

county town n. administrative capital of a county.

coup /kuː/ n. (pl. -s /kuːz/) 1 successful stroke or move. 2 = COUP D'ÉTAT. [medieval Latin *colpus* blow]

coup de grâce /ˌkuː də ˈgrɑːs/ n. finishing stroke. [French]

coup d'état /ˌkuː deɪˈtɑː/ n. (pl. *coups d'état* pronunc. same) violent or illegal seizure of power. [French]

coupé /ˈkuːpeɪ/ n. (US **coupe** /kuːp/) car with a hard roof, two doors, and usu. a sloping rear. [French *couper* cut]

couple /ˈkʌp(ə)l/ —n. 1 a two (*a couple of girls*). b about two (*a couple of hours*). 2 a two people who are married to, or in a sexual relationship with, each other. b pair of partners in a dance etc. —v. (-ling) 1 link together. 2 associate in thought or speech. 3 copulate. [Latin COPULA]

couplet /ˈkʌplɪt/ n. two successive lines of verse, usu. rhyming and of the same length. [French diminutive: related to COUPLE]

coupling /ˈkʌplɪŋ/ n. 1 link connecting railway carriages etc. 2 device for connecting parts of machinery.

coupon /ˈkuːpɒn/ n. 1 form etc. as an application for a purchase etc. 2 entry form for a football pool or other competition. 3 discount voucher given with a purchase. [French *couper* cut]

courage /ˈkʌrɪdʒ/ n. ability to disregard fear; bravery. □ **courage of one's convictions** courage to act on one's beliefs. [Latin *cor* heart]

courageous /kəˈreɪdʒəs/ adj. brave. □ **courageously** adv.

courgette /kʊəˈʒet/ n. small vegetable marrow. [French]

courier /ˈkʊərɪə(r)/ n. 1 person employed to guide and assist tourists. 2 special messenger. [Latin *curro curs-* run]

course /kɔːs/ —n. 1 onward movement or progression. 2 direction taken (*changed course*). 3 stretch of land or water for races; golf-course. 4 series of lessons etc. in a particular subject. 5 each successive part of a meal. 6 sequence of medical treatment etc. 7 line of conduct. 8 continuous horizontal layer of masonry, brick, etc. 9 channel in which water flows. —v. (-**sing**) 1 (esp. of liquid) run, esp. fast. 2 (also *absol.*) use hounds to hunt (esp. hares). □ **in course of** during. **of course** naturally; as is or was to be expected; admittedly. [Latin *cursus*: related to COURIER]

courser n. *poet.* swift horse.

court /kɔːt/ —n. 1 (in full **court of law**) a judicial body hearing legal cases. b = COURTROOM. 2 quadrangular area for games (*tennis-court*; *squash-court*). 3 a yard surrounded by masonry, brick, etc. b = COURTYARD. 4 a the residence, retinue, and courtiers of a sovereign. b sovereign and councillors, constituting the ruling power. c assembly held by a sovereign; State reception. 5 attention paid to a person whose favour etc. is sought (*paid court to her*). —v. 1 a try to win affection or favour of. b pay amorous attention to. 2 seek to win (applause, fame, etc.). 3 invite (misfortune) by one's actions. □ **go to court** take legal action. **out of court 1** without reaching trial. **2** not worthy of consideration. [Latin: related to COHORT]

court-card n. playing-card that is a king, queen, or jack.

courteous /ˈkɜːtɪəs/ adj. polite, considerate. □ **courteously** adv. **courteousness** n. [French related to COURT]

courtesan /ˌkɔːtɪˈzæn/ n. prostitute, esp. one with wealthy or upper-class clients. [Italian: related to COURT]

courtesy /ˈkɜːtəsɪ/ n. (pl. -**ies**) courteous behaviour or act. □ **by courtesy of** with the formal permission of. [French: related to COURTEOUS]

courtesy light n. light in a car switched on by opening a door.

court-house n. 1 building in which a judicial court is held. 2 US building containing the administrative offices of a county.

courtier /ˈkɔːtɪə(r)/ n. person who attends a sovereign's court. [Anglo-French: related to COURT]

courtly adj. (-**ier**, -**iest**) dignified, refined. □ **courtliness** n.

---

court martial /kɔːt ˈmɑːʃ(ə)l/ —n. (pl. **courts martial**) judicial court trying members of the armed services. —v. (**court-martial**) (-**ll**-; US -**l**-) try by this.

court order n. direction issued by a court or judge.

courtroom n. room in which a court of law meets.

courtship n. 1 courting, wooing. 2 courting behaviour of animals, birds, etc.

court shoe n. woman's light, high-heeled, shoe with a low-cut upper.

courtyard n. area enclosed by walls or buildings.

couscous /ˈkuːskuːs/ n. N. African dish of crushed wheat or coarse flour steamed over broth, often with meat or fruit added. [French from Arabic]

cousin /ˈkʌz(ə)n/ n. 1 (also **first cousin**) child of one's uncle or aunt. 2 person of a kindred race or nation. [Latin *consobrinus*]

□ **Usage** There is often some confusion as to the difference between *cousin*, *first cousin*, *second cousin*, *first cousin once removed*, etc. For definitions see *cousin*, *second cousin* and *remove* v. 5.

couture /kuːˈtjʊə(r)/ n. design and manufacture of fashionable clothes. [French]

couturier /kuːˈtjʊərɪeɪ/ n. fashion designer.

cove[1] —n. 1 small bay or creek. 2 sheltered recess. 3 moulding, esp. at the junction of a wall and a ceiling. —v. (-**ving**) 1 provide (a room etc.) with a cove. 2 slope (the sides of a fireplace) inwards. [Old English]

cove[2] n. *slang* fellow, chap. [cant: origin unknown]

coven /ˈkʌv(ə)n/ n. assembly of witches. [related to CONVENT]

covenant /ˈkʌvənənt/ —n. 1 agreement; contract. 2 *Law* sealed contract, esp. a deed of covenant. 3 (Covenant) *Bibl.* agreement between God and the Israelites. —v. agree, esp. by legal covenant. [French: related to CONVENE]

Coventry /ˈkɒvəntrɪ/ n. □ **send a person to Coventry** refuse to associate with or speak to a person. [*Coventry* in England]

cover /ˈkʌvə(r)/ —v. 1 (often foll. by *with*) protect or conceal with a cloth, lid, etc. 2 a extend over; occupy the whole surface of. b (often foll. by *with*) strew thickly or thoroughly. c lie over. 3 a protect. b (as **covered** adj.) wearing a hat; having a roof. 4 include; comprise; deal with. 5 travel (a specified distance). 6 describe as a reporter. 7 be enough to defray (*£20 should cover it*). 8 a *refl.* take

---

coverage measures to protect oneself. **b** (*absol.*; foll. by *for*) stand in for. **9 a** aim a gun etc. at. **b** (of a fortress, guns, etc.) command (territory). **c** protect (an exposed person etc.) by being able to return fire. **10 a** esp. *Cricket* stand behind (another player) to stop any missed balls. **b** mark (an opposing player). **11** (of a stallion etc.) copulate with. —*n.* **1** thing that covers, esp.: **a** lid. **b** book's binding. **c** either board of this. **d** envelope or wrapping (*under separate cover*). **2** shelter. **3 a** pretence; screen. **b** pretended identity. **c** *Mil.* supporting force protecting an advance party from attack. **4 a** funds, esp. obtainable from insurance to meet a liability or secure against loss. **b** insurance protection (*third-party cover*). **5** place-setting as a substitute. **6** place-setting at table. **7** *Cricket* = COVER-POINT. □ **cover up** completely cover or conceal. **take cover** find shelter. [Latin *cooperio*]

coverage *n.* **1** area or amount covered. **2** amount of publicity received by an event etc.

coverall *n.* esp. *US* **1** thing that covers entirely. **2** (usu. in *pl.*) full-length protective garment.

cover charge *n.* service charge per head in a restaurant, nightclub, etc.

cover girl *n.* female model appearing on magazine covers etc.

covering letter *n.* (also **covering note**) explanatory letter sent with an enclosure.

coverlet /'kʌvəlɪt/ *n.* bedspread. [Anglo-French: related to COVER, *lit* bed]

cover note *n.* temporary certificate of insurance.

cover-point *n.* *Cricket* **1** fielding position covering point. **2** fielder at this position.

cover story *n.* news story in a magazine that is advertised etc. on the front cover.

covert /'kʌvət/—*adj.* secret or disguised (*covert glance*). —*n.* **1** shelter, esp. a thicket hiding game. **2** feather covering the base of a bird's flight-feather. □ **covertly** *adv.* [French: related to COVER]

cover-up *n.* concealment of facts.

covet /'kʌvɪt/ *v.* (*-t-*) desire greatly (esp. a thing belonging to another person). [French: related to CUPID]

covetous /'kʌvɪtəs/ *adj.* (usu. foll. by *of*) coveting; grasping. □ **covetously** *adv.*

covey /'kʌvɪ/ *n.* (*pl.* *-s*) **1** brood of partridges. **2** small group of people. [Latin *cubo* lie]

cow¹ *n.* **1** fully grown female of any esp. domestic bovine animal, used as a source of milk and beef. **2** female of

other large animals, esp. the elephant, whale, and seal. **3** *derog. slang* woman. [Old English]

cow² *v.* intimidate or dispirit. [Old Norse]

coward /'kaʊəd/ *n.* person who is easily frightened. [Latin *cauda* tail]

cowardice /'kaʊədɪs/ *n.* lack of bravery.

cowardly *adj.* **1** of or like a coward; lacking courage. **2** (of an action) done against one who cannot retaliate.

cowbell *n.* bell worn round a cow's neck.

cowboy *n.* **1** (*fem.* **cowgirl**) person who tends cattle, esp. in the western US. **2** *colloq.* unscrupulous or incompetent person in business.

cower *v.* crouch or shrink back in fear or distress. [Low German]

cowherd *n.* person who tends cattle.

cowhide *n.* **1** cow's hide. **2** leather or whip made from this.

cowl *n.* **1** monk's cloak. **2** hood-shaped covering of a chimney or ventilating shaft. [Latin *cucullus*]

cow-lick *n.* projecting lock of hair.

cowling *n.* removable cover of a vehicle or aircraft engine.

co-worker /kəʊ'wɜːkə(r)/ *n.* person who works with another.

cow-parsley *n.* hedgerow plant with lacelike umbels of flowers.

cow-pat *n.* flat round piece of cow-dung.

cowpox *n.* disease of cows, whose virus was formerly used in smallpox vaccination.

cowrie /'kaʊrɪ/ *n.* **1** tropical mollusc with a bright shell. **2** its shell as money in parts of Africa and S. Asia. [Urdu and Hindi]

co-write /kəʊ'raɪt/ *v.* write with another person. □ **co-writer** *n.*

cowslip /'kaʊslɪp/ *n.* primula with small yellow flowers. [obsolete *slyppe* dung]

cox —*n.* coxswain, esp. of a racing-boat. —*v.* act as cox (of). [abbreviation]

coxcomb /'kɒkskəʊm/ *n.* ostentatiously conceited man. □ **coxcombry** *n.* (*pl.* **-ies**). [= *cock's comb*]

coxswain /'kɒks(ə)n/ —*n.* **1** person who steers, esp. a rowing-boat. **2** senior petty officer in a small ship. —*v.* act as coxswain (of). [*cock* ship's boat, SWAIN]

coy *adj.* **1** affectedly shy. **2** irritatingly reticent. □ **coyly** *adv.* **coyness** *n.* [French: related to QUIET]

coyote /kɔː'əʊtɪ/ *n.* (*pl.* same or **-s**) N. American wolflike wild dog. [Mexican Spanish]

coypu /'kɔɪpuː/ *n.* progress towards a climax. —*adv.* & *adj.* increasing in loudness. [Italian: related to CRESCENT]

cozen /ˈkʌz(ə)n/ v. literary 1 cheat, defraud. 2 beguile. 3 act deceitfully. □ **cozenage** n. [cant]

cozy US var. of cosy.

C.P. abbr. candlepower.

Cpl. abbr. Corporal.

cps abbr. (also **c.p.s.**) 1 Computing characters per second. 2 Sci. cycles per second.

CPU abbr. Computing central processing unit.

Cr symb. chromium.

crab¹ n. 1 a a ten-footed crustacean, with the first pair of legs as pincers. b crab as food. 2 (Crab) sign or constellation Cancer. 3 (in full **crab-louse**) (often in pl.) parasitic louse transmitted sexually to esp. pubic hair. 4 machine for hoisting heavy weights. □ **catch a crab** Rowing jam an oar or miss the water. □ **crablike** adj. [Old English]

crab² n. 1 (in full **crab-apple**) small sour apple. 2 (in full **crab tree** or **crab-apple tree**) tree (esp. uncultivated) bearing this. 3 sour person. [origin unknown]

crab³ v. (**-bb-**) colloq. 1 criticize; grumble. 2 spoil. [Low German krabben]

crabbed /ˈkræbɪd/ adj. 1 = CRABBY. 2 (of handwriting) ill-formed; illegible. [from CRAB²]

crabby adj. (**-ier**, **-iest**) irritable, morose. □ **crabbily** adv. **crabbiness** n.

crabwise adv. & attrib.adj. sideways or backwards.

crack —n. 1 a sharp explosive noise. b sudden harshness or change in vocal pitch. 2 sharp blow. 3 a narrow opening; break or split. b chink. 4 colloq. joke or malicious remark. 5 colloq. attempt. 6 slang crystalline form of cocaine broken into small pieces. —v. 1 break without separating the parts. 2 make or cause to make a sharp explosive sound. 3 break with a sharp sound. 4 give way or cause to give way (under torture etc.). 5 (of the voice) change pitch sharply. 6 colloq. find the solution to. 7 tell (a joke etc.). 8 colloq. hit sharply. 9 (as **cracked** adj.) crazy. 10 break (wheat) into coarse pieces. □ **crack down on** colloq. take severe measures against. **crack of dawn** daybreak. **crack up** colloq. 1 collapse under strain. 2 praise. **get cracking** colloq. begin promptly and vigorously. [Old English]

crack-brained adj. colloq. crazy.

crack-down n. colloq. severe measures against law-breakers.

cracker n. 1 paper cylinder pulled apart, esp. at Christmas, with a sharp noise and releasing a hat, joke, etc. 2 crackers predic.adj. slang crazy.

cracking slang —adj. 1 excellent. 2 (attrib.) fast and exciting. —adv. outstandingly.

crackle /ˈkræk(ə)l/ —v. (**-ling**) make repeated slight cracking sound (radio crackled; fire was crackling). —n. such a sound. □ **crackly** adj. [from CRACK]

crackling /ˈkræklɪŋ/ n. crisp skin of roast pork.

cracknel /ˈkræknəl/ n. light crisp biscuit. [Dutch: related to CRACK]

crackpot slang —n. eccentric person. —adj. mad, unworkable.

crack-up n. colloq. mental breakdown.

-cracy comb.form denoting a particular form of government etc. (bureaucracy). [Latin -cratia]

cradle /ˈkreɪd(ə)l/ —n. 1 a baby's bed or cot, esp. on rockers. b place in which something begins, esp. civilization (cradle of democracy). 2 supporting framework or structure. —v. (**-ling**) 1 contain or shelter as in a cradle. 2 place in a cradle. [Old English]

cradle-snatcher n. slang admirer or lover of a much younger person.

cradle-song n. lullaby.

craft /krɑːft/ —n. 1 special skill or technique. 2 occupation needing this. 3 (pl. **craft**) a boat or vessel. b aircraft or spacecraft. 4 cunning or deceit. —v. make in a skilful way. [Old English]

craftsman n. (fem. **craftswoman**) 1 skilled worker. 2 person who practises a craft. □ **craftsmanship** n.

crafty adj. (**-ier**, **-iest**) cunning, artful, wily. □ **craftily** adv. **craftiness** n.

craggy adj. (**-ier**, **-iest**) (of facial features, landscape etc.) rugged, rough, textured. □ **cragginess** n.

crake n. bird of the rail family, esp. the corncrake. [Old Norse, initiative of cry]

cram v. (**-mm-**) 1 a fill to bursting; stuff. b (foll. by in, into; also absol.) force (a thing) in or into. 2 prepare intensively for an examination. 3 (often foll. by with) feed to excess. [Old English]

crammer n. person or institution that crams pupils for examinations.

cramp —n. 1 painful involuntary muscular contraction. 2 (also **cramp-iron**) metal bar with bent ends for holding masonry etc. together. —v. 1 affect with cramp. 2 (often foll. by up) confine narrowly. 3 restrict. 4 fasten with a cramp. □ **cramp a person's style** prevent a person from acting freely or naturally. [Low German or Dutch]

cramped *adj.* **1** (of a space) too small. **2** (of handwriting) small and with the letters close together.

crampon /ˈkræmpən/ *n.* (*US* **crampoon** /-ˈpuːn/) (usu. in *pl.*) spiked iron plate fixed to a boot for climbing on ice. [French: related to CRAMP]

cranberry /ˈkrænbərɪ/ *n.* (*pl.* **-ies**) **1** shrub with small red acid berries. **2** this berry used in cookery. [German *Kranbeere* crane-berry]

crane —*n.* **1** machine with a long projecting arm for moving heavy objects. **2** tall wading bird with long legs, neck, and bill. —*v.* (**-ning**) (also *absol.*) stretch out (one's neck) in order to see something. [Old English]

crane-fly *n.* two-winged long-legged fly; also called DADDY-LONG-LEGS.

cranesbill *n.* wild geranium.

cranium /ˈkreɪnɪəm/ *n.* (*pl.* **-s** or **-nia**) **1** skull. **2** part of the skeleton enclosing the brain. □ **cranial** *adj.* **craniology** /-ˈblədʒɪ/ *n.* [medieval Latin from Greek]

crank —*n.* **1** part of an axle or shaft bent at right angles for converting reciprocal into circular motion or vice versa. **2** eccentric person. —*v.* cause to move by means of a crank. □ **crank up** start (a car engine) with a crank. [Old English]

crankcase *n.* case enclosing a crankshaft.

crankpin *n.* pin by which a connecting rod is attached to a crank.

crankshaft *n.* shaft driven by a crank.

cranky *adj.* (**-ier, -iest**) **1** *colloq.* eccentric. **2** working badly; shaky. **3** esp. *US* crotchety. □ **crankily** *adv.* **crankiness** *n.*

cranny /ˈkrænɪ/ *n.* (*pl.* **-ies**) chink, crevice. □ **crannied** *adj.* [French]

crap *coarse slang* —*n.* **1** (often as *int.* or *attrib.*) nonsense, rubbish. **2** faeces. —*v.* (**-pp-**) defecate. □ **crappy** *adj.* (**-ier, -iest**) [Dutch]

crape *n.* crêpe, usu. of black silk, formerly used for mourning. [from CRÊPE]

craps *n.pl.* (also **crap game**) *US* gambling dice game. [origin uncertain]

crapulent /ˈkræpjʊlənt/ *adj.* suffering the effects of drunkenness. □ **crapulence** *n.* **crapulous** *adj.* [Latin *crapula* inebriation]

crash¹ —*v.* **1** (cause to) make a loud smashing noise. **2** throw, drive, move, or fall with a loud smash. **3** (often foll. by *into*) collide or fall, or cause (a vehicle etc.) to collide or fall, violently; overturn at high speed. **4** collapse financially. **5** *colloq.* gatecrash. **6** *Computing* (of a machine or system) fail suddenly. **7** *colloq.* pass (a red traffic-light etc.). **8** (often foll. by *out*) *slang* sleep, esp. on a

floor etc. —*n.* **1** loud and sudden smashing noise. **2** violent collision or fall, esp. of a vehicle. **3** ruin, esp. financial. **4** *Computing* sudden failure of a machine or system. **5** (*attrib.*) done rapidly or urgently (*crash course in first aid*). —*adv.* with a crash (*go crash*). [imitative]

crash² *n.* coarse plain fabric of linen, cotton, etc. [Russian]

crash barrier *n.* barrier at the side or centre of a road etc.

crash-dive —*v.* **1 a** (of a submarine or its pilot) dive hastily in an emergency. **b** (of an aircraft or airman) dive and crash. **2** cause to crash-dive. —*n.* such a dive.

crash-helmet *n.* helmet worn esp. by motor cyclists.

crashing *adj. colloq.* overwhelming (*crashing bore*).

crash-land *v.* land or cause (an aircraft etc.) to land hurriedly with a crash. □ **crash landing** *n.*

crass *adj.* gross; grossly stupid. □ **crassly** *adv.* **crassness** *n.* [Latin *crassus* thick]

-crat *comb. form* member or supporter of a type of government etc.

crate —*n.* **1** slatted wooden case etc. for conveying esp. fragile goods. **2** *slang* old aircraft or other vehicle. —*v.* (**-ting**) pack in a crate. [perhaps from Dutch]

crater —*n.* **1** mouth of a volcano. **2** bowl-shaped cavity, esp. that made by a shell or bomb. **3** hollow on the surface of a planet or moon, caused by impact. —*v.* form a crater in. [Greek, = mixing-bowl]

-cratic *comb. form* (also **-cratical**) denoting a type of government etc. (*autocratic*). □ **-cratically** *comb. form* forming adverbs. [forming adverbs]

cravat /krəˈvæt/ *n.* man's scarf worn inside an open-necked shirt. [Serbo-Croatian, = Croat]

crave *v.* (**-ving**) (often foll. by *for*) long or beg for. [Old English]

craven /ˈkreɪv(ə)n/ *adj.* cowardly, abject. [probably French *cravané* defeated]

craving *n.* strong desire or longing.

craw *n.* crop of a bird or insect. □ **stick in one's craw** be unacceptable. [Low German or Dutch]

crawfish /ˈkrɔːfɪʃ/ *n.* (*pl.* same) large marine spiny lobster. [var. of CRAYFISH]

crawl¹ —*v.* **1** move slowly, esp. on hands and knees or with the body close to the ground etc. **2** walk or move slowly. **3** *colloq.* behave obsequiously. **4** (often foll. by *with*) be or appear to be covered or filled with crawling or moving things or people. **5** (esp. of the skin) creep. —*n.* **1**

crawling. 2 slow rate of movement. **3** high-speed overarm swimming stroke. [origin unknown]

crayfish /'kreɪfɪʃ/ n. (pl. same) **1** small lobster-like freshwater crustacean. **2** crawfish. [French crevice]

crayon /'kreɪən/ n. stick or pencil of coloured chalk, wax, etc. —v. draw with crayons. [French craie chalk]

craze —v. (-zing) **1** (usu. as **crazed** adj.) make insane (crazed with grief). **2** produce fine surface cracks on (pottery glaze etc.); develop such cracks. —n. **1** usu. temporary enthusiasm (craze for skateboarding). **2** object of this. [perhaps from Old Norse]

crazy adj. (-ier, -iest) **1** colloq. insane or mad; foolish. **2** (usu. foll. by about) colloq. extremely enthusiastic. **3** (attrib.) (of paving etc.) made up of irregular pieces. □ **crazily** adv. **craziness** n.

creak —n. harsh scraping or squeaking sound. —v. **1** make a creak. **2 a** move stiffly or with a creaking noise. **b** be poorly constructed (plot creaks). [imitative]

creaky adj. (-ier, -iest) **1** liable to creak. **2 a** stiff or frail. **b** decrepit, outmoded. □ **creakily** adv. **creakiness** n.

cream —n. **1** fatty part of milk. **2** its yellowish-white colour. **3** creamlike cosmetic etc. **4** food or drink like or containing cream. **5** (usu. prec. by the) best part of something. —v. **1** take cream from (milk). **2** make creamy. **3** treat (the skin etc.) with cosmetic cream. **4** form a cream or scum. —adj. pale yellowish white. □ **cream off** take (esp. the best part) from a whole. [Latin cramum and Church Latin chrisma oil for anointing]

cream cheese n. soft rich cheese made from cream and unskimmed milk.

creamer n. **1** cream-substitute for adding to coffee. **2** jug for cream.

creamery n. (pl. -ies) **1** factory producing butter and cheese. **2** dairy.

cream of tartar n. purified tartar, used in medicine, baking powder, etc.

cream soda n. carbonated vanilla-flavoured soft drink.

cream tea n. afternoon tea with scones, jam, and cream.

creamy adj. (-ier, -iest) **1** like cream. **2** rich in cream. □ **creamily** adv. **creaminess** n.

crease —n. **1** line caused by folding or crushing. **2** Cricket line marking the position of a bowler or batsman. —v. (-sing) **1** make creases in. **2** develop creases. **3** (often foll. by up) make or become incapable through laughter. [from CREST]

create /kriː'eɪt/ v. (-ting) **1** bring into existence; cause. **2** originate (actor creates a part). **3** invest with rank (created him a lord). **4** slang make a fuss. [Latin creo]

creation /kriː'eɪʃ(ə)n/ n. **1** creating or being created. **2 a** (usu. the Creation) God's creating of the universe. **b** (usu. Creation) all created things, the universe. **3** product of the imagination, art, fashion, etc.

creative adj. **1** inventive, imaginative. **2** able to create. □ **creatively** adv. **creativeness** n. **creativity** /-'tɪvɪtɪ/ n.

creative accounting n. exploitation of loopholes in financial legislation to gain maximum advantage or present figures in a misleadingly favourable light.

creator n. **1** person who creates. **2** (as **the Creator**) God.

creature /'kriːtʃər/ n. **1** any living being, esp. an animal. **2** person of a specified kind (poor creature). **3** subservient person. □ **creaturely** adj. [French from Latin: related to CREATE]

creature comforts n.pl. good food, warmth, etc.

crèche /kreʃ/ n. day nursery. [French]

credence /'kriːd(ə)ns/ n. belief. □ **give credence to** believe. [medieval Latin: related to CREDO]

credential /krɪ'denʃ(ə)l/ n. (usu. in pl.) **1** certificates, references, etc., attesting to a person's education, character, etc. **2** letter(s) of introduction. [medieval Latin: related to CREDO]

credibility /ˌkredɪ'bɪlɪtɪ/ n. **1** being credible. **2** reputation, status.

credibility gap n. apparent difference between what is said and what is true.

credible /'kredɪb(ə)l/ adj. believable or worthy of belief. [Latin: related to CREDO]

■ **Usage** Credible is sometimes confused with credulous.

credit /'kredɪt/ —n. **1** source of honour, pride, etc. (is a credit to the school). **2** acknowledgement of merit. **3** good reputation. **4** belief or trust. **5 a** person's financial standing. **b** power to obtain goods etc. before payment. **6** (usu. in pl.) acknowledgement of a contributor's services to a film etc. **7** grade above pass in an examination. **8** reputation for solvency and honesty in business. **9 a** entry in an account of a sum paid into it. **b** sum entered. **c** side of an account recording such entries. **10** educational course counting towards a degree. —v. (-t-) **1** believe (cannot credit it). **2** (usu. foll. by to, with) enter on the credit side

creditable of an account. □ **credit a person with** ascribe (a good quality) to a person. **do credit to** (or **do a person credit**) enhance the reputation of. **on credit** with an arrangement to pay later. **to one's credit** in one's favour. [Italian or Latin: related to CREDO]

creditable *adj.* bringing credit or honour. □ **creditably** *adv.*

credit card *n.* plastic card from a bank etc. authorizing the purchase of goods on credit.

credit note *n.* note with a specific monetary value given by a shop etc. for goods returned.

creditor *n.* person to whom a debt is owing. [Latin: related to CREDO]

credit rating *n.* estimate of a person's suitability for commercial credit.

creditworthy *adj.* considered suitable to receive commercial credit. □ **creditworthiness** *n.*

credo /ˈkriːdəʊ, ˈkreɪ-/ *n.* (*pl.* -s) creed. [Latin, = I believe]

credulous /ˈkredjʊləs/ *adj.* too ready to believe; gullible. □ **credulity** /krɪˈdjuːlɪtɪ/ *n.* **credulously** *adv.* [Latin: related to CREDO]

■ **Usage** *Credulous* is sometimes confused with *credible*.

creed *n.* **1** set of principles or beliefs. **2** system of religious belief. **3** (often **the creed**) formal summary of Christian doctrine. [Latin: related to CREDO]

creek *n.* **1 a** inlet on a sea-coast. **b** short arm of a river. **2** esp. *US, Austral., & NZ* tributary of a river; stream. □ **up the creek** *slang* **1** in difficulties. **2** crazy. [Old Norse and Dutch]

creel *n.* fisherman's large wicker basket. [origin unknown]

creep *—v.* (*past* and *past part.* **crept**) **1** move with the body prone and close to the ground. **2** move stealthily or timidly. **3** advance very gradually (*a feeling crept over her*). **4** *colloq.* act obsequiously in the hope of advancement. **5** (of a plant) grow along the ground or up a wall etc. **6** (as **creeping** *adj.*) developing slowly and steadily. **7** (of flesh) shiver or shudder from fear, horror, etc. *—n.* **1** act or spell of creeping. **2** (in *pl.*; prec. by *the*) *colloq.* feeling of revulsion or fear. **3** *slang* unpleasant person. **4** (of metals etc.) gradual change of shape under stress. [Old English]

creeper *n.* **1** climbing or creeping plant. **2** bird that climbs, esp. the treecreeper. **3** *slang* soft-soled shoe.

creepy *adj.* (-**ier**, -**iest**) *colloq.* feeling or causing horror or fear. □ **creepily** *adv.* **creepiness** *n.*

creepy-crawly /ˌkriːpɪˈkrɔːlɪ/ *n.* (*pl.* -ies) *colloq.* small crawling insect etc.

cremate /krɪˈmeɪt/ *v.* (-ting) burn (a corpse etc.) to ashes. □ **cremation** *n.* [Latin *cremo* burn]

crematorium /ˌkreməˈtɔːrɪəm/ *n.* (*pl.* -**ria** or -**s**) place where corpses are cremated.

crème /krem/ *n.* **1** = CREAM *n.* 4. **2** liqueur (*crème de cassis*). [French, = cream]

crème brûlée /bruːˈleɪ/ *n.* baked cream or custard pudding coated with caramel.

crème caramel *n.* custard coated with caramel.

crème de cassis /də kæˈsiːs/ *n.* blackcurrant liqueur.

crème de la crème /də lɑː ˈkrem/ *n.* best part; élite.

crème de menthe /də ˈmɒ̃t, ˈmɒnt/ *n.* peppermint liqueur.

crenellate /ˈkrenəleɪt/ *v.* (US **crenelate**) (-ting) provide (a tower etc.) with battlements. □ **crenellation** /-ˈleɪʃ(ə)n/ *n.* [French *crenel* embrasure]

Creole /ˈkriːəʊl/ *—n.* **1 a** descendant of European settlers in the W. Indies or Central or S. America. **b** White descendant of French settlers in the southern US. **c** person of mixed European and Black descent. **2** language formed from a European language and another (esp. African) language. *—adj.* **1** of Creoles. **2** (usu. **creole**) of Creole origin etc. (*creole cooking*). [French from Spanish]

creosote /ˈkrɪəˌsəʊt/ *—n.* **1** dark-brown oil distilled from coal tar, used as a wood-preservative. **2** oily fluid distilled from wood tar, used as an antiseptic. *—v.* (-ting) treat with creosote. [Greek *kreas* flesh, *sōtēr* preserver, because of its antiseptic properties]

crêpe /kreɪp/ *n.* **1** fine gauzy wrinkled fabric. **2** thin pancake with a savoury or sweet filling. **3** hard-wearing wrinkled sheet rubber used for the soles of shoes etc. □ **crêpey** *adj.* **crêpy** *adj.* [French, related to CRISP]

crêpe de Chine /də ˈʃiːn/ *n.* fine silk crêpe.

crêpe paper *n.* thin crinkled paper.

crêpe Suzette /suːˈzet/ *n.* small dessert pancake flamed in alcohol.

crept *past* and *past part.* of CREEP.

crepuscular /krɪˈpʌskjʊlə(r)/ *adj.* **1 a** of twilight. **b** dim. **2** *Zool.* appearing or active in twilight. [Latin *crepusculum* twilight]

Cres. *abbr.* Crescent.

cres. *abbr.* (also **cres.**) *Mus.* = CRESCENDO.

crescendo /krɪˈʃendəʊ/ *—n.* (*pl.* -s) **1** *Mus.* gradual increase in loudness. **2**

progress towards a climax. —*adv. & adj.* increasing in loudness. [Italian: related to CRESCENT]

■ **Usage** *Crescendo* is sometimes wrongly used to mean the climax itself rather than progress towards it.

crescent /'krez(ə)nt/ —*n.* **1** curved sickle shape as of the waxing or waning moon. **2** thing of this shape, esp. a street forming an arc. —*adj.* crescent-shaped. [Latin *cresco* grow]

cress *n.* any of various plants with pungent edible leaves. [Old English]

crest —*n.* **1** a comb or tuft etc. on a bird's or animal's head. **b** plume etc. on a helmet etc. **2** top of a mountain, wave, roof, etc. **3** *Heraldry* a device above a coat of arms; such a device on writing-paper etc. —*v.* **1** reach the crest of. **2** provide with a crest or serve as a crest to. **3** (of a wave) form a crest. □ **crested** *adj.* [Latin *crista*]

crestfallen *adj.* dejected, dispirited.

cretaceous /krɪˈteɪʃəs/ —*adj.* **1** of or like chalk. **2** (**Cretaceous**) *Geol.* of the last period of the Mesozoic era, with deposits of chalk. —*n.* (**Cretaceous**) *Geol.* this era or system. [Latin *creta* chalk]

cretin /'krɛtɪn/ *n.* **1** deformed and mentally retarded person, esp. as the result of thyroid deficiency. **2** *colloq.* stupid person. □ **cretinism** *n.* **cretinous** *adj.* [French *crétin*: related to CHRISTIAN]

cretonne /krɛˈtɒn/ *n.* (often *attrib.*) heavy cotton upholstery fabric, usu. with a floral pattern. [*Creton* in Normandy]

crevasse /krɪˈvæs/ *n.* deep open crack, esp. in a glacier. [Latin *crepo* crack]

crevice /'krɛvɪs/ *n.* narrow opening or fissure, esp. in rock etc. [French: related to CREVASSE]

crew[1] /kruː/ —*n.* (often treated as *pl.*) **1 a** people manning a ship, aircraft, train, etc. **b** these as distinct from the captain or officers. **c** people working together. **2** *colloq.* gang. —*v.* **1** supply or act as a crew or crew member for. **2** act as a crew. [Latin *cresco* increase]

crew[2] *past* of CROW[2].

crew cut *n.* close-cropped hairstyle.

crewel /'kruːəl/ *n.* thin worsted yarn for tapestry and embroidery. [origin unknown]

crewel-work *n.* design in crewel.

crew neck *n.* round close-fitting neck-line.

crib —*n.* **1 a** baby's small bed or cot. **b** model of the Nativity with a manger. **2** rack for animal fodder. **3** *colloq.* **a** translation of a text used by students. **b** plagiarized work etc. **4** *colloq.* a crib-bage. **b** set of cards given to the dealer at

cribbage. —*v.* (**-bb-**) (also *absol.*) **1** *colloq.* copy unfairly. **2** confine in a small space. [Old English]

cribbage /'krɪbɪdʒ/ *n.* card-game for up to four players. [origin unknown]

crick —*n.* sudden painful stiffness, esp. in the neck. —*v.* cause this in. [origin unknown]

cricket[1] /'krɪkɪt/ *n.* team game played on a grass pitch, with bowling at a wicket defended by a batting player of the other team. □ **not cricket** *colloq.* unfair behaviour. □ **cricketer** *n.* [origin uncertain]

cricket[2] /'krɪkɪt/ *n.* grasshopper-like chirping insect. [French imitative]

cri de cœur /ˌkriː də ˈkɜː(r)/ *n.* (*pl.* **cris de cœur** pronunc. same) passionate appeal, protest, etc. [French, = cry from the heart]

cried *past* and *past pt* of CRY.

crier /'kraɪə(r)/ *n.* (also **cryer**) **1** person who cries. **2** official making public announcements in a lawcourt or street. [related to CRY]

crikey /'kraɪkɪ/ *int.* *slang* expression of astonishment. [from CHRIST]

crime *n.* **1 a** offence punishable by law. **b** illegal acts (*resorted to crime*). **2** evil act (*crime against humanity*). **3** *colloq.* shameful act. [Latin *crimen*]

criminal /'krɪmɪn(ə)l/ —*n.* person guilty of a crime. —*adj.* **1** of, involving, or concerning crime. **2** guilty of crime. **3** *Law* of or concerning criminal offences (*criminal code; criminal lawyer*). **4** *colloq.* scandalous, deplorable. □ **criminality** /-ˈnælɪtɪ/ *n.* **criminally** *adv.* [Latin: related to CRIME]

criminology /ˌkrɪmɪˈnɒlədʒɪ/ *n.* the study of crime. □ **criminologist** *n.* [Latin *crimen* crime]

crimp —*v.* **1** press into small folds; corrugate. **2** make waves in (hair). —*n.* crimped thing or form. [Low German or Dutch]

Crimplene /'krɪmpliːn/ *n. propr.* synthetic crease-resistant fabric.

crimson /'krɪmz(ə)n/ —*adj.* of a rich deep red. —*n.* this colour. [ultimately from Arabic: related to KERMES]

cringe /krɪndʒ/ *v.* (**-ging**) **1** shrink in fear, cower. **2** (often *foll. by to*) behave obsequiously. [related to CRANK]

crinkle /'krɪŋk(ə)l/ —*n.* wrinkle or crease. —*v.* (**-ling**) form crinkles (in). □ **crinkly** *adj.* [related to CRINGE]

crinkle-cut *adj.* (of vegetables) with wavy edges.

crinoline /'krɪnəlɪn/ *n.* **1** *hist.* stiffened or hooped petticoat. **2** stiff fabric of horsehair etc. used for linings, hats, etc. [French, from Latin *crinis* hair, *linum* thread]

cripple /ˈkrɪp(ə)l/ —n. permanently lame person. —v. (-ling) 1 make a cripple of, lame. 2 disable, weaken, or damage seriously (crippled by strikes). [Old English]

crisis /ˈkraɪsɪs/ n. (pl. crises /-siːz/) 1 time of danger or great difficulty. 2 decisive moment; turning-point. [Greek, = decision]

crisp —adj. 1 hard but brittle. 2 a (of air) bracing. b (of style or manner) lively, brisk and decisive. c (of features etc.) neat, clear-cut. d (of paper) stiff and crackling. e (of hair) closely curling. —v. (in full potato crisp) potato sliced thinly, fried, and sold in packets. —v. make or become crisp. □ crisply adv. crispness n. [Latin crispus curled]

crispbread n. 1 thin crisp biscuit of crushed rye etc. 2 these collectively (packet of crispbread).

crispy adj. (-ier, -iest) crisp. □ crispiness n.

criss-cross —n. pattern of crossing lines. —adj. crossing; in cross lines. —adv. crosswise; at cross purposes. —v. 1 intersect repeatedly. b move crosswise. 2 mark or make with a criss-cross pattern. [Christ's cross]

criterion /kraɪˈtɪərɪən/ n. (pl. -ria) principle or standard of judgement. [Greek, = means of judging]

■ **Usage** The plural form of criterion, criteria, is often used incorrectly as the singular. In the singular criterion should always be used.

critic /ˈkrɪtɪk/ n. 1 person who criticizes. 2 person who reviews literary, artistic, etc. works. [Latin criticus from Greek kritēs judge]

critical adj. 1 a fault-finding, censorious. b expressing or involving criticism. 2 skilful at or engaged in criticism. 3 providing textual criticism (critical edition of Milton). 4 a of or at a crisis; dangerous, risky (in a critical condition). b decisive, crucial (at the critical moment). 5 a Math. & Physics marking a transition from one state etc. to another (critical angle). b (of a nuclear reactor) maintaining a self-sustaining chain reaction. □ critically adv. criticalness n.

critical path n. sequence of stages determining the minimum time needed for an operation.

criticism /ˈkrɪtɪsɪz(ə)m/ n. 1 a fault-finding; censure. b critical remark etc. 2 a work of a critic. b analytical article, essay, etc.

criticize /ˈkrɪtɪsaɪz/ v. (also -ise) (-zing or -sing) (also absol.) 1 find fault with; censure. 2 discuss critically.

critique /krɪˈtiːk/ n. critical analysis. [French: related to CRITIC]

croak —n. deep hoarse reptile sound, esp. of a frog. —v. 1 utter or speak with a croak. 2 slang die. [imitative]

croaky adj. (-ier, -iest) croaking; hoarse. □ croakily adv. croakiness n.

Croat /ˈkrəʊæt/ n. (also **Croatian** /krəʊˈeɪʃ(ə)n/) n. 1 a native of Croatia in SE Europe. b person of Croatian descent. 2 Slavonic dialect of the Croats. —adj. of the Croats or their dialect. [Serbo-Croatian Hrvat]

crochet /ˈkrəʊʃeɪ/ —n. needlework in which yarn is hooked into a lacy patterned fabric. —v. (crocheted /-ʃeɪd/; crocheting /-ʃeɪɪŋ/) (also absol.) make using crochet. [French: related to CROCHET]

crock[1] n. colloq. old or worn-out person or vehicle. [originally Scots]

crock[2] n. 1 earthenware pot or jar. 2 broken piece of this. [Old English]

crockery n. earthenware or china dishes, plates, etc. [related to CROCK[2]]

crocodile /ˈkrɒkədaɪl/ n. 1 a large tropical amphibious reptile with thick scaly skin, a long tail, and long jaws. b (often attrib.) its skin. 2 colloq. line of school-children etc. walking in pairs. [Greek krokodilos]

crocodile tears n.pl. insincere grief.

crocus /ˈkrəʊkəs/ n. (pl. -cuses) small plant with white, yellow, or purple flowers, growing from a corm. [Latin from Greek]

Croesus /ˈkriːsəs/ n. person of great wealth. [name of a king of ancient Lydia]

croft —n. 1 enclosed piece of (usu. arable) land. 2 small rented farm in Scotland or N. England. —v. farm a croft; live as a crofter. [Old English]

crofter n. person who farms a croft.

Crohn's disease /krəʊnz/ n. chronic inflammatory disease of the alimentary tract. [E. Crohn, name of a US pathologist]

croissant /ˈkrwɑːsɑ̃/ n. crescent-shaped breakfast roll. [French: related to CRESCENT]

cromlech /ˈkrɒmlek/ n. 1 dolmen. 2 prehistoric stone circle. [Welsh]

crone n. withered old woman. [Dutch croonje carcass]

crony /ˈkrəʊnɪ/ n. (pl. -ies) friend, companion. [Greek khronios long-lasting]

crook /krʊk/ —n. 1 hooked staff of a shepherd or bishop. 2 a bend, curve, or hook. b hooked or curved thing. 3 colloq. rogue; swindler; criminal. —v. bend, curve. [Old Norse]

crooked /ˈkrʊkɪd/ adj. (-er, -est) 1 not straight or level; bent. 2 colloq. not

straightforward; dishonest, criminal. □ **crookedly** *adv.* **crookedness** *n.*

croon —*v.* sing, hum, or say in a low sentimental voice. —*n.* such singing etc. □ **crooner** *n.* [Low German or Dutch]

crop —*n.* **1 a** produce of cultivated plants, esp. cereals. **b** season's yield. **2** group, yield, etc., of one time or place (*a new crop of students*). **3** handle or stock of a whip. **4 a** very short haircut. **b** cropping of hair. **5** pouch in a bird's gullet where food is prepared for digestion. —*v.* (*-pp-*) **1 a** cut off. **b** bite off. **2** cut (hair etc.) short. **3** (foll. by *with*) sow or plant (land) with a crop. **4** (of land) bear a crop. □ **crop up** occur unexpectedly. [Old English]

crop circle *n.* circle of crops that has been inexplicably flattened.

crop-eared *adj.* with the ears (esp. of animals) or hair cut short.

cropper *n.* crop-producing plant of a specified quality. □ **come a cropper** *slang* fall heavily; fail badly.

croquet /ˈkrəʊkeɪ/; —*n.* **1** lawn game in which wooden balls are driven through hoops with mallets. **2** act of croqueting a ball. —*v.* (**croqueted** /-keɪd/; **croqueting** /-keɪɪŋ/) drive away (an opponent's ball) by placing and then striking one's own against it. [perhaps a dial. form of French *crochet* hook]

croquette /krəˈket/ *n.* ball of breaded and fried mashed potato etc. [French *croquer* crunch]

crosier /ˈkrəʊzɪə(r)/ *n.* (also **crozier**) bishop's ceremonial hooked staff. [French *croisier* cross-bearer and *crossier* crook-bearer]

cross —*n.* **1** upright post with a transverse bar as used in antiquity for crucifixion. **2 a** (**the Cross**) cross on which Christ was crucified. **b** representation of this as an emblem of Christianity. **c** = SIGN OF THE CROSS. **3** staff surmounted by a cross, carried in a religious procession. **4** thing or mark like a cross, esp. two short intersecting lines (+ or x). **5** cross-shaped military etc. decoration. **6** (foll. by *between*) mixture of two things. **8** crosswise movement, pass in football, etc. **9** trial or affliction. —*v.* **1** (often foll. by *over*) go across. **2** intersect; (cause to) be across (*roads cross; cross one's legs*). **3 a** draw a line(s) across. **b** mark (a cheque) with two parallel lines to indicate that it cannot be cashed. **4** (foll. by *off, out, through*) cancel etc. by drawing lines across. **5** (often *refl.*) make the sign of the cross on or over. **6 a** pass in opposite directions. **b** (of letters etc.) be sent at the same time. **c** (of telephone lines) be connected to an

unwanted conversation. **7** a cause to interbreed. **b** cross-fertilize (plants). **8** oppose or thwart (*crossed in love*). —*adj.* **1** (often foll. by *with*) peevish, angry. **2** (usu. *attrib.*) transverse; reaching from side to side. **3** (usu. *attrib.*) intersecting. **4** (usu. *attrib.*) contrary, opposed, reciprocal. □ **at cross purposes** misunderstanding, conflicting. **cross one's fingers** (or **keep one's fingers crossed**) **1** put one finger across another to ward off bad luck. **2** trust in good luck. **cross one's heart** make a solemn pledge, esp. by crossing one's front. **cross one's mind** occur to one, esp. transiently. **cross swords** (often foll. by *with*) argue or dispute. **cross wires** (or **get one's wires crossed**) **1** become wrongly connected by telephone. **2** have a misunderstanding. □ **on the cross** diagonally. □ **crossly** *adv.* **crossness** *n.* [Latin *crux*]

crossbar *n.* horizontal bar, esp. that on a man's bicycle.

cross-bench *n.* seat in the House of Lords for non-party members. □ **cross-bencher** *n.*

crossbill *n.* finch with a bill with crossed mandibles for opening pine cones.

crossbones see SKULL AND CROSSBONES.

crossbow *n.* bow fixed on a wooden stock, with a groove for an arrow.

cross-breed —*n.* **1** hybrid breed of animals or plants. **2** individual hybrid. —*v.* produce by crossing.

cross-check —*v.* check by alternative method(s). —*n.* such a check.

cross-country —*adj.* & *adv.* **1** across open country. **2** not keeping to main roads. —*n.* (*pl.* **-ies**) cross-country race.

cross-cut —*adj.* cut across the grain. —*n.* diagonal cut, path, etc.

cross-cut saw *n.* saw for cross-cutting.

cross-dressing *n.* practice of dressing in the clothes of the opposite sex. □ **cross-dress** *v.*

crosse *n.* lacrosse stick. [French]

cross-examine *v.* question (esp. an opposing witness in a lawcourt). □ **cross-examination** *n.*

cross-eyed /ˈkrɒsaɪd/ *adj.* having one or both eyes turned inwards.

cross-fertilize *v.* (also **-ise**) **1** fertilize (an animal or plant) from one of a different species. **2** interchange ideas etc. □ **cross-fertilization** *n.*

crossfire *n.* **1** firing in two crossing directions simultaneously. **2 a** attack or criticism from all sides. **b** combative exchange of views etc.

cross-grain *n.* grain in timber, running across the regular grain.

cross-grained *adj.* **1** having a cross-grain. **2** perverse, intractable.

cross-hatch *v.* shade with crossing parallel lines.

crossing *n.* **1** place where things (esp. roads) cross. **2** place for crossing a street etc. **3** journey across water.

cross-legged /krɒsˈlegd/ *adj.* (sitting) with legs folded one across the other.

crossover —*n.* **1** point or place of crossing. **2** process of crossing over, esp. from one style or genre to another. —*attrib. adj.* that crosses over, esp. from one style or genre to another.

crosspatch *n. colloq.* bad-tempered person.

crosspiece *n.* transverse beam etc.

cross-ply *adj.* (of a tyre) having fabric layers with crosswise cords.

cross-question *v.* = CROSS-EXAMINE.

cross-refer *v.* (-**rr**-) refer from one part of a book etc. to another.

cross-reference —*n.* reference from one part of a book etc. to another. —*v.* provide with cross-references.

crossroad *n.* (usu. in *pl.*) intersection of two or more roads. □ **at the crossroads** at the critical point.

cross-section *n.* **1 a** plane surface so produced. **c** drawing etc. of this. **2** representative sample. □ **cross-sectional** *adj.*

cross-stitch *n.* cross-shaped stitch.

crosstalk *n.* **1** unwanted signals between communication channels. **2** witty repartee.

crossways *adv.* = CROSSWISE.

crosswind *n.* wind blowing across one's path etc.

crosswise *adj. & adv.* **1** in the form of a cross; intersecting. **2** diagonal or diagonally.

crossword *n.* (also **crossword puzzle**) printed grid of squares and blanks for vertical and horizontal words to be filled in from clues.

crotch *n.* fork, esp. between legs (of a person, trousers, etc.). [related to CROOK]

crotchet /ˈkrɒtʃɪt/ *n. Mus.* note equal to a quarter of a semibreve and usu. one beat. [French diminutive of *croc*: related to CROOK]

crotchety *adj.* peevish, irritable.

crouch —*v.* lower the body with limbs close to the chest; be in this position. —*n.* crouching; crouching position. [Old Norse: related to CROOK]

croup[1] /kruːp/ *n.* childhood inflammation of the larynx etc., with a hard cough. [imitative]

croup[2] /kruːp/ *n.* rump, esp. of a horse. [French: related to CROP]

croupier /ˈkruːpɪə(r)/ *n.* person running a gaming-table, raking in and paying out money etc. [French: related to CROUP[2]]

croûton /ˈkruːtɒn/ *n.* small cube of fried or toasted bread served with soup etc. [French: related to CRUST]

crow[1] /krəʊ/ *n.* **1** large black bird with a powerful black beak. **2** similar bird, e.g. the raven, rook, and jackdaw. □ **as the crow flies** in a straight line. [Old English]

crow[2] /krəʊ/ —*v.* **1** (*past* **crowed** or **crew** /kruː/) (of a cock) utter a loud cry. **2** (of a baby) utter happy cries. **3** (usu. foll. by *over*) gloat; show glee. —*n.* cry of a cock or baby. [Old English]

crowbar *n.* iron bar with a flattened end, used as a lever.

crowd —*n.* **1** large gathering of people. **2** spectators; audience. **3** *colloq.* particular set of people. **4** (prec. by *the*) majority. —*v.* **1 a** (cause to) come together in a crowd. **b** force one's way (*crowded into the cinema*). **2 a** (foll. by *into*) force or compress into a confined space. **b** (often foll. by *with*; usu. in *passive*) fill or make full of. **3** *colloq.* come aggressively close to. □ **crowd out** exclude by crowding.

crowdedness *n.* [Old English]

crown —*n.* **1** monarch's jewelled head-dress. **2** (**the Crown**) **a** monarch as head of State. **b** power or authority of the monarchy. **3 a** wreath for the head as an emblem of victory. **b** award or distinction, esp. in sport. **4** crown-shaped ornament etc. **5** top part of the head, a hat, etc. **6 a** highest or central part (*crown of the road*). **b** thing that completes or forms a summit. **7 a** part of a tooth visible outside the gum. **b** artificial replacement for this. **8** former British coin worth five shillings. —*v.* **1** put a crown on (a person or head). **2** invest with a royal crown or authority. **3** be a crown to; rest on top of. **4 a** (often as **crowning** *adj.*) (cause to) be the reward, summit, or finishing touch to (*crowning glory*). **b** bring to a happy outcome. **5** fit a crown to (a tooth). **6** *slang* hit on the head. **7** promote (a piece in draughts) to king. [Latin *corona*]

Crown Colony *n.* British colony controlled by the Crown.

Crown Court *n.* court of criminal jurisdiction in England and Wales.

Crown Derby *n.* porcelain made at Derby and often marked with a crown.

crown glass *n.* glass without lead or iron used formerly in windows, now as optical glass of low refractive index.

crown jewels *n.pl.* sovereign's State regalia etc.

Crown prince *n.* male heir to a throne.

Crown princess *n.* 1 wife of a Crown prince. 2 female heir to a throne.

crown wheel *n.* wheel with teeth at right angles to its plane.

crow's-foot *n.* wrinkle near the eye.

crow's-nest *n.* shelter at a sailing-ship's masthead for a lookout man.

crozier var. of CROSIER.

CRT *abbr.* cathode-ray tube.

cru /kru/ *n.* 1 French vineyard or wine region. 2 grade of wine. [French *cru* grown]

cruces *pl.* of CRUX.

crucial /ˈkruːʃ(ə)l/ *adj.* 1 decisive, critical. 2 very important. □ **crucially** *adv.* [Latin *crux crucis* cross]

■ **Usage** The use of *crucial* in sense 2 should be restricted to informal contexts.

crucible /ˈkruːsɪb(ə)l/ *n.* 1 melting-pot for metals etc. 2 severe test. [medieval Latin: related to CRUCIAL]

cruciferous /kruːˈsɪfərəs/ *adj.* having flowers with four petals arranged in a cross. [Latin: related to CRUCIAL]

crucifix /ˈkruːsɪfɪks/ *n.* model of a cross with the figure of Christ on it [Latin *cruci fixus* fixed to a cross]

crucifixion /kruːsɪˈfɪkʃ(ə)n/ *n.* 1 crucifying or being crucified. 2 (**Cruc-ifixion**) crucifixion of Christ. [Church Latin: related to CRUCIFIX]

cruciform /ˈkruːsɪfɔːm/ *adj.* cross-shaped. [Latin *crux crucis* cross]

crucify /ˈkruːsɪfaɪ/ *v.* (**-ies, -ied**) 1 put to death by fastening to a cross. 2 persecute, torment. 3 *slang* defeat thoroughly; humiliate. [French: related to CRUCIFIX]

crud *n. slang* 1 deposit of grease etc. 2 unpleasant person. □ **cruddy** *adj.* (**-ier, -iest**). [var. of CURD]

crude /kruːd/ —*adj.* 1 a in the natural state; not refined. b unpolished; lacking finish. 2 a rude, blunt. b offensive, indecent. 3 inexact. —*n.* natural mineral oil. □ **crudely** *adv.* **crudeness** *n.* **crudity** *n.* [Latin *crudus* raw]

crudités /ˈkruːdɪteɪ/ *n.pl.* hors d'oeuvre of mixed raw vegetables. [French]

cruel /ˈkruːəl/ *adj.* (**crueller, cruellest** or **crueler, cruelest**) 1 causing pain or suffering, esp. deliberately. 2 harsh, severe (*a cruel blow*). □ **cruelly** *adv.* **cruelness** *n.* **cruelty** *n.* (*pl.* **-ies**). [Latin: related to CRUDE]

cruet /ˈkruːɪt/ *n.* 1 set of small salt, pepper etc. containers for use at table. 2 such a container. [Anglo-French diminutive: related to CROCK²]

cruise /kruːz/ —*v.* (**-sing**) 1 a travel by sea for pleasure, calling at ports. b sail

about. 2 travel at a relaxed or economical speed. 3 achieve an objective, esp. win a race etc. with ease. 4 *slang* search for a sexual (esp. homosexual) partner in bars, streets, etc. —*n.* cruising voyage. [Dutch: related to CROSS]

cruise missile *n.* one able to fly low and guide itself.

cruiser *n.* 1 high-speed warship. 2 = CABIN CRUISER.

cruiserweight *n.* = LIGHT HEAVY-WEIGHT.

crumb /krʌm/ —*n.* 1 a small fragment, esp. of bread. b small particle (*crumb of comfort*). 2 bread without crusts. 3 *slang* objectionable person. —*v.* cover with or break into breadcrumbs. [Old English]

crumble /ˈkrʌmb(ə)l/ —*v.* (**-ling**) 1 break or fall into small fragments. 2 (of power etc.) gradually disintegrate. —*n.* dish of stewed fruit with a crumbly topping. □ **crumbly** *adj.* (**-ier, -iest**) consisting of, or apt to fall into, crumbs or fragments.

crumbs /krʌmz/ *int. slang* expressing dismay or surprise. [euphemism for CHRIST]

crumby /ˈkrʌmɪ/ *adj.* (**-ier, -iest**) 1 like or covered in crumbs 2 = CRUMMY.

crummy *adj.* (**-ier, -iest**) *slang* dirty, squalid; inferior, worthless. □ **crum-miness** *n.* [var. of CRUMBY]

crumpet /ˈkrʌmpɪt/ *n.* 1 soft flat yeasty cake toasted and buttered. 2 *joc.* or *offens.* sexually attractive woman or women. [origin uncertain]

crumple /ˈkrʌmp(ə)l/ —*v.* (**-ling**) (often foll. by *up*) 1 crush or become crushed into creases or wrinkles. 2 collapse, give way. —*n.* crease or wrinkle. [obsolete *crump* curl up]

crunch —*v.* 1 a crush noisily with the teeth. b grind under foot, wheels, etc. 2 (often foll. by *up, through*) make a crunching sound. —*n.* 1 crunching sound. 2 *colloq.* decisive event or moment. [imitative]

crunchy *adj.* (**-ier, -iest**) hard and crisp. □ **crunchiness** *n.*

crupper *n.* 1 strap looped under a horse's tail to hold the harness back. 2 hindquarters of a horse. [French: related to CROUP²]

crusade /kruːˈseɪd/ —*n.* 1 *hist.* any of several medieval military expeditions made by Europeans to recover the Holy Land from the Muslims. 2 vigorous campaign for a cause. —*v.* (**-ding**) engage in a crusade. □ **crusader** *n.* [French: related to CROSS]

cruse /kruːz/ *n. archaic* earthenware pot. [Old English]

crush –v. **1** compress with force or violence, so as to break, bruise, etc. **2** reduce to powder by pressure. **3** crease or crumple. **4** defeat or subdue completely. –n. **1** act of crushing. **2** crowded mass of people. **3** drink from the juice of crushed fruit. **4** (usu. foll. by on) *colloq.* infatuation. [French]

crust –n. **1 a** hard outer part of bread. **b** hard dry scrap of bread. **c** *slang* livelihood. **2** pastry covering of a pie. **3** hard casing over a soft thing. **4** outer portion of the earth. **5** deposit, esp. from wine on a bottle. –v. cover or become covered with or form into a crust. [Latin *crusta* rind, shell]

crustacean /krʌˈsteɪʃ(ə)n/ –n. esp. aquatic arthropod with a hard shell, e.g. the crab, lobster, and shrimp. –adj. of crustaceans.

crusty adj. (-ier, -iest) **1** having a crisp crust. **2** irritable, curt. □ **crustily** adv. **crustiness** n.

crutch n. **1** usu. T-shaped support for a lame person fitting under the armpit. **2** support, prop. **3** crotch. [Old English]

crux n. (pl. **cruxes** or **cruces** /ˈkruːsiːz/) decisive point at issue. [Latin, = cross]

cruzado /kruːˈzɑːdəʊ/ n. (pl. -s) chief monetary unit of Brazil. [Portuguese]

cruzeiro /kruːˈzeərəʊ/ n. (pl. -s) one-thousandth of a cruzado. [Portuguese]

cry /kraɪ/ –v. (**cries, cried**) **1** (often foll. by out) make a loud or shrill sound, esp. to express pain, grief, etc., or to appeal for help. **2** shed tears; weep. **3** (often foll. by out) say or exclaim loudly or excitedly. **4** (foll. by for) appeal, demand, or show a need for. **5** (of an animal, esp. a bird) make a loud call. –n. (pl. **cries**) **1** loud shout or scream of grief, pain, etc. **2** spell of weeping. **3** loud excited utterance. **4** urgent appeal. **5 a** public demand or opinion. **b** rallying call. **6** call of an animal. □ **cry down** disparage. **cry off** withdraw from an undertaking. **cry out for** need as an obvious requirement or solution. **cry wolf** see WOLF. [Latin *quirito*]

cry-baby n. person who weeps frequently.

cryer var. of CRIER.

crying attrib. adj. (of injustice etc.) flagrant, demanding redress.

cryogenics /kraɪəʊˈdʒenɪks/ n. branch of physics dealing with very low temperatures. □ **cryogenic** adj. [Greek *kruos* frost, *genēs* born]

crypt /krɪpt/ n. vault, esp. beneath a church, used usu. as a burial-place. [Latin *crypta* from Greek *kruptos* hidden]

cryptic adj. obscure in meaning; secret, mysterious. □ **cryptically** adv.

cryptogam /ˈkrɪptəˌɡæm/ n. plant with no true flowers or seeds, e.g. ferns, mosses, and fungi. □ **cryptogamous** /-ˈtɒɡəməs/ adj. [as CRYPT, Greek *gamos* marriage]

cryptogram /ˈkrɪptəˌɡræm/ n. text written in cipher. [related to CRYPT]

cryptography /krɪpˈtɒɡrəfɪ/ n. art of writing or solving ciphers. □ **cryptographer** n. **cryptographic** /-təˈɡræfɪk/ adj.

crystal /ˈkrɪst(ə)l/ –n. **1 a** transparent colourless mineral, esp. rock crystal. **b** piece of this. **2 a** highly transparent glass; flint glass. **b** articles of this. **3** crystalline piece of semiconductor. **4** aggregation of molecules with a definite internal structure and the external form of a solid enclosed by symmetrically arranged plane faces. –adj. (usu. attrib.) made of, like, or clear as crystal. [Greek *krustallos*]

crystal ball n. glass globe used in crystal-gazing.

crystal-gazing n. supposed foretelling of the future by gazing into a crystal ball.

crystalline /ˈkrɪstəˌlaɪn/ adj. **1** of, like, or clear as crystal. **2** having the structure and form of a crystal. □ **crystallinity** /-ˈlɪnɪtɪ/ n.

crystallize /ˈkrɪstəˌlaɪz/ v. (also -ise) (-zing or -sing) **1** form into crystals. **2** (often foll. by out) (of ideas or plans) make or become definite. **3** make or become coated or impregnated with sugar (*crystallized fruit*). □ **crystallization** /-ˈzeɪʃ(ə)n/ n.

crystallography /ˌkrɪstəˈlɒɡrəfɪ/ n. science of crystal formation and structure. □ **crystallographer** n.

crystalloid /ˈkrɪstəˌlɔɪd/ n. substance that in solution is able to pass through a semipermeable membrane.

Cs symb. caesium.

c/s abbr. cycles per second.

CSE abbr. hist. Certificate of Secondary Education.

■ **Usage** The CSE examination was replaced in 1988 by GCSE.

CS gas n. tear-gas used to control riots etc. [Corson and Stoughton, names of chemists]

CTC abbr. City Technology College.

Cu symb. copper. [Latin *cuprum*]

cu. abbr. cubic.

cub –n. **1** young of a fox, bear, lion, etc. **2** (**Cub**) (in full **Cub Scout**) junior Scout. **3** *colloq.* young newspaper reporter. –v. (-bb-) (also absol.) give birth to (cubs). [origin unknown]

cubby-hole /ˈkʌbɪˌhəʊl/ n. **1** very small room. **2** snug space. [Low German]

cube —n. 1 solid contained by six equal squares. 2 cube-shaped block. 3 product of a number multiplied by its square. —v. (-bing) 1 find the cube of (a number). 2 cut (food etc.) into small cubes. [Latin from Greek]

cube root n. number which produces a given number when cubed.

cubic adj. 1 cube-shaped. 2 of three dimensions. 3 involving the cube (and no higher power) of a number (cubic equation).

cubical adj. cube-shaped.

cubicle /ˈkjuːbɪk(ə)l/ n. 1 small screened compartment. 2 small separate sleeping-space. [Latin cubo lie]

cubic metre etc. n. volume of a cube whose edge is one metre etc.

cubism /ˈkjuːbɪz(ə)m/ n. style in art, esp. painting, in which objects are represented geometrically. □ **cubist** n. & adj.

cubit /ˈkjuːbɪt/ n. ancient measure of length, approximating to the length of a forearm. [Latin cubitum elbow]

cuboid /ˈkjuːbɔɪd/ —adj. cube-shaped; like a cube. —n. Geom. rectangular parallelepiped.

cuckold /ˈkʌkəʊld/ —n. husband of an adulteress. —v. make a cuckold of. □ **cuckoldry** n. [French]

cuckoo /ˈkʊkuː/ —n. bird having a characteristic cry, and laying its eggs in the nests of small birds. —predic. adj. slang crazy. [French, imitative]

cuckoo clock n. clock with the figure of a cuckoo emerging to make a call on the hour.

cuckoo-pint n. wild arum. [Old English]

cuckoo-spit n. froth exuded by insect larvae on leaves, stems, etc.

cucumber /ˈkjuːkʌmbə(r)/ n. 1 long green fleshy fruit, used in salads. 2 climbing plant yielding this. [French from Latin]

cud n. half-digested food returned to the mouth of ruminants for further chewing. [Old English]

cuddle /ˈkʌd(ə)l/ —v. (-ling) 1 hug, fondle. 2 nestle together, lie close and snug. —n. prolonged and fond hug. □ **cuddlesome** adj. [origin uncertain]

cuddly adj. (-ier, -iest) 1 of a person, toy, etc.) soft and yielding. 2 given to cuddling.

cudgel /ˈkʌdʒ(ə)l/ —n. short thick stick used as a weapon. —v. (-ll-; US -l-) beat with a cudgel. [Old English]

cue¹ —n. 1 a last words of an actor's speech as a signal to another to enter or speak. b similar signal to a musician etc. 2 a stimulus to perception etc. b signal for action. c hint on appropriate behaviour. 3 cueing audio equipment (see sense 2 of v.). —v. (cues, cued, cueing or

cuing) 1 give a cue to. 2 put (audio equipment) in readiness to play a particular section. □ **cue in** 1 insert a cue for. 2 give information to. **on cue** at the correct moment. [origin unknown]

cue² Billiards etc. —n. long rod for striking a ball. —v. (cues, cued, cueing or cuing) strike (a ball) with or use a cue. [var. of QUEUE]

cue-ball n. ball to be struck with a cue.

cuff¹ n. 1 end part of a sleeve. 2 US trouser turn-up. 3 (in pl.) colloq. handcuffs. □ **off the cuff** colloq. without preparation, ex-tempore. [origin unknown]

cuff² —v. strike with an open hand. —n. such a blow. [perhaps imitative]

cuff-link n. two joined studs etc. for fastening a cuff.

Cufic var. of KUFIC.

cuirass /kwɪˈræs/ n. armour breast-plate and back-plate fastened together. [Latin corium leather]

cuisine /kwɪˈziːn/ n. style or method of cooking. [French]

cul-de-sac /ˈkʌldəsæk/ n. (pl. **culs-de-sac** pronunc. same, or **cul-de-sacs**) 1 road etc. with a dead end. 2 futile course. [French, = sack-bottom]

-cule suffix forming (orig. diminutive) nouns (molecule). [Latin -culus]

culinary /ˈkʌlɪnərɪ/ adj. of or for cooking. [Latin culina kitchen]

cull —v. 1 select or gather (knowledge etc.). 2 pick (flowers etc.). 3 a select (animals), esp. for killing. b reduce the population of (an animal) by selective slaughter. —n. 1 culling or being culled. 2 animal(s) culled. [French: related to COLLECT]

culminate /ˈkʌlmɪneɪt/ v. (-ting) (usu. foll. by in) reach its highest or final point (culminate in war). □ **culmination** /-ˈneɪʃ(ə)n/ n. [Latin culmen -min-]

culotte /kjuːˈlɒts/ n.pl. women's trousers cut like a skirt. [French, = knee-breeches]

culpable /ˈkʌlpəb(ə)l/ adj. deserving blame. □ **culpability** /-ˈbɪlɪtɪ/ n. [Latin culpo blame]

culprit /ˈkʌlprɪt/ n. guilty person. [perhaps from Anglo-French culpable: see CULPABLE]

cult n. 1 religious system, sect, etc., esp. ritualistic. 2 a devotion to a person or thing (cult of aestheticism). b fashion. c (attrib.) fashionable (cult film). [Latin; related to CULTIVATE]

cultivar /ˈkʌltɪvɑː(r)/ n. plant variety produced by cultivation. [from CULTIVATE, VARIETY]

cultivate /ˈkʌltɪveɪt/ v. (-ting) 1 prepare and use (soil etc.) for crops or gardening. 2 a raise (crops). b culture

cultivator (bacteria etc.). **3 a** (often as **cultivated** *adj.*) improve (the mind, manners, etc.). **b** nurture (a person, friendship, etc.). □ **cultivable** *adj.* **cultivation** /-'veɪʃ(ə)n/ *n.* [Latin *colo cult-* till, worship]

cultivator /'kʌltɪveɪtə(r)/ *n.* **1** mechanical implement for breaking up the ground etc. **2** person or thing that cultivates.

cultural /'kʌltʃər(ə)l/ *adj.* of or relating to intellectual or artistic matters, or to a specific culture. □ **culturally** *adv.*

culture /'kʌltʃə(r)/ —*n.* **1 a** intellectual and artistic achievement or expression (*city lacking in culture*). **b** refined appreciation of the arts etc. (*person of culture*). **2** customs, achievements, etc. of a particular civilization or group (*Chinese culture*). **3** improvement by mental or physical training. **4** cultivation of plants; rearing of bees etc. **5** quantity of micro-organisms and nutrient material supporting their growth. —*v.* (**-ring**) maintain (bacteria etc.) in suitable growth conditions. [Latin: related to CULTIVATE]

cultured *adj.* having refined taste etc.

cultured pearl *n.* pearl formed by an oyster after the insertion of a foreign body into its shell.

culture shock *n.* disorientation felt by a person subjected to an unfamiliar way of life.

culture vulture *n. colloq.* person eager for cultural pursuits.

culvert /'kʌlvət/ *n.* underground channel carrying water under a road etc. [origin unknown]

cum *prep.* (usu. in *comb.*) with, combined with, also used as (*bedroom-cum-study*). [Latin]

cumbersome /'kʌmbəsəm/ *adj.* (also **cumbrous** /'kʌmbrəs/) inconveniently bulky etc.; unwieldy. [*cumber* hinder]

cumin /'kʌmɪn/ *n.* (also **cummin**) **1** plant with aromatic seeds. **2** these as flavouring. [Greek *kuminon*]

cummerbund /'kʌmə,bʌnd/ *n.* waist sash. [Hindustani and Persian]

cumquat var. of KUMQUAT.

cumulative /'kjuːmjʊlətɪv/ *adj.* **1** increasing or increased progressively in amount, force, etc. (*cumulative evidence*). **2** formed by successive additions (*learning is a cumulative process*). □ **cumulatively** *adv.*

cumulus /'kjuːmjʊləs/ *n.* (*pl.* **-li** /-ˌlaɪ/) cloud formation of rounded masses heaped upon a flat base. [Latin, = heap]

cuneiform /'kjuːnɪfɔːm/ —*adj.* **1** wedge-shaped. **2** of or using wedge-shaped writing. —*n.* cuneiform writing. [Latin *cuneus* wedge]

cunnilingus /ˌkʌnɪ'lɪŋgəs/ *n.* oral stimulation of the female genitals. [Latin *cunnus* vulva, *lingo* lick]

cunning —*adj.* (**-er, -est**) **1** deceitful, clever, or crafty. **2** ingenious (*cunning device*). **3** *US* attractive, quaint. —*n.* **1** craftiness; deception. **2** skill, ingenuity. □ **cunningly** *adv.* [Old Norse: related to CAN¹]

cunt *n. coarse slang* **1** female genitals. **2** *offens.* unpleasant person. [origin uncertain]

cup —*n.* **1** small bowl-shaped container for drinking from. **2 a** its contents. **b** = CUPFUL. **3** cup-shaped thing. **4** flavoured wine, cider, etc. usu. chilled. **5** cup-shaped trophy as a prize. **6** one's fate or fortune (*a bitter cup*). —*v.* (**-pp-**) **1** form (esp. the hands) into the shape of a cup. **2** take or hold as in a cup. □ **one's cup of tea** *colloq.* what interests or suits one. [medieval Latin *cuppa*]

cupboard /'kʌbəd/ *n.* recess or piece of furniture with a door and (usu.) shelves.

cupboard love *n.* false affection for gain.

Cup Final *n.* final match in a (esp. football) competition.

cupful *n.* (*pl.* **-s**) **1** amount held by a cup, esp. *US* a half-pint or 8-ounce measure. **2** full cup.

■ **Usage** A *cupful* is a measure, and so *three cupfuls* is a quantity regarded in terms of a cup; *three cups full* denotes the actual cups as in *brought in three cups full of water.*

Cupid /'kjuːpɪd/ *n.* **1** Roman god of love, represented as a naked winged boy archer. **2** (also **cupid**) representation of Cupid. [Latin *cupio* desire]

cupidity /kjuː'pɪdɪtɪ/ *n.* greed; avarice. [Latin: related to CUPID]

Cupid's bow *n.* upper lip etc. shaped like an archery bow.

cupola /'kjuːpələ/ *n.* **1** dome forming or adorning a roof. **2** revolving dome protecting mounted guns. **3** furnace for melting metals. □ **cupolaed** /-ləd/ *adj.* [Italian from Latin *cupa* cask]

cuppa /'kʌpə/ *n. colloq.* **1** cup of. **2** cup of tea. [corruption]

cupreous /'kjuːprɪəs/ *adj.* of or like copper. [Latin: related to COPPER¹]

cupric /'kjuːprɪk/ *adj.* of copper.

cupro-nickel /ˌkjuːprəʊ'nɪk(ə)l/ *n.* alloy of copper and nickel.

cup-tie *n.* match in a competition for a cup.

cur *n.* **1** mangy ill-tempered dog. **2** contemptible person. [perhaps from Old Norse *kurr* grumbling]

curable /'kjʊərəb(ə)l/ *adj.* able to be cured. □ **curability** /-'bɪlɪtɪ/ *n.*

curaçao /ˈkjʊərəsəʊ/ n. (pl. -s) orange-flavoured liqueur. [*Curaçao*, Caribbean island]

curacy /ˈkjʊərəsɪ/ n. (pl. -ies) curate's office or tenure of it.

curare /kjʊˈrɑːrɪ/ n. extract of various plants, used by American Indians to poison arrows. [Carib]

curate /ˈkjʊərət/ n. assistant to a parish priest. [medieval Latin *curatus*: related to CURE]

curate's egg n. thing that is good in parts.

curative /ˈkjʊərətɪv/ —adj. tending or able to cure. —n. curative agent [medieval Latin: related to CURATE]

curator /kjʊˈreɪtə(r)/ n. keeper or custodian of a museum etc. □ **curatorship** n. [Anglo-Latin: related to CURE]

curb —n. 1 check, restraint 2 strap etc. passing under a horse's lower jaw, used as a check 3 enclosing border, e.g. the frame round a well or a fender round a hearth. 4 = KERB. —v. 1 restrain 2 put a curb on (a horse). [French: related to CURVE]

curd n. (often in *pl.*) coagulated acidic milk product made into cheese or eaten as food. [origin unknown]

curd cheese n. soft smooth cheese made from skimmed milk curds.

curdle /ˈkɜːd(ə)l/ v. (-ling) form into curds; congeal. □ **make one's blood curdle** horrify one. [from CURD]

cure —v. (-ring) 1 (often foll. by *of*) restore to health; relieve (*cured of pleurisy*). 2 eliminate (disease, evil, etc.). 3 preserve (meat, fruit, etc.) by salting, drying, etc. 4 vulcanize (rubber); harden (plastic etc.). —n. 1 restoration to health. 2 thing effecting a cure. 3 course of treatment. 4 curacy. [Latin *cura* care]

curé /ˈkjʊəreɪ/ n. parish priest in France etc. [French]

cure-all n. panacea.

curette /kjʊˈret/ —n. surgeon's small scraping-instrument. —v. (-tt-ing) clean or scrape with this. □ **curettage** /-ˈretɪdʒ/ n. [French: related to CURE]

curfew /ˈkɜːfjuː/ n. 1 signal or time after which people must remain indoors. 2 *hist.* signal for extinction of fires at a fixed hour. [French: related to COVER, fire]

Curia /ˈkjʊərɪə/ n. (also **curia**) papal court; government departments of the Vatican. [Latin]

curie /ˈkjʊərɪ/ n. unit of radioactivity. [P. *Curie*, name of a scientist]

curio /ˈkjʊərɪəʊ/ n. (pl. -s) rare or unusual object. [abbreviation of CURIOSITY]

curiosity /kjʊərɪˈɒsɪtɪ/ n. (pl. -ies) 1 eager desire to know; inquisitiveness. 2 strange, rare, etc. object. [Latin: related to CURIOUS]

curious /ˈkjʊərɪəs/ adj. 1 eager to learn; inquisitive. 2 strange, surprising, odd. □ **curiously** adv. [Latin related to CURE]

curium /ˈkjʊərɪəm/ n. artificial radioactive metallic element. [M. and P. *Curie*, name of scientists]

curl —v. 1 (often foll. by *up*) bend or coil into a spiral 2 move in a spiral form 3 a (of the upper lip) be raised contemptuously. b cause (the lip) to do this. 4 play curling. —n. 1 lock of curled hair. 2 anything spiral or curved inwards. 3 a curling movement. b being curled. □ **curl one's lip** express scorn. **curl up** 1 lie or sit with the knees drawn up. 2 *colloq.* writhe in embarrassment etc. [Dutch]

curler n. pin or roller etc. for curling the hair.

curlew /ˈkɜːljuː/ n. wading bird, usu. with a long slender bill. [French]

curlicue /ˈkɜːlɪkjuː/ n. decorative curl or twist. [from CURLY, CUE² or Q²]

curling n. game resembling bowls, played on ice with round flat stones.

curly adj. (-ier, -iest) 1 having or arranged in curls. 2 moving in curves. □ **curliness** n.

curly kale n. = KALE.

curmudgeon /kɜːˈmʌdʒ(ə)n/ n. bad-tempered person. □ **curmudgeonly** adj. [origin unknown]

currant /ˈkʌrənt/ n. 1 small seedless dried grape. 2 a any of various shrubs producing red, white, or black berries. b such a berry. [Anglo-French from *Corinth* in Greece]

currency /ˈkʌrənsɪ/ n. (pl. -ies) 1 a money in use in a country. b other commodity used as money. 2 being current; prevalence (e.g. of words or ideas).

current —adj. 1 belonging to the present; happening now (*current events*). 2 (of money, opinion, rumour, etc.) in general circulation or use. —n. 1 body of moving water, air, etc., esp. passing through still water etc. 2 a ordered movement of electrically charged particles. b quantity representing the intensity of this. 3 (usu. foll. by *of*) general tendency or course (of events, opinions, etc.). □ **currentness** n. [Latin *currere* run]

current account n. instantly accessible bank account.

currently adv. at the present time; now.

curriculum /kəˈrɪkjʊləm/ n. (pl. -la) subjects included in a course of study. [Latin, = course]

curriculum vitae /viːtaɪ/ *n.* brief account of one's education, career, etc.

curry¹ /ˈkʌrɪ/ *n.* (*pl.* -**ies**) meat, vegetables, etc., cooked in a spicy sauce, usu. served with rice. —*v.* (-**ies**, -**ied**) prepare or flavour with a curry sauce. [Tamil]

curry² /ˈkʌrɪ/ *v.* (-**ies**, -**ied**) **1** groom (a horse) with a curry-comb. **2** treat (tanned leather) to improve it. □ **curry favour** ingratiate oneself. [Germanic: related to READY]

curry-comb *n.* metal serrated device for grooming horses.

curry-powder *n.* mixture of turmeric, cumin, etc. for making curry.

curse —*n.* **1** solemn invocation of divine wrath on a person or thing. **2** supposed resulting evil. **3** violent or profane exclamation or oath. **4** thing causing evil or harm. **5** (prec. by *the*) *colloq.* menstruation. —*v.* (-**sing**) **1 a** utter a curse against. **b** (in *imper.*) may God curse. **2** (usu. in *passive*, foll. by *with*) afflict with. **3** swear profanely. [Old English]

cursed /ˈkɜːsɪd/ *attrib. adj.* damned.

cursive /ˈkɜːsɪv/ —*adj.* (of writing) with joined characters. —*n.* cursive writing. [medieval Latin, = running: related to CURRENT]

cursor /ˈkɜːsə(r)/ *n.* **1** *Math.* etc. transparent slide with a hairline, forming part of a slide-rule. **2** *Computing* indicator on a VDU screen identifying the position that the program will operate on with the next keystroke. [Latin, = runner: related to CURSIVE]

cursory /ˈkɜːsərɪ/ *adj.* hasty, hurried. □ **cursorily** *adv.* **cursoriness** *n.* [Latin: related to CURSOR]

curt *adj.* noticeably or rudely brief. □ **curtly** *adv.* **curtness** *n.* [Latin *curtus* short]

curtail /kɜːˈteɪl/ *v.* cut short; reduce. □ **curtailment** *n.* [corruption of obsolete adj. *curtal*: related to CURT]

curtain /ˈkɜːt(ə)n/ —*n.* **1** piece of cloth etc. hung as a screen, esp. at a window. **2 a** rise or fall of a stage curtain between acts or scenes. **b** = CURTAIN-CALL. **3** partition or cover. **4** (in *pl.*) *slang* the end. —*v.* **1** provide or cover with curtain(s). **2** (foll. by *off*) shut off with curtain(s). [Latin *cortina*]

curtain-call *n.* audience's applause summoning actors to take a bow.

curtain-raiser *n.* **1** short play before the main performance. **2** preliminary event.

curtilage /ˈkɜːtɪlɪdʒ/ *n.* esp. *Law* area attached to a house and forming one enclosure with it. [French: related to COURT]

curtsy /ˈkɜːtsɪ/ (also **curtsey**) —*n.* (*pl.* -**ies** or -**eys**) bending of the knees and lowering the body made by a girl or woman in acknowledgement of applause or as a respectful greeting etc. —*v.* (-**ies**, -**ied** or -**eys**, -**eyed**) make a curtsy. [var. of COURTESY]

curvaceous /kɜːˈveɪʃəs/ *adj. colloq.* (esp. of a woman) having a shapely figure.

curvature /ˈkɜːvətʃə(r)/ *n.* **1** curving. **2** curved form. **3** deviation of a curve or curved surface from a plane. [French from Latin: related to CURVE]

curve —*n.* **1** line or surface of which no part is straight or flat. **2** curved form or thing. **3** curved line on a graph. —*v.* (-**ving**) bend or shape to form a curve. □ **curved** *adj.* [Latin *curvus* curved]

curvet /kɜːˈvet/ —*n.* horse's frisky leap. —*v.* (-tt- or -t-) perform a curvet. [Italian diminutive: related to CURVE]

curvilinear /ˌkɜːvɪˈlɪnɪə(r)/ *adj.* contained by or consisting of curved lines. □ **curvilinearly** *adv.* [from CURVE after *rectilinear*]

curvy *adj.* (-**ier**, -**iest**) **1** having many curves. **2** (of a woman's figure) shapely. □ **curviness** *n.*

cushion /ˈkʊʃ(ə)n/ —*n.* **1** bag stuffed with soft material, for sitting or leaning on etc. **2** protection against shock; measure to soften a blow. **3** padded rim of a billiard-table etc. **4** air supporting a hovercraft etc. —*v.* **1** provide or protect with cushion(s). **2** mitigate the adverse effects of. [Latin *cuxita* mattress]

cushy /ˈkʊʃɪ/ *adj.* (-**ier**, -**iest**) *colloq.* (of a job etc.) easy and pleasant. [Hindi *khush* pleasant]

cusp *n.* point at which two curves meet, e.g. the horn of a crescent moon etc. [Latin *cuspis* -id- point, apex]

cuss *colloq.* —*n.* **1** curse. **2** usu. *derog.* person; creature. —*v.* curse. [var. of CURSE]

cussed /ˈkʌsɪd/ *adj. colloq.* stubborn. □ **cussedness** *n.*

custard /ˈkʌstəd/ *n.* pudding or sweet sauce of eggs or flavoured cornflour and milk. [obsolete *crustade*: related to CRUST]

custodian /kʌˈstəʊdɪən/ *n.* guardian or keeper. □ **custodianship** *n.*

custody /ˈkʌstədɪ/ *n.* **1** guardianship; protective care. **2** imprisonment. □ **take into custody** arrest. □ **custodial** /kʌˈstəʊdɪəl/ *adj.* [Latin *custos* -od- guard]

custom /ˈkʌstəm/ *n.* **1 a** usual behaviour. **b** particular established way of behaving. **2** *Law* established usage having the force of law. **3** regular business dealings or customers. **4** (in *pl.*; also treated as *sing.*) **a** duty on imports and

exports. **b** official department administering this. **c** area at a port or frontier etc., dealing with customs etc. [Latin *consuetudo*]

customary *adj.* in accordance with custom; usual. □ **customarily** *adv.* □ **customariness** *n.* [medieval Latin: related to CUSTOM]

customer *n.* **1** person who buys goods or services from a shop or business. **2** *colloq.* person of a specified kind (*awkward customer*). [Anglo-French: related to CUSTOM]

custom-house *n.* customs office at a port or frontier etc.

customize *v.* (also *-ise*) (*-zing* or *-sing*) make or modify to order; personalize.

custom-built *adj.* (also **custom-made**) made to order.

cut —*v.* (**-tt-**; *past* and *past part.* **cut**) **1** (also *absol.*) penetrate or wound with a sharp-edged instrument. **2** (often foll. by *into*) divide or be divided with a knife etc. **3** trim or detach by cutting. **4** (foll. by *loose, open,* etc.) loosen etc. by cutting. **5** (esp. as **cutting** *adj.*) (*cutting remark*). **6** (often foll. by *down*) reduce (wages, time, etc.) or cease (services etc.) **7 a** make (a coat, gem, key, record etc.) by cutting. **b** make (a path, tunnel, etc.) by removing material. **8** perform, make (*cut a caper, cut a sorry figure*). **9** (also *absol.*) cross, intersect. **10** (foll. by *across, through,* etc.) traverse, esp. as a shorter way (*cut across verse*). **11 a** deliberately ignore (a person one knows). **b** renounce (a connection). **12** esp. *US* deliberately miss (a class etc.). **13** *Cards* **a** divide (a pack) into two parts. **b** do this to select a dealer etc. **14 a** edit (film or tape), **b** (often in *imper.*) stop filming or recording. **c** (foll. by *to*) go quickly to (another shot). **15** switch off (an engine etc.). □ —*n.* **1** cutting. **2** division or wound made by cutting. **3** stroke with a knife, sword, whip, etc. **4 a** reduction (in wages etc.). **b** cessation (of power supply etc.) **5** removal of lines etc. from a play, film, etc. **6** wounding remark or act. **7** style of hair, garment, etc. achieved by cutting. **8** particular piece of butchered meat. **9** *colloq.* commission; share of profits. **10** stroke made by cutting. **11** deliberate ignoring of a person. **12** = WOODCUT. □ **a cut above** *colloq.* noticeably superior to. **be cut out** (foll. by *for*; or *to* + infin.) be suited. **cut above** *colloq.* noticeably superior to. **cut across 1** *trans.* tend (normal limitations etc.). **2** see sense 10 of *v.* **cut and run** *slang* run away. **cut back 1** reduce (expenditure etc.). **2** prune (a tree etc.). **cut both ways 1** serve both sides of an argument etc. **2** (of an action) have both good and bad effects. **cut a corner** go across it. **cut corners** do perfunctorily or incompletely, esp. to save time. **cut a dash** make a brilliant show. **cut a person dead** deliberately ignore (a person one knows). **cut down 1** bring or throw down by cutting. **b** kill by sword or disease. **2** see sense 6 of *v.* **3** reduce the length of (*cut down trousers to make shorts*). **4** (often foll. by *on*) reduce consumption (*cut down on beer*). **cut a person down to size** *colloq.* deflate a person's pretensions. **cut in 1** interrupt. **2** pull in too closely in front of another vehicle. **cut it fine** allow very little margin of time etc. **cut it out** (usu. in *imper.*) *slang* stop doing that. **cut one's losses** abandon an unprofitable scheme. **cut no ice** *slang* have no influence. **cut off 1** remove by cutting. **2 a** (often in *passive*) bring to an abrupt end or (esp. early) death. **b** intercept, interrupt. **c** disconnect (a person on the telephone). **3 a** prevent from travelling. **b** (as **cut off** *adj.*) isolated or remote. **4** disinherit. **cut out 1** remove from inside by cutting. **2** make by cutting from a larger whole. **3** omit. **4** *colloq.* stop doing or using (something) (*cut out chocolate*). **5** (cause to) cease functioning (*engine cut out*). **6** outdo or supplant (a rival). **cut short** interrupt; terminate. **cut one's teeth on** acquire experience from. **cut a tooth** have it appear through the gum. **cut up 1** cut into pieces. **2** (usu. in *passive*) distress greatly. **cut up rough** *slang* show anger or resentment. [Old English]

cut and dried *adj.* **1** completely decided; inflexible. **2** (of opinions etc.) ready-made, lacking freshness.

cut and thrust *n.* lively argument etc.

cutaneous /kjuːˈteɪnɪəs/ *adj.* of the skin. [Latin: related to CUTIS]

cutaway *attrib. adj.* **1** (of a diagram etc.) with parts of the exterior left out to reveal the interior.

cut-back *n.* cutting back, esp. a reduction in expenditure.

cute *adj.* *colloq.* **1** esp. *US* attractive, quaint. **2** clever, ingenious. □ **cutely** *adv.* **cuteness** *n.* [shortening of ACUTE]

cut glass *n.* (often hyphenated when *attrib.*) glass with patterns cut on it.

cuticle /ˈkjuːtɪk(ə)l/ *n.* dead skin at the base of a fingernail or toenail. [Latin *cuticula*, diminutive of *cutis* skin]

cutis /ˈkjuːtɪs/ *n.* true skin, beneath the epidermis. [Latin]

cutlass /ˈkʌtləs/ *n.* *hist.* short sword with a slightly curved blade. [Latin *cultellus*: related to CUTLER]

cutler *n.* person who makes or deals in knives etc. [Latin *cultellus* diminutive: related to COULTER]

cutlery /ˈkʌtləri/ n. knives, forks, and spoons for use at table. [Anglo-French: related to CUTLER]

cutlet /ˈkʌtlɪt/ n. 1 neck-chop of mutton or lamb. 2 small piece of veal etc. for frying. 3 flat cake of minced meat or nuts and breadcrumbs etc. [French diminutive from Latin *costa* rib]

cut-off n. 1 (often *attrib.*) point at which something is cut off. 2 device for stopping a flow.

cut-out n. 1 figure cut out of paper etc. 2 device for automatic disconnection, the release of exhaust gases, etc.

cut-price *adj.* (also **cut-rate**) at a reduced price.

cutter n. 1 **a** person or thing that cuts. **b** (in *pl.*) cutting tool. 2 **a** small fast sailing-ship. **b** small boat carried by a large ship.

cutthroat −n. 1 murderer. 2 (in full **cutthroat razor**) razor with a long unguarded blade set in a handle. −*adj.* 1 (of competition) ruthless and intense. 2 (of a card-game) three-handed.

cutting −n. 1 piece cut from a newspaper etc. 2 piece cut from a plant for propagation. 3 excavated channel in a hillside etc. for a railway or road. −*adj.* see CUT v. 5. □ **cuttingly** *adv.*

cuttlefish /ˈkʌt(ə)lfɪʃ/ n. (*pl.* same or −es) mollusc with ten arms and ejecting a black fluid when threatened. [Old English]

cutwater n. 1 forward edge of a ship's prow. 2 wedge-shaped projection from a pier or bridge.

cuvée /kjuːˈveɪ/ n. blend or batch of wine. [French, = vatful]

c.v. *abbr.* (also **CV**) curriculum vitae.

cwm /kuːm/ n. (in Wales) = COOMB. [Welsh]

cwt *abbr.* hundredweight.

-cy *suffix* denoting state, condition, or status (*idiocy; captaincy*). [Latin *-cia*, Greek *-kia*]

cyanic acid /saɪˈænɪk/ n. unstable colourless pungent acid gas. [Greek *kuanos* a blue mineral]

cyanide /ˈsaɪənaɪd/ n. highly poisonous substance used in the extraction of gold and silver.

cyanogen /saɪˈænədʒ(ə)n/ n. highly poisonous gas used in fertilizers.

cyanosis /saɪəˈnəʊsɪs/ n. bluish skin due to oxygen-deficient blood.

cybernetics /saɪbəˈnetɪks/ n.pl. (usu. treated as *sing.*) science of communications and control systems in machines and living things. □ **cybernetic** *adj.* [Greek *kubernētēs* steersman]

cyberpunk /ˈsaɪbəpʌŋk/ n. science fiction writing combining high-tech plots

with unconventional or nihilistic social values. [from CYBERNETICS, PUNK]

cycad /ˈsaɪkæd/ n. palmlike plant often growing to a great height. [Greek *koix* Egyptian palm]

cyclamate /ˈsaɪkləmeɪt/ n. former artificial sweetener. [chemical name]

cyclamen /ˈsɪkləmən/ n. 1 plant with pink, red, or white flowers with backward-turned petals. 2 cyclamen red or pink. [Latin from Greek]

cycle /ˈsaɪk(ə)l/ −n. 1 **a** recurrent round or period (of events, phenomena, etc.). **b** time needed for this. 2 **a** *Physics* etc. recurrent series of operations or states. **b** *Electr.* = HERTZ. 3 series of related songs, poems, etc. 4 bicycle, tricycle, etc. −*v.* (-**ling**) 1 ride a bicycle etc. 2 move in cycles. [Greek *kuklos* circle]

cycle-track n. (also **cycle-way**) path or road for bicycles.

cyclic /ˈsaɪklɪk/ *adj.* (also **cyclical** /ˈsɪklɪk(ə)l/) 1 **a** recurring in cycles. **b** belonging to a chronological cycle. 2 with constituent atoms forming a ring. □ **cyclically** *adv.*

cyclist /ˈsaɪklɪst/ n. rider of a bicycle.

cyclo- *comb. form* circle, cycle, or cyclic.

cyclone /ˈsaɪkləʊn/ n. 1 winds rotating inwards to an area of low barometric pressure; depression. 2 violent hurricane of limited diameter. □ **cyclonic** /-ˈklɒnɪk/ *adj.* [Greek *kuklōma* wheel]

cyclotron /ˈsaɪkləˌtrɒn/ n. apparatus for the acceleration of charged atomic and subatomic particles revolving in a magnetic field.

cygnet /ˈsɪgnɪt/ n. young swan. [Latin *cygnus* swan from Greek]

cylinder /ˈsɪlɪndə(r)/ n. 1 uniform solid or hollow body with straight sides and a circular section. 2 thing of this shape, e.g. a container for liquefied gas, a piston-chamber in an engine. □ **cylindrical** /-ˈlɪndrɪk(ə)l/ *adj.* [Latin *cylindrus* from Greek]

cymbal /ˈsɪmb(ə)l/ n. concave disc, struck usu. with another to make a ringing sound. □ **cymbalist** n. [Latin from Greek]

cyme /saɪm/ n. flower cluster with a single terminal flower that develops first. □ **cymose** *adj.* [Greek *kuma* wave]

Cymric /ˈkɪmrɪk/ *adj.* Welsh. [Welsh *Cymru* Wales]

cynic /ˈsɪnɪk/ n. 1 person with a pessimistic view of human nature. 2 (**Cynic**) one of a school of ancient Greek philosophers showing contempt for ease and pleasure. □ **cynical** *adj.* **cynically** *adv.* **cynicism** /-ˌsɪz(ə)m/ n. [Greek *kuōn* dog]

cynosure /'saɪnə،zjuə(r)/ n. centre of attraction or admiration. [Greek, = dog's tail (name for Ursa Minor)]

cypher var. of CIPHER.

cypress /'saɪprəs/ n. conifer with hard wood and dark foliage. [Greek kuparissos]

Cypriot /'sɪprɪət/ (also Cypriote /-əʊt/) —n. native or national of Cyprus. —adj. of Cyprus. [Cyprus in E Mediterranean]

Cyrillic /sɪˈrɪlɪk/ —adj. of the alphabet used by the Slavonic peoples of the Orthodox Church, now used esp. for Russian and Bulgarian. —n. this alphabet. [St Cyril, d. 869]

cyst /sɪst/ n. sac formed in the body, containing liquid matter. [Greek kustis bladder]

cystic adj. 1 of the bladder. 2 like a cyst.

cystic fibrosis n. hereditary disease usu. with respiratory infections.

cystitis /sɪˈstaɪtɪs/ n. inflammation of the bladder usu. causing frequent painful urination.

-cyte comb. form mature cell (leucocyte). [Greek kutos vessel]

cytology /saɪˈtɒlədʒɪ/ n. the study of cells. □ **cytological** /-təˈlɒdʒɪk(ə)l/ adj.

cytoplasm /'saɪtəʊˌplæz(ə)m/ n. protoplasmic content of a cell apart from its nucleus. □ **cytoplasmic** /-'plæzmɪk/ adj.

czar var. of TSAR.

Czech /tʃek/ —n. 1 native or national of Czechoslovakia. 2 one of the two official languages of Czechoslovakia. —adj. of Czechoslovakia, its people, or language. [Bohemian Cech]

Czechoslovak /ˌtʃekəʊˈsləʊvæk/ (also **Czechoslovakian** /ˌtʃekəʊsləˈvækɪən/) —n. native or national of Czechoslovakia. —adj. of Czechoslovakia. [from Czech, SLOVAK]

D

D[1] /diː/ *n.* (also *d*) (*pl.* **Ds** or **D's**) **1** fourth letter of the alphabet. **2** *Mus.* second note of the diatonic scale of C major. **3** (as a Roman numeral) 500. **4** = DEE. **5** fourth highest class or category (of academic marks etc.).

D[2] *symb.* deuterium.

d. *abbr.* **1** died. **2** departs. **3** daughter. **4** (pre-decimal) penny. [sense 4 from Latin DENARIUS]

'd *v. colloq.* (usu. after pronouns) had, would (*I'd*; *he'd*). [abbreviation]

dab[1] —*v.* (**-bb-**) **1** (often foll. by *at*) repeatedly press briefly and lightly with a cloth etc. (*dabbed at her eyes*). **2** press (a cloth etc.) thus. **3** (foll. by *on*) apply by dabbing. **4** (often foll. by *at*) aim a feeble blow; strike lightly. —*n.* **1** dabbing. **2** small amount thus applied (*dab of paint*). **3** light blow. **4** (in *pl.*) *slang* fingerprints. [imitative]

dab[2] *n.* (*pl.* same) a kind of marine flatfish. [origin unknown]

dabble /'dæb(ə)l/ *v.* (**-ling**) **1** (usu. foll. by *in*, *at*) engage (in an activity etc.) superficially. **2** move the feet, hands, etc. in esp. shallow liquid. **3** wet partly; stain, splash. □ **dabbler** *n.* [from DAB[1]]

dabchick /'dæbtʃɪk/ *n.* = LITTLE GREBE. [Old English]

dab hand *n.* (usu. foll. by *a*) *colloq.* expert. [*dab* adept, origin unknown]

da capo /dɑː 'kɑːpəʊ/ *adv. Mus.* repeat from the beginning. [Italian]

dace *n.* (*pl.* same) small freshwater fish related to the carp. [French *dars*: related to DART]

dacha /'dætʃə/ *n.* Russian country cottage. [Russian]

dachshund /'dækshʊnd/ *n.* dog of a short-legged long-bodied breed. [German, = badger-dog]

dactyl /'dæktɪl/ *n.* metrical foot consisting of one long syllable followed by two short syllables (‒ ◡ ◡). □ **dactylic** /-'tɪlɪk/ *adj.* [Greek, = finger]

dad *n. colloq.* father. [imitative of a child's *da da*]

Dada /'dɑːdɑː/ *n.* early 20th-c. artistic and literary movement repudiating conventions. □ **Dadaism** /-də,ɪz(ə)m/ *n.* **Dadaist** /-daɪst/ *n.* & *adj.* **Dadaistic** /-'ɪstɪk/ *adj.* [French *dada* hobby-horse]

daddy /'dædɪ/ *n.* (*pl.* **-ies**) *colloq.* father. [from DAD]

daddy-long-legs *n.* (*pl.* same) cranefly.

dado /'deɪdəʊ/ *n.* (*pl.* **-s**) **1** lower, differently decorated, part of an interior wall. **2** plinth of a column. **3** cube of a pedestal between the base and the cornice. [Italian: related to DIE[2]]

daemon var. of DEMON 4.

daff *n. colloq.* = DAFFODIL. [abbreviation]

daffodil /'dæfədɪl/ *n.* spring bulb with a yellow trumpet-shaped flower. [related to ASPHODEL]

daft /dɑːft/ *adj. colloq.* silly, foolish, crazy. [Old English, = meek]

dagger *n.* **1** short pointed knife used as a weapon. **2** *Printing* = OBELUS. □ **at daggers drawn** in bitter enmity. □ **look daggers at** glare angrily at. [origin uncertain]

dago /'deɪgəʊ/ *n.* (*pl.* **-s**) *slang offens.* foreigner, esp. a Spaniard, Portuguese, or Italian. [Spanish *Diego* = James]

daguerreotype /də'gerəʊ,taɪp/ *n.* early photograph using a silvered plate and mercury vapour. [*Daguerre*, name of its inventor]

dahlia /'deɪlɪə/ *n.* large-flowered showy garden plant. [*Dahl*, name of a botanist]

Dáil /dɔɪl/ *n.* (in full **Dáil Éireann** /'erən/) lower house of parliament in the Republic of Ireland. [Irish, = assembly (of Ireland)]

daily /'deɪlɪ/ —*adj.* done, produced, or occurring every day or every weekday. —*adv.* **1** every day. **2** constantly. —*n.* (*pl.* **-ies**) *colloq.* **1** daily newspaper. **2** cleaning woman.

daily bread *n.* necessary food; livelihood.

dainty /'deɪntɪ/ —*adj.* (**-ier**, **-iest**) **1** delicately pretty. **2** delicate or small. **3** (of food) choice. **4** fastidious; discriminating. —*n.* (*pl.* **-ies**) choice delicacy. □ **daintily** *adv.* **daintiness** *n.* [Latin *dignitas* DIGNITY]

daiquiri /'daɪkərɪ/ *n.* (*pl.* **-s**) cocktail of rum, lime juice, etc. [*Daiquiri* in Cuba]

dairy /'deərɪ/ *n.* (*pl.* **-ies**) **1** place for processing, distributing, or selling milk and its products. **2** (*attrib.*) of, containing, or used for, dairy products (and sometimes eggs) (*dairy cow*). [Old English]

dairying *n.* dairy farming and distribution.

dairymaid *n.* woman employed in a dairy.

dairyman *n.* dealer in dairy products.

dais /'deɪs/ n. low platform, usu. at the upper end of a hall. [Latin discus disc, (later) table]

daisy /'deɪzɪ/ n. (pl. **-ies**) 1 small wild plant with white-petalled flowers. 2 plant with similar flowers. [Old English, = *day's eye*]

daisy wheel n. spoked disc bearing printing characters, used in word processors and typewriters.

dal var. of DHAL.

Dalai Lama /ˌdælaɪ 'lɑːmə/ n. spiritual head of Tibetan Buddhism. [Mongolian *dalai* ocean]

dale n. valley. [Old English]

dally /'dælɪ/ v. (**-ies, -ied**) 1 delay; waste time. 2 (often foll. by *with*) flirt, trifle. □ **dalliance** n. [French]

Dalmatian /dæl'meɪʃ(ə)n/ n. large white spotted short-haired dog. [*Dalmatia* in Croatia]

dal segno /dæl 'senjəʊ/ adv. Mus. repeat from the point marked by a sign. [Italian, = from the sign]

dam¹ —n. 1 barrier across river etc., forming a reservoir or preventing flooding. 2 barrier made by beaver. —v. (**-mm-**) 1 provide or confine with a dam. 2 (often foll. by *up*) block up; obstruct. [Low German or Dutch]

dam² n. mother, esp. of a four-footed animal. [var. of DAME]

damage /'dæmɪdʒ/ —n. 1 harm or injury. 2 (in pl.) Law financial compensation for loss or injury. 3 (prec. by *the*) slang cost. —v. (**-ging**) inflict damage on. [Latin *damnum*]

damascene /'dæməsiːn/ —v. (**-ning**) decorate (metal) by etching or inlaying esp. with gold or silver. —n. design or article produced in this way. —adj. of this process. [*Damascus* in Syria]

damask /'dæməsk/ —n. reversible figured woven fabric, esp. white table linen. —adj. 1 made of damask. 2 velvety pink. —v. weave with figured designs. [as DAMASCENE]

damask rose n. old sweet-scented rose used to make attar.

dame n. 1 (**Dame**) a title given to a woman holding any of several orders of chivalry. b woman holding this title. 2 comic middle-aged female pantomime character, usu. played by a man. 3 US slang woman. [Latin *domina* lady]

dame-school n. hist. primary school kept by an elderly woman.

damn /dæm/ —v. 1 (often *int. colloq.*) curse (a person or thing; = may God damn). 2 doom to hell; censure. 3 condemn, censure (*review damning the book*). 4 a (often as **damning** adj.) (of

circumstance, evidence, etc.) show or prove to be guilty. b be the ruin of. —n. 1 uttered curse. 2 slang negligible amount. —adj. & adv. colloq. = DAMNED. □ **damn all** slang nothing at all. **damn well** colloq. (for emphasis) simply (*damn well do as I say*). **damn with faint praise** commend feebly, and so imply disapproval. **I'm** (or **I'll be**) **damned if** colloq. I certainly do not, will not, etc. **not give a damn** see GIVE. **well, I'm** (or **I'll be**) **damned** colloq. exclamation of surprise etc. [Latin *damnum* loss]

damnable /'dæmnəb(ə)l/ adj. hateful, annoying. □ **damnably** adv.

damnation /dæm'neɪʃ(ə)n/ —n. eternal punishment in hell. —int. expressing anger.

damned /dæmd/ colloq. —attrib. adj. damnable. —adv. extremely (*damned hot*). □ **damned well** = damn well. **do one's damnedest** do one's utmost.

damp —adj. slightly wet, diffused or condensed moisture, esp. when unwelcome. —v. 1 make damp, moisten. 2 (often foll. by *down*) b make (a fire) burn less strongly by reducing the flow of air to it. 3 reduce or stop the vibration of (esp. strings of a musical instrument). □ **damply** adv. **dampness** n. [Low German]

damp course n. (also **damp-proof course**) layer of waterproof material in a wall near the ground, to prevent rising damp.

damp squib n. unsuccessful attempt to impress etc.

dampen v. 1 make or become damp. 2 (often foll. by *down*) = DAMP v. 2a.

damper n. 1 discouraging person or thing. 2 device that reduces shock or noise. 3 metal plate in a flue to control the draught. 4 Mus. pad silencing a piano string. □ **put a damper on** take the vigour or enjoyment out of.

damsel /'dæmz(ə)l/ n. archaic or literary young unmarried woman. [French diminutive: related to DAME]

damselfly n. insect like a dragonfly but with wings folded when resting.

damson /'dæmz(ə)n/ n. 1 (in full **damson plum**) small dark-purple plum. 2 dark-purple colour. [Latin: related to DAMASCENE]

dan n. 1 grade of proficiency in judo. 2 holder of such a grade. [Japanese]

dance /dɑːns/ —v. (**-cing**) 1 move rhythmically, usu. to music. 2 skip or jump about. 3 perform (a specified dance, role, etc.). 4 bob up and down. 5 dandle (a child). —n. 1 a dancing as an art form. b style or form of this. 2 social gathering

dancehall for dancing. **3** single round or turn of a dance. **4** music for dancing to. **5** lively motion. □ **dance attendance on** serve obsequiously. **lead a person a dance** (or **merry dance**) cause a person much trouble. □ **danceable** *adj*. **dancer** *n*. [French]

dancehall *n*. public hall for dancing.

d. and c. *n*. dilatation (of the cervix) and curettage (of the uterus).

dandelion /'dændɪˌlaɪən/ *n*. wild plant with jagged leaves, a yellow flower, and a fluffy seed-head. [French *dent-de-lion*, = lion's tooth]

dander *n*. *colloq*. temper, indignation. □ **get one's dander up** become angry. [origin uncertain]

dandify /'dændɪˌfaɪ/ *v*. (**-ies, -ied**) make a dandy.

dandle /'dænd(ə)l/ *v*. (**-ling**) bounce (a child) on one's knees etc. [origin unknown]

dandruff /'dændrʌf/ *n*. **1** flakes of dead skin in the hair. **2** this as a condition. [origin uncertain]

dandy /'dændɪ/ —*n*. (*pl*. **-ies**) **1** man greatly devoted to style and fashion. **2** *colloq*. excellent thing. —*adj*. (**-ier, -iest**) esp. *US colloq*. splendid. [perhaps from the name *Andrew*]

dandy-brush *n*. brush for grooming a horse.

Dane *n*. **1** native or national of Denmark. **2** *hist*. Viking invader of England in the 9th–11th c. [Old Norse]

danger /'deɪndʒə(r)/ *n*. **1** liability or exposure to harm. **2** thing that causes or may cause harm. □ **in danger of** likely to incur or to suffer from. [earlier = 'power', from Latin *dominus* lord]

danger list *n*. list of those dangerously ill.

danger money *n*. extra payment for dangerous work.

dangerous *adj*. involving or causing danger. □ **dangerously** *adv*.

dangle /'dæŋg(ə)l/ *v*. (**-ling**) **1** be loosely suspended and able to sway. **2** hold or carry thus. **3** hold out (hope, temptation, etc.) enticingly. [imitative]

Danish /'deɪnɪʃ/ —*adj*. of Denmark or the Danes. —*n*. **1** Danish language. **2** (prec. by *the*; treated as *pl*.) the Danish people. [Latin: related to DANE]

Danish blue *n*. white blue-veined cheese.

Danish pastry *n*. yeast cake topped with icing, fruit, nuts, etc.

dank *adj*. disagreeably damp and cold. □ **dankly** *adv*. **dankness** *n*. [probably Scandinavian]

daphne /'dæfnɪ/ *n*. any of various flowering shrubs. [Greek]

dapper *adj*. **1** neat and precise, esp. in dress. **2** sprightly. [Low German or Dutch *dapper* strong]

dapple /'dæp(ə)l/ —*v*. (**-ling**) mark or become marked with spots of colour or shade. —*n*. dappled effect. [origin unknown]

dapple-grey *adj*. (of an animal's coat) grey or white with darker spots.

dapple grey *n*. dapple-grey horse.

Darby and Joan /ˌdɑːbɪ ənd 'dʒəʊn/ *n*. devoted old married couple. [names of a couple in an 18th-c. poem]

Darby and Joan club *n*. club for pensioners.

dare —*v*. (**-ring**; *3rd sing. present* usu. **dare** before an expressed or implied infinitive without *to*) **1** (foll. by infin. with or without *to*) have the courage or impudence (to) (*dare he do it?; if they dare to come; how dare you?*). **2** (usu. foll. by *to* + infin.) defy or challenge (*I dare you to own up*). —*n*. **1** act of daring. **2** challenge, esp. to prove courage. □ **I dare say 1** (often foll. by *that*) it is probable. **2** probably; I grant that much. [Old English]

daredevil —*n*. recklessly daring person. —*adj*. recklessly daring. □ **daredevilry** *n*.

daring —*n*. adventurous courage. —*adj*. adventurous, bold; prepared to take risks. □ **daringly** *adv*.

dariole /'dɛərɪˌəʊl/ *n*. dish cooked and served in a small mould. [French]

dark —*adj*. **1** with little or no light. **2** of deep or sombre colour. **3** (of a person) with dark colouring. **4** gloomy, dismal. **5** evil, sinister. **6** sullen, angry. **7** secret, mysterious. **8** ignorant, unenlightened. —*n*. **1** absence of light. **2** lack of knowledge. **3** dark area or colour, esp. in painting. □ **after dark** after nightfall. **the Dark Ages** (or **Age**) **1** period of European history from the 5th–10th c. **2** period of supposed unenlightenment. **in the dark 1** lacking information. **2** with no light. □ **darkish** *adj*. **darkly** *adv*. **darkness** *n*. [Old English]

darken *v*. make or become dark or darker. □ **never darken a person's door** keep away permanently. □ **darkener** *n*.

dark glasses *n.pl*. spectacles with dark-tinted lenses.

dark horse *n*. little-known person who is unexpectedly successful.

darkie var. of DARKY.

darkroom *n*. darkened room for photographic work.

darky n. (also **darkie**) (pl. **-ies**) slang offens. Black person.

darling /'dɑːlɪŋ/ —n. 1 beloved, lovable, or endearing person or thing. 2 favourite. —adj. 1 beloved, lovable, charming or pretty. [Old English: related to DEAR]

darn[1] v. mend (cloth etc.) by filling a hole with stitching. —n. darned area. [origin uncertain]

darn[2] v., int., adj., & adv. colloq. = DAMN (in imprecatory senses). [corruption]

darned adj. & adv. colloq. = DAMNED.

darnel /'dɑːn(ə)l/ n. grass growing in cereal crops. [origin unknown]

darner n. needle for darning.

darning n. 1 act of darning. 2 things to be darned.

dart —n. 1 small pointed missile. 2 (in pl.; usu. treated as sing.) indoor game of throwing darts at a dartboard to score points. 3 sudden rapid movement. 4 tapering tuck in a garment. —v. 1 (often foll. by out, in, past, etc.) move, send, or go suddenly or rapidly. [French from Germanic]

dartboard n. circular target in darts.

Darwinian /dɑː'wɪnɪən/ —adj. of Darwin's theory of evolution. —n. adherent of this. □ **Darwinism** /'dɑː-/ n. **Darwinist** /'dɑː-/ n. [Darwin, name of a naturalist]

dash —v. 1 rush. 2 strike or fling forcefully, esp. so as to shatter (dashed it to the ground). 3 frustrate, dispirit (dashed their hopes). 4 colloq. (esp. dash it or dash it all) = DAMN v. 1. —n. 1 rush or onset; sudden advance. 2 horizontal stroke(-) in writing or printing to mark a pause etc. 3 impetuous vigour, capacity for or appearance of this. 4 US sprinting-race. 5 longer signal of two in Morse code (cf. DOT n. 2). 6 slight admixture, esp. of a liquid. 7 = DASHBOARD. □ **dash off** write or draw hurriedly. [imitative]

dashboard n. instrument panel of a vehicle or aircraft.

dashing adj. 1 spirited, lively. 2 showy. □ **dashingly** adv. **dashingness** n.

dastardly /'dæstədlɪ/ adj. cowardly, despicable. □ **dastardliness** n. [origin uncertain]

DAT /dæt/ abbr. digital audio tape.

data /'deɪtə/ n.pl. (also treated as sing., although the singular form is strictly datum) 1 known facts used for inference or in reckoning. 2 quantities or characters operated on by a computer etc. [Latin data from do give]

■ **Usage** (1) In scientific, philosophical, and general use, this word is usually considered as plural and, as is thus treated as plural with datum as the singular. (2) In computing and allied subjects (and sometimes in general use), it is treated as a mass (or collective) noun and used with words like this, that, and much, with singular verbs, e.g. useful data has been collected. Some people consider use (2) to be incorrect but it is more common than use (1). However, data is not a singular count noun and cannot be preceded by a, every, each, either, or neither, or be given a plural form datus.

data bank n. store or source of data.

database n. structured set of data held in a computer.

datable /'deɪtəb(ə)l/ adj. (often foll. by to) capable of being dated.

data capture n. entering of data into a computer.

data processing n. series of operations on data, esp. by a computer. □ **data processor** n.

date[1] —n. 1 day of the month, esp. as a number. 2 particular, esp. historical, day or year. 3 day, month, and year of writing etc. at the head of a document etc. 4 period to which a document etc. belongs. 5 time when an event takes place. 6 colloq. a appointment, esp. social with a person of the opposite sex. b US person to be met at this. —v. (-ting) 1 mark with a date. 2 a assign a date to (an object, event, etc.). b (foll. by to) assign to a particular time, period, etc. 3 (often foll. by from, back to, etc.) have its origins at a particular time. 4 appear or expose as old-fashioned (design that does not date; that hat dates you). 5 US colloq. a make a date with. b go out together as sexual partners. □ **out of date** (attrib. out-of-date) old-fashioned; obsolete. **to date** until now. **up to date** (attrib. up-to-date) modern; fashionable; current. [French; related to DATA]

date[2] n. 1 dark oval single-stoned fruit. 2 (in full **date-palm**) tree bearing it. [Greek; related to DACTYL, from the shape of the leaf]

date-line n. 1 north-south line partly along the meridian 180° from Greenwich, to the east of which the date is a day earlier than to the west. 2 date and place of writing at the head of a newspaper article etc.

date-stamp —n. adjustable rubber stamp etc. used to record a date. —v. mark with a date-stamp.

dative /'deɪtɪv/ Gram. —n. case expressing the indirect object or recipient.

—*adj.* of or in this case. [Latin: related to DATA]

datum /'dettəm/ see DATA.

daub /dɔːb/ —*v.* **1** spread (paint etc.) crudely or roughly. **2** coat or smear (a surface) with paint etc. **3** paint crudely or unskilfully. —*n.* **1** paint etc. daubed on a surface. **2** plaster, clay, etc., esp. coating laths or wattles to form a wall. **3** crude painting. [Latin: related to DE-, ALB]

daughter /'dɔːtə(r)/ *n.* **1** girl or woman in relation to her parent(s). **2** female descendant. **3** (foll. by *of*) female member of a family etc. **4** (foll. by *of*) female descendant or inheritor of a quality etc. □ **daughterly** *adj.* [Old English]

daughter-in-law *n.* (*pl.* **daughters-in-law**) son's wife.

daunt /dɔːnt/ *v.* discourage, intimidate. □ **daunting** *adj.* [Latin *domito* from *domo* tame]

dauntless *adj.* intrepid, persevering.

dauphin /'dɔːfɪn/ *n. hist.* eldest son of the King of France. [French from Latin *delphinus* DOLPHIN, as a family name]

Davenport /'dævən.pɔːt/ *n.* **1** small writing-desk with a sloping top. **2** *US* large sofa. [name of the maker]

davit /'dævɪt/ *n.* small crane on board ship, esp. for moving or holding a lifeboat. [French diminutive of *David*]

Davy /'deɪvɪ/ *n.* (*pl.* **-ies**) (in full **Davy lamp**) miner's safety lamp. [name of its inventor]

Davy Jones /deɪvɪ 'dʒəʊnz/ *n. slang* (in full **Davy Jones's locker**) bottom of the sea, esp. as the sailors' graveyard. [origin unknown]

daw *n.* = JACKDAW. [Old English]

dawdle /'dɔːd(ə)l/ *v.* (**-ling**) **1** walk slowly and idly. **2** waste time; procrastinate. [origin unknown]

dawn —*n.* **1** daybreak. **2** beginning or birth of something. —*v.* **1** (of a day) begin; grow light. **2** (often foll. by *on*, *upon*) begin to become obvious (to). [Old English]

dawn chorus *n.* bird-song at daybreak.

day *n.* **1** time between sunrise and sunset. **2 a** 24 hours as a unit of time. **b** corresponding period on other planets (*Martian day*). **3** daylight (*clear as day*). **4** time during which work is normally done (*eight-hour day*). **5 a** (also *pl.*) historical period (*in those days*). **b** (prec. by *the*) present time (*issues of the day*). **6** prime of a person's life (*have had my day; in my day*). **7** a future time (*will do it one day*). **8** date of a specific festival or event etc. (*graduation day; Christmas day*). **9** battle or contest (*win the day*). □ **all in a day's work** part of the normal routine. **at the end of the day** when all is said and done. **call it a day** end a period of activity. **day after day** without respite. **day by day** gradually. **day in, day out** routinely, constantly. **not one's day** day when things go badly (for a person). **one of these days** soon. **one of those days** day when things go badly, **that will be the day** *colloq.* that will never happen. [Old English]

day-bed *n.* bed for daytime rest.

day-boy *n.* (also **day-girl**) non-boarding pupil, esp. at a boarding school.

daybreak *n.* first light in the morning.

day care *n.* care of young children, the elderly, the handicapped, etc. during the working day.

day centre *n.* place for care of the elderly or handicapped during the day.

day-dream —*n.* pleasant fantasy or reverie. —*v.* indulge in this. □ **day-dreamer** *n.*

daylight *n.* **1** light of day. **2** dawn. **3** visible gap, e.g. between boats in a race. **4** (usu. in *pl.*) *slang* life or consciousness (*scared the daylights out of me; beat the living daylights out of them*).

daylight robbery *n. colloq.* blatantly excessive charge.

daylight saving *n.* longer summer evening daylight, achieved by putting clocks forward.

day nursery *n.* nursery for children of working parents.

day off *n.* day's holiday.

day of reckoning *n.* time when something must be atoned for or avenged.

day release *n.* part-time education for employees.

day return *n.* reduced fare or ticket for a return journey in one day.

day-room *n.* room, esp. in an institution, used during the day.

day-school *n.* school for pupils living at home.

daytime *n.* part of the day when there is natural light.

day-to-day *adj.* mundane, routine.

day-trip *n.* trip completed in one day. □ **day-tripper** *n.*

daze —*v.* (**-zing**) stupefy, bewilder. —*n.* state of bewilderment. [Old Norse]

dazzle /'dæz(ə)l/ —*v.* (**-ling**) **1** blind or confuse temporarily with a sudden bright light. **2** impress or overpower with knowledge, ability, etc. —*n.* bright confusing light. □ **dazzling** *adj.* **dazzlingly** *adv.* [from DAZE]

DBS *abbr.* **1** direct-broadcast satellite. **2** direct broadcasting by satellite.

DC *abbr.* **1** (also **dc**) direct current. **2** District of Columbia. **3** da capo.

DD *abbr.* Doctor of Divinity.

D-Day /'di:deɪ/ n. 1 day (6 June 1944) on which Allied forces invaded N France. 2 important or decisive day. [D for day]

DDT abbr. colourless chlorinated hydrocarbon used as insecticide. [from the chemical name]

de- prefix 1 forming verbs and their derivatives: a down, away (descend; deduct). b completely (denude). 2 added to verbs and their derivatives to form verbs and nouns implying removal or reversal (de-ice; decentralization). [Latin]

deacon /'di:kən/ n. (fem. in senses 2 and 3) deaconess /ˌ'nes/) 1 (in Episcopal churches) minister below bishop and priest. 2 (in Nonconformist churches) lay officer. 3 (in the early Church) minister of charity. [Greek diakonos servant]

deactivate /di:'æktɪveɪt/ v. (-ting) make inactive or less reactive.

dead /ded/ —adj. 1 no longer alive. 2 colloq. extremely tired or unwell. 3 numb (fingers are dead). 4 (foll. by to) insensitive. 5 no longer effective or in use; extinct. 6 (of a match, coal, etc.) extinguished. 7 inanimate 8 a lacking force or vigour. b (of sound) not resonant. 9 quiet, lacking activity (dead season). 10 (of a microphone, telephone, ball in a game) out of play. 12 abrupt, complete (come to a dead stop; a dead calm; dead certainty). —adv. 1 absolutely, completely (dead on target; dead tired). 2 colloq. very, extremely (dead easy). —n. time of silence or inactivity (dead of night). □ as dead as the (or a) dodo entirely obsolete. dead to the world colloq. fast asleep; unconscious. [Old English]

dead beat adj. colloq. exhausted.

dead-beat n. colloq. derelict; tramp.

dead duck n. slang unsuccessful or useless person or thing.

deaden v. 1 deprive of or lose vitality, force, brightness, sound, feeling, etc. 2 (foll. by to) make insensitive.

dead end n. 1 closed end of road, passage, etc. 2 (often with hyphen, attrib.) hopeless situation, job, etc.

deadhead n. 1 faded flower-head. 2 non-paying passenger or spectator. 3 useless person. —v. remove deadheads from (a plant).

dead heat n. 1 race in which competitors tie. 2 result of such a race.

dead language n. language no longer spoken, e.g. Latin.

dead letter n. law or practice no longer observed or recognized.

deadline n. time-limit.

deadlock —n. 1 state of unresolved conflict. 2 lock requiring a key to open

or close it. —v. bring or come to a standstill.

dead loss n. colloq. useless person or thing.

deadly —adj. (-ier, -iest) 1 causing or able to cause fatal injury or serious damage. 2 intense, extreme (deadly dullness). 3 (of aim etc.) true; effective. 4 deathlike (deadly pale). 5 colloq. dreary, dull. —adv. 1 like death; as if dead (deadly faint). 2 extremely (deadly serious).

deadly nightshade n. poisonous plant with purple-black berries.

dead man's handle n. (also dead man's pedal) device on an electric train disconnecting the power supply if released.

dead march n. funeral march.

dead on adj. exactly right.

deadpan adj. & adv. lacking expression or emotion.

dead reckoning n. calculation of a ship's position from the log, compass, etc., when visibility is bad.

dead set n. determined attack. □ be dead set against strongly oppose. be dead set on be determined to do or get.

dead shot n. person who shoots extremely accurately.

dead weight n. (also dead-weight) 1 a inert mass. b heavy burden. 2 debt not covered by assets. 3 total weight carried on a ship.

dead wood n. colloq. useless person(s) or thing(s).

deaf /def/ adj. 1 wholly or partly unable to hear. 2 (foll. by to) refusing to listen or comply. □ turn a deaf ear (usu. foll. by to) be unresponsive. □ deafness n. [Old English]

deaf-aid n. hearing-aid.

deaf-and-dumb adj. often offens. = d.

deaf-and-dumb alphabet n. (also deaf-and-dumb language) = SIGN LANGUAGE.

■ **Usage** *Sign language* is the preferred term in official use.

deafen v. (often as deafening adj.) overpower with noise or make deaf by noise, esp. temporarily. □ deafeningly adv.

deaf mute n. deaf and dumb person.

deal¹ —v. (past and past part. dealt /delt/) 1 (foll. by with): a take measures to resolve, placate, etc. b do business with; associate with. c discuss or treat (a subject). 2 (often foll. by with) behave in a specified way (dealt honourably by them). 3 (foll. by in) sell (deals in insurance). 4 (often foll. by out, round) distribute to several people etc. 5 (also absol.) distribute (cards) to players. 6 administer (was dealt a blow). 7 assign esp. providentially (were dealt much

deal

happiness). —*n.* 1 (usu. **a good** or **great deal**) *colloq.* **a** large amount (*good deal of trouble*). **b** considerably (*great deal better*). 2 *colloq.* business arrangement; transaction. 3 specified treatment (*a rough deal*). 4 **a** dealing of cards. **b** player's turn to do this. [Old English]

deal² *n.* 1 fir or pine timber, esp. as boards of a standard size. 2 board of this. [Low German]

dealer *n.* 1 trader in (esp. retail) goods (*car-dealer*; *dealer in tobacco*). 2 player dealing at cards. 3 jobber on the Stock Exchange.

■ **Usage** In sense 3, this name has been merged with *broker* since Oct. 1986 (see BROKER 2, JOBBER 2).

dealings *n.pl.* contacts, conduct, or transactions.

dealt *past* and *past part.* of DEAL¹.

dean¹ *n.* 1 **a** head of the chapter of a cathedral or collegiate church. **b** (usu. **rural dean**) clergyman supervising parochial clergy. 2 **a** college or university official with disciplinary and advisory functions. **b** head of a university faculty or department or of a medical school. [Latin *decanus*]

dean² var. of DENE.

deanery *n.* (*pl.* -ies) 1 dean's house or position. 2 parishes presided over by a rural dean.

dear —*adj.* 1 **a** beloved or much esteemed. **b** as a merely polite or ironic form (*my dear man*). 2 as a formula of address, esp. beginning a letter (*Dear Sir*). 3 (often foll. by *to*) precious; cherished. 4 (usu. in *superl.*) earnest (*my dearest wish*). 5 expensive (*my having high prices*). —*n.* (esp. as a form of address) dear person. —*adv.* at great cost (*will pay dear*). —*int.* expressing surprise, dismay, pity, etc. (*dear me!*; *oh dear!*). □ **for dear life** desperately. □ **dearly** *adv.* [Old English]

dearie *n.* my dear. □ **dearie me!** = **dearie me!** *int.* expressing surprise, dismay, etc.

dearth /dɜːθ/ *n.* scarcity, lack.

death /deθ/ *n.* 1 irreversible ending of life; dying or being killed. 2 instance of this. 3 destruction; ending (*death of our hopes*). 4 being dead (*eyes closed in death*). 5 (usu. **Death**) personification of death, esp. as a skeleton. 6 lack of spiritual life. □ **at death's door** close to death. **be the death of** 1 cause the death of. 2 be annoying or harmful to. **catch one's death** *colloq.* catch a serious chill etc. **do to death** 1 kill. 2 overdo. **fate worse than death** *colloq.* very unpleasant experience. **put to death** kill or cause to be killed. **to death** to the

utmost, extremely (*bored to death*). □

deathlike *adj.* [Old English]

deathblow *n.* 1 blow etc. causing death. 2 event etc. that destroys or ends something.

death certificate *n.* official statement of a person's death.

death duty *n. hist.* property tax levied after death.

■ **Usage** This term was replaced in 1975 by *capital transfer tax* and in 1986 by *inheritance tax*.

deathly —*adj.* (-ier, -iest) suggestive of death (*deathly silence*). —*adv.* in a deathly way (*deathly pale*).

death-mask *n.* cast taken of a dead person's face.

death penalty *n.* punishment by death.

death rate *n.* number of deaths per thousand of population per year.

death-rattle *n.* gurgling in the throat sometimes heard at death.

death row *n.* US part of a prison for those sentenced to death.

death squad *n.* armed paramilitary group.

death-trap *n. colloq.* dangerous building, vehicle, etc.

death-warrant *n.* 1 order of execution. 2 anything that causes the end of an established practice etc.

death-watch *n.* (in full **death-watch beetle**) small beetle which makes a ticking sound, said to portend death.

death-wish *n. Psychol.* alleged usu. unconscious desire for death.

deb *n. colloq.* debutante. [abbreviation]

débâcle /deɪˈbɑːk(ə)l/ *n.* (US **debacle**) 1 **a** utter defeat or failure. **b** sudden collapse. 2 confused rush or rout. [French]

debag /diːˈbæg/ *v.* (**-gg-**) *slang* remove the trousers of (a person), esp. as a joke.

debar /dɪˈbɑː(r)/ *v.* (**-rr-**) (foll. by *from club*). □ **debarment** *n.* [French: related to BAR¹]

debark /diːˈbɑːk/ *v.* land from a ship. □ **debarkation** /-ˈkeɪʃ(ə)n/ *n.* [French *débarquer*]

debase /dɪˈbeɪs/ *v.* (**-sing**) 1 lower in quality, value, or character. 2 depreciate (a coin) by alloying etc. □ **debasement** *n.* [from DE-, (A)BASE]

debatable /dɪˈbeɪtəb(ə)l/ *adj.* questionable; disputable. [related to DEBATE]

debate /dɪˈbeɪt/ —*v.* (**-ting**) 1 (also *absol.*) discuss or dispute, esp. formally. 2 consider aspects of (a question); ponder. —*n.* 1 formal discussion on a particular matter. 2 discussion (*open to debate*). [French: related to BATTLE]

debauch /dɪˈbɔːtʃ/ —v. 1 (as **debauched** *adj.*) dissolute. 2 corrupt, deprave. 3 debase (taste or judgement). —n. bout of sensual indulgence. [French]

debauchee /ˌdɔːbɔːˈtʃiː/ n. debauched person.

debauchery n. excessive sensual indulgence.

debenture /dɪˈbentʃə(r)/ n. acknowledgement of indebtedness, esp. a company bond providing for payment of interest at fixed intervals. [Latin *debentur* are owed]

debilitate /dɪˈbɪlɪteɪt/ v. (**-ting**) enfeeble, enervate. □ **debilitation** n. [Latin *debilis* weak]

debility /dɪˈbɪlɪtɪ/ n. feebleness, esp. of health.

debit /ˈdebɪt/ —n. 1 entry in an account recording a sum owed. 2 sum recorded. 3 total of such sums. 4 debit side of an account. —v. (-**t**-) (foll. by *against*, *to*) enter on the debit side of an account (*debit £50 to my account*). 2 (foll. by *with*) charge (a person) with a debt (*debited me with £500*). [Latin *debitum* DEBT]

debonair /ˌdebəˈneə(r)/ adj. 1 cheerful, self-assured. 2 pleasant-mannered. [French]

debouch /dɪˈbaʊtʃ/ v. 1 (of troops or a stream) come out into open ground. 2 (often foll. by *into*) (of a river, road, etc.) merge into a larger body or area. □ **debouchment** n. [French *bouche* mouth]

debrief /diːˈbriːf/ v. *colloq.* question (a diplomat, pilot, etc.) about a completed mission or undertaking. □ **debriefing** n.

debris /ˈdebriː/ n. 1 scattered fragments, esp. of wreckage. 2 accumulation of loose rock etc. [French *briser* break]

debt /det/ n. 1 money etc. owed (*debt of gratitude*). 2 state of owing (*in debt; get into debt*). 3 = DELOUSE. □ **in a person's debt** under obligation to a person. [Latin *debeo debit-* owe]

debt of honour n. debt not legally recoverable, esp. a sum lost in gambling.

debtor n. person owing money etc.

debug /diːˈbʌɡ/ v. (**-gg-**) *colloq.* 1 remove concealed microphones from (a room etc.). 2 remove defects from (a computer program etc.). 3 remove bugs (insects) from.

debunk /diːˈbʌŋk/ v. *colloq.* expose (a person, claim, etc.) as spurious or false. □ **debunker** n.

début /ˈdeɪbjuː/ n. (*US* **debut**) first public appearance (as a performer etc.). [French]

débutante /ˈdebjʊˌtɑːnt/ n. (*US* **debutante**) (usu. wealthy) young woman making her social début. [French *début* ten]

Dec. *abbr.* December.

deca- *comb. form* ten. [Greek *deka* ten]

decade /ˈdekeɪd, dɪˈkeɪd/ n. 1 period of ten years. 2 series or group of ten.

■ **Usage** The second pronunciation given, with the stress on the second syllable, is considered incorrect by some people, even though it is much used in broadcasting.

decadence /ˈdekəd(ə)ns/ n. 1 moral or cultural decline. 2 immoral behaviour. [Latin: related to DECAY]

decadent *adj.* & n. **decadently** *adv.*

decaffeinated /diːˈkæfɪˌneɪtɪd/ *adj.* with caffeine removed or reduced.

decagon /ˈdekəɡən/ n. plane figure with ten sides and angles. □ **decagonal** /dɪˈkæɡən(ə)l/ *adj.* [Greek: related to DECA-, *-gōnos* -angled]

decahedron /ˌdekəˈhiːdrən/ n. solid figure with ten faces. □ **decahedral** *adj.* [after POLYHEDRON]

decalitre /ˈdekəˌliːtə(r)/ n. (*US* **-liter**) metric unit of capacity, equal to 10 litres.

Decalogue /ˈdekəˌlɒɡ/ n. Ten Commandments. [Greek: related to DECA-, *logos* word, reason]

decametre /ˈdekəˌmiːtə(r)/ n. (*US* **-meter**) metric unit of length, equal to 10 metres.

decamp /dɪˈkæmp/ v. 1 depart suddenly; abscond. 2 break up or leave camp. □ **decampment** n. [French: related to CAMP[1]]

decanal /dɪˈkeɪn(ə)l/ *adj.* 1 of a dean. 2 of the south side of a choir (where the dean sits). [Latin: related to DEAN[1]]

decant /dɪˈkænt/ v. 1 gradually pour off (wine etc.), esp. leaving the sediment behind. 2 transfer as if by pouring. [Greek *kanthos* lip of jug]

decanter n. stoppered glass container for decanted wine or spirit.

decapitate /dɪˈkæpɪteɪt/ v. (**-ting**) behead. □ **decapitation** /-ˈteɪʃ(ə)n/ n. [Latin: related to CAPITAL]

decapod /ˈdekəˌpɒd/ n. 1 crustacean with ten limbs for walking, e.g. the shrimp. 2 ten-tentacled mollusc, e.g. the squid. [Greek: related to DECA-, *pous pod-* foot]

decarbonize /diːˈkɑːbəˌnaɪz/ v. (also **-ise**) (**-zing** or **-sing**) remove the carbon etc. from (an internal-combustion engine etc.). □ **decarbonization** /-ˈzeɪʃ(ə)n/ n.

decathlon /dɪˈkæθlən/ n. athletic contest of ten events for all competitors.

□ **decathlete** /-liːt/ *n.* [from DECA-, Greek *athlon* contest]

decay /drˈkeɪ/ —*v.* 1 (cause to) rot or decompose. 2 decline or cause to decline in quality, power, etc. 3 (usu. foll. by *to*) (of a substance) undergo change by radioactivity. —*n.* 1 rotten state; wasting away. 2 decline in health, quality, etc. 3 radioactive change. [Latin *cado* fall]

decease /drˈsiːs/ *formal esp. Law* —*n.* death. —*v.* (-sing) die. [Latin *cado* fall]

deceased *formal* —*adj.* dead. —*n.* (usu. prec. by *the*) person who has died, esp. recently.

deceit /drˈsiːt/ *n.* 1 deception, esp. by concealing the truth. 2 dishonest trick. [Latin *capio* take]

deceitful *adj.* using deceit. □ **deceitfully** *adv.* **deceitfulness** *n.*

deceive /drˈsiːv/ *v.* (-ving) 1 make (a person) believe what is false; purposely mislead. 2 be unfaithful to, esp. sexually. 3 use deceit. □ **deceive oneself** persist in a mistaken belief. □ **deceiver** *n.*

decelerate /diːˈseləˌreɪt/ *v.* (-ting) (cause to) reduce speed. □ **deceleration** /-ˈreɪʃ(ə)n/ *n.* [from DE-, ACCELERATE]

December /drˈsembə(r)/ *n.* twelfth month of the year. [Latin *decem* ten, originally 10th month of Roman year]

decency /ˈdiːsənsɪ/ *n.* (*pl.* -ies) 1 correct, honourable, or modest behaviour. 2 (in *pl.*) proprieties; manners. [Latin: related to DECENT]

decennial /drˈsenɪəl/ *adj.* lasting, recurring every, ten years. [Latin *decem* ten, *annus* year]

decent /ˈdiːs(ə)nt/ *adj.* 1 a conforming with standards of decency. b avoiding obscenity. 2 respectable. 3 acceptable, good enough. 4 kind, obliging. □ **decently** *adv.* [Latin *decet* is fitting]

decentralize /diːˈsentrəˌlaɪz/ *v.* (also -ise) (-zing or -sing) 1 transfer (power etc.) from central to local authority. 2 reorganize to give greater local autonomy. □ **decentralization** /-ˈzeɪʃ(ə)n/ *n.*

deception /drˈsepʃ(ə)m/ *n.* 1 deceiving or being deceived. 2 thing that deceives. [Latin: related to DECEIVE]

deceptive /drˈseptɪv/ *adj.* likely to deceive; misleading. □ **deceptively** *adv.* **deceptiveness** *n.*

deci- *comb. form* one-tenth. [Latin *decimus* tenth]

decibel /ˈdesɪˌbel/ *n.* unit used in the comparison of sound levels or power levels of electrical signals.

decide /drˈsaɪd/ *v.* (-ding) 1 (usu. foll. by *to*, *that*, or *on*, *about*) resolve or have consideration (*decided to stay*; *decided*

quickly; *weather decided me*; *decided on a blue hat*). 2 resolve or settle (an issue etc.). 3 (usu. foll. by *between*, *for*, *against*, *in favour of*, or *that*) give a judgement. □ **decidable** *adj.* [Latin *caedo* cut]

decided *adj.* 1 (usu. *attrib.*) definite, unquestionable (*decided tilt*). 2 positive, wilful, resolute.

decidedly *adv.* undoubtedly, undeniably.

decider *n.* 1 game, race, etc., as a tiebreak. 2 person or thing that decides.

deciduous /drˈsɪdjuəs/ *adj.* 1 (of a tree) shedding leaves annually. 2 (of leaves, horns, teeth, etc.) shed periodically. [Latin *cado* fall]

decigram /ˈdesɪɡræm/ *n.* (also **decigramme**) metric unit of mass, equal to 0.1 gram.

decilitre /ˈdesɪˌliːtə(r)/ *n.* (*US* -**liter**) metric unit of capacity, equal to 0.1 litre.

decimal /ˈdesɪm(ə)l/ —*adj.* 1 (of a system of numbers, weights, measures, etc.) based on the number ten. 2 of tenths or ten; reckoning or proceeding by tens. —*n.* decimal fraction. [Latin *decem* ten]

decimal fraction *n.* fraction expressed in tenths, hundredths, etc., esp. by units to the right of the decimal point (e.g. 0.61).

decimalize *v.* (also -**ise**) (-**zing** or -**sing**) 1 express as a decimal. 2 convert to a decimal system (esp. of coinage). □ **decimalization** /-ˈzeɪʃ(ə)n/ *n.*

decimal point *n.* dot placed before the fraction in a decimal fraction.

decimate /ˈdesɪˌmeɪt/ *v.* (-ting) 1 destroy a large proportion of. 2 orig. *Rom. Hist.* kill or remove one in every ten of. □ **decimation** /-ˈmeɪʃ(ə)n/ *n.*

■ **Usage** Sense 1 is now the usual sense, but it is considered inappropriate by some people. This word should not be used to mean 'defeat utterly'.

decimetre /ˈdesɪˌmiːtə(r)/ *n.* (*US* -**meter**) metric unit of length, equal to 0.1 metre.

decipher /drˈsaɪfə(r)/ *v.* 1 convert (coded information) into intelligible language. 2 determine the meaning of (unclear handwriting etc.). □ **decipherable** *adj.*

decision /drˈsɪʒ(ə)n/ *n.* 1 act or process of deciding. 2 resolution made after consideration (*made my decision*). 3 (often foll. by *of*) a settlement of a question. b formal judgement. 4 resoluteness. [Latin: related to DECIDE]

decisive /drˈsaɪsɪv/ *adj.* 1 conclusive, settling an issue. 2 quick to decide. □ **decisively** *adv.* **decisiveness** *n.* [medieval Latin: related to DECIDE]

deck –n. **1 a** a platform in a ship serving as a floor. **b** the accommodation on a particular deck of a ship. **2** floor or compartment of a bus etc. **3** section for playing discs or tapes etc. in a sound system. **4** esp. US pack of cards. **5** slang ground. –v. **1** (often foll. by out) decorate. **2** provide with or cover as a deck. □ **below deck(s)** in or into the space below the main deck. [Dutch, = cover]

deck-chair n. folding garden chair of wood and canvas.

-decker comb. form having a specified number of decks or layers (double-decker).

deck-hand n. cleaner on a ship's deck.

declaim /dɪˈkleɪm/ v. **1** speak or say as if addressing an audience. **2** (foll. by against) protest forcefully. □ **declamation** /ˌdeklǝˈmeɪʃ(ǝ)n/ n. **declamatory** /dɪˈklamǝtǝrɪ/ adj. [Latin: related to CLAIM]

declaration /ˌdeklǝˈreɪʃ(ǝ)n/ n. **1** declaring. **2** formal, emphatic, or deliberate statement. [Latin: related to DECLARE]

declare /dɪˈkleǝr/ v. (-ring) **1** announce openly or formally (declare war). **2** pronounce (declared it invalid). **3** (usu. foll. by that) assert emphatically. **4** acknowledge possession of (dutiable goods, income, etc.). **5** (as declared adj.) admitting to be such (declared atheist). **6** (also absol.) Cricket close (an innings) voluntarily before the team is out. **7** (also absol.) Cards name (the trump suit). □ **declare oneself** reveal one's intentions or identity. □ **declarative** /-ˈklarǝtɪv/ adj. **declaratory** /-ˈklarǝtǝrɪ/ adj. **declarer** n. [Latin clarus clear]

declassify /diːˈklasɪˌfaɪ/ v. (-ies, -ied) declare (information etc.) to be no longer secret. □ **declassification** /-fɪˈkeɪʃ(ǝ)n/ n.

declension /dɪˈklenʃ(ǝ)n/ n. **1** Gram. a variation of the form of a noun, pronoun, or adjective to show its grammatical case etc. **b** class of nouns with the same inflexions. **2** deterioration, declining. [Latin: related to DECLINE]

declination /ˌdeklɪˈneɪʃ(ǝ)n/ n. **1** downward bend or turn. **2** angular distance of a star etc. north or south of the celestial equator. **3** deviation of a compass needle from true north. □ **declinational** adj.

decline /dɪˈklaɪn/ –v. (-ning) **1** deteriorate; lose strength or vigour; decrease. **2** (also absol.) politely refuse (an invitation, challenge, etc.). **3** slope or bend downwards, droop. **4** Gram. state the forms of (a noun, pronoun, or adjective).

–n. **1** gradual loss of vigour or excellence. **2** deterioration. [Latin clino bend]

declining years n.pl. old age.

declivity /dɪˈklɪvɪtɪ/ n. (pl. -ies) downward slope. [Latin clivus slope]

declutch /diːˈklʌtʃ/ v. disengage the clutch of a motor vehicle.

decoction /dɪˈkɒkʃ(ǝ)n/ n. **1** boiling down to extract an essence. **2** the resulting liquid. [Latin coquo boil]

decode /diːˈkǝʊd/ v. decipher. □ **decoder** n.

decoke colloq. –v. /diːˈkǝʊk/ decarbonize. –n. /ˈdiːkǝʊk/ process of this.

décolletage /ˌdeɪkɒlˈtɑːʒ/ n. low neckline of a woman's dress etc. [French collet collar]

décolleté /deɪˈkɒlteɪ/ adj. (also **décolletée**) (of a dress, woman, etc.) having or wearing a low neckline. [French]

decompose /ˌdiːkǝmˈpǝʊz/ v. (-sing) **1** rot. **2** separate (a substance, light, etc.) into its elements. □ **decomposition** /diːˌkɒmpǝˈzɪʃ(ǝ)n/ n.

decompress /ˌdiːkǝmˈpres/ v. subject to decompression.

decompression /ˌdiːkǝmˈpreʃ(ǝ)n/ n. **1** release from compression. **2** gradual reduction of high pressure on a deep-sea diver etc.

decompression chamber n. enclosed space for decompression.

decompression sickness n. condition caused by the sudden lowering of air pressure.

decongestant /ˌdiːkǝnˈdʒest(ǝ)nt/ n. medicine etc. that relieves nasal congestion.

decontaminate /ˌdiːkǝnˈtamɪˌneɪt/ v. remove contamination from. □ **decontamination** /-ˈneɪʃ(ǝ)n/ n.

décor /ˈdeɪkɔːr/ n. furnishing and decoration of a room, stage set, etc. [French: related to DECORATE]

decorate /ˈdekǝˌreɪt/ v. (-ting) **1** beautify, adorn. **2** paint wallpaper, etc. (a room or building). **3** give a medal or award to. [Latin decus -oris beauty]

Decorated style n. Archit. highly ornamented late English Gothic style (14th c.).

decoration /ˌdekǝˈreɪʃ(ǝ)n/ n. **1** decorating. **2** thing that decorates. **3** medal etc. worn as an honour. **4** (in pl.) flags, tinsel, etc., put up on a festive occasion.

decorative /ˈdekǝrǝtɪv/ adj. pleasing in appearance. □ **decoratively** adv.

decorator n. person who decorates for a living.

decorous /ˈdekǝrǝs/ adj. having or showing decorum. □ **decorously** adv. **decorousness** n. [Latin decorus seemly]

decorum /dɪˈkɔːrəm/ n. polite dignified behaviour. [as DECOROUS]

decoy —n. /ˈdiːkɔɪ/ person or thing used as a lure, bait, enticement. —v. /dɪˈkɔɪ/ lure, esp. using a decoy. [Dutch]

decrease —v. /dɪˈkriːs/ (-sing) make or become smaller or fewer. —n. /ˈdiːkriːs/ 1 decreasing. 2 amount of this. □ **de-creasingly** adv. [Latin: related to DE-, cresco grow]

decree /dɪˈkriː/ —n. 1 official legal order. 2 legal judgement or decision, esp. in divorce cases. —v. (-ees, -eed, -eeing) ordain by decree. [Latin decretum from cerno sift]

decree absolute n. final order for completion of a divorce.

decree nisi /ˈnaɪsaɪ/ n. provisional order for divorce, made absolute after a fixed period. [Latin nisi unless]

decrepit /dɪˈkrepɪt/ adj. 1 weakened by age or infirmity. 2 dilapidated. □ **decrepitude** n. [Latin crepo creak]

decrescendo /diːkrɪˈʃendəʊ/ adv., adj., & n. (pl. -s) = DIMINUENDO. [Italian: related to DECREASE]

decretal /dɪˈkriːt(ə)l/ n. papal decree. [Latin: related to DECREE]

decriminalize /diːˈkrɪmɪnəlaɪz/ v. (also -ise) (-zing or -sing) cease to treat as criminal. □ **decriminalization** /-ˈzeɪʃ(ə)n/ n.

decry /dɪˈkraɪ/ v. (-ies, -ied) disparage, belittle.

dedicate /ˈdedɪkeɪt/ v. (-ting) (often foll. by to) 1 devote (esp. oneself) to a special task or purpose. 2 address (a book etc.) to a friend, patron, etc. 3 devote (a building etc.) to a deity, saint, etc. 4 (as **dedicated** adj.) a (of a person) single-mindedly loyal to an aim, vocation, etc. b (of equipment, esp. a computer) designed for or assigned to a specific task. □ **dedicator** n. **dedicatory** adj. [Latin dico declare]

dedication /dedɪˈkeɪʃ(ə)n/ n. 1 dedicating or being dedicated. 2 words with which a book etc. is dedicated. [Latin: related to DEDICATE]

deduce /dɪˈdjuːs/ v. (-cing) (often foll. by from) infer logically. □ **deducible** adj. [Latin duco duct- lead]

deduct /dɪˈdʌkt/ v. (often foll. by from) subtract, take away, or withhold (an amount, portion, etc.). [related to DE-DUCE]

deductible adj. that may be deducted, esp. from tax or taxable income.

deduction /dɪˈdʌkʃ(ə)n/ n. 1 a deducting. b amount deducted. 2 a inferring of particular instances from a general law or principle. b conclusion deduced. [Latin: related to DEDUCE]

deductive adj. of or reasoning by deduction. □ **deductively** adv. [medieval Latin: related to DEDUCE]

dee n. 1 letter D. 2 thing shaped like this. [name of the letter D]

deed n. 1 thing done intentionally or consciously. 2 brave, skilful, or conspicuous act. 3 action (kind in word and deed). 4 legal document used esp. for transferring ownership of property. [Old English: related to DO']

deed-box n. strong box for deeds etc.

deed of covenant n. agreement to pay a regular sum, esp. to charity.

deed poll n. deed made by one party only, esp. to change one's name.

deem v. formal consider, judge (deem it my duty). [Old English]

deemster n. judge in the Isle of Man. [from DEEM]

deep —adj. 1 extending far down or in (deep water; deep wound; deep shelf). 2 (predic.) a to or at a specified depth (water 6 feet deep). b in a specified number of ranks (soldiers drawn up six deep). 3 situated or coming from far down, back, or in (deep in his pockets; deep sigh). 4 low-pitched, full-toned (deep voice). 5 intense, extreme (deep sleep; deep colour; deep interest). 6 (pre-dic.) fully absorbed or overwhelmed (deep in a book; deep in debt). 7 pro-found; difficult to understand (too deep for me). —n. 1 (prec. by the) poet. sea, esp. when deep. 2 abyss, pit, cavity. 3 (prec. by the) Cricket position of a fielder distant from the batsman. 4 deep state (deep of the night). —adv. deeply; far down or in (dig deep). □ **go off the deep end** colloq. give way to anger or emotion. **in deep water** in trouble or difficulty. □ **deeply** adv. [Old English]

deep breathing n. breathing with long breaths, esp. as exercise.

deepen v. make or become deep or deeper.

deep-freeze —n. cabinet for freezing and keeping food for long periods. —v. freeze or store in a deep-freeze.

deep-fry v. immerse in boiling fat to cook.

deep-laid adj. (of a scheme) secret and elaborate.

deep-rooted adj. (also **deep-seated**) firmly established, profound.

deer n. (pl. same) four-hoofed grazing animal, the male of which usu. has antlers. [Old English]

deerskin n. (often attrib.) leather from a deer's skin.

deerstalker n. soft cloth peaked cap with ear-flaps.

de-escalate /diːˈeskəleit/ v. become less intense. □ **de-escalation** n.

def adj. slang excellent. [perhaps from DEFINITE or DEFINITIVE]

deface /dɪˈfeɪs/ v. disfigure. □ **defacement** n. [French: related to FACE]

de facto /dei ˈfæktəʊ/ —adv. (whether by right or not) —adj. existing or so in fact (a de facto ruler). [Latin]

defalcate /ˈdiːfælkeɪt/ v. (-ting) formal misappropriate, esp. money. □ **defalcator** n. [Latin defalcare lop, from falx sickle]

defalcation /ˌdiːfælˈkeɪʃ(ə)n/ n. formal **1 a** misappropriation of money. **b** amount misappropriated. **2** shortcoming.

defame /dɪˈfeɪm/ v. (-ming) libel; slander; speak ill of. □ **defamation** /ˌdefəˈmeɪʃ(ə)n/ n. **defamatory** /dɪˈfæmətərɪ/ adj. [Latin fama report]

default /dɪˈfɔːlt/ —n. 1 failure to appear, pay, or act as one should. 2 preselected option adopted by a computer program when no alternative is specified. —v. fail to fulfil (esp. a legal) obligation. □ **by default** because of lack of an alternative. **in default of** because of the absence of. [French: related to FAIL]

defeat /dɪˈfiːt/ —v. 1 overcome in battle, a contest, etc. 2 frustrate, baffle. 3 reject (a motion etc.) by voting. —n. defeating or being defeated. [Latin: related to DIS-, FACT]

defeatism n. excessive readiness to accept defeat. □ **defeatist** n. & adj.

defecate /ˈdefəkeit/ v. (-ting) evacuate the bowels. □ **defecation** /ˌdefəˈkeɪʃ(ə)n/ n. [Latin faex faecis dregs]

defect —n. /ˈdiːfekt/ fault, imperfection, shortcoming. —v. /dɪˈfekt/ leave one's country or cause for another. □ **defection** n. **defector** n. [Latin defectio -fect-]

defective /dɪˈfektɪv/ adj. having defect(s); imperfect. □ **defectiveness** n. [Latin: related to DEFECT]

defence /dɪˈfens/ n. (US **defense**) 1 defending, protection. 2 means of this. 3 justification, vindication. 4 defendant's case or counsel (in pl.). 5 fortifications. 6 defending play or players. □ **defenceless** adj. **defencelessly** adv. **defencelessness** n. [related to DEFEND]

defence mechanism n. 1 body's resistance to disease. 2 usu. unconscious mental process to avoid anxiety.

defend /dɪˈfend/ v. (also absol.) 1 resist an attack made on; protect. 2 uphold by argument. 3 conduct a defence in a lawsuit. 4 compete to retain (a title etc.) in a contest. □ **defender** n. [Latin defendo]

defendant n. person etc. sued or accused in a lawcourt. [French: related to DEFEND]

defense US var. of DEFENCE.

defensible /dɪˈfensɪb(ə)l/ adj. 1 justifiable; able to be defended by argument. 2 able to be defended militarily. □ **defensibility** /-ˈbɪlɪtɪ/ n. **defensibly** adv. [Latin: related to DEFEND]

defensive adj. 1 done or intended for defence. 2 over-reacting to criticism. □ **on the defensive** 1 expecting criticism. 2 Mil ready to defend. □ **defensively** adv. **defensiveness** n. [medieval Latin: related to DEFEND]

defer¹ /dɪˈfɜː(r)/ v. (-rr-) postpone. □ **deferment** n. **deferral** n. [originally the same as DEFER²]

defer² /dɪˈfɜː(r)/ v. (-rr-) (foll. by to) yield or make concessions to. [Latin defero carry away]

deference /ˈdefərəns/ n. 1 courteous regard, respect. 2 compliance with another's wishes. □ **in deference to** out of respect for.

deferential /ˌdefəˈrenʃ(ə)l/ adj. respectful. □ **deferentially** adv.

deferred payment n. payment by instalments.

defiance /dɪˈfaɪəns/ n. open disobedience; bold resistance. [French: related to DEFY]

defiant adj. showing defiance; disobedient. □ **defiantly** adv.

deficiency /dɪˈfɪʃənsɪ/ n. (pl. -ies) 1 being deficient. 2 (usu. foll. by of) lack or shortage. 3 thing lacking. 4 financial deficit. [Latin: related to DEFICIT]

deficiency disease n. disease caused by the lack of an essential element of diet.

deficient adj. (often foll. by in) incomplete or insufficient in quantity, quality, etc. [Latin: related to DEFICIT]

deficit /ˈdefɪsɪt/ n. 1 amount by which a thing (esp. money) is too small. 2 excess of liabilities over assets. [French from Latin deficit]

defile¹ /dɪˈfaɪl/ v. (-ling) 1 make dirty; pollute. 2 desecrate, profane. □ **defilement** n. [earlier defoul, from French défouler trample down]

defile² /dɪˈfaɪl/ —n. narrow gorge or pass. —v. /dɪˈfaɪl/ march in file. [French: related to FILE²]

define /dɪˈfaɪn/ v. (-ning) 1 give the meaning of (a word etc.). 2 describe or explain the scope of (define one's position). 3 outline clearly (well-defined image). 4 mark out the boundary of. □ **definable** adj. [Latin finis end]

definite /'defɪnɪt/ *adj.* **1** certain, sure. **2** clearly defined; not vague; precise. □ **definitely** *adv.* [Latin: related to DE-FINE]

■ **Usage** See note at *definitive*.

definite article *n.* the word (*the* in English) preceding a noun and implying a specific instance.

definition /defɪ'nɪʃ(ə)n/ *n.* **1 a** defining. **b** statement of the meaning of a word etc. **2** distinctness in outline, esp. of a photographic image. [Latin: related to DEFINE]

definitive /dɪ'fɪnɪtɪv/ *adj.* **1** (of an answer, verdict, etc.) decisive, unconditional, final. **2** (of a book etc.) most authoritative.

■ **Usage** In sense 1, this word is often confused with *definite*, which does not imply authority and conclusiveness. A *definite no* is an authoritative judgement or refusal, while a *definitive no* is not an authoritative judgement or decision that something is not the case.

deflate /dɪ'fleɪt/ *v.* (-ting) **1** empty (a tyre, balloon, etc.) of air, gas, etc.; be so emptied. **2** (cause to) lose confidence or conceit. **3 a** subject (a currency or economy) to deflation. **b** pursue this as a policy. [from DE-, INFLATE]

deflation /dɪ'fleɪʃ(ə)n/ *n.* **1** deflating or being deflated. **2** reduction of money in circulation, intended to combat inflation. □ **deflationary** *adj.*

deflect /dɪ'flekt/ *v.* **1** bend or turn aside from a course or purpose. **2** (often foll. by *from*) (cause to) deviate. □ **deflection** *n.* (also **deflexion**). **deflector** *n.* [Latin *flecto* bend]

deflower /dɪ'flaʊə(r)/ *v. literary* **1** deprive of virginity. **2** ravage, spoil. [Latin: related to FLOWER]

defoliate /diː'fəʊlɪˌeɪt/ *v.* (-ting) destroy the leaves of (trees or plants). □ **defoliant** *n.* **defoliation** /-'eɪʃ(ə)n/ *n.* [Latin: related to FOIL²]

deforest /diː'fɒrɪst/ *v.* clear of forests or trees. □ **deforestation** /-'steɪʃ(ə)n/ *n.*

deform /dɪ'fɔːm/ *v.* make ugly or misshapen, disfigure. □ **deformation** /ˌdiːfɔː'meɪʃ(ə)n/ *n.* [Latin: related to FORM]

deformed *adj.* (of a person or limb) misshapen.

deformity *n.* (*pl.* -ies) **1** being deformed. **2** malformation, esp. of a body or limb.

defraud /dɪ'frɔːd/ *v.* (often foll. by *of*) cheat by fraud. [Latin: related to FRAUD]

defray /dɪ'freɪ/ *v.* provide money for (a cost or expense). □ **defrayal** *n.* **defrayment** *n.* [medieval Latin *fredum* fine]

defrock /diː'frɒk/ *v.* deprive (esp. a priest) of office. [French: related to DE-, FROCK]

defrost /diː'frɒst/ *v.* **1** remove frost or ice from (a refrigerator, windscreen, etc.). **2** unfreeze (frozen food). **3** become unfrozen.

deft *adj.* neat; dexterous; adroit. □ **deftly** *adv.* **deftness** *n.* [var. of DAFT = meek']

defunct /dɪ'fʌŋkt/ *adj.* **1** no longer existing or used. **2** dead or extinct. □ **defunctness** *n.* [Latin *fungor* perform]

defuse /diː'fjuːz/ *v.* (-sing) **1** remove the fuse from (a bomb etc.). **2** reduce tension etc. in (a crisis, difficulty, etc.).

defy /dɪ'faɪ/ *v.* (-ies, -ied) **1** resist openly; refuse to obey. **2** (of a thing) present insuperable obstacles to (*defies solution*). **3** (foll. by *to* + infin.) challenge (a person) to do or prove something. [Latin *fides* faith]

degenerate —*adj.* /dɪ'dʒenərət/ **1** having lost its usual or good qualities; immoral, degraded. **2** *Biol.* having changed to a lower form. —*n.* /dɪ'dʒenərət/ degenerate person or animal. —*v.* /dɪ'dʒenəˌreɪt/ (-ting) become degenerate. □ **degeneracy** *n.* [Latin *genus* race]

degeneration /dɪˌdʒenə'reɪʃ(ə)n/ *n.* **1** becoming degenerate. **2** *Med.* morbid deterioration of body tissue etc. [Latin: related to DEGENERATE]

degrade /dɪ'greɪd/ *v.* (-ding) **1** humiliate, dishonour. **2** reduce to a lower rank. **3** *Chem.* reduce to a simpler molecular structure. □ **degradation** /ˌdegrə'deɪʃ(ə)n/ *n.* **degrading** *adj.* [Latin: related to GRADE]

degree /dɪ'griː/ *n.* **1** stage in a scale, series, or process. **2** stage in intensity or amount (*in some degree*). **3** unit of measurement of an angle or arc. **4** unit in a scale of temperature, hardness, etc. **5** extent of burns. **6** academic rank conferred by a polytechnic, university, etc. **7** grade of crime (*first-degree murder*). **8** step in direct genealogical descent. **9** social rank. □ **by degrees** gradually. [Latin *gradus* step]

degrees of comparison see COMPARISON 4.

dehisce /dɪ'hɪs/ *v.* (-cing) (esp. of a pod, cut, etc.) gape or burst open. □ **dehiscence** *n.* **dehiscent** *adj.* [Latin *hio* gape]

dehumanize /diː'hjuːməˌnaɪz/ *v.* (also **-ise**) (-zing or -sing) **1** take human qualities away from. **2** make impersonal. □ **dehumanization** /-'zeɪʃ(ə)n/ *n.*

dehydrate /ˌdiːhaɪ'dreɪt/ *v.* (-ting) **1** remove water from (esp. foods). **2** make or

de-ice /diːˈaɪs/ v. 1 remove ice from. 2 prevent the formation of ice on. □ **de-icer** n.

deity /ˈdiːɪtɪ, ˈdeɪ-/ n. (pl. -ies) 1 a god or goddess. b a divine status or nature. 2 (the Deity) God. [Latin *deus* god]

deign /deɪn/ v. (foll. by to + infin.) think fit, condescend. [Latin *dignus* worthy]

deism /ˈdiːɪz(ə)m/ n. reasoned belief in the existence of a god. □ **deist** n. **deistic** /-ˈɪstɪk/ adj. [Latin *deus* god]

deity /ˈdiːɪtɪ/ n. (pl. -ies) 1 god or goddess. 2 divine status or nature. 3 (the Deity) God. [French from Church Latin]

déjà vu /ˌdeɪʒɑː ˈvuː/ n. 1 feeling of having already experienced the present situation. 2 something tediously familiar. [French, = already seen]

deject /dɪˈdʒɛkt/ v. (usu. as **dejected** adj.) make sad, depress. □ **dejectedly** adv. **dejection** n. [Latin *jacio* throw]

de jure /deɪ ˈdʒʊərɪ/ adj. rightful. —adv. rightfully. by right. [Latin]

dekko /ˈdɛkəʊ/ n. (pl. -s) slang look, glance. [Hindi]

delay /dɪˈleɪ/ —v. 1 postpone, defer. 2 make or be late; loiter. —n. 1 delaying or being delayed. 2 time lost by this. 3 hindrance. [French]

delayed-action attrib. adj. (esp. of a bomb, camera, etc.) operating after a set interval.

delectable /dɪˈlɛktəb(ə)l/ adj. esp. liter-ary delightful, delicious. □ **delectably** adv. [Latin: related to DELIGHT]

delectation /ˌdiːlɛkˈteɪʃ(ə)n/ n. literary pleasure, enjoyment.

delegate —n. /ˈdɛlɪgət/ 1 elected repres-entative sent to a conference. 2 member of a committee or delegation. —v. /ˈdɛlɪgeɪt/ (-ting) 1 (often foll. by to) a commit (power etc.) to an agent or deputy. b entrust (a task) to another. 2 send or authorize (a person, as a repres-entative. [Latin: related to LEGATE]

delegation /ˌdɛlɪˈgeɪʃ(ə)n/ n. 1 group representing others. 2 delegating or being delegated.

delete /dɪˈliːt/ v. (-ting) remove (a letter, word, etc.), esp. by striking out. □ **dele-tion** n. [Latin *deleo*]

deleterious /ˌdɛlɪˈtɪərɪəs/ adj. harmful. [Latin from Greek]

---

delft n. (also **delftware**) glazed, usu. blue and white, earthenware. [*Delft* in Holland]

deli /ˈdɛlɪ/ n. (pl. -s) colloq. delicatessen shop. [abbreviation]

deliberate —adj. /dɪˈlɪbərət/ 1 a inten-tional. b considered, careful. 2 (of move-ment, thought, etc.) unhurried, cau-tious. —v. /dɪˈlɪbəˌreɪt/ (-ting) 1 think carefully. 2 discuss (jury delib-erated). □ **deliberately** /dɪˈlɪbərətlɪ/ adv. [Latin *libra* balance]

deliberation /dɪˌlɪbəˈreɪʃ(ə)n/ n. 1 care-ful consideration; discussion. 2 careful slowness.

deliberative /dɪˈlɪbərətɪv/ adj. (esp. of an assembly etc.) of or for deliberation or debate

delicacy /ˈdɛlɪkəsɪ/ n. (pl. -ies) 1 being delicate (in all senses). 2 a choice food.

delicate /ˈdɛlɪkət/ adj. 1 a fine in tex-ture, quality, etc.; slender, slight. b (of colour, flavour, etc.) subtle, hard to discern. 2 susceptible; weak, tender. 3 a requiring tact; tricky (delicate situ-ation). b (of an instrument) highly sens-itive. 4 deft (delicate touch). 5 modest. 6 (esp. of actions) considerate. □ **delic-ately** adv. [Latin]

delicatessen /ˌdɛlɪkəˈtɛs(ə)n/ n. 1 shop selling esp. exotic cooked meats, cheeses, etc. 2 (often attrib.) such foods. [French: related to DELICATE]

delicious /dɪˈlɪʃəs/ adj. highly enjoy-able, esp. to taste or smell. □ **deli-ciously** adv. [Latin *delicia* delights]

delight /dɪˈlaɪt/ —v. 1 (often as **delighted** adj.) please greatly (her sing-ing delighted us; delighted to help) 2 (foll. by in) take great pleasure in (de-lights in surprising everyone). —n. 1 great pleasure. 2 thing that delights. □ **delighted** adj. **delightful** adj. **delightfully** adv. [Latin *delecto*]

delimit /dɪˈlɪmɪt/ v. (-t-) fix the limits or boundary of. □ **delimitation** /-ˈteɪʃ(ə)n/ n. [Latin: related to LIMIT]

delineate /dɪˈlɪnɪeɪt/ v. (-ting) portray by drawing etc. or in words. □ **delin-eation** /-ˈeɪʃ(ə)n/ n. [Latin: related to LINE[1]]

delinquent /dɪˈlɪŋkwənt/ —adj. 1 guilty of a minor crime or misdeed. 2 failing in one's duty. —n. delinquent person. □ **delinquency** n. [Latin *delinquo* offend]

deliquesce /ˌdɛlɪˈkwɛs/ v. (-cing) 1 become liquid, melt. 2 dissolve in water absorbed from the air. □ **deliques-cence** n. **deliquescent** adj. [Latin: related to LIQUID]

226

delirious /dɪˈlɪrɪəs/ *adj.* **1** affected with delirium. **2** wildly excited, ecstatic. □ **deliriously** *adv.*

delirium /dɪˈlɪrɪəm/ *n.* **1** disorder involving incoherent speech, hallucinations, etc., caused by intoxication, fever, etc. **2** great excitement, ecstasy. [Latin *lira* ridge between furrows]

delirium tremens /ˈtriːmenz/ *n.* psychosis of chronic alcoholism involving tremors and hallucinations.

deliver /dɪˈlɪvə(r)/ *v.* **1 a** distribute (letters, goods, etc.) to their destination(s). **b** (often foll. by *to*) hand over. **2** (often foll. by *from*) save, rescue, or set free. **3 a** give birth to (*delivered a girl*). **b** assist at the birth of or in giving birth (*delivered six babies*). **4** utter (an opinion, speech, etc.). **5** (often foll. by *up*, *over*) abandon; resign (*delivered his soul up*). **6** launch or aim (a blow etc.). □ **be delivered of** give birth to. **deliver the goods** *colloq.* carry out an undertaking. [Latin *liber* free]

deliverance *n.* rescuing or being rescued.

delivery *n.* (*pl.* **-ies**) **1** delivering or being delivered. **2** regular distribution of letters etc. (*two deliveries a day*). **3** thing delivered. **4** childbirth. **5** deliverance. **6** style of throwing a ball, delivering a speech, etc. [Anglo-French: related to DELIVER]

dell *n.* small usu. wooded valley. [Old English]

delouse /diːˈlaʊs/ *v.* (**-sing**) rid of lice.

Delphic /ˈdelfɪk/ *adj.* (also **Delphian** /-fɪən/) **1** obscure, ambiguous, or enigmatic. **2** of the ancient Greek oracle at Delphi.

delphinium /delˈfɪnɪəm/ *n.* (*pl.* **-s**) garden plant with tall spikes of usu. blue flowers. [Greek: related to DOLPHIN]

delta /ˈdeltə/ *n.* **1** triangular area of earth, alluvium etc. at the mouth of a river, formed by its diverging outlets. **2 a** fourth letter of the Greek alphabet (Δ, δ). **b** fourth-class mark for work etc. [Greek]

delta wing *n.* triangular swept-back wing of an aircraft.

delude /dɪˈluːd/ *v.* (**-ding**) deceive, mislead. [Latin *ludo* mock]

deluge /ˈdeljuːdʒ/ *n.* **1** great flood. **2** (**the Deluge**) biblical Flood (Gen. 6-8). **3** overwhelming rush. **4** heavy fall of rain. —*v.* (**-ging**) flood or inundate (*deluged with complaints*). [Latin *diluvium*]

delusion /dɪˈluːʒ(ə)n/ *n.* **1** false belief, hope, etc. **2** hallucination. □ **delusive** *adj.* **delusory** *adj.* [related to DELUDE]

de luxe /də ˈlʌks/ *adj.* luxurious; superior; sumptuous. [French, = of luxury]

delve *v.* (**-ving**) **1** (often foll. by *in, into*) search or research energetically or deeply (*delved into his pocket, his family history*). **2** *poet.* dig. [Old English]

demagnetize /diːˈmæɡnɪtaɪz/ *v.* (also **-ise**) (**-zing** or **-sing**) remove the magnetic properties of. □ **demagnetization** /-ˈzeɪʃ(ə)n/ *n.*

demagogue /ˈdeməɡɒɡ/ *n.* (*US* **-gog**) political agitator appealing to mob instincts. □ **demagogic** /-ˈɡɒɡɪk/ *adj.* **demagogy** *n.* [Greek, = leader of the people]

demand /dɪˈmɑːnd/ —*n.* **1** insistent and peremptory request. **2** desire for a commodity (*no demand for fur coats*). **3** urgent claim (*makes demands on her*). —*v.* **1** (often foll. by *of*, *from*, or *to* + infin., or *that* + clause) ask for insistently (*demanded to know*). **2** require (*task demanded skill*). **3** insist on being told (*demanded her age*). **4** (as **demanding** *adj.*) requiring skill, effort, attention, etc. (*demanding job*; *demanding child*). □ **in demand** sought after. **on demand** as soon as requested (*payable on demand*). [French from Latin: related to MANDATE]

demand feeding *n.* feeding a baby when it cries.

demarcation /diːmɑːˈkeɪʃ(ə)n/ *n.* **1** marking of a boundary or limits. **2** trade-union practice of restricting a specific job to one union. □ **demarcate** /ˈdiː-/ *v.* (**-ting**). [Spanish *marcar* MARK]

dematerialize /diːməˈtɪərɪəlaɪz/ *v.* (also **-ise**) (**-zing** or **-sing**) make or become non-material; vanish. □ **dematerialization** /-ˈzeɪʃ(ə)n/ *n.*

demean /dɪˈmiːn/ *v.* (usu. *refl.*) lower the dignity of (*would not demean myself*). [from MEAN²]

demeanour /dɪˈmiːnə(r)/ *n.* (*US* **demeanor**) outward behaviour or bearing. [Latin *minor* threaten]

demented /dɪˈmentɪd/ *adj.* mad. □ **dementedly** *adv.* [Latin *mens* mind]

dementia /dɪˈmenʃə/ *n.* chronic insanity. [Latin: related to DEMENTED]

dementia praecox /ˈpriːkɒks/ *n.* *formal* schizophrenia.

demerara /deməˈreərə/ *n.* light-brown cane sugar. [*Demerara* in Guyana]

demerge /diːˈmɜːdʒ(r)/ *n.* dissolution of a commercial merger. □ **demerge** *v.* (**-ging**).

demerit /diːˈmerɪt/ *n.* fault; blemish.

demesne /dɪˈmiːn, -ˈmeɪn/ *n.* **1 a** territory; domain. **b** land attached to a mansion etc. **c** landed property. **2** (usu. foll. by *of*) region or sphere. **3** *Law hist.* possession (of real property) as one's

demi- | **demonstrator**

demi-. [Latin *dominicus* from *dominus* lord]

demi- *prefix* half; partly. [Latin *dimidius* half]

demigod /ˈdemɪgɒd/ *n.* **1 a** a partly divine being. **b** child of a god or goddess and a mortal. **2** *collog.* a godlike person.

demijohn /ˈdemɪdʒɒn/ *n.* large bottle usu. in a wicker cover. [French]

demilitarize /diːˈmɪlɪtəraɪz/ *v.* (also **-ise**) (**-zing** or **-sing**) remove an army etc. from (a frontier, zone, etc.). □ **demilitarization** /-ˈzeɪʃ(ə)n/ *n.*

demi-monde /ˈdemɪˌmɒnd/ *n.* **1** class of women considered to be of doubtful morality. **2** any semi-respectable group. [French, = half-world]

demise /dɪˈmaɪz/ *n.* **1** death; termination. **2** *Law* transfer of an estate, title, etc. by demising. —*v.* (**-sing**) *Law* transfer (an estate, title, etc.) by will, lease, or death. [Anglo-French: related to DISMISS]

demisemiquaver /ˌdemɪˈsemɪkweɪvə(r)/ *n. Mus.* note equal to half a semiquaver.

demist /diːˈmɪst/ *v.* clear mist from (a windscreen etc.). □ **demister** *n.*

demo /ˈdeməʊ/ *n.* (*pl.* **-s**) *collog.* = DEMONSTRATION 2, 3. [abbreviation]

demob /diːˈmɒb/ *collog.* —*v.* (**-bb-**) demobilize. —*n.* demobilization. [abbreviation]

demobilize /diːˈməʊbɪlaɪz/ *v.* (also **-ise**) (**-zing** or **-sing**) disband (troops, ships, etc.). □ **demobilization** /-ˈzeɪʃ(ə)n/ *n.*

democracy /dɪˈmɒkrəsɪ/ *n.* (*pl.* **-ies**) **1 a** government by the whole population, usu. through elected representatives. **b** State so governed. **2** classless and tolerant society. [Greek *dēmokratia* rule of the people]

democrat /ˈdeməkræt/ *n.* **1** advocate of democracy. **2** (**Democrat**) (in the US) member of the Democratic Party.

democratic /ˌdeməˈkrætɪk/ *adj.* **1** of, like, practising, or being a democracy. **2** favouring social equality. □ **democratically** *adv.*

Democratic Party *n.* more liberal of the two main US political parties.

democratize /dɪˈmɒkrətaɪz/ *v.* (also **-ise**) (**-zing** or **-sing**) make democratic. □ **democratization** /-ˈzeɪʃ(ə)n/ *n.*

demodulate /diːˈmɒdjʊleɪt/ *v.* (**-ting**) extract (a modulating signal) from its carrier. □ **demodulation** /diːˌmɒdjʊˈleɪʃ(ə)n/ *n.*

demography /dɪˈmɒgrəfɪ/ *n.* the study of the statistics of births, deaths, disease, etc. □ **demographic** /ˌdeməˈgræfɪk/ *adj.* **demographically** /ˌdeməˈgræfɪkəlɪ/ *adv.* [Greek *dēmos* the people, -GRAPHY]

demolish /dɪˈmɒlɪʃ/ *v.* **1 a** pull down (a building). **b** destroy. **2** overthrow (an institution). **3** refute (an argument, theory, etc.). **4** *joc.* eat up voraciously. □ **demolition** /ˌdeməˈlɪʃ(ə)n/ *n.* [Latin *moliri* mass]

demon /ˈdiːmən/ *n.* **1 a** evil spirit or devil. **b** personification of evil passion. **2** (often *attrib.*) forceful or skilful performer (*demon player*). **3** cruel person. **4** (also **daemon**) supernatural being in ancient Greece. □ **demonic** /dɪˈmɒnɪk/ *adj.* [Greek *daimōn* deity]

demonetize /diːˈmʌnɪtaɪz/ *v.* (also **-ise**) (**-zing** or **-sing**) withdraw (a coin etc.) from use. □ **demonetization** /-ˈzeɪʃ(ə)n/ *n.* [Latin: related to MONEY]

demoniac /dɪˈməʊnɪæk/ —*adj.* **1** fiercely energetic or frenzied. **2** supposedly possessed by an evil spirit. **3** of or like demons. —*n.* demoniac person. □ **demoniacal** /ˌdiːməˈnaɪək(ə)l/ *adj.* **demoniacally** /ˌdiːməˈnaɪəklɪ/ *adv.* [Church Latin: related to DEMON]

demonism /ˈdiːmənɪz(ə)m/ *n.* belief in or worship of demons. [from DEMON, Greek *latreuō* worship]

demonology /ˌdiːməˈnɒlədʒɪ/ *n.* the study of demons etc.

demonstrable /ˈdemənstrəb(ə)l, dɪˈmɒnstrəb(ə)l/ *adj.* able to be shown or proved. □ **demonstrably** *adv.*

demonstrate /ˈdemənstreɪt/ *v.* (**-ting**) **1** show (feelings etc.). **2** describe and explain by experiment, practical use, etc. **3** logically prove or be proof of the truth or existence of. **4** take part in a public demonstration. **5** act as a demonstrator. [Latin *monstro* show]

demonstration /ˌdemənˈstreɪʃ(ə)n/ *n.* **1** (foll. by *of*) show of feeling etc. **2** (esp. political) public meeting, march, etc. **3** the exhibiting etc. of specimens or experiments in esp. scientific teaching. **4** proof by logic, argument, etc. **5** *Mil.* display of military force.

demonstrative /dɪˈmɒnstrətɪv/ *adj.* **1** showing feelings readily; affectionate. **2** (usu. foll. by *of*) logically conclusive; giving proof (*demonstrative of their skill*). **3** *Gram.* (of an adjective or pronoun) indicating the person or thing referred to (e.g. *this, that, those*). □ **demonstratively** *adv.* **demonstrativeness** *n.*

demonstrator /ˈdemənstreɪtə(r)/ *n.* **1** person who demonstrates politically. **2** person who demonstrates machines etc to prospective customers. **3** person who teaches by esp. scientific demonstration.

demoralize /dɪˈmɒrəˌlaɪz/ v. (also **-ise**) (**-zing** or **-sing**) destroy the morale of; dishearten. □ **demoralization** /-ˈzeɪʃ(ə)n/ n. [French]

demote /dɪˈməʊt/ v. (**-ting**) reduce to a lower rank or class. □ **demotion** /-ˈməʊʃ(ə)n/ n. [from DE-, PROMOTE]

demotic /dɪˈmɒtɪk/ —n. **1** colloquial form of a language. **2** simplified form of ancient Egyptian writing (cf. HIERATIC). —adj. **1** (esp. of language) colloquial or vulgar. **2** of ancient Egyptian or modern Greek demotic. [Greek *dēmos* the people]

demotivate /diːˈməʊtɪˌveɪt/ v. (**-ting**) (also *absol.*) cause to lose motivation or incentive. □ **demotivation** /-ˈveɪʃ(ə)n/ n.

demur /dɪˈmɜː(r)/ —v. (**-rr-**) **1** (often foll. by *to, at*) raise objections. **2** *Law* put in a demurrer. —n. (usu. in *neg.*) objection; objecting (*agreed without demur*). [Latin *moror* delay]

demure /dɪˈmjʊə(r)/ adj. (**demurer, demurest**) **1** quiet, reserved; modest. **2** coy. □ **demurely** adv. **demureness** n. [French: related to DEMUR]

demurrer /dɪˈmʌrə(r)/ n. *Law* objection raised or exception taken.

demystify /diːˈmɪstɪˌfaɪ/ v. (**-ies, -ied**) remove the mystery from; clarify. □ **demystification** /-fɪˈkeɪʃ(ə)n/ n.

den n. **1** wild animal's lair. **2** place of crime or vice (*opium den*). **3** small private room. [Old English]

denarius /dɪˈneərɪəs/ n. (*pl.* **denarii** /-rɪˌaɪ/) ancient Roman silver coin. [Latin *deni* by tens]

denary /ˈdiːnərɪ/ adj. of ten; decimal. [Latin *deni* by tens]

denationalize /diːˈnæʃənəˌlaɪz/ v. (also **-ise**) (**-zing** or **-sing**) transfer (an industry etc.) from public to private ownership. □ **denationalization** /-ˈzeɪʃ(ə)n/ n.

denature /diːˈneɪtʃə(r)/ v. (**-ring**) **1** change the properties of (a protein etc.) by heat, acidity, etc. **2** make (alcohol) undrinkable. [French]

dendrochronology /ˌdendrəʊkrə-ˈnɒlədʒɪ/ n. **1** dating of trees by their annual growth rings. **2** the study of these. [Greek *dendron* tree]

dendrology /denˈdrɒlədʒɪ/ n. the study of trees. □ **dendrological** /ˌdrə-ˈlɒdʒɪk(ə)l/ adj. **dendrologist** n. [Greek *dendron* tree]

dene n. (also **dean**) narrow wooded valley. [Old English]

dengue /ˈdeŋgɪ/ n. infectious tropical viral fever. [W. Indian Spanish from Swahili]

deniable /dɪˈnaɪəb(ə)l/ adj. that may be denied.

denial /dɪˈnaɪəl/ n. **1** denying the truth or existence of a thing. **2** refusal of a request or wish. **3** disavowal of a leader etc.

denier /ˈdenjə(r)/ n. unit of weight measuring the fineness of silk, nylon, etc. [originally the name of a small coin, from Latin DENARIUS]

denigrate /ˈdenɪˌgreɪt/ v. (**-ting**) blacken the reputation of. □ **denigration** /-ˈgreɪʃ(ə)n/ n. **denigrator** n. **denigratory** /-ˈgreɪtərɪ/ adj. [Latin *niger* black]

denim /ˈdenɪm/ n. **1** (often *attrib.*) hard-wearing usu. blue cotton twill used for jeans, overalls, etc. **2** (in *pl.*) *colloq.* jeans etc. made of this. [French *de of*, *Nîmes* in France]

denizen /ˈdenɪz(ə)n/ n. **1** (usu. foll. by *of*) inhabitant or occupant. **2** foreigner having certain rights in an adopted country. **3** naturalized foreign word, animal, or plant. [Latin *de intus* from within]

denominate /dɪˈnɒmɪˌneɪt/ v. (**-ting**) give a name to, call, describe as. [Latin: related to NOMINATE]

denomination /dɪˌnɒmɪˈneɪʃ(ə)n/ n. **1** Church or religious sect. **2** class of measurement or money. **3** name, esp. a characteristic or class name. □ **denominational** adj. [Latin: related to DENOMINATE]

denominator /dɪˈnɒmɪˌneɪtə(r)/ n. number below the line in a vulgar fraction; divisor. [Latin *nomen* name]

denote /dɪˈnəʊt/ v. (**-ting**) **1** (often foll. by *that*) be a sign of; indicate; mean. **2** stand as a name for; signify. □ **denotation** /ˌdiːnəʊˈteɪʃ(ə)n/ n. [Latin: related to NOTE]

denouement /deɪˈnuːmɑ̃/ n. (also **dénouement**) **1** final unravelling of a plot or complicated situation. **2** final scene in a play, novel, etc. [French, from Latin *nodus* knot]

denounce /dɪˈnaʊns/ v. (**-cing**) **1** accuse publicly; condemn. **2** inform against. **3** announce withdrawal from (an armistice, treaty, etc.). □ **denouncement** n. [Latin *nuntius* messenger]

de novo /diː ˈnəʊvəʊ/ adv. starting again; anew. [Latin]

dense adj. **1** closely compacted; crowded together; thick. **2** *colloq.* stupid. □ **densely** adv. **denseness** n. [Latin *densus*]

density n. (*pl.* **-ies**) **1** denseness of thing(s) or a substance. **2** *Physics* degree of consistency measured by the quantity of mass per unit volume. **3** opacity of a photographic image.

dent —n. **1** slight hollow as made by a blow or pressure. **2** noticeable adverse

effect (*dent in our funds*). —*v.* 1 mark with a dent. 2 adversely affect. [from INDENT]

dental /'dent(ə)l/ *adj.* 1 of the teeth or dentistry. 2 (of a consonant) produced with the tongue-tip against the upper front teeth (as *th*) or the ridge of the teeth (as *n, s, t*). [Latin *dens dentis* tooth]

dental floss *n.* thread used to clean between the teeth.

dental surgeon *n.* dentist.

dentate /'denteɪt/ *adj.* toothed; with toothlike notches. [Latin]

dentifrice /'dentɪfrɪs/ *n.* toothpaste or tooth powder. [Latin: related to DENTAL, *frico* rub]

dentine /'dentiːn/ *n.* (US **dentin** /-tɪn/) hard dense tissue forming the bulk of a tooth.

dentist /'dentɪst/ *n.* person qualified to treat, extract, etc., teeth. □ **dentistry** *n.*

dentition /den'tɪʃ(ə)n/ *n.* 1 type, number, and arrangement of teeth in a species etc. 2 teething.

denture /'dentʃə(r)/ *n.* removable artificial tooth or teeth.

denuclearize /diː'njuːklɪəraɪz/ *v.* (also **-ise**) (**-zing** or **-sing**) remove nuclear weapons from (a country etc.). □ **denuclearization** /-'zeɪʃ(ə)n/ *n.*

denude /dɪ'njuːd/ *v.* 2 (foll. by *of*) strip of (covering, property, etc.). □ **denudation** /diːnjuː'deɪʃ(ə)n/ *n.* [Latin *nudus* naked]

denunciation /dɪnʌnsɪ'eɪʃ(ə)n/ *n.* denouncing; public condemnation. [Latin: related to DENOUNCE]

deny /dɪ'naɪ/ *v.* (**-ies, -ied**) 1 declare untrue or non-existent. 2 repudiate or disclaim. 3 (often foll. by *to*) withhold (a thing) from (*denied him the satisfaction; denied it to me*). □ **deny oneself** be abstinent. [Latin: related to NEGATE]

deodar /'diːədɑː(r)/ *n.* Himalayan cedar. [Sanskrit, = divine tree]

deodorant /diː'əʊdərənt/ *n.* (often *attrib.*) substance applied to the body or sprayed into the air to conceal smells. [related to ODOUR]

deodorize /diː'əʊdəraɪz/ *v.* (also **-ise**) (**-zing** or **-sing**) remove or destroy the smell of. □ **deodorization** /-'zeɪʃ(ə)n/ *n.*

deoxyribonucleic acid /diːɒksɪ-raɪbəʊnjuː'kleɪɪk/ see DNA [from DE-, OXYGEN, RIBONUCLEIC ACID]

dep. *abbr.* 1 departs. 2 deputy.

depart /dɪ'pɑːt/ *v.* 1 a (often foll. by *from*) go away; leave. b (usu. foll. by *for*) start; set out. 2 (usu. foll. by *from*) deviate (*departs from good taste*). 3 esp. *formal* or *literary* leave by death; die (*departed this life*). [Latin *dispertio* divide]

departed —*adj.* bygone. —*n.* (prec. by *the*) *euphem.* dead person or people.

department *n.* 1 separate part of a complex whole, esp.: **a** a branch of administration (*Housing Department*). **b** a division of a school, college, etc., by subject (*physics department*). **c** a section of a large store (*hardware department*). 2 *colloq.* area of special expertise. [French: related to DEPART]

departmental /ˌdiːpɑːt'ment(ə)l/ *adj.* of a department. □ **departmentally** *adv.*

department store *n.* large shop with many departments.

departure /dɪ'pɑːtʃə(r)/ *n.* 1 departing. 2 (often foll. by *from*) deviation (from the truth, a standard, etc.). 3 (often *attrib.*) departing of a train, aircraft, etc. (*departure lounge*). 4 new course of action or thought (*driving is rather a departure for him*).

depend /dɪ'pend/ *v.* 1 (often foll. by *on, upon*) be controlled or determined by (*it depends on luck*). 2 (foll. by *on, upon*) **a** need (*depends on his car*). **b** rely on (*I'm depending on good weather*). [Latin *pendeo* hang]

dependable *adj.* reliable. □ **dependability** /-'bɪlɪtɪ/ *n.* **dependableness** *n.* **dependably** *adv.*

dependant *n.* (*US* **dependent**) person supported, esp. financially, by another. [French: related to DEPEND]

dependence *n.* 1 depending or being dependent, esp. financially. 2 reliance; trust.

dependency *n.* (*pl.* **-ies**) country or province controlled by another.

dependent —*adj.* 1 (usu. foll. by *on, upon*) depending; conditional. 2 unable to do without (esp. a drug). 3 maintained at another's cost. 4 (of a clause etc.) subordinate to a sentence or word. —*n. US* var. of DEPENDANT.

depict /dɪ'pɪkt/ *v.* 1 represent in drawing or painting etc. 2 portray in words; describe. □ **depicter** *n.* **depictor** *n.* **depiction** *n.* [Latin: related to PICTURE]

depilate /'depɪleɪt/ *v.* (**-ting**) remove hair from. □ **depilation** /-'leɪʃ(ə)n/ *n.* [Latin *pilus* hair]

depilatory /dɪ'pɪlətərɪ/ —*adj.* removing unwanted hair. —*n.* (*pl.* **-ies**) depilatory substance.

deplete /dɪ'pliːt/ *v.* (**-ting**) (esp. in *passive*) reduce in numbers, force, or quantity; exhaust. □ **depletion** *n.* [Latin *pleo* fill]

deplorable /dɪ'plɔːrəb(ə)l/ *adj.* exceedingly bad. □ **deplorably** *adv.*

deplore /dɪˈplɔː(r)/ v. (-ring) 1 regret deeply. 2 find exceedingly bad. [Latin *ploro* wail]

deploy /dɪˈplɔɪ/ v. 1 spread out (troops) into a line ready for action. 2 use (arguments, forces, etc.) effectively. □ **deployment** n. [Latin *plico* fold]

depoliticize /diːpəˈlɪtɪˌsaɪz/ v. (also **-ise**) (**-zing** or **-sing**) make non-political. □ **depoliticization** /-ˈzeɪʃ(ə)n/ n.

deponent /dɪˈpəʊnənt/ —adj. (of esp. a Latin or Greek verb) passive in form but active in meaning. —n. 1 deponent verb. 2 person making deposition under oath. [Latin *depono* put down, lay aside]

depopulate /diːˈpɒpjʊˌleɪt/ v. (-ting) reduce the population of. □ **depopulation** /-ˈleɪʃ(ə)n/ n.

deport /dɪˈpɔːt/ v. 1 remove forcibly or exile to another country; banish. 2 *refl.* behave. (in a specified manner) *(deported himself well).* □ **deportation** /diːpɔːˈteɪʃ(ə)n/ n. (in sense 1). [Latin *porto* carry]

deportee /diːpɔːˈtiː/ n. deported person.

deportment /dɪˈpɔːtmənt/ n. bearing. demeanour. [French: related to DEPORT]

depose /dɪˈpəʊz/ v. (-sing) 1 remove from office, esp. dethrone. 2 *Law* (usu. foll. by *to*, or *that* + clause) testify. esp. on oath. [French from Latin: related to DEPOSIT]

deposit /dɪˈpɒzɪt/ —n. 1 a money in a bank account. b anything stored for safe keeping. 2 a payment made as a pledge for a contract or as an initial part payment for a thing bought. b returnable sum paid on the hire of an item. 3 a natural layer of sand, rock, coal, etc. b layer of accumulated matter on a surface. —v. (-t-) 1 a put or lay down *(deposited the book on the shelf).* b (of water etc.) leave (matter etc.) lying. 2 a store or entrust for keeping. b pay (a sum of money) into a bank account. 3 pay (a sum) as part of a larger sum or as a pledge for a contract. [Latin *pono posit-* put]

deposit account n. bank account that pays interest but is not usu. immediately accessible.

depositary n. (pl. **-ies**) person to whom a thing is entrusted. [Latin: related to DEPOSIT]

deposition /depəˈzɪʃ(ə)n/ n. 1 deposing. esp. dethronement. 2 sworn evidence; giving of this. 3 (**the Deposition**) taking down of Christ from the Cross. 4 depositing or being deposited. [Latin: related to DEPOSIT]

depositor n. person who deposits money, property, etc.

depository n. (pl. **-ies**) 1 a storehouse. b store (of wisdom. knowledge. etc.). 2 = DEPOSITARY. [Latin: related to DEPOSIT]

depot /ˈdepəʊ/ n. 1 a storehouse, esp. for military supplies. b headquarters of a regiment. 2 a place where vehicles, e.g. buses, are kept. b *US* railway or bus station. [French: related to DEPOSIT]

deprave /dɪˈpreɪv/ v. (-ving) corrupt, esp. morally. [Latin *pravus* crooked]

depravity /dɪˈprævɪtɪ/ n. (pl. **-ies**) moral corruption; wickedness.

deprecate /ˈdeprɪˌkeɪt/ v. (-ting) express disapproval of; deplore. □ **deprecation** /-ˈkeɪʃ(ə)n/ n. **deprecatory** /-ˈkeɪtərɪ/ adj. [Latin: related to PRAY]

■ **Usage** *Deprecate* is often confused with *depreciate*.

depreciate /dɪˈpriːʃɪˌeɪt/ v. (-ting) 1 diminish in value. 2 belittle. □ **depreciatory** /dɪˈpriːʃɪətərɪ/ adj. [Latin: related to PRICE]

depreciation /dɪˌpriːʃɪˈeɪʃ(ə)n/ n. 1 a decline in value, esp. due to wear and tear. b allowance made for this. 2 belittlement.

■ **Usage** *Depreciate* is often confused with *deprecate*.

depredation /ˌdepriˈdeɪʃ(ə)n/ n. (usu. in pl.) despoiling, ravaging. [Latin: related to PREY]

depress /dɪˈpres/ v. 1 make dispirited or sad. 2 push down; lower. 3 reduce the activity of (esp. trade). 4 (as **depressed** adj.) a miserable. b suffering from depression. □ **depressing** adj. **depressingly** adv. [Latin: related to PRESS[1]]

depressant —adj. reducing activity. —n. depressant substance.

depressed area n. area of economic depression.

depression /dɪˈpreʃ(ə)n/ n. 1 extreme melancholy, often with a reduction in vitality and physical symptoms. 2 *Econ.* long period of slump. 3 lowering of atmospheric pressure; winds etc. caused by this. 4 hollow on a surface. 5 pressing down.

depressive —adj. 1 tending to depress *(depressive drug, influence).* 2 of or tending towards depression *(depressive illness; depressive father).* —n. person suffering from depression.

deprivation /ˌdeprɪˈveɪʃ(ə)n/ n. depriving or being deprived *(suffered many deprivations).*

deprive /dɪˈpraɪv/ v. (-ving) 1 (usu. foll. by *of*) prevent from having or enjoying. 2 (as **deprived** adj.) lacking what is needed for well-being; underprivileged.

□ **deprival** *n.* [Latin: related to PRIVATION]

Dept. *abbr.* Department.

depth *n.* **1 a** deepness. **b** measurement from the top down, from the surface inwards, or from front to back. **2** difficulty; abstruseness. **3 a** wisdom. **b** intensity of emotion etc. **4** intensity of colour, darkness, etc. **5** (usu. in *pl.*) **a** deep water or place; abyss. **b** low, depressed state. **c** lowest, central, or inmost part (*depths of the country*; *depth of winter*). □ **in depth** thoroughly. **out of one's depth 1** in water over one's head. **2** engaged in a task etc. too difficult for one. [related to DEEP]

depth-charge *n.* bomb exploding under water.

deputation /ˌdepjʊˈteɪʃ(ə)n/ *n.* delegation. [Latin: related to DEPUTE]

depute /dɪˈpju:t/ *v.* (**-ting**) (often foll. by *to*) **1** delegate (a task, authority, etc.). **2** authorize as representative. [Latin *puto* think]

deputize /ˈdepjʊˌtaɪz/ *v.* (also **-ise**) (**-zing** or **-sing**) (usu. foll. by *for*) act as deputy.

deputy /ˈdepjʊtɪ/ *n.* (*pl.* **-ies**) **1** person appointed to act for another (also *attrib.*: *deputy manager*). **2** parliamentary representative in some countries. [var. of DEPUTE]

derail /di:ˈreɪl/ *v.* (usu. in *passive*) cause (a train etc.) to leave the rails. □ **derailment** *n.* [French: related to RAIL[1]]

derange /dɪˈreɪndʒ/ *v.* (**-ging**) **1** make insane. **2** disorder, disturb. □ **derangement** *n.* [French: related to RANK[1]]

Derby /ˈdɑ:bɪ/ *n.* (*pl.* **-ies**) **1 a** annual flat horse-race at Epsom. **b** similar race elsewhere. **2** important sporting contest. **3** (**derby**) *US* bowler hat. [Earl of *Derby*]

derecognize /di:ˈrekəgˌnaɪz/ *v.* (also **-ise**) (**-zing** or **-sing**) cease to recognize the status of (esp. a trade union). □ **derecognition** /-ˈnɪʃ(ə)n/ *n.*

deregulate /di:ˈregjʊˌleɪt/ *v.* (**-ting**) remove regulations from. □ **deregulation** /-ˈleɪʃ(ə)n/ *n.*

derelict /ˈderəlɪkt/ —*adj.* **1** (esp. of a property) dilapidated. **2** abandoned, ownerless. —*n.* **1** vagrant. **2** abandoned property. [Latin: related to RELINQUISH]

dereliction /ˌderəˈlɪkʃ(ə)n/ *n.* **1** (usu. foll. by *of*) neglect; failure to carry out obligations. **2** abandoning or being abandoned.

derestrict /ˌdi:rɪˈstrɪkt/ *v.* remove restrictions (esp. speed limits) from. □ **derestriction** *n.*

deride /dɪˈraɪd/ *v.* (**-ding**) mock. □ **derision** /-ˈrɪʒ(ə)n/ *n.* [Latin *rideo* laugh]

de rigueur /də rɪˈgɜ:(r)/ *predic. adj.* required by fashion or etiquette (*drugs were de rigueur*). [French]

derisive /dɪˈraɪsɪv/ *adj.* = DERISORY. □ **derisively** *adv.* [from DERIDE]

derisory /dɪˈraɪsərɪ/ *adj.* **1** scoffing, ironical (*derisory cheers*). **2** ridiculously small (*derisory offer*).

derivation /ˌderɪˈveɪʃ(ə)n/ *n.* **1** deriving or being derived. **2 a** formation of a word from another or from a root. **b** tracing of the origin of a word. **c** statement of this.

derivative /dɪˈrɪvətɪv/ —*adj.* derived; not original (*his music is derivative*). —*n.* **1** derived word or thing. **2** *Math.* quantity measuring the rate of change of another.

derive /dɪˈraɪv/ *v.* (**-ving**) **1** (usu. foll. by *from*) get or trace from a source (*derived satisfaction from work*). **2** (foll. by *from*) arise from, originate in (*happiness derives from many things*). **3** (usu. foll. by *from*) show or state the origin or formation of (a word etc.). [Latin *rivus* stream]

dermatitis /ˌdɜ:məˈtaɪtɪs/ *n.* inflammation of the skin. [Greek *derma* skin, -ITIS]

dermatology /ˌdɜ:məˈtɒlədʒɪ/ *n.* the study of skin diseases. □ **dermatological** /-təˈlɒdʒɪk(ə)l/ *adj.* **dermatologist** *n.* [from DERMATITIS, -LOGY]

dermis /ˈdɜ:mɪs/ *n.* **1** (in general use) the skin. **2** layer of living tissue below the epidermis. [from EPIDERMIS]

derogate /ˈderəˌgeɪt/ *v.* (**-ting**) (foll. by *from*) *formal* detract from (merit, right, etc.). □ **derogation** /-ˈgeɪʃ(ə)n/ *n.* [Latin *rogo* ask]

derogatory /dɪˈrɒgətərɪ/ *adj.* disparaging; insulting (*derogatory remark*). □ **derogatorily** *adv.*

derrick /ˈderɪk/ *n.* **1** crane for heavy weights, with a movable pivoted arm. **2** framework over an oil well etc., holding the drilling machinery. [*Derrick*, name of a hangman]

derring-do /ˌderɪŋˈdu:/ *n. literary joc.* heroic courage or actions. [*daring to do*]

derris /ˈderɪs/ *n.* **1** tropical climbing plant. **2** insecticide made from its root. [Latin from Greek]

derv *n.* diesel oil for road vehicles. [*d*iesel-*e*ngined *r*oad-*v*ehicle]

dervish /ˈdɜ:vɪʃ/ *n.* member of a Muslim fraternity vowed to poverty and austerity. [Turkish from Persian, = poor]

DES *abbr.* Department of Education and Science.

desalinate /di:ˈsælɪˌneɪt/ *v.* (**-ting**) remove the salt from (esp. sea water). □ **desalination** /-ˈneɪʃ(ə)n/ *n.* [from SALINE]

descale /di:ˈskeɪl/ *v.* (**-ling**) remove scale from.

descant —*n.* /'deskant/ **1** harmonizing treble melody above the basic melody, esp. of a hymn tune. **2** *poet.* melody; song. —*v.* /dis'kænt/ (foll. by *on, upon*) talk prosily, esp. in praise of. [Latin *cantus* song: related to CHANT]

descend /di'send/ *v.* **1** go or come down. **2** sink, fall. **3** slope downwards. **4** (usu. foll. by *on*) make a sudden attack or visit. **5** (of property etc.) be passed on by inheritance. **6 a** sink in rank, quality, etc. **b** (foll. by *to*) stoop to (an unworthy act). □ **be descended from** have as an ancestor. □ **descendent** *adj.* [Latin *scando* climb]

descendant *n.* person or thing descended from another. [French: related to DESCEND]

descent /di'sent/ *n.* **1** act or way of descending. **2** downward slope. **3** lineage, family origin. **4** decline; fall. **5** sudden attack.

describe /di'skraɪb/ *v.* (**-bing**) **1 a** state the characteristics, appearance, etc. of. **b** (foll. by *as*) assert to be; call (*described him as a liar*). **2 a** draw (esp. a geometrical figure). **b** move in (a specified way, esp. a curve) (*described a parabola through the air*). [Latin *scribo* write]

description /di'skrɪpʃ(ə)n/ *n.* **1 a** describing or being described. **b** representation, esp. in words. **2** sort, kind (*no food of any description*). [Latin: related to DESCRIBE]

descriptive /di'skrɪptɪv/ *adj.* describing, esp. vividly. [Latin: related to DESCRIBE]

descry /di'skraɪ/ *v.* (**-ies, -ied**) *literary* catch sight of; discern. [French: related to CRY]

desecrate /'desɪˌkreɪt/ *v.* (**-ting**) violate (a sacred place etc.) with violence, profanity, etc. □ **desecration** /-'kreɪʃ(ə)n/ *n.* **desecrator** *n.* [from DE-, CONSECRATE]

desegregate /diː'segrɪˌgeɪt/ *v.* (**-ting**) abolish racial segregation in. □ **desegregation** /-'geɪʃ(ə)n/ *n.*

deselect /ˌdiːsɪ'lekt/ *v.* reject (a selected candidate, esp. a sitting MP) in favour of another. □ **deselection** *n.*

desensitize /diː'sensɪˌtaɪz/ *v.* (also **-ise**) (**-zing** or **-sing**) reduce or destroy the sensitivity of. □ **desensitization** /-'zeɪʃ(ə)n/ *n.*

desert [1] /'dezət/ *v.* **1** leave without intending to return. **2** (esp. as **deserted** *adj.*) forsake, abandon. **3** run away from military service). □ **deserter** *n.* **desertion** *n.* [Latin *desero -sert-* leave]

desert [2] /'dezət/ —*n.* dry barren, esp. sandy, tract. —*adj.* uninhabited, desolate, barren. [Latin *desertus*: related to DESERT [1]]

desert [3] /di'zɜːt/ *n.* **1** (in *pl.*) deserved reward or punishment (*got his deserts*). **2** being worthy of reward or punishment. [French: related to DESERVE]

desert boot *n.* suede etc. ankle-high boot.

desertification /dɪˌzɜːtɪfɪ'keɪʃ(ə)n/ *n.* making or becoming a desert.

desert island *n.* (usu. tropical) uninhabited island.

deserve /di'zɜːv/ *v.* (**-ving**) (often foll. by *of*) worthy to + infin.), be worthy of (a reward, punishment, etc.) (*deserves a prize*). □ **deservedly** /-vɪdlɪ/ *adv.* [Latin *servio* serve]

deserving *adj.* (often foll. by *of*) worthy (esp. of help, praise, etc.).

déshabillé /ˌdeɪzæ'biːl/, **dishabille** /ˌdɪsæ'biːl/ *n.* (also **des-habille** /ˌdezæ'biːl/) state of partial undress. [French, = undressed]

desiccate /'desɪˌkeɪt/ *v.* (**-ting**) remove moisture from (esp. food) (*desiccated coconut*). □ **desiccation** /-'keɪʃ(ə)n/ *n.* [Latin *siccus* dry]

desideratum /dɪˌzɪdə'rɑːtəm/ *n.* (*pl.* **-ta**) something lacking but desirable. [Latin: related to DESIRE]

design /di'zaɪn/ —*n.* **1 a** preliminary plan or sketch for making something. **b** art of producing these. **2** lines or shapes forming a pattern or decoration. **3** plan, purpose, or intention. **4** arrangement or layout of a product. —*v.* **1** produce a version of a product. **b** established design for (a building, machine, etc.). **2** intend or plan (*designed for beginners*). **3** be a designer. □ **by design** on purpose. **have designs on** plan to appropriate, seduce, etc. [Latin *signum* mark]

designate —*v.* /'dezɪgˌneɪt/ (**-ting**) **1** (often foll. by *as*) appoint to an office or function. **2** specify (*designated times*). **3** (often foll. by *as*) serve as the name or symbol of. —*adj.* /'dezɪgnət/ (after the noun) appointed to office but not yet installed. [Latin: related to DESIGN]

designation /ˌdezɪg'neɪʃ(ə)n/ *n.* **1** name, description, or title. **2** designating.

designedly /dɪ'zaɪnɪdlɪ/ *adv.* on purpose.

designer *n.* **1** person who designs e.g. clothing, machines, theatre sets; draughtsman. **2** (*attrib.*) bearing the label of a famous designer; prestigious.

designer drug *n.* synthetic analogue of an illegal drug.

designing *adj.* crafty, scheming.

desirable /dɪˈzaɪərəb(ə)l/ *adj.* 1 worth having or doing. 2 sexually attractive. □ **desirability** /-ˈbɪlɪtɪ/ *n.* **desirableness** *n.* **desirably** *adv.*

desire /dɪˈzaɪə(r)/ — *n.* 1 a unsatisfied longing or wish. b expression of this; request. 2 sexual appetite. 3 something desired (*achieved his heart's desire*). — *v.* (-**ring**) 1 (often foll. by *to* + infin., or *that* + clause) long for; wish. 2 request (*desires a rest*). [Latin *desidero* long for]

desirous *predic. adj.* 1 (usu. foll. by *of*) desiring; wanting (*desirous of stardom*). 2 wanting; hoping (*desirous to do the right thing*).

desist /dɪˈzɪst/ *v.* (often foll. by *from*) abstain; cease. [Latin *desisto*]

desk *n.* 1 piece of furniture with a surface for writing on, and often drawers. 2 counter in a hotel, bank, etc. 3 specialized section of a newspaper office (*sports desk*). 4 unit of two orchestral players sharing a stand. [Latin: related to DISCUS]

desktop *n.* 1 working surface of a desk. 2 (*attrib.*) (esp. of a microcomputer) for use on an ordinary desk.

desktop publishing *n.* printing with a desktop computer and high-quality printer.

desolate — *adj.* /ˈdesələt/ 1 left alone; solitary. 2 uninhabited, ruined, dreary (*desolate moor*). 3 forlorn; wretched. — *v.* /ˈdesəleɪt/ (-**ting**) 1 depopulate, devastate; lay waste. 2 (esp. as **desolated** *adj.*) make wretched. □ **desolately** /-lətli/ *adv.* **desolateness** /-lətnɪs/ *n.* [Latin *solus* alone]

desolation /desəˈleɪʃ(ə)n/ *n.* 1 desolating or being desolated. 2 loneliness, grief, etc., caused by desertion. 3 neglected, ruined, or empty state.

despair /dɪˈspeə(r)/ — *v.* 1 complete loss or absence of hope. 2 cause of this. — *v.* (often foll. by *of*) lose or be without hope (*despaired of ever winning*). [Latin *spero* hope]

despatch var. of DISPATCH.

desperado /despəˈrɑːdəʊ/ *n.* (pl. -**es** or US -**s**) desperate or reckless criminal etc. [as DESPERATE]

desperate /ˈdespərət/ *adj.* 1 reckless from despair; violent and lawless. 2 a extremely dangerous, serious, or bad (*desperate situation*). b staking all on a small chance (*desperate remedy*). 3 (usu. foll. by *for*) needing or desiring very much (*desperate for recognition*). □ **desperately** *adv.* **desperateness** *n.* [Latin: related to DESPAIR]

despicable /dɪˈspɪkəb(ə)l, ˈdespɪk-/ *adj.* vile; contemptible. esp. morally. □ **despicably** *adv.* [Latin *specio* look at]

despise /dɪˈspaɪz/ *v.* (-**sing**) regard as inferior, worthless, or contemptible. [Latin: related to DESPICABLE]

despite /dɪˈspaɪt/ *prep.* in spite of. [Latin: related to DESPICABLE]

despoil /dɪˈspɔɪl/ *v. literary* (often foll. by *of*) plunder; rob; deprive. □ **despoliation** /dɪspəʊlɪˈeɪʃ(ə)n/ *n.* [Latin: related to SPOIL]

despondent /dɪˈspɒnd(ə)nt/ *adj.* in low spirits, dejected. □ **despondency** *n.* **despondently** *adv.* [Latin *spondeo* promise]

despot /ˈdespɒt/ *n.* 1 absolute ruler. 2 tyrant. □ **despotic** /-ˈspɒtɪk/ *adj.* **despotically** /-ˈspɒtɪkəlɪ/ *adv.* [Greek *despotēs* master]

despotism /ˈdespəˌtɪz(ə)m/ *n.* 1 rule by a despot; tyranny. 2 country ruled by a despot.

des res /dez ˈrez/ *n. slang* desirable residence. [abbreviation]

dessert /dɪˈzɜːt/ *n.* 1 sweet course of a meal. 2 fruit, nuts etc., served at the end of a meal. [French: related to DIS-, SERVE]

dessertspoon *n.* 1 medium-sized spoon for dessert. 2 amount held by this. □ **dessertspoonful** *n.* (pl. -**s**)

destabilize /diːˈsteɪbɪˌlaɪz/ *v.* (also -**ise**) (-**zing** or -**sing**) 1 make unstable. 2 subvert (esp. a foreign government). □ **destabilization** /-ˈzeɪʃ(ə)n/ *n.*

destination /destɪˈneɪʃ(ə)n/ *n.* place a person or thing is bound for. [Latin: related to DESTINE]

destine /ˈdestɪn/ *v.* (-**ning**) (often foll. by *to, for*; or *to* + infin.) appoint; preordain; intend (*destined him for the navy*). b destined to be fêted or preordained to. [French from Latin]

destiny /ˈdestɪnɪ/ *n.* (pl. -**ies**) 1 a fate. b this regarded as a power. 2 particular person's fate etc. [French from Latin]

destitute /ˈdestɪˌtjuːt/ *adj.* 1 without food, shelter, etc. 2 (usu. foll. by *of*) lacking (*destitute of friends*). □ **destitution** /-ˈtjuːʃ(ə)n/ *n.* [Latin]

destroy /dɪˈstrɔɪ/ *v.* 1 pull or break down; demolish. 2 kill (esp. an animal). 3 make useless; spoil. 4 ruin. esp. financially. 5 defeat. [Latin *struo struct-* build]

destroyer *n.* 1 person or thing that destroys. 2 fast armed warship escorting other ships.

destruct /dɪˈstrʌkt/ *US esp. Astronaut.* — *v.* destroy (one's own rocket etc.) or be destroyed deliberately, esp. for safety. — *n.* destructing.

destructible *adj.* able to be destroyed. [Latin: related to DESTROY]

destruction /dɪˈstrʌkʃ(ə)n/ *n.* **1** destroying or being destroyed. **2** cause of this. [Latin: related to DESTROY]

destructive *adj.* **1** (often foll. by *to, of*) destroying or tending to destroy. **2** negatively critical. □ **destructively** *adv.* **destructiveness** *n.*

desuetude /dɪˈsjuːɪˌtjuːd/ *n. formal* state of disuse (*fell into desuetude*). [Latin *suesco* be accustomed]

desultory /ˈdezəltərɪ/ *adj.* **1** constantly turning from one subject to another. **2** disconnected; unmethodical. □ **desultorily** *adv.* [Latin *desultorius* superficial]

detach /dɪˈtætʃ/ *v.* (often foll. by *from*) unfasten or disengage and remove. □ **detachable** *adj.* [French: related to ATTACH]

detachment *n.* **1 a** aloofness; indifference. **b** impartiality. **2** detaching or being detached. **3** troops etc. detached for a specific purpose. [French: related to DETACH]

detail /ˈdiːteɪl/ *n.* **1** small particular; item. **2 a** these collectively (*eye for detail*). **b** treatment of them (*detail was unconvincing*). **3 a** minor decoration on a building etc. **b** small part of a picture etc. shown alone. **4** small military detachment. —*v.* **1** give particulars of. **2** relate circumstantially. **3** assign for special duty. **4** (as **detailed** *adj.*) **a** (of a picture, story, etc.) containing many details. **b** itemized (*detailed list*). □ **in detail** item by item, minutely. [French: related to TAIL²]

detain /dɪˈteɪn/ *v.* **1** keep waiting; delay. **2** keep in custody, lock up. □ **detainment** *n.* [Latin *teneo* hold]

detainee /ˌdiːteɪˈniː/ *n.* person kept in custody, esp. for political reasons.

detect /dɪˈtekt/ *v.* **1** discover or perceive (*detected a note of sarcasm*). **2** (often foll. by *in*) discover (a criminal); solve (a crime). □ **detectable** *adj.* **detector** *n.* [Latin *tego tect-* cover]

detection /dɪˈtekʃ(ə)n/ *n.* **1** detecting or being detected. **2** work of a detective.

detective /dɪˈtektɪv/ *n.* person, esp. a police officer, investigating crimes.

détente /deɪˈtɑːt/ *n.* easing of strained, esp. international, relations. [French, = relaxation]

detention /dɪˈtenʃ(ə)n/ *n.* **1** detaining or being detained. **2** being kept late in school as a punishment. [Latin: related to DETAIN]

detention centre *n.* short-term prison for young offenders.

deter /dɪˈtɜː(r)/ *v.* (-rr-) (often foll. by *from*) discourage or prevent, esp. through fear. □ **determent** *n.* [Latin *terreo* frighten]

detergent /dɪˈtɜːdʒ(ə)nt/ —*n.* synthetic cleansing agent used with water. —*adj.* cleansing. [Latin *tergeo* wipe]

deteriorate /dɪˈtɪərɪəˌreɪt/ *v.* (-ting) become worse. □ **deterioration** /-ˈreɪʃ(ə)n/ *n.* [Latin *deterior* worse]

determinant /dɪˈtɜːmɪnənt/ —*adj.* determining. —*n.* **1** determining factor etc. **2** quantity obtained by the addition of products of the elements of a square matrix according to a given rule. [Latin: related to DETERMINE]

determinate /dɪˈtɜːmɪnət/ *adj.* limited, of definite scope or nature.

determination /dɪˌtɜːmɪˈneɪʃ(ə)n/ *n.* **1** firmness of purpose; resoluteness. **2** process of deciding or determining.

determine /dɪˈtɜːmɪn/ *v.* (-ning) **1** find out or establish precisely. **2** decide or settle; resolve. **3** be the decisive factor in regard to (*demand determines supply*). □ **be determined** be resolved. [Latin *terminus* boundary]

determined *adj.* showing determination; resolute, unflinching. □ **determinedly** *adv.*

determinism *n.* doctrine that human actions, events, etc. are determined by causes external to the will. □ **determinist** *n. & adj.* **deterministic** /-ˈnɪstɪk/ *adj.* **deterministically** /-ˈnɪstɪkəlɪ/ *adv.*

deterrent /dɪˈterənt/ —*adj.* deterring. —*n.* deterrent thing or factor (esp. nuclear weapons). □ **deterrence** *n.*

detest /dɪˈtest/ *v.* hate violently, loathe. □ **detestation** /ˌdiːteˈsteɪʃ(ə)n/ *n.* [Latin *detestor* from *testis* witness]

detestable *adj.* intensely disliked; hateful.

dethrone /diːˈθrəʊn/ *v.* (-ning) remove from a throne, depose. □ **dethronement** *n.*

detonate /ˈdetəˌneɪt/ *v.* (-ting) set off (an explosive charge); be set off. □ **detonation** /-ˈneɪʃ(ə)n/ *n.* [Latin *tono* thunder]

detonator *n.* device for detonating explosives.

detour /ˈdiːtʊə(r)/ *n.* divergence from a usual route; roundabout course. [French: related to TURN]

detoxify /diːˈtɒksɪˌfaɪ/ *v.* (-ies, -ied) remove poison or harmful substances from. □ **detoxification** /-fɪˈkeɪʃ(ə)n/ *n.* [Latin *toxicum* poison]

detract /dɪˈtrækt/ *v.* (foll. by *from*) take away (a part); diminish; make seem less

valuable or important. [Latin *traho traxi* draw]

detractor /dɪˈtræktə(r)/ *n.* person who criticizes unfairly. □ **detraction** *n.*

detriment /ˈdetrɪmənt/ *n.* 1 harm, damage. 2 cause of this. □ **detrimental** /-ˈment(ə)l/ *adj.* □ **detrimentally** *adv.* [Latin related to TRITE]

detritus /dɪˈtraɪtəs/ *n.* gravel, sand, etc. produced by erosion; debris. [Latin: related to DETRIMENT]

de trop /də ˈtrəʊ/ *predic. adj.* not wanted, in the way. [French]

deuce[1] /djuːs/ *n.* 1 two on dice or playing-cards. 2 *Tennis* score of 40 all. [Latin *duos* two]

deuce[2] /djuːs/ *n.* the Devil, esp. as an exclamation of surprise or annoyance (*who the deuce are you?*). [Low German *duus* two (being the worst throw at dice)]

deus ex machina /ˌderʊs eks ˈmækɪnə/ *n.* unlikely agent resolving a seemingly hopeless situation, esp. in a play or novel. [Latin, = god from the machinery, i.e. in a theatre]

deuterium /djuːˈtɪərɪəm/ *n.* stable isotope of hydrogen with a mass about double that of the usual isotope. [Greek *deuteros* second]

Deutschmark /ˈdɔɪtʃmɑːk/ *n.* (also **Deutsche Mark** /ˈdɔɪtʃə mɑːk/) chief monetary unit of Germany. [German: related to MARK[2]]

devalue /diːˈvæljuː/ *v.* (**-ues, -ued, -uing**) 1 reduce the value of 2 reduce the value of (a currency) in relation to others or to gold. □ **devaluation** /-ˈeɪʃ(ə)n/ *n.*

devastate /ˈdevəˌsteɪt/ *v.* (**-ting**) 1 lay waste; cause great destruction to. 2 (often in *passive*) overwhelm with shock or grief. □ **devastation** /-ˈsteɪʃ(ə)n/ *n.* [Latin *vasto* lay waste]

devastating *adj.* crushingly effective; overwhelming. □ **devastatingly** *adv.*

develop /dɪˈveləp/ *v.* (**-p-**) 1 a make or become bigger, fuller, more elaborate, etc. b bring or come to an active, visible, or mature state. 2 begin to exhibit or suffer from (*developed a rattle*). 3 a build on (land). b convert (land) to new use. 4 treat (photographic film etc.) to make the image visible. □ **developer** *n.* [French]

developing country *n.* poor or primitive country.

development *n.* 1 developing or being developed. 2 a stage of growth or advancement. b thing that has developed; new event or circumstance etc. (*latest developments*). 3 full-grown state. 4 developed land; group of buildings. □ **developmental** /-ˈment(ə)l/ *adj.*

development area *n.* area where new industries are encouraged by the State.

deviant /ˈdiːvɪənt/ *adj.* deviating from what is normal, esp. sexually. —*n.* deviant person or thing. □ **deviance** *n.* **deviancy** *n.*

deviate /ˈdiːvɪeɪt/ *v.* (**-ting**) (often foll. by *from*) turn aside or diverge (from a course of action, rule, etc.). □ **deviation** *n.*

device /dɪˈvaɪs/ *n.* 1 thing made or adapted for a special purpose. 2 plan, scheme, or trick. 3 design, esp. heraldic. □ **leave a person to his or her own devices** leave a person to do as he or she wishes. [French: related to DEVISE]

devil /ˈdev(ə)l/ —*n.* 1 (usu. **the Devil**) (in Christian and Jewish belief) supreme spirit of evil; Satan. 2 a evil spirit; demon. b personified evil. 3 a wicked person. b mischievously clever person. 4 *colloq.* person of a specified kind (*lucky devil*). 5 fighting spirit, mischief (*the devil is in him tonight*). 6 *colloq.* awkward thing. 7 (**the devil** or **the Devil**) *colloq.* used as an exclamation of surprise or annoyance (*who the devil are you?*). 8 literary hack. 9 junior legal counsel. —*v.* (**-ll-**; *US* **-l-**) 1 cook (food) with hot seasoning. 2 act as devil for an author or barrister. 3 *US* harass, worry. □ **between the devil and the deep blue sea** in a dilemma. a **devil of** *colloq.* considerable, difficult, or remarkable. **devil's own** *colloq.* very difficult or unusual (*the devil's own job*). **the devil to pay** trouble to be expected. **speak** (or **talk**) **of the devil** said when a person appears just after being mentioned. [Greek *diabolos* accuser, slanderer]

devilish —*adj.* 1 of or like a devil; wicked. 2 mischievous. —*adv. colloq.* very. □ **devilishly** *adv.*

devil-may-care *adj.* cheerful and reckless.

devilment *n.* mischief, wild spirits.

devilry *n.* (*pl.* **-ies**) 1 wickedness; reckless mischief. 2 black magic.

devil's advocate *n.* person who argues against a proposition to test it.

devils-on-horseback *n.pl.* savoury of prunes or plums wrapped in bacon.

devious /ˈdiːvɪəs/ *adj.* 1 not straightforward, underhand. 2 winding, circuitous. □ **deviously** *adv.* **deviousness** *n.* [Latin *via* way]

devise /dɪˈvaɪz/ *v.* (**-sing**) 1 carefully plan or invent. 2 *Law* leave (real estate) by will. [Latin: related to DIVIDE]

devoid /dɪˈvɔɪd/ *predic. adj.* (foll. by *of*) lacking or free from. [French: related to *you*]

devolution /ˌdiːvəˈluːʃ(ə)n/ n. delegation of power, esp. to local or regional administration. □ **devolutionist** n. & adj. [Latin: related to DEVOLVE]

devolve /dɪˈvɒlv/ v. (-ving) **1** (foll. by on, upon, etc.) pass (work or duties) or be passed to (a deputy etc.). **2** (foll. by on, to, upon) (of property etc.) descend to. □ **devolvement** n. [Latin volvo volut- roll]

Devonian /dɪˈvəʊnɪən/ –adj. of the fourth period of the Palaeozoic era. –n. this period. [Devon in England]

devote /dɪˈvəʊt/ v. (-ting) (often refl.; foll. by to) apply or give over to (a particular activity etc.). [Latin voveo vot- vow]

devoted adj. loving; loyal. □ **devotedly** adv.

devotee /ˌdevəˈtiː/ n. **1** (usu. foll. by of) zealous enthusiast or supporter. **2** pious person.

devotion /dɪˈvəʊʃ(ə)n/ n. **1** (usu. foll. by to) great love or loyalty. **2 a** religious worship. **b** (in pl.) prayers. □ **devotional** adj. [Latin: related to DEVOTE]

devour /dɪˈvaʊər/ v. **1** eat voraciously. **2** (of fire etc.) engulf, destroy. **3** take in eagerly (devoured the play). **4** preoccupy (devoured by fear). [Latin voro swallow]

devout /dɪˈvaʊt/ adj. earnestly religious or sincere. □ **devoutly** adv. **devoutness** n. [Latin: related to DEVOTE]

dew n. **1** condensed water vapour forming on cool surfaces at night. **2** similar glistening moisture. □ **dewy** adj. (-ier, -iest). [Old English]

dewberry n. (pl. -ies) bluish fruit like the blackberry.

dew-claw n. rudimentary inner toe on some dogs.

dewdrop n. drop of dew.

Dewey system /ˈdjuːɪ/ n. decimal system of library classification. [Dewey, name of a librarian]

dewlap n. loose fold of skin hanging from the throat of cattle, dogs, etc. [from DEW, LAP¹]

dew point n. temperature at which dew forms.

dexter adj. esp. Heraldry on or of the right-hand side (observer's left) of a shield etc. [Latin, = on the right]

dexterity /dekˈsterɪtɪ/ n. **1** skill in using one's hands. **2** mental adroitness. [Latin: related to DEXTER]

dexterous /ˈdekstrəs/ adj. (also **dextrous**) having or using dexterity. □ **dexterously** adv. **dexterousness** n.

dextrin /ˈdekstrɪn/ n. soluble gummy substance used as a thickening agent, adhesive, etc. [Latin dextra on or to the right]

dextrose /ˈdekstrəʊs/ n. form of glucose. [Latin dextra on or to the right]

DFC abbr. Distinguished Flying Cross.

DFM abbr. Distinguished Flying Medal.

dhal /dɑːl/ n. (also **dal**) **1** a kind of split pulse common in India. **2** dish made with this. [Hindi]

dharma /ˈdɑːmə/ n. Ind. **1** social custom; correct behaviour. **2** the Buddhist truth. **3** the Hindu moral law. [Sanskrit, = decree, custom]

dhoti /ˈdəʊtɪ/ n. (pl. -s) loincloth worn by male Hindus. [Hindi]

di-¹ comb. form two-, double. [Greek dis twice]

di-² prefix = DIS-.

di-³ prefix form of DIA- before a vowel.

dia. abbr. diameter.

dia- prefix (also **di-** before a vowel) **1** through (diaphanous). **2** apart (dia-critical). **3** across (diameter). [Greek dia through]

diabetes /ˌdaɪəˈbiːtiːz/ n. disease in which sugar and starch are not properly absorbed by the body. [Latin from Greek]

diabetic /ˌdaɪəˈbetɪk/ –adj. **1** of or having diabetes. **2** for diabetics. –n. person suffering from diabetes.

diabolical /ˌdaɪəˈbɒlɪk(ə)l/ adj. (also **diabolic**) **1** of the Devil. **2** devilish; inhumanly cruel or wicked. **3** extremely bad, clever, or annoying. □ **diabolically** adv. [Latin: related to DEVIL]

diabolism /daɪˈæb(ə)lɪz(ə)m/ n. **1** worship of the Devil. **2** sorcery. [Greek: related to DEVIL]

diachronic /ˌdaɪəˈkrɒnɪk/ adj. of a thing's historical development. □ **diachronically** adv. [Greek khronos time]

diaconal /daɪˈækən(ə)l/ adj. of a deacon. [Church Latin: related to DEACON]

diaconate /daɪˈækənət/ n. **1** position of deacon. **2** body of deacons.

diacritic /ˌdaɪəˈkrɪtɪk/ n. sign (e.g. an accent or cedilla) indicating different sounds or values of a letter. [Greek: related to CRITIC]

diacritical –adj. distinguishing, distinctive. –n. (in full **diacritical mark** or **sign**) = DIACRITIC.

diadem /ˈdaɪədem/ n. **1** crown or headband as a sign of sovereignty. **2** sovereignty. **3** crowning distinction. [Greek deō bind]

diaeresis /daɪˈɪərəsɪs/ n. (pl. **diaereses** /-ˌsiːz/) (US **dieresis**) mark (as in naïve) over a vowel to indicate that it is sounded separately. [Greek, = separation]

diagnose /ˈdaɪəgnəʊz/ v. (-sing) make a diagnosis of (a disease, fault, etc.).

diagnosis /ˌdaɪəgˈnəʊsɪs/ n. (pl. dia-gnoses /-ˌsiːz/) 1 a identification of a disease from its symptoms. b formal statement from its symptoms. 2 identification of the cause of a mechanical fault etc. [Greek gignōskō recognize]

diagnostic /ˌdaɪəgˈnɒstɪk/ —adj. of or assisting diagnosis. —n. symptom. □ **diagnostically** adv. **diagnostician** /-ɒˈstɪʃ(ə)n/ n. [Greek: related to DIA-GNOSIS]

diagnostics n. 1 (treated as pl.) Com-puting programs etc. used to identify faults in hardware or software. 2 (treated as sing.) science of diagnosing disease.

diagonal /daɪˈægən(ə)l/ —adj. 1 cross-ing a straight-sided figure from corner to corner. 2 slanting, oblique. —n. straight line joining two opposite corners. □ **diagonally** adv. [Greek gōnia angle]

diagram /ˈdaɪəgræm/ n. outline draw-ing, plan, or graphic representation of a machine, structure, process, etc. □ **dia-grammatic** /-grəˈmætɪk/ adj. **dia-grammatically** /-grəˈmætɪkəlɪ/ adv. [Greek: related to -GRAM]

dial /ˈdaɪ(ə)l/ —n. 1 plate with a scale for measuring weight, volume, etc., indi-cated by a pointer. 2 movable numbered disc on a telephone for making connec-tion. 3 face of a clock or watch, marking the hours etc. 4 a plate or disc etc. on a radio or television for selecting a wave-length or channel. b similar device on other equipment. —v. (-ll-; US -l-) 1 (also absol.) select (a telephone number) with a dial. 2 measure, indicate, or regulate with a dial. [medieval Latin diale from dies day]

dialect /ˈdaɪəlɛkt/ n. 1 regional form of speech. 2 variety of language with non-standard vocabulary, pronunciation, or grammar. □ **dialectal** /-ˈlɛkt(ə)l/ adj. [Greek legō speak]

dialectic /ˌdaɪəˈlɛktɪk/ n. 1 art of inves-tigating the truth by discussion and lo-gical argument. 2 process whereby con-tradictions merge to form a higher truth. 3 any situation or discussion involving the juxtaposition or conflict of opposites. [Greek: related to DIALECT]

dialectical adj. of dialectic. □ **dialect-ically** adv.

dialectical materialism n. Marxist theory that political and historical events are due to the conflict of social forces arising from economic con-ditions.

dialectics n. (treated as sing. or pl.) = DIALECTIC n. 1.

dialling tone n. sound indicating that a telephone caller may dial.

dialogue /ˈdaɪəlɒg/ n. (US dialog) 1 a conversation. b this in written form. 2 discussion between people with dif-ferent opinions. [Greek legō speak]

dialysis /daɪˈælɪsɪs/ n. (pl. dialyses /-ˌsiːz/) 1 separation of particles in a liquid by differences in their ability to pass through a membrane into another liquid. 2 purification of the blood by this technique. [Greek luō set free]

diamanté /ˌdaɪəˈmɒnteɪ/ adj. decorated with synthetic diamonds or another sparkling substance. [French diamant diamond]

diameter /daɪˈæmɪtə(r)/ n. 1 straight line passing through the centre of a circle or sphere to its edges; length of this. 2 transverse measurement, width, thickness. 3 unit of linear magnifying power. [Greek: related to -METER]

diametrical /ˌdaɪəˈmɛtrɪk(ə)l/ adj. (also **diametric**) 1 of or along a dia-meter. 2 (of opposites etc.) absolute. □ **diametrically** adv. [Greek: related to DIAMETER]

diamond /ˈdaɪəmənd/ n. 1 very hard transparent precious stone of pure crys-tallized carbon. 2 rhombus. 3 a playing card of the suit denoted by a red rhom-bus. b (in pl.) this suit. [Greek: related to ADAMANT]

diamond wedding n. 60th (or 75th) wedding anniversary.

dianthus /daɪˈænθəs/ n. flowering plant of the genus including the carnation. [Greek anthos flower or Zeus]

diapason /ˌdaɪəˈpeɪz(ə)n/ n. 1 compass of a voice or musical instrument. 2 fixed standard of musical pitch. 3 either of two main organ-stops. [Greek, = through all (notes)]

diaper /ˈdaɪəpə(r)/ n. US baby's nappy. [Greek aspros white]

diaphanous /daɪˈæfənəs/ adj. (of fabric etc.) light, delicate, and almost trans-parent. [Greek phainō show]

diaphragm /ˈdaɪəfræm/ n. 1 muscular partition between the thorax and abdo-men in mammals. 2 = DUTCH CAP. 3 a circular hole to cut off marginal beams of light. b vibrating disc in a micro-phone, telephone, loudspeaker, etc. 4 device for varying the lens aperture in a camera etc. 5 thin sheet as a partition etc. [Greek phragma fence]

diapositive /ˌdaɪəˈpɒzɪtɪv/ n. positive photographic slide or transparency. [DIA- + POSITIVE]

diarist /ˈdaɪərɪst/ n. person who keeps a diary.

diarrhoea /ˌdaɪəˈrɪə/ n. (esp. US **diarrhea**) condition of excessively frequent and loose bowel movements. [Greek rheō flow]

diary /ˈdaɪərɪ/ n. (pl. **-ies**) **1** daily record of events or thoughts. **2** book for this or for noting future engagements. [Latin *dies* day]

Diaspora /daɪˈæspərə/ n. **1** the dispersion of the Jews after their exile in 538 BC. **2** the dispersed Jews. [Greek]

diastase /ˈdaɪəsteɪz/ n. enzyme converting starch to sugar. [Greek *diastasis* separation]

diatom /ˈdaɪətəm/ n. one-cell alga found as plankton and forming fossil deposits. [Greek, = cut in half]

diatomic /daɪəˈtɒmɪk/ adj. consisting of two atoms.

diatonic /daɪəˈtɒnɪk/ adj. Mus. (of a scale, interval, etc.) involving only notes belonging to the prevailing key. [Greek: related to TONIC]

diatribe /ˈdaɪətraɪb/ n. forceful verbal attack or criticism; invective. [Greek *tribō* rub]

diazepam /daɪˈæzɪpæm/ n. a tranquillizing drug. [benzodiazepine + *am*]

dibble /ˈdɪb(ə)l/ —n. (also **dibber** /ˈdɪbə(r)/) hand tool for making holes for planting. —v. (**-ling**) sow, plant, or prepare (soil) with a dibble. [origin uncertain]

dice —n.pl. **1 a** small cubes with faces bearing 1–6 spots, used in games or gambling. **b** (treated as *sing.*) one of these cubes (see DIE²). **2** game played with dice. —v. (**-cing**) **1** take great risks, gamble (*dicing with death*). **2** cut into small cubes. [pl. of DIE²]

■ **Usage** See note at DIE².

dicey adj. (**dicier, diciest**) slang risky, unreliable.

dichotomy /daɪˈkɒtəmɪ/ n. (pl. **-ies**) division into two, esp. a sharply defined one. [Greek *dikho-* apart: related to TOME]

■ **Usage** The use of *dichotomy* to mean *dilemma* or *ambivalence* is considered incorrect in standard English.

dichromatic /daɪkrəˈmætɪk/ adj. **1** two-coloured. **2** having vision sensitive to only two of the three primary colours.

dick¹ n. **1** colloq. (in certain set phrases) person (*clever dick*). **2** coarse slang penis. [*Dick*, pet form of *Richard*]

dick² n. slang detective. [perhaps an abbreviation]

dickens /ˈdɪkɪnz/ n. (usu. prec. by *how, what, why*, etc., *the, the*) colloq. (esp. in exclamations) deuce; the Devil (*what the dickens is it*). [probably the name *Dickens*]

Dickensian /dɪˈkɛnzɪən/ adj. **1** of the 19th-c. novelist Dickens or his work. **2** resembling situations in Dickens's work, esp. poverty.

dickhead n. coarse slang idiot. [from DICK¹]

dicky /ˈdɪkɪ/ —n. (pl. **-ies**) colloq. false shirt-front. —adj. (**-ier, -iest**) slang unsound; unhealthy. [*Dicky*, pet form of *Richard*]

dicky-bird n. **1** child's word for a little bird. **2** word (*didn't say a dicky-bird*).

dicky bow n. colloq. bow-tie.

dicotyledon /ˌdaɪkɒtɪˈliːd(ə)n/ n. flowering plant having two cotyledons. □ **dicotyledonous** adj.

dicta pl. of DICTUM.

Dictaphone /ˈdɪktəˌfəʊn/ n. propr. machine for recording and playing back dictated words. [from DICTATE, PHONE]

dictate —v. /dɪkˈteɪt/ (**-ting**) **1** say or read aloud (material to be written down or recorded). **2** state or order authoritatively or peremptorily. —n. /ˈdɪk-/ (usu. in pl.) authoritative instruction or requirement (*dictates of conscience, fashion*). □ **dictation** /dɪkˈteɪʃ(ə)n/ n. [Latin *dicto* from *dico* say]

dictator /dɪkˈteɪtə(r)/ n. **1** usu. unelected omnipotent ruler. **2** omnipotent person in any sphere. **3** domineering person. □ **dictatorship** n. [Latin: related to DICTATE]

dictatorial /ˌdɪktəˈtɔːrɪəl/ adj. **1** of or like a dictator. **2** overbearing. □ **dictatorially** adv. [Latin: related to DICTATOR]

diction /ˈdɪkʃ(ə)n/ n. manner of enunciation in speaking or singing. [Latin *dictio* from *dico* dict- say]

dictionary /ˈdɪkʃənrɪ/ n. (pl. **-ies**) **1** book listing (usu. alphabetically) and explaining the words of a language or giving corresponding words in another language. **2** reference book explaining the terms of a particular subject. [medieval Latin: related to DICTION]

dictum /ˈdɪktəm/ n. (pl. **dicta** /-tə/ or **-s**) **1** formal expression of opinion. **2** a saying. [Latin, neuter past part. of *dico* say]

did past of DO¹.

didactic /dɪˈdaktɪk/ adj. **1** meant to instruct. **2** (of a person) tediously pedantic. □ **didactically** adv. **didacticism** /-ˌtɪˌsɪz(ə)m/ n. [Greek *didaskō* teach]

diddle /ˈdɪd(ə)l/ v. (**-ling**) colloq. swindle. [probably from *Diddler*, name of a character in a 19th-c. play]

diddums /ˈdɪdəmz/ int. often iron. expressing commiseration. [= *did 'em*, i.e. did they (tease you etc.)?]

didgeridoo /ˌdɪdʒərɪˈduː/ n. long tubular Australian Aboriginal musical instrument. [imitative]

didn't /ˈdɪd(ə)nt/ contr. did not.

die

die¹ /daɪ/ v. (dies, died, dying /daɪɪŋ/) 1 cease to live; expire, lose vital force. 2 a come to an end, fade away (*his interest died*). b cease to function. c (of a flame) go out. 3 (foll. by *on*) die or cease to function while in the presence or charge of (a person). 4 (usu. foll. by *of, from, with*) be exhausted or tormented (*near¹y died of boredom*). □ **be dying** (foll. by *for*, or *to* + infin.) wish for longingly or intently (*was dying for a drink*). **die away** fade to the point of extinction. **die back** (of a plant) decay from the tip towards the root. **die down** become fainter or weaker. **die hard** die reluctantly (*old habits die hard*). **die out** die one after another. **die out** become extinct, cease to exist. [Old Norse]

die² /daɪ/ n. 1 = DICE 1b. 2 (pl. **dies**) a engraved device for stamping coins, medals, etc. b device for stamping, cutting, or moulding material. □ **the die is cast** an irrevocable step has been taken. [Latin *datum* from *do* give].

■ **Usage** *Dice*, rather than *die*, is now the standard singular as well as plural form in the games sense (*one dice, two dice*).

die-casting n. process or product of casting from metal moulds.

die-hard n. conservative or stubborn person.

dielectric /ˌdaɪɪˈlektrɪk/ —adj. not conducting electricity. —n. dielectric substance.

dieresis *US* var. of DIAERESIS.

diesel /ˈdiːz(ə)l/ n. 1 (in full **diesel engine**) internal-combustion engine in which heat produced by the compression of air in the cylinder ignites the fuel. 2 vehicle driven by a diesel engine. 3 fuel for a diesel engine. [*Diesel*, name of an engineer]

diesel-electric adj. (of a locomotive etc.) driven by an electric current from a diesel-engined generator.

diesel oil n. heavy petroleum fraction used in diesel engines.

die-sinker n. engraver of dies.

die-stamping n. embossing paper etc. with die.

diet¹ /ˈdaɪət/ —n. 1 range of foods habitually eaten by a person or animal. 2 limited range of food to which a person is restricted. 3 thing regularly offered (*diet of half-truths*). —v. (-t-) restrict oneself to a special diet, esp. to slim. □ **dietary** adj. **dieter** n. [Greek *diaita* way of life]

diet² /ˈdaɪət/ n. 1 legislative assembly in certain countries. 2 *hist.* congress. [Latin *dieta*]

diffident

dietetic /ˌdaɪəˈtetɪk/ adj. of diet and nutrition. [Greek: related to DIET¹]

dietetics n.pl. (usu. treated as *sing.*) the study of diet and nutrition.

dietitian /ˌdaɪəˈtɪʃ(ə)n/ n. (also **dietician**) expert in dietetics.

dif- prefix = DIS-.

differ v. 1 (often foll. by *from*) be unlike or distinguishable. 2 (often foll. by *with*) disagree. [Latin *differo, dilat-* bring apart]

difference /ˈdɪfrəns/ n. 1 being different or unlike. 2 degree of this. 3 way in which things differ. 4 a quantity by which amounts differ. b remainder left after subtraction. 5 disagreement, dispute. □ **make a** (or **all the, no,** etc.) **difference** have a significant (or a very significant, or no) effect. **with a difference** having a new or unusual feature.

different adj. 1 (often foll. by *from* or *to*) unlike, of another nature. 2 distinct, separate. 3 unusual. □ **differently** adv.

■ **Usage** In sense 1, *different from* is more widely acceptable than *different to*, which is common in less formal use.

differential /ˌdɪfəˈrenʃ(ə)l/ —adj. 1 of, exhibiting, or depending on a difference. 2 *Math.* relating to infinitesimal differences. 3 constituting or relating to a specific difference. —n. 1 difference between things of the same kind. 2 difference in wages between industries or categories of employees in the same industry. 3 difference between rates of interest etc.

differential calculus n. method of calculating rates of change, maximum or minimum values, etc.

differential gear n. gear enabling a vehicle's rear wheels to revolve at different speeds on corners.

differentiate /ˌdɪfəˈrenʃɪeɪt/ v. (-ting) 1 constitute a difference between or in 2 recognize as different; distinguish. 3 become different during development. 4 *Math.* calculate the derivative of. □ **differentiation** /-ˈeɪʃ(ə)n/ n.

difficult /ˈdɪfɪk(ə)lt/ adj. 1 a needing much effort or skill. b troublesome, perplexing. 2 (of a person) demanding. 3 problematic.

difficulty n. (pl. -ies) 1 being difficult 2 a difficult thing; problem, hindrance. b (often in *pl.*) distress, esp. financial (*in difficulties*). [Latin *difficultas*; related to FACULTY]

diffident /ˈdɪfɪd(ə)nt/ adj. shy, lacking self-confidence; excessively reticent. □ **diffidence** n. **diffidently** adv. [Latin *diffido* distrust]

diffract /dɪˈfrækt/ v. break up (a beam of light) into a series of dark and light bands or coloured spectra, or (a beam of radiation or particles) into a series of high and low intensities. □ **diffraction** n. **diffractive** adj. [Latin diffringo: related to FRACTION]

diffuse —adj. /dɪˈfjuːs/ **1** spread out, not concentrated. **2** not concise, wordy. —v. /dɪˈfjuːz/ (**-sing**) **1** disperse or spread widely. **2** intermingle by diffusion. □ **diffusible** /dɪˈfjuːzɪb(ə)l/ adj. **diffusive** /dɪˈfjuːsɪv/ adj. [Latin: related to DIFFUSE]

diffusion /dɪˈfjuːʒ(ə)n/ n. **1** diffusing or being diffused. **2** interpenetration of substances by natural movement of their particles. [Latin: related to DIFFUSE]

dig —v. (**-gg-**; past and past part. **dug**) **1** (also absol.) break up and remove or turn over (ground etc.). **2** (foll. by up) break up the soil of (fallow land). **3** make (a hole, tunnel, etc.) by digging. **4** (often foll. by up, out) **a** obtain by digging. **b** (foll. by into) search for information in (a book etc.). **5** (also absol.) excavate (an archaeological site). **6** slang like; understand. **7** (foll. by in, into) thrust (a sharp object); prod or nudge. **8** (foll. by into, through, under) make one's way by digging. —n. **1** piece of digging. **2** thrust or poke. **3** colloq. pointed remark. **4** archaeological excavation. **5** (in pl.) colloq. lodgings. □ **dig in** colloq. begin eating. **dig one's heels in** be obstinate. **dig in** colloq. begin eating. **dig oneself in 1** prepare a defensive trench or pit. **2** establish one's position. [Old English]

digest —v. /daɪˈdʒest/ **1** assimilate (food) in the stomach and bowels. **2** understand and assimilate mentally. **3** summarize. —n. /ˈdaɪdʒest/ **1** periodical synopsis of current literature or news. **2** methodical summary, esp. of laws. **digestible** adj. [Latin digero -gest-]

digestion /daɪˈdʒestʃ(ə)n/ n. **1** process of digesting. **2** capacity to digest food.

digestive —adj. of or aiding digestion. —n. **1** substance aiding digestion. **2** (in full **digestive biscuit**) wholemeal biscuit.

digger n. **1** person or machine that digs, esp. a mechanical excavator. **2** colloq. Australian or New Zealander.

digit /ˈdɪdʒɪt/ n. **1** any numeral from 0 to 9. **2** finger or toe. [Latin, = finger, toe]

digital adj. **1** of digits. **2** (of a clock, watch, etc.) giving a reading by displayed digits. **3** (of a computer) operating on data represented by a series of digits. **4** (of a recording) with sound information represented by digits for

more reliable transmission. □ **digitally** adv. [Latin: related to DIGIT]

digital audio tape n. magnetic tape on which sound is recorded digitally.

digitalis /ˌdɪdʒɪˈteɪlɪs/ n. drug prepared from foxgloves, used to stimulate the heart. [related to DIGIT, from the form of the flowers]

digitize v. (also **-ise**) (**-zing** or **-sing**) convert (data etc.) into digital form, esp. for a computer. □ **digitization** /ˌ-ˈzeɪʃ(ə)n/ n.

dignified /ˈdɪɡnɪˌfaɪd/ adj. having or showing dignity.

dignify /ˈdɪɡnɪˌfaɪ/ v. (**-ies, -ied**) **1** confer dignity on; ennoble. **2** give a fine name to. [Latin dignus worthy]

dignitary /ˈdɪɡnɪtəri/ n. (pl. **-ies**) person of high rank or office. [from DIGNITY]

dignity /ˈdɪɡnɪti/ n. (pl. **-ies**) **1** composed and serious manner. **2** worthiness. **3** high rank or position. □ **beneath one's dignity** not worthy enough for one. **stand on** (or **upon**) **one's dignity** insist on being treated with respect. [Latin dignus worthy]

digraph /ˈdaɪɡrɑːf/ n. two letters representing one sound, e.g. ph, ey as in phone, key. [from DI-¹, -GRAPH]

■ **Usage** Digraph is sometimes confused with ligature, which means two or more letters joined together.

digress /daɪˈɡres/ v. depart from the main subject in speech or writing. □ **digression** n. [Latin digredior -gress-]

digs see DIG n. 5.

dike¹ var. of DYKE¹.

dike² var. of DYKE².

diktat /ˈdɪktæt/ n. categorical statement or decree. [German, = DICTATE]

dilapidated /dɪˈlæpɪˌdeɪtɪd/ adj. in disrepair or ruin. □ **dilapidation** /-ˈdeɪʃ(ə)n/ n. [Latin: related to DI-², lapis stone]

dilatation /ˌdaɪləˈteɪʃ(ə)n/ n. **1** dilating of the cervix, e.g. for surgical curettage. **2** dilation. [from DILATE]

dilate /daɪˈleɪt/ v. (**-ting**) **1** make or become wider or larger. **2** speak or write at length. □ **dilation** n. [Latin latus wide]

dilatory /ˈdɪlətəri/ adj. given to or causing delay. [Latin dilatorius: related to DIFFER]

dildo /ˈdɪldəʊ/ n. (pl. **-s**) artificial erect penis for sexual stimulation. [origin unknown]

dilemma /dɪˈlemə/ n. **1** situation in which a difficult choice has to be made. **2** difficult situation, predicament. [Greek lēmma premiss]

dilettante /dılı'tæntı/ n. (pl. dilettanti /-tı/ or -s) dabbler in a subject. □ dilettantism n. [Italian dilettare DELIGHT]

diligent /'dılıdʒ(ə)nt/ adj. 1 hardworking. 2 showing care and effort. □ diligence n. diligently adv. [French from Latin diligo love]

dill n. herb with aromatic leaves and seeds. [Old English]

dilly-dally /'dılı'dælı/ v. (-ies, -ied) colloq. 1 dawdle. 2 vacillate. [reduplication of DALLY]

dilute /dar'ljuːt/ —v. (-ting) 1 reduce the strength of (a fluid) by adding water etc. 2 weaken or reduce in effect. —adj. diluted. □ dilution n. [Latin diluo -lut- wash away]

diluvial /dar'luːvɪəl/ adj. of a flood, esp. of the Flood in Genesis. [Latin: related to DELUGE]

dim —adj. (dimmer, dimmest) 1 a faintly luminous or visible; not bright. b indistinct. 2 not clearly perceived or remembered. 3 colloq. stupid. 4 (of the eyes) not seeing clearly. —v. (-mm-) make or become dim. □ take a dim view of colloq. disapprove of. □ dimly adv. dimness n. [Old English]

dime n. US ten-cent coin. [Latin decima tenth (part)]

dimension /dar'menʃ(ə)n/ —n. 1 measurable extent, as length, breadth, depth, etc. 2 (in pl.) size (of huge dimensions). 3 aspect, facet (gained a new dimension). —v. (usu. as **dimensioned** adj.) mark the dimensions on (a diagram etc.). □ **dimensional** adj. [Latin metior mens- measure]

diminish /dı'mınıʃ/ v. 1 make or become smaller or less. 2 (often as **diminished** adj.) lessen the reputation of (a person); humiliate. □ **diminishing returns** fact that expenditure etc. beyond a certain point ceases to produce a proportionate yield. [Latin: related to MINUTE]

diminuendo /dı,mınjʊ'endəʊ/ —n. (pl. -s) gradual decrease in loudness. —adv. & adj. decreasing in loudness. [Italian: related to DIMINISH]

diminution /,dımı'njuːʃ(ə)n/ n. 1 diminishing or being diminished. 2 decrease. [Latin: related to DIMINISH]

diminutive /dı'mınjʊtıv/ —adj. 1 tiny. 2 (of a word or suffix) implying smallness or affection. —n. diminutive word or suffix.

dimmer n. 1 (in full **dimmer switch**) device for varying the brightness of an electric light. 2 US a (in pl.) small

241

parking lights on a vehicle. b headlight on low beam.

dimple /'dımp(ə)l/ —n. small hollow, esp. in the cheek or chin. —v. (-ling) form dimples (in). □ **dimply** adj. [probably Old English]

dim-witted adj. colloq. stupid person. □ **dim-witted** adj.

DIN n. any of a series of German technical standards designating electrical connections, film speeds, and paper sizes. [German, from Deutsche Industrie-Norm]

din —n. prolonged loud confused noise. —v. (-nn-) (foll. by into) force (information) into a person by constant repetition; make a din. [Old English]

dinar /'diːnɑː(r)/ n. chief monetary unit of Yugoslavia and several countries of the Middle East and N. Africa. [Arabic and Persian from Latin DENARIUS]

dine v. (-ning) 1 a eat dinner. b (foll. by on, upon) eat for dinner. 2 (esp. in phr. **wine and dine**) entertain with food. □ **dine out** dine away from home. [French diner as DIS-, Latin jejunus fasting]

diner n. 1 person who dines. 2 dining-car. 3 US small restaurant. 4 small dining-room.

dinette /dar'net/ n. small room or alcove for eating meals.

ding —v. make a ringing sound. —n. ringing sound. [imitative]

dingbat /'dıŋbæt/ n. slang US & Austral. stupid or eccentric person. [perhaps from ding to beat + BAT[1]]

ding-dong /'dıŋdɒŋ/ n. 1 sound of two chimes, esp. as a doorbell. 2 colloq. heated argument or fight. [imitative]

dinghy /'dıŋı/ n. (pl. -ies) 1 small boat carried by a ship. 2 small pleasure-boat. [Hindi]

dingle /'dıŋg(ə)l/ n. deep wooded valley or dell. [origin unknown]

dingo /'dıŋgəʊ/ n. (pl. -es) wild Australian dog. [Aboriginal]

dingy /'dındʒı/ adj. (-ier, -iest) dirty-looking, drab. □ **dingily** adv. **dinginess** n. [origin uncertain]

dining-car n. restaurant car on a train.

dining-room n. room in which meals are eaten.

dinkum /'dıŋkəm/ adj. Austral. & NZ colloq. genuine, honest, true. □ **dinkum** oil the honest truth. **fair dinkum** 1 fair play. 2 genuine(ly), honest(ly), true. [origin unknown]

dinky /'dıŋkı/ adj. (-ier, -iest) colloq. neat and attractive; small, dainty. [Scots dink]

dinner n. 1 main meal of the day, either at midday or in the evening. 2 (in full **dinner-party**) formal evening meal.

esp. with guests. [French: related to DINE]

dinner-dance n. formal dinner followed by dancing.

dinner-jacket n. man's short usu. black formal jacket for evening wear.

dinner lady n. woman who supervises school dinners.

dinner service n. set of matching crockery for dinner.

dinosaur /ˈdaɪnəˌsɔː(r)/ n. 1 extinct, often enormous, reptile of the Mesozoic era. 2 unwieldy or unchanging system or organization. [Greek *deinos* terrible, SAURIAN]

dint –n. dent. –v. mark with dints. □ **by dint of** by force or means of. [Old English and Old Norse]

diocese /ˈdaɪəsɪs/ n. district under the pastoral care of a bishop. □ **diocesan** /daɪˈɒsɪs(ə)n/ adj. [Greek *dioikēsis* administration]

diode /ˈdaɪəʊd/ n. 1 semiconductor allowing the flow of current in one direction only and having two terminals. 2 thermionic valve having two electrodes. [from DI-¹, ELECTRODE]

Dionysian /ˌdaɪəˈnɪzɪən/ adj. wildly sensual; unrestrained. [Greek *Dionusos* god of wine]

dioptre /daɪˈɒptə(r)/ n. (US **diopter**) unit of refractive power of a lens. [Greek: related to DIA, *opsis* sight]

diorama /ˌdaɪəˈrɑːmə/ n. 1 scenic painting lit to simulate sunrise etc. 2 small scene with three-dimensional figures, viewed through a window etc. 3 small-scale model or film-set. [from DIA, Greek *horaō* see]

dioxide /daɪˈɒksaɪd/ n. oxide containing two atoms of oxygen (*carbon dioxide*).

dip –v. (**-pp-**) 1 put or lower briefly into liquid etc.; immerse. 2 a go below a surface or level. b (of income, activity, etc.) decline slightly; drop. 3 slope or extend downwards (*road dips*). 4 go under water and emerge quickly. 5 (foll. by *into*) look cursorily into (a book, subject, etc.). 6 a (foll. by *into*) put a hand, ladle, etc., into (a container) to take something out. b use part of (one's resources) (*dipped into our savings*). 7 lower or be lowered, esp. in salute. 8 lower or be lowered, esp. in salute. 8 lower the beam of (headlights) to reduce dazzle. 9 colour (a fabric) by immersing it in dye. 10 wash (sheep) in disinfectant. –n. 1 dipping or being dipped. 2 liquid for dipping. 3 brief bathe in the sea etc. 4 downward slope or hollow in a road, skyline, etc. 5 sauce into which food is dipped. 6 candle made by dipping the wick in tallow. [Old English]

Dip. Ed. abbr. Diploma in Education.

diphtheria /dɪfˈθɪərɪə, dɪp-/ n. acute infectious bacterial disease with inflammation of a mucous membrane esp. of the throat. [Greek *diphthera* skin, hide]

diphthong /ˈdɪfθɒŋ/ n. two written or spoken vowels pronounced in one syllable (as in *coin*, *loud*, *toy*). [Greek *phthoggos* voice]

diplodocus /dɪˈplɒdəkəs/ n. (pl. **-cuses**) giant plant-eating dinosaur with a long neck and tail. [Greek *diplous* double, *dokos* wooden beam]

diploma /dɪˈpləʊmə/ n. 1 certificate of qualification awarded by a college etc. 2 document conferring an honour or privilege. [Greek, = folded paper, from *diploos* double]

diplomacy /dɪˈpləʊməsɪ/ n. 1 a management of international relations. b skill in this. 2 tact. [French: related to DIPLOMATIC]

diplomat /ˈdɪpləmæt/ n. 1 member of a diplomatic service. 2 tactful person.

diplomatic /ˌdɪpləˈmætɪk/ adj. 1 of or involved in diplomacy. 2 tactful. □ **diplomatically** adv. [French: related to DIPLOMA]

diplomatic bag n. container for dispatching official mail etc. to or from an embassy, usu. exempt from customs inspection.

diplomatic immunity n. exemption of diplomatic staff abroad from arrest, taxation, etc.

diplomatic service n. branch of the civil service concerned with the representation of a country abroad.

diplomatist /dɪˈpləʊmətɪst/ n. diplomat.

dipole /ˈdaɪpəʊl/ n. 1 two equal and oppositely charged or magnetized poles separated by a distance. 2 molecule in which a concentration of positive charges is separated from a concentration of negative charges. 3 aerial consisting of a horizontal metal rod with a connecting wire at its core.

dipper n. 1 diving bird, esp. the water ouzel. 2 ladle.

dippy /ˈdɪpɪ/ adj. (**-ier**, **-iest**) *slang* crazy, silly. [origin uncertain]

dipso /ˈdɪpsəʊ/ n. (pl. **-s**) *colloq.* alcoholic. [abbreviation]

dipsomania /ˌdɪpsəˈmeɪnɪə/ n. alcoholism. □ **dipsomaniac** /-nɪˌæk/ n. [Greek *dipsa* thirst]

dipstick n. rod for measuring the depth of esp. oil in a vehicle's engine.

dip-switch n. switch for dipping a vehicle's headlights.

■ **Usage** The second pronunciation is considered incorrect by some people.

dipterous /'dɪptərəs/ *adj.* (of an insect) having two wings. [Greek *pteron* wing]

diptych /'dɪptɪk/ *n.* painting, esp. an altarpiece, on two hinged panels closing like a book. [Greek, = pair of writing-tablets, from *ptukhē* fold]

dire *adj.* 1 a calamitous, dreadful. b ominous. c (*predic*) *colloq.* very bad. 2 urgent (*in dire need*). [Latin]

direct /daɪrekt, dɪ-/ —*adj.* 1 extending or moving in a straight line or by the shortest route; not crooked or circuitous. 2 straightforward; frank. 3 with nothing or no-one in between; personal (*direct line*). 4 (of descent) lineal, not collateral. 5 complete, greatest possible (*the direct opposite*). —*adv.* 1 in a direct way or manner (*dealt with them direct*). 2 by the direct route (*sen: direct to London*). —*v.* 1 control; govern or guide (*duty directs me*). 2 (foll. by *to* + infin. or *that* + clause) order (a person) to. 3 (foll. by *to*) a address (a person). b tell (a person) the way to (a place). 4 (foll. by *at, to, towards*) point, aim, or turn (a blow, attention, or remark). 5 (also *absol.*) supervise the performing, staging, etc., of (a film, play, etc.). □ *direct-* guide.

direct access *n.* facility of retrieving data immediately from any part of a computer file.

direct current *n.* electric current flowing in one direction only.

direct debit *n.* regular debiting of a bank account at the request of the payee.

direct-grant school *n.* school funded by the Government and not a local authority.

direction /daɪrek(ʃ)n dɪ-/ *n.* 1 directing; supervision. 2 (usu. in *pl.*) order or instruction. 3 line along which, or point to or from which, a person or thing moves or looks. 4 tendency or scope of a theme, subject, etc.

directional *adj.* 1 of or indicating direction. 2 sending or receiving radio or sound waves in one particular direction.

directive /daɪrektɪv, dɪ-/ —*n.* order from an authority. —*adj.* serving to direct.

directly —*adv.* 1 a at once; immediately. (*directly after lunch*). b presently, shortly. 2 exactly (*directly opposite*). 3 in a direct manner. —*conj. colloq.* as soon as (*will tell you directly they come*).

director *n.* 1 person who directs, esp. action of a transitive verb.

company. 2 person who directs a film, play, etc. □ **directorial** /ˌdaɪrektɔːrɪəl/ *adj.* **directorship** *n.*

directorate /daɪrektərət, dɪ-/ *n.* 1 board of directors. 2 office of director.

director-general *n.* chief executive of a large organization.

directory /daɪrektəri, dɪ-/ *n.* (*pl.* -ies) book with a list of telephone subscribers, inhabitants of a district, or members of a profession etc. [Latin: related to DIRECT]

directory enquiries *n.pl.* telephone service providing a subscriber's number on request.

direct speech *n.* words actually spoken, not reported.

direct tax *n.* tax that one pays directly to the Government, esp. on income.

dirge *n.* 1 lament for the dead. 2 any dreary piece of music. [Latin imperative *dir-ige* = direct, used in the Office for the Dead]

dirham /'dɪərəm, n. principal monetary unit of Morocco and the United Arab Emirates. [A-abic]

dirigible /'dɪrɪdʒɪb(ə)l/ —*adj.* capable of being guided. —*n.* dirigible balloon or airship. [related to DIRECT]

dirk *n.* short dagger. [origin unknown]

dirndl /'dɜːnd(ə)l/ *n.* 1 dress with a close-fitting bodice and full skirt. 2 full skirt of this kind. [German]

dirt *n.* 1 unclean matter that soils. 2 a earth, soil. b earth, cinders, etc., used to make the surface (of a road etc. (usu. *attrib. dirt track*). 3 foul or malicious words or talk. 4 excrement. □ **treat like dirt** treat with contempt. [Old Norse *drit* excrement]

dirt cheap *adj.* & *adv. colloq.* extremely cheap.

dirty —*adj.* (-ier, -iest) 1 soiled, unclean. 2 causing dirtiness (*dirty job*). 3 sordid, lewd, obscene. 4 unpleasant, dishonourable, unfair (*dirty trick*). 5 (of weather) rough, squally. 6 (of colour) muddied, dingy. —*adv. slang* 1 very (*a dirty great diamond*). 2 in a dirty manner (*talk dirty; act dirty*) (esp. in senses 3 and 4 of *adj.*). —*v.* (-ies, -ied) make or become dirty. □ **do the dirty on** *colloq.* play a mean trick on. □ **dirtily** *adv.* **dirtiness** *n.*

dirty look *n. colloq.* look of disapproval or disgust.

dirty old man *n. colloq.* lecherous man.

dirty weekend *n. colloq.* weekend spent with a lover.

dirty word *n.* 1 offensive or indecent word. 2 word for something disapproved of (*profit is a dirty word*).

dirty work *n.* dishonourable or illegal activity.

dis- *prefix* forming nouns, adjectives, and verbs implying: **1** negation or direct opposite (*dishonest; discourteous*). **2** reversal (*disengage; disorientate*). **3** removal of a thing or quality (*dismember; disable*). **4** separation (*distinguish*). **5** completeness or intensification (*disgruntled*). **6** expulsion from (*disbar*). [French *des-* or Latin *dis-*]

disability /ˌdɪsəˈbɪlɪtɪ/ *n.* (*pl.* **-ies**) **1** permanent physical or mental incapacity. **2** lack of some capacity etc., preventing action.

disable /dɪsˈeɪb(ə)l/ *v.* (**-ling**) **1** deprive of an ability or function. **2** (often as **disabled** *adj.*) physically incapacitate. □ **disablement** *n.*

disabuse /ˌdɪsəˈbjuːz/ *v.* (**-sing**) (usu. foll. by *of*) free from a mistaken idea; disillusion.

disadvantage /ˌdɪsədˈvɑːntɪdʒ/ *n.* **1** unfavourable circumstance or condition. **2** damage; loss.—*v.* (**-ging**) cause disadvantage to. □ **at a disadvantage** in an unfavourable position or aspect. □ **disadvantageous** /ˌdɪsædvɑːnˈteɪdʒəs/ *adj.*

disadvantaged *adj.* lacking normal opportunities through poverty, disability, etc.

disaffected /ˌdɪsəˈfektɪd/ *adj.* discontented (esp. politically); no longer loyal. □ **disaffection** *n.*

disagree /ˌdɪsəˈɡriː/ *v.* (**-ees**, **-eed**, **-eeing**) (often foll. by *with*) **1** hold a different opinion. **2** (of factors) not correspond. **3** upset (*onions disagree with me*). □ **disagreement** *n.*

disagreeable *adj.* **1** unpleasant. **2** bad-tempered. □ **disagreeably** *adv.*

disallow /ˌdɪsəˈlaʊ/ *v.* refuse to allow or accept; prohibit.

disappear /ˌdɪsəˈpɪə(r)/ *v.* **1** cease to be visible. **2** cease to exist or be in circulation or use. **3** (of a person) go missing. □ **disappearance** *n.*

disappoint /ˌdɪsəˈpɔɪnt/ *v.* **1** fail to fulfil the desire or expectation of. **2** frustrate (a hope etc.). □ **disappointed** *adj.* **disappointing** *adj.*

disappointment *n.* **1** person or thing that disappoints. **2** being disappointed.

disapprobation /ˌdɪsˌæprəˈbeɪʃ(ə)n/ *n. formal* disapproval.

disapprove /ˌdɪsəˈpruːv/ *v.* (**-ving**) (usu. foll. by *of*) have or express an unfavourable opinion. □ **disapproval** *n.*

disarm /dɪsˈɑːm/ *v.* **1** take weapons away from a person or give up one's own weapons. **3** defuse (a bomb etc.). **4** make less angry, hostile, etc; charm,

win over. □ **disarming** *adj.* (esp. in sense 4). □ **disarmingly** *adv.*

disarmament /dɪsˈɑːməmənt/ *n.* reduction by a State of its armaments.

disarrange /ˌdɪsəˈreɪndʒ/ *v.* (**-ging**) bring into disorder. □ **disarrangement** *n.*

disarray /ˌdɪsəˈreɪ/ —*n.* disorder. —*v.* throw into disorder.

disassociate /ˌdɪsəˈsəʊʃɪˌeɪt/ *v.* (**-ting**) = **disassociation** /ˌdɪsˌəsəʊsiˈeɪʃ(ə)n/.

disaster /dɪˈzɑːstə(r)/ *n.* **1** great or sudden misfortune; catastrophe. **2** *colloq.* complete failure. □ **disastrous** *adj.* **disastrously** *adv.* [Latin *astrum* star]

disavow /ˌdɪsəˈvaʊ/ *v.* disclaim knowledge of or responsibility for. □ **disavowal** *n.*

disband /dɪsˈbænd/ *v.* break up; disperse. □ **disbandment** *n.*

disbar /dɪsˈbɑː(r)/ *v.* (**-rr-**) deprive (a barrister) of the right to practise. □ **disbarment** *n.*

disbelieve /ˌdɪsbɪˈliːv/ *v.* (**-ving**) be unable or unwilling to believe; be sceptical. □ **disbelief** *n.* **disbelievingly** *adv.*

disburse /dɪsˈbɜːs/ *v.* (**-sing**) pay out (money). □ **disbursal** *n.* **disbursement** *n.* [French: related to DIS-, BOURSE]

disc *n.* (also **disk** esp. *US* and in sense 4a) **1 a** flat thin circular object. **b** round flat or apparently flat surface or mark. **2** layer of cartilage between vertebrae. **3** gramophone record. **4 a** (usu. **disk**; in full **magnetic disk**) flat circular computer storage device. **b** (in full **optical disc**) disc for data recorded and read by laser. [Latin DISCUS]

discard /dɪsˈkɑːd/ *v.* **1** reject as unwanted. **2** remove or put aside. [from DIS-, CARD[1]]

disc brake *n.* brake employing the friction of pads against a disc.

discern /dɪˈsɜːn/ *v.* **1** perceive clearly with the mind or senses. **2** make out with effort. □ **discernible** *adj.* [Latin *cerno cret-* separate]

discerning *adj.* having good judgement. □ **discerningly** *adv.* **discernment** *n.*

discharge —*v.* /dɪsˈtʃɑːdʒ/ (**-ging**) **1** release (a prisoner); allow (a patient, jury) to leave. **2** dismiss from office or employment. **3** fire (a gun etc.). **4** throw; eject. **5** emit, pour out (pus etc.). **6** (foll. by *into*) (of a river etc.) flow into (esp. the sea). **7 a** carry out (a duty or obligation). **b** relieve oneself of (a debt etc.). **c** relieve (a bankrupt) of residual liability. **8** *Law* cancel (an order of court). **9** release an electrical charge from. **10 a** relieve (a

ship etc.) of cargo. **b** unload (cargo). —*n.* 1 discharging or being discharged. 2 certificate of release, dismissal, etc. 3 matter discharged; pus etc. 4 release of an electric charge, esp. with a spark.

disciple /dɪˈsaɪp(ə)l/ *n.* follower of a leader, teacher, etc., esp. of Christ. [Latin *disco* learn]

disciplinarian /dɪsɪplɪˈneərɪən/ *n.* enforcer of or believer in firm discipline.

disciplinary /ˈdɪsɪplɪnərɪ/ *adj.* of or enforcing discipline.

discipline /ˈdɪsɪplɪn/ —*n.* 1 a control or order exercised over people or animals, e.g. over members of an organization. **b** system of rules for this. 2 training or way of life aimed at self-control and conformity. 3 branch of learning. 4 punishment. —*v.* (**-ning**) 1 punish. 2 control by training in obedience. [Latin *disciplina* from *disco* learn]

disc jockey *n.* presenter of recorded pop music.

disclaim /dɪsˈkleɪm/ *v.* 1 deny or disown. 2 renounce legal claim to.

disclaimer *n.* renunciation, statement disclaiming something.

disclose /dɪsˈkləʊz/ *v.* (**-sing**) make known; expose. □ **disclosure** *n.*

disco /ˈdɪskəʊ/ *colloq.* —*n.* (*pl.* **-s**) = DISCOTHEQUE. —*v.* (**-es, -ed**) dance to disco music. [abbreviation]

discolour /dɪsˈkʌlə(r)/ *v.* (*US* **discolor**) cause to change from its normal colour; stain; tarnish. □ **discoloration** /-ˈreɪʃ(ə)n/ *n.*

discomfit /dɪsˈkʌmfɪt/ *v.* (**-t-**) disconcert, baffle, frustrate. □ **discomfiture** *n.* [French: related to *dis-*, CONFECTION]

■ **Usage** *Discomfit* is sometimes confused with *discomfort*.

discomfort /dɪsˈkʌmfət/ —*n.* 1 lack of comfort; slight pain or unease. 2 cause of this. —*v.* make uncomfortable.

■ **Usage** As a verb, *discomfort* is sometimes confused with *discomfit*.

discompose /dɪskəmˈpəʊz/ *v.* (**-sing**) disturb the composure of. □ **discomposure** *n.*

disco music *n.* popular dance music with a heavy bass rhythm.

disconcert /dɪskənˈsɜːt/ *v.* disturb the composure of; fluster.

disconnect /dɪskəˈnekt/ *v.* 1 break the connection of. 2 put out of action by disconnecting the parts. □ **disconnection** *n.*

disconnected *adj.* incoherent and illogical.

disconsolate /dɪsˈkɒnsələt/ *adj.* forlorn, unhappy, disappointed. □ **disconsolately** *adv.* [Latin: related to DIS-, SOLACE]

discontent /dɪskənˈtent/ —*n.* lack of contentment; dissatisfaction, grievance. —*v.* (esp. as **discontented** *adj.*) make dissatisfied. □ **discontentment** *n.*

discontinue /dɪskənˈtɪnjuː/ *v.* (**-ues, -ued, -uing**) 1 come or bring to an end (*a discontinued line*). 2 give up, cease from (doing something). □ **discontinuance** *n.*

discontinuous *adj.* lacking continuity; intermittent. □ **discontinuity** /-kɒntɪˈnjuːɪtɪ/ *n.*

discord /ˈdɪskɔːd/ *n.* 1 disagreement; strife. 2 harsh noise; clashing sounds. 3 lack of harmony in a chord. [Latin: related to DIS-, *cor cord-* heart]

discordant /dɪsˈkɔːd(ə)nt/ *adj.* 1 disagreeing. 2 not in harmony; dissonant. □ **discordance** *n.* **discordantly** *adv.*

discotheque /ˈdɪskətek/ *n.* 1 nightclub etc. for dancing to pop records. 2 professional lighting and sound equipment used for this. 3 party with such equipment. [French; = record-library]

discount —*n.* /ˈdɪskaʊnt/ amount deducted from a full or normal price, esp. for prompt or advance payment. —*v.* /dɪsˈkaʊnt/ 1 disregard as unreliable or unimportant. 2 deduct an amount from (a price etc.). 3 give or get the present worth of (an investment certificate which has yet to mature). □ **at a discount** below the usual price or true value.

discountenance /dɪsˈkaʊntɪnəns/ *v.* (**-cing**) 1 disconcert. 2 refuse to approve of.

discourage /dɪsˈkʌrɪdʒ/ *v.* (**-ging**) 1 deprive of courage or confidence. 2 dissuade, deter. 3 show disapproval of. □ **discouragement** *n.*

discourse —*n.* /ˈdɪskɔːs/ 1 conversation. 2 lengthy treatment of a subject. 3 lecture, speech. —*v.* /dɪsˈkɔːs/ (**-sing**) 1 converse. 2 speak or write at length on a subject. [Latin *currō curs-* run]

discourteous /dɪsˈkɜːtɪəs/ *adj.* lacking courtesy. □ **discourteously** *adv.* **discourtesy** *n.* (*pl.* **-ies**).

discover /dɪsˈkʌvə(r)/ *v.* 1 **a** find out or become aware of, by intention or chance. **b** be first to find or find out (*who discovered America?*). 2 find and promote as a new performer. □ **discoverer** *n.* [Latin: related to DIS-, COVER]

discovery *n.* (*pl.* **-ies**) 1 discovering or being discovered. 2 person or thing discovered.

discredit /dɪs'kredɪt/ —n. 1 harm to reputation. 2 person or thing causing this. 3 lack of credibility. —v. (-t-) 1 harm the good reputation of. 2 cause to be disbelieved. 3 refuse to believe.

discreditable adj. bringing discredit; shameful. □ **discreditably** adv.

discreet /dɪs'kriːt/ adj. (-er, -est) 1 a circumspect. b tactful; judicious, prudent. 2 unobtrusive. □ **discreetly** adv. □ **discreetness** n. [Latin: related to DIS-CERN]

discrepancy /dɪs'krepənsɪ/ n. (pl. -ies) difference; inconsistency. □ **discrepant** adj. [Latin discrepo be discordant]

discrete /dɪs'kriːt/ adj. individually distinct; separate, discontinuous. □ **discreteness** n. [Latin: related to DISCERN]

discretion /dɪs'kreʃ(ə)n/ n. 1 being discreet. 2 prudence; good judgement. 3 freedom or authority to act according to one's judgement. □ **use one's discretion** act according to one's own judgement. □ **discretionary** adj. [Latin discrimino: related to DISCERN]

discriminate /dɪs'krɪmɪˌneɪt/ v. (-ting) 1 (often foll. by between) make or see a distinction. 2 (usu. foll. by against or in favour of) treat unfavourably or favourably, esp. on the basis of race, gender, etc. □ **discriminatory** /-nətərɪ/ adj. [Latin discrimino: related to DISCERN]

discriminating adj. showing good judgement or taste.

discrimination /dɪˌskrɪmɪ'neɪʃ(ə)n/ n. 1 unfavourable treatment based on racial, sexual, etc. prejudice. 2 good taste or judgement.

discursive /dɪs'kɜːsɪv/ adj. tending to digress, rambling. [Latin curro curs- run]

discus /'dɪskəs/ n. (pl. -cuses) heavy thick-centred disc thrown in athletic events. [Latin from Greek]

discuss /dɪ'skʌs/ v. 1 talk about (discussed their holidays). 2 talk or write about (a subject) in detail. □ **discussion** n. [Latin discutio -cuss- disperse]

disdain /dɪs'deɪn/ —n. scorn, contempt. —v. 1 regard with disdain. 2 refrain or refuse out of disdain. □ **disdainful** adj. □ **disdainfully** adv. [Latin: related to DE-, DEIGN]

disease /dɪ'ziːz/ n. 1 unhealthy condition of the body or mind, plants, society, etc. 2 particular kind of disease. □ **diseased** adj. [French: related to DIS-, EASE]

disembark /ˌdɪsɪm'bɑːk/ v. put or go ashore; get off an aircraft, bus, etc. □ **disembarkation** /-bɑː'keɪʃ(ə)n/ n.

disembarrass /ˌdɪsɪm'bærəs/ v. 1 (usu. foll. by of) relieve (of a load etc.). 2 free

from embarrassment. □ **disembarrassment** n.

disembodied /ˌdɪsɪm'bɒdɪd/ adj. 1 (of the soul etc.) freed from the body or concrete form. 2 lacking a body. □ **disembodiment** n.

disembowel /ˌdɪsɪm'baʊəl/ v. (-ll-; US -l-) remove the bowels or entrails of. □ **disembowelment** n.

disenchant /ˌdɪsɪn'tʃɑːnt/ v. disillusion. □ **disenchantment** n.

disencumber /ˌdɪsɪn'kʌmbə(r)/ v. free from encumbrance.

disenfranchise /ˌdɪsɪn'fræntʃaɪz/ v. (also **disfranchise**) (-sing) 1 deprive of the right to vote or be represented. 2 deprive of rights as a citizen or of a franchise held. □ **disenfranchisement** n.

disengage /ˌdɪsɪn'geɪdʒ/ v. (-ging) 1 detach, loosen, release. 2 remove (troops) from battle etc. 3 become detached. 4 (as **disengaged** adj.) a at leisure. b uncommitted. □ **disengagement** n.

disentangle /ˌdɪsɪn'tæŋg(ə)l/ v. (-ling) 1 free or become free of tangles or complications. □ **disentanglement** n.

disestablish /ˌdɪsɪ'stæblɪʃ/ v. 1 terminate (a Church) of State support. 2 terminate the establishment of. □ **disestablishment** n.

disfavour /dɪs'feɪvə(r)/ (US **disfavor**) —n. 1 disapproval or dislike. 2 being disliked. —v. regard or treat with disfavour.

disfigure /dɪs'fɪgə(r)/ v. (-ring) spoil the appearance of. □ **disfigurement** n.

disfranchise var. of DISENFRANCHISE.

disgorge /dɪs'gɔːdʒ/ v. (-ging) 1 eject from the throat. 2 pour forth. □ **disgorgement** n.

disgrace /dɪs'greɪs/ —n. 1 shame; ignominy. 2 shameful or very bad person or thing (disgraced my anger). —n. 1 a costume, make-up, etc., used to disguise. b action, manner, etc., used to deceive. 2 disguised state. 3 practice of disguising. [French: related to DIS-, GRACE]

disgraceful adj. shameful; causing disgrace. □ **disgracefully** adv.

disgruntled /dɪs'grʌnt(ə)ld/ adj. discontented, sulky. □ **disgruntlement** n. [from DIS-, GRUNT]

disguise /dɪs'gaɪz/ —v. (-sing) 1 conceal the identity of; make unrecognizable. 2 conceal (disguised my anger). —n. 1 a **in disguise** out of favour. □ **in disgrace** out of favour. □ [Latin: related to DIS-, GRACE]

disgust /dɪs'gʌst/ —n. strong aversion; repugnance. —v. cause disgust in. □ **disgustingly** adv. [French or Italian: related to DIS-, GUSTO]

dish —n. 1 a shallow flat-bottomed container for food. b its contents. c particular kind of food or food prepared to a particular recipe (*meat dish*). 2 (in *pl.*) crockery, pans, etc. after a meal (*wash the dishes*). 3 a dish-shaped object or cavity. b = SATELLITE DISH. 4 *colloq.* sexually attractive person.—v. 1 *colloq.* outmanoeuvre, frustrate. 2 make dish-shaped. □ **dish out** *colloq.* distribute. **dish up 1** put (food) in dishes for serving. 2 *colloq.* present as a fact or argument. [Old English from Latin DISCUS]

dishabille var. of DÉSHABILLÉ.

disharmony /dɪsˈhɑːmənɪ/ *n.* lack of harmony; discord. □ **disharmonious** /ˌmənɪəs/ *adj.*

dishcloth *n.* cloth for washing dishes.

dishearten /dɪsˈhɑːt(ə)n/ *v.* cause to lose courage, hope, or confidence. □ **disheartenment** *n.*

dishevelled /dɪˈʃev(ə)ld/ *adj.* (US **disheveled**) untidy; ruffled. □ **disheveled** *n.* [from *chevel* 'hair', from Latin *capillus*]

dishonest /dɪsˈɒnɪst/ *adj.* fraudulent or insincere. □ **dishonestly** *adv.* **dishonesty** *n.*

dishonour /dɪsˈɒnə(r)/ (US **dishonor**) —*n.* 1 loss of honour or respect; disgrace. 2 thing causing this. —*v.* 1 disgrace (*dishonoured his name*). 2 refuse to accept or pay (a cheque etc.). □ **dishonourable** *adj.* (US **dishonorable**) 1 causing disgrace; ignominious. 2 unprincipled. □ **dishonourably** *adv.*

dishwasher *n.* machine or person that washes dishes.

dishy *adj.* (**-ier, -iest**) *colloq.* sexually attractive.

disillusion /ˌdɪsɪˈluːʒ(ə)n/ —*v.* free from an illusion or mistaken belief. —*n.* disillusioned state. □ **disillusionment** *n.*

disincentive /ˌdɪsɪnˈsentɪv/ *n.* thing discouraging action, effort, etc.

disincline /ˌdɪsɪnˈklaɪn/ *v.* make unwilling or reluctant. □ **disinclination** /-klɪˈneɪʃ(ə)n/ *n.*

disinfect /ˌdɪsɪnˈfekt/ *v.* cleanse of infection, esp. with disinfectant. □ **disinfection** *n.*

disinfectant —*n.* substance that destroys germs etc.—*adj.* disinfecting.

disinformation /ˌdɪsɪnfəˈmeɪʃ(ə)n/ *n.* false information, propaganda.

disingenuous /ˌdɪsɪnˈdʒenjʊəs/ *adj.* insincere, not candid. □ **disingenuously** *adv.*

disinherit /ˌdɪsɪnˈherɪt/ *v.* (**-t-**) reject as one's heir; deprive of the right of inheritance. □ **disinheritance** *n.*

disintegrate /dɪsˈɪntɪˌɡreɪt/ *v.* (**-ting**) 1 separate into component parts or fragments; break up. 2 *colloq.* break down, collapse.

nuclei. □ **disintegration** /-ˈɡreɪʃ(ə)n/ *n.*

disinter /ˌdɪsɪnˈtɜː(r)/ *v.* (**-rr-**) dig up (esp. a corpse). □ **disinterment** *n.*

disinterested /dɪsˈɪntrɪstɪd/ *adj.* 1 impartial. 2 uninterested. □ **disinterestedly** *adv.*

■ **Usage** Use of *disinterested* in sense 2 is common in informal use, but is widely regarded as incorrect. The use of the noun *disinterest* to mean 'lack of interest' is also objected to but it is rarely used in any other sense and the alternative *uninterest* is rare.

disinvest /ˌdɪsɪnˈvest/ *v.* reduce or dispose of one's investment. □ **disinvestment** *n.*

disjoint /dɪsˈdʒɔɪnt/ *v.* 1 take apart at the joints. 2 (as **disjointed** *adj.*) incoherent; disconnected. 3 disturb the working of; disrupt.

disjunction /dɪsˈdʒʌŋkʃ(ə)n/ *n.* separation.

disjunctive /dɪsˈdʒʌŋktɪv/ *adj.* 1 involving separation. 2 (of a conjunction) expressing an alternative, e.g. *or* in *is it wet or dry?*

disk var. of DISC (esp. US & *Computing*).

disk drive *n.* *Computing* mechanism for rotating a disk and reading or writing data from or to it.

diskette /dɪˈsket/ *n.* *Computing* = FLOPPY *n.*

dislike /dɪsˈlaɪk/ —*v.* (**-king**) have an aversion to; not like. —*n.* 1 feeling of repugnance or not liking. 2 object of this.

dislocate /ˈdɪsləˌkeɪt/ *v.* (**-ting**) 1 disturb the normal connection of (esp. a joint in the body). 2 disrupt. □ **dislocation** /-ˈkeɪʃ(ə)n/ *n.*

dislodge /dɪsˈlɒdʒ/ *v.* (**-ging**) disturb or move. □ **dislodgement** *n.*

disloyal /dɪsˈlɔɪəl/ *adj.* not loyal; unfaithful. □ **disloyally** *adv.* **disloyalty** *n.*

dismal /ˈdɪzm(ə)l/ *adj.* 1 gloomy; miserable. 2 dreary; sombre. 3 *colloq.* feeble, inept (*dismal attempt*). □ **dismally** *adv.* [medieval Latin *dies mali* unlucky days]

dismantle /dɪsˈmænt(ə)l/ *v.* (**-ling**) 1 take to pieces; pull down. 2 deprive of defences or equipment.

dismay /dɪsˈmeɪ/ —*v.* fill with dismay. —*n.* intense disappointment or despair. [French from may, [French from Germanic: related to DIS, MAY]

(esp. mentally. 3 (of an atomic nucleus) emit particles or divide into smaller nuclei. □ **disintegration** /-ˈɡreɪʃ(ə)n/ *n.*

dismember /dɪsˈmembə(r)/ *v.* 1 remove the limbs from. 2 partition or divide up. □ **dismemberment** *n.*

dismiss /dɪsˈmɪs/ v. **1** send away, esp. from one's presence; disperse. **2** terminate the employment of, esp. dishonourably; sack. **3** put from one's mind or emotions. **4** consider not worth talking or thinking about; treat summarily. **5** Law refuse further hearing to (a case). **6** Cricket put (a batsman or side) out (usu. for a stated score). □ **dismissal** n. [Latin mitto miss- send]

dismissive adj. dismissing rudely or casually; disdainful. □ **dismissively** adv. **dismissiveness** n.

dismount /dɪsˈmaʊnt/ v. **1 a** alight from a horse, bicycle, etc. **b** unseat. **2** remove (a thing) from its mounting.

disobedient /ˌdɪsəˈbiːdɪənt/ adj. disobeying; rebellious. □ **disobedience** n. **disobediently** adv.

disobey /ˌdɪsəˈbeɪ/ v. refuse or fail to obey.

disoblige /ˌdɪsəˈblaɪdʒ/ v. (-ging) refuse to help or cooperate with (a person).

disorder /dɪsˈɔːdə(r)/ n. **1** lack of order; confusion. **2** public disturbance; riot. **3** ailment or disease. □ **disordered** adj.

disorderly adj. **1** untidy; confused. **2** riotous, unruly. □ **disorderliness** n.

disorganize /dɪsˈɔːɡənaɪz/ v. (also -ise) (-zing or -sing) **1** throw into confusion or disorder. **2** (as **disorganized** adj.) badly organized; untidy. □ **disorganization** /-ˈzeɪʃ(ə)n/ n.

disorient /dɪsˈɔːrɪənt/ v. = DISORIENT-ATE.

disorientate /dɪsˈɔːrɪənˌteɪt/ v. (also **disorient**) (-ting) confuse (a person), esp. as to his or her bearings. □ **disorientation** /-ˈteɪʃ(ə)n/ n.

disown /dɪsˈəʊn/ v. deny or give up any connection with; repudiate.

disparage /dɪsˈpærɪdʒ/ v. (-ging) **1** criticize; belittle. **2** bring discredit on. □ **disparagement** n. [French: related to DIS-, parage rank]

disparate /ˈdɪspərət/ adj. essentially different; not comparable. □ **disparateness** n. [Latin disparo separate]

disparity /dɪsˈpærɪtɪ/ n. (pl. -ies) inequality; difference; incongruity.

dispassionate /dɪsˈpæʃ(ə)nət/ adj. free from emotion; impartial. □ **dispassionately** adv.

dispatch /dɪsˈpætʃ/ (also **despatch**) —v. **1** send off to a destination or for a purpose. **2** perform (a task etc.) promptly; finish off. **3** kill, execute. **4** colloq. eat quickly. —n. **1** dispatching or being dispatched. **2 a** official written message, esp. military. **b** news report to a newspaper etc. **3** promptness, efficiency. [Italian dispacciare or Spanish despachar]

dispatch-box n. case for esp. parliamentary documents.

dispatch-rider n. messenger on a motor cycle.

dispel /dɪsˈpel/ v. (-ll-) drive away; scatter (fears etc.). [Latin pello drive]

dispensable /dɪsˈpensəb(ə)l/ adj. that can be dispensed with.

dispensary /dɪsˈpensərɪ/ n. (pl. -ies) place where medicines are dispensed.

dispensation /ˌdɪspenˈseɪʃ(ə)n/ n. **1** dispensing or distributing. **2** exemption from penalty, rule, etc. **3** ordering or management of the world by Providence.

dispense /dɪsˈpens/ v. (-sing) **1** distribute; deal out. **2** administer. **3** make up and give out (medicine etc.). **4** (foll. by with) do without; make unnecessary. [French from Latin pendo pens- weigh]

dispenser n. **1** person or thing that dispenses e.g. medicine, good advice. **2** automatic machine dispensing a specific amount.

disperse /dɪsˈpɜːs/ v. (-sing) **1** go, send, drive, or scatter widely or in different directions. **2** send to or station at different points. **3** disseminate. **4** Chem. distribute (small particles) in a medium. **5** divide (white light) into its coloured constituents. □ **dispersal** n. **dispersive** adj. [Latin: related to DIS-, SPARSE]

dispersion /dɪsˈpɜːʃ(ə)n/ n. **1** dispersing or being dispersed. **2** (the **Dispersion**) = DIASPORA.

dispirit /dɪsˈpɪrɪt/ v. (esp. as **dispiriting, dispirited** adj/s.) make despondent, deject.

displace /dɪsˈpleɪs/ v. (-cing) **1** move from its place. **2** remove from office. **3** take the place of; oust.

displaced person n. refugee in war etc. or from persecution.

displacement n. **1** displacing or being displaced. **2** amount of fluid displaced by an object floating or immersed in it.

display /dɪsˈpleɪ/ —v. **1** exhibit; show. **2** reveal; betray. —n. **1** displaying. **2 a** exhibition or show. **b** thing(s) displayed. **3** ostentation. **4** mating rituals of some birds etc. **5** what is shown on a visual display unit etc. [Latin plico fold]

displease /dɪsˈpliːz/ v. (-sing) make upset or angry; annoy. □ **displeasure** /-ˈpleʒ(ə)r/ n.

disport /dɪsˈpɔːt/ v. (often refl.) play, frolic, enjoy oneself. [Anglo-French porter carry, from Latin]

disposable /dɪsˈpəʊzəb(ə)l/ —adj. **1** intended to be used once and discarded. **2** able to be disposed of. —n. disposable article.

disposable income n. income after tax and other fixed payments.

disposal /dɪsˈpəʊz(ə)l/ n. disposing of, e.g. waste. □ **at one's disposal** available.

■ **Usage** *Disposal* is the noun corresponding to the verb *dispose of* (get rid of, deal with, etc.), *Disposition* is the noun from *dispose* (arrange, incline).

dispose /dɪsˈpəʊz/ v. (-sing) 1 (usu. foll. by *to*, or *to* + infin.) **a** make willing; incline (*was disposed to agree*). **b** tend (*wheel was disposed to buckle*). 2 arrange suitably. 3 (as **disposed** *adj.*) have a specified inclination (*ill-disposed; well-disposed*). 4 determine events (*man proposes, God disposes*). □ **dispose of 1 a** deal with. **b** get rid of. **c** finish. **d** kill. 2 sell. 3 prove (an argument etc.) incorrect. [French related to PURPOSE]

disposition /dɪspəˈzɪʃ(ə)n/ n. 1 natural tendency; temperament. 2 a arrangement (of parts etc.). **b** arrangement. 3 (usu. in *pl.*) preparations; plans.

■ **Usage** See note at *disposal*.

dispossess /dɪspəˈzes/ v. 1 (usu. foll. by *of*) (esp. as **dispossessed** *adj.*) deprive (a person) of. 2 dislodge; oust. □ **dispossession** /-ˈzeʃ(ə)n/ n.

disproof /dɪsˈpruːf/ n. refutation.

disproportion /dɪsprəˈpɔːʃ(ə)n/ n. lack of proportion. □ **disproportional** *adj.*

disproportionate *adj.* 1 out of proportion. 2 relatively too large or small etc. □ **disproportionately** *adv.*

disprove /dɪsˈpruːv/ v. (-ving) prove false.

disputable /dɪsˈpjuːtəb(ə)l/ *adj.* open to question; uncertain. □ **disputably** *adv.*

disputant /dɪsˈpjuːt(ə)nt/ n. person in a dispute.

disputation /ˌdɪspjuːˈteɪʃ(ə)n/ n. 1 debate, esp. formal. 2 argument; controversy.

disputatious *adj.* argumentative.

dispute /dɪsˈpjuːt/ —v. 1 (-ting) 1 debate, argue. 2 discuss, esp. heatedly; quarrel. 3 question the truth or validity of (a statement etc). 4 contend for (*disputed territory*). 5 resist, oppose. —n. 1 controversy; debate. 2 quarrel. 3 disagreement leading to industrial action. □ **in dispute** 1 being argued about. 2 (of a workforce) involved in industrial action. [Latin *puto* reckon]

disqualify /dɪsˈkwɒlɪfaɪ/ v. (-ies, -ied) 1 debar from a competition or pronounce ineligible as a winner. 2 make or pronounce ineligible, unsuitable, or unqualified (*disqualified from driving*). □ **disqualification** /-fɪˈkeɪʃ(ə)n/ n.

disquiet /dɪsˈkwaɪət/ —v. make anxious. —n. anxiety; uneasiness.

disquietude n. uneasiness.

disquisition /ˌdɪskwɪˈzɪʃ(ə)n/ n. discursive treatise or discourse. [Latin *quaero quaesit-* seek]

disregard /dɪsrɪˈɡɑːd/ —v. 1 ignore. 2 treat as unimportant. —n. indifference; neglect.

disrepair /dɪsrɪˈpeə(r)/ n. poor condition due to lack of repairs.

disreputable /dɪsˈrepjʊtəb(ə)l/ *adj.* 1 of bad reputation. 2 not respectable in character or appearance. □ **disreputably** *adv.*

disrepute /dɪsrɪˈpjuːt/ n. lack of good reputation; discredit.

disrespect /dɪsrɪˈspekt/ n. lack of respect; discourtesy. □ **disrespectful** *adj.* □ **disrespectfully** *adv.*

disrobe /dɪsˈrəʊb/ v. (-bing) *literary* undress.

disrupt /dɪsˈrʌpt/ v. 1 interrupt the continuity of; bring disorder to. 2 break apart. □ **disruption** n. □ **disruptive** *adj.* □ **disruptively** *adv.* [Latin: related to RUPTURE]

dissatisfy /dɪsˈsætɪsfaɪ/ v. (-ies, -ied) make discontented; fail to satisfy. □ **dissatisfaction** /-ˈfækʃ(ə)n/ n.

dissect /dɪsˈekt/ v. 1 cut into pieces, esp. for examination or post mortem. 2 analyse or criticize in detail. □ **dissection** n. [Latin: related to SECTION]

dissemble /dɪsˈemb(ə)l/ v. (-ling) 1 be hypocritical or insincere. 2 disguise or conceal (a feeling, intention, etc.). [Latin *simulo* SIMULATE]

disseminate /dɪsˈemɪneɪt/ v. (-ting) scatter about, spread (esp. ideas) widely. □ **dissemination** /-ˈneɪʃ(ə)n/ n. [Latin: related to *semen* SEMEN]

dissension /dɪsˈenʃ(ə)n/ n. angry disagreement. [Latin: related to DISSENT]

dissent /dɪsˈent/ —v. (often foll. by *from*) 1 disagree esp. openly. 2 differ, esp. from the established or official opinion. —n. 1 such difference. 2 expression of this. [Latin: related to DIS-, *sentio* feel]

dissenter n. 1 person who dissents. 2 (**Dissenter**) Protestant dissenting from the Church of England.

dissentient /dɪsˈenʃ(ə)nt/ —*adj.* disagreeing with the established or official view. —n. person who dissents.

dissertation /dɪsəˈteɪʃ(ə)n/ n. detailed discourse, esp. one submitted towards an academic degree. [Latin *disserto* discuss]

disservice /dɪsˈsɜːvɪs/ n. harmful action, harm.

dissident /ˈdɪsɪd(ə)nt/ —*adj.* disagreeing, esp. with the established government, system, etc. —n. dissident person.

□ **dissidence** n. [Latin: related to DIS-, *sedeo* sit]

dissimilar /dɪˈsɪmɪlə(r)/ adj. unlike, not similar. □ **dissimilarity** /-ˈlærɪtɪ/ n. (pl. -ies).

dissimulate /dɪˈsɪmjʊˌleɪt/ v. (-ting) dissemble. □ **dissimulation** /-ˈleɪʃ(ə)n/ n. [Latin: related to DISSEMBLE]

dissipate /ˈdɪsɪˌpeɪt/ v. (-ting) 1 disperse, disappear, dispel. 2 squander. 3 (as **dissipated** adj.) dissolute. [Latin *dissipare*-pat-]

dissipation /ˌdɪsɪˈpeɪʃ(ə)n/ n. 1 dissolute way of life. 2 dissipating or being dissipated.

dissociate /dɪˈsəʊʃɪˌeɪt/ v. (-ting) 1 disconnect or separate. 2 become disconnected. □ **dissociate oneself from** declare oneself unconnected with. □ **dissociation** /-ˈeɪʃ(ə)n/ n. **dissociative** /-ətɪv/ adj. [Latin: related to DIS-, ASSOCIATE]

dissoluble /dɪˈsɒljʊb(ə)l/ adj. that can be disintegrated, loosened, or disconnected.

dissolute /ˈdɪsəˌluːt/ adj. lax in morals; licentious. [Latin: related to DISSOLVE]

dissolution /ˌdɪsəˈluːʃ(ə)n/ n. 1 dissolving or being dissolved, esp. of a partnership or of parliament for a new election. 2 breaking up, abolition (of an institution). 3 death.

dissolve /dɪˈzɒlv/ v. (-ving) 1 make or become liquid, esp. by immersion or dispersion in a liquid. 2 (cause to) disappear gradually. 3 dismiss (an assembly, esp. Parliament). 4 annul or put an end to (a partnership, marriage, etc.). 5 (often foll. by *into*) be overcome (by tears, laughter, etc.). [Latin: related to DIS-, *solvo solut-* loosen]

dissonant /ˈdɪsənənt/ adj. 1 harsh-toned; discordant. 2 incongruous. □ **dissonance** n. [Latin: related to DIS-, *sono* SOUND[1]]

dissuade /dɪˈsweɪd/ v. (-ding) (often foll. by *from*) discourage (a person); persuade against. □ **dissuasion** /-ˈsweɪʒ(ə)n/ n. **dissuasive** adj. [Latin: related to DIS-, *suadeo* advise]

dissyllable var. of DISYLLABLE.

distaff /ˈdɪstɑːf/ n. cleft stick holding wool or flax for spinning by hand. [Old English]

distaff side n. female branch of a family.

distance /ˈdɪst(ə)ns/ —n. 1 being far off; remoteness. 2 space between two points. 3 distant point or place. 4 aloofness; reserve. 5 remoter field of vision (*in the distance*). 6 interval of time. —v. (-cing) (often *refl.*) 1 place or cause to seem far off; be aloof. 2 leave far behind in a race etc. □ **at a distance** far off. **keep one's**

distance remain aloof. [Latin: related to DIS-, *sto* stand]

distant adj. 1 far away; at a specified distance (*three miles distant*). 2 remote in time, relationship, etc. (*distant prospect*; *distant relation*). 3 aloof. 4 abstracted (*distant stare*). 5 faint (*distant memory*). □ **distantly** adv.

distaste /dɪsˈteɪst/ n. (usu. foll. by *for*) dislike; aversion. □ **distasteful** adj. **distastefully** adv. **distastefulness** n.

distemper[1] /dɪsˈtempə(r)/ —n. paint using glue or size as a base, for use on walls. —v. paint with this. [Latin, = soak: see DISTEMPER[2]]

distemper[2] /dɪsˈtempə(r)/ n. disease of esp. dogs, with coughing and weakness. [Latin: related to DIS-, *tempero* mingle]

distend /dɪsˈtend/ v. swell out by pressure from within (*distended stomach*). □ **distensible** /-ˈstensɪb(ə)l/ adj. **distension** /-ˈstenʃ(ə)n/ n. [Latin: related to TEND[1]]

distich /ˈdɪstɪk/ n. verse couplet. [Greek *stikhos* line]

distil /dɪsˈtɪl/ v. (US **distill**) (-ll-) 1 purify or extract the essence from (a substance) by vaporizing and condensing it and collecting the resulting liquid. 2 extract the essential essence of (an idea etc.). 3 make (whisky, essence, etc.) by distilling raw materials. 4 fall or cause to fall in drops. □ **distillation** /-ˈleɪʃ(ə)n/ n. [Latin: related to DE-, *stillo* drip]

distiller n. person who distils, esp. alcoholic liquor.

distillery n. (pl. -ies) place where alcoholic liquor is distilled.

distinct /dɪsˈtɪŋkt/ adj. 1 (often foll. by *from*) not identical; separate; different. 2 clearly perceptible. 3 unmistakable, decided (*distinct advantage*). □ **distinctly** adv. [Latin: related to DISTINGUISH]

distinction /dɪsˈtɪŋkʃ(ə)n/ n. 1 discriminating or distinguishing. 2 difference between two things. 3 thing that differentiates or distinguishes. 4 special consideration or honour (*treat with distinction*). 5 excellence (*person of distinction*). 6 title or mark of honour.

distinctive adj. distinguishing, characteristic. □ **distinctively** adv. **distinctiveness** n.

distingué /dɪˈstæŋɡeɪ/ adj. distinguished in appearance, manner, etc. [French]

distinguish /dɪsˈtɪŋɡwɪʃ/ v. 1 (often foll. by *from*, *between*) differentiate; see or draw distinctions. 2 be a mark or property of; characterize. 3 discover by listening, looking, etc. 4 (usu. *refl.*) often

distinguished foll. by *by*) make prominent (*distinguished himself by winning*). □ **distinguishable** *adj.* [Latin: related to DIS-, *stinguo stinct*- extinguish]

distinguished *adj.* 1 eminent; famous. 2 dignified.

distort /dɪˈstɔːt/ *v.* 1 pull or twist out of shape. 2 misrepresent (facts etc.). □ **distortion** *n.* [Latin *torqueo tort*- twist]

distract /dɪˈstrækt/ *v.* 1 (often foll. by *from*) draw away the attention of. 2 bewilder, perplex. 3 (as **distracted** *adj.*) confused, mad, or angry. 4 amuse, esp. to divert from pain etc. [Latin: related to DIS-, *traho tract*- draw]

distraction /dɪˈstrækʃ(ə)n/ *n.* 1 a distracting or being distracted. b thing that distracts. 2 relaxation; amusement. 3 confusion; frenzy; madness.

distrain /dɪˈstreɪn/ *v.* (usu. foll. by *upon*) impose distraint (on a person, goods, etc.). [Latin: related to DIS-, *stringo strict*- draw tight]

distraint /dɪˈstreɪnt/ *n.* seizure of goods to enforce payment.

distrait /ˈdɪstreɪ/ *adj.* (*fem.* **distraite** /-ˈstreɪt/) inattentive; distraught.

distraught /dɪˈstrɔːt/ *adj.* distracted with worry, fear, etc.; extremely agitated. [related to DISTRACT]

distress /dɪˈstres/ —*n.* 1 anguish or suffering caused by pain, sorrow, worry, etc. 2 poverty. 3 *Law* = DISTRAINT. —*v.* cause distress to, make unhappy. □ **in distress** suffering or in danger. □ **distressful** *adj.* [Romanic: related to DISTRAIN]

distressed *adj.* 1 suffering from distress. 2 impoverished. 3 (of furniture, clothing, etc.) aged, torn, etc. artificially.

distressed area *n.* region of high unemployment and poverty.

distribute /dɪˈstrɪbjuːt, ˈdɪs-/ *v.* (-ting) 1 give shares of; deal out. 2 scatter; put at different points. 3 arrange; classify. [Latin *tribuo -but-* assign]

■ **Usage** The stress on the first syllable, is considered incorrect by some people.

distribution /ˌdɪstrɪˈbjuːʃ(ə)n/ *n.* 1 distributing or being distributed. 2 a commercial dispersal of goods etc. b extent to which different classes etc. share in a nation's total wealth etc.

distributive /dɪˈstrɪbjʊtɪv/ —*adj.* 1 of or produced by distribution. 2 *Logic & Gram.* referring to each individual of a class, not to the class collectively (e.g.

each, either). —*n. Gram.* distributive word.

distributor *n.* 1 person or thing that distributes, esp. goods. 2 device in an internal-combustion engine for passing current to each spark-plug in turn.

district /ˈdɪstrɪkt/ *n.* 1 (often *attrib.*) area regarded as a geographical or administrative unit (*the Peak District; postal district; wine-growing district*). 2 administrative division of a county etc. [Latin: related to DISTRAIN]

district nurse *n.* nurse who makes home visits in an area.

district attorney *n.* (in the US) prosecuting officer of a district.

distrust /dɪsˈtrʌst/ —*n.* lack of trust; suspicion. —*v.* have no trust in. □ **distrustful** *adj.* **distrustfully** *adv.*

disturb /dɪˈstɜːb/ *v.* 1 break the rest, calm, or quiet of. 2 agitate; worry. 3 move from a settled position (*disturbed my papers*). 4 (as **disturbed** *adj.*) emotionally or mentally unstable. [Latin: related to DIS-, *turba* tumult]

disturbance *n.* 1 disturbing or being disturbed. 2 tumult; uproar; agitation.

disunion /dɪsˈjuːnjən/ *n.* lack of union; separation; dissension.

disunite /ˌdɪsjuːˈnaɪt/ *v.* (-ting) 1 remove the unity from. 2 separate.

disunity /dɪsˈjuːnɪtɪ/ *n.* lack of unity.

disuse —*n.* /dɪsˈjuːs/ disused state. —*v.* /-ˈjuːz/ cease to use. □ **disused** /-ˈjuːzd/ *adj.*

disyllable /daɪˈsɪləb(ə)l/ *n.* (also **dissyllable**) *Prosody* word or metrical foot of two syllables. □ **disyllabic** /-ˈlæbɪk/ *adj.*

ditch —*n.* long narrow excavation esp. for drainage or as a boundary. —*v.* 1 make or repair ditches (*hedging and ditching*). 2 *slang* abandon; discard. □ **dull as ditch-water** extremely dull. [Old English]

dither /ˈdɪðə(r)/ —*v.* 1 hesitate; be indecisive. 2 tremble; quiver. —*n. colloq.* state of agitation or hesitation. □ **ditherer** *n.* **dithery** *adj.* [var. of *didder* DODDER]

dithyramb /ˈdɪθɪˌræm/ *n.* 1 wild choral hymn in ancient Greece. 2 passionate or inflated poem etc. □ **dithyrambic** /ˌdɪθɪˈræmbɪk/ *adj.* [Latin from Greek]

ditto /ˈdɪtəʊ/ *n.* (*pl.* -s) 1 (in accounts, inventories, etc.) the aforesaid, the same. 2 *colloq.* (used to avoid repetition) the same (*came late today and ditto yesterday*). [Latin DICTUM]

■ **Usage** In sense 1, the word *ditto* is often replaced by - under the word or sum to be repeated.

ditto marks *n.pl.* inverted commas etc. representing 'ditto'.

ditty /dɪtɪ/ n. (pl. **-ies**) short simple song. [Latin: related to DICTATE]

diuretic /daɪjʊˈretɪk/ —adj. causing increased output of urine. —n. diuretic drug. [Greek: related to DIA-, *oureō* urinate]

diurnal /daɪˈɜːn(ə)l/ adj. 1 of the day or daytime. 2 daily. 3 occupying one day. □ **diurnally** adv. [Latin *diurnalis* from *dies* day]

diva /ˈdiːvə/ n. (pl. **-s**) great woman opera singer; prima donna. [Italian from Latin, = goddess]

divalent /daɪˈveɪlənt/ adj. Chem. having a valency of two.

divan /dɪˈvæn/ n. low couch or bed without a back or ends. [ultimately from Persian *dīvān* bench]

dive —v. (**-ving**) 1 plunge head first into water. 2 **a** (of an aircraft, person, etc.) plunge steeply downwards. **b** (of a submarine) submerge; go deeper. 3 (foll. by *into*) colloq. **a** put one's hand into (a pocket, handbag, etc.). **b** become enthusiastic about (a subject, meal, etc.). 4 move suddenly (*dived into a shop*). —n. 1 act of diving; plunge. 2 steep descent or fall. 3 colloq. disreputable nightclub, bar, etc. [Old English]

dive-bomb v. bomb (a target) from a diving aircraft. □ **dive-bomber** n.

diver n. 1 person who dives, esp. working under water. 2 diving bird.

diverge /daɪˈvɜːdʒ/ v. (**-ging**) 1 **a** spread out from a central point, become dispersed. **b** take different courses (*their interests diverged*). 2 **a** (often foll. by *from*) depart from a set course. **b** (often foll. by *into*) differ. □ **divergence** n. □ **divergent** adj. [Latin: related to DI-[2], *vergo* incline]

divers /ˈdaɪvəz/ adj. archaic various; several. [Latin: related to DIVERSE]

diverse /daɪˈvɜːs/ adj. varied. [Latin: related to DI-[2], *verto vers-* turn]

diversify /daɪˈvɜːsɪfaɪ/ v. (**-ies**, **-ied**) 1 make diverse; vary. 2 spread (investment) over several enterprises. 3 (often foll. by *into*) expand one's range of products. □ **diversification** /-fɪˈkeɪʃ(ə)n/ n.

diversion /daɪˈvɜːʃ(ə)n/ n. 1 diverting or being diverted. 2 a diverting of attention. **b** stratagem for this. 3 recreation, pastime. 4 alternative route when a road is temporarily closed. □ **diversionary** adj.

diversity /daɪˈvɜːsɪtɪ/ n. variety.

divert /daɪˈvɜːt/ v. 1 **a** turn aside; deflect. **b** distract (attention). 2 (often as **diverting** adj.) entertain; amuse. [Latin: related to DIVERSE]

divest /daɪˈvest/ v. (usu. foll. by *of*) 1 unclothe; strip. 2 deprive, rid. [Latin: related to VEST]

divide /dɪˈvaɪd/ —v. (**-ding**) 1 (often foll. by *in*, *into*) separate into parts; break up; split. 2 (often foll. by *out*) distribute; deal; share. 3 **a** separate (one thing) from another. **b** classify into parts or groups. 4 cause to disagree. 5 **a** find how many times (a number) contains or is contained in another (*divide 20 by 4*; *divide 4 into 20*). **b** (of a number) be contained in (a number) without remainder (*4 divides into 20*). 6 Parl. vote (by members entering either of two lobbies) (*the House divided*). —n. 1 dividing line. 2 watershed. [Latin *divido -vis-*]

dividend /ˈdɪvɪdend/ n. 1 share of profits paid to shareholders or to winners in a football pool etc. 2 number to be divided. 3 benefit from an action. [Anglo-French: related to DIVIDE]

divider n. 1 screen etc. dividing a room. 2 (in pl.) measuring-compasses.

divination /dɪvɪˈneɪʃ(ə)n/ n. supposed supernatural insight into the future etc. [Latin: related to DIVINE]

divine /dɪˈvaɪn/ —adj. (**diviner**, **divinest**) 1 **a** of, from, or like God or a god. **b** sacred. 2 colloq. excellent; delightful. —v. (**-ning**) 1 discover by intuition or guessing. 2 foresee. 3 practise divination. —n. theologian or clergyman. □ **divinely** adv. [Latin *divinus*]

diviner n. person who practises divination.

diving-bell n. open-bottomed enclosure, supplied with air, for descent into deep water.

diving-board n. elevated board for diving from.

diving-suit n. watertight suit, usu. with helmet and air-supply, for work under water.

divining-rod n. = DOWSING-ROD.

divinity /dɪˈvɪnɪtɪ/ n. (pl. **-ies**) 1 being divine. 2 god; godhead. 3 theology.

divisible /dɪˈvɪzɪb(ə)l/ adj. capable of being divided. □ **divisibility** /-ˈbɪlɪtɪ/ n.

division /dɪˈvɪʒ(ə)n/ n. 1 dividing or being divided. 2 dividing one number by another (*division of opinion*). 4 Parl. separation of members for counting votes. 5 one of two or more parts into which a thing is divided. 6 unit of administration, esp. a group of army brigades, regiments, or teams in a sporting league. □ **divisional** adj.

division sign n. sign (÷) indicating that one quantity is to be divided by another.

divisive /dɪˈvaɪsɪv/ adj. causing disagreement. □ **divisively** adv. **divisiveness** n. [Latin: related to DIVIDE]

divisor /dɪˈvaɪzə(r)/ n. number by which another is divided.

divorce /dɪˈvɔːs/ —n. 1 legal dissolution of a marriage. 2 separation (*divorce between thought and feeling*). —v. (-cing) 1 a (usu. as **divorced** adj.) (often foll. by *from*) legally dissolve the marriage of. b separate by divorce. c end one's marriage with. 2 separate (*divorced from reality*). [Latin: related to DIVERSE]

divorcee /dɪˌvɔːˈsiː/ n. divorced person.

divot /ˈdɪvət/ n. piece of turf cut out by a blow, esp. by the head of a golf club. [origin unknown]

divulge /daɪˈvʌldʒ/ v. (-ging) disclose, reveal (a secret etc.). □ **divulgence** n. [Latin *divulgo* publish]

divvy /ˈdɪvɪ/ colloq. —n. (pl. -ies) dividend. —v. (-ies, -ied) (often foll. by *up*) share out. [abbreviation]

Diwali /diːˈwɑːlɪ/ n. Hindu and Jainist festival with illuminations, held between September and November. [Sanskrit: *dīpa* lamp]

Dixie /ˈdɪksɪ/ n. southern States of the US. [origin uncertain]

dixie /ˈdɪksɪ/ n. large iron cooking-pot used by campers etc. [Hindustani from Persian]

Dixieland n. 1 = DIXIE. 2 traditional kind of jazz.

dizzy /ˈdɪzɪ/ —adj. (-ier, -iest) 1 a giddy. b feeling confused. 2 causing giddiness. —v. (-ies, -ied) 1 make dizzy. 2 bewilder. □ **dizzily** adv. **dizziness** n. [Old English]

DJ abbr. 1 dinner-jacket. 2 disc jockey.

djellaba /ˈdʒeləbə/ n. (also **jellaba**) loose hooded cloak (as) worn by Arab men. [Arabic]

dl abbr. decilitre(s).

D-layer n. lowest layer of the ionosphere. [D arbitrary]

D.Litt. abbr. Doctor of Letters. [Latin *Doctor Litterarum*]

DM abbr. Deutschmark.

dm abbr. decimetre(s).

DMus. abbr. Doctor of Music.

DNA abbr. deoxyribonucleic acid, esp. carrying genetic information in chromosomes.

D-notice n. government notice to news editors not to publish certain items for security reasons. [defence, NOTICE]

do¹ /duː/ —v. (3 sing. pres. **does** /dʌz/; past **did**; past part. **done** /dʌn/; pres. part. **doing**) 1 perform, carry out, achieve, complete (work etc.) (*did his homework; a lot to do*). 2 produce, make, provide (*doing a painting; we do lunches*). 3 grant, impart (*do me a favour*). 4 act, behave, proceed (*do as I do; would do well to wait*). 5 work at (*do carpentry; do chemistry*). 6 be suitable or acceptable; satisfy (*will never do; will do me nicely*). 7 deal with; attend to (*do one's hair*). 8 fare; get on (*did badly in the test*). 9 solve; work out (*did the sum*). 10 a traverse (a certain distance) (*did 50 miles today*). b travel at a specified speed (*was doing eighty*). 11 colloq. act or behave like; play the part of. 12 produce (a play, opera, etc.) (*will do Shakespeare*). 13 a colloq. finish (*I've done in the garden*). b (as **done** adj.) be finished (*day is done*). 14 cook, esp. completely (*do it in the oven; potatoes aren't done?*). 15 be in progress (*what's doing?*). 16 colloq. visit (*did the museums*). 17 colloq. (often as **done** adj.) exhaust; tire out. b defeat, kill, ruin. 18 (foll. by *into*) translate or transform. 19 colloq. cater for (*they do one very well here*). 20 slang rob (*did a big bank*). b swindle. 21 slang prosecute, convict (*done for shoplifting*). 22 slang undergo (a term of imprisonment). 23 slang take (an illegal drug). —v.aux. 1 in questions and negative statements or commands (*do you understand?; I don't smoke; don't be silly*). 2 ellipt. or in place of a verb (*you know her better than I do; I wanted to go and I did; tell me, do?; they did go*). 4 in inversion (*rarely does it happen*). —n. (pl. **dos** or **do's**) colloq. 1 elaborate party, operation, etc. 2 colloq. swindle. □ **be done with** see DONE. **be nothing to do with 1** be no business of. **2** be unconnected with. **be to do with** be concerned or connected with. **do away with** colloq. 1 get rid of; abolish. 2 kill. **do down** colloq. 1 cheat, swindle. 2 overcome. **do for 1** be satisfactory or sufficient for. **2** colloq. destroy, ruin. **3** colloq. act as cleaner etc. for. **do in 1** slang a kill. b ruin. **2** colloq. exhaust, tire out. **do justice to** see JUSTICE. **do nothing for** (or **to**) colloq. not flatter or enhance. **do or die** persist recklessly. **do out** colloq. clean or redecorate (a room). **do a person out of** colloq. cheat of. **do over 1** slang attack; beat up. **2** colloq. redecorate, refurbish. **do proud** see PROUD. **dos and don'ts** rules of behaviour. **do something for** (or **to**) colloq. enhance the appearance or quality of. **do up 1** fasten, secure. 2 colloq. refurbish, renovate. b adorn, dress up. **do with** (prec. by *could*) would be glad of; would profit by (*could do with a rest*). **do without** manage without; forgo. **to do with** in connection with; related to (*what has that to do*

with it*; *something to do with the weather*; □ **doable** *adj.* of DO.

do² *var. of* DOH.

doc² *abbr.* ditto.

Dobermann pinscher /ˈdəʊbəmən ˈpɪnʃə(r)/ *n.* large dog of a smooth-coated German breed with a docked tail. [German]

doc *n. colloq.* doctor. [abbreviation]

docile /ˈdəʊsaɪl/ *adj.* submissive, easily managed. □ **docilely** *adv.* **docility** /-ˈsɪltɪ/ *n.* [Latin *doceo* teach]

dock¹ —*n.* **1** enclosed harbour for the loading, unloading, and repair of ships. **2** (in *pl.*) docks with wharves and offices. —*v.* **1** bring or come into dock. **2 a** join (spacecraft) together in space. **b** be joined thus. [Dutch *docke*]

dock² *n.* enclosure in a criminal court for the accused. [Flemish *dok* cage]

dock³ *n.* weed with broad leaves. [Old English]

dock⁴ *v.* **1** cut short (an animal's tail). **2** take away part of, reduce (wages, supplies, etc.). [Old English]

docker *n.* person employed to load and unload ships.

docket /ˈdɒkɪt/ —*n.* document or label listing goods delivered, jobs done, contents of a package, etc. —*v.* (-t-) label with, or enter on, a docket. [origin unknown]

dockland *n.* district near docks or former docks.

dockyard *n.* area with docks and equipment for building and repairing ships.

doctor /ˈdɒktə(r)/ —*n.* **1** qualified practitioner of medicine; physician. **2** person who holds a doctorate. —*v. colloq.* **1** treat medically. **2** castrate or spay. **3** patch up (machinery etc.). **4** adulterate. **5** tamper with, falsify. □ **what the doctor ordered** *colloq.* something welcome. [Latin *doceo* teach]

doctoral *adj.* of or for the degree of doctor.

doctorate /ˈdɒktərət/ *n.* highest university degree in any faculty, often honorary.

doctrinaire /ˌdɒktrɪˈneə(r)/ *adj.* applying theory or doctrine dogmatically. [French: related to DOCTRINE]

doctrine /ˈdɒktrɪn/ *n.* **1** what is taught; body of instruction. **2 a** principle of religious or political etc. belief. **b** set of such principles. □ **doctrinal** /-ˈtraɪn(ə)l/ *adj.* [Latin: related to DOCTOR]

docudrama /ˈdɒkjʊˌdrɑːmə/ *n.* television drama based on real events. [from DOCUMENTARY, DRAMA]

document —*n.* /ˈdɒkjʊmənt/ thing providing a record or evidence of events, agreement, ownership, identification,

etc. —*v.* /ˈdɒkjʊˌment/ **1** prove by or support with documents. **2** record in a document. [Latin: related to DOCTOR]

documentary /ˌdɒkjʊˈmentərɪ/ —*adj.* **1** consisting of documents (*documentary evidence*). **2** providing a factual record or report. —*n.* (*pl.* -**ies**) documentary film etc.

documentation /ˌdɒkjʊmenˈteɪʃ(ə)n/ *n.* **1** collection and classification of information. **2** material so collected. **3** *Computing* etc. material explaining a system.

dodder¹ *v.* tremble or totter, esp. from age. □ **dodderer** *n.* **doddery** *adj.* [obsolete dial. *dadder*]

dodder² *n.* threadlike climbing parasitic plant. [origin unknown]

doddle /ˈdɒd(ə)l/ *n. colloq.* easy task. [perhaps from *doodle* = TODDLE]

dodecagon /dəʊˈdekəgən/ *n.* plane figure with twelve sides. [Greek *dōdeka* twelve, -*gōnos* angled]

dodecahedron /ˌdəʊdekəˈhiːdrən/ *n.* solid figure with twelve faces. [from DODECAGON, Greek *hedra* base]

dodge —*v.* (-ging) **1** (often foll. by *about, behind, round*) move quickly to elude a pursuer, blow, etc. **2** evade by cunning or trickery. —*n.* **1** quick movement to avoid something. **2** clever trick or expedient. □ **dodger** *n.* [origin unknown]

dodgem /ˈdɒdʒəm/ *n.* small electrically-driven car in an enclosure at a funfair, bumped into others for fun. [from DODGE, 'EM]

dodgy *adj.* (-ier, -iest) *colloq.* unreliable, risky.

dodo /ˈdəʊdəʊ/ *n.* (*pl.* -**s**) large extinct bird of Mauritius etc. [Portuguese *doudo* simpleton]

DoE *abbr.* Department of the Environment.

doe *n.* (*pl.* same or -**s**) female fallow deer, reindeer, hare, or rabbit. [Old English]

doer /ˈduːə(r)/ *n.* **1** person who does something. **2** person who acts rather than theorizing.

does see DO¹.

doesn't /ˈdʌz(ə)nt/ *contr.* does not.

doff *v.* remove (a hat or clothes). [from *do off*]

dog —*n.* **1** four-legged flesh-eating animal akin to the fox and wolf, and of many breeds. **2** male of this, or of the fox or wolf. **3** *colloq.* **a** despicable person. **b** person of a specified kind (*lucky dog*). **4** mechanical device for gripping. **5** (in *pl.*; prec. by *the*) *colloq.* greyhound-racing. —*v.* (-gg-) follow closely; pursue, track. □ **go to the dogs** *slang* deteriorate, be ruined. **like a dog's dinner** *colloq.* smartly or flashily (dressed etc.). **not a**

dogcart *n.* two-wheeled driving-cart with cross seats back to back.

dog-collar *n.* **1** collar for a dog. **2** *colloq.* clerical collar.

dog days *n.pl.* hottest period of the year.

doge /dəʊdʒ/ *n. hist.* chief magistrate of Venice or Genoa. [Italian from *dux* leader]

dog-eared *adj.* (of a book etc.) with bent or worn corners.

dog-eat-dog *adj. colloq.* ruthlessly competitive.

dog-end *n. slang* cigarette-end.

dogfight *n.* **1** close combat between fighter aircraft. **2** rough fight.

dogfish *n.* (*pl.* same or **-es**) a kind of small shark.

dogged /ˈdɒgɪd/ *adj.* tenacious; grimly persistent. □ **doggedly** *adv.* **doggedness** *n.*

doggerel /ˈdɒgər(ə)l/ *n.* poor or trivial verse. [apparently from *dog*]

doggo /ˈdɒgəʊ/ *adv.* □ **lie doggo** *slang* lie motionless or hidden.

doggy —*adj.* **1** of or like a dog. **2** devoted to dogs. —*n.* (also **doggie**) (*pl.* **-ies**) pet name for a dog.

doggy bag *n.* bag for leftovers given to a customer in a restaurant etc.

doggy-paddle *n.* (also **dog-paddle**) elementary swimming stroke like that of a dog.

doghouse *n. US & Austral.* dog's kennel. □ **in the doghouse** *slang* in disgrace.

dog in the manger *n.* person who stops others using a thing for which he or she has no use.

dogma /ˈdɒgmə/ *n.* **1** principle, tenet, or system of these, esp. of a Church or political party. **2** arrogant declaration of opinion. [Greek, = opinion]

dogmatic /dɒgˈmætɪk/ *adj.* asserting or imposing personal opinions; intolerant; authoritative; arrogant. □ **dogmatically** *adv.*

dogmatism /ˈdɒgmətɪz(ə)m/ *n.* tendency to be dogmatic. □ **dogmatist** *n.*

dogmatize /ˈdɒgmətaɪz/ *v.* (also **-ise**) (**-zing** or **-sing**) **1** speak dogmatically. **2** express (a principle etc.) as dogma.

do-gooder *n.* well-meaning but unrealistic or patronizing philanthropist or reformer.

dog-paddle var. of DOGGY-PADDLE.

dog-rose *n.* wild hedge-rose.

dogsbody *n.* (*pl.* **-ies**) *colloq.* drudge.

dog's breakfast *n.* (also **dog's dinner**) *colloq.* mess.

dog's life *n.* life of misery etc.

dog's chance *n.* no chance at all. [Old English]

dog-star *n.* chief star of the constellation Canis Major or Minor, esp. Sirius.

dog-tired *adj.* tired out.

dog-tooth *n.* V-shaped pattern or moulding; chevron.

dogtrot *n.* gentle easy trot.

dogwatch *n.* either of two short watches on a ship (4-6 or 6-8 p.m.).

dogwood *n.* shrub with dark-red branches, greenish-white flowers, and purple berries.

DoH *abbr.* Department of Health.

doh /dəʊ/ *n.* (also **do**) *Mus.* first note of a major scale. [Italian *do*]

doily /ˈdɔɪlɪ/ *n.* (also **doyley**) (*pl.* **-ies** or **-eys**) small lacey mat used on a plate for cakes etc. [*Doiley*, name of a draper]

doing /ˈduːɪŋ/ *pres. part.* of **do¹**. —*n.* **1 a** action (*famous for his doings*). **b** effort (*takes a lot of doing*). **2** (in *pl.*) *slang* unspecified things (*have we got all the doings?*).

doing-over *n. slang* attack, beating-up.

do-it-yourself —*adj.* (of work) done or to be done by a householder etc. —*n.* such work.

Dolby /ˈdɒlbɪ/ *n. propr.* electronic noise-reduction system used esp. in tape-recording to reduce hiss. [name of its inventor]

doldrums /ˈdɒldrəmz/ *n.pl.* (usu. prec. by *the*) **1** low spirits. **2** period of inactivity. **3** equatorial ocean region with little or no wind. [perhaps after *dull, tantrum*]

dole —*n.* **1** (usu. prec. by *the*) *colloq.* unemployment benefit. **2 a** charitable distribution. **b** thing given sparingly or reluctantly. —*v.* (**-ling**) (usu. foll. by *out*) distribute sparingly. □ **on the dole** *colloq.* receiving unemployment benefit. [Old English]

doleful /ˈdəʊlfʊl/ *adj.* **1** mournful, sad. **2** dreary, dismal. □ **dolefully** *adv.* **dolefulness** *n.* [Latin *doleo* grieve]

doll —*n.* **1** small model of esp. a child as a child's toy. **2** *colloq.* **a** pretty but silly young woman. **b** attractive woman. **3** ventriloquist's dummy. —*v.* (foll. by *up*) *colloq.* dress smartly. [pet form of *Dorothy*]

dollar /ˈdɒlə(r)/ *n.* chief monetary unit in the US, Australia, etc. [Low German *daler* from German *Taler*]

dollop /ˈdɒləp/ —*n.* shapeless lump of food etc. —*v.* (**-p-**) (usu. foll. by *out*) serve in dollops. [perhaps from Scandinavian]

dolly *n.* (*pl.* **-ies**) **1** child's name for a doll. **2** movable platform for a cinecamera etc. **3** easy catch in cricket.

dolly-bird *n. colloq.* attractive and stylish young woman.

dolma /ˈdɒlmə/ n. (pl. -s or **dolmades** /-ˈmɑːðez/) E. European delicacy of spiced rice or meat etc. wrapped in vine or cabbage leaves. [modern Greek]

dolman sleeve /ˈdɒlmən/ n. loose sleeve cut in one piece with a bodice. [Turkish]

dolmen /ˈdɒlmən/ n. megalithic tomb with a large flat stone laid on upright ones. [French]

dolomite /ˈdɒləmaɪt/ n. mineral or rock of calcium magnesium carbonate. [de *Dolomieu*, name c.a French geologist]

dolour /ˈdɒlə(r)/ n. (US **dolor**) literary sorrow, distress. □ **dolorous** adj. [Latin *dolor* pain]

dolphin /ˈdɒlfɪn/ n. large porpoise-like sea mammal with a slender pointed snout. [Greek *delphis* -in-]

dolphinarium /ˌdɒlfɪˈneərɪəm/ n. (pl. -s) public aquarium for dolphins.

dolt /dəʊlt/ n. stupid person. □ **doltish** adj. [apparently related to obsolete *dol* = DULL]

Dom n. title of some Roman Catholic dignitaries, and Benedictine and Carthusian monks. [Latin *dominus* master]

-dom suffix forming nouns denoting: **1** condition (*freedom*). **2** rank, domain (*earldom*; *kingdom*). **3** class of people (or associated attitudes etc.) regarded collectively (*officialdom*). [Old English]

domain /dəˈmeɪn/ n. **1** area under one rule; realm. **2** estate etc. under one control. **3** sphere of control or influence. [French: related to DEMESNE]

dome — n. **1** rounded (usu. hemispherical) vault forming a roof. **2** dome-shaped thing. — v. (-**ming**) (usu. as **domed** adj.) cover with or shape as a dome. [Latin *domus* house]

domestic /dəˈmestɪk/ — adj. **1** of the home, household, or family affairs. **2** of one's own country. **3** (of an animal) tamed, not wild. **4** fond of home life. — n. household servant. □ **domestically** adv. [Latin *domus* home]

domesticate /dəˈmestɪˌkeɪt/ v. (-**ting**) **1** tame (an animal) to live with humans. **2** accustom to housework etc. □ **domestication** /-ˈkeɪʃ(ə)n/ n. [medieval Latin: related to DOMESTIC]

domesticity /ˌdəʊmeˈstɪsɪtɪ/ n. **1** being domestic. **2** domestic or home life.

domestic science n. = HOME ECONOMICS.

domicile /ˈdɒmɪˌsaɪl/ — n. **1** dwelling-place. **2** Law a place of permanent residence. **b** residing. — v. (-**ling**) (usu. as **domiciled** adj.) (usu. foll. by *at, in*) settle in a place. [Latin *domus* home]

domiciliary /ˌdɒmɪˈsɪlɪərɪ/ adj. formal (esp. of a doctor's etc. visit) to, at, or of a

person's home. [medieval Latin: related to DOMICILE]

dominant /ˈdɒmɪnənt/ — adj. **1** dominating, prevailing, prevalent. **2** (of an inherited characteristic) appearing in offspring even when the opposite characteristic is also inherited. — n. Mus. fifth note of the diatonic scale of any key. □ **dominance** n. **dominantly** adv.

dominate /ˈdɒmɪˌneɪt/ v. (-**ting**) **1** command, control. **2** be the most influential or obvious. **3** (of a high place) overlook. □ **domination** /-ˈneɪʃ(ə)n/ n. [Latin *dominor* from *dominus* lord]

domineer /ˌdɒmɪˈnɪə(r)/ v. (often as **domineering** adj.) behave arrogantly or tyrannically. [French: related to DOMINATE]

Dominican /dəˈmɪnɪkən/ — adj. of St Dominic or his order. — n. Dominican friar or nun. [Latin *Dominicus* Dominic]

dominion /dəˈmɪnjən/ n. **1** sovereignty, control. **2** realm; domain. **3** hist. self-governing territory of the British Commonwealth. [Latin *dominus* lord]

domino /ˈdɒmɪˌnəʊ/ n. (pl. -es) **1** any of 28 small oblong pieces marked with 0-6 pips in each half. **2** (in pl.) game played with these. **3** loose cloak with a mask. [French, probably as DOMINION]

domino effect n. (also **domino theory**) effect whereby (or theory that) one event precipitates others in causal sequence.

don[1] n. **1** university teacher, esp. a senior member of a college at Oxford or Cambridge. **2** (**Don**) Spanish title prefixed to a forename. [Spanish from Latin *dominus* lord]

don[2] v. (-**nn**-) put on (clothing). [= *do on*]

donate /dəʊˈneɪt/ v. (-**ting**) give (money etc.), esp. to charity. [from DONATION]

donation /dəʊˈneɪʃ(ə)n/ n. **1** donating or being donated. **2** thing, esp. money, donated. [Latin *donum* gift]

done /dʌn/ adj. **1** completed. **2** cooked. **3** colloq. socially acceptable (*the done thing*). **4** (often with *in*) colloq. tired out. **5** (esp. as int. in reply to an offer etc.) accepted. □ **be done with** have or be finished with. **done for** colloq. in serious trouble. **have done with** be rid of; finish dealing with. [past part. of DO[1]]

doner kebab /ˈdɒnə, ˈdəʊ-/ n. spiced lamb cooked on a spit and served in slices, often with pitta bread. [Turkish: related to KEBAB]

donjon /ˈdʌndʒ(ə)n/ n. great tower or innermost keep of a castle. [archaic spelling of DUNGEON]

Don Juan /dʒuːən, ˈwɑːn/ n. seducer of women.

donkey /ˈdɒŋki/ n. (pl. -s) 1 domestic ass. 2 colloq. stupid person. [perhaps from Duncan; cf. NEDDY]

donkey jacket n. thick weatherproof workman's jacket or fashion garment.

donkey's years n.pl. colloq. very long time.

donkey-work n. laborious part of a job.

Donna /ˈdɒnə/ n. title of an Italian, Spanish, or Portuguese lady. [Latin domina mistress]

donnish adj. like a college don; pedantic.

donor /ˈdəʊnə(r)/ n. 1 person who donates (e.g. to charity). 2 person who provides blood, semen, or an organ or tissue for medical use.

donor card n. official card authorizing the use of organs, carried by a donor.

don't /dəʊnt/ —contr. do not. —n. prohibition (dos and don'ts).

doodle /ˈduːd(ə)l/ —v. (-ling) scribble or draw, esp. absent-mindedly. —n. such a scribble or drawing. [originally = foolish person]

doom —n. 1 a grim fate or destiny. b death or ruin. 2 condemnation. —v. 1 (usu. foll. by to) condemn or destine. 2 (esp. as **doomed** adj.) consign to misfortune or destruction. [Old English, = STATUTE]

doomsday n. day of the Last Judgement. □ **till doomsday** for ever.

door n. 1 a esp. hinged barrier for closing and opening the entrance to a building, room, cupboard, etc. b this as representing a house etc. (lives two doors away). 2 a entrance or exit; doorway. b means of access. □ **close** (or **open**) **the door to** exclude (or create) an opportunity for. [Old English]

doorbell n. bell on a door rung by visitors to signal arrival.

door-keeper n. = DOORMAN.

doorknob n. knob turned to open a door.

doorman n. person on duty at the door to a large building.

doormat n. 1 mat at an entrance, for wiping shoes. 2 colloq. submissive person.

doorpost n. upright of a door-frame, on which the door is hung.

doorstep n. 1 step or area in front of the outer door of a house etc. 2 slang thick slice of bread. —v. colloq. 1 go from door to door canvassing, selling, etc. 2 call upon or wait on the doorstep for (a person) in order to interview etc. □ **on one's doorstep** very near.

doorstop n. device for keeping a door open or to prevent it from striking the wall.

door-to-door adj. (of selling etc.) done at each house in turn.

doorway n. opening filled by a door.

dope —n. 1 a slang narcotic. b drug etc. given to a horse, athlete, etc., to improve performance. 2 thick liquid used as a lubricant etc. 3 varnish. 4 slang stupid person. 5 slang information. —v. (-ping) 1 give or add a drug to. 2 apply dope to. [Dutch, = sauce]

dopey adj. (also **dopy**) (**dopier, dopiest**) colloq. 1 half asleep or stupefied as if by a drug. 2 stupid. □ **dopily** adv. **dopiness** n.

doppelgänger /ˈdɒp(ə)lˌgeŋə(r)/ n. apparition of a living person. [German, = double-goer]

Doppler effect n. increase (or decrease) in the frequency of sound, light, etc. waves caused by moving nearer to (or further from) the source. [Doppler, name of a physicist]

dorado /dəˈrɑːdəʊ/ n. (pl. same or -s) sea-fish showing brilliant colours when dying out of water. [Spanish, = gilded]

Doric /ˈdɒrɪk/ —adj. 1 Archit. of the oldest and simplest of the Greek orders. 2 (of a dialect) broad, rustic. —n. rustic English or esp. Scots. [from Dōris in Greece]

dormant /ˈdɔːmənt/ adj. 1 lying inactive; sleeping. 2 temporarily inactive. 3 (of plants) alive but not growing. □ **dormancy** n. [Latin dormio sleep]

dormer n. (in full **dormer window**) projecting upright window in a sloping roof. [French: related to DORMANT]

dormitory /ˈdɔːmɪtri/ n. (pl. -ies) 1 sleeping-room with several beds, esp. in a school or institution. 2 (in full **dormitory town** etc.) small commuter town or suburb. [Latin: related to DORMER]

Dormobile /ˈdɔːməˌbiːl/ n. propr. motor caravan. [from DORMITORY, AUTOMOBILE]

dormouse /ˈdɔːmaʊs/ n. (pl. -mice) small mouselike hibernating rodent. [origin unknown]

dorsal /ˈdɔːs(ə)l/ adj. of or on the back. [Latin dorsum back]

dory /ˈdɔːri/ n. (pl. same or -ies) any of various edible marine fish, esp. the John Dory. [French dorée = gilded]

dosage /ˈdəʊsɪdʒ/ n. 1 size of a dose. 2 giving of a dose.

dose —n. 1 single portion of medicine. 2 experience of something (dose of flu, laughter). 3 amount of radiation received. 4 slang venereal infection. —v. (-sing) treat with or give doses of medicine to. [Greek dosis gift]

do-se-do /ˌdəʊsɪˈdəʊ/ n. (also **do-si-do**) (pl. -s) figure in which two dancers pass round each other back to back. [French dos-à-dos, = back to back]

dosh n. slang money. [origin unknown]

doss v. 1 (often foll. by down) slang sleep roughly or in a doss-house. 2 (often foll. by about, around) spend time idly. [probably originally = 'seat-back cover': from Latin dorsum back]

dosser n. slang 1 person who dosses. 2 = DOSS-HOUSE.

doss-house n. cheap lodging-house for vagrants.

dossier /ˈdɒsɪeɪ, -sɪə(r)/ n. file containing information about a person, event, etc. [French]

DoT abbr. Department of Transport.

dot —n. 1 a small spot or mark. b this as part of i or j, or as a decimal point etc. 2 shorter signal of the two in Morse code. —v. (-tt-) 1 a mark with dot(s). b place a dot over (a letter). 2 (often foll. by about) scatter like dots. 3 partly cover as with dots (sea dotted with ships). 4 slang hit. □ **dot the i's and cross the t's** colloq. 1 be minutely accurate. 2 add the final touches to a task etc. **on the dot** exactly on time. **the year dot** colloq. far in the past. [Old English]

dotage n. feeble-minded senility (in his dotage).

dotard /ˈdəʊtəd/ n. senile person.

dote v. (-ting) (foll. by on) be excessively fond of. □ **dotingly** adv. [origin uncertain]

dotted line n. line of dots on a document etc., esp. for writing a signature on.

dotterel /ˈdɒtər(ə)l/ n. small migrant plover. [from DOTE]

dottle /ˈdɒt(ə)l/ n. remnant of unburnt tobacco in a pipe. [from DOT]

dotty adj. (-ier, -iest) colloq. 1 crazy; eccentric. 2 (foll. by about) infatuated with. □ **dottiness** n.

double /ˈdʌb(ə)l/ —adj. 1 consisting of two parts or things; twofold. 2 twice as much or many (double thickness). 3 having twice the usual size, quantity, strength, etc. (double bed). 4 a being double in part. b (of a flower) with two or more circles of petals. 5 ambiguous, deceitful (double meaning; a double life). —adv. 1 at or to twice the amount etc. (counts double). 2 two together (sleep double). —n. 1 double quantity (of spirits etc.) or thing; twice as much or many. 2 counterpart; person who looks exactly like another. 3 (in pl.) game between two pairs of players. 4 pair of victories. 5 bet in which winnings and stake from the first bet are transferred

to the second. 6 doubling of an opponent's bid in bridge. 7 hit on the narrow ring between the two outer circles in darts. —v. (-ling) 1 make or become double; increase twofold; multiply by two. 2 amount to twice as much as. 3 fold or bend over on itself; become folded. 4 a act (two parts) in the same play etc. b (often foll. by for) be understudy etc. 5 (usu. foll. by as) play a twofold role. 6 turn sharply in flight or pursuit. 7 sail round (a headland). 8 make a call in bridge increasing the value of the points to be won or lost on (an opponent's bid). □ **at the double** running, hurrying. **bent double** stooping. **double back** turn back in the opposite direction. **double or quits** gamble to decide whether a player's loss or debt be doubled or cancelled. **double up 1** (cause to) bend or curl up with pain or laughter. 2 share or assign to a shared room, quarters, etc. □ **doubly** adv. [Latin duplus]

double act n. comedy act by a duo.

double agent n. spy working for rival countries.

double-barrelled adj. 1 (of a gun) having two barrels. 2 (of a surname) hyphenated.

double-bass n. largest instrument of the violin family.

double bluff n. genuine action or statement disguised as a bluff.

double-book v. reserve (the same seat, room, etc.) for two people at once.

double-breasted adj. (of a coat etc.) overlapping across the body.

double-check v. verify twice.

double chin n. chin with a fold of loose flesh below it.

double cream n. thick cream with a high fat-content.

double-cross —v. deceive or betray (a supposed ally). —n. act of doing this. □ **double-crosser** n.

double-dealing —n. deceit, esp. in business. —adj. practising deceit.

double-decker n. 1 bus having an upper and lower deck. 2 colloq. sandwich with two layers of filling.

double Dutch n. colloq. gibberish.

double eagle n. figure of a two-headed eagle.

double-edged adj. 1 presenting both a danger and an advantage. 2 (of a knife etc.) having two cutting-edges.

double entendre /ˌduːb(ə)l ɑːnˈtɑːndrə/ n. ambiguous phrase open to usu. indecent interpretation. [obsolete French]

double entry n. system of bookkeeping with entries debited in one account and credited in another.

double feature n. cinema programme with two full-length films.

double figures n.pl. numbers from 10 to 99.

double glazing n. two layers of glass in a window.

double helix n. pair of parallel helices with a common axis, esp. in the structure of a DNA molecule.

double-jointed adj. having joints that allow unusual bending.

double negative n. Gram. negative statement containing two negative elements (e.g. he didn't say nothing).

■ **Usage** The double negative is considered incorrect in standard English.

double-park v. (also absol.) park (a vehicle) alongside one already parked at the roadside.

double pneumonia n. pneumonia affecting both lungs.

double-quick adj. & adv. colloq. very quick or quickly.

double standard n. rule or principle not impartially applied.

doublet /ˈdʌblɪt/ n. 1 hist. man's short close-fitting jacket. 2 one of a pair of similar things. [French: related to DOUBLE]

double take n. delayed reaction to a situation etc.

double-talk n. (usu. deliberately) ambiguous or misleading speech.

double-think n. capacity to accept contrary opinions at the same time.

double time n. wages paid at twice the normal rate.

doubloon /dʌˈbluːn/ n. hist. Spanish gold coin. [French or Spanish: related to DOUBLE]

doubt /daʊt/ —n. 1 uncertainty; undecided state of mind. 2 cynicism. 3 uncertain state. 4 lack of full proof or clear indication. —v. 1 feel uncertain or undecided about. 2 hesitate to believe. 3 call in question. □ **in doubt** open to question. **no doubt** certainly; probably; admittedly. **without doubt** (or **a doubt**) certainly. [Latin dubito hesitate]

doubtful adj. 1 feeling doubt. 2 causing doubt. 3 unreliable. □ **doubtfully** adv.

doubtfulness n.

doubtless adv. certainly; probably.

douche /duːʃ/ —n. 1 jet of liquid applied to part of the body for cleansing or medicinal purposes. 2 device for producing such a jet. —v. (-ching) 1 treat with a douche. 2 use a douche. [Latin: related to DUCT]

dough /dəʊ/ n. 1 thick mixture of flour etc. and liquid for baking. 2 slang money. □ **doughy** adj. (-ier, -iest) [Old English]

doughnut n. (US **donut**) small fried cake of sweetened dough.

doughnutting n. the clustering of politicians round a speaker during a television debate to make him or her appear well supported.

doughty /ˈdaʊtɪ/ adj. (-ier, -iest) archaic valiant. □ **doughtily** adv. [Old English]

dour /dʊə(r)/ adj. severe, stern, obstinate. [probably Gaelic dúr dull, obstinate]

douse v. (also **dowse**) (-sing) 1 a throw water over. b plunge into water. 2 extinguish (a light). [origin uncertain]

dove /dʌv/ n. 1 bird with short legs, a small head, and a large breast. 2 gentle or innocent person. 3 advocate of peace or peaceful policies. [Old Norse]

dovecote /ˈdʌvkɒt/ n. (also **dovecot**) shelter with nesting-holes for domesticated pigeons.

dovetail —n. mortise and tenon joint shaped like a dove's spread tail. —v. 1 join with dovetails. 2 fit together; combine neatly.

dowager /ˈdaʊədʒə(r)/ n. 1 widow with a title or property from her late husband (dowager duchess). 2 colloq. dignified elderly woman. [French: related to DOWER]

dowdy /ˈdaʊdɪ/ adj. (-ier, -iest) 1 (of clothes) unattractively dull. 2 dressed dowdily. —v. □ **dowdily** adv. **dowdiness** n. [origin unknown]

dowel /ˈdaʊəl/ n. cylindrical peg for holding structural components together. —v. (-ll-; US -l-) fasten with a dowel. [Low German]

dowelling n. rods for cutting into dowels.

dower n. 1 widow's share for life of a husband's estate. 2 archaic dowry. [Latin dos dowry]

dower house n. smaller house near a big one, as part of a woman's dower.

Dow-Jones average /daʊˈdʒəʊnz/ n. (also **Dow-Jones Index**) a figure indicating the relative prices of shares on the New York Stock Exchange. [Dow and Jones, names of American economists]

down¹ —adv. 1 into or towards a lower place, esp. to the ground (blinds were down). 2 in a lower place or position (blinds were down). 3 to or in a place regarded as lower, esp. a southwards. b away from a major city or a university. 4 a in or into a low or weaker position or condition (hit a man when he's down; down with a cold). b losing by (three goals down). c (of a computer system) out of action. 5 from an earlier to a later time (down to 1600). 6 to a finer or thinner consistency or smaller amount

down-market *adj.* & *adv. colloq.* of or to the cheaper sector of the market.

down payment *n.* partial initial payment.

downpipe *n.* pipe to carry rainwater from a roof.

downpour *n.* heavy fall of rain.

downright —*adj.* 1 plain, straightforward. 2 utter (*downright nonsense*). —*adv.* thoroughly (*downright rude*).

Down's syndrome *n.* congenital disorder with mental retardation and physical abnormalities. [*Down*, name of a physician]

downstage *adj.* & *adv.* nearer the front of a theatre stage.

downstairs —*adv.* 1 down the stairs. 2 to or on a lower floor. —*attrib. adj.* situated downstairs. —*n.* lower floor.

downstream *adv.* & *adj.* in the direction in which a stream etc. flows.

down-to-earth *adj.* practical, realistic.

downtown *esp. US* —*attrib. adj.* of the lower or more central part of a town or city. —*n.* downtown area. —*adv.* in or into the downtown area.

downtrodden *adj.* oppressed; badly treated.

downturn *n.* decline, esp. in economic activity.

down under *adv. colloq.* in the antipodes, esp. Australia.

downward /'daunwəd/ —*adv.* (also downwards) towards what is lower, inferior, less important, or later. —*adj.* moving or extending downwards.

downwind *adj.* & *adv.* in the direction in which the wind is blowing.

downy *adj.* (-ier, -iest) 1 of, like, or covered with down. 2 soft and fluffy.

dowry /'dauərɪ/ *n.* (*pl.* -ies) property or money brought by a bride to her husband. [Anglo-French, = French *douaire* DOWER]

dowse /daus/ *v.* (-sing) search for underground water or minerals by holding a stick or rod which dips abruptly when over the right spot. □ dowser *n.* [origin unknown]

dowse var. of DOUSE.

dowsing-rod *n.* rod for dowsing.

doxology /dɒk'sɒlədʒɪ/ *n.* (*pl.* -ies) liturgical hymn etc. of praise to God. □ doxological /-sə'lɒdʒɪk(ə)l/ *adj.* [Greek *doxa* glory]

doyen /'dɔɪən/ *n.* (*fem.* doyenne /dɔɪ'en/) senior member of a group. [French: related to DEAN¹]

doyley var. of DOILY.

doz. *abbr.* dozen.

doze —*v.* (-zing) sleep lightly; be half asleep. —*n.* short light sleep. □ doze off fall lightly asleep. [origin unknown]

---

or size (*grind down; water down; boil down*). 7 cheaper (*bread is down; shares are down*). 8 into a more settled state (*calm down*). 9 in writing or recorded form (*copy it down; down on tape; down to speak next*). 10 paid or dealt with as a deposit or part (*£5 down, £20 to pay; three down, six to go*). 11 with the current or wind. 12 (of a crossword clue or answer) read vertically (*five down*). —*prep.* 1 downwards along, through, or into. 2 from the top to the bottom of. 3 along (*walk down the road*). 4 at or in a lower part of (*lives down the road*). —*attrib. adj.* 1 directed downwards (*a down draught*). 2 from a capital or centre (*down train; down platform*). —*v. colloq.* 1 knock or bring down. 2 swallow. —*n.* 1 act of putting down. 2 reverse of fortune (*ups and downs*). 3 *colloq.* period of depression. □ be down to 1 be the responsibility of. 2 have nothing left (*down to my last penny*). 3 be attributable to. down on one's luck *colloq.* temporarily unfortunate. down to the ground *colloq.* completely. down tools *colloq.* cease work, go on strike. down with expressing rejection of a specified person or thing. have a down on *colloq.* show hostility towards. [earlier *adown*: related to DOWN³]

down² *n.* 1 a first covering of young birds. b bird's under-plumage. c fine soft feathers or hairs. 2 fluffy substance. [Old Norse]

down³ *n.* 1 open rolling land. 2 (in *pl.*) chalk uplands, esp. in S. England. [Old English]

down-and-out *n.* destitute person. □ down and out *predic. adj.*

downbeat —*n. Mus.* accented beat, usu. the first of the bar. —*adj.* 1 pessimistic, gloomy. 2 relaxed.

downcast *adj.* 1 dejected. 2 (of eyes) looking downwards.

downer *n. slang* 1 depressant or tranquillizing drug. 2 depressing person or experience; failure. 3 = DOWNTURN.

downfall *n.* 1 fall from prosperity or power. 2 cause of this.

downgrade *v.* (-ding) reduce in rank or status.

downhearted *adj.* dejected. □ downheartedly *adv.* downheartedness *n.*

downhill *adv.* in a descending direction. —*adj.* sloping down, declining. —*n.* 1 downhill race in skiing. 2 downward slope. □ go downhill *colloq.* deteriorate.

down in the mouth *adj.* looking unhappy.

downland *n.* = DOWN³.

dozen /ˈdʌz(ə)n/ n. 1 (prec. by a or a number) (pl. dozen) twelve (a dozen eggs; two dozen eggs). 2 set of twelve (sold in dozens). 3 (in pl.; usu. foll. by of) colloq. very many (dozens of errors). □ talk nineteen to the dozen talk incessantly. [Latin duodecim twelve]

dozy adj. (-ier, -iest) 1 drowsy. 2 colloq. stupid or lazy.

D.Phil. abbr. Doctor of Philosophy.

DPP abbr. Director of Public Prosecutions.

Dr abbr. Doctor.

drab adj. (drabber, drabbest) 1 dull, uninteresting. 2 of a dull brownish colour. □ drably adv. drabness n. [obsolete drap cloth]

drachm /dræm/ n. weight formerly used by apothecaries, = ⅛ ounce. [Latin from Greek]

drachma /ˈdrækmə/ n. (pl. -s) 1 chief monetary unit of Greece. 2 silver coin of ancient Greece. [Greek drakhmē]

Draconian /drəˈkəʊnɪən/ adj. (of laws) very harsh, cruel. [Drakōn, name of an Athenian lawgiver]

draft /drɑːft/ n. 1 preliminary written version of a speech, document, etc., or outline of a scheme. 2 a written order for payment of money by a bank. b drawing of money by this. 3 a detachment from a larger group. b selection of this. 4 US conscription. 5 US = DRAUGHT. —v. 1 prepare a draft of (a document, scheme, etc.). 2 select for a special duty or purpose. 3 US conscript. [phonetic spelling of DRAUGHT]

draftsman n. 1 person who drafts documents. 2 = DRAUGHTSMAN 1. [phonetic spelling of DRAUGHTSMAN]

drafty US var. of DRAUGHTY.

drag —v. (-gg-) 1 pull along with effort. 2 a trail or allow to trail along the ground. b (often foll. by on) (of time, a meeting, etc.) go or pass slowly or tediously. 3 a use as a grapnel. b search the bottom of (a river etc.) with grapnels, nets, etc. 4 (often foll. by to) colloq. take (an esp. unwilling person) with one. 5 (foll. by on, at) draw on (a cigarette etc.). —n. 1 a obstruction to progress. b retarding force or motion. 2 colloq. boring or tiresome person, duty, etc. 3 a lure before hounds as a substitute for a fox. b hunt using this. 4 apparatus for dredging. 5 = DRAG-NET. 6 slang inhalation. 7 slang women's clothes worn by men. □ drag one's feet be deliberately slow or reluctant to act. drag in introduce (an irrelevant subject). drag out protract. drag up colloq. introduce or revive (an unwelcome subject). [Old English or Old Norse]

draggle /ˈdræg(ə)l/ v. (-ling) 1 make dirty, wet, or limp by trailing. 2 hang trailing. [from DRAG]

dragon /ˈdrægən/ n. 1 mythical usu. winged monster like a reptile, able to breathe fire. 2 fierce woman. [Greek, = serpent]

dragonfly n. large insect with a long body and two pairs of transparent wings.

dragoon /drəˈguːn/ n. 1 cavalryman. 2 fierce fellow. —v. (foll. by into) coerce or bully into. [French dragon: related to DRAGON]

drag queen n. slang derog. male homosexual transvestite.

drain —v. 1 draw off liquid from. 2 draw off (liquid). 3 flow or trickle away. 4 dry (land) or become dry as liquid flows away. 5 exhaust of strength or resources. 6 a drink to the dregs. b empty (a glass etc.) by drinking the contents. —n. 1 a channel, conduit, or pipe carrying off liquid, sewage, etc. b tube for drawing off discharge etc. 2 constant outflow or expenditure. □ down the drain colloq. lost, wasted. [Old English: related to DRY]

drainage n. 1 draining. 2 system of drains. 3 what is drained off.

draining-board n. sloping grooved surface beside a sink for draining washed dishes.

drainpipe n. 1 pipe for carrying off water etc. 2 (attrib.) (of trousers) very narrow. 3 (in pl.) very narrow trousers.

drake n. male duck. [origin uncertain]

Dralon /ˈdreɪlɒn/ n. propr. 1 synthetic acrylic fibre. 2 fabric made from this. [invented word, after NYLON]

dram n. 1 small drink of spirits, esp. whisky. 2 = DRACHM. [Latin from Greek drakhmē: related to DRACHM]

drama /ˈdrɑːmə/ n. 1 play for stage or broadcasting. 2 art of writing, acting, or presenting plays. 3 dramatic event or quality (the drama of the situation). [Latin from Greek draō do]

dramatic /drəˈmætɪk/ adj. 1 of drama. 2 sudden and exciting or unexpected. 3 vividly striking. 4 (of a gesture etc.) theatrical. □ dramatically adv. [Greek: related to DRAMA]

dramatis personae /ˌdræmætɪs pɜːˈsəʊnaɪ/ n.pl. 1 characters in a play. 2 list of these. [Latin, = persons of the drama]

dramatist /'dræmətɪst/ n. writer of dramas.

dramatize /'dræmə,taɪz/ v. (also **-ise**) (**-zing** or **-sing**) **1** turn (a novel etc.) into a play. **2** make a dramatic scene of. **3** behave dramatically. □ **dramatization** /-'zeɪʃ(ə)n/ n.

drank past of DRINK.

drape -v. (**-ping**) **1** hang or cover loosely, adorn with cloth etc. **2** arrange (hangings etc.) in folds. -n. (in pl.) US curtains. [Latin drappus cloth]

draper n. dealer in textile fabrics.

drapery n. (pl. **-ies**) **1** clothing or hangings arranged in folds. **2** draper's trade or fabrics.

drastic /'dræstɪk/ adj. far-reaching in effect; severe. □ **drastically** adv. [Greek drastikos: related to DRAMA]

drat colloq. -v. (**-tt-**) (usu. as int.) curse (drat the thing!). -int. expressing anger or annoyance. □ **dratted** adj. [(God) rot]

draught /drɑːft/ n. (US **draft**) **1** current of air in a room or chimney etc. **2** pulling, traction. **3** depth of water needed to float a ship. **4** drawing of liquor from a cask etc. **5 a** single act of drinking or inhaling. **b** amount drunk thus. **6** (in pl.) game for two with 12 pieces each on a draughtboard. **7 a** drawing in of a fishing-net. **b** fish so caught. □ **feel the draught** suffer from esp. financial hardship. [related to DRAW]

draught beer n. beer from the cask, not bottled or canned.

draughtboard n. = CHESSBOARD.

draught-horse n. horse for heavy work.

draughtsman n. **1** person who makes drawings, plans, or sketches. **2** piece in draughts. □ **draughtsmanship** n.

draughty adj. (US **drafty**) (**-ier, -iest**) (of a room etc.) letting in sharp currents of air. □ **draughtiness** n.

draw -v. (past **drew** /druː/; past part. **drawn**) **1** pull or cause to move towards or after one. **2** pull (a thing) up, over, or across. **3** pull (curtains etc.) open or shut. **4** take (a person) aside. **5** attract; bring; take in (drew a deep breath; felt drawn to her; drew my attention; drew a crowd). **6** (foll. by at, on) inhale from (a cigarette, pipe, etc.). **7** (also absol.) take out; remove (a tooth, gun, cork, card, etc.). **8** obtain or take from a source (draw a salary; draw inspiration; drew £100 out). **9 a** (also absol.) make (a line or mark). **b** produce (a picture) thus. **c** represent (something) thus. **10** (also absol.) finish (a contest or game) with equal scores. **11** proceed (drew near the bridge; draw to a close; drew level). **12** infer (a conclusion). **13 a** elicit, evoke (draw criticism). **b** induce (a person) to reveal facts etc. **14** haul up (water) from a well. **15** bring out (liquid from a tap etc. or blood from a wound). **16** extract a liquid essence from. **17** (of a chimney etc.) promote or allow a draught. **18** (of tea) infuse. **19 a** obtain by lot (drew the winner). **b** absol. draw lots. **20** (foll. by on) call on (a person or a person's skill etc.). **21** write out or compose (a cheque, document, etc.). **22** formulate or perceive (a comparison or distinction). **23** disembowel. **24** search (cover) for game. **25** drag (a badger or fox) from a hole. -n. **1** act of drawing. **2** person or thing attracting custom, attention, etc. **3** drawing of lots, raffle. **4** drawn game. **5** inhalation of smoke etc. □ **draw back** withdraw from an undertaking. **draw a bead on** see BEAD. **draw a blank** see BLANK. **draw in 1** (of days) become shorter. **2** persuade to join. **3** (of a train) arrive at a station. **draw in one's horns** become less assertive or ambitious. **draw the line at** set a limit of tolerance etc. at. **draw lots** see LOT. **draw on 1** approach, come near. **2** lead to. **3** allure. **4** put (gloves, boots, etc.) on. **draw out 1** prolong. **2** elicit. **3** induce to talk. **4** (of days) become longer. **5** (of a train) leave a station. **draw up 1** draft (a document etc.). **2** bring into order. **3** come to a halt. **4** make (oneself) erect. **quick on the draw** quick to react. [Old English]

drawback n. disadvantage.

drawbridge n. hinged retractable bridge over a moat.

drawer /'drɔː(r)/ n. **1** person or thing that draws, esp. a cheque etc. **2** also /drɔː(r)/ lidless boxlike storage compartment, sliding in and out of a table etc. (chest of drawers). **3** (in pl.) knickers, underpants.

drawing n. **1** art of representing by line with a pencil etc. **2** picture etc. made thus.

drawing-board n. board on which paper is fixed for drawing on.

drawing-pin n. flat-headed pin for fastening paper etc. to a surface.

drawing-room n. **1** room in a private house for sitting or entertaining in. **2** (attrib.) restrained, polite (drawing-room manners). [earlier withdrawing-room]

drawl -v. speak with drawn-out vowel sounds. -n. drawling utterance or way of speaking.

drawn adj. looking strained and tense.

drawstring n. string or cord threaded through a waistband, bag opening, etc.

dray n. low cart without sides for heavy loads, esp. beer-barrels. [related to DRAW]

dread /dred/ –v. fear greatly, esp. in advance. –n. great fear or apprehension. –adj. 1 dreaded. 2 archaic awe-inspiring, dreadful. [Old English]

dreadful adj. 1 terrible. 2 colloq. annoying, very bad. □ **dreadfully** adv.

dreadlocks n.pl. Rastafarian hairstyle with hair hanging in tight braids on all sides.

dream –n. 1 series of scenes or feelings in the mind of a sleeping person. 2 day-dream or ideal or fantasy. 3 ideal, aspiration. 4 beautiful or ideal person or thing. –v. (past and past part. **dreamt** /dremt/ or **dreamed**) 1 experience a dream. 2 imagine as in a dream. 3 (with neg.) consider possible (never dreamt that he would come; would not dream of it). 4 (foll. by away) waste (time). 5 be in-active or unpractical. □ **dream up** imagine, invent. **like a dream** colloq. easily, effortlessly. □ **dreamer** n. [Old English]

dreamboat n. colloq. sexually attractive or ideal person.

dreamland n. ideal or imaginary land.

dreamy adj. (-ier, -iest) 1 given to day-dreaming or fantasy. 2 dreamlike. vague. 3 colloq. delightful. □ **dreamily** adv. **dreaminess** n.

dreary adj. (-ier, -iest) dismal, dull, gloomy. □ **drearily** adv. **dreariness** n. [Old English]

dredge[1] –n. apparatus used to scoop up oysters etc., or to clear mud etc., from a river or sea bed. –v. (-ging) 1 (often foll. by up) a bring up or clear (mud etc.) with a dredge. b bring up (something forgotten) (dredged it all up). 2 clean with or use a dredge. [origin uncertain]

dredge[2] v. (-ging) sprinkle with flour, sugar, etc. [earlier = sweetmeat, from French]

dredger[1] n. 1 boat with a dredge. 2 dredge.

dredger[2] n. container with a perforated lid for sprinkling flour, sugar, etc.

dregs n.pl. 1 sediment; grounds, lees. 2 = SCUM n. 2 (dregs of humanity).

drench –v. 1 wet thoroughly. 2 force (an animal) to take medicine. –n. dose of medicine for an animal. [Old English]

dress –v. 1 a (also absol.) put clothes on. b have and wear clothes (dresses well). 2 put on evening dress. 3 arrange or adorn (hair, a shop window, etc.). 4 treat (a wound) esp. with a dressing. 5 a prepare (poultry, crab, etc.) for cooking or eating. b add dressing to (a salad etc.). 6 apply manure to. 7 finish the surface of

(fabric, leather, stone, etc.). 8 correct the alignment of (troops). 9 make (an artificial fly) for fishing. –n. 1 woman's garment of a bodice and skirt. 2 cloth-ing, esp. a whole outfit. 3 formal or ceremonial costume. 4 external cover-ing. □ **dress down** colloq. 1 reprimand or scold. 2 dress informally. **dress up** 1 put on special clothes. 2 make (a thing) more attract-ive or interesting. [French dress, ulti-mately related to DIRECT]

dressage /ˈdresɑːʒ/ n. training of a horse in obedience and deportment; dis-play of this. [French]

dress circle n. first gallery in a theatre.

dress coat n. man's swallow-tailed evening coat.

dresser[1] n. kitchen sideboard with shelves for plates etc. [French dresser = prepare]

dresser[2] n. 1 person who helps to dress actors or actresses. 2 surgeon's assist-ant at operations. 3 person who dresses in a specified way (snappy dresser).

dressing n. 1 putting one's clothes on. 2 a sauce, esp. of oil and vinegar etc., for salads (French dressing). b sauce or stuffing etc. for food. 3 bandage, oint-ment, etc., for a wound. 4 size or stiffen-ing used to coat fabrics. 5 compost etc. spread over land.

dressing-down n. colloq. scolding.

dressing-gown n. loose robe worn when one is not fully dressed.

dressing-room n. room for changing one's clothes, esp. in a theatre, or attached to a bedroom.

dressing-table n. table with a flat top, mirror, and drawers, used while apply-ing make-up etc.

dressmaker n. person who makes women's clothes, esp. for a living. □ **dressmaking** n.

dress rehearsal n. final rehearsal in full costume.

dress-shield n. waterproof material in the armpit of a dress to protect it from sweat.

dress-shirt n. man's shirt worn with evening dress, usu. white with con-cealed buttons or studs.

dressy adj. (-ier, -iest) colloq. (of clothes or a person) smart, elaborate, elegant. □ **dressiness** n.

drew past of DRAW.

dribble /ˈdrɪb(ə)l/ –v. (-ling) 1 allow saliva to flow from the mouth. 2 flow or allow to flow in drops. 3 (also absol.) esp. Football & Hockey move (the ball) for-ward with slight touches of the feet or

stick. —*n.* **1** act of dribbling. **2** dribbling flow. [obsolete *drib* = DRIP]

driblet /'driblit/ *n.* small quantity.

dribs and drabs *n.pl. colloq.* small scattered amounts.

dried *past* and *past part.* of DRY.

drier¹ *compar.* of DRY.

drier² /'draıə(r)/ *n.* (also **dryer**) device for drying hair, laundry, etc.

driest *superl.* of DRY.

drift —*n.* **1 a** slow movement or variation. **b** this caused by a current. **2** intention, meaning, etc. of what is said etc. **3** mass of snow etc. heaped up by the wind. **4** esp. *derog.* state of inaction. **5** slow deviation of a ship, aircraft, etc., from its course. **6** fragments of rock heaped up (*glacial drift*). **7** *S.Afr.* ford. —*v.* **1** be carried by or as if by a current of air or water. **2** progress casually or aimlessly (*drifted into teaching*). **3** pile or be piled into drifts. **4** (of a current) carry, cause to drift. [Old Norse and Germanic *trift* movement of cattle]

drifter *n.* **1** aimless person. **2** boat used for drift-net fishing.

drift-net *n.* net for sea fishing, allowed to drift.

driftwood *n.* wood floating on moving water or washed ashore.

drill¹ —*n.* **1** tool or machine for boring holes, sinking wells, etc. **2** instruction in military exercises. **3** routine procedure in an emergency (*fire-drill*). **4** thorough training, esp. by repetition. **5** *colloq.* recognized procedure (*what's the drill?*). —*v.* **1 a** make a hole in or through with a drill. **b** make a hole) with a drill. **2** train or be trained by drill. [Dutch]

drill² —*n.* **1** machine for making furrows, sowing, and covering seed. **2** small furrow. **3** row of seeds sown by a drill. —*v.* plant in drills. [origin unknown]

drill³ *n.* coarse twilled cotton or linen fabric. [Latin *trilix* having three threads]

drill⁴ *n.* W. African baboon related to the mandrill. [probably native]

drily *adv.* (also **dryly**) in a dry manner.

drink —*v.* (*past* **drank**; *past part.* **drunk**) **1 a** (also *absol.*) swallow (liquid). **b** swallow the contents of (a vessel). **2** take alcohol, esp. to excess. **3** (of a plant, sponge, etc.) absorb (moisture). **4** bring (oneself etc.) to a specified condition by drinking. **5** wish (a person good health etc.) by drinking (*drank his health*). —*n.* **1 a** liquid for drinking. **b** draught or specified amount of this. **2 a** alcoholic liquor. **b** portion, glass, etc. of this. **c** excessive use of alcohol (*took to drink*). **3** (**the drink**) *colloq.* the sea. □ **drink in** listen eagerly to. **drink to**

toast; wish success to. **drink up** (also *absol.*) drink all or the remainder of. □ **drinkable** *adj.* **drinker** *n.* [Old English]

drink-driver *n.* person who drives with excess alcohol in the blood. □ **drink-driving** *n.*

drip —*v.* (**-pp-**) **1** fall or let fall in drops. **2** (often foll. by *with*) be so wet as to shed drops. —*n.* **1 a** liquid falling in drops (*steady drip of rain*). **b** drop of liquid. **c** sound of dripping. **2** *colloq.* dull or ineffectual person. **3** = DRIP-FEED. □ **be dripping with** be full of or covered with. [Danish; cf. DROP]

drip-dry —*v.* dry or leave to dry crease-free when hung up. —*adj.* able to be drip-dried.

drip-feed —*v.* feed intravenously in drops. —*n.* **1** feeding thus. **2** apparatus for doing this.

dripping *n.* fat melted from roasted meat.

drippy *adj.* (**-ier**, **-iest**) *slang* ineffectual; sloppily sentimental.

drive —*v.* (**-ving**; *past* **drove**; *past part.* **driven** /'drɪv(ə)n/) **1** urge forward, esp. forcibly. **2 a** compel (*was driven to complain*). **b** force into a specified state (*drove him mad*). **c** (often *refl.*) urge to overwork. **3 a** operate and direct (a vehicle, locomotive, etc.). **b** convey or be conveyed in a vehicle. **c** be competent to drive (a vehicle) (*does he drive?*). **d** travel in a private vehicle. **4** (of wind etc.) carry along, propel, esp. rapidly (*driven snow*; *driving rain*). **5 a** (often foll. by *into*) force (a stake, nail, etc.) into place by blows. **b** bore (a tunnel etc.). **6** effect or conclude forcibly (*drove a hard bargain*; *drove his point home*). **7** (of power) operate (machinery). **8** (usu. foll. by *at*) work hard; dash, rush. **9** hit (a ball) forcibly. —*n.* **1** journey or excursion in a vehicle. **2 a** (esp. scenic) street or road. **b** private road through a garden to a house. **3 a** motivation and energy. **b** inner urge (*sex-drive*). **4** forcible stroke of a bat etc. **5** organized effort (*membership drive*). **6 a** transmission of power to machinery, wheels, etc. **b** position of the steering-wheel in a vehicle (*left-hand drive*). **c** *Computing* = DISK DRIVE. **7** organized whist, bingo, etc. competition. □ **drive at** seek, intend, or mean (*what is he driving at?*). [Old English]

drive-in —*attrib. adj.* (of a bank, cinema, etc.) used while sitting in one's car. —*n.* such a bank, cinema, etc.

drivel /'drɪv(ə)l/ —*n.* silly talk; nonsense. —*v.* (**-ll-**; *US* **-l-**, **-ling**) **1** talk drivel. **2** run at the mouth or nose. [Old English]

driven *past part.* of DRIVE.

drive-on *adj.* (of a ship) on to which vehicles may be driven.

driver *n.* 1 person who drives a vehicle. 2 golf-club for driving from a tee.

driveway *n.* = DRIVE *n.* 2b

driving-licence *n.* official test of competence to drive.

driving test *n.* official test of competence to drive.

driving-wheel *n.* wheel communicating motive power in machinery.

drizzle /ˈdrɪz(ə)l/ —*n.* very fine rain. —*v.* (-ling) (of rain) fall in very fine drops. □ **drizzly** *adj.* [Old English]

droll /drəʊl/ *adj.* quaintly amusing; strange, odd. □ **drollery** *n.* (*pl.* -ies). **drolly** /ˈdrəʊlli/ *adv.* [French]

dromedary /ˈdrɒmɪdərɪ/ *n.* (*pl.* -ies) one-humped (esp. Arabian) camel bred for riding. [Greek *dromas -ados* runner]

drone —*n.* 1 non-working male of the honey-bee. 2 idler. 3 deep humming sound. 4 monotonous speaking tone. 5 bass-pipe of bagpipes or its continuous note. —*v.* (-ning) 1 make a deep humming sound. 2 speak or utter monotonously. [Old English]

drool *v.* 1 slobber, dribble. 2 (often foll. by *over*) admire extravagantly. [from DRIVEL]

droop —*v.* 1 bend or hang down, esp. from weariness; flag. 2 (of the eyes) look downwards. —*n.* 1 drooping attitude. 2 loss of spirit. □ **droopy** *adj.* [Old Norse: related to DROP]

drop —*n.* 1 a globule of liquid that hangs, falls, or adheres to a surface. b very small amount of liquid (*just a drop left*). c glass etc. of alcohol. 2 a abrupt fall or slope. b amount of this (*drop of fifteen feet*). c act of dropping. d fall in prices, temperature, etc. e deterioration (*drop in status*). 3 drop-shaped thing, esp. a pendant or sweet. 4 curtain or scenery let down on to a stage. 5 (in *pl.*) liquid medicine used in drops (*eye drops*). 6 minute quantity. 7 *slang* hiding-place for stolen goods etc. 8 *slang* bribe. —*v.* (-pp-) 1 fall or let fall in drops; shed (tears, blood). 2 fall or allow to fall; let go. 3 a sink down from exhaustion or injury. b die. c fall naturally. 4 a (cause to) cease or lapse; abandon. b *colloq.* cease to associate with or discuss. 5 set down (a passenger etc.) (*drop me here*). 6 utter or be uttered casually (*dropped a hint*). 7 send casually (*drop a line*). 8 a fall or allow to fall in direction, amount, condition, degree, pitch, etc. b (*voice* *dropped; wind dropped; we dropped in price*). c (of a person) jump down lightly; let oneself fall. c allow (trousers etc.) to fall to the ground. 9 omit (a letter) in

speech (*drop one's h's*). 10 (as **dropped** *adj.*) in a lower position than usual (*dropped handlebars; dropped waist*). 11 give birth to (esp. a lamb). 12 lose (a game, point, etc.). 13 deliver by parachute etc. 14 *Football* send (a ball, or score (a goal), by a drop-kick. 15 *colloq.* dismiss or omit (*dropped from the team*). □ **at the drop of a hat** promptly, instantly. **drop back** (or **behind**) fall back; get left behind. **drop a brick** *colloq.* make an indiscreet or embarrassing remark. **drop a curtsy** curtsy. **drop in** (or **by**) *colloq.* visit casually. **drop off** 1 fall asleep. 2 drop (a passenger). **drop out** *colloq.* cease to participate. □ **droplet** *n.* [Old English]

drop-curtain *n.* painted curtain lowered on to a stage.

drop-kick *n. Football* kick as the ball touches the ground having been dropped.

drop-out *n. colloq.* person who has dropped out of conventional society, a course of study, etc.

dropper *n.* device for releasing liquid in drops.

droppings *n.pl.* 1 dung of animals or birds. 2 thing that falls or has fallen in drops.

drop scone *n.* scone made by dropping a spoonful of mixture into the pan etc.

drop-shot *n.* (in tennis) shot dropping abruptly over the net.

dropsy /ˈdrɒpsɪ/ *n.* = OEDEMA. □ **dropsical** *adj.* [earlier *hydropsy* from Greek *hudrōps*: related to HYDRO-]

drosophila /drəˈsɒfɪlə/ *n.* fruit fly used in genetic research. [Greek, = dew-loving]

dross *n.* 1 rubbish. 2 a scum from melted metals. b impurities. [Old English]

drought /draʊt/ *n.* prolonged absence of rain. [Old English]

drove *past* of DRIVE.

drove *n.* 1 a moving crowd. b (in *pl.*) (*droves*). 2 herd or flock driven or moving together. [Old English: related to DRIVE]

drover *n.* herder of cattle.

drown *v.* 1 kill or die by submersion in liquid. 2 submerge; flood; drench. 3 deaden (grief etc.) by drinking. 4 (often foll. by *out*) overpower (sound) with louder sound. [probably Old English]

drowse /draʊz/ *v.* (-sing) be lightly asleep. [from DROWSY]

drowsy /ˈdraʊzɪ/ *adj.* (-ier, -iest) very sleepy, almost asleep. □ **drowsily** *adv.* **drowsiness** *n.* [probably Old English]

drub *v.* (-bb-) 1 beat, thrash. 2 defeat thoroughly. □ **drubbing** *n.* [Arabic *ḍaraba* beat]

drudge —*n.* person who does dull, laborious, or menial work. —*v.* (-**ging**) work laboriously, toil. □ **drudgery** *n.* [origin uncertain]

drug —*n.* **1** medicinal substance. **2** addictive, narcotic, hallucinogen, or stimulant. —*v.* (-**gg**-) **1** add a drug to (food or drink). **2 a** give a drug to. **b** stupefy. [French]

druggist /ˈdrʌgɪt/ *n.* pharmacist. [related to DRUG]

drugget *n.* coarse woven fabric used for floor coverings etc. [French]

drugstore *n.* US combined chemist's shop and café.

Druid /ˈdruːɪd/ *n.* **1** priest of an ancient Celtic religion. **2** member of a modern Druidic order, esp. the Gorsedd. □ **Druidic** /-ˈɪdɪk/ *adj.* **Druidism** *n.* [Latin from Celtic]

drum —*n.* **1** hollow esp. cylindrical percussion instrument covered at the end(s) with plastic etc. **2** (often in *pl.*) percussion section of an orchestra etc. **3** sound made by a drum. **4** thing resembling a drum, esp. a container, etc. **5** segment of a pillar. **6** eardrum. —*v.* (-**mm**-) **1** play a drum. **2** beat or tap continuously with the fingers etc. **3** (of a bird or insect) make a loud noise with the wings. □ **drum into** drive (a lesson or facts) into (a person) by persistence. **drum out** dismiss with ignominy. **drum up** summon or get by vigorous effort (*drum up support*). [Low German]

drumbeat *n.* stroke or sound of a stroke on a drum.

drum brake *n.* brake in which brake shoes on a vehicle press against the brake drum on a wheel.

drumhead *n.* part of a drum that is hit.

drum kit *n.* set of drums in a band etc.

drum machine *n.* electronic device that simulates percussion.

drum major *n.* leader of a marching band.

drum majorette *n.* female baton-twirling member of a parading group.

drummer *n.* player of drums.

drumstick *n.* **1** stick for beating drums. **2** lower leg of a dressed fowl.

drunk —*adj.* **1** lacking control from drinking alcohol. **2** (often foll. by *with*) overcome with joy, success, power, etc. —*n.* person who is drunk, esp. habitually. [past part. of DRINK]

drunkard /ˈdrʌŋkəd/ *n.* person who is habitually drunk.

drunken *adj.* (usu. *attrib.*) **1** = DRUNK 1. **2** caused by or involving drunkenness (*drunken brawl*). **3** often drunk. □ **drunkenly** *adv.* **drunkenness** *n.*

drupe /druːp/ *n.* fleshy stone-fruit, e.g. the olive and plum. [Latin from Greek]

dry /draɪ/ —*adj.* (**drier**; **driest**) **1** free from moisture, esp. **a** with moisture having evaporated, drained away, etc. (*clothes are not dry yet*). **b** (of eyes) free from tears. **c** (of a climate etc.) with insufficient rain; not rainy (*dry spell*). **d** (of a river, well, etc.) dried up. **e** using or producing no moisture (*dry shampoo*; *dry cough*). **f** (of a shave) with an electric razor. **2** (of wine) not sweet (*dry sherry*). **3 a** plain, unelaborated (*dry facts*). **b** uninteresting (*dry book*). **4** (of a sense of humour) subtle, ironic, understated. **5** prohibiting the sale of alcohol (*a dry State*). **6** (of bread) without butter etc. **7** (of provisions etc.) solid, not liquid. **8** impassive. **9** (of a cow) not yielding milk. **10** *colloq.* thirsty (*feel dry*). —*v.* (**dries, dried**) **1** make or become dry. **2** (usu. as **dried** *adj.*) preserve (food etc.) by removing moisture. **3** (often foll. by *up*) *colloq.* forget one's lines. —*n.* (*pl.* **dries**) **1** process of drying. **2** dry ginger ale. **3** dry place (*come into the dry*). □ **dry out 1** make or become fully dry. **2** treat or be treated for alcoholism. **dry up 1** make or become utterly dry. **2** dry dishes. **3** *colloq.* cease talking. **4** become unproductive. **5** (esp. in *imper.*) run out. □ **dryness** *n.*

dryad /ˈdraɪæd/ *n.* wood nymph. [Greek *drus* tree]

dry battery *n.* (also **dry cell**) electric battery or cell in which electrolyte is absorbed in a solid.

dry-clean *v.* clean (clothes etc.) with solvents without water. □ **dry-cleaner** *n.*

dry dock *n.* dock that can be pumped dry for building or repairing ships.

dryer var. of DRIER².

dry-fly *attrib. adj.* (of fishing) with a floating artificial fly.

dry ice *n.* solid carbon dioxide used as a refrigerant.

dry land *n.* land as distinct from sea etc.

dryly var. of DRILY.

dry measure *n.* measure for dry goods.

dry rot *n.* decayed state of unventilated wood; fungi causing this.

dry run *n.* *colloq.* rehearsal.

dry-shod *adj.* & *adv.* without wetting one's shoes.

drystone *attrib. adj.* (of a wall etc.) built without mortar.

DSC *abbr.* Distinguished Service Cross.

D.Sc. *abbr.* Doctor of Science.

DSM *abbr.* Distinguished Service Medal.

DSO *abbr.* Distinguished Service Order.

DSS *abbr.* Department of Social Security (formerly DHSS).

DT abbr. (also **DT's** /diːˈtiːz/) delirium tremens.

DTI abbr. Department of Trade and Industry.

dual /ˈdjuːəl/ —adj. **1** in two parts; two-fold. **2** double (dual ownership). —n. Gram. dual number or form. □ **duality** /ˈæltɪ/ n. [Latin duo two]

dual carriageway n. road with a dividing strip between traffic flowing in opposite directions.

dual control n. two linked sets of controls, enabling operation by either of two persons.

dub[1] v. (**-bb-**) **1** make (a person) a knight by touching his shoulders with a sword. **2** give (a person) a name, nickname, etc. **3** smear (leather) with grease. [French]

dub[2] v. (**-bb-**) **1** provide (a film etc.) with an esp. translated alternative sound-track. **2** add (sound effects or music) to a film or broadcast. **3** transfer or make a copy of (recorded sound or images). [abbreviation of DOUBLE]

dubbin /ˈdʌbɪn/ n. (also **dubbing**) thick grease for softening and waterproofing leather. [see DUB[1] 3]

dubiety /djuːˈbaɪətɪ/ n. literary doubt. [Latin: related to DUBIOUS]

dubious /ˈdjuːbɪəs/ adj. **1** hesitating, doubtful. **2** questionable, suspicious. **3** unreliable. □ **dubiously** adv. **dubiousness** n. [Latin dubium doubt]

ducal /ˈdjuːk(ə)l/ adj. of or like a duke. [French: related to DUKE]

ducat /ˈdʌkət/ n. gold coin, formerly current in most of Europe. [medieval Latin ducatus DUCHY]

duchess /ˈdʌtʃɪs/ n. **1** duke's wife or widow. **2** woman holding the rank of duke. [medieval Latin ducissa: related to DUKE]

duchesse potatoes /duːˈʃes/ n.pl. mashed potatoes mixed with egg, baked or fried, and served as small cakes or used as piping. [French]

duchy /ˈdʌtʃɪ/ n. (pl. **-ies**) territory or dukedom of a duke or duchess; royal dukedom of Cornwall or Lancaster. [medieval Latin ducatus: related to DUKE]

duck[1] n. (pl. same or **-s**) **1 a** swimming-bird, esp. the domesticated form of the mallard or wild duck. **b** female of this. **c** its flesh as food. **2** score of 0 in cricket. **3** (also **ducks**) colloq. (esp. as a form of address) dear. —v. **1** bob down, esp. to avoid being seen or hit. **2 a** dip one's head briefly under water. **b** plunge (a person) briefly in water. **3** colloq. dodge (a task etc.). □ **like water off a duck's back** colloq. producing no effect. [Old English]

duck[2] n. **1** strong linen or cotton fabric. **2** (in pl.) trousers made of this. [Dutch]

duckbill n. (also **duck-billed platy-pus**) = PLATYPUS.

duckboard n. (usu. in pl.) path of wooden slats over muddy ground, in a trench, etc.

duckling n. young duck.

ducks and drakes n.pl. (usu. treated as sing.) game of making a flat stone skim the surface of water. □ **play ducks and drakes with** colloq. squander.

duckweed n. any of various plants growing on the surface of still water.

ducky n. (pl. **-ies**) colloq. (esp. as a form of address) dear.

duct n. channel or tube for conveying a fluid, cable, bodily secretions, etc. (tear ducts). —v. convey through a duct. [Latin ductus from duco duct- lead]

ductile /ˈdʌktaɪl/ adj. **1** (of metal) cap-able of being drawn into wire; pliable. **2** easily moulded. **3** docile. □ **ductility** /-ˈtɪlɪtɪ/ n. [Latin: related to DUCT]

ductless gland n. gland secreting directly into the bloodstream.

dud slang —n. **1** useless or broken thing. **2** counterfeit article. **3** (in pl.) clothes, rags. —adj. useless, defective. [origin unknown]

dude /djuːd/ n. slang **1** fellow. **2** US dandy. **3** US city-dweller staying on a ranch. [German dial. dude fool]

dudgeon /ˈdʌdʒ(ə)n/ n. resentment, in-dignation. □ **in high dudgeon** very angry. [origin unknown]

due —adj. **1** owing or payable. **2** (often foll. by to) merited; appropriate. **3** (foll. by to) that ought to be given or ascribed to (a person, cause, etc.) (first place is due to Milton; difficulty due to ignor-ance). **4** (often foll. by to + infin.) expected or under an obligation at a certain time (due to speak tonight; train due at 7.30). **5** suitable, right, proper (in due time). —n. **1** what one owes or is owed (give him his due). **2** (usu. in pl.) fee or amount payable. —adv. (of a com-pass point) exactly, directly (went due east). □ **due to** because of (he was late due to an accident). [French from Latin debeo owe]

■ **Usage** The use of **due to** to mean 'because of' as in the example given is regarded as unacceptable by some people and could be avoided by substi-tuting his lateness was due to an ac-cident. Alternatively, owing to could be used.

duel /ˈdjuːəl/ —n. **1** armed contest between two people, usu. to the death. **2** two-sided contest. —v. (**-ll-**; US **-l-**) fight a duel. □ **duellist** n. [Latin duellum war]

duenna /djuːˈenə/ *n.* older woman acting as a chaperon to girls, esp. in Spain. [Spanish from Latin *domina* DON[1]]

duet /djuːˈet/ *n.* musical composition for two performers. □ **duettist** *n.* [Latin *duo* two]

duff[1] *—n.* boiled pudding. *—adj. slang* worthless, counterfeit, useless. [var. of DOUGH]

duff[2] *v.* □ **duff up** *slang* beat; thrash. [perhaps from DUFFER]

duffer *n. colloq.* inefficient or stupid person; dunce. [origin uncertain]

duffle /ˈdʌf(ə)l/ *n.* (also **duffel**) heavy woollen cloth. [*Duffel* in Belgium]

duffle bag *n.* cylindrical canvas bag closed by a drawstring.

duffle-coat *n.* hooded overcoat of duffle, fastened with toggles.

dug[1] *past* and *past part.* of DIG.

dug[2] *n.* udder, teat. [origin unknown]

dugong /ˈduːɡɒŋ/ *n.* (*pl.* same or **-s**) Asian sea-mammal. [Malay]

dugout *n.* **1 a** a roofed shelter, esp. for troops in trenches. **b** underground shelter. **2** canoe made from a tree-trunk.

duke /djuːk/ *n.* **1** person holding the highest hereditary title of the nobility. **2** sovereign prince ruling a duchy or small State. □ **dukedom** *n.* [Latin *dux* leader]

dulcet /ˈdʌlsɪt/ *adj.* sweet-sounding. [Latin *dulcis* sweet]

dulcimer /ˈdʌlsɪmə(r)/ *n.* metal stringed instrument struck with two hand-held hammers. [Latin: related to DULCET, *melos* song]

dull *—adj.* **1** tedious; not interesting. **2** (of the weather) overcast. **3** (of colour, light, sound, etc.) not bright, vivid, or clear. **4** (of a pain) indistinct; not acute (*a dull ache*). **5** slow-witted; stupid. **6** (of a knife-edge etc.) blunt. **7 a** (of trade etc.) sluggish, slow. **b** listless; depressed. **8** (of the ears, eyes, etc.) lacking keenness. *—v.* make or become dull. □ **dullness** *n.* [Low German or Dutch]

dullard /ˈdʌləd/ *n.* stupid person.

duly /ˈdjuːlɪ/ *adv.* **1** in due time or manner. **2** rightly, properly.

dumb /dʌm/ *adj.* **1 a** unable to speak. **b** (of an animal) naturally dumb. **2** silenced by surprise, shyness, etc. **3** taciturn, reticent (*dumb insolence*). **4** suffered or done in silence (*dumb agony*). **5** *colloq.* stupid; ignorant. **6** disenfranchised (*dumb masses*). **7** (of a computer terminal etc.) able to transmit or receive but unable to process data. **8** giving no sound. [Old English]

dumb-bell *n.* **1** short bar with a weight at each end, for muscle-building etc. **2** *slang* stupid person, esp. a woman.

dumbfound /dʌmˈfaʊnd/ *v.* nonplus, make speechless with surprise. [from DUMB, CONFOUND]

dumbo /ˈdʌmbəʊ/ *n.* (*pl.* **-s**) *slang* stupid person. [from DUMB, -O]

dumb show *n.* gestures; mime.

dumbstruck *adj.* speechless with surprise.

dumb waiter *n.* small hand-operated lift for conveying food from kitchen to dining-room.

dumdum /ˈdʌmdʌm/ *n.* (in full **dumdum bullet**) soft-nosed bullet that expands on impact. [*Dum-Dum* in India]

dummy /ˈdʌmɪ/ *—n.* (*pl.* **-ies**) **1** model of a human figure, esp. as used to display clothes or by a ventriloquist or as a target. **2** (often *attrib.*) imitation object or a baby's rubber or plastic teat. **3** stupid person. **4** *colloq.* imaginary player in bridge etc., whose cards are exposed and played by a partner. *—attrib. adj.* sham; imitation. *—v.* (**-ies, -ied**) make a pretended pass or swerve in football etc. [from DUMB]

dummy run *n.* trial attempt; rehearsal.

dump *—n.* **1** place or heap for depositing rubbish. **2** *colloq.* unpleasant or dreary place. **3** temporary store of ammunition etc. *—v.* **1** put down firmly or clumsily. **2** deposit as rubbish. **3** *colloq.* abandon or get rid of. **4** sell (excess goods) to a foreign market at a low price. **5** copy (the contents of a computer memory etc.) as a diagnostic aid or for security. □ **dump on** esp. *US* criticize or abuse; get the better of. [origin uncertain]

dumpling /ˈdʌmplɪŋ/ *n.* **1** ball of dough boiled in stew or containing apple etc. **2** small fat person. [*dump* small round object]

dumps *n.pl.* (usu. in **down in the dumps**) *colloq.* low spirits. [Low German or Dutch: related to DAMP]

dump truck *n.* truck that tilts or opens at the back for unloading.

dumpy *adj.* (**-ier, -iest**) short and stout. □ **dumpily** *adv.* **dumpiness** *n.* [related to DUMPLING]

dun[1] *—adj.* greyish-brown. *—n.* **1** dun colour. **2** dun horse. [Old English]

dunce *n.* person slow at learning; dullard. [*Duns* Scotus, name of a philosopher]

dunce's cap *n.* paper cone worn by a dunce.

dunderhead /ˈdʌndəˌhed/ *n.* stupid person. [origin unknown]

dune *n.* drift of sand etc. formed by the wind. [Dutch: related to DOWN[3]]

dung —*n.* excrement of animals; manure. —*v.* apply dung to (land). [Old English]

dungaree /dʌŋgə'riː/ *n.* 1 coarse cotton cloth. 2 (in *pl.*) overalls or trousers of this. [Hindi]

dung-beetle *n.* beetle whose larvae develop in dung.

dungeon /'dʌndʒ(ə)n/ *n.* underground prison cell. [earlier *donjon* keep of a castle; ultimately from Latin *dominus* lord]

dunghill *n.* heap of dung or refuse.

dunk *v.* 1 dip (food) into liquid before eating. 2 immerse. [German *tunken* dip]

dunlin /'dʌnlɪn/ *n.* red-backed sandpiper. [probably from DUN]

dunnock /'dʌnək/ *n.* hedge sparrow. [apparently from DUN]

duo /'djuːəʊ/ *n.* (*pl.* **-s**) 1 pair of performers. 2 duet. [Italian from Latin, = two]

duodecimal /djuːə'desɪm(ə)l/ *adj.* 1 of twelfths or twelve. 2 in or by twelves. [Latin *duodecim* twelve]

duodenum /djuːə'diːnəm/ *n.* (*pl.* **-s**) first part of the small intestine immediately below the stomach. □ **duodenal** *adj.* [medieval Latin: related to DUODECIMAL]

duologue /'djuːəlɒg/ *n.* dialogue between two people. [from DUO, MONOLOGUE]

dupe —*n.* victim of deception. —*v.* (**-ping**) deceive, trick. [French]

duple /'djuːp(ə)l/ *adj.* of two parts. [Latin *duplus*]

duple time *n.* *Mus.* rhythm with two beats to the bar.

duplex /'djuːpleks/ —*n.* (often *attrib.*) esp. *US* 1 flat on two floors. 2 house subdivided for two families; semidetached house. —*adj.* 1 of two parts. 2 *Computing* (of a circuit) allowing simultaneous two-way transmission of signals. [Latin, = double]

duplicate —*adj.* /'djuːplɪkət/ 1 identical. 2 a having two identical parts. b doubled. 3 (of card-games) with the same hands played by different players. —*n.* /'djuːplɪkət/ 1 identical thing, esp. a copy. 2 copy of a letter etc. —*v.* /'djuːplɪ.keɪt/ (**-ting**) 1 multiply by two; double. 2 make or be an exact copy of. 3 repeat (an action etc.), esp. unnecessarily. □ **in duplicate** in two exact copies. □ **duplication** /-'keɪʃ(ə)n/ *n.* [Latin: related to DUPLEX]

duplicator *n.* machine for making multiple copies of a text etc.

duplicity /djuː'plɪsɪtɪ/ *n.* double-dealing; deceitfulness. □ **duplicitous** *adj.* [Latin: related to DUPLEX]

durable /'djʊərəb(ə)l/ —*adj.* 1 lasting; hard-wearing. 2 (of goods) with a relatively long useful life. —*n.* (in *pl.*) durable goods. □ **durability** /-'bɪlɪtɪ/ *n.* [Latin *durus* hard]

dura mater /ˌdjʊərə 'meɪtə(r)/ *n.* tough outermost membrane enveloping the brain and spinal cord. [medieval Latin = hard mother, translation of Arabic]

duration /djʊ'reɪʃ(ə)n/ *n.* 1 time taken by an event. 2 specified length of time (*duration of a minute*). □ **for the duration** 1 until the end of an event. 2 for a very long time. [medieval Latin: related to DURABLE]

duress /djʊə'res/ *n.* 1 compulsion, esp. illegal use of threats or violence (*under duress*). 2 imprisonment. [Latin *durus* hard]

Durex /'djʊəreks/ *n. propr.* condom. [origin uncertain]

during /'djʊərɪŋ/ *prep.* throughout or at some point in. [Latin: related to DURABLE]

dusk *n.* darker stage of twilight. [Old English]

dusky *adj.* (**-ier**, **-iest**) 1 shadowy; dim. 2 dark-coloured; dark-skinned. □ **duskily** *adv.* **duskiness** *n.*

dust —*n.* 1 finely powdered earth or other material etc. 2 dead person's remains. 3 confusion, turmoil. —*v.* 1 wipe the dust from (furniture etc.). 2 a sprinkle with powder, sugar, etc. b sprinkle (sugar, powder, etc.). □ **dust down 1** dust the clothes of. 2 *colloq.* reprimand. 3 = *dust off.* □ **dust off 1** remove the dust from. 2 use again after a long period. **when the dust settles** when things quieten down. [Old English]

dustbin *n.* container for household refuse.

dust bowl *n.* desert made by drought or erosion.

dustcart *n.* vehicle collecting household refuse.

dust cover *n.* 1 = DUST-SHEET. 2 = DUST-JACKET.

duster *n.* cloth for dusting furniture etc.

dust-jacket *n.* paper cover on a hardback book.

dustman *n.* person employed to collect household refuse.

dustpan *n.* pan into which dust is brushed from the floor.

dust-sheet *n.* protective cloth over furniture.

dust-up *n. colloq.* fight, disturbance.

dusty *adj.* (**-ier**, **-iest**) 1 full of or covered with dust. 2 (of a colour) dull or muted. □ **not so dusty** *slang* fairly good. □ **dustily** *adv.* **dustiness** *n.*

dusty answer *n. colloq.* curt refusal.

Dutch –adj. of the Netherlands or its people or language. –n. **1** the Dutch language. **2** (prec. by *the;* treated as *pl.*) the people of the Netherlands. □ **go Dutch** share expenses on an outing etc. [Dutch]

dutch n. slang wife. [abbreviation of DUCHESS]

Dutch auction n. one in which the price is progressively reduced.

Dutch barn n. roof for hay etc., set on poles.

Dutch cap n. dome-shaped contraceptive device fitting over the cervix.

Dutch courage n. courage induced by alcohol.

Dutch elm disease n. fungus disease of elms.

Dutchman n. (fem. **Dutchwoman**) person of Dutch birth or nationality.

Dutch oven n. **1** metal box with the open side facing a fire. **2** covered cooking-pot for braising etc.

Dutch treat n. party, outing, etc., at which people pay for themselves.

Dutch uncle n. kind but firm adviser.

duteous /ˈdjuːtɪəs/ adj. literary dutiful. □ **duteously** adv.

dutiable /ˈdjuːtɪəb(ə)l/ adj. requiring the payment of duty.

dutiful /ˈdjuːtɪfʊl/ adj. doing one's duty; obedient. □ **dutifully** adv.

duty /ˈdjuːtɪ/ n. (pl. **-ies**) **1 a** moral or legal obligation; responsibility. **b** binding force of what is right. **2** tax on certain goods, imports, etc. **3** job or function arising from a business or office (*playground duty*). **4** deference; respect due to a superior. □ **do duty for** serve as or pass for (something else). **on (or off) duty** working (or not working). [Anglo-French: related to DUE]

duty-bound adj. obliged by duty.

duty-free adj. (of goods) on which duty is not payable.

duty-free shop n. shop at an airport etc. selling duty-free goods.

duvet /ˈduːveɪ/ n. thick soft quilt used instead of sheets and blankets. [French]

dwarf /dwɔːf/ –n. (pl. **-s** or **dwarves** /dwɔːvz/) **1** person, animal, or plant much below normal size. **2** small mythological being with magical powers. **3** small usu. dense star. –v. **1** stunt in growth. **2** make seem small. □ **dwarfish** adj. [Old English]

■ **Usage** In sense 1, with regard to people, the term *person of restricted growth* is now often preferred.

dwell v. (*past* and *past part.* **dwelt** or **dwelled**) live, reside. □ **dwell on** (or **upon**) think, write, or speak at length on. □ **dweller** n. [Old English]

dwelling n. house, residence.

dwindle /ˈdwɪnd(ə)l/ v. (**-ling**) **1** become gradually less or smaller. **2** lose importance. [Old English]

Dy symb. dysprosium.

dye /daɪ/ –n. **1** substance used to change the colour of hair, fabric, etc. **2** colour so produced. –v. (**dyeing, dyed**) **1** colour with dye. **2** dye a specified colour (*dyed it yellow*). □ **dyer** n. [Old English]

dyed-in-the-wool adj. (usu. *attrib.*) out and out; unchangeable.

dying /ˈdaɪɪŋ/ *attrib.* adj. of, or at the time of, death (*dying words*).

dyke¹ /daɪk/ (also **dike**) –n. **1** embankment built to prevent flooding. **2** low wall of turf or stone. –v. (**-king**) provide or protect with dyke(s). [related to DITCH]

dyke² /daɪk/ n. (also **dike**) slang lesbian. [origin unknown]

dynamic /daɪˈnæmɪk/ adj. **1** energetic; active. **2** Physics **a** of motive force. **b** of force in actual operation. **3** of dynamics. □ **dynamically** adv. [Greek *dunamis* power]

dynamics n.pl. **1** (usu. treated as *sing.*) **a** mathematical study of motion and the forces causing it. **b** branch of any science concerned with forces or changes. **2** motive forces in any sphere. **3** *Mus.* variation in loudness.

dynamism /ˈdaɪnəmɪz(ə)m/ n. energy; dynamic power.

dynamite /ˈdaɪnəmaɪt/ –n. **1** high explosive mixture containing nitroglycerine. **2** potentially dangerous person etc. –v. (**-ting**) charge or blow up with dynamite.

dynamo /ˈdaɪnəməʊ/ n. (pl. **-s**) **1** machine converting mechanical into electrical energy, esp. by rotating coils of copper wire in a magnetic field. **2** colloq. energetic person. [abbreviation of *dynamo-electric machine*]

dynamometer /ˌdaɪnəˈmɒmɪtə(r)/ n. instrument measuring energy expended. [Greek: related to DYNAMIC]

dynast /ˈdɪnæst/ n. **1** ruler. **2** member of a dynasty. [Latin from Greek]

dynasty /ˈdɪnəstɪ/ n. (pl. **-ies**) **1** line of hereditary rulers. **2** succession of leaders in any field. □ **dynastic** /-ˈnæstɪk/ adj. [Latin from Greek]

dyne /daɪn/ n. *Physics* force required to give a mass of one gram an acceleration of one centimetre per second per second. [Greek *dunamis* force]

dys- *prefix* bad, difficult. [Greek]

dysentery /ˈdɪsəntrɪ/ n. inflammation of the intestines, causing severe diarrhoea. [Greek *entera* bowels]

dysfunction /dɪsˈfʌŋkʃ(ə)n/ n. abnormality or impairment of function.

dyslexia /dɪsˈlɛksɪə/ n. abnormal difficulty in reading and spelling. □ **dyslectic** /-ˈlɛktɪk/ adj. & n. **dyslexic** adj. & n. [Greek *lexis* speech]

dysmenorrhoea /ˌdɪsmɛnəˈrɪə/ n. painful or difficult menstruation.

dyspepsia /dɪsˈpɛpsɪə/ n. indigestion. □ **dyspeptic** adj. & n. [Greek *peptos* digested]

dysphasia /dɪsˈfeɪzɪə/ n. lack of coordination in speech, owing to brain damage. [Greek *dusphatos* hard to utter]

dysprosium /dɪsˈprəʊzɪəm/ n. metallic element of the lanthanide series. [Greek *dusprositos* hard to get at]

dystrophy /ˈdɪstrəfɪ/ n. defective nutrition. [Greek *-trophē* nourishment]

E

E[1] /iː/ *n.* (also **e**) (*pl.* **Es** or **E's**) **1** fifth letter of the alphabet. **2** *Mus.* third note of the diatonic scale of C major.

E[2] *abbr.* (also **E.**) **1** east, eastern. **2** see E-NUMBER.

e- *prefix* see EX-[1] before some consonants.

each —*adj.* every one of two or more persons or things, regarded separately (*five in each class*). —*pron.* each person or thing (*each of us*). [Old English]

each other *pron.* one another.

each way *adj.* (of a bet) backing a horse etc. to win or to come second or third.

eager /ˈiːgə(r)/ *adj.* keen, enthusiastic (*eager to learn; eager for news*). □ **eagerly** *adv.* **eagerness** *n.* [Latin *acer* keen]

eager beaver *n. colloq.* very diligent person.

eagle /ˈiːg(ə)l/ *n.* **1 a** large bird of prey with keen vision and powerful flight. **b** this as a symbol, esp. of the US. **2** score of two strokes under par at any hole in golf. [Latin *aquila*]

eagle eye *n.* keen sight, watchfulness. □ **eagle-eyed** *adj.*

eaglet /ˈiːglɪt/ *n.* young eagle.

E. & O. E. *abbr.* errors and omissions excepted.

ear[1] *n.* **1** organ of hearing, esp. its external part. **2** faculty for discriminating sounds (*an ear for music*). **3** attention, esp. sympathetic (*give ear to; have a person's ear*). □ **all ears** listening attentively. **have (or keep) an ear to the ground** be alert to rumours or trends. **up to one's ears** (often foll. by *in*) *colloq.* deeply involved or occupied. [Old English]

ear[2] *n.* seed-bearing head of a cereal plant. [Old English]

earache *n.* pain in the inner ear.

eardrum *n.* membrane of the middle ear.

earful *n.* (*pl.* **-s**) *colloq.* **1** prolonged amount of talking. **2** strong reprimand.

earl /ɜːl/ *n.* British nobleman ranking between marquis and viscount. □ **earldom** *n.* [Old English]

Earl Marshal *n.* president of the College of Heralds, with ceremonial duties.

early /ˈɜːlɪ/ —*adj.* & *adv.* (**-ier**, **-iest**) **1** before the due, usual, or expected time. **2 a** not far on in the day or night, or in time (*early evening; at the earliest opportunity*). **b** prompt (*early payment*

appreciated). **3** not far on in a period, development, or process of evolution; being the first stage (*Early English architecture; early spring*). **4** forward in flowering, ripening, etc. (*early peaches*). —*n.* (*pl.* **-ies**) (usu. in *pl.*) early fruit or vegetable. □ **earliness** *n.* [Old English: related to ERE]

early bird *n. colloq.* person who arrives, gets up, etc. early.

early days *n.pl.* too soon to expect results etc.

early on *adv.* at an early stage.

earmark —*v.* set aside for a special purpose. —*n.* identifying mark.

earn /ɜːn/ *v.* **1** bring in as income or interest. **2** be entitled to or obtain as the reward for work or merit. □ **earner** *n.* [Old English]

earnest /ˈɜːnɪst/ *adj.* intensely serious. □ **in earnest** serious, seriously, with determination. □ **earnestly** *adv.* **earnestness** *n.* [Old English]

earnings *n.pl.* money earned.

earphone *n.* device applied to the ear to receive a radio etc. communication.

earpiece *n.* part of a telephone etc. applied to the ear.

ear-piercing —*adj.* shrill. —*n.* piercing of the ears for wearing earrings.

earplug *n.* piece of wax etc. placed in the ear to protect against water, noise, etc.

earring *n.* jewellery worn on the ear.

earshot *n.* hearing-range (*within earshot*).

ear-splitting *adj.* excessively loud.

earth /ɜːθ/ —*n.* **1 a** (also **Earth**) the planet on which we live. **b** land and sea, as distinct from sky. **2 a** the ground (*fell to earth*). **b** soil, mould. **3** *Relig.* this world, as distinct from heaven or hell. **4** connection to the earth as the completion of an electrical circuit. **5** hole of a fox etc. **6** (prec. by *the*) *colloq.* huge sum; everything (*cost the earth; want the earth*). —*v.* **1** cover (plant-roots) with earth. **2** connect (an electrical circuit) to the earth. □ **come back (or down) to earth** return to realities. **gone to earth** in hiding. **on earth** *colloq.* existing anywhere; emphatically (*the happiest man on earth; looked like nothing on earth; what on earth have you done?*). **run to earth** find after a long search. □ **earthward** *adj.* & *adv.* **earthwards** *adv.* [Old English]

earthbound *adj.* **1** attached to the earth or earthly things. **2** moving towards the earth.

earthen *adj.* made of earth or baked clay.

earthenware *n.* pottery made of fired clay.

earthling *n.* inhabitant of the earth, esp. in science fiction.

earthly *adj.* **1** terrestrial. **2** (usu. with *neg.*) *colloq.* remotely possible (*is no earthly use; there wasn't an earthly reason*). □ **not an earthly** *colloq.* no chance or idea whatever.

earth mother *n.* sensual and maternal woman.

earthquake *n.* convulsion of the earth's surface as a result of faults in strata or volcanic action.

earth sciences *n.pl.* those concerned with the earth or part of it.

earth-shattering *adj. colloq.* traumatic, devastating. □ **earth-shatteringly** *adv.*

earthwork *n.* artificial bank of earth in fortification or road-building etc.

earthworm *n.* common worm living in the ground.

earthy *adj.* (**-ier**, **-iest**) **1** of or like earth or soil. **2** coarse, crude (*earthy humour*). □ **earthiness** *n.*

ear-trumpet *n.* trumpet-shaped device formerly used as a hearing-aid.

earwig *n.* small insect with pincers at its rear end. [from EAR, because they were once thought to enter the head through the ear]

ease /iːz/ —*n.* **1** facility, effortlessness. **2** freedom from pain or trouble. **b** freedom from constraint. —*v.* (**-sing**) **1** relieve from pain or anxiety. **2** (often foll. by *off, up*) **a** become less burdensome or severe. **b** begin to take it easy. **c** slow down; moderate one's behaviour etc. **3** **a** relax; slacken; make a less tight fit. **b** move or be moved carefully into place (*eased it into position*). □ **at ease 1** free from anxiety or constraint. **2** *Mil.* in a relaxed attitude, with the feet apart. [Latin: related to ADJACENT]

easel /ˈiːz(ə)l/ *n.* stand for an artist's work, a blackboard, etc. [Dutch *ezel* ass]

easement *n.* legal right of way or similar right over another's land. [French: related to EASE]

easily /ˈiːzɪli/ *adv.* **1** without difficulty. **2** by far (*easily the best*). **3** very probably (*it could easily snow*).

east —*n.* **1 a** point of the horizon where the sun rises at the equinoxes. **b** compass point corresponding to this. **c** (**the East**) countries to the east of Europe, esp. in science fiction.

b States of eastern Europe. **3** eastern part of a country, town, etc. —*adj.* **1** towards, at, near, or facing the east. **2** from the east (*east wind*). —*adv.* **1** towards, at, or near the east. **2** (foll. by *of*) further east than. □ **to the east** (often foll. by *of*) in an easterly direction. [Old English]

eastbound *adj.* travelling or leading eastwards.

East End *n.* part of London east of the City. □ **East Ender** *n.*

Easter *n.* festival (held on a variable Sunday in March or April) commemorating Christ's resurrection. [Old English]

Easter egg *n.* artificial usu. chocolate egg given at Easter.

easterly *adj. & adv.* **1** in an eastern position or direction. **2** (of a wind) from the east. —*n.* (*pl.* -**ies**) such a wind.

eastern *adj.* of or in the east. □ **eastermost** *adj.*

Eastern Church *n.* Orthodox Church.

easterner *n.* native or inhabitant of the east.

Easter *n.*

east-north-east *n.* point or direction midway between east and north-east.

east-south-east *n.* point or direction midway between east and south-east.

eastward —*adj. & adv.* (also **eastwards**) towards the east. —*n.* eastward direction or region.

easy /ˈiːzi/ —*adj.* (**-ier**, **-iest**) **1** not difficult; not requiring great effort. **2** free from pain, trouble, or anxiety. **3** free from constraint; relaxed and pleasant. **4** compliant. —*adv.* with ease; in an effortless or relaxed manner. —*int.* go or move carefully. □ **easy on the eye** (or ear etc.) *colloq.* pleasant to look at (or listen to etc.). **go easy** (foll. by *with, on*) be sparing or cautious. **I'm easy** *colloq.* I have no preference. **take it easy 1** proceed gently. **2** relax; work less. □ **easiness** *n.* [French: related to EASE]

easy chair *n.* large comfortable armchair.

easygoing *adj.* placid and tolerant.

Easy Street *n. colloq.* affluence.

eat —*v.* (*past* **ate** /et, eɪt/; *past part.* **eaten**) **1 a** take into the mouth, chew, and swallow (food). **b** consume food; take a meal. **c** devour (*eaten by a lion*). **2** (foll. by *away, at, into*) **a** destroy gradually, esp. by corrosion, disease, etc. **b** begin to consume or diminish (resources etc.). **3** *colloq.* trouble, vex (*what's eating you?*). —*n.* (in *pl.*) *colloq.* food. □ **eat one's heart out** suffer from excessive longing or envy. **eat out** have a meal away from home, esp. in a restaurant. **eat up 1** eat completely. **2** use or deal with rapidly or wastefully (*eats*

up petrol; eats up the miles). **3** pre-occupy (*eaten up with envy*). **eat one's words** retract them abjectly. [Old English]

eatable *—adj.* fit to be eaten. *—n.* (usu. in *pl.*) food.

eater *n.* **1** person who eats (*a big eater*). **2** eating apple etc.

eating apple etc. *n.* apple etc. suitable for eating raw.

eau-de-Cologne /ˌəʊdəkəˈləʊn/ *n.* toilet water orig. from Cologne. [French, = water of Cologne]

eaves /iːvz/ *n.pl.* underside of a projecting roof. [Old English]

eavesdrop *v.* (**-pp-**) listen to a private conversation. □ **eavesdropper** *n.*

ebb *—n.* movement of the tide out to sea. *—v.* (often foll. by *away*) **1** flow out to sea; recede. **2** decline (*life was ebbing away*). [Old English]

ebonite /ˈebəˌnaɪt/ *n.* vulcanite. [from EBONY]

ebony /ˈebənɪ/ *—n.* heavy hard dark wood of a tropical tree. *—adj.* **1** made of ebony. **2** black like ebony. [Greek *ebenos* ebony tree]

ebullient /ɪˈbʌlɪənt/ *adj.* exuberant. □ **ebullience** *n.* **ebulliency** *n.* **ebulliently** *adv.* [Latin: related to BOIL[1]]

EC *abbr.* **1** East Central. **2** European Community.

eccentric /ɪkˈsentrɪk/ *—adj.* **1** odd or capricious in behaviour or appearance. **2** (also **excentric**) **a** not placed, not having its axis placed, centrally. **b** (often foll. by *to*) (of a circle) not concentric (to another). **c** (of an orbit) not circular. *—n.* **1** eccentric person. **2** disc at the end of a shaft for changing rotatory into backward-and-forward motion. □ **eccentrically** *adv.* **eccentricity** /ˌeksenˈtrɪsətɪ/ *n.* [Greek: related to CENTRE]

Eccles cake /ˈek(ə)lz/ *n.* round cake of pastry filled with currants etc. [*Eccles* in N. England]

ecclesiastic /ɪˌkliːzɪˈæstɪk/ *—n.* clergyman. *—adj.* = ECCLESIASTICAL. [Greek *ekklēsia* church]

ecclesiastical *adj.* of the Church or clergy.

ECG *abbr.* electrocardiogram.

echelon /ˈeʃəˌlɒn/ *n.* **1** level in an organization, in society, etc.; those occupying it (*often in pl.: upper echelons*). **2** wedge-shaped formation of troops, aircraft, etc. [French, = ladder, from Latin *scala*]

echidna /ɪˈkɪdnə/ *n.* Australian egg-laying spiny mammal. [Greek, = viper]

echinoderm /ɪˈkaɪnəˌdɜːm/ *n.* (usu. spiny) sea animal of the group including the starfish and sea urchin. [Greek *ekhinos* sea-urchin, *derma* skin]

echo /ˈekəʊ/ *—n.* (*pl.* **-es**) **1 a** repetition of a sound by the reflection of sound waves. **b** sound so produced. **2** reflected radio or radar beam. **3** close imitation or imitator. **4** circumstance or event reminiscent of an earlier one. *—v.* (**-es**, **-ed**) **1 a** (of a place) resound with an echo. **b** (of a sound) be repeated; resound. **2** repeat (a sound) thus. **3 a** repeat (another's words). **b** imitate the opinions etc. of. [Latin from Greek]

echo chamber *n.* enclosure with sound-reflecting walls.

echoic /eˈkəʊɪk/ *adj.* (of a word) onomatopoeic.

echolocation *n.* location of objects by reflected sound.

echo-sounder *n.* depth-sounding device using timed echoes.

echt /ext/ *adj.* genuine. [German]

éclair /ɪˈkleə(r)/ *n.* small elongated iced cake of choux pastry filled with cream. [French, = lightning]

eclampsia /ɪˈklæmpsɪə/ *n.* convulsive condition occurring esp. in pregnant women. [ultimately from Greek]

éclat /eɪˈklɑː/ *n.* **1** brilliant display. **2** social distinction; conspicuous success. [French]

eclectic /ɪˈklektɪk/ *—adj.* selecting ideas, style, etc., from various sources. *—n.* eclectic person or philosopher. □ **eclectically** *adv.* **eclecticism** /-ˌsɪz(ə)m/ *n.* [Greek *eklegō* pick out]

eclipse /ɪˈklɪps/ *—n.* **1** obscuring of light from one heavenly body by another. **2** loss of light, importance, or prominence. *—v.* (**-sing**) **1** (of a heavenly body) cause the eclipse of (another). **2** intercept (light). **3** outshine, surpass. [Greek *ekleipsis*]

ecliptic /ɪˈklɪptɪk/ *n.* sun's apparent path among the stars during the year.

eclogue /ˈeklɒg/ *n.* short pastoral poem. [Greek: related to ECLECTIC]

eco- *comb. form* ecology, ecological (*ecoclimate*).

ecology /ɪˈkɒlədʒɪ/ *n.* **1** the study of the relations of organisms to one another and to their surroundings. **2** the study of the interaction of people with their environment. □ **ecological** /ˌiːkəˈlɒdʒɪk(ə)l/ *adj.* **ecologically** /ˌiːkə-ˈlɒdʒɪkəlɪ/ *adv.* **ecologist** *n.* [Greek *oikos* house]

economic /ˌiːkəˈnɒmɪk/ *adj.* **1** of economics. **2** profitable (*not economic to run buses on a Sunday*). **3** connected with trade and industry (*economic geography*). □ **economically** *adv.* [Greek: related to ECONOMY]

economical *adj.* sparing; avoiding waste. □ **economically** *adv.*

economics *n.pl.* (as *sing.*) 1 science of the production and distribution of wealth. 2 application of this to a particular subject (*the economics of publishing*).

economist /ɪˈkɒnəmɪst/ *n.* expert on or student of economics.

economize /ɪˈkɒnəmaɪz/ *v.* (also **-ise**) (**-zing** or **-sing**) 1 be economical; make economies; reduce expenditure. 2 (foll. by *on*) use sparingly.

economy /ɪˈkɒnəmɪ/ *n.* (*pl.* **-ies**) 1 a community's system of wealth creation. b particular kind of this (*a capitalist economy*). c administration or condition of this. 2 a careful management of (esp. financial) resources; frugality. b instance of this (*made many economies*). 3 sparing or careful use (*economy of language*). [Greek *oikonomia* household management]

economy class *n.* cheapest class of air travel.

economy-size *adj.* (of goods) contained in a larger quantity for a proportionally lower cost.

ecosystem /ˈiːkəʊsɪstəm/ *n.* biological community of interacting organisms and their physical environment.

ecstasy /ˈekstəsɪ/ *n.* (*pl.* **-ies**) 1 overwhelming joy or rapture. 2 *slang* type of hallucinogenic drug. □ **ecstatic** /ɪkˈstætɪk/ *adj.* **ecstatically** /-klɪ/ *adv.* [Greek *ekstasis* standing outside oneself]

ECT *abbr.* electroconvulsive therapy.

ecto- *comb. form* outside. [Greek *ektos*]

ectomorph /ˈektəʊmɔːf/ *n.* person with a lean body. [Greek *morphē* form]

-ectomy *comb. form* denoting the surgical removal of part of the body (*appendectomy*). [Greek *ektomē* excision]

ectoplasm /ˈektəʊplæz(ə)m/ *n.* supposed viscous substance exuding from the body of a spiritualistic medium during a trance. [from ECTO-, PLASMA]

ecu /ˈeɪkjuː, -kuː/ *n.* (also **Ecu**) (*pl.* **-s**) European Currency Unit. [abbreviation]

ecumenical /ˌiːkjuˈmenɪk(ə)l/ *adj.* 1 of or representing the whole Christian world. 2 seeking worldwide Christian unity. □ **ecumenically** *adv.* **ecumenism** /iːˈkjuːmənɪz(ə)m/ *n.* [Greek *oikoumenikos* of the inhabited earth]

eczema /ˈeksɪmə/ *n.* inflammation of the skin, with itching and discharge. [Latin from Greek]

-ed *suffix* forming adjectives: 1 from nouns, meaning 'having, wearing, etc.' (*talented; trousered*). 2 from phrases of adjective and noun (*good-humoured*).

-ed *suffix* forming 1 past tense and past participle of weak verbs (*needed*). 2 participial adjectives (*escaped prisoner*). [Old English]

Edam /ˈiːdæm/ *n.* round Dutch cheese with a red rind. [*Edam* in Holland]

eddy /ˈedɪ/ -*n.* (*pl.* **-ies**) 1 circular movement of water causing a small whirlpool. 2 movement (of wind, smoke, etc. resembling this. -*v.* (**-ies, -ied**) whirl round in eddies. [Old English *ed-* again, back]

edelweiss /ˈeɪd(ə)lvaɪs/ *n.* Alpine plant with white flowers. [German *ed-* noble, *weiss* white]

edema *US var. of* OEDEMA.

Eden /ˈiːd(ə)n/ *n.* place or state of great happiness, with reference to the abode of Adam and Eve at the Creation. [Hebrew, originally = delight]

edentate /iːˈdenteɪt/ -*adj.* having no or few teeth. -*n.* such a mammal. [Latin *dens dent-* tooth]

edge -*n.* 1 boundary-line or margin of an area or surface. 2 narrow surface of a thin object. 3 meeting-line of surfaces. 4 a sharpened side of a blade. b sharpness. 5 brink of a precipice. 6 edge-like thing, esp. the crest of a ridge. 7 effectiveness, incisiveness; excitement. -*v.* (**-ging**) 1 advance, esp. gradually or furtively. 2 a provide with an edge or border. b form a border to. 3 sharpen (a tool etc.). □ **have the edge on** (or **over**) have a slight advantage over. **on edge** tense and irritable; **set a person's teeth on edge** (of taste or sound) cause an unpleasant nervous sensation. **take the edge off** make less intense. [Old English]

edgeways *adv.* (also **edgewise**) with edge uppermost or foremost. □ **get a word in edgeways** contribute to a conversation when the dominant speaker pauses.

edging *n.* thing forming an edge or border.

edgy *adj.* (**-ier, -iest**) irritable; anxious. □ **edgily** *adv.* **edginess** *n.*

edible /ˈedɪb(ə)l/ *adj.* fit to be eaten. □ **edibility** /-ˈbɪlɪtɪ/ *n.* [Latin *edo* eat]

edict /ˈiːdɪkt/ *n.* order proclaimed by authority. [Latin *edico* proclaim]

edifice /ˈedɪfɪs/ *n.* building, esp. an imposing one. [Latin *aedis* dwelling]

edify /ˈedɪfaɪ/ *v.* (**-ies, -ied**) improve morally or intellectually. □ **edification** /-ˈkeɪʃ(ə)n/ *n.* [Latin *aedifico* build]

edit /ˈedɪt/ *v.* (**-t-**) 1 assemble, prepare, or modify (written material for publication). 2 be editor of (a newspaper etc.). 3

take extracts from and collate (a film etc.) to form a unified sequence. **4 a** prepare (data) for processing by a computer. **b** alter (a text entered in a word processor etc.). **5 a** reword in order to correct, or to alter the emphasis. **b** (foll. by *out*) remove (a part) from a text etc. [Latin *edo edit-* give out]

edition /ɪˈdɪʃ(ə)n/ n. **1** edited or published form of a book etc. **2** copies of a book, newspaper, etc. issued at one time. **3** instance of a regular broadcast. **4** person or thing similar to another (*a miniature edition of her mother*).

editor n. **1** person who edits. **2** person who directs the preparation of a newspaper or broadcast news programme or a particular section of one (*sports editor*). **3** person who selects or commissions material for publication. **4** computer program for entering and modifying textual data. □ **editorship** n. [Latin]

editorial /edɪˈtɔːrɪəl/ —adj. **1** of editing or editors. **2** written or approved by an editor. —n. article giving a newspaper's views on a current topic. □ **editorially** adv.

EDP abbr. electronic data processing.

educate /edjʊ,keɪt/ v. (-ting) **1** give intellectual, moral, and social instruction to. **2** provide education for. □ **educable** /-kəb(ə)l/ adj. **educability** /-kəˈbɪlɪtɪ/ n. **educative** /-keɪtɪv/ adj. **educator** n. [Latin *educo -are* rear]

educated adj. **1** having had an (esp. good) education. **2** resulting from this (*educated accent*). **3** based on experience or study (*educated guess*).

education /edjʊˈkeɪʃ(ə)n/ n. **1** systematic instruction. **2** particular kind of or stage in education (*a classical education; further education*). **3** development of character or mental powers. □ **educational** adj. **educationally** adv. **educationist** n. (also **educationalist**) expert in the theory or practice of education and teaching methods.

educe /ɪˈdjuːs/ v. (-cing) literary bring out or develop from latency. □ **eduction** /ɪˈdʌkʃ(ə)n/ n. [Latin *educo -ere* draw out]

Edwardian /edˈwɔːdiən/ —adj. of or characteristic of the reign of Edward VII (1901–10). —n. person of this period.

-ee suffix forming nouns denoting: **1** person affected by the verbal action (*employee; payee*). **2** person concerned with or described as (*absentee; refugee*). **3** object of smaller size (*bootee*). [French *-é* in past part.]

EEC abbr. European Economic Community.

EEG abbr. electroencephalogram.

eel n. snakelike fish. [Old English]

-eer suffix forming: **1** nouns meaning 'person concerned with' (*auctioneer*). **2** verbs meaning 'be concerned with' (*electioneer*). [French *-ier* from Latin *-arius*]

eerie /ˈɪərɪ/ adj. (**eerier, eeriest**) gloomy and strange; weird (*eerie silence*). □ **eerily** adv. **eeriness** n. [Old English]

ef- see EX-[1].

efface /ɪˈfeɪs/ v. (-cing) **1** rub or wipe out (a mark, recollection, etc.). **2** surpass, eclipse. **3** refl. (usu. as **self-effacing** adj.) treat oneself as unimportant. □ **effacement** n. [French: related to FACE]

effect /ɪˈfekt/ —n. **1** result or consequence of an action etc. **2** efficacy (*had little effect*). **3** impression produced on a spectator, hearer, etc. (*lights gave a pretty effect; said it just for effect*). **4** (in pl.) property. **5** (in pl.) lighting, sound, etc., giving realism to a play, film, etc. **6** physical phenomenon (*Doppler effect; greenhouse effect*). —v. bring about (a change, cure, etc.). □ **bring** (or **carry**) **into effect** accomplish. **give effect to** make operative. **in effect** for practical purposes. **take effect** become operative. **to the effect that** the gist being that. **to that effect** having that result or implication. **with effect from** coming into operation at (a stated time). [Latin: related to FACT]

effective adj. **1** producing the intended result. **2** impressive, striking. **3** actual, existing. **4** operative. □ **effectively** adv. **effectiveness** n.

effectual /ɪˈfektjʊəl/ adj. **1** producing the required effect. **2** valid. □ **effectually** adv.

effeminate /ɪˈfemɪnət/ adj. (of a man) womanish in appearance or manner. □ **effeminacy** n. **effeminately** adv. [Latin *femina* woman]

effervesce /,efəˈves/ v. (-cing) **1** give off bubbles of gas. **2** be lively. □ **effervescence** n. **effervescent** adj. [Latin: related to FERVENT]

effete /ɪˈfiːt/ adj. feeble, languid; effeminate. □ **effeteness** n. [Latin]

efficacious /,efɪˈkeɪʃəs/ adj. producing the desired effect. □ **efficacy** /ˈefɪkəsɪ/ n. [Latin *efficax*: related to EFFICIENT]

efficient /ɪˈfɪʃ(ə)nt/ adj. **1** productive with minimum waste or effort. **2** (of a person) capable; acting effectively. □ **efficiency** n. **efficiently** adv. [Latin *facio* make]

effigy /ˈefɪdʒɪ/ n. (pl. -ies) sculpture or model of a person. □ **burn in effigy** burn a model of a person. [Latin from *fingo* fashion]

effloresce /ˌefləˈres/ v. (-cing) 1 burst into flower. 2 a (of a substance) turn to a fine powder on exposure to air. b (of salts) come to the surface and crystallize. c (of a surface) become covered with salt particles. □ **efflorescence** n. □ **efflorescent** adj. [Latin: *flos* FLOWER]

effluence /ˈefluəns/ n. 1 flowing out of light, electricity, etc. 2 that which flows out. [Latin *fluo* flow]

effluent –adj. flowing out. –n. 1 sewage or industrial waste discharged into a river etc. 2 stream or lake flowing from a larger body of water.

effluvium /ɪˈfluːvɪəm/ n. (pl. -via) unpleasant or noxious outflow. [Latin: related to EFFLUENCE]

effort /ˈefət/ n. 1 use of physical or mental energy. 2 determined attempt. 3 force exerted. 4 colloq. something accomplished. [Latin *fortis* strong]

effortless adj. easily done, requiring no effort. □ **effortlessly** adv. **effortlessness** n.

effrontery /ɪˈfrʌntərɪ/ n. (pl. -ies) impudent audacity. [Latin *frons front-* forehead]

effulgent /ɪˈfʌldʒ(ə)nt/ adj. literary radiant. □ **effulgence** n. [Latin *fulgeo* shine]

effuse /ɪˈfjuːz/ v. (-sing) 1 pour forth (liquid, light, etc.). 2 give out (ideas etc.). [Latin *fundo fus-* pour]

effusion /ɪˈfjuːʒ(ə)n/ n. 1 outpouring. 2 derog. unrestrained flow of words. [Latin: related to EFFUSE]

effusive /ɪˈfjuːsɪv/ adj. gushing, demonstrative. □ **effusively** adv. **effusiveness** n.

EFL abbr. English as a foreign language.

eft n. newt. [Old English]

Efta /ˈeftə/ n. (also **EFTA**) European Free Trade Association. [abbreviation]

e.g. abbr. for example. [Latin *exempli gratia*]

egalitarian /ɪˌgælɪˈteərɪən/ –adj. of or advocating equal rights for all. –n. egalitarian person. □ **egalitarianism** n. [French *égal* EQUAL]

egg n. 1 a body produced by females of birds, insects, etc. and capable of developing into a new individual. b egg of the domestic hen, used for food. 2 Biol. ovum. 3 colloq. person or thing of a specified kind (*good egg*). □ **with egg on one's face** colloq. looking foolish. □ **eggy** adj. [Old Norse]

egg v. (foll. by on) urge. [Old Norse: related to EDGE]

eggcup n. cup for holding a boiled egg.

egg-flip n. (also **egg-nog**) drink of alcoholic spirit with beaten egg, milk, etc.

egghead n. colloq. intellectual; expert.

eggplant n. = AUBERGINE.

eggshell –n. shell of an egg. –adj. 1 (of china) thin and fragile. 2 (of paint) with a slight gloss.

egg-white n. white part round the yolk of an egg.

eglantine /ˈegləntaɪn/ n. sweet-brier. [Latin *acus* needle]

ego /ˈiːgəʊ/ n. (pl. -s) 1 the self; the part of the mind that reacts to reality and has a sense of individuality. 2 self-esteem; self-conceit. [Latin, = I]

egocentric /ˌiːgəʊˈsentrɪk/ adj. self-centred.

egoism /ˈiːgəʊɪz(ə)m/ n. 1 self-interest as the moral basis of behaviour. 2 systematic selfishness. 3 = EGOTISM. □ **egoist** n. **egoistic** /-ˈɪstɪk/ adj. **egoistical** /-ˈɪstɪk(ə)l/ adj.

■ **Usage** The senses of *egoism* and *egotism* overlap, but *egoism* alone is used as a term in philosophy and psychology to mean self-interest (often contrasted with *altruism*).

egotism /ˈiːgətɪz(ə)m/ n. 1 self-conceit. 2 selfishness. □ **egotist** n. **egotistic** /-ˈtɪstɪk/ adj. **egotistical** /-ˈtɪstɪk(ə)l/ adj. **egotistically** /-ˈtɪstɪkəlɪ/ adv.

■ **Usage** See note at *egoism*.

ego-trip n. colloq. activity to boost one's own self-esteem or self-conceit.

egregious /ɪˈgriːdʒəs/ adj. 1 extremely bad. 2 archaic remarkable. [Latin *grex greg-* flock]

egress /ˈiːgres/ n. formal 1 exit. 2 right of going out. [Latin *egredior -gress-* walk out]

egret /ˈiːgrɪt/ n. a kind of heron with long white feathers. [French *aigrette*]

Egyptian /ɪˈdʒɪpʃ(ə)n/ –adj. of Egypt. –n. 1 native of Egypt. 2 language of the ancient Egyptians.

Egyptology /ˌiːdʒɪpˈtɒlədʒɪ/ n. the study of the language, history, and culture of ancient Egypt. □ **Egyptologist** n.

eh /eɪ/ int. colloq. 1 expressing enquiry or surprise. 2 inviting assent 3 asking for repetition or explanation. [instinctive exclamation]

eider /ˈaɪdə(r)/ n. any of various large northern ducks. [Icelandic]

eiderdown n. quilt stuffed with soft material, esp. down.

eight /eɪt/ adj. & n. 1 one more than seven. 2 symbol for this (8, viii, VIII). 3 eight-oared boat or its crew. 4 eight-... size etc. denoted by eight.

rowing-boat or its crew. 5 eight o'clock. [Old English]

eighteen /eɪˈtiːn/ *adj. & n.* **1** one more than seventeen. **2** symbol for this (18, xviii, XVIII). **3** size etc. denoted by eighteen. **4** (**18**) (of films) suitable only for persons of 18 years and over. □ **eighteenth** *adj. & n.* [Old English]

eightfold *adj. & adv.* **1** eight times as much or as many. **2** consisting of eight parts.

eighth *adj. & n.* **1** next after seventh. **2** one of eight equal parts of a thing. □ **eighthly** *adv.*

eightsome *n.* (in full **eightsome reel**) lively Scottish dance for eight people.

eighty /ˈeɪtɪ/ *adj. & n.* (*pl.* **-ies**) **1** eight times ten. **2** symbol for this (80, lxxx, LXXX). **3** (in *pl.*) numbers from 80 to 89, esp. the years of a century or of a person's life. □ **eightieth** *adj. & n.* [Old English]

einsteinium /aɪnˈstaɪnɪəm/ *n.* artificial radioactive metallic element. [*Einstein*, name of a physicist]

eisteddfod /aɪˈstɛdfəd/ *n.* congress of Welsh singers and musicians; festival for musical competitions etc. [Welsh]

either /ˈaɪðə(r)/ *adj. & pron.* **1** one or the other of two (*either of you can go; you may have either book*). **2** each of two (*houses on either side of the road*). —*adv. & conj.* **1** as one possibility (*is either right or wrong*). **2** as one choice or alternative; which way you will (*either come in or go out*). **3** (with *neg.*) **a** any more than the other (*if you do not go, I shall not either*). **b** moreover (*there is no time to lose, either*). [Old English]

ejaculate /ɪˈdʒækjʊleɪt/ *v.* (**-ting**) (also *absol.*) **1** exclaim. **2** emit (semen) in orgasm. □ **ejaculation** /-ˈleɪʃ(ə)n/ *n.* **ejaculatory** /ɪˈdʒækjʊlətərɪ/ *adj.* [Latin *ejaculor* dart out]

eject /ɪˈdʒɛkt/ *v.* **1** expel, compel to leave. **2** (of a pilot etc.) cause oneself to be propelled from an aircraft as an emergency measure. **3** cause to be removed, drop out, or pop up automatically from a gun, cassette-player, etc. **4** dispossess (a tenant). **5** emit, send out. □ **ejection** *n.* [Latin *ejicio eject-* throw out]

ejector *n.* device for ejecting.

ejector seat *n.* device in an aircraft for the emergency ejection of a pilot etc.

eke *v.* (**eking**) □ **eke out 1** supplement (income etc.). **2** make (a living) or support (an existence) with difficulty. [Old English]

elaborate —*adj.* /ɪˈlæbərət/ **1** minutely worked out. **2** complicated. —*v.* /ɪˈlæbəreɪt/ (**-ting**) work out or explain in detail. □ **elaborately** /-rətlɪ/ *adv.*

elaborateness /-rətnɪs/ *n.* **elaboration** /-ˈreɪʃ(ə)n/ *n.* [Latin: related to LABOUR]

élan /eɪˈlɑː/ *n.* vivacity, dash. [French]

eland /ˈiːlənd/ *n.* (*pl.* same or **-s**) large African antelope. [Dutch]

elapse /ɪˈlæps/ *v.* (**-sing**) (of time) pass by. [Latin *elabor elaps-* slip away]

elastic /ɪˈlæstɪk/ —*adj.* **1** able to resume its normal bulk or shape after contraction, dilation, or distortion. **2** springy. **3** flexible, adaptable. —*n.* elastic cord or fabric, usu. woven with strips of rubber. □ **elastically** *adv.* **elasticity** /ˌiːlæˈstɪsɪtɪ/ *n.* [Greek *elastikos* propulsive]

elasticated /ɪˈlæstɪkeɪtɪd/ *adj.* (of fabric) made elastic by weaving with rubber thread.

elastic band *n.* = RUBBER BAND.

elastomer /ɪˈlæstəmə(r)/ *n.* natural or synthetic rubber or rubber-like plastic. [from ELASTIC, after *isomer*]

elate /ɪˈleɪt/ *v.* (**-ting**) (esp. as **elated** *adj.*) make delighted or proud. □ **elatedly** *adv.* **elation** *n.* [Latin *effero elat-* raise]

elbow /ˈɛlbəʊ/ —*n.* **1 a** joint between the forearm and the upper arm. **b** part of a sleeve covering the elbow. **2** elbow-shaped bend etc. —*v.* (foll. by *in, out, aside,* etc.) **1** jostle or thrust (a person or oneself). **2** make (one's way) thus. □ **give a person the elbow** *colloq.* dismiss or reject a person. [Old English: related to ELL, BOW[1]]

elbow-grease *n. colloq.* vigorous polishing; hard work.

elbow-room *n.* sufficient room to move or work in.

elder[1] —*attrib. adj.* (of persons, esp. when related) senior; of greater age. —*n.* **1** older of two persons (*is my elder by ten years*). **2** (in *pl.*) persons of greater age or venerable because of age. **3** official in the early Christian Church and some modern Churches. [Old English: related to OLD]

elder[2] *n.* tree with white flowers and dark berries. [Old English]

elderly *adj.* rather old; past middle age.

elder statesman *n.* influential experienced older person, esp. a politician.

eldest *adj.* first-born; oldest surviving.

eldorado /ˌɛldəˈrɑːdəʊ/ *n.* (*pl.* **-s**) **1** imaginary land of great wealth. **2** place of abundance or opportunity. [Spanish *el dorado* the gilded]

elecampane /ˌɛlɪkæmˈpeɪn/ *n.* plant with bitter aromatic leaves and roots. [Latin *enula* this plant, *campana* of the fields]

elect /ɪˈlekt/ –v. (usu. foll. by *to* + infin.)
1 choose. 2 choose by voting. —*adj.*
chosen. 2 select, choice. 3 (after the
noun) chosen but not yet in office (*president elect*). [Latin *eligo elect* pick out]

election /ɪˈlek(ʃ)ən/ n. 1 electing or
being elected. 2 occasion of this.

electioneer /ɪˌlekʃəˈnɪə(r)/ v. take part
in an election campaign.

elective /ɪˈlektɪv/ adj. 1 chosen by or
derived from election. 2 (of a body)
having the power to elect. 3 optional, not
urgently necessary.

elector n. 1 person who has the right to
vote in an election. 2 (**Elector**) *hist.* (in
German princes entitled to elect the
Emperor. □ **electoral** adj.
□ **electorally** adv. [from L]

electorate /ɪˈlektərət/ n. 1 body of all
electors. 2 *hist.* office or territories of a
German Elector.

electric /ɪˈlektrɪk/ –adj. 1 of, worked by,
or charged with electricity; producing,
or capable of generating electricity. 2
causing or charged with excitement. —*n.*
(in *pl.*) *colloq.* electrical equipment.
[Greek *elektron* amber]

electrical adj. of electricity.
□ **electrically** adv.

electric blanket n. blanket heated by
an internal electric element.

electric chair n. electrified chair used
for capital punishment.

electric eel n. eel-like fish able to give
an electric shock.

electric eye n. *colloq.* photoelectric cell
operating a relay when a beam of light is
broken.

electric fire n. electrically operated
portable domestic heater.

electric guitar n. guitar with a solid
body and built-in pick-up rather than a
soundbox.

electric shock n. effect of a sudden
discharge of electricity through the
body of a person etc.

electrician /ɪˌlekˈtrɪʃ(ə)n/ n. person
who installs or maintains electrical
equipment for a living.

electricity /ɪˌlekˈtrɪsɪtɪ/ n. 1 form of
energy occurring in elementary particles (electrons, protons, etc.) and
hence in larger bodies containing them.
2 science of electricity. 3 supply of
electricity. 4 excitement.

electrify /ɪˈlektrɪfaɪ/ v. (-**ies**, -**ied**) 1
charge with electricity. 2 convert to the
use of electric power. 3 cause sudden
excitement (*news was electrifying*). □
electrification /-fɪˈkeɪʃ(ə)n/ n.

electro- *comb. form* of, by, or caused by
electricity.

electrocardiogram
/ˈkɑːdɪəˌgræm/ n. record traced by an

electrocardiograph [German: related to
ELECTRO-]

electrocardiograph
/ˈkɑːdɪəˌgrɑːf/ n. instrument recording
the electric currents generated by a
heartbeat.

electroconvulsive /ɪˌlektrəʊkənˈ
ˈvʌlsɪv/ adj. (of therapy) using convulsive response to electric shocks.

electrocute /ɪˈlektrəkjuːt/ v. (-**ting**)
kill by electric shock. □ **electrocution**
/-ˈkjuː(ə)n/ n. [from **ELECTRO-**, after *execute*]

electrode /ɪˈlektrəʊd/ n. conductor
through which electricity enters or
leaves an electrolyte, gas, vacuum, etc.
[from **ELECTRIC**, Greek *hodos* way]

electroencephalogram /ɪˌlektrəʊ
ɛnˈsefələˌgræm/ n. record traced by an
electroencephalograph. [German: related to **ELECTRO-**]

electroencephalograph /ɪˌlektrəʊ
ɛnˈsefələˌgrɑːf/ n. instrument that records
the electrical activity of the brain.
□ **electrodynamic** adj.

electrodynamics /ɪˌlektrəʊdaɪˈ
ˈnæmɪks/ n.pl. (usu. treated as *sing.*)
the study of electricity in motion.

electrolyse /ɪˈlektrəlaɪz/ v. (*US* -**yze**)
(-**sing**, *US* -**zing**) subject to or treat by
electrolysis.

electrolysis /ɪˌlekˈtrɒlɪsɪs/ n. 1 chemical decomposition by electric action. 2
destruction of tumours, hair-roots, etc.,
by this process. □ **electrolytic**
/ɪˌlektrəʊˈlɪtɪk/ adj.

electrolyte /ɪˈlektrəlaɪt/ n. 1 solution
able to conduct electricity, esp. in an
electric cell or battery. 2 substance that
can dissolve to produce this.

electromagnet /ɪˌlektrəʊˈmægnɪt/ n.
soft metal core made into a magnet by
passing an electric current through a
coil surrounding it.

electromagnetic /ɪˌlektrəʊmæg
ˈnetɪk/ adj. having both electrical
and magnetic properties. □ **electro-
magnetically** adv.

electromagnetism /ɪˌlektrəʊ
ˈmægnɪˌtɪz(ə)m/ n. 1 magnetic forces
produced by electricity. 2 the study
of these.

electromotive /ɪˌlektrəʊˈməʊtɪv/ adj.
producing or tending to produce an
electric current.

electromotive force n. force set up in
an electric circuit by a difference in
potential.

electron /ɪˈlektrɒn/ n. stable elementary particle with a charge of negative
electricity, found in all atoms and acting
as the primary carrier of electricity in
solids.

electronic /ˌlek'trɒnɪk/ *adj.* **1 a** produced by or involving the flow of electrons. **b** of electrons or electronics **2** (of music) produced by electronic means and usu. recorded on tape. □ **electronically** *adv.*

electronic mail *n.* messages distributed by a computer system.

electronics *n.pl.* (treated as *sing.*) science of the movement of electrons in a vacuum, gas, semiconductor, etc., esp. in devices in which the flow is controlled and utilized.

electronic tagging *n.* the attaching of electronic markers to people or goods, enabling them to be tracked down.

electron lens *n.* device for focusing a stream of electrons by means of electric or magnetic fields.

electron microscope *n.* microscope with high magnification and resolution, using electron beams instead of light.

electronvolt /ɪˈlektrɒnˌvəʊlt/ *n.* a unit of energy, the amount gained by an electron when accelerated through a potential difference of one volt.

electroplate /ɪˈlektrəʊˌpleɪt/ —*v.* (-ting) coat with a thin layer of chromium, silver, etc, by electrolysis. —*n.* electroplated articles.

electroscope /ɪˈlektrəˌskəʊp/ *n.* instrument for detecting and measuring electricity, esp. as an indication of the ionization of air by radioactivity. □ **electroscopic** /-ˈskɒpɪk/ *adj.*

electro-shock /ɪˌlektrəʊˈʃɒk/ *attrib. adj.* (of therapy) by means of electric shocks.

electrostatics /ɪˌlektrəʊˈstætɪks/ *n.pl.* (treated as *sing.*) the study of electricity at rest.

electrotechnology /ɪˌlektrəʊtek-'nɒlədʒɪ/ *n.* science of the application of electricity in technology.

electrotherapy /ɪˌlektrəʊˈθerəpɪ/ *n.* treatment of diseases by use of electricity.

elegant /ˈelɪɡənt/ *adj.* **1** tasteful, refined, graceful. **2** ingeniously simple. □ **elegance** *n.* **elegantly** *adv.* [Latin: related to ELECT]

elegiac /elɪˈdʒaɪək/ —*adj.* **1** used for elegies. **2** mournful. —*n.* (in *pl.*) elegiac verses. □ **elegiacally** *adv.*

elegy /ˈelɪdʒɪ/ *n.* (*pl.* -**ies**) **1** sorrowful poem or song, esp. for the dead. **2** poem in elegiac metre. [Latin from Greek]

element /ˈelɪmənt/ *n.* **1** component part; contributing factor. **2** any of the substances that cannot be resolved by chemical means into simpler substances. **3 a** any of the four substances (earth, water, air, and fire) in ancient and medieval philosophy. **b** a being's

natural abode or environment. **4** *Electr.* wire that heats up in an electric heater, kettle, etc. **5** (in *pl.*) atmospheric agencies, esp. wind and storm. **6** (in *pl.*) rudiments of learning or of an art etc. **7** (in *pl.*) bread and wine of the Eucharist. □ **in one's element** in one's preferred situation, doing what one does well and enjoys. [French from Latin]

elemental /elɪˈment(ə)l/ *adj.* **1** of or like the elements or the forces of nature; powerful. **2** essential, basic.

elementary /elɪˈmentərɪ/ *adj.* **1** dealing with the simplest facts of a subject. **2** unanalysable.

elementary particle *n. Physics* subatomic particle, esp. one not known to consist of simpler ones.

elephant /ˈelɪf(ə)nt/ *n.* (*pl.* same or **-s**) largest living land animal, with a trunk and ivory tusks. [Greek *elephas*]

elephantiasis /ˌelɪfənˈtaɪəsɪs/ *n.* skin disease causing gross enlargement of limbs etc.

elephantine /ˌelɪˈfæntaɪn/ *adj.* **1** of elephants. **2 a** huge. **b** clumsy.

elevate /ˈelɪˌveɪt/ *v.* (-ting) **1** raise, lift up. **2** exalt in rank etc. **3** (usu. as **elevated** *adj.*) raise morally or intellectually. [Latin *levo* lift]

elevation /elɪˈveɪʃ(ə)n/ *n.* **1 a** elevating or being elevated. **b** angle with the horizontal. **c** height above sea level etc. **d** high position. **2** drawing or diagram showing one side of a building.

elevator *n.* **1** *US* lift. **2** movable part of a tailplane for changing an aircraft's altitude. **3** hoisting machine.

eleven /ɪˈlev(ə)n/ *adj.* & *n.* **1** one more than ten. **2** symbol for this (11, xi, XI). **3** size etc. denoted by eleven. **4** team of eleven players at cricket, football, etc. **5** eleven o'clock. [Old English]

elevenfold *adj.* & *adv.* **1** eleven times as much or as many. **2** consisting of eleven parts.

eleven-plus *n.* esp. *hist.* examination taken at age 11–12 to determine the type of secondary school a child would enter.

elevenses /ɪˈlevənzɪz/ *n. colloq.* light refreshment taken at about 11 a.m.

eleventh *adj.* & *n.* **1** next after tenth. **2** each of eleven equal parts of a thing. □ **eleventh hour** last possible moment.

elf *n.* (*pl.* **elves** /elvz/) mythological being, esp. one that is small and mischievous. □ **elfish** *adj.* **elvish** *adj.* [Old English]

elfin *adj.* of elves; elflike.

elicit /ɪˈlɪsɪt/ *v.* (-**t**-) draw out (facts, a response, etc.), esp. with difficulty. [Latin *elicio*]

elide /ɪˈlaɪd/ v. (**-ding**) omit (a vowel or syllable) in pronunciation. [Latin *elis* crush out]

eligible /ˈelɪdʒɪb(ə)l/ adj. **1** (often foll. by *for*) fit or entitled to be chosen (*eligible for a rebate*). **2** desirable or suitable, esp. for marriage. □ **eligibility** /-ˈbɪlɪtɪ/ n. [Latin related to ELECT]

eliminate /ɪˈlɪmɪˌneɪt/ v. (**-ting**) **1** remove, get rid of. **2** exclude from consideration. **3** exclude from a further stage of a competition through defeat etc. □ **elimination** /-ˈneɪʃ(ə)n/ n. **eliminator** n. [Latin *limen limin-* threshold]

elision /ɪˈlɪʒ(ə)n/ n. omission of a vowel or syllable in pronunciation (e.g. in *we'll*). [Latin: related to ELIDE]

elite /eɪˈliːt/ n. **1** (prec. by *the*) the best (of a group). **2** select group or class. **3** a size of letters in typewriting (12 per inch). [French: related to ELECT]

elitism n. recourse to or advocacy of leadership or dominance by a select group. □ **elitist** n. & adj.

elixir /ɪˈlɪksə(r)/ n. **1 a** alchemist's preparation supposedly able to change metals into gold or (in full **elixir of life**) to prolong life indefinitely. **b** remedy for all ills. **2** aromatic medicinal drug. [Latin from Arabic]

Elizabethan /ɪˌlɪzəˈbiːθ(ə)n/ —adj. of the time of Queen Elizabeth I or II. —n. person of this time.

elk n. (pl. same or **-s**) large deer of northern parts of Europe, N. America, and Asia. [Old English]

ell n. hist. measure = 45 in. [Old English, = forearm]

ellipse /ɪˈlɪps/ n. regular oval, resulting when a cone is cut obliquely by a plane. [Greek *ellipsis* deficit]

ellipsis /ɪˈlɪpsɪs/ n. (pl. **ellipses** /-siːz/) **1** omission of words needed to complete a construction or sense. **2** set of three dots etc. indicating omission.

ellipsoid /ɪˈlɪpsɔɪd/ n. solid of which all the plane sections through one axis are circles and all the other plane sections are ellipses.

elliptic /ɪˈlɪptɪk/ adj. (also **elliptical**) of or in the form of an ellipse. □ **elliptically** adv.

elm n. **1** tree with rough serrated leaves. **2** its wood. [Old English]

elocution /ˌeləˈkjuːʃ(ə)n/ n. art of clear and expressive speech. [Latin *loquor* speak]

elongate /ˈiːlɒŋˌgeɪt/ v. (**-ting**) lengthen, extend. □ **elongation** /-ˈgeɪʃ(ə)n/ n. [Latin *longus* long]

elope /ɪˈləʊp/ v. (**-ping**) run away to marry secretly. □ **elopement** n. [Anglo-French]

eloquence /ˈeləkwəns/ n. fluent and effective use of language. [Latin *loquor* speak]

eloquent adj. **1** having eloquence. **2** (often foll. by *of*) expressive. □ **eloquently** adv.

else adv. **1** (prec. by indefinite or interrog. pron.) besides (*someone else, nowhere else, who else?*). **2** instead (*what else could I say?*). **3** otherwise; if not (*run, (or) else you will be late*). □ **or else** see OR¹. [Old English]

elsewhere adv. in or to some other place.

elucidate /ɪˈluːsɪˌdeɪt/ v. (**-ting**) throw light on; explain. □ **elucidation** /-ˈdeɪʃ(ə)n/ n. **elucidatory** adj. [Latin: related to LUCID]

elude /ɪˈluːd/ v. (**-ding**) **1** escape adroitly from (danger, pursuit, etc.). **2** avoid compliance with (a law etc.) or fulfilment of (an obligation). **3** baffle (a person or memory etc.). □ **elusion** /-ʒ(ə)n/ n. [Latin *ludo* play]

elusive /ɪˈluːsɪv/ adj. **1** difficult to find or catch. **2** difficult to remember. **3** avoiding the point raised. □ **elusiveness** n.

elves pl. of ELF.

elvish see ELF.

Elysium /ɪˈlɪzɪəm/ n. **1** (also **Elysian Fields**) (in Greek mythology) abode of the blessed after death. **2** place of ideal happiness. □ **Elysian** adj. [Latin from Greek]

em n. *Printing* unit of measurement equal to the width of an M. [name of the letter M]

em-¹² see EN-¹².

'em /əm/ pron. colloq. them.

emaciate /ɪˈmeɪsɪˌeɪt/ v. (**-ting**) (esp. as **emaciated** adj.) make abnormally thin or feeble. □ **emaciation** /-ˈeɪʃ(ə)n/ n. [Latin *macies* leanness]

email /ˈiːmeɪl/ n. (also **e-mail**) = ELECTRONIC MAIL.

emanate /ˈeməˌneɪt/ v. (**-ting**) (usu. foll. by *from*) issue or originate (from a source). □ **emanation** /-ˈneɪʃ(ə)n/ n. [Latin *mano* flow]

emancipate /ɪˈmænsɪˌpeɪt/ v. (**-ting**) **1** free from social or political restraint. **2** (usu. as **emancipated** adj.) free from the inhibitions of moral or social conventions. **3** free from slavery. □ **emancipation** /-ˈpeɪʃ(ə)n/ n. **emancipatory** /-ˈpeɪt(ə)rɪ/ adj. [Latin, = free from possession, from *manus* hand, *capio* take]

emasculate —v. /ɪˈmæskjʊˌleɪt/ (**-ting**) **1** deprive of force or vigour. **2** castrate. —adj. /ɪˈmæskjʊlət/ **1** deprived of force.

castration. 3 effeminate. □ **emasculation** /-'leɪʃ(ə)n/ n. [Latin: related to MALE]

embalm /ɪm'bɑːm/ v. 1 preserve (a corpse) from decay. 2 preserve from oblivion. 3 make fragrant. □ **embalmment** n. [French: related to BALM]

embankment /ɪm'bæŋkmənt/ n. bank constructed to keep back water or carry a road, railway, etc.

embargo /ɪm'bɑːgəʊ/ –n. (pl. -es) 1 order forbidding foreign ships to enter, or any ships to leave, a country's ports. 2 official suspension of an activity. –v. (-es, -ed) place under embargo. [Spanish: related to BAR¹]

embark /ɪm'bɑːk/ v. 1 (often foll. by for) put or go on board a ship or aircraft (for a destination). 2 (foll. by on, in) begin an enterprise. □ **embarkation** /ˌembɑː'keɪʃ(ə)n/ n. (in sense 1). [French: related to BARQUE]

embarrass /ɪm'bærəs/ v. 1 make (a person) feel awkward or ashamed. 2 (as **embarrassed** adj.) encumbered with debts. 3 encumber. □ **embarrassment** n. [Italian imbarrare bar in]

embassy /'embəsɪ/ n. (pl. -ies) 1 a residence or offices of an ambassador. b ambassador and staff. 2 deputation to a foreign government. [French: related to AMBASSADOR]

embattled /ɪm'bæt(ə)ld/ adj. 1 prepared or arrayed for battle. 2 fortified with battlements. 3 under heavy attack or in trying circumstances.

embed /ɪm'bed/ v. (also **imbed**) (-dd-) (esp. as **embedded** adj.) fix firmly in a surrounding mass.

embellish /ɪm'belɪʃ/ v. 1 beautify, adorn. 2 enhance with fictitious additions. □ **embellishment** n. [French bel, BEAU]

ember n. (usu. in pl.) small piece of glowing coal etc. in a dying fire. [Old English]

ember days n.pl. days of fasting and prayer in the Christian Church, associated with ordinations. [Old English]

embezzle /ɪm'bez(ə)l/ v. (-ling) divert (money etc.) fraudulently to one's own use. □ **embezzlement** n. **embezzler** n. [Anglo-French]

embitter /ɪm'bɪtə(r)/ v. arouse bitter feelings in. □ **embitterment** n.

emblazon /ɪm'bleɪz(ə)n/ v. 1 portray or adorn conspicuously. 2 adorn (a heraldic shield). □ **emblazonment** n.

emblem /'embləm/ n. 1 symbol. 2 (foll. by of) type, embodiment (the very emblem of courage). 3 heraldic or representative device. □ **emblematic** /-'mætɪk/ adj. [Greek, = insertion]

embody /ɪm'bɒdɪ/ v. (-ies, -ied) 1 make (an idea etc.) actual or discernible. 2 (of a thing) be a tangible expression of. 3 include, comprise. □ **embodiment** n.

embolden /ɪm'bəʊld(ə)n/ v. make bold; encourage.

embolism /'embəˌlɪz(ə)m/ n. obstruction of an artery by a clot, air-bubble, etc. [Latin from Greek]

embolus /'embələs/ n. (pl. -li /-lɪ /-ˌlaɪ/) object causing an embolism.

emboss /ɪm'bɒs/ v. carve or decorate with a design in relief. □ **embossment** n. [related to BOSS²]

embouchure /ˌɒmbuːˈʃʊə(r)/ n. way of applying the mouth to the mouthpiece of a musical instrument. [French: related to EN-¹, bouche mouth]

embrace /ɪm'breɪs/ –v. (-cing) 1 a hold closely in the arms. b (absol., of two people) embrace each other. 2 clasp, enclose. 3 accept eagerly (an offer etc.). 4 adopt (a cause, idea, etc.). 5 include, comprise. 6 take in with the eye or mind. –n. act of embracing, clasp. □ **embraceable** adj. [Latin: related to BRACE]

embrasure /ɪm'breɪʒə(r)/ n. 1 bevelling of a wall at the sides of a window etc. 2 opening in a parapet for a gun etc. b splay. [French embraser splay]

embrocation /ˌembrə'keɪʃ(ə)n/ n. liquid for rubbing on the body to relieve muscular pain. [Greek embrokhē lotion]

embroider /ɪm'brɔɪdə(r)/ v. 1 decorate (cloth etc.) with needlework. 2 embellish (a narrative). □ **embroiderer** n. [Anglo-French from Germanic]

embroidery n. (pl. -ies) 1 art of embroidering. 2 embroidered work. 3 inessential ornament. 4 fictitious additions (to a story etc.).

embroil /ɪm'brɔɪl/ v. (often foll. by with) involve (a person etc.) in a conflict or difficulties. □ **embroilment** n. [French brouiller mix]

embryo /'embrɪəʊ/ n. (pl. -s) 1 a unborn or unhatched offspring. b human offspring in the first eight weeks from conception. 2 rudimentary plant in a seed. 3 thing in a rudimentary stage. 4 (attrib.) undeveloped, immature. □ **in embryo** undeveloped. □ **embryonic** /ˌembrɪ'ɒnɪk/ adj. [Greek bruō grow]

embryology /ˌembrɪ'ɒlədʒɪ/ n. the study of embryos.

emend /ɪ'mend/ v. edit (a text etc.) to make corrections. □ **emendation** /ˌiːmen'deɪʃ(ə)n/ n. [Latin menda fault]

■ **Usage** See note at **amend**.

emerald /'emər(ə)ld/ –n. 1 bright-green gem. 2 colour of this. –adj. bright green. [Greek smaragdos]

emerald green *adj.* & *n.* (as adj. often hyphenated) bright green.

Emerald Isle *n.* Ireland.

emerge /ɪˈmɜːdʒ/ *v.* (**-ging**) 1 come up or out into view. 2 (of facts etc.) become known, be revealed. 3 become recognized or prominent. 4 (of a question, difficulty, etc.) become apparent. □ **emergence** *n.* **emergent** *adj.* [Latin: related to MERGE]

emergency /ɪˈmɜːdʒənsɪ/ *n.* (*pl.* **-ies**) 1 sudden state of danger etc., requiring immediate action. 2 a condition requiring immediate treatment. b patient with this. 3 (*attrib.*) for use in an emergency. [medieval Latin: related to EMERGE]

emeritus /ɪˈmerɪtəs/ *adj.* retired but retaining one's title as an honour (*emeritus professor*). [Latin *mereor* earn]

emery /ˈemərɪ/ *n.* coarse corundum for polishing metal etc. [Greek *smēris* polishing powder]

emery-board *n.* emery-coated nail-file.

emetic /ɪˈmetɪk/ —*adj.* that causes vomiting. —*n.* emetic medicine. [Greek *emeō* vomit]

emf *abbr.* (also **e.m.f.**) electromotive force.

emigrant /ˈemɪɡrənt/ —*n.* person who emigrates. —*adj.* emigrating.

emigrate /ˈemɪɡreɪt/ *v.* (**-ting**) leave one's own country to settle in another. □ **emigration** /-ˈɡreɪʃ(ə)n/ *n.* [Latin: related to MIGRATE]

émigré /ˈemɪˌɡreɪ/ *n.* emigrant, esp. a political exile. [French]

eminence /ˈemɪnəns/ *n.* 1 distinction; recognized superiority. 2 piece of rising ground. 3 title used in addressing or referring to a cardinal (*Your Eminence*; *His Eminence*). [Latin: related to EMINENT]

éminence grise /ˌemɪnɑːs ˈɡriːz/ *n.* (*pl.* *éminences grises* pronunc. same) person who exercises power or influence without holding office. [French, = grey cardinal (orig. of Richelieu's secretary)]

eminent /ˈemɪnənt/ *adj.* distinguished, notable, outstanding. [Latin *emineo* jut out]

emir /eˈmɪə(r)/ *n.* (also **amir** /əˈmɪə(r)/) title of various Muslim rulers. [French: from Arabic '*amīr*']

emirate /ˈemɪrət/ *n.* rank, domain, or reign of an emir.

emissary /ˈemɪsərɪ/ *n.* (*pl.* **-ies**) person sent on a diplomatic mission. [Latin: related to EMIT]

emit /ɪˈmɪt/ *v.* (**-tt-**) give or send out (heat, light, a smell, sound, etc.); discharge. □ **emission** /-ˈʃ(ə)n/ *n.* [Latin *emitto emiss-*]

emollient /ɪˈmɒlɪənt/ —*adj.* that softens or soothes the skin, feelings, etc. —*n.* emollient substance. [Latin *mollis* soft]

emolument /ɪˈmɒljʊmənt/ *n.* fee from employment, salary. [Latin]

emote /ɪˈməʊt/ *v.* (**-ting**) show excessive emotion.

emotion /ɪˈməʊʃ(ə)n/ *n.* 1 strong instinctive feeling such as love or fear. 2 emotional intensity or sensibility (*spoke with emotion*). [Latin: related to MOTION]

emotional *adj.* 1 of or expressing emotions. 2 especially liable to emotion. 3 arousing emotion. □ **emotionalism** *n.* **emotionally** *adv.*

■ **Usage** See note at *emotive*.

emotive /ɪˈməʊtɪv/ *adj.* 1 arousing emotion. 2 of emotion. [Latin: related to MOTION]

■ **Usage** Although the senses of *emotive* and *emotional* overlap, *emotive* is more common in the sense 'arousing emotion', as in *an emotive issue*, and is not used at all in sense 2 of *emotional*.

empanel /ɪmˈpæn(ə)l/ *v.* (also **impanel**) (**-ll-**; *US* **-l-**) enter (a jury) on a panel.

empathize /ˈempəˌθaɪz/ *v.* (also **-ise**) (**-zing** or **-sing**) (usu. foll. by *with*) exercise empathy.

empathy /ˈempəθɪ/ *n.* ability to identify with a person or object. □ **empathetic** /-ˈθetɪk/ *adj.* [as PATHOS]

emperor /ˈempərə(r)/ *n.* sovereign of an empire. [Latin *impero* command]

emperor penguin *n.* largest known penguin.

emphasis /ˈemfəsɪs/ *n.* (*pl.* **emphases** /-ˌsiːz/) 1 importance or prominence attached to a thing (*emphasis on economy*). 2 stress laid on a word or syllable to make the meaning clear or to show importance, feeling, etc. 3 vigour or intensity of expression, feeling, etc. [Latin from Greek]

emphasize /ˈemfəˌsaɪz/ *v.* (also **-ise**) (**-zing** or **-sing**) put emphasis on, stress.

emphatic /ɪmˈfætɪk/ *adj.* 1 forcibly expressive. 2 of words: a bearing the stress. b used to give emphasis. □ **emphatically** *adv.*

emphysema /ˌemfɪˈsiːmə/ *n.* disease of the lungs causing breathlessness. [Greek *emphusaō* puff up]

empire /ˈempaɪə(r)/ *n.* 1 large group of States or countries under a single authority. 2 supreme dominion. 3 large commercial organization etc. owned or directed by one person. 4 (**the Empire**) *hist.* the British Empire. [Latin *imperium* cor inion]

empire-building

empire-building n. purposeful accumulation of territory, authority, etc.

empirical /ɪm'pɪrɪk(ə)l/ adj. (also **empiric**) based on observation, experience, or experiment, not on theory. □ **empirically** adv. **empiricism** /-sɪz(ə)m/ n. **empiricist** /-sɪst/ n. [Greek empeiria experience]

emplacement /ɪm'pleɪsmənt/ n. 1 putting in position. 2 platform for guns. [French: related to PLACE]

employ /ɪm'plɔɪ/ -v. 1 use the services of (a person) in return for payment. 2 use (a thing, time, energy, etc.) to good effect. 3 keep (a person) occupied. -n. (in phr. **in the employ of**) employed by. □ **employable** adj. **employer** n. [Latin implicor be involved]

employee /emplɔɪ'iː/ n. person employed.

employment n. 1 employing or being employed. 2 person's trade or profession.

employment office n. (formerly **employment exchange**) government office finding work for the unemployed.

emporium /em'pɔːrɪəm/ n. (pl. -s or **-ria**) 1 large shop or store. 2 centre of commerce, market. [Greek emporos merchant]

empower /ɪm'paʊə(r)/ v. give authority to.

empress /'emprɪs/ n. 1 wife or widow of an emperor. 2 woman emperor. [French: related to EMPEROR]

empty /'emptɪ/ -adj. (-ier, -iest) 1 containing nothing. 2 (of a house etc.) unoccupied or unfurnished. 3 (of a vehicle etc.) without passengers etc. 4 a hollow, insincere (empty threats). b without purpose (an empty existence). c vacuous (an empty head). 5 colloq. hungry. -v. (-ies, -ied) 1 remove the contents of. 2 (often foll. by into) transfer (contents). 3 become empty. 4 (of a river) discharge itself. -n. (pl. -ies) colloq. empty bottle etc. □ **emptiness** n. [Old English]

empty-handed adj. (usu. predic.) 1 bringing or taking nothing. 2 having achieved nothing.

empty-headed adj. foolish; lacking sense.

empyrean /empaɪ'riːən/ -n. the highest heaven, as the sphere of fire or abode of God. -adj. of the empyrean. □ **empyreal** adj. [Greek pur fire]

EMS abbr. European Monetary System.

EMU /iːem'juː, 'iːmjuː/ abbr. economic and monetary union; European monetary union.

emu /'iːmjuː/ n. (pl. -s) large flightless Australian bird. [Portuguese]

emulate /'emjʊleɪt/ v. (-ting) 1 try to equal or excel. 2 imitate. □ **emulation** /-'leɪʃ(ə)n/ n. **emulative** /-lətɪv/ adj. **emulator** n. [Latin aemulus rival]

emulsify /ɪ'mʌlsɪfaɪ/ v. (-ies, -ied) convert into an emulsion. □ **emulsification** /-fɪ'keɪʃ(ə)n/ n. **emulsifier** n.

emulsion /ɪ'mʌlʃ(ə)n/ n. 1 fine dispersion of one liquid in another, esp. as paint, medicine, etc. 2 mixture for coating photographic plate or film. 3 emulsion paint. [Latin mulgeo milk]

emulsion paint n. water-thinned paint.

en n. Printing unit of measurement equal to half an em. (name of the letter N]

en-¹ prefix (also **em-** before b, p) forming verbs, = IN-². 1 from nouns, meaning 'put into or on' (engulf; entrust; embed). 2 from nouns or adjectives, meaning 'bring into the condition of' (enslave), often with the suffix -en (enlighten). 3 from verbs: a in the sense 'in, into, on' (enfold). b as an intensifier (entangle). [French en-, Latin in-]

en-² prefix (also **em-** before b, p) in inside (energy; enthusiasm). [Greek]

-en suffix forming verbs: 1 from adjectives, usu. meaning 'make or become so or more so' (deepen; moisten). 2 from nouns (happen; strengthen). [Old English]

enable /ɪ'neɪb(ə)l/ v. (-ling) 1 (foll. by to + infin.) give (a person etc.) the means or authority. 2 make possible. 3 esp. Computing make (a device) operational; switch on.

enact /ɪ'nækt/ v. 1 a ordain, decree. b make (a bill etc.) law. 2 play (a part on stage or in life). □ **enactive** adj.

enactment n. 1 law enacted. 2 process of enacting.

enamel /ɪ'næm(ə)l/ -n. 1 glasslike opaque ornamental or preservative coating on metal etc. 2 a smooth hard coating. b a kind of hard gloss paint. c cosmetic simulating this, esp. nail varnish. 4 hard coating of a tooth. 4 painting done in enamel. -v. (-ll-; US -l-) inlay, coat, or portray with enamel. [Anglo-French from Germanic]

enamour /ɪ'næmə(r)/ v. (US **enamor**) (usu. in passive; foll. by of) inspire with love or delight. [French amour love]

en bloc /ɑ̃ 'blɒk/ adv. in a block; all at the same time. [French]

encamp /ɪn'kæmp/ v. settle in a (esp. military) camp. □ **encampment** n.

encapsulate /ɪn'kæpsjʊleɪt/ v. 1 enclose in or as in a capsule. 2 express briefly, summarize. □ **encapsulation** /-'leɪʃ(ə)n/ n. [related to CAPSULE]

encase /ɪn'keɪs/ v. (-sing) enclose in or as in a case. □ **encasement** n.

encaustic /ɪnˈkɔːstɪk/ —*adj.* (of painting etc.) using pigments mixed with hot wax, which are burned in as an inlay. —*n.* 1 art of encaustic painting. 2 product of this. [Greek: related to CAUSTIC]

-ence *suffix* forming nouns expressing: 1 a quality or state or an instance of this (*patience; an impertinence*). 2 an action (*reference*). [French -*ence*, Latin -*entia*]

encephalogram /enˈsefələgram/ *n.* = ELECTROENCEPHALOGRAM.

encephalograph /enˈsefələgrɑːf/ *n.* = ELECTROENCEPHALOGRAPH.

enchant /ɪnˈtʃɑːnt/ *v.* 1 charm, delight. 2 bewitch. □ **enchanted** *adj.* **enchanting** *adj.* **enchantingly** *adv.* [French *enchanter*, Latin *incanto*]

enchanter *n.* (*fem.* **enchantress**) person who enchants, esp. by using magic. □ **enchantment** *n.*

encircle /ɪnˈsɜːk(ə)l/ *v.* (-**ling**) 1 surround. 2 form a circle round. □ **encirclement** *n.*

enclave /ˈenkleɪv/ *n.* territory of one State surrounded by that of another. [Latin *clavis* key]

enclose /ɪnˈkləʊz/ *v.* (-**sing**) 1 a surround with a wall, fence, etc. **b** shut in. 2 put in a receptacle (esp. in an envelope with a letter). 3 (usu. as **enclosed** *adj.*) secude (a religious community) from the outside world. [Latin: related to INCLUDE]

enclosure /ɪnˈkləʊʒə(r)/ *n.* 1 act of enclosing. 2 enclosed space or area, esp. at a sporting event. 3 thing enclosed with a letter. [French: related to ENCLOSE]

encode /ɪnˈkəʊd/ *v.* (-**ding**) put into code.

encomium /enˈkəʊmɪəm/ *n.* (*pl.* -**s**) formal or high-flown praise. [Greek *kōmos* revelry]

encompass /ɪnˈkʌmpəs/ *v.* 1 contain; include. 2 surround.

encore /ˈɒŋkɔː(r)/ —*n.* 1 audience's demand for the repetition of an item, or for a further item. 2 such an item. —*v.* (-**ring**) 1 call for the repetition of (an item). 2 call back (a performer) for this. —*int.* /also ˈkɔː(r)/ again, once more. [French, = once again]

encounter /ɪnˈkaʊntə(r)/ —*v.* 1 meet unexpectedly. 2 meet as an adversary. —*n.* meeting by chance or in conflict. [Latin *contra* against]

encourage /ɪnˈkʌrɪdʒ/ *v.* (-**ging**) 1 give courage or confidence to. 2 urge. 3 promote. □ **encouragement** *n.*

encroach /ɪnˈkrəʊtʃ/ *v.* 1 (foll. by *on*, *upon*) intrude on another's territory etc.

2 advance gradually beyond due limits. □ **encroachment** *n.* [French *croc* crook]

encrust /ɪnˈkrʌst/ *v.* 1 cover with or form a crust. 2 coat with a hard casing or deposit, sometimes for decoration. [French: related to EN-[1]]

encumber /ɪnˈkʌmbə(r)/ *v.* 1 be a burden to. 2 hamper. [French from Romanic]

encumbrance /ɪnˈkʌmbrəns/ *n.* 1 burden. 2 impediment.

-ency *suffix* forming nouns denoting quality or state (*efficiency; fluency; presidency*). [Latin -*entia*]

encyclical /ɪnˈsɪklɪk(ə)l/ —*adj.* for wide circulation. —*n.* papal encyclical letter. [Greek: related to CYCLE]

encyclopedia /ɪnˌsaɪkləˈpiːdɪə/ *n.* (also **-paedia**) book, often in a number of volumes, giving information on many subjects, or on many aspects of one subject. [Greek *egk-uklios* all-round, *paideia* education]

encyclopedic *adj.* (also **-paedic**) (of knowledge or information) comprehensive.

end —*n.* 1 a extreme limit. **b** extremity (*to the ends of the earth*). 2 extreme part or surface of a thing (*strip of wood with a nail in one end*). 3 a finish (*no end to*). **b** latter part. **c** death, destruction (*met an untimely end*). **d** result. 4 goal (*will do anything to achieve his ends*). 5 remnant (*cigarette-end*). 6 (prec. by *the*) colloq. the limit of endurability. 7 half of a sports pitch etc. occupied by one team or player. 8 part with which a person is concerned (*no problem at my end*). —*v.* 1 bring or come to an end, finish. 2 (foll. by *in*) result. □ **end it all** (or **end it**) *colloq.* commit suicide. **end on** with the end facing one, or adjoining the end of the next object. **end to end** with the end of one adjoining the end of the next in a series. **end up** reach a specified state or action eventually (*ended up a drunkard; ended up making a fortune*). **in the end** finally. **keep one's end up** do one's part despite difficulties. **make ends meet** live within one's income. **no end** *colloq.* to a great extent. **no end of** *colloq.* much or many of. **on end** 1 upright (*hair stood on end*). 2 continuously (*for three weeks on end*). **put an end to** stop, abolish. [Old English]

endanger /ɪnˈdeɪndʒə(r)/ *v.* place in danger.

endangered species *n.* species in danger of extinction.

endear /ɪnˈdɪə(r)/ *v.* (usu. foll. by *to*) make dear. □ **endearing** *adj.*

endearment *n.* **1** an expression of affection. **2** liking, affection.

endeavour /ɪn'devər/ (/US/ **endeavor**) —*v.* (foll. by *to* + infin.) try earnestly. —*n.* earnest attempt. [from EN-¹, French *devoir* owe]

endemic /en'demɪk/ *adj.* (often foll. by *to*) regularly or only found among a particular people or in a particular region. □ **endemically** *adv.* [Greek *en-* in, *dēmos* the people]

ending *n.* **1** end or final part, esp. of a story. **2** inflected final part of a word.

endive /'endaɪv/ *n.* curly-leaved plant used in salads. [Greek *entubon*]

endless *adj.* **1** infinite; without end. **2** continual (*endless complaints*). **3** *colloq.* innumerable. **4** (of a belt, chain, etc.) having the ends joined for continuous action over wheels etc. □ **endlessly** *adv.* [Old English: related to END]

endmost *adj.* nearest the end.

endo- *comb. form* internal. [Greek *endon* within]

endocrine /'endəʊ,kraɪn/ *adj.* (of a gland) secreting directly into the blood. [Greek *krinō* sift]

endogenous /en'bdʒɪnəs/ *adj.* growing or originating from within.

endometrium /,endəʊ'miːtrɪəm/ *n.* membrane lining the womb. [Greek *mētra* womb]

endomorph /'endəʊ,mɔːf/ *n.* person with a soft round body. [Greek *morphē* form]

endorse /ɪn'dɔːs/ *v.* (also **indorse**) (**-sing**) **1** approve. **2** sign or write on (a document), esp. sign the back of (a cheque). **3** enter details of a conviction for an offence on (a driving-licence). □ **endorsement** *n.* [Latin *dorsum* back]

endoscope /'endəʊ,skəʊp/ *n.* instrument for viewing internal parts of the body.

endow /ɪn'daʊ/ *v.* **1** bequeath or give a permanent income to (a person, institution, etc.). **2** (esp. as **endowed** *adj.*) provide with talent, ability, etc. [Anglo-French: related to DOWER]

endowment *n.* **1** endowing. **2** endowed income. **3** (*attrib.*) denoting forms of life insurance with payment of a fixed sum on a specified date, or on the death of the insured person if earlier.

endowment mortgage *n.* mortgage linked to endowment insurance.

endpaper *n.* either of the blank leaves of paper at the beginning and end of a book.

end-product *n.* final product of manufacture etc.

endue /ɪn'djuː/ *v.* (also **indue**) (**-dues**, **-duing**) (foll. by *with*) provide (a

person) with (qualities etc.). [Latin *induo* put on clothes]

endurance /ɪn'djʊərəns/ *n.* **1** power of enduring. **2** ability to withstand prolonged strain. [French: related to EN-DURE]

endure /ɪn'djʊər/ *v.* (**-ring**) **1** undergo (a difficulty etc.). **2** tolerate. **3** last. [Latin *durus* hard]

endurable *adj.* that can be endured.

endways *adv.* (also **endwise**) **1** with end uppermost or foremost. **2** end to end.

enema /'enɪmə/ *n.* **1** introduction of fluid etc. into the rectum, esp. to flush out its contents. **2** fluid etc. used for this. [Greek *hiēmi* send]

enemy /'enəmɪ/ *n.* (*pl.* **-ies**) **1** person actively hostile to another. **2 a** (often *attrib.*) hostile nation or army. **b** member of this. **2** adversary or opponent (*enemy of progress*). [Latin: related to IN-², *amicus* friend]

energetic /,enə'dʒetɪk/ *adj.* full of energy, vigorous. □ **energetically** *adv.* [Greek: related to ENERGY]

energize /'enə,dʒaɪz/ *v.* (also **-ise**) (**-zing** or **-sing**) **1** give energy to. **2** provide (a device) with energy for operation.

energy /'enədʒɪ/ *n.* (*pl.* **-ies**) **1** capacity for activity, force, vigour. **2** capacity of matter or radiation to do work. [Greek *ergon* work]

enervate /'enə,veɪt/ *v.* (**-ting**) deprive of vigour or vitality. □ **enervation** /-'veɪʃ(ə)n/ *n.* [Latin: related to NERVE]

en famille /ā fæ'miː/ *adv.* in or with one's family. [French, = in family]

enfant terrible /ɑ̃fɑ̃ teˈriːbl/ *n.* (*pl.* **enfants terribles** pronunc. same) indiscreet or unruly person. [French, = terrible child]

enfeeble /ɪnˈfiːb(ə)l/ *v.* (**-ling**) make feeble. □ **enfeeblement** *n.*

enfilade /,enfɪˈleɪd/ —*n.* gunfire directed along a line from end to end. —*v.* (**-ding**) direct an enfilade at. [French: related to FILE¹]

enfold /ɪnˈfəʊld/ *v.* **1** (usu. foll. by *in*, *with*) wrap, envelop. **2** clasp, embrace.

enforce /ɪnˈfɔːs/ *v.* (**-cing**) **1** compel observance of (a law etc.). **2** (foll. by *on*) impose on a person's will, etc.) on. □ **enforceable** *adj.* **enforcement** *n.* **enforcer** *n.* [Latin: related to FORCE¹]

enfranchise /ɪnˈfræntʃaɪz/ *v.* (**-sing**) **1** give (a person) the right to vote. **2** give (a town) municipal rights, esp. representation in parliament. **3** *hist.* free (a slave etc.). □ **enfranchisement** /-ɪzmənt/ *n.* [French: related to FRANK]

engage /ɪnˈɡeɪdʒ/ *v.* (**-ging**) **1** employ or hire (a person). **2 a** (usu. in *passive*) occupy (*are you engaged tomorrow?*). **b** hold fast (a person's attention). **3** (usu.

in *passive*) bind by a promise, esp. of marriage. **4** arrange beforehand to occupy (a room, seat, etc.). **5 a** interlock (parts of a gear etc.). **b** (of a gear etc.) become interlocked. **6 a** come into battle with. **b** bring (troops) into battle with. **c** come into battle with (an enemy etc.). **7** take part (*engage in politics*). **8** (foll. by *that* + clause or *to* + infin.) undertake. [French: related to GAGE[1]]

engagement *n.* **1** pledged to marry. **2** of a person) occupied, busy. **3** (of a telephone line, toilet, etc.) in use.

engagement *n.* **1** engaging or being engaged. **2** appointment with another person. **3** betrothal. **4** battle.

engaging *adj.* attractive, charming. □ **engagingly** *adv.*

engender /in'dʒendə(r)/ *v.* give rise to; produce (a feeling etc.). [related to GENUS]

engine /'endʒin/ *n.* **1** mechanical contrivance of parts working together, esp. as a source of power (*steam engine*). **2 a** railway locomotive. **b** = FIRE-ENGINE. [Latin *ingenium* device]

engineer /endʒi'niə(r)/ *n.* **1** person skilled in a branch of engineering. **2** person who makes or is in charge of engines etc. (*ship's engineer*). **3** person who designs and constructs military works; soldier so trained. **4** contriver. —*v.* **1** contrive, bring about. **2** act as an engineer. **3** construct or manage as an engineer. [Medieval Latin: related to ENGINE]

engineering *n.* application of science to the design, building, and use of machines etc. (*civil engineering*).

English /'ɪŋglɪʃ/ —*adj.* of England or its people or language. —*n.* **1** language of England, now used in the UK, US, and most Commonwealth countries. **2** (prec. by *the*; treated as *pl.*) the people of England. [Old English]

Englishman *n.* (*fem.* **Englishwoman**) person who is English by birth or descent.

engorged /in'gɔːdʒd/ *adj.* **1** crammed full. **2** congested with fluid, esp. blood. [French: related to EN-[1], GORGE]

engraft /in'grɑːft/ *v.* (also **ingraft**) *Bot.* (usu. foll. by *into*, *on*) graft. **2** implant. **3** (usu. foll. by *into*) incorporate.

engrave /in'greɪv/ *v.* (-**ving**) **1** (often foll. by *on*) carve (a text or design) on a hard surface. **2** inscribe (a surface) thus. **3** (often foll. by *on*) impress deeply (on a person's memory). □ **engraver** *n.* [from GRAVE[3]]

engraving *n.* print made from an engraved plate.

tion of, occupy fully. **2** write out in larger letters or in legal form. □ **engrossment** *n.* [Anglo-French: related to EN-[1]]

engulf /in'gʌlf/ *v.* flow over and swamp; overwhelm. □ **engulfment** *n.*

enhance /in'hɑːns/ *v.* (-**cing**) intensify (qualities, powers, etc.); improve (something already good). □ **enhancement** *n.* [Anglo-French from Latin *altus* high]

enigma /i'nɪgmə/ *n.* **1** puzzling thing or person. **2** riddle or paradox. □ **enigmatic** /enɪg'mætɪk/ *adj.* **enigmatically** /enɪg'mætɪk-/ *adv.* [Latin from Greek]

enjoin /in'dʒɔɪn/ *v.* **1** command or order. **2** (often foll. by *on*) impose (an action). **3** (usu. foll. by *from*) *Law* prohibit by injunction (from doing a thing). [Latin *injungo* attach]

enjoy /in'dʒɔɪ/ *v.* **1** take pleasure in. **2** have the use or benefit of. **3** experience (*enjoy good health*). □ **enjoy oneself** experience pleasure. □ **enjoyment** *n.* [French]

enjoyable *adj.* pleasant. □ **enjoyably** *adv.*

enkephalin /en'kefəlɪn/ *n.* either of two morphine-like peptides in the brain thought to control levels of pain. [Greek *egkephalos* brain]

enkindle /in'kɪndl/ *v.* (-**ling**) cause to flare up, arouse.

enlarge /in'lɑːdʒ/ *v.* (-**ging**) **1** make or become larger or wider. **2** (often foll. by *on*, *upon*) describe in greater detail. **3** reproduce a photograph on a larger scale. □ **enlargement** *n.* [French: related to LARGE]

enlarger *n.* apparatus for enlarging photographs.

enlighten /in'laɪt(ə)n/ *v.* **1** (often foll. by *on*) inform (about a subject). **2** (as **enlightened** *adj.*) progressive.

enlightenment *n.* **1** enlightening or being enlightened. **2** (**the Enlightenment**) 18th-c. philosophy of reason and individualism.

enlist /in'lɪst/ *v.* **1** enrol in the armed services. **2** secure as a means of help or support. □ **enlistment** *n.*

enliven /in'laɪv(ə)n/ *v.* make lively or cheerful; brighten (a picture etc.); inspirit. □ **enlivenment** *n.*

en masse /ɑ̃ 'mæs/ *adv.* all together. [French]

enmesh /in'meʃ/ *v.* entangle in or as in a net.

enmity /'enmɪtɪ/ *n.* (*pl.* -**ies**) **1** state of being an enemy. **2** hostility. [Romanic: related to ENEMY]

ennoble /i'nəʊb(ə)l/ *v.* (-**ling**) **1** make noble. **2** make (a person) a noble. □

engross /in'grəʊs/ *v.* **1** absorb the atten-

ennui

emboblement n. [French: related to EN-¹]

ennui /ɒnwiː/ n. mental weariness from idleness or lack of interest; boredom. [French: related to ANNOY]

enormity /ɪˈnɔːmɪtɪ/ n. (pl. -ies) 1 monstrous wickedness; monstrous crime. 2 serious error. 3 great size. [Latin enor-mitas]

■ **Usage** Sense 3 is commonly found, but is regarded as incorrect by some people.

enormous /ɪˈnɔːməs/ adj. extremely large. □ **enormously** adv. [Latin enor-mis: related to NORM]

enough /ɪˈnʌf/ —adj. as much or as many as required (enough apples). —n. sufficient amount or quantity (we have enough). —adv. 1 adequately (warm enough). 2 fairly (sings well enough). 3 quite (you know well enough what I mean). □ **have had enough** of want no more of, be satiated with or tired of. **sure enough** as expected. [Old English]

en passant /ɑ̃ pæˈsɑ̃/ adv. in passing; casually (mentioned it en passant). [French, = in passing]

enprint /ˈenprɪnt/ n. standard-sized photograph. [enlarged print]

enquire /ɪnˈkwaɪə(r)/ v. (-ring) 1 seek information; ask; ask a question. 2 = INQUIRE. 3 (foll. by after, for) ask about (a person, a person's health, etc.). □ **enquirer** n. [Latin quaero quaesit-seek]

enquiry n. (pl. -ies) 1 act of asking or seeking information. 2 = INQUIRY.

enrage /ɪnˈreɪdʒ/ v. (-ging) make furious. [French: related to EN-¹]

enrapture /ɪnˈræptʃə(r)/ v. (-ring) delight intensely.

enrich /ɪnˈrɪtʃ/ v. 1 make rich or richer. 2 make more nutritive. 3 increase the strength, wealth, value, or contents of. □ **enrichment** n. [French: related to EN-¹]

enrol /ɪnˈrəʊl/ v. (US **enroll**) (-ll-) 1 enlist. 2 **a** write the name of (a person) on a list. **b** incorporate as a member. **c** enrol oneself, esp. for a course of study. □ **enrolment** n. [French: related to ROLL]

en route /ɑ̃ ˈruːt/ adv. on the way. [French]

ensconce /ɪnˈskɒns/ v. (-cing) (usu. refl. or in passive) establish or settle comfortably. [from sconce small fortification]

ensemble /ɒnˈsɒmb(ə)l/ n. 1 **a** thing viewed as the sum of its parts. **b** general effect of this. 2 set of clothes worn together. 3 group of performers working together. 4 Mus. concerted passage for an ensemble. [Latin simul at the same time]

enshrine /ɪnˈʃraɪn/ v. (-ning) 1 enclose in a shrine. 2 protect, make inviolable. □ **enshrinement** n.

enshroud /ɪnˈʃraʊd/ v. literary 1 cover with or as with a shroud. 2 obscure.

ensign /ˈensaɪn, -s(ə)n/ n. 1 banner or flag, esp. the military or naval flag of a nation. 2 standard-bearer. 3 **a** hist. lowest commissioned infantry officer. **b** US lowest commissioned naval officer. [French: related to INSIGNIA]

ensilage /ensɪlɪdʒ/ —n. = SILAGE. —v. (-ging) preserve (fodder) by ensilage. [French: related to SILO]

enslave /ɪnˈsleɪv/ v. (-ving) make (a person) a slave. □ **enslavement** n.

ensnare /ɪnˈsneə(r)/ v. (-ring) catch in or as in a snare. □ **ensnarement** n.

ensue /ɪnˈsjuː/ v. (-sues, -sued, -suing) happen later or as a result. [Latin sequor follow]

en suite /ɑ̃ ˈswiːt/ —adv. forming a single unit (bedroom with bathroom en suite). —adj. 1 forming a single unit (en suite bathroom). 2 with a bathroom attached (seven en suite bedrooms). [French, = in sequence]

ensure /ɪnˈʃʊə(r)/ v. (-ring) 1 make certain. 2 (usu. foll. by against) make safe (ensure against risks). □ **ensurer** n. [Anglo-French: related to ASSURE]

ENT abbr. related to ear, nose, and throat.

-ent suffix 1 forming adjectives denoting attribution of an action (consequent) or state (existent). 2 forming agent nouns (president). [Latin -ent- present participial stem of verbs]

entablature /ɪnˈtæblətʃə(r)/ n. upper part of a classical building supported by columns including an architrave, frieze, and cornice. [Italian: related to TABLE]

entail /ɪnˈteɪl/ —v. 1 necessitate or involve unavoidably (entails much effort). 2 Law bequeath (an estate) to a specified line of beneficiaries so that it cannot be sold or given away. —n. Law 1 entailed estate. 2 succession to such an estate. [related to TAIL²]

entangle /ɪnˈtæŋg(ə)l/ v. (-ling) 1 catch or hold fast in a snare, tangle, etc. 2 involve in difficulties. 3 complicate. □ **entanglement** n.

entente /ɒnˈtɒnt/ n. friendly understanding between States. [French]

entente cordiale n. entente, esp. between Britain and France from 1904.

enter v. 1 go or come in or into. 2 come on stage (also as a direction: enter Macbeth). 3 penetrate (bullet entered his arm). 4 write (name, details, etc.) in a list, book, etc. 5 register, record the

name of as a competitor (*entered for the long jump*). **6 a** become a member of (a society or profession). **b** enrol in a school etc. **7** make known; present for consideration (*enter a protest*). **8** record formally (*before a court of law etc.*). **9** (foll. by *into*) **a** engage in (conversation etc.). **b** subscribe to; bind oneself by (an agreement, contract, etc.). **c** form part of (a calculation, plan, etc.). **d** sympathize with (feelings). **10** (foll. by *on, upon*) **a** begin to deal with. **b** assume the functions of (an office) or possession of (property). [Latin *intra* within]

enteric /en'terik/ *adj.* of the intestines. □ **enteritis** /,entə'raitis/ *n.* [Greek *enteron* intestine]

enterprise /'entəpraiz/ *n.* **1** undertaking, esp. a challenging one. **2** readiness to engage in such undertakings. **3** business firm or venture. [Latin *prehendo* grasp]

enterprising *adj.* showing enterprise; resourceful, energetic. □ **enterprisingly** *adv.*

entertain /,entə'tein/ *v.* **1** occupy agreeably. **2 a** receive as a guest. **b** receive guests. **3** cherish, consider (an idea etc.). [Latin *teneo* hold]

entertainer *n.* person who entertains, esp. professionally.

entertaining *adj.* amusing, diverting. □ **entertainingly** *adv.*

entertainment *n.* **1** entertaining or being entertained. **2** thing that entertains; performance.

enthral /ɪn'θrɔːl/ *v.* (US **enthrall**) (**-ll-**) captivate, please greatly. □ **enthralment** *n.* [from EN-, THRALL]

enthrone /ɪn'θrəʊn/ *v.* (**-ning**) place on a throne, esp. ceremonially. □ **enthronement** *n.*

enthuse /ɪn'θjuːz/ *v.* (**-sing**) *colloq.* be or make enthusiastic.

enthusiasm /ɪn'θjuːzɪæz(ə)m/ *n.* **1** (often foll. by *for, about*) strong interest or admiration; great eagerness. **2** object of enthusiasm. [Greek *entheos* inspired by a god]

enthusiast *n.* person full of enthusiasm. [Church Latin: related to ENTHUSIASM]

enthusiastic /ɪn,θjuːzɪ'æstɪk/ *adj.* having enthusiasm. □ **enthusiastically** *adv.*

entice /ɪn'taɪs/ *v.* (**-cing**) attract by the offer of pleasure or reward. □ **enticement** *n.* enticing *adj.* **enticingly** *adv.* [French *enticier* probably from Romanic]

entire /ɪn'taɪə(r)/ *adj.* **1** whole, complete. **2** unbroken. **3** unqualified, absolute. **4** in one piece; continuous. [Latin: related to INTEGER]

entirely *adv.* **1** wholly. **2** solely.

entirety /ɪn'taɪərəti/ *n.* (*pl.* **-ies**) **1** completeness. **2** (usu. foll. by *of*) sum total. □ **in its entirety** in its complete form.

entitle /ɪn'taɪt(ə)l/ *v.* (**-ling**) **1** (usu. foll. by *to*) give (a person) a just claim or right. **2** give a title to. [Latin: related to TITLE]

entity /'entɪti/ *n.* (*pl.* **-ies**) **1** thing with distinct existence. **2** thing's existence in itself. [Latin *ens entis* being]

entomb /ɪn'tuːm/ *v.* **1** place in a tomb. **2** serve as a tomb for. □ **entombment** *n.* [French: related to TOMB]

entomology /,entə'mɒlədʒi/ *n.* the study of insects. □ **entomological** /-mə'lɒdʒɪk(ə)l/ *adj.* **entomologist** *n.* [Greek *entomon* insect]

entourage /'ɒntʊrɑːʒ/ *n.* people attending an important person. [French]

entr'acte /'ɒntrækt/ *n.* **1** interval between acts of a play. **2** music or dance performed during this. [French]

entrails /'entreɪlz/ *n.pl.* **1** bowels, intestines. **2** innermost parts of a thing. [Latin *inter* among]

entrance¹ /'entrəns/ *n.* **1** place for entering. **2** going or coming in. **3** right of admission. **4** coming of an actor on stage. **5** (in full **entrance fee**) admission fee. [French: related to ENTER]

entrance² /ɪn'trɑːns/ *v.* (**-cing**) **1** enchant, delight. **2** put into a trance. □ **entrancement** *n.* **entrancingly** *adv.*

entrant /'entrənt/ *n.* person who enters (an examination, profession, etc.).

entrap /ɪn'træp/ *v.* (**-pp-**) **1** catch in or as in a trap. **2** beguile. □ **entrapment** *n.* [related to EN-']

entreat /ɪn'triːt/ *v.* ask earnestly, beg. [related to EN-']

entreaty *n.* (*pl.* **-ies**) earnest request.

entrecôte /'ɒntrəkəʊt/ *n.* boned steak off the sirloin. [French, = between-rib]

entrée /'ɒntreɪ/ *n.* **1** dish served between the fish and meat courses. **2** US main dish. **3** right of admission. [French]

entrench /ɪn'trentʃ/ *v.* **1 a** establish firmly (in a position, office, etc.). **b** (as **entrenched** *adj.*) of an attitude etc. not easily modified. **2** surround with a trench as a fortification. □ **entrenchment** *n.*

entrepôt /'ɒntrəpəʊ/ *n.* warehouse for goods in transit. [French]

entrepreneur /,ɒntrəprə'nɜː(r)/ *n.* **1** person who undertakes a commercial venture. **2** contractor acting as an intermediary. □ **entrepreneurial** *adj.*

entrepreneurialism *n.* (also **entre-preneurism**). [French: related to ENTREPRENEUR]

entropy /'entrəpi/ *n.* **1** *Physics* measure of the disorganization or degradation of the universe, resulting in a decrease in available energy. **2** *Physics* measure of the unavailability of a system's thermal energy for conversion into mechanical work. [Greek: related to EN², *tropē* transformation]

entrust /ɪn'trʌst/ *v.* (also **intrust**) **1** (foll. by *to*) give (a person or thing) into the care of a person. **2** (foll. by *with*) assign responsibility for (a person or thing) to (a person) (*entrusted him with my camera*).

entry /'entri/ *n.* (*pl.* -**ies**) **1 a** going or coming in. **b** liberty to do this. **2** place of entrance, door, gate, etc. **3** passage between buildings. **4 a** item entered in a diary, list, etc. **b** recording of this. **5 a** person or thing competing in a race etc. **b** list of competitors. [Romanic: related to ENTER]

Entryphone *n. propr.* intercom at the entrance of a building or flat for callers to identify themselves.

entwine /ɪn'twaɪn/ *v.* (-**ning**) twine round, interweave.

E-number /'iːˌnʌmbə(r)/ *n.* E plus a number, the EC designation for food additives.

enumerate /ɪ'njuːməˌreɪt/ *v.* (-**ting**) **1** specify (items). **2** count. □ **enu-meration** /-'reɪʃ(ə)n/ *n.* **enumerative** /-rətɪv/ *adj.* [Latin: related to NUMBER]

enumerator *n.* person employed in census-taking.

enunciate /ɪ'nʌnsɪˌeɪt/ *v.* (-**ting**) **1** pronounce (words) clearly. **2** express in definite terms. □ **enunciation** /-'eɪʃ(ə)n/ *n.* [Latin *nuntio* announce]

enuresis /ˌenjʊə'riːsɪs/ *n.* involuntary urination. [Greek *enoureō* urinate in]

envelop /ɪn'veləp/ *v.* (-**p**-) **1** wrap up or cover completely. **2** completely surround. □ **envelopment** *n.* [French]

envelope /'envəˌləʊp/ *n.* **1** folded paper container for a letter etc. **2** wrapper, covering. **3** gas container of a balloon or airship.

enviable /'envɪəb(ə)l/ *adj.* likely to excite envy. □ **enviably** *adv.*

envious /'envɪəs/ *adj.* feeling or showing envy. □ **enviously** *adv.* [French: related to ENVY]

environment /ɪn'vaɪərənmənt/ *n.* **1** surroundings, esp. as affecting lives. **2** circumstances of living. **3** *Computing* overall structure within which a user, computer, or program operates. □ **environmental** /-'ment(ə)l/ *adj.*

environmentally /-'mentəlɪ/ *adv.* [French *environ* surroundings]

environmentalist /-'mentəlɪst/ *n.* person concerned with the protection of the natural environment. □ **environmental-ism** *n.*

environs /ɪn'vaɪərənz/ *n.pl.* district round a town etc.

envisage /ɪn'vɪzɪdʒ/ *v.* (-**ging**) **1** have a mental picture of (a thing not yet existing). **2** imagine as possible or desirable. [French *visage* face]

envoy /'envɔɪ/ *n.* **1** messenger or representative. **2** (in full **envoy extraordinary**) diplomatic agent ranking below ambassador. [French *envoyer* send, from Latin *via* way]

envy /'envi/ —*n.* (*pl.* -**ies**) **1** discontent aroused by another's better fortune etc. **2** object of this feeling. —*v.* (-**ies**, -**ied**) feel envy of (a person etc.). [Latin *invidia*, from *video* see]

enwrap /ɪn'ræp/ *v.* (-**pp**-) (often foll. by *in*) literary wrap, enfold.

enzyme /'enzaɪm/ *n.* protein catalyst of a specific biochemical reaction. [Greek *enzumos* leavened]

Eocene /'iːəʊˌsiːn/ *Geol.* —*adj.* of the second epoch of the Tertiary period. —*n.* this epoch. [Greek *ēōs* dawn, *kainos* new]

eolian harp *US* var. of AEOLIAN HARP.

eolithic /ˌiːə'lɪθɪk/ *adj.* of the period preceding the palaeolithic age. [Greek *ēōs* dawn, *lithos* stone]

eon var. of AEON.

EP *abbr.* extended-play (gramophone record).

epaulette /'epəˌlet/ *n.* (*US* **epaulet**) ornamental shoulder-piece on a coat etc., esp. on a uniform. [French *épaule* shoulder]

épée /eɪ'peɪ/ *n.* sharp-pointed sword, used (with the end blunted) in fencing. [French: related to SPATHE]

ephedrine /'efədrɪn/ *n.* alkaloid drug used to relieve asthma, etc. [*Ephedra*, genus of plants yielding it]

ephemera /ɪ'femərə/ *n.pl.* things of only short-lived relevance. [Latin: related to EPHEMERAL]

ephemeral /ɪ'femər(ə)l/ *adj.* lasting or of use for only a short time; transitory. [Greek: related to EPI, *hēmera* day]

epi- *prefix* **1** upon. **2** above. **3** in addition. [Greek]

epic /'epɪk/ —*n.* **1** long poem narrating the adventures or deeds of one or more heroic or legendary figures. **2** book or film based on an epic narrative. —*adj.* **1** of or like an epic, heroic. [Greek *epos* song]

epicene /ˈepɪsiːn/ —*adj.* 1 of, for, denoting, or used by both sexes. 2 having characteristics of both sexes or of neither sex. —*n.* epicene person. [Greek *koinos* common]

epicentre /ˈepɪsentə(r)/ *n.* (*US* **epicenter**) 1 point at which an earthquake reaches the earth's surface. 2 central point of a difficulty. [Greek: related to CENTRE]

epicure /ˈepɪkjʊə(r)/ *n.* person with refined tastes, esp. in food and drink. [related to EPICUREAN]

Epicurean /ˌepɪkjʊˈriːən/ —*n.* 1 disciple or student of the Greek philosopher Epicurus. 2 (**epicurean**) devotee of (esp. sensual) enjoyment. —*adj.* 1 of Epicurus or his ideas. 2 (**epicurean**) characteristic of an epicurean. □ **Epicureanism** *n.* [Latin from Greek]

epidemic /ˌepɪˈdemɪk/ —*n.* widespread occurrence of a disease in a community at a particular time. —*adj.* in the nature of an epidemic. [Greek *dēmos* the people]

epidemiology /ˌepɪdiːmɪˈɒlədʒɪ/ *n.* the study of epidemic diseases and their control. □ **epidemiologist** *n.* [from EPI-, *demos*, -LOGY]

epidermis /ˌepɪˈdɜːmɪs/ *n.* outer layer of the skin. □ **epidermal** *adj.* [Greek *derma* skin]

epidiascope /ˌepɪˈdaɪəskəʊp/ *n.* optical projector capable of giving images of both opaque and transparent objects. [from EPI-, DIA-, -SCOPE]

epidural /ˌepɪˈdjʊərəl/ —*adj.* (of an anaesthetic) introduced into the space around the dura mater of the spinal cord. —*n.* epidural anaesthetic. [from EPI-, DURA MATER]

epiglottis /ˌepɪˈglɒtɪs/ *n.* flap of cartilage at the root of the tongue, depressed during swallowing to cover the windpipe. □ **epiglottal** *adj.* [Greek *glōtta* tongue]

epigram /ˈepɪgræm/ *n.* 1 short poem with a witty ending. 2 pointed saying. □ **epigrammatic** /-grəˈmætɪk/ *adj.* [Greek: related to -GRAM]

epigraph /ˈepɪgrɑːf/ *n.* inscription. [Greek: related to -GRAPH]

epilepsy /ˈepɪlepsɪ/ *n.* nervous disorder with convulsions and often loss of consciousness. [Greek *lambanō* take]

epileptic /ˌepɪˈleptɪk/ —*adj.* of epilepsy. —*n.* person with epilepsy. [French: related to EPILEPSY]

epilogue /ˈepɪlɒg/ *n.* 1 speech addressed to the audience by an actor at the end of a play. 2 speech ending a literary work. [Greek *logos* speech]

epiphany /ɪˈpɪfənɪ/ *n.* (*pl.* **-ies**) 1 (**Epiphany**) a manifestation of Christ to the

Magi. **b** festival of this on 6 January. 2 manifestation of a god or demigod. [Greek *phainō* show]

episcopacy /ɪˈpɪskəpəsɪ/ *n.* (*pl.* **-ies**) 1 government by bishops. 2 (prec. by *the*) the bishops.

episcopal /ɪˈpɪskəp(ə)l/ *adj.* 1 of a bishop or bishops. 2 (of a Church) governed by bishops. □ **episcopally** *adv.*

Episcopalian /ɪˌpɪskəˈpeɪlɪən/ —*adj.* 1 of episcopacy. 2 of an episcopal Church (Episcopalian) the Episcopal Church. —*n.* 1 adherent of episcopacy. 2 (**Episcopalian**) member of the Episcopal Church. [Latin: related to EPISCOPAL]

episcopate /ɪˈpɪskəpət/ *n.* 1 the office or tenure of a bishop. 2 (prec. by *the*) bishops collectively. [Church Latin: related to BISHOP]

episiotomy /ɪˌpiːzɪˈɒtəmɪ/ *n.* (*pl.* **-ies**) surgical cut made at the vaginal opening during childbirth, to aid delivery. [Greek *epision* pubic region]

episode /ˈepɪsəʊd/ *n.* 1 event or group of events as part of a sequence. 2 each of the parts of a serial story or broadcast. 3 incident or set of incidents in a narrative. [Greek *eisodos* entry]

episodic /ˌepɪˈsɒdɪk/ *adj.* 1 consisting of separate episodes. 2 irregular, sporadic. □ **episodically** *adv.*

epistemology /ɪˌpɪstɪˈmɒlədʒɪ/ *n.* philosophy of knowledge. □ **epistemological** /-məˈlɒdʒɪk(ə)l/ *adj.* [Greek *epistēmē* knowledge]

epistle /ɪˈpɪs(ə)l/ *n.* 1 joc. letter. 2 (**Epistle**) any of the apostles' letters in the New Testament. 3 poem etc. in the form of a letter. [Greek *epistolē* from *stellō* send]

epistolary /ɪˈpɪstələrɪ/ *adj.* of or in the form of a letter or letters. [Latin: related to EPISTLE]

epitaph /ˈepɪtɑːf/ *n.* words written in memory of a dead person, esp. as a tomb inscription. [Greek *taphos* tomb]

epithelium /ˌepɪˈθiːlɪəm/ *n.* (*pl.* **-s** or **-lia** /-lɪə/) tissue forming the outer layer of the body and lining many hollow structures. □ **epithelial** *adj.* [Greek *thēlē* teat]

epithet /ˈepɪθet/ *n.* 1 adjective etc. expressing a quality or attribute. 2 this as a term of abuse. [Greek *tithēmi* place]

epitome /ɪˈpɪtəmɪ/ *n.* 1 person or thing embodying a quality etc. 2 thing representing another in miniature. [Greek *temnō* cut]

epitomize *v.* (also **-ise**) (**-zing** or **-sing**) make or be a perfect example of (a quality etc.).

EPNS *abbr.* electroplated nickel silver.

epoch /ˈiːpɒk/ n. 1 period of history etc. marked by notable events. 2 beginning of an era. 3 *Geol.* division of a period, corresponding to a set of strata. □ **epoch-making** *adj.* remarkable; very important.

eponym /ˈepənɪm/ n. 1 word, place-name, etc., derived from a person's name. 2 person whose name is used in this way. □ **eponymous** /ɪˈpɒnɪməs/ *adj.* [Greek *onoma* name]

EPOS /ˈiːpɒs/ *abbr.* electronic point-of-sale (equipment recording stock, sales, etc. in shops).

epoxy /ɪˈpɒksɪ/ *adj.* relating to or derived from a compound with one oxygen atom and two carbon atoms bonded in a triangle. [from EPI-, OXYGEN]

epoxy resin n. synthetic thermosetting resin.

epsilon /ˈepsɪlɒn/ n. fifth letter of the Greek alphabet (Ε, ε). [Greek]

Epsom salts /ˈepsəm/ n. magnesium sulphate used as a purgative etc. [*Epsom* in S. England]

equable /ˈekwəb(ə)l/ *adj.* 1 not varying. 2 moderate (*equable climate*). 3 (of a person) not easily disturbed. □ **equably** *adv.* [related to EQUAL]

equal /ˈiːkw(ə)l/ —*adj.* 1 (often foll. by *to, with*) the same in quantity, quality, size, degree, level, etc. 2 evenly balanced (*an equal contest*). 3 having the same rights or status (*human beings are essentially equal*). 4 uniform in application or effect. —*n.* person or thing equal to another, esp. in rank or quality. —*v.* (**-ll-**, US **-l-**) 1 be equal to. 2 achieve something that is equal to. □ **be equal to** have the ability or resources for. [Latin *aequalis*]

equality /ɪˈkwɒlɪtɪ/ n. being equal. [Latin: related to EQUAL]

equalize *v.* (also **-ise**) (**-zing** or **-sing**) 1 make or become equal. 2 reach one's opponent's score. □ **equalization** /-ˈzeɪʃ(ə)n/ n.

equalizer n. (also **-iser**) equalizing score or goal etc.

equally *adv.* 1 in an equal manner (*treated them equally*). 2 to an equal degree (*equally important*).

■ **Usage** In sense 2, construction with *as* (e.g. *equally as important as important*) is often found, but is considered incorrect by some people.

equal opportunity n. (often in *pl.*) opportunity to compete on equal terms, regardless of sex, race, etc.

equanimity /ˌekwəˈnɪmɪtɪ/ n. composure, evenness of temper, esp. in

adversity. [Latin *aequus* even, *animus* mind]

equate /ɪˈkweɪt/ *v.* (**-ting**) 1 (usu. foll. by *to, with*) regard as equal or equivalent to. 2 (foll. by *with*) be equal or equivalent to. □ **equatable** *adj.* [Latin *aequo aequat*: related to EQUAL]

equation /ɪˈkweɪʒ(ə)n/ n. 1 equating or making equal; being equal. 2 statement that two mathematical expressions are equal (indicated by the sign =). 3 formula indicating a chemical reaction by means of symbols.

equator n. 1 imaginary line round the earth or other body, equidistant from the poles. 2 = CELESTIAL EQUATOR. [medieval Latin: related to EQUATE]

equatorial /ˌekwəˈtɔːrɪəl/ *adj.* of or near the equator.

equerry /ˈekwərɪ/ n. (*pl.* **-ies**) officer attending the British royal family. [French *esquierie* stable]

equestrian /ɪˈkwestrɪən/ —*adj.* 1 of horse-riding. 2 on horseback. —*n.* rider or performer on horseback. □ **equestrianism** n. [Latin *equestris* from *equus* horse]

equi- *comb. form* equal. [Latin: related to EQUAL]

equiangular /ˌiːkwɪˈæŋɡjʊlə(r)/ *adj.* having equal angles.

equidistant /ˌiːkwɪˈdɪst(ə)nt/ *adj.* at equal distances.

equilateral /ˌiːkwɪˈlætər(ə)l/ *adj.* having all its sides equal in length.

equilibrium /ˌiːkwɪˈlɪbrɪəm/ n. (*pl.* **-ria** /-rɪə/ or **-s**) 1 state of physical balance. 2 state of composure. [Latin *libra* balance]

equine /ˈekwaɪn/ *adj.* of or like a horse. [Latin *equus* horse]

equinoctial /ˌiːkwɪˈnɒkʃ(ə)l/ —*adj.* happening at or near the time of an equinox. —*n.* (in full **equinoctial line**) = CELESTIAL EQUATOR. [Latin: related to EQUINOX]

equinox /ˈiːkwɪnɒks/ n. time or date (twice each year) at which the sun crosses the celestial equator, when day and night are of equal length. [Latin *nox noctis* night]

equip /ɪˈkwɪp/ *v.* (**-pp-**) supply with what is needed. [Old Norse *skipa* to man a ship]

equipage /ˈekwɪpɪdʒ/ n. 1 *archaic* **a** requisites. **b** outfit. 2 *hist.* carriage and horses with attendants. [French: related to EQUIP]

equipment n. 1 necessary articles, clothing, etc. 2 equipping or being equipped. [French: related to EQUIP]

equipoise /ˈekwɪˌpɔɪz/ n. 1 equilibrium. 2 counterbalancing thing.

equitable /ˈekwɪtəb(ə)l/ adj. 1 fair, just. 2 Law valid in equity as distinct from law. □ **equitably** adv. [French: related to EQUITY]

equitation /ˌekwɪˈteɪʃ(ə)n/ n. horsemanship; horse-riding. [Latin *equito* ride a horse]

equity /ˈekwɪtɪ/ n. (pl. -ies) 1 fairness. 2 principles of justice used to correct or supplement the law. 3 a value of a company's shares. **b** (in pl.) stocks and shares not bearing fixed interest. [Latin *aequitas*: related to EQUAL]

equivalent /ɪˈkwɪvələnt/ —adj. 1 (often foll. by to) equal in value, amount, importance, etc. 2 corresponding. 3 having the same meaning or result. —n. equivalent thing, amount, etc. □ **equivalence** n. [Latin: related to VALUE]

equivocal /ɪˈkwɪvək(ə)l/ adj. 1 of double or doubtful meaning. 2 of uncertain nature. 3 (of a person etc.) questionable. □ **equivocally** adv. [Latin *voco* call]

equivocate /ɪˈkwɪvəˌkeɪt/ v. (-ting) use ambiguity to conceal the truth. □ **equivocation** /-ˈkeɪʃ(ə)n/ n. **equivocator** n. [Latin: related to EQUIVOCAL]

ER abbr. Queen Elizabeth. [Latin *Elizabetha Regina*]

er /ɜː(r)/ int. expressing hesitation. [imitative]

-er[1] suffix forming nouns from nouns, adjectives, and verbs, denoting: 1 person, animal, or thing that does (*cobbler*; *poker*). 2 person or thing that is (*for-eigner*; *four-wheeler*). 3 person concerned with (*hatter*; *geographer*). 4 person from (*villager*; *sixth-former*). [Old English]

-er[2] suffix forming the comparative of adjectives (*wider*) and adverbs (*faster*). [Old English]

-er[3] suffix used in a slang distortion of the word (*rugger*). [probably an extension of ER[1]]

era /ˈɪərə/ n. 1 system of chronology reckoning from a noteworthy event (*Christian era*). 2 large period, esp. regarded historically. 3 date at which an era begins. 4 major division of geological time. [Latin, = number (pl. of *aes* money)]

eradicate /ɪˈrædɪˌkeɪt/ v. (-ting) root out; destroy completely. □ **eradicable** adj. **eradication** /-ˈkeɪʃ(ə)n/ n. **eradicator** n. [Latin *radix -icis* root]

erase /ɪˈreɪz/ v. (-sing) 1 rub out; obliterate. 2 remove all traces of. 3 remove recorded material from (magnetic tape or disk). [Latin *rado ras-* scrape]

eraser n. thing that erases, esp. a piece of rubber etc. for removing pencil etc. marks.

erasure /ɪˈreɪʒə(r)/ n. 1 erasing. 2 erased word etc.

ere /eə(r)/ prep. & conj. poet. or archaic before (of time) (*ere noon*; *ere they come*). [Old English]

erbium /ˈɜːbɪəm/ n. metallic element of the lanthanide series. [*Ytterby* in Sweden]

erect /ɪˈrekt/ —adj. 1 upright; vertical. 2 (of the penis etc.) enlarged and rigid, esp. in sexual excitement. 3 (of hair) bristling. —v. 1 set up; build. 2 establish. □ **erection** n. **erectly** adv. **erectness** n. [Latin *erigere erect-* set up]

erectile adj. that can become erect (esp. of body tissue in sexual excitement). [French: related to ERECT]

erg n. unit of work or energy. [Greek *ergon* work]

ergo /ˈɜːgəʊ/ adv. therefore. [Latin]

ergonomics /ˌɜːgəˈnɒmɪks/ n. the study of the relationship between people and their working environment. □ **ergonomic** adj. [Greek *ergon* work]

ergot /ˈɜːgət/ n. disease of rye etc. caused by a fungus. [French]

Erin /ˈɪərɪn/ n. poet. Ireland. [Irish]

ermine /ˈɜːmɪn/ n. (pl. same or -s) 1 stoat, esp. when white in winter. 2 its white fur, used to trim robes etc. [French]

Ernie /ˈɜːnɪ/ n. device for drawing prize-winning numbers of Premium Bonds. [Electronic Random Number Indicator Equipment]

erode /ɪˈrəʊd/ v. (-ding) wear away, destroy gradually. □ **erosion** n. **erosive** adj. [Latin *rodo ros-* gnaw]

erogenous /ɪˈrɒdʒɪnəs/ adj. (of a part of the body) particularly sensitive to sexual stimulation. [Greek (as EROTIC), -GENOUS]

erotic /ɪˈrɒtɪk/ adj. of or causing sexual love, esp. tending to arouse sexual desire or excitement. □ **erotically** adv. [Greek *erōs* sexual love]

erotica n.pl. erotic literature or art. [Greek *erōs* sexual love]

eroticism /ɪˈrɒtɪˌsɪz(ə)m/ n. 1 erotic character. 2 use of or response to erotic images or stimulation.

err /ɜː(r)/ v. 1 be mistaken or incorrect. 2 do wrong; sin. [Latin *erro* stray]

errand /ˈerənd/ n. 1 short journey, esp. on another's behalf, to take a message, collect goods, etc. 2 object of such a journey. [Old English]

errand of mercy n. journey to relieve suffering etc.

ERM abbr. Exchange Rate Mechanism.

errant /'erənt/ *adj.* **1** erring. **2** *literary* or *archaic* travelling in search of adventure (*knight errant*). □ **errantry** *n.* (in sense 2). [from ERR: sense 2 ultimately from Latin *iter* journey]

erratic /ɪ'rætɪk/ *adj.* **1** inconsistent in conduct, opinions, etc. **2** uncertain in movement. □ **erratically** *adv.* [Latin: related to ERR]

erratum /ɪ'rɑːtəm/ *n.* (*pl.* **errata**) error in printing or writing. [Latin: related to ERR]

erroneous /ɪ'rəʊnɪəs/ *adj.* incorrect. □ **erroneously** *adv.* [Latin: related to ERR]

error /'erə(r)/ *n.* **1** mistake. **2** condition of being morally wrong (*led into error*). **3** degree of inaccuracy in a calculation etc. (*2% error*). [Latin: related to ERR]

ersatz /'eəzæts/ *adj.* & *n.* substitute, imitation. [German]

Erse /ɜːs/ *adj.* Irish or Highland Gaelic. —*n.* the Gaelic language. [early Scots form of IRISH]

erstwhile /'ɜːstwaɪl/ —*adj.* former, previous. —*adv.* *archaic* formerly. [related to ERE]

eructation /ˌiːrʌk'teɪʃ(ə)n/ *n.* *formal* belching. [Latin *ructo* belch]

erudite /'eruːdaɪt/ *adj.* learned. □ **erudition** /-'dɪʃ(ə)n/ *n.* [Latin *eruditus* instructed: related to RUDE]

erupt /ɪ'rʌpt/ *v.* **1** break out suddenly or dramatically. **2** (of a volcano) eject lava etc. **3** (of a rash etc.) appear on the skin. □ **eruption** *n.* **eruptive** *adj.* [Latin *erumpo erupt-* break out]

-ery *suffix* (also **-ry**) forming nouns denoting: **1** class or kind (*greenery*). **2** employment (*dentistry; slavery*). **3** state or condition (*machinery; citizenry*). **4** behaviour (*mimicry*). **5** often *derog.* all that has to do with (*popery*). [French *-erie*]

erysipelas /ˌerɪ'sɪpɪləs/ *n.* disease causing fever and a deep red inflammation of the skin. [Latin from Greek]

erythrocyte /ɪ'rɪθrəʊˌsaɪt/ *n.* red blood cell. [Greek *eruthros* red, -CYTE]

Es *symb.* einsteinium.

escalate /'eskəˌleɪt/ *v.* (**-ting**) **1** increase or develop (usu. rapidly) by stages. **2** make or become more intense. □ **escalation** /-'leɪʃ(ə)n/ *n.* [from ESCALATOR]

escalator *n.* moving staircase consisting of a circulating belt forming steps. [Latin *scala* ladder]

escalope /'eskəˌlɒp/ *n.* thin slice of boneless meat, esp. veal. [French, originally = shell]

escapade /'eskəˌpeɪd/ *n.* piece of reckless behaviour. [French from Provençal or Spanish: related to ESCAPE]

escape /ɪ'skeɪp/ —*v.* (**-ping**) **1** (often foll. by *from*) get free of restriction or control. **2** (of gas etc.) leak. **3** succeed in avoiding punishment etc. **4** get free of (a person, grasp, etc.). **5** elude (a commitment, danger, etc.). **6** elude the notice or memory of (*nothing escapes you; name escaped me*). **7** (of words etc.) issue unawares from (a person etc.). —*n.* **1** act or instance of escaping. **2** means of escaping (often *attrib.: escape hatch*). **3** leakage of gas etc. **4** temporary relief from unpleasant reality. [Latin *cappa* cloak]

escape clause *n.* *Law* clause specifying conditions under which a contracting party is free from an obligation.

escapee /ɪˌskeɪ'piː/ *n.* person who has escaped.

escapement *n.* part of a clock etc. that connects and regulates the motive power. [French: related to ESCAPE]

escape velocity *n.* minimum velocity needed to escape from the gravitational field of a body.

escapism *n.* pursuit of distraction and relief from reality. □ **escapist** *n.* & *adj.*

escapology /ˌeskə'pɒlədʒi/ *n.* techniques of escaping from confinement, esp. as entertainment. □ **escapologist** *n.*

escarpment /ɪ'skɑːpmənt/ *n.* long steep slope at the edge of a plateau etc. [French from Italian: related to SCARP]

eschatology /ˌeskə'tɒlədʒi/ *n.* theology of death and final destiny. □ **eschatological** /-təˈlɒdʒɪk(ə)l/ *adj.* [Greek *eskhatos* last]

escheat /ɪs'tʃiːt/ *hist.* —*n.* **1** reversion of property to the State etc. in the absence of legal heirs. **2** property so affected. —*v.* **1** hand over (property) as an escheat. **2** confiscate. **3** revert by escheat. [Latin *cado fall*]

eschew /ɪs'tʃuː/ *v.* *formal* avoid; abstain from. □ **eschewal** *n.* [Germanic: related to SHY[1]]

escort —*n.* /'eskɔːt/ **1** one or more persons, vehicles, etc., accompanying a person, vehicle, etc., for protection or as a mark of status. **2** person accompanying a person of the opposite sex socially. —*v.* /ɪ'skɔːt/ act as an escort to. [French from Italian]

escritoire /ˌeskriː'twɑː(r)/ *n.* writing-desk with drawers etc. [French from Latin *scriptorium* writing-room]

escudo /e'skjuːdəʊ/ *n.* (*pl.* **-s**) chief monetary unit of Portugal. [Spanish and Portuguese from Latin *scutum* shield]

escutcheon /ɪ'skʌtʃ(ə)n/ *n.* shield or emblem bearing a coat of arms. [Latin *scutum* shield]

Eskimo /'eskɪməʊ/ —*n.* (*pl.* same or -s) **1** member of a people inhabiting N. Canada, Alaska, Greenland, and E. Siberia. **2** language of this people. —*adj.* of Eskimos or their language. [Algonquian]

■ **Usage** The people themselves prefer the name *Inuit*.

ESN *abbr.* educationally subnormal.

esophagus *US var.* of OESOPHAGUS.

esoteric /ˌesə'terɪk/ *adj.* intelligible only to those with special knowledge. □ **esoterically** *adv.* [Greek *esō* within]

ESP *abbr.* extrasensory perception.

espadrille /ˌespə'drɪl/ *n.* light canvas shoe with a plaited fibre sole. [Proven-çal: related to ESPARTO]

espalier /ɪ'spælɪə(r)/ *n.* **1** lattice-work along which the branches of a tree or shrub are trained. **2** tree or shrub so trained. [French from Italian]

esparto /e'spɑːtəʊ/ *n.* (*pl.* -s) (in full **esparto grass**) coarse grass of Spain and N. Africa, used to make good-quality paper etc. [Greek *sparton* rope]

especial /ɪ'speʃ(ə)l/ *adj.* notable. [Latin: related to SPECIAL]

especially *adv.* in particular. **2** much more than in other cases. **3** particularly.

Esperanto /ˌespə'ræntəʊ/ *n.* an artificial language designed for universal use. [Latin *spero* hope]

espionage /'espɪənɑːʒ/ *n.* spying or use of spies. [French: related to SPY]

esplanade /ˌesplə'neɪd/ *n.* **1** long open leve. area for walking cn. esp. beside the sea. **2** level space separating a fortress from a town. [Latin *planus* level]

espousal /ɪ'spaʊz(ə)l/ *n.* **1** (foll. by *of*) espousing (of a cause etc.). **2** *archaic* marriage, betrothal.

espouse /ɪ'spaʊz/ *v.* (**-sing**) **1** adopt or support (a cause, doctrine, etc.). **2** *archaic* **a** (usu. of a man) marry. **b** (usu. foll. by *to*) give (a woman) in marriage. [Latin *spondeo* betroth]

espresso /e'spresəʊ/ *n.* (also **expresso** /ek'spresəʊ/) (*pl.* -s) strong black coffee made under steam pressure. [Italian, = pressed out]

esprit /e'spriː/ *n.* sprightliness, wit. □ **esprit de corps** /də 'kɔː(r)/ devotion to and pride in one's group. [French: related to SPIRIT]

espy /ɪ'spaɪ/ *v.* (**-ies, -ied**) catch sight of. [French: related to SPY]

Esq. *abbr.* Esquire.

-esque *suffix* forming adjectives meaning in the style of or 'resembling' (*Kafkaesque*). [French from Latin *-iscus*]

esquire /ɪ'skwaɪə(r)/ *n.* **1** (usu. as abbr. **Esq.**) title added to a man's surname when no other title is used, esp. as a form of address for letters. **2** *archaic* squire. [French from Latin *scutum* shield]

-ess *suffix* forming nouns denoting females (*actress*, *lioness*). [Greek *-issa*]

essay —*n.* /'eseɪ/ **1** short piece of writing on a given subject. **2** (often foll. by *at*, *in*) *formal* attempt. —*v.* /e'seɪ/ attempt. □ **essayist** *n.* [Latin *exigo* weigh: cf. AS-SAY]

essence /'es(ə)ns/ *n.* **1** fundamental nature; inherent characteristics. **2 a** extract got by distillation etc. **b** perfume. □ **in essence** fundamentally. **in essence** indispensable. [Latin *esse* be]

essential /ɪ'senʃ(ə)l/ —*adj.* **1** necessary; indispensable. **2** of or constituting the essence of a person or thing. —*n.* (esp. in *pl.*) basic or indispensable element or thing. □ **essentially** *adv.* [Latin: related to ESSENCE]

essential oil *n.* volatile oil derived from a plant etc. with its characteristic odour.

-est *suffix* forming the superlative of adjectives (*widest*, *nicest*, *happiest*) and adverbs (*soonest*). [Old English]

establish /ɪ'stæblɪʃ/ *v.* **1** set up (a business, system, etc.) on a permanent basis. **2** (foll. by *in*) settle (a person or oneself) in some capacity. **3** (esp. as **established** *adj.*) **a** achieve permanent acceptance for (a custom, belief, etc.). **b** place (a fact etc.) beyond dispute. [Latin *stabilio* make firm]

Established Church *n.* the Church recognized by the State.

establishment *n.* **1** establishing or being established. **2 a** business organization or public institution. **b** place of business. **c** residence. **3 a** staff of an organization. **b** household. **4** organized body permanently maintained. **5** Church system organized by law. **6** (**the Establishment**) social group with authority or influence and resisting change.

estate /ɪ'steɪt/ *n.* **1** property consisting of much land and ust. a large house. **2** modern residential or industrial area with an integrated design or purpose. **3** person's assets and liabilities, esp. at death. **4** property where rubber, tea, grapes, etc., are cultivated. **5** order or class forming (or regarded as) part of the body politic. **6** *archaic* or *literary* state or position in life (*the estate of holy matrimony*). □ **the Three Estates** Lords Spiritual (the heads of the Church), Lords Temporal (the peerage), and the Commons. [French *estat*, from Latin *sto stat-* stand]

estate agent n. person whose business is the sale or lease of buildings and land on behalf of others.

estate car n. car with a continuous area for rear passengers and luggage.

estate duty n. hist. death duty.

■ **Usage** Estate duty was replaced in 1975 by *capital transfer tax* and in 1986 by *inheritance tax*.

esteem /ɪˈstiːm/ —v. 1 (usu. in *passive*) have a high regard for. 2 *formal* consider (*esteemed it an honour*). —n. high regard; favour. [Latin: related to ESTIMATE]

ester /ˈestə(r)/ n. *Chem.* a compound produced by replacing the hydrogen of an acid by an organic radical. [German]

estimable /ˈestɪməb(ə)l/ adj. worthy of esteem; admirable. [Latin: related to ESTEEM]

estimate —n. /ˈestɪmət/ 1 approximate judgement, esp. of cost, value, size, etc. 2 statement of approximate charge for work to be undertaken. —v. /ˈestɪmeɪt/ (-ting) (also *absol.*) 1 form an estimate or opinion of. 2 (foll. by *that*) make a rough calculation. 3 (often foll. by *at*) form an estimate; adjudge. □ **estimator** /ˌmeɪtə(r)/ n. [Latin *aestimo* fix the price of]

estimation /ˌestɪˈmeɪʃ(ə)n/ n. 1 estimating. 2 judgement of worth. [Latin: related to ESTIMATE]

estrogen US var. of OESTROGEN.

estrus US var. of OESTRUS.

estuary /ˈestjʊərɪ/ n. (pl. -ies) wide tidal river mouth. [Latin *aestus* tide]

ETA *abbr.* estimated time of arrival.

eta /ˈiːtə/ n. seventh letter of the Greek alphabet ($H, η$). [Greek]

et al. /et ˈæl/ *abbr.* and others. [Latin *et alii*]

etc. *abbr.* = ET CETERA.

et cetera /et ˈsetrə/ (also **etcetera**) —adv. 1 and the rest. 2 and so on. —n. (in *pl.*) the usual extras. [Latin]

etch v. 1 a reproduce (a picture etc.) by engraving on a metal plate with acid (esp. to print copies). b engrave (a plate) in this way. 2 practise this craft. 3 (foll.

by *on, upon*) impress deeply (esp. on the mind). □ **etcher** n. [Dutch *etsen*]

etching n. 1 print made from an etched plate. 2 art of producing these plates.

eternal /ɪˈtɜːn(ə)l/ adj. 1 existing always; without an end or (usu.) beginning. 2 unchanging. 3 *colloq.* constant; too frequent (*eternal nagging*). □ **eternally** adv. [Latin *aeternus*]

eternal triangle n. two people of one sex and one person of the other involved in a complex emotional relationship.

eternity /ɪˈtɜːnɪtɪ/ n. (pl. -ies) 1 infinite (esp. future) time. 2 endless life after death. 3 being eternal. 4 *colloq.* (often prec. by *an*) a very long time. [Latin: related to ETERNAL]

eternity ring n. finger-ring esp. set with gems all round.

-**eth** var. of -TH.

ethanal /ˈeθənæl/ n. = ACETALDEHYDE.

ethane /ˈiːθeɪn/ n. gaseous hydrocarbon of the alkane series. [from ETHER]

ether /ˈiːθə(r)/ n. 1 *Chem.* colourless volatile organic liquid used as an anaesthetic or solvent. 2 clear sky; upper regions of the air. 3 *hist.* a medium formerly assumed to permeate all space. b medium through which electromagnetic waves were formerly thought to be transmitted. [Greek *aithō* burn]

ethereal /ɪˈθɪərɪəl/ adj. 1 light, airy. 2 highly delicate, esp. in appearance. 3 heavenly. □ **ethereally** adv. [Greek: related to ETHER]

ethic /ˈeθɪk/ n. set of moral principles (*the Quaker ethic*). —adj. = ETHICAL. [Greek: related to ETHOS]

ethical adj. 1 relating to morals, esp. as concerning human conduct. 2 morally correct. 3 (of a drug etc.) not advertised to the general public, and usu. available only on prescription. □ **ethically** adv.

ethics n.pl. (also treated as *sing.*) 1 moral philosophy. 2 a moral principles. b set of these.

Ethiopian /ˌiːθɪˈəʊpɪən/ —n. 1 native or national of Ethiopia in NE Africa. 2 person of Ethiopian descent. —adj. of Ethiopia.

ethnic /ˈeθnɪk/ adj. 1 a (of a social group) having a common national or cultural tradition. b (of music, clothing, etc.) inspired by or resembling those of an exotic people. 2 denoting origin by birth or descent rather than nationality (*ethnic Turks*). □ **ethnically** adv. [Greek *ethnos* nation]

ethnology /eθˈnɒlədʒɪ/ n. the comparative study of peoples. □ **ethnological** /-nəˈlɒdʒɪk(ə)l/ adj. **ethnologist** n.

ethos /ˈiːθɒs/ n. characteristic spirit or attitudes of a community etc. [Greek *ēthos* character]

Estonian /eˈstəʊnɪən/ —n. 1 a native or national of Estonia in eastern Europe. b person of Estonian descent. 2 language of Estonia. —adj. of Estonia, its people, or language.

estrange /ɪˈstreɪndʒ/ v. (-ging) 1 (usu. in *passive*, often foll. by *from*) alienate; make hostile or indifferent. 2 (as **estranged** adj.) (of a husband or wife) no longer living with his or her spouse. □ **estrangement** n. [Latin: related to STRANGE]

ethyl /ˈeθl/ n. (attrib.) a radical derived from ethane, present in alcohol and ether. [German: related to ETHER]

ethylene /ˈeθɪliːn/ n. a hydrocarbon of the alkene series.

etiolate /ˈiːtɪəleɪt/ v. (-ting) 1 make (a plant) pale by excluding light. 2 give a sickly colour to (a person). □ **etiolation** /-ˈleɪʃ(ə)n/ n. [Latin stipula straw]

etiology US var. of AETIOLOGY.

etiquette /ˈetɪket/ n. conventional rules of social behaviour or professional conduct. [French: related to TICKET]

Etruscan /ɪˈtrʌskən/ —adj. of ancient Etruria in Italy. —n. 1 native of Etruria. 2 language of Etruria. [Latin Etruscus]

et seq. abbr. (also et seqq.) and the following (pages etc.). [Latin et sequentia]

-ette suffix forming nouns meaning: 1 small (kitchenette). 2 imitation or substitute (flannelette). 3 female (usherette). [French]

étude /erˈtjuːd/ n. = STUDY n. 6. [French, = study]

etymology /etɪˈmɒlədʒɪ/ n. (pl. -ies) 1 a derivation and development of a word in form and meaning. b account of these. 2 the study of word origins. □ **etymological** /-məˈlɒdʒɪk(ə)l/ adj. **etymologist** n. [Greek etumos true]

Eu symb. europium.

eu- comb. form well, easily. [Greek]

eucalyptus /juːkəˈlɪptəs/ n. (pl. -tuses or -ti /-taɪ/) (also **eucalypt** pl. -s) 1 tall evergreen Australian tree. 2 its oil, used as an antiseptic etc. [from Greek kaluptos covered]

Eucharist /ˈjuːkərɪst/ n. 1 Christian sacrament in which consecrated bread and wine are consumed. 2 consecrated elements, esp. the bread. □ **Eucharistic** /-ˈrɪstɪk/ adj. [Greek, = thanksgiving]

eugenics /juːˈdʒenɪks/ n.pl. (also treated as sing.) improvement of the qualities of a race by control of inherited characteristics. □ **eugenic** adj. [from EU, Greek gen- produce]

eukaryote /juːˈkærɪəʊt, n. organism consisting of a cell or cells in which the genetic material is contained within a distinct nucleus. □ **eukaryotic** /-ˈɒtɪk/ adj. [from EU, karyo- from Greek karuon kernel, -ote as in ZYGOTE]

eulogize /ˈjuːlədʒaɪz/ v. (also -ise) (-zing or -sing) praise in speech or writing. □ **eulogistic** /-ˈdʒɪstɪk/ adj.

eulogy /ˈjuːlədʒɪ/ n. (pl. -ies) 1 speech or writing in praise of a person. 2 expression of praise. [Latin from Greek]

eunuch /ˈjuːnək/ n. castrated man, esp. one formerly employed at an oriental harem or court. [Greek, = bedchamber attendant]

euphemism /ˈjuːfɪmɪz(ə)m/ n. 1 mild or vague expression substituted for a harsher or more direct one (e.g. pass over for die). 2 use of such expressions. □ **euphemistic** /-ˈmɪstɪk/ adj. **euphemistically** /-ˈmɪstɪkəlɪ/ adv. [Greek phēmē speaking]

euphonium /juːˈfəʊnɪəm/ n. brass instrument of the tuba family. [related to EUPHONY]

euphony /ˈjuːfənɪ/ n. (pl. -ies) 1 pleasantness of sound, esp. of a word or phrase. 2 pleasant sound. □ **euphonious** /-ˈfəʊnɪəs/ adj. [Greek phōnē sound]

euphoria /juːˈfɔːrɪə/ n. intense feeling of well-being and excitement. □ **euphoric** /-ˈfɒrɪk/ adj. [Greek pherō bear]

Eurasian /jʊəˈreɪʒ(ə)n/ —adj. 1 of mixed European and Asian parentage. 2 of Europe and Asia. —n. Eurasian person. [Greek]

eureka /jʊəˈriːkə/ int. I have found it! (announcing a discovery etc.). [Greek heurēka]

Euro- comb. form Europe, European. [abbreviation]

Eurodollar /ˈjʊərəʊdɒlə(r)/ n. dollar held in a bank outside the US.

European /jʊərəˈpɪən/ —adj. 1 of or in Europe. 2 originating in, native to, or characteristic of Europe. —n. 1 a native or inhabitant of Europe. b person descended from natives of Europe. 2 person favouring European integration. □ **Europeanize** v. (also -ise) (-zing or -sing). [Greek Eurōpē Europe]

europium /jʊəˈrəʊpɪəm/ n. metallic element of the lanthanide series. [from the name Europe]

Eustachian tube /juːˈsteɪʃ(ə)n/ n. tube from the pharynx to the cavity of the middle ear. [Eustachio, name of an anatomist]

euthanasia /juːθəˈneɪzɪə/ n. bringing about of a gentle death in the case of incurable and painful disease. [Greek thanatos death]

eV abbr. electronvolt.

evacuate /ɪˈvækjʊeɪt/ v. (-ting) 1 a remove (people) from a place of danger. b empty (a place) in this way. 2 make empty. 3 (of troops) withdraw from (a place). 4 empty (the bowels etc.). □ **evacuation** /-ˈeɪʃ(ə)n/ n. [Latin vacuus empty]

evacuee /ɪvækjʊˈiː/ n. person evacuated.

evade /ɪˈveɪd/ v. (-ding) 1 a escape from, avoid, esp. by guile or trickery. b avoid doing, esp. one's duty etc. c avoid answering (a question). 2 avoid paying (tax). [Latin evado escape]

evaluate /ɪˈvæljʊˌeɪt/ v. (**-ting**) **1** assess, appraise. **2** find or state the number or amount of. □ **evaluation** /-ˈeɪʃ(ə)n/ n. [French: related to VALUE]

evanesce /ˌevəˈnes/ v. (**-cing**) literary fade from sight. [Latin vanus empty]

evanescent /ˌevəˈnes(ə)nt/ adj. quickly fading. □ **evanescence** n.

evangelical /ˌiːvænˈdʒelɪk(ə)l/ —adj. **1** of or according to the teaching of the gospel. **2** of the Protestant school maintaining the doctrine of salvation by faith. —n. member of this. □ **evangelicalism** n. **evangelically** adv. [Greek: related to EU-, ANGEL]

evangelism /ɪˈvændʒəˌlɪz(ə)m/ n. preaching or spreading of the gospel.

evangelist n. **1** writer of one of the four Gospels. **2** preacher of the gospel. □ **evangelistic** /-ˈlɪstɪk/ adj.

evangelize v. (also **-ise**) (**-zing** or **-sing**) **1** (also absol.) preach the gospel to. **2** convert to Christianity. □ **evangelization** /-ˈzeɪʃ(ə)n/ n.

evaporate /ɪˈvæpəˌreɪt/ v. (**-ting**) **1** turn from solid or liquid into vapour. **2** (cause to) lose moisture as vapour. **3** (cause to) disappear. □ **evaporable** adj. **evaporation** /-ˈreɪʃ(ə)n/ n. [Latin: related to VAPOUR]

evaporated milk n. unsweetened milk concentrated by evaporation.

evasion /ɪˈveɪʒ(ə)n/ n. **1** evading. **2** evasive answer. [Latin: related to EVADE]

evasive /ɪˈveɪsɪv/ adj. **1** seeking to evade. **2** not direct in one's answers etc. □ **evasively** adv. **evasiveness** n.

eve n. **1** evening or day before a festival etc. (Christmas Eve; eve of the funeral). **2** time just before an event (eve of the election). **3** archaic evening. [= EVEN²]

even¹ /ˈiːv(ə)n/ —adj. (**evener, evenest**) **1** level, smooth. **2 a** uniform in quality; constant. **b** equal in amount or value etc. **c** equally balanced. **3** (of a person's temper etc.) equable, calm. **4 a** (of a number) divisible by two without a remainder. **b** bearing such a number (no parking on even dates). **c** not involving fractions; exact (in even dozens). —adv. **1** inviting comparison of the assertion, negation, etc., with an implied one that is less strong or remarkable (never even opened [let alone read] the letter; ran even faster [not just as fast as before]). **2** introducing an extreme case (even you must realize it). —v. (often foll. by up) make or become even. □ **even now 1** now as well as before. **2** at this very moment. **even so** nevertheless. **even though** despite the fact that. **get (or be) even with** have one's revenge on. □ **evenly** adv. **evenness** n. [Old English]

even² /ˈiːv(ə)n/ n. poet. evening. [Old English]

even chance n. equal chance of success or failure.

even-handed adj. impartial.

evening /ˈiːvnɪŋ/ n. end part of the day, esp. from about 6 p.m. to bedtime. [Old English: related to EVEN²]

evening primrose n. plant with pale-yellow flowers that open in the evening.

evening star n. planet, esp. Venus, conspicuous in the west after sunset.

even money n. betting odds offering the gambler the chance of winning the amount staked.

evens n.pl. = EVEN MONEY.

evensong n. service of evening prayer in the Church of England. [from EVEN²]

event /ɪˈvent/ n. **1** thing that happens. **2** fact of a thing's occurring. **3** item in a (esp. sports) programme. □ **at all events** (or **in any event**) whatever happens. **in the event** as it turns (or turned) out. **in the event of** if (a specified thing) happens. **in the event that** if it happens that. [Latin venio vent- come]

■ **Usage** The phrase in the event that is considered awkward by some people. It can usually be avoided by rephrasing, e.g. in the event that it rains can be replaced by in the event of rain.

eventful adj. marked by noteworthy events. □ **eventfully** adv.

eventide /ˈiːvɪˌtaɪd/ n. archaic or poet. = EVENING. [related to EVEN²]

eventing n. participation in equestrian competitions, esp. dressage and show-jumping. [see EVENT 3]

eventual /ɪˈventʃʊəl/ adj. occurring in due course, ultimate. □ **eventually** adv. [from EVENT]

eventuality /ɪˌventʃʊˈælɪtɪ/ n. (pl. **-ies**) possible event or outcome.

eventuate /ɪˈventʃʊˌeɪt/ v. (**-ting**) (often foll. by in) result.

ever /ˈevə(r)/ adv. **1** at all times; always (ever hopeful; ever after). **2** at any time (have you ever smoked?; nothing ever happens). **3** (used for emphasis) in any way; at all (how ever did you do it?). **4** (in comb.) constantly (ever-present). **5** (foll. by so, such) colloq. very; very much (ever so easy; thanks ever so). □ **did you ever?** colloq. did you ever hear or see the like? **ever since** throughout the period since. [Old English]

■ **Usage** When *ever* is used with a question word for emphasis it is written separately (see sense 2). When used with a question or adverb to give it indefinite or general force, *ever* is written as one word with the relative pronoun or adverb, e.g. *however it's done, it's difficult.*

evergreen –*adj.* retaining green leaves all year round. –*n.* evergreen plant.

everlasting –*adj.* 1 lasting for ever or for a long time. 2 (of flowers) keeping their shape and colour when dried. –*n.* 1 eternity. 2 everlasting flower.

evermore *adv.* for ever; always.

every /'evrɪ/ *adj.* 1 each single (*heard every word*) 2 each at a specified interval in a series (*comes every four days*) 3 all possible (*every prospect of success*). □ **every bit as** *colloq.* (in comparisons) quite as. **every now and again** (or **then**) from time to time. **every other** each second in a series (*every other day*). **every so often** occasionally. [Old English: related to EVER, EACH]

everybody *pron.* every person.

everyday *attrib. adj.* 1 occurring every day. 2 used on ordinary days. 3 commonplace.

Everyman *n.* ordinary or typical human being. [name of a character in a 15th-c. morality play]

everyone *pron.* everybody.

every one *n.* each one.

everything *pron.* 1 all things. 2 most important thing (*speed is everything*).

everywhere *adv.* 1 in every place. 2 *colloq.* in many places.

evict /ɪ'vɪkt/ *v.* expel (a tenant etc.) by legal process. □ **eviction** *n.* [Latin *evinco evict-* conquer]

evidence /'evɪd(ə)ns/ –*n.* 1 (often foll. by *for, of*) available facts, circumstances, etc. indicating whether or not a thing is true or valid. 2 *Law* a information tending to prove a fact or proposition. b statements or proof admissible as testimony in a lawcourt. –*v.* (-**cing**) be evidence of. □ **in evidence** conspicuous. **Queen's** (or **King's**) **evidence** *Law* evidence for the prosecution given by a participant in the crime at issue. [Latin *video* see]

evident *adj.* plain or obvious; manifest. [Latin: related to EVIDENCE]

evidential /evɪ'dɛnʃ(ə)l/ *adj.* of or providing evidence.

evidently *adv.* 1 seemingly; as it appears. 2 as shown by evidence.

evil /'iːv(ə)l, -ɪl/ –*adj.* 1 morally bad; wicked. 2 harmful. 3 disagreeable (*evil temper*). –*n.* 1 evil thing. 2 wickedness. □ **evilly** *adv.* [Old English]

evildoer *n.* sinner. □ **evildoing** *n.*

evil eye *n.* gaze that is superstitiously believed to cause harm.

evince /ɪ'vɪns/ *v.* (-**cing**) indicate, display (a quality, feeling, etc.). [Latin: related to EVICT]

eviscerate /ɪ'vɪsəreɪt/ *v.* (-**ting**) disembowel. □ **evisceration** /-'reɪʃ(ə)n/ *n.* [Latin: related to VISCERA]

evocative /ɪ'vɒkətɪv/ *adj.* evoking (esp. feelings or memories). □ **evocatively** *adv.* **evocativeness** *n.*

evoke /ɪ'vəʊk/ *v.* (-**king**) inspire or draw forth (memories, a response, etc.). □ **evocation** /evə'keɪʃ(ə)n/ *n.* [Latin *voco* call]

evolution /iːvə'luːʃ(ə)n/ *n.* 1 gradual development. 2 development of species from earlier forms, as an explanation of their origins. 3 unfolding of events etc. 4 change in the disposition of troops or ships. □ **evolutionary** *adj.* [Latin: related to EVOLVE]

evolutionist *n.* person who regards evolution as explaining the origin of species.

evolve /ɪ'vɒlv/ *v.* (-**ving**) 1 develop gradually and naturally. 2 devise (a theory, plan, etc.). 3 unfold. 4 give off (gas, heat etc.). [Latin *volvo volut-* roll]

ewe /juː/ *n.* female sheep. [Old English]

ewer /'juːə(r)/ *n.* water-jug with a wide mouth. [Latin *aqua* water]

ex[1] *prep.* (of goods) sold from (*ex-works*). [Latin, = out of]

ex[2] *n. colloq.* former husband or wife. [see EX-[1]]

ex-[1] *prefix* (also before some consonants **e-**, **ef-** before *f*) 1 (forming verbs meaning: **a** out, forth (*exclude; exit*). **b** upward (*extol*). **c** thoroughly (*excruciate*). **d** bring into a state (*exasperate*). **e** remove or free from (*expatriate; exonerate*). 2 forming nouns from titles of office, status, etc. meaning 'formerly' (*ex-president; ex-wife*). [Latin from *ex* out of]

ex-[2] *prefix* (*exodus*) [Greek]

exacerbate /ek'sæsə,beɪt/ *v.* (-**ting**) 1 make (pain etc.) worse. 2 irritate (a person). □ **exacerbation** /-'beɪʃ(ə)n/ *n.* [Latin *acerbus* bitter]

exact /ɪg'zækt/ –*adj.* 1 accurate, correct in all details (*exact description*). 2 precise. –*v.* 1 demand and enforce payment of (money etc.). 2 demand; insist on; require. □ **exactness** *n.* [Latin *exigo exact-* require]

exacting *adj.* 1 making great demands. 2 requiring much effort.

exaction /ɪg'zækʃ(ə)n/ *n.* 1 exacting or being exacted. 2 **a** illegal or exorbitant demand; extortion. **b** sum or thing exacted.

exactitude *n.* exactness, precision.

exactly *adv.* **1** precisely. **2** (said in reply) I quite agree.

exact science *n.* a science in which absolute precision is possible.

exaggerate /ɪɡˈzædʒəˌreɪt/ *v.* (**-ting**) **1** (also *absol.*) make (a thing) seem larger or greater etc. than it really is. **2** increase beyond normal or due proportions (*exaggerated politeness*). □ **exaggeration** /-ˈreɪʃ(ə)n/ *n.* [Latin *agger* heap]

exalt /ɪɡˈzɔːlt/ *v.* **1** raise in rank or power etc. **2** praise highly. **3** (usu. as **exalted** *adj.*) make lofty or noble (*exalted aims*; *exalted style*). □ **exaltation** /ˌeɡzɔːlˈteɪʃ(ə)n/ *n.* [Latin *altus* high]

exam /ɪɡˈzæm/ *n.* = EXAMINATION 3.

examination /ɪɡˌzæmɪˈneɪʃ(ə)n/ *n.* **1** examining or being examined. **2** detailed inspection. **3** test of proficiency or knowledge by questions. **4** formal questioning of a witness etc. in court. □ **examine** /ɪɡˈzæmɪn/ *v.* (**-ning**) **1** inquire into the nature or condition etc. of. **2** look closely at. **3** test the proficiency of. **4** check the health of (a patient). **5** formally question in court. □ **examinee** /-ˈniː/ *n.* **examiner** *n.* [Latin *examen* tongue of a balance]

example /ɪɡˈzɑːmp(ə)l/ *n.* **1** thing characteristic of its kind or illustrating a general rule. **2** person, thing, or piece of conduct, in terms of its fitness to be imitated. **3** circumstance or treatment seen as a warning to others. **4** problem or exercise designed to illustrate a rule. □ **for example** by way of illustration. [Latin *exemplum*: related to EXEMPT]

exasperate /ɪɡˈzɑːspəˌreɪt/ *v.* (**-ting**) irritate intensely. □ **exasperation** /-ˈreɪʃ(ə)n/ *n.* [Latin *asper* rough]

ex cathedra /ˌeks kəˈθiːdrə/ *adj.* & *adv.* with full authority (esp. of a papal pronouncement). [Latin, = from the chair]

excavate /ˈekskəˌveɪt/ *v.* (**-ting**) **1 a** make (a hole or channel) by digging. **b** dig out material from (the ground). **2** reveal or extract by digging. **3** (also *absol.*) *Archaeol.* dig systematically to explore (a site). □ **excavation** /-ˈveɪʃ(ə)n/ *n.* **excavator** *n.* [Latin *excavo*: related to CAVE]

exceed /ɪkˈsiːd/ *v.* **1** (often foll. by *by* an amount) be more or greater than. **2** go beyond or do more than is warranted by (a set limit, esp. of one's authority, instructions, or rights). **3** surpass. [Latin *excedo* -*cess*- go beyond]

exceedingly /ɪkˈsiːdɪŋlɪ/ *adv.* extremely.

excel /ɪkˈsel/ *v.* (**-ll-**) **1** surpass. **2** be preeminent. [Latin *excello* be eminent]

excellence /ˈeksələns/ *n.* outstanding merit or quality. [Latin: related to EXCEL]

Excellency *n.* (*pl.* **-ies**) (usu. prec. by *Your, His, Her, Their*) title used in addressing or referring to certain high officials.

excellent *adj.* extremely good.

eccentric var. of ECCENTRIC (in technical senses).

except /ɪkˈsept/ —*v.* exclude from a general statement, condition, etc. —*prep.* (often foll. by *for*) not including; other than (*all failed except him*; *is all right except that it is too long*). —*conj. archaic* unless (*except he be born again*). [Latin *excipio -cept-* take out]

excepting *prep.* = EXCEPT *prep.*

■ **Usage** *Excepting* should be used only after *not* and *always*; otherwise, *except* should be used.

exception /ɪkˈsepʃ(ə)n/ *n.* **1** excepting or being excepted. **2** thing that has been or will be excepted. **3** instance that does not follow a rule. □ **take exception** (often foll. by *to*) object. **with the exception of** except.

exceptionable *adj.* open to objection.

■ **Usage** *Exceptionable* is sometimes confused with *exceptional*.

exceptional *adj.* **1** forming an exception; unusual. **2** outstanding. □ **exceptionally** *adv.*

■ **Usage** See note at *exceptionable*.

excerpt —*n.* /ˈeksɜːpt/ short extract from a book, film, etc. —*v.* /ɪkˈsɜːpt/ (also *absol.*) take extracts from. □ **excerption** /-ˈsɜːpʃ(ə)n/ *n.* [Latin *carpo* pluck]

excess /ɪkˈses, ˈekses/ —*n.* **1** exceeding. **2** amount by which one thing exceeds another. **3 a** overstepping of accepted limits of moderation, esp. in eating or drinking. **b** (in *pl.*) immoderate behaviour. **4** part of an insurance claim to be paid by the insured. —*attrib. adj.* usu. /ˈekses/ **1** that exceeds a prescribed amount. **2** required as extra payment (*excess postage*). □ **in** (or **to**) **excess** exceeding the proper amount or degree. **in excess of** more than; exceeding. [Latin: related to EXCEED]

excess baggage *n.* (also **excess luggage**) baggage exceeding a weight allowance and liable to an extra charge.

excessive /ɪkˈsesɪv/ *adj.* too much or too great. □ **excessively** *adv.*

exchange /ɪksˈtʃeɪndʒ/ —*n.* **1** giving of one thing and receiving of another in its place. **2** giving of money for its equivalent in the money of another or another

exchange rate n. value of one currency in terms of another.

exchequer /ɪks'tʃekər/ n. 1 former government department in charge of national revenue. 2 royal or national treasury. 3 money of a private individual or group. [medieval Latin *scaccarium* chessboard]

■ **Usage** With reference to sense 1, the functions of this department in the UK now belong to the Treasury, although the name formally survives, e.g. in the title *Chancellor of the Exchequer*.

excise[1] /'eksaɪz/ n. tax on goods produced or sold within the country of origin. 2 tax on certain licences. —v. (-**sing**) 1 charge excise on. 2 force (a person) to pay excise. [Dutch *excijs* from Romanic: related to Latin CENSUS tax]

excise[2] /ɪk'saɪz/ v. (-**sing**) 1 remove (a passage from a book etc.). 2 cut out (an organ etc.) by surgery. □ **excision** /ɪk'sɪʒ(ə)n/ n. [Latin *excido* *cis* cut]

excitable /ɪk'saɪtəb(ə)l/ adj. easily excited. □ **excitability** /-'bɪlɪtɪ/ n.

excitably adv.

excite /ɪk'saɪt/ v. (-**ting**) 1 a rouse the emotions of (a person). b arouse (feelings etc.). c arouse sexually. 2 provoke (an action etc.). 3 stimulate (an organism, tissue, etc.) to activity. [Latin *cieo* stir up]

excitement n. 1 excited state of mind. 2 exciting thing.

exciting adj. arousing great interest or enthusiasm. □ **excitingly** adv.

exclaim /ɪks'kleɪm/ v. 1 cry out suddenly. 2 (foll. by *that*) utter by exclaiming. [Latin: related to CLAIM]

exclamation /ˌeksklə'meɪʃ(ə)n/ n. 1 exclaiming. 2 word(s) exclaimed. [Latin: related to EXCLAIM]

exclamation mark n. punctuation mark (!) indicating exclamation.

exclamatory /ɪk'sklæmətərɪ/ adj. of or serving as an exclamation.

exclude /ɪk'sklu:d/ v. (-**ding**) 1 keep out (a person or thing) from a place, group,

privilege, etc. 2 remove from consideration (*no theory can be excluded*). 3 make impossible, preclude (*excluded all doubt*). □ **exclusion** n. [Latin *excludo* -*clus*- shut out]

exclusive /ɪk'sklu:sɪv/ —adj. 1 excluding other things. 2 (*predic*; foll. by *of*) not including; except for. 3 tending to exclude others, esp. socially. 4 high-class. 5 not obtainable elsewhere or not published elsewhere. —n. article etc. published by only one newspaper etc. □ **exclusively** adv. **exclusiveness** n. **exclusivity** /-'sɪvɪtɪ/ n.

excommunicate —v. /ˌekskə'mju:nɪkeɪt/ (-**ting**) officially exclude (a person) from membership and esp. sacraments of the Church. —adj. /ˌekskə'mju:nɪkət/ excommunicated person. —n. /ˌekskə'mju:nɪkət/ excommunicated person. □ **excommunication** /-'keɪʃ(ə)n/ n. [Latin: related to COMMON]

excoriate /eks'kɔ:rɪeɪt/ v. (-**ting**) 1 a remove skin from (a person etc.) by abrasion. b strip off (skin). 2 censure severely. □ **excoriation** /-'eɪʃ(ə)n/ n. [Latin *corium* hide]

excrement /'ekskrɪmənt/ n. faeces. □ **excremental** /-'ment(ə)l/ adj. [Latin: related to EXCRETE]

excrescence /ɪk'skres(ə)ns/ n. 1 abnormal or morbid outgrowth on the body or a plant. 2 ugly addition. □ **excrescent** adj. [Latin *cresco* grow]

excreta /ɪk'skri:tə/ n.pl. faeces and urine. [Latin: related to EXCRETE]

excrete /ɪk'skri:t/ v. (-**ting**) (of an animal or plant) expel (waste matter). □ **excretion** n. **excretory** adj. [Latin *cerno cret-* sift]

excruciating /ɪk'skru:ʃɪeɪtɪŋ/ adj. causing acute mental or physical pain. □ **excruciatingly** adv. [Latin *crucio* torment]

exculpate /'ekskʌlpeɪt/ v. (-**ting**) *formal* free from blame, clear of a charge. □ **exculpation** /-'peɪʃ(ə)n/ n. **exculpatory** /-'kʌlpətərɪ/ adj. [Latin *culpa* blame]

excursion /ɪk'skɜ:ʃ(ə)n/ n. journey (usu. a day-trip) to a place and back, made for pleasure. [Latin *excurro* run out]

excursive /ɪk'skɜ:sɪv/ adj. *literary* digressive.

excuse —v. /ɪk'skju:z/ (-**sing**) 1 try to lessen the blame attaching to (a person, act, or fault). 2 (of a fact) serve as a reason to judge (a person or act) less severely. 3 (often foll. by *from*) release (a person) from a duty etc. 4 forgive (a fault or offence). 5 (foll. by *for*) forgive (a person) for (a fault). 6 *refl.* leave with

country. 3 centre where telephone connections are made. 4 place where charts, bankers, etc. transact business. 5 a office where information is given or a service provided. b employment office. 6 system of settling debts without the use of money, by bills of exchange. 7 short conversation. —v. (-**ging**) 1 (often foll. by *for*) give or receive (one thing) in place of another. 2 give and receive as equivalents. 3 (often foll. by *with*) make an exchange. □ **in exchange** (often foll. by *for*) as a thing exchanged (for). □ **exchangeable** adj. [French: related to CHANGE]

apologies. —*n.* **1** reason put forward to mitigate or justify an offence. **2** apology (*made my excuses*). □ **be excused** be allowed to leave the room etc. or be absent. **excuse me** polite preface to an interruption etc., or to disagreeing. □ **excusable** /-'kjuːzəb(ə)l/ *adj.* [Latin *causa* accusation]

ex-directory /ˌeksdəˈrektərɪ/ *adj.* not listed in a telephone directory, at one's own request.

execrable /ˈeksɪkrəb(ə)l/ *adj.* abominable. [Latin: related to EXECRATE]

execrate /ˈeksɪˌkreɪt/ *v.* (**-ting**) **1** express or feel abhorrence for. **2** (also *absol.*) curse (a person or thing). □ **execration** /-ˈkreɪʃ(ə)n/ *n.* [Latin *execror* curse: related to SACRED]

execute /ˈeksɪˌkjuːt/ *v.* (**-ting**) **1** carry out, perform (a plan, duty etc.). **2** carry out a design for (a product of art or skill). **3** carry out a death sentence on. **4** make (a legal instrument) valid by signing, sealing, etc. [Latin *sequor* follow]

execution /ˌeksɪˈkjuːʃ(ə)n/ *n.* **1** carrying out; performance. **2** technique or style of performance in the arts, esp. music. **3** carrying out of a death sentence. [Latin: related to EXECUTE]

executioner *n.* official who carries out a death sentence.

executive /ɪgˈzekjʊtɪv/ —*n.* **1** person or body with managerial or administrative responsibility. **2** branch of a government concerned with executing laws, agreements, etc. —*adj.* concerned with executing laws, agreements, etc., or with other administration or management. [medieval Latin: related to EXECUTE]

executor /ɪgˈzekjʊtə(r)/ *n.* (*fem.* **executrix** /-trɪks/) person appointed by a testator to administer his or her will. □ **executorial** /-ˈtɔːrɪəl/ *adj.*

exegesis /ˌeksɪˈdʒiːsɪs/ *n.* (*pl.* **exegeses** /-siːz/) critical explanation of a text, esp. of Scripture. □ **exegetic** /-ˈdʒetɪk/ *adj.* [Greek *hēgeomai* lead]

exemplar /ɪgˈzemplɑː(r)/ *n.* **1** model. **2** typical or parallel instance. [Latin: related to EXAMPLE]

exemplary /ɪgˈzemplərɪ/ *adj.* **1** fit to be imitated; outstandingly good. **2** serving as a warning. **3** illustrative. [Latin: related to EXAMPLE]

exemplify /ɪgˈzemplɪˌfaɪ/ *v.* (**-ies, -ied**) **1** illustrate by example. **2** be an example of. □ **exemplification** /-fɪˈkeɪʃ(ə)n/ *n.*

exempt /ɪgˈzempt/ —*adj.* (often foll. by *from*) free from an obligation or liability etc. imposed on others. —*v.* (foll. by *from*) make exempt. □ **exemption** *n.* [Latin *eximo -empt-* take out]

exercise /ˈeksəˌsaɪz/ —*n.* **1** activity requiring physical effort, done to sustain or improve health. **2** mental or spiritual activity, esp. as practice to develop a faculty. **3** task devised as exercise. **4** a use or application of a mental ability, right, etc. **b** practice of an ability, quality, etc. **5** (often in *pl.*) military drill or manoeuvres. —*v.* (**-sing**) **1** use or apply (a faculty, right, etc.). **2** perform (a function). **3 a** take (esp. physical) exercise. **b** provide (an animal) with exercise. **4 a** tax the powers of. **b** perplex, worry. [Latin *exerceo* keep busy]

exert /ɪgˈzɜːt/ *v.* **1** bring to bear, use (a quality, force, influence, etc.). **2** *refl.* (often foll. by *for,* or *to* + *infin.*) use one's efforts or endeavours; strive. □ **exertion** *n.* [Latin *exsero exsert-* put forth]

exeunt /ˈeksɪˌʌnt/ *v.* (as a stage direction) (actors) leave the stage. [Latin: related to EXIT]

exfoliate /eksˈfəʊlɪˌeɪt/ *v.* (**-ting**) **1** come off in scales or layers. **2** throw off layers of bark. □ **exfoliation** /-ˈeɪʃ(ə)n/ *n.* [Latin *folium* leaf]

ex gratia /eks ˈgreɪʃə/ —*adv.* as a favour; not from (esp. legal) obligation. —*attrib. adj.* granted on this basis. [Latin, = from favour]

exhale /eksˈheɪl/ *v.* (**-ling**) **1** breathe out. **2** give off or be given off in vapour. □ **exhalation** /ˌekshəˈleɪʃ(ə)n/ *n.* [French from Latin *halo* breathe]

exhaust /ɪgˈzɔːst/ —*v.* **1** consume or use up the whole of. **2** (often as **exhausted** *adj.* or **exhausting** *adj.*) tire out. **3** study or expound (a subject) completely. **4** (often foll. by *of*) empty (a vessel etc.) of its contents. —*n.* **1** waste gases etc. expelled from an engine after combustion. **2** (also **exhaust-pipe**) pipe or system by which these are expelled. **3** process of expulsion of these gases. □ **exhaustible** *adj.* [Latin *haurio haust-* drain]

exhaustion /ɪgˈzɔːstʃ(ə)n/ *n.* **1** exhausting or being exhausted. **2** total loss of strength.

exhaustive /ɪgˈzɔːstɪv/ *adj.* thorough, comprehensive. □ **exhaustively** *adv.* **exhaustiveness** *n.*

exhibit /ɪgˈzɪbɪt/ —*v.* (**-t-**) **1** show or reveal, esp. publicly. **2** display (a quality etc.). —*n.* item displayed, esp. in an exhibition or as evidence in a lawcourt. □ **exhibitor** *n.* [Latin *exhibeo -hibit-*]

exhibition /ˌeksɪˈbɪʃ(ə)n/ *n.* **1** display (esp. public) of works of art etc. **2** exhibiting or being exhibited. **3** scholarship, esp. from the funds of a school, college, etc.

exhibitioner n. student who has been awarded an exhibition.

exhibitionism n. 1 tendency towards attention-seeking behaviour. 2 Psychol. compulsion to display one's genitals in public. □ **exhibitionist** n.

exhilarate /ɪgˈzɪləreɪt/ v. (often as **exhilarating**, **exhilarated** adj.) enliven, gladden; raise the spirits of. □ **exhilaration** /-ˈreɪʃ(ə)n/ n. [Latin: related to HILARIS cheerful]

exhort /ɪgˈzɔːt/ v. (often foll. by to + infin.) urge strongly or earnestly. □ **exhortation** /ˌegzɔːˈteɪʃ(ə)n/ n. **ex-hortative** /-tətɪv/ adj. (also **ex-hortatory** /-tət(ə)rɪ/) [Latin exhortor encourage]

exhume /eks'hjuːm/ v. (-**ming**) dig up (esp. a buried corpse). □ **exhumation** /-'meɪʃ(ə)n/ n. [Latin humus ground]

exigency /ˈeksɪdʒənsɪ/ n. (pl. -**ies**) (also **exigence**) 1 urgent need or demand. 2 emergency. □ **exigent** adj. [Latin EXACT]

exiguous /egˈzɪgjʊəs/ adj. scanty, small. □ **exiguity** /ˌeksɪˈgjuːɪtɪ/ n. [Latin]

exile /ˈeksaɪl/ —n. 1 expulsion from one's native land or (**internal exile**) native town etc. 2 long absence abroad. 3 exiled person. —v. (-**ling**) send into exile. [French from Latin]

exist /ɪgˈzɪst/ v. 1 have a place in objective reality. 2 (of circumstances etc.) occur; be found. 3 live with no pleasure. 4 continue to live or be. [Latin existo]

existence n. 1 fact or manner of being or existing. 2 continuance in life or being. 3 all that exists. □ **existent** adj. [Latin existo]

existential /ˌegzɪˈstenʃ(ə)l/ adj. 1 of or relating to existence. 2 Philos. concerned with existence, esp. with human existence as viewed by existentialism. □ **existentially** adv.

existentialism /ˌegzɪˈstenʃəlɪz(ə)m/ n. philosophical theory emphasizing the existence of the individual as a free and self-determining agent. □ **existentialist** n. & adj.

exit /ˈeksɪt/ —n. 1 passage or door by which to leave a room etc. 2 act or right of going out. 3 place where vehicles can leave a motorway etc. 4 actor's departure from the stage. —v. (-**t**-) 1 go out of a room etc. 2 leave the stage (also as a direction: exit Macbeth). [Latin exeo exit-go out]

exit poll n. poll of people leaving a polling-station, asking how they voted.

exo- comb. form external. [Greek exō outside]

exocrine /ˈeksəʊˌkraɪn/ adj. (of a gland) secreting through a duct. [Greek krinō sift]

exodus /ˈeksədəs/ n. 1 mass departure. 2 (**Exodus**) Biblical departure of the Israelites from Egypt. [Greek hodos way]

ex officio /ˌeks əˈfɪʃɪəʊ/ adv. & attrib. adj. by virtue of one's office. [Latin]

exonerate /ɪgˈzɒnəreɪt/ v. (-**ting**) (often foll. by from) free or declare free from blame etc. □ **exoneration** /-ˈreɪʃ(ə)n/ n. [Latin onus oner- burden]

exorbitant /ɪgˈzɔːbɪt(ə)nt/ adj. (of a price, demand, etc.) grossly excessive. [Latin: related to ORBIT]

exorcize /ˈeksɔːˌsaɪz/ v. (also **-ise**) (-**zing**) 1 expel (a supposed evil spirit) by prayers etc. 2 (often foll. by of) free (a person or place) in this way. □ **exor-cism** n. **exorcist** n. [Greek horkos oath]

exordium /ekˈsɔːdɪəm/ n. (pl. -**s** or **-dia**) introductory part, esp. of a discourse or treatise. [Latin exo-dior begin]

exotic /ɪgˈzɒtɪk/ —adj. 1 introduced from a foreign country; not native. 2 strange or unusual. —n. exotic person or thing. □ **exotically** adv. [Greek exō outside]

exotica n.pl. strange or rare objects. [Greek]

expand /ɪkˈspænd/ v. 1 increase in size or importance. 2 (often foll. by on) give a fuller account. 3 become more genial. 4 set or write out in full. 5 spread out flat. □ **expandable** adj. [Latin pando pans-spread]

expanse /ɪkˈspæns/ n. wide continuous area of land, space, etc.

expansible adj. that can be expanded.

expansion /ɪkˈspænʃ(ə)n/ n. 1 expanding or being expanded. 2 enlargement of the scale or scope o: a business.

expansionism n. advocacy of expansion, esp. of a State's territory. □ **expansionist** n. & adj.

expansive /ɪkˈspænsɪv/ adj. 1 able or tending to expand. 2 extensive. 3 (of a person etc.) effusive, open. □ **expans-ively** adv. **expansiveness** n.

expat /eks'pæt/ n. & adj. colloq. expat-riate. [abbreviation]

expatiate /ɪkˈspeɪʃɪeɪt/ v. (-**ting**) (usu. foll. by on, upon) speak or write at length. □ **expatiation** /-ˈeɪʃ(ə)n/ n. [Latin spatium SPACE]

expatriate —adj. /eks'pætrɪət/ 1 living abroad. 2 exiled. —n. /eks'pætrɪət/ expatriate person. —v. /eks'pætrɪeɪt/ (-**ting**) 1 expel (a person) from his or her native country. 2 refl. renounce one's citizenship. □ **ex-patriation** /-ˈeɪʃ(ə)n/ n. [Latin patria native land]

expect /ɪkˈspekt/ v. 1 a regard as likely. b look for as appropriate or one's due (I expect cooperation). 2 colloq. think, suppose. □ **be expecting** colloq. be pregnant (with). [Latin specto look]

expectancy /ɪkˈspɛktənsɪ/ n. (pl. -ies) 1 state of expectation. 2 prospect. 3 (foll. by of) prospective chance.

expectant /ɪkˈspɛkt(ə)nt/ adj. 1 hopeful, expecting. 2 having an expectation. 3 pregnant. □ **expectantly** adv.

expectation /ˌɛkspɛkˈteɪʃ(ə)n/ n. 1 expecting or anticipation. 2 thing expected. 3 (foll. by of) probability of an event. 4 (in pl.) one's prospects of inheritance.

expectorant /ɛkˈspɛktərənt/ —adj. causing expectoration.—n. expectorant medicine.

expectorate /ɛkˈspɛktəˌreɪt/ v. (-ting) (also absol.) cough or spit out (phlegm etc.). □ **expectoration** /-ˈreɪʃ(ə)n/ n. [Latin pectus pector- breast]

expedient /ɪkˈspiːdɪənt/ —adj. advantageous; advisable on practical rather than moral grounds. —n. means of attaining an end; resource. □ **expedience** n. **expediency** n. [related to EXPEDITE]

expedite /ˈɛkspɪˌdaɪt/ v. (-ting) 1 assist the progress of. 2 accomplish (business) quickly. [Latin expedio from pes ped- foot]

expedition /ˌɛkspɪˈdɪʃ(ə)n/ n. 1 journey or voyage for a particular purpose, esp. exploration. 2 people etc. undertaking this. 3 speed. [Latin: related to EXPEDITE]

expeditionary adj. of or used in an expedition.

expeditious /ˌɛkspɪˈdɪʃəs/ adj. acting or done with speed and efficiency.

expel /ɪkˈspɛl/ v. (-ll-) (often foll. by from) 1 deprive (a person) of membership etc. of a school, society, etc. 2 force out, eject. 3 order or force to leave a building etc. [Latin pello puls- drive]

expend /ɪkˈspɛnd/ v. spend or use up (money, time, etc.). [Latin pendo pens- weigh]

expendable adj. that may be sacrificed or dispensed with; not worth preserving or saving.

expenditure /ɪkˈspɛndɪtʃə(r)/ n. 1 spending or using up. 2 thing (esp. money) expended.

expense /ɪkˈspɛns/ n. 1 cost incurred; payment of money. 2 (usu. in pl.) a costs incurred in doing a job etc. b amount paid to reimburse this. 3 thing on which money is spent. □ **at the expense of** so as to cause loss or harm to; costing. [Latin expensa: related to EXPEND]

expense account n. list of an employee's expenses payable by the employer.

expensive adj. costing or charging much. □ **expensively** adv. **expensiveness** n.

experience /ɪkˈspɪərɪəns/ —n. 1 observation of or practical acquaintance with facts or events. 2 knowledge or skill resulting from this. 3 event or activity participated in or observed (a rare experience). —v. (-cing) 1 have experience of; undergo. 2 feel. [Latin experior -pert- try]

experienced adj. 1 having had much experience. 2 skilled from experience (experienced driver).

experiential /ɪkˌspɪərɪˈɛnʃ(ə)l/ adj. involving or based on experience. □ **experientially** adv.

experiment /ɪkˈspɛrɪmənt/ —n. procedure adopted in the hope of success, or for testing a hypothesis etc., or to demonstrate a known fact. —v. /also -ˌmɛnt/ (often foll. by on, with) make an experiment. □ **experimentation** /-menˈteɪʃ(ə)n/ n. **experimenter** n. [Latin: related to EXPERIENCE]

experimental /ɪkˌspɛrɪˈmɛnt(ə)l/ adj. 1 based on or making use of experiment. 2 used in experiments. □ **experimentalism** n. **experimentally** adv.

expert /ˈɛkspɜːt/ —adj. 1 (often foll. by at, in) having special knowledge of or skill in a subject. 2 (attrib.) involving or resulting from this (expert advice). —n. (often foll. by at, in) person with special knowledge or skill. □ **expertly** adv. [Latin: related to EXPERIENCE]

expertise /ˌɛkspɜːˈtiːz/ n. expert skill, knowledge, or judgement. [French]

expiate /ˈɛkspɪˌeɪt/ v. (-ting) pay the penalty for or make amends for (wrongdoing). □ **expiable** /ˈɛkspɪəb(ə)l/ adj. **expiation** /-ˈeɪʃ(ə)n/ n. **expiatory** adj. [Latin expio: related to PIOUS]

expire /ɪkˈspaɪə(r)/ v. (-ring) 1 (of a period of time, validity, etc.) come to an end. 2 cease to be valid. 3 die. 4 (also absol.) breathe out (air etc.). □ **expiration** /ˌɛkspɪˈreɪʃ(ə)n/ n. **expiratory** adj. (in sense 4). [Latin spirare breathe]

expiry n. end of validity or duration.

explain /ɪkˈspleɪn/ v. 1 a make clear or intelligible (also absol.: let me explain). b make known in detail. 2 (foll. by that) say by way of explanation. 3 account for (one's conduct etc.). □ **explain away** minimize the significance of by explanation. **explain oneself** 1 make one's meaning clear. 2 give an account of one's motives or conduct. [Latin explano from planus flat]

explanation /ˌɛksplənˈeɪʃ(ə)n/ n. 1 explaining. 2 statement or circumstance that explains something.

explanatory /ɪkˈsplænət(ə)rɪ/ adj. serving or designed to explain.

expletive /ɪk'spli:tɪv/ n. swear-word or exclamation. [Latin *expleo* fill out]

expletive /ɪk'splɪkəb(ə)l/ adj. that can be explained.

explicate /'eksplɪˌkeɪt/ v. (-ting) 1 develop the meaning of (an idea etc.). 2 explain (esp. a literary text). □ **explica-tion** /-'keɪʃ(ə)n/ n. [Latin *explico* unfold]

explicit /ɪk'splɪsɪt/ adj. 1 expressly stated, not merely implied; stated in detail. 2 definite. 3 outspoken. □ **expli-citly** adv. **explicitness** n. [Latin: related to EXPLICATE]

explode /ɪk'spləʊd/ v. (-ding) 1 a expand suddenly with a loud noise owing to a release of internal energy. b cause (a bomb etc.) to explode. 2 give vent suddenly to emotion, esp. anger. 3 (of a population etc.) increase suddenly or rapidly. 4 show (a theory etc.) to be false or baseless. 5 (as **exploded** adj.) (of a drawing etc.) showing the components of a mechanism somewhat separated but in the normal relative positions. [Latin *explodo -plos-* hiss off the stage]

exploit –n. /'eksplɔɪt/ daring feat. –v. /ɪk'splɔɪt/ 1 make use of (a resource etc.). 2 usu. *derog.* utilize or take advantage of (esp. a person) for one's own ends. □ **exploitation** /ˌeksplɔɪ'teɪʃ(ə)n/ n. **exploitative** /ɪk'splɔɪtətɪv/ adj. **exploiter** n. [Latin: related to EXPLI-CATE]

explore /ɪk'splɔ:(r)/ v. (-ring) 1 travel through (a country etc.) to learn about it. 2 inquire into. 3 *Surgery* examine (a part of the body) in detail. □ **explora-tion** /ˌeksplə'reɪʃ(ə)n/ n. **exploratory** /-'splɒrətrɪ/ adj. **explorer** n. [Latin *exploro* search out]

explosion /ɪk'spləʊʒ(ə)n/ n. 1 explod-ing. 2 loud noise caused by this. 3 sud-den outbreak of feeling. 4 rapid or sud-den increase. [Latin: related to EXPLODE]

explosive /ɪk'spləʊsɪv/ –adj. 1 able, tending, likely to explode. 2 likely to cause a violent outburst etc.; danger-ously tense. –n. explosive substance. □ **explosiveness** n.

Expo /'ekspəʊ/ n. (also **expo**) (pl. **-s**) large international exhibition. [abbre-viation cf. EXPOSITION 4]

exponent /ɪk'spəʊnənt/ n. 1 person who promotes an idea etc. 2 practitioner of an activity, profession, etc. 3 person who explains or interprets something. 4 type or representative. 5 raised symbol beside a numeral indicating how many of the number are to be multiplied together (e.g. $2^3 = 2 \times 2 \times 2$). [Latin *expono* EXPOUND]

exponential /ˌekspə'nenʃ(ə)l/ adj. 1 of or indicated by a mathematical expo-nent 2 (of an increase etc.) more and more rapid.

export –v. /ɪk'spɔ:t, 'ek-/ sell or send (goods or services) to another country. –n. /'ekspɔ:t/ 1 exporting. 2 a exported article or service. b (in *pl.*) amount exported. □ **exportation** /-'teɪʃ(ə)n/ n. **exporter** /ɪk'spɔ:tə(r)/ n. [Latin *porto* carry]

expose /ɪk'spəʊz/ v. (-sing) (esp. as **exposed** adj.) 1 leave uncovered or unprotected, esp. from the weather. 2 (foll. by *to*) a put at risk of. b subject to (an influence etc.). 3 *Photog.* subject (a film) to light, esp. by operation of a camera. 4 reveal the identity or fact of. 5 exhibit, display. □ **expose oneself** dis-play one's body, esp. one's genitals, indecently in public. [Latin *pono* put]

exposé /ek'spəʊzeɪ/ n. 1 orderly state-ment of facts. 2 revelation of something discreditable. [French]

exposition /ˌekspə'zɪʃ(ə)n/ n. 1 explanatory account. 2 explanation or commentary. 3 *Mus.* part of a movement in which the principal themes are presented. 4 large public exhibition. [Latin: related to EXPOUND]

ex post facto /ˌeks pəʊst 'fæktəʊ/ adj. & adv. with retrospective action or force. [Latin, = in the light of subsequent events]

expostulate /ɪk'spɒstjʊˌleɪt/ v. (-ting) (often foll. by *with* a person) make a protest; remonstrate. □ **expostulation** /-'leɪʃ(ə)n/ n. **expostulatory** /-lətərɪ/ adj. [Latin: related to POSTULATE]

exposure /ɪk'spəʊʒə(r)/ n. (foll. by *to*) 1 exposing or being exposed. 2 physical condition resulting from being exposed to the elements. 3 *Photog.* a exposing a film etc. to the light. b duration of this. c section of film etc. affected by it.

expound /ɪk'spaʊnd/ v. 1 set out in detail. 2 explain or interpret. [Latin *pono posit-* place]

express /ɪk'spres/ –v. 1 represent or make known in words or by gestures, conduct, etc. 2 *refl.* communicate what one thinks, feels, or means. 3 esp. *Math.* represent by symbols. 4 squeeze out (liquid or air). 5 send by express service. –adj. 1 operating at high speed. 2 also /'ekspres/ definitely stated. 3 delivered by a specially fast service. –adv. 1 at high speed. 2 by express messenger or train. –n. 1 express train etc. 2 *US* service for the rapid transport of par-cels etc. □ **expressible** adj. expressly adv. (in sense 2 of adj.). [Latin *exprimo -press-* squeeze out]

expression /ɪkˈspreʃ(ə)n/ n. **1** expressing or being expressed. **2** word or phrase expressed. **3** person's facial appearance, indicating feeling. **4** conveying of feeling in music, speaking, dance, etc. **5** depiction of feeling etc. in art. **6** Math. collection of symbols expressing a quantity. □ **expressionless** adj. [French: related to EXPRESS]

expressionism n. style of painting, music, drama, etc., seeking to express emotion rather than the external world. □ **expressionist** n. & adj.

expressive /ɪkˈspresɪv/ adj. **1** full of expression (expressive look). **2** (foll. by of) serving to express. □ **expressively** adv. **expressiveness** n.

expresso var. of ESPRESSO.

expressway n. US motorway.

expropriate /ɪkˈsprəʊprɪˌeɪt/ v. (-ting) **1** take away (property) from its owner. **2** (foll. by from) dispossess. □ **expropriation** /-ˈeɪʃ(ə)n/ n. **expropriator** n. [Latin proprium property]

expulsion /ɪkˈspʌlʃ(ə)n/ n. expelling or being expelled. □ **expulsive** adj. [Latin: related to EXPEL]

expunge /ɪkˈspʌndʒ/ v. (-ging) **1** remove objectionable matter from (a book etc.). **2** remove (such matter). □ **expurgation** /-ˈgeɪʃ(ə)n/ n. **expurgator** n. [Latin: related to PURGE]

exquisite /ɪkˈskwɪzɪt/ adj. **1** extremely beautiful or delicate. **2** keenly felt (exquisite pleasure). **3** highly sensitive (exquisite taste). □ **exquisitely** adv. [Latin exquiro -quisit- seek out]

ex-serviceman /eksˈsɜːvɪsmən/ n. man formerly a member of the armed forces. **ex-servicewoman** /eksˈsɜːvɪsˌwʊmən/ n. woman formerly a member of the armed forces.

extant /ekˈstænt/ adj. still existing. [Latin ex(s)to exist]

extemporaneous /ɪkˌstempəˈreɪnɪəs/ adj. spoken or done without preparation. □ **extemporaneously** adv. [from EXTEMPORE]

extemporary /ɪkˈstempərərɪ/ adj. = EXTEMPORANEOUS. □ **extemporarily** adv.

extempore /ɪkˈstempərɪ/ adj. & adv. without preparation. [Latin]

extemporize /ɪkˈstempəˌraɪz/ v. (also -ise) (-zing or -sing) improvise. □ **extemporization** /-ˈzeɪʃ(ə)n/ n.

extend /ɪkˈstend/ v. **1** lengthen or make larger in space or time. **2** stretch or lay out at full length. **3** (foll. by to, over) reach or be or make continuous over a specified area. **4** (foll. by to) have a specified scope (permit does not extend to camping). **5** offer or accord (an invitation, hospitality, kindness, etc.). **6** (usu. refl. or in passive) tax the powers of (an athlete, horse, etc.). □ **extendible** adj. (also **extensible**). [Latin extendo -tens-: related to TEND¹]

extended family n. family including relatives living near.

extended-play adj. (of a gramophone record) playing for somewhat longer than most singles.

extension /ɪkˈstenʃ(ə)n/ n. **1** extending or being extended. **2** part enlarging or added on to a main building etc. **3** additional part. **4 a** subsidiary telephone on the same line as the main one. **b** its number. **5** additional period of time. **6** extramural instruction by a university or college.

extensive /ɪkˈstensɪv/ adj. **1** covering a large area. **2** far-reaching. □ **extensively** adv. **extensiveness** n. [Latin: related to EXTEND]

extent /ɪkˈstent/ n. **1** space over which a thing extends. **2** range, scope, degree. [Anglo-French: related to EXTEND]

extenuating /ɪkˈstenjʊˌeɪt/ v. (often as **extenuating** adj.) make (guilt or an offence) seem less serious by reference to another factor. □ **extenuation** /-ˈeɪʃ(ə)n/ n. [Latin tenuis thin]

exterior /ɪkˈstɪərɪə(r)/ -adj. **1** of or on the outer side. **2** coming from outside. -n. **1** outward aspect or surface of a building etc. **2** outward demeanour. **3** outdoor scene in filming. [Latin]

exterminate /ɪkˈstɜːmɪˌneɪt/ v. (-ting) destroy utterly (esp. a living thing). □ **extermination** /-ˈneɪʃ(ə)n/ n. **exterminator** n. [Latin: related to TERMINAL]

external /ɪkˈstɜːn(ə)l/ -adj. **1 a** of or on the outside or visible part. **b** coming from the outside or an outside source. **5** relating to a country's foreign affairs. **3** outside the conscious subject (the external world). **4** (of medicine etc.) for use on the outside of the body. **5** for students taking the examinations of a university without attending it. -n. **1** (in pl.) outward features or aspect. **2** external circumstances. **3** inessentials. □ **externality** /ˌekstəˈnælɪtɪ/ n. **externally** adv. [Latin externus outer]

externalize v. (also **-ise**) (-zing or -sing) give or attribute external existence to. □ **externalization** /-ˈzeɪʃ(ə)n/ n.

extinct /ɪkˈstɪŋkt/ adj. **1** that has died out. **2** no longer burning. **b** (of a volcano) that no longer erupts. **3** obsolete. [Latin ex(s)tinguo -stinct- quench]

extinction /ɪk'stɪŋkʃ(ə)n/ n. 1 making or becoming extinct. 2 extinguishing or being extinguished. 3 total destruction or annihilation.

extinguish /ɪk'stɪŋgwɪʃ/ v. 1 cause (a flame, light, etc.) to die out. (a debt). 3 terminate. 4 wipe out (a debt). □ **extinguishable** adj.

extinguisher n. = FIRE EXTINGUISHER.

extirpate /'ekstə,peɪt/ v. (-ting) root out; destroy completely. □ **extirpation** /-'peɪʃ(ə)n/ n. [Latin ex(s)tirpo from stirps stem of tree]

extol /ɪk'stəʊl/ v. (-ll-) praise enthusiastically. [Latin tollo raise]

extort /ɪk'stɔːt/ v. obtain by coercion. [Latin torqueo tort- twist]

extortion /ɪk'stɔːʃ(ə)n/ n. 1 act of extorting, esp. money. 2 illegal exaction. □ **extortioner** n. **extortionist** n.

extortionate /ɪk'stɔːʃənət/ adj. (of a price etc.) exorbitant. □ **extortionately** adv.

extra /'ekstrə/ —adj. additional; more than usual or necessary or expected. —adv. 1 more than usually. 2 additionally (was charged extra). —n. 1 extra thing. 2 thing for which an extra charge is made. 3 person engaged temporarily for a minor part in a film. 4 special issue of a newspaper etc. 5 Cricket run scored other than from a hit with the bat. [probably from EXTRAORDINARY]

extra- comb. form 1 outside. 2 beyond the scope of. [Latin extra outside]

extra cover n. Cricket 1 fielding position on a line between cover-point and mid-off, but beyond these. 2 fielder at this position.

extract —v. /ɪk'strækt/ 1 remove or take out, esp. by effort or force. 2 obtain (money, an admission, etc.) against a person's will. 3 obtain (a natural resource) from the earth. 4 select or reproduce for quotation or performance. 5 obtain (juice etc.) by pressure, distillation, etc. 6 derive (pleasure etc.). 7 find (the root of a number). —n. /'ekstrækt/ 1 short passage from a book etc. 2 preparation containing a concentrated constituent of a substance (malt extract). [Latin traho tract- draw]

extraction /ɪk'strækʃ(ə)n/ n. 1 extracting or being extracted. 2 removal of a tooth. 3 lineage, descent (of Indian extraction). [Latin traho tract- draw]

extractive /ɪk'stræktɪv/ adj. of or involving extraction.

extractor /ɪk'stræktə(r)/ n. 1 person or machine that extracts. 2 (attrib.) (of a device) that extracts bad air etc.

extracurricular /,ekstrəkə'rɪkjʊlə(r)/ adj. not part of the normal curriculum.

extraditable /'ekstrə,daɪtəb(ə)l/ adj. 1 liable to extradition. 2 (of a crime) warranting extradition.

extradite /'ekstrə,daɪt/ v. (-ting) hand over (a person accused or convicted of a crime) to the foreign State etc. in which the crime was committed. □ **extradition** /-'dɪʃ(ə)n/ n. [French: related to TRADITION]

extramarital /,ekstrə'mærɪt(ə)l/ adj. (esp. of sexual relations) occurring outside marriage.

extramural /,ekstrə'mjʊər(ə)l/ adj. additional to normal teaching or studies, esp. for non-resident students.

extraneous /ɪk'streɪnəs/ adj. 1 of external origin. 2 (often foll. by to) a separate from the object to which it is attached etc. b irrelevant, unrelated. [Latin extraneus]

extraordinary /ɪk'strɔːdɪn(ə)rɪ/ adj. 1 unusual or remarkable. 2 unusually great. 3 (of a meeting, official, etc.) additional; specially employed. □ **extraordinarily** adv. [Latin]

extrapolate /ɪk'stræpə,leɪt/ v. (-ting) (also absol.) calculate approximately from known data etc. (others which lie outside the range of those known). □ **extrapolation** /-'leɪʃ(ə)n/ n. [from EXTRA, INTERPOLATE]

extrasensory /,ekstrə'sensərɪ/ adj. derived by means other than the known senses, e.g. by telepathy.

extraterrestrial /,ekstrətə'restrɪəl/ —adj. outside the earth or its atmosphere. —n. (in science fiction) being from outer space.

extravagant /ɪk'strævəg(ə)nt/ adj. 1 spending money excessively. 2 excessive; absurd. 3 costing much. □ **extravagantly** adv. [Latin vagor wander]

extravaganza /ɪk,strævə'gænzə/ n. 1 spectacular theatrical or television production. 2 fanciful literary, musical, or dramatic composition. [Italian]

extreme /ɪk'striːm/ —adj. 1 of a high, or the highest, degree (extreme danger). 2 severe (extreme measures). 3 outermost. 4 on the far left or right of a political party. 5 utmost; last. —n. 1 (often in pl.) either of two things as remote or as different as possible. 2 thing at either end. 3 highest degree. 4 Math first or last term of a ratio or series. □ **go to extremes** take an extreme course of action. **in the extreme** to an extreme degree. □ **extremely** adv. [French from Latin]

extreme unction n. last rites in the Roman Catholic and Orthodox Churches.

extremist *n.* (also *attrib.*) person with extreme views. □ **extremism** *n.*

extremity /ɪk'strɛmɪtɪ/ *n.* (*pl.* **-ies**) **1** extreme point; very end. **2** (in *pl.*) the hands and feet. **3** condition of extreme adversity. [Latin: related to EXTREME]

extricate /'ɛkstrɪ,keɪt/ *v.* (**-ting**) (often foll. by *from*) free or disentangle from a difficulty etc. □ **extricable** *adj.* **extrication** /-'keɪʃ(ə)n/ *n.* [Latin *tricae* perplexities]

extrinsic /ɛk'strɪnsɪk/ *adj.* **1** not inherent or intrinsic. **2** (often foll. by *to*) extraneous; not belonging. □ **extrinsically** *adv.* [Latin *extrinsecus* outwardly]

extrovert /'ɛkstrə,vɜːt/ *—n.* **1** outgoing person. **2** person mainly concerned with external things. *—adj.* typical of or with the nature of an extrovert. □ **extroversion** /-'vɜːʃ(ə)n/ *n.* **extroverted** *adj.* [Latin *verto* turn]

extrude /ɪk'struːd/ *v.* (**-ding**) **1** (foll. by *from*) thrust or force out. **2** shape metal, plastics, etc. by forcing them through a die. □ **extrusion** *n.* **extrusive** *adj.* [Latin *extrudo -trus-* thrust out]

exuberant /ɪg'zjuːbərənt/ *adj.* **1** lively, high-spirited. **2** (of a plant etc.) prolific. **3** (of feelings etc.) abounding. □ **exuberance** *n.* **exuberantly** *adv.* [Latin *uber* fertile]

exude /ɪg'zjuːd/ *v.* (**-ding**) **1** ooze out. **2** emit (a smell). **3** display (an emotion etc.) freely. □ **exudation** /-'deɪʃ(ə)n/ *n.* [Latin *sudo* sweat]

exult /ɪg'zʌlt/ *v.* be joyful. □ **exultation** /-'teɪʃ(ə)n/ *n.* **exultant** *adj.* **exultantly** *adv.* [Latin *ex(s)ulto* from *salio salt-* leap]

-ey var. of **-y**[2].

eye /aɪ/ *—n.* **1** organ of sight. **2** eye characterized by the colour of the iris (*has blue eyes*). **3** region round the eye (*eyes swollen from weeping*). **4** (in *sing.* or *pl.*) sight. **5** particular visual ability (*a straight eye*). **6** thing like an eye, esp.: **a** a spot on a peacock's tail. **b** a leaf bud of a potato. **7** calm region at the centre of a hurricane etc. **8** hole of a needle. *—v.* (**eyes, eyed, eyeing** or **eying**) (often foll. by *up*) watch or observe closely, esp. admiringly or with suspicion. □ **all eyes** watching intently. **an eye for an eye** retaliation in kind. **have an eye for** be discerning about. **have one's eye on 1** watch. **2** wish or plan to procure. **have eyes for** wish to acquire. **keep an eye on 1** watch. **2** look after. **keep an eye open** (or *out*) (often foll. by *for*) watch carefully. **keep one's eyes open** (or *peeled* or *skinned*) watch out; be on the alert. **make eyes** (or *sheep's eyes*)

(foll. by *at*) look amorously or flirtatiously at. **one in the eye** (often foll. by *for*) disappointment or setback. **see eye to eye** (often foll. by *with*) agree. **set eyes on** see. **up to the** (or *one's*) **eyes in** deeply engaged or involved in. **with one's eyes shut** (or *closed*) with little effort. **with an eye to** with a view to. [Old English]

eyeball *—n.* ball of the eye within the lids and socket. *—v. US slang* look or stare (at)

eyeball to eyeball *adv. colloq.* confronting closely.

eyebath *n.* small vessel for applying lotion etc. to the eye.

eyebright *n.* plant used as a remedy for weak eyes.

eyebrow *n.* line of hair on the ridge above the eye-socket. □ **raise one's eyebrows** show surprise, disbelief, or disapproval.

eye-catching *adj. colloq.* striking.

eyeful *n.* (*pl.* **-s**) *colloq.* **1** (esp. in phr. **get an eyeful of**) good look; as much as the eye can take in. **2** visually striking person or thing. **3** thing thrown or blown into the eye.

eyeglass *n.* lens to assist defective sight.

eyehole *n.* hole to look through.

eyelash *n.* each of the hairs growing on the edges of the eyelids.

eyelet /'aɪlɪt/ *n.* **1** small hole for string or rope etc. to pass through. **2** metal ring strengthening this. [French *oillet* from Latin *oculus*]

eyelid *n.* either of the folds of skin closing to cover the eye.

eye-liner *n.* cosmetic applied as a line round the eye.

eye-opener *n. colloq.* enlightening experience; unexpected revelation.

eyepiece *n.* lens or lenses to which the eye is applied at the end of an optical instrument.

eye-shade *n.* device to protect the eyes, esp. from strong light.

eye-shadow *n.* coloured cosmetic applied to the eyelids.

eyesight *n.* faculty or power of seeing.

eyesore *n.* ugly thing.

eye strain *n.* fatigue of the eye muscles.

eye-tooth *n.* canine tooth in the upper jaw just under the eye.

eyewash *n.* **1** lotion for the eyes. **2** *slang* nonsense; insincere talk.

eyewitness *n.* person who saw a thing happen and can tell of it.

eyrie /'ɪərɪ/ *n.* **1** nest of a bird of prey, esp. an eagle, built high up. **2** house etc. perched high up. [French *aire* lair, from Latin *agrum* piece of ground]

F¹ /ef/ n. (also **f**) (pl. **Fs** or **F's**) **1** sixth letter of the alphabet. **2** Mus. fourth note of the diatonic scale of C major.

F² abbr. (also **F.**) **1** Fahrenheit. **2** farad(s).

F³ symb. fluorine.

f abbr. (also **f.**) **1** female. **2** feminine. **3** following page etc. **4** Mus. forte. **5** folio. **6** focal length.

FA abbr. Football Association.

fa var. of FAH.

fab adj. colloq. fabulous, marvellous. [abbreviation]

fable /'feɪb(ə)l/ n. **1 a** fictional, esp. supernatural, story. **b** moral tale, esp. with animals as characters. **2** legendary tales collectively (in fable). **3 a** lie. **b** thing only supposed to exist. [Latin fabula discourse]

fabled adj. celebrated; legendary.

fabric /'fæbrɪk/ n. **1** woven material; cloth. **2** walls, floor, and roof of a building. **3** essential structure. [Latin faber metal-worker]

fabricate /'fæbrɪkeɪt/ v. (-ting) **1** construct, esp. from components. **2** invent (a story etc.). **3** forge (a document). □ **fabrication** /-'keɪʃ(ə)n/ n. **fabricator** n. [Latin: related to FABRIC]

fabulous /'fæbjʊləs/ adj. **1** incredible. **2** colloq. marvellous. **3** legendary. □ **fabulously** adv. [Latin: related to FABLE]

façade /fə'sɑːd/ n. **1** face or front of a building. **2** outward appearance, esp. a deceptive one. [French: related to FACE]

face –n. **1** front of the head from forehead to chin. **2** facial expression. **3** coolness, effrontery. **4** surface, esp.: **a** solid. **d** the façade of a building. **e** dial of a clock etc. **5** functional side of a tool etc. **6** = TYPEFACE. **7** aspect (unacceptable face of capitalism). –v. (-cing) **1** look or be positioned towards or in a certain direction. **2** be opposite. **3** meet resolutely. **4** confront (faces us with a problem). **5 a** coat the surface of (a thing). **b** put a facing on (a garment). □ **face the music** colloq. take unpleasant consequences without flinching. **face up to** accept bravely. **have the face** be shameless enough. **in face of** despite. **lose face** be humiliated. **on the face of it** apparently. **put a bold (or brave) face on it** accept difficulty etc.

cheerfully. **save face** avoid humiliation. **set one's face against** oppose stubbornly. **to a person's face** openly in a person's presence. [Latin facies]

face-cloth n. cloth for washing one's face.

face-flannel n. = FACE-CLOTH.

faceless adj. **1** without identity; characterless. **2** purposely not identifiable.

face-lift n. **1** (also **face-lifting**) cosmetic surgery to remove wrinkles etc. **2** improvement to appearance, efficiency, etc.

face-pack n. skin preparation for the face.

facer n. colloq. sudden difficulty.

facet /'fæsɪt/ n. **1** aspect. **2** side of a cut gem etc. [French: related to FACE]

facetious /fə'siːʃəs/ adj. intending or intended to be amusing, esp. inappropriately. □ **facetiously** adv. [Latin facetia jest]

facia var. of FASCIA.

facial /'feɪʃ(ə)l/ –adj. of or for the face. –n. beauty treatment for the face. □ **facially** adv.

facile /'fæsaɪl/ adj. usu. derog. **1** easily achieved but of little value. **2** glib, fluent. [Latin facio do]

facilitate /fə'sɪlɪteɪt/ v. (-ting) ease (a process etc.). □ **facilitation** /-'teɪʃ(ə)n/ n. [Italian: related to FACILE]

facility /fə'sɪlɪtɪ/ n. (pl. -ies) **1** ease; absence of difficulty. **2** fluency, dexterity. **3** (esp. in pl.) opportunity or equipment for doing something. [Latin: related to FACILE]

facing n. **1** layer of material covering part of a garment etc. for contrast or strength. **2** outer covering on a wall etc.

facsimile /fæk'sɪmɪlɪ/ n. exact copy, esp. of writing, printing, a picture, etc. [Latin, = make like]

fact n. **1** thing that is known to exist or to be true. **2** (usu. in pl.) item of verified information. **3** truth, reality. **4** thing assumed as the basis for argument. □ **in point of fact** **1** in reality. **2** in short. **facia var. of FASCIA.** **in (or after) the fact** before (or after) the committing of a crime. [Latin factum from facio do]

faction /ˈfækʃ(ə)n/ n. small organized dissentient group within a larger one, esp. in politics. □ **factional** adj. [Latin: related to FACT]

-faction comb. form forming nouns of action from verbs in -fy (satisfaction). [Latin -factio]

factious /ˈfækʃəs/ adj. of, characterized by, or inclined to faction. [Latin: related to FACTION]

factitious /fækˈtɪʃəs/ adj. 1 specially contrived 2 artificial. [Latin: related to FACT]

fact of life n. something that must be accepted.

factor /ˈfæktə(r)/ n. 1 circumstance etc. contributing to a result. 2 whole number etc. that when multiplied with another produces a given number. 3 a business agent. b Scot. land-agent, steward. c agent, deputy. [Latin: related to FACT]

factorial /fækˈtɔːrɪəl/ —n. product of a number and all the whole numbers below it. —adj. of a factor or factorial. [ultimately from Latin factorium]

factorize v. (also -ise) (-zing or -sing) resolve into factors. □ **factorization** /-ˈzeɪʃ(ə)n/ n.

factory /ˈfækt(ə)rɪ/ n. (pl. -ies) building(s) in which goods are manufactured. [ultimately from Latin factorium]

factory farm n. farm using intensive or industrial methods of livestock rearing. □ **factory farming** n.

factotum /fækˈtəʊtəm/ n. (pl. -s) employee who does all kinds of work. [medieval Latin: related to FACT, TOTAL]

facts and figures n.pl. precise details.

factsheet n. information leaflet, esp. accompanying a television programme.

facts of life n.pl. (prec. by the) information about sexual functions and practices.

factual /ˈfæktʃʊəl/ adj. based on or concerned with fact. □ **factually** adv.

faculty /ˈfæk(ə)ltɪ/ n. (pl. -ies) 1 aptitude for a particular activity. 2 inherent mental or physical power. 3 a group of related university departments. b US teaching staff of a university or college. 4 authorization, esp. by a Church authority. [Latin: related to FACILE]

fad n. 1 craze. 2 peculiar notion. □ **faddish** adj. [probably from fiddle-faddle]

faddy adj. (-ier, -iest) having petty likes and dislikes. □ **faddiness** n.

fade —v. (-ding) 1 lose or cause to lose colour, light, or sound; slowly diminish. 2 lose freshness or strength. 3 (foll. by in, out) Cinematog. etc. cause (a picture or sound) to appear or disappear, increase or decrease, gradually. —n. action of fading. □ **fade away** 1 colloq.

languish, grow thin. 2 die away; disappear. [French fade dull]

faeces /ˈfiːsiːz/ n.pl. (US feces) waste matter discharged from the bowels. □ **faecal** /ˈfiːk(ə)l/ adj. [Latin]

faff v. colloq. (often foll. by about, around) fuss, dither. [imitative]

fag[1] —n. 1 colloq. tedious task. 2 slang cigarette. 3 (at public schools) junior boy who runs errands for a senior. —v. (-gg-) 1 (often foll. by out) colloq. exhaust. 2 (at public schools) act as a fag. [origin unknown]

fag[2] n. US slang offens. male homosexual. [abbreviation of FAGGOT]

fag-end n. slang cigarette-end.

faggot /ˈfægət/ n. (US fagot) 1 ball of seasoned chopped liver etc., baked or fried. 2 bundle of sticks etc. 3 slang offens. a unpleasant woman. b US male homosexual. [French from Italian]

fah /fɑː/ n. (also fa) Mus. fourth note of a major scale. [Latin famuli: see GAMUT]

Fahrenheit /ˈfærənˌhaɪt/ adj. of a scale of temperature on which water freezes at 32° and boils at 212°. [Fahrenheit, name of a physicist]

faience /faɪˈɑːs/ n. decorated and glazed earthenware and porcelain. [French from Faenza in Italy]

fail —v. 1 not succeed (failed to qualify). 2 be or judge to be unsuccessful in (an examination etc.). 3 be unable; neglect (failed to appear). 4 disappoint. 5 be absent or insufficient 6 become weaker; cease functioning (health is failing; engine failed). 7 become bankrupt. —n. failure in an examination. □ **without fail** for certain, whatever happens. [Latin fallo deceive]

failed adj. unsuccessful (failed actor).

failing —n. fault, weakness. —prep. in default of.

fail-safe adj. reverting to a safe condition when faulty etc.

failure /ˈfeɪljə(r)/ n. 1 lack of success; failing. 2 unsuccessful person or thing. 3 non-performance. 4 breaking down or ceasing to function (heart failure). 5 running short of supply etc. [Anglo-French: related to FAIL]

fain archaic —predic. adj. (foll. by to + infin.) willing or obliged to. —adv. gladly (esp. would fain). [Old English]

faint —adj. 1 indistinct; pale, dim. 2 weak or giddy. 3 slight. 4 feeble; timid. 5 (also feint) (of paper) with inconspicuous ruled lines. —v. 1 lose consciousness. 2 become faint. —n. act or state of fainting. □ **faintly** adv. **faintness** n. [French: related to FEIGN]

faint-hearted adj. cowardly, timid.

fair[1] —adj. 1 just, equitable; in accordance with the rules. 2 blond; light or

pale. **3 a** moderate in quality or amount. **b** satisfactory. **4** (of weather) fine; (of the wind) favourable. **5** clean, clear (*fair copy*). **6** *archaic* beautiful. —*adv.* **1** in a just manner. **2** exactly, completely. □ **in a fair way to** likely to. □ **fairness** *n.* [Old English]

fair² *n.* **1** stalls, amusements, etc., for public entertainment. **2** periodic market, often with entertainments. **3** exhibition, esp. commercial. [Latin *feriae* holiday]

fair and square *adv.* exactly; straightforwardly.

fair dinkum see DINKUM.

fair dos *n.pl.* (esp. as *int.*) *colloq.* fair shares; fair treatment.

fair game *n.* legitimate target or object.

fairground *n.* outdoor area where a fair is held.

fairing *n.* streamlining structure added to a ship, aircraft, vehicle, etc.

Fair Isle *n.* (also *attrib.*) multicoloured knitwear design characteristic of Fair Isle. [*Fair Isle* in the Shetlands]

fairly *adv.* **1** in a fair manner. **2** moderately (*fairly good*). **3** quite, rather (*fairly narrow*).

fair play *n.* just treatment or behaviour.

fair sex *n.* (prec. by *the*) women.

fairway *n.* **1** navigable channel. **2** part of a golf-course between a tee and its green, kept free of rough grass.

fair-weather friend *n.* unreliable friend or ally.

fairy *n.* (*pl.* **-ies**) **1** (often *attrib.*) small winged legendary being. **2** *slang offens.* male homosexual. [French: related to FAY, -ERY]

fairy cake *n.* small iced sponge cake.

fairy godmother *n.* benefactress.

fairyland *n.* **1** home of fairies. **2** enchanted region.

fairy lights *n.pl.* small decorative coloured lights.

fairy ring *n.* ring of darker grass caused by fungi.

fairy story *n.* (also **fairy tale**) **1** tale about fairies. **2** incredible story; lie.

fait accompli /ˌfeɪt əˈkɒmpliː/ *n.* thing that has been done and is not capable of alteration. [French]

faith *n.* **1** complete trust or confidence. **2** firm, esp. religious, belief. **3** religion or creed (*Christian faith*). **4** loyalty, trustworthiness. [Latin *fides*]

faithful *adj.* **1** showing faith. **2** (often foll. by *to*) loyal, trustworthy. **3** accurate (*faithful account*). **4** (**the Faithful**) the believers in a religion. □ **faithfulness** *n.*

faithfully *adv.* in a faithful manner. □ **Yours faithfully** formula for ending a

formal letter when it begins 'Dear Sir' or 'Dear Madam'.

faithless *adj.* **1** false, unreliable, disloyal. **2** without religious faith.

fake —*n.* **1** false or counterfeit thing or person. —*adj.* counterfeit, not genuine. —*v.* (**-king**) **1** make a fake or imitation of (*faked my signature*). **2** feign (a feeling, illness, etc.). [German *fegen* sweep]

fakir /ˈfeɪkɪə(r)/ *n.* Muslim or (rarely) Hindu religious beggar or ascetic. [Arabic, = poor man]

falcon /ˈfɔːlkən/ *n.* small hawk sometimes trained to hunt. [Latin *falco*]

falconry *n.* breeding and training of hawks.

fall /fɔːl/ —*v.* (*past* **fell**; *past part.* **fallen**) **1** go or come down freely; descend. **2** (often foll. by *over*) come suddenly to the ground from loss of balance etc. **3 a** hang or slope down. **b** (foll. by *into*) (of a river etc.) discharge into. **4 a** sink lower; decline. **b** in power, status, etc. **b** subside. **5** occur (*fals on a Monday*). **6** (of the face) show dismay or disappointment. **7** yield to temptation. **8** take or have a particular direction or place (*his eye fell on me; accent falls on the first syllable*). **9 a** find a place; be naturally divisible. **b** (foll. by *under, within*) be classed among. **10** come by chance or duty (*it fell to me to answer*). **11 a** pass into a specified condition (*fell ill*). **b** become (*fall asleep*). **12** be defeated or captured. **13** die. **14** (foll. by *on, upon*) **a** attack. **b** meet with. **c** embrace or embark on avidly. **15** (foll. by *to* + verbal noun) begin (*fell to wondering*). —*n.* **1** act of falling. **2** that which falls or has fallen, e.g. snow. **3** recorded amount of rainfall etc. **4** overthrow (*fall of Rome*). **5 a** succumbing to temptation. **b** (**the Fall**) Adam's sin and its results. **6** (also **Fall**) *US* autumn. **7** (esp. in *pl.*) waterfall etc. **8** wrestling-bout; throw in wrestling. □ **fall about** *colloq.* be helpless with laughter. **fall away 1** (of a surface) incline abruptly. **2** become few or thin; gradually vanish. **3** desert. **fall back** retreat. **fall back on** have recourse to in difficulty. **fall behind 1** be outstripped; lag. **2** be in arrears. **fall down** (often foll. by *on*) *colloq.* fail. **fall for** *colloq.* be captivated or deceived by. **fall foul of** come into conflict with. **fall in 1** take one's place in military formation. **2** collapse inwards. **fall in with 1** meet by chance. **2** agree with. **3** coincide with. **fall off 1** become detached. **2** decrease, deteriorate. **fall out 1** quarrel. **2** (of the hair, teeth, etc.) become detached. **3** *Mil.* come out of formation. **4** result; occur. **fall over backwards**

see BACKWARDS. **fall over oneself** *colloq.* **1** be eager. **2** stumble through haste, confusion, etc. **fall short** be deficient. **fall short of** fail to reach or obtain. **fall through** fail; miscarry. **fall to** begin, e.g. eating or working. [Old English]

fall guy n. slang easy victim; scapegoat.

fallible /ˈfælɪb(ə)l/ adj. capable of making mistakes. □ **fallibility** /-ˈbɪlɪtɪ/ n. **fallibly** adv. [medieval Latin: related to FALLACY]

falling star n. meteor.

Fallopian tube /fəˈləʊpɪən/ n. either of two tubes along which ova travel from the ovaries to the womb. [*Fallopius*, name of an anatomist]

fallout n. radioactive nuclear debris.

fallow /ˈfæləʊ/ —adj. **1** (of land) ploughed but left unsown. **2** uncultivated. —n. fallow land. [Old English]

fallow deer n. small deer with a white-spotted reddish-brown summer coat. [Old English *fallow* pale brownish or reddish yellow]

false /fɔːls/ adj. **1** wrong, incorrect. **2** spurious, artificial. **3** improperly so called (*false acacia*). **4** deceptive. **5** (foll. by *to*) deceitful, treacherous, or unfaithful. □ **falsely** adv. **falseness** n. [Latin *falsus*: related to FAIL]

false alarm n. alarm given needlessly.

false pretences n.pl. misrepresentations made with intent to deceive (esp. *under false pretences*).

falsetto /fɔːlˈsetəʊ/ n. male singing voice above the normal range. [Italian diminutive: related to FALSE]

falsies /ˈfɔːlsɪz/ n.pl. colloq. pads worn to make the breasts seem larger.

falsify /ˈfɔːlsɪ.faɪ/ v. (-ies, -ied) **1** fraudulently alter. **2** misrepresent. □ **falsification** /-fɪˈkeɪʃ(ə)n/ n. [French or medieval Latin: related to FALSE]

falsity n. being false.

falter /ˈfɔːltə(r)/ v. **1** stumble; go unsteadily. **2** lose courage. **3** speak hesitatingly. [origin uncertain]

fame n. **1** renown; being famous. **2** archaic reputation. [Latin *fama*]

famed adj. (foll. by *for*) famous; much spoken of.

familial /fəˈmɪlɪəl/ adj. of a family or its members.

esp. presumptuously so. —n. **1** close friend. **2** (in full **familiar spirit**) supposed attendant of a witch etc. □ **familiarity** /-ˈærɪtɪ/ n. **familiarly** adv. [Latin: related to FAMILY]

familiarize v. (also **-ise**) (-zing or -sing) (usu. foll. by *with*) make (a person or oneself) conversant or well acquainted. □ **familiarization** /-ˈzeɪʃ(ə)n/ n.

family /ˈfæmɪlɪ/ n. (pl. -ies) **1** set of relations, esp. parents and children. **2 a** members of a household. **b** person's children. **3** all the descendants of a common ancestor. **4** group of similar objects, people, etc. **5** group of related genera of animals or plants. □ **in the family way** colloq. pregnant. [Latin *familia*]

family allowance n. former name for CHILD BENEFIT.

family credit n. (also **family income supplement**) regular State payment to a low-income family.

family man n. man who has a wife and children, esp. one fond of family life.

family name n. surname.

family planning n. birth control.

family tree n. genealogical chart.

famine /ˈfæmɪn/ n. extreme scarcity, esp. of food. [Latin *fames* hunger]

famish /ˈfæmɪʃ/ v. (usu. in *passive*) make or become extremely hungry. □ **be famished** (or **famishing**) colloq. be very hungry. [Romanic: related to FAMINE]

famous /ˈfeɪməs/ adj. **1** (often foll. by *for*) celebrated; well-known. **2** colloq. excellent. □ **famously** adv. [Latin: related to FAME]

fan¹ —n. **1** apparatus, usu. with rotating blades, for ventilation etc. **2** folding semicircular device waved to cool oneself. **3** thing spread out like a fan (*fan tracery*). —v. (-nn-) **1** blow air on, with or as with a fan. **2** (of a breeze) blow gently on. **3** (usu. foll. by *out*) spread out like a fan. [Latin *vannus* winnowing-basket]

fan² n. devotee of a particular activity, performer, etc. (*film fan*). [abbreviation of FANATIC]

fanatic /fəˈnætɪk/ —n. person obsessively devoted to a belief, activity, etc. —adj. excessively enthusiastic. □ **fanatical** adj. **fanatically** adv. **fanaticism** /-ˌtɪ.sɪz(ə)m/ n. [Latin *fanum* temple]

fancier /ˈfænsɪə(r)/ n. connoisseur (*dog-fancier*).

fan belt n. belt driving a fan to cool the radiator in a vehicle.

fanciful /ˈfænsɪfʊl/ adj. **1** imaginary. **2** indulging in fancies. □ **fancifully** adv.

fan club n. club of devotees.

fancy /'fænsɪ/ —n. (pl. **-ies**) **1** inclination. **2** whim. **3** supposition. **4** a faculty of imagination. **b** mental image. —*adj.* (-**ier**, -**iest**) **1** ornamental. **2** extravag-ant. —*v.* (-**ies**, -**ied**) (foll. by *that*) be inclined to suppose. **2** *colloq.* feel a desire for *(fancy a drink?)*. **3** *colloq.* find sexually attractive. **4** *colloq.* value (one-self, one's ability, etc.). **5** (in *imper.*) exclamation of surprise. **6** imagine. □ **take a fancy to** become (esp. inexplicably) fond of. **take a person's fancy** suddenly attract or please. □ **fanciable** *adj.* (in sense 3 of *v.*). **fancily** *adv.* **fanciness** n. [contraction of FANT-ASY]

fancy dress n. costume for masquerad-ing at a party.

fancy-free *adj.* without (esp. emotion-al) commitments.

fancy man n. *slang derog.* **1** woman's lover. **2** pimp.

fancy woman n. *slang derog.* mistress.

fandango /fæn'dæŋgəʊ/ n. (pl. **-es** or **-s**) **1** lively Spanish dance for two. **2** music for this. [Spanish]

fanfare /'fænfeə(r)/ n. short showy or ceremonious sounding of trumpets etc. [French]

fang n. **1** canine tooth, esp. of a dog or wolf. **2** tooth of a venomous snake. **3** root of a tooth or its prong. [Old English]

fan-jet n. = TURBOFAN.

fanlight n. small, orig. semicircular, window over a door or another window.

fan mail n. letters from fans.

fanny n. (pl. **-ies**) *coarse slang* the female genitals. **2** *US slang* the but-tocks. [origin unknown]

fantail n. pigeon with a broad tail.

fantasia /fæn'teɪzɪə/ n. free or impro-visatory musical or other composition, or one based on familiar tunes. [Italian: related to FANTASY]

fantasize /'fæntəsaɪz/ v. (also **-ise**) (**-zing** or **-sing**) **1** day-dream. **2** imagine; create a fantasy about.

fantastic /fæn'tæstɪk/ *adj.* **1** *colloq.* ex-cellent, extraordinary. **2** extravagantly fanciful. **3** grotesque, quaint. □ **fant-astically** *adv.* [Greek: related to FANT-ASY]

fantasy /'fæntəsɪ/ n. (pl. **-ies**) **1** imagina-tion, esp. when unrelated to reality *(lives in the realm of fantasy)*. **2** mental image, day-dream. **3** fantastic invention or composition. [Greek *phantasia* appearance]

far (**further**, **furthest** or **farther**, **farthest**) —*adv.* **1** at, to, or by a great distance *(far away; far off; far out)*. **2** a long way (off) in space or time *(are you travelling far?)*. **3** to a great extent or degree; by much *(far better; far too*

early). —*adj.* **1** remote; distant *(far country).* **2** more distant *(far end of the hall).* **3** extreme *(far left).* □ **as far as 1** right up to (a place). **2** to the extent that. **by far** by a great amount. **a far cry** a long way. **far from** very different from; being, almost the opposite of *(far from being fat).* **go far 1** achieve much. **2** contribute greatly. **go too far** overstep the limit (of propriety etc.). **so far 1** to such an extent; to this point **2** until now. **so (or in so) far as** (or that) to the extent that. **so far so good** satisfactory up to now. [Old English]

farad /'færəd/ n. SI unit of capacitance. [Faraday, name of a physicist]

far and away *adv.* by a very large amount.

far-away *adj.* **1** remote. **2** (of a look or voice) dreamy, distant.

farce n. **1** a low comedy with a ludic-rously improbable plot. **b** this branch of drama. **2** absurdly futile proceedings; pretence. □ **farcical** *adj.* [Latin *farcio* to stuff, used metaphorically of interludes etc.]

fare —n. **1** a price of a journey on public transport. **b** fare-paying passenger. **2** range of food. —*v.* (-**ring**) progress; get on *(how did you fare?).* [Old English]

Far East n. (prec. by *the*) China, Japan, and other countries of E. Asia.

fare-stage n. **1** section of bus etc. route for which a fixed fare is charged. **2** stop marking this.

farewell /feə'wel/ —*int.* goodbye. —*n.* leave-taking.

far-fetched *adj.* unconvincing, incred-ible.

far-flung *adj.* **1** widely scattered. **2** re-mote.

far gone *adj. colloq.* very ill, drunk, etc.

farina /fə'riːnə/ n. = flour or meal of cereal, nuts, or starchy roots. **2** starch. □ **farinaceous** /,færɪ'neɪʃəs/ *adj.* [Latin]

farm —n. **1** land and its buildings under one management for growing crops, rearing animals, etc. **2** such land etc. for a specified purpose *(trout-farm).* **3** = FARMHOUSE. —*v.* **1 a** use (land) for grow-ing crops, rearing animals, etc. **b** be a farmer; work on a farm. **2** breed (fish etc.). commercially. **3** (often foll. by *out*) delegate or subcontract (work) to others. □ **farming** n. [French *ferme* from Latin *firma* fixed payment]

farmer n. owner or manager of a farm.

farm-hand n. worker on a farm.

farmhouse n. house attached to a farm.

farmstead /'fɑːmsted/ n. farm and its buildings.

farmyard n. yard attached to a farm-house.

far-off *adj.* remote.

far-out *adj.* 1 distant. 2 *slang* avant-garde, unconventional. 3 *slang* excellent.

farrago /fəˈraːgəʊ/ *n.* (*pl.* -s or *US* -es) medley, hotchpotch. [Latin, = mixed fodder, from *far* corn]

far-reaching *adj.* widely influential or applicable.

farrier /ˈfærɪə(r)/ *n.* smith who shoes horses. [Latin *ferrum* iron, horseshoe]

farrow /ˈfærəʊ/ —*n.* 1 litter of pigs. 2 birth of a litter. —*v.* (also *absol.*) (of a sow) produce (pigs). [Old English]

Farsi /ˈfaːsiː/ *n.* modern Persian language. [Persian]

far-sighted *adj.* 1 having foresight, prudent. 2 esp. *US* = LONG-SIGHTED.

fart *coarse slang* —*v.* 1 emit wind from the anus. 2 (foll. by *about, around*) behave foolishly. —*n.* 1 an emission of wind from the anus. 2 unpleasant or foolish person. [Old English]

farther var. of FURTHER (esp. of physical distance).

farthest var. of FURTHEST (esp. of physical distance).

farthing /ˈfaːðɪŋ/ *n. hist.* coin and monetary unit worth a quarter of an old penny. [Old English: related to FOURTH]

■ **Usage** The farthing was withdrawn from circulation in 1961.

farthingale /ˈfaːðɪŋgeɪl/ *n. hist.* hooped petticoat. [Spanish *verdugo* rod]

fasces /ˈfæsiːz/ *n.pl.* 1 *Rom. Hist.* bundle of rods with a projecting axe-blade, as a magistrate's symbol of power. 2 emblems of authority. [Latin, *pl.* of *fascis* bundle]

fascia /ˈfeɪʃə/ *n.* (also **facia**) (*pl.* -s) 1 a instrument panel of a vehicle. b similar panel over a shop-front. 2 long flat surface in classical architecture. b flat surface, usu. of wood, covering the ends of rafters. 4 stripe or band. [Latin, = band, door-frame]

fascicle /ˈfæsɪk(ə)l/ *n.* section of a book that is published in instalments. [Latin diminutive: related to FASCES]

fascinate /ˈfæsɪneɪt/ *v.* (-**ting**) 1 capture the interest of, attract. 2 paralyse (a victim) with fear. □ **fascination** /-ˈneɪʃ(ə)n/ *n.* [Latin *fascinum* spell]

Fascism /ˈfæʃɪz(ə)m/ *n.* 1 extreme totalitarian right-wing nationalist movement in Italy (1922–43). 2 (also **fascism**) any similar movement. □ **Fascist** *n. & adj.* (also **fascist**). **Fascistic** /-ˈʃɪstɪk/ *adj.* (also **fascistic**). [Italian *fascio* bundle, organized group]

fashion /ˈfæʃ(ə)n/ —*n.* 1 current popular custom or style, esp. in dress. 2 manner of doing something. —*v.* (often foll. by *into*) make or form. □ **after** (or **in**) **a fashion** to some extent, barely acceptably. **in** (or **out of**) **fashion** fashionable (or not fashionable). [Latin *factio*: related to FACT]

fashionable *adj.* 1 following or suited to current fashion. 2 of or favoured by high society. □ **fashionableness** *n.* **fashionably** *adv.*

fast¹ /faːst/ —*adj.* 1 rapid, quick-moving. 2 capable of or intended for high-speed (*fast car; fast road*). 3 (of a clock etc.) ahead of the correct time. 4 (of a film etc.) causing the ball to bounce quickly. 5 firm; firmly fixed or attached (*fast knot; fast friendship*). 6 (of a colour) not fading. 7 (of photographic film etc.) needing only short exposure. —*adv.* 1 quickly; in quick succession. 2 firmly, tightly (*stand fast*). 3 soundly, completely (*fast asleep*). □ **pull a fast one** *colloq.* perpetrate deceit. [Old English]

fast² /faːst/ —*v.* abstain from food, or certain food, for a time. —*n.* act or period of fasting. [Old English]

fastback *n.* 1 car with a sloping rear. 2 such a rear.

fast breeder *n.* (also **fast breeder reactor**) reactor using fast neutrons.

fasten /ˈfaːs(ə)n/ *v.* 1 make or become fixed or secure. 2 (foll. by *in, up*) lock securely; shut in. 3 (foll. by *on, upon*) direct (a look, thoughts, etc.) towards. 4 (foll. by *on, upon*) a take hold of. b single out. 5 (foll. by *off*) fix with a knot or stitches. □ **fastener** *n.* [Old English: related to FAST¹]

fastening /ˈfaːsnɪŋ/ *n.* device that fastens something; fastener.

fast food *n.* restaurant food that is quickly produced and served.

fastidious /fæˈstɪdɪəs/ *adj.* 1 excessively discriminatory; fussy. 2 easily disgusted; squeamish. □ **fastidiously** *adv.* **fastidiousness** *n.* [Latin *fastidium* loathing]

fastness /ˈfaːstnɪs/ *n.* stronghold. [Old English]

fast neutron *n.* neutron with high kinetic energy.

fast worker *n. colloq.* person who rapidly makes esp. sexual advances.

fat —*n.* 1 natural oily or greasy substance found esp. in animal bodies. 2 part of meat etc. containing this. —*adj.* (**fatter, fattest**) 1 corpulent; plump. 2 containing much fat. 3 fertile. 4 a thick (*fat book*). b substantial (*fat cheque*). 5 *colloq. iron.* very little; not much (*a fat chance; a fat lot*). —*v.* (-**tt-**) make or

become fat. □ **the fat is in the fire** trouble is imminent. **kill the fatted calf** celebrate, esp. at a prodigal's return (Luke 15). **live off** (or **on**) **the fat of the land** live luxuriously. □ **fatless** adj.

fatness n. [**fattish** adj.] [Old English]

fatal /ˈfeɪt(ə)l/ adj. 1 causing or ending in death (fatal accident). 2 (often foll. by to) ruinous (fatal mistake). 3 fateful. □ **fatally** adv. [Latin: related to FATE]

fatalism n. 1 belief in predetermination. 2 submissive acceptance. □ **fatalist** n. **fatalistic** /ˌfeɪtəˈlɪstɪk/ adj. **fatalistic-ally** /-ˈlɪstɪkəlɪ/ adv.

fatality /fəˈtælɪtɪ/ n. (pl. -ies) 1 death by accident or in war etc. 2 fatal influence. 3 predestined liability to disaster.

fate —n. 1 supposed power predetermining events. 2 a the future so determined. b individual's destiny or fortune. 3 death, destruction. —v. (-ting) 1 (usu. in passive) preordain (fated to win). 2 (as **fated** adj.) doomed. □ **fate worse than death** see DEATH. [Italian and Latin fatum]

fateful adj. important, decisive. □ **fatefully** adv.

fat-head n. colloq. stupid person. **fat-headed** adj. stupid.

father /ˈfɑːðə(r)/ —n. 1 male parent. 2 (usu. in pl.) forefather. 3 originator, early leader. 4 (**Fathers** or **Fathers of the Church**) early Christian theologians. 5 (also **Father**) priest. 6 (**the Father**) (in Christian belief) first person of the Trinity. 7 (**Father**) venerable person, esp. as a title in personifications (Father Time). 8 (usu. in pl.) elders (city fathers). —v. 1 beget. 2 originate (a scheme etc.). □ **fatherhood** n. **father-less** adj. [Old English]

father-figure n. older man respected and trusted like a father.

father-in-law n. (pl. **fathers-in-law**) father of one's husband or wife.

fatherland n. one's native country.

fatherly adj. like or of a father.

Father's Day n. day on which cards and presents are given to fathers.

fathom /ˈfæð(ə)m/ —n. (pl. often **fathom** when prec. by a number) measure of six feet, esp. in depth soundings. —v. 1 comprehend. 2 measure the depth of (water). □ **fathomable** adj. [Old English]

fathomless adj. too deep to fathom.

fatigue /fəˈtiːg/ —n. 1 extreme tiredness. 2 weakness in metals etc. caused by repeated stress. 3 a non-military army duty. b (in pl.) clothing worn for this. —v. (-gues, -gued, -guing) cause fatigue in (Latin fatigo exhaust]

fatstock n. livestock fattened for slaughter.

fatten v. make or become fat.

fatty adj. (-ier, -iest) like or containing fat.

fatty acid n. organic compound consisting of a hydrocarbon chain and a terminal carboxyl group.

fatuous /ˈfætjʊəs/ adj. vacantly silly; purposeless. □ **fatuity** /fəˈtjuːɪtɪ/ n. (pl. -ies) **fatuously** adv. **fatuousness** n. [Latin fatuus]

fatwa /ˈfætwɑː/ n. legal decision or ruling by an Islamic religious leader. [Arabic]

faucet /ˈfɔːsɪt/ n. esp. US tap. [French fausset vent-peg]

fault /fɔːlt/ —n. 1 defect or imperfection of character, structure, appearance, etc. 2 responsibility for wrongdoing, error, etc. (your own fault). 3 break in an electric circuit. 4 transgression, offence. 5 a Tennis etc. incorrect service. b (in showjumping) penalty for error. 6 break in rock strata. —v. 1 find fault with; blame. 2 Geol. a break the continuity of (strata). b show a fault. □ **at fault** guilty; to blame. **find fault** (often foll. by with) criticize; complain. □ **to a fault** excessively (generous to a fault). [Latin fallo deceive]

fault-finder n. complaining person.

fault-finding n. continual criticism.

faultless adj. perfect. □ **faultlessly** adv.

faulty adj. (-ier, -iest) having faults; imperfect. □ **faultily** adv. **faultiness** n.

faun /fɔːn/ n. Latin rural deity with goat's horns, legs, and tail. [Latin Faunus]

fauna /ˈfɔːnə/ n. (pl. -s or -nae /-niː/) animal life of a region or period. [Latin Fauna, name of a rural goddess]

faux pas /fəʊ ˈpɑː/ n. (pl. same /ˈpɑːz/) tactless mistake; blunder. [French, = false step]

favour /ˈfeɪvə(r)/ (US **favor**) —n. 1 kind act (did it as a favour). 2 approval, goodwill; friendly regard (gained their favour). 3 partiality. 4 badge, ribbon, etc., as an emblem of support. —v. 1 regard or treat with favour or partiality. 2 support, promote, prefer. 3 be to the advantage of, facilitate. 4 tend to confirm (an idea etc.). 5 (foll. by with) oblige. 6 (as **favoured** adj.) having special advantages. □ **in favour 1** approved of. 2 (foll. by of) a in support of. b to the advantage of. **out of favour** disapproved of. [Latin faveo be kind to]

favourable /ˈfeɪvərəb(ə)l/ adj. (US **favorable**) 1 well-disposed; propitious;

approving. 2 promising, auspicious. 3 helpful, suitable. □ **favourably** *adv.*

favourite /'fervrɪt/ (*US* **favorite**) —*adj.* preferred to all others (*favourite book*). —*n.* 1 favourite person or thing. 2 *Sport* competitor thought most likely to win. [Italian: related to FAVOUR]

favouritism *n.* (*US* **favoritism**) unfair favouring of one person etc. at the expense of another.

fawn[1] —*n.* 1 deer in its first year. 2 light yellowish brown. —*adj.* fawn-coloured. —*v.* (also *absol.*) give birth to (a fawn). [Latin: related to FOETUS]

fawn[2] *v.* 1 (often foll. by *on*, *upon*) behave servilely, cringe. 2 (of esp. a dog) show extreme affection. [Old English]

fax —*n.* 1 transmission of an exact copy of a document etc. electronically. 2 copy produced by this. —*v.* transmit in this way. [abbreviation of FACSIMILE]

fay *n. literary* fairy. [Latin *fata* pl., = goddesses of destiny]

faze *v.* (**-zing**) (often as **fazed** *adj.*) *colloq.* disconcert, disorientate. [origin unknown]

FBA *abbr.* Fellow of the British Academy.

FBI *abbr.* Federal Bureau of Investigation.

FC *abbr.* Football Club.

FCO *abbr.* Foreign and Commonwealth Office.

FE *abbr.* further education.

Fe *symb.* iron. [Latin *ferrum*]

fealty /'fiːəltɪ/ *n.* (*pl.* **-ies**) 1 *hist.* fidelity to a feudal lord. 2 allegiance. [Latin: related to FIDELITY]

fear —*n.* 1 a panic or distress caused by a sense of impending danger, pain, etc. **b** cause of this. **c** state of alarm (*in fear*). 2 (often foll. by *of*) dread, awe (*fear of heights*). 3 danger (*little fear of failure*). —*v.* 1 feel fear about or towards. 2 (foll. by *for*) feel anxiety about (*feared for my life*). 3 (often foll. by *that*) foresee (*I fear that you are wrong*). 4 (foll. by verbal noun) shrink from (*feared meeting his ex-wife*). 5 revere (esp. God). □ **for fear of** (*or that*) to avoid the risk of (*or that*). **no fear** *colloq.* certainly not! [Old English]

fearful *adj.* 1 (usu. foll. by *of* or *that*) afraid. 2 terrible, awful. 3 *colloq.* extreme, unpleasant (*fearful row*). □ **fearfully** *adv.* **fearfulness** *n.*

fearless *adj.* (often foll. by *of*) not afraid, brave. □ **fearlessly** *adv.* **fearlessness** *n.*

fearsome *adj.* frightening. □ **fearsomely** *adv.*

---

feasible /'fiːzɪb(ə)l/ *adj.* practicable, possible. □ **feasibility** /-'bɪlɪtɪ/ *n.* **feasibly** *adv.* [Latin *facio* do]

■ **Usage** *Feasible* should not be used to mean 'possible' or 'probable' in the sense 'likely'. 'Possible' or 'probable' should be used instead.

feast —*n.* 1 large or sumptuous meal. 2 sensual or mental pleasure. 3 religious festival. 4 annual village festival. —*v.* 1 (often foll. by *on*) partake of a feast, eat and drink sumptuously. 2 regale. □ **feast one's eyes on** look with pleasure at. [Latin *festus* joy]

feat *n.* remarkable act or achievement. [Latin: related to FACT]

feather /'feðə(r)/ —*n.* 1 one of the structures forming a bird's plumage, with a horny stem and fine strands. 2 (*collect.*) **a** plumage. **b** game-birds. —*v.* 1 cover or line with feathers. 2 turn (an oar) edgeways through the air. □ **feather in one's cap** a personal achievement. **feather one's nest** enrich oneself. **in fine** (or **high**) **feather** *colloq.* in good spirits. □ **feathery** *adj.* [Old English]

feather-bed *v.* (**-dd-**) cushion, esp. financially.

feather-bed *n.* bed with a feather-stuffed mattress.

feather-brain *n.* (also **feather-head**) silly or absent-minded person. □ **feather-brained** *adj.* (also **feather-headed**).

feathering *n.* 1 bird's plumage. 2 feathers of an arrow. 3 feather-like structure or marking.

featherweight *n.* 1 weight in certain sports between bantamweight and lightweight, in amateur boxing 54–57kg. **b** sportsman of this weight. 2 very light person or thing. 3 (usu. *attrib.*) unimportant thing.

feature /'fiːtʃə(r)/ —*n.* 1 distinctive or characteristic part of a thing. 2 (usu. in *pl.*) part of the face. 3 (esp. specialized) article in a newspaper etc. 4 (in full **feature film**) main film in a cinema programme. —*v.* (**-ring**) 1 make a special display of, emphasize. 2 have as or be a central participant or topic in a film, broadcast, etc. □ **featureless** *adj.* [Latin *factura* formation: related to FACT]

Feb. *abbr.* February.

febrifuge /'febrɪfjuːdʒ/ *n.* medicine or treatment for fever. [Latin *febris* fever]

febrile /'fiːbraɪl/ *adj.* of fever; feverish. [Latin *febris* fever]

February /'febrʊərɪ/ *n.* (*pl.* **-ies**) second month of the year. [Latin *februa* purification feast]

fecal *US* var. of FAECAL.

feces *US* var. of FAECES.

feckless /ˈfeklɪs/ *adj.* **1** feeble, inef-fective. **2** unthinking, irresponsible. [Scots *feck* from *effeck* var. of EFFECT]

fecund /ˈfiːkʌnd, ˈfek-/ *adj.* **1** prolific, fertile. **2** fertilizing. □ **fecundity** /fɪˈkʌndɪtɪ/ *n.* [Latin]

fecundate /ˈfiːkən.deɪt/ *v.* (-ting) **1** make fruitful. **2** fertilize. □ **fecundation** /-ˈdeɪʃ(ə)n/ *n.*

fed *past and past part.* of FEED. □ **fed up** (often foll. by *with*) discontented or bored.

federal /ˈfedər(ə)l/ *adj.* **1** of a system of government in which self-governing States unite for certain functions etc. **2** of such a federation (*federal laws*). **3** of or favouring centralized government. **4** (**Federal**) *US* of the Northern States in the Civil War. **5** comprising an associ-ation of largely independent units. □ **federalism** *n.* **federalist** *n.* **feder-alize** *v.* (also **-ise**) (**-zing** or **-sing**). □ **federalization** /-ˈzeɪʃ(ə)n/ *n.* **federally** *adv.* [Latin *foedus* covenant]

federal reserve *n.* (in the US) reserve cash available to banks.

federate —*v.* /ˈfedəreɪt/ (-ting) unite on a federal basis. —*adj.* /ˈfedərət/ federally organized. □ **federative** /ˈfedərətɪv/ *adj.*

federation /ˌfedəˈreɪʃ(ə)n/ *n.* **1** federal group. **2** act of federating. [Latin: related to FEDERAL]

fee *n.* **1** payment made for professional advice or services etc. **2** a charge for a privilege, examination, admission to a society, etc. (*enrolment fee*). **b** money paid for the transfer to another employer of a footballer etc. **3** (in *pl.*) regular payments (esp. to a school). **4** *Law* inherited estate, unlimited (**fee simple**) or limited (**fee tail**) as to cat-egory of heir. [medieval Latin *feudum*]

feeble /ˈfiːb(ə)l/ *adj.* (**feebler, feeblest**) **1** weak, infirm. **2** lacking strength, energy, or effectiveness. □ **feebly** *adv.* [Latin *flebilis* lamentable]

feeble-minded *adj.* mentally deficient.

feed —*v.* (*past and past part.* **fed**) **1 a** supply with food. **b** put food into the mouth of. **2** give as food, or to animals. **3** (usu. foll. by *on*) (of animals, or *colloq.* of people) eat. **4** (often foll. by *on*) nourish or be nourished by; benefit from. **5 a** keep (a fire, machine, etc.) supplied with fuel etc. **b** (foll. by *into*) supply (material) to a machine etc. **c** (often foll. by *into*) (of a river etc.) flow into a lake etc. **d** keep (a meter) supplied with coins to ensure continuity. **6** *colloq.* of people) eat. **7** *Sport* supply (an actor etc.) with cues. **8** *Sport* supply (a player to ...

(vanity etc.). **9** provide (advice, informa-tion, etc.) to. —*n.* **1** food, esp. for animals or infants. **2** feeding; giving of food. **3** *colloq.* meal. **4 a** raw material for a machine etc. **b** provision of or device for this. □ **feed back** produce feedback.

feedback *n.* **1** public response to an event, experiment etc. **2** *Electronics* **a** return of a fraction of an output signal to the input. **b** signal so returned.

feeder *n.* **1** person or thing that feeds, esp. in specified manner. **2** baby's feed-ing-bottle. **3** bib. **4** tributary stream. **5** branch road, railway line, etc. linking electricity to a distribution point. **7** feed-ing apparatus in a machine.

feel —*v.* (*past and past part.* **felt**) **1 a** examine or search for touch. **b** (*absol.*) have the sensation of touch (*unable to feel the warmth*). **3** experience, exhibit, or be affected by (an emotion, convic-tion, etc.) (*felt strongly about it; felt the rebuke*). **4** (foll. by *that*) have an impres-sion (*I feel that I am right*). **5** consider, think (*I feel it useful*). **6** seem (*air feels chilly*). **7** be consciously; consider one-self (*I feel happy*). **8** (foll. by *for, with*) have sympathy or pity. **9** (often foll. by *up*) *slang* fondle sexually. —*n.* **1** feeling; testing by touch. **2** sensation character-izing a material, situation, etc. **3** sense of touch. □ **feel like** have a wish or in-clination for. **feel up to** be ready to face or deal with. **feel one's way** proceed cautiously. **get the feel of** become ac-customed to using. [Old English]

feeler *n.* **1** organ in certain animals for touching or searching for food. **2** tent-ative proposal (*put out feelers*).

feeling —*n.* **1 a** capacity to feel; sense of touch (*lost all feeling*). **b** physical sensa-tion. **2 a** (often foll. by *of*) emotional reaction (*feeling of despair*). **b** (in *pl.*) emotional susceptibilities (*hurt my feel-ings*). **3** particular sensitivity (*feeling for literature*). **4 a** opinion or notion (*had a feeling she would*). **b** general sentiment. **5** sympathy or compassion. **6** emotional sensibility or intensity (*played with feeling*). —*adj.* sensitive, sympathetic; heartfelt. □ **feelingly** *adv.*

feet *pl.* of FOOT.

feign /feɪn/ *v.* simulate; pretend (*feign madness*). [Latin *fingo fict-* mould, con-trive]

feint /feɪnt/ —*n.* **1** sham attack or diver-sionary blow. **2** pretence. —*v.* make a feint. —*adj.* = FAINT *adj.* **5**. [French: related to FEIGN]

feldspar /'feldspɑː(r)/ *n.* (also **felspar**) common aluminium silicate of potassium, sodium, or calcium. □ **feldspathic** /-'spæθik/ *adj.* [German *Feld field*, *Spat(h) spar*³]

felicitate /fɪ'lɪsɪˌteɪt/ *v.* (**-ting**) *formal* congratulate. □ **felicitation** /-ˈteɪʃ(ə)n/ *n.* (usu. in *pl.*). [Latin *felix happy*]

felicitous /fɪ'lɪsɪtəs/ *adj. formal* apt; pleasantly ingenious; well-chosen.

felicity /fɪ'lɪsɪtɪ/ *n.* (*pl.* **-ies**) *formal* **1** intense happiness. **2 a** capacity for apt expression. **b** well-chosen phrase. [Latin *felix happy*]

feline /'fiːlaɪn/ —*adj.* **1** of the cat family. **2** catlike. —*n.* animal of the cat family. □ **felinity** /fɪ'lɪnɪtɪ/ *n.* [Latin *feles cat*]

fell¹ *past of* FALL *v.*

fell², **1** cut down (esp. a tree). **2** strike or knock down. **3** stitch down (the edge of a seam). [Old English]

fell³ *n. N.Engl.* **1** hill. **2** stretch of hills or moorland. [Old Norse]

fell⁴ *adj. poet. or rhet.* ruthless, destructive. □ **at** (or **in**) **one fell swoop** in a single (orig. deadly) action. [French: related to FELON]

fell⁵ *n.* animal's hide or skin with its hair. [Old English]

fellatio /fɪ'leɪʃɪəʊ/ *n.* oral stimulation of the penis. [Latin *fello suck*]

feller *n.* = FELLOW 1.

felloe /'feləʊ/ *n.* (also **felly** /'felɪ/) (*pl.* **-s** or **-ies**) outer circle (or a section of it) of a wheel. [Old English]

fellow /'feləʊ/ *n.* **1** *colloq.* man or boy (*poor fellow!*). **2** (usu. in *pl.*) person in a group etc.; comrade (*separated from their fellows*). **3** counterpart; one of a pair. **4** equal; peer. **5 a** incorporated senior member of a college. **b** elected graduate paid to do research. **6** member of a learned society. **7** (*attrib.*) of the same group etc. (*fellow-countryman*). [Old English from Old Norse]

fellow-feeling *n.* sympathy.

fellowship *n.* **1** friendly association with others, companionship. **2** body of associates. **3** status or income of a fellow of a college or society.

fellow-traveller *n.* **1** person who travels with another. **2** sympathizer with the Communist Party.

felly var. of FELLOE.

felon /'felən/ *n.* person who has committed a felony. [medieval Latin *fello*]

felony *n.* (*pl.* **-ies**) serious, usu. violent, crime. □ **felonious** /fɪ'ləʊnɪəs/ *adj.*

felspar var. of FELDSPAR.

felt¹ —*n.* cloth of matted and pressed fibres of wool etc. —*v.* **1** make into felt. **2** cover with felt. **3** become matted. [Old English]

felt² *past and past part.* of FEEL.

felt-tipped pen *n.* (also **felt-tip pen**) pen with a fibre point.

felucca /fɪ'lʌkə/ *n.* small Mediterranean coasting vessel with oars and/or sails. [Arabic *fulk*]

female /'fiːmeɪl/ —*adj.* **1** of the sex that can give birth or produce eggs. **2** (of plants) fruit-bearing. **3** of women or female animals or plants. **4** (of a screw, socket, etc.) hollow to receive an inserted part. —*n.* female person, animal, or plant. [Latin diminutive of *femina* woman, assimilated to *male*]

feminine /'femɪnɪn/ —*adj.* **1** of women. **2** having womanly qualities. **3** of or denoting the female gender. —*n.* feminine gender or word. □ **femininity** /-'nɪnɪtɪ/ *n.* [Latin: related to FEMALE]

feminism /'femɪnɪz(ə)m/ *n.* advocacy of women's rights and sexual equality. □ **feminist** *n. & adj.*

femme fatale /ˌfæm fæ'tɑːl/ *n.* (*pl.* ***femmes fatales*** pronunc. same) dangerously seductive woman. [French]

femur /'fiːmə(r)/ *n.* (*pl.* **-s** or **femora** /'femərə/) thigh-bone. □ **femoral** /'femər(ə)l/ *adj.* [Latin]

fen *n.* **1** low marshy land. **2** (**the Fens**) low-lying areas in Cambridgeshire etc. [Old English]

fence —*n.* **1** barrier, railing, etc., enclosing a field, garden, etc. **2** large upright jump for horses. **3** *slang* receiver of stolen goods. **4** guard or guide in machinery. —*v.* (**-cing**) **1** surround with or as with a fence. **2** (foll. by *in*, *off*, *up*) enclose, separate, or seal, with or as with a fence. **3** practise fencing with a sword. **4** be evasive. **5** *slang* deal in (stolen goods). □ **fencer** *n.* [from DEFENCE]

fencing *n.* **1** set of, or material for, fences. **2** sword-fighting, esp. as a sport.

fend *v.* **1** (foll. by *for*) look after (esp. oneself). **2** (usu. foll. by *off*) ward off. [from DEFEND]

fender *n.* **1** low frame bordering a fireplace. **2** *Naut.* padding protecting a ship against impact. **3** *US* vehicle's bumper.

fennel /'fen(ə)l/ *n.* yellow-flowered fragrant herb used for flavouring. [Latin *fenum* hay]

fenugreek /'fenjuˌɡriːk/ *n.* leguminous plant with aromatic seeds used for flavouring. [Latin, = Greek hay]

feral /'fer(ə)l/ *adj.* **1** wild; uncultivated. **2** (of an animal) escaped and living wild. **3** brutal. [Latin *ferus* wild]

ferial /'fɪərɪəl/ *adj. Eccl.* (of a day) not a festival or fast. [Latin *feria* FAIR²]

ferment —*n.* /'fɜːment/ **1** excitement, unrest. **2 a** fermentation. **b** fermenting-agent. —*v.* /fə'ment/ **1** undergo or subject

to fermentation. 2 excite; stir up. [Latin *fermentum*: related to FERVENT]

fermentation /fɜːmɛnˈteɪʃ(ə)n/ *n.* 1 breakdown of a substance by yeasts and bacteria etc., esp. of sugar in making alcohol. 2 agitation, excitement. □ **fermentative** /-ˈmɛntətɪv/ *adj.* [Latin: related to FERMENT]

fermium /ˈfɜːmɪəm/ *n.* transuranic artificial radioactive metallic element. [*Fermi*, name of a physicist]

fern *n.* (*pl.* same or **-s**) flowerless plant usu. having feathery fronds. □ **ferny** *adj.* [Old English]

ferocious /fəˈrəʊʃəs/ *adj.* fierce, savage. □ **ferociously** *adv.* **ferocity** /fəˈrɒsɪtɪ/ *n.* [Latin *ferox*]

-ferous *comb. form* (usu. **-iferous**) forming adjectives with the sense 'bearing', 'having' (*odoriferous*). [Latin *fero* bear]

ferret /ˈfɛrɪt/ —*n.* small polecat used in catching rabbits, rats, etc. —*v.* 1 hunt with ferrets. 2 (often foll. by *out, about,* etc.) rummage; search out (secrets, criminals, etc.). [Latin *fur* thief]

ferric /ˈfɛrɪk/ *adj.* 1 of iron. 2 containing iron in a trivalent form. [Latin *ferrum* iron]

Ferris wheel /ˈfɛrɪs/ *n.* tall revolving vertical wheel with passenger cars in fairgrounds etc. [*Ferris*, name of its inventor]

ferro- *comb. form* 1 iron. 2 (of alloys) containing iron. [related to FERRIC]

ferroconcrete /ˌfɛrəʊˈkɒŋkriːt/ —*n.* reinforced concrete. —*adj.* made of this.

ferrous /ˈfɛrəs/ *adj.* 1 containing iron. 2 containing iron in a divalent form.

ferrule /ˈfɛruːl/ *n.* (also **ferrel** /ˈfɛr(ə)l/) 1 ring or cap on the lower end of a stick, umbrella, etc. 2 band strengthening or forming a joint. [Latin *viriae* bracelet]

ferry —*n.* (*pl.* **-ies**) 1 boat or aircraft etc. for esp. regular transport, esp. across water. 2 place or service of ferrying. —*v.* (**-ies, -ied**) 1 convey or go in a ferry. 2 (of a boat etc.) cross water regularly. 3 transport, esp. regularly, from place to place. □ **ferryman** *n.* [Old Norse]

fertile /ˈfɜːtaɪl/ *adj.* 1 a (of soil) abundantly productive. **b** fruitful. 2 a (of a seed, egg, etc.) capable of growth. **b** (of animals and plants) able to reproduce. 3 (of the mind) inventive. 4 (of nuclear material) able to become fissile by the capture of neutrons. □ **fertility** /-ˈtɪlɪtɪ/ *n.* [French from Latin]

fertilize /ˈfɜːtɪlaɪz/ *v.* (also **-ise**) (**-zing** or **-sing**) 1 make (soil etc.) fertile. 2 cause (an egg, female animal, etc.) to develop by mating etc. □ **fertilization** /-ˈzeɪʃ(ə)n/ *n.*

fertilizer *n.* (also **-iser**) substance added to soil to make it more fertile.

fervent /ˈfɜːv(ə)nt/ *adj.* ardent, intense (*fervent admirer*). □ **fervency** *n.* **fervently** *adv.* [Latin *ferveo* boil]

fervid /ˈfɜːvɪd/ *adj.* ardent, intense. □ **fervidly** *adv.* [Latin: related to FERVENT]

fervour /ˈfɜːvə(r)/ *n.* (US **fervor**) passion, zeal. [Latin: related to FERVENT]

fescue /ˈfɛskjuː/ *n.* a pasture and fodder grass. [Latin *festuca* stalk, straw]

festal /ˈfɛst(ə)l/ *adj.* 1 joyous, merry. 2 of a feast or festiva. □ **festally** *adv.* [Latin: related to FEAST]

fester *v.* 1 make or become septic. 2 cause continuing anger or bitterness. 3 rot, stagnate. [Latin *fistula*]

festival /ˈfɛstɪv(ə)l/ *n.* 1 day or period of celebration. 2 series of cultural events in a town etc. (*Bath Festival*). [French: related to FESTIVE]

festive /ˈfɛstɪv/ *adj.* 1 of or characteristic of a festival. 2 joyous. □ **festively** *adv.* **festiveness** *n.* [Latin: related to FEAST]

festivity /fɛˈstɪvɪtɪ/ *n.* (*pl.* **-ies**) 1 gaiety, rejoicing. 2 (in *pl.*) celebration; party.

festoon /fɛˈstuːn/ —*n.* curved hanging chain of flowers, leaves, ribbons, etc. —*v.* (often foll. by *with*) adorn with or form into festoons; decorate elaborately. [Italian: related to FESTIVE]

Festschrift /ˈfɛstʃrɪft/ *n.* (also **festschrift**) (*pl.* **-en** or **-s**) collection of writings published in honour of a scholar. [German]

feta /ˈfɛtə/ *n.* soft white esp. ewe's-milk cheese made es□. in Greece. [Greek *phea*]

fetal US var. of FOETAL.

fetch —*v.* 1 go for and bring back (*fetch a doctor*). 2 be sold for (a price) (*fetched £10*). 3 cause (blood, tears, etc.) to flow. 4 draw (breath), heave (a sigh). 5 *colloq.* give (a blow etc.; *fetched him a slap*). —*n.* 1 act of fetching. 2 dodge, trick. □ **fetch and carry** do menial tasks. **fetch up** *colloq.* 1 arrive, come to rest. 2 vomit. [Old English]

fetching *adj.* attractive. □ **fetchingly** *adv.*

fête /feɪt/ —*n.* 1 outdoor fund-raising event with stalls and amusements etc. 2 festival. 3 saint's day. —*v.* (**-ting**) honour or entertain lavishly. [French: related to FEAST]

fetid /ˈfɛtɪd/ *adj.* (also **foetid**) stinking. [Latin *foeteo* stink]

fetish /ˈfɛtɪʃ/ *n.* 1 *Psychol.* abnormal object of sexual desire. 2 a object worshipped by primitive peoples. **b** obses-

sional cause (*makes a fetish of punctuality*). □ **fetishism** *n.* **fetishist** *n.* **fetishistic** /-'ɪstɪk/ *adj.* [Portuguese *feitiço* charm]

fetlock /'fetlɒk/ *n.* back of a horse's leg above the hoof with a tuft of hair. [ultimately related to FOOT]

fetter *−n.* **1** shackle for the ankles. **2** (in *pl.*) captivity. **3** restraint. *−v.* **1** put into fetters. **2** restrict. [Old English]

fettle /'fet(ə)l/ *n.* condition or trim (*in fine fettle*). [Old English]

fetus *US* var. of FOETUS.

feu /fju:/ *Scot. −n.* **1** perpetual lease at a fixed rent. **2** land so held. *−v.* (**feus, feued, feuing**) grant (land) on feu. [French: related to FEE]

feud[1] /fju:d/ *−n.* prolonged hostility, esp. between families, tribes, etc. *−v.* conduct a feud. [Germanic: related to FOE]

feud[2] /fju:d/ *n.* = FIEF. [medieval Latin *feudum* FEE]

feudal /'fju:d(ə)l/ *adj.* **1** of, like, or according to the feudal system. **2** reactionary (*feudal attitude*). □ **feudalism** *n.* **feudalistic** /-'ɪstɪk/ *adj.*

feudal system *n.* medieval system of land tenure with allegiance and service due to the landowner.

fever *−n.* **1 a** abnormally high temperature, often with delirium etc. **b** disease characterized by this (*scarlet fever*). **2** nervous excitement; agitation. *−v.* (esp. as **fevered** *adj.*) affect with fever or excitement. [Latin *febris*]

feverfew /'fi:vəfju:/ *n.* aromatic bushy plant, used formerly to reduce fever, now to cure migraine. [Latin *febrifuga*: related to FEVER, *fugo* drive away]

feverish *adj.* **1** having symptoms of fever. **2** excited, restless. □ **feverishly** *adv.* **feverishness** *n.*

fever pitch *n.* state of extreme excitement.

few *−adj.* not many (*few doctors smoke*). *−n.* (as *pl.*) **1** (prec. by *a*) some but not many (*a few of his friends were there*). **2** not many (*few are chosen*). **3** (prec. by *the*) **a** the minority. □ **a good few** *colloq.* fairly large number. **no fewer than** as many as (a specified number). **not a few** a considerable number. [Old English]

few and far between *predic. adj.* scarce.

fey /feɪ/ *adj.* **1** strange, other-worldly; whimsical. **b** clairvoyant. **2** *Scot.* fated to die soon. [Old English. = doomed to die]

fez *n.* (*pl.* **fezzes**) man's flat-topped conical red cap worn by some Muslims. [Turkish]

ff *abbr. Mus.* fortissimo.

ff. *abbr.* following pages etc.

fiancé /fɪ'ɒnseɪ/ *n.* (*fem.* **fiancée** pronunc. same) person one is engaged to. [French]

fiasco /fɪ'æskəʊ/ *n.* (*pl.* **-s**) ludicrous or humiliating failure or breakdown. [Italian, = bottle]

fiat /'faɪæt/ *n.* **1** authorization. **2** decree. [Latin, = let it be done]

fib *−n.* trivial lie. *−v.* (**-bb-**) tell a fib. □ **fibber** *n.* [perhaps from *fible-fable*, a reduplication of FABLE]

fibre /'faɪbə(r)/ *n.* (*US* **fiber**) **1** thread or filament forming tissue or textile. **2** piece of threadlike glass. **3** substance formed of fibres, or able to be spun, woven, etc. **4** structure; character (*moral fibre*). **5** roughage. [French from Latin *fibra*]

fibreboard *n.* (*US* **fiberboard**) board of compressed wood or other plant fibres.

fibreglass *n.* (*US* **fiberglass**) **1** fabric made from woven glass fibres. **2** plastic reinforced by glass fibres.

fibre optics *n.pl.* optics using thin glass fibres, usu. for the transmission of modulated light to carry signals.

fibril /'faɪbrɪl/ *n.* small fibre. [diminutive of FIBRE]

fibroid /'faɪbrɔɪd/ *−adj.* of, like, or containing fibrous tissue or fibres. *−n.* benign fibrous tumour growing in the womb.

fibrosis /faɪ'brəʊsɪs/ *n.* thickening and scarring of connective tissue. [from FIBRE, -OSIS]

fibrositis /ˌfaɪbrə'saɪtɪs/ *n.* rheumatic inflammation of fibrous tissue. [from FIBRE, -ITIS]

fibrous /'faɪbrəs/ *adj.* of or like fibres.

fibula /'fɪbjʊlə/ *n.* (*pl.* **fibulae** /-li:/ or **-s**) small outer bone between the knee and the ankle. □ **fibular** *adj.* [Latin, = brooch]

-fic *suffix* (usu. as **-ific**) forming adjectives meaning 'producing', 'making' (*prolific; pacific*). [Latin *facio* make]

-fication *suffix* (usu. as **-ification**) forming nouns of action from verbs in *-fy* (*purification; simplification*).

fiche /fiːʃ/ *n.* (*pl.* same or **-s**) microfiche. [abbreviation]

fickle /'fɪk(ə)l/ *adj.* inconstant, changeable, disloyal. □ **fickleness** *n.* **fickly** *adv.* [Old English]

fiction /'fɪkʃ(ə)n/ *n.* **1** non-factual literature, esp. novels. **2** invented idea, thing, etc. **3** generally accepted falsehood (*polite fiction*). □ **fictional** *adj.* **fictionalize** *v.* (also **-ise**) (**-zing** or **-sing**). [Latin: related to FEIGN]

fictitious /fɪk'tɪʃəs/ *adj.* imaginary, unreal; not genuine.

fiddle /'fɪd(ə)l/ *−n.* **1** *colloq.* or *derog.* stringed instrument played with a bow, esp. a violin. **2** *colloq.* cheat or fraud. **3**

fiddly task. —v. (**-ling**) **1 a** (often foll. by *about*) move aimlessly. **b** play restlessly. **c** (usu. foll. by *with*) adjust, tinker; tamper. **2** *slang* **a** cheat, swindle. **b** falsify. **c** get by cheating. **3** play (a tune) on the fiddle. □ **as fit as a fiddle** in very good health. **play second** (or **first**) **fiddle** take a subordinate (or leading) role. [Old English]

fiddle-faddle —*n.* trivial matters. —*v.* (**-ling**) fuss, trifle. —*int.* nonsense! [reduplication of FIDDLE]

fiddler *n.* **1** fiddle-player. **2** *slang* swindler, cheat. **3** small N. American crab.

fiddlesticks *int.* nonsense.

fiddling *adj.* **1** petty, trivial. **2** *colloq.* = FIDDLY.

fiddly *adj.* (**-ier, -iest**) *colloq.* awkward or tiresome to do or use.

fidelity /fɪˈdɛlɪti/ *n.* **1** faithfulness, loyalty. **2** strict accuracy. **3** precision in sound reproduction (*high fidelity*). [Latin *fides* faith]

fidget /ˈfɪdʒɪt/ —*v.* (**-t-**) **1** move or act restlessly or nervously. **2** be or make uneasy. —*n.* **1** person who fidgets. **2** (usu. in *pl.*) restless movements or mood. □ **fidgety** *adj.* [obsolete or dial. *fidge* twitch]

fiduciary /fɪˈdjuːʃərɪ/ —*adj.* **1 a** of a trust, trustee, or trusteeship. **b** held or given in trust. **2** (of paper currency) dependent on public confidence or securities. —*n.* (*pl.* **-ies**) trustee. [Latin *fiducia* trust]

fie /faɪ/ *int. archaic* expressing disgust, shame, etc. [French from Latin]

fief /fiːf/ *n.* **1** land held under the feudal system or in fee. **2** person's sphere of operation. [French: related to FEE]

field —*n.* **1** area of esp. cultivated enclosed land. **2** area, often in some natural product (*gas field*). **3** land for a game etc. (*football field*). **4** participants in a contest, race, or all except those specified. **5** *Cricket* **a** the side fielding. **b** fielder. **6** expanse of ice, snow, sea, sky, etc. **7 a** battlefield. **b** (*attrib.*) (of artillery etc.) light and mobile. **8** area of activity or study (*in his own field*). **9** *Physics* **a** region in which a force is effective (*gravitational field*). **b** force exerted in this. **10** range of perception (*field of view*). **11** (*attrib.*) **a** (of an animal or plant) wild (*field mouse*). **b** in the natural environment, not in a laboratory etc. (*field test*). **12 a** background of a picture, coin, flag, etc. **b** *Heraldry* surface of an escutcheon. **13** *Computing* part of a record representing an item of data. —*v.* **1 a** act as a fieldsman in cricket etc. **b** stop and return (the ball) in

cricket etc. **2** select to play in a game. **3** deal with (question, argument, etc.). □ **hold the field** not be superseded. **play the field** *colloq.* date many partners. **take the field** begin a campaign. [Old English]

field-day *n.* **1** exciting or successful time. **2** military exercise or review.

fielder *n.* = FIELDSMAN.

field events *n.pl.* athletic events other than races.

field-glasses *n.pl.* outdoor binoculars.

Field Marshal *n.* army officer of the highest rank.

field mouse *n.* small long-tailed rodent.

field officer *n.* army officer of field rank.

field of honour *n.* battlefield.

field rank *n.* army rank above captain and below general.

fieldsman *n. Cricket, Baseball,* etc. member (other than the bowler or pitcher) of the fielding side.

field sports *n.pl.* outdoor sports, esp. hunting, shooting, and fishing.

field telegraph *n.* movable military telegraph.

fieldwork *n.* **1** practical surveying, science, sociology, etc. conducted in the natural environment. **2** temporary fortification. □ **fieldworker** *n.*

fiend /fiːnd/ *n.* **1** evil spirit, demon. **2 a** wicked or cruel person. **b** mischievous or annoying person. **3** *slang* devotee (*fitness fiend*). **4** difficult or unpleasant thing. □ **fiendish** *adj.*; **fiendishly** *adv.* [Old English]

fierce *adj.* (**fiercer, fiercest**) **1** violently aggressive or frightening. **2** eager, intense. **3** unpleasantly strong or intense (*fierce heat*). □ **fiercely** *adv.*; **fierceness** *n.* [Latin *ferus* savage]

fiery /ˈfaɪərɪ/ *adj.* (**-ier, -iest**) **1** consisting of or flaming with fire. **2** bright red. **3** hot; burning. **4 a** flashing, ardent (*fiery eyes*). **b** pugnacious; spirited (*fiery temper*). □ **fierily** *adv.*; **fieriness** *n.* [from FIRE]

fiesta /fiˈɛstə/ *n.* holiday, festivity, or religious festival. [Spanish]

FIFA /ˈfiːfə/ *abbr.* International Football Federation. [French *Fédération Internationale de Football Association*]

fife *n.* small shrill flute used in military music. [German *Pfeife* pipe or French *fifre*]

fifteen /fɪfˈtiːn/ *adj. & n.* **1** one more than fourteen. **2** symbol for this (15, xv, XV). **3** size etc. denoted by fifteen. **4** team of fifteen players, esp. in Rugby. **5** (15) (of a film) for persons of 15 and over. □ **fifteenth** *adj. & n.* [Old English: related to FIVE, -TEEN]

fifth *adj. & n.* **1** next after fourth. **2** any of five equal parts of a thing. **3** *Mus.* interval or chord spanning five consecutive notes in a diatonic scale (e.g. C to G). □ **fifthly** *adv.* [Old English: related to FIVE]

fifth column *n.* traitorous group within a country at war etc. □ **fifth-columnist** *n.*

fifty /'fɪftɪ/ *adj. & n.* (*pl. -ies*) **1** five times ten. **2** symbol for this (50, l, L). **3** (in *pl.*) numbers from 50 to 59, esp. the years of a century or of a person's life. □ **fiftieth** *adj. & n.* [Old English]

fifty-fifty —*adj.* equal. —*adv.* equally, half and half.

fig¹ *n.* **1** soft pulpy fruit with many seeds. **2** (in full **fig tree**) tree bearing figs. □ **not care** (or **give**) **a fig** not care at all. [Latin *ficus*]

fig² *n.* **1** dress or equipment (*in full fig*). **2** condition or form (*in good fig*). [obsolete *feague*: related to FAKE]

fig. *abbr.* figure.

fight /faɪt/ —*v.* (*past* and *past part.* **fought** /fɔːt/) **1** (often foll. by *against*, *with*) contend or contend with in war, battle, single combat, etc. **2** engage in (a battle, duel, etc.). **3** contend (an election); maintain (a lawsuit, cause, etc.) against an opponent. **4** strive to achieve something or to overcome (disease, fire, etc.). **5** make (one's way) by fighting. —*n.* **1 a** combat. **b** boxing-match. **c** battle. **2** conflict, struggle, or effort. **3** power or inclination to fight (*no fight left*). □ **fight back 1** counter-attack. **2** suppress (tears etc.). **fight for 1** fight on behalf of. **2** fight to secure. **fight a losing battle** struggle without hope of success. **fight off** repel with effort. **fight out** (usu. **fight it out**) settle by fighting. **fight shy of** avoid. **put up a fight** offer resistance. [Old English]

fighter *n.* **1** person or animal that fights. **2** fast military aircraft designed for attacking other aircraft.

fighting chance *n.* slight chance of success if an effort is made.

fighting fit *n.* fit and ready; at the peak of fitness.

fig-leaf *n.* **1** leaf of a fig-tree. **2** concealing device, esp. for the genitals (Gen. 3:7).

figment /'fɪgmənt/ *n.* invented or imaginary thing. [Latin: related to FEIGN]

figuration /ˌfɪgjʊ'reɪʃ(ə)n/ *n.* **1 a** act or mode of formation; form. **b** shape or outline. **2** ornamentation. [Latin: related to FIGURE]

figurative /'fɪgərətɪv/ *adj.* **1** metaphorical, not literal. **2** characterized by

figures of speech. **3** of pictorial or sculptural representation. □ **figuratively** *adv.* [Latin: related to FIGURE]

figure /'fɪgə(r)/ —*n.* **1** external form or bodily shape. **2 a** silhouette, human form (*figure on the lawn*). **b** person of a specified kind or appearance (*public figure*; *cut a poor figure*). **3 a** human form in drawing, sculpture, etc. **b** image or likeness. **4** two- or three-dimensional space enclosed by lines or surface(s), e.g. a triangle or sphere. **5 a** numerical symbol or number, esp. 0-9. **b** amount; estimated value (*cannot put a figure on it*). **c** (in *pl.*) arithmetical calculations. **6** diagram or illustration. **7** decorative pattern. **8** movement or sequence in a set dance etc. **9** *Mus.* succession of notes from which longer passages are developed. **10** (in full **figure of speech**) metaphor, hyperbole, etc. —*v.* (*-ring*) **1** appear or be mentioned, esp. prominently. **2** represent pictorially. **3** imagine; picture mentally. **4** embellish with a pattern etc. (*figured satin*). **5** calculate; do arithmetic. **6** symbolize. **7** esp. *US* understand, consider. **b** *colloq.* make sense; be likely (*that figures*). □ **figure on** *US* count on, expect. **figure out** work out by arithmetic or logic. [Latin *figura*: related to FEIGN]

figured bass *n. Mus.* = CONTINUO.

figurehead *n.* **1** nominal leader. **2** wooden bust or figure at a ship's prow.

figure-skating *n.* skating in prescribed patterns. □ **figure-skater** *n.*

figurine /ˌfɪgjʊ'riːn/ *n.* statuette. [Italian: related to FIGURE]

filament /'fɪləmənt/ *n.* **1** threadlike body or fibre. **2** conducting wire or thread in an electric bulb etc. □ **filamentous** /-'mentəs/ *adj.* [Latin *filum* thread]

filbert /'fɪlbət/ *n.* **1** the cultivated hazel with edible nuts. **2** this nut. [Anglo-French, because ripe about St *Philibert's day*]

filch *v.* pilfer, steal. [origin unknown]

file¹ —*n.* **1** folder, box, etc., for holding loose papers. **2** papers kept in this. **3** *Computing* collection of (usu. related) data stored under one name. **4** line of people or things one behind another. —*v.* (*-ling*) **1** place (papers) in a file or among (esp. public) records. **2** submit (a petition for divorce, a patent application, etc.). **3** (of a reporter) send (copy) to a newspaper. **4** walk in a line. [Latin *filum* thread]

file² —*n.* tool with a roughened surface for smoothing or shaping wood, fingernails, etc. —*v.* (*-ling*) smooth or shape with a file. [Old English]

filial /ˈfɪlɪəl/ *adj.* of or due from a son or daughter. □ **filially** *adv.* [Latin *filius*, son, *daughter*]

filibuster *n.* obstruction of progress in a legislative assembly, esp. by prolonged speaking. 2 esp. *US* person who engages in this. —*v.* act as a filibuster (against). □ **filibus-terer** *n.* [Dutch: related to FREEBOOTER]

filigree /ˈfɪlɪgriː/ *n.* fine ornamental work in gold etc. wire. 2 similar delicate work. □ **filigreed** *adj.* [Latin *filum* thread, *granum* seed]

filing *n.* (usu. in *pl.*) particle rubbed off by a file.

filing cabinet *n.* cabinet with drawers for storing files.

Filipino /ˌfɪlɪˈpiːnəʊ/ *n.* (*pl.* -s) native or national of the Philippines. —*adj.* of the Philippines or Filipinos. [Spanish = Philippine]

fill —*v.* 1 (often foll. by *with*) make or become full. 2 occupy completely; spread over or through. 3 block up (a cavity in a tooth); drill and put a filling into (a decayed tooth) 4 appoint a person to or hold (a vacant post). 5 hold (an office) 6 carry out or supply (an order, commission, etc.) 7 occupy (vacant time). 8 (of a sail) be distended by wind. 9 (usu. as **filling** *adj.*) (esp. of food) satisfy, satiate. —*n.* 1 as much as one wants or can bear (*eat your fill*). 2 enough to fill something. □ **fill the bill** be suitable or adequate. **fill in 1** complete (a form, document, etc.) 2 a complete (a drawing etc.) within an outline. **b** fill (an outline) in this way. 3 fill (a hole etc.) completely. 4 (often foll. by *for*) act as a substitute. 5 occupy oneself during (spare time). 6 *colloq.* inform (a person more fully. 7 *slang* thrash, beat. **fill out 1** enlarge to the required size. 2 become enlarged or plump. 3 *US* fill in (a document etc.). **fill up 1** make or become completely full. 2 fill in (a document etc.). 3 fill the petrol tank of (a car etc.). [Old English]

filler *n.* 1 material used to fill a cavity or increase bulk. 2 small item filling space in a newspaper etc.

fillet /ˈfɪlɪt/ —*n.* 1 a boneless piece of meat or fish. **b** (in full **fillet steak**) undercut of a sirloin. 2 ribbon etc. binding the hair. 3 thin narrow strip or ridge. 4 narrow flat band between mouldings. —*v.* (-t-) 1 remove bones from (fish or meat) or divide into fillets. 2 bind or provide with fillet(s). [Latin *filum* thread]

filling *n.* material that fills a tooth, sandwich, pie, etc.

filling-station *n.* garage selling petrol etc.

fillip /ˈfɪlɪp/ —*n.* 1 stimulus, incentive. 2 flick with a finger or thumb. —*v.* (-p-) 1 stimulate. 2 flick. [imitative]

filly /ˈfɪlɪ/ *n.* (*pl.* -ies) 1 young female horse. 2 *colloq.* girl or young woman. [Old Norse]

film —*n.* 1 thin coating or covering layer. 2 strip or sheet of plastic etc. coated with light-sensitive emulsion for exposure in a camera. 3 a story, episode, etc., on film, with the illusion of movement. **b** (in *pl.*) the cinema industry. 4 slight veil or haze etc. 5 dimness or morbid growth affecting the eyes. —*v.* 1 make a photographic film of (a scene, story, etc.). 2 cover or become covered with or as with a film. [Old English]

film-goer *n.* person who frequents the cinema.

filmsetting *n.* typesetting by projecting characters on to photographic film. □ **film-set** *v.* **film-setter** *n.*

film star *n.* celebrated film actor or actress.

film-strip *n.* series of transparencies in a strip for projection.

filmy *adj.* (**-ier, -iest**) 1 thin and translucent. 2 covered with or as with a film. □ **filmily** *adv.* **filminess** *n.*

Filofax /ˈfaɪləʊfæks/ *n. propr.* a type of loose-leaf personal organizer. [from FILE, FACT]

filo pastry /ˈfiːləʊ, ˈfaɪ-/ *n.* (also **phyllo pastry**) leaved pastry like strudel pastry. [Greek *phyllon* leaf]

filter —*n.* 1 porous device for removing impurities etc. from a liquid or gas passed through it. 2 = FILTER TIP. 3 screen or attachment for absorbing or modifying light, X-rays, etc. 4 device for suppressing unwanted electrical or sound waves. 5 arrangement for filtering traffic. —*v.* 1 (cause to) pass through a filter. 2 (foll. by *through, into*, etc.) make way gradually. 3 (foll. by *out*) (cause to) leak. 4 allow (traffic) or (of traffic) be allowed to pass to the left or right at a junction. [Germanic: related to FELT¹]

filter tip *n.* 1 filter on a cigarette removing some impurities. 2 cigarette with this. □ **filter-tipped** *adj.*

filth *n.* 1 repugnant or extreme dirt. 2 obscenity. [Old English: related to FOUL]

filthy —*adj.* (**-ier, -iest**) 1 extremely or disgustingly dirty. 2 obscene. 3 *colloq.* (of weather) very unpleasant. —*adv.* 1 filthily (*filthy dirty*). 2 *colloq.* extremely (*filthy rich*). □ **filthily** *adv.* **filthiness** *n.*

filthy lucre *n.* 1 dishonourable gain. 2 *joc.* money.

filtrate /ˈfɪltreɪt/ —v. (**-ting**) filter. —n. filtered liquid. [related to FILTER]

fin n. 1 (usu. thin) flat external organ of esp. fish, for propelling, steering, etc. (*dorsal fin*). 2 similar stabilizing projection on an aircraft, car, etc. 3 underwater swimmer's flipper. □ **finned** adj. [Old English]

finagle /fɪˈneɪg(ə)l/ v. (**-ling**) colloq. act or obtain dishonestly. □ **finagler** n. [dial. *fainaigue* cheat]

final /ˈfaɪn(ə)l/ —adj. 1 situated at the end, coming last. 2 conclusive, decisive. —n. 1 last or deciding heat or game in sports etc. (*Cup Final*). 2 last daily edition of a newspaper. 3 (usu. in pl.) examinations at the end of a degree course. □ **finally** adv. [Latin *finis* end]

final cause n. Philos. ultimate purpose.

final clause n. Gram. clause expressing purpose.

finale /fɪˈnɑːlɪ/ n. last movement or section of a piece of music or drama etc. [Italian: related to FINAL]

finalist n. competitor in the final of a competition etc.

finality /faɪˈnælɪtɪ/ n. (pl. **-ies**) 1 fact of being final. 2 final act etc. [Latin: related to FINAL]

finalize v. (also **-ise**) (**-zing** or **-sing**) put into final form; complete. □ **finalization** /-ˈzeɪʃ(ə)n/ n.

final solution n. Nazi policy (1941–5) of exterminating European Jews.

finance /faɪˈnæns/ —n. 1 management of money (esp. public) money. 2 monetary support for an enterprise. 3 (in pl.) money resources of a State, company, or person. —v. (**-cing**) provide capital for. [French: related to FINE²]

finance company n. (also **finance house**) company providing money, esp. for hire-purchase transactions.

financial year n. year as reckoned for taxing or accounting, esp. from 6 April. [Old English]

financial /faɪˈnænʃ(ə)l/ adj. of finance. □ **financially** adv.

financier /faɪˈnænsɪə(r)/ n. capitalist; entrepreneur. [French: related to FINANCE]

finch n. small seed-eating bird, esp. a crossbill, canary, or chaffinch. [Old English]

find /faɪnd/ —v. (past and past part. **found**) 1 a discover or get by chance or effort (*found a key*). b become aware of (*idea found acceptance*). 2 a obtain, succeed in obtaining; receive (*found courage*). 3 seek out and provide or supply (*will find you a book*; *finds his own meals*). 4 discover by study etc. (*find the answer*). 5 a perceive or experience (*find no sense in it*). b (often in passive) discover to be present (*not found in Shakespeare*). c discover from experience (*finds England too cold*). 6 Law (of a jury, judge, etc.) decide and declare (*found him guilty*). 7 reach by a natural process (*water finds its own level*). —n. 1 discovery of treasure etc. 2 valued thing or person newly discovered. □ **all found** (of wages) with board and lodging provided free. **find fault** see FAULT. **find favour** prove acceptable. **find one's feet** 1 become able to walk. 2 develop independence. **find oneself** 1 discover that one is (*found herself agreeing*). 2 discover one's vocation. **find out** 1 discover or detect (a wrongdoer etc.). 2 (often foll. by *about*) get information. 3 discover (*find out where we are*). 4 (often foll. by *about*) discover the truth, a fact, etc. (*he never found out*). [Old English]

finder n. 1 person who finds. 2 small telescope attached to a large one to locate an object. 3 viewfinder.

finding n. (often in pl.) conclusion reached by an inquiry etc.

fine¹ —adj. 1 a of high quality; excellent (*fine painting*). b good, satisfactory (*that will be fine*). 2 a pure, refined. b (of gold or silver) containing a specified proportion of pure metal. 3 imposing, dignified (*fine buildings*). 4 in good health (*I'm fine*). 5 (of weather etc.) bright and clear. b thin; sharp. b in small particles. c worked in slender thread. 7 euphemistic; flattering (*fine words*). 8 ornate, showy. 9 fastidious, affectedly refined. —adv. 1 finely. 2 colloq. very well (*suits me fine*). —v. (**-ning**) 1 (often foll. by *away*, *down*, *off*) make or become finer, thinner, more tapering, or less coarse. 2 (often foll. by *down*) make or become clear (esp. of beer etc.). □ **not to put too fine a point on it** to speak bluntly. □ **finely** adv. **fineness** n. [French *fin* from Latin *finis* FINISH]

fine² —n. money to be paid as a penalty. —v. (**-ning**) punish by a fine (*fined him £5*). □ **in fine** in short. [French *fin* settlement of a dispute, from Latin *finis* end]

fine arts n.pl. poetry, music, and the visual arts, esp. painting, sculpture, and architecture.

fines herbes /fiːnz ˈɛəb/ n.pl. mixed herbs used in cooking. [French, = fine herbs]

fine-spun adj. 1 delicate. 2 (of theory etc.) too subtle, unpractical.

finesse /fɪˈnes/ —n. 1 refinement. 2 subtle manipulation. 3 artfulness; tact. 4 Cards attempt to win a trick with a card

that is not the highest h3ld. —*v.* (**-ssing**) make a finesse. **b** play (a card) as a finesse. [French: related to FINE[1]]

fine-tooth comb *n.* comb with close-set teeth. □ **go over with a fine-tooth comb** check or search thoroughly.

fine-tune *v.* make small adjustments to (a mechanism etc.).

finger /ˈfɪŋɡə(r)/ —*n.* **1** any of the terminal projections of the hand (usu. excluding the thumb). **2** part of a glove etc. for a finger. **3** finger-like object or structure (*fish finger*). **4** *colloq.* small measure of liquor. —*v.* touch, feel, or turn about with the fingers. □ **get** (or **pull**) **one's finger** out *slang* start to act. **lay a finger on** touch, however slightly. **put one's finger on** locate or identify exactly. □ **fingerless** *adj.* [Old English]

finger-board *n.* part of the neck of a stringed instrument on which the fingers press to vary the pitch.

finger-bowl *n.* (also **finger-glass**) small bowl for rinsing the fingers during a meal.

finger-dry *v.* dry and style (the hair) by running one's fingers through it.

fingering *n.* **1** technique etc. of using the fingers, esp. in playing music. **2** indication of this in a musical score.

finger-mark *n.* mark left by a finger.

fingernail *n.* nail of each finger.

finger-plate *n.* plate fixed to a door to prevent finger-marks.

fingerprint —*n.* impression of a finger-tip on a surface, used in detecting crime. —*v.* record the fingerprints of.

finger-stall *n.* protective cover for an injured finger.

fingertip *n.* tip of a finger. □ **have at one's fingertips** be thoroughly familiar with (a subject etc.).

finial /ˈfɪnɪəl/ *n.* ornamental top or end of a roof, gable, etc. [Anglo-French: related to FINE[1]]

finicky /ˈfɪnɪkɪ/ *adj.* (also **finical**, **finicking**) **1** over-particular, fastidious. **2** detailed; fiddly. □ **finickiness** *n.* [perhaps from FINE[1]]

finis /ˈfɪnɪs/ *n.* end; esp. of a book. [Latin]

finish /ˈfɪnɪʃ/ —*v.* **1 a** (often foll. by *off*) bring or come to an end or the end of; complete; cease. **b** (usu. foll. by *off*) *colloq.* kill; vanquish. **c** (often foll. by *up*) consume or complete consuming (food or drink). **2** treat the surface of (cloth, woodwork, etc.). —*n.* **1 a** end, last stage, completion. **b** point at which a race etc. ends. **2** method, material, etc. used for surface treatment of wood, cloth, etc. □ **finish off 1** by *in*, *by*) end (*finished up by crying*). **finish with** have no more to

do with, complete using etc. [Latin *finis* end]

finishing-school *n.* private college preparing girls for fashionable society.

finishing touch *n.* (also **finishing touches**) final enhancing details.

finite /ˈfaɪnaɪt/ *adj.* **1** limited; not infinite. **2** (of a part of a verb) having a specific number and person. [Latin: related to FINISH]

Finn *n.* native or national of Finland.

finnan /ˈfɪnən/ *n.* (in full **finnan haddock**) smoke-cured haddock. [*Findhorn*, *Findon*, in Scotland]

Finnic *adj.* of the group of peoples or languages related to the Finns or Finnish.

Finnish —*adj.* of the Finns or their language. —*n.* language of the Finns.

fino /ˈfiːnəʊ/ *n.* (*pl.* **-s**) light-coloured dry sherry. [Spanish, = fine]

fiord /fjɔːd/ *n.* (also **fjord**) long narrow sea inlet, as in Norway. [Norwegian]

fipple /ˈfɪp(ə)l/ *n.* plug at the mouth-end of a wind instrument. [origin unknown]

fipple flute *n.* flute played by blowing endwise, e.g. a recorder.

fir *n.* **1** (in full **fir-tree**) evergreen coniferous tree with needles growing singly on the stems. **2** its wood. □ **firry** *adj.* [Old Norse]

fir-cone *n.* fruit of the fir.

fire —*n.* **1 a** combustion of substances with oxygen, giving out light and heat. **b** flame or incandescence. **2** destructive burning (*forest fire*). **3 a** burning fuel in a grate, furnace, etc. **b** = ELECTRIC FIRE. **c** = GAS FIRE. **4** firing of guns. **5 a** fervour, spirit, vivacity. **b** poetic inspiration. **6** burning heat, fever. —*v.* (**-ring**) **1** (often foll. by *at*, *into*, *on*) **a** shoot (a gun, missile, etc.). **b** shoot a gun or missile etc. **2** produce (a broadside, salute, etc.) by shooting guns etc. **3** (of a gun etc.) be discharged. **4** explode or kindle (an explosive). **5** deliver or utter rapidly (*fired insults at us*). **6** *slang* dismiss (an employee). **7** set fire to intentionally. **8** catch fire. **9** (of esp. an internal-combustion engine) undergo ignition. **10** supply (a furnace, engine, etc.) with fuel. **11** stimulate; enthuse. **12** bake, dry, or cure (pottery, bricks, tea, tobacco, etc.). **13** become or cause to become heated, excited, red, or glowing. □ **catch fire** begin to burn. **fire away** *colloq.* begin; go ahead. **on fire 1** burning. **2** excited. **set fire to** (or **set on fire**) ignite, kindle. **set the world** (or **Thames) on fire** do something remarkable or sensational. **under fire 1** being shot at. **2** being rigorously criticized or questioned. [Old English]

fire-alarm n. device warning of fire.

fire and brimstone n. supposed torments of hell.

firearm n. (usu. in pl.) gun, pistol, or rifle.

fire-ball n. 1 large meteor. 2 ball of flame or lightning. 3 energetic person.

fire-bomb n. incendiary bomb.

firebox n. place where fuel is burned in a steam engine or boiler.

firebrand n. 1 piece of burning wood. 2 person causing trouble or unrest.

fire-break n. obstacle to the spread of fire in a forest etc., esp. an open space.

fire-brick n. fireproof brick in a grate.

fire brigade n. body of professional firefighters.

fireclay n. clay used to make firebricks.

firecracker n. US explosive firework.

firedamp n. miners' name for methane, which is explosive when mixed with air.

firedog n. andiron.

fire door n. fire-resistant door preventing the spread of fire.

fire-drill n. rehearsal of the procedures to be used in case of fire.

fire-eater n. 1 conjuror who appears to swallow fire. 2 quarrelsome person.

fire-engine n. vehicle carrying hoses, firefighters, etc.

fire-escape n. emergency staircase etc. for use in a fire.

fire extinguisher n. apparatus discharging foam etc. to extinguish a fire.

firefighter n. = FIREMAN 1.

firefly n. beetle emitting phosphorescent light, e.g. the glow-worm.

fire-guard n. protective screen placed in front of a fireplace.

fire-irons n.pl. tongs, poker, and shovel for a domestic fire.

firelight n. light from a fire in a fireplace.

fire-lighter n. inflammable material used to start a fire in a grate.

fireman n. 1 member of a fire brigade. 2 person who tends a steam engine or steamship furnace.

fireplace n. 1 place for a domestic fire, esp. a recess in a wall. 2 structure surrounding this.

fire-power n. destructive capacity of guns etc.

fire-practice n. fire-drill.

fireproof —adj. able to resist fire or great heat. —v. make fireproof.

fire-raiser n. arsonist. □ **fire-raising** n.

fire-screen n. 1 ornamental screen for a fireplace. 2 screen against the direct heat of a fire. 3 fire-guard.

fire-ship n. hist. ship set on fire and directed against an enemy's ships etc.

fireside n. 1 area round a fireplace. 2 home or home-life.

fire station n. headquarters of a fire brigade.

fire-storm n. high wind or storm following a fire caused by bombs.

fire-trap n. building without fire-escapes etc.

fire-watcher n. person keeping watch for fires, esp. those caused by bombs.

fire-water n. colloq. strong alcoholic liquor.

firewood n. wood as fuel.

firework n. 1 device that burns or explodes spectacularly when lit. 2 (in pl.) outburst of passion, esp. anger.

firing n. 1 discharge of guns. 2 fuel.

firing-line n. 1 front line in a battle. 2 centre of activity etc.

firing-squad n. 1 soldiers ordered to shoot a condemned person. 2 group firing the salute at a military funeral.

firm¹ —adj. 1 a solid or compact. b fixed, stable, steady. 2 a resolute, determined. b steadfast, constant (firm belief; firm friend). 3 (of an offer etc.) definite; not conditional. —adv. firmly (stand firm). —v. (often foll. by up) make or become firm, secure, compact, or solid. □ **firmly** adv. **firmness** n. [Latin firmus]

firm² n. business concern or its partners. [Latin firma: cf. FIRM¹]

firmament /ˈfɜːməmənt/ n. literary the sky regarded as a vault or arch. [Latin: related to FIRM¹]

firmware n. Computing permanent kind of software.

firry see FIR.

first —adj. 1 earliest in time or order (took the first bus). 2 foremost in rank or importance (First Lord of the Treasury). 3 most willing or likely (the first to admit it). 4 basic or evident (first principles). —n. 1 (prec. by the) person or thing first mentioned or occurring. 2 first occurrence of something notable. 3 place in the first class in an examination. 4 first gear. 5 a first place in a race. b winner of this. —adv. 1 before any other person or thing (first of all; first and foremost). 2 before someone or something else (get this done first). 3 for the first time (when did you first see her?). 4 in preference; rather (will see him damned first). □ **at first** at the beginning. **at first hand** directly from the original source. **first past the post** (of an electoral system) selecting a candidate or party by simple majority. **from the first** from the beginning. **in the first place** as first consideration. [Old English]

first aid n. emergency medical treatment.

first-born —*adj.* eldest. —*n.* person's eldest child.

first class —*n.* **1** best group or category. **2** best accommodation in a train, ship, etc. **3** mail given priority. **4** highest division in an examination. —*adj. & adv.* (**first-class**) **1** of or by the first class. **2** excellent.

first cousin see COUSIN.

first-day cover *n.* envelope with stamps postmarked on their first day of issue.

first-degree *adj.* denoting non-serious surface burns.

first finger *n.* finger next to the thumb.

first floor *n.* (*US* **second floor**) floor above the ground floor.

first-foot *Scot.* —*n.* first person to cross a threshold in the New Year. —*v.* be a first-foot.

first-fruit *n.* (usu. in *pl.*) **1** first agricultural produce of a season, esp. as offered to God. **2** first results of work etc.

firsthand *adj. & adv.* from the original source; direct.

First Lady *n.* (in the US) wife of the President.

first light *n.* dawn.

firstly *adv.* in the first place, first (cf. FIRST *adv.*).

first mate *n.* (on a merchant ship) second in command.

first name *n.* personal or Christian name.

first night *n.* first public performance of a play etc.

first offender *n.* criminal without previous convictions.

first officer *n.* = FIRST MATE.

first person see PERSON.

first post *n.* (also **last post**) bugle-call as a signal to retire for the night.

first-rate *adj.* **1** excellent. **2** *colloq.* very well (*feeling first-rate*).

first thing *adv. colloq.* before anything else; very early.

firth *n.* (also **frith**) **1** narrow inlet of sea. **2** estuary. [Old Norse: related to FIORD]

fiscal /'fisk(ə)l/ —*adj.* of public revenue. —*n.* **1** legal official in some countries. **2** *Scot.* = PROCURATOR FISCAL. [Latin *fiscus* treasury]

fiscal year *n.* = FINANCIAL YEAR.

fish¹ —*n.* (*pl.* same or **-es**) **1** vertebrate cold-blooded animal with gills and fins living wholly in water. **2** any of various non-vertebrate animals living wholly in water, e.g. the cuttlefish, shellfish, and jellyfish. **3** fish as food. **4** *colloq.* person of a specified, usu. unpleasant, kind (*an odd fish*). **5** (the **Fish** or **Fishes**) sign or constellation Pisces. —*v.* **1** try to catch fish. **2** fish in (a certain river, pool, etc.). **3** (foll. by *for*) **a** search for. **b** seek

indirectly (*fishing for compliments*). **4** (foll. by *up, out, etc.*) retrieve with effort. □ **drink like a fish** drink alcohol excessively. **fish out of water** person out of his or her element. **other fish to fry** other matters to attend to. [Old English]

fish² *n.* flat or curved plate of iron, wood, etc., used to strengthen a beam, joint, or mast. [French *fiche* fix, from Latin *figere* FIX]

fish-bowl *n.* (usu. round) glass bowl for pet fish.

fish cake *n.* breaded cake of fish and mashed potato, usu. fried.

fisher *n.* **1** animal that catches fish. **2** *archaic* fisherman. [Old English]

fisherman *n.* man who catches fish as a livelihood or for sport.

fishery *n.* (*pl.* **-ies**) **1** place where fish are caught or reared. **2** industry of fishing or breeding fish.

fish-eye lens *n.* very wide-angle lens with a highly-curved front.

fish farm *n.* place where fish are bred for food.

fish finger *n.* small oblong piece of fish in batter or breadcrumbs.

fish-hook *n.* barbed hook for catching fish.

fishing *n.* catching fish.

fishing-line *n.* thread with a baited hook etc. for catching fish.

fishing-rod *n.* tapering usu. jointed rod for fishing.

fish-kettle *n.* oval pan for boiling fish.

fish-knife *n.* knife for eating or serving fish.

fish-meal *n.* ground dried fish as fertilizer or animal feed.

fishmonger *n.* dealer in fish.

fishnet *n.* (often *attrib.*) open-meshed fabric (*fishnet stockings*).

fish-plate *n.* flat piece of iron etc. connecting railway rails or positioning masonry.

fish-slice *n.* flat slotted cooking utensil.

fishtail *n.* device etc. shaped like a fish's tail.

fishwife *n.* **1** coarse-mannered or noisy woman. **2** woman who sells fish.

fishy *adj.* (**-ier, -iest**) **1** of or like fish. **2** *slang* dubious, suspect. □ **fishily** *adv.* **fishiness** *n.*

fissile /'fisaIl/ *adj.* **1** capable of undergoing nuclear fission. **2** tending to split. [Latin: related to FISSURE]

fission /'fiʃ(ə)n/ —*n.* **1** splitting of a heavy atomic nucleus, with a release of energy. **2** cell division as a mode of reproduction. —*v.* (cause to) undergo fission. □ **fissionable** *adj.* [Latin: related to FISSURE]

fission bomb *n.* atomic bomb.

fissure /'fɪʃə(r)/ —n. crack or split, usu. long and narrow. —v. (-ring) split, crack. [Latin *findo fiss-* cleave]

fist n. tightly closed hand. □ **fistful** n. (pl. -s). [Old English]

fisticuffs /'fɪstɪ,kʌfs/ n.pl. fighting with the fists. [probably from obsolete *fisty* (from FIST), CUFF²]

fistula /'fɪstjʊlə/ n. (pl. -s or -lae /-,liː/) abnormal or artificial passage between an organ and the body surface or between two organs. □ **fistular** adj. **fistulous** adj. [Latin. = pipe]

fit¹ —adj. (**fitter**, **fittest**) **1 a** well suited. **b** qualified, competent, worthy. **c** in suitable condition, ready. **d** (foll. by *for*) good enough (*fit for a king*). **2** in good health or condition. **3** proper, becoming, right (*it is fit that*). —v. (**-tt-**) **1 a** (also *absol.*) be of the right shape and size for (*dress fits her; key doesn't fit*). **b** (often foll. by *in, into*) be correctly positioned (*that bit fits here*). **c** find room for (*fit another on here*). **2** make suitable or competent; adapt (*fitted for battle*). **3** (usu. foll. by *with*) supply. **4** fix in place (*fit a lock on the door*). **5** = FIT ON. **6** befit, become (*it fits the occasion*). —adv. in a way which (a garment, component, etc., fits (*tight fit*). —adv. (foll. by *to* + infin.) colloq. so that; likely (*laughing fit to bust*). □ **fit the bill** = FILL the bill. **fit in 1** (often foll. by *with*) be compatible; accommodate (*tried to fit in with their plans*). **2** find space or time for (*dentist fitted me in*). **fit on** try on (a garment). **fit out** (or **up**) (often foll. by *with*) equip. **see** (or **think**) **fit** (often foll. by *to* + infin.) decide or choose (a specified action). □ **fitly** adv. **fitness** n. [origin unknown]

fit² n. **1** sudden esp. epileptic seizure with unconsciousness or convulsions. **2** sudden brief bout or burst (*fit of giggles, fit of coughing*). □ **by** (or **in**) **fits and starts** spasmodically. **have a fit** colloq. be greatly surprised or outraged. [Old English]

fitful adj. spasmodic or intermittent. □ **fitfully** adv.

fitment n. (usu. in pl.) fixed item of furniture.

fitted adj. **1** made to fit closely or exactly (*fitted carpet*). **2** provided with built-in fittings etc. (*fitted kitchen*). **3** built-in (*fitted cupboards*).

fitter n. **1** mechanic who fits together and adjusts machinery. **2** supervisor of the cutting, fitting, etc. of garments.

fitting —n. **1** trying-on of a garment etc. for adjustment before completion. **2** (in pl.) fixtures and fitments of a building. —adj. proper, becoming, right. □ **fittingly** adv.

five adj. & n. **1** one more than four. **2** symbol for this (5, v, V). **3** size etc. denoted by five. **4** set or team of five. **5** five o'clock (*is it five yet?*). **6** *Cricket* hit scoring five runs. [Old English]

fivefold adj. & adv. **1** five times as much or as many. **2** consisting of five parts.

five o'clock shadow n. beard-growth visible in the latter part of the day.

fiver n. colloq. five-pound note.

fives n. game in which a ball is hit with a gloved hand or bat against the walls of a court.

five-star adj. of the highest class.

fivestones n. jacks played with five pieces of metal etc. and usu. no ball.

fix —v. **1** make firm or stable; fasten, secure. **2** decide, settle, specify (a price, date, etc.). **3** mend, repair. **4** implant in the mind. **5 a** (foll. by *on, upon*) direct (the eyes etc.) steadily, set. **b** attract and hold (the attention, eyes, etc.). **c** (foll. by *with*) single out with one's look etc. **6** place definitely, establish. **7** determine the exact nature, position, etc., of; refer (a thing) to a definite place or time; identify, locate. **8 a** make (the eyes, features, etc.) rigid. **b** (of eyes, features, etc.) become rigid. **9** US colloq. prepare (food or drink). **10** congeal or become congealed. **11** colloq. punish, kill, deal with (a person). **12** colloq. **a** bribe or threaten into supporting. **b** gain a fraudulent result of (a race etc.). **13** slang inject a narcotic. **14** make (a colour, photographic image, etc.) fast or permanent. **15** (of a plant etc.) assimilate (nitrogen or carbon dioxide). —n. **1** colloq. dilemma, predicament. **2 a** finding one's position by bearings etc. **b** position found in this way. **3** slang dose of an addictive drug. □ **be fixed** (usu. foll. by *for*) colloq. be situated (regarding) (*how is he fixed for money?*). **fix on** (or **upon**) choose, decide on. **fix up 1** arrange, organize. **2** accommodate. **3** (often foll. by *with*) provide (a person) (*fixed me up with a job*). □ **fixable** adj. [Latin *figo fix-*]

fixate /fɪk'seɪt/ v. (**-ting**) **1** direct one's gaze on. **2** *Psychol.* (usu. in *passive*; often foll. by *on, upon*) cause (a person) to become abnormally attached to a person or thing. [Latin: related to FIX]

fixation /fɪk'seɪʃ(ə)n/ n. **1** state of being fixated. **2** obsession, monomania. **3** co-agulation. **4** process of assimilating a gas to form a solid compound.

fixative /'fɪksətɪv/ —adj. tending to fix or secure. —n. fixative substance.

fixedly /'fɪksɪdlɪ/ adv. intently.

fixed star n. *Astron.* seemingly motionless star.

fixer n. 1 person or thing that fixes. 2 *Photog.* substance for fixing a photographic image etc. 3 *colloq* person who makes esp. illicit deals.

fixings n.pl. US 1 apparatus or equipment. 2 trimmings for a dish, dress, etc.

fixity n. fixed state; stability; permanence.

fixture /ˈfɪkstʃə(r)/ n. 1 a something fixed in position. b *colloq* seemingly immovable person or thing (*seems to be a fixture*). 2 a sporting event, esp. a match, race, etc. b date agreed for this. 3 (in *pl.*) articles attached to a house or land and regarded as legally part of it.

fizz —v. 1 make a hissing or spluttering sound. 2 (of a drink) effervesce. —n. 1 effervescence. 2 *colloq* effervescent drink, esp. champagne. [imitative]

fizzle /ˈfɪz(ə)l/ —v. (-ling) make a feeble hiss. —n. such a sound. □ **fizzle out** end feebly. [imitative]

fizzy adj. (-ier, -iest) effervescent. □ **fizziness** n.

fjord var. of FIORD.

fl. abbr. 1 floruit. 2 fluid.

flab n. *colloq* fat; flabbiness. [imitative, or from FLABBY]

flabbergast /ˈflæbəgɑːst/ v. (esp. as **flabbergasted** adj.) *colloq.* dumbfound. [origin uncertain]

flabby /ˈflæbɪ/ adj. (-ier, -iest) 1 (of flesh etc.) limp; flaccid. 2 feeble. □ **flabbiness** n. [alteration of *flappy*; related to FLAP]

flaccid /ˈflæksɪd/ adj. limp, flabby, drooping. □ **flaccidity** /-ˈsɪdɪtɪ/ n. [Latin *flaccus* limp]

flag¹ —n. 1 a usu. oblong or square piece of cloth, attachable by one edge to a pole or rope as a country's emblem or standard, a signal, etc. b small toy etc. resembling a flag. 2 adjustable strip of metal etc. indicating a taxi's availability for hire. —v. (-gg-) 1 a grow tired; lag (*was soon flagging*). b hang down; droop. 2 mark out with or as if with a flag or flags. 3 (often foll. by *that*) inform or communicate by flag-signals. □ **flag down** signal to stop. [origin unknown]

flag² —n. (also **flagstone**) 1 flat usu. rectangular paving-stone. 2 (in *pl.*) pavement of these. —v. (-gg-) pave with flags. [probably Scandinavian]

flag³ n. plant with a bladed leaf (esp. the iris). [origin unknown]

flag-day n. fund-raising day for a charity, esp. with the sale of small paper flags etc. in the street.

flagellant /ˈflædʒələnt/ —n. person who scourges himself, herself, or others as a religious discipline or as a sexual stimulus. —adj. of flagellation. [Latin *flagellum* whip]

flagellate /ˈflædʒəleɪt/ v. (-ting) scourge, flog. □ **flagellation** /-ˈleɪʃ(ə)n/ n.

flagellum /fləˈdʒeləm/ n. (pl. **-gella**) 1 long lashlike appendage on some microscopic organisms. 2 runner; creeping shoot. [Latin, = whip]

flageolet /ˌflædʒəˈlet/ n. small flute. [French from Provençal]

flag of convenience n. foreign flag under which a ship is registered, usu. to avoid regulations or financial charges.

flag-officer n. admiral, vice admiral, or rear admiral, or the commodore of a yacht-club.

flag of truce n. white flag requesting a truce.

flagon /ˈflæɡən/ n. 1 large bottle, usu. holding a quart (1 13 litres), esp. of wine, cider, etc. 2 large vessel for wine etc. usu. with a handle, spout, and lid. [Latin *flasco* FLASK]

flagrant /ˈfleɪɡr(ə)nt/ adj. blatant; notorious; scandalous. □ **flagrancy** n. **flagrantly** adv. [Latin *flagro* blaze]

flagship n. 1 ship with an admiral on board. 2 leader in a category etc.; exemplar.

flagstaff n. pole on which a flag may be hoisted.

flagstone n. = FLAG².

flag-waving n. populist agitation, chauvinism.

flail —n. wooden staff with a short heavy stick swinging from it, used for threshing. —v. 1 wave or swing wildly. 2 beat with or as with a flail. [Latin *flagellum*]

flair n. 1 natural talent in a specific area (*flair for languages*). 2 style, finesse. [French *flairer* to smell]

flak n. 1 anti-aircraft fire. 2 adverse criticism; abuse. [German, = *Fliegerabwehrkanone*, 'aviator-defence-gun']

flake —n. 1 small thin light piece of snow etc. 2 thin broad piece peeled or split off. —v. (-king) (often foll. by *away*, *off*) 1 take or come away in flakes. 2 sprinkle with or fall in flakes. □ **flake out** *colloq.* fall asleep or drop from exhaustion; faint. [origin unknown]

flak jacket n. protective reinforced military jacket.

flaky adj. (-ier, -iest) 1 of, like, or in flakes. 2 esp. US *slang* crazy, eccentric. □ **flakiness** n.

flaky pastry n. crumblier version of puff pastry.

flambé /ˈflɒmbeɪ/ adj. (of food) covered with alcohol and set alight briefly (following a noun: *pancakes flambé*). [French: related to FLAME]

flamboyant /flæm'bɔɪənt/ *adj.* 1 ostentatious; showy. 2 floridly decorated or coloured. □ **flamboyance** *n.* **flamboyantly** *adv.* [French: related to FLAMBÉ]

flame —*n.* 1 **a** ignited gas. **b** portion of this (*flame flickered; burst into flames*). 2 **a** bright light or colouring. **b** brilliant orange-red colour. 3 **a** strong passion, esp. love (*fan the flame*). **b** *colloq.* sweetheart. —*v.* 1 (often foll. by *away, forth, out, up*) burn; blaze. 2 (often foll. by *out, up*) break out. **b** (of a person) become angry. 3 shine or glow like flame. [Latin *flamma*]

flamenco /flə'meŋkəʊ/ *n.* (*pl.* -**s**) 1 style of Spanish Gypsy guitar music with singing. 2 dance performed to this. [Spanish = Flemish]

flame-thrower *n.* weapon for throwing a spray of flame.

flaming *adj.* 1 emitting flames. 2 very hot (*flaming June*). 3 *colloq.* **a** passionate (*flaming row*). **b** expressing annoyance (*that flaming dog*). 4 brightcoloured.

flamingo /flə'mɪŋgəʊ/ *n.* (*pl.* -**s** or -**es**) tall long-necked wading bird with mainly pink plumage. [Provençal: related to FLAME]

■ **Usage** *Flammable* is often used because *inflammable* can be mistaken for a negative (the true negative being *non-flammable*).

flammable /'flæməb(ə)l/ *adj.* inflammable. □ **flammability** /-'bɪlɪtɪ/ *n.* [Latin: related to FLAME]

flan *n.* 1 pastry case with a savoury or sweet filling. 2 sponge base with a sweet topping. [medieval Latin *flado -onis*]

flange /flændʒ/ *n.* projecting flat rim etc., for strengthening or attachment. [origin uncertain]

flank —*n.* 1 side of the body between ribs and hip. 2 side of a mountain, building, etc. 3 right or left side of an army etc. —*v.* (often in *passive*) be at or move along the side of (*road flanked by mountains*). [French from Germanic]

flannel /'flæn(ə)l/ —*n.* 1 **a** woven woollen usu. napless fabric. **b** (in *pl.*) flannel garments, esp. trousers. 2 face-cloth, esp. towelling. 3 *slang* nonsense; flattery. —*v.* (-**ll-**; *US* -**l-**) 1 *slang* flatter. 2 wash with a flannel. [Welsh *gwlanen* from *gwlân* wool]

flannelette /ˌflænə'let/ *n.* napped cotton fabric like flannel.

flap —*v.* (-**pp-**) 1 move or be moved up and down; beat. 2 *colloq.* be agitated or panicky. 3 sway; flutter. 4 (usu. foll. by *away, off*) strike (flies etc.) with flat object; drive. 5 *colloq.* (of ears) listen

intently. —*n.* 1 piece of cloth, wood, etc. attached by one side, esp. to cover a gap, e.g. a pocket-cover, the folded part of an envelope, a table-leaf. 2 motion of a wing, arm, etc. 3 *colloq.* agitation; panic (*in a flap*). 4 aileron. 5 light blow with something flat. □ **flappy** *adj.* [probably imitative]

flapdoodle /flæp'du:d(ə)l/ *n. colloq.* nonsense. [origin unknown]

flapjack *n.* 1 sweet oatcake. 2 esp. *US* pancake.

flapper *n.* 1 person apt to panic. 2 *slang* (in the 1920s) young unconventional woman.

flare —*v.* (-**ring**) 1 widen gradually (*flared trousers*). 2 (cause to) blaze brightly and unsteadily. 3 burst out, esp. angrily. —*n.* 1 **a** dazzling irregular flame. 2 flame or bright light used as a signal or to illuminate a target etc. 3 **a** gradual widening, esp. of a skirt or trousers. **b** (in *pl.*) wide-bottomed trousers. □ **flare up** burst into a sudden blaze, anger, activity, etc. [origin unknown]

flare-path *n.* line of lights on a runway to guide aircraft.

flare-up *n.* sudden outburst.

flash —*v.* 1 (cause to) emit a brief or sudden light; (cause to) gleam. 2 send or reflect like a sudden flame (*eyes flashed fire*). 3 **a** move suddenly into view or perception (*answer flashed upon me*). **b** move swiftly (*train flashed past*). 4 **a** send (news etc.) by radio, telegraph, etc. **b** signal to (a person) with lights. 5 *colloq.* show ostentatiously (*flashed her ring*). 6 *slang* indecently expose oneself. —*n.* 1 sudden bright light or flame, e.g. of lightning. 2 an instant (*in a flash*). 3 sudden brief feeling, display of wit, etc. (*flash of hope*). 4 = NEWSFLASH. 5 *Photog.* 1. = FLASHLIGHT 1. 6 *Mil.* coloured cloth patch on a uniform. 7 bright patch of colour. —*adj. colloq.* gaudy; showy; vulgar (*flash car*). [imitative]

flashback *n.* scene set in an earlier time than the main action.

flash bulb *n. Photog.* bulb for a flashlight.

flash-cube *n. Photog.* set of four flash bulbs in a cube, operated in turn.

flasher *n.* 1 *slang* man who indecently exposes himself. 2 automatic device for switching lights rapidly on and off.

flash-gun *n.* device operating a camera flashlight.

flashing *n.* (usu. metal) strip used to prevent water penetration at a roof-joint etc. [dial.]

flash in the pan *n.* promising start followed by failure.

flash-lamp n. portable flashing electric lamp.

flashlight n. 1 light giving an intense flash, used for night or indoor photography. 2 US electric torch.

flashpoint n. 1 temperature at which vapour from oil etc. will ignite in air. 2 point at which anger etc. is expressed.

flashy adj. (-ier, -iest) showy; gaudy; cheaply attractive. □ **flashily** adv. **flashiness** n.

flask /flɑːsk/ n. 1 narrow-necked bulbous bottle for wine etc. or used in chemistry. 2 = HIP-FLASK. 3 = VACUUM FLASK. [Latin flasca, flasco: cf. FLAGON]

flat¹ —adj. (**flatter**, **flattest**) 1 a horizontally level, b even; smooth; unbroken. c level and shallow (flat cap). 2 unqualified; downright (flat refusal). 3 a dull; lifeless; monotonous (in a flat tone). b dejected. 4 (of a drink) having lost its effervescence. 5 (of an accumulator, battery, etc.) having exhausted its charge. 6 Mus. a below true or normal pitch (violins are flat). b (of a key) having a flat or flats in the signature. c (as B, E, etc. flat) semitone lower than B, E, etc. 7 (of a tyre) punctured; deflated. —adv. 1 at full length, spread out (lay flat, flat against the wall). 2 collog. a completely, absolutely (flat broke). b exactly (in five minutes flat). 3 Mus. below the true or normal pitch (sings flat). —n. 1 flat part or thing (flat of the hand). 2 level ground, esp. a plain or swamp. 3 Mus. a note lowered a semitone below natural pitch. b sign (♭) indicating this. 4 (as the flat) flat racing or its season. 5 Theatr. flat scenery on a frame. 6 esp. US collog. flat tyre. □ flat out 1 at top speed. 2 using all one's strength etc. that's flat collog. that is definite. □ **flatly** adv. **flatness** n. **flattish** adj. [Old Norse]

flat² n. set of rooms, usu. on one floor, as a residence. □ **flatlet** n. [obsolete flet floor, dwelling, from Germanic: related to FLAT¹]

flat-fish n. sole, plaice, etc. with both eyes on one side of a flattened body.

flat foot n. foot with a flattened arch.

flat-footed adj. 1 having flat feet. 2 collog. a uninspired. b unprepared. c resolute.

flat-iron n. hist. domestic iron heated on a fire etc.

flatmate n. person sharing a flat.

flat race n. horse race without jumps.

flat rate n. unvarying rate or charge over level ground. □ **flat racing** n.

flat spin n. 1 Aeron. a nearly horizontal spin. 2 collog. state of panic.

flatten v. 1 make or become flat. 2 collog. a humiliate. b knock down.

flatter v. 1 compliment unduly, esp. for gain or advantage. 2 (usu. refl.; usu. foll. by that) congratulate or delude (oneself etc.) (the flatters himself that he can sing). 3 (of colour, style, portrait, painter etc.) enhance the appearance of (that blouse flatters you). 4 cause to feel honoured. □ **flatterer** n. **flattering** adj.; **flatteringly** adv. **flattery** n. exaggerated or insincere praise.

flatulent /flætjulənt/ adj. 1 a causing intestinal wind. b caused by or suffering from this. 2 (of speech etc.) inflated, pretentious. □ **flatulence** n. **flatulentus** blowing.

flatworm n. worm with a flattened body, e.g. flukes.

flaunt v. (often refl.) display proudly; show off, parade [origin unknown]

■ Usage Flaunt is often confused with flout which means 'to disobey contemptuously'.

flautist /flɔːtɪst/ n. flute-player. [Italian: related to FLUTE]

flavour /fleɪvə(r)/ (US flavor) —n. 1 mingled sensation of smell and taste (cheesy flavour). 2 characteristic quality (romantic flavour). 3 (usu. foll. by of) slight admixture (flavour of failure). —v. give flavour to; season. □ **flavour of the month** temporary trend or fashion.

flavouring n. (US flavoring) substance used to flavour food or drink. □ **flavoursome** adj. [French]

flaw¹ —n. 1 imperfection; blemish. 2 crack, chip, etc. 3 invalidating defect. —v. crack; damage; spoil. □ **flawless** adj. **flawlessly** adv. [Old Norse]

flaw² n. squall of wind. [Low German or Dutch]

flax n. 1 blue-flowered plant cultivated for its textile fibre and its seeds. 2 flax fibres. [Old English]

flaxen adj. 1 of flax. 2 (of hair) pale yellow.

flax-seed n. linseed.

flay v. 1 strip the skin or hide off, esp. by beating. 2 criticize severely. 3 peel off (skin, bark, peel, etc.). 4 extort money etc. from. [Old English]

flea n. small wingless jumping parasitic insect. □ **a flea in one's ear** sharp reproof. [Old English]

fleabag n. slang shabby or unattractive person or thing.

flea-bite n. 1 bite of a flea. 2 trivial injury or inconvenience.

flea-bitten adj. 1 bitten by or infested with fleas. 2 shabby.

flea market *n.* street market selling second-hand goods etc.

flea-pit *n.* dingy dirty cinema etc.

fleck —*n.* **1** small patch of colour or light. **2** particle, speck. —*v.* mark with flecks. [Old Norse, or Low German or Dutch]

flection *US* var. of FLEXION.

fled *past* and *past part.* of FLEE.

fledge *v.* (-ging) **1** provide or deck (an arrow etc.) with feathers. **2** bring up (a young bird) until it can fly. **3** (as **fledged** *adj.*) **a** able to fly. **b** independent; mature. [obsolete adj. *fledge* fit to fly]

fledgling /ˈfledʒlɪŋ/ *n.* (also **fledgeling**) **1** young bird. **2** inexperienced person.

flee *v.* (*past* and *past part.* **fled**) **1** (often foll. by *from*, *before*) **a** run away (from); leave abruptly (*fled the room*). **b** seek safety by fleeing. **2** vanish. [Old English]

fleece —*n.* **1 a** woolly coat of a sheep etc. **2** thing resembling a fleece, esp. soft fabric for lining etc. —*v.* (-cing) **1** (often foll. by *of*) strip of money, valuables, etc.; swindle. **2** shear (sheep etc.). **3** cover as if with a fleece (*sky fleeced with clouds*). □ **fleecy** *adj.* (-ier, -iest). [Old English]

fleet —*n.* **1 a** warships under one commander-in-chief. **b** (prec. by *the*) nation's warships etc.; navy. **2** number of vehicles in one company etc. —*adj. poet. literary* swift, nimble. [Old English]

fleeting *adj.* transitory; brief. □ **fleetingly** *adv.*

Fleming /ˈflemɪŋ/ *n.* **1** native of medieval Flanders. **2** member of a Flemish-speaking people of N. and W. Belgium. [Old English]

Flemish /ˈflemɪʃ/ —*adj.* of Flanders. —*n.* language of the Flemings. [Dutch]

flesh *n.* **1 a** soft, esp. muscular, substance between the skin and bones of an animal or a human. **b** plumpness; fat. **2** the body, esp. as sinful. **3** pulpy substance of a fruit etc. **4 a** visible surface of the human body. **b** (also **flesh-colour**) yellowish pink colour. **5** animal or human life. □ **all flesh** all animate creation. **flesh out** make or become substantial. **in the flesh** in person. **one's own flesh and blood** near relatives. [Old English]

flesh and blood —*n.* **1** the body or its substance. **2** humankind. **3** human nature, esp. as fallible. —*adj.* real, not imaginary.

fleshly *adj.* (-lier, -liest) **1** bodily; sensual. **2** mortal. **3** worldly.

fleshpots *n.pl.* luxurious living.

flesh-wound *n.* superficial wound.

fleshy *adj.* (-ier, -iest) of flesh; plump, pulpy. □ **fleshiness** *n.*

fleur-de-lis /ˌflɜːdəˈliː/ *n.* (also **fleur-de-lys**) (*pl.* **fleurs-** pronunc. same) **1** iris flower. **2** *Heraldry* **a** lily of three petals. **b** former royal arms of France. [French, = flower of lily]

flews *n.pl.* hanging lips of a bloodhound etc. [origin unknown]

flew *past* of FLY¹.

flex¹ *v.* **1** bend (a joint, limb, etc.) or be bent. **2** move (a muscle) or (of a muscle) be moved to bend a joint. [Latin *flecto flex-* bend]

flex² *n.* flexible insulated electric cable. [abbreviation of FLEXIBLE]

flexible /ˈfleksɪb(ə)l/ *adj.* **1** capable of bending without breaking; pliable. **2** manageable. **3** adaptable; variable (*works flexible hours*). □ **flexibility** /-ˈbɪlɪtɪ/ *n.* **flexibly** *adv.* [Latin: related to FLEX¹]

flexion /ˈflekʃ(ə)n/ *n.* (*US* **flection**) **1** bending or being bent, esp. of a limb or joint. **2** bent part; curve. [Latin *flexio*: related to FLEX¹]

flexitime /ˈfleksɪtaɪm/ *n.* system of flexible working hours. [from FLEXIBLE]

flibbertigibbet /ˌflɪbətɪˈdʒɪbɪt/ *n.* gossiping, frivolous, or restless person.

flick —*n.* **1 a** light sharp blow with a whip etc. **b** sudden release of a bent digit, esp. to propel a small object. **2** sudden movement or jerk, esp. of the wrist in throwing etc. **3** *colloq.* **a** cinema film. **b** (in *pl.*; prec. by *the*) the cinema. —*v.* **1** (often foll. by *away*, *off*) strike or move with a flick (*flicked the ash off*). **2** give a flick with (a whip etc.). □ **flick through 1** turn over (cards, pages, etc.). **2 a** turn over the pages etc. of, by a rapid movement of the fingers. **b** glance through (a book etc.). [imitative]

flicker —*v.* **1** (of light or flame) shine or burn unsteadily. **2** flutter. **3** (of hope etc.) waver. —*n.* **1** flickering movement or light. **2** brief spell (of hope etc.). □ **flicker out** die away. [Old English]

flick-knife *n.* knife with a blade that springs out when a button is pressed.

flier var. of FLYER.

flight¹ /flaɪt/ *n.* **1 a** act or manner of flying. **b** movement or passage through the air. **2 a** journey through the air or in space. **b** timetabled airline journey. **3** flock of birds, insects, etc. **4** (usu. foll. by *of*) series. **5** imaginative excursion or sally (*flight of fancy*). **6** (usu. foll. by *of*) volley (*flight of arrows*). **7** tail of a dart. [Old English: related to FLY¹]

flight² /flaɪt/ *n.* fleeing, hasty retreat. □ **put to flight** cause to flee. **take** (or **take to**) **flight** flee. [Old English]

flight bag n. small zipped shoulder bag for air travel.

flight-deck n. 1 deck of an aircraft-carrier. 2 control room of a large aircraft.

flightless adj. (of a bird etc.) unable to fly.

flight lieutenant n. RAF officer next below squadron leader.

flight path n. planned course of an aircraft etc.

flight-recorder n. device in an aircraft recording technical details of a flight.

flight sergeant n. RAF rank next above sergeant.

flighty adj. (-ier, -iest) (usu. of a girl) frivolous, fickle, changeable. □ **flightiness** n.

flimsy /'flimzi/ adj. (-ier, -iest) 1 insubstantial, rickety (flimsy structure). 2 (of an excuse etc.) unconvincing. 3 (of clothing) thin. □ **flimsily** adv. **flimsiness** n. [origin uncertain]

flinch v. draw back in fear etc.; wince. [French from Germanic]

fling — v. (past and past part. **flung**) 1 throw or hurl forcefully or hurriedly. 2 (foll. by on, off) put on or take off (clothes) carelessly or rapidly. 3 put or send suddenly or violently (was flung into jail). 4 rush, esp. angrily (flung out of the room). 5 (foll. by away) discard rashly. — n. 1 act of flinging. 2 bout of wild behaviour. 3 whirling Scottish dance, esp. the Highland fling. [Old Norse]

flint n. 1 a hard grey siliceous stone. b piece of this, esp. as a primitive tool or weapon. 2 piece of hard alloy used to give a spark. 3 anything hard and unyielding. □ **flinty** adj. (-ier, -iest). [Old English]

flintlock n. hist. old type of gun fired by a spark from a flint.

flip¹ — v. (-pp-) 1 flick or toss (a coin, pellet, etc.) so that it spins in the air. 2 turn (a small object) over; flick. 3 slang = flip one's lid. — n. 1 act of flipping. 2 colloq. short trip. —adj. colloq. flippant. □ **flip one's lid** slang lose self-control; go mad. **flip through** = flick through. [probably from FLIP²]

flip² n. 1 = EGG-FLIP. 2 drink of heated beer and spirit. [perhaps from FLIP¹]

flip chart n. large pad of paper on a stand.

flip-flop n. (usu. rubber) sandal with a thong between the toes. [imitative]

flippant /'flipant/ adj. offhand, disrespectful; frivolous. □ **flippancy** n. **flippantly** adv. [from FLIP¹]

flipper n. 1 broad flat limb of a turtle, penguin, etc., used in swimming. 2 sim-

ilar rubber foot attachment for under-water swimming. 3 slang hand.

flipping adj. & adv. slang expressing annoyance, or as an intensifier.

flip side n. colloq. 1 reverse side of a gramophone record. 2 reverse or less important side of something.

flirt — v. 1 (usu. foll. by with) try to attract sexually but without serious intent. 2 (usu. foll. by with) superficially engage in; trifle. — n. person who flirts. □ **flirtation** /-'teiʃ(ə)n/ n. **flirtatious** /-'teiʃəs/ adj. **flirtatiously** /-'teiʃəsli/ adv. **flirtatiousness** /-'teiʃəsnis/ n. [imitative]

flit — v. (-tt-) 1 move lightly, softly, or rapidly. 2 make short flights. 3 colloq. disappear secretly to escape creditors etc. — n. act of flitting. [Old Norse; related to FLEET]

flitch n. side of bacon. [Old English]

flitter v. flit about; flutter. [from FLIT]

flitter-mouse n. = BAT².

float — v. 1 a (cause to) rest or move on the surface of a liquid. b (often foll. by before) hover before the eye or mind. 3 (often foll. by in) move or be suspended freely in a liquid or gas. 4 a start or launch (a company, scheme, etc.). b offer (stock, shares, etc.) on the stock market. 5 Commerce cause or allow to have a fluctuating exchange rate. 6 circulate or cause (a rumour or idea) to circulate. — n. 1 thing that floats, esp.: a a raft. b a light object as an indicator of a fish biting or supporting a fishing-net. c a hollow structure enabling an aircraft to float on water. d a floating device on the surface of a liquid, as in a cistern. 2 small, esp. electrically-powered vehicle or cart (milk float). 3 decorated platform or tableau on a lorry in a procession etc. 4 a supply of loose change in a shop, at a fete, etc. b petty cash. 5 Theatr. (in sing. or pl.) footlights. 6 tool for smoothing plaster. □ **floatable** adj. [Old English]

floatation var. of FLOTATION.

floating adj. not settled; variable (floating population).

floating dock n. floating structure usable as a dry dock.

floating kidney n. abnormally movable kidney.

floating rib n. lower rib not attached to the breastbone.

floating voter n. voter without fixed allegiance.

floaty adj. (esp. of fabric) light and airy. [from FLOAT]

flocculent /ˈflɒkjʊlənt/ *adj.* like or in tufts of wool etc.; downy. □ **flocculence** *n.* [related to FLOCK²]

flock¹ —*n.* **1** animals of one kind as a group or unit. **2** large crowd of people. **3** people in the care of a priest or teacher etc. —*v.* (usu. foll. by *to, in, out, together*) congregate; mass; troop. [Old English]

flock² *n.* **1** lock or tuft of wool, cotton, etc. **2** (also in *pl.*; often *attrib.*) woolrefuse etc. used for quilting and stuffing. [Latin *floccus*]

flock-paper *n.* (also **flock-wallpaper**) wallpaper with a raised flock pattern.

floe *n.* sheet of floating ice. [Norwegian]

flog *v.* (**-gg-**) **1** beat with a whip, stick, etc. **b** make work through violent effort (*flogged the engine*). **2** (often foll. by *off*) *slang* sell. □ **flog a dead horse** waste one's efforts. **flog to death** *colloq.* talk about or promote at tedious length. [origin unknown]

flood /flʌd/ —*n.* **1 a** overflowing or influx of water, esp. over land; inundation. **b** the water that overflows. **2** outpouring; torrent (*flood of tears*). **3** inflow of the tide (also in *comb.*: *flood-tide*). **4** *colloq.* floodlight. **5** (**the Flood**) the flood described in Genesis. —*v.* **1** overflow or cover, or be covered with or as if with a flood (*bathroom flooded*; *flooded with enquiries*). **2** irrigate. **3** deluge (a mine etc.) with water. **4** (often foll. by *in, through*) come in great quantities (*complaints flooded in*). **5** overfill (a carburettor) with petrol. **6** have a uterine haemorrhage. □ **flood out** drive out (of one's home etc.) with a flood. [Old English]

floodgate *n.* **1** gate for admitting or excluding water, esp. in a lock. **2** (usu. in *pl.*) last restraint against tears, rain, anger, etc.

floodlight —*n.* large powerful light (usu. one of several) to illuminate a building, sports ground, etc. —*v.* illuminate with floodlights. □ **floodlit** *adj.*

flood-tide *n.* exceptionally high tide caused esp. by the moon.

floor /flɔː(r)/ —*n.* **1** lower supporting surface of a room. **2 a** bottom of the sea, a cave, etc. **b** any level area. **3** all the rooms etc. on one level of a building; storey. **4 a** (in a legislative assembly) place where members sit and speak. **b** right to speak next in a debate (*gave him the floor*). **5** minimum of prices, wages, etc. **6** *colloq.* ground. —*v.* **1** provide with a floor; pave. **2** knock or bring (a person) down. **3** *colloq.* confound, baffle. **4** *colloq.* overcome. **5** serve as the floor of (*lino floored the hall*). □ **from the floor** (of a speech etc.) given by a member of the

audience. **take the floor 1** begin to dance. **2** speak in a debate. [Old English]

floorboard *n.* long wooden board used for flooring.

floorcloth *n.* cloth for washing the floor.

flooring *n.* material of which a floor is made.

floor manager *n.* stage-manager of a television production.

floor plan *n.* diagram of the rooms etc. on one storey.

floor show *n.* nightclub entertainment.

floozie /ˈfluːzɪ/ *n.* (also **floozy**) (*pl.* **-ies**) *colloq.* esp. disreputable girl or woman. [origin unknown]

flop —*v.* (**-pp-**) **1** sway about heavily or loosely. **2** (often foll. by *down, on, into*) fall or sit etc. awkwardly or suddenly. **3** *slang* fail; collapse (*play flopped*). **4** make a dull soft thud or splash. —*n.* **1** flopping movement or sound. **2** *slang* failure. —*adv.* with a flop. [var. of FLAP]

floppy —*adj.* (**-ier**, **-iest**) tending to flop; flaccid. —*n.* (*pl.* **-ies**) (in full **floppy disk**) *Computing* flexible disc for the storage of data. □ **floppiness** *n.*

flora /ˈflɔːrə/ *n.* (*pl.* **-s** or **florae** /-riː/) **1** plant life of a region or period. **2** list or book of these. [Latin *Flora*, name of the goddess of flowers]

floral *adj.* of, decorated with, or depicting flowers. □ **florally** *adv.* [Latin]

Florentine /ˈflɒrəntaɪn/ —*adj.* of Florence in Italy. —*n.* native or citizen of Florence. [Latin]

floret /ˈflɒrɪt/ *n.* **1** each of the small flowers making up a composite flowerhead. **2** each stem of a head of cauliflower, broccoli, etc. **3** small flower. [Latin *flos* FLOWER]

floribunda /ˌflɒrɪˈbʌndə/ *n.* plant, esp. a rose, bearing dense clusters of flowers. [related to FLORET: cf. MORIBUND]

florid /ˈflɒrɪd/ *adj.* **1** ruddy (*florid complexion*). **2** elaborately ornate; showy. □ **floridly** *adv.* **floridness** *n.* [Latin: related to FLOWER]

florin /ˈflɒrɪn/ *n.* *hist.* **1** British twoshilling coin now worth 10 pence. **2** English or foreign gold or silver coin. [Italian *fiorino*: related to FLOWER]

florist /ˈflɒrɪst/ *n.* person who deals in or grows flowers. [Latin *flos* FLOWER]

floruit /ˈflɒruɪt/ —*v.* flourished; lived and worked (of a painter, writer, etc., whose exact dates are unknown). —*n.* period or date of working etc. [Latin, = he or she flourished]

floss —*n.* **1** rough silk of a silkworm's cocoon. **2** silk thread used in embroidery. **3** = DENTAL FLOSS. —*v.* (also *absol.*) clean (teeth) with dental floss. □ **flossy** *adj.* [French *floche*]

flotation /fləʊˈteɪʃ(ə)n/ n. (also **floata-tion**) launching or financing of a commercial enterprise or financing of a company.

flotilla /fləˈtɪlə/ n. 1 small fleet. 2 fleet of small ships. [Spanish]

flotsam /ˈflɒtsəm/ n. wreckage found floating. [Anglo-French: related to FLOAT]

flotsam and jetsam n. 1 odds and ends. 2 vagrants.

flounce[1] — v. (-cing) (often foll. by *away, about, off, out*) go or move angrily or impatiently. — n. flouncing movement. [origin unknown]

flounce[2] — n. frill on a dress, skirt, etc. — v. (-cing) trim with flounces. [alteration of *frounce* pleat, from French]

flounder[1] — v. 1 struggle helplessly as if wading in mud. 2 do a task clumsily. — n. act of floundering. [imitative]

flounder[2] n. (pl. same) 1 edible European flat-fish. [Anglo-French, probably Scandinavian]

flour — n. 1 meal or powder from ground wheat etc. 2 any fine powder. — v. sprinkle with flour. □ **floury** adj. (-ier, -iest). fleuriness n. [different spelling of FLOWER 'best part']

flourish /ˈflʌrɪʃ/ — v. 1 a grow vigorously. thrive. b prosper. c be in one's prime. 2 wave, brandish. — n. 1 showy gesture. 2 ornamental curve in handwriting. 3 Mus. ornate passage or fanfare. [Latin *floreo* from *flos* FLOWER]

flout — v. disobey (the law etc.) contemptuously; mock; insult. — n. flouting speech or act. [Dutch *fluiten* whistle: related to FLUTE]

■ **Usage** *Flout* is often confused with *flaunt* which means 'to display proudly, show off'.

flow /fləʊ/ — v. 1 glide along as a stream. 2 (of liquid, blood, etc.) gush out; be spilt. 3 (of blood, money, electric current, etc.) circulate. 4 move smoothly or steadily. 5 (of a garment, hair, etc.) hang gracefully. 6 (often foll. by *from*) be caused by. 7 (esp. of the tide) be in flood. 8 (of wine) be plentiful. 9 (foll. by *with*) archaic be plentifully supplied with (*flowing with milk and honey*). — n. 1 a flowing movement or mass. b flowing liquid (*stop the flow*). c outpouring; stream (*flow of and flow*). 2 rise of a tide or river (*flow and flow*/*ebb and flow*). [Old English]

flow chart n. (also **flow diagram** or **flow sheet**) diagram of the movement or action in a complex activity.

flower /ˈflaʊə(r)/ — n. 1 part of a plant from which the fruit or seed is developed. 2 blossom, esp. used for decoration. 3 plant cultivated for its flowers. — v. 1 bloom or cause (a plant) to bloom;

blossom. 2 reach a peak. □ **the flower of** the best of. **in flower** blooming. □ **flowered** adj. [Lat.n *flos flor-*]

flower-bed n. garden bed for flowers.

flower-head n. = HEAD n. 3 c.

flower people n. hippies with flowers as symbols of peace and love.

flowerpot n. pot for growing a plant in.

flower power n. peace and love, esp. as a political idea.

flowers of sulphur n. fine powder produced when sulphur evaporates and condenses.

flowery adj. 1 florally decorated. 2 (of style, speech, etc.) high-flown; ornate. 3 full of flowers. □ **floweriness** n.

flowing adj. 1 (of style etc.) fluent; easy. 2 (of a line, curve, etc.) smoothly continuous. 3 (of hair etc.) unconfined. □ **flowingly** adv.

flown past part. of FLY[1].

flu /fluː/ n. colloq influenza. [abbreviation]

fluctuate /ˈflʌktʃʊeɪt/ v. (-ting) vary irregularly; rise and fall. □ **fluctuation** /-ˈeɪʃ(ə)n/ n. [Latin *fluctus* wave]

flue /fluː/ n. 1 smoke-duct in a chimney. 2 channel for conveying heat. [origin unknown]

fluent /ˈfluːənt/ adj. 1 (of speech, style, etc.) flowing; natural 2 verbally facile, esp. in a foreign language (*fluent in German*). □ **fluency** n. **fluently** adv. [Latin *fluo* flow]

fluff — n. 1 soft fur, feathers, or fabric particles etc. 2 slang mistake in a performance etc. — v. 1 (often foll. by *up*) shake into or become a soft mass. 2 colloq. make a fluff; bungle. □ **bit of fluff** slang offens. attractive woman. □ **fluffy** adj. (-ier, -iest). fluffiness n.

flugelhorn /ˈfluːg(ə)lhɔːn/ n. valved brass wind instrument like a cornet. [German *Flügel* wing, *Horn* horn]

fluid /ˈfluːɪd/ — n. 1 substance, esp. a gas or liquid, whose shape is determined by its confines. 2 fluid part or secretion. — adj. 1 able to flow and alter shape freely. 2 constantly changing (*situation is fluid*). □ **fluidity** /-ˈɪdɪtɪ/ n. **fluidly** adv. **fluidness** n. [Latin: related to FLU-ENT]

fluid ounce n. one-twentieth, or US one-sixteenth, of a pint.

fluke[1] /fluːk/ — n. lucky accident (*won by a fluke*). — v. (-king) achieve by a fluke. □ **fluky** adj. (-ier, -iest). [origin uncertain]

fluke[2] /fluːk/ n. 1 parasitic flatworm, e.g. the liver fluke. 2 flat-fish, esp. a flounder. [Old English]

336

fluke³ /fluːk/ n. 1 broad triangular plate on an anchor arm. 2 lobe of a whale's tail. [perhaps from FLUKE²]

flummery /ˈflʌmərɪ/ n. (pl. -ies) 1 flattery; nonsense. 2 sweet dish made with beaten eggs, sugar, etc. [Welsh *llymru*]

flummox /ˈflʌməks/ v. colloq. bewilder, disconcert. [origin unknown]

flung past and past part. of FLING.

flunk v. US colloq. fail (esp. an exam). [origin unknown]

flunkey /ˈflʌŋkɪ/ n. (also **flunky**) (pl. -eys or -ies) usu. derog. 1 liveried footman. 2 toady; snob. 3 US cook, waiter, etc. [origin uncertain]

fluoresce /fluəˈres/ v. (-scing) be or become fluorescent. [from FLUOR-ESCENT]

fluorescence n. 1 light radiation from certain substances. 2 property of absorbing invisible light and emitting visible light. [from FLUORSPAR, after *opalescence*]

fluorescent adj. of, having, or showing fluorescence.

fluorescent lamp n. (also fluorescent bulb) esp. tubular lamp or bulb radiating largely by fluorescence.

fluoridate /ˈfluərɪˌdeɪt/ v. (-ting) add fluoride to (drinking-water etc.), esp. to prevent tooth decay. □ **fluoridation** /-ˈdeɪʃ(ə)n/ n.

fluoride /ˈfluəraɪd/ n. binary compound of fluorine.

fluorinate /ˈfluərɪˌneɪt/ v. (-ting) 1 = FLUORIDATE. 2 introduce fluorine into (a compound). □ **fluorination** /-ˈneɪʃ(ə)n/ n.

fluorine /ˈfluəriːn/ n. poisonous pale-yellow gaseous element. [French: related to FLUORSPAR]

fluorite /ˈfluəraɪt/ n. mineral form of calcium fluoride. [Italian: related to FLUORSPAR]

fluorocarbon /fluərəˈkɑːbən/ n. compound of a hydrocarbon with fluorine atoms.

fluorspar /ˈfluəspɑː(r)/ n. = FLUORITE. [*fluor* a mineral used as flux, from Latin *fluo* flow]

flurry /ˈflʌrɪ/ —n. (pl. -ies) 1 gust or squall (of snow, rain, etc.). 2 sudden burst of activity, excitement, etc.; commotion. —v. (-ies, -ied) confuse; agitate. [imitative]

flush¹ —v. 1 blush, redden, glow warmly (*he flushed with embarrassment*). 2 (usu. as **flushed** adj.) cause to glow or blush (often foll. by with: *he was flushed with pride*). 3 a cleanse (a drain, lavatory, etc.) by a flow of water. b (often foll. by away, down) dispose of in this way. 4 rush out, spurt. —n. 1 blush or glow. 2 a rush of water. b cleansing of

a drain, lavatory, etc. thus. 3 rush of esp. elation or triumph. 4 freshness; vigour. 5 (also **hot flush**) sudden feeling of heat during menopause. b feverish redness or temperature etc. —adj. 1 level, in the same plane. 2 colloq. having plenty of money. [perhaps = FLUSH³]

flush² n. hand of cards all of one suit, esp. in poker. [Latin *fluxus* FLUX]

flush³ v. 1 cause (esp. a game-bird) to fly up. 2 (of a bird) fly up and away. □ **flush out** 1 reveal. 2 drive out. [imitative]

fluster —v. 1 make or become nervous or confused (*he flusters easily*). 2 bustle. —n. confused or agitated state. [origin unknown]

flute /fluːt/ —n. 1 a high-pitched woodwind instrument held sideways. b any similar wind instrument. 2 ornamental vertical groove in a column. —v. (-ting) 1 play, or play (a tune etc.) on, the flute. 2 speak or sing etc. in a high voice. 3 make grooves in. □ **fluting** n. **fluty** adj. (in sense 1a of n.). [French]

flutter —v. 1 flap (the wings) in flying or trying to fly. 2 fall quiveringly (*fluttered to the ground*). 3 wave or flap quickly. 4 move about restlessly. 5 (of a pulse etc.) beat feebly or irregularly. —n. 1 act of fluttering. 2 tremulous excitement (*caused a flutter*). 3 slang small bet, esp. on a horse. 4 abnormally rapid heartbeat. 5 rapid variation of pitch, esp. of recorded sound. [Old English]

fluvial /ˈfluːvɪəl/ adj. of or found in rivers. [Latin *fluvius* river]

flux n. 1 process of flowing or flowing out. 2 discharge. 3 continuous change (*state of flux*). 4 substance mixed with a metal etc. to aid fusion. [Latin *fluxus* from *fluo* flux- flow]

fly¹ /flaɪ/ —v. (**flies**; past **flew** /fluː/; past part. **flown** /fləʊn/) 1 a (of an aircraft, bird, etc.) move through the air or space under control, esp. with wings. b travel through the air or space. 2 control the flight of or transport in (esp. an aircraft). 3 a cause to fly or remain aloft. b (of a flag, hair, etc.) wave or flutter. 4 pass, move, or rise quickly. 5 a flee; flee from. b colloq. depart hastily. 6 be driven, forced, or scattered (*sent me flying*). 7 (foll. by at, upon) a hasten or spring violently. b attack or criticize fiercely. —n. (pl. -ies) 1 (usu. in pl.) a concealing flap, esp. over a trouser-fastening. b this fastening. 2 flap at a tent entrance. 3 (in pl.) space above a stage where scenery and lighting are suspended. 4 act of flying. □ **fly high** be ambitious; prosper. **fly in the face of** disregard or disobey. **fly a kite** test opinion. **fly off the handle** colloq. lose one's temper. [Old English]

fly² /flaɪ/ n. (pl. **flies**) **1** insect with two usu. transparent wings. **2** other winged insect, e.g. a firefly. **3** disease of plants or animals caused by flies. **4** (esp. artificial) fly as bait in fishing. □ **like flies** in large numbers (usu. of people dying etc.). **no flies on** (him etc.), (he is) very astute. [Old English]

fly³ /flaɪ/ adj. slang knowing, clever, alert. [origin unknown]

fly-away adj. (of hair) fine and difficult to control.

fly-blown adj. tainted, esp. by flies.

fly-by-night adj. unreliable. —n. unreliable person.

flycatcher n. bird catching insects during short flights from a chosen perch.

flyer n. (also **flier**) colloq. **1** airman or airwoman. **2** thing that flies in a specified way (poor flyer). **3** fast-moving animal or vehicle. **4** ambitious or outstanding person. **5** small handbill.

fly-fish v. fish with a fly.

fly-half n. Rugby stand-off half.

flying —adj. **1** fluttering, waving, or hanging loose. **2** hasty, brief (flying visit). **3** designed for rapid movement. **4** (of an animal) leaping with winglike membranes etc. —n. flight, esp. in an aircraft. □ **with flying colours** with distinction.

flying boat n. boatlike seaplane.

flying buttress n. (usu. arched) buttress running from the upper part of a wall to an outer support and transmitting the thrust of the roof or vault.

flying doctor n. doctor who uses an aircraft to visit patients.

flying fish n. tropical fish with winglike fins for gliding through the air.

flying fox n. fruit-eating bat with a foxlike head.

flying officer n. RAF rank next below flight lieutenant.

flying picket n. mobile industrial strike picket.

flying saucer n. supposed alien spaceship.

flying squad n. rapidly mobile police detachment etc.

flying start n. **1** start (of a race etc.) in which the starting-point is crossed at full speed. **2** vigorous start (of an enterprise etc.).

fly in the ointment n. minor irritation or setback.

flyleaf n. blank leaf at the beginning or end of a book.

flyover n. bridge carrying one road or railway over another.

fly on the wall n. unnoticed observer.

fly-paper n. sticky treated paper for catching flies.

fly-past n. ceremonial flight of aircraft.

fly-post v. (posters etc.) illegally on walls etc.

flysheet n. **1** canvas cover over a tent for extra protection. **2** short tract or circular.

fly-tip v. illegally dump (waste). □ **fly-tipper** n.

flyweight n. **1** weight in certain sports between light flyweight and bantamweight, in amateur boxing 48–51 kg. **2** sportsman of this weight.

flywheel n. heavy wheel on a revolving shaft to regulate machinery or accumulate power.

FM abbr. **1** Field Marshal. **2** frequency modulation.

Fm symb. fermium

f-number /ˈefnʌmbə(r)/ n. ratio of the focal length to the effective diameter of a camera lens. [from focal]

FO abbr. Flying Officer.

foal —n. young of a horse or related animal. —v. give birth to (a foal). □ **in** (or **with**) **foal** (of a mare etc.) pregnant. [Old English]

foam —n. **1** mass of small bubbles formed on or in liquid by agitation, fermentation, etc. **2** froth of saliva or sweat. **3** substance resembling these, e.g. spongy rubber or plastic. —v. emit or run with foam; froth. □ **foam at the mouth** be very angry. □ **foamy** adj.

fob¹ n. **1** chain of a pocket-watch. **2** small pocket for a watch etc. **3** tab on a key-ring. [German]

fob² v. (-bb-) □ **fob off 1** (often foll. by with a thing) deceive into accepting something inferior. **2** (often foll. by on or on to a person) offload (an unwanted thing). [cf. obsolete fop dupe]

focal /ˈfəʊk(ə)l/ adj. of or at a focus. [Latin: related to focus]

focal distance n. (also **focal length**) distance between the centre of a mirror or lens and its focus.

focal point n. **1** = FOCUS n. 1. **2** centre of interest or activity.

fo'c's'le var. of FORECASTLE.

focus /ˈfəʊkəs/ —n. (pl. **focuses** or **foci** /ˈfəʊsaɪ/) **1 a** point at which rays or waves meet after reflection or refraction. **b** point from which rays etc. appear to proceed. **2 a** point at which an object must be situated for a lens or mirror to give a well-defined image. **b** adjustment of the eye or a lens to give a clear image. **c** state of clear definition. **3** (out of focus) **3** = FOCAL POINT 2. —v. (-s- or -ss-) **1** bring into focus. **2** adjust the focus of (a lens or eye). **3** (often foll. by on) concentrate or be concentrated on. **4** converge or make converge to a focus [Latin, = hearth]

fodder n. dried hay or straw etc. as animal food. [Old English]

FOE /collog. fəʊ/ abbr. var. of FETID.

foe n. esp. poet. enemy. [Old English]

foetid var. of FETID.

foetus /ˈfiːtəs/ n. (US **fetus**) (pl. **-tuses**) unborn mammalian offspring, esp. a human embryo of eight weeks or more. □ **foetal** adj. [Latin fetus offspring]

fog —n. 1 thick cloud of water droplets or smoke suspended at or near the earth's surface. 2 cloudiness on a photographic negative etc. 3 uncertain or confused position or state. —v. (**-gg-**) 1 cover or become covered with or as with fog. 2 perplex. □ **fogginess** n. [perhaps a back-formation from FOGGY]

fog-bank n. mass of fog at sea.

fog-bound adj. unable to travel because of fog.

foggy adj. (**-ier, -iest**) 1 full of fog. 2 of or like fog. 3 vague, indistinct. □ **not have the foggiest** collog. have no idea at all. □ **fogginess** n. [perhaps from fog long grass]

foghorn n. 1 horn warning ships in fog. 2 collog. loud penetrating voice.

fog-lamp n. powerful lamp for use in fog.

fogy /ˈfəʊɡɪ/ n. (also **fogey**) (pl. **-ies** or **-eys**) dull old-fashioned person (esp. old fogy). [origin unknown]

foible /ˈfɔɪb(ə)l/ n. minor weakness or idiosyncrasy. [French: related to FEEBLE]

foil[1] v. frustrate, baffle, defeat. [perhaps from French fouler trample]

foil[2] n. 1 metal rolled into a very thin sheet. 2 person or thing setting off another to advantage. [Latin folium leaf]

foil[3] n. light blunt fencing sword. [origin unknown]

foist v. (foll. by on) force (a thing or oneself) on to an unwilling person. [Dutch vuisten take in the hand]

fold[1] /fəʊld/ —v. 1 **a** bend or close (a flexible thing) over upon itself. **b** (foll. by back, over, down) bend part of (a thing) (fold down the flap). 2 become or be able to be folded. 3 (foll. by away, up) make compact by folding. 4 (often foll. by up) collog. collapse, cease to function. 5 enfold (esp. fold in the arms or to the breast). 6 (foll. by about, round) clasp (the arms). 7 (foll. by in) mix (an ingredient with others) gently. —n. 1 folding. 2 line made by folding. 3 folded part. 4 hollow among hills. 5 curvature of geological strata. □ **fold one's arms** place or entwine them across the chest. **fold one's hands** clasp them. [Old English]

fold[2] /fəʊld/ —n. 1 = SHEEPFOLD. 2 religious body or congregation. —v. enclose (sheep) in a fold. [Old English]

-fold suffix forming adjectives and adverbs from cardinal numbers, meaning: 1 in an amount multiplied by (repaid tenfold). 2 with so many parts (threefold blessing); (originally = 'folded in so many layers')

folder n. folding cover or holder for loose papers.

foliaceous /ˌfəʊlɪˈeɪʃəs/ adj. 1 of or like leaves. 2 laminated. [Latin: related to FOIL[2]]

foliage /ˈfəʊlɪdʒ/ n. leaves, leafage. [French feuillage from feuille leaf]

foliar /ˈfəʊlɪə(r)/ adj. of leaves. [as FOLIATE]

foliar feed n. fertilizer supplied to the leaves of plants.

foliate —adj. /ˈfəʊlɪət/ 1 leaflike. 2 having leaves. —v. /ˈfəʊlɪeɪt/ (**-ting**) split or beat into thin layers. □ **foliation** /ˌfəʊlɪˈeɪʃ(ə)n/ n. [Latin folium leaf]

folio /ˈfəʊlɪəʊ/ —n. (pl. **-s**) 1 leaf of paper etc., esp. numbered only on the front. 2 sheet of paper folded once making two leaves of a book. 3 book of such sheets. —adj. (of a book) made of folios, of the largest size. □ **in folio** made of folios. [Latin, ablative of folium leaf]

folk /fəʊk/ n. (pl. same or **-s**) 1 (treated as pl.) people in general or of a specified class (few folk about; townsfolk). 2 (in pl.) (usu. **folks**) one's parents or relatives. 3 (treated as sing.) a people or nation. 4 (in full **folk-music**) (treated as sing.) collog. traditional music or modern music in this style. 5 (attrib.) of popular origin (folk art). [Old English]

folk-dance n. dance of popular origin.

folklore n. traditional beliefs and stories of a people; the study of these.

folk-singer n. singer of folk-songs.

folk-song n. song of popular or traditional origin or style.

folksy /ˈfəʊksɪ/ adj. (**-ier, -iest**) 1 of or like folk art, culture, etc. 2 friendly, unpretentious. □ **folksiness** n.

folk-tale n. traditional story.

folkweave n. rough loosely woven fabric.

follicle /ˈfɒlɪk(ə)l/ n. small sac or vesicle in the body, esp. one containing a hair-root. □ **follicular** /fəˈlɪkjʊlə(r)/ adj. [Latin diminutive of follis bellows]

follow /ˈfɒləʊ/ v. 1 (often foll. by after) go or come after (a person or thing ahead). 2 go along (a road etc.). 3 come after in order or time (dessert followed; proceed as follows). 4 take as a guide or leader. 5 conform to. 6 practise (a trade or profession). 7 undertake (a course of study

etc.). **8** understand (a speaker, argument, etc.). **9** take an interest in (current affairs etc.). **10** (foll. by *with*) provide with a sequel or successor. **11** happen after something else; ensue. **12 a** be necessarily true as a consequence. **b** (foll. by *from*) result. □ **follow on 1** continue. **2** (of a cricket team) have to continue. **follow out** (instructions etc.). follow **suit 1** play a card of the suit led. **2** conform to another's actions. **follow through 1** continue to a conclusion. **2** continue the movement of a stroke after hitting the ball. **follow up** (foll. by *with*) **1** develop, supplement. **2** investigate further. [Old English]

follower *n.* **1** supporter or devotee. **2** person who follows.

following —*prep.* after in time; as a sequel to. —*n.* supporters or devotees. —*adj.* that follows or comes after. □ **the following 1** what follows. **2** now to be given or named (*answer the following*).

follow-on *n. Cricket* instance of following on.

follow-through *n.* action of following through.

follow-up *n.* subsequent or continued action.

folly *n.* (*pl.* -**ies**) **1** foolishness. **2** foolish act, behaviour, idea, etc. **3** fanciful ornamental building created for display. [French *folie* from *fol* mad, fool]

foment /fə'ment/ *v.* instigate or stir up (trouble, discontent, etc.). □ **fomentation** /ˌfəʊmen'teɪʃ(ə)n/ *n.* [Latin *foveo* heat, cherish]

fond *adj.* **1** (foll. by *of*) liking. **2 a** affectionate. **b** doting. **3** (of beliefs etc.) foolishly optimistic or credulous. □ **fondly** *adv.* **fondness** *n.* [obsolete *fon* fool, be foolish]

fondant /'fɒnd(ə)nt/ *n.* soft sugary sweet. [French = melting: related to FUSE¹]

fondle /'fɒnd(ə)l/ *v.* (-**ling**) caress. [related to FOND]

fondue /'fɒndjuː/ *n.* dish of melted cheese. [French, = melted: related to FUSE¹]

font¹ *n.* receptacle in a church for baptismal water. [Latin *fons font-* fountain]

font² var. of FOUNT¹.

fontanelle /ˌfɒntə'nel/ *n.* (*US* fontanel) membranous space in an infant's skull at the angles of the parietal bones. [Latin *fontanella* little FOUNTAIN]

food *n.* **1 a** substance taken in to maintain life and growth. **b** solid food (*food and drink*). **2** mental stimulus (*food for thought*). [Old English]

food additive *n.* substance added to food to colour or flavour it etc.

food-chain *n.* series of organisms each dependent on the next for food.

foodie /'fuːdɪ/ *n. colloq.* gourmet. [from FOOD]

food poisoning *n.* illness due to bacteria etc. in food.

food processor *n.* machine for chopping and mixing food.

foodstuff *n.* substance used as food.

food value *n.* nourishing power of a food.

fool¹ —*n.* **1** rash, unwise, or stupid person. **2** *hist.* jester, clown. **3** dupe. —*v.* **1** deceive. **2** (foll. by *into* or *out of*) trick; cheat. **3** joke or tease. **4** (foll. by *about, around*) play the fool or trifle. □ **act** (or **play**) **the fool** behave in a silly way. **be no** (or **nobody's**) **fool** be shrewd or prudent. **make a fool of** make (a person or oneself) look foolish; trick, deceive. [Latin *follis* bellows]

fool² *n.* dessert of fruit purée with cream or custard. [perhaps from FOOL¹]

foolery *n.* foolish behaviour.

foolhardy *adj.* (-**ier**, -**iest**) rashly or foolishly bold; rec**k**less. □ **foolhardily** *adv.* **foolhardiness** *n.*

foolish *adj.* lacking good sense or judgement; unwise. □ **foolishly** *adv.* **foolishness** *n.*

foolproof *adj.* (of a procedure, mechanism, etc.) incapable of misuse or mistake.

foolscap /'fuːlskæp/ *n.* large size of paper, about 330 x 200 (or 400) mm. [from a watermark of a *fool's cap*]

fool's paradise *n.* illusory happiness.

foot —*n.* (*pl.* **feet**) **1 a** part of the leg below the ankle. **b** part of a sock etc. covering this. **2 a** lowest part of a page, stairs, etc. **b** end of a bed where the feet rest. **c** part of a chair, appliance, etc. on which it rests. **3** step, pace, or tread (*fleet of foot*). **4** (*pl.* **feet** or **foot**) linear measure of 12 inches (30.48 cm). **5** metrical unit of verse forming part of a line. **6** *hist.* infantry. —*v.* **1** pay (a bill). **2** (usu. as **foot it**) go or traverse on foot. □ **feet of clay** fundamental weakness in a respected person. **have one's** (or **both**) **feet on the ground** be practical. **have one foot in the grave** be near death or very old. **my foot!** *int.* expressing strong contradiction. **on foot** walking. **put one's feet up** *colloq.* take a rest. **put one's foot down** *colloq.* **1** insist firmly. **2** accelerate a vehicle. **put one's foot in it** *colloq.* make a tactless blunder. **under one's feet** in the way. **under foot** on the ground. □ **footless** *adj.* [Old English]

footage *n.* **1** a length of TV or cinema film etc. **2** length in feet.

foot-and-mouth disease *n.* contagious viral disease of cattle etc.

football *n.* **1** large inflated ball of leather or plastic. **2** outdoor team game played with this. □ **footballer** *n.*

football pool *n.* (also **football pools** *pl.*) large-scale organized gambling on the results of football matches.

footbrake *n.* foot-operated brake on a vehicle.

footbridge *n.* bridge for pedestrians.

footfall *n.* sound of a footstep.

foot-fault *n.* (in tennis) placing of the foot over the baseline while serving.

foothill *n.* any of the low hills at the base of a mountain or range.

foothold *n.* **1** secure place for a foot when climbing etc. **2** secure initial position.

footing *n.* **1** foothold; secure position (*lost his footing*). **2** operational basis. **3** relative position or status (*on an equal footing*). **4** (often in *pl.*) foundations of a wall.

footle /'fuːt(ə)l/ *v.* (**-ling**) (usu. foll. by *about*) *colloq.* potter or fiddle about. [origin uncertain]

footlights *n.pl.* row of floor-level lights at the front of a stage.

footling /'fuːtlɪŋ/ *adj. colloq.* trivial, silly.

footloose *adj.* free to act as one pleases.

footman *n.* liveried servant.

footmark *n.* footprint.

footnote *n.* note printed at the foot of a page.

footpad *n. hist.* unmounted highwayman.

footpath *n.* path for pedestrians; pavement.

footplate *n.* platform for the crew in a locomotive.

footprint *n.* impression left by a foot or shoe.

footrest *n.* stool, rail, etc. for the feet.

Footsie /'fʊtsɪ/ *n.* = FT-SE. [respelling of FT-SE]

footsie /'fʊtsɪ/ *n. colloq.* amorous play with the feet.

footsore *adj.* with sore feet, esp. from walking.

footstep *n.* **1** step taken in walking. **2** sound of this. □ **follow in a person's footsteps** do as another did before.

footstool *n.* stool for resting the feet on when sitting.

footway *n.* path for pedestrians.

footwear *n.* shoes, socks, etc.

footwork *n.* use or agility of the feet in sports, dancing, etc.

fop *n.* dandy. □ **foppery** *n.* **foppish** *adj.* [perhaps from obsolete *fop* fool]

for /fə(r), fɔː(r)/ —*prep.* **1** in the interest or to the benefit of; intended to go to (*did it all for my country; these flowers are for you*). **2** in defence, support, or favour of (*a dance for beginners; not for me to say*). **4** in respect of or with reference to; regarding (*usual for ties to be worn; ready for bed*). **5** representing or in place of (*MP for Lincoln; here for my uncle*). **6** in exchange with, at the price of, corresponding to (*swapped it for a cake; give me £5 for it; bought it for £5; word for word*). **7** as a consequence of (*fined for speeding; decorated for bravery; here's £5 for your trouble*). **8 a** with a view to; in the hope or quest of; in order to get (*go for a walk; send for a doctor; did it for the money*). **b** on account of (*could not speak for laughing*). **9** to reach; towards (*left for Rome*). **10** so as to start promptly at (*meet at seven for eight*). **11** through or over (a distance or period); during (*walked for miles*). **12** as being (*for the last time; I for one refuse*). **13** in spite of, notwithstanding (*for all your fine words*). **14** considering or making due allowance in respect of (*good for a beginner*). —*conj.* because, since, seeing that. □ **be for it** *colloq.* be about to be punished etc. **for all** (that) in spite of, although. **for ever** for all time (cf. FOR-EVER). [Old English reduced form of FORE]

for- *prefix* forming verbs etc. meaning: **1** away, off (*forget, forgive*). **2** prohibition (*forbid*). **3** abstention or neglect (*forgo; forsake*). [Old English]

forage /'fɒrɪdʒ/ —*n.* **1** food for horses and cattle. **2** searching for food. —*v.* **1** search for food; rummage. **2** collect food from. **3** get by foraging. [Germanic: related to FODDER]

forage cap *n.* infantry undress cap.

forasmuch as /fərəz'mʌtʃ/ *conj. archaic* because, since. [from *for as much*]

foray /'fɒreɪ/ —*n.* sudden attack; raid. —*v.* make a foray. [French: related to FODDER]

forbade (also **forbad**) *past of* FORBID.

forbear[1] /fɔː'beə(r)/ *v.* (*past* **forbore**; *past part.* **forborne**) *formal* abstain or desist (from) (*could not forbear (from) speaking out; forbore to mention it*). [Old English: related to BEAR[1]]

forbear[2] *var. of* FOREBEAR.

forbearance *n.* patient self-control; tolerance.

forbid /fə'bɪd/ *v.* (**forbidding**; *past* **forbade** or **forbad**; *past part.* **forbidden**) **1** (foll. by *to* + infin.) order not (*I forbid you to go*). **2** refuse to allow (a thing, or a person to have a thing). **3** refuse a person entry to. □ **God forbid!** may it not happen! [Old English: related to BID]

forbidden degrees n.pl. (also **prohibited degrees**) family relationship too close for marriage to be permitted.

forbidden fruit n. something desired esp. because not allowed.

forbidding adj. stern, threatening. □ **forbiddingly** adv.

forbore past of FORBEAR¹.

forborne past part. of FORBEAR¹.

force¹ —n. 1 power, strength, impetus; intense effort. 2 coercion, compulsion. 3 a military strength. b organized body of soldiers, police, etc. 4 a moral, intellectual, or legal power, influence, or validity. b person etc. with such power (force for good). 5 effect; precise significance. 6 a influence tending to cause a change in the motion of a body. b intensity of this. —v. (-cing) 1 compel or coerce (a person) by force. 2 make a forcible entry into; break open by force. 3 drive or propel violently or against resistance. 4 make (a way) by force. 5 (foll. by on, upon) impose or press on (a person). 6 cause, produce, or attain by effort (forced a smile; forced an entry). 7 strain or increase to the utmost. 8 artificially hasten the growth of (a plant). 9 seek quick results from; accelerate (force the pace). □ **force a person's hand** make a person act prematurely or unwillingly. **force the issue** make an immediate decision necessary. **in force** 1 valid (laws now in force). 2 in great strength or numbers (attacked in force). [Latin fortis strong]

force² n. N.Engl. waterfall. [Old Norse]

forced labour n. compulsory labour, esp. in prison.

forced landing n. emergency landing of an aircraft.

forced march n. long and vigorous march, esp. by troops.

force-feed v. force (esp. a prisoner) to take food.

forceful adj. vigorous, powerful, impressive. □ **forcefully** adv. **forcefulness** n.

force majeure /ˌfɔːs mæˈʒɜː(r)/ n. 1 irresistible force. 2 unforeseeable circumstances excusing a person from the fulfilment of a contract. [French]

forcemeat n. minced seasoned meat for stuffing or garnish. [related to FARCE]

forceps /ˈfɔːseps/ n. (pl. same) surgical pincers. [Latin]

forcible adj. done by or involving force; forceful. □ **forcibly** adv. [French: related to FORCE¹]

ford —n. shallow place where a river or stream may be crossed by wading, in a vehicle, etc. —v. cross (water) at a ford. □ **fordable** adj. [Old English]

fore —adj. situated in front. —n. front part; bow of a ship. —int. (in golf) warning to a person in the path of a ball. □ **to the fore** in or into a conspicuous position. [Old English]

fore- prefix forming 1 verbs meaning: a beforehand (forewarn). b beforehand; in front (foreshorten). 2 nouns meaning: a situated in front of (forecourt). b front part of (forehead). c or near the bow of a ship (forecastle). d preceding (forerunner).

fore and aft —adv. at bow and stern; all over the ship. —adj. (fore-and-aft) (of a sail or rigging) lengthwise.

forearm¹ /ˈfɔːrɑːm/ n. the arm from the elbow to the wrist or fingertips.

forearm² /fɔːrˈɑːm/ v. arm beforehand; prepare.

forebear /ˈfɔːbeə(r)/ n. (also **forbear**) (usu. in pl.) ancestor. [from FORE, obsolete beer: related to BE]

forebode /fɔːˈbəʊd/ v. (-ding) 1 be an advance sign of; portend. 2 (often foll. by that) have a presentiment of (usu. evil).

foreboding n. expectation of trouble.

forecast —v. (past and past part. -cast or -casted) predict; estimate beforehand. —n. prediction, esp. of weather. □ **forecaster** n.

forecastle /ˈfəʊks(ə)l/ n. (also **fo'c's'le**) forward part of a ship, formerly the living quarters.

foreclose /fɔːˈkləʊz/ v. (-sing) 1 stop (a mortgage) from being redeemable. 2 repossess the mortgaged property of (a person) when a loan is not duly repaid. 3 exclude, prevent. □ **foreclosure** n. [Latin foris outside, CLOSE²]

forecourt n. 1 part of a filling-station with petrol pumps. 2 enclosed space in front of a building.

forefather n. (usu. in pl.) ancestor of a family or people.

forefinger n. finger next to the thumb.

forefoot n. front foot of an animal.

forefront n. 1 leading position. 2 foremost part.

forego var. of FORGO.

foregoing /fɔːˈgəʊɪŋ/ adj. preceding; previously mentioned.

foregone conclusion /ˈfɔːgɒn/ n. easily predictable result.

foreground n. 1 part of a view or picture nearest the observer. 2 most conspicuous position. [Dutch: related to FORE, GROUND¹]

forehand n. 1 (in tennis etc.) stroke played with the palm of the hand facing forward. 2 (attrib.) (also **forehanded**) of or made with a forehand.

forehead /ˈfɒrɪd, ˈfɔːhed/ n. the part of the face above the eyebrows.

foreign /ˈfɒrɪn/ adj. 1 of, from, in, or characteristic of, a country or language

other than one's own. **2** dealing with other countries (*foreign service*). **3** of another district, society, etc. **4** (often foll. by *to*) unfamiliar, alien. **5** coming from outside (*foreign body*). □ **foreignness** *n*. [Latin *foris* outside]

Foreign and Commonwealth Office *n*. British government department dealing with foreign affairs.

foreigner *n*. person born in or coming from another country.

foreign legion *n*. body of foreign volunteers in the (esp. French) army.

foreign minister *n*. (also **foreign secretary**) government minister in charge of foreign affairs.

Foreign Office *n*. *hist.* or *informal* = FOREIGN AND COMMONWEALTH OFFICE.

foreknow /fɔːˈnəʊ/ *v.* (*past* **-knew**, *past part.* **-known**) *literary* know beforehand. □ **foreknowledge** /fɔːˈnɒlɪdʒ/ *n.*

foreland *n.* cape, promontory.

foreleg *n.* front leg of an animal.

forelimb *n.* front limb of an animal.

forelock *n.* lock of hair just above the forehead. □ **touch one's forelock** defer to a person of higher social rank.

foreman *n.* **1** worker supervising others. **2** president and spokesman of a jury.

foremast *n.* mast nearest the bow of a ship.

foremost —*adj.* **1** most notable, best. **2** first, front. —*adv.* most importantly (*first and foremost*). [Old English]

forename *n.* first or Christian name.

forenoon *n.* morning.

forensic /fəˈrensɪk/ *adj.* **1** of or used in courts of law (*forensic science; forensic medicine*). **2** of or involving forensic science (*sent for forensic examination*). □ **forensically** *adv.* [Latin *forensis*: related to FORUM]

■ **Usage** Use of *forensic* in sense 2 is common but considered an illogical extension of sense 1 by some people.

foreordain /ˌfɔːrɔːˈdeɪn/ *v.* destine beforehand.

forepaw *n.* front paw of an animal.

foreplay *n.* stimulation preceding sexual intercourse.

forerunner *n.* **1** predecessor. **2** herald.

foresail /ˈfɔːseɪl/ *n.* principal sail on a foremast.

foresee /fɔːˈsiː/ *v.* (*past* **-saw**; *past part.* **-seen**) see or be aware of beforehand. □ **foreseeable** *adj.*

foreshadow /fɔːˈʃædəʊ/ *v.* be a warning or indication of (a future event).

foreshore *n.* shore between high- and low-water marks.

foreshorten /fɔːˈʃɔːt(ə)n/ *v.* show or portray (an object) with the apparent shortening due to visual perspective.

foresight *n.* **1** regard or provision for the future. **2** foreseeing. **3** front sight of a gun.

foreskin *n.* fold of skin covering the end of the penis.

forest —*n.* **1** (often *attrib.*) large area of trees and undergrowth. **2** trees in this. **3** large number or dense mass. —*v.* **1** plant with trees. **2** convert into a forest. [Latin *forestis*: related to FOREIGN]

forestall /fɔːˈstɔːl/ *v.* **1** prevent by advance action. **2** deal with beforehand. [from FORE-, STALL¹]

forester *n.* **1** person managing a forest or skilled in forestry. **2** dweller in a forest.

forestry *n.* science or management of forests.

foretaste *n.* small preliminary experience of something.

foretell /fɔːˈtel/ *v.* (*past* and *past part.* **-told**) **1** predict, prophesy. **2** indicate the approach of.

forethought *n.* **1** care or provision for the future. **2** deliberate intention.

forever /fəˈrevə(r)/ *adv.* continually, persistently (*is forever complaining*) (cf. *for ever*).

forewarn /fɔːˈwɔːn/ *v.* warn beforehand.

forewoman *n.* **1** female worker with supervisory responsibilities. **2** president and spokeswoman of a jury.

foreword *n.* introductory remarks at the beginning of a book, often not by the author.

forfeit /ˈfɔːfɪt/ —*n.* **1** penalty. **2** thing surrendered as a penalty. —*adj.* lost or surrendered as a penalty. —*v.* (**-t-**) lose the right to, surrender as a penalty. □ **forfeiture** *n.* [French *forfaire* transgress, from Latin *foris* outside, *facio* do]

forgather /fɔːˈɡæðə(r)/ *v.* assemble; associate. [Dutch]

forgave *past* of FORGIVE.

forge¹ —*v.* (**-ging**) **1** make or write in fraudulent imitation. **2** shape (metal) by heating and hammering. —*n.* **1** furnace or workshop etc. for melting or refining metal. **2** blacksmith's workshop; smithy. □ **forger** *n.* [Latin *fabrica*: related to FABRIC]

forge² *v.* (**-ging**) move forward gradually or steadily. □ **forge ahead 1** take the lead. **2** progress rapidly. [perhaps an alteration of FORCE¹]

forgery /ˈfɔːdʒərɪ/ *n.* (*pl.* **-ies**) **1** act of forging. **2** forged document etc.

forget /fəˈɡet/ *v.* (**forgetting**; *past* **forgot**; *past part.* **forgotten** or *US* **forgot**)

forget **1** (often foll. by *about*) lose remembrance of, not remember. **2** neglect or overlook. **3** cease to think of. □ **forget oneself 1** act without dignity. **2** act selfishly. □ **forgettable** *adj.* [Old English]

forgetful *adj.* **1** apt to forget, absent-minded. **2** (often foll. by *of*) neglectful. □ **forgetfully** *adv.* **forgetfulness** *n.*

forget-me-not *n.* plant with small blue flowers.

forgive /fə'gɪv/ *v.* (**-ving**; *past* **forgave**; *past part.* **forgiven**) **1** cease to feel angry or resentful towards; pardon. **2** remit (a debt). □ **forgivable** *adj.* [Old English]

forgiveness *n.* forgiving or being forgiven.

forgiving *adj.* inclined to forgive.

forgo /fɔː'gəʊ/ *v.* (also **forego**) (**-goes**; *past* **-went**; *past part.* **-gone**) go without; relinquish. [Old English]

forgot *past part. of* FORGET.

forgotten *past part. of* FORGET.

fork —*n.* **1** pronged item of cutlery. **2** similar large tool used for digging, lifting, etc. **3** forked support for a bicycle wheel. **4 a** divergence of a branch, road, etc. into two parts. **b** place of this. **c** either part. —*v.* **1** form a fork or branch by separating into two parts. **2** take one road at a fork. **3** dig, lift, etc., with a fork. □ **fork out** *slang* pay, esp. reluctantly. [Latin *furca* pitchfork]

fork-lift truck *n.* vehicle with a fork for lifting and carrying loads.

forlorn /fə'lɔːn/ *adj.* **1** sad and abandoned. **2** in a pitiful state. □ **forlornly** *adv.* [*forlorn* = *past part. of* obsolete *leese* LOSE]

forlorn hope *n.* faint remaining hope or chance. [Dutch *verloren hoop* lost troop]

form —*n.* **1** shape; arrangement of parts; visible aspect. **2** person or animal as visible or tangible. **3** mode of existence or manifestation. **4** kind or variety (*a form of art*). **5** printed document with blank spaces for information to be inserted. **6** class in a school. **7** customary method. **8** set order of words. **9** etiquette or specified adherence to it (*good or bad form*). **10** (prec. by *the*) correct procedure. **11 a** (of an athlete, horse, etc.) condition of health and training. **b** racing history of a horse etc. **12** state or disposition (*in great form*). **13** any of the spellings, inflections, etc. of a word. **14** arrangement and style in a literary or musical composition. **15** long low bench. **16** hare's lair. —*v.* **1** make or be made (*formed a straight line; pudding formed*). **2** make up or constitute. **3** develop or establish as a concept, institution, or practice (*form an idea; form a habit*). **4** (foll. by *into*) mould or organize to become (*formed ourselves into a circle*). **5** (often foll. by *up*) (of troops etc.) bring or move into formation. **6** train or instruct. □ **off form** not playing or performing well. **on form** playing or performing well. **out of form** not fit for racing etc. [Latin *forma*]

-form *comb. form* (usu. as **-iform**) forming adjectives meaning: **1** having the form of (*cruciform*). **2** having so many forms (*multiform*).

formal /ˈfɔːm(ə)l/ *adj.* **1** in accordance with rules, convention, or ceremony (*formal dress; formal occasion*). **2** precise or symmetrical (*formal garden*). **3** prim or stiff. **4** perfunctory, in form only. **5** drawn up etc. correctly; explicit (*formal agreement*). **6** of or concerned with (outward) form, not content or matter. □ **formally** *adv.* [Latin: related to FORM]

formaldehyde /fɔː'mald̩ɪˌhaɪd/ *n.* colourless pungent gas used as a disinfectant and preservative. [from FORMIC ACID, ALDEHYDE]

formalin /ˈfɔːməlɪn/ *n.* solution of formaldehyde in water.

formalism *n.* strict adherence to exterior form without regard to content, esp. in art. □ **formalist** *n.*

formality /fɔː'malɪtɪ/ *n.* (*pl.* **-ies**) **1 a** formal, esp. meaningless, act, regulation, or custom. **b** thing done simply to comply with a rule. **2** rigid observance of rules or convention.

formalize *v.* (also **-ise**) (**-zing** or **-sing**) **1** give definite (esp. legal) form to. **2** make formal. □ **formalization** /-'zeɪʃ(ə)n/ *n.*

format /ˈfɔːmæt/ —*n.* **1** shape and size (of a book, etc.). **2** style or manner of procedure. **3** *Computing* arrangement of data etc. —*v.* (**-tt-**) **1** arrange or put into a format. **2** *Computing* prepare (a storage medium) to receive data. [Latin *formatus* shaped: related to FORM]

formation /fɔː'meɪʃ(ə)n/ *n.* **1** forming. **2** thing formed. **3** particular arrangement (e.g. of troops). **4** rocks or strata with a common characteristic. [Latin: related to FORM]

formative /ˈfɔːmətɪv/ *adj.* serving to form or fashion; of formation (*formative years*).

forme *n.* *Printing* body of type secured in a chase ready for printing. [var. of FORM]

former *attrib. adj.* **1** of the past, earlier, previous (*in former times*). **2** (**the former**) (often *absol.*) the first or first-mentioned of two. [related to FOREMOST]

-former *comb. form* pupil in a specified form (*fourth-former*).

formerly *adv.* in former times.

Formica /fɔːˈmaɪkə/ *n. propr.* hard durable plastic laminate used for surfaces. [origin uncertain]

formic acid /ˈfɔːmɪk/ *n.* colourless irritant volatile acid contained in fluid emitted by ants; methanoic acid. [Latin *formica* ant]

formidable /ˈfɔːmɪdəb(ə)l, fɔːˈmɪd-/ *adj.* 1 inspiring dread, awe, or respect. 2 hard to overcome or deal with. □ **formidably** *adv.* [Latin *formido* fear]

■ **Usage** The second pronunciation given, with the stress on the second syllable, is common but considered incorrect by some people.

formless *adj.* without definite or regular form. □ **formlessness** *n.*

formula /ˈfɔːmjʊlə/ *n.* (*pl.* **-s** or (esp. in senses 1, 2) **-lae** /-liː/) 1 chemical symbols showing the constituents of a substance. 2 mathematical rule expressed in symbols. 3 **a** fixed form of esp. ceremonial or polite words. **b** words used to formulate a treaty etc. 4 **a** list of ingredients. **b** *US* infant's food. 5 classification of a racing car, esp. by engine capacity. □ **formulaic** /-ˈleɪk/ *adj.* [Latin, diminutive of *forma* FORM]

formulary /ˈfɔːmjʊlərɪ/ *n.* (*pl.* **-ies**) 1 collection of esp. religious formulas or set forms. 2 *Pharm.* compendium of drug formulae. [French or medieval Latin: related to FORMULA]

formulate /ˈfɔːmjʊleɪt/ *v.* (**-ting**) 1 express in a formula. 2 express clearly and precisely. □ **formulation** /-ˈleɪʃ(ə)n/ *n.*

fornicate /ˈfɔːnɪkeɪt/ *v.* (**-ting**) *archaic* or *joc.* (of people not married to each other) have sexual intercourse. □ **fornication** /-ˈkeɪʃ(ə)n/ *n.* **fornicator** *n.* [Latin *fornix* brothel]

forsake /fəˈseɪk/ *v.* (**-king**; *past* **forsook** /-sʊk/; *past part.* **forsaken**) *literary* 1 give up; renounce. 2 desert, abandon. [Old English]

forsooth /fəˈsuːθ/ *adv.* *archaic* or *joc.* truly; no doubt. [Old English: related to FOR, SOOTH]

forswear /fɔːˈsweə(r)/ *v.* (*past* **forswore**; *past part.* **forsworn**) 1 abjure; renounce. 2 (as **forsworn** *adj.*) perjured. □ **forswear oneself** perjure oneself. [Old English]

forsythia /fɔːˈsaɪθɪə/ *n.* shrub with bright yellow flowers in early spring. [*Forsyth*, name of a botanist]

fort *n.* fortified military building or position. [Latin *fortis* strong]

forte[1] /ˈfɔːteɪ/ *n.* person's strong point or speciality. [feminine of French *fort*]

forte[2] /ˈfɔːteɪ/ *Mus.* —*adj.* loud. —*adv.* loudly. —*n.* loud playing or passage. [Italian: related to FORT]

forth *adv.* *archaic* except in set phrases 1 forward; into view (*bring forth; come forth*). 2 onwards in time (*from this time forth*). 3 forwards (*back and forth*). 4 out from a starting-point (*set forth*). □ **and so forth** see so'. [Old English]

forthcoming /fɔːθˈkʌmɪŋ, ˈfɔːθ-/ *adj.* 1 coming or available soon. 2 produced when wanted. 3 (of a person) informative, responsive.

forthright *adj.* 1 outspoken; straightforward. 2 decisive. [Old English]

forthwith /fɔːθˈwɪθ/ *adv.* at once; without delay. [from FORTH]

fortification /ˌfɔːtɪfɪˈkeɪʃ(ə)n/ *n.* 1 act of fortifying. 2 (usu. in *pl.*) defensive works, walls, etc.

fortify /ˈfɔːtɪfaɪ/ *v.* (**-ies, -ied**) 1 provide with fortifications. 2 strengthen physically, mentally, or morally. 3 strengthen (wine) with alcohol. 4 increase the nutritive value of (food, esp. with vitamins). [Latin *fortis* strong]

fortissimo /fɔːˈtɪsɪməʊ/ *Mus.* —*adj.* very loud. —*adv.* very loudly. —*n.* (*pl.* **-s** or **-mi** /-miː/) very loud playing or passage. [Italian, superlative of FORTE[2]]

fortitude /ˈfɔːtɪtjuːd/ *n.* courage in pain or adversity. [Latin *fortis* strong]

fortnight /ˈfɔːtnaɪt/ *n.* two weeks. [Old English, = *fourteen nights*]

fortnightly —*adj.* done, produced, or occurring once a fortnight. —*adv.* every fortnight. —*n.* (*pl.* **-ies**) fortnightly magazine etc.

Fortran /ˈfɔːtræn/ *n.* (also FORTRAN) computer language used esp. for scientific calculations. [from *formula translation*]

fortress /ˈfɔːtrɪs/ *n.* fortified building or town. [Latin *fortis*]

fortuitous /fɔːˈtjuːɪtəs/ *adj.* happening by esp. lucky chance; accidental. □ **fortuitously** *adv.* **fortuitousness** *n.* **fortuity** *n.* (*pl.* **-ies**). [Latin *forte* by chance]

fortunate /ˈfɔːtʃənət/ *adj.* 1 lucky. 2 auspicious. □ **fortunately** *adv.* [Latin *fortunatus*: related to FORTUNE]

fortune /ˈfɔːtʃ(ə)n, -tʃuːn/ *n.* 1 **a** chance or luck in human affairs. **b** person's destiny. 2 (in *sing.* or *pl.*) luck that befalls a person or enterprise. 3 good luck. 4 prosperity. 5 *colloq.* great wealth. □ **make a (or one's) fortune** become very rich. [Latin *fortuna*]

fortune-teller *n.* person who claims to foretell one's destiny. □ **fortunetelling** *n.*

forty /ˈfɔːtɪ/ *adj. & n.* (*pl.* **-ies**) 1 four times ten. 2 symbol for this (40, xl, XL). 3 (in *pl.*) numbers from 40 to 49, esp. the

years of a century or of a person's life. □ **fortieth** *adj.* & *n.* [Old English: related to FOUR]

forty winks *n. colloq.* short sleep.

forum /ˈfɔːrəm/ *n.* **1** place of or meeting for public discussion. **2** court or tribunal. **3** *hist.* public square in an ancient Roman city used for judicial and other business.

forward /ˈfɔːwəd/ —*adj.* **1** onward; towards the front. **2** lying in the direction in which one is moving. **3** precocious; bold; presumptuous. **4** relating to the future *(forward contract)*. **5 a** approaching maturity or completion. **b** (of a plant etc.) early. —*n.* attacking player near the front in football, hockey, etc. —*adv.* **1** to the front; into prominence *(come forward)* **2** in advance *(sent them forward)*. **3** onward so as to make progress *(from this time forward)*. **4** towards the future *(from this time forward)*. **5** (also **forwards**) **a** towards the front in the direction one is facing. **b** in the normal direction of motion. **c** with continuous forward motion *(rushing forward)*. —*v.* **1 a** send (a letter etc.) on to a further destination. **b** dispatch (goods etc.). **2** help to advance; promote. [Old English]

forwent *past of* FORGO.

fosse /fɒs/ *n.* long ditch or trench, esp. in a fortification. [Latin *fossa*]

fossil /ˈfɒs(ə)l/ —*n.* **1 a** remains or impression of a (usu. prehistoric) plant or animal hardened in rock. **2** *colloq.* antiquated or unchanging person or thing. —*attrib. adj.* of or like a fossil, antiquated. □ **fossilize** *v.* (also **-ise**) (**-zing** or **-sing**) **fossilization** /-ˈzeɪʃ(ə)n/ *n.* [Latin *fodio foss-* dig]

fossil fuel *n.* natural fuel extracted from the ground.

foster —*v.* **1 a** promote the growth or development of. **b** encourage or harbour (a feeling). **2 a** bring up (another's child). **b** (of a local authority etc.) assign (a child) to be fostered. **3** (of circumstances) be favourable to. —*attrib. adj.* **1** having a family connection by fostering *(foster-brother, foster-parent)*. **2** concerned with fostering a child *(foster care, foster home)*. [Old English: related to FOOD]

fought *past and past part. of* FIGHT.

foul —*adj.* **1** offensive; loathsome, stinking. **2** soiled, filthy. **3** *colloq.* disgusting, awful. **4 a** noxious *(foul air)*. **b** clogged, choked. **5** obscenely abusive *(foul language)*. **6** unfair; against the rules *(by foul means or foul)*. **7** (of the weather) rough, stormy. **8** (of a rope etc.) entangled. —*n.* **1** *Sport* foul stroke or play. **2**

collision, entanglement, or unfairly. —*v.* **1** make or become foul. **2** (of an animal) foul with excrement. **3** *Sport* commit a foul against (a player). **4** (often foll. by *up*) **a** (cause to) become entangled or blocked. **b** bungle. **5** collide with. □ **foully** *adv.* **foulness** *n.* [Old English]

foul play *n.* **1** unfair play in games. **2** treacherous or violent act, esp. murder.

foul-up *n.* muddle, bungle.

found¹ *past and past part. of* FIND.

found² *v.* **1** establish (an institution etc.); initiate, originate. **2** be the original builder of (a town etc.). **3** lay the base of (a building). **4** (foll. by *on, upon*) construct or base (a story, theory, rule, etc.) on. □ **founder** *n.* [Latin *fundus* bottom]

found³ *v.* **1 a** melt and mould (metal). **b** fuse (materials for glass). **2** make by founding. □ **founder** *n.* [Latin *fundo fus-* pour]

foundation /faʊnˈdeɪʃ(ə)n/ *n.* **1 a** solid ground or base beneath a building. **b** (usu. in *pl.*) lowest part of a building, usu. below ground level. **2** material base. **3** basis, underlying principle. **4 a** establishing (esp. an endowed institution). **b** college, hospital, etc. so founded. **c** its revenues. **5** (in full **foundation garment**) woman's supporting undergarment, e.g. a corset. [Latin: related to FOUND²]

foundation-stone *n.* **1** stone laid ceremonially at the founding of a building. **2** basis.

founder *v.* **1** (of a ship) fill with water and sink. **2** (of a plan etc.) fail. **3** (of a horse or its rider) stumble, fall lame, stick in mud etc. [Latin: related to FOUND²]

founding father *n.* American statesman at the time of the Revolution.

foundling /ˈfaʊndlɪŋ/ *n.* abandoned infant of unknown parentage. [related to FIND]

foundry /ˈfaʊndrɪ/ *n.* (*pl.* **-ies**) workshop for or business of casting metal.

fount¹ *n.* *poet.* spring or fountain; source. [back-formation from FOUNTAIN]

fount² /fɒnt/ *n.* (also **font**) set of printing-type of same face and size. [French: related to FOUND³]

fountain /ˈfaʊntɪn/ *n.* **1 a** spouting jet or jets of water as an ornament or for drinking. **b** structure for this. **2** spring. **3** (often foll. by *of*) source. [Latin *fontana* from *fons font-* spring]

fountain-head *n.* source.

fountain-pen *n.* pen with a reservoir or cartridge for ink.

four /fɔː(r)/ *adj.* & *n.* **1** one more than three. **2** symbol for this (4, iv, IV). **3** size

fourfold *adj.* & *adv.* **1** four times as much or as many. **2** of four parts.

four-in-hand *n.* four-horse carriage with one driver.

four-letter word *n.* short obscene word.

four-poster *n.* bed with four posts supporting a canopy.

foursome *n.* **1** group of four people. **2** golf match between two pairs.

four-square *—adj.* **1** solidly based. **2** steady, resolute. *—adv.* steadily, resolutely.

four-stroke */fɔːˈtin/ adj.* (of an internal-combustion engine) having a cycle of four strokes of the piston with the cylinder firing once.

fourteen */fɔːˈtin/ adj.* & *n.* **1** one more than thirteen. **2** symbol for this (14, xiv, XIV). **3** size etc. denoted by fourteen. **fourteenth** *adj.* & *n.* [Old English: related to FOUR, -TEEN]

fourth *adj.* & *n.* **1** next after third. **2** any of four equal parts of a thing. □ **fourthly** *adv.* [Old English: related to FOUR]

fourth estate *n.* the press.

four-wheel drive *n.* drive acting on all four wheels of a vehicle.

fowl *—n.* (*pl.* same or *-s*) **1** chicken kept for eggs and meat. **2** poultry as food. **3** *archaic* (except in *comb.*) bird (*guineafowl*; *wildfowl*). *—v.* catch or hunt wildfowl. [Old English]

fox *—n.* **1 a** wild canine animal with a bushy tail and red or grey fur. **b** its fur. **2** cunning person. *—v.* **1** deceive, baffle, trick. **2** (usu. as **foxed** *adj.*) discolour (leaves of a book etc.) with brownish marks. □ **foxlike** *adj.* [Old English]

foxglove *n.* tall plant with purple or white flowers like glove-fingers.

foxhole *n.* hole in the ground used as a shelter etc. in battle.

foxhound *n.* a kind of hound bred and trained to hunt foxes.

fox-hunting *n.* hunting foxes with hounds.

fox-terrier *n.* a kind of short-haired terrier.

foxtrot *—n.* **1** ballroom dance with slow and quick steps. **2** music for this. *—v.* (*-tt-*) perform this.

foxy *adj.* (*-ier*, *-iest*) **1** foxlike. **2** sly or cunning. **3** reddish-brown. □ **foxily** *adv.* **foxiness** *n.*

foyer */ˈfɔɪeɪ/ n.* entrance-hall in a hotel, theatre, etc. [French, = hearth, home, from Latin focus]

FPA *abbr.* Family Planning Association.

Fr *symb.* francium.

Fr. *abbr.* **1** Father. **2** French.

fr. *abbr.* franc(s).

fracas */ˈfrækɑː/ n.* (*pl.* same /-kɑːz/) noisy disturbance or quarrel. [French from Italian]

fraction */ˈfrækʃ(ə)n/ n.* **1** part of a whole number (e.g. $\frac{1}{2}$, 0.5). **2** small part, piece, or amount. **3** portion of a mixture obtained by distillation etc. □ **fractional** *adj.* **fractionally** *adv.* [Latin *frango fract-* break]

fractious */ˈfrækʃəs/ adj.* irritable, peevish. [from FRACTION in obsolete sense 'brawling']

fracture */ˈfræktʃə(r)/ —n.* breakage, esp. of a bone or cartilage. *—v.* (*-ring*) cause a fracture in; suffer fracture. [Latin: related to FRACTION]

fragile */ˈfrædʒaɪl/ adj.* **1** easily broken; weak. **2** delicate; not strong. □ **fragility** */frəˈdʒɪlɪtɪ/ n.* [Latin: related to FRACTURE]

fragment *—n.* */ˈfrægmənt/* **1** part broken off. **2** extant remains or unfinished portion (of a book etc.). *—v.* */frægˈment/* break or separate into fragments. □ **fragmental** */-ˈment(ə)l/ adj.* **fragmentary** */ˈfrægməntərɪ/ adj.* **fragmentation** */-ˈteɪʃ(ə)n/ n.* [Latin: related to FRACTION]

fragrance */ˈfreɪgrəns/ n.* **1** sweetness of smell. **2** sweet scent. [Latin *fragro* smell sweet]

fragrant *adj.* sweet-smelling.

frail *adj.* **1** fragile, delicate. **2** morally weak. □ **frailly** *adv.* **frailness** *n.* [Latin: related to FRAGILE]

frailty *n.* (*pl.* *-ies*) **1** frail quality. **2** weakness, foible.

frame *—n.* **1** case or border enclosing a picture, window, door, etc. **2** basic rigid supporting structure of a building, vehicle, etc. **3** (in *pl.*) structure of spectacles holding the lenses. **4** human or animal body, esp. as large or small. **5 a** established order or system (*the frame of society*). **b** construction, build, structure. **6** temporary state (esp. in **frame of mind**). **7** single complete image on a cinema film or transmitted in a series of lines by television. **8 a** triangular structure for positioning balls in snooker etc. **b** round of play in snooker etc. **9** boxlike structure of glass etc. for protecting plants. **10** *US slang* = FRAME-UP. *—v.* (*-ming*) **1 a** set in a frame. **b** serve as a frame for. **2** construct, put together, devise. **3** (foll. by *to, into*) adapt or fit. **4** *slang* concoct a false charge or evidence against; devise a plot against. **5** articulate (words). [Old English, = be helpful]

frame *n.* 1 set of standards or principles governing behaviour, thought, etc. 2 system of geometrical axes for defining position.

frame of reference *n.* 1 set of standards, religious brotherhood. 2 group with common interests, or of the same professional class. 3 *US* male students' society. 4 brotherliness. [Latin: related to FRATERNAL]

framework *n.* 1 essential supporting structure. 2 basic system.

franc *n.* unit of currency of France, Belgium, Switzerland, etc. [French; related to FRANK]

frame-up *n. slang* conspiracy to convict an innocent person.

fraternize /ˈfrætəˌnaɪz/ *v.* (also **-ise**) (**-zing** *or* **-sing**) (often foll. by *with*) 1 associate; make friends. 2 enter into friendly relations with enemies etc. □ **fraternization** /-ˈzeɪʃ(ə)n/ *n.* [French fraterniser]

franchise /ˈfræntʃaɪz/ —*n.* 1 right to vote in State elections. 2 full membership of a corporation or State; citizenship. 3 authorization to sell a company's goods etc. in a particular area. 4 right or privilege granted to a person or corporation. —*v.* (**-sing**) grant a franchise to. [French *franc* FRANK]

fratricide /ˈfrætrɪˌsaɪd/ *n.* 1 killing of one's brother or sister. 2 person who does this. □ **fratricidal** /-ˈsaɪd(ə)l/ *adj.* [Latin *frater* brother]

Franciscan /frænˈsɪsk(ə)n/ —*adj.* 1 of St Francis or his order. —*n.* Franciscan friar or nun. [Latin *Franciscus* Francis]

Frau /frau/ *n.* (*pl.* **Frauen** /ˈfrauən/) (often as a title) married or widowed German-speaking woman. [German]

francium /ˈfrænkɪəm/ *n.* radioactive metallic element. [*France*, the discoverer's country]

fraud /frɔːd/ *n.* 1 criminal deception. 2 dishonest artifice or trick. 3 person or thing that is not what it claims to be. [Latin *fraus fraud-*]

Franco- *comb. form* French and (*Franco-German*). [Latin: related to FRANK]

fraudulent /ˈfrɔːdjʊlənt/ *adj.* of, involving, or guilty of fraud. □ **fraudulence** *n.* □ **fraudulently** *adv.* [Latin: related to FRAUD]

franglais /ˈfrɑ̃gleɪ/ *n.* corrupt version of French using many English words and idioms. [French *français* French, *anglais* English]

fraught /frɔːt/ *adj.* 1 (foll. by *with*) filled or charged with (danger etc.). 2 *colloq.* distressing; tense [Dutch *vracht* FREIGHT]

Frank —*n.* member of the Germanic people that conquered Gaul in the 6th c. □ **Frankish** *adj.* [Old English]

Fräulein /ˈfrɔɪlaɪn/ *n.* (often as a title or form of address) unmarried German-speaking woman. [German]

frank —*adj.* 1 candid, outspoken. 2 undisguised. 3 open. —*v.* mark (a letter) to record the payment of postage. —*n.* franking signature or mark. □ **frankly** *adv.* **frankness** *n.* [Latin *francus* free; related to FRANK]

fray *v.* 1 wear through or become worn. 2 (of woven material) unravel at the edge. 2 (of nerves, temper, etc.) become strained. [Latin *frico* rub]

fray *n.* 1 conflict, fight. 2 brawl. [related to AFFRAY]

Frankenstein /ˈfræŋkənˌstaɪn/ *n.* (in full **Frankenstein's monster**) thing that becomes terrifying to its maker. [*Frankenstein*, name of a character in and title of a novel by Mary Shelley]

frazzle /ˈfræz(ə)l/ *colloq.* —*n.* worn, exhausted, or shrivelled state (*burnt to a frazzle*). —*v.* (**-ling**) (usu. as **frazzled** *adj.*) wear out; exhaust. [origin uncertain]

frankfurter /ˈfræŋkfɜːtə(r)/ *n.* seasoned smoked sausage. [German from *Frankfurt* in Germany]

freak —*n.* 1 (often *attrib.*) monstrosity, abnormal person or thing (*freak storm*). 2 *colloq.* **a** unconventional person. **b** fanatic of a specified kind (*health freak*). **c** drug addict. —*v.* (often foll. by *out*) *colloq.* 1 become or make very angry. 2 (cause to) undergo hallucinations etc., esp. as a result of drug abuse. 3 adopt an unconventional lifestyle. □ **freakish** *adj.* **freaky** *adj.* (**-ier**, **-iest**). [probably from dial.]

frankincense /ˈfræŋkɪnˌsens/ *n.* aromatic gum resin burnt as incense. [French: related to FRANK in obsolete sense 'high quality', INCENSE]

frantic /ˈfræntɪk/ *adj.* 1 wildly excited; frenzied. 2 hurried, anxious; desperate, violent. 3 *colloq.* extreme. □ **frantically** *adv.* [Latin: related to FRENETIC]

freckle /ˈfrek(ə)l/ —*n.* small light brown spot on the skin. —*v.* (**-ling**) (usu. as **freckled** *adj.*) spot or be spotted with freckles. □ **freckly** *adj.* [Old Norse]

frappé /ˈfræpeɪ/ —*adj.* (of wine etc.) iced, cooled. —*n.* iced, cooled. [French]

free —*adj.* (**freer** /ˈfriːə(r)/; **freest** /ˈfriːɪst/) 1 not a slave or under another's control; having personal rights and social and political liberty. 2 (of a State,

fraternal /frəˈtɜːn(ə)l/ *adj.* 1 of brothers, brotherly; comradely. 2 (of twins) developed from separate ova and not necessarily similar. □ **fraternally** *adv.* [Latin *frater* brother]

-free its citizens, etc.) autonomous; democratic. **3 a** unrestricted; not confined or fixed. **b** not imprisoned. **c** released from duties etc. **d** independent (*free agent*). **4** (foll. by *of*, *from*) **a** exempt from (*tax etc.*). **b** not containing or subject to (*free of preservatives; free from disease*). **5** (foll. by *to* + infin.) permitted; at liberty to. **6** costing nothing. **7 a** clear of duties etc. (*am free tomorrow*). **b** not in use (*bathroom is free*). **8** spontaneous, unforced (*free offer*). **9** available to all. **10** lavish (*free with their money*). **11** frank, unreserved. **12** (of literary style) informal, unmetrical. **13** (of translation) not literal. **14** familiar, impudent. **15** (of stories etc.) slightly indecent. **16** *Chem.* not combined (*free oxygen*). **17** (of power or energy) disengaged, available. —*adv.* **1** freely. **2** without cost or payment. —*v.* (**frees, freed**) **1** make free; liberate. **2** (foll. by *of*, *from*) relieve from. **3** disentangle, clear. □ **for free** *colloq.* free of charge, gratis. **free on board** or **rail** without charge for delivery to a ship or railway wagon. □ **freely** *adv.* [Old English]

-free *comb. form* free of or from (*worry-free; duty-free*).

free and easy *adj.* informal, relaxed.

freebie /ˈfriːbɪ/ *n. colloq.* thing given free of charge.

freeboard *n.* part of a ship's side between the water-line and deck.

freebooter *n.* pirate. [Dutch *vrijbuiter*: related to **free, booty**]

free-born *adj.* not born a slave.

Free Church *n.* Nonconformist Church.

freedman *n.* emancipated slave.

freedom /ˈfriːdəm/ *n.* **1** condition of being free or unrestricted. **2** personal or civic liberty. **3** liberty of action (*freedom to leave*). **4** (foll. by *of*) **a** exemption from. **5** (foll. by *of*) **a** honorary membership or citizenship (*freedom of the city*). **b** unrestricted use of (a house etc.). [Old English]

freedom fighter *n.* terrorist or rebel claiming to fight for freedom.

free enterprise *n.* freedom of private business from State control.

free fall *n.* movement under the force of gravity only.

free fight *n.* general fight in which all present join.

freefone *n.* (also **Freefone, -phone**) system whereby certain telephone calls, esp. on business, can be made without cost to the caller.

free-for-all *n.* free fight, unrestricted discussion, etc.

free-form *attrib. adj.* of irregular shape or structure.

freehand —*adj.* (of a drawing etc.) done without special instruments. —*adv.* in a freehand manner.

free-handed *adj.* generous.

freehold —*n.* **1** complete ownership of property for an unlimited period. **2** such land or property. —*adj.* owned thus. □ **freeholder** *n.*

free house *n.* public house not controlled by a brewery.

free kick *n.* kick granted in football as a minor penalty.

freelance —*n.* **1** (also **freelancer**) person, usu. self-employed, working for several employers on particular assignments. **2** (*attrib.*) (*freelance editor*). —*v.* (-**cing**) act as a freelance. —*adv.* as a freelance. [*free lance*, a medieval mercenary]

freeloader *n. slang* sponger. □ **freeload** /-ˈləʊd/ *v.*

free love *n.* sexual freedom.

freeman *n.* **1** person who has the freedom of a city etc. **2** person who is not a slave or serf.

free market *n.* market governed by unrestricted competition.

Freemason /ˈfriːˌmeɪs(ə)n/ *n.* member of an international fraternity for mutual help and fellowship with elaborate secret rituals. □ **Freemasonry** *n.*

free port *n.* **1** port without customs duties. **2** port open to all traders.

freepost *n.* system of business post where postage is paid by the addressee.

free radical *n. Chem.* atom or group of atoms with one or more unpaired electrons.

free-range *adj.* **1** (of hens etc.) roaming freely; not kept in a battery. **2** (of eggs) produced by such hens.

freesia /ˈfriːzɪə/ *n.* African bulb with fragrant flowers. [*Freese*, name of a physician]

free speech *n.* right of expression.

free spirit *n.* independent or uninhibited person.

free-spoken *adj.* forthright.

free-standing *adj.* not supported by another structure.

freestyle *n.* **1** swimming race in which any stroke may be used. **2** wrestling allowing almost any hold.

freethinker /friːˈθɪŋkə(r)/ *n.* person who rejects dogma or authority, esp. in religious belief. □ **freethinking** *n.* & *adj.*

free trade *n.* trade without import restrictions etc.

free vote *n.* parliamentary vote not subject to party discipline.

freeway n. US motorway.

free wheel n. driving wheel of a bicycle. **free wheel** v. to revolve with the pedals at rest.

free-wheel v. 1 ride a bicycle with the pedals at rest. 2 act without constraint.

free will n. 1 power of acting independently of necessity or fate. 2 ability to act without coercion (*did it of my own free will*).

free world n. *hist.* non-Communist countries' collective name for themselves.

freeze —v. (*zing; past* **froze**; *past part.* **frozen**) 1 a turn into ice or another solid by cold. b make or become rigid from the cold. 2 be or feel very cold, or become covered with ice. 4 (foll. by *to, together*) adhere by frost. 5 refrigerate (food) below freezing point. 6 a make or become motionless through fear, surprise, etc. b (as **frozen** *adj.*) devoid of emotion (*frozen smile*). 7 make (assets etc.) unrealizable. 8 fix (prices, wages, etc.) at a certain level. 9 stop (the movement in a film). —n. 1 period or state of frost. 2 fixing or stabilization of prices, wages, etc. 3 (in full **freeze-frame**) still film-shot. □ **freeze up** obstruct or be obstructed by ice. [Old English]

freeze-dry v. preserve (food) by freezing and then drying in a vacuum.

freezer n. refrigerated cabinet etc. for preserving frozen food at very low temperatures.

freeze-up n. period or state of extreme cold.

freezing point n. temperature at which a liquid freezes.

freight /freɪt/ —n. 1 transport of goods in containers or by water or air, or (*US*) by land. 2 goods transported; cargo, load. 3 charge for the transport of goods. —v. transport as or load with freight. [Low German or Dutch *vrecht*]

freighter n. ship or aircraft for carrying freight. 2 *US* freight-wagon.

freightliner n. train carrying goods in containers.

French —adj. 1 of France, its people, or language. 2 having French characteristics. —n. 1 the French language. 2 (the French) (*pl.*) the people of France. 3 *colloq.* dry vermouth. □ **Frenchness** n. [Old English: related to **FRANK**]

French bean n. kidney or haricot bean as unripe sliced pods or ripe seeds.

French bread n. long crisp loaf.

French Canadian n. Canadian whose principal language is French.

French chalk n. a kind of talc used for marking cloth, as a dry lubricant, etc.

French dressing n. salad dressing of seasoned vinegar and oil.

French fried potatoes *n.pl.* (or **French fries**) *US* potato chips.

French horn n. coiled brass wind instrument with a wide bell.

Frenchify /ˈfrentʃɪfaɪ/ v. (**-ies, -ied**) (usu. as **French-fied** *adj.*) *colloq.* make French in form, manners, etc.

French kiss n. open-mouthed kiss.

French leave n. absence without permission.

French letter n. *colloq.* condom.

Frenchman n. man of French birth or nationality.

French polish n. shellac polish for wood. □ **French-polish** v.

French window n. glazed door in an outside wall.

Frenchwoman n. woman of French birth or nationality.

frenetic /frəˈnetɪk/ adj. (also **phrenetic**) 1 frantic, frenzied. 2 fanatic. □ **frenetically** adv. [Greek *phrēn* mind]

frenzy /ˈfrenzɪ/ —n. (*pl.* -ies) wild or delirious excitement, agitation, or fury. —v. (-ies, -ied) (usu. as **frenzied** *adj.*) drive to frenzy. □ **frenziedly** adv. [medieval Latin: related to **FRENETIC**]

frequency /ˈfriːkwənsɪ/ n. (*pl.* -ies) 1 commonness of occurrence. 2 frequent occurrence. 3 rate of recurrence (of a vibration etc.); number of repetitions in a given time, esp. per second. [related to **FREQUENT**]

frequency modulation n. *Electronics* modulation by varying carrier-wave frequency.

frequent —adj. 1 occurring often or in close succession. 2 habitual, constant. —v. /frɪˈkwent/ attend or go to habitually. □ **frequently** /ˈfriːkwəntlɪ/ adv. [Latin *frequens -ent-* crowded]

frequentative /frɪˈkwentətɪv/ *Gram.* —adj. (of a verb etc.) expressing frequent repetition or intensity. —n. frequentative verb e.c.

fresco /ˈfreskəʊ/ n. (*pl.* -s) painting done in water-colour on a wall or ceiling before the plaster is dry. [Italian, = fresh]

fresh —adj. 1 newly made or obtained. 2 other, different; new (*start a fresh page; fresh ideas*). 3 additional (*fresh supplies*). 4 (foll. by *from*) lately arrived. 4 not stale, musty, or faded. 5 (of food) not preserved; newly caught, grown, etc. 6 not salty (*fresh water*). 7 a pure, untainted, refreshing (*fresh air*). b bright and pure in colour (*fresh complexion*). 8 (of wine) brisk. 9 *colloq.* cheeky; amorously impudent. 10 inexperienced. —adv. newly, recently (esp. in comb.: *fresh-baked*). □ **freshly** adv. **freshness** n. [Old English *fersc* and French *freis*]

freshen v. **1** make or become fresh. **2** (foll. by *up*) a wash, tidy oneself, etc. **b** revive.

fresher n. *colloq.* first-year student at university or (*US*) high school.

freshet /freʃɪt/ n. **1** rush of fresh water flowing from the sea. **2** flood of a river.

freshman n. = FRESHER.

freshwater *attrib. adj.* (of fish etc.) not of the sea.

fret[1] –v. (**-tt-**) **1** be worried or distressed. **2** worry, vex. **3** wear or consume by gnawing or rubbing. –n. worry, vexation. [Old English: related to FOR, EAT]

fret[2] –n. ornamental pattern of straight lines joined usu. at right angles. –v. (**-tt-**) embellish with a fret or with carved or embossed work. [French *freter*]

fret[3] n. each of a series of bars or ridges on the finger-board of a guitar etc. to guide fingering. [origin unknown]

fretful *adj.* anxious, irritable. □ **fretfully** *adv.*

fretsaw n. narrow saw on a frame for cutting thin wood in patterns.

fretwork n. ornamental work in wood done with a fretsaw.

Freudian /frɔɪdɪən/ –*adj.* of Freud, his theories, or his method of psychoanalysis. –n. follower of Freud.

Freudian slip n. unintentional verbal error revealing subconscious feelings.

Fri. *abbr.* Friday.

friable /fraɪəb(ə)l/ *adj.* easily crumbled. □ **friability** /-'bɪlɪti/ n. [Latin *frio* crumble]

friar /fraɪə(r)/ n. member of a male non-enclosed Roman Catholic order, e.g. Carmelites and Franciscans. [Latin *frater* brother]

friar's balsam n. tincture of benzoin etc. used esp. as an inhalant.

friary /fraɪəri/ n. (*pl.* **-ies**) monastery for friars.

fricassee /'frɪkə,seɪ/ –n. pieces of meat served in a thick sauce. –v. (**fricassees, fricasseed**) make a fricassee of. [French]

fricative /'frɪkətɪv/ –*adj.* (of a consonant) sounded by friction of the breath in a narrow opening. –n. such a consonant (e.g. *f, th*). [Latin *frico* rub]

friction /'frɪkʃ(ə)n/ n. **1** rubbing of one object against another. **2** the resistance encountered in so moving. **3** clash of wills, opinions, etc. □ **frictional** *adj.* [Latin: related to FRICATIVE]

Friday /'fraɪdeɪ/ –n. day of the week following Thursday. –*adv. colloq.* **1** on Friday. **2** (**Fridays**) on Fridays; each Friday. [Old English]

fridge n. *colloq.* = REFRIGERATOR. [abbreviation]

fridge-freezer n. combined refrigerator and freezer.

friend /frend/ n. **1** person one likes and chooses to spend time with (usu. without sexual or family bonds). **2** sympathizer, helper. **3** ally or neutral person (*friend or foe?*). **4** person already mentioned (*our friend at the bank*). **5** regular supporter of an institution. **6** (**Friend**) Quaker. [Old English]

friendly –*adj.* (**-ier, -iest**) **1** outgoing, well-disposed, kindly. **2** a (often foll. by *with*) on amicable terms. **b** not hostile. **3** (in *comb.*) not harming; helping (*ozone-friendly; user-friendly*). **4** = USER-FRIENDLY. –n. (*pl.* **-ies**) = FRIENDLY MATCH. –*adv.* in a friendly manner. □ **friendliness** n.

friendly match n. match played for enjoyment rather than competition.

Friendly Society n. insurance society insuring against illness etc.

friendship n. friendly relationship or feeling.

frier var. of FRYER.

Friesian /'friːzɪən/ n. one of a breed of black and white dairy cattle orig. from Friesland. [var. of FRISIAN]

frieze /friːz/ n. **1** part of an entablature between the architrave and cornice. **2** horizontal band of sculpture filling this. **3** band of decoration, esp. at the top of a wall. [Latin *Phrygium (opus)* Phrygian (work)]

frig v. (**-gg-**) *coarse slang* **1** = FUCK v. **2** masturbate. [perhaps imitative]

frigate /'frɪgɪt/ n. **1** naval escort-vessel. **2** *hist.* warship. [French from Italian]

fright /fraɪt/ n. **1** a sudden or extreme fear. **b** instance of this (*gave me a fright*). **2** grotesque-looking person or thing. □ **take fright** become frightened. [Old English]

frighten v. **1** fill with fright (*the bang frightened me; frightened of dogs*). **2** (foll. by *away, off, out of, into*) drive by fright. □ **frightening** *adj.* **frighteningly** *adv.*

frightful /'fraɪtfʊl/ *adj.* **1** a dreadful, shocking. **b** ugly. **2** *colloq.* extremely bad. **3** *colloq.* extreme (*frightful rush*). □ **frightfully** *adv.*

frigid /'frɪdʒɪd/ *adj.* **1** unfriendly, cold (*frigid stare*). **2** (of a woman) sexually unresponsive. **3** (esp. of a climate or air) cold. □ **frigidity** /-'dʒɪdɪti/ n. [Latin *frigus* (n.) cold]

frill –n. **1** strip of gathered or pleated material as an ornamental edging. **2** (in *pl.*) unnecessary embellishments. –v. decorate with a frill. □ **frilly** *adj.* (**-ier, -iest**) [origin unknown]

fringe –n. **1** border of tassels or loose threads. **2** front hair hanging over the

forehead. **3** outer limit of an area, population, etc. (often *attrib.*: *fringe theatre*). **4** unimportant area or part. —*v.* (**-ging**) **1** adorn with a fringe. **2** serve as a fringe to. [Latin *fimbria*]

fringe benefit *n.* employee's benefit additional to salary.

frippery /ˈfrɪpərɪ/ *n.* (*pl.* **-ies**) **1** showy finery, esp. in dress. **2** empty display in speech, literary style, etc. **3** (usu. in *pl.*) knick-knacks. [French *friperie*]

Frisbee /ˈfrɪzbɪ/ *n. propr.* concave plastic disc for skimming through the air as an outdoor game. [perhaps from *Frisbie* bakery pie-tins]

Frisian /ˈfrɪzɪən/ —*adj.* of Friesland. —*n.* native or language of Friesland. [Latin *Frisii* (pl.) from Old Frisian *Frisa*]

frisk —*v.* **1** leap or skip playfully **2** *slang* search (a person) for a weapon etc. by feeling. —*n.* **1** playful leap or skip. **2** *slang* frisking of a person. [French *frisque* lively]

frisky *adj.* (**-ier, -iest**) lively, playful. □ **friskily** *adv.* **friskiness** *n.*

frisson /ˈfriːsɒn/ *n.* emotional thrill. [French]

frith var. of FIRTH.

fritillary /frɪˈtɪlərɪ/ *n.* (*pl.* **-ies**) **1** plant with bell-like flowers. **2** butterfly with red-brown wings chequered with black. [Latin *fritillus* dice-box]

fritter[1] *v.* (usu. foll. by *away*) waste (money, time, etc.) triflingly. [obsolete *fritter(s)* fragments]

fritter[2] *n.* fruit, meat, etc. coated in batter and fried. [French *friture* from Latin *frigo* FRY]

frivolous /ˈfrɪvələs/ *adj.* **1** not serious, silly, shallow. **2** paltry, trifling. □ **frivolity** /-ˈvɒlɪtɪ/ *n.* (*pl.* **-ies**). **frivolously** *adv.* **frivolousness** *n.* [Latin]

frizz —*v.* form (hair) into tight curls. —*n.* frizzed hair or state. [French *friser*]

frizzle[1] /ˈfrɪz(ə)l/ *v.* (**-ling**) **1** fry or cook with a sizzling noise. **2** (often foll. by *up*) burn or shrivel. [obsolete *frizz*: related to FRY, with imitative ending]

frizzle[2] /ˈfrɪz(ə)l/ —*v.* (**-ling**) form into tight curls. —*n.* frizzled hair. [perhaps related to FRIZZ]

frizzy *adj.* (**-ier, -iest**) in tight curls. □ **frizzily** *adv.* **frizziness** *n.*

fro *adv.* back (now only in *to and fro*; see TO). [Old Norse: related to FROM]

frock *n.* **1** woman's or girl's dress. **2** monk's or priest's gown. **3** smock. [French from Germanic]

frock-coat *n.* man's long-skirted coat. [French from Germanic]

frog[1] *n.* **1** small smooth tailless leaping amphibian. **2** (**Frog**) *slang offens.* Frenchman. □ **frog in one's throat** *colloq.* hoarseness. [Old English]

frog[2] *n.* horny substance in the sole of a horse's foot. [origin uncertain: perhaps a use of FROG[1]]

frog[3] *n.* ornamental coat-fastening of a button and loop. [origin unknown]

frogman *n.* person with a rubber suit, flippers, and an oxygen supply for underwater swimming.

frogmarch *v.* hustle forward with the arms pinned behind.

frog-spawn *n.* frog's eggs.

frolic /ˈfrɒlɪk/ —*v.* (**-ck-**) play about cheerfully. —*n.* **1** cheerful play. **2** prank. **3** merry party. [Dutch *vrolijk* (adj.) from *vro* glad]

frolicsome *adj.* merry, playful.

from /frɒm, from/ *prep.* expressing separation or origin, followed by: **1** person, place, time, etc., that is the starting point (*dinner is served from 8*; *from this point*). **2** place, object, etc. at a specified distance etc. (*10 miles from Rome*; *far from stare*). **3 a** source (*gravel from a pit*; *quotations from Shaw*). **b** giver or sender (*not heard from her*). **4** thing or person avoided, deprived, etc. (*released him from prison*; *took his gun from him*). **5** reason, cause, motive (*died from fatigue*; *did it from jealousy*). **6** thing distinguished or unlike (*know black from white*). **7** lower limit (*from 10 to 20 boats*). **8** state changed for another (*from being poor he became rich*). **9** adverb or preposition of time or place (*from long ago*; *from abroad*; *from under the bed*). □ **from time to time** occasionally. [Old English]

fromage frais /ˌfrɒmɑːʒ ˈfreɪ/ *n.* smooth low-fat soft cheese. [French]

frond *n.* leaflike part of a fern or palm. [Latin *frons frond-* leaf]

front /frʌnt/ —*n.* **1** side or part most prominent or important; the nearer the spectator or direction of motion (*front of the house*). **2 a** line of battle. **b** ground towards an enemy. **c** scene of actual fighting. **3 a** activity compared to a military front. **b** organized political group **4** demeanour, bearing. **5** forward or conspicuous position. **6 a** bluff. **b** pretext. **7** person etc. as a cover for subversive or illegal activities. **8** promenade. **9** forward edge of advancing cold or warm air. **10** auditorium of a theatre. **11** breast of a garment (*spilt food down his front*). —*attrib. adj.* **1** of the front. **2** situated in front. —*v.* **1** (foll. by *on, to, towards, upon*) have the front facing or directed towards. **2** (foll. by *for*) *slang* act as a front or cover for. **3** provide with or have a front (*fronted with stone*). **4** lead or have a front, organization, etc.). □ **in front** in an advanced or facing position.

in front of 1 ahead of, in advance of. 2 in the presence of. [Latin *frons front*: face]

frontage /ˈfrʌntɪdʒ/ n. 1 front of a building. 2 land next to a street or water etc. 3 extent of a front. 4 a the way a thing faces. b outlook.

frontal adj. 1 of or on the front (*frontal view*; *frontal attack*). 2 of the forehead (*frontal bone*).

front bench n. seats in Parliament occupied by leading members of the government and opposition.

front-bencher n. MP occupying the front bench.

frontier /ˈfrʌntɪə(r)/ n. 1 a border between two countries. b district on each side of this. 2 limits of attainment or knowledge in a subject. 3 US borders between settled and unsettled country. □ **frontiersman** n.

frontispiece /ˈfrʌntɪsˌpiːs/ n. illustration facing the title-page of a book. [Latin: related to FRONT, *specio* look]

front line n. foremost part of an army or group under attack.

front runner n. favourite in a race etc.

frost — n. 1 a frozen dew or vapour. b consistent temperature below freezing point. 2 cold dispiriting atmosphere. — v. 1 (usu. foll. by *over*, *up*) become covered with frost. 2 a cover with or as with frost. b injure (a plant etc.) with frost. 3 make (glass) non-transparent by roughening its surface. [Old English: related to FREEZE]

frostbite n. injury to body tissues due to freezing. □ **frostbitten** adj.

frosting n. icing.

frosty adj. (-ier, -iest) 1 cold with frost. 2 covered with or as with frost. 3 unfriendly in manner. □ **frostily** adv. **frostiness** n.

froth — n. 1 foam. 2 idle or amusing talk etc. — v. 1 emit or gather froth. 2 cause (beer etc.) to foam. □ **frothy** adj. (-ier, -iest). [Old Norse]

frown — v. 1 wrinkle one's brows, esp. in displeasure or concentration. 2 (foll. by *at*, *on*) disapprove of. — n. 1 act of frowning. 2 look of displeasure or concentration. [French]

frowsty /ˈfraʊstɪ/ adj. (-ier, -iest) fusty, stuffy. [var. of FROWZY]

frowzy /ˈfraʊzɪ/ adj. (also **frowsy**) (-ier, -iest) 1 fusty. 2 slatternly, dingy. [origin unknown]

froze past of FREEZE.

frozen past part. of FREEZE.

FRS abbr. Fellow of the Royal Society.

fructify /ˈfrʌktɪˌfaɪ/ v. (-ies, -ied) 1 bear fruit. 2 make fruitful. [Latin: related to FRUIT]

fructose /ˈfrʌktəʊz/ n. sugar in honey, fruits, etc. [Latin: related to FRUIT]

frugal /ˈfruːg(ə)l/ adj. 1 sparing or thrifty, esp. as regards food. 2 meagre, cheap. □ **frugality** /-ˈɡælɪtɪ/ n. **frugally** adv. [Latin]

fruit /fruːt/ — n. 1 a seed-bearing part of a plant or tree; this as food. b these collectively. 2 (usu. in pl.) vegetables, grains, etc. as food (*fruits of the earth*). 3 (usu. in pl.) profits, rewards. — v. (cause to) bear fruit. [Latin *fructus* from *fruor* enjoy]

fruit cake n. cake containing dried fruit.

fruit cocktail n. diced fruit salad.

fruiterer n. dealer in fruit.

fruitful adj. 1 producing much fruit. 2 successful, profitable. □ **fruitfully** adv.

fruition /fruːˈɪʃ(ə)n/ n. 1 bearing of fruit. 2 realization of aims or hopes. [Latin: related to FRUIT]

fruit juice n. juice of fruit, esp. as a drink.

fruitless adj. 1 not bearing fruit. 2 useless, unsuccessful. □ **fruitlessly** adv.

fruit machine n. coin-operated gaming machine using symbols representing fruit.

fruit sugar n. fructose.

fruity adj. (-ier, -iest) 1 a of fruit. b tasting or smelling like fruit. 2 (of a voice etc.) deep and rich. 3 colloq. slightly indecent or suggestive. □ **fruitily** adv. **fruitiness** n.

frump n. dowdy unattractive woman. □ **frumpish** adj. **frumpy** adj. (-ier, -iest). [perhaps dial. *frumple* wrinkle]

frustrate /frʌˈstreɪt/ v. (-ting) 1 make (efforts) ineffective. 2 prevent (a person) from achieving a purpose. 3 (as **frustrated** adj.) a discontented because unable to achieve one's aims. b sexually unfulfilled. □ **frustrating** adj. **frustratingly** adv. **frustration** n. [Latin *frustra* in vain]

frustum /ˈfrʌstəm/ n. (pl. **-ta** or **-s**) Geom. remaining part of a decapitated cone or pyramid. [Latin, = piece cut off]

fry¹ — v. (**fries**, **fried**) cook or be cooked in hot fat. — n. (pl. **fries**) 1 offal, usu. eaten fried (*lamb's fry*). 2 fried food, esp. meat. [Latin *frigo*]

fry² n. pl. young or newly hatched fishes. [Old Norse, = seed]

fryer n. (also **frier**) 1 person who fries. 2 vessel for frying fish.

frying-pan n. shallow pan used in frying. □ **out of the frying-pan into the fire** from a bad situation to a worse one.

fry-up n. colloq. fried bacon, eggs, etc.

ft abbr. foot, feet.

FT-SE abbr. Financial Times Stock Exchange 100 share index (based on the

share values of Britain's largest public companies).

fuchsia /ˈfjuːʃə/ n. shrub with drooping red, purple, or white flowers. [Fuchs, name of a botanist]

fuck coarse slang —v. **1** (often absol. or as int. expressing annoyance) curse (a person or thing). **2** have sexual intercourse (with). **3** (foll. by about, around) mess about; fool around. **4** (as **fucking** adj. adv.) expressing annoyance etc. —n. **1 a** act of sexual intercourse. **b** partner in this. **2** slightest amount (don't give a fuck). □ **fuck off** go away. **fuck up** bungle or disturb emotionally. □ **fucker** n. (often as a term of abuse). [origin unknown]

■ **Usage** Although widely used, fuck is still considered to be the most offensive word in the English language by many people. In discussions about bad language it is frequently referred to as the 'f word.'

fuck-up n. coarse slang bungle or muddle.

fuddle /ˈfʌd(ə)l/ —v. (**-ling**) confuse or stupefy, esp. with alcohol. —n. **1** confusion. **2** intoxication. [origin unknown]

fuddy-duddy /ˈfʌdɪˌdʌdɪ/ slang —adj. old-fashioned or quaintly fussy. —n. (pl. **-ies**) such a person. [origin unknown]

fudge —n. **1** soft toffee-like sweet made of milk, sugar, butter, etc. **2** piece of dishonesty or faking. —v. (**-ging**) make or do clumsily or dishonestly; fake (fudge the results). [origin uncertain]

fuehrer var. of FÜHRER.

fuel /ˈfjuːəl/ —n. **1** material for burning or as a source of heat, power, or nuclear energy. **2** food as a source of energy. **3** thing that sustains or inflames passion etc. —v. (**-ll-**; US **-l-**) **1** supply with, take in, or get, fuel. **2** inflame (feeling etc.). [French from Latin]

fuel cell n. cell producing electricity direct from a chemical reaction.

fug n. colloq. close stuffy atmosphere. □ **fuggy** adj. [origin unknown]

fugitive /ˈfjuːdʒɪtɪv/ —n. (often foll. by from) person who flees, e.g. from justice or an enemy. —adj. **1** fleeing. **2** transient, fleeting. [Latin fugio flee]

fugue /fjuːg/ n. piece of music in which a short melody or phrase is introduced by one part and taken up and developed by others. [Latin fuga flight]

führer /ˈfjʊərə(r)/ n. (also **fuehrer**) tyrannical leader. [German]

-ful comb. form forming: **1** adjectives from a nouns, meaning full of or having qualities of (beautiful; masterful). **b** adjectives (direful). **c** verbs, meaning 'apt

to (forgetful). **2** nouns (pl. **-s** or **-fuls**) meaning 'amount that fills' (handful; spoonful).

fulcrum /ˈfʌlkrəm/ n. (pl. **-s** or **-cra**) point on which a lever is supported. [Latin fulcio to prop]

fulfil /fʊlˈfɪl/ v. (US **fulfill**) (**-ll-**) **1** carry out (a task, prophecy, promise, etc.). **2 a** satisfy (conditions, a desire, prayer, etc.). **b** (as **fulfilled** adj.) completely happy. **3** answer (a purpose). □ **fulfil oneself** realize one's potential. □ **fulfilment** n. [Old English: related to FULL¹]

full¹ /fʊl/ —adj. **1** holding all it can (bucket is full; full of water). **2** having eaten all one can or wants. **3** abundant, copious, satisfying (a full life, full details). **4** (foll. by of) having an abundance of (full of oneself). **5** (foll. by of) engrossed in (full of himself). **6** complete, perfect (full membership; in full bloom). **7** (of tone) deep and clear. **8** plump, rounded (full figure). **9** (of clothes) ample, hanging in folds. —adv. **1** very (knows full well). **2** quite, fully (full six miles). **3** exactly (full on the nose). □ **full up** colloq. completely full. **in full 1** without abridgement. **2** to or for the full amount. **in full view** entirely visible. **to the full** to the utmost extent. [Old English]

full² /fʊl/ v. clean and thicken (cloth). [from FULLER]

full back n. defensive player near the goal in football, hockey, etc.

full-blooded adj. **1** vigorous, hearty, sensual. **2** not hybrid.

full-blown adj. fully developed.

full board n. provision of bed and all meals at a hotel etc.

full-bodied adj. rich in quality, tone, etc.

fuller n. person who fulls cloth. □ **fuller's earth** type of clay used in fulling. [Latin fullo]

full-frontal adj. **1** (of a nude figure) fully exposed at the front. **2** explicit, unrestrained.

full house n. **1** maximum attendance at a theatre etc. **2** hand in poker with three of a kind and a pair.

full-length adj. **1** not shortened. **2** (of a mirror, portrait, etc.) showing the whole figure.

full moon n. **1** moon with its whole disc illuminated. **2** time of this.

fullness n. being full. □ **the fullness of time** the appropriate or destined time.

full-scale adj. not reduced in size, complete.

full stop n. **1** punctuation mark (.) at the end of a sentence or an abbreviation. **2** complete cessation.

full term n. completion of a normal pregnancy.

full-time —adj. for or during the whole of the working week (full-time job). —adv. on a full-time basis (work full-time).

full-timer n. person who does a full-time job.

fully adv. 1 completely, entirely (am fully aware). 2 at least (fully 60).

fully-fashioned adj. (of women's clothing) shaped to fit closely.

fulmar /'fʊlmə(r)/ n. Arctic sea bird related to the petrel. [Old Norse: related to FOUL, mar gull]

fulminant /'fʊlmɪnənt/ adj. 1 fulminating. 2 (of a disease etc.) developing suddenly. [Latin: related to FULMINATE]

fulminate /'fʊlmɪˌneɪt/ v. (-ting) 1 criticize loudly and forcefully. 2 explode violently; flash. □ **fulmination** /-'neɪʃ(ə)n/ n. [Latin fulmen -min- lightning]

fulsome /'fʊlsəm/ adj. excessive, cloying, insincere (fulsome praise). □ **fulsomely** adv. [from FULL]

■ **Usage** The phrase fulsome praise is sometimes wrongly used to mean generous praise rather than excessive praise.

fumble /'fʌmb(ə)l/ —v. (-ling) 1 use the hands awkwardly, grope about. 2 handle clumsily or nervously (fumbled the ball). —n. act of fumbling. [Low German fummeln]

fume —n. (usu. in pl.) exuded gas, smoke, or vapour, esp. when harmful or unpleasant.—v. (-ming) 1 emit fumes or as fumes. 2 be very angry. 3 subject (oak, film, etc.) to fumes to darken. [Latin fumus smoke]

fumigate /'fjuːmɪˌɡeɪt/ v. (-ting) disinfect or purify with fumes. □ **fumigation** /-'ɡeɪʃ(ə)n/ n. **fumigator** n. [Latin: related to FUME]

fun —n. 1 lively or playful amusement. 2 source of this. 3 mockery, ridicule (figure of fun). —attrib. adj. colloq. amusing, enjoyable (a fun thing to do). □ **for fun** or **for the fun of it** not for a serious purpose. **in fun** as a joke, not seriously. **make fun of** (or **poke fun at**) ridicule, tease. [obsolete fun, fon: related to FOND]

function /'fʌŋkʃ(ə)n/ —n. 1 a attributive role, activity, or purpose. b official or professional duty. 2 public or social occasion. 3 Math. quantity whose value depends on the varying values of others. —v. fulfil a function, operate. [Latin fungor funct- perform]

functional adj. 1 of or serving a function. 2 practical rather than attractive. 3 affecting the function of a bodily organ but not its structure. □ **functionally** adv.

functionalism n. belief that a thing's function should determine its design. □ **functionalist** n. & adj.

functionary n. (pl. -ies) official performing certain duties.

fund —n. 1 permanently available stock (fund of knowledge). 2 sum of money, esp. set apart for a purpose. 3 (in pl.) money resources. —v. 1 provide with money. 2 make (a debt) permanent at fixed interest. □ **in funds** colloq. having money to spend. [Latin fundus bottom]

fundamental /ˌfʌndəˈment(ə)l/ —adj. of or being a base or foundation; essential, primary. —n. 1 (usu. in pl.) fundamental principle. 2 Mus. fundamental note. □ **fundamentally** adv. [Latin: related to FOUND²]

fundamentalism n. strict adherence to traditional religious beliefs or doctrines. □ **fundamentalist** n. & adj.

fundamental note n. Mus. lowest note of a chord.

fundamental particle n. elementary particle.

fund-raiser n. person raising money for a cause, enterprise, etc. □ **fund-raising** n.

funeral /'fjuːnər(ə)l/ —n. 1 ceremonial burial or cremation of a corpse. 2 slang one's (usu. unpleasant) concern (that's your funeral).—attrib. adj. of or used at funerals. [Latin funus funer-]

funeral director n. undertaker.

funeral parlour n. establishment where corpses are prepared for funerals.

funerary /'fjuːnərərɪ/ adj. of or used at funerals.

funereal /fjuːˈnɪərɪəl/ adj. 1 of or appropriate to a funeral. 2 dismal, dark. □ **funereally** adv.

funfair n. fair with amusements and sideshows.

fungicide /'fʌndʒɪˌsaɪd/ n. substance that kills fungus. □ **fungicidal** /-'saɪd(ə)l/ adj.

fungoid /'fʌŋɡɔɪd/ —adj. fungus-like. —n. fungoid plant.

fungus /'fʌŋɡəs/ n. (pl. -gi /-ɡi/ or -guses) 1 mushroom, toadstool, or allied plant, including moulds, feeding on organic matter. 2 Med. spongy morbid growth. □ **fungal** adj. **fungous** adj. [Latin]

funicular /fjuːˈnɪkjʊlə(r)/ —adj. (of a mountain railway) operating by cable

with ascending and descending cars, counterbalanced. —n. funicular railway. [Latin *funiculus* diminutive of *funis* rope]

funk¹ n. *slang* —n. 1 evade through fear. 2 be afraid (of). [origin uncertain]

funk² n. *slang* funky music. [origin uncertain]

funky adj. (**-ier, -iest**) *slang* (esp. of jazz or rock music) earthy, bluesy, with a heavy rhythm.

funnel /ˈfʌn(ə)l/ —n. 1 tube widening at the top, for pouring liquid etc. into a small opening. 2 metal chimney on a steam engine or steamship. —v. (**-ll-;** *US* **-l-**) guide or move through or as through a funnel. [Provençal *fonilh* from Latin *(in)fundibulum*]

funny /ˈfʌnɪ/ adj. (**-ier, -iest**) 1 amusing, comical. 2 strange, peculiar. 3 *colloq.* **a** slightly unwell. **b** eccentric. □ **funnily** adv. **funniness** n. [from FUN]

funny-bone n. part of the elbow over which a very sensitive nerve passes.

fun run n. *colloq.* uncompetitive sponsored run for charity.

fur —n. 1 **a** short fine soft animal hair. **b** hide with fur on it, used esp. for clothing. 2 garment of or lined with fur. 3 (*collect.*) animals with fur. 4 fur-like coating on the tongue, in a kettle, etc. —v. (**-rr-**) 1 (esp. as **furred** adj.) line or trim with fur. 2 (often foll. by *up*) (of a kettle etc.) become coated with fur. □ **make the fur fly** *colloq.* cause a disturbance, stir up trouble. [French from Germanic]

furbelow /ˈfɜːbɪləʊ/ n. 1 (in *pl.*) showy ornaments. 2 *archaic* gathered strip or border of a skirt or petticoat. [French *falbala*]

furbish /ˈfɜːbɪʃ/ v. (often foll. by *up*) = REFURBISH. [French from Germanic]

furcate /ˈfɜːkeɪt/ —v. (**-ting**) fork, divide. —adj. forked, branched. [Latin *furca* fork]

furcation /fɜːˈkeɪʃ(ə)n/ n. [Latin: related to FORK]

furious /ˈfjʊərɪəs/ adj. 1 very angry. 2 raging, frantic. □ **furiously** adv. [Latin: related to FURY]

furl v. 1 roll up and secure (a sail etc.). 2 become furled. [French *ferler*]

furlong /ˈfɜːlɒŋ/ n. eighth of a mile. [Old English: related to FURROW, LONG¹]

furlough /ˈfɜːləʊ/ n. leave of absence, esp. military. —v. *US* 1 grant furlough to. 2 spend furlough. [Dutch: related to FOR-, LEAVE¹]

furnace /ˈfɜːnɪs/ n. 1 enclosed structure for intense heating by fire, esp. of metals or water. 2 very hot place. [Latin *fornax* from *fornus* oven]

furnish /ˈfɜːnɪʃ/ v. 1 provide (a house, room, etc.) with furniture. 2 (often foll. by *with*) supply. [French from Germanic]

furnished adj. (of a house etc.) let with furniture.

furnisher n. 1 person who furnishes. 2 person who sells furniture.

furnishings n.pl. furniture and fittings in a house, room, etc.

furniture /ˈfɜːnɪtʃə(r)/ n. 1 movable equipment of a horse, room, etc., e.g. tables, beds. 2 *Naut.* ship's equipment. 3 accessories, e.g. the handles and lock on a door. [French: related to FURNISH]

furore /fjʊəˈrɔːrɪ/ n. (*US* **furor** /ˈfjʊərɔːr/) 1 uproar; fury. 2 enthusiastic admiration. [Italian from Latin: related to FURY]

furrier /ˈfʌrɪə(r)/ n. dealer in or dresser of furs. [French]

furrow /ˈfʌrəʊ/ —n. 1 narrow trench made by a plough. 2 rut, groove, wrinkle. 3 ship's track. —v. 1 plough. 2 make furrows in. [Old English]

furry /ˈfɜːrɪ/ adj. (**-ier, -iest**) like or covered with fur.

further /ˈfɜːðə(r)/ —adv. (also **farther**) 1 more distant in space or time. 2 to a greater extent, more (*will enquire further*). 3 in addition (*I may add further*). —adj. (also **farther**) 1 more distant or advanced. 2 more, additional (*further details*). —v. promote or favour (a scheme etc.). [Old English: related to FORTH]

■ **Usage** The form *farther* is used esp. with reference to physical distance, although *further* is preferred by many people even in this sense.

furtherance n. furthering of a scheme etc.

further education n. education for those above school age.

furthermore /fɜːðəˈmɔː(r)/ adv. in addition, besides.

furthest /ˈfɜːðɪst/ (also **farthest** /ˈfɑːðɪst/) —adj. most distant. —adv. to or at the greatest distance.

■ **Usage** The form *farthest* is used esp. with reference to physical distance, although *furthest* is preferred by many people even in this sense.

furtive /ˈfɜːtɪv/ adj. sly, stealthy. □ **furtively** adv. **furtiveness** n. [Latin *fur* thief]

fury /ˈfjʊərɪ/ n. (*pl.* **-ies**) 1 **a** wild and passionate anger. **b** fit of rage. 2 violence of a storm, disease, etc. 3 (**Fury**) (usu. in

pl.) (in Greek mythology) avenging goddess. **4** avenging spirit. **5** angry or malignant woman. □ **like fury** *colloq.* with great force or effort. [Latin *furia*]

furze *n.* = GORSE. □ **furzy** *adj.* [Old English]

fuse¹ /fjuːz/ —*v.* (**-sing**) **1** melt with intense heat. **2** blend into one whole by melting. **3** provide (an electric circuit with a fuse. **4 a** (of an appliance) fail owing to the melting of a fuse. **b** cause to do this. —*n.* device with a strip or wire of easily melted metal placed in an electric circuit so as to interrupt an excessive current by melting. [Latin *fundo fus-melt*]

fuse² /fjuːz/ (also **fuze**) —*n.* **1** device of combustible matter for igniting a bomb or explosive charge. **2** component made of this in a shell, mine, etc. —*v.* (**-sing**) fit a fuse to. [Latin *fusus* spindle]

fuselage /ˈfjuːzəˌlɑːʒ/ *n.* body of an aeroplane. [French from *fuseau* spindle]

fusible /ˈfjuːzɪb(ə)l/ *adj.* that can be melted. □ **fusibility** /-ˈbɪlɪtɪ/ *n.* [Latin: related to FUSE¹]

fusil /ˈfjuːzɪl/ *n. hist.* light musket. [Latin *focus* fire]

fusilier /ˌfjuːzɪˈlɪə(r)/ *n.* member of any of several British regiments formerly armed with fusils. [French: related to FUSIL]

fusillade /ˌfjuːzɪˈleɪd/ *n.* **1** period of continuous discharge of firearms. **2** sustained outburst of criticism etc.

fusion /ˈfjuːʒ(ə)n/ *n.* **1** fusing or melting. **2** blending. **3** coalition. **4** = NUCLEAR FUSION. [Latin: related to FUSE¹]

fuss —*n.* **1** excited commotion, bustle. **2** excessive concern about a trivial thing. **3** sustained protest or dispute. —*v.* **1** behave with nervous concern. **2** agitate, worry. □ **make a fuss** complain vigorously. **make a fuss of** (or **over**) treat (a person or animal) affectionately. □ **fusser** *n.* [origin unknown]

fusspot *n. colloq.* person given to fussing.

fussy *adj.* (**-ier**, **-iest**) **1** inclined to fuss. **2** over-elaborate. **3** fastidious. □ **fussily** *adv.* **fussiness** *n.*

fustian /ˈfʌstɪən/ —*n.* **1** thick usu. dark twilled cotton cloth. **2** bombast. —*adj.* **1** made of fustian. **2** bombastic. **3** worthless. [French]

fusty /ˈfʌstɪ/ *adj.* (**-ier**, **-iest**) **1** musty, stuffy. **2** antiquated. □ **fustiness** *n.* [French *fust* cask, from Latin *fustis* cudgel]

futile /ˈfjuːtaɪl/ *adj.* **1** useless, ineffectual. **2** frivolous. □ **futility** /-ˈtɪlɪtɪ/ *n.* [Latin *futilis* leaky, futile]

futon /ˈfuːtɒn/ *n.* Japanese quilted mattress used as a bed; this sold with a low wooden frame, often convertible into a couch. [Japanese]

future /ˈfjuːtʃə(r)/ —*adj.* **1** about to happen, be, or become. **2** of time to come. □ *n.* **1** time to come. **2** future events. **3** future condition of a person, country, etc. **4** prospect of success etc. **5** *Gram.* future tense. **6** (in *pl.*) *Stock Exch.* goods etc. sold for future delivery. □ **in future** from now onwards. [Latin *futurus*]

future perfect *n. Gram.* tense giving the sense 'will have done'.

futurism *n.* 20th-century artistic movement departing from traditional forms and celebrating technology and dynamism. □ **futurist** *n. & adj.*

futuristic /ˌfjuːtʃəˈrɪstɪk/ *adj.* **1** suitable for the future; ultra-modern. **2** of futurism.

futurity /fjuːˈtjʊərɪtɪ/ *n.* (*pl.* **-ies**) *literary* **1** future time. **2** (in *sing.* or *pl.*) future events.

futurology /ˌfjuːtʃəˈrɒlədʒɪ/ *n.* forecasting of the future, esp. from present trends.

fuze var. of FUSE².

fuzz *n.* **1** fluff. **2** fluffy or frizzed hair. **3** *slang* **a** (prec. by *the*) **b** police officer. [probably Low German or Dutch]

fuzzy *adj.* (**-ier**, **-iest**) **1** like fuzz, fluffy. **2** blurred, indistinct. □ **fuzzily** *adv.* **fuzziness** *n.*

-fy *suffix* forming: **1** verbs from nouns, meaning: **a** make, produce (*pacify*). **b** make into (*deify*; *petrify*). **2** verbs from adjectives, meaning 'bring or come into a state' (*Frenchify*; *solidify*). **3** verbs in a causative sense (*horrify*; *stupefy*). [French *-fier* from Latin *facio* make]

G¹ /dʒiː/ n. (also **g**) (pl. **Gs** or **G's**) **1** seventh letter of the alphabet. **2** Mus. fifth note of the diatonic scale of C major

G² abbr. (also **G.**) **1** gauss. **2** giga-. **3** gravitational constant.

g abbr. (also **g.**) **1** gram(s). **2 a** gravity. **b** acceleration due to gravity.

Ga symb. gallium.

gab n. colloq. talk, chatter. [var. of GOB¹]

gabardine /ˌgæbəˈdiːn/ n. (also **gaberdine**) **1** twill-woven cloth, esp. of worsted. **2** raincoat etc. made of this. [French gavardine]

gabble /ˈgæb(ə)l/ —v. **1** talk or utter unintelligibly or too fast. **2** read inaudibly. —n. fast unintelligible talk. [Dutch, imitative]

gable /ˈgeɪb(ə)l/ n. **1** triangular upper part of a wall at the end of a ridged roof. **2** gable-topped wall. □ **gabled** adj. [Old Norse and French]

gad v. (**-dd-**) (foll. by about) go about idly or in search of pleasure. [obsolete gadling companion]

gadabout /ˈgædəbaʊt/ n. person who gads about.

gadfly n. **1** fly that bites cattle and horses. **2** irritating person. [obsolete gad spike]

gadget /ˈgædʒɪt/ n. small mechanical device or tool. □ **gadgetry** n. [origin unknown]

gadolinium /ˌgædəˈlɪnɪəm/ n. metallic element of the lanthanide series. [Gadolin, name of a mineralogist]

gadwall /ˈgædwɔːl/ n. brownish-grey freshwater duck. [origin unknown]

Gael /geɪl/ n. **1** Scottish Celt. **2** Gaelic-speaking Celt. [Gaelic Gàidheal]

Gaelic /ˈgeɪlɪk, ˈgɑː-/ —n. Celtic language of Ireland and Scotland. —adj. of the Celts or the Celtic languages.

gaff¹ —n. **1 a** stick with an iron hook for landing large fish. **b** barbed fishing-spear. **2** spar to which the head of a fore-and-aft sail is bent. —v. seize (a fish) with a gaff. [Provençal gaf hook]

gaff² n. slang □ **blow the gaff** reveal a plot or secret. [origin unknown]

gaffe /gæf/ n. blunder; indiscreet act or remark. [French]

gaffer /ˈgæfə(r)/ n. **1** old fellow. **2** colloq. foreman, boss. **3** chief electrician in a film or television production unit. [probably from GODFATHER]

gag —n. **1** thing thrust into or tied across the mouth, esp. to prevent speaking or

crying out. **2** joke or comic scene. **3** parliamentary closure. **4** thing restricting free speech. —v. (**-gg-**) **1** apply a gag to. **2** silence; deprive of free speech. **3** choke, retch. **4** make gags as a comedian etc. [origin uncertain]

gaga /ˈgɑːgɑː/ adj. slang **1** senile. **2** slightly crazy. [French]

gage¹ n. **1** pledge; thing deposited as security. **2** symbol of a challenge to fight, esp. a glove thrown down. [German: related to WED, WAGE]

gage² US var. of GAUGE.

gaggle /ˈgæg(ə)l/ n. **1** flock of geese. **2** colloq. disorganized group of people. [imitative]

gaiety /ˈgeɪətɪ/ n. (US **gayety**) **1** being gay; mirth. **2** merrymaking. **3** bright appearance. [French: related to GAY]

gaily adv. in a gay or careless manner (gaily decorated; gaily announced their departure).

gain —v. **1** obtain or win (gain advantage, gain recognition). **2** acquire as profits etc., earn. **3** (often foll. by in) get more of, improve ('gain momentum; gain in experience'). **4** benefit, profit. **5** (of a clock etc.) become fast; become fast (often foll. by on, upon) come closer to a person or thing pursued. **7 a** reclaim (land from the sea). **b** win (a battle). **8** reach (a desired place). —n. **1** increase of wealth etc.; profit, improvement. **2** (in pl.) sums of money got by trade etc. **3** increase in amount. □ **gain ground 1** advance. **2** (foll. by on) catch up (a person pursued). [French from Germanic]

gainful adj. **1** (of employment) paid. **2** lucrative. □ **gainfully** adv.

gainsay /geɪnˈseɪ/ v. deny, contradict. [Old Norse: related to AGAINST, SAY]

gait n. manner of walking or forward motion. [Old Norse]

gaiter n. covering of cloth, leather, etc., for the lower leg. [French guêtre]

gal n. slang girl. [representing a variant pronunciation]

gal. abbr. (also **gall.**) gallon(s).

gala /ˈgɑːlə/ n. festive occasion or gathering (swimming gala). [ultimately from French gale rejoicing from German]

galactic /gəˈlæktɪk/ adj. of a galaxy or galaxies.

galantine /'gælən,tin/ n. white meat boned, stuffed, spiced, etc., and served cold. [French from Latin]

galaxy /'gæləksi/ n. (pl. -ies) 1 independent system of stars, gas, dust, etc., in space. 2 **(the Galaxy)** Milky Way. 3 (foll. by of) brilliant company (galaxy of talent). [Greek gala milk]

gale n. 1 very strong wind or storm. 2 outburst, esp. of laughter. [origin unknown]

gall[1] /gɔːl/ n. 1 slang impudence. 2 rancour. 3 bitterness. 4 bile. [Old Norse]

gall[2] /gɔːl/ –n. 1 sore made by chafing. 2 mental soreness or its cause. 3 place rubbed bare. –v. 1 rub sore. 2 vex, humiliate. [Low German or Dutch galle]

gall[3] /gɔːl/ n. growth produced by insects etc. on plants and trees, esp. on oak. [Latin galla]

gall. abbr. var. of GAL.

gallant –adj. /'gælənt/ 1 brave. 2 fine, stately. 3 /gə'lænt/ very attentive to women. –n. /gə'lænt/ ladies' man. □ **gallantly** /'gæləntli/ adv. [French galer make merry]

gallantry /'gæləntri/ n. (pl. -ies) 1 bravery. 2 devotion to women. 3 polite act or speech.

gall bladder n. organ storing bile.

galleon /'gæliən/ n. hist. warship (usu. Spanish). [French or Spanish: related to GALLEY]

galleria /,gælə'riːə/ n. collection of small shops under a single roof. [Italian]

gallery /'gæləri/ n. (pl. -ies) 1 room or building for showing works of art. 2 balcony, esp. in a church, hall, etc. (minstrels' gallery). 3 highest balcony in a theatre. 4 a covered walk partly open at the side; colonnade. b narrow passage in the thickness of a wall or on corbels, open towards the interior of the building. 5 long narrow room or passage (shooting-gallery). 6 horizontal underground passage in a mine etc. 7 group of spectators at a golf-match etc. □ **play to the gallery** seek to win approval by appealing to popular taste. [French galerie]

galley /'gæli/ n. (pl. -s) 1 hist. a long flat single-decked vessel usu. rowed by slaves or criminals. b ancient Greek or Roman warship. 2 ship's or aircraft's kitchen. 3 Printing (in full **galley proof**) proof in continuous form before division into pages. [Latin galea]

galley-slave n. drudge.

Gallic /'gælik/ adj. 1 French or typically French. 2 of Gaul or the Gauls. [Latin Gallicus]

Gallicism /'gæli,sɪz(ə)m/ n. French idiom. [related to GALLIC]

gallinaceous /,gælɪ'neɪʃəs/ adj. of the order including domestic poultry, pheasants, etc. [Latin gallina hen]

gallium /'gæliəm/ n. soft bluish-white metallic element. [Latin Gallia France: so named patriotically by its discoverer Lecoq]

gallivant /'gælɪ,vænt/ v. colloq. gad about. [origin uncertain]

Gallo- comb. form French. [Latin]

gallon /'gælən/ n. 1 measure of capacity equal to eight pints (4.5 litres; for wine, or US. 3.8 litres). 2 (in pl.) colloq. large amount. [French]

gallop /'gæləp/ –n. 1 fastest pace of a horse etc., with all the feet off the ground together in each stride. 2 ride at this pace. –v. (-p-) 1 a (of a horse etc. or its rider) go at a gallop. b make (a horse etc.) gallop. 2 read, talk, etc., fast. 3 progress rapidly (galloping inflation). [French: related to WALLOP]

gallows /'gæləʊz/ n.pl. (usu. treated as sing.) structure, usu. of two uprights and a crosspiece, for hanging criminals. [Old Norse]

gallstone n. small hard mass forming in the gall-bladder.

Gallup poll /'gæləp/ n. = OPINION POLL. [Gallup, name of a statistician]

galore /gə'lɔː(r)/ adv. in plenty (whisky galore). [Irish]

galosh /gə'lɒʃ/ n. (also **golosh**) (usu. in pl.) overshoe, usu. of rubber. [French]

galumph /gə'lʌmf/ v. (esp. as **galumphing** adj.) colloq. move noisily or clumsily. [coined by Lewis Carroll, perhaps from GALLOP, TRIUMPH]

galvanic /gæl'vænik/ adj. 1 a producing an electric current by chemical action. b (of electricity) produced by chemical action. 2 a sudden and remarkable (had a galvanic effect). b stimulating; full of energy. □ **galvanically** adv.

galvanize /'gælvə,naɪz/ v. (also **-ise**) (-zing or -sing) 1 (often foll. by into) rouse forcefully, esp. by shock or excitement (was galvanized into action). 2 stimulate by or as by electricity. 3 coat (iron) with zinc to protect against rust. □ **galvanization** /-'zeɪʃ(ə)n/ n. [Galvani, name of a physiologist]

galvanometer /,gælvə'nɒmɪtə(r)/ n. instrument for detecting and measuring small electric currents. □ **galvanometric** /-'metrik/ adj.

gambit /'gæmbit/ n. 1 chess opening in which a player sacrifices a piece or pawn to secure an advantage. 2 opening move in a discussion etc. 3 trick or device. [Italian gambetto tripping up]

gamble /'gæmb(ə)l/ –v. (-ling) 1 play games of chance for money. 2 a bet (a

sum of money) in gambling. **b** (often foll. by *away*) lose by gambling. **3** risk much in the hope of great gain. **4** (foll. by *on*) act in the hope of. —*v.* **1** risky undertaking. **2** spell of gambling. □ **gambler** *n.* [related to GAMBOL]

gamboge /gæmˈbəʊdʒ/ *n.* gum resin used as a yellow pigment and as a purgative. [*Cambodia* in SE Asia]

gambol /ˈgæmbəl/ —*v.* (-ll-; *US* -l-) skip or jump about playfully. —*n.* frolic, cape. [French *gambade* leap, from Italian *gamba* leg]

game¹ —*n.* **1** form of play or sport, esp. a competitive one with rules. **2** portion of play forming a scoring unit, e.g. in bridge or tennis. **3** (in *pl.*) series of athletic etc. contests (*Olympic Games*). **4 a** piece of fun, jest (*didn't mean to upset you; it was only a game*). **b** (in *pl.*) dodges, tricks (*none of your games*). **5** *colloq.* a scheme or business (*so that's your game*). **6** a type of activity or business (*have been in the antiques game a long time*). **6** wild animals or birds hunted for sport or food. **b** their flesh as food. —*adj.* spirited, eager and willing (*are you game for a walk?*). —*v.* (-ming) gamble for money stakes. □ **the game is up** the scheme is revealed or foiled. **on the game** *slang* involved in prostitution. □ **gamely** *adv.* [Old English]

game² *adj. colloq.* (of a leg, arm, etc.) crippled. [origin unknown]

gamecock *n.* cock bred and trained for cock-fighting.

gamekeeper *n.* person employed to breed and protect game.

gamelan /ˈgæməˌlæn/ *n.* **1** SE Asian orchestra mainly of percussion instruments. **2** type of xylophone used in this. [Javanese]

gamesmanship *n.* art of winning games by gaining psychological advantage.

gamester /ˈgeɪmstə(r)/ *n.* gambler.

gamete /ˈgæmiːt/ *n.* mature germ cell able to unite with another in sexual reproduction. □ **gametic** /gəˈmetɪk/ *adj.* [Greek, = wife]

gamin /ˈgæmɪn/ *n.* **1** street urchin. **2** impudent child. [French]

gamine /gæˈmiːn/ *n.* **1** girl gamin. **2** girl with mischievous charm. [French]

gamma /ˈgæmə/ *n.* **1** third letter of the Greek alphabet (Γ, γ). **2** third-class mark for a piece of work etc. [Greek]

gamma radiation *n.* (also **gamma rays**) electromagnetic radiation of shorter wavelength than X-rays. [Greek]

gammon /ˈgæmən/ *n.* **1** bottom piece of a flitch of bacon including a hind leg. **2** ham of a pig cured like bacon. [French: related to JAMB]

gammy /ˈgæmɪ/ *adj.* (-ier, -iest) *slang* = GAME². [dial. form of GAME²]

gamut /ˈgæmət/ *n.* entire range or scope. □ **run the gamut of** experience or perform the complete range of. [Latin *gamma ut*, words arbitrarily taken as names of notes]

gamy *adj.* (-ier, -iest) smelling or tasting like high game.

gander *n.* **1** male goose. **2** *slang* look, glance (*take a gander*). [Old English]

gang¹ *n.* **1** band of persons associating for some (usu. antisocial or criminal) purpose. **2** set of workers, slaves, or prisoners. □ **gang up** *colloq.* **1** (often foll. by *with*) act together. **2** (foll. by *on*) combine against. [Old Norse]

ganger *n.* foreman of a gang of workers.

gangling /ˈgæŋglɪŋ/ *adj.* (of a person) loosely built; lanky. [frequentative of Old English *gang* go]

ganglion /ˈgæŋglɪən/ *n.* (*pl.* **-lia** or **-s**) structure containing an assemblage of nerve cells. □ **ganglionic** /-ˈɒnɪk/ *adj.* [Greek]

gangly /ˈgæŋglɪ/ *adj.* (-ier, -iest) = GANGLING.

gangplank *n.* movable plank for boarding or disembarking from a ship etc.

gangrene /ˈgæŋgriːn/ *n.* death of body tissue, usu. resulting from obstructed circulation. □ **gangrenous** /-grɪnəs/ *adj.* [Greek *gaggraina*]

gangster *n.* member of a gang of violent criminals.

gangue /gæŋ/ *n.* valueless earth etc. in which ore is found. [German: related to GANG]

gangway *n.* **1** passage, esp. between rows of seats. **2 a** opening in a ship's bulwarks. **b** bridge from ship to shore. [Old Norse]

gannet /ˈgænɪt/ *n.* **1** large diving sea-bird. **2** *slang* greedy person. [Old English]

gantry /ˈgæntrɪ/ *n.* (*pl.* **-ies**) structure supporting a traveling crane, railway or road signals, rocket-launching equipment, etc. [probably *gawn*, a dial. form of GALLON, + TREE]

gaol var. of JAIL.

gaolbird var. of JAILBIRD.

gaolbreak var. of JAILBREAK.

gaoler var. of JAILER.

gap *n.* **1** empty space, interval; deficiency **2** breach in a hedge, fence, etc. **3** wide divergence in views etc. □ **gappy** *adj.* [Old Norse]

gape —*v.* (-ping) **1 a** open one's mouth wide. **b** be or become wide open; split. **2** (foll. by *at*) stare at. —*n.* **1** open-mouthed stare; open mouth. **2** rent, opening. [Old Norse]

garage /ˈgærɑːʒ, -rɪdʒ/ —n. **1** building for housing a vehicle. **2** establishment selling petrol etc., or repairing and keeping vehicles. —v. (**-ging**) put or keep in a garage. [French]

garb —n. clothing, esp. of a distinctive kind. —v. (usu. in *passive* or *refl.*) dress. [Germanic: related to GEAR]

garbage /ˈgɑːbɪdʒ/ n. **1** esp. *US* refuse. **2** *colloq.* nonsense. [Anglo-French]

garbled *adj.* (unintentionally) distort or confuse (facts, messages, etc.). **2** make a (usu. unfair) selection from (facts, statements, etc.). [Italian from Arabic]

garden /ˈgɑːd(ə)n/ —n. **1** piece of ground for growing flowers, fruit, or vegetables. **2** (esp. in *pl.*) grounds laid out for public enjoyment. **3** (*attrib.*) cultivated (*garden plants*). —v. cultivate or tend a garden. □ **gardening** n. [Germanic: related to YARD²]

garden centre n. place where plants and garden equipment are sold.

garden city n. town spaciously laid out with parks etc.

gardener n. person who gardens, esp. for a living.

gardenia /ɡɑːˈdiːnɪə/ n. tree or shrub with large fragrant flowers. [*Garden*, name of a naturalist]

garden party n. party held on a lawn or in a garden.

garfish /ˈgɑːfɪʃ/ n. (*pl.* same or **-es**) fish with a long spearlike snout. [Old English, = spear-fish]

gargantuan /gɑːˈgæntjʊən/ *adj.* gigantic. [from the name *Gargantua*, a giant in Rabelais]

gargle /ˈgɑːg(ə)l/ —v. (**-ling**) wash (the throat) with a liquid kept in motion by breathing through it. —n. liquid for gargling. [French: related to GARGOYLE]

gargoyle /ˈgɑːgɔɪl/ n. grotesque carved face or figure, esp. as a spout from the gutter of a building. [French, = throat]

garibaldi /ˌgærɪˈbɔːldɪ/ n. (*pl.* **-s**) biscuit containing a layer of currants. [*Garibaldi*, name of an Italian patriot]

garish /ˈgeərɪʃ/ *adj.* obtrusively bright; showy; gaudy. □ **garishly** *adv.* **garishness** n. [obsolete *gaure* stare]

garland /ˈgɑːlənd/ —n. wreath of flowers etc., worn on the head or hung as a decoration. —v. adorn or crown with a garland or garlands. [French]

garlic /ˈgɑːlɪk/ n. plant of the onion family with a pungent bulb used in cookery. □ **garlicky** *adj.* [Old English, = spear-leek]

garment /ˈgɑːmənt/ n. **1** article of dress. **2** outward covering. [French: related to GARNISH]

garner /ˈgɑːnə(r)/ —v. **1** collect. **2** store. —n. *literary* storehouse or granary. [Latin: related to GRANARY]

garnet /ˈgɑːnɪt/ n. glassy silicate mineral, esp. a red kind used as a gem. [medieval Latin *granatum* POMEGRANATE]

garnish /ˈgɑːnɪʃ/ —v. decorate (esp. food). —n. decoration, esp. to food. [French *garnir* from Germanic]

garotte var. of GAROTTE.

garret /ˈgærɪt/ n. attic or room in a roof. [French, = watch-tower: related to GARRISON]

garrison /ˈgærɪs(ə)n/ —n. troops stationed in a town etc. to defend it. —v. (**-n-**) **1** provide with or occupy as a garrison. **2** place on garrison duty. [French *garir* defend, from Germanic]

garrotte /ɡəˈrɒt/ (also **garotte**, *US* **garrote**) —v. (**-ting**) execute or kill by strangulation, esp. with a wire collar. —n. device used for this. [French or Spanish]

garrulous /ˈgærʊləs/ *adj.* talkative. □ **garrulity** /ɡəˈruːlɪtɪ/ n. **garrulousness** n. [Latin]

garter n. **1** band worn to keep a sock or stocking up. **2** (**the Garter**) a highest order of English knighthood. **b** badge or membership of this. [French]

garter stitch n. plain knitting stitch.

gas —n. (*pl.* **-es**) **1** any airlike substance (i.e. not solid or liquid) moving freely to fill any space available. **2** such a substance (esp. found naturally or extracted from coal) used as fuel (also *attrib.*: *gas cooker*; *gas industry*). **3** nitrous oxide or other gas as an anaesthetic. **4** poisonous gas used in war. **5** *US colloq.* petrol, gasoline. **6** *slang* idle talk; boasting. **7** *slang* enjoyable or amusing thing or person. —v. (**gases**, **gassed**, **gassing**) **1** expose to gas, esp. to kill. **2** *colloq.* talk idly or boastfully. [Dutch invented word based on Greek *khaos* = CHAOS]

gasbag n. *slang* idle talker.

gas chamber n. room filled with poisonous gas to kill people or animals.

gaseous /ˈgæsɪəs/ *adj.* of or like gas.

gas fire n. domestic heater burning gas.

gas-fired *adj.* using gas as fuel.

gash —n. long deep slash, cut, or wound. —v. make a gash in; cut. [French]

gasholder n. large receptacle for storing gas; gasometer.

gasify /ˈgæsɪfaɪ/ v. (**-ies**, **-ied**) convert into gas. □ **gasification** /-fɪˈkeɪʃ(ə)n/ n.

gasket /ˈgæskɪt/ n. sheet or ring of rubber etc., shaped to seal the junction of metal surfaces. [French *garcette*]

gaslight n. light from burning gas.

gasman n. man who installs or services gas appliances, or reads gas meters.

gas mask n. respirator as a protection against poison gas.

gasoline /ˈgæsəliːn/ n. (also **gasolene**) US petrol.

gasometer /gæˈsɒmɪtə(r)/ n. large tank from which gas is distributed by pipes. [French *gazomètre*: related to GAS, -METER]

gasp /ɡɑːsp/ —v. **1** catch one's breath with an open mouth as in exhaustion or astonishment **2** utter with gasps. —n. convulsive catching of breath. [Old Norse]

gas ring n. hollow ring perforated with gas jets, for cooking etc.

gassy adj. (-ier, -iest) **1 a** of or like gas. **b** full of gas. **2** colloq. verbose.

gastric /ˈgæstrɪk/ adj. of the stomach. [French: related to GASTRO-]

gastric flu n. colloq. intestinal disorder of unknown cause.

gastric juice n. digestive fluid secreted by the stomach glands.

gastritis /gæˈstraɪtɪs/ n. inflammation of the stomach.

gastro- comb. form stomach. [Greek *gastēr* stomach]

gastro-enteritis /ˌgæstrəʊˌentəˈraɪtɪs/ n. inflammation of the stomach and intestines.

gastronome /ˈgæstrənəʊm/ n. gourmet. [Greek *gastēr* stomach, *nomos* law]

gastronomy /gæˈstrɒnəmɪ/ n. science or art of good eating and drinking. □ **gastronomic** /ˌgæstrəˈnɒmɪk/ adj. **gastronomical** /ˌgæstrəˈnɒmɪk(ə)l/ adj. **gastronomically** /ˌgæstrəˈnɒmɪkəlɪ/ adv.

gastropod /ˈgæstrəˌpɒd/ n. (also **gasteropod**) mollusc that moves by means of a ventral muscular organ, e.g. a snail. [from GASTRO-, Greek *pous pod-* foot]

gasworks n. place where gas is manufactured for lighting and heating.

gate —n. **1** barrier, usu. hinged, used to close an opening made for entrance and exit through a wall, fence, etc. **2** such an opening. **3** means of entrance or exit. **4** numbered place of access to aircraft at an airport. **5** device regulating the passage of water in a lock etc. **6 a** number of people entering by payment at the gates of a sports ground etc. **b** amount of money taken thus. **7 a** electrical signal that causes or controls the passage of other signals. **b** electrical circuit with an output that depends on the combination of several inputs. —v. (**-ting**) confine to college or school as a punishment. □ **gated** adj. [Old English]

gateau /ˈgætəʊ/ n. (pl. **-s** or **-x** /-təʊz/) large rich cake filled with cream etc. [French]

gatecrasher n. uninvited guest at a party etc. □ **gatecrash** v.

gatehouse n. house standing by or over a gateway to a large house or park.

gateleg n. (in full **gateleg table**) table with folding flaps supported by legs swung open like a gate. □ **gatelegged** adj.

gatepost n. post at either side of a gate.

gateway n. **1** opening which can be closed with a gate. **2** means of access (*gateway to the South; gateway to success*).

gather /ˈgæðə(r)/ —v. **1** bring or come together; accumulate. **2** pick or collect as harvest. **3** infer or deduce. **4 a** increase (*gather speed*). **b** collect (*gather dust*). **5** summon up (energy etc.). **6** draw together in folds or wrinkles. **7** (often as **gathering** adj.) come to a head (*gathering storm*). **8** develop a purulent swelling. —n. fold or pleat. □ **gather up** bring together; pick up from the ground; draw into a small compass. [Old English]

gathering n. **1** assembly. **2** purulent swelling. **3** group of leaves taken together in bookbinding.

GATT /gæt/ abbr. General Agreement on Tariffs and Trade.

gauche /gəʊʃ/ adj. **1** socially awkward. **2** tactless. □ **gauchely** adv. **gaucheness** n. [French]

gaucherie /ˈgəʊʃəriː/ n. gauche manners or act. [French: related to GAUCHE]

gaucho /ˈgaʊtʃəʊ/ n. (pl. **-s**) cowboy from the S. American pampas. [Spanish from Quechua]

gaudy /ˈgɔːdɪ/ adj. (-ier, -iest) tastelessly showy. □ **gaudily** adv. **gaudiness** n. [obsolete *gaud* ornament, from Latin *gaudēre* rejoice]

gauge /ɡeɪdʒ/ (US **gage**: see also sense 6) —n. **1** standard measure, esp. of the capacity or contents of a barrel, fineness of a textile, diameter of a bullet, or thickness of sheet metal. **2** instrument for measuring pressure, width, length, thickness, etc. **3** distance between rails or opposite wheels. **4** capacity, extent. **5** criterion, test. **6** (usu. **gage**) Naut. position relative to the wind. —v. (**-ging**) **1** measure exactly. **2** measure the capacity or content of. **3** estimate (a person, situation, etc.). [French]

Gaul /ɡɔːl/ n. inhabitant of ancient Gaul. [French from Germanic]

Gaulish —adj. of the Gauls. —n. their language.

362

gaunt /gɔːnt/ *adj.* **1** lean, haggard. **2** grim, desolate. □ **gauntness** *n.* [origin unknown]

gauntlet[1] /ˈgɔːntlɪt/ *n.* **1** stout glove with a long loose wrist. **2** *hist.* armoured glove. □ **pick up** (or **take up**) **the gauntlet** accept a challenge. **throw down the gauntlet** issue a challenge. [French diminutive of *gant* glove]

gauntlet[2] /ˈgɔːntlɪt/ *n.* □ **run the gauntlet 1** undergo harsh criticism. **2** pass between two rows of people and receive blows from them, as a punishment or ordeal. [Swedish *gatlopp* from *gata* lane, *lopp* course]

gauss /gaus/ *n.* (*pl.* same) unit of magnetic flux density. [*Gauss*, name of a mathematician]

gauze /gɔːz/ *n.* **1** thin transparent fabric of silk, cotton, etc. **2** fine mesh of wire etc. □ **gauzy** *adj.* (**-ier, -iest**). [French from *Gaza* in Palestine]

gave *past* of GIVE.

gavel /ˈgæv(ə)l/ *n.* hammer used for calling attention by an auctioneer, chairman, or judge. [origin unknown]

gavotte /gəˈvɒt/ *n.* **1** old French dance. **2** music for this. [French from Provençal]

gawk –*v. colloq.* gawp. –*n.* awkward or bashful person. [obsolete *gaw* GAZE]

gawky *adj.* (**-ier, -iest**) awkward or ungainly. □ **gawkily** *adv.* **gawkiness** *n.*

gawp *v. colloq.* stare stupidly or obtrusively. [related to YELP]

gay –*adj.* **1** light-hearted, cheerful. **2** brightly coloured. **3** *colloq.* homosexual. **4** *colloq.* careless, thoughtless (*gay abandon*). –*n. colloq.* (esp. male) homosexual. □ **gayness** *n.* [French]

■ **Usage** Sense 3 is generally informal in tone, but is favoured by homosexual groups.

gayety US var. of GAIETY.

gaze –*v.* (**-zing**) (foll. by *at, into, on,* etc.) look fixedly. –*n.* intent look. [origin unknown]

gazebo /gəˈziːbəʊ/ *n.* (*pl.* **-s**) summer-house, turret, etc., with a wide view. [perhaps a fanciful formation from GAZE]

gazelle /gəˈzel/ *n.* (*pl.* same or **-s**) small graceful antelope. [Arabic *gazāl*]

gazette /gəˈzet/ –*n.* **1** newspaper (used esp. in the title). **2** official publication with announcements etc. –*v.* (**-tting**) announce or name in an official gazette. [French from Italian]

gazetteer /ˌgæzɪˈtɪə(r)/ *n.* geographical index. [Italian: related to GAZETTE]

gazpacho /gæˈspætʃəʊ/ *n.* (*pl.* **-s**) cold Spanish soup. [Spanish]

gazump /gəˈzʌmp/ *v. colloq.* **1** raise the price of a property after accepting an offer from (a buyer). **2** swindle. [origin unknown]

gazunder /gəˈzʌndə(r)/ *v. colloq.* lower an offer made to (a seller) for a property just before the exchange of contracts. [from GAZUMP, UNDER]

GB *abbr.* Great Britain.

GBH *abbr.* grievous bodily harm.

GC *abbr.* George Cross.

GCE *abbr.* General Certificate of Education.

GCHQ *abbr.* Government Communications Headquarters.

GCSE *abbr.* General Certificate of Secondary Education.

Gd *symb.* gadolinium.

GDP *abbr.* gross domestic product.

GDR *abbr. hist.* German Democratic Republic.

Ge *symb.* germanium.

gear –*n.* **1** (often in *pl.*) a set of toothed wheels that work together, esp. those connecting the engine of a vehicle to the road wheels. **b** particular setting of these (*first gear*). **2** equipment, apparatus, or tackle. **3** *colloq.* clothing. –*v.* **1** (often foll. by *to*) adjust or adapt to. **2** (often foll. by *up*) equip with gears. **3** (foll. by *up*) make ready or prepared. □ **in gear** with a gear engaged. **out of gear** with no gear engaged. [Old Norse]

gearbox *n.* **1** set of gears with its casing, esp. in a vehicle. **2** the casing itself.

gearing *n.* set or arrangement of gears.

gear lever *n.* (also **gear shift**) lever used to engage or change gear.

gearwheel *n.* toothed wheel in a set of gears.

gecko /ˈgekəʊ/ *n.* (*pl.* **-s**) tropical house-lizard. [Malay]

gee[1] *int.* (also **gee whiz** /wɪz/) esp. *US colloq.* expression of surprise etc. [perhaps an abbreviation of JESUS]

gee[2] *int.* (usu. foll. by *up*) command to a horse etc. to start or go faster. [origin unknown]

gee-gee /ˈdʒiːdʒiː/ *n. colloq.* (a child's word for) a horse.

geese *pl.* of GOOSE.

geezer /ˈgiːzə(r)/ *n. slang* person, esp. an old man. [dial. *guiser* mummer]

Geiger counter /ˈgaɪgə(r)/ *n.* device for detecting and measuring radioactivity. [*Geiger*, name of a physicist]

geisha /ˈgeɪʃə/ *n.* (*pl.* same or **-s**) Japanese woman trained to entertain men. [Japanese]

gel –*n.* **1** semi-solid jelly-like colloid. **2** jelly-like substance used for setting the hair. –*v.* (**-ll-**) **1** form a gel. **2** = JELL 2. [from GELATIN]

gelatin /ˈdʒelətɪn/ n. (also **gelatine** /-ˌtiːn/) transparent tasteless substance from skin, tendons, etc., used in cookery, photography, etc. □ **gelatinize** /dʒɪˈlætɪnaɪz/ v. (also -**ise**), (-**zing** or -**sing**). [Italian; related to JELLY]

gelatinous /dʒɪˈlætɪnəs/ adj. of a jelly-like consistency.

geld /geld/ v. castrate. [Old Norse]

gelding n. gelded animal, esp. a horse.

gelignite /ˈdʒelɪɡnaɪt/ n. explosive made from nitroglycerine. [from GELAT-IN, IGNEOUS]

gem n. **1** precious stone, esp. cut and polished or engraved. **2** thing or person of great beauty or worth. —v. (-**mm**-) adorn with or as with gems. [Latin *gemma* bud, jewel]

geminate —adj. /ˈdʒemɪnət/ combined in pairs. —v. /ˈdʒemɪneɪt/ (-**ting**) **1** double, repeat. **2** arrange in pairs. □ **gemination** /-ˈneɪʃ(ə)n/ n. [Latin related to GEMINI]

Gemini /ˈdʒemɪnaɪ/ n. (pl. -**s**) **1** constellation and third sign of the zodiac (the Twins). **2** person born when the sun is in this sign. [Latin, = twins]

gemma n. (pl. **gemmae** /-miː/) small cellular body in plants such as mosses, that separates a new one. □ **gemmation** /-ˈmeɪʃ(ə)n/ n. [Latin, see GEM]

gemstone n. precious stone used as a gem.

Gen. abbr. General.

gen slang —n. information. —v. (-**nn**-) [probably *general* information]

-gen comb. form Chem. that which produces (*hydrogen*; *antigen*). [Greek *-genes* born]

gender n. **1 a** classification roughly corresponding to the two sexes and sexlessness. **b** class of noun according to this classification (see MASCULINE, FEM-ININE, NEUTER). **2** a person's sex. [Latin GENUS]

gene /dʒiːn/ n. unit in a chromosome determining heredity. [German]

genealogy /dʒiːnɪˈælədʒɪ/ n. (pl. -**ies**) **1** descent traced continuously from an ancestor; pedigree. **2** study of pedigrees. **3** organism's line of development from earlier forms. □ **genealogical** /-əˈlɒdʒɪk(ə)l/ adj. **genealogically** adv. **genealogist** n.

general /ˈdʒen(ə)r(ə)l/ —adj. **1** including or affecting all or most parts or cases of things. **2** prevalent, usual (*the general*

feeling). **3** not partial or particular or local. **4** not limited in application, true of all or nearly all cases (*as a general rule*). **5** not restricted or specialized (*general knowledge*; *general hospital*). **6** not detailed (*general idea*). **7** vague (*spoke only in general terms*). **8** chief, head, having overall authority (*general manager*; *Secretary-General*). —n. **1 a** army officer next below Field Marshal. **b** = *lieutenant general* (see LIEUTENANT COLONEL). MAJOR-GENERAL. **2** commander of an army. **3** strategist (*a great general*). **4** head of a religious order, e.g. of Jesuits etc. □ **in general 1** as a normal rule; usually. **2** for the most part. [Latin *generalis*]

general anaesthetic n. anaesthetic affecting the whole body, usu. with loss of consciousness.

General Certificate of Education n. examination set esp. for secondary-school pupils at advanced level (and, formerly, ordinary level) in England, Wales and Northern Ireland.

General Certificate of Secondary Education n. examination replacing and combining the GCE ordinary level and CSE examinations.

general election n. national parliamentary election.

generalissimo /ˌdʒen(ə)rəˈlɪsɪməʊ/ n. (pl. -**s**) commander of a combined military and naval or air force, or of combined armies. [Italian superlative]

generality /ˌdʒenəˈrælɪtɪ/ n. (pl. -**ies**) **1** general statement or rule. **2** general applicability. **3** lack of detail. **4** (foll. by *of*) main body or majority.

generalize /ˈdʒenərəˌlaɪz/ v. (also -**ise**) (-**zing** or -**sing**) **1 a** speak in general or indefinite terms. **b** form general notions. **2** reduce to a general statement. **3** infer (a rule etc.) from particular cases. **4** bring into general use. □ **generalization** /-ˈzeɪʃ(ə)n/ n.

generally adv. **1** usually, in most respects or cases (*generally get up early*; *was generally well-behaved*). **2** in a general sense; without regard to particulars or exceptions (*generally speaking*). **3** for the most part (*not generally known*).

general meeting n. meeting open to all the members of a society etc.

general practice n. work of a general practitioner.

general practitioner n. community doctor treating cases of all kinds in the first instance.

general staff n. staff assisting a military commander at headquarters.

general strike n. simultaneous strike of workers in all or most trades.

generate /'dʒena,reit/ v. (-ting) bring into existence; produce. [Latin: related to GENUS]

generation /,dʒena'reiʃ(ə)n/ n. **1** all the people born at about the same time. **2** single stage in a family history (*three generations were present in the photograph*). **3** stage in (esp. technological development (*fourth-generation computers*). **4** average time in which children are ready to take the place of their parents (about 30 years). **5** production, esp. of electricity. **6** procreation. □ **first-** (or **second-, third-,** etc.) **generation** *attrib.* designating a person who emigrated to a place (or whose parents or grandparents etc. emigrated). [Latin: related to GENERATE]

generation gap n. differences of outlook between generations.

generative /'dʒenarətiv/ adj. **1** of procreation. **2** productive.

generator n. **1** machine for converting mechanical into electrical energy. **2** apparatus for producing gas, steam, etc.

generic /dʒi'nerik/ adj. **1** characteristic of or relating to a class; general, not specific or special. **2** *Biol.* characteristic of or belonging to a genus. □ **generically** adv. [Latin: related to GENUS]

generous /'dʒenaras/ adj. **1** giving freely. **2** magnanimous, unprejudiced. **3** abundant, copious. □ **generosity** /-'rɒsiti/ n. **generously** adv. [Latin: related to GENUS]

genesis /'dʒenisis/ n. **1** origin; mode of formation. **2** (**Genesis**) first book of the Old Testament, with an account of the Creation. [Greek *gen-* be produced]

gene therapy n. introduction of normal genes into cells in place of defective or missing ones in order to correct genetic disorders.

genetic /dʒi'netik/ adj. **1** of genetics or genes. **2** of or in origin. □ **genetically** adv. [from GENESIS]

genetic code n. arrangement of genetic information in chromosomes.

genetic engineering n. manipulation of DNA to modify hereditary features.

genetic fingerprinting n. (also **genetic profiling**) identifying individuals by DNA patterns.

genetics n.pl. (treated as *sing.*) the study of heredity and the variation of inherited characteristics. □ **geneticist** /-tisist/ n.

genial /'dʒi:nial/ adj. **1** jovial, sociable, kindly. **2** (of the climate) mild and warm; conducive to growth. **3** cheering. □ **geniality** /-'æliti/ n. **genially** adv. [Latin: related to GENIUS]

genie /'dʒi:ni/ n. (pl. **genii** /-ni,ai/) (in Arabian tales) spirit or goblin with

magical powers. [French *génie* GENIUS: cf. JINNEE]

genital /'dʒenit(ə)l/ adj. of animal reproduction or the reproductive organs. —n. (in *pl.*) external reproductive organs. [Latin *gigno geniti- beget*]

genitalia /,dʒen'teiliə/ n.pl. genitals. [Latin, neuter pl. of *genitalis*: see GENITAL]

genitive /'dʒenitiv/ *Gram.* —n. case expressing possession or close association, corresponding to *of, from,* etc. —adj. of or in this case. [Latin: related to GENTAL]

genius /'dʒi:nias/ n. (pl. **geniuses**) **1 a** exceptional intellectual or creative power or other natural ability or tendency. **b** person with this. **2** tutelary spirit of a person, place, etc. **3** person or spirit powerfully influencing a person for good or evil. **4** prevalent feeling or association etc. of a people or place. [Latin]

genocide /'dʒena,said/ n. deliberate extermination of a people or nation. □ **genocidal** /-'said(ə)l/ adj. [Greek *genos* race, -CIDE]

genome /'dʒi:nəum/ n. **1** the haploid set of chromosomes of an organism. **2** the genetic material of an organism.

-genous *comb. form* forming adjectives meaning 'produced' (*endogenous*).

genre /'ʒɑ̃rə/ n. **1** kind or style of art etc. **2** painting of scenes from ordinary life. [French: related to GENDER]

gent /dʒent/ n. *colloq.* **1** gentleman. **2** (**the Gents**) *colloq.* men's public lavatory. [shortening of GENTLEMAN]

genteel /dʒen'ti:l/ adj. **1** affectedly refined or stylish. **2** upper-class. □ **genteelly** adv. [French *gentil*: related to GENTLE]

gentian /'dʒenʃ(ə)n/ n. mountain plant usu. with blue flowers. [Latin *gentiana* from *Gentius*, king of Illyria]

Gentile /'dʒentail/ —adj. not Jewish; heathen. —n. person who is not Jewish. [Latin *gentilis* from *gens* family]

gentility /dʒen'tiliti/ n. **1** social superiority. **2** genteel manners or behaviour. [French: related to GENTLE]

gentle /'dʒent(ə)l/ adj. (**gentler, gentlest**) **1** not rough or severe; mild, kind (*a gentle nature*). **2** moderate (*gentle breeze*). **3** (of birth, pursuits, etc.) honourable, of or fit for gentlefolk. **4** quiet; requiring patience (*gentle art*). □ **gentleness** n. **gently** adv. [Latin: related to GENTLE]

gentlefolk n.pl. people of good family.

gentleman n. **1** man (in polite or formal use). **2** chivalrous well-bred man. **3** man of good social position (*country gentleman*). **4** man of gentle birth attached to a

royal household (*gentleman in waiting*). **5** (*in pl.*) (as a form of address) male audience or part of this.

gentleman.

gentleman's agreement *n.* (also **gentlemen's agreement**) agreement binding in honour but not enforceable.

gentlewoman *n. archaic* woman of good birth or breeding.

gentrification /ˌdʒentrɪfɪˈkeɪʃ(ə)n/ *n.* upgrading of a working-class urban area by the arrival of more affluent residents. □ **gentrify** /-faɪ/ *v.* (**-ies, -ied**).

gentry /ˈdʒentri/ *n.pl.* **1** people next below the nobility. **2** *derog.* people (*these gentry*). [French: related to GEN-TLE]

genuflect /ˈdʒenjuːflekt/ *v.* bend the knee, esp. in worship. □ **genuflection** /-ˈflekʃ(ə)n/ *n.* (also **genuflexion**). [Latin *genu* knee, *flecto* bend]

genuine /ˈdʒenjuːɪn/ *adj.* **1** really coming from its reputed source etc. **2** properly so called; not sham; sincere. □ **genuinely** *adv.* **genuineness** *n.* [Latin]

genus /ˈdʒiːnəs/ *n.* (*pl.* **genera** /ˈdʒenərə/) **1** taxonomic category of animals or plants with common structural characteristics, usu. containing several species. **2** (in logic) kind of things including subordinate kinds or species. **3** *colloq.* kind, class. [Latin *genus -eris*]

geo- *comb. form* earth. [Greek *gē*]

geocentric /ˌdʒiːəʊˈsentrɪk/ *adj.* **1** considered as viewed from the earth's centre. **2** having the earth as the centre. □ **geocentrically** *adv.*

geode /ˈdʒiːəʊd/ *n.* **1** cavity lined with crystals. **2** rock containing this. [Greek *geōdēs* earthy]

geodesic /ˌdʒiːəʊˈdiːzɪk/ *adj.* (also **geodetic** /-ˈdetɪk/) of geodesy. □ **geodesic line** *n.* shortest possible line between two points on a curved surface.

geodesy /dʒiːˈɒdɪsɪ/ *n.* the study of the shape and area of the earth. [Greek *geōdaisia*]

geographical /ˌdʒiːəˈɡræfɪk(ə)l/ *adj.* (also **geographic**) of geography. □ **geographically** *adv.*

geographical mile *n.* distance of one minute of longitude or latitude at the equator (about 1.85 km).

geography /dʒɪˈɒɡrəfɪ/ *n.* **1** science of the earth's physical features, resources, climate, population, etc. **2** features or arrangement of an area, rooms, etc. □ **geographer** *n.* [Latin from Greek]

geology /dʒɪˈɒlədʒɪ/ *n.* **1** science of the earth's crust, strata, origin of its rocks, etc. **2** geological features of a district. □

geological /ˌdʒɪəˈlɒdʒɪk(ə)l/ *adj.* **geologically** /ˌdʒɪəˈlɒdʒɪkəlɪ/ *adv.* **geologist** *n.*

Geordie /ˈdʒɔːdɪ/ *n.* native of Tyneside. [name *George*]

George Cross /dʒɔːdʒ/ *n.* decoration for bravery awarded esp. to civilians. [*George VI*]

georgette /dʒɔːˈdʒet/ *n.* thin dress-material similar to crêpe. [*Georgette de la Plante*, name of a dressmaker]

Georgian¹ /ˈdʒɔːdʒ(ə)n/ *adj.* of the time of Kings George I-IV or of George V and VI.

Georgian² /ˈdʒɔːdʒ(ə)n/ *—adj.* of Georgia in eastern Europe or the US. *—n.* **1** native or language of Georgia in eastern Europe. **2** native of Georgia in the US.

geranium /dʒɪˈreɪnɪəm/ *n.* (*pl.* **-s**) **1** (in general use) cultivated pelargonium. **2** herb or shrub bearing fruit shaped like a crane's bill. [Greek *geranos* crane]

gerbil /ˈdʒɜːbɪl/ *n.* (also **jerbil**) mouse-like desert rodent with long hind legs. [French: related to JERBOA]

geriatric /ˌdʒerɪˈætrɪk/ *—adj.* **1** of old people. **2** *colloq.* old, outdated. *—n.* old person. [Greek *gēras* old age, *iatros* doctor]

geriatrics *n.pl.* (usu. treated as *sing.*) branch of medicine or social science dealing with the health and care of old people. □ **geriatrician** /-əˈtrɪʃ(ə)n/ *n.*

germ *n.* **1** micro-organism, esp. one causing disease. **2** portion of an organism capable of developing into a new one; rudiment of an animal or plant in seed (*wheat germ*). **3** thing that may develop; elementary principle. □ **germy** *adj.* (**-ier, -iest**). [Latin *germen* sprout]

German /ˈdʒɜːmən/ *—n.* **1 a** native or national of Germany. **b** person of German descent. **2** language of Germany. *—adj.* of Germany, its people or language. [Latin *Germanus*]

german /ˈdʒɜːmən/ *adj.* (placed after *brother, sister, or cousin*) having both parents the same or both grandparents the same on one side (*brother german; cousin german*). [Latin *germanus*]

geometer /dʒɪˈɒmɪtə/ *n.*

geometric /ˌdʒɪəˈmetrɪk/ *adj.* (also **geometrical**) **1** of geometry. **2** (of a design etc.) with regular lines and shapes. □ **geometrically** *adv.*

geometric progression *n.* progression with a constant ratio between successive quantities, as 1, 3, 9, 27.

geometry /dʒɪˈɒmɪtrɪ/ *n.* science of the properties and relations of lines, surfaces, and solids. □ **geometrician** *n.*

geophysics /ˌdʒɪəʊˈfɪzɪks/ *n.pl.* (treated as *sing.*) physics of the earth. □ **geophysical** *adj.* **geophysicist** *n.*

germander /dʒɜː'mændə(r)/ n. plant of the mint family. [Greek, = ground-oak]

germane /dʒɜː'meɪn/ adj. (usu. foll. by to) relevant (to a subject). [var. of GERMAN]

Germanic /dʒɜː'mænɪk/ —adj. 1 having German characteristics. 2 hist. of the Germans. 3 of the Scandinavians, Anglo-Saxons, or Germans. —n. 1 the branch of Indo-European languages which includes English, German, Dutch, and the Scandinavian languages. 2 the primitive language of Germanic peoples. [related to GERMAN]

germanium /dʒɜː'meɪnɪəm/ n. brittle greyish-white semi-metallic element. [related to GERMAN]

German measles n.pl. disease like mild measles; rubella.

Germano- comb. form German.

German shepherd n. (also **German shepherd dog**) = ALSATIAN.

German silver n. white alloy of nickel, zinc, and copper.

germicide /'dʒɜːmɪsaɪd/ n. substance that destroys germs. □ **germicidal** /-'saɪd(ə)l/ adj.

germinal /'dʒɜːmɪn(ə)l/ adj. 1 of germs. 2 in the earliest stage of development. 3 productive of new ideas. □ **germinally** adv. [related to GERM]

germinate /'dʒɜːmɪˌneɪt/ v. (-ting) 1 sprout, bud, or develop. 2 cause to do this. □ **germination** /-'neɪʃ(ə)n/ n. **germinative** adj. [Latin: related to GERM]

germ warfare n. use of germs to spread disease in war.

gerontology /ˌdʒɛrɒn'tɒlədʒɪ/ n. the study of old age and the process of ageing. [Greek gerōn geront- old man]

gerrymander /'dʒɛrɪˌmændə(r)/ —v. manipulate the boundaries of (a constituency etc.) so as to give undue influence to some party or class. —n. this practice. [Governor Gerry of Massachusetts]

gerund /'dʒɛrənd/ n. verbal noun, in English ending in -ing (e.g. do you mind my asking you?). [Latin]

gesso /'dʒɛsəʊ/ n. (pl. -es) gypsum as used in painting or sculpture. [Italian: related to GYPSUM]

Gestapo /ge'stɑːpəʊ/ n. hist. Nazi secret police. [German, from Geheime Staatspolizei]

gestation /dʒe'steɪʃ(ə)n/ n. 1 a process of carrying or being carried in the uterus between conception and birth. b this period. 2 development of a plan, idea, etc. □ **gestate** v. (-ting). [Latin gesto carry]

gesticulate /dʒe'stɪkjʊˌleɪt/ v. (-ting) 1 use gestures instead of, or to reinforce, speech. 2 express thus. □ **gesticulation** /-'leɪʃ(ə)n/ n. [Latin: related to GESTURE]

gesture /'dʒɛstʃə(r)/ —n. 1 significant movement of a limb or the body. 2 use of such movements, esp. as a rhetorical device. 3 action to evoke a response or convey intention, usu. friendly. —v. (-ring) gesticulate. [Latin gestura from gero wield]

get /get/ v. (getting; past got; past part. got or US gotten) (and in comb.) 1 come into possession of; receive or earn (get a job; got £200 a week; got first prize). 2 fetch or procure (get my book for me; got a new car). 3 go to reach or catch (a bus, train, etc.). 4 prepare (a meal etc.). 5 (cause to) reach some state or become (get rich; get married; get to be famous; got them ready; got him into trouble). 6 obtain as a result of calculation. 7 contract (a disease etc.). 8 establish contact by telephone etc. with; receive (a broadcast signal). 9 experience or suffer; have inflicted on one; receive as one's lot or penalty (got four years in prison). 10 a succeed in bringing, placing, etc. (get it round the corner; get it on to the agenda). b (cause to) succeed in coming or going (will get you there somehow; got absolutely nowhere; got home). 11 (prec. by have) a possess (have not got a penny). b (foll. by to + infin.) be bound or obliged (have got to see you). 12 (foll. by to + infin.) induce; prevail upon (got them to help me). 13 colloq. understand (a person or an argument) (have you got that?; I get your point; do you get me?). 14 colloq. harm, injure, kill, etc. in retaliation (I'll get you for that). 15 colloq. a annoy. b affect emotionally. c attract. 16 (foll. by to + infin.) develop an inclination (am getting to like it). 17 (foll. by verbal noun) begin (get going). 18 establish (an idea etc.) in one's mind. 19 archaic beget. □ **get about 1** travel extensively or fast; go from place to place. 2 begin walking etc. (esp. after illness). **get across 1** communicate (an idea etc.). 2 (of an idea etc.) be communicated. **get ahead** make progress (esp. in a career etc.). **get along** (or **on**) (foll. by together, with) live harmoniously. **get around** = get about. **get at 1** reach; get hold of. 2 colloq. imply. 3 colloq. nag, criticize. **get away 1** escape. start. 2 (as int.) colloq. expressing disbelief or scepticism. 3 (foll. by with) escape blame or punishment for. **get back at** colloq. retaliate against. **get by** colloq. manage, even if with difficulty. **get cracking** see CRACK. **get down 1** alight, descend (from a vehicle, ladder, etc.). 2 record in writing. **get a person down** depress or deject him or her. **get down to** begin

working on. **get hold of** grasp, secure, acquire, obtain; make contact with (a person). **get in 1** arrive; make contact in a college etc. **2** be elected. **get it** *slang* be punished. **get off 1** *colloq.* (cause to) be acquitted; escape with little or no punishment. **2** start. **3** alight from (a bus etc.). **4** (foll. by *with*, *together*) *colloq.* form an amorous or sexual relationship. **get on 1** make progress; esp. manage. **2** enter (a bus etc.). **3** = *get along*. **4** (usu. as **getting on** adj.) grow old. **get on to** *colloq.* **1** make contact with. **2** understand; become aware of. **get out 1** leave or escape or help to do this. **2** manage to go outdoors. **3** alight from a vehicle. **4** transpire; become known. **get out of** avoid or escape (a duty etc.). **get over 1** recover from (an illness, upset, etc.). **2** overcome (a difficulty). **3** = *get across*. **get a thing over (or over with)** complete (a tedious task) quickly. **get one's own back** *colloq.* have one's revenge. **get rid of** see *rid*. **get round 1** coax or cajole (a person) esp. to secure a favour. **2** evade (a law etc.). **get round to** deal with (a task etc.) in due course. **get somewhere** make progress; be initially successful. **get there** *colloq.* **1** succeed. **2** understand what is meant. **get through 1** pass (an examination etc.). **2** finish or use up (esp. resources). **3** make contact by telephone. **4** (foll. by *to*) succeed in making (a person) understand. **get together** gather, assemble. **get up 1** rise from sitting etc., or from bed after sleeping etc. **2** (of wind etc.) begin to be strong. **3** prepare or organize. **4** produce or stimulate (*get up steam*). **5** (often *refl.*) dress or arrange elaborately; arrange the appearance of. **6** (foll. by *to*) *colloq.* indulge or be involved in (*always get- ting up to mischief*). [Old Norse]

get-at-able /getˈatəb(ə)l/ *adj. colloq.* accessible.

getaway *n.* escape, esp. after a crime.

get-out *n.* means of avoiding some- thing.

get-together *n. colloq.* social gather- ing.

get-up *n. colloq.* style or arrangement of dress etc.

get-up-and-go *n. colloq.* energy, en- thusiasm.

geyser /ˈgiːzə(r)/ *n.* **1** intermittent hot spring. **2** apparatus for heating water. [Icelandic *Geysir* from *geysa* to gush]

ghastly /ˈgɑːstlɪ/ *adj.* (-ier, -iest) **1** hor- rible, frightful. **2** *colloq.* unpleasant. **3** deathlike, pallid. □ **ghastliness** *n.*

ghee /giː/ *n.* Indian clarified butter. [Hindi from Sanskrit]

gherkin /ˈgɜːkɪn/ *n.* small pickled cucumber. [Dutch]

ghetto /ˈgetəʊ/ *n.* (*pl.* -s) **1** part of a city occupied by a minority group. **2** *hist.* Jewish quarter in a city. **3** segregated group or area. [Italian]

ghetto-blaster *n. slang* large portable radio, esp. for playing loud pop music.

ghillie var. of GILLIE.

ghost /gəʊst/ —*n.* **1** supposed apparition of a dead person or animal; disembodied spirit. **2** shadow or semblance (*not a ghost of a chance*). **3** secondary image in a defective telescope or television pic- ture. —*v.* (often foll. by *for*) act as ghost- writer of (a work). □ **ghostliness** *n.*

ghostly *adj.* (-ier, -iest) of, like, or char- acteristic of a 'ghost'. [Old English]

ghost town *n.* town with few or no remaining inhabitants.

ghost train *n.* (at a funfair) open- topped miniature railway in which the rider experiences ghoulish sights, sounds, etc.

ghost-writer *n.* person who writes on behalf of the credited author.

ghoul /guːl/ *n.* **1** person morbidly interested in death etc. **2** evil spirit or phantom. **3** spirit in Muslim folklore preying on corpses. □ **ghoulish** *adj.* **ghoulishly** *adv.* [Arabic]

ghyll var. of GILL³.

GHQ *abbr.* General Headquarters.

GI /dʒiːˈaɪ/ *n.* (often *attrib.*) soldier in the US army. [abbreviation of *government issue*]

giant /ˈdʒaɪənt/ —*n.* **1** (*fem.* **giantess**) imaginary or mythical being of human form but superhuman size. **2** person or thing of great size, ability, courage, etc. —*attrib. adj.* **1** gigantic. **2** of a very large kind. [Greek *gigas gigant-*]

gibber *v.* jabber inarticulately. [limit- ative]

gibberish *n.* unintelligible or meaning- less speech; nonsense.

gibbet /ˈdʒɪbɪt/ —*n. hist.* **1 a** gallows. **b** post with an arm on which an executed criminal was hung. **2** (prec. by *the*) death by hanging. —*v.* (-t-) **1** put to death by hanging. **2** expose or hang up on a gibbet. [French *gibet*]

gibbon /ˈgɪbən/ *n.* long-armed SE Asian anthropoid ape. [French]

gibbous /ˈgɪbəs/ *adj.* **1** convex. **2** (of a moon or planet) having the bright part greater than a semicircle and less than a circle. **3** humpbacked. [Latin *gibbus* hump]

gibe (also **jibe**) —*v.* (-**bing**) (often foll. by *at*) jeer; mock. —*n.* jeering remark, taunt. [perhaps from French *giber* handle roughly]

giblets /dʒɪblɪts/ n.pl. edible organs etc. of a bird, removed and usu. cooked separately. [French *gibelet* game stew]

giddy /gɪdɪ/ adj. (-ier, -iest) 1 dizzy, tending to fall or stagger. 2 a mentally intoxicated (*giddy with success*). b excitable, frivolous, flighty. 3 making dizzy (*giddy heights*). □ **giddily** adv. **giddiness** n. [Old English]

gift /gɪft/ n. 1 thing given; present. 2 natural ability or talent. 3 the power to give (*in his gift*). 4 giving. 5 *colloq.* easy task. [Old Norse: related to GIVE]

gifted adj. talented; intelligent.

gift of the gab n. *colloq.* eloquence, loquacity.

gift token n. (also **gift voucher**) voucher used as a gift and exchangeable for goods.

gift-wrap v. wrap attractively as a gift.

gig¹ /gɪg/ n. 1 light two-wheeled one-horse carriage. 2 light ship's boat for rowing or sailing. 3 rowing-boat esp. for racing. [probably imitative]

gig² /gɪg/ *colloq.* —n. engagement to play music etc., usu. for one night. —v. (-gg-) perform a gig. [origin unknown]

giga- *comb. form* one thousand million (10⁹). [Greek: related to GIANT]

gigantic /dʒaɪˈgæntɪk/ adj. huge, giant-like. □ **gigantically** adv. [Latin: related to GIANT]

giggle /gɪg(ə)l/ —v. (-ling) laugh in half-suppressed spasms. —n. 1 such a laugh. 2 *colloq.* amusing person or thing; joke (*did it for a giggle*). □ **giggly** adj. (-ier, -iest). [imitative]

gigolo /ˈʒɪgələʊ/ n. (pl. -s) young man paid by an older woman to be her escort or lover. [French]

gild¹ /gɪld/ v. (*past part.* **gilded** or as adj. in sense 1 **gilt**) 1 cover thinly with gold. 2 tinge with a golden colour. 3 give a false brilliance to. □ **gild the lily** try to improve what is already satisfactory. [Old English: related to GOLD]

gild² var. of GUILD.

gill¹ /gɪl/ n. (usu. in *pl.*) 1 respiratory organ in a fish etc. 2 vertical radial plate on the underside of a mushroom etc. 3 flesh below a person's jaws and ears. [Old Norse]

gill² /dʒɪl/ n. unit of liquid measure equal to ¼ pint. [French]

gill³ /gɪl/ n. (also **ghyll**) 1 deep usu. wooded ravine. 2 narrow mountain torrent. [Old Norse]

gillie /ˈgɪlɪ/ n. (also **ghillie**) *Scot.* man or boy attending a person hunting or fishing. [Gaelic]

gillyflower /ˈdʒɪlɪˌflaʊə(r)/ n. clove-scented flower, e.g. a wallflower or the clove-scented pink. [French *giloſre*]

gilt¹ /gɪlt/ —adj. 1 thinly covered with gold. 2 gold-coloured. —n. 1 gilding. 2 gilt-edged security. [from GILD¹]

gilt² /gɪlt/ n. young sow. [Old Norse]

gilt-edged adj. (of securities, stocks, etc.) having a high degree of reliability.

gimbals /ˈdʒɪmb(ə)lz/ n.pl. contrivance of rings and pivots for keeping instruments horizontal in ships, aircraft, etc. [var. of *gimmal* from French *gemel* double finger-ring]

gimcrack /ˈdʒɪmkræk/ —adj. showy but flimsy and worthless. —n. showy ornament; knick-knack. [origin unknown]

gimlet /ˈgɪmlɪt/ n. small tool with a screw-tip for boring holes. [French]

gimlet eye n. eye with a piercing glance.

gimmick /ˈgɪmɪk/ n. trick or device, esp. to attract attention or publicity. □ **gimmickry** n. **gimmicky** adj. [origin unknown]

gimp /gɪmp/ n. (also **gymp**) 1 twist of silk etc. with cord or wire running through it. 2 fishing-line of silk etc. bound with wire. [Dutch]

gin¹ n. spirit made from grain or malt and flavoured with juniper berries. [Dutch *geneva*: related to JUNIPER]

gin² —n. 1 snare, trap. 2 machine separating cotton from its seeds. 3 a kind of crane and windlass. —v. (-nn-) 1 treat (cotton) in a gin. 2 trap. [French: related to ENGINE]

ginger /ˈdʒɪndʒə(r)/ —n. 1 a hot spicy root usu. powdered for use in cooking, or preserved in syrup, or candied. b plant having this root. 2 light reddish-yellow. 3 spirit, mettle. —adj. of a ginger colour. —v. 1 flavour with ginger. 2 (foll. by *up*) enliven. □ **gingery** adj. [Old English and French, ultimately from Sanskrit]

ginger ale n. ginger-flavoured non-alcoholic drink.

ginger beer n. mildly alcoholic or non-alcoholic cloudy drink made from fermented ginger and syrup.

gingerbread —n. ginger-flavoured treacle cake. —attrib. adj. gaudy, tawdry.

ginger group n. group urging a party or movement to stronger policy or action.

gingerly —adv. in a careful or cautious manner. —adj. showing great care or caution. [perhaps from French *gensor* delicate]

ginger-nut n. ginger-flavoured biscuit.

gingham /ˈgɪŋəm/ n. plain-woven cotton cloth, esp. striped or checked. [Dutch from Malay]

gingivitis /ˌdʒɪndʒɪˈvaɪtɪs/ n. inflamma-tion of the gums. [Latin *gingiva* GUM², -ITIS]

ginkgo /ˈɡɪŋkgəʊ/ n. (pl. -s) tree with fan-shaped leaves and yellow flowers. [Chinese, = silver apricot]

ginormous /dʒaɪˈnɔːməs/ adj. slang enormous. [from GIANT, ENORMOUS]

gin rummy n. form of the card-game rummy.

ginseng /ˈdʒɪnseŋ/ n. 1 plant found in E. Asia and N. America. 2 root of this used as a medicinal tonic. [Chinese]

gippy tummy /ˈdʒɪpɪ/ n. colloq. dia-rrhoea affecting visitors to hot coun-tries. [from EGYPTIAN]

Gipsy var. of GYPSY.

giraffe /dʒɪˈrɑːf/ n. (pl. same or -s) large four-legged African animal with a long neck and forelegs. [French, ultimately from Arabic]

gird /ɡɜːd/ v. (past and past part. **girded** or **girt**) 1 encircle, attach, or secure with a belt or band. 2 enclose or en-circle. 3 (foll. by *round*) place (a cord etc.) round. □ **gird** (or **gird up) one's loins** prepare for action. [Old English]

girder n. iron or steel beam or com-pound structure for bridge-building etc. [from GIRD]

girdle¹ /ˈɡɜːd(ə)l/ —n. 1 belt or cord worn round the waist. 2 corset. 3 thing that surrounds. 4 bony support for the limbs (*pelvic girdle*). —v. (-**ling**) surround with a girdle. [Old English]

girdle² /ˈɡɜːd(ə)l/ n. Scot. & N.Engl. var. of GRIDDLE.

girl /ɡɜːl/ n. 1 female child, daughter. 2 colloq. young woman. 3 colloq. girl-friend. 4 female servant. □ **girlhood** n. **girlish** adj. **girly** adj. [origin uncer-tain]

girl Friday n. female helper or fol-lower.

girlfriend n. 1 person's regular female companion or lover. 2 female friend.

Girl Guide n. = GUIDE n. 8.

girlie adj. colloq. (of a magazine etc.) depicting young women in erotic poses.

girl scout n. = SCOUT n. 4.

giro /ˈdʒaɪrəʊ/ —n. (pl. -s) 1 system of credit transfer between banks, Post Offices, etc. 2 cheque or payment by giro. —v. (-es, -ed) pay by giro. [German from Italian]

girt see GIRD.

girth /ɡɜːθ/ n. 1 distance round a thing. 2 band round the body of a horse to secure the saddle etc. [Old Norse: related to GIRD]

gismo /ˈɡɪzməʊ/ n. (also **gizmo**) (pl. -s) slang gadget. [origin unknown]

gist n. substance or essence of a matter. [Latin *jaceo* LIE¹]

git /ɡɪt/ n. slang silly or contemptible person. [get (noun), = fool]

gîte /ʒiːt/ n. furnished holiday house in the French countryside. [French]

give /ɡɪv/ —v. (-**ving**; past **gave**; past part. **given** /ˈɡɪv(ə)n/) 1 transfer the possession of freely; hand over as a present; donate. 2 a transfer tempor-arily; provide with (*gave him the dog to hold*; *gave her a new hip*) b administer (*medicine*). c deliver (a message) 3 (usu. foll. by *for*) make over in exchange or payment. 4 a confer, grant (a benefit, honour, etc.). b accord; bestow (love, time, etc.). c pledge (*gave his word*). 5 a perform (an action etc.) (*gave a jump*; *gave a performance*; *gave an inter-view*). b utter; declare (*gave a shriek*; foll. by *to*; be inclined to or fond of (*is given to boasting*; *is given to strong drink*). 7 yield as a product or result (*gives an average of 7*). 8 (in *passive*; foll. by *to*) be inclined to or fond of (*is given to boasting*; *is given to strong drink*). 9 a consign, put (*gave him into custody*). b sanction the marriage of (a daughter etc.). 10 devote; dedicate (*gave his life to the cause*). 11 present, offer; show; hold out (*gives no sign of life*; *gave her his arm*; *give me an example*). 12 impart, be a source of, cause (*gave me a cold*; *gave me trouble*; *gave much pain*). 13 concede (*I give you that point*). 14 deliver (a judgement etc.) authoritatively. 15 pro-vide (a party, meal etc.) as host. 16 (in past part.) assume or grant or specify (*given the circumstances*; *in a given situation*; *given that we earn so little*). 17 (*absol.*) colloq. tell what one knows. —n. capacity to yield or comply; elasti-city. □ **give and take** v. 1 exchange (words, ideas, blows, etc.). 2 ability to compromise. **give away 1** transfer as a gift. 2 hand over (a bride) to a bride-groom. 3 reveal (a secret etc.). **give the game** (or **show**) **away** reveal a secret or intention. **give in 1** yield; acknowledge defeat. 2 hand in (a document etc.) to an official etc. **give it to** a person colloq. scold or punish. **give me** I prefer (*give me Greece any day*). **give off** emit (fumes etc.). **give oneself up to 1** aban-don oneself to (despair etc.). 2 addict oneself to. **give on to** (or **into**) (of a window, corridor, etc.) overlook or lead into. **give over** or take colloq. accepting as a margin of error in estimating. **give out 1** announce; emit; distribute. 2 be exhausted. 3 run short. **give over 1** colloq. stop or desist. 2 hand over. 3 devote. **give rise to** cause. **give a per-son to understand** inform or assure. **give up 1** resign; surrender. 2 part with. 3 deliver (a wanted person etc.). 4 pronounce incurable or insoluble; renounce hope of. 5 renounce or cease

give-away

(an activity). **give way** yield under pressure, give precedence. **not give a damn** (or **monkey's** or **toss** etc.) *colloq.* not care at all. □ **giver** *n.* [Old English]

give-away *n. colloq.* **1** unintentional revelation. **2** thing given as a gift or at a low price.

gizmo var. of GISMO.

gizzard /ˈgɪzəd/ *n.* **1** second part of a bird's stomach, for grinding food. **2** muscular stomach of some fish etc. [French]

glacé /ˈglæseɪ/ *adj.* **1** (of fruit, esp. cherries) preserved in sugar. **2** (of cloth etc.) smooth; polished. [French]

glacé icing *n.* icing made with icing sugar and water.

glacial /ˈgleɪʃ(ə)l/ *adj.* **1** of ice. **2** *Geol.* characterized or produced by ice. [Latin *glacies* ice]

glacial period *n.* period when an exceptionally large area was covered by ice.

glaciated /ˈgleɪsɪˌeɪtɪd/ *adj.* **1** marked or polished by the action of ice. **2** covered by glaciers or ice sheets. □ **glaciation** /ˌgleɪsɪˈeɪʃ(ə)n/ *n.* [*glaciate* freeze, from Latin: related to GLACIAL]

glacier /ˈglæsɪə(r)/ *n.* mass of land ice formed by the accumulation of snow on high ground. [French: related to GLACIAL]

glad *adj.* (**gladder**, **gladdest**) **1** (*predic.*) pleased. **2** expressing or causing pleasure (*glad cry; glad news*). **3** ready and willing (*am glad to help*). □ **be glad of** find useful. □ **gladly** *adv.* **gladness** *n.* [Old English]

gladden /ˈglæd(ə)n/ *v.* make or become glad.

glade *n.* open space in a forest. [origin unknown]

glad eye *n.* (prec. by *the*) *colloq.* amorous glance.

glad hand *n. colloq.* hearty welcome.

gladiator /ˈglædɪˌeɪtə(r)/ *n. hist.* trained fighter in ancient Roman shows. □ **gladiatorial** /ˌglædɪəˈtɔːrɪəl/ *adj.* [Latin *gladius* sword]

gladiolus /ˌglædɪˈəʊləs/ *n.* (*pl.* **-li** /-laɪ/) plant of the lily family with sword-shaped leaves and flower-spikes. [Latin, diminutive of *gladius* sword]

glad rags *n.pl. colloq.* best clothes.

gladsome *adj. poet.* cheerful, joyous.

Gladstone bag /ˈglædst(ə)n/ *n.* bag with two compartments joined by a hinge. [*Gladstone*, name of a statesman]

glair *n.* **1** white of egg. **2** adhesive preparation made from this. [French]

glam *adj. colloq.* glamorous. [abbreviation]

glamorize /ˈglæməˌraɪz/ *v.* (also **-ise**) (**-zing** or **-sing**) make glamorous or attractive.

glamour /ˈglæmə(r)/ *n.* (*US* **glamor**) **1** physical, esp. cosmetic, attractiveness. **2** alluring or exciting beauty or charm. □ **glamorous** *adj.* **glamorously** *adv.* [var. of GRAMMAR in obsolete sense 'magic']

glance /glɑːns/ *v.* (**-cing**) **1** (often foll. by *down, up, over*, etc.) look briefly, direct one's eye. **2** strike at an angle and glide off an object (*glancing blow; ball glanced off his bat*). **3** (usu. foll. by *over*) refer briefly or indirectly to a subject or subjects. **4** (of light etc.) flash or dart. —*n.* **1** brief look. **2** flash or gleam. **3** glancing stroke in cricket. □ **at a glance** immediately upon looking. [origin uncertain]

gland *n.* **1** organ or similar structure secreting substances for use in the body or for ejection. **2** *Bot.* similar organ in a plant. [Latin *glandulae* pl.]

glanders /ˈglændəz/ *n.pl.* contagious disease of horses. [French *glandre*: related to GLAND]

glandular /ˈglændjʊlə(r)/ *adj.* of a gland or glands.

glandular fever *n.* infectious disease with swelling of the lymph glands.

glare —*v.* (**-ring**) **1** look fiercely or fixedly. **2** shine dazzlingly or oppressively. —*n.* **1** a strong fierce light, esp. sunshine. **b** oppressive public attention (*glare of publicity*). **2** fierce or fixed look. **3** tawdry brilliance. [Low German or Dutch]

glaring *adj.* **1** obvious, conspicuous (*glaring error*). **2** shining oppressively. □ **glaringly** *adv.*

glasnost /ˈglæznɒst/ *n.* (in the former Soviet Union) policy of more open government and access to information. [Russian, = openness]

glass /glɑːs/ —*n.* **1 a** (often *attrib.*) hard, brittle, usu. transparent substance, made by fusing sand with soda and lime etc. **b** substance of similar properties. **2** glass objects collectively. **3 a** glass drinking vessel. **b** its contents. **4** mirror. **5** glazed frame for plants. **6** barometer. **7** covering of a watch-face. **8** lens. **9** (in *pl.*) **a** spectacles. **b** binoculars. —*v.* (usu. as **glassed** *adj.*) fit with glass. □ **glassful** *n.* (*pl.* **-s**). [Old English]

glass-blowing *n.* blowing semi-molten glass to make glassware.

glass fibre *n.* filaments of glass made into fabric or embedded in plastic as reinforcement.

glasshouse *n.* **1** greenhouse. **2** *slang* military prison.

glass-paper *n.* paper coated with glass particles, for smoothing and polishing.

glassware *n.* articles made of glass.

glass wool *n.* mass of fine glass fibres for packing and insulation.

glassy *adj.* (-ier, -iest) 1 like glass. 2 (of the eye, expression, etc.) abstracted; dull; fixed.

Glaswegian /glæzˈwiːdʒ(ə)n/ —*adj.* of Glasgow. —*n.* native of Glasgow. [after *Norwegian*]

glaucoma /ɡɔːˈkəʊmə/ *n.* eye-condition with increased pressure in the eyeball and gradual loss of sight. □ **glaucomatous** *adj.* [Greek *glaukos* greyish blue]

glaze —*v.* (-zing) 1 fit (a window etc.) with glass or (a building) with windows. 2 a cover (pottery etc.) with a glaze. b fix (paint) on pottery thus. 3 cover (pastry, cloth, etc.) with a glaze. 4 (often foll. by over) (of the eyes) become glassy. 5 give a glassy surface to. —*n.* 1 vitreous substance for glazing pottery. 2 smooth shiny coating on food etc. 3 thin coat of transparent paint to modify underlying tone. 4 surface formed by glazing. [from GLASS]

glazier /ˈɡleɪzɪə(r)/ *n.* person whose trade is glazing windows etc.

gleam —*n.* faint or brief light or show. —*v.* emit gleams, shine. [Old English]

glean *v.* 1 acquire (facts etc.) in small amounts. 2 gather (corn left by reapers). [French]

gleanings *n.pl.* things gleaned, esp. facts.

glebe *n.* piece of land as part of a clergyman's benefice and providing income. [Latin *gleba* clod, soil]

glee *n.* 1 mirth; delight. 2 part-song for three or more (esp. male) voices. [Old English]

gleeful *adj.* joyful. □ **gleefully** *adv.* **gleefulness** *n.*

glen *n.* narrow valley. [Gaelic]

glengarry /ɡlenˈɡærɪ/ *n.* (*pl.* -ies) brimless Scottish hat cleft down the centre and with ribbons at the back. [*Glengarry* in Scotland]

glib *adj.* (**glibber, glibbest**) speaking or spoken quickly or fluently but without sincerity. □ **glibly** *adv.* **glibness** *n.* [obsolete *glibbery* slippery, perhaps imitative]

glide —*v.* (**-ding**) 1 move smoothly and continuously. 2 (of an aircraft or pilot) fly without engine-power. 3 pass gradually or imperceptibly. 4 go stealthily. 5 cause to glide. —*n.* gliding movement. [Old English]

glide path *n.* aircraft's line of descent to land.

glider *n.* light aircraft without an engine.

glimmer —*v.* shine faintly or intermittently. —*n.* 1 feeble or wavering light. 2 (also **glimmering**) (usu. foll. by *of*) small sign (of hope etc.). [probably Scandinavian]

glimpse —*n.* (often foll. by *of, at*) 1 brief view or look. 2 faint transient appearance (*glimpses of the truth*). —*v.* (**-sing**) have a brief view of (*glimpsed his face in the crowd*). [related to GLIMMER]

glint —*v.* flash, glitter. —*n.* flash, sparkle. [probably Scandinavian]

glissade /ɡlɪsɑːd/ —*n.* 1 controlled slide down a snow slope in mountaineering. 2 gliding step in ballet. —*v.* (**-ding**) perform a glissade. [French]

glissando /ɡlɪˈsændəʊ/ *n.* (*pl.* -di/-di/ or -s) *Mus.* continuous slide of adjacent notes. [French *glissant* sliding; related to GLISSADE]

glisten —*v.* shine like a wet or polished surface. —*n.* glitter, sparkle. [Old English]

glitch *n. colloq.* sudden irregularity or malfunction (of equipment etc.). [origin unknown]

glitter —*v.* 1 shine with a bright reflected light; sparkle. 2 (usu. foll. by *with*) be showy or splendid. —*n.* 1 sparkle. 2 showiness. 3 tiny pieces of sparkling material as decoration etc. □ **glittery** *adj.* [Old Norse]

glitterati /ɡlɪtəˈrɑːtiː/ *n.pl. slang* rich fashionable people. [from GLITTER, LITERATI]

glitz *n. slang* showy glamour. □ **glitzy** *adj.* (**-ier, -iest**) [from GLITTER, RITZY]

gloaming /ˈɡləʊmɪŋ/ *n. Scot.* or *poet.* twilight. [Old English]

gloat —*v.* (often foll. by *over* etc.) look or consider with greed, malice, etc. —*n.* act of gloating. [origin unknown]

glob *n. colloq.* mass or lump of semi-liquid substance, e.g. mud. [perhaps from BLOB, GOB]

global /ˈɡləʊb(ə)l/ *adj.* 1 worldwide (*global conflict*). 2 all-embracing. □ **globally** *adv.* [related to GLOBE]

global warming *n.* increase in the temperature of the earth's atmosphere caused by the greenhouse effect.

globe *n.* 1 a (prec. by *the*) the earth. b spherical representation of it with a map on the surface. 2 spherical object, e.g. a fish-bowl, lamp, etc. [Latin *globus*]

globe artichoke *n.* the partly edible head of the artichoke plant.

globe-trotter *n. colloq.* person who travels widely. □ **globe-trotting** *n.* & *attrib.adj.*

globular /ˈɡlɒbjʊlə(r)/ *adj.* 1 globe-shaped. 2 composed of globules.

globule /ˈɡlɒbjuːl/ *n.* small globe or round particle or drop. [Latin *globulus*]

globulin /ˈglɒbjʊlɪn/ n. molecule-transporting protein in plant and animal tissues.

glockenspiel /ˈglɒkənˌspiːl/ n. musical instrument with bells or metal bars or tubes struck by hammers. [German, = bell-play]

gloom n. 1 darkness; obscurity. 2 melancholy; despondency. [origin unknown]

gloomy adj. (-ier, -iest) 1 dark; unlit. 2 depressed or depressing. □ **gloomily** adv. **gloominess** n.

glorify /ˈglɔːrɪfaɪ/ v. (-ies, -ied) 1 make glorious. 2 make seem better or more splendid than it is. 3 (as **glorified** adj.) invested with more attractiveness, importance, etc. than it has in reality (glorified waitress). 4 extol. □ **glorification** /-fɪˈkeɪʃ(ə)n/ n. [Latin: related to GLORY]

glorious /ˈglɔːrɪəs/ adj. 1 possessing or conferring glory; illustrious. 2 colloq. often iron. splendid, excellent (glorious day; glorious muddle). □ **gloriously** adv.

glory /ˈglɔːrɪ/ —n. (pl. -ies) 1 renown, honour. 2 adoring praise. 3 resplendent majesty, beauty, etc. 4 thing that brings renown, distinction, or pride. 5 heavenly bliss and splendour. 6 colloq. state of exaltation, prosperity, etc. 7 halo of a saint etc. —v. (-ies, -ied) (often foll. by in) pride oneself. [Latin gloria]

glory-hole n. colloq. untidy room, cupboard, etc.

gloss[1] —n. 1 surface shine or lustre. 2 deceptively attractive appearance. 3 (in full **gloss paint**) paint giving a glossy finish. —v. make glossy. □ **gloss over** seek to conceal, esp. by mentioning only briefly. [origin unknown]

gloss[2] —n. 1 explanatory comment added to a text, e.g. in the margin. 2 interpretation or paraphrase. —v. add a gloss to (a text, word, etc.). [Latin glossa tongue]

glossary /ˈglɒsərɪ/ n. (pl. -ies) 1 list or dictionary of technical or special words. 2 collection of glosses. [Latin: related to GLOSS[2]]

glossy —adj. (-ier, -iest) 1 smooth and shiny (glossy paper). 2 printed on such paper. —n. (pl. -ies) colloq. glossy magazine or photograph. □ **glossily** adv. **glossiness** n.

glottal /ˈglɒt(ə)l/ adj. of the glottis.

glottal stop n. sound produced by the sudden opening or shutting of the glottis.

glottis /ˈglɒtɪs/ n. opening at the upper end of the windpipe and between the vocal cords. [Greek]

Gloucester /ˈglɒstə(r)/ n. (usu. **double Gloucester**, orig. a richer kind) cheese made in Gloucestershire. [Gloucester in England]

glove /glʌv/ —n. 1 hand-covering for protection, warmth, etc., usu. with separate fingers. 2 boxing glove. —v. (-ving) cover or provide with gloves. [Old English]

glove compartment n. recess for small articles in the dashboard of a car etc.

glove puppet n. small puppet fitted on the hand and worked by the fingers.

glover n. glove-maker.

glow /glaʊ/ —v. 1 a emit light and heat without flame. b shine as if heated in this way. 2 (often foll. by with) a (of the body) be heated. b show or feel strong emotion (glowed with pride). 3 show a warm colour. 4 (as **glowing** adj.) expressing pride or satisfaction (glowing report). —n. 1 glowing state. 2 bright warm colour. 3 feeling of satisfaction or well-being. [Old English]

glower /ˈglaʊə(r)/ —v. 1 (often foll. by at) look angrily. 2 look dark or threatening. —n. glowering look. [origin uncertain]

glow-worm n. beetle whose wingless female emits light from the end of the abdomen.

gloxinia /glɒkˈsɪnɪə/ n. American tropical plant with large bell-shaped flowers. [Gloxin, name of a botanist]

glucose /ˈgluːkəʊz/ n. sugar found in the blood or in fruit juice etc., and as a constituent of starch, cellulose, etc. [Greek gleukos sweet wine]

glue /gluː/ —n. adhesive substance. —v. (**glues**, **glued**, **gluing** or **glueing**) 1 fasten or join with glue. 2 keep or put very close (eye glued to the keyhole). □ **gluey** /ˈgluːɪ/ adj. (**gluier**, **gluiest**). [Latin glus: related to GLUTEN]

glue ear n. blocking of the Eustachian tube, esp. in children.

glue-sniffing n. inhalation of fumes from adhesives as an intoxicant. □ **glue-sniffer** n.

glum adj. (**glummer**, **glummest**) dejected; sullen. □ **glumly** adv. **glumness** n. [var. of GLOOM]

glut —v. (-tt-) 1 feed (a person, one's stomach, etc.) or indulge (a desire etc.) to the full; satiate. 2 fill to excess. 3 overstock (a market). —n. 1 supply exceeding demand. 2 full indulgence; surfeit. [French gloutir swallow: related to GLUTTON]

glutamate /ˈgluːtəˌmeɪt/ n. salt or ester of glutamic acid, esp. a sodium salt used to enhance the flavour of food.

glutamic acid /gluːˈtæmɪk/ n. amino acid normally found in proteins. [from GLUTEN, AMINE]

gluten /ˈgluːt(ə)n/ n. mixture of proteins present in cereal grains; sticky protein substance left when starch is washed out of flour. [Latin *gluten -tin-* glue]

glutinous /ˈgluːtɪnəs/ adj. sticky; like glue. [Latin: related to GLUTEN]

glutton /ˈglʌt(ə)n/ n. **1** greedy eater. **2** (often foll. by *for*) colloq. person insatiably eager (*glutton for work*). **3** voracious animal of the weasel family. □ **gluttonous** adj. **gluttonously** adv. [Latin *gluttō* SWALLOW¹]

gluttony /ˈglʌtənɪ/ n. greed or excess in eating. [French: related to GLUTTON]

glycerine /ˈglɪsərɪn/ n. (also **glycerol**, US **glycerin** /-rɪn/) thick sweet colourless liquid used as medicine, ointment, etc., and in explosives. [Greek *glukeros* sweet]

glycerol /ˈglɪsərɒl/ n. = GLYCERINE.

glycogen /ˈglaɪkədʒ(ə)n/ n. polysaccharide serving as a store of carbohydrates, esp. in animal tissues.

glycolysis /glaɪˈkɒlɪsɪs/ n. breakdown of glucose by enzymes with the release of energy.

GM abbr. George Medal.

gm abbr. gram(s).

G-man /ˈdʒiːmæn/ n. US colloq. federal criminal-investigation officer. [from Government]

GMS abbr. grant maintained status.

GMT abbr. Greenwich Mean Time.

gnarled /nɑːld/ adj. (of a tree, hands, etc.) knobbly, twisted, rugged. [var. of *knarled*: related to KNURL]

gnash /næʃ/ v. **1** grind (the teeth). **2** (of the teeth) strike together. [Old Norse]

gnat /næt/ n. small two-winged biting fly. [Old English]

gnaw /nɔː/ v. **1 a** (usu. foll. by *away* etc.) wear away by biting. **b** (often foll. by *at, into*) bite persistently. **2 a** corrode: wear away. **b** (of pain, fear, etc.) torment. [Old English]

gneiss /naɪs/ n. coarse-grained metamorphic rock of feldspar, quartz, and mica. [German]

gnome /nəʊm/ n. **1 a** dwarfish legendary spirit or goblin living underground. **b** figure of this as a garden ornament. **2** (esp. in pl.) colloq. person with sinister influence, esp. financial (*gnomes of Zurich*). □ **gnomish** adj. [French]

gnomic /ˈnəʊmɪk/ adj. of aphorisms; sententious. [Greek *gnōmē* opinion]

gnomon /ˈnəʊmɒn/ n. rod or pin etc. on a sundial, showing the time by its shadow. [Greek, = indicator]

GNP abbr. gross national product.

gnu /nuː/ n. (pl. same or -s) oxlike antelope. [Bushman *nqu*]

go¹ /gəʊ/ -v. (3rd sing. present **goes** /gəʊz/; past went; past part. **gone** /gɒn/) **1 a** start moving or be moving from one place or point in time to another; travel, proceed. **b** (foll. by *and* + verb) colloq. expressing annoyance (*you went and told him*). **2** (foll. by *verbal noun*) make a special journey for; participate in (*went skiing; goes running*). **3** lie or extend in a certain direction (*the road goes to London*). **4** leave; depart (*they had to go*). **5** move, act, work, etc. (*clock doesn't go*). **6 a** make a specified movement (*go like this with your foot*). **b** make a sound (often of a specified kind) (*gun went bang; door bell went*). **c** (of an animal) make (its characteristic cry) (*the cow went 'moo'*). **d** colloq. say (so the cow went 'Why did I you like it?*). **7** be in a specified state (*go hungry; went in fear of his life*). **8 a** pass into a specified condition (*gone bad; went to sleep*). **b** colloq. die. **c** proceed or escape in a specified condition (*pret went unrecognized*). **9** (of time or distance) pass, elapse; be traversed (*ten days to go before Easter; the last mile went quickly*). **10 a** (of a document, verse, song, etc.) have a specified content or wording (*the tune goes like this*). **b** be current or accepted (*so the story goes*). **c** be suitable; fit; match (*the shoes don't go with the hat; those pinks don't go*). **d** be regularly kept or put (*the forks go here*). **e** find room; fit (*this won't go into the cupboard*). **11** a turn out, proceed; take a course or view (*things went well; make the party go*). **12 a** be sold (*went cheap*). **b** (of money) be spent. **13 a** be relinquished or abolished (*the car will have to go*). **b** fail, decline; give way, collapse (*his sight is going; the bulb has gone*). **14 a** be acceptable or permitted; be accepted without question (*anything goes; what I say goes*). **15** (often foll. by *by, with, on, upon*) be guided by; judge or act on or in harmony with (*have nothing to go on; a good rule to go by*). **16** attend regularly (*goes to school*). **17** (foll. by *pres. part.*) colloq.

go

gnosis /ˈnəʊsɪs/ n. knowledge of spiritual mysteries. [Greek]

gnostic /ˈnɒstɪk/ -adj. **1** of knowledge. **2** having special mystical knowledge. -n. (**Gnostic**) adherent of Gnosticism. □ **Gnosticism** /-sɪz(ə)m/ n. [Greek *gnōstikos*]

gnostic /ˈnɒstɪk/ -adj. **1** of knowledge. **2** having special mystical knowledge. -n. (**Gnostic**) concerning the Gnostics. (**Gnostic**) (usu. in pl.) early Christian heretic claiming mystical knowledge. □ **Gnosticism** /-sɪz(ə)m/ n. [Greek *gnōsis* knowledge]

proceed (often foolishly) to do (*went running to the police; don't go making him angry*). **18** act or proceed to a certain point (*will go so far and no further; went as high as £100*). **19** (of a number) be capable of being contained in another (*6 into 5 won't go*). **20** (usu. foll. by *to*) be allotted or awarded; pass (*first prize went to the girl*). **21** (foll. by *to, towards*) amount to; contribute to (*12 inches go to make a foot; this will go towards your holiday*). **22** (in *imper.*) begin motion (a starter's order in a race (*ready, steady, go!*). **23** (usu. foll. by *by, under*) be known or called (*goes by the name of Droopy*). **24** *colloq.* proceed to (*go jump in the lake*). **25** (foll. by *for*) apply to (*that goes for me too*). —*n.* (*pl.* **goes**) **1** mettle; animation (*has a lot of go in her*). **2** vigorous activity (*it's all go*). **3** *colloq.* success (*made a go of it*). **4** *colloq.* turn; attempt (*I'll have a go; it's my go*). —*adj. colloq.* functioning properly (*all systems are go*). □ **go about 1** set to work at. **2** be socially active. **3** (foll. by *pres. part.*) make a habit of doing. **go ahead** proceed without hesitation. **go along with** agree to or with. **go back on** fail to keep (a promise etc.). **go begging** see BEG. **go down 1 a** (of an amount) become less through use (*coffee has gone down*). **b** subside (*the flood went down*). **c** decrease in price. **2 a** (of a ship) sink. **b** (of the sun) set. **c** (of a curtain fall. **3** deteriorate; (of a computer system etc.) cease to function. **4** be recorded in writing. **5** be swallowed. **6** (often foll. by *with*) find acceptance. **7** *colloq.* leave university. **8** *colloq.* be sent to prison. **go down with** become ill with (a disease). **go far** see FAR. **go for 1** go to fetch. **2** pass or be accounted as (*went for nothing*). **3** prefer; choose. **4** *colloq.* strive to attain (*go for it!*). **5** *colloq.* attack (*the dog went, for him*). **go halves** (often foll. by *with*) share equally. **go in 1** enter a room, house, etc. **2** (of the sun etc.) become obscured by cloud. **go in for 1** enter as a competitor. **2** take as one's style, pursuit, etc. **go into 1** enter (a profession, hospital, etc.). **2** investigate. **go a long way 1** (often foll. by *towards*) have a great effect. **2** (of food, money, etc.) last a long time, buy much. **3** = **go far. go off 1** explode. **2** leave the stage. **3** wear off. **4** (esp. of foodstuffs) deteriorate. **5** go to sleep. **6** *colloq.* begin to dislike (*I've gone off him*). **go off well** (or **badly**) (of an enterprise etc.) be received well or accomplished well or badly etc.). **go on 1** (often foll. by *pres. part.*) continue, persevere (*decided to go on with it; went on trying*). **2** *colloq.* **a** talk at great length. **b** (foll. by *at*) nag. **3** (foll. by *to* + *infin.*) proceed (*went on to become a star*). **4** (also **go upon**) *colloq.* use as evidence. **go out 1** leave a room, house, etc. **2** be extinguished. **3** be broadcast. **4** (often foll. by *with*) be courting. **5** cease to be fashionable. **6** *colloq.* lose consciousness. **7** (usu. foll. by *to*) (of the heart etc.) expand with sympathy etc. towards (*my heart goes out to them*). **8** (of a tide) ebb to low tide. **go over 1** inspect the details of; rehearse; retouch. **2** (of a play etc.) be received, esp. favourably. **go round 1** spin, revolve. **2** (of food etc.) suffice for everybody. **3** (usu. foll. by *to*) visit informally. **go slow** work slowly, as a form of industrial action. **go through 1** be dealt with or completed. **2** discuss or scrutinize in detail. **3** perform. **4** undergo. **5** *colloq.* use up; spend (money etc.). **go through with** complete. **go to blazes** (or **hell**) *slang* exclamation of dismissal, contempt, etc. **go too far** see FAR. **go under** sink; fail; succumb. **go up 1** rise in price. **2** *colloq.* enter university. **3** be consumed (in flames etc.); explode. **go with 1** be harmonious with; match. **2** be courting. **go without** manage without; forgo (also *absol.*). **have a go at 1** attack. **2** attempt. **on the go** *colloq.* **1** in constant motion. **2** constantly working. [Old English: *went* is originally a past of WEND]

go² /gəʊ/ *n.* Japanese board-game. [Japanese]

goad —*v.* **1** urge on with a goad. **2** (usu. foll. by *on, into*) irritate; stimulate. —*n.* **1** spiked stick used for urging cattle (or ward. **2** anything that torments or incites. [Old English]

go-ahead —*n.* permission to proceed. —*adj.* enterprising.

goal *n.* **1** object of ambition or effort; destination. **2 a** structure into or through which the ball has to be sent to score in certain games. **b** point won. **3** point marking the finish of a race. [origin unknown]

goalie *n. colloq.* = GOALKEEPER.

goalkeeper *n.* player defending a goal.

goalpost *n.* either of the two upright posts of a goal.

goat *n.* **1** hardy domesticated mammal, with horns and (in the male) a beard. **2** *colloq.* foolish person. **3** *colloq.* lecherous man. **4** (the Goat) zodiacal sign or constellation Capricorn. □ **get a person's goat** *colloq.* irritate a person. [Old English]

goatee /gəʊˈtiː/ *n.* small pointed beard.

goatherd *n.* person who tends goats.

goatskin *n.* **1** skin of a goat. **2** garment or bottle made of goatskin.

gob¹ *n. slang* mouth. [origin unknown]

gob² *slang* —*n.* clot of slimy matter. —*v.* (**-bb-**) spit. [French *gobbe* mouthful]

gobbet /ˈgɒbɪt/ n. 1 piece or lump of flesh, food, etc. 2 extract from a text, esp. one set for translation or comment. [French diminutive of gobe GOB²]

gobble¹ /ˈgɒb(ə)l/ v. (-ling) 1 (of a turkeycock) make a characteristic guttural sound. 2 make such a sound when speaking. [imitative]

gobble² /ˈgɒb(ə)l/ v. (-ling) eat hurriedly and noisily. [from GOB²]

gobbledegook /ˈgɒbɪldɪguːk/ n. (also **gobbledygook**) colloq. pompous or unintelligible jargon. [probably imitative of a turkeycock]

go-between n. intermediary.

goblet /ˈgɒblɪt/ n. drinking-vessel with a foot and stem. [French diminutive of gobel cup]

goblin /ˈgɒblɪn/ n. mischievous ugly dwarflike creature of folklore. [Anglo-French]

gobsmacked adj. slang flabbergasted.

gob-stopper n. large hard sweet.

goby /ˈgəʊbɪ/ n. (pl. -ies) small fish with ventral fins joined to form a disc or sucker. [Greek kōbios GUDGEON¹]

go-by n. var. of GO-KART.

god n. 1 a (in many religions) super-human being or spirit worshipped as having power over nature, human fortunes, etc. b image, idol, etc. symbolizing a god. 2 (God) (in Christian and other monotheistic religions) creator and ruler of the universe. 3 adored or greatly admired person. 4 (in pl.) Theatr. gallery. □ **God forbid** may it not happen! **God knows 1** it is beyond all knowledge. 2 I call God to witness that. **God willing** if Providence allows. [Old English]

godchild n. person in relation to his or her godparent.

god-daughter n. female godchild.

goddess /ˈgɒdɪs/ n. 1 female deity. 2 adored woman.

godfather n. 1 male godparent. 2 esp. US person directing an illegal organization, esp. the Mafia.

God-fearing adj. earnestly religious.

God-forsaken adj. dismal.

godhead n. (also **Godhead**) 1 a state of being God or a god. b divine nature. 2 deity. 3 (the Godhead) God.

godless adj. 1 impious, wicked. 2 without a god. 3 not recognizing God. □ **godlessness** n.

godlike adj. resembling God or a god.

godly adj. (-ier, -iest) pious, devout. □ **godliness** n.

godmother n. female godparent.

godparent n. person who presents a child at baptism and responds on the child's behalf.

godsend n. unexpected but welcome event or acquisition.

godson n. male godchild.

Godspeed /gɒdˈspiːd/ int. expression of good wishes to a person starting a journey.

goer n. 1 person or thing that goes (slow goer). 2 (often in comb.) person who attends, regularly (churchgoer). 3 colloq. a lively or persevering person. b sexually promiscuous person.

go-getter n. colloq. aggressively enterprising person.

goggle /ˈgɒg(ə)l/ v. (-ling) 1 a (often foll. by at) look with wide-open eyes. b (of the eyes) be rolled about; protrude. 2 roll (the eyes). —adj. (usu. attrib.) (of the eyes) protuberant or rolling. —n. (in pl.) spectacles for protecting the eyes. [probably imitative]

goggle-box n. colloq. television set.

go-go adj. colloq. (of a dancer, music, etc.) in modern style; lively, erotic, and rhythmic.

going /ˈgəʊɪŋ/ —n. 1 act or process of going. 2 a condition of the ground for walking, riding, etc. b progress affected by this. —adj. 1 in or into action (set the clock going). 2 existing, available (there's cold beef going). 3 current, prevalent (the going rate). □ **get going** start steadily talking, working, etc. **going on fifteen** etc. esp. US approaching (a time, age, etc.). **going on for** approaching (a time, age, etc.). **going strong** continuing vigorously. **going to** intending to; about to. **to be going on with** to start with; for the time being. **while the going is good** while conditions are favourable.

going concern n. thriving business.

going-over n. (pl. **goings-over**) 1 colloq. inspection or overhaul. 2 slang thrashing.

goings-on n.pl. (esp. morally suspect) behaviour.

goitre /ˈgɔɪtə(r)/ n. (US **goiter**) morbid enlargement of the thyroid gland. [Latin guttur throat]

go-kart n. (also **go-cart**) miniature racing car with a skeleton body.

gold /gəʊld/ —n. 1 precious yellow metallic element. 2 colour of gold. 3 a coins or articles made of gold. b wealth. 4 something precious or beautiful. 5 = GOLD MEDAL. —adj. 1 made wholly or chiefly of gold. 2 coloured like gold. [Old English]

gold-digger n. slang woman who cultivates men to obtain money from them.

gold-dust n. gold in fine particles as often found naturally.

goldcrest n. tiny bird with a golden crest.

golden *adj.* **1 a** made or consisting of gold. **b** yielding gold. **2** coloured or shining like gold (*golden hair*). **3** precious; excellent.

golden age *n.* period of a nation's greatest prosperity, cultural merit, etc.

golden eagle *n.* large eagle with yellow-tipped head-feathers.

golden handshake *n. colloq.* payment given on redundancy or early retirement.

golden jubilee *n.* fiftieth anniversary.

golden mean *n.* the principle of moderation.

golden retriever *n.* retriever with a thick golden-coloured coat.

golden rod *n.* plant with a spike of yellow flowers.

golden rule *n.* basic principle of action, esp. 'do as you would be done by'.

golden wedding *n.* fiftieth anniversary of a wedding.

gold-field *n.* district in which gold occurs naturally.

goldfinch *n.* songbird with a yellow band across each wing.

goldfish *n.* (*pl.* same or **-es**) small reddish-golden Chinese carp.

gold foil *n.* gold beaten into a thin sheet.

gold leaf *n.* gold beaten into a very thin sheet.

gold medal *n.* medal of gold, usu. awarded as first prize.

gold-mine *n.* **1** place where gold is mined. **2** *colloq.* source of great wealth.

gold plate *n.* **1** vessels made of gold. **2** material plated with gold.

gold-plate *v.* plate with gold.

gold-rush *n.* rush to a newly-discovered gold-field.

goldsmith *n.* worker in gold.

gold standard *n.* system by which the value of a currency is defined in terms of gold.

golf —*n.* game in which a small hard ball is driven with clubs into a series of 18 or 9 holes with the fewest possible strokes. —*v.* play golf. □ **golfer** *n.* [origin unknown]

golf ball *n.* **1** ball used in golf. **2** *colloq.* small ball used in some electric typewriters to carry the type.

golf club *n.* **1** club used in golf. **2** association for playing golf. **3** premises of this.

golf-course *n.* (also **golf-links**) course on which golf is played.

golliwog /ˈgɒlɪwɒg/ *n.* black-faced soft doll with fuzzy hair. [origin uncertain]

golly[1] /ˈgɒlɪ/ *int.* expressing surprise. [euphemism for God]

golly[2] /ˈgɒlɪ/ *n.* (*pl.* **-ies**) *colloq.* = GOLLIWOG. [abbreviation]

golosh var. of GALOSH.

gonad /ˈgəʊnæd/ *n.* animal organ producing gametes, esp. the testis or ovary. [Greek *gone* seed]

gondola /ˈgɒndələ/ *n.* **1** light flat-bottomed boat used on Venetian canals. **2** car suspended from an airship or balloon, or attached to a ski-lift. [Italian]

gondolier /ˌgɒndəˈlɪə(r)/ *n.* oarsman on a gondola. [Italian: related to GONDOLA]

gone /gɒn/ *adj.* **1** (of time) past (*not until gone nine*). **2 a** lost; hopeless. **b** dead. **3** *colloq.* pregnant for a specified time (*already three months gone*). **4** *slang* completely enthralled or entranced, esp. by rhythmic music, drugs, etc. □ **be gone** depart; leave temporarily (cf. BEGONE). **gone on** *slang* infatuated with. [past part. of GO]

goner /ˈgɒnə(r)/ *n. slang* person or thing that is doomed or irrevocably lost.

gong *n.* **1** metal disc with a turned rim, giving a resonant note when struck. **2** saucer-shaped bell. **3** *slang* medal. [Malay]

gonorrhoea /ˌgɒnəˈrɪə/ *n.* (*US* **gonorrhea**) venereal disease with inflammatory discharge from the urethra or vagina. [Greek, = semen-flux]

goo *n. colloq.* **1** sticky or slimy substance. **2** sickly sentiment. [origin unknown]

good /gʊd/ —*adj.* (**better**, **best**) **1** having the right or desired qualities; adequate. **2 a** (of a person) efficient, competent (*good at French; good driver*). **b** effective, reliable (*good brakes*). **3 a** kind. **b** morally excellent; virtuous (*good deed*). **c** well-behaved (*good child*). **4** enjoyable, agreeable (*good party; good news*). **5** thorough, considerable (*a good wash*). **6 a** not less than (*waited a good hour*). **b** considerable in number, quality, etc. (*a good many people*). **7** benefical (*milk is good for you*). **8 a** valid, sound (*good reason*). **b** financially sound (*his credit is good*). **9** in exclamations of surprise (*good heavens!*). **10** (sometimes patronizing) commendable, worthy (*good old George; my good man*). **11** in courteous greetings and farewells (*good morning*). —*n.* **1** (only in *sing.*) that which is good; what is beneficial or morally right (*only good can come of it; what good will it do?*). **2** (in *pl.*) a movable property or merchandise. **b** things to be transported. **c** (prec. by *the*) *colloq.* what one has undertaken to supply (esp. *deliver the goods*). —*adv.* *US colloq.* well (*doing pretty good*). □ **as good as** practically (*be* (*a certain amount*) *to the good* have as net profit or advantage. **for good** (**and all**) finally, permanently. **good for 1** benefical to; having a good

effect on. **2** able to perform. **3** able to be trusted to pay. **good books on a person** DANCE. **have the goods on a person** *slang* have information about a person giving one an advantage over him or her. **in good faith** with honest or sincere intentions. **in good time 1** with no risk of being late. **2** (also **all in good time**) in due course but without haste. **to the good** having as profit or benefit. [Old English]

good book *n.* (prec. by *the*) the Bible.

goodbye /gud'baɪ/ (*US* **goodby**) —*int.* expressing good wishes on parting, ending a telephone conversation, etc. —*n.* (*pl.* -byes or *US* -bys) parting, farewell. [from *God be with you!*]

good faith *n.* sincerity of intention.

Good Friday *n.* Friday before Easter Sunday, commemorating the Crucifixion.

good-for-nothing —*adj.* worthless. —*n.* worthless person.

good-hearted *adj.* kindly, well-meaning.

good humour *n.* genial mood.

good-humoured *adj.* cheerful, amiable. □ **good-humouredly** *adv.*

goodie var. of GOODY *n.*

good job *n.* fortunate state of affairs.

good-looking *adj.* handsome.

goodly /'gudli/ *adj.* (-ier, -iest) **1** handsome. **2** of imposing size etc. □ **goodliness** *n.* [Old English]

good nature *n.* friendly disposition.

good-natured *adj.* kind, patient; easygoing. □ **good-naturedly** *adv.*

goodness —*n.* **1** virtue; excellence. **2** kindness (*had the goodness to wait*). **3** what is beneficial in a thing. —*int.* (esp. as a substitution for 'God') expressing surprise, anger, etc. (*goodness me!*; *goodness knows*). [Old English]

good-tempered *adj.* having a good temper; not easily annoyed.

goodwill *n.* **1** kindly feeling. **2** established reputation of a business etc. as enhancing its value. **3** willingness to undertake unpaid duties.

good will *n.* intention that good will result (see also GOODWILL).

goody —*n.* (also **goodie**) (*pl.* -ies) **1** *colloq.* good or favoured person. **2** (usu. in *pl.*) something good or attractive, esp. to eat. —*int.* expressing childish delight. —*adj.* = GOODY-GOODY *adj.*

goody-goody *colloq.* —*n.* (*pl.* -ies) smug or obtrusively virtuous person. —*adj.* obtrusively or smugly virtuous.

gooey *adj.* (**gooier**, **gooiest**) *slang* **1** viscous, sticky. **2** sentimental. [from GOO]

goof *slang* —*n.* **1** foolish or stupid person. **2** mistake. —*v.* **1** bungle. **2** blunder. [Latin *gufus* coarse]

goofy *adj.* (-ier, -iest) *slang* **1** stupid. **2** having protruding or crooked front teeth.

googly /'guːglɪ/ *n.* (*pl.* -ies) *Cricket* ball bowled so as to bounce in an unexpected direction. [origin unknown]

goon *n.* *slang* **1** stupid person. **2** esp. *US* ruffian hired by racketeers etc. [origin uncertain]

goose *n.* (*pl.* **geese**) **1 a** large water-bird with webbed feet and a broad bill. **b** female of this (opp. GANDER 1). **c** flesh of a goose as food. **2** *colloq.* simpleton. [Old English]

gooseberry /'guzbərɪ/ *n.* (*pl.* -ies) **1** yellowish-green berry with juicy flesh. **2** thorny shrub bearing this. [origin uncertain]

goose-flesh *n.* (also **goose-pimples**; *US* **goose-bumps**) bristling state of the skin produced by cold, fright, etc.

goose-step *n.* military marching step in which the knees are kept stiff.

gopher /'gəʊfə(r)/ *n.* American burrowing rodent, ground-squirrel, or burrowing tortoise. [origin uncertain]

Gordian /'ɡɔːdɪən/ *adj.* □ **cut the Gordian knot** solve a problem by force or by evasion. [*Gordius* king of Phrygia, who tied a knot later cut by Alexander the Great]

gore[1] *n.* blood shed and clotted. [Old English, = dirt]

gore[2] *v.* (-**ring**) pierce with a horn, tusk, etc. [origin unknown]

gore[3] —*n.* **1** wedge-shaped piece in a garment. **2** triangular or tapering piece in an umbrella etc. —*v.* (-**ring**) shape (a garment) with a gore. [Old English, = triangle of land]

gorge —*n.* **1** narrow opening between hills. **2** act of gorging. **3** contents of the stomach. —*v.* (-**ging**) **1** feed greedily. **2** (often *refl.*) satiate. **b** devour greedily. □ **one's gorge rises at** one is sickened by. [French, = throat]

gorgeous /'ɡɔːdʒəs/ *adj.* **1** richly coloured, sumptuous. **2** *colloq.* very pleasant, splendid (*gorgeous weather*). **3** *colloq.* strikingly beautiful. □ **gorgeously** *adv.* [French]

gorgon /'ɡɔːɡən/ *n.* **1** (in Greek mythology) each of three snake-haired sisters (esp. Medusa) with the power to turn anyone who looked at them to stone. **2** frightening or repulsive woman. [Greek *gorgos* terrible]

Gorgonzola /ˌɡɔːɡən'zəʊlə/ *n.* type of rich cheese with bluish-green veins. [*Gorgonzola* in Italy]

gorilla /gəˈrɪlə/ n. largest anthropoid ape, native to Africa. [Greek, perhaps from African = wild man]

gormless /ˈgɔːmlɪs/ adj. colloq. foolish, lacking sense. □ **gormlessly** adv. [originally gaumless from dial. gaum understanding]

gorse n. spiny yellow-flowered shrub; furze. □ **gorsy** adj. [Old English]

Gorsedd /ˈgɔːseð/ n. Druidic order, meeting before the eisteddfod. [Welsh, literally 'throne']

gory adj. (-**ier**, -**iest**) 1 involving bloodshed; bloodthirsty. 2 covered in gore. □ **gorily** adv. **goriness** n.

gosh int. expressing surprise. [euphemism for GOD]

goshawk /ˈgɒshɔːk/ n. large short-winged hawk. [Old English: related to GOOSE, HAWK¹]

gosling /ˈgɒzlɪn/ n. young goose. [Old Norse: related to GOOSE]

go-slow n. working slowly, as a form of industrial action.

gospel /ˈgɒsp(ə)l/ n. 1 teaching or revelation of Christ. 2 (**Gospel**) a record of Christ's life in the first four books of the New Testament. b each of these books. c portion from one of them read at a service. 3 (also **gospel truth**) thing regarded as absolutely true. 4 (in full **gospel music**) Black American religious singing. [Old English: related to GOOD, SPELL¹ = news]

gossamer /ˈgɒsəmə(r)/ n. 1 filmy substance of small spiders' webs. 2 delicate filmy material. —adj. light and flimsy as filmy material. [origin uncertain]

gossip /ˈgɒsɪp/ n. 1 a unconstrained talk or writing. b idle talk. 2 person who indulges in gossip. —v. (-**p**-) talk or write gossip. □ **gossipy** adj. [Old English, originally 'godparent', hence 'familiar acquaintance']

gossip column n. section of a newspaper devoted to gossip about well-known people. □ **gossip columnist** n.

got past and past part. of GET.

Goth n. 1 member of a Germanic tribe that invaded the Roman Empire in the 3rd–5th c. 2 uncivilized or ignorant person. [Old English Gota and Greek Gothoi]

goth n. 1 style of rock music with an intense or droning blend of guitars, bass, and drums, often with apocalyptic or mystical lyrics. 2 performer or devotee of this music, or member of the subculture favouring black clothing and white-painted faces with black make-up.

Gothic —adj. 1 of the Goths. 2 in the style of architecture prevalent in W.

Europe in the 12th–16th c., characterized by pointed arches. 3 (of a novel etc.) in a style popular in the 18th–19th c., with supernatural or horrifying events. 4 barbarous, uncouth. —n. 1 Gothic language. 2 Gothic architecture. [French from Italian]

gotten US past part. of GET.

gouache /guˈɑːʃ/ n. 1 method of painting in opaque pigments ground in water and thickened with a gluelike substance. 2 these pigments. [French from Italian]

Gouda /ˈgaʊdə/ n. flat round usu. Dutch cheese. [Gouda in Holland]

gouge /gaʊdʒ/ —n. chisel with a concave blade. —v. (-**ging**) 1 cut with or as with a gouge. 2 (foll. by out) force out (esp. an eye with the thumb) with or as with a gouge. [Latin gubia]

goulash /ˈguːlæʃ/ n. highly-seasoned Hungarian stew of meat and vegetables. [Magyar gulyás-hús, = herdsman's meat]

gourd /gʊəd/ n. 1 a fleshy usu. large fruit with a hard skin. b climbing or trailing plant of the cucumber family bearing this. 2 dried skin of the gourd-fruit, used as a drinking-vessel etc. [Latin cucurbita]

gourmand /ˈgʊəmənd/ n. 1 glutton. 2 gourmet. [French]

■ **Usage** The use of gourmand in sense 2 is considered incorrect by some people.

gourmandise /ˈgʊəmɒndiːz/ n. gluttony.

gourmet /ˈgʊəmeɪ/ n. connoisseur of good food. [French]

gout n. disease with inflammation of the smaller joints, esp. of the toe. □ **gouty** adj. [Latin gutta drop]

govern /ˈgʌv(ə)n/ v. 1 rule or control with authority; conduct the policy and affairs of 2 influence or determine (a person or course of action). 3 be a standard or principle for. 4 Gram. (esp. of a verb or preposition) have (a noun or pronoun or its case) depending on it. [Greek kubernaō steer]

governance /ˈgʌvənəns/ n. 1 act or manner of governing. 2 function of governing. [French: related to GOVERN]

governess /ˈgʌvənɪs/ n. woman employed to teach children in a private household.

government /ˈgʌvənmənt/ n. 1 act or system of governing. 2 manner of governing. 3 body of persons governing a State. b (usu. **Government**) particular ministry in

office. 4 the State as an agent. □ **governmental** adj.

governor n. 1 ruler. 2 **a** official governing a province, town, etc. **b** representative of the Crown in a colony. 3 executive head of each State of the US. 4 officer commanding a fortress etc. 5 head or member of the governing body of an institution. 6 official in charge of a prison. 7 **a** slang one's employer. **b** slang one's father. 8 Mech. automatic regulator controlling the speed of an engine etc. □ **governorship** n.

Governor-General n. representative of the Crown in a Commonwealth country that regards the Queen as Head of State.

gown n. 1 loose flowing garment, esp. a woman's long dress. 2 official robe of an alderman, judge, cleric, academic, etc. 3 surgeon's overall. [Latin gunna fur]

goy n. (pl. **-im** or **-s**) Jewish name for a non-Jew. [Hebrew, = people]

GP abbr. general practitioner.

GPO abbr. General Post Office.

gr abbr. (also **gr.**) 1 gram(s) 2 grains. 3 gross.

grab –v. (**-bb-**) 1 seize suddenly. 2 take greedily or unfairly. 3 slang attract the attention of, impress. 4 (foll. by at) snatch at. 5 (of brakes) act harshly or jerkily. –n. 1 sudden clutch or attempt to seize. 2 mechanical device for clutching. [Low German or Dutch]

grace –n. 1 attractiveness, esp. in elegance of proportion or manner or movement. 2 courteous good will (had the grace to apologize) 3 attractive feature; accomplishment (social graces). 4 **a** (in Christian belief) the unmerited favour of God. **b** state of receiving this. 5 goodwill, favour. 6 delay granted as a favour (a year's grace) 7 short thanks-giving before or after a meal. 8 (**Grace**) (in Greek mythology) each of three beautiful sister goddesses, bestowers of beauty and charm. 9 (**Grace**) (prec. by His, Her, Your) forms of description or address for a duke, duchess, or archbishop. –v. (**-cing**) (often foll. by with) add grace to; confer honour on (graced us with his presence). □ **with good** (or **bad**) **grace** as if willingly (or reluctantly). [Latin gratia]

graceful adj. having or showing grace or elegance. □ **gracefully** adv. **gracefulness** n.

graceless adj. lacking grace, elegance, or charm.

grace-note n. Mus. extra note as an embellishment.

gracious /'greɪʃəs/ –adj. 1 kind, indulgent and beneficent to inferiors. 2 (of God) merciful, benign. –int. expressing

379

surprise. □ **graciously** adv. **graciousness** n. [Latin: related to GRACE]

gracious living n. elegant way of life.

gradate /grə'deɪt/ v. (**-ting**) 1 (cause to) pass gradually from one shade to another. 2 arrange in steps or grades of size etc.

gradation /grə'deɪʃ(ə)n/ n. (usu. in pl.) 1 stage of transition or advance. 2 **a** certain degree in rank, intensity, etc. **b** arrangement in such degrees. □ **gradational** adj. [Latin: related to GRADE]

grade –n. 1 **a** certain degree in rank, merit, proficiency, etc. **b** class of persons or things of the same grade. 2 mark indicating the quality of a student's work. 3 US class in school. 4 gradient, slope. –v. (**-ding**) 1 arrange in grades. 2 (foll. by up, down, off, into, etc.) pass gradually between grades, or into a grade. 3 give a grade to (a student). 4 reduce (a road etc.) to easy gradients. [Latin gradus step]

gradient /'greɪdɪənt/ n. 1 stretch of road, railway, etc. that slopes. 2 amount of such a slope. [probably from GRADE after salient]

gradual /'grædʒʊəl/ adj. 1 progressing by degrees. 2 not rapid, steep, or abrupt. □ **gradually** adv. [Latin: related to GRADE]

gradualism /'grædʒʊəlɪz(ə)m/ n. policy of gradual reform.

graduate –n. /'grædʒʊət/ person holding an academic degree. –v. /'grædʒʊeɪt/ (**-ting**) 1 obtain an academic degree. 2 (foll. by to) move up to (a higher grade of activity etc.). 3 mark out in degrees or parts. 4 arrange in gradations; apportion (e.g. tax) according to a scale. □ **graduation** /ˌgrædʒʊ'eɪʃ(ə)n/ n. [medieval Latin graduor take a degree: related to GRADE]

graffiti /grə'fiːtiː/ n.pl. (sing. **graffito** /grə'fiːtəʊ/) writing or drawing scribbled, scratched, or sprayed on a surface. [Italian graffio a scratch]

■ **Usage** The singular or collective use of the form graffiti is considered incorrect by some people, but it is frequently found, e.g. graffiti was appeared.

graft[1] /grɑːft/ –n. 1 **a** shoot or scion inserted into a slit of stock, from which it receives sap. **b** place where a graft is inserted. 2 Surgery piece of living tissue, organ, etc., transplanted surgically. 3 slang hard work. –v. 1 (often foll. by into, on, together, etc.) insert (a scion) as a graft. 2 transplant (living tissue). 3 (foll. by in, on) insert or fix (a thing)

permanently to another. **4** *slang* work hard. [Greek *graphion* stylus]

graft² /graːft/ *colloq. —n.* **1** practices, esp. bribery, used to secure illicit gains in politics or business. **2** such gains. *—v.* seek or make such gains. [origin unknown]

Grail *n.* (in full **Holy Grail**) (in medieval legend) cup or platter used by Christ at the Last Supper. [medieval Latin *gradalis* dish]

grain *—n.* **1** fruit or seed of a cereal. **2** (*collect.*) wheat or any allied grass used as food; corn. **3** small hard particle of salt, sand, etc. **4** unit of weight, 0.0648 gram. **5** smallest possible quantity (*not a grain of truth in it*). **6** roughness of surface. **7** texture of skin, wood, stone, etc. **8** a pattern of lines of fibre in wood or paper. **b** lamination in stone etc. *—v.* **1** paint in imitation of the grain of wood etc. **2** give a granular surface to. **3** form into grains. □ **against the grain** contrary to one's natural inclination or feeling. □ **grainy** *adj.* (**-ier, -iest**) [Latin *granum*]

gram *n.* (also **gramme**) metric unit of mass equal to one-thousandth of a kilogram. [Greek *gramma* small weight]

-gram *comb. form* forming nouns denoting a thing written or recorded (often in a certain way) (*anagram; epigram; telegram*). [Greek *gramma* thing written]

graminaceous /ˌgræmɪˈneɪʃəs/ *adj.* of or like grass. [Latin *gramen* grass]

graminivorous /ˌgræmɪˈnɪvərəs/ *adj.* feeding on grass, cereals, etc.

grammar /ˈgræmə(r)/ *n.* **1** the study or rules of a language's inflections or other means of showing the relation between words. **2** observance or application of the rules of grammar (*bad grammar*). **3** book on grammar. [Greek *gramma* letter]

grammarian /grəˈmeərɪən/ *n.* expert in grammar or linguistics.

grammar school *n. esp. hist.* selective State secondary school with a mainly academic curriculum.

grammatical /grəˈmætɪk(ə)l/ *adj.* of or conforming to the rules of grammar. □ **grammatically** *adv.*

gramme var. of GRAM.

gramophone /ˈgræməfəʊn/ *n.* = RECORD-PLAYER. [inversion of *phonogram*: as PHONO-, -GRAM]

gramophone record = RECORD *n.* 3.

grampus /ˈgræmpəs/ *n.* (*pl.* **-puses**) a kind of dolphin with a blunt snout. [Latin *crassus piscis* fat fish]

gran *n. colloq.* grandmother. [abbreviation]

granadilla /ˌgrænəˈdɪlə/ *n.* passion-fruit. [Spanish, diminutive of *granada* pomegranate]

granary /ˈgrænərɪ/ *n.* (*pl.* **-ies**) **1** storehouse for threshed grain. **2** region producing, and esp. exporting, much corn. [Latin: related to GRAIN]

grand *—adj.* **1** splendid, magnificent, imposing, dignified. **2** main; of chief importance. **3** (**Grand**) of the highest rank (*Grand Duke*). **4** *colloq.* excellent, enjoyable. **5** belonging to high society. **6** (in *comb.*) (in names of family relationships) denoting the second degree of ascent or descent (*granddaughter*). *—n.* **1** = GRAND PIANO. **2** (*pl.* same) (usu. in *pl.*) *US slang* a thousand dollars or pounds. □ **grandly** *adv.* **grandness** *n.* [Latin *grandis* full-grown]

grandad *n.* (also **grand-dad**) *colloq.* **1** grandfather. **2** elderly man.

grandchild *n.* child of one's son or daughter.

granddaughter *n.* female grandchild.

grandee /grænˈdiː/ *n.* **1** Spanish or Portuguese nobleman of the highest rank. **2** person of high rank. [Spanish and Portuguese *grande*: related to GRAND]

grandeur /ˈgrændʒə(r)/ *n.* **1** majesty, splendour, dignity of appearance or bearing. **2** high rank, eminence. **3** nobility of character. [French: related to GRAND]

grandfather *n.* male grandparent.

grandfather clock *n.* clock in a tall wooden case, driven by weights.

grand jury *n. esp. US* jury selected to examine the validity of an accusation prior to trial.

grandiloquent /grænˈdɪləkwənt/ *adj.* pompous or inflated in language. □ **grandiloquence** *n.* [Latin: related to GRAND, -*loquus* from *loqui* speak]

grandiose /ˈgrændɪˌəʊs/ *adj.* **1** producing or meant to produce an imposing effect. **2** planned on an ambitious scale. □ **grandiosity** /-ˈɒsɪtɪ/ *n.* [Italian: related to GRAND]

grand mal /grɑ̃ ˈmæl/ *n.* serious form of epilepsy with loss of consciousness. [French, = great sickness]

grand master *n.* chess-player of the highest class.

grandmother *n.* female grandparent.

Grand National *n.* steeplechase held annually at Aintree, Liverpool.

grand opera *n.* opera on a serious theme, or in which the entire libretto (including dialogue) is sung.

grandpa /ˈgrænpɑː/ *n. colloq.* grandfather.

grandparent n. parent of one's father or mother.

grand piano n. large full-toned piano used as fruit and in making wine. [French, probably from *grappe* hook]

Grand Prix /grã'pri:/ n. any of several important international motor or motor-cycle racing events. [French, = great or chief prize]

grandsire n. *archaic* grandfather.

grand slam n. **1** *Sport* winning of all of a group of matches etc. **2** *Bridge* winning of 13 tricks.

grandson n. male grandchild.

grandstand n. main stand for spectators at a racecourse etc.

grand total n. sum of other totals.

grand tour n. *hist.* cultural tour of Europe.

grange /greindʒ/ n. country house with farm-buildings. [Latin *granica* related to GRAIN]

graniferous /grə'nifərəs/ adj. producing grain or a grainlike seed. [Latin: related to GRAIN]

granite /'grænit/ n. granular crystalline rock of quartz, mica, etc., used for building. [Italian *granito*: related to GRAIN]

granivorous /grə'nivərəs/ adj. feeding on grain. [Latin: related to GRAIN]

granny /'græni/ n. (also **grannie**) (pl. **-ies**) *colloq.* grandmother. [diminutive of *grannam* from archaic *grandam*: related to GRAND, DAME]

granny flat n. part of a house made into self-contained accommodation for an elderly relative.

granny knot n. reef-knot crossed the wrong way and therefore insecure.

grant /grɑːnt/ —v. **1 a** consent to fulfil (a request etc.). **b** allow (a person) to have (a thing). **2** give formally; transfer legally. **3** (often foll. by *that*) admit as true; concede. —n. **1** process of granting. **2** sum of money given by the State. **3** legal conveyance by written instrument. □ **take for granted 1** assume something to be true or valid. **2** cease to appreciate through familiarity. □ **grantor** /-'tɔː(r)/ n. (esp. in sense 2 of v.) [French *gr(é)anter* var. of *creanter* from Latin *credo* entrust]

grant-maintained adj. (of a school) funded by central rather than local government.

granular /'grænjʊlə(r)/ adj. of or like grains or granules. □ **granularity** /-'læriti/ n. [Latin: related to GRANULE]

granulate /'grænjʊleɪt/ v. (**-ting**) **1** form into grains. **2** roughen the surface of. □ **granulation** /-'leɪʃ(ə)n/ n.

granule /'grænjuːl/ n. small grain. [Latin diminutive of *granum* GRAIN]

grape n. berry (usu. green, purple, or black) growing in clusters on a vine, usu. yellow citrus fruit.

grapefruit n. (pl. same) large round usu. yellow citrus fruit.

grape hyacinth n. plant of the lily family, with clusters of usu. blue flowers.

grapeshot n. *hist.* small balls used as charge in a cannon and scattering when fired.

grapevine n. **1** vine. **2** *colloq.* the means of transmission of a rumour.

graph /grɑːf/ —n. diagram showing the relation between variable quantities, usu. of two variables, each measured along one of a pair of axes. —v. plot or trace on a graph. [abbreviation of *graphic formula*]

-graph comb. form forming nouns and verbs meaning: **1** thing written or drawn etc. in a specified way (*photograph*). **2** instrument that records (*seismograph*).

-grapher comb. form denoting a person concerned with a subject (*geographer*, *radiographer*). [Greek *-graphos* write]

graphic /'græfik/ adj. **1** of or relating to the visual or descriptive arts, esp. writing and drawing. **2** vividly descriptive. □ **graphically** adv. [Greek *graphē* writing]

graphic arts n.pl. visual and technical arts involving design or the use of lettering.

graphic novel n. novel in comic-strip format.

graphics n.pl. (usu. treated as *sing.*) **1** products of the graphic arts. **2** use of diagrams in calculation and design.

graphite /'græfaɪt/ n. crystalline allotropic form of carbon used as a lubricant, in pencils, etc. □ **graphitic** /-'fɪtɪk/ adj. [German *Graphit* from Greek *graphō* write]

graphology /grə'fɒlədʒɪ/ n. the study of handwriting, esp. as a supposed guide to character. □ **graphologist** n. [Greek: related to GRAPHIC]

graph paper n. paper printed with a network of lines as a basis for drawing graphs.

-graphy comb. form forming nouns denoting: **1** descriptive science (*geography*). **2** technique of producing images (*photography*). **3** style or method of writing etc. (*calligraphy*).

grapnel /'græpn(ə)l/ n. **1** device with iron claws, for dragging or grasping. **2**

small anchor with several flukes. [French *grapon*: related to GRAPE]

grapple /ˈgræp(ə)l/ —v. (-ling) 1 (often foll. by *with*) fight in close combat. 2 (foll. by *with*) try to manage (a difficult problem etc.). 3 a grip with the hands; come to close quarters with. b seize with or as with a grapnel. —n. 1 a hold or grip in or as in wrestling. b contest at close quarters. 2 clutching-instrument; grapnel. [French *grapil*: related to GRAPNEL]

grappling-iron n. (also **grappling-hook**) = GRAPNEL.

grasp /grɑːsp/ —v. 1 a clutch at; seize greedily. b hold firmly. 2 (foll. by *at*) try to seize; accept avidly. 3 understand or realize (a fact or meaning). —n. 1 firm hold; grip. 2 (foll. by *of*) a mastery (*a grasp of the situation*). b mental hold. □ **grasp the nettle** tackle a difficulty boldly. [earlier *grapse*: related to GROPE]

grasping adj. avaricious.

grass /grɑːs/ —n. 1 a any of a group of wild plants with green blades that are eaten by ruminants. b plant of the family which includes cereals, reeds, and bamboos. 2 pasture land. 3 grass-covered ground, lawn. 4 grazing (*out to grass*). 5 *slang* marijuana. 6 *slang* informer. —v. 1 cover with turf. 2 *US* provide with pasture. 3 *slang* a betray, esp. to the police. b inform the police. □ **grassy** adj. (-ier, -iest). [Old English]

grasshopper n. jumping and chirping insect.

grassland n. large open area covered with grass, esp. used for grazing.

grass roots n.pl. 1 fundamental level or source. 2 ordinary people; rank and file of an organization; esp. a political party.

grass snake n. common harmless European snake.

grass widow n. (also **grass widower**) person whose husband (or wife) is away for a prolonged period.

grate¹ v. (-ting) 1 reduce to small particles by rubbing on a serrated surface. 2 (often foll. by *against*, *on*) rub with a harsh scraping sound. 3 utter in a harsh tone. 4 (often foll. by *on*) a sound harshly. b have an irritating effect. 5 grind (one's teeth). 6 creak. [French from Germanic]

grate² n. 1 fireplace or furnace. 2 metal frame confining fuel in this. [Latin *cratis* hurdle]

grateful /ˈgreɪtfʊl/ adj. 1 thankful; feeling or showing gratitude. 2 pleasant, acceptable. □ **gratefully** adv. [obsolete *grate* from Latin *gratus*]

gratify /ˈgrætɪfaɪ/ v. (-ies, -ied) 1 a please, delight. b please by compliance.

2 yield to (a feeling or desire). □ **gratification** /-fɪˈkeɪʃ(ə)n/ n. [Latin: related to GRATEFUL]

grating n. 1 framework of parallel or crossed metal bars. 2 *Optics* set of parallel wires, lines ruled on glass, etc.

gratis /ˈɡrɑːtɪs/ adv. & adj. free; without charge. [Latin]

gratitude /ˈɡrætɪtjuːd/ n. being thankful; readiness to return kindness. [Latin: related to GRATEFUL]

gratuitous /ɡrəˈtjuːɪtəs/ adj. 1 given or done free of charge. 2 uncalled-for; lacking good reason. □ **gratuitously** adv. **gratuitousness** n. [Latin, = spontaneous]

gratuity /ɡrəˈtjuːɪtɪ/ n. (pl. -ies) = TIP³ n. 1. [Latin: related to GRATEFUL]

grave¹ n. 1 trench dug in the ground for the burial of a corpse; mound or memorial stone placed over this. 2 (prec. by *the*) death. [Old English]

grave² —adj. 1 a serious, weighty, important. b dignified, solemn, sombre. 2 extremely serious or threatening. —n. /grɑːv/ = GRAVE ACCENT. □ **gravely** adv. [Latin *gravis* heavy]

grave³ v. (-ving; *past part.* **graven** or **graved**) 1 (foll. by *in*, *on*) fix indelibly (on one's memory). 2 *archaic* engrave, carve. [Old English]

grave accent /grɑːv/ n. a mark (`) placed over a vowel to denote pronunciation, length, etc.

gravedigger n. person who digs graves.

gravel /ˈgræv(ə)l/ —n. 1 mixture of coarse sand and small stones, used for paths etc. 2 *Med.* aggregations of crystals formed in the urinary tract. —v. (-ll-; *US* -l-) lay or strew with gravel. [French diminutive, perhaps of *grave* shore]

gravelly adj. 1 of or like gravel. 2 (of a voice) deep and rough-sounding.

graven *past part.* of GRAVE³.

graven image n. idol.

Graves /grɑːv/ n. light usu. white wine from Graves in France.

gravestone n. stone (usu. inscribed) marking a grave.

graveyard n. burial ground.

gravid /ˈgrævɪd/ adj. pregnant. [Latin *gravidus*: related to GRAVE²]

gravimeter /grəˈvɪmɪtə(r)/ n. instrument measuring the difference in the force of gravity between two places. [Latin: related to GRAVE²]

gravimetry /grəˈvɪmɪtrɪ/ n. measurement of weight. □ **gravimetric** /ˌgrævɪˈmetrɪk/ adj.

gravitate /ˈgrævɪteɪt/ v. (-ting) 1 (foll. by *to*, *towards*) move or be attracted to. 2 a move or tend by force of gravity

towards. **b** sink by or as if by gravity. [related to GRAVE²]

gravitation /grævɪˈteɪʃ(ə)n/ *n. Phys-ics* **1** force of attraction between any particle of matter in the universe and any other. **2** effect of this, esp. the falling of bodies to the earth. □ **gravitational** *adj.*

gravity /ˈgrævɪtɪ/ *n.* **1 a** force that attracts a body to the centre of the earth etc. **b** degree of intensity of this. **c** grav-itational force. **2** property of having weight. **3 a** importance, seriousness. **b** solemnity. [Latin: related to GRAVE²]

gravy /ˈgreɪvɪ/ *n.* (*pl.* **-ies**) **1** juices exud-ing from meat during and after cooking. **2** sauce for this made from these etc. [perhaps from a misreading of French *gravé* from *grain* spice, GRAIN]

gravy-boat *n.* boat-shaped vessel for serving gravy.

gravy train *n. slang* source of easy financial benefit.

gray US var. of GREY.

grayling *n.* (*pl.* same) silver-grey fresh-water fish. [from GREY, -LING]

graze¹ *v.* (**-zing**) **1** (of cattle, sheep, etc.) eat growing grass. **b** feed (cattle etc.) on growing grass, **b** feed on (grass). **3** pasture cattle. [Old English: related to GRASS]

graze² —*v.* (**-zing**) **1** rub or scrape (part of the body, esp. the skin). **2 a** touch lightly in passing. **b** (foll. by *against, along,* etc.) move with a light passing contact. —*n.* abrasion. [perhaps from GRAZE¹, as if 'take off the grass close to the ground']

grazier /ˈgreɪzɪə(r)/ *n.* **1** person who feeds cattle for market. **2** Australian large-scale sheep-farmer etc. [from GRASS]

grazing *n.* grassland suitable for pas-turage.

grease /griːs/ —*n.* **1** oily or fatty matter, esp. as a lubricant. **2** melted fat of a dead animal. —*v.* (**-sing**) smear or lubricate with grease. □ **grease the palm of** *colloq.* bribe. [Latin *crassus* (adj.) fat]

greasepaint *n.* make-up used by actors.

greaseproof *adj.* impervious to grease.

greaser *n. slang* member of a gang of youths with long hair and motor cycles.

greasy *adj.* (**-ier, -iest**) **1 a** of or like grease. **b** smeared or covered with grease. **c** containing or having too much grease. **2 a** slippery. **b** (of a person or manner) unpleasantly unctuous. □ **greasily** *adv.* **greasiness** *n.*

great /greɪt/ —*adj.* **1 a** of a size, amount, extent, or intensity considerably above the normal or average (*a great hole; great fun*). **b** also with implied admira-tion or contempt, etc., esp. in exclama-tions (*you great idiot!; great stuff!*). **c**

reinforcing other words denoting size, quantity, etc. (*great big hole*). **2** import-ant, pre-eminent (*the great thing is not to get caught*). **3** grand, imposing (*great occasion*). **4** distinguished, remark-able in ability, character, etc. (*great men; great thinker*). **6** (foll. by *at, on*) competent, well-informed. **7** fully deserving the name of; doing a thing extensively (*great reader; great believer in tolerance*). **8** (also **greater**) the larger of two things, etc. (*great auk; greater celandine*). **9** *colloq.* very enjoyable or satisfactory (*had a great time*). **10** (in *comb.*) (in names of family relationships) denoting one de-gree further removed upwards or down-wards (*great-uncle; great-great-grand-mother*). —*n.* **1** greater or outstanding person or thing. **2** (in *pl.*) (**Greats**) *col-loq.* (at Oxford University) honours course or final examinations in classics and philosophy. □ **greatness** *n.* [Old English]

Great Bear see BEAR².

great circle *n.* circle on the surface of a sphere whose plane passes through the sphere's centre.

greatcoat *n.* heavy overcoat.

Great Dane *n.* dog of a large short-haired breed.

great deal *n.* = DEAL¹ *n.* 1.

greatly *adv.* much by a considerable amount (*greatly admired; greatly superior*).

great tit *n.* Eurasian songbird with black and white head markings.

Great War *n.* world war of 1914–18.

greave *n.* (usu. in *pl.*) armour for the shin. [French, = shin]

grebe *n.* a kind of diving bird. [French]

Grecian /ˈgriːʃ(ə)n/ *adj.* (of architecture or facial outline) Greek. [Latin *Graecia* Greece]

Grecian nose *n.* straight nose that continues the line of the forehead with-out a dip.

greed *n.* excessive desire, esp. for food or wealth. [from GREEDY]

greedy *adj.* (**-ier, -iest**) **1** having or showing greed. **2** (foll. by *for, or to* + infin.) very eager. □ **greedily** *adv.* **greediness** *n.* [Old English]

Greek —*n.* **1 a** native or national of Greece. **b** person of Greek descent. **2** language of Greece. —*adj.* of Greece or its people or language; Hellenic. □ **Greek to me** *colloq.* incomprehensible to me. [Old English ultimately from Greek *Graikoi*]

Greek cross *n.* cross with four equal arms.

green —*adj.* **1** of the colour between blue and yellow in the spectrum; coloured

like grass. **2** covered with leaves or grass. **3** (of fruit etc. or wood) unripe or unseasoned. **4** not dried, smoked, or tanned. **5** inexperienced, gullible. **6 a** (of the complexion) pale, sickly-hued. **b** jealous, envious. **7** young, flourishing. **8** not withered or worn out (*a green old age*). **9** (also **Green**) concerned with protection of the environment as a political principle; not harmful to the environment. —*n.* **1** green colour or pigment. **2** green clothes or material. **3 a** piece of public grassy land (*village green*). **b** grassy area used for a special purpose (*putting-green*). **4** (in *pl.*) green vegetables. **5** (also **Green**) supporter of an environmentalist group or party. —*v.* make or become green. □ **greenish** *adj.* **greenly** *adv.* **greenness** *n.* [Old English]

green belt *n.* area of open land round a city, designated for preservation.

green card *n.* international insurance document for motorists.

greenery *n.* green foliage or growing plants.

green-eyed *adj. colloq.* jealous.

greenfinch *n.* finch with green and yellow plumage.

green fingers *n. colloq.* skill in growing plants.

greenfly *n.* **1** green aphid. **2** these collectively.

greengage *n.* roundish green variety of plum. [Sir W. *Gage*, name of a botanist]

greengrocer *n.* retailer of fruit and vegetables.

greengrocery *n.* (*pl.* **-ies**) **1** greengrocer's business. **2** goods sold by a greengrocer.

greenhorn *n.* inexperienced person; new recruit.

greenhouse *n.* light structure with the sides and roof mainly of glass, for rearing plants.

greenhouse effect *n.* trapping of the sun's warmth in the lower atmosphere of the earth, caused by an increase in carbon dioxide, methane, etc.

greenhouse gas *n.* any of the gases, esp. carbon dioxide and methane, that contribute to the greenhouse effect.

green light *n.* **1** signal to proceed on a road, railway, etc. **2** *colloq.* permission to proceed with a project.

Green Paper *n.* preliminary report of Government proposals, for discussion.

green pound *n.* exchange rate for the pound for payments for agricultural produce in the EC.

green revolution *n.* greatly increased crop production in underdeveloped countries.

green-room *n.* room in a theatre for actors and actresses who are off stage.

green-stick fracture *n.* bone-fracture, esp. in children, in which one side of the bone is broken and one only bent.

greenstuff *n.* vegetation; green vegetables.

greensward *n.* expanse of grassy turf/ *n.*

green tea *n.* tea made from steam-dried leaves.

Greenwich Mean Time /grɛnɪtʃ/ *n.* local time on the meridian of Greenwich, used as an international basis of time-reckoning.

greenwood *n.* a wood in summer.

greeny *adj.* greenish.

greet[1] *v.* **1** address politely or welcomingly on meeting or arrival. **2** receive or acknowledge in a specified way. **3** (of a sight, sound, etc.) become apparent to or noticed by. [Old English]

greet[2] *v. Scot.* weep. [Old English]

greeting *n.* **1** act or instance of welcoming etc. **2** words, gestures, etc., used to greet a person. **3** (often in *pl.*) expression of goodwill.

greetings card *n.* decorative card sent to convey greetings.

gregarious /grɪ'gɛərɪəs/ *adj.* **1** fond of company. **2** living in flocks or communities. □ **gregariousness** *n.* [Latin *grex gregis* flock]

Gregorian calendar /grɪ'gɔːrɪən/ *n.* calendar introduced in 1582 by Pope Gregory XIII.

Gregorian chant /grɪ'gɔːrɪən/ *n.* plainsong ritual music, named after Pope Gregory I.

gremlin /'grɛmlɪn/ *n. colloq.* imaginary mischievous sprite regarded as responsible for mechanical faults etc. [origin unknown]

grenade /grɪ'neɪd/ *n.* small bomb thrown by hand (**hand-grenade**) or shot from a rifle. [French: related to POMEGRANATE]

grenadier /grɛnə'dɪə(r)/ *n.* **1** (**Grenadiers** or **Grenadier Guards**) first regiment of the royal household infantry. **2** *hist.* soldier armed with grenades.

grew *past of* GROW.

grey /greɪ/ (*US* **gray**) —*adj.* **1** of a colour intermediate between black and white. **2** dull, dismal. **3 a** (of hair) turning white with age etc. **b** having grey hair. **4** anonymous, unidentifiable. —*n.* **1 a** grey colour or pigment. **b** grey clothes or material (*dressed in grey*). **2** grey or white horse. —*v.* make or become grey. □ **greyish** *adj.* **greyness** *n.* [Old English]

grey area *n.* situation or topic not clearly defined.

Grey Friar *n.* Franciscan friar.

greyhound n. dog of a tall slender breed capable of high speed. [Old English, = bitch-hound]

greylag n. [in full **greylag goose**] European wild goose. [from GREY]

grey matter n. the darker tissues of the brain and spinal cord. 2 colloq. intelligence.

grey squirrel n. American squirrel brought to Europe in the 19th c.

grid n. 1 grating. 2 system of numbered squares printed on a map and forming the basis of map references. 3 network of lines, electric-power connections, gas-supply lines, etc. 4 pattern of lines marking the starting-places on a motorracing track. 5 perforated electrode controlling the flow of electrons in a thermionic valve etc. 6 arrangement of town streets in a rectangular pattern. [from GRIDIRON]

griddle /ˈgrid(ə)l/ n. circular iron plate placed over a source of heat for baking etc. [Latin cratis hurdle]

gridiron /ˈgridˌaiən/ n. cooking utensil of metal bars for broiling or grilling. [related to GRIDDLE]

grief n. 1 intense sorrow. 2 cause of this. □ **come to grief** meet with disaster. [French: related to GRIEVE]

grievance /ˈgriːv(ə)ns/ n. real or fancied cause for complaint. [French: related to GRIEVE]

grieve v. (-ving) 1 cause grief to. 2 suffer grief. [Latin: related to GRAVE²]

grievous adj. 1 (of pain etc.) severe. 2 causing grief. 3 injurious. 4 flagrant, heinous. □ **grievously** adv. [French: related to GRIEVE]

grievous bodily harm n. Law serious injury inflicted intentionally.

griffin /ˈgrifin/ n. (also **gryphon** /ˈg(r)ə)n/) fabulous creature with an eagle's head and wings and a lion's body. [Latin gryphus from Greek]

griffon /ˈgrif(ə)n/ n. 1 dog of a small terrier-like breed. 2 large vulture. 3 = GRIFFIN. [French, = GRIFFIN]

grill —n. 1 **a** device on a cooker for radiating heat downwards. **b** = GRIDIRON. 2 food cooked on a grill. 3 (in full **grill room**) restaurant specializing in grilled food. —v. 1 cook or be cooked under a grill or on a gridiron. 2 subject or be subjected to extreme heat. 3 subject to severe questioning. [French: related to GRIDDLE]

grille n. (also **grill**) 1 grating or latticed screen, used as a partition etc. 2 metal grid protecting the radiator of a vehicle.

grilse n. (pl. same or -s) young salmon that has returned to fresh water from the sea for the first time. [origin unknown]

grim adj. (**grimmer, grimmest**) 1 of stern or forbidding appearance. 2 harsh, merciless. 3 ghastly, joyless (has a grim truth in it). 4 unpleasant, unattractive. □ **grimly** adv. **grimness** n. [Old English]

grimace /ˈgriməs, ˈmeis/ —n. distortion of the face made in disgust etc. or to amuse. —v. (-cing) make a grimace. [French from Spanish]

grime —v. (-ming) blacken with grime; befoul. —n. soot or dirt ingrained in a surface. □ **griminess** n. **grimy** adj. [Low German or Dutch]

grin —v. (-nn-) 1 **a** smile broadly, showing the teeth. **b** make a forced, unrestrained, or stupid smile. 2 express by grinning. —n. act of grinning. □ **grin and bear it** take pain etc. stoically. [Old English]

grind /graind/ —v. (past and past part. **ground**) 1 reduce to small particles or powder by crushing. 2 **a** sharpen or smooth by friction. **b** rub or rub together gratingly. 3 (often foll. by down) oppress; harass with exactions. **a** (often foll. by away) work or study hard. **b** (foll. by out) produce with effort. colloq. work hard. —n. 1 act or instance of grinding. 2 colloq. hard dull work (the daily grind). 3 size of ground particles. □ **grind to a halt** stop laboriously. [Old English]

grinder n. 1 person or thing that grinds, esp. a machine. 2 molar tooth.

grindstone n. 1 thick revolving disc used for grinding, sharpening, and polishing. 2 a kind of stone used for this. □ **keep one's nose to the grindstone** work hard and continuously. [Old English]

grip —v. (**-pp-**) 1 **a** grasp tightly. **b** take a firm hold, esp. by friction. 2 compel the attention of. —n. 1 **a** firm hold; tight grasp. **b** manner of grasping or holding. 2 power of holding attention. 3 **a** intellectual mastery. **b** effective control of one's behaviour etc. (lose one's grip). 4 **a** part of a machine that grips. **b** part by which a weapon etc. is held. 5 = HAIRGRIP. 6 travelling bag. □ **come** (or **get**) **to grips with** approach purposefully; begin to deal with. [Old English]

gripe —v. (-ping) 1 colloq. complain. 2 affect with gastric pain. —n. 1 (usu. in pl.) colic. 2 colloq. complaint. 3 grip, clutch. [Old English]

Gripe Water n. propr. preparation to relieve colic in infants.

grisly /ˈgrizli/ adj. (-ier, -iest) causing horror, disgust, or fear. □ **grisliness** n. [Old English]

grist n. corn to grind. □ **grist to the** (or a **person's**) **mill** source of profit or advantage. [Old English: related to GRIND]

gristle /'grɪs(ə)l/ n. tough flexible animal tissue; cartilage. □ **gristly** /-slɪ/ adj. [Old English]

grit -n. 1 particles of stone or sand, esp. as irritating or hindering. 2 coarse sandstone. 3 colloq. pluck, endurance. -v. (-tt-) 1 spread grit on (icy roads etc.). 2 clench (the teeth). 3 make a grating sound. □ **gritter** n. **gritty** adj. (-ier, -iest). [Old English]

grits n.pl. 1 coarsely ground grain, esp. oatmeal. 2 oats that have been husked but not ground. [Old English]

grizzle /'grɪz(ə)l/ v. (-ling) colloq. 1 (esp. of a child) cry fretfully. 2 complain whiningly. □ **grizzly** adj. [origin unknown]

grizzled /'grɪz(ə)ld/ adj. 1 (of hair) grey or streaked with grey. 2 having grizzled hair. [grizzle grey from French grisel]

grizzly /'grɪzlɪ/ -adj. (-ier, -iest) grey, grey-haired. -n. (pl. -ies) (in full **grizzly bear**) large variety of brown bear, found in N. America and N. Russia.

groan -v. 1 a make a deep sound expressing pain, grief, or disapproval. b utter with groans. 2 (usu. foll. by under, beneath, with) be loaded or oppressed. -n. sound made in groaning. [Old English]

groat n. hist. silver coin worth four old pence. [Low German or Dutch: related to GREAT]

groats n.pl. hulled or crushed grain, esp. oats. [Old English]

grocer n. dealer in food and household provisions. [Anglo-French grosser from Latin grossus GROSS]

grocery n. (pl. -ies) 1 grocer's trade or shop. 2 (in pl.) goods, esp. food, sold by a grocer.

grog n. drink of spirit (orig. rum) and water. [origin uncertain]

groggy adj. (-ier, -iest) incapable or unsteady. □ **groggily** adv. **grogginess** n.

groin¹ -n. 1 depression between the belly and the thigh. 2 Archit. a edge formed by intersecting vaults. b arch supporting a vault. -v. Archit. build with groins. [origin uncertain]

groin² US var. of GROYNE.

grommet /'grɒmɪt/ n. (also **grummet** /'grʌmɪt/) 1 metal, plastic, or rubber eyelet placed in a hole to protect or insulate a rope or cable etc. passed through it. 2 tube passed through the eardrum to make a communication with the middle ear. [French]

groom -n. 1 person employed to take care of horses. 2 = BRIDEGROOM. 3 Mil. any of certain officers of the Royal Household. -v. 1 a curry or tend (a horse). b give a neat appearance to (a person etc.). 2 (of an ape etc.) clean and comb the fur of (its fellow). 3 prepare or train (a person) for a particular purpose or job. [origin unknown]

groove -n. 1 channel or elongated hollow, esp. one made to guide motion or receive a corresponding ridge. 2 spiral track cut in a gramophone record. -v. (-ving) 1 make a groove or grooves in. 2 slang enjoy oneself. [Dutch]

groovy adj. (-ier, -iest) 1 slang excellent. 2 of or like a groove.

grope -v. (-ping) 1 (usu. foll. by for) feel about or search blindly. 2 (foll. by for, after) search mentally. 3 feel (one's way) towards something. 4 slang fondle clumsily for sexual pleasure. -n. act of groping. [Old English]

grosgrain /'grəʊgreɪn/ n. corded fabric of silk etc. [French, = coarse grain: related to GROSS, GRAIN]

gros point /grəʊ 'pwæ̃/ n. cross-stitch embroidery on canvas. [French: related to GROSS, POINT]

gross /grəʊs/ -adj. 1 overfed, bloated. 2 (of a person, manners, or morals) coarse, unrefined, or indecent. 3 flagrant (gross negligence). 4 total; not net (gross tonnage). 5 (of the senses etc.) dull. -v. produce as gross profit. -n. (pl. same) amount equal to twelve dozen. □ **grossly** adv. **grossness** n. [Latin grossus]

gross domestic product n. total value of goods and services provided in a country in one year.

gross national product n. gross domestic product plus the total of net income from abroad.

grotesque /grəʊ'tesk/ -adj. 1 comically or repulsively distorted. 2 incongruous, absurd. -n. 1 decorative form interweaving human and animal features. 2 comically distorted figure or design. □ **grotesquely** adv. **grotesqueness** n. [Italian: related to GROTTO]

grotto /'grɒtəʊ/ n. (pl. -es or -s) 1 picturesque or artificial ornamental cave. 2 artificial cave. [Italian grotta from Greek kruptē CRYPT]

grotty /'grɒtɪ/ adj. (-ier, -iest) slang unpleasant, dirty, shabby, unattractive. [shortening of GROTESQUE]

grouch colloq. -v. grumble. -n. 1 discontented person. 2 fit of grumbling or the sulks. □ **grouchy** adj. (-ier, -iest). [related to GRUDGE]

ground¹ -n. 1 a surface of the earth, esp. as contrasted with the air around it. b part of this specified in some way (low ground). 2 a position, area, or distance on the earth's surface. b extent of a subject dealt with (the book covers a lot

ground *of ground*). **3** (often in *pl*.) reason, justification. **4** (*attrib.*) area of a special kind or use (often in comb.: *cricket-ground*; *fishing-grounds*). **5** (in *pl*.) enclosed land attached to a house etc. **6** area or basis for agreement etc. (*common ground*). **7** (in painting etc.) the surface giving the predominant colour. **8** (in *pl*.) solid particles, esp. of coffee. **9** = EARTH n. 4. **10** bottom of the sea. **11** floor of a room etc. **12** (in full **ground bass**) *Mus.* short theme in the bass constantly repeated with the upper parts of the music varied. **13** (*attrib.*) (of animals) living on or in the ground; (of plants) dwarfish or trailing. —*v.* **1** refuse authority (to a pilot or an aircraft) to fly. **2 a** run (a ship) aground; strand. **b** (of a ship) run aground. **3** (foll. by *in*) instruct thoroughly (in a subject). **4** (often as **grounded** *adj.*) (foll. by *on*) base (a principle, conclusion, etc.) on. **5** *US Electr.* = EARTH *v.* □ **break new** (or **fresh**) **ground** treat a subject previously not dealt with. **get off the ground** *colloq.* make a successful start. **give** (or **lose**) **ground** retreat, decline. **go to ground 1** (of a fox etc.) enter its earth etc. **2** (of a person) become inaccessible for a prolonged period. **hold one's ground** not retreat. **on the grounds of** because of. [Old English]

ground² *past and past part.* of GRIND.

ground control *n.* personnel directing the landing etc. of aircraft etc.

ground cover *n.* low-growing plants covering the surface of the earth.

ground elder *n.* garden weed spreading by means of underground stems.

ground floor *n.* floor of a building at ground level.

ground frost *n.* frost on the surface of the ground or in the top layer of soil.

ground glass *n.* **1** glass made nontransparent by grinding etc. **2** glass ground to a powder.

grounding *n.* basic training or instruction.

groundless *adj.* without motive or foundation.

groundnut *n.* = PEANUT 1, 2.

ground-plan *n.* **1** plan of a building at ground level. **2** general outline of a scheme.

ground-rent *n.* rent for land leased for building.

groundsel /'graʊns(ə)l/ *n.* wild plant with small yellow flowers, used as a food for cage-birds etc. [Old English]

groundsheet *n.* waterproof sheet for spreading on the ground.

groundsman *n.* person who maintains a sports ground.

ground speed *n.* aircraft's speed relative to the ground.

ground swell *n.* heavy sea caused by a distant or past storm or an earthquake.

groundwater *n.* water found in soil or in pores, crevices, etc., in rock.

groundwork *n.* preliminary or basic work.

group /gruːp/ —*n.* **1** number of persons or things located close together, or considered or classed together. **2** number of people working together etc. **3** number of commercial companies under common ownership. **4** ensemble playing popular music. **5** division of an air force. —*v.* **1** form or be formed into a group. **2** (often foll. by *with*) place in a group or groups. [Italian *gruppo*]

group captain *n.* RAF officer next below air commodore.

groupie *n. slang* ardent follower of touring pop groups, esp. a young woman seeking sexual relations with them.

group therapy *n.* therapy in which people are brought together to assist one another psychologically.

grouse¹ *n.* (*pl.* same) **1** game-bird with a plump body and feathered legs. **2** its flesh as food. [origin uncertain]

grouse² *colloq.* —*v.* (*-sing*) grumble or complain. —*n.* complaint. [origin unknown]

grout —*n.* thin fluid mortar. —*v.* provide or fill with grout. [origin uncertain]

grove *n.* small wood or group of trees. [Old English]

grovel /'grɒv(ə)l/ *v.* (*-ll-*; *US -l-*) **1** behave obsequiously. **2** lie prone in abject humility. □ **grovelling** *adj.* [obsolete *grovelling* (adv.) from Old Norse á grúfu face down]

grow /grəʊ/ *v.* (*past* **grew**; *past part.* **grown**) **1** increase in size, height, quantity, degree, etc. **2** develop or exist as a living plant or natural product. **3 a** produce (plants etc.) by cultivation. **b** allow (a beard etc.) to develop. **4** become gradually (*grow rich*). **5** (foll. by *on*) become gradually more favoured by. **6** (in *passive*; foll. by *over* etc.) be covered with a growth. □ **grow out of 1** become too large to wear. **2** become too mature to retain (a habit etc.). **3** develop from. **grow up 1** advance to maturity. **b** (of a custom) arise. [Old English]

grower *n.* **1** (often in *comb.*) person growing produce (*fruit-grower*). **2** plant that grows in a specified way (*fast grower*).

growing pains *n.pl.* **1** early difficulties in the development of a project etc. **2** neuralgic pain in children's legs due to fatigue etc.

growl –*v.* **1 a** (often foll. by *at*) make a low guttural sound, usu. of anger. **b** murmur angrily. **2** rumble. **3** (often foll. by *out*) utter with a growl. –*n.* **1** growling sound. **2** angry murmur. **3** rumble. [probably imitative]

grown *past part.* of GROW.

grown-up –*adj.* adult. –*n.* adult person.

growth /grəʊθ/ *n.* **1** act or process of growing. **2** increase in size or value. **3** something that has grown or is growing. **4** *Med.* morbid formation.

growth industry *n.* industry that is developing rapidly.

groyne *n.* (*US* **groin**) timber, stone, or concrete wall built at right angles to the coast to check beach erosion. [dial. *groin* snout, from French]

grub –*n.* **1** larva of an insect. **2** *colloq.* food. –*v.* (**-bb-**) **1** dig superficially. **2** (foll. by *up, out*) **a** extract by digging. **b** extract (information etc.) by searching in books etc. **3** rummage. [Old English]

grubby *adj.* (**-ier, -iest**) **1** dirty. **2** infested with grubs. □ **grubbiness** *n.*

grudge –*n.* persistent feeling of ill will or resentment. –*v.* (**-ging**) **1** be resentfully unwilling to give or allow. **2** (foll. by verbal noun or *to* + infin.) be reluctant to do. [French]

gruel /ˈgruːəl/ *n.* liquid food of oatmeal etc. boiled in milk or water. [French from Germanic]

gruelling *adj.* (*US* **grueling**) extremely demanding or tiring. □ **gruellingly** *adv.*

gruesome /ˈgruːsəm/ *adj.* horrible, grisly, disgusting. □ **gruesomely** *adv.* [Scandinavian]

gruff *adj.* **1 a** (of a voice) low and harsh. **b** (of a person) having a gruff voice. **2** surly. □ **gruffly** *adv.* **gruffness** *n.* [Low German or Dutch *grof* coarse]

grumble /ˈgrʌmb(ə)l/ –*v.* (**-ling**) **1** complain peevishly. **2** rumble. –*n.* **1** complaint. **2** rumble. □ **grumbler** *n.* [obsolete *grummel*]

grummet var. of GROMMET.

grumpy /ˈgrʌmpɪ/ *adj.* (**-ier, -iest**) morosely irritable. □ **grumpily** *adv.* **grumpiness** *n.* [imitative]

grunt –*n.* **1** low guttural sound made by a pig. **2** similar sound. –*v.* **1** make a grunt. **2** make a similar sound, esp. to express discontent. **3** utter with a grunt. [Old English, imitative]

Gruyère /ˈgruːjeə(r)/ *n.* a firm pale cheese. [*Gruyère* in Switzerland]

gryphon var. of GRIFFIN.

G7 *attrib. adj.* designating the world's seven richest nations. [Group of *Seven*]

G-string /ˈdʒiːstrɪŋ/ *n.* **1** *Mus.* string sounding the note G. **2** narrow strip of cloth etc. covering only the genitals and attached to a string round the waist.

G-suit /ˈdʒiːsuːt, -sjuːt/ *n.* garment with inflatable pressurized pouches, worn by pilots and astronauts to enable them to withstand high acceleration. [*g* = gravity, SUIT]

GT *n.* high-performance saloon car. [Italian *gran turismo* great touring]

guano /ˈgwɑːnəʊ/ *n.* (*pl.* **-s**) **1** excrement of sea birds, used as manure. **2** artificial manure, esp. that made from fish. [Spanish from Quechua]

guarantee /ˌɡærənˈtiː/ –*n.* **1 a** formal promise or assurance, esp. that something is of a specified quality and durability. **b** document giving such an undertaking. **2** = GUARANTY. **3** person making a guaranty or giving a security. –*v.* (**-tees, -teed**) **1 a** give or serve as a guarantee for. **b** provide with a guarantee. **2** give a promise or assurance. **3** (foll. by *to*) secure the possession of (a thing) for a person. [related to WARRANT]

guarantor /ˌɡærənˈtɔː(r)/ *n.* person who gives a guarantee or guaranty.

guaranty /ˈɡærəntɪ/ *n.* (*pl.* **-ies**) **1** written or other undertaking to answer for the payment of a debt or for the performance of an obligation by another person liable in the first instance. **2** thing serving as security.

guard /gɑːd/ –*v.* **1** (often foll. by *from, against*) watch over and defend or protect. **2** keep watch by (a door etc.) to control entry or exit. **3** supervise (prisoners etc.) and prevent from escaping. **4** keep (thoughts or speech) in check. **5** (foll. by *against*) take precautions. –*n.* **1** state of vigilance. **2** person who protects or keeps watch. **3** soldiers etc. protecting a place or person; escort. **4** official in general charge of a train. **5** part of an army detached for some purpose (*advance guard*). **6** (in *pl.*) (usu. **Guards**) body of troops nominally employed to guard a monarch. **7** thing that protects (*fire-guard*). **8** *US* prison warder. **9** defensive posture or motion in boxing etc. □ **be on** (or **keep** or **stand**) **guard** keep watch. **off** (or **off one's**) **guard** unprepared for some surprise or difficulty. **on** (or **on one's**) **guard** prepared for all contingencies. [Germanic: related to WARD]

guarded *adj.* (of a remark etc.) cautious. □ **guardedly** *adv.*

guardhouse *n.* building used to accommodate a military guard or to detain prisoners.

guardian /ˈgɑːdɪən/ *n.* **1** protector, keeper. **2** person having legal custody of

another, esp. a minor. □ **guardianship** *n.* [French: related to WARD, WARDEN]

guardroom *n.* room serving the same purpose as a guardhouse.

guardsman *n.* soldier belonging to a body of guards or regiment of Guards.

guava /ˈgwɑːvə/ *n.* 1 edible pale orange fruit with pink flesh. 2 tree bearing this. [Spanish]

gubernatorial /ˌgjuːbənəˈtɔːrɪəl/ *adj.* esp. *US* of or relating to a governor. [Latin *gubernator* governor]

gudgeon¹ /ˈgʌdʒ(ə)n/ *n.* small freshwater fish often used as bait. [French *goujon* from Latin *gobio* GOBY]

gudgeon² /ˈgʌdʒ(ə)n/ *n.* 1 a kind of pivot. 2 tubular part of a hinge. 3 socket for a rudder. 4 pin holding two blocks of stone etc. together. [French diminutive; related to GOUGE]

guelder rose /ˈgeldə(r)/ *n.* shrub with round bunches of creamy-white flowers. [Dutch from *Gelderland* in the Netherlands]

Guernsey /ˈgɜːnzɪ/ *n.* (*pl.* -s) 1 one of a breed of dairy cattle from Guernsey in the Channel Islands. 2 (**guernsey**) type of thick woollen sweater.

guerrilla /gəˈrɪlə/ *n.* (also **guerilla**) member of a small independently acting (usu. political) group taking part in irregular fighting. [Spanish diminutive: related to WAR]

guess /ges/ —*v.* 1 (often *absol.*) estimate without calculation or measurement. 2 form a hypothesis or opinion about; conjecture; think likely. 3 conjecture or estimate correctly. 4 (foll. by *at*) make a conjecture about. —*n.* estimate, conjecture. □ **I guess** *colloq.* I think it likely; I suppose. [origin uncertain]

guesswork *n.* process of or results got by guessing.

guest /gest/ *n.* 1 person invited to visit another's house or to have a meal etc. at another's expense. 2 person lodging at a hotel etc. 3 outside performer invited to take part with a regular body of performers. [Old Norse]

guest-house *n.* private house offering paid accommodation.

guestimate /ˈgestɪmət/ *n.* (also **guesstimate**) *colloq.* estimate based on a mixture of guesswork and calculation. [from GUESS, ESTIMATE]

guff *n. slang* empty talk. [imitative]

guffaw /gʌˈfɔː/ —*n.* boisterous laugh. —*v.* utter a guffaw. [imitative]

guidance /ˈgaɪd(ə)ns/ *n.* 1 advice or direction for solving a problem etc. 2 direction for being guided.

guide /gaɪd/ —*n.* 1 person who leads or shows the way. 2 person who conducts tours. 3 adviser. 4 directing principle. 5

book with essential information on a subject, esp. = GUIDEBOOK. 6 thing marking a position or guiding the eye. 7 bar etc. directing the motion of something. 8 (**Guide**) member of a girls' organization similar to the Scouts. —*v.* (-*ding*) 1 act as guide to. 2 be the principle or motive of. [French from Germanic]

guidebook *n.* book of information about a place for tourists etc.

guided missile *n.* missile under remote control or directed by equipment within itself.

guide-dog *n.* dog trained to guide a blind person.

guideline *n.* principle directing action.

Guider *n.* adult leader of Guides.

guild /gɪld/ *n.* (also **gild**) 1 association of people for mutual aid or the pursuit of a common goal. 2 medieval association of craftsmen or merchants. [Low German or Dutch *gilde*]

guilder /ˈgɪldə(r)/ *n.* chief monetary unit of the Netherlands. [alteration of Dutch *gulden* golden]

guildhall *n.* meeting-place of a medieval guild; town hall.

guile /gaɪl/ *n.* cunning or sly behaviour; treachery, deceit. □ **guileful** *adj.* **guileless** *adj.* [French from Scandinavian]

guillemot /ˈgɪlɪmɒt/ *n.* fast-flying sea bird nesting on cliffs etc. [French]

guillotine /ˈgɪlətiːn/ —*n.* 1 machine with a blade sliding vertically in grooves, used for beheading. 2 device for cutting paper etc. 3 method of preventing delay in the discussion of a legislative bill by fixing times at which various parts of it must be voted on. —*v.* (-*ning*) use a guillotine on. [*Guillotin*, name of a physician]

guilt /gɪlt/ *n.* 1 fact of having committed a specified or implied offence. 2 feeling of having done wrong. [Old English]

guiltless *adj.* (often foll. by *of*) innocent.

guilty *adj.* (-**ier**, -**iest**) 1 culpable of or responsible for a wrong. 2 conscious of or affected by guilt. 3 causing a feeling of guilt (*a guilty secret*). 4 (often foll. by *of*) having committed a (specified) offence. □ **guiltily** *adv.* **guiltiness** *n.* [Old English: related to GUILT]

guinea /ˈgɪnɪ/ *n.* 1 *hist.* sum of 21 old shillings (£1.05). 2 *hist.* former British gold coin first coined for the African trade. [*Guinea* in W. Africa]

guinea-fowl *n.* African fowl with slate-coloured white-spotted plumage.

guinea-pig *n.* 1 domesticated S. American cavy. 2 person used in an experiment.

guipure /giːˈpjʊə(r)/ n. heavy lace of linen pieces joined by embroidery. [French]

guise /gaɪz/ n. 1 assumed appearance; pretence. 2 external appearance. [Germanic: related to WISE²]

guitar /gɪˈtɑː(r)/ n. usu. six-stringed musical instrument played with the fingers or a plectrum. □ **guitarist** n. [Greek *kithara* harp]

Gujarati /ˌɡʊdʒəˈrɑːtɪ/ (also **Gujerati**) –n. (pl. -s) 1 native of Gujarat. 2 language of Gujarat, its people, or language. [*Gujarat*, State in India]

gulch n. US ravine, esp. one in which a torrent flows. [origin uncertain]

gulf n. 1 stretch of sea consisting of a deep inlet with a narrow mouth. 2 deep hollow; chasm. 3 wide difference of feelings, opinion, etc. [Greek *kolpos*]

Gulf Stream n. warm current flowing from the Gulf of Mexico to Newfoundland where it is deflected across the Atlantic Ocean.

gull¹ n. long-winged web-footed sea bird. [probably Welsh *gwylan*]

gull² v. dupe, fool. [perhaps from obsolete *gull* yellow from Old Norse]

gullet /ˈɡʌlɪt/ n. food-passage extending from the mouth to the stomach. [Latin *gula* throat]

gullible adj. easily persuaded or deceived. □ **gullibility** /ˈbɪlɪtɪ/ n. [from GULL²]

gully /ˈɡʌlɪ/ n. (pl. -ies) 1 water-worn ravine. 2 gutter or drain. 3 Cricket fielding position between point and slips. [French *goulet*: related to GULLET]

gulp –v. 1 (often foll. by down) swallow hastily, greedily, or with effort. 2 swallow gaspingly or with difficulty; choke. 3 (foll. by down, back) suppress (esp. tears). –n. 1 act of gulping. 2 large mouthful of a drink. [Dutch *gulpen*, imitative]

gum¹ –n. 1 a viscous secretion of some trees and shrubs. b adhesive substance made from this. 2 US chewing gum. 3 = GUMDROP. 4 = GUM ARABIC. 5 = GUMTREE. –v. (-mm-) 1 (usu. foll. by down, together, etc.) fasten with gum. 2 apply gum to. □ **gum up** colloq. interfere with the smooth running of. [Greek *kommi* from Egyptian *kemai*]

gum² n. (usu. in pl.) firm flesh around the roots of the teeth. [Old English]

gum³ n. □ **by gum!** colloq. by God! [corruption of *God*]

gum arabic n. gum exuded by some kinds of acacia.

gumboil n. small abscess on the gum.

gumboot n. rubber boot.

gumdrop n. hard translucent sweet made with gelatin etc.

gummy¹ adj. (-ier, -iest) 1 sticky. 2 exuding gum.

gummy² adj. (-ier, -iest) toothless.

gumption /ˈɡʌmpʃ(ə)n/ n. colloq. 1 resourcefulness, initiative. 2 common sense. [origin unknown]

gum-tree n. tree exuding gum, esp. a eucalyptus. □ **up a gum-tree** colloq. in great difficulties.

gun –n. 1 weapon consisting of a metal tube from which bullets or other missiles are propelled with great force, esp. by a contained explosion. 2 starting pistol. 3 device for discharging insecticide, grease etc., in the required direction. 4 member of a shooting-party. 5 US gunman. –v. (-nn-) 1 a (usu. foll. by down) shoot (a person) with a gun. b shoot at with a gun. 2 go shooting. 3 (foll by for) seek out determinedly to attack or rebuke. □ **go great guns** colloq. proceed vigorously or successfully. **stick to one's guns** colloq. maintain one's position under attack. [perhaps an abbreviation of the Scandinavian woman's name *Gunnhildr*, applied to cannon etc.]

gunboat n. small vessel with heavy guns.

gunboat diplomacy n. political negotiation backed by the threat of force.

gun-carriage n. wheeled support for a gun.

gun-cotton n. explosive made by steeping cotton in acids.

gun dog n. dog trained to retrieve game shot by sportsmen.

gunfight n. US fight with firearms. □ **gunfighter** n.

gunfire n. firing of a gun or guns.

gunge /ɡʌndʒ/ colloq. –n. sticky or viscous matter. –v. (-ging) (usu. foll. by up) clog with gunge. □ **gungy** adj. [origin uncertain]

gung-ho /ɡʌŋˈhəʊ/ adj. zealous, arrogantly eager. [Chinese *gonghe* work together]

gunman n. man armed with a gun, esp. when committing a crime.

gun-metal n. 1 a dull bluish-grey colour. 2 alloy formerly used for guns.

gunnel var. of GUNWALE.

gunner n. 1 artillery soldier (esp. as an official term for a private). 2 Naut. warrant-officer in charge of a battery, magazine, etc. 3 member of an aircraft crew who operates a gun.

gunnery n. 1 construction and management of large guns. 2 firing of guns.

gunny /ˈɡʌnɪ/ n. (pl. -ies) 1 coarse sacking, usu. of jute fibre. 2 sack made of this. [Hindi and Marathi]

gunpoint *n.* □ **at gunpoint** threatened with a gun or an ultimatum etc.

gunpowder *n.* explosive made of saltpetre, sulphur, and charcoal.

gunrunner *n.* person engaged in the illegal sale or importing of firearms. □ **gunrunning** *n.*

gunshot *n.* **1** shot fired from a gun. **2** range of a gun (*within gunshot*).

gunslinger *n.* esp. *US slang* gunman.

gunsmith *n.* maker and repairer of small firearms.

gunwale /ˈgʌn(ə)l/ *n.* (also **gunnel**) upper edge of the side of a boat or ship. [from GUN, WALE, because it was formerly used to support guns]

guppy /ˈgʌpɪ/ *n.* (*pl.* **-ies**) freshwater fish of the W. Indies and S. America frequently kept in aquariums. [*Guppy*, name of a clergyman]

gurgle /ˈgɜːg(ə)l/ —*v.* (**-ling**) **1** make a bubbling sound as of water from a bottle. **2** utter with such a sound. —*n.* gurgling sound. [probably imitative]

Gurkha /ˈgɜːkə/ *n.* **1** member of the dominant Hindu race in Nepal. **2** Nepalese soldier serving in the British army. [Sanskrit]

gurnard /ˈgɜːnəd/ *n.* (*pl.* same or **-s**) marine fish with a large spiny head and finger-like pectoral rays. [French]

guru /ˈgʊruː/ *n.* (*pl.* **-s**) **1** Hindu spiritual teacher or head of a religious sect. **2** influential or revered teacher. [Hindi]

gush —*v.* **1** emit or flow in a sudden and copious stream. **2** speak or behave effusively. —*n.* **1** sudden or copious stream. **2** effusive manner. [probably imitative]

gusher *n.* **1** oil well from which oil flows without being pumped. **2** effusive person.

gusset /ˈgʌsɪt/ *n.* **1** piece let into a garment etc. to strengthen or enlarge it. **2** bracket strengthening an angle of a structure. [French]

gust —*n.* **1** sudden strong rush of wind. **2** burst of rain, smoke, emotion, etc. —*v.* blow in gusts. □ **gusty** *adj.* (**-ier**, **-iest**). [Old Norse]

gusto /ˈgʌstəʊ/ *n.* zest; enjoyment. [Latin *gustus* taste]

gut —*n.* **1** the intestine. **2** (in *pl.*) bowel or entrails. **3** (in *pl.*) *colloq.* personal courage and determination, perseverance. **4** *slang* stomach, belly. **5** (in *pl.*) **a** contents. **b** essence. **6 a** material for violin strings etc. **b** material for fishing-lines made from the silk-glands of silkworms. **7** (*attrib.*) **a** instinctive (*a gut reaction*). **b** fundamental (*a gut issue*). —*v.* (**-tt-**) **1** remove or destroy the internal fittings of (a house etc.). **2** remove the guts of (a fish).

person's guts *colloq.* dislike a person intensely. [Old English]

gutless *adj. colloq.* lacking courage or energy.

gutsy *adj.* (**-ier**, **-iest**) *colloq.* **1** courageous. **2** greedy.

gutta-percha /ˌgʌtəˈpɜːtʃə/ *n.* tough rubbery substance obtained from latex. [Malay]

gutted *adj. slang* utterly exhausted or fed-up.

gutter —*n.* **1** shallow trough below the eaves of a house, or a channel at the side of a street, to carry off rainwater. **2** (prec. by *the*) poor or degraded background or environment. **3** open conduit. —*v.* (of a candle) burn unsteadily and melt away rapidly. [Latin *gutta* drop]

guttering *n.* **1** gutters of a building etc. **2** material for gutters.

gutter press *n.* sensational newspapers.

guttersnipe *n.* street urchin.

guttural /ˈgʌtər(ə)l/ —*adj.* **1** throaty, harsh-sounding. **2** *Phonet.* (of a consonant) produced in the throat or by the back of the tongue and palate. **3** of the throat. —*n. Phonet.* guttural consonant (e.g. *k, g*). □ **gutturally** *adv.* [Latin *guttur* throat]

guv *n. slang* = GOVERNOR 7. [abbreviation]

guy[1] /gaɪ/ —*n.* **1** *colloq.* man; fellow. **2** effigy of Guy Fawkes burnt on 5 Nov.—*v.* ridicule. [*Guy* Fawkes, name of a conspirator]

guy[2] /gaɪ/ —*n.* rope or chain to secure or steady a crane-load etc. —*v.* secure with a guy or guys. [probably Low German]

guzzle /ˈgʌz(ə)l/ *v.* (**-ling**) eat or drink greedily. [probably French *gosiller* from *gosier* throat]

gybe /dʒaɪb/ *v.* (*US* **jibe**) (**-bing**) **1** (of a fore-and-aft sail or boom) swing across. **2** cause (a sail) to do this. **3** (of a ship or its crew) change course so that this happens. [Dutch]

gym /dʒɪm/ *n. colloq.* **1** gymnasium. **2** gymnastics. [abbreviation]

gymkhana /dʒɪmˈkɑːnə/ *n.* horse-riding competition. [Hindustani *gendkhana* ball-house, assimilated to GYMNASIUM]

gymnasium /dʒɪmˈneɪzɪəm/ *n.* (*pl.* **-s** or **-sia**) room or building equipped for gymnastics. [Greek *gumnos* naked]

gymnast /ˈdʒɪmnæst/ *n.* person who does gymnastics, esp. an expert.

gymnastic /dʒɪmˈnæstɪk/ adj. of or involving gymnastics. □ **gymnastically** adv.

gymnastics n.pl. (also treated as sing.) 1 exercises performed in order to develop or display physical agility. 2 other forms of physical or mental agility.

gymnosperm /ˈdʒɪmnəʊˌspɜːm/ n. any of a group of plants having seeds unprotected by an ovary, including conifers, cycads, and ginkgos. [Greek gumnos naked]

gymp var. of GIMP.

gymslip n. sleeveless tunic worn by schoolgirls.

gynae /ˈɡaɪni/ n. (also **gynie**) colloq. gynaecology. [abbreviation].

gynaecology /ˌɡaɪnɪˈkɒlədʒɪ/ n. (US **gynecology**) science of the physiological functions and diseases of women. □ **gynaecological** /-kəˈlɒdʒɪk(ə)l/ adj. **gynaecologist** n. [Greek gunē gunaik-woman, -LOGY]

gypsum /ˈdʒɪpsəm/ n. mineral used esp. to make plaster of Paris. [Greek gupsos]

Gypsy n. (also **Gipsy**) (pl. -ies) member of a nomadic people of Europe and N. America, of Hindu origin with dark skin and hair. [from EGYPTIAN]

gyrate /dʒaɪəˈreɪt/ v. (-ting) move in a circle or spiral; revolve, whirl. □ **gyration** /-ˈreɪʃ(ə)n/ n. **gyratory** adj. [Greek: related to GYRO-]

gyrfalcon /ˈdʒɜːˌfɔːlkən/ n. large falcon of the northern hemisphere. [French from Old Norse]

gyro /ˈdʒaɪərəʊ/ n. (pl. -s) colloq. GYROSCOPE. [abbreviation]

gyro- comb. form rotation. [Greek guros ring]

gyrocompass /ˈdʒaɪərəʊˌkʌmpəs/ n. compass giving true north and bearings from it by means of a gyroscope.

gyroscope /ˈdʒaɪərəˌskəʊp/ n. rotating wheel whose axis is free to turn but maintains a fixed direction unless perturbed, esp. used for stabilization or with the compass in an aircraft, ship, etc.

H

H¹ /eɪtʃ/ n. (also h) (pl. **Hs** or **H's**) **1** eighth letter of the alphabet (see ARCH). **2** anything having the form of an H (esp. in comb.). [H-girder]

H² abbr. (also **H.**) hard. **2** (water) hydrant **3** (of a pencil-lead) hard.

H³ symb. hydrogen.

h abbr. h. **2** (also h) henry(s).

h. abbr. (also h.) hecto-. **2** (also h) height. **3** hot. **4** hour(s).

Ha symb. hahnium.

ha¹ /hɑː/ (also **hah**) int. expressing surprise, derision, triumph, etc. (cf. HA HA). —v. in **hum and ha**: see HUM. [imitative]

ha² abbr. hectare(s).

haberdasher /ˈhæbəˌdæʃə(r)/ n. dealer in dress accessories and sewing-goods. □ **haberdashery** n. (pl. -ies). [probably Anglo-French]

habiliment /həˈbɪlɪmənt/ n. (usu. in pl.) archaic clothes. [French from habiller fit out]

habit /ˈhæbɪt/ n. **1** settled or regular tendency or practice (often foll. by of + verbal noun: has a habit of ignoring me). **2** practice that is hard to give up. **3** mental constitution or attitude. **4** dress, esp. of a religious order. [Latin habit-have]

habitable adj. suitable for living in. □ **habitability** /-ˈbɪlɪti/ n. [Latin habito inhabit]

habitat /ˈhæbɪˌtæt/ n. natural home of an animal or plant. [Latin, = it dwells]

habitation /ˌhæbɪˈteɪʃ(ə)n/ n. **1** inhabiting (fit for habitation). **2** house or home.

habit-forming adj. causing addiction.

habitual /həˈbɪtʃʊəl/ adj. **1** done constantly or as a habit. **2** regular, usual. **3** given to a (specified) habit (habitual smoker). □ **habitually** adv.

habituate /həˈbɪtʃʊˌeɪt/ v. (-ting) (often foll. by to) accustom. □ **habituation** /-ˈeɪʃ(ə)n/ n. [Latin: related to HABIT]

habitué /həˈbɪtʃʊˌeɪ/ n. habitual visitor or resident. [French]

háček /ˈhɑːtʃek/ n. diacritic (ˇ) placed over a letter to modify its sound in some languages. [Czech, diminutive of hák hook]

hachures /hæˈʃjʊə(r)/ n.pl. parallel lines on a map indicating the degree of steepness of hills. [French: related to HATCH³]

hacienda /ˌhæsɪˈendə/ n. (in Spanish-speaking countries) estate with a dwelling-house. [Spanish, from Latin facienda things to be done]

hack¹ —v. **1** cut or chop roughly. **2** Football etc. kick the shin of (an opponent). **3** (often foll. by at) deliver cutting blows. **4** cut (one's way) through foliage etc. **5** colloq. gain or authorized access to (data in a computer). **6** slang manage, cope with; tolerate. **7** (as **hacking** adj.) (of a cough) short, dry, and frequent. —n. **1** kick with the toe of a boot. **2** gash or wound, esp. from a kick. **3** a mattock. **b** miner's pick. [Old English]

hack² —n. **1 a** = HACKNEY. **b** horse let out for hire. **2** person hired to do dull routine work, esp. writing. —attrib. adj. **1** used as a hack. **2** typical of a hack; commonplace (hack work). —v. ride on horseback on a road at an ordinary pace. [abbreviation of HACKNEY]

hacker n. **1** person or thing that hacks or cuts roughly. **2** colloq. a person whose hobby is computing or computer programming. **b** person who uses a computer to gain unauthorized access to a computer network.

hackle /ˈhæk(ə)l/ n. **1 a** (in pl.) erectile hairs on an animal's neck, rising when it is angry or alarmed. **b** feather(s) on the neck of a domestic cock etc. **2** steel comb for dressing flax. □ **make one's hackles rise** cause one to be angry or indignant. [Old English]

hackney /ˈhækni/ n. (pl. -s) horse for ordinary riding. [Hackney in London]

hackney carriage n. taxi.

hackneyed /ˈhæknid/ adj. (of a phrase etc.) made trite by overuse.

hacksaw n. saw with a narrow blade set in a frame, for cutting metal.

had pest and past part. of HAVE.

haddock /ˈhædək/ n. (pl. same) N. Atlantic marine **fish** used as food. [probably French]

Hades /ˈheɪdiːz/ n. (in Greek mythology) the underworld. [Greek, originally a name of Pluto]

hadj var. of HAJJ.

hadji var. of HAJI.

hadn't /ˈhæd(ə)nt/ contr. had not.

haemal /ˈhiːm(ə)l/ *adj.* (*US* **hem-**) of the blood. [Greek *haima* blood]

haematite /ˈhiːmətaɪt/ *n.* (*US* **hem-**) a ferric oxide ore. [Latin: related to HAE-MAL]

haematology /ˌhiːməˈtɒlədʒɪ/ *n.* (*US* **hem-**) the study of the blood. □ **haematologist** *n.*

haemoglobin /ˌhiːməˈɡləʊbɪn/ *n.* (*US* **hem-**) oxygen-carrying substance in the red blood cells of vertebrates. [from GLOBULIN]

haemophilia /ˌhiːməˈfɪlɪə/ *n.* (*US* **hem-**) hereditary failure of the blood to clot normally with the tendency to bleed severely from even a slight injury. [Greek *haima* blood, *philia* loving]

haemophiliac *n.* (*US* **hem-**) person with haemophilia.

haemorrhage /ˈhemərɪdʒ/ (*US* **hem-**) —*n.* **1** profuse loss of blood from a ruptured blood-vessel. **2** damaging loss, esp. of people or assets. —*v.* (**-ging**) suffer a haemorrhage. [Greek *haima* blood, *rhēgnumi* burst]

haemorrhoids /ˈhemərɔɪdz/ *n.pl.* (*US* **hem-**) swollen veins in the wall of the anus; piles. [Greek *haima* blood, *rhoos* -flowing]

hafnium /ˈhæfnɪəm/ *n.* silvery lustrous metallic element [Latin *Hafnia* Copenhagen]

haft /hɑːft/ *n.* handle of a dagger, knife, etc. [Old English]

hag *n.* **1** ugly old woman. **2** witch. [Old English]

haggard /ˈhæɡəd/ *adj.* looking exhausted and distraught. [French *hagard*]

haggis /ˈhæɡɪs/ *n.* Scottish dish of offal boiled in a sheep's stomach with suet, oatmeal, etc. [origin unknown]

haggle /ˈhæɡ(ə)l/ —*v.* (**-ling**) (often foll. by *about*, *over*) bargain persistently. —*n.* haggling. [Old Norse]

hagio- *comb. form* of saints. [Greek *hagios* holy]

hagiography /ˌhæɡɪˈɒɡrəfɪ/ *n.* writing about saints' lives. □ **hagiographer** *n.*

hagiology /ˌhæɡɪˈɒlədʒɪ/ *n.* literature dealing with the lives and legends of saints.

hagridden *adj.* afflicted by nightmares or anxieties.

hah var. of HA¹.

ha ha /hɑːˈhɑː/ *int.* representing laughter (*iron.* when spoken). [Old English]

ha-ha /ˈhɑːhɑː/ *n.* ditch with a wall in it, forming a boundary or fence without interrupting the view. [French]

hahnium /ˈhɑːnɪəm/ *n.* artificially produced radioactive element. [*Hahn*, name of a chemist]

haiku /ˈhaɪkuː/ *n.* (*pl.* same) Japanese three-part poem of usu. 17 syllables. [Japanese]

hail¹ —*n.* **1** pellets of frozen rain. **2** (foll. by *of*) barrage or onslaught. —*v.* **1 a** (prec. by *it* as subject) hail falls. **b** come down forcefully. **2** pour down (blows, words, etc.). [Old English]

hail² —*v.* **1** signal to (a taxi etc.) to stop. **2** greet enthusiastically. **3** acclaim (*hailed him king*). **4** (foll. by *from*) originate or come (*hails from Leeds*). —*int. archaic* or *joc.* expressing greeting. —*n.* act of hailing. [Old Norse *heill*: related to WAS-SAIL]

hail-fellow-well-met *adj.* friendly, esp. too friendly towards strangers.

Hail Mary *n.* the Ave Maria (see AVE).

hailstone *n.* pellet of hail.

hailstorm *n.* period of heavy hail.

hair *n.* **1 a** any of the fine threadlike strands growing from the skin of mammals, esp. from the human head. **b** these collectively (*has long hair*). **2** thing resembling a hair. **3** elongated cell growing from a plant. **4** very small quantity or extent (also *attrib.*: *hair crack*). □ **get in a person's hair** *colloq.* annoy a person. **keep one's hair on** *colloq.* keep calm; not get angry. **let one's hair down** *colloq.* enjoy oneself by abandoning restraint. **make one's hair stand on end** *colloq.* horrify one. **not turn a hair** remain unmoved or unaffected. □ **hairless** *adj.* [Old English]

hairbrush *n.* brush for tidying the hair.

haircloth *n.* stiff cloth woven from hair.

haircut *n.* **1** act of cutting the hair (*needs a haircut*). **2** style in which the hair is cut.

hairdo *n.* (*pl.* **-s**) style or act of styling the hair.

hairdresser *n.* **1** person who cuts and styles the hair, esp. for a living. **2** hairdresser's shop. □ **hairdressing** *n.*

hair-drier *n.* (also **hair-dryer**) device for drying the hair with warm air.

hairgrip *n.* flat hairpin with the ends close together.

hairline *n.* **1** edge of a person's hair, esp. on the forehead. **2** very narrow line, crack (usu. *hairline crack*), etc.

hairnet *n.* piece of netting for confining the hair.

hair of the dog *n.* further alcoholic drink taken to cure the effects of drink.

hairpiece *n.* quantity of hair augmenting a person's natural hair.

hairpin *n.* U-shaped pin for fastening the hair.

hairpin bend *n.* sharp U-shaped bend in a road.

hair-raising *adj.* terrifying.

hair's breadth *n.* a tiny amount or margin.

hair shirt *n.* shirt of haircloth, worn formerly by penitents and ascetics.

hair-slide *n.* clip for keeping the hair in place.

hair-splitting *adj.* & *n.* quibbling.

hairspray *n.* liquid sprayed on the hair to keep it in place.

hairspring *n.* fine spring regulating the balance-wheel in a watch.

hairstyle *n.* particular way of arranging the hair. □ **hairstylist** *n.*

hair-trigger *n.* trigger of a firearm set for release at the slightest pressure.

hairy *adj.* (**-ier, -iest**) **1** covered with hair. **2** *slang* frightening, dangerous. □ **hairiness** *n.*

hajj /hadʒ/ *n.* (also **haj**) Islamic pilgrimage to Mecca. [Arabic]

hajji /ˈhadʒɪ/ *n.* (also **haji**) (*pl.* **-s**) Muslim who has made the pilgrimage to Mecca. [Persian from Arabic]

haka /ˈhɑːkə/ *n. NZ* **1** Maori ceremonial war dance with chanting. **2** imitation of this by a sports team before a match. [Maori]

hake *n.* (*pl.* same) marine fish resembling the cod, used as food. [origin uncertain]

halal /hɑːˈlɑːl/ *n.* (also **hallal**) (often *attrib.*) meat from an animal killed according to Muslim law. [Arabic]

halberd /ˈhalbəd/ *n. hist.* combined spear and battleaxe. [French from German]

halcyon /ˈhalsɪən/ *adj.* calm, peaceful, happy. (*halcyon days*). [Greek, = kingfisher, because it was reputed to calm the sea at midwinter]

hale *adj.* strong and healthy (esp. in **hale and hearty**). [var. of WHOLE]

half /hɑːf/ *—n.* (*pl.* **halves** /hɑːvz/) **1** either of two (esp. equal) parts into which a thing is divided **2** *colloq.* half a pint, esp. of beer. **3** *Sport* either of two equal periods of play. **4** *colloq.* half-price fare or ticket, esp. for a child. **5** *colloq.* = HALF-BACK. *—adj.* **1** amounting to half (*half the men*). **2** forming a half (*a half share*). *—adv.* **1** (often in *comb.*) to the extent of half; partly (*half cooked*). **2** to some extent (*in idiomatic phrases*: *half dead; am half convinced*). **3** (in reckoning time) by the amount of half (an hour etc.) (*half past two*). □ **at half cock** see COCK. **by half** (prec. by *too* + *adj.*) excessively (*too clever by half*). **by halves** imperfectly or incompletely (*does nothing by halves*). **half a mind** see MIND. **half the time** see TIME. **not half** *slang* extremely, violently (*not didn't half swear*). **2** not nearly (*not*

half long enough). **3** *colloq.* not at all (*not half bad*). [Old English]

■ **Usage** In sense 3 of the adverb, the word 'past' is often omitted in colloquial usage, e.g. *came at half two.* In some parts of Scotland and Ireland this means 'half past one'.

half-and-half *adj.* being half one thing and half another.

half-back *n. Sport* player between the forwards and full backs.

half-baked *adj. colloq.* **1** not thoroughly thought out; foolish. **2** (of enthusiasm etc.) only partly committed.

half board *n.* provision of bed, breakfast, and one main meal at a hotel etc.

half-breed *n. offens.* = HALF-CASTE.

half-brother *n.* brother with whom one has only one parent in common.

half-caste *n. offens.* person of mixed race.

half-crown *n.* (also **half a crown**) former coin and monetary unit worth 2s. 6d. (12½p).

half-cut *adj. slang* fairly drunk.

half-dozen *n.* (also **half a dozen**) *colloq.* six, or about six.

half-duplex *n. Computing* (of a circuit) allowing the two-way transmission of signals but not simultaneously.

half-hardy *adj.* (of a plant) able to grow in the open except in severe frost.

half-hearted *adj.* lacking enthusiasm. □ **half-heartedly** *adv.* **half-heartedness** *n.*

half hitch *n.* knot formed by passing the end of a rope round its standing part and through the loop.

half holiday *n.* half a day as holiday.

half-hour *n.* **1** (also **half an hour**) period of 30 minutes. **2** point of time 30 minutes after any hour o'clock. □ **half-hourly** *adj.* & *adv.*

half-life *n.* time taken for radioactivity etc. to fall to half its original value.

half-light *n.* dim imperfect light.

half-mast *n.* position of a flag halfway down a mast, as a mark of respect for a deceased person.

half measures *n.pl.* unsatisfactory compromise or inadequate policy.

half moon *n.* **1** moon when only half its surface is illuminated. **2** time when this occurs. **3** semicircular object.

half nelson see NELSON.

halfpenny /ˈheɪpnɪ/ *n.* (*pl.* **-pennies** or **-pence** /ˈheɪpəns/) former coin worth half a penny.

■ **Usage** The *halfpenny* was withdrawn from circulation in 1984.

half-sister *n.* sister with whom one has only one parent in common.

half-term *n.* short holiday halfway through a school term.

half-timbered *adj.* having walls with a timber frame and a brick or plaster filling.

half-time *n.* 1 mid-point of a game or contest. 2 short break occurring at this time.

half-title *n.* title or short title of a book printed on the front of the leaf preceding the title-page.

halftone *n.* photographic illustration in which various tones of grey are produced from small and large black dots.

half-truth *n.* statement that (esp. deliberately) conveys only part of the truth.

half-volley *n.* (in ball games) playing of the ball as soon as it bounces off the ground.

halfway *—adv.* 1 at a point midway between two others (*halfway to Rome*). 2 to some extent, more or less (*is half-way acceptable*). *—adj.* situated halfway (*reached a halfway point*).

halfway house *n.* 1 compromise. 2 halfway point in a progression. 3 centre for rehabilitating ex-prisoners etc. 4 inn midway between two towns.

halfwit *n.* foolish or stupid person. □ **halfwitted** *adj.*

halibut /ˈhælɪbət/ *n.* (*pl.* same) large marine flat-fish used as food. [from HOLY (perhaps because eaten on holy days), *butt* flat-fish]

halitosis /ˌhælɪˈtəʊsɪs/ *n.* = BAD BREATH. [Latin *halitus* breath]

hall /hɔːl/ *n.* 1 area into which the front entrance of a house etc. opens. 2 large room or building for meetings, concerts, etc. 3 large country house or estate. 4 (in full **hall of residence**) residence for students. 5 (in a college etc.) dining-room. 6 premises of a guild (*Fishmongers' Hall*). 7 large public room in a palace etc. [Old English]

hallal var. of HALAL.

hallelujah var. of ALLELUIA.

halliard var. of HALYARD.

hallmark *—n.* 1 mark indicating the standard of gold, silver, and platinum. 2 distinctive feature. *—v.* stamp with a hallmark.

hallo var. of HELLO.

halloo /həˈluː/ *int.* inciting dogs to the chase or calling attention. [perhaps from *hallow* pursue with shouts]

hallow /ˈhæləʊ/ *v.* 1 make holy, consecrate. 2 honour as holy. [Old English: related to HOLY]

Hallowe'en /ˌhæləʊˈiːn/ *n.* eve of All Saints' Day, 31 Oct.

hallucinate /həˈluːsɪˌneɪt/ *v.* (**-ting**) experience hallucinations. □ **hallucinant** *adj.* & *n.* [Greek *alussō* be uneasy]

hallucination /həˌluːsɪˈneɪʃ(ə)n/ *n.* illusion of seeing or hearing something not actually present. □ **hallucinatory** /həˈluːsɪnətərɪ/ *adj.*

hallucinogen /həˈluːsɪnədʒ(ə)n/ *n.* drug causing hallucinations. □ **hallucinogenic** /-ˈdʒenɪk/ *adj.*

hallway *n.* entrance-hall or corridor.

halm var. of HAULM.

halo /ˈheɪləʊ/ *—n.* (*pl.* **-es**) 1 disc or circle of light shown surrounding the head of a sacred person. 2 glory associated with an idealized person etc. 3 circle of white or coloured light round a luminous body, esp. the sun or moon. *—v.* (**-es, -ed**) surround with a halo. [Greek *halōs* threshing-floor, disc of the sun or moon]

halogen /ˈhælədʒ(ə)n/ *n.* any of the non-metallic elements (fluorine, chlorine, bromine, iodine, and astatine) which form a salt (e.g. sodium chloride) when combined with a metal. [Greek *hals* *halos* salt, -GEN]

halon /ˈheɪlɒn/ *n.* any of various gaseous compounds of carbon, bromine, and other halogens, used to extinguish fires. [related to HALOGEN]

halt[1] /hɔːlt/ *n.* 1 stop (usu. temporary) (*come to a halt*). 2 minor stopping-place on a local railway line. *—v.* stop; come or bring to a halt. □ **call a halt** (to) decide to stop. [German: related to HOLD]

halt[2] /hɔːlt/ *—v.* (esp. as **halting** *adj.*) proceed hesitantly. *—adj.* *archaic* lame. □ **haltingly** *adv.* [Old English]

halter /ˈhɔːltə(r)/ *n.* 1 headstall and rope for leading or tying up a horse etc. 2 a strap round the neck holding a dress etc. up and leaving the shoulders and back bare. b (also **halterneck**) dress etc. held by this. [Old English]

halva /ˈhælvə/ *n.* confection of sesame flour and honey etc. [Yiddish from Turkish *helva* from Arabic *ḥalwā*]

halve /hɑːv/ *v.* (**-ving**) 1 divide into two halves or parts; share equally between two. 2 reduce by half. 3 *Golf* use the same number of strokes as one's opponent in (a hole or match).

halves *pl.* of HALF.

halyard /ˈhæljəd/ *n.* (also **halliard**) rope or tackle for raising or lowering a sail, yard, etc. [archaic *hale* drag forcibly]

ham *—n.* 1 a upper part of a pig's leg salted and dried or smoked for food. b meat from this. 2 back of the thigh; thigh and buttock. 3 *colloq.* (often *attrib.*) inexpert or unsubtle actor or piece of acting. 4 *colloq.* operator of an amateur radio station. *—v.* (**-mm-**) (usu. in **ham it up**) *colloq.* overact. [Old English]

log. clumsy.

hamburger /ˈhæmbɜːgə(r)/ *n.* cake of minced beef, usu. eaten in a soft bread roll. [*Hamburg* in Germany]

ham-fisted *adj.* (also **ham-handed**) *col-*

Hamitic /hæˈmɪtɪk/—*n.* group of African languages including ancient Egyptian and Berber. —*adj.* of this group. [from the name *Ham* (Gen. 1c:6 ff.)]

hamlet /ˈhæmlɪt/ *n.* small village, esp. without a church. [French *hamelet* di-minutive]

hammer—*n.* **1 a** tool with a heavy metal head at right angles to its handle, used for driving nails etc. **b** similar device, as for exploding the charge in a gun, striking the strings of a piano, etc. **2** auctioneer's mallet. **3** metal ball attached to a wire for throwing in an athletic contest. —*v.* **1 a** hit or beat with or as with a hammer. **b** strike loudly. **2 a** drive in (nails) with a hammer. **b** fasten or secure by hammering (*hammered the lid down*). **3** (usu. foll. by *in*) inculcate (ideas, knowledge, etc.) forcefully or repeatedly. **4** *colloq.* defeat utterly. **5** (foll. by *at, away at*) work hard or persistently at. □ **come under the hammer** be sold at auction. **hammer and sickle** *n.* symbols of the industrial worker and peasant used as an emblem of the former USSR and international communism.

hammer and tongs *adv. colloq.* with great vigour and commotion.

hammerhead *n.* shark with a flattened head and with eyes in lateral extensions of it.

hammerlock *n. Wrestling* hold in which the arm is twisted and bent behind the back.

hammer-toe *n.* toe bent permanently downwards.

hammock /ˈhæmək/ *n.* bed of canvas or rope network suspended by cords at the ends. [Spanish from Carib]

hammy *adj.* (**-ier, -iest**) *colloq.* over-theatrical.

hamper[1] *n.* large basket, usu. with a hinged lid and containing food. [French *hanap* goblet]

hamper[2] *v.* prevent the free movement of, hinder. [origin unknown]

hamster *n.* mouselike rodent with a short tail and large cheek-pouches for storing food. [German]

hamstring—*n.* **1** each of five tendons at the back of the knee. **2** great tendon at the back of the hock in quadrupeds. —*v.*

(*past* and *past part.* **-strung** or **-stringed**) **1** cripple by cutting the hamstrings of (a person or animal). **2** impair the activity or efficiency of.

hand—*n.* **1 a** end part of the human arm beyond the wrist. **b** (in other primates) end part of a forelimb. **2 a** (often in *pl.*) control, management, custody, disposal (*is in good hands*). **b** agency or influence (*suffered at their hands*). **c** share in an action; active support (*had a hand in it; give me a hand*). **3** thing like a hand, esp. the pointer of a clock. **4** right or left side or direction relative to a person or thing. **5 a** skill (*has a hand for making pastry*). **b** person skilful in some respect. **6** person who does or makes something, esp. distinctively (*picture by the same hand*). **7** person's writing or its style. **8** a person etc. as a source (*at first hand*). **9** pledge of marriage. **10** manual worker, esp. at a factory or farm; member of a ship's crew. **11 a** playing-cards dealt to a player. **b** round of play. **12** *colloq.* burst of applause. **13** unit of measure of a horse's height, 4 inches (10.16 cm). **14** forehock of pork. **15** (*attrib.*) operated by or held in the hand (*hand-drill*). **b** done by hand, not machine (*hand-knitted*). —*v.* **1** (foll. by *in, to, over,* etc.) deliver, transfer by hand or otherwise. **2** *colloq.* give away too readily (*handed them the advantage*). □ **all hands** entire crew or workforce. **at hand 1** close by. **2** about to happen. **by hand 1** by a person, not a machine. **2** delivered privately, not by post. **from hand to mouth** satisfying only one's immediate needs, get (or have or keep) one's hand in become (or be or remain) in practice. **hand down 1** pass ownership or use of to a later generation etc. **2** transmit (a decision) from a higher court etc. **b** *US* express (an opinion or verdict). **hand it to** *colloq.* award deserved praise to. **hand on** pass (a thing) to the next in a series. **hand out 1** serve, distribute. **2** award, allocate (*handed out stiff penalties*). **hand round** serve, distribute. **hands down** with no difficulty; completely. **in hand 1** receiving attention. **2** in reserve. **3** under control. **on hand** available. **on the one** (or **the other**) **hand** from one (or another) point of view. **out of hand 1** out of control. **2** peremptorily (*refused out of hand*). **put** (or **set**) **one's hand to** start work on. **to hand** within easy reach; available. **turn one's hand to** undertake (as a new activity). □ **-handed** *adj.*

handbag *n.* small bag carried esp. by a woman.

handball n. **1** game with a ball thrown by hand among players or against a wall. **2** Football intentional touching of the ball, constituting a foul.

handbell n. small bell for ringing by hand, esp. one of a set.

handbill n. printed notice distributed by hand.

handbook n. short manual or guidebook.

handbrake n. brake operated by hand.

h. & c. abbr. hot and cold (water).

handcart n. small cart pushed or drawn by hand.

handclap n. clapping of the hands.

handcraft n. = HANDICRAFT. —v. make by handicraft.

handcuff —n. each of a pair of linked metal rings for securing a prisoner's wrist(s). —v. put handcuffs on.

handful n. (pl. -s) **1** quantity that fills the hand. **2** small number or amount. **3** colloq. troublesome person or task.

hand-grenade see GRENADE.

handgun n. small firearm held in and fired with one hand.

handhold n. something for the hand to grip on (in climbing etc.).

handicap /ˈhændɪkæp/ —n. **1** physical or mental disability. **2** thing that makes progress or success difficult. **3** a disadvantage imposed on a superior competitor to make chances more equal. **b** race etc. in which this is imposed. **4** number of strokes by which a golfer normally exceeds par for a course. —v. (-pp-) **1** impose a handicap on. **2** place at a disadvantage. [hand i' (= in) cap describing a kind of sporting lottery]

handicapped adj. suffering from a physical or mental disability.

handicraft /ˈhændɪˌkrɑːft/ n. work requiring manual and artistic skill. [from earlier HANDCRAFT]

hand in glove adv. in collusion or association.

hand in hand adv. **1** in close association (power and money go hand in hand). **2** (hand-in-hand) holding hands.

handiwork /ˈhændɪˌwɜːk/ n. work done or a thing made by hand, or by a particular person. [Old English]

handkerchief /ˈhæŋkətʃɪf/ n. (pl. -s or -chieves /-tʃiːvz/) square of cloth for wiping one's nose etc.

handle /ˈhænd(ə)l/ —n. **1** part by which a thing is held, carried, or controlled. **2** fact that may be taken advantage of (gave a handle to his critics). **3** colloq. personal title. —v. (-ling) **1** touch, feel, operate, or move with the hands. **2** manage, deal with (can handle people).

3 deal in (goods). **4** treat (a subject). [Old English: related to HAND]

handlebar n. (usu. in pl.) steering-bar of a bicycle etc.

handlebar moustache n. thick moustache with curved ends.

handler n. **1** person who handles or deals in something. **2** person who trains and looks after an animal (esp. a police dog).

handmade adj. made by hand (as opposed to machine).

handmaid n. (also **handmaiden**) archaic female servant.

hand-me-down n. article of clothing etc. passed on from another person.

hand-out n. **1** thing given free to a needy person. **2** statement given to the press etc.; notes given out in a class etc.

hand-over n. handing over.

hand-over-fist adv. colloq. with rapid progress.

hand-pick v. choose carefully or personally.

handrail n. narrow rail for holding as a support.

handsaw n. saw worked by one hand.

handset n. telephone mouthpiece and earpiece as one unit.

handshake n. clasping of a person's hand as a greeting etc.

hands off —int. warning not to touch or interfere with something. —adj. & adv. (also **hands-off**) not requiring the manual use of controls.

handsome /ˈhænsəm/ adj. (**handsomer**, **handsomest**) **1** (usu. of a man) good-looking. **2** (of an object) imposing, attractive. **3** a generous, liberal (handsome present). **b** (of a price, fortune, etc.) considerable. □ **handsomely** adv. **handsomeness** n.

hands on (also **hands-on**) —adj. & adv. of or requiring personal operation at a keyboard. —attrib. adj. practical rather than theoretical (lacks hands-on experience).

handspring n. gymnastic feat consisting of a handstand, somersaulting, and landing in a standing position.

handstand n. supporting oneself on one's hands with one's feet in the air.

hand-to-hand adj. (of fighting) at close quarters.

handwork n. work done with the hands. □ **handworked** adj.

handwriting n. **1** writing done with a pen, pencil, etc. **2** person's particular style of this. □ **handwritten** adj.

handy adj. (-ier, -iest) **1** convenient to handle or use; useful. **2** ready to hand. **3** clever with the hands. □ **handily** adv. **handiness** n.

handyman n. person able to do occasional repairs etc.; odd-job man.

hang –*v.* (*past* and *past part.* **hung** except in sense 7) **1 a** secure or cause to be supported from above, with the lower part free. **b** (foll. by *up, on, on to*, etc.) attach by suspending from the top. **2** set up (a door etc.) on hinges. **3** place (a picture) on a wall or in an exhibition. **4** attach (wallpaper) to a wall. **5** (foll. by *on*) *colloq.* blame (a thing) on (a person) (*can't hang that on me*). **6** (foll. by *with*) decorate by suspending pictures etc. (*hall hung with tapestries*). **7** (*past* and *past part.* **hanged**) **a** suspend or be suspended by the neck with a noosed rope until dead, esp. as a form of capital punishment. **b** as a mild oath (*hang the expense*). **8** let droop (*hang one's head*). **9** suspend (meat or game) from a hook and leave until dry, tender, or high. **10** be or remain hung (in various senses). **11** remain static in the air. **12** (often foll. by *over*) be present or imminent esp. oppressively or threateningly (*a hush hung over the room*). **13** (foll. by *on*) **a** be contingent or dependent on (*everything hangs on his reply*). **b** listen closely to (*hangs on my every word*). —*n.* way a thing hangs or falls. □ **get the hang of** *colloq.* understand the technique or meaning of. **hang about** (or **around**) **1 a** stand about or spend time aimlessly. not move away. **b** linger near (a person or place). **2** (often foll. by *with*) *colloq.* associate with. **hang back** show reluctance to act or move. **hang fire** be slow in taking action or in progressing. **hang heavily** (or **heavy**) (of time) pass slowly. **hang in** *US colloq.* **1** persist, persevere. **2** linger. **hang on 1** (often foll. by *to*) continue to hold or grasp. **2** (foll. by *to*) retain; fail to give back. **3** *colloq.* **a** wait for a short time. **b** (in telephoning) not ring off during a pause in the conversation. **4** *colloq.* continue; persevere. **hang out 1** suspend from a window, clothes-line, etc. **2 a** protrude downwards. **b** (foll. by *of*) lean out of a window etc.). **3** *slang* frequent or live in a place. **hang together 1** make sense. **2** remain associated. **hang up 1** hang from a hook etc. **2** (often foll. by *on*) end a telephone conversation by replacing the receiver (*the hung up on me*). **3** (usu. in *passive*, foll. by *on*) *slang* be a psychological problem or obsession for (*is hung up on her father*). **not care** (or **give**) **a hang** *colloq.* not care at all. [Old English]

hangar /'hæŋə(r)/ *n.* building for housing aircraft etc. [French]

hangdog /'hæŋdɒg/ *adj.* shamefaced.

hanger *n.* **1** person or thing that hangs. **2** (in full **coat-hanger**) shaped piece of wood etc. for hanging clothes on.

hanger-on *n.* (*pl.* **hangers-on**) follower or dependant, esp. an unwelcome one.

hang-glider *n.* glider with a fabric wing on a light frame, from which the operator is suspended. □ **hang-glide** *v.*

hang-gliding ?

hanging *n.* **1** execution by suspending by the neck. **2** (usu. in *pl.*) draperies hung on a wall etc.

hangman *n.* **1** executioner. **2** word-game for two players, with failed guesses recorded by drawing a representation of a gallows.

hangnail *n.* = AGNAIL.

hang-out *n. slang* place frequented by a person; haunt.

hangover *n.* **1** severe headache etc. from drinking too much alcohol. **2** survival from the past.

hang-up *n. slang* emotional problem or inhibition.

hank *n.* coil or skein of wool or thread etc. [Old Norse]

hanker *v.* (foll. by *after*, or *to* + infin.) long for; crave. □ **hankering** *n.* [from obsolete *hank*]

hanky /'hæŋkɪ/ *n.* (also **hankie**) (*pl.* **-ies**) *colloq.* handkerchief. [abbreviation]

hanky-panky /ˌhæŋkɪˈpæŋkɪ/ *n. slang* **1** naughtiness; trickery. **2** double-dealing; trickery. [origin unknown]

Hanoverian /ˌhænəˈvɪərɪən/ *adj.* of British sovereigns from George 1 to Victoria. [*Hanover* in Germany]

Hansard /'hænsɑːd/ *n.* official verbatim record of debates in the British Parliament. [*Hansard*, name of its first printer]

Hansen's disease /'hæns(ə)nz/ *n.* leprosy. [*Hansen*, name of a physician]

hansom /'hænsəm/ *n.* (in full **hansom cab**) *hist.* two-wheeled horse-drawn cab. [*Hansom*, name of an architect]

Hanukkah /'hɑːnəkə/ *n.* Jewish festival of lights, commemorating the purification of the Temple in 165 BC. [Hebrew *ḥănukkāh* consecration]

haphazard /hæpˈhæzəd/ *adj.* done etc. by chance; random. □ **haphazardly** *adv.* [archaic *hap* chance, luck, from Old Norse *happ*]

hapless *adj.* unlucky.

haploid /'hæplɔɪd/ *adj.* (of an organism or cell) with a single set of chromosomes. [Greek *haplous* single, *eidos* form]

happen /'hæp(ə)n/ *v.* **1** occur (by chance or otherwise). **2** (foll. by *to* + infin.) have the (good or bad) fortune to (*I happened to meet her*). **3** (foll. by *to*) be the (esp. unwelcome) fate or experience of (*what happened to you?*). **4** (foll. by *on*)

encounter or discover by chance. □ **as it happens** in fact; in reality. [related to HAPHAZARD]

happening *n.* **1** event. **2** improvised or spontaneous theatrical etc. performance.

happy /ˈhæpɪ/ *adj.* (**-ier, -iest**) **1** feeling or showing pleasure or contentment. **2 a** fortunate; characterized by happiness. **b** (of words, behaviour, etc.) apt, pleasing. □ **happily** *adv.* **happiness** *n.*

happy-go-lucky *adj.* cheerfully casual.

happy hour *n.* time of the day when goods, esp. drinks, are sold at reduced prices.

happy medium *n.* compromise; avoidance of extremes.

hara-kiri /ˌhærəˈkɪrɪ/ *n.* ritual suicide by disembowelment with a sword, formerly practised by samurai to avoid dishonour. [Japanese *hara* belly, *kiri* cutting]

harangue /həˈræŋ/ —*n.* lengthy and earnest speech. —*v.* (**-guing**) make a harangue to; lecture. [French *arenge* from medieval Latin]

harass /ˈhærəs, həˈræs/ *v.* **1** trouble and annoy continually. **2** make repeated attacks on. □ **harassment** *n.* [French]

■ **Usage** The second pronunciation given, with the stress on the second syllable, is common, but is considered incorrect by some people.

harbinger /ˈhɑːbɪndʒə(r)/ *n.* **1** person or thing that announces or signals the approach of another. **2** forerunner. [Germanic: related to HARBOUR]

harbour /ˈhɑːbə(r)/ (*US* **harbor**) —*n.* **1** place of shelter for ships. **2** shelter; refuge. —*v.* **1** give shelter to (esp. a criminal). **2** keep in one's mind (esp. resentment etc.). [Old English, = army shelter]

harbour-master *n.* official in charge of a harbour.

hard —*adj.* **1** (of a substance etc.) firm and solid. **2 a** difficult to understand, explain, or accomplish. **b** (foll. by *to* + infin.) not easy to (*hard to please*). **3** difficult to bear (*a hard life*). **4** unfeeling; severely critical. **5** (of a season or the weather) severe. **6** unpleasant to the senses, harsh (*hard colours*). **7 a** strenuous, enthusiastic, intense (*a hard worker*). **b** severe, uncompromising (*a hard bargain*). **c** *Polit.* extreme; most radical (*the hard right*). **8 a** (of liquor) strongly alcoholic. **b** (of drugs) potent and addictive. **c** (of pornography) highly obscene. **9** (of water) containing mineral salts that make lathering difficult. **10** established; not disputable (*hard facts*).

11 (of currency, prices, etc.) high; not likely to fall in value. **12** (of a consonant) guttural (as *c* in *cat*, *g* in *go*). —*adv.* strenuously, intensely, copiously (*try hard; raining hard*). □ **be hard on 1** be difficult for. **2** be severe in one's treatment or criticism of. **3** be unpleasant to (the senses). **be hard put to it** (usu. foll. by *to* + infin.) find it difficult. **hard by** close to. **hard on** (or **upon**) close to in pursuit etc. □ **hardish** *adj.* **hardness** *n.* [Old English]

hard and fast *adj.* (of a rule or distinction) definite, unalterable, strict.

hardback —*adj.* bound in boards covered with cloth etc. —*n.* hardback book.

hardbitten *adj. colloq.* tough and cynical.

hardboard *n.* stiff board made of compressed and treated wood pulp.

hard-boiled *adj.* **1** (of an egg) boiled until the white and yolk are solid. **2** *colloq.* (of a person) tough, shrewd.

hard cash *n.* negotiable coins and banknotes.

hard copy *n.* material printed by a computer on paper.

hardcore *n.* solid material, esp. rubble, as road-foundation.

hard core *n.* **1** irreducible nucleus. **2** *colloq.* the most committed members of a society etc. **b** conservative or reactionary minority (see also HARDCORE).

hard-core *adj.* **1** forming a nucleus. **2** blatant, uncompromising. **3** (of pornography) explicit, obscene.

hard disk *n. Computing* large-capacity rigid usu. magnetic storage disk.

hard-done-by *adj.* unfairly treated.

harden *v.* **1** make or become hard or harder. **2** become, or make (one's attitude etc.), less sympathetic. **3** (of prices etc.) cease to fall or fluctuate. □ **harden off** inure (a plant) to the cold by gradually increasing its exposure.

hardening of the arteries *n.* = ARTERIOSCLEROSIS.

hard-headed *adj.* practical; not sentimental. □ **hard-headedness** *n.*

hard-hearted *adj.* unfeeling. □ **hard-heartedness** *n.*

hardihood /ˈhɑːdɪhʊd/ *n.* boldness, daring.

hard labour *n.* heavy manual work as a punishment, esp. in a prison.

hard line *n.* unyielding adherence to a policy. □ **hard-liner** *n.*

hard luck *n.* worse fortune than one deserves.

hardly *adv.* **1** scarcely; only just (*hardly knew me*). **2** only with difficulty (*can hardly see*). **3** surely not (*can hardly have realised*). □ **hardly any**

almost no; almost none. **hardly ever** very seldom.
hard-nosed *adj. colloq* realistic, uncompromising.
hard of hearing *adj.* somewhat deaf.
hard-on *n. coarse slang* erection of the penis.
hard pad *n.* form of distemper in dogs etc.
hard palate *n.* front part of the palate.
hard-pressed *adj.* 1 closely pursued. 2 burdened with urgent business.
hard roe see ROE.
hard sell *n.* aggressive salesmanship.
hardship *n.* 1 severe suffering or privation. 2 circumstance causing this.
hard shoulder *n.* hard surface along side a motorway for stopping on in an emergency.
hard tack *n. Naut.* ship's biscuit.
hardtop *n.* car with a rigid (usu. detachable) roof.
hard up *adj.* short of money.
hardware *n.* 1 tools and household articles of metal etc. 2 heavy machinery or armaments. 3 mechanical and electronic components of a computer etc.
hard-wearing *adj.* able to stand much wear.
hardwood *n.* wood from a deciduous broad-leaved tree.
hard-working *adj.* diligent.
hardy /ˈhɑːdɪ/ *adj.* (**-ier**, **-iest**) 1 robust; capable of enduring difficult conditions. 2 (of a plant) able to grow in the open air all year. □ **hardiness** *n.* [French *hardi* made bold]
hardy annual *n.* annual plant that may be sown in the open.
hare –*n.* mammal like a large rabbit, with long ears, short tail, and long hind legs. –*v.* (**-ring**) run rapidly. [Old English]
harebell *n.* plant with pale-blue bell-shaped flowers.
hare-brained *adj.* rash, wild.
harelip *n.* often *offens.* congenital cleft in the upper lip.
harem /ˈhɑːriːm/ *n.* 1 women of a Muslim household. 2 their quarters. [Arabic, = sanctuary]
haricot /ˈhærɪkəʊ/ *n.* (in full **haricot bean**) variety of French bean with small white seeds dried and used as a vegetable. [French]
hark *v.* (usu. in *imper.*) *archaic* listen attentively. □ **hark back** revert to earlier topic. [Old English]
harlequin /ˈhɑːlɪkwɪn/ –*n.* (**Harle-quin**) name of a mute character in pantomime, usu. masked and dressed in a diamond-patterned costume. –*attrib. adj.* in varied colours. [French]

harlequinade /ˌhɑːlɪkwɪˈneɪd/ *n.* 1 part of a pantomime featuring Harlequin. 2 piece of buffoonery.
harlot /ˈhɑːlət/ *n. archaic* prostitute. □ **harlotry** *n.* [French, = knave]
harm –*n.* hurt, damage. –*v.* cause harm to. □ **out of harm's way** in safety. [Old English]
harmful *adj.* causing or likely to cause harm. □ **harmfully** *adv.* **harmfulness** *n.*
harmless *adj.* 1 not able or likely to cause harm. 2 inoffensive. □ **harm-lessly** *adv.* **harmlessness** *n.*
harmonic /hɑːˈmɒnɪk/ –*adj.* of or relating to harmony; harmonious. –*n. Mus.* overtone accompanying (and forming a note with) a fundamental at a fixed interval. □ **harmonically** *adv.*
harmonica *n.* small rectangular musical instrument played by blowing and sucking air through it.
harmonious /hɑːˈməʊnɪəs/ *adj.* 1 sweet-sounding; tuneful. 2 forming a pleasing or consistent whole. 3 free from disagreement; harmonious. □ **har-moniously** *adv.*
harmonium /hɑːˈməʊnɪəm/ *n.* keyboard instrument in which the notes are produced by air driven through metal reeds by foot-operated bellows. [Latin: related to HARMONY]
harmonize /ˈhɑːmənaɪz/ *v.* (also **-ise**) (**-zing** or **-sing**) 1 add notes to (a melody) to produce harmony. 2 bring into or be in harmony. 3 make or form a pleasing or consistent whole. □ **harmonization** /-ˈzeɪʃ(ə)n/ *n.*
harmony /ˈhɑːmənɪ/ *n.* (*pl.* **-ies**) 1 combination of simultaneously sounded musical notes to produce chords and chord progressions, esp. as creating a pleasing effect. 2 **a** apt or aesthetic arrangement of parts. **b** pleasing effect of this. 3 agreement, concord. □ **in harmony** 1 in agreement. 2 (of singing etc.) producing chords; not discordant. [Greek *harmonia* joining]
harness /ˈhɑːnɪs/ –*n.* 1 equipment of straps etc. by which a horse is fastened to a cart etc. and controlled. 2 similar arrangement for fastening a thing to a person's body. –*v.* 1 **a** put a harness on. **b** (foll. by *to*) attach by harness to. 2 make use of (natural resources), esp. to produce energy. □ **in harness** in the routine of daily work. [French *harneis* military equipment]
harp –*n.* large upright stringed instrument plucked with the fingers. –*v.* (foll. by *on*, *on about*) talk repeatedly and tediously about. □ **harpist** *n.* [Old English]

402

harpoon /ˈhɑːˈpuːn/ —*n.* barbed spear-like missile with a rope attached, for catching whales etc. —*v.* spear with a harpoon. [Greek *harpē* sickle]

harpsichord /ˈhɑːpsɪkɔːd/ *n.* keyboard instrument with horizontal strings plucked mechanically. □ **harpsichordist** *n.* [Latin *harpa* harp, *chorda* string]

harpy /ˈhɑːpɪ/ *n.* (*pl.* -**ies**) **1** mythological monster with a woman's head and body and a bird's wings and claws. **2** grasping unscrupulous person. [Greek *harpuiai* snatchers]

harridan /ˈhærɪd(ə)n/ *n.* bad-tempered old woman. [origin uncertain]

harrier /ˈhærɪə(r)/ *n.* **1** hound used for hunting hares. **2** group of cross-country runners. **3** hawklike bird of prey. [from HARE, HARRY]

harrow /ˈhærəʊ/ —*n.* heavy frame with iron teeth dragged over ploughed land to break up clods etc. —*v.* **1** draw a harrow over (land). **2** (usu. as **harrowing** *adj.*) distress greatly. [Old Norse *herfi*]

harry /ˈhærɪ/ *v.* (-**ies**, -**ied**) **1** ravage or despoil **2** harass. [Old English]

harsh *adj.* **1** unpleasantly rough or sharp, esp. to the senses. **2** severe, cruel. □ **harshen** *v.* **harshly** *adv.* **harshness** *n.* [Low German]

hart *n.* (*pl.* same or -**s**) male of the (esp. red) deer, esp. after its 5th year. [Old English]

hartebeest /ˈhɑːtɪˌbiːst/ *n.* large African antelope with curving horns. [Afrikaans]

harum-scarum /ˌheərəmˈskeərəm/ *colloq.* —*adj.* wild and reckless. —*n.* such a person. [rhyming formation on HARE, SCARE]

harvest /ˈhɑːvɪst/ —*n.* **1 a** process of gathering in crops etc. **b** season of this. **2** season's yield. **3** product of any action. —*v.* gather as harvest, reap. [Old English]

harvester *n.* **1** reaper. **2** reaping-machine, esp. with sheaf-binding.

harvest festival *n.* Christian thanksgiving service for the harvest.

harvest moon *n.* full moon nearest to the autumn equinox (22 or 23 Sept.).

harvest mouse *n.* small mouse nesting in the stalks of growing grain.

has *3rd sing. present of* HAVE.

has-been *n. colloq.* person or thing of declined importance.

hash¹ —*n.* **1** dish of cooked meat cut into small pieces and reheated. **2 a** mixture; jumble. **b** mess. **3** recycled material. —*v.* (often foll. by *up*) recycle (old material). □ **make a hash of** *colloq.* make a mess

of; bungle. **settle a person's hash** *colloq.* deal with and subdue a person. [French *hacher* cut up]

hash² *n. colloq.* hashish. [abbreviation]

hashish /ˈhæʃɪʃ/ *n.* resinous product of hemp, smoked or chewed as a narcotic. [Arabic]

haslet /ˈhæzlɪt/ *n.* pieces of (esp. pig's) offal cooked together, usu. as a meat loaf. [French *hastelet*]

hasn't /ˈhæz(ə)nt/ *contr.* has not.

hasp /hɑːsp/ *n.* hinged metal clasp fitting over a staple and secured by a padlock. [Old English]

hassle /ˈhæs(ə)l/ *colloq.* —*n.* trouble; problem; argument. —*v.* (-**ling**) harass, annoy. [originally a dial. word]

hassock /ˈhæsək/ *n.* thick firm cushion for kneeling on. [Old English]

haste /heɪst/ —*n.* urgency of movement or action; excessive hurry. —*v.* (-**ting**) *archaic* = HASTEN 1. □ **in haste** quickly, hurriedly. **make haste** hurry; be quick. [French from Germanic]

hasten /ˈheɪs(ə)n/ *v.* **1** make haste; hurry. **2** cause to occur or be ready or be done sooner.

hasty /ˈheɪstɪ/ *adj.* (-**ier**, -**iest**) **1** hurried; acting too quickly. **2** said, made, or done too quickly or too soon; rash. □ **hastily** *adv.* **hastiness** *n.*

hat *n.* **1** (esp. outdoor) covering for the head. **2** *colloq.* person's present capacity (*wearing his managerial hat*). □ **keep it under one's hat** *colloq.* keep it secret. **pass the hat round** collect contributions of money. **take one's hat off to** *colloq.* acknowledge admiration for. [Old English]

hatband *n.* band of ribbon etc. round a hat above the brim.

hatbox *n.* box to hold a hat, esp. for travelling.

hatch¹ *n.* **1** opening in a wall between a kitchen and dining-room for serving food. **2** opening or door in an aircraft etc. **3 a** = HATCHWAY. **b** cover for this. [Old English]

hatch² —*v.* **1 a** (often foll. by *out*) (of a young bird or fish etc.) emerge from the egg. **b** (of an egg) produce a young animal. **2** incubate (an egg). **3** (also foll. by *up*) devise (a plot etc.). —*n.* **1** act of hatching. **2** brood hatched. [earlier *hacche*, from Germanic]

hatch³ *v.* mark with close parallel lines. □ **hatching** *n.* [French *hacher*: related to HASH¹]

hatchback *n.* car with a sloping back hinged at the top to form a door.

hatchet /ˈhætʃɪt/ *n.* light short-handled axe. [French *hachette*]

hatchet man n. person hired to kill, dismiss, or otherwise harm another.

hatchway n. opening in a ship's deck for raising and lowering cargo.

hate —v. (-ting) 1 dislike intensely. 2 colloq. a dislike (to do something). (*I hate to disturb you; I hate fighting*). —n. 1 hatred. 2 colloq. hated person or thing. [Old English]

hateful adj. arousing hatred.

hatpin n. long pin for securing a hat to the hair.

hatred /ˈheɪtrɪd/ n. extreme dislike or ill will.

hatstand n. stand with hooks for hanging hats etc. on.

hatter n. maker or seller of hats.

hat trick n. 1 Cricket taking of three wickets by the same bowler with three successive balls. 2 three consecutive successes etc.

haughty /ˈhɔːtɪ/ adj. (-ier, -iest) arrogant and disdainful. □ **haughtily** adv. **haughtiness** n. [haught, haut from French, = high]

haul /hɔːl/ —v. 1 pull or drag forcibly. 2 transport by lorry, cart, etc. 3 turn a ship's course. 4 colloq. (usu. foll. by up) bring for reprimand or trial. —n. 1 hauling. 2 amount gained or acquired. 3 distance to be traversed (*a short haul*). □ **haul over the coals** see COAL. [French haler from Old Norse hala]

haulage n. 1 commercial transport of goods. 2 charge for this.

haulier /ˈhɔːliə(r)/ n. person or firm engaged in the transport of goods.

haulm /hɔːm/ n. (also **halm**) 1 stalk or stem. 2 stalks or stems of peas, beans, etc. collectively. [Old English]

haunch /hɔːntʃ/ n. 1 fleshy part of the buttock with the thigh. 2 leg and loin of a deer etc. as food. [French from Germanic]

haunt /hɔːnt/ —v. 1 (of a ghost) visit (a place) regularly. 2 frequent (a place). 3 linger in the mind of. —n. place frequented by a person or animal. [French from Germanic]

haunting adj. (of a memory, melody, etc.) lingering in the mind; poignant, evocative.

haute couture /ˌəʊt kuːˈtjʊə(r)/ n. high fashion; leading fashion houses or their products. [French]

haute cuisine /ˌəʊt kwiːˈziːn/ n. high-class cookery. [French]

hauteur /əʊˈtɜː(r)/ n. haughtiness. [French]

have /hæv, həv/ —v. (-ving; 3rd sing. present **has** /hæz/; past and past part. **had**) 1 as an auxiliary verb with past part. or ellipt. to form the perfect, pluperfect, and future perfect tenses, and the conditional mood (*has, had, will have, seen; had I known, I would have gone; yes I have*) 2 own or be able to use, be provided with (*has a car; had no time*). 3 hold in a certain relationship (*has a sister; has ne equals*). 4 contain as a part or quality (*box has a lid; has big eyes*). 5 a experience (*had a good time, a shock, a pain*). b be subjected to a specified state (*had my car stolen; book has a page missing*). c cause (a person or thing) to be in a particular state or take particular action (*had him sacked; had us worried; had my hair cut; had them to stay*). 6 a engage in (an activity) (*have an argument, a game, a party, a swim*). b hold (a meeting, party, etc.) 7 eat or drink (*had a beer*). 8 (usu. in neg.) accept or tolerate; permit to (*I won't have it won't have you say that*). 9 a feel (*have no doubt; has nothing against me*). b show (*mercy, pity, etc.*). c (foll. by to + infin.) show by action that one is influenced by (a feeling, quality, etc.) (*have the sense to stop*). 10 a give birth to (offspring). b conceive mentally (an idea etc.). 11 receive, obtain (*had a letter from him; not a ticket to be had*). 12 be burdened with or committed to (*has a job to do*). 13 a have obtained; a qualification) (*has six O levels*). b know (a language) (*has no Latin*). 14 engage in sexual intercourse with. —n. (usu. in pl.) (usu. in passive) cheat, deceive (*you were had*). **have had it** colloq. 1 have missed one's chance. 2 have passed one's prime. 3 have been killed, defeated, etc. **have it** 1 (foll. by that) maintain that. 2 win a decision in a vote etc. 3 colloq. have found the answer. **have it away** (or **off**) coarse slang have sexual intercourse with. —n. 1 (usu. in pl.) colloq. person or resources 2 slang swindle. □ **had better** see BETTER. **had best** see BEST. **had better** see BETTER. **have got to** colloq. = have to. **have had it** colloq. 1 have missed one's chance. 2 **have it out** (often foll. by with) colloq. attempt to settle a dispute by argument. **have on** 1 wear (clothes.) 2 have (an engagement) 3 colloq. tease, hoax. **have to** be obliged to; must. **have up** colloq. bring (a person) before a judge, interviewer, etc. [Old English]

haven /ˈheɪv(ə)n/ n. 1 refuge. 2 harbour, port. [Old English]

have-not n. (usu. in pl.) colloq. person lacking wealth or resources.

haven't /ˈhæv(ə)nt/ v. contr. have not.

haver /ˈheɪvə(r)/ v. 1 vacillate, hesitate. 2 dial. talk foolishly. [origin unknown]

haversack /'hævəsæk/ n. stout canvas bag carried on the back or over the shoulder. [German *Habersack*, = oatssack]

havoc /'hævək/ n. widespread destruction; great disorder. [French *havo(t)*]

haw[1] n. hawthorn berry. [Old English]

haw[2] see HUM.

hawfinch n. large finch with a thick beak for cracking seeds. [from HAW[1], FINCH]

hawk[1] —n. 1 bird of prey with a curved beak, rounded short wings, and a long tail. 2 *Polit.* person who advocates aggressive policies. —v. hunt with a hawk. □ **hawkish** *adj.* [Old English]

hawk[2] v. carry about or offer (goods) for sale. [back-formation from HAWKER]

hawk[3] v. 1 clear the throat noisily. 2 (foll. by *up*) bring (phlegm etc.) up from the throat. [imitative]

hawk-eyed *adj.* keen-sighted.

hawker n. person who travels about selling goods. [Low German or Dutch]

hawser /'hɔːzə(r)/ n. thick rope or cable for mooring or towing a ship. [French, *haucier* hoist, from Latin *altus* high]

hawthorn n. thorny shrub with small dark-red berries. [related to HAW[1]]

hay n. grass mown and dried for fodder. □ **make hay (while the sun shines)** seize opportunities. [Old English]

haycock n. conical heap of hay.

hay fever n. allergy with asthmatic symptoms etc., caused by pollen or dust.

haymaking n. mowing grass and spreading it to dry. □ **haymaker** n.

haystack n. (also **hayrick**) packed pile of hay with a pointed or ridged top.

haywire *adj. colloq.* badly disorganized, out of control.

hazard /'hæzəd/ —n. 1 danger or risk. 2 source of this. 3 *Golf* obstacle, e.g. a bunker. —v. 1 venture (*hazard a guess*). 2 risk. [Arabic *az-zahr* chance, luck]

hazardous *adj.* risky.

haze n. 1 thin atmospheric vapour. 2 mental obscurity or confusion. [back-formation from HAZY]

hazel /'heɪz(ə)l/ n. 1 hedgerow shrub bearing round brown edible nuts. 2 greenish-brown. [Old English]

hazelnut n. nut of the hazel.

hazy *adj.* (-ier, -iest) 1 misty. 2 vague, indistinct. 3 confused, uncertain. □ **hazily** *adv.* **haziness** n. [origin unknown]

HB *abbr.* (of pencil-lead) hard black.

H-bomb /'eɪtʃbɒm/ n. = HYDROGEN BOMB. [from H[3]]

HCF *abbr.* highest common factor.

HE *abbr.* 1 His or Her Excellency. 2 His Eminence. 3 high explosive.

He *symb.* helium.

he /hiː/ —pron. (*obj.* **him**; *poss.* **his**; *pl.* **they**) 1 the man, boy, or male animal previously named or in question. 2 person of unspecified sex (*if anyone comes he will have to wait; he who hesitates*). —n. 1 male; man. 2 (in *comb.*) male (*he-goat*). [Old English]

head /hed/ —n. 1 upper part of the human body, or foremost or upper part of an animal's body, containing the brain, mouth, and sense-organs. 2 **a** seat of intellect (*if anyone comes he will have to wait; he who hesitates*). **b** mental aptitude or tolerance (*a good head for business; no head for heights*). 3 thing like a head in form or position, esp. **a** the operative part of a tool. **b** the top of a nail. **c** the leaves or flowers at the top of a stem. **d** foam on the top of a glass of beer etc. 4 **a** person in charge, esp. the principal teacher of a school. **b** position of command. 5 front part of a queue etc. 6 upper end of a table or bed etc. 7 top or highest part of a page, stairs, etc. 8 **a** individual person as a unit (*£10 per head*). **b** (*pl.* same) individual animal as a unit (*20 head*). 9 **a** side of a coin bearing the image of a head. **b** (usu. in *pl.*) this as a choice when tossing a coin. 10 **a** source of a river etc. **b** end of a lake at which a river enters it. 11 height or length of a head as a measure. 12 part of a machine in contact with or very close to what is being worked on, esp.: **a** the part of a tape recorder that touches the moving tape and converts signals. **b** the part of a record-player that holds the playing cartridge and stylus. 13 (usu. in *pl.*) promontory (*Beachy Head*). 16 heading or headline. 17 fully developed top of a boil etc. 18 *colloq.* headache. 19 (*attrib.*) chief, principal.—v. 1 be at the head or front of. 2 be in charge of. 3 provide with a head or heading. 4 (often foll. by *for*) face, move, or direct in a specified direction (*is heading for trouble*). 5 hit (a ball etc.). □ **above** (or **over**) **one's head** beyond one's understanding. **come to a head** reach a crisis. **get it into one's head** (foll. by *that*) 1 adopt a mistaken idea. 2 form a definite plan. **give a person his** (or *her*) **head** allow a person to act freely. **go to one's head 1** make one slightly drunk. 2 make one conceited. **head off 1** get ahead of so as to intercept and turn aside. 2 forestall. **keep** (or **lose**) **one's head** remain (or fail to remain) calm. **off one's head** *slang* crazy. **off the top of one's head** *colloq.* impromptu. **on one's** (or **one's own**) **head** as one's own responsibility.

out of one's head slang crazy. **over one's head 1** beyond one's understanding. **2** without one's rightful knowledge or involvement, consulting one's superior. **3** with disregard for one's own (stronger) claim (*was promoted over my head*). **put heads together** consult together. **take it into one's head** (by *that* + clause or *to* + infin.) decide, esp. impetuously. **turn a person's head** make a person conceited. [Old English]

headache n. **1** continuous pain in the head. **2** *colloq.* worrying problem. □ **headachy** adj.

headband n. band worn round the head as decoration or to confine the hair.

headbanger n. *slang* **1** person who shakes his or her head violently to the rhythm of music; fan of loud music. **2** crazy or eccentric person.

headboard n. upright panel at the head of a bed.

head-butt —n. thrust with the head into the chin or body of another person. —v. attack with a head-butt.

headcount n. **1** counting of individual people. **2** total number of people, esp. employees.

headdress n. covering for the head.

header n. **1** *Football* shot or pass made with the head. **2** *colloq.* headlong fall or dive. **3** brick etc. laid at right angles to the face of a wall. **4** (in full **header-tank**) tank of water etc. maintaining pressure in a plumbing system.

head first adv. **1** with the head foremost. **2** precipitately.

headgear n. hat or headdress.

head-hunting n. **1** collecting of the heads of dead enemies as trophies. **2** seeking of (esp. senior) staff by approaching people employed elsewhere. □ **head-hunt** v. **head-hunter** n.

heading n. **1 a** title at the head of a page or section of a book etc. **b** section of a subject of discourse etc. **2** horizontal passage made in preparation for building a tunnel, or in a mine.

head in the sand n. refusal to acknowledge danger or difficulty.

headlamp n. = HEADLIGHT.

headland n. promontory.

headlight n. **1** strong light at the front of a vehicle. **2** beam from this.

headline n. **1** heading at the top of an article or page, esp. in a newspaper **2** (in pl.) summary of the most important items in a news bulletin.

headlock n. *Wrestling* hold with an arm round the opponent's head.

headlong adv. & adj. **1** with the head foremost. **2** in a rush.

headman n. chief man of a tribe etc.

headmaster n. (*fem.* **headmistress**) = HEAD TEACHER.

head-on adj. & adv. **1** with the front foremost (*head-on crash*). **2** in direct confrontation.

head over heels —n. turning over completely in forward motion as in a somersault etc. —adv. utterly (*head over heels in love*).

headphones n.pl. set of earphones fitting over the head, for listening to audio equipment etc.

headquarters n. (as *sing.* or *pl.*) administrative centre of an organization.

headrest n. support for the head, esp. on a seat.

headroom n. space or clearance above a vehicle, person's head, etc.

headscarf n. scarf worn round the head and tied under the chin.

headset n. headphones, often with a microphone attached.

headship n. position of head or chief, esp. in a school.

headshrinker n. *slang* psychiatrist.

headstall n. part of a halter or bridle fitting round a horse's head.

head start n. advantage granted or gained at an early stage.

headstone n. stone set up at the head of a grave.

headstrong adj. self-willed.

head teacher n. teacher in charge of a school.

headwaters n.pl. streams flowing from the sources of a river.

headway n. **1** progress. **2** ship's rate of progress. **3** headroom.

head wind n. wind blowing from directly in front.

headword n. word forming a heading.

heady adj. (**-ier**, **-iest**) **1** (of liquor) potent. **2** intoxicating, exciting. **3** impulsive, rash. **4** headachy. □ **headily** adv. **headiness** n.

heal v. **1** (often foll. by *up*) become sound or healthy again. **2** cause to heal. **3** put right (differences etc.). **4** alleviate (sorrow etc.). □ **healer** n. [Old English: related to WHOLE]

health /helθ/ n. **1** state of being well in body or mind. **2** person's mental or physical condition. **3** soundness, esp. financial or moral. [Old English: related to WHOLE]

health centre n. building containing various local medical services and doctors' practices.

health farm n. establishment offering improved health by a regime of dieting, exercise, etc.

health food n. natural food, thought to promote good health.

healthful adj. conducive to good health; beneficial.

health service n. public service providing medical care.

health visitor n. trained nurse who visits mothers and babies, or the sick or elderly, at home.

healthy adj. (-ier, -iest) 1 having, showing, or promoting good health. 2 indicative of (esp. moral or financial) health (a healthy sign). 3 substantial (won by a healthy 40 seconds). □ **healthily** adv. **healthiness** n.

heap —n. 1 disorderly pile. 2 (esp. in pl.) colloq. large number or amount. 3 slang dilapidated vehicle. —v. 1 (foll. by up, together, etc.) collect or be collected in a heap. 2 (foll. by with) load copiously with. 3 (foll. by on, upon) give or offer copiously (heaped insults on them). [Old English]

hear v. (past and past part. **heard** /hɜːd/) 1 (also absol.) perceive with the ear. 2 listen to (heard them on the radio). 3 listen judicially to (a case etc.). 4 be told or informed. 5 (foll. by from) be contacted by, esp. by letter or telephone. 6 be ready to obey (an order). 7 grant (a prayer). □ **have heard of** be aware of the existence of. **hear! hear!** int. expressing agreement. **hear a person out** listen to all a person says. **will not hear of** will not allow. □ **hearer** n. [Old English]

hearing n. 1 faculty of perceiving sounds. 2 range within which sounds may be heard (within hearing). 3 opportunity to state one's case (a fair hearing). 4 trial of a case before a court.

hearing-aid n. small device to amplify sound, worn by a partially deaf person.

hearken /ˈhɑːkən/ v. archaic (often foll. by to) listen. [Old English: related to HARK]

hearsay n. rumour, gossip.

hearse /hɜːs/ n. vehicle for conveying the coffin at a funeral. [French herse harrow, from Latin hirpex large rake]

heart /hɑːt/ n. 1 hollow muscular organ maintaining the circulation of blood by rhythmic contraction and dilation. 2 region of the heart; the breast. 3 a centre of thought, feeling, and emotion (esp. love). b capacity for feeling emotion (has no heart). 4 a courage or enthusiasm (take heart). b mood or feeling (change of heart). 5 a central or innermost part of something. b essence (heart of the matter). 6 compact tender inner part of a lettuce etc. 7 a heart-shaped thing. b conventional representation of a heart with two equal curves meeting at a point at the bottom and a cusp at the top. 8 a playing-card of the suit denoted by a red figure of a heart. b (in pl.) this suit. □ **at heart** 1 in one's inmost feelings. 2 basically. **break a person's heart** overwhelm a person with sorrow. **by heart** from memory. **give (or lose) one's heart** (often foll. by to) fall in love (with). **have the heart** (usu. with neg.; foll. by to + infin.) be insensitive or hard-hearted enough (didn't have the heart to ask him). **take to heart** be much affected by. **to one's heart's content** see CONTENT[1]. **with all one's heart** sincerely; with all goodwill. [Old English]

heartache n. mental anguish.

heart attack n. sudden occurrence of coronary thrombosis.

heartbeat n. pulsation of the heart.

heartbreak n. overwhelming distress. □ **heartbreaking** adj. **heartbroken** adj.

heartburn n. burning sensation in the chest from indigestion.

hearten v. make or become more cheerful. □ **heartening** adj.

heart failure n. failure of the heart to function properly, esp. as a cause of death.

heartfelt adj. sincere; deeply felt.

hearth /hɑːθ/ n. 1 floor of a fireplace. 2 the home. [Old English]

hearthrug n. rug laid before a fireplace.

heartily adv. 1 in a hearty manner. 2 very (am heartily sick of it).

heartland n. central part of an area.

heartless adj. unfeeling, pitiless. □ **heartlessly** adv.

heart-lung machine n. machine that temporarily takes over the functions of the heart and lungs.

heart-rending adj. very distressing.

heart-searching n. examination of one's own feelings and motives.

heartsick adj. despondent.

heartstrings n.pl. one's deepest feelings.

heartthrob n. colloq. person for whom one has (esp. immature) romantic feelings.

heart-to-heart —attrib. adj. (of a conversation etc.) candid, intimate. —n. candid or personal conversation.

heart-warming adj. emotionally rewarding or uplifting.

heartwood n. dense inner part of a tree-trunk, yielding the hardest timber.

hearty adj. (-ier, -iest) 1 strong, vigorous. 2 (of a meal or appetite) large. 3 warm, friendly. □ **heartiness** n.

heat —n. 1 condition of being hot. 2 Physics form of energy arising from the motion of bodies' molecules. 3 hot weather. 4 warmth of feeling, anger or

excitement. **5** (foll. by *of*) most intense or period of activity (*heat of battle*). **6** (usu. preliminary or trial) round in a race etc. *-v.* **1** make or become hot or warm. **2** inflame. □ **on heat** (of mammals, esp. females) sexually receptive. [Old English]

heated *adj.* angry; impassioned. □ **heatedly** *adv.*

heater *n.* stove or other heating device.

heath *n.* **1** area of flattish uncultivated land with low shrubs. **2** plant growing on a heath, esp. heather. [Old English]

heathen /ˈhiːð(ə)n/ *-n.* **1** person not belonging to a predominant religion, esp. not a Christian, Jew, or Muslim. **2** person regarded as lacking culture or moral principles. *-adj.* **1** of heathens. **2** having no religion. [Old English]

heather /ˈhɛðə(r)/ *n.* any of various shrubs growing esp. on moors and heaths. [origin unknown]

Heath Robinson /hiːθ ˈrɒbɪns(ə)n/ *adj.* absurdly ingenious and impracticable. [name of a cartoonist]

heating *n.* **1** imparting or generation of heat. **2** equipment used to heat a building etc.

heatproof *-adj.* able to resist great heat. *-v.* make heatproof.

heat shield *n.* device to protect (esp. a spacecraft) from excessive heat.

heatwave *n.* period of unusually hot weather.

heave *-v.* (**-ving;** *past* and *past part.* **heaved** or esp. *Naut.* **hove** /həʊv/) **1** lift or haul with great effort. **2** utter with effort (*heaved a sigh*). **3** *colloq.* throw. **4** rise and fall rhythmically or spasmodically. **5** *Naut.* haul by rope. **6** retch. *-n.* heaving. □ **heave in sight** come into view. **heave to** esp. *Naut.* bring or be brought to a standstill. [Old English]

heaven /ˈhɛv(ə)n/ *n.* **1** place regarded in some religions as the abode of God and the angels, and of the blessed after death. **2** place or state of supreme bliss. **3** *colloq.* delightful thing. **4** (usu. **Heaven**) God, Providence (often as an exclamation or mild oath: *Heavens!*). **5** (**the heavens**) esp. *poet.* the sky as seen from the earth, in which the sun, moon, and stars appear. □ **heavenward** *adv. & adj.* (also **heavenwards** *adv.*). [Old English]

heavenly *adj.* **1** of heaven; divine. **2** of the heavens or sky. **3** *colloq.* very pleasing; wonderful.

heavenly bodies *n.pl.* the sun, stars, planets, etc.

heaven-sent *adj.* providential.

heavier-than-air *attrib. adj.* (of an aircraft) weighing more than the air it displaces.

heavy /ˈhɛvɪ/ *-adj.* (**-ier, -iest**) **1** of great or unusually high weight; difficult to lift. **2** of great density (*heavy metal*). **3** abundant, considerable (*heavy crop; heavy traffic*). **4** severe, intense, extensive (*heavy fighting; a heavy sleep*). **5** doing a thing to excess (*heavy drinker*). **6** striking or falling with force; causing strong impact (*heavy blows; heavy rain; heavy sea; a heavy fall*). **7** (of machinery, artillery, etc.) very large of its kind; large in calibre etc. **8** needing much physical effort (*the heavy bit*). **9** carrying heavy weapons (*heavy bri-gade*). **10** serious or sombre in tone or attitude; dull, tedious. **11 a** hard to digest. **b** hard to read or understand. **12** (of bread etc.) too dense from not having risen. **13** (of ground) difficult to traverse or work. **14** oppressive; hard to endure (*heavy demands*). **15 a** coarse, ungrace-ful (*heavy features*). **b** unwieldy. *-n.* (*pl.* **-ies**) **1** *colloq.* large violent person; thug (esp. hired). **2** villainous or tragic role or actor. **3** (usu. in *pl.*) *colloq.* serious news-paper. **4** anything large or heavy of its kind, e.g. a vehicle. *-adv.* heavily (esp. in *comb.*: *heavy-laden*). □ **heavy on** using a lot of (*heavy on petrol*). **heavy weather of** see WEATHER. □ **heavily** *adv.* **heaviness** *n.* **heavyish** *adj.* [Old English]

heavy-duty *adj.* intended to withstand hard use.

heavy going *n.* slow or difficult progress.

heavy-handed *adj.* **1** clumsy. **2** over-bearing, oppressive. □ **heavy-handedly** *adv.* **heavy-handedness** *n.*

heavy-hearted *adj.* sad, doleful.

heavy hydrogen *n.* = DEUTERIUM.

heavy industry *n.* industry producing metal, machinery, etc.

heavy metal *n.* **1** heavy guns. **2** metal of high density. **3** *colloq.* loud kind of rock music with a pounding rhythm.

heavy petting *n.* erotic fondling that stops short of intercourse.

heavy water *n.* water composed of deuterium and oxygen.

heavyweight *n.* **1 a** weight in certain sports, in amateur boxing over 81 kg. **b** sportsman of this weight. **2** person etc. of above average weight. **3** *colloq.* person of influence or importance.

hebdomadal /hɛbˈdɒməd(ə)l/ *adj. formal* weekly. [Greek *hepta* seven]

hebe /ˈhiːbiː/ *n.* evergreen flowering shrub from New Zealand. [Greek goddess *Hebe*]

Hebraic /hɪˈbreɪɪk/ *adj.* of Hebrew or the Hebrews.

Hebrew /ˈhiːbruː/ —n. **1** member of a Semitic people orig. centred in ancient Palestine. **2 a** their language. **b** modern form of this, used esp. in Israel. —adj. **1** of or in Hebrew. **2** of the Hebrews or the Jews. [Hebrew, = one from the other side of the river]

heck int. colloq. mild exclamation of surprise or dismay. [a form of HELL]

heckle /ˈhek(ə)l/ —v. (-ling) interrupt and harass (a public speaker). —n. act of heckling. □ **heckler** n. [var. of HACKLE]

hectare /ˈhekteə(r)/ n. metric unit of square measure, 100 ares (2.471 acres or 10,000 square metres). [French: related to HECTO-, ARE²]

hectic /ˈhektɪk/ adj. **1** busy and confused; excited. **2** feverish. □ **hectically** adv. [Greek hektikos habitual]

hecto- comb. form hundred. [Greek hekaton]

hectogram /ˈhektəˌgræm/ n. (also **hectogramme**) metric unit of mass equal to 100 grams.

hector /ˈhektə(r)/ —v. bully, intimidate. —n. bully. [from the name Hector in the Iliad]

he'd /hiːd/ contr. **1** he had. **2** he would.

hedge —n. **1** fence or boundary of dense bushes or shrubs. **2** protection against possible loss. —v. (-ging) **1** surround or bound with a hedge. **2** (foll. by in) enclose. **3 a** reduce one's risk of loss on (a bet or speculation) by compensating transactions on the other side. **b** avoid committing oneself. [Old English]

hedgehog n. small insect-eating mammal with a piglike snout and a coat of spines, rolling itself up into a ball when attacked.

hedge-hop v. fly at a very low altitude.

hedgerow n. row of bushes etc. forming a hedge.

hedge sparrow n. common grey and brown bird; the dunnock.

hedonism /ˈhiːdənɪz(ə)m/ n. **1** belief in pleasure as mankind's proper aim. **2** behaviour based on this. □ **hedonist** n. **hedonistic** /-ˈnɪstɪk/ adj. [Greek hēdonē pleasure]

heebie-jeebies /ˌhiːbɪˈdʒiːbɪz/ n.pl. (prec. by the) slang nervous anxiety, tension. [origin unknown]

heed —v. attend to; take notice of. —n. careful attention. □ **heedful** adj. **heedless** adj. **heedlessly** adv. [Old English]

hee-haw /ˈhiːhɔː/ —n. bray of a donkey. —v. make a braying sound. [imitative]

heel¹ —n. **1** back of the foot below the ankle. **2 a** part of a sock etc. covering this. **b** part of a shoe etc. supporting this. **3** thing like a heel in form or position. **4** crust end of a loaf of bread. **5** colloq. scoundrel. **6** (as int.) command to a dog to walk close to its owner's heel. —v. **1** fit or renew a heel on (a shoe etc.). **2** touch the ground with the heel as in dancing. **3** (foll. by out) Rugby pass the ball with the heel. □ **at heel 1** (of a dog) close behind. **2** (of a person etc.) under control. **at** (or **on**) **the heels of** following closely after (a person or event). **cool** (or **kick**) **one's heels** be kept waiting. **down at heel 1** (of a shoe) with the heel worn down. **2** (of a person) shabby. **take to one's heels** run away. **to heel 1** (of a dog) close behind. **2** (of a person etc.) under control. **turn on one's heel** turn sharply round. [Old English]

heel² —v. (often foll. by over) **1** (of a ship etc.) lean over. **2** cause (a ship etc.) to do this. —n. act or amount of heeling. [obsolete heeld, from Germanic]

heel³ var. of HELE.

heelball n. mixture of hard wax and lampblack used by shoemakers for polishing. **2** this or a similar mixture used in brass-rubbing.

hefty /ˈheftɪ/ adj. (-ier, -iest) **1** (of a person) big and strong. **2** (of a thing) large, heavy, powerful. □ **heftily** adv. **heftiness** n. [heft weight: related to HEAVE]

hegemony /hɪˈgeməni/ n. leadership, esp. by one State of a confederacy. [Greek hēgemōn leader]

Hegira /ˈhedʒɪrə/ n. (also **Hejira**) **1** Muhammad's flight from Mecca in AD 622. **2** Muslim era reckoned from this date. [Arabic hijra departure]

heifer /ˈhefə(r)/ n. young cow, esp. one that has not had more than one calf.

height /haɪt/ n. **1** measurement from base to top or head to foot. **2** elevation above the ground or a recognized level. **3** considerable elevation (situated at a height). **4** high place or area. **5** top. **6 a** most intense part or period (battle was at its height). **b** extreme example (the height of fashion). [Old English]

heighten v. make or become higher or more intense.

heinous /ˈheɪnəs/ adj. utterly odious or wicked. [French hair hate]

heir /eə(r)/ n. (fem. **heiress**) person entitled to property or rank as the legal successor of its former holder. [Latin heres hered-]

heir apparent n. heir whose claim cannot be set aside by the birth of another heir.

heirloom n. **1** piece of personal property that has been in a family for several generations. **2** piece of property as part of an inheritance.

heir presumptive *n.* heir whose claim may be set aside by the birth of another heir.

Hejira var. of HEGIRA.

held *past and past part.* of HOLD¹.

hele /hiːl/ *v.* (**-ling**) (also **heel**) (foll. by *in*) set (a plant) in the ground temporarily and cover its roots. [Old English]

helices *pl.* of HELIX.

helicopter /ˈhelɪkɒptə(r)/ *n.* wingless aircraft obtaining lift and propulsion from horizontally revolving overhead blades. [Greek: related to HELIX, *pteron* wing]

helio- *comb. form* sun. [Greek *hēlios* sun]

heliocentric /ˌhiːliəʊˈsentrɪk/ *adj.* 1 regarding the sun as centre. 2 considered as viewed from the sun's centre.

heliograph /ˈhiːliəgrɑːf/ *n.* 1 signalling apparatus reflecting sunlight in flashes. 2 message sent by means of this. —*v.* send (a message) by heliograph.

heliotrope /ˈhiːliətrəʊp/ *n.* plant with fragrant purple flowers. [Greek: related to HELIO-, *trepō* turn]

heliport /ˈhelɪpɔːt/ *n.* place where helicopters take off and land.

helium /ˈhiːliəm/ *n.* light inert gaseous element used in airships and as a refrigerant. [related to HELIO-]

helix /ˈhiːlɪks/ *n.* (*pl.* **helices** /ˈhiːlɪsiːz/) spiral curve (like a corkscrew) or coiled curve (like a watch spring). [Latin from Greek]

hell —*n.* 1 place regarded in some religions as the abode of the dead, or of devils and condemned sinners. 2 place or state of misery or wickedness. —*int.* expressing anger, surprise, etc. □ **the hell** (usu. prec. by *what, where, who,* etc.) expressing anger, disbelief, etc. (*who the hell is this?; the hell you are?*). **come hell or high water** no matter what the difficulties. **for the hell of it** *colloq.* just for fun. **get hell** *colloq.* be severely scolded or punished. **give a person hell** *colloq.* scold or punish a person. **a (or one) hell of a** *colloq.* outstanding example of (*a hell of a mess; one hell of a party*). **like hell** *colloq.* 1 not at all. 2 recklessly, exceedingly. [Old English]

he'll /hiːl/ *contr.* he will; he shall.

hell-bent *adj.* (foll. by *on*) recklessly determined.

hellebore /ˈhelɪbɔː(r)/ *n.* evergreen plant with usu. white, purple, or green flowers, e.g. the Christmas rose. [Greek (*h)eleboros*]

Hellene /ˈhelliːn/ *n.* 1 native of modern Greece. 2 ancient Greek. □ **Hellenic** /heˈlenɪk, -ˈliːnɪk/ *adj.* [Greek]

Hellenism /ˈhelɪnɪz(ə)m/ *n.* (esp. ancient) Greek character or culture.

Hellenist *n.*

Hellenistic /ˌhelɪˈnɪstɪk/ *adj.* of Greek history, language, and culture of the late 4th to the late 1st c. BC.

hell-fire *n.* fire(s) regarded as existing in hell.

hell for leather *adv.* at full speed.

hell-hole *n.* oppressive or unbearable place.

hellish —*adj.* 1 of or like hell. 2 extremely difficult or unpleasant. —*adv. colloq.* extremely (*hellish expensive*). □ **hellishly** *adv.*

hello /həˈləʊ/ (also **hallo, hullo**) —*int.* expression of informal greeting, or of surprise, or to call attention. —*n.* (*pl.* **-s**) cry of 'hello'. [var. of earlier *hollo*]

Hell's Angel *n.* member of a gang of male motor-cycle enthusiasts notorious for outrageous and violent behaviour.

helm *n.* tiller or wheel for controlling a ship's rudder. □ **at the helm** in control; at the head of an organization etc. [Old English]

helmet /ˈhelmɪt/ *n.* protective headcovering worn by a policeman, motorcyclist, etc. [French from Germanic]

helmsman /ˈhelmzmən/ *n.* person who steers a ship.

helot /ˈhelət/ *n.* serf, esp. (**Helot**) of a class in ancient Sparta. [Latin from Greek]

help —*v.* 1 provide with the means towards what is needed or sought (*helped me with my work; he helped me (to) pay my debts; helped him on with his coat*). 2 (often *absol.*) be of use or service to (*does that help?*). 3 contribute to alleviating (a pain or difficulty). 4 prevent or remedy (*it can't be helped*). 5 (usu. with *neg.*) **a** refrain from (*can't help it; could not help laughing*). **b** refrain from acting (*couldn't help himself*). 6 (often foll. by *to*) serve (a person with food). —*n.* 1 helping or being helped (*need your help; came to our help*). 2 person or thing that helps. 3 *colloq.* domestic assistant or assistance. 4 remedy or escape (*there is no help for it*). □ **help oneself** (often foll. by *to*) 1 serve oneself (with food etc.). 2 take without permission. **help a person out** give a person help, esp. in difficulty. □ **helper** *n.* [Old English]

helpful *adj.* giving help; useful. □ **helpfully** *adv.* **helpfulness** *n.*

helping *n.* portion of food at a meal.

helpless *adj.* **1** lacking help or protection; defenceless. **2** unable to act without help. □ **helplessly** *adv.* **helplessness** *n.*

helpline *n.* telephone service providing help with problems.

helpmate *n.* helpful companion or partner.

helter-skelter /,heltə'skeltə(r)/ —*adv. & adj.* in disorderly haste. —*n.* (at a fairground) external spiral slide round a tower. [imitative]

hem[1] —*n.* border of cloth where the edge is turned under and sewn down. —*v.* (**-mm-**) turn down and sew in the edge of (cloth etc.). □ **hem in** confine; restrict the movement of. [Old English]

hem[2] —*int.* calling attention or expressing hesitation by a slight cough. —*n.* utterance of this. —*v.* (**-mm-**) say *hem*; hesitate in speech. □ **hem and haw** = **hum and haw** (see HUM[1]). [imitative]

hemal var. of HAEMAL etc.

he-man *n.* masterful or virile man.

hemi- *comb. form* half [Greek, = Latin *semi-*]

hemipterous /he'mɪptərəs/ *adj.* of the insect order including aphids, bugs, and cicadas, with piercing or sucking mouthparts. [Greek *pteron* wing]

hemisphere /'hemɪsfɪə(r)/ *n.* **1** half a sphere. **2** half of the earth, esp. as divided by the equator (into *northern* and *southern hemisphere*) or by a line passing through the poles (into *eastern* and *western hemisphere*). □ **hemispherical** /-'sferɪk(ə)l/ *adj.* [Greek: related to HEMI-, SPHERE]

hemline *n.* lower edge of a skirt etc.

hemlock /'hemlɒk/ *n.* **1** poisonous plant with fernlike leaves and small white flowers. **2** poison made from this. [Old English]

hemp *n.* **1** (in full **Indian hemp**) Asian herbaceous plant. **2** its fibre used to make rope and stout fabrics. **3** narcotic drug made from the hemp plant. [Old English]

hempen *adj.* made of hemp.

hemstitch —*n.* decorative stitch. —*v.* hem with this stitch.

hen *n.* female bird, esp. of a domestic fowl. [Old English]

henbane *n.* poisonous hairy plant with an unpleasant smell.

hence *adv.* **1** from this time (*two years hence*). **2** for this reason (*hence we seem to be wrong*). **3** *archaic* from here. [Old English]

henceforth *adv.* (also **henceforward**) from this time onwards.

henchman *n. usu. derog.* trusted supporter. [Old English *hengst* horse, MAN]

henge /hendʒ/ *n.* prehistoric monument consisting of a circle of stone or wood uprights. [*Stonehenge* in S. England]

henna /'henə/ —*n.* **1** tropical shrub. **2** reddish dye made from it and used to colour hair. —*v.* (**hennaed, hennaing**) dye with henna. [Arabic]

hen-party *n. colloq.* social gathering of women only.

henpeck *v.* (usu. in *passive*) (of a wife) constantly nag her husband.

henry /'henrɪ/ *n.* (*pl.* **-s** or **-ies**) *Electr.* SI unit of inductance. [*Henry*, name of a physicist]

hep var. of HIP[4].

hepatic /hɪ'pætɪk/ *adj.* of the liver. [Greek *hēpar -atos* liver]

hepatitis /,hepə'taɪtɪs/ *n.* inflammation of the liver. [related to HEPATIC]

hepta- *comb. form* seven. [Greek]

heptagon /'heptəgən/ *n.* plane figure with seven sides and angles. □ **heptagonal** /'tægən(ə)l/ *adj.* [Greek: related to HEPTA-, *-gōnos* angled]

her —*pron.* **1** *objective case of* SHE (*I like her*). **2** *colloq.* she (*it's her all right; am older than her*). —*poss. pron.* (attrib.) of or belonging to her or herself (*her house; her own business*). [Old English dative and genitive of SHE]

herald /'her(ə)ld/ —*n.* **1** official messenger bringing news. **2** forerunner, harbinger. **3 a** *hist.* officer responsible for State ceremonial and etiquette. **b** official concerned with pedigrees and coats of arms. —*v.* proclaim the approach of; usher in. □ **heraldic** /hɪ'rældɪk/ *adj.* [French from Germanic]

heraldry *n.* **1** art or knowledge of a herald. **2** coats of arms.

herb *n.* **1** any non-woody seed-bearing plant. **2** plant with leaves, seeds, or flowers used for flavouring, food, medicine, scent, etc. □ **herby** *adj.* (**-ier, -iest**). [Latin *herba*]

herbaceous /hɜː'beɪʃəs/ *adj.* of or like herbs.

herbaceous border *n.* garden border containing esp. perennial flowering plants.

herbage *n.* vegetation collectively, esp. as pasture.

herbal —*adj.* of herbs in medicinal and culinary use. —*n.* book describing the medicinal and culinary uses of herbs.

herbalist *n.* **1** dealer in medicinal herbs. **2** writer on herbs.

herbarium /hɜː'beərɪəm/ *n.* (*pl.* **-ria**) **1** systematically arranged collection of dried plants. **2** book, room, etc. for these.

herbicide /'hɜːbɪsaɪd/ *n.* poison used to destroy unwanted vegetation.

herbivore /ˈhɜːbɪvɔː(r)/ n. animal that feeds on plants. □ **herbivorous** /-ˈbɪvərəs/ adj. [Latin ʋoro devour]

Herculean /ˌhɜːkjʊˈliːən/ adj. having or requiring great strength or effort. [from the name Hercules, Latin alteration of Greek Hēraklēs]

herd –n. 1 a number of animals, esp. cattle, feeding or travelling or kept together. 2 (prec. by the) derog. large number of people; mob (tends to follow the herd). –v. 1 (cause to) go in a herd (herded together for warmth; herded the cattle into the field). 2 look after (sheep, cattle, etc.). [Old English]

herd instinct n. (prec. by the) tendency to think and act as a crowd.

herdsman n. man who owns or tends a herd.

here –adv. 1 in or at or to this place or position (come here; sit here). 2 indicating a person's presence or a thing offered (my son here will show you; here is your coat). 3 at this point in the argument, situation, etc. (here I have a question). –n. this place (get out of here; lives near here; fill it up to here). –int. 1 calling attention: short for come here, look here, etc. (here, where are you going with that?). 2 indicating one's presence in a roll-call: short for I am here. □ **here goes** colloq. expression indicating the start of a bold act. **here's** to I drink to the health of. **here we are** colloq. said on arrival at one's destination. **here we go again** colloq. the same, usu. undesirable, events are recurring. **neither here nor there** of no importance. [Old English]

hereabout /ˈhɪərəbaʊt/ adv. (also **hereabouts**) near this place.

hereafter /hɪərˈɑːftə(r)/ –adv. 1 from now on; in the future. –n. 1 the future. 2 life after death.

here and now adv. at this very moment; immediately.

here and there adv. in various places.

hereby /hɪəˈbaɪ/ adv. by this means; as a result of this.

hereditable /hɪˈredɪtəb(ə)l/ adj. that can be inherited. [Latin: related to HEIR]

hereditary /hɪˈredɪtərɪ/ adj. 1 (of a disease, instinct, etc.) able to be passed down genetically from one generation to another. 2 **a** descending by inheritance. **b** holding a position by inheritance. [Latin: related to HEIR]

heredity /hɪˈredɪtɪ/ n. 1 **a** passing on of physical or mental characteristics genetically. **b** these characteristics. 2 genetic constitution.

411

Hereford /ˈhɛrɪfəd/ n. animal of a breed of red and white beef cattle. [Hereford in England]

herein /hɪəˈrɪn/ adv. formal in this matter, book, etc.

hereinafter /ˌhɪərɪnˈɑːftə(r)/ adv. esp. Law formal from this point on. 2 in a later part of this document etc.

hereof /hɪəˈrɒv/ adv. formal of this.

heresy /ˈhɛrəsɪ/ n. pl. -ies 1 esp. RC Ch. religious belief or practice contrary to orthodox doctrine. 2 opinion contrary to what is normally accepted or maintained. [Greek hairesis choice]

heretic /ˈhɛrətɪk/ n. 1 person believing in or practising religious heresy. 2 holder of an unorthodox opinion. □ **heretical** /hɪˈrɛtɪk(ə)l/ adj.

hereto /hɪəˈtuː/ adv. formal to this matter.

heretofore /ˌhɪətəˈfɔː(r)/ adv. formal before this time.

hereupon /ˌhɪərəˈpɒn/ adv. after this; in consequence of this.

herewith /hɪəˈwɪð/ adv. with this (esp. of an enclosure in a letter etc.).

heritable /ˈhɛrɪtəb(ə)l/ adj. 1 Law capable of being inherited or of inheriting. 2 Biol. genetically transmissible from parent to offspring. [French: related to HEIR]

heritage /ˈhɛrɪtɪdʒ/ n. 1 what is or may be inherited. 2 inherited circumstances, benefits, etc. 3 a nation's historic buildings, monuments, countryside, etc., esp. when regarded as worthy of preservation.

hermaphrodite /hɜːˈmæfrədaɪt/ –n. person, animal, or plant having both male and female reproductive organs. –adj. combining both sexes. □ **hermaphroditic** /-ˈdɪtɪk/ adj. [from Hermaphroditus, son of Hermes and Aphrodite who became jo ned in one body to a nymph]

hermetic /hɜːˈmɛtɪk/ adj. with an airtight closure. □ **hermetically** adv. [from the Greek g d Hermes, regarded as the founder of alchemy]

hermit /ˈhɜːmɪt/ n. person (esp. an early Christian) living in solitude and austerity. □ **hermitic** /ˈmɪtɪk/ adj. [Greek erēmos solitary]

hermitage n. 1 hermit's dwelling. 2 secluded dwelling.

hermit-crab n. crab that lives in a mollusc's cast-off shell.

hernia /ˈhɜːnɪə/ n. protrusion of part of an organ through the wall of the body cavity containing it. [Latin]

hero /ˈhɪərəʊ/ n. (pl. -es) 1 person noted or admired for nobility, courage, outstanding achievements, etc. 2 chief male

hero

heroic /hɪˈrəʊɪk/ —*adj.* of, fit for, or like a hero; very brave. —*n.* (in *pl.*) **1** high-flown language or sentiments. **2** unduly bold behaviour. □ **heroically** *adv.*

character in a play, story, etc. [Greek *hērōs*]

heroin /ˈhɛrəʊɪn/ *n.* addictive analgesic drug derived from morphine, often used as a narcotic. [German: related to HERO, from the effect on the user's self-esteem]

heroine /ˈhɛrəʊɪn/ *n.* **1** woman noted or admired for nobility, courage, outstanding achievements, etc. **2** chief female character in a play, story, etc. [Greek: related to HERO]

heroism /ˈhɛrəʊɪz(ə)m/ *n.* heroic conduct or qualities. [French *héroïsme*: related to HERO]

heron /ˈhɛrən/ *n.* long-legged wading bird with a long S-shaped neck. [French from Germanic]

hero-worship —*n.* idealization of an admired person. —*v.* idolize.

herpes /ˈhɜːpiːz/ *n.* virus disease causing skin blisters. [Greek *herpō* creep]

Herr /hɛə(r)/ *n.* (*pl.* **Herren** /ˈhɛrən/) **1** title of a German man; Mr. **2** German man. [German]

herring /ˈhɛrɪŋ/ *n.* (*pl.* same or **-s**) N. Atlantic fish used as food. [Old English]

herring-bone *n.* stitch or weave consisting of a series of small 'V' shapes making a zigzag pattern.

herring-gull *n.* large gull with dark wing-tips.

hers /hɜːz/ *poss. pron.* the one or ones belonging to or associated with her (*it is hers; hers are over there*). □ **of hers** of or belonging to her (*friend of hers*).

herself /hɜːˈsɛlf/ *pron.* **1 a** *emphat. form* of SHE or HER (*she herself will do it*). **b** *refl. form* of HER (*she has hurt herself*). **2** in her normal state of body or mind (*does not feel quite herself today*). □ **be herself** see ONESELF. **by herself** see by oneself. [Old English: related to HER, SELF]

hertz *n.* (*pl.* same) SI unit of frequency, equal to one cycle per second. [*Hertz*, name of a physicist]

he's /hiːz, hɪz/ *contr.* **1** he is. **2** he has.

hesitant /ˈhɛzɪt(ə)nt/ *adj.* hesitating; irresolute. □ **hesitance** *n.* **hesitancy** *n.* □ **hesitantly** *adv.*

hesitate /ˈhɛzɪteɪt/ *v.* (**-ting**) **1** show or feel indecision or uncertainty; pause in doubt (*hesitated over her choice*). **2** be reluctant (*I hesitate to say so*). □ **hesitation** /-ˈteɪʃ(ə)n/ *n.* [Latin *haereo haes-* stick fast]

hessian /ˈhɛsɪən/ *n.* strong coarse sacking made of hemp or jute. [*Hesse* in Germany]

hetero- *comb. form* other, different. [Greek *heteros* other]

heterodox /ˈhɛtərəˌdɒks/ *adj.* not orthodox. □ **heterodoxy** /-ˌdɒksɪ/ *n.* [from HETERO- Greek *doxa* opinion]

heterodyne /ˈhɛtərəˌdaɪn/ *adj. Radio* relating to the production of a lower frequency from the combination of two almost equal high frequencies. [from HETERO-, Greek *dunamis* force]

heterogeneous /ˌhɛtərəʊˈdʒiːnɪəs/ *adj.* **1** diverse in character. **2** varied in content. □ **heterogeneity** /-dʒɪˈniːɪtɪ/ *n.* [Latin from Greek *genos* kind]

heteromorphic /ˌhɛtərəʊˈmɔːfɪk/ *adj.* (also **heteromorphous** /-ˈmɔːfəs/) *Biol.* of dissimilar forms. □ **heteromorphism** *n.*

heterosexual /ˌhɛtərəʊˈsɛkʃʊəl/ —*adj.* feeling or involving sexual attraction to the opposite sex. —*n.* heterosexual person. □ **heterosexuality** /-ˈælɪtɪ/ *n.*

het up *predic. adj. colloq.* overwrought. [*het*, a dial. word = heated]

heuristic /hjʊəˈrɪstɪk/ *adj.* **1** allowing or assisting to discover. **2** proceeding to a solution by trial and error. [Greek *heuriskō* find]

hew *v.* (*past part.* **hewn** /hjuːn/ or **hewed**) **1** chop or cut with an axe, sword, etc. **2** cut into shape. [Old English]

hex —*v.* **1** practise witchcraft. **2** bewitch. —*n.* magic spell. [German]

hexa- *comb. form* six. [Greek]

hexadecimal /ˌhɛksəˈdɛsɪm(ə)l/ *adj.* esp. *Computing* of a system of numerical notation that has 16 (the figures 0 to 9 and the letters A to F) rather than 10 as a base.

hexagon /ˈhɛksəgən/ *n.* plane figure with six sides and angles. □ **hexagonal** /-ˈsægən(ə)l/ *adj.* [Greek: related to HEXA-, *-gōnos* angled]

hexagram /ˈhɛksəgræm/ *n.* figure formed by two intersecting equilateral triangles.

hexameter /hɛkˈsæmɪtə(r)/ *n.* line of verse with six metrical feet.

hey /heɪ/ *int.* calling attention or expressing joy, surprise, inquiry, etc. [imitative]

heyday /ˈheɪdeɪ/ *n.* time of greatest success or prosperity. [Low German]

hey presto! *int.* conjuror's phrase on completing a trick.

Hezbollah /ˌhɛzbəˈlɑː/ *n.* (also **Hiz-**) /huz-/ extreme Shiite Muslim group, active esp. in Lebanon. [Arabic *hizbul-lah* Party of God]

HF *abbr.* high frequency.

Hf *symb.* hafnium.

Hg *symb.* mercury.

hg *abbr.* hectogram(s).

HGV *abbr.* heavy goods vehicle.

HH *abbr.* 1 Her or His Highness. 2 His Holiness. 3 (of pencil-lead) double-hard.

hi /haɪ/ *int.* calling attention or as a greeting.

hiatus /haɪˈeɪtəs/ *n.* (*pl.* **-tuses**) 1 break or gap in a series or sequence. 2 break between two vowels coming together but not in the same syllable, as in *though* or *the ear.* [Latin *hio* gape]

hibernate /ˈhaɪbəˌneɪt/ *v.* (-ting) (of an animal) spend the winter in a dormant state. □ **hibernation** /-ˈneɪʃ(ə)n/ *n.* [Latin *hibernus* wintry]

Hibernian /haɪˈbɜːnɪən/ *archaic poet.* —*adj.* of Ireland. —*n.* native of Ireland. [Latin *Hibernia* Ireland]

hibiscus /hɪˈbɪskəs/ *n.* (*pl.* **-cuses**) cultivated shrub with large bright-coloured flowers. [Greek *hibiskos* marsh mallow]

hiccup /ˈhɪkʌp/ (also **hiccough**) —*n.* 1 involuntary spasm of the diaphragm causing a characteristic sound. 'hic'. 2 temporary or minor stoppage or difficulty. —*v.* (-**p**-) make a hiccup. [imitative]

hick *n.* (often *attrib.*) esp. *US colloq.* country bumpkin, provincial. [familiar form of *Richard*]

hickory /ˈhɪkərɪ/ *n.* (*pl.* **-ies**) 1 N. American tree yielding wood and nutlike edible fruits. 2 the tough heavy wood of this. [Virginian *pohickery*]

hid *past* of **HIDE**[1].

hidden *past part.* of **HIDE**[1].

hidden agenda *n.* secret motivation behind a policy statement, etc.; ulterior motive.

hide[1] —*v.* (-**ding**; *past* **hid**; *past part.* **hidden**) 1 put or keep out of sight. 2 conceal oneself. 3 (usu. foll. by *from*) keep (a fact) secret. 4 conceal. —*n.* camouflaged shelter used for observing wildlife. □ **hider** *n.* [Old English]

hide[2] *n.* 1 animal's skin, esp. when tanned or dressed. 2 *colloq.* the human skin. esp. the backside. [Old English]

hide-and-seek *n.* game in which players hide and another searches for them.

hideaway *n.* hiding-place or place of retreat.

hidebound *adj.* 1 narrow-minded. 2 constricted by tradition.

hideous /ˈhɪdɪəs/ *adj.* 1 very ugly, revolting. 2 *colloq.* unpleasant. □ **hideosity** /-ˈɒstɪ/ *n.* (*pl.* **-ies**). □ **hideously** *adv.* [Anglo-French *hidous*]

hide-out *n. colloq.* hiding-place.

hiding[1] *n. colloq.* a thrashing. □ **on a hiding to nothing** with no chance of succeeding. [from **HIDE**[2]]

hiding[2] *n.* 1 act of hiding. 2 state of remaining hidden (*go into hiding*). [from **HIDE**[1]]

hiding-place *n.* place of concealment.

hierarchy /ˈhaɪəˌrɑːkɪ/ *n.* (*pl.* **-ies**) system of grades of status or authority ranked one above the other. □ **hierarchical** /ˈraɪkɪk(ə)l/ *adj.* [Greek *hieros* sacred, *arkhō* rule]

hieratic /ˌhaɪəˈrætɪk/ *adj.* 1 of priests. 2 of the ancient Egyptian hieroglyphic writing as used by priests. [Greek *hieros* priest]

hieroglyph /ˈhaɪərəɡlɪf/ *n.* picture representing a word, syllable, or sound, as used in ancient Egyptian etc. [Greek *hieros* sacred, *gluphō* carve]

hieroglyphic /ˌhaɪərəˈɡlɪfɪk/ —*adj.* of or written in hieroglyphs. —*n.* (in *pl.*) hieroglyphs; hieroglyphic writing.

hi-fi /ˈhaɪfaɪ/ *colloq.* —*adj.* of high fidelity. —*n.* (*pl.* **-s**) set of high-fidelity equipment. [abbreviation]

higgledy-piggledy /ˌhɪɡəldɪˈpɪɡəldɪ/ *adv.* & *adj.* in confusion or disorder. [origin uncertain]

high /haɪ/ —*adj.* 1 a of great vertical extent (*high building*). b (*predic.*; often in *comb.*) of a specified height (*one inch high*; *waist-high*). 2 a far above ground or sea level etc. (*high altitude*). b inland. esp. when raised (*High Asia*). 3 extending above the normal level (*jersey with a high neck*). 4 a of exalted rank (*high society*; *is high in the Government*). 6 a great; intense; extreme; powerful (*high praise*; *high temperature*). b greater than normal (*high prices*). c extreme or very traditional in religious or political opinion (*high Tory*). 7 performed at, to, or from a considerable height (*high diving*; *high flying*). 8 (often foll. by *on*) *colloq.* intoxicated by alcohol or esp. drugs. 9 (of a sound etc.) of high frequency; shrill. 10 (of a period, age, time, etc.), at its peak (*high noon*; *high summer*; *High Renaissance*). 11 a (of meat etc.) beginning to go bad; off. b (of game) well-hung and slightly decomposed. —*n.* 1 high, or the highest, level or figure. 2 area of high pressure; anticyclone. 3 *slang* euphoric state, esp. drug-induced (*am on a high*). —*adv.* 1 far up; aloft (*flew the flag high*). 2 in or to a high degree. 3 at a high price. 4 (of a sound) at or to a high pitch. □ **high opinion of** favourable opinion of. **on high** in or to heaven or a high place. **on one's high horse** *colloq.* acting arrogantly. [Old English]

high altar *n.* chief altar in a church.

high and dry *adj.* 1 stranded; aground. 2 out of the current of events.

high and low *adv.* everywhere (*searched high and low*).

high and mighty *adj. colloq.* arrogant.

highball

highball *n. US* drink of spirits and soda etc., served with ice in a tall glass.

highbrow *colloq.* —*adj.* intellectual; cultured. —*n.* intellectual or cultured person.

high chair *n.* infant's chair with long legs and a tray for meals.

High Church *n.* section of the Church of England emphasizing ritual, priestly authority, and sacraments.

high-class *adj.* of high quality.

high colour *n.* flushed complexion.

high command *n.* army commander-in-chief and associated staff.

High Commission *n.* embassy from one Commonwealth country to another. □ **High Commissioner** *n.*

High Court *n.* (also in England **High Court of Justice**) supreme court of justice for civil cases.

high day *n.* festal day.

higher animal *n.* (also **higher plant**) animal or plant evolved to a high degree.

higher education *n.* education at university etc.

high explosive *n.* extremely explosive substance used in shells, bombs, etc.

highfalutin /ˌhaɪfəˈluːtɪn/ *adj.* (also **highfaluting** /-tɪŋ/) *colloq.* pompous, pretentious. [origin unknown]

high fidelity *n.* high-quality sound reproduction with little distortion.

high-flown *adj.* (of language etc.) extravagant, bombastic.

high-flyer *n.* (also **high-flier**) **1** ambitious person. **2** person or thing of great potential. □ **high-flying** *adj.*

high frequency *n.* frequency, esp. in radio, of 3 to 30 megahertz.

high gear *n.* gear such that the driven end of a transmission revolves faster than the driving end.

high-handed *adj.* disregarding others' feelings; overbearing. □ **high-handedly** *adv.* **high-handedness** *n.*

high heels *n.pl.* women's shoes with high heels.

high jinks *n.pl.* boisterous fun.

high jump *n.* **1** athletic event consisting of jumping over a high bar. **2** *colloq.* drastic punishment (*he's for the high jump*).

highland —*n.* (usu. in *pl.*) **1** area of high land. **2** (**the Highlands**) mountainous part of Scotland. —*adj.* of or in a highland or the Highlands. □ **highlander** *n.* (also **Highlander**). [Old English; = promontory: related to HIGH]

Highland cattle *n.* cattle of a shaggy-haired breed with long curved horns.

Highland fling see FLING *n.* 3.

high-level *adj.* **1** (of negotiations etc.) conducted by high-ranking people. **2** *Computing* (of a programming language) not machine-dependent and usu. at a level of abstraction close to natural language.

highlight —*n.* **1** moment or detail of vivid interest; outstanding feature. **2** (in a painting etc.) bright area. **3** (usu. in *pl.*) light streak in the hair produced by bleaching. —*v.* **1** bring into prominence; draw attention to. **2** mark with a highlighter.

highlighter *n.* marker pen for emphasizing a printed word etc. by overlaying it with colour.

highly /ˈhaɪli/ *adv.* **1** in a high degree (*highly amusing; commend it highly*). **2** favourably (*think highly of him*).

high-minded *adj.* having high moral principles. □ **high-mindedly** *adv.* **high-mindedness** *n.*

highness *n.* **1** state of being high (*high-ness of taxation*). **2** (**Highness**) title used when addressing or referring to a prince or princess (*Her Highness; Your Royal Highness*).

high-octane *adj.* (of fuel used in internal-combustion engines) not detonating readily during the power stroke.

high-pitched *adj.* **1** (of a sound) high. **2** (of a roof) steep.

high point *n.* the maximum or best state reached.

high-powered *adj.* **1** having great power or energy. **2** important or influential.

high pressure *n.* **1** high degree of activity or exertion. **2** atmospheric condition with the pressure above average.

high priest *n.* (*fem.* **high priestess**) **1** chief priest, esp. Jewish. **2** head of a cult.

high-ranking *adj.* of high rank, senior.

high-rise —*attrib. adj.* (of a building) having many storeys. —*n.* such a building.

high-risk *attrib. adj.* involving or exposed to danger (*high-risk sports*).

high road *n.* main road.

high school *n.* **1** grammar school. **2** *US & Scot.* secondary school.

high sea *n.* (also **high seas**) open seas not under any country's jurisdiction.

high season *n.* busiest period at a resort etc.

high-speed *attrib. adj.* operating at great speed.

high-spirited *adj.* vivacious; cheerful; lively.

high spot *n.* important place or feature.

high street *n.* principal shopping street of a town.

high table n. dining-table for the most important guests or members.

high tea n. evening meal usu. consisting of a cooked dish, bread and butter, tea, etc.

high-tech adj. 1 employing, requiring, or involved in high technology. 2 imitating styles more usual in industry etc.

high technology n. advanced technological development esp. in electronics.

high tension n. = HIGH VOLTAGE.

high tide n. time or level of the tide at its peak.

high time n. time that is overdue (it is *high time they arrived*).

high treason n. = TREASON.

high-up n. colloq. person of high rank.

high voltage n. electrical potential large enough to injure or damage.

high water n. = HIGH TIDE.

high-water mark n. level reached at high water.

highway n. 1 a public road. b main route. 2 direct course of action (*on the highway to success*).

Highway Code n. official booklet of guidance for road-users.

highwayman n. hist. robber of travellers etc. usu. mounted.

high wire n. high tightrope.

hijack /'hʌɪdʒæk/ —v. 1 seize control of (a vehicle etc.), esp. to force it to a different destination. 2 seize (goods) in transit. 3 take control of (talks etc.) by force or subterfuge. —n. a hijacking. □ **hijacker** n. [origin unknown]

hike —n. 1 long walk, esp. in the country for pleasure. 2 rise in prices etc. —v. (-king) 1 go for a hike. 2 walk laboriously. 3 (usu. foll. by *up*) hitch up (clothing etc.); become hitched up. 4 (usu. foll. by *up*) raise (prices etc.). □ **hiker** n. [origin unknown]

hilarious /hɪ'lɛːrɪəs/ adj. 1 exceedingly funny. 2 boisterously merry. □ **hilariously** adv. **hilarity** /-'lærɪtɪ/ n. [Greek *hilaros* cheerful]

hill n. 1 naturally raised area of land, lower than a mountain. 2 (often in comb.) heap, mound (*anthill*). 3 sloping piece of road. □ **over the hill** colloq. past the prime of life. [Old English]

hill-billy n. US colloq. often derog. person from a remote rural area in a southern State.

hillock /'hɪlək/ n. small hill, mound.

hillside n. sloping side of a hill.

hilltop n. top of a hill.

hillwalking n. hiking in hilly country. □ **hillwalker** n.

hilly adj. (-ier, -iest) having many hills. □ **hilliness** n.

hilt n. handle of a sword, dagger, etc. □ **up to the hilt** completely. [Old English]

him pron. 1 objective case of HE (*I saw him*). 2 colloq. he (*it's him again; taller than him*). [Old English, dative of HE]

himself /hɪm'sɛlf/ pron. 1 a emphat. form of HE or HIM (*he himself will do it*). b refl. form of HIM (*he has hurt himself*). 2 in his normal state of body or mind (*does not feel quite himself today*). □ **be himself** see ONESELF. **by himself** see by oneself. [Old English: related to HIM, SELF]

hind¹ /hʌɪnd/ adj. a the back (*hind leg*). [Old English *hindan* from behind]

hinder¹ /'hɪndə(r)/ v. impede; delay. [Old English]

hinder² /'hʌɪndə(r)/ adj. rear, hind (*the hinder part*). [Old English]

hind² /hʌɪnd/ n. female (esp. red) deer, esp. in and after the third year. [Old English]

Hindi /'hɪndɪ/ n. 1 group of spoken dialects of N. India. 2 literary form of Hindustani, an official language of India. [Urdu *Hind* India]

hindmost adj. furthest behind.

hindquarters n.pl. hind legs and rump of a quadruped.

hindrance /'hɪndrəns/ n. 1 hindering, being hindered. 2 thing that hinders.

hindsight n. wisdom after the event.

Hindu /'hɪnduː/ —n. (pl. -s) follower of Hinduism. —adj. of Hindus or Hinduism. [Urdu *Hind* India]

Hinduism /'hɪnduːɪz(ə)m/ n. main religious and social system of India, including the belief in reincarnation, several gods, and a caste system.

Hindustani /hɪndʊ'stɑːnɪ/ n. language based on Hindi, used as a lingua franca in much of India, from HINDU, *stān*

hinge /hɪndʒ/ —n. 1 movable joint on which a door, lid, etc. turns or swings. 2 principle on which all depends. —v. (-ging) 1 (foll. by *on*) depend (on a principle, an event, etc.). 2 attach or be attached by a hinge. [related to HANG]

hinny /'hɪnɪ/ n. (pl. -ies) offspring of a female donkey and a male horse. [Greek *hinnos*]

hint —n. 1 slight or indirect indication or suggestion. 2 small piece of practical information. 3 very small trace; suggestion (*a hint of perfume*). —v. suggest slightly or indirectly. □ **hint at** give a hint of; refer indirectly to. **take a hint** heed a hint. [obsolete *hent* grasp]

hinterland /'hɪntəland/ n. 1 district beyond a coast or river's banks. 2 area served by a port or other centre. [German]

hip¹ n. projection of the pelvis and the upper part of the thigh-bone. [Old English]

hip² *n.* fruit of a rose, esp. wild. [Old English]

hip³ *int.* introducing a united cheer (*hip, hip, hooray*). [origin unknown]

hip⁴ *adj.* (also **hep**) (**-pper, -ppest**) *slang* trendy, stylish. [origin unknown]

hip-bath *n.* portable bath in which one sits immersed to the hips.

hip-bone *n.* bone forming the hip.

hip-flask *n.* small flask for spirits.

hip hop *n.* (also **hip-hop**) subculture combining rap music, graffiti art, and break-dancing. [from HIP⁴]

hippie /'hɪpɪ/ *n.* (also **hippy**) (*pl.* **-ies**) *colloq.* (esp. in the 1960s) person rejecting convention, typically with long hair, jeans, beads, etc., and taking hallucinogenic drugs. [from HIP⁴]

hippo /'hɪpəʊ/ *n.* (*pl.* **-s**) *colloq.* hippopotamus. [abbreviation]

hip-pocket *n.* trouser-pocket just behind the hip.

Hippocratic oath /hɪpə'krætɪk/ *n.* statement of ethics of the medical profession. [*Hippocrates*, name of a Greek physician]

hippodrome /'hɪpədrəʊm/ *n.* **1** music-hall or dancehall. **2** (in classical antiquity) course for chariot races etc. [Greek *hippos* horse, *dromos* race]

hippopotamus /hɪpə'pɒtəməs/ *n.* (*pl.* **-muses** or **-mi** /-maɪ/) large African mammal with short legs and thick skin, living by rivers, lakes, etc. [Greek *hippos* horse, *potamos* river]

hippy¹ var. of HIPPIE.

hippy² *adj.* having large hips.

hipster¹ *attrib. adj.* (of a garment) hanging from the hips rather than the waist. —*n.* (in *pl.*) such trousers.

hipster² *n. slang* hip person.

hire —*v.* (**-ring**) **1** purchase the temporary use of (a thing) (*hired a van*). **2** esp. *US* employ (a person). —*n.* **1** hiring or being hired. **2** payment for this. □ **for** (or **on**) **hire** ready to be hired. **hire out** grant the temporary use of (a thing) for payment. □ **hireable** *adj.* **hirer** *n.* [Old English]

hireling *n.* usu. *derog.* person who works (only) for money.

hire purchase *n.* system of purchase by paying in instalments.

hirsute /'hɜːsjuːt/ *adj.* hairy. [Latin]

his /hɪz/ *poss. pron.* **1** (*attrib.*) of or belonging to him or himself (*his house; his own business*). **2** the one or ones belonging to or associated with him (*it is his; his are over there*). □ **of his** of or belonging to him (*friend of his*). [Old English, genitive of HE]

Hispanic /hɪ'spænɪk/ —*adj.* **1** of Spain or Spain and Portugal. **2** of Spain and other Spanish-speaking countries. —*n.*

Spanish-speaking person living in the US. [Latin *Hispania* Spain]

hiss —*v.* **1** make a sharp sibilant sound, as of the letter s. **2** express disapproval of by hisses. **3** whisper urgently or angrily. —*n.* **1** sharp sibilant sound as of the letter s. **2** *Electronics* interference at audio frequencies. [imitative]

histamine /'hɪstəmiːn/ *n.* chemical compound in body tissues etc., associated with allergic reactions. [from HIS-TOLOGY, AMINE]

histogram /'hɪstəgræm/ *n.* statistical diagram of rectangles with areas proportional to the value of a number of variables. [Greek *histos* mast]

histology /hɪ'stɒlədʒɪ/ *n.* the study of tissue structure. [Greek *histos* web]

historian /hɪ'stɔːrɪən/ *n.* **1** writer of history. **2** person learned in history.

historic /hɪ'stɒrɪk/ *adj.* **1** famous or important in history or potentially so (*historic moment*). **2** *Gram.* (of a tense) used to narrate past events.

historical *adj.* **1** of or concerning history (*historical evidence*). **2** (of the study of a subject) showing its development over a period. **3** factual, not fictional or legendary. **4** belonging to the past, not the present. **5** (of a novel etc.) dealing with historical events. □ **historically** *adv.*

historicism /hɪ'stɒrɪsɪz(ə)m/ *n.* **1** theory that social and cultural phenomena are determined by history. **2** belief that historical events are governed by laws.

historicity /ˌhɪstə'rɪsɪtɪ/ *n.* historical truth or authenticity.

historiography /hɪˌstɔːrɪ'ɒgrəfɪ/ *n.* **1** the writing of history. **2** the study of this. □ **historiographer** *n.*

history /'hɪst(ə)rɪ/ *n.* (*pl.* **-ies**) **1** continuous record of (esp. public) events. **2 a** the study of past events, esp. human affairs. **b** total accumulation of past events, esp. relating to human affairs or a particular nation, person, thing, etc. **3** eventful past (*this house has a history*). **4** (foll. by *of*) past record (*had a history of illness*). **5 a** systematic or critical account of natural or historical events etc. **b** similar record or account of natural phenomena. **6** historical play. □ **make history** do something memorable. [Greek *historia* inquiry]

histrionic /ˌhɪstrɪ'ɒnɪk/ —*adj.* (of behaviour) theatrical, dramatic. —*n.* (in *pl.*) insincere and dramatic behaviour designed to impress. [Latin *histrio* actor]

hit —*v.* (**-tt-**; *past* and *past part.* **hit**) **1 a** strike with a blow or missile. **b** (of a moving body) strike with force (*the*

plane hit the ground), **c** reach (a target etc.), with a directed missile (*hit the wicket*). **2** cause to suffer; affect adversely. **3** (often foll. by *against*) direct a blow. **4** (often foll. by *against*, *on*) knock (a part of the body) (*hit his head*). **5** achieve, reach (*hit the right tone; can't hit the high notes*). **6** *colloq.* **a** arrive at (*hit a snag*). **b** arrive at (*hit town*). **c** indulge heavily in, esp. liquor etc. (*hit the bottle*). **7** esp. *US slang* rob or kill. **8** occur forcefully to (*it only hit him later*). **9 a** propel (a ball etc.) with a bat etc. to score runs or points. **b** score in this way (*hit a six*). —n. **1 a** blow, stroke. **b** collision. **2** shot etc. that hits its target. **3** *colloq.* popular success. □ **hit back** retaliate. **hit below the belt 1** *esp. Boxing* give a foul blow. **2** treat or behave unfairly. **hit the hay** (or *sack*) *colloq.* go to bed. **hit it off** (often foll. by *with, together*) *colloq.* get on well (with a person). **hit the nail on the head** state the truth exactly. **hit on** (or *upon*) find by chance. **hit out** deal vigorous physical or verbal blows. **hit the road** *slang* depart. **hit the roof** see ROOF. [Old English from Old Norse]

hit-and-run *attrib.adj.* **1** (of a driver, raider, etc.) causing damage or injury and leaving the scene immediately. **2** (of an accident, attack, etc.) perpetrated by such a person or people.

hitch —v. **1** fasten or be fastened with a loop, hook, etc.; tether. **2** move (a thing) slightly or with a jerk. **3** *colloq.* **a** = HITCHHIKE. **b** obtain (a lift) by hitchhiking. —n. **1** temporary obstacle or snag. **2** abrupt pull or push. **3** noose or knot of various kinds. **4** *colloq.* free ride in a vehicle. □ **get hitched** *colloq.* marry. **hitch up** lift (esp. clothing) with a jerk. [origin uncertain]

hitchhike v. (**-king**) travel by seeking free lifts in passing vehicles. □ **hitch-hiker** n.

hi-tech /haɪtek/ *adj.* = HIGH-TECH. [abbreviation]

hither /ˈhɪðə(r)/ *adv. formal* to or towards this place. [Old English]

hither and thither *adv.* to and fro.

hitherto /hɪðəˈtuː/ *adv.* until this time, up to now.

hit list n. *slang* list of prospective victims.

hit man n. *slang* hired assassin.

hit-or-miss *adj.* liable to error; random.

hit parade n. *colloq.* list of the current best-selling pop records.

Hittite /ˈhɪtaɪt/ —n. member or language of an ancient people of Asia Minor and Syria. —adj. of the Hittites. [Hebrew]

HIV *abbr.* human immunodeficiency virus, either of two viruses causing Aids.

hive n. beehive. □ **hive off** (**-ving**) separate from a larger group. [Old English]

hives n.pl. skin-eruption, esp. nettle-rash. [origin unknown]

Hizbollah var. of HEZBOLLAH.

HM *abbr.* Her (or His) Majesty('s).

HMG *abbr.* Her (or His) Majesty's Government.

HMI *abbr.* Her (or His) Majesty's Inspector (of Schools).

HMS *abbr.* Her (or His) Majesty's Ship.

HMSO *abbr.* Her (or His) Majesty's Stationery Office.

HNC *abbr.* Higher National Certificate.

HND *abbr.* Higher National Diploma.

Ho *symb.* holmium.

ho /həʊ/ *int.* expressing triumph, derision, etc. or calling attention. [natural exclamation]

hoard —n. stock or store (esp. of money or food). —v. amass and store. □ **hoarder** n. [Old English]

hoarding n. **1** large, usu. wooden, structure used to carry advertisements etc. **2** temporary fence round a building site etc. [obsolete *hoard* from French: related to HOARD]

hoar-frost n. frozen water vapour on vegetation etc. [Old English]

hoarse *adj.* **1** (of the voice) rough and deep; husky; croaking. **2** having such a voice. □ **hoarsely** *adv.* **hoarseness** n. [Old Norse]

hoary *adj.* (**-ier**, **-iest**) **1 a** (of hair) grey or white with age. **b** having such hair. **2** old and trite (*hoary joke*). [Old English]

hoax —n. **1** humorous or malicious deception. —v. deceive (a person) with a hoax. [probably a shortening of *hocus* in HOCUS-POCUS]

hob n. **1** flat heating surface with hot-plates or burners, on a cooker or as a separate unit. **2** flat metal shelf at the side of a fireplace for heating a pan etc. [perhaps var. of HUB]

hobble /ˈhɒb(ə)l/ —v. (**-ling**) **1** walk lamely; limp. **2** tie together the legs of (a horse etc.) to prevent it from straying. —n. **1** uneven or infirm gait. **2** rope etc. for hobbling a horse etc. [probably Low German]

hobby /ˈhɒbɪ/ n. (pl. **-ies**) leisure-time activity pursued for pleasure. [from the name *Robin*]

hobby-horse n. **1** child's toy consisting of a stick with a horse's head. **2** favourite idea or subject or idea.

hobgoblin /ˈhɒbˌɡɒblɪn/ n. mischievous imp; bogy. [from HOBBY, GOBLIN]

hobnail *n.* heavy-headed nail for boot-soles. [from HOB]

hobnob /'hobnob/ *v.* (**-bb-**) (usu. foll. by *with*) mix socially or informally. [*hab nab* have or not have]

hobo /'haubau/ *n.* (*pl.* **-es** or **-s**) *US* wandering worker; tramp. [origin unknown]

Hobson's choice /'hobs(a)nz/ *n.* choice of taking the thing offered or nothing. [*Hobson*, name of a carrier who let out horses thus]

hock[1] *n.* joint of a quadruped's hind leg between the knee and the fetlock. [Old English]

hock[2] *n.* German white wine from the Rhineland. [*Hochheim* in Germany]

hock[3] *v.* esp. *US colloq.* pawn; pledge. □ **in hock 1** in pawn. **2** in debt. **3** in prison. [Dutch]

hockey /'hoki/ *n.* team game with hooked sticks and a small hard ball. [origin unknown]

hocus-pocus /,haukas'paukas/ *n.* deception; trickery. [sham Latin]

hod *n.* **1** V-shaped trough on a pole used for carrying bricks etc. **2** portable receptacle for coal. [French *hotte* pannier]

hodgepodge var. of HOTCHPOTCH.

Hodgkin's disease /'hodʒkɪnz/ *n.* malignant disease of lymphatic tissues, usu. characterized by enlargement of the lymph nodes. [*Hodgkin*, name of a physician]

hoe – *n.* long-handled tool with a blade, used for weeding etc. – *v.* (**hoes, hoed, hoeing**) weed (crops); loosen (earth); dig up with a hoe. [French from Germanic]

hog – *n.* **1** castrated male pig. **2** *colloq.* greedy person. – *v.* (**-gg-**) *colloq.* take greedily; hoard selfishly; monopolize. □ **go the whole hog** *colloq.* do something completely or thoroughly. □ **hoggish** *adj.* [Old English]

Hogmanay /'hogmə,neɪ/ *n. Scot.* New Year's Eve. [probably French]

hogshead *n.* **1** large cask. **2** liquid or dry measure (about 50 gallons). [from HOG: the reason for the name is unknown]

hogwash *n. colloq.* nonsense, rubbish.

ho-ho /hə'həu/ *int.* **1** representing a deep jolly laugh. **2** expressing surprise, triumph, or derision. [reduplication of HO]

hoick *v. colloq.* (often foll. by *out*) lift or pull, esp. with a jerk. [perhaps var. of HIKE]

hoi polloi /,hɔɪ pə'lɔɪ/ *n.* the masses; the common people. [Greek, = the many]

■ **Usage** This phrase is often preceded by *the*, which is, strictly speaking, unnecessary, since *hoi* means 'the'.

hoist – *v.* **1** raise or haul up. **2** raise by means of ropes and pulleys etc. – *n.* **1** act of hoisting, lift. **2** apparatus for hoisting. □ **hoist with one's own petard** caught by one's own trick etc. [earlier *hoise*, probably from Low German]

hoity-toity /,hɔɪtɪ'tɔɪtɪ/ *adj.* haughty. [obsolete *hoit* romp]

hokum /'haukəm/ *n. esp. US slang* **1** sentimental, sensational, or unreal material in a film or play etc. **2** bunkum; rubbish. [origin unknown]

hold[1] /həʊld/ – *v.* (*past* and *past part.* **held**) **1 a** keep fast; grasp (esp. in the hands or arms). **b** (also *refl.*) keep or sustain (a thing, oneself, one's head, etc.) in a particular position. **c** grip so as to control (*hold the reins*). **2** have the capacity for, contain (*holds two pints*). **3** possess, gain, or have, esp.: **a** be the owner or tenant of (land, property, stocks, etc.). **b** gain or have gained (a qualification, record, etc.). **c** have the position of (a place etc.). **d** keep possession of (a place etc.), esp. against attack. **4** remain unbroken; not give way (*roof held under the storm*). **5** celebrate or conduct (a meeting, festival, conversation, etc.). **6 a** keep (a person etc.) in a place or condition (*held him in suspense*). **b** detain, esp. in custody. **7 a** engross (*held the stage*). **b** dominate (*held him for hours*). **8** (foll. by *to*) keep (a person etc.) to (a promise etc.). **9** (of weather) continue fine. **10** think, believe; assert (*can't hold his drink*). **11** regard with a specified feeling (*held him in contempt*). **12** cease; restrain (*hold your fire*). **13** keep or reserve (*please hold over me*). **14** be able to drink (alcohol) without effect (*can't hold his drink*). **15** (of a court etc.) lay down; decide. **16** *Mus.* sustain (a note). – *n.* **1** *hold the line.* – *n.* **1** grasp (*take hold of him*). **4** (often in *comb.*) thing to hold by (*seized the hand-hold*). □ **hold (a thing) against (a person)** resent or regard it as discreditable to (a person). **hold back 1** impede the progress of; restrain. **2** keep for oneself. **3** (often foll. by *from*) hesitate; refrain. **hold one's breath** see BREATH. **hold down 1** repress. **2** *colloq.* be competent enough to keep (one's job etc.). **hold the fort 1** act as a temporary substitute. **2** cope in an emergency. **hold forth** speak at length or tediously. **hold one's ground** see GROUND[1]. **hold hands** grasp one another by the hand as a sign of affection or for support or guidance. **hold it** cease action or movement. **hold**

hold the line not ring off (in a telephone connection). **hold one's nose** compress the nostrils to avoid a bad smell. **hold off 1** delay, not begin. **2** keep one's distance. **hold on 1** keep one's grasp on something. **2** wait a moment. **3** = *hold the line.* **hold out 1** stretch forth etc.). **2** offer (an inducement etc.). **3** maintain resistance. **4** persist or last. **hold out for** continue to demand. **hold out on** *colloq.* refuse something to (a person). **hold over** postpone. **hold one's own** maintain one's position; not be beaten. **hold one's tongue** *colloq.* remain silent. **hold to ransom 1** keep a prisoner until a ransom is paid. **2** demand concessions from by threats. **hold up 1** support, sustain. **2** exhibit, display. **3** hinder, obstruct. **4** stop and rob by force. **hold water** (of reasoning) be sound, bear examination. **hold with** (usu. with *neg.*) *colloq.* approve of, on **3** holding the line. **take hold of** (of a custom or habit) become established. **with no holds barred** with no restrictions of method. □ **holder** *n.* [Old English]

hold² /həʊld/ *n.* cavity in the lower part of a ship or aircraft for cargo. [Old English: related to HOLLOW]

holdall *n.* large soft travelling bag.

holding *n.* **1** tenure of land. **2** stocks, property, etc. held.

holding company *n.* company created to hold the shares of other companies, which it then controls.

hold-up *n.* **1** stoppage or delay. **2** robbery by force.

hole *n.* **1 a** empty space in a solid body. **b** opening in or through something. **2** animal's burrow. **3** (in games) cavity or receptacle for a ball. **4** *colloq.* small or dingy place. **5** *colloq.* awkward situation. **6** *Golf* a point scored by a player who gets the ball from tee to hole in the fewest strokes. **b** terrain or distance from tee to hole. —*v.* **1** pierce with a hole or holes. **b** make a hole in. **2** put into a hole. □ **hole up** *US colloq.* hide oneself. **make a hole in** use a large amount of. □ **holey** *adj.* [Old English]

hole-and-corner *adj.* secret; underhand.

hole in the heart *n. colloq.* congenital defect in the heart membrane.

holiday /ˈhɒlɪdeɪ/ —*n.* **1** (often in *pl.*) extended period of recreation, esp. spent away from home or travelling; break from work. **2** day of festivity or recreation when no work is done, esp. a religious festival etc. —*v.* spend a holiday. [Old English: related to HOLY, DAY]

holiday camp *n.* place for holidaymakers with facilities on site.

holiday-maker *n.* person on holiday.

holier-than-thou *adj. colloq.* self-righteous.

holiness /ˈhəʊlɪnɪs/ *n.* **1** being holy or sacred. **2** (**Holiness**) title used when addressing or referring to the Pope. [Old English: related to HOLY]

holism /ˈhəʊlɪz(ə)m/ *n.* (also **wholism**) **1** *Philos.* theory that certain wholes are greater than the sum of their parts. **2** *Med.* treating of the whole person rather than the symptoms of a disease. □ **holistic** /-ˈlɪstɪk/ *adj.* [Greek *holos* whole]

hollandaise sauce /ˌhɒlənˈdeɪz/ *n.* creamy sauce of melted butter, egg-yolks, vinegar, etc. [French]

holler *v. & n. US colloq.* shout. [French *holà* hello!]

hollow /ˈhɒləʊ/ —*adj.* **1 a** having a cavity; not solid. **b** sunken (*hollow cheeks*). **2** (of a sound) echoing. **3** empty; hungry. **4** meaningless (*hollow victory*). **5** insincere (*hollow laugh*). —*n.* **1** hollow place; hole. **2** valley; basin. —*v.* (often foll. by *out*) make hollow; excavate. —*adv. colloq.* completely (*beaten hollow*). □ **hollowly** *adv.* **hollowness** *n.* [Old English]

holly /ˈhɒlɪ/ *n.* (*pl.* **-ies**) evergreen shrub with prickly leaves and red berries. [Old English]

hollyhock /ˈhɒlɪhɒk/ *n.* tall plant with showy flowers. [from HOLY, obsolete *hock* mallow]

holm /həʊm/ *n.* (in full **holm-oak**) green oak with holly-like young leaves. [dial. *holm* holly]

holmium /ˈhəʊlmɪəm/ *n.* metallic element of the lanthanide series. [Latin *Holmia* Stockholm]

holocaust /ˈhɒləkɔːst/ *n.* **1** large-scale destruction, esp. by fire or nuclear war. **2** (**the Holocaust**) mass murder of the Jews by the Nazis 1939–45. [Greek *holos* whole, *kaustos* burnt]

hologram /ˈhɒləgræm/ *n.* photographic pattern that gives a three-dimensional image when illuminated by coherent light. [Greek *holos* whole, -GRAM]

holograph /ˈhɒləgrɑːf/ —*adj.* wholly written by hand by the person named as the author. —*n.* holograph document. [Greek *holos* whole, -GRAPH]

holography /həˈlɒgrəfɪ/ *n.* the study or production of holograms.

hols /hɒlz/ *n.pl. colloq.* holidays. [abbreviation]

holster /ˈhəʊlstə(r)/ *n.* leather case for a pistol or revolver, worn on a belt etc. [Dutch]

holy /ˈhəʊlɪ/ *adj.* (**-er**, **-iest**) **1** morally and spiritually excellent or perfect; and to be revered. **2** belonging to or devoted

to God. **3** consecrated, sacred. [Old English: related to WHOLE]

Holy Communion see COMMUNION.

Holy Ghost *n.* = HOLY SPIRIT.

Holy Grail see GRAIL.

Holy Land *n.* area between the River Jordan and the Mediterranean Sea.

holy of holies *n.* **1** sacred inner chamber of the Jewish temple. **2** thing regarded as most sacred.

holy orders *n.pl.* the status of a bishop, priest, or deacon.

Holy Roman Empire *n.* Western part of the Roman Empire as revived by Charlemagne in 800 AD.

Holy See *n.* papacy or papal court.

Holy Spirit *n.* Third Person of the Trinity; God as spiritually acting.

Holy Week *n.* week before Easter.

Holy Writ *n.* holy writings, esp. the Bible.

homage /'hɒmɪdʒ/ *n.* tribute, expression of reverence (*pay homage to*). [Latin *homo* man]

Homburg /'hɒmbɜːg/ *n.* man's felt hat with a narrow curled brim and a lengthwise dent in the crown. [*Homburg* in Germany]

home — *n.* **1 a** place where one lives; fixed residence. **b** dwelling-house. **2** family circumstances (*comes from a good home*). **3** native land. **4** place caring for people or animals. **5** place where a thing originates, is kept, or is native or most common. **6 a** finishing point in a race. **b** (in games) place where one is safe; goal. **7** *Sport* home match or win. —*attrib. adj.* **1 a** of or connected with one's home, family, etc. **b** carried on, done, or made, at home. **2** in one's own country (*home industries; the home market*). **3** *Sport* played on one's own ground etc. (*home match*). —*adv.* **1** to, at, or in one's home or country (*go home; is he home yet?*). **2** to the point aimed at; completely (*drove the nail home*). —*v.* (-**ming**) **1** (esp. of a trained pigeon) return home. **2** (often foll. by *on, in on*) (of a vessel, missile, etc.) be guided towards a destination or target. **3** send or guide homewards. □ **at home 1** in one's house or native land. **2** at ease (*make yourself at home*). **3** (usu. foll. by *in, on, with*) familiar or well informed. **4** available to callers. [Old English]

home and dry *predic. adj.* having achieved one's aim.

home-brew *n.* beer or other alcoholic drink brewed at home.

home-coming *n.* arrival at home.

Home Counties *n.pl.* the counties closest to London.

home economics *n.pl.* the study of household management.

home farm *n.* principal farm on an estate, providing produce for the owner.

home-grown *adj.* grown or produced at home.

Home Guard *n. hist.* British citizen army organized for defence in 1940.

home help *n.* person helping with housework etc., esp. one provided by a local authority.

homeland *n.* **1** one's native land. **2** any of several partially self-governing areas in S. Africa reserved for Black South Africans (the official name for a Bantustan).

homeless *adj.* lacking a home. □ **homelessness** *n.*

homely *adj.* (-**ier, -iest**) **1** simple, plain, unpretentious. **2** *US* (of facial appearance) plain, unattractive. **3** comfortable, cosy. □ **homeliness** *n.*

home-made *adj.* made at home.

Home Office *n.* British government department dealing with law and order, immigration, etc., in England and Wales.

homeopathy *US* var. of HOMOEOPATHY.

Homeric /hɒˈmɛrɪk/ *adj.* **1** of, or in the style of, Homer. **2** of Bronze Age Greece as described in Homer's poems.

home rule *n.* government of a country or region by its own citizens.

Home Secretary *n.* Secretary of State in charge of the Home Office.

homesick *adj.* depressed by absence from home. □ **homesickness** *n.*

homespun —*adj.* **1** made of yarn spun at home. **2** plain, simple. —*n.* homespun cloth.

homestead /'hɒmstɛd/ *n.* house, esp. a farmhouse, and outbuildings.

home truth *n.* basic but unwelcome information about oneself.

homeward /'həʊmwəd/ —*adv.* (also **homewards**) towards home. —*adj.* going towards home.

homework *n.* **1** work to be done at home, esp. by a school pupil. **2** preparatory work or study.

homey *adj.* (also **homy**) (-**mier, -miest**) suggesting home; cosy.

homicide /'hɒmɪsaɪd/ *n.* **1** killing of a human being by another. **2** person who kills a human being. □ **homicidal** /-ˈsaɪd(ə)l/ *adj.* [Latin *homo* man]

homily /'hɒmɪlɪ/ *n.* (*pl.* -**ies**) **1** sermon. **2** tedious moralizing discourse. □ **homiletic** /-ˈlɛtɪk/ *adj.* [Greek *homilia*]

homing *attrib. adj.* **1** (of a pigeon) trained to fly home. **2** (of a device) for guiding to a target etc.

hominid /'hɒmɪnɪd/ —*adj.* of the primate family including humans and their fossil ancestors. —*n.* member of this family. [Latin *homo homin-* man]

hominoid /ˈhomɪˌnɔɪd/ —*adj.* like a human. —*n.* animal resembling a human.

homo /ˈhəʊməʊ/ *n.* (*pl.* -s) *colloq. offens.* homosexual. [abbreviation]

homo- *comb. form* same. [Greek *homos* same]

homoeopathy /ˌhəʊmɪˈɒpəθɪ/ *n.* (*US* **homeopathy**) treatment of disease by minute doses of drugs that in a healthy person would produce symptoms of the disease. □ **homoeopath** /ˈhəʊmɪəpæθ/ *n.* **homoeopathic** /ˌhəʊmɪəˈpæθɪk/ *adj.* [Greek *homoios* like: related to PATHOS]

homogeneous /ˌhəʊməˈdʒiːnɪəs/ *adj.* 1 of the same kind. 2 consisting of parts all of the same kind; uniform. □ **homogeneity** /ˌhɒmədʒɪˈniːɪtɪ/ *n.* **homogeneously** *adv.* [from HOMO-, Greek *genos* kind]

■ **Usage** *Homogeneous* is often confused with *homogenous* which is a term in biology meaning 'similar owing to common descent'.

homogenize /həˈmɒdʒɪˌnaɪz/ *v.* (also **-ise**) (-zing or -sing) 1 make homogeneous. 2 treat (milk) so that the fat droplets are emulsified and the cream does not separate.

homograph /ˈhɒməˌɡrɑːf/ *n.* word spelt like another but of different meaning or origin (e.g. POLE¹, POLE²).

homologous /həˈmɒləgəs/ *adj.* 1 a having the same relation, relative position, etc. b corresponding. 2 *Biol.* (of organs etc.) similar in position and structure but not necessarily in function. [from HOMO-, Greek *logos* ratio]

homology /həˈmɒlədʒɪ/ *n.* homologous state or relation; correspondence.

homonym /ˈhɒmənɪm/ *n.* 1 word spelt or pronounced like another but of different meaning; homograph or homophone. 2 namesake. [from HOMO-, *onoma* name]

homophobia /ˌhəʊməˈfəʊbɪə/ *n.* hatred or fear of homosexuals. □ **homophobe** /ˈhəʊm-/ *n.* **homophobic** *adj.*

homophone /ˈhɒməˌfəʊn/ *n.* word pronounced like another but of different meaning or origin (e.g. *pair, pear*). [from HOMO-, Greek *phōnē* sound]

Homo sapiens /ˈhəʊməʊ ˈsæpɪenz/ *n.* modern humans regarded as a species. [Latin, = wise man]

homosexual /ˌhəʊməˈsekʃʊəl/ —*adj.* feeling or involving sexual attraction only to people of the same sex. —*n.* homosexual person. □ **homosexuality** /ˌhəʊməsekʃʊˈælɪtɪ/ *n.* [from HOMO- SEXUAL]

Hon. *abbr.* 1 Honorary. 2 Honourable.

hone —*n.* whetstone for razors. —*v.* (-ning) sharpen on or as on a hone. [Old English]

honest /ˈɒnɪst/ —*adj.* 1 fair and just; not cheating or stealing. 2 free of deceit and untruthfulness; sincere. 3 fairly earned (*an honest living*). 4 blameless but undistinguished. —*adv. colloq.* genuinely, really. [Latin *honestus*]

honestly *adv.* 1 in an honest way. 2 really (*I don't honestly know*).

honesty *n.* 1 being honest. 2 truthfulness. 3 plant with purple or white flowers and flat round semi-transparent seed-pods.

honey /ˈhʌnɪ/ *n.* (*pl.* -s) 1 sweet sticky yellowish fluid made by bees from nectar. 2 colour of this. 3 a sweetness. b sweet thing. 4 *esp. US* (usu. as a form of address) darling. [Old English]

honey-bee *n.* common hive-bee.

honeycomb —*n.* 1 bees' wax structure of hexagonal cells for honey and eggs. 2 pattern arranged hexagonally. —*v.* 1 fill with cavities or tunnels; undermine. 2 mark with a honeycomb pattern. [Old English]

honeydew *n.* 1 sweet sticky substance excreted by aphids on leaves and stems. 2 variety of melon.

honeyed *adj.* (of words, flattery, etc.) sweet, sweet-sounding.

honeymoon —*n.* 1 holiday taken by a newly married couple. 2 initial period of enthusiasm or goodwill. —*v.* spend a honeymoon. □ **honeymooner** *n.*

honeysuckle *n.* climbing shrub with fragrant yellow or pink flowers.

honk —*n.* 1 sound of a car horn. 2 cry of a wild goose. —*v.* (cause to) make a honk. [imitative]

honky-tonk /ˈhɒŋkɪˌtɒŋk/ *n. colloq.* 1 ragtime piano music. 2 cheap or disreputable nightclub etc. [origin unknown]

honor *US* var. of HONOUR.

honorable *US* var. of HONOURABLE.

honorarium /ˌɒnəˈreərɪəm/ *n.* (*pl.* -s or -ria) fee, esp. a voluntary payment for professional services rendered without the normal fee. [Latin: related to HONOUR]

honorary /ˈɒnərərɪ/ *adj.* 1 conferred as an honour (*honorary degree*). 2 (of an office or its holder) unpaid.

honorific /ˌɒnəˈrɪfɪk/ *adj.* 1 conferring honour. 2 implying respect.

honour /ˈɒnə(r)/ (*US* **honor**) —*n.* 1 high respect; public regard. 2 adherence to what is right or an accepted standard of conduct. 3 nobleness of mind; magnanimity (*honour among thieves*). 4 thing conferred as a distinction, esp. an official award for bravery or achievement. 5 privilege, special right (*had the*

honour of being invited. **6 a** exalted position. **b** (**Honour**) (prec. by *your, his, to*) title of a circuit judge etc. **7** (foll. by *to*) person or thing that brings honour (*an honour to her profession*). **8 a** chastity (of a woman). **b** reputation for this. **9** (in *pl.*) specialized degree course or special distinction in an examination. **10** (in card-games) the four or five highest-ranking cards. **11** *Golf* the right of driving off first. —*v.* **1** respect highly. **2** confer honour on. **3** accept or pay (a bill or cheque) when due. □ **do the honours** perform the duties of a host to guests etc. **in honour of** as a celebration of. **on one's honour** (usu. foll. by *to* + infin.) under a moral obligation. [Latin *honor* repute]

honourable *adj.* (*US* **honorable**) **1** deserving, bringing, or showing honour. **2** (**Honourable**) title indicating distinction, given to certain high officials, the children of certain ranks of the nobility, and (in the House of Commons) to MPs. □ **honourably** *adv.*

hooch *n. US colloq.* alcoholic liquor, esp. inferior or illicit whisky. [Alaskan]

hood[1] /hʊd/ —*n.* **1 a** covering for the head and neck, esp. as part of a garment. **b** separate hoodlike garment. **2** folding top of a car etc. **3** *US* bonnet of a car etc. **4** protective cover. —*v.* cover with or as with a hood. [Old English]

hood[2] /hʊd/ *n. US slang* gangster, gunman. [abbreviation of HOODLUM]

-hood *suffix* forming nouns: **1** of condition or state (*childhood; falsehood*). **2** designating a group (*sisterhood; neighbourhood*). [Old English]

hooded *adj.* **1** having a hood. **2** (of an animal) having a hoodlike part (*hooded crow*).

hoodlum /ˈhuːdləm/ *n.* **1** street hooligan, young thug. **2** gangster. [origin unknown]

hoodoo /ˈhuːduː/ *n.* esp. *US* **1 a** bad luck. **b** thing or person that brings this. **2** voodoo. [alteration of VOODOO]

hoodwink *v.* deceive, delude. [from HOOD: originally = 'blindfold']

hoof /huːf/ *n.* (*pl.* **-s** or **hooves** /-vz/) horny part of the foot of a horse etc. □ **hoof it** *slang* go on foot. [Old English]

hoo-ha /ˈhuːhɑː/ *n. slang* commotion. [origin unknown]

hook /hʊk/ —*n.* **1 a** bent piece of metal etc. for catching hold or for hanging things on. **b** (in full **fish-hook**) bent piece of wire for catching fish. **2** curved cutting instrument (*reaping-hook*). **3** bend in a river, curved strip of land, etc. **4 a** hooking stroke. **b** *Boxing* short swinging blow. —*v.* **1** grasp or secure with hook(s). **2** catch with or as

with a hook. **3** *slang* steal. **4** (in sports) send (the ball) in a curve or deviating path. **5** *Rugby* secure (the ball) and pass it backward with the foot in the scrum. □ **by hook or by crook** by one means or another. **off the hook 1** *colloq.* out of difficulty or trouble. **2** (of a telephone receiver) not on its rest. [Old English]

hookah /ˈhʊkə/ *n.* oriental tobacco-pipe with a long tube passing through water for cooling the smoke as it is drawn through. [Urdu from Arabic, = casket]

hooked *adj.* **1** hook-shaped. **2** (often foll. by *on*) *slang* addicted or captivated.

hooker *n.* **1** *Rugby* player in the front row of the scrum who tries to hook the ball. **2** *slang* prostitute.

hookey /ˈhʊki/ *n. US* □ **play hookey** *slang* play truant. [origin unknown]

hook, line, and sinker *adv.* entirely.

hook-up *n.* connection, esp. of broadcasting equipment.

hookworm *n.* worm with hooklike mouthparts, infesting humans and animals.

hooligan /ˈhuːlɪgən/ *n.* young ruffian. □ **hooliganism** *n.* [origin unknown]

hoop *n.* **1** circular band of metal, wood, etc., esp. as part of a framework. **2** ring bowled along by a child, or for circus performers to jump through. **3** arch through which balls are hit in croquet. —*v.* bind or encircle with hoop(s). □ **be put** (or **go**) **through the hoop** (or **hoops**) undergo rigorous testing. [Old English]

hoop-la *n.* fairground game with rings thrown to encircle a prize.

hoopoe /ˈhuːpuː/ *n.* salmon-pink bird with black and white wings and a large erectile crest. [Latin *upupa* (imitative of its cry)]

hooray /hʊˈreɪ/ *int.* = HURRAH.

Hooray Henry /hʊˈreɪ/ *n. slang* loud upper-class young man.

hoot —*n.* **1** owl's cry. **2** sound made by a car's horn etc. **3** shout expressing scorn or disapproval. **4** *colloq.* **a** laughter. **b** cause of this. **5** (also **two hoots**) *slang* anything at all, in the slightest degree (*don't care a hoot; doesn't matter two hoots*). —*v.* **1** utter or make hoot(s). **2** greet or drive away with scornful hoots. **3** sound (a car horn etc.). [imitative]

hooter *n.* **1** thing that hoots, esp. a car's horn or a siren. **2** *slang* nose.

Hoover —*n. propr.* vacuum cleaner. —*v.* (**hoover**) **1** (also *absol.*) clean with a vacuum cleaner. **2** (foll. by *up*) **a** suck up with a vacuum cleaner. **b** clean a room etc. with a vacuum cleaner. [name of the manufacturer]

hooves pl. of HOOF.

hop[1] —v. (**-pp-**) **1** (of a bird, frog, etc.) spring with two or all feet at once. **2** (of a person) jump on one foot. **3** move or go quickly (*hopped over the fence*). **4** cross (a ditch etc.) by hopping. —n. **1** hopping movement. **2** colloq. informal dance. **3** short journey, esp. a flight. □ **hop in** (or **out**) colloq. get into (or out o) a car etc. **hop it** slang go away. **on the hop** colloq. unprepared (*caught on the hop*). [Old English]

hop[2] n. **1** climbing plant bearing cones. **2** (in pl.) its ripe cones, used to flavour beer. [Low German or Dutch]

hope —n. **1** expectation and desire for a thing. **2** person or thing giving cause for hope. **3** what is hoped for. —v. (**-ping**) **1** feel hope. **2** expect and desire. **3** feel fairly confident. □ **hope against hope** cling to a mere possibility. [Old English]

hopeful —adj. **1** feeling hope. **2** causing or inspiring hope. **3** likely to succeed. —n. person likely to succeed. [Old English]

hopefully adv. **1** in a hopeful manner. **2** it is to be hoped (*hopefully, we will succeed*).

■ **Usage** The use of *hopefully* in sense 2 is common, but is considered incorrect by some people.

hopeless adj. **1** feeling no hope. **2** admitting no hope (*hopeless case*). **3** incompetent. □ **hopelessly** adv. **hopelessness** n.

hopper[1] n. **1** container tapering downward to an opening for discharging its contents. **2** hopping insect.

hopper[2] n. hop-picker.

hopping mad predic. adj. colloq. very angry.

hopscotch n. children's game of hopping over squares marked on the ground to retrieve a stone etc. [from HOP[1], SCOTCH]

horde n. usu. derog. large group, gang. [Turkish *ordā* camp]

horehound /ˈhɔːhaʊnd/ n. herbaceous plant yielding a bitter aromatic juice used against coughs etc. [Old English, = hoary herb]

horizon /həˈraɪz(ə)n/ n. **1** line at which the earth and sky appear to meet. **2** limit of mental perception, experience, interest, etc. □ **on the horizon** (of an event) just imminent or becoming apparent. [Greek *horizō* bound]

horizontal /hɒrɪˈzɒnt(ə)l/ —adj. **1** parallel to the plane of the horizon, at right angles to the vertical. **2** of or concerned with the same work, status, etc. (*it was a horizontal move rather than promotion*). —n. horizontal line, plane, etc.

□ **horizontally** adv. **horizont-ally** adv.

hormone /ˈhɔːməʊn/ n. **1** regulatory substance produced in an organism and transported in tissue fluids to stimulate cells or tissues into action. **2** similar synthetic substance. □ **hormonal** /-ˈməʊn(ə)l/ adj. [Greek *hormaō* impel]

hormone replacement therapy n. treatment to relieve menopausal symptoms by boosting a woman's oestrogen levels.

horn n. **1 a** hard outgrowth, often curved and pointed, on the head of esp. hoofed animals. **b** each of two branched appendages on the head of (esp. male) deer. **c** hornlike projection on animals, e.g. a snail's tentacle. **2** substance of which horns are made. **3** *Mus.* **a** = FRENCH HORN. **b** wind instrument played by lip vibration, orig. made of horn, now usu. of brass. **4** instrument sounding a warning. **5** receptacle or instrument made of horn. **6** horn-shaped projection. **7** extremity of the moon or other crescent. **8** arm of a river etc. □ **horn in** slang intrude, interfere. □ **horned** adj. **hornist** n. (in sense 3 of n.). [Old English]

hornbeam n. tree with a hard tough wood.

hornbill n. bird with a hornlike excrescence on its large curved bill.

hornblende /ˈhɔːnblɛnd/ n. dark-brown, black, or green mineral occurring in many rocks. [German]

hornet /ˈhɔːnɪt/ n. large wasp capable of inflicting a serious sting. [Low German or Dutch]

horn of plenty n. a cornucopia.

hornpipe n. **1** lively dance (esp. associated with sailors). **2** music for this.

horn-rimmed adj. (esp. of spectacles) having rims made of horn or a similar substance.

horny adj. (**-ier**, **-iest**) **1** of or like horn. **2** hard like horn. **3** slang sexually excited. □ **horniness** n.

horology /həˈrɒlədʒɪ/ n. art of measuring time or making clocks, watches, etc. □ **horological** /hɒrəˈlɒdʒɪk(ə)l/ adj. [Greek *hōra* time]

horoscope /ˈhɒrəskəʊp/ n. **1** forecast of a person's future from a diagram showing the relative positions of the stars and planets at his or her birth. **2** such a diagram. [Greek *hōra* time, *skopos* observer]

horrendous /həˈrɛndəs/ adj. horrify-ing. □ **horrendously** adv. [Latin: related to HORRIBLE]

horrible /'hɒrɪb(ə)l/ adj. 1 causing or likely to cause horror. 2 colloq. unpleasant. □ **horribly** adv. [Latin horreo bristle, shudder at]

horrid /'hɒrɪd/ adj. 1 horrible, revolting. 2 colloq. unpleasant (horrid weather).

horrific /həˈrɪfɪk/ adj. horrifying. □ **horrifically** adv.

horrify /'hɒrɪfaɪ/ v. (-ies, -ied) arouse horror in; shock. □ **horrifying** adj.

horror /'hɒrə(r)/ —n. 1 painful feeling of loathing and fear. 2 a (often foll. by at) intense dislike. b (often foll. by of) intense dismay. 3 a person or thing causing horror. b colloq. bad or mischievous person etc. 4 (in pl.; prec. by the) fit of depression, nervousness, etc. —attrib. adj. (of films etc.) designed to interest by arousing feelings of horror.

hors d'œuvre /ɔːˈdɜːvr/ n. food served as an appetizer at the start of a meal. [French, = outside the work]

horse —n. 1 a large four-legged mammal with flowing mane and tail, used for riding and to carry and pull loads. b adult male horse, stallion or gelding. c (collect.; as sing.) cavalry. 2 vaulting-block. 3 supporting frame (clothes-horse). —v. (-sing) (foll. by around) fool about. □ **from the horse's mouth** colloq. (of information etc.) from the original or an authoritative source. [Old English]

horseback n. □ **on horseback** mounted on a horse.

horsebox n. closed vehicle for transporting horse(s).

horse-brass n. brass ornament orig. for a horse's harness.

horse chestnut n. 1 large tree with upright conical clusters of flowers. 2 dark brown fruit of this.

horse-drawn adj. (of a vehicle) pulled by a horse or horses.

horseflesh n. 1 flesh of a horse, esp. as food. 2 horses collectively.

horsefly n. any of various biting insects troublesome esp. to horses.

Horse Guards n.pl. cavalry brigade of the household troops.

horsehair n. hair from the mane or tail of a horse, used for padding etc.

horseman n. 1 rider on horseback. 2 skilled rider. □ **horsemanship** n.

horseplay n. boisterous play.

horsepower n. (pl. same) imperial unit of power (about 750 watts), esp. for measuring the power of an engine.

horse-race n. race between horses with riders. □ **horse-racing** n.

horseradish n. plant with a pungent root used to make a sauce.

horse sense n. colloq. plain common sense.

horseshoe n. 1 U-shaped iron shoe for a horse. 2 thing of this shape.

horsetail n. 1 horse's tail. 2 plant resembling it.

horsewhip —n. whip for driving horses. —v. (-pp-) beat with a horsewhip.

horsewoman n. 1 woman who rides on horseback. 2 skilled woman rider.

horsy adj. (-ier, -iest) 1 of or like a horse. 2 concerned with or devoted to horses.

horticulture /'hɔːtɪˌkʌltʃə(r)/ n. art of garden cultivation. □ **horticultural** /-ˈkʌltʃər(ə)l/ adj. **horticulturist** /-ˈkʌltʃərɪst/ n. [Latin hortus garden, CULTURE]

hosanna /həʊˈzænə/ n. & int. shout of adoration (Matt. 21:9, etc.). [Hebrew]

hose /həʊz/ —n. 1 (also **hose-pipe**) flexible tube for conveying water. 2 a (collect.; as pl.) stockings and socks. b hist. breeches (doublet and hose). —v. (-sing) (often foll. by down) water, spray, or drench with a hose. [Old English]

hosier /'həʊzɪə(r)/ n. dealer in hosiery.

hosiery n. stockings and socks.

hospice /'hɒspɪs/ n. 1 home for people who are ill (esp. terminally) or destitute. 2 lodging for travellers, esp. one kept by a religious order. [Latin: related to HOST²]

hospitable /hɒˈspɪtəb(ə)l/ adj. giving hospitality. □ **hospitably** adv. [Latin hospito entertain: related to HOST²]

hospital /'hɒspɪt(ə)l/ n. 1 institution providing medical and surgical treatment and nursing care for ill and injured people. 2 hist. hospice. [Latin: related to HOST²]

hospitality /hɒspɪˈtælɪtɪ/ n. friendly and generous reception and entertainment of guests or strangers.

hospitalize /'hɒspɪtəlaɪz/ v. (also -ise) (-zing or -sing) send or admit (a patient) to hospital. □ **hospitalization** /-ˈzeɪʃ(ə)n/ n.

host¹ /həʊst/ n. (usu. foll. by of) large number of people or things. [Latin hostis enemy, army]

host² /həʊst/ —n. 1 person who receives or entertains another as a guest. 2 compère. 3 Biol. animal or plant having a parasite. 4 recipient of a transplanted organ etc. 5 landlord of an inn. —v. be host to (a person) or of (an event). [Latin hospes hospitis host, guest]

host³ /həʊst/ n. (usu. prec. by the; often Host) bread consecrated in the Eucharist. [Latin hostia victim]

hostage /'hɒstɪdʒ/ n. person seized or held as security for the fulfilment of a condition. [Latin obses obsidis hostage]

hostel /hŏst(ə)l/ n. 1 house of residence or lodging for students, nurses, etc. 2 = YOUTH HOSTEL. [Medieval Latin: related to HOSPITAL]

hostelry n. (pl. -ies) archaic inn.

hostess /hóustis/ n. 1 woman who receives or entertains a guest. 2 woman employed to entertain customers at a nightclub etc. 3 stewardess on an aircraft etc. [related to HOST²]

hostile /hóstail/ adj. 1 of an enemy. 2 (often foll. by to) unfriendly, opposed. □ **hostilely** adv. [Latin: related to HOST¹]

hostility /hostíliti/ n. (pl. -ies) 1 being hostile, enmity. 2 state of warfare. 3 (in pl.) acts of warfare.

hot —adj. (hotter, hottest) 1 having a high temperature. 2 causing a sensation of heat (hot flush). 3 (of pepper, spices, etc.) pungent 4 (of a person) feeling heat. 5 a ardent, passionate, excited. b (often foll. by for, on) eager, keen (in hot pursuit). c angry or upset 6 (of news etc.) fresh, recent. 7 Hunting (of the scent) fresh, recent. 8 a (of a player, competitor, or feat) very skilful, formidable. b (foll. by on) knowledgeable about. 9 (esp. of jazz) strongly rhythmical. 10 slang (of stolen goods) difficult to dispose of because identifiable. 11 slang radioactive. —v. (-tt-) (usu. foll. by up) colloq. 1 make or become more active, exciting, or dangerous. □ **have the hots for** slang be sexually attracted to. **hot under the collar** angry, resentful, or embarrassed. **like hot cakes** see CAKE. **make it** (or **things**) **hot for a person** persecute a person. □ **hotly** adv. **hotness** n. **hottish** adj. [Old English]

hot air n. slang empty or boastful talk.

hot-air balloon n. balloon containing air heated by burners below it, causing it to rise.

hotbed n. 1 (foll. by of) environment conducive to (vice, intrigue, etc.). 2 bed of earth heated by fermenting manure.

hot-blooded adj. ardent, passionate.

hotchpotch /hóchpoch/ n. (also **hodgepodge** /hódʒpodʒ/) confused mixture or jumble, esp. of ideas. [French hochepot shake pot]

hot cross bun n. bun marked with a cross and traditionally eaten on Good Friday.

hot dog n. colloq. hot sausage in a soft roll.

hotel /həutél/ n. (usu. licensed) establishment providing accommodation and meals for payment. [French: related to HOSTEL]

hotelier /həutéliə(r)/ n. hotel-keeper.

hot flush see FLUSH¹.

hotfoot —adv. in eager haste. —v. hurry eagerly (esp. hotfoot it).

hot gospeller n. colloq. eager preacher of the gospel.

hothead n. impetuous person. □ **hotheaded** adj. **hotheadedness** n.

hothouse n. 1 heated (mainly glass) building for rearing tender plants. 2 environment conducive to the rapid growth or development of something.

hot line n. direct exclusive telephone etc. line, esp. for emergencies.

hot money n. capital frequently transferred.

hotplate n. heated metal plate etc. (or a set of these) for cooking food or keeping it hot.

hotpot n. casserole of meat and vegetables topped with potato.

hot potato n. colloq. contentious matter.

hot rod n. vehicle modified to have extra power and speed.

hot seat n. slang 1 position of difficult responsibility. 2 electric chair.

hot spot n. 1 small region that is relatively hot. 2 lively or dangerous place.

hot stuff n. colloq. 1 formidably capable or important person or thing. 2 sexually attractive person or thing. 3 erotic book, film, etc.

hot-tempered adj. impulsively angry.

Hottentot /hót(ə)ntot/ n. 1 member of a SW African Negroid people. 2 their language. [Afrikaans]

hot water n. colloq. difficulty or trouble.

hot-water bottle n. (usu. rubber) container filled with hot water to warm a bed.

houmous var. of HUMMUS.

hound —n. 1 dog used in hunting. 2 colloq. despicable man. —v. harass or pursue. [Old English]

hour /auə(r)/ n. 1 twenty-fourth part of a day and night, 60 minutes. 2 time of day, point in time (a late hour; what is the hour?). 3 (in pl. with preceding numerals in form 18.00, 20.30, etc.) this number of hours and minutes past midnight on the 24-hour clock (will assemble at 20.00 hours). 4 a period for a specific purpose (lunch hour; keep regular hours). b (in pl.) fixed working or open period (office hours; opening hours). 5 short period of time (an idle hour). 6 present time (question of the hour). 7 time for action etc. (the hour has come). 8 expressing distance by travelling time (we are an hour from London). 9 RC Ch. prayers to be said at one of seven fixed times of day (book of

hours', **10** (prec. by *the*) each time o'clock of a whole number of hours (*buses leave on the hour*; *on the half hour*; *at a quarter past the hour*). □ **after hours** after closing-time. [Greek *hōra*]

hourglass *n.* two vertically connected glass bulbs containing sand taking an hour to pass from upper to lower bulb.

houri /'hʊərɪ/ *n.* (*pl.* **-s**) beautiful young woman of the Muslim Paradise. [Persian from Arabic, = dark-eyed]

hourly —*adj.* **1** done or occurring every hour. **2** frequent. **3** reckoned hour by hour (*hourly wage*). —*adv.* **1** every hour. **2** frequently.

house —*n.* /haʊs/ (*pl.* /'haʊzɪz/) **1** building for human habitation. **2** building for a special purpose or for animals or goods (*opera-house*; *summer-house*; *hen-house*). **3 a** religious community. **b** its buildings. **4 a** body of pupils living in the same building at a boarding-school. **b** such a building. **c** division of a day-school for games, competitions, etc. **5** royal family or dynasty (*House of York*). **6 a** firm or institution. **b** its premises. **7 a** legislative or deliberative assembly. **b** building for this. **8** audience or performance in a theatre etc. **9** *Astrol.* twelfth part of the heavens. —*v.* /haʊz/ (*-sing*) **1** provide with a house or other accommodation. **2** store (goods etc.). **3** enclose or encase (a part or fitting). **4** fix in a socket, mortise, etc. □ **keep house** provide for or manage a household. **like a house on fire** **1** vigorously, fast. **2** successfully, excellently. **on the house** free. **put** (or **set**) **one's house in order** make necessary reforms. [Old English]

house-agent *n.* agent for the sale and letting of houses.

house arrest *n.* detention in one's own house, not in prison.

houseboat *n.* boat equipped for living in.

housebound *adj.* confined to one's house through illness etc.

housebreaking /'haʊsˌbreɪkɪŋ/ *n.* act of breaking into a building, esp. in daytime, to commit a crime. □ **housebreaker** *n.*

■ **Usage** In 1968 housebreaking was replaced as a statutory crime in English law by *burglary*.

housecoat *n.* woman's informal indoor coat or gown.

housefly *n.* common fly often entering houses.

household *n.* **1** occupants of a house as a unit. **2** house and its affairs.

householder *n.* **1** person who owns or rents a house. **2** head of a household.

household troops *n.pl.* troops nominally guarding the sovereign.

household word *n.* (also **household name**) **1** familiar name or saying. **2** familiar person or thing.

house-hunting *n.* seeking a house to buy or rent.

house-husband *n.* man who does a wife's traditional household duties.

housekeeper *n.* person, esp. a woman, employed to manage a household.

housekeeping *n.* **1** management of household affairs. **2** money allowed for this. **3** operations of maintenance, record-keeping, etc., in an organization.

house lights *n.pl.* lights in a theatre auditorium.

housemaid *n.* female servant in a house.

housemaid's knee *n.* inflammation of the kneecap.

houseman *n.* resident junior doctor at a hospital etc.

house-martin *n.* black and white bird nesting on house walls etc.

housemaster *n.* (*fem.* **housemistress**) teacher in charge of a house, esp. at a boarding-school.

house music *n.* style of pop music, typically using drum machines and synthesized bass lines with sparse repetitive vocals and a fast beat.

house of cards *n.* insecure scheme etc.

House of Commons *n.* elected chamber of Parliament.

House of Keys *n.* (in the Isle of Man) elected chamber of the Tynwald.

House of Lords *n.* chamber of Parliament that is mainly hereditary.

house party *n.* group of guests staying at a country house etc.

house-plant *n.* plant grown indoors.

house-proud *adj.* attentive to the care and appearance of the home.

houseroom *n.* space or accommodation in one's house. □ **not give houseroom to** not have in any circumstances.

housetop *n.* roof of a house. □ **shout** etc. **from the housetops** announce publicly.

house-trained *adj.* **1** (of animals) trained to be clean in the house. **2** *colloq.* well-mannered.

house-warming *n.* party celebrating a move to a new home.

housewife *n.* **1** woman who manages a household and usu. does not have a full-time paid job. **2** /'hʌzɪf/ case for needles, thread, etc. □ **housewifely** *adj.* [from HOUSE, WIFE = woman]

housework *n.* regular housekeeping work, e.g. cleaning and cooking.

housey-housey /ˈhaʊzɪˈhaʊzɪ/ n. (also **house-house**) *slang* gambling form of lotto.

housing /ˈhaʊzɪŋ/ n. **1 a** provision of houses, collectively. **b** houses collectively. **2** shelter, lodging. **3** rigid casing for machinery etc. **4** hole or niche cut in one piece of wood for another to fit into.

housing estate n. residential area planned as a unit.

hove *past of* HEAVE.

hovel /ˈhɒv(ə)l/ n. small miserable dwelling. [origin unknown]

hover /ˈhɒvə(r)/ v.i. **1** (of a bird etc.) remain in one place in the air. **2** (often foll. by *about*, *round*) wait close at hand, linger. **—n. 1** hovering. **2** state of suspense. [obsolete *hove* hover]

hovercraft n. (pl. same) vehicle travelling on a cushion of air provided by a downward blast.

hoverport n. terminal for hovercraft.

how *—interrog. adv.* **1** by what means, in what way (*how do you do it?; tell me the how you do it; how could *you?*). **2** in what condition, esp. of health (*how are you?; how do things stand?*). **3 a** to what extent (*how far is it?; how would you like to take my place?; how we laughed!*). **b** to what extent good or well, what ... like (*how was the film?; how did they play?*). *—rel. adv.* in whatever way, as (*do it how you can*). *—conj. colloq.* that (*told us how he'd been in India*). □ **how about** *colloq.* would you like (*how about a quick swim?*). **how do you do?** a formal greeting. **how many** what number. **how much** **1** what amount. **2** what price. **how's that?** **1** what is your opinion or explanation of that? **2** *Cricket* (said to an umpire) is the batsman out or not? [Old English]

howbeit /haʊˈbiːt/ adv. archaic nevertheless.

howdah /ˈhaʊdə/ n. (usu. canopied) seat for riding on an elephant or camel. [Urdu *hauda*]

however /haʊˈevə(r)/ adv. **1 a** in whatever way (*do it however you want*). **b** to whatever extent (*must go however inconvenient*). **2** nevertheless.

howitzer /ˈhaʊɪtsə(r)/ n. short gun for the high-angle firing of shells. [Czech *houfnice* catapult]

howl /haʊl/ n. **1** long loud doleful cry of a dog etc. **2** prolonged wailing noise. **3** loud cry of pain, rage, derision, or laughter. **—v. 1** make a howl. **2** weep loudly. **3** utter with a howl. □ **howl down** prevent (a speaker) from being heard by howls of derision. [imitative]

howler n. *colloq.* glaring mistake.

howsoever /haʊsəʊˈevə(r)/ adv. *formal* **1** in whatsoever way. **2** to whatsoever extent.

hoy int. used to call attention. [natural cry]

hoyden /ˈhɔɪd(ə)n/ n. boisterous girl. [Dutch *heiden*: related to HEATHEN]

h.p. abbr. (also **hp**) **1** horsepower. **2** hire purchase.

HQ abbr. headquarters.

hr. abbr. hour.

HRH abbr. Her or His Royal Highness.

hrs. abbr. hours.

HRT abbr. hormone replacement therapy.

HT abbr. high tension.

hub n. **1** central part of a wheel, rotating on or with the axle. **2** centre of interest, activity, etc. [origin uncertain]

hubble-bubble /ˈhʌb(ə)lˌbʌb(ə)l/ n. **1** simple hookah. **2** bubbling sound. **3** confused talk. [imitative]

hubbub /ˈhʌbʌb/ n. **1** confused noise of talking. **2** disturbance. [perhaps of Irish origin]

hubby /ˈhʌbɪ/ n. (pl. -ies) colloq. husband. [abbreviation]

hubris /ˈhjuːbrɪs/ n. arrogant pride or presumption. □ **hubristic** /-ˈbrɪstɪk/ adj. [Greek]

huckleberry /ˈhʌk(ə)lbərɪ/ n. **1** low-growing N. American shrub. **2** blue or black fruit of this. [probably an alteration of *hurtleberry*: see WHORTLEBERRY]

huckster —n. aggressive salesman; hawker. —v. **1** haggle. **2** hawk (goods). [Low German]

huddle /ˈhʌd(ə)l/ —v. **1** (often foll. by *up*) crowd together, nestle closely. **2** (often foll. by *up*) curl one's body into a small space. **3** heap together in a muddle. —n. **1** confused or crowded mass. **2** *colloq.* close or secret conference (esp. in **go into a huddle**). [perhaps from Low German]

hue n. **1** colour, tint **2** variety or shade of colour. [Old English]

hue and cry n. loud outcry. [French *huer* shout]

huff —n. *colloq.* fit of petty annoyance. —v. **1** blow air, steam, etc. **2** (esp. *huff* and *puff*) bluster self-importantly but ineffectually. **3** *Draughts* remove (an opponent's piece) as a forfeit. □ **in a huff** *colloq.* annoyed and offended. [imitative of blowing]

huffy adj. (**-ier, -iest**) *colloq.* **1** apt to take offence. **2** offended. □ **huffily** adv. **huffiness** n.

hug —v. (**-gg-**) **1** squeeze tightly in one's arms, esp. with affection. **2** (of a bear) squeeze (a person) between its forelegs. **3** keep close to, fit tightly around. —n. **1** strong clasp with the arms. **2** squeezing

grip in wrestling. [probably Scandinavian]

huge adj. **1** extremely large; enormous. **2** (of an abstract thing) very great. □ **hugeness** n. [French ahuge]

hugely adv. **1** extremely (hugely successful). **2** very much (enjoyed it hugely).

hugger-mugger /ˈhʌgəˌmʌgə(r)/ —adj. & adv. **1** in secret. **2** confused; in confusion. —n. **1** secrecy. **2** confusion. [origin uncertain]

Huguenot /ˈhjuːgəˌnəʊ/ n. hist. French Protestant. [French]

huh /hʌ/ int. expressing disgust, surprise, etc. [imitative]

hula /ˈhuːlə/ n. (also **hula-hula**) Polynesian dance performed by women, with flowing arm movements. [Hawaiian]

hula hoop n. large hoop spun round the body.

hulk n. **1** body of a dismantled ship. **2** colloq. large clumsy-looking person or thing. [Old English]

hulking adj. colloq. bulky; clumsy.

hull[1] n. body of a ship, airship, etc. [perhaps related to HOLD[2]]

hull[2] —n. outer covering of a fruit, esp. the pod of peas and beans, the husk of grain, or the green calyx of a strawberry. —v. remove the hulls from (fruit etc.). [Old English]

hullabaloo /ˌhʌləbəˈluː/ n. uproar. [reduplication of hallo, hullo, etc.]

hullo var. of HELLO.

hum —v. (-mm-) **1** make a low steady continuous sound like a bee. **2** sing with closed lips. **3** utter a slight inarticulate sound. **4** colloq. be active (really made things hum). **5** colloq. smell unpleasantly. —n. **1** humming sound. **2** colloq. bad smell. [imitative]

human /ˈhjuːmən/ —adj. **1** of or belonging to the species Homo sapiens. **2** consisting of human beings (the human race). **3** of or characteristic of humankind, esp. as being weak, fallible, etc. (is only human). **4** showing warmth, sympathy, etc. (is very human). —n. human being. [Latin humanus]

human being n. man, woman, or child.

human chain n. line of people formed for passing things along, as a protest, etc.

humane /hjuːˈmeɪn/ adj. **1** benevolent, compassionate. **2** inflicting the minimum of pain. **3** (of learning) tending to civilize. □ **humanely** adv. **humaneness** n.

humane killer n. instrument for the painless slaughter of animals.

humanism /ˈhjuːmənɪz(ə)m/ n. **1** non-religious philosophy based on liberal human values. **2** (often **Humanism**) literary culture, esp. that of the Renaissance. □ **humanist** n. **humanistic** /-ˈnɪstɪk/ adj.

humanitarian /hjuːˌmænɪˈteəriən/ —n. person who seeks to promote human welfare. —adj. of humanitarians. □ **humanitarianism** n.

humanity /hjuːˈmænɪtɪ/ n. (pl. **-ies**) **1 a** the human race. **b** human beings collectively. **c** being human. **2** humaneness, benevolence. **3** (in pl.) subjects concerned with human culture, e.g. language, literature, and history.

humanize v. (also **-ise**) (-zing or -sing) make human or humane. □ **humanization** /-ˈzeɪʃ(ə)n/ n. [French: related to HUMAN]

humankind n. human beings collectively.

humanly adv. **1** by human means (if it is humanly possible). **2** in a human manner.

human nature n. general characteristics and feelings of mankind.

human rights n.pl. rights held to be common to all.

human shield n. person(s) placed in the line of fire in order to discourage attack.

humble /ˈhʌmb(ə)l/ —adj. **1** having or showing low self-esteem. **2** of low social or political rank. **3** modest in size, pretensions, etc. —v. (-ling) **1** make humble; abase. **2** lower the rank or status of. □ **eat humble pie** apologize humbly; accept humiliation. □ **humbleness** n. **humbly** adv. [Latin humilis: related to HUMUS]

humbug /ˈhʌmbʌg/ —n. **1** lying or deception; hypocrisy. **2** impostor. **3** hard boiled striped peppermint sweet. —v. (**-gg-**) **1** be or behave like an impostor. **2** deceive, hoax. [origin unknown]

humdinger /ˈhʌmdɪŋə(r)/ n. slang excellent or remarkable person or thing. [origin unknown]

humdrum /ˈhʌmdrʌm/ adj. commonplace, dull, monotonous. [a reduplication of HUM]

humerus /ˈhjuːmərəs/ n. (pl. **-ri** /-raɪ/) bone of the upper arm. □ **humeral** adj. [Latin, = shoulder]

humid /ˈhjuːmɪd/ adj. (of the air or climate) warm and damp. [Latin humidus]

humidifier /hjuːˈmɪdɪˌfaɪə(r)/ n. device for keeping the atmosphere moist in a room etc.

humidify /hjuːˈmɪdɪˌfaɪ/ v. (**-ies**, **-ied**) make (air etc.) humid.

dampness. 2 degree of moisture, esp. in the atmosphere.

humiliate /hju:'mɪlɪeɪt/ v. (-ting) injure the dignity or self-respect of. □ **humiliating** adj. **humiliation** /-'eɪʃ(ə)n/ n. [Latin: related to HUMBLE]

humility /hju:'mɪlɪtɪ/ n. 1 humbleness, meekness. 2 humble condition. [French: related to HUMILIATE]

hummingbird n. small tropical bird that makes a humming sound with its wings when it hovers.

hummock /'hʌmək/ n. hillock or hump. [origin unknown]

hummus /'hʊmʊs/ n. (also **houmous**) dip or appetizer made from ground chick-peas, sesame oil, lemon, and garlic. [Turkish]

humoresque /ˌhju:məˈresk/ n. short lively piece of music. [German *Humoreske*]

humorist n. humorous writer, talker, or actor.

humorous /'hju:mərəs/ adj. showing humour or a sense of humour. □ **humorously** adv.

humour /'hju:mə(r)/ (*US* **humor**) —n. 1 a quality of being amusing or comic. b the expression of humour in literature, speech, etc. 2 (in full **sense of humour**) ability to perceive or express humour. 3 state of mind; inclination (*bad humour*). 4 (in full **cardinal humour**) *hist.* each of the four fluids (blood, phlegm, choler, melancholy), thought to determine a person's physical and mental qualities. —v. gratify or indulge (a person or taste etc.). □ **out of humour** displeased. □ **humourless** adj. [Latin *humor* moisture]

hump —n. 1 rounded protuberance on a camel's back, or as an abnormality on a person's back. 2 rounded raised mass of earth etc. 3 critical point in an undertaking. 4 (prec. by *the*) *slang* fit of depression or vexation (*gave me the hump*). —v. 1 (often foll. by *about*) *colloq.* lift or carry (heavy objects etc.) with difficulty. 2 make hump-shaped. [probably Low German or Dutch]

humpback n. 1 a deformed back with a hump. b person with this. 2 whale with a dorsal fin forming a hump. □ **humpbacked** adj.

humpback bridge n. small bridge with a steep ascent and descent.

humph /hʌmf/ int. & n. inarticulate sound of doubt or dissatisfaction. [imitative]

humus /'hju:məs/ n. organic constituent of soil formed by the decomposition of vegetation. [Latin, = soil]

Hun n. 1 *offens.* German (esp. in contexts). 2 member of a warlike nomadic people who ravaged Europe in the 4th–5th c. 2 vandal. □ **Hunnish** adj. [Old English]

hunch —v. bend or arch into a hump. —n. 1 intuitive feeling or idea. 2 hump. [origin unknown]

hunchback n. = HUMPBACK 1. □ **hunchbacked** adj.

hundred /'hʌndrəd/ adj. & n. (pl. **hundreds** or (in sense 1) **hundred**) (in sing., prec. by *a* or *one*) 1 ten times ten. 2 symbol for this (100, c, C). 3 (in sing. or pl.) *colloq.* a large number. 4 (in pl.) the years of a specific century (*the seventeen hundreds*). 5 *hist.* subdivision of a county or shire, having its own court. □ **hundredfold** adj. & adv. **hundredth** adj. & n. [Old English]

hundreds and thousands n.pl. tiny coloured sweets for decorating cakes etc.

hundredweight n. (pl. same or -s) 1 unit of weight equal to 112 lb. or US 100 lb. 2 unit of weight equal to 50 kg.

hung past and past part. of HANG.

Hungarian /hʌŋˈgeərɪən/ —n. 1 a native or national of Hungary. b person of Hungarian descent. 2 language of Hungary. —adj. of Hungary or its people or language. [medieval Latin]

hunger /'hʌŋgə(r)/ —n. 1 a lack of food. b feeling of discomfort or exhaustion caused by this. 2 (often foll. by *for, after*) strong desire. —v. 1 (often foll. by *for, after*) crave or desire. 2 feel hunger. [Old English]

hunger strike n. refusal of food as a protest.

hung-over adj. *colloq.* suffering from a hangover.

hung parliament n. parliament in which no party has a clear majority.

hungry /'hʌŋgrɪ/ adj. (-ier, -iest) 1 feeling or showing hunger; needing food. 2 inducing hunger (*hungry work*). 3 craving (*hungry for news*). □ **hungrily** adv. [Old English]

hunk n. 1 large piece cut off (*hunk of bread*). 2 *colloq.* sexually attractive man. □ **hunky** adj. (-ier, -iest) [probably Dutch]

hunky-dory /ˌhʌŋkɪ'dɔ:rɪ/ adj. esp. *US colloq.* excellent. [origin unknown]

hunt —v. 1 also *absol.*) a pursue and kill (wild animals, esp. foxes, or game) for sport or food. b use (a horse or hounds) for hunting. c (of an animal) chase (its prey). 2 (foll. by *after, for*) seek, search. 3 (of an engine etc.) run alternately too fast and too slow. 4 scour (a district) for game. 5 (as **hunted** adj.) (of a look etc.)

terrified as if being hunted. —*n.* 1 practice or instance of hunting. 2 a association of people hunting with hounds. b area for hunting. □ **hunt down** pursue and capture. □ **hunting** *n.* [Old English]

hunter *n.* 1 a (*fem.* **huntress**) person or animal that hunts. b horse used in hunting. 2 person who seeks something. 3 pocket-watch with a hinged cover protecting the glass.

hunter's moon *n.* next full moon after the harvest moon.

huntsman *n.* 1 hunter. 2 hunt official in charge of hounds.

hurdle /ˈhɜːd(ə)l/ —*n.* 1 a each of a series of light frames to be cleared by athletes in a race. b (in *pl.*) hurdle-race. 2 obstacle or difficulty. 3 portable rectangular frame used as a temporary fence etc. —*v.* (**-ling**) 1 run in a hurdle-race. 2 fence off etc. with hurdles. [Old English]

hurdler /ˈhɜːdlə(r)/ *n.* 1 athlete who runs in hurdle-races. 2 maker of hurdles.

hurdy-gurdy /ˈhɜːdɪˈɡɜːdɪ/ *n.* (*pl.* **-ies**) 1 droning musical instrument played by turning a handle. 2 *colloq.* barrel-organ. [imitative]

hurl —*v.* 1 throw with great force. 2 utter (abuse etc.) vehemently. —*n.* forceful throw. [imitative]

hurley /ˈhɜːlɪ/ *n.* 1 (also **hurling**) Irish game resembling hockey. 2 stick used in this.

hurly-burly /ˈhɜːlɪˈbɜːlɪ/ *n.* boisterous activity; commotion. [a reduplication of HURL]

hurrah /hʊˈrɑː/ *int.* & *n.* (also **hurray** /hʊˈreɪ/) exclamation of joy or approval. [earlier *huzza*, origin uncertain]

hurricane /ˈhʌrɪkən/ *n.* 1 storm with a violent wind, esp. a W. Indian cyclone. 2 *Meteorol.* wind of 65 knots (75 m.p.h.) or more, force 12 on the Beaufort scale. [Spanish and Portuguese from Carib]

hurricane-lamp *n.* oil-lamp designed to resist a high wind.

hurry /ˈhʌrɪ/ —*n.* 1 great or eager haste. 2 (with *neg.* or *interrog.*) need for haste (*there is no hurry*; *what's the hurry?*). —*v.* (**-ies, -ied**) 1 move or act hastily. 2 cause to hurry. 3 (as **hurried** *adj.*) hasty; done rapidly. □ **hurry along** (or **up**) (cause to) make haste. **in a hurry** 1 hurrying. 2 *colloq.* easily or readily (*you will not beat that in a hurry*). □ **hurriedly** *adv.* [imitative]

hurt —*v.* (*past* and *past part.* **hurt**) 1 (also *absol.*) cause pain or injury to. 2 cause mental pain or distress to. 3 suffer pain (*my arm hurts*). —*n.* 1 injury. 2 harm, wrong. [French *hurter* knock]

hurtful *adj.* causing (esp. mental) hurt. □ **hurtfully** *adv.*

hurtle /ˈhɜːt(ə)l/ *v.* (**-ling**) 1 move or hurl rapidly or noisily. 2 come with a crash. [from HURT in the obsolete sense 'strike hard']

husband /ˈhʌzbənd/ —*n.* married man, esp. in relation to his wife. —*v.* use (resources) economically; eke out. [Old English, = house-dweller]

husbandry *n.* 1 farming. 2 management of resources.

hush —*v.* make or become silent or quiet. —*int.* calling for silence. —*n.* expectant stillness or silence. □ **hush up** suppress public mention of (an affair). [*husht*, an obsolete exclamation, taken as a past part.]

hush-hush *adj. colloq.* highly secret, confidential.

hush money *n. slang* money paid to ensure discretion.

husk —*n.* 1 dry outer covering of some fruits or seeds. 2 worthless outside part of a thing. —*v.* remove husk(s) from. [probably Low German]

husky[1] /ˈhʌskɪ/ *adj.* (**-ier, -iest**) 1 (of a person or voice) dry in the throat; hoarse. 2 of or full of husks. 3 dry as a husk. 4 tough, strong, hefty. □ **huskily** *adv.* **huskiness** *n.*

husky[2] /ˈhʌskɪ/ *n.* (*pl.* **-ies**) dog of a powerful breed used in the Arctic for pulling sledges. [perhaps from corruption of ESKIMO]

huss *n.* dogfish as food. [origin unknown]

hussar /hʊˈzɑː(r)/ *n.* soldier of a light cavalry regiment. [Magyar *huszár*]

hussy /ˈhʌsɪ/ *n.* (*pl.* **-ies**) *derog.* impudent or promiscuous girl or woman. [contraction of HOUSEWIFE]

hustings /ˈhʌstɪŋz/ *n.* election campaign or proceedings. [Old English, = house of assembly, from Old Norse]

hustle /ˈhʌs(ə)l/ —*v.* (**-ling**) 1 jostle, bustle. 2 (foll. by *into*, *out of*, etc.) force, coerce, or hurry (*hustled them out of the room*; *was hustled into agreeing*). 3 *slang* a solicit business. b engage in prostitution. 4 *slang* obtain by energetic activity. —*n.* act or instance of hustling. □ **hustler** *n.* [Dutch]

hut *n.* small simple or crude house or shelter. [French *hutte* from Germanic]

hutch *n.* box or cage for rabbits etc. [French *huche*]

hyacinth /ˈhaɪəsɪnθ/ *n.* 1 bulbous plant with racemes of bell-shaped (esp. purplish-blue) fragrant flowers. 2 purplish-blue. [Greek *huakinthos*]

hyaena var. of HYENA.

hybrid /ˈhaɪbrɪd/ —*n.* 1 offspring of two plants or animals of different species or

varieties. **2** thing composed of diverse elements, e.g. a word with parts taken from different languages. —*adj.* **1** bred as a hybrid. **2** heterogeneous. □ **hybridism** *n.* [Latin]

hybridize *v.* (also **-ise**) :to crossbreeding. **2 a** produce hybrids. **b** (of an animal or plant) interbreed. □ **hybridization** /-ˈzeɪʃ(ə)n/ *n.*

hydra /ˈhaɪdrə/ *n.* **1** freshwater polyp with a tubular body and tentacles. **2** something hard to destroy. [Greek, a mythical snake with many heads that grew again when cut off]

hydrangea /haɪˈdreɪndʒə/ *n.* shrub with globular clusters of white, pink, or blue flowers. [Greek *hudōr* water, *aggos* vessel]

hydrant /ˈhaɪdrənt/ *n.* outlet (esp. in a street) with a nozzle for a hose, for drawing water from the main. [as HYDRO-]

hydrate /ˈhaɪdreɪt/ —*n.* compound in which water is chemically combined with another compound or an element. —*v.* (**-ting**) **1** combine chemically with water. **2** cause to absorb water. □ **hydration** /-ˈdreɪʃ(ə)n/ *n.* [French: related to HYDRO-]

hydraulic /haɪˈdrɔːlɪk/ *adj.* **1** (of water, oil, etc.) conveyed through pipes or channels. **2** (of a mechanism etc.) operated by liquid moving in this way (*hydraulic brakes*). □ **hydraulically** *adv.* [Greek *hudōr* water, *aulos* pipe]

hydraulics *n.pl.* (usu. treated as *sing.*) science of the conveyance of liquids through pipes etc. esp. as motive power.

hydride /ˈhaɪdraɪd/ *n.* compound of hydrogen with an element.

hydro /ˈhaɪdrəu/ *n.* (*pl.* **-s**) *colloq.* **1** hotel or clinic etc., orig. providing hydropathic treatment. **2** hydroelectric power plant. [abbreviation]

hydro- *comb. form* **1** having to do with water (*hydroelectric*). **2** combined with hydrogen (*hydrochloric*). [Greek *hudro-* from *hudōr* water]

hydrocarbon /haɪdrəˈkɑːbən/ *n.* compound of hydrogen and carbon.

hydrocephalus /haɪdrəˈsefələs/ *n.* accumulated fluid in the brain, esp. in young children. □ **hydrocephalic** /-sɪˈfælɪk/ *adj.* [Greek *kephalē* head]

hydrochloric acid /haɪdrəˈklɒrɪk/ *n.* solution of the colourless gas hydrogen chloride in water.

hydrocyanic acid /ˌhaɪdrəsaɪˈænɪk/ *n.* highly poisonous liquid smelling of bitter almonds; prussic acid.

hydrodynamics /ˈnaɪmɪks/ *n.pl.* (usu. treated as *sing.*) science of forces acting on or exerted by fluids (esp. liquids). □ **hydrodynamic** *adj.*

hydroelectric /haɪdrəuɪˈlektrɪk/ *adj.* **1** generating electricity by water-power. **2** (of electricity) so generated. □ **hydroelectricity** /-ˈtrɪsɪti/ *n.*

hydrofoil /ˈhaɪdrə,fɔɪl/ *n.* **1** boat equipped with planes for lifting its hull out of the water to increase its speed. **2** such a plane.

hydrogen /ˈhaɪdrədʒ(ə)n/ *n.* tasteless odourless gas, the lightest element, occurring in water and all organic compounds. □ **hydrogenous** /haɪˈdrɒdʒinəs/ *adj.* [French: related to HYDRO-, -GEN]

hydrogenate /haɪˈdrɒdʒineɪt/ *v.* (**-ting**) charge with or cause to combine with hydrogen. □ **hydrogenation** /haɪˌdrɒdʒiˈneɪʃ(ə)n/ *n.*

hydrogen bomb *n.* immensely powerful bomb utilizing the explosive fusion of hydrogen nuclei.

hydrogen peroxide *n.* viscous unstable liquid with strong oxidizing properties.

hydrogen sulphide *n.* poisonous unpleasant-smelling gas formed by rotting animal matter.

hydrography /haɪˈdrɒgrəfi/ *n.* science of surveying and charting seas, lakes, rivers, etc. □ **hydrographer** *n.* **hydrographic** /-drəˈgræfɪk/ *adj.*

hydrology /haɪˈdrɒlədʒi/ *n.* science of the properties of water, esp. of its movement in relation to land. □ **hydrologist** *n.*

hydrolyse /ˈhaɪdrəlaɪz/ *v.* (*US* **-lyze**) (**-sing** or **-zing**) decompose by hydrolysis.

hydrolysis /haɪˈdrɒlisɪs/ *n.* chemical reaction of a substance with water, usu. resulting in decomposition. [Greek *lusis* dissolving]

hydrometer /haɪˈdrɒmitə(r)/ *n.* instrument for measuring the density of liquids.

hydropathy /haɪˈdrɒpəθi/ *n.* (medically unorthodox) treatment of disease by water. □ **hydropathic** /haɪdrəˈpæθɪk/ *adj.* [related to PATHOS]

hydrophilic /haɪdrəˈfɪlɪk/ *adj.* **1** having an affinity for water. **2** wettable by water. [Greek *philos* loving]

hydrophobia /haɪdrəˈfəubiə/ *n.* **1** aversion to water, esp. as a symptom of rabies in humans. **2** rabies, esp. in humans. □ **hydrophobic** *adj.*

hydroplane /ˈhaɪdrə,pleɪn/ *n.* **1** light fast motor boat that skims over water. **2** finlike attachment enabling a submarine to rise and descend.

hydroponics /haɪdrəˈpɒnɪks/ *n.* growing plants without soil, in sand, gravel,

or liquid, with added nutrients. [Greek *ponos* labour]

hydrosphere /ˈhaɪdrəˌsfɪə(r)/ *n.* waters of the earth's surface.

hydrostatic /ˌhaɪdrəˈstætɪk/ *adj.* of the equilibrium of liquids and the pressure exerted by liquid at rest. [related to STATIC]

hydrostatics *n.pl.* (usu. treated as *sing.*) mechanics of the hydrostatic properties of liquids.

hydrotherapy /ˌhaɪdrəˈθerəpɪ/ *n.* use of water, esp. swimming, in the treatment of arthritis, paralysis, etc.

hydrous /ˈhaɪdrəs/ *adj.* containing water. [related to HYDRO-]

hydroxide /haɪˈdrɒksaɪd/ *n.* compound containing oxygen and hydrogen as either a hydroxide ion or a hydroxyl group.

hydroxyl /haɪˈdrɒksɪl/ *n.* (*attrib.*) univalent group containing hydrogen and oxygen.

hyena /haɪˈiːnə/ *n.* (also **hyaena**) doglike flesh-eating mammal. [Latin from Greek]

hygiene /ˈhaɪdʒiːn/ *n.* 1 conditions or practices, esp. cleanliness, conducive to maintaining health. 2 science of maintaining health. □ **hygienic** /-ˈdʒiːnɪk/ *adj.* **hygienically** /-ˈdʒiːnɪkəlɪ/ *adv.* **hygienist** *n.* [Greek *hugiēs* healthy]

hygrometer /haɪˈgrɒmɪtə(r)/ *n.* instrument for measuring the humidity of the air or a gas. [Greek *hugros* wet]

hygroscope /ˈhaɪgrəˌskəʊp/ *n.* instrument indicating but not measuring the humidity of the air.

hygroscopic /ˌhaɪgrəˈskɒpɪk/ *adj.* 1 of the hygroscope. 2 (of a substance) tending to absorb moisture from the air.

hymen /ˈhaɪmen/ *n.* membrane at the opening of the vagina, usu. broken at the first occurrence of sexual intercourse. [Greek *humēn* membrane]

hymenopterous /ˌhaɪməˈnɒptərəs/ *adj.* of an order of insects having four transparent wings, including bees, wasps, and ants. [Greek, = membrane-winged]

hymn /hɪm/ —*n.* 1 song of esp. Christian praise. 2 crusading theme (*hymn of freedom*). —*v.* praise or celebrate in hymns. [Greek *humnos*]

hymnal /ˈhɪmn(ə)l/ *n.* book of hymns. [medieval Latin: related to HYMN]

hymnology /hɪmˈnɒlədʒɪ/ *n.* (*pl.* **-ies**) 1 the composition or study of hymns. 2 hymns collectively. □ **hymnologist** *n.*

hyoscine /ˈhaɪəˌsiːn/ *n.* poisonous alkaloid found in plants of the nightshade family, used to prevent motion sickness etc. [Greek *huoskuamos* henbane from *hus huos* pig, *kuamos* bean]

hype /haɪp/ *slang* —*n.* extravagant or intensive promotion of a product etc. —*v.* (**-ping**) promote with hype. [origin unknown]

hyped up *adj. slang* nervously excited or stimulated. [shortening of HYPO-DERMIC]

hyper /ˈhaɪpə(r)/ *adj. slang* hyperactive, highly-strung. [abbreviation of HYPERACTIVE]

hyper- *prefix* meaning: 1 over, beyond, above (*hypersonic*). 2 too (*hypersensitive*). [Greek *huper* over]

hyperactive /ˌhaɪpərˈæktɪv/ *adj.* (of a person) abnormally active.

hyperbola /haɪˈpɜːbələ/ *n.* (*pl.* **-s** or **-lae** /-ˌliː/) plane curve produced when a cone is cut by a plane that makes a larger angle with the base than the side of the cone makes. □ **hyperbolic** /ˌhaɪpəˈbɒlɪk/ *adj.* [Greek *hyperbolē*, = excess: related to HYPER-, *ballō* throw]

hyperbole /haɪˈpɜːbəlɪ/ *n.* exaggeration, esp. for effect. □ **hyperbolical** /-ˈbɒlɪk(ə)l/ *adj.*

hyperbolic function *n.* function related to a rectangular hyperbola, e.g. a hyperbolic cosine or sine.

hypercritical /ˌhaɪpəˈkrɪtɪk(ə)l/ *adj.* excessively critical. □ **hypercritically** *adv.*

hyperglycaemia /ˌhaɪpəglaɪˈsiːmɪə/ *n.* (*US* **hyperglycemia**) excess of glucose in the bloodstream. [from HYPER-, Greek *glukus* sweet, *haima* blood]

hypermarket /ˈhaɪpəˌmɑːkɪt/ *n.* very large supermarket.

hypermedia /ˈhaɪpəˌmiːdɪə/ *n.* provision of several media (e.g. audio, video, and graphics) on one computer system, with cross-references from one to another (often *attrib.*: *hypermedia database*).

hypersensitive /ˌhaɪpəˈsensɪtɪv/ *adj.* excessively sensitive. □ **hypersensitivity** /-ˈtɪvɪtɪ/ *n.*

hypersonic /ˌhaɪpəˈsɒnɪk/ *adj.* 1 of speeds of more than five times that of sound. 2 of sound-frequencies above about a thousand million hertz.

hypertension /ˌhaɪpəˈten(ʃ)ən/ *n.* 1 abnormally high blood pressure. 2 great emotional tension.

hypertext /ˈhaɪpəˌtekst/ *n.* provision of several texts on one computer system, with cross-references from one to another.

hyperthermia /ˌhaɪpəˈθɜːmɪə/ *n.* abnormally high body-temperature. [from HYPER-, Greek *thermē* heat]

hyperthyroidism /ˌhaɪpəˈθaɪrɔɪˌdɪz(ə)m/ *n.* overactivity of the thyroid

gland, resulting in an increased rate of metabolism.

hyperventilation /ˌhaɪpəˌventɪˈleɪʃ(ə)n/ n. abnormally rapid breathing. □ **hyperventilate** v. (-ting).

hyphen /ˈhaɪf(ə)n/ —n. sign (-) used to join words semantically or syntactically (e.g. *fruit-tree, pick-me-up, rock-forming*), to indicate the division of a word at the end of a line, or to indicate a missing or implied element (as in *man- and womankind*). —v. = HYPHENATE. [Greek *huphen* together]

hyphenate /ˈhaɪfəneɪt/ v. (-ting) 1 write (a compound word) with a hyphen. 2 join (words) with a hyphen. □ **hyphenation** /-ˈneɪʃ(ə)n/ n.

hypnosis /hɪpˈnəʊsɪs/ n. 1 state like sleep in which the subject acts only on external suggestion. 2 artificially produced sleep. [Greek *hupnos* sleep]

hypnotherapy /ˌhɪpnəʊˈθerəpɪ/ n. treat- ment of mental disorders by hypnosis.

hypnotic /hɪpˈnɒtɪk/ —adj. 1 of or producing hypnosis. 2 inducing sleep.—n. hypnotic drug or influence. □ **hypnotically** adv. [Greek: related to HYPNOSIS]

hypnotism /ˈhɪpnətɪz(ə)m/ n. the study or practice of hypnosis. □ **hypnotist** n.

hypnotize /ˈhɪpnətaɪz/ v. (also -ise) (-zing or -sing) 1 produce hypnosis in 2 fascinate; capture the mind o:

hypo[1] /ˈhaɪpəʊ/ n. sodium thiosulphate (incorrectly called hyposulphite) used as a photographic fixer. [abbreviation]

hypo[2] /ˈhaɪpəʊ/ n. (pl. -s) slang = HYPO- DERMIC n. [abbreviation]

hypo- prefix 1 under (*hypodermic*). 2 below normal (*hypotension*). 3 slightly. [Greek *hupo* under]

hypocaust /ˈhaɪpəˌkɔːst/ n. space for underfloor hot-air heating in ancient Roman houses. [from HYPO-, Greek *kaustos* burnt]

hypochondria /ˌhaɪpəˈkɒndrɪə/ n. abnormal and ill-founded anxiety about one's health. [Latin from Greek, = soft parts of the body below the ribs, where melancholy was thought to arise]

hypochondriac /ˌhaɪpəˈkɒndrɪˌæk/ —n. person given to hypochondria.—adj. of or affected by hypochondria.

hypocrisy /hɪˈpɒkrɪsɪ/ n. (pl. -ies) 1 false claim to virtue; insincerity, pretence. 2 instance of this. [Greek, = acting, feigning]

hypocrite /ˈhɪpəkrɪt/ n. person given to hypocrisy. □ **hypocritical** /ˌhɪpəˈkrɪtɪk(ə)l/ adj; **hypocritically** /ˌhɪpəˈkrɪtɪk(ə)lɪ/ adv.

hypodermic /ˌhaɪpəˈdɜːmɪk/ —adj. 1 of the area beneath the skin. 2 a (of a syringe, etc.) used to do this. —n. hypodermic injection or syringe. [from HYPO-, Greek *derma* skin]

hypotension /ˌhaɪpəʊˈtenʃ(ə)n/ n. abnormally low blood pressure.

hypotenuse /haɪˈpɒtɪnjuːz/ n. side opposite the right angle of a right-angled triangle. [Greek, = subtending line]

hypothalamus /ˌhaɪpəˈθæləməs/ n. (pl. -mi /-maɪ/) region of the brain controlling body-temperature, thirst, hunger, etc. □ **hypothalamic** adj. [Latin: related to HYPO-, Greek *thalamos* inner room]

hypothermia /ˌhaɪpəˈθɜːmɪə/ n. abnormally low body-temperature. [from HYPO-, Greek *thermē* heat]

hypothesis /haɪˈpɒθɪsɪs/ n. (pl. -theses /-siːz/) proposition or supposition made as the basis for reasoning or investigation. [Greek, = foundation]

hypothesize /haɪˈpɒθɪsaɪz/ v. (also -ise) (-zing or -sing) form or assume a hypothesis.

hypothetical /ˌhaɪpəˈθetɪk(ə)l/ adj. 1 of, based on, or serving as a hypothesis. 2 supposed; not necessarily true. □ **hypothetically** adv.

hypothyroidism /ˌhaɪpəʊˈθaɪrɔɪdɪz(ə)m/ n. subnormal activity of the thyroid gland, resulting in cretinism. □ **hypothyroid** n. & adj.

hypoventilation /ˌhaɪpəʊventɪˈleɪʃ(ə)n/ n. abnormally slow breathing.

hysterectomy /ˌhɪstəˈrektəmɪ/ n. (pl. -ies) surgical removal of the womb. [Greek *hustera* womb, -ECTOMY]

hysteresis /ˌhɪstəˈriːsɪs/ n. phenomenon whereby changes in an effect lag behind changes in its cause. [Greek *husteros* coming after]

hysteria /hɪˈstɪərɪə/ n. 1 wild uncontrollable emotion or excitement. 2 functional disturbance of the nervous system, of psychoneurotic origin. [Greek *hustera* womb]

hysteric /hɪˈsterɪk/ n. 1 (in pl.) a fit of hysteria. b colloq. overwhelming laughter (*we were in hysterics*). 2 hysterical person.

hysterical adj. 1 of or affected with hysteria. 2 uncontrollably emotional. 3 colloq. extremely funny. □ **hysterically** adv.

Hz abbr. hertz.

I

I¹ /ai/ n. (also **l**) (pl. **Is** or **I's**) **1** ninth letter of the alphabet. **2** (as a Roman numeral) 1.

I² /ai/ pron. (obj. **me**; poss. **my, mine**; pl. **we**) used by a speaker or writer to refer to himself or herself. [Old English]

I³ symb. iodine.

I⁴ abbr. (also **I.**) **1** Island(s). **2** Isle(s).

-ial var. of **-AL**.

iambus /ai'æmbik/ *Prosody* —adj. of or using iambuses. —n. (usu. in pl.) iambic verse.

iambus /ai'æmbəs/ n. (pl. **-buses** or **-bi** /-bai/) metrical foot consisting of one short followed by one long syllable (⌣–). [Greek, = lampoon]

-ian var. of **-AN**.

IBA abbr. Independent Broadcasting Authority.

Iberian /ai'biəriən/ —adj. of Iberia, the peninsula comprising Spain and Portugal; of Spain and Portugal. —n. native or language of Iberia. [Latin *Iberia*]

ibex /'aibeks/ n. (pl. **-es**) wild mountain goat with thick curved ridged horns. [Latin]

ibid. /'ibid/ abbr. in the same book or passage etc. [Latin *ibidem* in the same place]

-ibility suffix forming nouns from, or corresponding to, adjectives in *-ible*.

ibis /'aibis/ n. (pl. **-es**) wading bird with a curved bill, long neck, and long legs. [Greek, from Egyptian]

-ible suffix forming adjectives meaning 'that may or may be' (*forcible; possible*). [Latin]

-ibly suffix forming adverbs corresponding to adjectives in *-ible*.

Ibo /'i:bəu/ n. (also **Igbo**) (pl. same or **-s**) **1** member of a Black people of SE Nigeria **2** their language. [native name]

-ic suffix **1** forming adjectives (*Arabic; classic; public*) and nouns (*critic; epic; mechanic; music*). **2** combined in higher valence or degree of oxidation (*ferric; sulphuric*). [Latin *-icus*, Greek *-ikos*]

-ical suffix forming adjectives corresponding to nouns or adjectives in *-ic* or *-y* (*classical; historical*).

ice —n. **1 a** frozen water. **b** sheet of this on water. **2** ice-cream or water-ice (*ate an ice*). —v. (**icing**) **1** mix with or cool in ice (*iced drinks*). **2** (often foll. by *over, up*) **a** cover or become covered with ice. **b** freeze. **3** cover (a cake etc.) with icing. □ **on ice 1** performed by skaters. **2** colloq.

in reserve. **on thin ice** in a risky situation. [Old English]

ice age n. glacial period.

ice-axe n. cutting tool used by mountaineers.

iceberg n. large floating mass of ice. □ **the tip of the iceberg** small perceptible part of something very large or complex. [Dutch]

iceberg lettuce n. crisp type of round lettuce.

ice blue adj. & n. (as adj. often hyphenated) very pale blue.

icebox n. **1** compartment in a refrigerator for making or storing ice. **2** US refrigerator.

ice-breaker n. **1** ship designed to break through ice. **2** joke, incident, etc. that breaks the ice.

ice bucket n. bucket holding ice, used to chill wine.

icecap n. permanent covering of ice, esp. in polar regions.

ice-cream n. sweet creamy frozen food, usu. flavoured.

ice-cube n. small block of ice for drinks etc.

ice-field n. expanse of ice, esp. in polar regions.

ice hockey n. form of hockey played on ice.

Icelander /'aisləndə(r)/ n. **1** native or national of Iceland. **2** person of Icelandic descent.

Icelandic /ais'lændik/ —adj. of Iceland. —n. language of Iceland.

ice lolly n. (also **iced lolly**) flavoured ice on a stick.

ice-pack n. **1** = PACK ICE. **2** ice applied to the body for medical purposes.

ice-pick n. tool with a spike for splitting up ice.

ice-plant n. plant with speckled leaves.

ice-rink n. **1** = RINK n. 1.

ice-skate —n. boot with a blade beneath, for skating on ice. —v. skate on ice. □ **ice-skater** n.

ichneumon /ik'nju:mən/ n. **1** (in full **ichneumon fly**) small wasp depositing eggs in or on the larva of another as food for its own larva. **2** mongoose noted for destroying crocodile eggs. [Greek from *ikhnos* footstep]

ichthyology /ˌikθi'ɒlədʒi/ n. the study of fishes. □ **ichthyological** /-ə'lɒdʒik(ə)l/ adj. **ichthyologist** n. [Greek *ikhthus* fish]

ichthyosaurus /ˌɪkθɪəˈsɔːrəs/ n. (also **ichthyosaur** /ˈɪkθɪəˌsɔːr/) (pl. -**saur-uses** or -**saurs**) extinct marine reptile with four flippers and usu. a large tail. [Greek *ikhthus* fish, *sauros* lizard]

-**ician** *suffix* forming nouns denoting persons skilled in subjects having nouns usu. ending in -**ic** or -**ics** (*magician*; *politician*). [French -*icien*]

icicle /ˈaɪsɪk(ə)l/ n. hanging tapering piece of ice, formed from dripping water. [from *ice*, obsolete *ickle* icicle]

icing n. 1 coating of sugar etc. on a cake or biscuit. 2 formation of ice on a ship or aircraft. □ **icing on the cake** inessential though attractive addition or enhancement.

icing sugar n. finely powdered sugar.

icon /ˈaɪkɒn/ n. (also **ikon**) 1 painting of Christ etc., esp. in the Eastern Church. 2 image or statue. 3 symbol on a VDU screen of a program, option, or window, esp. for selection. □ **iconic** /aɪˈkɒnɪk/ *adj*. [Greek *eikōn* image]

iconoclast /aɪˈkɒnəˌklæst/ n. 1 person who attacks cherished beliefs. 2 *hist.* person destroying religious images. □ **iconoclasm** n. **iconoclastic** /ˌ-ˈklæstɪk/ *adj*. [Greek: related to ICON, *klaō* break]

iconography /ˌaɪkəˈnɒɡrəfɪ/ n. 1 the illustration of a subject by drawings or figures. 2 the study of portraits, esp. of an individual, or of artistic images or symbols. [Greek: related to ICON]

iconostasis /ˌaɪkəˈnɒstəsɪs/ n. (pl. -**stases** /-ˌsiːz/) (in the Eastern Church) screen bearing icons. [Greek: related to ICON]

icosahedron /ˌaɪkəsəˈhiːdrən/ n. solid figure with twenty faces. [Greek *eikosi* twenty, *hedra* base]

-**ics** *suffix* (treated as *sing.* or *pl.*) forming nouns denoting arts, sciences, etc. (*athletics*; *politics*).

icy /ˈaɪsɪ/ *adj.* (**-ier**, **-iest**) 1 very cold. 2 covered with or abounding in ice. 3 (of a tone or manner) unfriendly, hostile. □ **icily** *adv.* **iciness** n.

ID *abbr.* identification, identity (*ID card*).

I'd /aɪd/ *contr.* 1 I had. 2 I should. 3 I would.

-ide *suffix Chem.* forming nouns denoting binary compounds of an element (*sodium chloride*; *lead sulphide*; *calcium carbide*). [extended from OXIDE]

idea /aɪˈdɪə/ n. 1 plan etc. formed by mental effort (*an idea for a book*). 2 a mental impression or concept. b vague belief or fancy (*had an idea you were married*). 3 intention or purpose (*the idea is to make money*). 4 archetype or pattern. 5 ambition or aspiration (*have ideas*; *put ideas into a person's head*). □ **have no idea** *colloq.* 1 not know at all. 2 be completely incompetent. **not one's idea of** *colloq.* not what one regards as (*not my idea of a holiday*). [Greek, = form, kind]

ideal /aɪˈdɪəl/ -*adj.* 1 answering to one's highest conception; perfect. 2 existing only in idea; visionary. -n. perfect type, thing, concept, principle, etc., esp. as a standard to emulate. [French: related to IDEA]

idealism n. 1 forming or pursuing ideals, esp. unrealistically. 2 representation of things in ideal form. 3 system of thought in which objects are held to be in some way dependent on the mind. □ **idealist** n. **idealistic** /-ˈlɪstɪk/ *adj*. **idealistically** /-ˈlɪstɪkəlɪ/ *adv.*

idealize v. (also **-ise**) (**-zing** or **-sing**) regard or represent as ideal or perfect. □ **idealization** /-ˈzeɪʃ(ə)n/ n.

ideally *adv.* 1 in ideal circumstances. 2 according to an ideal.

idée fixe /ˌiːdeɪ ˈfiːks/ n. (pl. **idées fixes** pronunc. same) dominating idea, obsession. [French, = fixed idea]

identical /aɪˈdentɪk(ə)l/ *adj.* 1 (often foll. by *with*) (of different things) absolutely alike. 2 one and the same. 3 (of twins) developed from a single ovum. □ **identically** *adv.* [Latin *identicus*]

identification /aɪˌdentɪfɪˈkeɪʃ(ə)n/ n. 1 identifying or being identified. 2 means of identifying (also *attrib.: identification card*).

identification parade n. group of people from whom a suspect is to be identified.

identify /aɪˈdentɪfaɪ/ v. (**-ies**, **-ied**) 1 establish the identity of; recognize. 2 select or discover (*identify the best solution*). 3 (also *refl.*, foll. by *with*) associate inseparably or very closely (with a party, policy, etc.). 4 (often foll. by *with*) treat as identical. 5 (foll. by *with*) put oneself in the place of (another person). □ **identifiable** *adj.* [medieval Latin *identifico*: related to IDENTITY]

Identikit /aɪˈdentɪkɪt/ n. (often *attrib.*) *propr.* picture of esp. a wanted suspect assembled from standard components using witnesses' descriptions. [from IDENTITY, KIT]

identity /aɪˈdentɪtɪ/ n. (pl. **-ies**) 1 a condition of being a specified person or thing. b individuality, personality (*felt he had lost his identity*). 2 identification or the result of it (*mistaken identity*; *identity card*). 3 absolute sameness (*identity of interests*). 4 *Algebra* **a** equality of two expressions for all values of the quantities. **b** equation

ideogram /ˈɪdəgræm/ *n.* character symbolizing a thing without indicating the sounds in its name (e.g. a numeral, Chinese characters). [Greek *idea* form, -GRAM]

□ **ideographic** /-ˈgræfɪk/ *adj.* **ideography** /ˌɪdɪˈɒgrəfɪ/ *n.*

ideologue /ˈaɪdɪəlɒg/ *n.* adherent of an ideology. [French: related to IDEA]

ideology /ˌaɪdɪˈɒlədʒɪ/ *n.* (*pl.* -ies) 1 ideas at the basis of an economic or political theory (*Marxist ideology*). 2 characteristic thinking of a class etc. (*bourgeois ideology*). □ **ideologically** /-əˈlɒdʒɪk(ə)l/ *adj.* **ideologist** *n.* /-əˈlɒdʒɪkəlɪ/ *adv.* [French: related to IDEA, -LOGY]

ides /aɪdz/ *n.pl.* day of the ancient Roman month (the 15th day of March, May, July, and October, the 13th of other months). [Latin *idus*]

idiocy /ˈɪdɪəsɪ/ *n.* (*pl.* -ies) 1 foolishness; foolish act. 2 extreme mental imbecility. [Latin *idus*]

idiom /ˈɪdɪəm/ *n.* 1 phrase etc. established by usage and not immediately comprehensible from the words used (e.g. *over the moon, see the light*). 2 form of expression peculiar to a language etc. 3 language of a people or country. 4 characteristic mode of expression in art etc. [Greek *idios* own]

idiomatic /ˌɪdɪəˈmætɪk/ *adj.* 1 relating or conforming to idiom. 2 characteristic of a particular language. □ **idiomatically** *adv.*

idiosyncrasy /ˌɪdɪəˈsɪŋkrəsɪ/ *n.* (*pl.* -ies) attitude, behaviour, or opinion peculiar to a person; anything highly individual or eccentric. □ **idiosyncratic** /-ˈkrætɪk/ *adj.* **idiosyncratically** /-ˈkrætɪkəlɪ/ *adv.* [Greek *idios* private, *sun* with, *krasis* mixture]

idiot /ˈɪdɪət/ *n.* 1 stupid person. 2 mentally deficient person incapable of rational conduct. □ **idiotic** /-ˈɒtɪk/ *adj.* **idiotically** /-ˈɒtɪkəlɪ/ *adv.* [Greek *idiotēs*, = private citizen, ignorant person]

idle /ˈaɪd(ə)l/ —*adj.* (**idler**, **idlest**) 1 lazy, indolent. 2 not in use; not working. 3 (of time etc.) unoccupied. 4 purposeless; groundless (*idle rumour*). 5 useless, ineffective (*idle protest*). —*v.* (-ling) 1 be idle. 2 (of an engine or (of an engine) run (an engine or (of an engine) be run slowly or without doing any work. 3 (foll. by *away*) pass (time etc.) in idleness. □ **idleness** *n.* **idler** *n.* **idly** *adv.* [Old English]

idol /ˈaɪd(ə)l/ *n.* 1 image of a deity etc. as an object of worship. 2 object of excessive or supreme adulation. [Greek *eidōlon* image, phantom]

idolater /aɪˈdɒlətə(r)/ *n.* 1 worshipper of idols. 2 devoted admirer. □ **idolatrous** *adj.* **idolatry** *n.* [related to IDOL, Greek *latreuō* worship]

idolize *v.* (also -ise) (-zing or -sing) 1 venerate or love excessively. 2 make an idol of. □ **idolization** /-zeɪʃ(ə)n/ *n.*

idyll /ˈɪdɪl/ *n.* 1 short description, esp. in verse, of a peaceful or romantic, esp. rural, scene or incident. 2 such a scene or incident. [Greek *eidullion*]

idyllic /ɪˈdɪlɪk/ *adj.* 1 blissfully peaceful and happy. 2 of or like an idyll. □ **idyllically** *adv.*

i.e. *abbr.* that is to say. [Latin *id est*]

-ie see -y².

if —*conj.* 1 introducing a conditional clause: **a** on the condition or supposition that; in the event that (*if he comes I will tell him*; *if you are tired we can rest*). **b** (with past tense) implying that the condition is not fulfilled (*if I knew I would say*). 2 even though (*I'll finish it, if it takes me all day*). 3 whenever (*if I am not sure I ask*). 4 whether (*see if you can find it*). 5 expressing a wish, surprise, or request (*if I could just try*; *if it isn't my old hat!*; *if you wouldn't mind?*). —*n.* condition, supposition (*too many ifs about it*). □ **if only 1** even if for no other reason than (*I'll come if only to see her*). 2 (often *ellipt.*) expression of regret; I wish that (*if only I had thought of it*). [Old English]

iffy *adj.* (**-ier**, **-iest**) *colloq.* uncertain; dubious.

Igbo var. of IBO.

igloo /ˈɪgluː/ *n.* Eskimo dome-shaped dwelling, esp. of snow. [Eskimo, = house]

igneous /ˈɪgnɪəs/ *adj.* 1 of fire; fiery. 2 (esp. of rocks) volcanic. [Latin *ignis* fire]

ignite /ɪgˈnaɪt/ *v.* (-ting) 1 set fire to. 2 catch fire. 3 provoke or excite (feelings etc.). [Latin *ignio ignit-* set on fire]

ignition /ɪgˈnɪʃ(ə)n/ *n.* 1 mechanism for, or the action of, starting combustion in an internal-combustion engine. 2 igniting or being ignited.

ignoble /ɪgˈnəʊb(ə)l/ *adj.* (-bler, -blest) 1 dishonourable. 2 of low birth, position, or reputation. □ **ignobly** *adv.* [Latin: related to IN-¹, NOBLE]

ignominious /ˌɪgnəˈmɪnɪəs/ *adj.* shameful, humiliating. □ **ignominiously** *adv.* [Latin: related to IGNOMINY]

ignominy /'ɪgnəmɪnɪ/ n. dishonour, infamy. [Latin: related to IN-[1], Latin (g)no-men name]

ignoramus /ˌɪgnə'reɪməs/ n. (pl. -muses) ignorant person. [Latin, = we do not know: related to IGNORE]

ignorance /'ɪgnərəns/ n. lack of knowledge. [French from Latin: related to IGNORE]

ignorant adj. 1 (often foll. by of, in) lacking knowledge (esp. of a fact or subject). 2 colloq. uncouth. □ **ignorantly** adv.

ignore /ɪg'nɔː(r)/ v. (-ring) refuse to take notice of; intentionally disregard. [Latin ignoro not know]

iguana /ɪg'wɑːnə/ n. large American, W. Indian, or Pacific lizard with a dorsal crest. [Spanish from Carib iwana]

iguanodon /ɪg'wɑːnədɒn/ n. large plant-eating dinosaur with small forelimbs. [from IGUANA, which it resembles, after mastodon etc.]

ikebana /ˌɪkɪ'bɑːnɑː/ n. art of Japanese flower arrangement. [Japanese, = living flowers]

ikon var. of ICON.

il- prefix assim. form of IN-[1], IN-[2] before l.

ileum /'ɪlɪəm/ n. (pl. ilea) third and last portion of the small intestine. [Latin ilium]

ilex /'aɪleks/ n. (pl. -es) 1 tree or shrub of the genus including the common holly. 2 holm-oak. [Latin]

iliac /'ɪlɪæk/ adj. of the lower body (iliac artery). [Latin ilia flanks]

ilk n. 1 colloq. usu. derog. sort, family, class, etc. 2 (in of that ilk) Scot. of the ancestral estate with the same name as the family (Guthrie of that ilk). [Old English]

ill —adj. (attrib. except in sense 1) 1 (usu. predic.) not in good health; unwell. 2 wretched, unfavourable (ill fortune, ill luck). 3 harmful (ill effects). 4 hostile, unkind (ill feeling). 5 faulty, unskilful (ill management). 6 (of manners or conduct) improper. —adv. 1 badly, wrongly, imperfectly (ill-matched; ill-provided). 2 scarcely (can ill afford it). 3 unfavourably (spoke ill of them). —n. 1 injury, harm. 2 evil. □ ill at ease embarrassed, uneasy. [Old Norse]

I'll /aɪl/ contr. I shall; I will.

ill-advised adj. foolish; imprudent.

ill-assorted adj. badly matched; mixed.

ill-bred adj. badly brought up; rude.

ill-defined adj. not clearly defined.

ill-disposed adj. 1 (often foll. by to-wards) unfavourably disposed. 2 mal-evolent.

illegal /ɪ'liːg(ə)l/ adj. 1 not legal. 2 criminal. □ **illegality** /-'gælɪtɪ/ n. (pl. -ies). **illegally** adv.

illegible /ɪ'ledʒɪb(ə)l/ adj. not legible. □ **illegibility** /-'bɪlɪtɪ/ n. **illegibly** adv.

illegitimate /ˌɪlɪ'dʒɪtɪmət/ adj. 1 born of parents not married to each other. 2 unlawful. 3 improper. 4 wrongly inferred. □ **illegitimacy** n. **illegitimately** adv.

ill-fated adj. destined to or bringing bad fortune.

ill-favoured adj. unattractive.

ill-founded adj. (of an idea etc.) baseless.

ill-gotten adj. gained unlawfully or wickedly.

ill health n. poor physical or mental condition.

ill humour n. irritability.

illiberal /ɪ'lɪbər(ə)l/ adj. 1 intolerant, narrow-minded 2 without liberal culture; vulgar. 3 stingy; mean. □ **illiberality** /-'rælɪtɪ/ n. **illiberally** adv.

illicit /ɪ'lɪsɪt/ adj. unlawful, forbidden. □ **illicitly** adv.

illiterate /ɪ'lɪtərət/ —adj. 1 unable to read. 2 uneducated. —n. illiterate person. □ **illiteracy** n. **illiterately** adv.

ill-natured adj. churlish, unkind.

illness n. 1 disease 2 being ill.

illogical /ɪ'lɒdʒɪk(ə)l/ adj. devoid of or contrary to logic. □ **illogicality** /-'kælɪtɪ/ n. (pl. -ies), **illogically** adv.

ill-omened adj. doomed.

ill-tempered adj. morose, irritable.

ill-timed adj. done or occurring at an inappropriate time.

ill-treat v. treat badly; abuse.

illuminate /ɪ'luːmɪneɪt/ v. (-ting) 1 light up; make bright. 2 decorate (buildings etc.) with lights. 3 decorate (a manuscript etc.) with gold, colour, etc. 4 help to explain (a subject etc.). 5 enlighten spiritually or intellectually. 6 shed lustre on. □ **illuminating** adj. **illumination** /-'neɪ∫(ə)n/ n. **illuminative** adj. [Latin lumen light]

illumine /ɪ'luːmɪn/ v. (-ning) literary 1 light up; make bright. 2 enlighten.

ill-use v. = ILL-TREAT.

illusion /ɪ'luːʒ(ə)n/ n. 1 false impression or belief. 2 state of being deceived by appearances. 3 figment of the imagination. □ **be under the illusion** (foll. by that) believe mistakenly. □ **illusive** adj. **illusory** adj. [Latin illudo mock]

illusionist n. conjuror.

illustrate /'ɪləstreɪt/ v. (-ting) 1 a provide (a book etc.) with pictures. b elucidate by drawings, pictures,

illustration 438

examples, etc. **2** serve as an example of. □ **illustrator** *n.* [Latin *lustro* light up]

illustration /ˌɪləˈstreɪʃ(ə)n/ *n.* **1** drawing or picture in a book, magazine, etc. **2** explanatory example. **3** illustrating.

illustrative /ˈɪləstrətɪv/ *adj.* (often foll. by *of*) explanatory; exemplary.

illustrious /ɪˈlʌstrɪəs/ *adj.* distinguished, renowned. [Latin *illustris*: related to ILLUSTRATE]

ill will *n.* bad feeling; animosity.

im- *prefix* assim. form of IN-¹, IN-² before *b, m,* or *p.*

I'm /aɪm/ *contr.* I am.

image /ˈɪmɪdʒ/ —*n.* **1** representation of an object, e.g. a statue. **2** reputation or persona of a person, company, etc. **3** appearance as seen in a mirror or through a lens. **4** mental picture or idea. **5** simile or metaphor. —*v.* (**-ging**) **1** make an image of; portray. **2** reflect, mirror. **3** describe or imagine vividly. □ **be the image of** be or look exactly like. [Latin *imago imagin-*]

imagery *n.* **1** figurative illustration, esp. in literature. **2** images; statuary, carving. **3** mental images collectively.

imaginary /ɪˈmædʒɪnərɪ/ *adj.* **1** existing only in the imagination. **2** *Math.* being the square root of a negative quantity. [Latin: related to IMAGE]

imagination /ɪˌmædʒɪˈneɪʃ(ə)n/ *n.* **1** mental faculty of forming images or concepts of objects or situations not existent or not directly experienced. **2** mental creativity or resourcefulness.

imaginative /ɪˈmædʒɪnətɪv/ *adj.* having or showing imagination. □ **imaginatively** *adv.* **imaginativeness** *n.*

imagine /ɪˈmædʒɪn/ *v.* (**-ning**) **1** a form a mental image or concept of. **b** picture to oneself. **2** think of as probable (*can't imagine he'd be so stupid*). **3** guess (*can't imagine what he is doing*). **4** suppose (*I imagine you'll need help*). □ **imaginable** *adj.* [Latin *imaginor*]

imago /ɪˈmeɪɡəʊ/ *n.* (*pl.* **-s** or **imagines** /ɪˈmædʒɪˌniːz/) fully developed stage of an insect, e.g. a butterfly. [Latin: see IMAGE]

imam /ɪˈmɑːm/ *n.* **1** leader of prayers in a mosque. **2** title of various Muslim leaders. [Arabic]

imbalance /ɪmˈbæləns/ *n.* **1** lack of balance. **2** disproportion.

imbecile /ˈɪmbɪˌsiːl/ —*n.* **1** *colloq.* stupid person. **2** person with a mental age of about five. —*adj.* mentally weak; stupid; idiotic. □ **imbecilic** /-ˈsɪlɪk/ *adj.* **imbecility** /-ˈsɪlɪtɪ/ *n.* (*pl.* **-ies**). [French from Latin]

imbed var. of EMBED.

imbibe /ɪmˈbaɪb/ *v.* (**-bing**) **1** drink (esp. alcohol). **2 a** assimilate (ideas etc.). **b**

absorb (moisture etc.). **3** inhale (air etc.). [Latin *bibo* drink]

imbroglio /ɪmˈbrəʊlɪəʊ/ *n.* (*pl.* **-s**) confused or complicated situation. **2** confused heap. [Italian: related to IN-², BROIL]

imbue /ɪmˈbjuː/ *v.* (**-bues**, **-bued**, **-buing**) (often foll. by *with*) **1** inspire or permeate (with feelings, opinions, or qualities). **2** saturate. **3** dye. [Latin *imbuo*]

IMF *abbr.* International Monetary Fund.

imitate /ˈɪmɪˌteɪt/ *v.* (**-ting**) **1** follow the example of; copy. **2** mimic. **3** make a copy of. **4** be like. □ **imitable** *adj.* **imitator** *n.* [Latin *imitor-tat-*]

imitation /ˌɪmɪˈteɪʃ(ə)n/ *n.* **1** imitating or being imitated. **2** copy. **3** counterfeit (often *attrib.*: *imitation leather*).

imitative /ˈɪmɪtətɪv/ *adj.* **1** (often foll. by *of*) imitating; following a model or example. **2** (of a word) reproducing a natural sound (e.g. *fizz*), or otherwise suggestive (e.g. *blob*).

immaculate /ɪˈmækjʊlət/ *adj.* **1** perfectly clean and tidy. **2** perfect (*immaculate timing*). **3** innocent, faultless. □ **immaculately** *adv.* **immaculateness** *n.* [Latin: related to IN-¹, *macula* spot]

Immaculate Conception *n.* *RC Ch.* doctrine that the Virgin Mary was without original sin from conception.

immanent /ˈɪmənənt/ *adj.* **1** (often foll. by *in*) naturally present, inherent. **2** (of God) omnipresent. □ **immanence** *n.* [Latin: related to IN-² *maneo* remain]

immaterial /ˌɪməˈtɪərɪəl/ *adj.* **1** unimportant; irrelevant. **2** not material; incorporeal. □ **immateriality** /-ˈælɪtɪ/ *n.*

immature /ˌɪməˈtjʊə(r)/ *adj.* **1** not mature. **2** undeveloped, esp. emotionally. **3** unripe. □ **immaturely** *adv.* **immaturity** *n.*

immeasurable /ɪˈmeʒərəb(ə)l/ *adj.* not measurable; immense. □ **immeasurably** *adv.*

immediate /ɪˈmiːdɪət/ *adj.* **1** occurring or done at once (*immediate reply*). **2** nearest, next; direct (*immediate vicinity*; *immediate future*; *immediate cause of death*). **3** most pressing or urgent (*our immediate concern*). □ **immediacy** *n.* **immediateness** *n.* [Latin: related to IN-¹, MEDIATE]

immediately —*adv.* **1** without pause or delay. **2** without intermediary. —*conj.* as soon as.

immemorial /ˌɪmɪˈmɔːrɪəl/ *adj.* ancient beyond memory or record (*from time immemorial*).

immense /ɪˈmens/ *adj.* **1** extremely large; huge. **2** considerable (*immense*

difference). □ **immenseness** *n.* **immensity** *n.* [Latin *metior mensus* measure]

immensely *adv.* 1 colloq. very much (*enjoyed myself immensely*). 2 to an immense degree (*immensely rich*).

immerse /ɪˈmɜːs/ *v.* (**-sing**) 1 **a** (often foll. by *in*) dip, plunge. **b** submerge (a person). 2 (often *refl.* or in *passive*; often foll. by *in*) absorb or involve deeply. 3 (often foll. by *in*) bury, embed. [Latin *mergo mers- dip*]

immersion /ɪˈmɜːʃ(ə)n/ *n.* 1 immersing or being immersed. 2 baptism by total bodily immersion. 3 mental absorption.

immersion heater *n.* electric device immersed in a liquid to heat it, esp. in a hot-water tank.

immigrant /ˈɪmɪɡrənt/ *n.* 1 person who immigrates. 2 of immigrants.

immigrate /ˈɪmɪɡreɪt/ *v.* come into a country and settle. –*adj.* 1 immigrating. 2 of immigrants. □ **immigration** /-ˈɡreɪʃ(ə)n/ *n.* [related to IN-², MIGRATE]

imminent /ˈɪmɪnənt/ *adj.* impending; about to happen (*war is imminent*). □ **imminence** *n.* **imminently** *adv.* [Latin *immineo* be impending]

immiscible /ɪˈmɪsɪb(ə)l/ *adj.* (often foll. by *with*) not able to be mixed. □ **immiscibility** /-ˈbɪlɪtɪ/ *n.*

immobile /ɪˈmaʊbaɪl/ *adj.* 1 not moving. 2 unable to move or be moved. □ **immobility** /-ˈbɪlɪtɪ/ *n.*

immobilize /ɪˈmaʊbɪˌlaɪz/ *v.* (also **-ise**) (**-zing** or **-sing**) 1 make or keep immobile. 2 keep (a limb or patient) still for healing purposes. □ **immobilization** /-ˈzeɪʃ(ə)n/ *n.*

immoderate /ɪˈmɒdərət/ *adj.* excessive; lacking moderation. □ **immoderately** *adv.*

immodest /ɪˈmɒdɪst/ *adj.* 1 lacking modesty; conceited. 2 shameless, indecent. □ **immodestly** *adv.* **immodesty** *n.*

immolate /ˈɪməˌleɪt/ *v.* (**-ting**) kill or offer as a sacrifice. □ **immolation** /-ˈleɪʃ(ə)n/ *n.* [Latin, = sprinkle with meal]

immoral /ɪˈmɒr(ə)l/ *adj.* 1 not conforming to accepted morality; morally wrong. 2 sexually promiscuous or deviant. □ **immorality** /ˌɪməˈrælɪtɪ/ *n.* (*pl.* **-ies**). **immorally** *adv.*

immortal /ɪˈmɔːt(ə)l/ –*adj.* 1 **a** living for ever; not mortal. **b** divine. 2 unfading; famous for all time. –*n.* 1 **a** immortal being. **b** (in *pl.*) gods of antiquity. 2 person, esp. an author, remembered long after death. □ **immortality** /ˌɪmɔːˈtælɪtɪ/ *n.* **immortalize** *v.* (also **-ise**) (**-zing** or **-sing**). **immortally** *adv.*

immovable /ɪˈmuːvəb(ə)l/ *adj.* (also **immoveable**) 1 not able to be moved. 2 steadfast, unyielding. 3 emotionless. 4 not subject to change (*immovable law*). 5 motionless. 6 (of property) consisting of land, houses, etc. □ **immovability** *n.* **immovably** *adv.*

immune /ɪˈmjuːn/ *adj.* 1 **a** (often foll. by *against, from, to*) protected against infection through inoculation etc. **b** relating to immunity (*immune system*). 2 (foll. by *from, to*) exempt from or proof against a charge, duty, criticism, etc. [Latin *immunis* exempt]

immunity *n.* (*pl.* **-ies**) 1 ability of an organism to resist infection by means of antibodies and white blood cells. 2 (often foll. by *from*) freedom or exemption.

immunize /ˈɪmjʊˌnaɪz/ *v.* (also **-ise**) (**-zing** or **-sing**) make immune, usu. by inoculation. □ **immunization** /-ˈzeɪʃ(ə)n/ *n.*

immunodeficiency /ˌɪmjʊnəʊ-/ *n.* reduction in normal immune defences.

immunoglobulin /ˌɪmjʊnəʊˈglobjʊlɪn/ *n.* any of a group of related proteins functioning as antibodies.

immunology /ˌɪmjʊˈnɒlədʒɪ/ *n.* the study of immunity. □ **immunological** /-nəˈlɒdʒɪk(ə)l/ *adj.* **immunologist** *n.*

immunotherapy /ˌɪmjʊnəʊˈθerəpɪ/ *n.* prevention or treatment of disease with substances that stimulate the immune response.

immure /ɪˈmjʊə(r)/ *v.* (**-ring**) 1 imprison. 2 *refl.* shut oneself away. [Latin *murus* wall]

immutable /ɪˈmjuːtəb(ə)l/ *adj.* unchangeable. □ **immutability** /-ˈbɪlɪtɪ/ *n.* **immutably** *adv.*

imp *n.* 1 mischievous child. 2 small devil or sprite. [Old English, = young shoot]

impact –*n.* /ˈɪmpækt/ 1 effect of sudden forcible contact; collision. 2 strong effect or impression. –*v.* /ɪmˈpækt/ 1 press or fix firmly. 2 (as **impacted** *adj.*) (of a tooth) wedged between another tooth and the jaw. 3 (often foll. by *on*) have an impact on. □ **impaction** /ɪmˈpækʃ(ə)n/ *n.*

impair /ɪmˈpeə(r)/ *v.* 1 damage, weaken. □ **impairment** *n.* [Latin: related to IMPEJOR]

impala /ɪmˈpɑːlə/ *n.* (*pl.* same or **-s**) small African antelope. [Zulu]

impale /ɪmˈpeɪl/ *v.* (**-ling**) transfix or pierce with a sharp stake etc. □ **impalement** *n.* [Latin *palus* FALE²]

impalpable /ɪmˈpælpəb(ə)l/ *adj.* 1 not easily grasped by the mind; intangible. 2 imperceptible to the touch. 3 (of powder)

impanel var. of EMPANEL.

very fine. □ **impalpability** /-ˈbɪlɪtɪ/ n. **impalpably** adv.

impanel var. of EMPANEL.

impart /ɪmˈpɑːt/ v. (often foll. by to) 1 communicate (news etc.) 2 give a share of (a thing). [Latin: related to PART]

impartial /ɪmˈpɑːʃ(ə)l/ adj. treating all alike; unprejudiced; fair. □ **impartiality** /-ʃɪˈælɪtɪ/ n. **impartially** adv.

impassable /ɪmˈpɑːsəb(ə)l/ adj. not able to be traversed. □ **impassability** /-ˈbɪlɪtɪ/ n. **impassableness** n. **impassably** adv.

impasse /ˈæmpɑːs, ˈɪm-/ n. deadlock. [French: related to PASS¹]

impassible /ɪmˈpæsɪb(ə)l/ adj. 1 impassive. 2 incapable of feeling, emotion, or injury. □ **impassibility** /-ˈbɪlɪtɪ/ n. **impassibly** adv. [Latin patior pass-suffer]

impassioned /ɪmˈpæʃ(ə)nd/ adj. filled with passion; ardent. [Italian impassionato: related to PASSION]

impassive /ɪmˈpæsɪv/ adj. incapable of or not showing emotion; serene. □ **impassively** adv. **impassiveness** n. **impassivity** /-ˈsɪvɪtɪ/ n.

impasto /ɪmˈpæstəʊ/ n. Art technique of laying on paint thickly. [Italian]

impatiens /ɪmˈpeɪʃɪˌenz/ n. any of several plants including the busy Lizzie. [Latin: related to IMPATIENT]

impatient /ɪmˈpeɪʃ(ə)nt/ adj. 1 lacking or showing a lack of patience or tolerance. 2 restlessly eager. 3 (foll. by of) intolerant of. □ **impatience** n. **impatiently** adv.

impeach /ɪmˈpiːtʃ/ v. 1 charge with a crime against the State, esp. treason. 2 US charge (a public official) with misconduct. 3 call in question; disparage. □ **impeachable** adj. **impeachment** n. [French empêcher from Latin pedica fetter]

impeccable /ɪmˈpekəb(ə)l/ adj. faultless; exemplary. □ **impeccability** /-ˈbɪlɪtɪ/ n. **impeccably** adv. [related to IN¹, Latin pecco sin]

impecunious /ˌɪmpɪˈkjuːnɪəs/ adj. having little or no money. □ **impecuniosity** /-ˈɒsɪtɪ/ n. **impecuniousness** n. [related to PECUNIARY]

impedance /ɪmˈpiːd(ə)ns/ n. total effective resistance of an electric circuit etc. to an alternating current. [from IMPEDE]

■ **Usage** Impedance is sometimes confused with impediment, which means 'a hindrance' or 'a speech defect'.

impede /ɪmˈpiːd/ v. (-**ding**) obstruct; hinder. [Latin impedio from pes ped-foot]

impediment /ɪmˈpedɪmənt/ n. 1 hindrance or obstruction. 2 speech defect,

e.g. a stammer. [Latin: related to IMPEDE]

■ **Usage** See note at impedance.

impedimenta /ɪmˌpedɪˈmentə/ n.pl. 1 encumbrances. 2 baggage, esp. of an army.

impel /ɪmˈpel/ v. (-**ll**-) 1 drive, force, or urge. 2 propel. [Latin pello drive]

impend /ɪmˈpend/ v. (often foll. by over) 1 (of a danger, event, etc.) be threatening or imminent. 2 hang. □ **impending** adj. [Latin pendeo hang]

impenetrable /ɪmˈpenɪtrəb(ə)l/ adj. 1 not able to be penetrated. 2 inscrutable. 3 inaccessible to ideas, influences, etc. □ **impenetrability** /-ˈbɪlɪtɪ/ n. **impenetrableness** n. **impenetrably** adv.

impenitent /ɪmˈpenɪt(ə)nt/ adj. not sorry, unrepentant. □ **impenitence** n.

imperative /ɪmˈperətɪv/ —adj. 1 urgent; obligatory. 2 commanding, peremptory. 3 Gram. (of a mood) expressing a command (e.g. come here!). —n. 1 Gram. imperative mood. 2 command. 3 essential or urgent thing. [Latin impero command]

imperceptible /ˌɪmpəˈseptɪb(ə)l/ adj. 1 not perceptible. 2 very slight, gradual, or subtle. □ **imperceptibility** /-ˈbɪlɪtɪ/ n. **imperceptibly** adv.

imperfect /ɪmˈpɜːfɪkt/ —adj. 1 not perfect; faulty, incomplete. 2 Gram. (of a tense) denoting action in progress but not completed (e.g. they were singing). —n. imperfect tense. □ **imperfectly** adv.

imperfection /ˌɪmpəˈfek(ʃ)ən/ n. 1 state of being imperfect. 2 fault, blemish.

imperial /ɪmˈpɪərɪəl/ adj. 1 of or characteristic of an empire or similar sovereign State. 2 a of an emperor. b majestic, august; authoritative. 3 (of non-metric weights and measures) statutory in the UK, esp. formerly (imperial gallon). □ **imperially** adv. [Latin imperium do-minion]

imperialism n. 1 imperial rule or system. 2 usu. derog. policy of dominating other nations by acquiring dependencies etc. □ **imperialist** n. & adj. **imperialistic** /-ˈlɪstɪk/ adj.

imperil /ɪmˈperɪl/ v. (-**ll**-; US -**l**-) endanger.

imperious /ɪmˈpɪərɪəs/ adj. overbearing, domineering. □ **imperiously** adv. **imperiousness** n.

imperishable /ɪmˈperɪʃəb(ə)l/ adj. not able to perish, indestructible.

impermanent /ɪmˈpɜːmənənt/ adj. not permanent. □ **impermanence** n. **impermanency** n.

impermeable /im'pɜːməb(ə)l/ adj. not permeable, not allowing fluids to pass through. □ **impermeability** /-'biliti/ n.

impermissible /ˌimpə'misib(ə)l/ adj. not allowable.

impersonal /im'pɜːsən(ə)l/ adj. 1 without personal reference or connection; objective, impartial. 2 without human attributes; cold, unfeeling. 3 Gram. a (of a verb) used esp. with it as a subject (it is snowing). b (of a pronoun) = INDEF. INTE. □ **impersonality** /-'næliti/ n. **impersonally** adv.

impersonate /im'pɜːsəneit/ v. (-ting) 1 pretend to be (another person), esp. as entertainment or fraud. 2 act (a character). □ **impersonation** /-'neiʃ(ə)n/ n. **impersonator** n. [from IN-², Latin PERSONA]

impertinent /im'pɜːtinənt/ adj. 1 insolent, disrespectful. 2 Law irrelevant. □ **impertinence** n. **impertinently** adv.

imperturbable /ˌimpə'tɜːbəb(ə)l/ adj. not excitable; calm. □ **imperturbability** /-'biliti/ n. **imperturbably** adv.

impervious /im'pɜːviəs/ adj. (usu. foll. by to) 1 impermeable. 2 not responsive (to argument etc.).

impetigo /ˌimpi'taigəʊ/ n. contagious skin infection forming pimples and sores. [Latin impeto assail]

impetuous /im'petjuəs/ adj. 1 acting or done rashly or with sudden energy. 2 moving forcefully or rapidly. □ **impetuosity** /-'ɒsiti/ n. **impetuously** adv. **impetuousness** n. [Latin: related to IMPETUS]

impetus /'impitəs/ n. 1 force with which a body moves. 2 driving force or impulse. [Latin impeto]

impiety /im'paiəti/ n. (pl. -ies) 1 lack of piety or reverence. 2 ac etc. showing this.

impinge /im'pindʒ/ v. (-ging) (usu. foll. by on, upon) 1 make an impact or effect. 2 encroach. □ **impingement** n. [Latin pango pact- fix]

impious /'impiəs/ adj. 1 not pious. 2 wicked, profane.

impish adj. of or like an imp. mischievous. □ **impishly** adv. **impishness** n.

implacable /im'plækəb(ə)l/ adj. unable to be appeased. □ **implacability** /-'biliti/ n. **implacably** adv.

implant —v. /im'plɑːnt/ 1 (often foll. by in) insert or fix. 2 (often foll. by in) instil (an idea etc.) in a person's mind. 3 plant. 4 a insert (tissue etc.) in a living body. b (in passive) (of a fertilized ovum) become attached to the wall of the womb. —n. /'implɑːnt/ thing implanted, esp. a piece of tissue. □ **implantation** /-'teiʃ(ə)n/ n. [Latin: related to PLANT]

implausible /im'plɔːzib(ə)l/ adj. not plausible. □ **implausibility** /-'biliti/ n. **implausibly** adv.

implement —n. /'impliment/ tool, instrument, utensil. —v. /'impliment/ put (a decision, plan, contract, etc.) into effect. □ **implementation** /ˌimplimen'teiʃ(ə)n/ n. [Latin impleo fulfil]

implicate /'implikeit/ v. (-ting) 1 (often foll. by in) show (a person) to be involved (in a crime etc.). 2 imply. [Latin plico fold]

implication /ˌimpli'keiʃ(ə)n/ n. 1 thing implied. 2 implicating or implying.

implicit /im'plisit/ adj. 1 implied though not plainly expressed. 2 absolute, unquestioning (implicit belief). □ **implicitly** adv. [Latin: related to IMPLICATE]

implode /im'pləʊd/ v. (-ding) (cause to) burst inwards. □ **implosion** /im'pləʊʒ(ə)n/ n. [from IN-², cf. EXPLODE]

implore /im'plɔː(r)/ v. (-ring) 1 (often foll. by to + infin.) entreat (a person). 2 beg earnestly for. [Latin ploro weep]

imply /im'plai/ v. (-ies, -ied) 1 (often foll. by that) strongly suggest or insinuate without directly stating (what are you implying?). 2 signify, esp. as a consequence (silence implies guilt). [Latin: related to IMPLICATE]

impolite /ˌimpə'lait/ adj. ill-mannered, uncivil, rude. □ **impolitely** adv. **impoliteness** n.

impolitic /im'pɒlitik/ adj. inexpedient, unwise. □ **impoliticly** adv.

imponderable /im'pɒndərəb(ə)l/ —adj. 1 not able to be estimated 2 very light; weightless. —n. (usu. in pl.) imponderable thing. □ **imponderably** adv.

import —v. /im'pɔːt, 'impɔːt/ 1 bring in (esp. foreign goods or services) to a country. 2 imply, indicate, signify. —n. /'impɔːt/ 1 (esp. in pl.) imported article or service. 2 importing. 3 what is implied; meaning. 4 importance. □ **importation** /ˌimpɔː'teiʃ(ə)n/ n. **importer** /im'pɔːtə(r)/ n. [Latin importo carry in]

important /im'pɔːt(ə)nt/ adj. 1 (often foll. by to) of great effect or concern. 2 (of a person) having high rank or authority. 3 pompous. □ **importance** n. **importantly** adv. [Latin importo carry in, signify]

importunate /im'pɔːtjunət/ adj. making persistent or pressing requests. □ **importunity** /ˌimpɔː'tjuːniti/ n. [Latin importunus inconvenient]

importune /ˌimpɔː'tjuːn/ v. (-ning) 1 pester (a person) with requests. 2 solicit (a person) for immoral purposes. [Latin: as IMPORTUNATE]

impose /im'pəʊz/ v. (-sing) 1 (often foll. by on, upon) lay (a tax, duty, charge, or...

imposing obligation) on. **2** enforce compliance with. **3** also *refl.* (foll. by *on, upon,* or *absol.*) take advantage of (*will not impose on you any longer*). **4** (often foll. by *on, upon*) inflict (a thing) on. [Latin *impono*]

'**imposing** *adj.* impressive, formidable, esp. in appearance.

imposition /ˌɪmpəˈzɪʃ(ə)n/ *n.* **1** imposing or being imposed. **2** unfair demand or burden. **3** tax, duty.

impossible /ɪmˈpɒsɪb(ə)l/ *adj.* **1** not possible. **2** *colloq.* not easy, convenient, or believable. **3** *colloq.* (esp. of a person) outrageous, intolerable. □ **impossibility** /-ˈbɪlɪtɪ/ *n.* (*pl.* **-ies**). **impossibly** *adv.*

impost¹ /ˈɪmpəʊst/ *n.* tax, duty, or tribute. [Latin *impono impost-* impose]

impost² /ˈɪmpəʊst/ *n.* upper course of a pillar, carrying an arch.

impostor /ɪmˈpɒstə(r)/ *n.* (also **imposter**) **1** person who assumes a false character or pretends to be someone else. **2** swindler.

imposture /ɪmˈpɒstʃə(r)/ *n.* fraudulent deception.

impotent /ˈɪmpət(ə)nt/ *adj.* **1** powerless, ineffective. **2** (of a male) unable to achieve an erection or orgasm. □ **impotence** *n.*

impound /ɪmˈpaʊnd/ *v.* **1** confiscate. **2** take legal possession of. **3** shut up (animals) in a pound.

impoverish /ɪmˈpɒvərɪʃ/ *v.* make poor. □ **impoverishment** *n.* [French: related to POVERTY]

impracticable /ɪmˈpræktɪkəb(ə)l/ *adj.* not practicable. □ **impracticability** /-ˈbɪlɪtɪ/ *n.* **impracticably** *adv.*

impractical /ɪmˈpræktɪk(ə)l/ *adj.* **1** not practical. **2** esp. *US* not practicable. □ **impracticality** /-ˈkælɪtɪ/ *n.* **impractically** *adv.*

imprecate /ˈɪmprɪˌkeɪt/ *v.* (**-ting**) *formal* oath, curse. [Latin *precor* pray]

imprecation /ˌɪmprɪˈkeɪʃ(ə)n/ *n.* oath, curse. [Latin *precor* pray]

imprecise /ˌɪmprɪˈsaɪs/ *adj.* not precise. □ **imprecisely** *adv.* **impreciseness** *n.*

imprecision /ˌɪmprɪˈsɪʒ(ə)n/ *n.*

impregnable /ɪmˈpregnəb(ə)l/ *adj.* strong enough to be secure against attack. □ **impregnability** /-ˈbɪlɪtɪ/ *n.* **impregnably** *adv.* [French: related to IN-, Latin *prehendo* take]

impregnate /ˈɪmpreɡˌneɪt/ *v.* (**-ting**) **1** (often foll. by *with*) fill or saturate. **2** (often foll. by *with*) imbue (with feelings etc.). **3 a** make (a female) pregnant. **b** fertilize (an ovum). □ **impregnation** /-ˈneɪʃ(ə)n/ *n.* [Latin: related to PREGNANT]

impresario /ˌɪmprɪˈsɑːrɪəʊ/ *n.* (*pl.* **-s**) organizer of public entertainment, esp. a theatrical etc. manager. [Italian]

impress —*v.* /ɪmˈpres/ **1** (often foll. by *with*) **a** affect or influence deeply. **b** affect (a person) favourably (*was most impressed*). **2** (often foll. by *on*) emphasize (an idea etc.) (*must impress on you the need to be prompt*). **3 a** (often foll. by *on*) imprint or make (a mark). **b** mark (a thing) with a stamp, seal, etc. —*n.* /ˈɪmpres/ **1** mark made by a seal, stamp, etc. **2** characteristic mark or quality. □ **impressible** /ɪmˈpresɪb(ə)l/ *adj.* [French: related to PRESS¹]

impression /ɪmˈpreʃ(ə)n/ *n.* **1** effect (esp. on the mind or feelings). **2** notion or belief (esp. vague or mistaken). **3** imitation of a person or sound, esp. as entertainment. **4 a** impressing. **b** mark impressed. **5** unaltered reprint from standing type or plates. **6** number of copies of a book etc. issued at one time. **7** print taken from a wood or copper engraving.

impressionable *adj.* easily influenced. □ **impressionability** /-ˈbɪlɪtɪ/ *n.* **impressionably** *adv.*

impressionism /ɪmˈpreʃəˌnɪz(ə)m/ *n.* **1** style or movement in art concerned with conveying the effect of natural light on objects. **2** style of music or writing seeking to convey esp. fleeting feelings or experience. □ **impressionist** *n.* **impressionistic** /-ˈnɪstɪk/ *adj.*

impressive /ɪmˈpresɪv/ *adj.* arousing respect, approval, or admiration. □ **impressively** *adv.* **impressiveness** *n.*

imprimatur /ˌɪmprɪˈmɑːtə(r)/ *n.* **1** *RC Ch.* licence to print (a religious book etc.). **2** official approval. [Latin, = let it be printed]

■ **Usage** *Imprimatur* is sometimes confused with sense 2 of *imprint.*

imprint —*v.* /ɪmˈprɪnt/ **1** (often foll. by *on*) impress firmly, esp. on the mind. **2 a** (often foll. by *on*) make a stamp or impression of (a figure etc.) on a thing. **b** make an impression on (a thing) with a stamp etc. —*n.* /ˈɪmprɪnt/ **1** impression, stamp. **2** printer's or publisher's name etc. printed in a book.

■ **Usage** See note at *imprimatur.*

imprison /ɪmˈprɪz(ə)n/ *v.* **1** put in prison. **2** confine. □ **imprisonment** *n.*

improbable /ɪmˈprɒbəb(ə)l/ *adj.* **1** unlikely. **2** difficult to believe. □ **improbability** /-ˈbɪlɪtɪ/ *n.* **improbably** *adv.*

improbity /ɪmˈprəʊbɪtɪ/ *n.* (*pl.* **-ies**) **1** wickedness; dishonesty. **2** wicked or dishonest act.

impromptu /ɪmˈprɒmptjuː/ —*adj.* & *adv.* extempore, unrehearsed. —*n.* (*pl.* **-s**) **1** extempore performance or speech.

improper

2 short, usu. solo, instrumental composition, often improvisatory in style. [French from Latin *in promptu* in readiness]

improper /ɪmˈprɒpə(r)/ *adj.* 1 unseemly; indecent. 2 inaccurate, wrong. □ **improperly** *adv.*

improper fraction *n.* fraction in which the numerator is greater than or equal to the denominator.

impropriety /ˌɪmprəˈpraɪətɪ/ *n.* (*pl.* **-ies**) 1 lack of propriety; indecency. 2 instance of this. 3 incorrectness.

improve /ɪmˈpruːv/ *v.* (**-ving**) 1 a make or become better. b (foll. by *on*, *upon*) produce something better than. 2 (as **improving** *adj.*) giving moral benefit (*improving literature*). □ **improvable** *adj.* **improvement** *n.* [Anglo-French *emprouer* from French *prou* profit]

improvident /ɪmˈprɒvɪd(ə)nt/ *adj.* 1 lacking foresight. 2 profligate; wasteful. 3 incautious. □ **improvidence** *n.* **improvidently** *adv.*

improvise /ˈɪmprəvaɪz/ *v.* (**-sing**) (also *absol.*) 1 compose or perform (music, verse, etc.) extempore. 2 provide or construct from materials not intended for the purpose. □ **improvisation** *n.* **improvisational** *adj.* **improvisatory** *adj.*

imprudent /ɪmˈpruːd(ə)nt/ *adj.* unwise, indiscreet. □ **imprudence** *n.* **imprudently** *adv.*

impudent /ˈɪmpjʊd(ə)nt/ *adj.* impertinent. □ **impudence** *n.* **impudently** *adv.*

impugn /ɪmˈpjuːn/ *v.* challenge or call in question. □ **impugnment** *n.* [Latin *pugno* fight]

impulse /ˈɪmpʌls/ *n.* 1 a sudden urge (*felt an impulse to laugh*). 2 tendency to follow such urges (*man of impulse*). 3 impelling; a push. 4 impetus. 5 *Physics* a large temporary force producing a change of momentum (e.g. a hammer blow). b wave of excitation in a nerve. □ **on impulse**.

impulse buying *n.* purchasing goods on impulse.

impulsion /ɪmˈpʌlʃ(ə)n/ *n.* 1 impelling. 2 mental impulse. 3 impetus.

impulsive /ɪmˈpʌlsɪv/ *adj.* 1 tending to act on impulse. 2 done on impulse. 3 tending to impel. □ **impulsively** *adv.* **impulsiveness** *n.*

impunity /ɪmˈpjuːnɪtɪ/ *n.* exemption from punishment, bad consequences, etc. □ **with impunity** without punishment etc. [Latin *poena* penalty]

impure /ɪmˈpjʊə(r)/ *adj.* 1 adulterated. 2 dirty. 3 unchaste.

impurity *n.* (*pl.* **-ies**) 1 being impure. 2 impure thing or part.

impute /ɪmˈpjuːt/ *v.* (**-ting**) (foll. by *to*) attribute (a fault etc.) to. □ **imputation** /-ˈteɪʃ(ə)n/ *n.* [Latin *puto* reckon]

In *symb.* indium.

in- *prep.* 1 expressing inclusion or position within limits of space, time, circumstance, etc. (*in England; in bed; in 1989; in the rain*). 2 a within (a certain time) (*finished it in two hours*). b after (a certain time) (*will be leaving in an hour*). 3 with respect to (*blind in one eye; good in parts*. 4 as a proportionate part of (*one in three failed; gradient of one in six*). 5 with the form or arrangement of (*packed in tens; falling in folds*). 6 as a member of (*in the army*). 7 involved with (*is in banking*). 8 as the content of (*there is something in what you say*). 9 within the ability of (*does he have it in him?*). 10 having the condition of; affected by (*in bad health; in danger*). 11 having as a purpose (*in search of; in reply to*). 12 by means of or using as material (*drawn in pencil; modelled in bronze*). 13 a using as the language of expression (*written in French*). b (of music) having as its key (*symphony in C*). 14 (of a word) having as a beginning or ending (*words in un-*). 15 wearing (*in blue; in a suit*). 16 with the identity of (*found a friend in Mary*). 17 (of an animal) pregnant with (*in calf*). 18 into (with a verb of motion or change; *put it in the box; cut it in two*). 19 introducing an indirect object after a verb (*believe in; engage in; share in*). 20 forming adverbial phrases (*in any case; in reality; in short*). —*adv.* expressing position within limits, or motion to such a position: 1 into a room, house, etc. (*come in*). 2 at home, in one's office, etc. (*is not in*). 3 so as to be enclosed (*locked in*). 4 in a publication (*is the advert in?*). 5 in or to the inward side (*rub it in*). 6 a in fashion or season (*long skirts are in*). b elected or in office (*Democrats got in*). 7 (of luck) favourable (*their luck was in*). 8 *Cricket* (of a player or side) batting. 9 (of transport) at the platform etc. (*the train is in*). 10 (of a season, harvest, order, etc.) having arrived or been received. 11 (of a fire) continuing to burn. 12 denoting effective action (*join in*). 13 (of the tide) at the highest point. 14 (*in comb.*) *collog.* denoting prolonged concerted action, esp. by large numbers (*sit-in; teach-in*). —*adj.* 1 internal; living in (*in-patient*). 2 fashionable (*the in thing to do*). 3 confined to a small group (*in-joke*). □ **in all** see ALL. **in between** see

in. BETWEEN *adv.* **in for 1** about to undergo or get. **2** competing in or for. **in on** sharing in; privy to. **ins and outs** (often foll. by *of*) all the details. **in so far as** see FAR. **in that** because; in so far as. **in with** on good terms with; favourably placed for (*in with a chance*). [Old English]

in., *abbr.* inch(es).

in-[1] *prefix* (also **il-**, **im-**, **ir-**) added to: **1** adjectives, meaning 'not' (*inedible*; *insane*). **2** nouns, meaning 'without, lacking' (*inaction*). [Latin]

in-[2] *prefix* (also **il-**, **im-**, **ir-**) in, on, into, towards, within (*induce*, *influx*, *insight*; *intrude*). [from IN, or from Latin *in* (prep.)]

inability /ˌɪnəˈbɪlɪtɪ/ *n.* **1** being unable. **2** lack of power or means.

in absentia /ˌɪn æbˈsentɪə/ *adv.* in (his, her, or their) absence. [Latin]

inaccessible /ˌɪnækˈsesɪb(ə)l/ *adj.* **1** not accessible. **2** (of a person) unapproachable. □ **inaccessibility** /-ˈbɪlɪtɪ/ *n.*

inaccurate /ɪnˈækjʊrət/ *adj.* not accurate. □ **inaccuracy** *n.* (*pl.* -ies). **inaccurately** *adv.*

inaction /ɪnˈækʃ(ə)n/ *n.* lack of action.

inactive /ɪnˈæktɪv/ *adj.* **1** not active. **2** not operating. **3** indolent. □ **inactivity** /-ˈtɪvɪtɪ/ *n.*

inadequate /ɪnˈædɪkwət/ *adj.* **1** not adequate; insufficient. **2** (of a person) incompetent; weak. □ **inadequacy** *n.* (*pl.* -ies). **inadequately** *adv.*

inadmissible /ˌɪnədˈmɪsɪb(ə)l/ *adj.* that cannot be admitted or allowed. □ **inadmissibility** /-ˈbɪlɪtɪ/ *n.* **inadmissibly** *adv.*

inadvertent /ˌɪnədˈvɜːt(ə)nt/ *adj.* **1** unintentional. **2** negligent, inattentive. □ **inadvertence** *n.* **inadvertently** *adv.* [from IN-[1], ADVERT[2]]

inadvisable /ˌɪnədˈvaɪzəb(ə)l/ *adj.* not advisable. □ **inadvisability** /-ˈbɪlɪtɪ/ *n.*

inalienable /ɪnˈeɪlɪənəb(ə)l/ *adj.* that cannot be transferred to another or taken away (*inalienable rights*).

inamorato /ɪnˌæməˈrɑːtəʊ/ *n.* (*fem.* **inamorata** /-s/) *literary* lover. [Italian *inamorato*: related to IN-[2], Latin *amor* love]

inane /ɪˈneɪn/ *adj.* **1** silly, senseless. **2** empty, void. □ **inanely** *adv.* **inanity** /-ˈænɪtɪ/ *n.* (*pl.* -ies). [Latin *inanis*]

inanimate /ɪnˈænɪmət/ *adj.* **1** not endowed with, or deprived of, animal life (*an inanimate object*). **2** spiritless, dull.

inapplicable /ˌɪnəˈplɪkəb(ə)l/ *adj.* (often foll. by *to*) not applicable or relevant. □ **inapplicability** /-ˈbɪlɪtɪ/ *n.*

inapposite /ɪnˈæpəzɪt/ *adj.* not apposite.

inappropriate /ˌɪnəˈprəʊprɪət/ *adj.* not appropriate. □ **inappropriately** *adv.* **inappropriateness** *n.*

inapt /ɪnˈæpt/ *adj.* **1** not apt or suitable. **2** unskilful. □ **inaptitude** *n.*

inarticulate /ˌɪnɑːˈtɪkjʊlət/ *adj.* **1** unable to express oneself clearly. **2** (of speech) not articulate; indistinct. **3** dumb. **4** esp. *Anat.* not jointed. □ **inarticulately** *adv.*

inasmuch /ˌɪnəzˈmʌtʃ/ *adv.* (foll. by *as*) **1** since, because. **2** to the extent that. [from *in as much*]

inattentive /ˌɪnəˈtentɪv/ *adj.* **1** not paying attention. **2** neglecting to show courtesy. □ **inattention** *n.* **inattentively** *adv.*

inaudible /ɪnˈɔːdɪb(ə)l/ *adj.* unable to be heard. □ **inaudibly** *adv.*

inaugural /ɪˈnɔːɡjʊr(ə)l/ *—adj.* of or for an inauguration. *—n.* inaugural speech, lecture, etc. [French from Latin *auguro* take omens: related to AUGUR]

inaugurate /ɪˈnɔːɡjʊreɪt/ *v.* (-ting) **1** admit formally to office. **2** begin (an undertaking) or initiate the public use of (a building etc.), with a ceremony. **3** begin, introduce. □ **inauguration** /-ˈreɪʃ(ə)n/ *n.* **inaugurator** *n.*

inauspicious /ˌɪnɔːˈspɪʃəs/ *adj.* **1** illomened, not favourable. **2** unlucky. □ **inauspiciously** *adv.* **inauspiciousness** *n.*

in-between *attrib. adj. colloq.* intermediate.

inboard /ˈɪnbɔːd/ *—adv.* within the sides or towards the centre of a ship, aircraft, or vehicle. *—adj.* situated inboard.

inborn /ɪnˈbɔːn, ˈɪnbɔːn/ *adj.* existing from birth; natural, innate.

inbred /ɪnˈbred/ *adj.* **1** inborn. **2** produced by inbreeding.

inbreeding /ˈɪnbriːdɪŋ/ *n.* breeding from closely related animals or persons. □ **inbreed** *v.* (*past* and *past part.* **-bred**).

inbuilt /ˈɪnbɪlt/ *adj.* built-in.

Inc. *abbr.* US Incorporated.

Inca /ˈɪŋkə/ *n.* member of a people of Peru before the Spanish conquest. [Quechua, = lord]

incalculable /ɪnˈkælkjʊləb(ə)l/ *adj.* **1** too great for calculation. **2** not calculable beforehand. **3** uncertain, unpredictable. □ **incalculability** /-ˈbɪlɪtɪ/ *n.* **incalculably** *adv.*

incandesce /ˌɪnkænˈdes/ *v.* (-cing) (cause to) glow with heat.

incandescent *adj.* **1** glowing white with heat. **2** shining. **3** (of artificial light) produced by a glowing filament etc. □ **incandescence** *n.* [Latin *candeo* be white]

incantation

incantation /ˌɪnkænˈteɪʃ(ə)n/ n. magical formula; spell, charm. □ **incantational** adj. [Latin canto sing]

incapable /ɪnˈkeɪpəb(ə)l/ adj. **1 a** not capable. **b** too honest, kind, etc. to do something (incapable of hurting anyone). **2** not capable of rational conduct (drunk and incapable). □ **incapability** /-ˈbɪlɪtɪ/ n. **incapably** adv.

incapacitate /ˌɪnkəˈpæsɪteɪt/ v.t. (-ting) make incapable or unfit.

incapacity /ˌɪnkəˈpæsɪtɪ/ n. **1** inability, lack of power. **2** legal disqualification.

incarcerate /ɪnˈkɑːsəreɪt/ v.t. (-ting) imprison. □ **incarceration** /-ˈreɪʃ(ə)n/ n. [medieval Latin carcer prison]

incarnate —adj. /ɪnˈkɑːneɪt/ embodied in flesh, esp. in human form (is the devil incarnate). —v. /ˈɪnkɑːneɪt/ ·ˈkɑːneɪt/ **1** embody in flesh. **2** put (an idea etc.) into concrete form. **3** be the living embodiment of (a quality). [Latin incarno -cens: set fire to]

incarnation /ˌɪnkɑːˈneɪʃ(ə)n/ n. **1 a** embodiment in (esp. human) flesh. **b** (the Incarnation) the embodiment of God in Christ. **2** (often foll. by of) living type (of a quality etc.).

incautious /ɪnˈkɔːʃəs/ adj. heedless, rash. □ **incautiously** adv.

incendiary /ɪnˈsendɪərɪ/ —adj. **1** (of a bomb) designed to cause fires. **2 a** of arson. **b** guilty of arson. **3** inflammatory. —n. (pl. -ies) **1** incendiary bomb. **2** arsonist. □ **incendiarism** n. [Latin incendo -cens set fire to]

incense¹ /ˈɪnsens/ n. **1** gum or spice producing a sweet smell when burned. **2** smoke of this, esp. in religious ceremonial. [Church Latin incensum]

incense² /ɪnˈsens/ v. (-sing) make angry. [Latin: related to INCENDIARY]

incentive /ɪnˈsentɪv/ —n. **1** motive or incitement. **2** payment or concession encouraging effort in work. —attrib. adj. serving to motivate or incite (incentive scheme). [Latin incentivus that sets the tune]

inception /ɪnˈsepʃ(ə)n/ n. beginning. [Latin incipio -cept- begin]

inceptive /ɪnˈseptɪv/ adj. **1 a** beginning. **b** initial. **2** (of a verb) denoting the beginning of an action.

incessant /ɪnˈses(ə)nt/ adj. unceasing, continual, repeated. □ **incessantly** adv. [Latin cesso cease]

incest /ˈɪnsest/ n. sexual intercourse between persons too closely related to marry. [Latin castus chaste]

incestuous /ɪnˈsestjʊəs/ adj. **1** of or guilty of incest. **2** having relationships restricted to a particular group or organization. □ **incestuously** adv.

inch —n. **1** linear measure of ¹/₁₂ of a foot (2.54 cm) **2** (as a unit of map-scale) depth of water. **3** (as a unit of rainfall) 1 inch of water. **4** small amount (usu. with neg.: would not yield an inch). —v. move gradually. □ **every inch** entirely (looked every inch a queen). **within an inch of** almost to the point of. [Old English from Latin uncia OUNCE]

incidence /ˈɪnsɪd(ə)ns/ n. **1** (often foll. by of) range, scope, extent, or rate of occurrence or influence (of disease, tax, etc.). **2** falling of a line, ray, particles, etc., on a surface. **3** coming into contact with a thing. [Latin cado fall]

incident —n. **1** occurrence, esp. a minor one. **2** public disturbance (the march took place without incident). **3** clash of armed forces (frontier incident). **4** distinct piece of action in a play, film, etc. —adj. **1** (often foll. by to) apt to occur; naturally attaching. **2** (often foll. by on, upon) (of light etc.) falling. [Latin cado fall]

incidental /ˌɪnsɪˈdent(ə)l/ —adj. (often foll. by to) **1** small and relatively unimportant; minor; supplementary. **2** not essential. —n. (usu. in pl.) minor detail, expense, event, etc.

incidentally adv. **1** by the way. **2** in an incidental way.

incidental music n. background music in a film, broadcast, etc.

incinerate /ɪnˈsɪnəreɪt/ v. (-ting) burn to ashes. □ **incineration** /-ˈreɪʃ(ə)n/ n. [medieval Latin cinis ciner- ashes]

incinerator n. furnace or device for incineration.

incipient /ɪnˈsɪpɪənt/ adj. **1** beginning. **2** in an early stage. [Latin incipio begin]

incise /ɪnˈsaɪz/ v.t. (-sing) **1** make a cut in. **2** engrave. [Latin caedo cut]

incision /ɪnˈsɪʒ(ə)n/ n. **1** cutting, esp. by a surgeon. **2** cut made in this way.

incisive /ɪnˈsaɪsɪv/ adj. **1** sharp. **2** clear and effective.

incisor /ɪnˈsaɪzə(r)/ n. cutting-tooth, esp. at the front of the mouth.

incite /ɪnˈsaɪt/ v.t. (-ting) (often foll. by to) urge or stir up. □ **incitement** n. [Latin cito rouse]

incivility /ˌɪnsɪˈvɪlɪtɪ/ n. (pl. -ies) **1** rudeness. **2** impolite act.

inclement /ɪnˈklemənt/ adj. (of the weather) severe or stormy. □ **in-**

■ **Usage** Inchoate is sometimes used incorrectly to mean 'chaotic' or 'incoherent'.

inchoate /ɪnˈkəʊeɪt/ adj. **1** just begun. **2** undeveloped. □ **inchoation** /-ˈeɪʃ(ə)n/ n. **inchoately** adv. [Latin inchoo, incoho begin]

inclination /ɪnklɪˈneɪʃ(ə)n/ n. 1 disposition or propensity. 2 liking, affection. 3 slope, slant. 4 angle between lines. 5 dip of a magnetic needle. 6 slow nod of the head. [Latin: related to INCLINE]

incline —v. /ɪnˈklaɪn/ (-ning) 1 (usu. in passive) a dispose or influence (am inclined to think so; does not incline me to agree; don't feel inclined). b have a specified tendency (the door is inclined to bang). 2 a be disposed (I incline to think so). b (often foll. by to, towards) tend. 3 (cause to) lean, usu. from the vertical; slope. 4 bend forward or downward. —n. /ˈɪnklaɪn/ slope. □ incline one's ear listen favourably. [Latin clino bend]

inclined plane n. sloping plane used e.g. to reduce work in raising a load.

include /ɪnˈkluːd/ v. (-ding) 1 comprise or reckon in as part of a whole. 2 (as including prep.) if we include (six, including me). 3 put in a certain category etc. □ **inclusion** /-ʒ(ə)n/ n. [Latin includo clus- enclose, from claudo shut]

inclusive /ɪnˈkluːsɪv/ adj. 1 (often foll. by of) including. 2 including the limits stated (pages 7 to 26 inclusive). 3 including all or much (inclusive terms). □ **inclusively** adv. **inclusiveness** n.

incognito /ɪnkɒɡˈniːtəʊ/ —predic. adj. & adv. with one's name or identity kept secret. —n. (pl. -s) 1 person who is incognito. 2 pretended identity. [Italian, = unknown: related to IN¹, COGNITION]

incognizant /ɪnˈkɒɡnɪz(ə)nt/ adj. formal unaware. □ **incognizance** n.

incoherent /ɪnkəʊˈhɪərənt/ adj. 1 unintelligible. 2 lacking logic or consistency; not clear. □ **incoherence** n. **incoherently** adv.

incombustible /ɪnkəmˈbʌstɪb(ə)l/ adj. that cannot be burnt.

income /ˈɪnkʌm/ n. money received, esp. periodically or in a year, from one's work, investments, etc. [from IN, COME]

income tax n. tax levied on income.

incoming —adj. 1 coming in (incoming telephone calls). 2 succeeding another (incoming tenant). —n. (usu. in pl.) revenue, income.

incommensurable /ɪnkəˈmenʃərəb(ə)l/ adj. (often foll. by with) 1 not commensurable. 2 having no common factor, integral or fractional. □ **incommensurability** /-ˈbɪlɪtɪ/ n.

incommensurate /ɪnkəˈmenʃərət/ adj. 1 (often foll. by with, to) out of proportion; inadequate. 2 = INCOMMENSURABLE.

incommode /ɪnkəˈməʊd/ v. (-ding) formal 1 inconvenience. 2 trouble, annoy. □ **incommodious** adj. formal too small for comfort; inconvenient.

incommunicable /ɪnkəˈmjuːnɪkəb(ə)l/ adj. that cannot be communicated.

incommunicado /ɪnkəˌmjuːnɪˈkɑːdəʊ/ adj. 1 without means of communication. 2 (of a prisoner) in solitary confinement. [Spanish incomunicado]

incommunicative /ɪnkəˈmjuːnɪkətɪv/ adj. uncommunicative.

incomparable /ɪnˈkɒmpərəb(ə)l/ adj. without an equal; matchless. □ **incomparability** /-ˈbɪlɪtɪ/ n. **incomparably** adv.

incompatible /ɪnkəmˈpatɪb(ə)l/ adj. not compatible. □ **incompatibility** /-ˈbɪlɪtɪ/ n.

incompetent /ɪnˈkɒmpɪt(ə)nt/ —adj. lacking the necessary skill. —n. incompetent person. □ **incompetence** n. **incompetency** n.

incomplete /ɪnkəmˈpliːt/ adj. not complete.

incomprehensible /ɪnˌkɒmprɪˈhensɪb(ə)l/ adj. that cannot be understood.

incomprehension /ɪnˌkɒmprɪˈhenʃ(ə)n/ n. failure to understand.

inconceivable /ɪnkənˈsiːvəb(ə)l/ adj. 1 that cannot be imagined. 2 colloq. most unlikely. □ **inconceivably** adv.

inconclusive /ɪnkənˈkluːsɪv/ adj. (of an argument, evidence, or action) not decisive or convincing.

incongruous /ɪnˈkɒŋɡrʊəs/ adj. 1 out of place; absurd. 2 (often foll. by with) out of keeping. □ **incongruity** /-ˈɡruːɪtɪ/ n. (pl. -ies). **incongruously** adv.

inconsequent /ɪnˈkɒnsɪkwənt/ adj. 1 irrelevant. 2 lacking logical sequence. 3 disconnected. □ **inconsequence** n.

inconsequential /ɪnˌkɒnsɪˈkwenʃ(ə)l/ adj. 1 unimportant. 2 = INCONSEQUENT. □ **inconsequentially** adv.

inconsiderable /ɪnkənˈsɪdərəb(ə)l/ adj. 1 of small size, value, etc. 2 not worth considering. □ **inconsiderably** adv.

inconsiderate /ɪnkənˈsɪdərət/ adj. (of a person or action) lacking regard for others; thoughtless. □ **inconsiderately** adv. **inconsiderateness** n.

inconsistent /ɪnkənˈsɪst(ə)nt/ adj. not consistent. □ **inconsistency** n. (pl. -ies). **inconsistently** adv.

inconsolable /ɪnkənˈsəʊləb(ə)l/ adj. (of a person, grief, etc.) that cannot be consoled. □ **inconsolably** adv.

inconspicuous /ɪnkənˈspɪkjʊəs/ adj. not conspicuous; not easily noticed. □ **inconspicuously** adv. **inconspicuousness** n.

inconstant /ɪnˈkɒnst(ə)nt/ adj. 1 fickle, changeable. 2 variable, not fixed. □ **inconstancy** n. (pl. -ies).

ncontestable /ˌɪnkən'testəb(ə)l/ *adj.* that cannot be disputed. □ **incontestably** *adv.*

ncontinent /ɪn'kɒntɪnənt/ *adj.* 1 unable to control the bowels or bladder. 2 lacking self-restraint (esp. in sexual matters). □ **incontinence** *n.*

ncontrovertible /ˌɪnkɒntrə'vɜːtɪb(ə)l/ *adj.* indisputable, undeniable. □ **incontrovertibly** *adv.*

inconvenience /ˌɪnkən'viːnɪəns/ —*n.* 1 lack of ease or comfort; trouble. 2 cause or instance of this. —*v.* (**-cing**) cause inconvenience to.

inconvenient *adj.* causing trouble, difficulty, or discomfort; awkward. □ **inconveniently** *adv.*

incorporate —*v.* /ɪn'kɔːpəreɪt/ (**-ting**) 1 include as a part or ingredient (*incorporated all the latest features*). 2 (often foll. by *in, with*) unite (in one body). 3 admit as a member of a company etc. 4 (esp. as **incorporated** *adj.*) form into a legal corporation. —*adj.* /ɪn'kɔːpərət/ incorporated. □ **incorporation** /-ˌreɪʃ(ə)n/ *n.* [Latin *corpus* body]

incorporeal /ˌɪnkɔː'pɔːrɪəl/ *adj.* without physical or material existence. □ **incorporeally** *adv.* **Incorporeity** /-pə'riːɪtɪ/ *n.*

incorrect /ˌɪnkə'rekt/ *adj.* 1 not correct or true. 2 improper, unsuitable. □ **incorrectly** *adv.*

incorrigible /ɪn'kɒrɪdʒɪb(ə)l/ *adj.* (of a person or habit) that cannot be corrected or improved. □ **incorrigibility** /-'bɪlɪtɪ/ *n.* **incorrigibly** *adv.*

incorruptible /ˌɪnkə'rʌptɪb(ə)l/ *adj.* 1 that cannot be corrupted, esp. by bribery. 2 that cannot decay. □ **incorruptibility** /-'bɪlɪtɪ/ *n.* **incorruptibly** *adv.*

increase —*v.* /ɪn'kriːs/ (**-sing**) make or become greater or more numerous. —*n.* /'ɪnkriːs/ 1 growth, enlargement. 2 (of people, animals, or plants) multiplication. 3 amount or extent of an increase. □ **on the increase** increasing. [Latin *cresco* grow]

increasingly /ɪn'kriːsɪŋlɪ/ *adv.* more and more.

incredible /ɪn'kredɪb(ə)l/ *adj.* 1 that cannot be believed. 2 *colloq.* amazing, extremely good. □ **incredibility** /-'bɪlɪtɪ/ *n.* **incredibly** *adv.*

incredulous /ɪn'kredjʊləs/ *adj.* unwilling to believe; showing disbelief. □ **incredulity** /ˌɪnkrɪ'djuːlɪtɪ/ *n.* **incredulously** *adv.*

increment /'ɪnkrɪmənt/ *n.* increase or added amount, esp. on a fixed salary scale. □ **incremental** /-'ment(ə)l/ *adj.* [Latin *cresco* grow]

incriminate /ɪn'krɪmɪneɪt/ *v.* (**-ting**) 1 make (a person) appear to be guilty. 2

charge with a crime. □ **incrimination** /-'neɪʃ(ə)n/ *n.* **incriminatory** *adj.* [Latin: related to CRIME]

incrustation /ˌɪnkrʌ'steɪʃ(ə)n/ *n.* 1 encrusting. 2 crust or hard coating. 3 deposit on a surface. [Latin: related to CRUST]

incubate /'ɪŋkjʊbeɪt/ *v.* (**-ting**) 1 hatch (eggs) by sitting on them or by artificial heat. 2 cause (micro-organisms) to develop. 3 develop slowly. [Latin *cubo* lie]

incubation /ˌɪŋkjʊ'beɪʃ(ə)n/ *n.* 1 incubating. 2 period between infection and the appearance of the first symptoms.

incubator *n.* apparatus providing artificial warmth for hatching eggs, rearing premature babies, or developing micro-organisms.

incubus /'ɪŋkjʊbəs/ *n.* (*pl.* **-buses** or **-bi** /-baɪ/) 1 demon formerly believed to have sexual intercourse with sleeping women. 2 nightmare. 3 oppressive person or thing. [Latin as INCUBATE]

inculcate /'ɪnkʌlkeɪt/ *v.* (**-ting**) (often foll. by *upon, in*) urge or impress (a habit or idea) persistently. □ **inculcation** /-'keɪʃ(ə)n/ *n.* [Latin *calco* tread]

incumbency /ɪn'kʌmbənsɪ/ *n.* (*pl.* **-ies**) office or tenure of an incumbent.

incumbent —*adj.* 1 resting as a duty (*it is incumbent on you to do it*). 2 (often foll. by *on*) lying, pressing, 3 currently holding office (*the incumbent president*). —*n.* holder of an office or post, esp. a benefice. [Latin *incumbo* lie upon]

incunabulum /ˌɪŋkjʊ'næbjʊləm/ *n.* (*pl.* **-la**) 1 early printed book, esp. from before 1501. 2 (in *pl.*) early stages of a thing. [Latin, (in *pl.*) = swaddling-clothes]

incur /ɪn'kɜː(r)/ *v.* (**-rr-**) bring on oneself (danger, blame, loss, etc.). [Latin *curro* run]

incurable /ɪn'kjʊərəb(ə)l/ —*adj.* that cannot be cured. —*n.* incurable person. □ **incurability** /-'bɪlɪtɪ/ *n.* **incurably** *adv.*

incurious /ɪn'kjʊərɪəs/ *adj.* lacking curiosity.

incursion /ɪn'kɜːʃ(ə)n/ *n.* invasion or attack, esp. sudden or brief. □ **incursive** *adj.* [Latin: related to INCUR]

incurve /ɪn'kɜːv/ *v.* (**-ving**) 1 bend into a curve. 2 (as **incurved** *adj.*) curved inwards. □ **incurvation** /-'veɪʃ(ə)n/ *n.*

indebted /ɪn'detɪd/ *adj.* (usu. foll. by *to*) owing gratitude or money. □ **indebtedness** *n.* [French *endetté*: related to DEBT]

indecent /ɪn'diːs(ə)nt/ *adj.* 1 offending against decency. 2 unbecoming, unsuitable (*indecent haste*). □ **indecency** *n.* (*pl.* **-ies**). **indecently** *adv.* **indecent assault** *n.* sexual attack not involving rape.

indecent exposure *n.* exposing one's genitals in public.

indecipherable /ˌɪndɪˈsaɪfərəb(ə)l/ *adj.* that cannot be deciphered.

indecision /ˌɪndɪˈsɪʒ(ə)n/ *n.* inability to decide; hesitation.

indecisive /ˌɪndɪˈsaɪsɪv/ *adj.* 1 (of a person) not decisive; hesitating. 2 not conclusive (*an indecisive battle*). □ **indecisively** *adv.* **indecisiveness** *n.*

indeclinable /ˌɪndɪˈklaɪnəb(ə)l/ *adj. Gram.* that cannot be declined; having no inflections.

indecorous /ɪnˈdekərəs/ *adj.* 1 improper, undignified. 2 in bad taste. □ **indecorously** *adv.*

indeed /ɪnˈdiːd/ —*adv.* 1 in truth; really. 2 admittedly. —*int.* expressing irony, incredulity, etc.

indefatigable /ˌɪndɪˈfatɪɡəb(ə)l/ *adj.* unwearying, unremitting. □ **indefatigably** *adv.*

indefeasible /ˌɪndɪˈfiːzɪb(ə)l/ *adj. literary* (esp. of a claim, rights, etc.) that cannot be forfeited or annulled. □ **indefeasibly** *adv.*

indefensible /ˌɪndɪˈfensɪb(ə)l/ *adj.* that cannot be defended or justified. □ **indefensibility** /-ˈbɪlɪtɪ/ *n.* **indefensibly** *adv.*

indefinable /ˌɪndɪˈfaɪnəb(ə)l/ *adj.* that cannot be defined; mysterious. □ **indefinably** *adv.*

indefinite /ɪnˈdefɪnɪt/ *adj.* 1 vague, undefined. 2 unlimited. 3 (of adjectives, adverbs, and pronouns) not determining the person etc. referred to (e.g. *some, someone, anyhow*).

indefinite article *n.* word (e.g. *a, an,* in English) preceding a noun and implying 'any of several'.

indefinitely *adv.* 1 for an unlimited time (*was postponed indefinitely*). 2 in an indefinite manner.

indelible /ɪnˈdelɪb(ə)l/ *adj.* that cannot be rubbed out or removed. □ **indelibly** *adv.* [Latin *deleo* efface]

indelicate /ɪnˈdelɪkət/ *adj.* 1 coarse, unrefined. 2 tactless. □ **indelicacy** *n.* (*pl.* **-ies**), **indelicately** *adv.*

indemnify /ɪnˈdemnɪfaɪ/ *v.* (**-ies, -ied**) 1 (often foll. by *from, against*) secure (a person) in respect of harm, a loss, etc. 2 (often foll. by *for*) exempt from a penalty. 3 compensate. □ **indemnification** /-fɪˈkeɪʃ(ə)n/ *n.* [Latin *indemnis* free from loss]

indemnity /ɪnˈdemnɪtɪ/ *n.* (*pl.* **-ies**) 1 a compensation for damage. b sum exacted by a victor in war. 2 security against loss. 3 exemption from penalties.

indent —*v.* /ɪnˈdent/ 1 make or impress marks, notches, dents, etc. in. 2 start (a

line of print or writing) further from the margin than others. 3 draw up (a legal document) in duplicate. 4 **a** (often foll. by *on, upon* a person, *for* a thing) make a requisition. **b** order (goods) by requisition. —*n.* /ˈɪndent/ 1 **a** order (esp. from abroad) for goods. **b** official requisition for stores. 2 indented line. 3 indentation. 4 indenture. [Latin *dens dentis* tooth]

indentation /ˌɪndenˈteɪʃ(ə)n/ *n.* 1 indenting or being indented. 2 notch.

indention /ɪnˈden(ʃ)(ə)n/ *n.* 1 indenting, esp. in printing. 2 notch.

indenture /ɪnˈdentʃə(r)/ —*n.* 1 (usu. in *pl.*) sealed agreement or contract. 2 formal list, certificate, etc. —*v.* (-ring) *hist.* bind by indentures, esp. as an apprentice. [Anglo-French: related to INDENT]

independent /ˌɪndɪˈpend(ə)nt/ —*adj.* 1 **a** (often foll. by *of*) not depending on authority or control. **b** self-governing. 2 **a** not depending on another person for one's opinions or livelihood. **b** (of income or resources) making it unnecessary to earn one's living. 3 unwilling to be under an obligation to others. 4 acting independently of any political party. 5 not depending on something else for its validity etc. (*independent proof*). 6 (of broadcasting, a school, etc.) not supported by public funds. —*n.* person who is politically independent. □ **independence** *n.* **independently** *adv.*

in-depth *adj.* thorough.

indescribable /ˌɪndɪˈskraɪbəb(ə)l/ *adj.* 1 too good or bad etc. to be described. 2 that cannot be described. □ **indescribably** *adv.*

indestructible /ˌɪndɪˈstrʌktɪb(ə)l/ *adj.* that cannot be destroyed. □ **indestructibility** /-ˈbɪlɪtɪ/ *n.* **indestructibly** *adv.*

indeterminable /ˌɪndɪˈtɜːmɪnəb(ə)l/ *adj.* that cannot be ascertained or settled. □ **indeterminably** *adv.*

indeterminate /ˌɪndɪˈtɜːmɪnət/ *adj.* 1 not fixed in extent, character, etc. 2 left doubtful; vague. 3 *Math.* of no fixed value. □ **indeterminacy** *n.*

indeterminate vowel *n.* vowel /ə/ heard in 'a moment ago'.

index /ˈɪndeks/ —*n.* (*pl.* **indexes** or **indices** /ˈɪndɪsiːz/) 1 alphabetical list of subjects etc. with references, usu. at the end of a book. 2 = CARD INDEX. 3 measure of prices or wages compared with a previous month, year, etc. (*retail price index*). 4 *Math.* exponent of a number. 5 pointer, sign, or indicator. —*v.* 1 provide (a book etc.) with an index. 2 enter in an index. 3 relate (wages etc.) to a price index. □ **indexation** /-ˈseɪʃ(ə)n/ *n.* (in sense 3 of *v.*). [Latin]

index finger n. forefinger.

index-linked adj. related to the value of a price index.

Indian /'ɪndɪən/ —n. 1 a native or national of India. b person of Indian descent. 2 (in full **American Indian**) a original inhabitant of America. b any of the languages of the American Indians. —adj. 1 of India or the subcontinent comprising India, Pakistan, and Bangladesh. 2 of the original peoples of America.

Indian corn n. maize.

Indian elephant n. the elephant of India, smaller than the African elephant.

Indian file n. = SINGLE FILE.

Indian hemp See HEMP 1.

Indian ink n. 1 black pigment. 2 ink made from this.

Indian summer n. 1 dry warm weather in late autumn. 2 late tranquil period of life.

indiarubber n. rubber for erasing pencil marks etc.

indicate /'ɪndɪkeɪt/ v. (-ting) (often foll. by that) 1 point out; make known. 2 be a sign of; show the presence of. 3 call for; require (stronger measures are indicated). 4 state briefly. 5 give as a reading or measurement. 6 point by hand; use a vehicle's indicator (failed to indicate). □ **indication** /-'keɪʃ(ə)n/ n. [Latin dico make known]

indicative /ɪn'dɪkətɪv/ —adj. 1 (foll. by of) suggestive; serving as an indication. 2 Gram. (of a mood) stating a fact. —n. Gram. 1 indicative mood. 2 verb in this mood.

indicator n. 1 flashing light on a vehicle showing the direction in which it is about to turn. 2 person or thing that indicates. 3 device indicating the condition of a machine etc. 4 recording instrument. 5 board giving information, esp. times of trains etc.

indicatory /ɪn'dɪkətəri/ adj. (often foll. by of) indicative.

indices pl. of INDEX.

indict /ɪn'daɪt/ v. accuse formally by legal process. [Anglo-French: related to IN-², DICTATE]

indictable adj. 1 (of an offence) making the doer liable to be charged with a crime. 2 (of a person) so liable.

indictment n. 1 a indicting; accusation. b document containing this. 2 thing that serves to condemn or censure (an indictment of society).

indie /'ɪndɪ/ colloq. —adj. (of a pop group or record label) independent, not

belonging to one of the major companies. —n. such a group or label. [abbreviation of INDEPENDENT]

indifference /ɪn'dɪfrəns/ n. 1 lack of interest or attention. 2 unimportance.

indifferent adj. 1 (foll. by to) showing indifference or lack of interest. 2 neither good nor bad. 3 of poor quality or ability. □ **indifferently** adv.

indigenous /ɪn'dɪdʒɪnəs/ adj. (often foll. by to) native or belonging naturally to a place. [Latin from a root gen- be born]

indigent /'ɪndɪdʒ(ə)nt/ adj. formal needy, poor. □ **indigence** n. [Latin ego need]

indigestible /ˌɪndɪ'dʒestɪb(ə)l/ adj. 1 difficult or impossible to digest. 2 too complex to read or understand. □ **indigestibility** /-'bɪlɪtɪ/ n.

indigestion /ˌɪndɪ'dʒestʃ(ə)n/ n. 1 difficulty in digesting food. 2 pain caused by this.

indignant /ɪn'dɪgnənt/ adj. feeling or showing indignation. □ **indignantly** adv. [Latin dignus worthy]

indignation /ˌɪndɪg'neɪʃ(ə)n/ n. anger at supposed injustice etc.

indignity /ɪn'dɪgnɪtɪ/ n. (pl. -ies) 1 humiliating treatment or quality. 2 insult.

indigo /'ɪndɪgəʊ/ n. (pl. -s) 1 colour between blue and violet in the spectrum. 2 dye of this colour. [Greek indikon Indian dye]

indirect /ˌɪndaɪ'rekt/ adj. 1 not going straight to the point. 2 (of a route etc.) not straight. 3 a not directly sought (indirect result). b not primary (indirect cause). □ **indirectly** adv.

indirect object n. Gram. person or thing affected by a verbal action but not primarily acted on (e.g. him in give him the book).

indirect question n. Gram. question in indirect speech.

indirect speech n. = REPORTED SPEECH

indirect tax n. tax on goods and services, not on income or profits.

indiscernible /ˌɪndɪ'sɜːnɪb(ə)l/ adj. that cannot be discerned.

indiscipline /ɪn'dɪsɪplɪn/ n. lack of discipline.

indiscreet /ˌɪndɪ'skriːt/ adj. 1 not discreet. 2 injudicious, unwary. □ **indiscreetly** adv.

indiscretion /ˌɪndɪ'skreʃ(ə)n/ n. indiscreet conduct or action.

indiscriminate /ˌɪndɪ'skrɪmɪnət/ adj. making no distinctions; done or acting at random (indiscriminate shooting). □ **indiscriminately** adv.

indispensable /ˌɪndɪˈspensəb(ə)l/ *adj.* that cannot be dispensed with; necessary. □ **indispensability** /-ˈbɪlɪtɪ/ *n.* **indispensably** *adv.*

indisposed /ˌɪndɪˈspəʊzd/ *adj.* **1** slightly unwell. **2** averse or unwilling. □ **indisposition** /-spəˈzɪʃ(ə)n/ *n.*

indisputable /ˌɪndɪˈspjuːtəb(ə)l/ *adj.* that cannot be disputed. □ **indisputably** *adv.*

indissoluble /ˌɪndɪˈsɒljʊb(ə)l/ *adj.* **1** that cannot be dissolved or broken up. **2** firm and lasting. □ **indissolubly** *adv.*

indistinct /ˌɪndɪˈstɪŋkt/ *adj.* **1** not distinct. **2** confused, obscure. □ **indistinctly** *adv.*

indistinguishable /ˌɪndɪˈstɪŋgwɪʃəb(ə)l/ *adj.* (often foll. by *from*) not distinguishable.

indite /ɪnˈdaɪt/ *v.* (-ting) *formal or joc.* **1** put (a speech etc.) into words. **2** write (a letter etc.). [French: related to INDICT]

indium /ˈɪndɪəm/ *n.* soft silvery-white metallic element occurring in zinc ores. [Latin *indicum* INDIGO]

individual /ˌɪndɪˈvɪdʒʊəl/ —*adj.* **1** of, for, or characteristic of, a single person etc. **2 a** single (*individual* words). **b** particular; not general. **3** having a distinct character. **4** designed for use by one person. —*n.* **1** single member of a class. **2** single human being. **3** *colloq.* person (*a tiresome individual*). **4** distinctive person. [medieval Latin: related to DIVIDE]

individualism *n.* **1** social theory favouring free action by individuals. **2** being independent or different. □ **individualist** *n.* **individualistic** /-ˈlɪstɪk/ *adj.*

individuality /ˌɪndɪvɪdʒʊˈælɪtɪ/ *n.* **1** individual character, esp. when strongly marked. **2** separate existence.

individualize *v.* (also **-ise**) (-**zing** or -**sing**) **1** give an individual character to. **2** (esp. as **individualized** *adj.*) personalize (*individualized notepaper*).

individually *adv.* **1** one by one. **2** personally. **3** distinctively.

indivisible /ˌɪndɪˈvɪzɪb(ə)l/ *adj.* not divisible.

Indo- *comb. form* Indian; Indian and.

indoctrinate /ɪnˈdɒktrɪneɪt/ *v.* (-ting) teach to accept a particular belief uncritically. □ **indoctrination** /-ˈneɪʃ(ə)n/ *n.*

Indo-European /ˌɪndəʊjʊərəˈpɪən/ —*adj.* **1** of the family of languages spoken over most of Europe and Asia as far as N. India. **2** of the hypothetical parent language of this family. —*n.* **1** Indo-European family of languages. **2** hypothetical parent language of these.

indolent /ˈɪndələnt/ *adj.* lazy; averse to exertion. □ **indolence** *n.* **indolently** *adv.* [Latin *doleo* suffer pain]

indomitable /ɪnˈdɒmɪtəb(ə)l/ *adj.* **1** unconquerable. **2** unyielding. □ **indomitably** *adv.* [Latin: related to IN-[1], *domito* tame]

indoor *adj.* of, done, or for use in a building or under cover.

indoors /ɪnˈdɔːz/ *adv.* into or in a building.

indorse var. of ENDORSE.

indrawn /ˈɪndrɔːn/ *adj.* (of breath etc.) drawn in.

indubitable /ɪnˈdjuːbɪtəb(ə)l/ *adj.* that cannot be doubted. □ **indubitably** *adv.* [Latin *dubito* doubt]

induce /ɪnˈdjuːs/ *v.* (-cing) **1** prevail on; persuade. **2** bring about. **3 a** bring on (labour) artificially. **b** bring on labour in (a mother). **c** speed up the birth of (a baby). **4** produce (a current) by induction. **5** infer; deduce. □ **inducible** *adj.* [Latin *duco duct-* lead]

inducement *n.* attractive offer; incentive; bribe.

induct /ɪnˈdʌkt/ *v.* (often foll. by *to, into*) **1** introduce into office, install (into a benefice etc.). **2** *archaic* lead (to a seat, into a room, etc.); install. [related to INDUCE]

inductance *n.* property of an electric circuit generating an electromotive force by virtue of the current flowing through it.

induction /ɪnˈdʌkʃ(ə)n/ *n.* **1** act of inducting or inducing. **2** act of bringing on (esp. labour) by artificial means. **3** inference of a general law from particular instances. **4** (often *attrib.*) formal introduction to a new job etc. (*induction course*). **5** *Electr.* **a** production of an electric or magnetic state by the proximity (without contact) of an electrified or magnetized body. **b** production of an electric current by a change of magnetic field. **6** drawing of the fuel mixture into the cylinders of an internal-combustion engine.

inductive /ɪnˈdʌktɪv/ *adj.* **1** (of reasoning etc.) based on induction. **2** of electric or magnetic induction.

inductor *n.* component (in an electric circuit) having inductance.

indue var. of ENDUE.

indulge /ɪnˈdʌldʒ/ *v.* (-ging) **1** (often foll. by *in*) take pleasure freely. **2** yield freely to (a desire etc.). **3** (also *refl.*) gratify the wishes of. **4** *colloq.* take alcoholic liquor. [Latin *indulgeo* give free rein to]

indulgence /ɪnˈdʌldʒ(ə)ns/ *n.* **1** indulging or being indulgent. **2** thing indulged in. **3** *RC Ch.* remission of punishment still due after absolution. **4** privilege granted.

indulgent *adj.* 1 lenient; ready to over-look faults etc. 2 indulging. □ **indul-gently** *adv.*

industrial /ɪnˈdʌstrɪəl/ *adj.* 1 of, en-gaged in, or for use in or serving the needs of industries. 2 (of a nation etc.) having developed industries. □ **indus-trially** *adv.*

industrial action *n.* strike or other disruptive action by workers as a pro-test.

industrial estate *n.* area of land zoned for factories etc.

industrialism *n.* system in which manufacturing industries are preva-lent.

industrialist *n.* owner or manager in industry.

industrialize *v.* (also **-ise**) (**-zing** or **-sing**) make (a nation etc.) industrial. □ **industrialization** /-ˈzeɪʃ(ə)n/ *n.*

industrial relations *n.pl.* relations between management and workers.

industrious /ɪnˈdʌstrɪəs/ *adj.* hard-working. □ **industriously** *adv.*

industry /ˈɪndəstrɪ/ *n.* (*pl.* **-ies**) 1 a branch of production or manufacture; commercial enterprise. **b** these collect-ively. 2 concerted activity (*a hive of industry*). 3 diligence. [Latin *industria*]

-ine *suffix* 1 forming adjectives, mean-ing 'belonging to, or of the nature of' (*Alpine; asinine*). 2 forming feminine nouns (*heroine*). [Latin *-inus*]

inebriate —*v.* /ɪˈniːbrɪeɪt/ (**-ting**) 1 make drunk. 2 excite. —*adj.* /ɪˈniːbrɪət/ drunken. —*n.* /ɪˈniːbrɪət/ drunkard. □ **inebriation** /-ˈeɪʃ(ə)n/ *n.* **inebriety** /-ˈbraɪətɪ/ *n.* [Latin *ebrius* drunk]

inedible /ɪnˈedɪb(ə)l/ *adj.* not suitable for eating.

ineducable /ɪnˈedjʊkəb(ə)l/ *adj.* in-capable of being educated.

ineffable /ɪnˈefəb(ə)l/ *adj.* 1 too great for description in words. 2 that must not be uttered. □ **ineffability** /-ˈbɪlɪtɪ/ *n.* **inef-fably** *adv.* [Latin *effor* speak out]

ineffective /ɪnɪˈfektɪv/ *adj.* not achiev-ing the desired effect or results. □ **inef-fectively** *adv.* **ineffectiveness** *n.*

ineffectual /ɪnɪˈfektʃʊəl/ *adj.* ineffect-ive, feeble. □ **ineffectually** *adv.* **inef-fectualness** *n.*

inefficient /ɪnɪˈfɪʃ(ə)nt/ *adj.* 1 not effi-cient or fully capable. 2 (of a machine etc.) wasteful. □ **inefficiency** *n.* **ineffi-ciently** *adv.*

inelegant /ɪnˈelɪɡ(ə)nt/ *adj.* 1 ungrace-ful. 2 unrefined. □ **inelegance** *n.* **inel-egantly** *adv.*

ineligible /ɪnˈelɪdʒɪb(ə)l/ *adj.* not eli-gible or qualified. □ **ineligibility** /-ˈbɪlɪtɪ/ *n.*

ineluctable /ɪnɪˈlʌktəb(ə)l/ *adj.* ines-capable, unavoidable. [Latin *luctor* strive]

inept /ɪˈnept/ *adj.* 1 unskilful. 2 absurd, silly. 3 out of place. □ **ineptitude** *n.* **ineptly** *adv.* [Latin related to APT]

inequable /ɪnˈekwəb(ə)l/ *adj.* 1 unfair. 2 not uniform.

inequality /ɪnɪˈkwɒlɪtɪ/ *n.* (*pl.* **-ies**) 1 lack of equality. 2 variability. 3 uneven-ness.

inequitable /ɪnˈekwɪtəb(ə)l/ *adj.* unfair, unjust.

inequity /ɪnˈekwɪtɪ/ *n.* (*pl.* **-ies**) unfair-ness, injustice.

ineradicable /ɪnɪˈrædɪkəb(ə)l/ *adj.* that cannot be rooted out.

inert /ɪˈnɜːt/ *adj.* 1 without inherent power of action, or motion, or resistance. 2 not reacting chemically with other sub-stances (*inert gas*). 3 sluggish, slow, lifeless. [Latin *iners -ert-*: related to ART]

inertia /ɪˈnɜːʃə/ *n.* 1 *Physics* property of matter by which it continues in its existing state of rest or motion unless an external force is applied 2 **a** inertness, lethargy. **b** tendency to remain unchanged (*inertia of the system*). □ **inertial** *adj.* [Latin related to INERT]

inertia reel *n.* reel allowing a seat-belt to unwind freely but locking on impact

inertia selling *n.* sending of unsoli-cited goods in the hope of making a sale.

inescapable /ɪnɪˈskeɪpəb(ə)l/ *adj.* that cannot be escaped or avoided.

inessential /ɪnɪˈsenʃ(ə)l/ —*adj.* not necessary; dispensable. —*n.* inessential thing.

inestimable /ɪnˈestɪməb(ə)l/ *adj.* too great, precious, etc., to be estimated. □ **inestimably** *adv.*

inevitable /ɪnˈevɪtəb(ə)l/ —*adj.* 1 unavoidable; sure to happen. 2 *colloq.* tiresomely familiar. —*n.* (prec. by *the*) inevitable fact, event, etc. □ **inevitab-ility** /-ˈbɪlɪtɪ/ *n.* **inevitably** *adv.* [Latin *evito* avoid]

inexact /ɪnɪɡˈzækt/ *adj.* not exact. □ **inexactitude** *n.* **inexactly** *adv.*

inexcusable /ɪnɪkˈskjuːzəb(ə)l/ *adj.* that cannot be excused or justified. □ **inexcusably** *adv.*

inexhaustible /ɪnɪɡˈzɔːstɪb(ə)l/ *adj.* that cannot be used up, endless.

inexorable /ɪnˈeksərəb(ə)l/ *adj.* relent-less; unstoppable. □ **inexorably** *adv.* [Latin *exoro* entreat]

inexpedient /ɪnɪkˈspiːdɪənt/ *adj.* not expedient.

inexpensive /ɪnɪkˈspensɪv/ *adj.* not ex-pensive.

452

inexperience /ˌɪnɪkˈspɪərɪəns/ n. lack of experience, knowledge, or skill. □ **inexperienced** adj.

inexpert /ˈɪnɛkspəːt/ adj. unskilful; lacking expertise.

inexpiable /ɪnˈɛkspɪəb(ə)l/ adj. that cannot be expiated or appeased.

inexplicable /ˌɪnɪkˈsplɪkəb(ə)l/ adj. that cannot be explained. □ **inexplicably** adv.

inexpressible /ˌɪnɪkˈsprɛsɪb(ə)l/ adj. that cannot be expressed. □ **inexpressibly** adv.

inextinguishable /ˌɪnɪkˈstɪŋgwɪʃəb(ə)l/ adj. that cannot be extinguished or destroyed.

in extremis /ˌɪn ɛkˈstriːmɪs/ adj. 1 at the point of death. 2 in great difficulties; in an emergency. [Latin]

inextricable /ˌɪnɪkˈstrɪkəb(ə)l/ adj. 1 inescapable. 2 that cannot be separated, loosened, or solved. □ **inextricably** adv.

INF abbr. intermediate-range nuclear forces.

infallible /ɪnˈfalɪb(ə)l/ adj. 1 incapable of error. 2 unfailing; sure to succeed. 3 (of the Pope) incapable of doctrinal error. □ **infallibility** /-ˈbɪlɪtɪ/ n. **infallibly** adv.

infamous /ˈɪnfəməs/ adj. notoriously bad. □ **infamously** adv. **infamy** /ˈɪnfəmɪ/ n. (pl. -ies).

infant /ˈɪnf(ə)nt/ n. 1 a child during the earliest period of its life. b schoolchild below the age of seven years. 2 (esp. attrib.) thing in an early stage of its development. 3 Law person under 18. □ **infancy** n. [Latin infans unable to speak]

infanta /ɪnˈfantə/ n. hist. daughter of a Spanish or Portuguese king. [Spanish and Portuguese: related to INFANT]

infanticide /ɪnˈfantɪˌsaɪd/ n. 1 killing of an infant, esp. soon after birth. 2 person who kills an infant.

infantile /ˈɪnf(ə)nˌtaɪl/ adj. 1 of or like infants, 2 childish, immature. □ **infantilism** /ˈɪnf(ə)ntɪˌlɪz(ə)m/ n.

infantile paralysis n. poliomyelitis.

infantry /ˈɪnf(ə)ntrɪ/ n. (pl. -ies) body of foot-soldiers; foot-soldiers collectively. [Italian infante youth, foot-soldier]

infantryman n. soldier of an infantry regiment.

infarct /ˈɪnfɑːkt/ n. small area of dead tissue caused by an inadequate blood supply. □ **infarction** /ɪnˈfɑːkʃ(ə)n/ n. [Latin farcio farct- stuff]

infatuate /ɪnˈfatjʊˌeɪt/ v. (-ting) (usu. as **infatuated** adj.) 1 inspire with intense usu. transitory fondness or admiration. 2 affect with extreme folly. □

infatuation /-ˈeɪʃ(ə)n/ n. [Latin: related to FATUOUS]

infect /ɪnˈfɛkt/ v. 1 affect or contaminate with a germ, virus, or disease. 2 imbue, taint. [Latin inficio fect- taint]

infection /ɪnˈfɛkʃ(ə)n/ n. 1 a infecting or being infected. b instance of this; disease. 2 communication of disease, esp. by air, water, etc.

infectious adj. 1 infecting. 2 (of a disease) transmissible by infection. 3 (of emotions etc.) quickly affecting or spreading to others. □ **infectiously** adv. **infectiousness** n.

infelicity /ˌɪnfɪˈlɪsɪtɪ/ n. (pl. -ies) 1 inapt expression etc. 2 unhappiness. □ **infelicitous** adj.

infer /ɪnˈfɜː(r)/ v. (-rr-) 1 deduce or conclude. 2 imply. □ **inferable** adj. [Latin fero bring]

■ **Usage** The use of infer in sense 2 is considered incorrect by some people.

inference /ˈɪnfərəns/ n. 1 act of inferring. 2 thing inferred. □ **inferential** /-ˈrɛnʃ(ə)l/ adj.

inferior /ɪnˈfɪərɪə(r)/ —adj. 1 (often foll. by to) lower in rank, quality, etc. 2 of poor quality. 3 situated below. 4 written or printed below the line. —n. person inferior to another, esp. in rank. [Latin, comparative of inferus]

inferiority /ɪnˌfɪərɪˈɒrɪtɪ/ n. being inferior.

inferiority complex n. feeling of inadequacy, sometimes marked by compensating aggressive behaviour.

infernal /ɪnˈfɜːn(ə)l/ adj. 1 of hell; hellish. 2 colloq. detestable, tiresome. □ **infernally** adv. [Latin infernus low]

inferno /ɪnˈfɜːnəʊ/ n. (pl. -s) 1 raging fire. 2 scene of horror or distress. 3 hell. [Italian: related to INFERNAL]

infertile /ɪnˈfɜːtaɪl/ adj. 1 not fertile. 2 unable to have offspring. □ **infertility** /-fəˈtɪlɪtɪ/ n.

infest /ɪnˈfɛst/ v. (esp. of vermin) overrun (a place). □ **infestation** /-ˈsteɪʃ(ə)n/ n. [Latin infestus hostile]

infidel /ˈɪnfɪd(ə)l/ —n. unbeliever in esp. the supposed true religion. —adj. 1 of infidels. 2 unbelieving. [Latin fides faith]

infidelity /ˌɪnfɪˈdɛlɪtɪ/ n. (pl. -ies). unfaithfulness, esp. adultery. [Latin: related to INFIDEL]

infield n. Cricket the part of the ground near the wicket.

infighting n. 1 conflict or competitiveness between colleagues. 2 boxing within arm's length.

infill /ˈɪnfɪl/ —n. 1 material used to fill a hole, gap, etc. 2 filling gaps (esp. in a row of buildings). —v. fill in (a cavity etc.).

infilling n. = INFILL.

infiltrate /'ɪnfɪltreɪt/ v. (-ting) 1 a enter (a territory, political party, etc.) gradually and imperceptibly. b permeate or infiltrate this. 2 permeate by filtration, or cause to do this. □ by *into*, *through*) introduce (fluid) by filtration. □ **infiltration** /-'treɪʃ(ə)n/ n. **infiltrator** n. [from IN-², FILTRATE]

infinite /'ɪnfɪnɪt/ adj. 1 boundless, endless. 2 very great or many. —n. 1 (the Infinite) God. 2 (the infinite) infinite space. □ **infinitely** adv. [Latin: related to IN-¹ FINITE]

infinitesimal /ˌɪnfɪnɪ'tesɪm(ə)l/ adj. infinitely or very small. —n. infinitesimal amount. □ **infinitesimally** adv.

infinitive /ɪn'fɪnɪtɪv/ —n. form of a verb expressing the verbal notion without a particular subject, tense, etc. (e.g. *see* in *we came to see*, *let him see*). —adj. having this form.

infinitude /ɪn'fɪnɪtjuːd/ n. *literary* = INFINITY 1, 2.

infinity /ɪn'fɪnɪtɪ/ n. (pl. -ies) 1 being infinite; boundlessness. 2 infinite number or extent. 3 infinite distance (*gaze into infinity*). 4 *Math.* infinite quantity.

infirm /ɪn'fɜːm/ adj. physically weak, esp. through age.

infirmary n. (pl. -ies) 1 hospital. 2 sickquarters in a school etc.

infirmity n. (pl. -ies) 1 being infirm. 2 particular physical weakness.

in flagrante delicto /ɪn flə'grantɪ dɪ'lɪktəʊ/ adv. in the very act of committing an offence. [Latin, = in blazing crime]

inflame /ɪn'fleɪm/ v. (-ming) 1 provoke to strong feeling, esp. anger. 2 cause inflammation in; make hot 3 aggravate. 4 catch or set on fire. 5 light up with or as with flames.

inflammable /ɪn'flaməb(ə)l/ adj. easily set on fire or excited. □ **inflammability** /-'bɪlɪtɪ/ n.

■ **Usage** Where there is a danger of *inflammable* being understood to mean the opposite, i.e. 'not easily set on fire', *flammable* can be used to avoid confusion.

inflammation /ˌɪnflə'meɪʃ(ə)n/ n. 1 inflaming. 2 bodily condition with heat, swelling, redness, and usu. pain.

inflammatory /ɪn'flamət(ə)rɪ/ adj. 1 tending to cause anger etc. 2 of inflammation.

inflatable /ɪn'fleɪtəb(ə)l/ adj. that can be inflated. —n. inflatable object.

inflate /ɪn'fleɪt/ v. (-ting) 1 distend with air or gas. 2 (usu. foll. by *with*; usu. in *passive*) puff up (with pride etc.), 3 a

cause inflation of (the currency). b raise (prices) artificially. 4 (as inflated adj.) (esp. of language, opinions, etc.) bombastic, overblown, exaggerated. [Latin *inflo-flat-*]

inflation /ɪn'fleɪʃ(ə)n/ n. 1 inflating. 2 *Econ.* a general increase in prices. b increase in the supply of money regarded as causing this. □ **inflationary** adj.

inflect /ɪn'flekt/ v. 1 change the form of (a word) to express grammatical relation. b undergo such a change. 2 change the pitch of (the voice). 3 bend, curve. □ **inflective** adj. [Latin *flecto/flex-* bend]

inflection /ɪn'flekʃ(ə)n/ n. (also **inflexion**) 1 inflecting or being inflected. 2 a inflected word. b suffix etc. used to inflect. 3 modulation of the voice. □ **inflectional** adj. [Latin: related to IN-FLECT]

inflexible /ɪn'fleksɪb(ə)l/ adj. 1 unbendable. 2 unbending. □ **inflexibility** /-'bɪlɪtɪ/ n. **inflexibly** adv.

inflexion var. of INFLECTION.

inflict /ɪn'flɪkt/ v. (usu. foll. by *on*) 1 deal (a blow etc.). 2 often *joc.* impose (suffering, oneself, etc.) on (*shall not inflict myself on you any longer*). □ **infliction** n. **inflictor** n. [Latin *fligo flict-* strike]

in-flight *attrib. adj.* occurring or provided during a flight.

inflorescence /ˌɪnflə'tres(ə)ns/ n. 1 a complete flower-head of a plant. b arrangement of this. 2 flowering. [Latin: related to IN-² FLOURISH]

inflow n. 1 flowing in 2 something that flows in.

influence /'ɪnfluəns/ —n. 1 (usu. foll. by *on*) effect a person or thing has on another. 2 (usu. foll. by *over*, *with*) moral ascendancy or power. 3 thing or person exercising this. —v. (-cing) exert influence on; affect. □ **under the influence** *colloq.* drunk. [Latin *influo flow in*]

influential /ˌɪnflu'enʃ(ə)l/ adj. having great influence. □ **influentially** adv.

influenza /ˌɪnflu'enzə/ n. virus infection causing fever, aches, and catarrh. [Italian: related to INFLUENCE]

influx /'ɪnflʌks/ n. flowing in, esp. of people or things into a place. [Latin: related to FLUX]

info /'ɪnfəʊ/ n. *colloq.* information. [abbreviation]

inform /ɪn'fɔːm/ v. 1 tell (*informed them of their rights*). 2 (usu. foll. by *against*, *on*) give incriminating information about a person to the authorities. [Latin: related to FORM]

informal /ɪn'fɔːm(ə)l/ adj. 1 without formality. 2 not formal. □ **informally** /-'mælɪtɪ/ n. (pl. -ies). **informally** adv.

informant *n.* giver of information.

information /ˌɪnfəˈmeɪʃ(ə)n/ *n.* **1 a** something told; knowledge. **b** items of knowledge; news. **2** charge or complaint lodged with a court etc.

information retrieval *n.* the tracing of information stored in books, computers, etc.

information technology *n.* the study or use of processes (esp. computers, telecommunications, etc.) for storing, retrieving, and sending information.

informative /ɪnˈfɔːmətɪv/ *adj.* giving information; instructive.

informed *adj.* **1** knowing the facts. **2** having some knowledge.

informer *n.* person who informs, esp. against others.

infra /ˈɪnfrə/ *adv.* below, further on (in a book etc.). [Latin, = below]

infra- *comb. form* below.

infraction /ɪnˈfrækʃ(ə)n/ *n.* infringement. [Latin: related to INFRINGE]

infra dig /ˌɪnfrə ˈdɪɡ/ *predic. adj. colloq.* beneath one's dignity. [Latin *infra dignitatem*]

infrared /ˌɪnfrəˈred/ *adj.* of or using rays with a wavelength just longer than the red end of the visible spectrum.

infrastructure /ˈɪnfrəˌstrʌktʃə(r)/ *n.* **1 a** basic structural foundations of a society or enterprise. **b** roads, bridges, sewers, etc., regarded as a country's economic foundation. **2** permanent installations as a basis for military etc. operations.

infrequent /ɪnˈfriːkwənt/ *adj.* not frequent. □ **infrequently** *adv.*

infringe /ɪnˈfrɪndʒ/ *v.* (**-ging**) **1** break or violate (a law, another's rights, etc.). **2** (usu. foll. by *on*) encroach; trespass. □ **infringement** *n.* [Latin *frango fract-* break]

infuriate /ɪnˈfjʊərɪeɪt/ *v.* make furious; irritate greatly. □ **infuriating** *adj.* **infuriatingly** *adv.* [medieval Latin: related to FURY]

infuse /ɪnˈfjuːz/ *v.* (**-sing**) **1** (usu. foll. by *with*) fill (with a quality). **2** steep (tea leaves etc.) in liquid to extract the content; be steeped thus. **3** (usu. foll. by *into*) instil (life etc.). [Latin *infundo fus-*: related to FOUND³]

infusible /ɪnˈfjuːzɪb(ə)l/ *adj.* that cannot be melted. □ **infusibility** /-ˈbɪlɪtɪ/ *n.*

infusion /ɪnˈfjuːʒ(ə)n/ *n.* **1 a** infusing. **b** liquid extract obtained thus. **2** infused element.

-ing¹ *suffix* forming nouns from verbs denoting: **1** verbal action or its result (*asking*). **2** material associated with a

process etc. (*piping; washing*). **3** occupation or event (*banking; wedding*). [Old English]

-ing² *suffix* forming the present participle of verbs (*asking; fighting*), often as adjectives (*charming; strapping*). **2** forming adjectives from nouns (*hulking*) and verbs (*balding*). [Old English]

ingenious /ɪnˈdʒiːnɪəs/ *adj.* **1** clever at inventing, organizing, etc. **2** cleverly contrived. □ **ingeniously** *adv.* [Latin *ingenium* cleverness]

■ **Usage** *Ingenious* is sometimes confused with *ingenuous.*

ingénue /ˌæ̃ʒeɪˈnjuː/ *n.* **1** unsophisticated young woman. **2** such a part in a play. [French: related to INGENUOUS]

ingenuity /ˌɪndʒɪˈnjuːɪtɪ/ *n.* inventiveness, cleverness.

ingenuous /ɪnˈdʒenjʊəs/ *adj.* **1** artless. **2** frank. □ **ingenuously** *adv.* [Latin *ingenuus* free-born, frank]

■ **Usage** *Ingenuous* is sometimes confused with *ingenious.*

ingest /ɪnˈdʒest/ *v.* **1** take in (food etc.). **2** absorb (knowledge etc.). □ **ingestion** /ɪnˈdʒestʃ(ə)n/ *n.* [Latin *gero* carry]

inglenook /ˈɪŋɡ(ə)lnʊk/ *n.* space within the opening on either side of a large fireplace. [perhaps Gaelic *aingeal* fire, light]

inglorious /ɪnˈɡlɔːrɪəs/ *adj.* **1** shameful. **2** not famous.

ingoing *adj.* going in.

ingot /ˈɪŋɡət/ *n.* (usu. oblong) piece of cast metal, esp. gold. [origin uncertain]

ingraft var. of ENGRAFT.

ingrained /ɪnˈɡreɪnd/ *adj.* **1** deeply rooted; inveterate. **2** (of dirt etc.) deeply embedded.

ingratiate /ɪnˈɡreɪʃɪeɪt/ *v.refl.* (**-ting**) (usu. foll. by *with*) bring oneself into favour. □ **ingratiating** *adj.* **ingratiatingly** *adv.* [Latin *in gratiam* into favour]

ingratitude /ɪnˈɡrætɪtjuːd/ *n.* lack of due gratitude.

ingredient /ɪnˈɡriːdɪənt/ *n.* component part in a mixture. [Latin *ingredior* enter into]

ingress /ˈɪŋɡres/ *n.* act or right of going in. [Latin *ingressus*: related to INGREDIENT]

ingrowing *adj.* (esp. of a toenail) growing into the flesh. □ **ingrown** *adj.*

inguinal /ˈɪŋɡwɪn(ə)l/ *adj.* of the groin. [Latin *inguen* groin]

inhabit /ɪnˈhæbɪt/ *v.* (**-t-**) dwell in; occupy. □ **inhabitable** *adj.* [Latin: related to HABIT]

inhabitant *n.* person etc. who inhabits a place.

inhalant /ɪnˈheɪlənt/ n. medicinal substance for inhaling.

inhale /ɪnˈheɪl/ v. (-ling) (often absol.) breathe in (air, gas, smoke, etc.). □ **inhalation** /-həˈleɪʃ(ə)n/ n. [Latin halo breathe]

inhaler n. device for administering an inhalant, esp. to relieve asthma.

inhere /ɪnˈhɪə(r)/ v. (-ring) be inherent. [Latin haereo haes- stick]

inherent /ɪnˈhɪərənt/ adj. (often foll. by in) existing in something as an essential or permanent attribute. □ **inherence** n. □ **inherently** adv.

inherit /ɪnˈherɪt/ v. (-t-) 1 receive (property, rank, title, etc.) by legal succession. 2 derive (a characteristic) from one's ancestors. 3 derive (a situation etc.) from a predecessor. □ **inheritable** adj. **inheritor** n. [Latin heres heir]

inheritance n. 1 thing that is inherited. 2 inheriting.

inheritance tax n. tax levied on property acquired by gift or inheritance.

■ **Usage** This tax was introduced in 1986 to replace capital transfer tax.

inhibit /ɪnˈhɪbɪt/ v. (-t-) 1 hinder, restrain, or prevent (action or progress). 2 (as inhibited adj.) suffering from inhibition. 3 (usu. foll. by from + verbal noun) prohibit (a person etc.). □ **inhibitory** adj. [Latin inhibeo -hibit- hinder]

inhibition /ˌɪnhɪˈbɪʃ(ə)n/ n. 1 Psychol. restraint on the direct expression of an instinct. 2 colloq. emotional resistance to a thought, action, etc. 3 inhibiting or being inhibited.

inhospitable /ˌɪnhɒˈspɪtəb(ə)l/ adj. 1 not hospitable. 2 (of a region etc.) not affording shelter, favourable conditions, etc. □ **inhospitably** adv.

in-house adj. & adv. within an institution, company, etc.

inhuman /ɪnˈhjuːmən/ adj. brutal; unfeeling; barbarous. □ **inhumanity** /ˌɪnhjuːˈmænɪtɪ/ n. (pl. -ies). **inhumanly** adv.

inhumane /ˌɪnhjuːˈmeɪn/ adj. = IN-HUMAN. □ **inhumanely** adv.

inimical /ɪˈnɪmɪk(ə)l/ adj. 1 hostile. 2 harmful. □ **inimically** adv. [Latin inimicus enemy]

inimitable /ɪˈnɪmɪtəb(ə)l/ adj. impossible to imitate. □ **inimitably** adv.

iniquity /ɪˈnɪkwɪtɪ/ n. (pl. -ies) 1 wickedness. 2 gross injustice. □ **iniquitous** adj. [French from Latin aequus just]

initial /ɪˈnɪʃ(ə)l/ —adj. 1 of or at the beginning. —n. initial letter, esp. (in pl.) those of a person's names. —v. (-ll-; US -l-) mark or sign with one's initials. □ **initially** adv. [Latin initium beginning]

initial letter n. first letter of a word.

initiate —v. /ɪˈnɪʃɪeɪt/ (-ting) 1 begin; set going, originate. 2 a admit (a person) into a society, office, etc., esp. with a ritual. b instruct (a person) in a subject. —n. /ɪˈnɪʃɪət/ (esp. newly) initiated person. □ **initiation** /-eɪʃ(ə)n/ n. **initiator** n. **initiatory** /ɪˈnɪʃɪətərɪ/ adj. [Latin initium beginning]

initiative /ɪˈnɪʃɪətɪv/ n. 1 ability to initiate things; enterprise (lacks initiative). 2 first step. 3 prec. by the (power or right to begin). □ **have the initiative** esp. Mil. be able to control the enemy's movements. [French: related to INITIATE]

inject /ɪnˈdʒekt/ v. 1 a (usu. foll. by into) drive (a solution, medicine, etc.) by or as if by a syringe. b (usu. foll. by with) fill (a cavity etc.) by injecting. c administer medicine etc. to (a person) by injection. 2 place (a quality, money, etc.) into something. □ **injection** n. **injector** n. [Latin injicere -ject- from jacio throw]

injudicious /ˌɪndʒuːˈdɪʃəs/ adj. unwise; ill-judged.

injunction /ɪnˈdʒʌŋk(ʃ)ən/ n. 1 authoritative order. 2 judicial order restraining a person or body from an act, or compelling redress to an injured party. [Latin: related to ENJOIN]

injure /ˈɪndʒə(r)/ v. (-ring) 1 harm or damage. 2 do wrong to. [back-formation from INJURY]

injured adj. 1 harmed or hurt. 2 offended.

injurious /ɪnˈdʒʊərɪəs/ adj. 1 hurtful. 2 (of language) insulting. 3 wrongful.

injury /ˈɪndʒərɪ/ n. (pl. -ies) 1 physical harm or damage. 2 offence or feelings etc. 3 esp. Law wrongful action or treatment. [Latin injuria]

injury time n. extra playing-time at a football etc. match to compensate for time lost in dealing with injuries.

injustice /ɪnˈdʒʌstɪs/ n. 1 lack of fairness. 2 unjust act. □ **do a person an injustice** judge a person unfairly.

ink —n. 1 coloured fluid or paste used for writing, printing, etc. 2 black liquid ejected by a cuttlefish etc. —v. 1 (usu. foll. by in, over, etc.) mark with ink. 2 cover (type etc.) with ink. [Greek egkauston purple ink used by Roman emperors]

inkling /ˈɪŋklɪŋ/ n. (often foll. by of) slight knowledge or suspicion; hint. [origin unknown]

inkstand n. stand for one or more ink bottles.

ink-well n. pot for ink, usu. housed in a hole in a desk.

inky adj. (-ier, -iest) of, as black as, or stained with ink. □ **inkiness** n.

inland —*adj.* /'ɪnlənd/ **1** in the interior of a country. **2** carried on within a country. —*adv.* /ɪn'lænd/ in or towards the interior of a country.

Inland Revenue *n.* government department assessing and collecting taxes.

in-law *n.* (often in *pl.*) relative by marriage.

inlay —*v.* /ɪn'leɪ/ (*past* and *past part.* **inlaid** /ɪn'leɪd/) **1** embed (a thing in another) so that the surfaces are even. **2** decorate (a thing with inlaid work). —*n.* /'ɪnleɪ/ **1** inlaid work. **2** material inlaid. **3** filling shaped to fit a tooth-cavity. [from IN-², LAY¹]

inlet /'ɪnlət/ *n.* **1** small arm of the sea, a lake, or a river. **2** piece inserted. **3** way of entry. [from IN, LET¹]

in loco parentis /ɪn ˌləʊkəʊ pə'rentɪs/ *adv.* (acting) for or instead of a parent. [Latin]

inmate *n.* occupant of a hospital, prison, institution, etc. [probably from INN, MATE¹]

in memoriam /ɪn mɪ'mɔːrɪˌæm/ *prep.* in memory of (a dead person). [Latin]

inmost *adj.* most inward. [Old English]

inn *n.* **1** pub, sometimes with accommodation. **2** *hist.* house providing accommodation, esp. for travellers. [Old English: related to IN]

innards /'ɪnədz/ *n.pl. colloq.* entrails. [special pronunciation of INWARD]

innate /ɪ'neɪt/ *adj.* inborn; natural. □ **innately** *adv.* [Latin *natus* born]

inner —*adj.* (usu. *attrib.*) **1** inside; interior. **2** (of thoughts, feelings, etc.) deeper. —*n.* **1** *Archery* **1** division of the target next to the bull's-eye. **2** shot striking this. □ **innermost** *adj.* [Old English, comparative of IN]

inner city *n.* central area of a city, esp. regarded as having particular problems (also with hyphen) *attrib.*: *inner-city housing*).

inner man *n.* (also **inner woman**) **1** soul or mind. **2** *joc.* stomach.

inner tube *n.* separate inflatable tube inside a pneumatic tyre.

innings *n.* (*pl.* same) **1** esp. *Cricket* part of a game during which a side is batting. **2** period during which a government, party, person, etc. is in office or can achieve something. [obsolete *in* (verb) = go in]

innkeeper *n.* person who keeps an inn.

innocent /'ɪnəs(ə)nt/ —*adj.* **1** free from moral wrong. **2** (usu. foll. by *of*) not guilty (of a crime etc.). **3** simple; guileless. **4** harmless. —*n.* innocent person, esp. a young child. □ **innocence** *n.* **innocently** *adv.* [Latin *noceo* hurt]

innocuous /ɪ'nɒkjuəs/ *adj.* harmless. [Latin *innocuus*: related to INNOCENT]

Inn of Court *n.* each of the four legal societies admitting people to the English bar.

innovate /'ɪnəˌveɪt/ *v.* (-ting) bring in new methods, ideas, etc.; make changes. □ **innovation** /-'veɪʃ(ə)n/ *n.* **innovative** *adj.* **innovator** *n.* **innovatory** *adj.* [Latin *novus* new]

innuendo /ˌɪnjʊ'endəʊ/ *n.* (*pl.* **-es** or **-s**) allusive remark or hint, usu. disparaging or with a double meaning. [Latin, = by nodding at: related to IN-², *nuo* nod]

Inuit var. of INUIT.

innumerable /ɪ'njuːmərəb(ə)l/ *adj.* too many to be counted. □ **innumerably** *adv.*

innumerate /ɪ'njuːmərət/ *adj.* having no knowledge of basic mathematics. □ **innumeracy** *n.*

inoculate /ɪ'nɒkjʊˌleɪt/ *v.* (-ting) treat (a person or animal) with vaccine or serum to promote immunity against a disease. □ **inoculation** /-'leɪʃ(ə)n/ *n.* [Latin *oculus* eye, bud]

inoffensive /ɪnə'fensɪv/ *adj.* not objectionable; harmless.

inoperable /ɪn'ɒpərəb(ə)l/ *adj. Surgery* that cannot successfully be operated on.

inoperative /ɪn'ɒpərətɪv/ *adj.* not working or taking effect.

inopportune /ɪn'ɒpəˌtjuːn/ *adj.* not appropriate, esp. not timely.

inordinate /ɪn'ɔːdɪnət/ *adj.* excessive. □ **inordinately** *adv.* [Latin: related to ORDAIN]

inorganic /ɪnɔː'gænɪk/ *adj.* **1** *Chem.* (of a compound) not organic, usu. of mineral origin. **2** without organized physical structure. **3** extraneous.

in-patient *n.* patient who lives in hospital while under treatment.

input /'ɪnpʊt/ —*n.* **1** what is put in or taken in. **2** place where energy, information, etc., enters a system. **3** action of putting in or feeding in. **4** contribution of information etc. —*v.* (**inputting**; *past* and *past part.* **input** or **inputted**) (often foll. by *into*) **1** put in. **2** supply (data, programs, etc., to a computer etc.).

inquest /'ɪnkwest/ *n.* **1** *Law* inquiry by a coroner's court into the cause of a death. **2** *colloq.* discussion analysing the outcome of a game, election, etc. [Romanic: related to INQUIRE]

inquietude /ɪn'kwaɪɪˌtjuːd/ *n.* uneasiness. [Latin: related to QUIET]

inquire /ɪn'kwaɪə(r)/ *v.* -ring) seek information formally; make a formal investigation. **2** = ENQUIRE. [Latin *quaero quaesit-* seek]

inquiry *n.* (*pl.* -**ies**) **1** investigation, esp. an official one. **2** = ENQUIRY.

inquisition /ˌɪnkwɪˈzɪʃ(ə)n/ *n.* **1** intensive search or investigation. **2** judicial or official inquiry. **3** (the Inquisition) *RC Ch. hist.* ecclesiastical tribunal for the violent suppression of heresy, esp. in Spain. □ **inquisitional** *adj.* [Latin: related to INQUIRE]

inquisitive /ɪnˈkwɪzɪtɪv/ *adj.* **1** unduly curious; prying. **2** seeking knowledge. □ **inquisitively** *adv.* **inquisitiveness** *n.*

inquisitor /ɪnˈkwɪzɪtə(r)/ *n.* **1** official investigator. **2** *hist.* officer of the Inquisition.

inquisitorial /ɪnˌkwɪzɪˈtɔːrɪəl/ *adj.* **1** of or like an inquisitor. **2** prying. □ **inquisitorially** *adv.*

inquorate /ɪnˈkwɔːreɪt/ *adj.* not constituting a quorum.

in re /ɪn ˈriː/ *prep.* = RE¹. [Latin]

INRI *abbr.* Jesus of Nazareth, King of the Jews. [Latin *Iesus Nazarenus Rex Iudaeorum*]

inroad *n.* **1** (often in *pl.*) encroachment; using up of resources etc. **2** hostile attack.

inrush *n.* rapid influx.

insalubrious /ˌɪnsəˈluːbrɪəs/ *adj.* (of a climate or place) unhealthy.

insane *adj.* **1** mad. **2** *colloq.* extremely foolish. □ **insanely** *adv.* **insanity** /ɪnˈsænɪtɪ/ *n.* (*pl.* -ies).

insanitary /ɪnˈsænɪtərɪ/ *adj.* not sanitary; dirty.

insatiable /ɪnˈseɪʃəb(ə)l/ *adj.* **1** unable to be satisfied. **2** extremely greedy. □ **insatiability** /-ˈbɪlɪtɪ/ *n.* **insatiably** *adv.*

insatiate /ɪnˈseɪʃɪət/ *adj.* never satisfied.

inscribe /ɪnˈskraɪb/ *v.* (-bing) **1 a** (usu. foll. by *in*, *on*) write or carve (words etc.) on a surface, page, etc. **b** (usu. foll. by *with*) mark (a surface) with characters. **2** (usu. foll. by *to*) write an informal dedication in or on (a book etc.). **3** enter the name of (a person) on a list or in a book. **4** *Geom.* draw (a figure) within another so that points of it lie on the boundary of the other. [Latin *scribo* write]

inscription /ɪnˈskrɪpʃ(ə)n/ *n.* **1** words inscribed. **2** inscribing. □ **inscriptional** *adj.* [Latin: related to INSCRIBE]

inscrutable /ɪnˈskruːtəb(ə)l/ *adj.* mysterious, impenetrable. □ **inscrutability** /-ˈbɪlɪtɪ/ *n.* **inscrutably** *adv.* [Latin *scrutor* search]

insect /ˈɪnsekt/ *n.* small invertebrate of a class characteristically having a head, thorax, abdomen, two antennae, three pairs of thoracic legs, and usu. one or two pairs of thoracic wings. [Latin: related to SECTION]

insecticide /ɪnˈsektɪsaɪd/ *n.* substance for killing insects.

insectivore /ɪnˈsektɪvɔː(r)/ *n.* **1** animal that feeds on insects. **2** plant which captures and absorbs insects. □ **insectivorous** /-ˈtɪvərəs/ *adj.* [from INSECT, Latin *voro* devour]

insecure /ˌɪnsɪˈkjʊə(r)/ *adj.* **1 a** unsafe; not firm. **b** (of a surface etc.) liable to give way. **2** uncertain; lacking confidence. □ **insecurity** /-ˈkjʊrɪtɪ/ *n.* [Latin: related to SECURE]

inseminate /ɪnˈsemɪneɪt/ *v.* (-ting) **1** introduce semen into. **2** sow (seed etc.). □ **insemination** /-ˈneɪʃ(ə)n/ *n.* [Latin: related to SEMEN]

insensate /ɪnˈsenseɪt/ *adj.* **1** without physical sensation. **2** without sensibility. **3** stupid. [Latin: related to SENSE]

insensible /ɪnˈsensɪb(ə)l/ *adj.* **1** unconscious. **2** (usu. foll. by *of*, *to*) unaware (*insensible of her needs*). **3** too small or gradual to be perceived. **4** without emotion. □ **insensibility** /-ˈbɪlɪtɪ/ *n.* **insensibly** *adv.*

insensitive /ɪnˈsensɪtɪv/ *adj.* (often foll. by *to*) **1** unfeeling; boorish: crass. **2** not sensitive to physical stimuli. □ **insensitively** *adv.* **insensitiveness** *n.* **insensitivity** /-ˈtɪvɪtɪ/ *n.*

insentient /ɪnˈsenʃ(ə)nt/ *adj.* not sentient; inanimate.

inseparable /ɪnˈsep(ə)rəb(ə)l/ *adj.* (esp. of friends) unable or unwilling to be separated. □ **inseparability** /-ˈbɪlɪtɪ/ *n.* **inseparably** *adv.*

insert —*v.* /ɪnˈsɜːt/ place or put (a thing) into another. —*n.* /ˈɪnsɜːt/ something inserted. [Latin *sero sert-* join]

insertion /ɪnˈsɜːʃ(ə)n/ *n.* **1** inserting. **2** thing inserted.

in-service *attrib. adj.* (of training) for those actively engaged in the profession or activity concerned.

inset —*n.* /ˈɪnset/ **1 a** extra section inserted in a book etc. **b** small map etc. within the border of a larger one. **2** piece let into a dress etc. —*v.* /ɪnˈset/ (**inset**ting; *past* and *past part.* **inset** or **inset**ted) **1** put in as an inset. **2** decorate with an inset.

inshore *adv. & adj.* at sea but close to the shore.

inside —*n.* /ɪnˈsaɪd/ **1 a** inner side. **b** inner part; interior. **2** (usu. in *pl.*) *colloq.* stomach and bowels. —*adj.* /ˈɪnsaɪd/ **1** situated on or in the inside. **2** *Football & Hockey* nearer to the centre of the field. —*adv.* /ɪnˈsaɪd/ **1** on, in, or to the inside. **2** *slang* in prison. —*prep.* /ɪnˈsaɪd/ **1** on the inner side of; within. **2** in less than (*inside an hour*). □ **inside out 1** with the inner

surface turned outwards. **2** thoroughly (*knew his subject inside out*).

inside information n. information not normally accessible to outsiders.

inside job n. *colloq.* crime committed by a person living or working on the premises burgled etc.

insider /ɪnˈsaɪdə(r)/ n. **1** person who is within an organization etc. **2** person privy to a secret.

insider dealing n. *Stock Exch.* illegal practice of trading to one's own advantage through having access to confidential information.

insidious /ɪnˈsɪdɪəs/ adj. **1** proceeding inconspicuously but harmfully. **2** crafty. □ **insidiously** adv. **insidiousness** n. [Latin *insidiae* ambush]

insight n. (usu. foll. by *into*) **1** capacity of understanding hidden truths etc. **2** instance of this.

insignia /ɪnˈsɪɡnɪə/ n. (treated as *sing.* or *pl.*) badge. [Latin *signum* sign]

insignificant /ɪnsɪɡˈnɪfɪkənt/ adj. **1** unimportant. **2** meaningless. □ **insignificance** n.

insincere /ɪnsɪnˈsɪə(r)/ adj. not sincere. □ **insincerely** adv. **insincerity** /-ˈserɪtɪ/ n. (pl. **-ies**).

insinuate /ɪnˈsɪnjʊeɪt/ v. (**-ting**) **1** hint obliquely, esp. unpleasantly. **2** (often *refl.*; usu. foll. by *into*) **a** introduce (a person etc.) into favour etc., by subtle manipulation. **b** introduce (a thing, oneself, etc.) deviously into a place. □ **insinuation** /-ˈeɪʃ(ə)n/ n. [Latin *sinuo* curve]

insipid /ɪnˈsɪpɪd/ adj. **1** lacking vigour or character; dull. **2** tasteless. □ **insipidity** /-ˈpɪdɪtɪ/ n. **insipidly** adv. [Latin *sapio* have savour]

insist /ɪnˈsɪst/ v. (usu. foll. by *on* or *that*; also *absol.*) maintain or demand assertively (*insisted on my going*; *insisted that he was innocent*). [Latin *sisto* stand]

insistent adj. **1** (often foll. by *on*) insisting. **2** forcing itself on the attention. □ **insistence** n. **insistently** adv.

in situ /ɪn ˈsɪtjuː/ adv. in its proper or original place. [Latin]

insobriety /ɪnsəˈbraɪətɪ/ n. intemperance, esp. in drinking.

insofar /ɪnsəʊˈfɑː(r)/ adv. = *in so far* (see FAR).

insole n. fixed or removable inner sole of a boot or shoe.

insolent /ˈɪnsələnt/ adj. impertinently insulting. □ **insolence** n. **insolently** adv. [Latin *soleo* be accustomed]

insoluble /ɪnˈsɒljʊb(ə)l/ adj. **1** incapable of being solved. **2** incapable of being dissolved. □ **insolubility** /-ˈbɪlɪtɪ/ n. **insolubly** adv.

insolvent /ɪnˈsɒlv(ə)nt/ —adj. unable to pay one's debts; bankrupt. —n. insolvent person. □ **insolvency** n.

insomnia /ɪnˈsɒmnɪə/ n. sleeplessness, esp. habitual. [Latin *somnus* sleep]

insomniac /ɪnˈsɒmnɪæk/ n. person suffering from insomnia.

insomuch /ɪnsəʊˈmʌtʃ/ adv. **1** (foll. by *that*) to such an extent. **2** (foll. by *as*) inasmuch. [originally *in so much*]

insouciant /ɪnˈsuːsɪənt/ adj. carefree; unconcerned. □ **insouciance** n. [French *souci* care]

inspect /ɪnˈspekt/ v. **1** look closely at. **2** examine officially. □ **inspection** n. [Latin *spicio spect-* look]

inspector n. **1** person who inspects. **2** official employed to supervise. **3** police officer next above sergeant in rank. □ **inspectorate** n.

inspector of taxes n. Inland Revenue official responsible for assessing taxes.

inspiration /ɪnspəˈreɪʃ(ə)n/ n. **1 a** creative force or influence. **b** person etc. stimulating creativity etc. **c** divine influence, esp. on the writing of Scripture etc. **2** sudden brilliant idea. □ **inspirational** adj.

inspire /ɪnˈspaɪə(r)/ v. (**-ring**) **1** stimulate (a person) to esp. creative activity. **2 a** (usu. foll. by *with*) animate (a person) with a feeling. **b** create (a feeling) in a person (*inspires confidence*). **3** prompt; give rise to (*a poem inspired by love*). **4** (as **inspired** adj.) characterized by inspiration. □ **inspiring** adj. [Latin *spiro* breathe]

inspirit /ɪnˈspɪrɪt/ v. (**-t-**) **1** put life into; animate. **2** encourage.

inst. abbr. = INSTANT adj. **4** (*the 6th inst.*).

instability /ɪnstəˈbɪlɪtɪ/ n. **1** lack of stability. **2** unpredictability in behaviour etc.

install /ɪnˈstɔːl/ v. (also **instal**) (**-ll-**) **1** place (equipment etc.) in position ready for use. **2** place (a person) in an office or rank with ceremony. **3** establish (oneself, a person, etc.). □ **installation** /ɪnstəˈleɪʃ(ə)n/ n. [Latin: related to STALL[1]]

instalment n. (*US* **installment**) **1** any of several usu. equal payments for something. **2** any of several parts, esp. of a broadcast or published story. [Anglo-French *estaler* fix]

instance /ˈɪnst(ə)ns/ —n. **1** example or illustration of (*that's a particular case* (*that's not true in this instance*). □ **for instance** as an example. **in the first** (or **second** etc.) **instance** in the first (or second etc.) place; at the first (or second etc.) stage

(of a proceeding). [French from Latin *instantia* contrary example]

instant —*adj.* **1** occurring immediately. **2** (of food etc.) processed for quick preparation. **3** urgent; pressing. **4** *Commerce* of the current month (*the 6th instant*). —*n.* **1** precise moment (*come here this instant*). **2** short space of time (*in an instant*). [Latin *insto* be urgent]

instantaneous /ˌɪnstənˈteɪnɪəs/ *adj.* occurring or done in an instant. □ **instantaneously** *adv.*

instantly *adv.* immediately; at once.

instead /ɪnˈstɛd/ *adv.* **1** (foll. by *of*) in place of. **2** as an alternative.

instep *n.* **1** inner arch of the foot between the toes and the ankle. **2** part of a shoe etc. over or under this. [ultimately from IN-², STEP]

instigate /ˈɪnstɪgeɪt/ *v.* (-**ting**) **1** bring about by incitement or persuasion. **2** urge on; incite. □ **instigation** /-ˈgeɪʃ(ə)n/ *n.* **instigator** *n.* [Latin *instigo* prick]

instil /ɪnˈstɪl/ *v.* (US **instill**) (-**ll**-) (often foll. by *into*) **1** introduce (a feeling, idea, etc.) into a person's mind etc. gradually. **2** put (a liquid) into something in drops. □ **instillation** /-ˈleɪʃ(ə)n/ *n.* **instilment** *n.* [Latin *stillo* drop]

instinct —*n.* /ˈɪnstɪŋkt/ **1 a** innate pattern of behaviour, esp. in animals. **b** innate impulse. **2** intuition. —*predic. adj.* /ɪnˈstɪŋkt/ (foll. by *with*) imbued, filled (with life, beauty, etc.). □ **instinctive** /ɪnˈstɪŋktɪv/ *adj.* **instinctively** *adv.* **instinctual** /ɪnˈstɪŋktjʊəl/ *adj.* [Latin *stinguo* prick]

institute /ˈɪnstɪtjuːt/ —*n.* **1** society or organization for the promotion of science, education, etc. **2** its premises. —*v.* (-**ting**) **1** establish; found. **2** initiate (an inquiry etc.). **3** (usu. foll. by *to*, *into*) appoint (a person) as a cleric in a church etc. [Latin *statuo* set up]

institution /ˌɪnstɪˈtjuːʃ(ə)n/ *n.* **1** organization or society founded for a particular purpose. **2** established law, practice, or custom. **3** *colloq.* (of a person etc.) familiar object. **4** instituting or being instituted.

institutional *adj.* **1** of or like an institution. **2** typical of institutions. □ **institutionally** *adv.*

institutionalize *v.* (also **-ise**) (-**zing** or **-sing**) **1** (as **institutionalized** *adj.*) made dependent after a long period in an institution. **2** place or keep (a person) in an institution. **3** make institutional.

instruct /ɪnˈstrʌkt/ *v.* **1** teach (a person) a subject etc.; train. **2** (usu. foll. by +infin.) direct; command. **3** *Law* **a** employ (a lawyer). **b** inform. □ **Instructor** *n.* [Latin *instruo -struct-* build, teach]

instruction /ɪnˈstrʌkʃ(ə)n/ *n.* **1** (often in *pl.*) **a** order. **b** direction (as to how a thing works etc.). **2** teaching (*course of instruction*). □ **instructional** *adj.*

instructive /ɪnˈstrʌktɪv/ *adj.* tending to instruct; enlightening.

instrument /ˈɪnstrəmənt/ *n.* **1** tool or implement, esp. for delicate or scientific work. **2** (in full **musical instrument**) device for producing musical sounds. **3 a** thing used in performing an action. **b** person made use of. **4** measuring device, esp. in an aeroplane. **5** formal, esp. legal, document. [Latin *instru- mentum*: related to INSTRUCT]

instrumental /ˌɪnstrəˈment(ə)l/ *adj.* **1** serving as an instrument or means. **2** (of music) performed on instruments. **3** of, or arising from, an instrument (*instru- mental error*).

instrumentalist *n.* performer on a musical instrument.

instrumentality /ˌɪnstrəmenˈtælɪtɪ/ *n.* agency or means.

instrumentation /ˌɪnstrəmenˈteɪʃ(ə)n/ *n.* **1 a** provision or use of instruments. **b** instruments collectively. **2** arrangement of music for instruments. **b** the particular instruments used in a piece.

insubordinate /ˌɪnsəˈbɔːdɪnət/ *adj.* disobedient; rebellious. □ **insubordina- tion** /-ˈneɪʃ(ə)n/ *n.*

insubstantial /ˌɪnsəbˈstænʃ(ə)l/ *adj.* **1** lacking solidity or substance. **2** not real.

insufferable /ɪnˈsʌf(ə)rəb(ə)l/ *adj.* **1** intolerable. **2** unbearably conceited etc. □ **insufferably** *adv.*

insufficient /ˌɪnsəˈfɪʃ(ə)nt/ *adj.* not sufficient; inadequate. □ **insufficiency** *n.* **insufficiently** *adv.*

insular /ˈɪnsjʊlə(r)/ *adj.* **1 a** of or like an island. **b** separated or remote. **2** narrow-minded. □ **insularity** /-ˈlærɪtɪ/ *n.* [Latin *insula* island]

insulate /ˈɪnsjʊleɪt/ *v.* (-**ting**) **1** prevent the passage of electricity, heat, or sound from (a thing, room, etc.) by interposing non-conductors. **2** isolate. □ **insulation** /-ˈleɪʃ(ə)n/ *n.* **insulator** *n.* [Latin *insula* island]

insulin /ˈɪnsjʊlɪn/ *n.* hormone regulating the amount of glucose in the blood, the lack of which causes diabetes. [Latin *insula* island]

insult —*v.* /ɪnˈsʌlt/ **1** speak to or treat with scornful abuse. **2** offend the self-respect or modesty of. —*n.* /ˈɪnsʌlt/ insulting remark or action. □ **insulting** *adj.* **insultingly** *adv.* [Latin *insulto* leap on, assail]

insuperable /ɪnˈsuːp(ə)rəb(ə)l/ *adj.* **1** (of a barrier) impossible to surmount. **2** (of a difficulty etc.) impossible to overcome.

□ **insuperability** /ˌ'bɪlɪtɪ/ n. **insuperably** adv. [Latin supero overcome]

insupportable /ˌɪnsə'pɔːtəb(ə)l/ adj. **1** unable to be endured. **2** unjustifiable.

insurance /ɪn'ʃʊərəns/ n. **1** insuring. **2 a** sum paid for this. **b** sum paid out as compensation for theft, damage, etc. [French: related to ENSURE]

insure /ɪn'ʃʊə(r)/ v. (-ring) (often foll. by against; also absol.) secure compensation in the event of loss or damage to (property, life, a person, etc.) by advance regular payments. [var. of ENSURE]

insured n. (usu. prec. by the) person etc. covered by insurance

insurer n. person or company selling insurance policies.

insurgent /ɪn'sɜːdʒ(ə)nt/ —adj. in active revolt. —n. rebel. □ **insurgence** n. [Latin surgo surrect- rise]

insurmountable /ˌɪnsə'maʊntəb(ə)l/ adj. unable to be surmounted or overcome.

insurrection /ˌɪnsə'rek(ʃ)ən/ n. rebellion. □ **insurrectionist** n. [Latin: related to INSURGENT]

insusceptible /ˌɪnsə'septɪb(ə)l/ adj. not susceptible.

intact /ɪn'tækt/ adj. **1** undamaged; entire. **2** untouched. □ **intactness** n. [Latin tango tact- touch]

intaglio /ɪn'tɑːlɪəʊ/ n. (pl. -s) **1** gem with an incised design. **2** engraved design. [Italian: related to TAIL²]

intake n. **1** action of taking in. **2 a** number (of people etc.), or amount, taken in or received. **b** such people etc. (this year's intake). **3** place where water is taken into a pipe, or fuel or air enters an engine etc.

intangible /ɪn'tændʒɪb(ə)l/ —adj. **1** unable to be touched. **2** unable to be grasped mentally. —n. thing that cannot be precisely assessed or defined. □ **intangibility** /ˌ'bɪlɪtɪ/ n. **intangibly** adv. [Latin: related to INTACT]

integer /'ɪntɪdʒə(r)/ n. whole number. [Latin, = untouched, whole]

integral /'ɪntɪɡr(ə)l/ —adj. also /-'teɡ-/ **1 a** of or necessary to a whole. **b** forming a whole. **c** complete. **2** of or denoted by an integer. —n. Math. quantity of which a given function is the derivative. □ **integrally** adv. [Latin: related to INTEGER]

■ **Usage** The alternative pronunciation given for the adjective, stressed on the second syllable, is considered incorrect by some people.

integral calculus n. mathematics concerned with finding integrals, their properties and application, etc.

integrate /'ɪntɪˌɡreɪt/ v. (-ting) **1 a** combine (parts) into a whole. **b** complete by the addition of parts. **2** bring or come into equal membership of society, a school, etc. **3** desegregate, esp. racially (a school etc.). **4** Math. find the integral of. □ **integration** /-'ɡreɪʃ(ə)n/ n.

integrated circuit n. Electronics small chip etc. replacing several separate components in a conventional electronic circuit.

integrity /ɪn'teɡrɪtɪ/ n. **1** moral excellence; honesty. **2** wholeness; soundness. [Latin: related to INTEGER]

integument /ɪn'teɡjʊmənt/ n. natural outer covering, as a skin, husk, rind, etc. [Latin tego cover]

intellect /'ɪntɪlekt/ n. **1 a** faculty of reasoning, knowing, and thinking. **b** understanding. **2** clever or knowledgeable person. [Latin: related to INTELLIGENT]

intellectual /ˌɪntɪ'lektʃʊəl/ —adj. **1** of or appealing to the intellect. **2** possessing a highly developed intellect. **3** requiring the intellect. —n. intellectual person. □ **intellectuality** /-'ælɪtɪ/ n. **intellectualize** v. (also -ise) (-zing or -sing), **intellectually** adv.

intelligence /ɪn'telɪdʒ(ə)ns/ n. **1 a** intellect; understanding. **b** quickness of understanding. **2 a** the collecting of information, esp. of military or political value. **b** information so collected. **c** people employed in this.

intelligence quotient n. number denoting the ratio of a person's intelligence to the average.

intelligent adj. **1** having or showing intelligence, esp. of a high level. **2** clever. □ **intelligently** adv. [Latin intelligo -lect- understand]

intelligentsia /ɪnˌtelɪ'dʒentsɪə/ n. class of intellectuals regarded as possessing culture and political initiative. [Russian intelligentsiya]

intelligible /ɪn'telɪdʒɪb(ə)l/ adj. able to be understood. □ **intelligibility** /-'bɪlɪtɪ/ n. **intelligibly** adv.

intemperate /ɪn'tempərət/ adj. **1** immoderate. **2 a** given to excessive drinking of alcohol. **b** excessively indulgent in one's appetites. □ **intemperance** n.

intend /ɪn'tend/ v. **1** have as one's purpose (we intend to go; we intend going). **2** (usu. foll. by for, as) design or destine (a person or a thing) (I intend him to go; I intend it as a warning). [Latin tendo stretch]

intended —adj. done on purpose. —n. colloq. one's fiancé or fiancée.

intense /ɪn'tens/ adj. (intenser, intensest) **1** existing in a high degree; violent;

forceful; extreme (*intense joy; intense cold*). 2 very emotional. □ **Intensely** *adv.* **Intenseness** *n.* [Latin *intensus* stretched]

■ **Usage** *Intense* is sometimes confused with *intensive*, and wrongly used to describe a course of study etc.

intensifier /in'tensɪ,faiǝ(r)/ *n.* 1 thing that makes something more intense. 2 word or prefix used to give force or emphasis, e.g. *thundering* in a *thundering nuisance*.

intensify *v.* (-ies, -ied) make or become more or less intense. □ **intensification** *n.*

intensity /in'tensɪtɪ/ *n.* (*pl.* -ies) 1 intenseness. 2 amount of some quality, e.g. force, brightness, etc.

intensive *adj.* 1 thorough, vigorous; directed to a single point, area, or subject (*intensive study; intensive bombardment*). 2 of or relating to intensity. 3 serving to increase production in relation to costs (*intensive farming*). 4 (usu. in comb.) *Econ.* making much use of (*labour-intensive*). 5 (of an adjective, adverb, etc.) expressing intensity, e.g. *really* in *my feet are really cold*. □ **intensively** *adv.* **intensiveness** *n.*

intensive care *n.* 1 constant monitoring etc. of a seriously ill patient. 2 part of a hospital devoted to this.

intent /in'tent/ —*n.* intention; purpose (*with intent to defraud*). —*adj.* 1 (usu. foll. by *on*) a resolved, determined. b attentively occupied. 2 (esp. of a look) earnest; eager. □ **to all intents and purposes** practically; virtually. □ **intently** *adv.* **intentness** *n.* [Latin *intentus*]

intention /in'tenʃ(ǝ)n/ *n.* 1 thing intended; aim, purpose. 2 intending (*done without intention*).

intentional *adj.* done on purpose. □ **intentionally** *adv.*

inter /in'tɜː(r)/ *v.* (-rr-) bury (a corpse etc.). [Latin *terra* earth]

inter- *comb. form* 1 between, among (*intercontinental*). 2 mutually, reciprocally (*interbreed*). [Latin *inter* between, among]

interact /,intǝr'ækt/ *v.* act on each other. □ **interaction** *n.*

interactive *adj.* 1 reciprocally active. 2 (of a computer or other electronic device) allowing a two-way flow of information between it and a user. □ **interactively** *adv.*

inter alia /,intǝr 'eiliǝ/ *adv.* among other things. [Latin]

interbreed /,intǝ'briːd/ *v.* (*past* and *past part.* -bred) 1 (cause to) breed with members of a different race or species to produce a hybrid. 2 breed within one family etc.

intercalary /in'tɜːkǝlǝri/ *attrib. adj.* 1 a (of a day or a month) inserted in the calendar to harmonize it with the solar year. b (of a year) having such an addition. 2 interpolated. [Latin *calo* proclaim]

intercede /,intǝ'siːd/ *v.* (-ding) (usu. foll. by *with*) intervene on behalf of another; plead. [Latin: related to CEDE]

intercept /,intǝ'sept/ *v.* 1 seize, catch, or stop (a person or thing) going from one place to another. 2 (usu. foll. by *from*) cut off (light etc.). □ **interception** *n.* **interceptor** *n.* [Latin *intercipio -cept-* from *capio* take]

intercession /,intǝ'seʃ(ǝ)n/ *n.* interceding. □ **intercessor** *n.* [Latin: related to INTERCEDE]

interchange —*v.* /,intǝ'tʃeindʒ/ (-ging) 1 (of two people) exchange (things) with each other. 2 put each of (two things) in the other's place. —*n.* /'intǝtʃeindʒ/ 1 (often foll. by *of*) exchange between two people etc. 2 alternation. 3 road junction where traffic streams do not cross.

interchangeable *adj.* that can be interchanged, esp. without affecting the way a thing works. □ **interchangeably** *adv.*

inter-city /,intǝ'siti/ *adj.* existing or travelling between cities.

intercom /'intǝkɒm/ *n. colloq.* 1 system of intercommunication by radio or telephone. 2 instrument used in this. [abbreviation]

intercommunicate /,intǝkǝ'mjuːni,keit/ *v.* 1 communicate reciprocally. 2 (of rooms etc.) open into each other. □ **intercommunication** /,intǝkǝ,mjuːni'keiʃ(ǝ)n/ *n.*

intercommunion /,intǝkǝ'mjuːniǝn/ *n.* 1 mutual communion. 2 mutual action or relationship, esp. between Christian denominations.

interconnect /,intǝkǝ'nekt/ *v.* connect with each other. □ **interconnection** /-'nekʃ(ǝ)n/ *n.*

intercontinental /,intǝ,kɒnti'nent(ǝ)l/ *adj.* connecting or travelling between continents.

intercourse /'intǝkɔːs/ *n.* 1 communication or dealings between individuals, nations, etc. 2 = SEXUAL INTERCOURSE. [Latin: related to COURSE]

interdenominational /,intǝdi,nɒmi'neiʃǝn(ǝ)l/ *adj.* concerning more than one (religious) denomination.

interdepartmental /,ɪntədɪ'pɑːt'ment(ə)l/ adj. concerning more than one department.

interdependent /,ɪntədɪ'pend(ə)nt/ adj. dependent on each other. □ **interdependence** n.

interdict —n. /'ɪntədɪkt/ 1 authoritative prohibition. 2 RC Ch. sentence debarring a person, or esp. a place, from ecclesiastical functions and privileges. —v. /,ɪntə'dɪkt/ 1 prohibit (an action). 2 forbid the use of 3 (usu. foll. by from + verbal noun) restrain (a person). 4 (usu. foll. by to) forbid (a thing) to a person. □ **interdiction** /-'dɪk(ə)n/ n. **interdictory** /-'dɪktəri/ adj. [Latin dico say]

interdisciplinary /,ɪntə'dɪsɪplɪnəri/ adj. of or between more than one branch of learning.

interest /'ɪntrɪst/ —n. 1 a concern; curiosity (have no interest in fishing). b quality exciting curiosity etc. (this book lacks interest). 2 subject, hobby, etc., in which one is concerned. 3 advantage or profit (it is in my interest to go). 4 a money paid for the use of money lent. 5 a thing in which one has a stake or concern (business interests). b financial stake (in an undertaking etc.). c legal concern, title, or right (in property). 6 a party or group with a common interest (the brewing interest). b principle or cause with which this is concerned. —v. 1 excite the curiosity or attention of. 2 (usu. foll. by in) cause (a person) to take a personal interest. 3 (as interested adj.) having a private interest; not impartial or disinterested. [Latin, = it matters]

interesting adj. causing curiosity; holding the attention. □ **interestingly** adv.

interface —n. 1 surface forming a boundary between two regions. 2 means or place of interaction between two systems etc.; interaction (the interface between psychology and education). 3 Computing apparatus for connecting two pieces of equipment so that they can be operated jointly. —v. (-cing) 1 connect with (another piece of equipment etc.) by an interface. 2 interact.

■ **Usage** The use of the noun and verb in sense 2 is deplored by some people.

interfacing n. stiffish material between two layers of fabric in collars etc.

interfere /,ɪntə'fɪə(r)/ v. (-ring) 1 (usu. foll. by with) a (of a person) meddle; obstruct a process etc. b (of a thing) be a hindrance. 2 (usu. foll. by in) intervene, esp. without invitation or necessity. 3 (foll. by with or euphem. molest or assault sexually. 4 (of light or other waves) combine so as to cause interference. [Latin ferio strike]

interference n. 1 act of interfering. 2 fading or disturbance of received radio signals. 3 Physics combination of two or more wave motions to form a resultant wave in which the displacement is reinforced or cancelled.

interferon /,ɪntə'fɪərɒn/ n. any of various proteins inhibiting the development of a virus in a cell etc.

interfuse /,ɪntə'fjuːz/ v. (-sing) 1 a (usu. foll. by with) mix (a thing) with; intersperse. b blend (things). 2 (of two things) blend with each other. □ **interfusion** /-'fjuːʒ(ə)n/ n. [Latin: related to fuse[1]]

intergalactic /,ɪntəgə'læktɪk/ adj. of or situated between galaxies.

interim /'ɪntərɪm/ —n. intervening time. —adj. provisional, temporary. [Latin, = in the interim]

interior /ɪn'tɪərɪə(r)/ —adj. 1 inner. 2 inland. 3 internal; domestic. 4 (usu. foll. by to) situated further in or away. 5 existing in the mind. 6 coming from inside. —n. 1 interior part; inside. 2 interior part of a region. 3 home affairs of a country (Minister of the Interior). 4 representation of the inside of a room etc. [Latin]

interior decoration n. decoration of the interior of a building etc. □ **interior decorator** n.

interior design n. design of the interior of a building. □ **interior designer** n.

interject /,ɪntə'dʒekt/ v. 1 utter (words) abruptly or parenthetically. 2 interrupt. [Latin jacio throw]

interjection /,ɪntə'dʒek(ə)n/ n. exclamation, esp. as a part of speech (e.g. ah!, dear me!).

interlace /,ɪntə'leɪs/ v. (-cing) 1 bind intricately together; interweave. 2 cross each other intricately. □ **interlacement** n.

interlard /,ɪntə'lɑːd/ v. (usu. foll. by with) mix (writing or speech) with unusual words or phrases. [French]

interleave /,ɪntə'liːv/ v. (-ving) insert (usu. blank) leaves between the leaves of (a book etc.).

interline /,ɪntə'laɪn/ v. (-ning) put an extra layer of material between the fabric (of a garment) and its lining.

interlink /,ɪntə'lɪŋk/ v. link or be linked together.

interlock /,ɪntə'lɒk/ —v. 1 engage with each other by overlapping. 2 lock or clasp within each other. —n. 1 machine-knitted fabric with fine stitches. 2 mechanism for preventing a set of

interlocutor /ˌɪntəˈlɒkjʊtə(r)/ n. person who takes part in a conversation. [Latin *loquor* speak]

interlocutory *adj. formal* 1 of dialogue. 2 (of a decree etc.) given provisionally in a legal action.

interloper /ˈɪntələʊpə(r)/ n. 1 intruder. 2 person who interferes in others' affairs, esp. for profit. [after *landloper* vagabond, from Dutch *loopen* run]

interlude /ˈɪntəluːd/ n. 1 a pause between the acts of a play. **b** something performed during this pause. 2 contrasting event, time, etc. in the middle of something (*comic interlude*), 3 piece of music played between other pieces etc. [medieval Latin *ludus* play]

intermarry /ˌɪntəˈmærɪ/ v. (-ies, -ied) (foll. by *with*) (of races, castes, families, etc.) become connected by marriage. □ **intermarriage** /-rɪdʒ/ n.

intermediary /ˌɪntəˈmiːdɪərɪ/ —n. (pl. -ies) intermediate person or thing, esp. a mediator. —*adj.* acting as intermediate.

intermediate /ˌɪntəˈmiːdɪət/ —*adj.* coming between two things in time, place, order, character, etc. —n. 1 intermediate thing. 2 chemical compound formed by one reaction and then used in another. [Latin *intermedius*]

interment /ɪnˈtɜːmənt/ n. burial.

■ **Usage** *Interment* is sometimes confused with *internment*, which means 'confinement'.

intermezzo /ˌɪntəˈmetsəʊ/ n. (pl. -mezzi /-tsɪ/ or -s) 1 a short connecting instrumental movement in a musical work. **b** similar independent piece. 2 short light dramatic or other performance inserted between the acts of a play. [Italian]

interminable /ɪnˈtɜːmɪnəb(ə)l/ *adj.* 1 endless. 2 tediously long. □ **interminably** *adv.*

intermingle /ˌɪntəˈmɪŋg(ə)l/ v. (-ling) mix together; mingle.

intermission /ˌɪntəˈmɪʃ(ə)n/ n. 1 pause or cessation. 2 interval in a cinema etc. [Latin: related to INTERMITTENT]

intermittent /ˌɪntəˈmɪt(ə)nt/ *adj.* occurring at intervals; not continuous. □ **intermittently** *adv.* [Latin *mitto miss-* let go]

intermix /ˌɪntəˈmɪks/ v. mix together.

intern —n. /ˈɪntɜːn/ (also **interne**) esp. *US* = HOUSEMAN. —v. /ɪnˈtɜːn/ oblige (a prisoner, alien, etc.) to reside within prescribed limits. □ **internment** n. [French: related to INTERNAL]

internal /ɪnˈtɜːn(ə)l/ *adj.* 1 of or situated in the inside or invisible part. 2 of the inside of the body (*internal injuries*). 3 of a nation's domestic affairs. 4 (of a student) attending a university etc. as well as taking its examinations. 5 used or applying within an organization. 6 **a** intrinsic. **b** of the mind or soul. □ **internality** /ˈnælɪtɪ/ n. **internally** *adv.* [medieval Latin *internus* internal]

internal-combustion engine n. engine with its motive power generated by the explosion of gases or vapour with air in a cylinder.

internal evidence n. evidence derived from the contents of the thing discussed.

internalize v. (also -ise) (-zing or -sing) *Psychol.* make (attitudes, behaviour, etc.) part of one's nature by learning or unconscious assimilation. □ **internalization** /-ˈzeɪʃ(ə)n/ n.

international /ˌɪntəˈnæʃ(ə)n(ə)l/ —*adj.* 1 existing or carried on between nations. 2 agreed on or used by all or many nations. —n. 1 a contest, esp. in sport, between teams representing different countries. **b** member of such a team. 2 (**International**) any of four successive associations for socialist or Communist action. □ **internationally** *adv.*

internationalism n. advocacy of a community of interests among nations. □ **internationalist** n.

internationalize v. (also -ise) (-zing or -sing) 1 make international. 2 bring under the protection or control of two or more nations.

interne var. of INTERN n.

internecine /ˌɪntəˈniːsaɪn/ *adj.* mutually destructive. [Latin *internecinus* deadly]

internee /ˌɪntəˈniː/ n. person interned.

interpenetrate /ˌɪntəˈpenɪtreɪt/ v. (-ting) 1 penetrate each other. 2 pervade. □ **interpenetration** /-ˈtreɪʃ(ə)n/ n.

interpersonal /ˌɪntəˈpɜːsən(ə)l/ *adj.* between persons; social (*interpersonal skills*).

interplanetary /ˌɪntəˈplænɪtərɪ/ *adj.* 1 between planets. 2 of travel between planets.

interplay /ˈɪntəpleɪ/ n. reciprocal action.

Interpol /ˈɪntəpɒl/ n. International Criminal Police Organization. [abbreviation]

■ **Usage** *Interment* is sometimes confused with *interment*, which means 'burial'.

interpolate /ɪnˈtɜːpəˌleɪt/ v. (-ting) **1 a** insert (words) in a book etc., esp. misleadingly. **b** make such insertions in (a book etc.). **2** interject (a remark) in a conversation. **3** estimate (values) between known ones in the same range. □ **interpolation** /-ˈleɪʃ(ə)n/ n. **interpolator** n. [Latin *interpolo* furbish]

interpose /ˌɪntəˈpəʊz/ v. (-sing) **1** (often foll. by *between*) insert (a thing) between others. **2** say (words) as an interruption; interrupt. **3** exercise or advance (a veto or objection) so as to interfere. **4** (foll. by *between*) intervene (between parties). □ **interposition** /-pəˈzɪʃ(ə)n/ n. [Latin *pono* put]

interpret /ɪnˈtɜːprɪt/ v. (-t-) **1** explain the meaning of (words, a dream, etc.). **2** make out or bring out the meaning of (creative work). **3** act as an interpreter. **4** explain or understand (behaviour etc.) in a specified manner. □ **interpretation** /-ˈteɪʃ(ə)n/ n. **interpretative** adj. **interpretive** adj. [Latin *interpres -pretis* explainer]

interpreter n. person who interprets, esp. one who translates foreign speech orally.

interracial /ɪntəˈreɪʃ(ə)l/ adj. between or affecting different races.

interregnum /ɪntəˈreɡnəm/ n. (pl. -s) **1** interval when the normal government or leadership is suspended, esp. between successive reigns or regimes. **2** interval, pause. [Latin *regnum* reign]

interrelate /ˌɪntərɪˈleɪt/ v. (-ting) **1** relate (two or more things) to each other. **2** (of two or more things) relate to each other. □ **interrelation** n. **interrelationship** n.

interrogate /ɪnˈterəˌɡeɪt/ v. (-ting) question (a person), esp. closely or formally. □ **interrogation** /-ˈɡeɪʃ(ə)n/ n. **interrogator** n. [Latin *rogo* ask]

interrogative /ˌɪntəˈrɒɡətɪv/ —adj. of, like, or used in a question. —n. interrogative word (e.g. *what?*).

interrogatory /ˌɪntəˈrɒɡətəri/ —adj. questioning (*interrogatory tone*). —n. (pl. -ies) formal set of questions.

interrupt /ˌɪntəˈrʌpt/ v. **1** break the continuous progress of (an action, speech, person speaking, etc.). **2** obstruct, person's view etc.). □ **interruption** n. [Latin: related to RUPTURE]

interrupter n. (also **interruptor**) **1** person or thing that interrupts. **2** device for interrupting, esp. an electric circuit.

intersect /ˌɪntəˈsekt/ v. **1** divide (a thing) by crossing it. **2** (of lines, roads, etc.) cross each other. [Latin: related to SECTION]

intersection /ˌɪntəˈsekʃ(ə)n/ n. **1** intersecting. **2** place where two roads intersect. **3** point or line common to lines or planes that intersect.

intersperse /ˌɪntəˈspɜːs/ v. (-sing) **1** (often *foll. by between, among*) scatter. **2** (foll. by *with*) vary (a thing) by scattering other things among it. □ **interspersion** n. [Latin: related to SPARSE]

interstate /ˈɪntəˌsteɪt/ adj. existing or carried on between States, esp. those of the US.

interstellar /ˌɪntəˈstelə(r)/ adj. between stars.

interstice /ɪnˈtɜːstɪs/ n. **1** intervening space. **2** chink or crevice. [Latin *interstitium* from *sisto* stand]

interstitial /ˌɪntəˈstɪʃ(ə)l/ adj. of, forming, or occupying interstices. □ **interstitially** adv.

intertwine /ˌɪntəˈtwaɪn/ v. (-ning) (often *foll. by with*) entwine (together).

interval /ˈɪntəv(ə)l/ n. **1** intervening time or space. **2** pause or break, esp. between the parts of a performance. **3** difference in pitch between two sounds. □ **at intervals** here and there; now and then. [Latin *intervallum* space between ramparts]

intervene /ˌɪntəˈviːn/ v. (-ning) **1** occur in time between events. **2** interfere; prevent or modify events. **3** be situated between things. **4** come in as an extraneous factor. [Latin *venio vent-* come]

intervention /ˌɪntəˈvenʃ(ə)n/ n. **1** intervening. **2** interference, esp. by a State. **3** mediation.

interventionist n. person who favours intervention.

interview /ˈɪntəˌvjuː/ —n. **1** oral examination of an applicant. **2** conversation with a reporter, for a broadcast or publication. **3** meeting face to face, esp. for consultation. —v. hold an interview with. □ **interviewee** /-vjuːˈiː/ n. **interviewer** n. [French *entrevue*: related to INTER-, *vue* sight]

interwar /ˌɪntəˈwɔː(r)/ attrib. adj. existing in the period between wars.

interweave /ˌɪntəˈwiːv/ v. (-ving; past -wove; past part. -woven) **1** weave together. **2** blend intimately.

intestate /ɪnˈtesteɪt/ —adj. not having made a will before death. —n. person who has died intestate. □ **intestacy** /-təsi/ n. [Latin: related to TESTAMENT]

intestine /ɪnˈtestɪn/ n. (in sing. or pl.) lower part of the alimentary canal. □ **intestinal** adj. [Latin *intus* within]

intifada /ˌɪntɪˈfɑːdə/ n. Arab uprising. [Arabic]

intimacy /ˈɪntɪməsɪ/ n. (pl. -ies) **1** state of being intimate. **2** intimate remark or act; sexual intercourse.

intimate¹ /ˈɪntɪmət/ —adj. 1 closely acquainted; familiar (intimate friend). 2 private and personal. 3 (usu. foll. by with) having sexual relations. 4 (of knowledge) detailed, thorough. 5 (of a relationship between things) close. —n. close friend. □ intimately adv. [Latin intimus inmost]

intimate² /ˈɪntɪmeɪt/ v. (-ting) 1 (often foll. by that) state or make known. 2 imply, hint. □ intimation /-ˈmeɪʃ(ə)n/ n. [Latin intimo announce: related to INTIMATE¹]

intimidate /ɪnˈtɪmɪdeɪt/ v. (-ting) 1 frighten or overawe, esp. to subdue or influence. □ intimidation /-ˈdeɪʃ(ə)n/ n. [medieval Latin: related to TIMID]

into /ˈɪntu, ˈɪntə/ prep. 1 expressing motion or direction to a point on or within (walked into a tree; ran into the house). 2 expressing direction of attention etc. (will look into it). 3 expressing a change of state (turned into a dragon; separated into groups). 4 after the beginning of (five minutes into the game). 5 colloq. interested in. [Old English]

intolerable /ɪnˈtɒlərəb(ə)l/ adj. that cannot be endured. □ intolerably adv. [Latin: related to IN², TO]

intolerant /ɪnˈtɒlər(ə)nt/ adj. not tolerant, esp. of others' beliefs or behaviour. □ intolerance n.

intonation /ˌɪntəˈneɪʃ(ə)n/ n. 1 modulation of the voice; accent. 2 intoning. 3 accuracy of musical pitch. [medieval Latin: related to INTONE]

intone /ɪnˈtəʊn/ v. (-ning) 1 recite (prayers etc.) with prolonged sounds, esp. in a monotone. 2 utter with a particular tone. [medieval Latin: related to TONE²]

in toto /ɪn ˈtəʊtəʊ/ adv. completely. [Latin]

intoxicant /ɪnˈtɒksɪk(ə)nt/ —adj. intoxicating. —n. intoxicating substance.

intoxicate /ɪnˈtɒksɪkeɪt/ v. (-ting) 1 make drunk. 2 excite or elate beyond self-control. □ intoxication /-ˈkeɪʃ(ə)n/ n. [medieval Latin: related to TOXIC]

intra- prefix on the inside, within. [Latin intra inside]

intractable /ɪnˈtræktəb(ə)l/ adj. 1 hard to control or deal with. 2 difficult, stubborn. □ intractability /-ˈbɪlɪtɪ/ n.

intramural /ˌɪntrəˈmjʊər(ə)l/ adj. 1 situated or done within the walls of an institution etc. 2 forming part of normal university etc. studies. □ intramurally adv. [Latin murus wall]

intramuscular /ˌɪntrəˈmʌskjʊlə(r)/ adj. in or into muscle tissue.

intransigent /ɪnˈtrænsɪdʒ(ə)nt/ —adj. uncompromising, stubborn. —n.

intransigent person. □ Intransigence n. [Spanish los intransigentes extremists]

intransitive /ɪnˈtrænsɪtɪv/ adj. (of a verb) not taking a direct object.

intrauterine /ˌɪntrəˈjuːtəraɪn/ adj. within the womb.

intravenous /ˌɪntrəˈviːnəs/ adj. in or into a vein or veins. □ intravenously adv.

in-tray n. tray for incoming documents.

intrepid /ɪnˈtrepɪd/ adj. fearless; very brave. □ intrepidity /-trɪˈpɪdɪtɪ/ n. intrepidly adv. [Latin trepidus alarmed]

intricate /ˈɪntrɪkət/ adj. very complicated; perplexingly detailed. □ intricacy /-kəsɪ/ n. (pl. -ies). intricately adv. [Latin intrico entangle]

intrigue —v. /ɪnˈtriːg/ (-gues, -gued, -guing) 1 (foll. by with) carry on an underhand plot or intrigue. 2 arouse the curiosity of. —n. /ˈɪntriːg/ 1 underhand plot or plotting. 2 secret arrangement (amorous intrigues). □ intriguing adj. esp. in sense 2 of v. intriguingly adv. [French from Italian intrigo]

intrinsic /ɪnˈtrɪnsɪk/ adj. inherent, essential (intrinsic value). □ intrinsically adv. [Latin intrinsecus inwardly]

intro /ˈɪntrəʊ/ n. (pl. -s) colloq. introduction. [abbreviation]

intro- comb. form into. [Latin]

introduce /ˌɪntrəˈdjuːs/ v. (-cing) 1 (foll. by to) make (a person or oneself) known by name to another, esp. formally. 2 announce or present to an audience. 3 bring (a custom etc.) into use. 4 bring (legislation etc.) before Parliament etc. 5 (foll. by to) initiate (a person) in a subject. 6 insert. 7 bring in; usher in; bring forward. 8 occur just before the start of. 9 put on sale for the first time. □ introducible adj. [Latin duco lead]

introduction /ˌɪntrəˈdʌkʃ(ə)n/ n. 1 introducing or being introduced. 2 formal presentation of one person to another. 3 explanatory section at the beginning of a book etc. 4 introductory treatise. 5 thing introduced.

introductory /ˌɪntrəˈdʌktərɪ/ adj. serving as an introduction; preliminary.

introit /ˈɪntrɔɪt/ n. psalm or antiphon sung or said as the priest approaches the altar for the Eucharist. [Latin introitus entrance]

introspection /ˌɪntrəˈspekʃ(ə)n/ n. examination of one's own thoughts. □ introspective adj. [Latin specio spect- look]

introvert /ˈɪntrəvɜːt/ —n. 1 person predominantly concerned with his or her own thoughts. 2 shy thoughtful person.

—*adj.* (also **introverted**) characteristic of an introvert. □ **introversion** /-'vɜːʃ(ə)n/ *n.*

intrude /ɪn'truːd/ *v.* (**-ding**) (foll. by *on, upon, into*) **1** come uninvited or unwanted. **2** force on a person. [Latin *trudo trus-* thrust]

intruder *n.* person who intrudes, esp. a trespasser.

intrusion /ɪn'truːʒ(ə)n/ *n.* **1** intruding. **2** influx of molten rock between existing strata etc. □ **intrusive** *adj.*

intrust var. of ENTRUST.

intuition /ˌɪntjuː'ɪʃ(ə)n/ *n.* immediate insight or understanding without conscious reasoning. □ **intuitional** *adj.* [Latin *tueor tuit-* look]

intuitive /ɪn'tjuːɪtɪv/ *adj.* of, possessing, or perceived by intuition. □ **intuitively** *adv.* **intuitiveness** *n.*

Inuit /'ɪnʊɪt/ *n.* (also **Innuit**) (*pl.* same or **-s**) N. American Eskimo. [Eskimo *inuit* people]

inundate /'ɪnʌndeɪt/ *v.* (**-ting**) **1** flood. **2** overwhelm. □ **inundation** /-'deɪʃ(ə)n/ *n.* [Latin *unda* wave]

inure /ɪ'njʊə(r)/ *v.* (**-ring**) **1** (often in *passive*; foll. by *to*) accustom (a person) to an esp. unpleasant thing. **2** *Law* take effect. □ **inurement** *n.* [Anglo-French related to IN, *eure* work, from Latin *opera*]

invade /ɪn'veɪd/ *v.* (**-ding**) **1** enter (a country etc.) under arms to control or subdue it. **2** swarm into. **3** (of a disease) attack. **4** encroach upon (a person's rights, esp. privacy). □ **invader** *n.* [Latin *vado vas-* go]

invalid¹ /'ɪnvəlɪd, -liːd/ —*n.* person enfeebled or disabled by illness or injury. —*attrib. adj.* **1** of or for invalids. **2** sick, disabled. —*v.* (**-d-**) **1** (often foll. by *out* etc.) remove (an invalid) from active service. **2** (usu. in *passive*) disable (a person) by illness. □ **invalidism** /ˌɪnvə'lɪdɪz/ *n.* [Latin: related to IN-¹]

invalid² /ɪn'vælɪd/ *adj.* not valid. □ **invalidity** /ˌɪnvə'lɪdɪtɪ/ *n.*

invalidate /ɪn'vælɪdeɪt/ *v.* (**-ting**) make (a claim etc.) invalid. □ **invalidation** /-'deɪʃ(ə)n/ *n.*

invaluable /ɪn'væljʊəb(ə)l/ *adj.* above valuation; very valuable. □ **invaluably** *adv.*

invariable /ɪn'veərɪəb(ə)l/ *adj.* **1** unchangeable. **2** always the same. **3** *Math.* constant. □ **invariably** *adv.*

invasion /ɪn'veɪʒ(ə)n/ *n.* invading or being invaded.

invasive /ɪn'veɪsɪv/ *adj.* **1** (of weeds, cancer cells, etc.) tending to spread. **2** (of surgery) involving large incisions etc. **3** tending to encroach.

invective /ɪn'vektɪv/ *n.* strong verbal attack. [Latin: related to INVEIGH]

inveigh /ɪn'veɪ/ *v.* (foll. by *against*) speak or write with strong hostility. [Latin *invehor vect-* assail]

inveigle /ɪn'veɪg(ə)l/ *v.* (**-ling**) (foll. by *into*, or *to* + infin.) entice; persuade by guile. □ **inveiglement** *n.* [Anglo-French from French *aveugler* to blind]

invent /ɪn'vent/ *v.* **1** create by thought, originate (a method, device, etc.). **2** concoct (a false story etc.). □ **inventor** *n.* [Latin *invenio -vent-* find]

invention /ɪn'venʃ(ə)n/ *n.* **1** inventing or being invented. **2** thing invented. **3** fictitious story. **4** inventiveness.

inventive *adj.* able to invent; imaginative. □ **inventively** *adv.* **inventiveness** *n.*

inventory /'ɪnvəntərɪ/ *n.* (*pl.* **-ies**) **1** complete list of goods etc. **2** goods listed in this. —*v.* (**-ies, -ied**) **1** make an inventory of. **2** enter (goods) in an inventory. [medieval Latin: related to INVENT]

inverse /ɪn'vɜːs/ —*adj.* inverted in position, order, or relation. —*n.* **1** inverted state. **2** (often foll. by *of*) the direct opposite. [Latin: related to INVERT]

inverse proportion *n.* (also **inverse ratio**) relation between two quantities such that one increases in proportion as the other decreases.

inversion /ɪn'vɜːʃ(ə)n/ *n.* **1** turning upside down. **2** reversal of a normal order, position, or relation.

invert /ɪn'vɜːt/ *v.* **1** turn upside down. **2** reverse the position, order, or relation of. [Latin *verto vers-* turn]

invertebrate /ɪn'vɜːtɪbrət/ —*adj.* (of an animal) not having a backbone. —*n.* invertebrate animal.

inverted commas *n.pl.* = QUOTATION MARKS.

invest /ɪn'vest/ *v.* **1 a** (often foll. by *in*) apply or use (money), esp. for profit. **b** (foll. by *in*) put money for profit into (stocks etc.) to an enterprise. **3** (foll. by *in*) *colloq.* buy (something useful). **4 a** (foll. by *with*) provide or credit (a person etc. with qualities) (*invested her with magical importance; invested his tone with irony*). **b** (foll. by *in*) attribute or endow (qualities or feelings) to (a person etc.) (*power invested in the doctor*). **5** (often foll. by *with, in*) clothe with the insignia of office; install in an office. [Latin *vestis* clothing]

investor *n.*

investigate /ɪn'vestɪgeɪt/ *v.* (**-ting**) **1** inquire into; examine. **2** make a systematic inquiry. □ **investigation** /-'geɪʃ(ə)n/ *n.* **investigative** /-'geɪtɪv/

adj. □ **investigator** n. **investigatory** /-gətəri/ adj. [Latin: related to vestigo track]

investiture /in'vestitʃə(r)/ n. formal investing of a person with honours or rank. [medieval Latin: related to INVEST]

investment n. 1 investing. 2 money invested. 3 property etc. in which money is invested.

investment trust n. trust that buys and sells shares in selected companies to make a profit for its members.

inveterate /in'vetərət/ adj. 1 (of a person) confirmed in a habit etc. 2 (of a habit etc.) long-established. □ **inveter-acy** n. [Latin vetus old]

invidious /in'vidiəs/ adj. likely to cause resentment or anger (invidious position; invidious task). [Latin invidiosus: related to ENVY]

invigilate /in'vidʒi,leit/ v. (-ting) supervise people taking an exam. □ **invigila-tion** /-'leiʃ(ə)n/ n. **invigilator** n. [Latin: related to VIGIL]

invigorate /in'vigə,reit/ v. (-ting) give vigour or strength to. □ **invigorating** adj. [medieval Latin: related to VIGOUR]

invincible /in'vinsib(ə)l/ adj. unconquerable. □ **invincibility** /-'biliti/ n. **invincibly** adv. [Latin vinco conquer]

inviolable /in'vaiələb(ə)l/ adj. not to be violated or dishonoured. □ **inviolab-ility** /-'biliti/ n. **inviolably** adv.

inviolate /in'vaiələt/ adj. 1 not violated. 2 safe (from violation or harm). □ **inviolacy** n.

invisible /in'vizib(ə)l/ adj. not visible to the eye. □ **invisibility** /-'biliti/ n. **invis-ibly** adv.

invisible exports n.pl. (also invisible imports etc.) intangible commodities, esp. services, involving payment between countries.

invitation /,invi'teiʃ(ə)n/ n. 1 inviting or being invited. 2 letter or card etc. used to invite.

invite -v. /in'vait/ (-ting) 1 (often foll. by to, or to + infin.) ask (a person) courteously to come, or to do something. 2 make a formal courteous request for. 3 tend to call forth unintentionally. 4 a attract. b be attractive. -n. /'invait/ colloq. invitation. [Latin invito]

inviting adj. 1 attractive. 2 tempting. □ **invitingly** adv.

in vitro /in 'vitrəu/ adv. (of biological processes) taking place in a test-tube or other laboratory environment. [Latin, = in glass]

invocation /,invə'keiʃ(ə)n/ n. 1 invoking or being invoked, esp. in prayer. 2 summoning of supernatural beings e.g. the Muses, for inspiration. 3 Eccl. the words 'In the name of the Father' etc. used to preface a sermon etc. □ **invoc-**

-atory /in'vokətər/ adj. [Latin: related to INVOKE]

invoice /'invois/ -n. bill for usu. item-ized goods or services. -v. (- cing) 1 send an invoice to. 2 make an invoice of. [earlier invoyes pl of invoy: related to ENVOY]

invoke /in'vəuk/ v. (-king) 1 call on (a deity etc.) in prayer or as a witness. 2 appeal to (the law, a person's authority, etc.). 3 summon (a spirit) by charms etc. 4 ask earnestly for (vengeance etc.). [Latin voco call]

involuntary /in'voləntəri/ adj. 1 done without exercising the will; uninten-tional. 2 (of a muscle) not under the control of the will. □ **involuntarily** adv. **involuntariness** n.

involute /'invə,lu:t/ adj. 1 involved, intricate. 2 curled spirally. [Latin: related to INVOLVE]

involuted adj. complicated, abstruse.

involution /,invə'lu:ʃ(ə)n/ n. 1 involv-ing. 2 intricacy. 3 curling inwards. 4 part that curls inwards.

involve /in'volv/ v. (-ving) 1 (often foll. by in) cause (a person or thing) to share the experience or effect (of a situation, activity, etc.). 2 imply, entail, make necessary. 3 (often foll. by in) implicate (a person) in a charge, crime, etc. 4 include or affect in its operations. 5 (as **involved** adj.) a (often foll. by in) con-cerned. b complicated in thought or form. c amorously associated. □ **in-volvement** n. [Latin volvo roll]

invulnerable /in'vʌlnərəb(ə)l/ adj. that cannot be wounded, damaged, or hurt, physically or mentally. □ **invul-nerability** /-'biliti/ n. **invulnerably** adv.

inward /'inwəd/ -adj. 1 directed to-wards the inside; going in. 2 situated within. 3 mental, spiritual. -adv. (also **inwards**) 1 towards the inside. 2 in the mind or soul. [Old English: related to IN, -WARD]

inwardly adv. 1 on the inside. 2 in the mind or soul. 3 not aloud.

inwards adv. = INWARD adv.

inwrought /in'ro:t/ adj. 1 (often foll. by with) (of a fabric) decorated (with a pattern). 2 (often foll. by in, on) (of a pattern) wrought (in or on a fabric).

iodide /'aiə,daid/ n. any compound of iodine with another element or group.

iodine /'aiə,di:n/ n. 1 black crystalline element forming a violet vapour. 2 solu-tion of this as an antiseptic. [French iode from Greek iōdēs violet-like]

IOM abbr. Isle of Man.

ion /'aiən/ n. atom or group of atoms that has lost one or more electrons (= CATION), or gained one or more elec-trons (= ANION). [Greek, = going]

-ion *suffix* (usu. as **-sion**, **-tion**, **-xion**) forming nouns denoting: **1** verbal action (*excision*). **2** instance of this (*a suggestion*). **3** resulting state or product (*vexation*; *concoction*). [Latin *-io*]

Ionic /aɪˈɒnɪk/ *adj.* of or of the order of Greek architecture characterized by a column with scroll-shapes on either side of the capital. [from *Ionia* in Greek Asia Minor]

ionic /aɪˈɒnɪk/ *adj.* of or using ions. □ **ionically** *adv.*

ionize *v.* (also **-ise**) (**-zing** or **-sing**) convert or be converted into an ion or ions. □ **ionization** /-ˈzeɪʃ(ə)n/ *n.*

ionizer *n.* device producing ions to improve the quality of the air.

ionosphere /aɪˈɒnəsfɪə(r)/ *n.* ionized region of the atmosphere above the stratosphere, reflecting radio waves. □ **ionospheric** /-ˈsferɪk/ *adj.*

iota /aɪˈəʊtə/ *n.* **1** ninth letter of the Greek alphabet (*I*, *ι*). **2** (usu. with *neg.*) a jot. [Greek *iōta*]

IOU /aɪəʊˈjuː/ *n.* signed document acknowledging a debt. [from *I owe you*]

IOW *abbr.* Isle of Wight.

IPA *abbr.* International Phonetic Alphabet.

ipecacuanha /ˌɪpɪkækjuˈɑːnə/ *n.* root of a S. American shrub, used as an emetic and purgative. [Portuguese from S. American Indian, = emetic creeper]

ipso facto /ˌɪpsəʊ ˈfæktəʊ/ *adv.* by that very fact. [Latin]

IQ *abbr.* intelligence quotient.

ir- *prefix* assim. form of IN-[1], [2] before *r*.

IRA *abbr.* Irish Republican Army.

Iranian /ɪˈreɪnɪən/ *—adj.* **1** of Iran (formerly Persia). **2** of the group of languages including Persian. *—n.* **1** native or national of Iran. **2** person of Iranian descent.

Iraqi /ɪˈrɑːkɪ/ *—adj.* of Iraq. *—n.* (*pl.* **-s**) **1 a** native or national of Iraq. **b** person of Iraqi descent. **2** the form of Arabic spoken in Iraq.

irascible /ɪˈræsɪb(ə)l/ *adj.* irritable; hot-tempered. □ **irascibility** /-ˈbɪlɪtɪ/ *n.* **irascibly** *adv.* [Latin *irascor* grow angry, from *ira* anger]

irate /aɪˈreɪt/ *adj.* angry, enraged. □ **irately** *adv.* **irateness** *n.* [Latin *iratus* from *ira* anger]

ire /aɪə(r)/ *n. literary* anger. [Latin *ira*]

iridaceous /ˌɪrɪˈdeɪʃəs/ *adj.* of the iris family of plants.

iridescent /ˌɪrɪˈdes(ə)nt/ *adj.* **1** showing rainbow-like luminous colours. **2** changing colour with position. □ **iridescence** *n.*

iridium /ɪˈrɪdɪəm/ *n.* hard white metallic element of the platinum group.

iris /ˈaɪərɪs/ *n.* **1** circular coloured membrane behind the cornea of the eye, with a circular opening (pupil) in the centre. **2** plant of a family with bulbs or tuberous roots, sword-shaped leaves, and showy flowers. **3** adjustable diaphragm for regulating the size of a central hole, esp. for the admission of light to a lens. [Greek *iris* rainbow]

Irish /ˈaɪərɪʃ/ *—adj.* of Ireland or its people. *—n.* **1** Celtic language of Ireland. **2** (prec. by *the*; treated as *pl.*) the people of Ireland. [Old English]

Irish bull *n.* = BULL[3].

Irish coffee *n.* coffee with a dash of whiskey and a little sugar, topped with cream.

Irishman *n.* man who is Irish by birth or descent.

Irish stew *n.* stew of mutton, potato, and onion.

Irishwoman *n.* woman who is Irish by birth or descent.

irk *v.* irritate, bore, annoy. [origin unknown]

irksome *adj.* annoying, tiresome. □ **irksomely** *adv.*

iron /ˈaɪən/ *—n.* **1** grey metallic element used for tools and constructions and found in some foods, e.g. spinach. **2** this as a symbol of strength or firmness (*man of iron*; *iron will*). **3** tool made of iron. **4** implement with a flat base which is heated to smooth clothes etc. **5** golf club with an iron or steel sloping face. **6** (usu. in *pl.*) fetter. **7** (usu. in *pl.*) stirrup. **8** (often in *pl.*) iron support for a malformed leg. *—adj.* **1** made of iron. **2** very robust. **3** unyielding, merciless. *v.* smooth (clothes etc.) with an iron. □ **iron out** remove (difficulties etc.). [Old English]

Iron Age *n.* period when iron replaced bronze in the making of tools and weapons.

ironclad *—adj.* **1** clad or protected with iron. **2** impregnable. *—n. hist.* warship protected by iron plates.

Iron Cross *n.* German military decoration.

Iron Curtain *n. hist.* former notional barrier to the passage of people and information between the Soviet bloc and the West.

ironic /aɪˈrɒnɪk/ *adj.* (also **ironical**) using or displaying irony. □ **ironically** *adv.*

ironing *n.* clothes etc. for ironing or just ironed.

ironing-board *n.* narrow folding table on which clothes etc. are ironed.

iron in the fire *n.* undertaking, opportunity (usu. in *pl.*: *too many irons in the fire*).

iron lung n. rigid case fitted over a patient's body for administering prolonged artificial respiration.

ironmaster n. manufacturer of iron.

ironmonger n. dealer in hardware etc. □ **ironmongery** n. (pl. -ies).

iron rations n.pl. small emergency supply of food.

ironstone n. 1 rock containing much iron. 2 a kind of hard white pottery.

ironware n. articles made of iron.

ironwork n. 1 things made of iron. 2 work in iron.

ironworks n. (as sing. or pl.) factory where iron is smelted or iron goods are made.

irony /'aɪərənɪ/ n. (pl. -ies) 1 expression of meaning, often humorous or sarcastic, using language of a different or opposite tendency. 2 apparent perversity of an event or circumstance in reversing human intentions. 3 Theatr. use of language with one meaning for a privileged audience and another for those addressed or concerned. [Greek eirōneia pretended ignorance]

irradiate /ɪ'reɪdɪeɪt/ v. (-ting) 1 subject to radiation. 2 shine upon; light up. 3 throw light on (a subject). □ **irradiation** /ɪˌreɪdɪ'eɪʃ(ə)n/ n. [Latin irradio shine or, from radius ray]

irrational /ɪˈræʃən(ə)l/ adj. 1 illogical; unreasonable. 2 not commensurate with reason. 3 Math. not commensurate with the natural numbers. □ **irrationality** /-ˈnælɪtɪ/ n. **irrationally** adv.

irreconcilable /ɪˈrekən,saɪləb(ə)l/ adj. 1 implacably hostile. 2 (of ideas etc.) incompatible. □ **irreconcilability** /-ˈbɪlɪtɪ/ n. **irreconcilably** adv.

irrecoverable /ˌɪrɪˈkʌvərəb(ə)l/ adj. not able to be recovered or remedied. □ **irrecoverably** adv.

irredeemable /ˌɪrɪˈdiːməb(ə)l/ adj. 1 not able to be redeemed. 2 hopeless. □ **irredeemably** adv.

irredentist /ˌɪrɪˈdentɪst/ n. person advocating the restoration to his or her country of any territory formerly belonging to it. □ **irredentism** n. [Italian irredenta unredeemed]

irreducible /ˌɪrɪˈdjuːsɪb(ə)l/ adj. not able to be reduced or simplified. □ **irreducibility** /-ˈbɪlɪtɪ/ n. **irreducibly** adv.

irrefutable /ɪˈrefjʊtəb(ə)l/ adj. that cannot be refuted. □ **irrefutably** adv.

irregular /ɪˈregjʊlə(r)/ adj. 1 not regular; unsymmetrical, uneven; varying in form. 2 not occurring at regular intervals. 3 contrary to a rule, principle, or custom; abnormal. 4 (of troops) not belonging to the regular army. 5 (of a verb, noun, etc.) not inflected according to the usual rules. 6 disorderly. □ -n (in pl.) irregular troops. □ **Irregularity** /-ˈlærɪtɪ/ n. (pl. -ies). **irregularly** adv.

irrelevant /ɪˈrelɪv(ə)nt/ adj. (often foll. by to) not relevant. □ **irrelevance** n. **irrelevancy** n. (pl. -ies).

irreligious /ˌɪrɪˈlɪdʒəs/ adj. lacking or hostile to religion; irreverent.

irremediable /ˌɪrɪˈmiːdɪəb(ə)l/ adj. that cannot be remedied. □ **irremediably** adv.

irremovable /ˌɪrɪˈmuːvəb(ə)l/ adj. that cannot be removed. □ **irremovably** adv.

irreparable /ɪˈrepərəb(ə)l/ adj. (of an injury, loss, etc.) that cannot be rectified or made good. □ **irreparably** adv.

irreplaceable /ˌɪrɪˈpleɪsəb(ə)l/ adj. that cannot be replaced.

irrepressible /ˌɪrɪˈpresɪb(ə)l/ adj. that cannot be repressed or restrained. □ **irrepressibly** adv.

irreproachable /ˌɪrɪˈprəʊtʃəb(ə)l/ adj. faultless; blameless. □ **irreproachably** adv.

irresistible /ˌɪrɪˈzɪstɪb(ə)l/ adj. too strong, delightful, or convincing to be resisted. □ **irresistibly** adv.

irresolute /ɪˈrezəluːt/ adj. 1 hesitant. 2 lacking in resoluteness. □ **irresolutely** adv. **irresoluteness** n. **irresolution** /-ˈluːʃ(ə)n/ n.

irrespective /ˌɪrɪˈspektɪv/ adj. (foll. by of) not taking into account; regardless of.

irresponsible /ˌɪrɪˈspɒnsɪb(ə)l/ adj. 1 acting or done without due sense of responsibility. 2 not responsible for one's actions. □ **irresponsibility** n. **irresponsibly** adv.

irretrievable /ˌɪrɪˈtriːvəb(ə)l/ adj. that cannot be retrieved or restored. □ **irretrievably** adv.

irreverent /ɪˈrevərənt/ adj. lacking reverence. □ **irreverence** n. **irreverently** adv.

irreversible /ˌɪrɪˈvɜːsɪb(ə)l/ adj. not reversible or alterable. □ **irreversibly** adv.

irrevocable /ɪˈrevəkəb(ə)l/ adj. 1 unalterable. 2 gone beyond recall. □ **irrevocably** adv.

irrigate /ˈɪrɪgeɪt/ v. (-ting) 1 a water (land) by means of channels etc. b (of a stream etc.) supply (land) with water. 2 supply (a wound etc.) with a constant flow of liquid. □ **irrigable** adj. **irrigation** /-ˈgeɪʃ(ə)n/ n. **irrigator** n. [Latin rigo moisten]

irritable /ˈɪrɪtəb(ə)l/ adj. 1 easily annoyed. 2 (of an organ etc.) very sensitive to contact. □ **irritability** /-ˈbɪlɪtɪ/ n. **irritably** adv. [Latin: related to IRRITATE]

irritant /'ɪrɪt(ə)nt/ —*adj.* causing irritation. —*n.* irritant substance.

irritate /'ɪrɪ,teɪt/ *v.* (-ting) **1** excite to anger; annoy. **2** stimulate discomfort in (a part of the body). **3** *Biol.* stimulate (an organ) to action. □ **irritating** *adj.* **irritation** /-'teɪʃ(ə)n/ *n.* **irritative** *adj.* [Latin *irrito*]

irrupt /ɪ'rʌpt/ *v.* (foll. by *into*) enter forcibly or violently. □ **irruption** *n.* [Latin: related to RUPTURE]

is *3rd sing. present* of BE.

ISBN *abbr.* international standard book number.

-ise var. of -IZE.

■ **Usage** See note at -IZE.

-ish *suffix* forming adjectives: **1** from nouns, meaning: **a** having the qualities of (*boyish*). **b** of the nationality of (*Danish*). **2** from adjectives, meaning 'somewhat' (*thickish*). **3** *colloq.* denoting an approximate age or time of day (*fortyish; six-thirtyish*). [Old English]

isinglass /'aɪzɪŋ,ɡlɑːs/ *n.* **1** gelatin obtained from fish, esp. sturgeon, and used in making jellies, glue, etc. **2** mica. [Dutch *huisenblas* sturgeon's bladder]

Islam /'ɪzlɑːm/ *n.* **1** the religion of the Muslims, proclaimed by Muhammad. **2** the Muslim world. □ **Islamic** /ɪz'læmɪk/ *adj.* [Arabic, = submission (to God)]

island /'aɪlənd/ *n.* **1** piece of land surrounded by water. **2** = TRAFFIC ISLAND. **3** detached or isolated thing. [Old English *īgland*; first syllable influenced by ISLE]

islander *n.* native or inhabitant of an island.

isle /aɪl/ *n. poet.* (and in place-names) island, esp. a small one. [French *île* from Latin *insula*]

islet /'aɪlɪt/ *n.* **1** small island. **2** *Anat.* structurally distinct portion of tissue. [French diminutive of ISLE]

ism /'ɪz(ə)m/ *n. colloq. usu. derog.* any distinctive doctrine or practice. [from -ISM]

-ism *suffix* forming nouns, esp. denoting: **1** action or its result (*baptism; organism*). **2** system or principle (*Conservatism; jingoism*). **3** state or quality (*heroism; barbarism*). **4** basis of prejudice or discrimination (*racism; sexism*). **5** peculiarity in language (*Americanism*). [Greek *ismos*]

isn't /'ɪz(ə)nt/ *contr.* is not.

iso- *comb. form* equal. [Greek *isos* equal]

isobar /'aɪsəʊ,bɑː(r)/ *n.* line on a map connecting places with the same atmospheric pressure. □ **isobaric** /-'bærɪk/ *adj.* [Greek *baros* weight]

isochronous /aɪ'sɒkrənəs/ *adj.* **1** occurring at the same time. **2** occupying equal time.

isolate /'aɪsə,leɪt/ *v.* (-ting) **1 a** place apart or alone. **b** place (a contagious or infectious patient etc.) in quarantine. **2** separate (a substance) from a mixture. **3** insulate (electrical apparatus), esp. by a physical gap; disconnect. □ **isolation** /-'leɪʃ(ə)n/ *n.* [Latin *insulatus* made into an island]

isolationism *n.* policy of holding aloof from the affairs of other countries or groups. □ **isolationist** *n.*

isomer /'aɪsəmə(r)/ *n.* one of two or more compounds with the same molecular formula but a different arrangement of atoms. □ **isomeric** /-'merɪk/ *adj.* **isomerism** /aɪ'sɒmə,rɪz(ə)m/ *n.* [Greek iso-, *meros* share]

isometric /,aɪsəʊ'metrɪk/ *adj.* **1** of equal measure. **2** (of muscle action) developing tension while the muscle is prevented from contracting. **3** (of a drawing etc.) with the plane of projection at equal angles to the three principal axes of the object shown. [Greek *isometria* equality of measure]

isomorphic /,aɪsəʊ'mɔːfɪk/ *adj.* (also **isomorphous** /-fəs/) exactly corresponding in form and relations. [from iso-, Greek *morphē* form]

isosceles /aɪ'sɒsɪ,liːz/ *adj.* (of a triangle) having two sides equal. [from iso-, Greek *skelos* leg]

isotherm /'aɪsə,θɜːm/ *n.* line on a map connecting places with the same temperature. □ **isothermal** /-'θɜːm(ə)l/ *adj.* [from iso-, Greek *thermē* heat]

isotope /'aɪsə,təʊp/ *n.* one of two or more forms of an element differing from each other in relative atomic mass, and in nuclear but not chemical properties. □ **isotopic** /-'tɒpɪk/ *adj.* [from iso-, Greek *topos* place]

isotropic /,aɪsəʊ'trɒpɪk/ *adj.* having the same physical properties in all directions. □ **isotropy** /aɪ'sɒtrəpɪ/ *n.* [from iso-, Greek *tropos* turn]

Israeli /ɪz'reɪlɪ/ —*adj.* of the modern State of Israel. —*n.* (*pl.* -**s**) **1** native or national of Israel. **2** person of Israeli descent. [Hebrew]

Israelite /'ɪzrɪə,laɪt/ *n. hist.* native of ancient Israel; Jew. [Hebrew]

issue /'ɪʃuː/ —*n.* **1 a** act of giving out or circulating shares, notes, stamps, etc. **b** quantity of coins, copies of a newspaper, etc., circulated at one time. **c** each of a regular series of a magazine etc. (*the May issue*). **2 a** outgoing, outflow. **b** way out, outlet, esp. the place of the emergence of a stream etc. **3** point in question; important subject of debate or

litigation. **4** result; outcome. **5** *Law* children; progeny (*without male issue*). —*v.* (issues, issued, issuing) **1** *literary* go or come out. **2 a** send forth; publish; put into circulation. **b** supply; officially or authoritatively (foll. by *to*, *with*; *issued passports to them*; *issued with passports*). **3 a** (often foll. by *from*) be derived or result. **b** (foll. by *in*) end, result. **4** (foll. by *from*) emerge from a condition. □ **at issue** under discussion; in dispute. **join** (or **take**) **issue** (foll. by *with* a person etc., *about*, *on*, *over* a subject) disagree or argue. [Latin *exitus* related to exIT]

-ist *suffix* forming personal nouns denoting: **1** adherent of a system etc. in -*ism* (*Marxist*, *fatalist*). **2** person pursuing, using, or concerned with something as an interest or profession (*balloonist*; *tobacconist*). **3** person who does something expressed by a verb in -*ize* (*plagiarist*). **4** person who subscribes to a prejudice or practises discrimination (*racist*, *sexist*). [Greek -*istēs*]

isthmus /ˈisməs/ *n.* (*pl.* -**es**) narrow piece of land connecting two larger bodies of land. [Greek *isthmos*]

IT *abbr.* information technology.

it *pron.* (poss. **its**; *pl.* **they**) **1** thing (or occasionally an animal or child) previously named or in question (*took a stone and threw it*). **2** person in question (*Who is it? It is I*). **3** as the subject of an impersonal verb (*it is raining*; *it is winter*; *it is two miles to Bath*). **4** as a substitute for a deferred subject or object (*it is silly to talk like that*; *I take it that you agree*). **5** as a substitute for a vague object (*brazen it out*). **6** as the antecedent to a relative word or clause (*it was an owl that I heard*). **7** exactly what is needed. **8** extreme limit of achievement. **9** *colloq.* **a** sexual intercourse. **b** sex appeal. **10** (in children's games) player who has to perform a required feat. □ **that's it** *colloq.* that is: **1** what is required. **2** the difficulty. **3** the end; enough. [Old English]

Italian /iˈtaljən/ —*n.* **1 a** native or national of Italy. **b** person of Italian descent. **2** Romance language of Italy. —*adj.* of or relating to Italy.

Italianate /iˈtaljəneit/ *adj.* of Italian style or appearance.

italic /iˈtalik/ —*adj.* **1 a** of the sloping kind of letters now used esp. for emphasis and in foreign words. **b** (of handwriting) compact and pointed like early Italian handwriting. **2** (**Italic**) of ancient Italy. —*n.* **1** letter in italic type. **2** this type. [Latin *italicus*: related to ITALIAN]

Italian vermouth *n.* sweet kind of vermouth.

italicize /iˈtalisaiz/ *v.* (also -**ise**) (-**zing**, -**sing**) print in italics.

itch —*n.* **1** irritation in the skin. **2** impatient desire. **3** (prec. by *the*) (in general use) scabies. —*v.* **1** feel an irritation in the skin. **2** feel a desire to do something (*itching to tell you*). [Old English]

itching palm *n.* avarice.

itchy *adj.* (-**ier**, -**iest**) having or causing an itch. □ **have itchy feet** *colloq.* **1** be restless. **2** have a strong urge to travel. □ **itchiness** *n.*

it'd /ˈitəd/ *contr. colloq.* **1** it had. **2** it would.

-ite *suffix* forming nouns meaning 'a person or thing connected with' (*Israelite*, *Trotskyite*, *dynamite*). [Greek -*itēs*]

item /ˈaitəm/ *n.* **1** any of a number of enumerated things **2** separate or distinct piece of news etc. [Latin, = in like manner]

itemize *v.* (also -**ise**) (-**zing** or -**sing**) state item by item. □ **itemization** *n.*

iterate /ˈitəreit/ *v.* (-**ting**) repeat; state repeatedly. □ **iteration** /-ˈreiʃ(ə)n/ *n.* **iterative** /-rətiv/ *adj.* [Latin *iterum* again]

-itis *suffix* forming nouns, esp. **1** names of inflammatory diseases (*appendicitis*). **2** *colloq.* with ref. to conditions compared to diseases (*electionitis*). [Greek]

it'll /ˈit(ə)l/ *contr. colloq.* it will; it shall.

its poss. *pron.* of it; of itself.

it's *contr.* **1** it is. **2** it has.

itself /itˈself/ *pron.* emphatic and refl. form of *n.* □ **be itself** function normally (*not yet itself*). **by itself** see *by oneself*. **in itself** viewed in its essential qualities (*not in itself a bad thing*). [Old English: related to IT, SELF]

ITV *abbr.* Independent Television.

-ity *suffix* forming nouns denoting: **1** quality or condition (*humility*; *purity*). **2** instance of this (*monstrosity*). [Latin -*itas*]

IUD *abbr.* intrauterine (contraceptive) device.

I've /aiv/ *contr.* I have.

-ive *suffix* forming adjectives meaning 'tending to', and corresponding nouns

-itis *suffix* forming adjectives and nouns corresponding to nouns in -*ite*, -*itis*, etc. (*Semitic*; *arthritic*). [Latin -*iticus*, Greek -*itikos*]

itinerant /aiˈtinərənt/ —*adj.* travelling from place to place. —*n.* itinerant person. [Latin *iter itiner-* journey]

itinerary /aiˈtinərəri/ *n.* (*pl.* -**ies**) **1** detailed route. **2** record of travel. **3** guidebook.

(*suggestive*; *corrosive*; *palliative*).
[Latin *-ivus*]

IVF *abbr. in vitro* fertilization.

ivory /ˈaɪvərɪ/ *n.* (*pl.* -**ies**) **1** hard substance of the tusks of an elephant etc. **2** creamy-white colour of this. **3** (usu. in *pl.*) **a** article made of or resembling ivory, esp. a piano key or a tooth. [Latin *ebur*]

ivory tower *n.* seclusion or withdrawal from the harsh realities of life (often *attrib.*: *ivory tower professors*).

ivy /ˈaɪvɪ/ *n.* (*pl.* -**ies**) climbing evergreen shrub with shiny five-angled leaves. [Old English]

-ize *suffix* (also **-ise**) forming verbs, meaning: **1** make or become such (*Americanize*; *realize*). **2** treat in such a way (*monopolize*; *pasteurize*). **3 a** follow a special practice (*economize*). **b** have a specified feeling (*sympathize*). □ **-ization** /-ˈzeɪʃ(ə)n/ *suffix* forming nouns. [Greek *-izō*]

■ **Usage** The form *-ize* has been in use in English since the 16th c.; it is widely used in American English, but is not an Americanism. The alternative spelling *-ise* (reflecting a French influence) is in common use, esp. in British English, and is obligatory in certain cases: (*a*) where it forms part of a larger word-element, such as *-mise* (= sending) in *compromise*, and *-prise* (= taking) in *surprise*; and (*b*) in verbs corresponding to nouns with *-s-* in the stem, such as *advertise* and *televise*.

J¹ /dʒeɪ/ n. (also **j**) (pl. **Js** or **J's**) tenth letter of the alphabet.

J² abbr. (also **J.**) joule(s).

jab —v. (**-bb-**) **1 a** poke roughly. **b** stab. **2** (foll. by into) thrust (a thing) hard or abruptly. —n. **1** abrupt blow, thrust, or stab. **2** colloq. hypodermic injection. [var. of job = prod]

jabber —v. **1** chatter volubly. **2** utter (words) in this way. —n. chatter; gabble. [imitative]

jabot /ˈʒæbəʊ/ n. ornamental frill etc. on the front of a shirt or blouse. [French]

jacaranda /ˌdʒækəˈrændə/ n. tropical American tree with trumpet-shaped blue flowers or hard scented wood. [Tupi]

jacinth /ˈdʒæsɪnθ/ n. reddish-orange zircon used as a gem. [Latin: related to HYACINTH]

jack —n. **1** device for raising heavy objects, esp. vehicles. **2** court-card with a picture of a soldier, page, etc. **3** ship's flag, esp. showing nationality. **4** device using a single-pronged plug to connect an electrical circuit. **5** small white tar- get ball in bowls. **6 a** = JACKSTONE. **b** (in pl.) game of jackstones. **7** (**Jack**) famil- iar form of John, esp. typifying the common man, male animal, etc. (I'm all right, Jack). —v. (usu. foll. by up) **1** raise with or as with a jack (in sense 1). **2** colloq. raise (e.g. prices). □ **every man jack** every person. **jack in** slang aban- don (an attempt etc.). [familiar form of the name John]

jackal /ˈdʒæk(ə)l/ n. **1** African or Asian wild animal of the dog family, scaveng- ing in packs for food. **2** colloq. menial. [Persian]

jackanapes /ˈdʒækəˌneɪps/ n. archaic rascal. [earlier Jack Napes, supposed to refer to the Duke of Suffolk]

jackass n. **1** male ass. **2** stupid person.

jackboot n. **1** military boot reaching above the knee. **2** this as a militaristic or fascist symbol.

jackdaw n. grey-headed bird of the crow family.

jacket /ˈdʒækɪt/ n. **1 a** short coat with sleeves. **b** protective or supporting gar- ment (life-jacket). **2** casing or covering round a boiler etc. **3** = DUSTJACKET. **4** skin of a potato. **5** animal's coat. [French]

jacket potato n. potato baked in its skin.

Jack Frost n. frost personified.

jack-in-the-box n. toy figure that springs out of a box.

jackknife —n. **1** large clasp-knife. **2** dive in which the body is bent and then straightened. —v. (**-fing**) (of an articu- lated vehicle) fold against itself in an accident.

jack of all trades n. multi-skilled person.

jack-o'-lantern n. **1** will-o'-the-wisp. **2** pumpkin lantern.

jack plane n. medium-sized joinery plane.

jack plug n. plug for use with a jack (see JACK n. 4).

jackpot n. large prize, esp. accumulated in a game, lottery, etc. □ **hit the jackpot** colloq. **1** win a large prize. **2** have re- markable luck or success.

Jack Russell /ˈdʒæk ˈrʌs(ə)l/ n. short- legged breed of terrier.

jackstone n. **1** metal etc. piece used in tossing-games. **2** (in pl.) game with a ball and jackstones.

Jack tar n. sailor.

Jacobean /ˌdʒækəˈbɪən/ —adj. **1** of the reign of James I. **2** (of furniture) heavy and dark in style. —n. Jacobean person. [Latin Jacobus James]

Jacobite /ˈdʒækəbaɪt/ n. hist. sup- porter of James II after his flight, or of the Stuarts.

Jacquard /ˈdʒækɑːd/ n. **1** apparatus with perforated cards, for weaving figured fabrics. **2** (in full **Jacquard loom**) loom with this. **3** fabric or article so made. [name of its inventor]

Jacuzzi /dʒəˈkuːzɪ/ n. (pl. **-s**) propr. large bath with massaging underwater jets of water. [name of its inventor and manu- facturers]

jade¹ n. **1** hard usu. green stone used for ornaments etc. **2** green colour of jade. [Spanish ijada from Latin ilia flanks]

jade² n. **1** inferior or worn-out horse. **2** derog. disreputable woman. [origin unknown]

jaded adj. tired out; surfeited.

j'adoube /ʒaˈduːb/ int. Chess declara- tion of the intention to adjust a piece without moving it. [French, = I adjust]

jag¹ —n. sharp projection of rock etc. —v. (**-gg-**) **1** cut or tear unevenly. **2** make indentations in. [imitative]

jag² *n. slang* **1** drinking bout. **2** period of indulgence in an activity, emotion, etc. [originally dial. = load]

jagged /ˈdʒægɪd/ *adj.* **1** unevenly cut or torn. **2** deeply indented. □ **Jaggedly** *adv.* **jaggedness** *n.*

jaguar /ˈdʒægjuə(r)/ *n.* large American flesh-eating spotted animal of the cat family. [Tupi]

jail (also **gaol**) —*n.* **1** place for the detention of prisoners. **2** confinement in a jail. —*v.* put in jail. [French *jaiole*, ultimately from Latin *cavea* cage]

jailbird *n.* (also **gaolbird**) prisoner or habitual criminal.

jailbreak *n.* (also **gaolbreak**) escape from jail.

jailer *n.* (also **gaoler**) person in charge of a jail or prisoners.

Jain /dʒaɪn/ —*n.* adherent of an Indian religion resembling Buddhism. —*adj.* of this religion. □ **Jainism** *n.* **Jainist** *n. & adj.* [Hindi]

jalap /ˈdʒæləp/ *n.* purgative drug from the tuberous roots of a Mexican climbing plant. [Spanish *Xalapa*, name of a Mexican city, from Aztec]

jalopy /dʒəˈlɒpɪ/ *n.* (*pl.* **-ies**) *colloq.* dilapidated old vehicle. [origin unknown]

jalousie /ˈʒæluːziː/ *n.* slatted blind or shutter to keep out rain etc. and control light. [French: see JEALOUSY]

jam¹ —*v.* (**-mm-**) **1 a** (usu. foll. by *into, together*, etc.) squeeze, cram, or wedge into a space. **b** become wedged. **2** cause (machinery etc.) to become wedged and (of machinery etc.) become wedged and unworkable. **3 a** block (a passage, road, etc.) by crowding etc. **b** (foll. by *in*) obstruct the exit of (*was jammed in*). **4** (usu. foll. by *on*) apply (brakes etc.) forcefully or abruptly. **5** make (a radio transmission) unintelligible by interference. **6** *colloq.* (in jazz etc.) improvise with other musicians. —*n.* **1** squeeze, crush. **2** crowded mass (*traffic jam*). **3** *colloq.* predicament. **4** stoppage (of a machine etc.) due to jamming. **5** (in full **jam session**) *colloq.* (in jazz etc.) improvised ensemble playing. [imitative]

jam² *n.* **1** conserve of boiled fruit and sugar. **2** *colloq.* easy or pleasant thing (*money for jam*). □ **jam tomorrow** promise of future treats etc. that never materialize. [perhaps from JAM¹]

jamb /dʒæm/ *n.* side post or side face of a doorway, window, or fireplace. [French *jambe* leg, from Latin]

jamboree /ˌdʒæmbəˈriː/ *n.* **1** celebration. **2** large rally of Scouts. [origin unknown]

jamjar *n.* glass jar for jam.

jammy *adj.* (**-ier, -iest**) **1** covered with jam. **2** *colloq.* **a** lucky. **b** profitable.

jam-packed *adj. colloq.* full to capacity.

Jan. *abbr.* January.

jangle /ˈdʒæŋg(ə)l/ —*v.* (**-ling**) **1** (cause to) make a (esp. harsh) metallic sound. **2** irritate (the nerves etc.) by discord etc. —*n.* harsh metallic sound. [French]

janitor /ˈdʒænɪtə(r)/ *n.* **1** doorkeeper. **2** caretaker. [Latin *janua* door]

January /ˈdʒænjʊərɪ/ *n.* (*pl.* **-ies**) first month of the year. [Latin *Janus*, guardian god of doors]

Jap *n. & adj. colloq. often offens.* = JAPANESE. [abbreviation]

japan /dʒəˈpæn/ —*n.* hard usu. black varnish, orig. from Japan. —*v.* (**-nn-**) **1** varnish with japan. **2** make black and glossy. [*Japan* in E. Asia]

Japanese /ˌdʒæpəˈniːz/ —*n.* (*pl.* same) **1 a** native or national of Japan. **b** person of Japanese descent. **2** language of Japan. —*adj.* of Japan, its people, or its language.

jape —*n.* practical joke. —*v.* (**-ping**) play a joke. [origin unknown]

japonica /dʒəˈpɒnɪkə/ *n.* flowering shrub with bright red flowers and round edible fruits. [Latinized name for *Japonicus*]

jar¹ *n.* **1 a** container, usu. of glass and cylindrical. **b** contents of this. **2** *colloq.* glass of beer. [French from Arabic]

jar² —*v.* (**-rr-**) **1** (often foll. by *on*) (of sound, manner, etc.) sound discordant, grate (on the nerves etc.). **2 a** (often foll. by *against, on*) (cause to) strike (esp. part of the body) with vibration or shock (*jarred his neck*). **b** vibrate with shock etc. **3** (often foll. by *with*) be at variance or in conflict. —*n.* **1** jarring sound or sensation. **2** physical shock or jolt. [imitative]

jar³ *n.* □ **on the jar** ajar. [obsolete *char* turn: see AJAR, CHAR²]

jardinière /ˌʒɑːdɪˈnjeə(r)/ *n.* **1** ornamental pot or stand for plants. **2** dish of mixed vegetables. [French]

jargon /ˈdʒɑːɡən/ *n.* **1** words or expressions used by a particular group or profession (*medical jargon*). **2** debased or pretentious language. [French]

jasmine /ˈdʒæzmɪn/ *n.* ornamental shrub with white or yellow flowers. [French from Arabic from Persian]

jasper /ˈdʒæspə(r)/ *n.* opaque quartz, usu. red, yellow, or brown. [French from Latin from Greek *iaspis*]

jaundice /ˈdʒɔːndɪs/ —*n.* **1** yellowing of the skin etc. caused by liver disease, bile disorder, etc. **2** disordered (esp. mental) vision. **3** envy. —*v.* (**-cing**) **1** affect with jaundice. **2** (esp. as **jaundiced** *adj.*) affect (a person) with envy, resentment, etc. [French *jaune* yellow]

jaunt /dʒɔːnt/ —n. short pleasure trip. —v. take a jaunt. [origin unknown]

jaunting car n. light horse-drawn vehicle formerly used in Ireland.

jaunty /dʒɔːntɪ/ adj. (-ier, -iest) 1 cheerful and self-confident. 2 sprightly. □ **jauntily** adv. **jauntiness** n. [French: related to GENTLE]

Javanese /dʒɑːvəˈniːz/ —n. (pl. same) 1 a native of Java. b person of Javanese descent. 2 language of Java. —adj. (also **Javan**) of Java, its people, or its language. [Java in Indonesia]

javelin /dʒævəlɪn/ n. light spear thrown in sport or, formerly, as a weapon. [French]

jaw —n. 1 a upper or lower bony structure in vertebrates containing the teeth. b corresponding parts of certain invertebrates. 2 a (in pl.) the mouth with its bones and teeth. b narrow mouth of a valley, channel, etc. c gripping parts of a tool etc. d grip (jaws of death). 3 colloq. tedious talk (hold your jaw). —v. colloq. speak, esp. at tedious length. [French]

jawbone n. lower jaw in most mammals.

jaw-breaker n. colloq. long or hard word.

jay n. noisy European bird of the crow family with vivid plumage. [Latin gaius, gaia, perhaps from the name Gaius; cf. jackdaw, robin]

jaywalk v. cross a road carelessly or dangerously. □ **jaywalker** n.

jazz —n. 1 rhythmic syncopated esp. improvised music of Black US origin. 2 slang pretentious talk or behaviour (all that jazz). —v. play or dance to jazz. □ **jazz up** brighten or enliven. □ **jazzer** n. [origin uncertain]

jazzman n. jazz-player.

jazzy adj. (-ier, -iest) 1 of or like jazz. 2 vivid, showy.

JCB n. propr. mechanical excavator with a shovel and a digging arm. [J. C. Bamford, name of the makers]

JCR abbr. Junior Common (or Combination) Room.

jealous /dʒeləs/ adj. 1 resentful of rivalry in love. 2 (often foll. by of) envious (of a person etc.), 3 (often foll. by of) fiercely protective (cf rights etc.). 4 (of God) intolerant of disloyalty. 5 (of inquiry, supervision, etc.) vigilant. □ **jealously** adv. [medieval Latin zelosus: related to ZEAL]

jealousy n. (pl. -ies) 1 jealous state or feeling. 2 instance of this. [French: related to JEALOUS]

jeans /dʒiːnz/ n.pl. casual esp. denim trousers. [earlier geane fustian, = material from Genoa]

Jeep n. propr. small sturdy esp. military vehicle with four-wheel drive. [originally US, from the initials of general purposes]

jeepers /dʒiːpəz/ int. US slang expressing surprise etc. [corruption of Jesus]

jeer —v. (often foll. by at) scoff derisively; deride. —n. taunt. □ **jeeringly** adv. [origin unknown]

Jehad var. of JIHAD.

Jehovah /dʒɪˈhəʊvə/ n. Hebrew name of God in the Old Testament. [Hebrew yəhōvāh]

Jehovah's Witness n. member of a millenarian Christian sect rejecting the supremacy of the State and religious institutions over personal conscience, faith, etc.

jejune /dʒɪˈdʒuːn/ adj. 1 intellectually unsatisfying, shallow, meagre, scanty, dry. 2 puerile. 3 (of land) barren. [Latin jejunus]

jejunum /dʒɪˈdʒuːnəm/ n. small intestine between the duodenum and ileum. [Latin, related to JEJUNE]

Jekyll and Hyde /dʒekɪl ənd ˈhaɪd/ n. person having opposing good and evil personalities. [names of a character in a story by R. L. Stevenson]

jell v. colloq. 1 a set as jelly. b (of ideas etc.) take a definite form. 2 cohere. [back-formation from JELLY]

jellaba var. of DJELLABA.

jelly /dʒelɪ/ —n. (pl. -ies) 1 a (usu. fruit-flavoured) translucent dessert set with gelatin. b similar preparation as a jam, condiment, or sweet (redcurrant jelly). c similar preparation from meat, bones, etc. and gelatin (marrowbone jelly). 2 any similar substance. 3 slang gelignite. —v. (-ies, -ied) (cause to) set as or in a jelly, congeal (jellied eels). □ **jelly-like** adj. [French gelée from Latin gelo freeze]

jelly baby n. jelly-like baby-shaped sweet.

jellyfish n. (pl. same or -es) marine animal with a jelly-like body and stinging tentacles.

jelly /dʒelɪ.fɑɪ/ v. (-ies, -ied) turn into jelly; make or become like jelly. □ **jellification** /-fɪˈkeɪʃ(ə)n/ n.

jemmy /dʒemɪ/ n. (pl. -ies) burglar's short crowbar. [from the name James]

jenny /dʒenɪ/ n. (pl. -ies) 1 hist. = SPINNING-JENNY. 2 female donkey. [from the name Jane]

jenny-wren n. female wren.

jeopardize /dʒepədaɪz/ v. (also -ise) (-zing or -sing) endanger.

jeopardy /dʒepədɪ/ n. danger, esp. severe. [obsolete French iu parti divided play]

jerbil var. of GERBIL.

jerboa /dʒɜːˈbəʊə/ n. small jumping desert rodent. [Arabic]

jeremiad /ˌdʒɛrɪˈmaɪæd/ n. doleful complaint or lamentation. [Church Latin: related to JEREMIAH]

Jeremiah /ˌdʒɛrɪˈmaɪə/ n. dismal prophet, denouncer of the times. [Lamentations of Jeremiah, in the Old Testament]

jerk¹ —n. 1 sharp sudden pull, twist, twitch, start, etc. 2 spasmodic muscular twitch. 3 (in pl.) colloq. exercises (physical jerks). 4 slang fool. —v. move, pull, thrust, twist, throw, etc., with a jerk. □ **jerk off** coarse slang masturbate. [imitative]

jerk² v. cure (beef) by cutting it in long slices and drying it in the sun. [Quechua echarqui dried fish in strips]

jerkin /ˈdʒɜːkɪn/ n. 1 sleeveless jacket. 2 hist. man's close-fitting, esp. leather, jacket. [origin unknown]

jerky adj. (-ier, -iest) 1 moving suddenly or abruptly. 2 spasmodic. □ **jerkily** adv. **jerkiness** n.

jeroboam /ˌdʒɛrəˈbəʊəm/ n. wine bottle of 4–12 times the ordinary size. [Jeroboam in the Old Testament]

Jerry /ˈdʒɛrɪ/ n. (pl. -ies) slang 1 German (esp. soldier). 2 Germans collectively. [probably an alteration of German]

jerry /ˈdʒɛrɪ/ n. (pl. -ies) slang chamber-pot. [probably an abbreviation of JEROBOAM]

jerry-builder n. incompetent builder using cheap materials. □ **jerry-building** n. **jerry-built** adj. [origin uncertain]

jerrycan n. (also **jerrican**) a kind of (orig. German) petrol- or water-can. [from JERRY]

jersey /ˈdʒɜːzɪ/ n. (pl. -s) 1 a knitted usu. woollen pullover. b plain-knitted (orig. woollen) fabric. 2 (Jersey) light brown dairy cow from Jersey. [Jersey in the Channel Islands]

Jerusalem artichoke /dʒəˈruːsələm/ n. 1 a kind of sunflower with edible tubers. 2 this as a vegetable. [corruption of Italian girasole sunflower]

jest —n. 1 joke; fun. 2 a raillery, banter. b object of derision. —v. joke; fool about. □ **in jest** in fun. [Latin gesta exploits]

jester n. hist. professional clown at a medieval court etc.

Jesuit /ˈdʒɛzjʊɪt/ n. member of the Society of Jesus, a Roman Catholic order. [Latin Jesus, founder of the Christian religion]

Jesuitical /ˌdʒɛzjʊˈɪtɪk(ə)l/ adj. 1 of the Jesuits. 2 often offens. equivocating, casuistic.

Jesus /ˈdʒiːzəs/ int. colloq. exclamation of surprise, dismay, etc. [name of the founder of the Christian religion]

jet¹ —n. 1 stream of water, steam, gas, flame, etc., shot esp. from a small opening. 2 spout or nozzle for this purpose. 3 jet engine or jet plane. —v. (-tt-) 1 spurt out in jets. 2 colloq. send or travel by jet plane. [French jeter throw, Latin jacto]

jet² n. (often attrib.) hard black lignite often carved and highly polished. [French jaiet from Gagai in Asia Minor]

jet-black adj. & n. (as adj. often hyphenated) deep glossy black.

jet engine n. engine using jet propulsion, esp. of an aircraft.

jet lag n. exhaustion etc. felt after a long flight across time zones.

jet plane n. plane with a jet engine.

jet-propelled adj. 1 having jet propulsion. 2 very fast.

jet propulsion n. propulsion by the backward ejection of a high-speed jet of gas etc.

jetsam /ˈdʒɛtsəm/ n. objects washed ashore, esp. jettisoned from a ship. [contraction of JETTISON]

jet set n. wealthy people who travel widely, esp. for pleasure. □ **jet-setter** n. **jet-setting** n. & attrib. adj.

jettison /ˈdʒɛtɪs(ə)n/ —v. 1 a throw (esp. heavy material) overboard to lighten a ship etc. b drop (goods) from an aircraft. 2 abandon; get rid of. —n. jettisoning. [Anglo-French getteson: related to JET²]

jetty /ˈdʒɛtɪ/ n. (pl. -ies) 1 pier or breakwater to protect or defend a harbour, coast, etc. 2 landing-pier. [French jetée: related to JET²]

Jew /dʒuː/ n. 1 person of Hebrew descent or whose religion is Judaism. 2 slang offens. miserly person. [Greek ioudaios]

■ **Usage** The stereotype conveyed in sense 2 is deeply offensive. It arose from historical associations of Jews as moneylenders in medieval England.

jewel /ˈdʒuːəl/ —n. 1 a precious stone. b this used in watchmaking. 2 jewelled personal ornament. 3 precious person or thing. —v. (-ll-; US -l-) (esp. as jewelled adj.) adorn or set with jewels. [French]

jeweller n. (US jeweler) maker of or dealer in jewels or jewellery.

jewellery /ˈdʒuːəlrɪ/ n. (also jewelry) rings, brooches, necklaces, etc., regarded collectively.

Jewess /ˈdʒuːes/ n. often offens. woman or girl of Hebrew descent or whose religion is Judaism.

Jewish adj. 1 of Jews. 2 of Judaism. **Jewishness** n.

Jewry /ˈdʒʊərɪ/ n. Jews collectively.

jew's harp n. small musical instrument held between the teeth.

Jezebel /'dʒezə,bel/ n. shameless or immoral woman. [*Jezebel* in the Old Testament]

jib¹ n. 1 triangular staysail. 2 projecting arm of a crane. [origin unknown]

jib² v. (**-bb-**) 1 (esp. of a horse) stop and refuse to go on. 2 (foll. by *at*) show aversion to. □ **jibber** n. [origin unknown]

jibe¹ US var. of GIBE.

jibe² US var. of GYBE.

jiff n. (also **jiffy**, *pl.* **-ies**) *colloq.* short time; moment (*in a jiffy*). [origin unknown]

jiffy bag /'dʒifi/ n. *propr.* padded envelope.

jig n. 1 a lively leaping dance. b music for this. 2 device that holds a piece of work and guides the tools operating on it. — v. (**-gg-**) 1 dance a jig. 2 (often foll. by *about*) move quickly and jerkily up and down; fidget. 3 work on or equip with a jig or jigs. [origin unknown]

jigger /'dʒigə(r)/ n. 1 *Billiards colloq.* cue-rest. 2 a measure of spirits etc. b small glass holding this. [partly from JIG]

jiggered /'dʒigəd/ *adj. colloq.* (as a mild oath) confounded (*I'll be jiggered*). [euphemism]

jiggery-pokery /,dʒigəri'pəukəri/ n. *colloq.* trickery; swindling. [origin uncertain]

jiggle /'dʒig(ə)l/ v. (**-ling**) (often foll. by *about* etc.) shake or jerk lightly; fidget. —n. light shake. [from JIG]

jigsaw n. 1 a (in full **jigsaw puzzle**) picture on board or wood etc. cut into irregular interlocking pieces to be reassembled as a pastime. b problem consisting of various pieces of information. 2 mechanical fretsaw with a fine blade.

jihad /dʒɪ'hæd/ n. (also **jehad**) Muslim holy war against unbelievers. [Arabic *jihād*]

jilt v. abruptly reject or abandon (esp. a lover). [origin unknown]

Jim Crow /'krəu/ n. US *colloq.* 1 segregation of Blacks. 2 offens. a Black. [nickname]

jim-jams /'dʒɪmdʒæmz/ n.pl. 1 *slang* = DELIRIUM TREMENS. 2 *colloq.* nervousness; depression. [fanciful reduplication]

jingle /'dʒɪŋg(ə)l/ n. 1 mixed ringing or clinking noise. 2 a repetition of sounds in a phrase etc. b short catchy verse or song in advertising etc. — v. (**-ling**) 1 (cause to) make a jingling sound. 2 (of writing) be full of alliteration, rhymes, etc. [imitative]

---

jingo /'dʒɪŋgəu/ n. (*pl.* **-es**) supporter of war; blustering patriot. □ **by jingo!** (originally Scots: imitative)

□ **jingoism** n. □ **jingoist** n. □ **jingoistic** /-'ɪstɪk/ *adj.* [conjuror's word]

jink v. move elusively; dodge. 2 elude by dodging. —n. dodging or eluding. [originally Scots: imitative]

jinnee /dʒɪ'niː/ n. (also **jinn**, **djinn** /dʒɪn/) (*pl.* **jinn** or **djinn**) (in Muslim mythology) spirit in human or animal form having power over people. [Arabic]

jinx *colloq.* —n. person or thing that seems to cause bad luck. —v. (esp. as **jinxed** *adj.*) subject to bad luck. [perhaps var. of *jynx* wryneck, charm]

jitter *colloq.* —n. (**the jitters**) extreme nervousness. —v. be nervous; act nervously. □ **jittery** *adj.* **jitteriness** n. [origin unknown]

jitterbug —n. 1 nervous person. 2 *hist.* fast popular dance. —v. (**-gg-**) *hist.* dance the jitterbug.

jive —n. 1 lively dance popular esp. in the 1950s. 2 music for this. —v. (**-ving**) dance to or play jive music. □ **jiver** n. [origin uncertain]

jiu-jitsu var. of JU-JITSU.

Jnr. *abbr.* Junior.

job —n. 1 piece of work to be done; task. 2 position in, or piece of, paid employment. 3 *colloq.* difficult task (*had a job to find it*). 4 *slang* crime, esp. a robbery. 5 state of affairs etc. (*bad job*). —v. (**-bb-**) 1 do piece-work. 2 deal in stocks; buy and sell (stocks or goods). 3 deal corruptly with (a matter). □ **just the job** *colloq.* exactly what is wanted. **make a job (or good job) of** do well. **on the job** *colloq.* 1 at work. 2 engaged in sexual intercourse. **out of a job** unemployed. [origin unknown]

jobber n. 1 person who jobs. 2 *hist.* principal or wholesaler on the Stock Exchange.

■ **Usage** Up to Oct. 1986 jobbers were permitted to deal only with brokers, not directly with the public. From Oct. 1986 the name ceased to be in official use (see BROKER 2).

jobbery n. corrupt dealing.

jobbing *attrib. adj.* freelance; piece-working (*jobbing gardener*).

jobcentre n. local government office advertising available jobs.

job-hunt v. *colloq.* seek employment.

jobless *adj.* unemployed. □ **jobless-ness** n.

job lot n. mixed lot bought at auction etc.

Job's comforter /dʒəʊbz/ n. person who intends to comfort but increases distress. [*Job* in the Old Testament]

jobs for the boys n.pl. colloq. appointments for members of one's own group etc.

job-sharing n. sharing of a full-time job by two or more people. □ **job-share** n. & v.

jobsheet n. sheet for recording details of jobs done.

Jock n. slang Scotsman. [Scots form of the name *Jack*]

jockey /dʒɒki/ —n. (pl. -s) rider in horse-races, esp. professional. —v. (-eys, -eyed) 1 trick, cheat, or outwit. 2 (foll. by *away, out, into*, etc.) manoeuvre (a person). □ **jockey for position** manoeuvre for advantage. [diminutive of JOCK]

jockstrap n. support or protection for the male genitals, worn esp. in sport. [slang *jock* genitals]

jocose /dʒəˈkəʊs/ adj. playful; jocular. □ **jocosely** adv. **jocosity** /-ˈkɒsɪtɪ/ n. (pl. -ies). [Latin *jocus* jest]

jocular /dʒɒkjʊlə(r)/ adj. 1 fond of joking. 2 humorous. □ **jocularity** /-ˈlærɪtɪ/ n. (pl. -ies). **jocularly** adv.

jocund /dʒɒkənd/ adj. literary merry, cheerful. □ **jocundity** /dʒəˈkʌndɪtɪ/ n. (pl. -ies). **jocundly** adv. [French from Latin *jucundus* pleasant]

jodhpurs /dʒɒdpəz/ n.pl. riding breeches tight below the knee. [*Jodhpur* in India]

Joe Bloggs n. colloq. hypothetical average man.

jog —v. (-gg-) 1 run slowly, esp. as exercise. 2 push or jerk, esp. unsteadily. 3 nudge, esp. to alert. 4 stimulate (the memory). 5 (often foll. by *on, along*) trudge; proceed ploddingly (*must jog on somehow*). 6 (of a horse) trot. —n. 1 spell of jogging; slow walk or trot. 2 push, jerk, or nudge. [probably imitative]

jogger n. person who jogs, esp. for exercise.

joggle /dʒɒg(ə)l/ —v. (-ling) move in jerks. —n. slight shake.

jogtrot n. slow regular trot.

John /dʒɒn/ n. US slang lavatory. [from the name *John*]

John Bull /bʊl/ n. England or the typical Englishman. [name of a character in an 18th-c. satire]

John Dory /dʒɒn ˈdɔːrɪ/ n. (pl. same or -ies) edible marine fish. [see DORY]

johnny /dʒɒnɪ/ n. (pl. -ies) 1 slang condom. 2 colloq. fellow, man. [diminutive of *John*]

johnny-come-lately n. colloq. newcomer; upstart.

joie de vivre /ʒwɑː də ˈviːvrə/ n. exuberance; high spirits. [French, = joy of living]

join —v. 1 (often foll. by *to, together*) put together; fasten, unite (with one or several things or people). 2 connect (points) by a line etc. 3 become a member of (a club, organization, etc.). 4 a take one's place with (a person, group, etc.). b (foll. by *in, for*, etc.) take part with (others) in an activity etc. (*joined them in prayer*). 5 (often foll. by *with, to*) come together; be united. 6 (of a river etc.) be or become connected or continuous with. —n. point, line, or surface at which things are joined. □ **join battle** begin fighting. **join forces** combine efforts. **join hands** 1 clasp hands. 2 combine in an action etc. **join in** (also *absol.*) take part in (an activity). **join up** 1 enlist for military service. 2 (often foll. by *with*) unite, connect. [Latin *jungo junct-*]

joiner n. 1 maker of finished wood fittings. 2 colloq. person who joins an organization or who readily joins societies etc. □ **joinery** n. (in sense 1).

joint —n. 1 place at which two or more things or parts of a structure are joined; device for joining these. 2 point at which two bones fit together. 3 division of an animal carcass as meat. 4 slang restaurant, bar, etc. 5 slang marijuana cigarette. 6 Geol. crack in rock. —adj. 1 held, done by, or belonging to, two or more persons etc. (*joint mortgage, joint author, joint favourite*). 2 sharing with another (*joint action*). —v. 1 connect by joint(s). 2 divide at a joint or into joints. □ **out of joint** 1 (of a bone) dislocated. 2 out of order. □ **jointly** adv. [French: related to JOIN]

joint stock n. capital held jointly; common fund.

joint-stock company n. company formed on the basis of a joint stock.

jointure /dʒɔɪntʃə(r)/ —n. estate settled on a wife by her husband for use after his death. —v. provide with a jointure. [Latin: related to JOIN]

joist n. supporting beam in a floor, ceiling, etc. [French *giste* from Latin *jaceo* lie]

jojoba /həʊˈhəʊbə/ n. plant with seeds yielding an oily extract used in cosmetics etc. [Mexican Spanish]

joke —n. 1 thing said or done to cause laughter; witticism. 2 ridiculous person or thing. —v. (-king) make jokes; tease (*only joking*). □ **no joke** colloq. serious matter. □ **jokingly** adv. **joky** adj. (also **jokey**). **jokily** adv. **jokiness** n. [probably Latin *jocus* jest]

joker *n.* **1** person who jokes. **2** *slang* person. **3** playing-card used in some games.

jollify /ˈdʒɒlɪfaɪ/ *v.* (-**ies**, -**ied**) make merry. □ **jollification** /-fɪˈkeɪʃ(ə)n/ *n.*

jollity /ˈdʒɒlɪtɪ/ *n.* (*pl.* -**ies**) merry-making, festivity. [French *jolliveté*; related to JOLLY]

jolly /ˈdʒɒlɪ/ —*adj.* (-**ier**, -**iest**) **1** cheerful; merry. **2** festive, jovial. **3** *colloq.* pleasant, delightful. —*adv.* *colloq.* very. —*v.* (-**ies**, -**ied**) (usu. foll. by *along*) *colloq.* coax, coax or humour in a friendly way. □ **jolly along** *colloq.* party or celebration. □ **jolliness** *n.* [French *joli* gay, pretty: perhaps related to YULE]

Jolly Roger *n.* pirates' black flag, usu. with skull and crossbones.

jolt /dʒəʊlt/ —*v.* **1** disturb or shake (esp. in a moving vehicle) with a jerk. **2** shock; perturb. **3** move along jerkily. —*n.* **1** jerk. **2** surprise or shock. □ **jolty** *adj.* (-**ier**, -**iest**). [origin unknown]

Jonah /ˈdʒəʊnə/ *n.* person who seems to bring bad luck. [*Jonah* in the Old Testament]

jonquil /ˈdʒɒŋkwɪl/ *n.* narcissus with small fragrant yellow or white flowers. [ultimately from Latin *juncus* rush plant]

josh *slang* —*v.* **1** tease, banter **2** indulge in ridicule. —*n.* good-natured or teasing joke. [origin unknown]

Joss *n.* Chinese idol. [ultimately from Latin *deus* god]

joss-stick *n.* incense-stick for burning. [*joss* /dʒɒs(ə)l/ —*v.* (-**ling**) **1** (often foll. by *away*, *from*, *against*, etc.) push roughly or in a crowd. **2** (foll. by *with*) struggle roughly. —*n.* jostling. [from JOUST]

jot —*v.* (-**tt-**) (usu. foll. by *down*) write briefly or hastily. —*n.* very small amount (*not one jot*). [Greek IOTA]

jotter *n.* small pad or notebook.

jotting *n.* (usu. in *pl.*) jotted note.

joule /dʒuːl/ *n.* SI unit of work or energy. [*Joule*, name of a physicist]

journal /ˈdʒɜːn(ə)l/ *n.* **1** newspaper or periodical. **2** daily record of events; diary. **3** book in which transactions and accounts are entered. **4** part of a shaft or axle that rests on bearings. [Latin *diurnalis* DIURNAL]

journalese /dʒɜːnəˈliːz/ *n.* hackneyed writing characteristic of newspapers.

journalism *n.* profession of writing for or editing newspapers etc.

journalist *n.* person writing for or editing newspapers etc. □ **journalistic** /-ˈlɪstɪk/ *adj.*

journey /ˈdʒɜːnɪ/ —*n.* (*pl.* -**s**) **1** act of going from one place to another, esp. at a long distance. **2** time taken for this (*a day's journey*). —*v.* (-**s**, -**ed**) make a journey. [French *journée* day, day's work or travel, from Latin *diurnus* daily]

journeyman *n.* **1** qualified mechanic or artisan who works for another. **2** derog. reliable but not outstanding worker.

joust /dʒaʊst/ *hist.* —*n.* combat between two knights on horseback with lances. —*v.* engage in a joust. □ **jouster** *n.* [French *jouste* from Latin *juxta* near]

Jove *n.* (in Roman mythology) Jupiter. □ **by Jove!** exclamation of surprise etc. [Latin *Jupiter Jov-*]

jovial /ˈdʒəʊvɪəl/ *adj.* merry, convivial, hearty. □ **joviality** /-ˈælɪtɪ/ *n.* **jovially** *adv.* [Latin *jovialis*: related to JOVE]

jowl[1] *n.* jaw or jawbone. [Old English]

jowl[2] *n.* loose hanging skin on the throat or neck. □ **jowly** *adj.* [Old English]

joy *n.* **1** (often foll. by *at*, *in*) pleasure; extreme gladness. **2** thing causing joy. **3** *colloq.* satisfaction, success (*got no joy*). □ **joyful** *adj.* **joyfully** *adv.* **joyfulness** *n.* **joyless** *adj.* **joyous** *adj.* **joyously** *adv.* [French *joie* from Latin *gaudium*]

joyride *colloq.* —*n.* pleasure ride in esp. a stolen car. —*v.* (-**ding**; *past* -**rode**; *past part.* -**ridden**) go for a joyride. □ **joy-rider** *n.*

joystick *n.* **1** *colloq.* control column of an aircraft. **2** lever controlling movement of an image on a VDU screen etc.

Jr. *abbr.* Junior.

JP *abbr.* Justice of the Peace.

jubilant /ˈdʒuːbɪlənt/ *adj.* exultant, rejoicing. □ **jubilance** *n.* **jubilantly** *adv.* [Latin *jubilo* shout]

jubilee /ˈdʒuːbɪliː/ *n.* **1** anniversary, esp. the 25th or 50th. **2** time of rejoicing. [Hebrew, ultimately, = ram's-horn trumpet]

Judaic /dʒuːˈdeɪɪk/ *adj.* of or characteristic of the Jews. [Greek: related to JEW]

Judaism /ˈdʒuːdeɪɪz(ə)m/ *n.* religion of the Jews.

Judas /ˈdʒuːdəs/ *n.* traitor. [*Judas* Iscariot who betrayed Christ]

judder —*v.* shake noisily or violently. —*n.* juddering. [imitative: cf. *shudder*]

judge /dʒʌdʒ/ —*n.* **1** public official appointed to hear and try legal cases. **2** person appointed to decide in a contest, dispute, etc. **3 a** person who decides a question. **b** person regarded as having judgement of a specified type (*am no*

judge; good judge of art.) —*v.* (**-ging**) **1** form an opinion or judgement (about); estimate, appraise. **2** act as a judge (of). **3 a** try (a case) at law. **b** pronounce sentence on. **4** (often foll. by *to* + infin. or *that* + clause) conclude, consider. □ [Latin *judex judicis*]

judgement *n.* (also **judgment**) **1** critical faculty; discernment (*error of judgement*). **2** good sense. **3** opinion or estimate (*in my judgement*). **4** sentence of a court of justice. **5** often *joc.* deserved misfortune. □ **against one's better judgement** contrary to what one really feels to be advisable.

judgemental /dʒʌdʒˈment(ə)l/ *adj.* (also **judgmental**) **1** of or by way of judgement. **2** condemning, critical. □ **judgementally** *adv.*

Judgement Day *n.* (in Judaism, Christianity, and Islam) day on which mankind will be judged by God.

judicature /dʒuːdɪkətʃə(r)/ *n.* **1** administration of justice. **2** judge's position. **3** judges collectively. [medieval Latin *judico* judge]

judicial /dʒuːˈdɪʃ(ə)l/ *adj.* **1** of, done by, or proper to a court of law. **2** having the function of judgement (*judicial assembly*). **3** of or proper to a judge. **4** impartial. □ **judicially** *adv.* [Latin *judicium* judgement]

judiciary /dʒuːˈdɪʃəri/ *n.* (*pl.* **-ies**) judges of a State collectively.

judicious /dʒuːˈdɪʃəs/ *adj.* sensible, prudent. □ **judiciously** *adv.*

judo /dʒuːdəʊ/ *n.* sport derived from ju-jitsu. [Japanese, = gentle way]

jug —*n.* **1** deep vessel for liquids, with a handle and a lip for pouring. **2** contents of this. **3** *slang* prison. —*v.* (**-gg-**) (usu. as **jugged** *adj.*) stew or boil (esp. hare) in a casserole etc. □ **jugful** *n.* (*pl.* **-s**). [origin uncertain]

juggernaut /dʒʌɡənɔːt/ *n.* **1** large heavy lorry etc. **2** overwhelming force or object. [Hindi *Jagannath*, = lord of the world]

juggle /dʒʌɡ(ə)l/ —*v.* (**-ling**) **1 a** (often foll. by *with*) keep several objects in the air at once by throwing and catching. **b** perform such feats with (balls etc.). **2** deal with (several activities) at once. **3** (often foll. by *with*) misrepresent or rearrange (facts) adroitly. —*n.* **1** juggling. **2** fraud. □ **juggler** *n.* [French from Latin *jocus* jest]

Jugoslav var. of YUGOSLAV.

jugular /dʒʌɡjʊlə(r)/ —*adj.* of the neck or throat. —*n.* = JUGULAR VEIN. [Latin *jugulum* collar-bone]

jugular vein *n.* any of several large veins in the neck carrying blood from the head.

juice /dʒuːs/ *n.* **1** liquid part of vegetables or fruit. **2** animal fluid, esp. a secretion (*gastric juice*). **3** *colloq.* petrol, electricity. [French from Latin]

juicy *adj.* (**-ier**, **-iest**) **1** full of juice; succulent. **2** *colloq.* interesting, racy, scandalous. **3** *colloq.* profitable. □ **juicily** *adv.* **juiciness** *n.*

ju-jitsu /dʒuːˈdʒɪtsuː/ *n.* (also **jiu-jitsu**, **ju-jutsu**) Japanese system of unarmed combat and physical training. [Japanese *jūjutsu* gentle skill]

ju-ju /dʒuːdʒuː/ *n.* **1** charm or fetish of some W. African peoples. **2** supernatural power attributed to this. [perhaps French *joujou* toy]

jujube /dʒuːdʒuːb/ *n.* small flavoured jelly-like lozenge. [Greek *zizuphon*]

ju-jutsu var. of JU-JITSU.

jukebox /dʒuːkbɒks/ *n.* coin-operated record-playing machine. [Black *juke* disorderly]

Jul. *abbr.* July.

julep /dʒuːlep/ *n.* **1 a** sweet drink, esp. as a vehicle for medicine. **b** medicated drink as a mild stimulant etc. **2** *US* iced and flavoured spirits and water (*mint julep*). [Persian *gulāb* rose-water]

Julian /dʒuːliən/ *adj.* of Julius Caesar. [Latin *Julius*]

Julian calendar *n.* calendar introduced by Julius Caesar, with a year of 365 days, every fourth year having 366.

julienne /dʒuːliˈen/ —*n.* vegetables cut into short thin strips. —*adj.* cut into thin strips. [French from name *Jules* or *Julien*]

Juliet cap /dʒuːliət/ *n.* small net skull-cap worn by brides etc. [*Juliet* in Shakespeare's *Romeo & Juliet*]

July /dʒuːˈlaɪ/ *n.* (*pl.* **Julys**) seventh month of the year. [Latin *Julius* Caesar]

jumble /dʒʌmb(ə)l/ —*v.* (**-ling**) (often foll. by *up*) confuse; mix up; muddle. —*n.* **1** confused state or heap; muddle. **2** articles in a jumble sale. [probably imitative]

jumble sale *n.* sale of second-hand articles, esp. for charity.

jumbo /dʒʌmbəʊ/ *n.* (*pl.* **-s**) *colloq.* **1** (*often attrib.*) large animal (esp. an elephant), person, or thing (*jumbo packet*). **2** (in full **jumbo jet**) large airliner for several hundred passengers. [probably from MUMBO-JUMBO]

■ **Usage** In sense 2, *jumbo* is usu. applied specifically to the Boeing 747.

jump —*v.* **1** rise off the ground etc. by sudden muscular effort in the legs. **2** (often foll. by *up*, *from*, *in*, *out*, etc.) move suddenly or hastily (*jumped into the car*). **3** jerk or twitch from shock or excitement etc. **4** a change suddenly, esp. advance

in status or rise, rapidly (*prices jumped*). **b** cause to do this. **5** (often foll. by *about*) change the subject etc. rapidly. **6** pass over (an obstacle etc.) by jumping. **7** skip (a passage in a book etc.). **8** cause (a horse etc.) to jump. **9** (foll. by *to*, *at*) reach (a conclusion hastily. **10** (of a train) leave (the rails). **11** pass (a red traffic-light etc.). **12** get on or off (a train etc.) quickly, esp. illegally or dangerously. **13** attack (a person) unexpectedly. —*n.* **1** act of jumping. **2** sudden jerk caused by shock or excitement. **3** abrupt rise in amount, value, status, etc. **4** obstacle to be jumped. **5 a** sudden transition. **b** gap in a series, logical sequence, etc. □ **jump at** accept eagerly. **jump bail** fail to appear for trial having been released on bail. **jump down a person's throat** *colloq.* reprimand or contradict a person fiercely. **jump the gun** *colloq.* begin prematurely. **jump on** *colloq.* attack or criticize severely. **jump out of one's skin** *colloq.* be extremely startled. **jump the queue** take unfair precedence. **jump ship** (of a seaman) desert. **jump to it** *colloq.* act promptly. **one jump ahead** one stage further on than a rival etc. [imitative]

jumped-up *adj. colloq.* upstart.

jumper¹ *n.* **1** knitted pullover. **2** loose outer jacket worn by sailors. **3** *US* pinafore dress. [probably *jump* short coat]

jumper² *n.* **1** person or animal that jumps. **2** short wire used to make or break an electrical circuit.

jumping bean *n.* seed of a Mexican plant that jumps with the movement of a larva inside.

jump-jet *n.* vertical take-off jet aircraft.

jump-lead *n.* cable for conveying current from the battery of one vehicle to that of another.

jump-off *n.* deciding round in show-jumping.

jump-start —*v.* start (a vehicle) by pushing it or with jump-leads. —*n.* act of jump-starting.

jump suit *n.* one-piece garment for the whole body.

jumpy *adj.* (**-ier**, **-iest**) **1** nervous, easily startled. **2** making sudden movements. □ **jumpiness** *n.*

Jun. *abbr.* **1** June. **2** Junior.

junction /ˈdʒʌŋkʃ(ə)n/ *n.* **1** joint; joining-point. **2** place where railway lines or roads meet. **3** joining. [Latin: related to JOIN]

junction box *n.* box containing a junction of electric cables etc.

juncture /ˈdʒʌŋktʃə(r)/ *n.* **1** critical convergence of events; point of time (*at this juncture*). **2** joining-point. **3** joining.

June *n.* sixth month of the year. [Latin *Junius* from *Juno* name of a goddess]

Jungian /ˈjʊŋɡiən/ —*adj.* of the Swiss psychologist Carl Jung or his theories. —*n.* supporter of Jung or of his theories. [Junius]

jungle /ˈdʒʌŋɡ(ə)l/ *n.* **1 a** land overgrown with tangled vegetation, esp. in the tropics. **b** an area of this. **2** wild tangled mass. **3** place of bewildering complexity, confusion, or struggle. □ **law of the jungle** state of ruthless competition. □ **jungly** *adj.* [Hindi from Sanskrit]

junior /ˈdʒuːniə(r)/ —*adj.* **1** (often foll. by *to*) inferior in age, standing, or position. **2** the younger (esp. appended to the name of a son for distinction from his father). **3** of the lower or lowest position (*junior partner*). **4** (of a school) for younger pupils, us1. aged 7–11. —*n.* **1** junior person. **2** person at the lowest level; (in an office etc.). [Latin, comparative of *juvenis* young]

junior common room *n.* (also **junior combination room**) **1** common-room for undergraduates in a college. **2** undergraduates of a college collectively.

juniper /ˈdʒuːnɪpə(r)/ *n.* evergreen shrub or tree with prickly leaves and dark-purple berry-like cones. [Latin *juniperus*]

junk¹ —*n.* **1** discarded articles; rubbish. **2** anything regarded as of little value. **3** *slang* narcotic drug esp. heroin. —*v.* discard as junk. [origin unknown]

junk² *n.* flat-bottomed sailing-vessel in the China seas. [Javanese *djong*]

junk bond *n.* bond bearing high interest but deemed to be a risky investment.

junket /ˈdʒʌŋkɪt/ —*n.* **1** pleasure outing. **2** official's tour at public expense. **3** sweetened and flavoured milk curds. **4** feast. —*v.* (**-t-**) feast, picnic. [French *jonquette* rush-basket (used for junket 3 and 4) from Latin *juncus* rush]

junk food *n.* food, such as sweets and crisps, with low nutritional value.

junkie *n. slang* drug addict.

junk mail *n.* unsolicited advertising matter sent by post.

junk shop *n.* second-hand or cheap antiques shop.

junta /ˈdʒʌntə/ *n.* (usu. military) clique taking power in a *coup d'état*. [Spanish: related to JOIN]

jural /ˈdʒʊər(ə)l/ *adj.* **1** of law. **2** of rights and obligations. [Latin *jus jur-* law, right]

Jurassic /dʒʊəˈræsɪk/ *Geol.* —*adj.* of the second period of the Mesozoic era. —*n.* this era or system. [French from *Jura* mountains]

juridical /dʒʊəˈrɪdɪk(ə)l/ *adj.* **1** of judicial proceedings. **2** relating to the law. [Latin *jus jur-* law, *dico* say]

jurisdiction /ˌdʒʊərɪsˈdɪkʃ(ə)n/ *n.* **1** (often foll. by *over*, *of*) administration of justice. **2 a** a legal or other authority. **b** extent of this; territory it extends over. □ **jurisdictional** *adj.*

jurisprudence /ˌdʒʊərɪsˈpruːd(ə)ns/ *n.* science or philosophy of law. □ **jurisprudential** /-ˈdenʃ(ə)l/ *adj.*

jurist /ˈdʒʊərɪst/ *n.* expert in law. □ **juristic** /-ˈrɪstɪk/ *adj.*

juror /ˈdʒʊərə(r)/ *n.* **1** member of a jury. **2** person taking an oath.

jury /ˈdʒʊərɪ/ *n.* (*pl.* -**ies**) **1** body of usu. twelve people giving a verdict in a court of justice. **2** body of people awarding prizes in a competition.

jury-box *n.* enclosure for the jury in a lawcourt.

jury-rigged /ˈdʒʊərɪrɪgd/ *adj. Naut.* having temporary makeshift rigging. [origin uncertain]

just *–adj.* **1** morally right or fair. **2** (of treatment etc.) deserved (*just reward*). **3** well-grounded; justified (*just anger*). **4** right in amount etc.; proper. *–adv.* **1** exactly (*just what I need*). **2** a little time ago; very recently (*has just seen them*). **3** *colloq.* simply, merely (*just good friends*; *just doesn't make sense*). **4** barely; no more than (*just managed it*). **5** *colloq.* positively; indeed (*just splendid*; *won't I just tell him!*). **6** quite (*not just yet*). □ **just about** *colloq.* almost completely. **just in case** as a precaution. **just now 1** at this moment. **2** a little time ago. **just the same = all the same. just so 1** exactly arranged (*everything just so*). **2** it is exactly as you say. □ **justly** *adv.* **justness** *n.* [Latin *justus* from *jus* right]

justice /ˈdʒʌstɪs/ *n.* **1** justness, fairness. **2** authority exercised in the maintenance of right. **3** judicial proceedings (*brought to justice*; *Court of Justice*). **4** magistrate; judge. □ **do justice to 1** treat fairly. **2** appreciate properly. **do oneself justice** perform at one's best. **with justice** reasonably. [Latin *justitia*]

Justice of the Peace *n.* unpaid lay magistrate appointed to hear minor cases.

justifiable /ˈdʒʌstɪˌfaɪəb(ə)l/ *adj.* able to be justified. □ **justifiably** *adv.*

justify /ˈdʒʌstɪˌfaɪ/ *v.* (-**ies**, -**ied**) **1** show the justice or correctness of (a person, act, assertion, etc.). **2** (esp. in *passive*) cite or constitute adequate grounds for (conduct, a claim, etc.); vindicate. **3** (as **justified** *adj.*) just, right (*justified in assuming*). **4** *Printing* adjust (a line of type) to give even margins. □ **justification** /-fɪˈkeɪʃ(ə)n/ *n.* **justificatory** /-fɪˌkeɪtərɪ/ *adj.*

jut *–v.* (**-tt-**) (often foll. by *out*, *forth*) protrude, project. *–n.* projection. [var. of JET¹]

jute *n.* **1** fibre from the bark of an E. Indian plant, used esp. for sacking, mats, etc. **2** plant yielding this. [Bengali]

juvenile /ˈdʒuːvəˌnaɪl/ *–adj.* **1 a** youthful. **b** of or for young people. **2** often *derog.* immature (*juvenile behaviour*). *–n.* **1** young person. **2** actor playing a juvenile part. [Latin *juvenis* young]

juvenile court *n.* court for children under 17.

juvenile delinquency *n.* offences committed by people below the age of legal responsibility. □ **juvenile delinquent** *n.*

juvenilia /ˌdʒuːvəˈnɪlɪə/ *n.pl.* author's or artist's youthful works.

juxtapose /ˌdʒʌkstəˈpəʊz/ *v.* (-**sing**) **1** place (things) side by side. **2** (foll. by *to*, *with*) place (a thing) beside another. □ **juxtaposition** /-pəˈzɪʃ(ə)n/ *n.* **juxtapositional** /-pəˈzɪʃən(ə)l/ *adj.* [Latin *juxta* next, *pono* put]

K

K¹ /keɪ/ n. (also **k**) (pl. **Ks** or **K's**) eleventh letter of the alphabet.

K² abbr. (also **K.**) **1** kelvin(s). **2** King, King's. **3** Köchel (catalogue of Mozart's works). **4** (also **k**) (prec. by a numeral) **a** Computing unit of 1,024 (i.e. 2¹⁰) bytes or bits, or loosely 1,000. **b** 1,000. [sense 4 as abbreviation of KILO-]

K³ symb. potassium. [Latin Kalium]

k abbr. **1** kilo. **2** knot(s).

Kaffir /ˈkæfə(r)/ n. **1** hist. member or language of a S. African people of the Bantu family. **2** S.Afr. offens. any Black African. [Arabic, = infidel]

Kafkaesque /ˌkæfkəˈɛsk/ adj. impenetrably oppressive or nightmarish, as in the fiction of Franz Kafka.

kaftan var. of CAFTAN.

kaiser /ˈkaɪzə(r)/ n. hist. emperor, esp. of Germany, Austria, or the Holy Roman Empire. [Latin CAESAR]

kalashnikov /kəˈlæʃnɪkɒf/ n. type of Soviet rifle or sub-machine-gun. [Russian]

kale n. variety of cabbage, esp. with wrinkled leaves and no heart. [northern var. of COLE]

kaleidoscope /kəˈlaɪdəˌskəʊp/ n. **1** tube containing mirrors and pieces of coloured glass etc. producing changing reflected patterns when shaken. **2** constantly changing pattern, group etc. □ **kaleidoscopic** /-ˈskɒpɪk/ adj. [Greek kalos beautiful, eidos form, -SCOPE]

kalends var. of CALENDS.

kaleyard /ˈkeɪljɑːd/ n. Scot. kitchen garden.

kamikaze /ˌkæmɪˈkɑːzɪ/ —n. hist. **1** explosive-laden Japanese aircraft deliberately crashed on a ship etc. during the war of 1939–45. **2** pilot of this. —attrib. adj. **1** of a kamikaze. **2** reckless, esp. suicidal. [Japanese, = divine wind]

kangaroo /ˌkæŋɡəˈruː/ n. (pl. **-s**) Australian marsupial with strong hind legs for jumping. [Aboriginal]

kangaroo court n. illegal court, e.g. held by strikers or mutineers.

kaolin /ˈkeɪəlɪn/ n. fine soft white clay used esp. for porcelain and in medicines. [Chinese kao-ling high hill]

kapok /ˈkeɪpɒk/ n. fine fibrous cotton-like substance from a tropical tree, used for padding. [Malay]

kappa /ˈkæpə/ n. tenth letter of the Greek alphabet (K, κ). [Greek]

kaput /kəˈpʊt/ predic. adj. slang broken, ruined. [German]

karabiner /ˌkærəˈbiːnə(r)/ n. coupling link used by mountaineers. [German, literally 'carbine']

karakul /ˈkærəˌkʊl/ n. (also **caracul**) **1** Asian sheep with a dark curled fleece when young. **2** fur of or like this. [Russian]

karaoke /ˌkærɪˈɒkɪ/ n. entertainment in nightclubs etc. with customers singing to a backing track. [Japanese, = empty orchestral]

karate /kəˈrɑːtɪ/ n. Japanese system of unarmed combat using the hands and feet as weapons. [Japanese, = empty hand]

karma /ˈkɑːmə/ n. Buddhism & Hinduism person's actions in previous lives, believed to decide his or her fate in future existences. [Sanskrit, = action, fate]

kauri /ˈkaʊrɪ/ n. (pl. **-s**) coniferous New Zealand tree yielding timber and resin. [Maori]

kayak /ˈkaɪæk/ n. **1** Eskimo one-man canoe of wood and sealskins. **2** small covered canoe. [Eskimo]

kazoo /kəˈzuː/ n. toy musical instrument into which the player sings or hums. [origin uncertain]

KBE abbr. Knight Commander of the Order of the British Empire.

KC abbr. King's Counsel.

kc/s abbr. kilocycles per second.

kea /ˈkiːə, ˈkeɪə/ n. New Zealand parrot with brownish-green and red plumage. [Maori, imitative]

kebab /kɪˈbæb/ n. pieces of meat, vegetables, etc. cooked on a skewer (cf. DONER KEBAB, SHISH KEBAB). [Urdu from Arabic]

kedge —v. (-**ging**) **1** move (a ship) by a hawser attached to a kedged anchor. **2** (of a ship) move in this way. —n. (in full **kedge-anchor**) small anchor for this purpose. [origin uncertain]

kedgeree /ˈkɛdʒəriː/ n. dish of fish, rice, hard-boiled eggs, etc. [Hindi]

keel —n. main lengthwise member of the base of a ship etc. —v. **1** (often foll. by over) (cause to) fall down or over. **2** turn keel upwards. □ **on an even keel** steady; balanced. [Old Norse]

keelhaul v. **1** drag (a person) under the keel of a ship as a punishment. **2** scold or rebuke severely.

keelson /ˈkiːls(ə)n/ n. (also **kelson** /ˈkɛls(ə)n/) line of timber fastening a

ship's floor-timbers to its keel. [origin uncertain]

keen[1] *adj.* 1 enthusiastic, eager. 2 (foll. by *on*) enthusiastic about, fond of. 3 (of the senses) sharp. 4 intellectually acute. 5 (of a knife etc.) sharp. 6 (of a sound, light, etc.) penetrating, vivid. 7 (of a wind etc.) piercingly cold. 8 (of a pain etc.) acute. 9 (of a price) competitive. □ **keenly** *adv.* **keenness** *n.* [Old English]

keen[2] —*n.* Irish wailing funeral song. —*v.* (often foll. by *over*, *for*) wail mournfully, esp. at a funeral. [Irish *caoine* from *caoinim* wail]

keep —*v.* (*past* and *past part.* **kept**) 1 have continuous charge of; retain possession of. 2 (foll. by *for*) retain or reserve for (a future time) (*kept it for later*). 3 retain or remain in a specified condition, position, place, etc. (*keep cool*; *keep out*; *keep them happy*; *knives are kept here*). 4 (foll. by *from*) restrain, hold back. 5 detain (*what kept you?*). 6 observe, honour, or respect (a law, custom, commitment, secret, etc.) (*keep one's word*; *keep the sabbath*). 7 own and look after (animals). 8 a clothe, feed, maintain, etc. (a person, oneself, etc.). b (foll. by *in*) maintain (a person) with a supply of. 9 carry on; manage (a business etc.). 10 maintain (a diary, house, accounts, etc.) regularly and in proper order. 11 normally have on sale (*do you keep buttons?*). 12 guard or protect (a person or place). 13 preserve (a verbal noun) continue; repeat habitually (*keeps telling me*). 15 continue to follow (a way or course). 16 a (esp. of food) remain in good condition. b (of news etc.) not suffer from delay in telling. 17 (often foll. by *to*) remain in (one's bed, room, etc.). 18 maintain (a person) as one's mistress etc. (*kept woman*). —*n.* 1 maintenance, food, etc. (*hardly earn your keep*). 2 *hist.* tower, esp. the central stronghold of a castle. □ **for keeps** *colloq.* permanently, indefinitely. **how are you keeping?** how are you? **keep at** (cause to) persist with. **keep away** (often foll. by *from*) avoid, prevent from being near. **keep back** 1 remain or keep at a distance. 2 retard the progress of. 3 conceal. 4 withhold (*kept back £50*). **keep down** 1 hold in subjection. 2 keep low in amount. 3 stay hidden. 4 not vomit (food eaten). **keep one's hair on** see HAIR. **keep one's hand in** see HAND. **keep in** with remain on good terms with. **keep off** 1 (cause to) stay away from. 2 ward off. 3 abstain from. 4 avoid (a subject) (*let's keep off religion*). **keep on** 1 continue; do continually (*kept on laughing*). 2 continue to employ. 3 (foll.

by *at*) nag. **keep out** 1 keep or remain outside. 2 exclude. **keep to** 1 adhere to (a course, promise, etc.). 2 confine oneself to. **keep to oneself** 1 avoid contact with others. 2 keep secret. **keep track of** see TRACK. **keep under** repress. **keep up** 1 maintain (progress, morale, etc.). 2 keep in repair etc. 3 carry on (a correspondence etc.). 4 prevent from going to bed. 5 (often foll. by *with*) not fall behind. **keep up with the Joneses** compete socially with one's neighbours. [Old English]

keeper *n.* 1 person who looks after or is in charge of animals, people, or a thing. 2 custodian of a museum, forest, etc. 3 **a** = WICKET-KEEPER. **b** = GOALKEEPER. **4 a** sleeper in a pierced ear. **b** ring that keeps another on the finger.

keep-fit *n.* regular physical exercises.

keeping *n.* 1 custody, charge (*in safe keeping*). 2 agreement, harmony (esp. *in* or *out of keeping (with)*).

keepsake *n.* souvenir, esp. of a person.

keg *n.* small barrel. [Old Norse]

keg beer *n.* beer kept in a metal keg under pressure.

kelp *n.* 1 large brown seaweed suitable for manure. 2 its calcined ashes, formerly a source of sodium, potassium, etc. [origin unknown]

kelpie /ˈkelpɪ/ *n. Scot.* 1 malevolent water-spirit, usu. in the form of a horse. 2 Australian sheepdog. [origin unknown]

kelson var. of KEELSON.

Kelt var. of CELT.

kelt *n.* salmon or sea trout after spawning. [origin unknown]

kelter var. of KILTER.

kelvin /ˈkelvɪn/ *n.* SI unit of thermodynamic temperature. [*Kelvin*, name of a physicist]

Kelvin scale *n.* scale of temperature with zero at absolute zero.

ken —*n.* range of knowledge or sight (*beyond my ken*). —*v.* (*-nn-*; *past* and *past part.* **kenned** or **kent**) *Scot. & N.Engl.* 1 recognize at sight. 2 know. [Old English, = make known: related to CAN[1]]

kendo /ˈkendəʊ/ *n.* Japanese fencing with two-handed bamboo swords. [Japanese, = sword-way]

kennel /ˈken(ə)l/ —*n.* 1 small shelter for a dog. 2 (in *pl.*) breeding or boarding place for dogs. —*v.* (-ll-; *US* -l-) put into or keep in a kennel. [French *chenil* from Latin *canis* dog]

kent *past* and *past part.* of KEN.

Kenyan /ˈkenjən/ —*adj.* of Kenya in E. Africa. —*n.* 1 native or national of Kenya. 2 person of Kenyan descent.

kepi /'keipi/ n. (pl. -s) French military cap with a horizontal peak. [French *képi*]

kept past and past part. of KEEP.

keratin /'kerətin/ n. fibrous protein in hair, feathers, hooves, claws, horns, etc. [Greek *keras* horn]

kerb n. stone edging to a pavement or raised path. [var. of CURB]

kerb-crawling n. *colloq.* driving slowly in order to engage a prostitute.

kerb drill n. precautions before crossing a road.

kerbstone n. stone forming part of a kerb.

kerchief /'kɜːtʃɪf/ n. 1 headscarf, neckerchief. 2 *poet.* handkerchief. [Anglo-French *courchef*; related to COVER, CHIEF]

kerfuffle /kə'fʌf(ə)l/ n. *colloq.* fuss, commotion. [originally Scots]

kermes /'kɜːmɪz/ n. 1 female of an insect with a berry-like appearance. 2 (in full **kermes oak**) evergreen oak on which this feeds. 3 red dye made from these insects dried. [Arabic]

kernel /'kɜːn(ə)l/ n. 1 (usu. soft) edible centre within the hard shell of a nut, fruit stone, seed, etc. 2 whole seed of a cereal. 3 essence of anything. [Old English: related to CORN]

kestrel /'kestr(ə)l/ n. small hovering falcon. [origin uncertain]

ketch n. small two-masted sailing-boat. [probably from CATCH]

ketchup /'ketʃəp/ n. (US **catsup** /'kætsəp/) spicy esp. tomato sauce used as a condiment. [Chinese]

ketone /'kiːtəʊn/ n. any of a class of organic compounds including propanone (acetone). [German *Keton*, alteration of *Aketon* ACETONE]

kettle /'ket(ə)l/ n. vessel for boiling water in. □ **a different kettle of fish** a different matter altogether. **a fine (or pretty) kettle of fish** *iron.* an awkward state of affairs. [Old Norse]

kettledrum n. large bowl-shaped drum.

key[1] /kiː/ n. (pl. -s) 1 (usu. metal) instrument for moving the bolt of a lock. 2 similar implement for operating a switch. 3 instrument for grasping screws, nuts, etc., or for winding a clock etc. 4 (often in *pl.*) finger-operated button or lever on a typewriter, piano, computer terminal, etc. 5 means of advance, access, etc. (*key to success*). 6 (*attrib.*) essential (*key element*). 7 a solution or explanation. b word or system

for solving a cipher or code. c explanatory list of symbols used in a map, table, etc. 8 *Mus.* system of notes related to each other and based on a particular note (*key of C major*). 9 tone or style of thought or expression. 10 piece of wood or metal inserted between and securing others. 11 coat of wall plaster between the laths securing other coats. 12 roughness of a surface helping the adhesion of plaster etc. 13 winged fruit of the sycamore etc. 14 device for making or breaking an electric circuit. —v. 1 (foll. by *in, on, etc.*) fasten with a pin, wedge, bolt, etc. 2 (often foll. by *in*) enter (data) by means of a keyboard. 3 roughen (a surface) to help the adhesion of plaster etc. 4 (foll. by *to*) align or link (one thing to another). □ **keyed up** tense, nervous, excited. [Old English]

key[2] /kiː/ n. low-lying island or reef, esp. in the W. Indies. [Spanish *cayo*]

keyboard —n. 1 set of keys on a typewriter, computer, piano, etc. 2 electronic musical instrument with keys arranged as on a piano. —v. enter (data) by means of a keyboard. □ **keyboarder** n. (in sense 1 of n.). **keyboardist** n. (in sense 2 of n.).

keyhole n. hole in a door etc. for a key.

keyhole surgery n. *colloq.* minimally invasive surgery carried out through a very small incision.

Keynesian /'keɪnzɪən/ *adj.* of the economic theories of J. M. Keynes, esp. regarding State intervention in the economy.

keynote n. 1 (esp. *attrib.*) prevailing tone or idea, esp. in a speech, conference, etc. 2 *Mus.* note on which a key is based.

keypad n. miniature keyboard etc. for a portable electronic device, telephone, etc.

keypunch —n. device for recording data by means of punched holes or notches on cards or paper tape. —v. record (data) thus.

key-ring n. ring for keeping keys on.

key signature n. *Mus.* any of several combinations of sharps or flats indicating the key of a composition.

keystone n. 1 central principle of a system, policy, etc. 2 central locking stone in an arch.

keystroke n. single depression of a key on a keyboard, esp. as a measure of work.

keyword n. 1 key to a cipher etc. 2 a word of great significance. b significant word used in indexing.

KG *abbr.* Knight of the Order of the Garter.

kg *abbr.* kilogram(s).

KGB *n.* State security police of the former USSR. [Russian abbreviation, = committee of State security]

khaki /'kɑːkɪ/ —*adj.* dull brownish-yellow. —*n.* (*pl.* -**s**) **1** khaki fabric or uniform. **2** dull brownish-yellow colour. [Urdu, = dusty]

khan /kɑːn/ *n.* title of rulers and officials in Central Asia, Afghanistan, etc. □ **khanate** *n.* [Turki, = lord]

kHz *abbr.* kilohertz.

kibbutz /kɪ'bʊts/ *n.* (*pl.* **kibbutzim** /-'tsiːm/) communal esp. farming settlement in Israel. [Hebrew, = gathering]

kibosh /'kaɪbɒʃ/ *n. slang* nonsense. □ **put the kibosh on** put an end to. [origin unknown]

kick —*v.* **1** strike, strike out, or propel forcibly, with the foot or hoof. **2** (often foll. by *at, against*) protest at; rebel against. **3** *slang* give up (a habit). **4** (often foll. by *out* etc.) expel or dismiss forcibly. **5** *refl.* be annoyed with oneself. **6** *Football* score (a goal) by a kick. —*n.* **1** kicking action or blow. **2** *colloq.* a sharp stimulant effect, esp. of alcohol. **b** (often in *pl.*) thrill (*did it for kicks*). **3** strength, resilience (*no kick left*). **4** *colloq.* specified temporary interest (*on a jogging kick*). **5** recoil of a gun when fired. □ **kick about** (or **around**) *colloq.* **1** be unused or unwanted. **2** a treat roughly. **b** discuss unsystematically. **kick the bucket** *slang* die. **kick one's heels** see HEEL. **kick off 1** a *Football* start or resume a match. **b** *colloq.* begin. **2** remove (shoes etc.) by kicking. **kick over the traces** see TRACE². **kick up** (or **kick up a fuss, dust**, etc.) *colloq.* create a disturbance; object. **kick a person upstairs** dispose of a person by promotion etc. [origin unknown]

kickback *n. colloq.* **1** recoil. **2** (usu. illegal) payment for help or favours, esp. in business.

kick-off *n. Football* start or resumption of a match.

kickstand *n.* rod for supporting a bicycle or motor cycle when stationary.

kick-start —*n.* (also **kick-starter**) device to start the engine of a motor cycle etc. by the downward thrust of a pedal. —*v.* start (a motor cycle etc.) in this way.

kid¹ —*n.* **1** young goat. **2** leather from this. **3** *colloq.* child. —*v.* (-**dd**-) (of a goat) give birth. □ **handle with kid gloves** treat carefully. [Old Norse]

kid² *v.* (also *refl.*) (-**dd**-) *colloq.* deceive, trick, tease (*don't kid yourself; only kidding*). □ **no kidding** *slang* that is the truth. [origin uncertain]

kiddie /'kɪdɪ/ *n.* (also **kiddy**) (*pl.* -**ies**) *slang* = KID¹ *n.* 3.

kiddo /'kɪdəʊ/ *n.* (*pl.* -**s**) *slang* = KID¹ *n.* 3.

kidnap *v.* (-**pp**-; *US* -**p**-) **1** abduct (a person etc.), esp. to obtain a ransom **2** steal (a child). □ **kidnapper** *n.* [from KID¹, *nap* = NAB]

kidney /'kɪdnɪ/ *n.* (*pl.* -**s**) **1** either of two organs in the abdominal cavity of vertebrates which remove nitrogenous wastes from the blood and excrete urine. **2** animal's kidney as food. [origin unknown]

kidney bean *n.* red-skinned dried bean.

kidney machine *n.* machine able to take over the function of a damaged kidney.

kidney-shaped *adj.* having one side concave and the other convex.

kill —*v.* **1** (also *absol.*) deprive of life or vitality; cause death or the death of. **2** destroy (feelings etc.). **3** *refl. colloq.* **a** overexert oneself (*don't kill yourself trying*). **b** laugh heartily. **4** *colloq.* overwhelm with amusement **5** switch off (a light, engine, etc.). **6** *Computing colloq.* delete. **7** *colloq.* cause pain or discomfort to (*my feet are killing me*). **8** pass (time, or a specified period) usu. while waiting (*an hour to kill before the interview*). **9** defeat (a bill in Parliament). **10** a *Tennis* etc. hit (the ball) so that it cannot be returned. **b** stop (the ball) dead. **11** make ineffective (taste, sound, pain, etc.) (*carpet killed the sound*). —*n.* **1** act of killing (esp. in hunting). **2** animal(s) killed, esp. by a hunter. **3** *colloq.* destruction or disablement of an enemy aircraft etc. □ **dressed to kill** dressed showily or alluringly. **in at the kill** present at a successful conclusion. **kill off 1** destroy completely. **2** (of an author) bring about the death of (a fictional character). **kill or cure** (usu. *attrib.*) (of a remedy) drastic, extreme. **kill two birds with one stone** achieve two aims at once. **kill with kindness** spoil with over-indulgence. [perhaps related to QUELL]

killer *n.* **1** a person, animal, or thing that kills. **b** murderer. **2** *colloq.* **a** impressive, formidable, or excellent thing. **b** hilarious joke.

killer instinct *n.* **1** innate tendency to kill. **2** ruthless streak.

killer whale *n.* dolphin with a prominent dorsal fin.

killing —*n.* **1** a causing of death. **b** instance of this. **2** *colloq.* great (esp. financial) success (*make a killing*). —*adj. colloq.* **1** very funny. **2** exhausting. □ **killjoy** *n.* gloomy or censorious person, esp. at a party etc.

kiln *n.* furnace or oven for burning, baking, or drying, esp. for calcining

lime or firing pottery etc. [Old English from Latin *culina* kitchen]

kilo /ˈkiːləʊ/ *n.* (*pl.* -s) kilogram. [French, abbreviation]

kilo- *comb. form* 1,000 (esp. in metric units). [Greek *khilioi*]

kilobyte /ˈkɪləbaɪt/ *n. Computing* 1,024 (i.e. 2^{10}) bytes as a measure of memory size etc.

kilocalorie /ˈkɪləˌkæləri/ *n.* = *large calorie* (see CALORIE).

kilocycle /ˈkɪləsaɪk(ə)l/ *n. hist.* kilohertz.

kilogram /ˈkɪləˌgram/ *n.* (also **-gramme**) SI unit of mass, approx. 2.205 lb.

kilohertz /ˈkɪləhɜːts/ *n.* 1,000 cycles per second.

kilojoule /ˈkɪləˌdʒuːl/ *n.* 1,000 joules, esp. as a measure of the energy value of foods.

kilolitre /ˈkɪləˌliːtə(r)/ *n.* (*US* **-liter**) 1,000 litres (220 imperial gallons).

kilometre /ˈkɪləˌmiːtə(r), kɪˈlɒmɪtə(r)/ *n.* 1,000 metres (approx. 0.62 miles). (*US* **-meter**.) □ **kilometric** /ˌkɪləˈmetrɪk/ *adj.*

■ **Usage** The second pronunciation given, with the stress on the second syllable, is considered incorrect by some people.

kiloton /ˈkɪləˌtʌn/ *n.* (also **kilotonne**) unit of explosive power equivalent to 1,000 tons of TNT.

kilovolt /ˈkɪləˌvəʊlt/ *n.* 1,000 volts.

kilowatt /ˈkɪləˌwɒt/ *n.* 1,000 watts.

kilowatt-hour *n.* electrical energy equivalent to a power consumption of 1,000 watts for one hour.

kilter /ˈkɪltə(r)/ *n.* (also **kelter**) good working order (esp. *out of kilter*). [origin unknown]

kimono /kɪˈməʊnəʊ/ *n.* (*pl.* -s) 1 long sashed Japanese robe. 2 similar dressing-gown. [Japanese]

kin *—n.* one's relatives or family. *—predic. adj.* related. [Old English]

-kin *suffix* forming diminutive nouns (*catkin; manikin*). [Dutch]

kind /kaɪnd/ *—n.* 1 race, species, or natural group of animals, plants, etc. 2 class, type, sort, variety. 3 natural way, fashion, etc. (*true to kind*). *—adj.* (often foll. by *to*) friendly, generous, or benevolent. □ **in kind 1** in the same form, likewise (*was insulted and replied in kind*). 2 (of payment) in goods or labour, not money. 3 character, quality (*differ in degree but not in kind*).

kind *of colloq.* to some extent (*I kind of expected it*). **a kind of** loosely resembling (*he's a kind of doctor*). [Old English]

■ **Usage** In sense 2 of the noun, *these kinds of* is usually preferred to *these kind of*.

kindergarten /ˈkɪndəˌgɑːt(ə)n/ *n.* class or school for very young children. [German, = children's garden]

kind-hearted *adj.* of a kind disposition. □ **kind-heartedness** *n.* **kind-heartedly** *adv.*

kindle /ˈkɪnd(ə)l/ *v.* (-**ling**) 1 light, catch, or set on fire. 2 arouse or inspire. 3 become aroused or animated. [Old Norse]

kindling *n.* small sticks etc. for lighting fires.

kindly¹ *adv.* 1 in a kind manner (*spoke kindly*). 2 often *iron.* please (*kindly go away*). □ **look kindly upon** regard sympathetically. **take kindly to** be pleased by; like.

kindly² *adj.* (-**ier**, -**iest**) 1 kind, kind-hearted. 2 (of a climate etc.) pleasant, mild. □ **kindlily** *adv.* **kindliness** *n.*

kindness *n.* 1 being kind, kind act.

kindred /ˈkɪndrɪd/ *—n.* 1 one's relations collectively. 2 blood relationship. 3 resemblance or similar. *—adj.* related, allied, similar. □ **kindred spirit** *n.* person like or in sympathy with oneself. [Old English, = kinship]

kinematics /ˌkɪnɪˈmætɪks/ *n.pl.* (usu. treated as *sing.*) branch of mechanics concerned with the motion of objects without reference to cause. □ **kinematic** *adj.* [Greek *kinēma -matos* motion]

kinetic /kɪˈnetɪk/ *adj.* of or due to motion. □ **kinetically** *adv.* [Greek *kineō* move]

kinetic art *n.* sculpture etc. designed to move.

kinetic energy *n.* energy of motion.

kinetics *n.pl.* 1 = DYNAMICS 1a. 2 (usu. treated as *sing.*) branch of physical chemistry measuring and studying rates of chemical reactions.

king *n.* 1 (as a title usu. **King**) male sovereign, esp. a hereditary ruler. 2 preeminent person or thing (*oil king*). 3 (*attrib.*) large (or the largest) kind of plant, animal, etc. (*king penguin*). 4 *Chess* piece which must be checkmated for a win. 5 crowned piece in draughts. 6 court-card depicting a king. 7 (**the King's**) national anthem when the sovereign is male. □ **kingly** *adj.* **kingship** *n.* [Old English]

King Charles spaniel n. small black and tan spaniel.

kingcup n. marsh marigold.

kingdom n. 1 territory or State ruled by a king or queen. 2 spiritual reign or sphere of God. 3 domain. 4 division of the natural world (*plant kingdom*). 5 specified sphere (*kingdom of the heart*). [Old English]

kingdom come n. *colloq.* the next world.

kingfisher n. small bird with brightly coloured plumage, diving for fish etc.

King of Arms n. a chief herald.

king of beasts n. lion.

king of birds n. eagle.

kingpin n. 1 main, large, or vertical bolt, esp. as a pivot. 2 essential person or thing.

king-post n. upright post from the tie-beam of a roof to the apex of a truss.

King's Counsel n. = QUEEN'S COUN-SEL.

King's English n. = QUEEN'S ENGLISH.

King's evidence see EVIDENCE.

King's Guide n. = QUEEN'S GUIDE.

King's highway n. = QUEEN'S HIGH-WAY.

king-size *adj.* (also -**sized**) very large.

King's Proctor n. = QUEEN'S PROC-TOR.

King's Scout n. = QUEEN'S SCOUT.

kink —n. 1 a twist or bend in wire etc. b tight wave in hair. 2 mental twist or quirk, esp. when perverse. —v. (cause to) form a kink. [Low German or Dutch]

kinky *adj.* (**-ier**, **-iest**) 1 *colloq.* a sexually perverted or unconventional. b (of clothing etc.) bizarre and sexually provocative. 2 having kinks. □ **kinkily** *adv.* **kinkiness** n.

kinsfolk n.pl. one's blood relations.

kinship n. 1 blood relationship. 2 likeness; sympathy.

kinsman n. (*fem.* **kinswoman**) 1 blood relation. 2 relation by marriage.

■ **Usage** Use of *kinsman* in sense 2 is considered incorrect by some people.

kiosk /'kiːɒsk/ n. 1 light open-fronted booth selling food, newspapers, tickets, etc. 2 telephone box. [Turkish from Persian]

kip *slang* —n. 1 sleep; nap. 2 bed or cheap lodgings. —v. (**-pp-**) (often foll. by *down*) sleep. [cf. Danish *kippe* mean hut]

kipper /'kɪpə(r)/ —n. fish, esp. a herring, split, salted, dried, and usu. smoked. —v. cure (a herring etc.) thus. [origin uncertain]

kir /kɜː(r)/ n. dry white wine with *crème de cassis*.

kirby-grip /'kɜːbɪgrɪp/ n. (also **Kirbigrip** *propr.*) type of sprung hairgrip. [*Kirby*, name of the manufacturer]

kirk n. *Scot. & N.Engl.* 1 church. 2 (**the Kirk** or **the Kirk of Scotland**) Church of Scotland. [Old Norse *kirkja* = CHURCH]

Kirk-session n. lowest court in the Church of Scotland.

kirsch /kɪəʃ/ n. brandy distilled from cherries. [German, = cherry]

kismet /'kɪzmet/ n. destiny; fate. [Turkish from Arabic]

kiss —v. 1 touch with the lips, esp. as a sign of love, affection, greeting, or reverence. 2 (of two people) touch each others' lips in this way. 3 lightly touch. —n. 1 touch with the lips. 2 light touch. □ **kiss and tell** recount one's sexual exploits. **kiss a person's arse** *coarse slang* toady to. **kiss the dust** submit abjectly. [Old English]

kiss-curl n. small curl of hair on the forehead, nape, etc.

kisser n. 1 person who kisses. 2 *slang* mouth; face.

kiss of death n. apparent good luck etc. which causes ruin.

kiss of life n. mouth-to-mouth resuscitation.

kissogram /'kɪsəgræm/ n. (also **Kissa-gram** *propr.*) novelty telegram or greeting delivered with a kiss.

kit —n. 1 articles, equipment, etc. for a specific purpose (*first-aid kit*). 2 specialized, esp. sports, clothing or uniform (*football kit*). 3 set of parts needed to assemble furniture, a model, etc. —v. (**-tt-**) (often foll. by *out*, *up*) equip with kit. [Dutch]

kitbag n. large usu. cylindrical bag used for a soldier's or traveller's kit.

kitchen /'kɪtʃɪn/ n. 1 place where food is prepared and cooked. 2 kitchen fitments (*half-price kitchens*). [Latin *coquina*]

kitchenette /ˌkɪtʃɪ'net/ n. small kitchen or cooking area.

kitchen garden n. garden with vegetables, fruit, herbs, etc.

kitchenware n. cooking utensils.

kite n. 1 light framework with a thin covering flown on a string in the wind. 2 soaring bird of prey. [Old English]

Kitemark n. official kite-shaped mark on goods approved by the British Standards Institution.

kith n. □ **kith and kin** friends and relations. [Old English, originally 'knowledge': related to CAN¹]

kitsch /kɪtʃ/ n. (often *attrib.*) vulgar, pretentious, or worthless art. □ **kitschy** *adj.* (**-ier**, **-iest**). [German]

kitten /'kɪt(ə)n/ —n. young cat, ferret, etc. —v. (of a cat etc.) give birth (to). □

have kittens *colloq.* be very upset or anxious. [Anglo-French diminutive of *chat* CAT]

kittenish *adj.* playful, lively, or flirtatious.

kittiwake /ˈkɪtɪweɪk/ *n.* a kind of small seagull. [imitative of its cry]

kitty[1] /ˈkɪtɪ/ *n.* (*pl.* -**ies**) 1 fund of money for communal use. 2 pool in some card-games. [origin unknown]

kitty[2] /ˈkɪtɪ/ *n.* (*pl.* -**ies**) childish name for a kitten or cat.

kiwi /ˈkiːwiː/ *n.* (*pl.* -**s**) 1 flightless long-billed New Zealand bird. 2 (**Kiwi**) *colloq.* New Zealander. [Maori]

kiwi fruit *n.* green-fleshed fruit of a climbing plant.

kJ *abbr.* kilojoule(s).

kl *abbr.* kilolitre(s).

Klaxon /ˈklæks(ə)n/ *n. propr.* horn or warning hooter. [name cf the manufacturer]

Kleenex /ˈkliːneks/ *n. propr.* disposable paper hand-
-nexes) *propr.* disposable paper handkerchief.

kleptomania /ˌkleptəˈmeɪnɪə/ *n.* obsessive apparently motiveless urge to steal. □ **kleptomaniac** /-nɪæk/ *n. & adj.* [Greek *kleptēs* thief]

km *abbr.* kilometre(s).

knack /næk/ *n.* 1 acquired faculty or trick of doing a thing. 2 habit (*a knack of offending people*). [origin unknown]

knacker —*n.* buyer of useless horses etc. for slaughter, or of old houses, ships, etc. for the materials. —*v. slang* (esp. as **knackered** *adj.*) exhaust, wear out. [origin unknown]

knapsack /ˈnæpsæk/ *n.* soldier's or hiker's usu. canvas bag carried on the back. [German *knappen* bite, SACK[1]]

knapweed /ˈnæpwiːd/ *n.* plant with thistle-like purple flowers. [from *knop* ornamental knob or tuft]

knave *n.* 1 rogue, scoundrel. 2 = JACK *n.* 2. □ **knavery** *n.* (*pl.* -**ies**). **knavish** *adj.* [Old English, originally = boy, servant]

knead *v.* 1 a work into a dough, paste, etc. by pummelling. **b** make (bread, pottery, etc.) thus. 2 massage (muscles etc.) as if kneading. [Old English]

knee —*n.* 1 a (often *attrib.*)) joint between the thigh and the lower leg in humans. **b** corresponding joint in other animals. **c** area around this. **d** lap (*sat on his knee*). 2 part of a garment covering the knee. —*v.* (**knees, kneed, kneeing**) 1 touch or strike with the knee (*kneed him in the groin*). 2 *colloq.* make (trousers) bulge at the knee. [Old English]

knee-bend *n.* bending of the knee, esp. as a physical exercise.

knees.

knee-deep *adj.* 1 (usu. foll. by *in*) **a** immersed up to the knees. **b** deeply involved. 2 so deep as to reach the knees.

knee-high *adj.* so high as to reach the knees.

knee-jerk *n.* 1 sudden involuntary kick caused by a blow on the tendon just below the knee. 2 (*attrib.*) predictable, automatic, stereotyped.

kneel *v.* (*past* and *past part.* **knelt** /nelt/ or esp. *US* **kneeled**) fall or rest on the knees or a knee. [Old English: related to KNEE]

knee-length *adj.* reaching the knees.

kneeler *n.* 1 cushion for kneeling on. 2 person who kneels.

knees-up *n. colloq.* lively party or gathering.

knell —*n.* 1 sound of a bell, esp. for a death or funeral. 2 announcement, event, etc. regarded as an ill omen. —*v.* 1 ring a knell. 2 proclaim by or as by a knell. [Old English]

knelt *past* and *past part.* of KNEEL.

knew *past* of KNOW.

knickerbocker /ˈnɪkəbɒkə(r)/ *n.* (in *pl.*) loose-fitting breeches gathered at the knee or calf. [the pseudonym of W. Irving, author of *History of New York*]

Knickerbocker Glory *n.* ice-cream served with fruit etc. in a tall glass.

knickers *n.pl.* woman's or girl's under-garment for the lower torso. [abbreviation of KNICKERBOCKER]

knick-knack /ˈnɪknæk/ *n.* (also **nick-nack**) trinket or small dainty ornament etc. [from KNACK in the obsolete sense 'trinket']

knife —*n.* (*pl.* **knives**) 1 metal blade for cutting or as a weapon with usu. one long sharp edge fixed in a handle. 2 cutting-blade in a machine. 3 (as *the knife*) surgical operation. —*v.* (*-fing/cut* or stab with a knife. □ **at knife-point** threatened with a knife or an ultimatum etc. **get** (or **have got**) **one's knife into** treat maliciously, persecute. [Old English]

knife-edge *n.* 1 edge of a knife. 2 position of extreme danger or uncertainty.

knife-pleat *n.* narrow flat usu. overlapping pleat on a skirt etc.

knight /naɪt/ —*n.* 1 man awarded a non-hereditary title (*Sir*) by a sovereign. 2

knee-breeches *n.pl.* close-fitting trousers to the knee or just below.

kneecap —*n.* 1 convex bone in front of the knee. 2 protective covering for the knee. —*v.* (**-pp-**) *slang* (of a terrorist) shoot (a person) in the knee or leg as a punishment.

man, noble, raised to honourable military rank after service

as a page and squire. **b** military follower, attendant, or lady's champion in a war or tournament. **3** man devoted to a cause, woman, etc. **4** *Chess* piece usu. shaped like a horse's head. —*v.* confer a knighthood on. □ **knighthood** *n.* **knightly** *adj. poet.* [Old English, originally = boy]

knight commander see COMMANDER.

knight errant *n.* **1** medieval knight in search of chivalrous adventures. **2** chivalrous or quixotic man. □ **knighterrantry** *n.*

knit *v.* (-**tt**-; *past* and *past part.* **knitted** or (esp. in senses 2-4) **knit**) **1** (also *absol.*) **a** make (a garment etc.) by interlocking loops of esp. wool with knitting-needles or a knitting-machine. **b** make (a plain stitch) in knitting (*knit one, purl one*). **2** momentarily wrinkle (the forehead) or (of the forehead) become momentarily wrinkled. **3** (often foll. by *together*) make or become close or compact. **4** (often foll. by *together*) (of a broken bone) become joined; heal. □ **knit up 1** make or repair by knitting. **knitter** *n.* [Old English]

knitting *n.* work being knitted.

knitting-needle *n.* thin pointed rod used esp. in pairs for knitting by hand.

knitwear *n.* knitted garments.

knives *pl.* of KNIFE.

knob *n.* **1** rounded protuberance, esp. at the end or on the surface of a thing, e.g. the handle of a door, drawer, etc. **2** small piece (of butter etc.). □ **with knobs on** *slang* that and more (*same to you with knobs on*). □ **knobby** *adj.* **knoblike** *adj.* [Low German *knobbe* knot, knob]

knobbly /'nɒblɪ/ *adj.* (**-ier, -iest**) hard and lumpy. [*knobble*, diminutive of KNOB]

knock —*v.* **1 a** strike with an audible sharp blow. **b** (often foll. by *at*) strike (a door etc.) to gain admittance. **2** make (a hole etc.) by knocking. **3** (usu. foll. by *in, out, off,* etc.) drive (a thing, person, etc.) by striking (*knocked the ball into the hole; knocked these ideas out of him*). **4** *slang* criticize. **5 a** (of an engine) make a thumping or rattling noise. **b** = PINK³. **6** *coarse slang offens.* = *knock off 6.* —*n.* **1** act or sound of knocking. **2** knocking sound in esp. an engine. □ **knock about** (or **around**) *colloq.* **1** strike repeatedly; treat roughly. **2 a** wander aimlessly or adventurously. **b** be present, esp. by chance (*a cup knocking about somewhere*). **c** (usu. foll. by *with*) be associated socially. **knock back 1** *slang* eat or drink, esp. quickly. **2** *slang* disconcert.

knock down 1 strike (esp. a person) to the ground. **2** demolish. **3** (usu. foll. by *to*) (at an auction) sell (an article) to a bidder by a knock with a hammer. **4** *colloq.* lower the price of (an article). **5** *US slang* steal. **knock off 1** strike off with a blow. **2** *colloq.* finish (work) (*knocked off at 5.30; knocked off work early*). **3** *colloq.* produce (a work of art etc.) or do (a task) rapidly. **4** (often foll. by *from*) deduct (a sum) from a price etc. **5** *slang* steal. **6** *coarse slang offens.* have sexual intercourse with (a woman). **7** *slang* kill. **knock on the head** *colloq.* put an end to (a scheme etc.). **knock on** (or **knock**) **wood** *US* = *touch wood.* **knock out 1** make unconscious by a blow on the head. **2** defeat (a boxer) by knocking him or her down for a count of 10. **3** defeat, esp. in a knockout competition. **4** *slang* astonish. **5** (often *refl.*) *colloq.* exhaust. **knock sideways** *colloq.* astonish, shock. **knock spots off** defeat easily. **knock together** assemble hastily. **knock up 1** make hastily. **2** waken by a knock at the door. **3** *US slang* make pregnant. **4** practise tennis etc. before formal play begins. [Old English]

knockabout *attrib. adj.* **1** (of comedy) boisterous; slapstick. **2** (of clothes) hardwearing.

knock-down *attrib. adj.* **1** overwhelming. **2** (of a price) very low. **3** (of a price at auction) reserve. **4** (of furniture etc.) easily dismantled and reassembled.

knocker *n.* **1** hinged esp. metal instrument on a door for knocking with. **2** (in *pl.*) *coarse slang* woman's breasts.

knocking-shop *n. slang* brothel.

knock knees *n.pl.* abnormal curvature of the legs inwards at the knee. □ **knock-kneed** *adj.*

knock-on effect *n.* secondary, indirect, or cumulative effect.

knockout *n.* **1** act of making unconscious by a blow. **2** (usu. *attrib.*) *Boxing* etc. such a blow. **3** competition in which the loser in each round is eliminated (also *attrib.: knockout round*). **4** *colloq.* outstanding or irresistible person or thing.

knock-up *n.* practice at tennis etc.

knoll /nəʊl/ *n.* hillock, mound. [Old English]

knot¹ —*n.* **1 a** intertwining of rope, string, hair, etc., so as to fasten. **b** set method of this (*reef knot*). **c** knotted ribbon etc. as an ornament. **d** tangle in hair, knitting, etc. **2** unit of a ship's or aircraft's speed, equivalent to one nautical mile per hour. **3** (usu. foll. by *of*) cluster (*knot of journalists*). **4** bond, esp. of marriage. **5** hard lump of organic

tissue. **6 a** a hard mass in a tree-trunk where a branch grows out. **b** round cross-grained piece in timber marking this. **7** central point in a problem etc. —*v.* **(-tt-) 1** tie in a knot. **2** entangle. **3** unite closely. □ **at a rate of knots** *colloq.* very fast. **tie in knots** *colloq.* baffle or confuse completely. [Old English]

knot² *n.* small sandpiper. [origin unknown]

knotgrass *n.* wild plant with creeping stems and small pink flowers.

knot-hole *n.* hole in timber where a knot has fallen out.

knotty *adj.* (**-ier, -iest**) **1** full of knots. **2** puzzling (*knotty problem*).

know /nəʊ/ *v.* (*past* **knew**; *past part.* **known**) **1** (often foll. by *that, how, what,* etc.) **a** have in the mind; have learnt; be able to recall (*knows a lot about cars*). **b** (also *absol.*) be aware of (a fact) (*I think he knows*). **c** have a good command of (*knew German; knows his tables*). **2** be acquainted or friendly with. **3 a** (often foll. by *that*) recognize; identify (*I knew him at once; knew them to be rogues*). **b** (foll. *from*) be able to distinguish (*did not know him from Adam*). **4** be subject to (*joy knew no bounds*). **5** have personal experience of (*fear etc.*). **6** (as **known** *adj.*) **a** publicly acknowledged (*known fact*). **b** *Math.* (of a quantity etc.) having a value that can be stated. **7** have understanding or knowledge. □ **in the know** *colloq.* having inside information. **know of** be aware of; have heard of (*not that I know of*). **know one's own mind** be decisive, not vacillate. **know what's what** have knowledge of the world, life, etc. **you know** *colloq.* 1 implying something generally known (*you know, the pub on the corner*). 2 expression used as a gap-filler in conversation. **you never know** it is possible. □ **knowable** *adj.* [Old English]

know-all *n. colloq.* person who claims or seems to know everything.

know-how *n.* practical knowledge; natural skill.

knowing *adj.* **1** suggesting that one has inside information (*a knowing look*). **2** showing knowledge; shrewd.

knowingly *adv.* **1** consciously; intentionally (*wouldn't knowingly hurt him*). **2** in a knowing manner (*smiled knowingly*).

knowledge /ˈnɒlɪdʒ/ *n.* **1 a** (usu. foll. by *of*) awareness or familiarity (of or with a person or thing) (*have no knowledge of that*). **b** person's range of information. **2 a** (usu. foll. by *of*) understanding of a subject etc. (*good knowledge of Greek*). **b** sum of what is known (*every branch of*

knowledge). □ **to my knowledge** as far as I know.

knowledgeable *adj.* (also **knowledgable**) well-informed; intelligent. □ **knowledgeability** /ˈblɪtɪ/ *n.* **knowledgeably** *adv.*

known *past part. of* KNOW.

knuckle /ˈnʌk(ə)l/ —*n.* **1** bone at a finger-joint, esp. that connecting the finger to the hand. **2 a** knee- or ankle-joint of a quadruped. **b** this as a joint of meat, esp. of bacon or pork. —*v.* (-ling) strike, press, or rub with the knuckles. □ **knuckle down** (often foll. by *to*) **1** apply oneself seriously (to a task etc.). **2** (also **knuckle under**) give in; submit. [Low German or Dutch]

knuckleduster *n.* metal guard worn over the knuckles in fighting, esp. in order to inflict greater damage.

knuckle sandwich *n. slang* punch in the mouth.

knurl /nɜːl/ *n.* small projecting knob, ridge, etc. [Low German or Dutch]

KO *abbr.* knockout

koala /kəʊˈɑːlə/ *n.* (in full **koala bear**) small Australian bearlike marsupial with thick grey fur [Aboriginal]

kohl /kəʊl/ *n.* black powder used as eye make-up, esp. in Eastern countries. [Arabic]

kohlrabi /kəʊlˈrɑːbɪ/ *n.* (*pl.* **-bies**) cabbage with an edible turnip-like swollen stem. [German, from Italian *cavolo rapa*]

kola var. of COLA.

kolkhoz /kɒlˈxɒz/ *n.* collective farm in the former USSR. [Russian]

koodoo var. of KUDU.

kook *n. US slang* crazy or eccentric person. □ **kooky** *adj.* (**-ier, -iest**). [probably from CUCKOO]

kookaburra /ˈkʊkəbʌrə/ *n.* Australian kingfisher with a strange laughing cry. [Aboriginal]

kopeck (also **kopek**) var. of COPECK.

koppie /ˈkɒpɪ/ *n.* (also **kopje**) *S.Afr.* small hill. [Afrikaans *kopje* little head]

Koran /kɔːˈrɑːn/ *n.* Islamic sacred book. [Arabic, = recitation]

Korean /kəˈrɪən/ —*n.* **1** native or national of N. or S. Korea. **2** language of Korea. —*adj.* of Korea, its people, or language.

kosher /ˈkəʊʃə(r)/ —*adj.* **1** (of food or a food-shop) fulfilling the requirements of Jewish law. **2** *colloq.* correct, genuine, legitimate. —*n.* kosher food or shop. [Hebrew, = proper]

kowtow /kaʊˈtaʊ/ —*n. hist.* Chinese custom of kneeling with the forehead touching the ground. —*v.* **1** *hist.*

touching the ground, esp. in submission. −v. **1** (usu. foll. by *to*) act obsequiously. **2** *hist.* perform the kowtow. [Chinese, = knock the head]

k.p.h. *abbr.* kilometres per hour.

Kr *symb.* krypton.

kraal /krɑːl/ *n. S.Afr.* **1** village of huts enclosed by a fence. **2** enclosure for cattle or sheep. [Afrikaans from Portuguese *curral*, of Hottentot origin]

Kraut /kraut/ *n. slang offens.* German. [shortening of SAUERKRAUT]

kremlin /'kremlɪn/ *n.* **1** (**the Kremlin**) **a** citadel in Moscow. **b** Russian Government housed within it. **2** citadel within a Russian town. [Russian]

krill *n.* tiny planktonic crustaceans. [Norwegian *kril* tiny fish]

krona /'krəʊnə/ *n.* **1** (*pl.* **kronor**) chief monetary unit of Sweden. **2** (*pl.* **kronur**) chief monetary unit of Iceland. [Swedish and Icelandic, = CROWN]

krone /'krəʊnə/ *n.* (*pl.* **kroner**) chief monetary unit of Denmark and Norway. [Danish and Norwegian, = CROWN]

krugerrand /'kruːgəˌrænt/ *n. S. African* gold coin. [*Kruger*, name of a S. African statesman]

krummhorn /'krʊmhɔːn/ *n.* (also **crumhorn**) medieval wind instrument. [German]

krypton /'krɪptɒn/ *n.* inert gaseous element used in fluorescent lamps etc. [Greek *kruptō* hide]

Kt. *abbr.* Knight.

kt. *abbr.* knot.

Ku *symb.* kurchatovium.

kudos /'kjuːdɒs/ *n. colloq.* glory; renown. [Greek]

kudu /'kuːduː/ *n.* (also **koodoo**) (*pl.* same or **-s**) African antelope with white stripes and corkscrew-shaped ridged horns. [Xhosa]

Kufic /'kjuːfɪk/ (also **Cufic**) −*n.* early angular form of the Arabic alphabet used esp. in decorative inscriptions. −*adj.* of or in this script. [from *Kufa*, city in Iraq]

Ku Klux Klan /ˌkuːklʌks'klæn/ *n.* secret White racist society in the southern US. [origin uncertain]

kümmel /'kʊm(ə)l/ *n.* sweet liqueur flavoured with caraway and cumin seeds. [German: related to CUMIN]

kumquat /'kʌmkwɒt/ *n.* (also **cumquat**) **1** small orange-like fruit. **2** shrub or small tree yielding this. [Chinese *kin kü* gold orange]

kung fu /kʌŋ 'fuː/ *n.* Chinese form of karate. [Chinese]

kurchatovium /ˌkɜːtʃə'təʊvɪəm/ *n.* = RUTHERFORDIUM. [*Kurchatov*, name of a Russian physicist]

kV *abbr.* kilovolt(s).

kW *abbr.* kilowatt(s).

kWh *abbr.* kilowatt-hour(s).

kyle /kaɪl/ *n.* (in Scotland) narrow channel, strait. [Gaelic *caol* strait]

L[1] /el/ n. (also **l**) (pl. **Ls** or **L's**) **1** twelfth letter of the alphabet. **2** (as a Roman numeral) 50.

L[2] abbr. (also **L.**) **1** learner driver. **2** Lake.

l abbr. (also **L.**) **1** left. **2** line. **3** litre(s).

£ abbr. (also **L.**) pound(s) (money). [Latin libra]

LA abbr. Los Angeles.

La symb. lanthanum.

la var. of LAH.

Lab. abbr. Labour.

lab n. colloq. laboratory. [abbreviation]

label /'leɪb(ə)l/ —n. **1** piece of paper etc. attached to an object to give information about it. **2** short classifying phrase applied to a person etc. **3** logo, title, or trademark of a company. —v. (**-l-**; US **-l-**) **1** attach a label to. **2** (usu. foll. by as) assign to a category. **3** replace (an atom) by an atom of a usu. radioactive isotope as a means of identification. [French]

labial /'leɪbɪəl/ —adj. **1 a** of the lips. **b** of, like, or serving as a lip. **2** (of a sound) requiring partial or complete closure of the lips. —n. labial sound (e.g. p, m, v). [Latin labia lips]

labium /'leɪbɪəm/ n. (pl. **labia**) (usu. in pl.) each fold of skin of the two pairs enclosing the vulva. [Latin, = lip]

laboratory /lə'bɒrətərɪ/ n. (pl. **-ies**) room, building, or establishment for scientific experiments, research, chemical manufacture, etc. [Latin: related to LABORIOUS]

laborious /lə'bɔːrɪəs/ adj. **1** needing hard work or toil. **2** (esp. of literary style) showing signs of toil. □ **laboriously** adv. [Latin: related to LABOUR]

labour /'leɪbə(r)/ (US & Austral. **labor**) —n. **1** physical or mental work; exertion. **2 a** workers, esp. manual, considered as a political and economic force. **b** (**Labour**) the Labour Party. **3** process of childbirth. **4** particular task. —v. **1** work hard; exert oneself. **2 a** elaborate needlessly (don't labour the point). **b** (as **laboured** adj.) done with great effort; not spontaneous. **3** (often foll. by under) suffer under (a delusion etc.). **4** proceed with trouble or difficulty. [French from Latin labor, -oris]

labour camp n. prison camp enforcing a regime of hard labour.

Labour Day n. May 1 (or in the US and Canada the first Monday in September), celebrated in honour of working people.

labourer n. (US **laborer**) person doing unskilled, usu. manual, work for wages.

Labour Exchange n. colloq. or hist. employment exchange.

Labour Party n. political party formed to represent the interests of working people.

labour-saving adj. designed to reduce or eliminate work.

Labrador /'læbrə,dɔː(r)/ n. retriever of a breed with a black or golden coat. [Labrador in Canada]

laburnum /lə'bɜːnəm/ n. tree with drooping golden flowers yielding poisonous seeds. [Latin]

labyrinth /'læbərɪnθ/ n. **1** complicated network of passages etc. **2** intricate or tangled arrangement **3** the complex structure of the inner ear. □ **labyrinthine** /,-'rɪnθaɪn/ adj. [Latin from Greek]

lac n. resinous substance secreted as a protective covering by a SE Asian insect. [Hindustani]

lace —n. **1** fine open fabric or trimming, made by weaving thread in patterns. **2** cord etc. passed through holes or hooks for fastening shoes etc. —v. (**-cing**) **1** (usu. foll. by up) fasten or tighten with a lace or laces. **2** add spirits to (a drink). **3** (often foll. by through) pass (a shoelace etc.) through. [Latin laqueus noose]

lacerate /'læsə,reɪt/ v. (**-ting**) **1** mangle or tear (esp. flesh etc.). **2** cause pain to (the feelings etc.). □ **laceration** /-'reɪʃ(ə)n/ n [Latin lacer torn]

lace-up n. shoe fastened with a lace. —attrib. adj. (of a shoe etc.) fastened by a lace or laces.

lachrymal /'lækrɪməl/ adj. (also **lacrimal**) of or for tears (lacrimal duct). [Latin lacrima tear]

lachrymose /'lækrɪməʊs/ adj. formal given to weeping; tearful. [Latin lacrima tear]

lack —n. (usu. foll. by of) want, deficiency. —v. be without or deficient in.

lackadaisical /,lækə'deɪzɪk(ə)l/ adj. unenthusiastic; listless; idle. □ **lackadaisically** adv. [from archaic lackaday]

lackey /'lækɪ/ n. (pl. **-s**) **1** servile follower; toady. **2** footman, manservant. [Catalan alacay]

lacking adj. absent or deficient (money was lacking; is lacking in determination).

lacklustre *adj.* (*US* **lackluster**) **1** lacking in vitality etc. **2** dull.

laconic /ləˈkɒnɪk/ *adj.* terse, using few words. □ **laconically** *adv.* [Greek *Lakōn* Spartan]

lacquer /ˈlækə(r)/ —*n.* **1** varnish made of shellac or a synthetic substance. **2** substance sprayed on the hair to keep it in place. —*v.* coat with lacquer. [French *lacre* LAC]

lacrimal var. of LACHRYMAL.

lacrosse /ləˈkrɒs/ *n.* game like hockey, but with the ball carried in a crosse. [French *la* the, CROSSE]

lactate¹ /lækˈteɪt/ *v.* (*-ting*) (of mammals) secrete milk. [as LACTATION]

lactate² /ˈlækteɪt/ *n.* salt or ester of lactic acid.

lactation /lækˈteɪʃ(ə)n/ *n.* **1** secretion of milk. **2** suckling. [Latin: related to LACTIC]

lacteal /ˈlæktɪəl/ —*adj.* **1** of milk. **2** conveying chyle etc. —*n.* (in *pl.*) *Anat.* vessels which absorb fats. [Latin *lacteus*: related to LACTIC]

lactic /ˈlæktɪk/ *adj.* of milk. [Latin *lac lactis* milk]

lactic acid *n.* acid formed esp. in sour milk.

lactose /ˈlæktəʊs/ *n.* sugar that occurs in milk.

lacuna /ləˈkjuːnə/ *n.* (*pl.* **lacunae** /-niː/ or **-s**) **1** gap. **2** missing portion etc., esp. in an ancient MS etc. [Latin: related to LAKE¹]

lacy /ˈleɪsɪ/ *adj.* (**-ier**, **-iest**) of or resembling lace fabric.

lad *n.* **1** boy, youth. **2** *colloq.* man. [origin unknown]

ladder —*n.* **1** set of horizontal bars fixed between two uprights and used for climbing up or down. **2** vertical strip of unravelled stitching in a stocking etc. **3** hierarchical structure, esp. as a means of career advancement. —*v.* **1** cause a ladder in (a stocking etc.). **2** develop a ladder. [Old English]

ladder-back *n.* upright chair with a back resembling a ladder.

lade *v.* (*-ding*; *past part.* **laden**) **1** a load (a ship). **b** ship (goods). **2** (as **laden** *adj.*) (usu. foll. by *with*) loaded, burdened. [Old English]

la-di-da /ˌlɑːdɪˈdɑː/ *adj. colloq.* pretentious or snobbish, esp. in manner or speech. [imitative]

ladies' man *n.* (also **lady's man**) man fond of female company.

ladle /ˈleɪd(ə)l/ —*n.* deep long-handled spoon used for serving liquids. —*v.* (*-ling*) (often foll. by *out*) transfer (liquid) with a ladle. [Old English]

lady /ˈleɪdɪ/ *n.* (*pl.* **-ies**) **1 a** woman regarded as being of superior social status or as having refined manners. **b** (**Lady**) title of peeresses, female relatives of peers, the wives and widows of knights, etc. **2** (often *attrib.*) woman; female (*ask that lady*; *lady butcher*). **3** *colloq.* wife, girlfriend. **4** ruling woman (*lady of the house*). **5** (**the Ladies** or **Ladies'**) women's public lavatory. [Old English, = loaf-kneader]

ladybird *n.* small beetle, usu. red with black spots.

Lady chapel *n.* chapel dedicated to the Virgin Mary.

Lady Day *n.* Feast of the Annunciation, 25 Mar.

lady-in-waiting *n.* lady attending a queen or princess.

ladykiller *n.* habitual seducer of women.

ladylike *adj.* like or befitting a lady.

ladyship *n.* □ **her** (or **your**) **ladyship** respectful form of reference or address to a Lady.

lady's slipper *n.* plant of the orchid family with a slipper-shaped lip on its flowers.

lag¹ —*v.* (**-gg-**) fall behind; not keep pace. —*n.* delay. [origin uncertain]

lag² —*v.* (**-gg-**) enclose in heat-insulating material. —*n.* insulating cover. [Old Norse]

lag³ *n. slang* habitual convict. [origin unknown]

lager /ˈlɑːgə(r)/ *n.* a kind of light effervescent beer. [German, = store]

lager lout *n. colloq.* youth behaving violently etc. as a result of excessive drinking.

laggard /ˈlægəd/ *n.* person who lags behind.

lagging *n.* material used to lag a boiler etc. against loss of heat.

lagoon /ləˈguːn/ *n.* stretch of salt water separated from the sea by a sandbank, reef, etc. [Latin LACUNA pool]

lah /lɑː/ *n.* (also **la**) *Mus.* sixth note of a major scale. [Latin *labii*, word arbitrarily taken]

laid *past* and *past part.* of LAY¹.

laid-back *adj.* relaxed; easygoing. [Old English]

laid paper *n.* paper with the surface marked in fine ribs.

laid up *adj.* confined to bed or the house.

lain *past part.* of LIE¹.

lair *n.* **1** wild animal's resting-place. **2** person's hiding-place. [Old English]

laird *n. Scot.* landed proprietor. [from LORD]

laissez-faire /ˌleseɪˈfeə(r)/ *n.* (also non-interference. [French, = let act]

laity /ˈleɪɪtɪ/ *n.* lay people, as distinct from the clergy. [from LAY²]

lake¹ *n.* large body of water surrounded by land. [Latin *lacus*]

lake² *n.* **1** reddish pigment orig. made from lac. **2** pigment obtained by combining an organic colouring matter with a metallic oxide, hydroxide, or salt. [var. of LAC]

Lake District *n.* (also **the Lakes**) region of lakes in Cumbria.

lakh /læk/ *n. Ind.* (usu. foll. by *of*) hundred thousand (rupees etc.). [Hindustani *lākh*]

lam *v.* (**-mm-**) *slang* thrash; hit. [perhaps Scandinavian]

lama /ˈlɑːmə/ *n.* Tibetan or Mongolian Buddhist monk. [Tibetan]

lamasery /ˈlɑːməsərɪ/ *n.* (*pl.* **-ies**) monastery of lamas. [French]

lamb /læm/ —*n.* **1** young sheep. **2** its flesh as food. **3** mild, gentle, or kind person. —*v.* give birth to lambs. □ **the Lamb (or Lamb of God)** name for Christ. [Old English]

lambada /læmˈbɑːdə/ *n.* fast erotic Brazilian dance with their stomachs touching each other. [Portuguese, = a beating]

lambast /læmˈbæst/ *v.* (also **-ing**) (also **lambaste** /læmˈbeɪst/) *colloq.* thrash, beat. [from LAM, BASTE]

lambda /ˈlæmdə/ *n.* eleventh letter of the Greek alphabet (Λ, λ). [Greek]

lambent /ˈlæmbənt/ *adj.* **1** of a flame or a light) playing on a surface. **2** (of the eyes, sky, wit, etc.) lightly brilliant. □ **lambency** *n.* [Latin *lambo lick*]

lambswool *n.* soft fine wool from a young sheep.

lame —*adj.* **1** disabled in the foot or leg. **2 a** (of an excuse etc.) unconvincing; feeble. **b** (of verse etc.) halting. —*v.* (**-ming**) make lame; disable. □ **lamely** *adv.* **lameness** *n.* [Old English]

lamé /ˈlɑːmeɪ/ *n.* fabric with gold or silver threads interwoven. [French]

lame duck *n.* helpless person or firm.

lament /ləˈment/ —*n.* **1** passionate expression of grief. **2** song etc. of mourning etc. —*v.* (also *absol.*) **1** express or feel grief for or about. **2** (as **lamented** *adj.*) used to refer to a recently dead person. □ **lament for (or over)** mourn or regret. [Latin *lamentor*]

lamentable /ˈlæməntəb(ə)l/ *adj.* deplorable, regrettable. □ **lamentably** *adv.*

lamentation /ˌlæmənˈteɪʃ(ə)n/ *n.* **1** lamenting. **2** lament.

lamina /ˈlæmɪnə/ *n.* (*pl.* **-nae** /-niː/) thin plate or scale. □ **laminar** *adj.* [Latin]

laminate —*v.* /ˈlæmɪneɪt/ (**-ting**) **1** beat or roll into thin plates. **2** overlay with metal plates, a plastic layer, etc. **3** split into layers. —*n.* /ˈlæmɪnət/ laminated

structure, esp. of layers fixed together. —*adj.* /ˈlæmɪnət/ in the form of thin plates. □ **lamination** /-ˈneɪʃ(ə)n/ *n.*

Lammas /ˈlæməs/ *n.* (in full **Lammas Day**) first day of August, formerly kept as harvest festival. [Old English: related to LOAF¹, MASS²]

lamp *n.* **1** device for producing a steady light, esp.: **a** an electric bulb, and usu. its holder. **b** an oil-lamp. **c** a gas-jet and mantle. **2** device producing esp. ultraviolet or infrared radiation. [Greek *lampas* torch]

lampblack *n.* pigment made from soot.

lamplight *n.* light from a lamp.

lamplighter *n. hist.* person who lit street-lamps.

lampoon /læmˈpuːn/ —*n.* satirical attack on a person etc. —*v.* satirize. □ **lampoonist** *n.* [French *lampon*]

lamppost *n.* tall post supporting a street-light.

lamprey /ˈlæmprɪ/ *n.* (*pl.* **-s**) eel-like aquatic animal with a sucker mouth. [Latin *lampreda*]

lampshade *n.* translucent cover for a lamp.

Lancastrian /læŋˈkæstrɪən/ —*n.* **1** native of Lancashire or Lancaster. **2** *hist.* member or supporter of the House of Lancaster in the Wars of the Roses. —*adj.* of or concerning Lancashire or Lancaster, or the House of Lancaster. [*Lancaster* in Lancashire]

lance /lɑːns/ —*n.* **1** long spear, esp. one used by a horseman. —*v.* (**-cing**) **1** prick or cut open with a lancet. **2** pierce with a lance. [French from Latin]

lance-corporal *n.* lowest rank of NCO in the Army.

lanceolate /ˈlɑːnsɪəleɪt/ *adj.* shaped like a lance-head, tapering at each end.

lancer *n.* **1** *hist.* soldier of a cavalry regiment armed with lances. **2** (in *pl.*) **a** quadrille. **b** music for this.

lancet /ˈlɑːnsɪt/ *n.* small broad two-edged surgical knife with a sharp point. □ **lancet arch** *n.* (also **lancet light** or **window**) narrow arch or window with a pointed head.

land —*n.* **1** solid part of the earth's surface. **2 a** expanse of country; ground, soil. **b** this in relation to its use, quality, etc., or as a basis for agriculture. **3** country, nation, State. **4 a** landed property. **b** (in *pl.*) estates. —*v.* **1 a** set or go ashore. **b** (often foll. by *at*) disembark. **2** bring (an aircraft) to the ground or another surface. **3** alight on the ground or find oneself in a certain situation or place. **4** bring (a fish) to land. **5** (also *refl.*; often foll. by *up*) *colloq.* bring to, reach, or find oneself in a certain situation or place. **6** *colloq.* **a** deal (a person etc. a blow etc.). **b** (foll. by *with*) present (a

person) with (a problem, job, etc.). **7** *colloq.* win or obtain (a prize, job, etc.). □ **how the land lies** what is the state of affairs. **land on one's feet** attain a good position, job, etc., by luck. □ **landless** *adj.* [Old English]

land-agent *n.* **1** steward of an estate. **2** agent for the sale of estates.

landau /ˈlændɔː/ *n.* four-wheeled enclosed carriage with a divided top. [*Landau* in Germany]

landed *adj.* **1** owning land. **2** consisting of land.

landfall *n.* approach to land, esp. after a sea or air journey.

landfill *n.* **1** waste material etc. used to landscape or reclaim land. **2** process of disposing of rubbish in this way.

land-girl *n.* woman doing farm work, esp. in wartime.

landing *n.* **1** platform at the top of or part way up a flight of stairs. **2** coming to land. **3** place where ships etc. land.

landing-craft *n.* craft designed for putting troops and equipment ashore.

landing-gear *n.* undercarriage of an aircraft.

landing-stage *n.* platform for disembarking goods and passengers.

landlady *n.* **1** woman who owns and lets land or premises. **2** woman who keeps a public house, boarding-house, etc.

land line *n.* means of telecommunication over land.

landlocked *adj.* almost or entirely enclosed by land.

landlord *n.* **1** man who owns and lets land or premises. **2** man who keeps a public house, boarding-house, etc.

landlubber *n.* person unfamiliar with the sea.

landmark *n.* **1** conspicuous object in a district, landscape, etc. **2** prominent and critical event etc.

land mass *n.* large area of land.

land-mine *n.* explosive mine laid in or on the ground.

landowner *n.* owner of (esp. much) land. □ **landowning** *adj.* & *n.*

landscape /ˈlændskeɪp/ —*n.* **1** scenery as seen in a broad view. **2** (often *attrib.*) picture representing this; this genre of painting. —*v.* (**-ping**) improve (a piece of land) by landscape gardening. [Dutch *landscap*]

landscape gardening *n.* laying out of grounds to resemble natural scenery.

landslide *n.* **1** sliding down of a mass of land from a mountain, cliff, etc. **2** overwhelming victory in an election.

landslip *n.* = LANDSLIDE 1.

lane *n.* **1** narrow road. **2** division of a road for a stream of traffic. **3** strip of track etc. for a competitor in a race. **4** path regularly followed by a ship, aircraft, etc. **5** gangway between crowds of people. [Old English]

language /ˈlæŋgwɪdʒ/ *n.* **1** use of words in an agreed way as a method of human communication. **2** system of words of a particular community or country etc. **3 a** faculty of speech. **b** style of expression; use of words, etc. (*poetic language*). **4** system of symbols and rules for writing computer programs. **5** any method of communication. **6** professional or specialized vocabulary. [Latin *lingua* tongue]

language laboratory *n.* room equipped with tape recorders etc. for learning a foreign language.

languid /ˈlæŋgwɪd/ *adj.* lacking vigour; idle; inert. □ **languidly** *adv.* [related to LANGUISH]

languish /ˈlæŋgwɪʃ/ *v.* lose or lack vitality. □ **languish** for droop or pine for. **languish under** suffer (depression, confinement, etc.) [Latin *langueo*]

languor /ˈlæŋgə(r)/ *n.* **1** lack of energy, idleness. **2** soft or tender mood or effect. **3** oppressive stillness. □ **languorous** *adj.*

lank *adj.* **1** (of hair, grass, etc.) long and limp. **2** thin and tall. [Old English]

lanky *adj.* (**-ier**, **-iest**) ungracefully thin and long or tall. □ **lankiness** *n.*

lanolin /ˈlænəlɪn/ *n.* fat found on sheep's wool and used in cosmetics etc. [Latin *lana* wool, *oleum* OIL]

lantern /ˈlænt(ə)n/ *n.* **1** lamp with a transparent case protecting a flame etc. **2** raised structure on a dome, room, etc., glazed to admit light. **3** light-chamber of a lighthouse. [Greek *lamptēr* torch]

lantern jaws *n.pl.* long thin jaws and chin.

lanthanide /ˈlænθənaɪd/ *n.* any element of the lanthanide series. [German: related to LANTHANUM]

lanthanide series *n. Chem.* series of 15 metallic elements from lanthanum to lutetium in the periodic table, having similar chemical properties.

lanthanum /ˈlænθənəm/ *n.* metallic element, first of the lanthanide series. [Greek *lanthanō* escape notice]

lanyard /ˈlænjəd/ *n.* **1** cord worn round the neck or the shoulder, to which a knife etc. may be attached. **2** *Naut.* short rope or line used for securing, tightening, etc. [French *laniere*, assimilated to YARD]

Laodicean /ˌleɪəʊdɪˈsiːən/ *adj.* half-hearted, esp. in religion or politics. [*Laodicea* in Asia Minor (Rev. 3:16)]

lap¹ n. **1** front of the body from the waist to the knees of a sitting person. **2** clothing covering this. □ **in the lap of the gods** beyond human control. **in the lap of luxury** in extreme.y luxurious surroundings. [Old English]

lap² n. **1 a** one circuit of a racetrack etc. **b** section of a journey etc. **2 a** amount of overlapping. **b** overlapping part. **3** single turn of thread etc. round a reel etc. —v. (**-pp-**) **1** lead or overtake (a competitor in a race) by one or more laps. **2** (often foll. by *about, round*) fold or wrap (a garment etc.) round. **3** (usu. foll. by *in*) enfold in wraps etc. **4** (as **lapped** *adj.*) (usu. foll. by *in*) enfold caressingly. **5** cause to overlap. [probably from LAP¹]

lap³ —v. (**-pp-**) **1 a** (esp. of an animal) drink with the tongue. **b** (usu. foll. by *up, down*) consume (liquid) greedily. **c** (usu. foll. by *up*) consume (gossip, praise, etc.) greedily. **2** (of waves etc.) ripple; make a lapping sound against (the shore). —n. **1 a** act of lapping. **b** amount of liquid taken up. **2** sound of wavelets. [Old English]

lap-dog n. small pet dog.

lapel /lə'pel/ n. part of either side of a coat-front etc., folded back against itself. [from LAP¹]

lapidary /'læpɪdərɪ/ —adj. **1** concerned with stone or stones. **2** engraved upon stone. **3** concise, well-expressed, epigrammatic. —n. (pl. **-ies**) cutter, polisher, or engraver, of gems. [Latin *lapis lapid-* stone]

lapis lazuli /ˌlæpɪs 'læzjʊlɪ/ n. **1** blue mineral used as a gemstone. **2** bright blue pigment. **3** its colour. [related to LAPIDARY, AZURE]

Laplander /'læplændə(r)/ n. native or inhabitant of Lapland: Lapp. (as LAPP)

lap of honour n. ceremonial circuit of a racetrack etc. by a winner.

Lapp n. **1** member of a Mongol people of N. Scandinavia and NW Russia. **2** their language. [Swedish]

lappet /'læpɪt/ n. **1** small flap or fold of a garment etc. **2** hanging piece of flesh. [from LAP¹]

lapse —n. **1** slight error; slip of memory etc. **2** weak or careless decline into an inferior state. **3** (foll. by *of*) passage of time. —v. (**-sing**) **1** fail to maintain a position or standard. **2** (foll. by *into*) fall back into an inferior or previous state. **3** (of a right or privilege etc.) become invalid through disuse, failure to renew, etc. **4** (as **lapsed** *adj.*) that has lapsed. [Latin *lapsus* from *labor laps-* slip]

laptop n. (often *attrib.*) portable microcomputer suitable for use while travelling.

lapwing /'læpwɪŋ/ n. plover with a shrill cry. [Old English: related to LEAP, WINK: from its mode of flight]

larboard /'lɑːbəd/ n. & adj. archaic = PORT³. [originally *ladboard*, perhaps 'side on which cargo was taken in': related to LADE]

larceny /'lɑːsənɪ/ n. (pl. **-ies**) theft of personal property. □ **larcenous** adj. [Anglo-French from Latin *latrocinium*]

■ **Usage** In 1968 *larceny* was replaced as a statutory crime in English law by *theft*.

larch n. **1** deciduous coniferous tree with bright foliage. **2** its wood. [Latin *larix -icis*]

lard —n. pig-fat used in cooking etc. —v. **1** insert strips of fat or bacon in (meat etc.) before cooking. **2** (foll. by *with*) garnish (talk etc.) with strange terms. [French]

larder n. room or large cupboard for storing food.

lardy adj. like lard.

lardy-cake n. cake made with lard, currants, etc.

large adj. **1** of relatively great size or extent. **2** of the larger kind (*large intestine*). **3** comprehensive. **4** pursuing an activity on a large scale (*large farmer*). □ **at large 1** at liberty. **2** as a body or whole. **3** at full length, with all details. □ **largeness** n. **largish** adj. [Latin *largus* copious]

large as life adj. *colloq.* in person, esp prominently.

largely adv. to a great extent (*largely my own fault*).

large-scale adj. made or occurring on a large scale.

largesse /lɑː'ʒes/ n. (also **largess**) money or gifts freely given. [Latin *largus*]

largo /'lɑːgəʊ/ *Mus.* —adv. & adj. in a slow tempo and dignified style. —n. (pl. **-s**) largo passage or movement. [Italian, = broad]

lariat /'lærɪət/ n. **1** lasso. **2** tethering rope. [Spanish *la reata*]

lark¹ n. small bird with a tuneful song. esp the skylark. [Old English]

lark² *colloq.* —n. **1** frolic; amusing incident. **2** type of activity (*fed up with this digging lark*). —v. (foll. by *about*) play tricks. [origin uncertain]

larkspur n. plant with a spur-shaped calyx.

larva /'lɑːvə/ n. (pl. **-rae** /-riː/) stage of an insect's development between egg and pupa. □ **larval** adj. [Latin, = ghost]

laryngeal /ləˈrɪndʒɪəl/ *adj.* of the larynx.

laryngitis /ˌlærɪnˈdʒaɪtɪs/ *n.* inflammation of the larynx.

larynx /ˈlærɪŋks/ *n.* (*pl.* **larynges** /ləˈrɪndʒiːz/ or **-xes**) hollow organ in the throat holding the vocal cords. [Latin from Greek]

lasagne /ləˈsænjə/ *n.* pasta in the form of sheets. [Italian pl., from Latin *lasanum* cooking-pot]

lascivious /ləˈsɪvɪəs/ *adj.* 1 lustful 2 inciting to lust. □ **lasciviously** *adv.* [Latin]

laser /ˈleɪzə(r)/ *n.* device that generates an intense beam of coherent light, or other electromagnetic radiation, in one direction. [*light amplification by stimulated emission of radiation*]

lash —*v.* 1 make a sudden whiplike movement. 2 beat with a whip etc. 3 (often foll. by *against*, *down*, etc.) (of rain etc.) beat, strike. 4 criticize harshly. 5 rouse, incite. 6 (foll. by *down*, *together*, etc.) fasten with a cord etc. —*n.* 1 sharp blow made by a whip etc. 2 flexible end of a whip. 3 eyelash. □ **lash out** 1 speak or hit out angrily. 2 *colloq.* spend money extravagantly. [imitative]

lashings *n.pl. colloq.* (foll. by *of*) plenty.

lass *n.* esp. *Scot.* & *N.Engl.* or *poet.* girl. [Old Norse]

Lassa fever /ˈlæsə/ *n.* acute febrile viral disease of tropical Africa. [*Lassa* in Nigeria]

lassitude /ˈlæsɪtjuːd/ *n.* 1 languour. 2 disinclination to exert oneself. [Latin *lassus* tired]

lasso /læˈsuː/ —*n.* (*pl.* **-s** or **-es**) rope with a noose at one end, esp. for catching cattle. —*v.* (**-es**, **-ed**) catch with a lasso. [Spanish *lazo*: related to LACE]

last¹ /lɑːst/ —*adj.* 1 after all others; coming at or belonging to the end. 2 most recent; next before a specified time (*last Christmas*). 3 only remaining (*last chance*). 4 (prec. by *the*) least likely or suitable (*the last person I'd want*). 5 lowest in rank (*last place*). —*adv.* 1 after all others (esp. in *comb.*: *last-mentioned*). 2 on the most recent occasion (*when did you last see him?*). 3 lastly. —*n.* 1 person or thing that is last, last-mentioned, most recent, etc. 2 (prec. by *the*) last mention or sight etc. (*shall never hear the last of it*). 3 last performance of certain acts (*breathed his last*). 4 (prec. by *the*) the end; death (*fighting to the last*). □ **at last** (or **long last**) in the end; after much delay. [Old English]

last² /lɑːst/ *v.* 1 remain unexhausted or alive for a specified or considerable time (*food to last a week*). 2 continue for a specified time (*match lasts an hour*). □ **last out** be strong enough or sufficient for the whole of a given period. [Old English]

last³ /lɑːst/ *n.* shoemaker's model for shaping a shoe etc. □ **stick to one's last** not meddle in what one does not understand. [Old English]

last-ditch *attrib. adj.* (of an attempt etc.) final, desperate.

lasting *adj.* permanent; durable.

lastly *adv.* finally; in the last place.

last minute *n.* (also **last moment**) the time just before an important event (often with hyphen) *attrib.*: *last-minute panic*).

last post *n.* bugle-call at military funerals or as a signal to retire for the night.

last rites *n.pl.* rites for a person about to die.

last straw *n.* (prec. by *the*) slight addition to a burden that makes it finally unbearable.

last trump *n.* (prec. by *the*) trumpet-blast to wake the dead on Judgement Day.

last word *n.* (prec. by *the*) 1 final or definitive statement. 2 (often foll. by *in*) latest fashion.

lat. *abbr.* latitude.

latch —*n.* 1 bar with a catch and lever as a fastening for a gate etc. 2 spring-lock preventing a door from being opened from the outside without a key. —*v.* fasten with a latch. □ **latch on** (often foll. by *to*) *colloq.* 1 attach oneself (to). 2 understand. □ **on the latch** fastened by the latch (sense 1) only. [Old English]

latchkey *n.* (*pl.* **-s**) key of an outer door.

late —*adj.* 1 after the due or usual time; occurring or done after the proper time. 2 far on in the day or night or in a specified period. b far on in development. 3 flowering or ripening towards the end of the season. 4 no longer alive; no longer having the specified status, former (*my late husband*; *the late prime minister*). 5 of recent date. —*adv.* 1 after the due or usual time. 2 far on in time. 3 at or till a late hour. 4 at a late stage of development. 5 formerly but not now (*late of the Scillies*). □ **late in the day** *colloq.* at a late stage in the proceedings. □ **lateness** *n.* [Old English]

latecomer *n.* person who arrives late.

lateen /ləˈtiːn/ *adj.* (of a ship) rigged with a lateen sail. [French *voile latine* Latin sail]

lateen sail *n.* triangular sail on a long yard at an angle of 45° to the mast.

lately *adv.* not long ago; recently. [Old English: related to LATE]

latent /ˈleɪt(ə)nt/ adj. existing but not developed or manifest; concealed, dormant. □ **latency** n. [Latin *lateo* be hidden]

latent heat n. Physics heat required to convert a solid into a liquid or vapour, or a liquid into a vapour, without change of temperature.

lateral /ˈlæt(ə)r(ə)l/ —adj. 1 of, at, towards, or from the side or sides. 2 descended from the sibling of a person in direct line. —n. lateral shoot or branch. □ **laterally** adv. [Latin *latus later-* side]

lateral thinking n. method of solving problems other than by using conventional logic.

latex /ˈleɪteks/ n. (pl. -**xes**) 1 milky fluid of esp. the rubber tree. 2 synthetic product resembling this. [Latin, = liquid]

lath /lɑːθ/ n. (pl. **laths** /lɑːðs, lɑːθs/) thin flat strip of wood. [Old English]

lathe /leɪð/ n. machine for shaping wood, metal, etc., by turning the article against cutting tools. [origin uncertain]

lather /ˈlɑːðə(r)/ —n. 1 froth produced by agitating soap etc. and water. 2 frothy sweat 3 state of agitation. —v. 1 (of soap etc.) form a lather. 2 cover with lather. 3 colloq. thrash. [Old English]

Latin /ˈlætɪn/ —n. language of ancient Rome and its empire. —adj. 1 of or in Latin. 2 of the countries or peoples using languages descended from Latin. 3 of the Roman Catholic Church. [Latin *Latium* district around Rome]

Latin America n. parts of Central and S. America where Spanish or Portuguese is the main language.

Latinate /ˈlætɪneɪt/ adj. having the character of Latin.

Latinize /ˈlætɪnaɪz/ v. (also -**ise**) (-**zing** or -**sing**) give a Latin form to. □ **Latinization** /-ˈzeɪʃ(ə)n/ n.

latish adj. & adv. fairly late.

latitude /ˈlætɪtjuːd/ n. 1 a angular distance on a meridian north or south of the equator. b (usu. in pl.) regions or climes. 2 tolerated variety of action or opinion. □ **latitudinal** /-ˈtjuːdɪn(ə)l/ adj. [Latin *latus* broad]

latitudinarian /ˌlætɪˌtjuːdɪˈneərɪən/ —adj. liberal, esp. in religion. —n. latitudinarian person.

latrine /ləˈtriːn/ n. communal lavatory, esp. in a camp. [Latin *latrina*]

latter adj. 1 a second-mentioned of two, or last-mentioned of three or more. b last-mentioned person or thing. 2 (prec. by *the* usu. *absol.*) the second- or last-mentioned. 3 nearer the end (*latter part of the year*). 4 of the end of a period, the recent, etc. [Old English, = later]

499

■ **Usage** The use of *latter* to mean 'last mentioned of three or more' is considered incorrect by some people.

latter-day attrib. adj. modern, contemporary.

Latter-day Saints n.pl. Mormons' name for themselves.

latterly adv. 1 recently. 2 in the latter part of life or a period.

lattice /ˈlætɪs/ n. 1 structure of crossed laths or bars with spaces between, used as a screen, fence, etc. 2 regular periodic arrangement of atoms, ions, or molecules. □ **latticed** adj. [French *lattis* from *latte* LATH]

lattice window n. window with small panes set in diagonally crossing strips of lead.

Latvian /ˈlætvɪən/ —n. 1 a native or national of Latvia in eastern Europe. b person of Latvian descent 2 language of Latvia. —adj. of Latvia, its people, or language.

laud /lɔːd/ —v. praise or extol. —n. 1 praise; hymn of praise. 2 (in pl.) the first morning prayer of the Roman Catholic Church. [Latin *laus laud-*]

laudable adj. commendable. □ **laudability** /-ˈbɪlɪ/ n. **laudably** adv.

■ **Usage** *Laudable* is sometimes confused with *laudatory*.

laudanum /ˈlɔːdnəm/ n. solution prepared from opium. [perhaps from medieval Latin]

laudatory /ˈlɔːdətərɪ/ adj. praising.

■ **Usage** See note at LAUDABLE.

laugh /lɑːf/ —v. 1 make the sounds and movements usual in expressing lively amusement, scorn, etc. 2 express by laughing. 3 (foll. by *at*) ridicule, make fun of. —n. 1 sound, act, or manner of laughing. 2 colloq. comical thing. □ **laugh off** get rid of (embarrassment or humiliation) by joking **laugh up one's sleeve** laugh secretly. [Old English]

laughable adj. ludicrous; amusing. □ **laughably** adv.

laughing n. laughter. □ **no laughing matter** serious matter. □ **laughingly** adv.

laughing-gas n. nitrous oxide as an anaesthetic.

laughing jackass n. = KOOKABURRA.

laughing stock n. person or thing open to general ridicule.

laughter /ˈlɑːftə(r)/ n. act or sound of laughing. [Old English]

launch¹ /lɔːntʃ/ —v. 1 set (a vessel) afloat. 2 hurl or send forth (a weapon, rocket, etc.). 3 start or set in motion (an

enterprise, person, etc.). **4** formally introduce (a new product) with publicity etc. **5** (foll. by *out*, *into*, etc.) **a** make a start on (an enterprise etc.). **b** burst into (strong language etc.). —*n.* act of launching. [Anglo-Norman *launcher*: related to LANCE]

launch² /lɔːntʃ/ *n.* **1** large motor boat. **2** man-of-war's largest boat. [Spanish *lancha*]

launcher *n.* structure to hold a rocket during launching.

launch pad *n.* (also **launching pad**) platform with a supporting structure, for launching rockets from.

launder /ˈlɔːndə(r)/ *v.* **1** wash and iron (clothes etc.). **2** *colloq.* transfer (funds) to conceal their origin. [French: related to LAVE]

launderette /lɔːnˈdret/ *n.* (also **laundrette**) establishment with coin-operated washing-machines and driers for public use.

laundress /ˈlɔːndrɪs/ *n.* woman who launders, esp. professionally.

laundry /ˈlɔːndrɪ/ *n.* (*pl.* -**ies**) **1 a** place for washing clothes etc. **b** firm washing clothes etc. commercially. **2** clothes or linen for laundering or newly laundered.

laureate /ˈlɒrɪət, ˈlɔː-/ —*adj.* wreathed with laurel as a mark of honour. —*n.* = POET LAUREATE. □ **laureateship** *n.* [related to LAUREL]

laurel /ˈlɒr(ə)l/ *n.* **1** = BAY². **2** (in *sing.* or *pl.*) wreath of bay-leaves as an emblem of victory or poetic merit. **3** any of various plants with dark-green glossy leaves. □ **look to one's laurels** beware of losing one's pre-eminence. **rest on one's laurels** see REST. [Latin *laurus* bay]

lav *n.* *colloq.* lavatory. [abbreviation]

lava /ˈlɑːvə/ *n.* matter flowing from a volcano and solidifying as it cools. [Latin *lavo* wash]

lavatorial /ˌlævəˈtɔːrɪəl/ *adj.* of or like lavatories; (esp. of humour) relating to excretion.

lavatory /ˈlævətərɪ/ *n.* (*pl.* -**ies**) receptacle for urine and faeces, usu. with a means of disposal. **2** room or compartment containing this. [Latin: related to LAVA]

lavatory paper *n.* = TOILET PAPER.

lave *v.* (-**ving**) *literary* **1** wash, bathe. **2** (of water) wash against; flow along. [Latin *lavo* wash]

lavender /ˈlævɪndə(r)/ *n.* **1 a** evergreen shrub with purple aromatic flowers. **b** its flowers and stalks dried and used to scent linen etc. **2** pale mauve colour. [Latin *lavandula*]

lavender-water *n.* light perfume made with distilled lavender.

laver /ˈleɪvə(r), ˈlɑː-/ *n.* edible seaweed. [Latin]

lavish /ˈlævɪʃ/ —*adj.* **1** giving or producing in large quantities; profuse. **2** generous. —*v.* (often foll. by *on*) bestow or spend (money, effort, praise, etc.) abundantly. □ **lavishly** *adv.* [French *lavasse* deluge: related to LAVE]

law *n.* **1 a** rule enacted or customary in a community and recognized as commanding or forbidding certain actions. **b** body of such rules. **2** controlling influence of laws; respect for laws. **3** laws collectively as a social system or subject of study. **4** binding force (*her word is law*). **5** (prec. by *the*) **a** the legal profession. **b** *colloq.* the police. **6** (in *pl.*) jurisprudence. **7 a** the judicial remedy. **b** the lawcourts as providing this (*go to law*). **8** rule of action or procedure. **9** regularity in natural occurrences (*laws of nature*; *law of gravity*). **10** divine commandments. □ **be a law unto oneself** do what one considers right; disregard custom. **lay down the law** be dogmatic or authoritarian. **take the law into one's own hands** redress a grievance by one's own means, esp. by force. [Old English from Old Norse, = thing laid down]

law-abiding *adj.* obedient to the laws.

lawbreaker *n.* person who breaks the law. □ **lawbreaking** *n.* & *adj.*

lawcourt *n.* court of law.

lawful *adj.* conforming with or recognized by law; not illegal. □ **lawfully** *adv.* **lawfulness** *n.*

lawgiver *n.* person who formulates laws; legislator.

lawless *adj.* **1** having no laws or law enforcement. **2** disregarding laws. □ **lawlessness** *n.*

Law Lord *n.* member of the House of Lords qualified to perform its legal work.

lawmaker *n.* legislator.

lawn¹ *n.* piece of closely-mown grass in a garden etc. [French *launde* glade]

lawn² *n.* fine linen or cotton. [probably from *Laon* in France]

lawnmower *n.* machine for cutting lawns.

lawn tennis *n.* tennis played with a soft ball on outdoor grass or a hard court.

lawrencium /ləˈrensɪəm/ *n.* artificially made transuranic metallic element. [*Lawrence*, name of a physicist]

lawsuit *n.* bringing of a dispute, claim, etc. before a lawcourt.

lawyer /ˈlɔːjə(r)/ *n.* legal practitioner, esp. a solicitor.

ax adj. 1 lacking care or precision. 2 not strict. □ laxity n. laxly adv. laxness n. [Latin laxus loose]

laxative /ˈlæksətɪv/ —adj. facilitating evacuation of the bowels. —n. laxative medicine. [Latin: related to LAX]

lay¹ —v. (past and past part. laid) 1 place on a surface, esp. horizontally or in the proper or specified place. 2 put or bring into the required position or state (lay carpet). 3 make by laying (lay foundations). 4 (often absol.) (of a hen bird) produce (an egg). 5 cause to subside or lie flat. 6 (usu. foll. by on) attribute or impute (blame etc.). 7 prepare or make ready (a plan or trap). 8 prepare (a table) for a meal. 9 arrange the material for (a fire). 10 put down as a wager; stake. 11 (foll. by with) coat or strew (a surface). 12 slang offens. have sexual intercourse with (esp. a woman). —n. 1 way, position, or direction in which something lies. 2 slang offens. partner (esp. female) in, or act of, sexual intercourse. □ lay about one hit out on all sides. lay aside 1 put to one side. 2 cease to consider. lay at the door of impute to. lay bare expose, reveal. lay claim to claim as one's own. lay down 1 put on a flat surface. 2 give up (an office). 3 formulate (a rule). 4 store (wine) for maturing. 5 sacrifice (one's life). lay (one's) hands on obtain, locate. lay hands on seize or attack. lay hold of seize. lay in provide oneself with a stock of. lay into colloq. punish or scold harshly. lay it on thick (or with a trowel) colloq. flatter or exaggerate grossly. lay low overthrow or humble. lay off 1 discharge (unneeded workers) temporarily; make redundant. 2 colloq. desist. lay on 1 provide. 2 impose. 3 inflict (blows). 4 spread on (paint etc.). lay open 1 break the skin of. 2 (foll. by to) expose (to criticism etc.). lay out 1 spread out, expose to view. 2 prepare (a corpse) for burial. 3 colloq. knock unconscious. 4 arrange (grounds etc.) according to a design. 5 expend (money). lay to rest bury in a grave. lay up store, save. lay waste ravage, destroy. [Old English]

■ Usage The intransitive use of lay, meaning lie, as in she was laying on the floor, is incorrect in standard English.

lay² adj. 1 a non-clerical. b not ordained into the clergy. 2 a not professionally qualified. b of or done by such persons. [Greek laos people]

lay³ n. 1 short poem meant to be sung. 2 song. [French]

lay⁴ past of LIE¹.

layabout n. habitual loafer or idler.

lay-by n. (pl. -bys) area at the side of a road where vehicles may stop.

layer —n. 1 thickness of matter, esp. one of several, covering a surface. 2 person or thing that lays. 3 hen that lays eggs. 4 shoot fastened down to take root while attached to the parent plant. —v. 1 arrange (a plant) by a layer. 3 propagate (a plant) by a layer. [Dutch]

layette /leɪˈet/ n. set of clothing etc. for a newborn child. [French from Dutch]

lay figure n. 1 jointed figure of a human body used by artists for arranging drapery on etc. 2 unrealistic character in a novel etc. [Dutch lad joint]

layman n. (fem. laywoman) 1 non-ordained member of a Church. 2 person without professional or specialized knowledge.

lay-off n. temporary discharge of workers; a redundancy.

layout n. 1 way in which land, a building, printed matter, etc., is arranged or set out. 2 something arranged in a particular way; display.

lay reader n. lay person licensed to conduct some religious services.

laze —v. (-zing) 1 spend time idly. 2 (foll. by away) pass (time) idly. —n. spell of lazing. [back-formation from LAZY]

LBC abbr. London Broadcasting Company.

lazy adj. (-ier, -iest) 1 disinclined to work, doing little work. 2 of or inducing idleness. □ lazily adv. laziness n. [perhaps from Low German]

lazybones n. (pl. same) colloq. lazy person.

L/Cpl abbr. Lance-Corporal.

l.b.w. abbr. leg before wicket.

l.c. abbr. 1 = LOC. CIT. 2 lower case.

LCD abbr. 1 liquid crystal display. 2 lowest (or least) common denominator.

LCM abbr. lowest (or least) common multiple.

Ld. abbr. Lord.

LEA abbr. Local Education Authority.

lea n. poet. meadow, field. [Old English]

leach v. 1 make (a liquid) percolate through some material. 2 subject (bark, ore, ash, or soil) to the action of percolating fluid. 3 (foll. by away, out) remove (soluble matter) or be removed in this way. [Old English]

lead¹ /liːd/ —v. (past and past part. led) 1 cause to go with one, esp. by guiding or going in front. 2 a direct the actions or opinions of. b (often foll. by to, or to + infin.) guide by persuasion or example (what led you to think that). 3 (also absol.) provide access to; bring to a certain position (gate leads you into a field; road leads to Lincoln). 4 pass or go

leading question *n.* question prompting the answer wanted.

■ **Usage** *Leading question* does not mean a 'principal' or 'loaded' or 'searching' question.

lead pencil *n.* pencil of graphite in wood.

lead-poisoning *n.* poisoning by absorption of lead into the body.

leaf —*n.* (*pl.* **leaves**) **1** each of several flattened usu. green structures of a plant, growing usu. on the side of a stem. **2 a** foliage regarded collectively. **b** state of bearing leaves (*tree in leaf*). **3** single thickness of paper. **4** very thin sheet of metal etc. **5** hinged part, extra section, or flap of a table etc. —*v.* **1** put forth leaves. **2** (foll. by *through*) turn over the pages of (a book etc.). □ **leafage** *n.* **leafy** *adj.* (**-ier**, **-iest**). [Old English]

leaflet /ˈliːflɪt/ —*n.* **1** sheet of paper, pamphlet, etc. giving information. **2** young leaf. **3** *Bot.* division of a compound leaf. —*v.* (**-t-**) distribute leaflets (to).

leaf-mould *n.* soil or compost consisting chiefly of decayed leaves.

leaf-stalk *n.* stalk joining a leaf to a stem.

league¹ /liːg/ —*n.* **1** people, countries, groups, etc., combining for a particular purpose. **2** agreement to combine in this way. **3** group of sports clubs which compete for a championship. **4** class of contestants etc. —*v.* (**-gues**, **-gued**, **-guing**) (often foll. by *together*) join in a league. □ **in league** allied, conspiring. [Latin *ligo* bind]

league² /liːg/ *n. hist.* varying measure of distance, usu. about three miles. [Latin from Celtic]

league table *n.* list in ranked order of success etc.

leak —*n.* **1 a** hole through which matter passes accidentally in or out. **b** matter passing through thus. **c** act of passing through thus. **2 a** similar escape of electrical charge. **b** charge that escapes. **3** disclosure of secret information. —*v.* **1 a** pass through a leak. **b** lose or admit through a leak. **2** disclose (secret information). **3** (often foll. by *out*) become known. □ **have** (or **take**) **a leak** *slang* urinate. □ **leaky** *adj.* (**-ier**, **-iest**). [Low German or Dutch]

leakage *n.* action or result of leaking.

lean¹ —*v.* (*past* and *past part.* **leaned** or **leant** /lent/) **1** (often foll. by *across, back, over,* etc.) be or place in a sloping position; incline from the perpendicular. **2** (foll. by *against, on, upon*) (cause to) rest for support against etc. **3** (foll. by *to, towards*)

through (a life etc. of a specified kind). **5 a** have the first place in. **b** (*absol.*) go first; be ahead in a race etc. **c** (*absol.*) be pre-eminent in some field. **6** be in charge of (*leads a team*). **7** (also *absol.*) play (a card) or a card of (a particular suit) as first player in a round. **8** (foll. by *to*) result in. **9** (foll. by *with*) (of a newspaper or news broadcast) have as its main story (*led with the royal wedding*). **10** (foll. by *through*) make (a liquid, strip of material, etc.) pass through a certain course. —*n.* **1** guidance given by going in front; example. **2 a** leading place (*take the lead*). **b** amount by which a competitor is ahead of the others. **3** clue. **4** strap etc. for leading a dog etc. **5** conductor (usu. a wire) conveying electric current to an appliance. **6 a** chief part in a play etc. **b** person playing this. **c** (*attrib.*) chief performer or instrument of a specified type (*lead guitar*). **7** *Cards* **a** act or right of playing first. **b** card led. □ **lead by the nose** cajole into compliance. **lead off** begin. **lead on** entice dishonestly. **lead up the garden path** *colloq.* mislead. **lead up to** form a preparation for; direct conversation towards. [Old English]

lead² /lɛd/ —*n.* **1** heavy bluish-grey soft metallic element. **2 a** graphite. **b** thin length of this in a pencil. **3** lump of lead used in sounding water. **4** (*in pl.*) **a** strips of lead covering a roof. **b** piece of lead covered roof. **5** (*in pl.*) lead frames holding the glass of a lattice etc. **6** blank space between lines of print. —*v.* **1** cover, weight, or frame with lead. **2** space (printed matter) with leads. [Old English]

leaden /ˈlɛd(ə)n/ *adj.* **1** of or like lead. **2** heavy or slow. **3** lead-coloured.

leader *n.* **1 a** person or thing that leads. **b** person followed by others. **2** principal player in a music group or of the first violins in an orchestra. **3** = LEADING ARTICLE. **4** shoot of a plant at the apex of a stem or of the main branch. □ **leader-ship** *n.*

lead-free *adj.* (of petrol) without added lead compounds.

lead-in *n.* introduction, opening, etc.

leading¹ *adj.* chief; most important.

leading² /ˈlɛdɪŋ/ *n. Printing* = LEAD² *n.* 6.

leading aircraftman *n.* rank above aircraftman in the RAF.

leading article *n.* newspaper article giving editorial opinion.

leading light *n.* prominent and influential person.

leading note *n. Mus.* seventh note of a diatonic scale.

be inclined or partial to. —n. deviation from the perpendicular; inclination. □ **lean on** *sl.* put pressure on (a person) to act in a certain way. **lean over backwards** see BACKWARDS. [Old English]

lean² —*adj.* **1** (of a person or animal) thin; having no superfluous fat. **2** (of meat) containing little fat. **3** meagre. —*n.* lean part of meat. [Old English]

leaning *n.* tendency or partiality.

lean-to *n.* (*pl.* -**tos**) building with its roof leaning against a larger building or a wall.

leap —*v.* (*past* and *past part.* **leaped** or **leapt** /lept/) jump or spring forcefully. —*n.* forceful jump. □ **by leaps and bounds** with startlingly rapid progress. **leap in the dark** daring step or enterprise. [Old English]

leap-frog —*n.* game in which players vault with parted legs over others bending down. —*v.* (**-gg-**) **1** perform such a vault (over). **2** overtake alternately.

leap year *n.* year with 366 days (including 29th Feb. as an intercalary day).

learn /lɜːn/ *v.* (*past* and *past part.* **learned** /lɜːnt, lɜːnd/ or **learnt**) **1** gain knowledge of or skill in. **2** commit to memory. **3** (foll. by *of*) be told about. **4** (foll. by *that, how,* etc.) become aware of. **5** *archaic* or *dial.* teach. [Old English]

learned /ˈlɜːnɪd/ *adj.* **1** having much knowledge acquired by study. **2** showing or requiring learning (a *learned work*). **3** (of a publication) academic. □ **learnedly** *adv.*

learner *n.* **1** person who is learning a subject or skill. **2** (in full **learner driver**) person who is learning to drive and has not yet passed a driving test.

learning *n.* knowledge acquired by study.

lease —*n.* contract by which the owner of property allows another to use it for a specified time, usu. in return for payment. —*v.* (**-sing**) grant or take on lease. □ **new lease of** (*US* **on**) **life** improved prospect of living, or of use after repair. [Anglo-French *lesser* let, from Latin *laxo* loosen]

leasehold *n.* **1** holding of property by lease. **2** property held by lease. □ **leaseholder** *n.*

leash —*n.* strap for holding a dog etc.; lead. —*v.* **1** put a leash on. **2** restrain. □ **straining at the leash** eager to begin. [French *lesse* related to LEASE]

least —*adj.* **1** smallest; slightest. **2** (of a species etc.) very small. —*n.* the least amount. —*adv.* in the least degree. □ **at least 1** at any rate. **2** (also **at the least**)

not less than. **in the least** (or the least) (usu. with *neg.*) at all (*not in the least offended*). **to say the least** putting the case moderately. [Old English, superlative of LESS]

least common denominator *n.* = LOWEST COMMON DENOMINATOR.

least common multiple *n.* = LOWEST COMMON MULTIPLE.

leather /ˈleðə(r)/ —*n.* **1** material made from the skin of an animal by tanning etc. **2** piece of leather for polishing with. **3** leather part(s) of a thing. **4** *slang* cricket-ball or football. **5** (in *pl.*) leather clothes. —*v.* **1** beat. **2** cover with leather. **3** polish or wipe with a leather. [Old English]

leather-jacket *n.* crane-fly grub with a tough skin.

leatherback *n.* large marine turtle with a leathery shell.

leather-bound *adj.* bound in leather.

leatherette /ˌleðəˈret/ *n.* imitation leather.

leathery *adj.* **1** like leather. **2** tough.

leave¹ *v.* (**-ving**; *past* and *past part.* **left**) **1 a** go away from. **b** (often foll. by *for*) depart. **2** cause to or let remain; depart without taking. **3** (also *absol.*) cease to reside at or belong to or work for. **4** abandon; cease to live with (one's family etc.). **5** have remaining after one's death. **6** bequeath. **7** (foll. by *to* + *infin.*) allow (a person or thing) to do something independently. **8** (foll. by *to*) commit to another person etc. (*leave that to me*). **9 a** abstain from consuming or dealing with. **b** (in *passive*; often foll. by *over*) remain over. **10 a** deposit or entrust (a thing) to be attended to in one's absence (*left a message with his secretary*). **b** depute (a person) to perform a function in one's absence. **11** allow to remain or cause to be in a specified state or position (*left the door open; left me exhausted*). □ **leave alone** not interfere with, not disturb. **leave a person cold** not impress or excite a person. **leave off 1** come to or make an end. **2** discontinue. **leave out** omit; exclude. [Old English]

leave² *n.* **1** (often foll. by *to* + *infin.*) permission. **2 a** (in full **leave of absence**) permission to be absent from duty. **b** period for which this lasts. □ **on leave** legitimately absent from duty. **take one's leave** (of) bid farewell (to). **take leave of one's senses** go mad. [Old English]

leaved *adj.* having a leaf or leaves, esp. (in *comb.*) of a specified kind or number (*four-leaved clover*).

leaven /'lev(ə)n/ —n. 1 substance causing dough to ferment and rise. 2 pervasive transforming influence; admixture. —v. 1 ferment (dough) with leaven. 2 permeate and transform; modify with a tempering element. [Latin *levo* lift]

leaves pl. of LEAF.

leave-taking n. act of taking one's leave.

leavings n.pl. things left over.

Lebanese /lebə'niːz/ —adj. of Lebanon. —n. (pl. same) 1 native or national of Lebanon. 2 person of Lebanese descent.

lech colloq. —v. (often foll. by after) lust. —n. 1 lecherous man. 2 lust. [back-formation from LECHER]

lecher n. lecherous man. [French *lechier* live in debauchery]

lecherous adj. lustful, having excessive sexual desire. □ **lecherously** adv.

lechery n. excessive sexual desire.

lectern /'lektə(r)n/ n. 1 stand for holding a book in a church etc. 2 similar stand for a lecturer etc. [Latin *lectrum* from *lego* read]

lecture /'lektʃə(r)/ —n. 1 talk giving specified information to a class etc. 2 long serious speech, esp. as a reprimand. —v. (-ring) 1 (often foll. by on) deliver lecture(s). 2 talk seriously or reprovingly to. □ **lectureship** n. [Latin: related to LECTERN]

lecturer n. person who lectures, esp. as a teacher in higher education.

LED abbr. light-emitting diode.

led past and past part. of LEAD¹.

lederhosen /'leidəhəʊz(ə)n/ n.pl. leather shorts as worn by some men in Bavaria etc. [German, = leather trousers]

ledge n. narrow horizontal or shelflike projection. [origin uncertain]

ledger n. main record of the accounts of a business. [Dutch]

lee n. 1 shelter given by a close object (*under the lee of*). 2 (in full **lee side**) side away from the wind. [Old English]

leech n. 1 bloodsucking worm formerly much used medically. 2 person who sponges on others. [Old English]

leek n. 1 plant of the onion family with flat leaves forming a cylindrical bulb, used as food. 2 this as a Welsh national emblem. [Old English]

leer —v. look slyly, lasciviously, or maliciously. —n. leering look. [perhaps from obsolete *leer* cheek]

leery adj. (-ier, -iest) slang 1 knowing, sly. 2 (foll. by of) wary.

lees /liːz/ n.pl. 1 sediment of wine etc. 2 dregs. [French]

leeward /'liːwəd, Naut. 'luːəd/ —adj. & adv. on or towards the side sheltered from the wind. —n. leeward region or side.

leeway n. 1 allowable scope of action. 2 sideways drift of a ship to leeward of the desired course.

left¹ —adj. 1 on or towards the west side of the human body, or of any object, when facing north. 2 (also **Left**) Polit. of the Left. —adv. on or to the left side. —n. 1 left-hand part, region, or direction. 2 Boxing **a** left hand. **b** blow with this. 3 (often **Left**) group or section favouring socialism; socialists collectively. [Old English, originally = 'weak, worthless']

left² past and past part. of LEAVE¹.

left bank n. bank of a river on the left facing downstream.

left-hand attrib. adj. 1 on or towards the left side of a person or thing. 2 done with the left hand. 3 (of a screw) = LEFT-HANDED 4b.

left-handed adj. 1 naturally using the left hand for writing etc. 2 (of a tool etc.) for use by the left hand. 3 (of a blow) struck with the left hand. 4 **a** turning to the left. **b** (of a screw) turned anticlockwise to tighten. 5 awkward, clumsy. 6 **a** (of a compliment) ambiguous. **b** of doubtful sincerity. □ **left-handedly** adv. **left-handedness** n.

left-hander n. 1 left-handed person. 2 left-handed blow.

leftism n. socialist political principles. □ **leftist** n. & adj.

left luggage n. luggage deposited for later retrieval

leftmost adj. furthest to the left.

leftover —n. (usu. in pl.) surplus item (esp. of food). —attrib. adj. remaining over, surplus.

leftward /'leftwəd/ —adv. (also **leftwards**) towards the left. —adj. going towards or facing the left.

left wing —n. 1 more socialist section of a political party or system. 2 left side of a football etc. team on the field. —adj. (**left-wing**) socialist, radical. □ **left-winger** n.

lefty /'lefti/ n. (pl. -ies) colloq. 1 Polit. often derog. left-winger. 2 left-handed person.

leg n. 1 each of the limbs on which a person or animal walks and stands. 2 leg of an animal or bird as food. 3 part of a garment covering a leg. 4 support of a chair, table, etc. 5 Cricket the half of the field (divided lengthways) in which the batsman's feet are placed. 6 **a** section of a journey. **b** section of a relay race. **c** stage in a competition. □ **leg it** (-gg-) colloq. walk or run hard. **not have a leg to stand on** be unable to support one's argument by facts or sound reasons. **on one's last legs** near death or the end of

usefulness etc. □ **legged** /legd, 'legid/ adj. (also in comb.). [Old Norse]

legacy /'legəsi/ n. (pl. -ies) 1 gift left in a will. 2 thing handed down by a predecessor. [Latin *lego* bequeath]

legal /'li:g(ə)l/ adj. 1 of or based on law; concerned with law. 2 appointed or required by law. 3 permitted by law. □ **legally** adv. [Latin *lex leg-* law]

legal aid n. State assistance for legal advice or action.

legalese /li:gə'li:z/ n. colloq. technical language of legal documents.

legalistic /li:gə'lɪstɪk/ adj. adhering excessively to a law or formula. □ **legalism** /'li:gəlɪz(ə)m/ n. **legalist** /'li:gəlɪst/ n.

legality /lɪ'gælɪtɪ/ n. (pl. -ies) lawfulness. 2 (in pl.) obligations imposed by law.

legalize /'li:gəlaɪz/ v. (also -ise) (-zing or -sing) 1 make lawful 2 bring into harmony with the law. □ **legalization** /-'zeɪʃ(ə)n/ n.

legal separation see SEPARATION.

legal tender n. currency that cannot legally be refused in payment of a debt.

legate /'legət/ n. ambassador of the Pope. [Latin *lego* depute]

legatee /legə'ti:/ n. recipient of a legacy. [Latin *lego* bequeath]

legation /lɪ'geɪʃ(ə)n/ n. 1 diplomatic minister and his or her staff. 2 this minister's official residence. [Latin: related to LEGATE]

legato /lɪ'gɑ:təʊ/ Mus. —adv. & adj. in a smooth flowing manner. —n. (pl. -s) 1 legato passage. 2 legato playing. [Italian, = bound, from *ligo* bind]

leg before —adj. & adv. (in full **leg before wicket**) Cricket (of a batsman) out because of stopping the ball, other than with the bat or hand, which would otherwise have hit the wicket —n. such a dismissal.

leg-bye n. Cricket run scored from a ball that touches the batsman.

legend /'ledʒ(ə)nd/ n. 1 **a** traditional story; myth. **b** these collectively. 2 colloq. famous or remarkable event or person. 3 inscription. 4 explanation on a map etc. of symbols used. [Latin *legenda* what is to be read]

legendary adj. 1 of, based on, or described in a legend. 2 colloq. remarkable.

legerdemain /ledʒədə'meɪn/ n. 1 sleight of hand. 2 trickery; sophistry. [French, = light of hand]

leger line /'ledʒə(r)/ n. Mus. short line added for notes above or below the range of a staff. [var. of LEDGER]

legging n. (usu. in pl.) 1 close-fitting knitted trousers for women or children.

2 stout protective outer covering for the lower leg.

leggy adj. (-ier, -iest) 1 long-legged. 2 long-stemmed and weak. □ **legginess** n.

legible /'ledʒɪb(ə)l/ adj. clear enough to read; readable. □ **legibility** /-'bɪlɪtɪ/ n. **legibly** adv. [Latin *lego* read]

legion /'li:dʒ(ə)n/ —n. 1 division of 3,000–6,000 men in the ancient Roman army. 2 large organized body. —predic. adj. great in number (*this good works were legion*). [Latin *lego* -onis]

legionary —adj. of a legion or legions. —n. (pl. -ies) member of a legion. [French *legio* -onis]

legionnaire /li:dʒə'neə(r)/ n. member of a legion. [French related to LEGION]

legionnaires' disease n. form of bacterial pneumonia.

legislate /'ledʒɪsleɪt/ v. (-ting) make laws. □ **legislator** n. [from LEGIS-LATION]

legislation /ledʒɪs'leɪʃ(ə)n/ n. 1 law-making. 2 laws collectively. [Latin *legis* law, *latus* past part. of *fero* carry]

legislative /'ledʒɪslətɪv/ adj. of or empowered to make legislation.

legislature /'ledʒɪsleɪtʃə(r), -lətʃə(r)/ n. legislative body of a State.

legit /lɪ'dʒɪt/ adj. colloq. legitimate (in sense 2). [abbreviation]

legitimate /lɪ'dʒɪtɪmət/ adj. 1 (of a child) born of parents married to each other. 2 lawful, proper, regular. 3 logically acceptable. □ **legitimacy** n. **legitimately** adv. [Latin *legitimo* legitimize, from *lex legis* law]

legitimatize /lɪ'dʒɪtɪmətaɪz/ v. (also -ise) (-zing or -sing) legitimize.

legitimize /lɪ'dʒɪtɪmaɪz/ v. (also -ise) (-zing or -sing) 1 make legitimate. 2 serve as a justification for. □ **legitimization** /-'zeɪʃ(ə)n/ n.

legless adj. 1 having no legs. 2 slang very drunk.

Lego /'legəʊ/ n. propr. toy consisting of interlocking plastic building blocks. [Danish *legetøj* toys]

leg-of-mutton sleeve n. sleeve which is full and loose on the upper arm but close-fitting on the forearm.

leg-pull n. colloq. hoax.

leg-room n. space for the legs of a seated person.

legume /'legju:m/ n. 1 leguminous plant. 2 edible part of a leguminous plant. [Latin *legumen -minis* from *lego* pick, because pickable by hand]

leguminous /lɪ'gju:mɪnəs/ adj. of the family of plants with seeds in pods (e.g. peas and beans).

leg up n. help given to mount a horse etc., or to overcome an obstacle or problem; boost.

leg warmer *n.* either of a pair of tubular knitted garments covering the leg from ankle to knee or thigh.

lei /'leɪ/ *n.* Polynesian garland of flowers. [Hawaiian]

leisure /'leʒə(r)/ *n.* 1 free time. 2 enjoyment of free time. □ **at leisure** 1 not occupied. 2 in an unhurried manner. **at one's leisure** when one has time. [Anglo-French *leisour* from Latin *licet* it is allowed]

leisure centre *n.* public building with sports facilities etc.

leisured *adj.* having ample leisure.

leisurely /'leʒəlɪ/ *—adj.* unhurried, relaxed. *—adv.* without hurry. □ **leisureliness** *n.*

leisurewear *n.* informal clothes, esp. sportswear.

leitmotif /'laɪtməʊˌtiːf/ *n.* (also **leitmotiv**) recurrent theme in a musical etc. composition representing a particular person, idea, etc. [German: related to LEAD¹, MOTIVE]

lemming /'lemɪŋ/ *n.* small Arctic rodent reputed to rush into the sea and drown during migration. [Norwegian]

lemon /'lemən/ *n.* 1 **a** yellow oval citrus fruit with acidic juice. **b** tree bearing it. 2 pale yellow colour. 3 *colloq.* person or thing regarded as a failure. □ **lemony** *adj.* [Arabic *laimūn*]

lemonade /ˌlemə'neɪd/ *n.* 1 drink made from lemon juice. 2 synthetic substitute for this.

lemon balm *n.* bushy plant smelling and tasting of lemon.

lemon curd *n.* (also **lemon cheese**) creamy preserve made from lemons.

lemon geranium *n.* lemon-scented pelargonium.

lemon sole /'lemən/ *n.* (*pl.* same or **-s**) flat-fish of the plaice family. [French *limande*]

lemur /'liːmə(r)/ *n.* tree-dwelling primate of Madagascar. [Latin *lemures* ghosts]

lend *v.* (*past* and *past part.* **lent**) 1 (usu. foll. by *to*) grant (to a person) the use of (a thing) on the understanding that it or its equivalent shall be returned. 2 allow the use of (money) at interest. 3 bestow or contribute (*lends a certain charm*). □ **lend an ear** listen. **lend a hand** help. **lend itself to** (of a thing) be suitable for. □ **lender** *n.* [Old English: related to LOAN]

length *n.* 1 measurement or extent from end to end. 2 extent in or of time. 3 distance a thing extends. 4 length of a horse, boat, etc., as a measure of the lead in a race. 5 long stretch or extent. 6 degree of thoroughness in action (*went to great lengths*). 7 piece of a certain length (*length of cloth*). 8 *Prosody* quantity of a vowel or syllable. 9 *Cricket* **a** distance from the batsman at which the ball pitches. **b** proper amount of this. 10 length of a swimming-pool as a measure of distance swum. □ **at length** 1 in detail. 2 after a long time. [Old English: related to LONG¹]

lengthen *v.* make or become longer.

lengthways *adv.* in a direction parallel with a thing's length.

lengthwise *—adv.* lengthways. *—adj.* lying or moving lengthways.

lengthy *adj.* (**-ier**, **-iest**) of unusual or tedious length. □ **lengthily** *adv.* **lengthiness** *n.*

lenient /'liːnɪənt/ *adj.* merciful, not severe. □ **lenience** *n.* **leniency** *n.* **leniently** *adv.* [Latin *lenis* gentle]

lens /lenz/ *n.* 1 piece of a transparent substance with one or (usu.) both sides curved for concentrating or dispersing light-rays esp. in optical instruments. 2 combination of lenses used in photography. 3 transparent substance behind the iris of the eye. 4 = CONTACT LENS. [Latin *lens lent-* lentil (from the similarity of shape)]

Lent *n. Eccl.* period of fasting and penitence from Ash Wednesday to Holy Saturday. □ **Lenten** *adj.* [Old English, = spring]

lent *past* and *past part.* of LEND.

lentil /'lentɪl/ *n.* 1 pea-like plant. 2 its seed, esp. used as food. [Latin *lens*]

lento /'lentəʊ/ *Mus.* *—adj.* slow. *—adv.* slowly. [Italian]

Leo /'liːəʊ/ *n.* (*pl.* **-s**) 1 constellation and fifth sign of the zodiac (the Lion). 2 person born when the sun is in this sign. [Latin]

leonine /'liːənaɪn/ *adj.* 1 like a lion. 2 of or relating to lions. [Latin: related to LEO]

leopard /'lepəd/ *n.* large African or Asian animal of the cat family with a black-spotted yellowish or all black coat, panther. [Greek *leōn* lion, *pardos* panther]

leotard /'liːətɑːd/ *n.* close-fitting one-piece garment worn by dancers etc. [*Léotard*, name of a trapeze artist]

leper /'lepə(r)/ *n.* 1 person with leprosy. 2 person who is shunned. [Greek *lepros* scaly]

lepidopterous /ˌlepɪ'dɒptərəs/ *adj.* of the order of insects with four scale-covered wings, including butterflies and moths. □ **lepidopterist** *n.* [Greek *lepis -idos* scale, *pteron* wing]

leprechaun /'leprəˌkɔːn/ *n.* small mischievous sprite in Irish folklore. [Irish *lu* small, *corp* body]

leprosy /ˈleprəsi/ n. contagious disease that damages the skin and nerves. [related to LEPER]

leprous adj.; [related to LEPER]

lesbian /ˈlezbɪən/ —n. homosexual woman. —adj. of female homosexuality. □ **lesbianism** n. [Lesbos, name of an island in the Aegean Sea]

lèse-majesty /liːz ˈmædʒɪstɪ/ n. 1 treason. 2 insult to a sovereign or ruler. [French lèse-majesté injured sovereignty]

lesion /ˈliːʒ(ə)n/ n. 1 damage. 2 injury. 3 morbid change in the functioning or texture of an organ etc. [Latin laedo laes- injure]

less —adj. 1 smaller in extent, degree, duration, number, etc. 2 of smaller quantity, not so much (less meat). 3 collog. fewer (less biscuits). —adv. to a smaller extent, in a lower degree. —n. smaller amount, quantity or number (will take less; for less than £10). —prep. minus (made £1,000 less tax). [Old English]

■ **Usage** The use of less to mean 'fewer', as in sense 3, is regarded as incorrect in standard English.

-less suffix forming adjectives and adverbs: 1 from nouns, meaning 'not having, without, free from' (powerless). 2 from verbs, meaning 'not accessible to, affected by, or performing the action of the verb' (fathomless; ceaseless). [Old English]

lessee /leˈsiː/ n. (often foll. by of) person holding a property by lease. [French: related to LEASE]

lessen /ˈles(ə)n/ v. make or become less, diminish.

lesser adj. (usu. attrib.) not so great as the other(s) (lesser evil; lesser mortals).

lesson /ˈles(ə)n/ n. 1 spell of teaching. 2 (in pl.; foll. by in) systematic instruction. 3 thing learnt by a pupil. 4 experience that serves to warn or encourage (let that be a lesson). 5 passage from the Bible read aloud during a church service. [French leçon from Latin lego lect-]

lessor /leˈsɔː(r)/ n. person who lets a property by lease. [Anglo-French: related to LEASE]

lest conj. formal 1 in order that not, for fear that (lest we should be late). [Old English: related to LESS]

let¹ —v. (-tt-; past and past part. let) 1 a allow to, not prevent or forbid. b cause to (let me know). 2 (foll. by into) allow to or (let the subjunctive (see examples above).

■ **Usage** Lest is followed by should or

enter. 3 grant the use of (rooms, land, etc.) for rent or hire. 4 allow or cause (liquid or air) to escape (let blood). 5 aux. supplying the first and third persons of the imperative in exhortations (let us pray), commands (let it be done at once; let there be light), assumptions, etc. (let AB equal CD). —n. act of letting a house, room, etc. □ **let alone** 1 not to mention, far less or more (hasn't got a television, let alone a video). 2 = let be. **let be** not interfere with, attend to, or do. **let down** 1 lower 2 fail to support or satisfy, disappoint 3 lengthen (a garment). 4 deflate (a tyre). **let down** gently reject or disappoint without humiliating. **let drop** (or fall) drop (esp. a word or hint) intentionally or by accident. **let go** 1 release. 2 a (often foll. by of) lose one's hold b lose hold of. **let off steam** release pent-up energy or feeling. **let on** collog. 1 reveal a secret. 2 pretend. **let out** 1 release. 2 reveal a secret etc. 3 make (a garment) looser. 4 put out to rent or □ contract. **let rip** 1 act without restraint. 2 speak violently. **let up** collog. 1 become less intense or severe. 2 relax one's efforts. **to let** available for rent. [Old English]

let² —n. obstruction of a ball or player in tennis etc., requiring the ball to be served again. —v. □ **-tt-**; past and past part. **letted** or **let**) archaic hinder, obstruct. □ **without let or hindrance** unimpeded. [Old English: related to LATE]

-let suffix forming nouns, usu. diminutive (flatlet) or denoting articles of ornament or dress (anklet). [French]

let-down n. disappointment.

lethal /ˈliːθ(ə)l/ adj. causing or sufficient to cause death. □ **lethally** adv. [Latin letum death]

lethargy /ˈleθədʒɪ/ n. 1 lack of energy. 2 morbid drowsiness. □ **lethargic** /lɪˈθɑːdʒɪk/ adj. **lethargically** /lɪˈθɑːdʒɪkəlɪ/ adv. [Greek lēthargos forgetful]

letter —n. 1 character representing one or more of the sounds used in speech. 2 a written or printed message, usu. sent

letter-bomb

in an envelope by post. **b** (in *pl.*) addressed legal or formal document. **3** precise terms of a statement, the strict verbal interpretation (*letter of the law*). **4** (in *pl.*) **a** literature. **b** acquaintance with books, erudition. —*v.* **1** inscribe letters on. **2** classify with letters. □ **to the letter** with adherence to every detail. [French from Latin *littera*]

letter-bomb *n.* terrorist explosive device in the form of a postal packet.

letter-box *n.* box or slot into which letters are posted or delivered.

lettered *adj.* well-read or educated.

letterhead *n.* **1** printed heading on stationery. **2** stationery with this.

letter of credit *n.* letter from a bank authorizing the bearer to draw money from another bank.

letterpress *n.* **1** printed words of an illustrated book. **2** printing from raised type.

lettuce /ˈletɪs/ *n.* plant with crisp leaves used in salads. [Latin *lactuca* from *lac lact-* milk]

let-up *n. colloq.* **1** reduction in intensity. **2** relaxation of effort.

leuco- *comb. form* white. [Greek *leukos* white]

leucocyte /ˈluːkəˌsaɪt/ *n.* white blood cell.

leukaemia /luːˈkiːmɪə/ *n.* (*US* **leukemia**) malignant disease in which the bone-marrow etc. produces too many leucocytes. [Greek *leukos* white, *haima* blood]

Levant /lɪˈvænt/ *n.* (prec. by *the*) *archaic* eastern Mediterranean countries. [French, = point of sunrise, from Latin *levo* lift]

Levantine /ˈlevəntaɪn/ —*adj.* of or trading to the Levant. —*n.* native or inhabitant of the Levant.

levee /ˈlevɪ/ *n. US* **1** embankment against river floods. **2** natural embankment built up by a river. **3** landing-place. [French *levée* past part. of *lever* raise: related to LEVY]

level /ˈlev(ə)l/ —*n.* **1** horizontal line or plane. **2** height or value reached; position on a real or imaginary scale (*eye level; sugar level; danger level*). **3** social, moral, or intellectual standard. **4** plane of rank or authority (*talks at Cabinet level*). **5** instrument giving a line parallel to the plane of the horizon. **6** level surface. **7** flat tract of land. —*adj.* **1** flat and even; not bumpy. **2** horizontal. **3** (often foll. by *with*) **a** on the same horizontal plane as something else. **b** having equality with something else. **4** even, uniform, equable, or well-balanced. —*v.* (**-ll-**; *US* **-l-**) **1** make level. **2** raze. **3** (also *absol.*) aim (a missile or

gun). **4** (also *absol.*; foll. by *at, against*) direct (an accusation etc.). □ **do one's level best** *colloq.* do one's utmost. **find one's level** reach the right social, intellectual, etc. position. **level down** bring down to a standard. **level off** make or become level. **level out** make or become level. **level up** bring up to a standard. **on the level 1** honestly, without deception. **2** honest, truthful. **on a level with 1** in the same horizontal plane as. **2** equal with. [Latin diminutive of *libra* balance]

level crossing *n.* crossing of a railway and a road, or two railways, at the same level.

level-headed *adj.* sensible, mentally well-balanced. □ **level-headedness** *n.*

leveller *n.* (*US* **leveler**) **1** person who advocates the abolition of social distinctions. **2** person or thing that levels.

level pegging *n.* equality of scores etc.

lever /ˈliːvə(r)/ —*n.* **1** bar resting on a pivot, used to prise. **2** bar pivoted about a fulcrum (fixed point) which can be acted upon by a force (effort) in order to move a load. **3** projecting handle moved to operate a mechanism. **4** means of exerting moral pressure. —*v.* **1** use a lever. **2** (often foll. by *away, out, up*, etc.). [Latin *levo* raise]

leverage *n.* **1** action or power of a lever. **2** power to accomplish a purpose.

leveraged buyout /ˈlevərɪdʒd/ *n.* buyout in which outside capital is used to enable the management to buy up the company.

■ **Usage** The pronunciation is American because the practice takes place mainly in the US.

leveret /ˈlevərɪt/ *n.* young hare, esp. one in its first year. [Latin *lepus lepor-* hare]

leviathan /lɪˈvaɪəθ(ə)n/ *n.* **1** *Bibl.* seamonster. **2** very large or powerful thing. [Latin from Hebrew]

Levis /ˈliːvaɪz/ *n.pl. propr.* type of (orig. blue) denim jeans or overalls reinforced with rivets. [*Levi* Strauss, name of the manufacturer]

levitate /ˈlevɪteɪt/ *v.* (**-ting**) **1** rise and float in the air (esp. with reference to spiritualism). **2** cause to do this. □ **levitation** /-ˈteɪʃ(ə)n/ *n.* [Latin *levis* light, after GRAVITATE]

levity /ˈlevɪtɪ/ *n.* lack of serious thought, frivolity. [Latin *levis* light]

levy /ˈlevɪ/ —*v.* (**-ies, -ied**) **1** impose or collect compulsorily (payment etc.). **2** enrol (troops etc.). **3** wage (war). —*n.* (*pl.* **-ies**) **1 a** collecting of a contribution, tax, etc. **b** contribution, tax, etc. levied. **2 a** an act of

enrolling troops etc. **b** (in *pl.*) troops enrolled. [Latin *levo* raise]

lewd /ljuːd/ *adj.* **1** lascivious. **2** obscene. [Old English, originally = lay, vulgar]

lexical /ˈleksɪk(ə)l/ *adj.* **1** of the words of a language. **2** of or as of a lexicon. [Greek *lexikos, lexikon*: see LEXICON]

lexicography /ˌleksɪˈkɒgrəfɪ/ *n.* compiling of dictionaries. □ **lexicographer** *n.* [from LEXICON, GRAPHY]

lexicon /ˈleksɪkən/ *n.* **1** dictionary, esp. of Greek, Hebrew, Syriac, or Arabic. **2** vocabulary of a person etc. [Greek *lexis* word]

Leydenjar /ˈlaɪd(ə)n/ *n.* early capacitor consisting of a glass jar with layers of metal foil on the outside and inside. [*Leyden* (now *Leiden*) in Holland]

Li *symb.* lithium.

liable /ˈlaɪəb(ə)l/ *predic. adj.* (usu. foll. by *to*) **1** legally bound. **2** (foll. by *to*) subject to. **3** (foll. by *to* + infin.) under an obligation. **4** (foll. by *to*) exposed or open to (something undesirable). **5** (foll. by *to* + infin.) apt. likely (*it is liable to rain*). **6** (foll. by *for*) answerable. [French *lier* bind, from Latin *ligo*]

liaise /lɪˈeɪz/ *v.* (**-sing**) (foll. by *with, between*) *colloq.* establish cooperation, act as a link. [back-formation from LIAISON]

liaison /lɪˈeɪzɒn/ *n.* **1** communication or cooperation. **2** illicit sexual relationship. [French *lier* bind: see LIABLE]

liana /lɪˈɑːnə/ *n.* climbing plant of tropical forests. [French]

liar /ˈlaɪə(r)/ *n.* person who tells a lie or lies.

Lib. *abbr.* Liberal.

lib *n. colloq.* (in names of political movements) liberation. [abbreviation]

libation /laɪˈbeɪʃ(ə)n/ *n.* **1** pouring out of a drink-offering to a god. **2** such a drink-offering. [Latin]

libel /ˈlaɪb(ə)l/ —*n.* **1** *Law* **a** published false statement that is damaging to a person's reputation. **b** act of publishing this. **2** false and defamatory misrepresentation or statement. —*v.* (-**l**-; *US* -**l**-) **1** defame by libellous statements. **2** *Law* publish a libel against. □ **libellous** *adj.* [Latin *libellus* diminutive of *liber* book]

liberal /ˈlɪbər(ə)l/ —*adj.* **1** ample. **2** giving freely, generous. **3** openminded. **4** not strict or rigorous. **5** for the

liberalism *n.* **liberality** /-ˈrælɪtɪ/ *n.* **liberally** *adv.* [Latin *liber* free]

general broadening of the mind (*liberal studies*). **6 a** favouring moderate political and social reform. **b** (Liberal) of or characteristic of Liberals. —*n.* **1** person of liberal views. **2** (Liberal) supporter or member of a Liberal Party. □

■ **Usage** In the UK the name *Liberal* was discontinued in official political use in 1988 when the party regrouped to form the *Social and Liberal Democratic Party*. In 1989 this name was officially replaced by *Liberal Democratic Party*.

Liberal Democrat *n.* member of the party formed from the Liberal Party and the Social Democratic Party.

■ **Usage** See note at *liberal*.

liberalize /ˈlɪbərəˌlaɪz/ *v.* (also -**ise**) (**-zing** or -**sing**) make or become more liberal or less strict. □ **liberalization** /-ˈzeɪʃ(ə)n/ *n.*

liberate /ˈlɪbəreɪt/ *v.* (**-ting**) **1** (often foll. by *from*) set free. **2** free (a country etc.). **3** (often as **liberated** *adj.*) free (a person) from rigid social conventions. □ **liberation** /-ˈreɪʃ(ə)n/ *n.* **liberator** *n.* [Latin *libero liberat-* from *liber* free]

libertine /ˈlɪbətiːn/ —*n.* licentious person, rake. —*adj.* licentious. [Latin, = freedman, from *liber* free]

liberty /ˈlɪbətɪ/ *n.* (*pl.* -**ies**) **1** freedom from captivity etc. **2** right or power to do as one pleases. **3** (usu. in *pl.*) right or privilege granted by authority. □ **at liberty 1** free. **2** (foll. by *to* + infin.) permitted. **take liberties** (often foll. by *with*) behave in an unduly familiar manner. [Latin: related to LIBERAL]

libidinous /lɪˈbɪdɪnəs/ *adj.* lustful. [Latin: related to LIBIDO]

libido /lɪˈbiːdəʊ/ *n.* (*pl.* -**s**) psychic drive or energy, esp. that associated with sexual desire. □ **libidinal** /lɪˈbɪdɪn(ə)l/ *adj.* [Latin, = lust]

Libra /ˈliːbrə/ *n.* **1** constellation and seventh sign of the zodiac (the Scales). **2** person born when the sun is in this sign. [Latin, = pound weight]

librarian /laɪˈbreərɪən/ *n.* person in charge of or assisting in a library. □ **librarianship** *n.*

library /ˈlaɪbrərɪ/ *n.* (*pl.* -**ies**) **1** collection of books. **2** room or building where these are kept. **3 a** similar collection of films, records, computer routines, etc. **b** place where these are kept. **4** set of books issued in similar bindings. [Latin *liber* book]

libretto /lɪˈbretəʊ/ n. (pl. **-ti** /-tɪ/ or **-s**) text of an opera etc. □ **librettist** n. [Italian, = little book]

lice pl. of LOUSE.

licence /ˈlaɪs(ə)ns/ n. (US **license**) **1** official permit to own or use something, do something, or carry on a trade. esp permission. **3** liberty of action. esp when excessive. **4** writer's or artist's deliberate deviation from fact, correct grammar, etc. (poetic licence). [Latin licet it is allowed]

license /ˈlaɪs(ə)ns/ v. (-sing) **1** grant a licence to. **2** authorize the use of (premises) for a certain purpose.

licensee /ˌlaɪsənˈsiː/ n. holder of a licence, esp. to sell alcoholic liquor.

licentiate /laɪˈsenʃɪət/ n. holder of a certificate of professional competence. [medieval Latin: related to LICENCE]

licentious /laɪˈsenʃəs/ adj. sexually promiscuous. [Latin: related to LICENCE]

lichee var. of LYCHEE.

lichen /ˈlaɪkən, ˈlɪtʃ(ə)n/ n. plant composed of a fungus and an alga in association, growing on and colouring rocks, tree-trunks, etc. [Greek leikhēn]

lich-gate n. (also **lych-gate**) roofed gateway to a churchyard where a coffin awaits the clergyman's arrival. [from lich = corpse]

licit /ˈlɪsɪt/ adj. formal permitted, lawful. [Latin: related to LICENCE]

lick –v. **1** pass the tongue over. **2** bring into a specified condition by licking (licked it all up; licked it clean). **3** (of a flame etc.) play lightly over. **4** colloq. defeat. **5** colloq. thrash. –n. **1** act of licking with the tongue. **2** colloq. fast pace (at a lick). **3** smart blow. □ **lick a person's boots** be servile. **lick into shape** make presentable or efficient. **lick one's lips** (or **chops**) look forward with relish. **lick one's wounds** be in retirement regaining strength etc. after defeat. [Old English]

lick and a promise n. colloq. hasty performance of a task, esp. washing oneself.

licorice var. of LIQUORICE.

lid n. **1** hinged or removable cover, esp. for a container. **2** = EYELID. □ **put the lid on** colloq. **1** be the culmination of. **2** put a stop to. □ **lidded** adj. (also in comb.). [Old English]

lido /ˈliːdəʊ, ˈlaɪ-/ n. (pl. **-s**) public open-air swimming-pool or bathing-beach. [Lido, name of a beach near Venice]

lie¹ /laɪ/ –v. (**lies**, **lying**; past lay; past part. **lain**) **1** be in or assume a horizontal position on a surface; be at rest on a surface. **3** remain undisturbed or undiscussed etc. (let matters lie). **4** a be kept, remain, or be in a specified state or place (lie hidden; lie in wait; books lay unread). **b** (of abstract things) exist; be in a certain position or relation (answer lies in education). **5 a** be situated (village lay to the east). **b** be spread out to view. –n. way, direction, or position in which a thing lies. □ **lie down** assume a lying position; have a short rest. **lie down under** accept (an insult etc.) without protest. **lie in** stay in bed late in the morning. **lie low 1** keep quiet or unseen. **2** be discreet about one's intentions. **lie with** be the responsibility of (a person) (decision lies with you). **take lying down** (usu. with neg.) accept (an insult etc.) without protest. [Old English]

■ **Usage** The transitive use of lie, meaning lay, as in lie her on the bed, is incorrect in standard English.

lie² /laɪ/ –n. **1** intentionally false statement (tell a lie). **2** something that deceives. –v. (**lies**, **lied**, **lying**) **1** tell a lie or lies. **2** (of a thing) be deceptive. □ **give the lie to** show the falsity of (a supposition etc.). [Old English]

lied /liːd/ n. (pl. **lieder**) German song, esp. of the Romantic period. [German]

lie-detector n. instrument supposedly determining whether a person is lying, by testing for certain physiological changes.

lie-down n. short rest.

liege usu. hist. –adj. entitled to receive, or bound to give, feudal service or allegiance. –n. **1** (in full **liege lord**) feudal superior or sovereign. **2** (usu. in pl.) vassal, subject. [medieval Latin laeticus, probably from Germanic]

lie-in n. prolonged stay in bed in the morning.

lien /ˈliːən/ n. Law right to hold another's property until a debt on it is paid. [Latin ligo bind]

lie of the land n. state of affairs.

lieu /ljuː/ n. □ **in lieu** instead. **2** (foll. by of) in the place of. [Latin locus place]

Lieut. abbr. Lieutenant.

lieutenant /lefˈtenənt/ n. **1 a** army officer next in rank below captain. **b** naval officer next in rank below lieutenant commander. **2** deputy. □ **lieutenancy** n. (pl. **-ies**). [French: related to LIEU place, TENANT holder]

lieutenant colonel n. (also **lieutenant commander** or **general**) officers ranking next below colonel, commander, or general.

life n. (pl. **lives**) **1** capacity for growth, functional activity, and continual change until death. **2** living things and their activity (insect life; is there life on Mars?). **3 a** period during which life

life assurance lasts, or the period from birth to the present time or from the present time to death (*have done it all my life*; *will regret it all my life*). **b** duration of a thing's existence or ability to function. **4 a** a person's state of existence as a living individual (*sacrificed their lives*). **b** living person (*many lives were lost*). **5 a** particular aspect of this (*private life*). **6** business and pleasures and interests of the world (*in Paris you really see life*) **7** energy, liveliness (*full of life*). **8** biography. **9** *colloq.* = LIFE SENTENCE. □ **for dear** (or **one's**) **life** as if or in order to escape death. **for life** for the rest of one's life. **not on your life** *colloq.* most certainly not. [Old English]

life assurance *n.* = LIFE INSURANCE.

lifebelt *n.* buoyant belt for keeping a person afloat.

lifeblood *n.* **1** blood, as being necessary to life. **2** vital factor or influence.

lifeboat *n.* **1** special boat for rescuing those in distress at sea. **2** ship's small boat for use in emergency.

lifebuoy *n.* buoyant support for keeping a person afloat.

life cycle *n.* series of changes in the life of an organism, including reproduction.

lifeguard *n.* expert swimmer employed to rescue bathers from drowning.

Life Guards *n.pl.* regiment of the royal household cavalry.

life insurance *n.* insurance for a sum to be paid after a set period or on the death of the insured person if earlier.

life-jacket *n.* buoyant jacket for keeping a person afloat.

lifeless *adj.* **1** dead. **2** unconscious. **3** lacking movement or vitality. □ **lifelessly** *adv.* [Old English]

lifelike *adj.* closely resembling life or the person or thing represented.

lifeline *n.* **1** rope etc. used for life-saving. **2** sole means of communication or transport.

lifelong *adj.* lasting a lifetime.

life peer *n.* peer whose title lapses on death.

life-preserver *n.* **1** short stick with a heavily loaded end. **2** life-jacket etc.

lifer *n.* *slang* person serving a life sentence.

life sciences *n.pl.* biology and related subjects.

life sentence *n.* sentence of imprisonment for an indefinite period.

life-size *adj.* (also **-sized**) of the same size as the person or thing represented.

lifestyle *n.* way of life of a person or group.

life-support machine *n.* respirator.

lifetime *n.* duration of a person's life.

lift −*v.* **1** (often foll. by *up*, *off*, etc.) raise or remove to a higher position. **2** go up; be raised; yield to an upward force. **3** give an upward direction to (the eyes or face). **4** elevate to a higher plane of thought or feeling. **5** (of fog etc.) rise, disperse. **6** remove (a barrier or restriction). **7** transport supplies, troops, etc.) by air. **8** *colloq.* **a** steal. **b** plagiarize (a passage of writing etc.). **9** dig up (esp. potatoes etc.). −*n.* **1** lifting or being lifted. **2** ride in another person's vehicle (*gave them a lift*). **3 a** apparatus for raising and lowering persons or things to different floors of a building etc. **b** apparatus for carrying persons up or down a mountain etc. **4 a** transport by air. **b** quantity of goods transported by air. **5** upward pressure which air exerts on an aerofoil. **6** supporting or elevating influence; feeling of elation. □ **lift down** pick up and bring to a lower position. **lift-off** *n.* vertical take-off of a spacecraft or rocket.

[Old Norse; related to LOFT]

ligament /'lɪgəm(ə)nt/ *n.* band of tough fibrous tissue linking bones. [Latin *ligo* bind]

ligature /'lɪgətʃ(ə)r/ −*n.* **1** tie or bandage. **2** *Mus.* slur, tie. **3** two or more letters joined, e.g. æ. **4** bond; thing that unites. −*v.* (**-ring**) bind or connect with a ligature. [Latin *ligo*]

■ **Usage** Sense 3 of this word is sometimes confused with *digraph*, which means 'two separate letters together representing one sound'.

light¹ /laɪt/ −*n.* **1** the natural agent (electromagnetic radiation) that stimulates sight and makes things visible. **2** the medium or condition of the space in which this is present (*just enough light to see*) **3** appearance of brightness (*saw a distant light*). **4** source of light, e.g. the sun, a lamp, fire, etc. **5** (often in *pl*) traffic-light. **6 a** flame or spark serving to ignite. **b** device producing this. **7** aspect in which a thing is regarded (*appeared in a new light*). **8 a** spiritual illumination by divine truth. **9** vivacity etc. in a person's face, esp. in the eyes. **10** eminent person (*leading light*). **11** bright parts of a picture etc. **12** window or opening in a wall to let light in. −*v.* (*past* lit; *past part.* lit or lighted) (*attrib.*) **1** set burning; begin to burn. **2** (often foll. by *up*) provide with light or lighting. **3** (often foll. by *up*) (of the face, eyes, etc.) brighten with pleasure etc. **4** (usu. foll. by *up*) (of

the face or eyes) brighten with animation, pleasure, etc. —*adj.* **1** well provided with light; not dark. **2** (of a colour) pale (*light blue*; *light-blue ribbon*). □ **bring** (or **come**) **to light** reveal or be revealed. **in a good** (or **bad**) **light** giving a favourable (or unfavourable) impression. **in the light of** taking account of. **light up 1** *colloq.* begin to smoke a cigarette etc. **2** = sense 2 of *v.* **3** = sense 4 of *v.* □ **lightish** *adj.* [Old English]

light² /laɪt/ —*adj.* **1** not heavy. **2 a** atively low in weight, amount, density, intensity, etc. (*light arms, traffic, metal, rain*). **b** deficient in weight (*light coin*). **3 a** carrying or suitable for small loads (*light railway*). **b** (of a ship) unladen. **c** carrying only light arms, armaments, etc. **4** (of food) easy to digest. **5** (of entertainment, music, etc.) intended for amusement only; not profound. **6** (of sleep or a sleeper) easily disturbed. **7** easily borne or done (*light duties*). **8** nimble; quick-moving (*light step*; *light rhythm*). **9** (of a building etc.) graceful, elegant. **10 a** free from sorrow; cheerful (*light heart*). **b** giddy (*light in the head*). —*adv.* **1** in a light manner (*tread light*; *sleep light*). **2** with a minimum load (*travel light*). —*v.* (*past* and *past part.* **lit** or **lighted**) (foll. by *on, upon*) come upon or find by chance. □ **make light of** treat as unimportant. □ **lightish** *adj.* **lightly** *adv.* **lightness** *n.* [Old English]

light-bulb *n.* glass bulb containing an inert gas and a metal filament, providing light when an electric current is passed through it.

lighten¹ *v.* **1 a** make or become lighter in weight. **b** reduce the weight or load of. **2** bring relief to (the mind etc.). **3** mitigate (a penalty).

lighten² *v.* **1** shed light on. **2** make or grow bright.

lighter¹ *n.* device for lighting cigarettes etc.

lighter² *n.* boat, usu. flat-bottomed, for transferring goods from a ship to a wharf or another ship. [Dutch: related to LIGHT² in the sense 'unload']

lighter-than-air *attrib. adj.* (of an aircraft) weighing less than the air it displaces.

light-fingered *adj.* given to stealing.

light flyweight *n.* **1** amateur boxing weight up to 48 kg. **2** amateur boxer of this weight.

light-footed *adj.* nimble.

light-headed *adj.* giddy, delirious. □

light-headedness *n.*

light-hearted *adj.* **1** cheerful. **2** (unduly) casual. □ **light-heartedly** *adv.*

light heavyweight *n.* **1** weight in certain sports between middleweight and heavyweight, in amateur boxing 75–81 kg; also called CRUISERWEIGHT. **2** sportsman of this weight.

lighthouse *n.* tower etc. containing a beacon light to warn or guide ships at sea.

light industry *n.* manufacture of small or light articles.

lighting *n.* **1** equipment in a room or street etc. for producing light. **2** arrangement or effect of lights.

lighting-up time *n.* time after which vehicles must show the prescribed lights.

light meter *n.* instrument for measuring the intensity of the light, esp. to show the correct photographic exposure.

light middleweight *n.* **1** weight in amateur boxing of 67–71 kg. **2** amateur boxer of this weight.

lightning —*n.* flash of bright light produced by an electric discharge between clouds or between clouds and the ground. —*attrib. adj.* very quick. [from LIGHTEN²]

lightning-conductor *n.* (also **lightning-rod**) metal rod or wire fixed to an exposed part of a building or to a mast to divert lightning into the earth or sea.

lights *n.pl.* lungs of sheep, pigs, etc., used as a food esp. for pets. [from LIGHT²: cf. LUNG]

lightship *n.* moored or anchored ship with a beacon light.

lightweight —*adj.* **1** of below average weight. **2** of little importance or influence. —*n.* **1** lightweight person, animal, or thing. **2** a weight in certain sports between featherweight and welterweight, in amateur boxing 57–60 kg. **b** sportsman of this weight.

light welterweight *n.* **1** weight in amateur boxing of 60–63.5 kg. **2** amateur boxer of this weight.

light-year *n.* distance light travels in one year, nearly 6 million million miles.

ligneous /ˈlɪɡnɪəs/ *adj.* **1** (of a plant) woody. **2** of the nature of wood. [Latin *lignum* wood]

lignite /ˈlɪɡnaɪt/ *n.* brown coal of woody texture.

lignum vitae /ˌlɪɡnəm ˈvaɪtɪ/ *n.* a hard-wooded tree. [Latin, = wood of life]

likable var. of LIKEABLE.

like¹ —*adj.* (**more like**, **most like**) **1 a** having some or all of the qualities of another, each other, or an original. **b** resembling in some way, such as (*good writers like Dickens*). **3** characteristic of (*not like them to be late*). **3** in a suitable state or mood for (*felt like*

working; *felt like a cup of tea*), in the manner of; to the same degree as (*drink like a fish; acted like an idiot*). —*adv.* 1 *slang* so to speak (*did a quick getaway, like*). 2 *colloq.* likely, probably (*cannot do it like you do*). 2 as if (*ate like they were starving*). —*n.* 1 counterpart; equal; similar person or thing. 2 (prec. by *the*) thing or things of the same kind (*will never do the like again*). like and similar things. like anything of *colloq*, very much, vigorously. the likes of *colloq*, a person such as. more like it *colloq*, nearer what is required. what is the *he* (or *it* etc.)? [Old English]

■ **Usage** The use of *like* as a conjunction is considered incorrect by some people.

like² —*v.* (**-king**) 1 find agreeable or enjoyable. 2 **a** choose to have; prefer (*like my tea weak*). **b** wish for or be inclined to (*would like a nap; should like to come*). 3 (in *pl.*) things one likes or prefers. [Old English]
-like *comb. form* forming adjectives from nouns, meaning 'similar to, characteristic of' (*doglike; shell-like; tortoise-like*).

■ **Usage** Usage in formations not generally current the hyphen should be used. It may be omitted when the first element is of one syllable, unless it ends in -*l*.

likeable *adj.* (also **likable**) pleasant; easy to like. □ **likeably** *adv.*
likelihood /ˈlaɪklɪhʊd/ *n.* probability. □ **in all likelihood** very probably.
likely /ˈlaɪklɪ/ —*adj.* (**-ier**, **-iest**) 1 probable; such as may well happen or be true. 2 to be reasonably expected (*not likely to come now*). 3 promising; apparently suitable (*a likely spot*). —*adv.* probably. □ **not likely!** *colloq.* certainly not, I refuse. [Old Norse: related to LIKE²]
liken *v.* (foll. by *to*) point out the resemblance of (a person or thing to another). [from LIKE²]
likeness *n.* 1 (usu. foll. by *between, to*) resemblance. 2 (foll. by *of*) semblance or guise (*in the likeness of a ghost*). 3 portrait; representation.
likewise *adv.* 1 also, moreover. 2 similarly (*do likewise*).
liking *n.* 1 what one likes; one's taste (*is it to your liking?*). 2 (foll. by *for*) regard or fondness; taste or fancy.
lilac /ˈlaɪlək/ —*n.* 1 shrub with fragrant pinkish-violet or white blossoms. 2 pale

pinkish-violet colour. —*adj.* of this colour. [Persian]
liliaceous /ˌlɪlɪˈeɪʃəs/ *adj.* of the lily family. [related to LILY]
Lilliputian /ˌlɪlɪˈpjuːʃ(ə)n/ —*n.* diminutive person or thing. —*adj.* diminutive. [*Lilliput* in Swift's *Gulliver's Travels*]
Lilo /ˈlaɪləʊ/ *n.* (also **Li-Lo** *propr.*) (*pl.* **-s**) type of inflatable mattress. [from *lie low*]
lilt —*n.* 1 light springing rhythm. 2 tune with this. —*v.* (esp. as **lilting** *adj.*) speak etc. with a lilt; have a lilt. [origin unknown]
lily /ˈlɪlɪ/ *n.* (*pl.* **-ies**) 1 bulbous plant with large trumpet-shaped flowers on a tall stem. 2 heraldic fleur-de-lis. [Latin *lilium*]
lily-livered *adj.* cowardly.
lily of the valley *n.* plant with white bell-shaped fragrant flowers.
lily-white *adj. & n.* (as *adj.* often hyphenated) pure white.
limb¹ /lɪm/ *n.* 1 arm, leg, or wing. 2 large branch of a tree. 3 branch of a cross. □ **out on a limb** isolated. [Old English]
limb² /lɪm/ *n.* specified edge of the sun, moon, etc. [Latin *limbus* hem, border]
limber¹ —*adj.* 1 lithe. 2 flexible. —*v.* (usu. foll. by *up*) 1 make (oneself or a part of the body etc.) supple. 2 warm up in preparation for athletic etc. activity. [origin uncertain]
limber² —*n.* detachable front part of a gun-carriage. —*v.* attach a limber to. [perhaps from Latin *limo-onis* shaft] .
limbo¹ /ˈlɪmbəʊ/ *n.* (*pl.* **-s**) 1 (in some Christian beliefs) supposed abode of the souls of unbaptized infants, and of the just who died before Christ. 2 intermediate state or condition of awaiting a decision etc. [Latin *in limbo*: related to LIMB²]
limbo² /ˈlɪmbəʊ/ *n.* (*pl.* **-s**) W. Indian dance in which the dancer bends backwards to pass under a horizontal bar which is progressively lowered. [W. Indian word, perhaps = LIMBER¹]
lime¹ —*n.* 1 (in full **quicklime**) white substance (calcium oxide) obtained by heating limestone. 2 (in full **slaked lime**) calcium hydroxide obtained by reacting quicklime with water, used as a fertilizer and in making mortar. —*v.* (**-ming**) treat with lime. □ **limy** *adj.* (**-ier**, **-iest**). [Old English]
lime² *n.* 1 **a** fruit like a lemon but green, rounder, smaller, and more acid. **b** tree which produces this fruit. 2 (in full **lime-green**) yellowish-green colour. [French from Arabic]
lime³ *n.* (in full **lime-tree**) tree with heart-shaped leaves and fragrant

creamy blossom. [alteration of *line* = Old English *lind* = LINDEN]

limekiln *n.* kiln for heating limestone.

limelight *n.* 1 intense white light used formerly in theatres. 2 (prec. by *the*) the glare of publicity.

limerick /ˈlɪmərɪk/ *n.* humorous five-line verse with a rhyme-scheme *aabba*. [origin uncertain]

limestone *n.* rock composed mainly of calcium carbonate.

Limey /ˈlaɪmɪ/ *n.* (*pl.* -s) *US slang offens.* British person (orig. a sailor) or ship. [from LIME², because of the former enforced consumption of lime juice in the British Navy]

limit /ˈlɪmɪt/ —*n.* 1 point, line, or level beyond which something does not or may not extend or pass. 2 greatest or smallest amount permissible. —*v.* (*-t-*) 1 set or serve as a limit to. 2 (foll. by *to*) restrict. □ **be the limit** *colloq.* be intolerable. **within limits** with some degree of freedom. □ **limitless** *adj.* [Latin *limes limit-* boundary, frontier]

limitation /ˌlɪmɪˈteɪʃ(ə)n/ *n.* 1 limiting or being limited. 2 limit (*of ability etc.*) (often in *pl.*: *know one's limitations*). 3 limiting circumstance.

limited *adj.* 1 confined within limits. 2 not great in scope or talents. 3 restricted to a few examples (*limited edition*). 4 (after a company name) being a limited company.

limited company *n.* (also **limited liability company**) company whose owners are legally responsible only to a specified amount for its debts.

limn /lɪm/ *v. archaic* paint. [French *luminer* from Latin *lumino* ILLUMINATE]

limo /ˈlɪməʊ/ *n.* (*pl.* -s) *US colloq.* limousine. [abbreviation]

limousine /ˌlɪmuːˈziːn/ *n.* large luxurious car. [French]

limp¹ /lɪmp/ —*v.* walk or proceed lamely or awkwardly. —*n.* lame walk. [perhaps from obsolete *limphalt*: related to HALT²]

limp² *adj.* 1 not stiff or firm. 2 without energy or will. □ **limply** *adv.* **limpness** *n.* [perhaps from LIMP¹]

limpet /ˈlɪmpɪt/ *n.* marine gastropod with a conical shell, sticking tightly to rocks. [Old English]

limpet mine *n.* delayed action mine attached to a ship's hull.

limpid /ˈlɪmpɪd/ *adj.* clear, transparent. □ **limpidity** /-ˈpɪdɪtɪ/ *n.* [Latin]

linage /ˈlaɪnɪdʒ/ *n.* 1 number of lines in printed or written matter. 2 payment by the line.

linchpin *n.* 1 pin passed through an axle-end to keep a wheel in position. 2 person or thing vital to an organization etc. [Old English *lynis* = **axle-tree**]

linctus /ˈlɪŋktəs/ *n.* syrupy medicine, esp. a soothing cough mixture. [Latin *lingo* lick]

linden /ˈlɪnd(ə)n/ *n.* lime-tree. [Old English *lind(e)*]

line¹ —*n.* 1 continuous mark made on a surface. 2 similar mark, esp. a furrow or wrinkle. 3 use of lines in art. 4 a straight or curved continuous extent of length without breadth. b track of a moving point. 5 contour or outline (*has a slimming line*). 6 a curve connecting all points having a specified common property. b (the Line) the Equator. 7 a limit or boundary. b mark limiting the area of play, the starting or finishing point in a race, etc. 8 a row of persons or things. b direction as indicated by them. c *US* queue. 9 a row of printed or written words. b portion of verse written in one line. 10 (in *pl.*) a piece of poetry. b words of an actor's part. c specified amount of text etc. to be written out as a school punishment. 11 short letter or note (*drop me a line*). 12 length of cord, rope, etc., usu. serving a specified purpose. 13 a wire or cable for a telephone or telegraph. b connection by means of this. 14 a single track of a railway system, or the whole system under one management. 15 a regular succession of buses, ships, aircraft, etc., plying between certain places. b company conducting this. 16 connected series of persons following one another in time (esp. several generations of a family); stock. 17 course or manner of procedure, conduct, thought, etc. (*along these lines*; *don't take that line*). 18 direction, course, or channel (*lines of communication*). 19 department of activity; branch of business. 20 type of product (*new line in hats*). 21 a connected series of military fieldworks. b arrangement of soldiers or ships side by side. 22 each of the very narrow horizontal sections forming a television picture. 23 level of the base of most letters in printing and writing. —*v.* (*-ning*) 1 mark with lines. 2 cover with lines. 3 position or stand at intervals along (*crowds lined the route*). □ **all along the line** at every point. **bring into line** make conform. **come into line** conform. **get a line on** *colloq.* get information about. **in line for** likely to receive. **in (or out of) line with** (or not in) accordance with. **lay (or put) it on the line** *colloq.* speak frankly. **line up** 1 arrange or be arranged in a line or lines. 2 have ready. **out of line** not in alignment; inappropriate. [Latin *linea* from *linum* flax]

line² v. (**-ning**) **1** cover the inside surface of (a garment, box, etc.) with a layer of usu. different material. **2** serve as a lining for. **3** *colloq.* fill, esp. plentifully. [obsolete *line* linen used for linings]

lineage /'lɪnɪdʒ/ n. lineal descent; ancestry. [Latin: related to LINE²]

lineal /'lɪnɪəl/ adj. in the direct line of descent or ancestry. □ **lineally** adv.

lineament /'lɪnɪəmənt/ n. (usu. in pl.) distinctive feature or characteristic, esp. of the face. [Latin: related to LINE²]

linear /'lɪnɪə(r)/ adj. **1** of or in lines. **2** long and narrow and of uniform breadth. □ **linearly** /-ɪərlɪ/ n.

Linear B n. form of Bronze Age writing found in Greece; an earlier undeciphered form (**Linear A**) also exists.

lineation /lɪnɪ'eɪʃ(ə)n/ n. marking with or division into lines.

line-drawing n. drawing in which images are produced with lines.

linen /'lɪnɪn/ —n. **1** cloth woven from flax. **2** (collect.) articles made or orig. made of linen, as sheets, shirts, underwear, etc. —adj. made of linen. [Old English: related to Latin *linum* flax]

linen basket n. basket for dirty washing.

line of fire n. expected path of gunfire etc.

line of vision n. straight line along which an observer looks.

line-out n. (in Rugby) parallel lines of opposing forwards at right angles to the touchline for the throwing in of the ball.

line printer n. machine that prints output from a computer a line at a time.

liner¹ n. ship or aircraft etc. carrying passengers on a regular line.

liner² n. removable lining.

linesman n. umpire's or referee's assistant who decides whether a ball has fallen within the playing area or not.

line-up n. **1** line of people for inspection. **2** arrangement of persons in a team, band, etc.

ling¹ n. (pl. same) long slender marine fish. [probably Dutch]

ling² n. any of various heathers. [Old Norse]

-ling suffix denoting a person or thing: **a** connected with (*hireling*). **b** having the property of being (*weakling*) or undergoing (*starveling*). **2** denoting a diminutive (*duckling*), often derogatory (*lordling*). [Old English]

linger /'lɪŋɡə(r)/ v. **1** stay about. **2** (foll. by *over, on,* etc.) dally (*linger over dinner; lingered on the final note*). **3** (esp. of an illness) be protracted. **4** (often foll. by

on) be slow in dying. [Old English *lengan*: related to LONG¹]

lingerie /'læʒərɪ/ n. women's underwear and nightclothes. [French *linge* linen]

lingo /'lɪŋɡəʊ/ n. (pl. **-s** or **-es**) *colloq.* **1** foreign language. **2** vocabulary of a special subject or group. [probably from Portuguese *lingoa* from Latin *lingua* tongue]

lingua franca /ˌlɪŋɡwə 'fræŋkə/ n. (pl. **lingua francas**) **1** language used in common by speakers with different native languages. **2** system for mutual understanding. [Italian, = Frankish tongue]

lingual /'lɪŋɡw(ə)l/ adj. **1** of or formed by the tongue. **2** of speech or languages. □ **lingually** adv. [Latin *lingua* tongue]

linguist /'lɪŋɡwɪst/ n. person skilled in languages or linguistics.

linguistic /lɪŋ'ɡwɪstɪk/ adj. of language or the study of languages. □ **linguistically** adv.

linguistics n. the study of language and its structure.

liniment /'lɪnɪmənt/ n. embrocation. [Latin *linio* smear]

lining n. material which lines a surface etc.

link —n. **1** one loop or ring of a chain etc. **2 a** connecting part; one in a series. **b** state or means of connection. —v. **1** (foll. by *together, to, with*) connect or join (two things or one to another). **2** clasp or intertwine (hands or arms). **3** (foll. by *on, to, in to*) be joined; attach oneself to (a system, company, etc.). □ **link up** (foll. by *with*) connect or combine. [Old Norse]

linkage n. **1** linking or being linked, esp. the linking of quite different political issues in negotiations. **2** link or system of links.

linkman n. person providing continuity in a broadcast programme.

links n.pl. (treated as *sing.* or *pl.*) golf course. [Old English, = rising ground]

link-up n. act or result of linking up.

Linnaean adj. of Linnaeus or his system of classifying plants and animals.
■ **Usage** This word is spelt *Linnean* in *Linnean Society*.

linnet /'lɪnɪt/ n. brown-grey finch. [French *linette* from *lin* flax, because it eats flax-seed]

lino /'laɪnəʊ/ n. (pl. **-s**) linoleum. [abbreviation]

linocut n. **1** design carved in relief on a block of linoleum. **2** print made from this.

linoleum /lɪˈnəʊlɪəm/ n. canvas-backed material thickly coated with a preparation of linseed oil and powdered cork etc., esp. as a floor covering. [Latin *linum* flax, *oleum* oil]

linseed /ˈlɪnsiːd/ n. seed of flax. [Old English: related to LINE¹]

linseed oil n. oil extracted from linseed and used in paint and varnish.

linsey-woolsey /ˌlɪnzɪˈwʊlzɪ/ n. fabric of coarse wool woven on a cotton warp. [probably from *Lindsey* in Suffolk + WOOL]

lint n. 1 linen or cotton with a raised nap on one side, used for dressing wounds. 2 fluff. [perhaps from French *linette* from *lin* flax]

lintel /ˈlɪnt(ə)l/ n. horizontal timber, stone, etc., across the top of a door or window. [French: related to LIMIT]

lion /ˈlaɪən/ n. 1 (*fem.* **lioness**) large tawny flesh-eating wild cat of Africa and S. Asia. 2 (**the Lion**) zodiacal sign or constellation Leo. 3 brave or celebrated person. [Latin *leo*]

lion-heart n. courageous person. □ **lion-hearted** *adj.*

lionize v. (also **-ise**) (**-zing** or **-sing**) treat as a celebrity.

lion's share n. largest or best part.

lip – n. 1 either of the two fleshy parts forming the edges of the mouth-opening. 2 edge of a cup, vessel, etc., esp. the part shaped for pouring from. 3 *colloq.* impudent talk. – v. (**-pp-**) 1 touch with the lips; apply the lips to. 2 touch lightly. □ **lipped** *adj.* (also in *comb.*). [Old English]

lip-read v. understand (speech) from observing a speaker's lip-movements.

lip-service n. insincere expression of support etc.

lipstick n. stick of cosmetic for colouring the lips.

liquefy /ˈlɪkwɪˌfaɪ/ v. (**-ies, -ied**) make or become liquid. □ **liquefaction** /ˌlɪkwɪˈfækʃ(ə)n/ n. [Latin: related to LIQUID]

liqueur /lɪˈkjʊə(r)/ n. any of several strong sweet alcoholic spirits. [French]

liquid /ˈlɪkwɪd/ –*adj.* 1 having a consistency like that of water or oil, flowing freely but of constant volume. 2 having the qualities of water in appearance. 3 (of sounds) clear and pure. 4 (of assets) easily converted into cash. – n. 1 liquid

substance. 2 *Phonet.* sound of *l* or *r*. [Latin *liqueo* be liquid]

liquidate /ˈlɪkwɪˌdeɪt/ v. (**-ting**) 1 wind up the affairs of (a firm) by ascertaining liabilities and apportioning assets. 2 pay off (a debt). 3 wipe out, kill. □ **liquidator** n. [Latin: related to LIQUID]

liquidation /ˌlɪkwɪˈdeɪʃ(ə)n/ n. liquidating, esp. of a firm. □ **go into liquidation** (of a firm etc.) be wound up and have its assets apportioned.

liquid crystal n. turbid liquid with some order in its molecular arrangement.

liquid crystal display n. visual display in electronic devices, in which the reflectivity of a matrix of liquid crystals changes as a signal is applied.

liquidity /lɪˈkwɪdɪtɪ/ n. (*pl.* **-ies**) 1 state of being liquid. 2 availability of liquid assets.

liquidize v. (also **-ise**) (**-zing** or **-sing**) reduce to a liquid state.

liquidizer n. (also **-iser**) machine for liquidizing foods.

liquor /ˈlɪkə(r)/ n. 1 alcoholic (esp. distilled) drink. 2 other liquid, esp. that produced in cooking. [Latin: related to LIQUID]

liquorice /ˈlɪkərɪs, -rɪʃ/ n. (also **licorice**) 1 black root extract used as a sweet and in medicine. 2 plant from which it is obtained. [Greek *glukus* sweet, *rhiza* root]

lira /ˈlɪərə/ n. (*pl.* **lire** pronunc. same or /-reɪ/) 1 chief monetary unit of Italy. 2 chief monetary unit of Turkey. [Latin *libra* pound]

lisle /laɪl/ n. fine cotton thread for stockings etc. [*Lille* in France]

lisp – n. speech defect in which *s* is pronounced like *th* in *thick* and *z* is pronounced like *th* in *this*. – v. speak or utter with a lisp. [Old English]

lissom /ˈlɪsəm/ *adj.* lithe, agile. [ultimately from LITHE]

list¹ n. 1 number of items, names, etc., written or printed together as a record or aid to memory. 2 (in *pl.*) palisades enclosing an area for a tournament. b scene of a contest. – v. 1 make a list of. 2 enter in a list. 3 (as **listed** *adj.*) a (of securities) approved for dealings on the Stock Exchange. b (of a building) of historical importance and officially protected. □ **enter the lists** issue or accept a challenge. [Old English]

list² – v. (of a ship etc.) lean over to one side. – n. process or instance of listing. [origin unknown]

listen /ˈlɪs(ə)n/ v. 1 a make an effort to hear something. b attentively hear a person speaking. 2 (foll. by *to*) a give

attention with the ear. **b** take notice of; heed. **3** (also **listen out**) (often foll. by *for*) seek to hear by waiting alertly. □ **listen in 1** tap a telephonic communication. **2** use a radio receiving set. [Old English]

listener *n*. **1** person who listens. **2** person who listens to the radio.

listeria /lɪˈstɪərɪə/ *n*. any of several bacteria infecting humans and animals eating contaminated food. [*Lister*, name of a surgeon]

listless *adj*. lacking energy or enthusiasm. □ **listlessly** *adv*. **listlessness** *n*. [from obsolete *list* inclination]

list price *n*. price of something as shown in a published list.

lit *past* and *past part*. of LIGHT[1], LIGHT[2].

litany /ˈlɪtənɪ/ *n*. (*pl*. **-ies**) **1 a** a series of supplications to God recited by a priest etc. with set responses by the congregation. **b** (**the Litany**) that in the Book of Common Prayer. **2** tedious recital (*litany of woes*). [Greek *litaneia* prayer]

litchi var. of LYCHEE.

liter *US* var. of LITRE.

literacy /ˈlɪtərəsɪ/ *n*. ability to read and write. [Latin *littera* letter]

literal /ˈlɪtər(ə)l/ —*adj*. **1** taking words in their basic sense without metaphor or allegory. **2** corresponding exactly to the original words (*literal translation*). **3** prosaic; matter-of-fact. **4** so called without exaggeration (*literal bankruptcy*). **5** of a letter or the letters of the alphabet. —*n*. misprint. □ **literally** *adv*. [Latin *littera* letter]

literalism *n*. insistence on a literal interpretation; adherence to the letter. □ **literalist** *n*.

literary /ˈlɪtərərɪ/ *adj*. **1** of or concerned with books or literature etc. **2** (of a word or idiom) used chiefly by writers; formal. □ **literariness** *n*. [Latin: related to LETTER]

literate /ˈlɪtərət/ —*adj*. able to read and write; educated. —*n*. literate person. [Latin: related to LETTER]

literati /lɪtəˈrɑːtɪ/ *n.pl*. the class of learned people.

literature /ˈlɪtrətʃ(ə)r/ *n*. **1** written works, esp. those valued for form and style. **2** writings of a country or period or on a particular subject. **3** literary production. **4** *colloq*. printed matter, leaflets, etc.

lithe /laɪð/ *adj*. flexible, supple. [Old English]

lithium /ˈlɪθɪəm/ *n*. soft silver-white metallic element. [Greek *lithion* from *lithos* stone]

litho /ˈlaɪθəʊ/ *colloq*. —*n*. = LITHO-GRAPHY. —*v*. (**-oes**, **-oed**) lithograph. [abbreviation]

lithograph /ˈlɪθəgrɑːf/ —*n*. lithographic print. —*v*. print by lithography. [Greek *lithos* stone]

lithography /lɪˈθɒgrəfɪ/ *n*. process of printing from a plate so treated that ink adheres only to the design to be printed. □ **lithographer** *n*. **lithographic** /ˌlɪθəˈgræfɪk/ *adj*. **lithographically** *adv*.

Lithuanian /ˌlɪθjuˈeɪnɪən/ —*n*. **1 a** native or national of Lithuania in eastern Europe. **b** person of Lithuanian descent. **2** language of Lithuania. —*adj*. of Lithuania, its people, or language.

litigant /ˈlɪtɪgənt/ —*n*. party to a lawsuit. —*adj*. engaged in a lawsuit. [related to LITIGATE]

litigate /ˈlɪtɪgeɪt/ *v*. (**-ting**) **1** go to law. **2** contest (a point) at law. □ **litigation** /-ˈgeɪʃ(ə)n/ *n*. **litigator** *n*. [Latin *lis lit-* lawsuit]

litigious /lɪˈtɪdʒəs/ *adj*. **1** fond of litigation. **2** contentious. [Latin: related to LITIGATE]

litmus /ˈlɪtməs/ *n*. dye from lichens, turned red by acid and blue by alkali.

litmus paper *n*. paper stained with litmus, used to test for acids or alkalis.

litmus test *n*. *colloq*. real or ultimate test.

litotes /laɪˈəʊtiːz/ *n*. (*pl*. same) ironic understatement, esp. using the negative (e.g. *I shan't be sorry for I shall be glad*). [Greek *litos* plain, meagre]

litre /ˈliːtə(r)/ *n*. (*US* **liter**) metric unit of capacity equal to 1 cubic decimetre (1.76 pints). [Greek *litra*]

Litt.D. *abbr*. Doctor of Letters. [Latin *Litterarum Doctor*]

litter —*n*. **1 a** refuse, esp. paper, discarded in a public place. **b** odds and ends lying about. **2** young animals brought forth at one birth. **3** vehicle containing a couch and carried on men's shoulders or by animals. **4 a** kind of stretcher for the sick and wounded. **5** straw etc., as bedding for animals. **6** granulated material for use as an animal's, esp. a cat's, toilet indoors. —*v*. **1** make (a place) untidy with refuse. **2** give birth to (whelps etc.). **3 a** provide (a horse etc.) with litter as bedding. **b** spread straw etc. on (a stable-floor etc.). [Latin *lectus* bed]

litterbug *n*. *colloq*. person who drops litter in the street etc.

litter-lout *n*. *colloq*. = LITTERBUG.

little /ˈlɪt(ə)l/ —*adj*. (**littler, littlest**; *less* or *lesser*, *least*) **1** small in size, amount, degree, etc.; often used affectionately or condescendingly (*friendly little chap*; *silly little fool*). **2 a** short in stature. **b** of short distance or duration. **3** (prec. by *a*)

a certain though small amount of (*give me a little butter*). **4** trivial (*questions every little thing*). **5** only a small amount (*had little sleep*). **6** operating on a small scale; humble, ordinary (*the little shopkeeper; the little man*). **7** smaller or the smallest of the name (*little hand of a clock; little auk*). **8** young or younger (*little boy; my little sister*). —*n.* **1** not much; only a small amount (*got little out of it; did what little I could*). **2** (usu. prec. by *a*) **a** a certain but no great amount (*knows a little of everything*). **b** short time or distance (*after a little*). —*adv.* (**less, least**) **1** to a small extent only (*little-known author; little more than speculation*). **2** not at all; hardly (*they little thought*). **3** (prec. by *a*) somewhat (*is a little deaf*). [Old English]

Little Bear see BEAR².

little by little *adv.* by degrees; gradually.

little end *n.* the smaller end of a connecting-rod, attached to the piston.

little grebe *n.* small water-bird of the grebe family.

little people *n.pl.* (prec. by *the*) fairies.

little woman *n.* (prec. by *the*) *colloq.* often *derog.* one's wife.

littoral /ˈlɪtər(ə)l/ —*adj.* of or on the shore. —*n.* region lying along a shore. [Latin *litus litor-* shore]

liturgy /ˈlɪtədʒɪ/ *n.* (*pl.* -**ies**) **1** prescribed form of public worship. **2** (**the Liturgy**) the Book of Common Prayer. □ **liturgical** /-ˈtɜːdʒɪk(ə)l/ *adj.* **liturgically** /-ˈtɜːdʒɪkəlɪ/ *adv.* [Greek *leitourgia* public worship]

livable var. of LIVEABLE.

live¹ /lɪv/ *v.* (-**ving**) **1** have life; be or remain alive. **2** have one's home (*lives up the road*). **3** (foll. by *on*) subsist or feed (*lives on fruit*). **4** (foll. by *on, off*) depend for subsistence (*lives off the State; lives on a pension*). **5** (foll. by *on, by*) sustain one's position (*live on their reputation; lives by his wits*). **6 a** spend or pass (*lived a full life*). **b** express in one's life (*lives his faith*). **7** conduct oneself, arrange one's habits, etc., in a specified way (*live quietly*). **8** (often foll. by *on*) (of a person or thing) survive, remain (*memory lived on*). **9** enjoy life to the full (*not really living*). □ **live and let live** condone others' failings so as to be similarly tolerated. **live down** cause (past guilt, a scandal, etc.) to be forgotten by blameless conduct thereafter. **live for** regard as one's life's purpose (*lives for her music*). **live in** (or **out**) reside on (or off) the premises of one's work. **live it up** *colloq.* live gaily and extravagantly. **live a lie** keep up a pretence. **live together** (esp. of a couple not married to each other) share a home and have a sexual relationship. **live up to** fulfil. **live with 1** share a home with. **2** tolerate. [Old English]

live² /laɪv/ —*adj.* **1** (*attrib.*) that is alive; living. **2** (of a broadcast, performance, etc.) heard or seen at the time of its performance or with an audience present. **3** of current interest or importance (*a live issue*). **4** glowing, burning (*live coals*). **5** (of a match, bomb, etc.) not yet kindled or exploded. **6** (of a wire etc.) charged with or carrying electricity. —*adv.* **1** in order to make a live broadcast (*going live now to the House of Commons*). **2** as a live performance etc. (*show went out live*). [from ALIVE]

liveable /ˈlɪvəb(ə)l/ *adj.* (also **livable**) **1** *colloq.* (usu. **liveable-in**) (of a house etc.) fit to live in. **2** (of a life) worth living. **3** *colloq.* (usu. **liveable-with**) (of a person) easy to live with.

lived-in *adj.* **1** (of a room etc.) showing signs of habitation. **2** *colloq.* (of a face) marked by experience.

live-in *attrib. adj.* (of a sexual partner, employee, etc.) cohabiting; resident.

livelihood /ˈlaɪvlɪhʊd/ *n.* means of living; job, income. [Old English: related to LIFE]

livelong /ˈlɪvlɒŋ/ *adj.* in its entire length (*the livelong day*). [from obsolete *lief*, assimilated to LIVE²]

lively /ˈlaɪvlɪ/ *adj.* (-**ier**, -**iest**) **1** full of life; vigorous, energetic. **2** vivid (*lively imagination*). **3** cheerful. **4** *joc.* exciting, dangerous (*made things lively for him*). □ **liveliness** *n.* [Old English]

liven /ˈlaɪv(ə)n/ *v.* (often foll. by *up*) *colloq.* make or become lively, cheer up.

liver¹ /ˈlɪvə(r)/ *n.* **1** large glandular organ in the abdomen of vertebrates. **2** liver of some animals as food. [Old English]

liver² /ˈlɪvə(r)/ *n.* person who lives in a specified way (*a fast liver*).

liveried /ˈlɪvərɪd/ *adj.* wearing livery.

liverish /ˈlɪvərɪʃ/ *adj.* **1** suffering from a liver disorder. **2** peevish, glum.

Liverpudlian /ˌlɪvəˈpʌdlɪən/ —*adj.* of Liverpool. —*n.* native of Liverpool. [*Liverpool* in NW England]

liver sausage *n.* sausage of cooked liver etc.

liverwort *n.* small mosslike or leafless plant sometimes lobed like a liver.

livery /ˈlɪvərɪ/ *n.* (*pl.* -**ies**) **1** distinctive uniform of a member of a City Company or of a servant. **2** distinctive guise or marking (*birds in their winter livery*). **3** distinctive colour scheme in which a company's vehicles etc. are painted. □ **at livery** (of a horse) kept for the owner

for a fixed charge. [Anglo-French *livere*, past part. of *livrer* DELIVER]

livery stable *n.* stable where horses are kept at livery or let out for hire.

lives *pl.* of LIFE.

livestock *n.* (usu. treated as *pl.*) animals on a farm, kept for use or profit.

live wire *n.* spirited person.

livid /ˈlɪvɪd/ *adj.* 1 *colloq.* furious. 2 of a bluish leaden colour (*livid bruise*). [Latin]

living /ˈlɪvɪŋ/ —*n.* 1 being alive (*that's what living is all about*). 2 livelihood. 3 position held by a clergyman, providing an income. —*adj.* 1 contemporary; now alive. 2 (of a likeness) exact, lifelike. 3 (of a language) still in vernacular use. □ **within living memory** within the memory of people still alive.

living wage *n.* wage on which one can live without privation

living-room *n.* room for general day use.

lizard /ˈlɪzəd/ *n.* reptile with usu. a long body and tail, four legs, and a rough or scaly hide. [Latin *lacerta*]

LJ *abbr.* (*pl.* **L JJ**) Lord Justice.

'll *v.* (usu. after pronouns) shall, will (*I'll, that'll*). [abbreviation]

llama /ˈlɑːmə/ *n.* S. American ruminant kept as a beast of burden and for its soft woolly fleece. [Spanish from Quechua]

LL.B *abbr.* Bachelor of Laws. [Latin *legum baccalaureus*]

LL.D *abbr.* Doctor of Laws. [Latin *legum doctor*]

LL.M *abbr.* Master of Laws. [Latin *legum magister*]

Lloyd's /lɔɪdz/ *n.* incorporated society of underwriters in London. [*Lloyd*, proprietor of the coffee-house where the society originally met]

Lloyd's List *n.* daily publication devoted to shipping-news.

Lloyd's Register *n.* annual classified list of all ships.

ln *abbr.* natural logarithm.

lo /ləʊ/ *int. archaic* look. □ **lo and behold** *joc.* formula introducing mention of a surprising fact. [Old English]

loach /ləʊtʃ/ *n.* (*pl.* same or **-es**) small freshwater fish. [French]

load —*n.* 1 **a** what is carried or to be carried. **b** amount usu. or actually carried. (often in *comb.*: *lorry-load of bricks*). 2 burden or commitment of work, responsibility, care, etc. 3 *colloq.* **a** (in *pl.*; often foll. by *of*) plenty. **b** (**a load of**) a quantity (*a load of money; people*), a lot (*loads of nonsense*). 4 amount of power carried by an electric circuit or supplied by a generating station. —*v.* 1 **a** put a load on or aboard. **b** place (a load) aboard a ship, on a vehicle, etc. 2 (often

foll. by *up*) (of a vehicle or person) take a load aboard. 3 (often foll. by *with*) burden, strain (*loaded with food*). 4 (also **load up** (foll. by *with*)) overburden, overwhelm (*loaded us with work, with abuse*). 5 **a** put ammunition in (a gun, etc.). **b** put (a film, cassette, etc.) into a camera, a cassette in (a tape recorder), a program in (a computer, etc.). **6** give a bias to. □ **get a load of** *slang* take note of. [Old English, = way]

loaded *adj.* 1 *slang* **a** rich. **b** drunk. **c** *US* drugged. 2 (of dice etc.) weighted. 3 (of a question or statement) carrying some hidden implication.

loader *n.* 1 loading-machine. 2 (in *comb.*) gun, machine, lorry, etc., loaded in a specified way (*breech-loader; front-loader*). □ **-loading** *adj.* (in *comb.*)

load line *n.* = PLIMSOLL LINE.

loadstone var. of LODESTONE.

loaf *n.* (*pl.* **loaves**) 1 unit of baked bread, usu. of a standard size or shape. 2 other food made in the shape of a loaf and cooked. 3 *slang* head as the seat of common sense. [Old English]

loaf *v.* (often foll. by *about, around*) spend time idly hang about. [back-formation from LOAFER]

loafer *n.* 1 idle person. 2 (**Loafer**) *propr.* flat soft-soled leather shoe. [origin uncertain]

loam *n.* rich soil of clay, sand, and humus. □ **loamy** *adj.* [Old English]

loan —*n.* 1 thing lent, esp. a sum of money. 2 lending or being lent. —*v.* lend (money, works of art, etc.). □ **on loan** being lent. [Old English]

loan shark *n. colloq.* person who lends money at exorbitant rates of interest.

loath *predic. adj.* (also **loth**) disinclined, reluctant (*loath to admit it*). [Old English]

loathe /ləʊð/ *v.* (-thing) detest, hate. □ **loathing** *n.* [Old English]

loathsome /ˈləʊðsəm/ *adj.* arousing hatred or disgust; repulsive.

loaves *pl.* of LOAF[1].

lob —*v.* (-bb-) hit or throw (a ball etc.) slowly or in a high arc. —*n.* such a ball. [probably Low German or Dutch]

lobar /ˈləʊbə(r)/ *adj.* of a lobe, esp. of the lung (*lobar pneumonia*).

lobate /ˈləʊbeɪt/ *adj.* having a lobe or lobes.

lobby /ˈlɒbɪ/ —*n.* (*pl.* **-ies**) 1 porch, anteroom, entrance-hall, or corridor. 2 **a** (the House of Commons) large hall used esp. for interviews between MPs and the public. **b** (also **division lobby**) each of two corridors **to** which MPs retire to

vote. 3 a body of lobbyists (*anti-abortion lobby*). b organized rally of lobbying members of the public. 4 (prec. by *the*) group of journalists who receive unattributable briefings from the government (*lobby correspondent*). —v. (-ies, -ied) 1 solicit the support of (an influential person). 2 (of members of the public) inform in order to influence (legislators, an MP, etc.). 3 frequent a parliamentary lobby. [Latin *labia* lodge]

lobbyist n. person who lobbies an MP etc., esp. professionally.

lobe n. 1 lower soft pendulous part of the outer ear. 2 similar part of other organs, esp. the brain, liver, and lung. □ **lobed** adj. [Greek *lobos* lobe, pod]

lobelia /lə'bi:liə/ n. plant with bright, esp. blue, flowers. [*Lobel*, name of a botanist]

lobotomy /lə'bɒtəmɪ/ n. (pl. -ies) incision into the frontal lobe of the brain, formerly used in some cases of mental disorder. [from LOBE]

lobscouse /'lɒbskaʊs/ n. sailor's dish of meat stewed with vegetables and ship's biscuit. [origin unknown]

lobster n. 1 marine crustacean with two pincer-like claws. 2 its flesh as food. [Latin *locusta* lobster, LOCUST]

lobster-pot n. basket for trapping lobsters.

lobworm n. large earthworm used as fishing-bait. [from LOB in obsolete sense 'pendulous object']

local /'ləʊk(ə)l/ —adj. 1 belonging to, existing in, or peculiar to a particular place (*local history*). 2 of the neighbourhood (*local paper*). 3 of or affecting a part and not the whole (*local anaesthetic*). 4 (of a telephone call) to a nearby place and charged at a lower rate. —n. 1 inhabitant of a particular place. 2 (often prec. by *the*) colloq. local public house. 3 local anaesthetic. □ **locally** adv. [Latin *locus* place]

local authority n. administrative body in local government.

local colour n. touches of detail in a story etc. designed to provide a realistic background.

locale /ləʊ'kɑːl/ n. scene or locality of an event or occurrence. [French *local*]

local government n. system of administration of a county, district, parish, etc., by the elected representatives of those who live there.

locality /ləʊ'kælɪtɪ/ n. (pl. -ies) 1 district. 2 site or scene of a thing. 3 thing's position. [Latin: related to LOCAL]

localize /'ləʊkə,laɪz/ v. (also **-ise**) (-zing or -sing) 1 restrict or assign to a particular place. 2 invest with the characteristics of a particular place. 3 decentralize.

local time n. time in a particular place.

local train n. train stopping at all the stations on its route.

locate /ləʊ'keɪt/ v. (-ting) 1 discover the exact place of. 2 establish in a place; situate. 3 state the locality of. [Latin: related to LOCAL]

■ **Usage** In standard English, it is not acceptable to use locate to mean merely 'find' as in *can't locate my key.*

location /ləʊ'keɪʃ(ə)n/ n. 1 particular place. 2 locating. 3 natural, not studio, setting for a film etc. (*filmed on location*).

loc. cit. abbr. in the passage cited. [Latin *loco citato*]

loch /lɒk, lɒx/ n. Scot. lake or narrow inlet of the sea. [Gaelic]

loci pl. of LOCUS.

lock¹ —n. 1 mechanism for fastening a door etc., with a bolt that requires a key of a particular shape to work it. 2 confined section of a canal or river within sluice-gates, for moving boats from one level to another. 3 a turning of a vehicle's front wheels. b (in full **full lock**) maximum extent of this. 4 interlocked or jammed state. 5 wrestling-hold that keeps an opponent's limb fixed. 6 (in full **lock forward**) player in the second row of a Rugby scrum. 7 mechanism for exploding the charge of a gun. —v. 1 a fasten with a lock. b (foll. by *up*) shut (a house etc.). 2 a (foll. by *up, in, into*) enclose (a person or thing) by locking. b (foll. by *up*) colloq. imprison (a person). 3 (often foll. by *up, away*) store inaccessibly (*capital locked up in land*). 4 (foll. by *in*) hold fast (in sleep, an embrace, a struggle, etc.). 5 (usu. in *passive*) (of land, hills, etc.) enclose. 6 make or become rigidly fixed. 7 (cause to) jam or catch. □ **lock on to** (of a missile etc.) automatically find and then track (a target). **lock out** 1 keep out by locking the door. 2 (of an employer) subject (employees) to a lockout. **under lock and key** locked up. □ **lockable** adj. [Old English]

lock² —n. 1 portion of hair that hangs together. 2 (in *pl.*) the hair of the head (*golden locks*). [Old English]

locker n. (usu. lockable) cupboard or compartment, esp. for public use.

locket /'lɒkɪt/ n. small ornamental case for a portrait or lock of hair, worn on a chain round the neck. [French diminutive of *loc* latch, LOCK¹]

lockjaw n. form of tetanus in which the jaws become rigidly closed.

lock-keeper n. person in charge of a river or canal lock.

lockout *n.* employer's exclusion of employees from the workplace until certain terms are agreed to.

locksmith *n.* maker and mender of locks.

lock, stock, and barrel *adv.* completely.

lock-up *n.* 1 house or room for the temporary detention of prisoners. 2 premises that can be locked up, esp. a small shop. *—attrib. adj.* that can be locked up (*lock-up garage*).

loco[1] /ˈləʊkəʊ/ *n.* (*pl.* **-s**) *colloq.* locomotive engine. [abbreviation]

loco[2] /ˈləʊkəʊ/ *predic. adj. slang* crazy. [Spanish]

locomotion   /ˌləʊkəˈməʊʃ(ə)n/ *n.* motion or the power of motion from place to place. [Latin LOCUS, MOTION]

locomotive /ˌləʊkəˈməʊtɪv/ *—n.* engine for pulling trains. *—attrib. adj.* of, having, or effecting locomotion.

locum tenens /ˌləʊkəm ˈtiːnenz, ˈte-/ *n.* (*pl.* **locum tenentes** /tɪˈnentiːz/) (also *colloq.* **locum**) deputy acting esp. for a doctor or clergyman. [Latin, = one holding a place]

locus /ˈləʊkəs/ *n.* (*pl.* **loci** /-saɪ/) 1 position or locality. 2 line or curve etc. formed by all the points satisfying certain conditions, or by the defined motion of a point, line, or surface. [Latin, = place]

locus classicus /ˌləʊkəs ˈklæsɪkəs/ *n.* (*pl.* **loci classici** /ˌləʊsaɪ ˈklæsɪsaɪ/) best known or most authoritative passage on a subject. [Latin: related to LOCUS]

locust /ˈləʊkəst/ *n.* African or Asian grasshopper migrating in swarms and consuming all vegetation. [Latin *locusta* LOBSTER]

locution /ləˈkjuːʃ(ə)n/ *n.* 1 word, phrase, or idiom. 2 style of speech. [Latin *loquor locut-* speak]

lode *n.* vein of metal ore. [var. of LOAD]

lodestar *n.* 1 star used as a guide in navigation, esp. the pole star. 2 a guiding principle. b object of pursuit. [from LODE in obsolete sense 'way, journey']

lodestone *n.* (also **loadstone**) 1 magnetic oxide of iron. 2 a piece of this used as a magnet. b thing that attracts.

lodge *—n.* 1 small house at the entrance to a park or grounds of a large house, occupied by a gatekeeper etc. 2 small house used in the sporting seasons (*hunting lodge*). 3 porter's room at the gate of a college, factory, etc. 4 members or meeting-place of a branch of a society such as the Freemasons. 5 beaver's or otter's lair. *—v.* (**-ging**) 1 a reside or live, esp. as a lodger. b provide with temporary accommodation. 2 submit or present (a complaint etc.) for attention. 3

become fixed or caught (*stick. 4 deposit* (money etc.) for security. 5 (foll. by *in, with*) place (power etc.) in a person. [French *loge*: related to LEAF]

lodger *n.* person paying for accommodation in another's house.

lodging *n.* 1 temporary accommodation (*a lodging for the night*). 2 (in *pl.*) room or rooms rented for lodging in.

loess /ˈləʊɪs/ *n.* deposit of fine wind-blown soil, esp. in the basins of large rivers. [Swiss German, = loose]

loft *—n.* 1 attic. 2 room over a stable. 3 gallery in a church or hall. 4 pigeon-house. 5 backward slope on the face of a golf-club. 6 lofting stroke. *—v.* send (a ball etc.) high up. [Old English, = air, upper room]

lofty *adj.* (**-ier, -iest**) 1 (of things) of imposing height. 2 haughty, aloof. 3 exalted, noble (*lofty ideals*). □ **loftily** *adv.* **loftiness** *n.*

log[1] *—n.* 1 unhewn piece of a felled tree; any large rough piece of wood, esp. cut for firewood. 2 *hist.* floating device for gauging a ship's speed. 3 record of events occurring during the voyage of a ship or aircraft. 4 any systematic record of deeds, experiences, etc. 5 = LOGBOOK. *—v.* (**-gg-**) 1 a enter (a ship's speed, or other transport details) in a logbook. b attain (a distance, speed, etc., thus recorded) (*had logged over 600 miles*). 3 cut into logs. □ **log in** = *log on.* **log on** (or **off**) open (or close) one's online access to a computer system. **sleep like a log** sleep soundly. [origin unknown]

log[2] *n.* logarithm. [abbreviation]

logan /ˈləʊɡən/ *n.* (in full **logan-stone**) poised heavy stone rocking at a touch. [= (dial.) *logging*, = rocking]

loganberry /ˈləʊɡənbərɪ/ *n.* (*pl.* **-ies**) dark red fruit, hybrid of a blackberry and a raspberry. [*Logan*, name of a horticulturalist]

logarithm /ˈlɒɡərɪð(ə)m/ *n.* one of a series of arithmetic exponents tabulated to simplify computation by making it possible to use addition and subtraction instead of multiplication and division. □ **logarithmic** /-ˈrɪðmɪk/ *adj.* **logarithmically** /-ˈrɪðmɪkəlɪ/ *adv.* [Greek *logos* reckoning, *arithmos* number]

logbook *n.* 1 book containing a detailed record or log. 2 vehicle registration document.

log cabin *n.* hut built of logs.

logger *n. US* lumberjack.

loggerhead *n.* (often foll. by *with*) disagreeing or disputing. [probably dial. from *logger* wooden block]

loggia /ˈlɒdʒə, ˈlɒb/ n. open-sided gallery or arcade. [Italian, = LODGE]

logging n. work of cutting and preparing forest timber.

logic /ˈlɒdʒik/ n. **1 a** science or method of reasoning. **2 a** chain of reasoning (regarded as sound or unsound). **3** inexorable force, compulsion, or consequence (*the logic of events*). **4 a** principles used in designing a computer etc. **b** circuits using this. □ **logician** /ləˈdʒiʃ(ə)n/ n. [related to -LOGIC]

-logic *comb. form* (also **-logical**) forming adjectives corresponding esp. to nouns in *-logy* (*pathological*; *zoological*). [Greek *-logikos*]

logical *adj.* **1** of or according to logic (*the logical conclusion*). **2** correctly reasoned. **3** defensible or explicable on the ground of consistency. **4** capable of correct reasoning. □ **logicality** /-ˈkælɪtɪ/ n. **logically** *adv.* [Greek *logos* word, reason]

-logist *comb. form* forming nouns meaning person skilled in *-logy* (*geologist*).

logistics /ləˈdʒɪstɪks/ *n.pl.* **1** organization of (orig. military) services and supplies. **2** organization of any complex operation. □ **logistic** *adj.* **logistical** *adj.* **logistically** *adv.* [French *logistique*]

log-jam n. deadlock.

logo /ˈlɒɡəʊ/ n. (pl. **-s**) emblem of an organization used in its display material etc. [abbreviation of *logotype* from Greek *logos* word]

-logy *comb. form* forming nouns denoting: **1** a subject of study (*biology*). **2** speech or discourse or a characteristic of this (*trilogy*; *tautology*; *phraseology*). [Greek *-logia* from *logos* word]

loin n. **1** (in *pl.*) side and back of the body between the ribs and the hip-bones. **2** joint of meat from this part of an animal. [French *loigne* from Latin *lumbus*]

loincloth n. cloth worn round the hips, esp. as a sole garment.

loiter v. **1** stand about idly; linger. **2** go slowly with frequent stops. □ **loiter with intent** linger in order to commit a felony. □ **loiterer** n. [Dutch]

loll v. **1** stand, sit, or recline in a lazy attitude. **2** hang loosely. [imitative]

lollipop /ˈlɒlɪpɒp/ n. hard sweet on a stick. [origin uncertain]

lollipop man n. (also **lollipop lady**) *colloq.* warden using a circular sign on a pole to stop traffic for children to cross the road.

lolly /ˈlɒlɪ/ n. (pl. **-ies**) **1** *colloq.* lollipop. **2** = ICE LOLLY. **3** *slang* money. [abbreviation]

London /ˈlʌndən(r)/ n. native or inhabitant of London.

London pride /ˈlʌnd(ə)n/ n. pink-flowered saxifrage.

lone *attrib. adj.* **1** solitary; without companions. **2** isolated. **3** unmarried, single (*lone parent*). [from ALONE]

lone hand n. **1** hand played or player playing against the rest at cards. **2** person or action without allies.

lonely /ˈləʊnlɪ/ *adj.* (**-ier**, **-iest**) **1** without companions (*lonely existence*). **2** sad because of this. **3** unfrequented, isolated, uninhabited. □ **loneliness** n.

lonely hearts *n.pl.* people seeking friendship or marriage through a newspaper column, club, etc.

loner n. person or animal that prefers to be alone.

lonesome /ˈləʊnsəm/ *adj.* esp. *US* **1** lonely. **2** making one feel forlorn (*a lonesome song*).

lone wolf n. loner.

long[1] *adj.* (**longer** /ˈlɒŋɡə(r)/; **longest** /ˈlɒŋɡɪst/) **1** measuring much from end to end in space or time. **2** (following a measurement) in length or duration (*2 metres long*; *two months long*). **3 a** consisting of many items (*a long list*). **b** seemingly more than the stated amount; tedious (*ten long miles*). **4** of elongated shape. **5** lasting or reaching far back or forward in time (*long friendship*). **6** far-reaching; acting at a distance; involving a great interval or difference. **7** (of a vowel or syllable) having the greater of the two recognized durations. **8** (of odds or a chance) reflecting a low level of probability. **9** (of stocks) bought in large quantities in advance, with the expectation of a rise in price. **10** (foll. by *on*) *colloq.* well supplied with. *—n.* long interval or period (*will not take long*; *won't be long*). *—adv.* (**longer** /ˈlɒŋɡə(r)/; **longest** /ˈlɒŋɡɪst/) **1** by or for a long time (*long before*; *long ago*). **2** (following nouns of duration) throughout a specified time (*all day long*). **3** (in *compar.*) after an implied point of time (*shall not wait any longer*). □ **as** (or **so**) **long as** provided that. **before long** soon. **in the long run** (or **term**) eventually, ultimately. **the long and the short of it** all that need be said. **2** the eventual outcome. **not by a long shot** (or **chalk**) by no means. □ **longish** *adj.* [Old English]

long[2] v. (foll. by *for* or *to* + *infin.*) have a strong wish or desire for. [Old English, = seem LONG[1] to]

long. abbr. longitude.

longboat n. sailing-ship's largest boat.

longbow n. bow drawn by hand and shooting a long feathered arrow.

long-distance –attrib. adj. travelling between distant places, or operating between distant places. –adv. between distant places (phone long-distance).

long division n. division of numbers with details of the calculations written down.

long-drawn adj. (also **long-drawn-out**) prolonged.

longeron /ˈlɒndʒərən/ n. longitudinal member of a plane's fuselage. [French]

longevity /lɒnˈdʒevɪtɪ/ n. long life. [Latin longus long, aevum age]

long face n. dismal expression.

longhand n. ordinary handwriting.

long haul n. 1 transport over a long distance. 2 prolonged effort or task.

longing /ˈlɒŋɪŋ/ —n. intense desire. —adj. having or showing this. □ **longingly** adv.

longitude /ˈlɒŋgɪtjuːd, ˈlɒndʒ-/ n. 1 angular distance east or west from a standard meridian such as Greenwich to the meridian of any place. 2 angular distance of a celestial body, esp. along the ecliptic. [Latin longitudo length, from longus long]

longitudinal /ˌlɒŋgɪˈtjuːdɪn(ə)l, ˌlɒndʒ-/ adj. 1 of or in length. 2 running lengthwise. 3 of longitude. □ **longitudinally** adv.

long johns n.pl. colloq. long underpants.

long jump n. athletic contest of jumping as far as possible along the ground in one leap.

long-life adj. (of milk etc.) treated to prolong its period of usability.

long-lived adj. having a long life, durable.

long-lost attrib. adj. that has been lost for a long time.

long-playing adj. (of a gramophone record) playing for about 20–30 minutes on each side.

long-range adj. 1 having a long range. 2 relating to a period of time far into the future (long-range weather forecast).

long-running adj. continuing for a long time (a long-running musical).

longshore attrib. adj. 1 existing on or frequenting the shore. 2 directed along the shore. [from along shore]

longshoreman n. US docker.

long shot n. 1 wild guess or venture. 2 bet at long odds.

long sight n. ability to see clearly only what is comparatively distant.

long-sighted adj. 1 having long sight. 2 far-sighted. □ **long-sightedness** n.

long-standing adj. that has long existed.

long-suffering adj. bearing provocation patiently.

long-term adj. of or for a long period of time (long-term plans).

long wave n. radio wave of frequency less than 300 kHz.

longways adv. (also **longwise**) = LENGTHWAYS.

long-winded adj. (of a speech or writing) tediously lengthy.

loo n. colloq. lavatory. [origin uncertain]

loofah /ˈluːfə/ n. rough bath-sponge made from the dried pod of a type of gourd. [Arabic]

look /lʊk/ —v. 1 a (often foll. by at, down, up, etc.) use one's sight; turn one's eyes in some direction. b turn one's eyes on; examine (looked me in the eyes; looked us up and down). 2 a make a visual or mental search (I'll look in the morning). b (foll. by at) consider; examine (must look at the facts). 3 (foll. by for) search for, seek, be on the watch for. 4 inquire (when one looks deeper). 5 have a specified appearance; seem (look a fool; future looks bleak). 6 (foll. by to) a consider; be concerned about (look to the future). b rely on (look to me for support). 7 (foll. by to + infin.) investigate. 8 (foll. by what, where, whether, etc.) ascertain or observe by sight. 9 (of a thing) face some direction. 10 indicate (emotion etc.) by one's looks. 11 (foll. by that) take care; make sure. 12 (foll. by to + infin.) aim (am looking to finish by eight). —n. 1 act of looking; gaze, glance. 2 (in sing. or pl.) appearance of a thing (by the look of it). 3 appearance of a face; expression (looked back). —int. (also **look here!**) calling attention, expressing a protest, etc. □ **look after** attend to; take care of. **look ahead** look to the future. **look back 1** (foll. by on, to) turn one's thoughts to (something past). 2 (usu. with neg.) cease to progress (he's never looked back). **look down on** (or **look down one's nose at**) regard with contempt or superiority. **look forward to** await (an expected event) eagerly or with specified feelings. **look in** make a short visit or call. **look on 1** (often foll. by as) regard. 2 be a spectator. **look oneself** appear well (esp. after illness etc.). **look out 1** direct one's sight or put one's head out of a window etc. 2 (often foll. by on, over, etc.) have a view or afford an outlook. 3 (foll. by for) be vigilant or prepared. 4 search for and produce. 5 (as imper.) warning of immediate danger

etc. **look over** inspect. **look smart** make haste. **look up 1** search for (esp. information in a book). **2** *colloq.* visit (a person). **3** improve in prospect. **look up to** respect or admire. **not like the look of** find alarming or suspicious. [Old English]

look-alike *n.* person or thing closely resembling another.

looker *n.* **1** person of a specified appearance (*good-looker*). **2** *colloq.* attractive woman.

looker-on *n.* (*pl.* **lookers-on**) spectator.

look-in *n. colloq.* chance of participation or success (*never gets a look-in*).

looking-glass *n.* mirror.

lookout *n.* **1** watch or looking out (*on the lookout*). **2 a** observation-post. **b** person etc. stationed to keep watch. **3** prospect (*it's a bad lookout*). **4** *colloq.* person's own concern (*that's your lookout*).

loom¹ *n.* apparatus for weaving. [Old English]

loom² *v.* **1** appear dimly, esp. as a vague and often threatening shape. **2** (of an event) be ominously close. [probably Low German or Dutch]

loon *n.* **1** a kind of diving bird. **2** *colloq.* crazy person (cf. LOONY). [Old Norse]

loony *slang* —*n.* (*pl.* **-ies**) lunatic. —*adj.* (**-ier, -iest**) crazy. □ **looniness** *n.* [abbreviation]

loony-bin *n. slang offens.* mental home or hospital.

loop —*n.* **1 a** figure produced by a curve, or a doubled thread etc., that crosses itself. **b** thing, path, etc., forming this figure. **2** similarly shaped attachment used as a fastening. **3** ring etc. as a handle etc. **4** contraceptive coil. **5** (in full **loop-line**) railway or telegraph line that diverges from a main line and joins it again. **6** skating or aerobatic manoeuvre describing a loop. **7** complete circuit for an electric current. **8** endless band of tape or film allowing continuous repetition. **9** sequence of computer operations repeated until some condition is satisfied. —*v.* **1** form or bend into a loop. **2** fasten with a loop or loops. **3** form a loop. **4** (also **loop the loop**) fly in a circle vertically. [origin unknown]

loophole *n.* **1** means of evading a rule etc. while infringing it. **2** narrow vertical slit in the wall of a fort etc.

loopy *adj.* (**-ier, -iest**) *slang* crazy, daft.

loose —*adj.* **1** not tightly held, fixed, etc. (*loose handle, loose stones*). **2** free from bonds or restraint. **3** not held together (*loose papers*). **4** not compact or dense (*loose soil*). **5** inexact (*loose translation*). **6** morally lax. **7** (of the tongue)

indiscreet. **8** tending to diarrhoea. **9** (in *comb.*) loosely (*loose-fitting*). —*v.* (**-sing**) **1** free; untie or detach; release. **2** relax (*loosed my hold*). **3** discharge (a missile). □ **at a loose end** unoccupied. **on the loose 1** escaped from captivity. **2** enjoying oneself freely. □ **loosely** *adv.* **looseness** *n.* **loosish** *adj.* [Old Norse]

loose cover *n.* removable cover for an armchair etc.

loose-leaf *adj.* (of a notebook etc.) with pages that can be removed and replaced.

loosen *v.* make or become loose or looser. □ **loosen a person's tongue** make a person talk freely. **loosen up 1** relax. **2** limber up.

loot —*n.* **1** spoil, booty. **2** *slang* money. —*v.* **1** rob or steal, esp. after rioting etc. **2** plunder. □ **looter** *n.* [Hindi]

lop *v.* (**-pp-**) **1 a** (often foll. by *off, away*) cut or remove (a part or parts) from a whole, esp. branches from a tree. **b** remove branches from (a tree). **2** (often foll. by *off*) remove (items) as superfluous. [Old English]

lope —*v.* (**-ping**) run with a long bounding stride. —*n.* long bounding stride. [Old Norse: related to LEAP]

lop-eared *adj.* having drooping ears.

lopsided *adj.* unevenly balanced. □ **lopsidedness** *n.* [related to LOB]

loquacious /ləˈkweɪʃəs/ *adj.* talkative. □ **loquacity** /-ˈkwæsɪtɪ/ *n.* [Latin *loquor* speak]

loquat /ˈləʊkwɒt/ *n.* **1** small yellow egg-shaped fruit. **2** tree bearing it. [Chinese]

lord —*n.* **1** master or ruler. **2** *hist.* feudal superior, esp. of a manor. **3** peer of the realm or person with the title *Lord*. **4** (**Lord**) (often prec. by *the*) God or Christ. **5** (**Lord**) **a** prefixed as the designation of a marquis, earl, viscount, or baron, or (to the Christian name) of the younger son of a duke or marquis. **b** (**the Lords**) = HOUSE OF LORDS. —*int.* (**Lord, good Lord**, etc.) expressing surprise, dismay, etc. □ **lord it over** domineer. [Old English, = bread-keeper: related to LOAF, WARD]

Lord Chamberlain *n.* official in charge of the Royal Household.

Lord Chancellor *n.* (also **Lord High Chancellor**) highest officer of the Crown, presiding in the House of Lords etc.

Lord Chief Justice *n.* president of the Queen's Bench Division.

Lord Lieutenant *n.* **1** chief executive authority and head of magistrates in each county. **2** *hist.* viceroy of Ireland.

ordly adj. (**-ier**, **-iest**) 1 haughty, imperious. 2 suitable for a lord. □ **lord- liness** n.

Lord Mayor n. title of the mayor in some large cities.

Lord Privy Seal n. senior Cabinet minister without official duties.

lords and ladies n. wild arum.

Lord's Day n. Sunday.

lordship n. (usu. **Lordship**) title used in addressing or referring to a man with the rank of Lord (*Your Lordship; His Lordship*). 2 (foll. by *over*) dominion, rule.

Lord's Prayer n. the Our Father.

Lords spiritual n.pl. bishops in the House of Lords.

Lord's Supper n. Eucharist.

Lords temporal n.pl. members of the House of Lords other than bishops.

lore n. a body of traditions and knowledge on a subject or held by a particular group (*bird lore, Gypsy lore*). [Old English: related to LEARN]

lorgnette /lɔːˈnjet/ n. pair of eyeglasses or opera-glasses on a long handle. [French *lorgner* to squint]

lorn adj. archaic desolate, forlorn. [Old English, past part. of LOSE]

lorry /ˈlɒrɪ/ n. (pl. **-ies**) large vehicle for transporting goods etc. [origin uncertain]

lose /luːz/ v. (**-sing**; past and past part. **lost**) 1 be deprived of or cease to have, esp. by negligence. 2 be deprived of (a person) by death. 3 become unable to find, follow, or understand (*lose one's way*). 4 let or have pass from one's control or reach (*lost my chance; lost his composure*). 5 be defeated in (a game, lawsuit, battle, etc.). 6 get rid of (*lost our pursuers; lose weight*). 7 forfeit (a right to a thing). 8 spend (time, efforts, etc.) to no purpose. 9 a suffer loss or detriment. **b** be worse off. 10 cause (a person) the loss of (*will lose you your job*). 11 (of a clock etc.) become slow. 12 (in passive) disappear, perish; be dead (*lost at sea; is a lost art*). □ **be lost** 1 be engrossed in. **be lost on** be wasted on, or not noticed or appreciated by. **be lost to** be no longer affected by or accessible to (*is lost to the world*). **be lost without** be dependent on (*am lost without my diary*). **get lost** slang (usu. in imper.) go away. **lose face** see FACE. **lose out** 1 (often foll. by *on*) colloq. be unsuccessful; not get a full chance or advantage (in). 2 (foll. by *to*) te beaten in competition or replaced by. [Old English]

loser n. 1 person or thing that loses, esp. a contest (*is a bad loser*). 2 colloq. person who regularly fails.

loss n. 1 losing or being lost. 2 thing or amount lost. 3 detriment resulting from losing. □ **at a loss** (sold etc.) for less than was paid for it. **be at a loss** be puzzled or uncertain. [probably back-formation from LOST]

loss-leader n. item sold at a loss to attract customers.

lost past and past part. of LOSE.

lost cause n. hopeless undertaking.

lot n. 1 colloq. (prec. by *a* or in *pl.*) a a large number or amount (*a lot of people; lots of milk*). b colloq. much (*a lot warmer; smiles a bit*). 2 a each of a set of objects used to make a chance selection. b this method of deciding (*chosen by lot*). 3 share or responsibility resulting from it. 4 person's destiny, fortune, or condition. 5 (esp. US) plot, allotment of land (*parking lot*). 6 article or set of articles for sale at an auction etc. 7 group of associated persons or things. □ **cast** (or **draw**) **lots** decide by lots. **throw in one's lot with** decide to share the fortunes of. **the** (or **the whole**) **lot** the total number or quantity. **a whole lot** colloq. very much (*is a whole lot better*). [Old English]

■ **Usage** In sense 1a, *a lot of* is somewhat informal, but acceptable in serious writing, whereas *lots of* is not acceptable.

loth var. of LOATH.

Lothario /ləˈθɑːrɪəʊ, -ˈθɛərɪəʊ/ n. (pl. **-s**) libertine [name of a character in a play]

lotion /ˈləʊʃ(ə)n/ n. medicinal or cosmetic liquid preparation applied externally. [Latin *lavo lot-* wash]

lottery /ˈlɒtərɪ/ n. (pl. **-ies**) 1 means of raising money by selling numbered tickets and giving prizes to the holders of numbers drawn at random. 2 thing whose success is governed by chance. [Dutch: related to LOT]

lotto /ˈlɒtəʊ/ n. game of chance like bingo, but with numbers drawn instead of called. [Italian]

lotus /ˈləʊtəs/ n. 1 legendary plant inducing luxurious languor when eaten. 2 a kind of water lily etc., esp. used symbolically in Hinduism and Buddhism. [Greek *lōtos*]

lotus-eater n. person given to indolent enjoyment.

lotus position n. cross-legged position of meditation with the feet resting on the thighs.

loud —adj. 1 strongly audible, noisy. 2 (of colours etc.) gaudy, obtrusive. —adv. loudly. □ **out loud** aloud. □ **loudish**

adj. **loudly** *adv.* **loudness** *n.* [Old English]

loud hailer *n.* electronic device for amplifying the voice.

loudspeaker *n.* apparatus that converts electrical signals into sound.

lough /lɒk, lɒx/ *n. Ir.* lake, arm of the sea. [Irish: related to LOCH]

lounge —*v.* (**-ging**) **1** recline comfortably, loll. **2** stand or move about idly. —*n.* **1** place for lounging, esp.: **a** a sitting-room in a house. **b** a public room (e.g. in a hotel). **c** a place in an airport etc. with seats for waiting passengers. **2** spell of lounging. [origin uncertain]

lounge bar *n.* more comfortable bar in a pub etc.

lounge suit *n.* man's suit for ordinary day (esp. business) wear.

lour *v.* (also **lower**) **1** frown; look sullen. **2** (of the sky etc.) look dark and threatening. [origin unknown]

louse —*n.* **1** (*pl.* **lice**) parasitic insect. **2** (*pl.* **louses**) *slang* contemptible person. —*v.* (**-sing**) delouse. □ **louse up** *slang* make a mess of. [Old English]

lousy /ˈlaʊzɪ/ *adj.* (**-ier**, **-iest**) **1** *colloq.* very bad; disgusting; ill (*feel lousy*). **2** (often foll. by *with*) *colloq.* well supplied, teeming. **3** infested with lice. □ **lousily** *adv.* **lousiness** *n.*

lout *n.* rough-mannered person. □ **loutish** *adj.* [origin uncertain]

louvre /ˈluːvə(r)/ *n.* (also **louver**) **1** each of a set of overlapping slats designed to admit air and some light and exclude rain. **2** domed structure on a roof with side openings for ventilation etc. □ **louvred** *adj.* [French *lover* skylight]

lovable /ˈlʌvəb(ə)l/ *adj.* (also **loveable**) inspiring love or affection.

lovage /ˈlʌvɪdʒ/ *n.* herb used for flavouring etc. [French *levesche* from Latin *ligusticum* Ligurian]

lovat /ˈlʌvət/ *n.* & *adj.* muted green. [*Lovat* in Scotland]

love /lʌv/ —*n.* **1** deep affection or fondness. **2** sexual passion. **3** sexual relations. **4 a** a beloved one; sweetheart (often as a form of address). **b** *colloq.* form of address regardless of affection. **5** *colloq.* person of whom one is fond. **6** affectionate greetings (*give him my love*). **7** (in games) no score; nil. —*v.* (**-ving**) **1** feel love or a deep fondness for. **2** delight in; admire; greatly cherish. **3** *colloq.* like very much (*loves books*). **4** (foll. by verbal noun, or *to* + infin.) be inclined, as a habit; greatly enjoy (*children love dressing up*; *loves to run*). □ **fall in love** (often foll. by *with*) suddenly begin to love. **for love** for pleasure not profit. **for the love of** for the sake of. **in love** (often foll. by *with*)

enamoured (of). **make love** (often foll. by *to*) **1** have sexual intercourse (with). **2** *archaic* pay amorous attention (to). **not for love or money** *colloq.* not in any circumstances. [Old English]

loveable var. of LOVABLE.

love affair *n.* romantic or sexual relationship between two people.

love-bird *n.* parrot, esp. one seeming to show great affection for its mate.

love bite *n.* bruise made by a partner's biting etc. during lovemaking.

love-child *n.* child of unmarried parents.

love-hate relationship *n.* intense relationship involving ambivalent emotions.

love-in-a-mist *n.* blue-flowered cultivated plant.

loveless *adj.* unloving or unloved or both.

love-lies-bleeding *n.* cultivated plant with drooping spikes of purple-red blooms.

lovelorn *adj.* pining from unrequited love.

lovely —*adj.* (**-ier**, **-iest**) **1** *colloq.* pleasing, delightful **2** beautiful. —*n.* (*pl.* **-ies**) *colloq.* pretty woman. □ **lovely and** *colloq.* delightfully (*lovely and warm*). □ **loveliness** *n.* [Old English]

lovemaking *n.* **1** sexual play, esp. intercourse. **2** *archaic* courtship.

love-nest *n. colloq.* secluded retreat for (esp. illicit) lovers.

lover *n.* **1** person in love with another. **2** person with whom another is having sexual relations. **3** (in *pl.*) unmarried couple in love or having sexual relations. **4** person who likes or enjoys a specified thing (*music lover*).

love-seat *n.* small sofa in the shape of an S, with two seats facing in opposite directions.

lovesick *adj.* languishing with love.

lovey-dovey /ˌlʌvɪˈdʌvɪ/ *adj. colloq.* fondly affectionate, sentimental.

loving —*adj.* feeling or showing love; affectionate. —*n.* affection; love. □ **lovingly** *adv.*

loving-cup *n.* two-handled drinking-cup.

low[1] /ləʊ/ —*adj.* **1** not high or tall (*low wall*). **2 a** not elevated in position (*low altitude*). **b** of or near the horizon. **2** of or in humble rank or position (*of low birth*). **4** of small or less than normal amount, extent, or intensity (*low temperature*; *low in calories*). **5** small or reduced in quantity (*stocks are low*). **6** coming below the normal level (*low neck*). **7** dejected; lacking vigour (*feeling low*). **8** (of a sound) not shrill or

loud. **9** not exalted or sublime; common-place. **10** unfavourable (*low opinion*). **11** abject, mean, vulgar (*low cunning*; *low slang*). **12** (of a computer language) —*n.* **1** low or the lowest level or number (*pound reached a new low*). **2** area of low pressure. —*adv.* **1** in or to a low position or state. **2** in a low tone (*speak low*). **3** (of a sound) at or to a low pitch. □ **lowish** *adj.* **lowness** *n.* [Old Norse]

low² /ləʊ/ —*n.* sound made by cattle; moo. —*v.* make this sound. [Old English]

low-born *adj.* of humble birth.

lowbrow —*adj.* not intellectual or cul-tured. —*n.* lowbrow person.

Low Church *n.* section of the Church of England attaching little importance to ritual, priestly authority, and the sacraments.

low-class *adj.* of low quality or social class.

low comedy *n.* comedy bordering on farce.

Low Countries *n.pl.* the Netherlands, Belgium, and Luxemburg.

low-down —*adj.* mean, dishonourable. —*n. colloq.* (prec. by *the*; usu. foll. by *on*) relevant information.

lower¹ —*adj.* (*compar.* of LOW), **1** less high in position or status. **2** situated below another part (*lower lip*). **3 a** situated on less high land (*Lower Egypt*). **b** (of a mammal, plant, etc.) evolved to only a slight degree. —*adv.* in or to a lower position, status, etc. □ **lower-most** *adj.*

lower² *v.* **1** let or haul down. **2** make or become lower. **3** degrade.

lower³ var. of LOUR.

lower case *n.* small letters.

lower class *n.* working class.

Lower House *n.* larger and usu. elected body in a legislature, esp. the House of Commons.

lowest *adj.* (*superl.* of LOW) least high in position or status.

lowest common denominator *n.* **1** *Math.* lowest common multiple of the denominators of several fractions. **2** the worst or most vulgar common feature of members of a group.

lowest common multiple *n. Math.* least quantity that is a multiple of two or more given quantities.

low frequency *n.* frequency, esp. in radio, 30 to 300 kilohertz.

low gear *n.* gear such that the driven end of a transmission revolves slower than the driving end.

low-grade *adj.* of low quality.

low-key *adj.* lacking intensity, re-strained.

lowland —*n.* (usu. in *pl.*) low-lying country. —*adj.* of or in lowland. □ **low-lander** *n.*

low-level *adj.* (of a computer language) close in form to machine code.

lowly *adj.* (**-ier, -iest**) humble; unpre-tentious. □ **lowliness** *n.*

low-lying *adj.* near to the ground or sea level.

low-pitched *adj.* **1** (of a sound) low. **2** (of a roof) having only a slight slope.

low pressure *n.* **1** low degree of ac-tivity or exertion. **2** atmospheric con-dition with the pressure below average.

low-rise —*adj.* (of a building) having few storeys. —*n.* such a building.

low season *n.* period of fewest visitors at a resort etc.

Low Sunday *n.* Sunday after Easter.

low tide *n.* (also **low water**) time or level of the tide at its ebb.

loyal /ˈlɔɪəl/ *adj.* **1** (often foll. by *to*) faithful. **2** steadfast in allegiance etc. □ **loyally** *adv.* **loyalty** *n.* (*pl.* **-ies**). [Latin: related to LEGAL]

loyalist *n.* **1** person who remains loyal to the legitimate sovereign etc. **2** (**Loyal-ist**) (esp. extremist) supporter of union between Great Britain and Northern Ireland. □ **loyalism** *n.*

loyal toast *n.* toast to the sovereign.

lozenge /ˈlɒzɪndʒ/ *n.* **1** rhombus. **2** small sweet or medicinal tablet to be dissolved in the mouth. **3** lozenge-shaped orna-ment. [French]

LP *abbr.* long-playing (record).

L-plate *n.* sign bearing the letter L, attached to a vehicle to show that it is being driven by a learner. [from PLATE]

LPO *abbr.* London Philharmonic Or-chestra.

LSD *abbr.* lysergic acid diethylamide, a powerful hallucinogenic drug.

l.s.d. /ˌeles'diː/ *n.* (also **£.s.d.**) **1** *hist.* pounds, shillings, and pence (in former British currency). **2** money, riches. [Latin *librae, solidi, denarii*]

LSE *abbr.* London School of Economics.

LSO *abbr.* London Symphony Orches-tra.

Ltd. *abbr.* Limited.

Lt. *abbr.* **1** Lieutenant. **2** light.

Lu *symb.* lutetium.

lubber *n.* clumsy fellow; lout. [origin uncertain]

lubricant /ˈluːbrɪkənt/ *n.* substance used to reduce friction.

lubricate /ˈluːbrɪkeɪt/ *v.* (**-ting**) **1** apply oil or grease etc. to. **2** make slippery. □ **lubrication** /-ˈkeɪʃ(ə)n/ *n.* **lubricator** *n.* [Latin *lubricus* slippery]

lubricious /luːˈbrɪʃəs/ *adj.* **1** slippery. **2** lewd. □ **lubricity** *n.* [Latin: related to LUBRICATE]

lucerne /luːˈsɜːn/ *n.* = ALFALFA. [Provençal, = glow-worm, referring to its shiny seeds]

lucid /ˈluːsɪd/ *adj.* **1** expressing or expressed clearly. **2** sane. □ **lucidity** /-ˈsɪdɪtɪ/ *n.* **lucidly** *adv.* **lucidness** *n.* [Latin *lux luc-* light]

Lucifer /ˈluːsɪfə(r)/ *n.* Satan. [Latin: related to LUCID, *fero* bring]

luck *n.* **1** good or bad fortune. **2** circumstances of life (beneficial or not) brought by this. **3** good fortune; success due to chance (*in luck; out of luck*). □ **no such luck** *colloq.* unfortunately not. [Low German or Dutch]

luckless *adj.* unlucky; ending in failure.

lucky *adj.* (**-ier, -iest**) **1** having or resulting from good luck. **2** bringing good luck (*lucky charm*). □ **luckily** *adv.*

lucky dip *n.* tub containing articles varying in value and chosen at random.

lucrative /ˈluːkrətɪv/ *adj.* profitable. □ **lucratively** *adv.* **lucrativeness** *n.* [Latin: related to LUCRE]

lucre /ˈluːkə(r)/ *n. derog.* financial gain. [Latin *lucrum* gain]

Luddite /ˈlʌdaɪt/ —*n.* **1** person opposed to industrial progress or new technology. **2** *hist.* member of a band of English artisans who destroyed machinery (1811–16). —*adj.* of the Luddites. □ **Luddism** *n.* [Ned *Lud*, destroyer of machinery]

ludicrous /ˈluːdɪkrəs/ *adj.* absurd, ridiculous, laughable. □ **ludicrously** *adv.* **ludicrousness** *n.* [Latin *ludicrum* stage play]

ludo /ˈluːdəʊ/ *n.* simple board-game played with dice and counters. [Latin, = I play]

luff *v.* (also *absol.*) **1** steer (a ship) nearer the wind. **2** raise or lower (a crane's jib). [French, probably from Low German]

lug —*v.* (**-gg-**) **1** drag or carry with effort. **2** pull hard. —*n.* **1** hard or rough pull. **2** *colloq.* ear. **3** projection on an object by which it may be carried, fixed in place, etc. [probably Scandinavian]

luggage /ˈlʌgɪdʒ/ *n.* suitcases, bags, etc., for a traveller's belongings. [from LUG]

lugger /ˈlʌgə(r)/ *n.* small ship with four-cornered sails. [from LUGSAIL]

lughole *n. slang* ear.

lugsail *n.* four-cornered sail on a yard. [probably from LUG]

lugubrious /luːˈguːbrɪəs/ *adj.* doleful. □ **lugubriously** *adv.* **lugubriousness** *n.* [Latin *lugeo* mourn]

lugworm *n.* large marine worm used as bait. [origin unknown]

lukewarm *adj.* **1** moderately warm; tepid. **2** unenthusiastic, indifferent. [Old English (now dial.) *luke* warm, WARM]

lull —*v.* **1** soothe or send to sleep. **2** (usu. foll. by *into*) deceive (a person) into undue confidence (*lulled into a false sense of security*). **3** allay (suspicions etc.), usu. by deception. **4** (of noise, a storm, etc.) abate or fall quiet. —*n.* temporary quiet period. [imitative]

lullaby /ˈlʌləbaɪ/ *n.* (*pl.* **-ies**) soothing song to send a child to sleep. [related to LULL]

lumbago /lʌmˈbeɪgəʊ/ *n.* rheumatic pain in the muscles of the lower back. [Latin *lumbus* loin]

lumbar /ˈlʌmbə(r)/ *adj.* of the lower back area. [as LUMBAGO]

lumbar puncture *n.* withdrawal of spinal fluid from the lower back for diagnosis.

lumber /ˈlʌmbə(r)/ —*n.* **1** disused and cumbersome articles. **2** partly prepared timber. —*v.* **1** (usu. foll. by *with*) leave (a person etc.) with something unwanted or unpleasant. **2** (usu. foll. by *up*) obstruct, fill inconveniently. **3** cut and prepare forest timber. **4** move in a slow clumsy way. [origin uncertain]

lumberjack *n.* person who fells and transports lumber.

lumber-jacket *n.* jacket of the kind worn by lumberjacks.

lumber-room *n.* room where disused things are kept.

luminary /ˈluːmɪnərɪ/ *n.* (*pl.* **-ies**) **1** *literary* natural light-giving body. **2** wise or inspiring person. **3** celebrated member of a group (*show-business luminaries*). [Latin *lumen lumin-* light]

luminescence /ˌluːmɪˈnes(ə)ns/ *n.* emission of light without heat. □ **luminescent** *adj.*

luminous /ˈluːmɪnəs/ *adj.* **1** shedding light. **2** phosphorescent, visible in darkness (*luminous paint*). □ **luminosity** /-ˈnɒsɪtɪ/ *n.*

lump[1] —*n.* **1** compact shapeless mass. **2** tumour, swelling, bruise. **3** heavy, dull, or ungainly person. **4** (prec. by *the*) *slang* casual workers in the building trade. —*v.* **1** (usu. foll. by *together* etc.) treat as all alike; put together in a lump. **2** (of sauce etc.) become lumpy. □ **lump in the throat** feeling of pressure there, caused by emotion. [Scandinavian]

lump[2] *v. colloq.* put up with ungraciously (*like it or lump it*). [imitative]

lumpectomy /lʌmˈpektəmɪ/ *n.* (*pl.* **-ies**) surgical removal of a lump from the breast.

lumpish *adj.* **1** heavy and clumsy. **2** stupid, lethargic.

lump sugar *n.* sugar in cubes.

lump sum *n.* **1** sum covering a number of items. **2** money paid down at once.

lumpy *adj.* (**-ier, -iest**) full of or covered with lumps. □ **lumpily** *adv.* **lumpiness** *n.*

lunacy /'lu:nəsi/ *n.* (*pl.* **-ies**) **1** insanity. **2** mental unsoundness. **3** great folly.

lunar /'lu:nə(r)/ *adj.* of, like, concerned with, or determined by the moon. [Latin *luna* moon]

lunar module *n.* small craft for travelling between the moon and a spacecraft in orbit around it.

lunar month *n.* **1** period of the moon's revolution, esp. the interval between new moons (about 29½ days). **2** (in general use) four weeks.

lunate /'lu:neit/ *adj.* crescent-shaped.

lunatic /'lu:nətik/ *n.* **1** insane person. **2** wildly foolish person. —*adj.* insane; extremely reckless or foolish. [related to LUNACY]

lunatic asylum *n. hist.* mental home or hospital.

lunatic fringe *n.* extreme or eccentric minority group.

lunation /lu:'neiʃ(ə)n/ *n.* interval between new moons, about 29½ days. [medieval Latin: related to LUNAR]

lunch —*n.* midday meal. —*v.* **1** take lunch. **2** entertain to lunch. [shortening of LUNCHEON]

luncheon /'lʌntʃ(ə)n/ *n. formal* lunch. [origin unknown]

luncheon meat *n.* tinned meat loaf of pork etc.

luncheon voucher *n.* voucher issued to employees and exchangeable for food at many restaurants and shops.

lung *n.* either of the pair of respiratory organs in humans and many other vertebrates. [Old English related to LIGHT²]

lunge —*n.* **1** sudden movement forward. **2** the basic attacking move in fencing. **3** long rope on which a horse is held and made to circle round its trainer. —*v.* (**-ging**) (usu. foll. by *at, out*) deliver or make a lunge. [French *allonger* from *long* LONG¹]

lupin /'lu:pin/ *n.* cultivated plant with long tapering spikes of flowers. [related to LUPINE]

lupine /'lu:pain/ *adj.* of or like wolves. [Latin *lupinus* from *lupus* wolf]

lupus /'lu:pəs/ *n.* autoimmune inflammatory skin disease. [Latin, = wolf]

lurch¹ —*n.* stagger; sudden unsteady movement or leaning. —*v.* stagger; move or progress unsteadily. [originally Naut., of uncertain origin]

lurch² *n.* □ **leave in the lurch** desert (a friend etc.) in difficulties. [obsolete French *lourche* a kind of backgammon]

lurcher /'lɜːtʃə(r)/ *n.* crossbred dog, usu. a dog crossed with a greyhound. [related to LURK]

lure —*v.* (**-ring**) (usu. foll. by *away, into*) entice. **2** recall with a lure. —*n.* **1** thing used to entice (usu. foll. by *of*) enticing quality. **2** (of a pursuit etc.) **3** falconer's apparatus for recalling a hawk. [French from Germanic]

Lurex /'ljuəreks/ *n. propr.* **1** type of yarn incorporating a glittering metallic thread. **2** fabric made from this.

lurid /'ljuərɪd/ *adj.* **1** bright and glaring in colour. **2** sensational, shocking (*lurid details*). **3** ghastly, wan (*lurid complexion*). □ **luridly** *adv.* [Latin]

lurk *v.* **1** linger furtively. **2** (as **lurking** *adj.*) dormant (*a lurking suspicion*). [perhaps from LOUR]

luscious /'lʌʃəs/ *adj.* **1** richly sweet in taste or smell. **2** (of style) over-rich. **3** voluptuously attractive. [perhaps related to DELICIOUS]

lush¹ *adj.* **1** (of vegetation) luxuriant and succulent. **2** luxurious. **3** *slang* excellent. [origin uncertain]

lush² *n. slang* alcoholic, drunkard. [origin uncertain]

lust —*n.* **1** strong sexual desire. **2** (usu. foll. by *for, of*) passionate desire for or enjoyment of (*lust for power, lust of battle*). **3** sensuous appetite regarded as sinful (*lusts of the flesh*). —*v.* (usu. foll. by *after, for*) have a strong or excessive desire. □ **lustful** *adj.* **lustfully** *adv.* [Old English]

lustre /'lʌstə(r)/ *n.* (*US* **luster**) **1** gloss, shining surface. **2** brilliance, splendour. **3** iridescent glaze on pottery and porcelain. □ **lustrous** *adj.* [Latin *lustro* illumine]

lusty *adj.* (**-ier, -iest**) **1** healthy and strong. **2** vigorous, lively. □ **lustily** *adv.* **lustiness** *n.* [from LUST]

lutanist var. of LUTENIST.

lute¹ /lu:t/ *n.* guitar-like instrument with a long neck and a pear-shaped body. [Arabic]

lute² /lu:t/ *n.* clay or cement for making joints airtight etc. —*v.* (**-ting**) apply lute to. [Latin *lutum* mud]

lutenist /'lu:tənɪst/ *n.* (also **lutanist**) lute-player. [related to LUTE¹]

lutetium /lu:'ti:ʃəm/ *n.* silvery metallic element, the heaviest of the lanthanide series. [*Lutetia*, ancient name of Paris]

Lutheran /'lu:θərən/ —*n.* **1** follower of Luther. **2** member of the Lutheran Church. —*adj.* of Luther, or the Protestant Reformation and the doctrines associated with him. □ **Lutheranism** *n.* [Martin *Luther*, religious reformer]

lux n. (pl. same) the SI unit of illumination. [Latin]

luxuriant /lʌgˈzjʊərɪənt/ adj. 1 growing profusely. 2 exuberant. 3 florid. □ **luxuriance** n. **luxuriantly** adv. [Latin: related to LUXURY]

■ **Usage** Luxuriant is sometimes confused with luxurious.

luxuriate /lʌgˈzjʊərɪˌeɪt/ v. (-ting) 1 (foll. by in) take self-indulgent delight in, enjoy as a luxury. 2 relax in comfort. [Latin]

luxurious /lʌgˈzjʊərɪəs/ adj. 1 supplied with luxuries. 2 extremely comfortable. 3 fond of luxury. □ **luxuriously** adv. [Latin: related to LUXURY]

■ **Usage** Luxurious is sometimes confused with luxuriant.

luxury /ˈlʌkʃərɪ/ n. (pl. -ies) 1 choice or costly surroundings, possessions, etc. 2 thing affording comfort or enjoyment but not essential. 3 (attrib.) comfortable and expensive (luxury flat). [Latin luxus abundance]

LV abbr. luncheon voucher.

Lw symb. lawrencium.

-ly[1] suffix forming adjectives, esp. from nouns, meaning: 1 having the qualities of (princely). 2 recurring at intervals of (daily). [Old English]

-ly[2] suffix forming adverbs from adjectives (boldly; happily). [Old English]

lychee /ˈlaɪtʃiː, ˈliː-/ n. (also **litchi**, **lichee**) 1 sweet white juicy fruit in a brown skin. 2 tree, orig. from China, bearing this. [Chinese]

lych-gate var. of LICH-GATE.

Lycra /ˈlaɪkrə/ n. propr. elastic polyurethane fabric used esp. for sportswear.

lye /laɪ/ n. 1 water made alkaline with wood ashes. 2 any alkaline solution for washing. [Old English]

lying pres. part. of LIE[1], LIE[2].

lymph /lɪmf/ n. 1 colourless fluid from the tissues of the body, containing white blood cells. 2 this fluid used as a vaccine. [Latin lympha]

lymphatic /lɪmˈfætɪk/ adj. 1 of, secreting, or conveying lymph. 2 (of a person) pale, flabby, or sluggish.

lymphatic system n. network of vessels conveying lymph.

lymph gland n. (also **lymph node**) small mass of tissue in the lymphatic system.

lymphoma /lɪmˈfəʊmə/ n. (pl. -s or -mata) tumour of the lymph nodes.

lynch /lɪntʃ/ v. (of a mob) put (a person) to death without a legal trial. □ **lynching** n. [originally US, after Lynch, 18th-c. Justice of the Peace in Virginia]

lynch law n. procedure followed when a person is lynched.

lynx /lɪŋks/ n. (pl. same or -es) wild cat with a short tail and spotted fur. [Greek lugx]

lynx-eyed adj. keen-sighted.

lyre /ˈlaɪə(r)/ n. ancient U-shaped stringed instrument. [Greek lura]

lyre-bird n. Australian bird, the male of which has a lyre-shaped tail display.

lyric /ˈlɪrɪk/ —adj. 1 (of poetry) expressing the writer's emotions, usu. briefly and in stanzas. 2 (of a poet) writing in this manner. 3 meant or fit to be sung, songlike. —n. 1 lyric poem. 2 (in pl.) words of a song. [Latin: related to LYRE]

lyrical adj. 1 = LYRIC. 2 resembling, or using language appropriate to, lyric poetry. 3 colloq. highly enthusiastic (wax lyrical about). □ **lyrically** adv.

lyricism /ˈlɪrɪˌsɪz(ə)m/ n. quality of being lyric.

lyricist /ˈlɪrɪsɪst/ n. writer of (esp. popular) lyrics.

lysergic acid diethylamide /laɪˈsɜːdʒɪk ˌdaɪəˈθaɪləˌmaɪd/ n. = LSD. [from hydrolysis, ergot, -IC]

-lysis comb. form forming nouns denoting disintegration or decomposition (electrolysis). [Greek lusis loosening]

-lyte suffix forming nouns denoting substances that can be decomposed (electrolyte). [Greek lutos loosened]

M¹ /em/ n. (pl. **Ms** or **M's**) **1** thirteenth letter of the alphabet. **2** (as a Roman numeral) 1,000.

M² abbr. (also **M.**) **1** Master. **2** Monsieur. **3** motorway. **4** mega-.

m abbr. (also **m.**) **1** male. **2** masculine. **3** married. **4** mile(s). **5** metre(s). **6** milli-.

MA abbr. Master of Arts.

ma /mɑː/ n. colloq. mother. [abbreviation of MAMA]

ma'am /mæm, mɑːm, məm/ n. madam (used esp. in addressing royalty). [contraction]

mac n. (also **mack**) colloq. mackintosh. [abbreviation]

macabre /məˈkɑːbr/ adj. grim, gruesome. [French]

macadam /məˈkædəm/ n. **1** broken stone as material for road-making. **2** = TARMACADAM. □ **macadamize** v. (also **-ise**) (**-zing** or **-sing**) [McAdam, name of a surveyor]

macadamia /ˌmækəˈdeɪmɪə/ n. edible seed of an Australian tree. [Macadam, name of a chemist]

macaque /məˈkæk/ n. a kind of monkey, e.g. the rhesus monkey and Barbary ape, with prominent cheek-pouches. [Portuguese, = monkey]

macaroni /ˌmækəˈrəʊnɪ/ n. small pasta tubes. [Italian from Greek]

macaroon /ˌmækəˈruːn/ n. small almond cake or biscuit. [Italian: related to MACARONI]

macaw /məˈkɔː/ n. long-tailed brightly coloured American parrot. [Portuguese macao]

McCarthyism /məˈkɑːθɪɪz(ə)m/ n. hist. hunting out and sacking of Communists in the US. [McCarthy, name of a senator]

McCoy /məˈkɔɪ/ n. □ **the real McCoy** colloq. the real thing; the genuine article. [origin uncertain]

mace¹ n. **1** staff of office, esp. symbol of the Speaker's authority in the House of Commons. **2** person bearing this. [French from Romanic]

mace² n. dried outer covering of the nutmeg as a spice. [Latin macir]

macédoine /ˈmæsɪdwɑːn/ n. mixed vegetables or fruit, esp. diced or jellied. [French]

macerate /ˈmæsəreɪt/ v. (**-ting**) **1** soften by soaking. **2** waste away by fasting. □ **maceration** /-ˈreɪʃ(ə)n/ n. [Latin]

Mach /mɑːk/ n. (in full **Mach number**) ratio of the speed of a body to the speed of sound in the surrounding medium. [Mach, name of a physicist]

machete /məˈʃetɪ/ n. broad heavy knife, esp. of Central America. [Spanish from Latin]

Machiavellian /ˌmækɪəˈvelɪən/ adj. elaborately cunning; scheming, unscrupulous. □ **Machiavellianism** n. [Machiavelli, name of a political writer]

machination /ˌmækɪˈneɪʃ(ə)n/ n. (usu. in pl.) intrigue. □ **machinate** /ˈmæk-/ v. (**-ting**). [Latin: related to MACHINE]

machine /məˈʃiːn/ n. & v. —n. **1** apparatus for applying mechanical power, having several interrelated parts. **2** particular machine, esp. a vehicle or an electrical or electronic apparatus. **3** controlling system of an organization etc. (party machine). **4** person who acts mechanically. **5** (esp. in comb.) mechanical dispenser with slots for coins (cigarette machine). —v. (**-ting**) make or operate on with a machine. [Greek mēkhanē]

machine code n. (also **machine language**) computer language for a particular computer.

machine-gun n. & v. —n. automatic gun giving continuous fire. —v. □ **-nn-** shoot at with a machine-gun.

machine-readable adj. in a form that a computer can process.

machinery n. (pl. **-ies**) **1** machines. **2** mechanism. **3** (usu. foll. by of) organized system. **4** (usu. foll. by for) means devised.

machine tool n. mechanically operated tool.

machinist n. **1** person who operates a machine, esp. a sewing-machine or a machine tool. **2** person who makes machinery.

machismo /məˈkɪzməʊ, -ˈtʃɪzməʊ/ n. being macho; masculine pride. [Spanish]

macho /ˈmætʃəʊ/ adj. aggressively masculine. [from MACHISMO]

Mach one n. (also **Mach two** etc.) the speed (or twice etc. the speed) of sound.

macintosh var. of MACKINTOSH.

mack var. of MAC.

mackerel /ˈmækr(ə)l/ n. (pl. same or **-s**) marine fish used as food. [Anglo-French]

mackerel sky *n.* sky dappled with rows of small white fleecy clouds.

mackintosh /'mækɪn,tɒʃ/ *n.* (also **macintosh**) 1 waterproof coat or cloak. 2 cloth waterproofed with rubber. [*Macintosh,* name of its inventor]

macramé /mə'krɑːmɪ/ *n.* 1 art of knotting cord or string in patterns to make decorative articles. 2 work so made. [Arabic, = bedspread]

macro- *comb. form* 1 long. 2 large, large-scale. [Greek *makros* long]

macrobiotic /,mækrəʊbaɪ'ɒtɪk/ *–adj.* of a diet intended to prolong life, esp. consisting of wholefoods. *–n.* (in *pl.*; treated as *sing.*) theory of such a diet. [Greek *bios* life]

macrocarpa /,mækrəʊ'kɑːpə/ *n.* evergreen tree, often cultivated for hedges or wind-breaks. [Greek MACRO-, *karpos* fruit]

macrocosm /'mækrəʊ,kɒz(ə)m/ *n.* 1 universe. 2 the whole of a complex structure. [from MACRO-, COSMOS]

macroeconomics /,mækrəʊiːkə-'nɒmɪks/ *n.* the study of the economy as a whole. □ **macroeconomic** *adj.*

macron /'mækrɒn/ *n.* mark (¯) over a long or stressed vowel. [Greek, neuter of *makros*]

macroscopic /,mækrəʊ'skɒpɪk/ *adj.* 1 visible to the naked eye. 2 regarded in terms of large units.

macula /'mækjʊlə/ *n.* (*pl.* **-lae** /-liː/) dark, esp. permanent, spot in the skin. □ **maculation** /-'leɪʃ(ə)n/ *n.* [Latin, = spot, mesh]

mad *adj.* (**madder, maddest**) 1 insane; frenzied. 2 wildly foolish. 3 (often foll. by *about, on*) *colloq.* wildly excited or enamoured. 4 *colloq.* angry. 5 (of an animal) rabid. 6 wildly light-hearted. □ **like mad** *colloq.* with great energy or enthusiasm. □ **madness** *n.* [Old English]

madam /'mædəm/ *n.* 1 polite or respectful form of address or mode of reference to a woman. 2 *colloq.* conceited or precocious girl or young woman. 3 woman brothel-keeper. [related to MADAME]

Madame /mə'dɑːm, 'mædəm/ *n.* 1 (*pl.* **Mesdames** /meɪ'dɑːm, -'dæm/) Mrs or madam (used of or to a French-speaking woman). 2 (**madame**) = MADAM 1. [French *ma dame* my lady]

madcap *–adj.* wildly impulsive. *–n.* wildly impulsive person.

mad cow disease *n. colloq.* = BSE.

madden *v.* 1 make or become mad. 2 irritate. □ **maddening** *adj.* **maddeningly** *adv.*

madder /'mædə(r)/ *n.* 1 herbaceous plant with yellowish flowers. 2 a red dye from its root. b its synthetic substitute. [Old English]

made *past* and *past part.* of MAKE. *–adj.* 1 built or formed (*well-made*). 2 successful (*self-made man; be made*). □ **have (or have got) it made** *colloq.* be sure of success. **made for** ideally suited to. **made of** consisting of. **made of money** *colloq.* very rich.

Madeira /mə'dɪərə/ *n.* 1 fortified white wine from Madeira. 2 (in full **Madeira cake**) a kind of sponge cake.

Mademoiselle /,mædəmwə'zel/ *n.* (*pl.* **Mesdemoiselles** /,meɪdm-/) 1 Miss or madam (used of or to an unmarried French-speaking woman). 2 (**mademoiselle**) a young Frenchwoman. b French governess. [French *ma my demoiselle* DAMSEL]

madly *adv.* 1 in a mad manner. 2 *colloq.* a passionately. b extremely.

madman *n.* man who is mad.

Madonna /mə'dɒnə/ *n.* 1 (prec. by *the*) the Virgin Mary. 2 (**madonna**) picture or statue of her. [Italian, = my lady]

madrigal /'mædrɪɡ(ə)l/ *n.* part-song usu. unaccompanied, for several voices. [Italian]

madwoman *n.* woman who is mad.

maelstrom /'meɪlstrɒm/ *n.* 1 great whirlpool. 2 state of confusion. [Dutch]

maenad /'miːnæd/ *n.* 1 bacchante. 2 frenzied woman. □ **maenadic** /-'nædɪk/ *adj.* [Greek *mainomai* rave]

maestro /'maɪstrəʊ/ *n.* (*pl.* **maestri** /-striː/ or **-s**) 1 distinguished musician, esp. a conductor, composer, or teacher. 2 great performer in any sphere. [Italian]

Mae West /meɪ 'west/ *n. slang* inflatable life-jacket. [name of a film actress]

Mafia /'mæfɪə/ *n.* 1 organized body of criminals, orig. in Sicily, now also in Italy and the US. 2 (**mafia**) group regarded as exerting an intimidating and corrupt power. [Italian dial., = bragging]

Mafioso /,mæfɪ'əʊsəʊ/ *n.* (*pl.* **Mafiosi** /-siː/) member of the Mafia. [Italian: related to MAFIA]

mag *n. colloq.* = MAGAZINE 1. [abbreviation]

magazine /,mægə'ziːn/ *n.* 1 illustrated periodical publication containing articles, stories, etc. 2 chamber holding cartridges to be fed automatically to the breech of a gun. 3 similar device in a slide projector etc. 4 military store for arms etc. 5 store for explosives. [Arabic *makazin*]

magenta /mə'dʒentə/ *–n.* 1 shade of crimson. 2 aniline crimson dye. *–adj.* of

or coloured with magenta. [*Magenta* in N. Italy]

maggot /'mægət/ *n.* larva, esp. of the housefly or bluebottle. □ **maggoty** *adj.* [perhaps an alteration of *maddock*, from Old Norse]

magi *pl.* of MAGUS.

magic /'mædʒɪk/ *n.* **1 a** supposed art of influencing or controlling events supernaturally. **b** witchcraft. **3** conjuring tricks. **3** inexplicable influence. **4** enchanting quality or phenomenon. —*adj.* **1** of magic. **2** producing surprising results. **3** *colloq.* wonderful, exciting. —*v.* (**-ck-**) change or create by or as if by magic. □ **like magic** very rapidly. **magic away** cause to disappear as if by magic. [Greek *magikos*]

magical *adj.* **1** of magic. **2** resembling, or produced as if by, magic. **3** wonderful, enchanting. □ **magically** *adv.*

magic eye *n.* photoelectric device used for detection, automatic control, etc.

magician /mə'dʒɪʃ(ə)n/ *n.* **1** person skilled in magic. **2** conjuror.

magic lantern *n.* primitive form of slide projector.

magisterial /ˌmædʒɪ'stɪərɪəl/ *adj.* **1** imperious. **2** authoritative. **3** of a magistrate. □ **magisterially** *adv.* [medieval Latin: related to MASTER]

magistracy /'mædʒɪstrəsɪ/ *n.* (*pl.* **-ies**) **1** magisterial office. **2** magistrates collectively.

magistrate /'mædʒɪˌstreɪt/ *n.* **1** civil officer administering the law. **2** official conducting a court for minor cases and preliminary hearings. [Latin: related to MASTER]

magma /'mægmə/ *n.* (*pl.* **-s**) molten rock under the earth's crust, from which igneous rock is formed by cooling. [Greek *massō* knead]

Magna Carta /ˌmægnə 'kɑːtə/ *n.* (also obtained from King John in 1215. [medieval Latin, = great charter]

magnanimous /mæg'nænɪməs/ *adj.* nobly generous; not petty in feelings or conduct. □ **magnanimity** /ˌmægnə'nɪmɪtɪ/ *n.* **magnanimously** *adv.* [Latin *magnus* great, *animus* mind]

magnate /'mægneɪt/ *n.* wealthy and influential person, usu. in business. [Latin *magnus* great]

magnesia /mæg'niːʃə, -ʒə/ *n.* **1** magnesium oxide. **2** hydrated magnesium carbonate, used as an antacid and laxative. [*Magnesia* in Asia Minor]

magnesium /mæg'niːzɪəm/ *n.* silvery metallic element.

magnet /'mægnɪt/ *n.* **1** piece of iron, steel, alloy, ore, etc., having the property of attracting iron and of pointing approximately north and south when suspended. **2** lodestone. **3** person or thing that attracts. [Greek *magnēs ēros* of Magnesia: related to MAGNESIA]

magnetic /mæg'retɪk/ *adj.* **1 a** having the properties of a magnet. **b** produced or acting by magnetism. **2** capable of being attracted by or acquiring the properties of a magnet. **3** strongly attractive (*magnetic personality*). □ **magnetically** *adv.*

magnetic field *n.* area of force around a magnet.

magnetic mine *n.* underwater mine detonated by the approach of a large mass of metal, e.g. a ship.

magnetic needle *n.* piece of magnetized steel used as an indicator on the dial of a compass etc.

magnetic north *n.* point indicated by the north end of a magnetic needle.

magnetic pole *n.* point near the north or south pole where a magnetic needle dips vertically.

magnetic storm *n.* disturbance of the earth's magnetic field by charged particles from the sun etc.

magnetic tape *n.* plastic strip coated with magnetic material for recording sound or pictures.

magnetism /'mægnɪˌtɪz(ə)m/ *n.* **1 a** magnetic phenomena and their science. **b** property of producing these. **2** attraction; personal charm.

magnetize /'mægnɪˌtaɪz/ *v.* (also **-ise**) (**-zing** or **-sing**) **1** give magnetic property to. **2** make into a magnet. **3** attract as a magnet does. □ **magnetization** /-'zeɪʃ(ə)n/ *n.* **magnetizable** *adj.*

magneto /mæg'niːtəʊ/ *n.* (*pl.* **-s**) electric generator using permanent magnets (esp. for the ignition of an internal-combustion engine). [abbreviation of *magneto-electric*]

Magnificat /mæg'nɪfɪˌkæt/ *n.* hymn of the Virgin Mary used as a canticle. [from its opening word]

magnification /ˌmægnɪfɪ'keɪʃ(ə)n/ *n.* **1** magnifying or being magnified. **2** degree of this.

magnificent /mæg'rɪfɪs(ə)nt/ *adj.* **1** splendid, stately. **2** *colloq.* fine, excellent. □ **magnificence** *n.* **magnificently** *adv.* [Latin *magnificus* from *magnus* great]

magnify /'mægnɪˌfaɪ/ *v.* (**-ies**, **-ied**) **1** make (a thing) appear larger than it is, as with a lens. **2** exaggerate. **3** intensify. **4** *archaic* extol. □ **magnifiable** *adj.* **magnifier** *n.* [Latin related to MAGNIFI-CENT]

magnifying glass n. lens used to magnify.

magnitude /ˈmæɡnɪtjuːd/ n. 1 largeness. 2 size. 3 importance. 4 a degree of brightness of a star. b class of stars arranged according to this (*of the third magnitude*). □ **of the first magnitude** very important. [Latin *magnus* great]

magnolia /mæɡˈnəʊlɪə/ n. 1 tree with dark-green foliage and waxy flowers. 2 creamy-pink colour. [*Magnol*, name of a botanist]

magnox /ˈmæɡnɒks/ n. magnesium-based alloy used to enclose uranium fuel elements in some nuclear reactors. [*magnesium no oxidation*]

magnum /ˈmæɡnəm/ n. (pl. **-s**) wine bottle twice the normal size. [Latin, neuter of *magnus* great]

magnum opus /ˌmæɡnəm ˈəʊpəs/ n. great work of art, literature, etc., esp. an artist's most important work. [Latin]

magpie /ˈmæɡpaɪ/ n. 1 a kind of crow with a long tail and black and white plumage. 2 chatterer. 3 indiscriminate collector. [from *Mag*, abbreviation of *Margaret*, PIE²]

magus /ˈmeɪɡəs/ n. (pl. **magi** /ˈmeɪdʒaɪ/) 1 priest of ancient Persia. 2 sorcerer. 3 (**the Magi**) the 'wise men' from the East (Matt. 2:1–12). [Persian *magus*]

Magyar /ˈmæɡjɑː(r)/ —n. 1 member of the chief ethnic group in Hungary. 2 their language. —adj. of this people. [native name]

maharaja /ˌmɑːhəˈrɑːdʒə/ n. (also **maharajah**) hist. title of some Indian princes. [Hindi, = great rajah]

maharanee /ˌmɑːhəˈrɑːniː/ n. (also **maharani**) (pl. **-s**) hist. maharaja's wife or widow. [Hindi, = great ranee]

maharishi /ˌmɑːhəˈrɪʃi/ n. (pl. **-s**) great Hindu sage. [Hindi]

mahatma /məˈhætmə/ n. 1 (in India etc.) revered person. 2 one of a class of persons supposed by some Buddhists to have preternatural powers. [Sanskrit, = great soul]

mah-jong /mɑːˈdʒɒŋ/ n. (also **-jongg**) game played with 136 or 144 pieces called tiles. [Chinese dial. *ma-tsiang* sparrows]

mahlstick var. of MAULSTICK.

mahogany /məˈhɒɡəni/ n. (pl. **-ies**) 1 reddish-brown tropical wood used for furniture. 2 its colour. [origin unknown]

mahonia /məˈhəʊnɪə/ n. evergreen shrub with yellow bell-shaped flowers. [French or Spanish]

mahout /məˈhaʊt/ n. (in India etc.) elephant-driver. [Hindi from Sanskrit]

maid n. 1 female servant. 2 archaic or poet. girl, young woman. [abbreviation of MAIDEN]

maiden /ˈmeɪd(ə)n/ n. 1 a archaic or poet. girl; young unmarried woman. b (attrib.) unmarried woman. 2 = MAIDEN OVER. 3 (attrib.) (of a female animal) unmated. 4 (often attrib.) a horse that has never won a race. b race open only to such horses. 5 (attrib.) first (*maiden speech; maiden voyage*). □ **maidenhood** n. **maidenly** adj. [Old English]

maidenhair n. fern with hairlike stalks and delicate fronds.

maidenhead n. 1 virginity. 2 hymen.

maiden name n. woman's surname before marriage.

maiden over n. over in cricket in which no runs are scored.

maid of honour n. 1 unmarried lady attending a queen or princess. 2 esp. US principal bridesmaid.

maidservant n. female servant.

mail¹ —n. 1 a letters and parcels etc. carried by post. b postal system. c one complete delivery or collection of mail. 2 email. —v. send by post or email. □ **mailbox** n. US letter-box. **wallet**] [French *maille* from Latin *macula*]

mail² n. armour of metal rings or plates.

mailbag n. large sack for carrying mail.

mailbox n. US letter-box.

mailing list n. list of people to whom advertising matter etc. is posted.

mailshot n. advertising material sent to potential customers.

mail order n. purchase of goods by post.

maim v. cripple, disable, mutilate.

main —adj. 1 chief, principal. 2 exerted to the full (*by main force*). —n. 1 principal duct etc. for water, sewage, etc. 2 (usu. in pl.; prec. by the) a central distribution network for electricity, gas, water, etc. b domestic electricity supply as distinct from batteries. 3 poet. high seas (*Spanish Main*). □ **in the main** mostly. [Old English]

main brace n. brace attached to the main yard.

main chance n. (prec. by the) one's own interests.

mainframe n. 1 central processing unit of a large computer. 2 (often attrib.) large computer system.

mainland n. large continuous extent of land, excluding neighbouring islands.

mainline v. (**-ning**) slang 1 take drugs intravenously. 2 inject (drugs) intravenously. □ **mainliner** n.

main line *n.* railway line linking large cities.

mainly /ˈmeɪnli/ *adv.* mostly; chiefly.

mainmast *n.* principal mast of a ship.

mainsail /ˈmeɪnseɪl, -s(ə)l/ *n.* 1 (in a square-rigged vessel) lowest sail on the mainmast. 2 (in a fore-and-aft rigged vessel) sail set on the after part of the mainmast.

mainspring *n.* 1 principal spring of a watch, clock, etc. 2 chief motivating force; incentive.

mainstay *n.* 1 chief support 2 stay from the maintop to the foot of the foremast.

mainstream *n.* 1 (often *attrib.*), ultimately prevailing trend in opinion, fashion, etc. 2 type of swing jazz, esp. with solo improvisation. 3 principal current of a river etc.

maintain /meɪnˈteɪn/ *v.* 1 cause to continue; keep up (an activity etc.). 2 support by work, expenditure, etc. 3 assert as true. 4 preserve (a house, machine, etc.) in good repair. 5 provide means for. [Latin *manus* hand, *teneo* hold]

maintained school *n.* school supported from public funds, State school.

maintenance /ˈmeɪntənəns/ *n.* 1 maintaining or being maintained. 2 a provision of the means to support life. b alimony. [French: related to MAINTAIN]

maintop *n.* platform above the head of the lower mainmast.

maintopmast *n.* mast above the head of the lower mainmast.

main yard *n.* yard on which the mainsail is extended.

maiolica /maɪˈɒlɪkə/ *n.* (also **majolica**) white tin-glazed earthenware decorated with metallic colours or enamelled. [Italian from former name of Majorca]

maisonette /ˌmeɪzəˈnɛt/ *n.* 1 flat on more than one floor. 2 small house. [French *maisonette* diminutive of *maison* house]

maize *n.* 1 cereal plant of N. America. 2 cobs or grain of this. [French or Spanish]

Maj. *abbr.* Major.

majestic /məˈdʒɛstɪk/ *adj.* stately and dignified; imposing. □ **majestically** *adv.*

majesty /ˈmædʒɪsti/ *n.* (*pl.* **-ies**) 1 stateliness, dignity, or authority, esp. of bearing, language, etc. 2 a royal power. b (**Majesty**) (prec. by *His, Her, Your*) forms of description or address for a sovereign or a sovereign's wife or widow (*Your Majesty; His, Her, Your Queen Mother*). [Latin *majestas*: related to MAJOR]

majolica var. of MAIOLICA.

major /ˈmeɪdʒə(r)/ —*adj.* 1 relatively great in size, intensity, scope, or importance. 2 (of surgery) serious. 3 *Mus.* a (of an interval) greater by a semitone than its minor. b (of a scale) having intervals of a semitone above its third and seventh notes. c (of a key) based on a major scale. 4 of full legal age. —*n.* 1 a army officer next below lieutenant-colonel. b officer in charge of a band section (*drum major*). 2 person of full legal age. 3 *US* a student's main subject or course. b student of this. —*v.* (foll. by *in*) *US* study or qualify in (a subject) as one's main subject. [Latin, comparative of *magnus* great]

major-domo /ˌmeɪdʒəˈdəʊməʊ/ *n.* (*pl.* **-s**) chief steward of a great household. [medieval Latin *major* or *domus* highest official of the household]

majorette /ˌmeɪdʒəˈrɛt/ *n.* = DRUM MAJORETTE.

major-general *n.* officer next below a lieutenant-general.

majority /məˈdʒɒrɪti/ *n.* (*pl.* **-ies**) 1 (usu. foll. by *of*) greater number or part. 2 a number of votes by which a candidate wins. b party etc. receiving the greater number of votes. 3 full legal age. 4 rank of major. [medieval Latin: related to MAJOR]

■ **Usage** In sense 1 *majority* is strictly used only with countable nouns, as in *the majority of people*, and not (e.g.) *the majority of the work*.

majority rule *n.* principle that the greater number should exercise the greater power.

make —*v.* (-king; *past* and *past part.* **made**) 1 construct; create; form from parts or other substances. 2 cause or compel (*made me do it*). 3 a cause to exist; bring about (*made a noise*). b cause to become or seem (*made him angry; made a fool of; made him a knight*). 4 compose; prepare; write (*made her will; made a film*). 5 constitute; amount to; be reckoned as (2 *and 2 make 4*). 6 a undertake (*made a promise; make an effort*). b perform (an action etc.) (*made a face; made a bow*). 7 gain, acquire, procure (money, a living, a profit, etc.). 8 prepare (tea, coffee, a meal, etc.) 9 a arrange (a bed) for use. b arrange and light materials for (a fire). 10 a proceed (*made towards the river*). b (foll. by *to* + infin.) act as if with the intention to (*he made to go*). 11 *colloq.* a arrive at (a place) or in time for (a train etc.). b manage to attend. c manage to attend. d manage to reach the rank of. e manage to (a certain day) or at (a certain time) (*couldn't make the meeting last time*).

make *(continued)*

week; can make any day except Friday). **c** achieve a place in (*made the first eleven*). **12** establish or enact (a distinction, rule, law, etc.). **13** consider to be; estimate as (*what do you make the total?*). **14** secure the success or advancement of (*his second novel made him; it made my day*). **15** accomplish (a distance, speed, score, etc.). **16 a** become by development (*made a great leader*). **b** serve as (*makes a useful seat*). **17** (usu. foll. by *out*) represent as (*makes him out a liar*). **18** form in the mind (*make a decision*). **19** (foll. by *it* + compl.) **a** determine, establish, or choose (*let's make it Tuesday*). **b** bring to (a chosen value etc.) (*make it a dozen*). —*n.* **1** type or brand of manufacture. **2** way a thing is made. □ **make away with 1** = make off with. **2** = do away with. **make believe** pretend. **make the best of** see BEST. **make a clean breast** see BREAST. **make a clean sweep** see SWEEP. **make a day (or night etc.) of it** devote a whole day (or night etc.) to an activity. **make do 1** manage with the inadequate means available. **2** (foll. by *with*) manage with (something) as an inferior substitute. **make for 1** tend to result in. **2** proceed towards (a place). **3** attack. **make good 1** repay, repair, or compensate for. **2** achieve (a purpose); be successful. **make the grade** succeed. **make it** *colloq.* **1** succeed in reaching, esp. in time. **2** succeed. **make it up 1** be reconciled. **2** remedy a deficit. **make it up to** remedy negligence, an injury, etc. to (a person). **make love** see LOVE. **make a meal of** see MEAL. **make merry** see MERRY. **make money** acquire wealth. **make the most of** see MOST. **make much (or little) of** treat as important (or unimportant). **make a name for oneself** see NAME. **make no bones about** see BONE. **make nothing of 1** treat as trifling. **2** be unable to understand, use, or deal with. **make of 1** construct from. **2** conclude from or about (*can you make anything of it?*). **make off** depart hastily. **make off with** carry away; steal. **make or break** cause the success or ruin of. **make out 1** discern or understand. **2** assert; pretend. **3** *colloq.* progress; fare. **4** write out (a cheque etc.) or fill in (a form). **make over 1** transfer the possession of. **2** refashion. **make up 1** act to overcome (a deficiency). **2** complete (an amount etc.). **3** (foll. by *for*) compensate for. **4** be reconciled. **5** put together; concoct (a story). **7** apply cosmetics (to). **8** prepare (a bed) with fresh linen. **make up one's mind** decide. **make up to**

curry favour with. **make water** urinate. **make way 1** (often foll. by *for*) allow room to pass. **2** (foll. by *for*) be superseded by. **make one's way** go; prosper. **on the make** *colloq.* intent on gain. [Old English]

make-believe —*n.* pretence. —*attrib. adj.* pretended.

maker *n.* **1** person who makes. **2** (**Maker**) God.

makeshift —*adj.* temporary. —*n.* temporary substitute or device.

make-up *n.* **1** cosmetics, as used generally or by actors. **2** character, temperament, etc. **3** composition (of a thing).

makeweight *n.* **1** small quantity added to make up the weight. **2** person or thing supplying a deficiency.

making *n.* (in *pl.*) **1** earnings; profit. **2** essential qualities or ingredients (*has the makings of a pilot*). □ **be the making of** ensure the success of. **in the making** in the course of being made or formed. [Old English: related to MAKE]

mal- *comb. form* **1 a** bad, badly (*malpractice; maltreat*). **b** faulty (*malfunction*). **2** not (*maladroit*). [French *mal* badly, from Latin *male*]

malachite /ˈmæləkaɪt/ *n.* green mineral used for ornament. [Greek *molokhitis*]

maladjusted /ˌmæləˈdʒʌstɪd/ *adj.* (of a person) unable to adapt to or cope with the demands of a social environment. □ **maladjustment** *n.*

maladminister /ˌmælədˈmɪnɪstə(r)/ *v.* manage badly or improperly. □ **maladministration** /-ˈstreɪʃ(ə)n/ *n.*

maladroit /ˌmælədˈdrɔɪt/ *adj.* clumsy; bungling. [French: related to MAL-]

malady /ˈmælədɪ/ *n.* (*pl.* -ies) ailment; disease. [French *malade* sick]

malaise /məˈleɪz/ *n.* **1** general bodily discomfort or lassitude. **2** feeling of unease or demoralization. [French: related to EASE]

malapropism /ˈmæləprɒpɪz(ə)m/ *n.* comical misuse of a word in mistake for one sounding similar, e.g. *alligator* for *allegory*. [Mrs *Malaprop*, name of a character in Sheridan's *The Rivals*]

malaria /məˈleərɪə/ *n.* recurrent fever caused by a parasite transmitted by a mosquito bite. □ **malarial** *adj.* [Italian, = bad air]

malarkey /məˈlɑːkɪ/ *n. colloq.* humbug; nonsense. [origin unknown]

Malay /məˈleɪ/ *n.* **1** member of a people predominating in Malaysia and Indonesia. **2** their language. —*adj.* of this people or language. □ **Malayan** *n.* & *adj.* [Malay *malāyu*]

malcontent /ˈmalkəntent/ —n. discontented person. —adj. discontented. [French: related to MAL]

male —adj. 1 of the sex that can beget offspring by fertilization. 2 of men or male animals, plants, etc.: masculine. 3 (of plants or flowers) containing stamens but no pistil. 4 of parts of machinery etc.) designed to enter or fill the corresponding hollow part (*male screw*). —n. male person or animal. □ **maleness** n. [Latin *masculus* from *mas* a male]

male chauvinist n. = CHAUVINIST 2.

malediction /ˌmalɪˈdɪkʃ(ə)n/ n. 1 curse. 2 utterance of a curse. □ **maledictory** adj. [Latin *maledictio*: related to MAL]

malefactor /ˈmalɪfaktə(r)/ n. criminal; evil-doer. □ **malefaction** /-ˈfakʃ(ə)n/ n. [Latin *male* badly, *facio facti* do]

male menopause n. colloq. crisis of potency, confidence, etc., supposed to afflict some men in middle life.

malevolent /məˈlevələnt/ adj. wishing evil to others. □ **malevolence** n. **malevolently** adv. [Latin *volo* wish]

malfeasance /malˈfiːz(ə)ns/ n. formal misconduct, esp. in an official capacity. [French related to MAL]

malformation /ˌmalfɔːˈmeɪʃ(ə)n/ n. faulty formation. □ **malformed** /-ˈfɔːmd/ adj.

malfunction /malˈfʌŋkʃ(ə)n/ —n. failure to function normally. —v. fail to function normally.

malice /ˈmalɪs/ n. 1 desire to harm or cause difficulty to others; ill-will. 2 Law harmful intent. [Latin *malus* bad]

malice aforethought n. Law intention to commit a crime, esp. murder.

malicious /məˈlɪʃəs/ adj. given to or arising from malice. □ **maliciously** adv.

malign /məˈlaɪn/ —adj. 1 (of a disease) very virulent or infectious. 2 (of a tumour) spreading or recurring; cancerous. 3 harmful; feeling or showing intense ill-will. □ **malignancy** n. **malignantly** adv. [Latin: related to MALIGN]

malign /məˈlaɪn/ —adj. 1 injurious. 2 (of a disease) malignant. 3 malevolent. —v. speak ill of; slander. □ **malignity** /məˈlɪɡnɪtɪ/ n. [Latin *malus* bad]

malignant /məˈlɪɡnənt/ adj. 1 a (of a disease) very virulent or infectious. b (of a tumour) spreading or recurring; cancerous. 2 harmful; feeling or showing intense ill-will. □ **malignancy** n. **malignantly** adv. [Latin: related to MALIGN]

malinger /məˈlɪŋɡə(r)/ v. pretend to be ill, esp. to escape work. □ **malingerer** n. [French *malingre* sickly]

mall /mal, mɔːl/ n. 1 sheltered walk or promenade. 2 shopping precinct. [*The Mall*, street in London]

mallard /ˈmalɑːd/ n. (pl. same) a kind of wild duck. [French]

malleable /ˈmalɪəb(ə)l/ adj. 1 (of metal etc.) that can be shaped by hammering. 2 easily influenced; pliable. □ **malleability** /-ˈbɪlɪtɪ/ n. **malleably** adv. [Medieval Latin: related to MALLET]

mallet /ˈmalɪt/ n. 1 hammer, usu. of wood. 2 implement for striking a croquet or polo ball. [Latin *malleus* hammer]

mallow /ˈmaləʊ/ n. plant with hairy stems and leaves and pink or purple flowers. [Latin *malva*]

malmsey /ˈmɑːmzɪ/ n. a strong sweet wine. [Low German or Dutch from *Monemvasia* in Greece]

malnourished /malˈnʌrɪʃt/ adj. suffering from malnutrition. □ **malnourishment** n.

malnutrition /ˌmalnjuːˈtrɪʃ(ə)n/ n. condition resulting from the lack of foods necessary for health.

malodorous /malˈəʊdərəs/ adj. evil-smelling.

malpractice /malˈpraktɪs/ n. improper, negligent, or criminal professional conduct.

malt /mɔːlt/ —n. 1 barley, or other grain, steeped, germinated, and dried, for brewing etc. 2 colloq. malt whisky. —v. convert (grain) into malt. □ **malty** adj. (-ier, -iest). [Old English]

malted milk n. drink made from dried milk and extract of malt.

Maltese /mɔːlˈtiːz/ —n. (pl. same) native or language of Malta. —adj. of Malta. [French related to MALTESE]

Maltese cross n. cross with the arms broadening outwards, often indented at the ends.

Malthusian /malˈθjuːzɪən/ adj. of Malthus's doctrine that the population should be restricted so as to prevent an increase beyond its means of subsistence. □ **Malthusianism** n. [*Malthus*, name of a clergyman]

maltose /ˈmɔːltəʊz/ n. sugar made from starch by enzymes in malt, saliva, etc. [French related to MALT]

maltreat /malˈtriːt/ v. ill-treat. □ **maltreatment** n. [French: related to MAL]

malt whisky n. whisky made solely from malted barley.

mama /məˈmɑː/ n. (also **mamma**) archaic mother. [imitative of child's *ma, ma*]

mamba /ˈmambə/ n. venomous African snake. [Zulu *imamba*]

mambo /ˈmambəʊ/ n. (pl. -s) Latin American dance like the rumba. [American Spanish]

mamma /ˈmamə/ n. var. of MAMA.

mammal /ˈmam(ə)l/ n. warm-blooded vertebrate of the class secreting milk to

mammary feed its young. □ **mammalian** /-'meɪlɪən/ *adj. & n.* [Latin *mamma* breast]

mammary /'mæmərɪ/ *adj.* of the breasts.

mammogram /'mæməˌgræm/ *n.* image obtained by mammography. [Latin *mamma* breast]

mammography /mæ'mɒgrəfɪ/ *n.* X-ray technique for screening the breasts for tumours etc.

Mammon /'mæmən/ *n.* wealth regarded as a god or evil influence. [Aramaic *māmōn*]

mammoth /'mæməθ/ —*n.* large extinct elephant with a hairy coat and curved tusks. —*adj.* huge. [Russian]

man —*n.* (*pl.* **men**) **1** adult human male. **2 a** human being; person. **b** the human race. **3 a** workman (*the manager spoke to the men*). **b** manservant, valet. **4** (usu. in *pl.*) soldiers, sailors, etc., esp. non-officers. **5** suitable or appropriate person; expert (*he is your man; the man for the job*). **6 a** husband (*man and wife*). **b** *colloq.* boyfriend, lover. **7** human being of a specified type or historical period (*Renaissance man; Peking man*). **8** piece in chess, draughts, etc. **9** *colloq.* as a form of address. **10** person pursued opponent (*police caught their man*). —*v.* (**-nn-**) **1** supply with a person or people for work or defence. **2** work, service, or defend (*man the pumps*). **3** fill (a post). □ **as one man** in unison. **be one's own man** be independent. **to a man** without exception. □ **manlike** *adj.* [Old English]

man about town *n.* fashionable socializer.

manacle /'mænək(ə)l/ —*n.* (usu. in *pl.*) **1** fetter for the hand; handcuff. **2** restraint. —*v.* (**-ling**) fetter with manacles. [Latin *manus* hand]

manage /'mænɪdʒ/ *v.* (**-ging**) **1** organize; regulate; be in charge of. **2** succeed in achieving; contrive (*managed to come; managed a smile; managed to ruin the day*). **3** (often foll. by *with*) succeed with limited resources etc.; be able to cope. **4** succeed in controlling. **5** (often prec. by *can* etc.) **a** cope with (*couldn't manage another bite*). **b** be free to attend on or at (*can manage Monday*). **6** use or wield (a tool etc.). □ **manageable** *adj.* [Latin *manus* hand]

management *n.* **1** managing or being managed. **2 a** administration of business or public undertakings. **b** people engaged in this, esp. those controlling a workforce.

manager *n.* **1** person controlling or administering a business or part of a business. **2** person controlling the affairs, training, etc. of a person or team in sports, entertainment, etc. **3** person of a specified level of skill in household or financial affairs etc. (*a good manager*). □ **managerial** /ˌmænə'dʒɪərɪəl/ *adj.*

manageress /ˌmænɪdʒə'res/ *n.* woman manager, esp. of a shop, hotel, etc.

managing director *n.* director with executive control or authority.

mañana /mæn'jɑːnə/ —*adv.* tomorrow (esp. to indicate procrastination). —*n.* indefinite future. [Spanish]

man-at-arms *n.* (*pl.* **men-at-arms**) *archaic* soldier.

manatee /ˌmænə'tiː/ *n.* large aquatic plant-eating mammal. [Spanish from Carib]

Mancunian /mæŋ'kjuːnɪən/ —*n.* native of Manchester. —*adj.* of Manchester. [Latin *Mancunium*]

mandala /'mændələ/ *n.* circular figure as a religious symbol of the universe. [Sanskrit]

mandamus /mæn'deɪməs/ *n.* judicial writ issued as a command to an inferior court, or ordering a person to perform a public or statutory duty. [Latin, = we command]

mandarin /'mændərɪn/ *n.* **1** (**Mandarin**) official language of China. **2** *hist.* Chinese official. **3** powerful person, esp. a top civil servant. **4** (in full **mandarin orange**) = TANGERINE 1. [Hindi *mantrī*]

mandate /'mændeɪt/ —*n.* **1** official command or instruction. **2** authority given by electors to a government, trade union, etc. **3** authority to act for another.—*v.* (**-ting**) instruct (a delegate) how to act or vote. [Latin *mandatum*, past part. of *mando* command]

mandatory /'mændətərɪ/ *adj.* **1** compulsory. **2** of or conveying a command. □ **mandatorily** *adv.* [Latin: related to MANDATE]

mandible /'mændɪb(ə)l/ *n.* **1** jaw, esp. the lower jaw in mammals and fishes. **2** upper or lower part of a bird's beak. **3** either half of the crushing organ in the mouth-parts of an insect etc. [Latin *mando* chew]

mandolin /ˌmændə'lɪn/ *n.* a kind of lute with paired metal strings plucked with a plectrum. □ **mandolinist** *n.* [French from Italian]

mandrake /'mændreɪk/ *n.* poisonous narcotic plant with large yellow fruit. [Greek *mandragoras*]

mandrel /'mændr(ə)l/ *n.* **1** lathe-shaft to which work is fixed while being turned. **2** cylindrical rod round which metal or other material is forged or shaped. [origin unknown]

mandrill /ˈmændrɪl/ n. large W. African baboon. [probably from MAN,
DRILL[4]]

mane n. 1 long hair on the neck of a
horse, lion, etc. 2 colloq. person's long
hair. [Old English]

manège /mæˈneɪʒ/ n. (also **manege**) 1
riding-school. 2 movements of a trained
horse. 3 horsemanship. [Italian: related
to MANAGE]

maneuver US var. of MANOEUVRE.

man Friday n. male helper or follower.

manful adj. brave; resolute. □ **man-
fully** adv.

manganese /ˈmæŋɡəniːz/ n. 1 grey
brittle metallic element. 2 black mineral
oxide of this used in glass-making etc.
[Italian: related to MAGNESIA]

mange /meɪndʒ/ n. skin disease in hairy
and woolly animals. [French mangeue
itch from Latin manduco chew]

mangel-wurzel /ˈmæŋɡ(ə)lwɜːz(ə)l/ n.
(also **mangold-** /ˈmæŋɡəld-/) large
beet used as cattle food. [German Man-
gold beet, Wurzel root]

manger /ˈmeɪndʒə(r)/ n. box or trough
for horses or cattle to feed from. [Latin:
related to MANGE]

mange-tout /mɑ̃ˈtuː/ n. a kind of pea
eaten in the pod. [French, = eat-all]

mangle[1] /ˈmæŋɡ(ə)l/ —n. machine of
two or more cylinders for squeezing
water from and pressing wet clothes.
—v. (-ling) press (clothes etc.) in a
mangle. [Dutch mangel]

mangle[2] /ˈmæŋɡ(ə)l/ v. (-ling) 1 hack or
mutilate by blows. 2 spoil (a text etc.) by
gross blunders. 3 cut roughly so as to
disfigure. [Anglo-French mc(ha)ngler:
probably related to MAIM]

mango /ˈmæŋɡəʊ/ n. (pl. **-es** or **-s**) 1
tropical fruit with yellowish flesh. 2 tree
bearing this. [Tamil mānkāy]

mangold-wurzel var. of MANGEL-
WURZEL.

mangrove /ˈmæŋɡrəʊv/ n. tropical tree
or shrub growing in shore-mud with
many tangled roots above ground. [ori-
gin unknown]

mangy /ˈmeɪndʒɪ/ adj. (-ier, -iest) 1
having mange. 2 squalid; shabby.

manhandle v. (-ling) 1 colloq. handle (a
person) roughly. 2 move by human
effort.

manhole n. covered opening in a pavement, sewer, etc. for workmen to gain
access.

manhood n. 1 state of being a man. 2 a
manliness; courage. **b** a man's sexual
potency. 3 men of a country etc.

man-hour n. work done by one person
in one hour.

manhunt n. organized search for a
person, esp. a criminal.

mania /ˈmeɪnɪə/ n. 1 mental illness
marked by excitement and violence. 2
(often foll. by for) excessive enthusiasm;
obsession. [Greek mainomai be mad]

-mania comb. form 1 denoting a special
type of mental disorder (megalomania).
2 denoting enthusiasm or admiration
(Beatlemania).

maniac /ˈmeɪnɪæk/ —n. 1 colloq. person
behaving wildly (too many maniacs on
the road). 2 colloq. obsessive enthusiast.
3 person suffering from mania. —adj. of
or behaving like a maniac. □ **maniacal**
/məˈnaɪək(ə)l/ adj. **maniacally** /mə
ˈnaɪəkəlɪ/ adv.

manic /ˈmænɪk/ adj. 1 of or affected by
mania. 2 colloq. wildly excited; frenzied;
excitable. □ **manically** adv.

manic-depressive —adj. relating to a
mental disorder with alternating
periods of elation and depression. —n.
person with such a disorder.

manicure /ˈmænɪkjʊə(r)/ —n. cosmetic
treatment of the hands and fingernails.
—v. (-ring) give a manicure to (the hands
or a person). □ **manicurist** n. [Latin
manus hand, cura care]

manifest /ˈmænɪfest/ —adj. clear or
obvious to the eye or mind. —v. 1 show (a
quality or feeling) by one's acts etc. 2
show plainly to the eye or mind. 3 be
evidence of; prove. 4 refl. (of a thing)
reveal itself. 5 (of a ghost) appear. —n.
cargo or passenger list. □ **manifestation** /-ˈsteɪʃ(ə)n/ n. **manifestly** adv.
[Latin manifestus]

manifesto /ˌmænɪˈfestəʊ/ n. (pl. **-s**) declaration of policies, esp. by a political
party. [Italian: related to MANIFEST]

manifold /ˈmænɪfəʊld/ —adj. 1 many
and various. 2 having various forms,
parts, applications, etc. —n. 1 manifold
thing. 2 pipe or chamber branching into
several openings. [Old English: related
to MANY, FOLD]

manikin /ˈmænɪkɪn/ n. little man;
dwarf. [Dutch]

Manila /məˈnɪlə/ n. 1 (in full Manila
hemp) strong fibre of a kind of tree
native to the Philippines. 2 (also
manila) strong brown paper made from
this. [Manila in the Philippines]

man in the street n. ordinary person.

manipulate /məˈnɪpjʊleɪt/ v. (-ting) 1
handle, esp. with skill. 2 manage (a
person, situation, etc.) to one's own
advantage, esp. unfairly. 3 move (part of
a patient's body) by hand in order to
increase flexion etc. 4 Computing edit or
move (text, data, etc.). □ **manipulable**

manipulative

/-lǝb(ǝ)l/ adj. **manipulation** /-ˈleɪʃ(ǝ)n/ n. **manipulator** n. [Latin manus hand]

manipulative /mǝˈnɪpjʊlǝtɪv/ adj. tending to exploit a situation, person, etc., for one's own ends. □ **manipulatively** adv.

mankind n. **1** human species. **2** male people.

manky /ˈmæŋkɪ/ adj. (-ier, -iest) colloq. **1** bad, inferior, defective. **2** dirty. [obsolete mank defective]

manly adj. (-ier, -iest) **1** having qualities associated with a man (e.g. strength and courage). **2** befitting a man. □ **manliness** n.

man-made adj. (of textiles) artificial, synthetic.

manna /ˈmænǝ/ n. **1** substance miraculously supplied as food to the Israelites in the wilderness (Exod. 16). **2** unexpected benefit (esp. manna from heaven). [Old English ultimately from Hebrew]

manned adj. (of a spacecraft etc.) having a human crew.

mannequin /ˈmænɪkɪn/ n. **1** fashion model. **2** window dummy. [French, = MANIKIN]

manner /ˈmænǝ(r)/ n. **1** way a thing is done or happens. **2** (in pl.) **a** social behaviour (good manners). **b** polite behaviour (has no manners). **c** modes of life; social conditions. **3** outward bearing, way of speaking, etc. **4** style (in the manner of Rembrandt). **5** kind, sort (not by any manner of means). □ **in a manner of speaking** in a way; so to speak. **to the manner born** colloq. naturally at ease in a particular situation etc. [Latin manus hand]

mannered adj. **1** (in comb.) having specified manners (ill-mannered). **2** esp. Art full of mannerisms.

mannerism n. **1** habitual gesture or way of speaking etc. **2 a** stylistic trick in art etc. **b** excessive use of these. □ **mannerist** n.

mannerly adj. well-mannered, polite.

mannish adj. **1** (of a woman) masculine in appearance or manner. **2** characteristic of a man. □ **mannishly** adv.

manoeuvre /mǝˈnuːvǝ(r)/ (US **maneuver**) —n. **1** planned and controlled movement of a vehicle or body of troops etc. **2** (in pl.) large-scale exercise of troops, ships, etc. **3** agile or skilful movement. **4** artful plan. —v. (-ring) **1** move (a thing, esp. a vehicle) carefully. **2** perform manoeuvres. **3 a** (usu. foll. by into, out of, etc.) manipulate (a person, thing, etc.) by scheming or adroitness. **b** use artifice. □ **manoeuvrable** adj. **manoeuvrability** /-vrǝˈbɪltɪ/ n.

[medieval Latin manu operor work with the hand]

man of letters n. scholar or author.

man of the world see WORLD.

man-of-war n. (pl. **men-of-war**) warship.

manor /ˈmænǝ(r)/ n. **1** (also **manor-house**) large country house with lands. **2** hist. feudal lordship over lands. **3** slang district covered by a police station. □ **manorial** /mǝˈnɔːrɪǝl/ adj. [Latin maneo remain]

manpower n. number of people available for work, service, etc.

manqué /ˈmɒŋkeɪ/ adj. (placed after noun) that might have been but is not (an actor manqué). [French]

mansard /ˈmænsɑːd/ n. roof with four sloping sides, each of which becomes steeper halfway down. [Mansart, name of an architect]

manse /mæns/ n. ecclesiastical residence, esp. a Scottish Presbyterian minister's house. [medieval Latin: related to MANOR]

manservant n. (pl. **menservants**) male servant.

mansion /ˈmænʃ(ǝ)n/ n. **1** large grand house. **2** (in pl.) large building divided into flats. [Latin: related to MANOR]

manslaughter n. unintentional but not accidental unlawful killing of a human being.

mantel /ˈmænt(ǝ)l/ n. mantelpiece or mantelshelf. [var. of MANTLE]

mantelpiece n. **1** structure of wood, marble, etc. above and around a fireplace. **2** = MANTELSHELF.

mantelshelf n. shelf above a fireplace.

mantilla /mænˈtɪlǝ/ n. lace scarf worn by Spanish women over the hair and shoulders. [Spanish: related to MANTLE]

mantis /ˈmæntɪs/ n. (pl. same or **mantises**) (in full **praying mantis**) predatory insect that holds its forelegs like hands folded in prayer. [Greek, = prophet]

mantissa /mænˈtɪsǝ/ n. part of a logarithm after the decimal point. [Latin, = makeweight]

mantle /ˈmænt(ǝ)l/ —n. **1** loose sleeveless cloak. **2** covering (mantle of snow). **3** fragile lacelike tube fixed round a gas-jet to give an incandescent light. **4** region between the crust and the core of the earth. —v. (-ling) clothe; conceal; envelop. [Latin mantellum cloak]

man to man adv. candidly.

mantra /ˈmæntrǝ/ n. **1** Hindu or Buddhist devotional incantation. **2** Vedic hymn. [Sanskrit, = instrument of thought]

mantrap n. trap for catching trespassers etc.

manual /'mænjʊəl/ *adj.* **1** of or done with the hands (*manual labour*). **2 a** worked by hand, not automatically (*manual gear-change*). **b** (of a vehicle) worked by manual gear-change. —*n.* **1** reference book. **2** organ keyboard played with the hands, not the feet. **3** *collog.* vehicle with manual transmission. □ **manually** *adv.* [Latin *manus* hand]

manufacture /ˌmænjʊ'fæktʃ(ə)r/ —*n.* **1** making of articles, esp. in a factory etc. **2** branch of industry (*woollen manufacture*). —*v.* (**-ring**) **1** make (articles), esp. on an industrial scale. **2** invent or fabricate (evidence, a story, etc.). □ **manufacturer** *n.* [Latin *manufactum* made by hand]

manure /mə'njʊə(r)/ —*n.* fertilizer, esp. dung. —*v.* (**-ring**) apply manure to (land etc.). [Anglo-French *maineuverer* MAN-OEUVRE]

manuscript /'mænjʊskrɪpt/ —*n.* **1** text written by hand, not typed. **2 a** written or typed text. **3** handwritten form (*produced in manuscript*). —*adj.* written by hand. [medieval Latin *manuscriptus* written by hand]

Manx /mæŋks/ —*adj.* of the Isle of Man. —*n.* **1** former Celtic language of the Isle of Man. **2** (prec. by *the*; treated as *pl.*) Manx people. [Old Norse]

Manx cat *n.* tailless variety of cat.

many /'menɪ/ —*adj.* (**more**; **most**) great in number; numerous (*many people*). —*n.* (as *pl.*) **1** many people or things. **2** (prec. by *the*) the majority of people. □ **a good** (or **great**) **many** a large number. **many a** (foll. by *sing.*) a large number of. **many's the time** often. **many a time** many times. [Old English]

Maoism /'maʊɪz(ə)m/ *n.* Communist doctrines of Mao Zedong. □ **Maoist** *n. & adj.* [*Mao* Zedong, name of a Chinese statesman]

Maori /'maʊrɪ/ —*n.* (*pl.* same or **-s**) **1** member of the aboriginal people of New Zealand. **2** their language. —*adj.* of this people. [native name]

map —*n.* **1 a** flat representation of the earth's surface, or part of it. **b** diagram of a route etc. **2** similar representation of the stars, sky, mocrn, etc. **3** diagram showing the arrangement or components of a thing. —*v.* (**-pp-**) **1** represent on a map. **2** *Math.* associate each element of (a set) with one element of another set. □ **map out** plan in detail. [Latin *mappa* napkin]

maple /'meɪp(ə)l/ *n.* **1** any of various trees or shrubs grown for shade, ornament, wood, or sugar. **2** its wood. [Old English]

maple-leaf *n.* emblem of Canada.

maple sugar *n.* sugar produced by evaporating the sap of some kinds of maple.

maple syrup *n.* syrup made by evaporating maple sap or dissolving maple sugar.

maquette /mæ'ket/ *n.* preliminary model or sketch. [Italian *macchia* spot]

Maquis /mæ'ki:, 'mæ-/ *n.* (*pl.* same) **1** French resistance movement during the German occupation (1940–45). **2** member of this. [French, = brushwood]

Mar. *abbr.* March.

mar *v.* (**-rr-**) spoil; disfigure. [Old English]

marabou /'mærəbu:/ *n.* **1** large W. Af. rican stork. **2** its down as trimming etc. [French from Arabic]

maraca /mə'rækə/ *n.* clublike bean-filled gourd etc., shaken rhythmically in pairs in Latin American music. [Portuguese]

maraschino /ˌmærə'ski:nəʊ/ *n.* (*pl.* **-s**) sweet liqueur made from black cherries. [Italian]

maraschino cherry *n.* cherry preserved in maraschino and used in cocktails etc.

marathon /'mærəθ(ə)n/ *n.* **1** long-distance running race, usu. of 26 miles 385 yards (42.195 km.). **2** long-lasting or difficult undertaking etc. [*Marathon* in Greece, scene of a decisive battle in 490 BC: a messenger supposedly ran with news of the outcome to Athens]

maraud /mə'rɔ:d/ *v.* **1** make a plundering raid (on). **2** pilfer systematically. □ **marauder** *n.* [French *maraud* rogue]

marble /'mɑ:b(ə)l/ —*n.* **1** crystalline limestone capable of taking a polish, used in sculpture and architecture. **2** (often *attrib.*) a anything like marble in hardness, coldness, etc. (*her features were marble*). **3 a** small, esp. glass, ball used as a toy. **b** (in *pl.*; treated as *sing.*) game using these. **4** (in *pl.*) *slang* one's mental faculties (*he's lost his marbles*). **5** (in *pl.*) collection of sculptures (*Elgin Marbles*). —*v.* (**-ling**) **1** (esp. as **marbled** *adj.*) stain or colour (paper, soap, etc.) to look like variegated marble. **2** (as **marbled** *adj.*) (of meat) striped with fat and lean. [Latin *marmor* from Greek]

marble cake *n.* mottled cake of light and dark sponge.

marbling *n.* **1** colouring or marking like marble. **2** streaks of fat in lean meat.

marcasite /'mɑːkəsaɪt/ *n.* **1** yellowish crystalline iron sulphide. **2** crystals of this used in jewellery. [Arabic *markas-hita*]

March *n.* third month of the year. [Latin *Martius* of Mars]

march¹ −*v.* **1** (cause to) walk in a military manner with a regular tread (*army marched past*; *marched him away*). **2 a** walk purposefully. **b** (often foll. by *on*) (of events etc.) continue unrelentingly (*time marches on*). **3** (foll. by *on*) advance towards (a military objective). −*n.* **1 a** act of marching. **2** uniform military step (*slow march*). **2** long difficult walk. **3** procession as a demonstration. **4** (usu. foll. by *of*) progress or continuity (*march of events*). **5 a** music to accompany a march. **b** similar musical piece. □ **marcher** *n.* [French *marcher*]

march² −*n. hist.* **1** (usu. in *pl.*) boundary, frontier (esp. between England and Scotland or Wales). **2** tract of land between two countries, esp. disputed. −*v.* (foll. by *upon, with*) (of a country, an estate, etc.) border on. [French *marche* from medieval Latin *marca*]

March hare *n.* hare exuberant in the breeding season (*mad as a March hare*).

marching orders *n.pl.* **1** order for troops to mobilize etc. **2** dismissal (*gave him his marching orders*).

marchioness /ˌmɑːʃəˈnes/ *n.* **1** wife or widow of a marquess. **2** woman holding the rank of marquess. [medieval Latin: related to MARCH²]

march past −*n.* marching of troops past a saluting-point at a review. −*v.* (of troops) carry out a march past.

Mardi Gras /ˌmɑːdɪ ˈɡrɑː/ *n.* **1 a** Shrove Tuesday in some Catholic countries. **b** merrymaking on this day. **2** last day of a carnival etc. [French, = fat Tuesday]

mare¹ *n.* female equine animal, esp. a horse. [Old English]

mare² /ˈmɑːreɪ/ *n.* (*pl.* **maria** /ˈmɑːrɪə/ or **-s**) **1** large dark flat area on the moon, once thought to be sea. **2** similar area on Mars. [Latin, = sea]

mare's nest *n.* illusory discovery.

mare's tail *n.* **1** tall slender marsh plant. **2** (in *pl.*) long straight streaks of cirrus cloud.

margarine /ˌmɑːdʒəˈriːn/ *n.* butter-substitute made from vegetable oils or animal fats with milk etc. [Greek *margaron* pearl]

marge *n. colloq.* margarine. [abbreviation]

margin /ˈmɑːdʒɪn/ −*n.* **1** edge or border of a surface. **2** blank border flanking print etc. **3** amount by which a thing exceeds, falls short, etc. (*won by a narrow margin*). **4** lower limit (*his effort fell below the margin*). −*v.* (**-n-**) provide with a margin or marginal notes. [Latin *margo ginis*]

marginal *adj.* **1** of or written in a margin. **2 a** of or at the edge. **b** insignificant (*of merely marginal interest*). **3** (of a parliamentary seat etc.) held by a small majority. **4** close to the limit, esp. of profitability. **5** (of land) difficult to cultivate; unprofitable. **6** barely adequate. □ **marginally** *adv.* [medieval Latin: related to MARGIN]

marginal cost *n.* cost added by making one extra copy etc.

marginalia /ˌmɑːdʒɪˈneɪlɪə/ *n.pl.* marginal notes.

marginalize /ˈmɑːdʒɪnəlaɪz/ *v.* (also **-ise**) (**-zing** or **-sing**) make or treat as insignificant. □ **marginalization** /-ˈzeɪʃ(ə)n/ *n.*

margin of error *n.* allowance for miscalculation etc.

marguerite /ˌmɑːɡəˈriːt/ *n.* ox-eye daisy. [Latin *margarita* pearl]

marigold *n.* plant with golden or bright yellow flowers. [*Mary* (probably the Virgin), *gold* (dial.) marigold]

marijuana /ˌmærɪˈhwɑːnə/ *n.* (also **marihuana**) dried leaves etc. of hemp, smoked in cigarettes as a drug. [American Spanish]

marimba /məˈrɪmbə/ *n.* **1** xylophone played by natives of Africa and Central America. **2** modern orchestral instrument derived from this. [Congo]

marina /məˈriːnə/ *n.* harbour for pleasure-yachts etc. [Latin: related to MARINE]

marinade /ˌmærɪˈneɪd/ −*n.* **1** mixture of wine, vinegar, oil, spices, etc., for soaking meat, fish, etc. before cooking. **2** meat, fish, etc., so soaked. −*v.* (**-ding**) soak in a marinade. [Spanish *marinar* pickle in brine: related to MARINE]

marinate /ˈmærɪneɪt/ *v.* (**-ting**) = MARINADE. □ **marination** /ˌmærɪˈneɪʃ(ə)n/ *n.*

marine /məˈriːn/ −*adj.* **1** of, found in, or produced by the sea. **2 a** of shipping or naval matters (*marine insurance*). **b** for use at sea. −*n.* **1** soldier trained to serve on land or sea. **2** country's shipping, fleet, or navy (*merchant marine*). [Latin *mare* sea]

mariner /ˈmærɪnə(r)/ *n.* seaman.

marionette /ˌmærɪəˈnet/ *n.* puppet worked by strings. [French: related to *Mary*]

marital /ˈmærɪt(ə)l/ *adj.* of marriage or marriage relations. [Latin *maritus* husband]

maritime /ˈmærɪtaɪm/ *adj.* **1** connected with the sea or seafaring (*maritime insurance*). **2** living or found near the sea. [Latin: related to MARINE]

marjoram /ˈmɑːdʒərəm/ n. aromatic herb used in cookery. [French from medieval Latin]

mark¹ —n. **1** spot, sign, stain, scar, etc. on a surface etc. **2** (esp. in *comb.*) a written or printed symbol (*question mark*). **b** number or letter denoting proficiency, conduct, etc. (*black mark*). *46 marks out of 50*). **3** (usu. foll. by *of*) sign of quality, character, feeling, etc. (*mark of respect*). **4 a** sign, seal, etc., of identification. **b** cross etc. made as a signature by an illiterate person. **5** lasting effect (*war left its mark*). **6** a target etc. (*missed the mark*). **b** standard, norm (*his work falls below the mark*). **7** line etc. indicating a position. **8** (usu. *Mark*) (followed by a numeral) particular design, model, etc., of a car, aircraft, etc. (*Mark 2 Ford Granada*). **9** runner's starting-point in a race. —v. **1** a make a mark on. **b** mark with initials, name, etc. to identify etc. **2** correct and assess (a student's work etc.). **3** attach a price to (*marked the doll at £5*). **4** notice or observe (*marked his agitation*). **5 a** characterize (*day was marked by storms*). **b** acknowledge, celebrate (*marked the occasion with a toast*). **6** name or indicate on a map etc. (*the pub isn't marked*). **7** keep close to (an opponent in sport) to hinder him. **8** (as **marked** *adj.*) have natural marks (*is marked with dark spots*). □ **beside** (or **off** or **wide**) **the mark 1** irrelevant. **2** not accurate. **make one's mark** attain distinction; make an impression. **one's mark** *colloq.* opponent, object, etc., of one's own size etc. (*the little one's more my mark*). **mark down 1** reduce the price of. **2** make a written note of. **3** reduce the examination marks of. **mark off** separate by a boundary etc. **mark out 1** plan (a course of action etc.). **2** destine (*marked out for success*). **mark time 1** march on the spot without moving forward. **2** act routinely while awaiting an opportunity to advance. **mark up 1** add a proportion to the price of (goods etc.) for profit. **2** mark or correct (text etc.). **off the mark 1** having made a start. **2** = *beside the mark*. **on the mark** ready to start. **on your mark** (or **marks**) get ready to start (esp. a race). **up to the mark** normal (esp. of health). [Old English]

mark² n. = DEUTSCHMARK. [German]

mark-down n. reduction in price.

marked *adj.* **1** having a visible mark (*marked difference*). **2** clearly noticeable (*marked difference*). □ **markedly** /-kɪdlɪ/ *adv.*

marked man n. person singled out, esp. for attack.

marker n. **1** thing marking a position etc. **2** person or thing that marks. **3** broad-tipped felt-tipped pen. **4** scorer in a game.

market /ˈmɑːkɪt/ —n. **1** gathering of buyers and sellers of provisions, live-stock, etc. **2** space for this. **3** (often foll. by *for*) demand for a commodity etc. (*no market for sheds*). **4** place or group providing such a demand. **5** conditions etc. for buying or selling; rate of purchase and sale (*market is sluggish*). **6** = STOCK MARKET. —v. (**-t-**) **1** offer for sale, esp. by advertising etc. **2** buy or sell goods in a market. □ **be in the market for** wish to buy. **be on the market** be offered for sale. **put on the market** offer for sale. □ **marketer** n.

marketable *adj.* able or fit to be sold. □ **marketability** /-ˈbɪlɪtɪ/ n.

marketeer /mɑːkɪˈtɪə(r)/ n. **1** supporter of the EC and British membership of it. **2** marketer.

market garden n. farm where vegetables and fruit are grown for sale in markets.

market-place n. **1** open space for a market. **2** commercial world.

market price n. price in current dealings.

market research n. surveying of consumers' needs and preferences.

market town n. town where a market is held.

market value n. value if offered for sale.

marking n. (usu. in *pl.*) **1** identification mark. **2** colouring of an animal's fur etc.

marksman n. skilled shot, esp. with a pistol or rifle. □ **marksmanship** n.

mark-up n. **1** amount added to a price by the retailer for profit. **2** corrections in a text.

marl —n. soil of clay and lime, used as fertilizer. —v. apply marl to. □ **marly** *adj.* [medieval Latin *margila*]

marlin /ˈmɑːlɪn/ n. (*pl.* same or **-s**) US long-nosed marine fish. [from MARLIN-SPIKE]

marlinspike n. pointed iron tool used to separate strands of rope etc. [*marling* from Dutch *marlen* from *marren* bind]

marmalade /ˈmɑːməleɪd/ n. preserve of citrus fruit, usu. oranges. [Portuguese *marmelo* quince]

Marmite /ˈmɑːmaɪt/ n. *propr.* thick brown spread made from yeast and vegetable extract. [French, = cooking-pot]

marked man n. person singled out, esp. for attack.

marker n. **1** thing marking a position etc. **2** person or thing that marks. **3** broad-tipped felt-tipped pen. **4** scorer in a game.

marmoreal /maːˈmɔːrɪəl/ *adj.* of or like marble. [Latin: related to MARBLE]

marmoset /ˈmaːmə,zet/ *n.* small monkey with a long bushy tail. [French]

marmot /ˈmaːmət/ *n.* heavy-set burrowing rodent with a short bushy tail. [Latin *mus* mouse, *mons* mountain]

marocain /ˈmærə,kein/ *n.* fabric of ribbed crêpe. [French, = Moroccan]

maroon¹ /məˈruːn/ *adj. & n.* brownish-crimson. [French *marron* chestnut]

maroon² /məˈruːn/ *v.* **1** leave (a person) isolated, esp. on an island. **2** (of weather etc.) cause (a person) to be forcibly detained. [French *marron* wild person, from Spanish *cimarrón*]

marque /maːk/ *n.* make of car, as distinct from a specific model (*the Jaguar marque*). [French, = MARK¹]

marquee /maːˈkiː/ *n.* large tent for social functions etc. [French *marquise*]

marquess /ˈmaːkwɪs/ *n.* British nobleman ranking between duke and earl. [var. of MARQUIS]

marquetry /ˈmaːkɪtrɪ/ *n.* inlaid work in wood, ivory, etc. [French: related to MARQUE]

marquis /ˈmaːkwɪs/ *n.* (*pl.* -quises) foreign nobleman ranking between duke and count. [French: related to MARCH²]

marquise /maːˈkiːz/ *n.* **1** wife or widow of a marquis. **2** woman holding the rank of marquis.

marram /ˈmærəm/ *n.* shore grass that binds sand. [Old Norse, = sea-haulm]

marriage /ˈmærɪdʒ/ *n.* **1** legal union of a man and a woman for cohabitation and often procreation. **2** act or ceremony marking this. **3** particular such union (*a happy marriage*). **4** intimate union, combination. [French *marier* MARRY]

marriageable *adj.* free, ready, or fit for marriage. □ **marriageability** /-ˈbɪltɪ/ *n.*

marriage bureau *n.* company arranging introductions with a view to marriage.

marriage certificate *n.* certificate verifying a legal marriage.

marriage guidance *n.* counselling of people with marital problems.

marriage licence *n.* licence to marry.

marriage lines *n.pl.* marriage certificate.

marriage of convenience *n.* loveless marriage for gain.

marriage settlement *n.* legal property arrangement between spouses.

married —*adj.* **1** united in marriage. **2** of marriage (*married name; married life*). —*n.* (usu. in *pl.*) married person (*young marrieds*).

marron glacé /ˌmærɒn ˈglæseɪ/ *n.* (*pl.* **marrons glacés** pronunc. same) chestnut preserved in syrup. [French]

marrow /ˈmærəʊ/ *n.* **1** large fleshy usu. striped gourd eaten as a vegetable. **2** soft fatty substance in the cavities of bones. **3** essential part. □ **to the marrow** right through. [Old English]

marrowbone *n.* bone containing edible marrow.

marrowfat *n.* a kind of large pea.

marry /ˈmærɪ/ *v.* (-ies, -ied) **1** take, join, or give in marriage. **2 a** enter into marriage. **b** (foll. by *into*) become a member of (a family) by marriage. **3 a** unite intimately, combine. **b** pair (socks etc.). □ **marry off** find a spouse for. **marry up** link, join. [Latin *maritus* husband]

Marsala /maːˈsaːlə/ *n.* a dark sweet fortified dessert wine. [*Marsala* in Sicily]

Marseillaise /ˌmaːseɪˈjeɪz/ *n.* French national anthem. [French *Marseille* in France]

marsh *n.* (often *attrib.*) low watery land. □ **marshy** *adj.* (-ier, -iest). **marshiness** *n.* [Old English]

marshal /ˈmaːʃ(ə)l/ —*n.* **1** (**Marshal**) high-ranking officer of state or in the armed forces (*Earl Marshal; Field Marshal*). **2** officer arranging ceremonies, controlling racecourses, crowds, etc. —*v.* (-ll-) **1** arrange (soldiers, one's thoughts, etc.) in due order. **2** conduct (a person) ceremoniously. [French *mareschal*]

marshalling yard *n.* yard for assembling goods trains etc.

Marshal of the Royal Air Force *n.* highest rank in the RAF.

marsh gas *n.* methane.

marshland *n.* land consisting of marshes.

marshmallow /maːʃˈmæləʊ/ *n.* soft sticky sweet made of sugar, albumen, gelatin, etc. [MARSH MALLOW]

marsh mallow *n.* shrubby herbaceous plant.

marsh marigold *n.* golden-flowered plant.

marsupial /maːˈsuːpɪəl/ —*n.* mammal giving birth to underdeveloped young subsequently carried in a pouch. —*adj.* of or like a marsupial. [Greek *marsupion* pouch]

mart *n.* **1** trade centre. **2** auction-room. **3** market. [Dutch: related to MARKET]

Martello /maːˈteləʊ/ *n.* (*pl.* -s) (also **Martello tower**) small circular coastal fort. [Cape *Mortella* in Corsica]

marten /ˈmaːtɪn/ *n.* weasel-like carnivore with valuable fur. [Dutch from French]

martial /ˈmɑːʃ(ə)l/ *adj.* **1** of warfare. **2** warlike. [Latin *martialis* of Mars]

martial arts *n.pl.* oriental fighting sports such as judo and karate.

martial law *n.* military government with ordinary law suspended.

Martian /ˈmɑːʃ(ə)n/ —*adj.* of the planet Mars. —*n.* hypothetical inhabitant of Mars. [Latin]

martin /ˈmɑːtɪn/ *n.* a kind of swallow, esp. the house-martin and sand-martin. [probably St *Martin*, name of a 4th-c. bishop]

martinet /ˌmɑːtɪˈnet/ *n.* strict disciplinarian. [*Martinet*, name of a drill-master]

martingale /ˈmɑːtɪngeɪl/ *n.* strap(s) preventing a horse from rearing etc. [French, origin uncertain]

Martini /mɑːˈtiːni/ *n.* (*pl.* -s) **1** *propr.* type of vermouth. **2** cocktail of gin and French vermouth. [*Martini* and Rossi, name of a firm selling vermouth]

Martinmas /ˈmɑːtɪnməs/ *n.* St Martin's day, 11 Nov. [from MASS¹]

martyr /ˈmɑːtə(r)/ —*n.* **1 a** person killed for persisting in a belief. **b** person who suffers for a cause etc. **c** person who suffers or pretends to suffer to get pity etc. **2** (foll. by *to*) *colloq.* constant sufferer from (an ailment). —*v.* **1** put to death as a martyr. **2** torment. □ **martyrdom** *n.* [Greek *martur* witness]

marvel /ˈmɑːv(ə)l/ —*n.* **1** wonderful thing. **2** (foll. by *of*) wonderful example of (a quality). —*v.* (**-ll-**; *US* **-l-**) (foll. by *at* or *that*) feel surprise or wonder. [Latin *miror* wonder at]

marvellous /ˈmɑːvələs/ *adj.* (*US* **marvelous**) **1** astonishing. **2** excellent. □ **marvellously** *adv.* [French: related to MARVEL]

Marxism /ˈmɑːksɪz(ə)m/ *n.* political and economic theories of Marx, predicting the overthrow of capitalism and common ownership of the means of production in a classless society. □ **Marxist** *n. & adj.*

Marxism-Leninism *n.* Marxism as developed by Lenin. □ **Marxist-Leninist** *n. & adj.*

marzipan /ˈmɑːzɪpæn/ —*n.* paste of ground almonds, sugar, etc., used in confectionery. —*v.* (**-nn-**) cover with marzipan. [German from Italian]

mascara /mæˈskɑːrə/ *n.* cosmetic for darkening the eyelashes. [Italian. = mask]

mascot /ˈmæskɒt/ *n.* person, animal, or thing supposed to bring luck. [Provençal *masco* witch]

masculine /ˈmæskjʊlɪn/ —*adj.* **1** of men. **2** having manly qualities. **3** of or denoting the male gender. —*n.* masculine gender or word. □ **masculinity** /-ˈlɪnɪtɪ/ *n.* [Latin: related to MALE]

maser /ˈmeɪzə(r)/ *n.* device used to amplify or generate coherent electromagnetic radiation in the microwave range. [*microwave amplification by stimulated emission of radiation*]

mash —*n.* **1** soft or confused mixture. **2** mixture of boiled grain, bran, etc., fed to horses etc. **3** *colloq.* mashed potatoes. **4** mixture of malt and hot water used in brewing. **5** soft pulp made by crushing, mixing with water, etc. —*v.* **1** crush (potatoes etc.) to a pulp. **2** *dial.* **a** brew (tea). **b** (of tea) draw. □ **masher** *n.* [Old English]

mask /mɑːsk/ —*n.* **1** covering for all or part of the face as a disguise or for protection against infection etc. **2** respirator. **3** likeness of a person's face, esp. one from a mould (*death-mask*). **4** disguise, pretence (*throw off the mask*). —*v.* **1** cover with a mask. **2** conceal. **3** protect. [Arabic *maskara* buffoon]

masking tape *n.* adhesive tape used in decorating to protect areas where paint is not wanted.

masochism /ˈmæsəkɪz(ə)m/ *n.* **1** sexual perversion involving one's own pain or humiliation. **2** *colloq.* enjoyment of what appears to be painful or tiresome. □ **masochist** *n.* **masochistic** /-ˈkɪstɪk/ *adj.* **masochistically** /-ˈkɪstɪkəlɪ/ *adv.* [von Sacher-*Masoch*, novelist]

mason /ˈmeɪs(ə)n/ *n.* **1** person who builds with stone. **2** (**Mason**) Freemason. [French]

Masonic /məˈsɒnɪk/ *adj.* of Freemasons.

masonry *n.* **1 a** stonework. **b** work of a mason. **2** (**Masonry**) Freemasonry.

masque /mɑːsk/ *n.* musical drama with mime, esp. in the 16th and 17th c. [var. of MASK]

masquerade /ˌmæskəˈreɪd/ —*n.* **1** false show, pretence. **2** masked ball. —*v.* (**-ding**; often foll. by *as*) appear falsely or in disguise. [Spanish *máscara* mask]

mass¹ —*n.* **1** shapeless body of matter. **2** dense aggregation of objects (*mass of fibres*). **3** (in *sing.* or *pl.* usu. foll. by *of*) large number or amount. **4** (usu. foll. by *of*) unbroken expanse (of colour etc.). **5** (prec. by *the*) **a** the majority. **b** (in *pl.*) ordinary people. **6** *Physics* quantity of matter a body contains. **7** (*attrib.*) on a large scale (*mass hysteria; mass audience*). —*v.* assemble into a mass or as one body. [Latin *massa* from Greek]

mass² n. (often **Mass**) **1** Eucharist, esp. in the Roman Catholic Church. **2** celebration of this. **3** liturgy used in this. **4** musical setting of parts of this. [Latin *missa* dismissal]

massacre /'mæsəkə(r)/ —n. **1** mass killing. **2** utter defeat or destruction. —v. (-ring) **1** kill (esp. many people) cruelly or violently. **2** colloq. defeat heavily. [French]

massage /'mæsɑːʒ/ —n. rubbing and kneading of the muscles and joints with the hands, to relieve stiffness, cure strains, stimulate, etc. —v. (-ging) **1** apply massage to. **2** manipulate (statistics etc.) to give an acceptable result. **3** flatter (a person's ego etc.). [French]

massage parlour n. **1** establishment providing massage. **2** euphem. brothel.

masseur /mæˈsɜː(r)/ n. (fem. **masseuse** /mæˈsɜːz/) person who gives massage for a living. [French: related to MASSAGE]

massif /'mæsiːf/ n. compact group of mountain heights. [French: related to MASSIVE]

massive /'mæsɪv/ adj. **1** large and heavy or solid. **2** (of the features, head, etc.) relatively large or solid. **3** exceptionally large or severe (*massive heart attack*). **4** substantial, impressive. □ **massively** adv. **massiveness** n. [Latin: related to MASS¹]

mass media n.pl. = MEDIA 2.

mass noun n. Gram. noun that is not normally countable and cannot be used with the indefinite article (e.g. *bread*).

mass production n. mechanical production of large quantities of a standardized article. □ **mass-produce** v.

mast¹ /mɑːst/ n. **1** long upright post of timber etc. on a ship's keel to support sails. **2** post etc. for supporting a radio or television aerial. **3** flag-pole (*half-mast*). □ **before the mast** as an ordinary seaman. □ **masted** adj. (also in comb.). [Old English]

mast² /mɑːst/ n. fruit of the beech, oak, etc., esp. as food for pigs. [Old English]

mastectomy /mæˈstektəmɪ/ n. (pl. -ies) surgical removal of a breast. [Greek *mastos* breast]

master /'mɑːstə(r)/ —n. **1** person having control or ownership (*master of the house; dog obeyed his master; master of the hunt*). **2** captain of a merchant ship. **3** male teacher. **4** prevailing person. **5 a** skilled tradesman able to teach others (often attrib.: *master carpenter*). **b** skilled practitioner (*master of innuendo*). **6** holder of a usu. post-graduate university degree. (*Master of Arts*). **7** revered teacher in philosophy etc. **8** great artist. **9** Chess etc. player at international level. **10** original copy of a film, recording, etc., from which others can be made. **11** (**Master**) title for a boy not old enough to be called *Mr*. **12** archaic employer. —attrib. adj. **1** commanding, superior (*master hand*). **2** main, principal (*master bedroom*). **3** controlling others (*master plan*). —v. **1** overcome, defeat. **2** gain full knowledge of or skill in. [Latin *magister*]

master-class n. class given by a famous musician etc.

masterful adj. **1** imperious, domineering. **2** masterly. □ **masterfully** adv.

■ Usage *Masterful* is normally used of a person, whereas *masterly* is used of achievements, abilities, etc.

master-key n. key that opens several different locks.

masterly adj. very skilful.

■ Usage See note at *masterful*.

mastermind —n. **1** person with an outstanding intellect. **2** person directing a scheme etc. —v. plan and direct (a scheme etc.)

Master of Ceremonies n. **1** person introducing speakers at a banquet or entertainers in a variety show. **2** person in charge of a ceremonial or social occasion.

Master of the Rolls n. judge who presides over the Court of Appeal.

masterpiece n. **1** outstanding piece of artistry or workmanship. **2** person's best work.

master-stroke n. skilful tactic etc.

master-switch n. switch controlling the supply of electricity etc. to an entire system.

mastery n. **1** control, dominance. **2** (often foll. by *of*) comprehensive knowledge or skill.

masthead n. **1** top of a ship's mast, esp. as a place of observation or punishment. **2** title of a newspaper etc. at the head of the front page or editorial page.

mastic /'mæstɪk/ n. **1** gum or resin from the mastic tree, used in making varnish. **2** (in full **mastic tree**) evergreen tree yielding this. **3** waterproof filler and sealant. [Greek *mastikhē*]

masticate /'mæstɪkeɪt/ v. (-ting) grind or chew (food) with one's teeth. □ **mastication** /-ˈkeɪʃ(ə)n/ n. **masticatory** adj. [Latin from Greek]

mastiff /'mæstɪf/ n. dog of a large strong breed with drooping ears. [Latin *mansuetus* tame]

mastitis /mæˈstaɪtɪs/ n. inflammation of the breast or udder. [Greek *mastos* breast]

mastodon /ˈmastədon/ n. (pl. same or -s) large extinct mammal resembling the elephant. [Greek *odous odontos* tooth]

mastoid /ˈmastoid/ *adj.* shaped like a breast. —n. 1 = MASTOID PROCESS. 2 (usu. in pl.) *colloq.* inflammation of the mastoid process. [Greek *mastos* breast]

mastoid process n. conical prominence on the temporal bone behind the ear.

masturbate /ˈmastəbeɪt/ v. (-ting) (usu. *absol.*) sexually arouse (oneself or another) by manual stimulation of the genitals. □ **masturbation** /-ˈbeɪʃ(ə)n/ n. [Latin]

mat¹ —n. 1 small piece of coarse material on a floor, esp. for wiping one's shoes on. 2 piece of cork, rubber, etc., to protect a surface from a hot dish etc. placed on it. 3 padded floor covering in gymnastics, wrestling, etc. —v. (-tt-) (esp. as **matted** *adj.*) entangle or become entangled in a thick mass (*matted hair*). □ **on the mat** *slang* being reprimanded. [Old English]

mat² var. of MATT.

matador /ˈmatədɔː(r)/ n. bullfighter whose task is to kill the bull [Spanish from *matar* kill: related to *mate* in CHECKMATE]

match¹ —n. 1 contest or game in which players or teams compete. 2 **a** person as an equal contender (*meet one's match*). **b** person or thing exactly like or corresponding to another. 3 marriage. 4 person viewed as a marriage prospect. —v. 1 correspond (to); be like or alike, harmonize (with) (*his socks do not match; curtains match the wallpaper*). 2 equal, rival (*can you match this silk?*). 3 (foll. by *against, with*) place in conflict or competition with. 4 find material etc. that matches (another) (*can you match this silk?*). 5 find a person or thing suitable for. □ **match up** (often foll. by *with*) fit to form a whole; tally. **match up to** be as good as or equal to. [Old English]

match² n. 1 short thin piece of wood etc. with a combustible tip. 2 wick or cord etc. for firing a cannon etc. [French *mesche*]

matchboard n. tongued and grooved board fitting with similar boards.

matchbox n. box for holding matches.

matchless *adj.* incomparable.

matchmaker n. person who arranges marriages or schemes to bring couples together. □ **matchmaking** n.

match point n. *Tennis* etc. 1 position when one side needs only one more point to win the match. 2 this point.

matchstick n. stem of a match.

matchwood n. 1 wood suitable for matches. 2 minute splinters.

mate¹ —n. 1 friend or fellow worker. 2 *colloq.* form of address, esp. to another man. 3 **a** each of a breeding pair, esp. of birds. **b** *colloq.* partner in marriage. **c** (in comb.) fellow member or joint occupant of (*team-mate; room-mate*). 4 officer on a merchant ship. 5 assistant to a skilled worker (*plumber's mate*). —v. (-ting) (often foll. by *with*) 1 come or bring together for breeding. 2 *Mech.* fit well. [Low German]

mate² n. & v. (-ting) *Chess* = CHECK-MATE.

■ **Usage** *Mater* is now only found in jocular or affected use.

material /məˈtɪərɪəl/ —n. 1 matter from which a thing is made. 2 cloth, fabric. 3 (in pl.) things needed for an activity (*building materials*). 4 person or thing of a specified kind or suitable for a purpose (*officer material*). 5 (in *sing.* or pl.) information etc. for a book etc. 6 (in *sing.* or pl., often foll. by *of*) elements, constituent parts, or substance. —*adj.* 1 of matter; corporeal; not spiritual. 2 of bodily comfort etc. (*material well-being*). 3 (often foll. by *to*) important, significant, relevant. [Latin *materia*]

materialism n. 1 greater interest in material possessions and comfort than in spiritual values. 2 *Philos.* theory that nothing exists but matter. □ **materialist** n. **materialistic** /-ˈlɪstɪk/ *adj.* **materialistically** /-ˈlɪstɪkəli/ *adv.*

materialize v. (also -ise) (-zing or -sing) 1 become actual fact; happen. 2 *colloq.* appear or be present. 3 represent in or assume bodily form. □ **materialization** /-ˈzeɪʃ(ə)n/ n.

materially *adv.* substantially, significantly.

matériel /məˌtɪərɪˈel/ n. means, esp. materials and equipment in warfare. [French]

maternal /məˈtɜːn(ə)l/ *adj.* 1 of or like a mother; motherly. 2 related through the mother (*maternal uncle*). 3 of the mother in pregnancy and childbirth. □ **maternally** *adv.* [Latin *mater* mother]

maternity /məˈtɜːnɪtɪ/ n. 1 motherhood. 2 motherliness. 3 (*attrib.*) for women during pregnancy and childbirth (*maternity leave; maternity dress*). [French from medieval Latin: related to MATERNAL]

matey (also **maty**) —*adj.* (-tier, -tiest) *colloq.* sociable, familiar, friendly. —n. (pl. -s) *colloq.* (as a form of address) mate. □ **mateyness** n. (also **matiness**), **matily** *adv.*

math *n. US colloq.* mathematics. [abbreviation]

mathematical /ˌmæθəˈmætɪk(ə)l/ *adj.* **1** of mathematics. **2** rigorously precise. □ **mathematically** *adv.*

mathematical tables *n.pl.* tables of logarithms and trigonometric values etc.

mathematics /ˌmæθəˈmætɪks/ *n.pl.* **1** (also treated as *sing.*) abstract science of number, quantity, and space. **2** (as *pl.*) use of this in calculation etc. □ **mathematician** /-məˈtɪʃ(ə)n/ *n.* [Greek *manthanō* learn]

maths *n. colloq.* mathematics. [abbreviation]

matinée /ˈmætɪˌneɪ/ *n. (US* **matinee)** afternoon performance in the theatre, cinema, etc. [French from *matin* morning: related to MATINS]

matinée coat *n.* (also **matinée jacket)** baby's short knitted coat.

matinée idol *n.* handsome actor.

matins /ˈmætɪnz/ *n.* (also **mattins)** (as *sing.* or *pl.*) morning prayer, esp. in the Church of England. [Latin *matutinus* of the morning]

matriarch /ˈmeɪtrɪˌɑːk/ *n.* female head of a family or tribe. □ **matriarchal** /ˌ-ˈɑːk(ə)l/ *adj.* [Latin *mater* mother]

matriarchy /ˈmeɪtrɪˌɑːkɪ/ *n.* (*pl.* **-ies)** female-dominated system of society, with descent through the female line.

matrices *pl.* of MATRIX.

matricide /ˈmeɪtrɪˌsaɪd, ˈmæ-/ *n.* **1** killing of one's mother. **2** person who does this. [Latin: related to MATER, -CIDE]

matriculate /məˈtrɪkjʊˌleɪt/ *v.* (**-ting)** enrol at a college or university. □ **matriculation** /-ˈleɪʃ(ə)n/ *n.* [medieval Latin: related to MATRIX]

matrimony /ˈmeɪtrɪˌmənɪ/ *n.* rite or state of marriage. □ **matrimonial** /-ˈməʊnɪəl/ *adj.* [Latin *matrimonium*: related to MATER]

matrix /ˈmeɪtrɪks/ *n.* (*pl.* **matrices** /-ˌsiːz/ *or* **-es) 1** mould in which a thing is cast or shaped. **2** place etc. in which a thing is developed. **3** rock in which gems, fossils, etc., are embedded. **4** *Math.* rectangular array of elements treated as a single element. [Latin, = womb]

matron /ˈmeɪtr(ə)n/ *n.* **1** woman in charge of nursing in a hospital. **2** married, esp. staid, woman. **3** woman nurse and housekeeper at a school etc. [Latin *matrona*: related to MATER]

■ **Usage** In sense 1, *senior nursing officer* is now the official term.

matronly *adj.* like a matron, esp. portly or staid.

matron of honour *n.* married woman attending the bride at a wedding.

matt (also **mat)** *—adj.* not shiny or glossy; dull. *—n.* (in full **matt paint)** paint giving a dull flat finish. [French: related to MATE²]

matter *—n.* **1** physical substance having mass and occupying space, as distinct from mind and spirit. **2** specified substance (*colouring matter*; *reading matter*). **3** (prec. by *the*; often foll. by *with*) (thing) amiss (*something the matter with him*). **4** content as distinct from style, form, etc. **5** (often foll. by *of, for*) situation etc. under consideration or as an occasion for (regret etc.) (*matter for concern*; *matter of discipline*). **6** pus or a similar substance discharged from the body. *—v.* (often foll. by *to*) be of importance; have significance; actually. **for that matter 1** as far as that is concerned. **2** and indeed also. **a matter of** approximately; amounting to (*a matter of 40 years*). **no matter 1** (foll. by *when, how,* etc.) regardless of. **2** it is of no importance. [Latin *materia* timber, substance]

matter of course *n.* natural or expected thing.

matter-of-fact *adj.* **1** unimaginative, prosaic. **2** unemotional. □ **matter-of-factly** *adv.* **matter-of-factness** *n.*

matter of life and death *n.* matter of vital importance.

matting *n.* fabric for mats.

mattins var. of MATINS.

mattock /ˈmætək/ *n.* agricultural tool like a pickaxe, with an adze and a chisel edge. [Old English]

mattress /ˈmætrɪs/ *n.* stuffed, or air- or water-filled cushion the size of a bed. [Arabic *almatrah*]

maturate /ˈmætjʊˌreɪt/ *v.* (**-ting)** (of a boil etc.) come to maturation. [Latin: related to MATURE]

maturation /ˌmætjʊˈreɪʃ(ə)n/ *n.* **1** maturing or being matured. **2** formation of pus. [French or medieval Latin: related to MATURE]

mature /məˈtjʊə(r)/ *—adj.* (**maturer, maturest) 1** a fully developed, adult. **b** sensible, wise. **2** ripe; seasoned. **3** (of thought etc.) careful, considered. **4** (of a bill, insurance policy, etc.) due, payable. *—v.* (**-ring) 1** develop fully; ripen. **2** perfect (a plan etc.). **3** (of a bill, insurance policy, etc.) become due or payable. □ **maturely** *adv.* **matureness** *n.* **maturity** *n.* [Latin *maturus* timely]

mature student *n.* adult student.

matutinal /ˌmætjuːˈtaɪn(ə)l, məˈtjuːtɪn(ə)l/ *adj.* of the morning; early. [Latin: related to MATINS]

maty var. of MATEY.

maudlin /ˈmɔːdlɪn/ *adj.* weakly or tearfully sentimental, esp. from drunkenness. [French *Madeleine*, referring to pictures of Mary Magdalen weeping]

maul /mɔːl/ *v.* **1** tear the flesh of; claw. **2** handle roughly. **3** damage by criticism. —*n.* **1** *Rugby* loose scrum. **2** brawl. **3** heavy hammer. [Latin *malleus* hammer]

maulstick /ˈmɔːlstɪk/ *n.* (also **mahlstick**) stick held to support the hand in painting. **2** move or act listlessly or idly. [Dutch *maalen* paint]

maunder /ˈmɔːndə(r)/ *v.* **1** talk ramblingly. **2** move or act listlessly or idly. [origin unknown]

Maundy /ˈmɔːndɪ/ *n.* distribution of Maundy money. [French *mandé* from Latin *mandatum* command]

Maundy money *n.* specially minted silver coins distributed by the British sovereign on Maundy Thursday.

Maundy Thursday *n.* Thursday before Easter.

mausoleum /ˌmɔːsəˈliːəm/ *n.* magnificent tomb. [from *Mausōlos*, king of Caria, whose tomb had this name]

mauve /məʊv/ *adj.* pale purple. —*n.* this colour. □ **mauvish** *adj.* [Latin: related to MALLOW]

maverick /ˈmævərɪk/ *n.* **1** unorthodox or independent-minded person. **2** *US* unbranded calf or yearling. [*Maverick*, name of an owner of unbranded cattle]

maw *n.* **1** stomach of an animal or *colloq.* greedy person. **2** jaws or throat of a voracious animal. [Old English]

mawkish /ˈmɔːkɪʃ/ *adj.* feebly sentimental; sickly. □ **mawkishly** *adv.* **mawkishness** *n.* [obsolete *mawk* MAGGOT]

max. *abbr.* maximum.

maxi /ˈmæksɪ/ *n.* (*pl.* **-s**) *colloq.* maxicoat, -skirt, etc. [abbreviation]

maxi- *comb. form* very large or long. [abbreviation of MAXIMUM; cf. MINI-]

maxilla /mækˈsɪlə/ *n.* (*pl.* **-llae** /-liː/) jaw or jawbone, esp. (in vertebrates) the upper jaw. □ **maxillary** *adj.* [Latin]

maxim /ˈmæksɪm/ *n.* general truth or rule of conduct briefly expressed. [French or medieval Latin: related to MAXIMUM]

maxima *pl.* of MAXIMUM.

maximal /ˈmæksɪm(ə)l/ *adj.* of or being a maximum.

maximize /ˈmæksɪmaɪz/ *v.* (also **-ise**) (**-zing** or **-sing**) make as large or great as possible. □ **maximization** /-ˈzeɪʃ(ə)n/ *n.* [Latin: related to MAXIMUM]

■ **Usage** *Maximize* should not be used in standard English to mean 'to make as good as possible' or 'to make the most of.'

maximum /ˈmæksɪməm/ —*n.* (*pl.* **-ma**) highest possible amount, size, etc. —*adj.* greatest in amount, size, etc. [Latin *maximus* greatest]

May *n.* **1** fifth month of the year. **2** (**may**) hawthorn, esp. in blossom. [Latin *Maius* or the goddess Maia]

may *v.aux.* (*3rd sing. present* **may**; *past* **might** /maɪt/) **1** expressing: **a** (often foll. by *well* for emphasis) possibility (*it may be true; you may well lose your way*). **b** permission (*may I come in?*). **c** a wish (*may he live to regret it*). **d** uncertainty or irony (*who may you be?; who are you, may I ask?*). **2** in purpose clauses and after *wish, fear,* etc. (*hope he may succeed*). □ **be that as it may** (or **that is as it may be**) it is possible (but) (*be that as it may I still want to go*); may as well = *may; I still want to move?* (see MIGHT). [Old English]

■ **Usage** In sense 1b, both *can* and *may* are used to express permission; in more formal contexts *may* is preferred since *can* also denotes capability (*can I move? = am I physically able to move?; may I move? = am I allowed to move?*).

Maya /ˈmaɪə/ *n.* **1** (*pl.* same or **-s**) member of an ancient Indian people of Central America. **2** their language. □ **Mayan** *adj. & n.* [native name]

maybe /ˈmeɪbiː/ *adv.* perhaps. [from *it may be*]

May Day *n.* **1** May as a Spring festival or international holiday in honour of workers.

mayday /ˈmeɪdeɪ/ *n.* international radio distress-signal. [representing pronunciation of French *m'aidez* help me]

mayfly *n.* a kind of insect living briefly that bloom in May.

mayhem /ˈmeɪhem/ *n.* destruction; havoc. [Anglo-French *mahem*: related to MAIM]

mayn't /ˈmeɪənt/ *contr.* may not.

mayonnaise /ˌmeɪəˈneɪz/ *n.* **1** thick creamy dressing of egg-yolks, oil, vinegar, etc. **2** dish dressed with this (*egg mayonnaise*). [French]

mayor /meə(r)/ *n.* **1** head of the corporation of a city or borough. **2** head of a district council with the status of a borough. □ **mayoral** *adj.* [Latin: related to MAJOR]

mayoralty /ˈmeərəltɪ/ *n.* (*pl.* **-ies**) **1** office of mayor. **2** period of this.

mayoress /ˈmeərɪs/ *n.* **1** woman mayor. **2** wife or official consort of a mayor.

maypole *n.* decorated pole for dancing round on May Day.

May queen n. girl chosen to preside over May Day festivities.

maze n. 1 network of paths and hedges designed as a puzzle for those who enter it. 2 labyrinth. 3 confused network, mass, etc. [related to AMAZE]

mazurka /məˈzɜːkə/ n. 1 lively Polish dance in triple time. 2 music for this. [French or German from Polish]

MB abbr. 1 Bachelor of Medicine. 2 Computing megabyte. [sense 1 from Latin Medicinae Baccalaureus]

MBA abbr. Master of Business Administration.

MBE abbr. Member of the Order of the British Empire.

MBO abbr. management buyout.

MC abbr. 1 Master of Ceremonies. 2 Military Cross. 3 Member of Congress.

MCC abbr. Marylebone Cricket Club.

McCarthyism, McCoy see at MCC.

MD abbr. 1 Doctor of Medicine. 2 Managing Director. [sense 1 from Latin Medicinae Doctor]

Md symb. mendelevium.

ME abbr. myalgic encephalomyelitis, a condition with prolonged flu-like symptoms and depression.

me¹ /miː/ pron. 1 objective case of I² (he saw me). 2 colloq. = I² (it's me all right; is taller than me). [Old English accusative and dative of I²]

me² /miː/ n. (also **mi**) Mus. third note of a major scale. [Latin mira, word arbitrarily taken]

mea culpa /ˌmeɪə ˈkʊlpə/ —n. acknowledgement of error. —int. expressing this. [Latin, = by my fault]

mead n. alcoholic drink of fermented honey and water. [Old English]

meadow /ˈmedəʊ/ n. 1 piece of grassland, esp. one used for hay. 2 low marshy ground, esp. near a river. □ **meadowy** adj. [Old English]

meadowsweet n. fragrant meadow and marsh plant with creamy-white flowers.

meagre /ˈmiːɡə(r)/ adj. (US **meager**) 1 scant in amount or quality. 2 lean, thin. [Anglo-French megre from Latin macer]

meal¹ n. 1 occasion when food is eaten. 2 the food eaten at a meal. □ **make a meal of** colloq. treat (a task etc.) too laboriously or fussily. [Old English]

meal² n. 1 grain or pulse ground to powder. 2 Scot. oatmeal. 3 US maize flour. [Old English]

meals on wheels n.pl. (usu. treated as sing.) regular voluntary esp. lunch deliveries to old people, invalids, etc.

meal-ticket n. colloq. person or thing that is a source of maintenance or income.

mealtime n. usual time of eating.

mealy adj. (**-ier**, **-iest**) 1 of, like, or containing meal. 2 (of a complexion) pale. □ **mealiness** n.

mealy-mouthed adj. afraid to speak plainly.

mean¹ v. (past and past part. **meant** /ment/) 1 have as one's purpose or intention (meant no harm by it; I didn't mean to break it). 2 design or destine for a purpose (meant to be used). 3 intend to convey or refer to (I mean Richmond in Surrey). 4 (often foll. by that) entail, involve, portend, signify (this means war; means that he is dead). 5 (of a word) have as its equivalent in the same or another language. 6 (foll. by to) be of specified importance to (that means a lot to me). □ **mean business** colloq. be in earnest. **mean it** not be joking or exaggerating. **mean well** have good intentions. [Old English]

mean² adj. 1 niggardly; not generous. 2 ignoble, small-minded. 3 (of capacity, understanding, etc.) inferior, poor. 4 shabby, inadequate (mean hovel). 5 a malicious, ill-tempered. b US vicious or aggressive in behaviour. 6 US colloq. skilful, formidable (a mean fighter). □ **no mean** a very good (no mean feat). □ **meanly** adv. **meanness** n. [Old English]

mean³ —n. 1 median point (mean between modesty and pride). 2 a term midway between the first and last terms of an arithmetical etc. progression. b quotient of the sum of several quantities and their number; average. —adj. 1 (of a quantity) equally far from two extremes. 2 calculated as a mean. [Latin medianus MEDIAN]

meander /mɪˈændə(r)/ —v. 1 wander at random. 2 (of a stream) wind about.—n. 1 (in pl.) sinuous windings of a river, path, etc. 2 circuitous journey. [Greek Maiandros, a winding river in ancient Phrygia]

meanie /ˈmiːnɪ/ n. (also **meany**) (pl. **-ies**) colloq. niggardly or small-minded person.

meaning —n. 1 what is meant. 2 significance. 3 importance. —adj. expressive, significant (meaning glance). □ **meaningly** adv.

meaningful adj. 1 full of meaning; significant. 2 Logic able to be interpreted. □ **meaningfully** adv. **meaningfulness** n.

meaningless adj. having no meaning or significance. □ **meaninglessly** adv. **meaninglessness** n.

means n.pl. (often treated as sing.) 1 action, agent, device, or method producing a result (means of quick travel). 2 a money resources (live beyond one's

mean sea level n. the mean level of the sea's surface, used in the reckoning of heights and as a barometric standard.

means *n.pl.* **b** wealth (*man of means*). **all means** certainly. **by means of** by the agency etc. of. **by no means** certainly not. [from MEAN³]

meant *past* and *past part.* of MEAN¹.

meantime —*adv.* = MEANWHILE. —*n.* intervening period (esp. *in the mean-time*).

■ **Usage** As an adverb, *meantime* is less common than *meanwhile*.

meanwhile —*adv.* **1** in the intervening period of time. **2** at the same time. —*n.* intervening period (esp. *in the mean-while*).

measles /ˈmiːz(ə)lz/ *n.pl.* (also treated as *sing.*) infectious viral disease marked by a red rash. [Low German *masele* or Dutch *masel*]

measly /ˈmiːzli/ *adj.* (**-ier**, **-iest**) *colloq.* meagre, contemptible.

measure /ˈmeʒə(r)/ —*n.* **1** size or quantity found by measuring. **2** system or unit of measuring (*liquid measure*, *measures of wheat*). **3** rod, tape, vessel, etc. for measuring. **4** (often foll. by *of*) degree, extent, or amount (*a measure of agreement*). **5** factor determining evaluation etc. (*sales are the measure of popular-ity*). **6** (usu. in pl.) suitable action to achieve some end. **7** legislative bill, act, etc. **8** prescribed extent or quantity. **9** poetic metre. **10** mineral stratum (*coal measures*). —*v.* (**-ring**) **1** ascertain the extent or quantity of (a thing) by com-parison with a known standard. **2** be of a specified size. **3** ascertain the size of (a person) for clothes. **4** estimate (a quality etc.) by some criterion. **5** (often foll. by *off*) mark (a line etc. of a given length) **6** (foll. by *out*) distribute in measured quantities. **7** (foll. by *with*, *against*) bring (oneself or one's strength etc.) into competition with. □ **beyond measure** excessively. **for good measure** as a finishing touch. **in some measure** partly. **measure up 1** take the measurements (of). **2** (often foll. by *to*) have the qualifications (for). □ **measur-able** *adj.* [Latin *mensura* from *metior* measure]

measured *adj.* **1** rhythmical; regular (*measured tread*). **2** (of language) care-fully considered.

measureless *adj.* not measurable; infinite.

measurement *n.* **1** measuring. **2** amount measured. **3** (in *pl.*) detailed dimensions.

meat *n.* **1** animal flesh as food. **2** (often foll. by *of*) substance; chief part. □ **meaty** *adj.* [Old English]

meatless *adj.* having no meat.

meatball *n.* small round ball of minced meat.

meat loaf *n.* mince meat etc. moulded and baked.

meat safe *n.* ventilated cupboard for storing meat.

meaty *adj.* (**-ier**, **-iest**) **1** full of meat; fleshy. **2** of or like meat. **3** substantial, full of interest, satisfying. □ **meatiness** *n.*

Mecca /ˈmekə/ *n.* **pla**ce one aspires to visit. [*Mecca*, Muslim holy city in Ara-bia]

mechanic /mɪˈkænɪk/ *n.* person skilled in using or repairing machinery. [Latin: related to MACHINE]

mechanical *adj.* **1** of machines or machinery. **2** working or produced by machinery. **3** (of an action etc.) auto-matic; repetitive. **4** (of an agency, prin-ciple, etc.) belonging to mechanics. **5** of mechanics as a science. □ **mechan-ically** *adv.* [Latin: related to MECHANIC]

mechanical engineer *n.* person qualified in the design, construction, etc. of machines.

mechanics *n.pl.* (usu. treated as *sing.*) **1** branch of applied mathematics deal-ing with motion etc. **2** science of machinery. **3** routine technical aspects of a thing (*mechanics of local govern-ment*).

mechanism /ˈmekəniz(ə)m/ *n.* **1** struc-ture or parts of a machine. **2** system of parts working together. **3** process; method (*defence mechanism*; *no mechanism for complaints*). □ **mechanistic** /-ˈnɪstɪk/ *adj.* [Greek: related to MACHINE]

mechanize /ˈmekənaɪz/ *v* (also **-ise**) (**-zing** or **-sing**) **1** introduce machines in (a factory etc.). **2** make mechanical. **3** equip with tanks, armoured cars, etc. □ **mechanization** /-ˈzeɪʃ(ə)n/ *n.*

Med *n. colloq.* Mediterranean Sea. [abbreviation]

medal /ˈmed(ə)l/ *n.* commemorative metal disc etc., esp. awarded for milit-ary or sporting prowess. [Latin: related to METAL]

medallion /mɪˈdæljən/ *n.* **1** large medal. **2** thing so shaped, e.g. a decorative panel etc. [Italian: related to MEDAL]

medallist /ˈmedəlɪst/ *n.* (US **medalist**) winner of a (specified) medal (*gold medallist*).

meddle /'med(ə)l/ v. (-ling) (often foll. by with, in) interfere in others' concerns. □ **meddler** n. [Latin: related to MIX]

meddlesome adj. interfering.

media /'miːdɪə/ n.pl. 1 pl. of MEDIUM. 2 (usu. prec. by the) mass communications (esp. newspapers and broadcasting) regarded collectively.

■ **Usage** Media is commonly used with a singular verb (e.g. the media is biased), but this is not generally accepted (cf. DATA).

mediaeval var. of MEDIEVAL.

medial /'miːdɪəl/ adj. = MEDIAN. □ **medially** adv. [Latin medius middle]

median /'miːdɪən/ adj. situated in the middle. —n. 1 straight line drawn from any vertex of a triangle to the middle of the opposite side. 2 middle value of a series. [Latin: related to MEDIAL]

mediate /'miːdɪ,eɪt/ v. (-ting) 1 (often foll. by between) intervene (between disputants) to settle a quarrel etc. 2 bring about (a result) thus. □ **mediation** /-'eɪʃ(ə)n/ n. **mediator** n. [Latin medius middle]

medic /'medɪk/ n. colloq. medical practitioner or student. [Latin medicus physician]

medical /'medɪk(ə)l/ —adj. of medicine in general or as distinct from surgery (medical ward). —n. colloq. medical examination. □ **medically** adv.

medical certificate n. certificate of fitness or unfitness for work etc.

medical examination n. examination to determine a person's physical fitness.

medical officer n. person in charge of the health services of a local authority etc.

medical practitioner n. physician or surgeon.

medicament /mɪ'dɪkəmənt/ n. = MEDICINE 2.

Medicare /'medɪˌkeə(r)/ n. US federally funded health insurance scheme for the elderly. [from MEDICAL, CARE]

medicate /'medɪˌkeɪt/ v. (-ting) 1 treat medically. 2 impregnate with medicine etc. □ **medicative** /-kətɪv/ adj. [Latin medicare medicat-]

medication /ˌmedɪ'keɪʃ(ə)n/ n. 1 = MEDICINE 2. 2 treatment using drugs.

medicinal /mɪ'dɪsɪn(ə)l/ adj. (of a substance) healing. □ **medicinally** adv.

medicine /'meds(ə)n/ n. 1 science or practice of the diagnosis, treatment, and prevention of disease, esp. as distinct from surgery. 2 drug etc. for the treatment or prevention of disease, esp.

taken by mouth. □ **take one's medicine** submit to something disagreeable [Latin medicina]

medicine man n. tribal, esp. N. American Indian, witch-doctor.

medieval /ˌmedɪ'iːv(ə)l/ adj. (also **mediaeval**) 1 of the Middle Ages. 2 colloq. old-fashioned. [Latin medium aevum middle age]

medieval history n. history of the 5th–15th c.

medieval Latin n. Latin of about AD 600–1500.

mediocre /ˌmiːdɪ'əʊkə(r)/ adj. 1 indifferent in quality. 2 second-rate. [Latin mediocris]

mediocrity /ˌmiːdɪ'ɒkrɪtɪ/ n. (pl. -ies) 1 being mediocre. 2 mediocre person.

meditate /'medɪˌteɪt/ v. (-ting) 1 (often foll. by on, upon) engage in (esp. religious) contemplation. 2 plan mentally. □ **meditation** /-'teɪʃ(ə)n/ n. **meditator** n. [Latin meditor]

meditative /'medɪtətɪv/ adj. 1 inclined to meditate. 2 indicative of meditation, thoughtful. □ **meditatively** adv. **meditativeness** n.

Mediterranean /ˌmedɪtə'reɪnɪən/ adj. of the sea bordered by S. Europe, SW Asia, and N. Africa, or its surrounding region (Mediterranean cookery). [Latin mediterraneus inland]

medium /'miːdɪəm/ —n. (pl. media or -s) 1 middle quality, degree, etc. between extremes (find a happy medium). 2 means of communication (medium of television). 3 substance, e.g. air, through which sense-impressions are conveyed. 4 physical environment etc. of a living organism. 5 means. 6 material or form used by an artist, composer, etc. 7 liquid (e.g. oil or gel) used for diluting paints. 8 (pl. -s) person claiming to communicate with the dead. —adj. 1 between two qualities, degrees, etc. 2 average (of medium height). [Latin medius middle]

medium-range adj. (of an aircraft, missile, etc.) able to travel a medium distance.

medium wave n. radio wave of frequency between 300 kHz and 3 MHz.

medlar /'medlə(r)/ n. 1 tree bearing small brown apple-like fruits, eaten when decayed. 2 such a fruit. [French medler from Greek mespilē]

medley /'medlɪ/ n. (pl. -s) 1 varied mixture. 2 collection of tunes etc. played as one piece. [French medlee]

medulla /mɪ'dʌlə/ n. 1 inner part of certain organs etc. 2 the kidney. 2 soft internal tissue of plants. □ **medullary** adj. [Latin]

nedulla oblongata /ˌnɪblɒŋˈgɑːtə/ n. lowest part of the brainstem, formed from a continuation of the spinal cord. [Old Norse]

nedusa /mɪˈdjuːsə/ n. (pl. **medusae** /-siː/ or -s) jellyfish. [Greek *Medousa*, name of a Gorgon]

neek adj. humble and submissive or gentle. □ **meekly** adv. **meekness** n. [Old Norse]

neerkat /ˈmɪəkat/ n. S. African mongoose. [Dutch, = sea-cat]

neerschaum /ˈmɪəʃəm, -ʃɔːm/ n. 1 soft white clay-like substance. 2 tobacco-pipe with its bowl made from this. [German, = sea-foam]

meet[1] -v. (past and past part. **met**) 1 encounter (a person etc.), or (of two or more people) come together by accident or design; come face to face (with) (*met on the bridge*). 2 be present by design at the arrival of (a person, train, etc.). 3 come or seem to come together or into contact (with); join (*where the sea and the sky meet; jacket won't meet*). 4 make the acquaintance of (*delighted to meet you, all met at Oxford*). 5 come together for business, worship, etc. (*union met to confront their death; met with hostility*). 6 a deal with or answer (a demand, objection, etc.) (*met the proposal with hostility*). **b** satisfy or conform with (*agreed to meet the new terms*). 7 pay (a bill etc.); honour (a cheque) (*meet the cost*). 8 (often foll. by *with*) experience, encounter, or receive (*met their death; met with hostility*). 9 (often foll. by *with*) collog. confront in battle etc. —n. 1 assembly for a hunt. 2 assembly for sport, esp. athletics. □ **make ends meet** see END. **meet the case** be adequate. **meet the eye** be visible or evident. **meet a person half way** compromise with. **meet up** collog. meet. **with 1** see sense 8 of v. 2 meet (a reaction) (*met with her approval*). 3 esp. US = sense 1 of v. [Old English]

meet[2] adj. archaic fitting, proper. [related to METE]

meeting n. 1 coming together. 2 assembly of esp. a society, committee, etc. 3 = RACE MEETING.

mega /ˈmɛgə/ slang —adj. 1 excellent. 2 enormous. —adv. extremely.

mega- comb. form 1 large. 2 one million (10^6) in the metric system of measurement. 3 slang excellent; very big (*omega-stupid; mega-project*). [Greek *megas* great]

megabuck /ˈmɛgəbʌk/ n. US slang million dollars.

megabyte /ˈmɛgəbʌɪt/ n. Computing 1,048,576 (i.e. 2^20) bytes as a measure of data capacity, or loosely 1,000,000. Lon dollars.

megadeath /ˈmɛgədɛθ/ n. death of one million people (in war).

megahertz /ˈmɛgəhɜːts/ n. (pl. same) one million hertz, esp. as a measure of radio frequency.

megalith /ˈmɛgəlɪθ/ n. large stone, esp. as a prehistoric monument or part of one. □ **megalithic** /-ˈlɪθɪk/ adj. [Greek *lithos* stone]

megalomania /ˌmɛgələˈmeɪnɪə/ n. 1 mental disorder producing delusions of grandeur. 2 passion for grandiose schemes. □ **megalomaniac** adj. & n. [Greek *megas* great, MANIA]

megalosaurus /ˌmɛgələˈsɔːrəs/ n. (pl. -ruses) large flesh-eating dinosaur with stout hind legs and small forelimbs. [Greek *megas* great, *sauros* lizard]

megaphone /ˈmɛgəfəʊn/ n. large funnel-shaped device for amplifying the voice. [Greek *megas* great, *phōnē* sound]

megastar /ˈmɛgəstɑː(r)/ n. collog. very famous entertainer etc.

megaton /ˈmɛgətʌn/ n. unit of explosive power equal to one million tons of TNT.

megavolt /ˈmɛgəvəʊlt/ n. one million volts, esp. as a unit of electromotive force.

megawatt /ˈmɛgəwɒt/ n. one million watts, esp. as a measure of electrical power.

megohm /ˈmɛgəʊm/ n. one million ohms.

meiosis /maɪˈəʊsɪs/ n. (pl. **meioses** /-siːz/) 1 cell division that results in gametes with half the normal chromosome number. 2 = LITOTES. [Greek *meiōn* less]

melamine /ˈmɛləmiːn/ n. 1 white crystalline compound producing resins. 2 (in full **melamine resin**) plastic made from this and used esp. for laminated coatings.

melancholia /ˌmɛlənˈkəʊlɪə/ n. depression and anxiety. [Latin: related to MELANCHOLY]

melancholy /ˈmɛlənkəlɪ/ —n. 1 pensive sadness. 2 a mental depression. b tendency to this. —adj. sad, saddening, depressing; expressing sadness. □ **melancholic** /-ˈkɒlɪk/ adj. [Greek *melas* black, *kholē* bile]

mélange /meɪˈlɑːʒ/ n. mixture, medley. [French *mêler* mix]

melanin /ˈmɛlənɪn/ n. dark pigment in the hair, skin, etc., causing tanning in sunlight. [Greek *melas* black]

melanoma /ˌmɛləˈnəʊmə/ n. malignant skin tumour.

Melba toast /ˈmɛlbə/ n. very thin crisp toast. [*Melba*, name of a soprano]

meld v. merge, blend. [origin uncertain]

554

mêlée /ˈmeleɪ/ n. (US **melee**) 1 confused fight, skirmish, or scuffle. 2 muddle. [French: related to MEDLEY]

mellifluous /mɪˈlɪfluəs/ adj. (of a voice etc.) pleasing, musical, flowing. □ **mellifluously** adv. **mellifluousness** n. [Latin mel honey, fluo flow]

mellow /ˈmeləʊ/ —adj. 1 (of sound, colour, light) soft and rich, free from harshness. 2 (of character) gentle; mature. 3 genial, jovial. 4 euphem. partly intoxicated. 5 (of fruit) soft, sweet, and juicy. 6 (of wine) well-matured, smooth. 7 (of earth) rich, loamy. —v. make or become mellow. □ **mellowly** adv. **mellowness** n. [origin unknown]

melodeon /mɪˈləʊdɪən/ n. (also **melodion**) 1 small organ similar to the harmonium. 2 small German accordion. [from MELODY, HARMONIUM]

melodic /mɪˈlɒdɪk/ adj. of melody; melodious. □ **melodically** adv. [Greek: related to MELODY]

melodious /mɪˈləʊdɪəs/ adj. 1 of, producing, or having melody. 2 sweetsounding. □ **melodiously** adv. **melodiousness** n. [French: related to MELODY]

melodrama /ˈmelədrɑːmə/ n. 1 sensational play etc. appealing blatantly to the emotions. 2 this type of drama. 3 theatrical language, behaviour, etc. □ **melodramatic** /-drəˈmætɪk/ adj. **melodramatically** /-drəˈmætɪkəlɪ/ adv. [Greek melos music, DRAMA]

melody /ˈmelədɪ/ n. (pl. -ies) 1 single notes arranged to make a distinctive recognizable pattern; tune. 2 principal part in harmonized music. 3 musical arrangement of words. 4 sweet music, tunefulness. [Greek melos song: related to ODE]

melon /ˈmelən/ n. 1 sweet fleshy fruit of various climbing plants of the gourd family. 2 such a gourd. [Greek mēlon apple]

melt v. 1 become liquefied or change to liquid by the action of heat; dissolve. 2 (as **molten** adj.) (esp. of metals etc.) liquefied by heat (molten lava; molten lead). 3 (of food) be delicious, seeming to dissolve in the mouth. 4 soften, or (of a person, the heart, etc.) be softened, by pity, love, etc. (a melting look). 5 (usu. foll. by into) merge imperceptibly. 6 (often foll. by away) (of a person) leave or disappear unobtrusively (melted into the background). □ **melt away** disappear by or as if by liquefaction. **melt down** 1 melt (esp. metal) for reuse. 2 become liquid and lose structure. [Old English]

meltdown n. 1 melting of a structure, esp. the overheated core of a nuclear reactor. 2 disastrous event, e.g. a rapid fall in share values.

melting point n. temperature at which a solid melts.

melting-pot n. place for mixing races, theories, etc.

member /ˈmembə(r)/ n. 1 person etc. belonging to a society, team, group, etc. 2 (**Member**) person elected to certain assemblies etc. 3 part of a larger structure, e.g. of a group of figures or a mathematical set. 4 a part or organ of the body, esp. a limb. b = PENIS. [Latin membrum limb]

membership n. 1 being a member. 2 number or body of members.

membrane /ˈmembreɪn/ n. 1 pliable sheetlike tissue connecting or lining organs in plants and animals. 2 thin pliable sheet or skin. □ **membranous** /ˈmembrənəs/ adj. [Latin membrana skin, parchment: related to MEMBER]

memento /mɪˈmentəʊ/ n. (pl. -es or -s) souvenir of a person or event. [Latin, imperative of memini remember]

memento mori /mɪˌmentəʊ ˈmɔːrɪ/ n. skull etc. as a reminder of death. [Latin, = remember you must die]

memo /ˈmeməʊ/ n. (pl. -s) colloq. memorandum. [abbreviation]

memoir /ˈmemwɑː(r)/ n. 1 historical account etc. written from personal knowledge or special sources. 2 (in pl.) autobiography, esp. partial or dealing with specific events or people. 3 essay on a learned subject. [French mémoire: related to MEMORY]

memorabilia /ˌmeməˈrəbɪlɪə/ n.pl. souvenirs of memorable events. [Latin: related to MEMORABLE]

memorable /ˈmemərəb(ə)l/ adj. 1 worth remembering. 2 easily remembered. □ **memorably** adv. [Latin memor mindful]

memorandum /ˌmeməˈrændəm/ n. (pl. -da or -s) 1 note or record for future use. 2 informal written message, esp. in business, diplomacy, etc. [see MEMORABLE]

memorial /mɪˈmɔːrɪəl/ —n. object etc. established in memory of a person or event. —attrib. adj. commemorating (memorial service). [Latin: related to MEMORY]

memorize /ˈmeməraɪz/ v. (also -ise) (-zing or -sing) commit to memory.

memory /ˈmemərɪ/ n. (pl. -ies) 1 faculty by which things are recalled to or kept in the mind. 2 a this in an individual (my memory is failing). b store of things remembered (deep in my memory). 3 recollection; remembrance, esp. of a

person etc.; person or thing remembered (*memory of better times; his mother's memory*). **5** posthumous reputation (*his memory lives on; of blessed memory*). **6** length of remembered time of a specific person, group, etc. (*within living memory*). **7** remembering (*deed worthy of memory*). □ **from memory** as remembered (without checking). **in memory of** to keep alive the remembrance of. [Latin *memoria* from *memor* mindful]

memory lane *n.* (usu. prec. by *down, along*) *joc.* sentimental remembering.

memsahib /ˈmemsɑːb/ *n. Anglo-Ind. hist.* Indian name for a European married woman 'in India. [from MA'AM, SAHIB]

men *pl.* of MAN.

menace /ˈmenɪs/ —*n.* **1** threat. **2** dangerous thing or person. **3** *joc.* pest, nuisance. —*v.* (**-cing**) threaten. □ **menacingly** *adv.* [Latin *minax* from *minor* threaten]

ménage /meɪˈnɑːʒ/ *n.* household. [French: related to MÉNAGE]

ménage à trois /meɪnɑːʒ ɑː ˈtrwɑː/ *n.* (*pl.* **ménages à trois**) household of three, usu. a married couple and a lover. [French, = household of three]

menagerie /mɪˈnædʒərɪ/ *n.* small zoo. [French: related to MÉNAGE]

mend —*v.* **1** restore to good condition; repair. **2** regain health. **3** improve (*mend matters*). —*n.* darn or repair in material etc. □ **mend one's ways** reform oneself. **on the mend** recovering, esp. in health. [Anglo-French: related to AMEND]

mendacious /menˈdeɪʃəs/ *adj.* lying, untruthful. □ **mendacity** /-ˈdæsɪtɪ/ *n.* (*pl.* **-ies**). [Latin *mendax*]

mendelevium /ˌmendɪˈliːvɪəm/ *n.* artificially made transuranic radioactive metallic element. [*Mendeleev*, name of a chemist]

Mendelian /menˈdiːlɪən/ *adj.* of Mendel's theory of heredity by genes. [*Mendel*, name of a botanist]

mendicant /ˈmendɪkənt/ —*adj.* **1** begging. **2** (of a friar) living solely on alms. —*n.* **1** beggar. **2** mendicant friar. [Latin *mendicus* beggar]

mending *n.* **1** action of repairing **2** things, esp. clothes, to be mended.

menfolk *n.pl.* men, esp. the men of a family.

menhir /ˈmenhɪə(r)/ *n.* usu. prehistoric monument of a tall upright stone. [Breton *men* stone, *hir* long]

menial /ˈmiːnɪəl/ —*adj.* (of esp. work) degrading, servile. —*n.* domestic servant. [Anglo-French *meinie* retinue]

meninges /mɪˈnɪndʒiːz/ *n.pl.* three membranes enclosing the brain and spinal cord. [Greek *mēnigx* membrane]

meningitis /ˌmenɪnˈdʒaɪtɪs/ *n.* (esp. viral) infection and inflammation of the meninges.

meniscus /mɪˈnɪskəs/ *n.* (*pl.* **menisci** /-saɪ/) **1** curved upper surface of liquid in a tube. **2** lens convex on one side and concave on the other. [Greek *mēniskos* crescent, from *mēnē* moon]

menopause /ˈmenəpɔːz/ *n.* **1** ceasing of menstruation. **2** period in a woman's life (usu. 45–55) when this occurs. □ **menopausal** /-ˈpɔːz(ə)l/ *adj.* [Greek *mēn* month, PAUSE]

menorah /mɪˈnɔːrə/ *n.* seven-branched Jewish candelabrum [Hebrew, = candlestick]

menses /ˈmensiːz/ *n.pl.* flow of menstrual blood etc. [Latin, pl. of *mensis* month]

mens rea /menz ˈriːə/ *n. Law* criminal intent. [Latin, = guilty mind]

menstrual /ˈmenstrʊəl/ *adj.* of menstruation. [Latin *menstruus* monthly]

menstrual cycle *n.* process of ovulation and menstruation.

menstruate /ˈmenstrʊeɪt/ *v.* (**-ting**) undergo menstruation.

menstruation /ˌmenstrʊˈeɪʃ(ə)n/ *n.* process of discharging blood etc. from the uterus, usu. at monthly intervals from puberty to menopause.

mensuration /ˌmensjʊˈreɪʃ(ə)n/ *n.* **1** measuring. **2** measuring of lengths, areas, and volumes. [Latin: related to MEASURE]

menswear *n.* clothes for men.

-ment *suffix* **1** forming nouns expressing the means or result of verbal action (*abridgement; embankment*). **2** forming nouns from adjectives (*merriment; oddment*). [Latin *-mentum*]

mental /ˈment(ə)l/ *adj.* **1** of, in, or done by the mind. **2** caring for mental patients. **3** *colloq.* insane. □ **mentally** *adv.* [Latin *mens ment-* mind]

mental age *n.* degree of mental development in terms of the average age at which such development is attained.

mental block *n.* inability due to subconscious mental factors.

mental deficiency *n.* abnormally low intelligence.

mentality /menˈtælɪtɪ/ *n.* (*pl.* **-ies**) mental character or disposition; kind or degree of intelligence.

mental patient *n.* sufferer from mental illness.

mental reservation *n.* silent qualification made while seeming to agree.

menthol /ˈmenθɒl/ *n.* mint-tasting organic alcohol found in oil of peppermint

etc., used as a flavouring and to relieve local pain. [Latin: related to MINT[1]]

mentholated /ˈmenθəˌleɪtɪd/ adj. treated with or containing menthol.

mention /ˈmenʃ(ə)n/ —v. 1 refer to briefly or by name. 2 reveal or disclose (do not mention this to anyone). 3 (usu. as mention in dispatches) award a minor military honour to in war. —n. 1 reference, esp. by name. 2 minor military or other honour. □ **don't mention it** polite reply to an apology or thanks. **not to mention** and also. [Latin mentio]

mentor /ˈmentɔː(r)/ n. experienced and trusted adviser. [Mentor in Homer's Odyssey]

menu /ˈmenjuː/ n. 1 list of dishes available in a restaurant etc., or to be served at a meal. 2 Computing list of options displayed on a VDU. [Latin: related to MINUTE[2]]

MEP abbr. Member of the European Parliament.

Mephistophelean /ˌmefɪstəfiːˈliːən/ adj. fiendish. [Mephistopheles, evil spirit to whom Faust sold his soul in German legend]

mercantile /ˈmɜːkənˌtaɪl/ adj. 1 of trade, trading. 2 commercial. [Latin: related to MERCHANT]

mercantile marine n. merchant shipping.

Mercator projection /mɑːˈkeɪtə/ n. (also **Mercator's projection**) map of the world projected on to a cylinder so that all the parallels of latitude have the same length as the equator. [Mercator, name of a geographer]

mercenary /ˈmɜːsɪnərɪ/ —adj. primarily concerned with or working for money etc. —n. (pl. -ies) hired soldier in foreign service. □ **mercenariness** n. [Latin from merces reward]

mercer n. dealer in textile fabrics. [Latin merx merc- goods]

mercerize /ˈmɜːsəˌraɪz/ v. (also **-ise**) (**-zing** or **-sing**) treat (cotton) with caustic alkali to strengthen and make lustrous. [Mercer, name of its alleged inventor]

merchandise /ˈmɜːtʃənˌdaɪz/ —n. goods for sale. —v. (**-sing**) 1 trade, traffic (in). 2 advertise or promote (goods, an idea, or a person). [French: related to MERCHANT]

merchant /ˈmɜːtʃ(ə)nt/ n. 1 wholesale trader, esp. with foreign countries. 2 esp. US & Scot. retail trader. 3 colloq. usu. derog. person devoted to a specified activity etc. (speed merchant). [Latin mercor trade (v.)]

merchantable adj. saleable, marketable.

merchant bank n. bank dealing in commercial loans and finance.

merchantman n. (pl. -men) merchant ship.

merchant navy n. nation's commercial shipping.

merchant ship n. ship carrying merchandise.

merciful /ˈmɜːsɪfʊl/ adj. showing mercy. □ **mercifulness** n.

mercifully adv. 1 in a merciful manner. 2 fortunately (mercifully, the sun came out).

merciless /ˈmɜːsɪləs/ adj. showing no mercy. □ **mercilessly** adv.

mercurial /mɜːˈkjʊərɪəl/ adj. 1 of a person) volatile. 2 of or containing mercury. [Latin: related to MERCURY]

mercury /ˈmɜːkjʊrɪ/ n. 1 silvery heavy liquid metallic element used in barometers, thermometers, etc. 2 (**Mercury**) planet nearest to the sun. □ **mercuric** /-ˈkjʊərɪk/ adj. **mercurous** adj. [Latin Mercurius, Roman messenger-god]

mercy /ˈmɜːsɪ/ —n. (pl. -ies) 1 compassion or forbearance towards defeated enemies or offenders or as a quality. 2 act of mercy. 3 (attrib.) done out of compassion (mercy killing). 4 thing to be thankful for (small mercies). —int. expressing surprise or fear. □ **at the mercy of** 1 in the power of. 2 liable to danger or harm from. **have mercy on** (or **upon**) show mercy to. [Latin merces reward, pity]

mere[1] /mɪə(r)/ attrib. adj. (**merest**) being solely or only what is specified (a mere boy; no mere theory). □ **merely** adv. [Latin merus unmixed]

mere[2] /mɪə(r)/ n. dial. or poet. lake. [Old English]

meretricious /ˌmerɪˈtrɪʃəs/ adj. showily but falsely attractive. [Latin meretrix prostitute]

merganser /mɜːˈɡænsə(r)/ n. (pl. same or **-s**) a diving duck. [Latin mergus diver, anser goose]

merge v. (**-ging**) 1 (often foll. by with) **a** combine. **b** join or blend gradually. 2 (foll. by in) (cause to) lose character and identity in (something else). [Latin mergo dip]

merger n. combining, esp. of two commercial companies etc. into one.

meridian /məˈrɪdɪən/ n. 1 **a** circle of constant longitude, passing through a given place and the terrestrial poles. **b** corresponding line on a map. 2 (often attrib.) prime; full splendour. [Latin meridies midday]

meridional adj. 1 of or in the south (esp. of Europe). 2 of a meridian.

meringue /məˈraŋ/ n. 1 sugar, whipped egg-whites, etc., baked crisp. 2 small cake of this, filled with whipped cream. [French]

merino /məˈriːnəʊ/ n. (pl. -s) 1 (in full **merino sheep**) variety of sheep with long fine wool. 2 soft cashmere-like material, orig. of merino wool. 3 fine woollen yarn. [Spanish]

merit /ˈmerɪt/ —n. 1 quality of deserving well. 2 excellence, worth. 3 (usu. in pl.) a thing that entitles one to reward or gratitude. b intrinsic rights and wrongs (merits of a case). —v. (-t-) deserve. [Latin meritum value, from mereor deserve]

meritocracy /ˌmerɪˈtɒkrəsɪ/ n. (pl. -ies) 1 government by those selected for merit. 2 group selected in this way. 3 society governed thus.

meritorious /ˌmerɪˈtɔːrɪəs/ adj. praise-worthy.

merlin /ˈmɜːlɪn/ n. small falcon. [Anglo-French]

mermaid n. legendary creature with a woman's head and trunk and a fish's tail. [from MERE² 'sea', MAID]

merry /ˈmerɪ/ adj. (-ier, -iest) 1 a joyous. b full of laughter or gaiety. 2 colloq. slightly drunk. □ **make merry** be festive. □ **merrily** adv. **merriment** n. [Old English]

merry-go-round n. 1 a fairground ride with revolving model horses or cars. b = ROUNDABOUT 2a. 2 cycle of bustling activity.

merrymaking n. festivity, fun. □ **merrymaker** n.

mésalliance /meɪˈzælɪɑ̃s/ n. marriage with a social inferior. [French]

mescal /ˈmeskæl/ n. peyote cactus. [Spanish from Nahuatl]

mescal buttons n.pl. disc-shaped dried tops from the mescal, esp. as an intoxicant.

mescaline /ˈmeskəlɪn/ n. (also **mescalin**) hallucinogenic alkaloid present in mescal buttons.

Mesdames pl. of MADAME.

Mesdemoiselles pl. of MADEMOISELLE.

mesembryanthemum /mɪˌzembrɪˈænθɪməm/ n. S. African fleshy-leaved plant with bright daisy-like flowers that open fully in sunlight. [Greek = noon flower]

mesh —n. 1 network fabric or structure. 2 each of the open spaces in a net or sieve etc. 3 (in pl.) a network. b snare. —v. 1 (often foll. by with) (of the teeth of a wheel) be engaged (of another). 2 be harmonious. 3 catch in a net. □ **in mesh** (of the teeth of wheels) engaged. [Dutch]

mesmerize /ˈmezməˌraɪz/ v. (also **-ise**) (**-zing** or **-sing**) 1 hypnotize. 2 fascinate.

spellbind. □ **mesmerism** n. **mesmerizingly** adv. [Mesmer, name of a physician]

meso- comb. form middle, intermediate. [Greek mesos middle]

mesolithic /ˌmesəˈlɪθɪk/ adj. of the part of the Stone Age between the palaeolithic and neolithic periods. [Greek lithos stone]

mesomorph /ˈmesəˌmɔːf/ n. person with a compact muscular body. [Greek morphē form]

meson /ˈmiːzɒn/ n. elementary particle believed to help hold nucleons together in the atomic nucleus. [from MESO-]

mesosphere /ˈmesəˌsfɪə(r)/ n. region of the atmosphere from the top of the stratosphere to an altitude of about 80 km.

Mesozoic /ˌmesəˈzəʊɪk/ —adj. of the geological era marked by the development of dinosaurs, and the first mammals, birds, and flowering plants. —n. this era. [Greek zōon animal]

mess —n. 1 dirty or untidy state of things. 2 state of confusion, embarrassment, or trouble. 3 something spilt etc. 4 disagreeable concoction. 5 a soldiers etc. dining together. b army dining-hall. c meal taken there. 6 domestic animal's pulpy food. 7 archaic portion of liquid or excreta. —v. 1 (often foll. by up) make a mess of; dirty; muddle. 2 US (foll. by with) interfere with. 3 take one's meals. 4 colloq. defecate. □ **make a mess of** bungle. **mess about** (or **around**) 1 potter; fiddle. 2 colloq. make things awkward or inconvenient for (a person). [Latin missus course of a meal: related to MESSAGE]

message /ˈmesɪdʒ/ n. 1 communication sent by one person to another. 2 exalted or spiritual communication. 3 (in pl.) Scot., Ir., & N.Engl. shopping. □ **get the message** colloq. understand (a hint etc.). [Latin mitto miss- send]

messenger /ˈmesɪndʒə(r)/ n. person who carries a message.

Messiah /mɪˈsaɪə/ n. 1 a promised deliverer of the Jews. b Christ regarded as this. 2 liberator of an oppressed people. [Hebrew, = anointed]

Messianic /ˌmesɪˈænɪk/ adj. 1 of the Messiah. 2 inspired by hope or belief in a Messiah. [French: related to MESSIAH]

Messieurs pl. of MONSIEUR.

messmate n. soldier's cooking and eating utensils.

Messrs /ˈmesəz/ pl. of MR. [abbreviation of MESSIEURS]

messy adj. (-ier, -iest) 1 untidy or dirty. 2 causing or accompanied by a mess. 3

difficult to deal with; awkward. □ **messily** adv. **messiness** n.

met[1] past and past part. of MEET[1].

met[2] adj. colloq. **1** meteorological. **2** (**the Met**) **a** (in full **the Met Office**) Meteorological Office. **b** Metropolitan Police in London. [abbreviation]

meta- comb. form **1** denoting change of position or condition (metabolism). **2** denoting position: **a** behind, after, or beyond (metaphysics). **b** of a higher or second-order kind (metalanguage). [Greek meta with, after]

metabolism /mɪˈtæbəlɪz(ə)m/ n. all the chemical processes in a living organism producing energy and growth. □ **metabolic** /ˌmetəˈbɒlɪk/ adj. [Greek metabolē throw]

metabolite /mɪˈtæbəlaɪt/ n. substance formed in or necessary for metabolism.

metabolize /mɪˈtæbəlaɪz/ v. (also **-ise**) (**-zing** or **-sing**) process or be processed by metabolism.

metacarpus /ˌmetəˈkɑːpəs/ n. (pl. **-carpi** /-paɪ/) **1** part of the hand between the wrist and the fingers. **2** set of five bones in this. □ **metacarpal** adj. [related to META-, CARPUS]

metal /ˈmet(ə)l/ —n. **1 a** any of a class of workable elements such as gold, silver, iron, or tin. usu. good conductors of heat and electricity and forming base oxides. **b** alloy of any of these. **2** molten material for making glass. **3** (in pl.) rails of a railway line. **4** = ROAD-METAL. —adj. made of metal. —v. (**-ll-**; US **-l-**) **1** make or mend (a road) with road-metal. **2** cover or fit with metal. [Greek metallon mine]

metalanguage /ˈmetəˌlæŋgwɪdʒ/ n. **1** form of language used to discuss language. **2** system of propositions about propositions.

metal detector n. electronic device for locating esp. buried metal.

metallic /mɪˈtælɪk/ adj. **1** of or like metal or metals (metallic taste). **2** sounding like struck metal. **3** shiny (metallic blue). □ **metallically** adv.

metalliferous /ˌmetəˈlɪfərəs/ adj. (of rocks) containing metal.

metalize /ˈmetəlaɪz/ v. (also **-ise**) **1** render metallic. **2** coat with a thin layer of metal.

metallography /ˌmetəˈlɒgrəfɪ/ n. descriptive science of metals.

metalloid /ˈmetəlɔɪd/ n. element intermediate in properties between metals and non-metals, e.g. boron, silicon, and germanium.

metallurgy /mɪˈtælədʒɪ, ˈmetəˌlɜːdʒɪ/ n. **1** science of metals and their application. **2** extraction and purification of metals. □ **metallurgic** /ˌmetəˈlɜːdʒɪk/ adj. **metallurgical** /ˌmetəˈlɜːdʒɪk(ə)l/ adj. **metallurgist** n. [Greek metallon, -ourgia working of]

metalwork n. **1** art of working in metal. **2** metal objects collectively. □ **metalworker** n.

metamorphic /ˌmetəˈmɔːfɪk/ adj. **1** of metamorphosis. **2** (of rock) transformed naturally, e.g. by heat or pressure. □ **metamorphism** n. [from META-, Greek morphē form]

metamorphose /ˌmetəˈmɔːfəʊz/ v. (**-sing**) (often foll. by to, into) change in form or nature.

metamorphosis /ˌmetəˈmɔːfəsɪs, -mɔːˈfəʊsɪs/ n. (pl. **-phoses** /-siːz/) **1** change of form, esp. from a pupa to an insect etc. **2** change of character, conditions, etc. [Greek morphē form]

metaphor /ˈmetəfə(r)/ n. **1** application of a name or description to something to which it is not literally applicable (e.g. a glaring error). **2** instance of this. □ **metaphoric** /-ˈfɒrɪk/ adj. **metaphorical** /-ˈfɒrɪk(ə)l/ adj. **metaphorically** /-ˈfɒrɪkəlɪ/ adv. [Greek]

metaphysic /ˌmetəˈfɪzɪk/ n. system of metaphysics.

metaphysical /ˌmetəˈfɪzɪk(ə)l/ adj. **1** of metaphysics. **2** colloq. excessively abstract or theoretical. **3** (of esp. 17th-c. English poetry) subtle and complex in imagery.

metaphysics /ˌmetəˈfɪzɪks/ n.pl. (usu. treated as sing.) **1** branch of philosophy dealing with the nature of existence, truth, and knowledge. **2** colloq. abstract talk; mere theory. [Greek, as having followed physics in Aristotle's works]

metastasis /meˈtæstəsɪs/ n. (pl. **-stases** /-siːz/) transference of a bodily function, disease, etc., from one part or organ to another. [Greek, = removal]

metatarsus /ˌmetəˈtɑːsəs/ n. (pl. **-tarsi** /-saɪ/) **1** part of the foot between the ankle and the toes. **2** set of five bones in this. □ **metatarsal** adj. [related to META-, TARSUS]

mete v. (**-ting**) (usu. foll. by out) literary apportion or allot (punishment or reward). [Old English]

meteor /ˈmiːtɪə(r)/ n. **1** small solid body from outer space that becomes incandescent when entering the earth's atmosphere. **2** streak of light from a meteor. [Greek meteōros lofty]

meteoric /miːtɪˈɒrɪk/ adj. **1** rapid; dazzling (meteoric rise to fame). **2** of meteors. □ **meteorically** adv.

meteorite /ˈmiːtɪəraɪt/ n. fallen meteor, or fragment of natural rock or metal from outer space.

meteoroid /ˈmiːtɪərɔɪd/ n. small body that becomes visible as it passes through the earth's atmosphere as a meteor.

meteorology /ˌmiːtɪəˈrɒlədʒɪ/ n. the study of atmospheric phenomena, esp. for forecasting the weather. □ **meteorological** /-rəˈlɒdʒɪk(ə)l/ adj.; **meteorologist** n. [Greek meteōrologia: related to METEOR]

meter[1] /ˈmiːtə(r)/ n. 1 instrument that measures or records, esp. electricity, etc. used, distance travelled, etc. 2 = PARKING-METER. — v. measure or record by meter. [from METE]

meter[2] US var. of METRE[1,2].

-meter comb. form 1 forming nouns denoting measuring instruments (barometer). 2 forming nouns denoting lines of poetry with a specified number of measures (pentameter). [Greek metron measure]

methadone /ˈmeθədəʊn/ n. narcotic analgesic drug used esp. as a substitute for morphine or heroin. [6-dimethyla-mino-4,4-diphenyl-3-heptanone]

methanal /ˈmeθən(ə)l/ n. = FORMAL-DEHYDE. [from METHANE, ALDEHYDE]

methane /ˈmiːθeɪn/ n. colourless odourless inflammable gaseous hydrocarbon, the main constituent of natural gas. [from METHYL]

methanoic acid /ˌmeθəˈnəʊɪk/ n. = FORMIC ACID. [related to METHANE]

methanol /ˈmeθənɒl/ n. colourless volatile inflammable liquid hydrocarbon, used as a solvent. [from METHANE, ALCOHOL]

methinks /mɪˈθɪŋks/ v. (past **me-thought** /mɪˈθɔːt/) archaic it seems to me. [Old English: related to ME[1], THINK]

method /ˈmeθəd/ n. 1 way of doing something; systematic procedure. 2 orderliness; regular habits. — **method in one's madness** sense in apparently foolish or strange behaviour. [Greek: related to META-, hodos way]

methodical /mɪˈθɒdɪk(ə)l/ adj. characterized by method or order. □ **methodically** adv.

Methodist /ˈmeθədɪst/ n. member of a Protestant denomination originating in the 18th-c. Wesleyan evangelistic movement. — adj. of Methodists or Methodism. □ **Methodism** n.

methodology /ˌmeθəˈdɒlədʒɪ/ n. (pl. -ies) 1 body of methods used in a particular activity. 2 science of method. □ **methodological** /-dəˈlɒdʒɪk(ə)l/ adj.; **methodologically** /-dəˈlɒdʒɪkəlɪ/ adv.

methought past of METHINKS.

meths n. colloq. methylated spirit. [abbreviation]

methyl /ˈmeθɪl, ˈmiːθaɪl/ n. univalent hydrocarbon radical CH_3, present in many organic compounds. [Greek methu wine, hulē wood]

methyl alcohol n. = METHANOL.

methylate /ˈmeθɪleɪt/ v. (-ting) 1 mix or impregnate with methanol. 2 introduce a methyl group into (a molecule or compound).

methylated spirit n. (also methyl-ated spirits n.pl.) alcohol treated to make it unfit for drinking and exempt from duty.

meticulous /məˈtɪkjʊləs/ adj. 1 giving great attention to detail. 2 very careful and precise. □ **meticulously** adv.; **meticulousness** n. [Latin metus fear]

métier /ˈmetjeɪ/ n. 1 one's trade, profession, or field of activity. 2 one's forte. [Latin: related to MINISTER]

metonymy /mɪˈtɒnɪmɪ/ n. substitution of the name of an attribute or adjunct for that of the thing meant (e.g. Crown for king, the turf for horse-racing). [Latin from Greek metōnumia name]

metre[1] /ˈmiːtə(r)/ n. (US **meter**) metric unit and the base SI unit of linear measure, equal to 39.4 inches. □ **meterage** /ˈmiːtərɪdʒ/ n. [Greek metron]

metre[2] /ˈmiːtə(r)/ n. (US **meter**) 1 **a** poetic rhythm, esp. as determined by the number and length of feet in a line. **b** metrical group or measure. 2 basic rhythm of music. [related to METRE[1]]

metre-kilogram-second n. denoting a system of measure using the metre, kilogram, and second.

metric /ˈmetrɪk/ adj. of or based on the metre. [French: related to METRE[1]]

-metric comb. form (also **-metrical**) forming adjectives corresponding to nouns in -meter and -metry (thermometric; geometric).

metrical adj. 1 of or composed in metre (metrical psalms). 2 cf. or involving measurement (metrical geometry). □ **metrically** adv. [Greek: related to METRE[2]]

metricate v. (-ting) convert to a metric system. □ **metrication** /ˌmetrɪˈkeɪʃ(ə)n/ n.

metric system n. decimal measuring system with the metre, litre, and gram (or kilogram) as units of length, volume, and mass.

metric ton n. (also **metric tonne**) 1,000 kilograms (2205 lb).

metro /ˈmetrəʊ/ n. (pl. -s) underground railway system, esp. in Paris. [French shortened from métropolitain metro-politan]

metronome /ˈmetrəˌnəʊm/ n. device ticking at a selected rate to mark time for musicians. [Greek *metron* measure, *nomos* law]

metropolis /mɪˈtrɒpəlɪs/ n. chief city, capital. [Greek *mētēr* mother, *polis* city]

metropolitan /ˌmetrəˈpɒlɪt(ə)n/ —adj. 1 of a metropolis. 2 of or forming a mother country as distinct from its colonies etc. (*metropolitan France*). —n. 1 bishop having authority over the bishops of a province. 2 inhabitant of a metropolis.

-metry *comb. form* forming nouns denoting procedures and systems involving measurement (*geometry*).

mettle /ˈmet(ə)l/ n. 1 quality or strength of character. 2 spirit, courage. □ **on one's mettle** keen to do one's best. □ **mettlesome** adj. [from METAL n.]

MeV abbr. mega-electronvolt(s).

mew[1] —n. characteristic cry of a cat, gull, etc. —v. utter this sound. [imitative]

mew[2] n. gull, esp. the common gull. [Old English]

mewl v. 1 whimper. 2 mew like a cat. [imitative]

mews /mjuːz/ n. (treated as *sing.*) stabling round a yard etc., now used esp. for housing. (originally *sing. mew* 'cage for hawks': French from Latin *muto* change)

Mexican /ˈmeksɪkən/ —n. 1 native or national of Mexico. 2 person of Mexican descent. —adj. of Mexico or its people. [Spanish]

mezzanine /ˈmetsəˌniːn, ˈmez-/ n. storey between two others (usu. between the ground and first floors). [Italian: related to MEDIAN]

mezzo /ˈmetsəʊ/ Mus. —adv. half, moderately. —n. (in full **mezzo-soprano**) (pl. **-s**) 1 female singing-voice between soprano and contralto. 2 singer with this voice. [Latin *medius* middle]

mezzo forte adj. & adv. fairly loud(ly).

mezzo piano adj. & adv. fairly soft(ly).

mezzotint /ˈmetsəʊtɪnt/ n. 1 method of printing or engraving in which a plate is roughened by scraping to produce tones and halftones. 2 print so produced. [Italian: related to MEZZO, TINT]

mf abbr. mezzo forte.

Mg symb. magnesium.

mg abbr. milligram(s).

Mgr. abbr. 1 Manager. 2 *Monseigneur.* 3 Monsignor.

MHz abbr. megahertz.

mi var. of ME[2].

mi. abbr. US mile(s).

miaow /mɪˈaʊ/ —n. characteristic cry of a cat. —v. make this cry. [imitative]

miasma /mɪˈæzmə/ n. (pl. **-mata** or **-s**) *archaic* infectious or noxious vapour. [Greek, = defilement]

mica /ˈmaɪkə/ n. silicate mineral found as glittering scales in granite etc. or in crystals separable into thin transparent plates. [Latin, = crumb]

mice pl. of MOUSE.

Michaelmas /ˈmɪkəlməs/ n. feast of St Michael, 29 September. [related to MASS[2]]

Michaelmas daisy n. autumn-flowering aster.

mick n. *slang offens.* Irishman. [pet form of *Michael*]

mickey /ˈmɪkɪ/ n. (also **micky**) □ **take the mickey** (often foll. by *out of*) *slang* tease, mock, ridicule. [origin uncertain]

Mickey Finn /ˌmɪkɪ ˈfɪn/ n. *slang* drugged drink intended to make the victim unconscious. [origin uncertain]

mickle /ˈmɪk(ə)l/ n. (also **muckle** /ˈmʌk(ə)l/) *archaic* or *Scot.* large amount. □ **many a little makes a mickle** (orig. *erroneously* **many a mickle makes a muckle**) small amounts accumulate. [Old Norse]

micky var. of MICKEY.

micro /ˈmaɪkrəʊ/ n. (pl. **-s**) *colloq.* 1 = MICROCOMPUTER. 2 = MICROPROCESSOR.

micro- *comb. form* 1 small (*microchip*). 2 denoting a factor of one millionth (10^{-6}) (*microgram*). [Greek *mikros* small]

microbe /ˈmaɪkrəʊb/ n. micro-organism (esp. a bacterium causing disease or fermentation). □ **microbial** /-ˈkrəʊbɪəl/ adj. **microbic** /-ˈkrəʊbɪk/ adj. [Greek *mikros* small, *bios* life]

microbiology /ˌmaɪkrəʊbaɪˈɒlədʒɪ/ n. the study of micro-organisms. □ **microbiologist** n.

microchip /ˈmaɪkrəʊtʃɪp/ n. small piece of semiconductor (usu. silicon) used to carry integrated circuits.

microcircuit /ˈmaɪkrəʊˌsɜːkɪt/ n. integrated circuit on a microchip.

microclimate /ˈmaɪkrəʊˌklaɪmɪt/ n. small localized climate, e.g. inside a greenhouse.

microcomputer /ˈmaɪkrəʊkəmˌpjuːtə(r)/ n. small computer with a microprocessor as its central processor.

microcosm /ˈmaɪkrəˌkɒz(ə)m/ n. (often foll. by *of*) miniature representation, e.g. mankind or a community seen as a small-scale model of the universe; epitome. □ **microcosmic** /-ˈkɒzmɪk/ adj. [from MICRO-, COSMOS]

microdot /ˈmaɪkrəʊˌdɒt/ n. microphotograph of a document etc. reduced to the size of a dot.

micro-electronics /ˈmaɪkrəʊɪlek-ˈtrɒnɪks/ n. design, manufacture, and use of microchips and microcircuits.

microfiche /ˈmaɪkrəʊfiːʃ/ n. (pl. same or -s) small flat piece of film bearing microphotographs of documents etc. [from MICRO-, French *fiche* slip of paper]

microfilm /ˈmaɪkrəʊfɪlm/ —n. length of film bearing microphotographs of documents etc. —v. photograph on microfilm.

microlight /ˈmaɪkrəʊlaɪt/ n. a kind of motorized hang-glider.

micromesh /ˈmaɪkrəʊmɛʃ/ n. (often *attrib.*) fine-meshed material, esp. nylon.

micrometer /maɪˈkrɒmɪtə(r)/ n. gauge for accurate small-scale measurement.

micron /ˈmaɪkrɒn/ n. one-millionth of a metre. [Greek *mikros* small]

micro-organism /ˌmaɪkrəʊˈɔːgə-nɪz(ə)m/ n. microscopic organism, e.g. bacteria, protozoa, and viruses.

microphone /ˈmaɪkrəfəʊn/ n. instrument for converting sound waves into electrical energy for reconversion into sound after transmission or recording. [from MICRO-, Greek *phōnē* sound]

microphotograph /ˌmaɪkrəʊˈfəʊtə-grɑːf/ n. photograph reduced to a very small size. [from MICRO-]

microprocessor /ˈmaɪkrəʊprəʊ-sesə(r)/ n. integrated circuit containing all the functions of a computer's central processing unit.

microscope /ˈmaɪkrəskəʊp/ n. instrument with lenses for magnifying objects or details invisible to the naked eye. [from MICRO-, -SCOPE]

microscopic /ˌmaɪkrəˈskɒpɪk/ adj. 1 visible only with a microscope. 2 extremely small. 3 of or by means of a microscope. □ **microscopically** adv.

microscopy /maɪˈkrɒskəpɪ/ n. use of microscopes.

microsecond /ˈmaɪkrəʊˌsekənd/ n. one-millionth of a second.

microsurgery /ˈmaɪkrəˌsɜːdʒərɪ/ n. intricate surgery using microscopes.

microwave /ˈmaɪkrəʊweɪv/ —n. 1 electromagnetic wave with a wavelength in the range 0.001–0.3m. 2 (in full **microwave oven**) oven using microwaves to cook or heat food quickly. —v. (**-ving**) cook in a microwave oven.

micturition /ˌmɪktjʊəˈrɪʃ(ə)n/ n. *formal* urination. [Latin]

mid *attrib. adj.* (usu. in *comb.*) the middle of (*mid-air*; *mid-June*). [Old English]

midday n. (often *attrib.*) middle of the day; noon. [Old English: related to MID, DAY]

midden /ˈmɪd(ə)n/ n. 1 dunghill. 2 refuse heap. [Scandinavian: related to MUCK]

middle /ˈmɪd(ə)l/ —*attrib. adj.* 1 at an equal distance, time, or number from

extremities; central. 2 intermediate in rank, quality, etc. 3 average (*of middle height*). —n. 1 (often foll. by *of*) middle point, position, or part. 2 waist. □ in the **middle of** 1 in the process of. 2 during. [Old English]

middle age n. period between youth and old age. □ **middle-aged** *adj.*

Middle Ages n. (prec. by *the*) period of European history from c.1000 to 1453.

middle-age spread n. (also **middle-aged spread**) increased bodily girth at middle age.

middlebrow *colloq.* —*adj.* having or appealing to non-intellectual or conventional tastes. —n. middlebrow person.

middle C n. C near the middle of the piano keyboard, (in notation) the note between the treble and bass staves.

middle class n. social class between the upper and the lower, including professional and business workers. □ **middle-class** *adj.*

middle distance n. 1 (in a landscape) part between the foreground and the background. 2 *Athletics* race distance of esp. 400 or 800 metres.

middle ear n. cavity behind the eardrum.

Middle East n. (prec. by *the*) area covered by countries from Egypt to Iran inclusive. □ **Middle Eastern** *adj.*

Middle English n. English language from c.1150 to 1500.

middle game n. central phase of a chess game.

middleman n. 1 trader who handles a commodity between producer and consumer. 2 intermediary.

middle name n. 1 name between first name and surname. 2 *colloq.* person's most characteristic quality (*tact is my middle name*).

middle-of-the-road *adj.* 1 moderate; avoiding extremes. 2 of general appeal.

middle school n. school for children from about 9 to 13 years.

middle-sized *adj.* of medium size.

middleweight n. 1 weight in certain sports between welterweight and light heavyweight, in amateur boxing 71–5 kg. 2 sportsman of this weight.

middling —*adj.* moderately good. —*adv.* fairly, moderately.

midfield n. *Football* central part of the pitch, away from the goals. □ **midfielder** n.

midge n. gnatlike insect [Old English]

midget /ˈmɪdʒɪt/ n. 1 extremely small person or thing. 2 (*attrib.*) very small.

MIDI /ˈmɪdɪ/ n. (also **midi**) an interface allowing electronic musical instruments, synthesizers, and computers to

be interconnected and used simultaneously. [abbreviation of *musical instrument digital interface*]

midi system *n.* set of compact stacking components of hi-fi equipment.

midland *n.* **1 (the Midlands)** inland counties of central England. **2** middle part of a country. —*adj.* of or in the midland or Midlands.

mid-life *n.* middle age.

mid-life crisis *n.* crisis of self-confidence in early middle age.

midnight *n.* middle of the night; 12 o'clock at night. [Old English]

midnight blue *adj.* & *n.* (as *adj.* often hyphenated) very dark blue.

midnight sun *n.* sun visible at midnight during the summer in polar regions.

mid-off *n. Cricket* position of the fielder near the bowler on the off side.

mid-on *n. Cricket* position of the fielder near the bowler on the on side.

midriff *n.* front of the body just above the waist. [Old English, = mid-belly]

midshipman *n.* naval officer ranking next above a cadet.

midships *adv.* = AMIDSHIPS.

midst —*prep. poet.* amidst. —*n.* middle. □ **in the midst of** among; in the middle of. **in our (or your or their) midst** among us (or you or them). [related to MID]

midstream —*n.* middle of a stream etc. —*adv.* (also **in midstream**) in the middle of an action etc. (*abandoned the project midstream*).

midsummer *n.* period of or near the summer solstice, about 21 June. [Old English]

Midsummer Day *n.* (also **Midsummer's Day**) 24 June.

midsummer madness *n.* extreme folly.

midway *adv.* in or towards the middle of the distance between two points.

Midwest *n.* region of the US adjoining the northern Mississippi.

midwicket *n. Cricket* position of a fielder on the leg side opposite the middle of the pitch.

midwife *n.* person trained to assist at childbirth. □ **midwifery** /-'wifəri/ *n.* [originally = with-woman]

midwinter *n.* period of or near the winter solstice, about 22 Dec. [Old English]

mien *n. literary* person's look or bearing. [probably obsolete *demean*]

miff *v. colloq.* (usu. as **miffed** *adj.*) offend. [origin uncertain]

M.I.5 *abbr.* UK department of Military Intelligence concerned with State security.

■ **Usage** This term is not in official use.

might[1] /mait/ *past of* MAY, used *esp.*: **1** in reported speech, expressing possibility (*said he might come*) or permission (*asked if I might leave*) (cf. MAY 1, 2). **2** (foll. by perfect infin.) expressing a possibility based on a condition not fulfilled (*if you'd looked you might have found it*). **3** (foll. by present infin. or perfect infin.) expressing complaint that an obligation or expectation is not or has not been fulfilled (*they might have asked*). **4** expressing a request (*you might call in at the butcher's*). **5** *colloq.* **a** = MAY 1d (*it might be true*). **b** (in tentative questions) = MAY 2 (*might I have the pleasure of this dance?*). **c** = MAY 1d (*who might you be?*). □ **might as well** expressing lukewarm acquiescence (*might as well try*).

might[2] /mait/ *n.* strength, power. □ **with might and main** with all one's power. [Old English: related to MAY]

might-have-been *n. colloq.* **1** past possibility that no longer applies. **2** person of unfulfilled promise.

might'n't /'mait(ə)nt/ *contr.* might not.

mighty —*adj.* (**-ier**, **-iest**) **1** powerful, strong. **2** massive, bulky. **3** *colloq.* great, considerable. —*adv. colloq.* very (*mighty difficult*). □ **mightily** *adv.* **mightiness** *n.* [Old English: related to MIGHT[2]]

mignonette /ˌmɪnjə'net/ *n.* plant with fragrant grey-green flowers. [French, diminutive of *mignon* small]

migraine /'mi:grein, 'mai-/ *n.* recurrent throbbing headache often with nausea and visual disturbance. [Greek *hēmikrania*: related to HEMI-, CRANIUM]

migrant /'maigrənt/ —*adj.* migrating. —*n.* migrant person or animal, *esp.* a bird.

migrate /mai'greit/ *v.* (**-ting**) **1** move from one place and settle in another, *esp.* abroad. **2** (of a bird or fish) change its habitation seasonally. **3** move under natural forces. □ **migration** /-'greiʃ(ə)n/ *n.* **migrator** *n.* **migratory** /'maigrətəri/ *adj.* [Latin *migro*]

mikado /mi'kɑːdəʊ/ *n.* (*pl.* **-s**) *hist.* emperor of Japan. [Japanese, = august door]

mike *n. colloq.* microphone. [abbreviation]

mil *n.* one-thousandth of an inch, as a unit of measure for the diameter of wire etc. [Latin *mille* thousand]

milady /mi'leidi/ *n.* (*pl.* **-ies**) (*esp.* as a form of address) English noblewoman. [French from *my* LADY]

milage var. of MILEAGE.

milch *adj.* giving milk. [Old English: related to MILK]

milch cow n. source of easy profit.

mild /maɪld/ adj. 1 (esp. of a person) gentle and conciliatory. 2 not severe or harsh. 3 (of the weather) moderately warm. 4 (of flavour etc.) not sharp or strong. 5 tame, feeble; lacking vivacity. —n. mild draught beer (cf. BITTER). □ **mildish** adj. **mildly** adv. **mildness** n. [Old English]

mildew /'mɪldjuː/ —n. 1 destructive growth of minute fungi on plants. 2 similar growth on damp paper, leather, etc. —v. taint or be tainted with mildew. □ **mildewy** adj. [Old English]

mildly adv. in a mild fashion. □ **put it mildly** as an understatement.

mild-mannered adj. = MILD 1.

mild steel n. strong and tough steel not readily tempered.

mile n. 1 (also **statute mile**) unit of linear measure equal to 1,760 yards (approx. 1.6 kilometres). 2 (in pl.) colloq. great distance or amount (miles better). 3 race extending over a mile. [Latin mille thousand]

mileage n. (also **milage**) 1 number of miles travelled, esp. by a vehicle per unit of fuel. 2 colloq. profit, advantage.

miler n. colloq. person or horse specializing in races of one mile.

milestone n. 1 stone beside a road marking a distance in miles. 2 significant event or point in a life, history, project, etc.

milfoil /'mɪlfɔɪl/ n. common yarrow with small white flowers. [Latin: related to MILLE, FOIL]

milieu /miː'ljɜː, 'miː-/ n. (pl. milieux or -s /-'ljɜːz/) person's environment or social surroundings. [French]

militant /'mɪlɪt(ə)nt/ —adj. 1 combative, aggressively active in support of a cause. 2 engaged in warfare. —n. militant person. □ **militancy** n. **militantly** adv. [Latin: related to MILITATE]

militarism /'mɪlɪtərɪz(ə)m/ n. 1 aggressively military policy etc. 2 military spirit. □ **militarist** n. **militaristic** /-'rɪstɪk/ adj.

militarize /'mɪlɪtəraɪz/ v. (also **-ise**) (**-zing** or **-sing**) 1 equip with military resources. 2 make military or warlike. 3 imbue with militarism. □ **militarization** /-'zeɪʃ(ə)n/ n.

military /'mɪlɪtəri/ —adj. of or characteristic of soldiers or armed forces. —n. (as sing. or pl.; prec. by the; the army). □ **militarily** adv. [Latin miles -lit- soldier]

military honours n.pl. burial rites of a soldier, royalty, etc., performed by the military.

military police n. (as pl.) army police force disciplining soldiers.

militate /'mɪlɪteɪt/ v. (-ting) (usu. foll. by against) have force or effect; tell. [Latin: related to MILITARY]

■ **Usage** Militate is often confused with mitigate.

militia /mɪ'lɪʃə/ n. military force, esp. one conscripted in an emergency. □ **militiaman** n. [Latin, = military service]

milk —n. 1 opaque white fluid secreted by female mammals for the nourishment of their young. 2 milk of cows, goats, or sheep as food. 3 milklike juice of the coconut etc. —v. 1 draw milk from (a cow etc.). 2 exploit (a person or situation) to the utmost. [Old English]

milk and water n. feeble or insipid writing, speech, etc.

milk chocolate n. chocolate made with milk.

milk float n. small usu. electric vehicle used in delivering milk.

milkmaid n. girl or woman who milks cows or works in a dairy.

milkman n. person who sells or delivers milk.

Milk of Magnesia n. propr. white suspension of magnesium hydroxide usu. in water, taken as an antacid or laxative.

milk-powder n. dehydrated milk.

milk pudding n. pudding, esp. of rice, baked with milk.

milk round n. 1 fixed route for milk delivery. 2 regular trip with calls at several places.

milk run n. routine expedition etc.

milk shake n. drink of whisked milk, flavouring, etc.

milksop n. weak or timid man or youth.

milk tooth n. temporary tooth in young mammals.

milky adj. (-ier, -iest) 1 of, like, or mixed with milk. 2 (of a gem or liquid) cloudy; not clear. □ **milkiness** n.

Milky Way n. luminous band of stars; the Galaxy.

mill —n. 1 a building fitted with a mechanical device for grinding corn. b such a device. 2 device for grinding any solid to powder etc. (pepper-mill). 3 a building fitted with machinery for manufacturing processes etc. (cotton-mill). b such machinery (puts the grist to the mill). —v. 1 grind (corn), produce (flour), or hull (seeds) in a mill. 2 (esp. as **milled** adj.) produce a ribbed edge on (a coin). 3 cut or shape (metal) with a rotating tool. 4 (often foll. by about, around) move aimlessly, esp. in a confused mass. □ **go** (or **put**) **through the mill** undergo (or cause to undergo)

intensive work, pain, training, etc. [Latin *molo* grind]

millefeuille /mi:lfɜj/ *n.* rich cake of puff pastry split and filled with jam, cream, etc. [French, = thousand-leaf]

millennium /mɪˈlenɪəm/ *n.* (*pl.* -s or **millennia** /mɪˈlenɪə/) **1** period of 1,000 years, esp. that of Christ's prophesied reign on earth (Rev. 20:1-5). **2** (esp. future) period of happiness and prosperity. □ **millennial** *adj.* [Latin *mille* thousand]

millepede var. of MILLIPEDE.

miller *n.* **1** proprietor or tenant of a mill, esp. a corn-mill. **2** person operating a milling machine. [related to MILL]

miller's thumb *n.* small spiny freshwater fish.

millesimal /mɪˈlesɪm(ə)l/ —*adj.* **1** thousandth. **2** of, belonging to, or dealing with, a thousandth or thousandths. —*n.* thousandth part. [Latin *mille* thousand]

millet /ˈmɪlɪt/ *n.* **1** cereal plant bearing small nutritious seeds. **2** seed of this. [Latin *milium*]

millet-grass *n.* tall woodland grass.

milli- *comb. form* thousand, esp. denoting a factor of one thousandth. [Latin *mille* thousand]

milliard /ˈmɪljɑːd/ *n.* one thousand million. [French *mille* thousand]

■ **Usage** *Milliard* is now largely superseded by *billion*.

millibar /ˈmɪlɪˌbɑː(r)/ *n.* unit of atmospheric pressure equivalent to 100 pascals.

milligram /ˈmɪlɪˌɡræm/ *n.* (also **-gramme**) one-thousandth of a gram.

millilitre /ˈmɪlɪˌliːtə(r)/ *n.* (*US* **-liter**) one-thousandth of a litre (0.002 pint).

millimetre /ˈmɪlɪˌmiːtə(r)/ *n.* (*US* **-meter**) one-thousandth of a metre (0.039 in.).

milliner /ˈmɪlɪnə(r)/ *n.* person who makes or sells women's hats. □ **millinery** *n.* [*Milan* in Italy]

million /ˈmɪljən/ *n.* & *adj.* (*pl.* same or (in sense 2) **-s**) (in *sing.* prec. by *a* or *one*) **1** thousand thousand. **2** (in *pl.*) *colloq.* very large number. **3** million pounds or dollars. □ **millionth** *adj.* & *n.* [French, probably from Italian *mille* thousand]

millionaire /ˌmɪljəˈneə(r)/ *n.* (*fem.* **millionairess** /-ˈneəres/) person who has over a million pounds, dollars, etc. [French *millionnaire*; related to MILLION]

millipede /ˈmɪlɪˌpiːd/ *n.* (also **millepede** /ˈmɪlɪˌpiːd/) small crawling invertebrate with a long segmented body with two pairs of legs on each segment. [Latin *mille* thousand, *pes ped-* foot]

millisecond /ˈmɪlɪˌsekənd/ *n.* one-thousandth of a second.

millpond *n.* pool of water retained by a dam for operating a mill-wheel. □ **like a millpond** (of water) very calm.

mill-race *n.* current of water that drives a mill-wheel.

millstone *n.* **1** each of two circular stones for grinding corn. **2** heavy burden or responsibility.

mill-wheel *n.* wheel used to drive a water-mill.

millworker *n.* factory worker.

millwright *n.* person who designs or builds mills.

milometer /marˈlɒmɪtə(r)/ *n.* instrument for measuring the number of miles travelled by a vehicle.

milord /mɪˈlɔːd/ *n.* (esp. as a form of address) English nobleman. [French from *my lord*]

milt *n.* **1** spleen in mammals. **2** sperm-filled reproductive gland or the sperm of a male fish. [Old English]

mime —*n.* **1** acting without words, using only gestures. **2** performance using mime. **3** (also **mime artist**) mime actor. —*v.* (**-ming**) **1** (also *absol.*) convey by mime. **2** (often foll. by *to*) mouth words etc. in time with a soundtrack (*mime to a record*). [Greek *mimos*]

mimeograph /ˈmɪmɪəˌɡrɑːf/ —*n.* **1** machine which duplicates from a stencil. **2** copy so produced. —*v.* reproduce by this process. [Greek *mimeomai* imitate]

mimetic /mɪˈmetɪk/ *adj.* of or practising imitation or mimicry. [Greek *mimētikos*: see MIMEOGRAPH]

mimic /ˈmɪmɪk/ —*v.* (**-ck-**) **1** imitate (a person, gesture, etc.) esp. to entertain or ridicule. **2** copy minutely or servilely. **3** resemble closely. —*n.* person skilled in imitation. □ **mimicry** *n.* [Greek *mimikos*: related to MIME]

mimosa /mɪˈməuzə/ *n.* **1** shrub with globular usu. yellow flowers. **2** acacia plant with showy yellow flowers. [Latin: related to MIME]

Min. *abbr.* **1** Minister. **2** Ministry.

min. *abbr.* **1** minute(s). **2** minimum. **3** minim (fluid measure).

mina var. of MYNA.

minaret /ˌmɪnəˈret/ *n.* slender turret next to a mosque, from which the muezzin calls at hours of prayer. [French or Spanish from Turkish from Arabic]

minatory /ˈmɪnətərɪ/ *adj. formal* threatening, menacing. [Latin *minor* threaten]

mince —*v.* (**-cing**) **1** cut up or grind (esp. meat) finely. **2** (usu. as **mincing** *adj.*) speak or esp. walk effeminately or affectedly. —*n.* minced meat. □ **mince matters** (or **one's words**) (usu. with *neg.*) speak evasively or unduly mildly.

□ **mincer** n. [Latin *minutia* something small]]

mincemeat n. mixture of currants, sugar, spices, suet, etc. □ **make mincemeat of** utterly defeat.

mince pie n. pie containing mincemeat.

mind /maɪnd/ —n. **1 a** seat of consciousness, thought, volition, and feeling. **b** attention, concentration (*mind keeps wandering*). **2** intellect. **3** memory (*can't call it to mind*). **4** opinion (*of the same mind*). **5** way of thinking or feeling (*the Victorian mind*). **6** focussed will (*put one's mind to it*). **7** sanity (*lose one's mind*). **8** person in regard to mental faculties (*a great mind*). —v. **1** object, be upset or annoyed by. **2** remember; take care (to) (*do you mind if I smoke?; mind you come on time; mind the step; mind how you go; mind out!*). **3** heed; take care (to). **4** apply oneself to, concern oneself with (*mind my own business*). □ **be in two minds** be undecided. **do you mind?** *iron.* expression of annoyance. **have a good** (or **half a**) **mind to** feel inclined to (*I've a good mind to report you*). **have** (it) **in mind** intend. **in one's mind's eye** in one's imagination. **mind one's P's & Q's** be careful in one's behaviour. **mind you** let alone; used to add a qualifying statement (*mind you, it wasn't easy*). **never mind** 1 let alone; not to mention. **2** used to comfort or console. **3** (also **never you mind**) used to evade a question. **to my mind** in my opinion. [Old English]

mind-blowing adj. *slang* 1 mind-boggling; overwhelming. **2** (esp. of drugs etc.) inducing hallucinations.

mind-boggling adj. *colloq.* unbelievable, startling.

minded adj. **1** (in comb.) **a** inclined to think in some specified way, or with a specified interest (*mathematically minded; fair-minded; car-minded*). **b** having a specified kind of mind (*high-minded*). **2** (usu. foll. by *to* + infin.) disposed or inclined.

minder n. **1** (often in comb.) person employed to look after a person or thing (*child minder*). **2** *slang* bodyguard.

mindful adj. (often foll. by *of*) taking heed or care; giving thought (to). □ **mindfully** adv.

mindless adj. **1** lacking intelligence; brutish (*mindless violence*). **2** not requiring thought or skill (*mindless work*). **3** (usu. foll. by *of*) heedless (*advice etc.*). □ **mindlessly** adv. **mindlessness** n.

mind-read v. discern the thoughts of (another person). □ **mind-reader** n.

mine¹ *poss. pron.* the one(s) of or belonging to me (*it is mine; mine are over there*). □ **of mine** of or belonging to me (*a friend of mine*). [Old English]

mine² —n. **1** excavation to extract metal, coal, salt, etc. **2** abundant source (of information etc.). **3** military explosive device placed in the ground or in the water. —v. **1** obtain (metal, coal, etc.) from a mine. **2** (also *absol.*, often foll. by *for*) dig in (the earth etc.) for ore etc. or to tunnel. **3** lay explosive mines under or in. □ **mining** n. [French]

minefield n. **1** area planted with explosive mines. **2** *colloq.* hazardous subject or situation.

minelayer n. ship or aircraft for laying explosive mines.

miner n. person who works in a mine.

mineral /'mɪnər(ə)l/ n. (often *attrib.*) **1** inorganic substance. **2** substance obtained by mining. **3** (often in *pl.*) artificial mineral water or similar carbonated drink. [French or medieval Latin: related to MINE²]

mineralize v. (also **-ise**) (**-zing** or **-sing**) impregnate (water etc.) with a mineral substance.

mineralogy /,mɪnə'rælədʒɪ/ n. the study of minerals. □ **mineralogical** /-rə'lɒdʒɪk(ə)l/ adj. **mineralogist** n.

mineral water n. **1** natural water often containing dissolved salts. **2** artificial imitation of this, esp. soda water.

minestrone /,mɪnɪ'strəʊnɪ/ n. soup containing vegetables and pasta, beans, or rice. [Italian]

minesweeper n. ship for clearing explosive mines from the sea.

mineworker n. miner.

Ming n. (often *attrib.*) Chinese porcelain made during the Ming dynasty (1368-1644).

mingle /'mɪŋg(ə)l/ v. (**-ling**) **1** mix, blend. **2** (often foll. by *with*) mix socially. [Old English]

mingy /'mɪndʒɪ/ adj. (**-ier**, **-iest**) *colloq.* mean, stingy. □ **mingily** adv. [probably from MEAN², STINGY]

mini /'mɪnɪ/ n. (pl. **-s**) *colloq.* miniskirt. **2** (**Mini**) *propr.* make of small car. [abbreviation]

mini- comb. form miniature; small of its kind (*minibus*).

miniature /'mɪnɪtʃ(ə)r/ —adj. **1** much smaller than normal. **2** represented on a small scale. —n. **1** any miniature object. **2** detailed small-scale portrait. **3** this genre. □ **in miniature** on a small scale. [Italian *miniatura* red lead]

miniaturist n. (in senses 2 and 3 of n.). [Latin *minium* red lead]

miniaturize v. (also **-ise**) (**-zing** or **-sing**) produce in a smaller version;

566

make small. □ **miniaturization** /-'zeɪʃ(ə)n/ n.

minibus /'mɪnɪ,bʌs/ n. small bus for about twelve passengers.

minicab /'mɪnɪ,kæb/ n. car used as a taxi, hireable only by telephone.

minicomputer /'mɪnɪkəm,pjuːtə(r)/ n. computer of medium power.

minim /'mɪnɪm/ n. 1 Mus. note equal to two crotchets or half a semibreve. 2 one-sixtieth of a fluid drachm, about a drop. [Latin minimus least]

minima pl. of MINIMUM.

minimal /'mɪnɪm(ə)l/ adj. 1 very minute or slight. 2 being a minimum. □ **minimally** adv.

minimalism /'mɪnɪmə,lɪz(ə)m/ n. 1 Art use of simple or primary forms, often geometric and massive. 2 Mus. repetition of short phrases incorporating changes very gradually. □ **minimalist** n. & adj.

minimize /'mɪnɪ,maɪz/ v. (also **-ise**) (**-zing** or **-sing**) 1 reduce to, or estimate at, the smallest possible amount or degree. 2 estimate or represent at less than true value or importance. □ **minimization** /-'zeɪʃ(ə)n/ n.

minimum /'mɪnɪməm/ n. (pl. **minima**) —n. least possible or attainable amount (reduced to a minimum). —adj. that is a minimum. [Latin: related to MINIM]

minimum wage n. lowest wage permitted by law or agreement.

minion /'mɪnjən/ n. derog. servile subordinate. [French mignon]

minipill /'mɪnɪpɪl/ n. contraceptive pill containing a progestogen only (not oestrogen).

miniseries /'mɪnɪ,stɪərɪz/ n. (pl. same) short series of related television programmes.

miniskirt /'mɪnɪ,skɜːt/ n. very short skirt.

minister /'mɪnɪstə(r)/ —n. 1 head of a government department. 2 clergyman, esp. in the Presbyterian and Nonconformist Churches. 3 diplomat, usu. ranking below an ambassador. —v. (usu. foll. by to) help, serve, look after (a person, cause, etc.). □ **ministerial** /-'stɪərɪəl/ adj. [Latin, = servant]

Minister of State n. government minister, esp. holding a rank below that of Head of Department.

Minister of the Crown n. Parl. member of the Cabinet.

Minister without Portfolio n. government minister not in charge of a specific department of State.

ministration /,mɪnɪ'streɪʃ(ə)n/ n. 1 (usu. in pl.) help or service (kind ministrations). 2 ministering, esp. in religious matters. 3 (usu. foll. by of) supplying of help, justice, etc. □ **ministrant** /'mɪnɪstrənt/ adj. & n. [Latin: related to MINISTER]

ministry /'mɪnɪstrɪ/ n. (pl. **-ies**) 1 a government department headed by a minister. b building for this. 2 a (prec. by the) vocation, office, or profession of a religious minister. b period of tenure of this. 3 (prec. by the) body of ministers of a government or religion. 4 period of government under one prime minister. 5 ministering, ministration. [Latin: related to MINISTER]

mink n. (pl. same or **-s**) 1 small semi-aquatic stoatlike animal bred for its thick brown fur. 2 this fur. 3 coat of this. [Swedish]

minnow /'mɪnəʊ/ n. small freshwater carp. [Old English]

Minoan /mɪ'nəʊən/ —adj. of the Bronze Age civilization centred on Crete (c.3000–1100 BC). —n. person of this civilization. [Minos, legendary king of Crete]

minor /'maɪnə(r)/ —adj. 1 lesser or comparatively small in size or importance (minor poet). 2 Mus. a (of a scale) having intervals of a semitone above its second, fifth, and seventh notes. b (of an interval) less by a semitone than a major interval. c (of a key) based on a minor scale. —n. 1 person under full legal age. 2 US student's subsidiary subject or course. —v. (foll. by in) US Study (as a subject) as a subsidiary. [Latin, = less]

minority /maɪ'nɒrɪtɪ/ n. (pl. **-ies**) 1 (often foll. by of) smaller number or part, esp. in politics. 2 state of having less than half the votes or support (in the minority). 3 small group of people differing from others in race, religion, language, etc. 4 (attrib.) of or done by the minority (minority interests). 5 a being under full legal age. b period of this. [French or medieval Latin: related to MINOR]

minster n. 1 large or important church. 2 church of a monastery. [Old English: related to MONASTERY]

minstrel /'mɪnstr(ə)l/ n. 1 medieval singer or musician. 2 (usu. in pl.) entertainer with a blacked face singing ostensibly Black songs in a group. [related to MINISTER]

mint[1] n. 1 aromatic herb used in cooking. 2 peppermint. 3 peppermint sweet. □ **minty** adj. (**-ier**, **-iest**). [Latin menta from Greek]

mint[2] —n. 1 (esp. State) establishment where money is coined. 2 colloq. vast

sum (*making a minh*). —*v.* 1 make (a coin) by stamping metal. 2 invent, coin (a word, phrase, etc.). □ **in mint condition** as new. [Latin *moneta*]

minuet /mɪnjʊˈet/ —*n.* 1 slow stately dance for two in triple time. 2 music for this, often as a movement in a suite etc. —*v.* (-t-) dance a minuet. [French diminutive]

minus /ˈmaɪnəs/ —*prep.* 1 with the subtraction of (*7 minus 4 equals 3*). 2 below zero (*minus 2°*). 3 *colloq.* lacking (*returned minus their dog*). —*adj.* 1 *Math.* negative. 2 *Electronics* having a negative charge. —*n.* 1 = MINUS SIGN. 2 *Math.* negative quantity. 3 *colloq.* disadvantage. [Latin, neuter of MINOR]

minuscule /ˈmɪnəskjuːl/ *adj. colloq.* extremely small or unimportant. [Latin diminutive related to MINUS]

minus sign *n.* the symbol –, indicating subtraction or a negative value.

minute¹ /ˈmɪnɪt/ —*n.* 1 sixtieth part of an hour. 2 distance covered in one minute (*ten minutes from the shops*). 3 a moment (*expecting her any minute*). b (prec. by *the*) *colloq.* present time (*not here at the minute*). c (prec. by *the* foll. by a clause) as soon as (*the minute you get back*). 4 sixtieth part of an angular degree. 5 (in *pl.*) summary of the proceedings of a meeting. 6 official memorandum authorizing or recommending a course of action. —*v.* (-ting) 1 record in minutes. 2 send the minutes of a meeting to. □ **up to the minute** completely up to date. [Latin *minuo* lessen]

minute² /maɪˈnjuːt/ *adj.* (-est) 1 very small. 2 accurate, detailed. □ **minutely** *adv.* [Latin *minutus* related to MINUTE¹]

minute steak *n.* thin quickly-cooked slice of steak.

minutiae /maɪˈnjuːʃiː/ *n.pl.* very small, precise, or minor details. [Latin related to MINUTE¹]

minx /mɪŋks/ *n.* pert, sly, or playful girl. [origin unknown]

Miocene /ˈmaɪəˌsiːn/ *Geol.* —*adj.* of the fourth epoch of the Tertiary period. —*n.* this epoch. [Greek *meiōn* less, *kainos* new]

miracle /ˈmɪrək(ə)l/ *n.* 1 extraordinary, supposedly supernatural event. 2 remarkable occurrence or development (*economic miracle*). 3 (usu. foll. by *of*) remarkable specimen (*a miracle of ingenuity*). [Latin *mirus* wonderful]

miracle play *n.* medieval play on biblical themes.

miraculous /mɪˈrækjʊləs/ *adj.* 1 being a miracle. 2 supernatural. 3 remarkable, surprising. □ **miraculously** *adv.* [French or medieval Latin: related to MIRACLE]

mirage /ˈmɪrɑːʒ/ *n.* 1 optical illusion caused by atmospheric conditions, esp. the appearance of a pool of water in a desert etc. from the reflection of light. 2 illusory thing. [Latin *miro* look at]

MIRAS /ˈmaɪræs/ *abbr.* mortgage interest relief at source.

mire —*n.* 1 area of swampy ground. 2 mud, dirt. —*v.* (-ring) 1 plunge or sink in a mire. 2 involve in difficulties. 3 bespatter, besmirch. □ **miry** *adj.* [Old Norse]

mirror /ˈmɪrə(r)/ —*n.* 1 polished surface, usu. of coated glass, reflecting an image. 2 anything reflecting or illuminating a state of affairs etc. —*v.* reflect in or as in a mirror. [Latin *miro* look at]

mirror image *n.* identical image or reflection with left and right reversed.

mirth *n.* merriment, laughter. □ **mirthful** *adj.* [Old English: related to MERRY]

mis-¹ *prefix* added to verbs and verbal derivatives: meaning 'amiss', 'badly', 'wrongly', 'unfavourably' (*mislead*; *misshapen*; *mistrust*). [Old English]

mis-² *prefix* occurring in some verbs, nouns, and adjectives meaning 'badly', 'wrongly', 'amiss', 'ill-', or having a negative force (*misadventure*; *mischief*). [Latin *minus*]

misadventure /ˌmɪsədˈventʃə(r)/ *n.* 1 bad luck. 2 *Law* accident without crime or negligence (*death by misadventure*). 2 bad luck. 3 a misfortune.

misalliance /ˌmɪsəˈlaɪəns/ *n.* unsuitable alliance, esp. a marriage.

misanthrope /ˈmɪsənˌθrəʊp/ *n.* (also **misanthropist** /mɪˈsænθrəpɪst/) 1 person who hates mankind. 2 person who avoids human society. □ **misanthropic** /ˌmɪsənˈθrɒpɪk/ *adj.* **misanthropically** /ˌmɪsənˈθrɒpɪkli/ *adv.* [Greek *misos* hatred, *anthrōpos* man]

misanthropy /mɪˈsænθrəpi/ *n.* condition or habits of a misanthrope.

misapply /ˌmɪsəˈplaɪ/ *v.* (-ies, -ied) apply (esp. funds) wrongly. □ **misapplication** /ˌmɪsæplɪˈkeɪʃ(ə)n/ *n.*

misapprehend /ˌmɪsæprɪˈhend/ *v.* misunderstand (words, a person). □ **misapprehension** /ˌmɪsæprɪˈhenʃ(ə)n/ *n.*

misappropriate /ˌmɪsəˈprəʊprɪeɪt/ *v.* (-ting) take (another's money etc.) for one's own use; embezzle. □ **misappropriation** /ˌmɪsəprəʊprɪˈeɪʃ(ə)n/ *n.*

misbegotten /ˌmɪsbɪˈɡɒt(ə)n/ *adj.* 1 illegitimate, bastard. 2 contemptible, disreputable.

misbehave /ˌmɪsbɪˈheɪv/ *v. & refl.* (-ving) behave badly. □ **misbehaviour** *n.*

misc. *abbr.* miscellaneous

miscalculate /ˌmɪsˈkælkjʊˌleɪt/ *v.* (-ting) calculate wrongly. □ **miscalculation** /ˌmɪskælkjʊˈleɪʃ(ə)n/ *n.*

miscarriage /mɪsˌkærɪdʒ/ n. spontaneous premature expulsion of a foetus from the womb.

miscarriage of justice n. failure of the judicial system to attain justice.

miscarry /mɪsˈkærɪ/ v. (-ies, -ied) 1 (of a woman) have a miscarriage. 2 (of a plan etc.) fail.

miscast /mɪsˈkɑːst/ v. (past and past part. -cast) allot an unsuitable part to (an actor) or unsuitable actors to (a play etc.).

miscegenation /ˌmɪsɪdʒɪˈneɪʃ(ə)n/ n. interbreeding of races, esp. of Whites and non-Whites. [related to MIX, GENUS]

miscellaneous /ˌmɪsəˈleɪnɪəs/ adj. 1 of mixed composition or character. 2 (foll. by a plural noun) of various kinds. □ **miscellaneously** adv. [Latin misceo mix]

miscellany /mɪˈselənɪ/ n. (pl. -ies) 1 mixture, medley. 2 book containing various literary compositions. [Latin: related to MISCELLANEOUS]

mischance /mɪsˈtʃɑːns/ n. 1 bad luck. 2 instance of this. [French: related to MIS-²]

mischief /ˈmɪstʃɪf/ n. 1 troublesome, but not malicious, conduct, esp. of children (get into mischief). 2 playfulness; malice (eyes full of mischief). 3 harm, injury (do someone a mischief). □ **make mischief** create discord. [French: related to MIS-², chever happen]

mischievous /ˈmɪstʃɪvəs/ adj. 1 (of a person) disposed to mischief. 2 (of conduct) playful; malicious. 3 harmful. □ **mischievously** adv. **mischievousness** n.

miscible /ˈmɪsɪb(ə)l/ adj. capable of being mixed. □ **miscibility** /-ˈbɪlɪtɪ/ n. [medieval Latin: related to MIX]

misconceive /ˌmɪskənˈsiːv/ v. (-ving) 1 (often foll. by of) have a wrong idea or conception. 2 (as **misconceived** adj.) badly planned, organized, etc. □ **misconception** /-ˈsep(ə)n/ n. [from MIS-¹]

misconduct /mɪsˈkɒndʌkt/ n. improper or unprofessional behaviour.

misconstrue /ˌmɪskənˈstruː/ v. (-strues, -strued, -struing) interpret wrongly. □ **misconstruction** /-ˈstrʌkʃ(ə)n/ n.

miscopy /mɪsˈkɒpɪ/ v. (-ies, -ied) copy inaccurately.

miscount /mɪsˈkaʊnt/ v. (also absol.) count inaccurately. —n. inaccurate count.

miscreant /ˈmɪskrɪənt/ n. vile wretch, villain. [French: related to MIS-², creant believer]

misdeed /mɪsˈdiːd/ n. evil deed, wrongdoing, crime. [Old English]

misdemeanour /ˌmɪsdɪˈmiːnə(r)/ n. (US **misdemeanor**) 1 misdeed. 2 hist indictable offence less serious than a felony. [from MIS-¹]

misdiagnose /ˌmɪsˈdaɪəɡnəʊz/ v. (-sing) diagnose incorrectly. □ **misdiagnosis** /-ˈnəʊsɪs/ n.

misdial /mɪsˈdaɪəl/ v. (also absol.) (-ll-; US -l-) dial (a telephone number etc.) incorrectly.

misdirect /ˌmɪsdaɪˈrekt/ v. direct wrongly. □ **misdirection** n.

misdoing /mɪsˈduːɪŋ/ n. misdeed.

miser /ˈmaɪzə(r)/ n. 1 person who hoards wealth and lives miserably. 2 avaricious person. □ **miserly** adj. [Latin, = wretched]

miserable /ˈmɪzərəb(ə)l/ adj. 1 wretchedly unhappy or uncomfortable. 2 contemptible, mean. 3 causing wretchedness or discomfort (miserable weather). □ **miserableness** n. **miserably** adv. [Latin: related to MISER]

misericord /mɪˈzerɪˌkɔːd/ n. projection under a choir stall seat serving (when the seat is turned up) to support a person standing. [Latin misericordia pity]

misery /ˈmɪzərɪ/ n. (pl. -ies) 1 condition or feeling of wretchedness. 2 cause of this. 3 colloq. constantly depressed or discontented person. [Latin: related to MISER]

misfield /mɪsˈfiːld/ —v. (also absol.) (in cricket, baseball, etc.) field (the ball) badly. —n. instance of this. [from MIS-¹]

misfire /mɪsˈfaɪə(r)/ —v. (-ring) 1 (of a gun, motor engine, etc.) fail to go off or start or function smoothly. 2 (of a plan etc.) fail to have the intended effect. —n. such failure.

misfit n. 1 person unsuited to an environment, occupation, etc. 2 garment etc. that does not fit.

misfortune /mɪsˈfɔːtʃ(ə)n/ n. 1 bad luck. 2 instance of this.

misgive /mɪsˈɡɪv/ v. (-ving; past -gave; past part. -given) (of a person's mind, heart, etc.) fill (a person) with suspicion or foreboding.

misgiving /mɪsˈɡɪvɪŋ/ n. (usu. in pl.) feeling of mistrust or apprehension.

misgovern /mɪsˈɡʌv(ə)n/ v. govern badly. □ **misgovernment** n.

misguided /mɪsˈɡaɪdɪd/ adj. mistaken in thought or action. □ **misguidedly** adv. **misguidedness** n.

mishandle /mɪsˈhænd(ə)l/ v. (-ling) 1 deal with incorrectly or inefficiently. 2 handle roughly or rudely.

mishap /ˈmɪshæp/ n. unlucky accident.

mishear /mɪsˈhɪə(r)/ v. (past and past part. -heard /-ˈhɜːd/) hear incorrectly or imperfectly.

mishit —v. /ˌmɪsˈhɪt/ (-tt-; *past and past part.* -hit) hit (a ball etc.) badly. —n. /ˈmɪshɪt/ faulty or bad hit.

mishmash n. confused mixture. [reduplication of MASH.]

misinform /ˌmɪsɪnˈfɔːm/ v. give wrong information to, mislead. □ **misinformation** /-fəˈmeɪʃ(ə)n/ n. [from MIS-¹]

misinterpret /ˌmɪsɪnˈtɜːprɪt/ v. (-t-) 1 interpret wrongly. 2 draw a wrong inference from. □ **misinterpretation** /-ˈteɪʃ(ə)n/ n.

M.I.6 abbr. UK department of Military Intelligence concerned with espionage.

■ **Usage** This term is not in official use.

misjudge /mɪsˈdʒʌdʒ/ v. (-ging) (also absol.) 1 judge wrongly. 2 have a wrong opinion of. □ **misjudgement** n. (also -judgment).

miskey /mɪsˈkiː/ v. (-keys, -keyed) key (data) wrongly.

mislay /mɪsˈleɪ/ v. (*past and past part.* -laid) accidentally put (a thing) where it cannot readily be found.

mislead /mɪsˈliːd/ v. (*past and past part.* -led) cause to infer what is not true; deceive. □ **misleading** adj. [Old English]

mismanage /ˌmɪsˈmænɪdʒ/ v. (-ging) manage badly or wrongly. □ **mismanagement** n. [from MIS-¹]

mismatch —v. /ˌmɪsˈmætʃ/ match unsuitably or incorrectly. —n. /ˈmɪsmætʃ/ bad match.

misnomer /mɪsˈnəʊmə(r)/ n. 1 name or term used wrongly. 2 wrong use of a name or term. [Anglo-French: related to MIS-², nommer to name]

misogynist /mɪˈsɒdʒɪnɪst/ n. misogyny. □ **misogynistic** /-ˈnɪstɪk/ adj. [Greek misos hatred, gunē woman]

misogyny /mɪˈsɒdʒɪnɪ/ n. hatred of women. □ **misogynistic** /-ˈnɪstɪk/ adj.

misplace /mɪsˈpleɪs/ v. (-cing) 1 put in the wrong place. 2 bestow (affections, confidence, etc.) on an inappropriate object. □ **misplacement** n.

misprint —n. /ˈmɪsprɪnt/ printing error. —v. /mɪsˈprɪnt/ print wrongly.

misprision /mɪsˈprɪʒ(ə)n/ n. Law 1 (in full misprision of a felony or of treason) deliberate concealment of one's knowledge of a crime, treason, etc. 2 wrong action or omission. [Anglo-French: related to MIS-², prendre take]

mispronounce /ˌmɪsprəˈnaʊns/ v. (-cing) pronounce (a word etc.) wrongly. □ **mispronunciation** /-ˌnʌnsɪˈeɪʃ(ə)n/ n. [from MIS-¹]

misquote /mɪsˈkwəʊt/ v. (-ting) quote inaccurately. □ **misquotation** /-ˈteɪʃ(ə)n/ n.

misread /mɪsˈriːd/ v. (*past and past part.* -read /-ˈred/) read or interpret wrongly.

misrepresent /ˌmɪsreprɪˈzent/ v. represent wrongly; give a false account or idea of. □ **misrepresentation** /-ˈteɪʃ(ə)n/ n.

misrule /mɪsˈruːl/ —n. bad government; disorder. —v. (-ling) govern badly.

miss¹ —v. 1 (also absol.) fail to hit, reach, find, catch, etc. (an object or goal) 2 fail to catch (a bus, train, etc.) or see (an event or meet (a person). 3 fail to seize (an opportunity etc.) (*missed my chance*). 4 fail to hear or understand (*missed what you said*). 5 a regret the loss or absence of (*did you miss me?*). b notice the loss or absence of (*won't be missed until evening*). 6 avoid (*go early to miss the traffic*). 7 (of an engine etc.) fail, misfire. —n. failure to hit, reach, attain, connect, etc. □ **be missing** not have (*am missing c page*) (see also MISSING). **give** (a thing) **a miss** colloq. not attend or partake of (*gave the party a miss*). **miss out** 1 omit, leave out. 2 (usu. foll. by on) colloq. fail to get or experience. [Old English]

miss² n. 1 (Miss) a title of an unmarried woman or girl. b title of a beauty queen (*Miss World*). 2 title used to address a female schoolteacher, shop assistant, etc. 3 girl or unmarried woman. [from MISTRESS]

missal /ˈmɪs(ə)l/ n. RC Ch. 1 book containing the texts for the Mass throughout the year. 2 book of prayers. [Latin missa MASS²]

missel thrush var. of MISTLE THRUSH.

misshapen /mɪsˈʃeɪpən/ adj. ill-shaped, deformed, distorted. [from MIS-¹, shapen (archaic) = shaped]

missile /ˈmɪsaɪl/ n. 1 object or weapon suitable for throwing at a target or for discharge from a machine. 2 weapon directed by remote control or automatically. [Latin mitto miss- send]

missing adj. 1 not in its place; lost. 2 (of a person) not yet traced or confirmed as alive but not known to be dead. 3 not present.

missing link n. 1 thing lacking to complete a series. 2 hypothetical intermediate type, esp. between humans and apes.

mission /ˈmɪʃ(ə)n/ n. 1 a task or goal assigned to a person or group. b journey undertaken as part of this. c person's vocation. 2 military or scientific operation or expedition. 3 body of persons sent to conduct negotiations or propagate a religious faith. 4 missionary post. [Latin: related to MISSILE]

missionary /ˈmɪʃənərɪ/ —*adj.* of or concerned with religious missions. —*n.* (*pl.* -**ies**) person doing missionary work. [Latin: related to MISSION]

missionary position *n. colloq.* position for sexual intercourse with the woman lying on her back and the man lying on top and facing her.

missis /ˈmɪsɪz/ *n.* (also **missus** /-səz/) *colloq.* or *joc.* **1** form of address to a woman. **2** wife. □ **the missis** my or your wife. [from MISTRESS]

missive /ˈmɪsɪv/ *n.* **1** *joc.* letter. **2** official letter. [Latin: related to MISSILE]

misspell /mɪsˈspel/ *v.* (*past* and *past part.* -**spelt** or -**spelled**) spell wrongly.

misspend /mɪsˈspend/ *v.* (*past* and *past part.* -**spent**) (esp. as **misspent** *adj.*) spend amiss or wastefully.

misstate /mɪsˈsteɪt/ *v.* (-**ting**) state wrongly or inaccurately. □ **misstatement** *n.*

mist *var.* of MISSIS.

mist —*n.* **1 a** water vapour near the ground in minute droplets limiting visibility. **b** condensed vapour obscuring glass etc. **2** dimness or blurring of the sight caused by tears etc. **3** cloud of particles resembling mist. —*v.* (usu. foll. by *up, over*) cover or become covered with mist or as with mist. [Old English]

mistake /mɪˈsteɪk/ —*n.* **1** incorrect idea or opinion; thing incorrectly done or thought. **2** error of judgement. —*v.* (-**king**; *past* **mistook** /-ˈstʊk/; *past part.* **mistaken**) **1** misunderstand the meaning of. **2** (foll. by *for*) wrongly take or identify (*mistook me for you*). **3** choose wrongly (*mistake one's vocation*). [Old Norse: related to MIS-¹, TAKE]

mistaken /mɪˈsteɪk(ə)n/ *adj.* **1** wrong in opinion or judgement. **2** based on or resulting from this (*mistaken loyalty, mistaken identity*). □ **mistakenly** *adv.*

mister /ˈmɪstə(r)/ *n. colloq.* or *joc.* form of address to a man. [from MASTER; cf. MR]

mistime /mɪsˈtaɪm/ *v.* (-**ming**) say or do at the wrong time. [related to MIS-¹]

mistle thrush /ˈmɪs(ə)l/ *n.* (also **missel thrush**) large thrush with a spotted breast, feeding on mistletoe berries. [Old English]

mistletoe /ˈmɪs(ə)l,təʊ/ *n.* parasitic plant with white berries growing on apple and other trees. [Old English]

mistook *past* of MISTAKE.

mistral /ˈmɪstr(ə)l/ *n.* cold N or NW wind in S. France. [Latin: related to MASTER]

mistreat /mɪsˈtriːt/ *v.* treat badly. □ **mistreatment** *n.*

mistress /ˈmɪstrɪs/ *n.* **1** female head of a household. **2 a** woman in authority. **b**

female owner of a pet. **3** female teacher. **4** woman having an illicit sexual relationship with a (usu. married) man. [French *maistre* MASTER, -ESS]

mistrial /mɪsˈtraɪəl/ *n.* trial rendered invalid by error.

mistrust /mɪsˈtrʌst/ —*v.* **1** be suspicious of. **2** feel no confidence in. —*n.* **1** suspicion. **2** lack of confidence. □ **mistrustful** *adj.* **mistrustfully** *adv.*

misty *adj.* (-**ier**, -**iest**) **1** of or covered with mist. **2** dim in outline. **3** obscure, vague (*misty idea*). □ **mistily** *adv.* **mistiness** *n.* [Old English: related to MIST]

misunderstand /mɪsˌʌndəˈstænd/ *v.* (*past* and *past part.* -**understood** /-ˈstʊd/) **1** understand incorrectly. **2** misinterpret the words or actions of (a person).

misunderstanding *n.* **1** failure to understand correctly. **2** slight disagreement or quarrel.

misusage /mɪsˈjuːsɪdʒ/ *n.* **1** wrong or improper usage. **2** ill-treatment.

misuse —*v.* /mɪsˈjuːz/ (-**sing**) **1** use wrongly; apply to the wrong purpose. **2** ill-treat. —*n.* /mɪsˈjuːs/ wrong or improper use or application.

MIT *abbr.* Massachusetts Institute of Technology.

mite¹ *n.* small arachnid, esp. of a kind found in cheese etc. [Old English]

mite² *n.* **1** any small monetary unit. **2** small object or person, esp. a child. **3** modest contribution. [probably the same as MITE¹]

miter *US var.* of MITRE.

mitigate /ˈmɪtɪˌgeɪt/ *v.* (-**ting**) make less intense or severe. □ **mitigation** /-ˈgeɪʃ(ə)n/ *n.* [Latin *mitis* mild]

mitigating circumstances *n.pl.* circumstances permitting greater leniency.

mitosis /maɪˈtəʊsɪs/ *n. Biol.* type of cell division that results in two nuclei each having the same number and kind of chromosomes as the parent nucleus. □ **mitotic** /-ˈtɒtɪk/ *adj.* [Greek *mitos* thread]

mitre /ˈmaɪtə(r)/ (*US* **miter**) —*n.* **1** tall deeply-cleft headdress worn by bishops and abbots, esp. as a symbol of office. **2** joint of two pieces of wood etc. at an angle of 90°, such that the line of junction bisects this angle. —*v.* (-**ring**) **1** bestow a mitre on. **2** join with a mitre. [Greek *mitra* turban]

mitt *n.* **1** (also **mitten**) glove with only two compartments, one for the thumb and the other for all four fingers. **2** glove leaving the fingers and thumb-tip exposed. **3** *slang* hand or fist. **4** baseball glove. [Latin: related to MOIETY]

mix –v. **1** combine or put together (two or more substances or things) so that the constituents of each are diffused among those of the other(s). **2** prepare (a compound, cocktail, e:c.) by combining the ingredients. **3** combine (activities etc.). (*mix business and pleasure*). **4 a** join, be mixed, or combine, esp. readily (*oil and water will not mix*). **b** be compatible. **c** be sociable (*must learn to mix*). **5 a** (foll. by *with*) have regular dealings with. **b** (foll. by *in*) participate in. **6** drink different kinds of (alcoholic liquor) in close succession. **7** combine (two or more sound signals) into one. –n. **1 a** mixing. mixture. **2** proportion of materials in a mixture, or elements. **2** containing persons from various backgrounds etc. **3** for persons of both sexes (*mixed school*). [Latin *misceo* mix]

mixed /mɪkst/ *adj.* **1** of diverse qualities making a cake, concrete, etc. **b** be involved in or with (esp. something undesirable). **mix it** *colloq.* start fighting. **mix up 1** mix thoroughly. **2** confuse. [back-formation from MIXED]

mixed /mɪkst/ *adj.* **1** of diverse qualities or elements. **2** containing persons from various backgrounds etc. **3** for persons of both sexes (*mixed school*). [Latin *misceo* mix]

mixed bag n. diverse assortment.

mixed blessing n. thing having advantages and disadvantages.

mixed doubles *n.pl. Tennis* doubles game with a man and a woman on each side.

mixed economy n. economic system combining private and State enterprise.

mixed farming n. farming of both crops and livestock.

mixed feelings *n.pl.* mixture of pleasure and dismay about something.

mixed grill n. dish of various grilled meats and vegetables etc.

mixed marriage n. marriage between persons of different race or religion.

mixed metaphor n. combination of inconsistent metaphors (e.g. *this tower of strength will forge ahead*).

mixed-up *adj. colloq.* mentally or emotionally confused, socially ill-adjusted.

mixer n. **1** machine for mixing foods etc. **2** person who manages socially in a specified way (*a good mixer*). **3** (usu. soft) drink to be mixed with another. **4** device that receives two or more separate signals from microphones etc. and combines them in a single output.

mixer tap n. tap through which both hot and cold water can be drawn together.

mixture /ˈmɪkstʃə(r)/ n. **1** process or result of mixing. **2** combination of ingredients, qualities, characteristics, etc. [Latin: related to MIXED]

mix-up n. confusion, misunderstanding.

mizzen /ˈmɪz(ə)n/ n. (also **mizzen**) (in full **mizzen-sail**) lowest fore-and-aft sail of a fully rigged ship's mizzen-mast. [Italian related to MEZZANINE]

mizzen-mast n. mast next aft of the mainmast.

ml *abbr.* **1** millilitre(s). **2** mile(s).

M.Litt. *abbr.* Master of Letters. [Latin *Magister Litterarum*]

Mlle *abbr.* (pl. **-s**) Mademoiselle.

MM *abbr.* (pl. **-s**) Messieurs. **2** Military Medal.

mm *abbr.* millimetre(s).

Mme *abbr.* (pl. **-s**) Madame.

Mn *symb.* manganese.

mnemonic /nɪˈmɒnɪk/ –*adj.* of or designed to aid the memory. –n. mnemonic word, verse, etc. □ **mnemonically** *adv.* [Greek *mnēmōn* mindful]

Mo *symb.* molybdenum.

mo /məʊ/ n. (pl. **-s**) *colloq.* moment. [abbreviation]

MO *abbr.* **1** Medical Officer. **2** money order.

moa /ˈmoʊə/ n. (pl. **-s**) extinct flightless New Zealand bird resembling the ostrich. [Maori]

moan –n. **1** long, murmur expressing physical or mental suffering or pleasure. **2** low plaintive sound of wind etc. **3** *colloq.* complaint, grievance. –v. **1** make a moan or moans. **2** *colloq.* complain, grumble. **3** utter with moans. □ **moaner** n. [Old English]

moat n. defensive ditch round a castle etc., usu. filled with water. [French *mote* mound]

mob –n. **1** disorderly crowd; rabble. **2** (prec. by *the*) usu. *derog.* the populace. **3** *colloq.* gang; group. –v. (**-bb-**) crowd round in order to attack or admire. [Latin *mobile vulgus* excitable crowd]

mob-cap n. *hist.* woman's large indoor cap covering all the hair. [obsolete *mob*, originally = slut]

mobile /ˈməʊbaɪl/ –*adj.* **1** movable; able to move easily or get out and about. **2** (of the face etc.) readily changing its expression. **3** (of a shop etc.) accommodated in a vehicle so as to serve various places. **4** (of a person) able to change his or her social status. –n. decoration that may be hung so as to turn freely. □ **mobility** /məˈbɪlɪtɪ/ n. [Latin *moveo* move]

mobile home n. large caravan usu. permanently parked and used as a residence.

mobilize /ˈməʊbɪˌlaɪz/ v. (also **-ise**) (**-zing** or **-sing**) esp. *Mil.* make or become ready for service or action. □ **mobilization** /-ˈzeɪʃ(ə)n/ n.

Möbius strip /ˈmɜːbɪəs/ n. *Math.* one-sided surface formed by joining the ends of a narrow rectangle after twisting one end through 180°. [*Möbius*, name of a mathematician]

mobster n. *slang* gangster.

moccasin /ˈmɒkəsɪn/ n. soft flat-soled shoe orig. worn by N. American Indians. [American Indian]

mocha /ˈmɒkə/ n. 1 coffee of fine quality. 2 flavouring made with this. [*Mocha*, port on the Red Sea]

mock –v. 1 (often foll. by *at*) ridicule; scoff (at); act with scorn or contempt for. 2 mimic contemptuously. 3 defy or delude contemptuously. –*attrib. adj.* 1 sham, imitation. 2 as a trial run (*mock exam*). –n. (in pl.) *colloq.* mock examinations. □ **mockingly** *adv.* [French *moquer*]

mocker n. person who mocks. □ **put the mockers on** *slang* 1 bring bad luck to. 2 put a stop to.

mockery n. (pl. **-ies**) 1 derision, ridicule. 2 counterfeit or absurdly inadequate representation. 3 ludicrously or insultingly futile action etc.

mockingbird n. bird that mimics the notes of other birds.

mock orange n. white-flowered heavy-scented shrub.

mock turtle soup n. soup made from a calf's head etc. to resemble turtle soup.

mock-up n. experimental model or replica of a proposed structure etc.

MOD *abbr.* Ministry of Defence.

mod *colloq. –adj.* modern. –n. young person (esp. in the 1960s) of a group known for its smart modern dress. [abbreviation]

modal /ˈməʊd(ə)l/ *adj.* 1 of mode or form, not of substance. 2 *Gram.* **a** of the mood of a verb. **b** (of an auxiliary verb, e.g. *would*) used to express the mood of another verb. 3 *Mus.* denoting a style of music using a particular mode. [Latin: related to MODE]

mod cons *n.pl.* modern conveniences.

mode n. 1 way in which a thing is done. 2 prevailing fashion or custom. 3 *Mus.* any of several types of scale. [French and Latin *modus* measure]

model /ˈmɒd(ə)l/ –n. 1 representation in three dimensions of an existing person or thing or of a proposed structure, esp. on a smaller scale (often *attrib.*: *model train*). 2 simplified description of a system etc. to assist calculations and predictions. 3 figure in clay, wax, etc., to be reproduced in another material. 4 particular design or style, esp. of a car. 5 **a** ideal, exemplary. **b** (*attrib.*) exemplary. 6 person employed to pose for an artist or photographer or to wear clothes etc. for display. 7 garment etc. by a well-known designer, or a copy of this. –v. (-**ll-**; *US* -**l-**) 1 **a** fashion or shape (a figure) in clay, wax, etc. **b** (foll. by *after*, *on*, etc.) form (a thing in imitation of). 2 **a** act or pose as a model. **b** (of a person acting as a model) display (a garment). [Latin: related to MODE]

modem /ˈməʊdem/ n. combined device for modulation and demodulation, e.g. between a computer and a telephone line. [portmanteau word]

moderate –*adj.* /ˈmɒdərət/ 1 avoiding extremes; temperate in conduct or expression. 2 fairly large or good. 3 (of the wind) of medium strength. 4 (of prices) fairly low. –n. /ˈmɒdərət/ person who holds moderate views, esp. in politics. –v. /ˈmɒdəˌreɪt/ (-**ting**) 1 make or become less violent, intense, rigorous, etc. 2 (also *absol.*) act as moderator of or to. □ **moderately** /-rətlɪ/ *adv.* **moderateness** /-rətnəs/ n. [Latin]

moderation /ˌmɒdəˈreɪʃ(ə)n/ n. 1 moderateness. 2 moderating. □ **in moderation** in a moderate manner or degree.

moderato /ˌmɒdəˈrɑːtəʊ/ *adj.* & *adv.* *Mus.* at a moderate pace. [Italian]

moderator n. 1 arbitrator, mediator. 2 Presbyterian minister presiding over an ecclesiastical body. 4 *Physics* substance used in a nuclear reactor to retard neutrons.

modern /ˈmɒd(ə)n/ –*adj.* 1 of present and recent times. 2 in current fashion; not antiquated. –n. person living in modern times. □ **modernity** /-ˈdɜːnɪtɪ/ n. [Latin *modo* just now]

modern English n. English from about 1500 onwards.

modernism n. modern ideas or methods, esp. in art. □ **modernist** n. & *adj.*

modernize v. (also **-ise**) (-**zing** or -**sing**) 1 make modern; adapt to modern needs or habits. 2 adopt modern ways or views. □ **modernization** /-ˈzeɪʃ(ə)n/ n.

modest /ˈmɒdɪst/ *adj.* 1 having or expressing a humble or moderate estimate of one's own merits. 2 diffident, bashful. 3 decorous. 4 moderate or restrained in amount, extent, severity, etc. 5 unpretentious, not extravagant. □ **modestly** *adv.* **modesty** n. [French from Latin]

modicum /ˈmɒdɪkəm/ n. (foll. by *of*) small quantity. [Latin: related to MODE]

modification /ˌmɒdɪfɪˈkeɪʃ(ə)n/ n. 1 modifying or being modified. 2 change

made. □ **modificatory** /-/ *adj.*

modifier /'mɒdɪfaɪə(r)/ *n.*

modify /'mɒdɪfaɪ/ *v.* (**-ies**, **-ied**) **1** make less severe or extreme. **2** make partial changes in. **3** *Gram.* qualify or expand the sense of (a word etc.). [Latin: related to MODE]

modish /'məʊdɪʃ/ *adj.* fashionable. □ **modishly** *adv.*

modiste /məʊ'diːst/ *n.* milliner; dressmaker. [French: related to MODE]

modulate /'mɒdjʊleɪt/ *v.* (**-ting**) **1 a** regulate or adjust. **b** moderate. **2** adjust or vary the tone or pitch of (the speaking voice). **3** alter the amplitude or frequency of (a wave) by using a wave of a lower frequency to convey a signal. **4** *Mus.* (cause to) change from one key to another. □ **modulation** /-'leɪʃ(ə)n/ *n.* [Latin: related to MODULUS]

module /'mɒdjuːl/ *n.* **1** standardized part or independent unit in construction, esp. of furniture, a building, or an electronic system. **2** independent self-contained unit of a spacecraft. **3** unit or period of training or education. □ **modular** *adj.* [Latin: related to MODULUS]

modulus /'mɒdjʊləs/ *n.* (*pl.* **moduli** /-laɪ/) *Math.* constant factor or ratio. [Latin = measure: related to MODE]

modus operandi /ˌməʊdəs ˌɒpəˈrandiː/ *n.* (*pl.* **modi operandi** /ˌməʊdiː/) method of working. [Latin, = way of operating]

modus vivendi /ˌməʊdəs vɪˈvendiː/ *n.* (*pl.* **modi vivendi** /ˌməʊdiː/) **1** way of living or coping. **2** arrangement between people who agree to differ. [Latin. = way of living]

mog *n.* (also **moggie**) *slang* cat. [originally a dial. word]

Mogadon /'mɒgədɒn/ *n. propr.* hypnotic drug used to treat insomnia. [origin uncertain]

mogul /'məʊg(ə)l/ *n.* **1** *colloq.* important or influential person. **2** (**Mogul**) *hist.* **a** Mongolian. **b** (often **the Great Mogul**) emperor of Delhi in the 16th–19th c. [Persian and Arabic from Mongol]

mohair /'məʊheə(r)/ *n.* **1** hair of the angora goat. **2** yarn or fabric from this. [ultimately from Arabic, = choice]

Mohammedan var. of MUHAMMADAN.

Mohican /məʊˈhiːkən/ —*adj.* (of a hairstyle) with the head shaved except for a strip of hair from the middle of the forehead to the back of the neck, often worn in long spikes. —*n.* such a hairstyle. [*Mohicans*, N. American Indian people]

moiety /'mɔɪətɪ/ *n.* (*pl.* **-ies**) *Law* or *literary* **1** half. **2** each of the two parts of a thing. [Latin *medietas* from *medius* middle]

moire /mwɑː(r)/ *n.* (in full **moire antique**) watered fabric, usu. silk. [French: related to MOHAIR]

moiré /'mwɑːreɪ/ *adj.* **1** (of silk) watered. **2** (of metal) having a clouded appearance. [French: related to MOIRE]

moiré pattern *n.* pattern observed when one pattern of lines etc. is superimposed on another.

moist *adj.* slightly wet; damp. [French]

moisten /'mɔɪs(ə)n/ *v.* make or become moist.

moisture /'mɔɪstʃə(r)/ *n.* water or other liquid diffused in a small quantity as vapour, or within a solid, or condensed on a surface.

moisturize *v.* (also **-ise**) (**-zing** or **-sing**) make less dry (esp. the skin by use of a cosmetic). □ **moisturizer** *n.*

molar /'məʊlə(r)/ —*adj.* (usu. of a mammal's back teeth) serving to grind. —*n.* molar tooth. [Latin *mola* millstone]

molasses /mə'læsɪz/ *n.pl.* (treated as *sing.*) **1** uncrystallized syrup extracted from raw sugar. **2** *US* treacle. [Portuguese from Latin *mel* honey]

mold *US* var. of MOULD[1], MOULD[2], MOULD[3].

molder *US* var. of MOULDER.

molding *US* var. of MOULDING.

moldy *US* var. of MOULDY.

mole[1] *n.* **1** small burrowing mammal with dark velvety fur and very small eyes. **2** *slang* spy established in a position of trust in an organization. [Low German or Dutch]

mole[2] *n.* small permanent dark spot on the skin. [Old English]

mole[3] *n.* **1** massive structure serving as a pier, breakwater, or causeway. **2** artificial harbour. [Latin *moles* mass]

mole[4] *n. Chem.* the SI unit of amount of substance equal to the quantity containing as many elementary units as there are atoms in 0.012 kg of carbon-12. [German: from *Mol* from MOLECULE]

molecular /mə'lekjʊlə(r)/ *adj.* of, relating to, or consisting of molecules. □ **molecularity** /-'lærɪtɪ/ *n.*

molecular weight *n.* = RELATIVE MOLECULAR MASS.

molecule /'mɒlɪkjuːl/ *n.* **1** smallest fundamental unit (usu. a group of atoms) of a chemical compound that can take part in a chemical reaction. **2** (in general use) small particle. [Latin diminutive: related to MOLE[4]]

molehill *n.* small mound thrown up by a mole in burrowing. □ **make a mountain out of a molehill** overreact to a minor difficulty.

molest /mə'lest/ *v.* **1** annoy or pester (a person). **2** attack or interfere with (a person), esp. sexually. □ **molestation**

/ˈsteɪ(r)ɑ(ə)n/ n. **molester** n. [Latin *molestus* troublesome]

moll n. *slang* **1** gangster's female companion. **2** prostitute. [pet form of *Mary*]

mollify /ˈmɒlɪfaɪ/ v. (**-ies, -ied**) appease. □ **mollification** /ˌfɪˈkeɪʃ(ə)n/ n. [Latin *mollis* soft]

mollusc /ˈmɒlʌsk/ n. (*US* **mollusk**) invertebrate with a soft body and usu. a hard shell, e.g. snails and oysters. [Latin *molluscus* soft]

mollycoddle /ˈmɒlɪˌkɒd(ə)l/ v. (**-ling**) coddle, pamper. [related to MOLL, CODDLE]

Molotov cocktail /ˈmɒlə.tɒf/ n. crude incendiary device, usu. a bottle filled with inflammable liquid. [*Molotov*, name of a Russian statesman]

molt *US* var. of MOULT.

molten /ˈməʊlt(ə)n/ adj. melted, esp. made liquid by heat. [from MELT]

molto /ˈmɒltəʊ/ adv. *Mus.* very. [Latin *multus* much]

molybdenum /məˈlɪbdɪnəm/ n. silverwhite metallic element added to steel to give strength and resistance to corrosion. [Greek *molubdos* lead]

mom n. *US colloq.* mother. [abbreviation of MOMMA]

moment /ˈməʊmənt/ n. **1** very brief portion of time. **2** an exact point of time (*I came the moment you called*). **3** importance (*of no great moment*). **4** product of a force and the distance from its line of action to a point. □ **at the moment** now. **in a moment** very soon. **man** (or **woman** etc.) **of the moment** the one of importance at the time in question. [Latin: related to MOMENTUM]

momentary adj. lasting only a moment; transitory. □ **momentarily** adv. [Latin: related to MOMENT]

moment of truth n. time of crisis or test.

momentous /məˈmentəs/ adj. very important. □ **momentously** adv. **momentousness** n.

momentum /məˈmentəm/ n. (pl. **momenta**) **1** quantity of motion of a moving body, the product of its mass and velocity. **2** impetus gained by movement. **3** strength or continuity derived from an initial effort. [Latin *moveo* move]

momma /ˈmɒmə/ n. *US colloq.* mother. [var. of MAMA]

mommy /ˈmɒmɪ/ n. (pl. **-ies**) esp. *US colloq.* = MUMMY.

Mon. *abbr.* Monday.

monad /ˈmɒnæd, ˈməʊ-/ n. **1** the number one; unit. **2** *Philos.* ultimate unit of being (e.g. a soul, an atom, a person, God). □ **monadic** /məˈnædɪk/ adj. [Greek *monas -ados* unit]

monarch /ˈmɒnək/ n. sovereign with the title of king, queen, emperor, empress, or equivalent. □ **monarchic** /məˈnɑːkɪk/ adj. **monarchical** /məˈnɑːkɪk(ə)l/ adj. [Greek: related to MONO-, *arkhō* rule]

monarchism n. the advocacy of monarchy. □ **monarchist** n. [French: related to MONARCH]

monarchy n. (pl. **-ies**) **1** form of government with a monarch at the head. **2** State with this. □ **monarchial** /məˈnɑːkɪəl/ adj. [Greek: related to MONARCH]

monastery /ˈmɒnəstrɪ/ n. (pl. **-ies**) residence of a community of monks. [Latin *monasterium* from Greek *monazō* alone]

monastic /məˈnæstɪk/ adj. of or like monasteries or monks, nuns, etc. □ **monastically** adv. **monasticism** /-ˌsɪz(ə)m/ n. [Greek: related to MONASTERY]

Monday /ˈmʌndeɪ/ n. day of the week following Sunday. —adv. *colloq.* **1** on Monday. **2** (**Mondays**) on Mondays; each Monday. [Old English]

monetarism /ˈmʌnɪtəˌrɪz(ə)m/ n. control of the supply of money as the chief method of stabilizing the economy. □ **monetarist** n. & adj.

monetary /ˈmʌnɪtərɪ/ adj. **1** of the currency in use. **2** of or consisting of money. [Latin: related to MONEY]

money /ˈmʌnɪ/ n. **1** coins and banknotes as a medium of exchange. **2** (pl. **-eys** or **-ies**) (in pl.) sums of money. **3 a** wealth. **b** wealth as power (*money talks*). **c** rich person or family (*married into money*). □ **for my money** in my opinion; for my preference. **in the money** *colloq.* having or winning a lot of money. **money for jam** (or **old rope**) *colloq.* profit for little or no trouble. [Latin *moneta*]

moneybags n.pl. (treated as *sing.*) *colloq.* usu. *derog.* wealthy person.

moneyed /ˈmʌnɪd/ adj. wealthy.

money-grubber n. *colloq.* person greedily intent on amassing money. □ **money-grubbing** n. & adj.

moneylender n. person who lends money at interest.

moneymaker n. **1** person who earns much money. **2** thing, idea, etc., that produces much money. □ **moneymaking** n. & adj.

money market n. trade in short-term stocks, loans, etc.

money order n. order for payment of a specified sum, issued by a bank or Post Office.

money-spinner n. thing that brings in a profit.

money's worth see ONE's, MONEY's WORTH.

monger /'mʌŋgə(r)/ n. (usu. in comb.) 1 dealer, trader (fishmonger). 2 usu. derog. promoter, spreader (warmonger, scaremonger). [Latin mango dealer]

Mongol /'mɒŋg(ə)l/ —adj. 1 of the Asian people. 2 resembling this people. 3 (mongol) often offens. suffering from Down's syndrome. —n. 1 Mongolian. 2 (mongol) often offens. person suffering from Down's syndrome. [native name: perhaps from mong brave]

Mongolian /mɒŋ'gəʊliən/ —n. 1 native or inhabitant of Mongolia. 2 language of Mongolia, or its people or language. —adj. of or relating to Mongolia or its people or language.

mongolism /'mɒŋgə,lız(ə)m/ n. = DOWN'S SYNDROME.

■ **Usage** The term Down's syndrome is now preferred.

Mongoloid /'mɒŋgə,lɔɪd/ —adj. 1 characteristic of the Mongolians, esp. in having a broad flat yellowish face. 2 (mongoloid) often offens. having the characteristic symptoms of Down's syndrome. —n. Mongoloid or mongoloid person.

mongoose /'mɒŋguːs/ n. (pl. -s) small flesh-eating civet-like mammal. [Marathi]

mongrel /'mʌŋgr(ə)l/ —n. 1 dog of no definable type or breed. 2 other animal or plant resulting from the crossing of different breeds or types. —adj. of mixed origin, nature, or character. [related to MINGLE]

monies see MONEY 2.

monism /'mɒnız(ə)m/ n. 1 doctrine that only one ultimate principle or being exists. 2 theory denying the duality of matter and mind. □ **monist** n. **monistic** /-'nıstık/ adj. [Greek monos single]

monitor /'mɒnıtə(r)/ —n. 1 person or device for checking or warning. 2 school pupil with disciplinary or other special duties. 3 a television receiver used in a studio to select or verify the picture being broadcast. b = VISUAL DISPLAY UNIT. 4 person who listens to and reports on foreign broadcasts etc. 5 detector of radioactive contamination. —v. 1 act as a monitor of. 2 maintain regular surveillance over. 3 regulate the strength of (a recorded or transmitted signal). [Latin moneo warn]

monitory /'mɒnıtərı/ adj. literary giving or serving as a warning. [Latin monitorius: related to MONITOR]

monk /mʌŋk/ n. member of a religious community of men living under vows. □ **monkish** adj. [Greek monachos from monos alone]

monkey /'mʌŋkı/ —n. (pl. -eys) 1 any of various primates, including marmosets, baboons etc., esp. a small long-tailed kind. 2 mischievous person, esp. a child. —v. (-eys, -eyed) 1 (often foll. by with) tamper or play mischievous tricks. 2 (foll. by around, about) fool around. [origin unknown]

monkey business n. colloq. mischief.

monkey-nut n. peanut.

monkey-puzzle n. tree with hanging prickly branches.

monkey tricks n.pl. colloq. mischief.

monkey wrench n. wrench with an adjustable jaw.

monkshood /'mʌŋkshʊd/ n. poisonous plant with hood-shaped flowers.

mono /'mɒnəʊ/ colloq. —adj. monophonic. —n. monophonic reproduction. [abbreviation]

mono- comb. form (usu. mon- before a vowel) one, alone, single. [Greek monos alone]

monochromatic /,mɒnəkrə'mætık/ adj. 1 (of light or other radiation) of a single colour or wavelength. 2 containing only one colour. □ **monochromatically** adv.

monochrome /'mɒnəkrəʊm/ —n. photograph or picture done in one colour or different tones of this, or in black and white only. —adj. having or using only one colour or in black and white only. [from MONO-, Greek khrōma colour]

monocle /'mɒnək(ə)l/ n. single eye-glass. □ **monocled** adj. [Latin: related to MONO, oculus eye]

monocotyledon /,mɒnə,kɒtı'liːd(ə)n/ n. flowering plant with one cotyledon. □ **monocotyledonous** adj.

monocular /mə'nɒkjʊlə(r)/ adj. with or for one eye. [related to MONOCLE]

monody /'mɒnədı/ n. (pl. -ies) 1 ode sung by a single actor in a Greek tragedy. 2 poem lamenting a person's death. □ **monodist** n. [Greek: related to MONO-, ODE]

monogamy /mə'nɒgəmı/ n. practice or state of being married to one person at a time. □ **monogamous** adj. [Greek gamos marriage]

monogram /'mɒnə,græm/ n. two or more letters, esp. a person's initials, interwoven as a device. □ **monogrammed** adj. [Greek]

monograph /'mɒnə,grɑːf/ n. treatise on a single subject.

monolingual /,mɒnəʊ'lɪŋgw(ə)l/ adj. speaking or using only one language.

monolith /'mɒnəlɪθ/ n. 1 single block of stone, esp. shaped into a pillar etc. 2 person or thing like a monolith in being

monologue /ˈmɒnəˌlɒg/ n. **1 a** scene in a drama in which a person speaks alone. **b** dramatic composition for one performer. **2** long speech by one person in a conversation etc. [French from Greek *monologos* speaking alone]

monomania /ˌmɒnəˈmeɪnɪə/ n. obsession by a single idea or interest. □ **monomaniac** n. & adj.

monophonic /ˌmɒnəˈfɒnɪk/ adj. (of sound-reproduction) using only one channel of transmission. [Greek *phōnē* sound]

monoplane /ˈmɒnəˌpleɪn/ n. aeroplane with one set of wings.

monopolist /məˈnɒpəlɪst/ n. person who has or advocates a monopoly. □ **monopolistic** /-ˈlɪstɪk/ adj.

monopolize /məˈnɒpəˌlaɪz/ v. (also **-ise**) (**-zing** or **-sing**) **1** obtain exclusive possession or control of (a trade or commodity etc.). **2** dominate or prevent others from sharing in (a conversation etc.). □ **monopolization** /-ˈzeɪʃ(ə)n/ n. **monopolizer** n.

monopoly /məˈnɒpəlɪ/ n. (pl. **-ies**) **1 a** exclusive possession or control of a trade in a commodity or service. **b** this conferred as a privilege by the State. **2** (foll. by *of*, *US on*) exclusive possession, control, or exercise. [Greek *pōleō* sell]

monorail /ˈmɒnəʊˌreɪl/ n. railway with a single-rail track.

monosodium glutamate /ˌmɒnəʊˈsəʊdɪəm ˈgluːtəˌmeɪt/ n. sodium salt of glutamic acid used to enhance the flavour of food. [Latin *gluten* glue]

monosyllable /ˈmɒnəˌsɪləb(ə)l/ n. word of one syllable. □ **monosyllabic** /-ˈlæbɪk/ adj.

monotheism /ˈmɒnəˌθiːɪz(ə)m/ n. doctrine that there is only one god. □ **monotheist** n. **monotheistic** /-ˈɪstɪk/ adj.

monotone /ˈmɒnəˌtəʊn/ —n. **1** sound or utterance continuing or repeated on one note without change of pitch. **2** sameness of style in writing. —adj. without change of pitch.

monotonous /məˈnɒtənəs/ adj. lacking in variety; tedious through sameness. □ **monotonously** adv. **monotony** n.

monovalent /ˌmɒnəˈveɪl(ə)nt/ adj. univalent.

monoxide /məˈnɒksaɪd/ n. oxide containing one oxygen atom.

Messeigneurs /ˌmeseɪnˈjɜː(r)/ n. (pl. of **Monseigneur** and **Monsieur**).

massive, immovable, or solidly uniform. □ **monolithic** /-ˈlɪθɪk/ adj. [Greek *lithos* stone]

Monsieur /məˈsjɜː(r)/ n. (pl. **Messieurs** /meˈsjɜː(r)/) title used of or to a French-speaking man, corresponding to Mr or sir. [French *mon* my, *sieur* lord]

Monsignor /mɒnˈsiːnjə(r)/ n. (pl. **-nori** /-ˈnjɔːrɪ/) title of various Roman Catholic priests and officials. [Italian: related to **Monseigneur**]

monsoon /mɒnˈsuːn/ n. **1** wind in S. Asia, esp. in the Indian Ocean. **2** rainy season accompanying the summer monsoon. [Arabic *mawsim*]

monster n. **1** imaginary creature, usu. large and frightening, made up of incongruous elements. **2** inhumanly cruel or wicked person. **3** misshapen animal or plant. **4** large, usu. ugly, animal or thing. **5** (attrib.) huge. [Latin *monstrum* from *moneo* warn]

monstrance n. RC Ch. vessel in which the host is exposed for veneration. [Latin *monstro* show]

monstrosity /mɒnˈstrɒsɪtɪ/ n. (pl. **-ies**) **1** huge or outrageous thing. **2** monstrousness. **3** = **MONSTER** 3. [Latin: related to **MONSTER**]

monstrous adj. **1** like a monster; abnormally formed. **2** huge. **3 a** outrageously wrong or absurd. **b** atrocious. □ **monstrously** adv. **monstrousness** n. [Latin: related to **MONSTER**]

montage /mɒnˈtɑːʒ/ n. **1** selection, cutting, and piecing together as a consecutive whole, of separate sections of cinema or television film. **2 a** composite whole made from juxtaposed photographs etc. **b** production of this. [French: related to **MOUNT**¹]

month /mʌnθ/ n. **1** (in full **calendar month**) **a** each of twelve periods into which a year is divided. **b** period of time between the same dates in successive calendar months. **2** period of 28 days. [Old English]

monthly —adj. done, produced, or occurring once every month. —adv. every month. —n. (pl. **-ies**) monthly periodical. **month of Sundays** n. colloq. very long period.

monument /ˈmɒnjʊmənt/ n. **1** anything enduring that serves to commemorate or celebrate, esp. a structure or building. **2** stone etc. placed over a grave or in a church etc. in memory of the dead. **3** ancient building or site etc. that has been preserved. **4** lasting reminder. [Latin *moneo* remind]

monumental /ˌmɒnjʊˈment(ə)l/ adj. **1 a** extremely great; stupendous (*monumental effort*). **b** (of a work of art etc.) massive and permanent. **2** of or serving as a monument. □ **monumentally** adv. **monumental mason** n. maker of tombstones etc.

moo –n. (pl. -s) cry of cattle. –v. (moos, mooed) make this sound. [imitative]

mooch v. colloq. 1 (usu. foll. by about, around) wander aimlessly around. 2 esp. US cadge; steal [probably from French muchier skulk]

mood¹ n. 1 state of mind or feeling. 2 fit of bad temper or depression. □ **in the mood** (usu. foll. by for, or to + infin.) inclined. [Old English]

mood² n. 1 Gram. form or set of forms of a verb indicating whether it expresses a fact, command, wish, etc. (subjunctive mood). 2 distinction of meaning expressed by different moods. [alteration of MODE]

moody –adj. (-ier, -iest) given to changes of mood; gloomy, sullen. □ **moodily** adv. **moodiness** n. [related to MOOD¹]

moon –n. 1 a a natural satellite of the earth, orbiting it monthly, illuminated by the sun and reflecting some light to the earth. b this regarded in terms of its waxing and waning in a particular month (new moon). c the moon when visible (there is no moon tonight). 2 satellite of any planet. 3 (prec. by the) colloq. something desirable but unattainable (promised me the moon). –v. 1 wander about aimlessly or listlessly. 2 slang expose one's buttocks. □ **many moons ago** a long time ago. **moon over** act dreamily thinking about (a loved one). **over the moon** colloq. extremely happy. □ **moonless** adj. [Old English]

moonbeam n. ray of moonlight.

moon boot n. thickly-padded boot for low temperatures.

moon-face n. round face.

Moonie /ˈmuːnɪ/ n. colloq. offens. member of the Unification Church. [Sun Myung Moon, name of its founder]

moonlight –n. 1 light of the moon. 2 (attrib.) lit by the moon. –v. (-lighted) colloq. have two paid occupations, esp. one by day and one by night. □ **moonlighter** n.

moonlight flit n. hurried departure by night, esp. to avoid paying a debt.

moonlit adj. lit by the moon.

moonscape n. 1 surface or landscape of the moon. 2 area resembling this; wasteland.

moonshine n. 1 foolish or unrealistic talk or ideas. 2 slang illicitly distilled or smuggled alcohol.

moonshot n. launching of a spacecraft to the moon.

moonstone n. feldspar of pearly appearance.

moonstruck adj. slightly mad.

moony adj. (-ier, -iest) listless; stupidly dreamy.

Moor /mʊə(r), mɔː(r)/ n. member of a Muslim people of NW Africa. □ **Moorish** adj. [Greek Mauros]

moor¹ /mʊə(r), mɔː(r)/ n. 1 open uncultivated upland, esp. when covered with heather. 2 tract of ground preserved for shooting. [Old English]

moor² /mʊə(r), mɔː(r)/ v. attach (a boat etc.) to a fixed object. □ **moorage** n. [probably Low German]

moorhen n. small waterfowl.

moorland n. extensive area of moor.

moose n. (pl. same) N. American deer. [Narragansett]

moot –adj. debatable, undecided (moot point). –v. raise (a question) for discussion. –n. hist. assembly. [Old English]

mop –n. 1 bundle of yarn or cloth or a sponge on the end of a stick, for cleaning floors etc. 2 similarly-shaped implement for various purposes. 3 thick mass of hair. 4 mopping or being mopped (gave it a mop). –v. (-pp-) 1 wipe or clean with or as with a mop. 2 wipe tears or sweat etc. from (one's face etc.). □ **mop up** 1 wipe up with or as with a mop. 2 colloq. absorb. 3 dispatch; make an end of. 4 a complete the occupation of (a district etc.) by capturing or killing enemy troops left there. b capture or kill (stragglers). [origin uncertain]

mope –v. (-ping) 1 be depressed or listless. 2 wander about listlessly. –n. person who mopes. □ **mopy** adj. (-ier, -iest). [origin unknown]

moped /ˈməʊpɛd/ n. two-wheeled low-powered motor vehicle with pedals. [Swedish: related to MOTOR, PEDAL]

moquette /mɒˈkɛt/ n. thick pile or looped material used for upholstery etc. [French]

moraine /məˈreɪn/ n. area of debris carried down and deposited by a glacier. [French]

moral /ˈmɒr(ə)l/ –adj. 1 a concerned with goodness or badness of human character or behaviour, or with the distinction between right and wrong. b concerned with accepted rules and standards of human behaviour. 2 a virtuous in general conduct. b capable of moral action. 3 (of rights or duties etc.) founded on moral not actual law. 4 associated with the psychological rather than the physical (moral courage, moral support). –n. 1 moral lesson of a fable, story, event, etc. 2 (in pl.) moral behaviour, e.g. in sexual conduct.

□ **morally** adv. [Latin mos mor- cus-tom]

morale /mə'rɑːl/ n. confidence, deter-mination, etc. of a person or group. [French moral: related to MORAL]

moralist /'mɒrəlist/ n. 1 person who practises or teaches morality. 2 person who follows a natural system of ethics. □ **moralistic** /-'lɪstɪk/ adj.

morality /mə'ræləti/ n. (pl. -ies) 1 de-gree of conformity to moral principles. 2 right moral conduct. 3 science of mor-als. 4 particular system of morals (com-mercial morality).

morality play n. hist. drama with personified abstract qualities and including a moral lesson.

moralize /'mɒrəlaɪz/ v. (also -ise) 1 (-zing or -sing) 1 (often foll. by on) indulge in moral reflection or talk. 2 make moral or more moral. □ **moral-ization** /-'zeɪʃ(ə)n/ n.

moral law n. the conditions to be satis-fied by any right course of action.

moral philosophy n. branch of philo-sophy concerned with ethics.

moral victory n. defeat that has some of the satisfactory elements of victory.

morass /mə'ræs/ n. 1 entanglement; confusion. 2 literary bog. [French mar-ais related to MARSH]

moratorium /ˌmɒrə'tɔːrɪəm/ n. (pl. -s or -ria) 1 (often foll. by on) temporary prohibition or suspension (of an ac-tivity). 2 a legal authorization to debtors to postpone payment. b period of this postponement. [Latin moror delay]

morbid adj. 1 a (of the mind, ideas, etc.) unwholesome. b given to morbid feel-ings. 2 colloq. melancholy. 3 Med. of the nature or indicative of disease. □ **morbidity** /-'bɪdɪtɪ/ n. **morbidly** adv. [Latin morbus disease]

mordant /'mɔːd(ə)nt/ —adj. 1 (of sar-casm etc.) caustic, biting. 2 pungent, smarting. 3 corrosive or cleansing. 4 serving to fix dye. —n. mordant sub-stance. [Latin mordeo bite]

more /mɔː(r)/ —adj. greater in quantity or degree; additional (more problems than last time; bring some more water). —n. greater quantity, number, or amount (more than three people; more to it than meets the eye). —adv. 1 to a greater degree or extent. 2 forming the comparative of adjectives and adverbs, esp. those of more than one syllable (more absurd; more easily). □ **more and more** to a greater extent. **more or less** approximately; effectively; nearly. **what is more** as an additional point. [Old English]

moreish /'mɔːrɪʃ/ adj. (also **morish**) colloq. (of food) causing a desire for more.

morello /mə'reləʊ/ n. (pl. -s) sour kind of dark cherry. [Italian, = blackish]

moreover /mɔːr'əʊvə(r)/ adv. besides, in addition to what has been said.

mores /'mɔːreɪz/ n.pl. customs or con-ventions of a community. [Latin, pl. of mos custom]

morganatic /ˌmɔːgə'nætɪk/ adj. 1 (of a marriage) between a person of high rank and one of lower rank, the spouse and children having no claim to the possessions or title of the person of higher rank. 2 (of a spouse) married in this way. [Latin morganaticus from Germanic, = 'morning gift', from a husband to his wife on the morning after consummation of a marriage]

morgue /mɔːg/ n. 1 mortuary. 2 (in a newspaper office) room or file of miscel-laneous information. [French, ori-ginally the name of a Paris mortuary]

moribund /'mɒrɪˌbʌnd/ adj. 1 at the point of death. 2 lacking vitality. [Latin morior die]

morish var. of MOREISH.

Mormon /'mɔːmən/ n. member of the Church of Jesus Christ of Latter-Day Saints. □ **Mormonism** n. [Mormon, name of the supposed author of the book on which Mormonism is founded]

morn n. poet. morning. [Old English]

mornay /'mɔːneɪ/ n. cheese-flavoured white sauce. [origin uncertain]

morning n. 1 early part of the day, ending at noon or lunch-time (this morning; during the morning). 2 attrib. taken, occurring, or appearing during the morning (morning coffee). □ **in the morning** colloq. tomorrow morning. [from MORN]

morning after n. colloq. = HANGOVER 1.

morning-after pill n. contraceptive pill taken some hours after intercourse.

morning coat n. coat with tails, and with the front cut away.

morning dress n. man's morning coat and striped trousers.

morning glory n. twining plant with trumpet-shaped flowers.

morning sickness n. nausea felt in the morning in esp. early pregnancy.

morning star n. planet, usu. Venus, seen in the east before sunrise.

morocco /mə'rɒkəʊ/ n. (pl. -s) fine flex-ible leather of goatskin tanned with sumac. [Morocco in NW Africa]

moron /'mɔːrɒn/ n. 1 colloq. very stupid person. 2 adult with a mental age of 8–12. □ **moronic** /mə'rɒnɪk/ adj. [Greek mōros foolish]

morose /məˈraʊs/ *adj.* sullen, gloomy. □ **morosely** *adv.* **moroseness** *n.* [Latin *mos mor-* manner]

morpheme /ˈmɔːfiːm/ *n. Linguistics* the smallest meaningful unit of a language that cannot be further divided (e.g. *in*, *come*, *-ing*, forming *incoming*) [Greek *morphē* form]

morphia /ˈmɔːfiə/ *n.* (in general use) = MORPHINE.

morphine /ˈmɔːfiːn/ *n.* narcotic drug from opium, used to relieve pain. [Latin *Morpheus* god of sleep]

morphology /mɔːˈfɒlədʒɪ/ *n.* the study of the forms of things, esp. of animals and plants and of words and their structure. □ **morphological** /-fəˈlɒdʒɪk(ə)l/ *adj.* [Greek *morphē* form]

morrow *n.* (usu. prec. by *the*) *literary* the following day. [related to MORN]

Morse /mɔːs/ *n.* (in full **Morse code**) code in which letters are represented by combinations of long and short light or sound signals. —*v.* (**-sing**) signal by Morse code. [*Morse*, name of an electrician]

morsel /ˈmɔːs(ə)l/ *n.* mouthful; small piece (esp. of food). [Latin *morsus* bite]

mortal —*adj.* **1** subject to death. **2** causing death; fatal. **3** (of combat) fought to the death. **4** associated with death (*mortal agony*). **5** (of an enemy) implacable. **6** (of pain, fear, an affront, etc.) intense, very serious. **7** *colloq.* long and tedious (*for two mortal hours*). **8** *colloq.* conceivable, imaginable (*every mortal thing*; *of no mortal use*). —*n.* human being. □ **mortally** *adv.* [Latin *mors mort-* death]

mortality /mɔːˈtælɪtɪ/ *n.* (*pl.* **-ies**) **1** being subject to death. **2** loss of life on a large scale. **3 a** number of deaths in a given period etc. **b** (in full **mortality rate**) death rate.

mortal sin *n.* sin that deprives the soul of divine grace.

mortar /ˈmɔːtə(r)/ —*n.* **1** mixture of lime or cement, sand, and water, for bonding bricks or stones. **2** short large-bore cannon for firing shells at high angles. **3** vessel in which ingredients are pounded with a pestle. —*v.* **1** plaster or join with mortar. **2** bombard with mortar shells. [Latin *mortarium*]

mortarboard *n.* **1** academic cap with a stiff flat square top. **2** flat board for holding mortar.

mortgage /ˈmɔːgɪdʒ/ —*n.* **1 a** conveyance of property to a creditor as security for a debt; usu. one incurred by the purchase of the property. **b** deed effecting this. **2** sum of money lent by this. —*v.* (**-ging**) convey (a property) by mortgage. □ **no-tgageable** *adj.* [French, = dead pledge: related to GAGE[1]]

mortgagee /ˌmɔːgɪˈdʒiː/ *n.* creditor in a mortgage.

mortgager /ˈmɔːgɪdʒə(r)/ *n.* (also **mortgagor** /ˈ-dʒɔː(r)/) debtor in a mortgage.

mortgage rate *n.* rate of interest charged by a mortgagee.

mortician /mɔːˈtɪʃ(ə)n/ *n. US* undertaker. [Latin *mors mort-* death]

mortice var. of MORTISE.

mortification /ˌmɔːtɪfɪˈkeɪʃ(ə)n/ *n.* **1 a** cause (a person) to feel shamed, humiliated, or sorry. **b** wound (a person's feelings). **2** bring (the body, a person's passions, etc.) into subjection by self-denial or discipline. **3** (of flesh) be affected by gangrene or necrosis. □ **mortifying** /ˈmɔːtɪfaɪ/ *v.* (**-ies, -ied**) **1 a mortifying** *adj.* [Latin: related to MORTIFY]

mortise /ˈmɔːtɪs/ (also **mortice**) —*n.* hole in a framework designed to receive the end of another part, esp. a tenon. —*v.* (**-sing**) **1** join securely, esp. by mortise and tenon. **2** cut a mortise in. [French from Arabic]

mortise lock *n.* lock recessed in the frame or a door etc.

mortuary /ˈmɔːtʃʊərɪ/ —*n.* (*pl.* **-ies**) room or building in which dead bodies are kept until burial or cremation. —*adj.* of death or burial. [medieval Latin *mortuarius*: related to MUSE[1]]

Mosaic /məʊˈzeɪɪk/ *adj.* of Moses. [French from *Moses* in the Old Testament]

mosaic /məʊˈzeɪɪk/ *n.* **1 a** picture or pattern produced by arranging small variously coloured pieces of glass or stone etc. **b** this as an art form. **2** diversified thing. **3** (*attrib.*) of or like a mosaic. [Greek: ultimately related to MUSE[1]]

Mosaic Law *n.* the laws attributed to Moses and listed in the Pentateuch.

Moselle /məʊˈzel/ *n.* dry white wine from the Moselle valley in Germany.

mosey /ˈməʊzɪ/ *v.* (**-eys, -eyed**) (often foll. by *along*) *slang* go in a leisurely manner. [origin unknown]

Moslem var. of MUSLIM.

mosque /mɒsk/ *n.* Muslim place of worship. [Arabic *masgid*]

mosquito /mɒsˈkiːtəʊ/ *n.* (*pl.* **-es**) biting insect, esp. one of which the female punctures the skin with a long proboscis to suck blood. [Spanish and Portuguese, diminutive of *mosca* fly]

mosquito-net *n.* net to keep off mosquitoes.

moss *n.* **1** small flowerless plant growing in dense clusters in bogs, on the ground, trees, stones, etc. **2** *Scot. & N.Engl.* bog, esp. a peatbog. □ **mossy** *adj.* (**-ier**, **-iest**). [Old English]

most /məʊst/ —*adj.* **1** greatest in quantity or degree. **2** the majority of (*most people think so*). —*n.* **1** greatest quantity or number (*this is the most I can do*). **2** the majority (*most of them are missing*). —*adv.* **1** in the highest degree. **2** forming the superlative of adjectives and adverbs, esp. those of more than one syllable (*most absurd*; *most easily*). **3** *US colloq.* almost. □ **at most** no more or better than (*this is at most a makeshift*). **at the most 1** as the greatest amount. **2** not more than. **for the most part 1** mainly. **2** usually. **make the most of** employ to the best advantage. [Old English]

-most *suffix* forming superlative adjectives and adverbs from prepositions and other words indicating relative position (*foremost*; *uttermost*). [Old English]

mostly *adv.* **1** mainly. **2** usually.

MOT *abbr.* (in full **MOT test**) compulsory annual test of vehicles of more than a specified age. [*Ministry of Transport*]

mot /məʊ/ *n.* (*pl.* **mots** pronunc. same) = BON MOT. [French: = word]

mote *n.* speck of dust. [Old English]

motel /məʊˈtel/ *n.* roadside hotel for motorists. [from *motor hotel*]

motet /məʊˈtet/ *n. Mus.* short religious choral work. [French: related to MOT]

moth *n.* **1** nocturnal insect like a butterfly but without clubbed antennae. **2** insect of this type breeding in cloth etc., on which its larva feeds. [Old English]

mothball *n.* ball of naphthalene etc. placed in stored clothes to deter moths. □ **in mothballs** stored unused for a considerable time.

moth-eaten *adj.* **1** damaged by moths. **2** time-worn.

mother /ˈmʌðə(r)/ —*n.* **1** female parent. **2** woman, quality, or condition etc. that gives rise to something else (*necessity is the mother of invention*). **3** (in full **Mother Superior**) head of a female religious community. —*v.* **1** treat as a mother does. **2** give birth to; be the mother or origin of. □ **motherhood** *n.* **motherless** *adj.* [Old English]

Mother Carey's chicken *n.* = STORM PETREL 1.

mother country *n.* country in relation to its colonies.

mother earth *n.* the earth as mother of its inhabitants.

Mothering Sunday *n.* = MOTHER'S DAY.

mother-in-law *n.* (*pl.* **mothers-in-law**) husband's or wife's mother.

motherland *n.* one's native country.

motherly *adj.* kind or tender like a mother. □ **motherliness** *n.*

mother-of-pearl *n.* smooth iridescent substance forming the inner layer of the shell of oysters etc.

Mother's Day *n.* day when mothers are honoured with presents, (in the UK) the fourth Sunday in Lent, (in the US) the second Sunday in May.

mother tongue *n.* native language.

mothproof —*adj.* (of clothes) treated so as to repel moths. —*v.* treat (clothes) in this way.

motif /məʊˈtiːf/ *n.* **1** theme in an artistic work. **2** decorative design or pattern. **3** ornament sewn separately on a garment. [French: related to MOTIVE]

motion /ˈməʊʃ(ə)n/ —*n.* **1** moving, changing position. **2** gesture. **3** formal proposal put to a committee, legislature, etc. **4** application to a court for an order. **5** an evacuation of the bowels. **b** (in *sing.* or *pl.*) faeces. —*v.* (often foll. by *to* + *infin.*) direct (a person) by a gesture. **2** (often foll. by *to* a person) make a gesture (*motioned to me to leave*). □ **go through the motions** do something perfunctorily or superficially. **in motion** moving; not at rest. **put** (or **set**) **in motion** set going or working. □ **motionless** *adj.* [Latin: related to MOVE]

motion picture *n.* (esp. US) cinema film.

motivate /ˈməʊtɪveɪt/ *v.* (**-ting**) **1** supply a motive to; be the motive of. **2** cause (a person) to act in a particular way. **3** stimulate the interest of (a person in an activity). □ **motivation** /-ˈveɪʃ(ə)n/ *n.*

motivational /-ˈveɪʃən(ə)l/ *adj.*

motive /ˈməʊtɪv/ —*n.* **1** what induces a person to act in a particular way. **2** = MOTIF. —*adj.* **1** tending to initiate movement. **2** concerned with movement. [Latin *motivus*: related to MOVE]

motive power *n.* moving or impelling power, esp. a source of energy used to drive machinery.

mot juste /məʊ ˈʒuːst/ *n.* (*pl.* **mots justes** pronunc. same) most appropriate expression.

motley /ˈmɒtli/ —*adj.* (**-lier**, **-liest**) **1** diversified in colour. **2** of varied character (*a motley crew*). —*n. hist.* jester's particoloured costume. [origin unknown]

moto-cross /ˈməʊtəʊkrɒs/ n. cross-country racing on motor cycles. [from MOTOR, CROSS]

motor /ˈməʊtə(r)/ —n. **1** thing that imparts motion. **2** machine (esp. one using electricity or internal combustion) supplying motive power for a vehicle or other machine. **3** = CAR 1. **4** (attrib.) **a** giving, imparting, or producing motion. **b** driven by a motor (motor-mower). **c** of or for motor vehicles. **d** Anat. relating to muscular movement or the nerves activating it. —v. **a** go or convey in a motor vehicle. [Latin: related to MOVE]

motor bike n. colloq. = MOTOR CYCLE.

motor boat n. motor-driven boat.

motorcade /ˈməʊtəkeɪd/ n. procession of motor vehicles. [from MOTOR, after cavalcade]

motor car n. = CAR 1.

motor cycle n. two-wheeled motor vehicle without pedal propulsion. □ **motor cyclist** n.

motorist n. driver of a car.

motorize v. (also **-ise**) (**-zing** or **-sing**) **1** provide (troops etc.) with motor transport. **2** provide with a motor.

motorman n. driver of an underground train, tram, etc.

motor scooter see SCOOTER.

motor vehicle n. road vehicle powered by an internal-combustion engine.

motorway n. road for fast travel, with separate carriageways and limited access.

Motown /ˈməʊtaʊn/ n. music with elements of rhythm and blues, associated with Detroit. [Motor Town, = Detroit in US]

mottle v. (**-ling**) (esp. as **mottled** adj.) mark with spots or smears of colour. [back-formation from MOTLEY]

motto /ˈmɒtəʊ/ n. (pl. **-es**) **1** maxim adopted as a rule of conduct. **2** phrase or sentence accompanying a coat of arms. **3** appropriate inscription. **4** joke, maxim etc. in a paper cracker. [Italian: related to MOT]

mould¹ /məʊld/ (US **mold**) —n. **1** hollow container into which a substance is poured or pressed to harden into a required shape. **2** a vessel for shaping puddings etc. **b** pudding etc. made in this way. **3** form or shape. **4** frame or template for producing mouldings. **5** character or type (in heroic mould). —v. **1** make(an object) in a required shape or from certain ingredients (moulded out of clay). **2** give shape to. **3** influence the development of. [French modle from Latin MODULUS]

mould² /məʊld/ n. (US **mold**) furry growth of fungi occurring esp. in moist warm conditions. [Old Norse]

mould³ /məʊld/ n. (US **mold**) **1** loose earth. **2** upper soil of cultivated land, esp. when rich in organic matter. [Old English]

moulder v. (US **molder**) **1** decay to dust. **2** (foll. by away) rot or crumble. **3** deteriorate. [from MOULD³]

moulding n. (US **molding**) **1** ornamentally shaped outline of plaster etc. as an architectural feature, esp. in a cornice. **2** similar feature in woodwork etc.

mouldy adj. (US **moldy**) (**-ier**, **-iest**) **1** covered with mould **2** stale; out of date. **3** colloq. dull, miserable. □ **mouldiness** n.

moult /məʊlt/ (US **molt**) —v. (also absol.) shed (feathers, hair, a shell etc.) in the process of renewing plumage, a coat, etc. —n. moulting. [Latin muto change]

mound n. **1** raised mass of earth, stones, etc. **2** heap or pile; large quantity. **3** hillock. [origin unknown]

mount¹ —v. **1** ascend; climb on to. **2** get up on (a horse etc.) to ride it. **b** set on horseback **c** (as mounted adj.) serving on horseback (mounted police). **3 a** (often foll. by up) accumulate. **b** (of a feeling) increase. **4** (often foll. by on, in) set (an object) on a support or in a backing, frame, etc., esp. for viewing. **5** organize, arrange, set in motion (a play, exhibition, attack, guard, etc.). **6** (of a male animal) get on to (a female) to copulate. —n. **1** backing etc. on which a picture etc. is set for display. **2** horse for riding. **3** setting for a gem etc. [Latin: related to MOUNT²]

mount² n. archaic (except before a name): mountain, hill (Mount Everest). [Latin mons montis]

mountain /ˈmaʊntɪn/ n. **1** large abrupt natural elevation of the ground. **2** large heap or pile; huge quantity. **3** large surplus stock (butter mountain). □ **make a mountain out of a molehill** see MOLEHILL. [Latin: related to MOUNT²]

mountain ash n. tree with scarlet berries; rowan.

mountain bike n. sturdy bike with many gears for riding over rough terrain.

mountaineer /maʊntɪˈnɪə(r)/ —n. person who practises mountain-climbing. —v. climb mountains as a sport. □ **mountaineering** n.

mountain lion n. puma.

mountainous adj. **1** having many mountains. **2** huge.

mountain range n. continuous line of mountains.

mountain sickness *n.* sickness caused by thin air at great heights.

mountainside *n.* sloping side of a mountain.

mountebank /ˈmauntɪbæŋk/ *n.* 1 swindler; charlatan. 2 *hist.* itinerant quack. [Italian, = mount on bench]

Mountie *n. colloq.* member of the Royal Canadian Mounted Police. [abbreviation]

mounting *n.* 1. = MOUNT¹ *n.* 1. 2 in senses of MOUNT¹ *v.*

mourn /mɔːn/ *v.* (often foll. by *for, over*) feel or show deep sorrow or regret for (a dead person, a lost thing, a past event, etc.). [Old English]

mourner *n.* person who mourns, esp. at a funeral.

mournful *adj.* doleful, sad, expressing mourning. □ **mournfully** *adv.* **mournfulness** *n.*

mourning *n.* 1 expressing of sorrow for a dead person, esp. by wearing black clothes. 2 such clothes.

mouse —*n.* (*pl.* **mice**) 1 small rodent, esp. of a kind infesting houses. 2 timid or feeble person. 3 (*pl.* **-s**) *Computing* small hand-held device controlling the cursor on a VDU screen. —*v.* (also **mauz**/ **-sing**) (of a cat, owl, etc.) hunt mice. □ **mouser** *n.* [Old English]

mousetrap *n.* 1 trap for catching mice. 2 (often *attrib.*) *colloq.* poor quality cheese.

moussaka /muːˈsɑːkə/ *n.* (also **mousaka**) Greek dish of minced meat, aubergine, etc. [Greek or Turkish]

mousse /muːs/ *n.* 1 a dessert of whipped cream, eggs, etc., usu. flavoured with fruit or chocolate. b meat or fish purée made with whipped cream etc. 2 foamy substance applied to the hair to enable styling. [French, = froth]

moustache /məˈstɑːʃ/ *n.* (US **mustache**) hair left to grow on a man's upper lip. [Greek *mustax*]

mousy /ˈmausɪ/ *adj.* (**-ier, -iest**) 1 of or like a mouse. 2 (of a person) timid, feeble. 3 nondescript light brown.

mouth —*n.* (*pl.* **mouths** /mauðz/) 1 a external opening in the head, through which most animals take in food and emit communicative sounds. b (in humans and some animals) cavity behind it containing the means of biting and chewing and the vocal organs. 2 opening of a container, cave, trumpet, etc. 3 place where a river enters the sea. 4 an individual as needing sustenance (*an extra mouth to feed*). 5 *colloq.* a meaningless or ineffectual talk. b (with * the definite article*) cheek; impudent talk; cheek. —*v.* /mauθ/ (**-thing**) 1 say or speak by moving the lips but with no sound. 2 utter or speak insincerely or

without understanding (*mouthing pla-titudes*). □ **put words into a person's mouth** represent a person as having said something. **take the words out of a person's mouth** say what another was about to say. [Old English]

mouthful *n.* (*pl.* **-s**) 1 quantity of food etc. that fills the mouth. 2 small quantity. 3 *colloq.* long or complicated word or phrase.

mouth-organ *n.* = HARMONICA.

mouthpiece *n.* 1 part of a musical instrument, telephone, etc., placed next to the lips. 2 *colloq.* person who speaks for another or others.

mouth-to-mouth *adj.* (of resuscitation) in which a person breathes into a subject's lungs through the mouth.

mouthwash *n.* liquid antiseptic etc. for rinsing the mouth or gargling.

mouth-watering *adj.* (of food etc.) having a delicious smell or appearance.

movable /ˈmuːvəb(ə)l/ *adj.* (also **moveable**) 1 that can be moved. 2 variable in date from year to year (*movable feast*). [related to MOVE]

move /muːv/ —*v.* (**-ving**) 1 (cause to) change position or posture. 2 put or keep in motion; rouse; stir. 3 a take a turn in a board-game. b change the position of (a piece) in a board-game. 4 (often foll. by *about, away, off*, etc.) go or proceed. 5 take action, esp. promptly (*moved to reduce crime*). 6 make progress (*project is moving fast*). 7 (also *absol.*) change (one's home or place of work). 8 (foll. by *in*) be socially active in (a specified group etc.) (*moves in the best circles*). 9 affect (a person) with (usu. tender) emotion. 10 (foll. by *to*) provoke (a person to laughter etc.) (*was moved to tears*). 11 (foll. by *to*, or *to* + infin.) prompt or incline (a person to a feeling or action). 12 (cause to) change one's attitude (*nothing can move me on this issue*). 13 a cause (the bowels) to be evacuated. b (of the bowels) be evacuated. 14 (often foll. by *that*) propose in a meeting, etc. 15 (foll. by *for*) make a formal request or application. 16 sell; be sold. —*n.* 1 act or process of moving. 2 change of house, premises, etc. 3 step taken to secure an object. 4 a changing of the position of a piece in a board-game. b player's turn to do this. □ **get a move on** *colloq.* hurry up. □ **make a move take action. move along (or on)** advance, progress, esp. to avoid crowding etc. **move away** go to live in another area. **move heaven and earth** (foll. by *to* + infin.) make extraordinary efforts. **move in** 1 take up residence in a new home. 2 get into a position of readiness or proximity (for an offensive action

etc.), **move in with** start to share accommodation with (an existing resident). **move out** leave one's home. **move over** (or **up**) adjust one's position to make room for another. [Latin *moveo*]

moveable var. of MOVABLE.

movement *n.* **1 a** a moving or being moved. **b** instance of this (*watched his every movement*). **2** moving parts of a mechanism (esp. a clock or watch). **3 a** body of persons with a common object (*peace movement*). **b** campaign undertaken by them. **4** (in *pl.*) person's activities and whereabouts. **5** *Mus.* principal division of a longer musical work. **6** motion of the bowels. **7** rise or fall in price(s) on the stock market. **8** progress.

mover *n.* **1** person, animal, or thing that moves or dances, esp. in a specified way. **2** person who moves a proposition. **3** (also **prime mover**) originator.

movie *n.* esp. US *colloq.* cinema film.

moving *adj.* emotionally affecting. □ **movingly** *adv.*

moving staircase *n.* escalator.

mow /mau/ *v.* (*past part.* **mowed** or **mown**) **1** (also *absol.*) cut (grass, hay, etc.) with a scythe or machine. **2** cut down the produce of (a field) or the grass etc. of (a lawn) by mowing. □ **mow down** kill or destroy randomly or in great numbers. **mower** *n.* [Old English]

mozzarella /ˌmɒtsəˈrelə/ *n.* Italian curd cheese, orig. of buffalo milk. [Italian]

mp *abbr.* mezzo piano.

MP *abbr.* Member of Parliament.

mp *abbr.* melting-point.

m.p.g. *abbr.* miles per gallon.

m.p.h. *abbr.* miles per hour.

M.Phil. *abbr.* Master of Philosophy.

Mr /ˈmɪstə(r)/ *n.* (*pl.* **Messrs**) **1** title of a man without a higher title (*Mr Jones*). **2** title prefixed to a designation of office etc. (*Mr President*; *Mr Speaker*). [abbreviation of MISTER]

Mrs /ˈmɪsɪz/ *n.* (*pl.* same) title of a married woman without a higher title (*Mrs Jones*). [abbreviation of MISTRESS]

Ms /mɪz, məz/ *n.* title of a married or unmarried woman without a higher title. [combination of Mrs and Miss²]

M.Sc. *abbr.* Master of Science.

MS-DOS /ˌemesˈdɒs/ *abbr. propr. Computing* Microsoft disk operating system.

Mt. *abbr.* Mount.

mu /mjuː/ *n.* twelfth Greek letter (M, μ). [Greek]

much -*adj.* **1** existing or occurring in a great quantity (*much trouble, too much noise*). **2** (prec. by *as, how, that,* etc.) with relative sense (*I don't know how much money you want*). -*n.* **1** a great quantity (*much of that is true*). **2** (prec. by *as, how, that,* etc.) with relative sense (*we do not need that much*). **3** (usu. in *neg.*) noteworthy or outstanding example (*not much to look at*). -*adv.* **1** in a great degree (*much to my surprise; is much the same; I much regret it; much annoyed; much better; much the best*). **2** for a large part of one's time; often (*the is not here much*). □ **as much** so (*I thought as much*). **much as** even though (*cannot come, much as I would like to*). **much of a muchness** very nearly the same. **not much of a** *colloq.* a rather poor. [from MICKLE]

mucilage /ˈmjuːsɪlɪdʒ/ *n.* **1** viscous substance obtained from plants. **2** adhesive gum. [Latin: related to MUCUS]

muck -*n.* **1** *colloq.* dirt or filth; anything disgusting. **2** farmyard manure. **3** *colloq.* mess. -*v.* **1** (usu. foll. by *up*) *colloq.* **a** bungle (a job). **b** make dirty or untidy. **2** (foll. by *out*) remove manure from. □ **make a muck of** *colloq.* bungle. **muck about** (or **around**) *colloq.* **1** potter or fool about. **2** (foll. by *with*) fool or interfere with. **muck in** (often foll. by *with*) *colloq.* share tasks etc. equally. [Scandinavian]

mucker *n. slang* friend, mate. [probably from *muck in*: related to MUCK]

muckle var. of MICKLE.

muckrake *v.* □ (-king) search out and reveal scandal. □ **muckraker** *n.* **muckraking** *n.*

muck-spreader *n.* machine for spreading dung. □ **muck-spreading** *n.*

mucky *adj.* (-ier, -iest) covered with muck, dirty.

mucous /ˈmjuːkəs/ *adj.* of or covered with mucus. □ **mucosity** /-ˈkɒsɪtɪ/ *n.* [Latin *mucosus*: related to MUCUS]

mucous membrane *n.* mucus-secreting tissue lining body cavities etc.

mucus /ˈmjuːkəs/ *n.* slimy substance secreted by a mucous membrane. [Latin]

mud *n.* soft wet earth. □ **fling** (or **sling** or **throw**) **mud** speak disparagingly or slanderously. **one's name is mud** one is in disgrace. [German]

muddle -*v.* (-ling) (often foll. by *up*) **1** bring into disorder. **2** bewilder, confuse. -*n.* **1** disorder. **2** confusion. □ **muddle along** (or **on**) progress in a haphazard way. **muddle through** succeed despite one's inefficiency. [perhaps Dutch, related to MUD]

muddle-headed *adj.* mentally disorganized, confused.

muddy -*adj.* (-ier, -iest) **1** like mud. **2** covered in or full of mud. **3** (of liquid,

mudflap *n.* flap hanging behind the wheel of a vehicle, to prevent splashes. **mud-flat** *n.* stretch of muddy land uncovered at low tide. **mudguard** *n.* curved strip over a bicycle wheel etc. to protect the rider from splashes. **mud pack** *n.* cosmetic paste applied thickly to the face. **mud-slinger** *n. colloq.* person given to making abusive or disparaging remarks. □ **mud-slinging** *n.*

muesli /ˈmuːzlɪ, ˈmjuː-/ *n.* breakfast food of crushed cereals, dried fruits, nuts, etc., eaten with milk. [Swiss German]

muezzin /muːˈezɪn/ *n.* Muslim crier who proclaims the hours of prayer. [Arabic]

muff¹ *n.* covering, esp. of fur, for keeping the hands or ears warm. [Dutch *mof*]

muff² *v. colloq.* **1** bungle. **2** miss (a catch, ball, etc.). [origin unknown]

muffin /ˈmʌfɪn/ *n.* **1** light flat round spongy cake, eaten toasted and buttered. **2** *US* similar round cake made from batter or dough. [origin unknown]

muffle *v.* (-**ling**) **1** (often foll. by *up*) wrap or cover for warmth, or to deaden sound. **2** (usu. as **muffled** *adj.*) stifle (an utterance). [perhaps French *moufle* thick glove, MUFF¹]

muffler *n.* **1** wrap or scarf worn for warmth. **2** thing used to deaden sound. **3** *US* silencer of a vehicle.

mufti /ˈmʌftɪ/ *n.* civilian clothes (*in mufti*). [Arabic]

mug¹ —*n.* **1** a drinking-vessel, usu. cylindrical with a handle and no saucer. **b** its contents. **2** *slang* gullible person. **3** *slang* face or mouth. —*v.* (-**gg**-) attack and rob, esp. in public. □ **a mug's game** *colloq.* foolish or unprofitable activity. □ **mugger** *n.* **mugful** *n.* (*pl.* -**s**). **mugging** *n.* [Scandinavian]

mug² *v.* (-**gg**-) (usu. foll. by *up*) *slang* learn (a subject) by concentrated study. [origin unknown]

muggins /ˈmʌgɪnz/ *n.* (*pl.* same or **mugginses**) *colloq.* gullible person (often meaning oneself: *so muggins had to pay*). [perhaps from the surname]

muggy *adj.* (-**ier**, -**iest**) (of weather etc.) oppressively humid. □ **mugginess** *n.* [Old Norse]

mug shot *n. slang* photograph of a face, esp. for police records.

Muhammadan /məˈhæməd(ə)n/ *n. & adj.* (also **Mohammedan**) = MUSLIM. [*Muhammad*, name of a prophet]

colour, or sound) not clear, impure. **4** vague, confused. —*v.* (-**ies**, -**ied**) make muddy. □ **muddiness** *n.*

■ **Usage** The term *Muhammadan* is not used by Muslims, and is often regarded as offensive.

mujahidin /mʊdʒəhɑːˈdiːn/ *n.pl.* (also **mujahedin**, -**deen**) guerrilla fighters in Islamic countries, esp. Muslim fundamentalists. [Persian and Arabic related to JIHAD]

mulatto /mjuːˈlætəʊ/ *n.* (*pl.* -**s** or -**es**) person of mixed White and Black parentage. [Spanish *mulato* young mule]

mulberry /ˈmʌlbərɪ/ *n.* (*pl.* -**ies**) **1** tree bearing edible purple or white berries and leaves used to feed silkworms. **2** its fruit. **3** dark-red or purple. [Latin *morum* mulberry, BERRY]

mulch —*n.* layer of wet straw, leaves, or plastic, etc., spread around or over a plant to enrich or insulate the soil. —*v.* treat with mulch. [Old English, = soft]

mule¹ *n.* **1** offspring of a male donkey and a female horse, or (in general use) of a female donkey and a male horse (cf. HINNY). **2** stupid or obstinate person. **3** (in full **spinning mule**) a kind of spinning-machine. [Latin *mulus*]

mule² *n.* backless slipper. [French]

muleteer /mjuːlɪˈtɪə(r)/ *n.* mule-driver. [French *muletier*: related to MULE¹]

mulish *adj.* stubborn.

mull¹ *v.* (often foll. by *over*) ponder, consider. [probably Dutch]

mull² *v.* warm (wine or beer) with added sugar, spices, etc. [origin unknown]

mull³ *n. Scot.* promontory. [origin uncertain]

mullah /ˈmʌlə/ *n.* Muslim learned in theology and sacred law. [ultimately Arabic *maulā*]

mullet *n.* (*pl.* same) any of several kinds of marine fish valued for food. [Greek *mullos*]

mulligatawny /ˌmʌlɪgəˈtɔːnɪ/ *n.* highly seasoned soup orig. from India. [Tamil, = pepper-water]

mullion /ˈmʌljən/ *n.* vertical bar dividing the lights in a window. □ **mullioned** *adj.* [probably French *moinel* middle: related to MEAN³]

multi- *comb. form* many. [Latin *multus* much, many]

multi-access /ˌmʌltɪˈækses/ *adj.* (of a computer system) allowing access to the central processor from several terminals simultaneously.

multicoloured /ˈmʌltɪˌkʌled/ *adj.* of many colours.

multicultural /ˌmʌltɪˈkʌltʃər(ə)l/ *adj.* of several cultural groups. □ **multiculturalism** *n.*

multidirectional /ˌmʌltɪdɪˈrekʃən(ə)l/ adj. of, involving, or operating in several directions.

multiform /ˈmʌltɪfɔːm/ adj. 1 having many forms. 2 of many kinds. [Latin multiformis]

multifarious /ˌmʌltɪˈfeərɪəs/ adj. 1 many and various. 2 of great variety. □ **multifariousness** n. [Latin multifarius]

multilateral /ˌmʌltɪˈlætər(ə)l/ adj. 1 (of an agreement etc.) in which three or more parties participate. 2 having many sides. □ **multilaterally** adv.

multilingual /ˌmʌltɪˈlɪŋgw(ə)l/ adj. in, speaking, or using several languages.

multimedia —attrib. adj. using more than one medium of communication.

multimillion /ˌmʌltɪˈmɪljən/ attrib. adj. costing or involving several million (pounds, dollars, etc.) (multimillion dollar fraud).

multimillionaire /ˌmʌltɪˌmɪljəˈneə(r)/ n. person with a fortune of several millions.

multinational /ˌmʌltɪˈnæʃ(ə)n(ə)l/ —adj. 1 operating in several countries. 2 of several nationalities. —n. multinational company.

multiple /ˈmʌltɪp(ə)l/ —adj. 1 having several parts, elements, or components. 2 many and various. —n. number that contains another without a remainder (56 is a multiple of 7). [Latin multiplus: related to MULTIPLEX]

multiple-choice adj. (of an examination question) accompanied by several possible answers from which the correct one has to be chosen.

multiple sclerosis see SCLEROSIS.

multiplex /ˈmʌltɪpleks/ adj. manifold; of many elements. [Latin: related to MULTI-, -plex -plicis -fold]

multiplicand /ˌmʌltɪplɪˈkænd/ n. quantity to be multiplied by another.

multiplication /ˌmʌltɪplɪˈkeɪʃ(ə)n/ n. multiplying.

multiplication sign n. sign (×) to indicate that one quantity is to be multiplied by another.

multiplication table n. list of multiples of a particular number, usu. from 1 to 12.

multiplicity /ˌmʌltɪˈplɪsɪtɪ/ n. (pl. -ies) 1 manifold variety. 2 (foll. by of) great number.

multiplier /ˈmʌltɪplaɪə(r)/ n. quantity by which a given number is multiplied.

multiply /ˈmʌltɪplaɪ/ v. (-ies, -ied) 1 (also absol.) obtain from (a number) another that is a specified number of times its value (multiply 6 by 4 and you get 24). 2 increase in number, esp. by procreation. 3 produce a large number of (instances etc.) 4 a breed (animals). b propagate (plants). [Latin multiplico:

multi-purpose /ˌmʌltɪˈpɜːpəs/ attrib. adj. having several purposes.

multiracial /ˌmʌltɪˈreɪʃ(ə)l/ adj. of several races.

multi-storey /ˌmʌltɪˈstɔːrɪ/ attrib. adj. having several storeys.

multi-user /ˌmʌltɪˈjuːzə(r)/ attrib. adj. (of a computer system) having a number of simultaneous users.

multitude /ˈmʌltɪtjuːd/ n. 1 (often foll. by of) great number. 2 large gathering of people; crowd. 3 (the multitude) the common people. [French from Latin]

multitudinous /ˌmʌltɪˈtjuːdɪnəs/ adj. 1 very numerous. 2 consisting of many individuals. [Latin: related to MULTITUDE]

mum¹ n. colloq. = MUMMY¹. [French mumble]

mum² adj. colloq. silent (keep mum). □ **mum's the word** say nothing. [imitative]

mumble —v. (-ling) speak or utter indistinctly. —n. indistinct utterance or sound. [related to MUM²]

mumbo-jumbo /ˌmʌmbəʊˈdʒʌmbəʊ/ n. (pl. -s) 1 meaningless or ignorant ritual. 2 meaningless or unnecessarily complicated language; nonsense. [Mumbo Jumbo, name of a supposed African idol]

mummer n. actor in a traditional mime. [French momeur: cf. MUM²]

mummery n. (pl. -ies) 1 ridiculous (esp. religious) ceremonial. 2 performance by mummers. [French momerie: related to MUMMER]

mummify /ˈmʌmɪfaɪ/ v. (-ies, -ied) preserve (a body) as a mummy. □ **mummification** /-fɪˈkeɪʃ(ə)n/ n.

mummy¹ /ˈmʌmɪ/ n. (pl. -ies) colloq. mother. [imitative of a child's pronunciation]

mummy² /ˈmʌmɪ/ n. (pl. -ies) body of a human being or animal embalmed for burial, esp. in ancient Egypt. [Persian mūm wax]

mumps n.pl. (treated as sing.) infectious disease with swelling of the neck and face. [imitative of mouth-shape]

munch v. eat steadily with a marked action of the jaws. [imitative]

mundane /mʌnˈdeɪn/ adj. 1 dull, routine. 2 of this world. □ **mundanely** adv. **mundanity** /-ˈdænɪtɪ/ n. [Latin mundus world]

mung n. (in full mung bean) leguminous Indian plant used as a food. [Hindi mūng]

municipal /mjʊˈnɪsɪp(ə)l/ adj. of a municipality or its self-government. □ **municipalize** v. (also -ise) (-zing or

-sing). **municipally** *adv.* [Latin *municipium* free city]

municipality /mjuːˌnɪsɪˈpælɪtɪ/ *n.* (*pl.* -ies) 1 town or district having local self-government. 2 governing body of this area.

munificent /mjuːˈnɪfɪs(ə)nt/ *adj.* (of a giver or of a gift) splendidly generous. □ **munificence** *n.* [Latin *munus* gift: related to -FIC]

muniment *n.* (usu. in *pl.*) document kept as evidence of rights or privileges etc. [Latin *munio* fortify]

munition /mjuːˈnɪʃ(ə)n/ *n.* (usu. in *pl.*) military weapons, ammunition etc. [Latin, = fortification: related to MUNIMENT]

muon /ˈmjuːɒn/ *n. Physics* unstable elementary particle like an electron, but with a much greater mass. [μ (MU), the symbol for it]

mural /ˈmjʊər(ə)l/ —*n.* painting executed directly on a wall. —*adj.* of, on, or like a wall. [Latin *murus* wall]

murder —*n.* 1 intentional unlawful killing of a human being by another. 2 *colloq.* unpleasant, troublesome, or dangerous state of affairs. —*v.* 1 kill (a human being) intentionally and unlawfully. 2 *colloq.* **a** utterly defeat. **b** spoil by a bad performance, mispronunciation, etc. □ **cry blue murder** *colloq.* make an extravagant outcry. **get away with murder** *colloq.* do whatever one wishes and escape punishment. □ **murderer** *n.* **murderess** *n.* [Old English]

murderous *adj.* 1 (of a person, weapon, action, etc.) capable of, intending, or involving murder or great harm. 2 *colloq.* extremely arduous or unpleasant. □ **murderously** *adv.* **murderousness** *n.*

murk *n.* darkness, poor visibility. [probably Scandinavian]

murky *adj.* (-ier, -iest) 1 dark, gloomy. 2 (of darkness, liquid, etc.) thick, dirty. 3 suspiciously obscure (*murky past*). □ **murkily** *adv.* **murkiness** *n.*

murmur /ˈmɜːmə(r)/ —*n.* 1 subdued continuous sound, as made by waves, a brook, etc. 2 softly spoken or nearly inarticulate utterance. 3 subdued expression of discontent. —*v.* 1 make a murmur. 2 utter (words) in a low voice. 3 (usu. foll. by *at, against*) complain in low tones, grumble. [Latin]

Murphy's Law /ˈmɜːfɪ/ *n. joc.* any of various maxims about the perverseness of things. [*Murphy*, Irish surname]

murrain /ˈmʌrɪn/ *n.* infectious disease of cattle. [Anglo-French *moryn*]

Mus.B. *abbr.* (also **Mus. Bac.**) Bachelor of Music. [Latin *Musicae Baccalaureus*]

Muscadet /ˈmʌskədeɪ/ *n.* 1 a dry white wine from the Loire region of France. 2

variety of grape used for this. [*Muscadet* grape]

muscat /ˈmʌskæt/ *n.* 1 sweet usu. fortified white wine made from musk-flavoured grapes. 2 this grape. [Provençal: related to MUSK]

muscatel /ˌmʌskəˈtel/ *n.* 1 = MUSCAT. 2 raisin from a muscat grape.

muscle /ˈmʌs(ə)l/ —*n.* 1 fibrous tissue producing movement in or maintaining the position of an animal body. 2 part of an animal body that is composed of muscles. 3 strength, power. —*v.* (-**ling**) (foll. by *in, in on*) *colloq.* force oneself on others; intrude by forceful means. □ **not move a muscle** be completely motionless. [Latin diminutive of *mus* mouse]

muscle-bound *adj.* with muscles stiff and inflexible through excessive exercise.

muscle-man *n.* man with highly developed muscles.

Muscovite /ˈmʌskəˌvaɪt/ —*n.* native or citizen of Moscow. —*adj.* of Moscow. [from *Muscovy*, principality of Moscow]

Muscovy duck /ˈmʌskəvɪ/ *n.* crested duck with red markings on its head. [*Muscovy*, principality of Moscow]

muscular /ˈmʌskjʊlə(r)/ *adj.* 1 of or affecting the muscles. 2 having well-developed muscles. 3 robust. □ **muscularity** /-ˈlærɪtɪ/ *n.*

muscular Christianity *n.* Christian life of cheerful physical activity as described in the writings of Charles Kingsley.

muscular dystrophy *n.* hereditary progressive wasting of the muscles.

musculature /ˈmʌskjʊlətʃə(r)/ *n.* muscular system of a body or organ. [Greek]

Mus.D. *abbr.* (also **Mus. Doc.**) Doctor of Music. [Latin *Musicae Doctor*]

muse[1] /mjuːz/ *v.* (-**sing**) 1 (usu. foll. by *on, upon*) ponder, reflect. 2 say meditatively. [French]

muse[2] /mjuːz/ *n.* 1 (in Greek and Roman mythology) any of the nine goddesses who inspire poetry, music, etc. 2 (usu. prec. by *the*) poet's inspiration. [Greek *Mousa*]

museum /mjuːˈzɪəm/ *n.* building used for storing and exhibiting objects of historical, scientific, or cultural interest. [Greek: related to MUSE[2]]

museum piece *n.* 1 specimen of art etc. fit for a museum. 2 *derog.* old-fashioned or quaint person or object.

mush[1] *n.* 1 soft pulp. 2 feeble sentimentality. 3 *US* maize porridge. [apparently var. of MASH]

mushroom —*n.* 1 edible fungus with a stem and domed cap 2 pinkish-brown colour of this. —*v.* appear or develop rapidly. [French *mousseron* from Latin]

mushroom cloud *n.* mushroom-shaped cloud from a nuclear explosion.

mushy /ˈmʌʃɪ/ *adj.* (**-ier**, **-iest**) **1** like mush; soft. **2** feebly sentimental. □ **mushiness** *n.*

music /ˈmjuːzɪk/ *n.* **1** art of combining vocal or instrumental sounds in a harmonious or expressive way. **2** sounds so produced. **3** musical composition. **4** written or printed score of this. **5** pleasant natural sound. □ **music to one's ears** something one is pleased to hear. [Greek: related to MUSE²]

musical —*adj.* **1** of music. **2** (of sounds etc.) melodious, harmonious. **3** fond of or skilled in music. **4** set to or accompanied by music. —*n.* musical film or play. □ **musically** *adv.*

musical box *n.* box containing a mechanism which plays a tune.

musical chairs *n.pl.* **1** party game in which the players compete in successive rounds for a decreasing number of chairs. **2** series of changes or political manoeuvring etc.

music centre *n.* equipment combining radio, record-player, tape recorder, etc.

music-hall *n.* **1** variety entertainment with singing, dancing, etc. **2** theatre for this.

musician /mjuːˈzɪʃ(ə)n/ *n.* person who plays a musical instrument, esp. professionally. □ **musicianly** *adj.* **musicianship** *n.* [French: related to MUSIC]

musicology /mjuːzɪˈkɒlədʒɪ/ *n.* the academic study of music. □ **musicological** /-kəˈlɒdʒɪk(ə)l/ *adj.* **musicologist** *n.*

music stand *n.* support for sheet music.

music stool *n.* piano stool.

musk *n.* **1** substance secreted by the male musk deer and used in perfumes. **2** plant which orig. had a smell of musk. □ **musky** *adj.* (**-ier**, **-iest**). **muskiness** *n.* [Latin *muscus* from Persian]

musk deer *n.* small hornless Asian deer.

musket *n.* *hist.* infantryman's (esp. smooth-bored) light gun. [Italian *moschetto* crossbow bolt]

musketeer /mʌskɪˈtɪə(r)/ *n.* *hist.* soldier armed with a musket.

musketry /ˈmʌskɪtrɪ/ *n.* **1** muskets; soldiers armed with muskets. **2** knowledge of handling small arms.

musk ox *n.* shaggy N. American ruminant with curved horns.

muskrat *n.* **1** large N. American aquatic rodent with a musky smell. **2** its fur.

musk-rose *n.* rambling rose smelling of musk.

Muslim /ˈmʊzlɪm, ˈmʌz-/ (also **Moslem** /ˈmɒzləm/) —*n.* follower of the Islamic religion. —*adj.* of the Muslims or their religion. [Arabic: related to ISLAM]

muslin /ˈmʌzlɪn/ *n.* fine delicately woven cotton fabric. [Italian *Mussolo* Mosul in Iraq]

musquash /ˈmʌskwɒʃ/ *n.* = MUSKRAT. [Algonquian]

mussel /ˈmʌs(ə)l/ *n.* bivalve mollusc, esp. of the kind used for food. [Old English: related to MUSCLE]

must¹ —*v.aux.* (*present* **must**; *past had to* or in indirect speech **must**) (foll. by *infin.*, or *absol.*) **1 a** be obliged to (*you must go to school*). **b** in ironic questions (*must you slam the door?*). **2** be certainly (*you must be her sister*). **3** ought to (*must see what can be done*). **4** expressing insistence (*must ask you to leave*). **5** (foll. by *not* + infin.) **a** not be permitted to, be forbidden to (*must not think he's angry; must not worry*). **c** expressing insistence that something should not be done (*they must not be told*). —*n. colloq.* thing that should not be missed (*this exhibition is a must*). □ **I must say** often *iron.* I cannot refrain from saying (*I must say he tries hard; a fine way to behave, I must say*). **must**

■ **Usage** In sense 1 a, the negative (i.e. lack of obligation) is expressed by *not have to* or *need not*, *must not* denotes positive forbidding, as in *you must not smoke.*

must² *n.* grape juice before fermentation is complete. [Old English from Latin]

mustache *US var.* of MOUSTACHE.

mustang *n.* small wild horse of Mexico and California. [Spanish]

mustard /ˈmʌstəd/ *n.* **1 a** plant with slender pods and yellow flowers. **b** seeds of this crushed into a paste and used as a spicy condiment. **2** plant eaten at the seedling stage, often with cress. **3** brownish-yellow colour. [Romanic: related to MUST²]

mustard gas *n.* colourless oily liquid, whose vapour is a powerful irritant.

muster —*v.* **1** collect (orig. soldiers) for inspection, to check numbers, etc. **2** collect, gather together. **3** summon (courage etc.). —*n.* assembly of persons for inspection. □ **pass muster** be accepted as adequate. [Latin *monstro* show]

musty *adj.* (**-ier**, **-iest**) **1** mouldy, stale. **2** dull, antiquated. □ **mustily** *adv.* **mustiness** *n.* [perhaps an alteration of MOIST]

mustn't /ˈmʌs(ə)nt/ *contr.* must not.

588

mutable /ˈmjuːtəb(ə)l/ *adj. literary* liable to change. □ **mutability** /-ˈbɪlɪtɪ/ *n*. [Latin *muto* change]

mutagen /ˈmjuːtədʒən/ *n*. agent promoting genetic mutation. □ **mutagenic** /-ˈdʒenik/ *adj*. **mutagenesis** /-ˈdʒenisis/ *n*. [from MUTATION, -GEN]

mutant /ˈmjuːt(ə)nt/ *—adj*. resulting from mutation. *—n*. mutant organism or gene.

mutate /mjuːˈteɪt/ *v*. (**-ting**) (cause to) undergo mutation.

mutation /mjuːˈteɪʃ(ə)n/ *n*. 1 change, alteration. 2 genetic change which, when transmitted to offspring, gives rise to heritable variations. 3 mutant. [Latin *muto* change]

mutatis mutandis /muːˈtɑːtɪs muːˈtændɪs/ *adv*. (in comparing cases) making the necessary alterations. [Latin]

mute /mjuːt/ *—adj*. 1 silent, refraining from or temporarily bereft of speech. 2 (of a person or animal) dumb. 3 not expressed in speech (*mute protest*). 4 (of a letter) not pronounced. *—n*. 1 dumb person. 2 device for damping the sound of a musical instrument. 3 unsounded consonant.*—v*. (**-ting**) 1 deaden or soften the sound of (esp. a musical instrument). 2 **a** tone down, make less intense. **b** (as **muted** *adj*.) (of colours etc.) subdued. □ **mutely** *adv*. **muteness** *n*. [Latin *mutus*]

mute button *n*. device on a telephone to temporarily prevent the caller from hearing what is being said at the receiver's end, or on a television etc. to temporarily turn off the sound.

mute swan *n*. common white swan.

mutilate /ˈmjuːtɪleɪt/ *v*. (**-ting**) 1 **a** deprive (a person or animal) of a limb or organ. **b** destroy the use of (a limb or organ). 2 excise or damage part of (a book etc.). □ **mutilation** /-ˈleɪʃ(ə)n/ *n*. [Latin *mutilus* maimed]

mutineer /ˌmjuːtɪˈnɪə(r)/ *n*. person who mutinies. [Romanic: related to MOVE]

mutinous /ˈmjuːtɪnəs/ *adj*. rebellious; ready to mutiny. □ **mutinously** *adv*.

mutiny /ˈmjuːtɪnɪ/ *—n*. (*pl*. **-ies**) open revolt, esp. by soldiers or sailors against their officers. *—v*. (**-ies**, **-ied**) (often foll. by *against*) revolt; engage in mutiny.

mutt *n*. 1 *slang* ignorant or stupid person. 2 *derog*. dog. [abbreviation of MUTTON-HEAD]

mutter *—v*. 1 (also *absol*.) utter (words) in a barely audible manner. 2 (often foll. by *against*, *at*) murmur or grumble. *—n*. 1 muttered words or sounds. 2 muttering. [related to MUTE]

mutton *n*. flesh of sheep as food. [medieval Latin *multo* sheep]

mutton dressed as lamb *n*. *colloq*. middle-aged or elderly woman dressed to appear younger.

mutton-head *n*. *colloq*. stupid person.

mutual /ˈmjuːtʃʊəl/ *adj*. 1 (of feelings, actions, etc.) experienced or done by each of two or more parties to or towards the other(s) (*mutual affection*). 2 *colloq*. common to two or more persons (*a mutual friend*). 3 having the same (specified) relationship to each other (*mutual well-wishers*). □ **mutuality** /-ˈælɪtɪ/ *n*. **mutually** *adv*. [Latin *mutuus* borrowed]

■ **Usage** The use of *mutual* in sense 2, although often found, is considered incorrect by some people, for whom *common* is preferable.

Muzak /ˈmjuːzæk/ *n*. 1 *propr*. system of piped music used in public places. 2 (**muzak**) recorded light background music. [fanciful var. of MUSIC]

muzzle *—n*. 1 projecting part of an animal's face, including the nose and mouth. 2 guard, usu. of straps or wire, put over an animal's nose and mouth to stop it biting or feeding. 3 open end of a firearm. *—v*. (**-ling**) 1 put a muzzle on. 2 impose silence on. [medieval Latin *musum*]

muzzy *adj*. (**-ier**, **-iest**) 1 mentally hazy. 2 blurred, indistinct. □ **muzzily** *adv*. **muzziness** *n*. [origin unknown]

MW *abbr*. 1 megawatt(s). 2 medium wave.

my /maɪ/ *poss. pron*. (*attrib*.) 1 of or belonging to me. 2 affectionate, patronizing, etc. form of address (*my dear boy*). 3 in expressions of surprise (*my God!*; *oh my!*). 4 *colloq*. indicating a close relative etc. of the speaker (*my Johnny's ill again*). □ **my Lady** (or **Lord**) form of address to certain titled persons. [from MINE[1]]

myalgia /maɪˈældʒə/ *n*. muscular pain.
□ **myalgic** *adj*. [Greek *mus* muscle]

mycelium /maɪˈsiːlɪəm/ *n*. (*pl*. **-lia**) microscopic threadlike parts of a fungus. [Greek *mukēs* mushroom]

Mycenaean /ˌmaɪsɪˈniːən/ *—adj*. of the late Bronze Age civilization in Greece (c.1500–1100 BC), depicted in the Homeric poems. *—n*. person of this civilization. [Latin *Mycenaeus*]

mycology /maɪˈkɒlədʒɪ/ *n*. 1 the study of fungi. 2 fungi of a particular region. □ **mycologist** *n*. [Greek *mukēs* mushroom]

myna /ˈmaɪnə/ *n*. (also **mynah**, **mina**) talking bird of the starling family. [Hindi]

myopia /maɪˈəʊpɪə/ *n*. 1 short-sightedness. 2 lack of imagination or insight. □

myopic /-ˈɒpɪk/ adj. **myopically** /-ˈɒpɪkli/ adv. [Greek muō shut, ōps eye]

myriad /ˈmɪrɪəd/ literary —n. an indefinitely great number. —adj. innumerable. [Greek muríoi 10,000]

myrrh /mɜː(r)/ n. gum resin used in perfume, medicine, incense, etc. [Latin myrrha from Greek]

myrtle /ˈmɜːt(ə)l/ n. evergreen shrub with shiny leaves and white scented flowers. [Greek murtos]

myself /maɪˈsɛlf/ pron. 1 emphat. form of I¹ or ME¹ (I saw it myself). 2 refl. form of ME¹ (I was angry with myself). □ **be myself** see ONESELF. **I myself** I for my part (I myself am doubtful). [Old English: related to ME¹, SELF]

mysterious /mɪˈstɪərɪəs/ adj. full of or wrapped in mystery. □ **mysteriously** adv. [French: related to MYSTERY]

mystery /ˈmɪstəri/ n. (pl. -ies) 1 secret, hidden, or inexplicable matter. 2 secrecy or obscurity. 3 (attrib.) secret, undisclosed (mystery guest). 4 practice of making a secret of things (engaged in mystery and intrigue). 5 (in full mystery story) fictional work dealing with a puzzling event, esp. a murder. 6 a religious truth divinely revealed. 7 (in pl.) a secret religious rites of the ancient Greeks, Romans, etc. b archaic Eucharist. [Greek mustērion: related to MYSTIC]

mystery play n. miracle play.

mystery tour n. pleasure trip to an unspecified destination.

mystic /ˈmɪstɪk/ —n. person who seeks by contemplation etc. to achieve unity with the Deity, or who believes in the spiritual apprehension of truths that are beyond the understanding. —adj. = MYSTICAL. □ **mysticism** /-ˌsɪz(ə)m/ n. [Greek mustēs initiated person]

mystical adj. 1 of mystics or mysticism. 2 mysterious; occult, of hidden meaning. 3 spiritually allegorical or symbolic. □ **mystically** adv.

mystify /ˈmɪstɪ,faɪ/ v. (-ies, -ied) 1 bewilder, confuse. 2 wrap in mystery. □ **mystification** /-fɪˈkeɪʃ(ə)n/ n. [French: related to MYSTIC or MYSTERY]

mystique /mɪˈstiːk/ n. atmosphere of mystery and veneration attending some activity, person, profession, etc. [French: related to MYSTIC]

myth /mɪθ/ n. 1 traditional story usu. involving supernatural or imaginary persons and embodying popular ideas on natural or social phenomena etc. 2 such narratives collectively. 3 widely held but false notion. 4 fictitious person, thing, or idea. 5 allegory (Platonic myth). □ **mythical** adj. **mythically** adv. [Greek muthos]

mythology /mɪˈθɒlədʒi/ n. (pl. -ies) 1 body of myths. 2 the study of myths. □ **mythological** /-əˈlɒdʒɪk(ə)l/ adj. **mythologize** v. (a.sc -ise) (-zing or -sing). [Greek: related to MYTH]

myxomatosis /ˌmɪksəməˈtəʊsɪs/ n. viral disease of rabbits. [Greek muxa mucus]

N

N¹ /en/ *n.* (also **n**) (*pl.* **Ns** or **N's**) **1** fourteenth letter of the alphabet. **2** (**n**) indefinite number. □ **to the nth degree** to the utmost.

N² *abbr.* (also **N.**) **1** North; Northern. **2** New.

N³ *symb.* nitrogen.

n *abbr.* (also **n.**) **1** name. **2** neuter.

Na *symb.* sodium.

NAAFI /ˈnæfɪ/ *abbr.* **1** Navy, Army, and Air Force Institutes. **2** canteen for servicemen run by the NAAFI.

nab *v.* (**-bb-**) *slang* **1** arrest; catch in wrongdoing. **2** grab. [origin unknown]

nacho /ˈnætʃəʊ, ˈnɑː-/ *n.* (*pl.* **-s**) tortilla chip, usu. topped with melted cheese and spices etc. [origin uncertain]

nacre /ˈneɪkə(r)/ *n.* mother-of-pearl from any shelled mollusc. □ **nacreous** /ˈneɪkrɪəs/ *adj.* [French]

nadir /ˈneɪdɪə(r)/ *n.* **1** part of the celestial sphere directly below an observer. **2** lowest point; time of deep despair. [Arabic, = opposite]

naevus /ˈniːvəs/ *n.* (*US* **nevus**) (*pl.* **naevi** /-vaɪ/) **1** raised red birthmark. **2** = MOLE². [Latin]

naff *adj. slang* **1** unfashionable. **2** rubbishy. [origin unknown]

nag¹ *v.* (**-gg-**) **1 a** persistently criticize or scold. **b** (often foll. by *at*) find fault or urge, esp. persistently. **2** (of a pain) be persistent. [originally a dial. word]

nag² *n. colloq.* horse. [origin unknown]

naiad /ˈnaɪæd/ *n.* water-nymph. [Latin from Greek]

nail *n.* **1** small metal spike hammered in to join things together or as a peg or decoration. **b** horny covering on the upper surface of the tip of the human finger or toe. — *v.* **1** fasten with a nail or nails. **2** secure or get hold of (a person or thing). **3** keep (attention etc.) fixed. **4** expose or discover (a lie or liar). □ **nail down 1** bind (a person) to a promise etc. **2** define precisely. **3** fasten (a thing) with nails. **nail in a person's coffin** something thought to increase the risk of death. **on the nail** (esp. of payment) without delay. [Old English]

nail-file *n.* roughened metal or emery strip used for smoothing the nails.

nail polish *n.* (also **nail varnish**) varnish, usu. coloured, applied to the nails.

naive /naɪˈiːv/ *adj.* (also **naïve**) **1** innocent; unaffected. **2** foolishly credulous. **3** (of art) produced in a sophisticated society but lacking conventional expertise. □ **naively** *adv.* **naivety** *n.* (also **naïveté**). [Latin *nativus* NATIVE]

naked /ˈneɪkɪd/ *adj.* **1** without clothes; nude. **2** without its usual covering. **3** undisguised (*the naked truth*). **4** (of a light, flame, sword, etc.) unprotected or unsheathed. □ **nakedly** *adv.* **nakedness** *n.* [Old English]

naked eye *n.* (prec. by *the*) unassisted vision, e.g. without a telescope etc.

namby-pamby /ˌnæmbɪˈpæmbɪ/ *—adj.* insipidly pretty or sentimental; weak. *—n.* (*pl.* **-ies**) namby-pamby person. [fanciful formulation on the name of the writer *Ambrose Philips*]

name — *n.* **1** word by which an individual person, family, animal, place, or thing is spoken of etc. **2 a** (usu. abusive) term used of a person etc. (*called him names*). **b** word denoting an object or esp. a class of objects etc. (*what is the name of those flowers?*). **3** famous person. **4** reputation, esp. a good one. — *v.* (**-ming**) **1** give a name to. **2** state the name of. **3** mention; specify; cite. **4** nominate. □ **have to one's name** possess. **in the name of** as representing; by virtue of (*in the name of the law*). **in name only** not in reality. **make a name for oneself** become famous. □ **nameable** *adj.* [Old English]

name-day *n.* feast-day of the saint after whom a person is named.

name-dropping *n.* familiar mention of famous people as a form of boasting.

nameless *adj.* **1** having or showing no name. **2** unnamed (*our informant, who shall be nameless*). **3** too horrific to be named (*nameless vices*).

namely *adv.* that is to say; in other words.

name-plate *n.* plate or panel bearing the name of an occupant of a room etc.

namesake *n.* person or thing having the same name as another. [probably from *for the name's sake*]

nan *n.* (also **nana, nanna** /ˈnænə/) *colloq.* grandmother. [childish pronunciation]

nancy /ˈnænsɪ/ *n.* (*pl.* **-ies**) (in full **nancy boy**) *slang offens.* effeminate man, esp. a homosexual. [pet form of *Ann*]

nanny /ˈnænɪ/ *n.* (*pl.* **-ies**) **1** child's nurse. **2** *colloq.* grandmother. **3** (in full

nanny-goat n. female goat. [related to NANCY]

nano- comb. form denoting a factor of 10^{-9} (nanosecond). [Greek nanos dwarf]

nap[1] —v. (-pp-) sleep lightly or briefly. —n. short sleep or doze, esp. by day. □ **catch a person napping** detect in negligence etc; catch off guard. [Old English]

nap[2] n. raised pile on textiles, esp. velvet. [Low German or Dutch]

nap[3] —n. 1 form of whist in which players declare the number of tricks they expect to take. 2 racing tip claimed to be almost a certainty. —v. (-pp-) name (a horse etc.) as a probable winner. □ **go nap 1** attempt to take all five tricks in nap. **2** risk everything. [Napoleon]

napalm /ˈneɪpɑːm/ —n. thick jellied hydrocarbon mixture used in bombs. —v. attack with napalm bombs. [from NAPHTHALENE, PALM[1]]

nape n. back of the neck. [origin unknown]

naphtha /ˈnæfθə/ n. inflammable hydrocarbon distilled from coal etc. [from Greek]

naphthalene /ˈnæfθəliːn/ n. white crystalline substance produced by distilling coal tar.

napkin /ˈnæpkɪn/ n. 1 piece of linen etc. for wiping the lips, fingers, etc. at meals. **2** baby's nappy. [French nappe from Latin mappa MAP]

nappy /ˈnæpɪ/ n. (pl. -ies) piece of towelling etc. wrapped round a baby to absorb or retain urine and faeces. [from NAPKIN]

narcissism /nɑːˈsɪsɪz(ə)m/ n. excessive or erotic interest in oneself. □ **narcissistic** /-ˈsɪstɪk/ adj. [Narcissus, name of a youth in Greek myth who fell in love with his reflection]

narcissus /nɑːˈsɪsəs/ n. (pl. **-cissi** /-saɪ/) any of several flowering bulbs, including the daffodil. [Latin from Greek]

narcosis /nɑːˈkəʊsɪs/ n. 1 state of insensibility. 2 induction of this. [Greek narkē numbness]

narcotic /nɑːˈkɒtɪk/ —adj. 1 (of a substance) inducing drowsiness etc. 2 (of a drug) affecting the mind. —n. narcotic substance, drug, or influence. [Greek narkōtikos]

nark slang —n. police informer or decoy. —v. annoy. [Romany nāk nose]

narrate /nəˈreɪt/ v. (-ting) 1 give a continuous story or account of. 2 provide a spoken accompaniment for (a film etc.). □ **narration** /nəˈreɪʃ(ə)n/ n. **narrator** n. [Latin narro]

narrative /ˈnærətɪv/ —n. ordered account of connected events. —adj. of or by narration.

narrow /ˈnærəʊ/ —adj. (-er, -est) 1 a of small width. b confined or confining (within narrow bounds). 2 of limited scope (in the narrowest sense). 3 with little margin (narrow escape). 4 precise; exact. 5 = NARROW-MINDED. —n. (usu. in pl.) narrow part of a strait, river, pass, street, etc. —v. become or make narrow; contract; lessen. □ **narrowly** adv. **narrowness** n. [Old English]

narrow boat n. canal boat.

narrow-minded adj. rigid or restricted in one's views, intolerant. □ **narrow-mindedness** n.

narwhal /ˈnɑːw(ə)l/ n. Arctic white whale, the male of which has a long tusk. [Dutch from Danish]

NASA /ˈnæsə/ abbr. (in the US) National Aeronautics and Space Administration.

nasal /ˈneɪz(ə)l/ —adj. 1 of the nose. 2 (of the breath passing through the nose, e.g. m, a letter or a sound) pronounced with the breath passing through the nose, e.g. m, n, ng. 3 (of the voice or speech) having many nasal sounds. —n. nasal letter or sound. □ **nasalize** v. (also **-ise**) (-zing or **-sing**) **nasally** adv. [Latin nasus nose]

nascent /ˈnæs(ə)nt/ adj. 1 in the act of being born. 2 just beginning to be, not yet mature. □ **nascency** /ˈnæsənsɪ/ n. [Latin: related to NATAL]

nasturtium /nəˈstɜːʃəm/ n. trailing plant with edible leaves and bright orange, yellow, or red flowers. [Latin]

nasty /ˈnɑːstɪ/ —adj. (**-ier**, **-iest**) 1 highly unpleasant. 2 difficult to negotiate. 3 (of a person or animal) ill-natured. —n. (pl. **-ies**) colloq. horror film, esp. one on video and depicting cruelty or killing. □ **nastily** adv. **nastiness** n. [origin unknown]

nasty piece of work n. colloq. unpleasant or contemptible person.

Nat. abbr. 1 National 2 Nationalist. 3 Natural.

natal /ˈneɪt(ə)l/ adj. of or from one's birth. [Latin natalis from nascor nat- be born]

nation /ˈneɪʃ(ə)n/ n. community of people of mainly common descent, history, language, etc., forming a State or inhabiting a territory. [Latin: related to NATAL]

national /ˈnæʃ(ə)n(ə)l/ —adj. 1 of a, or the, nation. 2 characteristic of a particular nation. —n. 1 citizen of a specified country. 2 fellow-countryman. 3 (the **National**) = GRAND NATIONAL. □

national anthem n. song adopted by a nation, intended to inspire patriotism.

national curriculum n. common programme of study for pupils in the maintained schools of England and Wales,

with tests at specified ages.

national debt n. money owed by a State because of loans to it.

National Front n. UK political party with extreme reactionary views on immigration etc.

national grid n. 1 network of high-voltage electric power lines between major power stations. 2 metric system of geographical coordinates used in maps of the British Isles.

National Health Service n. (also **National Health Service**) system of national medical care paid for mainly by taxation.

National Insurance n. system of compulsory payments by employed persons (supplemented by employers) to provide State assistance in sickness etc.

nationalism n. 1 patriotic feeling, principles, etc. 2 policy of national independence. □ **nationalist** n. & adj. **nationalistic** /ˌlɪstɪk/ adj.

nationality /næʃəˈnælɪtɪ/ n. (pl. -ies) 1 status of belonging to a particular nation (has British nationality). 2 condition of being national; distinctive national qualities. 3 ethnic group forming a part of one or more political nations.

nationalize v. (also -ise) (-zing or -sing) 1 take (railways, industry, land, etc.) into State ownership. 2 make national. □ **nationalization** /ˈzeɪʃ(ə)n/ n.

national park n. area of natural beauty protected by the State for the use of the public.

national service n. hist. conscripted peacetime military service.

nationwide adj. & adv. extending over the whole nation.

native /ˈneɪtɪv/ —n. 1 a (usu. foll. by of) person born in a specified place. b local inhabitant. 2 often offens. member of a non-White indigenous people, as regarded by colonial settlers. 3 (usu. foll. by of) indigenous animal or plant. —adj. 1 inherent; innate. 2 of one's birth (native country). 3 (usu. foll. by to) belonging to a specified place. 4 (esp. of a non-European) indigenous; born in a place. 5 (of metal etc.) found in a pure or uncombined state. [Latin: related to NATAL]

nativity /nəˈtɪvɪtɪ/ n. (pl. -ies) 1 (esp. **the Nativity**) a Christ's birth. b festival of Christ's birth. 2 birth. [Latin: related to NATIVE]

NATO /ˈneɪtəʊ/ abbr. (also **Nato**) North Atlantic Treaty Organization.

natter colloq. —v. chatter idly. —n. aimless chatter. [imitative, originally dial.]

natterjack /ˈnætədʒæk/ n. a kind of small toad. [perhaps from NATTER]

natty /ˈnætɪ/ adj. (-ier, -iest) colloq. trim; smart. □ **nattily** adv. [cf. NEAT]

natural /ˈnætʃ(ə)r(ə)l/ —adj. 1 a existing in or caused by nature (natural landscape). b uncultivated (in its natural state). 2 in the course of nature (died of natural causes). 3 not surprising; to be expected (natural for her to be upset). 4 unaffected, spontaneous. 5 innate (natural talent for music). 6 not disguised or altered (as by make-up etc.). 7 likely or suited by its or their nature to be such (natural enemies; natural leader). 8 physically existing (the natural world). 9 illegitimate. 10 Mus. (of a note) not sharpened or flattened (B natural). —n. 1 colloq. (usu. foll. by for) person or thing naturally suitable, adept, etc. 2 Mus. a sign (♮) denoting a return to natural pitch. b natural note. □ **naturalness** n. [Latin: related to NATURE]

natural gas n. gas found in the earth's crust, not manufactured.

natural history n. the study of animals or plants.

naturalism n. 1 theory or practice in art and literature of realistic representation. 2 a theory of the world that excludes the supernatural or spiritual. b moral or religious system based on this. □ **naturalistic** /ˈlɪstɪk/ adj.

naturalist n. 1 person who studies natural history. 2 adherent of naturalism.

naturalize v. (also -ise) (-zing or -sing) 1 admit (a foreigner) to citizenship. 2 successfully introduce (an animal, plant, etc.) into another region. 3 adopt (a foreign word, custom, etc.). □ **naturalization** /ˈzeɪʃ(ə)n/ n.

natural law n. 1 unchanging moral principles common to all human beings. 2 correct statement of an invariable sequence between specified conditions and a specified phenomenon.

naturally adv. 1 in a natural manner. 2 (qualifying a whole sentence) as might be expected; of course.

natural number n. whole number greater than 0.

natural resources n.pl. materials or conditions occurring in nature and capable of economic exploitation.

natural science n. 1 the study of the natural or physical world. 2 (in pl.) sciences used for this.

natural selection n. Darwinian theory of the survival and propagation of organisms best adapted to their environment.

nature /ˈneɪtʃ(ə)r/ n. 1 thing's or person's innate or essential qualities or character. 2 (often **Nature**) a physical

power causing all material phenomena. **b** these phenomena. **3** kind or class (*things of this nature*). **4** inherent impulses determining character or action. □ **by nature** innately. **in (or by the) nature of things 1** inevitable. **2** inevitably. [Latin *natura*: related to NATAL]

natured *adj.* (in *comb.*) having a specified disposition (*good-natured*).

nature reserve *n.* tract of land managed so as to preserve its flora, fauna, physical features, etc.

nature trail *n.* signposted path through the countryside designed to draw attention to natural phenomena.

naturism *n.* nudism. □ **naturist** *n.*

naught /nɔːt/ *archaic* or *literary* —*n.* nothing, nought. —*adj.* (usu. *predic.*) worthless; useless. □ **come to naught** come to nothing, fail. **set at naught** despise. [Old English: related to NO²]

naughty /ˈnɔːtɪ/ *adj.* (**-ier, -iest**) **1** (esp. of children) disobedient; badly behaved. **2** *colloq. joc.* indecent. □ **naughtily** *adv.* **naughtiness** *n.*

nausea /ˈnɔːsɪə/ *n.* **1** inclination to vomit. **2** revulsion. [Greek *naus* ship]

nauseate /ˈnɔːsɪeɪt/ *v.* (**-ting**) affect with nausea. □ **nauseating** *adj.* **nauseatingly** *adv.*

nauseous /ˈnɔːsɪəs/ *adj.* **1** causing nausea. **2** inclined to vomit (*feel nauseous*). **3** disgusting; loathsome. [Greek *nautēs* sailor]

nautical /ˈnɔːtɪk(ə)l/ *adj.* of sailors or navigation. [Greek: related to NAUTICAL]

nautical mile *n.* unit of approx. 2,025 yards (1,852 metres).

nautilus /ˈnɔːtɪləs/ *n.* (*pl.* **nautiluses** or **nautili** /-laɪ/) cephalopod mollusc with a spiral shell, esp. (**pearly nautilus**) one having a chambered shell. [Greek *nautilos*: related to NAUTICAL]

naval /ˈneɪv(ə)l/ *adj.* **1** of the or a navy. **2** of ships. [Latin *navis* ship]

nave¹ *n.* central part of a church, usu. excluding the side aisles. [Latin *navis* ship]

nave² *n.* hub of a wheel. [Old English]

navel /ˈneɪv(ə)l/ *n.* depression in the centre of the belly marking the site of attachment of the umbilical cord. [Old English]

navel orange *n.* orange with a navel-like formation at the top.

navigable /ˈnævɪgəb(ə)l/ *adj.* **1** (of a river etc.) suitable for ships to pass through. **2** seaworthy. **3** steerable. □ **navigability** /-ˈbɪlɪtɪ/ *n.* [Latin: related to NAVIGATE]

navigate /ˈnævɪˌgeɪt/ *v.* (**-ting**) **1** manage or direct the course of (a ship or aircraft) using maps and instruments. **2**

navigation /ˌnævɪˈgeɪʃ(ə)n/ *n.* **1** act or process of navigating. **2** art or science of navigating. □ **navigational** *adj.* [Latin *navis*]

NB *abbr.* note well. [Latin *nota bene*]

Nb *symb.* niobium.

NCB *abbr. hist.* National Coal Board.

■ **Usage** Since 1987 the official name has been *British Coal*.

NCO *abbr.* non-commissioned officer.

NCP *abbr.* National Car Parks.

Nd *symb.* neodymium.

NE *abbr.* **1** north-east. **2** north-eastern.

Ne *symb.* neon.

Neanderthal /nɪˈændə(r)ˌtɑːl/ *adj.* of the type of human widely distributed in palaeolithic Europe, with a retreating forehead and massive brow-ridges. [region in W. Germany]

neap *n.* (in full **neap tide**) tide at the times of the month when there is least difference between high and low water. [Old English]

Neapolitan /ˌnɪəˈpɒlɪt(ə)n/ —*n.* native or citizen of Naples. —*adj.* of Naples. [Greek *Neapolis* Naples]

a sail on (a sea, river, etc.). **b** fly through (the air). **3** (in a car etc.) assist the driver by map-reading etc. **4** sail a ship; sail in a ship. □ **navigator** *n.* [Latin *navigo* from *navis*]

navvy /ˈnævɪ/ —*n.* (*pl.* **-ies**) labourer employed in building or excavating roads, canals, etc. —*v.* (**-ies, -ied**) work as a navvy. [abbreviation of *navigator*]

navy /ˈneɪvɪ/ *n.* (*pl.* **-ies**) **1** (often **the Navy**) **a** whole body of a State's ships of war, including crews, maintenance systems, etc. **b** officers and men of a navy. **2** (in full **navy blue**) dark-blue colour as of naval uniforms. **3** *poet.* fleet of ships. [Romanic *navia* ship: related to NAVAL]

nay —*adv.* **1** or rather, and even; and more than that (*large, nay, huge*). **2** *archaic* = no² *adv.* —*n.* utterance of 'nay'; 'no' vote. [Old Norse, = not ever]

Nazarene /ˈnæzəriːn/ —*n.* **1 a** (prec. by the) Christ. **b** (esp. in Jewish or Muslim use) Christian. **2** native or inhabitant of Nazareth. —*adj.* of Nazareth. [Latin from Greek]

Nazi /ˈnɑːtsɪ/ —*n.* (*pl.* **-s**) *hist.* member of the German National Socialist party. —*adj.* of the Nazis or Nazism. □ **Nazism** *n.* [representing pronunciation of *Nati-* in German *Nationalsozialist*]

near —*adv.* **1** (often foll. by **to**) to or at a short distance in space or time. **2** closely (*as near as one can guess*). —*prep.* **1** to or at a short distance from (in space, time, condition, or resemblance). **2** (in *comb.*) almost (*near-hysterical*). —*adj.* **1** (*near*) not far (in place or time) (*my flat's very near; the man nearest you; in*

the near future). **2 a** closely related. **b** intimate. **3** (of a part of a vehicle, animal, or road) on the left side. **4** close; narrow (*near escape*). **5** similar (to) (*is nearer the original*). **6** *colloq.* niggardly. —*v.* approach, draw near to. □ **come** (or **go**) **near** (foll. by verbal noun, or *to* + verbal noun) be on the point of, almost succeed in. **near at hand** within easy reach. **near the knuckle** *colloq.* verging on the indecent. □ **nearish** *adj.* **nearness** *n.* [Old Norse, originally = nigher; related to NIGH]

nearby —*adj.* near in position. —*adv.* close; not far away.

Near East *n.* (prec. by *the*) region comprising the countries of the eastern Mediterranean. □ **Near Eastern** *adj.*

nearly *adv.* **1** almost. **2** closely. □ **not nearly** nothing like.

near miss *n.* **1** bomb etc. falling close to the target. **2** narrowly avoided collision. **3** not quite successful attempt.

nearside *n.* (often *attrib.*) left side of a vehicle, animal, etc.

near-sighted *adj.* = SHORT-SIGHTED.

near thing *n.* narrow escape.

neat *adj.* **1** tidy and methodical. **2** elegantly simple. **3** brief, clear, and pointed. **4 a** cleverly executed. **b** dexterous. **5** (of esp. alcoholic liquor) undiluted. □ **neatly** *adv.* **neatness** *n.* [French *net* from Latin *nitidus* shining]

neaten *v.* make neat.

neath *prep. poet.* beneath. [from BE-NEATH]

nebula /ˈnɛbjʊlə/ *n.* (*pl.* **nebulae** /-ˌliː/) cloud of gas and dust seen in the night sky, sometimes glowing and sometimes appearing as a dark silhouette. □ **nebular** *adj.* [Latin, = mist]

nebulous *adj.* **1** cloudlike. **2** indistinct, vague. [Latin: related to NEBULA]

NEC *abbr.* National Executive Committee.

necessary /ˈnɛsəsərɪ/ —*adj.* **1** requiring to be done; requisite, essential. **2** determined, existing, or happening by natural laws etc., not by free will; inevitable. —*n.* (*pl.* -**ies**) (usu. in *pl.*) any of the basic requirements of life. □ **the necessary** *colloq.* **1** money. **2** an action etc. needed for a purpose. □ **necessarily** /also ˌnɛs-, ˈsɛrɪlɪ/ *adv.* [Latin *necesse* needful]

necessitarian /nɪˌsɛsɪˈtɛərɪən/ —*n.* person who holds that all action is predetermined and free will is impossible. —*adj.* of such a person or theory. □ **necessitarianism** *n.*

necessitate /nɪˈsɛsɪteɪt/ *v.* (-**ting**) make necessary (esp. as a result) (*will necessitate some sacrifice*).

necessitous /nɪˈsɛsɪtəs/ *adj.* poor, needy.

necessity /nɪˈsɛsɪtɪ/ *n.* (*pl.* -**ies**) **1** indispensable thing. **2** pressure of circumstances. **3** imperative need. **4** want, poverty. **5** constraint or compulsion regarded as a natural law governing all human action. □ **of necessity** unavoidably.

neck —*n.* **1 a** part of the body connecting the head to the shoulders. **b** part of a garment round the neck. **2** something resembling a neck; narrow part of a cavity, vessel, or object such as a bottle or violin. **3** length of a horse's head and neck as a measure of its lead in a race. **4** flesh of an animal's neck as food. **5** *slang* impudence. —*v. colloq.* kiss and caress amorously. □ **get it in the neck** *colloq.* **1** be severely reprimanded or punished. **2** suffer a severe blow. **up to one's neck** (often foll. by *in*) *colloq.* very deeply involved; very busy. [Old English]

neck and neck *adj. & adv.* (running) level in a race etc.

neckband *n.* strip of material round the neck of a garment.

neckerchief *n.* square of cloth worn round the neck. [from KERCHIEF]

necklace /ˈnɛkləs/ *n.* **1** chain or string of beads, precious stones, etc., worn round the neck. **2** *S.Afr.* tyre soaked or filled with petrol, placed round a victim's neck, and set alight.

neckline *n.* edge or shape of a garment-opening at the neck.

necktie *n.* esp. *US* = TIE *n.* 2.

necro- *comb. form* corpse. [Greek *nekros* corpse]

necromancy /ˈnɛkrəʊˌmænsɪ/ *n.* **1** divination by supposed communication with the dead. **2** magic. □ **necromancer** *n.* [from NECRO-, *mantis* seer]

necrophilia /ˌnɛkrəˈfɪlɪə/ *n.* morbid and esp. sexual attraction to corpses.

necropolis /nɛˈkrɒpəlɪs/ *n.* ancient cemetery or burial place. [Greek: related to NECRO-, *polis* city]

necrosis /nɛˈkrəʊsɪs/ *n.* death of tissue. □ **necrotic** /-ˈkrɒtɪk/ *adj.* [Greek *nekroō* kill]

nectar /ˈnɛktə(r)/ *n.* **1** sugary substance produced by plants and made into honey by bees. **2** (in Greek and Roman mythology) the drink of the gods. **3** drink compared to this. □ **nectarous** *adj.* [Latin from Greek]

nectarine /ˈnɛktərɪn/ *n.* smooth-skinned variety of peach. [from NEC-TAR]

NEDC *abbr.* National Economic Development Council.

neddy /'nedi/ n. (pl. -ies) colloq. 1 donkey. 2 (**Neddy**) = NEDC. [pet form of Edward]

née /nei/ adj. (US **nee**) (used in adding a married woman's maiden name after her surname) born (Mrs Ann Hall, née Brown). [French, feminine past part. of naître be born]

need —v. 1 stand in want of; require. 2 (foll. by to + infin.; 3rd sing. present neg., or interrog. **need** without to) be under the necessity or obligation (needs to be done well; he need not come; need you ask?). —n. 1 requirement (my needs are few). 2 circumstances requiring some course of action (no need to worry; if need be). 3 destitution; poverty. 4 crisis; emergency (failed them in their need). □ **have need of** require. **need not have** did not need to (but did). [Old English]

needful adj. requisite. □ **needfully** adv.

needle /'ni:d(ə)l/ —n. 1 a very thin pointed rod of smooth steel etc. with a slit ('eye') for thread at the blunt end, used in sewing. b larger plastic, wooden, etc. slender rod without an eye, used in knitting etc. 2 pointer on a dial. 3 any of several small thin pointed instruments, esp.: a the end of a hypodermic syringe. b = STYLUS 1. 4 a obelisk (Cleopatra's Needle). b pointed rock or peak. 5 leaf of a fir or pine tree. 6 (the needle) slang fit of bad temper or nervousness. —v. (-ling) colloq. irritate; provoke. [Old English]

needle-cord n. fine-ribbed corduroy fabric.

needle-point n. 1 lace made with needles, not bobbins. 2 = GROS or PETIT POINT.

needless adj. 1 unnecessary. 2 uncalled for. □ **needlessly** adv.

needlewoman n. 1 seamstress. 2 woman or girl with specified sewing skill.

needlework n. sewing or embroidery.

needs adv. archaic (usu. prec. or foll. by must) of necessity.

needy adj. (-ier, -iest) poor; destitute. □ **neediness** n.

ne'er /neə(r)/ adv. poet. = NEVER. [contraction]

ne'er-do-well —n. good-for-nothing person. —adj. good-for-nothing.

nefarious /ni'feəriəs/ adj. wicked. [Latin nefas wrong n.]

neg. abbr. esp. Photog. negative.

negate /ni'geit/ v. (-ting) 1 nullify. 2 assert or imply the non-existence of. [Latin nego deny]

negation /ni'geiʃ(ə)n/ n. 1 absence or opposite of something actual or positive. 2 act of denying. 3 negative statement 4 negative or unreal thing.

negative /'negətiv/ —adj. 1 expressing or implying denial, prohibition, or refusal (negative answer). 2 (of a person or attitude) lacking positive attributes. 3 marked by the absence of qualities (negative reaction). 4 of the opposite nature to a thing regarded as positive. 5 (of a quantity) less than zero, to be subtracted from others or from zero. 6 Electr. a of the kind of charge carried by electrons. b containing or producing such a charge. —n. 1 negative statement or word. 2 Photog. a image with black and white reversed or colours replaced by complementary ones, from which positive pictures are obtained. b developed film or plate bearing such an image. —v. (-ving) 1 refuse to accept or countenance; veto. 2 disprove. 3 contradict (a statement). 4 neutralize (an effect). □ **in the negative** with negative effect. □ **negatively** adv. **negativity** /-'tivti/ n.

negativism n. negative attitude; extreme scepticism

neglect /ni'glekt/ —v. 1 fail to care for or to do; be remiss about. 2 (foll. by to + infin.) fail; overlook the need to. 3 not pay attention to; disregard. —n. 1 negligence. 2 neglecting or being neglected. (usu. foll. by of) disregard. □ **neglectful** adj. **neglectfully** adv. [Latin neglego neglect-]

negligee /'neglizei/ n. (also **negligee**, **négligé**) woman's flimsy dressing gown. [French, past part. of négliger NEGLECT]

negligence /'neglidʒ(ə)ns/ n. 1 lack of proper care and attention. 2 culpable carelessness. □ **negligent** adj. **negligently** adv. [Latin: related to NEGLECT]

negligible /'neglidʒib(ə)l/ adj. not worth considering; insignificant. □ **negligibly** adv. [French: related to NEGLECT]

negotiable /ni'gəuʃ(ə)b(ə)l/ adj. 1 open to discussion. 2 able to be negotiated.

negotiate /ni'gəuʃieit/ v. (-ting) 1 (usu. foll. by with) confer in order to reach an agreement. 2 arrange (an affair) or bring about (a result) by negotiating. 3 find a way over, through, etc. (an obstacle, difficulty, etc.). 4 convert (a cheque etc.) into money. □ **negotiation** /-ʃi'eiʃ(ə)n/ n. **negotiator** n. [Latin negotium business]

Negress /'ni:gris/ n. female Negro.

Negritude

■ **Usage** The term *Negress* is often considered offensive; *Black* is usually preferred.

Negritude /'negrɪˌtjuːd/ n. 1 state of being Black. 2 affirmation of Black culture. [French]

Negro /'niːgrəʊ/ n. (pl. -es) member of a dark-skinned race orig. native to Africa. —adj. 1 of Negroes. 2 (as negro) Zool. black or dark. [Latin niger nigri black]

■ **Usage** The term *Negro* is often considered offensive; *Black* is usually preferred.

Negroid /'niːgrɔɪd/ —adj. (of physical features etc.) characteristic of Black people. —n. Black.

neigh /neɪ/ —n. cry of a horse. —v. make a neigh. [Old English]

neighbour /'neɪbə(r)/ (US **neighbor**) —n. 1 person living next door to or near or nearest another. 2 fellow human being. 3 person or thing near or next to another. —v. border on; adjoin. [Old English: related to NIGH, BOOR]

neighbourhood n. (US **neighborhood**) 1 district; vicinity. 2 people of a district. □ **in the neighbourhood of** roughly; about.

neighbourhood watch n. organized local vigilance by householders to discourage crime.

neighbourly adj. (US **neighborly**) like a good neighbour; friendly; kind. □ **neighbourliness** n.

neither /'naɪðə(r), 'niːð-/ —adj. & pron. (foll. by sing. verb) not the one nor the other (of two things); not either (neither of the accusations is true; neither of them knows; neither wish was granted; neither went to the fair). —adv. 1 not either; not on the one hand (foll. by nor, introducing the first of two or more things in the negative: neither knowing nor caring; neither the teachers nor the parents nor the children). 2 also not (if you do not, neither shall I). —conj. archaic nor yet; nor (I know not, neither can I guess). [Old English: related to NO², WHETHER]

nelson /'nelsən/ n. wrestling-hold in which one arm is passed under the opponent's arm from behind and the hand is applied to the neck (**half nelson**), or both arms and hands are applied (**full nelson**). [apparently from the name Nelson]

nematode /'nemətəʊd/ n. worm with a slender unsegmented cylindrical shape. [Greek nēma thread]

nem. con. abbr. with no one dissenting. [Latin nemine contradicente]

nemesis /'neməsɪs/ n. (pl. **nemeses** /-ˌsiːz/) 1 retributive justice. 2 downfall caused by this. [Greek, = retribution]

neo- comb. form 1 new, modern. 2 new form of. [Greek neos new]

neoclassicism /ˌniːəʊˈklæsɪˌsɪz(ə)m/ n. revival of classical style or treatment in the arts. □ **neoclassical** /-k(ə)l/ adj.

neodymium /ˌniːəʊˈdɪmɪəm/ n. metallic element of the lanthanide series. [from NEO-, Greek didumos twin]

neolithic /ˌniːəˈlɪθɪk/ adj. of the later part of the Stone Age. [Greek lithos stone]

neologism /niːˈɒləˌdʒɪz(ə)m/ n. 1 new word. 2 coining of new words. [Greek logos word]

neon /'niːɒn/ n. inert gaseous element giving an orange glow when electricity is passed through it. [Greek, = new]

neophyte /'niːəˌfaɪt/ n. 1 new convert. 2 RC Ch. novice of a religious order. 3 beginner. [Greek phuton plant]

nephew /'nefjuː/ n. son of one's brother or sister or of one's spouse's brother or sister. [Latin nepos]

nephritic /nɪˈfrɪtɪk/ adj. 1 of or in the kidneys. 2 of nephritis. [Greek nephros kidney]

nephritis /nɪˈfraɪtɪs/ n. inflammation of the kidneys.

ne plus ultra /neɪ plʊs 'ʊltrɑ/ n. 1 furthest attainable point. 2 acme, perfection. [Latin, = not further beyond]

nepotism /'nepəˌtɪz(ə)m/ n. favouritism shown to relatives in conferring offices. [Italian nepote nephew]

neptunium /nepˈtjuːnɪəm/ n. transuranic metallic element produced when uranium atoms absorb bombarding neutrons. [Neptune, name of a planet]

nerd n. (also **nurd**) esp. US slang foolish, feeble, or uninteresting person. [origin uncertain]

nereid /'nɪərɪɪd/ n. sea-nymph. [Latin from Greek]

nerve —n. 1 a fibre or bundle of fibres that transmits impulses of sensation or motion between the brain or spinal cord and other parts of the body. b material constituting these. 2 a coolness in danger; bravery. b colloq. impudence. 3 (in pl.) nervousness; mental or physical stress. —v. (-ving) 1 (usu. refl.) brace (oneself) to face danger etc. 2 give strength, vigour, or courage to. □ **get on a person's nerves** irritate a person. [Latin nervus sinew, bowstring]

nerve-cell n. cell transmitting impulses in nerve tissue.

nerve-centre n. 1 group of closely connected nerve-cells. 2 centre of control.

nerve gas n. poisonous gas affecting the nervous system.

nervy adj. 1 lacking vigour. 2 (of style) diffuse.

nerve-racking adj. causing mental strain.

nervous adj. 1 easily upset, timid, highly strung. 2 anxious. 3 affecting the nerves. 4 (foll. by of + verbal noun) afraid (am nervous of meeting them). □ **nervously** adv. **nervousness** n.

nervous breakdown n. period of mental illness, usu. resulting from severe stress.

nervous system n. body's network of nerve cells.

nervy adj. (-ier, -iest) colloq. nervous; easily excited.

nescient /'nesiant/ adj. literary (foll. by of) lacking knowledge. □ **nescience** n. [Latin ne- not, scio know]

-ness suffix forming nouns from adjectives, expressing: 1 state or condition, or an instance of this (happiness; a kindness). 2 something in a certain state (wilderness). [Old English]

nest -n. 1 structure or place where a bird lays its eggs and shelters its young. 2 any creature's breeding-place or lair. 3 snug retreat or shelter. 4 brood or swarm. 5 group or set of similar objects, often of different sizes and fitting one inside the other (nest of tables). -v. 1 use or build a nest. 2 take w.ld birds' nests or eggs. 3 (of objects) fit together or one inside another. [Old English]

nest egg n. sum of money saved for the future.

nestle /'nes(ə)l/ v. (-ling) 1 (often foll. by down, in, etc.) settle oneself comfortably. 2 press oneself against another in affection etc. 3 (foll. by in, into, etc.) push (a head or shoulder etc.) affectionately or snugly. 4 lie half hidden or embedded. [Old English]

nestling /'nestlɪŋ/ n. bird too young to leave its nest.

net¹ -n. 1 open-meshed fabric of cord, rope, etc. 2 piece of net used esp. to restrain, contain, or delimit, or to catch fish etc. 3 structure with a net used in various games. -v. (-tt-) 1 a cover, confine, or catch with a net. b procure as with a net. 2 hit (a ball) into the net, esp. at a goal. [Old English]

net² (also **nett**) -adj. 1 (esp. of money) remaining after all necessary deductions. 2 (of a price) not reducible. 3 (of a weight) excluding that of the packaging etc. 4 (of an effect, result, etc.) ultimate, actual. -v. (-tt-) gain or yield (a sum) as net profit. [French: related to NEAT]

netball n. team game in which goals are scored by throwing a ball through a high horizontal ring from which a net hangs.

nether /'neðə(r)/ adj. archaic = LOWER¹. [Old English]

nether regions n.pl. (also **nether world**) hell; the underworld.

net profit n. actual gain after working expenses have been paid.

netting n. var. of NET¹.

nettle /'net(ə)l/ n. 1 nettle fabric. 2 piece of this.

nettle /'net(ə)l/ -n. 1 plant with jagged leaves covered with stinging hairs. 2 plant resembling this. -v. (-ling) irritate, provoke. [Old English]

nettle-rash n. skin eruption like nettle stings.

network -n. 1 arrangement of intersecting horizontal and vertical lines. 2 complex system of railways etc. 3 people connected by the exchange of information etc., professionally or socially. 4 system of connected electrical conductors. 5 group of broadcasting stations connected or the simultaneous broadcast of a programme. 6 chain of interconnected computers. -v. broadcast on a network.

neural /'njʊər(ə)l/ adj. of a nerve or the central nervous system. [Greek neuron nerve]

neuralgia /njʊə'rældʒə/ n. intense pain along a nerve, esp. in the head or face. □ **neuralgic** adj.

neuritis /njʊə'raɪtɪs/ n. inflammation of a nerve or nerves.

neuro- comb. form nerve or nerves.

neurology /njʊə'rɒlədʒɪ/ n. the study of nerve systems. □ **neurological** /-rə'lɒdʒɪk(ə)l/ adj. **neurological neurologist** n.

neuron /'njʊərɒn/ n. (also **neurone** /-rəʊn/) nerve-cell.

neurosis /njʊə'rəʊsɪs/ n. (pl. **neuroses** /-siːz/) irrational or disturbed behaviour pattern, associated with nervous distress.

neurosurgery /njʊərəʊ'sɜːdʒərɪ/ n. surgery on the nervous system, esp. the brain or spinal cord. □ **neurosurgical** adj. **neurosurgeon** n.

neurotic /njʊə'rɒtɪk/ -adj. 1 caused by or relating to neurosis. 2 suffering from neurosis. 3 colloq. abnormally sensitive or obsessive. -n. neurotic person. □ **neurotically** adv.

neuter /'njuːtə(r)/ -adj. 1 neither masculine nor feminine. 2 (of a plant) having neither pistils nor stamen. 3 (of an insect) sexually undeveloped. -n. 1 neuter gender or word. 2 a non-fertile insect, esp. a worker bee or ant. b castrated animal. -v. castrate or spay. [Latin]

neutral /'njuːtr(ə)l/ -adj. 1 not supporting either of two opposing sides, impartial. 2 belonging to a neutral State etc.

(*neutral ships*). **3** indistinct, vague, indeterminate. **4** (of a gear) in which the engine is disconnected from the driven parts. **5** (of colours) not strong or positive; grey or beige. **6** *Chem.* neither acid nor alkaline. **7** *Electr.* neither positive nor negative. **8** *Biol.* sexually undeveloped; asexual.—*n.* **1 a** a neutral State or person. **b** citizen of a neutral State. **2** neutral gear. □ **neutrality** /-'træltɪ/ *n.* [Latin *neutralis* of neuter gender]

neutralize *v.* (also **-ise**) (*-zing* or *-sing*) **1** make neutral. **2** make ineffective by an opposite force or effect. **3** exempt or exclude (a place) from the sphere of hostilities. □ **neutralization** /-'zeɪʃ(ə)n/ *n.*

neutrino /njuː'triːnəʊ/ *n.* (*pl.* **-s**) elementary particle with zero electric charge and probably zero mass. [Italian, diminutive of *neutro* neutral: related to NEUTER]

neutron /'njuːtrɒn/ *n.* elementary particle of about the same mass as a proton but without an electric charge. [from NEUTRAL]

neutron bomb *n.* bomb producing neutrons and little blast, destroying life but not property.

never /'nevə(r)/ *adv.* **1 a** at no time; on no occasion; not ever. **b** *colloq.* as an emphatic negative (*I never heard you come in*). **2** not at all (*never fear*). **3** *colloq.* (expressing surprise) surely not (*you never left the door open!*). □ **well I never!** expressing great surprise. [Old English, = not ever]

nevermore *adv.* at no future time.

never-never *n.* (often prec. by *the*) *colloq.* hire purchase.

nevertheless /ˌnevəðə'les/ *adv.* in spite of that; notwithstanding.

nevus *US* var. of NAEVUS.

new —*adj.* **1 a** of recent origin or arrival. **b** made, discovered, acquired, or experienced recently or now for the first time. **2** in original condition; not worn or used. **3 a** renewed; reformed (*new life; the new order*). **b** reinvigorated (*felt like a new person*). **4** different from a recent previous one (*has a new job*). **5** (often foll. by *to*) unfamiliar or strange (*all new to me*). **6** (usu. prec. by *the*) often *derog.* **a** later, modern. **b** newfangled. **c** given to new or modern ideas. **d** recently affected by social change (*the new rich*). **7** (often prec. by *the*) advanced in method or theory. **8** (in place-names) discovered or founded later than and named after (*New York*). —*adv.* (usu. in comb.) newly, recently (*new-found; new-baked*). □ **newish** *adj.*

newness *n.* [Old English]

New Age *n.* set of beliefs replacing traditional Western culture, with alternative approaches to religion, medicine, the environment, etc.

new arrival *n. colloq.* newborn child.

newborn *adj.* newly born.

new broom *n.* new employee etc. eager to make changes.

newcomer *n.* **1** person who has recently arrived. **2** beginner in some activity.

newel /'njuːəl/ *n.* **1** supporting central post of winding stairs. **2** (also **newel post**) top or bottom supporting post of a stair-rail. [Latin *nodus* knot]

newfangled /njuː'fæŋɡ(ə)ld/ *adj. derog.* different from what one is used to; objectionably new. [= new taken]

newly *adv.* **1** recently. **2** afresh, anew.

newly-wed *n.* recently married person.

new mathematics *n.pl.* (also **new maths**) (also treated as *sing.*) system of elementary maths teaching with an emphasis on investigation and set theory.

new moon *n.* **1** moon when first seen as a crescent after conjunction with the sun. **2** time of its appearance.

new potatoes *n.pl.* earliest potatoes of a new crop.

news /njuːz/ *n.pl.* (usu. treated as *sing.*) **1** information about important or interesting recent events, esp. when published or broadcast. **2** (prec. by *the*) broadcast report of news. **3** newly received or noteworthy information. [from NEW]

newsagent *n.* seller of or shop selling newspapers etc.

newscast *n.* radio or television broadcast of news reports.

newscaster *n.* = NEWSREADER.

news conference *n.* press conference.

newsflash *n.* single item of important news, broadcast urgently and often interrupting other programmes.

newsletter *n.* informal printed report issued periodically to members of a club etc.

newspaper *n.* **1** printed publication of loose folded sheets containing news, advertisements, correspondence, etc. **2** paper forming this (*wrapped in newspaper*).

Newspeak *n.* ambiguous euphemistic language used esp. in political propaganda. [an artificial official language in Orwell's *Nineteen Eighty-Four*]

newsprint *n.* low-quality paper on which newspapers are printed.

newsreader *n.* person who reads out broadcast news bulletins.

newsreel *n.* short cinema film of recent events.

ews room n. room in a newspaper or broadcasting office where news is processed.

ews-sheet n. simple form of newspaper; newsletter.

ews-stand n. stall for the sale of newspapers.

ew star n. nova.

ew style n. dating reckoned by the Gregorian Calendar.

ews-vendor n. newspaper-seller.

ewsworthy adj. topical; noteworthy.

ewsy adj. (-ier, -iest) colloq. full of news.

ewt n. small amphibian with a well-developed tail. [eut, with n from an. var. of ever EFT]

ew Testament n. part of the Bible concerned with the life and teachings of Christ and his earliest followers.

ewton /'njuːt(ə)n/ n. SI unit of force. [Newton, name of a scientist]

ew town n. town planned and built all at once with government funds.

ew Wave n. a style of rock music.

ew World n. North and South America.

ew year n. year just begun or about to begin; first few days of a year.

New Year's Day n. 1 January.

New Year's Eve n. 31 December.

ext –adj. 1 (often foll. by to) being positioned, or living nearest 2 nearest in order of time; soonest encountered (next Friday; ask the next person you see). –adv. 1 (often foll. by to) in the nearest place or degree (put it next to mine). 2 on the first or soonest occasion (when we next meet). –n. next person or thing. –prep. colloq. next to. □ **next to** almost nothing (next to nothing left). [Old English superlative of NIGH]

ext-best adj. the next in order of preference.

ext door adj. & adv. (as adj. often hyphenated) in the next house or room.

ext of kin n.sing. & pl. closest living relative(s).

ext world n. (prec. by the) life after death.

exus /'neksəs/ n. (pl. same) connected group or series. [Latin necto nex- bird]

NHS abbr. National Health Service.

NI abbr. 1 Northern Ireland. 2 National Insurance.

Ni symb. nickel.

niacin /'naɪəsɪn/ n. = NICOTINIC ACID. [shortening]

nib n. 1 pen-point. 2 (in pl.) shelled and crushed coffee or cocoa beans. [Low German or Dutch]

nibble /'nɪb(ə)l/ –v. (-ling) 1 (foll. by at) a take small bites at. b take cautious interest in. 2 eat in small amounts. 3 bite at gently, cautiously, or playfully. –n. 1 act of nibbling. 2 very small amount of food. [Low German or Dutch]

nibs n. □ **his nibs** joc. colloq. mock title used with reference to an important or self-important person. [origin unknown]

nice adj. 1 pleasant, satisfactory. 2 (of a person) kind, good-natured. 3 iron. bad or awkward (nice mess). 4 fine or subtle (nice distinction). 5 fastidious; delicately sensitive. 6 (foll. by an adj., often with and) satisfactory in terms of the quality described (a nice long time; nice and warm). □ **nicely** adv. **niceness** n. **nicish** adj. (also **niceish**). [originally = foolish, from Latin nescius ignorant]

nicety /'naɪsɪtɪ/ n. (pl. -ies) 1 subtle distinction or detail. 2 precision. □ **to a nicety** with exactness.

niche /niːtʃ/ n. 1 shallow recess, esp. in a wall. 2 comfortable or apt position in life or employment. 3 position from which an entrepreneur exploits a gap in the market; profitable corner of the market. [Latin nidus nest]

nick n. 1 small cut or notch. 2 slang a prison. b police station. 3 colloq. condition (in good nick). –v. 1 make a nick or nicks in. 2 slang a steal. b arrest, catch. □ **in the nick of time** only just in time. [origin uncertain]

nickel /'nɪk(ə)l/ n. 1 silver-white metallic element, used esp. in magnetic alloys. 2 colloq. US five-cent coin. [German]

nickel silver n. = GERMAN SILVER.

nickel steel n. type of stainless steel with chromium and nickel.

nicker n. (pl. same) slang pound sterling. [origin unknown]

nick-nack var. of KNICK-KNACK.

nickname /'nɪkneɪm/ –n. familiar or humorous name given to a person or thing instead of or as well as the real name. –v. (-ming) 1 give a nickname to. 2 call by a nickname. [earlier eke-name, with n from an. eke = addition, from Old English: related to EKE]

nicotine /'nɪkətiːn/ n. poisonous alkaloid present in tobacco. [French from Nicot, introducer of tobacco into France]

nicotinic acid /ˌnɪkə'tɪnɪk/ n. vitamin of the B complex.

nictitate /'nɪktɪteɪt/ v. (-ting) blink or wink. □ **nictitation** /-'teɪʃ(ə)n/ n. [Latin]

nictitating membrane *n.* transparent third eyelid in amphibians, birds, and some other animals.

niece *n.* daughter of one's brother or sister or of one's spouse's brother or sister. [Latin *neptis* granddaughter]

niff /nif/ *n. & v. colloq.* smell, stink. □ **niffy** *adj.* (-ier, -iest). [originally a dial. word]

nifty /ˈnɪftɪ/ *adj.* (-ier, -iest) *colloq.* 1 clever, adroit. 2 smart, stylish. [origin uncertain]

niggard /ˈnɪɡəd/ *n.* stingy person. [probably of Scandinavian origin]

niggardly *adj.* stingy. □ **niggardliness** *n.*

nigger *n. offens.* Black or dark-skinned person. [Spanish NEGRO]

niggle /ˈnɪɡ(ə)l/ *v.* (-ling) 1 be over-attentive to details. 2 find fault in a petty way. 3 *colloq.* irritate; nag pettily. □ **niggling** *adj.* [origin unknown]

nigh /naɪ/ *adv., prep., & adj. archaic* or *dial.* near. [Old English]

night /naɪt/ *n.* 1 period of darkness between one day and the next; time from sunset to sunrise. 2 nightfall. 3 darkness of night. 4 night or evening appointed for some activity regarded in a certain way (*last night of the Proms*). [Old English]

nightbird *n.* person who is most active at night.

nightcap *n.* 1 *hist.* cap worn in bed. 2 hot or alcoholic drink taken at bedtime.

nightclub *n.* club providing refreshment and entertainment late at night.

nightdress *n.* woman's or child's loose garment worn in bed.

nightfall *n.* end of daylight.

nightgown *n.* = NIGHTDRESS.

nightie *n. colloq.* nightdress.

nightingale /ˈnaɪtɪŋɡeɪl/ *n.* small reddish-brown bird, of which the male sings melodiously, esp. at night. [Old English; = night-singer]

nightjar *n.* nocturnal bird with a characteristic harsh cry.

night-life *n.* entertainment available at night in a town.

night-light *n.* dim light kept burning in a bedroom at night.

night-long *adj. & adv.* throughout the night.

nightly —*adj.* 1 happening, done, or existing in the night. 2 recurring every night. —*adv.* every night.

nightmare *n.* 1 frightening dream. 2 *colloq.* frightening or unpleasant experience or situation. 3 haunting fear. □ **nightmarish** *adj.* [evil spirit (incubus) once thought to lie on and suffocate sleepers: Old English *mære* incubus]

night safe *n.* safe with access from the outer wall of a bank for the deposit of money etc. when the bank is closed.

night school *n.* institution providing classes in the evening.

nightshade *n.* any of various plants with poisonous berries. [Old English]

nightshirt *n.* long shirt worn in bed.

nightspot *n.* nightclub.

night-time *n.* time of darkness.

night-watchman *n.* 1 person employed to keep watch at night. 2 *Cricket* inferior batsman sent in near the close of a day's play.

nihilism /ˈnaɪ(h)ɪlɪz(ə)m/ *n.* 1 rejection of all religious and moral principles. 2 belief that nothing really exists. □ **nihilist** *n.* **nihilistic** /-ˈlɪstɪk/ *adj.* [Latin *nihil* nothing]

-nik *suffix* forming nouns denoting person associated with a specified thing or quality (*beatnik*). [Russian (as SPUTNIK) and Yiddish]

Nikkei index /ˈnɪkeɪ/ *n.* (also **Nikkei average**) a figure indicating the relative price of representative shares on the Tokyo Stock Exchange. [Japanese]

nil *n.* nothing; no number or amount (esp. as a score in games). [Latin]

nimble /ˈnɪmb(ə)l/ *adj.* (-bler, -blest) quick and light in movement or function; agile. □ **nimbly** *adv.* [Old English; = quick to seize]

nimbus /ˈnɪmbəs/ *n.* (*pl.* **nimbi** /-baɪ/ or **nimbuses**) 1 halo. 2 rain-cloud. [Latin = cloud]

Nimby /ˈnɪmbɪ/ —*adj.* objecting to the siting of unpleasant developments in one's own locality. —*n.* (*pl.* -ies) person who so objects. [not in *my back yard*]

nincompoop /ˈnɪŋkəmpuːp/ *n.* foolish person. [origin unknown]

nine *adj. & n.* 1 one more than eight. 2 symbol for this (9, ix, IX). 3 size etc denoted by nine. [Old English]

nine days' wonder *n.* person or thing that is briefly famous.

ninefold *adj. & adv.* 1 nine times as much or as many. 2 consisting of nine parts.

ninepin *n.* 1 (in *pl.*; usu. treated as *sing.*) game in which nine pins are bowled at. 2 pin used in this game.

nineteen /naɪnˈtiːn/ *adj. & n.* 1 one more than eighteen. 2 symbol for this (19, xix, XIX). 3 size etc. denoted by nineteen. □ **talk nineteen to the dozen** see DOZEN □ **nineteenth** *adj. & n.* [Old English]

ninety /ˈnaɪntɪ/ *adj. & n.* (*pl.* -ies) 1 product of nine and ten. 2 symbol for this (90, xc, XC). 3 (in *pl.*) numbers or of a person's life. □ **ninetieth** *adj. & n.* [Old English]

ninny /ˈnɪnɪ/ n. (pl. -ies) foolish person. [origin uncertain]

ninth /naɪnθ/ adj. & n. 1 next after eighth. 2 any of nine equal parts of a thing. □ **ninthly** adv.

niobium /naɪˈəʊbɪəm/ n. rare metallic element occurring naturally. [*Niobe* in Greek legend]

Nip n. slang offens. Japanese person. [abbreviation of *Nipponese* from Japanese *Nippon* Japan]

nip¹ -v. (-pp-) 1 pinch, squeeze, or bite sharply. 2 (often foll. by *off*) remove by pinching etc. 3 (of the cold etc.) cause pain or harm to. 4 (foll. by *in, out,* etc.) colloq. go nimbly or quickly. -n. 1 a pinch, sharp squeeze. b bite. 2 biting cold. □ **nip in the bud** suppress or destroy (esp. an idea) at an early stage. [Low German or Dutch]

nip² n. small quantity of spirits. [from *nipperkin* small measure]

nipper n. 1 person or thing that nips. 2 claw of a crab etc. 3 colloq. young child. 4 (in pl.) any tool for gripping or cutting.

nipple /ˈnɪp(ə)l/ n. 1 small projection in which the mammary ducts of either sex of mammals terminate and from which in females milk is secreted for the young. 2 teat of a feeding-bottle. 3 device like a nipple in function. 4 nipple-like protuberance. [perhaps from *neb* tip]

nippy adj. (-ier, -iest) colloq. 1 quick, nimble. 2 chilly. [from *nip¹*]

nirvana /nɪəˈvɑːnə, nɜː-/ n. (in Buddhism) perfect bliss attained by the extinction of individuality. [Sanskrit, = extinction]

nit-picking n. & adj. colloq. fault-finding in a petty manner.

Nissen hut /ˈnɪs(ə)n/ n. tunnel-shaped hut of corrugated iron with a cement floor. [*Nissen*, name of an engineer]

nit n. 1 egg or young form of a louse or other parasitic insect. 2 slang stupid person. [Old English]

nitrate -n. 1 any salt or ester of nitric acid. 2 potassium or sodium nitrate as a fertilizer. -v. /naɪˈtreɪt/ (-ting) treat, combine, or impregnate with nitric acid. □ **nitration** /naɪˈtreɪʃ(ə)n/ n. [French: related to NITRE]

nitre /ˈnaɪtə(r)/ n. (US **niter**) saltpetre. [Greek *nitron*]

nitric acid n. colourless corrosive poisonous liquid.

nitride /ˈnaɪtraɪd/ n. binary compound of nitrogen. [from NITRE]

nitrify /ˈnaɪtrɪfaɪ/ v. (-ies, -ied) 1 impregnate with nitrogen. 2 convert into nitrites or nitrates. □ **nitrification** /ˌnaɪtrɪfɪˈkeɪʃ(ə)n/ n. [French: related to NITRE]

nitrite /ˈnaɪtraɪt/ n. any salt or ester of nitrous acid. [from NITRE]

nitro- comb. form of or containing nitric acid, nitre, or nitrogen. [Greek: related to NITRE]

nitrogen /ˈnaɪtrədʒ(ə)n/ n. gaseous element that forms four-fifths of the atmosphere. □ **nitrogenous** /-ˈtrɒdʒɪnəs/ adj. [French]

nitroglycerine /ˌnaɪtrəʊˈglɪsərɪn/ n. (US **nitroglycerin**) explosive yellow liquid made by reacting glycerol with a mixture of concentrated sulphuric and nitric acids.

nitrous oxide /ˈnaɪtrəs/ n. colourless gas used as an anaesthetic. [Latin: related to NITRE]

nitty-gritty /ˌnɪtɪˈgrɪtɪ/ n. slang realities or practical details of a matter. [origin uncertain]

nitwit n. colloq. stupid person. [perhaps from NIT, WIT]

No. abbr. number. [Latin *numero*, ablative of *numerus* number]

no¹ /nəʊ/ adj. 1 not any (*there is no excuse*). 2 not a, quite other than (*is no food*). 3 hardly any (*did it in no time*). 4 used elliptically in a notice etc., to forbid etc. the thing specified (*no parking*). □ **no way** colloq. 1 it is impossible. 2 I will not agree etc. **no wonder** see WONDER. [related to NONE]

NNE abbr. north-north-east.

NNW abbr. north-north-west.

No¹ symb. nobelium.

No² var. of NOH.

no² /nəʊ/ -adv. 1 indicating that the answer to the question is negative, the statement etc. made or course of action intended or conclusion arrived at is not correct or satisfactory, the request or command will not be complied with, or the negative statement made is correct. 2 (foll. by compar.) by no amount; not at all (*no better than before*). -n. (pl. **noes**) 1 utterance of the word no. 2 denial or refusal. 3 'no' vote. □ **no longer** not now or henceforth as formerly. **or no** or not (*pleasant or no, it is true*). [Old English]

nob¹ n. slang person of wealth or high social position. [origin unknown]

nob² n. slang head. [from KNOB]

no-ball n. Cricket unlawfully delivered ball.

nobble /ˈnɒb(ə)l/ v. (-ling) slang 1 try to influence (e.g. a judge), esp. unfairly. 2 tamper with (a racehorse) □ prevent its winning. 3 steal. 4 seize, catch. [dial. *knobble* beat]

nobelium /nəʊˈbiːlɪəm/ n. artificially produced radioactive transuranic

metallic element. [from *Nobel*: see NOBEL PRIZE]

Nobel prize /nəʊˈbel/ *n.* any of six international prizes awarded annually for physics, chemistry, physiology or medicine, literature, economics, and the promotion of peace. [from *Nobel*, Swedish chemist and engineer, who endowed them]

nobility /nəʊˈbɪlɪtɪ/ *n.* (*pl.* -ies) 1 nobleness of character, mind, birth, or rank. 2 class of nobles, highest social class.

noble /ˈnəʊb(ə)l/ —*adj.* (**nobler, noblest**) 1 belonging to the aristocracy. 2 of excellent character; magnanimous. 3 of imposing appearance. —*n.* nobleman, noblewoman. □ **nobleness** *n.* **nobly** *adv.* [Latin *gynobilis*]

noble gas *n.* any of a group of gaseous elements that almost never combine with other elements.

nobleman *n.* peer.

noblesse oblige /nəʊˌbles əˈbliːʒ/ *n.* privilege entails responsibility. [French]

noblewoman *n.* peeress.

no claim bonus *n.* (also **no claims bonus**) reduction of an insurance premium after an agreed period without a claim.

nocturnal /nɒkˈtɜːn(ə)l/ *adj.* of or in the night; done or active by night. [Latin *nox noct-* night]

nocturne /ˈnɒktɜːn/ *n.* 1 *Mus.* short romantic composition, usu. for piano. 2 picture of a night scene. [French]

nod —*v.* (**-dd-**) 1 incline one's head slightly and briefly in assent, greeting, or command. 2 let one's head fall forward in drowsiness; be drowsy. 3 incline (one's head). 4 signify (assent etc.) by a nod. 5 (of flowers, plumes, etc.) bend downwards and sway. 6 make a mistake due to a momentary lack of alertness or attention. —*n.* nodding of the head. □ **nod off** *colloq.* fall asleep. [origin unknown]

noddle /ˈnɒd(ə)l/ *n. colloq.* head. [origin unknown]

noddy *n.* (*pl.* -ies) 1 simpleton. 2 tropical sea bird. [origin unknown]

node *n.* 1 **a** part of a plant stem from which leaves emerge. **b** knob on a root or branch. 2 natural swelling. 3 either of two points at which a planet's orbit intersects the plane of the ecliptic or the celestial equator. 4 point of minimum disturbance in a standing wave system. 5 point at which a curve intersects itself. 6 component in a computer network. □ **nodal** *adj.* [Latin *nodus* knot]

nodule /ˈnɒdjuːl/ *n.* 1 small rounded lump of anything. 2 small tumour, node or ganglion, or a swelling on the root of a legume containing bacteria etc. □ **nodular** *adj.* [Latin diminutive: related to NODE]

Noel /nəʊˈel/ *n.* Christmas. [related to NATAL]

noggin /ˈnɒgɪn/ *n.* 1 small mug. 2 small measure, usu. ¼ pint, of spirits. 3 *slang* head. [origin unknown]

no go *adj.* (usu. hyphenated when *attrib.*) *colloq.* impossible, hopeless; forbidden (*tried to get him to agree, but it was no go; no-go area*).

Noh /nəʊ/ *n.* (also **No**) traditional Japanese drama. [Japanese]

noise /nɔɪz/ —*n.* 1 sound, esp. a loud or unpleasant one. 2 series or confusion of loud sounds. 3 irregular fluctuations accompanying a transmitted signal. 4 (in *pl.*) conventional remarks, or speechlike sounds without actual words (*made sympathetic noises*). —*v.* (-sing) (usu. in *passive*) make public; spread abroad (a person's fame or a fact). [Latin NAUSEA]

noiseless *adj.* making little or no noise. □ **noiselessly** *adv.*

noisome /ˈnɔɪsəm/ *adj. literary* 1 harmful, noxious. 2 evil-smelling. [from ANNOY]

noisy *adj.* (-ier, -iest) 1 making much noise. 2 full of noise. □ **noisily** *adv.* **noisiness** *n.*

nomad /ˈnəʊmæd/ *n.* 1 member of a tribe roaming from place to place for pasture. 2 wanderer. □ **nomadic** /-ˈmædɪk/ *adj.* [Greek *nomas nomad-* from *nemō* to pasture]

no man's land *n.* 1 space between two opposing armies. 2 area not assigned to any owner.

nom de plume /ˌnɒm də ˈpluːm/ *n.* (*pl. noms de plume* pronunc. same) writer's assumed name. [sham French, = penname]

nomen /ˈnəʊmen/ *n.* ancient Roman's second or family name, as in Marcus *Tullius* Cicero. [Latin, = name]

nomenclature /nəʊˈmenklət[ʃ]ə(r)/ *n.* 1 person's or community's system of names for things. 2 terminology of a science etc. [Latin *nomen* name. *calo* call]

nominal /ˈnɒmɪn(ə)l/ *adj.* 1 existing in name only; not real or actual. 2 (of a sum of money etc.) very small. 3 of or in names (*nominal and essential distinctions*). 4 of, as, or like a noun. □ **nominally** *adv.* [Latin *nomen* name]

nominalism *n.* doctrine that universals or general ideas are mere names.

nominalist n. **nominalistic** /-'lɪstɪk/ adj.

nominal value n. face value.

nominate /'nɒmɪneɪt/ v. (-ting) 1 propose (a candidate) for election. 2 appoint to an office. □ **nomination** n. **nominator** n. [Latin: related to NOMINAL]

nominative /'nɒmɪnətɪv/ Gram. —n. case expressing the subject of a verb. —adj. of or in this case.

nominee /ˌnɒmɪ'niː/ n. person who is nominated.

non- prefix giving the negative sense of words with which it is combined. [Latin non not]

■ **Usage** The number of words that can be formed from the suffix non- is unlimited; consequently, only the most current and noteworthy can be given here.

nonagenarian /ˌnəʊnədʒɪ'neərɪən/ n. person from 90 to 99 years old. [Latin nonageni ninety each]

non-aggression /ˌnɒnə'greʃ(ə)n/ n. lack of or restraint from aggression (often attrib.: non-aggression pact).

nonagon /'nɒnəgən/ n. plane figure with nine sides and angles. [Latin nonus ninth, after HEXAGON]

non-alcoholic /ˌnɒnalkə'hɒlɪk/ adj. containing no alcohol.

non-aligned /ˌnɒnə'laɪnd/ adj. (of a State) not aligned with a major power. □ **non-alignment** n.

non-belligerent /ˌnɒnbɪ'lɪdʒərənt/ —adj. not engaged in hostilities. —n. non-belligerent State etc.

nonce n. □ **for the nonce** for the present occasion; for the time being. [from for than ones = for the one occasion]

nonce-word n. word coined for one occasion.

nonchalant /'nɒnʃələnt/ adj. calm and casual. □ **nonchalance** n. **nonchalantly** adv. [French chaloir be concerned]

non-com /'nɒnkɒm/ n. colloq. noncommissioned officer. [abbreviation]

non-combatant /nɒn'kɒmbət(ə)nt/ n. person not fighting in a war, esp. a civilian, army chaplain, etc.

non-commissioned /ˌnɒnkə'mɪʃ(ə)nd/ adj. (of an officer) not holding a commission.

noncommittal /ˌnɒnkə'mɪt(ə)l/ adj. avoiding commitment to a definite opinion or course of action.

non compos mentis /ˌnɒn kɒmpɒs 'mentɪs/ adj. (also **non compos**) not in one's right mind. [Latin, = not having control of one's mind]

non-conductor /ˌnɒnkən'dʌktə(r)/ n. substance that does not conduct heat or electricity.

nonconformist /ˌnɒnkən'fɔːmɪst/ n. 1 person who does not conform to the doctrine or discipline of an established Church, esp. (Nonconformist) member of a (usu. Protestant) sect dissenting from the Anglican Church. 2 person who does not conform to a prevailing principle.

nonconformity /ˌnɒnkən'fɔːmɪtɪ/ n. 1 nonconformists as a body, or their principles. 2 (usu. foll. by to) failure to conform. 3 lack of correspondence between things.

non-contributory /ˌnɒnkən'trɪbjʊtərɪ/ adj. not involving contributions.

non-cooperation /ˌnɒnkəʊˌɒpə'reɪʃ(ə)n/ n. failure to cooperate.

nondescript /'nɒndɪskrɪpt/ —adj. lacking distinctive characteristics, not easily classified. —n. nondescript person or thing. [related to DESCRIBE]

non-driver /nɒn'draɪvə(r)/ n. person who does not drive a motor vehicle.

non-drinker /nɒn'drɪŋkə(r)/ n. person who does not drink alcoholic liquor.

none /nʌn/ —pron. 1 (foll. by of) a not any (none of this concerns me, none of them have found it). b not any one of (none of them has come). 2 a no persons (none but fools believe it). b no person (none but a fool believes it). 3 (usu. with the preceding noun implied) not any (you have money and I have none). —adv. (foll. by the + compar. or so, too) by no amount; not at all (am none the wiser). [Old English, = not one]

■ **Usage** In sense 1b the verb following none can be singular or plural according to meaning.

nonentity /nɒ'nentɪtɪ/ n. (pl. -ies) 1 person or thing of no importance. 2 a non-existence. b non-existent thing. [medieval Latin]

nones /nəʊnz/ n.pl. day of the ancient Roman month (the 7th day of March, May, July, and October, the 5th of other months). [Latin nonus ninth]

non-essential /ˌnɒnɪ'senʃ(ə)l/ —adj. not essential. —n. non-essential thing.

nonetheless /ˌnʌnðə'les/ adv. (also **none the less**) nevertheless.

non-event /ˌnɒnɪ'vent/ n. insignificant event, esp. contrary to hopes or expectations.

non-existent /ˌnɒnɪg'zɪst(ə)nt/ adj. not existing.

non-fattening /nɒn'fæt(ə)nɪŋ/ adj. (of food) not containing many calories.

non-ferrous /nɒnˈferəs/ *adj.* (of a metal) other than iron or steel.

non-fiction /nɒnˈfɪkʃ(ə)n/ *n.* literary work other than fiction.

non-flammable /nɒnˈflæməb(ə)l/ *adj.* not inflammable.

non-interference /ˌnɒnɪntəˈfɪərəns/ *n.* = NON-INTERVENTION.

non-intervention /ˌnɒnɪntəˈvenʃ(ə)n/ *n.* (esp. political) principle or practice of not becoming involved in others' affairs.

non-member *n.* person who is not a member.

non-nuclear /nɒnˈnjuːklɪə(r)/ *adj.* 1 not involving nuclei or nuclear energy. 2 (of a State etc.) not having nuclear weapons.

non-observance /ˌnɒnəbˈzɜːv(ə)ns/ *n.* failure to observe (an agreement, requirement, etc.).

non-operational /ˌnɒnɒpəˈreɪʃən(ə)l/ *adj.* 1 that does not operate. 2 out of order.

nonpareil /ˌnɒnpəˈreɪl, ˈnɒnpər(ə)l/ *adj.* unrivalled or unique. —*n.* such a person or thing. [French *pareil*]

non-partisan /ˌnɒnpɑːtɪˈzæn/ *adj.* not partisan.

non-party /nɒnˈpɑːti/ *adj.* independent of political parties.

non-payment /nɒnˈpeɪmənt/ *n.* failure to pay; lack of payment.

nonplus /nɒnˈplʌs/ *v.* (-ss-) completely perplex. [Latin *non plus* not more]

non-profit-making /nɒnˈprɒfɪtˌmeɪkɪŋ/ *adj.* (of an enterprise) not conducted primarily to make a profit.

non-proliferation /ˌnɒnprəˌlɪfəˈreɪʃ(ə)n/ *n.* prevention of an increase in something, esp. possession of nuclear weapons.

non-resident /nɒnˈrezɪd(ə)nt/ —*adj.* 1 not residing in a particular place. 2 (of a post) not requiring the holder to reside at the place of work. —*n.* non-resident person. □ **non-residential** /ˈdenʃ(ə)l/ *adj.*

non-resistance /ˌnɒnrɪˈzɪst(ə)ns/ *n.* practice or principle of not resisting authority.

non-returnable /ˌnɒnrɪˈtɜːnəb(ə)l/ *adj.* that is not to be returned.

non-sectarian /ˌnɒnsekˈteərɪən/ *adj.* not sectarian.

nonsense /ˈnɒns(ə)ns/ *n.* 1 (often as *int.*) absurd or meaningless words or ideas. 2 foolish or extravagant conduct. □ **nonsensical** /-ˈsensɪk(ə)l/ *adj.* **nonsensically** /-ˈsensɪkəli/ *adv.*

non sequitur /nɒn ˈsekwɪtə(r)/ *n.* conclusion that does not logically follow from the premises. [Latin, = it does not follow]

non-slip /nɒnˈslɪp/ *adj.* 1 that does not slip. 2 that inhibits slipping.

non-smoker /nɒnˈsməʊkə(r)/ *n.* 1 person who does not smoke. 2 train compartment etc. where smoking is forbidden. □ **non-smoking** *adj.*

non-specialist /nɒnˈspeʃəlɪst/ *n.* person who is not a specialist (in a particular subject).

non-specific /ˌnɒnspɪˈsɪfɪk/ *adj.* that cannot be specified.

non-standard /nɒnˈstændəd/ *adj.* not standard.

non-starter /nɒnˈstɑːtə(r)/ *n. colloq.* person or scheme that is unlikely to succeed.

non-stick /nɒnˈstɪk/ *adj.* that does not allow things to stick to it.

non-stop /nɒnˈstɒp/ —*adj.* 1 (of a train etc.) not stopping at intermediate places. 2 done without a stop or intermission. —*adv.* without stopping.

non-swimmer /nɒnˈswɪmə(r)/ *n.* person who cannot swim.

non-toxic /nɒnˈtɒksɪk/ *adj.* not toxic.

non-transferable /ˌnɒntrænsˈfɜːrəb(ə)l/ *adj.* that may not be transferred.

non-U /nɒnˈjuː/ *adj. colloq.* not characteristic of the upper class. [from U²]

non-union /nɒnˈjuːnɪən/ *adj.* 1 not belonging to a trade union. 2 not done or made by trade-union members.

non-verbal /nɒnˈvɜːb(ə)l/ *adj.* not involving words or speech.

non-violence /nɒnˈvaɪələns/ *n.* avoidance of violence, esp. as a principle. □ **non-violent** *adj.*

non-voting /nɒnˈvəʊtɪŋ/ *adj.* 1 not having or using a vote. 2 (of shares) not entitling the holder to vote.

non-White /nɒnˈwaɪt/ —*adj.* not White. —*n.* non-White person.

noodle¹ /ˈnuːd(ə)l/ *n.* strip or ring of pasta. [German]

noodle² /ˈnuːd(ə)l/ *n.* 1 simpleton. 2 *slang* head. [origin unknown]

nook /nʊk/ *n.* corner or recess; secluded place. [origin unknown]

noon *n.* twelve o'clock in the day, midday. [Latin *nona* (*hora*) ninth (hour): originally = 3 p.m.]

noonday *n.* midday.

no one *n.* no person; nobody.

noose —*n.* 1 loop with a running knot. 2 snare, bond. —*v.* (-sing) catch with or enclose in a noose. [French *no(u)s* from Latin *nodus* NODE]

nor *conj.* and not; and not either (*neither one thing nor the other*; *can neither read nor write*). [contraction of obsolete *nother*: related to NO², WHETHER]

nor' /nɔː(r)/ *n., adj., & adv.* (esp. in compounds). = NORTH (*nor'wester*).

nor' (abbreviation).

Nordic /ˈnɔːdɪk/ —*adj.* of the tall blond long-headed Germanic people of Scandinavia. —*n.* Nordic person. [French *nord* north]

Norfolk jacket /ˈnɔːfək/ *n.* man's loose belted jacket with box pleats. [*Norfolk* in England]

norm *n.* 1 standard, pattern, or type. 2 standard amount of work etc. [Latin *norma* carpenter's square]

normal /ˈnɔːm(ə)l/ —*adj.* 1 conforming to a standard; regular, usual, typical. 2 free from mental or emotional disorder. 3 *Geom.* (of a line) at right angles, perpendicular. —*n.* 1 a normal value of a temperature etc. b usual state, level, etc. 2 line at right angles. □ **normalcy** *n.* esp. *US.* **normality** /-ˈmælɪtɪ/ *n.* [Latin: related to NORM]

normal distribution *n.* function that represents the distribution of many random variables as a symmetrical bell-shaped graph.

normalize *v.* (also **-ise**) (**-zing** or **-sing**) 1 make or become normal. 2 cause to conform. □ **normalization** /-ˈzeɪʃ(ə)n/ *n.*

normally *adv.* 1 in a normal manner. 2 usually.

Norman /ˈnɔːmən/ —*n.* 1 native or inhabitant of medieval Normandy. 2 descendant of the people of mixed Scandinavian and Frankish origin established there in the 10th c. 3 Norman French. 4 style of architecture found in Britain under the Normans. —*adj.* 1 of the Normans. 2 of the Norman style of architecture. [Old Norse, = NORTH-MAN]

Norman Conquest *n.* conquest of England by William of Normandy, in 1066.

Norman French *n.* French as spoken by the Normans or (after 1066) in English lawcourts.

Norse —*n.* 1 Norwegian language. 2 Scandinavian language-group. —*adj.* of ancient Scandinavia, esp. Norway. □ **Norseman** *n.* [Dutch *noor(d)sch* northern]

north —*n.* 1 a point of the horizon 90° anticlockwise from east. b compass point corresponding to this. c direction in which this lies. 2 (usu. **the North**) a part of a country or town lying to the north. b the industrialized nations. —*adj.* 1 towards, at, near, or facing the north. 2 from the north (*north wind*). —*adv.* 1 towards, at or near the north. 2 (foll. by *of*) further north than. □ **to the north** (often foll. by *of*) in a northerly direction. [Old English]

North American —*adj.* of North America. —*n.* native or inhabitant of North America, esp. a citizen of the US or Canada.

northbound *adj.* travelling or leading northwards.

north country *n.* northern England.

North-East *n.* part of a country or town to the north-east.

north-east —*n.* 1 point of the horizon midway between north and east. 2 direction in which this lies. —*adj.* of, towards, or coming from the north-east. —*adv.* towards, at, or near the north-east.

north-easter /nɔːθˈiːstə(r)/ *n.* north-east wind.

north-easterly *adj. & adv.* = NORTH-EAST.

north-eastern *adj.* on the north-east side.

northerly /ˈnɔːðəlɪ/ —*adj. & adv.* 1 in a northern position or direction. 2 (of wind) from the north. —*n.* (*pl.* **-ies**) such a wind.

northern /ˈnɔːð(ə)n/ *adj.* of or in the north. □ **northernmost** *adj.* [Old English]

northerner *n.* native or inhabitant of the north.

Northern hemisphere *n.* the half of the earth north of the equator.

northern lights *n.pl.* aurora borealis.

Northman *n.* native of Scandinavia, esp. Norway. [Old English]

north-north-east *n.* point or direction midway between north and north-east.

north-north-west *n.* point or direction midway between north and north-west.

North Pole *n.* northernmost point of the earth's axis of rotation.

North Star *n.* pole star.

northward /ˈnɔːθwəd/ —*adj. & adv.* (also **northwards**) towards the north. —*n.* northward direction or region.

North-West *n.* part of a country or town to the north-west.

north-west —*n.* 1 point of the horizon midway between north and west. 2 direction in which this lies. —*adj.* of, towards, or coming from the north-west. —*adv.* towards, at, or near the north-west.

northwester /nɔːθˈwestə(r)/ *n.* north-west wind.

north-westerly *adj. & adv.* = NORTH-WEST.

north-western

north-western *adj.* on the north-west side.

Norwegian /nɔːˈwiːdʒ(ə)n/ —*adj.* **1 a** native or national of Norway. **b** person of Norwegian descent. **2** language of Norway. —*adj.* of or relating to Norway. [medieval Latin *Norvegia* from Old Norse, = northway]

nor'wester /nɔːˈwestə(r)/ *n.* north-wester.

Nos. *pl.* of No.

nose /nəʊz/ —*n.* **1** organ above the mouth of a human or animal, used for smelling and breathing. **2 a** sense of smell. **b** ability to detect a particular thing (*a nose for scandal*). **3** odour or perfume of wine etc. **4** front end or projecting part of a thing, e.g. of a car or aircraft. —*v.* (**-sing**) **1** (usu. foll. by *about, around*, etc.) pry or search. **2** (often foll. by *out*) **a** perceive the smell of, discover by smell. **b** detect. **3** thrust one's nose against or into. **4** make one's way cautiously forward. □ **by a nose** by a very narrow margin. **get up a person's nose** *slang* annoy a person. **keep one's nose clean** *slang* stay out of trouble. **put a person's nose out of joint** *colloq.* annoy; make envious. **turn up one's nose** (usu. foll. by *at*) *colloq.* show disdain. **under a person's nose** *colloq.* right before a person. **with one's nose in the air** haughtily. [Old English]

nosebag *n.* bag containing fodder, hung on a horse's head.

noseband *n.* lower band of a bridle, passing over the horse's nose.

nosebleed *n.* bleeding from the nose.

nosedive —*n.* **1** steep downward plunge by an aeroplane. **2** sudden plunge or drop. —*v.* (**-ving**) make a nosedive.

nosegay *n.* small bunch of flowers.

nose-to-tail *adj. & adv.* (of vehicles) one close behind another.

nosh *slang* —*v.* eat. —*n.* **1** food or drink. **2** US snack. [Yiddish]

nosh-up *n. slang* large meal.

nostalgia /mɒˈstældʒə/ *n.* **1** (often foll. by *for*) yearning for a past period. **2** severe homesickness. □ **nostalgic** *adj.* **nostalgically** *adv.* [Greek *nostos* return home]

nostril /ˈnɒstr(ə)l/ *n.* either of the two openings in the nose. [Old English. = nose-hole]

nostrum /ˈnɒstrəm/ *n.* **1** quack remedy, patent medicine. **2** pet scheme, esp. for political or social reform. [Latin, = 'of our own make']

nosy *adj.* (**-ier, -iest**) *colloq.* inquisitive, prying. □ **nosily** *adv.* **nosiness** *n.*

Nosy Parker *n. colloq.* busybody.

not *adv.* expressing negation, esp.: **1** (also **n't** joined to a preceding verb)

following an auxiliary verb or *be* or (in question) the subject of such a verb (*cannot say; she isn't there; am I not right?*). **2** used elliptically for a negative phrase etc. (*Is she coming? — I hope not; Do you want it? — Certainly not!*). □ **not at all** (in polite reply to thanks) there is no need for thanks. **not half** *see* HALF. **not quite 1** almost. **2** noticeably not (*not quite proper*). [contraction of NOUGHT]

■ **Usage** The use of *not* with verbs other than auxiliaries or *be* is now archaic except with participles and infinitives (*not knowing, I cannot say; u asked them not to come*).

notable /ˈnəʊtəb(ə)l/ —*adj.* worthy o note; remarkable, eminent. —*n.* eminent person. □ **notability** /-ˈbɪlɪtɪ/ *n.* **no ably** *adv.* [Latin *noto* NOTE]

notary /ˈnəʊtərɪ/ *n.* (*pl.* -**ies**) (in fu **notary public**) solicitor etc. who attest or certifies deeds etc. □ **notaria** /nəʊˈteərɪəl/ *adj.* [Latin *notarius* se retary]

notation /nəʊˈteɪʃ(ə)n/ *n.* **1** representa tion of numbers, quantities, the pitch and duration of musical notes, etc., b symbols. **2** any set of such symbols [Latin: related to NOTE]

notch —*n.* V-shaped indentation on a edge or surface. —*v.* **1** make notches in. **2** (usu. foll. by *up*) record or score with o as with notches. [Anglo-French]

note —*n.* **1** brief written record as an aid to memory (often in *pl.*: *make notes*). **2** observation, usu. unwritten, of ex periences etc. (*compare notes*). **3** shor or informal letter. **4** formal diplomatic communication. **5** short annotation o additional explanation in a book etc. **6 a** = BANKNOTE. **b** written promise of pay ment. **7 a** notice, attention (*worthy of note*). **b** eminence (*person of note*). **8 a** single musical tone of definite pitch. **b** written sign representing its pitch and duration. **c** key of a piano etc. **9** quality or tone of speaking, expressing mood or attitude etc. (*note of optimism*). —*v.* (**-ting**) **1** observe, notice; give attention to. **2** (often foll. by *down*) record as a thing to be remembered or observed. **3** (in passive; often foll. by *for*) be well known. □ **hit** (or **strike**) **the right note** speak or act in exactly the right man ner. [Latin *nota* mark (n.), *noto* mark (v.)]

notebook *n.* small book for making notes in.

notecase *n.* wallet for holding bank notes.

notelet /ˈnəʊtlɪt/ n. small folded usu. decorated sheet of paper for an informal letter.

notepaper n. paper for writing letters.

noteworthy adj. worthy of attention; remarkable.

nothing /ˈnʌθɪŋ/ —n. 1 not anything (*nothing has been done*). 2 no thing or thing or thing of no importance. 4 non-existence; what does not exist. 5 no amount; nought. —adv. not at all; in no way. □ **be** (or **have**) **nothing to do with** 1 have no connection with. 2 not be involved or associated with. **for nothing** 1 at no cost. 2 to no purpose. **have nothing on** 1 be naked. 2 have no engagements. **nothing doing** colloq. 1 no prospect of success or agreement. 2 I refuse. [Old English: related to NO, THING]

nothingness n. 1 non-existence. 2 worthlessness, triviality.

notice /ˈnəʊtɪs/ —n. 1 attention, observation (*escaped my notice*). 2 displayed sheet etc. bearing an announcement. 3 a intimation or warning, esp. a formal one. b formal announcement or declaration of intention to end an agreement or leave employment at a specified time. 4 short published review of a new play, book, etc. —v. (-**cing**) (often foll. by *that*, *how*, etc.) perceive, observe. □ **at short notice** with little warning. **take notice** (or **no notice**) show signs (or no signs) of interest. **take notice of** 1 observe. 2 act upon. [Latin *notus* known]

noticeable adj. perceptible; noteworthy. □ **noticeably** adv.

notice-board n. board for displaying notices.

notifiable /ˈnəʊtɪfaɪəb(ə)l/ adj. (of a disease etc.) that must be notified to the health authorities.

notify /ˈnəʊtɪfaɪ/ v. (-**ies**, -**ied**) 1 (often foll. by *of* or *that*) inform or give formal notice to (a person). 2 make known. □ **notification** /-fɪˈkeɪʃ(ə)n/ n. [Latin *notus* known]

notion /ˈnəʊʃ(ə)n/ n. 1 a concept or idea; conception. b opinion. c vague view or understanding. 2 inclination or intention. [Latin *notio*: related to NOTIFY]

notional adj. hypothetical, imaginary. □ **notionally** adv.

notorious /nəʊˈtɔːrɪəs/ adj. well-known, esp. unfavourably. □ **notoriety** /-təˈraɪətɪ/ n. **notoriously** adv. [Latin *notus* known]

notwithstanding /ˌnɒtwɪðˈstændɪŋ/ —prep. in spite of; without prevention by. —adv. nevertheless. [from NOT, WITHSTAND]

nougat /ˈnuːgɑː/ n. sweet made from sugar or honey, nuts, and egg-white. [French from Provençal]

nought /nɔːt/ n. 1 digit 0; cipher. 2 poet. or archaic nothing. [Old English: related to NOT, AUGHT]

noughts and crosses n.pl. pencil-and-paper game in which players seek to complete a row of three noughts or three crosses.

noun n. word used to name a person, place, or thing. [Latin *nomen* name]

nourish /ˈnʌrɪʃ/ v. 1 sustain with food. 2 foster or cherish (a feeling etc.). □ **nourishing** adj. [Latin *nutrio* to feed]

nourishment n. sustenance, food.

nous /naʊs/ n. 1 colloq. common sense; gumption. 2 Philos. mind, intellect. [Greek]

nouveau riche /ˌnuːvəʊ ˈriːʃ/ n. (pl. **nouveaux riches** pronunc. same) person who has recently acquired (usu. ostentatious) wealth [French, = new rich]

nouvelle cuisine /ˌnuːvel kwɪˈziːn/ n. modern style of cookery avoiding heaviness and emphasizing presentation. [French, = new cookery]

Nov. abbr. November.

nova /ˈnəʊvə/ n. (pl. **novae** /-viː/ or -**s**) star showing a sudden burst of brightness and then subsiding. [Latin, = new]

novel¹ /ˈnɒv(ə)l/ n. fictitious prose story of book length. [Latin *novus* new]

novel² /ˈnɒv(ə)l/ adj. of a new kind or nature. [Latin *novus* new]

novelette /ˌnɒvəˈlet/ n. short novel.

novelist /ˈnɒvəlɪst/ n. writer of novels.

novella /nəʊˈvelə/ n. (pl. -**s**) short novel or narrative story. [Italian: related to NOVEL¹]

novelty /ˈnɒvəltɪ/ n. (pl. -**ies**) 1 newness. 2 new or unusual thing or occurrence. 3 small toy or trinket. [related to NOVEL²]

November /nəʊˈvembə(r)/ n. eleventh month of the year. [Latin *novem* nine, originally the 9th month of the Roman year]

novena /nəʊˈviːnə/ n. RC Ch. devotion consisting of special prayers or services on nine successive days. [Latin *novem* nine]

novice /ˈnɒvɪs/ n. 1 a probationary member of a religious order. b new convert. 2 beginner. [Latin *novus* new]

noviciate /nəʊˈvɪʃɪət/ n. (also **novitiate**) 1 period of being a novice. 2 religious novice. 3 novices' quarters. [medieval Latin *novicius*]

now —adv. 1 at the present or mentioned time. 2 immediately (*I must go now*). 3 by this time. 4 under the present circumstances (*I cannot now agree*). 5 on

this further occasion (*what do you want now?*). **6** in the immediate past (*just now*). **7** (esp. in a narrative) then, next (*the police now arrived*). **8** (without reference to time, giving various tones to a sentence) surely, I insist, I wonder, etc. (*now what do you mean by that?; oh come now!*). (often foll. by *that*) as a consequence of the fact (*now that I am older*). —*conj.* this time; the present. —*n.* until a later time (*goodbye for now*). **now and again** (or **then**) from time to time; intermittently. [Old English]

nowadays /ˈnaʊədeɪz/ —*adv.* at the present time or age; in these times. —*n.* the present time.

nowhere /ˈnəʊweə(r)/ —*adv.* in or to no place. —*pron.* no place. **get nowhere** make no progress. **nowhere near** not nearly. [Old English]

no-win *attrib. adj.* of or designating a situation in which success is impossible.

nowt *n. colloq.* or *dial.* nothing. [from NOUGHT]

noxious /ˈnɒkʃəs/ *adj.* harmful, unwholesome. [Latin *noxa* harm]

nozzle /ˈnɒz(ə)l/ *n.* spout on a hose etc. from which a jet issues. [diminutive of NOSE]

Np *symb.* neptunium.

nr. *abbr.* near.

NS *abbr.* new style.

NSPCC *abbr.* National Society for the Prevention of Cruelty to Children.

NSW *abbr.* New South Wales.

NT *abbr.* **1** New Testament. **2** Northern Territory (of Australia). **3** National Trust.

n't see NOT.

nth see N[1].

nu /njuː/ *n.* thirteenth letter of the Greek alphabet (N, ν). [Greek]

nuance /ˈnjuːɑːs/ *n.* subtle shade of meaning, feeling, colour, etc. [Latin *nubes* cloud]

nub *n.* **1** point or gist (of a matter or story). **2** (also **nubble**) small lump, esp. of coal. □ **nubbly** *adj.* [related to KNOB]

nubile /ˈnjuːbaɪl/ *adj.* (of a woman) marriageable or sexually attractive. □ **nubility** /-ˈbɪlɪtɪ/ *n.* [Latin *nubo* become the wife of]

nuclear /ˈnjuːklɪə(r)/ *adj.* **1** of, relating to, or constituting a nucleus. **2** using nuclear energy.

nuclear bomb *n.* bomb using the release of energy by nuclear fission or fusion or both.

nuclear energy *n.* energy obtained by nuclear fission or fusion.

nuclear family *n.* a couple and their child or children.

nuclear fission *n.* nuclear reaction in which a heavy nucleus splits spontaneously or on impact with another particle, with the release of energy.

nuclear fuel *n.* source of nuclear energy.

nuclear fusion *n.* nuclear reaction in which atomic nuclei of low atomic number fuse to form a heavier nucleus with the release of energy.

nuclear physics *n.pl.* (treated as *sing.*) physics of atomic nuclei.

nuclear power *n.* **1** power generated by a nuclear reactor. **2** country that has nuclear weapons.

nuclear reactor *n.* device in which a nuclear fission chain reaction is used to produce energy.

nuclear weapon *n.* weapon using the release of energy by nuclear fission or fusion or both.

nucleate /ˈnjuːklɪeɪt/ —*adj.* having a nucleus. —*v.* (**-ting**) form or form into a nucleus. [Latin: related to NUCLEUS]

nucleic acid /njuːˈkliːɪk/ *n.* either of two complex organic molecules (DNA and RNA), present in all living cells.

nucleon /ˈnjuːklɪɒn/ *n.* proton or neutron.

nucleus /ˈnjuːklɪəs/ *n.* (*pl.* **nuclei** /-klɪaɪ/) **1** a central part or thing round which others are collected. **b** kernel of an aggregate or mass. **2** initial part meant to receive additions. **3** central core of an atom. **4** large dense part of a cell, containing the genetic material. [Latin, = kernel, diminutive of *nux nuc-* nut]

nude —*adj.* naked, bare, unclothed. —*n.* **1** painting, sculpture, etc. of a nude human figure. **2** nude person. □ **in the nude** naked. □ **nudity** *n.* [Latin *nudus*]

nudge —*v.* (**-ging**) **1** prod gently with the elbow to attract attention. **2** push gradually. —*n.* prod; gentle push. [origin unknown]

nudist /ˈnjuːdɪst/ *n.* person who advocates or practises going unclothed. □ **nudism** *n.*

nugatory /ˈnjuːgətərɪ/ *adj.* **1** futile, trifling. **2** inoperative; not valid. [Latin *nugae* jests]

nugget /ˈnʌgɪt/ *n.* **1** lump of gold etc., as found in the earth. **2** lump of anything. **3** something valuable. [apparently from dial. *nug* lump]

nuisance /ˈnjuːs(ə)ns/ *n.* person, thing, or circumstance causing trouble or annoyance. [French, = hurt, from *nuire nuis-* injure, from Latin *noceo* to hurt]

nuke *colloq.* —*n.* nuclear weapon. —*v.* (**-king**) attack with nuclear weapons. [abbreviation]

null *adj.* **1** (esp. **null and void**) invalid. **2** non-existent. **3** without character or

expression. □ **nullity** n. [Latin *nullus* none]

nullify /ˈnʌlɪfaɪ/ v. (-ies, -ied) neutralize, invalidate. □ **nullification** n. [Latin]

numb /nʌm/ —adj. (often foll. by *with*) deprived of feeling; paralysed. —v. 1 make numb. 2 stupefy, paralyse. □ **numbness** n. [obsolete *nome* past part. of *nim* take: related to NIMBLE]

number —n. 1 a arithmetical value representing a particular quantity. b word, symbol, or figure representing this. c arithmetical value showing position in a series (*registration number*). 2 (often foll. by *of*) total count or aggregate (*the number of accidents has decreased*). 3 numerical reckoning (*the laws of number*). 4 a (in *sing.* or *pl.*) quantity, amount (*a large number of people; only in small numbers*). b (**a number of**) several (*of*). c (in *pl.*) numerical preponderance (*force of numbers*). 5 person or thing having a place in a series, esp. a single issue of a magazine, an item in a programme, etc. 6 company, collection, group (*among our number*). 7 *Gram.* a classification of words by their singular or plural forms. b such a form. —v. 1 include (*I number you among my friends*). 2 assign a number or numbers to. 3 amount to (*a specified number*). 4 count. □ **one's days are numbered** one does not have long to live. **have a person's number** *colloq.* understand a person's real motives, character, etc. **one's number is up** *colloq.* one is doomed to die soon. **without number** innumerable. [Latin *numerus*]

■ **Usage** In sense 4b *a number of* is normally used with a plural verb: *a number of problems remain*.

number crunching n. *colloq.* process of making complex calculations.
numberless adj. innumerable.
number one —n. *colloq.* oneself. —adj. most important (*the number one priority*).
number-plate n. plate on a vehicle showing its registration number.
numerable /ˈnjuːmərəb(ə)l/ adj. that can be counted. [Latin: related to NUMBER]
numeral /ˈnjuːmər(ə)l/ —n. symbol or group of symbols denoting a number. —adj. of or denoting a number. [Latin: related to NUMBER]
numerate /ˈnjuːmərət/ adj. acquainted with the basic principles of mathematics. □ **numeracy** n. [Latin *numerus* number, after *literate*]

numeration /ˌnjuːməˈreɪʃ(ə)n/ n. method or process of numbering. [Latin: related to NUMBER]
numerator /ˈnjuːməreɪtə(r)/ n. number above the line in a vulgar fraction showing how many of the parts indicated by the denominator are taken (e.g. 2 in 2/3). [Latin: related to NUMBER]
numerical /njuːˈmerɪk(ə)l/ adj. of or relating to a number or numbers. □ **numerically** adv. [medieval Latin: related to NUMBER]
numerology /ˌnjuːməˈrɒlədʒɪ/ n. the study of the supposed occult significance of numbers.
numerous /ˈnjuːmərəs/ adj. 1 many. 2 consisting of many. [Latin: related to NUMBER]
numinous /ˈnjuːmɪnəs/ adj. 1 indicating the presence of a divinity. 2 spiritual, awe-inspiring. [Latin *numen* deity]
numismatic /ˌnjuːmɪzˈmætɪk/ adj. of coins or medals. [Greek *nomisma* coin]
numismatics n.pl. (usu. treated as *sing.*) the study of coins or medals. □ **numismatist** /-ˈmɪzmətɪst/ n. [from NUMB]
numskull n. stupid person. [from NUMB]
nun n. member of a religious community of women living under certain vows. [Latin *nonna*]
nuncio /ˈnʌnsɪəʊ/ n. (pl. -s) papal ambassador. [Latin *nuntius* messenger]
nunnery n. (pl. -ies) religious house of nuns.
nuptial /ˈnʌpʃ(ə)l/ —adj. of marriage or weddings. —n. (usu. in *pl.*) wedding. [Latin *nubo nupt-* wed]
nurd var. of NERD.
nurse /nɜːs/ —n. 1 person trained to care for the sick or infirm and assist doctors or dentists. 2 = NURSEMAID. —v. (-sing) 1 a attend to (a sick person). b work as a nurse. 2 feed or be fed at the breast. 3 hold or treat carefully. 4 a foster; promote the development of. b harbour (a grievance etc.). [Latin related to NOURISH]
nursemaid n. woman in charge of a child or children.
nurseling var. of NURSLING.
nursery /ˈnɜːsərɪ/ n. (pl. -ies) 1 a room or place equipped for young children. b = DAY NURSERY. 2 place where plants are reared for sale. [probably Anglo-French: related to NURSE]
nurseryman n. owner of or worker in a plant nursery.
nursery rhyme n. simple traditional song or rhyme for children.
nursery school n. school for children between the ages of three and five.

nursery slopes *n.pl.* gentle slopes for novice skiers.

nursing home *n.* privately run hospital or home for invalids, old people, etc.

nursling /ˈnɜːslɪŋ/ *n.* (also **nurseling**) infant that is being suckled.

nurture /ˈnɜːtʃə(r)/ —*n.* **1** bringing up, fostering care. **2** nourishment. —*v.* (-ring) bring up; rear. [French: related to NOURISH]

nut *n.* **1 a** fruit consisting of a hard or tough shell around an edible kernel. **b** this kernel. **2** pod containing hard seeds. **3** small usu. hexagonal flat piece of metal etc. with a threaded hole through it for screwing on the end of a bolt to secure it. **4** *slang* person's head. **5** *slang* crazy or eccentric person. **6** small lump (of coal etc.). **7** (in *pl.*) *coarse slang* testicles. □ **do one's nut** *slang* be extremely angry. [Old English]

nutcase *n.* *slang* crazy person.

nutcracker *n.* (usu. in *pl.*) device for cracking nuts.

nuthatch *n.* small bird which climbs up and down tree-trunks.

nutmeg *n.* **1** hard aromatic seed used as a spice and in medicine. **2** E. Indian tree bearing this. [French *nois* nut, *mugue* MUSK]

nutria /ˈnjuːtrɪə/ *n.* coypu fur. [Spanish, = otter]

nutrient /ˈnjuːtrɪənt/ —*n.* substance that provides essential nourishment. —*adj.* serving as or providing nourishment. [Latin *nutrio* nourish]

nutriment /ˈnjuːtrɪmənt/ *n.* **1** nourishing food. **2** intellectual or artistic etc. nourishment.

nutrition /njuːˈtrɪʃ(ə)n/ *n.* food, nourishment. □ **nutritional** *adj.* **nutritionist** *n.*

nutritious /njuːˈtrɪʃəs/ *adj.* efficient as food.

nutritive /ˈnjuːtrɪtɪv/ *adj.* **1** of nutrition. **2** nutritious.

nuts about (or **on**) *colloq.* be very fond of. [*pl.* of NUT]

nuts and bolts *n.pl.* *colloq.* practical details.

nutshell *n.* hard exterior covering of a nut. □ **in a nutshell** in a few words.

nutter *n.* *slang* crazy person.

nutty *adj.* (-ier, -iest) **1 a** full of nuts. **b** tasting like nuts. **2** *slang* crazy. □ **nuttiness** *n.*

nux vomica /nʌks ˈvɒmɪkə/ *n.* **1** E. Indian tree. **2** seeds of this tree, containing strychnine. [Latin, = abscess nut]

nuzzle /ˈnʌz(ə)l/ *v.* (-ling) **1** prod or rub gently with the nose. **2** (foll. by *into*, *against*, *up to*) press the nose gently. **3** nestle; lie snug. [from NOSE]

NW *abbr.* **1** north-west. **2** north-western.

NY *abbr.* US New York.

nylon /ˈnaɪlɒn/ *n.* **1** tough light elastic synthetic fibre. **2** nylon fabric. **3** (in *pl.*) stockings of nylon. [invented word]

nymph /nɪmf/ *n.* **1** mythological semi-divine spirit regarded as a maiden and associated with an aspect of nature, esp. rivers and woods. **2** *poet.* beautiful young woman. **3** immature form of some insects. [Greek *numphē* nymph, bride]

nympho /ˈnɪmfəʊ/ *n.* (*pl.* -**s**) *colloq.* nymphomaniac. [abbreviation]

nymphomania /ˌnɪmfəˈmeɪnɪə/ *n.* excessive sexual desire in a woman. □ **nymphomaniac** *n.* & *adj.* [from NYMPH, -MANIA]

NZ *abbr.* New Zealand.

O

O[1] /əʊ/ n. (also **o**) (pl. **Os** or **O's**) **1** fifteenth letter of the alphabet. **2** (0) nought, zero.

O[2] abbr. (also **O.**) Old.

O[3] symb. oxygen.

O[4] /əʊ/ int. **1** var. of OH. **2** prefixed to a name in the vocative (O God). [natural exclamation]

o' /ə/ prep. of, on (esp. in phrases: o'clock; will-o'-the-wisp). [abbreviation]

-o suffix forming usu. slang or colloq. variants or derivatives (beano; wino). [perhaps from OH]

-o- suffix terminal vowel of comb. forms (neuro-; Franco-). [originally Greek]

■ **Usage** This suffix is often elided before a vowel, as in neuralgia.

oaf n. (pl. **-s**) awkward lout. **2** stupid person. □ **oafish** adj. **oafishly** adv. **oafishness** n. [Old Norse: related to ELF]

oak n. **1** acorn-bearing tree with lobed leaves. **2** its durable wood. **3** (attrib.) of oak. **4** (**the Oaks**) (treated as sing.) annual race at Epsom for fillies. [Old English]

oak-apple n. (also **oak-gall**) a kind of growth formed on oak trees by the larvae of certain wasps.

oakum /ˈəʊkəm/ n. loose fibre obtained by picking old rope to pieces and used esp. in caulking. = OF-. comb]

OAP abbr. old-age pensioner.

oar /ɔː(r)/ n. **1** pole with a blade used to propel a boat by leverage against the water. **2** rower. □ **put one's oar in** interfere. [Old English]

oarsman n. (fem. **oarswoman**) rower. □ **oarsmanship** n.

oasis /əʊˈeɪsɪs/ n. (pl. **oases** /-siːz/) **1** fertile place in a desert. **2** area or period of calm in the midst of turbulence. [Latin from Greek]

oast n. kiln for drying hops. [Old English]

oast-house n. building containing an oast.

oat n. **1 a** hardy cereal plant grown as food. **b** (in pl.) grain yielded by this. **2** oat plant or a variety of it. **3** (in pl.) slang sexual gratification. □ **off one's oats** colloq. not hungry. □ **oaten** adj. [Old English]

oatcake n. thin oatmeal biscuit.

oath n. (pl. **-s** /əʊðz/) **1** solemn declaration naming God etc. as witness. **2** profanity, curse. □ **on** (or **under**) **oath** having sworn a solemn oath. [Old English]

oatmeal n. **1** meal ground from oats. **2** greyish-fawn colour flecked with brown.

OAU abbr. Organization of African Unity.

OB abbr. outside broadcast.

ob. abbr. he or she died. [Latin obiit]

ob- prefix (also **oc-** before c, **of-** before f, **op-** before p) esp. in words from Latin, meaning: **1** exposure. **2** meeting or facing. **3** direction. **4** resistance. **5** hindrance or concealment. **6** finality or completeness. [Latin ob towards, against, in the way of]

obbligato /ˌɒblɪˈɡɑːtəʊ/ n. (pl. **-s**) Mus. accompaniment forming an integral part of a composition. [Italian, = obliged]

obdurate /ˈɒbdjʊərət/ adj. **1** stubborn. **2** hardened. □ **obduracy** n. [Latin duro harden]

OBE abbr. Officer of the Order of the British Empire.

obedient /əˈbiːdɪənt/ adj. **1** obeying or ready to obey. **2** submissive to another's will. □ **obedience** n. **obediently** adv. [Latin: related to OBEY]

obeisance /əʊˈbeɪs(ə)ns/ n. **1** bow, curtsy, or other respectful gesture. **2** homage. □ **obeisant** adj. [French: related to OBEY]

obelisk /ˈɒbəlɪsk/ n. tapering usu. four-sided stone pillar as a monument or landmark. [Greek diminutive: related to OBELUS]

obelus /ˈɒbələs/ n. (pl. **obeli** /-laɪ/) dagger-shaped reference mark (†). [Greek, = pointed pillar, spit]

obese /əʊˈbiːs/ adj. very fat. □ **obesity** n. [Latin edo eat]

obey /əˈbeɪ/ v. **1 a** carry out the command of. **b** carry out (a command). **2** do what one is told to do. **3** be actuated by (a force or impulse). [Latin obedio from audio hear]

obfuscate /ˈɒbfʌskeɪt/ v. (**-ting**) **1** obscure or confuse (a mind, topic, etc.). **2** stupefy, bewilder. □ **obfuscation** n. [Latin fuscus dark]

obituary /əˈbɪtjʊərɪ/ n. (pl. **-ies**) **1** notice of a death or deaths. **2** account of the life of a deceased person. **3** (attrib.) of or

serving as an obituary. [Latin *obitus* death]

object —n. /ˈɒbdʒɪkt/ **1** material thing that can be seen or touched. **2** person or thing to which action or feeling is directed (*object of attention*). **3** thing sought or aimed at. **4** *Gram.* noun or its equivalent governed by an active transitive verb or by a preposition. **5** *Philos.* thing external to the thinking mind or subject. —v. /əbˈdʒekt/ (often foll. by *to*, *against*) **1** express opposition, disapproval, or reluctance. **2** protest. □ **no object** not forming an important or restricting factor (*money no object*). □ **objector** /əbˈdʒektə(r)/ n. [Latin *jacio* throw]

objectify /əbˈdʒektɪfaɪ/ v. (-ies, -ied) present as an object; express in concrete form.

objection /əbˈdʒekʃ(ə)n/ n. **1** expression or feeling of opposition or disapproval. **2** objecting. **3** adverse reason or statement. [Latin: related to OBJECT]

objectionable adj. **1** unpleasant, offensive. **2** open to objection. □ **objectionably** adv.

objective /əbˈdʒektɪv/ —adj. **1** external to the mind; actually existing. **2** dealing with outward things or exhibiting facts uncoloured by feelings or opinions. **3** *Gram.* (of a case or word) in the form appropriate to the object. —n. **1** something sought or aimed at. **2** *Gram.* objective case. □ **objectively** adv. **objectivity** /ˌɒbdʒekˈtɪvɪtɪ/ n. [medieval Latin: related to OBJECT]

object-lesson n. striking practical example of some principle.

objet d'art /ˌɒbʒeɪ ˈdɑː/ n. (pl. **objets d'art** pronunc. same) small decorative object. [French, = object of art]

oblate /ˈɒblet/ adj. *Geom.* (of a spheroid) flattened at the poles. [Latin: related to OB-; cf. PROLATE]

oblation /əʊˈbleɪʃ(ə)n/ n. thing offered to a divine being. [Latin: related to OFFER]

obligate /ˈɒblɪgeɪt/ v. (-ting) bind (a person) legally or morally (*was obligated to attend*). [Latin: related to OBLIGE]

obligation /ˌɒblɪˈgeɪʃ(ə)n/ n. **1** constraining power of a law, duty, contract, etc. **2** duty, task. **3** binding agreement. **4** indebtedness for a service or benefit (*be under an obligation*). [Latin: related to OBLIGE]

obligatory /əˈblɪgətərɪ/ adj. binding. □ **obligatorily** adv. [Latin: related to OBLIGE]

oblige /əˈblaɪdʒ/ v. (-ging) **1** constrain, compel. **2** be binding on. **3** do (a person) a small favour, help. **4** (as **obliged** adj.)

indebted, grateful. □ **much obliged** thank you. [Latin *obligo* bind]

obliging adj. accommodating, helpful. □ **obligingly** adv.

oblique /əˈbliːk/ —adj. **1** slanting; at an angle. **2** not going straight to the point; indirect. **3** *Gram.* (of a case) other than nominative or vocative. —n. oblique stroke (/). □ **obliquely** adv. **obliqueness** n. **obliquity** /əˈblɪkwɪtɪ/ n. [French from Latin]

obliterate /əˈblɪtəˌreɪt/ v. (-ting) blot out, destroy, leave no clear traces of. □ **obliteration** /-ˈreɪʃ(ə)n/ n. [Latin *oblitero* erase, from *litera* letter]

oblivion /əˈblɪvɪən/ n. state of having or being forgotten. [Latin *obliviscor* forget]

oblivious /əˈblɪvɪəs/ adj. unaware or unconscious. □ **obliviously** adv. **obliviousness** n.

oblong /ˈɒblɒŋ/ —adj. rectangular with adjacent sides unequal. —n. oblong figure or object. [Latin *oblongus* longish]

obloquy /ˈɒbləkwɪ/ n. **1** being generally ill spoken of. **2** abuse. [Latin *obloquium* contradiction, from *loquor* speak]

obnoxious /əbˈnɒkʃəs/ adj. offensive, objectionable. □ **obnoxiously** adv. **obnoxiousness** n. [Latin *noxa* injury]

oboe /ˈəʊbəʊ/ n. woodwind double-reed instrument with a piercing plaintive tone. □ **oboist** /ˈəʊbəʊɪst/ n. [French *hautbois* from *haut* high, *bois* wood]

obscene /əbˈsiːn/ adj. **1** offensively indecent. **2** *colloq.* highly offensive. **3** *Law* (of a publication) tending to deprave or corrupt. □ **obscenely** adv. **obscenity** /-ˈsenɪtɪ/ n. (pl. **-ies**). [Latin *obsc(a)enus* abominable]

obscurantism /ˌɒbskjʊəˈræntɪz(ə)m/ n. opposition to knowledge and enlightenment. □ **obscurantist** n. & adj. [Latin *obscurus* dark]

obscure /əbˈskjʊə(r)/ —adj. **1** not clearly expressed or easily understood. **2** unexplained. **3** dark. **4** indistinct. **5** hidden; unnoticed. **6** (of a person) undistinguished, hardly known. —v. (-ring) **1** make obscure or unintelligible. **2** conceal. □ **obscurity** n. [French from Latin]

obsequies /ˈɒbsɪkwɪz/ n.pl. funeral rites. [Latin *obsequiae*]

obsequious /əbˈsiːkwɪəs/ adj. servile, fawning. □ **obsequiously** adv. **obsequiousness** n. [Latin *obsequor* comply with]

observance /əbˈzɜːv(ə)ns/ n. **1** keeping or performing of a law, duty, etc. **2** rite or ceremony.

observant adj. **1** acute in taking notice. **2** attentive in observance. □ **observantly** adv.

observation /ˌɒbzəˈveɪʃ(ə)n/ n. 1 observing or being observed 2 power of perception. 3 remark, comment 4 thing observed by esp. scientific study. □ **observational** adj.

observatory /əbˈzɜːvətəri/ n. (pl. -ies) building for astronomical or other observation.

observe /əbˈzɜːv/ v. (-ving) 1 perceive, become aware of. 2 watch carefully. 3 a follow or keep (rules etc.). b celebrate or perform (an occasion, rite, etc.). 4 remark. 5 take note of scientifically. □ **observable** adj. [Latin servo watch, keep]

observer n. 1 person who observes. 2 interested spectator. 3 person who attends a meeting etc. to note the proceedings but does not participate.

obsess /əbˈses/ v. fill the mind of (a person) continually; preoccupy. □ **obsessive** adj. & n. [Latin obsideo obsess: besiege]

obsession /əbˈseʃ(ə)n/ n. 1 obsessing or being obsessed. 2 persistent idea dominating a person's mind. □ **obsessional** adj. □ **obsessionally** adv.

obsidian /əbˈsɪdɪən/ n. dark glassy rock formed from lava. [Latin from Obsius, discoverer of a similar stone]

obsolescent /ˌɒbsəˈles(ə)nt/ adj. becoming obsolete. □ **obsolescence** n. [Latin soleo be accustomed]

obsolete /ˈɒbsəˌliːt/ adj. no longer used, antiquated.

obstacle /ˈɒbstək(ə)l/ n. thing that obstructs progress. [Latin obsto stand in the way]

obstetrician /ˌɒbstɪˈtrɪʃ(ə)n/ n. specialist in obstetrics.

obstetrics /əbˈstetrɪks/ n.pl. (treated as sing.) branch of medicine and surgery dealing with childbirth. □ **obstetric** adj. [Latin obstetrix midwife, from obsto be present]

obstinate /ˈɒbstɪnət/ adj. 1 stubborn, intractable. 2 firmly continuing in one's action or opinion despite advice. □ **obstinacy** n. **obstinately** adv. [Latin obstino persist]

obstreperous /əbˈstrepərəs/ adj. 1 turbulent, unruly. 2 noisy. □ **obstreperously** adv. **obstreperousness** n. [Latin obstrepo shout at]

obstruct /əbˈstrʌkt/ v. 1 block up; make hard or impossible to pass along or through. 2 prevent or retard the progress of. [Latin obstruo obstruct: block up]

obstruction /əbˈstrʌkʃ(ə)n/ n. 1 obstructing or being obstructed. 2 thing that obstructs, blockage. 3 Sport act of unlawfully obstructing another player.

□ **obstructive** adj. causing or intended to cause an obstruction. □ **obstructively** adv. **obstructiveness** n.

obtain /əbˈteɪn/ v. 1 acquire, secure, have granted to one, get. 2 be in vogue, prevail. □ **obtainable** adj. [Latin teneo hold]

obtrude /əbˈtruːd/ v. (-ding) 1 be or become obtrusive. 2 (often foll. by on, upon) thrust (oneself, a matter, etc.) importunately forward. □ **obtrusion** n. [Latin obtrudo thrust: against]

obtrusive /əbˈtruːsɪv/ adj. 1 unpleasantly noticeable. 2 obtruding oneself. □ **obtrusively** adv. **obtrusiveness** n.

obtuse /əbˈtjuːs/ adj. 1 dull-witted. 2 (of an angle) between 90° and 180°. 3 of blunt form; not sharp-pointed or sharp-edged. □ **obtuseness** n. [Latin obtundo obtus-beat against, blunt]

obverse /ˈɒbvɜːs/ n. 1 counterpart, opposite. 2 side of a coin or medal etc. bearing the head or principal design. 3 front, proper, or top side of a thing. [Latin obverto obvers- turn towards]

obviate /ˈɒbvɪˌeɪt/ v. (-ting) get round or do away with (a need, inconvenience, etc.). [Latin obvio prevent]

obvious /ˈɒbvɪəs/ adj. easily seen, recognized, or understood. □ **obviously** adv. **obviousness** n. [Latin ob viam in the way]

OC abbr. Officer Commanding.

oc- see **ob-**.

ocarina /ˌɒkəˈriːnə/ n. small egg-shaped musical wind-instrument. [Italian oca goose]

occasion /əˈkeɪʒ(ə)n/ n. —n. 1 a special event or happening. b time of this. 2 reason, need. 3 suitable juncture, opportunity. 4 immediate but subordinate cause. —v. cause, esp. incidentally. □ **on occasion** now and then; when the need arises. [Latin occido occas- go down]

occasional /əˈkeɪʒən(ə)l/ adj. 1 happening irregularly and infrequently. 2 made or meant for, or acting on, a special occasion. □ **occasionally** adv.

occasional table n. small table for use as required.

Occident /ˈɒksɪd(ə)nt/ n. poet. or rhet. 1 (prec. by the) West. 2 western Europe. 3 Europe and America as distinct from the Orient. [Latin occideus -entis setting, sunset, west]

occidental /ˌɒksɪˈdent(ə)l/ —adj. 1 of the Occident. 2 western. —n. native of the Occident.

occiput /ˈɒksɪˌpʌt/ n. back of the head. □ **occipital** /-ˈsɪpɪt(ə)l/ adj. [Latin caput head]

occlude /əˈkluːd/ v. (-ding) 1 stop up or close. 2 Chem. absorb and retain (gases). 3 (as **occluded** adj.) Meteorol. (of a

occult

frontal system) formed when a cold front overtakes a warm front, raising warm air from ground level. □ **occlusion** n. [Latin occludo occlus- close up]

occult /ɒˈkʌlt, ˈɒ-/ adj. **1** involving the supernatural; mystical. **2** esoteric. □ **the occult** occult phenomena generally. [Latin occulo occult- hide]

occupant /ˈɒkjʊpənt/ n. person who occupies, esp. lives in, a place etc. □ **occupancy** n. (pl. -ies). [Latin: related to occupy]

occupation /ˌɒkjʊˈpeɪʃ(ə)n/ n. **1** person's employment or profession. **2** pastime. **3** occupying or being occupied. **4** taking or holding of a country etc. by force.

occupational adj. **1** of or connected with one's occupation. **2** (of a disease, hazard, etc.) connected with one's occupation.

occupational therapy n. programme of mental or physical activity to assist recovery from disease or injury.

occupier /ˈɒkjʊpaɪə(r)/ n. person living in a house etc. as its owner or tenant.

occupy /ˈɒkjʊpaɪ/ v. (-ies, -ied) **1** live in; be the tenant of **2** take up or fill (space, time, or a place). **3** hold (a position or office). **4** take military possession of **5** place oneself in (a building etc.) forcibly or without authority as a protest. **6** keep busy or engaged. [Latin occupo seize]

occur /əˈkɜː(r)/ v. (-rr-) **1** come into being as an event or process. **2** exist or be encountered in some place or conditions. **3** (foll. by to) come into the mind of. [Latin occurro befall]

occurrence /əˈkʌrəns/ n. **1** occurring. **2** incident or event.

ocean /ˈəʊʃ(ə)n/ n. **1** large expanse of sea, esp. each of the main areas called the Atlantic, Pacific, Indian, Arctic, and Antarctic Oceans. **2** (often in pl.) colloq. very large expanse or quantity. □ **oceanic** /ˌəʊʃɪˈænɪk/ adj. [Greek ōkeanos]

ocean-going adj. (of a ship) able to cross oceans.

oceanography /ˌəʊʃəˈnɒɡrəfɪ/ n. the study of the oceans. □ **oceanographer** n.

ocelot /ˈɒsɪlɒt/ n. leopard-like cat of S. and Central America. [French from Nahuatl]

ochre /ˈəʊkə(r)/ n. (US **ocher**) **1** earth used as yellow, brown, or red pigment. **2** pale brownish-yellow colour. □ **ochreous** /ˈəʊkrɪəs/ adj. [Greek ōkhra]

o'clock /əˈklɒk/ adv. of the clock (used to specify the hour) (6 o'clock).

Oct. abbr. October.

octa- comb. form (also **oct-** before vowel) eight. [Latin octo, Greek oktō eight]

octagon /ˈɒktəɡən/ n. plane figure with eight sides and angles. □ **octagonal** /-ˈtæɡən(ə)l/ adj. [Greek: related to octa-, -gōnos -angled]

octahedron /ˌɒktəˈhiːdrən/ n. (pl. -s) solid figure contained by eight (esp. triangular) plane faces. □ **octahedral** adj. [Greek]

octane /ˈɒkteɪn/ n. colourless inflammable hydrocarbon occurring in petro [from octa-]

octane number n. (also **octane rating**) figure indicating the antiknock properties of a fuel.

octave /ˈɒktɪv/ n. **1** Mus. **a** interval between (and including) two notes, one having twice or half the frequency of vibration of the other. **b** eight note occupying this interval. **c** each of the two notes at the extremes of this interval. **2** eight-line stanza. [Latin octavus eighth]

octavo /ɒkˈteɪvəʊ/ n. (pl. -s) **1** size of book or page given by folding a sheet of standard size three times to form eight leaves. **2** book or sheet of this size. [Latin: related to octave]

octet /ɒkˈtet/ n. (also **octette**) **1 a** musical composition for eight performers. **b** the performers. **2** group of eight. [Italian or German: related to octa-]

octo- comb. form (also **oct-** before a vowel) eight. [see octa-]

October /ɒkˈtəʊbə(r)/ n. tenth month of the year. [Latin octo eight, originally the 8th month of the Roman year]

octogenarian /ˌɒktəʊdʒɪˈneərɪən/ n. person from 80 to 89 years old. [Latin octogeni 80 each]

octopus /ˈɒktəpəs/ n. (pl. -puses) sea mollusc with eight suckered tentacles [Greek: related to octo-, pous foot]

ocular /ˈɒkjʊlə(r)/ adj. of, for, or by the eyes; visual. [Latin oculus eye]

oculist /ˈɒkjʊlɪst/ n. specialist in the treatment of the eyes.

OD /əʊˈdiː/ slang -n. drug overdose. -v. (OD's, OD'd, OD'ing) take an overdose. [abbreviation]

odd /ɒd/ adj. **1** strange, remarkable, eccentric. **2** casual, occasional (odd jobs; odd moments). **3** not normally considered; unconnected (in some odd corner; picks up odd bargains). **4 a** (of numbers) not integrally divisible by two, e.g. 1, 3, 5. **b** bearing such a number (no parking on odd dates). **5** left over when the rest have been matched or divided into pairs (odd sock). **6** detached from a set or series (odd volumes). **7** (appended to a number, sum, weight, etc.) somewhat

more than (*forty odd*; *forty-odd people*).
8 by which a round number, given sum,
etc., is exceeded (*we have 102 – do you
want the odd 2?*). [Old Norse *oddi* angle, point, third or
odd number]

oddball *n. colloq.* eccentric person.

oddity /'ɒdɪtɪ/ *n.* (*pl.* **-ies**) **1** strange
person, thing, or occurrence. **2** peculiar
trait. **3** strangeness.

odd man out *n.* person or thing differing from the others in a group in some
respect.

oddment *n.* **1** odd article; something left
over. **2** (in *pl.*) miscellaneous articles.

odds *n.pl.* **1** ratio between the amounts
staked by the parties to a bet, based on
the expected probability either way. **2**
balance of probability or advantage (*the
odds are against it*; *the odds are in
your favour*). **3** difference giving an
advantage (*it makes no odds*). □ **at odds**
(often foll. by *with*) in conflict or at
variance. **over the odds** above the normal price etc. [apparently from ODD]

odds and ends *n.pl.* miscellaneous
articles or remnants.

odds-on *n.* state when success is more
likely than failure. —*adj.* (of a chance)
better than even; likely.

ode *n.* lyric poem of exalted style and
tone. [Greek *ōidē* song]

odious /'əʊdɪəs/ *adj.* hateful, repulsive.
□ **odiously** *adv.* **odiousness** *n.*
[related to ODIUM]

odium /'əʊdɪəm/ *n.* widespread dislike
or disapproval of a person or action.
[Latin, = hatred]

odometer /əʊˈdɒmɪtə(r), ɒ-/ *n.* =
MILOMETER. [Greek *hodos* way]

odoriferous /əʊdəˈrɪfərəs/ *adj.* diffusing a (usu. agreeable) odour. [Latin:
related to ODOUR]

odour /'əʊdə(r)/ *n.* (US **odor**) **1** smell or
fragrance. **2** quality or trace (*an odour
of intolerance*). **3** regard, repute (*in bad
odour*). □ **odorous** *adj.* **odourless** *adj.*
[Latin *odor*]

odyssey /'ɒdɪsɪ/ *n.* (*pl.* **-s**) long adventurous journey. [title of the Homeric epic
poem on the adventures of Odysseus]

OECD *abbr.* Organization for Economic
Cooperation and Development.

oedema /ɪˈdiːmə/ *n.* (US **edema**)
accumulation of excess fluid in body
tissues, causing swelling. [Greek
oideō swell]

Oedipus complex /'iːdɪpəs/ *n.* child's,
esp. a boy's, subconscious sexual desire
for the parent of the opposite sex. □
Oedipal *adj.* [Greek *Oidipous*, who
unknowingly married his mother]

o'er /ɔː(r)/ *adv. & prep. poet.* = OVER.
[contraction]

oesophagus /iːˈsɒfəgəs/ *n.* (US **esophagus**) (*pl.* **-gi** /-gaɪ/ or **-guses**) passage
from the mouth to the stomach; gullet.
[Greek]

oestrogen /'iːstrədʒ(ə)n/ *n.* (US **estrogen**) **1** sex hormone developing and
maintaining female characteristics of
the body. **2** this produced artificially for
use in medicine. [Greek *oistros* frenzy,
-GEN]

oestrus /'iːstrəs/ *n.* (also **oestrum**, US
estrus) recurring period of sexual
receptivity in many female mammals.
□ **oestrous** *adj.* [Greek *oistros* frenzy]

œuvre /'ɜːvr/ *n.* works of a creative artist
regarded collectively. [French, = work,
from Latin *opera*]

of /ɒv, əv/ *prep.* expressing: **1** origin or
cause (*paintings of Turner*; *died of
cancer*). **2** material or substance (*house
of cards*; *built of bricks*). **3** belonging or
connection (*thing of the past*; *articles of
clothing*; *head of the business*). **4** identity or close relation (*city of Rome*; *a
pound of apples*; *a fool of a man*). **5**
removal or separation (*north of the city*;
got rid of them; *robbed us of £1000*). **6**
reference or direction (*beware of the
dog*; *suspected of lying*; *very good of
you*; *short of money*). **7** objective relation (*love of music*; *in search of
peace*). **8** partitive, classification, or
inclusion (*no more of that*; *part of the
story*; *this sort of look*). **9** description,
quality, or condition (*the hour of
prayer*; *person of tact*; *girl of ten*; *on the
point of leaving*). **10** US time in relation
to the following hour (*a quarter of
three*). □ **be of** possess, give rise to (*is of
great interest*). **of an evening** (or
morning etc.) *colloq.* **1** on most evenings (or mornings etc.). **2** at some time in
the evenings (or mornings etc.). **of late**
recently. **of old** formerly. [Old English]

OFF. *abbr.* **1** Office. **2** Officer.

off —*adv.* **1** away; a: or to a distance
(*drove off*; *3 miles off*). **2** out of position;
not on, touching, or attached: loose,
separate, gone (*has come off*; *take your
coat off*). **3** so as to be rid of (*sleep it off*). **4**
so as to break continuity or continu-
ance; discontinued, stopped (*turn off the
radio*; *take a day off*; *the game is off*). **5**
not available on a menu etc. (*chips are
off*). **6** to the end; entirely; so as to be
clear (*clear off*; *finish off*; *pay off*). **7**
situated as regards money; supplies,
etc. (*well off*). **8** off stage (*noises off*). **9**
1a from; away, down, or up from (*fell off
the chair*; *took something off the price*).
2 a temporarily
relieved of or abstaining from (*off duty*).
b not on (*off the pitch*). **2 a**

b temporarily not attracted by (*off his food*). **c** not achieving (*off form*). **3** using as a source or means of support (*live off the land*). **4** leading from; not far from (*a street off the Strand*). **5** at a short distance to sea from (*sank off Cape Horn*). —*adj.* **1** far, further (*off side of the wall*). **2** (of a part of a vehicle, animal, or road) right (*the off front wheel*). **3** *Cricket* designating the half of the field (as divided lengthways through the pitch) to which the striker's feet are pointed. **4** *colloq.* **a** annoying, unfair (*that's really off*). **b** somewhat unwell (*feeling a bit off*). —*n.* **1** the off side in cricket. **2** start of a race. □ **off and on** intermittently; now and then. **off the cuff** see CUFF. **off the peg** see REG. [var. of OF]

■ **Usage** The use of *off of* for the preposition *off* (sense 1a), e.g. *picked it up off of the floor*, is non-standard and should be avoided.

offal /ˈɒf(ə)l/ *n.* **1** less valuable edible parts of a carcass, esp. the heart, liver, etc. **2** refuse; scraps. [Dutch *afval*: related to OFF, FALL]

offbeat —*adj.* **1** not coinciding with the beat. **2** eccentric, unconventional. —*n.* any of the unaccented beats in a bar.

off-centre *adj.* & *adv.* not quite centrally placed.

off chance *n.* (prec. by *the*) remote possibility.

off colour *predic. adj.* **1** unwell. **2** *US* somewhat indecent.

offcut *n.* remnant of timber, paper, etc., after cutting.

off-day *n. colloq.* day when one is not at one's best.

offence /əˈfens/ *n.* (*US* **offense**) **1** illegal act; transgression. **2** upsetting of feelings; insult; umbrage (*give offence*; *take offence*). **3** aggressive action. [related to OFFEND]

offend /əˈfend/ *v.* **1** cause offence to; upset. **2** displease, anger. **3** (often foll. by *against*) do wrong; transgress. □ **offending** *adj.* **offendedly** *adv.*

offender *n.* offending *adj.* [Latin *offendo offens-* strike against, displease]

offense *US* var. of OFFENCE.

offensive /əˈfensiv/ —*adj.* **1** causing offence, insulting. **2** disgusting. **3 a** aggressive, attacking. **b** (of a weapon) for attacking. —*n.* aggressive action, attitude, or campaign. □ **offensively** *adv.* **offensiveness** *n.*

7 present itself; occur (*as opportunity offers*). **8** attempt (violence, resistance, etc.). —*n.* **1** expression of readiness to do or give if desired, or to buy or sell. **2** amount offered. **3** proposal (esp. of marriage). **4** bid. □ **on offer** for sale at a certain (esp. reduced) price. [Latin *offero oblat-*]

offering *n.* **1** contribution or gift, esp. of money. **2** thing offered as a sacrifice etc.

offertory /ˈɒfətəri/ *n.* (*pl.* **-ies**) **1** offering of the bread and wine at the Eucharist. **2** collection of money at a religious service. [Church Latin: related to OFFER]

offhand —*adj.* curt or casual in manner. —*adv.* without preparation or thought (*can't say offhand*). □ **offhanded** *adj.* **offhandedly** *adv.* **offhandedness** *n.*

office /ˈɒfɪs/ *n.* **1** room or building used as a place of business, esp. for clerical or administrative work. **2** room or area for a particular business (*ticket office*). **3** local centre of a large business (*our London office*). **4** position with duties attached to it. **5** tenure of an official position (*hold office*). **6** (**Office**) quarters, staff, or collective authority of a Government department etc. (*Foreign Office*). **7** duty, task, function. **8** (usu. in *pl.*) piece of kindness; service (esp. *through the good offices of*). **9** authorized form of worship. [Latin *officium* from *opus* work, *facio fac-* do]

officer /ˈɒfɪsə(r)/ *n.* **1** person holding a position of authority or trust, esp. one with a commission in the army, navy, air force, etc. **2** policeman or policewoman. **3** holder of a post in a society (e.g. the president or secretary).

official /əˈfɪʃ(ə)l/ —*adj.* **1** of an office or its tenure. **2** characteristic of officials and bureaucracy. **3** properly authorized. —*n.* person holding office or engaged in official duties. □ **officialdom** *n.* **officially** *adv.*

officialese /ə,fɪʃəˈliːz/ *n. derog.* language characteristic of official documents.

official secrets *n.pl.* confidential information involving national security.

officiate /əˈfɪʃɪeɪt/ *v.* (**-ting**) **1** act in an official capacity. **2** conduct a religious service. □ **officiation** /-ˈeɪʃ(ə)n/ *n.* **officiator** *n.*

officious /əˈfɪʃəs/ *adj.* **1** domineering. **2** intrusive in correcting etc. □ **officiously** *adv.* **officiousness** *n.*

offing *n.* more distant part of the sea in view. □ **in the offing** not far away; likely to appear or happen soon. [probably from OFF]

off-key *adj.* & *adv.* **1** out of tune. **2** not quite fitting.

off-licence n. **1** shop selling alcoholic drink. **2** licence for this.

offline *Computing* —*adj*. not online. —*adv*. with a delay between the production of data and its processing; not under direct computer control.

offload *v.* get rid of; (esp. something unpleasant) by passing it to someone else.

off-peak *adj.* used or for use at times other than those of greatest demand.

off-piste *adj.* (of skiing) away from prepared ski runs.

offprint *n.* printed copy of an article etc. originally forming part of a larger publication.

offscreen *adj.* & *adv.* **1** beyond the range of a film camera etc.; when not being filmed.

off-season n. time of the year when business etc. is slack.

offset —*n.* **1** side-shoot from a plant serving for propagation. **2** compensation, consideration or amount diminishing or neutralizing the effect of a contrary one. **3** sloping ledge in a wall etc. **4** bend in a pipe etc. to carry it past an obstacle. **5** (often *attrib.*) method of printing in which ink is transferred from a plate or stone to a rubber surface and from there to paper etc. (*offset litho*). —*v.* (**-setting**; *past* and *past part.* **-set**) **1** counterbalance, compensate. **2** print by the offset process.

offshoot n. **1** side-shoot or branch. **2** derivative.

offshore *adj.* **1** at sea some distance from the shore. **2** (of the wind) blowing seawards.

offside —*adj.* (of a player in a field game) in a position where he or she may not play the ball. —*n.* (often *attrib.*) right side of a vehicle, animal, etc.

offspring n. (*pl.* same) **1** person's child, children, or descendants. **2** animal's young or descendants. **3** result. [Old English: see OFF, SPRING]

off-stage *adj.* & *adv.* not on the stage; not visible to the audience.

off-street *adj.* (esp. of parking) other than on a street.

off-the-wall *adj. slang* crazy, absurd, outlandish.

off white *adj.* & *n.* (as *adj.* often hyphenated) white with a grey or yellowish tinge.

oft *adv. archaic* often. [Old English]

often /ˈɒf(ə)n/ *adv.* (**oftener, oftenest**) **1** a frequently; many times. **b** at short intervals. **2** in many instances.

oft-times *adv. archaic* often.

ogee /ˈəʊdʒiː/ n. S-shaped line or moulding. [apparently from OGIVE]

ogive /ˈəʊdʒaɪv/, n. **1** pointed arch. **2** diagonal rib of a vault. [French]

ogle /ˈəʊg(ə)l/ —*v.* (**-ling**) look amorously or lecherously (at). —*n.* amorous or lecherous look. [probably Low German or Dutch]

ogre /ˈəʊgə(r)/ n. (*fem.* **ogress** /-grɪs/) **1** man-eating giant in folklore. **2** terrifying person. □ **ogreish** /ˈəʊgərɪʃ/ *adj.* (also **ogrish**). [French]

oh /əʊ/ *int.* (also **O**) expressing surprise, pain, entreaty, etc. □ **oh** (or **o) for** I wish I had. [var. of O¹]

ohm /əʊm/ n. SI unit of electrical resistance. [Ohm, name of a physicist]

OHMS *abbr.* on Her (or His) Majesty's Service.

oho /əʊˈhəʊ/ *int.* expressing surprise or exultation. [from O¹, HO]

OHP *abbr.* overhead projector.

oi *int.* calling attention or expressing alarm etc. [var. of HOY]

-oid *suffix* forming adjectives and nouns, denoting form or resemblance (*asteroid; rhomboid, thyroid*). [Greek *eidos* form]

oil —*n.* **1** any of various viscous, usu. inflammable liquids insoluble in water (*cooking oil; drill/or oil*). **2** petroleum. **3** (in *comb.*) using oil as fuel (*oil-heater*). **4 a** (usu. in *pl.*) = OIL-PAINT. **b** picture painted in oil-paints. —*v.* **1** apply oil to; lubricate. **2** impregnate or treat with oil (*oiled silk*). □ **oil the wheels** help make things go smoothly. [Latin *oleum* olive oil]

oilcake n. compressed linseed from which the oil has been extracted, used as fodder or manure.

oilcan n. can with a long nozzle for oiling machinery.

oilcloth n. fabric, esp. canvas, waterproofed with oil or another substance.

oil-colour var. of OIL-PAINT.

oiled *adj. slang* drunk.

oilfield n. area yielding mineral oil.

oil-fired *adj.* using oil as fuel.

oil of turpentine n. volatile pungent oil distilled from turpentine, used as a solvent in mixing paints and varnishes, and in medicine.

oil-paint n. (also **oil-colour**) paint made by mixing powdered pigment in oil. □ **oil-painting** n.

oil rig n. structure with equipment for drilling an oil well.

oilskin n. **1** cloth waterproofed with oil. **2 a** garment of this. **b** (in *pl.*) suit of this.

oil slick n. patch of oil, esp. on the sea.

oilstone n. fine-grained flat stone used with oil for sharpening flat tools, e.g. chisels, planes, etc.

oil well n. well from which mineral oil is drawn.

oily *adj.* (**-ier**, **-iest**) **1** of or like oil. **2** covered or soaked with oil. **3** (of a manner etc.) fawning, unctuous, ingratiating. □ **oiliness** *n.*

ointment /'ɔɪntmənt/ *n.* smooth greasy healing or cosmetic preparation for the skin. [Latin *unguo* anoint]

OK /əʊˈkeɪ/ (also **okay**) *colloq.* –*adj.* (often as *int.*) all right; satisfactory. –*adv.* well, satisfactorily. –*n.* (*pl.* **OKs**) approval, sanction. –*v.* (**OK's**, **OK'd**, **OK'ing**) approve, sanction. [originally US: probably abbreviation of *orl* (or *oll*) *korrect*, jocular form of 'all correct']

okapi /əʊˈkɑːpɪ/ *n.* (*pl.* same or **-s**) African giraffe-like mammal but with a shorter neck and striped body. [Mbuba]

okay var. of OK.

okra /ˈəʊkrə/ *n.* tall, orig. African plant with long ridged seed-pods used for food. [West African native name]

-ol *suffix* in the names of alcohols or analogous compounds. (from ALCOHOL and Latin *oleum* oil]

old /əʊld/ *adj.* (**older**, **oldest**) **1 a** advanced in age; far on in the natural period of existence. **b** not young or near its beginning. **2** made long ago. **3** long in use. **4** worn, dilapidated, or shabby from the passage of time. **5** having the characteristics of age (*child has an old face*). **6** practised, inveterate (*old offender*). **7** belonging to the past; lingering on; former (*old times*; *old memories*; *our old house*). **8** dating from far back; long established or known; ancient, primeval (*an old family*; *old friends*, *old as the hills*). **9** (appended to a period of age (*is four years old*; *four-year-old boy*; *a four-year-old*). **10** (of a language) as used in former or earliest times. **11** *colloq.* as a term of affection or casual reference (*good old Charlie*, *old thing*). □ **oldish** *adj.* **oldness** *n.* [Old English]

old age *n.* later part of normal life.

old-age pension *n.* = RETIREMENT PENSION. □ **old-age pensioner** *n.*

Old Bill *n.* *slang* **1** the police. **2** a policeman.

old boy *n.* **1** former male pupil of a school. **2** *colloq.* **a** elderly man. **b** (as a form of address) = OLD MAN.

old boy network *n.* *colloq.* preferment in employment, esp. of fellow ex-pupils of public schools.

old country *n.* (prec. by *the*) native country of colonists etc.

olden *attrib. adj. archaic* old; of old.

old-fashioned *adj.* showing or favouring the tastes of former times.

old girl *n.* **1** former female pupil of a school. **2** *colloq.* **a** elderly woman. **b**

affectionate term of address to a girl or woman.

Old Glory *n.* *US* US national flag.

old gold *adj.* & *n.* (as *adj.* often hyphenated) dull brownish-gold colour.

old guard *n.* original, past, or conservative members of a group.

old hand *n.* person with much experience.

old hat *adj. colloq.* hackneyed.

oldie *n. colloq.* old person or thing.

old lady *n. colloq.* one's mother or wife.

old maid *n.* **1** *derog.* elderly unmarried woman. **2** prim and fussy person.

old man *n. colloq.* **1** one's husband or father. **2** affectionate form of address to a boy or man.

old man's beard *n.* wild clematis, with grey fluffy hairs round the seeds.

old master *n.* **1** great artist of former times, esp. of the 13th–17th c. in Europe. **2** painting by such a painter.

Old Nick *n. colloq.* the Devil.

Old Norse *n.* **1** Germanic language from which the Scandinavian languages are derived. **2** language of Norway and its colonies until the 14th c.

old school *n.* traditional attitudes or people having them.

old school tie *n.* excessive loyalty to traditional values and to former pupils of one's own, esp. public, school.

old soldier *n.* (also **old stager** or **timer**) experienced person.

old style *n.* dating reckoned by the Julian calendar.

Old Testament *n.* part of the Bible containing the scriptures of the Hebrews.

old-time *attrib. adj.* belonging to former times (*old-time dancing*).

old timer var. of OLD SOLDIER.

old wives' tale *n.* unscientific belief.

old woman *n. colloq.* **1** one's wife or mother. **2** fussy or timid man.

Old World *n.* Europe, Asia, and Africa.

old year *n.* year just ended or ending.

oleaginous /ˌəʊlɪˈædʒɪnəs/ *adj.* **1** like or producing oil. **2** oily. [Latin: related to OIL]

oleander /ˌəʊlɪˈændə(r)/ *n.* evergreen flowering Mediterranean shrub. [Latin]

O level *n. hist.* = ORDINARY LEVEL. [abbreviation]

olfactory /ɒlˈfæktərɪ/ *adj.* of the sense of smell (*olfactory nerves*). [Latin *oleo* smell, *facio* make]

oligarch /ˈɒlɪɡɑːk/ *n.* member of an oligarchy. [Greek *oligoi* few]

oligarchy /ˈɒlɪɡɑːkɪ/ *n.* (*pl.* **-ies**) **1** government, or State governed, by a small group of people. **2** members of such a government. □ **oligarchic** /-ˈɡɑːkɪk/ *adj.* **oligarchical** /-ˈɡɑːkɪk(ə)l/ *adj.*

Oligocene /'ɒlɪgəˌsiːn/ —n. the third geological epoch of the Tertiary period. —adj. of this epoch. [Greek *oligos* little, *kainos* new]

olive /'ɒlɪv/ —n. **1** small oval hard-stoned fruit, green when unripe and bluish-black when ripe. **2** tree bearing this. **3** its wood. **4** olive green. —adj. (also **olive-green**) of the complexion) yellowish-brown. [Latin *oliva* from Greek]

olive branch *n.* gesture of reconciliation or peace.

olive green *adj.* & *n.* (as adj. often hyphenated) dull yellowish green.

olive oil *n.* cooking-oil extracted from olives.

olivine /'ɒlɪˌviːn/ *n.* mineral, usu. olive-green, composed of magnesium-iron silicate.

Olympiad /ə'lɪmpɪˌæd/ *n.* **1 a** period of four years between Olympic games, used by the ancient Greeks in dating events. **b** four-yearly celebration of the ancient Olympic Games. **2** celebration of the modern Olympic Games. **3** regular international contest in chess etc. [Greek *Olympias Olympiad-*: related to OLYMPIC]

Olympian /ə'lɪmpɪən/ —adj. **1 a** of Olympus. **b** celestial. **2** (cf. manners etc.) magnificent, condescending, superior. **3** = OLYMPIC. —n. **1** Greek god dwelling on Olympus. **2** person of superhuman ability or calm. **3** competitor in the Olympic games. [from Mt. *Olympus* in Greece, or as OLYMPIC]

Olympic /ə'lɪmpɪk/ —adj. of the Olympic games. —n.pl. (**the Olympics**) Olympic games. [Greek from *Olympia* in S. Greece]

Olympic games *n.pl.* **1** ancient Greek athletic festival held at Olympia every four years. **2** modern international revival of this.

OM *abbr.* Order of Merit.

ombudsman /'ɒmbʊdzmən/ *n.* (*pl.* **-men**) official appointed to investigate complaints against public authorities. [Swedish, = legal representative]

omega /'əʊmɪgə/ *n.* **1** last (24th) letter of the Greek alphabet (Ω, ω). **2** last of a series; final development. [Greek *ō mega* = great O]

omelette /'ɒmlɪt/ *n.* beaten eggs fried and often folded round a savoury filling. [French]

omen /'əʊmen/ —n. **1** event or object portending good or evil. **2** prophetic significance (*of good omen*). —v. (usu. in *passive*) portend. [Latin]

omicron /əʊ'maɪkrɒn, 'ɒmɪ-/ *n.* fifteenth letter of the Greek alphabet (O, o). [Greek *o mikron* = small o]

ominous /'ɒmɪnəs/ *adj.* **1** threatening. **2** of evil omen; inauspicious. □ **ominously** *adv.* [Latin: related to OMEN]

omission /əʊ'mɪʃ(ə)n/ *n.* **1** omitting or being omitted. **2** thing omitted. [Latin: related to OMIT]

omit /əʊ'mɪt/ *v.* (**-tt-**) **1** leave out; not insert or include. **2** leave undone. **3** (foll. by verbal noun or *to* + infin.) fail or neglect. [Latin *omitto omiss-*]

omni- *comb. form* all. [Latin *omnis* all]

omnibus /'ɒmnɪbəs/ —n. **1** *formal* bus. **2** volume containing several literary works previously published separately. —adj. **1** serving several purposes at once. **2** comprising several items. [Latin, = for all]

omnipotent /ɒm'nɪpət(ə)nt/ *adj.* having great or absolute power. □ **omnipotence** /-t(ə)ns/ *n.* [Latin: related to POTENT]

omnipresent /ˌɒmnɪ'prez(ə)nt/ *adj.* present everywhere. □ **omnipresence** *n.* [Latin: related to PRESENT]

omniscient /ɒm'nɪsɪənt/ *adj.* knowing everything or much. □ **omniscience** *n.* [Latin *scio* know]

omnivorous /ɒm'nɪvərəs/ *adj.* **1** feeding on both plant and animal material. **2** reading, observing, etc. everything that comes one's way. □ **omnivore** /'ɒmnɪˌvɔː(r)/ *n.* **omnivorousness** *n.* [Latin *voro* devour]

on —*prep.* **1** (so as to be) supported by, attached to, covering, or enclosing (*sat on a chair; stuck on the wall; rings on her fingers; leaned on his elbow*). **2** carried with; about the person of (*have you a pen on you?*). **3** (of time) exactly at; during (*on 29 May; on the hour; on schedule; closed on Tuesday*). **4** immediately after or before (*I saw them on my return*). **5** as a result of (*on further examination*). **6** (so as to be) having membership etc. of or residence at or in (*is on the board of directors; lives on the continent*). **7** supported, succoured, or fuelled by (*lives on a grant; lives on sandwiches; runs on the sea; lives on to; just by (*house on the main road*). **9** in the direction of, against. **10** so as to threaten; touching or striking (*advanced on Rome; pulled a knife on me; a punch on the nose*). **11** having as an axis or pivot (*turned on his heels*). **12** having as a basis or motive (*works on a ratchet; arrested on suspicion*). **13** having as a standard, confirmation, or guarantee (*had it on good authority; did it on purpose; I promise on my word*). **14** concerning or about (*writes on frogs*). **15** using or engaged with (*is on the pill; here on business*). **16** so as to effect (*walked out on her*). **17** at the expense of (*the drinks are on me; the joke is on him*). **18** added

to (*disaster on disaster; ten pence on a pint of beer*). **19** in a specified manner or state (*on the cheap; on the run*). —*adv.* **1** (so as to be) covering or in contact (*put your boots on*). **2** in the appropriate direction; towards something (*look on*). **3** further forward; in an advanced position or state (*time is getting on*). **4** with continued movement or action (*play on; chase was on*). **5** in operation or activity (*light is on; the party still on?*). **6** due to take place as planned (*is the party still on?*). **7** *colloq.* **a** willing to participate or approve, make a bet, etc. (*you're on*). **b** practicable or acceptable (*that's just not on*). **8** forward (*head on*). **9** on stage. **10** on duty. **11** forward (*head on*). —*adj.* *Cricket* designating the part of the field on the striker's side and in front of the wicket. —*n.* *Cricket* the on side. □ **be on about** *colloq.* discuss, esp. tediously. **be on at** *colloq.* nag or grumble at. **be on to 1** *colloq.* realize the significance or intentions of. **on and off** intermittently; now and then. **on and on** continually; at tedious length. **on time** punctual, punctually. **on to** on to a position on. [Old English]

onanism /ˈəʊnə,nɪz(ə)m/ *n. literary* masturbation. [*Onan*, biblical person]

ONC *abbr.* Ordinary National Certificate.

once /wʌns/ —*adv.* **1** on one occasion only. **2** at some point or period in the past. **3** ever or at all (*if you once forget it*). **4** multiplied by one. —*conj.* as soon as. —*n.* one time or occasion (*just the once*). □ **all at once 1** suddenly. **2** all together. **at once 1** immediately. **2** simultaneously. **for once** on this (or that) occasion, even if at no other. **once again** (or **more**) another time. **once and for all** (or **once for all**) in a final manner, esp. after much hesitation. **once** (or **every one**) **in a while** from time to time. **once or twice** a few times. **once upon a time** at some unspecified time in the past. [originally genitive of ONE]

once-over *n. colloq.* rapid inspection.

oncogene /ˈɒnkə,dʒiːn/ *n.* gene which can transform a cell into a cancer cell. [Greek *ogkos* mass]

oncology /ɒŋˈkɒlədʒɪ/ *n.* the study of tumours. [Greek *ogkos* mass]

oncoming *adj.* approaching from the front.

OND *abbr.* Ordinary National Diploma.

one /wʌn/ —*adj.* **1** single and integral in number. **2** (with a noun implied) a single person or thing of the kind expressed or implied (*one of the best; a nasty one*). **3** particular but undefined, esp. as contrasted with another (*that is one view; one night last week*). **4** only such (*the one man who can do it*). **5** forming a unity (*one and undivided*). **6** identical; the same (*of one opinion*). —*n.* **1 a** lowest cardinal number. **b** thing numbered with it. **2** unity; a unit (*one is half of two; came in ones and twos*). **3** single thing, person, or example (often referring to a noun previously expressed or implied: *the big dog and the small one*). **4** *colloq.* drink (*a quick one; have one on me*). **5** story or joke (*the one about the parrot*). —*pron.* **1** person of a specified kind (*loved ones; like one possessed*). **2** any person, as representing people in general (*one is bound to lose in the end*). **3** I, me. □ **all one** (often foll. by *to*) a matter of indifference. **at one** in agreement. **one and all** everyone. **one by one** singly, successively. **one day 1** on an unspecified day. **2** at some unspecified future date. **one or two** *colloq.* a few [Old English]

■ **Usage** The use of the pronoun *one* to mean 'I' or 'me' (e.g. *one would like to help*) is often regarded as an affectation.

one another *pron.* each the other or others (as a formula of reciprocity: *love one another*).

one-armed bandit *n. colloq.* fruit machine with a long handle.

one-horse *attrib. adj.* **1** using a single horse. **2** *colloq.* small, poorly equipped.

one-horse race *n.* contest in which one competitor is far superior to all the others.

one-liner *n.* short joke or remark in a play, comedy routine, etc.

one-man *attrib. adj.* involving or operated by only one man.

oneness *n.* **1** singleness. **2** uniqueness. **3** agreement. **4** sameness.

one-night stand *n.* **1** single performance of a play etc. in a place. **2** *colloq.* sexual liaison lasting only one night.

one-off —*attrib. adj.* made or done as the only one; not repeated. —*n.* one-off occurrence, achievement, etc.

onerous /ˈəʊnərəs/ *adj.* burdensome. □ **onerousness** *n.* [Latin: related to ONUS]

oneself *pron.* reflexive and emphatic form of *one* (*kill oneself; do it oneself*). □ **be oneself** act in one's normal unconstrained manner.

one-sided *adj.* unfair, partial. □ **one-sidedly** *adv.* **one-sidedness** *n.*

one's money's-worth *n.* good value for one's money.

one-time *attrib. adj.* former.

one-to-one *adj. & adv.* **1** involving or between only two people. **2** with one

one-track mind *n.* mind preoccupied with one subject.

member of one group corresponding to one of another.

one-up *adj. colloq.* having a particular advantage. □ **one-upmanship** *n.*

one-way *adj.* allowing movement, travel, etc., in one direction only.

ongoing *adj.* 1 continuing. 2 in progress.

onion /ˈʌnjən/ *n.* vegetable with an edible bulb of a pungent smell and flavour. □ **oniony** *adj.* [Latin *unio -onis*]

online *Computing* —*adj.* directly connected, so that a computer immediately receives an input from or sends an output to a peripheral process etc.; carried out while so connected or under direct computer control. —*adv.* with the processing of data carried out simultaneously with its production; while connected to a computer; under direct computer control.

onlooker *n.* spectator. □ **onlooking** *adj.*

only /ˈəʊnlɪ/ —*adv.* 1 solely, merely, exclusively; and no one or nothing more besides (*needed six only; is only a child*). 2 no longer ago than (*saw them only yesterday*). 3 not until (*arrives only on Tuesday*). 4 with no better result than (*hurried home only to find her gone*). —*attrib. adj.* 1 existing alone of its or their kind (*their only son*). 2 best or alone worth considering (*the only place to eat*). —*conj. colloq.* except that; but (*I would go, only I feel ill*). [Old English: related to ONE]

only too *adv.* extremely.

o.n.o. *abbr.* or near offer.

onomatopoeia /ˌɒnəmætəˈpiːə/ *n.* formation of a word from a sound associated with what is named (e.g. *cuckoo, sizzle*). □ **onomatopoeic** *adj.* [Greek *onoma* name, *poieō* make]

onrush *n.* onward rush.

onscreen *adj. & adv.* within the range of a film camera etc. when being filmed.

onset *n.* 1 attack. 2 impetuous beginning.

onshore *adj.* 1 on the shore. 2 (of the wind) blowing landwards from the sea.

onside *adj.* (of a player in a field game) not offside.

onslaught /ˈɒnslɔːt/ *n.* fierce attack. [Dutch: related to ON, *slag* blow]

on-street *adj.* (esp. of parking) along a street.

onto *prep.* = on to.

■ **Usage** The form *onto* is still not fully accepted in the way that *into* is, although it is in wide use. It is however useful in distinguishing sense as between *we drove on to the beach* (i.e. in that direction) and *we drove onto the beach* (i.e. in contact with it).

ontology /ɒnˈtɒlədʒɪ/ *n.* branch of metaphysics dealing with the nature of being. □ **ontological** /-təˈlɒdʒɪk(ə)l/ *adj.* **ontologically** /-təˈlɒdʒɪkəlɪ/ *adv.* **ontologist** *n.* [Greek *ont-* being]

onus /ˈəʊnəs/ *n.* (*pl.* **onuses**) burden, duty, responsibility. [Latin]

onward /ˈɒnwəd/ —*adv.* (also **onwards**) 1 forward, advancing. 2 into the future (*from 1985 onwards*). —*adj.* forward, advancing.

onyx /ˈɒnɪks/ *n.* semiprecious variety of agate with coloured layers. [Greek *onux*]

oodles /ˈuːd(ə)lz/ *n.pl. colloq.* very great amount. [origin unknown]

ooh /uː/ *int.* expressing surprise, delight, pain, etc. [natural exclamation]

oolite /ˈəʊəlaɪt/ *n.* granular limestone. □ **oolitic** /-ˈlɪtɪk/ *adj.* [Greek *ōion* egg]

oompah /ˈʊmpɑː/ *n. colloq.* rhythmical sound of deep brass instruments. [imitative]

oomph /ʊmf/ *n. slang* 1 energy, enthusiasm. 2 attractiveness, esp. sex appeal. [origin uncertain]

oops /ʊps/ *int. colloq.* on making an obvious mistake. [natural exclamation]

ooze —*v.* (-*zing*) 1 trickle or leak slowly out. 2 (of a substance) exude fluid. 3 (often foll. by *with*) exude (a feeling) freely (*oozed (with) charm*). —*n.* sluggish flow (*oozed with charm*). [Old English]

ooze[2] *n.* wet mud. □ **oozy** *adj.* [Old English]

op *n. colloq.* operation. [abbreviation]

op. *abbr.* opus.

OP see OB.

opacity /əʊˈpæsɪtɪ/ *n.* opaqueness. [Latin: related to OPAQUE]

opal /ˈəʊp(ə)l/ *n.* semiprecious stone usu. of a milky or bluish colour and sometimes showing changing colours. [Latin]

opalescent /ˌəʊpəˈles(ə)nt/ *adj.* iridescent. □ **opalescence** *n.*

opaline /ˈəʊpəˌlaɪn/ *adj.* opal-like, opalescent.

opaque /əʊˈpeɪk/ —*adj.* (**opaquer, opaquest**) 1 not transmitting light. 2 impenetrable to sight. 3 unintelligible.

4 unintelligent, stupid. □ **opaquely** adv. **opaqueness** n. [Latin opacus shaded]

op art n. colloq. = OPTICAL ART. [abbreviation]

op. cit. abbr. in the work already quoted. [Latin opere citato]

OPEC /ˈəʊpek/ abbr. Organization of Petroleum Exporting Countries.

open /ˈəʊpən/ —adj. 1 not closed, locked, or blocked up; allowing access. 2 unenclosed, unconfined, unobstructed (the open road; open views). 3 a uncovered, bare, exposed (open drain; open wound). b (of a goal etc.) unprotected, undefended. 4 undisguised, public, manifest (open hostilities). 5 expanded, unfolded, or spread out (had the map open on the table). 6 (of a fabric) not close, with gaps. 7 a frank and communicative. b open-minded. 8 a accessible to visitors or customers; ready for business. b (of a meeting) admitting all, not restricted to members etc. 9 (of a race, competition, scholarship, etc.) unrestricted as to who may compete. 10 (foll. by to) a willing to receive (is open to offers). b (of a choice, offer, or opportunity) available (three courses open to us). c vulnerable to, allowing of (open to abuse; open to doubt). 11 (of a return ticket) not restricted as to the day of travel. —v. 1 make or become open or more open. 2 (foll. by into, on to, etc.) (of a door, room, etc.) give access as specified (opened on to a patio). 3 a start, establish, or set going (a business, activity, etc.) (opened a new shop; opened fire). b start (conference opens today). 4 (often foll. by with) start; begin speaking, writing, etc. (show opens with a song; he opened with a joke). 5 ceremonially declare (a building etc.) in use. —n. 1 (prec. by the) a open space, country, or air. b public notice; general attention (esp. into the open). 2 open championship or competition etc. □ **open a person's eyes** enlighten a person. **open out** 1 unfold. 2 develop, expand. 3 become communicative. **open up** 1 unlock (premises). 2 make accessible. 3 reveal; bring to notice. 4 accelerate. 5 begin shooting or sounding. □ **openness** n. [Old English]

open air n. outdoors. □ **open-air** attrib. adj.

open-and-shut adj. straightforward.

open book n. person who is easily understood.

opencast adj. (of a mine or mining) with removal of the surface layers and working from above, not from shafts.

Open College n. college offering training and vocational courses mainly by correspondence.

open day n. day when the public may visit a place normally closed to them.

open-door attrib. adj. open, accessible.

open-ended adj. having no predetermined limit.

opener n. 1 device for opening tins, bottles, etc. 2 colloq. first item on a programme etc.

open-handed adj. generous.

open-hearted adj. frank and kindly.

open-heart surgery n. surgery with the heart exposed and the blood made to bypass it.

open house n. hospitality for all visitors.

opening —n. 1 aperture or gap. 2 opportunity. 3 beginning; initial part. —attrib. adj. initial, first (opening remarks).

opening-time n. time at which public houses may legally open for custom.

open letter n. letter of protest etc. addressed to an individual and published in a newspaper etc.

openly adv. 1 frankly. 2 publicly.

open-minded adj. accessible to new ideas; unprejudiced.

open-mouthed adj. aghast with surprise.

open-plan adj. (of a house, office, etc.) having large undivided rooms.

open prison n. prison with few restraints on prisoners' movements.

open question n. matter on which different views are legitimate.

open sandwich n. sandwich without a top slice of bread.

open sea n. expanse of sea away from land.

open secret n. supposed secret known to many.

open society n. society with freedom of belief.

Open University n. university teaching mainly by broadcasting and correspondence, and open to those without academic qualifications.

open verdict n. verdict affirming that a crime has been committed but not specifying the criminal or (in case of violent death) the cause.

openwork n. pattern with intervening spaces in metal, leather, lace, etc.

opera¹ /ˈɒpərə/ n. 1 a drama set to music for singers and instrumentalists. b this as a genre. 2 opera-house. [Italian from Latin, = labour, work]

opera² pl. of OPUS.

operable /ˈɒpərəb(ə)l/ adj. 1 that can be operated. 2 suitable for treatment by surgical operation. [Latin: related to OPERATE]

opera-glasses *n.pl.* small binoculars for use at the opera or theatre.

opera-house *n.* theatre for operas.

operate /'ɒpəreɪt/ *v.* (-ting) 1 work, control. 2 be in action. function. 3 a perform a surgical operation. b conduct a military etc. action. c be active in business etc. 4 bring about. [Latin *operor* work: related to opus]

operatic /ɒpə'rætɪk/ *adj.* of or like an opera or opera singer (*an operatic voice*). □ **operatically** *adv.*

operatics /ɒpə'rætɪks/ *n.pl.* production and performance of operas.

operating system *n.* basic software that enables the running of a computer program.

operating theatre *n.* room for surgical operations.

operation /ˌɒpə'reɪʃ(ə)n/ *n.* 1 action, scope, or method of working or operating. 2 active process. 3 piece of work, esp. one in a series (*begin operations*). 4 act of surgery on a patient. 5 military manoeuvre. 6 financial transaction. 7 *Math.* subjection of a number etc. to a process affecting its value or form, e.g. multiplication. [Latin: related to OPERATE]

operational *adj.* 1 of or engaged in or used for operations. 2 able or ready to function. □ **operationally** *adv.*

operational research *n.* the application of scientific principles to business etc. management.

operations research *n.* = OPERA-TIONAL RESEARCH.

operative /'ɒpərətɪv/ —*adj.* 1 in operation; having effect. 2 having the main relevance (*'may' is the operative word*). 3 of or by surgery. —*n.* worker, esp. a skilled one. [Latin: related to OPERATE]

operator *n.* 1 person operating a machine etc., esp. connecting lines in a telephone exchange. 2 person engaging in business. 3 *colloq.* person acting in a specified way (*smooth operator*) 4 symbol or function denoting an operation in mathematics, computing, etc.

operculum /ə'pɜːkjʊləm/ *n.* (*pl.* -cula)1 fish's gill-cover. 2 any of various other parts covering or closing an aperture in an animal or plant. [Latin *operio* cover (v.)]

operetta /ˌɒpə'retə/ *n.* 1 light opera. 2 one-act or short opera. [Italian, diminutive of OPERA]

ophidian /əʊ'fɪdɪən/ —*n.* member of a suborder of reptiles including snakes. —*adj.* 1 of this order. 2 snakelike. [Greek *ophis* snake]

ophthalmia /ɒf'θælmɪə/ *n.* inflammation of the eye. [Greek *ophthalmos* eye]

ophthalmic /ɒf'θælmɪk/ *adj.* of or relating to the eye and its diseases.

ophthalmic optician *n.* optician qualified to prescribe as well as dispense spectacles etc.

ophthalmology /ˌɒfθæl'mɒlədʒɪ/ *n.* the study of the eye. □ **ophthalmologist** *n.*

ophthalmoscope /ɒf'θælmə,skəʊp/ *n.* instrument for examining the eye.

opiate /'əʊpɪət/ —*adj.* 1 containing opium. 2 narcotic, soporific. —*n.* 1 drug containing opium, esp. to ease pain or induce sleep. 2 soothing influence. [Latin: related to OPIUM]

opine /əʊ'paɪn/ *v.* (-ning) (often foll. by *that*) *literary* hold or express as an opinion. [Latin *opinor* believe]

opinion /ə'pɪnjən/ *n.* 1 unproven belief. 2 view held as probable. 3 what one thinks about something. 4 piece of professional advice (*low opinion of*). 5 estimation (*a second opinion*). [Latin: related to OPINE]

opinionated /ə'pɪnjə,neɪtɪd/ *adj.* dogmatic in one's opinions.

opinion poll *n.* assessment of public opinion by questioning a representative sample.

opium /'əʊpɪəm/ *n.* drug made from the juice of a certain poppy used esp. as an analgesic and narcotic. [Latin from Greek *opion*]

opossum /ə'pɒsəm/ *n.* 1 tree-living American marsupial. 2 *Austral. & NZ* = POSSUM 2. [Virginian Indian]

opp. *abbr.* opposite.

opponent /ə'pəʊnənt/ *n.* person who opposes. [Latin *oppono opposit-* set against]

opportune /'ɒpə,tjuːn/ *adj.* 1 well-chosen or especially favourable (*opportune moment*). 2 (of an action or event) well-timed. [Latin *opportunus* (of the wind) driving towards the PORT]

opportunism /ˌɒpə'tjuːnɪz(ə)m, 'ɒp-/ *n.* adaptation of one's policy or judgement to circumstances or opportunity, esp. regardless of principle. □ **opportunist** *n.* □ **opportunistic** /-'nɪstɪk/ *adj.* □ **opportunistically** /-'nɪstɪkəlɪ/ *adv.*

opportunity /ˌɒpə'tjuːnɪtɪ/ *n.* (*pl.* -ies) favourable chance or opening offered by circumstances.

opposable /ə'pəʊzəb(ə)l/ *adj.* *Zool.* (of the thumb in primates) capable of facing and touching the other digits on the same hand.

oppose /ə'pəʊz/ *v.* (-sing) 1 set oneself against; resist; argue or compete against. 2 (foll. by *to*) place in opposition or contrast. □ **as opposed to** in contrast with. □ **opposer** *n.* [Latin: related to OPPONENT]

opposite /'ɒpəzɪt/ —adj. 1 facing, on the other side (opposite page; the house opposite). 2 (often foll. by to, from) contrary, diametrically different (opposite opinion). —n. opposite thing, person, or term. —adv. facing, on the other side (lives opposite). —prep. 1 facing (sat opposite me). 2 in a complementary role to (another actor etc.).

opposite number n. person holding an equivalent position in another group etc.

opposite sex n. (prec. by the) either sex in relation to the other.

opposition /ˌɒpə'zɪʃ(ə)n/ n. 1 resistance, antagonism. 2 being hostile or in conflict or disagreement. 3 contrast, antithesis. 4 a group or party of opponents or competitors. b (the Opposition) chief parliamentary party opposed to that in office. 5 act of placing opposite. 6 diametrically opposite position of two celestial bodies. [Latin: related to POSITION]

oppress /ə'pres/ v. 1 keep in subservience. 2 govern or treat cruelly. 3 weigh down (with cares or unhappiness). □ **oppression** n. **oppressor** n. [Latin: related to PRESS¹]

oppressive adj. 1 oppressing. 2 (of weather) close and sultry. □ **oppressively** adv. **oppressiveness** n.

opprobrious /ə'prəʊbrɪəs/ adj. (of language) very scornful; abusive.

opprobrium /ə'prəʊbrɪəm/ n. 1 disgrace. 2 cause of this. [Latin, = infamy, reproach]

oppugn /ə'pjuːn/ v. literary controvert, call in question. [Latin oppugno fight against]

opt v. (usu. foll. by for) make a choice, decide. □ **opt out** (often foll. by of) choose not, to participate (in). [Latin opto choose, wish]

optative /'ɒptətɪv/ Gram. —adj. (esp. of a mood in Greek) expressing a wish. —n. optative mood or form. [Latin: related to OPT]

optic /'ɒptɪk/ adj. of the eye or sight (optic nerve). [Greek optos seen]

optical adj. 1 of sight; visual. 2 of or according to optics. 3 aiding sight. □ **optically** adv.

optical art n. art using contrasting colours to create the illusion of movement.

optical disc see DISC.

optical fibre n. thin glass fibre through which light can be transmitted to carry signals.

optical illusion n. 1 image which deceives the eye. 2 mental misapprehension caused by this.

optician /ɒp'tɪʃ(ə)n/ n. 1 maker, seller, or prescriber of spectacles and contact lenses etc. 2 person trained in the detection and correction of poor eyesight. [medieval Latin: related to OPTIC]

optics n.pl. (treated as sing.) science of light and vision.

optimal /'ɒptɪm(ə)l/ adj. best or most favourable. [Latin optimus best]

optimism /'ɒptɪmɪz(ə)m/ n. 1 inclination to hopefulness and confidence. 2 Philos. belief that this world is as good as it could be or that good must ultimately prevail over evil. □ **optimist** n. **optimistic** /-'mɪstɪk/ adj. **optimistically** /-'mɪstɪkəlɪ/ adv. [Latin optimus best]

optimize /'ɒptɪmaɪz/ v. (also -ise) (-zing or -sing) make the best or most effective use of. □ **optimization** /-'zeɪʃ(ə)n/ n.

optimum /'ɒptɪməm/ —n. (pl. optima) most favourable conditions (for growth etc.). 2 best practical solution. —adj. = OPTIMAL. [Latin, neuter of optimus best]

option /'ɒpʃ(ə)n/ n. 1 a choosing; choice. b thing that is or may be chosen. 2 liberty to choose. 3 right to buy or sell at a specified price within a set time. □ keep (or leave) one's options open not commit oneself. [Latin: related to OPT]

optional adj. not obligatory. □ **optionally** adv.

optional extra n. item costing extra if one chooses to have it.

opulent /'ɒpjʊlənt/ adj. 1 wealthy. 2 luxurious. 3 abundant. □ **opulence** n. [Latin opes wealth]

opus /'əʊpəs/ n. (pl. opuses or opera /'ɒpərə/) 1 musical composition numbered as one of a composer's works (Beethoven, opus 15). 2 any artistic work (cf. MAGNUM OPUS). [Latin, = work]

or¹ conj. 1 introducing an alternative (white or black; take it or leave it; whether or not). 2 introducing an alternative name (the lapwing or peewit). 3 introducing an afterthought (came in laughing - or was it crying?). 4 = or else 1 (run or you'll be late). □ or else 1 otherwise (run, or else you will be late). 2 colloq. expressing a warning or threat (be good or else). [Old English]

or² n. Heraldry gold. [Latin aurum gold]

-or suffix forming nouns denoting esp. an agent (actor, escalator) or condition (error, horror). [Latin]

oracle /'ɒrək(ə)l/ n. 1 a place at which divine advice or prophecy was sought in classical antiquity. b response given. c prophet or prophetess at an oracle. 2 person or thing regarded as a source of wisdom etc. 3 (Oracle) propr. teletext

service provided by Independent Television. □ **oracular** /ɒˈrækjʊlə(r)/ adj. [Latin oraculum from oro speak]

oral /ˈɔːr(ə)l/ —adj. 1 by word of mouth; spoken; not written (oral examination; oral sex). 2 done or taken by the mouth (oral sex; oral contraceptive). —n. colloq. spoken examination. □ **orally** adv. [Latin os oris mouth]

orange /ˈɒrɪndʒ/ —n. 1 a roundish reddish-yellow juicy citrus fruit. b tree bearing this. 2 its colour. —adj. orange-coloured. [Arabic nāranj]

orangeade /ˌɒrɪndʒˈeɪd/ n. orange-flavoured, usu. fizzy, drink.

Orangeman n. member of a political society formed in 1795 to support Protestantism in Ireland. [William of Orange]

orangery /ˈɒrɪndʒərɪ/ n. (pl. -ies) place, esp. a building, where orange-trees are cultivated.

orang-utan /ɔːˌræŋuːˈtæn/ n. (also **orang-outang** /-ˈuːtæŋ/) large reddish-haired long-armed anthropoid ape of the E. Indies. [Malay, = wild man]

oration /ɔːˈreɪʃ(ə)n/ n. formal or ceremonial speech. [Latin oratio discourse, prayer, from oro speak, pray]

orator /ˈɒrətə(r)/ n. 1 person making a formal speech. 2 eloquent public speaker. [Latin: related to ORATION]

oratorio /ˌɒrəˈtɔːrɪəʊ/ n. (pl. -s) semi-dramatic work for orchestra and voices, esp. on a sacred theme. [Church Latin]

oratory /ˈɒrətərɪ/ n. (pl. -ies) 1 art of or skill in public speaking. 2 small private chapel. [French and Latin oro speak, pray] □ **oratorical** /-ˈtɒrɪk(ə)l/ adj. [Latin orbis ring]

orb n. 1 globe surmounted by a cross as part of coronation regalia. 2 sphere, globe. 3 poet. celestial body. 4 poet. eye. [Latin orbis ring]

orbicular /ɔːˈbɪkjʊlə(r)/ adj. formal circular or spherical. [Latin orbiculus diminutive of orbis ring]

orbit /ˈɔːbɪt/ —n. 1 a curved course of a planet, satellite, etc. b one complete passage around a body. 2 range or sphere of action. 3 eye socket. —v. (-t-) 1 move in orbit round. 2 put into orbit. □ **orbiter** n. [Latin orbita circular]

orbital adj. 1 of an orbit or orbits. 2 (of a road) passing round the outside of a town.

orca /ˈɔːkə/ n. any of various cetaceans, esp. the killer whale. [Latin]

Orcadian /ɔːˈkeɪdɪən/ —adj. of Orkney. —n. native of Orkney. [Latin Orcades Orkney Islands]

orch. abbr. 1 orchestrated by. 2 orchestra.

orchard /ˈɔːtʃəd/ n. piece of enclosed land with fruit-trees. [Latin hortus garden]

orchestra /ˈɔːkɪstrə/ n. 1 large group of instrumentalists combining strings, woodwinds, brass, and percussion. 2 (in full orchestra pit) part of a theatre etc. where the orchestra plays, usu. in front of the stage and on a lower level. □ **orchestral** /ˈkestr'əl/ adj. [Greek, = area for the chorus in drama]

orchestrate /ˈɔːkɪstreɪt/ v. (-ting) 1 arrange or compose for orchestral performance. 2 arrange (elements) to achieve a desired result. □ **orches-tration** /-ˈstreɪʃ(ə)n/ n.

orchid /ˈɔːkɪd/ n. any of various plants with brilliant flowers. [Greek orkhis, originally = testicle]

ordain /ɔːˈdeɪn/ v. 1 confer holy orders on. 2 decree, order. [Latin ordino:]

ordeal /ɔːˈdiːl/ n. 1 painful or horrific experience; severe trial. 2 hist. test of an accused person by subjection to severe pain, with survival taken as proof of innocence. [Old English]

order —n. 1 a condition in which every part, unit, etc. is in its right place; tidiness. b specified sequence, succession, etc. (alphabetical order; the order of events). 2 authoritative command, direction, instruction, etc. 3 state of obedience to law, authority, etc. 4 a direction to supply or pay something, b goods etc. to be supplied. 5 social class; sort (talents of a high order; the lower orders). 6 kind; sort or nature of order; (the order of things). 8 taxonomic rank below a class and above a family. 9 religious fraternity with a common rule of life. 10 grade of the Christian ministry. 11 any of the five classical styles of architecture (Doric order). 12 a company of persons distinguished by a particular honour (Order of the Garter). b insignia worn by its members. 13 Eccl. the stated form of divine service (the order of confirmation). 14 system of rules or procedure (at meetings etc.) (point of order). —v. 1 command; bid; prescribe. 2 command or direct (a person) to a specified destination (ordered them home). 3 direct (a waiter, tradesman, etc. to supply (often as ordered adj.) put in order; regulate (an ordered life). 5 (of God, fate, etc.) ordain. □ **in** (or **out** of) **order** 1 in (or not in) the correct or incorrect sequence or for use. 3 **in order that** with the according (or not according) to the rules at a meeting etc. **in order that** with the

Order in Council

intention; so that. **in order to** with the purpose of doing; with a view to. **of** (or **in**) **the order of** approximately. **on order** ordered but not yet received. **to order** as specified by the customer.
[Latin *ordo ordin-* row, command, etc.]

Order in Council *n.* executive order, often approved by Parliament but not debated.

orderly —*adj.* **1** methodically arranged or inclined, tidy. **2** well-behaved. —*n.* (*pl.* **-ies**) **1** male cleaner in a hospital. **2** soldier who carries orders for an officer etc. □ **orderliness** *n.*

orderly room *n.* room in a barracks used for company business.

order of the day *n.* **1** prevailing state of things. **2** principal action, procedure, or programme.

order-paper *n.* written or printed order of the day's proceedings, esp. in Parliament.

ordinal /ˈɔːdɪn(ə)l/ *n.* (in full **ordinal number**) number defining position in a series, e.g. 'first', 'second', 'third', etc. [Latin: related to ORDER]

ordinance /ˈɔːdɪnəns/ *n.* **1** decree. **2** religious rite. [Latin: related to ORDAIN]

ordinand /ˈɔːdɪnænd/ *n.* candidate for ordination. [Latin: related to ORDAIN]

ordinary /ˈɔːdɪnərɪ/ —*adj.* **1** normal, usual. **2** commonplace, unexceptional. —*n.* (*pl.* **-ies**) *RC Ch.* **1** parts of a service that do not vary from day to day. **2** rule or book laying down the order of service. □ **in the ordinary way** in normal circumstances. □ **ordinarily** *adv.* **ordinariness** *n.* [Latin: related to ORDER]

ordinary level *n. hist.* lowest level of the GCE examination.

ordinary seaman *n.* sailor of the lowest rank.

ordinate /ˈɔːdɪnət/ *n. Math.* coordinate measured usu. vertically. [Latin: related to ORDAIN]

ordination /ˌɔːdɪˈneɪʃ(ə)n/ *n.* conferring of holy orders, ordaining.

ordnance /ˈɔːdnəns/ *n.* **1** artillery; military supplies. **2** government service dealing with these. [contraction of ORDINANCE]

Ordnance Survey *n.* official survey of the UK producing detailed maps.

Ordovician /ˌɔːdəˈvɪʃən/ —*adj.* of the second period in the Palaeozoic era. —*n.* this period. [Latin *Ordovices*, an ancient British tribe in N. Wales]

ordure /ˈɔːdjʊə(r)/ *n.* dung. [Latin *horridus*: related to HORRID]

ore /ɔː(r)/ *n.* solid rock or mineral from which metal or other valuable minerals may be extracted. [Old English]

oregano /ˌɒrɪˈgɑːnəʊ/ *n.* dried wild marjoram as seasoning. [Spanish, = ORIGAN]

organ /ˈɔːgən/ *n.* **1 a** musical instrument having pipes supplied with air from bellows and operated by keyboards and pedals. **b** instrument producing similar sounds electronically. **c** harmonium. **2 a** part of an animal or plant body serving a particular function (*vocal organs; digestive organs*). **b** esp. *joc.* penis. **3** medium of communication, esp. a newspaper representing a party or interest. [Greek *organon* tool]

organdie /ˈɔːgəndɪ/ *n.* fine translucent muslin, usu. stiffened. [French]

organ-grinder *n.* player of a barrel-organ.

organic /ɔːˈgænɪk/ *adj.* **1** of or affecting a bodily organ or organs. **2** (of a plant or animal) having organs or an organized physical structure. **3** produced without the use of artificial fertilizers, pesticides, etc. **4** (of a chemical compound etc.) containing carbon. **5 a** structural, inherent. **b** constitutional. **6** organized or systematic (*an organic whole*). □ **organically** *adv.* [Greek: related to ORGAN]

organic chemistry *n.* chemistry of carbon compounds.

organism /ˈɔːgənɪz(ə)m/ *n.* **1** individual plant or animal. **2** living being with interdependent parts. **3** system made up of interdependent parts. [French: related to ORGANIZE]

organist /ˈɔːgənɪst/ *n.* organ-player.

organization /ˌɔːgənaɪˈzeɪʃ(ə)n/ *n.* (also **-isation**) **1** organizing or being organized. **2** organized body, system, or society. □ **organizational** *adj.*

organize /ˈɔːgənaɪz/ *v.* (also **-ise**) (**-zing** or **-sing**) **1 a** give an orderly structure to, systematize. **b** make arrangements for (a person or oneself). **2** initiate, arrange for. **3** (often *absol.*) **a** enlist (a person or group) in a trade union, political party, etc. **b** form (a trade union etc.). **4** (esp. as **organized** *adj.*) make organic; make into living tissue. □ **organizer** *n.* [Latin: related to ORGAN]

organ-loft *n.* gallery for an organ.

organza /ɔːˈgænzə/ *n.* thin stiff transparent silk or synthetic dress fabric. [origin uncertain]

orgasm /ˈɔːgæz(ə)m/ —*n.* climax of sexual excitement. —*v.* have a sexual orgasm. □ **orgasmic** /-ˈgæzmɪk/ *adj.* [Greek, = excitement]

orgy /ˈɔːdʒɪ/ *n.* (*pl.* **-ies**) **1** wild party with indiscriminate sexual activity. **2** excessive indulgence in an activity. □ **orgiastic** /-ˈæstɪk/ *adj.* [Greek *orgia* pl.]

oriel /ˈɔːrɪəl/ n. (in full **oriel window**) projecting window of an upper storey. [French]

orient /ˈɔːrɪənt/ n. (the Orient) countries east of the Mediterranean, esp. E. Asia. —v. **1 a** place or determine the position of with the aid of a compass; find the bearings of. **b** (often foll. by *towards*) direct. **2** place (a building etc.) to face east. **3** turn eastward or in a specified direction. □ **orient oneself** determine how one stands in relation to one's surroundings. [Latin *oriens -entis* rising, sunrise, east]

oriental /ˌɔːrɪˈent(ə)l/ (often **Oriental**) —*adj*. of the East, esp. E. Asia; of the Orient. —*n*. native of the Orient. [Latin: related to ORIENT]

orientate /ˈɔːrɪəntˌeɪt/ v. (also **orient**) = ORIENT v. [apparently from ORIENT]

orientation /ˌɔːrɪənˈteɪʃ(ə)n/ n. **1** orienting or being oriented. **2 a** relative position. **b** person's attitude or adjustment in relation to circumstances. **3** introduction to a subject or situation; briefing. □ **orientational** *adj*.

orienteering /ˌɔːrɪənˈtɪərɪŋ/ n. competitive sport in which runners cross open country with a map, compass, etc. [Swedish]

orifice /ˈɒrɪfɪs/ n. opening, esp. the mouth of a cavity. [Latin *os or-* mouth, *facio* make]

origami /ˌɒrɪˈɡɑːmɪ/ n. art of folding paper into decorative shapes. [Japanese]

origan /ˈɒrɪɡən/ n. (also **origanum** /əˈrɪɡənəm/) wild marjoram. [Latin from Greek]

origin /ˈɒrɪdʒɪn/ n. **1** starting-point; source. **2** (often in *pl.*) ancestry; parentage. **3** *Math*. point from which coordinates are measured. [Latin *origo origin-* from *orior* rise]

original /əˈrɪdʒɪn(ə)l/ —*adj*. **1** existing from the beginning; earliest; innate. **2** inventive; creative; not derivative or imitative. **3** not copied or translated by the artist etc. himself (*in the original Rembrandt*). —*n*. original model, pattern, picture, etc. from which another is copied or translated. □ **originality** /-ˈnælɪtɪ/ n. **originally** *adv*.

original sin n. innate human sinfulness held to be a result of the Fall.

originate /əˈrɪdʒɪˌneɪt/ v. (-ting) **1** cause to begin; initiate. **2** have as an origin; begin. □ **origination** /-ˈneɪʃ(ə)n/ n. **originator** n.

oriole /ˈɔːrɪəʊl/ n. (in full **golden oriole**) bird with black and yellow plumage in the male. [Latin *aurum* gold]

ormolu /ˈɔːməˌluː/ n. **1** (often *attrib.*) gilded bronze; gold-coloured alloy. **2** articles made of or decorated with ormolu. [French *or moulu* gold]

ornament /ˈɔːnəmənt/ —*n*. **1 a** thing used to adorn or decorate. **b** quality or person bringing honour or distinction. **2** decoration, esp. on a building (*tower rich in ornament*). **3** musical embellishment. —*v*. /-ˌment/ adorn; beautify. □ **ornamentation** /-menˈteɪʃ(ə)n/ n. [Latin *orno* adorn]

ornamental /ˌɔːnəˈment(ə)l/ *adj*. serving as an ornament; decorative. □ **ornamentally** *adv*.

ornate /ɔːˈneɪt/ *adj*. **1** elaborately adorned. **2** (of literary style) convoluted; flowery. □ **ornately** *adv*. **ornateness** n. [Latin: related to ORNAMENT]

ornithology /ˌɔːnɪˈθɒlədʒɪ/ n. the study of birds. □ **ornithological** /-θəˈlɒdʒɪk(ə)l/ *adj*. **ornithologist** n. [Greek *ornis ornith-* bird]

orotund /ˈɒrəˌtʌnd/ *adj*. **1** (of the voice) full, round, imposing. **2** (of writing, style, etc.) pompous, pretentious. [Latin *ore rotundo* with rounded mouth]

orphan /ˈɔːf(ə)n/ —*n*. child whose parents are dead. —v. bereave (a child) of its parents. [Latin from Greek, = bereaved]

orphanage n. home for orphans.

orrery /ˈɒrərɪ/ n. (pl. -ies) clockwork model of the solar system. [Earl of *Orrery*]

orris /ˈɒrɪs/ n. **1** a kind of iris. **2** = ORRIS ROOT. [alteration of IRIS]

orris root n. fragrant iris root used in perfumery etc.

ortho- *comb. form* **1** straight. **2** right; correct. [Greek *orthos* straight]

orthodontics /ˌɔːθəˈdɒntɪks/ n.pl. (treated as *sing.*) correction of irregularities in the teeth and jaws. □ **orthodontic** *adj*. **orthodontist** n. [Greek *odous odont-* tooth]

orthodox /ˈɔːθəˌdɒks/ *adj*. **1** holding usual or accepted opinions, esp. on religion, morals, etc. **2** generally approved; conventional (*orthodox medicine*). **3** (also **Orthodox**) (of Judaism) strictly traditional. □ **orthodoxy** n. [Greek *doxa* opinion]

Orthodox Church n. Eastern Church with the Patriarch of Constantinople as its head, and including the national Churches of Russia, Romania, Greece, etc.

orthography /ɔːˈθɒɡrəfɪ/ n. (pl. -ies) spelling (esp. with reference to its correctness). □ **orthographic** /-ˈɡræfɪk/ *adj*. [Greek *orthographia*]

orthopaedics /ˌɔːθəˈpiːdɪks/ n.pl. (US **-pedics**) branch of medicine dealing with the correction of diseased, deformed, or injured bones or

muscles. □ **orthopaedic** *adj*. **orthopaedist** *n*. [Greek *pais paid-* child]

ortolan /ˈɔːtələn/ *n*. European bunting, eaten as a delicacy. [Latin *hortus* garden]

-ory *suffix* **1** forming nouns denoting a place (*dormitory; refectory*). **2** forming adjectives and nouns relating to or involving a verbal action (*accessory; compulsory*). [Latin *-orius, -orium*]

Os *abbr*. **1** old style. **2** ordinary seaman. **3** Ordnance Survey. **4** outsize.

Os *symb*. osmium.

Oscar /ˈɒskə(r)/ *n*. any of the statuettes awarded by the US Academy of Motion Picture Arts and Sciences for excellence in film acting, directing, etc. [man's name]

oscillate /ˈɒsɪleɪt/ *v*. (**-ting**) **1** (cause to) swing to and fro. **2** vacillate; vary between extremes. **3** (of an electric current) undergo high-frequency alternations. □ **oscillation** /-ˈleɪʃ(ə)n/ *n*.

oscillator *n*. [Latin *oscillo* swing]

oscillo- *comb. form* oscillation, esp. of an electric current.

oscilloscope /əˈsɪləˌskəʊp/ *n*. device for viewing oscillations by a display on the screen of a cathode-ray tube.

-ose *suffix* forming adjectives denoting possession of a quality (*grandiose; verbose*). [Latin *-osus*]

osier /ˈəʊzɪə(r)/ *n*. **1** willow used in basketwork. **2** shoot of this. [French]

-osis *suffix* denoting a process or condition (*apotheosis; metamorphosis*), esp. a pathological state (*neurosis; thrombosis*). [Latin or Greek]

-osity *suffix* forming nouns from adjectives in *-ose* and *-ous* (*verbosity; curiosity*). [Latin *-ositas*]

osmium /ˈɒzmɪəm/ *n*. heavy hard bluish-white metallic element. [Greek *osmē* smell]

osmosis /ɒzˈməʊsɪs/ *n*. **1** passage of a solvent through a semi-permeable partition into another solution. **2** process by which something is acquired by absorption. □ **osmotic** /-ˈmɒtɪk/ *adj*. [Greek *ōsmos* push]

osprey /ˈɒspreɪ/ *n*. (*pl*. **-s**) large bird of prey feeding on fish. [Latin *ossifraga* from *os* bone, *frango* break]

osseous /ˈɒsɪəs/ *adj*. **1** of bone. **2** bony. [Latin *os* oss- bone]

ossicle /ˈɒsɪk(ə)l/ *n*. small bone or piece of bonelike substance. [Latin diminutive: related to OSSEOUS]

ossify /ˈɒsɪfaɪ/ *v*. (**-ies, -ied**) **1** turn into bone; harden. **2** make or become rigid, callous, or unprogressive. □ **ossification** /-ˈkeɪʃ(ə)n/ *n*. [Latin: related to OSSEOUS]

ostensible /ɒˈstensɪb(ə)l/ *adj*. concealing the real; professed. □ **ostensibly** *adv*. [Latin *ostendo ostens-* show]

ostensive /ɒˈstensɪv/ *adj*. directly showing.

ostentation /ˌɒstenˈteɪʃ(ə)n/ *n*. **1** pretentious display of wealth etc. **2** showing off. □ **ostentatious** *adj*. **ostentatiously** *adv*.

osteo- *comb. form* bone. [Greek *osteon*]

osteoarthritis /ˌɒstɪəʊɑːˈθraɪtɪs/ *n*. degenerative disease of joint cartilage. □ **osteoarthritic** /-ˈθrɪtɪk/ *adj*.

osteopathy /ˌɒstɪˈɒpəθɪ/ *n*. treatment of disease through the manipulation of bones. □ **osteopath** /ˈɒstɪəˌpæθ/ *n*.

osteoporosis /ˌɒstɪəʊpəˈrəʊsɪs/ *n*. condition of brittle bones caused esp. by hormonal changes or deficiency of calcium or vitamin D.

ostler /ˈɒslə(r)/ *n. hist.* stableman at an inn. [related to HOSTEL]

ostracize /ˈɒstrəˌsaɪz/ *v*. (also **-ise**) (**-zing** or **-sing**) exclude from society; refuse to associate with. □ **ostracism** /-sɪz(ə)m/ *n*. [Greek (*ostrakon* potsherd, on which a vote was recorded in ancient Athens to expel a powerful or unpopular citizen)]

ostrich /ˈɒstrɪtʃ/ *n*. **1** large African swift-running flightless bird. **2** person who refuses to acknowledge an awkward truth. [Latin *avis* bird, *struthio* (from Greek) ostrich]

OT *abbr*. Old Testament.

other /ˈʌðə(r)/ *-adj*. **1** not the same as one or some already mentioned or implied; separate in identity or distinct in kind (*other people; use other means*). **2 a** further; additional (*a few other examples*). **b** second of two (*open your other eye*). **3** (prec. by *the*) only remaining (*must be in the other pocket; where are the other two?*). **4** (foll. by *than*) apart from. *–n*. or *pron*. other person or thing. (*some others have come; give me one other; where are the others?*). □ **other than 1** except (*never speaks to me other than to insult me; has no friends other than me*). **2** differently; not (*cannot do other than laugh; never appears other than happy*). [Old English]

■ **Usage** In sense 2 of *other than*, *otherwise* is standard except in less formal use.

other day *n*. (also **other night**) (prec. by *the*) a few days (or nights) ago.

other half *n. colloq.* one's wife or husband.

otherwise *-adv*. **1** or else; in different circumstances (*hurry, otherwise we'll be late*). **2** in other respects (*is otherwise very suitable*). **3** in a different way

(*could not have acted otherwise*). **4** as an alternative (*otherwise known as Jack*). □ *adj.* (*predic*). different (*the matter is quite otherwise*). [Old English: related to WISE¹]

other woman *n.* (prec. by *the*) married man's mistress.

other-worldly *adj.* **1** of another world. **2** dreamily distracted from mundane life.

otiose /ˈəʊtɪəʊs/ *adj.* serving no practical purpose; not required. [Latin *otium* leisure]

OTT *abbr. colloq.* over-the-top.

otter /ˈɒtə(r)/ *n.* **1** aquatic fish-eating mammal with webbed feet and thick brown fur. **2** its fur. [Old English]

Ottoman /ˈɒtəmən/ —*adj.* **1** of the dynasty of Osman (or Othman) I or the empire ruled by his descendants. **2** Turkish. —*n.* (*pl.* **-s**) **1** Turk of the Ottoman period. **2** (**ottoman**) upholstered seat without back or arms, sometimes a box with a padded top. [French from Arabic]

OU *abbr.* **1** Open University **2** Oxford University.

oubliette /ˌuːblɪˈet/ *n.* secret dungeon with a trapdoor entrance. [French *oublier* forget]

ouch *int.* expressing sharp or sudden pain. [imitative]

ought /ɔːt/ *v.aux.* (as present and past, the only form now in use) **1** expressing duty or rightness (*we ought to be thankful; it ought to have been done long ago*). **2** expressing advisability (*you ought to see a dentist*). **3** probability (*it ought to rain soon*). □ **ought not** negative form of *ought* (*he ought not to have stolen it*). [Old English, past of OWE]

Ouija /ˈwiːdʒə/ *n.* (in full **Ouija board**) *propr.* board marked with letters or signs and used with a movable pointer to try to obtain messages at a seance. [French *oui* + German *ja*, yes]

ounce *n.* **1** unit of weight, ¹⁄₁₆ lb or approx. 28 g. **2** very small quantity. [Latin *uncia* twelfth part of a pound or a foot]

our *poss. pron.* **1** of or belonging to us or ourselves (*our children's future*). **2** *colloq.* indicating a relative, friend, etc. of the speaker (*our Barry works there; our friend here*). [Old English]

Our Father *n.* prayer beginning with these words (Matt. 6:9-13).

Our Lady *n.* Virgin Mary.

Our Lord *n.* Christ.

ours *poss. pron.* the one or ones belonging to or associated with us (*it is ours; ours are best; a friend of ours*).

ourself *pron. archaic* = MYSELF as used by a sovereign etc.

ourselves *pron.* **1 a** *emphat.* form of WE or US (*we did it ourselves*). **b** *refl.* form of US (*we are pleased with ourselves*). **2** in our normal state of body or mind (*not quite ourselves today*). □ **be ourselves** see ONESELF. **by ourselves** see *by oneself*.

-ous *suffix* **1** forming adjectives meaning 'abounding in, characterized by, of the nature of' (*envious; glorious; mountainous; poisonous*). **2** *Chem.* denoting a state of lower valence than -ic (*ferrous; sulphurous*). [Anglo-French *-ous* from Latin *-osus*]

ousel *var.* of OUZEL.

oust *v.* drive out or expel, esp. by seizing the place of. [Latin *obsto* oppose]

out —*adv.* **1** away from or not in or at a place etc. (*keep him out; get out; tide is out*). **2** indicating: **a** dispersal away from a centre etc. (*share out*). **b** coming or bringing into the open (*call out; will look it out for you*). **c** need for attentiveness (*watch out; listen out*). **3** not in one's house, office etc. (*tell them I'm out*). **4** to or at an end, completely (*tired out; die out; fight it out; my luck was out; typed it out*). **5** (of a fire, candle, etc.) not burning. **6** in error (*was 3% out*). **7** *colloq.* unconscious (*is out cold*). **8** (of a limb etc.) dislocated (*put his arm out*). **9** (of a political party etc.) not in office. **10** (of workers) on strike. **11** (of a flower) open. **12** (of a secret) revealed. **13** (of a book, record, etc.) published, on sale. **15** (of a star) visible after dark. **16** no longer in fashion (*turn-ups are out*). **17** (of a batsman etc.) dismissed from batting. **18** not worth considering (*that idea is out*). **19** (prec. by *superl.*) *colloq.* known to exist (*the best game out*). **20** (of a mark etc.) removed (*washed the stain out*). —*prep.* out of (*looked out the window*). —*n.* way of escape. —*v.* come or go out; *colloq.* (*murder will out*). □ **out for** intent on, determined to get. **out of 1** from within. **2** not within. **3** from among. **4** beyond the range of (*out of reach*). **5** so as to be without, lacking (*was swindled out of his money; out of sugar*). **6** from (*get money out of him*). **7** because of (*asked out of curiosity*). **8** by the use of (*what did you make it out of?*). **out of bounds** see BOUND². **out of date** see DATE¹. **out of order** see ORDER. **out of pocket** see POCKET. **out of the question** see QUESTION. **out of sorts** see SORT. **out of this world** see WORLD. **out of the way** see WAY. **out to** determined to. [Old English]

■ **Usage** The use of *out* as a preposition, e.g. *he walked out the room*, is nonstandard. *Out of* should be used.

out- *prefix* in senses 1 so as to surpass or exceed (*outdo*). **2** external, separate (*outline*). **3** out of; away from; outward (*outgrowth*).

outage /'aʊtɪdʒ/ *n.* period during which a power-supply etc. is not operating.

out and about *adj.* active outdoors (esp. after an illness etc.).

out and out —*adj.* thorough; complete. —*adv.* thoroughly.

outback *n.* remote inland areas of Australia.

outbalance /aʊt'bæləns/ *v.* (**-cing**) outweigh.

outbid /aʊt'bɪd/ *v.* (**-bidding**; *past* and *past part.* **-bid**) bid higher than.

outboard motor *n.* portable engine attached to the outside of a boat.

outbreak *n.* sudden eruption of anger, war, disease, fire, etc.

outbuilding *n.* shed, barn, etc. detached from a main building.

outburst *n.* **1** verbal explosion of anger etc. **2** bursting out (*outburst of steam*).

outcast —*n.* person rejected by family or society. —*adj.* rejected; homeless.

outclass /aʊt'klɑːs/ *v.* surpass in quality.

outcome *n.* result.

outcrop *n.* **1 a** emergence of a stratum etc. at a surface. **b** stratum etc. emerging. **2** noticeable manifestation.

outcry *n.* (*pl.* **-ies**) strong public protest.

outdated /aʊt'deɪtɪd/ *adj.* out of date; obsolete.

outdistance /aʊt'dɪst(ə)ns/ *v.* (**-cing**) leave (a competitor) behind completely.

outdo /aʊt'duː/ *v.* (**-doing**; *3rd sing. present* **-does**; *past* **-did**; *past part.* **-done**) exceed, excel, surpass.

outdoor *attrib. adj.* **1** done, existing, or used out of doors. **2** fond of the open air (*an outdoor type*).

outdoors /aʊt'dɔːz/ —*adv.* in or into the open air. —*n.* the open air.

outer *adj.* **1** outside; external (*pierced the outer layer*). **2** farther from the centre or the inside. □ **outermost** *adj.*

outer space *n.* universe beyond the earth's atmosphere.

outface /aʊt'feɪs/ *v.* (**-cing**) disconcert by staring or by a display of confidence.

outfall *n.* outlet of a river, drain, etc.

outfield *n.* outer part of a cricket or baseball pitch. □ **outfielder** *n.*

outfit *n.* **1** set of clothes or equipment. **2** *colloq.* group of people regarded as an organization.

outfitter *n.* supplier of clothing.

outflank /aʊt'flæŋk/ *v.* **1** extend beyond the flank of (an enemy). **2** outmanoeuvre, outwit.

outflow *n.* **1** outward flow. **2** amount that flows out.

outfox /aʊt'fɒks/ *v.* outwit.

outgoing —*adj.* **1** friendly. **2** retiring from office. **3** going out. —*n.* (in *pl.*) expenditure.

outgrow /aʊt'grəʊ/ *v.* (*past* **-grew**; *past part.* **-grown**) **1** grow too big for. **2** leave behind (a childish habit etc.). **3** grow faster or taller than.

outgrowth *n.* **1** offshoot. **2** natural product or development.

outhouse *n.* small building adjoining or apart from a house.

outing *n.* pleasure trip, excursion.

outlandish /aʊt'lændɪʃ/ *adj.* bizarre, strange. □ **outlandishly** *adv.* **outlandishness** *n.* [Old English, from *outland* foreign country]

outlast /aʊt'lɑːst/ *v.* last longer than.

outlaw —*n.* **1** fugitive from the law. **2** *hist.* person deprived of the protection of the law. —*v.* **1** declare (a person) an outlaw. **2** make illegal; proscribe.

outlay *n.* expenditure.

outlet *n.* **1** means of exit or escape. **2** means of expressing feelings. **3 a** market for goods. **b** shop (*retail outlet*).

outline —*n.* **1** rough draft. **2** summary. **3** sketch consisting of only contour lines. **4** (in *sing.* or *pl.*) **a** lines enclosing or indicating an object. **b** contour. **c** external boundary. **5** (in *pl.*) main features or principles. —*v.* (**-ning**) **1** draw or describe in outline. **2** mark the outline of.

outlive /aʊt'lɪv/ *v.* (**-ving**) **1** live longer than (a person). **2** live beyond (a period or date).

outlook *n.* **1** prospect, view. **2** mental attitude.

outlying *adj.* far from a centre; remote.

outmanoeuvre /aʊtmə'nuːvə(r)/ *v.* (**-ring**) secure an advantage over by skilful manoeuvring.

outmatch /aʊt'mætʃ/ *v.* be more than a match for.

outmoded /aʊt'məʊdɪd/ *adj.* **1** outdated. **2** out of fashion.

outnumber /aʊt'nʌmbə(r)/ *v.* exceed in number.

out of doors *adj.* & *adv.* in or into the open air.

out of it *predic. adj.* **1** (of a person) not included; forlorn. **2** *colloq.* unconscious, dazed.

outpace /aʊt'peɪs/ *v.* (**-cing**) **1** go faster than. **2** outdo in a contest.

outpatient *n.* non-resident hospital patient.

outplacement n. assistance in finding a new job after redundancy.

outpost n. 1 detachment posted at a distance from an army. 2 distant branch or settlement (*outpost of empire*).

outpouring n. (usu. in pl.) copious expression of emotion.

output –n. 1 amount produced (by a machine, worker, etc.). 2 electrical power etc. delivered by an apparatus. 3 printout, results, etc. from a computer. 4 place where energy, information, etc. leaves a system. –v. (-**ti-**; past and past part. **-put** or **-putted**) (of a computer) supply (results etc.).

outrage –n. 1 extreme violation of others' rights, sentiments, etc. 2 gross offence or indignity. 3 fierce resentment. –v. (**-ging**) 1 subject to outrage. 2 commit an outrage against. 3 shock and anger. [French *outrer* exceed, from Latin *ultra* beyond]

outrageous /aʊtˈreɪdʒəs/ adj. 1 immoderate. 2 shocking. 3 immoral offensive. □ **outrageously** adv.

outrank /aʊtˈræŋk/ v. be superior in rank to.

outré /ˈuːtreɪ/ adj. eccentric. unconventional. [French, past part of *outrer*: see OUTRAGE]

outrider n. mounted guard or motor cyclist riding ahead of a procession etc.

outrigger n. 1 spar or framework projecting over the side of a ship. racing boat, or canoe to give stability. 2 boat fitted with this.

outright –adv. 1 altogether, entirely. 2 not gradually. 3 without reservation, openly. –adj. 1 downright, complete. 2 undisputed (*outright winner*).

outrun /aʊtˈrʌn/ v. (**-nn-**; past **-ran**; past part. **-run**) 1 run faster or farther than. 2 go beyond (a point or limit).

outsell /aʊtˈsɛl/ v. (past and past part. **-sold**) 1 sell more than. 2 be sold in greater quantities than.

outset n. 1 at (or from) the **outset** from the beginning.

outshine /aʊtˈʃaɪn/ v. (-**ning**, past and past part. **-shone**) 1 shine brighter than. 2 surpass in excellence etc.

outside –n. /aʊtˈsaɪd, ˈaʊtsaɪd/ 1 external side or surface; outer parts. 2 external appearance; outward aspect. 3 position on the outer side (*gate opens from the outside*). –adj. /ˈaʊtsaɪd/ 1 a of, on, or nearer the outside; outer. b not in the main building (*outside toilet*). 2 not belonging to a particular group or organization (*outside help*). 3 (of a chance, estimate etc.) remote; very unlikely. 4 (of an estimate etc.) the greatest or highest possible (*the outside price*). 5 (of a player in football etc.) positioned

nearest to the edge of the field (*outside-left*). –adv. /aʊtˈsaɪd/ 1 on or to the outside. 2 in or to the open air. 3 not within, enclosed, or included. 4 slang not in prison. –prep. /aʊtˈsaɪd/ 1 not in; to or at the exterior of. 2 external to, not included in, beyond the limits of. □ **at the outside** (of an estimate etc.) at the most. **from the outside from an object-ive or impartial standpoint.

outside broadcast n. one not made in a studio.

outside interest n. hobby etc. not connected with one's work.

outsider /aʊtˈsaɪdə(r)/ n. 1 non-member of some group, organization, profession, etc. 2 competitor thought to have little chance.

outside world n. society outside the confines of an institution etc.

outsize adj. unusually large.

outskirts n.pl. outer area of a town etc.

outsmart /aʊtˈsmɑːt/ v. outwit, be cleverer than.

outspoken /aʊtˈspəʊkən/ adj. saying openly what one thinks; frank. □ **outspokenly** adv. **outspokenness** n.

outspread /aʊtˈsprɛd/ –adj. spread out; expanded. –v. spread out; expand.

outstanding /aʊtˈstændɪŋ/ adj. 1 conspicuous because of excellence. 2 a (of a debt) not yet settled. b still to be dealt with (*work outstanding*). □ **outstandingly** adv.

outstation n. remote branch or outpost.

outstay /aʊtˈsteɪ/ v. stay longer than (one's welcome etc.).

outstretched /aʊtˈstrɛtʃt/ adj. stretched out.

outstrip /aʊtˈstrɪp/ v. (**-pp-**) 1 go faster than. 2 surpass, esp. competitively.

out-take n. film or tape sequence rejected in editing.

out-tray n. tray for outgoing documents etc.

outvote /aʊtˈvəʊt/ v. defeat by a majority of votes.

outward /ˈaʊtwəd/ –adj. 1 situated on or directed towards the outside. 2 going out. 3 bodily, external, apparent. –adv. (also **outwards**) in an outward direction; towards the outside. [Old English related to OUT, -WARD]

outward bound adj. going away from home.

outwardness n. external existence; objectivity.

outwards var. of OUTWARD adv.

outweigh /aʊtˈweɪ/ v. exceed in weight, value, importance, or influence.

outwit /aʊtˈwɪt/ v. (-**tt-**) be too clever for; overcome by greater ingenuity.

outwork n. **1** advanced or detached part of a fortification. **2** work done off the premises of the firm etc. which supplies it. □ **outworker** n. (in sense 2).

ouzel /ˈuːz(ə)l/ n. (also **ousel**) **1** (in full **ring ouzel**) white-breasted thrush. **2** (in full **water ouzel**) diving bird; dipper. [Old English; = blackbird]

ouzo /ˈuːzəʊ/ n. (pl. **-s**) Greek aniseed-flavoured spirit. [Greek]

ova pl. of OVUM.

oval /ˈəʊv(ə)l/ —adj. **1** egg-shaped, ellipsoidal. **2** having the outline of an egg, elliptical. —n. **1** egg-shaped or elliptical closed curve. **2** thing with an oval outline. [Latin: related to OVUM]

ovary /ˈəʊvəri/ n. (pl. **-ies**) **1** each of the female reproductive organs in which ova are produced. **2** hollow base of the carpel of a flower. □ **ovarian** /əˈveəriən/ adj.

ovation /əʊˈveɪʃ(ə)n/ n. enthusiastic reception, esp. applause. [Latin ovo exult]

oven /ˈʌv(ə)n/ n. enclosed compartment for heating or cooking food etc. [Old English]

ovenproof adj. suitable for use in an oven; heat-resistant.

oven-ready adj. (of food) prepared before sale for immediate cooking in the oven.

ovenware n. dishes for cooking food in the oven.

over —adv. expressing movement, position, or state above or beyond something stated or implied: **1** outward and downward from a brink or from any erect position (knocked me over). **2** so as to cover or touch a whole surface (paint it over). **3** so as to produce a fold or reverse position (bend it over; turn it over). **4 a** across a street or other space (cross over; came over from France). **b** for a visit etc. (invited them over). **5** with transference or change from one hand, part, etc., to another (went over to the enemy; swapped them over). **6** with motion above something (climb over, fly over, boil over). **7** from beginning to end, with repetition or detailed consideration (think it over; did it six times over). **8** in excess, in addition, besides (left over). **9** for or until a later time (hold it over). **10** at an end; settled; completely finished (crisis is over; it's over between us; get it over with). **11** (in full **over to you**) (as int.) (in radio conversations etc.) it is your turn to speak. **12** umpire's call to change ends in cricket. —prep. **1** above, in, or to a position higher than. **2** out and down from; down from the edge of (fell over the cliff). **3** so as to cover or across (hat over his eyes). **4** above and across; so as to

clear; on or to the other side of (flew over Scotland; bridge over the Avon; look over the wall). **5** concerning; while occupied with (laughed over it; fell asleep over a book). **6** in superiority of; superior to; in charge of (victory over them; reign over two kingdoms). **b** in preference to. **7 a** throughout (travelled over most of Africa). **b** so as to deal with completely (went over the plans). **8 a** for or through the duration of (stay over Monday night; over the year's). **b** during the course of (did it over the weekend). **9** beyond; more than (bids of over £50; is he over 18?). **10** transmitted by (heard it over the radio). **11** in comparison with (gained 20% over last year). **12** recovered from (am over my cold; got over it in time). —n. **1** sequence of six balls in cricket bowled from one end of the pitch. **2** play resulting from this. —adj. (see also OVER-). **1** upper, outer. **2** superior. **3** extra. □ **over again** once again, again from the beginning. **over against** in contrast with. **over all** taken as a whole. **over and above** in addition to; not to mention. **over and over** repeatedly. **over one's head** see HEAD. **over the hill** see HILL. **over the moon** see MOON. **over the way** (in a street etc.) facing or opposite. [Old English]

over- prefix **1** excessively. **2** upper, outer. **3** = OVER in various senses (overshadow). **4** completely (overawe, overjoyed).

over-abundance /ˌəʊvərəˈbʌnd(ə)ns/ n. excessive quantity. □ **over-abundant** adj.

overact /ˌəʊvərˈækt/ v. act (a role) in an exaggerated manner.

over-active /ˌəʊvərˈæktɪv/ adj. excessively active.

overall —attrib. adj. /ˈəʊvərɔːl/ **1** total, inclusive of all (overall cost). **2** taking everything into account, general (over all improvement). —adv. /ˌəʊvərˈɔːl/ **1** including everything (cost £50 overall). **2** on the whole, generally (did well overall). —n. /ˈəʊvərɔːl/ **1** protective outer garment. **2** (in pl.) protective outer trousers or suit.

overambitious /ˌəʊvəræmˈbɪʃəs/ adj. excessively ambitious.

over-anxious /ˌəʊvərˈæŋkʃəs/ adj. excessively anxious.

overarm adj. & adv. with the hand above the shoulder (bowl overarm; overarm service).

overate past of OVEREAT.

overawe /ˌəʊvərˈɔː/ v. (-wing) overcome with awe.

overbalance /ˌəʊvəˈbæləns/ v. (-cing) **1** lose balance and fall. **2** cause to do this.

overbear /ˌəʊvəˈbeə(r)/ v. (past bore; past part. -borne) 1 (as overbearing adj.) a domineering, bullying. b overpowering. 2 bear down by weight, force, or emotion. 3 repress by power or authority.

overbid – v. (-dd-; past and past part. -bid) make a higher bid than. –n. /ˈəʊvəbɪd/ bid that is higher than another, or higher than is justified or pretentious.

overblown /ˌəʊvəˈbləʊn/ adj. 1 inflated or pretentious. 2 (of a flower) past its prime.

overboard adv. from a ship into the water (fall overboard). □ **go overboard** colloq. 1 be highly enthusiastic. 2 behave immoderately.

overbook /ˌəʊvəˈbʊk/ v. (also absol.) make too many bookings for (an aircraft, hotel, etc.).

overbore past of OVERBEAR.

overborne past part. of OVERBEAR.

overburden /ˌəʊvəˈbɜːd(ə)n/ v. burden (a person, thing, etc.) to excess.

overcame past of OVERCOME.

overcast /ˈəʊvəkɑːst/ adj. 1 (of the sky) covered with cloud. 2 (in sewing) edged with stitching to prevent fraying.

overcautious /ˌəʊvəˈkɔːʃəs/ adj. excessively cautious.

overcharge /ˌəʊvəˈtʃɑːdʒ/ v. (-ging) 1 charge too high a price to (a person). 2 put too much charge into (a battery, gun, etc.). 3 put excessive detail into (a description, picture, etc.)

overcoat n. warm outdoor coat.

overcome /ˌəʊvəˈkʌm/ v. (-ming; past -came; past part. -come) 1 prevail over, master; be victorious. 2 (usu. as overcome adj.) a make faint (overcome by smoke). b (usu. foll. by with, by) make weak or helpless (overcome with grief).

overcompensate /ˌəʊvəˈkɒmpənseɪt/ v. (-ting) 1 (usu. foll. by for) compensate excessively. 2 strive exaggeratedly to make amends etc.

overconfident /ˌəʊvəˈkɒnfɪd(ə)nt/ adj. excessively confident.

overcook /ˌəʊvəˈkʊk/ v. cook too much or for too long.

overcrowd /ˌəʊvəˈkraʊd/ v. (usu. as overcrowded adj.) fill beyond what is usual or comfortable. □ **overcrowding** n.

overdevelop /ˌəʊvədɪˈveləp/ v. (-p-) 1 develop too much 2 Photog. treat with developer for too long.

overdo /ˌəʊvəˈduː/ v. (-does; past -did; past part. -done) 1 carry to excess, go too far. 2 (esp. as overdone adj.) overcook. □ **overdo it** (or **things**) colloq. exhaust oneself.

overdose n. excessive dose of a drug etc.

overdraft n. 1 overdrawing of a bank account. 2 amount by which an account is overdrawn.

overdraw /ˌəʊvəˈdrɔː/ v. (past -drew; past part. -drawn) 1 draw more from (a bank account) than the amount credited. 2 (as overdrawn adj.) having overdrawn one's account.

overdress /ˌəʊvəˈdres/ v. dress with too much formality.

overdrive n. 1 mechanism in a vehicle providing a gear above top gear for economy at high speeds. 2 state of high activity.

overdue /ˌəʊvəˈdjuː/ adj. past the due time for payment, arrival, return, etc.

overeager /ˌəʊvərˈiːgə(r)/ adj. excessively eager.

overeat /ˌəʊvərˈiːt/ v. (past -ate; past part. -eaten) eat too much.

overemphasize /ˌəʊvərˈemfəsaɪz/ v. (also -ise) (-zing or -sing) give too much emphasis to.

overenthusiasm /ˌəʊvərɪnˈθjuːzɪæz(ə)m/ n. excessive enthusiasm. □ **overenthusiastic** /-ˈæstɪk/ adj. **overenthusiastically** /-ˈæstɪkəlɪ/ adv.

overestimate –v. /ˌəʊvərˈestɪmeɪt/ (-ting) form too high an estimate of. –n. /ˌəʊvərˈestɪmət/ too high an estimate. □ **overestimation** /-ˈmeɪʃ(ə)n/ n.

overexcite /ˌəʊvərɪkˈsaɪt/ v. (-ting) excite excessively. □ **overexcitement** n.

overexert /ˌəʊvərɪgˈzɜːt/ v. exert too much. □ **overexertion** /-ɪgˈzɜːʃ(ə)n/ n.

overexpose /ˌəʊvərɪkˈspəʊz/ v. (-sing) 1 expose too much to the public. 2 expose (film) too long. □ **overexposure** n.

overfeed /ˌəʊvəˈfiːd/ v. (past and past part. -fed) feed excessively.

overfish /ˌəʊvəˈfɪʃ/ v. deplete (a stream etc.) by too much fishing.

overflow –v. /ˌəʊvəˈfləʊ/ 1 flow over (the brim etc.) 2 a (of a receptacle etc.) be so full that the contents overflow. b (of contents) overflow a container. 3 (of a crowd etc.) extend beyond the limits of (a room etc.). 4 flood (a surface or area). 5 (of kindness, a harvest, etc.) be very abundant. –n. /ˈəʊvəfləʊ/ 1 what overflows or is superfluous. 2 outlet for excess water etc.

overfly /ˌəʊvəˈflaɪ/ v. (-flies; past -flew; past part. -flown) fly over or beyond (a place or territory).

overfond /ˌəʊvəˈfɒnd/ adj. (often foll. by of) having too great an affection or liking for (overfond of chocolate, overfond parent).

overfull /ˌəʊvəˈfʊl/ *adj.* filled excessively.

overground *adj.* 1 raised above the ground. 2 not underground.

overgrown /ˌəʊvəˈgrəʊn/ *adj.* 1 grown too big. 2 wild; covered with weeds etc. □ **overgrowth** *n.*

overhang –*v.* /ˌəʊvəˈhæŋ/ (*past* and *past part.* **-hung**) project or hang over. –*n.* /ˈəʊvəˌhæŋ/ 1 overhanging. 2 overhanging part or amount.

overhaul –*v.* /ˌəʊvəˈhɔːl/ 1 thoroughly examine the condition of and repair if necessary. 2 overtake. –*n.* /ˈəʊvəˌhɔːl/ thorough examination, with repairs if necessary.

overhead –*adv.* /ˌəʊvəˈhed/ 1 above head height. 2 in the sky. –*adj.* /ˈəʊvəˌhed/ placed overhead. –*n.* /ˈəʊvəˌhed/ (in *pl.*) routine administrative and maintenance expenses of a business.

overhead projector *n.* projector for producing an enlarged image of a transparency.

overhear /ˌəʊvəˈhɪər/ *v.* (*past* and *past part.* **-heard**) (also *absol.*) hear unintentionally or as an eavesdropper.

overheat /ˌəʊvəˈhiːt/ *v.* 1 make or become too hot. 2 cause inflation (in) by placing excessive pressure on resources at a time of expanding demand. 3 (as **overheated** *adj.*) overexcited.

overindulge /ˌəʊvərɪnˈdʌldʒ/ *v.* (**-ging**) indulge to excess. □ **overindulgence** *n.* **overindulgent** *adj.*

overjoyed /ˌəʊvəˈdʒɔɪd/ *adj.* filled with great joy.

overkill *n.* 1 excess of capacity to kill or destroy. 2 excess.

overland –*v.* /ˌəʊvəˈlænd, -ˈlænd/ *adj.* & *adv.* /ˈəʊvəˌlænd/ 1 by land. 2 not by sea.

overlap –*v.* /ˌəʊvəˈlæp/ (**-pp-**) 1 (cause to) partly cover and extend beyond (*don't overlap them*). 2 (of two things) be placed so that one overlaps the other (*overlapping tiles*). 3 partly coincide. –*n.* /ˈəʊvəˌlæp/ 1 overlapping. 2 overlapping part or amount.

overleaf /ˈəʊvəˌliːf/ *adv.* on the other side of the leaf of a book.

overlie /ˌəʊvəˈlaɪ/ *v.* (**-lying**; *past* **-lay**; *past part.* **-lain**) 1 lie on top of. 2 smother (a child etc.) thus.

overload –*v.* /ˌəʊvəˈləʊd/ 1 load excessively (with baggage, work, etc.). 2 put too great a demand on (an electrical circuit etc.). –*n.* /ˈəʊvəˌləʊd/ excessive quantity or demand.

over-long /ˌəʊvəˈlɒŋ/ *adj.* & *adv.* too long.

overlook /ˌəʊvəˈlʊk/ *v.* 1 fail to notice; tolerate. 2 have a view of from above. 3 supervise.

overlord *n.* supreme lord.

overly *adv.* excessively; too.

overman /ˌəʊvəˈmæn/ *v.* (**-nn-**) provide with too large a crew, staff, etc.

over-much /ˌəʊvəˈmʌtʃ/ –*adv.* to too great an extent. –*adj.* excessive.

overnight /ˌəʊvəˈnaɪt/ –*adv.* 1 for a night. 2 during the night. 3 instantly, suddenly. –*adj.* 1 done or for use etc. overnight. 2 instant (*overnight success*).

over-particular /ˌəʊvəpəˈtɪkjʊlə(r)/ *adj.* excessively particular or fussy.

overpass *n.* road or railway line that passes over another by means of a bridge.

overpay /ˌəʊvəˈpeɪ/ *v.* (*past* and *past part.* **-paid**) pay too highly or too much. □ **overpayment** *n.*

overplay /ˌəʊvəˈpleɪ/ *v.* give undue importance to; overemphasize. □ **overplay one's hand** act on an unduly optimistic estimation of one's chances.

overpopulated /ˌəʊvəˈpɒpjʊˌleɪtɪd/ *adj.* having too large a population. □ **overpopulation** /-ˈleɪʃ(ə)n/ *n.*

overpower /ˌəʊvəˈpaʊə(r)/ *v.* 1 subdue, conquer. 2 (esp. as **overpowering** *adj.*) be too intense or overwhelming for (*overpowering smell*). □ **overpoweringly** *adv.*

overprice /ˌəʊvəˈpraɪs/ *v.* (**-cing**) price too highly.

overprint –*v.* /ˌəʊvəˈprɪnt/ print over (a surface already printed). –*n.* /ˈəʊvəˌprɪnt/ words etc. overprinted.

overproduce /ˌəʊvəprəˈdjuːs/ *v.* (**-cing**) 1 (often *absol.*) produce more of (a commodity) than is wanted. 2 to produce (a play, recording, etc.) to an excessive degree. □ **overproduction** /-ˈdʌkʃ(ə)n/ *n.*

overprotective /ˌəʊvəprəˈtektɪv/ *adj.* excessively protective.

overqualified /ˌəʊvəˈkwɒlɪˌfaɪd/ *adj.* too highly qualified for a particular job etc.

overrate /ˌəʊvəˈreɪt/ *v.* (**-ting**) 1 assess or value too highly. 2 (as **overrated** *adj.*) not as good as it is said to be.

overreach /ˌəʊvəˈriːtʃ/ *v.* outwit, cheat. □ **overreach oneself** fail by attempting too much.

overreact /ˌəʊvərɪˈækt/ *v.* respond more forcibly than is justified. □ **overreaction** *n.*

override –*v.* /ˌəʊvəˈraɪd/ (**-ding**; *past* **-rode**; *past part.* **-ridden**) 1 (often as **overriding** *adj.*) have priority over

(*overriding consideration*.) **2 a** intervene and make ineffective. **b** interrupt
the action of (an automatic device), esp.
to take manual control. —*n.* **1** suspension of an automatic function. **2**
device for this.

overrider *n.* each of a pair of projecting
pieces on the bumper of a car.

overripe /ˌəʊvəˈraɪp/ *adj.* excessively
ripe.

overrule /ˌəʊvəˈruːl/ *v.* (**-ling**) **1** set
aside (a decision etc.) by superior authority. **2** reject a proposal of (a person)
in this way.

overrun /ˌəʊvəˈrʌn/ *v.* (**-nn-**; *past* **-ran**;
past part. **-run**) **1** swarm or spread over.
2 conquer (a territory) by force. **3** (usu.
absol.) exceed (an allotted time).

overseas —*adv.* /ˌəʊvəˈsiːz/ across the
sea; abroad. —*attrib. adj.* /ˈəʊvəˌsiːz/ of
places across the sea; foreign.

oversee /ˌəʊvəˈsiː/ *v.* (**-sees**; *past* **-saw**;
past. part. **-seen**) officially supervise
(workers etc.); superintend. □ **overseer** *n.*

over-sensitive /ˌəʊvəˈsɛnsɪtɪv/ *adj.*
excessively sensitive; easily hurt or
quick to react. □ **over-sensitiveness** *n.*
over-sensitivity /ˈtɪvɪtɪ/ *n.*

oversew *v.* (*past part.* **-sewn** or **-sewed**)
sew (two edges) with stitches passing
over the join.

oversexed /ˌəʊvəˈsɛkst/ *adj.* having
unusually strong sexual desires.

overshadow /ˌəʊvəˈʃædəʊ/ *v.* **1** appear
much more prominent or important
than. **2** cast into the shade.

overshoe *n.* outer protective shoe worn
over an ordinary one.

overshoot /ˌəʊvəˈʃuːt/ *v.* (*past and past
part.* **-shot**) **1** pass or send beyond (a
target or limit). **2** fly beyond or taxi too
far along (the runway) when landing or
taking off. □ **overshoot the mark** go
beyond what is intended or proper.

oversight *n.* **1** failure to do or notice
something. **2** inadvertent mistake. **3**
supervision.

oversimplify /ˌəʊvəˈsɪmplɪfaɪ/ *v.* (**-ies,
-ied**) (also *absol.*) distort (a problem
etc.) by stating it in too simple terms. □
oversimplification /-fɪˈkeɪʃ(ə)n/ *n.*

oversize *adj.* (also **-sized**) of greater
than the usual size.

oversleep /ˌəʊvəˈsliːp/ *v.* (*past and past
part.* **-slept**) sleep beyond the intended
time of waking.

overspecialize /ˌəʊvəˈspɛʃəlaɪz/ *v.*
(also **-ise**) (**-zing** or **-sing**) concentrate
too much on one aspect or area. □
overspecialization /-ˈzeɪʃ(ə)n/ *n.*

overspend /ˌəʊvəˈspɛnd/ *v.* (*past and
past part.* **-spent**) spend too much or
beyond one's means.

overspill *n.* **1** what is spilt over or
overflows. **2** surplus population moving
to a new area.

overspread /ˌəʊvəˈsprɛd/ *v.* (*past and
past part.* **-spread**) **1** cover the surface
of. **2** (as **overspread** *adj.*) (usu. foll. by
with) covered.

overstate /ˌəʊvəˈsteɪt/ *v.* (**-ting**) **1** state
too strongly. **2** exaggerate. □ **overstate-
ment** *n.*

overstay /ˌəʊvəˈsteɪ/ *v.* stay longer than
(one's welcome etc.).

oversteer —*n.* /ˈəʊvəˌstɪə(r)/ tendency
of a vehicle to turn more sharply than
was intended. —*v.* /ˌəʊvəˈstɪə(r)/ (of a
vehicle) exhibit oversteer.

overstep /ˌəʊvəˈstɛp/ *v.* (**-pp-**) pass beyond (a permitted or acceptable limit). □
overstep the mark violate conventional behaviour etc.

overstock /ˌəʊvəˈstɒk/ *v.* stock excessively.

overstrain /ˌəʊvəˈstreɪn/ *v.* strain too
much.

overstretch /ˌəʊvəˈstrɛtʃ/ *v.* **1** stretch
too much. **2** (esp. as **overstretched** *adj.*)
make excessive demands on (resources,
a person, etc.).

overstrung *adj.* **1** /ˌəʊvəˈstrʌŋ/ (of a
person, nerves, etc.) too highly strung. **2**
/ˈəʊvəˌstrʌŋ/ (of a piano) with strings in
sets crossing each other obliquely.

overstuffed /ˌəʊvəˈstʌft/ *adj.* **1** (of
furniture) made soft and comfortable
by thick upholstery. **2** stuffed too full.

oversubscribe /ˌəʊvəsəbˈskraɪb/ *v.*
(**-bing**) (usu. as **oversubscribed** *adj.*)
subscribe for more than the amount
available of (shares, tickets, places,
etc.).

overt /əʊˈvɜːt/ *adj.* done openly; unconcealed. □ **overtly** *adv.* [French, past
part. of *ouvrir* open]

overtake /ˌəʊvəˈteɪk/ *v.* (**-king**; *past
-took; *past part.* **-taken**) **1** (also *absol.*)
catch up with and pass while travelling
in the same direction. **2** (of misfortune
etc.) come suddenly upon.

overtax /ˌəʊvəˈtæks/ *v.* **1** make excessive demands on. **2** tax too heavily.

over-the-top *adj. colloq.* excessive.

overthrow —*v.* /ˌəʊvəˈθrəʊ/ **1** remove
forcibly from power. **2** conquer, overcome. —*n.* /ˈəʊvəˌθrəʊ/ defeat, downfall.

overtime —*n.* /ˈəʊvəˌtaɪm/ **1** time wo-ked in addition
to regular hours. **2** payment for this.
—*adv.* in addition to regular hours.

overtone *n.* **1** *Mus.* any of the tones
above the lowest in a harmonic series. **2**
subtle extra quality or implication.

overture /ˈəʊvəˌtjʊə(r)/ *n.* **1** orchestral
piece opening an opera etc. **2** composition in this style. **3** (usu. in *pl.*) **a** opening

of negotiations. **b** formal proposal or offer. [French: related to OVERT]

overturn /əʊvəˈtɜːn/ v. **1** over down or over. **2** reverse; overthrow.

overuse – v. /ˌəʊvəˈjuːz/ use too much. – n. /ˌəʊvəˈjuːs/ excessive use.

overview n. general survey.

overweening /əʊvəˈwiːnɪŋ/ adj. arrogant, presumptuous.

overweight – adj. /ˌəʊvəˈweɪt/ above an allowed or suitable weight. – n. /ˈəʊvəweɪt/ excess weight; preponderance.

overwhelm /ˌəʊvəˈwelm/ v. **1** overpower with emotion or a burden. **2** overcome by force of numbers. **3** bury or drown beneath a huge mass.

overwhelming adj. **1** too great to resist or overcome (*an overwhelming desire to laugh*). **2** by a great number (*the overwhelming majority*). □ **overwhelmingly** adv.

overwork /ˌəʊvəˈwɜːk/ – v. **1** (cause to) work too hard. **2** weary or exhaust with too much work. **3** (esp. as **overworked** adj.) make excessive use of (*an overworked phrase*). – n. excessive work.

overwrought /ˌəʊvəˈrɔːt/ adj. **1** overexcited, nervous, distraught. **2** too elaborate.

ovi- comb. form egg, ovum. [from OVUM]

oviduct /ˈəʊvɪdʌkt/ n. tube through which an ovum passes from the ovary.

oviform /ˈəʊvɪfɔːm/ adj. egg-shaped.

ovine /ˈəʊvaɪn/ adj. of or like sheep. [Latin *ovis* sheep]

oviparous /əʊˈvɪpərəs/ adj. producing young from eggs hatching after leaving the body. [from OVUM, Latin -*parus* bearing]

ovoid /ˈəʊvɔɪd/ adj. (of a solid) egg-shaped. [related to OVUM]

ovulate /ˈɒvjʊleɪt/ v. (-**ting**) produce ova or ovules, or discharge them from the ovary. □ **ovulation** /-ˈleɪʃ(ə)n/ n. [related to OVULE]

ovule /ˈɒvjuːl/ n. structure that contains the germ cell in a female plant. [related to OVUM]

ovum /ˈəʊvəm/ n. (pl. **ova**) female egg-cell from which young develop after fertilization. [Latin, = egg]

ow int. expressing sudden pain. [natural exclamation]

owe /əʊ/ v. (**owing**) **1 a** be under obligation (to a person etc.) to pay or repay (money, gratitude, etc.). **b** (usu. foll. by *for*) be in debt. **2** have a duty to render (*owe allegiance*). **3** (usu. foll. by *to*) be

indebted to a person or thing for (*we owe our success to the weather*). [Old English]

owing /ˈəʊɪŋ/ predic. adj. **1** owed; yet to be paid. **2** (foll. by *to*) **a** caused by. **b** (as prep.) because of.

■ **Usage** The use of *owing to* as a preposition meaning 'because of' is entirely acceptable (e.g. *couldn't come owing to the snow*), unlike this use of *due to*.

owl n. **1** nocturnal bird of prey with large eyes and a hooked beak. **2** solemn or wise-looking person. □ **owlish** adj. [Old English]

owlet n. small or young owl.

own /əʊn/ – adj. **1** (prec. by possessive) **1 a** belonging to oneself or itself; not another's (*saw it with my own eyes*). **b** individual, peculiar, particular (*has its own charm*). **2** used to emphasize identity rather than possession (*cooks his own meals*). **3** (absol.) private property (*is it your own?*). – v. **1** have as property; possess. **2** admit as valid, true, etc. **3** acknowledge paternity, authorship, or possession of. □ **come into one's own 1** receive one's due. **2** achieve recognition. **get one's own back** get revenge. **hold one's own** maintain one's position. **of one's own** belonging to oneself. **on one's own 1** alone, independent. **2** independently, without help. **own up** (often foll. by *to*) confess frankly. □ **-owned** adj. (in comb.). [Old English]

own brand n. (often *attrib.*) goods manufactured specially for a retailer and bearing the retailer's name.

owner n. person who owns something. □ **ownership** n.

owner-occupier n. person who owns and occupies a house.

own goal n. **1** goal scored by mistake against the scorer's own side. **2** act etc. that has the unintended effect of harming one's own interests.

owt n. colloq. or dial. anything. [var. of AUGHT]

ox n. (pl. **oxen**) **1** large usu. horned ruminant used for draught, milk, and meat. **2** castrated male of a domesticated species of cattle. [Old English]

oxalic acid /ɒkˈsælɪk/ n. very poisonous and sour acid found in sorrel and rhubarb leaves. [Greek *oxalis* wood sorrel]

oxbow n. loop formed by a horseshoe bend in a river.

Oxbridge n. (also *attrib.*) Oxford and Cambridge universities regarded together, esp. in contrast to newer ones. [portmanteau word]

oxen pl. of OX.

ox-eye daisy n. daisy with white petals and a yellow centre.

Oxf. abbr. Oxford.

Oxfam abbr. Oxford Committee for Famine Relief.

Oxford blue /ˈɒksfəd/ adj. & n. (as adj. often hyphenated) a dark blue, often with a purple tinge.

oxhide n. 1 hide of an ox. 2 leather from this.

oxidation /ˌɒksɪˈdeɪʃ(ə)n/ n. process of oxidizing. [French: related to OXIDE]

oxide /ˈɒksaɪd/ n. binary compound of oxygen. [French: related to OXYGEN]

oxidize /ˈɒksɪdaɪz/ v. (also -ise) (-zing or -sing) 1 combine with oxygen. 2 make or become rusty. 3 coat (metal) with oxide. □ **oxidization** /-ˈzeɪʃ(ə)n/ n.

Oxon abbr. (esp. in degree titles) of Oxford University. [Latin Oxoniensis: related to OXONIAN]

Oxonian /ɒkˈsəʊnɪən/ —n. 1 member of Oxford University. 2 native or inhabitant of Oxford. [Oxonia Latinized name of Oxenford]

oxtail n. tail of an ox, often used in making soup.

oxyacetylene /ˌɒksɪəˈsetɪliːn/ adj. of or using a mixture of oxygen and acetylene, esp. in cutting or welding metals.

oxygen /ˈɒksɪdʒ(ə)n/ n. tasteless odourless gaseous element essential to plant and animal life. [Greek oxus sharp, -GEN (because it was thought to be present in all acids)]

oxygenate /ˈɒksɪdʒəˌneɪt/ v. (-ting) supply, treat, or mix with oxygen; oxidize.

oxygen tent n. tentlike enclosure supplying a patient w. th air rich in oxygen.

oxymoron /ˌɒksɪˈmɔːrɒn/ n. figure of speech in which a pparently contradictory terms appear in conjunction (e.g. faith unfaithful kept him falsely true). [Greek, = pointedly foolish, from oxus sharp, mōros dull]

oyez /əʊˈjes/ int. (also oyes) uttered, usu. three times, by a public crier or a court officer to command attention. [Anglo-French, = hear!, from Latin audio]

oyster —n. 1 bivalve mollusc, esp. an edible kind, sometimes producing a pearl. 2 symbol of all one desires (the world is my oyster) —adj. oyster-white. [Greek ostreon]

oyster-catcher n. wading sea bird.

oyster white adj. & n. (as adj. often hyphenated) greyish white.

oz abbr. ounce(s). [Italian onza ounce]

ozone /ˈəʊzəʊn/ n. 1 Chem. unstable form of oxygen with three atoms in a molecule, having a pungent odour. 2 colloq. a invigorating air at the seaside etc. b exhilarating influence. [Greek ozō smell (v.)]

ozone-friendly adj. not containing chemicals destructive to the ozone layer.

ozone layer n. layer of ozone in the stratosphere that absorbs most of the sun's ultraviolet radiation.

P

P¹ /piː/ n. (also **p**) (pl. **Ps** or **P's**) sixteenth letter of the alphabet.

P² abbr. (also **P.**) 1 (on road signs) parking. 2 Chess pawn. 3 (also ℗) proprietary.

P³ symb. phosphorus.

p abbr. (also **p.**) 1 penny, pence. 2 page. 3 piano (softly).

PA abbr. 1 personal assistant. 2 public address (system).

Pa symb. protactinium.

pa /pɑː/ n. colloq. father. [abbreviation of PAPA]

p.a. abbr. per annum.

pabulum /ˈpæbjʊləm/ n. food, esp. for the mind. [Latin]

pace¹ —n. **1 a** a single step in walking or running. **b** distance covered in this. **2** speed in walking or running. **3** rate of movement or progression. **4** way of walking or running; gait (ambling pace). —v. (**-cing**) **1 a** walk slowly and evenly (pace up and down). **b** (of a horse) amble. **2** traverse by pacing. **3** set the pace for (a rider, runner, etc.). **4** (foll. by out) measure by pacing. □ **keep pace** (often foll. by with) advance at an equal rate (to). **put a person etc. through his** (or **her**) **paces** test a person's qualities in action etc. **set the pace** determine the speed; lead. [French pas from Latin passus]

pace² /ˈpɑːtʃeɪ, ˈpeɪsɪ/ prep. (in stating a contrary opinion) with due respect to (the person named). [Latin, ablative of pax peace]

pace bowler n. Cricket fast bowler.

pacemaker n. **1** competitor who sets the pace in a race. **2** natural or artificial device for stimulating the heart muscle.

pace-setter n. **1** leader. **2** = PACEMAKER 1.

pachyderm /ˈpækɪˌdɜːm/ n. thick-skinned mammal, esp. an elephant or rhinoceros. □ **pachydermatous** /ˌ-ˈdɜːmətəs/ adj. [Greek pakhus thick, derma skin]

pacific /pəˈsɪfɪk/ —adj. **1** peaceful; tranquil. **2** (**Pacific**) of or adjoining the Pacific. —n. (**the Pacific**) ocean between America to the east and Asia to the west. [Latin pax pacis peace]

pacifier /ˈpæsɪˌfaɪə(r)/ n. **1** person or thing that pacifies. **2** US baby's dummy.

pacifism /ˈpæsɪˌfɪz(ə)m/ n. belief that war and violence are morally unjustifiable. □ **pacifist** n. & adj.

pacify /ˈpæsɪˌfaɪ/ v. (**-ies, -ied**) **1** appease (a person, anger, etc.). **2** bring (a country etc.) to a state of peace. □ **pacification** /-fɪˈkeɪʃ(ə)n/ n. **pacificatory** /-ˈfɪkətəri/ adj.

pack¹ —n. **1 a** a collection of things wrapped up or tied together for carrying. **b** = BACKPACK. **2** set of packaged items. **3** usu. derog. lot or set (pack of lies; pack of thieves). **4** set of playing cards. **5** group of hounds, wild animals, etc. **6** organized group of Cub Scouts or Brownies. **7** Rugby team's forwards. **8** = FACE-PACK. **9** = PACK ICE. —v. **1** (often foll. by up) **a** fill (a suitcase, bag, etc.) with clothes etc. **b** put (things) in a bag or suitcase, esp. for travelling. **2** (often foll. by in, into) crowd or cram (packed a lot into a few hours; packed in like sardines). **3** (esp. in passive, often foll. by with) fill (restaurant was packed; fans packed the stadium; packed with information). **4** cover (a thing) with packaging. **5** be suitable for packing. **6** colloq. **a** carry (a gun etc.). **b** be capable of delivering (a forceful punch). **7** (of animals or Rugby forwards) form a pack. □ **pack in** colloq. stop, give up (packed in his job). **pack it in** (or **up**) colloq. end or stop it. **pack off** send (a person) away, esp. summarily. **pack them in** fill a theatre etc. with a capacity audience. **pack up** colloq. **1** stop functioning; break down. **2** retire from an activity, contest, etc. **send packing** colloq. dismiss summarily. [Low German or Dutch]

pack² v. select (a jury etc.) or fill (a meeting) so as to secure a decision in one's favour. [probably from PACT]

package —n. **1** a bundle of things packed. **b** parcel, box, etc., in which things are packed. **2** (in full **package deal**) set of proposals or items offered or agreed to as a whole. **3** Computing piece of software suitable for a wide range of users. **4** colloq. = PACKAGE HOLIDAY. —v. (**-ging**) make up into or enclose in a package. □ **packager** n.

package holiday n. (also **package tour**) holiday (or tour) with travel, hotels, etc. at an inclusive price.

packaging n. **1** wrapping or container for goods. **2** process of packing goods.

packed lunch n. lunch of sandwiches etc. prepared and packed to be eaten away from home.

packed out adj. full, crowded.

packer n. person or thing that packs, esp. a dealer who prepares and packs food.

packet /'pækɪt/ n. 1 small package. 2 colloq. large sum of money won, lost, or spent. 3 (in full **packet-boat**) hist. mail-boat or passenger ship.

packhorse n. horse for carrying loads.

pack ice n. crowded floating ice in the sea.

packing n. material used to pack esp. fragile articles.

packthread n. stout thread for sewing or tying up packs.

pact n. agreement; treaty. [Latin *pactum*]

pad¹ —n. 1 thick piece of soft material used to protect, fill out hollows, hold or absorb liquid, etc. 2 sheets of blank paper fastened together at one edge, for writing or drawing on. 3 fleshy under-part of an animal's foot or of a human finger. 4 guard for the leg and ankle in sports. 5 flat surface for helicopter take-off or rocket-launching. 6 slang lodgings, flat, etc. 7 floating leaf of a water lily. —v. (-dd-) 1 provide with a pad or padding; stuff. 2 (foll. by out) lengthen or fill out (a book etc.) with unnecessary material. [probably Low German or Dutch]

pad² —v. (-dd-) 1 walk with a soft dull steady step. 2 travel, or tramp along (a road etc.), on foot. —n. 7 sound of soft steady steps. [Low German *pad* PATH]

padded cell n. room with padded walls in a mental hospital.

padding n. soft material used to pad or stuff.

paddle¹ /'pæd(ə)l/ —n. 1 short broad-bladed oar used without a rowlock. 2 paddle-shaped instrument. 3 fin, flip-per. 4 board on a paddle-wheel. 5 action or spell of paddling. —v. (-ling) 1 move on water or propel a boat by paddles. 2 row gently. [origin unknown]

paddle² /'pæd(ə)l/ —v. (-ling) 1 walk bare-foot, or dabble the feet or hands, in shallow water. —n. act of paddling. [probably Low German or Dutch]

paddle-boat n. (also **paddle-steamer**) boat (or steamer) propelled by a paddle-wheel.

paddle-wheel n. wheel for propelling a ship, with boards round the circum-ference.

paddock /'pædək/ n. 1 small field, esp. for keeping horses in. 2 turf enclosure at a racecourse for horses or cars. [*par-rock*, var. of PARK]

Paddy /'pædɪ/ n. (pl. **-ies**) colloq. often offens. Irishman. [Irish *Pádraig* Patrick]

paddy¹ /'pædɪ/ n. (pl. **-ies**) 1 (in full **paddy-field**) field where rice is grown. 2 rice before threshing or in the husk. [Malay]

paddy² /'pædɪ/ n. (pl. **-ies**) colloq. rage; fit of temper. [from PADDY]

padlock /'pædlɒk/ —n. detachable lock hanging by a pivoted hook on the object fastened. —v. secure with a padlock. [origin unknown]

padre /'pɑːdrɪ/ n. chaplain in the army etc. [Italian, Spanish, and Portuguese, = father, priest]

paean /'piːən/ n. (US **pean**) song of praise or triumph. [Latin from Greek]

paederast, paederasty var. of PEDERAST, PEDERASTY.

paediatrics /ˌpiːdɪˈætrɪks/ n.pl. (treated as sing.) (US **pediatrics**) branch of medicine dealing with chil-dren and their diseases. □ **paediatric** adj. **paediatrician** /-trɪʃ(ə)n/ n. [from paedo-, Greek *iatros* physician]

paedo- comb. form (US **pedo-**) child. [Greek *pais paid-* child]

paedophile /'piːdəfaɪl/ n. (US **pedo-phile**) person who displays paedophilia.

paedophilia /ˌpiːdəˈfɪlɪə/ n. (US **pedo-philia**) sexual attraction felt towards children.

paella /paɪˈelə/ n. Spanish dish of rice, saffron, chicken, seafood, etc., cooked and served in a large shallow pan. [Latin PATELLA]

paeony var. of PEONY.

pagan /'peɪgən/ —n. non-religious per-son, pantheist, or heathen, esp. in pre-Christian times. —adj. 1 a of pagans. b irreligious. 2 pantheistic. □ **paganism** n. [Latin *paganus* from *pagus* country district]

page¹ —n. 1 a leaf of a book, periodical, etc. b each side of this. c what is written or printed on this. 2 episode; memorable event. —v. (-ging) paginate. [Latin *pagina*]

page² —n. 1 liveried boy or man employed to run errands, attend to a door, etc. 2 boy as a personal attendant of a bride etc. —v. (-ging) 1 (in hotels, airports, etc.) summon, esp. by making an announcement. 2 summon by pager. [French]

pageant /'pædʒ(ə)nt/ n. 1 a brilliant spectacle, esp. an elaborate parade. b spectacular procession or play illustrat-ing historical events. c tableau etc. on a fixed stage or moving vehicle. 2 empty or specious show. [origin unknown]

pageantry n. (esp. on State occasions) spectacular show; pomp.

page-boy n. 1 = PAGE² n. 2. 2 woman's hairstyle with the hair bobbed and rolled under.

pager n. bleeping radio device, calling its wearer to the telephone etc.

paginate /ˈpædʒɪneɪt/ v. (-ting) assign numbers to the pages of (a book etc.). □ **pagination** /-ˈneɪʃ(ə)n/ n. [Latin: related to PAGE¹]

pagoda /pəˈɡəʊdə/ n. 1 Hindu or Buddhist temple etc., esp. a many-tiered tower, in India and the Far East. 2 ornamental imitation of this. [Portuguese]

pah /pɑː/ int. expressing disgust or contempt. [natural exclamation]

paid past and past part. of PAY¹.

paid-up adj. having paid one's subscription to a trade-union, club, etc., or having done what is required to be considered a full member of a particular group (paid-up feminist).

pail n. 1 bucket. 2 amount contained in this. □ **pailful** n. (pl. -s). [Old English]

pain — n. 1 any unpleasant bodily sensation produced by illness, accident, etc. 2 mental suffering. 3 (also **pain in the neck** or **arse**) colloq. troublesome person or thing; nuisance. — v. 1 cause pain to. 2 (as **pained** adj.) expressing pain (pained expression). □ **be at** (or **take**) **pains** take great care. **in pain** suffering pain. **on** (or **under**) **pain of** with (death etc.) as the penalty. [Latin poena penalty]

painful adj. 1 causing bodily or mental pain. 2 (esp. of part of the body) suffering pain. 3 causing trouble or difficulty; laborious (painful climb). □ **painfully** adv.

painkiller n. drug for alleviating pain. □ **painkilling** adj.

painless adj. not causing pain. □ **painlessly** adv.

painstaking /ˈpeɪnzˌteɪkɪn/ adj. careful, industrious, thorough. □ **painstakingly** adv.

paint — n. 1 pigment, esp. in liquid form, for colouring a surface. 2 this as a dried film or coating (paint peeled off). — v. 1 **a** cover (a wall, object, etc.) with paint. **b** apply paint of a specified colour to (paint the door green). 2 depict (an object, scene, etc.) in paint; produce (a picture) thus. 3 describe vividly (painted a gloomy picture). 4 joc. or archaic **a** apply make-up to (the face, skin, etc.). **b** apply (a liquid to the skin etc.). □ **paint out** efface with paint. **paint the town red** colloq. enjoy oneself flamboyantly. [Latin pingo pict-]

paintbox n. box holding dry paints for painting pictures.

paintbrush n. brush for applying paint.

painted lady n. orange-red spotted butterfly.

painter¹ n. person who paints; artist or decorator.

painter² n. rope attached to the bow of a boat for tying it to a quay etc. [origin unknown]

painterly adj. 1 characteristic of a painter or paintings; artistic. 2 (of a painting) lacking clearly defined outlines.

painting n. 1 process or art of using paint. 2 painted picture.

paint shop n. part of a factory where cars etc. are sprayed or painted.

paintwork n. painted, esp. wooden, surface or area in a building etc.

painty adj. of or covered in paint (painty smell).

pair — n. 1 set of two people or things used together or regarded as a unit. 2 article (e.g. scissors, trousers, or pyjamas) consisting of two joined or corresponding parts. 3 **a** engaged or married couple. **b** mated couple of animals. 4 two horses harnessed side by side (coach and pair). 5 member of a pair in relation to the other (cannot find its pair). 6 two playing-cards of the same denomination. 7 either or both of two MPs etc. on opposite sides agreeing not to vote on certain occasions. — v. 1 (often foll. by off) arrange or be arranged in couples. 2 **a** join or be joined in marriage. **b** (of animals) mate. [Latin paria: related to PAR]

pair of scales n. simple balance.

Paisley /ˈpeɪzlɪ/ n. (pl. -s) (often attrib.) 1 pattern of curved feather-shaped figures. 2 soft woollen shawl etc. having this pattern. [Paisley in Scotland]

pajamas US var. of PYJAMAS.

Paki /ˈpækɪ/ n. (pl. -s) slang offens. person of Pakistani descent. [abbreviation]

Pakistani /pɑːkɪˈstɑːnɪ/ — n. (pl. -s) 1 native or national of Pakistan. 2 person of Pakistani descent. — adj. of Pakistan.

pal — n. colloq. friend, mate, comrade. — v. (-ll-) (usu. foll. by up) associate; form a friendship. [Romany]

palace /ˈpælɪs/ n. 1 official residence of a sovereign, president, archbishop, or bishop. 2 splendid or spacious building. [Latin palatium]

palace revolution n. (also **palace coup**) (usu. non-violent) overthrow of a sovereign, government, etc. by a bureaucracy.

palaeo- comb. form (US **paleo-**) ancient; prehistoric. [Greek palaios]

Palaeocene /ˈpælɪəˌsiːn/ (US **Paleocene**) Geol. — adj. of the earliest epoch of

the Tertiary period. —n. this epoch or system. [from PALAEO-. Greek *kainos* new]

palaeography /ˌpælɪˈɒgrəfɪ/ n. (US **paleography**) the study of ancient writing and documents. □ **palaeographer** n. [French: related to PALAEO-]

palaeolithic /ˌpælɪəˈlɪθɪk/ adj. (US **paleolithic**) of the early part of the Stone Age. [Greek *lithos* stone]

palaeontology /ˌpælɪɒnˈtɒlədʒɪ/ n. (US **paleontology**) the study of life in the geological past. □ **palaeontologist** n. [Greek *ōn ont-* being]

Palaeozoic /ˌpælɪəʊˈzəʊɪk/ —adj. (US **Paleozoic**) of an era of geological time marked by the appearance of plants and animals, esp. invertebrates. —n. this era. [Greek *zōion* animal]

palais /ˈpæleɪ/ n. *colloq.* public dance-hall. [French, = hall]

palanquin /ˌpælənˈkiːn/ n. (also **palankeen**) (in India and the East) covered litter for one. [Portuguese]

palatable /ˈpælətəb(ə)l/ adj. 1 pleasant to taste. 2 (of an idea etc.) acceptable, satisfactory.

palatal /ˈpælət(ə)l/ —adj. 1 of the palate. 2 (of a sound) made by placing the tongue against the hard palate (e.g. *y* in *yes*). —n. palatal sound.

palate /ˈpælət/ n. 1 structure closing the upper part of the mouth cavity in vertebrates. 2 sense of taste. 3 mental taste; liking. [Latin *palatum*]

palatial /pəˈleɪʃ(ə)l/ adj. (of a building) like a palace; spacious and splendid. □ **palatially** adv. [Latin: related to PALACE]

palatinate /pəˈlætɪneɪt/ n. territory under the jurisdiction of a Count Palatine.

palatine /ˈpælətaɪn/ adj. (also **Palatine**) *hist.* 1 (of an official etc.) having local authority that elsewhere belongs only to a sovereign (*Count Palatine*). 2 (of a territory) subject to this authority. [Latin: related to PALACE]

palaver /pəˈlɑːvə(r)/ n. *colloq.* tedious fuss and bother. [Latin: related to PARABLE]

pale¹ —adj. 1 (of a person, colour, or complexion) light or faint, whitish, ashen. 2 of faint lustre; dim. —v. (-ling) 1 grow or make pale. 2 (often foll. by *before, beside*) seem feeble in comparison (with). □ **palely** adv. **paleness** n. [Latin *pallidus*]

pale² n. 1 pointed piece of wood for fencing etc.; stake. 2 boundary. □ **beyond the pale** outside the bounds of acceptable behaviour. [Latin *palus*]

paleface n. name supposedly used by N. American Indians for the White man.

palette /ˈpælɪt/ n. 1 artist's thin board or slab for laying and mixing colours on. 2 range of colours used by an artist. [French from Latin *pala* spade]

palette-knife n. 1 thin flexible steel blade with a handle for mixing colours or applying or removing paint. 2 blunt round-ended flexible kitchen knife.

palimony /ˈpælɪmənɪ/ n. esp. *US colloq.* allowance paid by either partner of a separated unmarried couple to the other. [from PAL, ALIMONY]

palimpsest /ˈpælɪmpsɛst/ n. 1 writing-material or manuscript on which the original writing has been effaced for reuse. 2 monumental brass turned and re-engraved on the reverse side. [Greek *palin* again, *psēstos* rubbed]

palindrome /ˈpælɪndrəʊm/ n. word or phrase reading the same backwards as forwards (e.g. *nurses run*). □ **palindromic** /-ˈdrɒmɪk/ adj. [Greek *palindromos* running back: related to PALIMPSEST, *drom-* run]

paling n. 1 fence of pales. 2 pale.

palisade /ˌpælɪˈseɪd/ —n. 1 fence of pales or iron railings. 2 strong pointed wooden stake. —v. (-ding) enclose or provide with a palisade. [French: related to PALE²]

pall¹ /pɔːl/ n. 1 cloth spread over a coffin etc. 2 shoulder-band with pendants, worn as an ecclesiastical vestment and sign of authority. 3 dark covering (*pall of darkness*). [Latin *pallium* cloak]

pall² /pɔːl/ v. (often foll. by *on*) become uninteresting (to). [from APPAL]

palladium /pəˈleɪdɪəm/ n. rare white metallic element used as a catalyst and in jewellery. [*Pallas*: name of an asteroid]

pallbearer n. person helping to carry or escort a coffin at a funeral.

pallet¹ /ˈpælɪt/ n. 1 straw mattress. 2 mean or makeshift bed. [Latin *palea* straw]

pallet² /ˈpælɪt/ n. portable platform for transporting and storing loads. [French: related to PALETTE]

palliasse /ˈpælɪæs/ n. straw mattress. [Latin: related to PALLET¹]

paleo- comb. form US var. of PALAEO-.

Paleocene US var. of PALAEOCENE.

paleography US var. of PALAEO-GRAPHY.

paleolithic US var. of PALAEOLITHIC.

paleontology US var. of PALAEON-TOLOGY.

Paleozoic US var. of PALAEOZOIC.

Palestinian /ˌpælɪˈstɪnɪən/ —adj. of Palestine. —n. 1 native of Palestine. 2 Arab, or a descendant of one, born or living in the area formerly called Palestine.

palliate /ˈpælɪeɪt/ v. (-ting) **1** alleviate (disease) without curing it. **2** excuse, extenuate. □ **palliative** /-ətɪv/ n. & adj. [Latin pallio cloak: related to PALL¹]

pallid /ˈpælɪd/ adj. pale, esp. from illness. [Latin: related to PALE¹]

pallor /ˈpælə(r)/ n. paleness. [Latin palleo be pale]

pally adj. (-ier, -iest) colloq. friendly.

palm¹ /pɑːm/ n. **1** (also **palm-tree**) (usu. tropical) tree-like plant with no branches and a mass of large leaves at the top. **2** leaf of this as a symbol of victory. [Latin palma]

palm² /pɑːm/ -n. **1** inner surface of the hand between the wrist and fingers. **2** part of a glove that covers this. -v. conceal in the hand. □ **palm off 1** (often foll. by on) impose fraudulently (on a person) (palmed my old car off on him). **2** (often foll. by with) cause (a person) to accept unwillingly or unknowingly (palmed him off with my old car). [Latin palma]

palmate /ˈpælmeɪt/ adj. **1** shaped like an open hand. **2** having lobes etc. like spread fingers. [Latin palmatus: related to PALM²]

palmetto /pælˈmetəʊ/ n. (pl. -s) small palm-tree. [Spanish palmito diminutive of palma PALM¹]

palmistry /ˈpɑːmɪstrɪ/ n. fortune-telling from lines etc. on the palm of the hand. □ **palmist** n.

Palm oil n. oil from various palms.

Palm Sunday n. Sunday before Easter, celebrating Christ's entry into Jerusalem.

palmy /ˈpɑːmɪ/ adj. (-ier, -iest) **1** of, like, or abounding in palms. **2** triumphant, flourishing (palmy days).

palomino /ˌpæləˈmiːnəʊ/ n. (pl. -s) golden or cream-coloured horse with light-coloured mane and tail. [Latin palumba dove]

palpable /ˈpælpəb(ə)l/ adj. **1** able to be touched or felt. **2** readily perceived. □ **palpably** adv. [Latin palpo caress]

palpate /ˈpælpeɪt/ v. (-ting) examine (esp. medically) by touch. □ **palpation** /-ˈpeɪʃ(ə)n/ n.

palpitate /ˈpælpɪteɪt/ v. (-ting) pulsate, throb, tremble. [Latin palpito frequentative of palpo touch gently]

palpitation /ˌpælpɪˈteɪʃ(ə)n/ n. **1** throbbing, trembling. **2** (often in pl.) increased rate of heartbeat due to exertion, agitation, or disease.

palsy /ˈpɔːlzɪ/ -n. (pl. -ies) paralysis, esp. with involuntary tremors. -v. (-ies, -ied) affect with palsy. [French: related to PARALYSIS]

paltry /ˈpɔːltrɪ/ adj. (-ier, -iest) worthless, contemptible, trifling. □ **paltriness** n. [from palt rubbish]

pampas /ˈpæmpəs/ n.pl. large treeless plains in S. America. [Spanish from Quechua]

pampas-grass n. tall S. American ornamental grass.

pamper v. overindulge (a person, taste, etc.); spoil. [obsolete pamp cram]

pamphlet /ˈpæmflɪt/ -n. small usu. unbound booklet or leaflet. -v. (-t-) distribute pamphlets to. [Pamphilus, name of medieval poem]

pamphleteer /ˌpæmflɪˈtɪə(r)/ n. writer of (esp. political) pamphlets.

pan¹ -n. **1 a** broad usu. metal vessel used for cooking etc. **b** contents of this. **2** panlike vessel in which shallow container are heated etc. **3** similar shallow container, e.g. the bowl of a pair of scales. **4** lavatory bowl. **5** part of the lock in old guns. **6** hollow in the ground (salt-pan). -v. (-nn-) **1** colloq. criticize severely. **2 a** (foll. by off, out) wash (gold-bearing gravel) in a pan. **b** search for gold thus. □ **pan out 1** (of an action etc.) turn out; work out well or in a specified way. **2** (of gravel) yield gold. □ **panful** n. (pl. -s).

panlike adj. [Old English]

pan² -v. (-nn-) **1** swing (a film camera) horizontally to give a panoramic effect or to follow a moving object. **2** (of a camera) be moved thus. -n. panning movement. [from PANORAMA]

pan- comb. form **1** all; the whole of. **2** relating to the whole of a continent, racial group, religion, etc. (pan-American). [Greek pan, neuter of pas pantos all]

panacea /ˌpænəˈsɪə/ n. universal remedy. [Greek: related to PAN-, akos remedy]

panache /pəˈnæʃ/ n. assertive flamboyance; confidence of style or manner. [French, = plume]

Panama /ˈpænəmɑː/ n. straw hat with a brim and indented crown. [Panama in Central America]

panatella /ˌpænəˈtelə/ n. long thin cigar. [American Spanish, = long thin biscuit]

pancake n. **1** thin flat cake of fried batter usu. rolled up with a filling. **2** flat cake of make-up etc.

Pancake Day n. Shrove Tuesday (when pancakes are traditionally eaten).

pancake landing n. colloq. emergency aircraft landing with the undercarriage still retracted.

panchromatic /ˌpænkrəʊˈmætɪk/ adj. (of a film etc.) sensitive to all visible colours of the spectrum.

pancreas /ˈpæŋkrɪəs/ n. gland near the stomach supplying digestive fluid and secreting insulin. □ **pancreatic** /-ˈætɪk/ adj. [Greek *kreas* flesh]

panda /ˈpændə/ n. 1 (also **giant panda**) large bearlike black and white mammal native to China and Tibet. 2 (also **red panda**) reddish-brown Himalayan racoon-like mammal. [Nepali]

panda car n. police patrol car.

pandemic /pænˈdemɪk/ adj. (of a disease etc.) widespread; universal. [Greek *dēmos* people]

pandemonium /ˌpændɪˈməʊnɪəm/ n. 1 uproar; utter confusion. 2 scene of this. [place in hell in Milton's *Paradise Lost*]

pander /ˈpændə(r)/ –v. (foll. by *to*) gratify or indulge (a person or weakness etc.). –n. 1 procurer; pimp 2 person who encourages coarse desires. [*Pandarus*, name of a character in the story of Troilus and Cressida]

pandit var. of PUNDIT 1.

Pandora's box /pænˈdɔːrə/ n. process that once begun will generate many unmanageable problems. [a box in Greek mythology from which many ills were released on mankind]

p. & p. abbr. postage and packing.

pane n. single sheet of glass in a window or door. [Latin *pannus* a cloth]

panegyric /ˌpænɪˈdʒɪrɪk/ n. eulogy; speech or essay of praise. [Greek *agora* assembly]

panel /ˈpæn(ə)l/ –n. 1 distinct, usu. rectangular, section of a surface (e.g. of a wall, door, or vehicle). 2 strip of material in a garment. 3 team in a broadcast game, discussion, etc. 4 a list of available jurors. b jury. –v. (-ll-; US -l-) fit, cover, or decorate with panels. [Latin diminutive of *pannus*: related to PANE]

panel-beater n. person who beats out the metal panels of vehicles.

panel game n. broadcast quiz etc. played by a panel.

panelling n. (US **paneling**) 1 panelled work. 2 wood for making panels. [panel]

panellist n. (US **panelist**) member of a panel.

pang n. (often in *pl.*) sudden sharp pain or painful emotion. [obsolete *pronge*]

pangolin /pæŋˈɡəʊlɪn/ n. scaly Asian and African anteater. [Malay]

panic /ˈpænɪk/ –n. 1 sudden uncontrollable fear. 2 infectious fright, esp. in commercial dealings. –v. (-ck-) (often foll. by *into*) affect or be affected with panic (*was panicked into buying*). □ **panicky** adj. [Greek *Pan*, rural god]

panicle /ˈpænɪk(ə)l/ n. loose branching cluster of flowers, as in oats. [Latin *paniculum* diminutive of *panus* thread]

panic stations n.pl. colloq. state of emergency.

panic-stricken adj. (also **panic-struck**) affected with panic.

panjandrum /pænˈdʒændrəm/ n. 1 mock title for an important person. 2 pompous official etc. [invented word]

pannier /ˈpænɪə(r)/ n. basket, bag, or box, esp. one of a pair carried by a donkey etc., bicycle, or motor cycle. [Latin *panis* bread]

panoply /ˈpænəplɪ/ n. (pl. **-ies**) 1 complete or splendid array. 2 complete suit of armour. [Greek *hopla* arms]

panorama /ˌpænəˈrɑːmə/ n. 1 unbroken view of a surrounding region. 2 complete survey of a subject, series of events, etc. 3 picture or photograph containing a wide view. 4 continuous passing scene. □ **panoramic** /-ˈræmɪk/ adj. [Greek *horama* view]

pan-pipes n.pl. musical instrument made of a series of short graduated pipes fixed together. [from Pan, Greek rural god]

pansy /ˈpænzɪ/ n. (pl. **-ies**) 1 cultivated plant with flowers of various rich colours. 2 colloq. offens. a effeminate man. b male homosexual. [French *pensée* thought, pansy]

pant –v. 1 breathe with short quick breaths. 2 (often foll. by *out*) utter breathlessly. 3 (usu. foll. by *for*) yearn, crave. 4 (of the heart etc.) throb violently. –n. 1 panting breath. 2 throb. [Greek: related to FANTASY]

pantaloons /ˌpæntəˈluːnz/ n.pl. (esp. women's) baggy trousers gathered at the ankles. [French from Italian]

pantechnicon /pænˈteknɪkən/ n. large furniture removal van. [from TECHNIC: originally as the name of a bazaar]

pantheism /ˈpænθɪɪz(ə)m/ n. 1 belief that God is in all nature. 2 worship that admits or tolerates all gods. □ **pantheist** n. **pantheistic** /-ˈɪstɪk/ adj. [Greek *theos* god]

pantheon /ˈpænθɪən/ n. 1 building in which illustrious dead are buried or have memorials. 2 temple of a people collectively. 3 temple dedicated to all the gods. [Greek *theion* divine]

panther /ˈpænθə(r)/ n. 1 leopard, esp. with black fur. 2 US puma. [Greek *panthēr*]

pantie-girdle n. woman's girdle with a crotch shaped like the pants.

panties /ˈpæntɪz/ n.pl. colloq. short-legged or legless undergarments worn by women and girls. [diminutive of PANTS]

pantihose /ˈpæntɪˌhəʊz/ n. (usu. treated as pl.) US women's tights.

pantile /ˈpæntaɪl/ n. curved roof-tile. [from PAN[1]]

panto /ˈpæntəʊ/ *n.* (*pl.* -s) *colloq.* = PANTOMIME. [abbreviation]

pantograph /ˈpæntəˌgrɑːf/ *n.* **1** instrument with jointed rods for copying a plan or drawing etc. on a different scale. **2** jointed framework conveying a current to an electric vehicle from overhead wires. [from PAN-, -GRAPH]

pantomime /ˈpæntəˌmaɪm/ *n.* **1** Christmas theatrical entertainment based on a fairy tale. **2** gestures and facial expression conveying meaning, esp. in drama and dance. **3** *colloq.* absurd or outrageous piece of behaviour. [Greek: related to PAN-, MIME]

pantry /ˈpæntrɪ/ *n.* (*pl.* -ies) **1** small room or cupboard in which crockery, cutlery, table linen, etc., are kept. **2** larder. [Latin *panis* bread]

pants *n.pl.* **1** underpants or knickers. **2** *US* trousers. □ **bore** (or **scare** etc.) **the pants off** *colloq.* bore, scare, etc., greatly. **with one's pants down** *colloq.* in an embarrassingly unprepared state. [abbreviation of PANTALOONS]

pap[1] *n.* **1** soft or semi-liquid food for infants or invalids. **2** light or trivial reading matter. [Low German or Dutch]

pap[2] *n. archaic* or *dial.* nipple. [Scandinavian]

papa /pəˈpɑː/ *n. archaic* father (esp. as a child's word). [Greek *papas*]

papacy /ˈpeɪpəsɪ/ *n.* (*pl.* -ies) **1** pope's office or tenure. **2** papal system. [medieval Latin *papatia*: related to POPE]

papal /ˈpeɪp(ə)l/ *adj.* of a pope or the papacy. [medieval Latin: related to POPE]

paparazzo /ˌpæpəˈrætsəʊ/ *n.* (*pl.* **-zzi** /-tsiː/) freelance photographer who pursues celebrities to photograph them. [Italian]

papaw var. of PAWPAW.

papaya var. of PAWPAW. [earlier form of PAWPAW]

paper —*n.* **1** material made in thin sheets from the pulp of wood etc., used for writing, drawing, or printing on, or as wrapping material etc. **2** (*attrib.*) **a** made of or using paper. **b** flimsy like paper. **3** = NEWSPAPER. **4 a** printed document. **b** (in *pl.*) identification etc. documents. **c** (in *pl.*) documents of a specified kind (*divorce papers*). **5** *Commerce* **a** negotiable documents, e.g. bills of exchange. **b** (*attrib.*) not actual; theoretical (*paper profits*). **6 a** set of printed questions in an examination. **b** written answers to these. **7** = WALLPAPER. **8** essay or dissertation. **9** piece of paper, esp. as a wrapper etc. —*v.* **1** decorate (a wall etc.) with wallpaper. **2** (foll. by *over*) **a** cover (a hole or blemish) with paper. **b** disguise or try to hide (a fault etc.). □

on paper 1 in writing. **2** in theory; from written or printed evidence. [Latin PAPYRUS]

paperback *n.* (often *attrib.*) book bound in paper or card, not boards.

paper-boy *n.* (also **paper-girl**) boy or girl who delivers or sells newspapers.

paper-chase *n.* cross-country run following a trail of torn-up paper.

paper-clip *n.* clip of bent wire or plastic for fastening papers together.

paper-hanger *n.* person who hangs wallpaper, esp. for a living.

paper-knife *n.* blunt knife for opening letters etc.

paper-mill *n.* mill in which paper is made.

paper money *n.* banknotes.

paper round *n.* **1** job of regularly delivering newspapers. **2** route for this.

paper tiger *n.* apparently threatening, but ineffectual, person or thing.

paperweight *n.* small heavy object for keeping loose papers in place.

paperwork *n.* routine clerical or administrative work.

papery *adj.* like paper in thinness or texture.

papier mâché /ˌpæpɪeɪ ˈmæʃeɪ/ *n.* paper pulp moulded into boxes, trays, etc. [French; = chewed paper]

papilla /pəˈpɪlə/ *n.* (*pl.* **papillae** /-liː/) small nipple-like protuberance in or on the body, as at the base of a hair, feather, etc. □ **papillary** *adj.* [Latin]

papist /ˈpeɪpɪst/ *n.* often *derog.* **1** (also *attrib.*) Roman Catholic. **2** *hist.* advocate of papal supremacy. [related to POPE]

papoose /pəˈpuːs/ *n.* N. American Indian young child. [Algonquian]

paprika /ˈpæprɪkə/ *n.* **1** red pepper. **2** condiment made from this. [Magyar]

Pap test *n.* cervical smear test. [*Papanicolaou*, name of a US scientist]

papyrus /pəˈpaɪərəs/ *n.* (*pl.* **papyri** /-raɪ/) **1** aquatic plant of N. Africa. **2 a** writing-material made in ancient Egypt from the pithy stem of this. **b** text written on this. [Latin from Greek]

par *n.* **1** average or normal amount, degree, condition, etc. (*feel below par*). **2** equality; equal status or footing (*on a par with*). **3** *Golf* number of strokes a first-class player should normally require for a hole or course. **4** face value of stocks and shares etc. (*at par*). **5** (in full **par of exchange**) recognized value of one country's currency in terms of another's. □ **par for the course** *colloq.* what is normal or to be expected. [Latin, = equal]

par- var. of PARA.[1] before a vowel or *h* (*parody*).

para /ˈpærə/ n. colloq. **1** paragraph. **2** paratrooper. **2** paragraph. [abbreviation]

para-[1] comb. form protect, ward off, defend)

para-[2] comb. form **1** beside (*para-military*). **2** beyond (*paranormal*). [Greek]

parable /ˈpærəb(ə)l/ n. **1** story used to illustrate a moral or spiritual lesson. **2** allegory. [Greek *parabolē* comparison]

parabola /pəˈræbələ/ n. open plane curve formed by the intersection of a cone with a plane parallel to its side. □ **parabolic** /ˌpærəˈbɒlɪk/ adj. [Greek: related to PARABLE]

paracetamol /ˌpærəˈsiːtəmɒl/ n. drug used to relieve pain and reduce fever. **2** tablet of this. [from *para-acetylamino-phenol*]

parachute /ˈpærəʃuːt/ n. rectangular or umbrella-shaped apparatus allowing a slow and safe descent esp. from an aircraft, or used to retard forward motion etc. (often *attrib.*: *parachute troops*). —v. (-ting) convey or descend by parachute. □ **parachutist** n. [French: related to PARA-[2], CHUTE[1]]

parade /pəˈreɪd/ —n. **1** public procession. **2 a** ceremonial muster of troops for inspection. **b** = PARADE-GROUND. **3** ostentatious display (*made a parade of their wealth*). **4** public square, promenade, or row of shops. —v. (-ding) **1** march ceremonially. **2** assemble for parade. **3** display ostentatiously. **4** march through (streets etc.) in procession. □ **on parade 1** taking part in a parade. **2** on display. [Latin *paro* prepare]

parade-ground n. place for the muster and drilling of troops.

paradiddle /ˈpærədɪd(ə)l/ n. drum roll with alternate beating of sticks. [imitative]

paradigm /ˈpærədaɪm/ n. example or pattern, esp. a set of noun or verb inflections. □ **paradigmatic** /ˌpærədɪɡˈmætɪk/ adj. [Greek]

paradise /ˈpærədaɪs/ n. **1** (in some religions) heaven. **2** place or state of complete happiness. **3** (in full **earthly paradise**) abode of Adam and Eve; garden of Eden. □ **paradisaical** /-dɪˈseɪɪk(ə)l/ adj., **paradisal** /-dɪˈsaɪk(ə)l/ adj., **paradisiacal** /-dɪˈsaɪək(ə)l/ adj., **paradisiac** /-ˈdaɪsɪæk/ adj. [Greek *paradeisos*]

paradox /ˈpærədɒks/ n. **1 a** seemingly absurd or contradictory though often true statement. **b** self-contradictory or absurd statement. **2** person or thing having contradictory qualities etc. **3** paradoxical quality. □ **paradoxical** /-ˈdɒksɪk(ə)l/ adj., **paradoxically** /-ˈdɒksɪk(ə)l/ adv.

paraffin /ˈpærəfɪn/ n. **1** inflammable waxy or oily hydro-carbon distilled from petroleum or shale, used in liquid form esp. as a fuel. **2** *Chem.* = ALKANE. [Latin, = having little affinity]

paraffin wax n. paraffin in its solid form.

paragon /ˈpærəgən/ n. (often foll. by *of*) model of excellence etc. [Greek *par-akonē*]

paragraph /ˈpærəgrɑːf/ —n. **1** distinct section of a piece of writing, beginning on a new often indented line. **2** symbol (usu. ¶) used to mark a new paragraph, or as a reference mark. **3** short item in a newspaper. —v. arrange (a piece of writing) in paragraphs [Greek: related to PARA-[2], -GRAPH]

parakeet /ˈpærəkiːt/ n. small usu. long-tailed parrot. [French: related to PARROT]

parallax /ˈpærəlæks/ n. **1** apparent difference in the position or direction of an object caused when the observer's position is changed. **2** angular amount of this. [Greek, = change]

parallel /ˈpærəlel/ —adj. **1 a** (of lines or planes) continuously side by side and equidistant. **b** (foll. by *to*, *with*) (of a line or plane) having this relation (to or with another). **2** (of circumstances etc.) precisely similar, analogous, or corresponding. **3 a** (of processes etc.) occurring or performed simultaneously. **b** *Computing* involving the simultaneous performance of operations. —n. **1** person or thing precisely analogous to another. **2** comparison (*drew a parallel between them*). **3** (in full **parallel of latitude**) each of the imaginary parallel circles of constant latitude on the earth's surface. **b** corresponding line on a map (*49th parallel*). **4** *Printing* two parallel lines (‖) as a reference mark. —v. (-l-) **1** be parallel, or correspond, to. **2** represent as similar, compare. **3** cite as a parallel instance. □ **in parallel** (of electric circuits) arranged so as to join at common points at each end. □ **parallelism** n. [Greek, = alongside one another]

parallel bars n.pl. pair of parallel rails on posts for gymnastics.

parallelepiped /ˌpærəlelˈepɪped, -lɪˈpaɪpd/ n. solid body of which each face is a parallelogram. [Greek: related to PARALLEL, *epipedon* plane surface]

parallelogram /ˌpærəˈleləɡræm/ n. four-sided plane rectilinear figure with opposite sides parallel.

paralyse /ˈpærəlaɪz/ v. (US **paralyze**) (**-sing** or **-zing**) **1** affect with paralysis. **2**

render powerless; cripple. [Greek: related to PARA-¹, *luō* loosen]

paralysis /pəˈræləsɪs/ *n.* **1** impairment or loss of esp. the motor function of the nerves, causing immobility. **2** powerlessness.

paralytic /ˌpærəˈlɪtɪk/ —*adj.* **1** affected by paralysis. **2** *slang* very drunk. —*n.* person affected by paralysis.

paramedic /ˌpærəˈmedɪk/ *n.* paramedical worker.

paramedical *adj.* (of services etc.) supplementing and assisting medical work.

parameter /pəˈræmɪtə(r)/ *n.* **1** *Math.* quantity constant in the case considered but varying in different cases. **2 a** (esp. measurable or quantifiable) characteristic or feature. **b** (loosely) limit or boundary, esp. of a subject for discussion. [Greek PARA-¹, -METER]

paramilitary /ˌpærəˈmɪlɪtərɪ/ —*adj.* (of forces) organized on military lines. —*n.* (*pl.* -**ies**) member of an unofficial paramilitary organization, esp. in N. Ireland.

paramount /ˈpærəmaʊnt/ *adj.* **1** supreme; most important. **2** in supreme authority. [Anglo-French *par* by, *amont* above: see AMOUNT]

paramour /ˈpærəmʊə(r)/ *n. archaic* or *derog.* illicit lover of a married person. [French *par amour* by love]

paranoia /ˌpærəˈnɔɪə/ *n.* **1** mental disorder with delusions of persecution and self-importance. **2** abnormal suspicion and mistrust. □ **paranoiac** *adj.* & *n.* **paranoiacally** *adv.* **paranoic** /-ˈnəʊɪk, -ˈnɔɪk/ *adj.* **paranoically** /-ˈnəʊɪkəlɪ, -ˈnɔɪkəlɪ/ *adv.* **paranoid** /ˈpærənɔɪd/ *adj.* & *n.* [Greek: related to NOUS]

paranormal /ˌpærəˈnɔːm(ə)l/ *adj.* beyond the scope of normal scientific investigation or explanation.

parapet /ˈpærəpɪt/ *n.* **1** low wall at the edge of a roof, balcony, bridge, etc. **2** defence of earth or stone. [French or Italian: related to PARA-², *petto* breast]

paraphernalia /ˌpærəfəˈneɪlɪə/ *n.pl.* (also treated as *sing.*) miscellaneous belongings, equipment, accessories, etc. [Greek: related to PARA-¹, *pherna* dower]

paraphrase /ˈpærəfreɪz/ —*n.* expression of the meaning of (a passage) in other words. —*v.* (-**sing**) express the meaning of (a passage) thus. [Greek: related to PARA-¹]

paraplegia /ˌpærəˈpliːdʒə/ *n.* paralysis below the waist. □ **paraplegic** *adj.* & *n.* [Greek: related to PARA-¹, *plēssō* strike]

parapsychology /ˌpærəsaɪˈkɒlədʒɪ/ *n.* the study of mental phenomena outside the sphere of ordinary psychology (hypnosis, telepathy, etc.).

paraquat /ˈpærəkwɒt/ *n.* a quick-acting highly toxic herbicide. [from PARA-¹, QUATERNARY]

parascending /ˈpærəˌsendɪŋ/ *n.* sport in which participants wearing open parachutes are towed behind a vehicle or motor boat to gain height before release for a conventional descent. □

parasite /ˈpærəsaɪt/ *n.* **1** organism living in or on another and feeding on it. **2** person exploiting another or others. □ **parasitic** /-ˈsɪtɪk/ *adj.* **parasitically** /-ˈsɪtɪkəlɪ/ *adv.* **parasitism** *n.* [Greek: related to PARA-¹, *sitos* food]

parasol /ˈpærəsɒl/ *n.* light umbrella giving shade from the sun. [Italian: related to PARA-², *sole* sun]

paratrooper /ˈpærəˌtruːpə(r)/ *n.* member of a body of paratroops.

paratroops /ˈpærəˌtruːps/ *n.pl.* parachute troops. [contraction]

paratyphoid /ˌpærəˈtaɪfɔɪd/ *n.* (often *attrib.*) fever resembling typhoid.

par avion /pɑːr æˈvjɔ̃/ *adv.* by airmail. [French, = by aeroplane]

parboil /ˈpɑːbɔɪl/ *v.* boil until partly cooked. [Latin *par-* = PER-, confused with PART]

parcel /ˈpɑːs(ə)l/ —*n.* **1** goods etc. wrapped up in a package for posting or carrying. **2** piece of land. **3** quantity dealt with in one commercial transaction. —*v.* (-**ll**-; *US* -**l**-) **1** (foll. by *up*) wrap as a parcel. **2** (foll. by *out*) divide into portions. [Latin: related to PARTICLE]

parch *v.* **1** make or become hot and dry. **2** roast (peas, corn, etc.) slightly. [origin unknown]

parchment /ˈpɑːtʃmənt/ *n.* **1** a skin, esp. of sheep or goat, prepared for writing or painting on. **b** manuscript written on this. **2** high-grade paper resembling parchment. [Latin *Pergamum*, now *Bergama* in Turkey]

pardon /ˈpɑːd(ə)n/ —*n.* **1** forgiveness for an offence, error, etc. **2** (in full **free pardon**) remission of the legal consequences of a crime or conviction. —*v.* **1** forgive or excuse. **2** release from the legal consequences of an offence, error, etc. —*int.* (also **pardon me** or **I beg your pardon**) **1** formula of apology or disagreement. **2** request to repeat something said. □ **pardonable** *adj.* [Latin *perdono*: related to PER-, *dono* give]

pare /peə(r)/ *v.* (-**ring**) **1 a** trim or shave by cutting away the surface or edge. **b** (often foll. by *off*, *away*) cut off (the surface or edge). **2** (often foll. by *away*, *down*) diminish little by little. [Latin *paro* prepare]

parent /ˈpeərənt/ —*n.* **1** person who has or adopts a child; father or mother. **2** animal or plant from which others are

derived. 3 (often *attrib*) source, origin, etc. — v. (also *absol.*) be the parent of. □ **through parents.**

parent company n. company of which others are subsidiaries.

parenthesis /pəˈrenθɪsɪs/ n. (pl. **parentheses** /-siːz/) **1 a** explanatory or qualifying word, clause, or sentence inserted into a sentence etc., and usu. marked off by brackets, dashes, or commas. **b** (in *pl.*) round brackets ( ) used for this. **2** interlude or interval. □ **parenthetic** /pærənˈθetɪk/ *adj.* **parenthetical** /pærənˈθetɪk(ə)l/ *adv.* **parenthetically** /-kəlɪ/ *adv.* [Greek: related to PARA-, EN-, THESIS]

parenting n. (skill of) bringing up children.

parent-teacher association n. social and fund-raising organization of a school's parents and teachers.

par excellence /paːr eksˈlɑ̃s/ *adv.* being the supreme example of its kind (*the short story par excellence*). [French]

parfait /ˈpaːfeɪ/ n. **1** rich iced pudding of whipped cream, eggs, etc. **2** layers of ice-cream, meringue, etc., served in a tall glass. [French *parfait* PERFECT]

pariah /pəˈraɪə/ n. **1** social outcast. **2** *hist.* member of a low caste or of no caste in S. India. [Tamil]

parietal /pəˈraɪɪt(ə)l/ *adj.* of the wall of the body or any of its cavities. [Latin *paries* wall]

parietal bone n. either of a pair of bones in the skull.

paring n. strip or piece cut off.

parish /ˈpærɪʃ/ n. **1** area having its own church and clergyman. **2** (in full **civil parish**) local government district. **3** inhabitants of a parish. [Latin *parochia* from Greek *oikos* dwelling]

parish clerk n. official performing various duties for a church.

parish council n. administrative body in a civil parish.

parishioner /pəˈrɪʃənə(r)/ n. inhabitant of a parish. [obsolete *parishen*: related to PARISH]

parish register n. book recording christenings, marriages, and burials, at a parish church.

parity /ˈpærɪtɪ/ n. **1** equality, equal status or pay. **2** parallelism or analogy (*parity of reasoning*). **3** equivalence of one currency with another; being at par. [Latin *paritas*: related to PAR]

park — n. **1** large public garden in a town, for recreation. **2** land attached to a country house etc. **3** a large area of

uncultivated land for public recreational use. **b** large enclosed area where wild animals are kept in captivity (*wild-life park*). **4** area for parking vehicles etc. (*car park*). **5** a-ea for a specified purpose (*business park*). **6** a US sports ground. **b** (usu. prec. by *the*) football pitch. — v. **1** (also *absol.*) leave (a vehicle) usu. temporarily. **2** *colloq* deposit and leave, usu. temporarily. □ **park oneself** *colloq.* sit down. [French from Germanic]

parka /ˈpaːkə/ n. **1** long usu. green anorak with fur round the hood. **2** hooded skin jacket worn by Eskimos. [Aleutian]

parkin /ˈpaːkɪn/ n. cake of ginger, oatmeal, treacle, etc. [origin uncertain]

parking-lot n. US outdoor car park.

parking-meter n. coin-operated meter allocating a length of time for which a vehicle may be parked in a street.

parking-ticket n. notice of a penalty imposed for parking illegally.

parkland n. open grassland with trees etc.

parky /ˈpaːkɪ/ *adj.* (**-ier, -iest**) *colloq.* or *dial.* chilly. [origin unknown]

Parkinsonism /ˈpaːkɪns(ə)nɪz(ə)m/ n. (also **Parkinson's disease**) progressive disease of the nervous system with tremor, muscular rigidity, and emaciation. [*Parkinson*, name of a surgeon]

Parkinson's disease n. = PARKINSONISM.

Parkinson's law /ˈpaːkɪns(ə)nz/ n. notion that work expands to fill the time available for it. [*Parkinson*, name of a writer]

parlance /ˈpaːləns/ n. vocabulary or idiom of a particular subject, group, etc. [French from *parler* speak]

parley /ˈpaːlɪ/ — n. (pl. **-eys**) conference of disputants, esp. to discuss peace terms etc. — v. (**-leys, -leyed**) (often foll. by *with*) hold a parley. [French *parler* related to PARLANCE]

parliament /ˈpaːləmənt/ n. **1** (**Parliament**) **a** (in the UK) highest legislature, consisting of the Sovereign, the House of Lords, and the House of Commons. **b** members of this for a particular period. **2** similar legislature in other States. [French: related to PARLANCE]

parliamentarian /paːləmenˈteərɪən/ n. member of a parliament, esp. an expert in its procedures.

parliamentary /paːləˈmentərɪ/ *adj.* **1** of a parliament. **2** enacted or established by a parliament. **3** (of language, behaviour, etc.) polite.

parlour /ˈpaːlə(r)/ n. (US **parlor**) **1** *archaic* sitting-room in a private house. **2** esp. *US* shop providing specified goods or services (*beauty parlour, ice-cream*

parlour). [Anglo-French: related to PARLEY]

parlour game *n.* indoor game, esp. a word-game.

parlous /ˈpɑːləs/ *adj. archaic* or *joc.* dangerous or difficult. [from PERILOUS]

Parmesan /ˌpɑːmɪˈzæn/ *n.* hard dry cheese made orig. at Parma and usu. used grated. [Italian *parmegiano* of Parma]

parochial /pəˈrəʊkɪəl/ *adj.* **1** of a parish. **2** (of affairs, views, etc.) merely local, narrow, or provincial. □ **parochialism** *n.* **parochially** *adv.* [Latin: related to PARISH]

parody /ˈpærədɪ/ *–n.* (*pl.* **-ies**) **1** humorous exaggerated imitation of an author, literary work, style, etc. **2** feeble imitation, travesty. *–v.* (**-ies**, **-ied**) **1** compose a parody of. **2** mimic humorously. □ **parodist** *n.* [Latin or Greek: related to PARA-¹, ODE]

parole /pəˈrəʊl/ *–n.* **1** temporary or permanent release of a prisoner before the expiry of a sentence, on the promise of good behaviour. **2** such a promise. *–v.* (**-ling**) put (a prisoner) on parole. [French, = word: related to PARLANCE]

parotid /pəˈrɒtɪd/ *–adj.* situated near the ear. *–n.* (in full **parotid gland**) salivary gland in front of the ear. [Greek: related to PARA-¹, *ous ōt-* ear]

paroxysm /ˈpærəkˌsɪz(ə)m/ *n.* **1** (often foll. by *of*) sudden attack or outburst (of rage, coughing, etc.). **2** fit of disease. □ **paroxysmal** /-ˈsɪzm(ə)l/ *adj.* [Greek *oxus* sharp]

parquet /ˈpɑːkeɪ/ *–n.* **1** flooring of wooden blocks arranged in a pattern. **2** *US* stalls of a theatre. *–v.* (**-eted** /-etd/, **-eting** /-eɪɪŋ/) floor (a room) thus. [French, diminutive of *parc* PARK]

parquetry /ˈpɑːkɪtrɪ/ *n.* use of wooden blocks to make floors or inlay for furniture.

parr /pɑː(r)/ *n.* young salmon. [origin unknown]

parricide /ˈpærɪˌsaɪd/ *n.* **1** murder of a near relative, esp. of a parent. **2** person who commits parricide. □ **parricidal** /-ˈsaɪd(ə)l/ *adj.* [Latin: see PATER-, -CIDE]

parrot /ˈpærət/ *–n.* **1** mainly tropical bird with a short hooked bill, often vivid plumage, and the ability to mimic the human voice. **2** person who mechanically repeats another's words or actions. *–v.* (**-t-**) repeat mechanically. [French, diminutive of *Pierre* Peter]

parrot-fashion *adv.* (learning or repeating) mechanically, by rote.

parry /ˈpærɪ/ *–v.* (**-ies**, **-ied**) **1** avert or ward off (a weapon or attack), esp. with a countermove. **2** deal skilfully with (an awkward question etc.). *–n.* (*pl.* **-ies**) act of parrying. [Italian *parare* ward off]

parse /pɑːz/ *v.* (**-sing**) **1** describe (a word in context) grammatically, stating its inflection, relation to the sentence, etc. **2** resolve (a sentence) into its component parts and describe them grammatically. [perhaps from French *pars* parts: related to PART]

parsec /ˈpɑːsek/ *n.* unit of stellar distance, equal to about 3.25 light-years. [from PARALLAX, SECOND²]

parsimonious /ˌpɑːsɪˈməʊnɪəs/ *adj.* carefulness in the use of money etc.; stinginess. □ **parsimoniously** *adv.* [Latin *parco pars-* spare]

parsimony /ˈpɑːsɪmənɪ/ *n.* carefulness in the use of money etc.; stinginess. [Latin *parco pars-* spare]

parsley /ˈpɑːslɪ/ *n.* herb with crinkly aromatic leaves, used to season and garnish food. [Greek *petra* rock, *selinon* parsley]

parsnip /ˈpɑːsnɪp/ *n.* **1** plant with a pale-yellow tapering root. **2** this root eaten as a vegetable. [Latin *pastinaca*]

parson /ˈpɑːs(ə)n/ *n.* **1** rector. **2** *vicar;* clergyman. [Latin: related to PERSON]

parsonage *n.* church house provided for a parson.

parson's nose *n.* fatty flesh at the rump of a cooked fowl.

part *–n.* **1** some but not all of a thing or group of things. **2** essential member, constituent, or component (*part of the family; spare parts*). **3** portion of a human or animal body. **4** division of a book, broadcast serial, etc., esp. issued or broadcast at one time. **5** each of several equal portions of a whole (*3 parts sugar to 2 parts flour*). **6** allotted share. **b** person's share in an action etc. (*had no part in it*). **c** duty (*not my part to interfere*). **7 a** character assigned to, or words spoken by, an actor on stage. **b** melody line, etc., assigned to a particular voice or instrument. **c** printed or written copy of an actor's or musician's part. **8** side in an agreement or dispute. **9** (in *pl.*) region or district (*am not from these parts*). **10** (in *pl.*) abilities (*man of many parts*). *–v.* **1** divide or separate into parts (*crowd parted*). **2 a** leave one another's company (*parted the best of friends*). **b** (foll. by *with*) say goodbye to. **3** (foll. by *with*) give up; hand over. **4** separate (hair of the head) to make a parting. *–adv.* in part; partly (*part iron and part wood*). □ **for the most part** see MOST. **for one's part** as far as one is concerned. **in part** (or **parts**) partly. **on the part of** made or done by (*no objection on my part*). **part and parcel** (usu. foll. by *of*) see COMPANY. **play a part 1** be significant or contributory. **2** act deceitfully. **3** perform a theatrical role. **take**

in good part not be offended by; take part (often foll. by *in*) assist or have a share (in). **take the part of** support; side with. [Latin *pars part-*]

partake /pɑːˈteɪk/ v. (**-king**, *past* **partook**, *past part.* **partaken**) 1 (foll. by *of*, *in*) take a share or part. 2 (foll. by *of*) eat or drink some or *colloq.* all (of a thing). [back-formation from *partaker* = *partaker*]

parterre /pɑːˈteə(r)/ n. 1 level space in a formal garden occupied by flower-beds. 2 *US* pit of a theatre. [French, = on the ground]

part-exchange —n. transaction in which goods are given as part of the payment. —v. give (goods) thus.

parthenogenesis /ˌpɑːθɪnəʊˈdʒenɪsɪs/ n. reproduction without fertilization, esp. in invertebrates and lower plants. [Greek *parthenos* virgin]

Parthian shot n. remark or glance etc. on leaving. [*Parthia*, ancient kingdom in W. Asia: from the custom of a retreating Parthian horseman firing a shot at the enemy]

partial /ˈpɑːʃ(ə)l/ adj. 1 not complete; forming only part. 2 biased 3 (foll. by *to*) having a liking for. □ **partiality** /-ʃɪˈælɪtɪ/ n. **partially** adv. **partialness** n. [Latin: related to PART]

partial eclipse n. eclipse in which only part of the luminary is covered.

participant /pɑːˈtɪsɪpənt/ n. participator.

participate /pɑːˈtɪsɪpeɪt/ v. (**-ting**) (often foll. by *in*) take part or a share (in). □ **participation** /-ˈpeɪʃ(ə)n/ n. **participator** n. **participatory** adj. [Latin *particeps -cip-* taking part]

participle /ˈpɑːtɪsɪp(ə)l/ n. word formed from a verb (e.g. *going, gone, being, been*) and used in compound verb forms (e.g. *is going, has been*) or as an adjective (e.g. *working woman, burnt toast*). □ **participial** /-ˈsɪpɪəl/ adj. [Latin: related to PARTICIPLE]

particle /ˈpɑːtɪk(ə)l/ n. 1 minute portion of matter. 2 smallest possible amount (*particle of sense*). 3 a minor part of speech, esp. a short undeclinable one. b common prefix or suffix such as *in-*, *-ness*. [Latin *particula* diminutive of *pars* PART]

particoloured /ˈpɑːtɪˌkʌləd/ adj. (*US* **-colored**) of more than one colour. [related to PART, COLOUR]

particular /pəˈtɪkjʊlə(r)/ —adj. 1 relating to or considered as one thing or person as distinct from others; individual (*in this particular case*). 2 more than is usual; special (*took particular care*). 3 scrupulously exact; fastidious. 4 detailed (*full and particular account*). —n. 1 detail; item. 2 (in *pl.*) information, detailed account. □ **in particular** especially, specifically. [Latin: related to PARTICLE]

particularity /pəˌtɪkjʊˈlærɪtɪ/ n. 1 quality of being individual or particular. 2 fullness or minuteness of detail.

particularize /pəˈtɪkjʊləˌraɪz/ v. (also **-ise**) (**-zing** or **-sing**) (also *absol.*) 1 name specially or one by one. 2 specify (items). □ **particularization** n.

particularly /pəˈtɪkjʊləlɪ/ adv. 1 especially, very. 2 specifically (*particularly asked for you*). 3 in a particular or fastidious manner.

parting n. 1 leave-taking or departure (often *attrib.*: *parting words*). 2 dividing line of combed hair. 3 division; separating.

parting shot n. = PARTHIAN SHOT.

partisan /ˌpɑːtɪˈzæn/ (also **partizan**) —n. 1 strong, esp. unreasoning, supporter of a party, cause, etc. 2 guerrilla. —adj. 1 of partisans. 2 biased. □ **partisanship** n. [Italian: related to PART]

partition /pɑːˈtɪʃ(ə)n/ —n. 1 structure dividing a space, esp. a light interior wall. 2 division into parts, esp. *Polit.* of a country. —v. 1 divide into parts. 2 (foll. by *off*) separate (part of a room etc.) with a partition. [Latin *partior* divide]

partitive /ˈpɑːtɪtɪv/ —adj. (of a word, form, etc.) denoting part of a collective group or quantity. —n. partitive word (e.g. *some, any*) or form. [French or medieval Latin: related to PARTITION]

partly adv. 1 with respect to a part or parts. 2 to some extent.

partner /ˈpɑːtnə(r)/ —n. 1 person who shares or takes part with another or others, esp. in a business. 2 companion in dancing. 3 player (esp. one of two) on the same side in a game. 4 either member of a married or unmarried couple. —v. be the partner of. [alteration of *parcener* joint heir]

partnership n. 1 state of being a partner or partners. 2 joint business. 3 pair or group of partners.

part of speech n. grammatical class of words (in English noun, pronoun, adjective, adverb, verb, etc.).

partook past of PARTAKE.

partridge /ˈpɑːtrɪdʒ/ n. (pl. same or **-s**) game-bird, esp. European or Asian. [Greek *perdix*]

part-song n. song with three or more voice-parts, often unaccompanied.

part-time —adj. (esp. of a job) occupying less than the normal working week etc. —adv. (also **part time**) as a part-time activity (*works part time*).

part-timer *n.* person employed in part-time work.

parturient /pɑːˈtjʊərɪənt/ *adj. formal* about to give birth. [Latin *pario* bring forth]

parturition /ˌpɑːtjʊˈrɪʃ(ə)n/ *n. formal* giving birth.

party /ˈpɑːtɪ/ —*n.* (*pl.* -**ies**) **1** social gathering, usu. of invited guests. **2** people working or travelling together (*search party*). **3** political group putting forward candidates in elections and usu. organized on a national basis. **4** each side in an agreement or dispute. **5** (foll. by *to*) *Law* person. —*v.* (-**ies**, -**ied**) attend a party; celebrate. [Romanic: related to PART]

party line *n.* **1** policy adopted by a political party etc. **2** shared telephone line.

party-wall *n.* wall common to adjoining buildings or rooms.

parvenu /ˈpɑːvənjuː/ *n.* (*pl.* -**s**; *fem.* **parvenue**) (often *attrib.*) newly rich social climber; upstart. [Latin: related to PER, *venio* come]

pas /pɑː/ *n.* (*pl.* same) step, esp. in ballet. [French, = step]

pascal *n.* **1** (**Pascal**) /ˈpæsk(ə)l/ SI unit of pressure. **2** (**Pascal**) /pæsˈkɑːl/ *Computing* programming language used esp. in education. [*Pascal*, name of a scientist]

paschal /ˈpæsk(ə)l/ *adj.* **1** of the Jewish Passover. **2** of Easter. [Hebrew *pesaḥ*]

pas de deux /ˌpɑː də ˈdɜː/ *n.* dance for two. [French, = step for two]

pash *n. slang* brief infatuation. [abbreviation of PASSION]

pasha /ˈpɑːʃə/ *n. hist.* title (placed after the name) of a Turkish military commander, governor, etc. [Turkish]

Pashto /ˈpʌʃtəʊ/ —*n.* language of Afghanistan, parts of Pakistan, etc. —*adj.* of or in this language. [Pashto]

paso doble /ˌpɑːsəʊ ˈdəʊbleɪ/ *n.* Latin-American ballroom dance. [Spanish, = double step]

pasque-flower /ˈpæsk/ *n.* a kind of anemone with bell-shaped purple flowers. [French *passe-fleur*]

pass¹ /pɑːs/ —*v.* **1** (often foll. by *along, by, down, on*, etc.) move onward, esp. past something. **2 a** go past. **b** overtake, esp. in a vehicle. **3** (cause to) be transferred from one person or place to another (*title passes to his son*; *pass the butter*). **4** surpass; exceed (*passes all understanding*). **5** get through. **6 a** go unremarked or uncensured (*let the matter pass*). **b** (foll. by *as, for*) be accepted or known as. **7** move; cause to go (*passed her hand over her face*). **8 a** be successful or adequate, esp. in an examination. **b** be

successful in (an examination). **c** (of an examiner) judge (a candidate) to be satisfactory. **9 a** (of a bill) be approved by (Parliament etc.). **b** cause or allow (a bill) to proceed. **c** (of a bill or proposal be approved. **10** occur, elapse; happen (*time passes slowly*; *heard what passed*). **11** (cause to) circulate; be current. **12** spend (time or a period) (*passed the afternoon reading*). **13** (also *absol.*) (in field games) send (the ball) to a team-mate. **14 a** forgo one's turn or chance. **b** leave a quiz question etc. unanswered. **15** (foll. by *to, into, from*) change (from one form or state to another). **16** come to an end. **17** discharge (esp. faeces or urine) from the body. **18** (foll. by *on, upon*) utter (legal sentence, criticism) upon; adjudicate. —*n.* **1** act of passing. **2 a** success in an examination. **b** university degree without honours. **3 a** permit, esp. for admission, leave, etc. **b** ticket or permit giving free entry, access, travel, etc. **4** (in field games) transference of the ball to a team-mate. **5** desperate position (*come to a fine pass*). □ **in passing** in the course of conversation etc. **make a pass at** *colloq.* make sexual advances to. **pass away 1** *euphem.* die. **2** cease to exist. **pass by 1** go past. **2** disregard, omit. **pass muster** see MUSTER. **pass off 1** (of feelings etc.) disappear gradually. **2** (of proceedings) be carried through (in a specified way). **3** (foll. by *as*) misrepresent or disguise (a person or thing) as something else. **4** evade or lightly dismiss (an awkward remark etc.). **pass on 1** proceed. **2** *euphem.* die. **3** transmit to the next person in a series. **pass out 1** become unconscious. **2** complete military training. **pass over 1** omit, ignore, or disregard. **2** ignore the claims of (a person) to promotion etc. **3** *euphem.* die. **pass round 1** distribute. **2** give to one person after another. **pass the time of day** see TIME. **pass up** *colloq.* refuse or neglect (an opportunity etc.). **pass water** urinate. [Latin *passus* PACE¹]

pass² /pɑːs/ *n.* narrow way through mountains. [var. of PACE¹]

passable *adj.* **1** barely satisfactory; adequate. **2** (of a road, pass, etc.) that can be traversed. □ **passably** *adv.*

passage /ˈpæsɪdʒ/ *n.* **1** process or means of passing; transit. **2** = PASSAGEWAY. **3** liberty or right to pass through. **4** journey by sea or air. **5** transition from one state to another. **6** short extract from a book, piece of music, etc. **7** passing of a bill etc. into law. **8** duct etc. in the body. [French: related to PASS¹]

passageway *n.* narrow path or way; corridor.

passbook n. book issued to an account-holder recording deposits and withdrawals.

passé /'pæsei/ adj. (fem. **passée**) 1 old-fashioned 2 past its prime. [French]

passenger /'pæsindʒə(r)/ n. 1 (often attrib.) traveller in or on a vehicle (other than the driver, pilot, crew, etc.). 2 colloq. idle member of a team, crew, etc. [French passager: related to PASSAGE]

passer-by n. (pl. **passers-by**) person who goes past, esp. by chance. [PASS]

passerine /'pæsəri:n/ -n. perching bird such as the sparrow and most land birds. -adj. of passerines. [Latin passer sparrow]

passim /'pæsim/ adv. throughout; at several points in a book, article, etc. [Latin]

passion /'pæʃ(ə)n/ n. 1 strong emotion. 2 outburst of anger (flew into a passion). 3 intense sexual love. 4 a strong enthusiasm (passion for football). b object arousing this. 5 (the Passion) a suffering of Christ during his last days. b Gospel account of this. c musical setting of this. □ **passionless** adj. [Latin pation pass- suffer]

passionate /'pæʃənət/ adj. dominated, displaying, or caused by strong emotion. □ **passionately** adv.

passion-flower n. climbing plant with a flower supposedly suggestive of the instruments of the Crucifixion.

passion-fruit n. edible fruit of some species of passion-flower.

passion-play n. miracle play representing the Passion.

Passion Sunday n. fifth Sunday in Lent.

passive /'pæsiv/ adj. 1 acted upon, not acting. 2 showing no interest or initiative; submissive. 3 Chem. not active, inert. 4 Gram. indicating that the subject undergoes the action of the verb (e.g. they were seen). □ **passively** adv. **passivity** /-'siviti/ n. [Latin: related to PASSION]

passive resistance n. non-violent refusal to cooperate.

passive smoking n. involuntary inhalation of others' cigarette smoke.

passkey n. 1 private key to a gate etc. 2 master-key.

Passover /'pɑ:s,əuvə(r)/ n. Jewish spring festival commemorating the Exodus from Egypt. [from PASS¹ OVER]

passport n. 1 official document certifying the holder's identity and citizenship, and authorizing travel abroad. 2 (foll. by to) thing that ensures admission or attainment (passport to success). [French passeport: related to PASS¹, PORT¹]

password n. prearranged selected word or phrase securing recognition, admission, etc.

past /pɑ:st/ -adj. 1 gone by in time (in past years; the time is past). 2 recently gone by (the past month). 3 of a former time (past president). 4 Gram. expressing a past action or state. -n. 1 (prec. by the) a past time. b past events (cannot undo the past). 2 person's past life, esp. if discreditable (man with a past). 3 past tense or form. -prep. 1 beyond in time or place (is past two o'clock; lives just past the pub). 2 beyond the range, duration, or compass of (past endurance). -adv. so as to pass by (ran past). □ **not put it past** believe it possible of (a person). **past it** colloq. old and useless. [from PASS¹]

pasta /'pæstə/ n. dried flour paste in various shapes (e.g. lasagne or spaghetti). [Italian: related to PASTE]

paste /peist/ -n. 1 any moist fairly stiff mixture, esp. of powder and liquid. 2 dough of flour with fat, water, etc. 3 liquid adhesive used for sticking paper etc. 4 meat or fish spread (anchovy paste). 5 hard glasslike composition used for imitation gems. -v. (-ting) 1 fasten or coat with paste. 2 slang a beat or thrash. b bomb or bombard heavily. □ **pasting** n. (esp. in sense 2 of v.). [Latin pasta lozenge, from Greek]

pasteboard n. 1 stiff material made by pasting together sheets of paper. 2 (attrib.) flimsy, unsubstantial.

pastel /'pæst(ə)l/ n. 1 (often attrib.) light shade of a colour (pastel blue). 2 crayon of powdered pigments bound with a gum solution. 3 drawing in pastel. [French pastel, or Italian pastello diminutive of PASTA]

pastern /'pæstən/ n. part of a horse's foot between fetlock and hoof. [French from Latin]

paste-up n. document prepared for copying etc. by pasting sections on to a backing.

pasteurize /'pɑ:stʃə,raiz/ v. (also **-ise**) (-zing or -sing) partially sterilize (milk etc.) by heating. □ **pasteurization** /-'zeiʃ(ə)n/ n. [Pasteur, name of a chemist]

pastiche /pæ'sti:ʃ/ n. 1 picture or musical composition from or imitating various sources. 2 literary or other work composed in the style of a well-known author etc. [Latin pasta PASTE]

pastille /'pæstil/ n. small sweet or lozenge. [French from Latin]

pastime /ˈpɑːstaɪm/ n. recreation, hobby. [from PASS', TIME]

past master n. expert.

pastor /ˈpɑːstə(r)/ n. minister, esp. of a Nonconformist church. [Latin *pasco past-* feed]

pastoral /ˈpɑːstər(ə)l/ —adj. 1 of shepherds, flocks, or herds. 2 (of land) used for pasture. 3 (of a poem, picture, etc.) portraying (esp. romanticized) country life. 4 of a pastor. —n. 1 pastoral poem, play, picture, etc. 2 letter from a pastor (esp. a bishop) to the clergy or people. [Latin *pastoralis*: related to PASTOR]

pastorale /ˌpæstəˈrɑː/ n. (pl. -s or -li /-liː/) musical work with a rustic theme or atmosphere. [Italian: related to PASTORAL]

pastorate /ˈpɑːstərət/ n. 1 office or tenure of a pastor. 2 body of pastors.

pastrami /pæˈstrɑːmɪ/ n. seasoned smoked beef. [Yiddish]

pastry /ˈpeɪstrɪ/ n. (pl. -ies) 1 dough of flour, fat, and water used as a base and covering for pies etc. 2 cake etc. made wholly or partly of this. [from PASTE]

pastry-cook n. cook who specializes in pastry.

pasturage /ˈpɑːstʃərɪdʒ/ n. 1 land for pasture. 2 pasturing of cattle etc.

pasture /ˈpɑːstʃə(r)/ —n. 1 grassland suitable for grazing. 2 herbage for animals. —v. (-ring) 1 put (animals) to pasture. 2 (of animals) graze. [Latin: related to PASTOR]

pasty¹ /ˈpeɪstɪ/ n. (pl. -ies) pastry shaped around esp. a meat and vegetable filling. [Latin: related to PASTE]

pasty² /ˈpeɪstɪ/ adj. (-ier, -iest) unhealthily pale (*pasty-faced*). □ **pastiness** n.

Pat. abbr. Patent.

pat¹ —v. (-tt-) 1 strike gently with a flat palm, esp. in affection, sympathy, etc. 2 flatten or mould by patting. —n. 1 light stroke or tap, esp. with the hand in affection etc. 2 sound made by this. 3 small mass (esp. of butter) formed by patting. □ **pat on the back** congratulatory gesture. [probably imitative]

pat² —adj. 1 prepared or known thoroughly, apposite or opportune, esp. glibly so (*a pat answer*). —adv. 1 in a pat manner. 2 appositely. □ **have off pat** know or have memorized perfectly. [related to PAT¹]

patch —n. 1 material used to mend a hole or as reinforcement. 2 shield protecting an injured eye. 3 large or irregular distinguishable area. 4 colloq. period of a specified, esp. unpleasant, kind (*went through a bad patch*). 5 piece of ground. 6 colloq. area assigned to, or patrolled by, esp. a police officer. 7 plants growing in one place (*cabbage patch*). 8 scrap, remnant. —v. 1 (often foll. by *up*) repair with a patch or patches. 2 (of material) serve as a patch to. 3 (often foll. by *up*) put together, esp. hastily. 4 (foll. by *up*) settle (a quarrel etc.), esp. hastily or temporarily. □ **not a patch on** colloq. greatly inferior to. [perhaps French, var. of PIECE]

patchboard n. board with electrical sockets linked by movable leads to enable changeable permutations of connection.

patchouli /ˈpætʃʊlɪ/ n. 1 strongly scented E. Indian plant. 2 perfume from this. [native name in Madras]

patch pocket n. piece of cloth sewn on a garment as a pocket.

patch test n. test for allergy by applying patches of allergenic substances to the skin.

patchwork n. 1 (often attrib.) stitching together of small pieces of variegated cloth to form a pattern (*patchwork quilt*). 2 thing composed of fragments etc.

patchy adj. (-ier, -iest) 1 uneven in quality. 2 having or existing in patches. □ **patchily** adv. **patchiness** n.

pate n. archaic or colloq. head. [origin unknown]

pâté /ˈpæteɪ/ n. paste of mashed and spiced meat or fish etc. [French, = PASTY¹]

pâté de foie gras /ˌpæteɪ də fwɑː ˈɡrɑː/ n. fatted goose liver pâté. [French]

patella /pəˈtelə/ n. (pl. **patellae** /-liː/) kneecap. □ **patellar** adj. [Latin, = pan, diminutive of *patina*: related to PATEN]

paten /ˈpæt(ə)n/ n. shallow dish for bread at the Eucharist. [Latin *patina*]

patent /ˈpeɪt(ə)nt, ˈpæt-/ —n. 1 official document conferring a right or title, esp. the sole right to make, use, or sell a specified invention. 2 invention or process so protected. —adj. 1 /ˈpeɪt(ə)nt/ obvious, plain. 2 conferred or protected by patent. 3 a proprietary. b to which one has a proprietary claim. —v. obtain a patent for (an invention). □ **patently** /ˈpeɪtəntlɪ/ adv. (in sense 1 of adj.). [Latin *pateo* lie open]

patentee /ˌpeɪtənˈtiː/ n. 1 person who takes out or holds a patent. 2 person entitled temporarily to the benefit of a patent.

patent leather n. glossy leather.

patent medicine n. proprietary medicine available without prescription.

patent office n. office issuing patents.

pater /ˈpeɪtə(r)/ n. colloq. father. [Latin]

■ **Usage** *Pater* is now only found in jocular or affected use.

paterfamilias /ˌpeɪtəfəˈmɪlɪæs/ n. male head of a family or household. [Latin, = father of the family]

paternal /pəˈtɜːn(ə)l/ adj. 1 of, like, or appropriate to a father; fatherly. 2 related through the father. 3 (of a government etc.) limiting freedom and responsibility by well-meant regulations. □ **paternally** adv. [Latin: related to PATER]

paternalism n. policy of governing or behaving in a paternal way. □ **paternalistic** /-ˈlɪstɪk/ adj.

paternity /pəˈtɜːnɪtɪ/ n. 1 fatherhood. 2 one's paternal origin.

paternity suit n. lawsuit held to determine if a certain man is the father of a certain child.

paternoster /ˌpætəˈnɒstə(r)/ n. Lord's Prayer, esp. in Latin. [Latin pater noster our father]

path /pɑːθ/ n. (pl. **paths** /pɑːðz/) 1 way or track made for or by walking. 2 line along which a person or thing moves (flight path). 3 course of action. [Old English]

pathetic /pəˈθetɪk/ adj. 1 arousing pity, sadness, or contempt. 2 colloq. miserably inadequate. □ **pathetically** adv. [Greek pathos suffering]

pathetic fallacy n. attribution of human emotions to inanimate things, esp. in literature.

pathfinder n. explorer; pioneer.

pathogen /ˈpæθədʒ(ə)n/ n. agent causing disease. □ **pathogenic** /-ˈdʒenɪk/ adj. [Greek pathos suffering, -GEN]

pathological /ˌpæθəˈlɒdʒɪk(ə)l/ adj. 1 of pathology. 2 of or caused by physical or mental disorder (pathological fear of spiders). □ **pathologically** adv.

pathology /pəˈθɒlədʒɪ/ n. the study or symptoms of disease. □ **pathologist** n.

pathos /ˈpeɪθɒs/ n. evocation of pity or sadness in speech, writing, etc. [Greek: related to PATHETIC]

pathway n. path or its course.

patience /ˈpeɪʃ(ə)ns/ n. 1 ability to endure delay, hardship, provocation, etc. 2 perseverance or forbearance. 3 solo card-game. [Latin: related to PASSION]

patient —adj. having or showing patience. —n. person receiving or registered to receive medical treatment. □ **patiently** adv.

patina /ˈpætɪnə/ n. 1 film. usu. green, formed on old bronze. 2 similar film on other surfaces. 3 gloss produced by age on woodwork. [Latin: related to PATEN]

patio /ˈpætɪəʊ/ n. (pl. -s) 1 paved usu. roofless area adjoining a house. 2 inner roofless court in a Spanish or Spanish-American house. [Spanish]

patisserie /pəˈtiːsərɪ/ n. 1 shop where pastries are made and sold. 2 pastries collectively. [Latin: related to PASTE]

patois /ˈpætwɑː/ n. (pl. same /-wɑːz/) regional dialect, differing from the literary language. [French]

patna rice /ˈpætnə/ n. rice with long firm grains. [from Patna in India]

patriarch /ˈpeɪtrɪˌɑːk/ n. 1 male head of a family or tribe. 2 (often in pl.) any of those regarded as fathers of the human race, esp. the sons of Jacob, or Abraham, Isaac, and Jacob, and their forefathers. 3 Eccl. a chief bishop in the Orthodox Church. b RC Ch. bishop ranking immediately below the pope. 4 venerable old man. □ **patriarchal** /-ˈɑːk(ə)l/ adj. [Greek patria family, arkhēs ruler]

patriarchate /ˈpeɪtrɪˌɑːkət/ n. 1 office, see, or residence of a Church patriarch. 2 rank of a tribal patriarch.

patriarchy /ˈpeɪtrɪˌɑːkɪ/ n. (pl. -ies) male-dominated social system, with descent through the male line.

patrician /pəˈtrɪʃ(ə)n/ —n. hist. member of the nobility in ancient Rome. —adj. 1 aristocratic. 2 hist. of the ancient Roman nobility. [Latin patricius: related to PATER]

patricide /ˈpætrɪsaɪd/ n. = PARRICIDE (esp. with reference to the killing of one's father). □ **patricidal** /-ˈsaɪd(ə)l/ adj. [Latin: alteration of parricida]

patrimony /ˈpætrɪmənɪ/ n. (pl. -ies) 1 property inherited from one's father or ancestor. 2 heritage. □ **patrimonial** /-ˈməʊnɪəl/ adj. [Latin: related to PATER]

patriot /ˈpeɪtrɪət, ˈpæt-/ n. person devoted to and ready to defend his or her country. □ **patriotic** /-ˈɒtɪk/ adj. **patriotically** /-ˈɒtɪklɪ/ adv. **patriotism** n. [Greek patris fatherland]

patristic /pəˈtrɪstɪk/ adj. of the early Christian writers or their work. [Latin: related to PATER]

patrol /pəˈtrəʊl/ —n. 1 act of walking or traveling around an area, esp. regularly, for security or supervision. 2 guards, police, etc. sent out on patrol. 3 a troops sent out to reconnoitre. b such reconnaissance. 4 unit of six to eight Scouts or Guides. —v. (-ll-) 1 carry out a patrol of. 2 act as a patrol. [German Patrolle from French]

patrol car n. police car used for patrols.

patron /ˈpeɪtr(ə)n/ n. (fem. **patroness**) 1 person financially supporting a person, cause, etc. 2 customer of a shop etc. [Latin patronus: related to PATER]

patronage /ˈpætrənɪdʒ/ n. 1 patron's or customer's support. 2 right or control of

appointments to office, privileges, etc. 3 condescending manner.

patronize /ˈpætrəˌnaɪz/ *v.* (also **-ise**) (**-zing** or **-sing**) 1 treat condescendingly. 2 be a patron or customer of. □ **patronizing** *adj.* **patronizingly** *adv.*

patron saint *n.* saint regarded as protecting a person, place, activity, etc.

patronymic /ˌpætrəˈnɪmɪk/ *n.* name derived from the name of a father or ancestor (e.g. *Johnson, O'Brien, Ivanovich*). [Greek *patēr* father, *onoma* name]

patten /ˈpæt(ə)n/ *n. hist.* shoe or clog with a raised sole or set on an iron ring, for walking in mud etc. [French *patin*]

patter[1] *—n.* sound of quick light steps or taps. *—v.* make this sound (*rain pattering on the window-panes*). [from PAT[1]]

patter[2] *—n.* 1 rapid speech used by a comedian. 2 salesman's persuasive talk. *—v.* talk or say glibly or mechanically. [originally *pater*, = PATERNOSTER]

pattern /ˈpæt(ə)n/ *—n.* 1 repeated decorative design on wallpaper, cloth, etc. 2 regular or logical form, order, etc. (*behaviour pattern*). 3 model, design, or instructions for making something (*knitting pattern*). 4 excellent example, model (*pattern of elegance*). 5 wooden or metal shape from which a mould is made for a casting. 6 random combination of shapes or colours. *—v.* 1 (usu. foll. by *after, on*) model (a thing) on a design etc. 2 decorate with a pattern. [from PATRON]

patty /ˈpætɪ/ *n.* (*pl.* **-ies**) little pie or pasty. [French PÂTÉ, after PASTY[1]]

paucity /ˈpɔːsɪtɪ/ *n.* smallness of number or quantity. [Latin *paucus* few]

paunch /pɔːntʃ/ *n.* belly, stomach, esp. when protruding. □ **paunchy** *adj.* (**-ier, -iest**). [Anglo-French *pa(u)nche* from Latin *pantices* bowels]

pauper /ˈpɔːpə(r)/ *n.* poor person. □ **pauperism** *n.* [Latin, = poor]

pause /pɔːz/ *—n.* 1 temporary stop or rest that is to be lengthened. *—v.* (**-sing**) make a pause; wait. □ **give pause to** cause to hesitate. [Greek *pauō* stop]

pavane /pəˈvɑːn/ *n.* (also **pavan** /ˈpæv(ə)n/) *hist.* 1 a kind of stately dance. 2 music for this. [French from Spanish]

pave *v.* (**-ving**) cover (a street, floor, etc.) with a durable surface. □ **pave the way** (usu. foll. by *for*) make preparations. □ **paving** *n.* [Latin *pavio* ram (v.)]

pavement *n.* 1 raised path for pedestrians beside a road. 2 covering of a street, floor, etc., made of usu. rectangular stones. [Latin *pavimentum*: related to PAVE]

pavement artist *n.* artist who draws in chalk on paving-stones for tips.

pavilion /pəˈvɪljən/ *n.* 1 building at a sports ground for changing, refreshments, etc. 2 summerhouse or decorative shelter in a park. 3 large tent at a show, fair, etc. 4 building or stand for entertainments, at an exhibition, etc. [Latin *papilio* butterfly]

paving-stone *n.* large flat stone for paving.

pavlova /pævˈləʊvə/ *n.* meringue cake with cream and fruit. [*Pavlova*, name of a ballerina]

Pavlovian /pævˈləʊvɪən/ *adj.* 1 reacting predictably to a stimulus. 2 of such a stimulus or response. [*Pavlov*, name of a physiologist]

paw *—n.* 1 foot of an animal having claws or nails. 2 *colloq.* person's hand. *—v.* 1 strike or scrape with a paw or foot. 2 *colloq.* fondle awkwardly or indecently. [French *poue* from Germanic]

pawl[1] *n.* 1 lever with a catch for the teeth of a wheel or bar. 2 *Naut.* short bar used to lock a capstan, windlass, etc. [Low German or Dutch]

pawn[1] *n.* 1 *Chess* piece of the smallest size and value. 2 person used by others for their own ends. [French *poun* from Latin *pedo -onis* foot-soldier]

pawn[2] *—v.* 1 deposit (a thing) with a pawnbroker as security for money lent. 2 pledge or wager (one's life, honour, etc.). *—n.* object left in pawn. □ **in pawn** held as security. [French *pan* from Germanic]

pawnbroker *n.* person who lends money at interest on the security of personal property.

pawnshop *n.* pawnbroker's shop.

pawpaw /ˈpɔːpɔː/ *n.* (also **papaw** /pəˈpɔː/, **papaya** /pəˈpaɪə/) 1 elongated melon-shaped fruit with orange flesh. 2 tropical tree bearing this. [Spanish and Portuguese *papaya*]

pax *n.* 1 kiss of peace. 2 (as *int.*) *slang* call for a truce (used esp. by schoolchildren). [Latin, = peace]

pay *—v.* (*past* and *past part.* **paid**) 1 (also *absol.*) give (a person etc.) what is due for services done, goods received, debts incurred, etc. (*paid him in full*). 2 a give (a usu. specified amount) for work done, a debt, etc. (*they pay £6 an hour*). b (foll. by *to*) hand over the amount of (a debt, wages, etc.) □ to (*paid the money to the assistant*). 3 a give, bestow, or express (attention, a compliment, etc.) (*paid them no heed*). b make (a visit) (*paid a call on their uncle*). 4 (also *absol.*) be profitable or advantageous to (a person etc.). 5 reward or punish (*shall pay you for that*).

6 (usu. as **paid** adj.). recompense (work, time, etc.) □ (paid holiday). **7** (usu. foll. by out, away) let out (a rope) by slackening it. —n. wages. □ **in the pay of** employed by. **pay back 1** repay. **2** punish or have revenge on. **pay for 1** hand over the money for. **2** bear the cost of 3 suffer or be punished for (a fault etc.). **pay in** pay (money) into a bank etc. account. **pay its** (or **one's**) **way** cover costs. **pay one's last respects** attend a funeral to show respect. **pay off 1** dismiss. **2** colloq. yield good results; succeed. **3** pay (a debt) in full. **pay one's respects** make a polite visit. **pay through the nose** colloq. pay much more than a fair price. **pay up** pay the full amount (ob). **put paid to** colloq. 1 deal effectively with (a person). **2** terminate (hopes etc.). □ **payee** /peɪˈiː/ n. [Latin paco appease: related to PEACE]

payable adj. that must or may be paid; due (payable in April).

pay-as-you-earn n. deduction of income tax from wages at source.

pay-bed n. private hospital bed.

pay-claim n. (esp. a trade union's) demand for a pay increase.

pay-day n. day on which wages are paid.

PAYE abbr. pay-as-you-earn.

paying guest n. boarder.

payload n. 1 part of an aircraft's load yielding revenue. 2 explosive warhead carried by a rocket etc. 3 goods carried by a road vehicle.

paymaster n. 1 official who pays troops, workmen, etc. 2 usu. derog. person, organization, etc., to whom another owes loyalty because of payment given. □ **Paymaster General** n. (in full **Paymaster General**) Treasury minister responsible for payments.

payment n. 1 paying. 2 amount paid. 3 reward, recompense.

pay-off n. slang 1 payment. 2 climax. 3 final reckoning.

payola /peɪˈəʊlə/ n. esp. US slang bribe offered for unofficial promotion of a product etc. in the media.

pay-packet n. envelope etc. containing an employee's wages.

pay phone n. coin-box telephone.

payroll n. list of employees receiving regular pay.

Pb symb. lead. [Latin plumbum]

PC abbr. 1 police constable. 2 Privy Councillor. 3 personal computer.

p.c. abbr. 1 per cent. 2 postcard.

PCB abbr. 1 polychlorinated biphenyl, any of several toxic aromatic compounds formed as waste in industrial processes. 2 Computing printed circuit board.

Pd symb. palladium.

pd. abbr. paid.

p.d.q. abbr. colloq pretty damn quick.

PE abbr. physical education.

pea n. 1 a hardy climbing plant with edible seeds growing in pods. b its seed. 2 similar plant (sweet pea; chick-pea). [from PEASE taken as a plural]

peace n. 1 a quiet; tranquillity. b mental calm; serenity. 2 a (often attrib.) freedom from or the cessation of war (peace talks). b (esp. Peace) treaty of peace between States etc. at war. 3 freedom from civil disorder. □ **at peace 1** in a state of friendliness. 2 serene. 3 euphem. dead. **hold one's peace** keep silent. **keep the peace** prevent, or refrain from, strife. **make one's peace** (often with) re-establish friendly relations. **make peace** agree to end a war or quarrel. [Latin pax pac-]

peaceable adj. 1 disposed to peace. 2 peaceful; tranquil. □ **peaceably** adv. [Latin placibilis pleasing: related to PLEASE]

peaceful adj. 1 characterized by peace; tranquil. 2 not infringing peace (peaceful coexistence). □ **peacefully** adv. **peacefulness** n.

peacemaker n. person who brings about peace. □ **peacemaking** n. & adj.

peace dividend n. public money which becomes available when defence spending is reduced.

peace-offering n. propitiatory or conciliatory gift.

peace-pipe n. tobacco-pipe as a token of peace among N. American Indians.

peacetime n. period when a country is not at war.

peach¹ n. 1 a round juicy fruit with downy yellow or pink skin. b tree bearing this. 2 yellowish-pink colour. 3 colloq. a person or thing of superlative quality. b attractive young woman. □ **peachy** adj. (-ier, -iest). [Latin persica Persian (apple)]

peach² v.intr. (usu. foll. by against, on) colloq. turn informer; inform. (from obsolete appeach: related to IMPEACH]

peach Melba n. dish of peaches, ice-cream, and raspberry sauce.

peacock n. (pl. same or -s) male peafowl, with brilliant plumage and an erectile fanlike tail with eyelike markings. [from Latin pavo peacock, COCK']

peacock blue adj. & n. (as adj. often hyphenated) lustrous greenish blue of a peacock's neck.

peacock butterfly n. butterfly with eyelike wing markings.

peafowl n. a kind of pheasant; peacock, peahen.

pea green adj. & n. (as adj. often hyphenated) bright green.

peahen n. female peafowl.

peak[1] – n. **1** projecting usu. pointed part, esp.: **a** the pointed top of a mountain. **b** a mountain with a peak. **c** a stiff brim at the front of a cap. **2 a** highest point of a curve, graph, etc. (*peak of the wave*). **b** time of greatest success, fitness, etc. **3** *attrib.* maximum, busiest (*peak viewing; peak hours*). – v. reach its highest value, quality, etc. (*output peaked*). □ **peaked** *adj.* [related to PICK[2]]

peak[2] v. **1** waste away. **2** (as **peaked** *adj.*) sharp-featured; pinched. [origin unknown]

peak-load n. maximum of electric power demand etc.

peaky *adj.* (**-ier, -iest**) **1** sickly; puny. **2** white-faced.

peal – n. **1 a** loud ringing of a bell or bells, esp. a series of changes. **b** set of bells. **2** loud repeated sound, esp. of thunder, laughter, etc. – v. **1** (cause to) sound in a peal. **2** utter sonorously. [from APPEAL]

pean *US* var. of PAEAN.

peanut n. **1** plant of the pea family bearing pods underground that contain seeds used for food and oil. **2** seed of this. **3** (in *pl.*) *colloq.* paltry thing or amount, esp. of money.

peanut butter n. paste of ground roasted peanuts.

pear /peə(r)/ n. **1** yellowish or greenish fleshy fruit, tapering towards the stalk. **2** tree bearing this. [Latin *pirum*]

pearl /pɜːl/ – n. **1 a** (often *attrib.*) rounded usu. white or bluish-grey lustrous solid formed within the shell of certain oysters, highly prized as a gem. **b** imitation of this. **c** (in *pl.*) necklace of pearls. **2** precious thing; finest example. **3** thing like a pearl, e.g. a dewdrop or tear. – v. **1** *poet.* form or sprinkle with pearly drops. **2** reduce (barley etc.) to small rounded grains. **3** fish for pearls. [Italian *perla*, from Latin *perna* leg]

pearl barley n. barley ground to small rounded grains.

pearl bulb n. translucent electric light bulb.

pearl button n. mother-of-pearl button, or an imitation of it.

pearl-diver n. person who dives for pearl-oysters.

pearlite var. of PERLITE.

pearly – *adj.* (**-ier, -iest**) like, containing, or adorned with pearls; lustrous. – n. (*pl.* **-ies**) **1** pearly king or queen. **2** (in *pl.*) pearly king's or queen's clothes.

Pearly Gates *n.pl. colloq.* gates of Heaven.

pearly king n. (also **pearly queen**) London costermonger (or his wife)

wearing clothes covered with pearl buttons.

pearly nautilus see NAUTILUS.

peasant /ˈpez(ə)nt/ n. **1** (in some rural agricultural countries) small farmer; agricultural worker. **2** *derog.* lout; boor. □ **peasantry** n. (*pl.* **-ies**). [Anglo-French *paisant* from *païs* country]

pease /piːz/ *n.pl. archaic* peas. [Latin *pisa*]

pease-pudding n. boiled split peas (served esp. with boiled beef or ham).

peashooter n. small tube for blowing dried peas through as a toy.

pea-souper n. *colloq.* thick yellowish fog.

peat n. **1** partly carbonized vegetable matter used for fuel, in horticulture, etc. **2** cut piece of this. □ **peaty** *adj.* [perhaps Celtic: related to PIECE]

peatbog n. bog composed of peat.

pebble /ˈpeb(ə)l/ n. small stone worn smooth esp. by the action of water. □ **pebbly** *adj.* [Old English]

pebble-dash n. mortar with stone chippings in it as a coating for external walls.

pecan /ˈpiːkən/ n. **1** pinkish-brown smooth nut with an edible kernel. **2** type of hickory producing this. [Algonquian]

peccadillo /ˌpekəˈdɪləʊ/ n. (*pl.* **-es** or **-s**) trifling offence; venial sin. [Spanish *pecadillo*, from Latin *pecco* to sin (v.)]

peck[1] – v. **1** strike or bite with a beak. **2** kiss hastily or perfunctorily. **3** make (a hole) by pecking. **b** (foll. by *out*, *off*) remove or pluck out by pecking. **4** (also *absol.*) colloq. eat listlessly; nibble at. – n. **1** stroke, mark, or bite made by a beak. **2** hasty or perfunctory kiss.

peck at **1** eat (food) listlessly; nibble. **2** carp at; nag. **3** strike repeatedly with a beak. [probably Low German]

peck[2] n. measure of capacity for dry goods, equal to 2 gallons or 8 quarts. □ **a peck of** large number or amount of. [Anglo-French]

pecker n. *US coarse slang* penis. □ **keep your pecker up** *colloq.* remain cheerful.

pecking order n. social hierarchy, orig. as observed among hens.

peckish *adj. colloq.* hungry.

pectin /ˈpektɪn/ n. soluble gelatinous carbohydrate found in ripe fruits etc. and used as a setting agent in jams and jellies. □ **pectic** *adj.* [Greek *pēgnumi* make solid]

pectoral /ˈpektər(ə)l/ – *adj.* of or worn on the breast or chest (*pectoral fin; pectoral muscle; pectoral cross*). – n. pectoral muscle or fin. [Latin *pectus -tor-* chest]

peculate /'pekjʊleɪt/ v. (-ting) embezzle (money). □ **peculation** /-'leɪʃ(ə)n/ n. **peculator** n. [Latin: related to PECULIAR]

peculiar /prɪ'kjuːlɪə(r)/ adj. 1 strange; odd; unusual. 2 a (usu. foll. by to) belonging exclusively (peculiar to the time). b belonging to the individual (in their own peculiar way). 3 particular; special (point of peculiar interest). [Latin peculium private property, from pecu cattle]

peculiarity /prɪˌkjuːlɪ'ærɪtɪ/ n. (pl. -ies) 1 idiosyncrasy; oddity. 2 characteristic. 3 being peculiar.

peculiarly /prɪ'kjuːlɪəlɪ/ adv. 1 more than usually, especially (peculiarly annoying). 2 oddly.

pecuniary /prɪ'kjuːnɪərɪ/ adj. 1 of or concerning money. 2 (of an offence) entailing a money penalty. [Latin pecunia money, from pecu cattle]

pedagogue /'pedəgɒg/ n. archaic or derog. schoolmaster; teacher. □ **pedagogic** /-'gɒgɪk/ adj. **pedagogical** /-'gɒgɪk(ə)l/ adj. [Greek pais paid- child, agō lead]

pedagogy /'pedəgɒdʒɪ, -gɒgɪ/ n. science of teaching.

pedal -n. /'ped(ə)l/ lever or key operated by foot, esp. in a vehicle, on a bicycle, or on some musical instruments (e.g. the organ). -v. /'ped(ə)l/ (-ll-; US -l-) 1 operate the pedals of a bicycle, organ, etc. 2 propel (a bicycle etc.) with the pedals. -adj. /'piːd(ə)l/ of the foot or feet. [Latin pes ped- foot]

pedalo /'pedələʊ/ n. (pl. -s) pedal-operated pleasure-boat.

pedant /'ped(ə)nt/ n. derog. person who insists on adherence to formal rules or literal meaning. □ **pedantic** /prɪ'dæntɪk/ adj. **pedantically** /prɪ'dæntɪkəlɪ/ adv. **pedantry** n. [French from Italian]

peddle /'ped(ə)l/ v. (-ling) 1 a sell (goods) as a pedlar. b advocate or promote. 2 sell (drugs) illegally. 3 engage in selling, esp. as a pedlar. [back-formation from PEDLAR]

peddler n. 1 person who sells drugs illegally. 2 US var. of PEDLAR.

pederast /'pedəræst/ n. (also **paederast**) man who engages in pederasty.

pederasty /'pedəræstɪ/ n. (also **paederasty**) anal intercourse between a man and a boy. [Greek pais paid- boy, erastēs lover]

pedestal /'pedɪst(ə)l/ n. 1 base supporting a column or pillar. 2 stone etc. base of a statue etc. □ **put on a pedestal** admire disproportionately, idolize. [Italian piedestallo = foot of stall]

pedestrian /prɪ'destrɪən/ -n. 1 (often attrib.) person who is walking, esp. in a

---

town. -adj. prosaic; dull; uninspired. □ **pedestrianize** v. (also -ise) (-zing or -sing). [Latin: related to PEDAL] **pedestrian crossing** n. part of a road where crossing pedestrians have right of way.

pediatrics US var. of PAEDIATRICS.

pedicure /'pedɪkjʊə(r)/ n. 1 care or treatment of the feet, esp. the toenails. 2 person practising this for a living. [Latin pes ped- foot, cura care]

pedigree /'pedɪgriː/ n. 1 (often attrib.) recorded line of descent (esp. a distinguished one) of a person or pure-bred animal. 2 genealogical table. 3 colloq. 'life history' of a person, thing, idea, etc. □ **pedigreed** adj. [probably from French pie de grue (unrecorded) crane's foot, a mark denoting succession in pedigrees]

pediment /'pedɪmənt/ n. triangular part crowning the front of a building, esp. over a portico. [from periment, perhaps a corruption of PYRAMID]

pedlar /'pedlə(r)/ n. (US **peddler**) 1 travelling seller of small items. 2 (usu. foll. by of) retailer (of gossip etc.). [alteration of pedder from ped pannier]

pedo- US var. of PAEDO-.

pedometer /prɪ'dɒmɪtə(r)/ n. instrument for estimating distance walked by recording the number of steps taken. [Latin pes ped- foot: related to -METER]

pedophile US var. of PAEDOPHILE.

pedophilia US var. of PAEDOPHILIA.

peduncle /prɪ'dʌŋk(ə)l/ n. stalk of a flower, fruit, or cluster. 2 main stalk bearing a solitary flower or subordinate stalks. □ **peduncular** /-'dʌŋkjʊlə(r)/ adj. [related to PEDUNCLE: related to PEDAL]

pee colloq. -v. (**pees**, **peed**) urinate. -n. 1 act of urinating. 2 urine. [from PISS]

peek -v. (usu. foll. by in, out, at) peep slyly; glance. -n. quick or sly look. [origin unknown]

peel -v. 1 a strip the skin, rind, wrapping, etc. from. b (usu. foll. by off) strip (skin, peel, wrapping, etc.). 2 a become bare of skin, paint, etc. b (often foll. by off) (of skin, paint, etc.) flake off. 3 (often foll. by off) colloq. (of a person) strip ready for exercise etc. -n. outer covering of a fruit, vegetable, etc.; rind. □ **peel off** veer away and detach oneself from a group etc. □ **peeler** n. [Old English from Latin pilo strip of hair]

peeling n. (usu. in pl.) stripped-off piece of peel.

peen n. wedge-shaped or thin or curved end of a hammer-head. [origin unknown]

peep[1] -v. 1 (usu. foll. by at, in, out, into) look through a narrow opening; look furtively. 2 (usu. foll. by out) come slowly into view; emerge. -n. 1 furtive

peep

or peering glance. **2** first appearance (*peep of day*). [origin unknown]

peep² *v.* make a shrill feeble sound as of young birds, mice, etc. —*n.* **1** such a sound **2** slight sound, utterance, or complaint (*not a peep out of them*). [imitative]

peep-hole *n.* small hole for peeping through.

peeping Tom *n.* furtive voyeur.

peep-show *n.* small exhibition of pictures etc. viewed through a lens or hole set into a box etc.

peer¹ *v.* (usu. foll. by *into, at*, etc.) look closely or with difficulty. [origin unknown]

peer² *n.* **1 a** (*fem.* **peeress**) member of one of the degrees of the nobility in Britain or Ireland, i.e. a duke, marquis, earl, viscount, or baron. **b** noble of any country. **2** person who is equal in ability, standing, rank, or value. [Latin *par* equal]

peerage *n.* **1** peers as a class; the nobility. **2** rank of peer or peeress.

peer group *n.* group of people of the same age, status, etc.

peerless *adj.* unequalled, superb.

peer of the realm *n.* peer entitled to sit in the House of Lords.

peeve *colloq.* —*v.* (**-ving**) (usu. as **peeved** *adj.*) irritate, annoy. —*n.* cause or state of irritation. [back-formation from PEEVISH]

peevish *adj.* irritable. □ **peevishly** *adv.* [origin unknown]

peewit /'piːwɪt/ *n.* (also **pewit**) lapwing. [a sound imitative of its cry]

peg —*n.* **1** pin or bolt of wood, metal, etc., for holding things together, hanging garments on, holding up a tent, etc. **2** each of the pins used to tighten or loosen the strings of a violin etc. **3** pin for marking position, e.g. on a cribbage-board. **4** = CLOTHES-PEG. **5** occasion or pretext (*peg to hang an argument on*). **6** drink, esp. of spirits. —*v.* **1** (usu. foll. by *down, in, out*, etc.) fix (a thing) with a peg. **2** stabilize (prices, wages, etc.). **3** mark (the score) with pegs on a cribbage-board. □ **off the peg** (of clothes) ready-made. **peg away** (often foll. by *at*) work consistently. **peg out 1** *slang* die. **2** mark the boundaries of. **square peg in a round hole** misfit. **take a person down a peg or two** humble a person. [probably Low German or Dutch]

pegboard *n.* board with small holes for pegs, used for displays, games, etc.

peg-leg *n. colloq.* **1** artificial leg. **2** person with this.

pen

pejorative /prˈdʒɒrətɪv/ —*adj.* derogatory. —*n.* derogatory word. [Latin *pejor* worse]

peke *n. colloq.* Pekingese. [abbreviation]

Pekingese /ˌpiːkɪˈniːz/ *n.* (also **Pekinese**) (*pl.* same) lap-dog of a short-legged breed with long hair and a snub nose. [from *Peking* (Beijing) in China]

pelargonium /ˌpɛləˈɡəʊnɪəm/ *n.* plant with red, pink, or white flowers and, often, fragrant leaves; geranium. [Greek *pelargos* stork]

pelf *n. derog.* or *joc.* money; wealth. [French: related to PILFER]

pelican /'pɛlɪkən/ *n.* large water-bird with a large bill and a pouch in its throat for storing fish. [Greek *pelekan*]

pelican crossing *n.* pedestrian crossing with traffic-lights operated by pedestrians.

pelisse /pɛˈliːs/ *n. hist.* **1** woman's long cloak with armholes or sleeves. **2** fur-lined cloak as part of a hussar's uniform. [Latin *pellicia* (garment) of fur, from *pellis* skin]

pellagra /pəˈlæɡrə/ *n.* disease with cracking of the skin and often ending in insanity. [Italian from *pelle* skin]

pellet /'pɛlɪt/ *n.* **1** small compressed ball of paper, bread, etc. **2** pill. **3** piece of small shot. [French *pelote* from Latin *pila* ball]

pellicle /'pɛlɪk(ə)l/ *n.* thin skin, membrane, or film. [Latin diminutive of *pellis* skin]

pell-mell /pɛlˈmɛl/ *adv.* **1** headlong, recklessly. **2** in disorder or confusion. [French *pêle-mêle*]

pellucid /prˈluːsɪd/ *adj.* **1** transparent. **2** (of style, speech, etc.) clear. [Latin: related to PER-]

pelmet /'pɛlmɪt/ *n.* narrow border of cloth, wood, etc. fitted esp. above a window to conceal the curtain rail. [probably French]

pelt¹ —*v.* **1** (usu. foll. by *with*) strike repeatedly with thrown objects. **2** (usu. foll. by *down*) (of rain etc.) fall quickly and torrentially. **3** run fast. —*n.* pelting. □ **at full pelt** as fast as possible. [origin unknown]

pelt² *n.* undressed skin, usu. of a fur-bearing mammal. [French, ultimately from Latin *pellis* skin]

pelvis /'pɛlvɪs/ *n.* basin-shaped cavity in most vertebrates, formed from the hip-bone with the sacrum and other vertebrae. □ **pelvic** *adj.* [Latin, = basin]

pen¹ —*n.* **1** instrument for writing etc. with ink. **2** (**the pen**) occupation of writing. —*v.* (**-nn-**) write. [Latin *penna* feather]

pen² —*n.* small enclosure for cows, sheep, poultry, etc. —*v.* (-nn-) (often foll. by *in*, *up*) enclose or shut up, esp. in a pen. [Old English]

pen³ *n.* female swan. [origin unknown]

penal /ˈpiːn(ə)l/ *adj.* 1 of or concerning punishment or its infliction. 2 (of an offence) punishable, esp. by law. □ **penally** *adv.* [Latin *poena* PAIN]

penalize *v.* (also **-ise**) (**-zing** or **-sing**) 1 subject (a person) to a penalty or disadvantage. 2 make or declare (an action) penal.

penalty /ˈpen(ə)ltɪ/ *n.* (*pl.* **-ies**) 1 punishment for breaking a law, rule, or contract. 2 disadvantage, loss, etc., esp. as a result of one's own actions. 3 *Sport* disadvantage imposed for a breach of the rules etc. [medieval Latin: related to PENAL]

penalty area *n. Football* ground in front of the goal in which a foul by defenders involves the award of a penalty kick.

penalty kick *n. Football* free kick at the goal resulting from a foul in the penalty area.

penance /ˈpenəns/ *n.* 1 act of self-punishment as reparation for guilt. 2 a (in the Roman Catholic and Orthodox Church) sacrament including confession of and absolution for sins. b penalty imposed, esp. by a priest, for a sin. □ **do penance** perform a penance. [related to PENITENT]

pence *pl.* of PENNY.

penchant /ˈpɒ̃ʃɒ̃/ *n.* (followed by *for*) inclination or liking. [French]

pencil /ˈpens(ə)l/ —*n.* 1 instrument for writing or drawing, usu. a thin rod of graphite etc. enclosed in a wooden cylinder or metal case. 2 (*attrib.*) resembling a pencil in shape (*pencil skirt*). —*v.* (**-ll-**; *US* **-l-**) 1 write, draw, or mark with a pencil. 2 (usu. foll. by *in*) write note, or arrange provisionally. [Latin *penicillum* paintbrush]

pendant /ˈpend(ə)nt/ *n.* hanging jewel etc., esp. one attached to a necklace, bracelet, etc. [French *pendre* hang]

pendent /ˈpend(ə)nt/ *adj. formal* 1 a overhanging. b overhanging. 2 undecided, pending. □ **pendency** *n.*

pending —*predic. adj.* 1 awaiting decision or settlement, undecided 2 about to come into existence (*patent pending*). —*prep.* 1 during (*pending inquiries*). 2 until (*pending further trial*). [after French: see PENDANT]

pendulous /ˈpendjʊləs/ *adj.* hanging down; drooping and swinging. [Latin *pendulus* from *pendeo* hang]

pendulum /ˈpendjʊləm/ *n.* (*pl.* **-s**) weight suspended so as to swing freely, esp. a rod with a weighted end and regulating a clock. [Latin neuter adjective: related to PENDULOUS]

penetrate /ˈpenɪtreɪt/ *v.* (**-ting**) 1 a find access into or through. b (usu. foll. by *with*) imbue with; permeate. 2 see into, find out, or discern. 3 see through (darkness, fog, etc.). 4 be absorbed by the mind. 5 (as **penetrating** *adj.*) a having or suggesting sensitivity or insight. b (of a voice etc.) easily heard through or above other sounds; piercing. □ **penetrable** /-trəb(ə)l/ *adj.* **penetrability** /-ˈbɪlɪtɪ/ *n.* **penetration** *n.* **penetrative** /-trətɪv/ *adj.* [Latin]

penguin /ˈpeŋgwɪn/ *n.* flightless black and white sea bird of the southern hemisphere, with wings developed into flippers for swimming underwater. [origin unknown]

penicillin /ˌpenɪˈsɪlɪn/ *n.* antibiotic, produced naturally by mould or synthetically. [Latin *penicillum*: related to PENCIL]

peninsula /pɪˈnɪnsjʊlə/ *n.* piece of land almost surrounded by water or projecting far into a sea etc. □ **peninsular** *adj.* [Latin *paene* almost, *insula* island]

penis /ˈpiːnɪs/ *n.* male organ of copulation and (in mammals) urination. [Latin]

penitent /ˈpenɪt(ə)nt/ —*adj.* repentant. —*n.* 1 repentant sinner. 2 person doing penance under the direction of a confessor. □ **penitence** *n.* **penitently** *adv.* [Latin *paenitet* repent]

penitential /ˌpenɪˈtenʃ(ə)l/ *adj.* of penitence or penance.

penitentiary /ˌpenɪˈtenʃərɪ/ —*n.* (*pl.* **-ies**) *US* federal or State prison. —*adj.* 1 of penance. 2 of reformatory treatment. [Latin: related to PENITENT]

penknife *n.* small folding knife.

pen-name *n.* literary pseudonym.

pennant /ˈpenənt/ *n.* 1 tapering flag, esp. that flown at the masthead of a vessel in commission. 2 = PENNON. [blend of PENDANT and PENNON]

penniless /ˈpenɪlɪs/ *adj.* having no money; destitute.

pennon /ˈpenən/ *n.* 1 long narrow flag, triangular or swallow-tailed. 2 long pointed streamer on a ship. [Latin *penna* feather]

penny /ˈpenɪ/ *n.* (*pl.* for separate coins **-ies**, for a sum of money **pence** /pens/) 1 British coin and monetary unit equal to one-hundredth of a pound. 2 *hist.* British bronze coin and monetary unit equal to one-two-hundred-and-fortieth of a pound. □ **in for a penny, in for a pound** exhortation to total commitment

to an undertaking. **pennies from heaven** unexpected benefits. **the penny drops** colloq. one understands at last. **penny wise and pound foolish** mean in small expenditures but wasteful of large amounts. **a pretty penny** a large sum of money. **two a penny** easily obtained and so almost worthless. [Old English]

penny black n. first adhesive postage stamp (1840, price one penny).

penny farthing n. early type of bicycle with a large front and small rear wheel. □ **penny-pinching** –n. meanness. –adj. mean. □ **penny-pincher** n.

pennyroyal /ˌpenɪˈrɔɪəl/ n. creeping kind of mint. [Anglo-French puliol real royal thyme]

penny whistle n. tin pipe with six finger holes.

pennywort n. wild plant with rounded leaves, growing esp. in marshy places

pennyworth n. as much as can be bought for a penny.

penology /piːˈnɒlədʒɪ/ n. the study of the punishment of crime and prison management. □ **penologist** n. [Latin poena penalty]

pen-pal n. colloq. = PEN-FRIEND.

pen-pushing n. colloq. derog. clerical work. □ **pen-pusher** n.

pension¹ /ˈpenʃ(ə)n/ –n. **1** regular payment made by a government to people above a specified age, to widows, etc., or to the disabled. **2** similar payments made by an employer, private pension fund, etc. on the retirement of an employee. –v. grant a pension to. □ **pension off 1** dismiss with a pension. **2** cease to employ or use. [Latin pendo pens- pay]

pension² /pɑ̃ˈsjɔ̃/ n. European, esp. French, boarding-house. [French: related to PENSION¹]

pensionable adj. **1** entitled to a pension. **2** (of a service, job, etc.) entitling an employee to a pension.

pensioner n. recipient of a pension, esp. the retirement pension. [French: related to PENSION¹]

pensive /ˈpensɪv/ adj. deep in thought. □ **pensively** adv. [French penser think]

pent adj. (often foll. by in, up) closely confined; shut in (pent-up feelings). [from PEN²]

penta- comb. form five. [Greek pente five]

pentacle /ˈpentək(ə)l/ n. figure used as a symbol, esp. in magic, e.g. a pentagram. [medieval Latin pentaculum: related to PENTA-]

pentagon /ˈpentəɡən/ n. **1** plane figure with five sides and angles. **2** (**the Pentagon**) **a** pentagonal Washington headquarters of the US forces. **b** leaders of

the US forces. □ **pentagonal** /penˈtæɡən(ə)l/ adj. [Greek pentagōnon: related to PENTA-]

pentagram /ˈpentəˌɡræm/ n. five-pointed star. [Greek: see PENTA-, -GRAM]

pentameter /penˈtæmɪtə(r)/ n. line of verse with five metrical feet. [Greek: see PENTA-, -METER]

Pentateuch /ˈpentətjuːk/ n. first five books of the Old Testament. [Greek teukhos book]

pentathlon /penˈtæθlən/ n. athletic event comprising five different events for each competitor. □ **pentathlete** /-ˈtæθliːt/ n. [Greek: see PENTA-, athlon contest]

pentatonic /ˌpentəˈtɒnɪk/ adj. consisting of five musical notes.

Pentecost /ˈpentɪˌkɒst/ n. **1** Whit Sunday. **2** Jewish harvest festival, on the fiftieth day after the second day of Passover. [Greek pentēkostē fiftieth (day)]

Pentecostal /ˌpentɪˈkɒst(ə)l/ adj. (of a religious group) emphasizing the divine gifts, esp. the power to heal the sick, and often fundamentalist.

penthouse /ˈpenthaʊs/ n. (esp. luxurious) flat on the roof or top floor of a tall building. [Latin: related to APPEND]

penultimate /pɪˈnʌltɪmət/ adj. & n. last but one. [Latin paenultimus from paene almost, ultimus last]

penumbra /pɪˈnʌmbrə/ n. (pl. -s or -brae /-briː/) **1** partly shaded region around the shadow of an opaque body, esp. that around the shadow of the moon or earth in an eclipse. **2** partial shadow. □ **penumbral** adj. [Latin paene almost, UMBRA]

penurious /pɪˈnjʊərɪəs/ adj. **1** poor. **2** stingy; grudging. **3** scanty. [medieval Latin: related to PENURY]

penury /ˈpenjʊrɪ/ n. (pl. -ies) **1** destitution; poverty. **2** lack; scarcity. [Latin]

peon /ˈpiːɒn/ n. Spanish American day-labourer. [Portuguese and Spanish: related to PAWN¹]

peony /ˈpiːənɪ/ n. (also paeony) (pl. -ies) plant with large globular red, pink, or white flowers. [Greek paiōnia]

people /ˈpiːp(ə)l/ –n.pl. except in sense 2. **1** persons in general or of a specified kind (people don't like rudeness; famous people). **2** persons composing a community, tribe, race, nation, etc. (a warlike people; peoples of the Commonwealth). **3** (**the people**) **a** the mass of people in a country etc. not having special rank or position. **b** these as an electorate. **4** parents or other relatives (my people disapprove). **5 a** subjects, armed followers, etc. **b** congregation of a parish priest etc. –v. (-ling) (usu. foll. by with) **1** fill with people, animals, etc.;

populate. **2** (esp. as **peopled** *adj.*) inhabit. [Latin *populus*]

PEP /pep/ *abbr.* Personal Equity Plan.

pep *colloq.* —*n.* vigour, spirit. —*v.* (**-pp-**) (usu. foll. by *up*) fill with vigour. [abbreviation of PEPPER]

pepper —*n.* **1** hot aromatic condiment from the dried berries of certain plants. **2** anything pungent. **3 a** capsicum plant, grown as a vegetable. **b** its fruit. —*v.* **1** sprinkle or treat with or as if with pepper. **2** pelt with missiles. [Sanskrit *pippali*]

pepper-and-salt *adj.* with small patches of dark and light colour intermingled.

peppercorn *n.* **1** dried pepper berry. **2** (in full **peppercorn rent**) nominal rent.

pepper-mill *n.* device for grinding pepper by hand.

peppermint *n.* **1 a** mint plant grown for its strong-flavoured oil. **b** this oil. **2** sweet flavoured with peppermint.

pepperoni /pepə'rəʊni/ *n.* beef and pork sausage seasoned with pepper. [Italian *peperone* chilli]

pepper-pot *n.* small container with a perforated lid for sprinkling pepper.

peppery *adj.* **1** of, like, or containing pepper. **2** hot-tempered **3** pungent.

pep pill *n.* pill containing a stimulant drug.

peppy *adj.* (**-ier, -iest**) *colloq.* vigorous, energetic, bouncy.

pepsin /'pepsɪn/ *n.* enzyme contained in the gastric juice. [Greek *pepsis* digestion]

pep talk *n.* (usu. short) talk intended to enthuse, encourage, etc.

peptic /'peptɪk/ *adj.* concerning or promoting digestion. [Greek *peptikos* able to digest]

peptic ulcer *n.* ulcer in the stomach or duodenum.

peptide /'peptaɪd/ *n. Biochem.* compound consisting of two or more amino acids bonded in sequence. [Greek *peptos* cooked]

per *prep.* **1** for each (*two sweets per child; five miles per hour*). **2** by means of; through (*per post*). **3** (in full **as per**) in accordance with (*as per instructions*). □ **as per usual** *colloq.* as usual. [Latin]

per- *prefix* **1** through; all over (*pervade*). **2** completely; very (*perturb*). **3** to the bad (*perdition; pervert*). [Latin *per-*: related to FER]

peradventure /pɜːrəd'ventʃə(r)/ *adv. archaic* or *joc.* perhaps. [French related to FER, ADVENTURE]

perambulate /pə'ræmbjʊleɪt/ *v.* (**-ting**) **1** walk through, over, or about (streets, the country, etc.), **2** walk from

place to . to place. □ **perambulation** /-'leɪʃ(ə)n/ *n.* [Latin *perambulo*: related to AMBLE]

perambulator *n. formal* = PRAM. [Latin]

per annum /pər 'ænəm/ *adv.* for each year. [Latin]

percale /pə'keɪl/ *n.* closely woven cotton fabric. [French]

per capita /pə 'kæpɪtə/ *adv. & adj.* (also **per caput** /'kæpʊt/) for each person. [Latin: = by heads]

perceive /pə'siːv/ *v.* (**-ving**) **1** apprehend, esp. through the sight, observe. **2** (usu. foll. by *that, how,* etc.) apprehend with the mind; understand; see or regard. □ **perceivable** *adj.* [Latin *percipio -cept-* seize, understand]

per cent /pə 'sent/ (*US* **percent**) —*adv.* in every hundred. —*n.* **1** percentage. **2** one part in every hundred (*half a per cent*).

percentage *n.* **1** rate or proportion per cent. **2** proportion.

percentile /pə'sentaɪl/ *n. Statistics* **1** each of 99 points at which a range of data is divided to make 100 groups of equal size. **2** each of these groups.

perceptible /pə'septɪb(ə)l/ *adj.* capable of being perceived by the senses or intellect. □ **perceptibility** /-'bɪlɪtɪ/ *n.* **perceptibly** *adv.* [Latin: related to PERCEIVE]

perception /pə'sepʃ(ə)n/ *n.* **1** act or faculty of perceiving. **2** (often foll. by *of*) intuitive recognition of a truth, aesthetic quality, etc.; way of seeing, understanding. □ **perceptual** /pə'septjʊəl/ *adj.*

perceptive /pə'septɪv/ *adj.* **1** sensitive; discerning **2** capable of perceiving. □ **perceptively** *adv.* **perceptiveness** *n.* **perceptivity** /'tɪvɪtɪ/ *n.*

perch[1] —*n.* **1** bar, branch, etc. used by a bird to rest on. **2** high place for a person or thing to rest on. **3** *Hist.* measure of length, esp. for land, of 5½ yards. —*v.* (usu. foll. by *on*) settle or rest on or as on a perch etc. [Latin *pertica* pole]

perch[2] *n.* (*pl.* same or **-es**) edible European spiny-finned freshwater fish. [Latin *perca* from Greek]

perchance /pə'tʃɑːns/ *adv. archaic* or *poet.* **1** by chance. **2** maybe. [Anglo-French *par* by]

percipient /pə'sɪpɪənt/ *adj.* able to perceive; conscious. □ **percipience** *n.* [Latin: related to PERCEIVE]

percolate /'pɜːkəleɪt/ *v.* (**-ting**) **1** (often foll. by *through*) **a** (of liquid etc.) filter or ooze gradually. **b** (of an idea etc.) permeate gradually. **2** prepare (coffee) in a percolator. **3** strain (a liquid, powder,

etc.) through a fine mesh etc. □ **percolation** /ˌʔɜːˈleɪʃ(ə)n/ n. [Latin *colum* strainer]

percolator n. machine making coffee by circulating boiling water through ground beans.

percussion /pəˈkʌʃ(ə)n/ n. **1 a** (often *attrib.*) playing of music by striking instruments with sticks etc. (*percussion instrument*). **b** such instruments collectively. **2** gentle tapping of the body in medical diagnosis. **3** forcible striking of one esp. solid body against another. □ **percussionist** n. **percussive** *adj.* [Latin *percutio -cuss-* strike]

percussion cap n. small amount of explosive powder contained in metal or paper and exploded by striking.

perdition /pəˈdɪʃ(ə)n/ n. eternal death; damnation. [Latin *perdo -dit-* destroy]

peregrine /ˈperɪgrɪn/ n. (in full **peregrine falcon**) a kind of falcon much used for hawking. [Latin *peregrinus* foreign]

peremptory /pəˈrempt(ə)rɪ/ *adj.* **1** (of a statement or command) admitting no denial or refusal. **2** (of a person, manner, etc.) imperious; dictatorial. □ **peremptorily** *adv.* **peremptoriness** n. [Latin *peremptorius* deadly, decisive]

perennial /pəˈrenɪəl/ —*adj.* **1** lasting through a year or several years. **2** (of a plant) lasting several years. **3** lasting a long time or for ever. —n. perennial plant. □ **perennially** *adv.* [Latin *perennis* from *annus* year]

perestroika /ˌperəˈstrɔɪkə/ n. (in the former USSR) reform of the economic and political system. [Russian, = restructuring]

perfect /ˈpɜːfɪkt/ —*adj.* **1** complete; not deficient. **2** faultless. **3** very enjoyable, excellent (*perfect evening*). **4** exact, precise (*perfect circle*). **5** entire, unqualified (*perfect stranger*). **6** *Gram.* (of a tense) denoting a completed action or event (e.g. *he has gone*). —v. /pəˈfekt/ **1** make perfect. **2** complete. —n. *Gram.* the perfect tense. □ **perfectible** /pəˈfektɪb(ə)l/ *adj.* **perfectibility** /pəˌfektɪˈbɪlɪtɪ/ n. [Latin *perficere fect-* complete (v.)].

perfection /pəˈfekʃ(ə)n/ n. **1** making, becoming, or being perfect. **2** faultlessness. **3** perfect person, thing, or example. □ **to perfection** exactly; completely. [Latin: related to PERFECT]

perfectionism n. uncompromising pursuit of excellence. □ **perfectionist** n. & *adj.*

perfectly *adv.* **1** completely; quite. **2** in a perfect way.

perfect pitch n. = ABSOLUTE PITCH.

perfidy /ˈpɜːfɪdɪ/ n. breach of faith; treachery. □ **perfidious** /-ˈfɪdɪəs/ *adj.* [Latin *perfidia* from *fides* faith]

perforate /ˈpɜːfəreɪt/ v. (-ting) **1** make a hole or holes through; pierce. **2** make a row of small holes in (paper etc.) so that a part may be torn off easily. □ **perforation** /-ˈreɪʃ(ə)n/ n. [Latin *perforo* pierce through]

perforce /pəˈfɔːs/ *adv.* archaic unavoidably; necessarily. [French *par force* by FORCE¹]

perform /pəˈfɔːm/ v. **1** (also *absol.*) carry into effect; do. **2** act in a function, play, piece of music, etc.). **3** act in a play; play music, sing, etc.; execute tricks. **4** function. □ **performer** n. [Anglo-French: related to PER-, FURNISH]

performance /pəˈfɔːməns/ n. **1** (usu. foll. by *of*) **a** act, process, or manner of performing or functioning. **b** execution (of a duty etc.). **2** performing of a play, music, etc.; instance of this. **3** *colloq.* fuss; emotional scene.

performing arts n.pl. drama, music, dance, etc.

perfume /ˈpɜːfjuːm/ n. **1** sweet smell. **2** fluid containing the essence of flowers etc.; scent. —v. /also pəˈfjuːm/ (-ming) impart a sweet scent to. [Italian *parfumare* smoke through]

perfumer /pəˈfjuːmə(r)/ n. maker or seller of perfumes. □ **perfumery** n. (pl. -ies).

perfunctory /pəˈfʌŋktərɪ/ *adj.* done merely out of duty; superficial, careless. □ **perfunctorily** *adv.* **perfunctoriness** n. [Latin: related to FUNCTION]

pergola /ˈpɜːgələ/ n. arbour or covered walk formed of growing plants trained over trellis-work. [Italian]

perhaps /pəˈhæps/ *adv.* it may be; possibly.

peri- *prefix* round, about. [Greek]

perianth /ˈperɪænθ/ n. outer part of a flower. [Greek *anthos* flower]

pericardium /ˌperɪˈkɑːdɪəm/ n. (pl. -dia) membranous sac enclosing the heart. [Greek *kardia* heart]

perigee /ˈperɪdʒiː/ n. point of a planet's or comet's orbit where it is nearest the earth. [Greek *perigeion*]

perihelion /ˌperɪˈhiːlɪən/ n. (pl. -lia) point of a planet's or comet's orbit where it is nearest the sun's centre. [related to PERI-, Greek *hēlios* sun]

peril /ˈperɪl/ n. serious and immediate danger. □ **perilous** *adj.* **perilously** *adv.* [Latin *peric(u)lum*]

perimeter /pəˈrɪmɪtə(r)/ n. **1 a** circumference or outline of a closed figure. **b** length of this. **2** outer boundary of an

perineum /ˌperiˈniːəm/ n. (pl. **-nea**) region of the body between the anus and the scrotum or vulva. □ **perineal** adj. [Latin from Greek]

period /ˈpɪəriəd/ n. **1** length or portion of time. **2** distinct portion of history, a person's life, etc. **3** time forming part of a geological era. **4** interval between recurrences of an astronomical or other phenomenon. **5** time allowed for a lesson in school. **6** occurrence of menstruation (often attrib.: period pains). **7** complete sentence, esp. one consisting of several clauses. **8** esp. US a = FULL STOP 1. **b** colloq. used at the end of a statement to indicate finality (I'm not going, period). —adj. characteristic of some past period (period furniture). [Greek hodos way]

periodic /pɪərɪˈɒdɪk/ adj. appearing or occurring at intervals. □ **periodicity** /-rɪəˈdɪsɪtɪ/ n.

periodical —n. newspaper, magazine, etc. issued at regular intervals. —adj. periodic. □ **periodically** adv.

periodic table n. arrangement of elements in order of increasing atomic number and in which elements of similar chemical properties appear at regular intervals.

periodontics /ˌperɪəˈdɒntɪks/ n.pl. (treated as sing.) branch of dentistry concerned with the structures surrounding and supporting the teeth. □ **periodontal** adj.

peripatetic /ˌperɪpəˈtetɪk/ —adj. **1** (of a teacher) working in more than one school or college etc. **2** going from place to place; itinerant. —n. peripatetic person, esp. a teacher. [Greek pateō walk]

peripheral /pəˈrɪf(ə)r(ə)l/ —adj. **1** of the minor importance; marginal. **2** of the periphery. —n. any input, output, or storage device that can be controlled by a computer's central processing unit, e.g. a floppy disk or printer.

peripheral nervous system n. nervous system outside the brain and spinal cord.

periphery /pəˈrɪfərɪ/ n. (pl. **-ies**) **1** boundary of an area or surface. **2** outer or surrounding region. [Greek pherō bear]

periphrasis /pəˈrɪfrəsɪs/ n. (pl. **-phrases** /-ˌsiːz/) **1** roundabout way of speaking; circumlocution. **2** roundabout phrase. □ **periphrastic** /ˌperɪˈfræstɪk/ adj. [Greek: related to PHRASE]

periscope /ˈperɪˌskəʊp/ n. apparatus with a tube and mirrors or prisms, by which an observer in a trench, submerged submarine, or at the back of a crowd etc., can see things otherwise out of sight. □ **periscopic** /ˌperɪˈskɒpɪk/ adj.

perish /ˈperɪʃ/ v. **1** be destroyed; suffer death or ruin. **2 a** (esp. of rubber) lose its normal qualities; deteriorate, rot. **b** cause to rot or deteriorate. **3** (in passive) suffer from cold. [Latin pereo]

perishable —adj. liable to perish; subject to rapid decay. —n. thing, esp. a foodstuff, subject to rapid decay.

perisher n. slang annoying person.

perishing colloq. —adj. **1** confounded. **2** freezing cold. —adv. confoundedly.

peristalsis /ˌperɪˈstælsɪs/ n. involuntary muscular wavelike movement by which the contents of the digestive tract are propelled along it. □ **peristaltic** adj. [Greek peristellō wrap around]

peritoneum /ˌperɪtəˈniːəm/ n. (pl. **-s** or **-nea**) membrane lining the cavity of the abdomen. □ **peritoneal** adj. [Greek peritonos stretched around]

peritonitis /ˌperɪtəˈnaɪtɪs/ n. inflammatory disease of the peritoneum.

periwig /ˈperɪwɪg/ n. esp. hist. wig. [alteration of PERUKE]

periwinkle[1] /ˈperɪˌwɪŋk(ə)l/ n. evergreen trailing plant with blue, purple, or white flowers. [Latin pervinca]

periwinkle[2] /ˈperɪˌwɪŋk(ə)l/ n. = WINKLE. [origin unknown]

perjure /ˈpɜːdʒə(r)/ v.refl. (-ring) wilfully tell a lie when on oath. **2** (as **perjured** adj.) guilty of or involving perjury. □ **perjurer** n. [Latin iuro swear]

perjury n. (pl. **-ies**) Law act of wilfully telling a lie when on oath.

perk[1] v. □ **perk up 1** recover confidence, courage, life, or zest. **2** restore courage, life, or liveliness in. **3** smarten up. **4** raise (one's head etc.) briskly. [origin unknown]

perk[2] n. colloq. perquisite. [abbreviation]

perky adj. (**-ier, -iest**) lively; cheerful. □ **perkily** adv. **perkiness** n.

perlite /ˈpɜːlaɪt/ n. (also **pearlite**) glassy type of vermiculite used for insulation etc. [French perle pear]

perm[1] —n. permanent wave. —v. give a permanent wave to. [abbreviation]

perm[2] colloq. —n. permutation. —v. make a permutation of. [abbreviation]

permafrost /ˈpɜːməˌfrɒst/ n. subsoil which remains frozen all year, as in polar regions. [from PERMANENT, FROST]

permanent /ˈpɜːmənənt/ adj. lasting, or intended to last or function, indefinitely. □ **permanence** n. **permanency** n. **permanently** adv. [Latin permaneo remain to the end]

permanent wave n. long-lasting artificial wave in the hair.

permeable /'pɜːmɪəb(ə)l/ adj. capable of being permeated. □ **permeability** /-'bɪlɪtɪ/ n. [related to PERMEATE]

permeate /'pɜːmɪˌeɪt/ v. (-ting) 1 penetrate throughout; pervade; saturate. 2 (usu. foll. by through, among, etc.) diffuse itself. □ **permeation** /-'eɪʃ(ə)n/ n. [Latin permeo pass through]

Permian /'pɜːmɪən/ —adj. of the last period of the Palaeozoic era. —n. this period. [Perm in Russia]

permissible /pə'mɪsɪb(ə)l/ adj. allowable. □ **permissibility** /-'bɪlɪtɪ/ n. [French or medieval Latin: related to PERMIT]

permission /pə'mɪʃ(ə)n/ n. (often foll. by to + infin.) consent; authorization. [Latin permissio: related to PERMIT]

permissive /pə'mɪsɪv/ adj. 1 tolerant or liberal, esp. in sexual matters. 2 giving permission. □ **permissiveness** n. [French or medieval Latin: related to PERMIT]

permit —v. /pə'mɪt/ (-tt-) 1 give permission or consent to; authorize. 2 a allow; give an opportunity to. b give an opportunity (circumstances permitting). 3 (foll. by of) admit. —n. /'pɜːmɪt/ 1 a document giving permission to act. b document etc. which allows entry. 2 formal permission. [Latin permitto miss- allow]

permutation /pɜːmjʊ'teɪʃ(ə)n/ n. 1 one of the possible ordered arrangements or groupings of a set of things. 2 combination or selection of a specified number of things from a larger group, esp. matches in a football pool. [Latin permuto change thoroughly]

pernicious /pə'nɪʃəs/ adj. very harmful or destructive; deadly. [Latin pernicies ruin]

pernicious anaemia n. defective formation of red blood cells through lack of vitamin B.

pernickety /pə'nɪkɪtɪ/ adj. colloq. fastidious; over-precise. [origin unknown]

peroration /ˌperə'reɪʃ(ə)n/ n. concluding part of a speech. [Latin oro speak]

peroxide /pə'rɒksaɪd/ —n. 1 a (often attrib.) solution of hydrogen peroxide used esp. to bleach the hair. 2 compound of oxygen with another element containing the greatest possible proportion of oxygen. —v. (-ding) bleach (the hair) with peroxide. [from PER-, OXIDE]

perpendicular /ˌpɜːpən'dɪkjʊlə(r)/ —adj. 1 a (usu. foll. by to) at right angles (to a given line, plane, or surface). b at right angles to the plane of the horizon. 2 upright, vertical. 3 (of a slope etc.) very steep. 4 (**Perpendicular**) Archit. of the third stage of English Gothic (15th–16th c.) with vertical tracery in large windows. —n. 1 perpendicular line or direction (prec. by the) perpendicular line or direction (is out of the perpendicular). □ **perpendicularity** /-'lærɪtɪ/ n. [Latin perpendiculum plumb-line]

perpetrate /'pɜːpɪˌtreɪt/ v. (-ting) commit (a crime, blunder, or anything outrageous). □ **perpetration** /-'treɪʃ(ə)n/ n. **perpetrator** n. [Latin perpetro perform]

perpetual /pə'petjʊəl/ adj. 1 lasting for ever or indefinitely. 2 continuous, uninterrupted. 3 colloq. frequent (perpetual interruptions). □ **perpetually** adv. [Latin perpetuus continuous]

perpetual motion n. motion of a hypothetical machine which once set in motion would run for ever unless subject to an external force or to wear.

perpetuate /pə'petjʊˌeɪt/ v. (-ting) 1 make perpetual. 2 preserve from oblivion. □ **perpetuation** /-'eɪʃ(ə)n/ n. **perpetuator** n. [Latin perpetuo]

perpetuity /ˌpɜːpɪ'tjuːɪtɪ/ n. (pl. -ies) 1 state or quality of being perpetual. 2 perpetual annuity. 3 perpetual possession or position. □ **in perpetuity** for ever. [Latin: related to PERPETUAL]

perplex /pə'pleks/ v. 1 puzzle, bewilder, or disconcert. 2 complicate or confuse (a matter). □ **perplexedly** /-ɪdlɪ/ adv. **perplexing** adj. [Latin perplexus involved]

perplexity /pə'pleksɪtɪ/ n. (pl. -ies) 1 state of being perplexed. 2 thing that perplexes.

per pro. /pɜː 'prəʊ/ abbr. through the agency of (used in signatures). [Latin per procurationem]

■ **Usage** The correct sequence is A per pro. B, where B is signing on behalf of A.

perquisite /'pɜːkwɪzɪt/ n. 1 extra profit or allowance additional to a main income etc. 2 customary extra right or privilege. [Latin perquiro-quisit- search diligently for]

■ **Usage** Perquisite is sometimes confused with prerequisite, which means 'thing required as a precondition'.

perry /'perɪ/ n. (pl. -ies) drink made from fermented pear juice. [French peré: related to PEAR]

per se /pɜː 'seɪ/ adv. by or in itself; intrinsically. [Latin]

persecute /'pɜːsɪˌkjuːt/ v. (-ting) 1 subject (a person etc.) to hostility or ill-treatment, esp. on grounds of political or religious belief. 2 harass, worry. □ **persecution** /-'kjuːʃ(ə)n/ n. **persecutor** n. [Latin persequor-secut- pursue]

persevere /ˌpɜːsɪˈvɪə(r)/ v. (-ring) (often foll. by in, with) continue steadfastly or determinedly; persist. □ **perseverance** n. [Latin: related to SEVERE]

Persian /ˈpɜːʃ(ə)n/ —n. 1 native or inhabitant of ancient or modern Persia (now Iran); person of Persian descent. 2 language of ancient or modern Iran. 3 (in full Persian cat) cat of a breed with long silky hair. —adj. of, relating to Persia or its people or language.

■ **Usage** The preferred terms for the noun and adjective in sense 2 of the noun are Iranian and Farsi respectively.

Persian lamb n. silky tightly curled fur of a young karakul, used in clothing.

persiflage /ˈpɜːsɪflɑːʒ/ n. light raillery, banter. [French]

persimmon /pɜːˈsɪmən/ n. 1 tropical evergreen tree. 2 its edible tomato-like fruit. [Algonquian]

persist /pəˈsɪst/ v. 1 (often foll. by in) continue firmly or obstinately (in an opinion or action) esp. despite obstacles, remonstrance etc. 2 (of a phenomenon etc.) continue in existence; survive. □ **persistence** n. **persistent** adj. **persistently** adv. [Latin sisto stand]

person /ˈpɜːs(ə)n/ n. 1 individual human being. 2 living body of a human being (found on my person). 3 Gram. any of three classes of personal pronouns, verb-forms, etc.: the person speaking (first person); the person spoken to (second person); the person spoken of (third person). 4 (in comb.) used to replace -man in offices open to either sex (salesperson). 5 (in Christianity) God as Father, Son, or Holy Ghost. □ in person physically present. [Latin: related to PERSONA]

persona /pəˈsəʊnə/ n. (pl. -nae /-niː/) aspect of the personality as shown to or perceived by others. [Latin, = actor's mask]

personable adj. pleasing in appearance and behaviour.

personage n. person, esp. of rank or importance.

persona grata /pəˈsəʊnə ˈɡrɑːtə/ n. (pl. personae gratae /-niː, -tiː/) person acceptable to certain others.

personal /ˈpɜːsən(ə)l/ adj. 1 one's own; individual; private. 2 done or made in person (my personal attention). 3 directed to or concerning an individual (personal letter). 4 referring (esp. in a hostile way) to an individual's private life or concerns (personal remarks; no need to be personal). 5 of the body and clothing (personal hygiene). 6 existing as a person (a personal God). 7 Gram. of

or denoting one of the three persons (personal pronoun).

personal column n. part of a newspaper devoted to private advertisements and messages.

personal computer n. computer designed for use by a single individual.

personal equity plan n. scheme for tax-free personal investments through financial institutions.

personality /ˌpɜːsəˈnælɪtɪ/ n. (pl. -ies) 1 a person's distinctive character or qualities (has a strong personality). b socially attractive qualities (was clever but had no personality). 3 (in pl.) personal remarks.

personalize v. (also -ise) (-zing or -sing) 1 make personal, esp. by marking with one's name etc. 2 personify.

personally adv. 1 in person (see to it personally). 2 for one's own part (speaking personally). 3 in a personal manner (took the criticism personally).

personal organizer n. means of keeping track of personal affairs, esp. a loose-leaf notebook divided into sections.

personal pronoun n. pronoun replacing the subject, object, etc., of a clause etc., e.g. I, we, you, them, us.

personal property n. Law all one's property except land and those interests in land that pass to one's heirs.

personal stereo n. small portable cassette player, often with radio or CD player, used with lightweight headphones.

persona non grata /pəˈsəʊnə nɒn ˈɡrɑːtə/ n. (pl. personae non gratae /-niː/) unacceptable person.

personify /pəˈsɒnɪfaɪ/ v. (-ies, -ied) 1 represent (an abstraction or thing) as having human characteristics. 2 symbolize (a quality etc.) by a figure in human form. 3 (usu. as personified adj.) be a typical example of; embody (she personifies youthful arrogance; he was niceness personified). □ **personification** /-fɪˈkeɪʃ(ə)n/ n.

personnel /ˌpɜːsəˈnel/ n. staff of an organization, the armed forces, a public service, etc. [French, = personal]

personnel department n. part of an organization concerned with the appointment, training, and welfare of employees.

perspective /pəˈspektɪv/ —n. 1 a art of drawing solid objects on a two-dimensional surface so as to give the right impression of relative positions, size, etc. b picture so drawn. 2 apparent relation between visible objects as to position, distance, etc. 3 mental view of

the relative importance of things. **4** view, esp. stretching into the distance. □ **in** (or **out of**) **perspective 1** drawn or viewed according (or not according) to the rules of perspective. **2** correctly (or incorrectly) regarded in terms of relative importance. [Latin *perspicio -spect-* look at]

Perspex /ˈpɜːspeks/ *n.* propr. tough light transparent thermoplastic. [related to PERSPECTIVE]

perspicacious /ˌpɜːspɪˈkeɪʃəs/ *adj.* having mental penetration or discernment. □ **perspicacity** /-ˈkæsɪtɪ/ *n.* [Latin *perspicax*: related to PERSPICACIOUS]

■ **Usage** *Perspicacious* is sometimes confused with *perspicuous*.

perspicuous /pəˈspɪkjʊəs/ *adj.* **1** easily understood, clearly expressed. **2** expressing things clearly. □ **perspicuity** /-ˈkjuːɪtɪ/ *n.* [Latin: related to PERSPECTIVE]

■ **Usage** *Perspicuous* is sometimes confused with *perspicacious*.

perspiration /ˌpɜːspɪˈreɪʃ(ə)n/ *n.* **1** sweat. **2** sweating. [French: related to PERSPIRE]

perspire /pəˈspaɪə(r)/ *v.* (**-ring**) sweat. [Latin *spiro* breathe]

persuade /pəˈsweɪd/ *v.* (**-ding**) **1** (often foll. by *of* or *that*) cause (another person or oneself) to believe; convince. **2** (often foll. by *to* + infin.) induce. □ **persuadable** *adj.* **persuasible** *adj.* [Latin *persuadeo -suas-* induce]

persuasion /pəˈsweɪʒ(ə)n/ *n.* **1** persuading. **2** persuasiveness. **3** belief or conviction. **4** religious belief, or the group or sect holding it. [Latin: related to PERSUADE]

persuasive /pəˈsweɪsɪv/ *adj.* good at persuading. □ **persuasively** *adv.* **persuasiveness** *n.* [French or medieval Latin: related to PERSUADE]

pert *adj.* **1** saucy, impudent. **2** jaunty. □ **pertly** *adv.* **pertness** *n.* [Latin *apertus* open]

pertain /pəˈteɪn/ *v.* **1** (foll. by *to*) **a** relate or have reference to. **b** belong to as a part, appendage, or accessory. **2** (usu. foll. by *to*) be appropriate to. [Latin *pertineo* belong to]

pertinacious /ˌpɜːtɪˈneɪʃəs/ *adj.* stubborn; persistent (in a course of action etc.). □ **pertinacity** /-ˈnæsɪtɪ/ *n.* [Latin *pertinax*]

pertinent /ˈpɜːtɪnənt/ *adj.* (often foll. by *to*) relevant. □ **pertinence** *n.* **pertinency** *n.* [Latin: related to PERTAIN]

perturb /pəˈtɜːb/ *v.* **1** disturb mentally; agitate. **2** throw into confusion or disorder. □ **perturbation** /-ˈbeɪʃ(ə)n/ *n.* [French from Latin]

peruke /pəˈruːk/ *n. hist.* wig. [French from Italian]

peruse /pəˈruːz/ *v.* (**-sing**) **1** read or study carefully. **2** *joc.* read or look at desultorily. □ **perusal** *n.* [originally = 'use up']

pervade /pəˈveɪd/ *v.* (**-ding**) **1** spread throughout, permeate. **2** be rife among or through. □ **pervasion** *n.* **pervasive** *adj.* [Latin *pervado* penetrate]

perverse /pəˈvɜːs/ *adj.* **1** deliberately or stubbornly departing from what is reasonable or required. **2** intractable. □ **perversely** *adv.* **perversity** *n.* (*pl.* **-ies**). [Latin: related to PERVERT]

perversion /pəˈvɜːʃ(ə)n/ *n.* **1** perverting or being perverted. **2** preference for an abnormal form of sexual activity. [Latin: related to PERVERT]

pervert *-v.* /pəˈvɜːt/ **1** turn (a person or thing) aside from its proper use or nature. **2** misapply (words etc.). **3** lead astray from right conduct or (esp. religious) beliefs; corrupt. **4** (as *perverted adj.*) showing perversion. *-n.* /ˈpɜːvɜːt/ perverted person, esp. sexually. [Latin *verto vers-* turn]

pervious /ˈpɜːvɪəs/ *adj.* **1** permeable. **2** (usu. foll. by *to*) **a** affording passage. **b** accessible (to reason etc.). [Latin *via* road]

peseta /pəˈseɪtə/ *n.* chief monetary unit of Spain. [Spanish]

pesky /ˈpeskɪ/ *adj.* (**-ier, -iest**) esp. *US colloq.* troublesome; annoying. [origin unknown]

peso /ˈpeɪsəʊ/ *n.* (*pl.* **-s**) chief monetary unit of several Latin American countries and of the Philippines. [Spanish]

pessary /ˈpesərɪ/ *n.* (*pl.* **-ies**) **1** device worn in the vagina to support the uterus or as a contraceptive. **2** vaginal suppository. [Latin from Greek]

pessimism /ˈpesɪmɪz(ə)m/ *n.* **1** tendency to be gloomy or expect the worst. **2** *Philos.* belief that this world is as bad as it could be or that all things tend to evil. □ **pessimist** *n.* **pessimistic** /-ˈmɪstɪk/ *adj.* **pessimistically** /-ˈmɪstɪkəlɪ/ *adv.* [Latin *pessimus* worst]

pest *n.* **1** troublesome or annoying person or thing. **2** destructive animal, esp. one which attacks food sources. [Latin *pestis* plague]

pester *v.* trouble or annoy, esp. with frequent or persistent requests. [probably French *empestrer* encumber: influenced by PEST]

pesticide /ˈpestɪsaɪd/ *n.* substance for destroying pests, esp. insects.

pestilence /ˈpestɪləns/ n. fatal epidemic disease, esp. bubonic plague. [Latin *pestis* plague]

pestilent adj. 1 deadly. 2 harmful or morally destructive. 3 colloq. trouble-some, annoying.

pestilential /ˌpestɪˈlenʃ(ə)l/ adj. 1 of or relating to pestilence. 2 pestilent.

pestle /ˈpes(ə)l/ n. club-shaped instrument for pounding substances in a mortar. [Latin *pistillum* from *pinso* pound]

pet /pet/ —n. 1 domestic or tamed animal kept for pleasure or companionship. 2 darling, favourite. —attrib. adj. 1 kept as a pet (*pet lamb*). 2 of or for pet animals (*pet food*). 3 often joc. favourite or particular (*pet hate*). 4 expressing fondness or familiarity (*pet name*). —v. (**-tt-**) 1 fondle erotically. 2 treat as a pet; stroke, pat. [origin unknown]

pet[2] n. fit of ill-humour. [origin unknown]

petal /ˈpet(ə)l/ n. each of the parts of the corolla of a flower. □ **petalled** adj. [Greek *petalon* leaf]

petard /pɪˈtɑːd/ n. hist. small bomb used to blast down a door etc. [French]

peter /ˈpiːtə(r)/ v. □ **peter out** diminish, come to an end. [origin unknown]

Peter Pan n. person who remains youthful or is immature. [hero of J. M. Barrie's play (1904)]

petersham /ˈpiːtəʃəm/ n. thick corded silk ribbon. [Lord *Petersham*, name of an army officer]

pethidine /ˈpeθɪdiːn/ n. synthetic soluble analgesic used esp. in childbirth. [perhaps from the chemical *piperidine*]

petiole /ˈpetɪəʊl/ n. slender stalk joining a leaf to a stem. [French from Latin]

petits bourgeois /ˌpetiː ˈbʊəʒwɑː/ n. (pl. **petits bourgeois** pronunc. same) member of the lower middle classes. [French]

petite /pəˈtiːt/ adj. (of a woman) of small and dainty build. [French, = little]

petit four /ˌpeti ˈfɔː(r)/ n. (pl. **petits fours** /ˈfɔːz/) very small fancy cake. [French, = small oven]

petition /pɪˈtɪʃ(ə)n/ —n. 1 supplication, request. 2 formal written request, esp. one signed by many people, appealing to an authority. 3 Law application to a court for a writ etc. —v. 1 make or address a petition to. 2 (often foll. by *for*, *to*) appeal earnestly or humbly. [Latin *peto petit-* ask]

petit mal /ˌpeti ˈmæl/ n. mild form of epilepsy. [French, = little sickness]

petit point /ˌpeti ˈpwæ̃/ n. embroidery on canvas using small stitches. [French, = little point]

petrel /ˈpetr(ə)l/ n. sea bird, usu. flying far from land. [origin unknown]

Petri dish /ˈpiːtrɪ/ n. shallow covered dish used for the culture of bacteria etc. [*Petri*, name of a bacteriologist]

petrify /ˈpetrɪfaɪ/ v. (**-ies, -ied**) 1 paralyse with fear, astonishment, etc. 2 change (organic matter) into a stony substance. 3 become like stone. □ **petrifaction** /-ˈfækʃ(ə)n/ n. [Latin *petra* rock, from Greek]

petrochemical /ˌpetrəʊˈkemɪk(ə)l/ n. substance industrially obtained from petroleum or natural gas.

petrodollar /ˈpetrəʊdɒlə(r)/ n. notional unit of currency earned by a petroleum-exporting country.

petrol /ˈpetr(ə)l/ n. 1 refined petroleum used as a fuel in motor vehicles, aircraft, etc. 2 (attrib. concerned with the supply of petrol (*petrol pump*). [Latin: related to PETROLEUM]

petroleum /pɪˈtrəʊlɪəm/ n. hydrocarbon oil found in the upper strata of the earth, refined for use as fuel etc. [Latin *petra* rock, *oleum* oil]

petroleum jelly n. translucent solid mixture of hydrocarbons used as a lubricant, ointment, etc.

pet shop n. shop selling animals to be kept as pets.

petticoat /ˈpetɪkəʊt/ n. 1 woman's or girl's undergarment hanging from the waist or shoulders. 2 (attrib.) often derog. feminine (*petty coat*)

pettifog /ˈpetɪfɒg/ v. (**-gg-**) 1 practise legal trickery. 2 quibble or wrangle about trivial points. [origin unknown]

pettish adj. peevish, petulant; easily put out. [from PET[2]]

petty adj. (**-ier, -iest**) 1 unimportant, trivial. 2 small-minded. 3 minor, inferior, on a small scale. 4 Law (of a crime) of lesser importance. □ **pettily** adv. **pettiness** n. [French *petit* small]

petty cash n. money from or for small items of receipt or expenditure.

petty officer n. naval NCO.

petulant /ˈpetjʊlənt/ adj. peevishly impatient or irritable. □ **petulance** n. **petulantly** adv. [Latin *peto* seek]

petunia /pɪˈtjuːnɪə/ n. cultivated plant with white, purple, red, etc., funnel-shaped flowers. [French *petun* tobacco]

pew n. 1 (in a church) long bench with a back; enclosed compartment. 2 colloq. seat (esp. *take a pew*). [Latin PODIUM]

pewit var. of PEEWIT.

pewter /ˈpjuːtə(r)/ n. 1 grey alloy of tin, antimony, and copper. 2 utensils made of this. [French *peutre*]

peyote /peɪˈəʊtɪ/ n. 1 Mexican cactus. 2 hallucinogenic drug prepared from this. [American Spanish from Nahuatl]

pfennig /ˈfenɪg/ n. one-hundredth of a Deutschmark. [German]

668

PG *abbr.* (of a film) classified as suitable for children subject to parental guidance.

pH /piːˈeɪtʃ/ *n.* measure of the acidity or alkalinity of a solution. [German *Potenz* power, *H* (symbol for hydrogen)]

phagocyte /ˈfæɡəˌsaɪt/ *n.* leucocyte capable of engulfing and absorbing foreign matter. [Greek *phag-* eat, *kutos* cell]

phalanx /ˈfælæŋks/ *n.* (*pl.* **phalanxes** or **phalanges** /fəˈlændʒiːz/) **1** *Gk Antiq.* line of battle, esp. a body of infantry drawn up in close order. **2** set of people etc. forming a compact mass, or banded for a common purpose. [Latin from Greek]

phallus /ˈfæləs/ *n.* (*pl.* **phalli** /-laɪ/ or **phalluses** (esp. erect) **penis. 2** image of this as a symbol of natural generative power. □ **phallic** *adj.* [Latin from Greek]

phantasm /ˈfæntæz(ə)m/ *n.* illusion, phantom. □ **phantasmal** /-ˈtæzm(ə)l/ *adj.* [Latin: related to PHANTOM]

phantasmagoria /ˌfæntæzməˈɡɔːrɪə/ *n.* shifting series of real or imaginary figures as seen in a dream. □ **phantasmagoric** /-ˈɡɒrɪk/ *adj.* [probably from French *fantasmagorie*: related to PHANTASM]

phantom /ˈfæntəm/ *n.* **1** ghost, apparition, spectre. **2** mental illusion.—*attrib. adj.* illusory. [Greek *phantasma*]

Pharaoh /ˈfeərəʊ/ *n.* **1** ruler of ancient Egypt. **2** title of this ruler. [Old English from Church Latin *Pharao*, ultimately from Egyptian]

Pharisee /ˈfærɪˌsiː/ *n.* **1** member of an ancient Jewish sect, distinguished by strict observance of the traditional and written law. **2** self-righteous person; hypocrite. □ **Pharisaic** /-ˈseɪk/ *adj.* [Hebrew *pārûš*]

pharmaceutical /ˌfɑːməˈsjuːtɪk(ə)l/ *adj.* **1** of or engaged in pharmacy. **2** of the use or sale of medicinal drugs. [Latin from Greek *pharmakon* drug]

pharmaceutics *n.pl.* (usu. treated as *sing.*) = PHARMACY 1.

pharmacist /ˈfɑːməsɪst/ *n.* person qualified to prepare and dispense drugs.

pharmacology /ˌfɑːməˈkɒlədʒɪ/ *n.* the study of the action of drugs on the body. □ **pharmacological** /-kəˈlɒdʒɪk(ə)l/ *adj.* **pharmacologist** *n.*

pharmacopoeia /ˌfɑːməkəˈpiːə/ *n.* **1** book, esp. one officially published, containing a list of drugs with directions for use. **2** stock of drugs. [Greek *pharmako-poios* drug-maker]

pharmacy /ˈfɑːməsɪ/ *n.* (*pl.* **-ies**) **1** preparation and (esp. medicinal) dispensing of drugs. **2** pharmacist's shop, dispensary.

pharynx /ˈfærɪŋks/ *n.* (*pl.* **pharynges** /-rɪnˌdʒiːz/ or **-xes**) cavity behind the nose and mouth. □ **pharyngeal** /-rɪnˈdʒiːəl/ **pharyngitis** /-rɪnˈdʒaɪtɪs/ *n.* [Latin from Greek]

phase /feɪz/ —*n.* **1** stage in a process of change or development. **2** each of the aspects of the moon or a planet, according to the amount of its illumination. **3** *Physics* stage in a periodically recurring sequence, esp. the wave-form of alternating electric currents or light. —*v.* (-**sing**) carry out (a programme etc.) in phases or stages. □ **phase in** (or **out**) bring gradually into (or out of) use. [Greek *phasis* appearance]

Ph.D. *abbr.* Doctor of Philosophy. [Latin *philosophiae doctor*]

pheasant /ˈfez(ə)nt/ *n.* long-tailed game-bird. [Greek *Phasianos* of Phasis, name of a river associated with the bird]

phenobarbitone /ˌfiːnəʊˈbɑːbɪˌtəʊn/ *n.* narcotic and sedative barbiturate drug used esp. to treat epilepsy. [from PHENOL, BARBITURATE]

phenol /ˈfiːnɒl/ *n.* **1** hydroxyl derivative of benzene. **2** any hydroxyl derivative of an aromatic hydrocarbon. [French]

phenomenal /fɪˈnɒmɪn(ə)l/ *adj.* **1** extraordinary, remarkable. **2** of the nature of a phenomenon. □ **phenomenally** *adv.*

phenomenon /fɪˈnɒmɪnən/ *n.* (*pl.* **-mena**) **1** fact or occurrence that appears or is perceived, esp. one of which the cause is in question. **2** remarkable person or thing. [Greek *phainō* show]

■ **Usage** The plural form of this word, *phenomena*, is often used mistakenly for the singular. This should be avoided.

pheromone /ˈferəˌməʊn/ *n.* substance secreted and released by an animal for detection and response by another usu. of the same species. [Greek *pherō* convey, HORMONE]

phew /fjuː/ *int.* expression of relief, astonishment, weariness, etc. [imitative]

phi /faɪ/ *n.* twenty-first letter of the Greek alphabet (Φ, φ).

phial /ˈfaɪəl/ *n.* small glass bottle, esp. for liquid medicine. [Greek *phiale* broad flat dish]

phil- var. of PHILO-.

-phil- var. of -PHILE.

philadelphus /ˌfɪləˈdelfəs/ *n.* flowering shrub, esp. the mock orange. [Latin from Greek]

philander /fɪˈlændə(r)/ *v.* flirt or have casual affairs with women. □ **philanderer** *n.* [Greek *anēr andr-* male person]

philanthropy /fɪˈlænθrəpɪ/ *n.* **1** love of mankind. **2** practical benevolence. □

philanthropic /ˌfɪlənˈθrɒpɪk/ *adj.* **philanthropist** *n.* [Greek *anthrōpos* human being]

philately /fɪˈlætəlɪ/ *n.* the study and collecting of postage stamps. □ **philatelist** *n.* [Greek *atelēs* tax-free]

-phile *comb. form* (also **-phil**) forming nouns and adjectives denoting fondness for what is specified (*bibliophile*). [Greek *philos* loving]

philharmonic /ˌfɪlhɑːˈmɒnɪk/ *adj.* fond of music (usu. in the names of orchestras etc.). [Italian: related to HARMONIC]

philippic /fɪˈlɪpɪk/ *n.* bitter verbal attack. [Greek from *Philip* II of Macedon]

Philistine /ˈfɪlɪstaɪn/ *-n.* 1 member of a people of ancient Palestine. 2 (usu. **philistine**) person who is hostile or indifferent to culture. *-adj.* (usu. **philistine**) hostile or indifferent to culture. □ **philistinism** /-stɪnɪz(ə)m/ *n.* [Hebrew *pĕlištī*]

Phillips /ˈfɪlɪps/ *n.* (usu. *attrib.*) *propr.* denoting a screw with a cross-shaped slot, or a corresponding screwdriver. [name of the US manufacturer]

philo- *comb. form* (also **phil-** before a vowel or *h*) denoting a liking for what is specified. [Greek *philos* friend]

philodendron /ˌfɪləˈdendrən/ *n.* (*pl.* **-s** or **-dra**) tropical evergreen climber cultivated as a house-plant. [Greek *dendron* tree]

philology /fɪˈlɒlədʒɪ/ *n.* the study of language, esp. in its historical and comparative aspects. □ **philological** /-ləˈdʒɪk(ə)l/ *adj.* **philologist** *n.* [French from Latin from Greek: related to PHILO-, -LOGY]

philosopher /fɪˈlɒsəfə(r)/ *n.* 1 expert in or student of philosophy 2 person who lives by a philosophy or is wise. □ **philosopher's stone** *n.* (also **philosopher's stone**) supreme object of alchemy, a substance supposed to change other metals into gold or silver.

philosophical /ˌfɪləˈsɒfɪk(ə)l/ *adj.* (also **philosophic**) 1 of or according to philosophy. 2 skilled in or devoted to philosophy. 3 calm in adversity. □ **philosophically** *adv.*

philosophize /fɪˈlɒsəfaɪz/ *v.* (also **-ise**) 1 reason like a philosopher. 2 speculate; theorize. □ **philosophizer** *n.*

philosophy /fɪˈlɒsəfɪ/ *n.* (*pl.* **-ies**) 1 use of reason and argument in seeking truth and knowledge of reality, esp knowledge of the causes and nature of things and of the principles governing existence. 2 **a** particular system or set of beliefs reached by this. **b** personal rule of life. [Greek: related to PHILO-: *sophia* wisdom]

philtre /ˈfɪltə(r)/ *n.* (US **philter**) love-potion. [Greek *philēō* to love]

phlebitis /flɪˈbaɪtɪs/ *n.* inflammation of a vein. □ **phlebitic** /-ˈbɪtɪk/ *adj.* [Greek *phleps phleb-* vein]

phlegm /flem/ *n.* 1 thick viscous substance secreted by the mucous membranes of the respiratory passages, discharged by coughing. 2 **a** calmness. **b** sluggishness. 3 *hist.* phlegm regarded as one of the four bodily humours. [Greek *phlegma*]

phlegmatic /flegˈmætɪk/ *adj.* calm, unexcitable. □ **phlegmatically** *adv.* [Greek *phlegma* bark]

phloem /ˈfləʊem/ *n.* tissue conducting sap in plants. [Greek *phloos* bark]

phlox /flɒks/ *n.* (*pl.* same or **-es**) plant with scented clusters of esp. white, blue, or red flowers. [Greek *phlox*, name of a plant (literally 'flame')]

-phobe *comb. form* forming nouns denoting a person with a specified fear or aversion (*xenophobe*). [Greek *phobos* fear]

phobia /ˈfəʊbɪə/ *n.* abnormal or morbid fear or aversion. □ **phobic** *adj.* & *n.* [from -PHOBIA]

-phobia *comb. form* forming nouns denoting a specified fear or aversion (*agoraphobia*). □ **-phobic** *comb. form* forming adjectives.

phoenix /ˈfiːnɪks/ *n.* mythical bird, the only one of its kind, that burnt itself on a pyre and rose from the ashes to live again. [Greek *phoinix*]

phone *n.* & *v.* (**-ning**) *colloq.* = TELEPHONE. [abbreviation]

phone book *n.* = TELEPHONE DIRECTORY.

phonecard *n.* card containing prepaid units for use with a cardphone.

phone-in *n.* broadcast programme during which listeners or viewers telephone the studio and participate.

phoneme /ˈfəʊniːm/ *n.* unit of sound in a specified language that distinguishes one word from another (e.g. *p*, *b*, *d*, *t* as in *pad*, *pat*, *bad*, *bat*, in English). □ **phonemic** /-ˈniːmɪk/ *adj.* [Greek *phōnēma* speak]

phonetic /fəˈnetɪk/ *adj.* 1 representing vocal sounds. 2 (of spelling etc.) corresponding to pronunciation. □ **phonetically** *adv.* [Greek related to PHONE]

phonetics *n.pl.* (usu. treated as *sing.*) 1 vocal sounds. 2 the study of these. □ **phonetician** /ˌfəʊnɪˈtɪʃ(ə)n/ *n.*

phoney /ˈfəʊnɪ/ (also **phony**) *colloq.* *-adj.* (**-ier**, **-iest**) 1 sham; counterfeit. 2 fictitious. *-n.* (*pl.* **-eys** or **-ies**) phoney person or thing. □ **phoniness** *n.* [origin unknown]

phonic /ˈfəʊnɪk/ *adj.* of sound; of vocal sounds. [Greek *phōnē* voice]

phono- *comb. form* sound. [Greek *phōnē* voice, sound]

phonograph /ˈfəʊnəˌɡrɑːf/ *n.* **1** early form of gramophone. **2** *US* gramophone.

phonology /fəˈnɒlədʒɪ/ *n.* the study of sounds in language or a particular language; a language's sound system. □ **phonological** /ˌfəʊnəˈlɒdʒɪk(ə)l, ˌfɒn-/ *adj.*

phony var. of PHONEY.

phosphate /ˈfɒsfeɪt/ *n.* salt or ester of phosphoric acid, esp. used as a fertilizer. [French: related to PHOSPHORUS]

phosphor /ˈfɒsfə(r)/ *n.* synthetic fluorescent or phosphorescent substance. [Latin PHOSPHORUS]

phosphorescence /ˌfɒsfəˈres(ə)ns/ *n.* **1** radiation similar to fluorescence but detectable after excitation ceases. **2** emission of light without combustion or perceptible heat. □ **phosphoresce** *v.* (**-cing**). **phosphorescent** *adj.*

phosphorus /ˈfɒsfərəs/ *n. Chem.* non-metallic element existing in allotropic forms, esp. as a whitish waxy substance burning slowly and so luminous in the dark. □ **phosphoric** /-ˈfɒrɪk/ *adj.* **phosphorous** *adj.* [Greek *phōs* light, *-phoros* -bringing]

photo /ˈfəʊtəʊ/ *n.* (*pl.* **-s**) = PHOTOGRAPH *n.* [abbreviation]

photo- *comb. form* denoting: **1** light. **2** photography. [Greek *phōs phōt-* light]

photochemistry /ˌfəʊtəʊˈkemɪstrɪ/ *n.* the study of the chemical effects of light.

photocopier /ˈfəʊtəʊˌkɒpɪə(r)/ *n.* machine for producing photocopies.

photocopy *-n.* (*pl.* **-ies**) photographic copy of printed or written material. *-v.* (**-ies, -ied**) make a photocopy of.

photoelectric /ˌfəʊtəʊɪˈlektrɪk/ *adj.* marked by or using emissions of electrons from substances exposed to light. □ **photoelectricity** /-ˈtrɪsɪtɪ/ *n.*

photoelectric cell *n.* device using the effect of light to generate current.

photo finish *n.* close finish of a race or contest, where the winner is distinguishable only on a photograph.

photofit *n.* reconstructed picture of a suspect made from composite photographs.

photogenic /ˌfəʊtəʊˈdʒenɪk/ *adj.* **1** looking attractive in photographs. **2** *Biol.* producing or emitting light.

photograph /ˈfəʊtəˌɡrɑːf/ *-n.* picture formed by means of the chemical action of light or other radiation on sensitive film. *-v.* (also *absol.*) take a photograph of (a person etc.). □ **photographer** /fəˈtɒɡrəfə(r)/ *n.* **photographic** /-ˈɡræfɪk/ *adj.* **photographically** /-ˈɡræfɪkəlɪ/ *adv.*

photography /fəˈtɒɡrəfɪ/ *n.* the taking and processing of photographs.

photogravure /ˌfəʊtəʊɡrəˈvjʊə(r)/ *n.* **1** image produced from a photographic negative transferred to a metal plate and etched in. **2** this process. [French *gravure* engraving]

photojournalism /ˌfəʊtəʊˈdʒɜːnəˌlɪz(ə)m/ *n.* the relating of news by photographs, esp. in magazines etc. □ **photojournalist** *n.*

photolithography /ˌfəʊtəʊlɪˈθɒɡrəfɪ/ *n.* lithography using plates made photographically.

photometer /fəʊˈtɒmɪtə(r)/ *n.* instrument for measuring light. □ **photometric** /ˌfəʊtəʊˈmetrɪk/ *adj.* **photometry** /-ˈtɒmɪtrɪ/ *n.*

photon /ˈfəʊtɒn/ *n.* quantum of electromagnetic radiation energy, proportional to the frequency of radiation. [after *electron*]

photo opportunity *n.* organized opportunity for the press etc. to photograph a celebrity.

photosensitive /ˌfəʊtəʊˈsensɪtɪv/ *adj.* reacting to light.

Photostat /ˈfəʊtəʊˌstæt/ *-n. propr.* **1** type of photocopier. **2** copy made by it. *-v.* (**photostat**) (**-tt-**) make a Photostat of.

photosynthesis /ˌfəʊtəʊˈsɪnθɪsɪs/ *n.* process in which the energy of sunlight is used by organisms, esp. green plants, to synthesize carbohydrates from carbon dioxide and water. □ **photosynthesize** *v.* (also **-ise**) (**-zing** or **-sing**). **photosynthetic** /-ˈθetɪk/ *adj.*

phrase /freɪz/ *-n.* **1** group of words forming a conceptual unit, but not a sentence. **2** idiomatic or short pithy expression. **3** mode of expression. **4** *Mus.* group of notes forming a distinct unit within a melody. *-v.* (**-sing**) **1** express in words. **2** *Mus.* divide (music) into phrases, esp. in performance. □ **phrasal** *adj.* [Greek *phrasis* from *phrazō* tell]

phrase book *n.* book for travellers, listing useful expressions with their foreign equivalents.

phraseology /ˌfreɪzɪˈɒlədʒɪ/ *n.* (*pl.* **-ies**) **1** choice or arrangement of words. **2** mode of expression. □ **phraseological** /-zɪəˈlɒdʒɪk(ə)l/ *adj.*

phrenetic var. of FRENETIC.

phrenology /frɪˈnɒlədʒɪ/ *n. hist.* the study of the shape and size of the cranium as a supposed indication of character and mental faculties. □ **phrenological** /-nəˈlɒdʒɪk(ə)l/ *adj.* **phrenologist** *n.* [Greek *phrēn* mind]

phut /fʌt/ *n.* dull abrupt sound as of impact or an explosion. □ **go phut** *colloq.*

(esp. of a plan) collapse, break down. [perhaps from Hindi *phaṭnā* to burst]

phylactery /fɪˈlæktərɪ/ *n.* (*pl.* -**ies**) small leather box containing Hebrew texts, worn by Jewish men at prayer. [Greek *phulaktērion*]

phyllo pastry *var.* of FILO PASTRY.

phylum /ˈfaɪləm/ *n.* (*pl.* **phyla**) *Biol.* taxonomic rank below a kingdom, comprising a class or classes and subordinate taxa. [Greek *phulon* race]

physic /ˈfɪzɪk/ *n. archaic* 1 medicine. 2 art of healing. 3 medical profession. [Greek *phusikē* of nature]

physical /ˈfɪzɪk(ə)l/ *adj.* 1 of the body (*physical exercise*). 2 of matter; material. 3 **a** of, or according to, the laws of nature. **b** of physics. 4 US medical examination. □ **physically** *adv.*

physical chemistry *n.* application of physics to the study of chemical behaviour.

physical geography *n.* branch of geography dealing with natural features.

physical jerks *n.pl. colloq.* physical exercises.

physical science *n.* science(s) used in the study of inanimate natural objects.

physician /fɪˈzɪʃ(ə)n/ *n.* doctor, esp. a specialist in medical diagnosis and treatment.

physicist /ˈfɪzɪsɪst/ *n.* person skilled in physics.

physics /ˈfɪzɪks/ *n.pl.* (treated as *sing.*) branch of science dealing with the properties and interactions of matter and energy. [Latin *physica* (pl.) from Greek: related to PHYSIC]

physio /ˈfɪzɪəʊ/ *n.* (*pl.* -**s**) *colloq.* 1 physiotherapy. 2 physiotherapist.

physiognomy /ˌfɪzɪˈɒnəmɪ/ *n.* (*pl.* -**ies**) 1 **a** cast or form of a person's features, expression, etc. **b** supposed art of judging character from facial character. 2 external features of a landscape etc. [Greek: related to PHYSIC, GNOMON]

physiology /ˌfɪzɪˈɒlədʒɪ/ *n.* 1 science of the functions of living organisms and their parts. 2 these functions. □ **physiological** /-zɪəˈlɒdʒɪk(ə)l/ *adj.*; **physiologist** *n.* [Latin: related to PHYSIC, -LOGY]

physiotherapy /ˌfɪzɪəʊˈθerəpɪ/ *n.* treatment of disease, injury, deformity, etc., by physical methods including massage, heat treatment, remedial exercise, etc. □ **physiotherapist** *n.* [related to PHYSIC, THERAPY]

physique /fɪˈziːk/ *n.* bodily structure and development. [French: related to PHYSIC]

pi /paɪ/ *n.* 1 sixteenth letter of the Greek alphabet (Π, π). 2 (as π) the symbol of the

ratio of the circumference of a circle to its diameter (approx. 3.14). [Greek]

pia mater /ˌpaɪə ˈmeɪtə(r)/ *n.* delicate innermost membrane enveloping the brain and spinal cord. [Latin, = tender mother]

pianissimo /ˌpɪəˈnɪsɪməʊ/ *Mus.* –*adj.* very soft. –*adv.* very softly. –*n.* (*pl.* -**s** or -**mi** /-miː/) very soft playing or passage. [Italian, superlative of PIANO²]

pianist /ˈpɪənɪst/ *n.* piano-player.

piano¹ /ˈpɪænəʊ/ *n.* (*pl.* -**s**) keyboard instrument with metal strings struck by hammers. [Italian, abbreviation of PIANOFORTE]

piano² /ˈpjɑːnəʊ/ *Mus.* –*adj.* soft. –*adv.* softly. –*n.* (*pl.* -**s** or -**ni** /-niː/) soft playing or passage. [Latin *planus* flat, (of sound) soft]

piano-accordion *n.* accordion with a small keyboard like that of a piano.

pianoforte /ˌpɪænəʊˈfɔːtɪ/ *n. formal* or *archaic* = PIANO¹. [Italian, earlier *piano e forte* soft and loud]

Pianola /pɪəˈnəʊlə/ *n. propr.* a kind of automatic piano. [diminutive]

piazza /pɪˈætsə/ *n.* public square or market-place. [Italian: related to PLACE]

pibroch /ˈpiːbrɒk/ *n.* martial or funerary bagpipe music. [Gaelic]

pica /ˈpaɪkə/ *n.* 1 unit of type-size (¹⁄₆ inch). 2 size of letters in typewriting (10 per inch). [Latin: related to PIE²]

picador /ˈpɪkədɔː(r)/ *n.* mounted man with a lance in a bullfight. [Spanish]

picaresque /ˌpɪkəˈresk/ *adj.* (of a style of fiction) dealing with the episodic adventures of rogues etc. [Spanish *picaro* rogue]

■ **Usage** *Picaresque* is sometimes used to mean 'transitory' or 'roaming', but this is considered incorrect in standard English.

picayune /ˌpɪkəˈjuːn/ *US colloq.* –*n.* 1 small coin. 2 insignificant person or thing. –*adj.* mean; contemptible; petty. [French *picaillon*]

piccalilli /ˈpɪkəlɪlɪ/ *n.* (*pl.* -**s**) pickle of chopped vegetables, mustard, and hot spices. [origin unknown]

piccaninny /ˈpɪkənɪnɪ/ *n.* (*US* **pickaninny**) (*pl.* -**ies**) *offens.* small Black or Australian Aboriginal child. [West Indian Negro from Spanish *pequeño* or Portuguese *pequeno* little]

piccolo /ˈpɪkələʊ/ *n.* (*pl.* -**s**) small flute sounding an octave higher than the ordinary one. [Italian, = small]

pick¹ –*v.* 1 (also *absol.*) choose carefully. 2 detach or pluck (a flower, fruit, etc.) from a stem, tree, etc. 3 **a** probe (a tooth etc.) with the finger, an instrument, etc. to remove unwanted matter. **b** clear (a

pick

bone, carcass, etc.) of scraps of meat etc. **4** (also *absol.*) (of a person) eat (food, a meal, etc.) in small bits. —*n.* **1** act of picking. **2 a** selection, choice. **b** right to select (*had first pick of the prizes*). **3** (usu. foll. by *of*) best (*the pick of the bunch*). □ **pick and choose** select fastidiously. **pick at 1** eat (food) without interest. **2** find fault with. **pick a person's brains** extract ideas, information, etc. from a person for one's own use. **pick holes in** find fault with (an idea etc.). **pick a lock** open a lock with an instrument other than the proper key, esp. with criminal intent. **pick off 1** pluck (leaves etc.) off. **2** select. **pick on 1** find fault with; nag at. **2** select. **pick out 1** take from a larger number. **2** distinguish from surrounding objects; identify. **3** play (a tune) by ear on the piano etc. **4** (often foll. by *in*, *with*) accentuate (decoration, a painting, etc.) with a contrasting colour. **pick over** select the best from. **pick a person's pockets** steal from a person's pockets. **pick a quarrel** start an argument deliberately. **pick to pieces** = *take to pieces* (see PIECE). **pick up 1** grasp and raise. **2 a** acquire by chance or without effort. **b** learn effortlessly. **3** stop for and take along with one. **4** become acquainted with (a person) casually, esp for sexual purposes. **5** (of one's health, weather, share prices, etc.) recover, improve, etc. **6** (of an engine etc.) recover speed. **7** (of the police etc.) arrest. **8** detect by scrutiny or with a telescope, radio, etc. **9** accept the responsibility of paying (a bill etc.). **10** resume, take up anew (*picked up where we left off*). □

pick² *n.* **1** long-handled tool with a usu. curved iron bar pointed at one or both ends, used for breaking up hard ground etc. **2** *colloq.* plectrum. **3** any instrument for picking. [from PIKE]

pickaback var. of PIGGYBACK.

pickaninny *US* var. of PICCANINNY.

pickaxe /'pikæks/ *n.* (*US* **pickax**) = PICK² 1. [French: related to PIKE]

picket /'pikit/ —*n.* **1** one or more persons stationed outside a place of work to persuade others not to enter during a strike etc. **2** pointed stake driven into the ground. **3 a** small body of troops sent out to watch for the enemy. **b** group of sentries. —*v.* (-t-) **1 a** station or act as a picket. **b** beset or guard with a picket or pickets. **2** secure (a place) with stakes. **3** tether (an animal). [French *piquer* prick]

picket line *n.* boundary established by workers on strike, esp. at the entrance to the place of work, which others are asked not to cross.

pickings *n.pl.* **1** profits or gains acquired easily or dishonestly. **2** leftovers.

pickle /'pik(ə)l/ —*n.* **1 a** (often in *pl.*) food, esp. vegetables, preserved in brine, vinegar, mustard, etc. **b** the liquid used for this. **2** *colloq.* plight (*in a pickle*). —*v.* (-ling) **1** preserve in or treat with pickle. **2** (as **pickled** *adj.*) *slang* drunk. [Low German or Dutch *pekel*]

pick-me-up *n.* **1** tonic for the nerves etc. **2** a good experience that cheers.

pickpocket *n.* person who steals from people's pockets.

pick-up *n.* **1** *slang* person met casually, esp. for sexual purposes. **2** small open motor truck. **3** part of a record-player carrying the stylus. **4** device on an electric guitar etc. that converts string vibrations into electrical signals. **5** act of picking up.

picky *adj.* (-ier, -iest) *colloq.* excessively fastidious.

pick-your-own *adj.* (usu. *attrib.*) (of fruit and vegetables) dug or picked by the customer at the farm etc.

picnic /'piknik/ —*n.* **1** outing including an outdoor meal. **2** meal eaten out of doors. **3** (usu. with *neg.*) *colloq.* something agreeable or easily accomplished etc. —*v.* (-ck-) take part in a picnic. [French *pique-nique*]

pico- *comb. form* denoting a factor of 10^{-12} (*picometre*). [Spanish *pico* beak, peak, little bit]

Pict *n.* member of an ancient people of N. Britain. □ **Pictish** *adj.* [Latin]

pictograph /'piktəgra:f/ *n.* (also **pictogram** /-græm/) **1** pictorial symbol for a word or phrase. **2** pictorial representation of statistics etc. □ **pictographic** /-'græfik/ *adj.* [Latin *pingo pict-* paint]

pictorial /pik'tɔ:riəl/ —*adj.* **1** of or expressed in pictures or pictures. **2** illustrated. —*n.* periodical with pictures as the main feature. □ **pictorially** *adv.* [Latin *pictor* painter: related to PICTURE]

picture /'piktʃə(r)/ —*n.* **1 a** (often *attrib.*) painting, drawing, photograph, etc., esp. as a work of art. **b** portrait. **c** beautiful object. **2** total mental or visual impression produced; scene. **3 a** film. **b** (**the pictures**) cinema; cinema performance. —*v.* (-ring) **1** (also *refl.*; often foll. by *to*) imagine (*pictured it to herself*). **2** represent in a picture. **3** describe graphically. □ **get the picture** *colloq.* grasp the drift of information etc. **in the picture** *colloq.* fully informed. [Latin *pingo pict-* paint]

picture postcard *n.* postcard with a picture on one side.

picturesque /ˌpɪktʃəˈresk/ adj. 1 beautiful or striking to look at. 2 (of language etc.) strikingly graphic. [Italian pittoresco, assimilated to PICTURE]

picture window n. large window of one pane of glass.

piddle /ˈpɪd(ə)l/ v. (-ling) 1 colloq. urinate. 2 (as **piddling** adj.) colloq. trivial; trifling. 3 (foll. by about, around) work or act in a trifling way. [origin unknown]

pidgin /ˈpɪdʒɪn/ n. simplified language used between people not having a common language. [corruption of business] □ **pidgin English** n. pidgin in which the chief language is English, used orig. between Chinese and Europeans.

pie¹ /paɪ/ n. 1 baked dish of meat, fish, fruit, etc., usu. with a top and base of pastry. 2 thing resembling a pie (mud pie). □ **easy as pie** very easy. [origin uncertain]

pie² /paɪ/ n. archaic magpie. [Latin pica]

piebald /ˈpaɪbɔːld/ adj. (esp. of a horse) having irregular patches of two colours, esp. black and white. —n. piebald animal. [from PIE², BALD]

piece /piːs/ n. 1 a (often foll. by of) distinct portion forming part of or broken off from a larger object. b each of the parts of which a set or category is composed (five-piece band). 2 coin. 3 (usu. short) literary or musical composition; picture; play. 4 item or instance (piece of news; piece of impudence). 5 a object used to make moves in a board-game. b chessman (strictly, other than a pawn). 6 definite quantity in which a thing is sold. 7 (often foll. by of) enclosed portion (of land etc.). 8 slang derog. woman. —v. (-cing) (usu. foll. by together) form into a whole, put together; join. □ **go to pieces** collapse emotionally. **in** (or **all in**) **one piece** 1 unbroken. 2 unharmed. **of a piece** (often foll. by with) uniform, consistent. **a piece of cake** see CAKE. **a piece of one's mind** sharp rebuke or lecture. **say one's piece** give one's opinion or make a prepared statement. **take to pieces** 1 break up or dismantle. 2 criticize harshly. [Anglo-French, probably from Celtic]

pièce de résistance /ˌpjes də reˈzistɑ̃s/ n. (pl. **pièces de résistance** pronunc. same) most important or remarkable item, esp. a dish at a meal. [French]

piecemeal —adv. piece by piece; gradually. —adj. gradual; unsystematic. [from PIECE, MEAL]

piece-work n. work paid for according to the amount produced.

pie chart n. circle divided into sectors to represent relative quantities.

piecrust n. baked pastry crust of a pie.

pied /paɪd/ adj. particoloured. [from PIE²]

pied-à-terre /ˌpjeɪdɑːˈteə(r)/ n. (pl. **pieds-à-terre** pronunc. same) (usu. small) flat, house, etc. kept for occasional use. [French, literally 'foot to earth']

pie-eyed adj. slang drunk.

pie in the sky n. (used without an article) unrealistic prospect of future happiness.

pier n. 1 a structure built out into the sea, a lake, etc., as a promenade and landing-stage. b breakwater. 2 a support of an arch or of the span of a bridge; pillar. b solid masonry between windows etc. [Latin pera]

pierce v. (-cing) 1 (of a sharp instrument etc.) penetrate. b (often foll. by with) make a hole in or through with a sharp-pointed instrument. c make (a hole etc.). 2 (as **piercing** adj.) (of a glance, sound, light pain, cold, etc.) keen, sharp, or unpleasantly penetrating. 3 (often foll. by through, into) force a way through or into, penetrate. [French percer from Latin pertundo bore through]

pier-glass n. large mirror, used orig. to fill wall-space between windows.

pierrot /ˈpɪərəʊ/ n. (fem. **pierrette** /pɪəˈret/) 1 white-faced entertainer in pier shows etc. with a loose white clown's costume. 2 French pantomime character so dressed. [French, diminutive of Pierre Peter]

pietà /pɪeˈtɑː/ n. representation of the Virgin Mary holding the dead body of Christ on her lap. [Italian = PIETY]

pietism /ˈpaɪətɪz(ə)m/ n. 1 pious sentiment. 2 exaggerated or affected piety. [German: related to PIETY]

piety /ˈpaɪətɪ/ n. (pl. **-ies**) 1 quality of being pious. 2 pious act. [Latin: related to PIOUS]

piffle /ˈpɪf(ə)l/ colloq. —n. nonsense; empty speech. —v. (-ling) talk or act feebly; trifle. [imitative]

piffling adj. colloq. trivial; worthless.

pig n. 1 omnivorous hoofed bristly broad-snouted mammal, esp. a domesticated kind. 2 its flesh as food. 3 colloq. greedy, dirty, or unpleasant person. 4 oblong mass of metal (esp. iron or lead) from a smelting-furnace. 5 slang derog. police officer. —v. (-gg-) colloq. eat (food) greedily. □ **buy a pig in a poke** acquire something without previous sight or knowledge of it. **pig it** colloq. live in a disorderly or filthy fashion. **pig out** esp. US slang eat gluttonously. [Old English]

pigeon /ˈpɪdʒ(ə)n/ n. bird of the dove family. [Latin *pipio -onis*]

pigeon-hole –n. each of a set of compartments on a wall etc. for papers, letters, etc. –v. 1 assign to a preconceived category. 2 deposit in a pigeon-hole. 3 put aside for future consideration.

pigeon-toed adj. having the toes turned inwards.

piggery n. (pl. -ies) 1 pig farm. 2 = PIGSTY.

piggish adj. greedy; dirty; mean.

piggy –n. (pl. -ies) colloq. little pig. –adj. (-ier, -iest) 1 like a pig. 2 (of features etc.) like those of a pig.

piggyback (also **pickaback** /ˈpɪkəbæk/) –n. ride on the back and shoulders of another person. –adv. on the back and shoulders of another person. [origin unknown]

piggy bank n. pig-shaped money box.

pigheaded adj. obstinate. □ **pigheadedness** n.

pig-iron n. crude iron from a smelting-furnace.

piglet /ˈpɪɡlɪt/ n. young pig.

pigment /ˈpɪɡmənt/ –n. 1 colouring-matter used as paint or dye. 2 natural colouring-matter of animal or plant tissue. –v. colour with or as if with pigment. □ **pigmentary** adj. [Latin *pingo paint*]

pigmentation /pɪɡmənˈteɪʃ(ə)n/ n. 1 natural colouring of plants, animals, etc. 2 excessive colouring of tissue by the deposition of pigment.

pigmy var. of PYGMY.

pigskin n. 1 hide of a pig. 2 leather made from this.

pigsty n. (pl. -ies) 1 pen for pigs. 2 filthy house, room, etc.

pigswill /ˈpɪɡswɪl/ n. kitchen refuse and scraps fed to pigs.

pigtail n. plait of hair hanging from the back of the head.

pike n. (pl. same or -s) 1 large voracious freshwater fish with a long narrow snout. 2 hist. weapon with a pointed metal head on a long wooden shaft. [Old English]

pikestaff n. wooden shaft of a pike. □ **plain as a pikestaff** quite plain or obvious.

pilaster /pɪˈlæstə(r)/ n. rectangular column projecting slightly from a wall. □ **pilastered** adj. [Latin *pila pillar*]

pilau /prˈlaʊ/ n. (also **pilaff**, **pilaf** /prˈlæf/) Middle Eastern or Indian dish of rice boiled with meat, vegetables, spices, etc. [Turkish]

pilchard /ˈpɪltʃəd/ n. small marine fish of the herring family. [origin unknown]

pile¹ –n. 1 heap of things laid upon one another. 2 large imposing building. 3 colloq. a large quantity. b large amount of money. 4 a series of plates of dissimilar metals laid one on another alternately to produce an electric current. b = NUCLEAR REACTOR. 5 funeral pyre. –v. (-ling) 1 a (often foll. by up, on) heap up. b (foll. by with) load. 2 (foll. by in, into, on, out of, etc.) crowd hurriedly or tightly. □ **pile it on** colloq. exaggerate. **pile up** (or **pile it on** colloq.) accumulate; heap up. 2 colloq. cause (a vehicle etc.) to crash. [Latin *pila*]

pile² n. 1 heavy beam driven vertically into the ground to support a bridge, the foundations of a house, etc. 2 pointed stake or post. [Latin *pilum javelin*]

pile³ n. soft projecting surface on a carpet, velvet, etc. [Latin *pilus* hair]

pile-driver n. machine for driving piles into the ground.

piles n.pl. colloq. haemorrhoids. [Latin *pila* ball]

pile-up n. colloq. multiple crash of road vehicles.

pilfer /ˈpɪlfə(r)/ v. (also absol.) steal (objects), esp. in small quantities. [French *pelfre*]

pilgrim /ˈpɪlɡrɪm/ n. 1 person who journeys to a sacred place for religious reasons. 2 traveller. [Latin: related to PEREGRINE]

pilgrimage n. 1 pilgrim's journey. 2 any journey taken for sentimental reasons.

Pilgrim Fathers n.pl. English Puritans who founded the colony of Plymouth, Massachusetts, in 1620.

pill n. 1 a ball or flat disc of solid medicine for swallowing whole. b (usu. prec. by the) colloq. contraceptive pill. 2 unpleasant or painful necessity. [Latin *pila* ball]

pillage /ˈpɪlɪdʒ/ –v. (-ging) (also absol.) plunder, sack. –n. pillaging, esp. in war. [French *piller* plunder]

pillar /ˈpɪlə(r)/ n. 1 slender vertical structure of stone etc. used as a support or for ornament. 2 person regarded as a mainstay (*pillar of the faith*). 3 upright mass of air, water, rock, etc. □ **from pillar to post** (rushing etc.) from one place to another. [Latin *pila* pillar]

pillar-box n. public postbox shaped like a pillar.

pillar-box red adj. & n. bright red.

pillbox n. 1 shallow cylindrical box for holding pills. 2 hat of a similar shape. 3 Mil. small partly underground enclosed concrete fort.

pillion /ˈpɪljən/ n. seating for a passenger behind a motor cyclist. □ **ride**

pillion travel seated behind a motor cyclist. [Gaelic *pillean* small cushion]

pillory /'pɪlərɪ/ —*n.* (*pl.* -ies) *hist.* wooden framework with holes for the head and hands, holding a person and allowing him or her to be publicly ridiculed. —*v.* (-ies, -ied) **1** expose to ridicule. **2** *hist.* put in the pillory. [French]

pillow /'pɪləʊ/ —*n.* **1** soft support for the head esp. in bed. **2** pillow-shaped block or support. —*v.* rest on or as if on a pillow. [Latin *pulvinus* cushion]

pillowcase *n.* (also **pillowslip**) washable cover for a pillow.

pilot /'paɪlət/ —*n.* **1** person who operates the controls of an aircraft. **2** person qualified to take charge of a ship entering or leaving harbour. **3** (usu. *attrib.*) experimental undertaking or test (*pilot scheme*). **4** guide. —*v.* (-t-) **1** act as a pilot of **2** conduct or initiate as a pilot. [Greek *pēdon*]

pilot-light *n.* **1** small gas burner kept alight to light another. **2** electric indicator light or control light.

pilot officer *n.* lowest commissioned rank in the RAF.

pimento /pɪ'mentəʊ/ *n.* (*pl.* -s) **1** tree native to Jamaica. **2** berries of this, usu. crushed for culinary use; allspice. **3** = PIMIENTO. [Latin: related to PIGMENT]

pi meson var. of PION.

pimiento /pɪmɪ'entəʊ/ *n.* (*pl.* -s) = PIMENTO. [Latin *piper* PEPPER]

pimp —*n.* man who lives off the earnings of a prostitute or a brothel. —*v.* act as a pimp. [origin unknown]

pimpernel /'pɪmpənel/ *n.* = SCARLET PIMPERNEL. [Latin *piper* PEPPER]

pimple /'pɪmp(ə)l/ *n.* **1** small hard inflamed spot on the skin. **2** anything resembling a pimple. □ **pimply** *adj.* [Old English]

PIN /pɪn/ *abbr.* personal identification number (for use with a cashcard etc.).

pin —*n.* **1** small thin pointed piece of metal with a round or flattened head used (esp. in sewing) for holding things in place, attaching one thing to another, etc. **2** peg of wood or metal for various purposes. **3** (in idioms) something of small value (*not worth a pin*). **4** (in *pl.*) *colloq.* legs. —*v.* (-nn-) **1 a** (often foll. by *to, up, together*) fasten with a pin or pins. **b** transfix with a pin, lance, etc. **2** (usu. foll. by *on*) put (blame, responsibility, etc.) on (a person etc.). **3** (often foll. by *down*) seize and hold fast. □ **pin down** *v.* **1** (often foll. by *to*) bind (a person etc.) to a promise, arrangement, etc. **2** force (a person) to declare his or her intentions. **3** restrict the actions of (an enemy etc.). **4** specify (a thing) precisely. **pin one's faith** (or **hopes** etc.)

675

on rely implicitly on. [Latin *pinna* point etc.]

piña colada /ˌpiːnə kə'lɑːdə/ *n.* cocktail of pineapple juice, rum, and coconut. [Spanish]

pinafore /'pɪnəfɔː(r)/ *n.* **1** apron, esp. with a bib. **2** (in full **pinafore dress**) collarless sleeveless dress worn over a blouse or jumper. [from PIN, AFORE]

pinball *n.* game in which small metal balls are shot across a board to strike pins.

pince-nez /pæns'neɪ/ *n.* (*pl.* same) pair of eyeglasses with a nose-clip. [French, = pinch-nose]

pincer movement *n.* movement by two wings of an army converging to surround an enemy.

pincers /'pɪnsəz/ *n.pl.* **1** (also **pair of pincers**) gripping-tool resembling scissors but with blunt jaws. **2** front claws of lobsters and some other crustaceans. [related to PINCH]

pinch —*v.* **1 a** squeeze tightly, esp. between finger and thumb. **b** (often *absol.*) (of a shoe etc.) constrict painfully. **2** (of cold, hunger, etc.) affect painfully. **3** *slang* **a** steal. **b** arrest. **4** (as **pinched** *adj.*) (of the features) drawn. **5** (usu. foll. by *in, of, for*, etc.) stint. **6** (usu. foll. by *out, back, down*) remove (leaves, buds, etc.) to encourage bushy growth. —*n.* **1** act of pinching. **2** amount that can be taken up with fingers and thumb (*pinch of snuff*). **3** the stress caused by poverty etc. □ **at** (or **in**) **a pinch** in an emergency. [French *pincer*]

pinchbeck —*n.* gold-like alloy of copper and zinc used in cheap jewellery etc. —*adj.* counterfeit, sham. [*Pinchbeck*, name of a watchmaker]

pincushion *n.* small pad for holding pins.

pine[1] *n.* **1** evergreen coniferous tree with needle-shaped leaves growing in clusters. **2** its wood. **3** (*attrib.*) made of pine. [Latin *pinus*]

pine[2] *v.* (-ning) **1** (often foll. by *away*) decline or waste away from grief etc. **2** long eagerly. [Old English]

pineal /'pɪnɪəl/ *adj.* shaped like a pine cone. [Latin *pinea*: related to PINE[1]]

pineal body *n.* (also **pineal gland**) conical gland in the brain, secreting a hormone-like substance.

pineapple /'paɪnæp(ə)l/ *n.* **1** large juicy tropical fruit with yellow flesh and tough segmented skin. **2** plant bearing this. [from PINE[1], APPLE]

pine cone *n.* fruit of the pine.

pine nut *n.* edible seed of various pines.

676

ping *n.* single short high ringing sound. —*v.* (cause to) make a ping. [imitative]

ping-pong *n. colloq.* = TABLE TENNIS. [imitative]

pinhead *n.* 1 head of a pin. 2 very small thing or spot. 3 *colloq.* stupid person.

pinhole *n.* 1 hole made by a pin. 2 hole into which a peg fits.

pinhole camera *n.* camera with a pinhole aperture and no lens.

pinion[1] /ˈpɪnjən/ —*n.* 1 outer part of a bird's wing. 2 *poet.* wing; flight-feather. —*v.* 1 cut off the pinion of (a wing or bird) to prevent flight. 2 a bind the arms of (a person). b (often foll. by *to*) bind (the arms, a person, etc.) fast to a thing. [Latin *pinna*]

pinion[2] /ˈpɪnjən/ *n.* 1 small cog-wheel engaging with a larger one. 2 cogged spindle engaging with a wheel. [Latin *pinea* pine-cone: related to PINE[1]]

pink[1] —*n.* 1 pale red colour. 2 cultivated plant with fragrant flowers. 3 (prec. by *the*) the most perfect condition, the peak (*the pink of health*). 4 person with socialist tendencies. —*adj.* 1 of a pale red colour. 2 tending to socialism. □ **in the pink** *colloq.* in very good health. □ **pinkish** *adj.* **pinkness** *n.* **pinky** *adj.* [origin unknown]

pink[2] *v.* 1 pierce slightly. 2 cut a scalloped or zigzag edge on. [perhaps from Low German or Dutch]

pink[3] *v.* (of a vehicle engine) emit high-pitched explosive sounds caused by faulty combustion. [imitative]

pink gin *n.* gin flavoured with angostura bitters.

pinking shears *n.pl.* dressmaker's serrated shears for cutting a zigzag edge.

pinko /ˈpɪŋkəʊ/ *adj.* (*pl.* -s) *esp. US slang* socialist.

pin-money *n.* 1 *hist.* allowance to a woman from her husband. 2 very small sum of money.

pinnace /ˈpɪnɪs/ *n.* ship's small boat. [French]

pinnacle /ˈpɪnək(ə)l/ *n.* 1 culmination or climax. 2 natural peak. 3 small ornamental turret crowning a buttress, roof, etc. [Latin *pinna* PIN]

pinnate /ˈpɪneɪt/ *adj.* (of a compound leaf) having leaflets on either side of the leaf-stalk. [Latin *pinnatus* feathered: related to PINNACLE]

pinny /ˈpɪnɪ/ *n.* (*pl.* -ies) *colloq.* pinafore. [abbreviation]

pinpoint —*n.* 1 point of a pin. 2 something very small or sharp. 3 (*attrib.*) precise, accurate. —*v.* locate with precision.

pinprick *n.* trifling irritation.

pins and needles *n.pl.* tingling sensation in a limb recovering from numbness.

pinstripe *n.* 1 (often *attrib.*) narrow stripe in cloth (*pinstripe suit*). 2 (in *sing.* or *pl.*) pinstripe suit (*came wearing his pinstripes*). □ **pinstriped** *adj.*

pint /paɪnt/ *n.* 1 measure of capacity for liquids etc., ⅛ gal. (0.57, *US* 0.47, litre). 2 a *colloq.* pint of beer. b pint of a liquid, esp. milk. 3 measure of shellfish containable in a pint mug. [French]

pinta /ˈpaɪntə/ *n. colloq.* pint of milk. [corruption of *pint of*]

pin-table *n.* table used in playing pinball.

pintail *n.* duck or grouse with a pointed tail.

pintle /ˈpɪnt(ə)l/ *n.* pin or bolt, esp. one on which some other part turns. [Old English]

pint-sized *adj. colloq.* very small.

pin-tuck *n.* very narrow ornamental tuck.

pin-up *n.* 1 photograph of a popular or sexually attractive person, hung on the wall. 2 person in such a photograph.

pin-wheel *n.* small Catherine wheel.

Pinyin /pɪnˈjɪn/ *n.* system of romanized spelling for transliterating Chinese. [Chinese]

pion /ˈpaɪɒn/ *n.* (also **pi meson**) subatomic particle having a mass many times greater than that of an electron. [from PI]

pioneer /ˌpaɪəˈnɪə(r)/ —*n.* 1 initiator of an enterprise; investigator of a subject etc. 2 explorer or settler; colonist. —*v.* 1 initiate (an enterprise etc.) for others to follow. 2 be a pioneer. [French *pionnier*: related to PAWN[1]]

pious /ˈpaɪəs/ *adj.* 1 devout; religious. 2 sanctimonious. 3 dutiful. □ **piously** *adv.* **piousness** *n.* [Latin]

pip[1] —*n.* seed of an apple, pear, orange, grape, etc. —*v.* (-**pp**-) remove the pips from (fruit etc.). □ **pipless** *adj.* [abbreviation of PIPPIN]

pip[2] *n.* short high-pitched sound, usu. electronically produced, esp. as a time signal. [imitative]

pip[3] *v.* (-**pp**-) *colloq.* 1 hit with a shot. 2 (also **pip at the post**) defeat narrowly or at the last moment. [origin unknown]

pip[4] *n.* 1 any of the spots on a playing-card, dice, or domino. 2 star (1–3 according to rank) on the shoulder of an army officer's uniform. [origin unknown]

pip[5] *n.* 1 disease of poultry etc. 2 *colloq.* fit of disgust or bad temper (*esp. give one the pip*). [Low German or Dutch]

pipe —*n.* **1** tube of metal, plastic, etc. used to convey water, gas, etc. **2 a** narrow tube with a bowl at one end and containing tobacco for smoking. **b** quantity of tobacco held by this. **3 a** wind instrument of a single tube. **b** any of the tubes by which sound is produced in an organ. **c** (in *pl.*) = BAGPIPES. **4** tubular organ, vessel, etc. in an animal's body. **5** high note or song, esp. of a bird. **6 a** boatswain's whistle. **b** sounding of this. **7** cask for wine, esp. as a measure, usu. = 105 gal. (about 477 litres).—*v.* (**-ping**) **1 a** convey (oil, water, gas, etc.) by pipes. **b** provide with pipes. **2** (esp. as **piped** *adj.*) transmit (recorded music etc.) by wire or cable. **3** (esp. as **piped** *adj.*) *Naut.* **a** summon (a crew) etc. by wire or cable. **4** (usu. foll. by *up, on, to,* etc.) **b** signal the arrival of (an officer etc.) on board. **5** utter in a shrill voice. **6** decorate or trim with piping. **7** lead or bring (a person etc.) by the sound of a pipe or pipes. □ **pipe down** *colloq.* be quiet or less insistent. **pipe up** begin to play, sing, speak, etc. □ **pipeful** *n.* (*pl.* **-s**). [Latin *pipo* chirp]

pipeclay *n.* fine white clay used for tobacco-pipes, whitening leather, etc.

pipe-cleaner *n.* piece of flexible tufted wire for cleaning a tobacco-pipe.

pipedream *n.* unattainable or fanciful hope or scheme. [originally as experienced when smoking an opium pipe]

pipeline *n.* **1** long, usu. underground, pipe for conveying esp. oil. **2** channel supplying goods, information, etc. □ **in the pipeline** being dealt with or prepared; under discussion, on the way.

piper *n.* person who plays a pipe, esp. the bagpipes.

pipette /pɪˈpet/ *n. Chem* slender tube for transferring or measuring small quantities of liquids. [French diminutive: related to PIPE]

piping *n.* **1** pipelike fold or cord for edging or decorating clothing, upholstery, etc. **2** ornamental lines of icing, cream, potato, etc. on a cake etc. **3** lengths of pipe, system of pipes. □ **piping hot** (of food, water, etc.) very hot.

pipit /ˈpɪpɪt/ *n.* small bird resembling a lark. [imitative]

pippin /ˈpɪpɪn/ *n.* **1** apple grown from seed. **2** red and yellow eating apple. [French]

pipsqueak *n. colloq.* insignificant or contemptible person or thing. [imitative]

piquant /ˈpiːkənt, -kɑːnt/ *adj.* **1** agreeably pungent, sharp, or appetizing. **2** pleasantly stimulating to the mind. □ **piquancy** *n.* [French *piquer* prick]

pique /piːk/ —*v.* (**piques, piqued, piquing**) **1** wound the pride of, irritate. **2** arouse (curiosity, interest, etc.). —*n.* resentment; hurt pride. [French: related to PIQUANT]

piquet /pɪˈket/ *n.* card-game for two players with a pack of 32 cards. [French]

piracy /ˈpaɪrəsɪ/ *n.* (*pl.* **-ies**) robbery of ships at sea. **2** similar practice, esp. hijacking. **3** infringement of copyright etc. [related to PIRATE]

piranha /pɪˈrɑːnə/ *n.* voracious S. American freshwater fish. [Portuguese]

pirate /ˈpaɪərət/ —*n.* **1** seafaring robber attacking ships. **b** ship used by pirates. **2** (often *attrib.*) person who infringes another's copyright or business rights or who broadcasts without official authorization (*pirate radio station*).—*v.* (**-ting**) reproduce (a book etc.) or trade (goods) without permission. □ **piratical** /-ˈrætɪk(ə)l/ *adj.* [Latin *pirata* from Greek]

pirouette /pɪrʊˈet/ —*n.* dancer's spin on one foot or the point of the toe. —*v.* (**-ting**) perform a pirouette. [French, = spinning-top]

piscatorial /pɪskəˈtɔːrɪəl/ *adj.* of fishermen or fishing. □ **piscatorially** *adv.* [Latin *piscator* angler from *piscis* fish]

Pisces /ˈpaɪsiːz/ *n.* (*pl.* same) **1** constellation and twelfth sign of the zodiac (the Fish or Fishes). **2** person born when the sun is in this sign. [Latin, pl. of *piscis* fish]

piscina /pɪˈsiːnə/ *n.* (*pl.* **-nae** /-niː/ or **-s**) **1** stone basin near the altar in a church for draining water used in rinsing the chalice etc. **2** fish-pond. [Latin, from *piscis* fish]

piss *coarse slang* —*v.* **1** urinate. **2** discharge (blood etc.) with urine. **3** (as **pissed** *adj.*) drunk. —*n.* **1** urine. **2** act of urinating. □ **piss about** (or **around**) fool or mess about. **piss down** rain heavily. **piss off** (often as *int.*) go away. **2** (often as **pissed off** *adj.*) annoy; depress. **piss on** (a person or thing) show utter contempt for. **take the piss** (often foll. by *out of*) mock; make fun of. [French: imitative]

piss artist *n.* **1** drunkard. **2** person who fools about.

piss-taking *n.* mockery. □ **piss-taker** *n.*

piss-up *n.* drinking spree.

pistachio /pɪˈstɑːʃɪəʊ/ *n.* (*pl.* **-s**) **1** edible pale-green nut. **2** tree yielding this. [Persian *pistaẕ*]

piste /piːst/ *n.* ski-run of compacted snow. [French, = racetrack]

pistil /ˈpɪstɪl/ *n.* female organs of a flower, comprising the stigma, style, and ovary. □ **pistillate** *adj.* [Latin: related to PESTLE]

pistol /ˈpɪst(ə)l/ n. small handgun. [Czech *pišt'al*]

piston /ˈpɪst(ə)n/ n. 1 sliding cylinder fitting closely in a tube in which it moves up and down, used in an internal-combustion engine to impart motion, or in a pump to receive motion. 2 sliding valve in a trumpet etc. [Italian: related to PESTLE]

piston-ring n. ring on a piston sealing the gap between piston and cylinder wall.

piston-rod n. rod or crankshaft by which a piston imparts motion.

pit¹ —n. 1 a deep hole in the ground, usu. large. b coalmine. c covered hole as a trap for animals. 2 hollow on a surface, esp. an indentation of the skin. 3 a = *orchestra pit* (see ORCHESTRA 2). b usu. *hist.* seating at the back of the stalls. 4 (**the pits**) *slang* worst imaginable place, situation, person, etc. 5 a area at the side of a track where racing cars are serviced and refuelled. b sunken area in a workshop floor for access to a car's underside. —v. (-tt-) 1 (usu. foll. by *against*) set (one's wits, strength, etc.) in competition. 2 (usu. as **pitted** *adj.*) make pits, scars, craters, etc. in. 3 put into a pit. [Old English from Latin *puteus* well]

pit² v. (-tt-) (usu. as **pitted** *adj.*) remove stones from (fruit). [origin uncertain]

pita var. of PITTA.

pit-a-pat /ˈpɪtə.pæt/ (also **pitter-patter**) —adv. 1 with a sound like quick light steps. 2 falteringly (*heart went pit-a-pat*). —n. such a sound. [imitative]

pit bull terrier n. small American dog noted for ferocity.

pitch¹ —v. 1 erect and fix (a tent, camp, etc.). 2 throw. 3 fix in a definite position. 4 express in a particular style or at a particular level. 5 (often foll. by *against, into,* etc.) fall heavily, esp. headlong. 6 (of a ship etc.) plunge backwards and forwards in a lengthwise direction. 7 *Mus.* set at a particular pitch. 8 *Cricket* a cause (a bowled ball) to strike the ground at a specified point etc. b (of a ball) strike the ground thus. —n. 1 area of play in a field-game. 2 height, degree, intensity, etc. (*excitement had reached such a pitch*). 3 degree of slope, esp. of a roof. 4 *Mus.* quality of a sound governed by the rate of vibrations producing it; highness or lowness of a note. 5 act of throwing. 6 pitching motion of a ship etc. 7 *colloq.* salesman's persuasive talk. 8 place where a street vendor is stationed. 9 distance between successive points, lines, etc. (e.g. character spacing on a typewriter). □ **pitch in** *colloq.* set to work vigorously. **pitch into** *colloq.* 1 attack forcibly. 2 assail (food, work, etc.) vigorously. [origin uncertain]

pitch² —n. dark resinous substance from the distillation of tar or turpentine, used for making ships watertight etc. —v. coat with pitch. □ **pitchy** *adj.* (-ier, -iest). [Latin *pix pic-*]

pitch-black adj. (also **pitch-dark**) very or completely dark.

pitchblende /ˈpɪtʃblend/ n. uranium oxide occurring in pitchlike masses and yielding radium. [German: related to PITCH²]

pitched battle n. 1 vigorous argument etc. 2 planned battle between sides in prepared positions and on chosen ground.

pitched roof n. sloping roof.

pitcher¹ n. large jug with a lip and a handle. [related to BEAKER]

pitcher² n. player who delivers the ball in baseball.

pitchfork —n. long-handled two-pronged fork for pitching hay etc. —v. 1 throw with or as if with a pitchfork. 2 (usu. foll. by *into*) thrust (a person) forcibly into a position, office, etc.

pitch-pine n. pine-tree yielding much resin.

piteous /ˈpɪtɪəs/ adj. deserving or arousing pity; wretched. □ **piteously** adv. **piteousness** n. [Romanic: related to PITY]

pitfall n. 1 unsuspected danger or drawback. 2 covered pit for trapping animals.

pith n. 1 spongy white tissue lining the rind of an orange etc. 2 essential part. 3 spongy tissue in the stems and branches of plants. 4 strength; vigour; energy. [Old English]

pit-head n. 1 top of a mineshaft. 2 area surrounding this (also *attrib.: pit-head ballot*).

pith helmet n. protective sun-helmet made of dried pith from plants.

pithy adj. (-ier, -iest) 1 (of style, speech, etc.) terse and forcible. 2 of or like pith. □ **pithily** adv. **pithiness** n.

pitiable /ˈpɪtɪəb(ə)l/ adj. deserving or arousing pity or contempt. □ **pitiably** adv. [French: related to PITY]

pitiful /ˈpɪtɪfʊl/ adj. 1 causing pity. 2 contemptible. □ **pitifully** adv.

pitiless /ˈpɪtɪlɪs/ adj. showing no pity (*pitiless heat*). □ **pitilessly** adv.

pit of the stomach n. depression below the breastbone.

piton /ˈpiːtɒn/ n. peg driven into rock or a crack to support a climber or rope. [French]

pitta /ˈpɪtə/ n. (also **pita**) flat hollow unleavened bread which can be split and filled [modern Greek, = a kind of cake]

pittance /ˈpɪt(ə)ns/ n. very small allowance or remuneration. [Romanic: related to PITY]

pitter-patter var. of PIT-A-PAT.

pituitary /prˈtjuːɪtərɪ/ n. (pl. -ies) (also **pituitary gland** an small ductless gland at the base of the brain. [Latin *pituita* phlegm]

pity /ˈpɪtɪ/ n. & v. 1 sorrow and compassion for another's suffering. 2 cause for regret (*what a pity!*). —v. (-ies, -ied) feel (often contemptuous) pity for. □ **take** (or **have**) **pity on** help out of pity for. □ **pitying** adj. **pityingly** adv. [Latin: related to PIETY]

pivot /ˈpɪvət/ n. & v. 1 shaft or pin on which something turns or oscillates. 2 crucial or essential person, point, etc. —v. (-t-) 1 turn on or as on a pivot. 2 provide with a pivot. □ **pivotal** adj. [French]

pixel /ˈpɪks(ə)l/ n. any of the minute areas of uniform illumination of which an image on a display screen is composed. [abbreviation of *picture element*]

pixie /ˈpɪksɪ/ n. (also **pixy**) (pl. -ies) fairy-like being. [origin unknown]

pizza /ˈpiːtsə/ n. Italian dish of a layer of dough baked with a topping of tomatoes, cheese, etc. [Italian, = pie]

pizzeria /ˌpiːtsəˈriːə/ n. pizza restaurant.

pizzicato /ˌpɪtsɪˈkɑːtəʊ/ Mus. —adv. plucking. —adj. (of a note, passage, etc.) performed pizzicato. —n. (pl. -s or -ti /-tɪ/) note, passage, etc. played pizzicato. [Italian]

pl. abbr. 1 plural. 2 (usu. **Pl.**) place. 3 plate.

placable /ˈpleɪkəb(ə)l/ adj. easily placated; mild; forgiving. □ **placability** /-ˈbɪlɪtɪ/ n. [Latin *placo* appease]

placard /ˈplækɑːd/ —n. large notice for public display. —v. set up placards on (a wall etc.). [French from Dutch *placken* glue (v.)]

placate /pləˈkeɪt/ v. (-ting) pacify; conciliate. □ **placatory** /pləˈkeɪtərɪ/ adj. [Latin *placo* appease]

place —n. 1 a particular portion of space. b portion of space occupied by a person or thing. c proper or natural position. 2 city, town, village, etc. 3 residence, home. 4 group of houses in a town etc., esp. a square. 5 (esp. large) country house. 6 rank or status. 7 space, esp. a seat, for a person. 8 building or area for a specific purpose (*place of worship*). 9 point reached in a book etc. (*lost my place*). 10 particular spot on a surface, esp. of the skin (*sore place*). 11 a employment or office. b duties or entitlements of office etc. **b** duties or entitlements of office etc. 12 position as a member of a team, student in a college, etc. 13 any of the

first three (or four) positions in a race, esp. other than the winner. 14 position of a digit in a series indicated in decimal or similar notation. —v. (-cing) 1 put in a particular place or state or order; arrange. 2 identify, classify, or remember correctly. 3 assign to a particular place, class, or rank; locate. 4 find employment or a living etc. for. 5 make or state (an order or bet etc.). 6 (often foll. by in, on, etc.) have (confidence etc.). 7 state the position of (any of the first three or four runners) in a race. 8 (as **placed** adj.) among the first three (or four) in a race. □ **give place to 1** make room for. 2 yield precedence to. 3 be succeeded by. **go places** colloq. be successful. **in place** in the right position; suitable. **in place of** in exchange for; instead of. **in places** at only some places or parts. **out of place 1** in the wrong position. 2 unsuitable. **put a person in his** (or **her**) **place** deflate a person. **take place** occur. **take the place of** be substituted for. □ **place-** **ment** n. [Latin *platea* broad way]

place-kick n. kick in football with the ball placed on the ground.

place-mat n. small table-mat for a person's plate.

place-name n. name of a town, village, etc.

placenta /pləˈsentə/ n. (pl. -tae /-tiː/ or -s) organ in the uterus of pregnant mammals nourishing the foetus through the umbilical cord and expelled after birth. □ **placental** adj. [Greek, = flat cake]

placer /ˈpleɪsə(r)/ n. deposit of sand, gravel, etc. containing valuable minerals in particles. [American Spanish]

place-setting n. set of cutlery etc. for one person at a table.

placid /ˈplæsɪd/ adj. 1 calm; not easily excited or irritated. 2 tranquil, serene. □ **placidity** /pləˈsɪdɪtɪ/ n. **placidly** adv. **placidness** n. [Latin *placeo* please]

placket /ˈplækɪt/ n. 1 opening or slit in a garment, for fastenings or access to a pocket. 2 flap of fabric under this. [var. of PLACARD]

plagiarize /ˈpleɪdʒəraɪz/ v. (also -ise) (-zing or -sing) 1 (also *absol.*) take and pass off (another's thoughts, writings, etc.) as one's own. 2 pass off the thoughts etc. of (another person) as one's own. □ **plagiarism** n. **plagiarist** n. **plagiarizer** n. [Latin *plagiarius* kidnapper]

plague /pleɪg/ —*n.* **1** deadly contagious disease. **2** (foll. by *of*) *colloq.* infestation of a pest etc. **3** great trouble or affliction. **4** *colloq.* nuisance. —*v.* (**plagues, plagued, plaguing**) **1** *colloq.* pester, annoy. **2** afflict, hinder (*plagued by back pain*). **3** affect with plague. [Latin *plaga* stroke, infection]

plaice /pleɪs/ *n.* (*pl.* same) marine flat-fish used as food. [Latin *platessa*]

plaid /plad/ *n.* **1** (often *attrib.*) chequered or tartan, esp. woollen, twilled cloth (*plaid skirt*). **2** long piece of this worn over the shoulder in Highland Scottish costume. [Gaelic]

plain —*adj.* **1** clear, evident. **2** readily understood, simple. **3** (of food, decoration, etc.) simple. **4** not beautiful or distinguished-looking. **5** outspoken; straightforward. **6** unsophisticated; not luxurious (*a plain man; plain living*). —*adv.* **1** clearly. **2** simply. —*n.* **1** level tract of country. **2** basic knitting stitch. □ **plainly** *adv.* **plainness** *n.* [Latin *planus*]

plainchant *n.* = PLAINSONG.

plain chocolate *n.* dark chocolate without added milk.

plain clothes *n.pl.* ordinary clothes, not uniform (*plain-clothes police*).

plain dealing *n.* candour; straight-forwardness.

plain flour *n.* flour containing no rais-ing agent.

plain sailing *n.* uncomplicated situa-tion or course of action.

plainsong *n.* unaccompanied church music sung in unison in medieval modes and in free rhythm correspond-ing to the accentuation of the words.

plain-spoken *adj.* frank.

plaint *n.* **1** *Law* accusation; charge. **2** *literary* complaint, lamentation. [French *plainte* from Latin *plango* lament]

plaintiff /ˈpleɪntɪf/ *n.* person who brings a case against another into court. [French *plaintif*: related to PLAINTIVE]

plaintive /ˈpleɪntɪv/ *adj.* expressing sorrow; mournful-sounding. □ **plain-tively** *adv.* [French: related to PLAINT]

plait /plat/ —*n.* length of hair, straw, etc., in three or more interlaced strands. —*v.* **1** weave (hair etc.) into a plait. **2** make by interlacing strands (*plaited belt*). [French *pleit* from Latin *plico* fold]

plan —*n.* **1** method or procedure for doing something; design, scheme, or intention. **2** drawing etc. of a building or structure, made by projection on to a horizontal plane. **3** map of a town or district. **4** scheme of an arrangement (*seating plan*). —*v.* (**-nn-**) **1** arrange (a procedure etc.) beforehand; form a plan;

intend. **2** make a plan of or design for. **3** (as **planned** *adj.*) in accordance with a plan (*planned parenthood*). **4** make plans. □ **plan on** (often foll. by *pres. part.*) *colloq.* aim at; intend. □ **planning** *n.* [French]

planchette /plɑːnˈʃet/ *n.* small board on castors with a pencil, said to write spirit messages when a person's fingers rest lightly on it. [French diminutive: related to PLANK]

plane[1] —*n.* **1** flat surface such that a straight line joining any two points on it lies wholly in it. **2** level surface. **3** *colloq.* = AEROPLANE. **4** flat surface producing lift by the action of air or water over and under it (usu. in *comb.*: *hydroplane*). **5** (often foll. by *of*) level of attainment, knowledge, etc. —*adj.* **1** (of a surface etc.) perfectly level. **2** (of an angle, figure, etc.) lying in a plane. —*v.* (**-ning**) glide. [Latin *planus* PLAIN]

plane[2] —*n.* tool for smoothing a usu. wooden surface by paring shavings from it. —*v.* (**-ning**) **1** smooth with a plane. **2** (often foll. by *away, down*) pare with a plane. [Latin: related to PLANE[1]]

plane[3] *n.* tall tree with maple-like leaves and bark which peels in uneven patches. [Greek *platanos*]

planet /ˈplanɪt/ *n.* celestial body orbit-ing round a star. □ **planetary** *adj.* [Greek = wanderer]

planetarium /ˌplanɪˈteərɪəm/ *n.* (*pl.* **-s** or **-ria**) **1** domed building in which images of stars, planets, constellations, etc. are projected. **2** device for such projection.

plangent /ˈplandʒ(ə)nt/ *adj.* *literary* **1** loud and reverberating. **2** plaintive. [Latin: related to PLAINT]

plank —*n.* **1** long flat piece of timber. **2** item in a political or other programme. —*v.* **1** provide or cover with planks. **2** (usu. foll. by *down*) *colloq.* **a** put down or deposit roughly or violently. **b** pay (money) on the spot. □ **walk the plank** *hist.* be made to walk blindfold along a plank over the side of a ship to one's death in the sea. [Latin *planca*]

planking *n.* planks as flooring etc.

plankton /ˈplaŋkt(ə)n/ *n.* chiefly microscopic organisms drifting in the sea or fresh water. [Greek, = wander-ing]

planner *n.* **1** person who plans new towns etc. **2** person who makes plans. **3** list, table, etc., with information helpful in planning.

planning permission *n.* formal per-mission for building etc., esp. from a local authority.

plant /plɑːnt/ —*n.* **1 a** organism usu. containing chlorophyll enabling it to

live wholly on inorganic substances, and lacking the power of voluntary movement. **b** small organism of this kind, as distinguished from a shrub or tree. **2 a** machinery, fixtures, etc., used in industry. **b** factory. **3** *colloq.* something deliberately placed so as to incriminate another. —*v.* **1** place, fix (plants, etc.) in soil for growing. **2** (often foll. by *in*, *on*, etc.) put or fix in position. **3** (often *refl.*) station (a person etc.), esp. as a spy. **4** cause (an idea etc.) to be established, esp. in another person's mind. **5** deliver (a blow, kiss, etc.) with a deliberate aim. **6** *colloq.* place (something incriminating) for later discovery. □ **plant out** transfer from a pot or frame to the open ground; set out (seedlings) at intervals. □ **plantlike** *adj.* [Latin *planta*]

plantain[1] /ˈplæntɪn/ *n.* plant with broad flat leaves spread close to the ground and seeds used as food for birds. [Latin *plantāgo*]

plantain[2] /ˈplæntɪn/ *n.* **1 a** kind of banana plant, grown for its fruit. **2** banana-like fruit of this. [Spanish]

plantation /plɑːnˈteɪʃ(ə)n, plæn-/ *n.* **1** estate on which cotton, tobacco, etc. is cultivated. **2** area planted with trees etc. **3** *hist.* colony. [Latin: related to PLANT]

planter *n.* **1** manager or owner of a plantation. **2** container for house-plants.

plaque /plæk, plɑːk/ *n.* **1** commemorative tablet, esp. fixed to a building. **2** deposit on teeth where bacteria proliferate. [Dutch *plak* related to PLACARD]

plasma /ˈplæzmə/ *n.* (also **plasm** /ˈplæz(ə)m/) **1 a** colourless fluid part of blood, lymph, or milk, in which corpuscles or fat-globules are suspended. **b** this taken from blood for transfusions. **2** = PROTOPLASM. **3** gas of positive ions and free electrons in about equal numbers. □ **plasmic** *adj.* [Greek plasma shape (v.)]

plaster[2] /ˈplɑːstə(r)/ —*n.* **1** soft mixture of lime, sand, and water etc., applied to walls, ceilings, etc. to dry into a smooth hard surface. **2** = STICKING-PLASTER. **3** = PLASTER OF PARIS. —*v.* **1** cover (a wall etc.) with plaster. **2** coat, daub, cover thickly. **3** stick or apply (a thing) thickly like plaster. **4** (often foll. by *down*) smooth (esp. hair) with water etc. **5** (as **plastered** *adj.*) *slang* drunk. □ **plasterer** *n.* [Greek *emplastron*]

plasterboard *n.* two boards with a filling of plaster for partitions, walls, etc.

plaster cast *n.* **1** bandage stiffened with plaster of Paris and applied to a broken

limb etc. **2** statue or mould made of plaster.

plaster of Paris *n.* fine white gypsum paste for plaster casts etc.

plastic /ˈplæstɪk/ —*n.* **1** synthetic resinous substance that can be given any shape. **2** (in full **plastic money**) *colloq.* credit card(s). —*adj.* **1** made of plastic. **2** capable of being moulded; pliant, supple. **3** giving form to clay, wax, etc. □ **plasticity** /ˈtɪsɪtɪ/ *n.* **plasticize** /-ˌsaɪz/ *v.* (also **-ise**) (**-zing** or **-sing**). **plasticizer** /-ˌsaɪzə(r)/ *n.* (also **-iser**). **plasticky** *adj.* [Greek: related to PLASMA]

plastic arts *n.pl.* arts involving modelling or the representation of solid objects.

plastic bomb *n.* bomb containing plastic explosive.

plastic explosive *n.* putty-like explosive.

Plasticine /ˈplæstɪsiːn/ *n. propr.* pliant material used for modelling.

plastic surgery *n.* reconstruction or repair of damaged or unsightly skin, muscle, etc., esp. by the transfer of tissue. □ **plastic surgeon** *n.*

plate —*n.* **1 a** shallow usu. circular vessel from which food is eaten or served. **b** contents of this. **2** similar vessel used for a collection in church or other receptacle. **3** (*collect.*) a utensils of silver, gold, etc. **b** objects of plated metal. **4** piece of metal with a name or inscription for affixing to a door etc. **5** illustration on special paper in a book. **6** thin sheet of metal, glass, etc., coated with a sensitive film for photography. **7** flat thin usu. rigid sheet of metal etc., often as part of a mechanism. **8 a** smooth piece of metal etc. for engraving. **b** impression from this. **9 a** silver or gold cup as a prize for a horse-race etc. **b** race for this as a prize. **10 a** thin piece of plastic material, moulded to the shape of the mouth, on which artificial teeth are mounted. **b** *colloq.* denture. **11** each of several rigid sheets of rock thought to form the earth's outer crust. **12** thin flat organic structure or formation. —*v.* (*-ting*) **1** apply a thin coat esp. of silver, gold, or tin to (another metal). **2** cover (esp. a ship) with plates of metal for protection. □ **on a plate** *colloq.* available with little trouble to the recipient. **on one's plate** *colloq.* for one to deal with. □ **plateful** *n.* (*pl.* **-s**). [Latin *platta* from *pictus* flat]

plateau /ˈplætəʊ/ —*n.* (*pl.* **-x** or **-s** /-əʊz/) **1** area of fairly level high ground. **2** state of little variation after an increase. —*v.* (**plateaus**, **plateaued**, **plateauing**, **plateaus**, **plateaued**) (often foll. by *out*) reach a level or static

state after an increase. [French: related to PLATE]

plate glass *n.* thick fine-quality glass for shop windows etc.

platelayer *n.* person employed in fixing and repairing railway rails.

platelet /ˈpleɪtlɪt/ *n.* small colourless disc of protoplasm found in blood and involved in clotting.

platen /ˈplæt(ə)n/ *n.* **1** plate in a printing-press which presses the paper against the type. **2** cylindrical roller in a typewriter etc. against which the paper is held. [French *platine*: related to PLATE]

plate-rack *n.* rack in which plates are placed to drain.

plate tectonics *n.pl.* (usu. treated as *sing.*) the study of the earth's surface based on the concept of moving 'plates' (see sense 11 of PLATE) forming its structure.

platform /ˈplætfɔːm/ *n.* **1** raised level surface, esp. one from which a speaker addresses an audience or one alongside the line at a railway station. **2** floor area at the entrance to a bus etc. **3** thick sole of a shoe. **4** declared policy of a political party. [French: related to PLATE, FORM]

platinum /ˈplætɪnəm/ *n. Chem.* white heavy precious metallic element that does not tarnish. [earlier *platina* from Spanish, diminutive from *plata* silver]

platinum blonde (also **platinum blond**) *—adj.* silvery-blond. *—n.* person with such hair.

platitude /ˈplætɪtjuːd/ *n.* commonplace remark, esp. one solemnly delivered. □ **platitudinous** /-ˈtjuːdɪnəs/ *adj.* [French: related to PLATE]

Platonic /pləˈtɒnɪk/ *adj.* **1** of Plato or his ideas. **2** (**platonic**) (of love or friendship) not sexual. [Greek *Platōn* (5th-4th c. BC), name of a Greek philosopher]

Platonism /ˈpleɪtənɪz(ə)m/ *n.* philosophy of Plato or his followers. □ **Platonist** *n.*

platoon /pləˈtuːn/ *n.* **1** subdivision of a military company. **2** group of persons acting together. [French *peloton* diminutive of *pelote* PELLET]

platter *n.* large flat dish or plate. [Anglo-French *plater*: related to PLATE]

platypus /ˈplætɪpəs/ *n.* (*pl.* **-puses**) Australian aquatic egg-laying mammal, with a ducklike bill and flat tail. [Greek, = flat foot]

plaudit /ˈplɔːdɪt/ *n.* (usu. in *pl.*) **1** round of applause. **2** expression of approval. [Latin *plaudite*, imperative of *plaudo plaus-* clap]

plausible /ˈplɔːzɪb(ə)l/ *adj.* **1** (of a statement etc.) reasonable or probable. **2** (of a person) persuasive but deceptive.

□ **plausibility** /ˈblɪtɪ/ *n.* **plausibly** *adv.* [Latin: related to PLAUDIT]

play *—v.* **1** (often foll. by *with*) occupy or amuse oneself pleasantly. **2** (foll. by *with*) act light-heartedly or flippantly with (a person's feelings etc.). **3 a** perform on or be able to perform on (a musical instrument). **b** perform (a piece of music etc.). **c** (also *absol.*) cause (a record, record-player, etc.) to produce sounds. **4 a** (foll. by *in*) perform a role in (a drama etc.). **b** perform (a drama or role) on stage etc. **c** give a dramatic performance at (a particular theatre or place). **5** act in real life the part of (*play truant*; *play the fool*). **6** (foll. by *on*) perform (a trick or joke etc.) on (a person). **7** *colloq.* cooperate; do what is wanted (*they won't play*). **8** gamble, gamble on. **9 a** take part in (a game or recreation). **b** compete with (another player or team) in a game. **c** occupy (a specified position) in a team for a game. **d** assign (a player) to a position. **10** move (a piece) or display (a playing-card) in one's turn in a game. **11** (also *absol.*) strike (a ball etc.) or execute (a stroke) in a game. **12** move about in a lively manner; flit, dart. **13** (often foll. by *on*) **a** emit light, water, etc. (*fountains gently playing*). **b** touch gently. **14** allow (a fish) to exhaust itself pulling against a line. **15** (often foll. by *at*) **a** engage half-heartedly (in an activity). **b** pretend to be. *—n.* **1** recreation, amusement, esp. as the spontaneous activity of children. **2 a** playing of a game. **b** action or manner of this. **3** activity or operation (*the play of fancy*). **5 a** freedom of movement. **b** space or scope for this. **6** brisk, light, or fitful movement. **7** gambling. □ **in** (or **out of**) **play** *Sport* (of the ball etc.) in (or not in) a position to be played according to the rules. **make a play for** *colloq.* make a conspicuous attempt to acquire. **make play with** use ostentatiously. **play about** (or **around**) behave irresponsibly. **play along** pretend to cooperate. **play back** play (sounds recently recorded). **play ball** *colloq.* cooperate. **play by ear 1** perform (music) without having seen it written down. **2** (also **play it by ear**) *colloq.* proceed step by step according to results. **play one's cards right** (or **well**) *colloq.* make good use of opportunities; act shrewdly. **play down** minimize the importance of. **played out** exhausted of energy or usefulness. **play fast and loose** act unreliably. **play the field** see FIELD. **play for time** seek to gain time by delaying. **play the game** observe the rules; behave honourably. **play havoc** (or **hell**) **with**

play-act *colloq.* cause great confusion or difficulty: disrupt. **play into a person's hands** act so as unwittingly to give a person an advantage. **play it cool** *colloq.* be relaxed or apparently indifferent. **play the market** speculate in stocks etc. **play off** (usu. foll. by *against*) 1 oppose (one person against another), esp. for one's own advantage. 2 play an extra match to decide a draw or tie. **play on** 1 continue to play. 2 take advantage of (a person's feelings etc.). **play safe** (or **for safety**) avoid risks. **play up** 1 behave mischievously. 2 annoy in this way. 3 cause trouble; be irritating. **play up to** flatter, esp. to win favour. **play with fire** take foolish risks. [Old English]

play-act *v.* 1 act in a play. 2 pretend; behave insincerely. □ **play-acting** *n.*

playbill *n.* poster advertising a play.

play-back *n.* playing back of a sound.

playboy *n.* wealthy pleasure-seeking man.

player *n.* 1 participant in a game. 2 person playing a musical instrument. 3 actor.

playfellow *n.* playmate.

playful *adj.* 1 fond of or inclined to play. 2 done in fun. □ **playfully** *adv.* **playfulness** *n.*

playgoer *n.* person who goes often to the theatre.

playground *n.* outdoor area for children to play in.

playgroup *n.* organized regular meeting of preschool children for supervised play.

playhouse *n.* theatre.

playing-card *n.* one of a set of usu. 52 oblong cards, divided into four suits and used in games.

playing-field *n.* field for outdoor games.

playlet *n.* short play.

playmate *n.* child's companion in play.

play-off *n.* match played to decide a draw or tie.

play on words *n.* pun.

play-pen *n.* portable enclosure for a young child to play in.

play school *n.* nursery school or kindergarten.

plaything *n.* 1 toy or other thing to play with. 2 person used merely as an object of amusement or pleasure.

playtime *n.* time for play or recreation.

playwright *n.* person who writes plays.

plc *abbr.* (also **PLC**) Public Limited Company.

plea *n.* 1 appeal, entreaty. 2 *Law* formal statement by or on behalf of a defendant. 3 excuse. [Latin *placitum* decree; related to PLEASE]

pleach *v.* entwine or interlace (esp. branches to form a hedge). [Latin: related to PLEXUS]

plead *v.* 1 (foll. by *with*) make an earnest appeal to. 2 (of an advocate) address a lawcourt. 3 maintain (a cause) in a lawcourt. 4 (foll. by *guilty* or *not guilty*) declare oneself to be guilty or not guilty of a charge. 5 allege as an excuse (*plead insanity*). 6 (often as **pleading** *adj.*) make an appeal or entreaty (*in a pleading voice*). [Anglo-French *pleder*]

pleading *n.* (usu. in *pl.*) formal statement of the cause of an action or defence.

pleasant /ˈplez(ə)nt/ *adj.* (**-er**, **-est**) pleasing to the mind, feelings, or senses. □ **pleasantly** *adv.* [French: related to PLEASE]

pleasantry *n.* (*pl.* **-ies**) 1 amusing or polite remark. 2 humorous speech. 3 jocularity.

please /pliːz/ *v.* (**-sing**) 1 be agreeable to; make glad; give pleasure. 2 (in *passive*) **a** (foll. by *to* + infin.) be glad or willing to (*am pleased to help*). **b** (often foll. by *about, at, with*) derive pleasure or satisfaction (from). 3 (with *it* as subject) be the inclination or wish of (*it did not please him to attend*). 4 think fit (*take as many as you please*). 5 used in polite requests (*come in, please*). □ **if you please** if you are willing, esp. iron. to indicate unreasonableness (*then, if you please, we had to pay*). **please oneself** do as one likes. [French *plaisir* from Latin *placeo*]

pleasurable /ˈpleʒərəb(ə)l/ *adj.* causing pleasure. □ **pleasurably** *adv.*

pleasure /ˈpleʒə(r)/ *n.* 1 feeling of satisfaction or joy. 2 enjoyment. 3 source of pleasure or gratification. 4 one's will or desire (*what is your pleasure?*). 5 sensual gratification. 6 (*attrib.*) done or used for pleasure. [French: related to PLEASE]

pleat *n.* fold or crease, esp. a flattened fold in cloth doubled upon itself. —*v.* make a pleat or pleats in. [from PLAIT]

pleb *n. colloq. usu. derog.* = PLEBEIAN 2. □ **plebby** *adj.* [abbreviation of PLEBEIAN]

plebeian /plɪˈbiːən/ —*n.* 1 commoner, esp. in ancient Rome. 2 working-class person, an uncultured one. —*adj.* 1 of the common people. 2 uncultured, coarse. [Latin *plebs plebis* common people]

684

plebiscite /'pleb,sart/ n. referendum. [Latin *plebiscitum*: related to PLEBEIAN]

plectrum /'plɛktrəm/ n. (pl. -s or -tra) thin flat piece of plastic etc. for plucking the strings of a guitar etc. [Greek *plēssō* strike]

pledge —n. 1 solemn promise. 2 thing given as security against a debt etc. 3 thing put in pawn. 4 thing given as a token of favour etc., or of something to come. 5 drinking of a person's health, toast. 6 solemn promise to abstain from alcohol (*sign the pledge*). —v. (-ging) 1 a pawn. 2 promise solemnly by the pledge of (one's honour, word, etc.). 3 bind by a solemn promise. 4 drink to the health of. □ **pledge one's troth** see TROTH. [French *plege*]

Pleiades /'plaɪə,diːz/ n.pl. cluster of seven stars in the constellation Taurus. [Latin from Greek]

Pleistocene /'plaɪstə,siːn/ *Geol.* —adj. of the first epoch of the Quaternary period. —n. this epoch. [Greek *pleistos* nost, *kainos* new]

plenary /'pliːnərɪ/ adj. 1 (of an assembly) to be attended by all members. 2 entire, unqualified (*plenary indulgence*). [Latin *plenus* full]

plenipotentiary /,plɛnɪpə'tɛnʃərɪ/ —n. (pl. -ies) person (esp. a diplomat) invested with full authority to act. —adj. having this power. [Latin: related to PLENARY, POTENT]

plenitude /'plɛnɪ,tjuːd/ n. *literary* 1 fullness, completeness. 2 abundance. [Latin: related to PLENARY]

plenteous /'plɛntɪəs/ adj. *literary* plentiful. [French *plentivous*: related to PLENTY]

plentiful /'plɛntɪfʊl/ adj. abundant, copious. □ **plentifully** adv.

plenty /'plɛntɪ/ —n. (often foll. by *of*) abundance, sufficient quantity or number (*we have plenty*; *plenty of time*; *a time of plenty*). —adj. *colloq.* plentiful. —adv. *colloq.* fully, quite. [Latin *plenitas*: related to PLENARY]

plenum /'pliːnəm/ n. full assembly of people or a committee etc. [Latin, neuter of *plenus* full]

pleonasm /'pliːə,næz(ə)m/ n. use of more words than are needed (e.g. *see with one's eyes*). □ **pleonastic** /'næstɪk/ adj. [Greek *pleon* more]

plethora /'plɛθərə/ n. over-abundance. [Greek, = fullness]

pleura /'plʊərə/ n. (pl. **rae** /-riː/) membrane enveloping the lungs. □ **pleural** adj. [Latin *pleura* rib]

pleurisy /'plʊərəsɪ/ n. inflammation of the pleura. □ **pleuritic** /-'rɪtɪk/ adj. [Greek: related to PLEURA]

plexus /'plɛksəs/ n. (pl. same or **plexuses**) *Anat.* network of nerves or vessels (*solar plexus*). [Latin *plecto* plex- plait]

pliable /'plaɪəb(ə)l/ adj. 1 bending easily; supple. 2 yielding, compliant. □ **pliability** /-'bɪlɪtɪ/ n. [French: related to PLY[^1]]

pliant /'plaɪənt/ adj. = PLIABLE 1. □ **pliancy** n.

pliers /'plaɪəz/ n.pl. pincers with parallel flat surfaces for holding small objects, bending wire, etc. [from dial. *ply* bend: related to PLIABLE]

plight[^1] /plaɪt/ n. unfortunate condition or state. [Anglo-French *plit* PLAIT]

plight[^2] /plaɪt/ v. *archaic* 1 pledge. 2 (foll. by *to*) engage (oneself) in marriage. —n. pledge. □ **plight one's troth** see TROTH. [Old English]

plimsoll /'plɪmsəl/ n. (also **plimsole**) rubber-soled canvas sports shoe. [from PLIMSOLL LINE]

Plimsoll line /'plɪms(ə)l/ n. (also **Plimsoll mark**) marking on a ship's side showing the limit of legal submersion under various conditions. [*Plimsoll*, name of a politician]

plinth n. 1 lower square slab at the base of a column. 2 base supporting a vase or statue etc. [Greek, = tile]

Pliocene /'plaɪə,siːn/ *Geol.* —adj. of the last epoch of the Tertiary period. —n. this epoch. [Greek *pleiōn* more, *kainos* new]

PLO abbr. Palestine Liberation Organization.

plod —v. (-dd-) 1 walk doggedly or laboriously; trudge. 2 work slowly and steadily. —n. spell of plodding. □ **plodder** n. [probably imitative]

plonk[^1] —v. 1 set down hurriedly or clumsily. 2 (usu. foll. by *down*) set down firmly. —n. heavy thud. [imitative]

plonk[^2] n. *colloq.* cheap or inferior wine. [origin unknown]

plonker n. *coarse slang* 1 fool. 2 penis.

plop —n. sound as of a smooth object dropping into water without a splash. —v. (-pp-) fall or drop with a plop. —adv. with a plop. [imitative]

plosive /'pləʊsɪv/ —adj. pronounced with a sudden release of breath. —n. plosive sound. [from EXPLOSIVE]

plot —n. 1 defined and usu. small piece of land. 2 interrelationship of the main events in a play, novel, film, etc. 3 conspiracy or secret plan. —v. (-tt-) 1 make a plan or map of. 2 (also *absol.*) plan or contrive secretly (a crime etc.). 3 mark on a chart or diagram. 4 make (a curve etc.) by marking out a number of points. 5 provide (a play, novel, film,

etc.) with a plot. □ **plotter** n. [Old English and French *complot*]

plough /plaʊ/ (US **plow**) —n. **1** implement for cutting furrows in the soil and turning it up. **2** implement resembling this (*snowplough*). **3** (**the Plough**) the Great Bear (see **BEAR**) or its seven bright stars. —v. **1** (also *absol.*) turn up (the earth) with a plough. **2** (foll. by *up*, etc.) turn or extract with a plough. **3** furrow or scratch (a surface) as with a plough. **4** produce (a furrow or line) thus. **5** (foll. by *through*) advance laboriously, esp. through work, a book, etc. **6** (foll. by *through*, *into*) move violently like a plough. **7** *colloq.* fail in an examination. □ **plough back 1** plough (grass etc.) into the soil to enrich it. **2** re-invest (profits) into the business producing them. [Old English]

ploughman n. (US **plowman**) person who uses a plough.

ploughman's lunch n. meal of bread and cheese with pickle and salad.

ploughshare n. (US **plowshare**) cutting blade of a plough.

plover /ˈplʌvə(r)/ n. plump-breasted wading bird, e.g. the lapwing. [Latin *pluvia* rain]

plow US var. of PLOUGH.

plowman US var. of PLOUGHMAN.

plowshare US var. of PLOUGHSHARE.

ploy n. cunning manoeuvre to gain advantage. [origin unknown]

PLR *abbr.* Public Lending Right.

pluck —v. **1** pick or pull out or away. **2** strip (a bird) of feathers. **3** pull at, twitch. **4** (foll. by *at*) tug or snatch at. **5** sound (the string of a musical instrument) with a finger or plectrum. **6** plunder. —n. **1** courage, spirit. **2** pluck-ing; twitch. **3** animal's heart, liver, and lungs as food. □ **pluck up** summon up (one's courage etc.). [Old English]

plucky *adj.* (**-ier**, **-iest**) brave, spirited. □ **pluckily** *adv.* **pluckiness** n.

plug —n. **1** piece of solid material fitting tightly into a hole, used to fill a gap or cavity or act as a wedge or stopper. **2 a** device of metal pins in an insulated casing, fitting into holes in a socket for making an electrical connection. **b** *colloq.* electric socket. **3** = SPARK-PLUG. **4** *colloq.* piece of free publicity for an idea, product, etc. **5** cake or stick of tobacco; piece of this for chewing. —v. (**-gg-**) **1** (often foll. by *up*) stop (a hole etc.) with a plug. **2** *slang* shoot or hit (a person etc.). **3** *colloq.* seek to popularize (an idea, product, etc.) by constant recommendation. **4** *colloq.* (foll. by *away* (*at*)) work steadily (at). □ **plug in** connect electrically by inserting a plug into a socket. [Low German or Dutch]

plug-hole n. hole, esp. in a sink or bath, which can be closed by a plug.

plug-in *attrib. adj.* designed to be plugged into a socket.

plum n. **1 a** small sweet oval fleshy fruit with a flattish pointed stone. **b** tree bearing this. **2** reddish-purple colour. **3** raisin used in cooking. **4** *colloq.* something prized (often *attrib.*: *plum job*). □ **have a plum in one's mouth** have an affectedly rich voice. [Latin: related to PRUNE²]

plumage /ˈpluːmɪdʒ/ n. bird's feathers. [French: related to PLUME]

plumb /plʌm/ —n. lead ball, esp. attached to the end of a line for finding the depth of water or testing whether a wall etc. is vertical. —*adv.* **1** exactly (*plumb in the centre*). **2** vertically. **3** US *slang* quite, utterly (*plumb crazy*). —*adj.* vertical. —v. **1 a** provide with plumbing. **b** (often foll. by *in*) fit as part of a plumbing system. **c** work as a plumber. **2** sound or test with a plumb. **3** reach or experience (an extreme feeling) (*plumb the depths of fear*). **4** learn in detail the facts about (a matter). □ **out of plumb** not vertical. [Latin *plumbum* lead]

plumber n. person who fits and repairs the apparatus of a water-supply, heating, etc.

plumb-line n. line with a plumb attached.

plume /pluːm/ —n. **1** feather, esp. a large one used for ornament. **2** ornament of feathers etc. worn on a helmet or hat or in the hair. **3** something resembling this (*plume of smoke*). —v. (**-ming**) **1** decorate or provide with a plume or plumes. **2** *refl.* (foll. by *on*, *upon*) pride (oneself) on esp. something trivial. **3** (of a bird) preen (itself or its feathers). [Latin *pluma*]

plummet /ˈplʌmɪt/ —n. **1** plumb, plumb-line. **2** sounding-line. **3** weight attached to a fishing-line to keep the float upright. —v. (**-t-**) fall or plunge rapidly. [French: related to PLUMB]

plummy *adj.* (**-ier**, **-iest**) **1** abounding or rich in plums. **2** *colloq.* (of a voice) sounding affectedly rich in tone. **3** *colloq.* good, desirable.

plump¹ —*adj.* full or rounded in shape; fleshy. —v. (often foll. by *up*, *out*) make or become plump (*p'umped up the cushion*). □ **plumpness** n. [Low German or Dutch *plomp* blunt]

plump² —v. **1** (foll. by *for*) decide on, choose. **2** (often foll. by *down*) drop or fall abruptly. —n. abrupt or heavy fall.

—adv. colloq. with a plump. [Low German or Dutch *plompen,* imitative]

plum pudding *n.* = CHRISTMAS PUDDING.

plumy /ˈpluːmɪ/ *adj.* (-ier, -iest) **1** plumelike, feathery. **2** adorned with plumes.

plunder /ˈplʌndə(r)/ *—v.* **1** rob or steal, esp. in wartime; loot. **2** exploit (another person's or common property) for one's own profit. *—n.* **1** activity of plundering. **2** property so acquired. [German *plündern*]

plunge *—v.* (**-ging**) **1** (usu. foll. by *in, into*) **a** thrust forcefully or abruptly. **b** dive. **c** (cause to) enter a condition suddenly or abruptly (*they plunged into marriage; the room was plunged into darkness*). **2** immerse completely. **3 a** move suddenly and dramatically downward. **b** (foll. by *down, into,* etc.) move with a rush (*plunged down the stairs*). **4** *colloq.* run up gambling debts. *—n.* plunging action or movement; dive. □ **take the plunge** *colloq.* take a decisive step. [Romanic: related to PLUMB]

plunger *n.* **1** part of a mechanism that works with a plunging or thrusting movement. **2** rubber cup on a handle for clearing blocked pipes by a plunging and sucking action.

pluperfect /pluːˈpɜːfɪkt/ *Gram. —adj.* (of a tense) denoting an action completed prior to some past point of time (e.g. *he had gone by then*). *—n.* pluperfect tense. [Latin *plus quam perfectum* more than perfect]

plural /ˈplʊər(ə)l/ *—adj.* **1** more than one in number. **2** *Gram.* (of a word or form) denoting more than one. *—n. Gram.* **1** plural word or form. **2** plural number. [Latin: related to PLUS]

pluralism *n.* **1** form of society embracing many minority groups and cultural traditions. **2** the holding of more than one office at a time, esp. in the Church. □ **pluralist** *n.* **pluralistic** /-ˈlɪstɪk/ *adj.*

plurality /plʊəˈrælɪtɪ/ *n.* (*pl.* **-ies**) **1** state of being plural. **2** = PLURALISM **2**. **3** large number. **4** *US* majority that is not absolute.

pluralize /ˈplʊərəˌlaɪz/ *v.* (also **-ise**) (**-zing** or **-sing**) make plural, express in the plural.

plus *—prep.* **1** with the addition of (symbol +). **2** (of temperature) above zero (*plus 2°*). **3** *colloq.* with; having gained; newly possessing. *—adj.* **1** (after a number) at least (*fifteen plus*). **2** (after a grade etc.) rather better than (*beta plus*). **3** *Math.* positive. **4** having a positive electrical charge. **5** (*attrib.*) additional, extra. *—n.* **1** the symbol +. **2**

additional or positive quantity. **3** advantage. *—conj. colloq.* also; and furthermore. [Latin, = more]

■ **Usage** The use of *plus* as a conjunction, as in *they arrived late, plus they wanted a meal,* is considered incorrect by some people.

plus-fours *n.pl.* men's long wide knickerbockers. [the length was increased by 4 inches to create an overhang]

plush *—n.* cloth of silk or cotton etc. with a long soft nap. *—adj.* **1** made of plush. **2** *colloq.* = PLUSHY. □ **plushly** *adv.* **plushness** *n.* [Latin: related to PILE³]

plushy *adj.* (**-ier, -iest**) *colloq.* stylish, luxurious. □ **plushiness** *n.*

Pluto /ˈpluːtəʊ/ *n.* outermost known planet of the solar system. [Greek *Ploutōn,* god of the underworld]

plutocracy /pluːˈtɒkrəsɪ/ *n.* (*pl.* **-ies**) **1 a** government by the wealthy. **b** State so governed. **2** wealthy élite. □ **plutocratic** /-təˈkrætɪk/ *adj.* [Greek *ploutos* wealth]

plutocrat /ˈpluːtəˌkræt/ *n.* **1** member of a plutocracy. **2** wealthy person.

plutonic /pluːˈtɒnɪk/ *adj.* formed as igneous rock by solidification below the surface of the earth. [Latin *Pluto,* god of the underworld]

plutonium /pluːˈtəʊnɪəm/ *n.* radioactive metallic element. [*Pluto,* name of a planet]

pluvial /ˈpluːvɪəl/ *adj.* **1** of rain; rainy. **2** *Geol.* caused by rain. [Latin *pluvia* rain]

ply¹ /plaɪ/ *n.* (*pl.* **-ies**) **1** thickness or layer of cloth or wood etc. **2** strand of yarn or rope etc. [French *pli:* related to PLY²]

ply² /plaɪ/ *v.* (**-ies, -ied**) **1** use or wield (a tool, weapon, etc.). **2** work steadily at (*ply one's trade*). **3** (foll. by *with*) **a** supply continuously (with food, drink, etc.). **b** approach repeatedly (with questions, etc.). **4 a** (often foll. by *between*) (of a vehicle etc.) travel regularly to and fro. **b** work (a route) thus. **5** (of a taxi-driver etc.) attend regularly for custom (*ply for hire*). [from APPLY]

Plymouth Brethren /ˈplɪməθ/ *n.pl.* Calvinistic religious body with no formal creed and no official order of ministers. [*Plymouth* in Devon]

plywood *n.* strong thin board made by gluing layers of wood with the direction of the grain alternating.

PM *abbr.* **1** prime minister. **2** post-mortem.

Pm *symb.* promethium.

p.m. *abbr.* after noon. [Latin *post meridiem*]

PMS *abbr.* premenstrual syndrome.

PMT *abbr.* premenstrual tension.

pneumatic /njuːˈmætɪk/ adj. 1 filled with air or wind (pneumatic tyre). 2 operated by compressed air (pneumatic drill). [Greek pneuma wind]

pneumoconiosis /ˌnjuːməʊˌkəʊniˈəʊsis/ n. lung disease caused by the inhalation of dust or small particles. [Greek pneumōn lung, konis dust]

pneumonia /njuːˈməʊnɪə/ n. inflammation of one or both lungs. [Greek pneumōn lung]

PO abbr. 1 Post Office. 2 postal order. 3 Petty Officer. 4 Pilot Officer.

Po symb. polonium.

po /pəʊ/ n. (pl. -s) colloq. chamber-pot. [from POT?]

poach¹ v. 1 cook (an egg) without its shell in or over boiling water. 2 cook (fish etc.) by simmering in a small amount of liquid. □ **poacher** n. [French pocher: related to POKE²]

poach² v. 1 (also absol.) catch (game or fish) illegally. 2 (often foll. by on) trespass or encroach on (another's property, territory, etc.). 3 appropriate (another's ideas, staff, etc.). □ **poacher** n. [earlier poche: related to POACH¹]

pock n. (also **pock-mark**) small pustule on the skin, esp. caused by chickenpox or smallpox. □ **pock-marked** adj. [Old English]

pocket /ˈpɒkɪt/ —n. 1 small bag sewn into or on clothing, for carrying small articles. 2 pouchlike compartment in a suitcase, car door, etc. 3 one's financial resources (beyond my pocket). 4 isolated group or area (pockets of resistance). 5 cavity in the earth containing ore, esp. gold. 6 pouch at the corner or on the side of a billiard- or snooker-table into which balls are driven. 7 = AIR POCKET. 8 (attrib.) a small enough or intended for carrying in a pocket. b smaller than the usual size. —v. (-t-) 1 put into one's pocket. 2 appropriate, esp. dishonestly. 3 confine as in a pocket. 4 submit to (an injury or affront). 5 conceal or suppress (one's feelings). 6 Billiards etc. drive (a ball) into a pocket. □ **in pocket** having gained in a transaction. **in a person's pocket** 1 under a person's control. 2 close to or intimate with a person. **out of pocket** having lost in a transaction. □ pocket having lost in a transaction. related to POKE²]

pocketbook n. 1 notebook. 2 folding case for papers or money carried in a pocket.

pocketful n. (pl. -s) as much as a pocket will hold.

pocket knife n. = PENKNIFE.

pocket money n. money for minor expenses, esp. given to children.

pod —n. long seed-vessel, esp. of a pea or bean. —v. (-dd-) 1 bear or form pods. 2 remove (peas etc.) from pods. [origin unknown]

podgy /ˈpɒdʒɪ/ adj. (-ier, -iest) 1 short and fat. 2 plump, fleshy. □ **podginess** n. [podge short fat person]

podium /ˈpəʊdɪəm/ n. (pl. -s or **podia**) rostrum. [Greek podion diminutive of pous pod- foot]

poem /ˈpəʊɪm/ n. 1 metrical composition, usu. concerned with feeling or imaginative description. 2 elevated composition in verse or prose. 3 something with poetic qualities (a poem in stone). [Greek poiō make]

poesy /ˈpəʊɪzɪ/ n. archaic poetry. [French, ultimately as POEM]

poet /ˈpəʊɪt/ n. (fem. **poetess**) 1 writer of poems. 2 highly imaginative or expressive person. [Greek poiētēs: related to POEM]

poetaster /ˌpəʊɪˈtæstə(r)/ n. inferior poet. [from POET, Latin -aster derog.]

poetic /pəʊˈetɪk/ adj. (also **poetical**) of or like poetry or poets. □ **poetically** adv.

poetic justice n. very appropriate punishment or reward.

poetic licence n. writer's or artist's transgression of established rules for effect.

Poet Laureate n. (pl. Poets Laureate) poet appointed to write poems for State occasions.

poetry /ˈpəʊɪtrɪ/ n. 1 art or work of a poet. 2 poems collectively. 3 poetic or tenderly pleasing quality. [medieval Latin: related to POEM]

po-faced adj. 1 solemn-faced, humourless. 2 smug. [perhaps from PO, influenced by poker-faced]

pogo /ˈpəʊgəʊ/ n. (pl. -s) (also **pogo stick**) stiltlike toy with a spring, used for jumping about on. [origin uncertain]

pogrom /ˈpɒgrəm/ n. organized massacre (orig. of Jews in Russia). [Russian]

poignant /ˈpɔɪnjənt/ adj. 1 painfully sharp to the emotions or senses; deeply moving. 2 arousing sympathy. 3 sharp or pungent in taste or smell. 4 pleasantly piquant. □ **poignance** n. **poignancy** n. **poignantly** adv. [Latin: related to POINT]

poinsettia /pɔɪnˈsetɪə/ n. plant with large scarlet bracts surrounding small yellow flowers. [Poinsett, name of a diplomat]

point —n. 1 sharp or tapered end of a tool, weapon, pencil, etc. 2 tip or extreme end. 3 that which in geometry has position but not magnitude. 4 particular place or position. 5 precise or

critical moment (*when it came to the point, he refused*). **6** very small mark on a surface. **7** dot or other punctuation mark. **8** = DECIMAL POINT. **9** stage or degree in progress or increase (*abrupt to the point of rudeness*). **10** temperature at which a change of state occurs (*freezing point*). **11** single item or particular (*explained it point by point*). **12** unit of scoring in games or of measuring value etc. **13** significant or essential thing; what is intended or under discussion (*the point of my question; get to the point*). **14** sense, purpose; advantage, value (*saw no point in staying*). **15** characteristic (*tact is not his strong point*). **16 a** each of 32 directions marked at equal distances round a compass. **b** corresponding direction towards the horizon. **17** (usu. in *pl.*) pair of movable tapering rails that allow a train to pass from one line to another. **18** = POWER POINT. **19** (usu. in *pl.*) electrical contact in the distributor of a vehicle. **20** *Cricket* **a** fielder on the off side near the batsman. **b** this position. **21** tip of the toe in ballet. **22** promontory. **23** (usu. in *pl.*) extremities of a dog, horse, etc. —*v.* **1** (usu. foll. by *to*, *at*) **a** direct or aim (a finger, weapon, etc.). **b** direct attention. **2** (foll. by *at*, *towards*) aim or be directed to. **3** (foll. by *to*) indicate; be evidence of (*it all points to murder*). **4** give force to (words or actions). **5** fill the joints of (brickwork) with smoothed mortar or cement. **6** (also *absol.*) (of a dog) indicate the presence of (game) by acting as pointer. □ **at** (or **on**) **the point of** on the verge of; ready to do. **beside the point** irrelevant. **in point** relevant (*the case in point*). **in point of fact** see FACT. **make a point of** insist on (doing etc.); treat or regard as essential; call particular attention to (an action). **point out** indicate; draw attention to. **point up** emphasize. **to the point** relevant; relevantly. **up to a point** to some extent but not completely. [Latin *pungo punct-* prick]

point-blank —*adj.* **1 a** (of a shot) aimed or fired at very close range. **b** (of a range) very close. **2** (of a remark etc.) blunt, direct. —*adv.* **1** at very close range. **2** directly, bluntly.

point-duty *n.* traffic control by a police officer, esp. at a road junction.

pointed *adj.* **1** sharpened or tapering to a point. **2** (of a remark etc.) having point; cutting. **3** emphasized. □ **pointedly** *adv.*

pointer *n.* **1** thing that points, e.g. the index hand of a gauge. **2** rod for pointing to features on a chart etc. **3** *colloq.* hint. **4** dog of a breed that on scenting game stands rigid looking towards it. **5** (in *pl.*)

two stars in the Great Bear in line with the pole star.

pointillism /ˈpwæntɪˌlɪz(ə)m/ *n.* technique of impressionist painting using tiny dots of pure colour which become blended in the viewer's eye. □ **pointillist** *n. & adj.* [French *pointiller* mark with dots]

pointing *n.* **1** cement filling the joints of brickwork. **2** facing produced by this.

pointless *adj.* lacking purpose or meaning; ineffective, fruitless. □ **pointlessly** *adv.* **pointlessness** *n.*

point of honour *n.* thing of great importance to one's reputation or conscience.

point of no return *n.* point in a journey or enterprise at which it becomes essential or more practical to continue to the end.

point of order *n.* query in a debate etc. as to whether correct procedure is being followed.

point-of-sale *adj.* (usu. *attrib.*) of the place at which goods are retailed.

point of view *n.* **1** position from which a thing is viewed. **2** way of considering a matter.

point-to-point *n.* steeplechase for hunting horses.

poise /pɔɪz/ —*n.* **1** composure, self-possession. **2** equilibrium. **3** carriage (of the head etc.). —*v.* (-sing) **1** balance; hold suspended or supported. **2** be balanced or suspended. [Latin *pendo pens-* weigh]

poised *adj.* **1 a** composed, self-assured. **b** carrying oneself gracefully or with dignity. **2** (often foll. by *for*, or *to* + infin.) ready for action.

poison /ˈpɔɪz(ə)n/ —*n.* **1** substance that when introduced into or absorbed by a living organism causes death or injury, esp. one that kills by rapid action even in a small quantity. **2** *colloq.* harmful influence. —*v.* **1** administer poison to. **2** kill, injure, or infect with poison. **3** treat (a weapon) with poison. **4** corrupt or pervert (a person or mind). **5** spoil or destroy (a person's pleasure etc.). □ **poisoner** *n.* **poisonous** *adj.* [Latin: related to POTION]

poison ivy *n.* N. American climbing plant secreting an irritant oil from its leaves.

poison-pen letter *n.* malicious anonymous letter.

poke[1] —*v.* (-king) **1 a** thrust or push with the hand, a stick, etc. **b** (foll. by *out*, *up*, etc.) be thrust forward, protrude. **2** (foll. by *at* etc.) make thrusts. **3** thrust the end of a finger etc. against. **4** (foll. by *in*) produce (a hole etc. in a thing) by poking. **5** stir (a fire) with a poker. **6 a** (often foll. by *about*, *around*) potter. **b**

(foll. by *about*, *into*) pry; search. **7** *coarse slang* have sexual intercourse with. □~, **1** act of poking. **2** thrust, nudge. □ **poke fun at** ridicule. **poke one's nose into** *colloq* pry or intrude into. [German or Dutch]

poke² *n. dial.* bag, sack. □ **buy a pig in a poke** see PIG. [French *dial.*]

poker¹ *n.* metal rod for stirring a fire.

poker² *n.* card-game in which the bluff is used as players bet on the value of their hands. [origin unknown]

poker-face *n.* impassive countenance assumed by a poker-player. □ **poker-faced** *adj.*

poky /ˈpəʊkɪ/ *adj.* (**-ier**, **-iest**) (of a room etc.) small and cramped. □ **pokiness** *n.* [from POKE¹]

polar /ˈpəʊlə(r)/ **1** *adj.* of or near a pole of the earth or of the celestial sphere. **2** having magnetic or electric polarity. **3** directly opposite in character. [Latin: related to POLE²]

polar bear *n.* large white bear living in the Arctic regions.

polar circle *n.* each of the circles parallel to the equator at 23° 27′ from either pole.

polarity /pəˈlærɪtɪ/ *n.* (*pl.* **-ies**) **1** tendency of a magnet etc. to point with its extremities to the magnetic poles of the earth, or of a body to lie with its axis in a particular direction. **2** state of having two poles with contrary qualities. **3** state of having two opposite tendencies, opinions, etc. **4** electrical condition of a body (positive or negative). **5** attraction towards an object.

polarize /ˈpəʊləraɪz/ *v.* (also **-ise**) **1** restrict the vibrations of (light-waves etc.) to one direction. **2** give magnetic or electric polarity to. **3** divide into two opposing groups. □ **polarization** /-ˈzeɪʃ(ə)n/ *n.*

Polaroid /ˈpəʊləraɪd/ *n. propr.* **1** material in thin sheets polarizing light passing through it. **2** camera with internal processing that produces a print rapidly after each exposure. **3** (in *pl.*) sunglasses with Polaroid lenses.

polder /ˈpəʊldə(r)/ *n.* piece of land reclaimed from the sea or a river, esp. in the Netherlands. [Dutch]

Pole *n.* **1** native or national of Poland. **2** person of Polish descent. [German from Polish]

pole¹ *n.* **1** long slender rounded piece of wood, metal, etc., esp. with the end placed in the ground as a support etc. **2** = PERCH¹ 3. □ **up the pole** *slang* **1** crazy. **2** in difficulty. [Latin *palus* stake]

pole² *n.* **1** (in full **north pole**, **south pole**) **a** each of the two points in the celestial sphere about which the stars

appear to revolve. **b** each of the ends of the axis of rotation of the earth (*North Pole*, *South Pole*). **2** each of the two opposite points on the surface of a magnet at which magnetic forces are strongest. **3** each of two terminals (positive and negative) of an electric cell or battery etc. **4** each of two opposed principles. □ **be poles apart** differ greatly. [Greek, = axis]

■ **Usage** The spelling is *North Pole* and *South Pole* when used as geographical designations.

poleaxe /ˈpəʊlæks/ (*US* **-ax**) *n.* **1** *hist.* = BATTLEAXE 1. **2** butcher's axe. ―*v.* (**-xing**) **1** hit or kill with a poleaxe. **2** (esp. as **poleaxed** *adj.*) *colloq.* dumbfound; overwhelm. [Low German or Dutch; related to POLL, AXE]

polecat /ˈpəʊlkæt/ *n.* **1** small brownish-black mammal of the weasel family. **2** *US* skunk. [origin unknown]

pole-jump var. of POLE-VAULT.

polemic /pəˈlemɪk/ ―*n.* **1** forceful verbal or written controversy or argument. **2** (in *pl.*) art or practice of controversial discussion. ―*adj.* (also **polemical**) involving dispute; controversial. □ **polemically** *adv.* [Greek *polemos* war]

polemicist /pəˈlemɪsɪst/ *n.* [Greek *polemos* war]

pole star *n.* **1** star in the Little Bear, near the North Pole in the sky. **2** thing serving as a guide.

pole-vault (also **pole-jump**) ―*n.* vault, or sport of vaulting, over a high bar with the aid of a pole held in the hands. ―*v.* perform this. □ **pole-vaulter** *n.*

police /pəˈliːs/ ―*n.* (as *pl.*) **1** (usu. prec. by *the*) the civil force responsible for maintaining public order. **2** its members. **3** (as *pl.*) its members. ―*v.* (**-cing**) **1** keep (a place or people) in order by means of police or a similar body. **2** provide with police. **3** keep in order, administer, control. [Latin related to POLICY¹]

police constable see CONSTABLE.

police dog *n.* dog, esp. an Alsatian, used in police work.

police force *n.* body of police of a country, district, or town.

policeman *n.* member of a police force.

police officer *n.* member of a police force.

police State *n.* totalitarian State controlled by political police.

police station *n.* office of a local police force.

policy¹ /ˈpɒlɪsɪ/ *n.* (*pl.* **-ies**) **1** course of action adopted by a government, business, individual, etc. **2** prudent conduct; sagacity. [Latin *politia* POLITY]

■ **Usage** See note at *polity*.

policy² /ˈpɒlɪsɪ/ *n.* (*pl.* -**ies**) **1** contract of insurance. **2** document containing this. [French *police*, ultimately from Greek *apodeixis* proof]

policyholder *n.* person or body holding an insurance policy.

polio /ˈpəʊlɪəʊ/ *n.* = POLIOMYELITIS. [abbreviation]

poliomyelitis /ˌpəʊlɪəʊˌmaɪəˈlaɪtɪs/ *n.* infectious viral disease of the grey matter of the central nervous system with temporary or permanent paralysis. [Greek *polios* grey; *muelos* marrow]

Polish /ˈpəʊlɪʃ/ —*adj.* **1** of Poland. **2** of the Poles or their language. —*n.* language of Poland.

polish /ˈpɒlɪʃ/ —*v.* (often foll. by *up*) **1** make or become smooth or glossy by rubbing. **2** (esp. as **polished** *adj.*) refine or improve; add the finishing touches to. —*n.* **1** substance used for polishing. **2** smoothness or glossiness produced by friction. **3** refinement, elegance. □ **polish off** finish (esp. food) quickly. [Latin *polio*]

polite /pəˈlaɪt/ *adj.* (**politer**, **politest**) **1** having good manners; courteous. **2** cultivated, refined. □ **politely** *adv.* **politeness** *n.* [Latin *politus*: related to POLISH]

politic /ˈpɒlɪtɪk/ —*adj.* **1** (of an action) judicious, expedient. **2** (of a person) prudent, sagacious. **3** political (now only in *body politic*). —*v.* (-**ck**-) engage in politics. [Greek: related to POLITY]

political /pəˈlɪtɪk(ə)l/ *adj.* **1 a** of or concerning the State or its government. **b** of or belonging to public affairs generally. **c** relating to or engaged in politics. **2** taking or belonging to a side in politics. **3** concerned with seeking power, status, etc. (*political decision*). □ **politically** *adv.* [Latin: related to POLITIC]

political asylum *n.* State protection given to a political refugee from another country.

political economy *n.* the study of the economic aspects of government.

political geography *n.* geography dealing with boundaries and the possessions of States.

political prisoner *n.* person imprisoned for political reasons.

political science *n.* the study of political activity and systems of government.

politician /ˌpɒlɪˈtɪʃ(ə)n/ *n.* **1** person involved in politics, esp. professionally as an MP. **2** *US derog.* person who manoeuvres; schemer; time-server.

politicize /pəˈlɪtɪˌsaɪz/ *v.* (also -**ise**) (-**zing** or -**sing**) **1 a** give a political character to. **b** make politically aware. **2** engage in or talk politics. □ **politicization** /-ˈzeɪʃ(ə)n/ *n.*

politico /pəˈlɪtɪˌkəʊ/ *n.* (*pl.* -**s**) *colloq.* politician or political enthusiast. [Spanish]

politics /ˈpɒlɪtɪks/ *n.pl.* **1** (treated as *sing.* or *pl.*) **a** art and science of government. **b** public life and affairs. **2** (usu. treated as *pl.*) political principles or practice (*what are his politics?*). **3** activities concerned with seeking power, status, etc.

polity /ˈpɒlɪtɪ/ *n.* (*pl.* -**ies**) **1** form or process of civil government. **2** organized society; State. [Greek *politēs* citizen, from *polis* city]

■ **Usage** This word is sometimes confused with *policy*.

polka /ˈpɒlkə/ —*n.* **1** lively dance of Bohemian origin. **2** music for this. —*v.* (-**kas**, -**kaed** /-kəd/ or -**ka'd**, -**kaing** /-kəɪŋ/) dance the polka. [Czech *pilka*]

polka dot *n.* round dot as one of many forming a regular pattern on a textile fabric etc.

poll /pəʊl/ —*n.* **1 a** (often in *pl.*) voting or the counting of votes at an election (*go to the polls*). **b** result of voting or number of votes recorded. **2** = OPINION POLL. **3** human head. —*v.* **1 a** take the vote or votes of. **b** receive (so many votes). **c** give (a vote). **2** record the opinion of (a person or group) in an opinion poll. **3** cut off the top of (a tree or plant), esp. make a pollard of. **4** (esp. as **polled** *adj.*) cut the horns of (cattle). [perhaps from Low German or Dutch]

pollack /ˈpɒlək/ *n.* (also **pollock**) (*pl.* same or -**s**) edible marine fish related to the cod. [origin unknown]

pollard /ˈpɒləd/ —*n.* **1** animal that has lost or cast its horns; ox, sheep, or goat of a hornless breed. **2** tree whose branches have been cut back to encourage the dense growth of young branches. —*v.* make (a tree) a pollard. [from POLL]

pollen /ˈpɒlən/ *n.* fine dustlike grains discharged from the male part of a flower, each containing the fertilizing element. [Latin]

pollen count *n.* index of the amount of pollen in the air, published as a warning to hay fever sufferers.

pollinate /ˈpɒlɪˌneɪt/ *v.* (-**ting**) (also *absol.*) convey pollen to or sprinkle (a stigma) with pollen. □ **pollination** /-ˈneɪʃ(ə)n/ *n.* **pollinator** *n.*

polling *n.* registering or casting of votes.

polling-booth *n.* compartment in which a voter stands to mark the ballot paper.

polling-day n. election day.

polling-station n. building, often a school, used for voting at an election.

pollock var. of POLLACK.

pollster n. person who organizes an opinion poll.

poll tax n. 1 *informal* = COMMUNITY CHARGE. 2 *hist.* tax levied on every adult.

pollute /pə'luːt/ v. (-ting) 1 contaminate (the environment, esp. water). 2 make foul or impure. □ **pollutant** adj. & n. **polluter** n. **pollution** n. [Latin *polluo -lut-*]

polo /'pəʊləʊ/ n. game like hockey played on horseback with a long-handled mallet. [Balti = ball]

polonaise /ˌpɒlə'neɪz/ n. 1 slow dance of Polish origin. 2 music for this. [French: related to POLE]

polo-neck n. 1 high round turned-over collar. 2 sweater with this.

polonium /pə'ləʊnɪəm/ n. radioactive metallic element, occurring naturally in uranium ores. [medieval Latin *Polonia* Poland]

poltergeist /'pɒltəˌɡaɪst/ n. noisy mischievous ghost, esp. one causing physical damage. [German]

poltroon /pɒl'truːn/ n. spiritless coward. □ **poltroonery** n. [Italian *poltro* sluggard]

poly /'pɒlɪ/ n. (pl. -s) colloq. polytechnic. [abbreviation]

poly- comb. form 1 many (*polygamy*). 2 polymerized (*polyunsaturated polyester*). [Greek *polus* many]

polyandry /'pɒlɪˌændrɪ/ n. polygamy in which a woman has more than one husband. □ **polyandrous** adj. [Greek *anēr andr-* male]

polyanthus /ˌpɒlɪ'ænθəs/ n. (pl. -thuses) flowering plant cultivated from hybridized primulas. [Greek *anthos* flower]

polychromatic /ˌpɒlɪkrəʊ'mætɪk/ adj. 1 many-coloured. 2 (of radiation) containing more than one wavelength.

polychromatism /ˌpɒlɪ'krəʊmə,tɪz(ə)m/ n.

polychrome /'pɒlɪ,krəʊm/ —adj. in many colours. —n. polychrome work of art. [Greek: related to POLY-, CHROME]

polyester /ˌpɒlɪ'estə(r)/ n. synthetic fibre or resin.

polyethene /'pɒlɪ,θiːn/ n. = POLYTHENE.

polyethylene /ˌpɒlɪ'eθɪˌliːn/ n. = POLYTHENE.

polygamy /pə'lɪɡəmɪ/ n. practice of having more than one wife or (less usu.) husband at once. □ **polygamist** n. **polygamous** adj. [Greek *gamos* marriage]

polyglot /'pɒlɪˌɡlɒt/ —adj. knowing, using, or written in several languages.

—n. polyglot person. [Greek *glōtta* tongue]

polygon /'pɒlɪɡən/ n. figure with many (usu. five or more) sides and angles. □ **polygonal** /pə'lɪɡən(ə)l/ adj. [Greek *gōnos* angled]

polygraph /'pɒlɪˌɡrɑːf/ n. machine for reading physiological characteristics (e.g. pulse-rate); lie-detector.

polygyny /pə'lɪdʒɪnɪ/ n. polygamy in which a man has more than one wife. □ **polygynous** /pə'lɪdʒɪnəs/ adj. [Greek *gunē* woman]

polyhedron /ˌpɒlɪ'hiːdrən/ n. (pl. -dra) solid figure with many (usu. more than six) faces. □ **polyhedral** adj. [Greek *hedra* base]

polymath /'pɒlɪˌmæθ/ n. person of great or varied learning. [Greek *manthanō* learn]

polymer /'pɒlɪmə(r)/ n. compound of one or more large molecules formed from repeated units of smaller molecules. □ **polymeric** /-'merɪk/ adj. **polymerize** v. (also -ise) (-zing or -sing). **polymerization** n. [Greek *polumeros* having many parts]

polymorphous /ˌpɒlɪ'mɔːfəs/ adj. (also **polymorphic**) passing through various forms in successive stages of development.

polynomial /ˌpɒlɪ'nəʊmɪəl/ —n. expression of more than two algebraic terms. —adj. of, being a polynomial. [from POLY-, BINOMIAL]

polyp /'pɒlɪp/ n. 1 simple organism with a tube-shaped body. 2 small usu. benign growth on a mucous membrane. [Greek *pous* foot]

polyphony /pə'lɪfənɪ/ n. (pl. -ies) *Mus.* contrapuntal music. □ **polyphonic** /ˌpɒlɪ'fɒnɪk/ adj. [Greek *phōnē* sound]

polypropene /ˌpɒlɪ'prəʊpiːn/ n. = POLYPROPYLENE.

polypropylene /ˌpɒlɪ'prəʊpɪˌliːn/ n. any polymer of propylene, including thermoplastic materials used for films, fibres, or moulding materials.

polysaccharide /ˌpɒlɪ'sækəˌraɪd/ n. any of a group of complex carbohydrates, e.g. starch. [see SACCHARIN]

polystyrene /ˌpɒlɪ'staɪˌriːn/ n. a polymer of styrene, a kind of hard plastic, often foamed for packaging. [styrene from Greek *sturax* a resin]

polysyllabic /ˌpɒlɪsɪ'læbɪk/ adj. 1 having many syllables. 2 using words of many syllables. [medieval Latin from Greek]

polysyllable /'pɒlɪˌsɪləb(ə)l/ n. polysyllabic word.

polytechnic /ˌpɒlɪ'teknɪk/ —n. college offering courses in many (esp. vocational) subjects up to degree level. —adj.

polytheism giving instruction in various vocational or technical subjects. [Greek *teknē* art]

polytheism /'pɒlɪθi:ɪz(ə)m/ *n.* belief in or worship of more than one god. □ **polytheist** *n.* **polytheistic** /-'ɪstɪk/ *adj.* [Greek *theos* god]

polythene /'pɒlɪθi:n/ *n.* a tough light plastic. [from POLYETHYLENE]

polyunsaturated /ˌpɒlɪʌn'sætʃəreɪtɪd/ *adj.* (of a fat or oil) having a chemical structure capable of further reaction and not contributing to the accumulation of cholesterol in the blood.

polyurethane /ˌpɒlɪ'jʊərəˌθeɪn/ *n.* synthetic resin or plastic used esp. in paints or foam. [related to UREA, ETHANE]

polyvinyl chloride /ˌpɒlɪ'vaɪnɪl/ *n.* a vinyl plastic used for electrical insulation or as a fabric etc.; PVC.

Pom *n. Austral. & NZ slang offens.* = POMMY. [abbreviation]

pomace /'pʌmɪs/ *n.* crushed apples in cider-making. [Latin *pomum* apple]

pomade /pə'mɑ:d/ *n.* scented ointment for the hair and head. [Italian: related to POMACE]

pomander /pə'mændə(r)/ *n.* 1 ball of mixed aromatic substances. 2 container for this. [Anglo-French from medieval Latin]

pomegranate /'pɒmɪˌgrænɪt/ *n.* 1 tropical fruit with a tough rind, reddish pulp, and many seeds. 2 tree bearing this. [French *pome grenate* from Romanic; = many-seeded apple]

pomelo /'pɒməˌləʊ/ *n.* (*pl.* -s) = GRAPEFRUIT. 2 *US* = SHADDOCK. [origin unknown]

pommel /'pʌm(ə)l/ *n.* 1 knob, esp. at the end of a sword-hilt. 2 upward projecting front of a saddle. —*v.* (-ll-; *US* -l-) = PUMMEL. [Latin *pomum* apple]

Pommy /'pɒmɪ/ *n.* (also **pommie**) (*pl.* -ies) *Austral. & NZ slang offens.* British person, esp. a recent immigrant. [origin uncertain]

pomp *n.* 1 splendid display; splendour. 2 specious glory. [Latin from Greek *pompē*]

pom-pom /'pɒmpɒm/ *n.* automatic quick-firing gun. [imitative]

pompon /'pɒmpɒn/ *n.* (also **pompom**) 1 ornamental tuft or bobble on a hat, shoes, etc. 2 (often *attrib.*) dahlia etc. with small tightly-clustered petals. [French]

pompous /'pɒmpəs/ *n.* self-important, affectedly grand or solemn. □ **pomposity** /pɒm'pɒsɪtɪ/ *n.* (*pl.* -ies). **pompously** *adv.* **pompousness** *n.* [Latin: related to POMP]

ponce *slang* —*n.* 1 man who lives off a prostitute's earnings; pimp. 2 *offens.*

homosexual or effeminate man. —*v.* (-cing) act as a ponce. □ **ponce about** move about effeminately or ineffectually. [origin unknown]

poncho /'pɒntʃəʊ/ *n.* (*pl.* -s) cloak of a usu. blanket-like piece of cloth with a slit in the middle for the head. [South American Spanish]

pond *n.* small body of still water. [var. of POUND³]

ponder *v.* 1 think over; consider. 2 muse, be deep in thought. [Latin *pondero* weigh]

ponderable *adj. literary* having appreciable weight or significance. [Latin: related to PONDER]

ponderous /'pɒndərəs/ *adj.* 1 slow and awkward, esp. because of great weight. 2 (of style etc.) laborious; dull. □ **ponderously** *adv.* **ponderousness** *n.* [Latin *pondus -der-* weight]

pondweed *n.* aquatic plant growing in still water.

pong *v. colloq.* stink. □ **pongy** *adj.* (-ier, -iest). [origin unknown]

poniard /'pɒnjəd/ *n.* dagger. [French *poignard* from Latin *pugnus* fist]

pontiff /'pɒntɪf/ *n.* Pope. [Latin *pontifex -fic-* priest]

pontifical /pɒn'tɪfɪk(ə)l/ *adj.* 1 papal. 2 pompously dogmatic. □ **pontifically** *adv.*

pontificate —*v.* /pɒn'tɪfɪˌkeɪt/ (-ting) 1 be pompously dogmatic. 2 play the pontiff. —*n.* /pɒn'tɪfɪkət/ 1 office of a bishop or pope. 2 period of this.

pontoon¹ /pɒn'tu:n/ *n.* card-game in which players try to acquire cards with a face value totalling 21. [probably a corruption of VINGT-ET-UN]

pontoon² /pɒn'tu:n/ *n.* 1 flat-bottomed boat. 2 each of several boats etc. used to support a temporary bridge. [Latin *ponto ponton-* punt]

pony /'pəʊnɪ/ *n.* (*pl.* -ies) horse of any small breed. [perhaps from French *poulenet* foal]

pony-tail *n.* hair drawn back, tied, and hanging down behind the head.

pony-trekking *n.* travelling across country on ponies for pleasure.

poodle /'pu:d(ə)l/ *n.* 1 dog of a breed with a curly coat that is usually clipped. 2 servile follower. [German *Pudel*]

poof /pʊf/ *n.* (also **poofter**) *slang offens.* effeminate or homosexual man. [origin unknown]

pooh /pu:/ *int.* expressing impatience, contempt, or disgust at a bad smell. [imitative]

pooh-pooh /pu:'pu:/ *v.* express contempt for, ridicule. [reduplication of POOH]

pool¹ n. 1 small body of still water. 2 small shallow swimming-pool. 4 deep place in a river. [Old English]

pool² –n. 1 a common supply of persons, vehicles, commodities, etc. for sharing by a group of people. b group of persons sharing duties etc. 2 common fund, e.g. of profits of separate firms or of players' stakes in gambling. 3 arrangement between competing parties to fix prices and share business. 4 US a game on a billiard-table with 16 balls. b game on a billiard-table in which each player has a ball of a different colour with which he or she tries to pocket the others in fixed order, the winner taking all of the stakes.—v.1 put into a common fund. 2 share in common. [French *poule*]

pools n.pl. (prec. by *the*) = FOOTBALL POOL.

poop n. stern of a ship; the deck which is furthest aft and highest. [Latin *puppis*]

poor adj. 1 without enough money to live comfortably. 2 (foll. by *in*) deficient in (a possession or quality). 3 a scanty, inadequate. b less good than is usual or expected (*poor visibility; is a poor driver*). c paltry; interior (*came a poor third*). 4 deserving pity or sympathy; unfortunate (*you poor thing!*). 5 spiritless, despicable. □ **poor man's** inferior or cheaper substitute for. [French *pauper*]

poorhouse n. *hist.* = WORKHOUSE.

poor law n. *hist.* law concerning public support of the poor.

poorly –adv. in a poor manner, badly. –predic. adj. unwell.

poor relation n. inferior or subordinate member of a family etc.

pop¹ –n. 1 sudden sharp explosive sound as of a cork when drawn. 2 *colloq.* effervescent drink. –v. (-pp-) 1 (cause to) make a pop. 2 (foll. by *in, out, up,* etc.) go, move, come, or put unexpectedly or abruptly (*pop out to the shop*). 3 *slang* pawn. –adv. with the sound of a pop (*go pop*). □ **pop off** *colloq.* die. **pop the question** *colloq.* propose marriage. [imitative]

pop² *n. colloq.* 1 (in full **pop music**) highly successful commercial music, esp. since the 1950s. 2 (*attrib.*) of or relating to pop music (*pop concert, group, song*). 3 pop record or song (*top of the pops*). [abbreviation]

pop³ *n. esp. US colloq.* father. [from PAPA]

pop. *abbr.* population.

popadam var. of POPPADAM.

pop art n. art based on modern popular culture and the mass media.

popcorn n. maize which bursts open when heated.

pop culture n. commercial culture based on popular taste.

pope n. (also **Pope**) head of the Roman Catholic Church (*the Pope; we have a new pope*). [Greek *papas* patriarch]

popery /'pəʊpərɪ/ n. *derog.* papal system; Roman Catholicism.

pop-eyed adj. *colloq.* 1 having bulging eyes. 2 wide-eyed (with surprise etc.).

popgun n. child's toy gun shooting pellets etc. by the compression of air.

popinjay /'pɒpɪndʒeɪ/ n. *esp.* conceited person. [Arabic *babagha* parrot]

popish /'pəʊpɪʃ/ *adj. derog.* Roman Catholic.

poplar /'pɒplə(r)/ n. tall slender tree with a straight trunk and often tremulous leaves. [Latin *populus*]

poplin /'pɒplɪn/ n. plain-woven fabric usu. of cotton, with a corded surface. [French *papeline*]

poppadam, poppadom /'pɒppədæm/ n. (also **poppadom, poppadam**) *Ind.* thin, crisp, spiced bread eaten with curry etc. [Tamil]

popper n. 1 *colloq.* press-stud. 2 thing that pops (*party popper*).

poppet /'pɒpɪt/ n. *colloq.* (esp. as a term of endearment) small or dainty person. [Latin *pup(p)a* doll]

popping-crease n. *Cricket* line in front of and parallel to the wicket, within which the batsman stands. [from POP¹]

poppy /'pɒpɪ/ n. (pl. -ies) 1 plant with showy esp. scarlet flowers and a milky sap. 2 artificial poppy worn on Remembrance Sunday. [Latin *papaver*]

poppycock n. *slang* nonsense. [Dutch *pappekak*]

Poppy Day n. = REMEMBRANCE SUNDAY.

populace /'pɒpjʊləs/ n. the common people. [Italian: relate to POPULAR]

popular /'pɒpjʊlə(r)/ adj. 1 liked by many people. 2 a of or for the general public. b prevalent among the general public. (*popular fallacies*) 3 (sometimes *derog.*) adapted to the understanding, taste, or means of the people (*popular science; the popular press*). □ **popular front** n. party or coalition combining left-wing groups. **popularity** /-'lærɪtɪ/ n. popularly adv. [Anglo-Latin *populus* PEOPLE]

popularize v. (also **-ise**) (**-zing** or **-sing**) 1 make popular. 2 present (a difficult subject) in a readily understandable form. □ **popularization** /-'zeɪʃ(ə)n/ n.

popular music n. any music that appeals to a wide public.

populate /'pɒpjʊleɪt/ v. (-ting) 1 supply (an area) with a population. 2 inhabit; form the population of. [medieval Latin:

population /ˌpɒpjʊ'leɪʃ(ə)n/ n. 1 inhabitants of a place, country, etc. 2 total number of these or any group of living things.

population explosion n. sudden large increase of population.

populist /'pɒpjʊlɪst/ n. politician claiming to represent the ordinary people. [Latin *populus* people]

populous /'pɒpjʊləs/ adj. thickly inhabited.

pop-up adj. involving parts that pop up automatically (*pop-up toaster*; *pop-up book*).

porcelain /'pɔːsəlɪn/ n. 1 hard fine translucent ceramic with a transparent glaze. 2 objects made of this. [Italian *porcellana*]

porch n. covered entrance to a building. [Latin *porticus*]

porcine /'pɔːsaɪn/ adj. of or like pigs. [Latin: related to PORK]

porcupine /'pɔːkjʊpaɪn/ n. rodent with a body and tail covered with erectile spines. [Provençal: related to PORK, SPINE]

pore[1] n. esp. *Biol.* minute opening in a surface through which fluids etc. may pass. [Greek *poros*]

pore[2] v. (-ring) (foll. by *over*) 1 be absorbed in studying (a book etc.). 2 meditate on. [origin unknown]

pork n. flesh (esp. unsalted) of a pig, used as food. [Latin *porcus* pig]

porker n. pig raised for food.

pork pie n. pie of minced pork etc. eaten cold.

pork pie hat n. hat with a flat crown and a brim turned up all round.

porky adj. (-ier, -iest) 1 *colloq.* fat. 2 of or like pork.

porn (also **porno**) — n. *colloq.* pornography. —*attrib. adj.* pornographic. [abbreviation]

pornography /pɔː'nɒgrəfɪ/ n. 1 explicit representation of sexual activity in literature, films, etc., intended to stimulate erotic rather than aesthetic or emotional feelings. 2 literature etc. containing this. □ **pornographic** /-nə'græfɪk/ adj. [Greek *pornē* prostitute]

porous /'pɔːrəs/ adj. 1 full of pores. 2 letting through air, water, etc. □ **porosity** /pɔː'rɒsɪtɪ/ n. [Latin: related to PORE[1]]

porphyry /'pɔːfɪrɪ/ n. (pl. -ies) hard rock composed of crystals of white or red feldspar in a red matrix. □ **porphyritic** /-'rɪtɪk/ adj. [Greek: related to PURPLE]

porpoise /'pɔːpəs/ n. sea mammal of the whale family, with a blunt rounded snout. [Latin *porcus* pig, *piscis* **fish**]

porridge /'pɒrɪdʒ/ n. 1 dish of oatmeal or cereal boiled in water or milk. 2 *slang* imprisonment. [alteration of POTTAGE]

porringer /'pɒrɪndʒə(r)/ n. small bowl, often with a handle, for soup etc. [French *potager*: related to POTTAGE]

port[1] n. 1 harbour. 2 town possessing a harbour. [Latin *portus*]

port[2] n. a kind of sweet fortified wine. [*Oporto* in Portugal]

port[3] — n. left-hand side of a ship or aircraft looking forward. —v. (also *absol.*) turn (the helm) to port. [probably originally the side turned to PORT[1]]

port[4] n. 1 opening in the side of a ship for entrance, loading, etc. 2 porthole. [Latin *porta* gate]

portable /'pɔːtəb(ə)l/ —adj. 1 easily movable, convenient for carrying. 2 (of a right, opinion, etc.) capable of being transferred or adapted in altered circumstances (*portable pension*). —n. portable version of an item, e.g. a television. □ **portability** /ˌpɔːtə'bɪlɪtɪ/ n. [Latin *porto* carry]

portage /'pɔːtɪdʒ/ —n. 1 carrying of boats or goods overland between two navigable waters. 2 place where this is necessary. —v. (-ging) convey (a boat or goods) over a portage. [Latin *porto* carry]

Portakabin /'pɔːtəˌkæbɪn/ n. *propr.* prefabricated room or small building. [from PORTABLE, CABIN]

portal /'pɔːt(ə)l/ n. doorway or gate etc., esp. an elaborate one. [Latin: related to PORT[1]]

portcullis /pɔːt'kʌlɪs/ n. strong heavy grating lowered to block a gateway in a fortress etc. [French, = sliding door]

portend /pɔː'tend/ v. 1 foreshadow as an omen. 2 give warning of. [Latin *portendo*: related to PRO-[1], TEND]

portent /'pɔːtent/ n. 1 omen, significant sign of something to come. 2 prodigy; marvellous thing. [Latin *portentum*: related to PORTEND]

portentous /pɔː'tentəs/ adj. 1 like or being a portent. 2 pompously solemn.

porter[1] n. 1 person employed to carry luggage etc. 2 dark beer brewed from charred or browned malt. [Latin *porto* carry]

porter[2] n. gatekeeper or doorman, esp. of a large building. [Latin: related to PORT[4]]

porterage n. 1 hire of porters. 2 charge for this. [from PORTER[1]]

porterhouse steak n. choice cut of beef.

portfolio /pɔːt'fəʊlɪəʊ/ n. (pl. -s) 1 **a** folder for loose sheets of paper, drawings, etc. **b** samples of an artist's work. 2 range of investments held by a person,

company, etc. **3** office of a minister of State (cf. MINISTER WITHOUT PORT-FOLIO). [Italian *portafogli* sheet-carrier]

porthole *n.* aperture (esp. glazed) in a ship's side for letting in light.

portico /ˈpɔːtɪkəʊ/ *n.* (*pl.* -es or -s) colon-nade; roof supported by columns at regular intervals, usu. attached to a porch to a building. [Latin *porticus* porch]

portion /ˈpɔːʃ(ə)n/ — *n.* **1** part or share. **2** amount of food allotted to one person. **3** one's destiny or lot. — *v.* **1** divide (a thing) into portions. **2** (foll. by *out*) distribute. [Latin *portio*]

Portland cement /ˈpɔːtlənd/ *n.* cement manufactured from chalk and clay. [Isle of *Portland* in Dorset]

Portland stone /ˈpɔːtlənd/ *n.* building limestone from the Isle of Portland.

portly /ˈpɔːtlɪ/ *adj.* (-ier, -iest) corpu-lent; stout. [Latin *porto* carry]

portmanteau /pɔːtˈmæntəʊ/ *n.* (*pl.* -s or -x /-təʊz/) trunk for clothes etc., opening into two equal parts. [Latin *porto* carry: related to MANTLE]

portmanteau word *n.* word combin-ing the sounds and meanings of two others (e.g. *motel*, *Oxbridge*).

port of call *n.* place where a ship or a person stops on a journey.

portrait /ˈpɔːtrɪt/ *n.* **1** drawing, paint-ing, photograph, etc. of a person or animal, esp. of the face. **2** description in words. □ **portraitist** *n.* [French: related to PORTRAY]

portraiture /ˈpɔːtrɪtʃə(r)/ *n.* **1** making portraits. **2** description in words. **3** por-trait.

portray /pɔːˈtreɪ/ *v.* **1** make a likeness of. **2** describe in words. □ **portrayal** *n.* **portrayer** *n.* [French *portraire -trait-* depict]

Portuguese /ˌpɔːtjʊˈɡiːz/ — *n.* (*pl.* same) **1 a** native or national of Portugal. **b** person of Portuguese descent. **2** lan-guage of Portugal. — *adj.* of Portugal, its people, or language. [medieval Latin]

Portuguese man-of-war *n.* (*pl.* men-) jellyfish with a large crest and poisonous sting.

pose /pəʊz/ — *v.* (-sing) **1** assume a cer-tain attitude of the body, esp. when being photographed or painted **2** (foll. by *as*) pretend to be (another person etc.). (*posing as a celebrity*). **3** behave affectedly to impress others. **4** put for-ward or present (a question etc.). **5** place (an artist's model etc.) in a certain attitude. — *n.* **1** attitude of body or mind. **2** affectation, pretence. [Latin *pauso* PAUSE, confused with Latin *pono* place]

poser *n.* **1** poseur. **2** *colloq.* puzzling question or problem.

poseur /pəʊˈzɜː(r)/ *n.* person who be-haves affectedly. [French *poser* POSE]

posh /pɒʃ/ *colloq.* — *adj.* smart; upper-class. — *adv.* in an upper-class way (*talk posh*). □ **posh up** smarten up. □ **poshly** *adv.* **poshness** *n.* [perhaps from slang *posh* a dandy; money]

posit /ˈpɒzɪt/ *v.* (-t-) assume as a fact, postulate. [Latin: related to POSITION]

position /pəˈzɪʃ(ə)n/ — *n.* **1** place occu-pied by a person or thing. **2** way in which a thing or its parts are placed or arranged. **3** proper place (*in position*). **4** advantage (*jockeying for position*). **5** attitude; view on a question. **6** situation in relation to others (*puts one in an awkward position*). **7** rank; status; social standing. **8** paid employment. **9** place where troops etc. are posted for strategical purposes. — *v.* place in posi-tion. □ **in a position to** able to. □ **positional** *adj.* [Latin *pono posit-* place]

positive /ˈpɒzɪtɪv/ — *adj.* **1** explicit; de-finite, unequivocal (*positive proof*). **2** (of a person) convinced, confident, or overconfident in an opinion. **3 a** abso-lute; not relative. **b** *Gram.* (of an adject-ive or adverb) expressing a simple quality without comparison. **4** *colloq.* downright (*it was a positive miracle*). **5** constructive (*positive thinking*). **6** marked by the presence and not ab-sence of qualities (*positive reaction*). **7** esp. *Philos.* dealing only with matters of fact; practical. **8** tending in a direction naturally or arbitrarily taken as that of increase or progress. **9** greater than zero. **10** *Electr.* of, containing, or produc-ing the kind of electrical charge pro-duced by rubbing glass with silk; lack-ing electrons. **11** (of a photographic image) showing lights and shades or colours unreversed. — *n.* positive adject-ive, photograph, quantity, etc. □ **posit-ively** *adv.* **positiveness** *n.* [Latin: related to POSITION]

positive discrimination *n.* practice of making distinctions in favour of groups considered to be underpriv-ileged.

positive vetting *n.* inquiry into the background etc. of a candidate for a post involving national security.

positivism *n.* philosophical system recognizing only facts and observable phenomena. □ **positivist** *n. & adj.*

positron /ˈpɒzɪtrɒn/ *n. Physics* ele-mentary particle with the same mass as an electron, but opposite (positive) charge to an electron. [positive electron]

posse /ˈpɒsɪ/ *n.* **1** strong force or com-pany. **2** body of law-enforcers. [Latin, = be able]

possess /pə'zes/ v. 1 hold as property; own. 2 have (a faculty, quality, etc.). 3 occupy or dominate the mind of (*possessed by the devil*; *possessed by fear*). □ **be possessed of** own, have. **what possessed you?** an expression of incredulity. □ **possessor** n. [Latin *possideo possess-*]

possession /pə'ze[ə]n/ n. 1 possessing or being possessed. 2 thing possessed. 3 holding or occupancy. 4 *Law* power or control similar to ownership but which may exist separately from it (*prosecuted for possession of drugs*). 5 (in *pl.*) property, wealth, subject territory, etc. 6 *Football* etc. control of the ball by a player.

possessive /pə'zesɪv/ —*adj.* 1 wanting to retain what one has, reluctant to share. 2 jealous and domineering. 3 *Gram.* indicating possession. —*n.* (in full **possessive case**) *Gram.* case of nouns and pronouns expressing possession. □ **possessiveness** n.

possibility /ˌpɒsɪ'bɪlɪtɪ/ n. (*pl.* **-ies**) 1 state or fact of being possible. 2 thing that may exist or happen. 3 (usu. in *pl.*) capability of being used; potential (*have possibilities*). [Latin *posse* be able]

possible /'pɒsɪb(ə)l/ —*adj.* 1 capable of existing, happening, being done, etc. 2 potential (*a possible way of doing it*). —*n.* 1 possible candidate, member of a team, etc. 2 highest possible score, esp. in shooting.

possibly *adv.* 1 perhaps. 2 in accordance with possibility (*cannot possibly go*).

possum /'pɒsəm/ n. 1 *colloq.* = OPOSSUM 1. 2 *Austral. & NZ colloq.* marsupial resembling an American opossum. □ **play possum** *colloq.* pretend to be unconscious; feign ignorance. [abbreviation]

post[1] /pəʊst/ —*n.* 1 long stout piece of timber or metal set upright in the ground etc. to support something, mark a position or boundary, etc. 2 pole etc. marking the start or finish of a race. —*v.* 1 (often foll. by *up*) attach (a notice etc.) in a prominent place. 2 announce or advertise by poster or list. [Latin *postis*]

post[2] /pəʊst/ —*n.* 1 official conveyance of parcels, letters, etc. (*send it by post*). 2 single collection or delivery of these; the letters etc. dispatched (*has the post arrived?*). 3 place where letters etc. are collected (*take it to the post*). —*v.* 1 put (a letter etc.) in the post. 2 (esp. as **posted** *adj.*) (often foll. by *up*) supply with information (*keep me posted*). 3 a enter (an item) in a ledger. b (often foll. by *up*) complete (a ledger) in this way. [Latin: related to POSITION]

post[3] /pəʊst/ —*n.* 1 place where a soldier is stationed or which he or she patrols. 2 place of duty. 3 a position taken up by a body of soldiers. b force occupying this. c fort. 4 job, paid employment. 5 = TRADING POST. —*v.* 1 place (soldiers, an employee, etc.). 2 appoint to a post or command. [French: related to POST[2]]

post- *prefix* after, behind. [Latin *post* (adv. and prep.)]

postage n. charge for sending a letter etc. by post.

postage stamp n. official stamp affixed to a letter etc., showing the amount of postage paid.

postal *adj.* of or by post. [French: related to POST[2]]

postal code n. = POSTCODE.

postal order n. money order issued by the Post Office.

postbag n. = MAILBAG.

postbox n. public box for posting mail.

postcard n. card for sending by post without an envelope.

postcode n. group of letters and figures in a postal address to assist sorting.

post-coital /pəʊst'kɔɪt(ə)l/ *adj. formal* occurring after sexual intercourse.

postdate /pəʊst'deɪt/ v. (**-ting**) 1 give a date later than the actual one to (a document etc.). 2 follow in time.

poster n. 1 placard in a public place. 2 large printed picture.

poste restante /ˌpəʊst re'stɑ̃t/ n. department in a post office where letters are kept till called for. [French]

posterior /pɒ'stɪərɪə(r)/ —*adj.* 1 later; coming after. 2 at the back. —*n.* (in *sing.* or *pl.*) buttocks. [Latin, comparative of *posterus*: related to POST-]

posterity /pɒ'sterɪtɪ/ n. 1 succeeding generations. 2 person's descendants. [Latin: related to POSTERIOR]

postern /'pɒst(ə)n/ n. *archaic* back door; side way or entrance. [Latin: related to POSTERIOR]

poster paint n. gummy opaque paint.

post-free *adj.* & *adv.* carried by post free of charge, or with postage prepaid.

postgraduate /pəʊst'grædjʊət/ —*n.* person engaged in a course of study after taking a first degree. —*adj.* of or concerning postgraduates.

post-haste *adv.* with great speed.

posthumous /'pɒstjʊməs/ *adj.* 1 occurring after death. 2 (of a book etc.) published after the author's death. 3 (of a child) born after the death of its father. □ **posthumously** *adv.* [Latin *postumus* last]

postillion /pɒ'stɪljən/ n. (also **postilion**) person riding on the near horse of a team drawing a coach when there is no coachman. [Italian: related to POST[3]]

post-impressionism /ˌpəʊstɪmˈprɛʃənɪz(ə)m/ n. art intending to express the individual artist's conception of the objects represented. □ **post-impressionist** n. & adj.

post-industrial /ˌpəʊstɪnˈdʌstrɪəl/ adj. of a society or economy which no longer relies on heavy industry.

postman n. (fem. **postwoman**) person employed to deliver and collect letters etc.

postmark –n. official mark on a letter, giving the place, date, etc., and cancelling the stamp. –v. mark (an envelope etc.) with this.

postmaster n. (fem. **postmistress**) official in charge of a post office.

post-modern /pəʊstˈmɒd(ə)n/ adj. (in the arts etc.) of the movement reacting against modernism, esp. by drawing attention to former conventions. □ **post-modernism** n. **post-modernist** n. & adj.

post-mortem /pəʊstˈmɔːtəm/ –n. 1 examination made after death, esp. to determine its cause. 2 colloq. discussion after a game, election, etc. –adv. & adj. after death. [Latin]

postnatal /pəʊstˈneɪt(ə)l/ adj. of the period after childbirth.

Post Office n. 1 public department or corporation responsible for postal services. 2 (**post office**) room or building where postal business is carried on. **post-office box** n. numbered place in a post office where letters are kept until called for.

post-paid adj. & adv. on which postage has been paid.

postpone /pəʊsˈpəʊn/ v. (**-ning**) cause or arrange (an event etc.) to take place at a later time. □ **postponement** n. [Latin pono place]

postprandial /pəʊstˈprandɪəl/ adj. formal or joc. after dinner or lunch. [Latin prandium a meal]

postscript /ˈpəʊstskrɪpt/ n. additional paragraph or remark, usu. at the end of a letter after the signature and introduced by 'PS'.

postulant /ˈpɒstjʊlənt/ n. candidate, esp. for admission to a religious order. [Latin: related to POSTULATE]

postulate –v. /ˈpɒstjʊleɪt/ (**-ting**) 1 (often foll. by that) assume as a necessary condition, esp. as a basis for reasoning; take for granted. 2 claim. –n. /ˈpɒstjʊlət/ 1 thing postulated. 2 prerequisite or condition. □ **postulation** /ˌpɒstjʊˈleɪʃ(ə)n/ n. [Latin postulo]

posture /ˈpɒstʃə(r)/ –n. 1 relative position of parts, esp. of the body; carriage; bearing. 2 mental attitude. 3 condition or state (of affairs etc.). –v. (**-ring**) 1

assume a mental or physical attitude, esp. for effect. 2 pose (a person). □ **postural** adj. [Latin: related to POSITION]

postwar /pəʊstˈwɔː(r), ˈpəʊst-/ adj. occurring or existing after a war.

posy /ˈpəʊzɪ/ n. (pl. **-ies**) small bunch of flowers. [alteration of POESY]

pot [1] –n. 1 rounded ceramic, metal, or glass vessel for holding liquids or solids, or for cooking in. 2 flowerpot, teapot, etc. 3 contents of a pot. 4 chamber-pot; child's potty. 5 total amount bet in a game etc. 6 (usu. in pl.) colloq. large sum (pots of money). 7 string silver cup etc. as a trophy. –v. (**-tt-**) 1 place in a pot. 2 (usu. as **potted** adj.) preserve in a pot. 3 sit (a child) on a chamber-pot. 4 pocket (a ball) in billiards etc. 5 shoot at, hit, or kill (an animal) with a pot-shot. 6 seize or secure. □ **go to pot** colloq. deteriorate; be ruined. □ **potful** n. (pl. **-s**). [Old English from Latin]

pot [2] n. slang marijuana. [Mexican Spanish potiguaya]

potable /ˈpəʊtəb(ə)l/ adj. drinkable. [Latin poto drink]

potage /pɒˈtɑːʒ/ n. thick soup. [French: related to POT[1]]

potash /ˈpəʊtaʃ/ n. an alkaline potassium compound. [Dutch: related to POT[1], ASH[1]]

potassium /pəˈtasɪəm/ n. soft silver-white metallic element. [from POTASH]

potation /pəʊˈteɪʃ(ə)n/ n. 1 a drink. 2 drinking. [Latin: related to POTION]

potato /pəˈteɪtəʊ/ n. (pl. **-es**) 1 starchy plant tuber used for food. 2 plant bearing this. [Spanish patata from Taino batata]

potato crisp n. = CRISP.

pot-belly n. 1 protruding stomach. 2 person with this.

pot-boiler n. piece of art, writing, etc. done merely to earn money.

pot-bound adj. (of a plant) with roots filling the flowerpot, leaving no room to expand.

poteen /pɒˈtʃiːn/ n. Ir. illicit alcoholic spirit. [Irish poitín diminutive of pota pot[1]]

potent /ˈpəʊt(ə)nt/ adj. 1 powerful; strong. 2 (of a reason) cogent; forceful. 3 (of a male) capable of sexual erection or orgasm. □ **potency** n. [Latin potens = being able or powerful]

potentate /ˈpəʊtənteɪt/ n. monarch or ruler. [Latin: related to POTENT]

potential /pəˈtɛnʃ(ə)l/ –adj. capable of coming into being or action; latent. –n. 1 capacity for use or development. 2 usable resources. 3 Physics quantity determining the energy of mass in a gravitational field or of charge in an electric field. □ **potentiality** /ˌfraltɪ/

potential *adv.* **potentially** *adv.* [Latin: related to POTENT]

potential difference *n.* difference of electric potential between two points.

pother /ˈpɒðə(r)/ *n. literary* noise, commotion, fuss. [origin unknown]

pot-herb *n.* herb grown in a kitchen garden.

pothole *n.* **1** deep hole or cave system in rock. **2** hole in a road surface. □ **potholer** *n.* **potholing** *n.*

pot-hook *n.* **1** hook over a hearth for hanging or lifting a pot. **2** curved stroke in handwriting.

pot-hunter *n.* **1** person who hunts for game at random. **2** person who competes merely for the prize.

potion /ˈpəʊʃ(ə)n/ *n.* dose of a liquid medicine, drug, poison, etc. [Latin *poto* drink]

pot luck *n.* whatever is available.

pot plant *n.* plant grown in a flowerpot.

pot-pourri /pəʊˈpʊəri/ *n.* (*pl.* **-s**) **1** scented mixture of dried petals and spices. **2** musical or literary medley. [French, = rotten pot]

pot roast *n.* piece of meat cooked slowly in a covered dish. □ **pot-roast** *v.*

potsherd /ˈpɒtʃɜːd/ *n.* esp. *Archaeol.* broken piece of ceramic material.

pot-shot *n.* **1** random shot. **2** casual attempt.

pottage /ˈpɒtɪdʒ/ *n. archaic* soup, stew. [French: related to POT¹]

potter¹ *v.* (*US* **putter**) **1** (often foll. by *about, around*) work or occupy oneself in a desultory manner. **2** go slowly, dawdle, loiter (*pottered up to the pub*). [dial. *pote* push]

potter² *n.* maker of ceramic vessels. [Old English: related to POT¹]

potter's wheel *n.* horizontal revolving disc to carry clay during moulding. [French: related to POTTER²]

pottery *n.* (*pl.* **-ies**) **1** vessels etc. made of fired clay. **2** potter's work. **3** potter's workshop. [French: related to POTTER²]

potting shed *n.* shed in which plants are potted and tools etc. are stored.

potty¹ *adj.* (**-ier, -iest**) *slang* **1** foolish, crazy. **2** insignificant, trivial. □ **pottiness** *n.* [origin unknown]

potty² *n.* (*pl.* **-ies**) *colloq.* chamber-pot, esp. for a child.

pouch —*n.* **1** small bag or detachable outside pocket. **2** baggy area of skin under the eyes etc. **3 a** pocket-like receptacle in various animals, e.g. in the cheeks of rodents. **b** similar structure in marsupials. —*v.* **1** put or make into a pouch. **2** take possession of, pocket. [French]

pouffe /puːf/ *n.* large firm cushion used as a low seat or footstool. [French]

poult /pəʊlt/ *n.* young domestic fowl, turkey, pheasant, etc. [contraction of PULLET]

poulterer /ˈpəʊltərə(r)/ *n.* dealer in poultry and usu. game. [*poulter*: related to POULT]

poultice /ˈpəʊltɪs/ —*n.* soft medicated usu. heated mass applied to the body and kept in place with muslin etc., to relieve soreness and inflammation. —*v.* (**-cing**) apply a poultice to. [Latin *puls* pottage]

poultry /ˈpəʊltri/ *n.* domestic fowls (ducks, geese, turkeys, chickens, etc.), esp. as a source of food. [French: related to POULT]

pounce —*v.* (**-cing**) **1** spring or swoop, esp. as in capturing prey. **2** (often foll. by *on, upon*) **a** make a sudden attack. **b** seize eagerly upon a remark etc. —*n.* act of pouncing. [origin unknown]

pound¹ *n.* **1** unit of weight equal to 16 oz avoirdupois (0.4536 kg), 12 oz troy (0.3732 kg). **2** (in full **pound sterling**) (*pl.* same or **-s**) chief monetary unit of the UK etc. [Latin *pondo*]

pound² *v.* **1** crush or beat with repeated blows. **2** (foll. by *at, on*) deliver heavy blows or gunfire. **3** (foll. by *along* etc.) make one's way heavily or clumsily. **4** (of the heart) beat heavily. [Old English]

pound³ *n.* enclosure where stray animals or officially removed vehicles are kept until claimed. [Old English]

poundage *n.* commission or fee of so much per pound sterling or weight.

pound coin *n.* (also **pound note**) coin or note worth one pound.

pounder *n.* (usu. in *comb.*) **1** thing or person weighing a specified number of pounds (*a five-pounder*). **2** gun firing a shell of a specified number of pounds.

pound of flesh *n.* any legal but morally offensive demand.

pour /pɔː(r)/ *v.* **1** (usu. foll. by *down, out, over,* etc.) flow or cause to flow esp. downwards in a stream or shower. **2** dispense (a drink) by pouring. **3** rain heavily. **4** (usu. foll. by *in, out,* etc.) come or go in profusion or rapid succession (*the crowd poured out; letters poured in*). **5** discharge or send freely. **6** (often foll. by *out*) utter at length or in a rush (*poured out their story*). [origin unknown]

pourboire /pʊəˈbwɑː(r)/ *n.* gratuity, tip. [French]

pout —*v.* **1** push the lips forward as a sign of displeasure or sulking. **2** (of the lips) be pushed forward. —*n.* this action. [origin unknown]

pouter *n.* a kind of pigeon that is able to inflate its crop.

poverty /ˈpɒvətɪ/ n. **1** being poor; want. **2** (often foll. by *of*, *in*) scarcity or lack. **3** inferiority; poorness. [Latin *pauper*]

poverty line n. minimum income needed for the necessities of life.

poverty-stricken adj. very poor.

poverty trap n. situation in which an increase of income incurs a loss of State benefits, making real improvement impossible.

POW abbr. prisoner of war.

pow int. expressing the sound of a blow or explosion. [imitative]

powder —n. **1** mass of fine dry particles. **2** medicine or cosmetic in this form. **3** = GUNPOWDER. —v. **1** apply powder to. **2** (esp. as **powdered** adj.) reduce to a fine powder (*powdered milk*). □ **powdery** adj. [Latin *pulvis -ver-* dust]

powder blue adj. & n. (as adj. often hyphenated) pale blue.

powder-puff n. soft pad for applying powder to the skin, esp. the face.

powder-room n. euphem. women's lavatory in a public building.

power —n. **1** ability to do or act. **2** particular faculty of body or mind. **3 a** influence, authority. **b** ascendancy, control (*the party in power*). **4** authorization; delegated authority. **5** influential person, body, or thing. **6** State having international influence. **7** vigour, energy. **8** active property or function (*heating power*). **9** colloq. large number or amount (*did me a power of good*). **10** capacity for exerting mechanical force or doing work (*horsepower*). **11** (often attrib.) mechanical or electrical energy as distinct from manual labour. **12 a** electricity supply. **b** particular source or form of energy (*hydroelectric power*). **13** Physics rate of energy output. **14** product obtained when a number is multiplied by itself a certain number of times (*2 to the power of 3 = 8*). **15** magnifying capacity of a lens. **16** deity. —v. **1** supply with mechanical or electrical energy. **2** (foll. by *up*, *down*) increase or decrease the power supplied to (a device); switch on or off. □ **the powers that be** those in authority. [Latin *posse* be able]

powerboat n. powerful motor boat.

power cut n. temporary withdrawal or failure of an electric power supply.

powerful adj. having much power or influence. □ **powerfully** adv. **powerfulness** n.

powerhouse n. **1** = POWER STATION. **2** person or thing of great energy.

powerless adj. **1** without power. **2** wholly unable. □ **powerlessness** n.

power line n. conductor supplying electrical power, esp. one supported by pylons or poles.

power of attorney n. authority to act for another person in legal and financial matters.

powerplant n. installation which provides power.

power point n. socket in a wall etc. for connecting an electrical device to the mains.

power-sharing n. coalition government, esp. as preferred on principle.

power station n. building where electrical power is generated for distribution.

powwow —n. meeting for discussion (orig. among N. American Indians). —v. hold a powwow. [Algonquian]

pox n. **1** virus disease leaving pockmarks. **2** colloq. = SYPHILIS. [alteration of *pocks* pl. of POCK]

poxy adj. (*-ier*, *-iest*) **1** infected by pox. **2** slang of poor quality; worthless.

pp abbr. pages.

p.p. abbr. (also **pp**) per pro.

ppm abbr. parts per million.

PPS abbr. **1** Parliamentary Private Secretary. **2** additional postscript. [sense 2 from *post-postscript*]

PR abbr. **1** public relations. **2** proportional representation.

Pr symb. praseodymium.

pr. abbr. pair.

practicable /ˈpræktɪkəb(ə)l/ adj. **1** that can be done or used. **2** possible in practice. □ **practicability** /-ˈbɪlɪtɪ/ n. [French: related to PRACTICAL]

practical /ˈpræktɪk(ə)l/ —adj. **1** of or concerned with practice rather than theory (*practical difficulties*). **2** suited to use; functional (*practical shoes*). **3** (of a person) good at making, organizing, or mending things. **4** sensible, realistic. **5** that is such in effect, virtual (*in practical control*). —n. practical examination or lesson. □ **practicality** /-ˈkælɪtɪ/ n. (pl. *-ies*). [Greek *praktikos* from *prassō* do]

practical joke n. humorous trick played on a person.

practically adv. **1** virtually, almost. **2** in a practical way.

practice /ˈpræktɪs/ —n. **1** habitual action or performance. **2 a** repeated activity undertaken in order to improve a skill. **b** session of this. **3** action as opposed to theory. **4** the work, business, or place of business of a doctor, lawyer, etc. (*has a practice in town*). **5** procedure. —v. US var. of PRACTISE. □ **in practice 1** when actually applied; in

reality. **2** skilful from recent practice. **out of practice** lacking a former skill from lack of practice. [from PRACTISE]

practise /'præktɪs/ v. (US **practice**) (**-sing** or US **-cing**) **1** perform habitually; carry on in action. **2** do repeatedly as an exercise to improve a skill; exercise oneself in or on (an activity requiring skill). **3** (as **practised** adj.) experienced, expert. **4** (also absol.) be engaged in (a profession, religion, etc.). [Latin: related to PRACTICAL]

practitioner /præk'tɪʃənə(r)/ n. person practising a profession, esp. medicine.

praenomen /priː'nəʊmen/ n. ancient Roman's first or personal name (e.g. Marcus Tullius Cicero). [Latin: related to PRE-, NOMEN]

praesidium var. of PRESIDIUM.

praetor /'priːtə(r)/ n. ancient Roman magistrate below consul. [Latin]

praetorian guard /priː'tɔːrɪən/ n. bodyguard of the ancient Roman emperor.

pragmatic /præg'mætɪk/ adj. dealing with matters from a practical point of view. □ **pragmatically** adv. [Greek pragma-mat-deed]

pragmatism /'prægmə,tɪz(ə)m/ n. **1** pragmatic attitude or procedure. **2** philosophy that evaluates assertions solely by their practical consequences and bearing on human interests. □ **pragmatist** n. [Greek pragma: related to PRAGMATIC]

prairie /'preərɪ/ n. large area of treeless grassland, esp. in N. America. [Latin pratum meadow]

prairie dog n. N. American rodent making a barking sound.

prairie oyster n. seasoned raw egg, swallowed without breaking the yolk.

prairie wolf n. = COYOTE.

praise /preɪz/ -v. (**-sing**) **1** express warm approval or admiration of. **2** glorify (God) in words. -n. praising; commendation. [French preisier from Latin pretium price]

praiseworthy adj. worthy of praise.

praline /'prɑːliːn/ n. sweet made by browning nuts in boiling sugar. [French]

pram n. four-wheeled conveyance for a baby, pushed by a person on foot. [abbreviation of PERAMBULATOR]

prance /prɑːns/ -v. (**-cing**) **1** (of a horse) raise the forelegs and spring from the hind legs. **2** walk or behave in an elated or arrogant manner. -n. prancing, prancing movement. [origin unknown]

prang slang -v. **1** crash (an aircraft or vehicle). **2** damage by impact. **3** bomb (a target) successfully. -n. act of pranging. [imitative]

prank n. practical joke; piece of mischief. [origin unknown]

prankster n. practical joker.

praseodymium /,preɪzɪə'dɪmɪəm/ n. soft silvery metallic element of the lanthanide series. [Greek prasios green]

prat n. slang **1** fool. **2** buttocks. [origin unknown]

prate -v. (**-ting**) **1** chatter; talk too much. **2** talk foolishly or irrelevantly. -n. prating; idle talk. [Low German or Dutch]

prattle /'præt(ə)l/ -v. (**-ling**) chatter in a childish or inconsequential way. -n. childish or inconsequential chatter. [Low German pratelen: related to PRATE]

prawn n. edible shellfish like a large shrimp. [origin unknown]

pray v. (often foll. by for or to + infin. or that + clause) **1** say prayers; make devout supplication. **2 a** entreat. **b** ask earnestly (prayed to be released). **3** (as imper.) archaic please (pray tell me). [Latin precor]

prayer¹ /'preə(r)/ n. **1 a** request or thanksgiving to God or an object of worship. **b** formula used in praying (the Lord's Prayer). **c** act of praying. **d** religious service consisting largely of prayers (morning prayers). **2** entreaty to a person. [Latin: related to PRECARIOUS]

prayer² /'preɪə(r)/ n. person who prays.

prayer-book n. book of set prayers.

prayer-mat n. small carpet on which Muslims kneel to pray.

prayer-wheel n. revolving cylindrical box inscribed with or containing prayers, used esp. by Tibetan Buddhists.

praying mantis see MANTIS.

pre- prefix before (in time, place, order, degree, or importance). [Latin prae before]

preach v. **1** (also absol.) deliver (a sermon); proclaim or expound (the gospel etc.). **2** give moral advice in an obtrusive way. **3** advocate or inculcate (a quality or practice etc.). □ **preacher** n. [Latin praedico proclaim]

preamble /priː'æmb(ə)l/ n. **1** preliminary statement. **2** introductory part of a statute or deed etc. [Latin: related to AMBLE]

pre-amp /'priː,æmp/ n. = PREAMPLIFIER. [abbreviation]

preamplifier /priː'æmplɪfaɪə(r)/ n. electronic device that amplifies a weak signal (e.g. from a microphone or pickup) and transmits it to a main amplifier.

prearrange /,priːə'reɪndʒ/ v. (**-ging**) arrange beforehand. □ **prearrangement** n.

prebend /ˈprebend/ n. 1 stipend of a canon or member of chapter. 2 portion of land or tithe from which this is drawn. □ **prebendal** /priˈbend(ə)l/ adj. [Latin praebeo grant]

prebendary /ˈprebəndəri/ n. (pl. -ies) holder of a prebend; honorary canon. [medieval Latin: related to PREBEND]

Precambrian /priːˈkæmbrɪən/ Geol. —adj. of the earliest geological era. —n. this era.

precarious /prɪˈkeərɪəs/ adj. 1 uncertain; dependent on chance. 2 insecure; perilous. □ **precariously** adv. **precariousness** n. [Latin precarius: related to PRAY]

precast /priːˈkɑːst/ adj. (of concrete) cast in its final shape before positioning.

precaution /prɪˈkɔːʃ(ə)n/ n. action taken beforehand to avoid risk or ensure a good result. □ **precautionary** adj. [Latin: related to CAUTION]

precede /prɪˈsiːd/ v. (-ding) 1 come or go before in time, order, importance, etc. 2 (foll. by by) cause to be preceded. [Latin: related to CEDE]

precedence /ˈpresɪd(ə)ns/ n. 1 priority in time, order, importance, etc. 2 right of preceding others. □ **take precedence** (often foll. by over, of) have priority (over).

precedent —n. /ˈpresɪd(ə)nt/ previous case etc. taken as a guide for subsequent cases or as a justification. —adj. /prɪˈsiːd(ə)nt, ˈpresi-/ preceding in time, order, importance, etc. [French related to PRECEDE]

precentor /prɪˈsentə(r)/ n. person who leads the singing or (in a synagogue) the prayers of a congregation. [Latin praecentor from cano sing]

precept /ˈpriːsept/ n. 1 rule or guide, esp. for conduct. 2 lawful demand, esp. from one authority to another to levy rates. [Latin praeceptum maxim, order]

preceptor /prɪˈseptə(r)/ n. teacher, instructor. □ **preceptorial** /priː-sepˈtɔːrɪəl/ adj. [Latin: related to PRECEPT]

precession /prɪˈseʃ(ə)n/ n. slow movement of the axis of a spinning body around another axis. [Latin: related to PRECEDE]

precession of the equinoxes n. 1 slow retrograde motion of the equinoctial points along the ecliptic. 2 resulting earlier occurrence of equinoxes in each successive sidereal year.

pre-Christian /priːˈkrɪstʃ(ə)n/ adj. before Christianity.

precinct /ˈpriːsɪŋkt/ n. 1 enclosed area, e.g. around a cathedral, college, etc. 2 designated area in a town, esp. where traffic is excluded. 3 (in pl.) environs. [Latin praecingo-cincti encircle]

preciosity /preʃɪˈɒsɪtɪ/ n. affected refinement in art etc., esp. in the choice of words. [related to PRECIOUS]

precious /ˈpreʃəs/ —adj. 1 of great value or worth. 2 beloved; much prized (precious memories). 3 affectedly refined. 4 colloq. often iron. □ considerable (a precious lot of good). b expressing contempt or disdain (keep your precious flowers!). —adv. colloq. extremely, very (had precious little left). □ **precious** ness n. [Latin pretium price]

precious metals n. pl. gold, silver, and platinum.

precious stone n. piece of mineral of great value, esp. as used in jewellery.

precipice /ˈpresɪpɪs/ n. 1 vertical or steep face of a rock, cliff, mountain, etc. 2 dangerous situation. [Latin praeceps -cipit- headlong]

precipitate —v. (-ting) /prɪˈsɪpɪteɪt/ 1 hasten the occurrence of; cause to occur prematurely. 2 (foll. by into) send rapidly into a certain state or condition (was precipitated into war). 3 throw down headlong. 4 Chem. cause (a substance) to be deposited in solid form from a solution. 5 Physics condense (vapour) into drops and so deposit it. —adj. /prɪˈsɪpɪtət/ 1 headlong; violently hurried (precipitate departure). 2 (of a person or act) hasty, rash. —n. /prɪˈsɪpɪtət/ 1 Chem. substance precipitated from a solution. 2 Physics moisture condensed from vapour, e.g. rain, dew.

precipitation /prɪˌsɪpɪˈteɪʃ(ə)n/ n. 1 precipitating or being precipitated. 2 rash haste. 3 a rain or snow etc. falling to the ground. b quantity of this.

precipitous /prɪˈsɪpɪtəs/ adj. 1 a of or like a precipice. b dangerously steep. 2 = PRECIPITATE adj.

précis /ˈpreɪsiː/ —n. (pl. same /-siːz/) summary, abstract. —v. (-cises /-siːz/; -cised /-siːd/; -cising /-siːɪŋ/) make a précis of. [French]

precise /prɪˈsaɪs/ adj. 1 a accurately expressed. b definite, exact. 2 punctilious; scrupulous in being exact. [Latin praecido cut short]

precisely adv. 1 in a precise manner; exactly. 2 (as a reply) quite so, as you say.

precision /prɪˈsɪʒ(ə)n/ n. 1 accuracy. 2 degree of refinement in measurement etc. 3 (attrib.) marked by or adapted for precision (precision instruments).

preclinical /priːˈklɪnɪk(ə)l/ adj. of the first, chiefly theoretical, stage of a medical education.

preclude /prɪˈkluːd/ v. (**-ding**) **1** (foll. by *from*) prevent. **2** make impossible. [Latin *praecludo*: related to CLOSE]

precocious /prɪˈkəʊʃəs/ adj. **1** often *derog.* (of esp. a child) prematurely developed in some respect. **2** (of an action etc.) indicating such development. □ **precociously** adv. **precociousness** n. **precocity** /-ˈkɒsɪtɪ/ n. [Latin *praecox -cocis* early ripe]

precognition /ˌpriːkɒgˈnɪʃ(ə)n/ n. supposed foreknowledge, esp. of a supernatural kind.

preconceive /ˌpriːkənˈsiːv/ v. (**-ving**) form (an idea or opinion etc.) beforehand.

preconception /ˌpriːkənˈsepʃ(ə)n/ n. preconceived idea, prejudice.

precondition /ˌpriːkənˈdɪʃ(ə)n/ n. condition that must be fulfilled in advance. □

precursor /prɪˈkɜːsə(r)/ n. **1 a** forerunner. **b** person who precedes in office etc. **2** harbinger. [Latin *praecurro -curs-* run before]

predate /priːˈdeɪt/ v. (**-ting**) precede in time.

predator /ˈpredətə(r)/ n. predatory animal. [Latin]

predatory /ˈpredətərɪ/ adj. **1** (of an animal) preying naturally upon others. **2** plundering or exploiting others.

predecease /ˌpriːdɪˈsiːs/ v. (**-sing**) die earlier than (another person).

predecessor /ˈpriːdɪˌsesə(r)/ n. **1** former holder of an office or position with respect to a later holder. **2** ancestor. **3** thing to which another has succeeded. [Latin *decessor*: related to DECEASE]

predestine /priːˈdestɪn/ v. (**-ning**) **1** determine beforehand. **2** ordain in advance by divine will or as if by fate. □ **predestination** /-ˈneɪʃ(ə)n/ n. [French or Church Latin: related to PRE-]

predetermine /ˌpriːdɪˈtɜːmɪn/ v. (**-ning**) **1** decree beforehand. **2** predestine.

predicament /prɪˈdɪkəmənt/ n. difficult or unpleasant situation. [Latin: related to PREDICATE]

predicant /ˈpredɪkənt/ *hist.* —adj. (of a religious order) engaged in preaching. —n. predicant person, esp. a Dominican. [Latin: related to PREDICATE]

predicate —v. /ˈpredɪˌkeɪt/ **1** (also *absol.*) assert (something) about the subject of a proposition. **2** (foll. by *on*) found or base (a statement etc.) on. —n. /ˈpredɪkət/ *Gram. & Logic* what is said about the subject of a sentence or proposition etc. (e.g. *went home* in *John went home*). □ **predicable** /ˈpredɪkəb(ə)l/ adj. **predication** /-ˈkeɪʃ(ə)n/ n. [Latin *praedico -dicat-* declare]

predicative /prɪˈdɪkətɪv/ adj. **1** *Gram.* (of an adjective or noun) forming or contained in the predicate, as *old* in *the dog is old*. **2** that predicates. [Latin: related to PREDICATE]

predict /prɪˈdɪkt/ v. (often foll. by *that*) foretell, prophesy. □ **predictor** n. [Latin *praedico -dict-* foretell]

predictable adj. that can be predicted or is to be expected. □ **predictability** /-ˈbɪlɪtɪ/ n. **predictably** adv.

prediction /prɪˈdɪkʃ(ə)n/ n. **1** predicting or being predicted. **2** thing predicted.

predilection /ˌpriːdɪˈlekʃ(ə)n/ n. (often foll. by *for*) preference or special liking. [Latin *praediligo* prefer]

predispose /ˌpriːdɪˈspəʊz/ v. (**-sing**) **1** influence favourably in advance. **2** (foll. by *to*, or *to* + infin.) render liable or inclined beforehand. □ **predisposition** /-pəˈzɪʃ(ə)n/ n.

predominant /prɪˈdɒmɪnənt/ adj. **1** predominating. **2** being the strongest or main element. □ **predominance** n. **predominantly** adv.

predominate /prɪˈdɒmɪˌneɪt/ v. (**-ting**) **1** (foll. by *over*) have control. **2** be superior. **3** be the strongest or main element.

pre-echo /priːˈekəʊ/ n. (pl. **-es**) **1** faint copy heard just before an actual sound in a recording, caused by the accidental transfer of signals. **2** foreshadowing.

pre-embryo /priːˈembrɪəʊ/ n. (pl. **-s**) potential human embryo in the first fourteen days after fertilization.

pre-eminent /priːˈemɪnənt/ adj. **1** excelling others. **2** outstanding. □ **pre-eminence** n. **pre-eminently** adv.

pre-empt /priːˈempt/ v. **1 a** forestall. **b** appropriate in advance. **2** obtain by pre-emption. [back-formation from PRE-EMPTION]

■ **Usage** *Pre-empt* is sometimes used to mean *prevent*, but this is considered incorrect in standard English.

pre-emption /priːˈempʃ(ə)n/ n. purchase or taking by one person or party before the opportunity is offered to others. [medieval Latin *emo empt-* buy]

pre-emptive /priːˈemptɪv/ adj. **1** pre-empting. **2** (of military action) intended to prevent attack by disabling the enemy.

preen v. **1** (of a bird) tidy (the feathers or itself) with its beak. **2** (of a person) smarten or admire (oneself, one's hair, clothes, etc.). **3** (often foll. by *on*) congratulate or pride (oneself). [origin unknown]

prefab /ˈpriːfæb/ n. *colloq.* prefabricated building. [abbreviation]

prefabricate /priː'fæbrɪˌkeɪt/ v. (-ting) manufacture sections of (a building etc.) prior to their assembly on site.

preface /'prɛfəs/ —n. 1 introduction to a book stating its subject, scope, etc. 2 preliminary part of a speech. —v. (-cing) 1 (foll. by with) introduce or begin (a speech or event). 2 provide (a book etc.) with a preface. 3 (of an event etc.) lead up to (another). □ **prefatory** /-təri/ adj. [Latin praefatio]

prefect /'priːfɛkt/ n. 1 chief administrative officer of a district, esp. in France. 2 senior pupil in a school, helping to maintain discipline. [Latin praeficio -fect- set in authority over]

prefecture /'priːfɛktjʊər/ n. 1 district under the government of a prefect. 2 prefect's office or tenure. [Latin: related to PREFECT]

prefer /prɪ'fɜː(r)/ v. (-rr-) 1 (often foll. by to, or to + infin.) like better (prefers coffee to tea). 2 submit (information, an accusation, etc.) for consideration. 3 promote or advance (a person). [Latin praefero -lat-]

preferable /'prɛfərəb(ə)l/ adj. to be preferred; more desirable. □ **preferably** adv.

preference /'prɛfərəns/ n. 1 preferring or being preferred. 2 thing preferred. 3 favouring of one person etc. before others. 4 prior right, esp. to the payment of debts. □ **in preference to** as a thing preferred over (another).

preference shares n.pl. (also **preference stock** n.sing.) shares or stock whose entitlement to dividend takes precedence over that of ordinary shares.

preferential /ˌprɛfə'rɛnʃ(ə)l/ adj. 1 of or involving preference. 2 giving or receiving a favour. □ **preferentially** adv.

preferment /prɪ'fɜːmənt/ n. formal promotion to a higher office.

prefigure /priː'fɪɡə(r)/ v. formal (-ring) represent or imagine beforehand.

prefix /'priːfɪks/ —n. 1 verbal element placed at the beginning of a word to qualify its meaning (e.g. ex-, non-). 2 title before a name (e.g. Mr). —v. (often foll. by to) 1 add as an introduction. 2 join (a word or element) as a prefix.

pregnant /'prɛɡnənt/ adj. 1 having a child or young developing in the uterus. 2 full of meaning; significant; suggestive (a pregnant pause). □ **pregnancy** n. (pl. -ies). [Latin praegnans] **preheat** /priː'hiːt/ v. heat beforehand. **prehensile** /prɪ'hɛnsaɪl/ adj. Zool. (of a tail or limb) capable of grasping. [Latin prehendo -hens- grasp]

prehistoric /ˌpriːhɪ'stɒrɪk/ adj. 1 of the period before written records. 2 colloq. utterly out of date. □ **prehistory** /-'hɪstəri/ n.

prejudge /priː'dʒʌdʒ/ v. (-ging) form a premature judgement on (a person, issue, etc.).

prejudice /'prɛdʒʊdɪs/ —n. 1 a preconceived opinion. b (foll. by against, in favour of) bias, partiality. 2 harm that results or may result from some action or judgement (to the prejudice of). —v. (-cing) 1 impair the validity or force of (a right, claim, statement, etc.). 2 (esp. as **prejudiced** adj.) cause (a person) to have a prejudice. □ **without prejudice** (often foll. by to) without detriment (to an existing right or claim). [Latin: related to JUDGE]

prejudicial /ˌprɛdʒʊ'dɪʃ(ə)l/ adj. (often foll. by to) causing prejudice; detrimental.

prelacy /'prɛləsi/ n. (pl. -ies) 1 church government by prelates. 2 (prec. by the) prelates collectively. 3 office or rank of prelate. [Anglo-French from medieval Latin: related to PRELATE]

prelate /'prɛlət/ n. high ecclesiastical dignitary, e.g. a bishop. [Latin: related to PREFER]

prelim /'priːlɪm/ n. colloq. 1 preliminary university examination. 2 (in pl.) pages preceding the main text of a book. [abbreviation]

preliminary /prɪ'lɪmɪnəri/ —adj. introductory, preparatory. —n. (pl. -ies) (usu. in pl.) 1 preliminary action or arrangement (dispense with the preliminaries). 2 preliminary trial or contest. [Latin limen threshold]

prelude /'prɛljuːd/ —n. (often foll. by to) 1 action, event, or situation serving as an introduction. 2 introductory part of a poem etc. 3 Mus. a introductory piece to a fugue, suite, etc. b short piece of a similar type. —v. (-ding) 1 serve as a prelude to. 2 introduce with a prelude. [Latin ludo lus- play]

premarital /priː'mærɪt(ə)l/ adj. existing or (esp. of sexual relations) occurring before marriage.

premature /'prɛmətjʊə(r)/ adj. 1 a occurring or done before the usual or proper time (a premature decision). b too hasty. 2 (of a baby) born (esp. three or more weeks) before the end of gestation. □ **prematurely** adv. [Latin: related to PRE-, MATURE]

premed /priː'mɛd/ n. colloq. = PREMEDICATION. [abbreviation]

premedication /ˌpriːmɛdɪ'keɪʃ(ə)n/ n. medication to prepare for an operation etc.

premeditate /priːˈmedɪteɪt/ v. (-ting) think out or plan beforehand (*premeditated murder*). □ **premeditation** /-ˈteɪʃ(ə)n/ n. [Latin: related to MEDITATE]

premenstrual /priːˈmenstruəl/ adj. of the time shortly before each menstruation (*premenstrual tension*).

premier /ˈpremɪə(r)/ —n. prime minister or other head of government. —adj. first in importance, order, or time. □ **premiership** n. [French]

première /ˈpremɪˌeə(r)/ —n. first performance or showing of a play or film. —v. (-ring) give a première of. [French feminine: related to PREMIER]

premise /ˈpremɪs/ n. **1** Logic = PREMISS. **2** (in pl.) **a** house or other building with its grounds, outbuildings, etc. **b** Law houses, lands, or tenements previously specified in a document etc. □ **on the premises** in the building etc. concerned. [Latin *praemissa* set in front]

premiss /ˈpremɪs/ n. Logic previous statement from which another is inferred. [var. of PREMISE]

premium /ˈpriːmɪəm/ n. **1** amount to be paid for a contract of insurance. **2** sum added to interest, wages, price, etc. **3** reward or prize. **4** (attrib.) (of a commodity) of the best quality and therefore more expensive. □ **at a premium 1** highly valued; above the usual or nominal price. **2** scarce and in demand. [Latin *praemium* reward]

Premium Bond n. (also **Premium Savings Bond**) government security without interest but with a draw for cash prizes.

premolar /priːˈməʊlə(r)/ n. (in full **premolar tooth**) tooth between the canines and molars.

premonition /ˌpriːməˈnɪʃ(ə)n/ n. forewarning; presentiment. □ **premonitory** /prɪˈmɒnɪtərɪ/ adj. [Latin *moneo* warn]

prenatal /priːˈneɪt(ə)l/ adj. of the period before childbirth.

preoccupy /priːˈɒkjʊpaɪ/ v. (-ies, -ied) **1** (of a thought etc.) dominate the mind of (a person) to the exclusion of all else. **2** (as **preoccupied** adj.) otherwise engrossed; mentally distracted. □ **preoccupation** /-ˈpeɪʃ(ə)n/ n. [Latin *prae-occupo* seize beforehand]

preordain /ˌpriːɔːˈdeɪn/ v. ordain or determine beforehand.

prep n. colloq. **1** homework, esp. in boarding-schools. **2** period when this is done. [abbreviation of PREPARATION]

prepack /priːˈpæk/ v. (also **pre-package** /-ˈpækɪdʒ/) pack (goods) on the site of production or before retail.

prepaid past and past part. of PREPAY.

preparation /ˌprepəˈreɪʃ(ə)n/ n. **1** preparing or being prepared. **2** (often in pl.) something done to make ready. **3** specially prepared substance. **4** = PREP.

preparatory /prɪˈpærətərɪ/ —adj. (often foll. by to) serving to prepare; introductory. —adv. (often foll. by to) in a preparatory manner (*was packing preparatory to departure*).

preparatory school n. private primary school or US secondary school.

prepare /prɪˈpeə(r)/ v. (-ring) **1** make or get ready for use, consideration, etc. **2** assemble (a meal etc.). **3 a** make (a person or oneself) ready or disposed in some way (*prepared them for a shock*). **b** get ready (*prepare to jump*). □ **be prepared** (often foll. by for, or to + infin.) be disposed or willing to. [Latin *paro* make ready]

preparedness /prɪˈpeərɪdnɪs/ n. readiness, esp. for war.

prepay /priːˈpeɪ/ v. (past and past part. **prepaid**) **1** pay (a charge) in advance. **2** pay postage on (a letter etc.) before posting. □ **prepayment** n.

preplan /priːˈplæn/ v. (-nn-) plan in advance.

preponderate /prɪˈpɒndəreɪt/ v. (-ting) (often foll. by over) be greater in influence, quantity, or number; predominate. □ **preponderance** n. **preponderant** adj. [Latin *pondus -der- weight*]

preposition /ˌprepəˈzɪʃ(ə)n/ n. Gram. word governing (and usu. preceding) a noun or pronoun and expressing a relation to another word, as in: 'the man on the platform', 'came after dinner', 'went by train'. □ **prepositional** adj. [Latin *praepono -posit-* place before]

prepossess /ˌpriːpəˈzes/ v. **1** (usu. in passive) (of an idea, feeling, etc.) take possession of (a person). **2 a** prejudice (usu. favourably and spontaneously). **b** (as **prepossessing** adj.) attractive; appealing. □ **prepossession** /-ˈzeʃ(ə)n/ n.

preposterous /prɪˈpɒstərəs/ adj. **1** utterly absurd; outrageous. **2** contrary to nature, reason, or sense. □ **preposterously** adv. [Latin, = before behind]

preppy n. (pl. -ies) US colloq. student of an expensive private school or similar-looking person. [from PREP]

prepuce /ˈpriːpjuːs/ n. **1** = FORESKIN. **2** fold of skin surrounding the clitoris. [Latin *praeputium*]

Pre-Raphaelite /priːˈræfəˌlaɪt/ —n. member of a group of 19th-c. artists emulating Italian art before the time of Raphael. —adj. **1** of the Pre-Raphaelites. **2** (**pre-Raphaelite**) (esp. of a woman) like a type painted by the Pre-

Raphaelites (e.g. with long thick curly auburn hair).

pre-record /ˌpriːrɪˈkɔːd/ v. record (esp. material for broadcasting) in advance.

prerequisite /ˌpriːˈrekwɪzɪt/ —adj. required as a precondition. —n. prerequisite thing.

■ **Usage** *Prerequisite* is sometimes confused with *perquisite* which means 'an extra profit, allowance, or right'.

prerogative /prɪˈrɒgətɪv/ n. right or privilege exclusive to an individual or class. [Latin *praerogo* ask first]

Pres. *abbr.* President.

presage /ˈpresɪdʒ/ —n. 1 omen, portent. 2 presentiment, foreboding. —v. (-ging) 1 portend, foreshadow. 2 give warning of (an event etc.) by natural means. 3 (of a person) predict or have a presentiment of. [Latin *praesagium*]

presbyopia /ˌprezbɪˈəʊpɪə/ n. long-sightedness caused by loss of elasticity of the eye lens, occurring esp. in old age. [Greek *presbus* old man, *ōps* eye]

presbyter /ˈprezbɪtə(r)/ n. 1 (in the Episcopal Church) minister of the second order; priest 2 (in the Presbyterian Church) elder. [Church Latin from Greek, = elder]

Presbyterian /ˌprezbɪˈtɪərɪən/ —adj. (of a church) governed by elders all of equal rank, esp with ref. to the Church of Scotland. —n. member of a Presbyterian Church. □ **Presbyterianism** n.

presbytery /ˈprezbɪtərɪ/ n. (pl. -ies) 1 eastern part of a chancel. 2 body of presbyters, esp. a court next above a Kirk-session. 3 house of a Roman Catholic priest.

preschool /ˈpriːskuːl/ adj. of the time before a child is old enough to go to school.

prescient /ˈpresɪənt/ adj. having foreknowledge or foresight. □ **prescience** n. [Latin *praescio* know before]

prescribe /prɪˈskraɪb/ v. (-bing) 1 a advise the use of (a medicine etc.). b recommend, esp. as a benefit. 2 lay down or impose authoritatively. [Latin *praescribo*]

■ **Usage** *Prescribe* is sometimes confused with *proscribe.*

prescript /ˈpriːskrɪpt/ n. ordinance, law, command. [Latin related to PRE-SCRIBE]

prescription /prɪˈskrɪpʃ(ə)n/ n. 1 act of prescribing. 2 a doctor's (usu. written) instruction for the supply and use of a medicine. b medicine prescribed.

prescriptive /prɪˈskrɪptɪv/ adj. 1 prescribing, laying down rules. 2 arising from custom.

presence /ˈprez(ə)ns/ n. 1 being present. 2 place where a person is (*admitted to their presence*). 3 person's appearance or bearing, esp. when imposing. 4 person or spirit tha: is present (*the royal presence; aware of a presence in the room*). [Latin, related to PRESENT¹]

presence of mind n. calmness and quick-wittedness in sudden difficulty etc.

present¹ /ˈprez(ə)nt/ —adj. 1 (usu. predic.) being in the place in question. 2 a now existing, occurring, or being such. b now being considered etc. (*in the present case*). 3 *Gram.* expressing an action etc. now going on or habitually performed (*present participle*). —n. time now passing (*no time like the present*). 2 *Gram.* present tense. □ **at present** now. **by these presents** *Law* by this document. **for the present** just now; for the time being. [Latin *praesens -ent-*]

present² /prɪˈzent/ v. 1 introduce, offer, or exhibit for attention or considera-tion. 2 a (with a thing as object, foll. by *to*) offer or give as a gift (to a person, company, producer etc.) put (a piece of entertainment) before the public. 3 a (of a performer, compere, etc.) introduce. 4 introduce (a person, formally (*may I present my fiancé?*). 5 a (of a circum-stance) reveal (some quality etc) (*this presents some difficulty*). b exhibit (an appearance etc.). 6 (of an idea etc.) offer or suggest itself. 7 deliver (a cheque, bill, etc.) for acceptance or payment. 8 a (usu. foll. by *at*) aim (a weapon) b hold out (a weapon) in position for aiming. □ **present arms** hold a rifle etc. vertically in front of the body as a salute. □ **presenter** n. (in sense 3b). [Latin *prae-sento*: related to PRESENT¹]

present³ /ˈprez(ə)nt/ n. thing given, gift. [French: related to PRESENT¹]

presentable /prɪˈzentəb(ə)l/ adj. of good appearance; fit to be presented. □ **presentability** /-ˈbɪlɪtɪ/ n. **present-ably** adv.

presentation /ˌprez(ə)nˈteɪʃ(ə)n/ n. 1 a presenting or being presented. b thing presented. 2 manner or quality of pre-senting. 3 demonstration or display of materials, information, etc.; lecture. **present-day** attrib. adj. of this time; modern.

presentiment /prɪˈzentɪmənt/ *n.* vague expectation; foreboding (esp. of misfortune).

presently *adv.* 1 soon; after a short time. 2 esp. *US & Scot.* at the present time; now.

preservative /prɪˈzɜːvətɪv/ —*n.* substance for preserving perishable foodstuffs, wood, etc. —*adj.* tending to preserve.

preserve /prɪˈzɜːv/ —*v.* (-ving) 1 keep safe or free from decay etc. 2 maintain (a thing) in its existing state. 3 retain (a quality or condition). 4 treat (food) to prevent decomposition or fermentation. 5 keep (game etc.) undisturbed for private use. —*n.* (in *sing.* or *pl.*) 1 preserved fruit; jam. 2 place where game etc. is preserved. 3 sphere of activity regarded as a person's own. □ **preservation** /ˌprezəˈveɪʃ(ə)n/ *n.* [Latin *servo* keep]

pre-set /priːˈset/ *v.* (-**tt-**; *past* and *past part.* -**set**) set or fix (a device) in advance of its operation.

preshrunk /priːˈʃrʌŋk/ *adj.* (of fabric etc.) treated so that it shrinks during manufacture and not in use.

preside /prɪˈzaɪd/ *v.* (-**ding**) 1 (often foll. by *at, over*) be chairperson or president of a meeting etc. 2 exercise control or authority. [Latin *sedeo* sit]

presidency /ˈprezɪdənsɪ/ *n.* (*pl.* -**ies**) 1 office of president. 2 period of this.

president /ˈprezɪd(ə)nt/ *n.* 1 head of a republican State. 2 head of a society or council etc. 3 head of certain colleges. 4 *US* head of a university, company, etc. 5 person in charge of a meeting. □ **presidential** /-ˈdenʃ(ə)l/ *adj.*

presidium /prɪˈsɪdɪəm/ *n.* (also **praesidium**) standing committee in a Communist country. [Latin: related to PRESIDE]

press¹ —*v.* 1 apply steady force to (a thing in contact). 2 **a** compress or squeeze a thing to flatten, shape, or smooth it. **b** squeeze (a fruit etc.) to extract its juice. 3 (foll. by *out of, from*, etc.) squeeze (juice etc.). 4 embrace or caress by squeezing (*pressed my hand*). 5 (foll. by *on, against*, etc.) exert pressure. 6 be urgent; demand immediate action. 7 (foll. by *for*) make an insistent demand. 8 (foll. by *up, round*, etc.) crowd. 9 (foll. by *on, forward*, etc.) hasten insistently. 10 (often in *passive*) (of an enemy etc.) bear heavily on. 11 (often foll. by *for*, or *to* + infin.) urge or entreat (*pressed me to stay; pressed me for an answer*). 12 (foll. by *on, upon*) urge (an opinion, claim, or course of action). **b** force (an offer, a gift, etc.). 13 insist on (*did not press the point*). 14 manufacture (a gramophone record, car

part, etc.) by using pressure to shape and extract from a sheet of material. —*n.* 1 act of pressing (*give it a press*). 2 device for compressing, flattening, shaping, extracting juice, etc. 3 = PRINTING-PRESS. 4 (prec. by *the*) **a** art or practice of printing. **b** newspapers etc. generally or collectively. 5 notice or publicity in newspapers etc. (*got a good press*). 6 (**Press**) printing or publishing company. 7 **a** crowding. **b** crowd (of people etc.). 8 the pressure of affairs. 9 esp. *Ir. & Scot.* large usu. shelved cupboard. □ **be pressed for** have barely enough (time etc.). **go** (or **send**) **to press** go or send to be printed. [Latin *premo press*]

press² *v.* 1 *hist.* force to serve in the army or navy. 2 bring into use as a makeshift (*was pressed into service*). [obsolete *prest* from French, = loan]

press agent *n.* person employed to obtain advertising and press publicity.

press conference *n.* interview given to a number of journalists.

press gallery *n.* gallery for reporters, esp. in a legislative assembly.

press-gang —*n.* 1 *hist.* body of men employed to press men into army or navy service. 2 any group using coercive methods. —*v.* force into service.

pressie /ˈprezɪ/ *n.* (also **prezzie**) *colloq.* present, gift. [abbreviation]

pressing —*adj.* 1 urgent. 2 urging strongly (*pressing invitation*). —*n.* 1 thing made by pressing, e.g. a gramophone record. 2 series of these made at one time. 3 act of pressing (*all at one pressing*). □ **pressingly** *adv.*

press release *n.* statement issued to newspapers.

press-stud *n.* small fastening device engaged by pressing its two halves together.

press-up *n.* exercise in which the prone body is raised from the ground by placing the hands on the floor and straightening the arms.

pressure /ˈprɛʃə(r)/ —*n.* 1 **a** exertion of continuous force on or against a body by another in contact with it. **b** force exerted. **c** amount of this (expressed by the force or its weight per unit area) (*atmospheric pressure*). 2 urgency (*work under pressure*). 3 affliction or difficulty (*under financial pressure*). 4 constraining influence (*put pressure on us*). —*v.* (-**ring**) (often foll. by *into*) apply (esp. moral) pressure to; coerce; persuade. [Latin: related to PRESS¹]

pressure-cooker *n.* airtight pan for cooking quickly under steam pressure. □ **pressure-cook** *v.*

pressure group n. group formed to influence public policy.

pressure point n. point where an artery can be pressed against a bone to inhibit bleeding.

pressurize v. (also -**ise**) (-**zing** or -**sing**)
1 (esp. as **pressurized** adj.) maintain normal atmospheric pressure in (an aircraft cabin etc.) at a high altitude. 2 raise to a high pressure. 3 pressure (a person). □ **pressurization** /-'zeɪʃ(ə)n/ n.

pressurized-water reactor n. nuclear reactor with water at high pressure as the coolant.

Prestel /'prestel/ n. propr. computerized visual information system operated by British Telecom. [from PRESS, TELECOMMUNICATION]

prestidigitator /ˌprestɪ'dɪdʒɪteɪtə(r)/ n. formal conjuror. □ **prestidigitation** /-'teɪʃ(ə)n/ n. [French: related to PRESTO, DIGIT]

prestige /pre'stiːʒ/ n. 1 respect or reputation derived from achievements, power, associations, etc. 2 (attrib.) having or conferring prestige. □ **prestigious** /-'stɪdʒəs/ adj. [Latin prastigiae juggler's tricks]

presto /'prestəʊ/ Mus. —adv. & adj. in quick tempo. —n. (pl. -**s**) presto passage or movement. [Latin praestus quick]

prestressed /priː'strest/ adj. (of concrete) strengthened by stretched wires within it.

presumably /prɪ'zjuːməbli/ adv. as may reasonably be presumed.

presume /prɪ'zjuːm/ v. (-**ming**) 1 (often foll. by that) suppose to be true; take for granted. 2 (often foll. by to + infin.) a take the liberty; be impudent enough (presumed to question their authority). b dare, venture (may I presume to ask?). 3 be presumptuous. 4 (foll. by on, upon) take advantage of or make unscrupulous use of (a person's good nature etc.). [Latin praesumo]

presumption /prɪ'zʌmpʃ(ə)n/ n. 1 arrogance, presumptuous behaviour. 2 a presuming a thing to be true. b that is or may be presumed to be true. 3 ground for presuming. [Latin: related to PRESUME]

presumptive /prɪ'zʌmptɪv/ adj. giving grounds for presumption (presumptive evidence).

presumptuous /prɪ'zʌmptjʊəs/ adj. unduly or overbearingly confident. □ **presumptuously** adv. **presumptuousness** n.

presuppose /ˌpriːsə'pəʊz/ v. (-**sing**) 1 assume beforehand. 2 imply. □ **presup-position** /-'sʌpəˈzɪʃ(ə)n/ n.

pre-tax /'priː-/ adj. (of income etc.) before deduction of taxes.

pretence /prɪ'tens/ n. (US **pretense**) 1 pretending, make-believe. 2 a pretext, excuse. b false show of intentions or motives. 3 (foll. by to) claim, esp. a false one (to merit etc.). 4 display; ostentation. [Anglo-Latin: related to PRETEND]

pretend /prɪ'tend/ —v. 1 claim or assert falsely so as to deceive (pretend know-ledge; pretended to be rich). 2 imagine to oneself in play (pretended it was night). 3 (as **pretended** adj.) falsely claim to be such (a pretended friend). 4 (foll. by to) profess to have (a quality etc.). —adj. colloq. pretended; in pretence (pretend money). [Latin praetendo: related to TEND[1]]

pretender n. person who claims a throne, title, etc.

pretension /prɪ'tenʃ(ə)n/ n. 1 (often foll. by to) a assertion of a claim. b justifiable claim. 2 pretentiousness.

pretentious /prɪ'tenʃəs/ adj. 1 making an excessive claim to merit or import-ance. 2 ostentatious. □ **pretentiously** adv. **pretentiousness** n.

preterite /'pretərɪt/ (US **preterit**) Gram. —adj. expressing a past action or state. —n. preterite tense or form. [Latin praeteritum past]

preternatural /ˌpriːtə'nætʃ(ə)r(ə)l/ adj. extraordinary, exceptional; supernat-ural. [Latin praeter beyond]

pretext /'priːtekst/ n. ostensible reason; excuse offered. [Latin praetextus: related to TEXT]

pretty /'prɪtɪ/ —adj. (-**ier**, -**iest**) 1 attract-ive in a delicate way (pretty girl; pretty dress). 2 fine or good of its kind. 3 iron. considerable, fine (a pretty penny). —adv. colloq. fairly, moderately. □ **pretty much** (or **nearly** or **well**) colloq. almost, very nearly. □ **prettily** adv. **prettiness** n. [Old Eng-lish]

pretty-pretty adj. colloq. too pretty.

pretzel /'prets(ə)l/ n. crisp knot-shaped salted biscuit. [German]

prevail /prɪ'veɪl/ v. 1 (often foll. by against, over) be victorious or gain mas-tery. 2 be the more usual or predom-inant. 3 exist or occur in general use or experience. 4 (foll. by on, upon) per-suade. [Latin praevaleo: related to AVAIL]

prevalent /'prevalent/ *adj.* 1 generally existing or occurring. 2 predominant. □ **prevalence** *n.* [related to PREVAIL]

prevaricate /pri'værɪkeɪt/ *v.* (-ting) 1 speak or act evasively or misleadingly. 2 quibble, equivocate. □ **prevarication** /-'keɪʃ(ə)n/ *n.* **prevaricator** *n.* [Latin, = walk crookedly]

■ **Usage** *Prevaricate* is often confused with *procrastinate*, which means 'to defer or put off action'.

prevent /pri'vent/ *v.* (often foll. by *from* + verbal noun) stop from happening or doing something; hinder; make impossible (*the weather prevented me from going*). □ **preventable** *adj.* (also **preventible**). **prevention** *n.* [Latin *praevenio -vent-* hinder]

■ **Usage** The use of *prevent* without 'from' as in *prevented me going* is informal. An acceptable alternative is *prevented my going*.

preventative /pri'ventətɪv/ *adj. & n.* = PREVENTIVE.

preventive /pri'ventɪv/ *adj.* preventive to prevent, esp. disease. —*n.* preventive agent, measure, drug, etc.

preview /'priːvjuː/ —*n.* showing of a film, play, exhibition, etc., before it is seen by the general public. —*v.* see or show in advance.

previous /'priːvɪəs/ —*adj.* 1 (often foll. by *to*) coming before in time or order. 2 *colloq.* hasty, premature. —*adv.* (foll. by *to*) before. □ **previously** *adv.* [Latin *praevius* from *via* way]

pre-war /priː'wɔː(r)/ *adj.* existing or occurring before a war.

prey /preɪ/ —*n.* 1 animal that is hunted or killed by another for food. 2 (often foll. by *to*) person or thing that is influenced by or vulnerable to (something undesirable) (*prey to morbid fears*). —*v.* (foll. by *on, upon*) 1 seek or take as prey. 2 (of a disease, emotion, etc.) exert a harmful influence (*it preyed on his mind*). [Latin *praeda*]

prezzie var. of PRESSIE.

price —*n.* 1 amount of money for which a thing is bought or sold. 2 what is or must be given, done, sacrificed, etc., to obtain or achieve something (*peace at any price*). 3 odds in betting. —*v.* (-cing) 1 fix or find the price of (a thing for sale). 2 estimate the value of. □ **at a price** at a high cost. **price on a person's head** reward for a person's capture or death. **what price ... ?** (often foll. by verbal noun) *colloq.* 1 what is the chance of ... ? (*what price your finishing the course?*). 2 *iron.* the much boasted ... proves

disappointing (*what price your friend... ship now?*). [Latin *pretium*]

price-fixing *n.* maintaining of prices at a certain level by agreement between competing sellers.

priceless *adj.* 1 invaluable. 2 *colloq.* very amusing or absurd.

price tag *n.* 1 label on an item showing its price. 2 cost of an undertaking.

price war *n.* period of fierce competition among traders cutting prices.

pricey *adj.* (**-cier**, **-ciest**) *colloq.* expensive.

prick —*v.* 1 pierce slightly; make a small hole in. 2 (foll. by *off, out*) mark with small holes or dots. 3 trouble mentally (*my conscience pricked me*). 4 tingle. 5 (foll. by *out*) plant (seedlings etc.) in small holes. —*n.* 1 act of pricking. 2 small hole or mark made by pricking. 3 pain caused as by pricking. 4 mental pain. 5 *coarse slang* penis. **b** *derog.* contemptible man. □ **prick up one's ears** 1 (of a dog etc.) make the ears erect when alert. 2 (of a person) become suddenly attentive. [Old English]

prickle /'prɪk(ə)l/ —*n.* 1 small thorn. 2 hard-pointed spine of a hedgehog etc. 3 pricking sensation. —*v.* (-ling) affect or be affected with a sensation of multiple pricking. [Old English]

prickly *adj.* (**-ier**, **-iest**) 1 having prickles. 2 (of a person) ready to take offence. 3 tingling. □ **prickliness** *n.*

prickly heat *n.* itchy inflammation of the skin, causing a tingling sensation and common in hot countries.

prickly pear *n.* 1 cactus with pear-shaped prickly fruit. 2 its fruit.

pride —*n.* 1 **a** elation or satisfaction at one's achievements, qualities, possessions, etc. **b** object of this feeling; the flower or best. 2 high or overbearing opinion of one's worth or importance. 3 (in full **proper pride**) proper sense of what befits one's position; self-respect. 4 group (of certain animals, esp. lions). 5 best condition, prime. —*v.refl.* (-ding) (foll. by *on, upon*) be proud of. □ **take pride** (or **a pride**) **in** 1 be proud of. 2 maintain in good condition or appearance. [Old English: related to PROUD]

pride of place *n.* most important or prominent position.

prie-dieu /priː'djɜː/ *n.* (*pl.* **prie-dieux** pronunc. same) kneeling-desk for prayer. [French, = pray God]

priest *n.* 1 ordained minister of the Roman Catholic or Orthodox Church, or of the Anglican Church (above a deacon and below a bishop). 2 (*fem.* **priestess**) official minister of a non-

prig n. Christian religion. □ **priestly** adj. [Latin PRESBYTER]

prig n. self-righteous or moralistic person. □ **priggish** adj. **priggishness** n. [origin unknown]

prim adj. (**primmer**, **primmest**) formal and precise; prudish. □ **primly** adv. **primness** n. [French: related to PRIME¹]

prima ballerina /ˌpriːmə ˌbæləˈriːnə/ n. chief female dancer in a ballet. [Italian]

primacy /ˈpraɪməsɪ/ n. (pl. **-ies**) 1 pre-eminence. 2 office of a primate. [Latin: related to PRIMATE]

prima donna /ˌpriːmə ˈdɒnə/ n. (pl. **prima donnas**) 1 chief female singer in an opera. 2 temperamentally self-important person. □ **prima donna-ish** adj. [Italian]

prima facie /ˌpraɪmə ˈfeɪʃɪ/ —adv. at first sight. —adj. (of evidence) based on the first impression. [Latin]

primal /ˈpraɪm(ə)l/ adj. 1 primitive, primeval. 2 chief, fundamental. [Latin: related to PRIME¹]

primary /ˈpraɪmərɪ/ —adj. 1 a of the first importance, chief. b fundamental, basic. 2 earliest, original; first in a series. 3 of the first rank in a series; not derived. 4 designating any of the colours red, green, and blue, or (for pigments) red, blue, and yellow, of which all other colours are mixtures. 5 (of education) for children below the age of 11. 6 (**Primary**) Geol. of the lowest series of strata. 7 Biol. of the first stage of development. —n. (pl. **-ies**) 1 thing that is primary. 2 (in full **primary election**) (in the US) preliminary election to appoint party conference delegates or to select candidates for a principal (esp. presidential) election. 3 = PRIMARY FEATHER. □ **primarily** /ˈpraɪmərɪlɪ, praɪˈmeərɪlɪ/ adv. [Latin: related to PRIME¹]

primary feather n. large flight-feather of a bird's wing.

primary school n. school for children below the age of 11.

primate /ˈpraɪmeɪt/ n. 1 member of the highest order of mammals, including apes, monkeys, and man. 2 (also /-mət/) archbishop. [Latin primas -at- chief]

prime¹ —adj. 1 chief, most important. 2 first-rate, excellent. 3 primary, fundamental. 4 Math. a (of a number etc.) divisible only by itself and unity (e.g. 2, 3, 5, 7, 11). b (of numbers) having no common factor but unity. —n. 1 state of the highest perfection (prime of life). 2 (prec. by the; foll. by of) the best part. [Latin primus first]

prime² v. (**-ming**) 1 prepare (a thing) for use or action. 2 prepare (a gun) for firing or (an explosive) for detonation. 3 pour (liquid) into a pump to enable it to work. 4 prepare (wood etc.) for painting by applying a substance that prevents paint from being absorbed. 5 equip (a person) with information etc. 6 ply (a person) with food or drink in preparation for something. [origin unknown]

prime minister n. head of an elected government; principal minister.

primer¹ n. substance used to prime wood etc.

primer² n. 1 elementary textbook for teaching children to read. 2 introductory book. [Latin: related to PRIME¹]

prime time n. (in broadcasting) time when audiences are largest.

primeval /praɪˈmiːv(ə)l/ adj. 1 of the first age of the world. 2 ancient, primitive. □ **primevally** adv. [Latin: related to PRIME¹, aevum age]

primitive /ˈprɪmɪtɪv/ —adj. 1 at an early stage of civilization (primitive man). 2 undeveloped, crude, simple (primitive methods). —n. 1 untutored painter with a direct naïve style. 2 picture by such a painter. □ **primitively** adv. **primitiveness** n. [Latin: related to PRIME¹]

primogeniture /ˌpraɪməʊˈdʒenɪtʃə(r)/ n. 1 fact of being the first-born child. 2 (in full **right of primogeniture**) right of succession belonging to the first-born. [medieval Latin: related to PRIME¹, Latin genitura birth]

primordial /praɪˈmɔːdɪəl/ adj. existing at or from the beginning; primeval. [Latin: related to PRIME¹, ordior begin]

primp v. 1 make (the hair, clothes, etc.) tidy. 2 refl. make (oneself) smart. [var. of PRIM]

primrose /ˈprɪmrəʊz/ n. 1 a wild plant bearing pale yellow spring flowers. b its flower. 2 pale yellow colour. [French and medieval Latin, = first rose]

primrose path n. pursuit of pleasure.

primula /ˈprɪmjʊlə/ n. cultivated plant bearing primrose-like flowers in a wide variety of colours. [Latin diminutive: related to PRIME¹]

Primus /ˈpraɪməs/ n. propr. portable cooking stove burning vaporized oil. [Latin, = first]

prince n. (as a title usu. **Prince**) 1 male member of a royal family other than the reigning king. 2 ruler of a small State. 3 noble man in some countries. 4 (often foll. by of) chief or greatest (the prince of novelists). [Latin princeps -cp-]

Prince Consort n. (title conferred on) the husband of a reigning queen who is himself a prince.

princeling n. young or petty prince.

princely *adj.* (**-ier, iest**) **1** of or worthy of a prince. **2** sumptuous, generous, splendid.

Prince of Wales *n.* (title conferred on) the eldest son and heir apparent of the British monarch.

Prince Regent *n.* prince who acts as regent, esp. the future George IV.

Princess /prin'ses/ *n.* (as a title usu. /prin'ses/) **1** wife of a prince. **2** female member of a royal family other than a queen. [French: related to PRINCE]

Princess Royal *n.* (title conferred on) the British monarch's eldest daughter.

principal /'prinsip(ə)l/ —*adj.* **1** (usu. *attrib.*) first in rank or importance; chief. **2** main, leading. —*n.* **1** chief person. **2** head of some schools, colleges, and universities. **3** leading performer in a concert, play, etc. **4** capital sum as distinct from interest or income. **5** person for whom another is agent etc. **6** civil servant of the grade below Secretary. **7** person directly responsible for a crime. □ **principally** *adv.* [Latin: related to PRINCE]

principal boy *n.* leading male role in a pantomime, usu. played by a woman.

Principality /ˌprinsi'paliti/ *n.* (*pl.* **-ies**) **1** State ruled by or government of a prince. **2** (**the Principality**) Wales.

principal parts *n.pl. Gram.* parts of a verb from which all other parts can be deduced.

principle /'prinsip(ə)l/ *n.* **1** fundamental truth or law as the basis of reasoning or action. **2** a personal code of conduct (*person of high principle*). **b** (in *pl.*) personal rules of conduct (*has no principles*). **3** general law in physics etc. **4** law of nature forming the basis for the construction or working of a machine etc. **5** fundamental source; primary element. □ **in principle** in theory. **on principle** on the basis of a moral attitude. [Latin *principium* source]

principled *adj.* based on or having (esp. praiseworthy) principles of behaviour.

prink *v.* **1 a** (usu. *refl.*; often foll. by *up*) smarten (oneself) up. **b** dress oneself up. **2** (of a bird) preen. [origin unknown]

print —*v.* **1** produce or cause (a book, picture, etc.) to be produced by applying inked types, blocks, or plates, to paper, etc. **2** express or publish in print. **3 a** (often foll. by *on, in*) impress or stamp (a mark on a surface). **b** (often foll. by *with*) impress or stamp (a surface with a seal, die, etc.). **4** (often *absol.*) write (letters) without joining them up. **5** (often foll. by *off, out*) produce (a photograph) from a

negative. **6** (usu. foll. by *out*) (of a computer etc.) produce output in printed form. **7** mark (a textile fabric) with a coloured design. **8** (foll. by *on*) impress (an idea, scene, etc. on the mind or memory). —*n.* **1** indentation or mark on a surface left by the pressure of a thing in contact with it. **2 a** printed lettering or writing. **b** words in printed form. **c** printed publication, esp. a newspaper. **3** picture or design printed from a block or plate. **4** photograph produced on paper from a negative. **5** printed cotton fabric. □ **in print 1** (of a book etc.) available from the publisher. **2** in printed form. **out of print** no longer available from the publisher. [Latin *premo*: related to PRESS[1]]

printed circuit *n.* electric circuit with thin strips of conductor printed on a flat insulating sheet.

printer *n.* **1** person who prints books etc. **2** owner of a printing business. **3** device that prints, esp. from a computer.

printing *n.* **1** production of printed books etc. **2** copies of a book printed at one time. **3** printed letters or writing imitating them.

printing-press *n.* machine for printing from types or plates etc.

printout *n.* computer output in printed form.

prior /'praiə(r)/ —*adj.* **1** earlier. **2** (often foll. by *to*) coming before in time, order, or importance. —*adv.* (foll. by *to*) before (*left prior to his arrival*). —*n.* (*fem.* **prioress**) **1** superior of a religious house or order. **2** (in an abbey) deputy of an abbot. [Latin, = earlier]

priority /prai'ɒriti/ *n.* (*pl.* **-ies**) **1** thing that is regarded as more important than others. **2** high(est) place among various things to be done (*gave priority to*). **3** right to proceed ahead of other traffic. **5** (state of) being more important. □ **prioritize** *v.* (also **-ise**) (**-zing** or **-sing**) [medieval Latin: related to PRIOR]

priory /'praiəri/ *n.* (*pl.* **-ies**) monastery governed by a prior or nunnery governed by a prioress. [Anglo-French and medieval Latin: related to PRIOR]

prise *v.* (also **prize**) (**-sing** or **-zing**) force open or out by leverage. [French: related to PRIZE[2]]

prism /'priz(ə)m/ *n.* **1** solid figure whose two ends are equal parallel rectilinear figures, and whose sides are parallelograms. **2** transparent body in this form, usu. triangular with refracting surfaces at an acute angle with each other, which separates white light into a spectrum of

colours. [Greek *prisma* thing sawn]

prismatic /prɪzˈmætɪk/ *adj.* 1 of, like, or using a prism. 2 (of colours) distributed (as if) by a transparent prism. [Greek: related to PRISM]

prison /ˈprɪz(ə)n/ *n.* 1 place of captivity. 2 a building to which persons are committed while awaiting trial or for punishment. 2 custody, confinement. [Latin *prehendo* seize]

prisoner /ˈprɪznə(r)/ *n.* 1 person kept in prison. 2 (in full **prisoner at the bar**) person in custody on a criminal charge and on trial. 3 person or thing confined by illness, another's grasp, etc. 4 (in full **prisoner of war**) person captured in war. □ **take prisoner** seize and hold as a prisoner. [Anglo-French: related to PRISON]

prissy /ˈprɪsɪ/ *adj.* (**-ier, -iest**) prim, prudish. □ **prissily** *adv.* **prissiness** *n.* [perhaps from PRIM, SISSY]

pristine /ˈprɪstiːn/ *adj.* 1 in its original condition; unspoilt. 2 spotless; fresh as if new. 3 ancient, primitive. [Latin *pristinus* former]

prisoner of conscience see CONSCIENCE.

■ **Usage** The use of *pristine* in sense 2 is considered incorrect by some people.

privacy /ˈprɪvəsɪ/ *n.* 1 a being private and undisturbed. b right to this. 2 freedom from intrusion or public attention.

private /ˈpraɪvət/ *adj.* 1 belonging to an individual; one's own, personal (*private property*). 2 confidential, not to be disclosed to others (*private talks*). 3 kept or removed from public knowledge or observation. 4 not open to the public. 5 (of a place) secluded. 6 (of a person) not holding public office or an official position. 7 (of education or medical treatment) conducted outside the State system, at the individual's expense. —*n.* 1 private soldier. 2 (in *pl.*) *colloq.* genitals. □ **in private** privately. □ **privately** *adv.* [Latin *privo* deprive]

private bill *n.* parliamentary bill affecting an individual or corporation only.

private company *n.* company with restricted membership and no public share issue.

private detective *n.* detective engaged privately, outside an official police force.

private enterprise *n.* businesses not under State control.

privateer /praɪvəˈtɪə(r)/ *n.* 1 privately owned and officered warship holding a government commission. 2 its commander.

private eye *n. colloq.* private detective.

private hotel *n.* hotel not obliged to take all comers.

private means *n.pl.* income from investments etc., apart from earned income.

private member *n.* MP not holding government office.

private member's bill *n.* bill introduced by a private member, not part of government legislation.

private parts *n.pl. euphem.* genitals.

private sector *n.* the part of the economy free of direct State control.

private soldier *n.* ordinary soldier other than the officers.

private view *n.* viewing of an exhibition (esp. of paintings) before it opens to the public.

privation /praɪˈveɪʃ(ə)n/ *n.* lack of the comforts or necessities of life. [Latin: related to PRIVATE]

privative /ˈprɪvətɪv/ *adj.* 1 consisting in or marked by loss or absence. 2 *Gram.* expressing privation. [Latin: related to PRIVATE]

privatize /ˈpraɪvətaɪz/ *v.* (also **-ise**) (**-zing** or **-sing**) transfer (a business etc.) from State to private ownership. □ **privatization** /-ˈzeɪʃ(ə)n/ *n.*

privet /ˈprɪvɪt/ *n.* bushy evergreen shrub used for hedges. [origin unknown]

privilege /ˈprɪvɪlɪdʒ/ —*n.* 1 right, advantage, or immunity, belonging to a person, class, or office. 2 special benefit or honour (*a privilege to meet you*). —*v.* (**-ging**) invest with a privilege. □ **privileged** *adj.* [Latin: related to PRIVY, *lex leg-* law]

privy /ˈprɪvɪ/ —*adj.* 1 (foll. by *to*) sharing in the secret (of a person's plans etc.). 2 *archaic* private, hidden, secret. —*n.* (*pl.* **-ies**) lavatory, esp. an outside one. [French *privé* private place]

Privy Council *n.* body of advisers appointed by the sovereign (now chiefly honorary). □ **Privy Councillor** *n.* (also **Privy Counsellor**).

privy purse *n.* allowance from the public revenue for the monarch's private expenses.

privy seal *n.* seal formerly affixed to minor State documents.

prize /praɪz/ —*n.* 1 something that can be won in a competition, lottery, etc. 2 reward given as a symbol of victory or worth. 3 something striven for or worth striving for. 4 (*attrib.*) a to which a prize is awarded (*prize poem*). b excellent of its kind. —*v.* (**-zing**) value highly (*a much prized possession*). [French: related to PRAISE]

prize² n. ship or property captured in naval warfare. [French *prise* from Latin *prehendo* seize]

prize³ var. of PRISE.

prizefight n. boxing-match fought for a prize of money. □ **prizefighter** n.

prize-giving n. awarding of prizes, esp. formally at a school etc.

prizewinner n. winner of a prize. □ **prizewinning** attrib. adj.

PRO abbr. **1** Public Record Office. **2** public relations officer.

pro¹ /prəʊ/ n. (pl. -s) colloq. professional. [abbreviation]

pro² /prəʊ/ —adj. (of an argument or reason) in favour. —n. (pl. -s) reason in favour. —prep. in favour of. [Latin, = for, on behalf of]

pro-¹ prefix **1** favouring or supporting (*pro-government*). **2** acting as a substitute or deputy for (*proconsul*). **3** forwards (*produce*). **4** forwards and downwards (*prostrate*). **5** onwards (*progress*). **6** in front of (*protect*). [Latin *pro* in front (of)]

pro-² prefix before in time, place, order, etc. [Greek *pro* before]

proactive /prəʊˈæktɪv/ adj. (of a person, policy, etc.) taking the initiative. [from PRO-², after REACTIVE]

probability /ˌprɒbəˈbɪlɪtɪ/ n. (pl. -ies) **1** being probable. **2** likelihood of something happening. **3** probable or most probable event. **4** Math. extent to which an event is likely to occur, measured by the ratio of the favourable cases to the total number of possible cases. □ **in all probability** most probably.

probable /ˈprɒbəb(ə)l/ —adj. (often foll. by *that*) that may be expected to happen or prove true; likely (*the probable explanation; it is probable that they forgot*). —n. probable candidate, member of a team, etc. □ **probably** adv. [Latin: related to PROVE]

probate /ˈprəʊbeɪt/ n. **1** official proving of a will. **2** verified copy of a will with a certificate as handed to executors. [Latin *probo* PROVE]

probation n. **1** Law system of supervising and monitoring the behaviour of (esp. young) offenders, as an alternative to prison. **2** period of testing the character or abilities of esp. a new employee. □ **on probation** undergoing probation. □ **probationary** adj. [Latin: related to PROVE]

probationer n. person on probation.

probation officer n. official supervising offenders on probation.

probative /ˈprəʊbətɪv/ adj. formal affording proof. [Latin: related to PROVE]

probe —n. **1** penetrating investigation. **2** small device, esp. an electrode, for measuring, testing, etc. **3** blunt-ended surgical instrument for exploring a wound etc. **4** (in full **space probe**) unmanned exploratory spacecraft transmitting information about its environment. —v. (-**bing**) **1** examine or enquire into closely. **2** explore with a probe. [Latin *probo*: related to PROVE]

probity /ˈprəʊbɪtɪ/ n. uprightness, honesty. [Latin *probus* good]

problem /ˈprɒbləm/ n. **1** doubtful or difficult matter requiring a solution or accomplish. **3** (attrib.) causing problems (*problem child*). **4** puzzle or question for solution; exercise. [Greek *problēma -mat-*]

problematic /ˌprɒbləˈmætɪk/ adj. (also **problematical**) attended by difficulty; doubtful or questionable. □ **problematically** adv. [Greek: related to PROBLEM]

proboscis /prəˈbɒsɪs/ n. (pl. -sces) **1** long flexible trunk or snout of some mammals, e.g. an elephant or tapir. **2** elongated mouth parts of some insects. [Greek *boskō* feed]

proboscis monkey n. monkey of Borneo, the male of which has a large pendulous nose.

procedure /prəˈsiːdʒə(r)/ n. **1** way of acting or advancing, esp. in business or legal action. **2** way of performing a task. **3** series of actions conducted in a certain order or manner. □ **procedural** adj. [French: related to PROCEED]

proceed /prəˈsiːd/ v. **1** (often foll. by *to*) go forward or on further; make one's way. **2** (often foll. by *with*, or *to* + infin.) continue with an activity; go on to do something (*proceeded with their work; proceeded to beg me*). **3** (of an action) be carried on or continued (*the case will now proceed*). **4** adopt a course of action (*how shall we proceed?*). **5** go on to say. **6** (foll. by *against*) start a lawsuit against (a person). **7** (often foll. by *from*) originate (*trouble proceeded from ill-ness*). [Latin *cedo cess-* go]

proceeding n. **1** action or piece of conduct (*high-handed proceeding*). **2** (in pl.) (in full **legal proceedings**) lawsuit. **3** (in pl.) published report of discussions or a conference.

proceeds /ˈprəʊsiːdz/ n.pl. profits from sale etc. [pl. of obsolete *proceed* (n.) from PROCEED]

process¹ /ˈprəʊses/ —n. **1** course of action or proceeding; a series of stages in manufacture etc. **2** progress or course (*in process of construction*). **3** natural or involuntary course or

change (*process of growing old*). **4** action at law; summons or writ, etc. **5** natural projection of a bone, stem, etc. —*v.* **1** deal with by a particular process. **2** (as **processed** *adj.*) treat (food, esp. to prevent decay) (*processed cheese*) [Latin: related to PROCEED]

process² /prəˈses/ *v.* walk in procession. [back-formation from PROCESSION]

procession /prəˈseʃ(ə)n/ *n.* **1** people or vehicles etc. advancing in orderly succession, esp. at a ceremony, demonstration, or festivity. **2** movement of such a group (*go in procession*). [Latin: related to PROCEED]

processional —*adj.* **1** of processions. **2** used, carried, or sung in processions. —*n. Eccl.* processional hymn or hymn book.

processor /ˈprəʊsesə(r)/ *n.* machine that processes things, esp.:**1** = CENTRAL PROCESSOR. **2** = FOOD PROCESSOR.

proclaim /prəˈkleɪm/ *v.* **1** (often foll. by *that*) announce or declare (publicly or officially). **2** declare to be (king, a traitor, etc.). □ **proclamation** /ˌprɒkləˈmeɪʃ(ə)n/ *n.* [Latin: related to CLAIM]

proclivity /prəˈklɪvɪtɪ/ *n.* (*pl.* **-ies**) tendency, inclination. [Latin *clivus* slope]

procrastinate /prəˈkræstɪneɪt/ *v.* (**-ting**) defer action. □ **procrastination** *n.* [Latin *cras* tomorrow]

■ **Usage** *Procrastinate* is often confused with *prevaricate* which means 'to be evasive, quibble'.

procreate /ˈprəʊkrɪeɪt/ *v.* (**-ting**) (often *absol.*) produce (offspring) naturally. □ **procreation** /-ˈeɪʃ(ə)n/ *n.* **procreative** *adj.* [Latin: related to CREATE]

Procrustean /prəʊˈkrʌstɪən/ *adj.* seeking to enforce uniformity ruthlessly or violently. [Greek *Prokroustēs*, name of a robber who fitted his victims to a bed by stretching them or cutting bits off them]

proctor /ˈprɒktə(r)/ *n.* disciplinary officer, one of two, at certain universities. □ **proctorial** /-ˈtɔːrɪəl/ *adj.* **proctorship** *n.* [from PROCURATOR]

procuration /ˌprɒkjʊˈreɪʃ(ə)n/ *n.* **1** formal act of procuring. **2** function or authorized action of an attorney. [Latin: related to PROCURE]

procurator /ˈprɒkjʊreɪtə(r)/ *n.* agent or proxy, esp. with power of attorney. [Latin *procurator* agent]

procurator fiscal *n.* (in Scotland) local coroner and public prosecutor.

procure /prəˈkjʊə(r)/ *v.* (**-ring**) **1** obtain, acquire (*managed to procure a copy*). **2** bring about (*procured their dismissal*). **3** (also *absol.*) obtain (women) for prostitution. □ **procurement** *n.* [Latin *in curo* look after]

procurer /prəˈkjʊərə(r)/ *n.* (*fem.* **procuress**) person who obtains women for prostitution. [Latin PROCURATOR]

prod —*v.* (**-dd-**) **1** poke with a finger, stick, etc. **2** stimulate to action. **3** (foll. by *at*) make a prodding motion. —*n.* **1** poke, thrust. **2** stimulus to action. [origin unknown]

prodigal /ˈprɒdɪg(ə)l/ —*adj.* **1** recklessly wasteful. **2** (foll. by *of*) lavish. —*n.* **1** prodigal person. **2** (in full **prodigal son**) repentant wastrel, returned wanderer, etc. (*Luke* 15:11–2). □ **prodigality** /-ˈgælɪtɪ/ *n.* [Latin *prodigus* lavish]

prodigious /prəˈdɪdʒəs/ *adj.* **1** marvellous or amazing. **2** enormous. **3** abnormal. [Latin: related to PRODIGY]

prodigy /ˈprɒdɪdʒɪ/ *n.* (*pl.* **-ies**) **1** exceptionally gifted or able person, esp. a precocious child. **2** marvellous, esp. extraordinary thing. **3** (foll. by *of*) wonderful example (of a quality). [Latin *prodigium* portent]

produce —*v.* /prəˈdjuːs/ (**-cing**) **1** manufacture or prepare (goods etc.). **2** bring forward for consideration, inspection, or use (*will produce evidence*). **3** bear, yield, or bring into existence (offspring, fruit, a harvest, etc.). **4** cause or bring about (a reaction, sensation, etc.). **5** *Geom.* extend or continue (a line). **6** supervise the production of (a play, film, broadcast, record, etc.). —*n.* /ˈprɒdjuːs/ **1 a** what is produced, esp. agricultural products collectively (*dairy produce*). **b** amount of this. **2** (often foll. by *of*) result (of labour, efforts, etc.). □ **producible** /prəˈdjuːsɪb(ə)l/ *adj.* [Latin *duco duct* lead]

producer /prəˈdjuːsə(r)/ *n.* **1** person who produces goods etc. **2** person who supervises the production of a play, film, broadcast, etc.

product /ˈprɒdʌkt/ *n.* **1** thing or substance produced, esp. by manufacture. **2** result. **3** quantity obtained by multiplying. [Latin: related to PRODUCE]

production /prəˈdʌkʃ(ə)n/ *n.* **1** producing or being produced, esp. in large quantities (*go into production*). **2** total yield. **3** thing produced, esp. a film, play, book, etc. [Latin: related to PRODUCE]

production line *n.* systematized sequence of operations involved in producing a commodity.

productive /prəˈdʌktɪv/ *adj.* **1** of or producing. **2** producing much (*productive writer*). **3** engaged in the production of goods. **2** producing commodities of exchangeable value (*productive labour*). **4** (foll.

by of) producing or giving rise to (*pro-ductive of great annoyance*). □ **produc-tively** *adv.* **productiveness** *n.* [Latin: related to PRODUCE]

productivity /ˌprɒdʌkˈtɪvɪtɪ/ *n.* 1 being productive, capacity to produce. 2 amount produced by an industry, work-force, etc.

proem /ˈprəʊɪm/ *n.* preface etc. to a book or speech. [Latin from Greek]

Prof. *abbr.* Professor.

profane /prəˈfeɪn/ —*adj.* 1 a irreverent, blasphemous. b (of language) obscene. 2 not sacred or biblical; secular. —*v.* (-ning) 1 treat (esp. a sacred thing) irreverently; disregard. 2 violate or pol-lute. □ **profanation** /ˌprɒfəˈneɪʃ(ə)n/ *n.* [Latin *fanum* temple]

profanity /prəˈfænɪtɪ/ *n.* (*pl.* -ies) 1 profane act or language; blasphemy. 2 swear-word.

profess /prəˈfes/ *v.* 1 claim openly to have (a quality or feeling). 2 (often foll. by *to* + infin.) pretend, declare (*profess ignorance*). 3 affirm one's faith in or allegiance to. [Latin *profiteor -fess-* de-clare]

professed *adj.* 1 self-acknowledged (*professed Christian*). 2 alleged, ostens-ible. □ **professedly** /-sɪdlɪ/ *adv.*

profession /prəˈfeʃ(ə)n/ *n.* 1 vocation or calling, esp. learned or scientific (*medical profession*). 2 people in a pro-fession. 3 declaration or avowal. □ **the oldest profession** *colloq.* prostitution.

professional —*adj.* 1 of, belonging to, or connected with a profession. 2 a skilful, competent. b worthy of a profes-sional (*professional conduct*). 3 en-gaged in a specified activity as one's main paid occupation (*professional boxer*). 4 *derog.* engaged in a specified activity, esp. fanatically (*professional agitator*). —*n.* professional person. □ **professionally** *adv.*

professionalism *n.* qualities associ-ated with a profession, esp. competence, skill, etc.

professor /prəˈfesə(r)/ *n.* 1 a (often as a title) highest-ranking academic teach-ing in a university department; holder of a university chair. b *US* university teacher. 2 person who professes a reli-gion etc. □ **professorial** /ˌprɒfɪˈsɔːrɪəl/ *adj.* **professorship** *n.*

proffer *v.* offer. [French: related to PRO-¹, OFFER]

proficient /prəˈfɪʃ(ə)nt/ *adj.* (often foll. by *in, at*) adept, expert. □ **proficiency** *n.* **proficiently** *adv.* [Latin *proficio fect-* advance]

profile /ˈprəʊfaɪl/ —*n.* 1 a outline, esp. of a human face, as seen from one side. b representation of this. 2 short biograph-ical or character sketch. —*v.* (-ling) represent or describe by a profile. □ **keep a low profile** remain inconspicu-ous. [Italian *profilare* draw in outline]

profit /ˈprɒfɪt/ —*n.* 1 advantage or bene-fit. 2 financial gain; excess of returns over outlay. —*v.* (-t-) 1 (also *absol.*) be beneficial to. 2 obtain advantage or benefit (*profited by the experience*). □ **at a profit** with financial gain. [Latin *pro-fectus*: related to PROFICIENT]

profitable *adj.* 1 yielding profit. 2 bene-ficial. □ **profitability** /-ˈbɪlɪtɪ/ *n.* **profit-ably** *adv.*

profit and loss account *n.* account showing net profit or loss at any time.

profiteer /ˌprɒfɪˈtɪə(r)/ —*v.* make or seek excessive profits, esp. illegally or on the black market. —*n.* person who profit-eers.

profit margin *n.* profit after the deduc-tion of costs.

profiterole /prəˈfɪtərəʊl/ *n.* small hol-low choux bun, usu. filled with cream and covered with chocolate. [French diminutive: related to PROFIT]

profit-sharing *n.* sharing of profits, esp. between employer and employees.

profligate /ˈprɒflɪɡət/ —*adj.* 1 recklessly extravagant. 2 licentious, dissolute. —*n.* profligate person. □ **profligacy** *n.* **prof-ligately** *adv.* [Latin *profligo* ruin]

pro forma /prəʊ ˈfɔːmə/ —*adv. & adj.* as or being a matter of form. —*n.* (in full **pro-forma invoice**) invoice sent in ad-vance of goods supplied. [Latin]

profound /prəˈfaʊnd/ *adj.* (-er, -est) 1 having or demanding great knowledge, study, or insight (*profound treatise; profound doctrines*). 2 intense, unquali-fied, thorough (*a profound sleep; pro-found indifference*). 3 deep (*profound crevasses*). □ **profoundly** *adv.* **pro-foundness** *n.* **profundity** /prəˈfʌndɪtɪ/ *n.* (*pl.* -ies). [Latin *profundus*]

profuse /prəˈfjuːs/ *adj.* 1 (often foll. by *in, of*) lavish; extravagant. 2 exuber-antly plentiful; copious (*profuse vari-ety*). □ **profusely** *adv.* **profusion** /-ˈfjuːʒ(ə)n/ *n.* [Latin *fundo fus-* pour]

progenitor /prəʊˈdʒenɪtə(r)/ *n.* 1 an-cestor. 2 predecessor. 3 original. [Latin *progigno beget*]

progeny /ˈprɒdʒɪnɪ/ *n.* 1 offspring; des-cendant(s). 2 outcome, issue. [Latin: related to PROGENITOR]

progesterone /prəʊˈdʒestərəʊn/ *n.* a steroid hormone which stimulates the preparation of the uterus for pregnancy and maintains the uterus in the event of fertilization. [German: related to PRO-¹, GESTATION]

progestogen /prəʊˈdʒestədʒɪn/ *n.* 1 a steroid hormone (e.g. progesterone)

prognosis

maintaining pregnancy and preventing further ovulation. **2** similar synthetic hormone.

prognosis /prog'nəusıs/ n. (pl. **-noses** /-siːz/) forecast, esp. of the course of a disease. [Greek *gignōskō* know]

prognostic /prog'nostik/ —n. **1** (often foll. by *of*) advance indication, esp. of the course of a disease. **2** prediction, forecast. —adj. (often foll. by *of*) foretelling, predictive. [Latin: related to PRO-GNOSIS]

prognosticate /prog'nosti,keɪt/ v. (**-ting**) **1** (often foll. by *that*) foretell, foresee, prophesy. **2** (of a thing) betoken, indicate. □ **prognostication** /-'keɪʃ(ə)n/ n. **prognosticator** n. [medieval Latin: related to PROGNOSTIC]

programme /'prəʊgræm/ (US **program**) —n. **1** list of events, etc. at a public function etc. **2** radio or television broadcast. **3** plan of events (*programme is dinner and an early night*). **4** course or series of studies, lectures, etc. **5** (usu. **program**) series of coded instructions for a computer etc. —v. (**-mm-**; *US* **-m-**) **1** make a programme of. **2** (usu. **program**) express (a problem) or instruct (a computer) by means of a program. □ **programmable** *adj*. **programmatic** /-grə'mætɪk/ *adj*. **programmer** n. (in sense 5 of n.). [Greek *graphō* write]

progress —n. /'prəʊgres/ **1** forward or onward movement towards a destination. **2** advance or development; improvement (*made little progress*). **3** *hist.* State tour, esp. by royalty. —v. /prə'gres/ **1** move or be moved forward or onward; continue. **2** advance, develop, or improve (*science progresses*). □ **in progress** developing; going on. [Latin *progredior -gress-* go forward]

progression /prə'greʃ(ə)n/ n. **1** progressing. **2** succession; series. [Latin: related to PROGRESS]

progressive /prə'gresɪv/ —adj. **1** moving forward. **2** proceeding step by step; cumulative (*progressive drug use*). **3 a** favouring rapid political or social reform. **b** modern; efficient (*a progressive company*). **4** (of disease, violence, etc.) increasing in severity or extent. **5** (of taxation) increasing with the sum taxed. **6** (of a card-game, dance, etc.) with periodic changes of partners. **7** *Gram.* (of a tense) expressing action in progress, e.g. *am writing, was writing*. —n. (also **Progressive**) advocate of progressive political policies. □ **progressively** *adv*. **progressiveness** n. [French or medieval Latin: related to PROGRESS]

prohibit /prə'hɪbɪt/ v. (**-t-**) (often foll. by *from*) **1** forbid. **2** prevent.

□ **prohibiter** n. **prohibitory** *adj*. [Latin *prohibeo -hibit-*]

prohibited degrees var. of FORBID-DEN DEGREES.

prohibition /ˌprəʊɪ'bɪʃ(ə)n, ˌprəʊhɪ-/ n. **1** forbidding or being forbidden. **2** edict or order that forbids. **3** (usu. **Pro-hibition**) legal ban on the manufacture and sale of alcohol, esp. in the US (1920–33). □ **prohibitionist** n. (in sense 3).

prohibitive /prə'hɪbɪtɪv/ *adj*. **1** prohibiting. **2** (of prices, taxes, etc.) extremely high (*prohibitive price*). □ **prohibitively** *adv*.

project —n. /'prɒdʒekt/ **1** plan; scheme. **2** extensive essay, piece of research, etc. by a student. —v. /prə'dʒekt/ **1** protrude; jut out. **2** throw; cast; impel. **3** extrapolate (results etc.) to a future time; forecast. **4** plan or contrive (a scheme etc.). **5** cause (light, shadow, images, etc.) to fall on a surface. **6** cause (a sound, voice) to be heard at a distance. **7** (often *refl.* or *absol.*) express or promote forcefully or effectively. **8** make a projection of (the earth, sky, etc.). **9 a** (also *absol.*) attribute (an emotion etc.) to an external object or person, esp. unconsciously. **b** (*refl.*) imagine (oneself) having another's feelings, being in the future, etc. [Latin *projicio -ject-* throw forth]

projectile /prə'dʒektaɪl/ —n. **1** missile, esp. fired by a rocket. **2** bullet, shell, etc. —adj. **1** capable of being projected by force, esp. from a gun. **2** projecting or impelling.

projection /prə'dʒekʃ(ə)n/ n. **1** projecting or being projected. **2** thing that projects or obtrudes. **3** presentation or an image etc. on a surface. **4** forecast or estimate (*projection of next year's profits*). **5 a** mental image viewed as an objective reality. **b** unconscious transfer of feelings etc to external objects or persons. **6** representation on a plane surface of any part of the surface of the earth or a celestial sphere (*Mer-cator projection*). □ **projectionist** n. (in sense 3).

projector /prə'dʒektə(r)/ n. apparatus for projecting slides or film on to a screen.

prokaryote /prəʊ'kærɪət/ n. organ-ism in which the chromosomes are not separated from the cytoplasm by a membrane; bacterium. [from PRO-², *karyo-* from Greek *karuon* kernel, *-ote* as in ZYGOTE]

prolactin /prəʊ'læktɪn/ n. hormone that stimulates milk production after childbirth. [from PRO-¹, LACTATION]

prolapse /ˈprəʊlæps/ *n.* (also **prolapsus** /-ˈlæpsəs/) **1** forward or downward displacement of a part or organ. **2** prolapsed womb, rectum, etc. —*v.* (**-sing**) undergo prolapse. [Latin: related to LAPSE]

prolate /ˈprəʊleɪt/ *adj. Geom.* (of a spheroid) lengthened in the direction of a polar diameter. [Latin, = brought forward, prolonged]

prole *adj. & n. derog. colloq.* proletarian. [abbreviation]

prolegomenon /ˌprəʊliˈgɒmɪnən/ *n.* (*pl.* **-mena**) (usu. in *pl.*) preface to a book etc., esp. when critical or discursive. [Greek *legō* say]

proletariat /ˌprəʊliˈteərɪət/ *n.* member of the proletariat. —*n.* member of the proletariat. [Latin *proles* offspring]

proletariat /ˌprəʊliˈteərɪət/ *n.* **1** wage-earners collectively. **2** esp. *derog.* lowest, esp. uneducated, class. [French: related to PROLETARIAN]

proliferate /prəˈlɪfəˌreɪt/ *v.* (**-ting**) **1** reproduce; produce (cells etc.) rapidly. **2** increase rapidly in numbers. □ **proliferation** /-ˈreɪʃ(ə)n/ *n.* [Latin *proles* offspring]

prolific /prəˈlɪfɪk/ *adj.* **1** producing many offspring or much output. **2** (often foll. by *of*) abundantly productive. **3** (often foll. by *in*) abounding, copious. □ **prolifically** *adv.* [medieval Latin: related to PROLIFERATE]

prolix /ˈprəʊlɪks/ *adj.* (of speech, writing, etc.) lengthy; tedious. □ **prolixity** /-ˈlɪksɪtɪ/ *n.* [Latin]

prologue /ˈprəʊlɒg/ *n.* **1** preliminary speech, poem, etc., esp. of a play. **2** (usu. foll. by *to*) introductory event. [Greek *logos* word]

prolong /prəˈlɒŋ/ *v.* **1** extend in time or space. **2** (as **prolonged** *adj.*) lengthy, esp. tediously so. □ **prolongation** /ˌprəʊlɒŋˈgeɪʃ(ə)n/ *n.* [Latin *longus* long]

prom *n. colloq.* **1** = PROMENADE *n.* 1. **2** = PROMENADE CONCERT. [abbreviation]

promenade /ˌprɒməˈnɑːd/ *n.* **1** paved public walk, esp. along the sea front at a resort. **2** walk, ride, or drive, taken esp. for display or pleasure. —*v.* (**-ding**) **1** make a promenade (through). **2** lead (a person etc.) about, esp. for display. [French]

promenade concert *n.* concert with restricted seating and a large area for standing.

promenade deck *n.* upper deck on a passenger ship.

promenader *n.* **1** person who promenades. **2** regular attender at promenade concerts.

Promethean /prəˈmiːθɪən/ *adj.* daring or inventive. [*Prometheus*, a mortal punished by the Greek gods for stealing fire]

promethium /prəˈmiːθɪəm/ *n.* radioactive metallic element of the lanthanide series, found in nuclear waste. [*Prometheus*: see PROMETHEAN]

prominence /ˈprɒmɪnəns/ *n.* **1** being prominent. **2** jutting outcrop, mountain, etc. [Latin: related to PROMINENT]

prominent /ˈprɒmɪnənt/ *adj.* **1** jutting out, projecting. **2** conspicuous. **3** distinguished, important. [Latin *promineo* project]

promiscuous /prəˈmɪskjʊəs/ *adj.* **1** having frequent, esp. casual, sexual relationships. **2** mixed and indiscriminate. **3** *colloq.* carelessly irregular; casual. □ **promiscuity** /ˌprɒmɪˈskjuːɪtɪ/ *n.* **promiscuously** *adv.* [Latin *misceo* mix]

promise /ˈprɒmɪs/ —*n.* **1** assurance that one will or will not undertake a certain action etc. (*promise of help*). **2** sign of future achievements, good results, etc. (*writer of great promise*). —*v.* (**-sing**) **1** (usu. foll. by *to* + infin., or *that* + clause; also *absol.*) make a promise (*promise not to be late*). **2** (often foll. by *to* + infin.) seem likely (to) (*promises to be a good book*). **3** *colloq.* assure (*I promise you, it will not be easy*). □ **promise well** (or ill etc.) hold out good (or bad etc.) prospects. [Latin *promissum* from *mitto miss-* send]

promised land *n.* (prec. by *the*) **1** *Bibl.* Canaan (Gen. 12:7 etc.). **2** any desired place, esp. heaven.

promising *adj.* likely to turn out well; hopeful, full of promise (*promising start*). □ **promisingly** *adv.*

promissory /ˈprɒmɪsərɪ/ *adj.* conveying or implying a promise. [medieval Latin: related to PROMISE]

promissory note *n.* signed document containing a written promise to pay a stated sum.

promo /ˈprəʊməʊ/ *n.* (*pl.* **-s**) *colloq.* **1** (often *attrib.*) promotion, advertising (*promo video*). **2** promotional video, trailer, etc. [abbreviation]

promontory /ˈprɒməntərɪ/ *n.* (*pl.* **-ies**) point of high land jutting out into the sea etc.: headland. [Latin]

promote /prəˈməʊt/ *v.* (**-ting**) **1** (often foll. by *to*) raise (a person) to a higher office, rank, etc. (*promoted to captain*). **2** help forward; encourage (a cause, process, etc.). **3** publicize and sell (a product). **4** *Chess* raise (a pawn) to the rank of queen etc. □ **promotion** /-ˈməʊʃ(ə)n/ *n.* **promotional**

promoter /prɪˈmɔːtə(r)/ adj. [Latin *promoveo -mot-*]

promoter n. 1 person who promotes, esp. a sporting event, theatrical production. 2 (in full **company promoter**) person who promotes the formation of a joint-stock company. [medieval Latin: related to PROMOTE]

prompt —adj. acting, made, or done with alacrity; ready (*prompt reply*). 2 punctually (*at six o'clock promptly*). —v. 1 (usu. foll. by *to*, or infin.) incite; urge (*prompted them to action*). 2 a (also *absol.*) supply a forgotten word etc. to (an actor etc.). b assist (a hesitating speaker) with a suggestion. 3 give rise to; inspire (feeling, thought, action, etc.). —n. 1 a act of prompting. b thing said to prompt an actor etc. c = PROMPTER. 2 *Computing* sign on a VDU screen to show that the system is waiting for input. □ **promptitude** n. **promptly** adv. **promptness** n. [Latin *promptus*]

prompter n. person who prompts actors.

promulgate /ˈprɒməlɡeɪt/ v. (**-ting**) 1 make known to the public; disseminate; promote. 2 proclaim (a decree, news, etc.). □ **promulgation** /-ˈɡeɪʃ(ə)n/ n. **promulgator** n. [Latin]

prone adj. 1 a lying face downwards. b lying flat, prostrate. c having the front part downwards, esp. the palm 2 (usu. foll. by *to*, or *to* + infin.) disposed or liable (*prone to bite his nails*). 3 (usu. in comb.) likely to suffer (*accident-prone*). □ **proneness** n. [Latin]

prong n. each of two or more projecting pointed parts at the end of a fork etc. [origin unknown]

pronominal /prəˈnɒmɪn(ə)l/ adj. of, concerning, or being, a pronoun. [Latin: related to PRONOUN]

pronoun /ˈprəʊnaʊn/ n. word used instead of and to indicate a noun already mentioned or known, esp. to avoid repetition (e.g. *we, their, this, ourselves*). [from PRO-¹, NOUN]

pronounce /prəˈnaʊns/ v. (**-cing**) 1 (also *absol.*) utter or speak (words, sounds, etc.) in a certain, or esp. in the approved, way. 2 utter or proclaim (a judgement, sentence, etc.) officially, formally, or solemnly (*I pronounce you man and wife*). 3 state as one's opinion (*pronounced the beef excellent*). 4 (usu. foll. by *on, for, against, in favour of*) pass judgement (*pronounced for the defendant*). □ **pronounceable** adj. **pronouncement** n. [Latin *nuntio* announce]

pronounced adj. strongly marked; noticeable (*pronounced limp*).

pronto /ˈprɒntəʊ/ adv. *colloq.* promptly, quickly. [Latin: related to PROMPT]

pronunciation /prənʌnsɪˈeɪʃ(ə)n/ n. 1 way of pronouncing a word, esp. with reference to a standard. 2 act of pronouncing. 3 way of pronouncing words etc. [Latin: related to PRONOUNCE]

proof —n. 1 facts, evidence, reasoning, etc. establishing or helping to establish a fact (*no proof that he was there*). 2 demonstration, proving (*not capable of proof*). 3 test, trial (*put them to the proof*). 4 standard of strength of distilled alcohol. 5 trial impression from type or film, for correcting before final printing. 6 step by step resolution of a mathematical or philosophical problem. 7 photographic print made for selection etc. —adj. 1 (often in comb.) impervious to penetration, ill effects, etc. esp. by a specified agent (*proof against corruption; childproof*). 2 being of proof alcoholic strength. —v. 1 make proof of (a printed work). [Latin *proba*: related to PROVE]

proofread v. (past and past part. **-read** /-red/) read and correct (printer's proofs). □ **proofreader** n.

prop¹ —n. 1 rigid, esp. separate, support. 2 person or thing that supports, comforts, etc. —v. (**-pp-**) (often foll. by *against, up*, etc.) support with or as if with a prop. [Low German or Dutch]

prop² n. *colloq.* = PROPERTY 3. [abbreviation]

prop³ n. *colloq.* propeller. [abbreviation]

propaganda /prɒpəˈɡændə/ n. 1 organized propagation of a doctrine by use of publicity, selected information, etc. 2 usu. *derog.* ideas etc. so propagated. □ **propagandist** n. & adj. **propagandize** v. (also **-ise**) (**-zing** or **-sing**). [Latin]

propagate /ˈprɒpəɡeɪt/ v. (**-ting**) 1 a breed (a plant, animal, etc.) from the parent stock. b (*refl.* or *absol.*) (of a plant, animal, etc.) reproduce itself. 2 disseminate (a belief, theory, etc.). 3 transmit (a vibration, earthquake, etc.). □ **propagation** /-ˈɡeɪʃ(ə)n/ n. [Latin *propago*]

propagator n. 1 person or thing that propagates. 2 small heated box for germinating seeds or raising seedlings.

propane /ˈprəʊpeɪn/ n. gaseous hydrocarbon used as bottled fuel. [*propionic acid*: related to PRO-², Greek *piōn* fat]

propanone /ˈprəʊpənəʊn/ n. *Chem.* = ACETONE. [from PROPANE]

propel /prəˈpel/ v. (**-ll-**) drive or push forward; urge on. □ **propellant** n. & adj. [Latin *pello puls-* drive]

propeller *n.* revolving shaft with blades, esp. for propelling a ship or aircraft.

propene /ˈprəʊpiːn/ *n. Chem.* = PROPYLENE. [from PROPANE, ALKENE]

propensity /prəˈpensɪtɪ/ *n.* (*pl.* -ies) inclination, tendency. [Latin *propensus* inclined]

proper /ˈprɒpə(r)/ *adj.* 1 a accurate, correct (*gave him the proper amount*). b fit, suitable, right (*at the proper time*). 2 decent; respectable, esp. excessively so (*not quite proper*). 3 (usu. foll. by *to*) belonging or relating (*respect proper to them*). 4 (usu. placed after the noun) strictly so called; genuine (*this is the crypt, not the cathedral proper*). 5 *colloq.* thorough; complete (*a proper row*). [Latin *proprius* one's own]

proper fraction *n.* fraction less than unity, with the numerator less than the denominator.

properly *adv.* 1 fittingly, suitably (*do it properly*). 2 accurately, correctly (*properly speaking*). 3 rightly. 4 with decency; respectably (*behave properly*). 5 *colloq.* thoroughly (*properly puzzled*).

proper noun *n.* (also **proper name**) capitalized name for an individual person, place, animal, country, title, etc., e.g. *Jane*, *Everest*.

propertied /ˈprɒpətɪd/ *adj.* having property, esp. land.

property /ˈprɒpətɪ/ *n.* (*pl.* -ies) 1 a thing(s) owned; possession, esp. a house, land, etc. (*has money in property*). 2 attribute, quality, or characteristic (*property of dissolving grease*). 3 movable object used on a theatre stage or in a film. [Latin *proprietas*: related to PROPER]

prophecy /ˈprɒfɪsɪ/ *n.* (*pl.* -ies) 1 a prophetic utterance, esp. biblical. b prediction of future events. 2 faculty, practice, etc. of prophesying (*gift of prophecy*). [Greek: related to PROPHET]

prophesy /ˈprɒfɪsaɪ/ *v.* (-ies, -ied) (usu. foll. by *that, who*, etc.) foretell (an event etc.). 2 speak as a prophet; foretell the future. [French *profecier*: related to PROPHECY]

prophet /ˈprɒfɪt/ *n.* (*fem.* **prophetess**) 1 teacher or interpreter of the supposed will of God. 2 a person who foretells events. b spokesman; advocate (*the Prophet of the new order*). 3 (**the Prophet**) Muhammad. [Greek *prophētēs* spokesman]

prophetic /prəˈfetɪk/ *adj.* 1 (often foll. by *of*) containing a prediction; predicting. 2 of a prophet. □ **prophetically** *adv.* [Latin: related to PROPHET]

prophylactic /ˌprɒfɪˈlæktɪk/ *—adj.* tending to prevent disease etc. *—n.* 1

preventive medicine or action. 2 esp. *US* condom. [Greek, = keeping guard before]

prophylaxis /ˌprɒfɪˈlæksɪs/ *n.* preventive treatment against disease. [from PRO-[2], Greek *phulaxis* guarding]

propinquity /prəˈpɪŋkwɪtɪ/ *n.* 1 nearness in space; proximity. 2 close kinship. 3 similarity. [Latin *prope* near]

propitiate /prəˈpɪʃɪeɪt/ *v.* (-ting) appease (an offended person etc.). □ **propitiable** *adj.* **propitiation** /-ˈeɪʃ(ə)n/ *n.* **propitiator** *n.* **propitiatory** /-ʃətərɪ/ *adj.* [Latin: related to PROPITIOUS]

propitious /prəˈpɪʃəs/ *adj.* 1 (of an omen etc.) favourable, auspicious. 2 (often foll. by *for, to*) suitable, advantageous. [Latin *propitius*]

proponent /prəˈpəʊnənt/ *n.* person advocating a motion, theory, or proposal. [Latin: related to PROPOSE]

proportion /prəˈpɔːʃ(ə)n/ *—n.* 1 a comparative part or share (*large proportion of the profits*). b comparative ratio (*proportion of births to deaths*). 2 correct or pleasing relation of things or parts of a thing (*has fine proportions*; *exaggerated out of all proportion*). 3 (in *pl.*) dimensions; size (*large proportions*). 4 *Math.* equality of ratios between two pairs of quantities, e.g. 3:5 and 9:15. *—v.* (usu. foll. by *to*) make proportionate (*proportion the punishment to the crime*). [Latin: related to PORTION]

proportional *adj.* in due proportion; comparable (*proportional increase in the expense*). □ **proportionally** *adv.*

proportional representation *n.* electoral system in which parties gain seats in proportion to the number of votes cast for them.

proportionate /prəˈpɔːʃənət/ *adj.* = PROPORTIONAL. □ **proportionately** *adv.*

proposal /prəˈpəʊz(ə)l/ *n.* 1 a act of proposing something. b course of action etc. proposed. 2 offer of marriage.

propose /prəˈpəʊz/ *v.* (-sing) 1 (also *absol.*) put forward for consideration or as a plan; suggest. 2 (usu. foll. by + infin., or verbal noun) intend; purpose (*propose to open a café*). 3 (usu. foll. by *to*) offer oneself in marriage. 4 nominate (a person) as a member of a society, for an office, etc. □ **propose a toast** (or **somebody's health**) ask people to drink to someone's health. □ **proposer** *n.* [Latin *pono posit-* place]

proposition /ˌprɒpəˈzɪʃ(ə)n/ *—n.* 1 statement, assertion. 2 scheme proposed; proposal. 3 *Logic* statement subject to proof or disproof. 4 *colloq.* problem,

opponent, prospect, etc. for considera-tion (*difficult proposition*). **5** *Math.* for-mal statement of a theorem or problem. **6 a** often including the demonstration. **6 b** likely commercial etc. enterprise etc. **b** person regarded similarly. **7** *colloq.* sex-ual proposal. —*v. colloq.* make a (esp. sexual) proposal to (*the propositioned her*). [Latin: related to PROPOSE]

propound /prə'paʊnd/ *v.* offer for con-sideration; propose. [*propo(u)ne* from Latin: related to PROPOSE]

proprietary /prə'praɪətəri/ *adj.* **1 a** of or holding property (*proprietary classes*). **b** of a proprietor (*proprietary rights*). **2** held in private ownership. [Latin *proprietarius*: related to PROP-ERTY]

proprietary medicine *n.* drug, med-icine, etc. produced by a company, usu. under a trade name.

proprietary name *n.* (also **propriet-ary term**) registered name of a product etc. as a trade mark.

proprietor /prə'praɪətə(r)/ *n.* (*fem.* **pro-prietress**) **1** holder of property. **2** owner of a business etc., esp. of a hotel. □ **proprietorial** /-'tɔːrɪəl/ *adj.* [related to PROPRIETARY]

propriety /prə'praɪətɪ/ *n.* (*pl.* **-ies**) **1** fitness; rightness. **2** correctness of be-haviour or morals. **3** (in *pl.*) details of correct conduct. [French: related to PROPERTY]

propulsion /prə'pʌlʃ(ə)n/ *n.* **1** driving or pushing forward. **2** impelling influence. □ **propulsive** /-'pʌlsɪv/ *adj.* [related to PROPEL]

propylene /'prəʊpɪliːn/ *n.* gaseous hy-drocarbon used in the manufacture of chemicals. [from *propyl,* a univalent radical of propane]

pro rata /prəʊ 'rɑːtə/ —*adj.* propor-tional. —*adv.* proportionally. [Latin]

prorogue /prə'rəʊg/ *v.* (**-gues, -gued, -guing**) **1** discontinue the meetings of (a parliament etc.) without dissolving it. **2** (of a parliament etc.) be prorogued. □ **prorogation** /ˌprəʊrə'geɪʃ(ə)n/ *n.* [Latin *prorogo* extend]

prosaic /prə'zeɪɪk/ *adj.* **1** like prose, lacking poetic beauty. **2** unromantic; dull; commonplace. □ **prosaically** *adv.* [Latin: related to PROSE]

pros and cons *n.pl.* reasons or con-siderations for and against a proposi-tion etc.

proscenium /prə'siːnɪəm/ *n.* (*pl.* **-s** or **-nia**) part of the stage in front of the curtain and the enclosing arch. [Greek: related to SCENE]

proscribe /prə'skraɪb/ *v.* (**-bing**) **1** for-bid, esp. by law. **2** reject or denounce (a practice etc.). **3** outlaw (a person). □

proscription /-'skrɪp(ʃ)(ə)n/ *n.* **pro-scriptive** /-'skrɪptɪv/ *adj.* [Latin. = pub-lish in writing]

■ **Usage** *Proscribe* is sometimes con-fused with *prescribe.*

prose /prəʊz/ —*n.* **1** ordinary written or spoken language not in verse. **2** passage of prose, esp. for translation into a foreign language. **3** dull or matter-of-fact quality (*prose of existence*). —*v.* (**-sing**) talk tediously. [Latin *prosa* from *oratio* straightforward (discourse)]

prosecute /'prɒsɪkjuːt/ *v.* (**-ting**) **1 a** (also *absol.*) institute legal proceedings against (a person), or with reference to (a claim, crime, etc.) (*decided not to prosecute*). **2** *formal* carry on (a trade, pursuit, etc.). □ **prosecutor** *n.* [Latin *prosequor -secut-* pursue]

prosecution /ˌprɒsɪ'kjuːʃ(ə)n/ *n.* **1 a** institution and continuation of (esp. criminal) legal proceedings. **b** prosecut-ing party in a court case. **2** prosecuting or being prosecuted (*in the prosecution of his hobby*).

proselyte /'prɒsɪlaɪt/ *n.* **1** person con-verted, esp. recently, from one opinion, creed, party, etc., to another. **2** convert to Judaism. □ **proselytism** /-la,tɪz(ə)m/ *n.* [Latin *proselytus* from Greek]

proselytize /'prɒsɪlɪˌtaɪz/ *v.* (also **-ise**) (**-zing** or **-sing**) (also *absol.*) convert or seek to convert from one belief etc. to another.

prose poem *n.* piece of poetic writing in prose.

prosody /'prɒsədɪ/ *n.* **1** science of versi-fication. **2** the study of speech-rhythms. □ **prosodic** /prə'sɒdɪk/ *adj.* **prosodist** *n.* [Greek *pros* to: related to ODE]

prospect —*n.* /'prɒspekt/ **1 a** (often in *pl.*) expectation, esp. of success in a career etc. (*job with no prospects*). **b** something one expects or looks for (*a prospect of meeting him*). **2** extensive view of landscape etc. (*striking pro-spect*). **3** mental picture. **4** possible or probable customer, subscriber, etc. —*v.* /prə'spekt/ (usu. foll. by *for*) explore, search (esp. a region) for gold etc. □ **prospector** /prə'spektə(r)/ *n.* [Latin: related to PROSPECTUS]

prospective /prə'spektɪv/ *adj.* some day to be; expected; future (*prospective bridegroom*). [Latin: related to PRO-SPECT]

prospectus /prə'spektəs/ *n.* (*pl.* **-tuses**) printed document advertising or de-scribing a school, commercial enter-prise, forthcoming book, etc. [Latin. = prospect, from *prospicio -spect-* look forward]

prosper *v.* be successful, thrive. [Latin *prospero*]

prosperity /prɒˈspɛrɪtɪ/ *n.* prosperous state; wealth; success.

prosperous /ˈprɒspərəs/ *adj.* **1** successful; rich; thriving. **2** auspicious (*prosperous wind*). □ **prosperously** *adv.* [French from Latin]

prostate /ˈprɒsteɪt/ *n.* (in full **prostate gland**) gland round the neck of the bladder in male mammals, releasing part of the semen. □ **prostatic** /-ˈstætɪk/ *adj.* [Greek *prostatēs* one who stands before]

prosthesis /prɒsˈθiːsɪs/ *n.* (*pl.* **-theses** /-siːz/) **1** artificial leg etc; false tooth, breast, etc. **2** branch of surgery dealing with prostheses. □ **prosthetic** /-ˈθetɪk/ *adj.* [Greek, = placing in addition]

prostitute /ˈprɒstɪtjuːt/ —*n.* **1** woman who engages in sexual activity for payment. **2** (usu. **male prostitute**) man or boy who engages in sexual activity, esp. with homosexual men, for payment. —*v.* (**-ting**) **1** (esp. *refl.*) make a prostitute of (esp. oneself). **2** misuse or offer (one's talents, skills, name, etc.) for money etc. □ **prostitution** /-ˈtjuːʃ(ə)n/ *n.* [Latin *prostitu-tut-* offer for sale]

prostrate —*adj.* /ˈprɒstreɪt/ **1 a** lying face downwards, esp. in submission. **b** lying horizontally. **2** overcome, esp. by grief, exhaustion, etc. **3** growing along the ground. —*v.* /prɒˈstreɪt/ (**-ting**) **1** lay or throw (esp. a person) flat. **2** *refl.* throw (oneself) down in submission etc. **3** overcome; make weak. □ **prostration** /-ˈstreɪʃ(ə)n/ *n.* [Latin *prostra-strat-* throw in front]

prosy /ˈprəʊzɪ/ *adj.* (**-ier, -iest**) tedious, commonplace, dull (*prosy talk*). □ **prosily** *adv.* **prosiness** *n.*

protactinium /ˌprəʊtækˈtɪnɪəm/ *n.* radioactive metallic element. [German: related to ACTINIUM]

protagonist /prəˈtæɡənɪst/ *n.* **1** chief person in a drama, story, etc. **2** leading person in a contest etc.; principal performer. **3** (usu. foll. by *of, for*) advocate or champion of a cause etc. (*protagonist of women's rights*). [Greek: related to PROTO-, *agōnistēs* actor]

■ **Usage** The use of *protagonist* in sense 3 is considered incorrect by some people.

protean /prəʊˈtiːən/ *adj.* variable, taking many forms; versatile. [*Proteus*, Greek sea-god who took various shapes]

protect /prəˈtekt/ *v.* **1** (often foll. by *from, against*) keep (a person, thing, etc.) safe; defend, guard. **2** shield (home industry) from competition with import duties. [Latin *tego tect-* cover]

protection /prəˈtekʃ(ə)n/ *n.* **1 a** protecting or being protected; defence. **b** thing, person, or animal that protects. **2** (also **protectionism**) theory or practice of protecting home industries. **3** *colloq.* **a** immunity from violence etc. obtained by payment to gangsters etc. **b** (in full **protection money**) money so paid. □ **protectionist** *n. & adj.*

protective /prəˈtektɪv/ *adj.* protecting; intended or tending to protect. □ **protectively** *adv.* **protectiveness** *n.*

protective custody *n.* detention of a person for his or her own protection.

protector *n.* (*fem.* **protectress**) **1** person or thing that protects. **2** *hist.* regent ruling during the minority or absence of the sovereign. □ **protectorship** *n.*

protectorate /prəˈtektərət/ *n.* **1 a** State that is controlled and protected by another. **b** this relation. **2** *hist.* office of the protector of a kingdom or State. **b** period of this, esp. in England 1653–9.

protégé /ˈprɒtɪˌʒeɪ/ *n.* (*fem.* **protégée** pronunc. same) person under the protection, patronage, tutelage, etc. of another. [French: related to PROTECT]

protein /ˈprəʊtiːn/ *n.* any of a group of organic compounds composed of one or more chains of amino acids and forming an essential part of all living organisms. [Greek *prōtos* first]

pro tem /prəʊ ˈtem/ *adj. & adv. colloq.* = PRO TEMPORE. [abbreviation]

pro tempore /prəʊ ˈtempərɪ/ *adj. & adv.* for the time being. [Latin]

Proterozoic /ˌprɒtərəʊˈzəʊɪk/ *Geol.* —*adj.* of the later part of the Precambrian era. —*n.* this time. [Greek *proteros* former, *zōē* life]

protest —*n.* /ˈprəʊtest/ **1** statement or act of dissent or disapproval. **2** *Law* written declaration that a bill has been presented and payment or acceptance refused. —*v.* /prəˈtest/ **1** (usu. foll. by *against, at, about, etc.*) make a protest. **2** affirm (one's innocence etc.) solemnly. **3** *Law* write or obtain a protest in regard to (a bill). **4** *US* object to (a decision etc.). □ **under protest** unwillingly. □ **protester** *n.* (also **protestor**). [Latin *protestor* declare formally]

Protestant /ˈprɒtɪst(ə)nt/ —*n.* member or follower of any of the Churches separating from the Roman Catholic Church after the Reformation. —*adj.* of the Protestant Churches or their members etc. □ **Protestantism** *n.* [related to PROTEST]

protestation /ˌprɒtɪˈsteɪʃ(ə)n/ *n.* **1** strong affirmation. **2** protest. [Latin: related to PROTEST]

protium /ˈprəʊtɪəm/ *n.* ordinary isotope of hydrogen. [Latin: related to PROTO-]

proto- *comb. form* first. [Greek *prōtos*]

protocol /ˈprəutəkɒl/ —*n.* **1** official formality and etiquette, esp. as observed on State occasions etc. **2** original draft of esp. the terms of a treaty. **3** formal statement of a transaction. —*v.* (-ll-) draw up or record in a protocol. [Greek *kolla* glue]

proton /ˈprəutɒn/ *n.* elementary particle with a positive electric charge equal to that of an electron, and occurring in all atomic nuclei. [Greek *prōtos* first]

protoplasm /ˈprəutəˌplæz(ə)m/ *n.* material comprising the living part of a cell, consisting of a nucleus and membrane-enclosed cytoplasm. □ **protoplasmic** /-ˈplæzmɪk/ *adj.* [Greek: related to PROTO-, PLASMA]

prototype /ˈprəutətaɪp/ *n.* **1** original as a pattern for imitations, improved forms, representations, etc. **2** trial model or preliminary version of a vehicle, machine, etc. □ **prototypic** /-ˈtɪpɪk/ *adj.* **prototypical** /-ˈtɪpɪk(ə)l/ *adj.* [Greek: related to PROTO-]

protozoon /ˌprəutəˈzəuɒn/ *n.* (also **protozoan** /-ˈzəuən/) (*pl.* **protozoa** /-ˈzəuə/ or **-s**) unicellular microscopic organism, e.g. the amoeba. □ **protozoic** *adj.* (also **protozoan** *adj.*) of this group. [from PROTO-, Greek *zōion* animal]

protract /prəˈtrækt/ *v.* (often as **protracted** *adj.*) prolong or lengthen. □ **protraction** *n.* [Latin *traho tract-* draw]

protractor *n.* instrument for measuring angles, usu. in the form of a graduated semicircle.

protrude /prəˈtruːd/ *v.* (**-ding**) thrust forward; stick out; project. □ **protrusion** *n.* **protrusive** *adj.* [Latin *trudo trus-* thrust]

protuberant /prəˈtjuːbərənt/ *adj.* bulging out; prominent. □ **protuberance** *n.* [Latin: related to TUBER]

proud *adj.* **1** feeling greatly honoured or pleased (*proud to know him*). **2 a** (often foll. by *of*) haughty, arrogant (*too proud to speak to us*). **b** (often in *comb.*) having a proper pride; satisfied (*house-proud; proud of a job well done*). **3 a** of an occasion, action, etc.) justly arousing or showing pride (*proud day; proud smile*). **4** imposing, splendid. **5** (often foll. by *of*) slightly projecting (*nail stood proud of the plank*). □ **do proud** *colloq.* treat with lavish generosity or honour (*did us proud*). □ **proudly** *adv.* [French *prud* valiant]

prove /pruːv/ *v.* (**-ving;** *past part.* **proved** or **proven** /ˈpruːv(ə)n, ˈprəu-/) **1** (often foll. by *that*) demonstrate the truth of by evidence or argument. **2 a** (usu. foll. by *to* + infin.) be found (*it proved to be untrue*). **b** emerge as (*will prove the winner*). **3** test the accuracy of (a calculation). **4** establish the validity of (a will). **5** (of dough) rise in breadmaking. □ **not proven** (in Scottish Law) verdict that there is insufficient evidence to establish guilt or innocence. **prove oneself** show one's abilities, courage, etc. □ **provable** *adj.* [Latin *probo* test, approve]

■ **Usage** The use of *proven* as the past participle is uncommon except in certain expressions, such as of *proven ability*. It is, however, standard in Scots and American English.

provenance /ˈprɒvɪnəns/ *n.* origin or place of origin; history. [French *provenir* from Latin]

Provençal /ˌprɒvɒnˈsɑːl/ —*adj.* of Provence. —*n.* native or language of Provence. [French: related to PROVINCE]

provender /ˈprɒvɪndə(r)/ *n.* **1** animal fodder. **2** *joc.* food. [Latin: related to PREBEND]

proverb /ˈprɒvɜːb/ *n.* short pithy saying in general use, held to embody a general word). [Latin *proverbium* from *verbum* word]

proverbial /prəˈvɜːbɪəl/ *adj.* **1** (esp. of a characteristic) well known; notorious (*his proverbial honesty*). **2** of or referred to in a proverb (*proverbial ill-wind*). □ **proverbially** *adv.* [Latin: related to PROVERB]

provide /prəˈvaɪd/ *v.* (**-ding**) **1** supply; furnish (*provided me with food; provided a chance*). **2 a** (usu. foll. by *for, against*) take due preparation. **b** (usu. foll. by *for*) take care of a person etc. with money, food, etc. (*provides for a large family*). **3** (usu. foll. by *that*) stipulate in a will, statute, etc. □ **provider** *n.* [Latin *provideo -vis-* foresee]

provided *conj.* (often foll. by *that*) on the condition or understanding that.

providence /ˈprɒvɪdəns/ *n.* **1** protective care of God or nature. **2** (**Providence**) God in this aspect. **3** foresight; thrift. [Latin: related to PROVIDE]

provident /ˈprɒvɪd(ə)nt/ *adj.* having or showing foresight; thrifty. [Latin: related to PROVIDE]

providential /ˌprɒvɪˈdenʃ(ə)l/ *adj.* **1** of or by divine foresight or interposition. **2** opportune, lucky. □ **providentially** *adv.*

Provident Society *n.* = FRIENDLY SOCIETY.

providing *conj.* = PROVIDED.

province /ˈprɒvɪns/ *n.* **1** principal administrative division of a country etc. **2** (**the provinces**) country outside a capital city, esp. regarded as uncultured or unsophisticated. **3** sphere of action.

provincial

business (*outside my province*). **4** branch of learning etc. (*in the province of aesthetics*). **5** district under an archbishop or metropolitan. **6** territory outside Italy under an ancient Roman governor. [Latin *provincia*]

provincial /prə'vɪnʃ(ə)l/ —*adj.* **1** of a province or provinces. **2** unsophisticated or uncultured. —*n.* **1** inhabitant of a province or the provinces. **2** unsophisticated or uncultured person. □ **provincialism** *n.*

provision /prə'vɪʒ(ə)n/ —*n.* **1 a** act of providing (*provision of nurseries*). **b** preparation, esp. for the future (*made provision for their old age*). **2** (in *pl.*) food, drink, etc., esp. for an expedition. **3** legal or formal stipulation or proviso. —*v.* supply with provisions. [Latin: related to PROVIDE]

provisional —*adj.* **1** providing for immediate needs only; temporary. **2** (**Provisional**) of the unofficial wing of the IRA, using terrorism. —*n.* (**Provisional**) member of the Provisional wing of the IRA. □ **provisionally** *adv.*

proviso /prə'vaɪzəʊ/ *n.* (*pl.* -**s**) **1** stipulation. **2** clause containing this. □ **provisory** *adj.* [Latin, = it being provided] **Provo** /'prəʊvəʊ/ *n.* (*pl.* -**s**) *colloq.* Provisional. [abbreviation]

provocation /ˌprɒvə'keɪʃ(ə)n/ *n.* **1** provoking or being provoked (*did it under severe provocation*). **2** cause of annoyance.

provocative /prə'vɒkətɪv/ *adj.* **1** (usu. foll. by *of*) tending to provoke, esp. anger or sexual desire. **2** intentionally annoying or controversial. □ **provocatively** *adv.* **provocativeness** *n.*

provoke /prə'vəʊk/ *v.* (-**king**) **1** (often foll. by *to*, or *to* + infin.) rouse or incite (*provoked him to fury*). **2** call forth; instigate; cause (indignation, an inquiry, process, etc.). **3** (usu. foll. by *into* + verbal noun) irritate or stimulate (a person) (*provoked him into retaliating*). **4** tempt; allure. [Latin *provoco* call forth]

provost /'prɒvəst/ *n.* **1** head of some (esp. Oxbridge) colleges. **2** head of a cathedral chapter. **3** = PROVOST MARSHAL. [Latin *propositus* from *pono* place]

provost marshal /prə'vəʊ/ *n.* head of military police in camp or on active service.

prow *n.* **1** fore-part or bow of a ship. **2** pointed or projecting front part. [French *proue* from Greek *prōira*]

prowess /'praʊɪs/ *n.* **1** skill, expertise. **2** valour, gallantry. [French: related to PROUD]

prowl —*v.* (often foll. by *about*, *around*) roam (a place) esp. stealthily or restlessly or in search of prey, plunder, etc. —*n.* act of prowling. □ **on the prowl** prowling. □ **prowler** *n.* [origin unknown]

prox. *abbr.* proximo.

proximate /'prɒksɪmət/ *adj.* **1** nearest or next before or after (in place, order, time, causation, thought process, etc.). **2** approximate. [Latin *proximus* nearest]

proximity /prɒk'sɪmɪtɪ/ *n.* nearness in space, time, etc. (*in close proximity*). [Latin: related to PROXIMATE]

proximo /'prɒksɪˌməʊ/ *adj. Commerce* of next month (*the third proximo*). [Latin, = in the next (*mense* month)]

proxy /'prɒksɪ/ *n.* (*pl.* -**ies**) (also *attrib.*) **1** authorization for esp. voting or deputy (*proxy vote; married by proxy*). **2** person authorized to act thus. **3 a** written authorization for esp. proxy voting. **b** proxy vote. [obsolete *procuracy* procuration]

prude /pruːd/ *n.* excessively (often affectedly) squeamish or sexually modest person. □ **prudery** *n.* **prudish** *adj.* **prudishly** *adv.* **prudishness** *n.* [French: related to PROUD]

prudent /'pruːd(ə)nt/ *adj.* cautious; politic. □ **prudence** *n.* **prudently** *adv.* [Latin *prudens* -*ent*-: related to PROVIDENT]

prudential /pruː'denʃ(ə)l/ *adj.* of or showing prudence. □ **prudentially** *adv.*

prune[1] /pruːn/ *n.* dried plum. [Latin *prunum* from Greek]

prune[2] /pruːn/ *v.* (-**ning**) **1 a** (often foll. by *down*) trim (a bush etc.) by cutting away dead or overgrown branches etc. **b** (usu. foll. by *off*, *away*) lop (branches etc.) thus. **2** reduce (costs etc.) (*prune expenses*). **3 a** (often foll. by *of*) clear or remove superfluities from. **b** remove (superfluities). [French *prooignier* from Romanic: related to ROUND]

prurient /'prʊərɪənt/ *adj.* having or encouraging unhealthy sexual curiosity. □ **prurience** *n.* [Latin *prurio* itch]

Prussian /'prʌʃ(ə)n/ —*adj.* of Prussia, or esp. its rigidly militaristic tradition. —*n.* native of Prussia. [*Prussia*, former German state]

Prussian blue *n.* & *adj.* (as adj. often hyphenated) deep blue (pigment).

prussic acid /'prʌsɪk/ *n.* hydrocyanic acid. [French]

pry /praɪ/ *v.* (**pries**, **pried**) **1** (usu. foll. by *into*) inquire impertinently. **2** (usu. foll. by *into*, *about*, etc.) look or peer inquisitively. [origin unknown]

PS *abbr.* postscript.

salm /sɑːm/ n. **1** (also **Psalm**) sacred song, esp. from the Book of Psalms, esp. numerically chanted in a service. **2** (the **Psalms** or **the book of Psalms**) Old Testament book containing the Psalms. [Latin *psalmus* from Greek]

salmist n. composer of a psalm.

salmody /ˈsɑːmədi, ˈsæl-/ n. practice or art of singing psalms, hymns, etc., esp. in public worship. [Greek: related to PSALM]

salter /ˈsɔːltə(r)/ n. **1** the Book of Psalms. **2** (**psalter**) version or copy of this. [Old English and French from Greek *psalterion* stringed instrument]

saltery /ˈsɔːltəri/ n. (pl. **-ies**) ancient and medieval instrument like a dulcimer but played by plucking the strings. [Latin: related to PSALTER]

sephology /sɪˈfɒlədʒi/ n. the statistical study of voting etc. □ **psephologist** n. [Greek *psēphos* pebble, vote]

seud /sjuːd/ colloq. = adj. Greek intellec-tually pretentious: not genuine. —n. such a person; poseur. [from PSEUDO-]

seudo /ˈsjuːdəʊ/ adj. & n. (pl. **-s**) = PSEUD.

seudo- comb. form (also **pseud-** before a vowel) **1** false; not genuine (*pseudo-intellectual*). **2** resembling or imitating (*pseudo-acid*). [Greek *pseudēs* false]

seudonym /ˈsjuːdənɪm/ n. fictitious name, esp. of an author. [Greek: related to PSEUDO-, *onoma* name]

si /psaɪ, saɪ/ n. twenty-third letter of the Greek alphabet (Ψ, ψ). [Greek]

si² abbr. pounds per square inch.

sittacosis /ˌsɪtəˈkəʊsɪs/ n. contagious viral disease of esp. parrots, transmissible to human beings. [Greek *psittakos* parrot]

soriasis /səˈraɪəsɪs/ n. skin disease marked by red scaly patches. [Greek *psōra* itch]

sst int. (also **pst**) whispered exclama-tion to attract a person's attention. [imitative]

PSV abbr. public service vehicle.

psych /saɪk/ v. colloq. **1** (usu. foll. by **up**; often refl.) prepare (oneself or another) mentally for an ordeal etc. **2** (often foll. by **out**) intimidate or frighten (a person). **3** esp. for one's own advantage. **3** (usu. foll. by **out**) analyse (a person's motiva-tion etc.; for one's own advantage (*can't psych him out*)). [abbreviation]

psyche /ˈsaɪki/ n. the soul, spirit, or mind. [Latin from Greek]

psychedelia /ˌsaɪkəˈdiːliə/ n. pl. **1** psy-chedelic culture. **2** subculture as-sociated with these.

psychedelic /ˌsaɪkəˈdelɪk/ adj. **1 a** expanding the mind's awareness etc., esp. with hallucinogenic drugs. **b**

hallucinatory: bizarre. **c** (of a drug) pro-ducing hallucinations. **2** colloq. **a** produ-cing a hallucinatory effect: vivid in col-our or design etc. **b** (of colours, patterns, etc.) bright, bold, and often abstract. [Greek *psukhē* mind *dēlos* clear]

psychiatry /saɪˈkaɪətri/ n. the study and treatment of mental disease. □ **psy-chiatric** /ˌ-kiˈætrɪk/ adj. **psychiatrist** n. [from PSYCHO-, Greek *iatros* phys-ician]

psychic /ˈsaɪkɪk/ —adj. **1 a** (of a person) considered to have occult powers such as telepathy, clairvoyance, etc. **b** super-natural. **2** of the soul or mind. —n. person considered to have psychic powers: medium. [Greek *psukhē* soul, mind]

psychical adj. **1** concerning psychic phenomena or faculties (*psychical re-search*). **2** of the soul or mind. □ **psych-ically** adv.

psycho /ˈsaɪkəʊ/ colloq. —n. (pl. **-s**) psy-chopath. —adj. psychopathic. [abbrevia-tion]

psycho- comb. form of the mind or psychology. [Greek: related to PSYCHE]

psychoanalysis /ˌsaɪkəʊəˈnæləsɪs/ n. treatment of mental disorders by bringing repressed fears and conflicts into the conscious mind over a long course of interviews. □ **psychoanalyse** /-ˈænəˌlaɪz/ v. (-sing). **psychoanalyst** /-ˈænəlɪst/ n. **psychoanalytic** /-ˌænəˈlɪtɪk/ adj. **psychoanalytical** /-ˌænəˈlɪtɪk(ə)l/ adj.

psychokinesis /ˌsaɪkəʊkɪˈniːsɪs/ n. movement of objects supposedly by tele-pathy or mental effort.

psychological /ˌsaɪkəˈdʒɪk(ə)l/ adj. **1** of or arising in the mind. **2** of psycho-logy. **3** colloq. (of an ailment etc.) imaginary (*her cold is psychological*). □ **psychologically** adv.

psychological block n. mental inhibi-tion caused by emotional factors.

psychological moment n. best time for achieving a particular effect or pur-pose.

psychological warfare n. campaign directed at reducing enemy morale.

psychology /saɪˈkɒlədʒi/ n. (pl. **-ies**) **1** the study of the human mind. **2** treatise on or theory of this. **3 a** mental charac-teristics etc. of a person or group. **b** mental aspects of an activity, situation, etc. (*psychology of crime*). □ **psycho-logist** n.

psychopath /ˈsaɪkəˌpæθ/ n. **1** mentally deranged person, esp. showing abnor-mal or violent social behaviour. **2** men-tally or emotionally unstable person. □ **psychopathic** /-ˈpæθɪk/ adj.

psychopathology /ˌsaɪkəʊpəˈθɒlədʒɪ/ n. 1 the study of mental disorders. 2 mentally or behaviourally disordered state.

psychopathy /saɪˈkɒpəθɪ/ n. psychopathic or psychologically abnormal behaviour.

psychosis /saɪˈkəʊsɪs/ n. (pl. **-choses** /-siːz/) severe mental disorder with loss of contact with reality. [Greek: related to PSYCHE]

psychosomatic /ˌsaɪkəʊsəˈmætɪk/ adj. 1 (of a bodily disorder) mental, not physical, in origin. 2 of the mind and body together.

psychotherapy /ˌsaɪkəʊˈθerəpɪ/ n. treatment of mental disorder by psychological means. □ **psychotherapeutic** /-ˈpjuːtɪk/ adj. **psychotherapist** n.

psychotic /saɪˈkɒtɪk/ —adj. of or suffering from a psychosis. —n. psychotic person.

PT abbr. physical training.

Pt symb. platinum.

pt abbr. 1 part. 2 pint. 3 point. 4 Naut. port.

PTA abbr. parent-teacher association.

ptarmigan /ˈtɑːmɪgən/ n. game-bird with a grouselike appearance. [Gaelic]

Pte. abbr. Private (soldier).

pteridophyte /ˈterɪdəˌfaɪt/ n. flowerless plant, e.g. ferns, club-mosses, etc. [Greek pteris fern]

pterodactyl /ˌterəˈdæktɪl/ n. large extinct flying reptile. [Greek pteron wing, DACTYL]

pterosaur /ˈterəˌsɔː(r)/ n. flying reptile with large batlike wings. [Greek pteron wing, saura lizard]

PTO abbr. please turn over.

Ptolemaic /ˌtɒlɪˈmeɪɪk/ adj. hist. of Ptolemy or his theories. [Greek Ptolemaios, name of a 2nd-c. astronomer]

Ptolemaic system n. theory that the earth is the stationary centre of the universe.

ptomaine /ˈtəʊmeɪn/ n. any of various esp. toxic amine compounds in putrefying matter. [Greek ptōma corpse]

Pu symb. plutonium.

pub n. colloq. public house. [abbreviation]

pub-crawl n. colloq. drinking tour of several pubs.

puberty /ˈpjuːbətɪ/ n. period of sexual maturation. □ **pubertal** adj. [Latin puber adult]

pubes[1] /ˈpjuːbiːz/ n. (pl. same) 1 lower part of the abdomen at the front of the pelvis. 2 colloq. pubic hair. [Latin]

pubes[2] pl. of PUBIS.

pubescence /pjuːˈbes(ə)ns/ n. 1 beginning of puberty. 2 soft down on plants, or on animals, esp. insects. □ **pubescent** adj. [Latin: related to PUBES]

pubic /ˈpjuːbɪk/ adj. of the pubes or pubis.

pubis /ˈpjuːbɪs/ n. (pl. **pubes** /-biːz/) either of a pair of bones forming the two sides of the pelvis. [Latin os pubis bone of the PUBES]

public /ˈpʌblɪk/ —adj. 1 of the people as a whole (public holiday). 2 open to or shared by all (public baths). 3 done or existing openly (public apology). 4 (of a service, funds, etc.) provided by or concerning government (public money; public records). 5 of or involved in the affairs, esp. the government or entertainment, of the community (distinguished public career; public figures). —n. 1 (as sing. or pl.) community, or members of it, in general. 2 specified section of the community (reading public; my public). □ **go public** 1 become a public company. 2 reveal one's plans etc. in public openly, publicly. □ **publicly** adv. [Latin]

public-address system n. set of loudspeakers, microphones, amplifiers, etc., used in addressing large audiences.

publican /ˈpʌblɪkən/ n. keeper of a public house. [Latin: related to PUBLIC]

publication /ˌpʌblɪˈkeɪʃ(ə)n/ n. 1 a preparation and issuing of a book, newspaper, etc. to the public. b book etc. so issued. 2 making something publicly known. [Latin: related to PUBLIC]

public bar n. less or least expensive bar in a public house.

public company n. company that sells shares on the open market.

public convenience n. public lavatory.

public enemy n. notorious wanted criminal.

public figure n. famous person.

public health n. provision of adequate sanitation, drainage, etc. by government.

public house n. inn providing alcoholic drinks for consumption on the premises.

publicist /ˈpʌblɪsɪst/ n. publicity agent or public relations officer.

publicity /pʌbˈlɪsɪtɪ/ n. 1 public exposure. 2 a advertising. b material used for this. [French: related to PUBLIC]

publicize /ˈpʌblɪˌsaɪz/ v. (also **-ise**) (**-zing** or **-sing**) advertise; make publicly known.

public lending right n. right of authors to payment when their books etc. are lent by public libraries.

public opinion n. views, esp. moral, that are generally prevalent.

public ownership n. State ownership of the means of production, distribution, or exchange.

public prosecutor n. law officer acting on behalf of the State or in the public interest.

public relations n.pl. (usu. treated as sing.) professional promotion of a favourable public image, esp. by a company, famous person, etc.

public relations officer n. person employed to promote public relations.

public school n. 1 private fee-paying secondary school, esp. for boarders. 2 US, Austral., & Scot. non-fee-paying school.

public sector n. State-controlled part of an economy, industry, etc.

public servant n. State official.

public spirit n. willingness to engage in community action. □ **public-spirited** adj.

public transport n. buses, trains, etc., charging set fares and running on fixed routes.

public utility n. organization supplying water, gas, etc. to the community.

public works n.pl. building operations etc. done by or for the State.

publish /ˈpʌblɪʃ/ v. 1 (also absol.) prepare and issue (a book, newspaper, etc.) for public sale. 2 make generally known. 3 announce formally. [Latin: related to PUBLIC]

publisher n. person or (esp.) company that publishes books etc. for sale.

puce adj. & n. dark red or purple-brown. [Latin pulex flea]

puck[1] n. rubber disc used as a ball in ice hockey. [origin unknown]

puck[2] n. mischievous or evil sprite. □ **puckish** adj. **puckishly** adv. **puckishness** n. [Old English]

pucker —v. (often foll. by up) gather into wrinkles, folds, or bulges (this seam is puckered up). —n. such a wrinkle, bulge, fold, etc. [origin unknown]

pud /pʊd/ n. colloq. = PUDDING. [abbreviation]

pudding /ˈpʊdɪŋ/ n. 1 a any of various sweet cooked dishes (rice pudding). b savoury dish containing flour, suet, etc. (steak and kidney pudding). c sweet course of a meal. d any of various sausages stuffed with oatmeal, spices, blood, etc. (black pudding). 2 colloq. plump, stupid, or lazy person. □ **puddingy** adj. [Latin botellus sausage]

puddle /ˈpʌd(ə)l/ —n. 1 small pool, esp. of rainwater. 2 clay and sand worked with water used as a watertight covering for embankments etc. —v. (-ling) 1 knead (clay and sand) into puddle. 2 stir (molten iron) to produce wrought iron.

by expelling carbon. □ **puddly** adj. [Old English]

pudendum /pjuˈdendəm/ n. (pl. pudenda) (usu. in pl.) genitals, esp. of a woman. [Latin pudeo be ashamed]

pudgy /ˈpʌdʒɪ/ adj. (-ier, -iest) colloq. (esp. of a person) plump, podgy. □ **pudginess** n.

puerile /ˈpjʊəraɪl/ adj. childish, immature. □ **puerility** /-ˈrɪlɪtɪ/ n. (pl. -ies). [Latin puer boy]

puerperal /pjuːˈɜːrp(ə)r(ə)l/ adj. of or caused by childbirth. [Latin puer boy, pario bear]

puerperal fever n. fever following childbirth and caused by uterine infection.

puff —n. 1 a short quick blast of breath or wind. b sound of or like this. c small quantity of vapour, smoke, etc., emitted in one blast (puff of smoke). 2 light pastry cake containing jam, cream, etc. 3 gathered material in a dress etc. (usu. in passive; often foll. by out) colloq. 4 extravagantly enthusiastic review, advertisement, etc., esp. in a newspaper. 5 = POWDER-PUFF. —v. 1 emit a puff of air or breath; blow with short blasts. 2 (usu. foll. by away, out, etc.) emit or move with puffs (puffing away at his cigar; train puffed out). 3 breathe hard; pant. 5 (usu. foll. by up, out) inflate; swell (his eye was puffed up). 6 (usu. foll. by cut up, away) blow or emit (dust, smoke, etc.) with a puff. 7 smoke (a pipe etc.) in puffs. 8 (usu. as **puffed up** adj.) elate; make proud or boastful. 9 advertise or promote with exaggerated or false praise. □ **puff up** = sense 8 of v. [imitative]

puff-adder n. large venomous African viper which inflates the upper part of its body.

puffball n. ball-shaped fungus emitting clouds of spores.

puffin /ˈpʌfɪn/ n. N Atlantic and N. Pacific sea bird with a large head and brightly coloured triangular bill. [origin unknown]

puff pastry n. leaved pastry made light and flaky by rolling and folding the dough many times.

puffy adj. (-ier, -iest) 1 swollen, puffed out. 2 colloq. short-winded. □ **puffily** adv. **puffiness** n.

pug n. (in full **pug-dog**) dog of a dwarf breed with a broad flat nose and wrinkled face. [origin unknown]

pugilist /ˈpjuːdʒɪlɪst/ n. (esp. professional) boxer. □ **pugilism** n. **pugilistic** /-ˈlɪstɪk/ adj. [Latin pugil boxer]

pugnacious /pʌgˈneɪʃəs/ *adj.* quarrelsome, disposed to fight. □ **pugnaciously** *adv.* **pugnacity** /-ˈnæsɪtɪ/ *n.* [Latin *pugnax -acis* from *pugno* fight]

pug-nose *n.* short squat or snub nose. □ **pug-nosed** *adj.*

puissance /ˈpwiːsɑ̃s/ *n.* competitive jumping of large obstacles in show-jumping. [French: related to PUISSANT]

puissant /ˈpwiːsənt/ *adj. literary* or *archaic* powerful; mighty. [Romanic: related to POTENT]

puke *v. & n.* (**-king**) *slang* vomit. □ **pukey** *adj.* [imitative]

pukka /ˈpʌkə/ *adj. Anglo-Ind. colloq.* **1** genuine. **2** of good quality; reliable (*a pukka job*). [Hindi]

pulchritude /ˈpʌlkrɪtjuːd/ *n. literary* beauty. □ **pulchritudinous** /-ˈtjuːdɪnəs/ *adj.* [Latin *pulcher* beautiful]

pule *v.* (**-ling**) *literary* cry querulously or weakly; whimper. [imitative]

pull /pʊl/ *v. & n.* — *v.* **1** exert force upon (a thing, person, etc.) to move it to oneself or the origin of the force (*pulled it nearer*). **2** exert a pulling force (*engine will not pull*). **3** extract (a cork or tooth) by pulling. **4** damage (a muscle etc.) by abnormal strain. **5 a** move (a boat) by pulling on the oars. **b** (of a boat etc.) be caused to move, esp. in a specified direction. **6** (often foll. by *up*) proceed with effort (up a hill etc.). **7** (foll. by *on*) bring out (a weapon) for use against (a person). **8** check the speed of (a horse), esp. to lose a race. **9** attract (custom or support). **10** draw (liquor) from a barrel etc. **11** (foll. by *at*) tear or pluck at. **12** (often foll. by *on*, *at*) inhale or drink deeply; draw or suck (on a pipe etc.). **13** (often foll. by *up*) remove (a plant) by the root. **14 a** *Cricket* strike (the ball) to the leg side. **b** *Golf* strike (the ball) widely to the left. **15** print (a proof etc.). **16** *slang* succeed in attracting sexually. — *n.* **1** act of pulling. **2** force exerted by this. **3** influence; advantage. **4** attraction or attention-getter. **5** deep draught of liquor **6** prolonged effort, e.g. in going up a hill. **7** handle etc. for applying a pull. **8** printer's rough proof. **9** *Cricket* & *Golf* pulling stroke. **10** suck at a cigarette. □ **pull about 1** treat roughly. **2** pull from side to side. **pull apart** = *take to pieces* (see PIECE). **pull back 1** (cause to) retreat. **pull down 1** demolish (a building). **2** humiliate. **pull a face** distort the features, grimace. **pull a fast one** see FAST[1]. **pull in 1** (of a bus, train, etc.) arrive to take passengers. **2** (of a vehicle) move to the side of or off the road. **3** *colloq.* earn or acquire. **4** *colloq.* arrest. **pull a person's**

leg deceive playfully. **pull off 1** remove by pulling. **2** succeed in achieving or winning. **pull oneself together** recover control of oneself; recover. **pull the other one** *colloq.* expressing disbelief (with ref. to *pull a person's leg*). **pull out 1** take out by pulling. **2** depart. **3** withdraw from an undertaking. **4** (of a bus, train, etc.) leave a station, stop, etc. **5** (of a vehicle) move out from the side of the road, or to overtake. **pull over** (of a vehicle) pull in. **pull one's punches** avoid using one's full force. **pull the plug on** put an end to (by withdrawing resources etc.). **pull rank** take unfair advantage of one's seniority. **pull round** (or **through**) (cause to) recover from an illness. **pull strings** exert (esp. clandestine) influence. **pull together** work in harmony. **pull up 1** (cause to) stop moving. **2** pull out of the ground. **3** reprimand. **pull one's weight** (often *ref.*) do one's fair share of work. [Old English]

pullet /ˈpʊlɪt/ *n.* young hen, one less than one year old. [Latin *pullus*]

pulley /ˈpʊlɪ/ *n.* (*pl.* **-s**) **1** grooved wheel or wheels for a cord etc. to pass over, set in a block and used for changing the direction of a force. **2** wheel or drum fixed on a shaft and turned by a belt, used esp. to increase speed or power. [French *poulie*: related to POLE[2]]

pull-in *n.* roadside café or other stopping-place.

Pullman /ˈpʊlmən/ *n.* (*pl.* **-s**) **1** luxurious railway carriage or motor coach. **2** sleeping-car. [*Pullman*, name of the designer]

pull-out *n.* removable section of a magazine etc.

pullover *n.* knitted garment put on over the head and covering the top half of the body.

pullulate /ˈpʌljʊleɪt/ *v.* (**-ting**) **1** (of a seed, shoot, etc.) bud, sprout. **2** swarm, teem. **3** develop; spring up. **4** (foll. by *with*) abound. □ **pullulation** /-ˈleɪʃ(ə)n/ *n.* [Latin *pullulo* sprout]

pulmonary /ˈpʌlmənərɪ/ *adj.* **1** of the lungs. **2** having lungs or lunglike organs. **3** affected with or susceptible to lung disease. [Latin *pulmo -onis* lung]

pulp — *n.* **1** soft fleshy part of fruit etc. **2** soft thick wet mass, esp. from rags, wood, etc., used in paper-making. **3** (often *attrib.*) cheap fiction etc., orig. printed on rough paper. — *v.* reduce to or become pulp. □ **pulpy** *adj.* **pulpiness** *n.* [Latin]

pulpit /ˈpʊlpɪt/ *n.* **1** raised enclosed platform in a church etc. from which the preacher delivers a sermon. **2** (prec. by

the) preachers collectively; preaching. [Latin *pulpitum* platform]

pulpwood *n.* timber suitable for making paper-pulp.

pulsar /'pʌlsɑ:(r)/ *n.* cosmic source of regular rapid pulses of radiation, e.g. a rotating neutron star. [from *pulsating star*, after *quasar*]

pulsate /pʌl'seɪt/ *v.* (-ting) 1 expand and contract rhythmically; throb. 2 vibrate, quiver, thrill. □ **pulsation** *n.* **pulsatory** *adj.* [Latin: related to PULSE¹]

pulse¹ *-n.* 1 a rhythmical throbbing of the arteries as blood is propelled through them, esp. in the wrists, temples, etc. b each beat of the arteries or heart. 2 throb or thrill of life or emotion. 3 general feeling or opinion. 4 single vibration of sound, electric current, light, etc., esp. as a signal. 5 rhythmical beat, esp. of music. *-v.* (-sing) pulsate. [Latin *pello puls-* drive, beat]

pulse² *n.* (as *sing.* or *pl.*) 1 edible seeds of various leguminous plants, e.g. chickpeas, lentils, beans, etc. 2 plant producing these. [Latin *puls*]

pulverize *v.* (also **-ise**) (-zing or -sing) 1 reduce or crumble to fine particles or dust. 2 *colloq.* demolish, defeat utterly. □ **pulverization** *n.* [Latin *pulvis -ver-* dust]

puma /'pju:mə/ *n.* wild American greyish-brown cat. [Spanish from Quechua]

pumice /'pʌmɪs/ *n.* (in full **pumice-stone**) 1 light porous volcanic rock used in cleaning or polishing. 2 piece of this used for removing hard skin etc. [Latin *pumex pumic-*]

pummel /'pʌm(ə)l/ *v.* (-ll-; US -l-) strike repeatedly, esp. with the fists. [from POMMEL]

pump¹ *-n.* 1 machine or device for raising or moving liquids, compressing gases, inflating tyres, etc. 2 act of pumping; stroke of a pump. *-v.* 1 (often foll. by *up*) fill (a tyre etc.) with air. 2 (often foll. by *in, out, into, up*, etc.) with a pump. 3 remove (water etc.) with a pump. 4 work a pump 5 (often foll. by *out*) (cause to) move, pour forth, etc., as if by pumping. 6 persistently question (a person) to obtain information. 7 a move vigorously up and down. b shake (a person's hand) effusively. □ **pump iron** *colloq.* exercise with weights. [origin uncertain]

pump² *n.* 1 plimsoll. 2 light dancing shoe. 3 *US* court shoe. [origin unknown]

pumpernickel /'pʌmpə,nɪk(ə)l/ *n.* German wholemeal rye bread. [German]

pumpkin /'pʌmpkɪn/ *n.* 1 large rounded yellow or orange fruit cooked as a vegetable. 2 large-leaved tendrilled plant bearing this. [Greek *pepōn* melon]

pun *-n.* humorous use of a word or words with two or more meanings; play on words. *-v.* (-nn-) (foll. by *on*; also *absol.*) make a pun or puns with (words). [origin unknown]

punch¹ *-v.* 1 strike, esp. with a closed fist. 2 a pierce a hole in (metal, paper, etc.) as or with a punch. b pierce (a hole) thus. *-n.* 1 blow with a fist. 2 ability to deliver this. 3 *colloq.* vigour, momentum; effectiveness. 4 tool, machine, or device for punching holes or impressing a design in leather, metal, etc. □ **puncher** *n.* [var. of *pounce* emboss]

punch² *n.* drink of wine or spirits mixed with water, fruit juices, spices, etc., usu. served hot. [origin unknown]

punch³ *n.* (**Punch**) grotesque humpbacked puppet in *Punch and Judy* shows. □ **as pleased as Punch** extremely pleased. [abbreviation of *Punchinello*, name of the chief character in an Italian puppet-show]

punchball *n.* stuffed or inflated ball on a stand for punching as exercise or training.

punch-bowl *n.* 1 bowl for punch. 2 deep round hollow in a hill.

punch card *n.* (also **punched card** or **tape**) card etc. perforated according to a code, for conveying instructions or data to a data processor etc.

punch-drunk *adj.* stupefied from or as if from a series of heavy blows.

punch-line *n.* words giving the point of a joke or story.

punch-up *n. colloq.* fist-fight; brawl.

punchy *adj.* (-ier, -iest) vigorous; forceful.

punctilio /pʌŋk'tɪlɪəʊ/ *n.* (*pl.* -s) 1 delicate point of ceremony or honour. 2 etiquette of such points. 3 petty formality. [Italian and Spanish: related to POINT]

punctilious /pʌŋk'tɪlɪəs/ *adj.* 1 attentive to formality or etiquette. 2 precise in behaviour. □ **punctiliously** *adv.* **punctiliousness** *n.* [Italian: related to PUNCTILIO]

punctual /'pʌŋktʃʊəl/ *adj.* keeping to the appointed time; prompt. □ **punctuality** /-'ælɪtɪ/ *n.* **punctually** *adv.* [medieval Latin: related to POINT]

punctuate /'pʌŋktʃʊeɪt/ *v.* (-ting) 1 insert punctuation marks in. 2 interrupt at intervals (*punctuated his tale with heavy sighs*). [medieval Latin: related to PUNCTUAL]

punctuation /pʌŋktʃʊ'eɪʃ(ə)n/ *n.* 1 system of marks used to punctuate a

written passage. **2** use of, or skill in using, these.

punctuation mark *n.* any of the marks (e.g. full stop and comma) used in writing to separate sentences etc. and clarify meaning.

puncture /ˈpʌŋktʃə(r)/ —*n.* **1** prick or pricking, esp. the accidental piercing of a pneumatic tyre. **2** hole made in this way. —*v.* (**-ring**) **1** make or undergo a puncture (in). **2** prick, pierce, or deflate (pomposity etc.). [Latin *punctura*: related to POINT]

pundit /ˈpʌndɪt/ *n.* **1** (also **pandit**) learned Hindu. **2** often *iron.* expert. □ **punditry** *n.* [Hindustani from Sanskrit]

pungent /ˈpʌndʒ(ə)nt/ *adj.* **1** sharp or strong in taste or smell, esp. producing a smarting or pricking sensation. **2** (of remarks) penetrating, biting, caustic. **3** mentally stimulating. □ **pungency** *n.* [Latin: related to POINT]

punish /ˈpʌnɪʃ/ *v.* **1** inflict retribution on (an offender) or for (an offence). **2** *colloq.* inflict severe blows on (an opponent). **3** tax, abuse, or treat severely or improperly. □ **punishable** *adj.* □ **punishing** *adj.* [Latin *punio*]

punishment /ˈpʌnɪʃm(ə)nt/ *n.* **1** punishing or being punished. **2** loss or suffering inflicted in this. **3** *colloq.* severe treatment or suffering.

punitive /ˈpjuːnɪtɪv/ *adj.* **1** inflicting or intended to inflict punishment. **2** (of taxation etc.) extremely severe. [French or medieval Latin: related to PUNISH]

Punjabi /pʊnˈdʒɑːbɪ/ —*n.* (*pl.* **-s**) native of Punjab. **2** language of Punjab. —*adj.* of Punjab, its people, or language. [*Punjab*, State in India and province in Pakistan]

punk *n.* **1 a** (in full **punk rock**) anti-establishment and deliberately outrageous style of rock music. **b** (in full **punk rocker**) devotee of this. **2** esp. *US* young hooligan or petty criminal; lout. **3** soft crumbly fungus-infested wood used as tinder. [origin unknown]

punkah /ˈpʌŋkə/ *n.* large swinging cloth fan on a frame, worked by a cord or electrically. [Hindi]

punnet /ˈpʌnɪt/ *n.* small light basket or container for fruit or vegetables. [origin unknown]

punster *n.* person who makes puns, esp. habitually.

punt[1] —*n.* square-ended flat-bottomed pleasure boat propelled by a long pole. —*v.* **1** propel (a punt) with a pole. **2** travel or convey in a punt. □ **punter** *n.* [Low German or Dutch]

punt[2] —*v.* kick (a ball, esp. in Rugby) after it has dropped from the hands and

before it reaches the ground. —*n.* such a kick. [origin unknown]

punt[3] *v.* **1** *colloq.* **a** bet on a horse etc. **b** speculate in shares etc. **2** (in some card-games) lay a stake against the bank. [French *ponter*]

punt[4] /pʊnt/ *n.* chief monetary unit of the Republic of Ireland. [Irish, = pound]

punter *n. colloq.* **1** person who gambles or lays a bet. **2 a** customer or client; member of an audience. **b** prostitute's client.

puny /ˈpjuːnɪ/ *adj.* (**-ier**, **-iest**) **1** undersized. **2** weak, feeble. [French *puisné* born afterwards]

pup —*n.* young dog, wolf, rat, seal, etc. —*v.* (**-pp-**) (also *absol.*) (of a bitch etc.) bring forth (young). [from PUPPY]

pupa /ˈpjuːpə/ *n.* (*pl.* **pupae** /-piː/) insect in the stage between larva and imago. □ **pupal** *adj.* [Latin, = doll]

pupil[1] /ˈpjuːpɪl/ *n.* person taught by another, esp. a schoolchild or student. [Latin *pupillus*, *-illa* diminutives of *pupus* boy, *pupa* girl]

pupil[2] *n.* dark circular opening in the centre of the iris of the eye. [related to PUPIL[1]]

puppet /ˈpʌpɪt/ *n.* **1** small figure moved esp. by strings as entertainment. **2** person controlled by another. □ **puppetry** *n.* [var. of POPPET]

puppet State *n.* country that is nominally independent but actually under the control of another power.

puppy /ˈpʌpɪ/ *n.* (*pl.* **-ies**) **1** young dog. **2** conceited or arrogant young man. [French: related to POPPET]

puppy-fat *n.* temporary fatness of a child or adolescent.

puppy love *n.* = CALF-LOVE.

purblind /ˈpɜːblaɪnd/ *adj.* **1** partly blind; dim-sighted. **2** obtuse, dim-witted. □ **purblindness** *n.* [from *pur(e)* (= 'utterly') *blind*]

purchase /ˈpɜːtʃəs/ —*v.* (**-sing**) **1** buy. **2** (often foll. by *with*) obtain or achieve at some cost. —*n.* **1** buying. **2** thing bought. **3 a** firm hold to prevent slipping; leverage. **b** device or tackle for moving heavy objects. **4** annual rent or return from land. □ **purchaser** *n.* [Anglo-French: related to PRO-[1], CHASE[1]]

purdah /ˈpɜːdə/ *n. Ind.* screening of women from strangers by a veil or curtain in some Muslim and Hindu societies. [Urdu]

pure /pjʊə(r)/ *adj.* **1** unmixed, unadulterated (*pure white*; *pure malice*). **2** of unmixed origin or descent (*pure-blooded*). **3** chaste. **4** not morally corrupt. **5** guiltless. **6** sincere. **7** (of a sound) perfectly in tune. **8** (of a subject of study) abstract,

not applied. □ **pureness** n. [Latin purus]

purée /'pjuareı/ —n. smooth pulp of vegetables or fruit etc. —v. (-ees, -eed) make a purée of. [French]

purely adv. 1 in a pure manner. 2 merely, solely, exclusively.

purgative /'pз:gətıv/ —adj. 1 serving to purify. 2 strongly laxative. —n. 1 purgative thing. 2 laxative. [Latin: related to PURGE]

purgatory /'pз:gətərı/ —n. (pl. -ies) 1 RC Ch. supposed place or state of expiation of petty sins after death and before entering heaven. 2 place or state of temporary suffering or expiation. —adj. purifying. □ **purgatorial** /-'tɔ:rıəl/ adj. [medieval Latin: related to PURGE]

purge —v. (-ging) 1 (often foll. by of, from) make physically or spiritually clean. 2 remove by cleansing. 3 rid (an organization, party, etc.) of unacceptable members. 4 a empty (the bowels). b empty the bowels of (a person). 5 Law atone for (an offence, esp. contempt of court). —n. 1 act of purging. 2 purgative. [Latin purgo purify]

purify /'pjuarıfaı/ v. (-ies, -ied) 1 clear of extraneous elements; make pure. 2 (often foll. by of, from) make ceremonially pure or clean. □ **purification** /-fı'keıʃ(ə)n/ n. **purificatory** /-fı,keıtərı/ adj. **purifier** n.

purist /'pjuarıst/ n. advocate of scrupulous purity, esp. in language or art. □ **purism** n. **puristic** /-'rıstık/ adj.

puritan /'pjuarıt(ə)n/ —n. 1 (**Puritan**) hist. member of a group of English Protestants who sought to simplify and regulate forms of worship after the Reformation. 2 purist member of any party. 3 strict observer of religion or morals. —adj. 1 (**Puritan**) hist. of the Puritans. 2 scrupulous and austere in religion or morals. □ **puritanism** n. [Latin: related to PURE]

puritanical /,pjuarı'tænık(ə)l/ adj. strictly religious or moral in behaviour. □ **puritanically** adv.

purity /'pjuarıtı/ n. pureness, cleanness.

purl[1] —n. 1 knitting stitch, made by putting the needle through the front of the previous stitch and passing the yarn round the back of the needle. 2 chain of minute loops decorating the edges of lace etc. —v. (also absol.) knit with a purl stitch. [origin unknown]

purl[2] v. (of a brook etc.) flow with a babbling sound. [imitative]

purler n. colloq. headlong fall. [purl]

purlieu /'pз:lju:/ n. (pl. -s) 1 person's bounds, limits, or usual haunts. 2 hist. tract on the border of a forest. 3 (in pl.) outskirts, outlying region. [Anglo-French puralé from aller go]

purlin /'pз:lın/ n. horizontal beam along the length of a roof. [Anglo-Latin perlio]

purloin /pə'lɔın/ v. formal or joc. steal, pilfer. [Anglo-French: related to loign far]

purple /'pз:p(ə)l/ —n. 1 colour between red and blue. 2 (in full **Tyrian purple**) crimson dye obtained from some molluscs. 3 purple robe, esp. of an emperor or senior magistrate. 4 scarlet official dress of a cardinal. 5 (prec. by the) position of rank, authority, or privilege. —adj. of a purple colour. —v. (-ling) make or become purple. □ **purplish** adj. [Greek porphura a shellfish yielding dye]

purple heart n. colloq. heart-shaped stimulant tablet, esp. of amphetamine.

purple passage n. (also **purple patch**) ornate or elaborate literary passage.

purport —v. /pə'pɔ:t/ 1 profess; be intended to seem (purports to be an officer). 2 (often foll. by that) (of a document or speech) have as its meaning. —n. /'pз:pɔ:t/ 1 ostensible meaning. 2 sense or tenor (cf a document or statement). □ **purportedly** /pə'pɔ:tıdlı/ adv. [Latin: related to PRO-, porto carry]

purpose /'pз:pəs/ —n. 1 object to be attained; thing intended. 2 intention to act. 3 resolution, determination. —v. (-sing) have as one's purpose; design, intend. □ **on purpose** intentionally. **to no purpose** with no result or effect. **to the purpose** 1 relevant. 2 useful. [Latin proporto PROPOSE]

purpose-built adj. (also **purpose-made**) built or made for a specific purpose.

purposeful adj. 1 having or indicating purpose. 2 intentional. 3 resolute. □ **purposefully** adv. **purposefulness** n.

purposeless adj. having no aim or plan.

purposely adv. on purpose.

purpose-made adj. var. of PURPOSE-BUILT.

purposive /'pз:pəsıv/ adj. 1 having, serving, or done with a purpose. 2 purposeful; resolute.

purr /pз:(r)/ v. 1 (of a cat) make a low vibratory sound expressing content-ment. 2 (of machinery etc.) run smoothly and quietly. 3 (of a person) express pleasure; utter purringly. —n. purring sound. [imitative]

purse —n. 1 small pouch for carrying money, on the person. 2 US handbag. 3 money, funds. 4 sum as a present or prize in a contest. —v. (-sing) 1 (often foll. by up) pucker or contract (the lips etc.). 2 become wrinkled. □ **hold the**

purse-strings have control of expenditure. [Greek, = leather bag]

purser *n.* officer on a ship who keeps the accounts, esp. the head steward in a passenger vessel.

pursuance /pəˈsjuːəns/ *n.* (foll. by *of*) carrying out or observance (of a plan, idea, etc.).

pursuant *adv.* (foll. by *to*) in accordance with. [French: related to PURSUE]

pursue /pəˈsjuː/ *v.* (-sues, -sued, -suing) **1** follow with intent to overtake, capture, or do harm to; go in pursuit. **2** continue or proceed along (a route or course of action). **3** follow or engage in (study or other activity). **4** proceed according to (a plan etc.). **5** seek after, aim at. **6** continue to investigate or discuss (a topic). **7** importune (a person) persistently. **8** (of misfortune etc.) persistently assail. □ **pursuer** *n.* [Latin *sequor* follow]

pursuit /pəˈsjuːt/ *n.* **1** act of pursuing. **2** occupation or activity pursued. □ **in pursuit of** in pursuit of. [French: related to SUIT]

pursuivant /ˈpɜːsɪv(ə)nt/ *n.* officer of the College of Arms below a herald. [French: related to PURSUE]

purulent /ˈpjʊərʊlənt/ *adj.* of, containing, or discharging pus. □ **purulence** *n.* [Latin: related to PUS]

purvey /pəˈveɪ/ *v.* provide or supply (food etc.) as one's business. □ **purveyor** *n.* [Latin: related to PROVIDE]

purview /ˈpɜːvjuː/ *n.* **1** scope or range of a document, scheme, etc. **2** range of physical or mental vision. [Anglo-French past part.: related to PURVEY]

pus *n.* thick yellowish or greenish liquid produced from infected tissue. [Latin *pus puris*]

push /pʊʃ/ *-v.* **1** exert a force on (a thing) to move it or cause it to move away. **2** exert such a force (*do not push against the door*). **3 a** thrust forward or upward. **b** (cause to) project (*pushes out new roots*). **4** move forward or make (one's way) by force or persistence. **5** exert oneself, esp. to surpass others. **6** (often foll. by *to*, *into*, or *to* + infin.) urge, impel, or press (a person) hard; harass. **7** (often foll. by *for*) pursue or demand (a claim etc.) persistently. **8** promote, e.g. by advertising. **9** *colloq.* sell (a drug) illegally. *-n.* **1** act of pushing; shove, thrust. **2** force exerted in this. **3** vigorous effort. **4** military attack in force. **5** enterprise, ambition. **6** use of influence to advance a person. □ **be pushed for** *colloq.* have very little of (esp. time). **give** (or **get**) **the push** *colloq.* dismiss or send (or be dismissed or sent) away. **push about** = **push around**. **push**

along (often in *imper.*) *colloq.* depart, leave. **push around** *colloq.* bully. **push one's luck** **1** take undue risks. **2** act presumptuously. **push off** **1** push with an oar etc. to get a boat out into a river etc. **2** (often in *imper.*) *colloq.* go away. **push through** get (a scheme, proposal, etc.) completed or accepted quickly. [Latin: related to PULSATE]

push-bike *n.* *colloq.* bicycle.

push-button *n.* **1** button to be pushed, esp. to operate an electrical device. **2** (*attrib.*) operated thus.

pushchair *n.* folding chair on wheels, for pushing a young child along in.

pusher *n.* *colloq.* seller of illegal drugs.

pushful *adj.* pushy; arrogant. □ **pushfully** *adv.*

pushing *adj.* **1** pushy. **2** *predic colloq.* having nearly reached (a specified age).

pushover *n.* *colloq.* **1** something easily done. **2** person easily persuaded, defeated, etc.

push-start *-n.* starting of a vehicle by pushing it to turn the engine. *-v.* start (a vehicle) in this way.

Pushtu /ˈpʌʃtuː/ *n. & adj.* = PASHTO. [Persian]

push-up *n.* = PRESS-UP.

pushy *adj.* (-ier, -iest) *colloq.* excessively self-assertive. □ **pushily** *adv.* **pushiness** *n.*

pusillanimous /ˌpjuːsɪˈlænɪməs/ *adj. formal* cowardly; timid. □ **pusillanimity** /-ləˈnɪmɪtɪ/ *n.* [Church Latin *pusillanimis* from *pusillus* very small, *animus* mind]

puss /pʊs/ *n.* *colloq.* **1** cat (esp. as a form of address). **2** sly or coquettish girl. [Low German or Dutch]

pussy /ˈpʊsɪ/ *n.* (*pl.* -ies) **1** (also **pussy-cat**) *colloq.* cat. **2** *coarse slang* vulva.

pussyfoot *v. colloq.* **1** move stealthily. **2** equivocate; stall.

pussy willow *n.* willow with furry catkins.

pustulate /ˈpʌstjʊleɪt/ *v.* (-ting) form into pustules. [Latin: related to PUSTULE]

pustule /ˈpʌstjuːl/ *n.* pimple containing pus. □ **pustular** *adj.* [Latin *pustula*]

put /pʊt/ *-v.* (-tt-; *past* and *past part.* **put**) **1** move to or cause to be in a specified place or position (*put it in your pocket*; *put the children to bed*). **2** bring into a specified condition or state (*puts me in great difficulty*). **3** (often foll. by *on, to*) impose, enforce, assign, or apply (*put a tax on beer*; *where do you put the blame?*; *put a stop to it*; *put it to good use*). **4** place (a person) or (*refl.*) imagine (oneself) in a specified position (*put them at their ease*; *put yourself in my shoes*). **5** (foll. by *for*) substitute (one

put

thing) for (another). **6** express in a specified way (*to put it mildly*). **7** (foll. by *at*) estimate (an amount etc.) at so much (*put the cost at £50*). **8** (foll. by *into*) express or translate (in words, or another language). **9** (foll. by *into*) invest (money in an asset, e.g. land). **10** (foll. by *on*) stake (money) on (a horse etc.). **11** (foll. by *to*) submit for attention (*put it to a vote*). **12** throw (esp. a shot or weight) as a sport. **13** (foll. by *back*, *off*, *out to sea*, etc.) (of a ship etc.) proceed in a specified direction. —*n.* throw of the shot etc. □ **put about 1** spread (information, a rumour, etc.). **2** *Naut.* turn round; put (a ship) on the opposite tack. **put across 1** communicate (an idea etc.) effectively. **2** (often in **put it** or **one across**) achieve by deceit. **put away 1** restore (a thing) to its usual or former place. **2** lay (money etc.) aside for future use. **3** imprison or commit to a home etc. **4** consume (food and drink), esp. in large quantities. **5** = *put down* 7. **put back 1** change (a meeting etc.) to a later date or time. **3** move back the hands of (a clock or watch). **put a bold face** etc. on (a difficulty etc.): see BOLD. **put by** = *put away* 2. **put down 1** suppress by force. **2** *colloq.* snub, humiliate. **3** record or enter in writing. **4** enter the name of (a person) on a list. **5** (foll. by *as*, *for*) account or reckon. **6** (foll. by *to*) attribute (*put it down to bad planning*). **7** put (an old or sick animal) to death. **8** pay as a deposit. **9** stop to let (passengers) get off. **put an end to see** END. **put one's foot down see** FOOT. **put one's foot in it see** FOOT. **put forth 1** (of a plant) send out (buds or leaves). **put forward 1** suggest or propose. **2** advance the time shown on (a clock or watch); put in **1 a** enter or submit (a claim etc.). **b** (foll. by *for*) submit a claim for (a specified thing). **2** (foll. by *for*) be a candidate for (an appointment, election, etc.). **3** spend (time). **4** interpose (a remark, blow, etc.). **put it to a person** (often foll. by *that*) challenge a person to deny. **put off 1 a** postpone. **b** postpone an engagement with (a person). **2** (often foll. by *with*) evade (a person) with an excuse etc. **3** hinder, dissuade; offend, disconcert. **put on 1** clothe oneself with (a light etc.) to function. **3** cause (transport) to be available. **4** stage (a play, show, etc.). **5** advance the hands of a clock or watch). **6 a** pretend to (an emotion), **b** assume, take on (a character or appearance). **c** (**put it on**) exaggerate one's feelings etc. **7** increase one's weight by (a specified amount). **8** (foll. by *to*) make aware of or put in

touch with (*put us on to their new accountant*). **put on weight** increase one's weight. **put out 1 a** put as put out (a hand etc.) disconcert or annoy. **b** (often *refl.*) inconvenience (*don't put yourself out*). **2** extinguish (a fire or light). **3** cause (a batsman or side) to be out. **4** allocate (work, to be done off the premises. **5** blind (a person's eyes). **put over** = *put across*. **put a sock in it see** SOCK. **put through 1** carry out or complete. **2** (often foll. by *to*) connect by telephone. **put to flight see** FLIGHT. **put together 1** assemble (a whole) from parts. **2** combine (parts) to form a whole. **put under** make unconscious. **put up 1** build, erect. **2** raise (a price etc.). **3** take up for the night). **4** engage in (a defensive fight, struggle, etc.). **5** present (a proposal). **6** present oneself; or propose. **put up to** (usu. foll. by verbal noun) instigate a person to (*put them up to stealing*). **put up with** endure, tolerate. **put the wind up see** WIND. **put a person wise see** WISE. **put words into a person's mouth see** MOUTH. [Old English]

putative /ˈpjuːtətɪv/ *adj. formal* reputed, supposed (*this putative father*). [Latin *puto* think]

put-down *n. colloq.* snub.

put-on *n. colloq.* deception or hoax.

putrefy /ˈpjuːtrɪfaɪ/ *v.* (**-ies**, **-ied**) **1** become or make putrid; go bad. **2** fester, suppurate. **3** become morally corrupt. □ **putrefaction** /-ˈfækʃ(ə)n/ *n.* **putrefactive** *adj.* [Latin *puter putris* rotten]

putrescent /pjuːˈres(ə)nt/ *adj.* rotting. □ **putrescence** *n.* [Latin: related to PUTRID]

putrid /ˈpjuːtrɪd/ *adj.* **1** decomposed, rotten. **2** foul, noxious. **3** corrupt. **4** *slang* of poor quality; contemptible; very unpleasant. □ **putridity** /-ˈtrɪdɪtɪ/ *n.* [Latin *putreo* rot]

putsch /pʊtʃ/ *n.* attempt at political revolution; violent uprising. [Swiss German]

putt —*v.* (**-tt-**) strike (a golf ball) gently on a putting-green —*n.* putting stroke. [from PUT]

puttee /ˈpʌtiː/ *n.* long strip of cloth wound round the leg from ankle to knee for protection and support, worn esp. by soldiers. [Hindi]

putter[1] *n.* golf club for putting.

putter[2] US var. of POTTER[1].

putting-green *n.* (in golf) smooth area of grass round a hole.

putty /ˈpʌtɪ/ —*n.* cement of whiting and linseed oil, used for fixing panes of glass, filling holes, etc. —*v.* (-ies, -ied) cover, fix, join, or fill with putty. [French *potée*: related to POT]

put-up job *n. colloq.* fraudulent scheme.

puzzle /ˈpʌz(ə)l/ —*n.* **1** difficult or confusing problem. **2** problem or toy designed to test knowledge or ingenuity. —*v.* (-ling) **1** confound or disconcert mentally. **2** (usu. foll. by *over* etc.) be perplexed (about). **3** (usu. as **puzzling** *adj.*) require much mental effort (*puzzling situation*). **4** (foll. by *out*) solve or understand by hard thought. □ **puzzlement** *n.* [origin unknown]

puzzler *n.* difficult question or problem.

PVC *abbr.* polyvinyl chloride.

PW *abbr.* policewoman.

PWR *abbr.* pressurized-water reactor.

pyaemia /paɪˈiːmɪə/ *n.* (*US* **pyemia**) blood-poisoning caused by pus-forming bacteria in the bloodstream. [Greek *puon* pus, *haima* blood]

pygmy /ˈpɪgmɪ/ *n.* (also **pigmy**) (*pl.* -ies) (often *attrib.*) **1** member of a dwarf people of esp. equatorial Africa. **2** very small person, animal, or thing. **3** insignificant person. [Latin from Greek]

pyjamas /pəˈdʒɑːməz/ *n.pl.* (*US* **pajamas**) **1** suit of loose trousers and jacket for sleeping in. **2** loose trousers worn by both sexes in some Asian countries. **3** (**pyjama**) (*attrib.*) of either part of a pair of pyjamas (*pyjama jacket*). [Urdu, = leg-clothing]

pylon /ˈpaɪlɒn/ *n.* tall structure, esp. as a support for electric-power cables etc. [Greek *pulē* gate]

pyorrhoea /paɪəˈrɪə/ *n.* (*US* **pyorrhea**) **1** gum disease causing loosening of the teeth. **2** discharge of pus. [Greek *puon* pus, *rheō* flow]

pyracantha /paɪərəˈkænθə/ *n.* evergreen thorny shrub with white flowers and bright red or yellow berries. [Latin from Greek]

pyramid /ˈpɪrəmɪd/ *n.* **1** monumental, esp. stone, structure, with a square base and sloping triangular sides meeting at an apex, esp. an ancient Egyptian royal tomb. **2** solid of this shape with esp. a square or triangular base. **3** pyramid-shaped thing or pile of things. □ **pyramidal** /-ˈræmɪd(ə)l/ *adj.* [Greek *puramis-mid-*]

pyramid selling *n.* system of selling goods in which agency rights are sold to an increasing number of distributors at successively lower levels.

pyre /ˈpaɪə(r)/ *n.* heap of combustible material, esp. for burning a corpse. [Greek: related to PYRO-]

pyrethrum /paɪˈriːθrəm/ *n.* **1** aromatic chrysanthemum. **2** insecticide from its dried flowers. [Latin from Greek]

pyretic /paɪˈretɪk/ *adj.* of, for, or producing fever. [Greek *puretos* fever]

Pyrex /ˈpaɪəreks/ *n. propr.* hard heat-resistant glass, used esp. for ovenware. [invented word]

pyrexia /paɪˈreksɪə/ *n. Med.* = FEVER. [Greek *purexis*]

pyrites /paɪˈraɪtiːz/ *n.* (in full **iron pyrites**) lustrous yellow mineral that is a sulphide of iron. [Greek: related to PYRE]

pyro- *comb. form* **1** denoting fire. **2** denoting a mineral etc. changed under the action of heat, or fiery in colour. [Greek *pur* fire]

pyromania /paɪərəʊˈmeɪnɪə/ *n.* obsessive desire to start fires. □ **pyromaniac** *n. & adj.*

pyrotechnics /paɪərəʊˈtekniks/ *n.pl.* **1** art of making fireworks. **2** display of fireworks. **3** any brilliant display. □ **pyrotechnic** *adj.*

pyrrhic /ˈpɪrɪk/ *adj.* (of a victory) won at too great a cost. [*Pyrrhus* of Epirus, who defeated the Romans in 279 BC, but suffered heavy losses]

Pythagoras' theorem /paɪˈθægərəs/ *n.* theorem that the square on the hypotenuse of a right-angled triangle is equal to the sum of the squares on the other two sides. [*Pythagoras* (6th c. BC), name of a Greek philosopher]

python /ˈpaɪθ(ə)n/ *n.* large tropical constricting snake. [Greek *Puthōn*, name of a monster]

pyx /pɪks/ *n.* vessel for the consecrated bread of the Eucharist. [Greek *puxis* BOX¹]

Q

Q¹ /kjuː/ n. (also **q**) (pl. **Qs** or **Q's**) seventeenth letter of the alphabet.

Q² abbr. (also **Q.**) **1** Queen('s). **2** question.

Q.C. abbr. Queen's Counsel.

QED abbr. which was to be proved. [Latin *quod erat demonstrandum*]

QM abbr. quartermaster.

qr. abbr. quarter(s).

qt abbr. quart(s).

qua /kwɑː, kweɪ/ conj. in the capacity of. [Latin... = in the way in which]

quack¹ /kwæk/ n. harsh sound made by ducks. —v. utter this sound. [imitative]

quack² n. **1** unqualified practitioner, esp. of medicine; charlatan (often attrib.: *quack cure*). **2** slang any doctor. □ **quackery** n. [abbreviation of *quacksalver* from Dutch: probably related to QUACK¹, SALVE¹]

quad¹ /kwɒd/ n. colloq. quadrangle. [abbreviation]

quad² /kwɒd/ n. colloq. quadruplet. [abbreviation]

quad³ /kwɒd/ colloq. —n. quadraphonics. —adj. quadraphonic. [abbreviation]

Quadragesima /ˌkwɒdrəˈdʒesɪmə/ n. first Sunday in Lent. [Latin *quadragesimus* fortieth]

quadrangle /ˈkwɒdræŋg(ə)l/ n. **1** four-sided plane figure, esp. a square or rectangle. **2** four-sided court, esp. in colleges. □ **quadrangular** /-ˈræŋɡjʊlə(r)/ adj. [Latin: related to QUADRI-, ANGLE¹]

quadrant /ˈkwɒdrənt/ n. **1** quarter of a circle's circumference. **2** quarter of a circle enclosed by two radii at right angles. **3** quarter of a sphere etc. **4** any of four parts of a plane divided by two lines at right angles. **5 a** graduated quarter-circular strip of metal etc. **b** instrument graduated (esp. through an arc of 90°) for measuring angles. [Latin *quadrans -ant-*]

quadraphonic /ˌkwɒdrəˈfɒnɪk/ adj. (of sound reproduction) using four transmission channels. □ **quadraphonically** adv. **quadraphonics** n.pl. [from QUADRI-, STEREOPHONIC]

quadrate —adj. /ˈkwɒdreɪt, esp. Anat. & Zool. square or rectangular. —n. /ˈkwɒdreɪt, -drət/ rectangular object. —v. /kwɒˈdreɪt/ (-ting) make square. [Latin *quadro* make square]

quadratic /kwɒˈdrætɪk/ Math —adj. involving the square (and no higher power) of an unknown quantity or variable (*quadratic equation*). —n. quadratic equation.

quadri- comb. form four. [Latin *quattuor* four]

quadriceps /ˈkwɒdrɪseps/ n. four-headed muscle at the front of the thigh. [from QUADRI-, BICEPS]

quadrilateral /ˌkwɒdrɪˈlætər(ə)l/ —adj. having four sides. —n. four-sided figure.

quadrille /kwəˈdrɪl/ n. **1** a kind of square dance. **2** music for this. [French]

quadriplegia /ˌkwɒdrɪˈpliːdʒə/ n. paralysis of all four limbs. □ **quadriplegic** adj. & n. [from QUADRI-, Greek *plēgē* a blow]

quadruped /ˈkwɒdrʊped/ n. four-footed animal, esp. a mammal. [Latin: related to QUADRI-, *pes ped-* foot]

quadruple /ˈkwɒdrʊp(ə)l/ —adj. **1** fourfold. having four parts. **2** (of time in music) having four beats in a bar. —n. fourfold number or amount. —v. (-ling) multiply by four. [Latin: related to QUADRI-]

quadruplet /ˈkwɒdrʊplɪt/ n. each of four children born at one birth.

quadruplicate —adj. /kwɒˈdruːplɪkət/ **1** fourfold. **2** of which four copies are made. —v. /kwɒˈdruːplɪkeɪt/ (-ting) multiply by four.

quaff /kwɒf/ v. literary **1** drink deeply. **2** drain (a cup etc.) in long draughts. □ **quaffable** adj. [perhaps imitative]

quagmire /ˈkwæɡmaɪə(r), ˈkwɒɡ-/ n. **1** muddy or boggy area. **2** hazardous situation. [from *quag* b c g, MIRE]

quail¹ /kweɪl/ n. (pl. same or -s) small game-bird related to the partridge. [French *quaille*]

quail² v. flinch; show fear. [origin unknown]

quaint adj. attractively odd or old-fashioned. □ **quaintly** adv. **quaintness** n. [French *cointe* from Latin *cognosco* ascertain]

quake —v. (-king) shake, tremble. —n. colloq. earthquake. [Old English]

Quaker n. member of the Society of Friends. □ **Quakerism** n.

qualification /ˌkwɒlɪfɪˈkeɪʃ(ə)n/ n. **1** accomplishment fitting a person for a position or purpose. **2** thing that modifies or limits (*statement had many qualifications*). **3** qualifying or being qualified.

qualificatory /ˈkwɒlɪ...

adj. [French or medieval Latin: related to QUALIFY]

qualify /'kwɒlɪfaɪ/ *v.* (**-ies**, **-ied**) **1** (often as **qualified** *adj.*) make competent or fit for a position or purpose. **2** make legally entitled. **3** (usu. foll. by *for*) (of a person) satisfy conditions or requirements. **4** modify or limit (a statement etc.) (*qualified approval*). **5** *Gram.* (of a word) attribute a quality to esp. a noun. **6** moderate, mitigate; make less severe. **7** (foll. by *as*) be describable as, count as (*a grunt hardly qualifies as conversation*). □ **qualifier** *n.* [Latin *qualis* such as, of what kind]

qualitative /'kwɒlɪtətɪv/ *adj.* of quality as opposed to quantity. □ **qualitatively** *adv.* [Latin: related to QUALITY]

quality /'kwɒlɪtɪ/ *n.* (*pl.* **-ies**) **1** degree of excellence. **2 a** general excellence (*has quality*). **b** (*attrib.*) of high quality (*a quality product*). **3** attribute, faculty (*has many good qualities*). **4** relative nature or character. **5** timbre of a voice or sound. **6** *archaic* high social standing (*people of quality*). [Latin *qualis* such as, of what kind]

quality control *n.* maintaining of standards in products or services by testing samples.

qualm /kwɑːm/ *n.* **1** misgiving; uneasy doubt. **2** scruple of conscience. **3** momentary faint or sick feeling. [origin uncertain]

quandary /'kwɒndərɪ/ *n.* (*pl.* **-ies**) **1** perplexed state. **2** practical dilemma. [origin uncertain]

quango /'kwæŋgəʊ/ *n.* (*pl.* **-s**) semi-public body with financial support from and senior appointments made by the government. [abbreviation of *quasi* (or *quasi*-autonomous) *non-government(al)* organization]

quanta *pl.* of QUANTUM.

quantify /'kwɒntɪfaɪ/ *v.* (**-ies**, **-ied**) **1** determine the quantity of. **2** express as a quantity. □ **quantifiable** *adj.* **quantification** /ˌkwɒntɪfɪ'keɪʃ(ə)n/ *n.* [medieval Latin: related to QUANTITY]

quantitative /'kwɒntɪtətɪv/ *adj.* **1** of quantity as opposed to quality. **2** measured or measurable by quantity.

quantity /'kwɒntɪtɪ/ *n.* (*pl.* **-ies**) **1** property of things that is measurable. **2** size, extent, weight, amount, or number. **3** specified or considerable portion, number, or amount (*buys in quantity*; *small quantity of food*). **4** (in *pl.*) large amounts or numbers; an abundance. **5** length or shortness of vowel sounds or syllables. **6** *Math.* value, component, etc. that may be expressed in numbers. [Latin *quantus* how much]

quantity surveyor *n.* person who measures and prices building work.

quantum /'kwɒntəm/ *n.* (*pl.* **quanta**) **1** *Physics* discrete amount of energy proportional to the frequency of radiation it represents. **2** a required or allowed amount. [Latin *quantus* how much]

quantum jump *n.* (also **quantum leap**) **1** sudden large increase or advance. **2** *Physics* abrupt transition in an atom or molecule from one quantum state to another.

quantum mechanics *n.pl.* (usu. treated as *sing.*) (also **quantum theory**) *Physics* theory assuming that energy exists in discrete units.

quarantine /'kwɒrəntiːn/ *n.* **1** isolation imposed on persons or animals to prevent infection or contagion. **2** period of this. □ *v.* (**-ning**) put in quarantine. [Italian *quaranta* forty]

quark[1] /kwɑːk/ *n. Physics* component of elementary particles. [word used by Joyce in *Finnegans Wake* (1939)]

quark[2] /kwɑːk/ *n.* a kind of low-fat curd cheese. [German]

quarrel /'kwɒr(ə)l/ *n.* **1** severe or angry dispute or contention. **2** break in friendly relations. **3** cause of complaint (*have no quarrel with him*). □ *v.* (**-ll-**; *US* **-l-**) **1** (often foll. by *with*) find fault. **2** dispute; break off friendly relations. [Latin *querela* from *queror* complain]

quarrelsome *adj.* given to quarrelling.

quarry[1] /'kwɒrɪ/ *n.* (*pl.* **-ies**) place from which stone etc. may be extracted. □ *v.* (**-ies**, **-ied**) extract (stone) from a quarry. [Latin *quadrum* square]

quarry[2] /'kwɒrɪ/ *n.* (*pl.* **-ies**) **1** intended victim or prey. **2** object of pursuit. [Latin *cor* heart]

quarry tile *n.* unglazed floor-tile.

quart /kwɔːt/ *n.* liquid measure equal to a quarter of a gallon; two pints (0.946 litre). [Latin *quartus* fourth]

quarter /'kwɔːtə(r)/ *n.* **1** each of four equal parts into which a thing is divided. **2** period of three months. **3** point of time 15 minutes before or after any hour. **4 a** 25 US or Canadian cents. **b** coin for this. **5** part of a town, esp. as occupied by a particular class (*residential quarter*). **6 a** point of the compass. **b** region at this. **7** direction, district, or source of supply (*help from any quarter*). **8** (in *pl.*) **a** lodgings. **b** accommodation of troops etc. **9 a** one fourth of a lunar month. **b** moon's position between the first and second (**first quarter**) or third and fourth (**last quarter**) of these. **10 a** each of the four parts into which a carcass is divided. **b** (in *pl.*) = HINDQUARTERS. **11** mercy towards an enemy etc. on condition of

surrender. **12 a** a grain measure equivalent to 8 bushels. **b** one-fourth of a hundredweight. **c** colloq. one-fourth of a pound weight. **13** each of four divisions on a shield. —v. **1** divide into quarters. **2** hist. divide (the body of an executed person) in this way. **3 a** put (troops etc.) into quarters. **b** provide with lodgings. **4** Heraldry place (coats of arms) on the four quarters of a shield. [Latin quartarius; related to QUART]

quarterback n. player in American football who directs attacking play.

quarter day n. one of four days on which quarterly payments are due, tenancies begin and end, etc.

quarterdeck n. part of a ship's upper deck near the stern, usu. reserved for officers.

quarter-final n. match or round preceding the semifinal.

quarter-hour n. **1** period of 15 minutes. **2** = QUARTER n. 3.

quarter-light n. small pivoted window in the side of a car, carriage, etc.

quarterly —adj. produced or occurring once every quarter of a year. —adv. once every quarter of a year. —n. (pl. -ies) quarterly journal.

quartermaster n. **1** regimental officer in charge of quartering, rations, etc. **2** naval petty officer in charge of steering, signals, etc.

quarter sessions n.pl. hist. court of limited criminal and civil jurisdiction, usu. held quarterly.

quarterstaff /kwɔːtəstɑːf/ n. hist. stout pole 6-8 feet long, formerly used as a weapon.

quartet /kwɔːˈtet/ n. **1** Mus. **a** composition for four performers. **b** the performers. **2** any group of four. [Latin quartus]

quarto /ˈkwɔːtəʊ/ n. (pl. -s) **1** size of a book or page given by folding a sheet of standard size twice to form four leaves. **2** book or page of this size. [Latin: related to QUART]

quartz /kwɔːts/ n. silica in various mineral forms. [German from Slavonic]

quartz clock n. (also **quartz watch**) clock or watch operated by vibrations of an electrically driven quartz crystal.

quasar /ˈkweɪzɑː(r)/ n. Astron. starlike object with a large redshift. [from quasistellar]

quash /kwɒʃ/ v. **1** annul; reject as invalid, esp. by a legal procedure. **2** suppress, crush. [French quasser from Latin]

quasi- /ˈkweɪzaɪ/ comb. form **1** seemingly, not really. **2** almost. [Latin quasi as if]

quaternary /kwəˈtɜːnərɪ/ —adj. **1** having four parts. **2** (**Quaternary**) Geol. of

the most recent period in the Cenozoic era. —n. (**Quaternary**) Geol. this period. [Latin quaterni four each]

quatrain /ˈkwɒtreɪn/ n. four-line stanza. [French quatre four]

quatrefoil /ˈkætrəfɔɪl/ n. four-pointed or -leafed figure, esp. as an architectural ornament. [Anglo-French quatre four: related to FOIL²]

quattrocento /ˌkwætrəʊˈtʃentəʊ/ n. 15th-c. Italian art. [Italian = 400, used for the years 1400-99]

quaver —v. **1** (esp. of a voice or sound) vibrate, shake, tremble. **2** sing or say with a quavering voice. —n. **1** Mus. note half as long as a crotchet. **2** trill in singing. **3** tremble in speech. □ **quavery** adj. [probably imitative]

quay /kiː/ n. artificial landing-place for loading and unloading ships. [French]

quayside n. land forming or near a quay.

queasy /ˈkwiːzɪ/ adj. (-ier, -iest) **1 a** (of a person) nauseous. **b** (of the stomach) easily upset, weak of digestion. **2** (of the conscience etc.) overscrupulous. □ **queasily** adv. **queasiness** n. [origin uncertain]

queen —n. **1** (as a title usu. **Queen**) female sovereign. **2** (in full **queen consort**) king's wife. **3** woman, country, or thing pre-eminent of its kind. **4** fertile female among ants, bees, etc. **5** most powerful piece in chess. **6** court-card depicting a queen. **7** (**the Queen**) national anthem when the sovereign is female. **8** slang offens. male homosexual. **9** belle or mock sovereign for some event (Queen of the May). —v. Chess convert (a pawn) into a queen when it reaches the opponent's side of the board. □ **queenly** adj. (-ier, -iest). [Old English]

Queen-Anne n. (often attrib.) style of English architecture, furniture, etc., in the early 18th c.

queen bee n. **1** fertile female bee. **2** woman who behaves as if she is the most important person in a group.

queen mother n. dowager who is mother of the sovereign.

Queen of the May n. = MAY QUEEN.

queen-post n. either of two upright timbers between the tie-beam and main rafters of a roof-truss.

Queensberry Rules /ˈkwiːnzbərɪ/ n.pl. standard rules, esp. of boxing. [from the name Marquis of Queensberry]

Queen's Counsel n. counsel to the Crown, taking precedence over other barristers.

Queen's English n. (prec. by *the*) English language correctly written or spoken.

Queen's evidence see EVIDENCE.

Queen's Guide n. Guide who has reached the highest rank of proficiency.

Queen's highway n. public road, regarded as being under the sovereign's protection.

Queen's Proctor n. official who has the right to intervene in probate, divorce, and nullity cases when collusion or the suppression of facts is alleged.

Queen's Scout n. Scout who has reached the highest standard of proficiency.

queer –adj. 1 strange, odd, eccentric. 2 shady, suspect, of questionable character. 3 slightly ill; faint. 4 *slang offens.* (esp. of a man) homosexual. –n. *slang offens.* homosexual. –v. *slang* spoil, put out of order. □ **in Queer Street** *slang* in difficulty, esp. in debt. **queer a person's pitch** *colloq.* spoil a person's chances. [origin uncertain]

quell v. 1 crush or put down (a rebellion etc.). 2 suppress (fear etc.). [Old English]

quench v. 1 satisfy (thirst) by drinking. 2 extinguish (a fire or light). 3 cool, esp. with water. 4 esp. *Metallurgy* cool (a hot substance) in cold water etc. 5 stifle or suppress (desire etc.). [Old English]

quern n. hand-mill for grinding corn. [Old English]

querulous /ˈkwerʊləs/ adj. complaining, peevish. □ **querulously** adv. [Latin *queror* complain]

query /ˈkwɪərɪ/ –n. (pl. -ies) 1 question. 2 question mark or the word *query* as a mark of interrogation. –v. (-ies, -ied) 1 ask or inquire. 2 call in question. 3 dispute the accuracy of. [Latin *quaere* imperative of *quaero* inquire]

quest –n. 1 search or seeking. 2 thing sought, esp. by a medieval knight. –v. (often foll. by *about*) go about in search of something (esp. of dogs seeking game). [Latin *quaero quaesit-* seek]

question /ˈkwestʃ(ə)n/ –n. 1 sentence worded or expressed so as to seek information or an answer. 2 a doubt or dispute about a matter (*no question that he is dead*). b raising of such doubt etc. 3 matter to be discussed or decided. 4 problem requiring a solution. –v. 1 ask questions of; interrogate; subject (a person) to examination. 2 throw doubt upon; raise objections to. □ **be just a question of time** be certain to happen sooner or later. **be a question of** be at issue, be a problem (*it's a question of money*). **call in** (or **into**) **question** express doubts about. **in question** that is

being discussed or referred to (*the person in question*). **out of the question** not worth discussing; impossible. □ **questioner** n. **questioning** adj. & n. **questioningly** adv. [Latin: related to QUEST]

questionable adj. doubtful as regards truth, quality, honesty, wisdom, etc. □ **question mark** n. punctuation mark (?) indicating a question.

question-master n. person presiding over a quiz game etc.

questionnaire /ˌkwestʃəˈneər/ n. formulated series of questions, esp. for statistical analysis. [French: related to QUESTION]

question time n. period in Parliament when MPs may question ministers.

queue /kjuː/ –n. line or sequence of persons, vehicles, etc. waiting their turn. –v. (**queues**, **queued**, **queuing** or **queueing**) (often foll. by *up*) form or join a queue. [Latin *cauda* tail]

queue-jump v. push forward out of turn in a queue.

quibble /ˈkwɪb(ə)l/ –n. 1 petty objection; trivial point of criticism. 2 evasion; argument relying on ambiguity. 3 *archaic* pun. –v. (**-ling**) use quibbles. □ **quibbling** adj. [origin uncertain]

quiche /kiːʃ/ n. savoury flan. [French]

quick –adj. 1 taking only a short time (*quick worker*). 2 arriving after a short time, prompt. 3 with only a short interval (*in quick succession*). 4 lively, intelligent, alert. 5 (of a temper) easily roused. 6 *archaic* alive (*the quick and the dead*). –adv. (also as *int.*) quickly. –n. 1 soft sensitive flesh, esp. below the nails. 2 seat of emotion (*cut to the quick*). □ **quickly** adv. [Old English]

quicken v. 1 make or become quicker, accelerate. 2 give life or vigour to; rouse. 3 a (of a woman) reach a stage in pregnancy when movements of the foetus can be felt. b (of a foetus) begin to show signs of life.

quick-fire attrib. adj. rapid; in rapid succession.

quick-freeze v. freeze (food) rapidly so as to preserve its natural qualities.

quickie n. *colloq.* thing done or made quickly.

quicklime n. = LIME[1].

quick one n. *colloq.* drink (usu. alcoholic) taken quickly.

quicksand n. (often in *pl.*) 1 area of loose wet sand that sucks in anything placed on it. 2 treacherous situation etc.

quickset –attrib. adj. (of a hedge etc.) formed of cuttings, esp. hawthorn. –n. hedge formed in this way.

quicksilver n. mercury.

quickstep n. fast foxtrot.

quick-tempered *adj.* easily angered.

quick-witted *adj.* quick to grasp a situation, make repartee, etc. □ **quick-wittedness** *n.*

quid¹ *n.* (*pl.* same) *slang* one pound sterling. □ **quids in** *slang* in a position of profit. [probably from Latin *quid* what]

quid² *n.* lump of tobacco for chewing. [a dialect word, = CUD]

quiddity /ˈkwɪdɪtɪ/ *n.* (*pl.* -**ies**) 1 *Philos.* essence of a thing. 2 quibble; trivial objection. [Latin *quidditas* from *quid* what]

quid pro quo /ˌkwɪd prəʊ ˈkwəʊ/ *n.* (*pl.* **quid pro quos**) return made (for a gift, favour, etc.). [Latin, = something for something]

quiescent /kwɪˈes(ə)nt/ *adj.* inert, dormant. □ **quiescence** *n.* [related to QUIET]

quiet /ˈkwaɪət/ —*adj.* 1 with little or no sound or motion. 2 of gentle or peaceful disposition; disguised; not showy. 4 not overt; disguised. 5 undisturbed, uninterrupted; free or far from vigorous action. 6 informal (*quiet wedding*). 7 enjoyed in quiet (*quiet smoke*). 8 not anxious or remorseful. 9 not busy (*it is very quiet at work*). 10 peaceful (*all quiet on the frontier*). —*n.* 1 silence; stillness. 2 undisturbed state; tranquillity. —*v.* (often foll. by *down*) make or become quiet or calm. □ **be quiet** (esp. in *imper.*) cease talking etc. **keep quiet** (often foll. by *about*) say nothing. **on the quiet** secretly. □ **quietly** *adv.* **quietness** *n.* [Latin *quiesco* become calm]

quieten *v.* (often foll. by *down*) *v.*

quietism *n.* passive contemplative attitude towards life, esp. as a form of mysticism. □ **quietist** *n.* & *adj.* [Italian: related to QUIET]

quietude /ˈkwaɪətjuːd/ *n.* state of quiet.

quietus /kwaɪˈiːtəs/ *n.* release from life; death, final riddance (*will get its quietus*). [medieval Latin: related to QUIET]

quiff *n.* 1 man's tuft of hair, brushed upward over the forehead. 2 curl plastered down on the forehead. [origin unknown]

quill *n.* 1 (in full **quill-feather**) large feather in a wing or tail. 2 hollow stem of this. 3 (in full **quill pen**) pen made of a quill. 4 (usu. in *pl.*) porcupine's spine. [probably Low German *quiele*]

quilt —*n.* coverlet, esp. of quilted material. —*v.* line a coverlet or garment with padding enclosed between layers of cloth by lines of stitching. □ **quilter** *n.* **quilting** *n.* [Latin *culcita* cushion]

quim *n.* *coarse slang* female genitals. [origin unknown]

quin *n.* *colloq.* quintuplet. [abbreviation]

quince *n.* 1 acid pear-shaped fruit used in jams etc. 2 tree bearing this. [originally a plural, from French *cooin*, from *Cydonia* in Crete]

quincentenary /ˌkwɪnsenˈtiːnərɪ/ —*n.* (*pl.* -**ies**) 500th anniversary; celebration of this. —*adj.* of this anniversary. [Latin *quinque* five]

quincunx /ˈkwɪnkʌŋks/ *n.* five objects, esp. trees, at the corners and centre of a square or rectangle. [Latin, = five-twelfths]

quinine /ˈkwɪniːn/ *n.* bitter drug obtained from cinchona bark, used as a tonic and to reduce fever. [Spanish *quina* cinchona bark, from Quechua *kina* bark]

Quinquagesima /ˌkwɪŋkwəˈdʒesɪmə/ *n.* Sunday before Lent. [Latin *quinquagesimus* fiftieth]

quinquennial /kwɪŋˈkwenɪəl/ *adj.* 1 lasting five years. 2 recurring every five years. □ **quinquennially** *adv.* [Latin *quinque* five, *annus* year]

quinquennium /kwɪŋˈkwenɪəm/ *n.* (*pl.* -**ia** or -**iums**) period of five years. [Latin *quinquennis* from *quinque* five, *annus* year]

quinquereme /ˈkwɪŋkwɪriːm/ *n.* ancient Roman galley with five files of oarsmen on each side. [Latin *quinque* five, *remus* oar]

quinquina /kwɪŋˈkwiːnə/ *n.* 1 (usu. foll. by *of*) purest and most perfect form, manifestation, or embodiment of a quality etc. 2 highly refined extract. □ **quintessential** /ˌkwɪntɪˈsen(ʃ)(ə)l/ *adj.* **quintessentially** *adv.* [Latin *quinta essentia* fifth substance (underlying the four elements)]

quintet /kwɪnˈtet/ *n.* 1 *Mus.* a composition for five performers. b the performers. 2 any group of five. [Latin *quintus*]

quintuple /ˈkwɪntjʊp(ə)l/ —*adj.* fivefold; having five parts. —*n.* fivefold number or amount. —*v.* (-**ling**) multiply by five. [Latin *quintus* fifth]

quintuplet /ˈkwɪntjʊplɪt/ *n.* each of five children born at one birth.

quintuplicate —*adj.* /kwɪnˈtjuːplɪkət/ 1 fivefold. 2 of which five copies are made. —*v.* /kwɪnˈtjuːplɪkeɪt/ (-**ting**) multiply by five.

quip —*n.* clever saying; epigram. —*v.* (-**pp**-) make quips. [perhaps from Latin *quippe* forsooth]

quire *n.* 25 (formerly 24) sheets of paper. [Latin: related to QUATERNARY]

quirk *n.* 1 peculiar feature, peculiarity. 2 trick of fate. □ **quirky** *adj.* (-**ier**, -**iest**). [origin unknown]

quisling /ˈkwɪzlɪŋ/ *n.* traitor, collaborator. [*Quisling*, name of a Norwegian officer and collaborator with the Nazis]

quit —v. (-tting; past and past part. **quitted** or **quit**) **1** (also absol.) give up, let go, abandon (a task etc.). **2** US cease, stop (quit grumbling). **3** leave or depart from. —predic. adj. (foll. by of) rid of (glad to be quit of the problem). [Latin: related to QUIET]

quitch n. (in full **quitch-grass**) = COUCH². [Old English]

quite adv. **1** completely, entirely, wholly. **2** to some extent, rather. **3** (often foll. by so) said to indicate agreement. □ **quite a** (or **some**) remarkable or outstanding (thing). **quite a few** colloq. a fairly large number of. **quite something** colloq. remarkable thing or person. [var. of QUIT]

quits predic. adj. on even terms by retaliation or repayment. □ **call it quits** acknowledge that things are now even; agree to stop quarrelling. [probably related to QUIT]

quitter n. **1** person who gives up easily. **2** shirker.

quiver¹ /ˈkwɪvə(r)/ —v. tremble or vibrate with a slight rapid motion. —n. quivering motion or sound. [obsolete quiver nimble]

quiver² /ˈkwɪvə(r)/ n. case for arrows. [Anglo-French from Germanic]

quixotic /kwɪkˈsɒtɪk/ adj. extravagantly and romantically chivalrous. □ **quixotically** adv. [Don Quixote, in Cervantes' romance]

quiz —n. (pl. **quizzes**) **1** test of knowledge, esp. as entertainment. **2** interrogation, examination. —v. (-zz-) examine by questioning. [origin unknown]

quizzical /ˈkwɪzɪk(ə)l/ adj. expressing or done with mild or amused perplexity. □ **quizzically** adv.

quod n. slang prison. [origin unknown]

quoin /kɔɪn/ n. **1** external angle of a building. **2** cornerstone. **3** wedge used in printing and gunnery. [var. of COIN]

quoit /kɔɪt/ n. **1** ring thrown to encircle an iron peg. **2** (in pl.) game using these. [origin unknown]

quondam /ˈkwɒndæm/ attrib. adj. that once was, sometime, former. [Latin adv., = formerly]

quorate /ˈkwɔːreɪt/ adj. constituting or having a quorum. [from QUORUM]

quorum /ˈkwɔːrəm/ n. minimum number of members that must be present to constitute a valid meeting. [Latin, = of whom]

quota /ˈkwəʊtə/ n. **1** share or number contributed to, or received from, a total. **2** number of goods, people, etc., stipulated or permitted. [Latin quotus from quot how many]

quotable /ˈkwəʊtəb(ə)l/ adj. worth quoting.

quotation /kwəʊˈteɪʃ(ə)n/ n. **1** passage or remark quoted. **2** quoting or being quoted. **3** contractor's estimate. [medieval Latin: related to QUOTE]

quotation marks n.pl. inverted commas (' ' or " ") used at the beginning and end of a quotation etc.

quote —v. (-ting) **1** cite or appeal to (an author, book, etc.) in confirmation of some view. **2** a repeat or copy out passage from. **b** (foll. by from) cite (an author, book, etc.). **3** (foll. by as) cite (an author etc.) as proof, evidence, etc. **4** enclose (words) in quotation marks. —n. (as int.) verbal formula indicating opening quotation marks (he said, quote, shall stay). **5** (often foll. by at, also absol.) state the price of. —n. colloq. **1** passage quoted. **2** price quoted. **3** (usu. in pl.) quotation marks. [Latin quoto mark with numbers]

quoth /kwəʊθ/ v. (only in 1st and 3rd person) archaic said. [Old English]

quotidian /kwɒˈtɪdɪən/ adj. **1** occurring or recurring daily. **2** commonplace, trivial. [Latin cotidie daily]

quotient /ˈkwəʊʃ(ə)nt/ n. result of a division sum. [Latin quotiens -ent- how many times]

q.v. abbr. which see (in references). [Latin quod vide]

qwerty /ˈkwɜːtɪ/ attrib. adj. denoting the standard keyboard on English language typewriters etc., with q, w, e, r, t, and y as the first keys on the top row of letters.

R

R¹ /ɑː(r)/ n. (also **r**) (pl. **Rs** or **R's**) eighteenth letter of the alphabet.

R² abbr. (also **®**) 1 Regina (Elizabeth R). 2 Rex. 3 River. 4 (also ®) registered as a trademark. 5 Chess rook.

r. abbr. (also **r**) 1 right. 2 radius.

RA abbr. 1 a Royal Academy. b Royal Academician. 2 Royal Artillery.

Ra symb. radium.

rabbet /'ræbɪt/ n. — v. step-shaped channel cut along the edge or face of a length of wood etc. usu. to receive the edge or tongue of another piece. — v. 1 join or fix with a rabbet. 2 make a rabbet in. [French rab(b)at: related to REBATE¹]

rabbi /'ræbaɪ/ n. (pl. -s) 1 Jewish scholar or teacher, esp. of the law. 2 Jewish religious leader. □ **rabbinical** /rə-'bɪnɪk(ə)l/ adj. [Hebrew, = my master]

rabbit /'ræbɪt/ n. 1 a burrowing plant-eating mammal of the hare family. b US hare. 2 its fur. —v. (-t-) 1 hunt rabbits. 2 (often foll. by on, away) colloq. talk pointlessly; chatter. [origin uncertain]

rabbit punch n. short chop with the edge of the hand to the nape of the neck.

rabble /'ræb(ə)l/ n. 1 disorderly crowd; mob. 2 contemptible or inferior set of people. 3 (prec. by the) the lower or disorderly classes of the populace. [origin uncertain]

rabble-rouser n. person who stirs up the rabble or a crowd, esp. to agitate for social change.

Rabelaisian /ˌræbə'leɪziən/ adj. 1 of or like the French satirist Rabelais or his writings. 2 marked by exuberant imagination and coarse humour.

rabid /'ræbɪd, 'reɪ-/ adj. 1 affected with rabies; mad. 2 violent; fanatical. □ **rabidity** /rə'bɪdɪtɪ/ n. [Latin rabio rave]

rabies /'reɪbiːz/ n. contagious viral disease of esp. dogs, transmissible through saliva to humans etc. and causing madness; hydrophobia. [Latin: related to RABID]

RAC abbr. Royal Automobile Club.

raccoon var. of RACOON.

race¹ — n. 1 contest of speed between runners, horses, vehicles, ships, etc. 2 (in pl.) series of these for horses, dogs, etc., at a fixed time on a regular course. 3 contest between persons to be first to achieve something. 4 a strong current in the sea or a river. b channel (mill-race). — v. (-cing) 1 take part in a race with. 3 try to surpass in

speed. 4 (foll. by with) compete in speed with. 5 cause □ race. 6 a go at full or excessive speed. b cause to do this. 7 (usu. as **racing** adj.) follow or take part in horse-racing (a racing man). [Old Norse]

race² n. 1 each of the major divisions of humankind, each having distinct physical characteristics. 2 fact or concept of division into races. 3 genus, species, breed, or variety of animals, or plants 4 group of persons, animals, or plants connected by common descent. 5 any great division of living creatures (the human race). [Italian razza]

racecourse n. ground for horse-racing.

racegoer n. person who frequents horse-races.

racehorse n. horse bred or kept for racing.

raceme /rə'siːm/ n. flower cluster with separate flowers attached by short stalks at equal distances along the stem. [Latin racemus grape-bunch]

race meeting n. sequence of horse-races at one place.

race relations n.pl. relations between members of different races in the same country.

race riot n. outbreak of violence due to racial antagonism.

racetrack n. 1 = RACECOURSE. 2 track for motor racing.

racial /'reɪʃ(ə)l/ adj. 1 of or concerning race. 2 on the grounds of or connected with difference in race. □ **racially** adv.

racialism /'reɪʃəˌlɪz(ə)m/ n. = RACISM. □ **racialist** n. & adj.

racing car n. motor car built for racing.

racing driver n. driver of a racing car.

racism n. 1 belief in the superiority of a particular race; prejudice based on this. 2 antagonism towards other races. □ **racist** n. & adj.

rack¹ — n. 1 framework, usu. with rails, bars, etc., for holding things. 2 cogged or toothed bar or rail engaging with a wheel or pinion etc. 3 hist. instrument of torture stretching the victim's joints. — v. 1 (of disease or pain) inflict suffering on. 2 hist. torture (a person) on the rack. 3 place in or on a rack. 4 shake violently. 5 injure by straining. □ **on the rack** suffering acute mental or physical pain. **rack one's brains** make a great mental effort. [Low German or Dutch]

rack² n. destruction (esp. *rack and ruin*). [from WRACK]

rack³ v. (often foll. by *off*) draw off (wine, beer, etc.) from the lees. [Provençal *arracar* from *raca* stems and husks of grapes, dregs]

racket¹ /'rækɪt/ n. (also **racquet**) 1 bat with a round or oval frame strung with catgut, nylon, etc., used in tennis, squash, etc. 2 (in *pl.*) game like squash, played in a court of four plain walls. [French *raquette* from Arabic *rahat* palm of the hand]

racket² /'rækɪt/ n. 1 disturbance, uproar, din. 2 *slang* a scheme for obtaining money etc. by dishonest means. b dodge; sly game. 3 *colloq.* line of business. [perhaps imitative]

racketeer /ˌrækɪ'tɪə(r)/ n. person who operates a dishonest business. □ **racketeering** n.

rack-rent n. extortionate rent.

raconteur /ˌrækɒn'tɜː(r)/ n. teller of anecdotes. [French: related to RECOUNT]

raccoon /rə'kuːn/ n. (also **racoon**) (*pl.* same or **-s**) 1 N. American mammal with a bushy tail and sharp snout. 2 its fur. [Algonquian]

racquet var. of RACKET¹.

racy *adj.* (**-ier, -iest**) 1 lively and vigorous in style. 2 risqué. 3 of distinctive quality (*a racy wine*). □ **raciness** n. [from RACE²]

RADA /'rɑːdə/ *abbr.* Royal Academy of Dramatic Art.

radar /'reɪdɑː(r)/ n. 1 system for detecting the direction, range, or presence of objects, by sending out pulses of high frequency electromagnetic waves which they reflect. 2 apparatus for this. [from *radio detection and ranging*]

radar trap n. device using radar to detect speeding vehicles.

raddle /'ræd(ə)l/ —n. red ochre. —v. (**-ling**) 1 colour with raddle or too much rouge. 2 (as **raddled** *adj.*) worn out. [related to RUDDY]

radial /'reɪdɪəl/ —*adj.* 1 of or in rays. 2 a arranged like rays or radii. b having spokes or radiating lines. c acting or moving along lines diverging from a centre. 3 (in full **radial-ply**) (of a tyre) having the fabric layers arranged radially and the tread strengthened. —n. radial-ply tyre. □ **radially** *adv.* [related to RADIUS]

radian /'reɪdɪən/ n. SI unit of angle, equal to an angle at the centre of a circle the arc of which is equal in length to the radius (1 radian is approx. 57°).

radiant /'reɪdɪənt/ —*adj.* 1 emitting rays of light. 2 (of eyes or looks) beaming with joy, hope, or love. 3 (of beauty) splendid or dazzling. 4 (of light) issuing in rays. —n. point or object from which light or heat radiates. □ **radiance** n. **radiantly** *adv.*

radiant heat n. heat transmitted by radiation.

radiate —v. /'reɪdɪeɪt/ (**-ting**) 1 a emit rays of light, heat, etc. b (of light or heat) be emitted in rays. 2 emit (light, heat, etc.) from a centre. 3 transmit or demonstrate (joy etc.). 4 diverge or spread from a centre. —*adj.* /'reɪdɪət/ having divergent rays or parts radially arranged.

radiation /ˌreɪdɪ'eɪʃ(ə)n/ n. 1 radiating or being radiated. 2 *Physics* a emission of energy as electromagnetic waves or as moving particles, e.g. X-rays or ultraviolet light.

radiation sickness n. sickness caused by exposure to radiation, such as gamma rays.

radiation therapy treatment of cancer etc. using radiation, e.g. X-rays or ultraviolet light.

radiator /'reɪdɪeɪtə(r)/ n. 1 device for heating a room etc., consisting of a metal case through which hot water or steam circulates. 2 engine-cooling device in a motor vehicle or aircraft.

radical /'rædɪk(ə)l/ —*adj.* 1 fundamental (*a radical error*). 2 far-reaching; thorough (*radical change*). 3 advocating thorough reform; revolutionary. 4 forming the basis; primary. 5 of the root of a number or quantity. 6 (of surgery etc.) seeking to ensure the removal of all diseased tissue. 7 of the roots of words. 8 *Bot.* of the root. —n. 1 person holding radical views or belonging to a radical party. 2 *Chem.* **a** = FREE RADICAL. **b** atom or a group of these normally forming part of a compound and remaining unaltered during the compound's ordinary chemical changes. 3 root of a word. 4 *Math.* quantity forming or expressed as the root of another. □ **radicalism** n. **radically** *adv.* [Latin: related to RADIX]

radicchio /rə'diːkɪəʊ/ n. (*pl.* **-s**) chicory with reddish-purple leaves. [Italian, = chicory]

radicle /'rædɪk(ə)l/ n. part of a plant embryo that develops into the primary root; rootlet. [Latin: related to RADIX]

radii *pl.* of RADIUS.

radio /'reɪdɪəʊ/ —n. (*pl.* **-s**) 1 (often *attrib.*) a transmission and reception of sound messages etc. by electromagnetic waves of radio frequency. b apparatus

radio- for receiving, broadcasting, or transmitting radio signals. **2** a sound broadcasting (*prefers the radio*). **b** broadcasting station or channel (*Radio One*). —*v.* **(-es, -ed) 1 a** send (a message) by radio. **b** send a message to (a person) by radio. **2** communicate or broadcast by radio. [short for *radio-telegraphy* etc.]

radio- *comb. form* **1** denoting radio or broadcasting. **2** connected with rays or radiation.

radioactive /ˌreɪdɪəʊˈæktɪv/ *adj.* of or exhibiting radioactivity.

radioactivity /ˌreɪdɪəʊækˈtɪvɪtɪ/ *n.* spontaneous disintegration of atomic nuclei, with the emission of usu. penetrating radiation or particles.

radiocarbon /ˈreɪdɪəʊˈkɑːbən/ *n.* radioactive isotope of carbon.

radio-controlled /ˌreɪdɪəʊkənˈtrəʊld/ *adj.* controlled from a distance by radio.

radio frequency *n.* (*pl.* **-ies**) frequency band of telecommunication, ranging from 10^4 to 10^{11} or 10^{12} Hz.

radiogram /ˈreɪdɪəʊˌgræm/ *n.* **1** combined radio and record-player. **2** picture obtained by X-rays etc. **3** telegram sent by radio.

radiograph /ˈreɪdɪəʊˌgrɑːf/ —*n.* **1** instrument recording the intensity of radiation. **2** = RADIOGRAM 2. —*v.* obtain a picture of by X-ray, gamma ray, etc. □ **radiographer** /-ˈɒgrəfə(r)/ *n.* **radiography** /-ˈɒgrəfɪ/ *n.*

radioisotope /ˌreɪdɪəʊˈaɪsətəʊp/ *n.* radioactive isotope.

radiology /ˌreɪdɪˈɒlədʒɪ/ *n.* the study of X-rays and other high-energy radiation, esp. as used in medicine. □ **radiologist** *n.*

radiophonic /ˌreɪdɪəʊˈfɒnɪk/ *adj.* of or relating to electronically produced sound, esp. music.

radioscopy /ˌreɪdɪˈɒskəpɪ/ *n.* examination by X-rays etc. of objects opaque to light.

radio-telegraphy /ˌreɪdɪəʊtɪˈlegrəfɪ/ *n.* telegraphy using radio. □ **radio-telegram** *n.*

radio-telephone /ˌreɪdɪəʊˈtelɪfəʊn/ *n.* telephone using radio. □ **radio-telephony** /ˌreɪdɪəʊtɪˈlefənɪ/ *n.*

radio telescope *n.* directional aerial system for collecting and analysing radiation in the radio frequency range from stars etc.

radiotherapy /ˌreɪdɪəʊˈθerəpɪ/ *n.* treatment of disease by X-rays or other forms of radiation.

radish /ˈrædɪʃ/ *n.* **1** plant with a fleshy pungent root. **2** this root, eaten esp. raw. [Latin RADIX]

radium /ˈreɪdɪəm/ *n.* radioactive metallic element orig. obtained from pitchblende etc., used esp. in radiotherapy.

radius /ˈreɪdɪəs/ *n.* (*pl.* **radii** /-dɪaɪ/ or **radiuses**) **1 a** straight line from the centre to the circumference of a circle or sphere. **b** length of this. **2** distance from a centre (*within a radius of 20 miles*). **3 a** thicker and shorter of the two bones in the human forearm. **b** corresponding bone in a vertebrate's foreleg or a bird's wing. [Latin]

radix /ˈreɪdɪks/ *n.* (*pl.* **radices** /-dɪsiːz/) *Math.* number or symbol used as the basis of a numeration scale (e.g. ten in the decimal system). [Latin, = root]

radon /ˈreɪdɒn/ *n.* gaseous radioactive inert element arising from the disintegration of radium.

RAF *abbr.* [colloq. raf] Royal Air Force.

raffia /ˈræfɪə/ *n.* **1** palm-tree native to Madagascar. **2** fibre from its leaves, used for weaving and for tying plants etc. [Malagasy]

raffish /ˈræfɪʃ/ *adj.* **1** disreputable, rakish. **2** tawdry. [*raff* rubbish]

raffle /ˈræf(ə)l/ —*n.* fund-raising lottery with prizes. —*v.* (-ling) (often foll. by *off*) sell by means of a raffle. [French *rafl(e)*, a dice-game]

raft /rɑːft/ *n.* flat floating structure of timber or other materials for conveying persons or things. [Old Norse]

rafter /ˈrɑːftə(r)/ *n.* each of the sloping beams forming the framework of a roof. [Old English]

rag [1] *n.* **1** torn, frayed, or worn piece of woven material. **2** (in *pl.*) old or worn clothes. **3** (*collect.*) scraps of cloth used as material for paper, stuffing, etc. **4** *derog.* newspaper. □ **in rags** much torn. **rags to riches** poverty to affluence. [probably a back-formation from RAGGED]

rag [2] —*n.* **1** fund-raising programme of stunts, parades, and entertainment organized by students. **2** prank. **3 a** rowdy celebration. **b** noisy disorderly scene. —*v.* (**-gg-**) **1** tease; play rough jokes on. **2** engage in rough play; be noisy and riotous. [origin unknown]

rag [3] *n.* ragtime composition. [abbreviation]

ragamuffin /ˈrægəˌmʌfɪn/ *n.* child in ragged dirty clothes. [probably from RAG [1]]

rag-and-bone man *n.* itinerant dealer in old clothes, furniture, etc.

rag-bag *n.* **1** bag for scraps of fabric etc. **2** miscellaneous collection.

rag doll *n.* stuffed cloth doll.

rage —*n.* **1** fierce or violent anger. **2** fit of this. **3** violent action of a natural force. —*v.* (**-ging**) **1** be full of anger. **2** (often foll.

by (*at*, *against*) speak furiously or madly. 3 (of wind, battle, etc.) be violent; be at its height. 4 (as **raging** *adj.*) extreme, very painful (*raging thirst*; *raging headache*). □ **all the rage** very popular, fashionable. [Latin RABIES]

ragged /ˈragɪd/ *adj.* 1 torn; frayed. 2 in ragged clothes. 3 with a broken or jagged outline or surface. 4 faulty, imperfect; lacking finish, smoothness, or uniformity. [Old Norse]

ragged robin *n.* pink-flowered campion with tattered petals.

raglan /ˈraglən/ —*adj.* (of a sleeve) running up to the neck of a garment. —*n.* (often *attrib.*) overcoat without shoulder seams, the sleeves running up to the neck. [Lord *Raglan*]

ragout /raˈguː/ *n.* meat stewed with vegetables and highly seasoned. [French]

ragtag *n.* (in full **ragtag and bobtail**) *derog.* rabble or common people. [from RAG¹]

ragtime *n.* form of highly syncopated early jazz, esp. for the piano.

rag trade *n.* *colloq.* the clothing business.

ragwort /ˈragwəːt/ *n.* yellow-flowered ragged-leaved plant.

raid —*n.* 1 rapid surprise attack, esp.: **a** in warfare. **b** in order to commit a crime, steal, or do harm. 2 surprise attack by police etc. to arrest suspected persons or seize illicit goods. —*v.* make a raid on. □ **raider** *n.* [Scots form of ROAD]

rail¹ —*n.* 1 level or sloping bar or series of bars: **a** used to hang things on. **b** as the top of banisters. **c** forming part of a fence or barrier as protection. 2 steel bar or continuous line of bars laid on the ground, usu. as a railway. 3 (often *attrib.*) railway. —*v.* 1 furnish with a rail or rails. 2 (usu. foll. by *in*, *off*) enclose with rails. □ **off the rails** disorganized; out of order; deranged. [French *reille* from Latin *regula* RULE]

rail² *v.* (often foll. by *at*, *against*) complain or protest strongly; rant. [French *railler*]

rail³ *n.* wading bird often inhabiting marshes. [French]

railcar *n.* single powered railway coach.

railcard *n.* pass entitling the holder to reduced rail fares.

railing *n.* (usu. in *pl.*) fence or barrier made of rails.

raillery /ˈreɪlərɪ/ *n.* good-humoured ridicule. [French *raillerie*: related to RAIL²]

railman *n.* = RAILWAYMAN.

railroad —*n.* esp. *US* = RAILWAY. —*v.* (often foll. by *into*, *through*, etc.) coerce;

rush (*railroaded into agreeing*; *railroaded through the Cabinet*).

railway *n.* 1 track or set of tracks of steel rails upon which trains run. 2 such a system worked by a single company. 3 organization and personnel required for its working.

railwayman *n.* railway employee.

raiment /ˈreɪmənt/ *n.* *archaic* clothing. [*arrayment*: related to ARRAY]

rain —*n.* 1 **a** condensed atmospheric moisture falling in drops. **b** (*the*) rainy season. **b** rainfalls. 3 **a** falling liquid or solid particles or objects. **b** rainlike descent of these. —*v.* 1 (prec. by *it* as subject) rain falls. 2 **a** fall like rain. **b** (prec. by *it* as subject) send in large quantities. 3 send down like rain; lavishly bestow (*rained blows upon him*). 4 (of the sky, clouds, etc.) send down rain. □ **rain off** (or *US* **out**) (esp. in *passive*) cause (an event etc.) to be cancelled because of rain. [Old English]

rainbow /ˈreɪnbəʊ/ —*n.* arch of colours formed in the sky by reflection, refraction, and dispersion of the sun's rays in falling rain or in spray or mist. —*adj.* many-coloured. [Old English: related to RAIN, BOW¹]

rainbow trout *n.* large trout orig. of the Pacific coast of N. America.

rain check *n.* esp. *US* ticket given for later use when an outdoor event is interrupted or postponed by rain. □ **take a rain check on** reserve the right not to take up (an offer) until convenient.

raincoat *n.* waterproof or water-resistant coat.

raindrop *n.* single drop of rain.

rainfall *n.* 1 fall of rain. 2 quantity of rain falling within a given area in a given time.

rainforest *n.* luxuriant tropical forest with heavy rainfall.

rainproof *adj.* impervious to rain.

rainstorm *n.* storm with heavy rain.

rainwater *n.* water collected from fallen rain.

rainwear *n.* clothes for wearing in the rain.

rainy *adj.* (**-ier**, **-iest**) (of weather, a climate, day, etc.) in or on which rain is falling or much rain usually falls. [Old English: related to RAIN]

rainy day *n.* time of special need in the future.

raise /reɪz/ —*v.* (**-sing**) 1 put or take into a higher position. 2 (often foll. by *up*) cause to rise or stand up or be vertical. 3 increase the amount, value, or strength of. 4 (often foll. by *up*) construct or build up. 5 levy, collect, or bring together

(*raise money*), **6** cause to be heard or considered (*raise an objection*). **7** set going or bring into being (*raise hopes*). **8** bring up, educate. **9** breed, grow. **10** promote to a higher rank **11** (foll. by *to*) multiply a quantity to a power. **12** cause (bread) to rise. **13** *Cards* bet more than (another player). **14** end (a siege etc.). **15** remove (a barrier etc.). **18** rouse from sleep or death, or from a lair. **17** *colloq. US* increase in salary. —*n.* **1** act of raising. **2** *esp. US* increase in salary. [Old French]. □ **raise Cain** *colloq.* = **raise the roof**. **raise from the dead** restore to life. **raise a laugh** cause others to laugh. **raise the roof** *colloq.* cause an uproar. [Old Norse]

raisin /'reɪz(ə)n/ *n.* dried grape. [French]

raison d'être /ˌreɪzɒ̃ 'detr/ *n.* (*pl.* **raisons d'être** pronunc. same) purpose or reason that accounts for, justifies, or originally caused a thing's existence. [French]

raj /rɑːdʒ/ *n.* (prec. by *the*) *hist.* British sovereignty in India. [Hindi]

raja /'rɑːdʒə/ *n.* (also **rajah**) *hist.* **1** Indian king or prince. **2** petty dignitary or noble in India. [Hindi from Sanskrit]

rake¹ —*n.* **1** implement consisting of a pole with a toothed crossbar at the end for drawing together hay etc. or smoothing loose soil or gravel. **2** similar implement used (e.g.) at a gaming-table. —*v.* (**-king**) **1** collect or gather with or as with a rake. **2** make tidy or smooth with a rake. **3** use a rake. **4** search thoroughly, ransack. **5** direct gunfire along (a line) from end to end. **6** scratch or scrape. □ **rake in** *colloq.* amass (profits etc.). **rake up** revive the (unwelcome) memory of. [Old English]

rake² *n.* dissolute man of fashion. [*rake-hell*: related to RAKE¹, HELL]

rake³ —*v.* (**-king**) **1** set or be set at a sloping angle. **2** (of a mast or funnel) incline from the perpendicular towards the stern. —*n.* **1** raking position or build. **2** amount by which a thing rakes. [origin unknown]

rake-off *n. colloq.* commission or share.

rakish *adj.* **1** dashing; jaunty. **2** dissolute. □ **rakishly** *adv.* [from RAKE²]

rallentando /ˌrælən'tændəʊ/ *Mus.* —*adv. & adj.* with a gradual decrease of speed. —*n.* (*pl.* **-s** or **-di** /-diː/) passage to be performed in this way. [Italian]

rally¹ /'rælɪ/ —*v.* (**-ies, -ied**) **1** (often foll. by *round*) bring or come together as support for or for action. **2** bring or come together again after a rout or dispersion. **3** recover again after illness etc., revive. **4** revive (courage etc.). **5** (of share-prices etc.) increase after a fall. —*n.* (*pl.* **-ies**) **1** rallying or being rallied. **2** mass meeting of supporters or persons with a common interest. **3** competition for motor vehicles, mainly over public roads. **4** (in tennis etc.) extended exchange of strokes. [French *rallier*: related to RE-, ALLY¹]

rally² /'rælɪ/ *v.* (**-ies -ied**) ridicule good-humouredly. [French *railler*: related to RAIL²]

rallycross *n.* motor racing over roads and cross-country.

RAM *abbr.* **1** Royal Academy of Music. **2** random-access memory.

ram —*n.* **1** uncastrated male sheep. **2** (the Ram) zodiacal sign or constellation Aries. **3** *hist.* = BATTERING-RAM. **4** falling weight of a pile-driving machine. **5** hydraulically operated water pump. —*v.* (**-mm-**) **1** force or squeeze into place by pressure. **2** (usu. foll. by *down, in*, etc.) beat down or drive in by heavy blows. **3** (of a ship, vehicle, etc.) strike violently, crash against. **4** (foll. by *against, into*) dash or violently impel. [Old English]

Ramadan /ˌræmə'dæn/ *n.* ninth month of the Muslim year, with strict fasting from sunrise to sunset. [Arabic]

ramble /'ræmb(ə)l/ —*v.* (**-ling**) **1** walk for pleasure. **2** talk or write incoherently. —*n.* walk taken for pleasure. [Dutch *rammelen*]

rambler *n.* **1** person who rambles. **2** straggling or spreading rose.

rambling *adj.* **1** wandering. **2** disconnected, incoherent. **3** (of a house, street, etc.) irregularly arranged. **4** (of a plant) straggling, climbing.

rambutan /ræm'buːt(ə)n/ *n.* **1** red plum-sized prickly fruit. **2** E. Indian tree bearing this. [Malay]

RAMC *abbr.* Royal Army Medical Corps.

ramekin /'ræmɪkɪn/ *n.* **1** small dish for baking and serving an individual portion of food. **2** food served in this. [French *ramequin*]

ramification /ˌræmɪfɪ'keɪʃ(ə)n/ *n.* **1** consequence. **2** subdivision of a complex structure or process. [French: related to RAMIFY]

ramify /'ræmɪfaɪ/ *v.* (**-ies, -ied**) (cause to) form branches, subdivisions, or offshoots; branch out. [Latin *ramus* branch]

ramp —*n.* **1** slope, esp. joining two levels of ground, floor, etc. **2** movable stairs for entering or leaving an aircraft. **3** transverse ridge in a road making vehicles slow down. —*v.* **1** furnish or build with a ramp. **2 a** assume a threatening posture.

b (often foll. by *about*) storm, rage. [French *ramper* crawl]

rampage –*v.* /ræmˈpeɪdʒ/ (**-ging**) **1** (often foll. by *about*) rush wildly or violently about. **2** rage, storm. –*n.* /ˈræmpeɪdʒ/ wild or violent behaviour. □ **on the rampage** rampaging. [perhaps from RAMP]

rampant /ˈræmpənt/ *adj.* **1** unchecked, flourishing excessively. **2** rank, luxuriant. **3** (placed after the noun) *Heraldry* (of an animal) standing on its left hind foot with its forepaws in the air (*lion rampant*). **4** violent, fanatical. □ **rampancy** *n.* [French: related to RAMP]

rampart /ˈræmpɑːt/ *n.* **1 a** a defensive wall with a broad top and usu. a stone parapet. **b** walkway on top of this. **2** defence, protection. [French *remparer* fortify]

ramrod *n.* **1** rod for ramming down the charge of a muzzle-loading firearm. **2** thing that is very straight or rigid.

ramshackle /ˈræmˌʃæk(ə)l/ *adj.* tumbledown, rickety. [related to RANSACK]

ran *past of* RUN.

ranch /rɑːntʃ/ –*n.* **1** cattle-breeding establishment, esp. in the US and Canada. **2** farm where other animals are bred (*mink ranch*). –*v.* farm on a ranch. □ **rancher** *n.* [Spanish *rancho* group of persons eating together]

rancid /ˈrænsɪd/ *adj.* smelling or tasting like rank stale fat. □ **rancidity** /-ˈsɪdɪtɪ/ *n.* [Latin *rancidus* stinking]

rancour /ˈræŋkə(r)/ *n.* (*US* **rancor**) inveterate bitterness, malignant hate. □ **rancorous** *adj.* [Latin *rancor*: related to RANCID]

rand *n.* chief monetary unit of South Africa. [*the Rand*, gold-field district near Johannesburg]

R & B *abbr.* rhythm and blues.

R & D *abbr.* research and development.

random /ˈrændəm/ *adj.* made, done, etc., without method or conscious choice. □ **at random** without a particular aim. □ **randomize** *v.* (also **-ise**) (**-zing** *or* **-sing**). **randomization** /-ˈzeɪʃ(ə)n/ *n.* **randomly** *adv.* **randomness** *n.* [French *random* from *randir* gallop]

random-access *adj.* *Computing* (of a memory or file) having all parts directly accessible, so that it need not read sequentially.

randy /ˈrændɪ/ *adj.* (**-ier, -iest**) eager for sexual gratification, lustful. □ **randily** *adv.* **randiness** *n.* [perhaps related to RANT]

ranee /ˈrɑːnɪ/ *n.* (also **rani**) (*pl.* **-s**) *hist.* raja's wife or widow. [Hindi]

rang *past of* RING².

range /reɪndʒ/ –*n.* **1 a** region between limits of variation, esp. scope of effective operation. **b** such limits. **2** area attainable by a gun or projectile. **b** distance attainable by a gun or projectile and its objective. **4** row, series, etc., esp. of mountains. **5** area with targets or objective. **6** fireplace with ovens and hotplates for cooking. **7** area over which a thing is distributed. **8** distance that can be covered by a vehicle without refuelling. **9** distance between a camera and the subject to be photographed. **10** large area of open land for grazing or hunting. –*v.* (**-ging**) **1** reach; lie spread out; extend; be found over a specified district; vary between limits. **2** (usu. in *passive* or *refl.*) line up, arrange. **3** rove, wander. **4** traverse in all directions. [French: related to RANK¹]

rangefinder *n.* instrument for estimating the distance of an object to be shot at or photographed.

ranger *n.* **1** keeper of a royal or national park, or of a forest. **2** member of a body of mounted soldiers. **3** (**Ranger**) senior Guide.

rangy /ˈreɪndʒɪ/ *adj.* (**-ier, -iest**) tall and slim.

rani *var. of* RANEE.

rank¹ –*n.* **1 a** position in a hierarchy, grade of advancement. **b** distinct social class; grade of dignity or achievement. **c** high social position. **d** place in a scale. **2** row or line. **3** single line of soldiers drawn up abreast. **b** row where taxis await customers. **5** order, array. –*v.* **1** have a certain rank or place. **2** classify, give a certain grade to. **3** arrange (esp. soldiers) in rank. □ **close ranks** maintain solidarity. **the ranks** common soldiers. [French *ranc*]

rank² *adj.* **1** luxuriant, coarse; choked with or apt to produce weeds or excessive foliage. **2 a** foul-smelling. **b** loathsome, corrupt. **3** flagrant, virulent, gross, complete (*rank outsider*). [Old English]

rank and file *n.* (usu. treated as *pl.*) ordinary members of an organization.

rankle /ˈræŋk(ə)l/ *v.* (**-ling**) (of envy, disappointment, etc., or their cause) cause persistent annoyance or resentment. [French (*d*)*rancler* fester, from medieval Latin *dra(cu)nculus* little serpent]

ransack /ˈrænsæk/ *v.* **1** pillage or plunder (a house, country, etc.). **2** thoroughly search. [Old Norse *rannsaka* from *rann* house, *-saka* seek]

ransom /ˈrænsəm/ –*n.* **1** money demanded or paid for the release of a prisoner. **2** liberation of a prisoner in

return for this.—v. 1 buy the freedom or restoration of; redeem. 2 = **hold to ransom** (see HOLD[1]). 3 release for a ransom. [Latin: related to REDEMPTION]

rant —v. speak loudly, bombastically, violently, or theatrically. —n. piece of ranting. □ **rant and rave** express anger noisily and forcefully. [Dutch]

ranunculus /rəˈnʌŋkjʊləs/ n. (pl. **-luses** or **-li** /-laɪ/) plant cf the genus including buttercups. [Latin, diminutive of rana frog]

RAOC abbr. Royal Army Ordnance Corps.

rap[1] —n. 1 smart slight blow. 2 knock, sharp tapping sound 3 slang blame, punishment. 4 a rhythmic monologue recited to music. b (in full **rap music**) style of rock music with words recited. —v. (**-pp-**) 1 strike smartly. 2 knock; make a sharp tapping sound 3 criticize adversely. 4 perform a rap. □ **take the rap** suffer the consequences. □ **rapper** n. [probably imitative]

rap[2] n. small amount, the least bit (don't care a rap). [Irish ropaire counterfeit coin]

rapacious /rəˈpeɪʃəs/ adj. grasping, extortionate, predatory. □ **rapacity** /rəˈpæstɪ/ n. [Latin rapax: related to RAPE[1]]

rape[1] —n. 1 a act of forcing a woman or girl to have sexual intercourse against her will. b forcible sodomy. 2 (often foll. by of) violent assault or plunder. forcible interference. —v. (**-ping**) commit rape on. [Latin rapio seize]

rape[2] n. plant grown as fodder, and for its seed from which oil is extracted. [Latin rapum, rapa turnip]

rapid /ˈræpɪd/ —adj. (**-er, -est**) 1 quick, swift. 2 acting or completed in a short time. 3 (of a slope) descending steeply. —n. (usu. in pl.) steep descent in a river-bed, with a swift current. □ **rapidity** /rəˈpɪdɪtɪ/ n. **rapidly** adv. **rapidness** n. [Latin: related to RAPE[1]]

rapid eye movement n. type of jerky movement of the eyes during dreaming.

rapier /ˈreɪpɪə(r)/ n. 1 light slender sword for thrusting. 2 (attrib.) sharp (rapier wit). [French rapière]

rapine /ˈræpaɪn/ n. rhet. plundering. [Latin: related to RAPE[1]]

rapist n. person who commits rape.

rapport /ræˈpɔː(r)/ n. relationship or communication, esp. when useful and harmonious. [Latin porto carry]

rapprochement /ræˈprɒʃmɑ̃/ n. resumption of harmonious relations, esp. between States. [French: related to APPROACH]

rapscallion /ræpˈskæljən/ n. archaic or joc. rascal. [perhaps from RASCAL]

rapt adj. 1 fully absorbed or intent, enraptured. 2 carried away with feeling or lofty thought. [Latin raptus: related to RAPE[1]]

rapture /ˈræptʃə(r)/ n. 1 ecstatic delight. 2 (in pl.) great pleasure or enthusiasm or the expression of it. □ **rapturous** adj. [French or medieval Latin: related to RAPE[1]]

rare[1] adj. (**rarer, rarest**) 1 seldom done, found, or occurring. uncommon, unusual. 2 exceptionally good. 3 of less than the usual density. □ **rareness** n. [Latin rarus]

rare[2] adj. (**rarer, rarest**) (of meat) cooked so that the inside is still red and juicy. underdone. [Old English]

rarebit n. = WELSH RABBIT. [from RARE[1]]

rare earth n. lanthanide element.

rarefy /ˈreərɪfaɪ/ v. (**-ies, -ied**) 1 make or become less dense or solid. 2 purify or refine (a person's nature etc.). 3 make (an idea etc.) subtle. □ **rarefaction** /-ˈfæk(ʃ)ən/ n. [French or medieval Latin: related to RARE[1]]

rarely adv. 1 seldom, not often. 2 exceptionally.

raring /ˈreərɪŋ/ adj. colloq. enthusiastic, eager (raring to go). [participle of rare, dial. var. of RCAR or REAR[2]]

rarity /ˈreərɪtɪ/ n. (pl. **-ies**) 1 rareness. 2 uncommon thing. [Latin: related to RARE[1]]

rascal /ˈrɑːsk(ə)l/ n. dishonest or mischievous person. □ **rascally** adj. [French rascaille rabble]

rase var. of RAZE.

rash[1] adj. reckless, impetuous, hasty. □ **rashly** adv. **rashness** n. [probably Old English]

rash[2] n. 1 eruption of the skin in spots or patches. 2 (usu. foll. by of) sudden widespread phenomenon (rash of strikes). [origin uncertain]

rasher n. thin slice of bacon or ham. [origin unknown]

rasp —n. 1 coarse kind of file having separate teeth. 2 grating noise or utterance. —v. 1 a scrape with a rasp. b scrape roughly. 2 a make a grating sound. b say gratingly. 3 grate upon (a person or feelings). [French raspe(r)]

raspberry /ˈrɑːzbərɪ/ n. (pl. **-ies**) 1 a red blackberry-like fruit. b bramble bearing this. 2 colloq. sound made by blowing through the lips, expressing derision or disapproval. [origin unknown]

raspberry-cane n. raspberry plant.

Rasta /ˈræstə/ n. = RASTAFARIAN (also attrib.).

Rastafarian /ˌræstəˈfeərɪən/ n. member of a Jamaican sect, often having dreadlocks and regarding Haile Selassie of Ethiopia

as God. —*adj.* of this sect. [*Ras Tafari*, title of former Emperor Haile Selassie]

rat —*n.* **1 a** rodent like a large mouse. **b** similar rodent (*muskrat; water-rat*). **2** turncoat. **3** *colloq.* unpleasant or treacherous person. **4** (in *pl.*) *slang* exclamation of annoyance etc. —*v.* (**-tt-**) **1** hunt or kill rats. **2** (also foll. by *on*) inform (on); desert, betray. [Old English]

ratable var. of RATEABLE.

ratatat (also **rat-a-tat**) var. of RAT-TAT.

ratatouille /ˌrætəˈtuːɪ, -ˈtwiː/ *n.* dish of stewed onions, courgettes, tomatoes, aubergines, and peppers. [French dial.]

ratbag *n. slang* obnoxious person.

ratchet /ˈrætʃɪt/ *n.* **1** set of teeth on the edge of a bar or wheel with a catch ensuring motion in one direction only. **2** (in full **ratchet-wheel**) wheel with a rim so toothed. [French *rochet* lance-head]

rate¹ —*n.* **1** numerical proportion between two sets of things (*moving at a rate of 50 m.p.h.*) or as the basis of calculating an amount or value (*charge, cost, or value; measure of this (*postal rates; the rate for the job*. **3** pace of movement or change (*prices increasing at a great rate*). **4** (in *comb.*) class or rank (*first-rate*). **5** (in *pl.*) tax levied by local authorities on businesses (and formerly on private individuals) according to the value of buildings and land occupied. —*v.* (**-ting**) **1 a** estimate the worth or value of. **b** assign a value to. **2** consider, regard as. **3** (foll. by *as*) rank or be considered. **4 a** subject to the payment of a local rate. **b** value for the purpose of assessing rates. **5** be worthy of, deserve. ◻ **at any rate** in any case, whatever happens. **at this rate** if this example is typical. [Latin *rata*: related to RATIO]

■ **Usage** See note at *community charge.*

rate² *v.* (**-ting**) scold angrily. [origin unknown]

rateable *adj.* (also **ratable**) liable to rates.

rateable value *n.* value at which a business etc. is assessed for rates.

rate-capping *n. hist.* imposition of an upper limit on local authority rates. ◻ **rate-cap** *v.*

ratepayer *n.* person liable to pay rates.

rather /ˈrɑːðə(r)/ *adv.* **1** by preference (*would rather not go*). **2** (usu. foll. by *than*) more truly; as a more likely alternative (*is stupid rather than dishonest*). **3** more precisely (*a book, or rather, a pamphlet*). **4** slightly, to some extent (*became rather drunk*). **5** /rɑːˈðɜː(r)/ (as an emphatic response)

assuredly (*Did you like it? —Rather!*). ◻ **had rather** would rather. [Old English comparative of *rathe* early]

ratify /ˈrætɪfaɪ/ *v.* (**-ies, -ied**) confirm or accept (an agreement made in one's name) by formal consent, signature, etc. ◻ **ratification** /-fɪˈkeɪʃ(ə)n/ *n.* [medieval Latin: related to RATE¹]

rating *n.* **1** placing in a rank or class. **2** estimated standing of a person as regards credit etc. **3** non-commissioned sailor. **4** amount fixed as a local rate. **5** relative popularity of a broadcast programme as determined by the estimated size of the audience.

ratio /ˈreɪʃɪəʊ/ *n.* (*pl.* **-s**) quantitative relation between two similar magnitudes expressed as the number of times one contains the other (*in the ratio of three to two*). [Latin *reor rat-* reckon]

ratiocinate /ˌrætɪˈɒsɪneɪt/ *v.* (**-ting**) *literary* reason, esp. using syllogisms. ◻ **ratiocination** /-ˈneɪʃ(ə)n/ *n.* [Latin: related to RATIO]

ration /ˈræʃ(ə)n/ —*n.* **1** official allowance of food, clothing, etc., in a time of shortage. **2** (in *pl.*) fixed daily allowance of food, esp. in the armed forces. —*v.* **1** limit (persons or provisions) to a fixed ration. **2** (usu. foll. by *out*) share out (food etc.) in fixed quantities. [Latin: related to RATIO]

rational /ˈræʃən(ə)l/ *adj.* **1** of or based on reason. **2** sensible. **3** endowed with reason. **4** rejecting what is unreasonable or cannot be tested by reason in religion or custom. **5** (of a quantity or ratio) expressible as a ratio of whole numbers. ◻ **rationality** /-ˈnæltɪ/ *n.* **rationally** *adv.* [Latin: related to RATIO]

rationale /ˌræʃəˈnɑːl/ *n.* fundamental reason, logical basis. [neuter of Latin *rationalis*: related to RATIONAL]

rationalism /ˈræʃənəˌlɪz(ə)m/ *n.* practice of treating reason as the basis of belief and knowledge. ◻ **rationalist** *n.* & *adj.* **rationalistic** /-ˈlɪstɪk/ *adj.*

rationalize *v.* (also **-ise**) (**-zing** or **-sing**) **1** (often foll. by *away*) offer a rational but specious explanation of (one's behaviour or attitude). **2** make logical and consistent. **3** make (a business etc.) more efficient by reorganizing it to reduce or eliminate waste. ◻ **rationalization** /-ˈzeɪʃ(ə)n/ *n.*

ratline /ˈrætlɪn/ *n.* (also **ratlin**) (usu. in *pl.*) any of the small lines fastened across a sailing-ship's shrouds like ladder-rungs. [origin unknown]

rat race *n. colloq.* fiercely competitive struggle for position, power, etc.

ratsbane *n.* anything poisonous to rats, esp. a plant.

attan /rəˈtæn/ n. **1** climbing palm with long thin jointed pliable stems, used for furniture etc. **2** piece of rattan stem used as a walking-stick etc. [Malay]

at-tat /ˈrætˈtæt/ n. (also **rat-tat-tat**, **rat-a-tat** /ˌrætəˈtæt/) rapping sound, esp. of a knocker. [imitative]

attle /ˈræt(ə)l/ —v. (-ling) **1 a** give out a rapid succession of short sharp hard sounds. **b** cause to do this. **c** cause such sounds by shaking something. **2** (often foll. by *along*) **a** move with a rattling noise. **b** move or travel rapidly. **3 a** (usu. foll. by *on*) talk in a lively thoughtless way. **4** colloq. disconcert, alarm. —n. **1** rattling sound. **2** device or plaything made to rattle. □ **rattly** adj. [probably Low German or Dutch]

attlesnake n. poisonous American snake with a rattling structure of horny rings on its tail.

atting —adj. **1** that rattles. **2** brisk, vigorous (*rattling pace*). —adv. colloq. remarkably (*rattling good story*).

atty adj. (-ier, -iest) **1** relating to or infested with rats. **2** colloq. irritable, bad-tempered. □ **rattiness** n.

raucous /ˈrɔːkəs/ adj. harsh-sounding, loud and hoarse. □ **raucously** adv. **raucousness** n. [Latin]

raunchy /ˈrɔːntʃi/ adj. (-ier, -iest) colloq. coarse, earthy, sexually boisterous. □ **raunchily** adv. **raunchiness** n. [origin unknown]

ravage /ˈrævɪdʒ/ —v. (-ging) devastate, plunder. —n. **1** devastation. **2** (usu. in *pl.*, foll. by *of*) destructive effect. [French alteration from *ravine* rush of water]

rave —v. (-ving) **1** talk wildly or furiously in or as in delirium. **2** (usu. foll. by *about*, *over*) speak with rapturous admiration; go into raptures. **3** colloq. enjoy oneself freely (esp. *rave it up*). —n. **1** (usu. *attrib.*) colloq. highly enthusiastic review. **2** (also **rave-up**) colloq. lively party. **3** slang craze. [probably French dial. *raver*]

ravel /ˈræv(ə)l/ v. (-l-; US -l-) **1** entangle or become entangled. **2** fray out. **3** (often foll. by *out*) disentangle, unravel, separate into threads. [probably Dutch *rave-ler*]

raven /ˈreɪv(ə)n/ —n. large glossy black crow with a hoarse cry. —adj. glossy black. [Old English]

ravening /ˈreɪvənɪŋ/ adj. hungrily seeking prey, voracious. [French *raviner* from Latin: related to RAPINE]

ravenous /ˈrævənəs/ adj. **1** very hungry. **2** voracious. **3** rapacious. □

ravenously adv. [obsolete *raven*, *ravener* from French *raviner* ravage]

raver n. colloq. uninhibited pleasure-loving person.

ravine /rəˈviːn/ n. deep narrow gorge. [Latin: related to RAPINE]

raving —n. (usu. in *pl.*) wild or delirious talk. —adj. & adv. colloq. as an intensifier (*a raving beauty*; *raving mad*).

ravioli /ˌrævɪˈəʊli/ n. small pasta envelopes containing minced meat etc. [Italian]

ravish /ˈrævɪʃ/ v. **1** archaic rape (a woman). **2** enrapture. □ **ravishment** n. [Latin: related to RAPE]

ravishing adj. lovely, beautiful. □ **ravishingly** adv.

raw adj. **1** uncooked. **2** in the natural state; not processed or manufactured. **3** inexperienced, untrained. **4 a** stripped of skin; with the flesh exposed. **b** sensitive to the touch from being so exposed. **5** (of the atmosphere, day, etc.) cold and damp. **6** crude in artistic quality; lacking finish. **7** (of the edge of cloth) without hem or selvage. □ **in the raw 1** in its natural state without mitigation (*life in the raw*). **2** naked. **touch on the raw** upset (a person) on a sensitive matter. [Old English]

raw-boned adj. gaunt.

raw deal n. harsh or unfair treatment.

rawhide n. **1** untanned hide. **2** rope or whip of this.

Rawlplug /ˈrɔːlplʌɡ/ n. propr. cylindrical plug for holding a screw or nail in masonry. [*Rawlings*, name of the engineers]

raw material n. material from which manufactured goods are made.

ray¹ n. **1** single line or narrow beam of light from a small or distant source. **2** straight line in which radiation travels to a given point. **3** (in *pl.*) radiation of a specified type (*X-rays*). **4** trace or beginning of an enlightening or cheering influence (*ray of hope*). **5** any of a set of radiating lines, parts, or things. **6** marginal floret of a composite flower, e.g. a daisy. [Latin RADIUS]

ray² n. large edible marine fish with a flat body and a long slender tail. [Latin *raia*]

ray³ n. (also **re**) Mus. second note of a major scale. [Latin *resonare*, word arbitrarily taken]

rayon /ˈreɪɒn/ n. textile fibre or fabric made from cellulose. [from RAY¹]

raze v. (also **rase**) (-zing or -sing) completely destroy; tear down (esp. *raze to the ground*). [Latin *rado ras-* scrape]

razor /ˈreɪzə(r)/ n. instrument with a sharp blade used in cutting hair, esp. shaving. [French *rasor*: related to RAZE]

razor-bill *n.* auk with a sharp-edged bill.

razor-blade *n.* flat piece of metal with a sharp edge, used in a safety razor.

razor-edge *n.* (also **razor's edge**) **1** keen edge. **2** sharp mountain-ridge. **3** critical situation. **4** sharp line of division.

razzle-dazzle /ˈræzəlˌdæz(ə)l/ *n.* (also **razzle**) *colloq.* **1 a** excitement; bustle. **b** spree (esp. *on the razzle*). **2** extravagant publicity. [reduplication of DAZZLE]

razzmatazz /ˌræzməˈtæz/ *n. colloq.* **1** glamorous excitement; bustle. **2** spree. **3** insincere actions. [probably an alteration of RAZZLE-DAZZLE]

Rb *symb.* rubidium.

RC *abbr.* Roman Catholic.

Rd. *abbr.* Road.

RE *abbr.* **1** Religious Education. **2** Royal Engineers.

Re *symb.* rhenium.

re[1] /riː/ *prep.* **1** in the matter of (as the first word in a heading). **2** *Commerce* about, concerning (in letters). [Latin, ablative of *res* thing]

re[2] var. of RAY[3].

re- *prefix* **1** attachable to almost any verb or its derivative, meaning: **a** once more; afresh, anew. **b** back; with return to a previous state. **2** (also **red-** before a vowel, as in *redolent*) in verbs and verbal derivatives denoting: **a** in return; mutually (*react*). **b** opposition (*resist*). **c** behind or after (*relic*). **d** retirement or secrecy (*recluse*). **e** off, away, down (*recede; relegate; repress*). **f** frequentative or intensive force (*redouble; resplendent*). **g** negative force (*recant; reveal*). [Latin]

■ **Usage** In sense 1, a hyphen is normally used when the word begins with *e* (*re-enact*), or to distinguish the compound from a more familiar one-word form (*re-form* = form again).

reach —*v.* **1** (often foll. by *out*) stretch out, extend. **2** (often foll. by *for*) stretch out the hand etc.; make a stretch or effort. **3** get as far as. **4** get to or attain. **5** make contact with the hand etc., or by telephone etc. (*reach me that book*). **6** hand, pass (*reach me that book*). **7** take with an outstretched hand. **8** *Naut.* sail with the wind abeam or abaft the beam. —*n.* **1** extent to which a hand etc. can be reached out, influence exerted, motion carried out, or mental powers used. **2** act of reaching out. **3** continuous extent, esp. of river between two bends or of canal between locks. **4** *Naut.* distance traversed in reaching. □ **reachable** *adj.* [Old English]

reach-me-down *n. colloq.* **1** ready-made garment. **2** = HAND-ME-DOWN.

reacquaint /ˌriːəˈkweɪnt/ *v.* make acquainted again. □ **reacquaintance** *n.*

react /rɪˈækt/ *v.* **1** (often foll. by *to*) respond to a stimulus; change or behave differently due to some influence (*reacted badly to the news*). **2** (often foll. by *against*) respond with repulsion to; tend in a reverse or contrary direction. **3** (foll. by *with*) (of a substance or particle) be the cause of chemical activity or interaction with another (*nitrous oxide reacts with the metal*). **4** (foll. by *with*) cause (a substance) to react with another.

reaction /rɪˈækʃ(ə)n/ *n.* **1** reacting, response. **2** bad physical response to a drug etc. **3** occurrence of a condition after a period of its opposite. **4** tendency to oppose change or reform. **5** interaction of substances undergoing chemical change.

reactionary —*adj.* tending to oppose (esp. political) change or reform. —*n.* (*pl.* -ies) reactionary person.

reactivate /rɪˈæktɪˌveɪt/ *v.* (-ting) restore to a state of activity. □ **reactivation** /-ˈveɪʃ(ə)n/ *n.*

reactive /rɪˈæktɪv/ *adj.* **1** showing reaction. **2** reacting rather than taking the initiative. **3** susceptible to chemical reaction.

reactor *n.* **1** person or thing that reacts. **2** = NUCLEAR REACTOR.

read —*v.* (*past* and *past part.* **read** /red/) **1** (also *absol.*) reproduce mentally or (often foll. by *aloud, out, off,* etc.) vocally the written or printed words of (a book, author, etc.). **2** convert or be able to convert into the intended words or meaning (written or other symbols or the things expressed in this way) (*can't read music*). **3** understand by observing; interpret (*read me like a book; read his silence as consent; read my mind; reads tea-leaves*). **4** find (a thing) stated in print etc. (*read that you were leaving*). **5** (often foll. by *into*) assume as intended or deducible (*read too much into it*). **6** bring into a specified state by reading (*read myself to sleep*). **7 a** (of a recording instrument) show (a specified figure etc.). **b** interpret (a recording instrument) (*read the meter*). **8** convey meaning when read; have a certain wording (*it reads persuasively; reads from left to right*). **9** sound or affect a hearer or reader when read (*the book reads like a parody*). **10** study by reading (esp. a subject at university). **11** (as **read** /red/ *adj.*) versed in a subject (esp.

literature. by reading (*well-read person*). 12 (of a computer) copy or transfer (data). 13 hear and understand (over a radio) (*are you reading me?*), 14 replace (a word etc.) with the correct one(s) (*for 'this' read 'these'*). —n. 1 spell of reading. 2 *colloq.* book etc. as regards readability (*is a good read*). □ **read between the lines** look for or find hidden meaning. **read up** (often followed by **on**) make a special study of a subject; **take as read** treat (a thing) as if it has been agreed. [Old English]

readable *adj.* 1 able to be read. 2 interesting to read. □ **readability** /-'bɪlɪtɪ/ *n.*

readdress /riːə'dres/ *v.* 1 change the address of (an item for posting). 2 address (a problem etc.) anew. 3 speak or write to anew.

reader *n.* 1 person who reads. 2 book intended to give reading practice, esp. in a foreign language. 3 device for producing an image that can be read from microfilm etc. 4 (also **Reader**) university lecturer of the highest grade below professor. 5 publisher's employee who reports on submitted manuscripts. 6 printer's proof-corrector. 7 person appointed to read aloud, esp. in church.

readership *n.* 1 readers of a newspaper etc. 2 (also **Readership**) position of Reader.

readily /'redɪlɪ/ *adv.* 1 without showing reluctance, willingly. 2 without difficulty.

readiness *n.* 1 ready or prepared state. 2 willingness. 3 facility; promptness in argument or action.

reading *n.* 1 a act of reading (*reading of the will*). b matter to be read (*made exciting reading*). 2 (in *comb.*) used for reading (*reading-lamp; reading-room*). 3 literary knowledge. 4 entertainment at which a play, poems, etc., are read. 5 figure etc. shown by a recording instrument. 6 interpretation or view taken (*what is your reading of the facts?*). 7 interpretation made (of drama, music, etc.). 8 each of the successive occasions on which a bill must be presented to a legislature for acceptance. [Old English: related to READ]

readjust /riːə'dʒʌst/ *v.* adjust again or to a former state. □ **readjustment** *n.*

readmit /riːəd'mɪt/ *v.* (-tt-) admit again. □ **readmission** *n.*

readopt /riːə'dɒpt/ *v.* adopt again. □ **readoption** *n.*

ready /'redɪ/ —*adj.* (-ier, -iest) (usu. *predic.*) 1 with preparations complete (*dinner is ready*). 2 in a fit state. 3 willing, inclined, or resolved (*he is always ready to complain*). 4 within reach; easily secured (*ready source of*

income). 5 fit for immediate use. 6 immediate, unqualified (*found ready acceptance*). 7 prompt (*is always ready with excuses*). 8 (foll. by **to** + infin.) about to (*ready to burst*). 9 provided beforehand. —*adv.* (usu. in *comb.*) beforehand, so as not to require doing when the time comes for use etc. (*is ready packed; ready-mixed concrete; ready-made family*). —*n.* (*pl.* -ies) *slang* (prec. by *the*) = READY MONEY. —*v.* (-ies, -ied) make ready, prepare. □ **at the ready** ready for action. □ **make ready** prepare. [Old English]

ready-made *adj.* (also **ready-to-wear**) (esp. of clothes) made in a standard size, not to measure.

ready money *n.* 1 actual coin or notes.

ready reckoner *n.* book or table listing standard numerical calculations as used esp. in commerce.

reaffirm /riːə'fɜːm/ *v.* affirm again. □ **reaffirmation** /-æfə'meɪʃ(ə)n/ *n.*

reafforest /riːə'fɒrɪst/ *v.* replant (former forest land) with trees. □ **reafforestation** /-steɪʃ(ə)n/ *n.*

reagent /rɪ'eɪdʒ(ə)nt/ *n. Chem.* substance used to cause a reaction, esp. to detect another substance.

real /rɪəl/ —*adj.* 1 actually existing or occurring. 2 genuine; rightly so called; not artificial. 3 *Law* consisting of immovable property such as land or houses (*real estate*). 4 appraised by purchasing power (*real value*). 5 *Math.* (of a quantity) having no imaginary part (see IMAGINARY 2). —*adv. Scot. & US colloq.* really, very. □ **for real** *colloq.* seriously, in earnest; **the real thing** (of an object or emotion) genuine, not inferior. [Anglo-French and Latin *realis* from *res* thing]

real² /reɪ'ɑːl/ *n. hist.* coin and monetary unit in Spanish-speaking countries. [Spanish: related to ROYAL]

real ale *n.* beer regarded as brewed in a traditional way.

realign /rɪə'laɪn/ *v.* 1 align again. 2 regroup in politics etc. □ **realignment** *n.*

realism *n.* 1 practice of regarding things in their true nature and dealing with them as they are. 2 fidelity to nature in representation; the showing of life etc. as it is. 3 *Philos.* doctrine that abstract concepts have an objective existence. □ **realist** *n.*

realistic /rɪə'lɪstɪk/ *adj.* 1 regarding things as they are; following a policy of realism. 2 based on facts rather than ideals. □ **realistically** *adv.*

reality /rɪˈæltɪ/ *n.* (*pl.* **-ies**) **1** what is real or existent or underlies appearances. **2** (foll. by *of*) the real nature of. **3** real existence; state of being real. **4** resemblance to an original. □ **in reality** in fact. [Medieval Latin or French: related to REAL[1]]

realize *v.* (also **-ise**) (**-zing** or **-sing**) **1** (often foll. by *that*) be fully aware of; conceive as real. **2** understand clearly. **3** present as real. **4** convert into actuality. **5** a convert into money. **b** acquire (profit). **c** be sold for (a specified price). □ **realizable** *adj.* **realization** /-ˈzeɪʃ(ə)n/ *n.*

real life *n.* **1** life lived by actual people. **2** (*attrib.*) (**real-life**) actual, not fictional (*her real-life husband*).

reallocate /riːˈæləkeɪt/ *v.* (**-ting**) allocate again or differently. □ **reallocation** /-ˈkeɪʃ(ə)n/ *n.*

really /ˈrɪəlɪ/ *adv.* **1** in reality. **2** very (*really useful*). **3** indeed. I assure you. **4** expression of mild protest or surprise.

realm /rɛlm/ *n.* **1** *formal* kingdom. **2** domain (*realm of myth*). [Latin REGIMEN]

real money *n.* current coin; cash.

real tennis *n.* original form of tennis played on an indoor court.

real time *n.* **1** actual time during which a process occurs. **2** (*attrib.*) (**real-time**) *Computing* (of a system) in which the response time is the actual time during which an event occurs.

realty /ˈrɪəltɪ/ *n.* real estate.

ream *n.* **1** twenty quires of paper. **2** (in *pl.*) large quantity of writing. [Arabic, = bundle]

reanimate /riːˈænɪmeɪt/ *v.* (**-ting**) **1** restore to life. **2** restore to activity or liveliness. □ **reanimation** *n.*

reap *v.* **1** cut or gather (esp. grain) as a harvest. **2** harvest the crop of (a field etc.). **3** receive as a result of one's own or others' actions. [Old English]

reaper *n.* **1** person who reaps. **2** reaping machine. **3** (**the Reaper** or **grim Reaper**) death personified.

reappear /riːəˈpɪə(r)/ *v.* appear again or as previously. □ **reappearance** *n.*

reapply /riːəˈplaɪ/ *v.* (**-ies, -ied**) apply again, esp. submit a further application (for a position etc.). □ **reapplication** /-æplɪˈkeɪʃ(ə)n/ *n.*

reappoint /riːəˈpɔɪnt/ *v.* appoint to a position previously held. □ **reappointment** *n.*

reapportion /riːəˈpɔːʃ(ə)n/ *v.* apportion again or differently.

reappraise /riːəˈpreɪz/ *v.* (**-sing**) appraise or assess again or differently. □ **reappraisal** *n.*

rear[1] *–n.* **1** back part of anything. **2** space behind, or position at the back of anything. **3** *colloq.* buttocks. *–adj.* at the back. □ **bring up the rear** come last [probably from REARWARD or REAR GUARD]

rear[2] *v.* **1** a bring up and educate (children). **b** breed and care for (animals). **c** cultivate (crops). **2** (of a horse etc.) raise itself on its hind legs. **3 a** set upright. **b** build. **c** hold upwards. **4** extend to a great height. [Old English]

rear admiral *n.* naval officer ranking below vice admiral.

rearguard *n.* body of troops detached to protect the rear, esp. in retreats. [French *rereguarde*]

rearguard action *n.* **1** engagement undertaken by a rearguard. **2** defensive stand or struggle, esp. when losing.

rear-lamp *n.* (also **rear-light**) usu. red light at the rear of a vehicle.

rearm /riːˈɑːm/ *v.* (also *absol.*) arm again, esp. with improved weapons. □ **rearmament** *n.*

rearmost *adj.* furthest back.

rearrange /riːəˈreɪndʒ/ *v.* (**-ging**) arrange again in a different way. □ **rearrangement** *n.*

rearrest /riːəˈrest/ *–v.* arrest again. *–n.* rearresting or being rearrested.

rearward /ˈrɪəwəd/ *–n.* (esp. in prepositional phrases) rear (*to the rearward of*; *in the rearward*). *–adj.* to the rear. *–adv.* (also **rearwards**) towards the rear. [Anglo-French *rerewarde* = REARGUARD]

reason /ˈriːz(ə)n/ *–n.* **1** motive, cause, or justification. **2** fact adduced or serving as this. **3** intellectual faculty by which conclusions are drawn from premises. **4** sanity (*lost his reason*). **5** sense; sensible conduct; what is right, practical, or practicable; moderation. *–v.* **1** form or try to reach conclusions by connected thought. **2** (foll. by *with*) use argument with (a person) by way of persuasion. **3** (foll. by *that*) conclude or assert in argument. **4** (foll. by *into*, *out of*) persuade or move by argument. **5** (foll. by *out*) think out (consequences etc.). **6** (often as **reasoned** *adj.*) express in a logical way. **7** embody reason in (an amendment etc.). □ **by reason of** owing to. **in** (or **within**) **reason** within the bounds of moderation. **with reason** justifiably. [Latin *ratio*]

reasonable *adj.* **1** having sound judgement; moderate; ready to listen to reason. **2** not absurd. **3** a not greatly less or more than might be expected. **b** inexpensive. **c** tolerable, fair. □ **reasonableness** *n.* **reasonably** *adv.*

reassemble /ˌriːəˈsemb(ə)l/ v. (-ling) assemble again or into a former state. □ **reassembly** n.

reassert /ˌriːəˈsɜːt/ v. assert again, esp. with renewed emphasis. □ **reassertion** n.

reassess /ˌriːəˈses/ v. assess again or differently. □ **reassessment** n.

reassign /ˌriːəˈsaɪn/ v. assign again or differently. □ **reassignment** n.

reassure /ˌriːəˈʃʊə(r)/ v. (-ring) 1 restore confidence to; dispel the apprehensions of. 2 confirm in an opinion or impression. □ **reassurance** n. **reassuring** adj.

reawaken /ˌriːəˈweɪkən/ v. awaken again.

rebate¹ /ˈriːbeɪt/ n. 1 partial refund. 2 deduction from a sum to be paid; discount. [French rabattre: related to RE-, ABATE]

rebate² /ˈriːbeɪt/ n. & v. = RABBET.

rebel —n. /ˈreb(ə)l/ 1 person who fights against, resists, or refuses allegiance to, the established government 2 person or thing that resists authority or control. —attrib.adj. /ˈreb(ə)l/ 1 rebellious. 2 of rebels. 3 in rebellion. —v. /rɪˈbel/ (-ll-; US -l-) (usu. foll. by against) 1 act as a rebel; revolt. 2 feel or display repugnance. [Latin: related to RE-, bellum war]

rebellion /rɪˈbeljən/ n. open resistance to authority, esp. organized armed resistance to an established government. [Latin: related to REBEL]

rebellious /rɪˈbeljəs/ adj. 1 tending to rebel. 2 in rebellion. 3 defying lawful authority. 4 (of a thing; unmanageable, refractory. □ **rebelliously** adv. **rebelliousness** n.

rebid —v. /riːˈbɪd/ v. also riːˈbɪd/ (-dd-; past and past part. rebid) bid again. —n.1 act of rebidding. 2 bid so made. [Latin: related tc REBEL]

rebind /riːˈbaɪnd/ v. (past and past part. rebound) bind (esp. a book) again or differently.

rebirth /riːˈbɜːθ/ n. 1 new incarnation. 2 spiritual enlightenment. 3 revival. □ **reborn** /riːˈbɔːn/ adj.

reboot /riːˈbuːt/ v. (often absol.) Computing boot up (a system) again.

rebound —v. /rɪˈbaʊnd/ 1 spring back after impact. 2 (foll. by upon) (of an action) have an adverse effect upon (the doer). —n. /ˈriːbaʊnd/ act of rebounding; recoil, reaction. □ **on the rebound** while still recovering from an emotional shock, esp. rejection by a lover. [French rebonder: related to BOUND³]

rebroadcast /riːˈbrɔːdkɑːst/ —v. (past and past part. -cast or -casted; past part. broadcast again. —n. repeat broadcast.

rebuff /rɪˈbʌf/ —n. 1 rejection of one who makes advances, proffers help, shows interest, makes a request, etc. 2 snub. —v. give a rebuff to. [French from Italian]

rebuild /riːˈbɪld/ v. (past and past part. rebuilt) build again or differently.

rebuke /rɪˈbjuːk/ —v. (-king) express sharp disapproval to (a person) for a fault; censure. —n. rebuking or being rebuked. [Anglo-French]

rebus /ˈriːbəs/ n. (pl. rebuses) representation of a word (esp. a name) by pictures etc. suggesting its parts. [Latin rebus, ablative pl. of res thing]

rebut /rɪˈbʌt/ v. (-tt-) 1 refute or disprove (evidence or a charge). 2 force or turn back. [Anglo-French rebuter: related to BUTT¹]

rec n. colloq. recreation ground. [abbreviation]

recalcitrant /rɪˈkælsɪtrənt/ adj. 1 obstinately disobedient. 2 objecting to restraint. □ **recalcitrance** n. [Latin recalcitro kick out, from calx heel]

recall /rɪˈkɔːl/ —v. 1 summon to return. 2 recollect, remember. 3 bring back to memory; serve as a reminder of. 4 revoke or annul (an action or decision). 5 revive, resuscitate. 6 take back (a gift). —n. /ˈriːkɔːl/ 1 summons to come back. 2 act of remembering. 3 ability to remember. 4 possibility of recalling, esp. in the sense of revoking (beyond recall).

recant /rɪˈkænt/ v. (also absol.) withdraw and renounce (a former belief or statement as erroneous or heretical. □ **recantation** /ˌriːkænˈteɪʃ(ə)n/ n. [Latin: related to CHANT]

recap /ˈriːkæp/ colloq. —v. (-pp-) recapitulate. —n. recapitulation. [abbreviation]

recapitulate /ˌriːkəˈpɪtjʊleɪt/ v. (-ting) 1 go briefly through again; summarize. 2 go over the main points or headings of. [Latin: related to CAPITAL]

recapitulation /ˌriːkəpɪtjʊˈleɪʃ(ə)n/ n. 1 act of recapitulating. 2 Mus. part of a movement in which themes are restated. [Latin: related to RECAPITULATE]

recapture /riːˈkæptʃə(r)/ —v. (-ring) 1 capture again; recover by capture. 2 re-experience (a past emotion etc.). —n. act of recapturing.

recast /riːˈkɑːst/ —v. (past and past part. recast) 1 cast again (a play, net, votes, etc.). 2 put into a new form; improve the arrangement of. —n. 1 recasting. 2 recast form.

recce /ˈrekɪ/ colloq. —n. reconnaissance. —v. (recced, recceing) reconnoitre. [abbreviation]

recede /rɪ'siːd/ v. (-ding) 1 go or shrink back or further off. 2 be left at an increasing distance by an observer's motion. 3 slope backwards (*a receding chin*). 4 decline in force or value. [Latin *recedere -cess-*: related to CEDE]

receipt /rɪ'siːt/ —n. 1 receiving or being received. 2 written acknowledgement of payment received. 3 (usu. in *pl.*) amount of money etc. received. 4 *archaic* recipe. —v. place a written or printed receipt on (a bill). □ **in receipt of** having received. [Anglo-French *receite*: related to RECEIVE]

receive /rɪ'siːv/ v. (-ving) 1 take or accept (a thing offered, sent, or given). 2 acquire; be provided with. 3 have conferred or inflicted on one. 4 react to (news, a play, etc.) in a particular way. 5 a stand the force or weight of b bear up against; encounter with opposition. 6 consent to hear (a confession or oath) or consider (a petition). 7 (also *absol.*) accept (stolen goods knowingly). 8 admit; consent or prove able to hold; provide accommodation for. 9 (of a receptacle) be able to hold. 10 greet or welcome, esp. in a specified manner. 11 entertain as a guest etc. 12 admit to membership. 13 convert (broadcast signals) into sound or pictures. 14 (often as **received** *adj.*) give credit to; accept as authoritative or true. □ **be at** (or **on**) **the receiving end** *colloq.* bear the brunt of something unpleasant. [Latin *recipio -cept-* get back again]

received pronunciation *n.* the form of educated spoken English used in southern England.

receiver *n.* 1 person or thing that receives. 2 part of a machine or instrument that receives something (esp. the part of a telephone that contains the earpiece). 3 (in full **official receiver**) person appointed by a court to administer the property of a bankrupt or insane person, or property under litigation. 4 radio or television receiving apparatus. 5 person who receives stolen goods.

receivership *n.* 1 office of official receiver. 2 state of being dealt with by a receiver (esp. *in receivership*).

recent /'riːs(ə)nt/ —*adj.* 1 not long past; that happened, began to exist, or existed, lately. 2 not long established; lately begun; modern. 3 (**Recent**) *Geol.* of the most recent epoch of the Quaternary period. —*n.* (**Recent**) *Geol.* this epoch. □ **recently** *adv.* [Latin *recens -ent-*]

receptacle /rɪ'septək(ə)l/ *n.* 1 containing vessel, place, or space. 2 *Bot.* enlarged and modified area of the stem

apex which bears the flower. [Latin: related to RECEIVE]

reception /rɪ'sep∫(ə)n/ *n.* 1 receiving or being received. 2 way in which a person or thing is received (*cool reception*). 3 social occasion for receiving guests, esp. after a wedding. 4 place where guests or clients etc. report on arrival at a hotel, office, etc. 5 a receiving of broadcast signals. b quality of this. [Latin: related to RECEIVE]

receptionist *n.* person employed to receive guests, clients, etc.

reception room *n.* room for receiving guests, clients, etc.

receptive /rɪ'septɪv/ *adj.* able or quick to receive impressions or ideas. □ **receptively** *adv.* **receptiveness** *n.* **receptivity** /ˌriːsep'tɪvɪtɪ/ *n.* [French or medieval Latin: related to RECEIVE]

recess /rɪ'ses, 'riːses, 'rɪses/ —*n.* 1 space set back in a wall. 2 (often in *pl.*) remote or secret place. 3 temporary cessation from work, esp. of Parliament. —*v.* 1 make a recess in. 2 place in a recess. 3 *US* take a recess; adjourn. [Latin *recessus*: related to RECEDE]

recession /rɪ'se∫(ə)n/ *n.* 1 temporary decline in economic activity or prosperity. 2 receding or withdrawal from a place or point. [Latin: related to RECEDE]

recessional —*adj.* sung while the clergy and choir withdraw after a service. —*n.* recessional hymn.

recessive /rɪ'sesɪv/ *adj.* 1 tending to recede. 2 (of an inherited characteristic) appearing in offspring only when not masked by an inherited dominant characteristic.

recharge —*v.* /riː't∫ɑːdʒ/ charge (a battery etc.) again or be recharged. —*n.* /'riːt∫ɑːdʒ/ recharging or being recharged. □ **rechargeable** /riː't∫ɑːdʒəb(ə)l/ *adj.*

recheck —*v.* /riː't∫ek/ check again. —*n.* /'riːt∫ek/ further check or inspection.

recherché /rə'∫eə∫eɪ/ *adj.* 1 carefully sought out; rare or exotic. 2 far-fetched. [French]

rechristen /riː'krɪs(ə)n/ *v.* 1 christen again. 2 give a new name to.

recidivist /rɪ'sɪdɪvɪst/ *n.* person who relapses into crime. □ **recidivism** *n.* [Latin *recidivus* falling back: related to RECIDE]

recipe /'resɪpɪ/ *n.* 1 statement of the ingredients and procedure required for preparing a cooked dish. 2 (foll. by *for*) certain means to (an outcome) (*recipe for disaster*). [2nd sing. imperative of Latin *recipio* RECEIVE]

recipient /rɪ'sɪpɪənt/ *n.* person who receives something. [Italian or Latin: related to RECEIVE]

reciprocal /rɪ'sɪprək(ə)l/ —*adj.* 1 in return (*a reciprocal greeting*). 2 mutual. 3 *Gram.* (of a pronoun) expressing mutual relation (as in *each other*). —*n. Math.* expression or function so related to another that their product is unity (½ *is the reciprocal of* 2). □ **reciprocally** *adv.* [Latin *reciprocus* moving to and fro]

reciprocate /rɪ'sɪprə,keɪt/ *v.* (-**ting**) 1 requite (affection etc.). 2 (foll. by *with*) give in return. 3 give and receive mutually; interchange. 4 (of a part of a machine) move backwards and forwards. □ **reciprocation** /-'keɪʃ(ə)n/ *n.*

reciprocity /,resɪ'prosɪtɪ/ *n.* 1 condition of being reciprocal 2 mutual action. 3 give and take, esp. the interchange of privileges.

recital /rɪ'saɪt(ə)l/ *n.* 1 reciting or being recited. 2 concert of classical music given by a soloist or small group. 3 (foll. by *of*) detailed account of (connected things or facts); narrative.

recitation /,resɪ'teɪʃ(ə)n/ *n.* 1 reciting. 2 thing recited.

recitative /,resɪtə'tiːv/ *n.* musical declamation in the narrative and dialogue parts of opera and oratorio. [Italian *recitativo*: related to RECITE]

recite /rɪ'saɪt/ *v.* (-**ting**) 1 repeat aloud or declaim (a poem or passage) from memory. 2 give a recitation. 3 enumerate. [Latin *recito* read out]

reckless /'reklɪs/ *adj.* disregarding the consequences or danger etc.; rash. □ **recklessly** *adv.* **recklessness** *n.* [Old English *reck* concern oneself]

reckon /'rekən/ *v.* 1 (often foll. by *that*) be of the considered opinion; think. 2 consider or regard (*reckoned to be the best*). 3 count or compute by calculation. 4 (foll. by *in*) count in or include in computation. 5 make calculations; add up an account or sum. 6 (foll. by *on*) rely on, count on, or base plans on. 7 (foll. by *with* or *without*) take (or fail to take) into account. [Old English]

reckoning *n.* 1 counting or calculating. 2 consideration or opinion. 3 settlement of an account.

reclaim /rɪ'kleɪm/ *v.* 1 seek the return of (one's property, rights, etc.). 2 bring (land) under cultivation, esp. from being under water. 3 win back or away from vice, error, or a waste condition. □ **reclaimable** *adj.* **reclamation** /,reklə'meɪʃ(ə)n/ *n.* [Latin *reclamare* cry out against]

reclassify /riː'klæsɪ,faɪ/ *v.* (-**ies**, -**ied**) classify again or differently. □ **reclassification** /-fɪ'keɪʃ(ə)n/ *n.*

recline /rɪ'klaɪn/ *v.* (-**ning**) assume or be in a horizontal or re-axed leaning position. [Latin *reclino*]

reclothe /riː'kləʊð/ *v.* (-**thing**) clothe again or differently.

recluse /rɪ'kluːs/ *n.* person given to or living in seclusion or isolation; hermit. □ **reclusive** *adj.* [Latin *recludo -clus-* shut away]

recognition /,rekəg'nɪʃ(ə)n/ *n.* recognizing or being recognized. [Latin: related to RECOGNIZE]

recognizance /rɪ'kɒgnɪz(ə)ns/ *n.* 1 bond by which a person undertakes before a court or magistrate to observe some condition, e.g. to appear when summoned. 2 sum pledged as surety for this. [French: related to RECOGNIZE]

recognize /'rekəg,naɪz/ *v.* (also -**ise**) (-**zing** or -**sing**) 1 identify as already known. 2 realize or discover the nature of 3 (foll. by *that*) realize or admit. 4 acknowledge the existence, validity, character, or claims of 5 show appreciation of; reward. 6 (foll. by *as, for*) treat. [Latin *recognosco*] □ **recognizable** *adj.* [Latin *recognosco*]

recoil /rɪ'kɔɪl/ —*v.* 1 suddenly move or spring back in fear, horror, or disgust. 2 shrink mentally in this way. 3 rebound after an impact. 4 (foll. by *on, upon*) have an adverse reactive effect on (the originator). 5 (of a gun) be driven backwards by its discharge. —*n.* /also 'riːkɔɪl/ act or sensation of recoiling. [French *reculer* from Latin *culus* buttocks]

recollect /,rekə'lekt/ *v.* 1 remember. 2 succeed in remembering; call to mind. [Latin *recolligo*: related to COLLECT]

recollection /,rekə'lekʃ(ə)n/ *n.* 1 act or power of recollecting. 2 thing recollected. 3 a person's memory. **b** time over which memory extends (*happened within my recollection*). [French or medieval Latin: related to RECOLLECT]

recolour /riː'kʌlə(r)/ *v.* colour again or differently.

recombine /,riːkəm'baɪn/ *v.* (-**ning**) combine again or differently.

recommence /,riːkə'mens/ *v.* (-**cing**) begin again. □ **recommencement** *n.*

recommend /,rekə'mend/ *v.* 1 suggest as fit for some purpose or use. 2 advise as a course of action etc. 3 (of qualities, conduct, etc.) make acceptable or desirable. 4 (foll. by *to*) commend or entrust (to a person or a person's care). □ **recommendation** /-'deɪʃ(ə)n/ *n.* [medieval Latin: related to RE-]

recompense /'rekəm,pens/ —*v.* (-**sing**) 1 make amends to (a person) or for (a loss etc.). 2 requite; reward or punish (a person or action). —*n.* 1 reward, requital. 2 retribution. [Latin: related to COMPENSATE]

reconcile /'rekən,saıl/ v. (-ling) 1 make friendly again after an estrangement. 2 (usu. in *refl.* or *passive*; foll. by *to*) make acquiescent or contentedly submissive to (something disagreeable). 3 settle (a quarrel etc.). 4 a harmonize, make compatible. b show the compatibility of by argument or in practice. □ **reconcilable** *adj.* **reconciliation** /-,sılı'reıʃ(ə)n/ *n.* [Latin: related to CONCILIATE]

recondite /'rekən,daıt/ *adj.* 1 (of a subject or knowledge) abstruse, out of the way, little known. 2 (of an author or style) dealing in abstruse knowledge or allusions, obscure. [Latin *recondo -dit-* put away]

recondition /,ri:kən'dıʃ(ə)n/ *v.* overhaul, renovate, make usable again.

reconnaissance /rı'kɒnıs(ə)ns/ *n.* 1 survey of a region, esp. to locate an enemy or ascertain strategic features. 2 preliminary survey. [French: related to RECONNOITRE]

reconnect /,ri:kə'nekt/ *v.* connect again. □ **reconnection** *n.*

reconnoitre /,rekə'nɔıtə(r)/ *v.* (US **reconnoiter**) (-ring) make a reconnaissance (of). [French: related to RECOGNIZE]

reconquer /ri:'kɒŋkə(r)/ *v.* conquer again. □ **reconquest** *n.*

reconsider /,ri:kən'sıdə(r)/ *v.* consider again, esp. for a possible change of decision. □ **reconsideration** /-'reıʃ(ə)n/ *n.*

reconstitute /ri:'kɒnstı,tju:t/ *v.* (-ting) 1 reconstruct. 2 reorganize. 3 rehydrate (dried food etc.). □ **reconstitution** /-'tju:ʃ(ə)n/ *n.*

reconstruct /,ri:kən'strʌkt/ *v.* 1 build again. 2 a form an impression of (past events) by assembling the evidence for them. b re-enact (a crime). 3 reorganize. □ **reconstruction** *n.*

reconvene /,ri:kən'vi:n/ *v.* (-ning) convene again, esp. after a pause in proceedings.

reconvert /,ri:kən'vɜ:t/ *v.* convert back to a former state. □ **reconversion** *n.*

recopy /ri:'kɒpı/ *v.* (-ies, -ied) copy again.

record –*n.* /'rekɔ:d/ 1 a piece of evidence or information constituting an (esp. official) account of something that has occurred, been said, etc. b document etc. preserving this. 2 state of being set down or preserved in writing etc. 3 (in full **gramophone record**) disc carrying recorded sound in grooves on each surface, for reproduction by a recordplayer. 4 official report of the proceedings and judgement in a court of justice. 5 a facts known about a person's past. b list of a person's previous criminal convictions. 6 (often *attrib.*) best performance (esp. in sport) or most remarkable event of its kind on record. 7 object serving as a memorial; portrait. –*v.* /rı'kɔ:d/ 1 set down in writing or some other permanent form for later reference. 2 convert (sound, a broadcast, etc.) into permanent form for later reproduction. □ **for the record** as an official statement etc. **go on record** state one's opinion openly, so that it is recorded. **have a record** have a recorded criminal conviction or convictions. **off the record** unofficially, confidentially. **on record** officially recorded; publicly known. [Latin *cor cordis* heart]

record-breaking *attrib. adj.* that breaks a record.

recorded delivery *n.* Post Office service in which the dispatch and receipt of an item are recorded.

recorder /rı'kɔ:də(r)/ *n.* 1 apparatus for recording, esp. a video or tape recorder. 2 (also **Recorder**) barrister or solicitor of at least ten years' standing, serving as a part-time judge. 3 wooden or plastic wind instrument with holes covered by the fingers. 4 keeper of records.

record-holder *n.* person who holds a record.

recording *n.* 1 process by which audio or video signals are recorded for later reproduction. 2 material or a programme recorded.

recordist *n.* person who records sound.

record-player *n.* apparatus for reproducing sound from gramophone records.

recount /rı'kaʊnt/ *v.* 1 narrate. 2 tell in detail. [Anglo-French *reconter*: related to RE-, COUNT[1]]

re-count –*v.* /ri:'kaʊnt/ count again. –*n.* /'ri:kaʊnt/ re-counting, esp. of votes in an election.

recoup /rı'ku:p/ *v.* 1 recover or regain (a loss). 2 compensate or reimburse for a loss. □ **recoupment** *n.* [French *recouper* cut back]

recourse /rı'kɔːs, 'riː-/ *n.* 1 resort to a possible source of help. 2 person or thing resorted to. □ **have recourse to** turn to (a person or thing) for help. [Latin: related to COURSE]

recover /rı'kʌvə(r)/ *v.* 1 regain possession, use, or control of. 2 return to health, consciousness, or to a normal state or position. 3 obtain or secure by legal process. 4 retrieve or make up for (a loss, setback, etc.). 5 *refl.* regain composure, consciousness, or control of one's limbs. 6 retrieve (reusable substances) from waste. □ **recoverable** *adj.* [Latin: related to RECUPERATE]

re-cover /ˌriːˈkʌvə(r)/ v. 1 cover again. 2 provide (a chair etc.) with a new cover.

recovery n. (pl. -ies) recovering or being recovered. [Anglo-French re-coverie: related to RECOVER]

recreant /ˈrekriənt/ literary —adj. craven, cowardly. —n. coward. [medieval Latin: related to CREED]

re-create /ˌriːkriˈeɪt/ v. (-ting) create over again, reproduce. □ **re-creation** n.

recreation /ˌrekriˈeɪʃ(ə)n/ n. 1 process or means of refreshing or entertaining oneself. 2 pleasurable activity. □ **recreational** adj. [Latin: related to CREATE]

recreation ground n. public land used for sports or games.

recriminate /rɪˈkrɪmɪneɪt/ v. (-ting) make mutual or counter accusations. □ **recrimination** /-ˈneɪʃ(ə)n/ n. **recriminatory** /-nətəri/ adj. [medieval Latin: related to CRIME]

recross /riːˈkrɒs/ v. cross again.

recrudesce /ˌriːkruːˈdes/ v. (-cing) formal (of a disease, problem, etc.) break out again. □ **recrudescence** n. **recrudescent** adj. [Latin: related to CRUDE]

recruit /rɪˈkruːt/ —n. 1 newly enlisted serviceman or servicewoman. 2 new member of a society etc. 3 beginner. —v. 1 enlist (a person) as a recruit. 2 form (an army etc.) by enlisting recruits. 3 get or seek recruits. 4 replenish or reinvigorate (numbers, strength, etc.). □ **recruitment** n. [French dial. recrute: related to CREW']

rectal /ˈrekt(ə)l/ adj. of or by means of the rectum.

rectangle /ˈrekˌtæŋɡ(ə)l/ n. plane figure with four straight sides and four right angles, esp. other than a square. □ **rectangular** /-ˈtæŋɡjʊlə(r)/ adj. [French or medieval Latin]

rectify /ˈrektɪfaɪ/ v. (-ies, -ied) 1 adjust or make right. 2 purify or refine, esp. by repeated distillation. 3 convert (alternating current) to direct current. □ **rectifiable** adj. **rectification** /-fɪˈkeɪʃ(ə)n/ n. **rectifier** n. [Latin rectus straight, right]

rectilinear /ˌrektɪˈlɪnɪə(r)/ adj. 1 bounded or characterized by straight lines. 2 in or forming a straight line. [Latin: related to RECTIFY]

rectitude /ˈrektɪtjuːd/ n. 1 moral uprightness, righteousness. 2 correctness. [Latin rectus right]

recto /ˈrektəʊ/ n. (pl. -s) 1 right-hand page of an open book. 2 front of a printed leaf. [Latin = on the right]

rector /ˈrektə(r)/ n. 1 (in the Church of England) incumbent of a parish where

all tithes formerly passed to the incumbent (cf. VICAR). 2 RC Ch. priest in charge of a church or religious institution. 3 head of some universities and colleges. □ **rectorship** n. [Latin rego rect- rule]

rectory n. (pl. -ies) rector's house. [French or medieval Latin: related to RECTOR]

rectum /ˈrektəm/ n. (pl. -s) final section of the large intestine, terminating at the anus. [Latin, = straight]

recumbent /rɪˈkʌmbənt/ adj. lying down, reclining. [Latin cumbo lie]

recuperate /rɪˈkuːpəreɪt/ v. (-ting) 1 recover from illness, exhaustion, loss, etc. 2 regain (health, a loss, etc.). □ **recuperation** /-ˈreɪʃ(ə)n/ n. **recuperative** /-rətɪv/ adj. [Latin recupero]

recur /rɪˈkɜː(r)/ v. (-rr-) 1 occur again; be repeated. 2 (foll. by to) go back in thought or speech. 3 (as recurring adj.) (of a decimal fraction) repeated indefinitely (1.66 recurring). [Latin curro run]

recurrent /rɪˈkʌrənt/ adj. recurring; happening repeatedly. □ **recurrence** n. **recurrent** adj. [Latin]

recusant /ˈrekjʊz(ə)nt/ —n. person who refuses submission to an authority or compliance with a regulation, esp. hist. one who refused to attend services of the Church of England. —adj. of or being a recusant. □ **recusancy** n. [Latin recuso refuse]

recycle /riːˈsaɪk(ə)l/ v. (-ling) convert (waste) to reusable material. □ **recyclable** adj.

red —adj. (redder, reddest) 1 of the colour ranging from that of blood to deep pink or orange 2 flushed in the face with shame, anger, etc. 3 (of the eyes) bloodshot or red-rimmed. 4 (of hair) reddish-brown, tawny. 5 having to do with bloodshed, burning, violence, or revolution. 6 colloq. Communist or socialist. 7 hist. (Red) Russian, Soviet. —n. 1 red colour or pigment. 2 red clothes or material. 3 colloq. Communist or socialist. □ **in the red** in debt or deficit. □ **reddish** adj. **redness** n. [Old English]

red admiral n. butterfly with red bands.

red-blooded adj. virile, vigorous.

redbreast n. colloq. robin.

redbrick adj. (of a university founded in the 19th or early 20th c.).

redcap n. member of the military police.

red card n. Football card shown by the referee to a player being sent off.

red carpet n. privileged treatment of an eminent visitor.

red cell *n.* (also **red corpuscle**) erythrocyte.

redcoat *n. hist.* British soldier.

Red Crescent *n.* equivalent of the Red Cross in Muslim countries.

Red Cross *n.* international organization bringing relief to victims of war or disaster.

redcurrant *n.* **1** small red edible berry. **2** shrub bearing this.

redden *v.* **1** make or become red. **2** blush.

redecorate /riːˈdekəˌreɪt/ *v.* (**-ting**) decorate (a room etc.) again or differently. □ **redecoration** /-ˈreɪʃ(ə)n/ *n.*

redeem /rɪˈdiːm/ *v.* **1** recover by expenditure of effort or by a stipulated payment. **2** make a single payment to cancel (a regular charge or obligation). **3** convert (tokens or bonds etc.) into goods or cash. **4** deliver from sin and damnation. **5** make up for; be a compensating factor in (*has one redeeming feature*). **6** (foll. by *from*) save from (a defect). **7** *refl.* save (oneself) from blame. **8** purchase the freedom of (a person). **9** save (a person's life) by ransom. **10** save or rescue or reclaim. **11** fulfil (a promise). □ **redeemable** *adj.* [Latin *emo* buy]

redeemer *n.* **1** person who redeems. **2** (**the Redeemer**) Christ.

redefine /ˌriːdɪˈfaɪn/ *v.* (**-ning**) define again or differently. □ **redefinition** /-defɪˈnɪʃ(ə)n/ *n.*

redemption /rɪˈdempʃ(ə)n/ *n.* **1** redeeming or being redeemed. **2** thing that redeems. [Latin: related to REDEEM]

redeploy /ˌriːdɪˈplɔɪ/ *v.* send (troops, workers, etc.) to a new place or task. □ **redeployment** *n.*

redesign /ˌriːdɪˈzaɪn/ *v.* design again or differently.

redevelop /ˌriːdɪˈveləp/ *v.* replan or rebuild (esp. an urban area). □ **redevelopment** *n.*

re₋ flag *n.* **1** symbol o₋ socialist revolution. **2** warning of danger.

red-handed *adv.* in the act of committing a crime, doing wrong, etc.

red hat *n.* **1** cardinal's hat. **2** symbol of a cardinal's office.

redhead *n.* person with red hair.

red herring *n.* misleading clue; distraction.

red-hot *adj.* **1** heated until red. **2** *colloq.* highly exciting. **3** *colloq.* (of news) fresh; completely new. **4** intensely excited. **5** enraged.

red-hot poker *n.* cultivated plant with spikes of usu. red or yellow flowers.

redial /riːˈdaɪəl/ *v.* (**-ll-**; *US* **-l-**) dial again.

rediffusion /ˌriːdɪˈfjuːʒ(ə)n/ *n.* relaying of broadcast programmes, esp. by cable from a central receiver.

Red Indian *n. offens.* American Indian.

redirect /ˌriːdaɪˈrekt, -dɪˈrekt/ *v.* **1** direct again; send in a different direction. **2** readdress (a letter etc.).

rediscover /ˌriːdɪˈskʌvə(r)/ *v.* discover again. □ **rediscovery** *n.* (*pl.* **-ies**).

redistribute /ˌriːdɪˈstrɪbjuːt, riːˈdɪs-/ *v.* (**-ting**) distribute again or differently. □ **redistribution** /-ˈbjuːʃ(ə)n/ *n.*

■ **Usage** The second pronunciation given, with the stress on the second syllable, is considered incorrect by some people.

redivide /ˌriːdɪˈvaɪd/ *v.* (**-ding**) divide again or differently.

red lead *n.* red form of lead oxide used as a pigment.

red-letter day *n.* day that is pleasantly noteworthy or memorable (orig. a festival marked in red on the calendar).

red light *n.* **1** signal to stop on a road, railway, etc. **2** warning.

red-light district *n.* district where many prostitutes work.

red meat *n.* meat that is red when raw (e.g. beef or lamb).

redneck *n. US often derog.* politically conservative working-class White in the southern US.

redo /riːˈduː/ *v.* (**redoing**; *3rd sing. present* **redoes**; *past* **redid**; *past part.* **redone**) **1** do again. **2** redecorate.

redolent /ˈredələnt/ *adj.* **1** (foll. by *of*, *with*) strongly reminiscent, suggestive, or smelling. **2** fragrant. □ **redolence** *n.* [Latin *oleo* smell]

redouble /riːˈdʌb(ə)l/ —*v.* (**-ling**) **1** make or grow greater or more intense or numerous. **2** *Bridge* double again a bid already doubled by an opponent. —*n. Bridge* redoubling of a bid.

redoubt /rɪˈdaʊt/ *n. Mil.* outwork or fieldwork without flanking defences. [French *redoute*: related to REDUCE]

redoubtable /rɪˈdaʊtəb(ə)l/ *adj.* formidable.

redound /rɪˈdaʊnd/ *v.* **1** (foll. by *to*) make a great contribution to (one's credit or advantage etc.). **2** (foll. by *upon*, *on*) come back or recoil upon. [Latin *unda* wave]

red pepper *n.* **1** cayenne pepper. **2** ripe red fruit of the capsicum plant.

redpoll *n.* finch with a red forehead, similar to a linnet.

redraft /riːˈdrɑːft/ *v.* draft (a text) again, usu. differently.

red rag *n.* something that excites a person's rage.

redraw /riːˈdrɔː/ v. (past **redrew**; past part. **redrawn**) draw again or differently.

redress /rɪˈdres/ —v. 1 remedy or rectify (a wrong or grievance etc.). 2 readjust, set straight again. —n. 1 reparation for a wrong. 2 (foll. by *of*) redressing (a grievance etc.). □ **redress the balance** restore equality. [French: related to DRESS]

redshank n. sandpiper with bright-red legs.

redshift n. displacement of the spectrum to longer wavelengths in the light coming from receding galaxies etc.

redskin n. colloq. offens. American Indian.

red squirrel n. native British squirrel with reddish fur.

redstart n. red-tailed songbird. [from RED, obsolete *steort* tail]

red tape n. excessive bureaucracy or formality; esp. in public business.

reduce /rɪˈdjuːs/ v. (**-cing**) 1 make or become smaller or less. 2 (foll. by *to*) bring by force or necessity (to some undesirable state or action) (*reduced them to tears; reduced to begging*). 3 convert to another (esp. simpler) form (*reduced it to a powder*). 4 convert (a fraction) to the form with the lowest terms. 5 (foll. by *to*) bring, simplify, or adapt by classification or analysis (*the dispute may be reduced to three issues*). 6 make lower in status or rank. 7 lower the price of. 8 lessen one's weight or size. 9 weaken (*is in a very reduced state*). 10 impoverish. 11 subdue, bring back to obedience. 12 *Chem.* a (cause to) combine with hydrogen. b (cause to) undergo reduction of electrons. 13 a (in surgery) restore (a dislocated etc. part) to its proper position. b remedy (a dislocation etc.) in this way. □ **reducible** adj. [Latin *duco* bring]

reduced circumstances n.pl. poverty after relative prosperity.

reductio ad absurdum /rɪˌdʌktɪəʊ æd æbˈzɜːdəm/ n. proof of the falsity of a premiss by showing that its logical consequence is absurd. [Latin, = reduction to the absurd]

reduction /rɪˈdʌkʃ(ə)n/ n. 1 reducing or being reduced. 2 amount by which prices etc. are reduced. 3 smaller copy of a picture etc. □ **reductive** adj.

redundant /rɪˈdʌnd(ə)nt/ adj. 1 superfluous. 2 that can be omitted without any loss of significance. 3 (of a person) no longer needed at work and therefore unemployed. □ **redundancy** n. (pl. **-ies**). [Latin: related to REDOUND]

red rose n. emblem of Lancashire or the Lancastrians.

reduplicate /rɪˈdjuːplɪkeɪt/ v. (**-ting**) 1 make double. 2 repeat. 3 repeat (a letter or syllable or word) exactly or with a slight change (e.g. *hurly-burly, see-saw*). □ **reduplication** /-ˈkeɪʃ(ə)n/ n.

redwing n. thrush with red under-wings.

redwood n. very large Californian conifer yielding red wood.

re-echo /riːˈekəʊ/ v. (**-es, -ed**) echo repeatedly; resound.

re-educate /riːˈedjʊkeɪt/ v. (**-ting**) educate again, esp. to change a person's views. □ **re-education** /-ˈkeɪʃ(ə)n/ n.

reed n. 1 a a water or marsh plant with a firm stem. b tall straight stalk of this. 2 a strip of cane etc. vibrating to produce the sound in some wind instruments. b (esp. in *pl.*) such an instrument. □ **reeded** adj. [Old English]

reed-bed n. bed or growth of reeds.

reedy adj. (**-ier, -iest**) 1 full of reeds. 2 like a reed. 3 (of a voice) like a reed instrument in tone. □ **reediness** n.

reef¹ —n. 1 ridge of rock or coral etc. at or near the surface of the sea. 2 a lode of ore. b bedrock surrounding this. [Dutch from Norse *rif*]

reef² —n. each of several strips across a sail, for taking it in or rolling it up to reduce its surface area in a high wind. —v. take in a reef or reefs (of a sail). [Old Norse]

reefer n. 1 *slang* marijuana cigarette. 2 thick double-breasted jacket. [from REEF²]

reef-knot n. symmetrical double knot.

reek —v. (often foll. by *of*) 1 smell strongly and unpleasantly. 2 have unpleasant or suspicious associations (*reeks of corruption*). —n. 1 foul or stale smell. 2 esp. *Scot.* smoke. 3 vapour, visible exhalation. [Old English]

reel —n. 1 cylindrical device on which thread, silk, yarn, paper, film, wire, etc., are wound. 2 quantity of thread etc. wound on a reel. 3 device for winding and unwinding a line as required, esp. in fishing. 4 revolving part in various machines. 5 a lively folk or Scottish dance. b music for this. —v. 1 wind (thread, silk, fishing-line, etc.) on a reel. 2 (foll. by *in, up*) draw (fish etc.) in or up with a reel. 3 stand, walk, or run unsteadily. 4 be shaken mentally or physically. 5 rock from side to side, or swing violently. 6 dance a reel. □ **reel off** say or recite very rapidly and without apparent effort. [Old English]

re-elect /ˌriːɪˈlekt/ v. elect again. □ **re-election** /ˌriːɪˈlekʃ(ə)n/ n.

re-embark /ˌriːɪmˈbɑːk/ v. go or put on board ship again.

re-emerge /ˌriːɪˈmɜːdʒ/ v. (**-ging**) emerge again; come back out. □ **re-emergence** n.

re-emphasize /riːˈemfəˌsaɪz/ v. (also **-ise**) (**-zing** or **-sing**) place renewed emphasis on.

re-employ /ˌriːɪmˈplɔɪ/ v. employ again. □ **re-employment** n.

re-enact /ˌriːɪˈnækt/ v. act out (a past event). □ **re-enactment** n.

re-engage /ˌriːɪnˈɡeɪdʒ/ v. (**-ging**) engage again.

re-enlist /ˌriːɪnˈlɪst/ v. enlist again, esp. in the armed services.

re-enter /riːˈentə(r)/ v. enter again; go back in.

re-entrant /riːˈentrənt/ adj. (of an angle) pointing inwards, reflex.

re-entry /riːˈentri/ n. (pl. **-ies**) act of entering again, esp. (of a spacecraft, missile, etc.) re-entering the earth's atmosphere.

re-equip /ˌriːɪˈkwɪp/ v. (**-pp-**) provide or be provided with new equipment.

re-establish /ˌriːɪˈstæblɪʃ/ v. establish again or anew. □ **re-establishment** n.

reeve[1] n. hist. **1** chief magistrate of a town or district. **2** official supervising a landowner's estate. [Old English]

reeve[2] v. (past **rove** or **reeved**) Naut. **1** (usu. foll. by through) thread (a rope or rod etc.) through a ring or other aperture. **2** fasten (a rope or block) in this way. [probably Dutch reven]

reeve[3] n. female ruff. [origin unknown]

re-examine /ˌriːɪɡˈzæmɪn/ v. (**-ning**) examine again or further. □ **re-examination** /-neɪʃ(ə)n/ n.

ref[1] n. colloq. referee in sports. [abbreviation]

ref[2] n. Commerce reference. [abbreviation]

reface /riːˈfeɪs/ v. (**-cing**) put a new facing on (a building).

refashion /riːˈfæʃ(ə)n/ v. fashion again or differently.

refectory /rɪˈfektəri/ n. (pl. **-ies**) dining-room, esp. in a monastery or college. [Latin reficio renew]

refectory table n. long narrow table.

refer /rɪˈfɜː(r)/ v. (**-rr-**) (usu. foll. by to) **1** make an appeal or have recourse to (some authority or source of information) (referred to his notes). **2** send on or direct (a person, or a question for decision). **3** (of a person speaking) make an allusion or direct the hearer's or reader's attention (did not refer to our problems). **4** (of a statement etc.) be relevant; relate (these figures refer to last year). **5** send (a person) to a medical specialist etc. **6** (foll. by back to) a return (a document etc.) to its sender for clarification. **b** send (a proposal etc.) back to

(a lower body, court, etc.). **7** fail (a candidate in an examination). □ **referable** /rɪˈfɜːrəb(ə)l/ adj. [Latin refero relat- carry back]

referee /ˌrefəˈriː/ —n. **1** umpire, esp. in football or boxing. **2** person referred to for a decision in a dispute etc. **3** person willing to testify to the character of an applicant for employment etc. —v. (**-rees, -reed**) act as referee (for).

reference /ˈrefərəns/ n. **1** referring of a matter for decision or settlement or consideration to some authority. **2** scope given to this authority. **3** (foll. by to) **a** relation, respect, or correspondence. **b** allusion. **c** direction to a book etc. (or a passage in it) where information may be found. **d** book or passage so cited. **4** act of looking up a passage etc., or referring to a book or person for information. **5 a** written testimonial supporting an applicant for employment etc. **b** person giving this. □ **with** (or **in**) **reference to** regarding; as regards; about. □ **referential** /-ˈrenʃ(ə)l/ adj.

reference book n. book intended to be consulted for occasional information rather than to be read continuously.

referendum /ˌrefəˈrendəm/ n. (pl. **-s** or **-da**) vote on an important political question open to all the electors of a State. [Latin: related to REFER]

referral /rɪˈfɜːr(ə)l/ n. referring of a person to a medical specialist etc.

referred pain n. pain felt in a part of the body other than its actual source.

refill —v. /riːˈfɪl/ fill again. —n. /ˈriːfɪl/ **1** thing that refills, esp. another drink. **2** act of refilling. □ **refillable** /-ˈfɪləb(ə)l/ adj.

refine /rɪˈfaɪn/ v. (**-ning**) **1** free from impurities or defects. **2** make or become more polished, elegant, or cultured.

refined adj. polished, elegant, cultured.

refinement /rɪˈfaɪnmənt/ n. **1** refining or being refined. **2** fineness of feeling or taste. **3** polish or elegance in behaviour or manner. **4** added development or improvement (car with several refinements). **5** subtle reasoning; fine distinction.

refiner n. person or firm whose business is to refine crude oil, metal, sugar, etc.

refinery n. (pl. **-ies**) place where oil, sugar, etc. is refined.

refit —v. /riːˈfɪt/ (**-tt-**) esp. Naut. make or become serviceable again by repairs, renewals, etc. —n. /ˈriːfɪt/ refitting.

reflate /riːˈfleɪt/ v. (**-ting**) cause reflation (of a currency or economy etc.). [from RE-, after inflate, deflate]

reflation /riːˈfleɪʃ(ə)n/ n. inflation of a financial system to restore its previous

condition after deflation. □ **reflation-ary** *adj.* [from RE-, after *inflation*, *deflation*]

reflect /rɪˈflekt/ *v.* 1 (of a surface or body) throw back (heat, light, sound, etc.). 2 (of a mirror) show an image of, reproduce or effect to (*their* correspond in appearance or effect to (*their behaviour reflects their upbringing*). 4 **a** (of an action, result, etc.) show or bring (credit, discredit, etc.). **b** (*absol.*) usu. foll. by *on*, *upon*) bring discredit on; consider; remind oneself [Latin *flecto flex-* bend]

reflective *adj.* 1 (of a surface etc.) reflecting. 2 (of mental faculties) concerned in reflection or thought. 3 (of a person or mood etc.) thoughtful; given to meditation. □ **reflectively** *adv.* **reflectiveness** *n.*

reflector *n.* 1 piece of glass or metal etc. for reflecting light in a required direction, e.g. a red one on the back of a motor vehicle or bicycle. 2 **a** telescope etc. using a mirror to produce images. **b** the mirror itself.

reflex /ˈriːfleks/ —*adj.* 1 (of an action) independent of the will, as an automatic response to the stimulation of a nerve. 2 (of an angle) exceeding 180°. —*n.* 1 reflex action. 2 sign or secondary manifestation (*law is a reflex of public opinion*). 3 reflected light or image. [Latin: related to REFLECT]

reflex camera *n.* camera in which the viewed image is formed by a mirror, enabling the scene to be correctly composed and focused.

reflexion var. of REFLECTION.

reflexive /rɪˈfleksɪv/ *Gram.* —*adj.* 1 (of a word or form, esp. of a pronoun) referring back to the subject of a sentence (e.g. *myself*). 2 (of a verb) having a reflexive pronoun as its object (as in *to wash oneself*). —*n.* reflexive word or form, esp. a pronoun (e.g. *myself*).

reflexology /ˌriːflekˈsɒlədʒɪ/ *n.* massage through points on the feet, hands, and head, to relieve tension and treat illness. □ **reflexologist** *n.*

refloat /riːˈfləʊt/ *v.* set (a stranded ship) afloat again.

refocus /riːˈfəʊkəs/ *v.* (**-s-** or **-ss-**) focus again or anew.

reforest /riːˈfɒrɪst/ *v.* = REAFFOREST. □ **reforestation** /-steɪʃ(ə)n/ *n.*

reforge /riːˈfɔːdʒ/ *v.* (**-ging**) forge again or differently.

reform /rɪˈfɔːm/ —*v.* 1 make or become better by the removal of faults and errors. 2 abolish or cure (an abuse or malpractice). —*n.* 1 removal of faults or abuses, esp. mora, political, or social. 2 improvement made or suggested. □ **reformative** *adj.*

re-form /riːˈfɔːm/ *v.* form again. □ **re-formation** /-ˈmeɪʃ(ə)n/ *n.*

reformat /riːˈfɔːmæt/ *v.* (**-tt-**) format anew.

reformation /ˌrefəˈmeɪʃ(ə)n/ *n.* 1 reforming or being reformed, esp. a radical change for the better in political, religious, or socia. affairs. 2 (**the Reformation**) *hist.* 16th-c. movement for the reform of abuses in the Roman Church ending in the establishment of the Reformed or Protestant Churches.

reformatory /rɪˈfɔːmətərɪ/ —*n.* (*pl.* **-ies**) *US & hist.* institution for the reform of young offenders. —*adj.* producing reform.

Reformed Church *n.* a Protestant (esp. Calvinist) Church.

reformer *n.* person who advocates or brings about (esp. political or social) reform.

reformism /rɪˈfɔːmɪz(ə)m/ *n.* policy of reform rather than abolition or revolution. □ **reformist** *n. & adj.*

reformulate /riːˈfɔːmjʊleɪt/ *v.* (**-ting**) formulate again or differently. □ **re-formulation** /-ˈleɪʃ(ə)n/ *n.*

refract /rɪˈfrækt/ *v.* (of water, air, glass, etc.), deflect (a ray of light etc.) at a certain angle when it enters obliquely from another medium. □ **refraction** *n.* **refractive** *adj.* [Latin *refringo -fract-* break open]

refractor *n.* 1 refracting medium or lens. 2 telescope using a lens to produce an image.

refractory /rɪˈfræktərɪ/ *adj.* 1 stubborn, unmanageable, rebellious. 2 (of a wound, disease, etc.) not yielding to treatment. 3 (of a substance) hard to fuse or work. [Latin: related to REFRACT]

refrain[1] /rɪˈfreɪn/ *v.* (foll. by *from*) avoid doing (an action) (*refrain from smoking*). [Latin *frenum* bridle]

refrain[2] /rɪˈfreɪn/ *n.* 1 recurring phrase or lines, esp. at the ends of stanzas. 2 music accompanying this. [Latin: related to REFRACT]

refrangible /rɪˈfrændʒɪb(ə)l/ *adj.* that can be refracted. [Latin: related to REFRACT]

refreeze /riːˈfriːz/ v. (-zing; past **refroze**; past part. **refrozen**) freeze again.

refresh /rɪˈfreʃ/ v. **1** give new spirit or vigour to. **2** revive (the memory), esp. by consulting the source of one's information. □ **refreshing** adj. **refreshingly** adv. [French: related to FRESH]

refresher n. **1** something that refreshes, esp. a drink. **2** Law extra fee payable to counsel in a prolonged case. **refresher course** n. course reviewing or updating previous studies.

refreshment n. **1** refreshing or being refreshed. **2** (usu. in pl.) food or drink.

refrigerant /rɪˈfrɪdʒərənt/ —n. substance used for refrigeration. —adj. cooling. [Latin: related to REFRIGERATE]

refrigerate /rɪˈfrɪdʒəˌreɪt/ v. (-ting) **1** make or become cool or cold. **2** subject (food etc.) to cold in order to freeze or preserve it. □ **refrigeration** /-ˈreɪʃ(ə)n/ n. [Latin refrigero from frigus cold]

refrigerator n. cabinet or room in which food etc. is kept cold.

refroze past of REFREEZE.

refrozen past part. of REFREEZE.

refuel /riːˈfjuːəl/ v. (-ll-; US -l-) replenish a fuel supply; supply with more fuel.

refuge /ˈrefjuːdʒ/ n. **1** shelter from pursuit, danger, or trouble. **2** person or place etc. offering this. [Latin refugium from fugio flee]

refugee /ˌrefjʊˈdʒiː/ n. person taking refuge, esp. in a foreign country, from war, persecution, or natural disaster. [French réfugié: related to REFUGE]

refulgent /rɪˈfʌldʒ(ə)nt/ adj. literary shining, gloriously bright. □ **refulgence** n. [Latin refulgeo shine brightly]

refund —v. /rɪˈfʌnd/ (also absol.) **1** pay back (money or expenses). **2** reimburse (a person). —n. /ˈriːfʌnd/ **1** act of refunding. **2** sum refunded. □ **refundable** /rɪˈfʌndəb(ə)l/ adj. [Latin fundo pour]

refurbish /riːˈfɜːbɪʃ/ v. **1** brighten up. **2** restore and redecorate. □ **refurbishment** n.

refurnish /riːˈfɜːnɪʃ/ v. furnish again or differently.

refusal /rɪˈfjuːz(ə)l/ n. **1** refusing or being refused. **2** (in full **first refusal**) right or privilege of deciding to take or leave a thing before it is offered to others.

refuse[1] /rɪˈfjuːz/ v. (-sing) **1** withhold acceptance of or consent to (refuse an offer, orders). **2** (often foll. by to + infin.) indicate unwillingness or inability (I refuse to go; car refuses to start; I refuse). **3** (often with double object) not grant (a request) made by (a person). **4** (also absol.) (of a horse) be unwilling to jump (a fence etc.). [French refuser]

refuse[2] /ˈrefjuːs/ n. items rejected as worthless; waste. [French: related to REFUSE[1]]

refusenik /rɪˈfjuːznɪk/ n. hist. Soviet Jew who has been refused permission to emigrate to Israel.

refute /rɪˈfjuːt/ v. (-ting) **1** prove the falsity or error of (a statement etc. or the person advancing it). **2** rebut by argument. **3** deny or contradict (without argument). □ **refutation** /ˌrefjʊˈteɪʃ(ə)n/ n. [Latin refuto]

■ **Usage** The use of refute in sense 3 is considered incorrect by some people. It is often confused in this sense with repudiate.

reg /red͡ʒ/ n. colloq. = REGISTRATION MARK. [abbreviation]

regain /rɪˈɡeɪn/ v. obtain possession or use of after loss (regain consciousness).

regal /ˈriːɡ(ə)l/ adj. **1** of or by a monarch or monarchs. **2** fit for a monarch; magnificent. □ **regally** adv. [Latin rex reg- king]

regale /rɪˈɡeɪl/ v. (-ling) **1** entertain lavishly with feasting. **2** (foll. by with) entertain with (talk etc.). [French régaler: related to GALLANT]

regalia /rɪˈɡeɪlɪə/ n.pl. **1** insignia of royalty used at coronations. **2** insignia of an order or of civic dignity. [medieval Latin: related to REGAL]

regard /rɪˈɡɑːd/ —v. **1** gaze on steadily (usu. in a specified way) (regarded them suspiciously). **2** heed; take into account. **3** look upon or think of in a specified way (regard it as an insult). —n. **1** gaze; steady or significant look. **2** (foll. by for) attention or care. **3** (foll. by for) esteem; kindly feeling; respectful opinion. **4** respect; point attended to (in this regard). **5** (in pl.) expression of friendliness in a letter etc.; compliments. □ **as regards** about, concerning; in respect of. **in (or with) regard to** as concerns; in respect of. [French regard(er): related to GUARD]

regardful adj. (foll. by of) mindful of.

regarding prep. about, concerning; in respect of.

regardless —adj. (foll. by of) without regard or consideration for. —adv. without paying attention.

regatta /rɪˈɡætə/ n. event consisting of rowing or yacht races. [Italian]

regency /ˈriːdʒənsɪ/ n. (pl. -ies) office of regent. **2** commission acting as regent. **3 a** period of office of a regent or regency commission. **b** (**Regency**) (in the UK) 1811 to 1820. [medieval Latin regentia: related to REGENT]

regenerate —v. /rɪˈdʒenəˌreɪt/ (-ting) **1** bring or come into renewed existence;

generate again. 2 improve the moral condition of. 3 impart new, more vigorous, or spiritually higher life or nature to. 4 *Biol.* regrow or cause (new tissue) to regrow. —*adj.* /rɪˈdʒenərət/ spiritually born again, reformed. □ **regenerative** /-rətɪv/ *adj.*

regent /ˈriːdʒ(ə)nt/ —*n.* person appointed to administer a State because the monarch is a minor or is absent or incapacitated. —*adj.* (after the noun) acting as regent (*Prince Regent*). [Latin *rego* rule]

reggae /ˈregeɪ/ *n.* W. Indian style of music with a strongly accented subsidiary beat. [origin unknown]

regicide /ˈredʒɪsaɪd/ *n.* **1** person who kills or helps to kill a king. **2** killing of a king. [Latin *rex reg- king*, CIDE]

regime /reɪˈʒiːm/ *n.* (also **régime**) **1** method or system of government. **2** prevailing order or system of things. **3** = REGIMEN. [French: related to REGIMEN]

regimen /ˈredʒɪmən/ *n.* prescribed course of exercise, way of life, and diet. [Latin *rego* rule]

regiment —*n.* /ˈredʒɪmənt/ **1 a** permanent unit of an army, usu. commanded by a colonel and divided into several companies, troops, or batteries. **b** operational unit of artillery etc. **2** (usu. foll. by *of*) large or formidable array or number. —*v.* /ˈredʒɪment/ **1** organize (esp. oppressively) in groups or according to a system. **2** form into a regiment or regiments. □ **regimentation** /ˌredʒɪmenˈteɪʃ(ə)n/ *n.* [Latin: related to REGIMEN]

regimental /ˌredʒɪˈment(ə)l/ —*adj.* of a regiment. —*n.* (in *pl.*) military uniform, esp. of a particular regiment. □ **regimentally** *adv.*

Regina /rɪˈdʒaɪnə/ *n.* **1** (after the name) reigning queen (*Elizabeth Regina*). **2** *Law* the Crown (*Regina v. Jones*). [Latin, = queen: related to REX]

region /ˈriːdʒ(ə)n/ *n.* **1** geographical area or division, having definable boundaries or characteristics (*fertile region*). **2** administrative area, esp. in Scotland. **3** part of the body (*lumbar region*). **4** sphere or realm (*region of metaphysics*). □ **in the region of** approximately. □ **regional** *adj.* **regionally** *adv.* [Latin *regio* rule]

register /ˈredʒɪstə(r)/ —*n.* **1** official list, e.g. of births, marriages, and deaths, of children in a class, of shipping, of professionally qualified persons, or of qualified voters in a constituency. **2** book in which items are recorded for reference. **3** device recording speed, force, etc. **4 a** compass of a voice or instrument. **b** part of this compass (*lower register*). **5** adjustable plate for

widening or narrowing an opening and regulating a draught, esp. in a fire-grate. **6 a** set of organ pipes. **b** sliding device controlling this. **7** = CASH REGISTER. **8** form of a language (colloquial, literary, etc.) used in particular circumstances. **9** *Computing* a memory location having specific properties and quick access time. —*v.* **1** set down (a name, fact, complaint, etc.) formally: record in writing. **2** enter or cause to be entered in a particular register. **3** commit (a letter etc.) to registered post. **4** (of an instrument) record automatically; indicate. **5** (of a person or feature) express (an emotion) facially: indicate. **6** make an impression on a person's mind. [Latin *regero -gest-* transcribe, record]

registered nurse *n.* nurse with a State certificate of competence.

registered post *n.* postal procedure with special precautions for safety and for compensation in case of loss.

register office *n.* State office where civil marriages are conducted.

■ **Usage** *Register office* is the official name, although *registry office* is often heard in colloquial usage.

registrar /ˌredʒɪˈstrɑː(r)/ *n.* **1** official responsible for keeping a register. **2** chief administrator in a university, college, etc. **3** hospital doctor training as a specialist. [medieval Latin: related to REGISTER]

registration /ˌredʒɪˈstreɪʃ(ə)n/ *n.* registering or being registered. [French or medieval Latin: related to REGISTER]

registration mark *n.* (also **registration number**) combination of letters and numbers identifying a vehicle etc.

registry /ˈredʒɪstrɪ/ *n.* (*pl.* **-ies**) place where registers or records are kept. [medieval Latin: related to REGISTER]

registry office *n.* = REGISTER OFFICE.

Regius professor /ˈriːdʒəs/ *n.* holder of a chair founded by a sovereign (esp. one at Oxford or Cambridge instituted by Henry VIII) or filled by Crown appointment. [Latin *regius* royal]

regrade /riːˈgreɪd/ *v.* (**-ding**) grade again or differently.

regress —*v.* /rɪˈgres/ **1** move backwards; return to a former, esp. worse, state. **2** *Psychol.* (cause to) return mentally to a former stage of life. —*n.* /ˈriːgres/ act of regressing. □ **regression** /rɪˈgreʃ(ə)n/ *n.* **regressive** /rɪˈgresɪv/ *adj.* [Latin *regredior -gress-* go back]

regret /rɪˈgret/ —*v.* (**-tt-**) **1** feel or express sorrow, repentance, or distress over (an

action or loss etc.) **2** acknowledge with sorrow or remorse (*regret to say*). —*n.* feeling of sorrow, repentance, etc., over an action or loss etc. □ **give** (or **send**) **one's regrets** formally decline an invitation. [French *regretter*]

regretful *adj.* feeling or showing regret. □ **regretfully** *adv.*

regrettable *adj.* (of events or conduct) undesirable, unwelcome; deserving censure. □ **regrettably** *adv.*

regroup /riːˈɡruːp/ *v.* **1** group or arrange again or differently. **2** *Mil.* prepare for a fresh attack.

regrow /riːˈɡrəʊ/ *v.* grow again, esp. after an interval. □ **regrowth** *n.*

regular /ˈreɡjʊlə(r)/ —*adj.* **1** acting, done, or recurring uniformly or calculably in time or manner; habitual, constant, orderly. **2** conforming to a rule or principle; systematic. **3** harmonious, symmetrical. **4** conforming to a standard of etiquette or procedure. **5** properly constituted or qualified; pursuing an occupation as one's main pursuit (*regular soldier*). **6** *Gram.* (of a noun, verb, etc.) following the normal type of inflection. **7** *colloq.* thorough, absolute (*a regular hero*). **8** (before or after the noun) bound by religious rule; belonging to a religious or monastic order (*canon regular*). **9** (of a person) defecating or menstruating at predictable times. —*n.* **1** regular soldier. **2** *colloq.* regular customer, visitor, etc. **3** one of the regular clergy. □ **regularity** /-ˈlærɪtɪ/ *n.* **regularize** *v.* (also **-ise**) (**-zing** or **-sing**) **regularly** *adv.* [Latin *regula* rule]

regulate /ˈreɡjʊˌleɪt/ *v.* (**-ting**) **1** control by rule. **2** subject to restrictions. **3** adapt to requirements. **4** alter the speed of (a machine or clock) so that it works accurately. □ **regulator** *n.* **regulatory** /-lətərɪ/ *adj.* [Latin: related to REGULAR]

regulation /ˌreɡjʊˈleɪʃ(ə)n/ *n.* **1** regulating or being regulated. **2** prescribed rule. **3** (*attrib.*) **a** in accordance with regulations; of the correct type etc. **b** *colloq.* usual.

regulo /ˈreɡjʊˌləʊ/ *n.* (usu. foll. by a numeral) each of the numbers of a scale denoting temperature in a gas oven (*cook at regulo 6*). [*Regulo*, propr. term for a thermostatic gas oven control]

regurgitate /rɪˈɡɜːdʒɪˌteɪt/ *v.* (**-ting**) **1** bring (swallowed food) up again to the mouth. **2** reproduce, rehash (information etc.). □ **regurgitation** /-ˈteɪʃ(ə)n/ *n.* [Latin *gurges git.* whirlpool]

rehabilitate /ˌriːhəˈbɪlɪˌteɪt/ *v.* (**-ting**) **1** restore to effectiveness or normal life by training etc., esp. after imprisonment or illness. **2** restore to former privileges or reputation or a proper condition. □ **rehabilitation** /-ˈteɪʃ(ə)n/ *n.* [medieval Latin: related to RE- ABILITY]

rehang /riːˈhæŋ/ *v.* (*past and past part.* **rehung**) hang again or differently.

rehash —*v.* /riːˈhæʃ/ put (old material) into a new form without significant change or improvement. —*n.* /ˈriːhæʃ/ **1** material rehashed. **2** rehashing.

rehear /riːˈhɪə(r)/ *v.* (*past and past part.* **reheard** /-ˈhɜːd/) hear (esp. a judicial case) again.

rehearsal /rɪˈhɜːs(ə)l/ *n.* **1** trial performance or practice of a play, music, etc. **2** process of rehearsing.

rehearse /rɪˈhɜːs/ *v.* (**-sing**) **1** practise (a play, music, etc.) for later public performance. **2** hold a rehearsal. **3** train (a person) by rehearsal. **4** recite or say over. **5** give a list of, enumerate. [Anglo-French: related to HEARSE]

reheat /riːˈhiːt/ *v.* heat again.

rehouse /riːˈhaʊz/ *v.* (**-sing**) house elsewhere.

rehung *past and past part.* of REHANG.

Reich /raɪx/ *n.* the former German State, (in the **Third Reich.** [German = empire]

reign /reɪn/ —*v.* **1** be king or queen. **2** prevail (*confusion reigns*). **3** (as **reigning** *attrib. adj.*) (of a winner, champion, etc.) currently holding the title etc. —*n.* **1** sovereignty, rule. **2** period during which a sovereign rules. [Latin *regnum*: related to Rex]

reimburse /ˌriːɪmˈbɜːs/ *v.* (**-sing**) **1** repay (a person who has expended money). **2** repay (a person's expenses). □ **reimbursement** *n.*

reimpose /ˌriːɪmˈpəʊz/ *v.* (**-sing**) impose again, esp. after a lapse.

rein /reɪn/ —*n.* (in *sing.* or *pl.*) **1** long narrow strap with each end attached to the bit, used to guide or check a horse etc. **2** similar device used to restrain a child. **3** means of control. —*v.* **1** check or manage with reins. **2** (foll. by *up, back*) pull up or back with reins. **3** (foll. by *in*) hold in as with reins. **4** govern, restrain, control. □ **give free rein to** allow freedom of action or expression. **keep a tight rein on** allow little freedom to. [French *rene* from Latin *retinēre* RE-TAIN]

reincarnation /ˌriːɪnkɑːˈneɪʃ(ə)n/ *n.* rebirth of a soul in a new body. □ **reincarnate** /-ˈkɑːneɪt/ *v.* (**-ting**). **reincarnate** /-ˈkɑːnət/ *adj.*

reindeer /ˈreɪndɪə(r)/ *n.* (*pl.* same or **-s**) subarctic deer with large antlers. [Old Norse]

reinforce /ˌriːɪnˈfɔːs/ *v.* (**-cing**) strengthen or support, esp. with additional personnel or material or by

an increase of numbers or quantity or size etc. [French *renforcer*]

reinforced concrete *n.* concrete with metal bars or wire etc. embedded to increase its strength.

reinforcement *n.* **1** reinforcing or being reinforced. **2** thing that reinforces. **3** (in *pl.*) reinforcing personnel or equipment etc.

reinsert /ˌriːɪnˈsɜːt/ *v.* insert again. □ **reinsertion** *n.*

reinstate /ˌriːɪnˈsteɪt/ *v.* (**-ting**) **1** replace in a former position. **2** restore (a person etc.) to former privileges. □ **reinstatement** *n.*

reinsure /ˌriːɪnˈʃʊə(r)/ *v.* (**-ring**) insure again (esp. of an insurer transferring risk to another insurer). □ **reinsurance** *n.*

reinterpret /ˌriːɪnˈtɜːprɪt/ *v.* (**-t-**) interpret again or differently. □ **reinterpretation** /-ˈteɪʃ(ə)n/ *n.*

reintroduce /ˌriːɪntrəˈdjuːs/ *v.* (**-cing**) introduce again. □ **reintroduction** /-ˈdʌk(ʃ)ən/ *n.*

reinvest /ˌriːɪnˈvest/ *v.* invest again (esp. proceeds or interest). □ **reinvestment** *n.*

reissue /riːˈɪʃuː/ *v.* (**-ues, -ued, -uing**) issue again or in a different form. —*n.* new issue, esp. of a previously published book.

reiterate /riːˈɪtəreɪt/ *v.* (**-ting**) say or do again or repeatedly. □ **reiteration** *n.*

reject —*v.* /rɪˈdʒekt/ **1** put aside or send back as not to be used, done, or complied with etc. **2** refuse to accept or believe in. **3** rebuff or withhold affection from (a person). **4** show an immune response to (a transplant) so that it fails. —*n.* /ˈriːdʒekt/ thing or person rejected as unfit or below standard. □ **rejection** /rɪˈdʒek(ʃ)ən/ *n.* [Latin *rejicio -ject-* throw back]

rejig /riːˈdʒɪg/ *v.* (**-gg-**) **1** re-equip (a factory etc.) for a new kind of work. **2** rearrange.

rejoice /rɪˈdʒɔɪs/ *v.* (**-cing**) **1** feel great joy. **2** be glad. **3** (foll. by *in, at*) take delight. [French *rejoir*: related to JOY]

rejoin¹ /riːˈdʒɔɪn/ *v.* **1** join together again; reunite. **2** join (a companion etc.) again.

rejoin² /rɪˈdʒɔɪn/ *v.* **1** say in answer, retort. **2** reply to a charge or pleading in a lawsuit. [French *rejoindre*: related to JOIN]

rejoinder /rɪˈdʒɔɪndə(r)/ *n.* what is said in reply; retort. [Anglo-French related to REJOIN²]

rejuvenate /rɪˈdʒuːvəneɪt/ *v.* (**-ting**) make (as if) young again. □ **rejuvenation** /-ˈneɪʃ(ə)n/ *n.* [Latin *juvenis* young]

rekindle /riːˈkɪnd(ə)l/ *v.* (**-ling**) kindle again.

relabel /riːˈleɪb(ə)l/ *v.* (**-ll-; US -l-**) label (esp. a commodity) again or differently.

relapse /rɪˈlæps/ —*v.* (**-sing**) (usu. foll. by *into*) fall back or sink again (into a worse state after improvement). —*n.* /also rɪˈlaps/ relapsing, esp. a deterioration in a patient's condition after partial recovery. [Latin *labor laps-* slip]

relate /rɪˈleɪt/ *v.* (**-ting**) **1** narrate or recount **2** (usu. foll. by *to, with*) connect (two things) in thought or meaning. **3** (foll. by *to*) have reference to. **4** (foll. by *to*) be connected or sympathetic to. [Latin: related to REFER]

related *adj.* connected, esp. by blood or marriage.

relation /rɪˈleɪʃ(ə)n/ *n.* **1 a** the way in which one person or thing is related or connected to another. **b** connection, correspondence, contrast, or feeling prevailing between persons or things (*bears no relation to the facts; enjoyed good relations for many years*). **2** relative. **3** (in *pl.*) **a** (foll. by *with*) dealings (with others). **b** sexual intercourse. **4** = RELATIONSHIP. **5 a** narration. **b** narrative. □ **in relation to** as regards. [Latin: related to REFER]

relationship *n.* **1** state or instance of being related. **2 a** connection or association (*good working relationship*). **b** emotional (esp. sexual) association between two people.

relative /ˈrelətɪv/ —*adj.* **1** considered in relation to something else (*relative velocity*). **2** (foll. by *to*) proportioned to (something else) (*growth is relative to input*). **3** implying comparison or contextual relation (*'heat' is a relative word*). **4** comparative (*their relative merits*). **5** having mutual relations; corresponding in some way; related to each other. **6** (foll. by *to*) having reference to the issue; relating to (*the focus relative to the issue*). **7** *Gram.* **a** (of a word, esp. a pronoun) referring to an expressed or implied antecedent and attaching a subordinate clause to it, e.g. *which, who*, **b** (of a clause) attached to an antecedent by a relative word. —*n.* **1** person connected by blood or marriage. **2** species related to another by blood or marriage. **3** *Gram.* relative word, esp. a pronoun. [Latin: related to REFER]

relatively *adv.*

relative atomic mass *n.* the ratio of the average mass of one atom of an element to one-twelfth of the mass of an atom of carbon-12.

relative density *n.* the ratio between the mass of a substance and that of the

same volume of a substance used as a standard (usu. water or air).

relative molecular mass n. the ratio of the average mass of one molecule of an element or compound to one-twelfth of the mass of an atom of carbon-12.

relativity /ˌrelə'trɪvɪtɪ/ n. **1** being relative. **2** *Physics* a (**special theory of relativity**) theory based on the principle that all motion is relative and that light has a constant velocity. b (**general theory of relativity**) theory extending this to gravitation and accelerated motion.

relax /rɪ'læks/ v. **1** make or become less stiff, rigid, or tense. **2** make or become less formal or strict (*rules were relaxed*). **3** reduce or abate (one's attention, efforts, etc.). **4** cease work or effort. **5** (**as relaxed** adj.) at ease; unperturbed. [Latin *relaxo*: related to LAX]

relaxation /ˌriːlæk'seɪʃ(ə)n/ n. **1** relaxing or being relaxed. **2** recreation.

relay /'riːleɪ/ —n. **1** fresh set of people etc. substituted for tired ones. **2** supply of material similarly used. **3** = RELAY RACE. **4** device activating an electric circuit etc. in response to changes affecting itself. **5** a device to receive, reinforce, and transmit a message, broadcast, etc. b relayed message or transmission. —v. /also rɪ'leɪ/ receive (a message, broadcast, etc.) and transmit it to others. [French *relai* from Latin *laxo*: see LAX]

re-lay /riː'leɪ/ v. (*past* and *past part.* **re-laid**) lay again or differently.

relay race n. race between teams of which each member in turn covers part of the distance.

relearn /riː'lɜːn/ v. learn again.

release /rɪ'liːs/ —v. (-**sing**) **1** (often foll. by *from*) set free; liberate, unfasten. **2** allow to move from a fixed position. **3** a make (information, a recording, etc.) publicly available. b issue (a film etc.) for general exhibition. —n. **1** liberation from a restriction, duty, or difficulty. **2** handle or catch that releases part of a mechanism. **3** news item etc. made available for publication (*press release*). **4** a film or record etc. that is released. b releasing or being released in this way. [French *relesser* from Latin *relaxo* RELAX]

relegate /'relɪgeɪt/ v. (-**ting**) **1** consign or dismiss to an inferior position. **2** transfer (a sports team) to a lower division of a league etc. **3** banish. □ **relegation** /-'geɪʃ(ə)n/ n. [Latin *relego* send away]

relent /rɪ'lent/ v. relax severity, abandon a harsh intention, yield to compassion. [medieval Latin *lentus* flexible]

relentless adj. unrelenting, oppressively constant. □ **relentlessly** adv.

re-let /riː'let/ —v. (-**tt-**; *past* and *past part.* **-let**) let (a property) for a further period or to a new tenant. —n. re-let property.

relevant /'relɪv(ə)nt/ adj. (often foll. by *to*) bearing on or having reference to the matter in hand. □ **relevance** n. [Latin *relevo*: related to RELIEVE]

reliable /rɪ'laɪəb(ə)l/ adj. of consistently good character or quality; dependable. □ **reliability** /-'bɪlɪtɪ/ n. **reliably** adv.

reliance /rɪ'laɪəns/ n. (foll. by *in, on*) trust, confidence. □ **reliant** adj.

relic /'relɪk/ n. **1** object that is interesting because of its age or association. **2** part of a dead holy person's body or belongings kept as an object of reverence. **3** surviving custom or belief etc. from a past age. **4** memento or souvenir. **5** (in *pl.*) what has survived. **6** (in *pl.*) dead body or remains of a person. [Latin *reliquiae* remains: related to RELINQUISH]

relict /'relɪkt/ n. object surviving in its primitive form. [French *relicte*: related to RELIC]

relief /rɪ'liːf/ n. **1** a alleviation of or deliverance from pain, distress, anxiety, etc. b feeling accompanying such deliverance. **2** feature etc. that diversifies monotony or relaxes tension. **3** assistance (esp. financial) given to those in special need or difficulty. **4** a replacing of a person or persons on duty by another or others. b person or persons replacing others in this way. **5** (usu. *attrib.*) thing supplementing another in some service (*relief bus*). **6** a method of moulding, carving, or stamping in which the design stands out from the surface. b piece of sculpture etc. in relief. c representation of relief given by an arrangement of line, colour, or shading. **7** vividness, distinctness (*brings the facts out in sharp relief*). **8** (foll. by *of*) reinforcement (esp. the raising of a siege) of a place. **9** esp. *Law* redress of a hardship or grievance. [French and Italian: related to RELIEVE]

relief map n. map indicating hills and valleys by shading etc. rather than by contour lines alone.

relief road n. road taking traffic around a congested area.

relieve /rɪ'liːv/ v. (-**ving**) **1** bring or give relief to. **2** mitigate the tedium or monotony of. **3** release (a person) from a duty by acting as or providing a substitute. **4** (foll. by *of*) take (esp. a burden or duty) away from (a person). □ **relieve one's**

feelings use strong language or vigorous behaviour when annoyed. **relieve oneself** urinate or defecate. □ **relieved** *adj.* [Italian *rillievo*: related to RELIEVE]

relievo /rɪˈliːvəʊ/ *n.* (*pl.* -**s**) = RELIEF 6.

relight /riːˈlaɪt/ *v.* (*past and past. -lit*) light (a fire etc.) again.

religion /rɪˈlɪdʒ(ə)n/ *n.* **1** belief in a superhuman controlling power, esp. in a personal God or gods entitled to obedience and worship. **2** expression of this in worship. **3** particular system of faith and worship. **4** life under monastic vows. **5** thing that one is devoted to. [Latin *religio* bond]

religiosity /rɪˌlɪdʒɪˈɒsɪtɪ/ *n.* state of being religious or too religious. [Latin: related to RELIGIOUS]

religious /rɪˈlɪdʒəs/ —*adj.* **1** devoted to religion, pious, devout. **2** of or concerned with religion. **3** of or belonging to a monastic order. **4** scrupulous, conscientious. —*n.* (*pl.* same) person bound by monastic vows. □ **religiously** *adv.* [Latin *religiosus*: related to RELIGION]

reline /riːˈlaɪn/ *v.* (-**ring**) put a new lining in (a garment etc.).

relinquish /rɪˈlɪŋkwɪʃ/ *v.* **1** surrender or resign (a right or possession). **2** give up or cease from (a habit, plan, belief, etc.). **3** relax hold of. □ **relinquishment** *n.* [Latin *relinquo*: related to RELIC hind]

reliquary /ˈrɛlɪkwərɪ/ *n.* (*pl.* -**ies**) esp. *Relig.* receptacle for a relic or relics. [French *reliquaire*: related to RELIC]

relish /ˈrɛlɪʃ/ —*n.* **1** (often foll. by *for*) great liking or enjoyment. **2 a** appetizing flavour. **b** attractive quality. **3** condiment eaten with plainer food to add flavour. **4** (foll. by *of*) distinctive taste or tinge. —*v.* **1** get pleasure out of, enjoy greatly. **2** anticipate with pleasure. [French *reles* remainder: related to RELEASE]

relive /riːˈlɪv/ *v.* (-**ving**) live (an experience etc.) over again, esp. in the imagination.

reload /riːˈləʊd/ *v.* (also *absol.*) load (esp. a gun) again.

relocate /ˌriːləʊˈkeɪt/ *v.* (-**ting**) **1** locate in a new place. **2** move to a new place (esp. to live or work). □ **relocation** /-ˈkeɪʃ(ə)n/ *n.*

reluctant /rɪˈlʌkt(ə)nt/ *adj.* (often foll. by *to* + infin.) unwilling or disinclined. □ **reluctance** *n.* **reluctantly** *adv.* [Latin *luctor* struggle]

rely /rɪˈlaɪ/ *v.* (-**ies**, -**ied**) (foll. by *on*, *upon*) **1** depend on with confidence or assurance. **2** be dependent on. [Latin *religo* bind closely]

REM *abbr.* rapid eye movement.

remade *past and past part.* of REMAKE.

remain /rɪˈmeɪn/ *v.* **1** be left over after others or other parts have been removed, used, or dealt with. **2** be in the same place or condition during further time, stay (*remained at home*). **3** (foll. by *compl.*) continue to be (*remained calm*). [Latin *remaneo*]

remainder —*n.* **1** residue. **2** remaining persons or things. **3** number left after subtraction. **4** copies of a book left unsold when demand has almost ceased. —*v.* dispose of (a remainder of books) at a reduced price. [Anglo-French: related to REMAIN]

remains *n.pl.* **1** what remains after other parts have been removed or used etc. **2** relics of antiquity, esp. of buildings. **3** dead body.

remake —*v.* /riːˈmeɪk/ (-**king**; *past and past part.* remade) make again or differently. —*n.* /ˈriːmeɪk/ thing that has been remade, esp. a cinema film.

remand /rɪˈmɑːnd/ —*v.* return (a prisoner) to custody, esp. to allow further inquiry. —*n.* recommittal to custody. □ **on remand** in custody pending trial. [Latin *remando*]

remand centre *n.* institution to which accused persons are remanded.

remark /rɪˈmɑːk/ —*v.* **1** (often foll. by *that*) **a** say by way of comment. **b** *archaic* take notice of, regard with attention. **2** (usu. foll. by *on*, *upon*) make a comment. —*n.* **1** written or spoken comment; anything said. **2 a** noticing (*worthy of remark*). **b** commenting (*let it pass without remark*). [French *remarquer*: related to MARK]

remarkable *adj.* worth notice; exceptional, striking. □ **remarkably** *adv.* [French: related to REMARK]

remarriage *n.*

remarry /riːˈmærɪ/ *v.* (-**ies**, -**ied**) marry again. □ **remarriage** *n.*

REME /riːm/ *abbr.* Royal Electrical and Mechanical Engineers.

remeasure /riːˈmɛʒə(r)/ *v.* (-**ring**) measure again.

remedial /rɪˈmiːdɪəl/ *adj.* **1** affording or intended as a remedy. **2** (of teaching etc.) for slow or disadvantaged pupils. [Latin: related to REMEDY]

remedy /ˈrɛmɪdɪ/ —*n.* (*pl.* -**ies**) (often foll. by *for*, *against*) **1** medicine or treatment. **2** means of counteracting or removing anything undesirable. **3** redress; legal or other reparation. —*v.* (-**ies**, -**ied**) rectify; make good. □ **remediable** /rɪˈmiːdɪəb(ə)l/ *adj.* [Latin *remedium* from *medeor* heal]

remember /rɪˈmɛmbə(r)/ *v.* **1** (often foll. by *to* + infin. or *that* + clause) keep in the memory; not forget. **2** (also *absol.*)

bring back into one's thoughts. **3** think of or acknowledge (a person), esp. in making a gift etc. **4** (foll. by *to*) convey greetings from (one person) to (another) (*remember me to John*). [Latin: related to MEMORY]

remembrance /rɪˈmembrəns/ *n.* **1** remembering or being remembered. **2** a memory or recollection. **3** keepsake, souvenir. **4** (in *pl.*) greetings conveyed through a third person. [French: related to REMEMBER]

Remembrance Day *n.* **1** = REMEMBRANCE SUNDAY. **2** *hist.* Armistice Day.

Remembrance Sunday *n.* Sunday nearest 11 Nov., when those killed in the wars of 1914–18 and 1939–45 and later conflicts are commemorated.

remind /rɪˈmaɪnd/ *v.* (usu. foll. by *of* or *to* + infin. or *that* + clause) cause (a person) to remember or think of (*reminds me of her father; reminded them of the time*).

reminder *n.* **1** thing that reminds, esp. a repeat letter or bill. **2** (often foll. by *of*) memento.

reminisce /remɪˈnɪs/ *v.* (-**cing**) indulge in reminiscence.

reminiscence /remɪˈnɪs(ə)ns/ *n.* **1** remembering things past. **2** (in *pl.*) collection on literary form of incidents and experiences remembered. [Latin *reminiscor* remember]

reminiscent *adj.* **1** (foll. by *of*) reminding or suggestive of. **2** concerned with reminiscence.

remiss /rɪˈmɪs/ *adj.* careless of duty; lax, negligent. [Latin: related to REMIT]

remission /rɪˈmɪʃ(ə)n/ *n.* **1** reduction of a prison sentence on account of good behaviour. **2** remitting of a debt or penalty etc. **3** diminution of force, effect, or degree (*esp. of disease or pain*). **4** (often foll. by *of*) forgiveness (of sins etc.). [Latin: related to REMIT]

remit –*v.* /rɪˈmɪt/ (-**tt**-) **1** cancel or refrain from exacting or inflicting (a debt, punishment, etc.). **2** abate or slacken; cease partly or entirely. **3** send (money etc.) in payment. **4 a** (foll. by *to*) refer (a matter for decision etc.) to some authority. **b** send back (a case) to a lower court. **5** postpone or defer. **6** pardon (sins etc.). –*n.* /ˈriːmɪt/ **1** terms of reference of a committee etc. **2** item referred for consideration. [Latin *remitto* -*miss*-]

remittance *n.* **1** money sent, esp. by post. **2** sending of money.

remittent *adj.* (of a fever or disease) abating at intervals.

remix –*v.* /riːˈmɪks/ mix again. –*n.* /ˈriːmɪks/ remixed recording.

remnant /ˈremnənt/ *n.* **1** small remaining quantity. **2** piece of cloth etc. left when the greater part has been used or sold. [French: related to REMAIN]

remodel /riːˈmɒd(ə)l/ *v.* (-**ll**-; *US* -**l**-) **1** model again or differently. **2** reconstruct.

remold *US var.* of REMOULD.

remonstrate /ˈremənstreɪt/ *v.* (-**ting**) (foll. by *with*) make a protest; argue forcibly. □ **remonstrance** /rɪˈmɒnstrəns/ *n.* **remonstration** /-ˈstreɪʃ(ə)n/ *n.* [medieval Latin *monstro* show]

remorse /rɪˈmɔːs/ *n.* **1** deep regret for a wrong committed. **2** compunction; compassion, mercy (*without remorse*). [medieval Latin *mordeo mors-* bite]

remorseful *adj.* filled with repentance. □ **remorsefully** *adv.*

remorseless *adj.* without compassion. □ **remorselessly** *adv.*

remortgage /riːˈmɔːgɪdʒ/ –*v.* (-**ging**) (also *absol.*) mortgage again; revise the terms of an existing mortgage on (a property). –*n.* different or altered mortgage.

remote /rɪˈməʊt/ *adj.* (**remoter**, **remotest**) **1** far away, far apart, distant. **2** isolated; secluded. **3** distantly related (*remote ancestor*). **4** slight, faint (*a remote hope; not the remotest chance*). **5** aloof; not friendly. □ **remotely** *adv.* **remoteness** *n.* [Latin *remotus*: related to REMOVE]

remote control *n.* **1** control of an apparatus from a distance by means of signals transmitted from a radio or electronic device. **2** such a device.

remould (*US* **remold**) –*v.* /riːˈməʊld/ **1** mould again; refashion. **2** re-form the tread of (a tyre). –*n.* /ˈriːməʊld/ remoulded tyre.

removal /rɪˈmuːv(ə)l/ *n.* **1** removing or being removed. **2** transfer of furniture etc. on moving house.

remove /rɪˈmuːv/ –*v.* (-**ving**) **1** take off or away from the place occupied. **2 a** convey to another place; change the situation of. **b** get rid of; dismiss. **3** cause to be no longer present or available; take away (*privileges were removed*). **4** (in *passive*; foll. by *from*) distant or remote in condition (*country is not far removed from anarchy*). **5** (as **removed** *adj.*) (esp. of cousins) separated by a specified number of steps of descent (*a first cousin twice removed* = a grand child of a first cousin). –*n.* **1** degree of remoteness; distance. **2** stage in a gradation; degree (*several removes from what I expected*). **3** form or division in some schools. □ **removable** *adj.* [Latin *removeo -mot-*]

remunerate /rɪˈmjuːnəˌreɪt/ v. (-ting) 1 reward; pay for services rendered. 2 serve as or provide recompense for (work etc.) or to (a person). □ **remuneration** /-ˈreɪʃ(ə)n/ n. **remunerative** /-rətɪv/ adj. [Latin munus -eris gift]

Renaissance /rɪˈneɪs(ə)ns/ n. 1 revival of art and literature in the 14th-16th c. 2 period of this. 3 (often attrib.) style of art, architecture, etc. developed by it. 4 (renaissance) any similar revival. [French naissance birth]

Renaissance man n. person with many talents or pursuits, esp. in the humanities.

renal /ˈriːn(ə)l/ adj. of the kidneys. [Latin renes kidneys]

rename /riːˈneɪm/ v. (-ming) name again; give a new name to.

renascent /rɪˈnæs(ə)nt/ adj. springing up anew; being reborn. □ **renascence** n.

renationalize /riːˈnæʃənəˌlaɪz/ v. (also **-ise**) (-zing or -sing) nationalize again (an originally nationalized and more recently privatized industry etc.). □ **renationalization** /-ˈzeɪʃ(ə)n/ n.

rend v. (past and past part. **rent**) archaic tear or wrench forcibly. [Old English]

render v. 1 cause to be or become (rendered us helpless). 2 give or pay (money, service, etc.), esp. in return or as a thing due. 3 (often foll. by to) a give (assistance). b show (obedience etc.). c do (a service etc.). 4 submit; send in; present (an account, reason, etc.). 5 a represent or portray. b act (a role). c Mus. perform; execute. 6 translate. 7 (often foll. by down) melt down (fat etc.). 8 cover (stone or brick) with a coat of plaster. □ **rendering** n. [Latin reddo give back]

rendezvous /ˈrɒndɪˌvuː/ n. (pl. same /-ˌvuːz/) 1 agreed or regular meeting place. 2 meeting by arrangement. —v. (**rendezvouses** /-ˌvuːz/; **rendezvoused** /-ˌvuːd/; **rendezvousing** /-ˌvuːɪŋ/) meet at a rendezvous. [French, = present yourselves]

rendition /renˈdɪʃ(ə)n/ n. interpretation or rendering of a dramatic role, piece of music, etc. [French related to RENDER]

renegade /ˈrenɪˌgeɪd/ n. person who deserts a party or principles. [medieval Latin: related to RENEGE]

renege /rɪˈniːg, -ˈneɪg/ v. (**-ging**) (often foll. by on) go back on (one's word etc.). [Latin nego deny]

renegotiate /ˌriːnɪˈgəʊʃɪˌeɪt/ v. (-ting) negotiate again or on different terms. □ **renegotiation** /-ˈeɪʃ(ə)n/ n.

renew /rɪˈnjuː/ v. 1 revive; make new again; restore to the original state. 2 reinforce resupply; replace. 3 repeat or re-establish; resume after an interruption (renewed our acquaintance). 4 (also absol.) grant or be granted continuation of (a licence, subscription, lease, etc.). 5 recover (strength etc.). □ **renewable** adj. **renewal** n.

rennet /ˈrenɪt/ n. 1 curdled milk found in the stomach of an unweaned calf. 2 preparation made from the stomach-membrane of a calf or from certain fungi, used in making cheese. [probably Old English: related to RUN]

renounce /rɪˈnaʊns/ v. (-cing) 1 consent formally to abandon (a claim, right, etc.). 2 repudiate; refuse to recognize any longer. 3 decline further association or disclaim relationship with. [Latin nuntio announce]

renovate /ˈrenəˌveɪt/ v. (-ting) restore to good condition; repair. □ **renovation** /-ˈveɪʃ(ə)n/ n. **renovator** n. [Latin novus new]

renown /rɪˈnaʊn/ n. fame, high distinction. [French renom make famous]

renowned adj. famous, celebrated.

rent¹ —n. 1 tenant's periodical payment for the use of land or premises. 2 payment for the use of equipment etc. —v. 1 (often foll. by from) take, occupy, or use at a rent. 2 (often foll. by out) let or hire (a thing) for rent. 3 (foll. by at) be let at a specified rate. [French rente: related to RENDER]

rent² n. 1 large tear in a garment etc. 2 opening in clouds etc. [from REND]

rent³ past and past part. of REND.

rental /ˈrent(ə)l/ n. 1 amount paid or received as rent. 2 act of renting. [Anglo-French or Anglo-Latin: related to RENT¹]

rent-boy n. young male prostitute.

rentier /ˈrɒntɪˌeɪ/ n. person living on income from property, investments, etc. [French]

renumber /riːˈnʌmbə(r)/ v. change the number or numbers given or allocated to.

renunciation /rɪˌnʌnsɪˈeɪʃ(ə)n/ n. 1 renouncing or giving up. 2 self-denial. [related to RENOUNCE]

reoccupy /riːˈɒkjʊˌpaɪ/ v. (-ies, -ied) occupy again. □ **reoccupation** /-ˈpeɪʃ(ə)n/ n.

reoccur /ˌriːəˈkɜː(r)/ v. (-rr-) occur again or habitually. □ **reoccurrence** /-ˈkʌrəns/ n.

reopen /riːˈəʊpən/ v. open again.

reorder /riːˈɔːdə(r)/ —v. 1 order again. 2 put into a new order. —n. renewed or repeated order for goods.

reorganize /riːˈɔːgənaɪz/ v. (also -ise) (-zing or -sing) organize differently. □ **reorganization** /ˈzeɪʃ(ə)n/ n.

reorient /riːˈɔːrɪˌent/ v. 1 give a new direction or outlook to (ideas, a person, etc.). 2 help a (person) find his or her bearings again. 3 (refl., often foll. by to) adjust oneself to or come to terms with something.

reorientate /riːˈɔːrɪənˌteɪt/ v. (-ting) = REORIENT. □ **reorientation** /-ˈteɪʃ(ə)n/ n.

rep[1] n. colloq. representative, esp. a commercial traveller. [abbreviation]

rep[2] n. colloq. 1 repertory. 2 repertory theatre or company. [abbreviation]

repack /riːˈpæk/ v. pack again.

repackage /riːˈpækɪdʒ/ v. (-ging) 1 package again or differently. 2 present in a new form.

repaid past and past part. of REPAY.

repaint –v. /riːˈpeɪnt/ 1 paint again or differently. 2 restore the paint or colouring of. –n. /ˈriːpeɪnt/ act of repainting.

repair[1] /rɪˈpeə(r)/ –v. 1 restore to good condition after damage or wear. 2 set right or make amends for (a loss, wrong, error, etc.). –n. 1 restoring to sound condition (in need of repair). 2 result of this (the repair hardly shows). 3 good or relative condition for working or using (in bad repair). □ **repairable** adj. **repairer** n. [Latin paro make ready]

repair[2] /rɪˈpeə(r)/ v. (foll. by to) resort; have recourse; go. [Latin: related to REPATRIATE]

repaper /riːˈpeɪpə(r)/ v. paper (a wall etc.) again.

reparable /ˈrepərəb(ə)l/ adj. (of a loss etc.) that can be made good. [Latin: related to REPAIR[1]]

reparation /ˌrepəˈreɪʃ(ə)n/ n. 1 making amends. 2 (esp. in pl.) compensation for war damages.

repartee /ˌrepɑːˈtiː/ n. 1 practice or skill of making witty retorts. 2 conversation characterized by such retorts. [French repartir from repartir reply promptly: related to PART]

repast /rɪˈpɑːst/ n. formal 1 meal. 2 food and drink for this. [Latin repasco -past-feed]

repatriate –v. /riːˈpætrɪˌeɪt/ (-ting) return (a person) to his or her native land. –n. /riːˈpætrɪət/ repatriated person. □ **repatriation** /-ˈeɪʃ(ə)n/ n. [Latin repatrio native rio go back home, from patria native land]

repay /riːˈpeɪ/ v. (past and past part. repaid) 1 pay back (money). 2 make repayment to (a person). 3 requite, reward (a service, action, etc.) (repaid

their kindness; book repays study). □ **repayable** adj. **repayment** n.

repeal /rɪˈpiːl/ –v. revoke or annul (a law etc.). –n. repealing. [French: related to APPEAL]

repeat /rɪˈpiːt/ –v. 1 say or do over again. 2 recite, rehearse, or report (something learnt or heard). 3 recur; appear again. 4 (of food) be tasted after being swallowed due to belching. –n. 1 a repeating. b thing repeated (often attrib.: repeat prescription). 2 repeated broadcast. 3 Mus. a passage intended to be repeated. b mark indicating this. 4 pattern repeated in wallpaper etc. □ **repeat itself** recur in the same form. **repeat oneself** say or do the same thing over again. □ **repeatable** adj. **repeatedly** adv. [Latin peto seek]

repeater n. 1 person or thing that repeats. 2 firearm which fires several shots without reloading. 3 watch or clock which repeats its last strike when required. 4 device for the re-transmission of an electrical message.

repel /rɪˈpel/ v. (-ll-) 1 drive back; ward off (repel an attacker). 2 refuse to accept (repelled offers of help). 3 be repulsive or distasteful to. 4 resist mixing with or admitting (oil and water repel each other; surface repels water). 5 (of a magnetic pole) push away from itself (like poles repel). □ **repellent** adj. & n. [Latin repello -puls-]

repent /rɪˈpent/ v. (often foll. by of) feel deep sorrow about one's actions etc. 2 (also absol.) wish one had not done; resolve not to continue (a wrongdoing etc.). □ **repentance** n. **repentant** adj. [Latin paeniteo]

repercussion /ˌriːpəˈkʌʃ(ə)n/ n. 1 indirect effect or reaction following an event or act. 2 recoil after impact. 3 echo. [Latin: related to RE-]

repertoire /ˈrepətwɑː(r)/ n. 1 stock of works that a performer etc. knows or is prepared to perform. 2 stock of techniques etc. (repertoire of excuses). [Latin: related to REPERTORY]

repertory /ˈrepətəri/ n. (pl. -ies) 1 performance of various plays for short periods by one company. 2 repertory theatres collectively. 3 store or collection, esp. of information, instances, etc. 4 = REPERTOIRE. [Latin reperio find]

repertory company n. theatrical company that performs plays from a repertoire.

repetition /ˌrepɪˈtɪʃ(ə)n/ n. 1 a repeating or being repeated. b thing repeated. 2 copy. □ **repetitious** adj. **repetitive** /rɪˈpetətɪv/ adj.

repetitive strain injury *n.* painful or arm condition resulting from prolonged repetitive movements.

rephrase /riːˈfreɪz/ *v.* (-**sing**) express differently.

repine /rɪˈpaɪn/ *v.* (-**ning**) (often foll. by *at, against*) fret; be discontented. [from PINE², after *repent*]

replace /rɪˈpleɪs/ *v.* (-**cing**) 1 put back in place. 2 take the place of; succeed; be substituted for. 3 find or provide a substitute for. 4 (often foll. by *with, by*) fill up the place of. □ **replaceable** *adj.*

replacement *n.* 1 replacing or being replaced. 2 person or thing that replaces another.

replant /riːˈplɑːnt/ *v.* 1 transfer (a plant etc.). 2 plant (ground) again.

replay —*v.* /riːˈpleɪ/ play (a match, recording, etc.) again. —*n.* /ˈriːpleɪ/ replaying of a match, recorded incident in a game, etc.

replenish /rɪˈplɛnɪʃ/ *v.* 1 (often foll. by *with*) fill up again. 2 renew (a supply etc.). □ **replenishment** *n.* [French *plenir* from *plein* full]

replete /rɪˈpliːt/ *adj.* (often foll. by *with*) 1 well-fed, gorged. 2 filled or well-supplied. □ **repletion** *n.* [Latin *pleo* fill]

replica /ˈrɛplɪkə/ *n.* 1 exact copy, esp. on a duplicate of a work, made by the original artist. [Italian *replicare* REPLY]

reply /rɪˈplaɪ/ —*v.* (-**ies**, -**ied**) 1 (often foll. by *to*) make an answer, respond in word or action. 2 say in answer. —*n.* (*pl.* -**ies**) 1 replying (*what did they say in reply?*). 2 what is replied; response. [Latin *replico* fold back]

repoint /riːˈpɔɪnt/ *v.* point (esp. brickwork) again.

repopulate /riːˈpɒpjʊleɪt/ *v.* (-**ting**) populate again or increase the population of.

report /rɪˈpɔːt/ —*v.* 1 **a** bring back or give an account of. **b** state as fact or news, narrate or describe or repeat, esp. as an eyewitness or hearer etc. **c** relate as spoken by another. 2 make an official or formal statement about. 3 (often foll. by *to*) bring (an offender or offence) to the attention of the authorities. 4 (often foll. by *to*) present oneself to a person as having returned or arrived. 5 (also *absol.*) take down word for word, summarize, or write a description of for publication. 6 make or send in a report. —*n.* 1 account given or opinion formally expressed after investigation or consideration. 2 description, summary, or reproduction of a scene,

speech, law case, etc., esp. for newspaper publication or broadcast. 3 common talk; rumour. 4 way a person or thing is spoken of (*hear a good report of you*). 5 periodical statement on (esp. a school pupil's) work, conduct, etc. 6 sound of a gunshot etc. □ **reportedly** *adv.* [Latin *porto* bring]

reportage /rɛpɔːˈtɑːʒ/ *n.* 1 reporting of news for the media. 2 typical style of journalistic material in a book etc. [from REPORT, after French]

reported speech *n.* speaker's words with the person, tense, etc. adapted, e.g. *he said that he would go*.

reporter *n.* person employed to report news etc. for the media.

repose¹ /rɪˈpəʊz/ —*n.* 1 cessation of activity, excitement, or toil. 2 sleep. 3 peaceful or quiescent state; tranquillity. —*v.* (-**sing**) 1 (also *refl.*) lie down in rest. 2 (often foll. by *in, on*) lie, be lying or laid, esp. in sleep or death. [Latin: related to PAUSE]

repose² /rɪˈpəʊz/ *v.* (foll. by *in*) place (trust etc.) in. [from RE-, POSE]

reposeful *adj.* showing or inducing repose. □ **reposefully** *adv.* [from RE-POSE¹]

reposition /riːpəˈzɪʃ(ə)n/ *v.* 1 move or place in a different position. 2 alter one's position.

repository /rɪˈpɒzɪtəri/ *n.* (*pl.* -**ies**) 1 place where things are stored or may be found, esp. a warehouse or museum. 2 receptacle. 3 (often foll. by *of*) a book, person, etc. regarded as a store of information etc. **b** recipient of secrets etc. [Latin: related to REPOSE²]

repossess /riːpəˈzɛs/ *v.* 1 regain possession of (esp. goods on which payment is in arrears). □ **repossession** *n.*

repot /riːˈpɒt/ *v.* (-**tt-**) move (a plant) to another, esp. larger, pot.

reprehend /rɛprɪˈhɛnd/ *v.* formal rebuke; find fault with. [Latin *prehendo* seize]

reprehensible /rɛprɪˈhɛnsɪb(ə)l/ *adj.* blameworthy.

represent¹ /rɛprɪˈzɛnt/ *v.* 1 stand for or correspond to. 2 (often in *passive*) be a specimen of. 3 embody; symbolize. 4 place a likeness of before the mind or senses. 5 (often foll. by *as, to be*) describe or depict as; declare. 6 (foll. by *that*) allege. 7 show, or play the part of, on stage. 8 be a substitute or deputy for; be entitled to act or speak for. 9 be elected as a member of a legislature etc. by. [Latin: related to PRESENT¹]

represent² /riːprɪˈzɛnt/ *v.* submit (a cheque etc.) again for payment.

representation /rɛprɪzɛnˈteɪʃ(ə)n/ *n.* 1 representing or being represented. 2

thing that represents another. **3** (esp. in *pl.*) statement made of allegations or opinions.

representational *adj. Art* depicting a subject as it appears to the eye.

representative /ˌreprɪˈzentətɪv/ —*adj.* **1** typical of a class. **2** containing typical specimens of all or many classes (*representative sample*). **3 a** consisting of elected deputies etc. **b** based on representation by these (*representative government*). **4** (foll. by *of*) serving as a portrayal or symbol of. —*n.* **1** (foll. by *of*) sample, specimen, or typical embodiment of. **2 a** agent of a person or society. **b** commercial traveller. **3** delegate; substitute. **4** deputy etc. in a representative assembly. [French or medieval Latin: related to REPRESENT¹]

repress /rɪˈpres/ *v.* **1 a** keep under; quell. **b** suppress; prevent from sounding, rioting, or bursting out. **2** *Psychol.* actively exclude (an unwelcome thought) from conscious awareness. **3** (usu. as **repressed** *adj.*) subject (a person) to the suppression of his or her thoughts or impulses. □ **repression** *n.* **repressive** *adj.* [Latin: related to PRESS¹]

reprieve /rɪˈpriːv/ —*v.* **1** remit or postpone the execution of (a condemned person). **2** give respite to. —*n.* **1 a** reprieving or being reprieved. **b** warrant for this. **2** respite. [French *reprendre -pris* take back]

reprimand /ˈreprɪmɑːnd/ —*n.* (esp. official) rebuke. —*v.* administer this to. [Latin: related to REPRESS]

reprint —*v.* /riːˈprɪnt/ print again. —*n.* /ˈriːprɪnt/ **1** reprinting of a book etc. **2** book etc. reprinted. **3** quantity reprinted.

reprisal /rɪˈpraɪz(ə)l/ *n.* act of retaliation. [medieval Latin: related to REPREHEND]

reprise /rɪˈpriːz/ *n.* **1** repeated passage in music. **2** repeated item in a musical programme. [French: related to REPRIEVE]

repro /ˈriːprəʊ/ *n.* (*pl.* **-s**) (often *attrib.*) *colloq.* reproduction or copy. [abbreviation]

reproach /rɪˈprəʊtʃ/ —*v.* express disapproval to (a person or oneself) for a fault. —*n.* **1** rebuke or censure. **2** (often foll. by *to*) thing that brings disgrace or discredit. **3** state of disgrace or discredit. □ **above** (or **beyond**) **reproach** perfect; blameless. [French *reprocher*]

reproachful *adj.* full of or expressing reproach. □ **reproachfully** *adv.*

reprobate /ˈreprəbeɪt/ *n.* unprincipled or immoral person. [Latin: related to PROVE]

reprocess /riːˈprəʊses/ *v.* process again or differently.

reproduce /ˌriːprəˈdjuːs/ *v.* (**-cing**) **1** produce a copy or representation of. **2** cause to be seen or heard etc. again (*tried to reproduce the sound exactly*). **3** produce further members of the same species by natural means. **4** *refl.* produce offspring. □ **reproducible** *adj.*

reproduction /ˌriːprəˈdʌkʃ(ə)n/ *n.* **1** reproducing or being reproduced, esp. the production of further members of the same species. **2** copy of a work of art. **3** (*attrib.*) (of furniture etc.) imitating an earlier style. **4** quality of reproduced sound. □ **reproductive** *adj.*

reprogram /riːˈprəʊgræm/ *v.* (also **reprogramme**) (**-mm-**; *US* **-m-**) program (esp. a computer) again or differently. □ **reprogramable** *adj.* (also **reprogrammable**)

reproof /rɪˈpruːf/ *n. formal* **1** blame (*glance of reproof*). **2** rebuke. [French *reprove*: related to REPROVE]

reprove /rɪˈpruːv/ *v.* (**-ving**) *formal* rebuke (a person, conduct, etc.). [Latin: related to REPROBATE]

reptile /ˈreptaɪl/ *n.* **1** cold-blooded scaly animal of a class including snakes, lizards, crocodiles, turtles, tortoises, etc. **2** mean, grovelling, or repulsive person. □ **reptilian** /-ˈtɪlɪən/ *adj. & n.* [Latin *repo rept-* creep]

republic /rɪˈpʌblɪk/ *n.* State in which supreme power is held by the people or their elected representatives or by an elected or nominated president, not by a monarch etc. [Latin *res* concern: related to PUBLIC]

republican —*adj.* **1** of or constituted as a republic. **2** characteristic of a republic. **3** advocating or supporting republican government. —*n.* **1** person advocating or supporting republican government. **2** (**Republican**) a *US* supporter of the Republican Party. **b** *Ir.* supporter of the IRA or Sinn Féin. □ **republicanism** *n.*

republish /riːˈpʌblɪʃ/ *v.* publish again or in a new edition etc. □ **republication** /-ˈkeɪʃ(ə)n/ *n.*

repudiate /rɪˈpjuːdɪeɪt/ *v.* (**-ting**) **1 a** disown, disavow, reject. **b** refuse dealings with. **c** deny. **2** refuse to recognize or obey (authority or a treaty). **3** refuse to discharge (an obligation or debt). □ **repudiation** /-ˈeɪʃ(ə)n/ *n.* [Latin *repudium* divorce]

■ **Usage** See note at *refute*.

repugnance /rɪˈpʌgnəns/ n. 1 antipathy; aversion. 2 incompatibility of ideas etc. [Latin *pugno* fight]

repugnant adj. 1 extremely distasteful. 2 contradictory.

repulse /rɪˈpʌls/ -v. (-sing) 1 drive back by force of arms. 2 a rebuff. b refuse. -n. 1 repulsing or being repulsed. 2 rebuff. [Latin: related to REPEL]

repulsion /rɪˈpʌlʃ(ə)n/ n. 1 aversion; disgust. 2 *Physics* tendency of bodies to repel each other.

repulsive /rɪˈpʌlsɪv/ adj. causing aversion or loathing; disgusting. □ **repulsively** adv. [French *repulsif* or REPULSE]

reputable /ˈrepjʊtəb(ə)l/ adj. of good repute; respectable. [French or medieval Latin: related to REPUTE]

reputation /ˌrepjʊˈteɪʃ(ə)n/ n. 1 what is generally said or believed about a person's or thing's character (*reputation for honesty*; *reputation of being a crook*). 2 state of being well thought of, respectability (*lost its reputation*).

repute /rɪˈpjuːt/ -n. reputation. -v. (as **reputed** adj.) 1 be generally considered (*is reputed to be the best*). 2 passing as, but probably not (*his reputed father*). □ **reputedly** adv. [Latin *puto* think]

request /rɪˈkwest/ -n. 1 act of asking for something (*came at his request*). 2 thing asked for. -v. 1 ask to be given, allowed, or favoured with 2 (foll. by *to* + infin.) ask (a person) to do something. 3 (foll. by *that*) ask that. □ **by** (or **on**) **request** in response to an expressed wish. [Latin: related to REQUIRE]

request stop n. bus-stop at which a bus stops only if requested.

requiem /ˈrekwɪəm/ n. 1 (**Requiem**) (also *attrib.*) chiefly *RC Ch.* mass for the repose of the souls of the dead. 2 music for this. [Latin, = rest]

require /rɪˈkwaɪə(r)/ v. (-ring) 1 need; depend on, for success or fulfilment (*the work requires patience*). 2 lay down as an imperative (*required by law*). 3 command; instruct (a person etc.). 4 order; insist on (an action or measure). □ **requirement** n. [Latin *requiro -quisi-* seek]

requisite /ˈrekwɪzɪt/ -adj. required by circumstances; necessary to success etc. -n. (often foll. by *for*) thing needed (for some purpose). [Latin: related to REQUIRE]

requisition /ˌrekwɪˈzɪʃ(ə)n/ -n. 1 official order laying claim to the use of property or materials. 2 formal written demand that some duty should be performed. 3 being called or put into service. -v. demand the use or supply of, esp. by requisition order. [Latin: related to REQUIRE]

requite /rɪˈkwaɪt/ v. (-ting) 1 make return for (a service). 2 reward or avenge (a favour or injury). 3 (often foll. by *for*) make return to (a person). 4 repay with good or evil. □ **requital** n. [from RE-, *quite* = QUIT]

reran past of RERUN.

reread /riːˈriːd/ -v. (*past* and *past part.* **reread** /-ˈred/) read again. -n. [/-ˈriːd/] act of reading again.

rerecord /ˌriːrɪˈkɔːd/ v. record again.

reredos /ˈrɪədɒs/ n. ornamental screen covering the wall at the back of an altar. [Anglo-French: related to ARREARS, *dos* back]

re-release /ˌriːrɪˈliːs/ -v. (-sing) release (a record, film, etc.) again. -n. rereleased record, film, etc.

re-route /ˌriːˈruːt/ v. (-teing) send or carry by a different route.

rerun -v. /riːˈrʌn/ (-nn-; *past* **reran**; *past part.* **rerun**) 1 run (a race, film, etc.) again. 2 repeat (a course of action). -n. /ˈriːrʌn/ 1 act of rerunning. 2 film etc. shown again. 3 repetition (of events).

resale /ˈriːseɪl/ n. sale of a thing previously bought.

resat past and past part. of RESIT.

reschedule /riːˈʃedjuːl/ v. (-ling) alter the schedule of; replan.

rescind /rɪˈsɪnd/ v. abrogate, revoke, cancel. □ **rescission** /-ˈsɪʒ(ə)n/ n. [Latin *rescindo -sciss-* cut off]

rescript /ˈriːskrɪpt/ n. 1 Roman emperor's or Pope's written reply to an appeal for a decision. 2 official edict or announcement. [Latin *rescribo -script-* reply in writing]

rescue /ˈreskjuː/ -v. (-ues, -ued, -uing) (often foll. by *from*) save or set free from danger or harm. -n. rescuing or being rescued. □ **rescuer** n. [Romanic]

reseal /riːˈsiːl/ v. seal again. □ **resealable** adj.

research /rɪˈsɜːtʃ, ˈriːsɜːtʃ/ -n. (often *attrib.*) systematic investigation and study of materials, sources, etc., in order to establish facts and reach conclusions. -v. do research into or for. □ **researcher** n. [French: related to SEARCH]

■ **Usage** The second pronunciation, with the stress on the first syllable, is considered incorrect by some people.

research and development *n.* work directed towards the innovation, introduction, and improvement of products and processes.

resell /riːˈsel/ *v.* (*past* and *past part.* **resold**) sell (an object etc.) after buying it.

resemblance /rɪˈzembləns/ *n.* likeness or similarity. [Anglo-French: related to RESEMBLE]

resemble /rɪˈzemb(ə)l/ *v.* (-**ling**) be like; have a similarity to, or the same appearance as. [French *sembler* seem]

resent /rɪˈzent/ *v.* feel indignation at; be aggrieved by (a circumstance, action, or person). [French *sentio* feel]

resentful *adj.* feeling resentment. □ **resentfully** *adv.*

resentment *n.* indignant or bitter feelings. [Italian or French: related to RESENT]

reservation /ˌrezəˈveɪʃ(ə)n/ *n.* 1 reserving or being reserved. 2 thing booked, e.g. a room in a hotel. 3 spoken or unspoken limitation or exception to an agreement etc. 4 (in full **central reservation**) strip of land between the carriageways of a road. 5 area of land reserved for occupation by American Indians etc. [Latin: related to RESERVE]

reserve /rɪˈzɜːv/ —*v.* (-**ving**) 1 put aside, keep back for a later occasion or special use. 2 order to be specially retained or allocated for a particular person or at a particular time. 3 retain or secure (*reserve the right to*). —*n.* 1 thing reserved for future use; extra amount. 2 limitation or exception attached to something. 3 self-restraint; reticence; lack of cordiality. 4 company's profit added to capital. 5 (in *sing.* or *pl.*) assets kept readily available. 6 (in *sing.* or *pl.*) **a** troops withheld from action to reinforce or protect others. **b** forces in addition to the regular army etc., but available in an emergency. 7 member of the military reserve. 8 extra player chosen as a possible substitute in a team. 9 land reserved for special use, esp. as a habitat (*nature reserve*). □ **in reserve** unused and available if required. **reserve judgement** postpone giving one's opinion. [Latin *servo* keep]

reserved *adj.* 1 reticent; slow to reveal emotion or opinions; uncommunicative. 2 set apart, destined for a particular use.

reserve price *n.* lowest acceptable price stipulated for an item sold at auction.

reservist *n.* member of the military reserve.

reservoir /ˈrezəvwɑː(r)/ *n.* 1 large natural or artificial lake as a source of

water supply. 2 receptacle for fluid. 3 supply of information etc. [French: related to RESERVE]

reset /riːˈset/ *v.* (-**tt**-; *past* and *past part.* **reset**) set (a bone, gems, a clock etc.) again or differently.

resettle /riːˈset(ə)l/ *v.* (-**ling**) settle again or elsewhere. □ **resettlement** *n.*

reshape /riːˈʃeɪp/ *v.* (-**ping**) shape or form again or differently.

reshuffle /riːˈʃʌf(ə)l/ —*v.* (-**ling**) 1 shuffle (cards) again. 2 change the posts of (government ministers etc.). —*n.* act of reshuffling.

reside /rɪˈzaɪd/ *v.* (-**ding**) 1 have one's home, dwell permanently. 2 (foll. by *in*) (of power, a right, etc.) be vested in. 3 (foll. by *in*) (of a quality) be present or inherent in. [Latin *sedeo* sit]

residence /ˈrezɪd(ə)ns/ *n.* 1 process of residing or being resident. 2 **a** place where a person resides. **b** house, esp. one of pretension. □ **in residence** living or working at a specified place, esp. for the performance of duties (*artist in residence*).

residency /ˈrezɪdənsɪ/ *n.* (*pl.* -**ies**) 1 = RESIDENCE 1, 2a. 2 permanent or regular engagement of a musician, artist, etc., in one place.

resident —*n.* 1 (often foll. by *of*) a permanent inhabitant. **b** non-migratory species of bird. 2 guest in a hotel etc. staying overnight. —*adj.* 1 residing. 2 having quarters at one's workplace etc. (*resident housekeeper*). 3 located in. 4 (of birds etc.) non-migratory.

residential /ˌrezɪˈdenʃ(ə)l/ *adj.* 1 suitable for or occupied by dwellings (*residential area*). 2 used as a residence (*residential hotel*). 3 based on or connected with residence (*residential course*).

residual /rɪˈzɪdjʊəl/ —*adj.* left as a residue or residuum. —*n.* residual quantity.

residuary /rɪˈzɪdjʊərɪ/ *adj.* 1 of the residue of an estate (*residuary bequest*). 2 residual.

residue /ˈrezɪdjuː/ *n.* 1 what is left over or remains; remainder. 2 what remains of an estate after the payment of charges, debts, and bequests. [Latin *residuum*: related to RESIDUUM]

residuum /rɪˈzɪdjʊəm/ *n.* (*pl.* -**dua**) 1 substance left after combustion or evaporation. 2 residue. [Latin]

resign /rɪˈzaɪn/ *v.* 1 (often foll. by *from*) give up office, one's employment, etc. 2 relinquish, surrender (a right, task, etc.). 3 *refl.* (usu. foll. by *to*) reconcile (oneself etc.) to the inevitable. [Latin *signo* sign]

re-sign /riːˈsaɪn/ v. sign again.

resignation /ˌrezɪɡˈneɪʃ(ə)n/ n. 1 resigning, esp. from one's job or office. 2 letter etc. conveying this. 3 reluctant acceptance of the inevitable. [medieval Latin: related to RESIGN]

resigned adj. 1 (often foll. by to) having resigned oneself; resolved to endure. 2 indicative of this □ **resignedly** /-nɪdlɪ/ adv.

resilient adj. 1 resuming its original shape after compression etc. 2 readily recovering from a setback. □ **resilience** n. [Latin: related to SALIENT]

resin /ˈrezɪn/ n. 1 adhesive substance secreted by some plants and trees. 2 (in full **synthetic resin**) organic compound made by polymerization etc. and used in plastics. —v. (-**n**-) rub or treat with resin. □ **resinous** adj. [Latin]

resist /rɪˈzɪst/ —v. 1 withstand the action or effect of. 2 stop the course or progress of. 3 abstain from (pleasure, temptation, etc.). 4 strive against; try to impede; refuse to comply with (resist arrest). 5 offer opposition; refuse to comply. —n. protective coating of a resistant substance. □ **resistible** adj. [Latin sisto stop]

resistance n. 1 resisting; refusal to comply. 2 power of resisting. 3 ability to withstand disease. 4 impeding or stopping effect exerted by one thing on another. 5 Physics property of hindering the conduction of electricity, heat, etc. 6 resistor. 7 secret organization resisting a regime, esp. in an occupied country. □ **resistant** adj. [Latin: related to RESIST]

resistor n. device having resistance to the passage of an electric current.

resit —v. /riːˈsɪt/ (-**tt**-; past and past part. **resat**) sit (an examination) again after failing. —n. /ˈriːsɪt/ 1 resitting of an examination. 2 examination specifically for this.

resold past and past part. of RESELL.

resoluble /rɪˈzɒljʊb(ə)l/ adj. 1 that can be resolved. 2 (foll. by into) analysable into. [Latin: related to RESOLVE]

resolute /ˈrezəluːt/ adj. determined, decided; firm of purpose. □ **resolutely** adv. [Latin: related to RESOLVE]

resolution /ˌrezəˈluːʃ(ə)n/ n. 1 resolute temper or character. 2 thing resolved on; intention. 3 formal expression of opinion or intention by a legislative body or public meeting. 4 (usu. foll. by of) solving of a doubt, problem, or question. 5 separation into components. 6 (foll. by into) conversion into another form. 7 Mus. causing discord to pass into concord. 8 a smallest interval

resolve /rɪˈzɒlv/ —v. (-**ving**) 1 make up one's mind; decide firmly (resolved to leave, on leaving). 2 cause (a person) to do this (events resolved him to leave). 3 solve, explain, or settle (a doubt, argument, etc.). 4 (foll. by that) (of an assembly or meeting) pass a resolution by vote. 5 (often foll. by into) (cause to) separate into constituent parts; analyse. 6 (foll. by into) reduce by mental analysis into. 7 Mus. convert or be converted into concord. —n. firm mental decision or intention; determination. [Latin: related to SOLVE]

resolved adj. resolute, determined.

resonant /ˈrezənənt/ adj. 1 (of sound) echoing, resounding; continuing to sound; reinforced or prolonged by reflection or vibration. 2 (of a body, room, etc.) tending to reinforce or prolong sounds, esp. by vibration. 3 (often foll. by with) (of a place) resounding. □ **resonance** n. □ **resonantly** adv. [Latin: related to RESOUND]

resonate /ˈrezəneɪt/ v. (-**ting**) produce or show resonance; resound. □ **resonator** n. [Latin: related to RESONANT]

resort /rɪˈzɔːt/ —n. 1 place frequented esp. for holidays or for a specified purpose or quality (seaside resort; health resort). 2 a thing to which one has recourse; expedient measure. b (foll. by to) recourse to; use of (without resort to violence). —v. 1 (foll. by to) turn to as an expedient (resorted to force). 2 (foll. by to) go often or in large numbers to. □ **in the** (or **as a**) **last resort** when all else has failed. [French sortir go out]

re-sort /riːˈsɔːt/ v. sort again or differently.

resound /rɪˈzaʊnd/ v. 1 (often foll. by with) (of a place) ring or echo. 2 (of a voice, instrument, sound, etc.) produce echoes; go on sounding; fill a place with sound. 3 a (of a reputation etc.) be much talked of. b (foll. by through) produce a sensation. 4 (of a place) re-echo (a sound). [Latin: related to SOUND]

resounding adj. 1 ringing, echoing. 2 notable, emphatic (a resounding success).

resource /rɪˈzɔːs/ —n. 1 expedient or device. 2 (often in pl.) means available; stock or supply that can be drawn on; asset. 3 (in pl.) country's collective wealth. 4 skill in devising expedients (person of great resource). 5 (in pl.) one's inner strength, ingenuity, etc. —v. (-**cing**) provide with resources. □ **resourceful** adj. (in sense 4). **resourcefully** adv. **resourcefulness** n. [French: related to SOURCE]

measurable by a scientific instrument. **b** resolving power.

[Latin: related to RESIGN]

respect /rɪˈspekt/ —n. 1 deferential esteem felt or shown towards a person or quality. 2 (foll. by *of*, *for*) heed or regard. 3 aspect, detail, etc. (*correct in all respects*). 4 reference, relation (*with respect to*). 5 (in *pl.*) polite messages or attentions (*give her my respects*). —v. 1 regard with deference or esteem. 2 **a** avoid interfering with or harming. **b** treat with consideration. **c** refrain from offending (a person, feelings, etc.). □ **in respect of** (or **with respect to**) as concerns. □ **respecter** *n*. [Latin *respicio -spect-* look back at]

respectable *adj.* 1 of acceptable social standing, decent and proper in appearance or behaviour. 2 fairly competent (*a respectable try*). 3 reasonably good in condition, appearance, number, size, etc. □ **respectability** /-ˈbɪlɪtɪ/ *n*. **respectably** *adv*.

respectful *adj.* showing deference. □ **respectfully** *adv*.

respecting *prep.* with regard to; concerning.

respective *adj.* of or relating to each of several individually (*go to your respective seats*). [French or medieval Latin: related to RESPECT]

respectively *adv.* for each separately or in turn, and in the order mentioned (*she and I gave £10 and £1 respectively*).

respell /riːˈspel/ *v*. (*past* and *past part.* **respelt** or **respelled**) spell again or differently, esp. phonetically.

respiration /ˌrespəˈreɪʃ(ə)n/ *n*. 1 **a** breathing. **b** single breath in or out. 2 *Biol.* (in living organisms) the absorption of oxygen and the release of energy and carbon dioxide. [Latin *spiro* breathe]

respirator /ˈrespəˌreɪtə(r)/ *n*. 1 apparatus worn over the face to warm, filter, or purify inhaled air. 2 apparatus for maintaining artificial respiration.

respire /rɪˈspaɪə(r)/ *v.* (-**ring**) 1 (also *absol.*) breathe (air etc.); inhale and exhale. 2 (of a plant) carry out respiration. □ **respiratory** /rɪˈspɪrətərɪ/ *adj*.

respite /ˈrespaɪt/ *n.* 1 interval of rest or relief. 2 delay permitted before the discharge of an obligation or the suffering of a penalty. [Latin: related to RESPECT]

resplendent /rɪˈsplend(ə)nt/ *adj.* brilliant, dazzlingly or gloriously bright. □ **resplendence** *n*. [Latin *resplendeo* shine]

respond /rɪˈspɒnd/ *v.* 1 answer, reply. 2 act or behave in a corresponding manner. 3 (usu. foll. by *to*) show sensitiveness to by behaviour or change (*does not respond to kindness*). 4 (of a congregation) make set answers to a priest etc. [Latin *respondeo -spons-*]

respondent —*n*. defendant, esp. in an appeal or divorce case. —*adj.* in the position of defendant.

response /rɪˈspɒns/ *n*. 1 answer given in a word or act; reply. 2 feeling, movement, or change caused by a stimulus or influence. 3 (often in *pl.*) any part of the liturgy said or sung in answer to the priest. [Latin: related to RESPOND]

responsibility /rɪˌspɒnsəˈbɪlɪtɪ/ *n.* (*pl.* -**ies**) 1 **a** (often foll. by *for*, *of*) being responsible. **b** authority; managerial freedom (*job with more responsibility*). 2 person or thing for which one is responsible; duty, commitment. 3 capacity for rational conduct (*diminished responsibility*).

responsible /rɪˈspɒnsəb(ə)l/ *adj.* 1 (often foll. by *to*, *for*) liable to be called to account (to a person or for a thing). 2 morally accountable for one's actions; capable of rational conduct. 3 of good credit, position, or repute; respectable; evidently trustworthy. 4 (often foll. by *for*) being the primary cause. 5 involving responsibility. □ **responsibly** *adv*.

responsive /rɪˈspɒnsɪv/ *adj.* 1 (often foll. by *to*) responding readily (to some influence). 2 sympathetic. 3 **a** answering. **b** by way of answer. □ **responsiveness** *n*.

respray —*v*. /riːˈspreɪ/ spray again (esp. a vehicle with paint). —*n.* /ˈriːspreɪ/ act of respraying.

rest¹ —*v*. 1 cease from exertion, action, etc. 2 be still or asleep, esp. to refresh oneself or recover strength. 3 give relief or repose to; allow to rest. 4 (foll. by *on*, *upon*, *against*) lie on; be supported by. 5 (foll. by *on*, *upon*) depend or be based on. 6 (foll. by *on*, *upon*) (of a look) alight or be steadily directed on. 7 (foll. by *on*, *upon*) place for support or foundation on. 8 (of a problem or subject) be left without further investigation or discussion (*let the matter rest*). 9 **a** lie in death. **b** (foll. by *in*) lie buried in (a churchyard etc.). 10 (as **rested** *adj.*) refreshed by resting. —*n*. 1 repose or sleep. 2 cessation of exertion, activity, etc. 3 period of resting. 4 support for holding or steadying something. 5 *Mus.* **a** interval of silence. **b** sign denoting this. □ **at rest** not moving; not agitated or troubled; dead. **be resting** *euphem.* (of an actor) be out of work. **rest one's case** conclude one's argument etc. **rest on one's laurels** not seek further success. **rest on one's oars** relax one's efforts. **set at rest** settle or relieve (a question, a person's mind, etc.). [Old English]

rest² —*n.* (prec. by *the*) the remaining part or parts; the others; the remainder

of some quantity or number. —v. 1 remain in a specified state (*rest assured*). 2 (foll. by *with*) be left in the hands or charge of (*the final arrangements rest with you*). □ **for the rest** as regards anything else. [French *rester* remain]

restart —v. /riː'stɑːt/ start again. —n. /'riːstɑːt/ act of restarting.

restate /riː'steɪt/ v. (**-ting**) express again or differently, esp. for emphasis. □ **restatement** n.

restaurant /'restərɒnt/ n. public or private place where meals may be bought and eaten. [French from *restaurer* RESTORE]

restaurant car n. dining-car.

restaurateur /ˌrestərə'tɜː(r)/ n. restaurant-keeper.

rest-cure n. rest usu. of some weeks as a medical treatment.

restful adj. giving rest or a feeling of rest; quiet, undisturbed. □ **restfully** adv. **restfulness** n.

rest home n. place where old or convalescent people are cared for.

restitution /ˌrestɪ'tjuːʃ(ə)n/ n. 1 restoring of a thing to its proper owner. 2 reparation for an injury (esp. *make restitution*). [Latin]

restive /'restɪv/ adj. 1 fidgety; restless. 2 (of a horse) jibbing; refractory. 3 (of a person) resisting control. □ **restively** adv. **restiveness** n. [French: related to REST[2]]

restless adj. 1 without rest or sleep. 2 uneasy; agitated. 3 constantly in motion, fidgeting, etc. □ **restlessly** adv. **restlessness** n. [Old English: related to REST[1]]

restock /riː'stɒk/ v. (also absol.) stock again or differently.

restoration /ˌrestə'reɪʃ(ə)n/ n. 1 restoring or being restored. 2 model or representation of the supposed original form of a thing. 3 (**Restoration**) hist. a (prec. by *the*) re-establishment of the British monarchy in 1660. b (often *attrib.*) literary period following this (*Restoration comedy*).

restorative /rɪ'stɒrətɪv/ —adj. tending to restore health or strength. —n. restorative medicine, food, etc.

restore /rɪ'stɔː(r)/ v. (**-ring**) 1 bring back to the original state by rebuilding, repairing, etc. 2 bring back to health etc. 3 give back to the original owner etc. 4 reinstate. 5 replace; put back; bring back to a former condition. 6 make a representation of the supposed original state of (a ruin, extinct animal, etc.). □ **restorer** n. [Latin *restauro*]

restrain /rɪ'streɪn/ v. 1 (often *refl.*, usu. foll. by *from*) check or hold in; keep in check, under control, or within bounds.

2 repress, keep down. 3 confine, imprison. [Latin *restringo -strict-*]

restraint n. 1 restraining or being restrained. 2 restraining agency or influence. 3 moderation; self-control. 4 reserve of manner. 5 confinement, esp. because of insanity.

restrict /rɪ'strɪkt/ v. 1 confine, limit. 2 withhold from general circulation or disclosure. □ **restriction** n. [Latin: related to RESTRAIN]

restrictive /rɪ'strɪktɪv/ adj. restricting. □ **restrictively** adv. [French or medieval Latin: related to RESTRICT]

restrictive practice n. agreement that limits competition or output in industry.

rest room n. esp. US public lavatory.

restructure /riː'strʌktʃə(r)/ v. (**-ring**) give a new structure to; rebuild; rearrange.

restyle /riː'staɪl/ v. (**-ling**) reshape; remake in a new style.

result /rɪ'zʌlt/ —n. 1 consequence, issue, outcome or outcome of something. 2 satisfactory outcome (*gets results*) 3 end product of calculation. 4 (in *pl.*) list of scores or winners etc. in examinations or sporting events. —v. 1 (often foll. by *from*) arise as the actual, or follow as a logical, consequence 2 (often foll. by *in*) have a specified end or outcome (*resulted in a large profit*). [Latin *resulto* spring back]

resultant —adj. resulting, esp. as the total outcome of more or less opposed forces. —n. force etc. equivalent to two or more acting in different directions at the same point.

resume /rɪ'zjuːm/ v. (**-ming**) 1 begin again or continue after an interruption. 2 begin to speak, work or use again; recommence. 3 get back; take back (*resume one's seat*). [Latin *sumo sumpt-* take]

résumé /'rezjʊmeɪ/ n. summary. [French: related to RESUME]

resumption /rɪ'zʌmpʃ(ə)n/ n. resuming. □ **resumptive** adj. Latin: related to RESUME]

resurface /riː'sɜːfɪs/ v. (**-cing**) 1 lay a new surface on (a road etc.). 2 return to the surface. 3 turn up again.

resurgent /rɪ'sɜːdʒ(ə)nt/ adj. rising or arising again. □ **resurgence** n. [Latin *resurgo -surrect-* rise again]

resurrect /ˌrezə'rekt/ v. 1 colloq. revive the practice, use, or memory of 2 raise or rise from the dead. [back-formation from RESURRECTION]

resurrection /ˌrezə'rekʃ(ə)n/ n. 1 rising from the dead. 2 (**Resurrection**) Christ's rising from the dead. 3 revival after disuse, inactivity, or decay. [Latin: related to RESURGENT]

resuscitate /rɪ'sʌsɪˌteɪt/ v. (**-ting**) re-vive from unconsciousness or apparent death. 2 revive, restore. □ **resuscitation** /-'teɪʃ(ə)n/ n. [Latin *suscito* raise]

retail /'riːteɪl/ —n. sale of goods in small quantities to the public, and usu. not for resale. —adj. & adv. by retail; at a retail price. —v. 1 sell (goods) by retail. 2 (often foll. by *at, of*) (of goods) be sold in this way (esp. for a specified price). 3 /also rɪ'teɪl/ recount; relate details of. □ **retailer** n. [French *taillier* cut: related to TALLY]

retain /rɪ'teɪn/ v. 1 a keep possession of, not lose; continue to have. b not abolish, discard, or alter. 2 keep in one's memory. 3 keep in place; hold fixed. 4 secure the services of (a person, esp. a barrister) with a preliminary payment. [Latin *retineo -tent-*]

retainer n. 1 fee for securing a person's services. 2 faithful servant (esp. *old retainer*). 3 reduced rent paid to retain unoccupied accommodation. 4 person or thing that retains.

retake —v. /riː'teɪk/ (-**king**; *past* **retook**; *past part.* **retaken**) 1 take (a photo-graph, exam, etc.) again. 2 recapture. —n. /'riːteɪk/ 1 act of filming a scene or recording music etc. again. 2 film or recording obtained in this way. 3 act of taking an exam etc. again.

retaliate /rɪ'tælɪeɪt/ v. (-**ting**) repay an injury, insult, etc. in kind; attack in return. □ **retaliation** /-'eɪʃ(ə)n/ n. **re-taliatory** /-'tælɪətərɪ/ adj. [Latin *talis* such]

retard /rɪ'tɑːd/ v. 1 make slow or late. 2 delay the progress or accomplishment of. □ **retardant** adj. & n. **retardation** /ˌriːtɑː'deɪʃ(ə)n/ n. [Latin *tardus* slow]

retarded adj. backward in mental or physical development.

retch v. make a motion of vomiting, esp. involuntarily and without effect. [Old English]

retell /riː'tel/ v. (*past* and *past part.* **retold**) tell again or differently.

retention /rɪ'tenʃ(ə)n/ n. 1 retaining or being retained. 2 condition of retain-ing bodily fluid (esp. urine) normally evacuated. [Latin: related to RETAIN]

retentive /rɪ'tentɪv/ adj. 1 tending to retain. 2 (of memory etc.) not forgetful. [French or medieval Latin: related to RETAIN]

retexture /riː'tekstʃə(r)/ v. (-**ring**) treat (material, a garment, etc.) so as to re-store its original texture.

rethink —v. /riː'θɪŋk/ (*past* and *past part.* **rethought**) consider again, esp. with a view to making changes. —n. /'riːθɪŋk/ reassessment; rethinking.

reticence /'retɪs(ə)ns/ n. 1 avoidance of saying all one feels, or feels, or more than is necessary. 2 disposition to silence; taciturnity. □ **reticent** adj. [Latin *reticeo* keep silent]

reticulate —v. /rɪ'tɪkjʊˌleɪt/ (-**ting**) di-vide or be divided in fact or appearance into a network. —adj. /rɪ'tɪkjʊlət/ reticu-lated. □ **reticulation** /-'leɪʃ(ə)n/ n. [Latin *reticulum* diminutive of *rete* net]

retie /riː'taɪ/ v. (**retying**) tie again.

retina /'retɪnə/ n. (pl. **-s** or **-nae** /-ˌniː/) layer at the back of the eyeball sensitive to light. □ **retinal** adj. [Latin *rete* net]

retinue /'retɪˌnjuː/ n. body of attendants accompanying an important person. [French: related to RETAIN]

retire /rɪ'taɪə(r)/ v. (-**ring**) 1 a leave office or employment, esp. because of age. b cause (a person) to retire from work. 2 withdraw, go away, retreat. 3 seek seclusion or shelter. 4 go to bed. 5 *Cricket* (of a batsman) voluntarily end or be compelled to suspend one's innings. □ **retire into oneself** become uncommunicative or unsociable. [French *tirer* draw]

retired adj. 1 having retired from em-ployment. 2 withdrawn from society or observation; secluded.

retirement n. 1 a retiring. b period of a retiring person. 2 seclu-sion.

retirement pension n. pension paid by the State to retired people above a certain age.

retiring adj. shy; fond of seclusion.

retold *past* and *past part.* of RETELL.

retook *past* of RETAKE.

retort¹ /rɪ'tɔːt/ —n. incisive, witty, or angry reply. —v. 1 a say by way of a retort. b make a retort. 2 repay (an insult or attack) in kind. [Latin *retor-queo -tort-* twist]

retort² /rɪ'tɔːt/ —n. 1 vessel with a long neck turned downwards, used in distil-ling liquids. 2 vessel for heating coal to generate gas. —v. purify (mercury) by heating in a retort. [medieval Latin: related to RETORT¹]

retouch /riː'tʌtʃ/ v. improve (a picture, photograph, etc.) by minor alterations.

retrace /rɪ'treɪs/ v. (-**cing**) 1 go back over (one's steps etc.). 2 trace back to a source or beginning. 3 recall the course of (a thing) in one's memory.

retract /rɪ'trækt/ v. 1 withdraw (a state-ment or undertaking). 2 draw or be drawn back or in. □ **retractable** adj. **retraction** n. [Latin *retraho -tract-* draw back]

retractile /rɪ'træktaɪl/ adj. capable of being retracted.

retrain /ri:'trein/ v. train again or further, esp. for new work.

retread –v. /ri:'tred/ **1** (*past* **retrod**; *past part.* **retrodden**) tread (a path etc.) again. **2** (*past, past part.* **retreaded**) put a fresh tread on (a tyre). –n. /'ri:tred/ retreaded tyre.

retreat /ri'tri:t/ –v. **1** (esp. of military forces) go back, retire; relinquish a position. **2** recede. –n. **1 a** act of retreat. **b** *Mil.* signal for this. **2** withdrawal into privacy or security. **3** piece of shelter or seclusion. **4** period of seclusion for prayer and meditation. **5** *Mil.* bugle-call at sunset. [Latin: related to RETRACT]

retrench /ri'trentʃ/ v. **1** cut down expenses; introduce economies. **2** reduce the amount of (costs). □ **retrenchment** n. [French: related to TRENCH]

retrial /ri:'traiəl/ n. second or further (judicial) trial.

retribution /ˌretri'bju:ʃ(ə)n/ n. requital, usu. for evil done; vengeance. □ **retributive** /ri'tribjutiv/ adj. [Latin: related to TRIBUTE]

retrieve /ri'tri:v/ –v. (**-ving**) **1 a** regain possession of. **b** recover by investigation or effort of memory. **2** obtain (information stored in a computer etc.). **3** (of a dog) find and bring in (killed or wounded game etc.). **4** (foll. by *from*) rescue (esp. from a bad state). **5** restore to a flourishing state; revive. **6** repair or set right (a loss or error etc.) –n. possibility of recovery. (*beyond retrieve*). □ **retrievable** adj. **retrieval** n. [French *trouver* find]

retriever n. dog of a breed used for retrieving game.

retro /'retrəʊ/ *slang* –adj. reviving or harking back to the past. –n. retro fashion or style.

retro- *comb. form* **1** denoting action back or in return. **2** *Anat. & Med.* denoting location behind. [Latin]

retroactive /ˌretrəʊ'æktiv/ adj. (esp. of legislation) effective from a past date.

retrod *past* of RETREAD.

retrodden *past part.* of RETREAD.

retrograde /'retrə.greid/ –adj. **1** directed backwards. **2** reverting, esp. to an inferior state; declining. **3** reversed (*retrograde order*). –v. **1** move backwards; recede. **2** decline, revert. [Latin]

retrogress /ˌretrə'gres/ v. **1** move backwards. **2** deteriorate. □ **retrogression** /-'greʃ(ə)n/ n. **retrogressive** adj.

retrorocket /'retrəʊ.rɒkit/ n. auxiliary rocket for slowing down a spacecraft etc.

retrospect /'retrə.spekt/ n. □ **in retrospect** when looking back. [from RETRO-, PROSPECT]

retrospection /ˌretrə'spekʃ(ə)n/ n. looking back into the past.

retrospective /ˌretrə'spektiv/ –adj. **1** looking back on or dealing with the past. **2** (of a statute etc.) applying to the past as well as the future. –n. exhibition, recital, etc. showing an artist's development over his or her lifetime. □ **retrospectively** adv.

retroussé /rə'tru:sei/ adj. (of the nose) turned up at the tip. [French]

retroverted /'retrəʊ.vɜ:tid/ adj. (of the womb) inclined backwards. [Latin: related to RETRO-, *verto* turn]

retrovirus /'retrəʊ.vaiərəs/ n. any of a group of RNA viruses which form DNA from RNA viruses which form DNA and during the replication of their RNA, and so transfer genetic material into the DNA of host cells. [from the initial letters of *reverse transcriptase* + VIRUS]

retry /ri:'trai/ v. (**-ies, -ied**) try (a defendant or lawsuit) a second or further time.

retsina /ret'si:nə/ n. Greek white wine flavoured with resin. [modern Greek]

retune /ri:'tju:n/ v. (**-ning**) **1** tune (a musical instrument, again or differently. **2** tune (a radio etc.) to a different frequency.

return /ri'tɜ:n/ –v. **1** come or go back. **2** bring, put, or send back. **3** pay back or reciprocate; give in response. **4** yield (a profit). **5** say in reply; retort. **6** (in cricket or tennis etc.) hit or send (the ball) back. **7** state, mention, or describe officially, esp. in answer to a writ or formal demand. **8** (of an electorate) elect as an MP. government etc. –n. **1** coming or going back. **2 a** giving, sending, putting, or paying back. **b** going back. **3** thing given or sent back **3** (in full **return ticket**) ticket for a journey to a place and back to the starting-point **4** (in *sing.* or *pl.*) **a** proceeds or profit of an undertaking. **b** acquisition of these. **5** formal statement compiled or submitted by order (*income-tax return*). **6** (in full **return match** or **game**) second match etc. between the same opponents. **7 a** person's election as an MP etc. **b** returning officer's announcement of this. □ **by return** (**of post**) by the next available post in the return direction. **in return** as an exchange or reciprocal action. **many happy returns (of the day)** greeting on a birthday. □ **returnable** adj. [Romanic: related to TURN]

returnee /ˌritə'ni:/ n. person who returns home from abroad esp. after war service.

returning officer *n.* official conducting an election in a constituency and announcing the results.

retying *pres. part. of* RETIE.

retype /riː'taɪp/ *v.* (**-ies, -ied**) retype again, esp. to correct errors.

reunify /riː'juːnɪfaɪ/ *v.* (**-ies, -ied**) restore (esp. separated territories) to a political unity. □ **reunification** /-fɪ'keɪʃ(ə)n/ *n.*

reunion /riː'juːnjən/ *n.* **1** reuniting or being reunited. **2** social gathering, esp. of people formerly associated.

reunite /riːjuː'naɪt/ *v.* (**-ting**) (cause to) come together again.

reupholster /riːʌp'həʊlstə(r)/ *v.* upholster anew.

reuse –*v.* /riː'juːz/ (**-sing**) use again. –*n.* /riː'juːs/ second or further use. □ **reusable** /-'juːzəb(ə)l/ *adj.*

Rev. *abbr.* Reverend.

rev *colloq.* –*n.* (in *pl.*) number of revolutions of an engine per minute. –*v.* (**-vv-**) **1** (of an engine) revolve; turn over. **2** (also *absol.*; often foll. by *up*) cause (an engine) to run quickly. [abbreviation]

revalue /riː'væljuː/ *v.* (**-ues, -ued, -uing**) give a different, esp. higher, value to (a currency etc.). □ **revaluation** /-'eɪʃ(ə)n/ *n.*

revamp /riː'væmp/ *v.* **1** renovate, revise, improve. **2** patch up.

Revd *abbr.* Reverend.

reveal /rɪ'viːl/ *v.* **1** display or show; allow to appear. **2** (often as **revealing** *adj.*) disclose, divulge, betray (*revealing remark*). **3** (in *refl.* or *passive*) come to sight or knowledge. [Latin *velum* veil]

reveille /rɪ'vælɪ/ *n.* military waking-signal. [French *réveillez* wake up]

revel /'rev(ə)l/ *v.* (**-ll-**; *US* **-l-**) **1** have a good time; be extravagantly festive. **2** (foll. by *in*) take keen delight in. –*n.* (in *sing.* or *pl.*) revelling. □ **reveller** *n.* **revelry** *n.* (*pl.* **-ies**). [Latin: related to REBEL]

revelation /revə'leɪʃ(ə)n/ *n.* **1 a** revealing, esp. the supposed disclosure of knowledge to man by a divine or supernatural agency. **b** knowledge disclosed in this way. **2** striking disclosure. **3** (**Revelation** or *colloq.* **Revelations**) (in full **the Revelation of St John the Divine**) last book of the New Testament.

revenge /rɪ'vendʒ/ –*n.* **1** retaliation for an offence or injury. **2** act of retaliation **3** desire for this; vindictive feeling. **4** (in games) win after an earlier defeat. –*v.* (**-ging**) **1** (in *refl.* or *passive*; often foll. by *on, upon*) inflict retaliation for (an offence). **2** avenge (a person). [Latin: related to VINDICATE]

revengeful *adj.* eager for revenge. □ **revengefully** *adv.*

revenue /'revə,njuː/ *n.* **1 a** income, esp. a substantial one. **b** (in *pl.*) items constituting this. **2** State's annual income from which public expenses are met. **3** department of the civil service collecting this. [French *revenu* from Latin *revenio* return]

reverberate /rɪ'vɜːbə,reɪt/ *v.* (**-ting**) **1** (of sound, light, or heat) be returned, echoed, or reflected repeatedly. **2** return (a sound etc.) in this way. **3** (of an event etc.) produce a continuing effect, shock, etc. □ **reverberant** *adj.* **reverberation** /-'reɪʃ(ə)n/ *n.* **reverberative** /-rətɪv/ *adj.* [Latin *verbero* beat]

revere /rɪ'vɪə(r)/ *v.* (**-ring**) hold in deep and usu. affectionate or religious respect. [Latin *vereor* fear]

reverence /'revərəns/ –*n.* **1** revering or being revered. **2** capacity for revering. –*v.* (**-cing**) regard or treat with reverence. [Latin: related to REVERE]

reverend /'revərənd/ *adj.* (esp. as the title of a clergyman) deserving reverence. [Latin *reverendus*: related to REVERE]

Reverend Mother *n.* Mother Superior of a convent.

reverent /'revərənt/ *adj.* feeling or showing reverence. □ **reverently** *adv.* [Latin: related to REVERE]

reverential /,revə'ren(ʃ)(ə)l/ *n.* of the nature of, due to, or characterized by reverence. □ **reverentially** *adv.* [medieval Latin: related to REVERENCE]

reverie /'revərɪ/ *n.* fit of abstracted musing, day-dream. [French]

revers /rɪ'vɪə(r)/ *n.* (*pl.* same /-'vɪəz/) **1** turned-back edge of a garment revealing the undersurface. **2** material on this surface. [French: related to REVERSE]

reverse /rɪ'vɜːs/ –*v.* (**-sing**) **1** turn the other way round or up or inside out. **2** change to the opposite character or effect. **3** (cause to) travel backwards. **4** make (an engine etc.) work in a contrary direction. **5** revoke or annul (a decree, act, etc.). –*adj.* **1** backwards or upside down. **2** opposite or contrary in character or order; inverted. –*n.* **1** opposite or contrary (*the reverse is the case*). **2** contrary of the usual manner (*printed in reverse*). **3** piece of misfortune; disaster; defeat. **4** reverse gear or motion. **5** reverse side. **6** side of a coin etc. bearing the secondary design. **7** verso of a printed leaf. □ **reverse arms** hold a rifle with the butt upwards. **reverse the charges** have the recipient of a telephone call pay for it. □ **reversal** *n.* [Latin *verto vers-* turn]

reversible *adj.* [Latin

reverse gear n. gear used to make a vehicle etc. go backwards.

reversing light n. white light at the rear of a vehicle showing that it is in reverse gear.

reversion /rɪˈvɜːʃ(ə)n/ n. 1 return to a previous state, habit, etc. 2 *Biol.* return to ancestral type. 3 legal right (esp. of the original owner, or his or her heirs) to possess or succeed to property on the death of the present possessor. [Latin: related to REVERSE]

revert /rɪˈvɜːt/ v. 1 (foll. by *to*) return to a former state, practice, opinion, etc. 2 (of property, an office, etc.) return by reversion. □ **revertible** *adj.* (in sense 2). [Latin *reverto*]

revetment /rɪˈvɛtm(ə)nt/ n. a facing of masonry etc. supporting a wall.

review /rɪˈvjuː/ —n. 1 general survey or assessment of a subject or thing. 2 survey of the past. 3 revision or reconsideration (*is under review*). 4 display and formal inspection of troops etc. 5 published criticism of a book, play, etc. 6 periodical with critical articles on current events, the arts, etc. —v. 1 survey or look back on. 2 reconsider or revise. 3 hold a review of (troops etc.). 4 write a review of (a book, play, etc.). □ **reviewer** n. [French *revoir*: related to VIEW]

revile /rɪˈvaɪl/ v. (-ling) abuse verbally. [French: related to VILE]

revise /rɪˈvaɪz/ v. (-sing) 1 examine and improve or amend (esp. written or printed matter). 2 consider and alter (an opinion etc.). 3 (also *absol.*) go over (work learnt or done) again, esp. for an examination. □ **revisory** *adj.* [Latin *reviso* from *video vis-* see]

Revised Standard Version n. revision published in 1946–57 of the American Standard Version of the Bible (itself based on the English RV).

Revised Version n. revision published in 1881–95 of the Authorized Version of the Bible.

revision /rɪˈvɪʒ(ə)n/ n. 1 revising or being revised. 2 revised edition or form. [Latin: related to REVISE]

revisionism n. often *derog.* revision or modification of an orthodoxy, esp. of Marxism. □ **revisionist** n. & *adj.*

revisit /riːˈvɪzɪt/ v. (-t-) visit again.

revitalize /riːˈvaɪtəˌlaɪz/ v. (also **-ise**) (-zing or -sing) imbue with new life and vitality.

revival /rɪˈvaɪv(ə)l/ n. 1 reviving or being revived. 2 new production of an old play etc. 3 revived use of an old practice, style, etc. 4 a reawakening of religious fervour. **b** campaign to promote this.

revivalism n. promotion of a revival, esp. of religious fervour. □ **revivalist** n. & *adj.*

revive /rɪˈvaɪv/ v. (-ving) 1 come or bring back to consciousness, life, or strength. 2 come or bring back to existence, use or notice etc. [Latin *vivo* live]

revivify /rɪˈvɪvɪˌfaɪ/ v. (-ies, -ied) restore to animation, vigour, or life. □ **revivification** /-fɪˈkeɪʃ(ə)n/ n. [Latin: related to VIVIFY]

revoke /rɪˈvəʊk/ —v. (-king) 1 rescind, withdraw, or cancel. 2 *Cards* fail to follow suit when able to do so. —n. *Cards* revoking. □ **revocable** /ˈrevəkəb(ə)l/ *adj.* **revocation** /ˌrevəˈkeɪʃ(ə)n/ n. [Latin *voco* call]

revolt /rɪˈvəʊlt/ —v. 1 rise in rebellion. 2 **a** affect with strong disgust. **b** (often foll. by *at, against*) feel strong disgust. —n. 1 act of rebelling. 2 state of insurrection. 3 sense of disgust. 4 mood of protest or defiance. [Italian: related to REVOLVE]

revolting *adj.* disgusting, horrible. □ **revoltingly** *adv.*

revolution /ˌrevəˈluːʃ(ə)n/ n. 1 forcible overthrow of a government or social order. 2 any fundamental change or reversal of conditions. 3 revolving. 4 **a** single completion of an orbit or rotation. **b** time taken for this. 5 cyclic recurrence. [Latin: related to REVOLVE]

revolutionary —*adj.* 1 involving great and often violent change. 2 of or causing political revolution. —n. (*pl.* -ies) instigator or supporter of political revolution.

revolutionize v. (also **-ise**) (-zing or -sing) change fundamentally.

revolve /rɪˈvɒlv/ v. (-ving) 1 (cause to) turn round, esp. on an axis, rotate. 2 move in a circular orbit. 3 ponder (a problem etc.) in the mind. 4 (foll. by *around*) have as its chief concern; be centred upon (*his life revolves around his job*). [Latin *revolvo -volut-*]

revolver n. pistol with revolving chambers enabling several shots to be fired without reloading.

revolving door n. door with usu. four partitions turning round a central axis.

revue /rɪˈvjuː/ n. entertainment of short usu. satirical sketches and songs. [French: related to REVIEW]

revulsion /rɪˈvʌlʃ(ə)n/ n. 1 abhorrence. 2 sudden violent change of feeling. [Latin *vello vuls-* pull]

reward /rɪˈwɔːd/ —n. 1 **a** return or recompense for service or merit. **b** requital for good or evil. 2 sum offered for the detection of a criminal, restoration of lost property, etc. —v. give a reward to (a person) or for (a service etc.). [Anglo-French *reward(er)* REGARD]

rewarding *adj.* (of an activity etc.) worthwhile; satisfying.

rewind /riːˈwaɪnd/ v. (past and past part. **rewound**) wind (a film or tape etc.) back.

rewire /riːˈwaɪə(r)/ v. (-**ring**) provide with new electrical wiring.

reword /riːˈwɜːd/ v. express in different words.

rework /riːˈwɜːk/ v. revise; refashion; remake. □ **reworking** n.

rewrite —v. /riːˈraɪt/ (-**ting**; past **rewrote**; past part. **rewritten**) write again or differently. —n. /ˈriːraɪt/ **1** rewriting. **2** thing rewritten.

Rex n. **1** (after the name) reigning king (George Rex). **2** Law the Crown (Rex v. Jones). [Latin]

Rf symb. rutherfordium.

RFC abbr. Rugby Football Club.

Rh symb. rhodium.

r.h. abbr. right hand.

rhapsodize /ˈræpsədaɪz/ v. (also -**ise**) (-**zing** or -**sing**) talk or write rhapsodies.

rhapsody /ˈræpsədɪ/ n. (pl. -**ies**) **1** enthusiastic or extravagant speech or composition. **2** piece of music in one movement, often based on national, folk, or popular melodies. □ **rhapsodic** /ræpˈsɒdɪk/ adj. [Greek rhaptō stitch: related to ODE]

rhea /ˈrɪə/ n. S. American flightless ostrich-like bird. [Greek Rhea mother name of Zeus]

rhenium /ˈriːnɪəm/ n. rare metallic element occurring naturally in molybdenum ores. [Latin Rhenus Rhine]

rheostat /ˈriːəstæt/ n. instrument used to control an electric current by varying the resistance. [Greek rheos stream]

rhesus /ˈriːsəs/ n. (in full **rhesus monkey**) small N. Indian monkey. [Rhesus, mythical king of Thrace]

rhesus factor n. antigen occurring on the red blood cells of most humans and some other primates.

rhesus negative adj. lacking the rhesus factor.

rhesus positive adj. having the rhesus factor.

rhetoric /ˈretərɪk/ n. **1** art of effective or persuasive speaking or writing. **2** language designed to persuade or impress (esp. seen as overblown and meaningless). [Greek rhētōr orator]

rhetorical /rɪˈtɒrɪk(ə)l/ adj. **1** expressed artificially or extravagantly. **2** of the nature or art of rhetoric. □ **rhetorically** adv. [Greek: related to RHETORIC]

rhetorical question n. question used for effect but not seeking an answer (e.g. who cares? for nobody cares).

rheumatic /ruːˈmætɪk/ adj. of, suffering from, producing, or produced by rheumatism. —n. person suffering from rheumatism. □ **rheumatically** adv. **rheumaticky** adj. colloq. [Greek rheuma stream]

rheumatic fever n. fever with inflammation and pain in the joints.

rheumatics n.pl. (treated as sing.; often prec. by the) colloq. rheumatism.

rheumatism /ˈruːmə.tɪz(ə)m/ n. disease marked by inflammation and pain in the joints, muscles, or fibrous tissue, esp. rheumatoid arthritis.

rheumatoid /ˈruːmə.tɔɪd/ adj. having the character of rheumatism.

rheumatoid arthritis n. chronic progressive disease causing inflammation and stiffening of the joints.

rhinestone n. imitation diamond. [river Rhine in Germany]

rhino /ˈraɪnəʊ/ n. (pl. same or -s) colloq. rhinoceros. [abbreviation]

rhinoceros /raɪˈnɒsərəs/ n. (pl. same or -roses) large thick-skinned mammal with usu. one horn on its nose. [Greek rhis rhin- nose, keras horn]

rhizome /ˈraɪzəʊm/ n. underground rootlike stem bearing both roots and shoots. [Greek rhizoma]

rho /rəʊ/ n. seventeenth letter of the Greek alphabet (Ρ, ρ). [Greek]

rhodium /ˈrəʊdɪəm/ n. hard white metallic element used in making alloys and plating jewellery. [Greek rhodon rose]

rhododendron /ˌrəʊdəˈdendrən/ n. (pl. -s or -dra) evergreen shrub with large clusters of bell-shaped flowers. [Greek rhodon rose, dendron tree]

rhomboid /ˈrɒmbɔɪd/ —adj. (also **rhomboidal** /-ˈbɔɪd(ə)l/) like a rhombus. —n. quadrilateral of which only the opposite sides and angles are equal. [Greek: related to RHOMBUS]

rhombus /ˈrɒmbəs/ n. (pl. -**buses** or -**bi** /-baɪ/) Geom. parallelogram with oblique angles and equal sides. [Greek rhombos]

RHS abbr. Royal Horticultural Society.

rhubarb /ˈruːbɑːb/ n. **1 a** plant with long fleshy dark-red leaf-stalks cooked as a dessert. **b** these stalks. **2 a** colloq. indistinct conversation or noise, from the repeated use of the word 'rhubarb' by a crowd. **b** slang nonsense. [Greek rha rhubarb, barbaros foreign]

rhyme /raɪm/ —n. **1** identity of sound between words or their endings, esp. in verse. **2** (in sing. or pl.) verse or a poem having rhymes. **3** word providing a rhyme. —v. (-**ming**) **1 a** (of words or lines) produce a rhyme. **b** (foll. by with) act as or treat (a word) as a rhyme (with another). **2** make or write rhymes. **3** put or make (a story etc.) into

rhyme. □ **rhyme or reason** sense, logic. [Latin related to RHYTHM]

hymester n. writer of (esp. simple) rhymes.

hyming slang n. slang that replaces words by rhyming words or phrases, e.g. *suit* by *whistle and flute*.

hythm /ˈrɪð(ə)m/ n. **1 a** periodical accent and the duration of notes in music, esp. as beats in a bar. **b** type of structure formed by this (*samba rhythm*). **2** measured regular flow of verse or prose determined by the length of and stress on syllables. **3** *Physiol.* pattern of successive strong and weak movements. **4** regularly recurring sequence of events. □ **rhythmic** adj. **rhythmical** adj. **rhythmically** adv. [Greek *rhuthmos*]

rhythm and blues n. popular music with blues themes and a strong rhythm.

rhythm method n. abstention from sexual intercourse near the time of ovulation, as a method of birth control.

rhythm section n. piano or guitar etc.), bass, and drums in a dance or jazz band.

rib – n. **1** each of the curved bones joined to the spine in pairs and protecting the chest. **2** joint of meat from this part of an animal. **3** supporting ridge, timber, rod, etc. across a surface or through a structure. **4** *Knitting* combination of plain and purl stitches producing a ribbed design. – v. **(-bb-) 1** provide with ribs; act as the ribs of. **2** *colloq.* make fun of, tease. **3** mark with ridges. [Old English]

ribald /ˈrɪb(ə)ld/ adj. coarsely or disrespectfully humorous; obscene. [French *riber* be licentious]

ribaldry /ˈrɪb(ə)ldri/ n. ribald talk or behaviour.

riband /ˈrɪband/ n. ribbon. [French *riban*]

ribbed adj. having ribs or riblike markings.

ribbing n. ribs or a riblike structure. **2** *colloq.* teasing.

ribbon /ˈrɪb(ə)n/ n. **1 a** narrow strip or band of fabric, used esp. for trimming or decoration. **b** material in this form. **2** ribbon worn to indicate some honour or membership of a sports team etc. **3** long narrow strip of anything (*typewriter ribbon*). **4** (in pl.) ragged strips (*torn to ribbons*). [var. of RIBAND]

ribbon development n. building of houses one house deep along a road leading out of a town or village.

ribcage n. wall of bones formed by the ribs round the chest.

riboflavin /ˌraɪbəˈfleɪvɪn/ n. (also **riboflavine** /-viːn/) vitamin of the B complex, found in liver, milk, and eggs. [ribose sugar, Latin *flavus* yellow]

ribonucleic acid /ˌraɪbəʊnjuːˈkliːɪk/ n. nucleic acid in living cells, involved in protein synthesis. [ribose sugar]

rib-tickler n. something amusing, joke.

rice n. **1** swamp grass cultivated in esp. Asian marshes. **2** grains of this, used as food. [French *ris* ultimately from Greek *oruza*]

rice-paper n. edible paper made from the pith of an oriental tree and used for painting and in cookery.

rich adj. **1** having much wealth. **2** splendid, costly, elaborate. **3** valuable (*rich offerings*). **4** copious, abundant, ample (*rich supply of ideas*. **5** (often foll. by *in*, *with*) (of soil or a region etc.) fertile; abundant in resources etc. (*rich in nutrients*). **6** (of food or diet) containing much fat or spice etc. **7** (of the mixture in an internal-combustion engine) containing a high proportion of fuel. **8** (of colour, sound, or smell) mellow and deep, strong and full. **9** highly amusing or ludicrous; outrageous. □ **richness** n. [Old English and French]

riches n.pl. abundant means, valuable possessions. [French *richesse*: related to RICH]

richly adv. **1** in a rich way. **2** fully, thoroughly (*richly deserves success*).

Richter scale /ˈrɪktə/ n. scale of 0-10 for representing the strength of an earthquake. [*Richter* name of a seismologist]

rick[1] n. stack of hay etc. [Old English]

rick[2] (also **wrick**) – v. **1.** slight sprain or strain. – v. sprain or strain slightly. [Low German *wricken*]

rickets /ˈrɪkɪts/ n. (treated as *sing.* or *pl.*) deficiency disease of children with softening of the bones. [origin uncertain]

rickety /ˈrɪkɪtɪ/ adj. **1** insecure, shaky. **2** suffering from rickets. □ **ricketiness** n.

rickrack var. of RICRAC.

rickshaw /ˈrɪkʃɔː/ n. (also **ricksha** /-ʃə/) light two-wheeled hooded vehicle drawn by one or more persons. [abbreviation of *jinrickshaw* from Japanese]

ricochet /ˈrɪkəʃeɪ/ – n. **1** rebounding of esp. a shell or bullet off a surface. **2** hit made after this. – v. (**-cheted** /-ʃeɪd/; **-cheting** /-ʃeɪɪŋ/) or (**-chetted** /-ʃetɪd/; **-chetting** /-ʃetɪŋ/) (of a projectile) make a ricochet. [French]

ricotta /rɪˈkɒtə/ n. soft Italian cheese. [Latin related to RE-, ?*coquo* cook]

ricrac /ˈrɪkræk/ n. (also **rickrack**) zigzag braided trimming for garments. [from RACK[1]]

rid v. (**-dd-**; past and past part. **rid**) (foll. by *of*) free (a person or place) of something unwanted. □ **be** (or **get**) **rid of** be

riddance column:

freed or relieved of, dispose of. [Old Norse]

riddance /ˈrɪd(ə)ns/ n. getting rid of something. □ **good riddance** expression of relief at getting rid of something. **ridden** past part. of RIDE.

riddle[1] /ˈrɪd(ə)l/ —n. 1 verbal puzzle or test, often with a trick answer. 2 puzzling fact, thing, or person. —v. (-**ling**) speak in riddles. [Old English: related to READ]

riddle[2] /ˈrɪd(ə)l/ —v. (-**ling**) (usu. foll. by **with**) 1 make many holes in, esp. with gunshot. 2 (in *passive*) fill; permeate (*riddled with errors*). 3 pass through a riddle. —n. coarse sieve. [Old English]

ride —v. (-**ding**; past **rode**; past part. **ridden** /ˈrɪd(ə)n/) 1 (often foll. by *on, in*) travel or be carried on (a bicycle etc.) or esp. US in (a vehicle); be conveyed (*rode her bike; rode on her bike; rode the tram*). 2 (often foll. by *on*; also *absol.*) be carried by (a horse etc.). 3 be carried or supported by (*ship rides the waves*). 4 traverse or take part in on horseback etc. (*ride 50 miles; rode the prairie*). 5 a lie at anchor; float buoyantly. b (of the moon) seem to float. 6 yield to (a blow) so as to reduce its impact. 7 give a ride to; cause to ride (*rode me home*). 8 (of a rider) (*rode their horses at the fence*). 9 (as **ridden** adj.) (foll. by *by, with*, or in *comb.*) be dominated by; be infested with (*ridden with guilt; rat-ridden cellar*). —n. 1 journey or spell of riding in a vehicle, or on a horse, bicycle, person's back, etc. 2 path (esp. through woods) for riding on. 3 specified kind of ride (*bumpy ride*). 4 amusement for riding on at a fairground etc. □ **let a thing ride** leave it undisturbed. **ride again** reappear as strong etc. as ever. **ride high** be elated or successful. **ride out** come safely through (a storm, danger, etc.). **ride roughshod over** see ROUGHSHOD. **ride up** (of a garment) work upwards out of place. **take for a ride** *colloq.* hoax or deceive. [Old English]

rider n. 1 person who rides (esp. a horse). 2 additional remark following a statement, verdict, etc. □ **riderless** adj.

ridge —n. 1 line of the junction of two surfaces sloping upwards towards each other (*ridge of a roof*). 2 long narrow hilltop, mountain range, or watershed. 3 any narrow elevation across a surface. 4 elongated region of high barometric pressure. 5 raised strip of esp. ploughed land. —v. (-**ging**) mark with ridges. □ **ridgy** adj. [Old English]

ridge-pole n. horizontal roof pole of a long tent.

ridgeway n. road or track along a ridge.

ridicule /ˈrɪdɪkjuːl/ —n. derision, mockery. —v. (-**ling**) make fun of; mock; laugh at. [Latin *rideo* laugh]

ridiculous /rɪˈdɪkjʊləs/ adj. 1 deserving or inviting ridicule. 2 unreasonable. □ **ridiculously** adv. **ridiculousness** n.

riding[1] /ˈraɪdɪŋ/ n. sport or pastime of travelling on horseback.

riding[2] /ˈraɪdɪŋ/ n. *hist.* former administrative division (**East, North, West Riding**) of Yorkshire. [Old English from Old Norse, = third part]

riding-light n. light shown by a ship at anchor.

riding-school n. establishment teaching horsemanship.

Riesling /ˈriːzlɪŋ/ n. 1 a kind of grape. 2 white wine made from this. [German]

rife predic. adj. 1 of common occurrence; widespread. 2 (foll. by *with*) abounding in. [Old English, probably from Old Norse]

riff n. short repeated phrase in jazz etc. [abbreviation of RIFFLE]

riffle /ˈrɪf(ə)l/ —v. (-**ling**) 1 (often foll. by *through*) leaf quickly through (pages). 2 a turn (pages) in quick succession. b shuffle (playing-cards), esp. by flexing and combining the two halves of a pack. —n. 1 act of riffling. 2 US **a** shallow disturbed part of a stream. **b** patch of waves or ripples. [perhaps var. of RUFFLE]

riff-raff /ˈrɪfræf/ n. (often prec. by *the*) rabble; disreputable people. [French *rif et raf*]

rifle[1] /ˈraɪf(ə)l/ —n. 1 gun with a long rifled barrel, esp. one fired from the shoulder. 2 (in *pl.*) riflemen. —v. (-**ling**) make spiral grooves in (a gun, its barrel, or its bore) to make a projectile spin. [French]

rifle[2] /ˈraɪf(ə)l/ v. (-**ling**) (often foll. by *through*) 1 search and rob. 2 carry off as booty. [French]

rifleman n. soldier armed with a rifle.

rifle-range n. place for rifle-practice.

rifle-shot n. 1 shot fired with a rifle. 2 distance coverable by this.

rifling n. arrangement of grooves on the inside of a gun's barrel.

rift —n. 1 crack, split; break (in cloud etc.). 2 disagreement; breach. 3 cleft in earth or rock. —v. tear or burst apart. [Scandinavian: related to RIVEN]

rift-valley n. steep-sided valley formed by subsidence between nearly parallel faults.

rig[1] —v. (-**gg-**) 1 provide (a ship) with sails, rigging, etc. 2 (often foll. by *out, up*) fit with clothes or other equipment. 3 (foll. by *up*) set up hastily or as a makeshift. 4 assemble and adjust the parts of (an aircraft). —n. 1 arrangement

of a ship's masts, sails, etc. **2** equipment for a special purpose, e.g. a radio transmitter. **3** = OIL RIG. **4** colloq. style of dress; uniform (in full rig). [perhaps from Scandinavian]

rig² v. (**-gg-**) manage or fix (a result etc.) fraudulently (rigged the election). —n. trick, dodge, or way of swindling. □ **rig the market** cause an artificial rise or fall in prices. □ **rigger** n. [origin unknown]

rigger n. **1** worker on an oil rig. **2** person who rigs or who arranges rigging.

rigging n. ship's spars, ropes, etc.

right /rʌɪt/ —adj. **1** (of conduct) just, morally or socially correct (do the right thing). **2** true, correct (which is the right way?). **3** suitable or preferable (right person for the job). **4** sound or normal; healthy; satisfactory (engine doesn't sound right). **5** on or towards the east side of the human body, or of any object etc., when facing north. **6** (of a side of fabric etc.) meant for display or use. **7** colloq. real; complete (made a right mess of it). **8** (also **Right**) Polit. of or the Right. —n. **1** that which is correct or just; fair treatment (often in pl.: rights and wrongs of the case). **2** justification or fair claim (has no right to speak). **3** legal or moral entitlement to act (human rights; right of reply). **4** right-hand part, region, or direction. **5** (often **Right**) **a** right hand. **b** Boxing a right hand. **b** blow with this. **6** (often **Right**) **a** conservative political group or section. **b** conservatives collectively. **7** side of a stage to the right of a person facing the audience. —v. **1** (of a person etc.) restore to a proper, straight, or vertical position. **2** correct or avenge (mistakes, wrongs, etc.); set in order; make reparation. —int. colloq. expressing agreement or assent. □ **by right** (or **rights**) if right were done. **do right by** act dutifully towards (a person). **in the right** having justice or truth on one's side. **in one's own right** through one's own position or effort etc. **on the right side of 1** in the favour of (a person etc.). **2** somewhat less than (a specified age). **put (or set) right 1** restore to order,

health, etc. **2** correct the mistaken impression etc. of (a person). **put (or set) to rights** make correct or well ordered. **right away** (or **off**) immediately. **right it** (or **hot**) = RIGHTO. **right on!** slang expression of strong approval or encouragement. **a right one** colloq. foolish or funny person. **right you are!** colloq. exclamation of assent. **too right** slang expression of agreement. □ **rightness** n. [Old English]

right angle n. angle of 90°.

right arm n. one's most reliable helper.

right bank n. bank of a river on the right facing downstream.

righten v. make right or correct.

righteous /ˈrʌɪtʃəs/ adj. (of a person or conduct) morally right; virtuous, lawabiding. □ **righteously** adv. **righteousness** n. [Old English]

rightful adj. **1 a** (of a person) legitimately entitled to a position etc.) (rightful heir). **b** (of status or property etc.) that one is entitled to. **2** (of an action etc.) equitable, fair. □ **rightfully** adv. [Old English]

right hand n. = RIGHT-HAND MAN.

right-hand attrib. adj. **1** on or towards the right side of a person or thing. **2** done with the right hand. **3** (of a screw) = RIGHT-HANDED 4b.

right-handed adj. **1** naturally using the right hand for writing etc. **2** (of a tool or blow) for use by the right hand. **3** (of a blow) struck with the right hand. **4 a** turning to the right. **b** (of a screw) turned clockwise to tighten. □ **right-handedly** adv. **right-handedness** n.

right-hander n. **1** right-handed person. **2** right-handed blow.

right-hand man n. indispensable or chief assistant.

Right Honourable n. title given to certain high officials, e.g. Privy Councillors.

rightism n. political conservatism. □ **rightist** n. & adj.

rightly adv. justly, properly, correctly, justifiably.

right-minded adj. (also **right-thinking**) having sound views and principles.

rightmost adj. furthest to the right.

righto /rʌɪˈtəʊ/ int. colloq. expressing agreement or assent.

right of way n. **1** right established by usage to pass over another's ground. **2** path subject to such a right. **3** right of a vehicle to precede another. **4** precedence.

Right Reverend n. bishop's title.

right turn n. turn of 90 degrees to the right.

rightward /ˈraɪtwəd/ (also **rightwards**) towards the right. —*adj.* going towards or facing the right.

right wing —*n.* 1 more conservative section of a political party or system. 2 right side of a football team etc. on the field. —*adj.* (**right-wing**) conservative or reactionary. □ **right-winger** *n.*

rigid /ˈrɪdʒɪd/ *adj.* 1 not flexible; unbendable. 2 (of a person, conduct, etc.) inflexible, unbending, harsh. □ **rigidity** /ˈdʒɪdɪtɪ/ *n.* **rigidly** *adv.* **rigidness** *n.* [Latin *rigidus* from *rigeo* be stiff]

rigmarole /ˈrɪgmərəʊl/ *n.* 1 lengthy and complicated procedure. 2 rambling or meaningless talk or tale. [originally *ragman roll* catalogue]

rigor /ˈrɪgə(r), ˈraɪgɔː(r)/ *n.* feeling of cold with shivering and a rise in temperature, preceding a fever etc. [Latin *rigeo* be stiff]

rigor² *US* var. of RIGOUR.

rigor mortis /ˌrɪgə ˈmɔːtɪs/ *n.* stiffening of the body after death.

rigorous /ˈrɪgərəs/ *adj.* 1 firm; strict, severe. 2 strictly exact or accurate. □ **rigorously** *adv.* **rigorousness** *n.* [related to RIGOUR]

rigour /ˈrɪgə(r)/ *n.* (*US* **rigor**) 1 a severity, strictness, harshness. **b** (in *pl.*) harsh measures or conditions. 2 logical exactitude. 3 strict enforcement of rules etc. (*utmost rigour of the law*). 4 austerity of life. [Latin: related to RIGOR¹]

rig-out *n. colloq.* outfit of clothes.

rile *v.* (-ling) *colloq.* anger, irritate. [French from Latin]

rill *n.* small stream. [probably Low German or Dutch]

rim *n.* 1 edge or border, esp. of something circular. 2 outer edge of a wheel, holding the tyre. 3 part of spectacle frames around the lens. □ **rimless** *adj.* **rimmed** *adj.* (also in *comb.*). [Old English]

rime¹ —*n.* 1 frost. 2 hoar-frost. —*v.* (**-ming**) cover with rime. [Old English]

rime² *archaic* var. of RHYME.

rind /raɪnd/ *n.* tough outer layer or covering of fruit and vegetables, cheese, bacon, etc. [Old English]

ring¹ —*n.* 1 circular band, usu. of metal, worn on a finger. 2 circular band of any material. 3 rim of a cylindrical or circular object, or a line or band round it. 4 mark etc. resembling a ring (*rings round his eyes*; *smoke rings*). 5 ring in the cross-section of a tree, produced by one year's growth. 6 a enclosure for a circus performance, boxing, betting at races, showing of cattle, etc. **b** (prec. by *the*) bookmakers collectively. 7 a people or things in a circle. **b** such an arrangement. 8 traders, spies, politicians, etc.,

combined illicitly for profit etc. 9 circular or spiral course. 10 = GAS RING. 11 a thin disc of particles etc. round a planet. **b** halo round the moon. —*v.* 1 (often foll. by *round*, *about*, *in*) make or draw a circle round; encircle. 2 put a ring on (a bird etc.) or through the nose of (a pig, bull, etc.). □ **run** (or **make**) **rings round** *colloq.* outclass or outwit (another person). [Old English]

ring² —*v.* (*past* **rang**; *past part.* **rung**) 1 (often foll. by *out* etc.) give a clear resonant or vibrating sound of or as of a bell. 2 a make (esp. a bell) ring. **b** (*absol.*) call by ringing a bell (*you rang, sir?*). 3 (also *absol.*; often foll. by *up*) call by telephone (*will ring you*). 4 (usu. foll. by *with*, *to*) (of a place) resound with a sound, fame, etc. (*theatre rang with applause*). 5 (of the ears) be filled with a sensation of ringing. 6 a sound (a peal etc.) on bells. **b** (of a bell) sound (the hour etc.). 7 (foll. by *in*, *out*) usher in or out with bell-ringing (*rang out the Old Year*). 8 convey a specified impression (*words rang true*). —*n.* 1 ringing sound or tone. 2 act or sound of ringing a bell. 3 *colloq.* telephone call (*give me a ring*). 4 specified meaning conveyed by words etc. (*had a melancholy ring*). 5 set of espe. church bells. □ **ring back** make a return telephone call to. **ring a bell** *colloq.* begin to revive a memory. **ring down** (or **up**) **the curtain** 1 cause the curtain to be lowered or raised. 2 (foll. by *on*) mark the end or the beginning of (an enterprise etc.). **ring in** report or make contact by telephone. **ring off** end a telephone call. **ring round** telephone several people. **ring up** 1 call by telephone. 2 record (an amount etc.) on a cash register. [Old English]

ring-binder *n.* loose-leaf binder with ring-shaped clasps.

ring-dove *n.* woodpigeon.

ringer *n.* bell-ringer. □ **be a ringer** (or **dead ringer**) **for** *slang* resemble (a person) exactly.

ring-fence *v.* (**-cing**) protect or guarantee (funds).

ring finger *n.* third finger, esp. of the left hand, on which a wedding ring is usu. worn.

ringing tone *n.* sound heard after dialling an unengaged number.

ringleader *n.* leading instigator of a crime, mischief, etc.

ringlet /ˈrɪŋlɪt/ *n.* curly lock of esp. long hair. □ **ringleted** *adj.*

ringmaster *n.* person directing a circus performance.

ring-pull *attrib. adj.* (of a tin) having a ring for pulling to break its seal.

ring road *n.* bypass encircling a town.

ringside n. area immediately beside a boxing or circus ring etc. (often *attrib.*: *ringside view*).

ringworm n. fungal skin infection causing circular inflamed patches, esp. on the scalp.

rink n. 1 area of ice for skating or curling etc. 2 enclosed area for roller skating. 3 building containing either of these. 4 strip of bowling-green. 5 team in bowls or curling. [apparently from French *renc* RANK[1]]

rinse –v. (-sing) (often foll. by *through*, *out*) 1 wash or treat with clean water etc. 2 wash lightly. 3 put (clothes etc.) through clean water after washing. 4 (foll. by *out*, *away*) clear ('impurities) by rinsing. –n. 1 rinsing (*give it a rinse*). 2 temporary hair tint (*blue rinse*). [French *rincer*]

riot /'raɪət/ –n. 1 a violent disturbance by a crowd of people. b (*attrib.*) involved in suppressing riots (*riot police*). 2 loud uncontrolled revelry. 3 (foll. by *of*) lavish display or sensation (*riot of colour and sound*). 4 *colloq.* very amusing thing or person. –v. make or engage in a riot. □ **read the Riot Act** firmly to suppress insubordination; give warning. **run riot** 1 throw off all restraint. 2 (of plants) grow or spread uncontrolled. □ **rioter** n. **riotous** *adj.* [French]

RIP *abbr.* may he, she, or they rest in peace. [Latin *requiesca(n)t in pace*]

rip¹ –v. (**-pp-**) 1 tear or cut a (thing) quickly or forcibly away or apart (*ripped out the lining*). 2 a make (a hole etc.) by ripping. b make a long tear or cut in. 3 come violently apart; split. 4 rush along. –n. 1 long tear or cut. 2 act of ripping. □ **let rip** *colloq.* 1 (allow to) proceed or act without restraint or interference. 2 speak violently. **rip into** *colloq.* attack (a person) verbally. **rip off** *colloq.* 1 swindle. 2 steal. [origin unknown]

rip² n. stretch of rough water caused by meeting currents. [origin uncertain]

rip³ n. 1 dissolute person; rascal. 2 worthless horse. [origin uncertain]

riparian /raɪ'peərɪən/ *adj.* of or on a river-bank (*riparian rights*). [Latin *ripa* bank]

ripcord n. cord for releasing a parachute from its pack.

ripe *adj.* 1 (of grain, fruit, cheese, etc.) ready to be reaped, picked, or eaten. 2 mature, fully developed (*ripe in judgement*). 3 (of a person's age) advanced. 4 (often foll. by *for*) fit or ready (*ripe for development*). □ **ripeness** n. [Old English]

ripen v. make or become ripe.

rip-off n. *colloq.* swindle, financial exploitation.

riposte /rɪ'pɒst/ –n. 1 quick retort. 2 quick return thrust in fencing. –v. (-ting) deliver a riposte. [Italian: related to RESPOND]

ripper n. 1 person or thing that rips. 2 murderer who mutilates the victims' bodies.

ripple /'rɪp(ə)l/ –n. 1 ruffling of the water's surface; small wave or waves. 2 gentle lively sound, e.g. of laughter or applause. 3 wavy appearance in hair, material, etc. 4 slight variation in the strength of a current etc. 5 ice-cream with veins of syrup (*raspberry ripple*). –v. (-ling) 1 (cause to) form or flow in ripples. 2 show or sound like ripples. □ **ripply** *adj.* [origin unknown]

rip-roaring *adj.* 1 wildly noisy or boisterous. 2 excellent, first-rate.

ripsaw n. coarse saw for sawing wood along the grain.

rise /raɪz/ –v. (-sing; *past* **rose** /rəʊz/; *past part.* **risen** /'rɪz(ə)n/) 1 come or go up. 2 grow, project, or incline upwards; become higher. 3 appear or be visible above the horizon. 4 get up from lying, sitting, kneeling, or from bed; become erect. 5 (of a meeting etc.) adjourn. 6 reach a higher position, level, amount, intensity, etc. 7 make progress socially etc. (*rose from the ranks*). 8 a come to the surface of liquid. b (of a person) react to provocation (*rise to the bait*). 9 come to life again 10 (of dough) swell by the action of yeast etc. 11 (often foll. by *up*) rebel (*rise up against them*). 12 originate (*river rises in the mountains*). 13 (of wind) start to blow. 14 (of a person's spirits) become cheerful. –n. 1 rising. 2 upward slope, hill, or movement. 3 a increase in amount, extent, sound, pitch, etc. b increase in status or power; upward progress. 5 movement of fish to the surface. 4 increase in salary. 4 a vertical height of a step, arch, incline etc. b = RISER 2. □ **get** (or **take**) **a rise out of** *colloq.* provoke a reaction from (a person), esp. by teasing. **on the rise** on the increase. **rise above** be superior to (petty feelings, difficulties, etc.). **rise to** develop powers equal to (an occasion). [Old English]

riser n. 1 person who rises from bed (*early riser*). 2 vertical section between the treads of a staircase.

risible /'rɪzɪb(ə)l/ *adj.* laughable, ludicrous. [Latin *rideo ris-* laugh]

rising –*adj.* 1 advancing to maturity or high standing (*rising young lawyer*). 2 approaching a specified age (*rising*

five). **3** (of ground) sloping upwards. —*n.* revolt or insurrection.

rising damp *n.* moisture absorbed from the ground into a wall.

risk —*n.* **1** chance or possibility of danger, loss, injury, etc. (*health risk; risk of fire*). **2** person or thing causing a risk or regarded in relation to risk (*is a poor risk*). —*v.* **1** expose to risk. **2** accept the chance of (*risk getting wet*). **3** venture on. □ **at risk** exposed to danger. **at one's (own) risk** accepting responsibility, agreeing to make no claims. **at the risk of** with the possibility of (an adverse consequence). **put at risk** expose to danger. **run a** (or **the**) **risk** (often foll. by *of*) expose oneself to danger or loss etc. **take a risk** (or **risks**) chance the possibility of danger etc. [French *risque(r)* from Italian]

risky *adj.* (**-ier**, **-iest**) **1** involving risk. **2** = RISQUÉ. □ **riskily** *adv.* **riskiness** *n.*

risotto /rɪˈzɒtəʊ/ *n.* (*pl.* **-s**) Italian savoury rice dish cooked in stock. [Italian]

risqué /ˈrɪskeɪ, ˈriː-/ *adj.* (of a story etc.) slightly indecent. [French: related to RISK]

rissole /ˈrɪsəʊl/ *n.* cake of spiced minced meat, coated in breadcrumbs and fried. [French]

rit. *abbr. Mus.* ritardando.

ritardando /ˌrɪtɑːˈdændəʊ/ *adv.* & *n.* (*pl.* **-s** or **-di** /-diː/) *Mus.* = RALLENTANDO. [Italian]

rite *n.* **1** religious or solemn observance, act, or procedure (*burial rites*). **2** body of customary observances characteristic of a Church etc. (*Latin rite*). [Latin *ritus*]

rite of passage *n.* (often in *pl.*) event marking a change or stage in life, e.g. marriage.

ritual /ˈrɪtjʊəl/ —*n.* **1 a** prescribed order of a ceremony etc. **b** solemn or colourful pageantry etc. **2** procedure regularly followed. —*adj.* of or done as a ritual or rite (*ritual murder*). □ **ritually** *adv.* [Latin: related to RITE]

ritualism *n.* regular or excessive practice of ritual. □ **ritualist** *n.* **ritualistic** /-ˈlɪstɪk/ *adj.* **ritualistically** /-ˈlɪstɪkəlɪ/ *adv.*

ritzy /ˈrɪtsɪ/ *adj.* (**-ier**, **-iest**) *colloq.* high-class, luxurious, showily smart. [from *Ritz*, name of luxury hotels]

rival /ˈraɪv(ə)l/ —*n.* (often *attrib.*) **1** person competing with another. **2** person or thing that equals another in quality. —*v.* (**-ll-**; *US* **-l-**) be, seem, or claim to be the rival of or comparable to. [Latin *rivus* stream]

rivalry *n.* (*pl.* **-ies**) being rivals; competition.

riven /ˈrɪv(ə)n/ *adj. literary* split, torn. [past part. of *rive* from Old Norse]

river /ˈrɪvə(r)/ *n.* **1** copious natural stream of water flowing to the sea or a lake etc. **2** copious flow (*rivers of blood*). □ **sell down the river** *colloq.* betray or let down. [Latin *ripa* bank]

riverside *n.* (often *attrib.*) ground along a river-bank.

rivet /ˈrɪvɪt/ —*n.* nail or bolt for joining metal plates etc., with the headless end beaten out when in place. —*v.* (**-t-**) **1 a** join or fasten with rivets. **b** beat out or press down the end of (a nail or bolt). **c** fix, make immovable. **2 a** (foll. by *on*, *upon*) direct intently (one's eyes or attention etc.). **b** engross (a person or the attention). □ **riveting** *adj.* engross (a person or the attention). [French *river* fasten]

riviera /ˌrɪvɪˈeərə/ *n.* coastal subtropical region, esp. that of SE France and NW Italy. [Italian, = sea-shore]

rivulet /ˈrɪvjʊlɪt/ *n.* small stream. [Latin *rivus* stream]

RM *abbr.* Royal Marines.

rm. *abbr.* room.

RMA *abbr.* Royal Military Academy.

RN *abbr.* Royal Navy.

Rn *symb.* radon.

RNA *abbr.* ribonucleic acid.

RNLI *abbr.* Royal National Lifeboat Institution.

roach *n.* (*pl.* same or **-es**) small freshwater fish of the carp family. [French]

road *n.* **1 a** way with a prepared surface, for vehicles, pedestrians, etc. **b** part of this for vehicles only (*step out into the road*). **2** one's way or route. **3** (usu. in *pl.*) piece of water near the shore in which ships can ride at anchor. □ **any road** *dial.* = ANYWAY 2, 3. **get out of the** (or **my** etc.) **road** stop obstructing a person. **in the** (or **one's**) **road** *dial.* forming an obstruction. **one for the road** *colloq.* final (esp. alcoholic) drink before departure. **on the road** travelling, esp. as a firm's representative, itinerant performer, or vagrant. **the road to** way of getting to or achieving (*road to London; road to ruin*). [Old English: related to RIDE]

roadbed *n.* **1** foundation structure of a railway. **2** foundation material for a road. **3** *US* part of a road on which vehicles travel.

roadblock *n.* barrier set up on a road in order to stop and examine traffic.

road fund licence *n.* disc displayed on a vehicle certifying payment of road tax.

road-hog *n. colloq.* reckless or inconsiderate road-user.

road-holding *n.* stability of a moving vehicle.

road-house n. inn or club on a major road.

roadie n. collog. assistant of a touring band etc., erecting and maintaining equipment.

road-making n. etc.

road-metal n. broken stone used in road-making etc.

road sense n. capacity for safe behaviour in traffic etc.

roadshow n. 1 television or radio series broadcasting each programme from a different venue 2 any touring political or advertising campaign or touring entertainment etc.

roadside n. (often attrib.) strip of land beside a road.

road sign n. sign giving information or instructions to road users.

roadstead n. = ROAD 3.

roadster n. open car without rear seats.

road tax n. periodic tax payable on road vehicles.

road test —n. test of a vehicle's roadworthiness. —v. (**road-test**) test (a vehicle) on the road.

roadway n. 1 road. 2 part of a road intended for vehicles.

roadworks n.pl. construction, repair, etc. of roads.

roadworthy adj. fit to be used on the road. □ **roadworthiness** n.

roam —v. 1 ramble, wander. 2 travel unsystematically over, through, or about. —n. act of roaming; ramble. □ **roamer** n. [origin unknown]

roan adj. (of esp. a horse) having a coat thickly interspersed with hairs of another colour. —n. roan animal. [French]

roar —n. 1 a loud deep hoarse sound, as made by a lion. b similar sound. 2 loud laugh. —v. 1 (often foll. by out) utter loudly or make a roar, roaring laugh, etc. 2 travel in a vehicle at high speed, esp. with the engine roaring. [Old English]

roaring drunk predic. adj. very drunk and noisy.

roaring forties n.pl. stormy ocean tracts between lat. 40° and 50° S.

roaring success n. great success.

roaring trade n. (also **roaring business**) very brisk trade or business.

roaring twenties n.pl. decade of the 1920s.

roast —v. 1 a cook (food, esp. meat) or (of food) be cooked in an oven or by open heat (roast chestnuts). b heat (coffee beans) before grinding. 2 refl. expose (oneself etc.) to fire or heat. 3 criticize severely, denounce. —attrib. adj. roasted (roast beef). —n. 1 a roast meat. b dish of this. c piece of meat for

roasting. 2 process of roasting. [French rost(ir) from Germanic]

roasting —adj. very hot. —n. severe criticism or denunciation.

roaster n. 1 oven, dish, apparatus, etc. for roasting. 2 fowl, potato, etc. for roasting.

rob v. (-bb-) (often foll. by of) 1 (also absol.) take unlawfully from, esp. by force or threat (robbed the safe; robbed her of her jewels). 2 deprive of what is due or normal (robbed of sleep). □ **robber** n. [French rob(b)er from Germanic]

robbery n. (pl. -ies) 1 act of robbing. 2 collog. excessive charge or cost.

robe —n. 1 a long loose outer garment. b (often in pl.) this worn as an indication of rank, office, profession, etc. 2 esp. US dressing-gown. —v. (-bing) clothe in a robe; dress. [French]

robin /'rɒbɪn/ n. 1 (also **robin redbreast**) small brown red-breasted bird. 2 US red-breasted thrush. [pet form of Robert]

Robin Hood n. person who steals from the rich to give to the poor.

robinia /rə'bɪnɪə/ n. any of various N. American trees or shrubs, e.g. a locust tree or false acacia. [Robin, name of a French gardener]

robot /'rəʊbɒt/ n. 1 machine resembling or functioning like a human. 2 machine automatically completing a mechanical process. 3 person who acts mechanically. □ **robotic** /-'bɒtɪk/ adj. robotize v. (also **-ise**) (**-zing** or **-sing**). [Czech]

robotics /rəʊ'bɒtɪks/ n.pl. (usu. treated as sing.) art, science, or study of robot design and operation.

robust /rəʊ'bʌst/ adj. (**-er**, **-est**) 1 strong and sturdy, esp. in physique or construction. 2 (of exercise, discipline, etc.) vigorous, requiring strength. 3 (of mental attitude, argument, etc.) straightforward, vigorous. 4 (of a statement, reply, etc.) bold, firm, unyielding □ **robustly** adv. **robustness** n. [Latin robur strength]

roc n. gigantic bird of Eastern legend. [Spanish from Arabic]

rochet /'rɒtʃɪt/ n. surplice-like vestment of a bishop or abbot. [French from Germanic]

rock n. 1 a hard material of the earth's crust, often exposed on the surface. b similar material on other planets. 2 Geol. any natural material, hard or soft (e.g. clay), consisting of one or more minerals. 3 a projecting rock forming a hill, cliff, reef, etc. b (the Rock) Gibraltar. 4 large detached stone. 5 US stone of any size. 6 firm and dependable support or protection. 7 hard sweet usu. in the

form of a peppermint-flavoured stick. **8** *slang* precious stone. **□** a diamond. **□** **get one's rocks off** *coarse slang* achieve (esp. sexual) satisfaction. **on the rocks** *colloq.* **1** short of money. **2** (of a marriage etc.) broken down. **3** (of a drink) served neat with ice-cubes. [French *roque*, *roche*]

rock² –*v.* **1** move gently to and fro; set, maintain, or be in, such motion. **2** (cause to) sway; shake, oscillate, reel. **3** distress, perturb (*rocked by the news*). –*n.* **1** rocking movement. **2** spell of this. **3 a** = ROCK AND ROLL. **b** rock and roll-influenced popular music. **□ rock the boat** *colloq.* disturb a stable situation. [Old English]

rockabilly /'rɒkə,bɪlɪ/ *n.* rock and roll combined with hill-billy music.

rock and roll *n.* (also **rock 'n' roll**) popular dance-music originating in the 1950s with a heavy beat and often a blues element.

rock-bottom –*adj.* (of prices etc.) the very lowest. –*n.* very lowest level.

rock-cake *n.* small rough-surfaced spicy currant bun.

rock-crystal *n.* transparent colourless quartz, usu. in hexagonal prisms.

rocker *n.* **1** curved bar etc. on which something can rock. **2** rocking-chair. **3** devotee of rock music, esp. a leather-clad motor cyclist. **4 a** device for rocking. **b** pivoted switch operating between 'on' and 'off' positions. **□ off one's rocker** *slang* crazy.

rockery *n.* (*pl.* -**ies**) construction of stones with soil between them for growing rock-plants on.

rocket /'rɒkɪt/ –*n.* **1** cylindrical firework or signal etc. propelled to a great height after ignition. **2** engine operating on the same principle, providing thrust but not dependent on air intake. **3** rocket-propelled missile, spacecraft, etc. **4** *slang* severe reprimand. –*v.* (-t-) **1** a move rapidly upwards or away. **b** increase rapidly (*prices rocketed*). **2** bombard with rockets. [French *roquette* from Italian]

rocketry *n.* science or practice of rocket propulsion.

rock-face *n.* vertical surface of natural rock.

rockfall *n.* descent or mass of loose fallen rocks.

rock-garden *n.* = ROCKERY.

rocking-chair *n.* chair mounted on rockers or springs for gently rocking in.

rocking-horse *n.* toy horse on rockers or springs.

rock-plant *n.* plant growing on or among rocks.

rock-salmon *n.* any of several fishes, esp. the catfish and dogfish.

rock-salt *n.* common salt as a solid mineral.

rocky¹ *adj.* (-**ier**, -**iest**) of, like, or full of rock or rocks. **□ rockiness** *n.*

rocky² *adj.* (-**ier**, -**iest**) *colloq.* unsteady, tottering, unstable. **□ rockiness** *n.*

rococo /rə'kəʊkəʊ/ –*adj.* **1** of a late baroque style of 18th-c. decoration. **2** (of literature, music, architecture, etc.) highly ornate. –*n.* this style. [French]

rod *n.* **1** slender straight cylindrical bar or stick. **2** a cane for flogging. **b** (*prec. by the*) use of this. **3** = FISHING-ROD. **4** *hist.* (as a measure) perch or square perch (see PERCH). **□ make a rod for one's own back** make trouble for oneself. [Old English]

rode *past of* RIDE.

rodent /'rəʊd(ə)nt/ *n.* mammal with strong incisors and no canine teeth, e.g. the rat, mouse, squirrel, beaver, and porcupine. [Latin *rodo* gnaw]

rodeo /'rəʊdɪəʊ, rə'deɪəʊ/ *n.* (*pl.* -**s**) **1** exhibition of cowboys' skills in handling animals. **2** round-up of cattle on a ranch for branding etc. [Spanish]

rodomontade /,rɒdəmɒn'teɪd/ *n.* boastful talk or behaviour. [French from Italian]

roe¹ *n.* **1** (also **hard roe**) mass of eggs in a female fish's ovary. **2** (also **soft roe**) milt of a male fish. [Low German or Dutch]

roe² /rəʊ/ *n.* (*pl.* same or -**s**) (also **roe-deer**) small kind of deer. [Old English]

roebuck *n.* male roe-deer.

roentgen /'rʌntjən/ *n.* (also **röntgen**) unit of ionizing radiation. [*Röntgen*, name of a physicist]

rogation /rəʊ'geɪʃ(ə)n/ *n.* (usu. in *pl.*) litany of the saints chanted on the three days before Ascension day. [Latin *rogo* ask]

Rogation Days *n.pl.* the three days before Ascension Day.

roger /'rɒdʒə(r)/ *int.* **1** your message has been received and understood (used in radio communication etc.). **2** *slang* I agree. [from the name, code for R]

rogue /rəʊg/ *n.* **1** dishonest or unprincipled person. **2** *joc.* mischievous person, esp. a child. **3** (usu. *attrib.*) wild fierce animal driven away or living apart from others (*rogue elephant*). **4** (often *attrib.*) inexplicably aberrant result or phenomenon; inferior or defective specimen. [origin unknown]

roguery /'rəʊgərɪ/ *n.* (*pl.* -**ies**) conduct or action characteristic of rogues.

rogues' gallery *n. colloq.* collection of photographs of known criminals etc., used for identification.

roguish *adj.* 1 playfully mischievous. 2 characteristic of rogues. □ **roguishly** *adv.* **roguishness** *n.*

roister *v.* (esp. as **roistering** *adj.*) revel noisily; be uproarious. □ **roisterer** *n.* [Latin: related to RUSTIC]

role *n.* (also **rôle**) 1 actor's part in a play, film, etc. 2 person's or thing's function. [French: related to ROLL]

role model *n.* person on whom others model themselves.

role-playing *n.* (also **role-play**) acting of characters or situations as an aid in psychotherapy, language-teaching, etc. □ **role-play** *v.*

roll /rəʊl/ —*v.* 1 (cause to) move or go in some direction by turning on an axis (*ball rolled under the table; rolled the barrel into the cellar*). 2 a make cylindrical or spherical by revolving between two surfaces or over on itself (*rolled a newspaper*). **b** make thus or shape (*rolled the dough into a ball; rolled himself into a ball*). 3 (often foll. by *along, by, etc.*) (cause to) move, advance, or be conveyed on or (of time etc.) as if on wheels etc. (*years rolled past; rolled by in his car*). 4 flatten or form by passing a roller etc. over or by passing between rollers (*roll the lawn; roll pastry*). 5 rotate (*his eyes rolled; he rolled his eyes*). 6 a wallow (*in the dust*). **b** (of a horse etc.) lie on its back and kick about. 7 (of a moving ship, aircraft, vehicle, or person) sway to and fro sideways or walk unsteadily (*rolled out of the pub*). 8 a undulate (*rolling hills; rolling mist*). **b** carry or propel with undulations (*river rolls its waters to the sea*). 9 (cause to) start functioning or moving (*cameras rolled*). 10 sound or utter with vibrations or a trill (*thunder rolled; rolls his rs*). —*n.* 1 rolling motion or gait; undulation (*roll of the hills*). 2 a spell of rolling (*roll in the mud*). **b** gymnastic exercise in which the body rolls in a forward or backward circle. **c** (esp. **a roll in the hay**) *colloq.* sexual intercourse etc. 3 rhythmic rumbling sound of thunder etc. 4 complete revolution of an aircraft about its longitudinal axis. 5 anything forming a cylinder by being turned over on itself without folding (*roll of carpet; sausage roll*). 6 a small portion of bread individually baked. **b** this with a specified filling. 7 thing cylindrical in shape (*rolls of fat; roll of hair*). 8 a official list or register (*electoral roll*). **b** total numbers on this. □ **be rolling in** *colloq.* have plenty of (esp. money). **rolled into one** combined in one person or thing.

roll *n.* arrive in great numbers or quantity. **roll on 1** put on or apply by rolling. **2** (in *imper.*) *colloq.* come quickly (*roll on Friday!*). **roll up 1** *colloq.* arrive in or form a roll. **strike off the rolls** debar (esp. a solicitor) from practising. [Latin *rotulus* diminutive: related to ROTA]

roll-call *n.* calling out a list of names to establish who is present.

rolled gold *n.* thin coating of gold applied to a base metal by rolling.

rolled oats *n.pl.* husked and crushed oats.

roller *n.* 1 a revolving cylinder for smoothing, spreading, crushing, stamping, hanging a towel on, etc., used alone or in a machine. **b** cylinder for diminishing friction when moving a heavy object. 2 small cylinder on which hair is rolled for setting. 3 long swelling wave. **4** bearing but with small cylinders instead of balls.

roller blind *n.* blind on a roller.

roller-coaster *n.* 1 switchback at a fair etc. 2 (*attrib.*) (of emotions etc.) uncontrollable, unstable.

roller-skate —*n.* metal frame with small wheels, fitted to shoes for riding on a hard surface. —*v.* (*-ting*) move on roller-skates. □ **roller-skater** *n.*

roller towel *n.* towel with the ends joined, hung on a roller.

rollicking /ˈrɒlɪkɪŋ/ *adj.* jovial, exuberant. [origin unknown]

rolling drunk *predic. adj.* swaying or staggering from drunkenness.

rolling-mill *n.* machine or factory for rolling metal into shape.

rolling-pin *n.* cylinder for rolling out pastry, dough, etc.

rolling-stock *n.* 1 locomotives, carriages, etc. used on a railway. 2 US road vehicles of a company.

rolling stone *n.* unsettled rootless person.

rollmop *n.* rolled uncooked pickled herring fillet. [German *Rollmops*]

roll-neck *adj.* (of a garment) having a high loosely turned-over neck.

roll of honour *n.* list of those honoured, esp. the dead in war.

roll-on —*attrib. adj.* (of deodorant etc.) applied by means of a rotating ball in the neck of the container. —*n.* light elastic corset.

roll-on roll-off *adj.* (of a ship, etc.) in which vehicles are driven directly on and off.

roll-top desk *n.* desk with a flexible cover sliding in curved grooves.

roll-up *n.* (also **roll-your-own**) hand-rolled cigarette.

roly-poly /ˌrəʊlɪˈpəʊlɪ/ *–n.* (*pl.* **-ies**) (also **roly-poly pudding**) pudding made of a rolled strip of suet pastry covered with jam etc. and boiled or baked. *–adj.* podgy. plump. [probably from ROLL]

ROM *n. Computing* read-only memory. [abbreviation]

rom. *abbr.* roman (type).

Roman /ˈrəʊmən/ *–adj.* **1** of ancient Rome, its territory, people, etc. **2** of medieval or modern Rome. **3** = ROMAN CATHOLIC. **4** (**roman**) (of type) plain and upright, used in ordinary print. **5** (of the alphabet, etc.) based on the ancient Roman system with letters A–Z. *–n.* **1** citizen or soldier of the ancient Roman Republic or Empire. **2** citizen of modern Rome. **3** = ROMAN CATHOLIC. **4** (**roman**) roman type. [Latin]

Roman candle *n.* firework discharging flaming coloured balls.

Roman Catholic *–adj.* of the part of the Christian Church acknowledging the Pope as its head. *–n.* member of this Church. □ **Roman Catholicism** *n.*

romance /rəʊˈmæns/ *–n.* /also ˈrəʊ-/ **1** idealized, poetic, or unworldly atmosphere or tendency. **2 a** love affair. **b** mutual attraction in this. **c** sentimental or idealized love. **3 a** literary genre concerning romantic love, stirring action, etc. **b** work of this genre. **4** medieval, esp. verse, tale of chivalry, etc. **5 a** exaggeration, lies. **b** instance of this. **6** (**Romance**) (often *attrib.*) languages descended from Latin. **7** *Mus.* short informal piece. *–v.* (**-cing**) **1** exaggerate, distort the truth, fantasize. **2** court, woo. [Romanic: related to ROMANIC]

■ **Usage** The alternative pronunciation given for the noun, with the stress on the first syllable, is considered incorrect by some people.

Roman Empire *n. hist.* that established by Augustus in 27 BC and divided by Theodosius in AD 395.

Romanesque /ˌrəʊməˈnesk/ *–n.* style of European architecture c. 900–1200, with massive vaulting and round arches. *–adj.* of this style.

Romanian /rəʊˈmeɪnɪən/ (also **Rumanian** /ruː-/) *–n.* **1 a** native or national of Romania. **b** person of Romanian descent. **2** language of Romania. *–adj.* of Romania, its people, or language.

Romanic /rəʊˈmænɪk/ *–n.* = ROMANCE *n.* **6.** *–adj.* **1 a** of Romance. **b** Romance-speaking. **2** descended from, or inheriting the civilization etc. of, the ancient

Romans. [Latin *Romanicus*: related to ROMAN]

romanize /ˈrəʊmənaɪz/ *v.* (also **-ise**) (**-zing** or **-sing**) **1** make Roman or Roman Catholic in character. **2** put into the Roman alphabet or roman type. □ **romanization** /-ˈzeɪʃ(ə)n/ *n.*

Roman law *n.* law-code of ancient Rome, forming the basis of many modern codes.

Roman nose *n.* aquiline high-bridged nose.

roman numeral *n.* any of the Roman letters representing numbers: I = 1, V = 5, X = 10, L = 50, C = 100, D = 500, M = 1000.

Romano- *comb. form* Roman; Roman and (**Romano-British**).

romantic /rəʊˈmæntɪk/ *–adj.* **1** of, characterized by, or suggestive of romance (*romantic picture*). **2** inclined towards or suggestive of romance in love (*romantic evening; romantic words*). **3** (of a person) imaginative, visionary, idealistic. **4 a** (of style in art, music, etc.) concerned more with feeling and emotion than with form and aesthetic qualities. **b** (also **Romantic**) of the 18th–19th-c. romantic movement or style in the European arts. **5** (of a project etc.) impractical, fantastic. *–n.* **1** romantic person. **2** romanticist. □ **romantically** *adv.* [French: related to ROMANCE]

romanticism *n.* (also **Romanticism**) adherence to a romantic style in art, music, etc.

romanticist *n.* (also **Romanticist**) writer or artist of the romantic school.

romanticize *v.* (also **-ise**) (**-zing** or **-sing**) **1** make romantic; exaggerate (*romanticized account*). **2** indulge in romantic thoughts or actions.

Romany /ˈrɒmənɪ/ *–n.* (*pl.* **-ies**) **1** Gypsy. **2** language of the Gypsies. *–adj.* of Gypsies or the Romany language. [Romany *Rom* Gypsy]

Romeo /ˈrəʊmɪəʊ/ *n.* (*pl.* **-s**) passionate male lover or seducer. [name of a character in Shakespeare]

romp *–v.* **1** play roughly and energetically. **2** (foll. by *along, past*, etc.) *colloq.* proceed without effort. *–n.* spell of romping. □ **romp in** (or **home**) *colloq.* win easily. [perhaps from RAMP]

rompers *n. pl.* (also **romper suit**) young child's one-piece garment covering the legs and trunk.

rondeau /ˈrɒndəʊ/ *n.* (*pl.* **rondeaux** pronunc. same or /-əʊz/) poem of ten or thirteen lines with only two rhymes throughout and with the opening words used twice as a refrain. [French: related to RONDEL]

rondel /ˈrondəl/ n. rondeau, esp. one of special form. [French: related to ROUND: cf. ROUNDEL]

rondo /ˈrondəʊ/ n. (pl. -s) musical form with a recurring leading theme. [French RONDEAU]

röntgen var. of ROENTGEN.

rood n. 1 crucifix, esp. one raised on a rood-screen. 2 quarter of an acre. [Old English]

rood-screen n. carved screen separating nave and chancel.

roof –n. (pl. -s) 1 a upper covering of a building. b top of a covered vehicle. c top inner surface of an oven, refrigerator, etc. 2 overhead rock in a cave or mine etc. –v. 1 (often foll. by in, over) cover with or as with a roof. 2 be the roof of. □ **go through the roof** colloq. (of prices etc.) rise dramatically. **hit** (or **go through**) **the roof** colloq. become very angry. [Old English]

roof-garden n. garden on the flat roof of a building.

roofing n. material for a roof.

roof of the mouth n. palate.

roof-rack n. framework for luggage on top of a vehicle.

rooftop n. 1 outer surface of a roof. 2 (in pl.) tops of houses etc. □ **shout it from the rooftops** make a thing embarrassingly public.

roof-tree n. ridge-piece of a roof.

rook¹ /rʊk/ –n. black bird of the crow family nesting in colonies. –v. 1 colloq. charge (a customer) extortionately. 2 win money at cards etc. by swindling. [Old English]

rook² /rʊk/ n. chess piece with a battlement-shaped top. [French from Arabic]

rookery n. (pl. -ies) colony of rooks, penguins, or seals.

rookie /ˈrʊkɪ/ n. slang new recruit. [corruption of recruit]

room /ruːm/ –n. 1 space for, or occupied by, something; capacity (takes up too much room; room for improvement). 2 a part of a building enclosed by walls, floor, and ceiling. b (in pl.) apartments or lodgings. c people in a room (room fell silent). –v. US have room(s); lodge, board. [Old English]

rooming-house n. lodging house.

room-mate n. person sharing a room.

room service n. provision of food etc. in a hotel bedroom.

roomy adj. (-ier, -iest) having much room, spacious. □ **roominess** n.

roost –n. branch or perch for a bird, esp. to sleep. –v. settle for rest or sleep. □ **come home to roost** (of a scheme etc.) recoil unfavourably. [Old English]

rooster n. domestic cock.

root¹ –n. 1 a part of a plant normally below the ground, conveying nourishment from the soil. b (in pl.) branches or fibres of this. c small plant with a root for transplanting. 2 a plant with an edible root. b such a root. 3 (in pl.) emotional attachment or family ties to a place or community. 4 a embedded part of a hair, tooth, nail, etc. b part of a thing attaching it to a greater whole. 5 (often attrib.) basic cause, source, nature, or origin (root of all evil; roots in the distant past; root cause; the root of things). 6 a number that when multiplied by itself a usu. specified number of times gives a specified number or quantity (cube root of eight is two). b square root, c value of an unknown quantity satisfying a given equation. 7 core of a word, without prefixes, suffixes, etc. –v. 1 (cause to) take root; grow roots (root them firmly). 2 (esp. as rooted adj.) fix firmly; establish (rooted objection; reaction rooted in fear). 3 (usu. foll. by out, up) drag or dig up by the roots. □ **root and branch** thoroughly, radical(ly). **root out** find and get rid of. **strike** (or **take**) **root** 1 begin to grow and draw nourishment from the soil. 2 become established. □ **rootless** adj. [Old English]

root² v. 1 (also absol.) (often foll. by up) turn up (the ground) with the snout, beak, etc., in search of food. 2 a (foll. by around, in, etc.) rummage. b (foll. by out or up) find or extract by rummaging. 3 (foll. by for) US slang encourage or applaud (a person or team). [Old English and Old Norse]

rootstock n. 1 rhizome. 2 plant into which a graft is inserted. 3 primary form from which offshoots have arisen.

rope –n. 1 a stout cord made by twisting together strands of hemp, wire, etc. b piece of this. 2 (foll. by of) quantity of onions, pearls, etc. strung together. 3 (prec. by the) a halter for hanging a person. b execution by hanging. –v. (-ping) 1 fasten, secure, or catch with rope. 2 (usu. foll. by off, in) enclose with rope. 3 Mountaineering connect with or attach to a rope. □ **know** (or **learn** or **show**) **the ropes** know or learn or show how to do a thing properly. **rope in** persuade to take part. **rope into** persuade to take part in (roped into washing up). [Old English]

rope-ladder n. two ropes with crosspieces, used as a ladder.

ropy adj. (also **ropey**) (-ier, -iest) colloq. poor in quality. □ **ropiness** n.

Roquefort /ˈrɒkfɔː(r)/ n. propr. soft blue cheese made from ewes' milk. [Roquefort in France]

ro-ro /ˈrəʊrəʊ/ *attrib. adj.* roll-on roll-off. [abbreviation]

rorqual /ˈrɔːkw(ə)l/ *n.* whale with a dorsal fin. [French from Norwegian]

Rorschach test /ˈrɔːʃɑːk/ *n.* personality test based on the subject's interpretation of a standard set of ink-blots. [*Rorschach*, name of a psychiatrist]

rosaceous /rəʊˈzeɪʃəs/ *adj.* of a large plant family including the rose. [Latin: related to ROSE¹]

rosary /ˈrəʊzəri/ *n.* (*pl.* **-ies**) **1** *RC Ch.* repeated sequence of prayers. **2** string of beads for keeping count in this. [Latin *rosarium* rose-garden]

rose¹ /rəʊz/ *n.* **1** prickly bush or shrub bearing usu. fragrant red, pink, yellow, or white flowers. **2** this flower. **3** flowering plant resembling this (*Christmas rose*). **4 a** pinkish-red colour. **b** (usu. in *pl.*) rosy complexion (*roses in her cheeks*). **5** sprinkling-nozzle of a watering-can etc. **6** circular electric light mounting on a ceiling. **7 a** representation of a rose in heraldry etc. **b** rose-shaped design. **8** (in *pl.*) used to express luck, ease, success, etc. (*roses all the way; everything's roses*). —*adj.* = ROSE-COLOURED 1. [Latin *rosa*]

rose² *past of* RISE.

rosé /ˈrəʊzeɪ/ *n.* light pink wine. [French]

rosebowl *n.* bowl for cut roses, esp. as a prize in a competition.

rosebud *n.* **1** bud of a rose. **2** pretty young woman.

rose-bush *n.* rose plant.

rose-coloured *adj.* **1** pinkish-red. **2** optimistic, cheerful (*wears rose-coloured glasses*).

rose-hip *n.* = HIP².

rosemary /ˈrəʊzməri/ *n.* evergreen fragrant shrub used as a herb. [*rosmarine* from Latin *ros* dew: related to MARINE]

rosette /rəʊˈzet/ *n.* **1** rose-shaped ornament of ribbon etc., esp. as a supporter's badge or as a prize in a competition. **2** rose-shaped carving. [French diminutive: related to ROSE¹]

rose-water *n.* perfume made from roses.

rose-window *n.* circular window with roselike tracery.

rosewood *n.* any of several fragrant close-grained woods used in making furniture.

rosin /ˈrɒzɪn/ —*n.* resin, esp. in solid form. —*v.* (**-n-**) rub (esp. a violin bow etc.) with rosin. [alteration of RESIN]

RoSPA /ˈrɒspə/ *abbr.* Royal Society for the Prevention of Accidents.

roster /ˈrɒstə(r)/ —*n.* list or plan of turns of duty etc. —*v.* place on a roster. [Dutch *rooster*, literally gridiron]

rostrum /ˈrɒstrəm/ *n.* (*pl.* **rostra** or **-s**) platform for public speaking, an orchestral conductor, etc. [Latin]

rosy /ˈrəʊzi/ *adj.* (**-ier**, **-iest**) **1** pink or red. **2** optimistic, hopeful (*rosy future*). □ **rosily** *adv.* **rosiness** *n.*

rot —*v.* (**-tt-**) **1** (of animal or vegetable matter) lose its original form by the chemical action of bacteria, fungi, etc.; decay. **2** gradually perish or waste away (*left to rot in prison*). **3** cause to rot, make rotten. —*n.* **1** rotting; decay. **2** *slang* nonsense (*talks rot*). **3** decline in standards etc. (*rot set in*). —*int.* expressing incredulity or ridicule. [Old English]

rota /ˈrəʊtə/ *n.* list of duties to be done or names of people to do them in turn; roster. [Latin, = wheel]

Rotarian /rəʊˈteəriən/ —*n.* member of Rotary. —*adj.* of Rotary.

rotary /ˈrəʊtəri/ —*adj.* acting by rotation (*rotary drill*). —*n.* (*pl.* **-ies**) **1** rotary machine. **2** (**Rotary**) (in full **Rotary International**) worldwide charitable society of businessmen, orig. entertaining in rotation. [medieval Latin: related to ROTA]

Rotary Club *n.* local branch of Rotary.

rotate /rəʊˈteɪt/ *v.* (**-ting**) **1** move round an axis or centre, revolve. **2** take or arrange (esp. crops) in rotation. **3** act or take place in rotation (*chairmanship will rotate*). □ **rotatable** *adj.* **rotatory** /ˈrəʊtətəri, -ˈteɪtəri/ *adj.* [Latin: related to ROTA]

rotation /rəʊˈteɪʃ(ə)n/ *n.* **1** rotating or being rotated. **2** recurrence, recurrent series or period; regular succession. **3** the growing of different crops in regular order to avoid exhausting the soil. □ **rotational** *adj.*

Rotavator /ˈrəʊtəveɪtə(r)/ *n.* (also **Rotovator**) *propr.* machine with a rotating blade for breaking up or tilling the soil. [from ROTARY, CULTIVATOR]

rote *n.* (usu. prec. by *by*; also *attrib.*) mechanical or habitual repetition (in order to memorize) (*rote learning*). [origin unknown]

rot-gut *n.* *slang* cheap harmful alcohol.

rotisserie /rəʊˈtɪsəri/ *n.* **1** restaurant etc. where meat is roasted or barbecued. **2** rotating spit for roasting or barbecuing meat. [French: related to ROAST]

rotor /ˈrəʊtə(r)/ *n.* **1** rotary part of a machine. **2** rotary aerofoil on a helicopter, providing lift. [related to ROTATE]

Rotovator *var. of* ROTAVATOR.

rotten /ˈrɒt(ə)n/ *adj.* (**-er**, **-est**) **1** rotting or rotted; fragile from age or use. **2** morally or politically corrupt. **3** *slang* **a** disagreeable, unpleasant, bad (*had a rotten time*). **b** worthless (*rotten idea*). **c**

ill (*feel rotten*). □ **rottenly** *adv.* **rottenness** *n.* [Old Norse: related to ROT]

rotten borough *n. hist.* (before 1832) English borough electing an MP though having very few voters.

rotter *n. slang* nasty or contemptible person. [from ROT]

Rottweiler /'rɒtvaɪlər, -waɪlər)/ *n.* black-and-tan dog noted for ferocity. [*Rottweil* in Germany]

rotund /rəʊ'tʌnd/ *adj.* 1 plump, podgy. 2 (of speech etc.) sonorous, grandiloquent. □ **rotundity** *n.* [Latin *rotundus*: related to ROTA]

rotunda /rəʊ'tʌndə/ *n.* circular building, hall or room, esp. domed. [Italian *rotonda*: related to ROTUND]

rouble /'ruːb(ə)l/ *n.* (also **ruble**) chief monetary unit of Russia etc. [French from Russian]

roué /'ruːeɪ/ *n.* (esp. elderly) debauchee. [French]

rouge /ruːʒ/ —*n.* red cosmetic for colouring the cheeks. —*v.* (**-ging**) 1 colour with or apply rouge. 2 become red, blush. [Latin *rubeus* red]

rough /rʌf/ —*adj.* 1 uneven or bumpy, not smooth, level, or polished. 2 shaggy or coarse-haired. 3 boisterous, coarse, violent, not mild, quiet, or gentle (*rough fellow; rough play; rough sea*). 4 (of wine etc.) sharp or harsh in taste. 5 harsh, insensitive (*rough words; rough treatment*). 6 a unpleasant, severe, demanding (*had a rough time*). b unfortunate; undeserved (*had rough luck*). c (often foll. by *on*) hard or unfair (towards). 7 lacking finish etc. 8 incomplete, rudimentary, approximate (*rough attempt; rough sketch; rough estimate*). 9 (of stationery etc) used for rough notes etc. 10 *colloq.* unwell; depressed (*feeling rough*). —*adv.* in a rough manner (*play rough*). —*n.* 1 (usu. prec. by *the*) hardship (*take the rough with the smooth*). 2 rough ground, esp. on a golf-course (*went into the rough*). 3 violent person (*bunch of roughs*). 4 unfinished or natural state (*written it in rough*). —*v.* 1 (foll. by *up*) ruffle (feathers, hair, etc., esp. by rubbing). 2 (foll. by *out, in*) shape, plan, or sketch roughly. □ **rough it** *colloq.* do without basic comforts. **rough up** *slang* attack violently. □ **roughish** *adj.* **roughness** *n.* [Old English]

roughage *n.* coarse fibrous material in food, stimulating intestinal action.

rough-and-ready *adj.* crude but effective; not over-particular.

rough-and-tumble —*adj.* irregular, scrambling, disorderly. —*n.* disorderly fight; scuffle.

roughcast —*n.* (often *attrib.*) plaster of lime and gravel, used on outside walls. —*adj.* (of a plan etc.) roughly formed, preliminary. —*v.* (*past* and *past part.* **-cast**) 1 coat with roughcast. 2 prepare in outline.

rough diamond *n.* 1 uncut diamond 2 rough-mannered but honest person.

rough-dry *v.* dry (clothes) without ironing.

roughen *v.* make or become rough.

rough-hewn *adj.* uncouth, unrefined.

rough house *n. slang* disturbance or row; boisterous play.

rough justice *n.* 1 treatment that is approximately fair. 2 unjust treatment.

roughly *adv.* 1 in a rough manner. 2 approximately (*roughly 20 people*). □ **roughly speaking** approximately.

roughneck *n. colloq.* 1 worker on an oil rig. 2 rough or rowdy person.

rough-rider *n.* person who breaks in or rides unbroken horses.

roughshod *adj.* (of a horse) having shoes with nail-heads projecting to prevent slipping. □ **ride roughshod over** treat inconsiderately or arrogantly.

roulade /ruː'lɑːd/ *n.* 1 rolled piece of meat, sponge, etc. with a filling. 2 quick succession of notes, esp. sung to one syllable. [French *rouler* roll]

roulette /ruː'let/ *n.* gambling game in which a ball is dropped on to a revolving numbered wheel. [French, = little wheel]

round —*adj.* 1 shaped like a circle, sphere, or cylinder; convex; circular, curved, not angular. 2 gone with or involving circular motion. 3 entire, continuous, complete (*round dozen*). 4 candid, outspoken 5 (usu. *attrib.*) (of a number) expressed for brevity as a complete number (*£297.32 or in round figures £300*). 6 (of a voice, style, etc.) flowing, sonorous. —*n.* 1 round object or form. 2 a revolving motion or course (*yearly round*). b recurring series of activities, meetings, etc. (*continuous round of pleasure; round of talks*). 3 a fixed route for deliveries (*milk round*). b route for deliveries or inspection (*watchman's round, doctor's round*). 4 drink e.t.c. for each member of a group. 5 a one bullet, shell, etc. b act of firing this. 6 a slice from a loaf of bread. b sandwich made from two slices. c joint of beef from the haunch. 7 set, series, or sequence of actions in turn esp.: a one spell of play in a game etc. b one stage in a competition. 8 *Golf* playing of all the holes in a course once. 9 song for unaccompanied voices overlapping at intervals. 10 rung of a ladder. 11 (foll. by *of*) circumference or extent of (*in all the*

round of Nature). —adv. **1** with circular motion (wheels go round). **2** with return to the starting-point or an earlier state (summer soon comes round). **3** with change to an opposite position, opinion, etc. (turned round to look; soon won them round). **4** to, at, or affecting a circumference, area, group, etc. (tea was handed round; may I look round?). **5** in every direction within a radius (spread destruction round). **6** circuitously (go the long way round). **7** to a person's house, a convenient place, etc. (ask him round; will be round soon; brought the car round). **8** measuring (a specified distance) in girth. —prep. **1** so as to encircle or enclose (a blanket round him). **2** at or to points on the circumference of (sat round the table). **3** with successive visits to (hawks them round the cafés). **4** within a radius of (towns round Birmingham). **5** having as an axis or central point (planned a book round the War). **6 a** so as to pass in a curved course (go round the corner). **b** having so passed (be round the corner). **c** in the resulting position (find them round the corner). —v. **1** give or take a round shape. **2** pass round (a corner, cape, etc.). **3** (usu. foll. by up, down) express (a number) approximately, for brevity. □ **go the round** (or **rounds**) (of news etc.) be passed on in **the round 1** with all features shown; all things considered. **2** with the audience on at least three sides of the stage. **3** (of sculpture) with all sides shown. **round about 1** all round; on all sides (of). **2** approximately (round about £50). **round and round** several times round. **round the bend** see BEND¹. **round off** make complete or less angular. **round on** attack unexpectedly, esp. verbally. **round out 1** provide with more details. **2** complete, finish. **round the twist** see TWIST. **round up 1** collect or bring together. **2** = sense 3 of v. □ **roundish** adj. **roundness** n. [Latin: related to ROTUND]

roundabout —n. **1** road junction at which traffic circulates in one direction round a central island. **2 a** large revolving device for children to ride on in a playground. **b** = MERRY-GO-ROUND 1. —adj. circuitous.

round brackets n.pl. brackets of the form ( ).

round dance n. dance in which couples move in circles or dancers form one large circle.

roundel /ˈraʊnd(ə)l/ n. **1** circular mark, esp. identifying military aircraft. **2** small disc, esp. a medallion. [French rondel(le): related to ROUND]

roundelay /ˈraʊndɪleɪ/ n. short simple song with a refrain. [alteration of French rondelet diminutive: related to ROUNDEL]

rounder n. **1** (in pl.; treated as sing.) ball game in which players hit the ball and run through a round of bases. **2** complete run as a unit of scoring in rounders.

Roundhead n. hist. member of the Parliamentary party in the English Civil War.

roundly adv. bluntly, severely. (told them roundly).

round robin n. **1** petition, esp. with signatures in a circle to conceal the order of writing. **2** US tournament in which each competitor plays every other.

round-shouldered adj. having shoulders bent forward and a rounded back.

roundsman n. tradesman's employee delivering goods.

Round Table n. **1** international charitable association. **2** (**round table**) assembly for discussion, esp. at a conference (often attrib.: round-table talks).

round trip n. trip to one or more places and back again.

round-up n. **1** systematic rounding up. **2** summary or résumé.

roundworm n. worm with a rounded body.

rouse /raʊz/ v. (-sing) **1** (cause to) wake. **2** (often foll. by up, often refl.) stir up, make or become active or excited (was roused to protest). **3** anger (terrible when roused). **4** evoke (feelings). [origin unknown]

rousing adj. exciting, stirring (rousing song).

roustabout /ˈraʊstəˌbaʊt/ n. **1** labourer on an oil rig. **2** unskilled or casual labourer. [roust rout out, rouse]

rout¹ —n. **1** disorderly retreat of defeated troops (put them to rout). **2** overthrow, defeat. —v. (-ting) send, forward, or direct by a particular route. [French route road, from Latin rupta (via)]

route /ruːt/ —n. way or course taken (esp. regularly) from one place to another. —v. (-teing) send, forward, or direct by a particular route. [French route road, from Latin rupta (via)]

route march n. training-march for troops.

routine /ruːˈtiːn/ —n. **1** regular course or procedure, unvarying performance of certain acts. **2** set sequence in a dance, comedy act, etc. **3** Computing sequence of instructions for a particular task. —adj. **1** performed as part of a routine (routine duties). **2** of a customary or

standard. kind. □ **routinely** adv.

roux /ruː/ n. (pl. same) mixture of fat and flour used in sauces etc. [French]

rove[1] v. (-ving) 1 wander without settling; roam, ramble. 2 (of eyes) look about. [probably Scandinavian]

rove[2] past of REEVE[2].

rover[1] n. wanderer.

rover[2] n. pirate. [Low German or Dutch]

roving eye n. tendency to infidelity.

row[1] /rəʊ/ n. 1 line of persons or things. 2 line of seats across a theatre etc. 3 street with houses along one or each side. □ **in a row** 1 forming a row. 2 colloq. in succession (two days in a row). [Old English]

row[2] /rəʊ/ v. (-ving) 1 propel (a boat) with oars 2 convey (a passenger) thus. —n. 1 spell of rowing. 2 trip in a rowing-boat. □ **rower** n. [Old English]

row[3] /raʊ/ colloq. —n. 1 loud noise or commotion. 2 fierce quarrel or dispute. 3 severe reprimand. —v. 1 make or engage in a row. 2 reprimand. [origin unknown]

rowan /ˈrəʊən/ n. (in full **rowan-tree**) 1 mountain ash. 2 (in full **rowan-berry**) its scarlet berry. [Scandinavian]

row-boat n. US = ROWING-BOAT.

rowdy /ˈraʊdɪ/ —adj. (-ier, -iest) noisy and disorderly. —n. (pl. -ies) rowdy person. □ **rowdily** adv. **rowdiness** n. **rowdyism** n. [origin unknown]

rowel /ˈraʊəl/ n. spiked revolving disc at the end of a spur. [Latin rotella dimin. of ROTA]

rowing-boat n. small boat propelled by oars.

rowlock /ˈrɒlək/ n. device on a boat's side for holding an oar in place. [earlier from Old English: related to OAR, LOCK[1]]

royal /ˈrɔɪəl/ —adj. 1 of, suited to, or worthy of a king or queen. 2 in the service or under the patronage of a king or queen. 3 of the family of a king or queen. 4 majestic, splendid. 5 exceptional, first-rate (had a royal time). —n. colloq. member of the royal family. □ **royally** adv. [Latin: related to REGAL]

royal blue adj. & n. (as adj. often hyphenated) deep vivid blue.

Royal British Legion n. national association of ex-members of the armed forces, founded in 1921.

Royal Commission n. commission of inquiry appointed by the Crown at the request of Government.

royal family n. family of a sovereign.

royal flush n. straight poker flush headed by an ace.

royal icing n. hard white icing for cakes.

royalist n. supporter of monarchy, or hist. of the roya. side in the English Civil War. □ **royalism** n.

royal jelly n. substance secreted by worker bees and fed by them to future queen bees.

Royal Marine n. British marine (see MARINE n. 1).

Royal Navy n. British navy.

royalty n. (pl. -ies) 1 royal office, dignity, or power; being royal. 2 a royal persons. b member of a royal family. 3 percentage of profit from a book, public performance, patent, etc. paid to the author etc. 4 a royal right (now esp. over minerals) granted by the sovereign. b payment made by a producer of minerals etc. to the owner of the site etc. [French: related to ROYAL]

royal warrant n. warrant authorizing a tradesperson to supply goods to a specified royal person.

royal 'we' n. use of 'we' instead of 'I' by a single person.

RP abbr. received pronunciation.

RPI abbr. retail price index.

rpm abbr. revolutions per minute.

RPO abbr. Royal Philharmonic Orchestra.

RSA abbr. 1 Royal Society of Arts. 2 Royal Scottish Academy; Royal Scottish Academician.

RSC abbr. Royal Shakespeare Company.

RSJ abbr. rolled steel joist.

RSM abbr. Regimental Sergeant-Major.

RSPB abbr. Royal Society for the Protection of Birds.

RSPCA abbr. Royal Soc.ety for the Prevention of Cruelty to Animals.

RSV abbr. Revised Standard Version (of the Bible).

RSVP abbr. (in an invitation etc.) please answer. [French répondez s'il vous plaît]

rt. abbr. right.

Rt. Hon. abbr. Right Honourable.

Rt. Revd. abbr. (also **Rt. Rev.**) Right Reverend.

RU abbr. Rugby Union.

Ru symb. ruthenium.

rub —v. (-bb-) 1 move something, esp. one's hand, with firm pressure over the surface of. 2 (usu. foll. by against, in, on, over) apply (one's hand etc.) in this way. 3 clean, polish, chafe, or make dry, sore, or bare by rubbing. 4 (foll. by in, into, through, over) apply (polish etc.) by rubbing. 5 (often foll. by together, against, on) move with contact or friction. 6 (of cloth, skin, etc.) become frayed, worn, sore, or bare with friction.

rubato —*n.* **1** act or spell of rubbing (*give it a rub*). **2** impediment or difficulty (*there's the rub*). □ **rub along** *colloq.* cope or manage routinely. **rub down** dry, smooth, or clean by rubbing. **rub it in** (or **rub a person's nose in it**) emphasize or repeat an embarrassing fact etc. **rub off 1** (usu. foll. by *on*) be transmitted by contact, be transmitted (*his attitudes have rubbed off on me*). **2** remove by rubbing. **rub out** erase with a rubber. **rub shoulders with** associate with. **rub up 1** polish. **2** brush up (a subject or one's memory). **rub up the wrong way** irritate. [Low German]

rubato /ruːˈbɑːtəʊ/ *n. Mus.* (*pl.* -s or -ti /-ti/) temporary disregarding of strict tempo. [Italian, = robbed]

rubber[1] *n.* **1** tough elastic substance made from the latex of plants or synthetically. **2** piece of this or a similar substance for erasing esp. pencil marks. **3** *colloq.* condom. **4** (in *pl.*) *US* galoshes. □ **rubbery** *adj.* **rubberiness** *n.* [from RUB]

rubber[2] *n.* match of esp. three successive games between the same sides or persons at whist, bridge, cricket, etc. [origin unknown]

rubber band *n.* loop of rubber for holding papers etc. together.

rubberize *v.* (also **-ise**) (**-zing** or **-sing**) treat or coat with rubber.

rubberneck *colloq.* —*n.* inquisitive person, esp. a tourist or sightseer. —*v.* behave like a rubberneck.

rubber plant *n.* **1** evergreen tropical plant often cultivated as a house-plant. **2** (also **rubber tree**) tropical tree yielding latex.

rubber stamp —*n.* **1** device for inking and imprinting on a surface. **2** a person who mechanically copies or endorses others' actions. **b** indication of such endorsement. —*v.* (**rubber-stamp**) approve automatically.

rubbing *n.* impression or copy made by rubbing.

rub-down *n.* rubbing down.

rubella /ruːˈbelə/ *n. formal* German measles. [Latin *rubellus* reddish]

Rubicon /ˈruːbɪ.kən/ *n.* boundary; point from which there is no going back. [*Rubicon*, river on ancient frontier of Italy]

rubicund /ˈruːbɪ.kənd/ *adj.* (of a face, complexion, etc.) ruddy, high-coloured. [Latin *rubor* be red]

rubidium /ruːˈbɪdɪəm/ *n.* soft silvery metallic element. [Latin *rubidus* red]

Rubik's cube /ˈruːbɪks/ *n.* cube-shaped puzzle in which composite faces must be restored to single colours by rotation. [*Rubik*, name of its inventor]

ruble var. of ROUBLE.

rubric /ˈruːbrɪk/ *n.* **1** heading or passage in red or special lettering. **2** explanatory words. **3** established custom or rule. **4** direction for the conduct of divine service in a liturgical book. [Latin *ruber* red]

ruby /ˈruːbɪ/ —*n.* (*pl.* -ies) **1** rare precious stone varying in colour from deep crimson to pale rose. **2** deep red colour. —*adj.* of this colour. [Latin *rubeus* red]

ruby wedding *n.* fortieth wedding anniversary.

RUC *abbr.* Royal Ulster Constabulary.

ruche /ruːʃ/ *n.* frill or gathering of lace etc. □ **ruched** *adj.* [French, = beehive]

ruck[1] *n.* **1** (prec. by *the*) main body of competitors not likely to overtake the leaders. **2** undistinguished crowd or group. **3** *Rugby* loose scrum. [apparently Scandinavian]

ruck[2] —*v.* (often foll. by *up*) make or become creased or wrinkled. —*n.* crease or wrinkle. [Old Norse]

rucksack /ˈrʌksæk/ *n.* bag carried on the back, esp. by hikers. [German]

ruckus /ˈrʌkəs/ *n. US informal* row, commotion. [perhaps from RUCTION or RUMPUS]

ruction /ˈrʌkʃ(ə)n/ *n. colloq.* **1** disturbance or tumult. **2** (in *pl.*) row, heated arguments. [origin unknown]

rudder *n.* flat piece hinged vertically to the stern of a ship or on the tailplane of an aircraft etc., for steering. □ **rudderless** *adj.* [Old English]

ruddy /ˈrʌdɪ/ *adj.* (**-ier**, **-iest**) **1** (of a person, complexion, etc.) freshly or healthily red. **2** reddish. **3** *colloq.* bloody, damnable. □ **ruddily** *adv.* **ruddiness** *n.* [Old English]

rude *adj.* **1** impolite or offensive. **2** roughly made or done; crude (*rude plough*). **3** primitive or uneducated (*rude simplicity*). **4** abrupt, sudden, startling (*rude awakening*). **5** *colloq.* indecent, lewd (*rude joke*). **6** vigorous or hearty (*rude health*). □ **rudely** *adv.* **rudeness** *n.* [Latin *rudis*]

rudiment /ˈruːdɪmənt/ *n.* **1** (in *pl.*) elements or first principles of a subject. **2** (in *pl.*) imperfect beginning of something undeveloped or yet to develop. **3** vestigial or undeveloped part or organ.

□ **rudimentary** /ˌ-ˈmentəri/ *adj.* [Latin: related to RUDE]

rue¹ *v.* (**rues, rued, rueing** or **ruing**) repent of; wish to be undone or non-existent (esp. *rue the day*). [Old English]

rue² *n.* evergreen shrub with bitter strong-scented leaves. [Greek *rhutē*]

rueful *adj.* genuinely or humorously sorrowful. □ **ruefully** *adv.* **ruefulness** *n.* [from RUE¹]

ruff¹ *n.* 1 projecting starched frill worn round the neck, esp. in the 16th c. 2 projecting or coloured ring of feathers or hair round a bird's or animal's neck. 3 domestic pigeon. 4 (*fem.* **reeve** /reev/) wading bird with a ruff. [perhaps = ROUGH]

ruff² *v. & n.* trump at cards. □ trumping. [French *ro(u)fle*]

ruffian /ˈrʌfiən/ *n.* violent lawless person. [Italian *ruffiano*]

ruffle /ˈrʌf(ə)l/ —*v.* (**-ling**) 1 a disturb the smoothness or tranquility of. b undergo this. 2 gather (lace etc.) into a ruffle. 3 (often foll. by *up*) (of a bird) erect (its feathers) in anger, display, etc. —*n.* frill of lace etc., esp. round the wrist or neck. [origin unknown]

rufous /ˈruːfəs/ *adj.* (esp. of animals) reddish-brown. [Latin *rufus*]

rug *n.* 1 thick floor covering, usu. smaller than a carpet. 2 thick woollen coverlet or wrap. □ **pull the rug from under** deprive of support; weaken, unsettle. [probably Scandinavian]

Rugby /ˈrʌgbi/ *n.* (in full **Rugby football**) team game played with an oval ball that may be kicked or carried. [*Rugby school*, where it was first played]

Rugby League *n.* partly professional Rugby with teams of 13.

Rugby Union *n.* amateur Rugby with teams of 15.

rugged /ˈrʌgɪd/ *adj.* 1 (esp. of ground) rough, uneven. 2 (of features) wrinkled, furrowed, irregular. 3 a unpolished, lacking refinement (*rugged grandeur*). b harsh in sound. 4 robust, hardy. □ **ruggedly** *adv.* **ruggedness** *n.* [probably Scandinavian]

rugger /ˈrʌgə(r)/ *n. colloq.* Rugby.

ruin /ˈruːɪn/ —*n.* 1 destroyed, wrecked, or spoiled state. 2 downfall or elimination (*ruin of my hopes*). 3 complete loss of one's property or position (*bring to ruin*). 4 (in *sing.* or *pl.*) remains of a building etc. that has suffered ruin. 5 cause of ruin (*the ruin of us*). —*v.* 1 a bring to ruin (*extravagance has ruined me*). b spoil, damage. 2 (esp. as **ruined** *adj.*) reduce to ruins. □ **in ruins** completely wrecked (*hopes were in ruins*). [Latin *ruo* fall]

ruination /ˌruːɪˈneɪʃ(ə)n/ *n.* 1 bringing to ruin. 2 ruining or being ruined.

ruinous *adj.* 1 bringing ruin; disastrous (*ruinous expense*). 2 dilapidated. □ **ruinously** *adv.*

rule —*n.* 1 compulsory principle or standard. 2 prevailing custom or standard; normal state of things. 3 government or dominion (*under British rule*). 4 graduated straight measure; ruler. 5 code of discipline or a religious order. 6 order made by a judge or court with reference to a particular case only. 7 *Printing* thin line or dash. —*v.* (**-ling**) 1 dominate; keep under control. 2 (often foll. by *over*) have sovereign control of (*rules over a vast kingdom*). 3 (often foll. by *that*) pronounce authoritatively. 4 a make parallel lines across (paper). b make (a straight line) with a ruler etc. □ **as a rule** usually. **rule out** exclude; pronounce irrelevant or ineligible. **rule the roost** be in control. [Latin *regula*]

rule of thumb *n.* rule based on experience or practice rather than theory.

ruler *n.* 1 person exercising government or dominion. 2 straight usu. graduated strip of wood, metal, or plastic used to draw or measure.

ruling *n.* authoritative pronouncement.

rum¹ *n.* spirit distilled from sugar-cane or molasses. [origin unknown]

rum² *adj.* (**rummer, rummest**) *colloq.* odd, strange, queer. [origin unknown]

rumba /ˈrʌmbə/ *n.* 1 Latin American ballroom dance orig. from Cuba. 2 music for this. [American Spanish]

rum baba *n.* sponge cake soaked in rum syrup.

rumble /ˈrʌmb(ə)l/ —*v.* (**-ling**) 1 make a continuous deep resonant sound as of distant thunder. 2 (foll. by *along, by, past,* etc.) (esp. of a vehicle) move with a rumbling noise. 3 (often *colloq.*) *slang* find out the esp. discreditable truth about. —*n.* rumbling sound. [probably Dutch *rommelen*]

rumbustious /rʌmˈbʌstʃəs/ *adj. colloq.* boisterous, noisy, uproarious. [probably var. of *robustious* from ROBUST]

ruminant /ˈruːmɪnənt/ —*n.* animal that chews the cud. —*adj.* 1 of ruminants. 2 meditative. [related to RUMINATE]

ruminate /ˈruːmɪneɪt/ *v.* (**-ting**) 1 meditate, ponder. 2 chew the cud. □ **rumination** /-ˈneɪʃ(ə)n/ *n.* **ruminative** /-nətɪv/ *adj.* [Latin *rumen* throat]

rummage /ˈrʌmɪdʒ/ —*v.* (**-ging**) 1 search, esp. unsystematically. 2 (foll. by *out, up*) find among other things. —*n.* rummaging. [French *arrumage* from *arrumer* stow cargo]

rummage sale n. esp. US jumble sale.

rummy /ˈrʌmɪ/ n. card-game played usu. with two packs. [origin unknown]

rumour /ˈruːmə(r)/ (US **rumor**) —n. (often foll. by of or that) general talk, assertion, or hearsay of doubtful accuracy (heard a rumour that you are leaving). —v. (usu. in passive) report by way of rumour (it is rumoured that you are leaving). [Latin rumor noise]

rump n. 1 hind part of a mammal or bird, esp. the buttocks. 2 remnant of a parliament etc. [probably Scandinavian]

rumple /ˈrʌmp(ə)l/ v. (-**ling**) crease, ruffle. [Dutch rompelen]

rump steak n. cut of beef from the rump.

rumpus /ˈrʌmpəs/ n. colloq. disturbance, brawl, row, or uproar. [origin unknown]

run —v. (-**nn**-; past **ran**; past part. **run**) 1 go with quick steps, never having both or all feet on the ground at once. 2 flee, abscond. 3 go or travel hurriedly or briefly (I'll just run down to the shops) 4 a advance by or as by rolling or on wheels, or smoothly or easily. b (cause to) be in action or operation or go in a specified way (left the engine running; ran the car into a tree). 5 be current or operative (lease runs for 99 years). 6 travel on its route (train is running late). 7 (of a play etc.) be staged or presented (now running at the Apollo). 8 extend; have a course, order, or tendency (road runs by the coast; prices are running high). 9 a (often absol.) compete in (a race). b finish a race in a specified position. 10 (often foll. by for) seek election (ran for president). 11 flow (with) or be wet; drip (with) (walls running with condensation). 12 a cause (water etc.) to flow. b fill (a bath) thus. 13 spread rapidly (ink ran over the table). 14 traverse (a course, race, or distance). 15 perform (an errand). 16 publish (an article etc.) in a newspaper etc. 17 direct or manage (a business etc.). 18 own and use (a vehicle) regularly. 19 transport in a private vehicle (ran me to the station). 20 enter (a horse etc.) for a race. 21 smuggle (guns etc.). 22 chase or hunt. 23 allow (an account) to accumulate before paying. 24 (of a dyed colour) spread from the dyed parts. 25 a (of a thought, the eye, the memory, etc.) pass quickly (ideas ran through my mind). b pass (one's eye) quickly (ran my eye down the page). 26 (of tights etc.) ladder. 27 (of esp. the eyes or nose) exude liquid. —n. 1 running. 2 short excursion. 3 distance travelled. 4 general tendency. 5 regular route. 6 continuous stretch, spell, or

course (run of bad luck). 7 (often foll. by on) high general demand (run on the dollar). 8 quantity produced at one time (print run). 9 average type or class (general run of customers). 10 point scored in cricket or baseball. 11 (foll by of) free use of or access to (run of the house). 12 a animal's regular track. b enclosure for fowls etc. c range of pasture. 13 ladder in tights etc. 14 Mus. rapid scale passage. 15 (in full the runs) colloq. diarrhoea. □ on the run fleeing. **run about 1** bustle, hurry. 2 (esp. of children) play freely. **run across** happen to meet or find. **run after 1** pursue at a run. 2 pursue, esp. sexually. **run along** colloq. depart. **run around** 1 take from place to place by car etc. 2 (often foll. by with) slang engage in esp. promiscuous sexual relations. **run away 1** flee, abscond. 2 (often foll. by from) flee, abscond. **run away with 1** carry off. 2 win easily. 3 deprive of self-control, carry away. 4 consume (money etc.). 5 (of a horse) bolt with (a rider etc.). 6 leave home to have a relationship with (esp. another person's husband or wife). **run down 1** knock down. 2 reduce the numbers etc. of. 3 (of an unwound clock etc.) stop. 4 discover after a search. 5 colloq. disparage. **run dry 1** cease to flow. 2 = run out 1. **run for it** seek safety by fleeing. **run (or good run) for one's money 1** vigorous or close competition. 2 some return for outlay or effort. **run the gauntlet** see GAUNTLET². **run high** (of feelings) be strong. **run in 1** run (an engine or vehicle) carefully when new. 2 colloq. arrest. **run in the family** (of a trait) be common in a family. **run into 1** collide with. 2 encounter. 3 reach as many as (a run away with 6. **run on 1** continue in operation. 2 speak volubly or incessantly. 3 continue on the same line as the preceding matter. **run out 1** come to an end. 2 (foll. by of) exhaust one's stock of. 3 put down the wicket of (a running batsman). **run out on** colloq. desert (a person). **run over 1** (of a vehicle etc.) knock down or crush. 2 overflow. 3 study or repeat quickly (ran my eye down the page). **run ragged** exhaust (a person). **run rings round** see RING¹. **run riot** see RIOT. **run through 1** examine or rehearse briefly. 2 peruse. 3

colloq. high figure). **run into the ground** colloq. bring (a person) to exhaustion etc. **run low** (or **short**) become depleted, have too little. **run off 1** flee. 2 produce (copies etc.) on a machine. 3 decide (a race etc.) after heats or a tie. 4 (cause to) flow away. 5 write or recite fluently. **run off with 1** steal. 2 = run

deal, successively with. **4** spend money rapidly or recklessly. **5** pervade. **6** pierce with a sword etc. **run** to **1** have the money, resources, or ability for. **2** reach (an amount or number). **3** (of a person) show a tendency to (*runs to* fat). **run to earth** see EARTH. **run to seed** see SEED. **run up 1** accumulate (a debt etc.). **2** build or make hurriedly. **3** raise (a flag). **run up against** meet with (a difficulty etc.). [Old English]

runabout *n.* light car or aircraft.

run-around *n.* (esp. in phr. **give a person the run-around**) *colloq.* deceit or evasion.

runaway *n.* **1** fugitive. **2** bolting animal, vehicle out of control. **3** (*attrib.*) that is running away, or out of control (*runaway slave; runaway inflation*).

run-down *n.* **1** reduction in numbers. **2** detailed analysis. —*adj.* **1** decayed, dilapidated. (from over-work, illness, etc.).

rune *n.* **1** letter of the earliest Germanic alphabet. **2** similar mark of mysterious or magic significance. □ **runic** *adj.* [Old Norse]

rung[1] *n.* **1** step of a ladder. **2** strengthening crosspiece in a chair etc. [Old English]

rung[2] *past part.* of RING[2].

run-in *n.* **1** approach to an action or event. **2** *colloq.* quarrel.

runnel /ˈrʌn(ə)l/ *n.* **1** brook. **2** gutter. [Old English]

runner *n.* **1** person, horse, etc. that runs, esp. in a race. **2** creeping rooting plant-stem. **3** rod, groove, roller, or blade on which a thing, e.g. a sledge, slides. **4** sliding ring on a rod etc. **5** messenger. **6** (in full **runner bean**) twining bean plant with long flat green edible seed pods. **7** long narrow ornamental cloth or rug. □ **do a runner** *slang* leave hastily, flee.

runner-up *n.* (*pl.* **runners-up** or **runner-ups**) competitor or team taking second place.

running —*n.* **1** action of runners in a race etc. **2** way a race etc. proceeds. —*adj.* **1** continuous (*running battle*). **2** consecutive (*three days running*). **3** done with a run (*running jump*). **4** (*in* or *out of*) **the running** (of a competitor) with a good (or poor) chance of success. **make** (*or* **take up**) **the running** take the lead; set the pace. **take a running jump** (esp. as *int.*) *slang* go away.

running-board *n.* footboard on either side of a vehicle.

running commentary *n.* verbal description of an esp. sporting event.

running knot *n.* knot that slips along a rope etc. to allow tightening etc.

running mate *n.* US **1** candidate for vice-president etc. **2** horse intended to set the pace for another horse in a race.

running repairs *n.pl.* minor or temporary repairs etc.

running sore *n.* suppurating sore; festering situation etc.

running water *n.* flowing water, esp. on tap.

runny *adj.* (**-ier**, **-iest**) **1** tending to run or flow. **2** excessively fluid.

run-off *n.* additional election, race, etc., after a tie.

run-of-the-mill *adj.* ordinary, undistinguished.

run-out *n.* dismissal of a batsman by being Run out.

runt *n.* **1** smallest pig etc. in a litter. **2** weakling; undersized person. [origin unknown]

run-through *n.* **1** rehearsal. **2** brief survey.

run-up *n.* (often foll. by *to*) preparatory period.

runway *n.* specially prepared surface for aircraft taking off and landing.

rupee /ruːˈpiː/ *n.* chief monetary unit of India, Pakistan, etc. [Hindustani]

rupiah /ruːˈpiːə/ *n.* chief monetary unit of Indonesia. [related to RUPEE]

rupture /ˈrʌptʃə(r)/ —*n.* **1** breaking, breach. **2** breach in a relationship; disagreement and parting. **3** abdominal hernia. —*v.* (**-ring**) **1** burst (a cell or membrane etc.). **2** sever (a connection). **3** affect with or suffer a hernia. [Latin *rumpo rupt-* break]

rural /ˈrʊər(ə)l/ *adj.* in of, or suggesting the country (*rural seclusion*). [Latin *rus rur-* the country]

rural dean see DEAN[1].

rural district *n. hist.* group of country parishes with an elected council.

ruse /ruːz/ *n.* stratagem, trick. [French]

rush[1] —*v.* **1** go, move, flow, or act precipitately or with great haste (*was rushed to hospital*). **3** (foll. by *at*) **a** move suddenly towards. **b** begin or attack impetuously. **4** perform or deal with hurriedly (*don't rush your dinner*). **5** force or induce (a person) to act hastily. **6** attack or capture by sudden assault. **7** *slang* overcharge (a customer). —*n.* **1 a** rushing; violent or speedy advance or attack. **b** sudden flow. flood. **2** period of great activity. **3** (*attrib.*) done with great haste or speed (*a rush job*). **4** sudden migration of large numbers. **5** (foll. by *on*, *for*) sudden strong demand for a commodity. **6** (in *pl.*) *colloq.* first uncut

prints of a film. [French *ruser*: related to RUSE]

rush² *n.* **1** marsh plant with slender tapering pith-filled stems, used for making chair-bottoms, baskets, etc. **2** stem of this. □ **rushy** *adj.* [Old English]

rush candle *n.* candle made of rush pith dipped in tallow.

rush hour *n.* (often hyphenated when *attrib.*) time(s) each day when traffic is heaviest.

rushlight *n.* rush candle.

rusk *n.* slice of bread rebaked as a light biscuit, esp. as baby food. [Spanish or Portuguese *rosca* twist]

russet /'rʌsɪt/ —*adj.* reddish-brown. —*n.* **1** russet colour. **2** rough-skinned russet-coloured apple. [Latin *russus*]

Russian /'rʌʃ(ə)n/ —*n.* **1 a** native or national of Russia or (loosely) the former Soviet Union. **b** person of Russian descent. **2** language of Russia. —*adj.* **1** of Russia or (loosely) the former Soviet Union or its people. **2** of or in Russian.

Russian roulette *n.* firing of a revolver, with one chamber loaded, at one's head, after spinning the chamber.

Russian salad *n.* salad of mixed diced vegetables with mayonnaise.

Russo- *comb. form* Russian; Russian and.

rust —*n.* **1** reddish corrosive coating formed on iron, steel, etc. by oxidation, esp. when wet. **2** fungal plant-disease with rust-coloured spots. **3** impaired state due to disuse or inactivity. **4** reddish-brown. —*v.* **1** affect or be affected with rust. **2** become impaired through disuse. [Old English]

rustic /'rʌstɪk/ —*adj.* **1** of or like country people or country life. **2** unsophisticated. **3** of rude or rough workmanship. **4** made of untrimmed branches or rough timber (*rustic bench*). **5** *Archit.* with a roughened or rough-hewn surface. —*n.* country person, peasant. □ **rusticity** /-'tɪstɪ/ *n.* [Latin *rus* the country]

rusticate /'rʌstɪ.keɪt/ *v.* (**-ting**) **1** send down (a student) temporarily from university. **2** retire to or live in the country. **3** make rustic. □ **rustication** /-'keɪʃ(ə)n/ *n.*

rustle /'rʌs(ə)l/ —*v.* (**-ling**) **1** (cause to) make a gentle sound as of dry blown leaves. **2** (also *absol.*) steal (cattle or horses). —*n.* rustling sound. □ **rustle up** *colloq.* produce at short notice. □ **rustler** *n.* (esp. in sense 2 of *v.*). [limitative]

rustproof —*adj.* not susceptible to corrosion by rust. —*v.* make rustproof.

rusty *adj.* (**-ier**, **-iest**) **1** rusted or affected by rust **2** stiff with age or disuse. **3** (of knowledge etc.) impaired, lost by neglect (*my French is rusty*). **4** rust-coloured. **5** (of black clothes) discoloured by age. □ **rustiness** *n.*

rut¹ —*n.* **1** deep track made by the passage of wheels. **2** established (esp. tedious) practice or routine (*in a rut*). —*v.* (**-tt-**) mark with ruts. [probably French: related to ROUTE]

rut² —*n.* periodic sexual excitement of a male deer etc. —*v.* (**-tt-**) be affected with rut. [Latin *rugio* roar]

ruthenium /ruː'θiːnɪəm/ *n.* rare hard white metallic element from platinum ores. [medieval Latin *Ruthenia* Russia]

rutherfordium /ˌrʌðə'fɔːdɪəm/ *n.* artificial metallic element. [*Rutherford*, name of a physicist]

ruthless /'ruːθlɪs/ *adj.* having no pity or compassion. □ **ruthlessly** *adv.* **ruthlessness** *n.* [*ruth* pity, from RUE¹]

RV *abbr.* Revised Version (of the Bible).

-ry *suffix* = -ERY (*infantry; rivalry*).

rye /raɪ/ *n.* **1 a** cereal plant. **b** grain of this used for bread and fodder. **2** (in full **rye whisky**) whisky distilled from fermented rye. [Old English]

ryegrass *n.* forage or coarse lawn grass. [alteration of *ray-grass*]

S

S¹ /es/ *n.* (also **s**) (*pl.* **Ss** or **S's**) **1** nineteenth letter of the alphabet. **2** S-shaped thing.

S² *abbr.* (also **S**) **1** Saint. **2** South, Southern.

S³ *symb.* sulphur.

s. *abbr.* **1** second(s). **2** *hist.* shilling(s). **3** son. [sense 2 originally from Latin *solidus*]

-s¹ *suffix* denoting the plural of most nouns ending in *-s* (*the boys' shoes*).

's¹ *suffix* denoting the possessive case of singular nouns and sometimes of plural nouns ending in *-s* (*the boys' shoes*; *Charles' book*). [Old English inflection]

's² *abbr.* **1** is; has (*he's*; *she's got it*; *John's*; *Charles's*). **2** us (*let's*).

's³ *suffix* denoting the possessive case of singular nouns and of plural nouns not ending in *-s* (*John's book*; *book's cover*; *children's shoes*).

SA *abbr.* **1** Salvation Army. **2** South Africa. **3** South Australia.

sabbath /ˈsæbəθ/ *n.* religious day of rest kept by Christians on Sunday and Jews on Saturday. [Hebrew, = rest]

sabbatical /səˈbætɪk(ə)l/ —*adj.* (of leave) granted at intervals to a university teacher for study or travel. —*n.* period of sabbatical leave. [Greek: related to SABBATH]

sable /ˈseɪb(ə)l/ —*n.* (*pl.* same or **-s**) **1** small brown-furred mammal of N. Europe and N. Asia. **2** its skin or fur. —*adj.* **1** (of) black. **2** *poet.* gloomy. [Slavonic]

sabot /ˈsæbəʊ/ *n.* **1** shoe carved from wood. **2** wooden-soled shoe. [French]

sabotage /ˈsæbətɑːʒ/ —*n.* deliberate damage to productive capacity, esp. as a political act. —*v.* (**-ging**) **1** commit sabotage on. **2** destroy, spoil. [French: related to SABOT]

saboteur /sæbəˈtɜː(r)/ *n.* person who commits sabotage. [French]

sabre /ˈseɪbə(r)/ *n.* (*US* **saber**) **1** curved cavalry sword. **2** light tapering fencing-sword. [French from German *Sabel*]

sabre-rattling *n.* display or threat of military force.

sac *n.* membranous bag in an animal or plant. [Latin: related to SACK¹]

saccharin /ˈsækərɪn/ *n.* a sugar substitute. [medieval Latin *saccharum* sugar]

saccharine /ˈsækəriːn/ *adj.* excessively sentimental or sweet.

sacerdotal /sækəˈdəʊt(ə)l/ *adj.* of priests or priestly office. [Latin *sacerdos -dot-* priest]

sachet /ˈsæʃeɪ/ *n.* **1** small bag or packet containing shampoo etc. **2** small scented bag for perfuming drawers etc. [French diminutive: related to SAC]

sack¹ —*n.* **1 a** large strong bag for storage or conveyance. **b** quantity contained in a sack. **2** (prec. by *the*) *colloq.* dismissal from employment. **3** (prec. by *the*) *US slang* bed. —*v.* **1** put into a sack or sacks. **2** *colloq.* dismiss from employment. [Latin *saccus*]

sack² —*v.* plunder and destroy (a captured town etc.). —*n.* such sacking. [French *mettre à sac* put in a sack]

sack³ *n. hist.* white wine from Spain and the Canaries. [French *vin sec* dry wine]

sackbut /ˈsækbʌt/ *n.* early form of trombone. [French]

sackcloth *n.* **1** coarse fabric of flax or hemp used for sacks. **2** clothing for penance or mourning (esp. *sackcloth and ashes*).

sacking *n.* material for making sacks; sackcloth.

sacral /ˈseɪkr(ə)l/ *adj.* **1** *Anat.* of the sacrum. **2** of or for sacred rites. [Latin *sacrum* sacred]

sacrament /ˈsækrəmənt/ *n.* **1** symbolic Christian ceremony, e.g. baptism and Eucharist. **2** (also **Blessed** or **Holy Sacrament**) (prec. by *the*) Eucharist. **3** sacred thing. □ **sacramental** /-ˈment(ə)l/ *adj.* [Latin: related to SACRED]

sacred /ˈseɪkrɪd/ *adj.* **1 a** (often foll. by *to*) dedicated to a god. **b** connected with religion (*sacred music*). **2** safeguarded or required esp. by tradition; inviolable. [Latin *sacer* holy]

sacred cow *n. colloq.* traditionally hallowed idea or institution.

sacrifice /ˈsækrɪfaɪs/ —*n.* **1 a** voluntary relinquishing of something valued. **b** the loss entailed. **c** thing so relinquished. **2 a** slaughter of an animal or person or surrender of a possession, as an offering to a deity. **b** animal, person, or thing so offered. **3** (a thing) as a sacrifice. —*v.* (**-cing**) **1** give up (a thing) as a sacrifice. **2** (foll. by *to*) devote or give over to. **3** (also *absol.*) offer or kill as a sacrifice. □ **sacrificial** /-ˈfɪʃ(ə)l/ *adj.* [Latin: related to SACRED]

sacrilege /ˈsækrɪlɪdʒ/ n. violation of what is regarded as sacred. □ **sacrilegious** /-ˈlɪdʒəs/ adj. [Latin: related to SACRED, lego take]

sacristan /ˈsækrɪst(ə)n/ n. person in charge of a sacristy and church contents. [medieval Latin: related to SACRED]

sacristy /ˈsækrɪstɪ/ n. (pl. -ies) room in a church where vestments, sacred vessels, etc., are kept. [medieval Latin: related to SACRED]

sacrosanct /ˈsækrəʊˌsæŋkt/ adj. most sacred; inviolable. □ **sacrosanctity** /-ˈsæŋkt-/ n. [Latin: related to SACRED, SAINT]

sacrum /ˈseɪkrəm/ n. (pl. **sacra** or **-s**) triangular bone between the two hip-bones. [Latin os sacrum sacred bone]

sad adj. (**sadder**, **saddest**) 1 unhappy. 2 causing sorrow. 3 regrettable. 4 shameful, deplorable. □ **sadden** v. **sadly** adv. **sadness** n. [Old English]

saddle /ˈsæd(ə)l/ —n. 1 seat of leather etc. strapped on a horse etc. for riding. 2 bicycle etc. seat. 3 joint of meat consisting of the two loins. 4 ridge rising to a summit at each end. —v. (**-ling**) 1 put a saddle on (a horse etc.). 2 (foll. by with) burden (a person) with a task etc. □ **in the saddle** 1 mounted. 2 in office or control. [Old English]

saddleback n. 1 roof of a tower with two opposite gables. 2 hill with a concave upper outline. 3 black pig with a white stripe across the back. □ **saddlebacked** adj.

saddle-bag n. 1 each of a pair of bags laid across the back of a horse etc. 2 bag attached to a bicycle saddle etc.

saddler n. maker of or dealer in saddles etc.

saddlery /ˈsædlərɪ/ n. (pl. **-ies**) saddler's goods, trade, or premises.

Sadducee /ˈsædjʊˌsiː/ n. member of a Jewish sect of the time of Christ that denied the resurrection of the dead. [Hebrew]

sadhu /ˈsɑːduː/ n. (in India) holy man, sage, or ascetic. [Sanskrit]

sadism /ˈseɪdɪz(ə)m/ n. 1 colloq. enjoyment of cruelty to others. 2 sexual perversion characterized by this. □ **sadist** n. **sadistic** /səˈdɪstɪk/ adj. **sadistically** /səˈdɪstɪkəlɪ/ adv. [de Sade, name of an author]

sado-masochism /ˌseɪdəʊˈmæsəkɪz(ə)m/ n. sadism and masochism in one person. □ **sado-masochist** n. **sado-masochistic** /-ˈkɪstɪk/ adj.

s.a.e. abbr. stamped addressed envelope.

safari /səˈfɑːrɪ/ n. (pl. **-s**) expedition, esp. in Africa, to observe or hunt animals (go on safari). [Swahili from Arabic safara to travel]

safari park n. park where wild animals are kept in the open for viewing from vehicles.

safe —adj. 1 free of danger or injury. 2 secure, not risky (in a safe place). 3 reliable, certain. 4 prevented from escaping or doing harm (have got him safe). 5 (also safe and sound) uninjured, with no harm done. 6 cautious, unenterprising. —n. 1 strong lockable cabinet etc. for valuables. 2 = MEAT SAFE. □ **on the safe side** with a margin for error. □ **safely** adv. [French sauf from Latin salvus]

safe conduct n. 1 immunity given from arrest or harm. 2 document securing this.

safe deposit n. building containing strongrooms and safes for hire.

safeguard —n. protecting proviso, circumstance, etc. —v. guard or protect (rights etc.).

safe house n. place of refuge etc. for spies, terrorists, etc.

safe keeping n. preservation in a safe place.

safe period n. time during the month when conception is least likely.

safe sex n. sexual activity in which precautions are taken against sexually transmitted diseases, esp. Aids.

safety n. being safe; freedom from danger or risk.

safety-belt n. 1 = SEAT-BELT. 2 belt or strap worn to prevent injury.

safety-catch n. device preventing a gun-trigger or machinery from being operated accidentally.

safety curtain n. fireproof curtain between a stage and auditorium.

safety lamp n. miner's lamp so protected as not to ignite firedamp.

safety match n. match igniting only on a specially prepared surface.

safety net n. net placed to catch an acrobat etc. in case of a fall.

safety pin n. pin with a guarded point.

safety razor n. razor with a guard to prevent cutting the skin.

safety-valve n. 1 (in a steam boiler) automatic valve relieving excess pressure. 2 means of venting excitement etc. harmlessly.

saffron /ˈsæfrən/ —n. 1 deep yellow food colouring and flavouring made from dried crocus stigmas. 2 colour of this. —adj. deep yellow. [French from Arabic]

sag —v. (**-gg-**) 1 sink or subside, esp. unevenly. 2 have a downward bulge or curve in the middle. 3 fall in price. —n. state or extent of sagging. □ **saggy** adj. [Low German or Dutch]

saga /ˈsɑːgə/ n. 1 long heroic story, esp. medieval Icelandic or Norwegian. 2 series of connected novels concerning a family's history etc. 3 long involved story. [Old Norse: related to saw³]

sagacious /səˈgeɪʃəs/ adj. showing insight or good judgement. □ **sagacity** /səˈgæsɪtɪ/ n. [Latin sagax -acis]

sage¹ n. culinary herb with dull greyish-green leaves. [French from Latin SAPIVA]

sage² —n. often iron. wise man. —adj. wise, judicious, experienced. □ **sagely** adv. [French from Latin sapio be wise]

sagebrush n. growth of shrubby aromatic plants in some semi-arid regions of western N. America.

Sagittarius /ˌsædʒɪˈteərɪəs/ n. (pl. -es) 1 constellation and ninth sign of the zodiac (the Archer). 2 person born when the sun is in this sign. □ **Sagittarian** adj. & n. [Latin, = archer]

sago /ˈseɪgəʊ/ n. (pl. -s) 1 a starch used in puddings etc. 2 (in full **sago palm**) any of several tropical palms and cycads yielding this. [Malay]

sahib /sɑːb/ n. hist. (in India) form of address to European man. [Arabic, = lord]

said past and past part. of SAY.

sail —n. 1 piece of material extended on rigging to catch the wind and propel a boat or ship. 2 ship's sails collectively. 3 voyage or excursion in a sailing-boat. 4 wind-catching apparatus of a windmill. —v. 1 travel on water by the use of sails or engine-power. 2 begin a voyage (sails at nine). 3 a navigate (a ship etc.). b travel on (a sea). 4 set (a toy boat) afloat. 5 glide or move smoothly or in a stately manner. 6 (often foll. by through) colloq. succeed easily (sailed through the exams). □ **sail close to the wind** 1 sail as nearly against the wind as possible. 2 come close to indecency or dishonesty. **sail into** colloq. attack physically or verbally. **under sail** with sails set. [Old English]

sailboard n. board with a mast and sail, used in windsurfing. □ **sailboarder** n. **sailboarding** n.

sailcloth n. 1 material used for sails. 2 canvas-like dress material.

sailing-boat n. (also **sailing-ship**) vessel driven by sails.

sailor n. 1 member of a ship's crew, esp. one below the rank of officer. 2 person considered with regard to seasickness (a good sailor). [originally sailer: see -ER]

sailplane n. glider designed for sustained flight.

803

sainfoin /ˈsænfɔɪn/ n. pink-flowered fodder-plant. [Latin sanctus holy, foenum hay]

saint /semt, before a name usu. sant/ —n. (abbr. **St** or **S**; pl. **Sts** or **SS**) 1 holy or (in some Churches) formally canonized person regarded as worthy of special veneration. 2 very virtuous person. —v. (as **sainted** adj.) saintly. □ **sainthood** n. **saintlike** adj. [Latin sanctus holy]

St Bernard /ˈbɜːnəd/ n. (in full **St Bernard dog**) very large log of a breed orig. kept in the Alps to rescue travellers.

St John's wort /dʒɒnz/ n. yellow-flowered plant.

St Leger /ˈledʒə(r)/ n. horse-race at Doncaster for three-year-olds. [from the name of the founder]

saintly adj. (-ier, -iest) very holy or virtuous. □ **saintliness** n.

St Vitus's dance /ˈvaɪtəsɪz/ n. disease producing involuntary convulsive movements of the body.

sake¹ /seɪk/ n. □ **for Christ's (or God's or goodness' or Heaven's or Pete's etc.) sake** expression of impatience, supplication, anger, etc. **for the sake of** (or **for one's sake**) out of consideration for; in the interest of; because of, in order to please, honour, get, or keep. [Old English]

sake² /ˈsɑːkɪ/ n. Japanese rice wine. [Japanese]

salaam /səˈlɑːm/ —n. 1 (chiefly as a Muslim greeting) Peace! 2 Muslim low bow with the right palm on the forehead. 3 (in pl.) respectful compliments. —v. make a salaam (to). [Arabic]

salacious /səˈleɪʃəs/ adj. 1 indecently erotic. 2 lecherous. □ **salaciously** adv. **salaciousness** n. [Latin salax -acis: related to SALIENT]

salad /ˈsæləd/ n. cold mixture of usu. raw vegetables, often with a dressing. [French salade from Latin sal salt]

salad cream n. creamy salad-dressing.

salad days n. period of youthful inexperience.

salad-dressing n. = DRESSING 2a.

salamander /ˈsælə,mændə(r)/ n. 1 tailed newtlike amphibian once thought able to endure fire. 2 similar mythical creature. [Greek salamandra]

salami /səˈlɑːmɪ/ n. (pl. -s) highly-seasoned Italian sausage. [Italian]

sal ammoniac /ˌsæl əˈməʊnɪˌæk/ n. ammonium chloride, a white crystalline salt. [Latin sal salt, armoniacus of Jupiter Ammon]

salary /ˈsælərɪ/ —n. (pl. -ies) fixed regular wages, usu. monthly or quarterly, esp. for white-collar work. —v. (-ies, -ied) (usu. as **salaried** adj.) pay a salary

sale to. [Latin *salarium* money for buying salt]

sale *n.* **1** exchange of a commodity for money etc.; act or instance of selling. **2** amount sold (*sales were enormous*). **3** temporary offering of goods at reduced prices. **4 a** event at which goods are sold. **b** public auction. □ **on** (or **for**) **sale** offered for purchase. [Old English]

saleable *adj.* fit or likely to be sold. □ **saleability** /-'bɪlɪtɪ/ *n.*

sale of work *n.* sale of home-made goods etc. for charity.

sale or return *n.* arrangement by which a purchaser may return surplus goods to the supplier without payment.

saleroom *n.* room where auctions are held.

salesman *n.* **1** man employed to sell goods. **2** *US* commercial traveller.

salesmanship *n.* skill in selling.

salesperson *n.* salesman or saleswoman.

sales talk *n.* persuasive talk promoting goods or an idea etc.

saleswoman *n.* woman employed to sell goods.

salicylic acid /ˌsælɪ'sɪlɪk/ *n.* chemical used as a fungicide and in aspirin and dyes. □ **salicylate** /sə'lɪsɪ,leɪt/ *n.* [Latin *salix* willow]

salient /'seɪlɪənt/ —*adj.* **1** prominent, conspicuous. **2** (of an angle, esp. in fortification) pointing outwards. —*n.* salient angle or part of a fortification; outward bulge in a military line. [Latin *salio* leap]

saline /'seɪlaɪn/ —*adj.* **1** containing salt or salts. **2** tasting of salt. **3** of chemical salts. **4** of the nature of a salt. —*n.* **1** salt lake, spring, etc. **2** saline solution. □ **salinity** /sə'lɪnɪtɪ/ *n.* [Latin *sal* salt]

saliva /sə'laɪvə/ *n.* colourless liquid secreted into the mouth by glands. □ **salivary** /sə'laɪ-, 'sælə-/ *adj.* [Latin]

salivate /'sælɪ,veɪt/ *v.* (-**ting**) secrete saliva, esp. in excess. □ **salivation** /-'veɪʃ(ə)n/ *n.* [Latin *salivare*: related to SALIVA]

sallow[1] /'sæləʊ/ *adj.* (-**er**, -**est**) (esp. of the skin) yellowish. [Old English]

sallow[2] /'sæləʊ/ *n.* **1** low-growing willow. **2** a shoot or the wood of this. [Old English]

sally /'sælɪ/ (*pl.* -**ies**) —*n.* **1** sudden military charge; sortie. **2** excursion. **3** witticism. —*v.* (-**ies**, -**ied**) **1** (usu. foll. by *out*, *forth*) set out on a walk, journey, etc. **2** (usu. foll. by *out*) make a military sally. [French *saillie* from Latin *salio* leap]

salmon /'sæmən/ —*n.* (*pl.* usu. same or -**s**) large expensive edible fish with orange-pink flesh. —*adj.* salmon-pink. [Latin *salmo*]

salmonella /ˌsælmə'nelə/ *n.* (*pl.* -**llae** /-liː/) **1** bacterium causing food poisoning. **2** such food poisoning. [*Salmon*, name of a veterinary surgeon]

salmon pink *adj.* & *n.* (as *adj.* often hyphenated) orange-pink colour of salmon flesh.

salmon trout *n.* large silver-coloured trout.

salon /'sælɒn/ *n.* **1** room or establishment of a hairdresser, beautician, etc. **2** *hist.* meeting of eminent people in the home of a lady of fashion. **3** reception room, esp. of a continental house. [French: related to SALOON]

saloon /sə'luːn/ *n.* **1 a** large room or hall on a ship, in a hotel, etc. **b** public room for a specified purpose (*billiard-saloon*). **2** (in full **saloon car**) (usu. four-seater) car with the body closed off from the luggage area. **3** *US* drinking-bar. **4** (in full **saloon bar**) more comfortable bar in a public house. [French *salon*]

salsa /'sælsə/ *n.* a kind of dance music of Cuban origin, with jazz and rock elements. [Spanish: related to SAUCE]

salsify /'sælsɪfɪ/ *n.* (*pl.* -**ies**) plant with long fleshy edible roots. [French from Italian]

SALT /sɔːlt, sɒlt/ *abbr.* Strategic Arms Limitation Talks (or Treaty).

salt /sɔːlt, sɒlt/ —*n.* **1** (also **common salt**) sodium chloride, esp. mined or evaporated from sea water, and used for seasoning or preserving food. **2** chemical compound formed from the reaction of an acid with a base. **3** piquancy; wit. **4** (in *sing.* or *pl.*) substance resembling salt in taste, form, etc. (*bath salts*). **5** (esp. in *pl.*) substance used as a laxative. **6** = SALT-CELLAR. —*adj.* containing, tasting of, or preserved with salt. —*v.* **1** cure, preserve, or season with salt or brine. **2** sprinkle (a road etc.) with salt. □ **salt away** (or **down**) *slang* put (money etc.) by. **the salt of the earth** most admirable or honest person or people (Matt. 5:13). **take with a pinch** (or **grain**) **of salt** regard sceptically. **worth one's salt** efficient, capable. [Old English]

salt-cellar *n.* container for salt at table. [earlier *salt saler* from French *salier* salt-box]

salting *n.* (esp. in *pl.*) marsh overflowed by the sea.

saltire /'sɔːl,taɪə(r)/ *n.* X-shaped cross dividing a shield in four. [French *sautoir* stile]

salt-lick *n.* place where animals lick salt from the ground.

salt-mine *n.* mine yielding rock-salt.

salt-pan *n.* vessel, or depression near the sea, used for getting salt by evaporation.

salt-water *adj.* of or living in the sea.

salty *adj.* (-ier, -iest) 1 tasting of or containing salt. 2 (of wit etc.) piquant. □ **saltiness** *n.*

salubrious /sə'lu:briəs/ *adj.* health-giving; healthy. □ **salubrity** *n.* [Latin *salus* health]

saluki /sə'lu:ki/ *n.* (pl. -s) dog of a tall slender silky-coated breed. [Arabic]

salutary /'sæljutəri/ *adj.* having a good effect. [Latin: related to SALUTE]

salutation /ˌsælju:'teɪʃ(ə)n/ *n. formal* sign or expression of greeting.

salute /sə'lu:t/ —*n.* 1 gesture of respect, homage, greeting etc. 2 *Mil. & Naut.* prescribed gesture or use of weapons or flags as a sign of respect etc. 3 ceremonial discharge of a gun or guns.—*v.* (-ting) 1 a make a salute to. b (often foll. by *to*) perform a salute. 2 greet. 3 commend. [Latin *salus -ut-* health]

salvage /'sælvɪdʒ/ —*n.* 1 rescue of property from the sea, a fire, etc. 2 property so saved. 3 a saving and use of waste materials. b materials salvaged.—*v.* (-ging) 1 save from a disaster etc. 2 retrieve from a disaster etc. [Latin: related to SAVE¹] □ **salvageable** *adj.* [Latin: related to SAVE¹]

salvation /sæl'veɪʃ(ə)n/ *n.* 1 saving or being saved. 2 deliverance from sin and damnation. 3 religious conversion. 4 person or thing that saves. □ **Salvationist** *n.* (esp. with ref. to the Salvation Army). [Latin: related to SAVE¹]

Salvation Army *n.* worldwide evangelical Christian quasi-military organization helping the poor.

salve¹ —*n.* 1 healing ointment. 2 (often foll. by *for*) thing that soothes or consoles.—*v.* (-ving) soothe. [Old English]

salve² *v.* (-ving) save from wreck or fire etc. □ **salvable** *adj.* [back-formation from SALVAGE]

salver *n.* tray, esp. silver, for drinks, letters, etc. [Spanish *salva* assaying of food]

salvia /'sælvɪə/ *n.* garden plant of the sage family with red or blue flowers. [Latin, = SAGE¹]

salvo /'sælvəʊ/ *n.* (pl. -es or -s) 1 simultaneous discharge of guns etc. 2 round of applause. [Italian *salva*]

sal volatile /ˌsæl və'lætɪlɪ/ *n.* solution of ammonium carbonate used as smelling-salts. [Latin, = volatile salt]

SAM *abbr.* surface-to-air missile.

Samaritan /sə'mærɪt(ə)n/ *n.* 1 (in full **good Samaritan**, charitable or helpful person (Luke 10:33 etc.). 2 member of a counselling organization. [originally = inhabitant of ancient Samaria]

samarium /sə'meərɪəm/ *n.* metallic element of the lanthanide series. [ultimately from *Samarski*, name of an official]

samba /'sæmbə/ —*n.* 1 ballroom dance of Brazilian origin. 2 music for this.—*v.* (-bas, -ba'd or -baed /-bæd/, -baing /-bæɪŋ/) dance the samba. [Portuguese]

same —*adj.* 1 (often prec. by *the*) identical; not different (*on the same bus*). 2 unvarying (*same old story*). 3 (usu. prec. by *this, these, that, those*) just mentioned (*this same man later died*).—*pron.* (prec. by *the*) 1 the same person or thing. 2 *Law* or *archaic* the person or thing just mentioned.—*adv.* (usu. prec. by *the*) similarly; in the same way (*feel the same*). □ **all (or just) the same 1** at the same time 1 simultaneously. 2 nevertheless. 2 emphatically the same. **be all (or just) the same to** make no difference to. **same here** *colloq.* the same applies to me. □ **sameness** *n.* [Old Norse]

samizdat /ˌsæmɪz'dæt/ *n.* clandestine publication of banned literature. [Russian]

samosa /sə'məʊsə/ *n.* fried triangular pastry containing spiced vegetables or meat. [Hindustani]

samovar /'sæməvɑ:(r)/ *n.* Russian tea-urn. [Russian]

Samoyed /'sæmɔɪed/ *n.* 1 member of a people of northern Siberia. 2 (also **samoyed**) dog of a white Arctic breed. [Russian]

sampan /'sæmpæn/ *n.* small boat used in the Far East. [Chinese]

samphire /'sæmfaɪə(r)/ *n.* edible maritime rock-plant. [French, = St Peter's herb]

sample /'sɑːmp(ə)l/ —*n.* 1 small representative part or quantity. 2 specimen. 3 illustrative or typical example.—*v.* (-ling) 1 take or give samples of. 2 try the qualities of. 3 experience briefly. [Anglo-French: related to EXAMPLE]

sampler *n.* piece of embroidery using various stitches as a specimen of proficiency. [French: related to EXEMPLAR]

sampler² *n.* 1 person or thing that samples. 2 *US* collection of representative items etc.

sampling *n.* technique of digitally encoding a piece of sound and re-using it as part of a composition or recording.

Samson /ˈsæms(ə)n/ n. person of great strength. [*Samson* in the Old Testament]

samurai /ˈsæmʊˌraɪ/ n. (pl. same) **1** Japanese army officer. **2** hist. member of a Japanese military caste. [Japanese]

sanatorium /ˌsænəˈtɔːrɪəm/ n. (pl. -s or -ria) **1** residential clinic, esp. for convalescents and the chronically sick. **2** room etc. for sick people in a school etc. [Latin *sano* heal]

sanctify /ˈsæŋktɪˌfaɪ/ v. (-ies, -ied) **1** consecrate; treat as holy. **2** free from sin. **3** justify; sanction. □ **sanctification** /ˌfɪkeɪʃ(ə)n/ n. [Latin *sanctus* holy]

sanctimonious /ˌsæŋktɪˈməʊnɪəs/ adj. ostentatiously pious. □ **sanctimoniously** adv. **sanctimoniousness** n. [Latin *sanctimonia* sanctity]

sanction /ˈsæŋkʃ(ə)n/ —n. **1** approval by custom or tradition; express permission. **2** confirmation of a law etc. **3** penalty for disobeying a law or rule, or a reward for obeying it. **4** *Ethics* moral force encouraging obedience to any rule of conduct. **5** (esp. in pl.) (esp. economic) action by a State against another to abide by an international agreement etc. —v. **1** authorize or agree to (an action etc.). **2** ratify; make (a law etc.) binding. [Latin *sancio sanct-* make sacred]

sanctity /ˈsæŋktɪtɪ/ n. holiness, sacredness; inviolability. [Latin *sanctus* holy]

sanctuary /ˈsæŋktjʊərɪ/ n. (pl. -ies) **1** holy place. **2 a** holiest part of a temple etc. **b** chancel. **3** place where birds, wild animals, etc., are bred and protected. **4** place of refuge.

sanctum /ˈsæŋktəm/ n. (pl. -s) **1** holy place. **2** colloq. study, den.

sand —n. **1** fine loose grains resulting from the erosion of esp. siliceous rocks and forming the seashore, deserts, etc. **2** (in pl.) **a** grains of sand. **b** expanse of sand. —v. **1** smooth with sandpaper or sand. **2** sprinkle or cover with sand. [Old English]

sandal¹ /ˈsænd(ə)l/ n. shoe with an open-work upper or no upper, usu. fastened by straps. [Latin from Greek]

sandal² /ˈsænd(ə)l/ n. = SANDALWOOD. [Sanskrit *candana*]

sandal-tree n. tree yielding sandalwood.

sandalwood n. **1** scented wood of a sandal-tree. **2** perfume from this.

sandbag —n. bag filled with sand, used for temporary defences etc. —v. (-gg-) **1** defend or hit with sandbag(s).

sandbank n. sand forming a shallow place in the sea or a river.

sandblast —v. roughen, treat, or clean with a jet of sand driven by compressed air or steam. —n. this jet. □ **sandblaster** n.

sandboy n. □ **happy as a sandboy** extremely happy or carefree. [probably = a boy hawking sand for sale]

sandcastle n. model castle made of sand at the seashore.

sand-dune n. (also **sand-hill**) = DUNE.

sander n. power tool for sanding.

sandman n. imaginary person causing tiredness in children.

sand-martin n. bird nesting in sandy banks.

sandpaper —n. paper with an abrasive coating for smoothing or polishing. —v. rub with this.

sandpiper n. wading bird frequenting wet sandy areas.

sandpit n. pit containing sand, for children to play in.

sandstone n. sedimentary rock of compressed sand.

sandstorm n. storm with clouds of sand raised by the wind.

sandwich /ˈsænwɪdʒ/ —n. **1** two or more slices of bread with a filling. **2** layered cake with jam or cream. —v. **1** put (a thing, statement, etc.) between two of another character. **2** squeeze in between others (*sat sandwiched in the middle*). [from the Earl of *Sandwich*]

sandwich-board n. each of two boards worn front and back to carry advertisements.

sandwich course n. course with alternate periods of study and work experience.

sandy adj. (-ier, -iest) **1** having much sand. **2 a** (of hair) reddish. **b** sand-coloured. □ **sandiness** n.

sane adj. **1** of sound mind; not mad. **2** (of views etc.) moderate, sensible. [Latin *sanus* healthy]

sang past of SING.

sang-froid /sɑ̃ˈfrwɑː/ n. calmness in danger or difficulty. [French, = cold blood]

sangria /sæŋˈɡriːə/ n. Spanish drink of red wine with lemonade, fruit, etc. [Spanish, = bleeding]

sanguinary /ˈsæŋɡwɪnərɪ/ adj. **1** bloody. **2** bloodthirsty. [Latin *sanguis sanguin-* blood]

sanguine /ˈsæŋɡwɪn/ adj. **1** optimistic, confident. **2** (of the complexion) florid, ruddy.

Sanhedrin /ˈsænɪdrɪn/ n. highest court of justice and the supreme council in ancient Jerusalem. [Greek *sunedrion* council]

sanitarium /ˌsænɪˈteərɪəm/ n. (pl. -s or -ria) *US* = SANATORIUM. [related to SANITARY]

sanitary /'sænɪtərɪ/ *adj.* **1** (of conditions etc.) affecting health. **2** hygienic. □ **sanitariness** *n.* [Latin *sanitas*: related to SANE]

sanitary towel *n.* (*US* **sanitary napkin**) absorbent pad used during menstruation.

sanitation /ˌsænɪ'teɪʃ(ə)n/ *n.* **1** sanitary conditions. **2** maintenance etc. of these.

3 disposal of sewage and refuse etc.

sanitize /'sænɪtaɪz/ *v.* (also **-ise**) (**-zing**) **1** make sanitary; disinfect. **2** *colloq.* censor (information etc.) to make it more acceptable.

sanity /'sænɪtɪ/ *n.* **1** being sane. **2** moderation. [Latin *sanitas*: related to SANE]

sank *past of* SINK.

sansculotte /ˌsænzkjʊ'lɒt/ *n.* (esp. in the French Revolution) extreme republican. [French, literally = 'without knee-breeches']

sanserif /sæn'serɪf/ *n.* (also **sans-serif**) form of type without serifs. [apparently from *sans* without, SERIF]

Sanskrit /'sænskrɪt/ —*n.* ancient and sacred language of the Hindus in India. —*adj.* of or in this language. [Sanskrit, = composed]

Santa Claus /'sæntə ˌklɔːz/ *n.* person said to bring children presents on Christmas Eve. [Dutch, = St Nicholas]

sap[1] —*n.* **1** vital juice circulating in plants. **2** vigour, vitality. **3** *slang* foolish person. —*v.* (**-pp-**) **1** drain or dry (wood) of sap. **2** weaken. [Old English]

sap[2] —*n.* tunnel or trench dug to get nearer to the enemy. —*v.* (**-pp-**) **1** dig saps. **2** undermine. [French *sappe* or Italian *zappa* spade]

sapient /'seɪpɪənt/ *adj. literary* **1** wise. **2** aping wisdom. □ **sapience** *n.* [Latin *sapio* be wise]

sapling *n.* young tree. [from SAP[1]]

sapper *n.* **1** person who digs saps. **2** soldier of the Royal Engineers (esp. as the official term for a private).

Sapphic /'sæfɪk/ *adj.* **1** of Sappho or her poetry. **2** lesbian. [Greek *Sapphō*, poetess of Lesbos]

sapphire /'sæfaɪə(r)/ —*n.* **1** transparent blue precious stone. **2** its bright blue colour. —*adj.* (also **sapphire blue**) bright blue. [Greek *sappheiros* lapis lazuli]

sappy *adj.* (**-ier**, **-iest**) **1** full of sap. **2** young and vigorous.

saprophyte /'sæprəfaɪt/ *n.* plant or micro-organism living on dead or decayed organic matter. [Greek *sapros* rotten, *phuto* grow]

saraband /'særəˌbænd/ *n.* **1** slow stately Spanish dance. **2** music for this. [Spanish *zarabanda*]

Saracen /'særəs(ə)n/ *n. hist.* Arab or Muslim at the time of the Crusades. [Greek *sarakēnos*]

sarcasm /'sɑːkæz(ə)m/ *n.* ironically scornful language. □ **sarcastic** /-'kæstɪk/ *adj.* **sarcastically** /-'kæstɪkəlɪ/ *adv.* [Greek *sarkazō* speak bitterly]

sarcoma /sɑː'kəʊmə/ *n.* (*pl.* **-s or -mata**) malignant tumour of connective tissue. [Greek *sarx sark-* flesh]

sarcophagus /sɑː'kɒfəgəs/ *n.* (*pl.* **-gi** /-gaɪ/) stone coffin. [Greek, = flesh-consumer]

sardine /sɑː'diːn/ *n.* (*pl.* same or **-s**) young pilchard etc. sold in closely packed tins. □ **like sardines** crowded close together. [French from Latin]

sardonic /sɑː'dɒnɪk/ *adj.* bitterly mocking or cynical. □ **sardonically** *adv.* [Greek *sardonios* Sardinian]

sardonyx /'sɑːdənɪks/ *n.* onyx in which white layers alternate with yellow or orange ones. [Greek *sardi-onux*]

sargasso /sɑː'gæsəʊ/ *n.* (*pl.* **-s or -es**) (also **sargassum**) seaweed with berry-like air-vessels. [Portuguese]

sarge *n. slang* sergeant. [abbreviation]

sari /'sɑːrɪ/ *n.* (*pl.* **-s**) length of cloth draped round the body, traditionally worn by women of the Indian subcontinent. [Hindi]

sarky /'sɑːkɪ/ *adj.* (**-ier**, **-iest**) *slang* sarcastic. [abbreviation]

sarnie /'sɑːnɪ/ *n. colloq.* sandwich. [abbreviation]

sarong /sə'rɒŋ/ *n.* Malay and Javanese garment of a long strip of cloth tucked round the waist or under the armpits. [Malay]

sarsaparilla /ˌsɑːsəpə'rɪlə/ *n.* **1** preparation of the dried roots of various plants, esp. smilax, used to flavour some drinks and medicines and formerly as a tonic. **2** plant yielding this. [Spanish]

sarsen /'sɑːs(ə)n/ *n.* sandstone boulder carried by ice during a glacial period. [from SARACEN]

sarsenet /'sɑːsnɪt/ *n.* soft silk material used esp. for linings. [Anglo-French from *sarzin* SARACEN]

sartorial /sɑː'tɔːrɪəl/ *adj.* of men's clothes or tailoring. □ **sartorially** *adv.* [Latin *sartor* tailor]

SAS *abbr.* Special Air Service.

sash[1] *n.* strip or loop of cloth etc. worn over one shoulder or round the waist. [Arabic, = muslin]

sash[2] *n.* frame holding the glass in a sash-window. [from CHASSIS]

sashay /'sæʃeɪ/ *v. esp. US colloq.* walk or move ostentatiously, casually, or diagonally. [French *chassé*]

sash-cord n. strong cord attaching the sash-weights to a window sash.

sash-weight n. weight attached to each end of a window sash.

sash-window n. window sliding up and down in grooves.

sass US colloq. —n. impudence, cheek. —v. be impudent to. [var. of SAUCE]

sassafras /ˈsæsəfræs/ n. 1 small N. American tree. 2 medicinal preparation from its leaves or bark. [Spanish or Portuguese]

Sassenach /ˈsæsənak/ n. Scot. & Ir. usu. derog. English person. [Gaelic Sasunnoch]

sassy adj. (-ier, -iest) esp. US colloq. impudent, cheeky. [var. of SAUCY]

SAT /sæt/ abbr. standard assessment task.

Sat. abbr. Saturday.

sat past and past part. of SIT.

Satan /ˈseɪt(ə)n/ n. the Devil; Lucifer. [Hebrew, = enemy]

satanic /səˈtænɪk/ adj. of or like Satan; hellish; evil. □ **satanically** adv.

Satanism /ˈseɪtəˌnɪz(ə)m/ n. 1 worship of Satan. 2 pursuit of evil. □ **Satanist** n. & adj.

satchel /ˈsætʃ(ə)l/ n. small shoulder-bag for carrying school-books etc. [Latin: related to SACK¹]

sate v. (-ting) formal gratify fully; surfeit. [probably dial. sade satisfy]

sateen /sæˈtiːn/ n. glossy cotton fabric like satin. [satin after velveteen]

satellite /ˈsætəˌlaɪt/ —n. 1 celestial or artificial body orbiting the earth or another planet. 2 (in full **satellite State**) small country controlled by another. —attrib. adj. transmitted by satellite (satellite television). [Latin satelles -lit- attendant]

satellite dish n. dish-shaped aerial for receiving satellite television.

satiate /ˈseɪʃɪˌeɪt/ v. (-ting) = SATE. □ **satiation** /-ˈeɪʃ(ə)n/ n. [Latin satis enough]

satiable /ˈseɪʃ(ə)l/ adj.

satiety /səˈtaɪɪtɪ/ n. formal being sated. [Latin: related to SATIATE]

satin /ˈsætɪn/ —n. silk etc. fabric glossy on one side. —adj. smooth as satin. □ **satiny** adj. [Arabic zaitūnī]

satinwood n. a kind of yellow glossy timber.

satire /ˈsætaɪə(r)/ n. 1 ridicule, irony, etc., used to expose folly or vice etc. 2 work using this. □ **satirical** /səˈtɪrɪk(ə)l/ adj. **satirically** /səˈtɪrɪkəlɪ/ adv. [Latin satira medley]

satirist /ˈsætərɪst/ n. 1 writer of satires. 2 satirical person.

satirize /ˈsætəˌraɪz/ v. (also -ise) (-zing or -sing) attack or describe with satire.

satisfaction /ˌsætɪsˈfæk(ʃ)ən/ n. 1 satisfying or being satisfied (derived great satisfaction). 2 thing that satisfies (is a great satisfaction to me). 3 (foll. by for) atonement; compensation (demanded satisfaction).

satisfactory /ˌsætɪsˈfæktərɪ/ adj. adequate; giving satisfaction. □ **satisfactorily** adv.

satisfy /ˈsætɪsˌfaɪ/ v. (-ies, -ied) 1 a meet the expectations or desires of. b be adequate. 2 meet (an appetite or want). 3 rid a (a person) of such an appetite or want. 4 pay (a debt or creditor). 5 adequately fulfil or comply with (conditions etc.). 6 (often foll. by of, that) convince, esp. with proof etc. □ **satisfy oneself** (often foll. by that) become certain. [Latin satisfacio]

satrap /ˈsætrap/ n. 1 provincial governor in the ancient Persian empire. 2 subordinate ruler. [Persian, = protector of the land]

satsuma /satˈsuːmə/ n. variety of tangerine. [Satsuma, province in Japan]

saturate /ˈsætʃəˌreɪt/ v. (-ting) 1 fill with moisture. 2 (often foll. by with) fill to capacity. 3 cause (a substance etc.) to absorb, hold, etc. as much as possible of another substance etc. 4 supply (a market) beyond demand. 5 (as **saturated** adj.) (of fat molecules) containing the greatest number of hydrogen atoms. [Latin satur full]

saturation /ˌsætʃəˈreɪʃ(ə)n/ n. saturating or being saturated.

saturation point n. stage beyond which no more can be absorbed or accepted.

Saturday /ˈsætədeɪ/ —n. day of the week following Friday. —adv. colloq. 1 on Saturday. 2 (**Saturdays**) on Saturdays; each Saturday. [Latin: related to SATURN]

Saturn /ˈsætə(r)/ n. 1 (in Greek and Roman mythology) woodland god with some horselike or goatlike features. 2 lecherous man. [Greek saturos]

Saturnalia /ˌsætəˈneɪlɪə/ n. (pl. same or -s) 1 (usu. **Saturnalia**) Rom. Hist. festival of Saturn in December, the predecessor of Christmas. 2 (as sing. or pl.) scene of wild revelry. [Latin, pl. from Saturnus Roman god]

saturnine /ˈsætəˌnaɪn/ adj. of gloomy temperament or appearance.

satyr /ˈsætə(r)/ n. 1 (in Greek and Roman mythology) woodland god with some horselike or goatlike features. 2 lecherous man. [Greek saturos]

sauce /sɔːs/ —n. 1 liquid or viscous accompaniment to a dish. 2 something adding piquancy or excitement. 3 colloq. impudence, impertinence, cheek. —v. (-cing) colloq. be impudent to; cheek. [Latin salsus salted]

sauce-boat n. jug or dish for serving sauces etc.

saucepan *n.* cooking pan, usu. round with a lid and a projecting handle, used on a hob.

saucer *n.* 1 shallow circular dish for standing a cup on. 2 thing of this shape. □ **saucerful** *n.* (*pl.* -s).

saucy *adj.* (-ier, -iest) impudent, cheeky. □ **saucily** *adv.* **sauciness** *n.* [French *sauce*]

sauerkraut /'saʊəkraʊt/ *n.* German dish of pickled cabbage. [German]

sauna /'sɔːnə/ *n.* 1 period spent in a special steam-heated very hot room to clean the body. 2 such a room. [Finnish]

saunter /'sɔːntə(r)/ —*v.* walk slowly; stroll. —*n.* leisurely walk. [origin unknown]

saurian /'sɔːrɪən/ *adj.* of or like a lizard. [Greek *saura* lizard]

sausage /'sɒsɪdʒ/ *n.* 1 a seasoned minced meat etc. in a cylindrical edible skin. b piece of this. 2 sausage-shaped object. □ **not a sausage** *colloq.* nothing at all. [French *saussiche*]

sausage meat *n.* minced meat used in sausages etc.

sausage roll *n.* sausage meat in a pastry roll.

sauté /'səʊteɪ/ —*attrib. adj.* (esp. of potatoes) fried quickly in a little fat. —*n.* food so cooked. —*v.* (**sautéed** or **sautéd**) cook in this way. [French *sauter* jump]

Sauternes /səʊ'tɜːn/ *n.* sweet white wine from Sauternes in the Bordeaux region of France. [*Sauternes* in France]

savage /'sævɪdʒ/ —*adj.* 1 fierce; cruel. 2 wild; primitive. —*n.* 1 *derog.* member of a primitive tribe. 2 cruel or barbarous person. —*v.* (-**ging**) 1 attack and maul. 2 attack verbally. □ **savagely** *adv.* **savagery** *n.* (*pl.* -**ies**). [French from Latin *silva* a wood]

savannah /sə'vænə/ *n.* (also **savanna**) grassy plain in tropical and subtropical regions. [Spanish]

savant /'sævənt, sæ'vɑ̃/ *n.* (*fem.* **savante** /'sævə(n)t, sæ'vɑ̃t/) learned person. [French]

save[1] —*v.* (-**ving**) 1 (often foll. by *from*) rescue or keep from danger, harm, etc. 2 (often foll. by *up*) keep (esp. money) for future use. 3 a (often *refl.*) relieve (another or oneself) from spending (money, time, trouble, etc.). b prevent the need for. 4 preserve from danger, harm, etc. 5 a avoid losing (a game, match, etc.). b prevent (a goal etc.) from being scored. —*n.* *Football* etc. prevention of a goal etc. (also **saveable** *adj.* (also **savable** *adj.*)) safe). [Latin *salvo* from *salvus* safe]

save[2] *archaic or poet* —*prep.* except; but. —*conj.* (often foll. by *for*) except; but.

[Latin *salvo, salva*, ablative sing. of *salvus* safe]

save-as-you-earn *n.* saving by regular deduction from earnings at source.

saveloy /'sævə,lɔɪ/ *n.* seasoned dried smoked sausage. [Italian *cervellata*]

saving —*adj.* (often in *comb.*) making economical use of (*labour-saving*). —*n.* 1 anything that is saved. 2 an economy (*a saving in expenses*). 3 (usu. in *pl.*) money saved. 4 act of preserving or rescuing. —*prep.* 1 except. 2 without offence to (*saving your presence*).

saving grace *n.* redeeming quality.

savings bank *n.* bank paying interest on small deposits.

savings certificate *n.* interest-bearing Government certificate issued to savers.

saviour /'seɪvjə(r)/ *n.* (*US* **savior**) 1 person who saves from danger etc. 2 (**Saviour**) (prec. by *the*, *our*) Christ. [Latin: related to SAVE[1]]

savoir faire /,sævwɑː 'feə(r)/ *n.* ability to behave appropriately; tact. [French *sapori*]

savor *US* var. of SAVOUR.

savory[1] /'seɪvərɪ/ *n.* (*pl.* -**ies**) aromatic herb used esp. in cookery. [Latin *satureia*]

savory[2] *US* var. of SAVOURY.

savour /'seɪvə(r)/ (*US* **savor**) —*n.* 1 characteristic taste, flavour, etc. 2 hint of a different quality etc. ir something. —*v.* 1 appreciate and enjoy (food, an experience, etc.). 2 (foll. by *of*) imply or suggest (a specified quality). [Latin *sapor*]

savoury /'seɪvərɪ/ (*US* **savory**) —*adj.* 1 having an appetizing taste or smell. 2 (of food) salty or piquant, not sweet. 3 pleasant; acceptable. —*n.* (*pl.* -**ies**) savoury dish. □ **savouriness** *n.* [French]

Savoy /sə'vɔɪ/ *n.* cabbage with wrinkled leaves. [*Savoy* in SE France]

savvy /'sævɪ/ *slang* —*v.* (-**ies**, -**ied**) know. —*n.* knowingness; understanding. —*adj.* (-ier, -iest) *US* knowing; wise. [Pidgin alteration of Spanish *sabe usted* you know]

---

saw[1] —*n.* 1 hand tool with a toothed blade used to cut esp. wood with a to-and-fro movement. 2 power tool with a toothed rotating disk or moving band, for cutting. —*v.* (*past part.* **sawn** or **sawed**) 1 cut (wood etc.) or make (boards etc.) with a saw. 2 use a saw. 3 a move with a saw. 2 use a saw. 3 a move with a sawing motion (*sawing away on his violin*). b divide (the air etc.) with gesticulations. [Old English]

saw[2] *past of* SEE[1].

saw³ *n.* proverb; maxim. [Old English: related to SAY]

sawdust *n.* powdery wood particles produced in sawing.

sawfish *n.* (*pl.* same or *-es*) large marine fish with a toothed flat snout.

sawmill *n.* factory for sawing planks.

sawn *past part.* of SAW¹.

sawn-off *adj.* (*US* **sawed-off**) (of a shotgun) with part of the barrel sawn off.

sawtooth *adj.* (also **sawtoothed**) serrated.

sawyer *n.* person who saws timber, esp. for a living.

sax *n. colloq.* saxophone. [abbreviation]

saxe /saeks/ *n.* & *adj.* (in full **saxe blue**; as adj. often hyphenated) light greyish-blue colour. [French, = Saxony]

saxifrage /ˈsæksɪˌfreɪdʒ/ *n.* rock-plant with small white, yellow, or red flowers. [Latin *saxum* rock, *frango* break]

Saxon /ˈsæks(ə)n/ —*n.* **1** *hist.* a member of the Germanic people that conquered parts of England in 5th–6th c. **b** (usu. = ANGLO-SAXON. —*adj.* **1** *hist.* of the Saxons. **2** = ANGLO-SAXON. [Latin *Saxo -onis*]

saxophone /ˈsæksəˌfəʊn/ *n.* metal woodwind reed instrument used esp. in jazz. □ **saxophonist** /-ˈsɒfənɪst/ *n.* [*Sax*, name of the maker]

say —*v.* (*3rd sing. present* **says** /sez/; *past and past part.* **said** /sed/) **1** (often foll. by *that*) utter (specified words); remark. **b** express (*say what you feel*). **2** (often foll. by *that*) a state; promise or prophesy. **b** have specified wording; indicate (*clock says ten to six*). **3** (in *passive*; usu. foll. by *to* + infin.) be asserted (*is said to be old*). **4** (foll. by *to* + infin.) *colloq.* tell to do (*he said to hurry*). **5** convey (information) (*spoke, but said little*). **6** offer as an argument or excuse (*much to be said in favour of it*). **7** (often *absol.*) give an opinion or decision as to (*hard to say*). **8** take as an example or as near enough (*paid, say, £20*). **9** recite or repeat (prayers, Mass, tables, a lesson, etc.). **10** convey (inner meaning etc.) (*what is the poem saying?*). **11** (the said) *Law* or *joc.* the previously mentioned. —*n.* **1** opportunity to express a view (*let him have his say*). **2** share in a decision (*had no say in it*). □ **I'll say** *colloq.* yes indeed. **I say!** exclamation of surprise etc. or drawing attention. **that is to say** in other words, more explicitly. [Old English]

SAYE *abbr.* save-as-you-earn.

saying *n.* maxim, proverb, etc. □ **go without saying** be too obvious to need mention.

say-so *n. colloq.* **1** power of decision. **2** mere assertion (*his say-so is not enough*).

Sb *symb.* antimony. [Latin *stibium*]

S-bend *n.* S-shaped bend in a road or pipe.

Sc *symb.* scandium.

sc. *abbr.* scilicet.

s.c. *abbr.* small capitals.

scab —*n.* **1** crust over a healing cut, sore, etc. **2** (often *attrib.*) *colloq. derog.* blackleg. **3** skin disease, esp. in animals. **4** fungous plant disease. —*v.* (**-bb-**) **1** *colloq. derog.* act as a blackleg. **2** form a scab, heal over. □ **scabby** *adj.* (**-ier**, **-iest**) cf. SHABBY]

scabbard /ˈskæbəd/ *n. hist.* sheath of a sword etc. [Anglo-French]

scabies /ˈskeɪbɪːz/ *n.* contagious skin disease causing itching. [Latin]

scabious /ˈskeɪbɪəs/ *n.* plant with esp. blue pincushion-shaped flowers. [medieval Latin *scabiosa* (*herba*) named as curing scabies]

scabrous /ˈskeɪbrəs/ *adj.* **1** rough, scaly. **2** indecent, salacious. [Latin]

scaffold /ˈskæfəʊld/ *n.* **1** *hist.* platform for the execution of criminals. **2** = SCAFFOLDING. [Romanic: related to EX-¹, CATAFALQUE]

scaffolding *n.* **1** a temporary structure of poles, planks, etc., for building work. **b** materials for this. **2** any temporary framework.

scalar /ˈskeɪlə(r)/ *Math. & Physics* —*adj.* (of a quantity) having only magnitude, not direction. —*n.* scalar quantity. [Latin: related to SCALE³]

scalawag var. of SCALLYWAG.

scald /skɔːld, skɒld/ —*v.* **1** burn (the skin etc.) with hot liquid or steam. **2** heat (esp. milk) to near boiling point. **3** (usu. foll. by *out*) clean with boiling water. —*n.* burn etc. caused by scalding. [Latin *excaldo* from *calidus* hot]

scale¹ —*n.* **1** each of the thin horny plates protecting the skin of fish and reptiles. **2** something resembling this. **3** white deposit formed in a kettle etc. by hard water. **4** tartar formed on teeth. —*v.* (**-ling**) **1** remove scale(s) from. **2** form or come off in scales. □ **scaly** *adj.* (**-ier**, **-iest**) [French *escale*]

scale² *n.* **1** a (often in *pl.*) weighing machine. **b** (also **scale-pan**) each of the dishes on a simple balance. **2** (**the Scales**) zodiacal sign or constellation Libra. □ **tip** (or **turn**) **the scales 1** be the decisive factor. **2** (usu. foll. by *at*) weigh. [Old Norse *skál* bowl]

scale³ —*n.* **1** graded classification system (*high on the social scale*). **2** a (often *attrib.*) ratio of reduction or enlargement in a map, model, picture, etc. (*on a*

scale of one inch to the mile; a scale model), **b** relative dimensions. **3** Mus. set of notes at fixed intervals, arranged in order of pitch. **4** a set of marks on a line used in measuring etc. **b** rule determining the distances between these. **c** rod etc. on which these are marked. —v. **climb** (a wall, height, etc.). **b** climb (the social scale, heights of ambition, etc.). **2** represent proportionally; reduce to a common scale. □ **in scale** in proportion. **scale down** (or up) make or become smaller (or larger) in proportion. **to scale** uniformly in proportion. [Latin *scala* ladder]

scalene /'skeɪliːn/ adj. (esp. of a triangle) having unequal sides. [Greek *skalēnos* unequal]

scallion /'skæljən/ n. esp. US shallot; spring onion etc. [Latin from Ascalon in ancient Palestine]

scallop /'skɒləp, 'skɒl-/ (also **scollop** /'skɒl-/) —n. **1** edible mollusc with two fan-shaped ridged shells. **2** (in full **scallop shell**) single shell of a scallop, often used for cooking or serving food in. **3** (in pl.) ornamental edging of semicircular curves. —v. (-p-) ornament with scallops. □ **scalloping** n. (in sense 3 of n.). [French ESCALOPE]

scallywag /'skælɪwæg/ n. (also **scalawag** /'skæləwæg/) scamp, rascal. [origin unknown]

scalp —n. **1** skin on the head, with the hair etc. attached. **2** hist. this cut off as a trophy by an American Indian. —v. **1** hist. take the scalp of (an enemy). **2** US colloq. resell (shares etc.) at a high or quick profit. [probably Scandinavian]

scalpel /'skælp(ə)l/ n. surgeon's small sharp knife. [Latin *scalpo* scratch]

scam n. US slang trick, fraud. [origin unknown]

scamp n. colloq. rascal; rogue. [probably Dutch]

scamper —v. run and skip. —n. act of scampering. [perhaps from SCAMP]

scampi /'skæmpɪ/ n.pl. large prawns. [Italian]

scan —v. (-nn-) **1** look at intently or quickly. **2** (of a verse etc.) be metrically correct. **3 a** examine (a surface etc.) to detect radioactivity etc. **b** traverse (a particular region) with a radar etc. beam. **4** resolve (a picture) into its elements of light and shade for esp. television transmission. **5** analyse the metrical structure of (verse). **6** obtain an image of (part of the body) using a scanner. —n. **1** scanning. **2** image obtained by scanning. [Latin *scando* climb, scan]

scandal /'skænd(ə)l/ n. **1** cause of public outrage etc. so caused. **2** outrage etc. so caused. **3** malicious gossip. □ **scandalous** adj. **scandalously** adv. [Greek *skandalon*, = snare]

scandalize v. (also **-ise**) (**-zing** or **-sing**) offend morally; shock.

scandalmonger n. person who habitually spreads scandal.

Scandinavian /skændɪ'neɪvɪən/ —n. **1 a** native or inhabitant of Scandinavia (Denmark, Norway, Sweden, and Iceland). **b** person of Scandinavian descent. **2** family of languages of Scandinavia. —adj. of Scandinavia. [Latin]

scandium /'skændɪəm/ n. metallic element occurring naturally in lanthanide ores. [Latin *Scandia* Scandinavia]

scanner n. **1** device for scanning or systematically examining all the parts of something. **2** machine for measuring radiation, ultrasound reflections, etc. from the body as a diagnostic aid.

scansion /'skænʃ(ə)n/ n. metrical scanning of verse. [Latin related to SCAN]

scant adj. barely sufficient; deficient. [Old Norse]

scanty adj. (-ier, -iest) **1** of small extent or amount. **2** barely sufficient. □ **scantily** adv. **scantiness** n.

scapegoat /'skeɪpɡəʊt/ —n. person blamed for others' shortcomings (with ref. to Lev. 16). [obsolete *scape* escape]

scapula /'skæpjʊlə/ n. (pl. **-lae** /-liː/ or **-s**) shoulder-blade. [Latin]

scapular /'skæpjʊlə(r)/ —adj. of the shoulder or shoulder-blade. —n. short monastic cloak.

scar[1] —n. **1** usu. permanent mark on the skin from a wound etc. **2** emotional damage from grief etc. **3** sign of damage. **4** mark left on a plant by the loss of a leaf etc. —v. (-rr-) **1** (esp. as **scarred** adj.) mark with a scar or scars (*scarred for life*). **2** form a scar. [French *eschar(r)e*]

scar[2] n. (also **scaur**) steep craggy outcrop of a mountain or cliff. [Old Norse, = reef]

scarab /'skærəb/ n. **1 a** sacred dung-beetle of ancient Egypt. **b** a kind of beetle. **2** ancient Egyptian gem cut in the form of a beetle. [Latin *scarabaeus* from Greek]

scarce /skeəs/ —adj. **1** (usu. predic.) (esp. of food, money, etc.) in short supply. **2** rare. —adv. archaic or literary scarcely. □ **make oneself scarce** colloq. keep out of the way; surreptitiously disappear. [French *scars* Latin *excerpo* EXCERPT]

scarcely adv. **1** hardly, only just (*had scarcely arrived*). **2** surely not (*can scarcely have said so*). **3** esp. iron. not (*scarcely expected to be ill-treated*).

scarcity n. (pl. **-ies**) (often foll. by of) lack or shortage, esp. of food.

scare /skeə(r)/ —v. (-**ring**) **1** frighten, esp. suddenly. **2** (as **scared** adj.) (usu. foll. by of, or to + infin.) frightened; terrified. **3** (usu. foll. by away, off, up, etc.) drive away by frightening. **4** become scared (they don't scare easily). —n. **1** sudden attack of fright. **2** alarm caused by rumour etc. (a measles scare). [Old Norse]

scarecrow n. **1** human figure dressed in old clothes and set up in a field to scare birds away. **2** colloq. badly dressed, grotesque-looking, or very thin person.

scaremonger n. person who spreads alarming rumours. □ **scaremongering** n.

scarf[1] n. (pl. **scarves** /skɑːvz/ or -s) piece of material worn esp. round the neck or over the head, for warmth or ornament. [French escarpe]

scarf[2] —v. join the ends of (timber etc.) by bevelling or notching them to fit and then bolting them etc. —n. (pl. -s) joint made by scarfing. [probably French escarf]

scarify[1] /ˈskærɪfaɪ/ v. (-**ies**, -**ied**) **1 a** make slight incisions in. **b** cut off skin from. **2** hurt by severe criticism etc. **3** loosen (soil). □ **scarification** /-fɪˈkeɪʃ(ə)n/ n. [Greek skariphos stylus]

scarify[2] /ˈskærɪfaɪ/ v. (-**ies**, -**ied**) colloq. scare.

scarlatina /ˌskɑːləˈtiːnə/ n. = SCARLET FEVER. [Italian: related to SCARLET]

scarlet /ˈskɑːlət/ —adj. of brilliant red tinged with orange. —n. **1** scarlet colour or pigment. **2** scarlet clothes or material (dressed in scarlet). [French escarlate]

scarlet fever n. infectious bacterial fever with a scarlet rash.

scarlet pimpernel n. wild plant with small esp. scarlet flowers.

scarlet woman n. derog. promiscuous woman, prostitute.

scarp —n. steep slope, esp. the inner side of a ditch in a fortification. —v. make perpendicular or steep. [Italian scarpa]

scarper v. slang run away, escape. [probably Italian scappare escape]

scarves pl. of SCARF.

scary /ˈskeərɪ/ adj. (-**ier**, -**iest**) colloq. frightening.

scat[1] v. (-**tt**-) (usu. in imper.) colloq. depart quickly. [perhaps an abbreviation of SCATTER]

scat[2] —n. wordless jazz singing. —v. (-**tt**-) sing scat. [probably imitative]

scathing /ˈskeɪðɪŋ/ adj. witheringly scornful. □ **scathingly** adv. [Old Norse]

scatology /skæˈtɒlədʒɪ/ n. excessive interest in excrement or obscenity. □

scatological /ˌskætəˈlɒdʒɪk(ə)l/ adj. [Greek skōr skat- dung]

scatter —v. **1 a** throw about; strew. **b** cover by scattering. **2 a** (cause to) move in flight etc.; disperse. **b** disperse or cause (hopes, clouds, etc.) to disperse. **3** (as **scattered** adj.) wide apart or sporadic (scattered villages). **4** Physics deflect or diffuse (light, particles etc.). —n. **1** act of scattering. **2** small amount scattered. **3** extent of distribution. [probably var. of SHATTER]

scatterbrain n. person lacking concentration. □ **scatterbrained** adj.

scatty /ˈskætɪ/ adj. (-**ier**, -**iest**) colloq. scatterbrained. □ **scattily** adv. **scattiness** n.

scaur var. of SCAR[2].

scavenge /ˈskævɪndʒ/ v. (-**ging**) (usu. foll. by for; also absol.) search for and collect (discarded items). [back-formation from SCAVENGER]

scavenger n. **1** person who scavenges. **2** animal feeding on carrion, refuse, etc. [Anglo-French scavager: related to SHOW]

Sc.D. abbr. Doctor of Science. [Latin scientiae doctor]

SCE abbr. Scottish Certificate of Education.

scenario /sɪˈnɑːrɪəʊ/ n. (pl. -s) **1** outline of the plot of a play, film, etc. **2** postulated sequence of future events. [Italian]

■ **Usage** Scenario should not be used in standard English to mean 'situation', as in it was an unpleasant scenario.

scene /siːn/ n. **1** place in which events, real or fictional, occur. **2 a** incident, real or fictional. **b** description of this. **3** public display of emotion, temper, etc. (made a scene in the restaurant). **4 a** continuous portion of a play in a fixed setting; subdivision of an act. **b** similar section of a film, book, etc. **5 a** piece of scenery used in a play. **b** these collectively. **6** landscape or view. **7** colloq. **a** area of interest (not my scene). **b** milieu (well-known on the jazz scene). □ **behind the scenes 1** offstage. **2** secret; secretly. **set the scene** describe the location of events. [Greek skēnē tent, stage]

scene-shifter n. person who moves scenery in a theatre.

scenery n. **1** natural features of a landscape, esp. when picturesque. **2** painted backcloths, props, etc., used as the background in a play etc. [Italian: related to SCENARIO]

scenic adj. **1 a** picturesque. **b** of natural scenery. **2** of or on the stage. □ **scenically** adv.

scent /sent/ —n. **1** distinctive, esp. pleasant, smell **2** = PERFUME 2. **3 a** perceptible smell left by an animal. **b** clues etc. leading to a discovery. **c** power of detecting esp. smells. —v. **1 a** discern by scent. **b** sense (*scented danger*). **2** (esp. as **scented** *adj.*) make fragrant (*scented soap*). □ **put** (or **throw**) **off the scent** deceive by false clues etc. **scent out** discover or search by smelling or searching. [French *sentir* perceive]

scepter US var. of SCEPTRE.

sceptic /'skeptik/ n. (US **skeptic**) **1** person inclined to doubt accepted opinions. **2** person who doubts the truth of religions. **3** philosopher who questions the possibility of knowledge. □ **scepticism** /-,siz(ə)m/ n. [Greek *skeptomai* observe]

sceptical /'skeptik(ə)l/ adj. (US **skeptical**) inclined to doubt accepted opinions; critical; incredulous. □ **sceptically** adv.

sceptre /'septə(r)/ n. (US **scepter**) staff as a symbol of sovereignty. [Greek *skēptō* lean on]

schadenfreude /'ʃɑːd(ə)n,frɔɪdə/ n. malicious enjoyment of another's misfortunes. [German *Schaden* harm *Freude* joy]

schedule /'ʃedjuːl/ —n. **1 a** list of intended events, times, etc. **b** plan of work. **2** list of rates or prices. **3** US timetable. **4** tabulated list. —v. (-ling) **1** include in a schedule. **2** make a schedule of. **3** list (a building) for preservation as planned; on time. [Latin *schedula* slip of paper]

scheduled flight n. (also **scheduled service** etc.) regular public flight, service, etc.

schema /'skiːmə/ n. (pl. **schemata** or **-s**) synopsis, outline, or diagram. [Greek *skhēma -at-* form, figure]

schematic /skɪ'mætɪk/ —adj. of or as a scheme or schema; diagrammatic. —n. diagram, esp. of an electronic circuit. □ **schematically** adv.

schematize /'skiːmə,taɪz/ v. (also **-ise**) (-zing or -sing) put in schematic form. [to SCHEMA]

scheme /skiːm/ —n. **1** systematic plan or arrangement (*colour scheme*). **2** artful plot. **3** timetable, outline, syllabus, etc. —v. (-ming) plan, esp. secretly or deceitfully. □ **scheming** adj. & n. [Greek: related to SCHEMA]

scherzo /'skeətsəʊ/ n. (pl. **-s**) Mus. vigorous, often playful, piece, esp. as part of a larger work. [Italian, = jest]

schism /'sɪz(ə)m/ n. division of a group (esp. religious) into sects etc. usu. over doctrine. □ **schismatic** /-'mætɪk/ adj. & n. [Greek *skhizō* to split]

schist /ʃɪst/ n. layered crystalline rock. [Greek *skhizō* to split]

schizo /'skɪtsəʊ/ colloq. —adj. schizophrenic. —n. (pl. **-s**) schizophrenic person. [abbreviation]

schizoid /'skɪtsɔɪd/ —adj. tending to schizophrenia but usu. without delusions. —n. schizoid person.

schizophrenia /,skɪtsə'friːnɪə/ n. mental disease marked by a breakdown in the relation between thoughts, feelings, and actions, and often with delusions and retreat from social life. □ **schizophrenic** /-'frenɪk/ adj. & n. [Greek]

schlock /ʃlɒk/ n. US colloq. trash. [Yiddish *shlak* a blow]

schmaltz /ʃmɔːlts/ n. colloq. esp. US sentimentality, esp. in music, drama, etc. □ **schmaltzy** adj. [Yiddish]

schmuck /ʃmʌk/ n. esp. US foolish or contemptible person. [Yiddish]

schnapps /ʃnæps/ n. any of various spirits drunk in N. Europe. [German]

schnitzel /'ʃnɪts(ə)l/ n. escalope of veal. [German]

scholar /'skɒlə(r)/ n. **1** learned person, academic. **2** holder of a scholarship. **3** person of specified academic ability (*poor scholar*). □ **scholarly** adj. [Latin: related to SCHOOL]

scholarship n. **1 a** academic achievement, esp. of a high level. **b** standards of a good scholar (*shows great scholarship*). **2** financial award for a student, given for scholarly achievement.

scholastic /skə'læstɪk/ adj. **1** of schools, education, etc.; academic. **2** hist. of scholasticism. [Greek: related to SCHOOL]

scholasticism /skə'læstɪsɪz(ə)m/ n. hist. medieval western Church philosophy.

school[1] /skuːl/ —n. **1 a** educational institution for pupils up to 19 years of age, or (US) including college or university level. **b** (attrib.) of or for use in school (*school dinners*). **2 a** school buildings, pupils, staff, etc. **b** time of teaching; teaching itself (*no school today*). **3** university department or faculty. **4 a** group of similar artists etc., esp. followers of an artist etc. **b** group of likeminded people (*belongs to the old school*). **5** group of card-players etc. **6** colloq. instructive circumstances etc. (*school of adversity*). —v. **1** send to school; educate. **2** (often foll. by *to*) discipline, train, control. **3** (as **schooled** adj.) (foll. by *in*) educate or trained (*schooled in humility*). □ **at** (US **in**) **school** attending lessons etc. **go to school** attend lessons etc. [Greek *skholē*]

school[2] /skuːl/ n. (often foll. by *of*) shoal of fish, whales, etc. [Low German or Dutch]

school age *n.* age-range of school attendance.

schoolboy *n.* boy attending school.

schoolchild *n.* child attending school.

schoolgirl *n.* girl attending school.

schoolhouse *n.* school building, esp. in a village.

schooling *n.* education, esp. at school.

school-leaver *n.* person finishing secondary school (esp. considered as joining the job market).

schoolmaster *n.* head or assistant male teacher.

schoolmistress *n.* head or assistant female teacher.

schoolroom *n.* room used for lessons.

schoolteacher *n.* teacher in a school.

school year *n.* period from September to July.

schooner /ˈskuːnə(r)/ *n.* 1 fore-and-aft rigged ship with two or more masts. 2 **a** measure or glass for esp. sherry. **b** *US & Austral.* tall beer-glass. [origin uncertain]

schottische /ʃɒˈtiːʃ/ *n.* 1 a kind of slow polka. 2 music for this. [German, = Scottish]

sciatic /saɪˈætɪk/ *adj.* 1 of the hip. 2 of the sciatic nerve. 3 suffering from or liable to sciatica. [Greek *iskhion* hip]

sciatica /saɪˈætɪkə/ *n.* neuralgia of the hip and leg. [Latin: related to SCIATIC]

sciatic nerve *n.* largest nerve, running from pelvis to thigh.

science /ˈsaɪəns/ *n.* 1 branch of knowledge involving systematized observation and experiment. 2 **a** knowledge so gained, or on a specific subject. **b** pursuit or principles of this. 3 skilful technique. [Latin *scio* know]

science fiction *n.* fiction with a scientific theme, esp. concerned with the future, space, other worlds, etc.

science park *n.* area containing science-based industries.

scientific /ˌsaɪənˈtɪfɪk/ *adj.* 1 **a** following the systematic methods of science. **b** systematic, accurate. 2 of, used in, or engaged in science. □ **scientifically** *adv.*

scientist /ˈsaɪəntɪst/ *n.* student or expert in science.

Scientology /ˌsaɪənˈtɒlədʒɪ/ *n.* system of religious philosophy based on self-improvement and graded courses of study and training. □ **Scientologist** *n. & adj.* [Latin *scientia* knowledge]

sci-fi /ˈsaɪfaɪ/ *n.* (often *attrib.*) *colloq.* science fiction. [abbreviation]

scilicet /ˈsaɪlɪsɛt/ *adv.* that is to say (used esp. in explanation of an ambiguity). [Latin]

scimitar /ˈsɪmɪtə(r)/ *n.* curved oriental sword. [French and Italian]

scintilla /sɪnˈtɪlə/ *n.* trace. [Latin, = spark]

scintillate /ˈsɪntɪˌleɪt/ *v.* (**-ting**) 1 (esp. as **scintillating** *adj.*) talk cleverly; be brilliant. 2 sparkle; twinkle. □ **scintillation** /-ˈleɪʃ(ə)n/ *n.* [Latin: related to SCINTILLA]

scion /ˈsaɪən/ *n.* 1 shoot of a plant etc., esp. one cut for grafting or planting. 2 descendant; younger member of (esp. a noble) family. [French]

scirocco var. of SIROCCO.

scissors /ˈsɪzəz/ *n.pl.* (also **pair of scissors** *sing.*) hand-held cutting instrument with two pivoted blades opening and closing. [Latin *caedo* cut: related to CHISEL]

sclerosis /skləˈrəʊsɪs/ *n.* 1 abnormal hardening of body tissue. 2 (in full **multiple** or **disseminated sclerosis**) serious progressive disease of the nervous system. □ **sclerotic** /-ˈrɒtɪk/ *adj.* [Greek *sklēros* hard]

scoff[1] — *v.* (usu. foll. by *at*) speak scornfully; mock. —*n.* mocking words; taunt. [perhaps from Scandinavian]

scoff[2] *colloq.* —*v.* eat greedily. —*n.* food; a meal. [Afrikaans *schoff* from Dutch]

scold /skəʊld/ —*v.* 1 rebuke (esp. a child). 2 find fault noisily. —*n.* *archaic* nagging woman. □ **scolding** *n.* [probably Old Norse]

scollop var. of SCALLOP.

sconce *n.* wall-bracket for a candle-stick or light-fitting. [Latin *(ab)sconsa* covered (light)]

scone /skɒn, skəʊn/ *n.* small cake of flour, fat, and milk, baked quickly. [origin uncertain]

scoop —*n.* 1 spoon-shaped object, esp.: **a** a short-handled deep shovel for loose materials. **b** a large long-handled ladle for liquids. **c** the excavating part of a digging-machine etc. **d** an instrument for serving ice-cream etc. 2 quantity taken up by a scoop. 3 scooping movement. 4 exclusive news item. 5 large profit made quickly. —*v.* 1 (usu. foll. by *out*) hollow out (as if) with a scoop. 2 (usu. foll. by *up*) lift (as if) with a scoop. 3 forestall (a rival newspaper etc.) with a scoop. 4 secure (a large profit etc.), esp. suddenly. [Low German or Dutch]

scoot *v.* (esp. in *imper.*) *colloq.* depart quickly, flee. [origin unknown]

scooter *n.* 1 child's toy with a footboard on two wheels and a long steering-handle. 2 (in full **motor scooter**) low-powered motor cycle with a shieldlike protective front.

scope *n.* 1 range or opportunity (*beyond the scope of our research*). 2 extent of mental ability, outlook, etc. (*intellect limited in its scope*). [Greek, = target]

-scope comb. form forming nouns denoting: **1** device looked at or through (*telescope*). **2** instrument for observing or showing (*oscilloscope*). □ **-scopic** showing corresponding adjectives. [Greek *skopeō* look at]

-scopy comb. form indicating viewing or observation, usu. with an instrument ending in *-scope* (*microscopy*).

scorbutic /skɔːˈbjuːtɪk/ adj. of, like, or affected with scurvy. [Latin *scorbutus* scurvy]

scorch –v. **1** burn or discolour the surface of with dry heat. **2** become so discoloured etc. **3** (as **scorching** adj.) colloq. **a** (of the weather) very hot. **b** (of criticism etc.) stringent; harsh. —n. mark made by scorching. [origin unknown]

scorched earth policy n. policy of destroying anything that might be of use to an invading enemy.

scorcher n. colloq. very hot day.

score –n. **1 a** number of points, goals, runs, etc., made by a player or side in some games. **b** respective numbers of points etc. at the end of a game (*score was five-nil*). **c** act of gaining esp. a goal. **2** (pl. same or -s) twenty or a set of twenty. **3** (in pl.) a great many (*rejected on that score*). **5** Mus. a copy of a composition showing all the vocal and instrumental parts arranged one below the other. **b** music for a film or play, esp. for a musical. **6** notch, line, etc. cut or scratched into a surface. **7** record of money owing. —v. (-ring) **1 a** win or gain (a goal, points, success, etc.). **b** count for advantage (*that is where he scores*). **5** Mus. (often foll. by *for*) orchestrate or arrange (a piece of music). **6** slang **a** obtain drugs illegally. **b** make a sexual conquest. □ **keep score** (or **the score**) register scores as they are made. **know the score** colloq. be aware of the essential facts. **on that score** so far as that is concerned. **score off** (or **score points off**) colloq. humiliate, esp. verbally. **score out** delete. □ **scorer** n. [Old Norse: related to SHEAR]

scoreboard n. large board for displaying the score in a game or match.

score-book n. (also **score-card** or **-sheet**) printed book etc. for entering esp. cricket scores in.

scoria /ˈskɔːrɪə/ n. (pl. **scoriae** /-riˌiː/) **1** cellular lava, or fragments of it. **2** slag or dross of metals. □ **scoriaceous** /-ˈeɪʃəs/ adj. [Greek *skōria* refuse]

Scot n. **1** native of Scotland. **2** person of Scottish descent. [Latin *Scottus*]

Scotch –adj. var. of SCOTTISH or SCOTS. —n. **1** var. of SCOTTISH or SCOTS. **2** Scotch whisky. [from SCOTTISH]

■ **Usage** *Scots* or *Scottish* is preferred to *Scotch* in Scotland, except in the compound nouns *Scotch broth*, *egg*, *fir*, *mist*, *terrier*, and *whisky*.

scotch v. **1** put an end to; frustrate. **2** *archaic* wound without killing. [origin unknown]

Scotch broth n. meal soup with pearl barley etc.

Scotch egg n. hard-boiled egg in sausage meat.

Scotch fir n. (also **Scots fir**) = Scots PINE.

Scotch mist n. thick drizzly mist.

Scotch terrier n. (also **Scottish terrier**) small rough-haired terrier.

Scotch whisky n. whisky distilled in Scotland.

scot-free adv. unharmed, unpunished. [obsolete *scot* tax]

Scots (also **Scotch**) esp. *Scot.* —adj. **1** = SCOTTISH. **2** in the dialect, accent, etc., of (esp. Lowland) Scotland. —n. **1** = SCOTTISH. **2** form of English spoken in (esp. Lowland) Scotland. [var. of SCOTTISH]

Scots fir var. of SCOTCH FIR.

Scotsman n. (fem. **Scotswoman**) = Scot.

Scottie n. (also **Scottie dog**) colloq. Scotch terrier.

Scottish (also **Scotch**) —adj. of Scotland or its inhabitants. —n. (prec. by *the*; treated as pl.) people of Scotland.

Scottish pine var. of SCOTS PINE.

Scottish terrier var. of SCOTCH TERRIER.

scoundrel /ˈskaʊndr(ə)l/ n. unscrupulous villain; rogue. [origin unknown]

scour[1] v. **1 a** cleanse by rubbing. **b** (usu. foll. by *away*, *off*, etc.) clear (rust, stains, etc.) by rubbing. **c** clear out (a pipe, channel, etc.) by flushing through.

scorn –n. disdain, contempt, derision. –v. **1** hold in contempt. **2** reject or refuse to do as unworthy. [French *escarnir*]

scornful adj. (often foll. by *of*) contemptuous. □ **scornfully** adv.

Scorpio /ˈskɔːpɪəʊ/ n. (pl. -s) constellation and eighth sign of the zodiac (the Scorpion). **2** person born when the sun is in this sign. [Greek *skorpios* scorpion]

scorpion /ˈskɔːpɪən/ n. **1** arachnid with pincers and a jointed stinging tail. **2** (the **Scorpion**) zodiacal sign or constellation Scorpio.

—n. scouring or being scoured. □ **scourer** n. [French *écurer*]

scour² v. search thoroughly, esp. by scanning (*scoured the streets for him*; *scoured the newspaper*). [origin unknown]

scourge n. 1 person or thing seen as causing suffering. 2 whip. —v. (-ging) 1 whip. 2 punish, oppress. [Latin *corrigia* whip]

Scouse *colloq.* —n. 1 Liverpool dialect. 2 (also **Scouser**) native of Liverpool. —adj. of Liverpool. [from LOBSCOUSE]

scout —n. 1 soldier etc. sent ahead to get esp. military intelligence. 2 search for this. 3 = TALENT-SCOUT. 4 (also **Scout**) member of the Scout Association, an (orig. boys') association intended to develop character. —v. 1 (often foll. by *for*) go about searching for information etc. 2 (foll. by *about, around*) make a search. 3 (often foll. by *out*) *colloq.* explore to get information about (territory etc.). □ **scouting** n. [French *écoute(r)* from Latin *ausculto* listen]

Scouter n. adult leader of Scouts.

Scoutmaster n. person in charge of a group of Scouts.

scow n. esp. US flat-bottomed boat. [Dutch]

scowl —n. severe frowning or sullen expression. —v. make a scowl. [Scandinavian]

scrabble /'skræb(ə)l/ —v. (-ling) scratch or grope about, esp. in search of something. —n. 1 act of scrabbling. 2 (**Scrabble**) *propr.* game in which players build up words from letter-blocks on a board. [Dutch]

scrag —n. 1 (also **scrag-end**) inferior end of a neck of mutton. 2 skinny person or animal. —v. (-gg-) *slang* 1 strangle, hang. 2 handle roughly, beat up. [origin uncertain]

scraggy adj. (-ier, -iest) thin and bony. □ **scragginess** n.

scram v. (-mm-) (esp. in *imper.*) *colloq.* go away. [perhaps from SCRAMBLE]

scramble /'skræmb(ə)l/ —v. (-ling) 1 clamber, crawl, climb, etc., esp. hurriedly or anxiously. 2 (foll. by *for, at*) struggle with competitors (for a thing or share). 3 mix together indiscriminately. 4 cook (eggs) by stirring them in a pan over heat. 5 change the speech frequency of (a broadcast transmission or telephone conversation) so as to make it unintelligible without a decoding device. 6 (of fighter aircraft or pilots) take off quickly in an emergency or for action. —n. 1 act of scrambling. 2 difficult climb or walk. 3 (foll. by *for*) eager struggle or competition. 4 motor-cycle race over rough ground. 5 emergency take-off by fighter aircraft. [imitative]

scrambler n. device for scrambling telephone conversations.

scrap¹ —n. 1 small detached piece; fragment. 2 rubbish or waste material. 3 discarded metal for reprocessing (often *attrib. scrap metal*). 4 (with *neg.*) smallest piece or amount. 5 (in *pl.*) a odds and ends. b uneaten food. —v. (-pp-) discard as useless. [Old Norse: related to SCRAPE]

scrap² *colloq.* —n. fight or rough quarrel. —v. (-pp-) have a scrap. [perhaps from SCRAPE]

scrapbook n. blank book for sticking cuttings, drawings, etc., in.

scrape —v. (-ping) 1 a move a hard or sharp edge across (a surface), esp. to make smooth. b apply (a hard or sharp edge) in this way. 2 (foll. by *away, off,* etc.) remove by scraping. 3 a rub (a surface) harshly against another. b scratch or damage by scraping. 4 make (a hollow) by scraping. 5 a draw or move with a scraping sound. b make such a sound. c produce such a sound from. 6 (often foll. by *along, by, through,* etc.) move almost touching surrounding obstacles etc. (*scraped through the gap*). 7 narrowly achieve (a living, an examination pass, etc.). a barely manage. b pass an examination etc. with difficulty. 9 (foll. by *together, up*) bring, provide, or amass with difficulty. 10 be economical. 11 draw back a foot in making a clumsy bow. 12 (foll. by *back*) draw (the hair) tightly back. —n. 1 act or sound of scraping. 2 scraped place; graze. 3 *colloq.* predicament caused by rashness etc. □ **scrape the barrel** *colloq.* be reduced to a limited choice etc. [Old Norse]

scraper n. device for scraping, esp. paint etc. from a surface.

scrap heap n. 1 pile of scrap. 2 state of being discarded as useless.

scrapie /'skreɪpɪ/ n. viral disease of sheep, characterized by lack of coordination.

scraping n. (esp. in *pl.*) fragment produced by scraping.

scrap merchant n. dealer in scrap.

scrappy adj. (-ier, -iest) 1 consisting of scraps. 2 incomplete; carelessly arranged or put together.

scrapyard n. place where (esp. metal) scrap is collected for reuse.

scratch —v. 1 score, mark, or wound superficially, esp. with a sharp object. 2 (also *absol.*) scrape, esp. with the nails to relieve itching. 3 make or form by scratching. 4 (foll. by *together, up,* etc.)

= SCRAPE 9. 5 (foll. by *out*, *off*, *through*) strike (out) (writing etc.). 6 (also *absol.*) withdraw (a competitor, oneself, etc.) from a race or competition. 7 (often foll. by *about*, *around*, etc.) **a** search haphazardly (*scratching about for evidence*). —*n*. 1 mark or wound made by scratching. 2 sound of scratching. 3 spell of scratching oneself. 4 *colloq.* superficial wound. 5 line from which competitors in a race (esp. those not receiving a handicap) start. —*attrib.adj.* 1 collected by chance. 2 collected or made from whatever is available; heterogeneous. 3 (of a drawing etc.) causing itching. —*n*. 1 example of untidy manner of writing. 2 example of this. □ **scrawly** *adj.* (*-ier*, *-iest*) lean, scraggy. [dial.]

scratchy *adj.* (*-ier*, *-iest*) 1 tending to make scratches or a scratching noise. 2 causing itching. 3 (of a drawing etc.) untidy, careless. □ **scratchily** *adv.* **scratchiness** *n.*

scrawl —*v.* 1 write or make (marks) in a hurried untidy way. 2 (foll. by *out*) cross out by scrawling over. —*n.* 1 hurried untidy manner of writing. 2 example of this. □ **scrawly** *adj.* (*-ier*, *-iest*). [origin uncertain]

scrawny *adj.* (*-ier*, *-iest*) lean, scraggy. [dial.]

scream —*n.* 1 loud high-pitched cry of fear, pain, etc. 2 similar sound or cry. 3 *colloq.* hilarious occurrence or person. —*v.* 1 emit a scream. 2 speak or sing (words etc.) in a screaming tone. 3 make or move with a screaming sound. 4 laugh uncontrollably. 5 be blatantly obvious. [Old English]

scree *n.* (in *sing.* or *pl.*) 1 small loose stones. 2 mountain slope covered with these. [Old Norse. = landslip]

screech —*n.* harsh piercing scream. —*v.* utter with or make a screech. □ **screechy** *adj.* (*-ier*, *-iest*). [Old English (imitative)]

screech-owl *n.* owl that screeches, esp. a barn-owl.

screed *n.* 1 long usu. tiresome piece of writing or speech. 2 layer of cement etc. applied to level a surface. [probably from SHRED]

screen —*n.* 1 fixed or movable upright partition for separating, concealing, or protecting from heat etc. 2 thing used to conceal or shelter. 3 **a** concealing stratagem. **b** protection thus given. 4 **a** blank surface on which a photographic image is projected (in *prec.* by *the*) the cinema industry; films collectively. 5 surface of

a cathode-ray tube etc., esp. of a television, on which images appear. 6 = SIGHT-SCREEN. 7 = WINDSCREEN. 8 frame with fine netting to keep out insects etc. 9 large sieve or riddle. 10 system of checking for disease, an ability, attribute, etc. —*v.* 1 (often foll. by *from*) **a** shelter; hide. **b** protect from detection, censure, etc. 2 (foll. by *off*) conceal behind a screen. 3 show (a film, television programme, etc.). 4 prevent from causing, or protect from, electrical interference. 5 test or check (a person or group) for a disease, reliability, loyalty, etc. 6 sieve. [French]

screenplay *n.* film script.

screen printing *n.* printing process with ink forced through a prepared sheet of fine material.

screen test *n.* audition for a part in a film.

screenwriter *n.* person who writes for the cinema.

screw /skruː/ —*n.* 1 thin cylinder or cone with a spiral ridge or thread running round the outside (**male screw**) or the inside (**female screw**). 2 (in full **wood-screw**) metal male screw with a slotted head and a sharp point. 3 (in full **screw-bolt**) blunt metal male screw on which a nut is threaded to bolt things together. 4 straight screw used to exert pressure. 5 (in *sing.* or *pl.*) instrument of torture acting in this way. 6 (in full **screw-propeller**) propeller with twisted blades acting like a screw on the water or air. 7 one turn of a screw. 8 (foll. by *of*) small twisted-up paper (*of* tobacco etc.). 9 (in billiards etc.) oblique curling motion of the ball. 10 *slang* prison warder. 11 *coarse slang* act of sexual intercourse. **b** partner in this. —*v.* 1 fasten or tighten with a screw or screws. 2 turn (a screw). 3 twist or turn round like a screw. 4 (of a ball etc.) swerve. 5 (foll. by *out of*) extort (consent, money, etc.) from. 6 (also *absol.*) *coarse slang* have sexual intercourse with. 7 swindle. □ **have a screw loose** *colloq.* be slightly crazy. **put the screws on** *colloq.* pressurize, intimidate. **screw up** 1 contract and crush (a piece of paper etc.) into a tight mass. 3 summon up one's courage etc.). 4 *slang* **a** bungle. **b** spoil (an opportunity, etc.). **c** upset, disturb mentally. [French *escroue*]

screwball *n. US slang* crazy or eccentric person.

screwdriver *n.* tool with a tip that fits into the head of a screw, to turn it.

screw top *n.* (also (with hyphen) *attrib.*) screwed-on cap or lid.

screw-up *n. slang* bungle mess.

screwy *adj.* (**-ier, -iest**) *slang* **1** crazy or eccentric. **2** absurd. □ **screwiness** *n.*

scribble /ˈskrɪb(ə)l/ —*v.* (**-ling**) **1** write or draw carelessly or hurriedly. **2** *joc.* be an author or writer. —*n.* **1** scrawl. **2** hasty note etc. [Latin *scribillo* diminutive: related to SCRIBE]

scribe —*n.* **1** ancient or medieval copyist of manuscripts. **2** ancient Jewish record-keeper or professional theologian and jurist. **3** pointed instrument for making marks on wood etc. **4** (also *colloq.* writer, esp. a journalist. —*v.* (**-bing**) mark with a scribe. □ **scribal** *adj.* [Latin *scriba* from *scribo* write]

scrim *n.* open-weave fabric for lining or upholstery etc. [origin unknown]

scrimmage /ˈskrɪmɪdʒ/ —*n.* tussle; brawl. —*v.* (**-ging**) engage in this. [from SKIRMISH]

scrimp *v.* skimp. [origin unknown]

scrip *n.* **1** provisional certificate of money subscribed, entitling the holder to dividends. **2** (*collect.*) such certificates. **3** extra share or shares instead of a dividend. [abbreviation of *subscription receipt*]

script —*n.* **1** text of a play, film, or broadcast. **2** handwriting, written characters. **3** type imitating handwriting. **4** alphabet or system of writing. **5** examinee's written answers. —*v.* write a script for (a film etc.). [Latin *scriptum* from *scribo* write]

scripture /ˈskrɪptʃə(r)/ *n.* **1** sacred writings. **2** (**Scripture** or **the Scriptures**) the Bible. □ **scriptural** *adj.* [Latin: related to SCRIPT]

scriptwriter *n.* person who writes scripts for films, TV, etc. □ **scriptwriting** *n.*

scrivener /ˈskrɪvənə(r)/ *n. hist.* **1** copyist or drafter of documents. **2** notary. [French *escrivein*]

scrofula /ˈskrɒfjʊlə/ *n.* disease with glandular swellings, probably a form of tuberculosis. □ **scrofulous** *adj.* [Latin *scrofa* a sow]

scroll /skrəʊl/ —*n.* **1** roll of parchment or paper, esp. written on. **2** book in the ancient roll form. **3** ornamental design imitating a roll of parchment. —*v.* (often foll. by *down, up*) move (a display on a VDU screen) to view earlier or later material. [originally (*sc*)*rowle* ROLL]

scrolled *adj.* having a scroll ornament.

Scrooge /skruːdʒ/ *n.* miser. [name of a character in Dickens]

scrotum /ˈskrəʊtəm/ *n.* (*pl.* **scrota** or **-s**) pouch of skin containing the testicles. □ **scrotal** *adj.* [Latin]

scrounge *v.* (**-ging**) (also *absol.*) obtain by cadging. □ **on the scrounge** scrounging. □ **scrounger** *n.* [dial. *scrunge* steal]

scrub¹ —*v.* (**-bb-**) **1** clean by rubbing, esp. with a hard brush and water. **2** (often foll. by *up*) (of a surgeon etc.) clean and disinfect the hands and arms before operating. **3** *colloq.* scrap or cancel. **4** use water to remove impurities from (gases etc.). —*n.* scrubbing or being scrubbed. [Low German or Dutch]

scrub² *n.* **1** a brushwood or stunted forest growth. **b** land covered with this. **2** (*attrib.*) small or dwarf variety (*scrub pine*). □ **scrubby** *adj.* [from SHRUB]

scrubber *n.* **1** *slang* promiscuous woman. **2** apparatus for purifying gases etc.

scruff¹ *n.* back of the neck (esp. *scruff of the neck*). [perhaps from Old Norse *skoft* hair]

scruff² *n. colloq.* scruffy person. [origin uncertain]

scruffy *adj.* (**-ier, -iest**) *colloq.* shabby, slovenly, untidy. □ **scruffily** *adv.* □ **scruffiness** *n.*

scrum *n.* **1** scrummage. **2** *colloq.* = SCRIMMAGE. [abbreviation]

scrum-half *n.* half-back who puts the ball into the scrum.

scrummage *n. Rugby* massed forwards on each side pushing to gain possession of the ball thrown on the ground between them. [related to SCRIMMAGE]

scrump *v. colloq.* steal from an orchard or garden. [related to SCRUMPY]

scrumptious /ˈskrʌmpʃəs/ *adj. colloq.* **1** delicious. **2** delightful. [origin unknown]

scrumpy /ˈskrʌmpɪ/ *n. colloq.* rough cider. [dial. *scrump* small apple]

scrunch —*v.* **1** (usu. foll. by *up*) crumple. **2** crunch. —*n.* crunching sound. [var. of CRUNCH]

scruple /ˈskruːp(ə)l/ —*n.* **1** (often in *pl.*) moral concern. **2** doubt caused by this. —*v.* (**-ling**) (foll. by *to* + infin.; usu. with *neg.*) hesitate because of scruples. [Latin]

scrupulous /ˈskruːpjʊləs/ *adj.* **1** conscientious, thorough. **2** careful to avoid doing wrong. **3** punctilious; over-attentive to details. □ **scrupulously** *adv.* [Latin: related to SCRUPLE]

scrutineer /ˌskruːtɪˈnɪə(r)/ *n.* person who scrutinizes ballot-papers.

scrutinize /ˈskruːtɪnaɪz/ *v.* (also **-ise**) (**-zing** or **-sing**) subject to scrutiny.

scrutiny /ˈskruːtɪnɪ/ *n.* (*pl.* **-ies**) **1** critical gaze. **2** close investigation. **3** official examination of ballot-papers. [Latin *scrutinium* from *scrutor* examine]

scuba /ˈskuːbə/ *n.* (*pl.* **-s**) aqualung. [acronym of *self-contained underwater breathing apparatus*]

scuba-diving n. swimming under-water using a scuba. □ **scuba-diver** n.

scuba-diver n.

scud – v. (-dd-) 1 move straight and fast; skim along (*scudding clouds*). 2 *Naut.* run before the wind. —n. 1 spell of scudding. 2 scudding motion. 3 vapoury driving clouds or shower. [perhaps an alteration of scut]

scuff – v. 1 graze or brush against. 2 mark or wear out (shoes) in this way. 3 shuffle or drag the feet. —n. mark of scuffing. [imitative]

scuffle /'skʌf(ə)l/ —n. confused struggle or fight at close quarters. —v. (-ling) engage in a scuffle. [probably Scandinavian: related to SHOVE]

scull —n. 1 either of a pair of small oars. 2 oar over the stern of a boat to propel it, usu. by a twisting motion. 3 (in *pl.*) sculling race. —v. (often *absol.*) propel (a boat) with sculls. [origin unknown]

sculler n. 1 user of sculls. 2 boat for sculling.

scullery /'skʌləri/ n. (pl. **-ies**) back kit-chen; room for washing dishes etc. [Anglo-French *squillerie*]

scullion /'skʌljən/ n. *archaic* 1 cook's boy. 2 person who washes dishes etc. [origin unknown]

sculpt v. sculpture. [shortening of SCULPTOR]

sculptor n. (*fem.* **sculptress**) artist who sculptures. [Latin: related to scul-TURE]

sculpture /'skʌlptʃə(r)/ —n. 1 art of making three-dimensional or relief forms, by chiselling, carving, model-ling, casting, etc. 2 work of sculpture. —v. (-ring) 1 represent in or adorn with sculpture. 2 practise sculpture. □ **sculptural** adj. [Latin *sculpo sculpt-* carve]

scum —n. 1 layer of dirt, froth, etc. at the top of liquid. 2 *derog.* worst part, person, or group (*scum of the earth*). —v. (-mm-) 1 remove scum from. 2 form a scum (on). □ **scummy** adj. (-ier, -iest). [Low German or Dutch]

scupper¹ n. hole in a ship's side to drain water from the deck. [French *escupir* to spit]

scupper² v. *slang* 1 sink (a ship or its crew). 2 defeat or ruin (a plan etc.). 3 kill. [origin unknown]

scurf n. dandruff. □ **scurfy** adj. [Old English]

scurrilous /'skʌrɪləs/ adj. grossly or indecently abusive. □ **scurrility** /skə'rɪlɪtɪ/ n. (pl. **-ies**). **scurrilously** adv. **scurrilousness** n. [Latin *scurra* buffoon]

scurry /'skʌrɪ/ —v. (-ies, -ied) run or move hurriedly, esp. with short quick steps; scamper. —n. (pl. **-ies**) 1 act or sound of scurrying. 2 flurry of rain or snow. [abbreviation of *hurry-scurry*]

scurvy /'skɜːvɪ/ —n. disease caused by a deficiency of vitamin C. —adj. (-ier, -iest) paltry, contemptible. □ **scurvily** adv. [from SCURF]

scut n. short tail, esp. of a hare, rabbit, or deer. [origin unknown]

scutter v. & n. *colloq.* scurry. [perhaps an alteration of SCUTTLE²]

scuttle¹ n. 1 = COAL-SCUTTLE. 2 part of a car body between the wind-screen and the bonnet. [Old English from Latin *scutella* dish]

scuttle² /'skʌt(ə)l/ —v. (-ling) scurry; flee from danger etc. —n. hurried gait; precipitate flight. [perhaps related to dial. *scuddle* frequentative of scud]

scuttle³ /'skʌt(ə)l/ —n. 1 hole with a lid in a ship's deck or side. —v. let water into (a ship) to sink it. [Spanish *escotilla* hatch-way]

Scylla and Charybdis /ˌsɪlə, kə'rɪbdɪs/ n.pl. two dangers or extremes such that one can be avoided only by approaching the other. [names of a monster and a whirlpool in Greek mythology]

scythe /saɪð/ —n. mowing and reaping implement with a long handle and curved blade swung over the ground. —v. (-thing) cut with a scythe. [Old English]

SDI abbr. strategic defence initiative.

SDLP abbr. (in N. Ireland) Social Demo-cratic and Labour Party.

SDP abbr. *hist.* Social Democratic Party.

SE abbr. 1 south-east. 2 south-eastern.

Se symb. selenium.

sea n. 1 expanse of salt water that covers most of the earth's surface. 2 any part of this. 3 named tract of this partly or wholly enclosed by land (*North Sea*). 4 waves of the sea; their motion or state (*choppy sea*). 6 (foll. by *of*) vast quantity or expanse. 7 (*attrib.*) living or used in, on, or near the sea (often prefixed to the name of a marine animal, plant, etc., having a superficial resemblance to what it is named after) (*sea lettuce*). □ **at sea** 1 in a ship on the sea. 2 perplexed, confused. **by sea** in a ship or ships. **go to sea** become a sailor. **on the sea** 1 = **at sea** 1. 2 on the coast. [Old English]

sea anchor n. bag to retard the drifting of a ship.

sea anemone *n.* marine animal with tube-shaped body and petal-like tentacles.

seabed *n.* ocean floor.

sea bird *n.* bird living near the sea.

seaboard *n.* 1 seashore or coastline. 2 coastal region.

seaborne *adj.* transported by sea.

sea change *n.* notable or unexpected transformation.

sea cow *n.* 1 sirenian. 2 walrus.

sea dog *n.* old sailor.

seafarer *n.* 1 sailor. 2 traveller by sea. □ **seafaring** *adj. & n.*

seafood *n.* (often *attrib.*) edible sea fish or shellfish (*seafood restaurant*).

sea front *n.* part of a town directly facing the sea.

seagoing *adj.* (of ships) fit for crossing the sea.

sea green *adj. & n.* (as *adj.* often hyphenated) bluish-green.

seagull *n.* = GULL¹.

sea horse *n.* 1 small upright fish with a head like a horse's. 2 mythical creature with a horse's head and fish's tail.

seakale *n.* plant with young shoots used as a vegetable.

seal¹ —*n.* 1 piece of stamped wax, lead, paper, etc., attached to a document or to a receptacle, envelope, etc., to guarantee authenticity or security. 2 engraved piece of metal etc. for stamping a design on a seal. 3 substance or device used to close a gap etc. 4 anything regarded as a confirmation or guarantee (*seal of approval*). 5 decorative adhesive stamp. —*v.* 1 close securely or hermetically. 2 stamp, fasten, or fix with a seal. 3 certify as correct with a seal or stamp. 4 (often foll. by *up*) confine securely. 5 settle or decide (*their fate is sealed*). 6 (foll. by *off*) prevent entry to or exit from (an area). □ **set one's seal to** (or **on**) authorize or confirm. [Latin *sigillum*]

seal² —*n.* fish-eating amphibious marine mammal with flippers. —*v.* hunt for seals. [Old English]

sealant *n.* material for sealing, esp. to make airtight or watertight.

sea legs *n.pl.* ability to keep one's balance and avoid seasickness at sea.

sea level *n.* mean level of the sea's surface, used in reckoning the height of hills etc. and as a barometric standard.

sealing-wax *n.* mixture softened by heating and used to make seals.

sea lion *n.* large, eared seal.

Sea Lord *n.* naval member of the Admiralty Board.

sealskin *n.* 1 skin or prepared fur of a seal. 2 (often *attrib.*) garment made from this.

seals of office *n.pl.* seals held, esp. by the Lord Chancellor or a Secretary of State.

seam —*n.* 1 line where two edges join, esp. of cloth or boards. 2 fissure between parallel edges. 3 wrinkle. 4 stratum of coal etc. —*v.* 1 join with a seam. 2 (esp. as **seamed** *adj.*) mark or score with a seam. □ **seamless** *adj.* [Old English]

seaman *n.* 1 person whose work is at sea. 2 sailor, esp. one below the rank of officer.

seamanship *n.* skill in managing a ship or boat.

seam bowler *n. Cricket* bowler who makes the ball deviate by bouncing it off its seam.

sea mile *n.* = unit varying between approx. 2,014 yards (1,842 metres) and 2,035 yards (1,861 metres).

seamstress /'semstris/ *n.* (also **sempstress**) woman who sews, esp. for a living. [Old English: related to SEAM]

seamy *adj.* (**-ier**, **-iest**) 1 disreputable or sordid (esp. *the seamy side*). 2 marked with or showing seams. □ **seaminess** *n.*

seance /'seiɒs/ *n.* meeting at which a spiritualist attempts to make contact with the dead. [French]

sea pink *n.* maritime plant with bright pink flowers.

seaplane *n.* aircraft designed to take off from and land on water.

seaport *n.* town with a harbour.

sear *v.* 1 scorch, cauterize. 2 cause anguish to. 3 brown (meat) quickly at a high temperature to retain its juices in cooking. [Old English]

search /sɜːtʃ/ —*v.* 1 (also *absol.*) look through or go over thoroughly to find something. 2 examine or feel over (a person) to find anything concealed. 3 probe (*search one's conscience*). 4 (foll. by *for*) look thoroughly in order to find. 5 (as **searching** *adj.*) (of an examination) thorough; keenly questioning (*searching gaze*). 6 (foll. by *out*) look for; seek out. —*n.* 1 act of searching. 2 investigation. □ **in search of** trying to find. **search me!** *colloq.* I do not know. □ **searcher** *n.* **searchingly** *adv.* [Anglo-French *cercher*]

searchlight *n.* 1 powerful outdoor electric light with a concentrated beam that can be turned in any direction. 2 light or beam from this.

search-party *n.* group of people conducting an organized search.

search warrant *n.* official authorization to enter and search a building.

sea room *n.* space at sea for a ship to turn etc.

sea salt *n.* salt produced by evaporating sea water.

seascape n. picture or view of the sea.

Sea Scout n. member of the maritime branch of the Scout Association.

seashell n. shell of a salt-water mollusc.

seashore n. land next to the sea.

seasick adj. nauseous from the motion of a ship at sea. □ **seasickness** n.

seaside n. sea-coast, esp. as a holiday resort.

season /'siːz(ə)n/ —n. 1 each of the climatic divisions of the year (spring, summer, autumn, winter). 2 proper or suitable time. 3 time when something is plentiful, active, etc. 4 (usu. prec. by the) indefinite period; London in the season. —v. 1 flavour (food) with salt, herbs, etc. 2 enhance with wit etc. 3 moderate. 4 (esp. as **seasoned** adj.) make or become suitable by exposure to the weather or experience (seasoned wood; seasoned campaigner). □ **in season** 1 (of food) plentiful and good. 2 (of an animal) on heat. [Latin satio sowing]

seasonable adj. 1 suitable or usual to the season. 2 opportune. 3 apt.

■ **Usage** Seasonable is sometimes confused with seasonal.

seasonal adj. of, depending on, or varying with the season. □ **seasonally** adv.

seasoning n. salt, herbs, etc. added to food to enhance its flavour.

season ticket n. ticket entitling the holder to unlimited travel, access, etc., in a given period.

seat —n. 1 thing made or used for sitting on. 2 a buttocks. b part of a garment covering them. 3 part of a chair etc. on which the seat of a person rests 4 place for one person in a theatre etc. 5 position as an MP, committee member, etc., or the right to occupy it. 6 supporting or guiding part of a machine. 7 location (seat of learning). 8 country mansion. 9 manner of sitting on a horse etc. —v. 1 cause to sit. 2 provide sitting accommodation for (bus seats 50). 3 (as **seated** adj.) sitting. 4 put or fit in position. □ **be seated** sit down. **by the seat of one's pants** colloq. by instinct rather than knowledge. **take a seat** sit down. [Old Norse related to sit]

seat-belt n. belt securing motor vehicle or aircraft passengers.

-seater comb. form having a specified number of seats.

seating n. 1 seats collectively. 2 sitting accommodation.

sea urchin n. small marine animal with a spiny shell.

sea wall n. wall built to stop flooding or erosion by the sea.

seaward /'siːwəd/ —adv. (also **seawards**) towards the sea. —adj. going or facing towards the sea.

seaway n. 1 inland waterway open to seagoing ships. 2 ship's progress. 3 ship's path across the sea.

seaweed n. plant growing in the sea or on rocks on a shore.

seaworthy adj. fit to put to sea. □ **seaworthiness** n.

sebaceous /sɪ'beɪʃəs/ adj. fatty, secreting oily matter. [Latin sebum tallow]

Sec. abbr. (also **sec**) secretary.

sec[1] abbr. secant.

sec[2] n. colloq. (in phrases) second, moment (wait a sec). [abbreviation]

sec. abbr. second(s).

secant /'siːkænt/ n. Math. 1 ratio of the hypotenuse to the shorter side adjacent to an acute angle (in a right-angled triangle). 2 line cutting a curve at one or more points. [French]

secateurs /sekə'tɜːz/ n.pl. pruning clippers used with one hand. [French]

secede /sɪ'siːd/ v. (-**ding**) withdraw formally from a political federation or religious body. [Latin secedo cess-]

secession /sɪ'seʃ(ə)n/ n. act of seceding. [Latin related to SECEDE] □ **secessionist** n. & adj.

seclude /sɪ'kluːd/ v. (-**ding**) (also refl.) 1 keep (a person or place) away from others. 2 (esp. as **secluded** adj.) screen from view. [Latin secludo clus-]

seclusion /sɪ'kluːʒ(ə)n/ n. secluded state or place.

second[1] —adj. 1 next after first. 2 additional (ate a second cake). 3 subordinate; inferior. 4 Mus. performing a lower or subordinate part (second violins). 5 such as to be comparable to (a second Callas). —n. 1 runner-up. 2 person or thing besides the first or previously mentioned one. 3 second gear. 4 second helping or course. 5 (in pl.) colloq. second helping or course 5 assistant to a duellist, boxer, etc. —v. 1 support; back up. 2 formally support (a nomination, resolution, or its proposer). □ **at second hand** indirectly. [Latin secundus from sequor follow]

second[2] /'sekənd/ n. 1 sixtieth of a minute of time or of an angle. 2 colloq. very short time (wait a second). [medieval Latin secunda (minuta) secondary (minute)]

second[3] /sɪ'kɒnd/ v. transfer (a person) temporarily to another department etc. □ **secondment** n. [French en second in the second rank]

secondary /ˈsekəndəri/ *–adj.* **1** coming after or next below what is primary. **2** derived from or supplementing what is primary. **3** (of education, a school, etc.) following primary, esp. from the age of 11. *–n.* (*pl.* **-ies**) secondary thing. □ **secondarily** *adv.* [Latin: related to SECOND]

secondary colour *n.* result of mixing two primary colours.

secondary picketing *n.* picketing of premises of a firm not directly involved in an industrial dispute.

second-best *adj.* & *n.* next after best.

second chamber *n.* upper house of a parliament.

second class *–n.* second-best group, category, postal service, or accommodation. *–adj.* & *adv.* (**second-class**) of or by the second class (*second-class citizens; travelled second-class*).

second cousin *n.* son or daughter of one's parent's cousin.

second-degree *adj.* denoting burns that cause blistering but not permanent scars.

second fiddle see FIDDLE.

second-guess *v. colloq.* **1** anticipate by guesswork. **2** criticize with hindsight.

second-hand *–adj.* **1 a** having had a previous owner; not new. **b** (*attrib.*) (of a shop etc.) where such goods can be bought. **2** (of information etc.) indirect, not from one's own observation etc. *–adv.* **1** on a second-hand basis. **2** indirectly.

second lieutenant *n.* army officer next below lieutenant.

secondly *adv.* **1** furthermore. **2** as a second item.

second nature *n.* acquired tendency that has become instinctive.

second officer *n.* assistant mate on a merchant ship.

second person see PERSON.

second-rate *adj.* mediocre; inferior.

second sight *n.* clairvoyance.

second string *n.* alternative course of action etc.

second thoughts *n.pl.* revised opinion or resolution.

second wind *n.* **1** recovery of normal breathing during exercise after initial breathlessness. **2** renewed energy to continue.

secrecy /ˈsiːkrəsi/ *n.* state of being secret; habit or faculty of keeping secrets (*done in secrecy*).

secret /ˈsiːkrɪt/ *–adj.* **1** kept or meant to be kept private, unknown, or hidden. **2** acting or operating secretly. **3** fond of secrecy. *–n.* **1** thing kept or meant to be kept secret. **2** mystery. **3** effective but not generally known method (*what's*

their secret?; the secret of success). □ **in secret** secretly. □ **secretly** *adv.* [Latin *secerno secret-* separate]

secret agent *n.* spy.

secretaire /sekrɪˈteə(r)/ *n.* escritoire. [French: related to SECRETARY]

secretariat /sekrɪˈteəriət/ *n.* **1** administrative office or department. **2** its members or premises. [medieval Latin: related to SECRETARY]

secretary /ˈsekrɪtəri/ *n.* (*pl.* **-ies**) **1** employee who assists with correspondence, records, making appointments, etc. **2** official of a society or company who writes letters, organizes papers, etc. **3** principal assistant of a government minister, ambassador, etc. □ **secretarial** /-ˈteəriəl/ *adj.* □ **secretaryship** *n.* [Latin *secretarius*: related to SECRET]

secretary bird *n.* long-legged crested African bird.

Secretary-General *n.* principal administrator of an organization.

Secretary of State *n.* **1** head of a major government department. **2** *US* = FOREIGN MINISTER.

secret ballot *n.* ballot in which votes are cast in secret.

secrete /sɪˈkriːt/ *v.* (**-ting**) **1** (of a cell, organ, etc.) produce and discharge (a substance). **2** conceal. □ **secretory** *adj.* [from SECRET]

secretion /sɪˈkriːʃ(ə)n/ *n.* **1 a** process of secreting. **b** secreted substance. **2** act of concealing. [Latin: related to SECRET]

secretive /ˈsiːkrətɪv/ *adj.* inclined to make or keep secrets; uncommunicative. □ **secretively** *adv.* □ **secretiveness** *n.*

secret police *n.* police force operating secretly for political ends.

secret service *n.* government department concerned with espionage.

secret society *n.* society whose members are sworn to secrecy about it.

sect *n.* **1** group sharing (usu. unorthodox) religious, political, or philosophical doctrines. **2** (esp. exclusive) religious denomination. [Latin *sequor* *secut-* follow]

sectarian /sekˈteəriən/ *–adj.* **1** of a sect. **2** devoted, esp. narrow-mindedly, to one's sect. *–n.* member of a sect. □ **sectarianism** *n.* [medieval Latin *sectarius* adherent]

section /ˈsekʃ(ə)n/ *–n.* **1** each of the parts of a thing or out of which a thing can be fitted together. **2** part cut off. **3** subdivision of a town. **4** *US* area of land. **b** district of a town. **5** act of cutting or separating surgically. **6 a** resulting figure or area. *–v.* **1** arrange in or divide into sections. **2** compulsorily commit to a

psychiatric hospital. [Latin *seco sect-* cut]

sectional /ˈsekʃən(ə)l/ *adj.* **1 a** of a social group (*sectional interests*). **b** partisan. **2** made in sections. **3** local rather than general. □ **sectionally** *adv.*

sector /ˈsektə(r)/ *n.* **1** distinct part of an enterprise, society, the economy, etc. **2** military subdivision of an area. **3** plane figure enclosed by two radii of a circle, ellipse, etc., and the arc between them. [Latin: related to SECTION]

secular /ˈsekjʊlə(r)/ *adj.* **1** not concerned with religion; not sacred; worldly (*secular education; secular music*). **2** (of clerics) not monastic. □ **-ise** (*also* **-ize**) *v.* **secularism** *n.* **secularize** *v.* (*also* **-ise**) (-*zing or* -*sing*). **secularization** /-ˈzeɪʃ(ə)n/ *n.* [Latin *saeculum* an age]

secure /sɪˈkjʊə(r)/ *adj.* **1** untroubled by danger or fear. **2** safe. **3** reliable; stable; fixed. —*v.* (-*ring*) **1** make secure or safe. **2** fasten or close securely. **3** succeed in obtaining. □ **securely** *adv.* [Latin *se-* without, *cura* care]

security risk *n.* person or thing that threatens security.

security *n.* (*pl.* -**ies**) **1** secure condition or feeling. **2** thing that guards or guarantees. **3 a** safety against espionage, theft, etc. **b** organization for ensuring this. **4** thing deposited as a guarantee of an undertaking or loan, to be forfeited in case of default. **5** (often in *pl.*) document as evidence of a loan, certificate of stock, bonds, etc.

sedan /sɪˈdæn/ *n.* **1** (in full **sedan chair**) *hist.* enclosed chair for one, carried on poles by two men. **2** *US* enclosed car with four or more seats. [origin uncertain]

sedate /sɪˈdeɪt/ —*adj.* tranquil and dignified; serious. —*v.* (-*ting*) put under sedation. □ **sedately** *adv.* **sedateness** *n.* [Latin *sedo* settle, calm]

sedation /sɪˈdeɪʃ(ə)n/ *n.* act of calming, esp. by sedatives. [Latin: related to SEDATE]

sedative /ˈsedətɪv/ —*n.* calming drug or influence. —*adj.* calming, soothing. [medieval Latin: related to SEDATE]

sedentary /ˈsedəntərɪ/ *adj.* **1** sitting. **2** (of work etc.) done while sitting. **3** (of a person) disinclined to exercise. [Latin *sedeo* sit]

sedge *n.* waterside or marsh plant resembling coarse grass. □ **sedgy** *adj.* [Old English]

sediment /ˈsedɪmənt/ *n.* **1** grounds; dregs. **2** matter deposited on the land by water or wind. □ **sedimentary** /-ˈmentərɪ/ *adj.* **sedimentation** /-ˈteɪʃ(ə)n/ *n.* [Latin *sedeo* sit]

sedition /sɪˈdɪʃ(ə)n/ *n.* conduct or speech inciting to rebellion. □ **seditious** *adj.* [Latin *seditio*]

seduce /sɪˈdjuːs/ *v.* (-*cing*) **1** entice into sexual activity or wrongdoing. **2** coax or lead astray. □ **seducer** *n.* [Latin *se-* away, *duco duct-* lead]

seduction /sɪˈdʌkʃ(ə)n/ *n.* **1** seducing or being seduced. **2** thing that tempts or attracts.

seductive /sɪˈdʌktɪv/ *adj.* alluring, enticing. □ **seductively** *adv.* **seductiveness** *n.*

seductress /sɪˈdʌktrɪs/ *n.* female seducer. [obsolete *seductor* male seducer, related to SEDUCE]

sedulous /ˈsedjʊləs/ *adj.* persevering, diligent, painstaking. □ **sedulity** /sɪˈdjuːlɪtɪ/ *n.* **sedulously** *adv.* [Latin *sedulus* zealous]

sedum /ˈsiːdəm/ *n.* fleshy-leaved plant with yellow, pink, or white flowers, e.g. the stonecrop. [Latin = houseleek]

see *v.* (*past* **saw**; *past part.* **seen**) **1** perceive with the eyes. **2** have or use this power. **3** discern mentally; understand. **4** watch (a film, game, etc.). **5** ascertain, learn (*will see if he's here*). **6** imagine, foresee (*see trouble ahead*). **7** look at for information (*see page 15*). **8** meet and recognize (*I saw your mother in town*). **9 a** meet socially or on business; visit or be visited by (*is too ill to see anyone; must see a doctor*). **b** meet regularly as a boyfriend or girlfriend. **10** reflect, wait for clarification (*use shall have to see*). **11** experience (*I never thought to see it*). **12** find attractive (*can't think what she sees in him*). **13** escort, conduct (*saw them home*). **14** witness (an event etc.). (*see the New Year in*). **15** ensure (*see that it is done*). **16 a** (in poker etc.) equal (a bet). **b** equal the bet of (a player). □ **see about 1** attend to. **2** consider. **see the back of** *colloq.* be rid of. **see fit** *see* FIT. **see the light 1** realize one's mistakes etc. **2** undergo religious conversion. **see off 1** be present at the departure of (a person). **2** *colloq.* ward off, get the better of. **see out 1** accompany out of a building etc. **2** finish (a project etc.). **3** survive (a period etc.). **see over** inspect; tour. **see red** *colloq.* become enraged. **see stars** *colloq.* see lights as a result of a blow on the head. **see through 1** detect the truth or true nature of, not be deceived by. **2** penetrate visually. **see a person through** support a person during a difficult time. **see a thing through** finish it completely. **see to** it (foll. by *that*) ensure. [Old English]

see² n. 1 area under the authority of a bishop or archbishop. 2 his office or jurisdiction. [Latin *sedes* seat]

seed —n. 1 a a part of a plant capable of developing into another such plant. b seeds collectively, esp. for sowing. 2 semen. 3 prime cause, beginning. 4 offspring, descendants. 5 (in tennis etc.) seeded player. —v. 1 a place seeds in. b sprinkle (as) with seed. 2 sow seeds. 3 produce or drop seed. 4 remove seeds from (fruit etc.). 5 place a crystal etc. in (a cloud) to produce rain. 6 *Sport* a so position (a strong competitor in a knockout competition) that he or she will not meet other strong competitors in early rounds. b arrange (the order of play) in this way. □ **go** (or **run**) **to seed 1** cease flowering as seed develops. 2 become degenerate, unkempt, etc. □ **seedless** adj. [Old English]

seed-bed n. 1 bed prepared for sowing. 2 place of development.

seedling n. young plant raised from seed rather than from a cutting etc.

seed-pearl n. very small pearl.

seed-potato n. potato kept for seed.

seedsman n. dealer in seeds.

seedy adj. (**-ier**, **-iest**) 1 shabby, unkempt. 2 *colloq.* unwell. 3 full of or going to seed. □ **seediness** n.

seeing conj. (usu. foll. by *that*) considering that, inasmuch as, because.

seek v. (*past* and *past part.* **sought** /sɔːt/) 1 (often foll. by *for, after*) search or inquire. 2 try or want to find or get or reach (*sought my hand*). b request (*sought help*). 3 endeavour (*seek to please*). □ **seek out 1** search for and find. 2 single out as a friend etc. □ **seeker** n. [Old English]

seem v. (often foll. by *to* + infin.) appear or feel (*seems ridiculous*). □ **I** etc. **can't seem to** I etc. appear unable to (*can't seem to manage it*). **it seems** (or **would seem**) (often foll. by *that*) it appears to be the case. [Old Norse]

seeming adj. apparent but perhaps doubtful (*his seeming interest*). □ **seemingly** adv.

seemly adj. (**-ier**, **-iest**) in good taste; decorous. □ **seemliness** n. [Old Norse: related to SEEM]

seen *past part.* of SEE¹.

seep v. ooze out; percolate. [Old English]

seepage n. 1 act of seeping. 2 quantity that seeps out.

seer n. 1 person who sees. 2 prophet; visionary.

seersucker /ˈsɪəsʌkə(r)/ n. linen, cotton, etc. fabric with a puckered surface. [Persian]

see-saw /ˈsiːsɔː/ —n. 1 a a long plank balanced on a central support, for children to sit on at each end and move up and down alternately. b this game. 2 up-and-down or to-and-fro motion. 3 close contest with alternating advantage. —v. 1 play on a see-saw. 2 move up and down. 3 vacillate in policy, emotion, etc. —adj. & adv. with up-and-down or backward-and-forward motion. [reduplication of SAW¹]

seethe /siːð/ v. (**-thing**) 1 boil, bubble over. 2 be very angry, resentful, etc. [Old English]

see-through adj. (esp. of clothing) translucent.

segment /ˈsɛgmənt/ —n. 1 each part into which a thing is or can be divided. 2 part of a circle or sphere etc. cut off by an intersecting line or plane. —v. usu. /ˈment/ divide into segments. □ **segmental** /-ˈment(ə)l/ adj. **segmentation** /-ˈteɪʃ(ə)n/ n. [Latin *seco* cut]

segregate /ˈsɛgrɪgeɪt/ v. (**-ting**) 1 put apart; isolate. 2 separate (esp. an ethnic group) from the rest of the community. [Latin *grex greg-* flock]

segregation /ˌsɛgrɪˈgeɪʃ(ə)n/ n. 1 enforced separation of ethnic groups in a community etc. 2 segregating or being segregated. □ **segregationist** n. & adj.

seigneur /seɪnˈjɜː(r)/ n. feudal lord. □ **seigneurial** adj. [French from Latin *senior* SENIOR]

seine /seɪn/ —n. fishing-net with floats at the top and weights at the bottom edge. —v. (**-ning**) fish or catch with a seine. [Old English *segne*]

seise var. of SEIZE 6.

seismic /ˈsaɪzmɪk/ adj. of earthquakes. [Greek *seismos* earthquake]

seismograph /ˈsaɪzməˌɡrɑːf/ n. instrument that records the force, direction, etc., of earthquakes. □ **seismographic** /-ˈɡræfɪk/ adj.

seismology /saɪzˈmɒlədʒɪ/ n. the study of earthquakes. □ **seismological** /-məˈlɒdʒɪk(ə)l/ adj. **seismologist** n.

seize /siːz/ v. (**-zing**) 1 (often foll. by *on, upon*) take hold of forcibly or suddenly. 2 take possession of forcibly or by legal power. 3 affect suddenly (*panic seized us*). 4 (often foll. by *on, upon*) take advantage of (an opportunity etc.). 5 (often foll. by *on, upon*) comprehend quickly or clearly. 6 (also **seise**) (usu. foll. by *of*) *Law* put in possession of. □ **seized** (or **seised**) **of 1** possessing legally. 2 aware or informed of. □ **seize up 1** (of a mechanism) become jammed. 2 (of part of the body etc.) become stiff. [French *saisir*]

seizure /'siːʒə(r)/ n. 1 seizing or being seized. 2 sudden attack, esp. of epilepsy or apoplexy.

seldom /'seldəm/ adv. rarely, not often. [Old English]

select /sɪ'lekt/ —v. choose. esp. with care. —adj. 1 chosen for excellence or suitability. 2 (of a society etc.) exclusive. [Latin *seligo -lect-*]

select committee n. small parliamentary committee conducting a special inquiry.

selection /sɪ'lekʃ(ə)n/ n. 1 selecting or being selected. 2 selected person or thing. 3 things from which a choice may be made. 4 evolutionary process by which some species thrive better than others.

selective adj. 1 of or using selection (*selective schools*). 2 able to select 3 (of memory etc.) selecting what is convenient. □ **selectively** adv. **selectivity** /-'tɪvɪtɪ/ n.

selector n. 1 person who selects, esp. a team. 2 device in a vehicle, machinery, etc. that selects the required gear etc.

selenium /sɪ'liːnɪəm/ n. non-metallic element occurring naturally in various metallic sulphide ores. [Greek *selēnē* moon]

self n. (pl. **selves**) 1 individuality, personality, or essence (*showed his true self*; *is her old self again*). 2 object of introspection or reflexive action. 3 a one's own interests or pleasure. b concentration on these. 4 *Commerce* or *colloq.* myself, yourself, etc. (*cheque drawn to self*). [Old English]

self- comb. form expressing reflexive action: 1 of or directed at oneself (*self-locking*). 2 on, in, for, or of oneself or itself (*self-absorbed*).

self-abasement /,self ə'beɪsmənt/ n. self-humiliation; cringing.

self-absorption /,selfəb'zɔːpʃ(ə)n/ n. absorption in oneself. □ **self-absorbed** adj.

self-abuse /,self ə'bjuːs/ n. masturbation.

self-addressed /,selfə'drest/ adj. (of an envelope) bearing one's own address for a reply.

self-adhesive /,selfəd'hiːsɪv/ adj. (of an envelope, label, etc.) adhesive, esp. without wetting.

self-advancement /,selfəd'vɑːnsmənt/ n. advancement of oneself.

self-aggrandizement /,selfə'grændɪzmənt/ n. process of enriching oneself or making oneself powerful. □ **self-aggrandizing** /-'grændaɪzɪŋ/ adj.

self-analysis /,selfə'næləsɪs/ n. analysis of oneself, one's motives, character, etc.

self-appointed /,selfə'pɔɪntɪd/ adj. designated so by oneself, not by others (*self-appointed critic*).

self-assembly /,selfə'semblɪ/ adj. assembled by the buyer from a kit.

self-assertive /,selfə'sɜːtɪv/ adj. confident or aggressive in promoting oneself, one's rights, etc. □ **self-assertion** n.

self-assured /,selfə'ʃʊəd/ adj. self-confident. □ **self-assurance** n.

self-aware /,selfə'weə(r)/ adj. conscious of one's character, feelings, motives, etc. □ **self-awareness** n.

self-catering /,self'keɪtərɪŋ/ adj. (of a holiday, accommodation etc.) with cooking facilities provided, but no food.

self-censorship /self'sensəʃɪp/ n. censoring of oneself.

self-centred /,self'sentəd/ adj. (US **-centered**) preoccupied with oneself, selfish. □ **self-centredly** adv. **self-centredness** n.

self-cleaning /,self'kliːnɪŋ/ adj. (esp. of an oven) cleaning itself when heated.

self-conceit /,self'kɒnsiːt/ n. high or exaggerated opinion of oneself.

self-confessed /,self'kɒnfest/ adj. openly admitting oneself to be.

self-confident /,self'kɒnfɪd(ə)nt/ adj. having confidence in oneself. □ **self-confidence** n. **self-confidently** adv.

self-congratulatory /,selfkəŋ'grætjʊlətərɪ/ adj. = SELF-SATISFIED.

self-conscious /,self'kɒnʃəs/ adj. nervous, shy, or embarrassed. □ **self-consciously** adv. **self-consciousness** n.

self-consistent /,self kən'sɪst(ə)nt/ adj. (of parts of the same whole etc.) consistent; not conflicting. □ **self-consistency** n.

self-contained /,self kən'teɪnd/ adj. 1 (of a person) uncommunicative; independent. 2 (of accommodation) complete in itself, having no shared entrance or facilities.

self-control /,self kən'trəʊl/ n. power of controlling one's behaviour, emotions, etc. □ **self-controlled** adj.

self-critical /,self'krɪtɪk(ə)l/ adj. critical of oneself, one's abilities, etc. □ **self-criticism** /-'sɪz(ə)m/ n.

self-deception /,self dɪ'sepʃ(ə)n/ n. deceiving of oneself esp. about one's motives or feelings. □ **self-deceit** /-dɪ'siːt/ n.

self-defeating /,self dɪ'fiːtɪŋ/ adj. (of an action etc.) doomed to failure because of internal inconsistencies; achieving the opposite of what is intended.

self-defence /,self dɪ'fens/ n. (US **-defense**) physical or verbal defence of

one's body, property, rights, reputation, etc.

self-denial /ˌselfdɪˈnaɪəl/ n. asceticism, esp. to discipline oneself. □ **self-deny-ing** adj.

self-deprecation /ˌselfdepraˈkeɪʃ(ə)n/ n. belittling of oneself. □ **self-depreca-ting** /ˈdepri,keitin/ adj.

self-destruct /ˌselfdɪˈstrʌkt/ —v. (of a spacecraft, bomb, etc.) explode or disin-tegrate automatically, esp. when pre-set to do so.—attrib. adj. enabling a thing to self-destruct (self-destruct device).

self-destruction /ˌselfdɪˈstrʌkʃ(ə)n/ n. 1 destroying of itself or oneself or one's chances, happiness, etc. 2 act of self destructing. □ **self-destructive** adj.

self-determination /ˌselfdɪtɜːmɪˈneɪʃ(ə)n/ n. 1 nation's right to determine its own government etc. 2 ability to act with free will

self-discipline /selfˈdɪsɪplɪn/ n. 1 abil-ity to apply oneself. 2 self-control. □ **self-disciplined** adj.

self-discovery /ˌselfdɪˈskʌvəri/ n. pro-cess of acquiring insight into one's character, desires, etc.

self-doubt /selfˈdaʊt/ n. lack of confid-ence in oneself

self-drive /selfˈdraɪv/ adj. (of a hired vehicle) driven by the hirer.

self-educated /selfˈedjʊˌkeɪtɪd/ adj. educated by one's own reading etc., without formal instruction.

self-effacing /ˌselfɪˈfeɪsɪŋ/ adj. retiring; modest. □ **self-effacement** n.

self-employed /ˌselfɪmˈplɔɪd/ adj. working as a freelance or for one's own business etc. □ **self-employment** n.

self-esteem /ˌselfɪˈstiːm/ n. good opin-ion of oneself.

self-evident /selfˈevɪd(ə)nt/ adj. ob-vious, without the need of proof or further explanation. □ **self-evidence** n. **self-evidently** adv.

self-examination /ˌselfɪgˌzæmɪˈneɪʃ(ə)n/ n. 1 the study of one's own conduct etc. 2 examining of one's own body for signs of illness.

self-explanatory /ˌselfɪkˈsplænətəri/ adj. not needing explanation.

self-expression /ˌselfɪkˈspreʃ(ə)n/ n. artistic or free expression.

self-financing /ˌselfˈfaɪnænsɪŋ/ adj. (of an institution or undertaking) that pays for itself with-out subsidy.

self-fulfilling /ˌselfˈfʊlfɪlɪŋ/ adj. (of a prophecy etc.) bound to come true as a result of its being made.

self-fulfilment /ˌselfˈfʊlfɪlmənt/ n. ful-filment of one's ambitions etc.

self-governing /ˌselfˈgʌvənɪŋ/ adj. governing itself or oneself. □ **self--government** n.

self-help /selfˈhelp/ n. (often attrib.) use of one's own abilities, resources, etc. to solve one's problems etc. (formed a self-help group)

self-image /selfˈɪmɪdʒ/ n. one's concep-tion of oneself.

self-important /ˌselfɪmˈpɔːt(ə)nt/ adj. conceited; pompous. □ **self--importance** n.

self-imposed /ˌselfɪmˈpəʊzd/ adj. (of a task etc.) imposed on and by oneself.

self-improvement /ˌselfɪmˈpruːv-mənt/ n. improvement of oneself or one's life etc. by one's own efforts.

self-induced /ˌselfɪnˈdjuːst/ adj. in-duced by oneself or itself.

self-indulgent /ˌselfɪnˈdʌldʒ(ə)nt/ adj. 1 indulging in one's own pleasure, feelings, etc. 2 (of a work of art etc.) lacking economy and control. □ **self--indulgence** n.

self-inflicted /ˌselfɪnˈflɪktɪd/ adj. in-flicted by and on oneself.

self-interest /selfˈɪntrest/ n. one's per-sonal interest or advantage. □ **self-interested** adj.

selfish adj. concerned chiefly with one's own interests or pleasure; actuated by or appealing to self-interest. □ **self-ishly** adv. **selfishness** n.

self-justification /ˌselfdʒʌstɪfɪ-ˈkeɪʃ(ə)n/ n. justification or excusing of oneself.

self-knowledge /selfˈnɒlɪdʒ/ n. under-standing of oneself.

selfless adj. unselfish. □ **selflessly** adv. **selflessness** n.

self-made adj. successful or rich by one's own effort.

self-opinionated /ˌselfəˈpɪnjə,neɪtɪd/ adj. stubbornly adhering to one's opin-ions.

self-perpetuating /ˌselfpəˈpetjuːˌeɪtɪŋ/ adj. perpetuating itself or oneself with-out external agency.

self-pity /selfˈpɪti/ n. feeling sorry for oneself. □ **self-pitying** adj.

self-pollination /ˌselfpɒlɪˈneɪʃ(ə)n/ n. pollination of a flower by pollen from the same plant. □ **self-pollinating** adj.

self-portrait /selfˈpɔːtrɪt/ n. portrait or description of oneself by oneself.

self-possessed /ˌselfpəˈzest/ adj. calm and composed. □ **self-possession** /-ˈzeʃ(ə)n/ n.

self-preservation /ˌselfprezəˈveɪʃ(ə)n/ n. 1 keeping oneself safe. 2 instinct for this

self-proclaimed /ˌselfprəˈkleɪmd/ adj. proclaimed by oneself or itself to be such.

self-propelled /ˌselfprəˈpeld/ adj. (of a vehicle etc.) propelled by its own power. □ **self-propelling** adj.

self-raising /ˈselfreɪzɪŋ/ adj. (of flour) containing a raising agent.

self-realization /ˌselfrɪəlaɪˈzeɪʃ(ə)n/ n. development of one's abilities etc.

self-regard /ˌselfrɪˈɡɑːd/ n. proper regard for oneself.

self-regulating /ˈselfreɡjuleɪtɪŋ/ adj. regulating oneself or itself without intervention. □ **self-regulation** /-ˈleɪʃ(ə)n/ n. **self-regulatory** /-ˈleɪt(ə)rɪ/ adj.

self-reliance /ˌselfrɪˈlaɪəns/ n. reliance on one's own resources etc.; independence. □ **self-reliant** adj.

self-reproach /ˌselfrɪˈprəʊtʃ/ n. reproach directed at oneself.

self-respect /ˌselfrɪˈspekt/ n. respect for oneself. □ **self-respecting** adj.

self-restraint /ˌselfrɪˈstreɪnt/ n. self-control.

self-righteous /selfˈraɪtʃəs/ adj. smugly sure of one's rightness. □ **self-righteously** adv. **self-righteousness** n.

selfsame adj. (prec. by the) very same, identical.

self-satisfied /selfˈsætɪsfaɪd/ adj. complacent, self-righteous. □ **self-satisfaction** /-ˈfækʃ(ə)n/ n.

self-sealing /selfˈsiːlɪŋ/ adj. 1 (of a tyre etc.) automatically able to seal small punctures. 2 (of an envelope) self-adhesive.

self-seed /selfˈsiːd/ v. (of a plant) propagate itself by seed. □ **self-seeder** n.

self-seeking /selfˈsiːkɪŋ/ adj. & n. self-ish.

self-service /selfˈsɜːvɪs/ —adj. (often attrib.) (of a shop, restaurant, etc.) allowing customers serving themselves and paying at a checkout etc. —n. colloq. self-service restaurant etc.

self-starter /selfˈstɑːtə(r)/ n. 1 electrical appliance for starting an engine. 2 ambitious person with initiative.

self-styled adj. called so by oneself.

self-sufficient /ˌselfsəˈfɪʃ(ə)nt/ adj. able to supply one's own needs; independent. □ **self-sufficiency** n.

self-supporting /ˌselfsəˈpɔːtɪŋ/ adj. financially self-sufficient.

self-taught /selfˈtɔːt/ adj. self-educated.

self-willed /selfˈwɪld/ adj. obstinately pursuing one's own wishes.

self-worth /selfˈwɜːθ/ n. = SELF-ESTEEM.

sell —v. (past and past part. **sold** /səʊld/) 1 exchange or be exchanged for money (these sell well). 2 stock for sale (do you sell eggs?). 3 (foll. by at, for) have a specified price (sells at £5). 4 (also refl.) betray or prostitute for money etc. 5 (also refl.) advertise or publicize (a product, oneself, etc.). **6** cause to be sold (name alone will sell it). 7 colloq. make (a person) enthusiastic about (an idea etc.). —n. colloq. 1 manner of selling (soft sell). 2 deception; disappointment. □ **sell down the river** see RIVER. **sell off** sell at reduced prices. **sell out 1** (also absol.) sell (all one's stock, shares, etc.). 2 betray; be treacherous or disloyal. **sell up** sell one's business, house, etc. [Old English]

sell-by date n. latest recommended date of sale.

seller n. 1 person who sells. 2 thing that sells well or badly.

seller's market n. (also **sellers' market**) trading conditions favourable to the seller.

selling-point n. advantageous feature.

Sellotape /ˈseləteɪp/ —n. propr. adhesive usu. transparent tape. —v. (sello-tape) (-ping) fix with Sellotape. [from CELLULOSE]

sell-out n. 1 commercial success, esp. the selling of all tickets for a show. 2 betrayal.

selvage /ˈselvɪdʒ/ n. (also **selvedge**) fabric edging woven to prevent cloth from fraying. [from SELF, EDGE]

selves pl. of SELF.

semantic /sɪˈmæntɪk/ adj. of meaning in language. □ **semantically** adv. [Greek sēmainō to mean]

semantics n.pl. (us. treated as sing.) branch of linguistics concerned with meaning.

semaphore /ˈseməfɔː(r)/ —n. 1 system of signalling with the arms or two flags. 2 railway signalling apparatus consisting of a post with a movable arm or arms etc. —v. (-ring) signal or send by semaphore. [Greek sēma sign, pherō bear]

semblance /ˈsembləns/ n. (foll. by of) appearance; show (a semblance of anger). [French sembler resemble]

semen /ˈsiːmen/ n. reproductive fluid of males. [Latin semen semin- seed]

semester /sɪˈmestə(r)/ n. half-year course or term in (esp. US) universities. [Latin semestris from sex six, mensis month]

semi /ˈsemɪ/ n. (pl. -s) colloq. detached house. [abbreviation]

semi- prefix 1 half. 2 partly

semibreve /'semɪbriːv/ n. Mus. note equal to four crotchets.

semicircle /'semɪsɜːk(ə)l/ n. half of a circle or of its circumference. □ **semicircular** /ˌ'sɜːkjʊlə(r)/ adj.

semicolon /ˌsemɪ'kəʊlən/ n. punctuation mark (;) of intermediate value between a comma and full stop.

semiconductor /semɪkən'dʌktə(r)/ n. substance that in certain conditions has electrical conductivity intermediate between insulators and metals.

semi-conscious /ˌsemɪ'kɒnʃəs/ adj. partly or imperfectly conscious.

semi-detached /ˌsemɪdɪ'tætʃt/ —adj. (of a house) joined to one other on one side only. —n. such a house.

semifinal /ˌsemɪ'faɪn(ə)l/ n. match or round preceding the final. □ **semifinalist** n.

seminal /'semɪn(ə)l/ adj. 1 of seed, semen, or reproduction; germinal. 2 (of ideas etc.) forming a basis for future development. [Latin: related to SEMEN]

seminar /'semɪnɑː(r)/ n. 1 small discussion class at a university etc. 2 short intensive course of study. 3 conference of specialists. [German: related to SEMINARY]

seminary /'semɪnərɪ/ n. (pl. -ies) training-college for priests or rabbis etc. □ **seminarist** n. [Latin: related to SEMEN]

semiotics /ˌsemɪ'ɒtɪks/ n. the study of signs and symbols and their use, esp. in language. □ **semiotic** adj. [Greek sēmeiōtikos of signs]

semi-permeable /ˌsemɪ'pɜːmɪəb(ə)l/ adj. (of a membrane etc.) allowing small molecules to pass through.

semiprecious /ˌsemɪ'preʃəs/ adj. (of a gem) less valuable than a precious stone.

semi-professional /ˌsemɪprə'feʃən(ə)l/ —adj. 1 (of a footballer, musician, etc.) paid for an activity but not relying on it for a living. 2 of semi-professionals. —n. semi-professional person.

semiquaver /'semɪkweɪvə(r)/ n. Mus. note equal to half a quaver.

semi-skilled /ˌsemɪ'skɪld/ adj. (of work or a worker) needing or having some training.

semi-... mmed /ˌsemɪ'skɪmd/ adj. (of ... which some of the cream has ...ed.

semi-...mart /... mart/ n. member of the ... o be descended from Shem ... ...uding esp. the Jews and ... Sem Shem]

... ... /... k/ adj. 1 of the Semites, ... of languages of the ... ...lebrew and Arabic.

semibreve /'semɪbriːv/ n. half a tone in the musical scale.

semitone /'semɪtəʊn/ n. half a tone in the musical scale.

semitropical /ˌsemɪ'trɒpɪk(ə)l/ adj. = SUBTROPICAL.

semivowel /'semɪvaʊəl/ n. 1 sound intermediate between a vowel and a consonant. 2 letter representing this. (e.g. w, y)

semolina /ˌsemə'liːnə/ n. 1 hard grains left after the milling of flour, used in milk puddings etc. 2 pudding of this. [Italian semolino]

sempstress var. of SEAMSTRESS.

Semtex n. malleable odourless plastic explosive. [from Semtín in Czechoslovakia, where it was originally made]

SEN abbr. State Enrolled Nurse.

Sen. abbr. 1 Senior. 2 Senator.

senate /'senɪt/ n. 1 legislative body, esp. the upper and smaller assembly in the US, France, etc. 2 governing body of a university or (US) a college. 3 ancient Roman State council. [Latin senatus from senex old man]

senator /'senətə(r)/ n. member of a senate. □ **senatorial** /ˌ'tɔːrɪəl/ adj. [Latin: related to SENATE]

send v. (past and past part. sent) 1 a order or cause to go or be conveyed. b propel (sent him flying). c cause to become (sent me mad). 2 send a message etc. (he sent to warn me). 3 (of God, etc.) grant, bestow, or inflict; bring about; cause to be. 4 slang put into ecstasy. □ **send away for** order or cause (goods) by post. **send down 1** rusticate or expel from a university. **2** send to prison. **send for 1** summon. **2** order by post. **send in 1** cause to go in. **2** submit (an entry etc.) for a competition etc. **send off 1** dispatch (a letter, parcel, etc.). **2** attend the departure of (a person) as a sign of respect etc. **3** Sport (of a referee) order (a player) to leave the field. **send off for** = send away for. **send on** transmit further or in advance of oneself. **send up 1** cause to go up. **2** transmit to a higher authority. **3** colloq. ridicule by mimicking. **send word** send information. □ **sender** n. [Old English]

send-off n. party etc. at the departure of a person, start of a project, etc.

send-up n. colloq. satire, parody.

senescent /sɪ'nes(ə)nt/ adj. growing old. □ **senescence** n. [Latin senex old]

seneschal /'senɪʃ(ə)l/ n. steward of a medieval great house. [French, = old servant]

senile /'siːnaɪl/ adj. 1 of old age. 2 mentally or physically infirm because of old age. □ **senility** /sɪ'nɪlɪtɪ/ n. [Latin: related to SENESCENT]

senile dementia n. illness of old people with loss of memory and control of bodily functions etc.

senior /'siːnɪə(r)/ —adj. 1 more or most advanced in age, standing, or position. 2 a relative of the same name senior to a person. 2 one's elder or superior. □ **seniority** /-'ɒrɪtɪ/ n. [Latin comparative of senex old]

senior citizen n. old-age pensioner.

senior nursing officer n. person in charge of nursing services in a hospital.

senior school n. school for children esp. over the age of 11.

senior service n. Royal Navy.

senna /'senə/ n. 1 cassia. 2 laxative from the dried pod of this. [Arabic]

señor /sen'jɔː(r)/ n. (pl. señores /-reɪz/) title used of or to a Spanish-speaking man. [Spanish from Latin SENIOR]

señora /sen'jɔːrə/ n. title used of or to a Spanish-speaking esp. married woman.

señorita /ˌsenjɔː'riːtə/ n. title used of or to a young esp. unmarried Spanish-speaking woman.

sensation /sen'seɪʃ(ə)n/ n. 1 feeling in one's body (sensation of warmth). 2 awareness, impression (sensation of being watched). 3 a intense interest, shock, etc. felt among a large group. b person, event, etc. causing this. 4 sense of touch. [medieval Latin: related to SENSE]

sensational adj. 1 causing or intended to cause great public excitement etc. 2 dazzling; wonderful (you look sensational). □ **sensationalize** v. (also -ise) (-zing or -sing) **sensationally** adv.

sensationalism n. use of or interest in the sensational. □ **sensationalist** n. & adj.

sense —n. 1 a any of the five bodily faculties transmitting sensation. b sensitiveness of all or any of these (good sense of smell). 2 ability to perceive or feel. 3 (foll. by of) consciousness; awareness (sense of guilt). 4 quick or accurate appreciation, understanding, or instinct (sense of humour). 5 practical wisdom, common sense. 6 a meaning of a word etc. b intelligibility or coherence. 7 prevailing opinion (sense of the meeting). 8 (in pl.) sanity ability to think. —v. (-sing) 1 perceive by a sense or senses. 2 be vaguely aware of. 3 realize. 4 (of a machine etc.) detect. □ **come to one's senses** 1 regain consciousness. 2 regain common sense. in a (or one) **sense** if the statement etc. is understood in a particular way. **make sense** be intelligible or practicable.

make sense of show or find the meaning of. **take leave of one's senses** go mad. [Latin sensus from sentio sens-]

senseless adj. 1 pointless; foolish. 2 unconscious. □ **senselessly** adv. **senselessness** n.

sense-organ n. bodily organ conveying external stimuli to the sensory system.

sensibility /ˌsensɪ'bɪlɪtɪ/ n. (pl. -ies) 1 capacity to feel. 2 e sensitiveness. b exceptional degree of this. 3 (in pl.) tendency to feel offended etc.

■ **Usage** Sensibility should not be used in standard English to mean 'possession of good sense'.

sensible /'sensɪb(ə)l/ adj. 1 having or showing wisdom or common sense. 2 a perceptible by the senses. b great enough to be perceived. 3 (of clothing etc.) practical. 4 (foll. by of) aware. □ **sensibly** adv.

sensitive /'sensɪtɪv/ adj. 1 (often foll. by to) acutely susceptible to external stimuli or impressions; having sensibility. 2 easily offended or hurt. 3 (often foll. by to) (of an instrument etc.) responsive to or recording slight changes. 4 (of photographic materials) responding (esp. rapidly) to light. 5 (of a topic etc.) requiring tactful treatment or secrecy. □ **sensitively** adv. **sensitiveness** n.

sensitivity /ˌsensɪ'tɪvɪtɪ/ n.

sensitize /'sensɪtaɪz/ v. (also -ise) (-zing or -sing) make sensitive. □ **sensitization** /-'zeɪʃ(ə)n/ n.

sensor n. device for detecting or measuring a physical property. [from SENSORY]

sensory adj. of sensation or the senses. [Latin sentio sens- feel]

sensual /'sensjʊəl/ adj. 1 a of physical, esp. sexual, pleasure. b enjoying or giving this, voluptuous. 2 showing sensuality (sensual lips). □ **sensualism** n. **sensually** adv. [Latin related to SENSE]

■ **Usage** Sensual is sometimes confused with sensuous, which does not have the sexual overtones of sensual.

sensuality /ˌsensjʊ'ælɪtɪ/ n. (esp. sexual) gratification of the senses.

sensuous /'sensjʊəs/ adj. of or affecting the senses, esp. aesthetically. □ **sensuously** adv. **sensuousness** n. [Latin: related to SENSE]

■ **Usage** See note at sensual.

sent past and past part. of SEND.

sentence /'sent(ə)ns/ —n. 1 statement, question, exclamation, or command containing a subject and predicate (e.g. I went; come here!). 2 a

sententious /sen'tenfəs/ adj. 1 pompously moralizing. 2 affectedly formal in style. 3 aphoristic; using maxims. □ **sententiously** adv. **sententiousness** n. [Latin: related to SENTENCE]

sentient /'senf(ə)nt/ adj. capable of perception and feeling. □ **sentience** n. **sentiency** n. **sentiently** adv. [Latin sentio feel]

sentiment /'sentiment/ n. 1 mental feeling. 2 (often in pl.) what one feels, opinion. 3 opinion or feeling, as distinct from its expression (the sentiment is good). 4 emotional or irrational view. 5 such views collectively, esp. as an influence. 6 tendency to be swayed by feeling. 7 a mawkish or exaggerated emotion. b display of this.

sentimental /,sentr'ment(ə)l/ adj. 1 of or showing sentiment. 2 showing or affected by emotion rather than reason. □ **sentimentalism** n. **sentimentalist** n. **sentimentality** /-'tælrtr/ n. **sentimentalize** v. (also -ise) (-zing or -sing). **sentimentally** adv.

sentimental value n. value given to a thing because of its associations.

sentinel /'sentrn(ə)l/ n. sentry or lookout. [French from Italian]

sentry /'sentrr/ n. (pl. -ies) soldier etc. stationed to keep guard. [perhaps from obsolete centrinel, var. of SENTINEL]

sentry-box n. cabin for sheltering a standing sentry.

sepal /'sep(ə)l/ n. division or leaf of a calyx. [perhaps from SEPARATE, PETAL]

separable /'separəb(ə)l/ adj. able to be separated. □ **separability** /-'bɪlrtɪ/ n. [Latin: related to SEPARATE]

separate —adj. /'separat/, v. /'separeɪt/ —adj. forming a unit by itself, existing apart; disconnected, distinct, or individual. —n. /'separat/ (in pl.) trousers, skirts, etc. that are not parts of suits. —v. /'separeɪt/ (-ting) 1 make separate, sever. 2 prevent union or contact of. 3 go different ways. 4 (esp. as separated adj.) cease to live with one's spouse. 5 (foll. by from) secede. 6 a divide or sort into parts or sizes. b (often foll. by out) extract or remove (an ingredient etc.). □ **separately** adv. [Latin separo (v.)]

separation n. /,sepa'reɪʃ(ə)n/ n. 1 separating or being separated. 2 (in full **judicial** or **legal separation**) legal arrangement by which a couple remain married but live apart. [Latin: related to SEPARATE]

separatist /'separatist/ n. person who favours separation, esp. political independence. □ **separatism** n.

separator /'sepa,reɪtə(r)/ n. machine for separating, e.g. cream from milk.

Sephardi /sɪ'fɑːdɪ/ n. (pl. **Sephardim**) Jew of Spanish or Portuguese descent. □ **Sephardic** adj. [Hebrew, = Spaniard]

sepia /'siːpɪə/ n. 1 dark reddish-brown colour or paint. 2 brown tint used in photography. [Greek, = cuttlefish]

sepoy /'siːpɔɪ/ n. hist. native Indian soldier under European, esp. British, discipline. [Persian sipāhī soldier]

sepsis /'sepsɪs/ n. septic condition. [Greek: related to SEPTIC]

Sept. abbr. September.

sept n. clan, esp. in Ireland. [alteration of SECT]

September /sep'tembə(r)/ n. ninth month of the year. [Latin septem seven, originally the 7th month of the Roman year]

septennial /sep'tenɪəl/ adj. 1 lasting for seven years. 2 recurring every seven years.

septet /sep'tet/ n. 1 Mus. a composition for seven performers. b the performers. 2 any group of seven. [Latin septem seven]

septic /'septɪk/ adj. contaminated with bacteria, putrefying. [Greek sēpō rot]

septicaemia /,septɪ'siːmɪə/ n. (US **septicemia**) blood-poisoning. □ **septicaemic** adj. [from SEPTIC, Greek haima blood]

septic tank n. tank in which sewage is disintegrated through bacterial activity.

septuagenarian /,septjuədʒɪ'neərɪən/ n. person from 70 to 79 years old. [Latin -arius from septuaginta seventy]

Septuagesima /,septjuə'dʒesɪmə/ n. Sunday before Sexagesima. [Latin, = seventieth]

Septuagint /'septjuə,dʒɪnt/ n. Greek version of the Old Testament including the Apocrypha. [Latin septuaginta seventy]

septum /'septəm/ n. (pl. **septa**) partition such as that between the nostrils or the chambers of a poppy-fruit or of a shell. [Latin s(a)eptum from saepio enclose]

septuple /'septjup(ə)l/ —adj. 1 sevenfold, having seven parts. 2 seven times as many or as much. —n. sevenfold number or amount. [Latin septem seven]

sepulchral /sɪ'pʌlkr(ə)l/ adj. 1 of a tomb or interment. 2 funereal, gloomy. [Latin: related to SEPULCHRE]

sepulchre /ˈsepəlkə(r)/ (US **sepulcher**) —n. tomb, esp. cut in rock or built of stone or brick. —v. (-**ring**) 1 place in a sepulchre. 2 serve as a sepulchre for. [Latin *sepelio* bury]

sepulture /ˈsepəltʃə(r)/ n. burying, interment. [Latin: related to SEPULCHRE]

sequel /ˈsiːkw(ə)l/ n. 1 what follows (esp. as a result). 2 novel, film, etc. that continues the story of an earlier one. [Latin *sequor* follow]

sequence /ˈsiːkwəns/ n. 1 succession. 2 order of succession. 3 set of things belonging next to one another. 4 part of a film dealing with one scene or topic. [Latin: related to SEQUEL]

sequencer n. programmable electronic device for storing sequences of musical notes, chords, etc., and transmitting them when required to an electronic musical instrument. □ **sequencing** n.

sequential /sɪˈkwenʃ(ə)l/ adj. forming a sequence or consequence. □ **sequentially** adv. [from SEQUENCE]

sequester /sɪˈkwestə(r)/ v. 1 (esp. as **sequestered** adj.) seclude, isolate. 2 = SEQUESTRATE. [Latin *sequester* trustee]

sequestrate /ˈsiːkwɪstreɪt, sɪˈkwe-/ v. (-**ting**) 1 confiscate. 2 take temporary possession of (a debtor's estate etc.). □ **sequestration** /ˌsiːkwɪˈstreɪʃ(ə)n/ n.

sequestrator /ˈsiːkwɪˌstreɪtə(r)/ n. [Latin: related to SEQUESTER]

sequin /ˈsiːkwɪn/ n. circular spangle, esp. sewn on to clothing. □ **sequinned** adj. (also **sequined**). [Italian *zecchino* a gold coin]

sequoia /sɪˈkwɔɪə/ n. extremely tall Californian evergreen conifer. [*Sequoiah*, name of a Cherokee]

seraglio /səˈrɑːlɪəʊ/ n. (pl. -**s**) 1 harem. 2 hist. Turkish palace. [Italian *serraglio* from Turkish]

seraph /ˈserəf/ n. (pl. -**im** or -**s**) angelic being of the highest order of the celestial hierarchy. □ **seraphic** /səˈræfɪk/ adj. [Hebrew]

Serb —n. 1 native of Serbia in SE Europe. 2 person of Serbian descent. —adj. = SERBIAN. [Serbian *Srb*]

Serbian /ˈsɜːbɪən/ —n. 1 dialect of the Serbs. 2 = SERB. —adj. of Serbia.

Serbo-Croat /ˌsɜːbəʊˈkrəʊæt/ (also **Serbo-Croatian** /ˌsɜːbəʊkrəʊˈeɪʃ(ə)n/) —n. main official language of Yugoslavia, combining Serbian and Croatian. —adj. of this language.

serenade /ˌserɪˈneɪd/ —n. 1 piece of music performed at night, esp. beneath a lover's window. 2 orchestral suite for a small ensemble. —v. (-**ding**) perform a serenade to. □ **serenader** n. [Italian: related to SERENE]

serendipity /ˌserənˈdɪpɪtɪ/ n. faculty of making happy discoveries by accident. □ **serendipitous** adj. [coined by Horace Walpole]

serene /sɪˈriːn/ adj. (-**ner**, -**nest**) 1 clear and calm. 2 tranquil, unperturbed. □ **serenely** adv. **sereneness** n. **serenity** /sɪˈrenɪtɪ/ n. [Latin]

serf n. 1 hist. labourer who was not allowed to leave the land on which he worked. 2 oppressed person, drudge. □ **serfdom** n. [Latin *servus* slave]

serge n. durable twilled worsted etc. fabric. [French *sarge*, *serge*]

sergeant /ˈsɑːdʒ(ə)nt/ n. 1 non-commissioned Army or RAF officer next below warrant-officer. 2 police officer below inspector. [French *sergent* from Latin *serviens-enti-* servant]

sergeant-major n. (in full **regimental sergeant-major**) warrant-officer assisting the adjutant of a regiment or battalion.

serial /ˈsɪərɪəl/ —n. 1 (also *attrib.*) story etc. published, broadcast, or shown in instalments. —adj. 1 of, in, or forming a series. 2 *Mus.* using transformations of a fixed series of notes (see SERIES 4). □ **serially** adv. [from SERIES]

serialize v. (also **-ise**) (-**zing** or **-sing**) publish or produce in instalments. □ **serialization** /-ˈzeɪʃ(ə)n/ n.

serial killer n. person who murders continually with no apparent motive.

serial number n. number identifying an item in a series.

series /ˈsɪəriːz, -rɪz/ n. (pl. same) 1 number of similar or related things, events, etc.; succession, row, or set. 2 set of related but individual programmes. 3 set of related geological strata. 4 arrangement of the twelve notes of the chromatic scale as a basis for serial music. 5 set of electrical circuits or components arranged so that the same current passes through each successively. □ **in series** in ordered succession. [Latin *sero* join]

serif /ˈserɪf/ n. slight projection at the extremities of a printed letter (as in 'T' contrasted with 'T') (cf. SANSERIF). [origin uncertain]

serio-comic /ˌsɪərɪəʊˈkɒmɪk/ adj. combining the serious and the comic.

serious /ˈsɪərɪəs/ adj. 1 thoughtful, earnest. 2 important, demanding consideration. 3 not negligible; dangerous, frightening (*serious injury*). 4 sincere, in earnest, not frivolous. 5 (of music, literature, etc.) intellectual in content or appeal; not popular. □ **seriously** adv. **seriousness** n. [Latin *seriosus*]

serjeant /ˈsɑːdʒ(ə)nt/ n. (in full **serjeant-at-law**, pl. **serjeants-at-law**) hist. barrister of the highest rank. [var. of SERGEANT]

serjeant-at-arms n. (pl. **serjeants-at-arms**) official of a court, city, or parliament, with ceremonial duties.

sermon /ˈsɜːmən/ n. 1 spoken or written discourse on religion or morals etc., esp. delivered in church. 2 admonition, reproof. [Latin sermo -onis speech]

sermonize v. (also **-ise**) (**-zing** or **-sing**) moralize (to).

serous /ˈsɪərəs/ adj. 1 of or like serum; watery. 2 (of a gland or membrane) having a serous secretion. □ **serosity** /-ˈrɒsɪtɪ/ n. [related to SERUM]

serpent /ˈsɜːp(ə)nt/ n. 1 snake, esp. large. 2 sly or treacherous person. [Latin serpo creep]

serpentine /ˈsɜːpəntaɪn/ adj. 1 of or like a serpent. 2 coiling, meandering. 3 cunning, treacherous. —n. soft usu. dark-green rock, sometimes mottled.

SERPS abbr. State earnings-related pension scheme.

serrated /səˈreɪtɪd/ adj. with a sawlike edge. □ **serration** n. [Latin serra saw]

serried /ˈserɪd/ adj. (of ranks of soldiers etc.) close together. [French serrer to close]

serum /ˈsɪərəm/ n. (pl. **sera** or **-s**) 1 liquid that separates from a clot when blood coagulates, esp. used for inoculation. 2 watery fluid in animal bodies. [Latin, = whey]

servant /ˈsɜːv(ə)nt/ n. 1 person employed to do domestic duties, esp. in a wealthy household. 2 devoted follower or helper. [French: related to SERVE]

serve —v. (**-ving**) 1 do a service for (a person, community, etc.). 2 be a servant to. 3 carry out duties (served on six committees). 4 (foll. by in) be employed in (esp. the armed forces) (served in the navy). 5 a be useful to or serviceable for. b meet requirements; perform a function. 6 a go through a due period of (apprenticeship), a prison sentence, etc.). b go through (a due period) to eat. 8 (in full **serve at table**) act as a waiter. 9 a attend to (a customer etc.). b (foll. by with) supply with (goods). 10 treat (a person) in a specified way. 11 a (often foll. by on) deliver (a writ etc.). b (foll. by with) deliver a writ etc. to. 12 (also absol.) (in tennis etc.) deliver (a ball etc.) to begin or resume play. 13 (of an animal) copulate with (a female). —n. = SERVICE n. 16a, b. □ **serve a person right** be deserved punishment etc. **serve up** derog. offer (served up the same old excuses). [Latin servio]

server n. 1 a person who serves. b utensil for serving food. 2 celebrant's assistant at a mass etc.

servery n. (pl. **-ies**) room or counter from which meals etc. are served.

service /ˈsɜːvɪs/ —n. 1 work, or the doing of work, for another or for a community etc. (often in pl.: the services of a lawyer). 2 work done by a machine etc. (has given good service). 3 assistance or benefit given. 4 provision or supplying of a public need, e.g. transport, or (often in pl.) of water, gas, electricity, etc. 5 employment as a servant. 6 state or period of employment (resigned after 15 years' service). 7 public or Crown department or organization (civil service). 8 (in pl.) the armed forces. 9 (attrib.) of the kind issued to the armed forces (service revolver). 10 a ceremony of worship. b form of liturgy for this. 11 a provision for the maintenance of a machine etc. b routine maintenance of a vehicle etc. 12 assistance given to customers. 13 a serving of food, drinks, etc.; quality of this. b extra charge nominally made for this. 14 (in pl.) = SERVICE AREA (motorway services). 15 set of dishes, plates, etc. for serving meals (dinner service). 16 a act of serving in tennis etc. b person's turn to serve. c (in full **service game**) game in which a specified player serves. —v. (**-cing**) 1 maintain or repair (a car, machine, etc.). 2 supply with a service. □ **at a person's service** ready to serve a person. **be of service** be helpful or useful. **in service** 1 employed as a servant. 2 in use. **out of service** not available for use, not working. [Latin servitium from servus slave]

serviceable adj. 1 useful or usable; able to render service. 2 durable but plain. □ **serviceability** /-ˈbɪlɪtɪ/ n.

service area n. area beside a major road providing petrol, refreshments, toilet facilities, etc.

service charge n. additional charge for service in a restaurant etc.

service flat n. flat in which domestic service and sometimes meals are provided for an extra fee.

service industry n. industry providing services, not goods.

serviceman n. 1 man in the armed forces. 2 man providing service or maintenance.

service road n. road serving houses, shops, etc., lying back from the main road.

service station n. = GARAGE n. 2.

servicewoman n. woman in the armed forces.

serviette

serviette /sɜːˈvjet/ n. table-napkin. [French: related to SERVE]

servile /ˈsɜːvaɪl/ adj. 1 of or like a slave. 2 fawning; subservient. □ **servility** /-ˈvɪlɪtɪ/ n. [Latin servus slave]

serving n. quantity of food for one person.

servitor /ˈsɜːvɪtə(r)/ n. archaic servant, attendant. [Latin: related to SERVE]

servitude /ˈsɜːvɪtjuːd/ n. slavery, subjection. [Latin servus slave]

servo /ˈsɜːvəʊ/ n. (pl. -s) 1 powered mechanism producing motion at a higher level of energy than the input level. 2 (in comb.) involving this. [Latin servus slave]

sesame /ˈsesəmɪ/ n. 1 E. Indian plant with oil-yielding seeds. 2 its seeds. □ **open sesame** magic phrase for opening a locked door or gaining access. [Greek]

sesqui- /ˈseskwɪ/ comb. form denoting one and a half. [Latin]

sessile /ˈsesaɪl/ adj. 1 (of a flower, leaf, eye, etc.) attached directly by its base without a stalk or peduncle. 2 fixed in one position; immobile. [Latin: related to SESSION]

session /ˈseʃ(ə)n/ n. 1 period devoted to an activity (recording session). 2 assembly of a parliament, court, etc. 3 single meeting or period for this. 4 period during which these are regularly held. 5 academic year. □ **in session** assembled for business; not on vacation. □ **sessional** adj. [Latin sedeo sess- sit]

sestet /seˈstet/ n. 1 last six lines of a sonnet. 2 sextet. [Italian sesto sixth]

set¹ /set/ v. (-tt-; past and past part. set) 1 put, lay, or stand in a certain position etc. 2 apply (one thing) to (another) (set pen to paper). 3 a fix ready or in position. b dispose suitably for use, action, or display. 4 a adjust (a clock or watch) to show the right time. b adjust (an alarm clock) to sound at the required time. 5 a fix, arrange, or mount b insert (a jewel) in a ring etc. 6 make (a device) ready to operate. 7 lay (a table) for a meal. 8 style (the hair) while damp. 9 (foll. by with) ornament or provide (a surface). 10 make or bring into a specified state; cause to be (set things in motion; set it on fire). 11 (of jelly, cement, etc.) harden or solidify. 12 (of the sun, moon, etc.) move towards or below the earth's horizon. 13 show (a story etc.) as happening in a certain time or place. 14 a (foll. by to + infin.) cause (a person or oneself) to do a specified thing. b (foll. by pres. part.) start (a person or thing) doing something. 15 give as work to be done or a matter to be dealt with. 16 exhibit as a model etc. (set an example). 17 initiate, lead (set the fashion; set the pace). 18

833

set

establish (a record etc.). 19 determine or decide. 20 appoint or establish (set them in authority). 21 a put parts of (a broken or dislocated bone limb, etc.) together for healing. b deal with (a fracture etc.) in this way. 22 (in full **set to music**) provide (words etc.) with music for singing. 23 a compose the type etc. for (a book etc.). b compose (type etc.) 24 (of a tide, current, etc.) have a certain motion or direction. 25 (of a face) assume a hard expression. 26 a cause (a hen) to sit on eggs. b place (eggs) for a hen to sit on. 27 (of eyes etc.) become motionless. 28 fee, or show a certain tendency (opinion's setting against it). 29 a (of blossom) form into fruit. b (of fruit) develop from blossom. c (of a tree) develop fruit. 30 (of a dancer) take a position facing another. 31 (of a bone) hunting dog) take a rigid attitude indicating the presence of game. 32 dial or steps towards. □ **set about** 1 begin or take steps towards. 2 colloq. attack. **set against** 1 cons ider or reckon as a set-off to 4. (foll. by to) explain as set oppose. **set apart** separate, reserve, differentiate. **set aside** 1 put to one side. 2 keep for future use. 3 disregard or reject. **set back** 1 place further back in place or time. 2 impede or reverse the progress of. 3 colloq. cost (a person) a specified amount. **set down** 1 record in writing. 2 allow to alight. 3 (foll. by to) attribute to. 4. (foll. by to) explain as set eyes on see EYE. **set foot on** (or in) enter or go to (a place etc.). **set forth** 1 begin a journey. 2 expound. **set in** 1 (of weather etc.) begin, become established. 2 insert. **set off** 1 begin a journey. 2 detonate (a bomb etc.). 3 initiate, stimulate. 4 cause (a person) to start laughing, talking, etc. 5 adorn; enhance 6 (foll. by against) use as a compensating item. **set on** (or **upon**) 1 attack violently. 2 cause or urge to attack. **set oneself up** as pretend or claim to be. **set out** 1 begin a journey. 2 (foll. by to + infin.) intend. 3 demonstrate, arrange, or exhibit. 4 mark out. 5 declare. **set sail** hoist the sails, begin a voyage. **set to** begin vigorously, esp. fighting, arguing, or eating. **set up** 1 place in position or view. 2 start (a business etc.) 3 establish in some capacity. 4 supply the needs of. 5 begin making (a loud sound). 6 cause (a condition or situation). 7 prepare (a task etc. for another). 8 restore the health of (a person). 9 establish (a record). 10 colloq. frame or cause (a person) to look foolish; cheat. [Old English]

set² n. 1 group of linked or similar things or persons. 2 section of society. 3 collection of objects for a specified purpose

set *(cricket set; teasel).* **4** radio or television receiver. **5** (in tennis etc.) group of games counting as a unit towards winning a match. **6** *Math.* collection of things sharing a property. **7** direction or position in which something sets or is set. **8** slip, shoot, bulb, etc., for planting. **9** setting, stage furniture, etc., for a play or film etc. **10** styling of the hair while damp. **11** (also **sett**) badger's burrow. **12** (also **sett**) granite paving-block. [senses 1–6 from French *sette*; senses 7–12 from SET¹]

set³ *adj.* **1** prescribed or determined in advance; fixed *(a set meal).* **2** (of a phrase or speech etc.) having invariable or predetermined wording; not extempore. **3** prepared for action. **4** (foll. by *on*, *upon*) determined to get or achieve etc. [past part. of SET¹]

set-back *n.* reversal or arrest of progress; relapse.

set piece *n.* **1** formal or elaborate arrangement, esp. in art or literature. **2** fireworks arranged on scaffolding etc.

set square *n.* right-angled triangular plate for drawing lines, esp. at 90°, 45°, 60°, or 30°.

sett var. of SET² 11, 12.

settee /seˈtiː/ *n.* = SOFA. [origin uncertain]

setter *n.* dog of a long-haired breed trained to stand rigid when scenting game.

set theory *n.* the study or use of sets in mathematics.

setting *n.* **1** position or manner in which a thing is set. **2** immediate surroundings of a house etc. **3** period, place, etc., of a story, drama, etc. **4** frame etc. for a jewel. **5** music to which words are set. **6** cutlery etc. for one person at a table. **7** level at which a machine is set to operate *(on a high setting).*

settle¹ /ˈset(ə)l/ *v.* (-ling) **1** (often foll. by *down*, *in*) establish or become established in an abode or lifestyle. **2** (often foll. by *down*) **a** regain calm after disturbance; come to rest. **b** adopt a regular or secure style of life. **c** (foll. by *to*) apply oneself *(settled down to work).* **3** (cause to) sit, alight, or come down to stay for some time. **4** make or become composed, certain, quiet, or fixed. **5** determine, decide, or agree upon. **6** resolve (a dispute, matter, etc.). **7** agree to terminate (a lawsuit). **8** (foll. by *for*) accept or agree to. (esp. a less desirable alternative). **9** **10** (as **settled** *adj.*) established *(settled weather).* **11** calm (nerves, the stomach, etc.). **12 a** colonize. **b** establish colonists in. **13** subside; fall to the bottom or on to a surface. □ **settle up** (also *absol.*) pay

(an account, debt, etc.). **settle with 1** pay (a creditor). **2** get revenge on. [Old English; related to SIT]

settle² /ˈset(ə)l/ *n.* high-backed wooden bench, often with a box below the seat. [Old English]

settlement *n.* **1** settling or being settled. **2 a** place occupied by settlers. **b** small village. **3** a political or financial etc. agreement ending a dispute. **4** a terms on which property is given to a person. **b** deed stating these. **c** amount or property given.

settler *n.* person who settles abroad.

set-to *n.* (*pl.* -tos) *colloq.* fight, argument.

set-up *n.* **1** arrangement or organization. **2** manner, structure, or position of this. **3** instance of setting a person up (see *set up* 10).

seven /ˈsev(ə)n/ *adj. & n.* **1** one more than six. **2** symbol for this (7, vii, VII). **3** size etc. denoted by seven. **4** seven o'clock. [Old English]

sevenfold *adj. & adv.* **1** seven times as much or as many. **2** consisting of seven parts.

seven seas *n.* (prec. by *the*) the oceans of the world.

seventeen /ˌsevənˈtiːn/ *adj. & n.* **1** one more than sixteen. **2** symbol for this (17, xvii, XVII). **3** size etc. denoted by seventeen. □ **seventeenth** *adj. & n.* [Old English]

seventh *adj. & n.* **1** next after sixth. **2** one of seven equal parts of a thing. □ **seventhly** *adv.*

Seventh-Day Adventists *n.pl.* sect of Adventists observing the sabbath on Saturday.

seventh heaven *n.* state of intense joy.

seventy /ˈsevəntiː/ *adj. & n.* (*pl.* -ies) **1** seven times ten. **2** symbol for this (70, lxx, LXX). **3** (in *pl.*) numbers from 70 to 79, esp. the years of a century or of a person's life. □ **seventieth** *adj. & n.* [Old English]

sever /ˈsevə(r)/ *v.* divide, break, or make separate, esp. by cutting *(severed artery).* [Anglo-French *severer* from Latin *separo*]

several /ˈsev(ə)l/ —*adj. & pron.* more than two but not many; a few. —*adj. formal* separate or respective *(went their several ways).* □ **severally** *adv.* [Latin *separ* distinct]

severance *n.* **1** act of severing. **2** severed state.

severance pay *n.* payment made to an employee on termination of a contract.

severe /siˈviə(r)/ *adj.* **1** rigorous and harsh *(severe critic).* **2** serious *(severe shortage).* **3** forceful *(severe storm).* **4** extreme *(severe winter).* **5** exacting

Seville orange /'sevil/ n. bitter orange used for marmalade. [*Seville* in Spain.]

sew /sau/ v. (*past part.* **sewn** or **sewed**) fasten, join, etc., with a needle and thread or a sewing-machine. □ **sew up 1** join or enclose by sewing. **2** (esp. in *passive*) *colloq.* satisfactorily arrange or finish; gain control of. [Old English]

sewage /'suːɪdʒ/ n. waste matter conveyed in sewers. [from SEWER]

sewage farm n. (also **sewage works**) place where sewage is treated.

sewer /'suːə(r)/ n. conduit, usu. underground, for carrying off drainage water and sewage. [Anglo-French *sever*(*e*): related to EX-[1], *aqua* water]

sewerage /'suːərɪdʒ/ n. system of, or drainage by, sewers.

sewing /'səʊɪŋ/ n. material or work to be sewn.

sewing-machine n. machine for sewing or stitching.

sewn *past part.* of SEW.

sex –n. **1** each of the main groups (male and female) into which living things are categorized on the basis of their reproductive functions (*what sex is your dog?*). **2** sexual instincts, desires, etc., or their manifestation. **3** *colloq.* sexual intercourse. **4** (*attrib.*) of or relating to sex or sexual differences. –v. **1** determine the sex of. **2** (as **sexed** *adj.*) having a specified sexual appetite (*highly sexed*) [Latin *sexus*]

sexagenarian /ˌseksədʒɪ'neərɪən/ n. person from 60 to 69 years old. [Latin *-arius* from *sexaginta* sixty]

Sexagesima /ˌseksə'dʒesɪmə/ n. Sunday before Quinquagesima. [Latin, = sixtieth]

sex appeal n. sexual attractiveness.

sex change n. apparent change of sex by hormone treatment and surgery.

sex chromosome n. chromosome determining the sex of an organism.

sexism n. prejudice or discrimination, esp. against women, on the grounds of sex. □ **sexist** *adj.* & n.

sexless *adj.* **1** neither male nor female. **2** lacking sexual desire or attractiveness.

sex life n. person's sexual activity.

sex maniac n. *colloq.* person obsessed with sex.

sex object n. person regarded as an object of sexual gratification.

sex offender n. person who commits a sexual crime.

sexology /sek'sɒlədʒɪ/ n. the study of sexual relationships or practices. □ **sex-ologist** n.

sex symbol n. person widely noted for sex appeal.

sextant /'sekst(ə)nt/ n. instrument with a graduated arc of 60°, used in navigation and surveying for measuring the angular distance of objects by means of mirrors. [Latin *sexta-ntis* sixth part]

sextet /sek'stet/ n. **1** *Mus.* a composition for six performers. **b** the performers. **2** any group of six. [alteration of SESTET after Latin *sex* six]

sexton /'sekst(ə)n/ n. person who looks after a church and churchyard, often acting as bell-ringer and gravedigger. [Medieval Latin from Latin *sacrista-nus*]

sextuple /'sekstjʊp(ə)l/ –*adj.* **1** sixfold. **2** having six parts. **3** being six times as much or as many. –n. sixfold number or amount. [medieval Latin from Latin *sex* six]

sextuplet /'sekstjʊplɪt, -'tjuːplɪt/ n. each of six children born at one birth. [French *segerstein* from Latin *sacrista-nus*]

sexual /'seksjʊəl/ *adj.* of sex, the sexes, or relations between them. □ **sexuality** /-'ælɪtɪ/ n. **sexually** *adv.*

sexual intercourse n. method of reproduction involving insertion of the penis into the vagina usu. followed by ejaculation.

sexy *adj.* (**-ier, -iest**) sexually attractive, stimulating, or aroused. **2** *colloq.* (of a project etc.) exciting, trendy. □ **sexily** *adv.* **sexiness** n.

Sgt. *abbr.* Sergeant.

sh *int.* = HUSH.

shabby /'ʃæbɪ/ *adj.* (**-ier, -iest**) **1** faded and worn; dingy, dilapidated. **2** contemptible (*a shabby trick*). □ **shabbily** *adv.* **shabbiness** n. [related to SCAB]

shack –n. roughly built hut or cabin. –v. (foll. by *up*) *slang* cohabit, esp. as lovers. [perhaps from Mexican *jacal* wooden hut]

shackle /'ʃæk(ə)l/ –n. **1** metal loop or link, closed by a bolt, used to connect chains etc. **2** fetter for the ankle or wrist. **3** (usu. in *pl.*) restraint, impediment. –v. fetter, impede, restrain. [Old English]

shad n. (*pl.* same or **-s**) large edible marine fish. [Old English]

shaddock /'ʃædək/ n. **1** largest citrus fruit, with a thick yellow skin and bitter pulp. **2** tree bearing these. [Capt. *Shaddock*, who introduced it to the W. Indies in the 17th c.]

si *abbr.* storzando.

sforzando /sfɔː'tsændəʊ/ *Mus.* –*adj.* & *adv.* with sudden emphasis. –n. (*pl.* **-s** or **-di** /-diː/) **1** suddenly emphasized note or group of notes. **2** increase in emphasis and loudness. [Italian]

SF *abbr.* science fiction.

shade —n. **1** comparative darkness (and usu. coolness) given by shelter from direct light and heat. **2** area so sheltered. **3** darker part of a picture etc. **4** colour, esp. as darker or lighter than one similar. **5** comparative obscurity. **6** slight amount (*a shade better*). **7** lampshade. **8** screen against the light. **9** (in *pl.*) esp. *US colloq.* sunglasses. **10** *literary* ghost. **11** (in *pl.*; foll. by *of*) reminder of, suggesting (esp. something undesirable) (*shades of Hitler!*). —v. (**-ding**) **1** screen from light. **2** cover, moderate, or exclude the light of **3** darken, esp. with parallel lines to show shadow etc. **4** (often foll. by *away, off, into*) pass or change gradually. [Old English]

shading n. light and shade shown on a map or drawing by parallel lines etc.

shadow /ˈʃædəʊ/ —n. **1** shade; patch of shade. **2** dark shape projected by a body intercepting rays of light. **3** inseparable attendant or companion. **4** person secretly following another. **5** slightest trace (*not a shadow of doubt*). **6** weak or insubstantial remnant (*a shadow of his former self*). **7** (*attrib.*) denoting members of an Opposition party holding posts parallel to those of the government (*shadow Cabinet*). **8** shaded part of a picture. **9** gloom or sadness. —v. **1** cast a shadow over. **2** secretly follow and watch. [Old English: related to SHADE]

shadow-boxing n. boxing with an imaginary opponent as training.

shadowy adj. **1** like or having a shadow. **2** vague, indistinct.

shady /ˈʃeɪdɪ/ adj. (**-ier, -iest**) **1** giving shade. **2** situated in shade. **3** disreputable; of doubtful honesty. □ **shadily** *adv.* **shadiness** n.

shaft /ʃɑːft/ n. **1** narrow usu. vertical space, for access to a mine, or (in a building) for a lift, ventilation, etc. **2** (foll. by *of*) **a** a ray (of light). **b** bolt (of lightning). **3** stem or handle of a tool etc. **4** long narrow part supporting, connecting, or driving thicker part(s) etc. **5 a** *archaic* arrow, spear. **b** its long slender stem. **6** hurtful or provocative remark (*shafts of wit*). **7** each of the pair of poles between which a horse is harnessed to a vehicle. **8** central stem of a feather. **9** column, esp. between the base and capital. [Old English]

shag¹ n. **1** coarse kind of cut tobacco. **2 a** rough mass of hair etc. **b** (*attrib.*) (of a carpet) with a long rough pile **3** cormorant, esp. the crested cormorant. [Old English]

shag² v. (**-gg-**) *coarse slang* **1** have sexual intercourse with. **2** (usu. in *passive*; often foll. by *out*) exhaust, tire out. [origin unknown]

shaggy adj. (**-ier, -iest**) **1** hairy, rough-haired. **2** unkempt. □ **shagginess** n.

shaggy-dog story n. long rambling joke, amusing only by its pointlessness.

shagreen /ʃæˈgriːn/ n. **1** a kind of untanned granulated leather. **2** sharkskin. [var. of CHAGRIN]

shah n. *hist.* former monarch of Iran. [Persian]

shake —v. (**-king**; *past* **shook** /ʃʊk/; *past part.* **shaken**) **1** move forcefully or quickly up and down or to and fro. **2** (cause to) tremble or vibrate. **3** agitate, shock, or upset the composure of **4** weaken or impair in courage, effectiveness, etc. **5** (of a voice, note, etc.) tremble; trill. **6** gesture with (one's fist, a stick, etc.) **7** *colloq.* shake hands (*they shook on the deal*). —n. **1** shaking or being shaken. **2** jerk or shock. **3** (in *pl.*; prec. by *the*) *colloq.* fit of trembling. **4** *Mus.* trill **5** = MILK SHAKE. □ **no great shakes** *colloq.* mediocre, poor. **shake down 1** settle or cause to fall by shaking. **2** settle down; become established. **shake hands** (often foll. by *with*) clasp hands as a greeting, farewell, in congratulation, as confirmation of a deal, etc. **shake one's head** turn one's head from side to side in refusal, denial, disapproval, or concern. **shake off** get rid of or evade (a person or thing). **shake out 1** empty by shaking. **2** open (a sail, flag, etc.) by shaking. **shake up 1** mix by shaking. **2** restore to shape by shaking. **3** disturb or make uncomfortable; rouse from apathy, conventionality, etc. [Old English]

shaker n. **1** person or thing that shakes. **2** container for shaking together the ingredients of cocktails etc.

Shakespearian /ʃeɪkˈspɪərɪən/ adj. (also **Shakespearean**) of Shakespeare.

shake-up n. upheaval or drastic reorganization.

shako /ˈʃækəʊ/ n. (*pl.* **-s**) cylindrical plumed peaked military hat. [Hungarian *csákó*]

shaky adj. (**-ier, -iest**) **1** unsteady; trembling. **2** unsound, infirm. **3** unreliable. □ **shakily** *adv.* **shakiness** n.

shale n. soft rock of consolidated mud or clay that splits easily. □ **shaly** *adj.* [German: related to SCALE²]

shall /ʃæl, ʃ(ə)l/ v.aux. (*3rd sing. present* **shall**; *archaic 2nd sing. present* **shalt**; *past* **should** /ʃʊd, ʃəd/) (foll. by infin. without *to*, or *absol.*; present and past only in use) **1** (in the 1st person) expressing the future tense or (with *shall* stressed) emphatic intention (*I shall return soon*). **2** (in the 2nd and 3rd

persons) expressing a strong assertion, command, or duty (*they shall go to the party; thou shalt not steal; they shall obey*). **3** (in 2nd-person questions) expressing an enquiry, esp. to avoid the form of a request (*shall you go to France?*). □ **shall I?** (or **we**) do you want me (or us) to? [Old English]

shallot /ʃəˈlɒt/ *n.* onion-like plant with a cluster of small bulbs. [French: related to SCALLION]

shallow /ˈʃæləʊ/ —*adj.* **1** of little depth. **2** superficial, trivial. —*n.* (often in *pl.*) shallow place. □ **shallowness** *n.* [English]

shalom /ʃəˈlɒm/ *n. & int.* Jewish salutation at meeting or parting. [Hebrew]

shalt *archaic 2nd person sing. of* SHALL.

sham —*v.* (**-mm-**) **1** feign, pretend. **2** pretend to be. —*n.* **1** imposture, pretence. **2** bogus or false person or thing. —*adj.* pretended, counterfeit. [origin unknown]

shaman /ˈʃeɪmən/ *n.* witch-doctor or priest claiming to communicate with gods etc. □ **shamanism** *n.* [Russian]

shamble /ˈʃæmb(ə)l/ —*v.* (**-ling**) walk or run awkwardly, dragging the feet. —*n.* shambling gait. [perhaps related to SHAMBLES]

shambles *n.pl.* (usu. treated as *sing.*) **1** *colloq.* mess, muddle. **2** butcher's slaughterhouse. **3** scene of carnage. [pl. of *shamble* table for selling meat]

shambolic /ʃæmˈbɒlɪk/ *adj. colloq.* chaotic, unorganized. [from SHAMBLES after *symbolic*]

shame —*n.* **1** distress or humiliation caused by consciousness of one's guilt, dishonour, or folly **2** capacity for feeling this. **3** state of disgrace or discredit. **4** a person or thing that brings disgrace etc. **b** thing that is wrong or regrettable. —*v.* (**-ming**) **1** bring shame on; make ashamed; put to shame. **2** (foll. by *into, out of*) force by shame (*shamed into confessing*). □ **for shame!** reproof to a shameless person. **put to shame** humiliate by being greatly superior. [Old English]

shamefaced *adj.* **1** showing shame. **2** bashful, shy. □ **shamefacedly** /also -stlɪ/ *adv.*

shameful *adj.* disgraceful, scandalous. □ **shamefully** *adv.* **shamefulness** *n.*

shameless *adj.* **1** having or showing no shame. **2** impudent. □ **shamelessly** *adv.*

shammy /ˈʃæmɪ/ *n.* (*pl.* **-ies**) (in full **shammy leather**) *colloq.* = CHAMOIS 2. [representing corrupted pronunciation]

shampoo /ʃæmˈpuː/ —*n.* **1** liquid for washing the hair. **2** similar substance for washing cars, carpets, etc. —*v.*

(**-poos, -pooed**) wash with shampoo. [Hindustani]

shamrock /ˈʃæmrɒk/ *n.* trefoil, used as an emblem of Ireland. [Irish]

shandy /ˈʃændɪ/ *n.* (*pl.* **-ies**) beer with lemonade or ginger beer. [origin unknown]

shanghai /ʃæŋˈhaɪ/ *v.* (**-hais, -haied, -haiing**) *colloq.* trick or force someone into doing something. **2** trick or force (a person) into serving as a sailor. [*Shanghai* in China]

shank *n.* **1** a leg. **3** lower part of the leg. **c** shin-bone. **2** shaft or stem, esp. the part of a tool etc. joining the handle to the working end. [Old English]

shank's mare *n.* (also **shanks's pony**) one's own legs as transport.

shan't /ʃɑːnt/ *contr.* shall not.

shantung /ʃænˈtʊŋ/ *n.* soft undressed Chinese silk. [*Shantung,* Chinese province]

shanty¹ /ˈʃæntɪ/ *n.* (*pl.* **-ies**) **1** hut or cabin. **2** shack. [origin unknown]

shanty² /ˈʃæntɪ/ *n.* (*pl.* **-ies**) (in full **sea shanty**) sailors' work song. [probably French *chanter:* related to CHANT]

shanty town *n.* area with makeshift housing.

shape —*n.* **1** effect produced by a thing's outline. **2** external form or appearance. **3** specific form or guise (*in the shape of an excuse*). **4** good or specified condition (*back in shape; in poor shape*). **5** person or thing seen in outline or indistinctly. **6** mould or pattern. **7** moulded jelly etc. **8** piece of material, paper, etc., made or cut in a particular form. —*v.* (**-ping**) **1** give a certain shape or form to; fashion, create. **2** influence (one's life, course, etc.). **3** (usu. foll. by *up*) show signs of developing; show promise. **4** (foll. by *to*) adapt or make conform. □ **in any shape or form** in any form at all (*don't like jazz in any shape or form*). **take shape** take on a definite form. [Old English]

shapeless *adj.* lacking definite or attractive shape. □ **shapelessness** *n.*

shapely *adj.* (**-ier, -iest**) pleasing in appearance, elegant, well-proportioned. □ **shapeliness** *n.*

shard *n.* broken piece of pottery or glass etc. [Old English]

share —*n.* **1** portion of a whole allotted to or taken from a person. **2** each of the equal parts into which a company's capital is divided, entitling its owner to a proportion of the profits. —*v.* (**-ring**) **1** (also *absol.*) have or use with another or others; get, have, or give a share of (*we shared his food*). **2** (foll. by *in*) participate. **3** (often foll. by *out*) divide and distribute (*let's share the last cake*). **4**

share

have in common (*shared the same belief*). [Old English: related to SHEAR]

share² *n.* = PLOUGHSHARE. [Old English: related to SHEAR¹]

shareholder *n.* owner of shares in a company.

share-out *n.* act of sharing out, distribution.

shark¹ *n.* large voracious marine fish. [origin unknown]

shark² *n. colloq.* swindler, profiteer. [origin unknown]

sharkskin *n.* 1 skin of a shark. 2 smooth slightly shiny fabric.

sharp —*adj.* 1 having an edge or point able to cut or pierce. 2 tapering to a point or edge. 3 abrupt, steep, angular. 4 well-defined, clean-cut. 5 a severe or intense. b (of food etc.) pungent, acid. 6 (of a voice etc.) shrill and piercing. 7 (of words or temper etc.) harsh. 8 acute; quick to understand. 9 artful, unscrupulous. 10 vigorous or brisk. 11 *Mus.* above the normal pitch; a semitone higher than a specified pitch (*C sharp*). —*n.* 1 *Mus.* a note a semitone above natural pitch, b sign (#) indicating this. 2 *colloq.* swindler, cheat. —*adv.* 1 punctually (*at nine o'clock sharp*). 2 suddenly (*pulled up sharp*). 3 at a sharp angle. 4 *Mus.* above true pitch (*sings sharp*). □ **sharply** *adv.* **sharpness** *n.* [Old English]

sharpen *v.* make or become sharp. □ **sharpener** *n.*

sharper *n.* swindler, esp. at cards.

sharpish *colloq.* —*adj.* fairly sharp. —*adv.* 1 fairly sharply. 2 quite quickly.

sharp practice *n.* dishonest or dubious dealings.

sharpshooter *n.* skilled marksman.

sharp-witted *adj.* keenly perceptive or intelligent.

shat *past* and *past. part.* of SHIT.

shatter *v.* 1 break suddenly in pieces. 2 severely damage or destroy. 3 (esp. in *passive*) greatly upset or discompose. 4 (usu. as **shattered** *adj.*) *colloq.* exhaust. [origin unknown]

shave —*v.* (*-ving*; *past part.* **shaved** or (as *adj.*) **shaven**) 1 remove (bristles or hair) with a razor. 2 (also *absol.*) remove bristles or hair with a razor from (a person, face, leg, etc.). 3 reduce by a small amount. 4 pare (wood etc.) to shape it. 5 miss or pass narrowly. —*n.* 1 shaving or being shaved. 2 narrow miss or escape. 3 tool for shaving wood etc. [Old English]

shaver *n.* 1 thing that shaves. 2 electric razor. 3 *colloq.* young lad.

Shavian /ˈʃeɪvɪən/ —*adj.* of or like the writings of G. B. Shaw. —*n.* admirer of

Shaw. [*Shavius*, Latinized form of *Shaw*]

shaving *n.* thin strip cut off wood etc.

shawl *n.* large usu. rectangular piece of fabric worn over the shoulders or head, or wrapped round a baby. [Urdu from Persian *shāl*]

she /ʃiː/ —*pron.* (*obj.* **her**; *poss.* **her**; *pl.* **they**) the woman, girl, female animal, ship, or country, etc. previously named or in question. —*n.* 1 female; woman. 2 (in *comb.*) female (*she-goat*). [Old English]

s/he *pron.* written representation of 'he or she' used to indicate either sex.

sheaf —*n.* (*pl.* **sheaves**) bundle of things laid lengthways together and usu. tied, esp. reaped corn or a collection of papers. —*v.* make into sheaves. [Old English]

shear —*v.* (*past* **sheared**; *past. part.* **shorn** or **sheared**) 1 (also *absol.*) clip the wool off (a sheep etc.). 2 remove or take off by cutting. 3 cut with scissors or shears etc. 4 (foll. by *of*) a strip bare. b deprive. 5 (often foll. by *off*) distort; be distorted, or break, from structural strain. —*n.* 1 strain produced by pressure in the direction of a substance. 2 (in *pl.*) (also **pair of shears** *sing.*) large scissor-shaped clipping or cutting instrument. □ **shearer** *n.* [Old English]

sheath *n.* (*pl.* **-s** /ʃiːðz, ʃiːθs/) 1 close-fitting cover, esp. for the blade of a knife or sword. 2 condom. 3 enclosing case, covering, or tissue. 4 woman's close-fitting dress. [Old English]

sheathe /ʃiːð/ *v.* (*-thing*) 1 put into a sheath. 2 encase; protect with a sheath.

sheath knife *n.* dagger-like knife carried in a sheath.

sheave *v.* (*-ving*) make into sheaves.

sheaves *pl.* of SHEAF.

shebeen /ʃɪˈbiːn/ *n.* esp. *Ir.* unlicensed drinking place. [Irish]

shed¹ *n.* one-storeyed usu. wooden structure for storage or shelter, or as a workshop. [from SHADE]

shed² *v.* (*-dd-*; *past* and *past part.* **shed**) 1 let, or cause to, fall off (*trees shed their leaves*). 2 take off (clothes). 3 reduce (an electrical power load) by disconnection etc. 4 cause to fall or flow (*shed blood*; *shed tears*). 5 disperse, diffuse, radiate (*shed light*). 6 get rid of (*IBM are shedding 5000 jobs*; *shed your inhibitions*). □ **shed light on** help to explain. [Old English]

she'd /ʃiːd/ *contr.* 1 she had. 2 she would.

sheen *n.* 1 gloss or lustre. 2 brightness. □ **sheeny** *adj.* [Old English, = beautiful]

sheep *n.* (*pl.* same) 1 mammal with a thick woolly coat, esp. kept for its wool

or meat. **2** timid, silly, or easily-led person. **3** (usu. in *pl.*) member of a minister's congregation. [Old English]

sheep-dip *n.* preparation or place for cleansing sheep of vermin by dipping.

sheepdog *n.* **1** dog trained to guard and herd sheep. **2** dog of a breed suitable for this.

sheepfold *n.* pen for sheep.

sheepish *adj.* embarrassed or shy; ashamed. □ **sheepishly** *adv.*

sheepshank *n.* knot for shortening a rope temporarily.

sheepskin *n.* **1** (often *attrib.*) sheep's skin with the wool on. **2** leather from sheep's skin.

sheer[1] —*adj.* **1** mere, complete (*sheer luck*). **2** (of a cliff etc.) perpendicular. **3** (of a textile) diaphanous. —*adv.* directly, perpendicularly. [Old English]

sheer[2] *v.* **1** esp. *Naut.* swerve or change course. **2** (foll. by *away, off*) turn away, esp. from a person or topic one dislikes or fears. [origin unknown]

sheet[1] *n.* **1** large rectangle of cotton etc. used esp. in pairs as inner bedclothes. **2** broad usu. thin flat piece of paper, metal, etc. **3** wide expanse of water, ice, flame, falling rain, etc. **4** page of unseparated postage stamps. **5** *derog.* newspaper. —*v.* **1** provide or cover with sheets. **2** form into sheets. **3** (of rain etc.) fall in sheets. [Old English]

sheet[2] *n.* rope or chain attached to the lower corner of a sail to hold or control it. [Old English: related to SHEET[1]]

sheet anchor *n.* **1** emergency reserve anchor. **2** person or thing depended on in the last resort.

sheeting *n.* material for making bed linen.

sheet metal *n.* metal rolled or hammered etc. into thin sheets.

sheet music *n.* music published in sheets, not bound.

sheikh /ʃeɪk/ *n.* **1** chief or head of an Arab tribe, family, or village. **2** Muslim leader. □ **sheikhdom** *n.* [Arabic]

sheila /ˈʃiːlə/ *n. Austral. & NZ slang* girl, young woman. [origin uncertain]

shekel /ˈʃek(ə)l/ *n.* **1** chief monetary unit of modern Israel. **2** *hist.* silver coin and unit of weight in ancient Israel etc. **3** (in *pl.*) *colloq.* money; riches. [Hebrew]

shelduck /ˈʃeldʌk/ *n.* (*pl.* same or **-s**; *masc.* **sheldrake**, *pl.* same or **-s**) bright-plumaged wild duck. [probably from dial. *sheld* pied, DUCK']

shelf *n.* (*pl.* **shelves**) **1** wooden etc. board projecting from a wall, or as part of a unit, used to store things. **2 a** projecting horizontal ledge in a cliff face etc. **b** reef or sandbank. □ **on the shelf 1** (of a woman) regarded as too old to hope

for marriage. **2** (esp. of a retired person) put aside as if no longer useful. [Low German]

shelf-life *n.* time for which a stored item remains usable.

shelf-mark *n.* code on a library book showing where it is kept.

shell —*n.* **1 a** hard outer case of many molluscs, the tortoise, etc. **b** hard but fragile case of an egg, nut, etc. **2 a** explosive projectile for use in a big gun etc. **b** hollow container for fireworks, cartridges, etc. **3** shell-like thing, esp.: **a** a light racing-boat. **b** the metal framework of a vehicle etc. **c** the walls of an unfinished or gutted building, ship, etc. —*v.* **1** remove the shell or pod from. **2** bombard with shells. □ **come out of one's shell** become less shy. **shell out** *colloq.* pay (money). □ **shell-less** *adj.* **shell-like** *adj.* [Old English]

she'll /ʃiːl/ *contr.* she will; she shall.

shellac /ʃəˈlæk/ —*n.* resin used for making shellac. [from SHEL, LAC]

shelled *adj.* **1** having a shell. **2** with its shell removed.

shellfish *n.* (*pl.* same) **1** aquatic mollusc with a shell. **2** crustacean.

shell-shock *n.* nervous breakdown caused by warfare. □ **shell-shocked** *adj.*

Shela /ˈʃeɪlə/ *n.* ancient hybrid secret language used by Irish tinkers, Gypsies, etc.

shelter —*n.* **1** protection from danger, bad weather, etc. **2** place giving shelter or commotion. —*v.* **1** act or serve as a shelter to; protect; conceal; defend. **2** find refuge; take cover. [origin unknown]

shelve *v.* (**-ving**) **1** put aside, esp. temporarily. **2** put (books etc.) on a shelf. **3** fit with shelves. **4** (of ground etc.) slope. □ **shelving** *n.*

shelves *pl.* of SHELF

shemozzle /ʃɪˈmɒz(ə)l/ *n. slang* **1** brawl or commotion. **2** muddle. [Yiddish]

shenanigan /ʃɪˈnænɪɡən/ *n.* (esp. in *pl.*) *colloq.* mischievous or dubious behaviour, carryings-on. [origin unknown]

shepherd /ˈʃepəd/ —*n.* **1** (*fem.* **shepherdess**) person employed to tend sheep. **2** member of the clergy in charge of a congregation. —*v.* **1 a** tend (sheep etc.). **b** guide (followers etc.) **2** marshal or drive (a crowd etc.) as sheep. [Old English: related to SHEEP, HERD]

shepherd's pie *n.* = COTTAGE PIE.

Sheraton /ˈʃerətən/ *n.* (often *attrib.*) style of English furniture c.1790. [name of a furniture-maker]

sherbet /ˈʃɜːbət/ *n.* **1** flavoured sweet effervescent powder or drink. **2** drink of

sweet diluted fruit juices. [Turkish and Persian from Arabic]

sherd n. = POTSHERD. [Old English]

sheriff /ˈʃerɪf/ n. 1 a (also **High Sheriff**) chief executive officer of the Crown in a county, administering justice etc. b honorary officer elected annually in some towns. 2 US elected chief law-enforcing officer in a county. 3 (also **sheriff-depute**) Scot. chief judge of a county or district. [Old English: related to SHIRE, REEVE¹]

Sherpa n. (pl. same or -s) member of a Himalayan people living on the borders of Nepal and Tibet. [native name]

sherry /ˈʃerɪ/ n. (pl. -ies) 1 fortified wine orig. from S. Spain. 2 glass of this. [Xeres in Andalusia]

she's /ʃiːz, ʃɪz/ contr. 1 she is. 2 she has.

Shetland pony /ˈʃetlənd/ n. pony of a small hardy rough-coated breed. [Shetland Islands, NNE of Scotland]

shew archaic var. of SHOW.

shiatsu /ʃiˈætsuː/ n. Japanese therapy in which pressure is applied, chiefly with fingers and hands, to specific points on the body. [Japanese, = finger pressure]

shibboleth /ˈʃɪbəleθ/ n. long-standing formula, doctrine, or phrase, etc., held to be true by a party or sect. [Hebrew (Judg. 12:6)]

shield /ʃiːld/ n. & v. —n. 1 a piece of armour held in front of the body for protection when fighting. b person or thing giving protection. 2 shield-shaped trophy. 3 protective plate or screen in machinery etc. 4 Heraldry stylized representation of a shield for displaying a coat of arms etc. —v. protect or screen. [Old English]

shier compar. of SHY¹.

shiest superl. of SHY¹.

shift —v. 1 (cause to) change or move from one position to another. 2 remove. 3 slang a hurry. b consume (food or drink). 4 US change (gear) in a vehicle. —n. 1 act of shifting. 2 a relay of workers. b time for which they work. 3 a device, stratagem, or expedient. b trick or evasion. 4 woman's straight unwaisted dress or petticoat. 5 Physics displacement of a spectral line. 6 key on a keyboard used to switch between lower and upper case etc. 7 US a gear lever in a vehicle. b mechanism for this. □ **make shift** manage; get along somehow. **shift for oneself** rely on one's own efforts. **shift one's ground** take up a new position in an argument etc. [Old English]

shiftless adj. lacking resourcefulness; lazy.

shifty adj. colloq. (-ier, -iest) evasive; deceitful. □ **shiftily** adv. **shiftiness** n.

Shiite /ˈʃiːaɪt/ n. & adj. —n. adherent of the branch of Islam rejecting the first three Sunni caliphs. —adj. of this branch. [Arabic Shīah, = party]

shillelagh /ʃɪˈleɪlə, -lɪ/ n. Irish cudgel. [Shillelagh in Ireland]

shilling /ˈʃɪlɪŋ/ n. 1 hist. former British coin and monetary unit worth one-twentieth of a pound. 2 monetary unit in Kenya, Tanzania, and Uganda. [Old English]

shilly-shally /ˈʃɪlɪˌʃælɪ/ v. (-ies, -ied) be undecided; vacillate. [from shall I?]

shim —n. thin wedge in machinery etc. to make parts fit. —v. (-mm-) fit or fill up with a shim. [origin unknown]

shimmer —v. shine tremulously or faintly. —n. tremulous or faint light. [Old English]

shin —n. 1 front of the leg below the knee. 2 cut of beef from this part. —v. (-nn-) (usu. foll. by up, down) climb quickly by clinging with the arms and legs. [Old English]

shin-bone n. = TIBIA.

shindig /ˈʃɪndɪɡ/ n. colloq. 1 lively noisy party. 2 = SHINDY 1. [probably from SHINDY]

shindy /ˈʃɪndɪ/ n. (pl. -ies) colloq. 1 brawl, disturbance, or noise. 2 = SHIN-DIG 1. [perhaps an alteration of SHINTY]

shine —v. (-ning; past and past part. shone /ʃɒn/ or shined) 1 emit or reflect light; be bright; glow. 2 (of the sun, a star, etc.) be visible. 3 cause (a lamp etc.) to shine. 4 (past and past part. shined) polish. 5 be brilliant; excel. —n. 1 light; brightness. 2 high polish; lustre. □ **take a shine to** colloq. take a fancy to. [Old English]

shiner n. colloq. black eye.

shingle¹ /ˈʃɪŋɡ(ə)l/ n. small smooth pebbles, esp. on the sea-shore. □ **shingly** adj. [origin uncertain]

shingle² /ˈʃɪŋɡ(ə)l/ —n. 1 rectangular wooden tile used on roofs etc. 2 archaic a shingled hair. b shingling of hair. —v. (-ling) 1 roof with shingles. 2 archaic a cut (a woman's hair) short. b cut the hair of (a person or head) in this way. [Latin scindula]

shingles /ˈʃɪŋɡ(ə)lz/ n.pl. (usu. treated as sing.) acute painful viral inflammation of the nerve ganglia, with a rash often encircling the body. [Latin cingulum girdle]

Shinto /ˈʃɪntəʊ/ n. Japanese religion with the worship of ancestors and nature-spirits. □ **Shintoism** n. **Shintoist** n. [Chinese, = way of the gods]

shinty /'ʃɪntɪ/ n. (pl. **-ies**) **1** game like hockey, but with taller goalposts. **2** stick or ball used in this. [origin uncertain]

shiny adj. (**-ier**, **-iest**) **1** having a shine. **2** (of clothing) with the nap worn off. □ **shininess** n.

ship —n. **1** large seagoing vessel. **2** US aircraft. **3** spaceship. —v. (**-pp-**) **1** put, take, or send away in a ship. **2 a** take in (water) over a ship's side etc. **b** lay (oars) at the bottom of a boat. **c** fix (a rudder etc.) in place. **3 a** embark. **b** (of a sailor etc.) take service on a ship. **4** deliver (goods) to an agent for forwarding. □ **ship off** send away (or in) when a person's ship comes home (or in) when a person's fortune is made. [Old English]

-ship suffix forming nouns denoting: **1** quality or condition (*friendship*; *hardship*). **2** status, office, etc. (*authorship*; *lordship*). **3** tenure of office (*chairmanship*). **4** specific skill (*workmanship*). **5** members of a group (*readership*). [Old English]

shipboard attrib. adj. used or occurring on board a ship.

shipbuilder n. person, company, etc. that constructs ships. □ **shipbuilding** n.

ship-canal n. canal large enough for ships.

shipload n. as many goods or passengers as a ship can hold.

shipmate n. fellow member of a ship's crew.

shipment n. **1** amount of goods shipped. **2** act of shipping goods etc.

shipowner n. owner of a ship, ships, or shares in ships.

shipper n. person or company that ships goods. [Old English]

shipping n. **1** transport of goods etc. **2** ships, esp. a navy.

ship's boat n. small boat carried on board a ship.

shipshape adj. trim, neat, tidy.

shipwreck —n. **1 a** destruction of a ship by a storm, foundering, etc. **b** ship so destroyed. **2** (often foll. by *of*) ruin of hopes, dreams, etc. —v. **1** inflict shipwreck on. **2** suffer shipwreck.

shipwright n. **1** shipbuilder. **2** ship's carpenter.

shipyard n. place where ships are built etc.

shire n. county. [Old English]

shire-horse n. heavy powerful draught-horse.

shirk v. (also *absol.*) avoid (duty, work, etc.). □ **shirker** n. [German *Schurke* scoundrel]

shirr —n. elasticated gathered threads in a garment etc. forming smocking. —v.

gather (material) with parallel threads. □ **shirring** n. [origin unknown]

shirt n. upper-body garment of cotton etc., usu. front-opening. □ **keep one's shirt on** *colloq.* keep one's temper. **put one's shirt on** *colloq.* bet all one has on. □ **shirting** n. **shirtless** adj. [Old English]

shirtsleeve n. (usu. in pl.) sleeve of a shirt. □ **in shirtsleeves** without one's jacket on.

shirt-tail n. curved part of a shirt below the waist.

shirtwaister n. woman's dress with a bodice like a shirt.

shirty adj. (**-ier**, **-iest**) *colloq.* angry, annoyed. □ **shirtily** adv. **shirtiness** n.

shish kebab /ˌʃɪʃ kɪˈbæb/ n. pieces of meat and vegetables grilled on skewers. [Turkish: related to KEBAB]

shit *coarse slang* —n. **1** faeces. **2** act of defecating. **3** contemptible person. **4** nonsense. —*int.* exclamation of anger etc. —v. (**-tt-**; *past* and *past part.* **shitted**, **shat** or **shit**) defecate or cause the defecation of (faeces etc.). [Old English]

shitty adj. (**-ier**, **-iest**) *coarse slang* **1** disgusting, contemptible. **2** covered with excrement.

shiver[1] /ˈʃɪvə(r)/ —v. tremble with cold, fear, etc. —n. **1** momentary shivering movement. **2** (in *pl.*, prec. by *the*) attack of shivering. □ **shivery** adj. [origin uncertain]

shiver[2] /ˈʃɪvə(r)/ —n. (esp. in *pl.*) small fragment or splinter. —v. break into shivers. [related to dial. *shive* slice]

shoal[1] —n. multitude, esp. of fish swimming together. —v. (of fish) form shoals. [Dutch: cf. SCHOOL[2]]

shoal[2] —n. **1** area of shallow water. **b** submerged sandbank visible at low water. **2** (esp. in *pl.*) hidden danger. —v. (of water) get shallower. [Old English]

shock[1] —n. **1** violent collision, impact, tremor, etc. **2** sudden and disturbing effect on the emotions etc. **3** acute prostration following a wound, pain, etc. **4** = ELECTRIC SHOCK. **5** disturbance in the stability of an organization etc. —v. **1 a** horrify; outrage. **b** (*absol.*) cause shock. **2** affect with an electric or pathological shock. [French *choc*, *choquer*]

shock[2] —n. group of corn-sheaves in a field. —v. arrange (corn) in shocks. [origin uncertain]

shock[3] n. unkempt or shaggy mass of hair. [origin unknown]

shock absorber n. device on a vehicle etc. for absorbing shocks, vibrations, etc.

shocker n. *colloq.* **1** shocking person or thing. **2** sensational novel etc.

shocking adj. **1** causing shock; scandalous. **2** colloq. very bad. □ **shockingly** adv.

shocking pink adj. & n. (as adj. often hyphenated) vibrant shade of pink.

shockproof adj. resistant to the effects of (esp. physical) shock.

shock therapy n. (also **shock treatment**) treatment of depressive patients by electric shock etc.

shock troops n.pl. troops specially trained for assault.

shock wave n. **1** moving region of high air pressure caused by an explosion or by a supersonic body. **2** wave of emotional shock (the news sent shock waves throughout the region).

shod past and past part. of SHOE.

shoddy /ˈʃɒdɪ/ adj. (-ier, -iest) **1** poorly made. **2** counterfeit. □ **shoddily** adv. **shoddiness** n. [origin unknown]

shoe /ʃuː/ –n. **1** protective foot-covering of leather etc., esp. one not reaching above the ankle. **2** protective metal rim for a horse's hoof. **3** thing like a shoe in shape or use. **4** = BRAKE SHOE. –v. (shoes, shoeing; past and past part. shod) **1** fit (esp. a horse etc.) with a shoe or shoes. **2** (as shod adj.) (in comb.) having shoes etc. of a specified kind (roughshod). □ **be in a person's shoes** be in his or her situation, difficulty, etc. [Old English]

shoehorn n. curved implement for easing the heel into a shoe.

shoelace n. cord for lacing up shoes.

shoemaker n. maker of boots and shoes. □ **shoemaking** n.

shoestring n. **1** shoelace. **2** colloq. small esp. inadequate amount of money.

shoe-tree n. shaped block for keeping a shoe in shape.

shone past and past part. of SHINE.

shoo –int. exclamation used to frighten away animals etc. –v. (**shoos, shooed**) **1** (usu. foll. by away) drive away 'shoo!'. **2** (usu. foll. by away) utter the word 'shoo!'. [imitative]

shook past of SHAKE.

shoot –v. (past and past part. **shot**) **1 a** (also absol.) cause (a weapon) to fire. **b** kill or wound with a bullet, arrow, etc. **2** send out, discharge, etc., esp. swiftly. **3** (often foll. by out, along, forth, etc.) come or go swiftly or vigorously. **4 a** (of a plant etc.) put forth buds etc. **b** (of a bud etc.) appear. **5** hunt game etc. with a gun. **6** film or photograph. **7** (also absol.) esp. Football **a** score (a goal). **b** take a shot at (the goal). **8** (of a boat) sweep swiftly down or under (a bridge, rapids, etc.). **9** (usu. foll. by through, up, etc.) (of a pain) seem to stab. **10** (often foll. by up; also absol.) slang inject (a drug). –n. **1 a**

young branch or sucker. **b** new growth of a plant. **2 a** hunting party, expedition, etc. **b** land shot over for game. **3** = CHUTE[1]. –int. colloq. invitation to ask questions etc. □ **shoot down 1** kill by shooting. **2** cause (an aircraft etc.) to crash by shooting. **3** argue effectively against. **shoot one's bolt** colloq. do all that is in one's power. **shoot one's mouth off** slang talk too much or indiscreetly. **shoot up 1** grow rapidly. **2** rise suddenly. **3** terrorize by indiscriminate shooting. **the whole shoot** (or the **whole shooting match**) colloq. everything. [Old English]

shooting-brake n. archaic estate car.

shooting star n. small rapidly moving meteor.

shooting-stick n. walking-stick with a foldable seat.

shop –n. **1** place for the retail sale of goods or services. **2** act of going shopping (did a big shop). **3** place for manufacture or repair (engineering-shop). **4** one's profession etc. as a subject of conversation (talk shop). **5** colloq. institution, place of business, etc. –v. (**-pp-**) **1** (often foll. by for) go to a shop or shops to buy goods. **2** slang inform against (a criminal etc.). □ **all over the shop** colloq. **1** in disorder. **2** everywhere. **shop around** look for the best bargain. □ **shopper** n. [French eschoppe]

shop assistant n. person serving in a shop.

shop-floor n. **1** production area in a factory etc. **2** workers as distinct from management.

shopkeeper n. owner or manager of a shop.

shoplift v. steal goods while appearing to shop. □ **shoplifter** n.

shopping n. **1** (often attrib.) purchase of goods etc. **2** goods purchased.

shopping centre n. area or complex of shops.

shop-soiled adj. soiled or faded by display in a shop.

shop steward n. elected representative of workers in a factory etc.

shopwalker n. supervisor in a large shop.

shore[1] n. **1** land adjoining the sea, a lake etc. **2** (usu. in pl.) country (foreign shores). □ **on shore** ashore. [Low German or Dutch]

shore[2] –n. prop or beam set against a ship, wall, etc., as a support. –v. (**-ring**) (often foll. by up) support (as if) with a shore or shores; hold up. [Low German or Dutch]

shoreline n. line where shore and water meet.

shorn past part. of SHEAR.

short —*adj.* **1 a** measuring little from head to foot, top to bottom, or end to end; not long. **b** not long in duration. **c** seeming (*short years of happiness*). **2 a** (usu. foll. by *of*) deficient; scanty (*short of spoons*). **b** not far-reaching, acting or being near at hand (*short range*). **3 a** concise; brief. **b** curt; uncivil. **4** (of the memory) unable to remember distant events. **5** (of a vowel or syllable) having the lesser of the two recognized durations. **6** (of pastry) easily crumbled. **7** (of stocks etc.) sold or selling when the amount is not in hand, with reliance on getting the deficit at a lower price in time for delivery. **8** (of a drink of spirits) undiluted. **9** (of odds or a chance) nearly even. —*adv.* **1** before the natural or expected time or place; abruptly. **2** rudely. —*n.* **1** short circuit. **2** *colloq.* short drink. **3** short film. —*v.* short-circuit. □ **be caught (or taken) short 1** be put at a disadvantage. **2** *colloq.* urgently need to use the lavatory. **be short for** be an abbreviation for. **come short of** = *fall short of.* **for short** as a short name (*Tom for short*). **in short** briefly. **short of 1** see sense 2a of *adj.* **2** less than (*nothing short of a miracle*). **3** distant from (*two miles short of home*). **4** without going so far as (*did everything short of resigning*). **short on** *colloq.* see sense 2a of *adj.* **shortish** *adj.* **shortness** *n.* [Old English]

shortage *n.* (often foll. by *of*) deficiency; lack.

short back and sides *n.* short simple haircut.

shortbread *n.* rich biscuit of butter, flour, and sugar.

shortcake *n.* **1** = SHORTBREAD. **2** cake of short pastry filled with fruit and cream.

short-change *v.* cheat, esp. by giving insufficient change.

short circuit —*n.* electric circuit through small resistance, esp. instead of the resistance of a normal circuit —*v.* (**short-circuit**) **1** cause a short circuit (in). **2** shorten or avoid by taking a more direct route etc.

shortcoming *n.* deficiency; defect.

shortcrust *n.* (in full **shortcrust pastry**) a type of crumbly pastry.

short cut *n.* **1** route shorter than the usual one. **2** quick method.

shorten *v.* become or make shorter or short.

shortening *n.* fat for pastry.

shortfall *n.* deficit.

shorthand *n.* (often *attrib.*) system of rapid writing using special symbols. **2** abbreviated or symbolic mode of expression.

short-handed *adj.* understaffed.

shorthand typist *n.* typist qualified in shorthand.

shorthorn *n.* animal of a breed of cattle with short horns.

shortie var. of SHORTY.

short list —*n.* list of selected candidates from which a final choice is made. —*v.* (**short-list**) put on a short list.

short-lived *adj.* ephemeral.

shortly *adv.* **1** (often foll. by *before, after*) soon. **2** in a few words; curtly. [Old English]

short-range *adj.* **1** having a short range. **2** relating to the immediate future.

shorts *n.pl.* **1** trousers reaching to the knees or higher. **2** *US* underpants.

short shrift *n.* curt or dismissive treatment. [Old English *shrift* confession: related to SHRIVE]

short sight *n.* inability to focus on distant objects.

short-sighted *adj.* **1** having short sight. **2** lacking imagination or foresight. □ **short-sightedly** *adv.* **short-sightedness** *n.*

short-staffed *adj.* understaffed.

short temper *n.* temper easily lost. □ **short-tempered** *adj.*

short-term *adj.* of or for a short period of time.

short wave *n.* radio wave of frequency greater than 3 MHz.

short weight *n.* weight less than it is alleged to be.

short-winded *adj.* easily becoming breathless.

shorty *n.* (also **shortie**) (*pl.* **-ies**) *colloq.* person or garment shorter than average.

shot¹ *n.* **1** firing of a gun, cannon, etc. **2** attempt to hit by shooting or throwing etc. **3 a** single nonexplosive missile for a gun etc. **b** (*pl.* same or **-s**) small lead pellet used in quantity in a single charge. **c** (as *pl.*) these collectively. **4 a** photograph. **b** continuous film sequence. **5 a** stroke or a kick in a ball game. **b** *colloq.* attempt, guess (*had a shot at it*). **6** *colloq.* person of specified shooting skill (*a good shot*). **7** ball thrown by a shot-putter. **8** launch of a space rocket. **9** range etc. to or at which a thing will carry or act. **10** *colloq.* **a** drink of esp. spirits. **b** injection of a drug etc. □ **like a shot** *colloq.* without hesitation; willingly. [Old English]

shot² *past* and *past part.* of SHOOT. —*adj.* (of coloured material) woven so as to show different colours at different

844

angles. □ **shot through** (usu. foll. by *with*) permeated or suffused.

shotgun *n.* gun for firing small shot at short range.

shotgun wedding *n. colloq.* wedding enforced because of the bride's pregnancy.

shot in the arm *n. colloq.* stimulus or encouragement.

shot in the dark *n.* mere guess.

shot-put *n.* athletic contest in which a shot is thrown. □ **shot-putter** *n.*

should /ʃʊd, ʃəd/ *v.aux.* (*3rd sing.* **should**) *past of* SHALL, used esp.: **1** in reported speech (*I said I should be home soon*). **2** a to express obligation or likelihood (*I should tell you; you should have read it; they should have arrived by now*). **b** to express a tentative suggestion (*I should like to add*). **3** a expressing the conditional mood in the 1st person (*I should have been killed if I had gone*). **b** forming a conditional clause (*if you should see him*).

shoulder /ˈʃəʊldə(r)/ —*n.* **1** part of the body at which the arm, foreleg, or wing is attached. **2** either of the two projections below the neck. **3** upper foreleg of an animal regarded as supportive, comforting, etc. (*a shoulder to cry on; has broad shoulders*). **5** strip of land next to a road. **6** the part of a garment covering the shoulder. —*v.* **1** a push with the shoulder. **b** make one's way thus. **2** take on (a burden etc.). □ **put one's shoulder to the wheel** make a great effort. **shoulder arms** hold a rifle with the barrel against the shoulder and the butt in the hand. **shoulder to shoulder 1** side by side. **2** with united effort. [Old English]

shoulder bag *n.* bag hung from the shoulder by a strap.

shoulder-blade *n.* either of the large flat bones of the upper back.

shoulder-length *adj.* (of hair etc.) reaching to the shoulders.

shoulder-pad *n.* pad in a garment to bulk out the shoulder.

shoulder-strap *n.* **1** strip of cloth going over the shoulder from front to back of a garment. **2** strap suspending a bag etc. from the shoulder. **3** strip of cloth from shoulder to collar, esp. on a military uniform.

shouldn't /ˈʃʊd(ə)nt/ *contr.* should not.

shout —*v.* **1** speak or cry loudly. **2** say or express loudly. —*n.* **1** loud cry of joy etc., or calling attention. **2** *colloq.* one's turn to buy a round of drinks etc. □ **shout down** reduce to silence by shouting. [perhaps related to SHOUT]

shove /ʃʌv/ —*v.* (**-ving**) **1** (also *absol.*) push vigorously. **2** *colloq.* put casually (*shoved it in a drawer*). —*n.* act of shoving. □ **shove off 1** start from the shore in a boat. **2** *slang* depart. [Old English]

shove-halfpenny *n.* form of shovelboard played with coins etc. on a table.

shovel /ˈʃʌv(ə)l/ —*n.* **1** spadelike tool with raised sides, for shifting coal etc. **2** (part of) a machine with a similar form or function. —*v.* (**-ll-**; *US* **-l-**) **1** move (as if with a shovel. **2** *colloq.* move in large quantities or roughly (*shovelled peas into his mouth*). □ **shovelful** *n.* (*pl.* **-s**). [Old English]

shovelboard *n.* game played esp. on a ship's deck by pushing discs over a marked surface.

shoveller /ˈʃʌvələ(r)/ *n.* (also **shoveler**) duck with a shovel-like beak.

show /ʃəʊ/ —*v.* (*past part.* **shown** or **showed**) **1** be, allow, or cause to be, visible; manifest (*buds are beginning to show; white shows the dirt*). **2** (often foll. by *to*) offer for scrutiny etc. (*show your tickets please*). **3** a indicate (one's feelings) (*showed his anger*). **b** accord, grant (favour, mercy, etc.). **4** (of feelings etc.) be manifest (*his dislike shows*). **5** a demonstrate; point out; prove (*showed it to be false; showed his competence*). **b** (usu. foll. by *how to* + infin.) instruct by example (*showed them how to knit*). **6** (*refl.*) exhibit oneself (as being) (*showed herself to be fair*). **7** exhibit in a show. **8** (often foll. by *in, out, up, round*, etc.) conduct or lead (*showed them to their rooms*). **9** *colloq.* = *show up* 3 (*he didn't show*). —*n.* **1** showing. **2** spectacle, display, exhibition, etc. **3** public entertainment or performance. **4** a outward appearance or display. **b** empty appearance; mere display. **5** *colloq.* undertaking, business, affair. **6** *Med.* discharge of blood etc. at the onset of childbirth. □ **good** (or **bad** or **poor**) **show!** *colloq.* that was well (or badly) done. **on show** being exhibited. **show one's hand** disclose one's plans. **show off 1** display to advantage. **2** *colloq.* act pretentiously. **show up 1** make or be conspicuous or clearly visible. **2** expose or humiliate. **3** *colloq.* appear; arrive. **show willing** show a willingness to help etc. [Old English]

showbiz *n. colloq.* = SHOW BUSINESS.

show business *n. colloq.* theatrical profession.

showcase —*n.* **1** glass case for exhibiting goods etc. **2** event etc. designed to exhibit someone or something to advantage. —*v.* (**-sing**) display in or as if in a showcase.

showdown n. final test or confrontation.

shower /ˈʃaʊə(r)/ n. 1 brief fall of rain, snow, etc. 2 a brisk flurry of bullets, dust, etc. b sudden copious arrival of gifts, honours, etc. 3 (in full **shower-bath**) a cubicle, bath, etc. in which one stands under a spray of water. b apparatus etc. used for this. c act of bathing in a shower. 4 US party for giving presents to a prospective bride etc. 5 derog contemptible person or group. —v. 1 discharge (water, missiles, etc.) in a shower. 2 take a shower 3 (usu. foll. by on, upon) lavishly bestow (gifts etc.) 4 descend in a shower. □ **showery** adj. [Old English]

showerproof adj. resistant to light rain.

showgirl n. female singer and dancer in musicals, variety shows, etc.

show house n. (also **show flat**) furnished and decorated new house etc., on show to prospective buyers.

showing n. 1 display, performance. 2 quality of performance. 3 presentation of a case; evidence.

showjumping n. sport of riding horses competitively over a course of fences etc. □ **showjumper** n.

showman n. 1 proprietor or manager of a circus, show. 2 person skilled in publicity, esp. self-advertisement. □ **showmanship** n.

shown past part. of SHOW.

show-off n. colloq. person who shows off.

show of hands n. raised hands indicating a vote for or against.

show-piece n. 1 item presented for display. 2 outstanding specimen.

show-place n. tourist attraction.

showroom n. room used to display goods for sale.

show-stopper n. colloq. act in a show receiving prolonged applause.

show trial n. judicial trial designed to frighten or impress the public.

showy adj. (-ier, -iest) 1 brilliant; gaudy. 2 striking. □ **showily** adv. **showiness** n.

shrank past of SHRINK.

shrapnel /ˈʃræpn(ə)l/ n. 1 fragments of an exploded bomb etc. 2 shell containing pieces of metal etc., timed to burst short of impact. [Shrapnel, name of the inventor of the shell]

shred —n. 1 scrap or fragment. 2 least amount (not a shred of evidence). —v. (-dd-) tear or cut into shreds. □ **shredder** n. [Old English]

shrew /ʃruː/ n. 1 small mouselike long-nosed mammal. 2 bad-tempered or scolding woman. □ **shrewish** adj. (in sense 2). [Old English]

shrewd /ʃruːd/ adj. astute; clever and judicious. □ **shrewdly** adv. **shrewdness** n. [perhaps from obsolete shrew to curse, from SHREW]

shriek n. shrill scream or sound. —v. make or utter in a shriek. [Old Norse]

shrike n. bird with a strong hooked and toothed bill. [Old English]

shrill —adj. 1 piercing and high-pitched in sound. 2 derog. sharp, unrestrained. —v. utter with or make a shrill sound. □ **shrillness** n. **shrilly** adv. [origin uncertain]

shrimp —n. 1 (pl. same or -s) small edible crustacean, turning pink when boiled. 2 colloq. very small person. —v. try to catch shrimps. [origin uncertain]

shrine n. 1 esp. RC Ch. a place for special worship or devotion. b tomb or reliquary. 2 place hallowed by some memory or association. [Latin scrinium bookcase]

shrink —v. (past **shrank**; past part. **shrunk** or (esp. as adj.) **shrunken**) 1 make or become smaller, esp. from moisture, heat, or cold 2 (usu. foll. by from) recoil; flinch. —n. 1 act of shrinking. 2 slang psychiatrist. [Old English]

shrinkage n. 1 process or degree of shrinking. 2 allowance made by a shop etc. for loss by wastage, theft, etc.

shrink-wrap v. enclose (an article) in film that shrinks tightly on to it.

shrive v. (-ving; past **shrove**; past part. **shriven**) RC Ch. archaic 1 (of a priest) hear and absolve (a penitent). 2 (refl.) submit oneself to a priest for confession as penance. [Old English scrīfan impose as penance]

shrivel /ˈʃrɪv(ə)l/ v. (-ll-; US -l-) contract into a wrinkled or dried-up state. [perhaps from Old Norse]

shroud —n. 1 wrapping for a corpse. 2 thing that conceals. 3 (in pl.) ropes supporting a mast. —v. 1 clothe (a body) for burial. 2 cover or conceal. [Old English; = garment]

shrove past of SHRIVE.

Shrovetide n. Shrove Tuesday and the two days preceding it.

Shrove Tuesday n. day before Ash Wednesday.

shrub n. any woody plant smaller than a tree and with branches near the ground. □ **shrubby** adj. [Old English]

shrubbery n. (pl. -ies) area planted with shrubs.

shrug —v. (-gg-) (often absol.) slightly and momentarily raise (the shoulders) to express indifference, doubt, etc. —n. act of shrugging. □ **shrug off** dismiss as unimportant. [origin unknown]

shrunk (also **shrunken**) *past part.* of SHRINK.

shudder —*v.* **1** shiver, esp. convulsively, from fear, cold, etc. **2** feel strong repugnance, fear, etc. (*shudder at the thought*). **3** vibrate. —*n.* **1** act of shuddering. **2** (in *pl.*; prec. by *the*) *colloq.* state of shuddering. [Low German or Dutch]

shuffle /ˈʃʌf(ə)l/ —*v.* (**-ling**) **1** (also *absol.*) drag (the feet) in walking etc. **2** (also *absol.*) rearrange or intermingle (esp. cards or papers). **3 a** prevaricate, be evasive. **b** keep shifting one's position. —*n.* **1** act of shuffling; shuffling walk or movement. **2** change of relative positions. **3** shuffling dance. □ **shuffle off** remove, get rid of. [Low German]

shufti /ˈʃʊftɪ/ *n.* (*pl.* **-s**) *colloq.* look, glimpse. [Arabic *ṣafṭa* try to see]

shun *v.* (**-nn-**) avoid; keep clear of. [Old English]

shunt —*v.* **1** move (a train) between sidings etc.; (of a train) be shunted. **2** move or put aside; redirect. —*n.* **1** shunting or being shunted. **2** *Electr.* conductor joining two points of a circuit, through which current may be diverted. **3** *Surgery* alternative path for the circulation of the blood. **4** *slang* collision of vehicles, esp. one behind another. [perhaps from SHUN]

shush /ʃʊʃ, ʃʌʃ/ —*int.* hush! —*v.* **1** quieten (a person or people) by saying "shush". **2** fall silent. [imitative]

shut *v.* (**-tt-**; *past* and *past part.* **shut**) **1 a** move (a door, window, lid, etc.) into position to block an opening. **b** close or seal (a room, box, eye, etc.) by moving a door etc. **2** become or be capable of being closed or sealed. **3** become or make closed for trade. **4** fold or contract (a book, telescope, etc.). **5** (usu. foll. by *in*, *out*) keep in or out of a room etc. **6** (usu. foll. by *in*) catch (a finger, dress, etc.) by shutting something on it. **7** bar access to. □ **be** (or **get**) **shut of** (or **get**) **rid of** slang be or get rid of. **shut down 1** stop (a factory etc.) from operating. **2** (of a factory etc.) stop operating. **shut off 1** stop the flow of (water, gas, etc.). **2** separate from (a person or people). **shut out 1** exclude. **2** screen from view. **3** prevent. **4** block from the mind. **shut up 1** close all doors and windows of. **2** imprison. **3** put (a thing) away in a box etc. **4** (esp. in *imper.*) *colloq.* stop talking. **shut up shop** close a business, shop, etc., temporarily or permanently. [Old English]

shut-down *n.* closure of a factory etc.

shut-eye *n. colloq.* sleep.

shutter —*n.* **1** movable hinged cover for a window. **2** device that exposes the film in a camera. —*v.* provide with shutters.

shuttle /ˈʃʌt(ə)l/ —*n.* **1 a** (in a loom) instrument pulling the weft-thread between the warp-threads. **b** (in a sewing-machine) bobbin carrying the lower thread. **2** train, bus, etc. used in a shuttle service. **3** = SPACE SHUTTLE. —*v.* (**-ling**) (cause to) move to and fro like a shuttle. [Old English: related to SHOOT]

shuttlecock *n.* cork with a ring of feathers, or a similar plastic device, struck to and fro in badminton.

shuttle diplomacy *n.* negotiations conducted by a mediator travelling between disputing parties.

shuttle service *n.* transport service operating to and fro over a short route.

shy[1] /ʃaɪ/ —*adj.* (**shyer**, **shyest** or **shier**, **shiest**) **1 a** timid and nervous in company; self-conscious. **b** (in *comb.*) disliking or fearing (*work-shy*). —*v.* (**shies**, **shied**) **1** (usu. foll. by *at*) (esp. of a horse) turn suddenly aside in fright. **2** (usu. foll. by *away from*, *at*) avoid involvement. —*n.* sudden startled movement. □ **shyly** *adv.* (also **shily**). **shyness** *n.* [Old English]

shy[2] —*v.* (**shies**, **shied**) (also *absol.*) fling, throw. —*n.* (*pl.* **shies**) fling, throw. [origin unknown]

Shylock /ˈʃaɪlɒk/ *n.* hard-hearted money-lender. [name of a character in a play by Shakespeare]

shyster /ˈʃaɪstə(r)/ *n.* esp. *US colloq.* unscrupulous or unprofessional person. [origin uncertain]

SI *abbr.* the international system of units of measurement. [French *Système International*]

Si *symb.* silicon.

si /siː/ *n.* = TE. [French from Italian]

Siamese /saɪəˈmiːz/ —*n.* (*pl.* same) **1** native or language of Siam (now Thailand) in Asia. **2** (in full **Siamese cat**) cat of a cream-coloured short-haired breed with dark markings and blue eyes. —*adj.* of Siam, its people, or language.

Siamese twins *n.pl.* **1** twins joined at some part of the body. **2** any closely associated pair.

sibilant /ˈsɪbɪlənt/ —*adj.* **1** sounded with a hiss. **2** hissing. —*n.* sibilant letter or sound. □ **sibilance** *n.* **sibilancy** *n.* [Latin]

sibling *n.* each of two or more children having one or both parents in common. [Old English, = akin]

sibyl /ˈsɪbɪl/ *n.* pagan prophetess. [Greek *sibulla*]

sibylline /ˈsɪbɪˌlaɪn/ *adj.* **1** of or from a sibyl. **2** oracular; prophetic. [Latin: related to SIBYL]

sic /sɪk/ *adv.* (usu. in brackets) used, spelt, etc., as written (confirming, or

sick emphasizing: the quoted or copied words). [Latin. = so]

sick —*adj.* **1** esp. *US* unwell. ill. **2** vomiting or likely to vomit. **3** (often foll. by *of*) *colloq.* **a** disgusted; surfeited. **b** angry. esp. because of surfeit. **4** *colloq.* (of a joke etc.) cruel, morbid, perverted, offensive. **5 a** mentally disordered. **b** (esp. in *comb.*) pining (*lovesick*). —*n. colloq.* vomit. —*v.* (usu. foll. by *up*) *colloq.* vomit. □ **take** (or **fall**) **sick** *colloq.* be taken ill. [Old English]

sickbay *n.* room, cabin, etc. for those who are sick.

sickbed *n.* invalid's bed.

sicken *v.* **1** affect with disgust etc. **2 a** (often foll. by *for*) show symptoms of illness. **b** (often foll. by *at*, or *to* + infin.) feel nausea or disgust. **3** (as **sickening** *adj.*) **a** disgusting. **b** *colloq.* very annoying. □ **sickeningly** *adv.*

sickle /'sik(ə)l/ *n.* short-handled tool with a semicircular blade, used for reaping etc. [Old English]

sick-leave *n.* leave granted because of illness.

sickle-cell *n.* sickle-shaped blood cell, esp. as found in a type of severe hereditary anaemia.

sickly *adj.* (**-ier, -iest**) **1 a** weak; apt to be ill. **b** languid, faint, or pale. **2** causing ill health. **3** sentimental or mawkish. **4** of or inducing nausea. [related to sick]

sickness *n.* **1** being ill; disease. **2** vomiting or a tendency to vomit.

sick-pay *n.* pay given during sick-leave.

side —*n.* **1 a** each of the surfaces bounding an object. **b** vertical inner or outer surface. **c** such a surface as distinct from the top or bottom, front or back. **2 a** right or left part of a person or animal, esp. of the torso. **b** left or right half or a specified part of a thing. **c** (often in *comb.*) adjoining position (*seaside; stood at my side*). **3 a** either surface of a thing (*sides*). **b** direction (*from all sides*). **3 a** either surface of a thing regarded as having two surfaces. **b** writing filling one side of a sheet of paper. **4** aspect of a question, character, etc. (*look on the bright side*). **5 a** each of two competing groups in war, politics, games, etc. **b** cause etc. regarded as being in conflict with another. **6 a** part or region near the edge. **b** (*attrib.*) subordinate, peripheral, or detached part (*side-road; side-table*). **7** *colloq.* television channel. **8** each of the boundary lines of a plane rectilinear figure. **9** position nearer or farther than, or right or left of, a given dividing line. **10** line of descent through one parent. **11** (in full **side spin**) spin given to a billiard-ball etc. by hitting it on one side. **12** *slang* cheek; pretensions (*has no side about him*). —*v.i.* **-ding**) (usu. foll. by *with*) take part or be on the same side. □ **by the side of 1** close to. **2** compared with. **let the side down** embarrass or fail one's colleagues. **on one side 1** not in the main or central position. **2** aside. **on the side 1** as a sideline. **2** illicitly. **3** *US* as a side dish **side by side** standing close together, esp. for mutual support. **take sides** support one or other cause etc. [Old English]

sideboard *n.* table or esp. a flat-topped cupboard for dishes, table linen, etc.

sideboards *n.pl. colloq.* hair grown by a man down the sides of his face.

sideburns *n.pl.* = SIDEBOARDS. [earlier *burnsides*, after General *Burnside* (d. 1881)]

side-car *n.* passenger compartment attached to the side of a motor cycle.

sided *adj.* **1** having sides. **2** (in *comb.*) having a specified number or type of sides.

side-door *n.* **1** door at the side of a building. **2** indirect means of access.

side-drum *n.* small double-headed drum.

side-effect *n.* secondary (usu. undesirable) effect.

sidekick *n. colloq.* friend, associate; henchman.

sidelight *n.* **1** light from the side. **2** small light at the front of a vehicle. **3** *Naut.* light on the side of a moving ship.

sideline *n.* **1** work etc. done in addition to one's main activity. **2** (usu. in *pl.*) **a** line bounding the side of a hockey-pitch etc. **b** space next to these where spectators etc. sit. □ **on the sidelines** not directly concerned.

sidelong —*adv.* (esp. of a glance) obliquely. —*adv.* obliquely.

sidereal /saɪˈdɪərɪəl/ *adj.* of the constellations or fixed stars. [Latin *sidus sider-star*]

sidereal day *n.* time between successive meridional transits of a star etc.

side-road *n.* minor road, esp. branching from a main road.

side-saddle —*n.* saddle for a woman riding with both legs on the same side of the horse. —*adv.* riding in this position.

sideshow *n.* **1** small show or stall in an exhibition, fair, etc. **2** minor incident or issue.

sidesman *n.* assistant churchwarden who takes the collection etc.

side-splitting *adj.* causing violent laughter.

sidestep —*n.* step to the side. —*v.* (**-pp-**) **1** avoid by stepping sideways. **2** evade.

side-swipe —n. **1** glancing blow on or from the side. **2** incidental criticism etc. —v. hit (as if) with a side-swipe.

sidetrack v. divert or diverge from the main course or issue.

sidewalk n. US pavement.

sideways —adv. **1** to or from a side. **2** with one side facing forward. —adj. to or from a side.

side-whiskers n.pl. whiskers on the cheeks.

side wind n. wind from the side.

siding n. short track at the side of a railway line, used for shunting.

sidle /ˈsaɪd(ə)l/ v. (-ling) (usu. foll. by along, up) walk timidly or furtively. [shortening of SIDELONG]

SIDS abbr. sudden infant death syndrome; cot-death.

siege n. **1** surrounding and blockading of a town, castle, etc. **2** similar operation by police etc. to force an armed person out of a building. □ **lay siege to** conduct the siege of. **raise the siege of** abandon, or cause the abandonment of, an attempted siege of. [French sege seat]

siemens /ˈsiːmənz/ n. SI unit of conductance, equal to one reciprocal ohm. [von Siemens, name of an engineer]

sienna /sɪˈenə/ n. **1** a kind of earth used as a pigment. **2** its colour of yellowish-brown (**raw sienna**) or reddish-brown (**burnt sienna**). [Siena in Tuscany]

sierra /sɪˈerə/ n. long jagged mountain chain, esp. in Spain or Spanish America. [Spanish from Latin serra saw]

siesta /sɪˈestə/ n. afternoon sleep or rest, esp. in hot countries. [Spanish from Latin sexta (hora) sixth hour]

sieve /sɪv/ —n. utensil with a network of wire or plastic, or a perforated or meshed utensil for separating solids or coarse material from liquids or fine particles, or for pulping. —v. (-ving) sift. [Old English]

sift v. **1** put through a sieve. **2** (usu. foll. by from, out) separate (finer or coarser parts) from material. **3** sprinkle (esp. sugar) from a perforated container. **4** examine (evidence, facts, etc.). **5** (of snow, light, etc.) fall as if from a sieve. [Old English]

sigh /saɪ/ —v. **1** emit an audible breath in sadness, weariness, relief, etc. **2** (foll. by for) yearn for. **3** express with sighs. **4** make a sighing sound. —n. **1** act of sighing. **2** sound made in sighing. [Old English]

sight /saɪt/ —n. **1** a faculty of seeing or being seen. **2** thing seen. **3** opinion (in my sight). **4** range of vision (out of sight). **5** (usu. in pl.) noteworthy features of a place. **6** a device on a gun, telescope, etc., for assisting aim or observation. **b** aim or observation so

gained. **7** colloq. unsightly person or thing (looked a sight). **8** colloq. great deal (a sight too clever). —v. **1** get sight of, observe the presence of (they sighted land). **2** aim (a gun etc.) with a sight. □ **at first sight** on first glimpse or impression. **at** (or **on**) **sight** as soon as a person or a thing has been seen. **catch** (or **lose**) **sight of** begin (or cease) to see or be aware of. **in sight 1** visible. **2** near at hand. **set one's sights on** aim at. [Old English: related to SEE[1]]

sighted adj. **1** not blind. **2** (in comb.) having specified vision (long-sighted).

sight for sore eyes n. colloq. welcome person or thing.

sightless adj. blind.

sightly adj. attractive to look at.

sight-read v. read (music) at sight.

sight-screen n. Cricket large white screen placed near the boundary in line with the wicket to help the batsman see the ball.

sightseer n. person visiting the sights of a place. □ **sightseeing** n.

sight unseen adv. without previous inspection.

sigma /ˈsɪgmə/ n. eighteenth letter of the Greek alphabet (Σ, σ, or, when final, ς). [Latin from Greek]

sign /saɪn/ —n. **1** thing indicating a quality, state, future event, etc. (sign of weakness). **2** mark, symbol, etc. **3** gesture or action conveying an order etc. **4** signboard; signpost. **5** each of the twelve divisions of the zodiac. —v. **1** a (also absol.) write (one's name) on a document etc. as authorization. **b** sign (a document) as authorization. **2** communicate by gesture (signed to me to come). **3** engage or be engaged by signing a contract etc. (see also sign on, sign up). □ **sign away** relinquish (property etc.) by signing. **sign in** sign a register on arrival. **2** get (a person) admitted by signing a register. **sign off 1** end work, broadcasting, etc. **2** withdraw one's claim to unemployment benefit after finding work. **sign on 1** agree to a contract etc. **2** employ (a person). **3** register as unemployed. **sign out** sign a register on departing. **sign up 1** engage (a person). **2** enlist in the armed forces. **3** enrol. [Latin signum]

signal /ˈsɪgn(ə)l/ —n. **1** a sign (usu. prearranged) conveying information etc. **b** message of such signs. **2** immediate cause of action etc. (her death was a signal for hope). **3** a electrical impulse or impulses or radio waves transmitted on a railway giving instructions or warnings to train-drivers etc. —v. (-ll-; US -l-) **1** make signals. **2** a (often foll. by

signal

to + infin.) make signals to; direct. **b** transmit or express by signal; announce. □ **signaller** *n.* [Latin *signum*]

signal² /'sɪgn(ə)l/ *attrib. adj.* remarkable, noteworthy. □ **signally** *adv.* [French *signalé*: related to SIGNAL¹]

signal-box *n.* building beside a railway track from which signals are controlled.

signalize *v.* (also **-ise**) (**-zing** or **-sing**) 1 make noteworthy or remarkable. 2 indicate.

signalman *n.* railway signal operator.

signatory /'sɪgnətərɪ/ —*n.* (*pl.* **-ies**) party that has signed an agreement, esp. a treaty. —*adj.* having signed such an agreement etc. [Latin: related to SIGN]

signature /'sɪgnətʃə(r)/ *n.* 1 **a** a person's name, initials, etc. used in signing. **b** act of signing. 2 *Mus.* **a** = KEY SIGNATURE. **b** = TIME SIGNATURE. 3 *Printing* section of a book made from one sheet folded and cut. [medieval Latin: related to SIGNATORY]

signature tune *n.* tune used regularly to introduce a particular broadcast or performer.

signboard *n.* board displaying a name or symbol etc. outside a shop or hotel etc.

signet /'sɪgnɪt/ *n.* small seal. [French or medieval Latin: related to SIGN]

signet-ring *n.* ring with a seal set in it.

significance /sɪg'nɪfɪkəns/ *n.* 1 importance. 2 meaning. 3 being significant. 4 extent to which a result deviates from a hypothesis such that the difference is due to more than errors in sampling. [Latin: related to SIGNIFY]

significant *adj.* 1 having a meaning; indicative. 2 noteworthy; important. □ **significantly** *adv.* [Latin: related to SIGNIFY]

significant figure *n.* digit conveying information about a number containing it.

signify /'sɪgnɪfaɪ/ *v.* (**-ies**, **-ied**) 1 be a sign or indication of. 2 mean; symbolize. 3 make known. 4 be of importance; matter. □ **signification** /-fɪ'keɪʃ(ə)n/ *n.* [Latin: related to SIGN]

sign language *n.* system of communication by gestures, used esp. by the deaf.

sign of the cross *n.* Christian sign made by tracing a cross with the hand.

signor /'siːnjɔː(r)/ *n.* (*pl.* **-nori** /-'njɔːriː/) title used of or to an Italian-speaking man. [Latin *senior* SENIOR]

signora /siː'njɔːrə/ *n.* title used of or to an Italian-speaking esp. married woman.

signorina /siːnjə'riːnə/ *n.* title used or to an Italian-speaking esp. unmarried woman.

signpost —*n.* 1 post on a road etc. indicating direction etc. 2 indication, guide. —*v.* provide with a signpost or signposts.

signwriter *n.* person who paints signboards etc.

Sikh /siːk, sɪk/ *n.* member of an Indian monotheistic sect [Hindi, = disciple]

silage /'saɪlɪdʒ/ *n.* 1 green fodder stored in a silo. 2 storage in a silo. [alteration of ENSILAGE after SILO]

silence /'saɪləns/ —*n.* 1 absence of sound. 2 abstinence from speech or noise. 3 avoidance of mentioning a thing, betraying a secret, etc.—*v.* (**-cing**) make silent, esp. by force or superior argument. □ **in silence** without speech or other sound. [Latin: related to SILENT]

silencer *n.* device for reducing the noise of a vehicle's exhaust, a gun, etc.

silent *adj.* not speaking, not making or accompanied by any sound. □ **silently** *adv.* [Latin *sileo* be silent]

silent majority *n.* the mass of allegedly moderate people who rarely express an opinion

silhouette /sɪlu'et/ —*n.* 1 picture showing the outline only, usu. in black on white or cut from paper. 2 dark shadow or outline against a lighter background. —*v.* (**-ting**) represent or (usu. in *passive*) show in silhouette. [*Silhouette*, name of a politician]

silica /'sɪlɪkə/ *n.* silicon dioxide, occurring as quartz etc. and as a main constituent of sandstone and other rocks. □ **siliceous** /-'ʃəs/ *adj.* [Latin *silex -lic-* flint]

silica gel *n.* hydrated silica in a hard granular form used as a drying agent.

silicate /'sɪlɪkeɪt/ *n.* compound of a metal with silicon and oxygen.

silicon /'sɪlɪkən/ *n.* non-metallic element occurring widely in silica and silicates.

silicon chip *n.* silicon microchip.

silicone /'sɪlɪkəʊn/ *n.* any organic compound of silicon, with high resistance to cold, heat, water, etc.

silicosis /ˌsɪlɪ'kəʊsɪs/ *n.* lung fibrosis caused by inhaling dust containing silica.

silk *n.* 1 fine soft lustrous fibre produced by silkworms. 2 (often *attrib.*) thread or cloth from this. 3 (in *pl.*) cloth or garments of silk, esp. as worn by a jockey. 4 *colloq.* Queen's (or King's) Counsel, as having the right to wear a silk gown. 5 fine soft thread (*embroidery silk*). □ **take silk** become a Queen's (or King's) Counsel. [Old English *sioloc*]

Sn adj. **1** made of silk. **2** soft or ...trous.

...k-screen printing n. = SCREEN PRINTING.

silkworm n. caterpillar that spins a cocoon of silk.

silky adj. (**-ier**, **-iest**) **1** soft and smooth like silk. **2** suave. □ **silkily** adv. **silkiness** n.

sill n. slab of stone, wood, or metal at the foot of a window or doorway. [Old English]

sillabub var. of SYLLABUB.

silly /'sɪlɪ/ –adj. (**-ier**, **-iest**) **1** foolish, imprudent. **2** weak-minded. **3** Cricket (of a fielder or position) very close to the batsman. –n. (pl. **-ies**) colloq. foolish person. □ **sillily** adv. **silliness** n. [Old English; = happy]

silo /'saɪləʊ/ n. (pl. **-s**) **1** pit or airtight barn etc. in which green crops are kept for fodder. **2** pit or tower for storing grain, cement, etc. **3** underground storage chamber for a guided missile. [Spanish from Latin]

silt –n. sediment in a channel, harbour, etc. –v. (often foll. by up) choke or be choked with silt. [perhaps Scandinavian]

Silurian /saɪ'ljʊərɪən/ Geol. –adj. of the third period of the Palaeozoic era. –n. this period. [Silures, people of ancient Wales]

silvan var. of SYLVAN.

silver –n. **1** greyish-white lustrous precious metallic element. **2** colour of this. **3** silver or cupro-nickel coins. **4** household cutlery. **5** = SILVER MEDAL. –adj. of or coloured like silver. –v. **1** coat or plate with silver. **2** provide (a mirror-glass) with a backing of tin amalgam etc. **3** make silvery. **4** turn grey or white. [Old English]

silver band n. band playing silver-plated instruments.

silver birch n. common birch with silver-coloured bark.

silverfish n. (pl. same or **-es**) **1** small silvery wingless insect. **2** silver-coloured fish.

silver jubilee n. 25th anniversary.

silver lining n. consolation or hope in misfortune.

silver medal n. medal of silver, usu. awarded as second prize.

silver paper n. aluminium foil.

silver plate n. vessels, cutlery, etc., plated with silver. □ **silver-plated** adj.

silver sand n. fine pure sand used in gardening.

silver screen n. (usu. prec. by the) cinema films collectively.

silverside n. upper side of a round of beef.

silversmith n. worker in silver.

silver tongue n. eloquence.

silverware n. articles of or plated with silver.

silver wedding n. 25th anniversary of a wedding.

silvery adj. **1** like silver in colour or appearance. **2** having a clear gentle ringing sound.

silviculture /'sɪlvɪˌkʌltʃə(r)/ n. (also **sylviculture**) cultivation of forest trees. [Latin silva a wood: related to CULTURE]

simian /'sɪmɪən/ –adj. **1** of the anthropoid apes. **2** like an ape or monkey. –n. ape or monkey. [Latin simia ape]

similar /'sɪmɪlə(r)/ adj. **1** like, alike. **2** (often foll. by to) having a resemblance. **3** Geom. shaped alike. □ **similarity** /-'lærɪtɪ/ n. (pl. **-ies**). **similarly** adv. [Latin similis like]

simile /'sɪmɪlɪ/ n. **1** esp. poetical comparison of one thing with another using the words 'like' or 'as' (e.g. as brave as a lion). **2** use of this. [Latin, neuter of similis like]

similitude /sɪ'mɪlɪtjuːd/ n. **1** guise, appearance. **2** comparison; expression of a comparison. [Latin: related to SIMILE]

simmer –v. **1** bubble or boil gently. **2** be in a state of suppressed anger or excitement. –n. simmering condition. □ **simmer down** become less agitated. [perhaps imitative]

simnel cake /'sɪmn(ə)l/ n. rich fruit cake, usu. with a marzipan layer and decoration, eaten esp. at Easter. [Latin simila fine flour]

simony /'saɪmənɪ/ n. buying or selling of ecclesiastical privileges. [from Simon Magus (Acts 8:18)]

simoom /sɪ'muːm/ n. hot dry dust-laden desert wind. [Arabic]

simper –v. **1** smile in a silly or affected way. **2** express by or with simpering. –n. such a smile. [origin unknown]

simple /'sɪmp(ə)l/ adj. (**simpler**, **simplest**) **1** understood or done easily and without difficulty. **2** not complicated or elaborate; plain. **3** not compound or complex. **4** absolute, unqualified, straightforward (the simple truth). **5** foolish; gullible; feeble-minded. □ **simpleness** n.

simple fracture n. fracture of the bone only without a wound.

simple interest n. interest payable on a capital sum only.

simple-minded adj. foolish; feeble-minded. □ **simple-mindedness** n.

simpleton n. gullible or halfwitted person.

□ simplification /-fɪ'keɪʃ(ə)n/ n.

simplify /'sɪmplɪfaɪ/ v. (-ies, -ied) make simple or simpler. □ **simplification**

simplistic /sɪm'plɪstɪk/ adj. excessively or affectedly simple. □ **simplistically** adv.

simply adv. 1 in a simple manner. 2 absolutely (simply astonishing). 3 merely (was simply trying to please).

simulate /'sɪmjʊleɪt/ v. (-ting) 1 pretend to be, have, or feel. 2 imitate or counterfeit. 3 reproduce the conditions of (a situation etc.), e.g. for training. 4 produce a computer model of (a process). □ **simulation** /-'leɪʃ(ə)n/ n. **simulator** n. [Latin related to SIMILAR]

simultaneous /sɪməl'teɪnɪəs/ adj. (often foll. by with) occurring or operating at the same time. □ **simultaneously** adv. **simultaneity** /-tə'neɪtɪ/ n. [Latin simul at the same time]

sin[1] —n. 1 a breaking of divine or moral law, esp. deliberately. b such an act. 2 offence against good taste or propriety etc. —v. (-nn-) 1 commit a sin. 2 (foll. by against) offend. [Old English]

sin[2] /saɪn/ abbr. sine.

sin bin n. colloq. Ice Hockey penalty box.

since —prep. throughout or during the period after (has been here since June; happened after (has been here since June; during or in the time after (what have you done since we met?). 2 because. —adv. 1 from that time or event until now (many years since). 2 ago (many years since). [Old English, = after that]

sincere /sɪn'sɪə(r)/ adj. (sincerer, sincerest) 1 free from pretence. 2 genuine, honest, frank. □ **sincerity** /-'serɪtɪ/ n. [Latin]

sincerely adv. in a sincere manner. □ **yours sincerely** formula for ending an informal letter.

sine n. ratio of the side opposite a given angle (in a right-angled triangle) to the hypotenuse. [Latin sinus]

sinecure /'saɪnɪkjʊə(r), 'sɪn-/ n. profitable or prestigious position requiring little or no work. [Latin sine cura without care]

sine die /ˌsaɪnɪ 'daɪiː, ˌsɪneɪ 'diːeɪ/ adv. formal indefinitely (postponed sine die). [Latin]

sine qua non /ˌsɪneɪ kwɑː 'nəʊn/ n. indispensable condition or qualification. [Latin, = without which not]

sinew /'sɪnjuː/ n. 1 tough fibrous tissue uniting muscle to bone; a tendon. 2 (in pl.) muscles; bodily strength. 3 (in pl.) strength or framework of a thing. □ **sinewy** adj. [Old English]

sinful adj. committing or involving sin. □ **sinfully** adv. **sinfulness** n.

sing —v. (past **sang**; past part. **sung**) 1 utter musical sounds, esp. words with a set tune. 2 utter or produce by singing. 3 (of the wind, a kettle etc.) hum, buzz, or whistle. 4 (of the ears) hear a humming sound. 5 slang turn informer. 6 (foll. by of) literary celebrate in verse. —n. act or spell of singing. □ **sing out** shout. **sing the praises of** praise enthusiastically. □ **singer** n. [Old English]

singe /sɪndʒ/ v. (-geing) 1 burn superficially; scorch. 2 burn off the tips of (hair). —n. superficial burn. [Old English]

singer-songwriter n. person who sings and writes songs.

Singhalese var. of SINHALESE.

single /'sɪŋg(ə)l/ —adj. 1 one only, not double or multiple. 2 united or undivided. 3 for or done by one person etc. 4 one by itself (a single tree). 5 regarded separately (every single thing). 6 not married. 7 (with neg. or interrog.) even one (not a single car). 8 (of a flower) having only one circle of petals. —n. 1 single thing, esp. a single room in a hotel. 2 (in full **single ticket**) ticket valid for an outward journey only. 3 pop record with one item on each side. 4 Cricket hit for one run. 5 (usu. in pl.) game with one player on each side. 6 (in pl.) unmarried people. —v. (foll. by out) choose for special attention etc. □ **singly** adv. [Latin singulus]

single-breasted adj. (of a coat etc.) having only one vertical row of buttons and overlapping little down the front.

single combat n. duel.

single cream n. thin cream with a relatively low fat content.

single-decker n. bus with only one deck.

single file n. line of people one behind another. —adv. one behind the other.

single-handed adv. without help. □ **single-handedly** adv.

single-minded adj. having or intent on only one aim. □ **single-mindedly** adv. **single-mindedness** n.

single parent n. person bringing up a child or children alone.

singlet /'sɪŋglɪt/ n. sleeveless vest. [after doublet]

singleton /'sɪŋg(ə)lt(ə)n/ n. 1 one card only of a suit in a player's hand. 2 single person or thing. [after singleton]

singsong —n. informal singing party. —adj. monotonously rising and falling. [from SING, SONG]

singular /'sɪŋgjʊlə(r)/ —adj. 1 unique; outstanding; extraordinary, strange. 2 Gram. (of a word or form) denoting a

single person or thing. —*n. Gram.* **1** singular word or form. **2** the singular number. □ **singularity** /-'lærɪtɪ/ *n.* **singularly** *adv.* [Latin: related to SINGLE]

sinh /sɑɪn, sɑɪnetʃ/ *abbr. Math.* hyperbolic sine. [sine, hyperbolic]

Sinhalese /sɪnhə'liːz, sɪnə'liːz/ (also **Singhalese** /sɪŋg-/) —*n.* (*pl.* same) **1** member of a N. Indian people now forming the majority of the population of Sri Lanka. **2** their language. —*adj.* of this people or language. [Sanskrit]

sinister /'sɪnɪstə(r)/ *adj.* **1** evil or villainous in appearance or manner. **2** wicked, criminal. **3** ominous. **4** *Heraldry* of or on the left-hand side of a shield etc. (i.e. to the observer's right). [Latin, = left]

sink —*v.* (*past* **sank** or **sunk**; *past part.* **sunk** or as *adj.* **sunken**) **1** fall or come slowly downwards. **2** disappear below the horizon. **3 a** go or penetrate below the surface esp. of a liquid. **b** (of a ship) go to the bottom of the sea etc. **4** settle comfortably. **5 a** decline in strength etc. **b** (of the voice) descend in pitch or volume. **6** cause or allow to sink or penetrate. **7** cause (a plan, person, etc.) to fail. **8** dig (a well) or bore (a shaft). **9** engrave (a die). **10** invest (money). **11 a** knock (a ball) into a pocket or hole in billiards, golf, etc. **b** achieve this by a stroke). **12** overlook or forget (*sank their differences*). —*n.* **1** plumbed-in basin, esp. in a kitchen. **2** place where foul liquid collects. **3** place of vice. □ **sink in 1** penetrate or permeate. **2** become understood. [Old English]

sinker *n.* weight used to sink a fishing-line or sounding-line.

sinking fund *n.* money set aside gradually for the eventual repayment of a debt.

sinner *n.* person who sins, esp. habitually.

Sinn Fein /ʃɪn 'feɪn/ *n.* political wing of the IRA. [Irish, = we ourselves]

Sino- *comb. form* Chinese; Chinese and (*Sino-American*). [Greek *Sinai* the Chinese]

sinology /sɑɪ'nɒlədʒɪ/ *n.* the study of the Chinese language, Chinese history, etc. □ **sinologist** *n.*

sinuous /'sɪnjʊəs/ *adj.* having many curves; undulating. □ **sinuosity** /-'ɒsɪtɪ/ *n.* [Latin: related to SINUS]

sinus /'sɑɪnəs/ *n.* cavity of bone or tissue, esp. in the skull connecting with the nostrils. [Latin, = bosom, recess]

sinusitis /ˌsɑɪnə'sɑɪtɪs/ *n.* inflammation of a sinus.

-sion see -ION.

sip —*v.* (**-pp-**) drink in small mouthfuls. —*n.* **1** small mouthful of liquid. **2** act of taking this. [perhaps var. of SUP[1]]

siphon /'sɑɪf(ə)n/ —*n.* **1** tube shaped like an inverted V or U with unequal legs, used to convey liquid from a container to a lower level by atmospheric pressure. **2** bottle from which aerated water is forced by the pressure of gas. —*v.* (often foll. by *off*) **1** (cause to) flow through a siphon. **2** divert or set aside (funds etc.). [Greek, = pipe]

sir *n.* **1** polite form of address or reference to a man. **2** (**Sir**) title prefixed to the forename of a knight or baronet. [from SIRE]

sire —*n.* **1** male parent of an animal, esp. a stallion. **2** *archaic* form of address to a king. **3** *archaic* father or male ancestor. —*v.* (esp. of an animal) beget.

siren /'sɑɪərən/ *n.* **1** device for making a loud wailing or warning sound. **b** this sound. **2** (in Greek mythology) woman or winged creature whose singing lured unwary sailors on to rocks. **3** (often *attrib.*) temptress; seductress. [Greek *seirēn*]

sirenian /sɑɪ'riːnɪən/ *n.* any one of an order of large aquatic plant-eating mammals.

sirloin /'sɜːlɔɪn/ *n.* upper and choicer part of a loin of beef. [French: related to SUR-[1], LOIN]

sirocco /sɪ'rɒkəʊ/ *n.* (also **scirocco**) (*pl.* **-s**) **1** Saharan simoom. **2** warm sultry wind in S. Europe. [Arabic *sharik*]

sirup US var. of SYRUP.

sis *n. colloq.* sister. [abbreviation]

sisal /'sɑɪs(ə)l/ *n.* **1** fibre made from a Mexican agave. **2** this plant. [*Sisal*, the port of Yucatan]

siskin /'sɪskɪn/ *n.* yellowish-green songbird. [Dutch]

sissy /'sɪsɪ/ (also **cissy**) *colloq.* —*n.* (*pl.* **-ies**) effeminate or cowardly person. —*adj.* (**-ier**, **-iest**) effeminate; cowardly. [from SIS]

sister *n.* **1** woman or girl in relation to her siblings. **2** female fellow member of a trade union, feminist group, etc. **3** senior female nurse. **4** member of a female religious order. **5** (often *attrib.*) of the same type, design, or origin etc. (*sister ship; prose, the younger sister of verse*). □ **sisterly** *adj.* [Old English]

sisterhood *n.* **1** relationship between or as between sisters. **2** society of esp. religious or charitable women. **3** community of feeling between women.

sister-in-law *n.* (*pl.* **sisters-in-law**) **1** sister of one's wife or husband. **2** wife of one's brother.

Sisyphean /ˌsɪsɪˈfiːən/ adj. (of toil) endless and fruitless like that of Sisyphus (who endlessly pushed a stone uphill in Hades). [Latin from Greek]

sit v. (-tt-; past and past part. sat) 1 support the body by resting the buttocks on the ground or a seat etc. 2 cause to sit; place in a sitting position. 3 a (of a bird) perch or warm the eggs in its nest. b (of an animal) rest with the hind legs bent and the buttocks on the ground. 4 (of a committee etc.) be in session. 5 (usu. foll. by for) pose (for a portrait). 6 (foll. by for) be a Member of Parliament (for a constituency). 7 (often foll. by for) take (an examination). 8 be in a more or less permanent position or condition (left sitting in Rome; parcel sitting on the doorstep). 9 (of clothes etc.) fit or hang in a certain way. 10 babysit. □ **be sitting pretty** be comfortably placed. **sit at a person's feet** be a person's pupil. **sit back** relax one's efforts. **sit down** 1 sit after standing 2 cause to sit. 3 (foll. by under) submit tamely to (an insult etc.). **sit in** 1 occupy a place as a protest. 2 (foll. by for) take the place of 3 (foll. by on) be present as a guest or observer at (a meeting etc.). **sit in judgement** be censorious or self-righteous. **sit on** 1 be a member of (a committee etc.). 2 hold a session or inquiry concerning. 3 colloq. delay action about. 4 colloq. repress, rebuke, or snub. **sit on the fence** remain neutral or undecided. **sit out** 1 take no part in (a dance etc.). 2 stay till the end of (esp. an ordeal). 3 sit outdoors. **sit tight** colloq. 1 remain firmly in one's place. 2 not yield. **sit up** 1 rise from lying to sitting. 2 sit firmly upright. 3 go to bed late. 4 colloq. become interested or aroused etc. **sit well on** suit or fit. [Old English]

sitar /sɪˈtɑː(r)/ n. long-necked Indian lute. [Hindi]

sitcom n. colloq. situation comedy. [abbreviation]

sit-down —attrib. adj. 1 (of a meal) eaten sitting at a table. 2 (of a protest etc.) with demonstrators occupying their workplace or sitting down on the ground in a public place. —n. 1 spell of sitting. 2 sit-down protest etc.

site —n. 1 ground chosen or used for a town or building. 2 place of or for some activity (camping site). —v. (-ting) locate, place. [Latin situs]

sit-in n. protest involving sitting in.

Sitka /ˈsɪtkə/ n. (in full **Sitka spruce**) fast-growing spruce yielding timber. [Sitka in Alaska]

sits vac /sɪts ˈvæk/ abbr. situations vacant.

sitter n. 1 person who sits, esp. for a portrait. 2 = BABYSITTER (see BABYSIT).

sitting —n. 1 continuous period spent engaged in an activity (finished the book in one sitting). 2 time during which an assembly is engaged in business. 3 session in which a meal is served. —adj. 1 having sat down. 2 (of an animal or bird) still. 3 (cf an MP etc.) current.

sitting duck n. (also **sitting target**) colloq. easy target.

sitting-room n. room for relaxed sitting in.

sitting tenant n. tenant occupying premises.

situate /ˈsɪtjʊeɪt/ v. (-ting) (usu. in passive) 1 put in a certain position or circumstances. 2 establish or indicate the place of; put in a context. [Latin situs: related to SITE]

situation /ˌsɪtjʊˈeɪʃ(ə)n/ n. 1 place and its surroundings. 2 circumstances; position; state of affairs. 3 formal paid job. □ **situation comedy** n. broadcast comedy based on characters dealing with awkward domestic situations. **situational** adj.

sit-up n. physical exercise of sitting up from a supine position without using the arms or hands.

sit-upon n. colloq. buttocks.

six adj. & n. 1 one more than five. 2 symbol for this (6, vi, VI). 3 size etc. denoted by six. 4 Cricket hit scoring six runs. 5 six o'clock. □ **at sixes and sevens** in confusion or disagreement. **knock** (or **hit**) **for six** colloq. utterly surprise or overcome. [Old English]

sixer n. 1 Cricket hit for six runs. 2 Brownie or Cub in charge of a group of six.

sixfold adj. & adv. 1 six times as much or as many. 2 consisting of six parts.

sixpence /ˈsɪkspəns/ n. 1 sum of six pence. 2 hist. coin worth this.

sixpenny adj. costing or worth sixpence, esp. before decimalization.

six-shooter n. (also **six-gun**) revolver with six chambers.

sixteen /sɪksˈtiːn, ˈsɪks-/ adj. & n. 1 one more than fifteen. 2 symbol for this (16, xvi, XVI). 3 size etc. denoted by sixteen. □ **sixteenth** adj. & n.

sixth adj. & n. 1 next after fifth. 2 any of six equal parts of a thing. □ **sixthly** adv.

sixth form n. form in a secondary school for pupils over 16.

sixth-form college n. separate college for pupils over 16.

sixth former n. sixth-form pupil.

sixth sense n. supposed intuitive or extrasensory faculty.

sixty /'siksti/ *adj. & n. (pl. -ies)* **1** six times ten. **2** symbol for this (60, lx, LX). **3** (in *pl.*) numbers from 60 to 69, esp. the years of a century or of a person's life. □ **sixtieth** *adj. & n.* [Old English]

sizable var. of SIZEABLE.

size[1] —*n.* **1** relative dimensions, magnitude. **2** each of the classes into which similar things are divided according to size. —*v.* (-zing) sort in sizes or according to size. □ **the size of it** *colloq.* the truth of the matter. **size up** *colloq.* form a judgement of. □ **sized** *adj.* (also in *comb.*). [French *sise*]

size[2] —*n.* sticky solution used in glazing paper, stiffening textiles, etc. —*v.* (-zing) treat with size. [perhaps = SIZE[1]]

sizeable *adj.* (also **sizable**) large or fairly large.

sizzle /'sIz(ə)l/ —*v.* (-ling) **1** sputter or hiss, esp. in frying. **2** *colloq.* be very hot or excited etc. —*n.* sizzling sound. □ **sizzling** *adj. & adv.* [imitative]

SJ *abbr.* Society of Jesus.

ska /skɑ:/ *n.* a kind offast orig. Jamaican pop music. [origin unknown]

skate[1] —*n.* **1** boot with a blade attached for gliding on ice; this blade. **2** = ROLLER-SKATE. —*v.* (-ting) **1 a** move on skates. **b** perform (a specified figure) on skates. **2** (foll. by *over*) refer fleetingly to, disregard. □ **get one's skates on** *slang* make haste. **skate on thin ice** behave rashly, risk danger. □ **skater** *n.* [Dutch *schaats* from French]

skate[2] *n.* (*pl.* same or **-s**) large flat marine fish used as food. [Old Norse]

skateboard —*n.* short narrow board on two pairs of trucks, for riding on while standing. —*v.* ride on a skateboard. □ **skateboarder** *n.*

skedaddle /skI'dæd(ə)l/ *v.* (-ling) *colloq.* depart quickly, flee. [origin unknown]

skein /skeIn/ *n.* **1** loosely-coiled bundle of yarn or thread. **2** flock of wild geese etc. in flight. [French *escaigne*]

skeleton /'skelIt(ə)n/ *n.* **1** hard framework of bones etc. of an animal. **2** supporting framework or structure of a thing. **3** very thin person or animal. **4** useless or dead remnant. **5** outline sketch, epitome. **6** (*attrib.*) having only the essential or minimum number of persons, parts, etc. (*skeleton staff*). □ **skeletal** *adj.* [Greek *skelētō* dry up]

skeleton in the cupboard *n.* discreditable or embarrassing secret.

skeleton key *n.* key designed to fit many locks.

skeptic *US* var. of SCEPTIC.

skeptical *US* var. of SCEPTICAL.

skerry /'skerI/ *n.* (*pl.* -ies) *Scot.* reef, rocky island. [Old Norse]

sketch —*n.* **1** rough or unfinished drawing or painting. **2** rough draft or general outline. **3** short usu. humorous play. **4** short descriptive essay etc. —*v.* **1** make or give a sketch of. **2** draw sketches. **3** (often foll. by *in*, *out*) outline briefly. [Greek *skhedios* extempore]

sketch-book *n.* (also **sketch-block**) pad of drawing-paper for sketching.

sketch-map *n.* roughly-drawn map with few details.

sketchy *adj.* (-ier, -iest) **1** giving only a rough outline, like a sketch. **2** *colloq.* unsubstantial or imperfect, esp. through haste. □ **sketchily** *adv.* **sketchiness** *n.*

skew —*adj.* oblique, slanting, set askew. —*n.* slant. —*v.* **1** make skew. **2** distort. **3** move obliquely. □ **on the skew** askew.

skewbald /'skju:bɔ:ld/ —*adj.* (esp. of a horse) with irregular patches of white and another colour. —*n.* skewbald animal. [origin uncertain]

skewer /'skju:ə(r)/ —*n.* long pin designed for holding meat together while cooking. —*v.* fasten together or pierce (as) with a skewer. [origin uncertain]

skew-whiff *adj. & adv. colloq.* askew.

ski /ski:/ —*n.* (*pl.* **-s**) each of a pair of long narrow pieces of wood etc., fastened under the feet for travelling over snow. **2** similar device under a vehicle or aircraft. —*v.* (**skis, ski'd** or **skied** /ski:d/; **skiing**) travel on skis. □ **skier** *n.* [Norwegian from Old Norse]

skid —*v.* (**-dd-**) **1** (of a vehicle etc.) slide on slippery ground, esp. sideways or obliquely. **2** cause (a vehicle) to skid. —*n.* **1** act of skidding. **2** runner beneath an aircraft for use when landing. □ **on the skids** *colloq.* about to be discarded or defeated. **put the skids under** *colloq.* hasten the downfall or failure of. [origin unknown]

skid-pan *n.* slippery surface for drivers to practise control of skidding.

skid row *n. US slang* part of a town frequented by vagrants.

skiff *n.* light rowing- or sculling-boat. [French *esquif*; related to SHIP]

ski-jump *n.* steep slope levelling off before a sharp drop to allow a skier to leap through the air. □ **ski-jumping** *n.*

skilful *adj.* (*US* **skillful**) (often foll. by *at, in*) having or showing skill. □ **skilfully** *adv.*

ski-lift *n.* device for carrying skiers up a slope, usu. a cable with hanging seats.

skill *n.* (often foll. by *in*) ability to do something well; technique, expertise. [Old Norse, = difference]

skilled *adj.* 1 (often foll. by *in*) skilful. 2 having skill or special training.

skillet /ˈskilit/ *n.* 1 small long-handled metal cooking-pot. 2 *US* frying-pan. [French]

skilful *US* var. of SKILFUL.

skim *v.* (**-mm-**) 1 a take a floating layer from the surface of (a liquid). b take (cream etc.) from the surface of a liquid. 2 a barely touch (a surface) in passing over. b (often followed by *over*) deal with or treat (a matter) superficially. 3 (often foll. by *over*, *along*) go or glide lightly. 4 (often followed by *through*) read or look over cursorily. —*n.* skimming. [French: related to SCUM]

skimmia /ˈskimiə/ *n.* evergreen shrub with red berries. [Japanese]

skim milk *n.* (also **skimmed milk**) milk from which the cream has been removed.

skimp *v.* 1 (often followed by *on*) economize; use a meagre or insufficient amount of, stint. 2 (often foll. by *in*) supply (a person etc.) meagrely with food etc. 3 do hastily or carelessly. [cf. SCRIMP]

skimpy *adj.* (**-ier, -iest**) meagre; insufficient. □ **skimpiness** *n.*

skin —*n.* 1 flexible covering of a body. 2 a skin of a flayed animal with or without the hair etc. b material prepared from skins. 3 complexion of the skin. 4 outer layer or covering, esp. of a fruit, sausage, etc. 5 film like skin on a liquid etc. 6 container for liquid, made of an animal's skin. 7 *slang* skinhead. —*v.* (**-nn-**) 1 remove the skin from. 2 graze (part of the body). 3 *slang* swindle. □ **be skin and bone** be very thin. **by (or with) the skin of one's teeth** by a very narrow margin. **get under a person's skin** *colloq.* interest or annoy a person intensely. **have a thick (or thin) skin** be insensitive (or sensitive). **no skin off one's nose** *colloq.* of no consequence to one. □ **skinless** *adj.* [Old Norse]

skin-deep *adj.* superficial.

skin-diver *n.* underwater swimmer without a diving-suit, usu. with aqualung and flippers. □ **skin-diving** *n.*

skinflint *n.* miser.

skinful *n. colloq.* enough alcohol to make one drunk.

skin-graft *n.* 1 surgical transplanting of skin. 2 skin transferred in this way.

skinhead *n.* youth with a shaven head, esp. one of an aggressive gang.

skinny *adj.* (**-ier, -iest**) thin or emaciated. □ **skinniness** *n.*

skint *adj. slang* having no money left. [= *skinned*]

skin-tight *adj.* (of a garment) very close-fitting.

skip¹ —*v.* (**-pp-**) 1 a move along lightly, esp. with alternate hops. b jump lightly, esp. over a skipping-rope. c gambol, caper, frisk. 2 (often foll. by *from*, *off*, *to*) move quickly from one point, subject, etc. to another. 3 (also *absol.*) omit parts of (a text, subject, etc.). 4 *colloq.* miss intentionally, not attend. 5 *colloq.* leave hurriedly. —*n.* skipping movement or action. □ **skip it** *colloq.* abandon a topic, action. [probably Scandinavian]

skip² *n.* 1 large container for building or raising materials in mining etc. 2 container for transporting refuse etc. [Old Norse]

skijack *n.* (in full **skijack tuna**) (*pl.* same or **-s**) small striped Pacific tuna used as food. [from SKIP¹, JACK]

skipper —*n.* 1 captain of a ship or aircraft. 2 captain of a sporting team. —*v.* be the captain of. [Low German or Dutch *schipper*]

skipping-rope *n.* length of rope turned over the head and under the feet while jumping it as a game or exercise.

skirl —*n.* shrill sound, esp. of bagpipes. —*v.* make a skirl. [probably Scandinavian]

skirmish /ˈskɜːmiʃ/ —*n.* 1 minor battle. 2 short argument or contest of wit etc. —*v.* engage in a skirmish. [French from Germanic]

skirt —*n.* 1 woman's garment hanging from the waist. 2 the part of a coat etc. hanging below the waist. 3 hanging part at the base of a hovercraft. 4 (in *sing.* or *pl.*) edge, border, extreme part. 5 (also *bit of skirt*) *slang offens.* woman. 6 (in full *skirt of beef* etc.) cut of meat from the flank or diaphragm. —*v.* (often foll. by *around*) 1 go or lie along or round the edge of. 2 avoid dealing with (an issue etc.). [Old Norse: related to SHIRT]

skirting-board *n.* narrow board etc. along the bottom of a room-wall.

ski-run *n.* slope prepared for skiing.

skit *n.* light, usu. short, piece of satire or burlesque. [perhaps from Old Norse: related to SHOOT]

skittish *adj.* 1 lively, playful. 2 (of a horse etc.) nervous, inclined to shy. [perhaps related to SKIT]

skittle /ˈskit(ə)l/ *n.* 1 pin used in skittles. 2 (in *pl.*; usu. treated as *sing.*) game of trying to bowl down usu. nine wooden pins. [origin unknown]

skive *v.* (**-ving**) (often followed by *off*) *slang* evade work; play truant. □ **skiver** *n.* [Old Norse]

skivvy /ˈskivi/ —*n.* (*pl.* **-ies**) *colloq. derog.* female domestic servant. —*v.*

(-ies, -ied) work as a skivvy. [origin unknown]

skua /'skju:ə/ n. large predatory sea bird. [Old Norse]

skulduggery /skʌl'dʌgəri/ n. trickery; unscrupulous behaviour. [origin unknown]

skulk v. move stealthily; lurk, hide. [Scandinavian]

skull n. **1** bony case of the brain of a vertebrate. **2** bony skeleton of the head. **3** head as the seat of intelligence. [origin unknown]

skull and crossbones n.pl. representation of a skull with two crossed thigh-bones as an emblem of piracy or death.

skullcap n. peakless cap covering the crown only.

skunk n. (pl. same or **-s**) **1** black and white striped mammal emitting a powerful stench when attacked. **2** colloq. contemptible person. [American Indian]

sky /skaɪ/ -n. (pl. **skies**) (in sing. or pl.) atmosphere and outer space as seen from the earth. -v. (**skies**, **skied**) Cricket etc. hit (a ball) high. □ **to the skies** without reserve (praise to the skies). [Old Norse]

sky blue adj. & n. (as adj. often hyphenated) bright clear blue.

skydiving n. sport of performing acrobatic manoeuvres under free fall before opening a parachute. □ **skydiver** n.

sky-high adv. & adj. very high.

skyjack v. slang hijack (an aircraft).

skylark n. lark that sings while soaring. -v. play tricks, frolic.

skylight n. window in a roof.

skyline n. outline of hills, buildings, etc. against the sky.

sky-rocket -n. = ROCKET 1. -v. (esp. of prices) rise very rapidly.

skyscraper n. very tall building.

skyward /'skaɪwəd/ -adv. (also **skywards**) towards the sky. -adj. moving skyward.

sky-writing n. writing in aeroplane smoke-trails.

slab n. **1** flat thick esp. rectangular piece of solid material, esp. stone. **2** mortuary table. [origin unknown]

slack -adj. **1** (of rope etc.) not taut. **2** inactive or sluggish. **3** negligent, remiss. **4** (of tide etc.) neither ebbing nor flowing. -n. **1** slack part of a rope (haul in the slack). **2** slack period. **3** (in pl.) informal trousers. -v. **1** loosen (rope etc.). **2** colloq. take a rest, be lazy. □ **slack off 1** loosen. **2** (also **slack up**) reduce one's level of activity; reduce speed. □ **slackness** n. [Old English]

slack² n. coal-dust or fragments of coal. [probably Low German or Dutch]

slacken v. make or become slack. □ **slacken off** = slack off (see SLACK¹).

slacker n. shirker.

slag -n. **1** refuse left after smelting etc. **2** slang derog. prostitute; promiscuous woman. -v. (**-gg-**) **1** form slag. **2** (often foll. by **off**) slang insult, slander. □ **slaggy** adj. [Low German]

slag-heap n. hill of refuse from a coal-mine, steelworks, etc.

slain past part. of SLAY¹.

slake v. (**-king**) **1** assuage or satisfy (thirst, a desire, etc.). **2** temper (quicklime) by combination with water. [Old English: related to SLACK¹]

slalom /'slɑːləm/ n. **1** ski-race down a zigzag obstacle course. **2** obstacle race in canoes etc. [Norwegian]

slam¹ -v. (**-mm-**) **1** shut forcefully and loudly. **2** put down loudly. **3** put or go suddenly (slam the brakes on; car slammed to a halt). **4** slang criticize severely. **5** slang hit. **6** slang conquer easily. -n. sound or action of slamming. [probably Scandinavian]

slam² n. Cards winning of every trick in a game. [origin uncertain]

slander -n. **1** false and damaging utterance about a person. **2** uttering of this. -v. utter slander about. □ **slanderous** adj. [French esclandre: related to SCANDAL]

slang -n. very informal words, phrases, or meanings, not regarded as standard and often used by a specific profession, class, etc. -v. use abusive language (to). □ **slangy** adj. [origin unknown]

slanging-match n. prolonged exchange of insults.

slant /slɑːnt/ -v. **1** slope; lie or (cause to) go obliquely. **2** (often as **slanted** adj.) present (information) in a biased or particular way. -n. **1** slope; oblique position. **2** point of view, esp. a biased one. -adj. sloping, oblique. □ **on a** (or **the**) **slant** aslant. [Scandinavian]

slantwise adv. aslant.

slap -v. (**-pp-**) **1** strike with the palm or a flat object, or so as to make a similar noise. **2** lay forcefully (slapped it down). **3** put hastily or carelessly (slap paint on). **4** (often foll. by **down**) colloq. reprimand or snub. -n. **1** blow with the palm or a flat object. **2** slapping sound. -adv. suddenly, fully, directly (ran slap into him). [Low German, imitative]

slap and tickle n. colloq. sexual horseplay.

slap-bang adv. colloq. violently, headlong.

slapdash -adj. hasty and careless. -adv. in this manner.

slap-happy *adj. colloq.* cheerfully casual or flippant.

slap in the face *n.* rebuff or affront.

slap on the back *n.* congratulations.

slapstick *n.* boisterous comedy.

slap-up *attrib. adj. colloq.* excellent, lavish.

slash —*v.* **1** cut or gash with a knife etc. **2** (often foll. by *at*) deliver or aim cutting blows. **3** reduce (prices etc.) drastically. **4** censure vigorously. —*n.* **1** slashing cut or stroke. **2** *Printing* oblique stroke; solidus. **3** *slang* act of urinating. [origin unknown]

slat *n.* thin narrow piece of wood, plastic, or metal, esp. as in a fence or Venetian blind. [French *esclat* splinter]

slate —*n.* **1** (esp. bluish-grey) metamorphic rock easily split into flat smooth plates. **2** piece of this as a tile or slab, for writing on. **3** bluish-grey colour of slate. **4** list of nominees for office etc. —*v.* (**-ting**) **1** roof with slates. **2** *colloq.* criticize severely. **3** *US* make arrangements for (an event etc.). **4** *US* nominate for office etc. —*adj.* of slate or the colour of slate. □ **on the slate** on (usu. informal) credit. □ **slating** *n.* **slaty** *adj.* [French *esclat*, feminine of *esclat*: related to **slat**]

slattern *n.* slovenly woman. □ **slatternly** *adj.* [origin uncertain]

slaughter /ˈslɔːtə(r)/ —*n.* **1** kill (animals) for food or skins or because of disease. **2** kill (people) ruthlessly or on a great scale. **3** *colloq.* defeat utterly. —*v.* act of slaughtering. □ **slaughterer** *n.* [Old Norse: related to **slay**]

slaughterhouse *n.* place for the slaughter of animals as food.

Slav /slɑːv/ —*n.* member of a group of peoples in central and eastern Europe speaking Slavonic languages. —*adj.* of the Slavs. [Latin *Sclavus*, ethnic name]

slave —*n.* **1** person who is owned by and has to serve another. **2** drudge; hard worker. **3** (foll. by *of, to*) obsessive devotee (*slave of fashion*). **4** machine, or part of one, directly controlled by another. —*v.* (**-ving**) (often foll. by *at, over*) work very hard. [French *esclave* from Latin *Sclavus* Slav (captive)]

slave-driver *n.* **1** overseer of slaves. **2** demanding boss.

slave labour *n.* forced labour.

slaver[1] *n. hist.* ship or person engaged in the slave-trade.

slaver[2] /ˈslævə(r)/ —*v.* **1** dribble. **2** (foll. by *over*) drool over. —*n.* **1** dribbling saliva. **2** a fulsome flattery. b drivel, nonsense. [Low German or Dutch]

slavery /ˈsleɪvərɪ/ *n.* **1** condition of a slave. **2** drudgery. **3** practice of having slaves.

slave-trade *n. hist.* dealing in slaves, esp. African Blacks.

Slavic /ˈslɑːvɪk/ *adj. & n.* = SLAVONIC.

slavish *adj.* **1** like slaves. **2** without originality. □ **slavishly** *adv.*

Slavonic /sləˈvɒnɪk/ —*adj.* **1** of the group of languages including Russian, Polish, and Czech. **2** of the Slavs. —*n.* Slavonic language-group. [related to SLAV]

slay *v.* (*past* **slew** /sluː/; *past part.* **slain**) **1** *literary* = KILL 1 **2** = KILL 4. □ **slayer** *n.* [Old English]

sleaze *n. colloq.* sleaziness. [back-formation from SLEAZY]

sleazy *adj.* (**-ier, -iest**) squalid, tawdry. □ **sleazily** *adv.* **sleaziness** *n.* [origin unknown]

sled *US* —*n.* sledge. —*v.* (**-dd-**) ride on a sledge. [Low German]

sledge —*n.* vehicle on runners for use on snow. —*v.* (**-ging**) travel or convey by sledge. [Dutch *sleedse*]

sledgehammer /ˈslɛdʒhæmə(r)/ *n.* **1** large heavy long-handled hammer used to break stone etc. **2** (*attrib.*) heavy or powerful (*sledgehammer blow*). [Old English *slecg*: related to SLAY]

sleek —*adj.* **1** (of hair, skin, etc.) smooth and glossy. **2** looking well-fed and comfortable. —*v.* make sleek. □ **sleekly** *adv.* **sleekness** *n.* [var. of SLICK]

sleep —*n.* **1** natural recurring condition of suspended consciousness, with the eyes closed and the muscles relaxed. **2** period of sleep (*had a sleep*). **3** state like sleep; rest, quiet, death. —*v.* (*past and past part.* **slept**) **1** a be in a state of sleep. b fall asleep. **2** (foll. by *at, in,* etc.) spend the night. **3** provide beds etc. for (*house sleeps six*). **4** (foll. by *with, together*) have sexual intercourse, esp. in bed. **5** (foll. by *on*) put off (a decision) until the next day. **6** (foll. by *through*) fail to be woken by. **7** be inactive or dead. **8** (foll. by *off*) remedy by sleeping. □ **get to sleep** manage to fall asleep. **go to sleep 1** begin to sleep. **2** (of a limb) become numb. **put to sleep 1** anaesthetize. **2** put down (an animal). **sleep around** *colloq.* be sexually promiscuous. **sleep in** sleep later than usual in the morning. [Old English]

sleeper *n.* **1** person or animal that sleeps. **2** horizontal beam supporting a railway track. **3** a sleeping-car. b berth in this. **4** ring or stud worn in a pierced ear to keep the hole open.

sleeping-bag *n.* padded bag to sleep in when camping etc.

sleeping-car *n.* (also **sleeping-carriage**) railway coach with berths.

sleeping partner *n.* partner not sharing in the actual work of a firm.

sleeping-pill n. pill to induce sleep.

sleeping policeman n. ramp etc. in the road to make traffic slow down.

sleeping sickness n. tropical disease causing extreme lethargy.

sleepless adj. 1 lacking sleep (sleepless night). 2 unable to sleep. 3 continually active. □ **sleeplessness** n.

sleepwalk v. walk about while asleep. □ **sleepwalker** n.

sleepy adj. (-ier, -iest) 1 drowsy. 2 quiet, inactive (sleepy town). □ **sleepily** adv. **sleepiness** n.

sleet —n. 1 snow and rain falling together. 2 hail or snow melting as it falls (it is sleeting). —v. (prec. by it as subject) sleet falls (it is sleeting). □ **sleety** adj. [Old English]

sleeve n. 1 part of a garment that encloses an arm. 2 cover of a gramophone record. 3 tube enclosing a rod etc. □ **up one's sleeve** in reserve. □ **sleeved** adj. (also in comb.). **sleeveless** adj. [Old English]

sleigh /slei/ —n. sledge, esp. for riding on. —v. travel on a sleigh. [Dutch slee: related to SLEDGE]

sleight of hand /slait/ n. dexterity, esp. in conjuring. [Old Norse: related to SLY]

slender adj. (-er, -est) 1 a of small girth or breadth. b gracefully thin. 2 relatively small, scanty, inadequate. [origin unknown]

slept past and past part. of SLEEP.

sleuth /sluːθ/ colloq. —n. detective. —v. investigate crime etc. [Old Norse]

slew¹ /sluː/ (also **slue**) —v. (often foll. by round) turn or swing forcibly to a new position. —n. such a turn. [origin unknown]

slew² past of SLAY.

slice —n. 1 thin flat piece or wedge of esp. food cut off or out. 2 share; part. 3 long-handled kitchen utensil with a broad flat perforated blade. 4 Sport stroke that sends the ball obliquely. —v. (-cing) 1 (often foll. by up) cut into slices. 2 (foll. by off) cut off. 3 (foll. by into, through) cut (as) with a knife. 4 strike (a ball) with a slice. [French esclice from Germanic]

slick —adj. colloq. 1 a skilful or efficient. b superficially or pretentiously smooth and dexterous; glib. 2 sleek, smooth. —n. large patch of oil etc., esp. on the sea. —v. colloq. 1 (usu. foll. by back, down) flatten (one's hair etc.). 2 (usu. foll. by up) make sleek or smart. □ **slickly** adv. **slickness** n. [Old English]

slide —v. (past and past part. slid) 1 move along a smooth surface with continuous contact on the same part of the thing moving. 2 move quietly or smoothly; glide. 3 glide over ice without skates. 4 (foll. by over) barely touch upon (a delicate subject etc.). 5 (often foll. by into) move quietly or unobtrusively. —n. 1 act of sliding. 2 rapid decline. 3 inclined plane down which children, goods, etc., slide. 4 track made by or for sliding, esp. on ice. 5 part of a machine or instrument that slides. 6 a mounted transparency viewed with a projector. b piece of glass holding an object for a microscope. 7 = HAIR-SLIDE. □ **let things slide** be negligent; allow deterioration. [Old English]

slide-rule n. ruler with a sliding central strip, graduated logarithmically for making rapid calculations.

sliding scale n. scale of fees, taxes, wages, etc., that varies according to some other factor.

slight /slait/ —adj. 1 a small; insignificant. b inadequate. 2 slender, frail-looking. 3 (in superl.) any whatever (if there were the slightest chance). —v. treat disrespectfully; ignore. —n. act of slighting. □ **slightly** adv. **slightness** n. [Old Norse]

slim —adj. (slimmer, slimmest) 1 not fat, slender. 2 small, insufficient (slim chance). —v. (-mm-) (often foll. by down) 1 become slimmer by dieting, exercise, etc. 2 make smaller (slimmed it down to 40 pages). □ **slimmer** n. **slimming** n. & adj. **slimmish** adj. [Low German or Dutch]

slime n. thick slippery mud or sticky substance produced by an animal or plant. [Old English]

slimline adj. 1 of slender design. 2 (of a drink) not fattening.

slimy adj. (-ier, -iest) 1 like, covered with, or full of slime. 2 colloq. disgustingly obsequious. □ **sliminess** n.

sling¹ —n. 1 strap etc. used to support or raise a thing. 2 bandage supporting an injured arm from the neck. 3 strap etc. for firing a stone etc. by hand. —v. (past and past part. slung) 1 colloq. throw. 2 suspend with a sling. □ **sling one's hook** slang go away. [Old Norse or Low German or Dutch]

sling² n. sweetened drink of spirits (esp. gin) and water. [origin unknown]

sling-back n. shoe held in place by a strap above the heel.

slink v. (past and past part. slunk) (often foll. by off, away, by) move in a stealthy or guilty manner. [Old English]

slinky adj. (-ier, -iest) (of a garment) close-fitting and sinuous.

slip¹ —v. (-pp-) 1 slide unintentionally or momentarily; lose one's footing, or balance. 2 go or move with a sliding motion. 3 escape or fall from being slippery or not being held properly. 4

slip (often foll. by *in, out, away*) go unobserved or quietly. **5 a** make a careless or slight error. **5** fall below standard. **6** place or slide stealthily or casually (*slipped a coin to him*). **7** release from restraint or connection. **8** move (a stitch) to the other needle without knitting it. **9** (foll. by *on, off*) pull a (garment) easily or hastily on or off. **10** escape from; evade (*dog slipped its collar; slipped my mind*). —*n*. **1** act of slipping. **2** careless or slight error. **3 a** pillowcase. **b** petticoat. **4** (in *sing.* or *pl.*) = SLIPWAY. **5** *Cricket* a fielder stationed for balls glancing off the bat to the off side. **b** (in *sing.* or *pl.*) this position. □ **give a person the slip** escape from; evade. **let slip 1** utter inadvertently. **2** miss (an opportunity). **3** release, esp. from a leash. **slip up** *colloq.* make a mistake. [probably from Low German *slippen*]

slip² *n*. **1** small piece of paper, esp. for writing on. **2** piece cut from a plant for grafting or planting. □ **slip of a** small and slim (*slip of a girl*). [Low German or Dutch]

slip³ *n*. clay and water mixture for decorating earthenware. [Old English, = slime]

slip-knot *n*. **1** knot that can be undone by a pull. **2** running knot.

slip of the pen *n*. (also **slip of the tongue**) small written (or spoken) mistake.

slip-on —*attrib. adj.* easily slipped on and off. —*n.* slip-on shoe or garment.

slippage *n*. act or an instance of slipping.

slipped disc *n*. displaced disc between vertebrae causing lumbar pain.

slipper *n*. light loose soft indoor shoe.

slippery *adj.* **1** difficult to grasp, stand on, etc. because smooth or wet. **2** unreliable, unscrupulous. □ **slipperiness** *n*. [Old English]

slippery slope *n.* course leading eventually to disaster.

slippy *adj.* (**-ier, -iest**) *colloq.* slippery. □ **look** (or **be**) **slippy** make haste.

slip-road *n.* road for entering or leaving a motorway etc.

slipshod *adj.* careless, slovenly.

slipstream *n.* current of air or water driven back by a revolving propeller or a moving vehicle.

slip-up *n. colloq.* mistake.

slipway *n.* ramp for building ships or landing boats.

slit —*n.* straight narrow incision or opening. —*v.* (**-tt-**; *past* and *past part.* **slit**) **1** make a slit in. **2** cut into strips. [Old English]

slither /ˈslɪðə(r)/ —*v.* slide unsteadily. —*n.* act of slithering. □ **slithery** *adj.* [var. of *slidder*: related to SLIDE]

sliver /ˈslɪvə(r)/ —*v.* **1** break or form into slivers. [Old English] or split off. —*v.* **1** break or form into slivers. [Old English]

Sloane /sləʊn/ *n.* (in full **Sloane Ranger**) *slang* fashionable and conventional upper-class young person. □ **Sloaney** *adj.* [*Sloane* Square in London, and *Lone Ranger*, cowboy hero]

slob *n. colloq. derog.* lazy, untidy, or fat person. [Irish *slab* mud]

slobber —*v.* **1** dribble. **2** (foll. by *over*) drool over. —*n.* dribbling saliva. □ **slobbery** *adj.* [Dutch]

sloe /sləʊ/ *n.* **1** = BLACKTHORN. **2** its small sour bluish-black fruit. [Old English]

slog —*v.* (**-gg-**) **1** hit hard and usu. wildly. **2** work or walk doggedly. —*n.* **1** hard random hit. **2 a** hard steady work or walk. **b** spell of this. [origin unknown]

slogan /ˈsləʊɡən/ *n.* **1** catchy phrase used in advertising etc. **2** party cry; war cry. [Gaelic, = war cry]

sloop *n.* small one-masted fore-and-aft rigged vessel. [Dutch *sloep*]

slop —*v.* (**-pp-**) **1** (often foll. by *over*) spill over the edge of a vessel. **2** wet (the floor etc.) by slopping. —*n.* **1** liquid spilled or splashed. **2** sloppy language. **3** (in *pl.*) dirty waste water or wine etc. from a kitchen, bedroom, or prison vessels. **4** (in *sing.* or *pl.*) unappetizing weak liquid food. [Dutch *sloep*] □ **slop about** move about in a slovenly manner. **slop out** carry slops out (in prison etc.). [Old English]

slope —*n.* **1** inclined position, direction, or state. **2** piece of rising or falling ground. **3** difference in level between the two ends or sides of a thing. **4** place for skiing on a mountain etc. —*v.* **1** have or take a slope, slant. **2** cause to slope. □ **slope arms** place one's rifle in a sloping position against one's shoulder. **slope off** *slang* go away, esp. to evade work etc. [*aslope* crosswise]

sloppy *adj.* (**-ier, -iest**) **1** wet, watery. **2** careless, untidy. **3** foolishly sentimental. □ **sloppily** *adv.* **sloppiness** *n.*

slosh —*v.* **1** (often foll. by *about*) splash or flounder. **2** *slang* hit, esp. heavily. **3** *colloq.* (usu. foll. by *on*) pour liquid on. —*n.* **1** slush. **2** act or sound of splashing. **3** *slang* heavy blow. [var. of SLUSH]

sloshed *predic. adj. slang* drunk.

slot —*n.* **1** slit in a machine etc. for a thing, esp. a coin, to be inserted. **2** slit, groove, etc. for a thing. **3** allotted place in a schedule, esp. in broadcasting. —*v.* (**-tt-**) **1** (often foll. by *in, into*) place or be

sloth placed (as if) into a slot. **2** provide with slots. [French *esclot* hollow of breast]

sloth /sləυθ/ n. **1** laziness, indolence. **2** slow-moving S. American mammal that hangs upside down in trees. [from SLOW]

slothful adj. lazy. □ **slothfully** adv.

slot-machine n. machine worked by the insertion of a coin, esp. selling small items or providing amusement.

slouch —v. stand, move, or sit in a drooping fashion. —n. **1** slouching posture or movement. **2** slang incompetent or slovenly worker etc. [origin unknown]

slouch hat n. hat with a wide flexible brim.

slough[1] /slaυ/ n. swamp, miry place. [Old English]

slough[2] /slʌf/ —n. part that an animal casts or moults, esp. a snake's cast skin. —v. (often foll. by *off*) cast or drop off as a slough. [origin unknown]

Slough of Despond n. state of hopeless depression.

Slovak /sláυvæk/ —n. **1** native of Slovakia in Czechoslovakia. **2** language of Slovakia, one of the two official languages of Czechoslovakia. —adj. of the Slovaks or their language. [native name]

sloven /slʌv(ə)n/ n. untidy or careless person. [origin uncertain]

slovenly —adj. careless and untidy; unmethodical. —adv. in a slovenly manner. □ **slovenliness** n.

slow /sláυ/ —adj. **1 a** taking a relatively long time to do a thing (also foll. by *of slow of speech*). **b** acting, moving, or done without speed, not quick. **2** not conducive to speed (*slow route*). **3** (of a clock etc.) showing a time earlier than is correct. **4** (of a person) not understanding or learning readily. **5** dull, tedious. **6** slack, sluggish (*business is slow*). **7** (of a fire or oven) giving little heat. **8** *Photog.* (of a film) needing long exposure. **9** reluctant; not hasty (*slow to anger*). —adv. slowly (also in *comb.: slow-moving traffic*). —v. (usu. foll. by *down, up*) **1** reduce one's speed or the speed of (a vehicle etc.). **2** reduce one's pace of life. □ **slowish** adj. **slowly** adv. **slowness** n. [Old English]

slowcoach n. colloq. slow person.

slow-down n. action of slowing down.

slow motion n. **1** speed of a film at which actions etc. appear much slower than usual. **2** simulation of this in real action.

slow-worm n. small European legless lizard. [Old English *slow* of uncertain origin]

sludge n. **1** thick greasy mud or sediment. **2** sewage. □ **sludgy** adj. [cf. SLUSH]

slue var. of SLEW[1].

slug[1] n. **1** small shell-less mollusc often destroying plants. **2** a bullet, esp. of irregular shape. **b** missile for an airgun. **3** *Printing* metal bar used in spacing. **4** mouthful of drink (esp. spirits). [Scandinavian]

slug[2] *US* —v. (**-gg-**) hit hard. —n. hard blow. □ **slug it out** fight it out. [origin unknown]

sluggard /slʌɡəd/ n. lazy person. [related to SLUG[1]]

sluggish adj. inert; slow-moving. □ **sluggishly** adv. **sluggishness** n.

sluice /sluːs/ —n. **1** (also **sluice-gate**, **sluice-valve**) sliding gate or other contrivance for regulating the volume or flow of water so regulated. **3** (**sluice-way**) artificial water-channel, esp. for washing ore. **4** place for rinsing. **5** act of rinsing. —v. (**-cing**) **1** provide or wash with a sluice or sluices. **2** rinse, esp. with running water. **3** (foll. by *out, away*) wash out or away with a flow of water. **4** (of water) rush out (as if) from a sluice. [French *escluse*]

slum —n. **1** house unfit for human habitation. **2** (often in *pl.*) overcrowded and squalid district in a city. —v. (**-mm-**) visit slums, esp. out of curiosity. □ **slum it** *colloq.* put up with conditions less comfortable than usual. □ **slummy** adj. [originally cant]

slumber v. & n. *poet.* or *joc.* sleep. [Old English]

slump —n. sudden severe or prolonged fall in prices and trade, usu. bringing widespread unemployment. —v. **1** undergo a slump. **2** sit or fall heavily or limply. [imitative]

slung *past* and *past part.* of SLING[1].

slunk *past* and *past part.* of SLINK.

slur —v. (**-rr-**) **1** pronounce indistinctly with sounds running into one another. **2** *Mus.* perform (notes) legato. **3** *archaic* or *US* put a slur on (a person or a person's character). **4** (usu. foll. by *over*) pass over (a fact, fault, etc.) lightly. —n. **1** imputation of wrongdoing. **2** act of slurring. **3** *Mus.* curved line joining notes to be slurred. [origin unknown]

slurp *colloq.* —v. eat or drink noisily. —n. sound of this. [Dutch]

slurry /slʌrɪ/ n. thin semi-liquid cement, mud, manure, etc. [related to dial. *slur* thin mud]

slush n. **1** thawing muddy snow. **2** silly sentimentality. □ **slushy** adj. (**-ier**, **-iest**) [origin unknown]

slush fund n. reserve fund, esp. for political bribery.

slut n. derog. slovenly or promiscuous woman. □ **sluttish** adj. [origin unknown]

sly /slaɪ/ adj. (**slyer, slyest**) 1 cunning, crafty, wily. 2 secretive. 3 knowing, insinuating. □ **on the sly** secretly. □ **slyly** adv. **slyness** n. [Old Norse; related to SLAY]

Sm symb. samarium.

smack¹ n. 1 sharp slap or blow. 2 hard hit at cricket etc. 3 loud kiss. 4 loud sharp sound. —v. 1 slap. 2 part (one's lips) noisily in anticipation of food. 3 move, hit, etc., with a smack. —adv. colloq. 1 with a smack. 2 suddenly; directly; violently. □ **a smack in the eye (or face)** colloq. rebuff, setback. [imitative]

smack² n. (foll. by of) —v. 1 have a flavour of, taste of 2 suggest (smacks of nepotism). —n. 1 flavour 2 barely discernible quality. [Old English]

smack³ —n. 1 single-masted sailing-boat. [Low German or Dutch]

smack⁴ n. slang heroin or other hard drug. [probably alteration of Yiddish schmeck sniff]

smacker n. slang 1 loud kiss. 2 a £1. b US $1.

small /smɔːl/ —adj. 1 not large or big. 2 not great in importance, amount, number, power, etc. 3 not much; little (paid small attention). 4 insignificant (from small beginnings). 5 of small particles (small shot). 6 on a small scale (small farmer). 7 poor or humble. 8 mean; ungenerous. 9 young (small child). —v. 1 slenderest part of a thing. esp. of the back. 2 (in pl.) colloq. underwear, esp. as laundry. □ **feel (or look) small** be humiliated or ashamed. □ **smallish** adj. **smallness** n. [Old English]

small arms n.pl. portable firearms.

small beer n. trifling thing.

small change n.pl. coins, not notes.

small fry n. unimportant people; children.

smallholder n. farmer of a smallholding.

smallholding n. agricultural holding smaller than a farm.

small hours n.pl. period soon after midnight.

small-minded adj. petty; narrow in outlook.

smallpox n. hist. acute contagious disease with fever and pustules, usu. leaving scars.

small print n. unfavourable clauses etc. in a contract, usu. printed small.

small-scale adj. made or occurring on a small scale.

small talk n. light social conversation.

small-time adj. colloq unimportant, petty.

smarm —v. colloq 1 (often foll. by down) smooth, plaster flat (hair etc.). 2 be ingratiating. —n. colloq. obsequiousness n. [dial.]

smarmy adj. (**-ier, -iest**) colloq. ingratiating. □ **smarmily** adv. **smarminess** n.

smart —adj. 1 well-groomed, neat. 2 brightly coloured newly painted, etc. 3 stylish, fashionable. 4 (esp. US) clever, ingenious, quickwitted. 5 quick, brisk. 6 painfully severe; sharp, vigorous. —v. 1 feel or give pain. 2 rankle. 3 (foll. by for) suffer the consequences of. —n. sharp pain; stinging sensation. —adv. smartly. □ **smartish** adj. & adv. **smartly** adv. **smartness** n. [Old English]

smart alec n. (also **smart aleck**) colloq. conceited know-all.

smart money n. money invested by people with expert knowledge.

smarten v. (usu. foll. by up) make or become smart.

smash —v. 1 (often foll. by up) a break into pieces; shatter. b bring or come to sudden destruction, defeat, or disaster. 2 (foll. by into, through) move with great force. 3 (foll. by in) break with a crushing blow. 4 hit (a ball etc.) with great force, esp. downwards. —n. 1 act of smashing, collision. 2 sound of this. 3 (in full **smash hit**) very successful play, song, performer, etc. —adv. with a smash. [imitative]

smash-and-grab n. robbery in which a shop-window is smashed and goods seized.

smasher n. colloq. beautiful or pleasing person or thing.

smashing adj. colloq. excellent, wonderful.

smash-up n. violent collision.

smattering n. slight superficial knowledge of a language etc. [origin unknown]

smear —v. 1 daub or mark with grease etc. 2 smudge. 3 defame. —n. 1 act of smearing. 2 smudge. 3 Med. a material smeared on a microscopic slide etc. for examination. b specimen of this. □ **smeary** adj. [Old English]

smear test n. = CERVICAL SMEAR.

smell —n. 1 faculty of perceiving odours. 2 quality in substances that is perceived by this. 3 unpleasant odour. 4 act of inhaling to ascertain smell. —v. (past and past part. **smelt** or **smelled**) 1 perceive or examine by smell. 2 emit an odour. stink. 3 seem by smell to (smells sour). 4 (foll. by of) a emit the odour of (smells of fish). b be suggestive

of (*smells of dishonesty*). **5** perceive; detect (*smell a bargain*). **6** have or use a sense of smell. □ **smell a rat** suspect trickery etc. **smell out** detect by smell or investigation. [Old English]

smelling-salts *n.pl.* sharp-smelling substances sniffed to relieve faintness etc.

smelly *adj.* (**-ier, -iest**) having a strong or unpleasant smell. □ **smelliness** *n.*

smelt¹ *v.* **1** extract metal from (ore) by melting. **2** extract (metal) in this way. □ **smelter** *n.* [Low German or Dutch *smelten*]

smelt² *past* and *past part.* of SMELL.

smelt³ *n.* (*pl.* same or **-s**) small edible green and silver fish. [Old English]

smidgen /'smɪdʒ(ə)n/ *n.* (also **smidgin**) *colloq.* small bit or amount. [perhaps from *smitch* in the same sense]

smilax /'smaɪlaks/ *n.* any of several climbing shrubs. [Greek, = bindweed]

smile *v.* (**-ling**) **1** have or assume a happy, kind or amused expression, with the corners of the mouth turned up. **2** express by smiling (*smiled a welcome*). **3** give (a smile) of a specified kind (*smiled a sardonic smile*). **4** (foll. by *on, upon*) favour (*fortune smiled on me*). —*n.* **1** act of smiling. **2** smiling expression or aspect. [perhaps from Scandinavian]

smirch —*v.* soil; discredit. —*n.* spot, stain. [origin unknown]

smirk —*n.* conceited or silly smile. —*v.* give a smirk. [Old English]

smite *v.* (**-ting**; *past* **smote**; *past part.* **smitten** /'smɪt(ə)n/) **1** *archaic* or *literary* **a** hit. **b** chastise; defeat. **2** (*in passive*) affect strongly; seize (*smitten with regret; smitten by her beauty*). [Old English]

smith *n.* **1** blacksmith. **2** (esp. in *comb.*) worker in metal (*goldsmith*). **3** (esp. in *comb.*) craftsman (*wordsmith*). [Old English]

smithereens /ˌsmɪðə'riːnz/ *n.pl.* small fragments. [dial. *smithers*]

smithy /'smɪðɪ/ *n.* (*pl.* **-ies**) blacksmith's workshop, forge. [related to SMITH]

smitten *past part.* of SMITE.

smock —*n.* **1** loose shirtlike garment often ornamented with smocking. **2** loose overall. —*v.* adorn with smocking. [Old English]

smocking *n.* ornamental effect on cloth made by gathering it tightly with stitches.

smog *n.* smoke-laden fog. □ **smoggy** *adj.* (**-ier, -iest**). [portmanteau word]

smoke —*n.* **1** visible vapour from a burning substance. **2** act of smoking tobacco. **3** *colloq.* cigarette or cigar. —*v.* (**-king**) **1 a** inhale and exhale the smoke of (a cigarette etc.). **b** do this habitually. **2** emit smoke or visible vapour. **3** darken or preserve with smoke (*smoked salmon*). □ **go up in smoke** *colloq.* come to nothing. **smoke out 1** drive out by means of smoke. **2** drive out of hiding etc. [Old English]

smoke bomb *n.* bomb that emits dense smoke on exploding.

smoke-free *adj.* **1** free from smoke. **2** where smoking is not permitted.

smokeless *adj.* producing little or no smoke; free from smoke.

smokeless zone *n.* district where only smokeless fuel may be used.

smoker *n.* **1** person who habitually smokes. **2** compartment on a train where smoking is allowed.

smokescreen *n.* **1** cloud of smoke concealing (esp. military) operations. **2** ruse for disguising one's activities.

smokestack *n.* **1** chimney or funnel of a locomotive or steamer. **2** tall chimney.

smoky *adj.* (**-ier, -iest**) **1** emitting, filled with, or obscured by, smoke. **2** stained with or coloured like smoke. **3** having the flavour of smoked food. □ **smokiness** *n.*

smolder *US* var. of SMOULDER.

smooch *colloq.* —*n.* **1** period of slow close dancing. **2** period of kissing and caressing. —*v.* engage in a smooch. □ **smoochy** *adj.* [imitative]

smooth /smuːð/ —*adj.* **1** having an even surface; free from projections, dents, and roughness. **2** that can be traversed without check. **3** (of the sea etc.) calm, flat. **4** (of a journey etc.) easy. **5** not harsh in sound or taste. **6** suave, conciliatory; slick. **7** not jerky. —*v.* **1** (often foll. by *out, down*) make or become smooth. **2** (often foll. by *out, down, over, away*) reduce or get rid of (differences, faults, difficulties, etc.) in fact or appearance. —*n.* smoothing touch or stroke. —*adv.* smoothly. □ **smoothly** *adv.* **smoothness** *n.* [Old English]

smoothie /'smuːðɪ/ *n.* *colloq.* often *derog.* smooth person.

smooth-tongued *adj.* insincerely flattering.

smorgasbord /'smɔːgəsˌbɔːd/ *n.* various esp. savoury dishes as hors d'oeuvres or a buffet meal. [Swedish]

smote *past* of SMITE.

smother /'smʌðə(r)/ *v.* **1** suffocate, stifle. **2** (foll. by *in, with*) overwhelm or cover with (kisses, gifts, kindness, etc.). **3** extinguish (a fire) by covering it. **4 a** die of suffocation. **b** have difficulty breathing. **5** (often foll. by *up*) suppress or conceal. [Old English]

smoulder /'sməʊldə(r)/ (*US* **smolder**) —*v.* **1** burn slowly without flame or

internally. **2** (of emotions) be fierce but suppressed. **3** (of a person) show silent emotion. —*n.* smouldering. [origin unknown]

smudge —*n.* blurred or smeared line, mark, blot, etc. —*v.* (**-ging**) **1** make a smudge on or of. **2** become smeared or blurred. □ **smudgy** *adj.* [origin unknown]

smug *adj.* (**smugger, smuggest**) self-satisfied. □ **smugly** *adv.* **smugness** *n.* [Low German *smuk* pretty]

smuggle /ˈsmʌg(ə)l/ *v.* (**-ling**) **1** (also *absol.*) import or export illegally, esp. without paying duties. **2** (foll. by *in, out*) convey secretly. □ **smuggler** *n.* **smuggling** *n.* [Low German]

smut —*n.* **1** small flake of soot etc. **2** spot or smudge made by this. **3** obscene talk, pictures, or stories. **4** fungous disease of cereals. —*v.* (**-tt-**) mark with smuts. □ **smutty** *adj.* (**-ier, -iest**). [origin unknown]

Sn *symb.* tin. [Latin *stannum*]

snack —*n.* **1** light, casual, or hurried meal. **2** small amount of food eaten between meals. [Dutch]

snack bar *n.* place where snacks are sold.

snaffle /ˈsnæf(ə)l/ —*n.* (in full **snaffle-bit**) simple bridle-bit without a curb. —*v.* (**-ling**) *colloq.* steal; seize. [Low German or Dutch perhaps from *snavel* beak]

snafu /snæˈfuː/ *slang* —*adj.* in utter confusion. —*n.* this state. [acronym of 'situation normal: all fouled (or fucked) up']

snag —*n.* **1** unexpected obstacle or drawback. **2** jagged projection. **3** tear in material etc. —*v.* (**-gg-**) catch or tear on a snag. [probably Scandinavian]

snail *n.* slow-moving gastropod mollusc with a spiral shell. [Old English]

snail's pace *n.* very slow movement.

snake —*n.* **1** long limbless reptile. **2** (also **snake in the grass**) traitor; secret enemy. —*v.* (**-king**) move or twist like a snake. [Old English]

snake-charmer *n.* person appearing to make snakes move by music etc.

snakes and ladders *n.pl.* (usu. treated as *sing.*) board-game with counters moved up 'ladders' and down 'snakes'.

snakeskin —*n.* skin of a snake. —*adj.* made of snakeskin.

snaky *adj.* **1** of or like a snake. **2** winding, sinuous. **3** cunning, treacherous.

snap —*v.* (**-pp-**) **1** break suddenly or with a cracking sound. **2** (cause to) emit a sudden sharp crack. **3** open or close with a snapping sound **4** speak or say irritably. **5** (often foll. by *at*) make a sudden audible bite. **6** move quickly (*snap into*

action). **7** photograph. —*n.* **1** act or sound of snapping. **2** crisp biscuit (*brandy snap*). **3** snapshot. **4** (in full **cold snap**) sudden brief spell of cold weather. **5 a** card-game in which players call 'snap' when two similar cards are exposed. **b** (as *int.*) on noticing an (often unexpected) similarity. **6** vigour, liveliness. —*adj.* done without forethought (*snap decision*). —*adv.* with a snap (*heard it go snap*). □ **snap out of it** *slang* get rid of (a mood, etc.) by a sudden effort. **snap up** accept (an offer etc.) quickly or eagerly. [Low German or Dutch *snappen*]

snapdragon *n.* plant with a two-lipped flower.

snap-fastener *n.* = PRESS-STUD.

snapper *n.* any of several edible marine fish.

snappish *adj.* **1** curt, ill-tempered; sharp. **2** inclined to snap.

snappy *adj.* (**-ier, -iest**) *colloq.* **1** brisk, lively. **2** neat and elegant (*snappy dresser*). **3** snappish. □ **make it snappy** be quick. □ **snappily** *adv.*

snapshot *n.* casual or informal photograph.

snare /sneə(r)/ —*n.* **1** trap, esp. with a noose, for birds or animals. **2** trap, trick, or temptation. **3** (in *sing.* or *pl.*) twisted strings of gut, hide or wire stretched across the lower head of a side-drum to produce a rattle. **4** (in full **snare drum**) drum fitted with snares. —*v.* (**-ring**) catch in a snare; trap. [Old Norse]

snarl[1] —*v.* **1** growl with bared teeth. **2** speak, say, or express angrily. —*n.* act or sound of snarling. [*snar* from Low German]

snarl[2] —*v.* (often foll. by *up*) twist; entangle; hamper the movement of (traffic etc.); become entangled or congested. —*n.* knot, tangle. [from SNARE]

snarl-up *n.* *colloq.* traffic jam; muddle.

snatch —*v.* **1** (often foll. by *away, from*) seize or remove quickly, eagerly, or unexpectedly. **2 a** steal (a handbag etc.) by grabbing. **b** (foll. by *at*) try to seize. **b** (take an offer etc.) eagerly. —*n.* **1** act of snatching. **2** fragment of a song or talk etc. **3** *US slang* kidnapping. **4** short spell of activity etc. [related to SNACK]

snazzy *adj.* (**-ier, -iest**) *slang* smart, stylish, showy. □ **snazzily** *adv.* **snazziness** *n.* [origin unknown]

sneak —*v.* **1** (foll. by *in, out, past, away,* etc.) go or convey furtively. **2** *slang* steal unobserved. **3** *slang* tell tales; turn informer. **4** (as **sneaking** *adj.*) **a** furtive (*sneaking affection*). **b** persistent and puzzling (*sneaking feeling*). —*n.* **1** mean-spirited underhand person. **2** *slang* tell-

tale; informer. —*adj.* acting or done without warning; secret. □ **sneaky** *adj.* (**-ier, -iest**). [origin uncertain]

sneaker *n.* *slang* soft-soled canvas shoe.

sneak-thief *n.* thief who steals without breaking in.

sneer —*n.* contemptuous smile or remark. —*v.* **1** (often foll. by *at*) smile or speak derisively. **2** say with a sneer. □ **sneering** *adj.*; **sneeringly** *adv.* [origin unknown]

sneeze —*n.* sudden loud involuntary expulsion of air from the nose and mouth caused by irritation of the nostrils. —*v.* (**-zing**) make a sneeze. □ **not to be sneezed** at *colloq.* worth having or considering. [Old English]

snick —*v.* **1** make a small notch or incision in. **2** *Cricket* deflect (the ball) slightly with the bat. —*n.* **1** small notch or cut. **2** *Cricket* slight deflection of the ball. [*snickersnee* long knife, ultimately from Dutch]

snicker *n.* & *v.* = SNIGGER. [imitative]

snide *adj.* sneering; slyly derogatory. [origin unknown]

sniff —*v.* **1** inhale air audibly through the nose. **2** (often foll. by *up*) draw in through the nose. **3** smell the scent of by sniffing. —*n.* **1** act or sound of sniffing. **2** amount of air etc. sniffed up. □ **sniff at** show contempt for. **sniff out** = *smell out*. [imitative]

sniffer *n.* person who sniffs, esp. a drug etc. (often in *comb.*: *glue-sniffer*).

sniffer-dog *n.* *colloq.* dog trained to sniff out drugs or explosives.

sniffle /ˈsnɪf(ə)l/ —*v.* (**-ling**) sniff slightly or repeatedly. —*n.* **1** act of sniffling. **2** (in *sing.* or *pl.*) cold in the head causing sniffling. [imitative: cf. SNIVEL]

sniffy *adj.* *colloq.* (**-ier, -iest**) disdainful. □ **sniffily** *adv.* **sniffiness** *n.*

snifter *n.* *slang* small alcoholic drink. [*dial. snift* sniff]

snigger —*n.* half-suppressed laugh. —*v.* utter this. [var. of SNICKER]

snip —*v.* (**-pp-**) (also *absol.*) cut with scissors etc., esp. in small quick strokes. —*n.* **1** act of snipping. **2** piece snipped off. **3** *slang* **a** something easily done. **b** bargain. [Low German or Dutch *snip-pen*]

snipe —*n.* (*pl.* same or **-s**) wading bird with a long straight bill. —*v.* (**-ping**) **1** fire shots from hiding, usu. at long range. **2** (often foll. by *at*) make a sly critical attack. □ **sniper** *n.* (in sense 1 of *v.*) [probably Scandinavian]

snippet /ˈsnɪpɪt/ *n.* **1** small piece cut off. **2** (usu. in *pl.*) **a** scrap of information etc. **b** short extract from a book etc.

snitch *slang* —*v.* **1** steal. **2** (often foll. by *on*) inform on a person. —*n.* informer. [origin unknown]

snivel /ˈsnɪv(ə)l/ —*v.* (**-ll-**; *US* **-l-**) **1** weep with sniffling. **2** run at the nose; sniffle. **3** show weak or tearful sentiment. —*n.* act of snivelling. [Old English]

snob *n.* person who despises those inferior in social position, wealth, intellect, taste, etc. (*intellectual snob*). □ **snobbery** *n.* **snobbish** *adj.* **snobby** *adj.* (**-ier, -iest**). [origin unknown]

snog *slang* —*v.* (**-gg-**) engage in kissing and caressing. —*n.* period of this. [origin unknown]

snood *n.* ornamental hairnet, worn usu. at the back of the head. [Old English]

snook *n.* *slang* contemptuous gesture with the thumb to the nose and the fingers spread. □ **cock a snook** (often foll. by *at*) **1** make this gesture. **2** register one's contempt. [origin unknown]

snooker —*n.* **1** game played on an oblong cloth-covered table with a cue-ball, 15 red, and 6 coloured balls. **2** position in a game in which a direct shot would lose points. —*v.* **1** (also *refl.*) subject (oneself or an opponent) to a snooker. **2** (esp. as **snookered** *adj.*) *slang* thwart, defeat. [origin unknown]

snoop *colloq.* —*v.* **1** pry into another's affairs. **2** (often foll. by *about, around*) investigate transgressions of rules, the law, etc.—*n.* act of snooping. □ **snooper** *n.* **snoopy** *adj.* [Dutch]

snooty *adj.* (**-ier, -iest**) *colloq.* supercilious; conceited; snobbish. □ **snootily** *adv.* [origin unknown]

snooze *colloq.* —*n.* short sleep, nap. —*v.* (**-zing**) take a snooze. [origin unknown]

snore —*n.* snorting or grunting sound of breathing during sleep. —*v.* (**-ring**) make this sound. [imitative]

snorkel /ˈsnɔːk(ə)l/ —*n.* **1** breathing-tube for an underwater swimmer. **2** device for supplying air to a submerged submarine. —*v.* (**-ll-**; *US* **-l-**) use a snorkel. [German *Schnorchel*]

snort —*n.* **1** explosive sound made esp. by horses by the sudden forcing of breath through the nose. **2** similar human sound showing contempt, incredulity, etc. **3** *colloq.* small drink of liquor. **4** *slang* inhaled dose of powdered cocaine etc. —*v.* **1** make a snort. **2** (also *absol.*) *slang* inhale (esp. cocaine). **3** express or utter with a snort. [imitative]

snot *n.* *slang* nasal mucus. [probably Low German or Dutch: related to SNOUT]

snotty *adj.* (**-ier, -iest**) *slang* **1** running or covered with nasal mucus. **2** snooty. **3** mean, contemptible. □ **snottily** *adv.* **snottiness** *n.*

snout n. 1 projecting nose and mouth of an animal. 2 derog. person's nose. 3 pointed front of a thing. [Low German or Dutch]

snow /snəʊ/ —n. 1 frozen atmospheric vapour falling to earth in light white flakes. 2 fall or layer of this. 3 thing resembling snow in whiteness or texture etc. 4 slang cocaine. —v. 1 (prec. by it as subject) snow falls (it is snowing; if it snows). 2 (foll. by in, over, up, etc.) confine or block with snow. □ be snowed under be overwhelmed, esp. with work. [Old English]

snowball —n. ball of compressed snow for throwing in play. —v. 1 throw or pelt with snowballs. 2 increase rapidly.

snowball-tree n. guelder rose.

snowberry n. (pl. -ies) shrub with white berries.

snow-blind adj. temporarily blinded by the glare from snow.

snowblower n. machine that clears snow by blowing.

snowbound adj. prevented by snow from going out or travelling.

snowcap n. snow-covered mountain peak. □ **snowcapped** adj.

snowdrift n. bank of snow heaped up by the wind.

snowdrop n. early spring plant with white drooping flowers.

snowfall n. 1 fall of snow. 2 amount of this.

snowflake n. each of the flakes in which snow falls.

snow goose n. white Arctic goose.

snowline n. level above which snow never melts entirely.

snowman n. figure resembling a human, made of compressed snow.

snowmobile /'snəʊməbiːl/ n. motor vehicle, esp. with runners or Caterpillar tracks, for travel over snow.

snowplough n. (US **snowplow**) device or vehicle for clearing roads of thick snow.

snowshoe n. racket-shaped attachment to a boot for walking on snow without sinking in.

snowstorm n. heavy fall of snow, esp. with a high wind.

snow white adj. & n. (as adj. often hyphenated) pure white.

snowy adj. (-ier -iest) 1 of or like snow. 2 (of the weather etc.) with much snow.

snowy owl n. large white Arctic owl.

SNP abbr. Scottish National Party.

Snr. abbr. Senior.

snub —v. 1 (-bb-) rebuff or humiliate with sharp words or coldness. —n. act of snubbing. —adj. short and blunt in shape. [Old Norse, = chide]

snub nose n. short turned-up nose. □ **snub-nosed** adj.

snuff¹ —v. trim the snuff from (a candle). □ **snuff it** slang d.e. **snuff out** 1 extinguish (a candle flame). 2 put an end to (hopes etc.). [origin unknown]

snuff² —n. powdered tobacco or medicine taken by sniffing. —v. take snuff. [Dutch]

snuffbox n. small box for holding snuff.

snuffer n. device for snuffing or extinguishing a candle.

snuffle —v. (-ling) 1 make sniffing sounds 2 speak or say nasally or whiningly. 3 breathe noisily, esp. with a blocked nose. —n. snuffling sound or tone. □ **snuffly** adj. [Low German or Dutch snuffelen]

snug —adj. (**snugger**, **snuggest**) 1 cosy, comfortable, sheltered. 2 close-fitting. —n. small room in a pub. □ **snugly** adv. [probably Low German or Dutch]

snuggery n. (pl. -ies) snug place, den.

snuggle /'snʌg(ə)l/ v. (-ling) settle or draw into a warm comfortable position.

so¹ /səʊ/ —adv. 1 to such an extent (stop complaining so; so small as to be invisible; not so late as I expected). 2 in this or that way; in the manner, position, or state described or implied (place your feet so; am not cold but may become so). 3 also (he went and so did I). 4 indeed, actually (you said it was good, and so it is). 5 very (I am so glad). 6 (with verbs of saying or thinking etc.) thus, this, that (I think so; so he said). —conj. (often foll. by that) 1 consequently (was ill, so couldn't come). 2 in order that (came early so that I could see you). 3 and then; as the next step (so then I gave up; and so to bed). 4 (introducing a question) then; after that (so what did you do?). □ and so on (or forth) 1 and others of the same kind. 2 and in other similar ways. or so approximately (50 or so). so as to in order to. so be it expression of acceptance or resignation. so long! colloq. goodbye. so much for 1 = certain amount (of). 2 nothing but (so much nonsense). so much for that is all that need be done or said about (a thing). so so adj. & adv. colloq. only moderately good or well. so what? colloq. that is not significant. [Old English]

-so² var. of SOH.

so³ comb. form = -SOEVER.

soak —v. 1 make or become thoroughly wet through saturation 2 (of rain etc.) drench. 3 (foll. by in, up; absorb (liquid, knowledge, etc.). 4 refl. (often foll. by in) steep (oneself) in a subject etc. 5 (foll. by

866

in, into, through) (of liquid) go or penetrate by saturation. **6** *colloq.* drink money from. **7** *colloq.* drink heavily. —*n.* **1** act of soaking; prolonged spell in a bath. **2** *colloq.* hard drinker. [Old English]

soakaway *n.* pit into which liquids may flow and then percolate slowly into the subsoil.

soaking *adj.* (in full **soaking wet**) wet through.

so-and-so /'səuən,səu/ *n.* (*pl.* -**so's**) **1** particular but unspecified person or thing. **2** *colloq.* objectionable person.

soap —*n.* **1** cleansing agent yielding lather when rubbed in water. **2** *colloq.* = SOAP OPERA. —*v.* apply soap to. [Old English]

soapbox *n.* makeshift stand for a speaker in the street etc.

soap flakes *n.pl.* thin flakes of soap for washing clothes etc.

soap opera *n.* broadcast drama serial with domestic themes (orig. sponsored in the US by soap manufacturers).

soap powder *n.* powdered soap, esp. with additives, for washing clothes etc.

soapstone *n.* steatite.

soapsuds *n.pl.* = SUDS.

soapwort *n.* plant with pink or white flowers, and leaves yielding a soapy substance.

soapy *adj.* (-**ier**, -**iest**) **1** of or like soap. **2** containing or smeared with soap. **3** unctuous, flattering. □ **soapily** *adv.* **soapiness** *n.*

soar *v.* **1** fly or rise high. **2** reach a high level or standard. **3** fly without flapping the wings or using power. [French *essorer*]

sob —*v.* (-**bb**-) **1** inhale convulsively, usu. with weeping. **2** utter with sobs. —*n.* act or sound of sobbing. [imitative]

sober —*adj.* (**soberer**, **soberest**) **1** not drunk. **2** not given to drink. **3** moderate, tranquil, sedate, serious. **4** not exaggerated. **5** (of a colour etc.) quiet; dull. —*v.* (often foll. by *down*, *up*) make or become sober. □ **soberly** *adv.* **soberness** *n.* [Latin]

sobriety /sə'braɪətɪ/ *n.* being sober. [Latin: related to SOBER]

sobriquet /'səubrɪˌkeɪ/ *n.* (also **soubriquet** /'suː-/) nickname. [French]

sob story *n. colloq.* story or explanation appealing for sympathy.

Soc. *abbr.* **1** Socialist. **2** Society.

so-called *adj.* commonly called, often incorrectly.

soccer /'sɒkə(r)/ *n.* Association football. [from Assoc.]

sociable /'səʊʃəb(ə)l/ *adj.* liking company, gregarious; friendly. □ **sociability** /-'bɪlɪtɪ/ *n.* **sociably** *adv.* [Latin *socius* companion]

social /'səʊʃ(ə)l/ —*adj.* **1** of society or its organization, esp. of the relations of people or classes of people. **2** living in organized communities. **3** needing companionship; gregarious. —*n.* social gathering, esp. of a club. □ **socially** *adv.* [Latin: related to SOCIABLE]

social climber *n.* person anxious to gain a higher social status.

social contract *n.* agreement between the State and population for mutual advantage.

social democracy *n.* political system favouring a mixed economy and democratic social change. □ **social democrat** *n.*

socialism *n.* **1** political and economic theory advocating State ownership and control of the means of production, distribution, and exchange. **2** social system based on this. □ **socialist** *n.* & *adj.* **socialistic** /-'lɪstɪk/ *adj.* [French: related to SOCIAL]

socialite /'səʊʃəˌlaɪt/ *n.* person moving in fashionable society.

socialize /'səʊʃəˌlaɪz/ *v.* (also -**ise**) (-**zing** or -**sing**) **1** mix socially. **2** make social. **3** organize on socialistic principles. □ **socialization** /-'zeɪʃ(ə)n/ *n.*

social science *n.* the study of society and social relationships. □ **social scientist** *n.*

social security *n.* State assistance to the poor and unemployed etc.

social services *n.pl.* welfare services provided by the State, esp. education, health, and housing.

social work *n.* professional or voluntary work with disadvantaged groups. □ **social worker** *n.*

society /sə'saɪətɪ/ *n.* (*pl.* -**ies**) **1** organized and interdependent community. **2** system and organization of this. **3** aristocratic part of this; its members (*polite society; society would not approve*). **4** mixing with others; companionship, company. **5** club, association (*music society; building society*). □ **societal** *adj.* [Latin *societas*]

Society of Friends *n.* pacifist Christian sect with no written creed or ordained ministers; Quakers.

Society of Jesus see JESUIT.

socio- *comb. form* of society or sociology (and) (*socio-economic*). [Latin: related to SOCIAL]

sociology /ˌsəʊsɪ'blədʒɪ/ *n.* the study of society and social problems. □ **sociological** /-ə'lɒdʒɪk(ə)l/ *adj.* **sociologist** *n.* [French: related to SOCIAL]

sock¹ /n. 1 Knitted covering for the foot and lower leg. 2 insole. □ **pull one's socks up** *colloq.* make an effort to improve. **put a sock in it** *slang* be quiet. [Old English *socc* from Greek *sukkhos* slipper]

sock² *colloq.* —*v.* hit hard.—*n.* hard blow. □ **sock it to** attack or address (a person or people) vigorously. [origin unknown]

socket /'sɒkɪt/ *n.* hollow for something to fit into etc., esp. a device receiving an electric plug, light-bulb, etc. [Anglo-French]

Socratic /sə'kratɪk/ *adj.* of Socrates or his philosophy.

Socratic irony *n.* pose of ignorance to entice others into refutable statements.

Socratic method *n.* dialectic, proceeding by question and answer.

sod¹ *n.* 1 turf, piece of turf. 2 surface of the ground. [Low German or Dutch]

sod² *coarse slang* —*n.* 1 unpleasant or awkward person or thing. 2 fellow (*lucky sod*). —*v.* (**-dd-**) 1 damn (*sod them!*). 2 (as **sodding** *adj.*) damned. □ **sod off** go away. [abbreviation of SODOMITE]

soda /'səʊdə/ *n.* 1 compound of sodium in common use. 2 (in full **soda water**) effervescent water used esp. with spirits etc. as a drink. [perhaps from Latin *sodanum* from Arabic]

soda bread *n.* bread leavened with baking-soda.

soda fountain *n.* 1 device supplying soda water. 2 shop or counter with this.

sodden /'sɒd(ə)n/ *adj.* 1 saturated, soaked through. 2 stupid or dull etc. with drunkenness. [archaic past part. of SEETHE]

sodium /'səʊdɪəm/ *n.* soft silver-white metallic element. [from SODA]

sodium bicarbonate *n.* white crystalline compound used in baking-powder.

sodium chloride *n.* common salt.

sodium hydroxide *n.* strongly alkaline compound used in soap etc.; caustic soda.

sodium lamp *n.* lamp using sodium vapour and giving a yellow light.

sodium nitrate *n.* yellow powdery compound used in fertilizers etc.

sodomite /'sɒdəmaɪt/ *n.* person who practises sodomy. [Greek: related to SODOMY]

sodomy /'sɒdəmɪ/ *n.* = BUGGERY. □ **sodomize** *v.* (also **-ise**) (-zing or -sing). [Latin from *Sodom*: Gen. 18,19]

Sod's Law *n.* = MURPHY'S LAW.

soever /səʊ'evə(r)/ *adv.* literary of any kind; to any extent (*how great soever it may be*).

-soever *comb. form* of any kind; to any extent (*whatsoever, howsoever*).

---

sofa /'səʊfə/ *n.* long upholstered seat with a back and arms. [Arabic *shuffa*]

sofa bed *n.* sofa that can be converted into a bed.

soffit /'sɒfɪt/ *n.* undersurface of an arch, lintel, etc. [French *soffite*, Italian *soffitta*]

soft —*adj.* 1 not hard; easily cut or dented; malleable. 2 (of cloth etc.) smooth; fine; not rough. 3 (of wind etc.) mild, gentle. 4 (of water) low in mineral salts and lathering easily. 5 (of light or colour etc.) not brilliant or glaring. 6 (of sound) gentle, not loud. 7 (of a consonant) sibilant (as *c* in *ice*, *s* in *pleasure*). 8 (of an outline etc.) vague, blurred. 9 *colloq.* (of a job etc.) easy. 13 (of drugs) not highly addictive. 14 (also **soft-core**) (of pornography) not highly obscene. 15 (of currency) likely to fall in value; not readily exchangeable into other currencies. —*adv.* softly. □ **be soft on** *colloq.* 1 be lenient towards. 2 be infatuated with. **have a soft spot for** be fond of. □ **softish** *adj.*; **softly** *adv.*

softball *n.* form of baseball using a softer and larger ball.

soft-boiled *adj.* (of an egg) boiled leaving the yolk soft.

soft-centred *adj.* 1 (of a sweet) having a soft centre. 2 soft-hearted; sentimental.

soft drink *n.* non-alcoholic drink.

soften /'sɒf(ə)n/ *v.* 1 make or become soft or softer. 2 (often foll. by *up*) **a** make weaker by preliminary attack. **b** make (a person) more receptive to persuasion. □ **softener** *n.*

soft fruit *n.* small stoneless fruit (a strawberry or currant).

soft furnishings *n.pl.* curtains, rugs, etc.

soft-hearted *adj.* tender, compassionate. □ **soft-heartedness** *n.*

softie *n.* (also **softy**) (*pl.* **-ies**) *colloq.* weak, silly, or soft-hearted person.

softly-softly *adj.* (also **softly, softly**) (of strategy) cautious and cunning.

soft option *n.* easier alternative.

soft palate *n.* rear part of the palate.

soft pedal —*n.* piano pedal that softens the tone. —*v.* (**soft-pedal**) (-**ll-**; *US* **-l-**) refrain from emphasizing, be restrained.

soft roe see ROE¹.

soft sell *n.* restrained salesmanship.

soft soap —*n.* *colloq.* persuasive flattery. —*v.* (**soft-soap**) *colloq.* persuade with flattery.

soft-spoken *adj.* having a gentle voice.

soft target *n.* vulnerable person or thing.

soft touch n. colloq. gullible person, esp. over money.

software n. programs for a computer.

softwood n. easily sawn wood of deciduous trees.

softy var. of SOFTIE.

soggy /'sɒgɪ/ adj. (**-ier**, **-iest**) sodden, saturated; too moist (*soggy bread*). □ **sogginess** n. [dial. sog marsh]

soh /səʊ/ n. (also **so**) Mus. fifth note of a major scale. [arbitrarily taken]

soigné /'swɑːnjeɪ/ adj. (fem. **soignée** pronunc. same) well-groomed. [French]

soil¹ n. 1 upper layer of earth in which plants grow. 2 ground belonging to a nation; territory (*on French soil*). [Latin *solium* seat, *solum* ground]

soil² -v. 1 make dirty; smear or stain. 2 defile; discredit. -n. 1 dirty mark. 2 filth; refuse. [French *soill(i)er*]

soil pipe n. discharge-pipe of a lavatory.

soirée /'swɑːreɪ/ n. evening party, usu. for conversation or music. [French]

soixante-neuf /ˌswɑːsɑ̃tnɜːf/ n. slang mutual oral stimulation of the genitals. [French, = sixty-nine]

sojourn /'sɒdʒ(ə)n/ -n. temporary stay. -v. stay temporarily. [French *sojorner*]

sola /'səʊlə/ n. pithy-stemmed E. Indian swamp plant. [Urdu]

solace /'sɒləs/ -n. comfort in sadness, disappointment, or tedium. -v. (**-cing**) give solace to. [Latin *solatium*]

solan /'səʊlən/ n. (in full **solan goose**) large gooseli ʒ gannet. [Old Norse]

solar /'səʊlə(r)/ adj. of or reckoned by the sun. [Latin *sol* sun]

solar battery n. (also **solar cell**) device converting solar radiation into electricity.

solar day n. interval between meridian transits of the sun.

solarium /sə'leərɪəm/ n. (pl. **-ria**) room with sun-lamps or a glass roof etc. [Latin: related to SOLAR]

solar panel n. panel that absorbs the sun's rays as an energy source.

solar plexus n. complex of nerves at the pit of the stomach.

solar system n. the sun and the celestial bodies whose motion it governs.

solar year n. time taken for the earth to travel once round the sun.

sola topi n. sun-helmet made from the pith of the sola plant.

sold past and past part. of SELL. -adj. (foll. by **on**) colloq. enthusiastic about.

solder /'sɒlda(r), 'səʊ-/ -n. fusible alloy used to join metals or wires etc. -v. join with solder. [Latin: related to SOLID]

soldering iron n. heated tool for melting and applying solder.

soldier /'səʊldʒə(r)/ -n. 1 member of an army. 2 (in full **common soldier**) private or NCO in an army. 3 colloq. finger of bread for dipping into egg. -v. serve as a soldier. □ **soldier on** colloq. persevere doggedly. □ **soldierly** adj. [French *soulde*, originally = soldier's pay]

soldier of fortune n. mercenary.

soldiery n. soldiers, esp. of a specified character.

sole¹ -n. 1 undersurface of the foot. 2 part of a shoe, sock, etc., under the foot, esp. other than the heel. 3 lower surface or base of a plough, golf-club head, etc. -v. (**-ling**) provide (a shoe etc.) with a sole. □ **-soled** adj. (in comb.). [Latin *solea* sandal]

sole² n. (pl. same or **-s**) flat-fish used as food. [Latin *solea* sandal, which the shape of fish resembles]

sole³ adj. one and only; single, exclusive. [French from Latin *solus*]

solecism /'sɒlˌsɪz(ə)m/ n. 1 mistake of grammar or idiom. 2 offence against etiquette. □ **solecistic** /-'sɪstɪk/ adj. [Greek *soloikos* speaking incorrectly]

solely /'səʊlli/ adv. 1 alone (*solely responsible*). 2 only (*did it solely out of duty*).

solemn /'sɒləm/ adj. 1 serious and dignified. 2 formal. 3 awe-inspiring. 4 (of a person) serious or cheerless in manner. 5 grave, sober (*solemn promise*). □ **solemnly** adv. **solemnness** n. [Latin *solemnis*]

solemnity /sə'lemnɪtɪ/ n. (pl. **-ies**) 1 being solemn. 2 rite, ceremony.

solemnize /'sɒləm,naɪz/ v. (also **-ise**) (**-zing** or **-sing**) 1 duly perform (esp. a marriage ceremony). 2 make solemn. □ **solemnization** /-'zeɪʃ(ə)n/ n.

solenoid /'səʊlə,nɔɪd/ n. cylindrical coil of wire acting as a magnet when carrying electric current. [French from Greek *sōlēn* tube]

sol-fa /'sɒlfɑ/ n. system of syllables representing musical notes. [*sol* var. of SOH, FA]

soli pl. of SOLO.

solicit /sə'lɪsɪt/ v. (**-t-**) 1 seek (esp. business) repeatedly or earnestly. 2 (also *absol.*) accost as a prostitute. □ **solicitation** /-'teɪʃ(ə)n/ n. [Latin *sollicitus* anxious]

solicitor n. lawyer qualified to advise clients and instruct barristers. [French: related to SOLICIT]

Solicitor-General n. (pl. **Solicitors-General**) law officer below the Attorney-General or the Lord Advocate.

solicitous adj. 1 showing interest or concern. 2 (foll. by **to** + infin.) eager,

anxious. □ **solicitously** *adv.* [Latin: related to SOLICIT]

solicitude *n.* being solicitous. [Latin: related to SOLICITOUS]

solid /ˈsɒlɪd/ —*adj.* (**-der**, **-dest**) **1** firm and stable in shape; not liquid or fluid. **2** of such material throughout; not hollow. **3** of the same substance throughout (*solid silver*). **4** sturdily built; not flimsy or slender. **5 a** three-dimensional. **b** of solids (*solid geometry*). **6 a** sound, reliable (*solid arguments*). **b** dependable (*solid friend*). **7** sound but unexciting (*solid piece of work*). **8** financially sound. **9** uninterrupted (*four solid hours*). **10** unanimous, undivided. **11** (of printing) without spaces. —*n.* **1** solid substance or body. **2** (in *pl.*) solid food. **3** *Geom.* three-dimensional body or magnitude. —*adv.* solidly (*jammed solid*). □ **solidly** *adv.* **solidness** *n.* [Latin *solidus*]

solidarity /ˌsɒlɪˈdærɪtɪ/ *n.* **1** unity, esp. political or in an industrial dispute. **2** mutual dependence. [French: related to SOLID]

solidify /səˈlɪdɪfaɪ/ *v.* (**-ies**, **-ied**) make or become solid. □ **solidification** /-fɪˈkeɪʃ(ə)n/ *n.* being solid; firmness.

solid-state *adj.* using the electronic properties of solids (e.g. a semiconductor) to replace those of valves.

solidus /ˈsɒlɪdəs/ *n.* (*pl.* **solidi** /-daɪ/) oblique stroke (/). [Latin: related to SOLID]

soliloquy /səˈlɪləkwɪ/ *n.* (*pl.* **-quies**) **1** talking without or regardless of hearers, esp. in a play. **2** this part of a play. □ **soliloquist** *n.* **soliloquize** *v.* (also **-ise**) (**-zing** or **-sing**). [Latin *solus* alone, *loquor* speak]

solipsism /ˈsɒlɪpsɪz(ə)m/ *n.* philosophical theory that the self is all that exists or can be known. □ **solipsist** *n.* [Latin *solus* alone, *ipse* self]

solitaire /ˌsɒlɪˈteə(r)/ *n.* **1** jewel set by itself. **2** ring etc. with this. **3** game for one player in which pegs etc. are removed from a board by jumping others over them. **4** *US* = PATIENCE 3. [French: see SOLITARY]

solitary /ˈsɒlɪtərɪ/ —*adj.* **1** living or being alone; not gregarious; lonely. **2** secluded. **3** single, sole. —*n.* (*pl.* **-ies**) **1** recluse. **2** *colloq.* = SOLITARY CONFINEMENT. □ **solitarily** *adv.* **solitariness** *n.* [Latin *solitarius* from *solus* alone]

solitary confinement *n.* isolation in a separate prison cell.

solitude /ˈsɒlɪtjuːd/ *n.* **1** being solitary. **2** lonely place. [Latin *solitudo*: related to SOLITARY]

solo /ˈsəʊləʊ/ —*n.* (*pl.* **-s** or **soli** /-liː/) **1** musical piece or passage, or a dance, performed by one person. **2** thing done by one person, esp. an unaccompanied flight. **3** (in full **solo whist**) type of whist in which one player may oppose the others. —*v.* (**-es**, **-ed**) perform a solo. —*adv.* unaccompanied, alone. [Italian from Latin: related to SOLE[1]]

soloist /ˈsəʊləʊɪst/ *n.* performer of a solo, esp. in music.

Solomon's seal *n.* flowering plant with drooping green and white flowers. [*Solomon*, king of Israel]

solstice /ˈsɒlstɪs/ *n.* either of the times when the sun is furthest from the equator. [Latin *solstitium* 'the sun standing still']

soluble /ˈsɒljʊb(ə)l/ *adj.* **1** that can be dissolved, esp. in water. **2** solvable. □ **solubility** /-ˈbɪlɪtɪ/ *n.* [Latin *solvo solut-* release]

solute /ˈsɒljuːt/ *n.* dissolved substance. [Latin]

solution /səˈluːʃ(ə)n/ *n.* **1** solving or means of solving a problem. **2 a** conversion of a solid or gas into a liquid by mixture with a liquid. **b** state resulting from this. **3** dissolving or being dissolved.

solve *v.* (**-ving**) answer, remove, or effectively deal with (a problem). □ **solvable** *adj.*

solvent *adj.* **1** able to pay one's debts; not in debt. **2** able to dissolve or form a solution with something. —*n.* solvent liquid etc. □ **solvency** *n.* (in sense 2 of *adj.*).

somatic /səˈmætɪk/ *adj.* of the body, not of the mind. □ **somatically** *adv.* [Greek *sōma -mat-* body]

sombre /ˈsɒmbə(r)/ *adj.* (also *US* **somber**) dark, gloomy, dismal. □ **sombrely** *adv.* **sombreness** *n.* [Latin *sub umbra* under shade]

sombrero /sɒmˈbreərəʊ/ *n.* (*pl.* **-s**) broad-brimmed hat worn esp. in Latin America. [Spanish: related to SOMBRE]

some /sʌm/ —*adj.* **1** unspecified amount or number of (*some water*; *some apples*; *some of them*). **2** unknown or unspecified (*some day*; *some fool broke it*). **3** approximately (*some ten days*). **4** considerable (*went to some trouble*; *at some cost*). **5** (usu. stressed) **a** at least a modicum of (*have some consideration*). **b** such up to a point (*that is some help*). **c** *colloq.* remarkable (*i call that some story*). —*pron.* some people or things, some number or amount (*I have some already*). —*adv.* *colloq.* to some extent (*do it some more*). [Old English]

-some suffix forming adjectives meaning **1** producing (*fearsome*). **2** characterized by being (*gladsome*). **3** apt to

(tiresome, meddlesome). **4** suitable for (cuddlesome). [Old English]

-some² suffix forming nouns from numerals, meaning 'a group of' (foursome). [Old English]

somebody –pron. some person. –n. (pl. -ies) important person.

someday adv. at some time in the future.

somehow adv. **1** for some reason or other (somehow I don't trust him). **2** in some way; by some means.

someone n. & pron. = SOMEBODY.

someplace adv. US colloq. = SOMEWHERE.

somersault /'sʌməsɒlt/ –n. leap or roll with the body turning through a circle. –v. perform this. [French sobre above, saut jump]

something n. & pron. **1** unspecified or unknown thing (something has happened). **2** unexpressed or intangible quantity, quality, or extent (something strange about it). **3** colloq. notable person or thing. □ **something else** colloq. something exceptional. **something like** approximately. **something of** to some extent (something of an expert). [Old English: related to SOME, THING]

sometime –adv. **1** at some time. **2** formerly. –attrib. adj. former.

sometimes adv. occasionally.

somewhat adv. to some extent.

somewhen adv. colloq. at some time.

somewhere –adv. in or to some place. –pron. some unspecified place.

somnambulism /sɒm'næmbjʊlɪz(ə)m/ n. sleepwalking. □ **somnambulist** n. [Latin somnus sleep, ambulo walk]

somnolent /'sɒmnələnt/ adj. **1** sleepy, drowsy. **2** inducing drowsiness. □ **somnolence** n. [Latin: related to SOMNAMBULISM]

son /sʌn/ n. **1** boy or man in relation to his parent(s). **2** male descendant. **3** (foll. by of) male member of a family, etc. **4** male descendant or inheritor of a quality etc. (sons of freedom). **5** form of address, esp. to a boy. [Old English]

sonar /'səʊnɑː(r)/ n. **1** system for the underwater detection of objects by reflected sound. **2** apparatus for this. [sound navigation and ranging]

sonata /sə'nɑːtə/ n. composition for one or two instruments, usu. in three or four movements. [Italian, = sounded]

sonatina /ˌsɒnə'tiːnə/ n. simple or short sonata. [Italian, diminutive of SONATA]

son et lumière /ˌsɒn eɪ 'luːmjeə(r)/ n. entertainment by night at a historic building etc., using lighting effects and recorded sound to give a dramatic narrative of its history. [French, = sound and light]

song n. **1** words set to music or meant to be sung. **2** vocal music. **3** musical composition suggestive of a song. **4** cry of some birds. □ **for a song** colloq. very cheaply. [Old English: related to SING]

song and dance n. colloq. fuss, commotion.

songbird n. bird with a musical call.

songbook n. book of song lyrics and music.

song cycle n. set of linked songs.

songster n. (fem. **songstress**) **1** singer. **2** songbird.

song thrush n. common thrush, noted for singing.

songwriter n. writer of songs or the music for them.

sonic /'sɒnɪk/ adj. of or using sound or sound waves. [Latin sonus sound]

sonic bang n. (also **sonic boom**) noise made when an aircraft passes the speed of sound.

sonic barrier n. = SOUND BARRIER.

son-in-law n. (pl. **sons-in-law**) daughter's husband.

sonnet /'sɒnɪt/ n. poem of 14 lines with a fixed rhyme-scheme and, in English, usu. ten syllables per line. [French sonnet or Italian sonetto]

sonny /'sʌnɪ/ n. colloq. familiar form of address to a young boy.

sonorous /'sɒnərəs/ adj. **1** having a loud, full, or deep sound; resonant. **2** (of language, style, etc.) imposing. □ **sonority** /sə'nɒrɪtɪ/ n. [Latin]

soon adv. **1** in a short time (shall soon know). **2** relatively early (must you go so soon?). **3** readily or willingly (would sooner go; would as soon stay). □ **as (or so) soon as** at the moment that; not later than; as early as (came as soon as I could). **sooner or later** at some future time; eventually. □ **soonish** adv. [Old English]

soot /sʊt/ n. black powdery deposit from smoke. [Old English]

sooth n. archaic truth. [Old English]

soothe /suːð/ v. (-thing) **1** calm (a person, feelings, etc.). **2** soften or mitigate (pain etc.). [Old English]

soothsayer /'suːθseɪə(r)/ n. seer, prophet.

sooty adj. (-ier, -iest) **1** covered with soot. **2** black or brownish-black.

sop –n. **1** thing given or done to pacify or bribe. **2** piece of bread etc. dipped in gravy etc. –v. (-pp-) **1** (as sopping adj.) drenched (came home sopping; sopping wet clothes). **2** (foll. by up) soak up or mop up. [Old English]

sophism /'sɒfɪz(ə)m/ n. false argument, esp. one intended to deceive. [Greek]

sophist /'sɒfɪst/ n. captious or clever but fallacious reasoner. □ **sophistic** /sə'fɪstɪk/ adj. [Greek: related to SOPHISM]

sophisticate /sə'fɪstɪkət/ n. sophisticated person. [medieval Latin: related to SOPHISM]

sophisticated /sə'fɪstɪkeɪtɪd/ adj. 1 (of a person) worldly-wise; cultured; eleg- ant. 2 (of a thing, idea, etc.) highly developed and complex. □ **sophistica- tion** /-'keɪʃ(ə)n/ n.

sophistry /'sɒfɪstrɪ/ n. (pl. -ies) 1 use of sophisms. 2 a sophism.

sophomore /'sɒfəmɔː(r)/ n. US second- year university or high-school student.

soporific /ˌsɒpə'rɪfɪk/ —adj. inducing sleep. —n. soporific drug or influence. □ **soporifically** adv. [Latin sopor sleep]

sopping see SOP.

soppy adj. (-ier, -iest) colloq. mawk- ishly sentimental; silly; infatuated. □ **soppily** adv. **soppiness** n. [from SOP]

soprano /sə'prɑːnəʊ/ n. (pl. -s) 1 a high- est singing-voice. b female or boy singer with this voice. 2 instrument of a high or the highest pitch in its family. [Italian sopra above]

sorbet /'sɔːbeɪ/ n. 1 water-ice. 2 sherbet. [Arabic sharba to drink]

sorcerer /'sɔːsərə(r)/ n. (fem. sorcer- ess) magician, wizard. □ **sorcery** n. (pl. -ies). [French sourcier: related to sorɪ]

sordid /'sɔːdɪd/ adj. 1 dirty, squalid. 2 ignoble, mercenary. □ **sordidly** adv. **sordidness** n. [Latin sordidus]

sore —adj. 1 (of a part of the body) painful. 2 suffering pain 3 aggrieved, vexed. 4 archaic grievous or severe (in sore need). —n. 1 inflamed place on the skin or flesh. 2 source of distress or annoyance. —adv. archaic grievously, severely. □ **soreness** n. [Old English]

sorely adv. extremely (sorely tempted; sorely vexed).

sore point n. subject causing distress or annoyance.

sorghum /'sɔːgəm/ n. tropical cereal grass. [Italian sorgo]

sorority /sə'rɒrɪtɪ/ n. (pl. -ies) US female students' society in a university or college. [Latin soror sister]

sorrel¹ /'sɒr(ə)l/ n. sour-leaved herb. [Germanic: related to SOUR]

sorrel² /'sɒr(ə)l/ —adj. of a light reddish- brown colour. —n. 1 this colour. 2 sorrel animal, esp. a horse. [French]

sorrow /'sɒrəʊ/ —n. 1 mental distress caused by loss or disappointment etc. 2

cause of sorrow. —v. feel sorrow, mourn. [Old English]

sorrowful adj. feeling, causing, or showing sorrow. □ **sorrowfully** adv.

sorry /'sɒrɪ/ —adj. (-ier, -iest) 1 pained, regretful, penitent (sorry about the mess). 2 (foll. by for) feeling pity or sympathy for. 3 (attrib.) wretched (a sorry sight). —int. expression of apo- logy. □ **sorry for oneself** dejected. [Old English: related to SORE]

sort —n. 1 group or similar things etc.; class or kind. 2 colloq. person of a specified kind (a good sort). —v. (often foll. by out, over) arrange systematic- ally; put in order. □ **of a sort** (or of **sorts**) colloq. barely deserving the name (a holiday of sort). **out of sorts** slightly unwell; in low spirits. **sort of** colloq. as it were; to some extent. **sort out 1** separate into sets. 2 select from a varied group. 3 disentangle or put into order. 4 solve. 5 colloq. deal with or reprimand. [Latin sors sort- lot]

sortie /'sɔːtiː/ —n. 1 sally, esp. from a besieged garrison. 2 operational milit- ary flight. —v. (-ties, -tied, -tieing) make a sortie. [French]

SOS /ˌesəʊ'es/ n. (pl. SOSs) 1 inter- national code-signal of extreme dis- tress. 2 urgent appeal for help. [letters easily recognized in Morse]

sostenuto /ˌsɒstɪ'nuːtəʊ/ Mus. —adv. & adj. in a sustained or prolonged man- ner. —n. (pl. -s) passage to be played in this way. [Italian]

sot n. habitual drunkard. □ **sottish** adj. [Old English]

sotto voce /ˌsɒtəʊ 'vəʊtʃɪ/ adv. in an undertone. [Italian]

sou /suː/ n. 1 colloq. very small sum of money. 2 hist. former French coin of low value. [French from Latin: related to SOLD]

soubrette /suː'bret/ n. 1 pert maidser- vant etc. in a comedy. 2 actress taking this part. [French]

soubriquet var. of SOBRIQUET.

soufflé /'suːfleɪ/ n. light spongy sweet or savoury dish usu. made with stiffly beaten egg-whites and gelatine. [French, = blown]

sough /saʊ, sʌf/ —v. moan or whisper like the wind in trees etc. —n. this sound. [Old English]

sought past and past part. of SEEK.

sought-after adj. generally desired.

souk /suːk/ n. market-place in Muslim countries. [Arabic]

soul /səʊl/ n. 1 spiritual or immaterial part of a person, often regarded as

soul-destroying (cont.)

immortal. **2** moral, emotional, or intellectual nature of a person. **3** personification or pattern (*the very soul of discretion*). **4** an individual (*not a soul in sight*). **5** person regarded with familiarity or pity etc. (*the poor soul; a good soul*). **6** person regarded as an animating or essential part (*life and soul*). **7** energy or intensity, esp. in a work of art. **8** = SOUL MUSIC. □ **upon my soul** exclamation of surprise. [Old English]

soul-destroying *adj.* (of an activity etc.) tedious, monotonous.

soul food *n.* traditional food of American Blacks.

soulful *adj.* having, expressing, or evoking deep feeling. □ **soulfully** *adv.*

soulless *adj.* **1** lacking sensitivity or noble qualities. **2** undistinguished or uninteresting.

soul mate *n.* person ideally suited to another.

soul music *n.* Black American music with rhythm and blues, gospel, and rock elements.

soul-searching *n.* introspection.

sound[1] –*n.* **1** sensation caused in the ear by the vibration of the surrounding air or other medium. **2** vibrations causing this sensation. **3** what is or may be heard. **4** idea or impression conveyed by words (*don't like the sound of that*). **5** mere words. –*v.* **1** (cause to) emit sound. **2** utter, pronounce (*sound a warning note*). **3** convey an impression when heard (*sounds worried*). **4** give an audible signal for (an alarm etc.). **5** test (the lungs etc.) by the sound produced. □ **sound off** talk loudly or express one's opinions forcefully. □ **soundless** *adj.* [Latin *sonus*]

sound[2] –*adj.* **1** healthy; not diseased, injured, or rotten. **2** (of an opinion, policy, etc.) correct, well-founded. **3** financially secure. **4** undisturbed (*sound sleeper*). **5** thorough (*sound thrashing*). –*adv.* soundly (*sound asleep*). □ **soundly** *adv.* **soundness** *n.* [Old English]

sound[3] *v.* **1** test the depth or quality of the bottom of (the sea or a river etc.). **2** (often foll. by *out*) inquire (esp. discreetly) into the opinions or feelings of (a person). [French *sonder* from Latin *sub unda* under the wave]

sound[4] *n.* strait (of water). [Old English, = swimming]

sound barrier *n.* high resistance of air to objects moving at speeds near that of sound.

sound bite *n.* short pithy extract from an interview, speech, etc., as part of a news etc. broadcast.

soundbox *n.* the hollow body of a stringed musical instrument, providing resonance.

sound effect *n.* sound other than speech or music made artificially for a film, broadcast, etc.

sounding[1] *n.* **1** measurement of the depth of water. **2** (in *pl.*) region close enough to the shore for sounding. **3** (in *pl.*) cautious investigation.

sounding-balloon *n.* balloon used to obtain information about the upper atmosphere.

sounding-board *n.* **1** a means of disseminating opinions etc. **b** means of testing opinion. **2** canopy directing sound towards an audience.

sounding-line *n.* line used in sounding.

sounding-rod *n.* rod used in sounding water in a ship's hold.

soundproof –*adj.* impervious to sound. –*v.* make soundproof.

sound system *n.* equipment for sound reproduction.

soundtrack *n.* **1** the sound element of a film or videotape. **2** recording of this made available separately. **3** any single track in a multi-track recording.

sound wave *n.* wave of compression and rarefaction, by which sound is transmitted in the air etc.

soup /su:p/ –*n.* liquid food made by boiling meat, fish, or vegetables. –*v.* (usu. foll. by *up*) *colloq.* **1** increase the power of (an engine). **2** enliven (*a souped-up version of the original*). □ **in the soup** *colloq.* in difficulties. [French]

soupçon /ˈsuːpsɔ̃/ *n.* small quantity; trace. [French: related to SUSPICION]

soup-kitchen *n.* place dispensing soup etc. to the poor.

soup-plate *n.* deep wide-rimmed plate.

soup-spoon *n.* large round-bowled spoon.

soupy *adj.* (-ier, -iest) **1** like soup. **2** sentimental.

sour –*adj.* **1** acid in taste or smell, esp. because unripe or fermented. **2** morose; bitter. **3** (of a thing) unpleasant; distasteful. **4** (of the soil) dank. –*v.* make or become sour. □ **go** (or **turn**) **sour 1** turn out badly. **2** lose one's keenness. □ **sourly** *adv.* **sourness** *n.* [Old English]

source /sɔ:s/ *n.* **1** place from which a river or stream issues. **2** place of origination. **3** person or document etc. providing information. □ **at source** at the point of origin or issue. [French: related to SURGE]

sour grapes *n.pl.* resentful disparagement of something one covets.

sourpuss *n.* *colloq.* sour-tempered person.

souse /saus/ *v.* (-sing) 1 immerse in pickle or other liquid 2 (as **soused** *adj.*) *colloq.* drunk. 3 (usu. foll. by *in*) soak (a thing) in liquid. —*n.* 1 **a** pickle made with salt. **b** *US* food in pickle. 2 plunge or drench in water. [French *sous*]

soutane /suːˈtɑːn/ *n.* cassock worn by a Roman Catholic priest. [French from Italian *sotto* under]

south —*n.* 1 point of the horizon 90° clockwise from east. 2 compass point corresponding to this. 3 direction in which this lies. 4 (usu. **the South**) part of the world, a country, or a town to the south. —*adj.* 1 towards, at, near, or facing the south. 2 from the south (*south wind*). —*adv.* 1 towards, at, or near the south. 2 (foll. by *of*) further south than. □ **to the south** (often foll. by *of*) in a southerly direction. [Old English]

South African —*adj.* of the republic of South Africa. —*n.* 1 native or national of South Africa. 2 person of South African descent.

South American —*adj.* of South America. —*n.* native or national of a South American country.

southbound *adj.* travelling or leading southwards.

South-East *n.* part of a country or town to the south-east.

south-east —*n.* 1 point of the horizon midway between south and east. 2 direction in which this lies. —*adj.* of, towards, or coming from the south-east. —*adv.* towards, at, or near the south-east. —southeast **southeaster** /sauˈθiːstə(r)/ *n.* south-east wind.

south-easterly *adj.* & *adv.* = SOUTH-EAST.

south-eastern *adj.* on the south-east side.

southerly /ˈsʌðəlɪ/ —*adj.* & *adv.* 1 in a southern position or direction. 2 (of a wind) from the south. —*n.* (*pl.* -**ies**) such a wind.

southern /ˈsʌð(ə)n/ *adj.* of or in the south. □ **southernmost** *adj.*

Southern Cross *n.* southern constellation in the shape of a cross.

southerner *n.* native or inhabitant of the south.

Southern hemisphere *n.* the half of the earth south of the equator.

southern lights *n.pl.* aurora australis.

southpaw *colloq.* —*n.* left-handed person, esp. in boxing. —*adj.* left-handed.

south pole see POLE².

South Sea *n.* (also **South Seas**) southern Pacific Ocean.

south-south-east *n.* point or direction midway between south and south-east.

south-south-west *n.* point or direction midway between south and south-west.

southward /ˈsauθwəd/ *adj.* & *adv.* (also **southwards**) towards the south. —*n.* southward direction or region.

South-West *n.* part of a country or town to the south-west.

south-west —*n.* 1 point of the horizon midway between south and west. 2 direction in which this lies. —*adj.* of, towards, or coming from the south-west. —*adv.* towards, at, or near the south-west.

south-western *adj.* on the south-west side.

south-westerly *adj.* & *adv.* = SOUTH-WEST.

southwester /sauˈθwestə(r)/ *n.* south-west wind.

souvenir /ˌsuːvəˈnɪə(r)/ *n.* memento of an occasion, place, etc. [French]

sou'wester /sauˈwestə(r)/ *n.* 1 waterproof hat with a broad flap covering the neck. 2 south-west wind. [from SOUTH-WESTER]

sovereign /ˈsɒvrɪn/ —*n.* 1 supreme ruler, esp. a monarch. 2 *hist.* British gold coin nominally worth £1. —*adj.* 1 supreme (*sovereign power*). 2 self-governing (*sovereign State*). 3 royal (*our sovereign lord*). 4 excellent; effective (*sovereign remedy*). 5 unmitigated (*sovereign contempt*). [French *so(u)ver-ain*: *g-* by association with *reign*]

sovereignty *n.* (*pl.* -**ies**) 1 supremacy. 2 self-government. **b** self-governing State.

Soviet /ˈsəuvɪət, ˈsɒv-/ *hist.* —*adj.* (the) USSR or its people. —*n.* 1 citizen of the USSR. 2 (**soviet**) elected council in the USSR. 3 revolutionary council of workers, peasants, etc. [Russian]

sow¹ /səu/ *v.* (*past* **sowed**; *past part.* **sown** or **sowed**) 1 (also *absol.*) **a** scatter (seed) on or in the earth. **b** (often foll. by *with*) plant with seed. 2 initiate (*sow hatred*). □ **sow one's wild oats** indulge in youthful excess or promiscuity. [Old English]

sow² /sau/ *n.* adult female pig. [Old English]

soy *n.* 1 (in full **soy sauce**) sauce from pickled soya beans. 2 (in full **soy bean**) = SOYA 1. [Japanese]

soya /ˈsɔɪə/ *n.* 1 (in full **soya bean**) **a** leguminous plant yielding edible oil and flour and used to replace animal protein. **b** seed of this. 2 (in full **soya sauce**) = SOY 1. [Malay: related to SOY]

sozzled /ˈsɒz(ə)ld/ *adj. colloq.* very drunk. [dial. *sozzle* mix sloppily, imitative]

spa /spɑː/ n. 1 curative mineral spring. 2 resort with this. [*Spa* in Belgium]

space —n. 1 a continuous expanse in which things exist and move. b amount of this taken by a thing or available. 2 interval between points or objects. 3 empty area (*make a space*). 4 a outdoor urban recreation area (*open space*). b large unoccupied region (*wide open spaces*). 5 = OUTER SPACE. 6 interval of time (*in the space of an hour*). 7 amount of paper used in writing, available for advertising, etc. 8 a blank between printed, typed, or written words, etc. b piece of metal providing this. 9 freedom to think, be oneself, etc. (*need my own space*). —v. (-cing) 1 set or arrange at intervals. 2 put spaces between. 3 (as **spaced** *adj.*) (often foll. by *out*) *slang* euphoric, esp. from taking drugs. □ **space out** spread out (more) widely. □ **spacer** n. [Latin *spatium*]

space age n. era of space travel. **—attrib. adj.** (**space-age**) very modern.

spacecraft n. vehicle for travelling in outer space.

Space Invaders n.pl. computer game in which players combat aliens.

spaceman n. (*fem.* **spacewoman**) astronaut.

space-saving *adj.* occupying little space or helping to save space.

spaceship n. spacecraft.

space shuttle n. spacecraft for repeated use, esp. between the earth and a space station.

space station n. artificial satellite as a base for operations in outer space.

spacesuit n. sealed pressurized suit for an astronaut in outer space.

space-time n. fusion of the concepts of space and time as a four-dimensional continuum.

spacious /ˈspeɪʃəs/ *adj.* having ample space; roomy. □ **spaciously** *adv.* **spaciousness** n. [Latin: related to SPACE]

spade[1] n. long-handled digging tool with a broad sharp-edged metal blade. □ **call a spade a spade** speak bluntly. □ **spadeful** n. (*pl.* -s). [Old English]

spade[2] n. 1 a playing-card of a suit denoted by black inverted heart-shaped figures with short stalks. b (in *pl.*) this suit. 2 *slang offens.* Black person. [Italian *spada* sword: related to SPADE[1]]

spadework n. hard preparatory work.

spaghetti junction n. multi-level road junction, esp. on a motorway.

spaghetti western n. cowboy film made cheaply in Italy.

spaghetti Bolognese /ˌbɒləˈneɪz/ n. spaghetti with a meat and tomato sauce.

spaghetti /spəˈɡetɪ/ n. pasta in long thin strands. [Italian]

874

Spam n. *propr.* tinned meat made from ham. [spiced *ham*]

span[1] —n. 1 full extent from end to end. 2 each part of a bridge between supports. 3 maximum lateral extent of an aeroplane or its wing, or a bird's wing, etc. 4 a maximum distance between the tips of the thumb and little finger. b this as a measure of 9 in. —v. (-nn-) 1 stretch from side to side of; extend across. 2 bridge (a river etc.). [Old English]

span[2] see SPICK AND SPAN.

spandrel /ˈspændrɪl/ n. space between the curve of an arch and the surrounding rectangular moulding, or between the curves of adjoining arches and the moulding above. [origin uncertain]

spangle /ˈspæŋɡ(ə)l/ —n. small piece of glittering material, esp. one of many used to ornament a dress etc.; sequin. —v. (-ling) (esp. as **spangled** *adj.*) cover with or as with spangles (*star-spangled*). [obsolete *spang* from Dutch]

Spaniard /ˈspænjəd/ n. 1 native or national of Spain. 2 person of Spanish descent. [French *Espaigne* Spain]

spaniel /ˈspænj(ə)l/ n. dog of a breed with a long silky coat and drooping ears. [French *espaignol* Spanish (dog)]

Spanish /ˈspænɪʃ/ —*adj.* of Spain, its people, or language. —n. 1 the language of Spain and Spanish America. 2 (**the Spanish**) (*pl.*) the people of Spain. [*Spain* in Europe]

Spanish Main n. *hist.* NE coast of S. America and adjoining parts of the Caribbean Sea.

Spanish omelette n. omelette with chopped vegetables in the mix.

Spanish onion n. large mild-flavoured onion.

spank —v. 1 slap, esp. on the buttocks as punishment. 2 (of a horse etc.) move briskly. —n. slap, esp. on the buttocks. [imitative]

spanker n. *Naut.* fore-and-aft sail set on the after side of the mizen-mast.

spanking —*adj.* 1 brisk. 2 *colloq.* striking; excellent. —*adv.* *colloq.* very (*spanking new*). —n. slapping on the buttocks.

spanner n. tool for turning a nut on a bolt etc. [German]

spanner in the works n. *colloq.* impediment.

spar[1] n. stout pole, esp. as a ship's mast etc. 2 main longitudinal beam of an aeroplane wing. [Old Norse *sperra* or French *esparre*]

spar[2] —v. (-rr-) 1 make the motions of boxing without heavy blows. 2 argue. —n. 1 sparring motion. 2 boxing-match. [Old English]

spar³ n. easily split crystalline mineral. [Low German]

spar⁴ —adj. 1 a not required for normal movement or emergency or immediate use; extra. b for emergency or occasional use. 2 lean; thin. 3 frugal. —n. spare part. —v. (ring.) 1 afford to give, do without; dispense with (*spared me ten minutes*). 2 a refrain from killing, hurting, etc. b abstain from inflicting (*spare me this task*). 3 be frugal or grudging of (*no expense spared*). □ **go spare** colloq. become very angry or distraught. **not spare oneself** exert one's utmost efforts. **spare a person's life** not kill him or her. **to spare** left over; additional (*an hour to spare*). □ **sparely** adv. **spareness** n. [Old English]

spare part n. duplicate, esp. as a replacement.

spare-rib n. closely-trimmed ribs of esp. pork. [Low German *ribbesper*, associated with SPARE]

spare time n. leisure.

spare tyre n. colloq. roll of fat round the waist.

sparing adj. 1 frugal; economical. 2 restrained. □ **sparingly** adv.

spark¹ —n. 1 fiery particle thrown from a fire, alight in ashes, or produced by a flint, match, etc. 2 (often foll. by *of*) small amount (*spark of interest*). 3 a flash of light between electric conductors etc. b this serving to ignite the explosive mixture in an internal-combustion engine. 4 a flash of wit etc. b (also **bright spark**) witty or lively person. —v. 1 emit a spark or sparks. 2 (often foll. by *off*) stir into activity; initiate. □ **sparky** adj. [Old English]

spark² n. colloq. lively young person. [probably from SPARK¹]

sparkle /spaːk(ə)l/ —v. (-ling) 1 a emit or seem to emit sparks; glitter, glisten. b be witty; scintillate. 2 (of wine etc.) effervesce. —n. 1 glitter. 2 lively quality (*the song lacks sparkle*). □ **sparkly** adj.

sparkler n. 1 hand-held sparkling firework. 2 colloq. diamond.

spark-plug n. (also **sparking-plug**) device for making a spark in an internal-combustion engine.

sparring partner n. 1 boxer employed to spar with another as training. 2 person with whom one enjoys arguing.

sparrow /ˈspærəʊ/ n. small brownish-grey bird. [Old English]

sparrowhawk n. small hawk.

sparse adj. thinly dispersed or scattered. □ **sparsely** adv. **sparseness** n. **sparsity** n. [Latin *spargo spars-* scatter]

Spartan /ˈspɑːt(ə)n/ —adj. 1 of Sparta in ancient Greece. 2 austere, rigorous, frugal. —n. citizen of Sparta. [Latin]

spasm /ˈspæz(ə)m/ n. 1 sudden involuntary muscular contraction. 2 convulsive movement or emotion etc. 3 (usu. foll. by *of*) colloq. brief spell. [Greek *spaō* pull]

spasmodic /spæzˈmɒdɪk/ adj. of or in spasms, intermittent. □ **spasmodically** adv. [Greek: related to SPASM]

spastic /ˈspæstɪk/ —adj. 1 suffering from cerebral palsy. —n. 1 spastic person. 2 slang offens. stupid or incompetent person. [Greek: related to SPASM]

spat¹ past and past part. of SPIT¹.

spat² n. (usu. in pl.) hist. short gaiter covering a shoe. [abbreviation of *spatterdash*: related to SPATTER]

spat³ n. colloq. petty or brief quarrel. [probably imitative]

spat⁴ n. spawn of shellfish, esp. the oyster. [Anglo-French, of unknown origin]

spate n. 1 river-flood (*river in spate*), 2 unexpected occurrence of similar events (*spate of car thefts*). [origin unknown]

spathe /speɪð/ n. large bract(s) enveloping a flower-cluster. [Greek *spathē* broad blade]

spatial /ˈspeɪʃ(ə)l/ adj. of space. □ **spatially** adv. [Latin: related to SPACE]

spatter —v. splash or scatter in drips. —n. 1 splash. 2 pattering. [imitative]

spatula /ˈspætjʊlə/ n. broad-bladed flexible implement used for spreading, stirring, mixing paints, etc. [Latin diminutive: related to SPATHE]

spawn v. 1 a (of a fish, frog, etc.) produce (eggs). b be produced as eggs or young. 2 a produce or generate in large numbers. —n. 1 eggs of fish, frogs, etc. 2 mycelium of mushrooms or other fungi. [Anglo-French *espaundre*: related to EXPAND]

spay v. sterilize (a female animal) by removing the ovaries. [Anglo-French, related to ÉPÉE]

speak v. (*past* **spoke**; *past part.* **spoken**) 1 utter words (in an ordinary voice). 2 utter (words; the truth, etc.) 3 a converse; talk (*spoke to her earlier, had to speak to the children about rudeness*). b (foll. by *of*, *about*) mention in writing etc. c (foll. by *for*) act as spokesman for. 4 (foll. by *to*) speak with reference to use (a specified language); 5 make a speech. 6 use or be able to use (a specified language); convey an idea (*actions speak louder than words*). b (usu. foll. by *to*) communicate feeling etc.; affect, touch (*the sunset spoke to her*). □ **generally** (or **strictly** etc.) **speaking** in the general (or strict etc.) sense. **not** (or **nothing**) **to**

speak of not (or nothing) worth mentioning. **on speaking terms** friendly enough to converse. **speak for itself** be sufficient evidence. **speak out** (often followed by *against*) give one's opinion courageously. **speak up 1** speak loudly or freely. **2** (followed by *for*) defend. **speak volumes** be very significant. [Old English]

-speak *comb. form* jargon (*Newspeak; computer speak*).

speakeasy *n.* (*pl.* -**ies**) *US hist. slang* place where alcoholic liquor was sold illicitly.

speaker *n.* **1** person who speaks, esp. in public. **2** person who speaks a specified language (esp. in *comb.*: *a French speaker*). **3** (**Speaker**) presiding officer in a legislative assembly, esp. the House of Commons. **4** = LOUDSPEAKER.

speaking clock *n.* telephone service announcing the correct time.

spear –*n.* **1** thrusting or throwing weapon with a long shaft and a pointed usu. steel tip. **2 a** tip and stem of asparagus, broccoli, etc. **b** blade of grass etc. –*v.* pierce or strike (as) with a spear. [Old English]

spearhead –*n.* **1** point of a spear. **2** person or group leading an attack etc. –*v.* act as the spearhead of (an attack etc.).

spearmint *n.* common garden mint, used in cookery and to flavour chewing-gum etc.

spearwort *n.* aquatic plant with narrow spear-shaped leaves and yellow flowers.

spec¹ *n. colloq.* speculation. □ **on spec** as a gamble. [abbreviation]

spec² *n. colloq.* detailed working description; specification. [abbreviation of SPE-CIFICATION]

special /ˈspeʃ(ə)l/ –*adj.* **1 a** exceptional. **b** peculiar; specific. **2** for a particular purpose. **3** for children with special needs (*special school*). –*n.* special constable, train, edition of a newspaper, dish on a menu, etc. □ **specially** *adv.* **specialness** *n.* [Latin: related to SPE-CIES]

Special Branch *n.* police department dealing with political security.

special constable *n.* person trained to assist the police in routine duties or in an emergency.

special correspondent *n.* journalist writing on special events or a special subject.

special delivery *n.* delivery of mail outside the normal delivery schedule.

special edition *n.* extra late edition of a newspaper.

special effects *n.pl.* illusions created by props, camera-work, etc.

specialist *n.* **1** person trained in a particular branch of a profession, esp. medicine. **2** person who specially studies a subject or area.

speciality /ˌspeʃɪˈælɪtɪ/ *n.* (*pl.* -**ies**) **1** special subject, product, activity, etc. **2** special feature or skill.

specialize /ˈspeʃəlaɪz/ *v.* (also -**ise**) (-*zing* or -*sing*) **1** (often foll. by *in*) **a** be or become a specialist. **b** devote oneself to an interest, skill, etc. (*specializes in insulting people*). **2** (esp. in *passive*) adapt for a particular purpose (*specialized organs*). **3** (as **special-ized** *adj.*) of a specialist (*specialized work*). □ **specialization** *n.* [French: related to SPECIAL]

special licence *n.* licence allowing immediate marriage without banns.

special pleading *n.* biased reasoning.

specialty /ˈspeʃəltɪ/ *n.* (*pl.* -**ies**) esp. *US* = SPECIALITY.

specie /ˈspiːʃiː, -ʃiː/ *n.* coin as opposed to paper money. [related to SPECIES]

species /ˈspiːʃiːz, -ʃɪz, -siːz/ *n.* (*pl.* same) **1** class of things having some common characteristics. **2** group of animals or plants within a genus, differing only slightly from others and capable of interbreeding. **3** kind, sort. [Latin *specio* look]

specific /spəˈsɪfɪk/ –*adj.* **1** clearly defined (*a specific purpose*). **2** relating to a particular subject; peculiar. **3** exact, giving full details (*was specific about his wishes*). **4** *archaic* (of medicine etc.) having a distinct effect in curing a certain disease. –*n.* **1** *archaic* specific medicine or remedy. **2** specific aspect or factor (*discussed specifics; from the general to the specific*). □ **specifically** *adv.* **specificity** /-ˈfɪsɪtɪ/ *n.* [Latin: related to SPECIES]

specification /ˌspesɪfɪˈkeɪʃ(ə)n/ *n.* **1** act of specifying. **2** (esp. in *pl.*) detail of the design and materials etc. of work done or to be done. [medieval Latin: related to SPECIFY]

specific gravity *n.* = RELATIVE DEN-SITY.

specific heat capacity *n.* heat required to raise the temperature of the unit mass of a given substance by a given amount (usu. one degree).

specify /ˈspesɪfaɪ/ *v.* (-**ies**, -**ied**) **1** (also *absol.*) name or mention explicitly or as a condition (*specified a two-hour limit*). **2** include in specifications. [Latin: related to SPECIFIC]

specimen /ˈspesɪmɪn/ *n.* **1** individual or sample taken as an example of a class or

whole, esp. in experiments etc. **2** sample of urine for testing. **3** colloq. usu. derog. person of a specified sort. [Latin specio look]

specious /'spiːʃəs/ adj. plausible but wrong (specious argument). [Latin specio look]

speck –v. **1** small spot or stain. **2** particle. –v. (esp. as **specked** adj.) marked with specks. [Old English]

speckle /'spek(ə)l/ –n. speck, esp. one of many markings. –v. (-ling) (esp. as **speckled** adj.) mark with speckles. [Dutch spekkel]

specs n.pl. colloq. = SPECTACLES. [abbreviation]

spectacle /'spektək(ə)l/ n. **1** striking, impressive, or ridiculous sight. **2** public show. **3** object of public attention. [Latin specio spect- look]

spectacled adj. wearing spectacles.

spectacles n.pl. pair of lenses in a frame resting on the nose and ears, used to correct defective eyesight.

spectacular /spek'tækjʊlə(r)/ –adj. striking, impressive, lavish. –n. spectacular show. □ **spectacularly** adv.

spectator n. person who watches a show, game, incident, etc. □ **spectate** v. (-ting) informal. [Latin: related to SPECTACLE]

spectator sport n. sport attracting many spectators.

specter US var. of SPECTRE.

spectra pl. of SPECTRUM.

spectral /'spektr(ə)l/ adj. **1** of or like a spectre, ghostly. **2** of the spectrum or spectra. □ **spectrally** adv.

spectre /'spektə(r)/ n. (US **specter**) **1** ghost. **2** haunting presentiment (spectre of war). [Latin spectrum from specio look]

spectrometer /spek'trɒmɪtə(r)/ n. instrument for measuring observed spectra.

spectroscope /'spektrəskəʊp/ n. instrument for recording spectra for examination. □ **spectroscopic** /-'skɒpɪk/ adj. **spectroscopy** /-'trɒskəpɪ/ n.

spectrum /'spektrəm/ n. (pl. **-tra**) **1** band of colours as seen in a rainbow etc. **2** entire or wide range of a subject, emotion, etc. **3** distribution of electromagnetic radiation in which the parts are arranged according to wavelength. [Latin specio look]

specula pl. of SPECULUM.

speculate /'spekjʊleɪt/ v. (-ting) **1** (usu. foll. by on, upon, about) theorize, conjecture. **2** deal in a commodity or asset in the hope of profiting from fluctuating prices. □ **speculation** /-'leɪʃ(ə)n/ n. **speculative** /-lətɪv/ adj. **speculator** n. [Latin specula watch-tower, from specio look]

speculum /'spekjʊləm/ n. (pl. **-la**) **1** instrument for dilating orifices of the body. **2** mirror of polished metal in a telescope. [Latin, = mirror]

sped past and past part. of SPEED.

speech n. **1** faculty, act, or manner of speaking. **2** formal public address. **3** language of a nation, group, etc. [Old English: related to SPEAK]

speech day n. school celebration with speeches, prize-giving, etc.

speechify /'spiːtʃɪfaɪ/ v. (-ies, -ied) joc. make esp. boring or long speeches.

speechless adj. temporarily silent because of emotion etc.

speech therapy n. treatment for defective speech.

speed –n. **1** rapidity of movement. **2** rate of progress or motion. **3** gear appropriate to a range of speeds of a bicycle. **4** Photog. **a** sensitivity of film to light. **b** light-gathering power of a lens. **c** duration of an exposure. **5** slang amphetamine drug. **6** archaic success, prosperity. –v. (past and past part. **sped**) **1** go or send quickly. **2** (past and past part. **speeded**) travel at an illegal or dangerous speed. **3** archaic be or make prosperous or successful. □ **at speed** moving quickly. **speed up** move or work faster. [Old English]

speedboat n. high-speed motor boat.

speed limit n. maximum permitted speed on a road etc.

speedo /'spiːdəʊ/ n. (pl. **-s**) colloq. = SPEEDOMETER. [abbreviation]

speedometer /spiː'dɒmɪtə(r)/ n. instrument on a vehicle indicating its speed.

speedway n. **1 a** motor-cycle racing. **b** arena for this. **2** US road or track for fast traffic.

speedwell n. small plant with bright blue flowers. [from SPEED, WELL¹]

speedy adj. (-ier, -iest) **1** rapid. **2** done without delay; prompt. □ **speedily** adv. **speediness** n.

speleology /ˌspiːlɪ'ɒlədʒɪ/ n. the study of caves. [Greek spēlaion cave]

spell¹ v. (past and past part. **spelt** or **spelled**) **1** (also absol.) write or name correctly the letters of (a word etc.). **2 a** (of letters) form (a word etc.). **b** result in (spell ruin). □ **spell out 1** make out (words etc.) letter by letter. **2** explain in detail. □ **speller** n. [French espeler]

spell² n. **1** words used as a charm or incantation etc. **2** effect of these. **3** fascination exercised by a person, activity, etc. [Old English]

spell³ *n.* **1** short or fairly short period (*a cold spell*). **2** period of some activity or work. [Old English, = substitute]

spellbind /'spelbaɪnd/ *v.* (*past* and *past part.* **spellbound**) **1** (esp. as **spellbinding** *adj.*) hold the attention as if with a spell; entrance. **2** (as **spellbound** *adj.*) entranced, fascinated.

spelling *n.* **1** way a word is spelt. **2** ability to spell.

spelt¹ *past* and *past part.* of **SPELL**¹.

spelt² *n.* a kind of wheat giving very fine flour. [Old English]

spend *v.* (*past* and *past part.* **spent**) **1** pay out (money). **2 a** use or consume (time or energy). **b** use up (material etc.). **3** (as **spent** *adj.*) having lost its original force or strength; exhausted. □ **spend a penny** *colloq.* go to the lavatory. □ **spender** *n.* [Latin: related to **EXPEND**]

spendthrift –*n.* extravagant person. –*adj.* extravagant.

sperm *n.* (*pl.* same or **-s**) **1** = SPERMATOZOON. **2** semen. [Greek *sperma -mat-*]

spermaceti /ˌspɜːmə'setɪ/ *n.* white waxy substance from the sperm whale, used for ointments etc. [medieval Latin, = whale sperm]

spermatozoon /ˌspɜːmətəʊ'zəʊən/ *n.* (*pl.* **-zoa**) mature sex cell in semen. [from SPERM, Greek *zōion* animal]

sperm bank *n.* store of semen for artificial insemination.

sperm count *n.* number of spermatozoa in one ejaculation or a measured amount of semen.

spermicide /'spɜːmɪsaɪd/ *n.* substance able to kill spermatozoa. □ **spermicidal** /-'saɪd(ə)l/ *adj.*

sperm whale *n.* large whale yielding spermaceti.

spew *v.* (also **spue**) **1** (often foll. by *up*) vomit. **2** (often foll. by *out*) (cause to) gush. [Old English]

sphagnum /'sfægnəm/ *n.* (*pl.* **-na**) (in full **sphagnum moss**) moss growing in bogs, used as packing etc. [Greek *sphagnos*]

sphere *n.* **1** solid figure with every point on its surface equidistant from its centre; its surface. **2** ball, globe. **3** a field of action, influence, etc. **b** social class. **4** *hist.* each of the revolving shells in which celestial bodies were thought to be set. [Greek *sphaira* ball]

spherical /'sferɪk(ə)l/ *adj.* **1** shaped like a sphere. **2** of spheres. □ **spherically** *adv.*

spheroid /'sfɪərɔɪd/ *n.* spherelike but not perfectly spherical body. □ **spheroidal** /-'rɔɪd(ə)l/ *adj.*

sphincter /'sfɪŋktə(r)/ *n.* ring of muscle surrounding and closing an opening in the body. [Greek *sphiŋgō* bind tight]

sphinx /sfɪŋks/ *n.* **1** (**Sphinx**) (in Greek mythology) winged monster with a woman's head and a lion's body, whose riddle Oedipus guessed. **2** *Antiq.* **a** ancient Egyptian stone figure with a lion's body and a human or animal head. **b** (**the Sphinx**) huge sphinx near the Pyramids at Giza. **3** inscrutable person. [Greek]

spice –*n.* **1** aromatic or pungent vegetable substance used to flavour food. **2** spices collectively. **3 a** piquant quality. **b** (foll. by *of*) slight flavour or suggestion. –*v.* (**-cing**) **1** flavour with spice. **2** (foll. by *with*) enhance (*spiced with wit*). [French *espice*]

spick and span *adj.* **1** neat and clean. **2** smart and new. [earlier *span and span new*, fresh and new like a shaved chip]

spicy *adj.* (**-ier**, **-iest**) **1** of or flavoured with spice. **2** piquant; sensational, improper. □ **spiciness** *n.*

spider /'spaɪdə(r)/ *n.* eight-legged arthropod of which many species spin webs esp. to capture insects as food. [Old English: related to SPIN]

spider crab *n.* crab with long thin legs.

spider monkey *n.* monkey with long limbs and a prehensile tail.

spider plant *n.* house plant with long narrow striped leaves.

spidery *adj.* elongated and thin (*spidery handwriting*).

spiel /ʃpiːl/ *n.* slang glib speech or story; sales pitch. [German, = game]

spigot /'spɪgət/ *n.* **1** small peg or plug, esp. in a cask. **2** device for controlling the flow of liquid in a tap. [related to SPIKE²]

spike¹ –*n.* **1 a** a sharp point. **b** pointed piece of metal, esp. the top of an iron railing. **2 a** metal point in the sole of a running-shoe to prevent slipping. **b** (in *pl.*) spiked running-shoes. **3** pointed metal rod used for filing rejected news items. **4** large nail. –*v.* (**-king**) **1** put spikes on or into. **2** fix on a spike. **3** *colloq.* lace (a drink) with alcohol etc. **4 b** contaminate with something added. **4** *colloq.* reject (a newspaper story). □ **spike a person's guns** spoil his or her plans. [Low German or Dutch: related to SPOKE¹]

spike² *n.* cluster of flower-heads on a long stem. [Latin *spica*]

spikenard /'spaɪknɑːd/ *n.* **1** tall sweet-smelling Indian plant. **2** *hist.* perfumed ointment formerly made from this. [medieval Latin *spica nardi*]

spiky *adj.* (**-ier**, **-iest**) **1** like a spike; having or sticking up in spikes. **2** *colloq.*

spill touchy, irritable. □ **spikily** *adv.* **spiki-ness** *n.*

spill[1] −*v.* (*past* and *past part.* **split** or **spilled**) **1** fall or run out or cause (liquid, powder, etc.) to fall or run out of a container, esp. accidentally. **2 a** throw from a vehicle, saddle, etc. **b** (foll. by *into*, *out* etc.) (esp. of a crowd) leave a place quickly. **3** *slang* d.sclose (informa-tion etc.). **4** shed (blood). −*n.* **1** spilling or being split. **2** tumble, esp. from a horse, bicycle, etc. □ **spill the beans** *colloq.* divulge information etc. **spill over** overflow. □ **spillage** *n.* [Old English]

spill[2] *n.* thin strip of wood or paper etc. for lighting a fire, pipe, etc. [Low Ger-man or Dutch]

spillikin /spilikin/ *n.* **1** splinter of wood etc. **2** (in *pl.*) game in which thin rods are removed one at a time from a heap without moving the others. [from spill[2]]

spillway *n.* passage for surplus water from a dam.

spin −*v.* (**-nn-**; *past* and *past part.* **spun**) **1** (cause to) turn or whirl round quickly. **2** (also *absol.*) **a** draw out and twist (wool, cotton, etc.) into threads. **b** make (yarn, etc.) in this way. **3** (of a spider, silk-worm, etc.) make (a web, cocoon, etc.) by extruding a fine viscous thread. **4** (esp. of the head) be dizzy through excitement etc. **5** tell or write (a story etc.). **6** (as **spun** *adj.*) made into threads (*spun glass; spun gold*). **7** toss (a coin). −*n.* **1** spinning motion; whirl. **2** rotating dive o.' an aircraft. **3** secondary twisting motion, e.g. of a ball in flight. **4** *colloq.* brief drive, esp. in a car. □ **spin out** prolong. **spin a yarn** tell a story. [Old English]

spina bifida /spainə 'bifidə/ *n.* congen-ital spinal defect in which part of the spinal cord protrudes. [Latin, = cleft spine]

spinach /spinidʒ/ *n.* green vegetable with edible leaves. [French *espinache*]

spinal column *n.* spine.

spinal cord *n.* cylindrical nervous structure within the spine.

spin bowler *n. Cricket* bowler who imparts spin to a ball.

spindle /spind(ə)l/ *n.* **1** slender rod or bar, often tapered, for twisting and winding thread. **2** pin or axis that re-volves or on which something revolves. **3** turned piece of wood used as a banis-ter, chair leg, etc. [Old English: related to SPIN]

spindle tree *n.* tree with hard wood used for spindles.

spindly *adj.* (**-ier, -iest**) long or tall and thin; thin and weak.

spin-drier *n.* (also **spin-dryer**) machine for drying clothes by spinning them in a rapidly revolving drum. □ **spin-dry** *v.*

spindrift *n.* spray on the surface of the sea [Scots var. of *spoon-drift* from obsolete *spoon* scud]

spine *n.* **1** vertebrae extending from the skull to the coccyx; backbone. **2** needle-like outgrowth of an animal or plant. **3** part of a book enclosing the page-fastening. **4** sharp ridge or projection. [Latin *spina*]

spine-chiller *n.* frightening and usu. exciting story, film, etc. □ **spine-chill-ing** *adj.*

spineless *adj.* **1** having no spine; inver-tebrate. **2** lacking resolve, feeble.

spinet /spinet/ *n.* *Hist.* small harpsi-chord with oblique strings. [Italian *spinetta*]

spinnaker /spinəkə(r)/ *n.* large tri-angular sail oppos.te the mainsail of a racing-yacht. [*Sphinx*, name of the yacht first using it]

spinner *n.* **1** spin bowler. **2** person or thing that spins, esp. a manufacturer engaged in cotton-spinning. **3** revolving bait.

spinneret /spinə, ret/ *n.* **1** spinning-organ in a spider etc. **2** device for form-ing synthetic fibre.

spinney /spini/ *n.* (*pl.* **-s**) small wood; thicket. [Latin *spinetum* from *spina* thorn]

spinning-jenny *n.* *hist.* unmarried woman. esp. from technology.

spinning-jenny *n. hist.* machine for spinning fibres with more than one spindle at a time.

spinning wheel *n.* household device for spinning yarn or thread, with a spindle driven by a wheel with a crank or treadle.

spin-off *n.* incidental result or benefit.

spinster *n.* 1 *formal* unmarried woman. **2** woman, esp. elderly, thought unlikely to marry. □ **spinsterish** *adj.* [originally = woman who spins]

spiny *adj.* (**-ier, -iest**) having many spines.

spiny anteater *n.* = ECHIDNA.

spiraea /spaiˈriə/ *n.* (*US* **spirea**) shrub with clusters of small white or pink flowers. [Greek: related to SPIRAL]

spiral /ˈspaiər(ə)l/ *−adj.* **1** coiled in a plane or as round a cylinder or cone. **2** having this shape. −*n.* **1** spiral curve or thing (*spiral of smoke*). **2** progressive rise or fall of two or more quantities alternately because each depends on the other(s). −*v.* (**-ll-**; *US* **-l-**) **1** move in a spiral course. **2** (of prices, wages, etc.) rise or fall continuously. □ **spirally** *adv.* [Greek *speira* coil]

880

spiral staircase *n.* circular staircase round a central axis.

spirant /'spaɪərənt/ *adj.* uttered with a continuous expulsion of breath. —*n.* such a consonant. [Latin *spiro* breathe]

spire *n.* 1 tapering structure, esp. on a church tower. 2 any tapering thing. [Old English]

spirea US var. of SPIRAEA.

spirit /'spɪrɪt/ —*n.* 1 person's essence or intelligence; soul. 2 a rational or intelligent being without a material body. **b** ghost. 3 a person's character (*an unbending spirit*). **b** attitude (*took it in the wrong spirit; a free spirit; a kindred spirit*). **d** prevailing tendency (*spirit of the age*). 4 a (usu. in *pl.*) strong distilled liquor, e.g. whisky or gin. **b** distilled volatile liquid (*wood spirit*). **c** purified alcohol (*methylated spirit*). 5 a courage, vivacity. **b** (in *pl.*) state of mind, mood (*in high spirits; his spirits were dashed*). 6 essential as opposed to formal meaning (*the spirit of the law*). —*v.* (-t-) (usu. foll. by *away, off,* etc.) convey rapidly or mysteriously. □ **in spirit** inwardly. [Latin *spiritus*: related to SPIRANT]

spirited *adj.* 1 lively, courageous. 2 (in *comb.*) in a specified mood (*high-spirited*). □ **spiritedly** *adv.*

spirit gum *n.* quick-drying gum for attaching false hair.

spirit-lamp *n.* lamp burning methylated spirit etc. instead of oil.

spiritless *adj.* lacking vigour.

spirit-level *n.* device with a glass tube nearly filled with alcohol, used to test horizontality.

spiritual /'spɪrɪtʃʊəl/ —*adj.* 1 of the spirit or soul (*spiritual relationship; spiritual home*). 2 religious, divine, inspired. 3 refined, sensitive. —*n.* (also **Negro spiritual**) religious song orig. of American Blacks. □ **spirituality** /-'ælɪtɪ/ *n.* **spiritually** *adv.*

spiritualism *n.* belief in, and supposed practice of, communication with the dead, esp. through mediums. □ **spiritualist** *n.* **spiritualistic** /-'lɪstɪk/ *adj.*

spirituous /'spɪrɪtʃʊəs/ *adj.* 1 very alcoholic. 2 distilled as well as fermented.

spirochaete /'spaɪərəʊ,kiːt/ *n.* any of various flexible spiral-shaped bacteria. [Latin from Greek *speira* coil, *khaitē* long hair]

spirogyra /,spaɪərəʊ'dʒaɪərə/ *n.* freshwater alga containing spiral bands of chlorophyll. [Greek *speira* coil, *guros* round]

spit¹ —*v.* (-tt-; *past* and *past part.* **spat** or **spit**) 1 a (also *absol.*) eject (esp. saliva) from the mouth. **b** do this in contempt or anger. 2 utter vehemently. 3 (of a fire,

gun, etc.) throw out with an explosion. 4 (of rain) fall lightly. 5 make a spitting noise. —*n.* 1 spittle. 2 act of spitting. □ **spit it out** *colloq.* say it quickly and concisely. [Old English]

spit² —*n.* 1 rod for skewering meat for roasting on a fire etc. 2 point of land projecting into the sea. —*v.* (-tt-) pierce (as) with a spit. [Old English]

spit and polish *n. colloq.* esp. military cleaning and polishing.

spite —*n.* ill will, malice. —*v.* (-ting) hurt, harm, or frustrate (a person) through spite. □ **in spite of** notwithstanding. [French: related to DESPITE]

spiteful *adj.* malicious. □ **spitefully** *adv.*

spitfire *n.* person of fiery temper.

spit-roast *v.* roast on a spit.

spitting distance *n. colloq.* very short distance.

spitting image *n.* (foll. by *of*) *colloq.* double (of a person).

spittle /'spɪt(ə)l/ *n.* saliva. [related to SPIT¹]

spittoon /spɪ'tuːn/ *n.* vessel to spit into.

spiv *n. colloq.* man, esp. a flashily-dressed one, living from shady dealings. □ **spivvish** *adj.* **spivvy** *adj.* [origin unknown]

splash —*v.* 1 scatter or cause (liquid) to scatter in drops. 2 wet with spattered liquid etc. 3 a (usu. foll. by *across, along, about,* etc.) move while spattering liquid etc. **b** jump or fall into water etc. with a splash. 4 display (news) prominently. 5 decorate with scattered colour. 6 spend (money) ostentatiously. —*n.* 1 act or noise of splashing. 2 quantity of liquid splashed. 3 mark etc. made by splashing. 4 prominent news feature, display, etc. 5 patch of colour. 6 *colloq.* small quantity of soda water etc. (in drink). □ **make a splash** attract attention. **splash out** *colloq.* spend money freely. □ **splashy** *adj.* (-ier, -iest). [imitative]

splashback *n.* panel behind a sink etc. to protect the wall from splashes.

splashdown *n.* landing of a spacecraft on the sea. □ **splash down** *v.*

splat *colloq.* —*n.* sharp splattering sound. —*adv.* with a splat. —*v.* (-tt-) fall or hit with a splat. [abbreviation of SPLATTER]

splatter —*v.* splash esp. with a continuous noisy action; spatter. —*n.* noisy splashing sound. [imitative]

splay —*v.* 1 spread apart. 2 (of an opening) have its sides with divergent sides. 3 construct (an opening) with divergent sides. —*n.* surface at an oblique angle to another. —*adj.* splayed. [from DISPLAY]

spleen n. 1 abdominal organ regulating the quality of the blood. 2 moroseness, irritability (from the earlier belief that the spleen was the seat of such feelings). [Greek *splēn*]

spleenwort n. evergreen fern formerly used as a remedy.

splendid /splendid/ adj. 1 magnificent, sumptuous. 2 impressive, glorious, dignified (*splendid isolation*). 3 excellent; fine. □ **splendidly** adv. [Latin: related to SPLENDOUR]

splendiferous /splendifərəs/ adj. colloq. splendid. [from SPLENDOUR]

splendour /splendər/ n. (US **splendor**) dazzling brightness; magnificence. [Latin *splendeo* shine]

splenetic /splinetik/ adj. bad-tempered; peevish. □ **splenetically** adv. [Latin: related to SPLEEN]

splenic /splinik, splen-/ adj. of or in the spleen. [Latin from Greek: related to SPLEEN]

splice —v. (-cing) 1 join (ropes) by interweaving strands. 2 join (pieces of wood or tape etc.) by overlapping 3 (esp. as **spliced** adj.) colloq. join in marriage. —n. join made by splicing. □ **splice the main brace** *Naut. hist. slang* issue an extra tot of rum. [probably Dutch *splissen*]

splint —n. strip of wood etc. bound to a broken limb while it sets. —v. secure with a splint. [Low German or Dutch]

splinter —n. small sharp fragment of wood, stone, glass, etc. —v. break into splinters; shatter. □ **splintery** adj. [Dutch: related to SPLINT]

splinter group n. breakaway political group.

split —v. (-tt-; past and past part. split) 1 a break, esp. with the grain or into halves; break forcibly. b (often foll. by up) divide into parts, esp. equal shares (*they split the money*). 2 (often foll. by off, away) remove or be removed by breaking or dividing. 3 a (usu. foll. by on, over, etc.) divide into disagreeing or hostile parties (*split on the question of picketing*). b (foll. by with) quarrel or cease association with. 4 cause the fission of (an atom). 5 slang leave, esp. suddenly. 6 (usu. foll. by on) colloq. inform. 7 a (as **splitting** adj.) (of a headache) severe. b (of the head) suffer from a severe headache, noise, etc. —n. 1 act or result of splitting. 2 disagreement; schism. 3 (in pl.) feat of leaping in the air or sitting down with the legs at right angles to the body in front and behind or on either side. 4 dish of split bananas

split-level adj. (of a room etc.) with more than one level.

split pea n. pea dried and split in half for cooking.

split personality n. condition in which a person seems to have two alternating personalities.

split pin n. metal cotter passed through a hole and held by the pressing back of the two ends.

split-screen n. screen on which two or more separate images are displayed.

split second —n. 1 very brief moment. 2 (**split-second**) adj. 1 very rapid. 2 (of timing) very accurate.

splodge colloq. —n. daub, blot, or smear. —v. (-ging) make a splodge on. □ **splodgy** adj. [alteration of SPLOTCH]

splosh colloq. —v. move with a splashing sound. —n. 1 splash. 2 splash of water etc. [imitative]

splotch n. & v. = SPLODGE. □ **splotchy** adj. [origin uncertain]

splurge colloq. —n. 1 sudden extravagance. 2 ostentatious display or effort. —v. (-ging) (usu. foll. by on) spend large sums of money or make a great effort. [probably imitative]

splutter —v. 1 a speak, say, or express in a choking manner. b emit spitting sounds. 2 speak rapidly or incoherently. —n. spluttering speech or sound. [from SPUTTER]

spoil —v. (past and past part. spoilt or spoiled) 1 a make or become useless or unsatisfactory. b reduce the enjoyment etc. of (*the news spoiled his dinner*). 2 make (esp. a child) unpleasant by overindulgence. 3 (of food) go bad. 4 render (a ballot-paper) invalid by improper marking. —n. (usu. in pl.) 1 plunder, stolen goods. 2 profit or advantage from success or position. □ **be spoiling for** aggressively seek (a fight etc.). **spoil for choice** having so many choices that it is difficult to choose. [Latin *spolio*]

spoilage n. 1 paper broken in printing. 2 spoiling of food etc. by decay.

spoiler n. 1 retarding device on an aircraft, interrupting the air flow. 2 similar device on a vehicle to increase contact with the ground at speed.

spoilsport n. person who spoils others'

etc. with ice-cream. □ **split the difference** take the average of two proposed amounts. **split hairs** make insignificant distinctions. **split one's sides** laugh uncontrollably. **split up** separate, end a relationship. [Dutch]

split infinitive n. infinitive with an adverb etc. inserted between to and the verb.

spollt *past* and *past part.* of SPOIL.

spoke[1] *n.* each of the rods running from the hub to the rim of a person's wheel. □ **put a spoke in a person's wheel** thwart or hinder a person. □ **spoked** *adj.* [Old English]

spoke[2] *past* of SPEAK.

spoken *past part.* of SPEAK. *adj.* (in *comb.*) speaking in a specified way (*well-spoken*). □ **spoken for** claimed (*this seat is spoken for*).

spokeshave *n.* tool for planing curved surfaces. [from SPOKE[1]]

spokesman *n.* (*fem.* **spokeswoman**) person speaking for a group etc. [from SPOKE[2]]

spokesperson *n.* (*pl.* -s or -people) spokesman or spokeswoman.

spoliation /spəʊlɪˈeɪʃ(ə)n/ *n.* plundering, pillage. [Latin: related to SPOIL]

spondee /ˈspɒndiː/ *n.* metrical foot consisting of two long syllables (- -). □ **spondaic** /-ˈdeɪɪk/ *adj.* [Greek *spondē* libation, with which songs in this metre were associated]

sponge /spʌndʒ/ —*n.* 1 sea animal with a porous body wall and a rigid internal skeleton. 2 this skeleton or a piece of porous rubber etc. used in bathing, cleaning, etc. 3 thing like a sponge in consistency etc., esp. a sponge cake. 4 act of sponging. —*v.* (**-ging**) 1 wipe or cleanse with a sponge. 2 (often foll. by *out*, *away*, etc.) wipe off or efface (as) with a sponge. 3 (often foll. by *up*) absorb (as) with a sponge. 4 (often foll. by *on*, *off*) live as a parasite. □ **spongiform** *adj.* (esp. in senses 1, 2 of the *n.*). [Latin *spongia*]

sponge bag *n.* waterproof bag for toilet articles.

sponge cake *n.* light spongy cake.

sponge pudding *n.* light spongy pudding.

sponger *n.* parasitic person.

sponge rubber *n.* porous rubber.

spongy *adj.* (-ier, -iest) like a sponge, porous, elastic, absorbent. □ **sponginess** *n.*

sponsor /ˈspɒnsə(r)/ —*n.* 1 person who pledges money to a charity etc. in return for another person fulfilling a sporting etc. challenge. 2 a patron of an artistic or sporting activity etc. **b** company etc. supporting a broadcast in return for advertising time. 3 person who introduces legislation. 4 godparent at a baptism or (esp. *RC Ch.*) person who presents a candidate for baptism. —*v.* be a sponsor for. □ **sponsorial** /-ˈsɔːrɪəl/ *adj.* **sponsorship** *n.* [Latin *spondeo* sponsus pledge]

spontaneous /spɒnˈteɪnɪəs/ *adj.* 1 acting, done, or occurring without external

cause. 2 instinctive, automatic, natural. 3 (of style or manner) gracefully natural. □ **spontaneity** /ˌspɒntəˈneɪɪtɪ/ *n.* **spontaneously** *adv.* [Latin *sponte* of one's own accord]

spontaneous combustion *n.* ignition of a substance from internal heat.

spoof *n.* & *v. colloq.* 1 parody. 2 hoax, swindle. [invented word]

spook —*n. colloq.* ghost. —*v.* esp. *US* frighten, unnerve. ['Low German or Dutch]

spooky *adj.* (-ier, -iest) *colloq.* ghostly, eerie. □ **spookily** *adv.* **spookiness** *n.*

spool —*n.* 1 reel for winding magnetic tape, yarn, etc., on. 2 revolving cylinder of an angler's reel. —*v.* wind on a spool. [French *espole* or Germanic *spole*]

spoon —*n.* 1 **a** utensil with a bowl and a handle for lifting food to the mouth, stirring, etc. **b** spoonful, esp. of sugar. 2 spoon-shaped thing, esp. (in full spoon-bait) a revolving metal fish-lure. —*v.* 1 (often foll. by *up*, *out*) take (liquid etc.) with a spoon. 2 hit (a ball) feebly upwards. 3 *colloq.* kiss and cuddle. □ **spoonful** *n.* (*pl.* -s). [Old English]

spoonbill *n.* wading bird with a broad flat-tipped bill.

spoonerism /ˈspuːnərɪz(ə)m/ *n.* (usu. accidental) transposition of the initial letters etc. of two or more words. [*Spooner*, name of a scholar]

spoonfeed *v.* (*past* and *past part.* **-fed**) 1 feed with a spoon. 2 give such extensive help etc. to (a person) that he or she need make no effort.

spoor *n.* animal's track or scent. [Dutch]

sporadic /spəˈrædɪk/ *adj.* occurring only sparsely or occasionally. □ **sporadically** *adv.* [Greek *sporas* -*ad*- scattered]

spore *n.* reproductive cell of many plants and micro-organisms. [Greek *spora* seed]

sporran /ˈspɒrən/ *n.* pouch worn in front of the kilt. [Gaelic *sporan*]

sport —*n.* 1 **a** game or competitive activity, usu. played outdoors and involving physical exertion, e.g. cricket, football, racing. **b** these collectively. 2 (in *pl.*) meeting for competing in sports, esp. athletics. 3 amusement, fun. 4 *colloq.* **a** fair, generous, or sporting person. **b** person with a specified attitude to games, rules, etc. 5 animal or plant deviating from the normal type. —*v.* 1 amuse oneself, play about. 2 wear or exhibit, esp. ostentatiously. □ **in sport** jestingly. **make sport of** ridicule. [from DISPORT]

sporting *adj.* 1 interested or concerned in sport. 2 generous, fair. □ **a sporting**

sportive chance some possibility of success. □ **sportively** *adv.*

sportive *adj.* playful.

sports car *n.* low-built fast car.

sports coat *n.* (also **sports jacket**) man's informal jacket.

sports ground *n.* piece of land used for sports.

sportsman *n.* (*fem.* **sportswoman**) **1** person who takes part in sport, esp. professionally. **2** fair and generous person. □ **sportsmanlike** *adj.* **sportsmanship** *n.*

sportswear *n.* clothes for sports or informal wear.

sporty *adj.* (**-ier, -iest**) *colloq.* **1** fond of sport. **2** rakish, showy. □ **sportily** *adv.* **sportiness** *n.*

spot —*n.* **1** small roundish area or mark differing in colour, texture, etc., from the surface it is on. **2** pimple or blemish. **3** moral blemish or stain. **4** particular place, locality. **5** particular part of one's body or aspect of one's character. **6** *colloq.* one's esp. regular position in an organization, programme, etc. **7** a *colloq.* small quantity (*spot of trouble*). **b** drop (*spot of rain*). **8** = SPOTLIGHT. **9** (usu. *attrib.*) money paid or goods delivered immediately after a sale (*spot cash*). —*v.* (**-tt-**) **1** *colloq.* pick out, recognize, catch sight of. **2** watch for and take note of (trains, talent, etc.). **3** (as **spotted** *adj.*) marked or decorated with spots. **4** make spots, rain slightly. □ **in a spot** (or **in a tight** etc. **spot**) *colloq.* in difficulty. □ **on the spot 1** at the scene of an event. **2** *colloq.* in a position demanding response or action. **3** without delay. **4** without moving forwards or backwards (*running on the spot*). [perhaps from Low German or Dutch]

spot check *n.* sudden or random check.

spotless *adj.* absolutely clean or pure. □ **spotlessly** *adv.*

spotlight —*n.* **1** beam of light directed on a small area. **2** lamp projecting this. **3** full publicity. —*v.* (*past* and *past part.* **-lighted** or **-lit**) **1** direct a spotlight on. **2** draw attention to.

spot on *adj. colloq.* precise; on target.

spotted dick *n.* suet pudding containing currants.

spotter *n.* **1** (often in *comb.*) person who spots people or things (*train-spotter*). **2** (in full **spotter plane**) aircraft used to locate enemy positions etc.

spotty *adj.* (**-ier, -iest**) **1** marked with spots. **2** patchy, irregular. □ **spottiness** *n.*

spot-weld *v.* join (two metal surfaces) by welding at discrete points. □ **spot welder** *n.* **spot welding** *n.*

spouse /spauz/ *n.* husband or wife. [Latin *sponsus sponsa* betrothed]

spout —*n.* **1** projecting tube or lip used for pouring from a teapot, kettle, jug, etc., or on a fountain, roof-gutter, etc. **2** jet or column of liquid etc. —*v.* **1** discharge or issue forcibly in a jet. **2** utter or speak at length or pompously. □ **up the spout** *slang* **1** useless, ruined. **2** pregnant. [Dutch]

sprain —*v.* wrench (an ankle, wrist, etc.), causing pain or swelling. —*n.* such a wrench. [origin unknown]

sprang *past* of SPRING.

sprat *n.* small edible marine fish. [Old English]

sprawl —*v.* **1** sit, lie, or fall with limbs flung out untidily. **b** spread (one's limbs) thus. **2** (of writing, a plant, a town, etc.) be irregular or straggling. —*n.* **1** sprawling movement, position, or mass. **2** straggling urban expansion. [Old English]

spray[1] —*n.* **1** water etc. flying in small drops. **2** liquid sprayed with an aerosol etc. **3** device for this. —*v.* **1** (also *absol.*) throw (liquid) as spray. **2** (also *absol.*) sprinkle (an object) thus, esp. with insecticide. **3** (of a tom-cat) mark its environment with urine, to attract females. □ **sprayer** *n.* [origin uncertain]

spray[2] *n.* **1** sprig of flowers or leaves, or a small branch; decoratively arranged bunch of flowers. **2** ornament in a similar form. [Old English]

spray-gun *n.* device for spraying paint etc.

spread /spred/ —*v.* (*past* and *past part.* **spread**) **1** (often foll. by *out*) **a** open, extend, or unfold. **b** cause to cover a surface or larger area. **c** display thus. **2** (often foll. by *out*) have a wide, specified, or increasing extent. **3** become or make widely known, felt, etc. (*rumours are spreading*). **4 a** cover (*spread the wall with paint*). **b** lay (a table). —*n.* **1** act of spreading. **2** capability or extent of spreading. **3** diffusion (*spread of learning*). **4** breadth. **5** increased girth (*middle-aged spread*). **6** difference between two rates, prices, etc. **7** *colloq.* elaborate meal. **8** paste for spreading on bread etc. **9** bedspread. **10** printed matter spread across more than one column. □ **spread oneself** be lavish or discursive. **spread one's wings** develop one's powers fully. [Old English]

spread eagle —*n.* figure of an eagle with legs and wings extended as an emblem. —*v.* (**spread-eagle**) **1** (usu. as **spread-eagled** *adj.*) place (a person) with arms and legs spread out. **2** defeat utterly.

spreadsheet n. computer program for the manipulation and retrieval of esp. tabulated figures, esp. for accounting.

spree n. colloq. **1** extravagant outing (*shopping spree*). **2** bout of fun or drinking etc. [origin unknown]

sprig –n. **1** small branch or shoot. **2** ornament resembling this, esp. on fabric. –v. (**-gg-**) ornament with sprigs (*sprigged muslin*). [*sprick*]

sprightly /ˈspraɪtlɪ/ adj. (**-ier**, **-iest**) vivacious, lively, brisk. □ **sprightliness** n. [from *spright*, var. of SPRITE]

spring –v. (past **sprang**; past part. **sprung**) **1** rise rapidly or suddenly, leap, jump. **2** move rapidly by or as by the action of a spring. **3** (usu. foll. by *from*) originate (from ancestors, a source, etc.). **4** act or appear suddenly or unexpectedly (*a breeze sprang up*; *spring to mind*; *spring to life*). **5** (often foll. by *on*) present (a thing or circumstance etc.) suddenly or unexpectedly (*sprang it on me*). **6** slang contrive the escape of (a person from prison etc.). **7** rouse (game) from a covert etc. **8** (usu. as **sprung** adj.) provide (a mattress etc.) with springs. –n. **1** jump, leap. **2** recoil. **3** elastic device, usu. of coiled metal, used esp. to drive clockwork or for cushioning in furniture or vehicles. **5 a** (often attrib.) the first season of the year, in which new vegetation begins to appear. **b** (often foll. by *of*) early stage of life etc. **6** place where water, oil, etc., wells up from the earth; basin or flow so formed. **7** motive for or origin of an action, custom, etc. □ **spring a leak** develop a leak. **spring up** come into being, appear. □ **springlike** adj. [Old English]

spring balance n. balance that measures weight by the tension of a spring.

springboard n. **1** flexible board for leaping or diving from. **2** source of impetus.

springbok /ˈsprɪŋbɒk/ n. (pl. same or **-s**) S. African gazelle. [Afrikaans]

spring chicken n. **1** young fowl for eating. **2** youthful person.

spring-clean –n. (also **spring-cleaning**) thorough cleaning of a house, esp. in spring. –v. clean (a house) thus.

spring equinox n. (also **vernal equinox**) equinox about 20 March.

spring fever n. restlessness or lethargy associated with spring.

spring greens n.pl. young cabbage leaves.

spring onion n. young onion eaten raw.

spring roll n. Chinese fried pancake filled with vegetables.

spring tide n. tide just after the new and the full moon when there is the greatest difference between high and low water.

springtime n. season of spring.

springy adj. (**-ier**, **-iest**) springing back quickly when squeezed, bent, etc.; elastic. □ **springiness** n.

sprinkle /ˈsprɪŋk(ə)l/ –v. (**-ling**) **1** scatter in small drops or particles. **2** (often foll. by *with*) subject to sprinkling with liquid etc. **3** (of liquid etc.) fall on in this way. **4** distribute in small amounts. –n. (usu. foll. by *of*) **1** light shower. **2** = SPRINKLING. [origin uncertain]

sprinkler n. device for sprinkling lawn or extinguishing fires.

sprinkling n. small sparse number or amount.

sprint –v. **1** run a short distance at full speed. **2** run (a specified distance) thus. –n. **1** such a run. **2** short burst in cycling, swimming, etc. □ **sprinter** n. [Old Norse]

sprit n. small diagonal spar from the mast to the upper outer corner of a sail. [Old English]

sprite n. elf, fairy. [*sprit*, contraction of SPIRIT]

spritsail /ˈsprɪts(ə)l/ n. sail extended by a sprit.

spritzer /ˈsprɪtsə(r)/ n. drink of wine with soda water. [German, = a splash]

sprocket /ˈsprɒkɪt/ n. each of several teeth on a wheel engaging with links of a chain. [origin unknown]

sprout –v. **1** put forth (shoots, hair, etc.). **2** begin to grow. –n. **1** shoot of a plant. **2** = BRUSSELS SPROUT. [Old English]

spruce[1] /spruːs/ –adj. neatly dressed etc.; smart. –v. (**-cing**) (usu. foll. by *up*) make or become smart. □ **sprucely** adv. **spruceness** n. [perhaps from SPRUCE[2]]

spruce[2] /spruːs/ n. **1** conifer with dense conical foliage. **2** its wood. [obsolete *Pruce* Prussia]

sprung see SPRING.

spry /spraɪ/ adj. (**spryer**, **spryest**) lively, nimble. □ **spryly** adv. [origin unknown]

spud –n. **1** colloq. potato. **2** small narrow spade for weeding. –v. (**-dd-**) (foll. by *up*, *out*) remove with a spud. [origin unknown]

spue var. of SPEW.

spumante /spuːˈmæntɪ/ n. Italian sparkling white wine. [Italian, = sparkling]

spume *n. & v.* (-ming) froth, foam. □ **spumy** *adj.* (-ier, -iest). [Latin *spuma*]

spun *past* and *past part.* of SPIN.

spunk /spʌŋk/ *n.* 1 *colloq.* courage, mettle, spirit. 2 *coarse slang* semen. 3 touchwood. [origin unknown]

spunky *adj.* (-ier, -iest) *colloq.* brave, spirited.

spun silk *n.* cheap material containing waste silk.

spur –*n.* 1 small spike or spiked wheel worn on a rider's heel for urging on a horse. 2 stimulus, incentive. 3 spur-shaped thing, esp.: **a** a projection from a mountain or mountain range. **b** a branch road or railway. **c** a hard projection on a cock's leg. –*v.* (-rr-) 1 prick (a horse) with spurs. 2 incite or stimulate. □ **on the spur of the moment** on an impulse. [Old English]

spurge *n.* plant with an acrid milky juice. [Latin *expurgare* to clean out]

spurious /ˈspjʊəriəs/ *adj.* not genuine, fake. [Latin]

spurn *v.* reject with disdain or contempt. [Old English]

spurt –*v.* 1 (cause to) gush out in a jet or stream. 2 make a sudden effort. –*n.* 1 sudden gushing out, jet. 2 short burst of speed, growth, etc. [origin unknown]

sputnik /ˈspʌtnɪk, ˈspʊt-/ *n.* Russian artificial satellite orbiting the earth. [Russian]

sputter –*v.* make a series of quick explosive sounds, splutter. –*n.* this sound. [Dutch (imitative)]

sputum /ˈspjuːtəm/ *n.* (*pl.* **sputa**) 1 saliva. 2 expectorated matter, used esp. in diagnosis. [Latin]

spy /spaɪ/ –*n.* (*pl.* **spies**) 1 person who secretly collects and reports information for a government, company, etc. 2 person watching others secretly. –*v.* (**spies, spied**) 1 discern, see. 2 (often foll. by *on*) act as a spy. 3 (often foll. by *into*) pry. □ **spy out** explore or discover, esp. secretly. [French *espie, espier*]

spyglass *n.* small telescope.

spyhole *n.* peep-hole.

sq. *abbr.* square.

Sqn. Ldr. *abbr.* Squadron Leader.

squab /skwɒb/ –*n.* 1 young (esp. unfledged) pigeon or other bird. 2 short fat person. 3 stuffed cushion, esp. as part of a car-seat. 4 sofa, ottoman. –*adj.* short and fat, squat. [perhaps from Scandinavian]

squabble /ˈskwɒb(ə)l/ –*n.* petty or noisy quarrel. –*v.* (-ling) engage in this. [probably imitative]

squad /skwɒd/ *n.* 1 small group sharing a task etc., esp. of soldiers or policemen (*drug squad*). 2 *Sport* team. [French *escouade*]

squad car *n.* police car.

squaddie *n.* (also **squaddy**) (*pl.* -ies) *slang* recruit; private.

squadron /ˈskwɒdrən/ *n.* 1 unit of the RAF with 10–18 aircraft. 2 detachment of warships employed on a particular duty. 3 organized group etc., esp. a cavalry division of two troops. [Italian *squadrone* related to SQUAD]

squadron leader *n.* commander of an RAF squadron, next below Wing Commander.

squalid /ˈskwɒlɪd/ *adj.* 1 filthy, dirty. 2 mean or poor in appearance. [Latin]

squall /skwɔːl/ –*n.* 1 sudden or violent wind, esp. with rain, snow, or sleet. 2 discordant cry; scream (esp. of a baby). –*v.* 1 utter a squall; scream. 2 utter with a squall. □ **squally** *adj.* [probably alteration of SQUEAL after BAWL]

squalor /ˈskwɒlə(r)/ *n.* filthy or squalid state. [Latin]

squander /ˈskwɒndə(r)/ *v.* spend wastefully. [origin unknown]

square /skweə(r)/ –*n.* 1 rectangle with four equal sides. 2 object of (approximately) this shape. 3 open (usu. four-sided area surrounded by buildings. 4 product of a number multiplied by itself (*16 is the square of 4*, 5, L, or T-shaped instrument for obtaining or testing right angles. 6 *slang* old-fashioned or conventional person. –*adj.* 1 square-shaped. 2 having or in the form of a right angle (*square corner*). 3 angular, not round. 4 designating a unit of measure equal to the area of a square whose side is one of the unit specified (*square metre*). 5 (often foll. by *with*) level, parallel. 6 (usu. foll. by *to*) at right angles. 7 sturdy, squat (*a man of square frame*). 8 arranged; settled (*get things square*). 9 (also **all square**) **a** with no money owed. **b** (of scores) equal. 10 fair and honest. 11 direct (*met with a square refusal*). 12 *slang* conventional or old-fashioned. –*adv.* 1 squarely (*hit me square on the jaw*). 2 fairly, honestly. –*v.* (-ring) 1 make square. 2 multiply (a number) by itself. 3 usu. foll. by *to, with*) adjust; make or be suitable or consistent; reconcile. 4 mark out in squares. 5 settle or pay (a bill etc.). 6 place (one's shoulders etc.) squarely facing forwards. 7 *colloq.* pay or bribe (a person). 8 (also *absol.*) make the scores of (a match etc.) equal. □ **back to square one** *colloq.* back to the starting point with no progress made. **out of square** not at right angles. **square the circle** 1 construct a square equal in area to a given circle. 2 do what is impossible. **square peg in a round hole** see PEG. **square up** settle an account etc. **square**

up to 1 move threateningly towards (a person). 2 face and tackle (a difficulty etc.) resolutely. □ **squarely** adv. **squareness** n. **squarish** adj. [French esquare, Latin quadra]

square-bashing n. slang military drill on a barrack-square.

square dance n. dance with usu. four couples inwards from four sides.

square deal n. fair bargain or treatment.

square leg n. fielding position in cricket at some distance on the batsman's leg side and nearly opposite the stumps.

square meal n. substantial meal.

square measure n. measure expressed in square units.

square-rigged adj. with the principal sails at right angles to the length of the ship.

square root n. number that multiplied by itself gives a specified number.

squash[1] /skwɒʃ/ -v. 1 crush or squeeze, esp. flat or into pulp. 2 (often foll. by into) colloq. put or make one's way by squeezing. 3 belittle, bully (a person). 4 suppress (a proposal, allegation, etc.). -n. 1 crowd, crowded state. 2 drink made of crushed fruit. 3 (in full **squash rackets**) game played with rackets and a small ball in a closed court. □ **squashy** adj. (-ier, -iest). [French esquasser, related to EX-[1], QUASH]

squash[2] /skwɒʃ/ n. (pl. same or -es) 1 trailing annual plant. 2 edible gourd of this. [Narragansett]

squat /skwɒt/ -v. (-tt-) 1 sit on one's heels or on the ground with the knees drawn up. 2 colloq. sit down. 3 occupy a building as a squatter. -adj. (**squatter**, **squattest**) short and thick, dumpy. -n. 1 squatting posture. 2 place occupied by squatters. [French esquatir flatten]

squatter n. person who inhabits unoccupied premises without permission.

squaw n. N. American Indian woman or wife. [Narragansett]

squawk -n. 1 loud harsh cry, esp. of a bird. 2 complaint. -v. utter a squawk. [imitative]

squeak -n. 1 short high-pitched cry or sound. 2 (also **narrow squeak**) narrow escape. -v. 1 make a squeak. 2 utter (words) shrilly. 3 (foll. by by, through) colloq. pass narrowly. 4 slang turn informer. [imitative: related to SQUEAL, SHRIEK]

squeaky adj. (-ier, -iest) making a squeaking sound. □ **squeakily** adv. **squeakiness** n.

squeaky clean adj. (usu. hyphenated when attrib.) colloq. 1 completely clean. 2 above criticism.

squeal -n. prolonged shrill sound or cry. -v. 1 make, or utter with, a squeal. 2 slang turn informer. 3 colloq. protest vociferously. [imitative]

squeamish /'skwi:mɪʃ/ adj. 1 easily nauseated or disgusted. 2 fastidious. □ **squeamishly** adv. **squeamishness** n. [Anglo-French escoymos]

squeegee /'skwi:dʒi:/ n. rubber-edged implement on a handle, for cleaning windows etc. [squeege, alteration of SQUEEZE]

squeeze -v. (-zing) 1 (often foll. by out) a exert pressure on, esp. to extract moisture etc. b extract (moisture) by squeezing. 2 reduce in size or alter in shape by squeezing. 3 force or push into or through a small or narrow space. 4 a harass or pressure (a person). b (usu. foll. by out of) obtain by extortion, entreaty, etc. 5 press (a person's hand) in sympathy etc. -n. 1 squeezing or being squeezed. 2 close embrace. 3 crowd, crowded state. 4 small quantity produced by squeezing (*squeeze of lemon*). 5 restriction on borrowing, investment, etc., in a financial crisis. □ **put the squeeze on** colloq. coerce or pressure. [origin unknown]

squeeze-box n. colloq. accordion or concertina.

squelch -v. 1 a make a sucking sound as of treading in thick mud. b move with a squelching sound. 2 disconcert, silence. -n. act or sound of squelching. □ **squelchy** adj. [imitative]

squib n. 1 small hissing firework that finally explodes. 2 satirical essay. [perhaps imitative]

squid n. (pl. same or -s) ten-armed marine cephalopod used as food. [origin unknown]

squidgy /'skwɪdʒɪ/ adj. (-ier, -iest) colloq. squashy, soggy. [imitative]

squiffy /'skwɪfɪ/ adj. (-ier, -iest) slang slightly drunk. [origin unknown]

squiggle /'skwɪg(ə)l/ n. short curly line, esp. in handwriting. □ **squiggly** adj. [imitative]

squill n. bulbous plant resembling a bluebell. [Latin squilla]

squint -v. 1 have eyes that do not move together but look in different directions. 2 (often foll. by at) look obliquely or with half-closed eyes. -n. 1 condition causing squinting. 2 stealthy or sidelong glance. 3 colloq. glance, look. 4 oblique opening in a church wall affording a view of the altar. [obsolete asquint, perhaps from Dutch schuinte slant]

squire —n. 1 country gentleman, esp. the chief landowner of a district. 2 *hist.* knight's attendant. —v. (of a man) attend or escort (a woman). [related to ESQUIRE]

squirearchy /'skwaɪərɑːrkɪ/ n. (pl. -ies) landowners collectively.

squirm —v. 1 wriggle, writhe. 2 show or feel embarrassment. —n. squirming movement. [imitative]

squirrel /'skwɪr(ə)l/ —n. 1 bushy-tailed usu. tree-living rodent. 2 its fur. 3 hoarder. —v. (-ll-; *US* -l-) 1 (often foll. by *away*) hoard. 2 (often foll. by *around*) bustle about. [Greek *skiouros*, from *skia* shade, *oura* tail]

squirt —v. 1 eject (liquid etc.) in a jet. 2 be ejected in this way. 3 splash with a squirted substance. —n. 1 a jet of water etc. b small quantity squirted. 2 syringe. 3 *colloq.* insignificant but self-assertive person. [imitative]

squish *colloq.* —n. 1 slight squelching sound. —v. move with a squish. □ **squishy** *adj.* (-ier, -iest). [imitative]

Sr *symb.* strontium.

Sr. *abbr.* 1 Senior. 2 Señor. 3 Signor.

SRN *abbr.* State Registered Nurse.

SS *abbr.* 1 steamship. 2 *hist.* Nazi special police force. 3 Saints. [sense 2 from German *Schutz-Staffel*]

SSE *abbr.* south-south-east.

SSW *abbr.* south-south-west.

St. *abbr.* Saint.

St. *abbr.* Street.

st. *abbr.* stone (in weight).

stab —v. (-bb-) 1 pierce or wound with a knife etc. 2 (often foll. by *at*) aim a blow with such a weapon. 3 cause a sensation like being stabbed (*stabbing pain*). 4 hurt or distress (a person, feelings, etc.). —n. 1 act of stabbing. 2 wound from this. 3 *colloq.* attempt. [origin unknown]

stab in the back n. treacherous attack. —v. betray.

stable /'steɪb(ə)l/ —adj. (-bler, -blest) 1 firmly fixed or established; not likely to move or change. 2 (of a person) not easily upset or disturbed. —n. 1 building for keeping horses. 2 establishment for training racehorses. 3 racehorses from one stable. 4 persons, products, etc., having a common origin or affiliation. 5 such an origin or affiliation. —v. (-ling)

put or keep in a stable. □ **stably** *adv.* [Latin *stabilis* from *sto* to stand]

stable-companion n. (also **stable-mate**) 1 horse of the same stable. 2 member of the same organization.

stabling n. accommodation for horses.

staccato /stə'kɑːtəʊ/ esp. *Mus.* —*adv.* & *adj.* with each sound or note sharply distinct. —n. (pl. **-s**) staccato passage or delivery. [Italian]

stack —n. 1 (esp. orderly) pile or heap. 2 *colloq.* large quantity (*a stack of work*; *stacks of money*). 4 a = CHIMNEY-STACK. b = SMOKESTACK. c tall factory chimney. 5 stacked group of aircraft. 6 part of a library where books are compactly stored. 7 high detached rock, esp. off the coast of Scotland. —v. 1 pile in a stack or stacks. 2 a arrange (cards) secretly for cheating. b manipulate (circumstances etc.) to suit one. 3 cause (aircraft) to fly in circles while waiting to land. [Old Norse]

stadium /'steɪdɪəm/ n. (pl. **-s**) athletic or sports ground with tiered seats for spectators. [Greek *stadion*]

staff /stɑːf/ —n. 1 a stick or pole for use in walking or as a weapon. b stick or rod as a sign of office etc. c person or thing that supports. 2 a people employed in a business etc. b those in authority in a school etc. c body of officers assisting an officer in high command (*general staff*). 3 (pl. **-s** or **staves**) *Mus.* set of usu. five parallel lines on or between which notes are placed to indicate their pitch. —v. provide (an institution etc.) with staff. [Old English]

staff college n. college where officers are trained for staff duties.

staff nurse n. nurse ranking just below a sister.

staff sergeant n. senior sergeant of a non-infantry company.

stag n. 1 adult male deer. 2 *Stock Exch. slang* person who applies for new shares, intending to sell at once for a profit. [Old English]

stag beetle n. beetle with branched mandibles like antlers.

stage —n. 1 point or period in a process or development. 2 a raised platform, esp. for performing plays etc. on. b (prec. by *the*) theatrical profession, drama. c scene of action. 3 a regular stopping-place on a route. b distance between two of these. 4 *Aeronaut.* section of a rocket with a separate engine. —v. (-ging) 1 present (a play etc.) on stage. 2 arrange, organize (*staged a demonstration*). [French *estage*, ultimately from Latin *sto* stand]

stagecoach n. hist. large closed horse-drawn coach running on a regular route by stages.

stagecraft n. theatrical skill or experience.

stage direction n. instruction in a play as to actors' movements, sound effects, etc.

stage fright n. performer's fear of an audience.

stage-hand n. person moving stage scenery etc.

stage-manage v. 1 be the stage-manager of. 2 arrange and control for effect.

stage-manager n. person responsible for lighting and mechanical arrangements etc. on stage.

stage-struck adj. obsessed with becoming an actor.

stage whisper n. 1 an aside. 2 loud whisper meant to be overheard.

stagey var. of STAGY.

stagflation /stægˈfleɪʃ(ə)n/ n. Econ. state of inflation without a corresponding increase of demand and employment. [blend of stagnation, inflation]

stagger –v. 1 (cause to) walk unsteadily. 2 shock, confuse. 3 arrange (events etc.) so that they do not coincide. 4 arrange (objects) so that they are not in line. –n. 1 tottering movement. 2 (in pl.) disease, esp. of horses and cattle, causing staggering. [Old Norse]

staggering adj. astonishing, bewildering. □ **staggeringly** adv.

staghound n. large dog used for hunting deer.

stagy /ˈsteɪdʒɪ/ adj. (also **stagey**) (-**ier**, -**iest**) theatrical, artificial, exaggerated. □ **stagily** adv. **staginess** n.

staid adj. of quiet and steady character; sedate. [= stayed, past part. of STAY]

stain –v. 1 discolour or be discoloured by the action of liquid sinking in. 2 spoil (a reputation, character, etc.). 3 colour (wood, glass, etc.) with a penetrating substance. 4 impregnate (a specimen) with a colouring agent for microscopic examination. –n. 1 discoloration;

spot, mark. 2 blot, blemish; damage to a reputation etc. 3 substance used in staining. [earlier distain from French desteindre]

stained glass n. coloured glass in a leaded window etc.

stainless adj. 1 without stains. 2 not liable to stain.

stainless steel n. chrome steel resisting rust or tarnish.

stair n. 1 each of a set of fixed indoor steps. 2 (usu. in pl.) set of these. [Old English]

staircase n. flight of stairs and the supporting structure.

stair-rod n. rod securing a carpet between two steps.

stairway n. = STAIRCASE.

stairwell n. shaft for a staircase.

stake[1] –n. 1 stout sharpened stick driven into the ground as a support, boundary mark, etc. 2 hist. a post to which a condemned person was tied to be burnt alive. b (prec. by the) such death as a punishment. –v. (**king**) 1 secure or support with a stake or stakes. 2 (foll. by off, out) mark off (an area) with stakes. 3 establish (a claim). □ **stake out** colloq. place under surveillance. [Old English]

stake[2] –n. 1 sum of money etc. wagered on an event. 2 (often foll. by in) interest or concern, esp. financial. 3 (in pl.) a prize-money, esp. in a horse-race. b such a race. –v. 1 wager. 2 US colloq. support, esp. financially. □ **at stake** risked, to be won or lost. [Old English]

stakeholder n. independent party with whom money etc. is deposited.

stake-out n. esp. US colloq. period of surveillance.

Stakhanovite /stæˈkɑːnəˌvaɪt/ n. (often attrib.) exceptionally productive worker. [Stakhanov, name of a Russian coalminer]

stalactite /ˈstælakˌtaɪt/ n. icicle-like deposit of calcium carbonate hanging from the roof of a cave etc. [Greek stalaktos dripping]

stalagmite /ˈstælagˌmaɪt/ n. icicle-like deposit of calcium carbonate rising from the floor of a cave etc. [Greek stalagma a drop]

stale –adj. 1 a not fresh. b musty, insipid, or otherwise the worse for age or use. 2 trite, unoriginal (stale joke). 3 (of an athlete or performer) impaired by excessive training. –v. (-**ling**) make or become stale. □ **staleness** n. [Anglo-French estaler halt]

stalemate –n. 1 Chess position counting as a draw, in which a player cannot move except into check. 2 deadlock. –v. (-**ting**) 1 Chess bring (a player) to a

staging /ˈsteɪdʒɪŋ/ n. 1 presentation of a play etc. 2 a platform or support, esp. temporary. b shelves for plants in a greenhouse.

staging post n. regular stopping-place, esp. on an air route.

stagnant /ˈstægnənt/ adj. 1 (of liquid) motionless, having no current. 2 dull, sluggish. □ **stagnancy** n. [Latin stagnum pool]

stagnate /stægˈneɪt/ v. (-**ting**) be or become stagnant. □ **stagnation** n.

stag-party n. colloq. all-male celebration held esp. for a man about to marry.

Stalinism stalemate. **2** bring to a deadlock. [obsol-ete *stale*: related to STALE, MATE²]

Stalinism /ˈstɑːlɪnɪz(ə)m/ *n.* central-ized authoritarian form of socialism associated with Stalin. □ **Stalinist** *n. & adj.* [*Stalin*, a Soviet statesman]

stalk¹ /stɔːk/ *n.* **1** main stem of a herb-aceous plant. **2** slender attachment or support of a leaf, flower, fruit, etc. **3** similar support for an organ etc. in an animal. [diminutive of (now dial.) *stale* rung]

stalk² /stɔːk/ –*v.* **1** pursue (game or an enemy) stealthily. **2** stride, walk in a haughty manner. **3** *formal* or *rhet.* move silently or threateningly through (a place). (*fear stalked the land*). –*n.* **1** stalking of game. **2** haughty gait. [Old English: related to STEAL]

stalking-horse *n.* **1** horse concealing a hunter. **2** pretext concealing one's real intentions or actions. **3** weak political candidate forcing an election in the hope of a more serious contender com-ing forward.

stall¹ /stɔːl/ –*n.* **1** trader's booth or table in a market etc. **2** compartment for one animal in a stable or cowhouse. **3** fixed, usu. partly enclosed, seat in the choir or chancel of a church. **4** (usu. in *pl.*) each of the seats on the ground floor of a theatre. **5 a** compartment for one person in a shower-bath etc. **b** compartment for one horse at the start of a race. **6 a** stalling of an engine or aircraft **b** con-dition resulting from this. –*v.* **1** (of a vehicle or its engine) stop because of an overload on the engine or an inadequate supply of fuel to it. **2** (of an aircraft or its pilot) lose control because the speed is too low. **3** cause to stall. [Old English]

stall² /stɔːl/ *v.* **1** play for time when being questioned etc. **2** delay, obstruct. [*stall* 'decoy': probably related to STALL¹]

stallholder *n.* person in charge of a stall at a market etc.

stallion /ˈstæljən/ *n.* uncastrated adult male horse. [French *estalon*]

stalwart /ˈstɔːlwət/ –*adj.* **1** strong, sturdy. **2** courageous, resolute, reliable. –*n.* stalwart person, esp. a loyal com-rade. [Old English, = place, WORTH]

stamen /ˈsteɪmən/ *n.* organ producing pollen in a flower. [Latin, = warp, thread]

stamina /ˈstæmɪnə/ *n.* physical or men-tal endurance. [Latin, pl. of STAMEN]

stammer –*v.* **1** speak haltingly, esp. with pauses or rapid repetitions of the same syllable. **2** (often foll. by *out*) utter (words) in this way. –*n.* **1** tendency to stammer. **2** instance of stammering. [Old English]

stamp –*v.* **1 a** bring down (one's foot) heavily, esp. on the ground. **b** (often foll. by *on*) crush or flatten in this way. **c** walk heavily. **2 a** impress (a design, mark, etc.) on a surface. **b** impress (a surface) with a pattern etc. **3** affix a postage or other stamp to. **4** assign a specific character to; mark out. –*n.* **1** instrument for stamping. **2 a** mark or design made by this. **b** impression of an official mark required to be made on deeds, bills of exchange, etc., as evid-ence of payment of tax. **3** small adhesive piece of paper indicating that payment has been made, esp. a postage stamp. **4** mark or label etc. on a commodity as evidence of quality etc. **5** act or sound of stamping the foot. **6** characteristic mark or quality. □ **stamp on 1** impress (an idea etc.) on (the memory etc.). **2** sup-press, stamp out **1** produce by cutting out with a die etc. **2** put an end to, destroy. [Old English]

stamp-collector *n.* philatelist.

stamp-duty *n.* duty imposed on certain legal documents.

stampede /stæmˈpiːd/ –*n.* **1** sudden flight or hurried movement of animals or people. **2** response of many persons at once to a common impulse. –*v.* (**-ding**) (cause to) take part in a stampede. [Spanish *estampida* crash, uproar]

stamping-ground *n.* *colloq.* favourite haunt.

stance /stɑːns, stæns/ *n.* **1** standpoint; attitude. **2** attitude or position of the body, esp. when hitting a ball etc. [It-alian *stanza* standing]

stanch /stɑːntʃ/, /ˈstɑːntʃ/ *v.* (also **staunch**) **1** restrain the flow of (esp. blood). **2** restrain the flow from (esp. a wound). [French *estanchier*]

stanchion /ˈstænʃ(ə)n/ *n.* **1** upright post or support. **2** upright bar or frame for confining cattle in a stall. [Anglo-French]

stand –*v.* (*past* and *past part.* **stood** /stʊd/) **1** have, take, or maintain an upright position, esp. on the feet or a base. **2** be situated (*here once stood a village*). **3** be of a specified height. **4** be in a specified state (*stands accused; it stands as follows*). **5** set in an upright or specified position (*stood it against the wall*). **6 a** move to and remain in a specified position (*stand aside*). **b** take a specified attitude (*stand clear*). **7** main-tain a position; avoid falling, moving, or being moved. **8** assume a stationary position; cease to move. **9** remain valid or unaltered. **10** *Naut.* hold a course. **11** endure, tolerate. **12** provide at one's own expense (*stood him a*

drink). **13** (often foll. by *for*) be a candidate (for office etc.) (*stood for Parliament*). **14** act in a specified capacity (*stood proxy*). **15** undergo (trial). —*n.* **1** cessation from progress, stoppage. **2 a** *Mil.* halt made to repel an attack. **b** resistance to attack or compulsion (esp. *make a stand*). **c** *Cricket* prolonged period at the wicket by two batsmen. **3** position taken up; attitude adopted. **4** rack, set of shelves, etc. for storage. **5** open-fronted stall or structure for a trader, exhibitor, etc. **6** standing-place for vehicles. **7 a** raised structure to sit or stand on. **b** *US* witness-box. **8** each halt made for a performance on a tour. **9** group of growing plants (*stand of trees*). □ **as it stands 1** in its present condition. **2** in the present circumstances. **stand by 1** stand nearby, look on without interfering. **2** uphold, support (a person). **3** adhere to (a promise etc.). **4** be ready for action. **stand a chance** see CHANCE. **stand corrected** accept correction. **stand down** withdraw from a position or candidacy. **stand for 1** represent, signify, imply. **2** *colloq.* endure, tolerate. **stand one's ground** not yield. **stand in** (usu. foll. by *for*) deputize. **stand off 1** move or keep away. **2** temporarily dismiss (an employee). **stand on** insist on, observe scrupulously. **stand on one's own feet** (or **own two feet**) be self-reliant or independent. **stand out 1** be prominent or outstanding. **2** (usu. foll. by *against, for*) persist in opposition or support. **stand to 1** *Mil.* stand ready for an attack. **2** abide by. **3** be likely or certain to. **stand to reason** be obvious. **stand up 1 a** rise to one's feet. **b** come to, remain in, or place in a standing position. **2** (of an argument etc.) be valid. **3** *colloq.* fail to keep an appointment with. **stand up for** support, side with. **stand up to 1** face (an opponent) courageously. **2** be resistant to (wear, use, etc.). **take one's stand on** base one's argument etc. on, rely on. [Old English]

standard /'stændəd/ —*n.* **1** object, quality, or measure serving as a basis, example, or principle to which others conform or should conform or by which others are judged. **2 a** level of excellence etc. required or specified (*not up to standard*). **b** average quality (*of a low standard*). **3** ordinary procedure etc. **4** distinctive flag. **5 a** upright support. **b** upright pipe. **6 a** tree or shrub that stands without support. **b** shrub grafted on an upright stem and trained in tree form. **7** tune or song of established popularity. —*adj.* **1** serving or used as a standard. **2** of a normal or prescribed quality, type, or size. **3** of recognized and permanent value; authoritative (*standard book on jazz*). **4** (of language) conforming to established educated usage. [Anglo-French: related to EXTEND, and in senses 5 and 6 of *n.* influenced by STAND]

standard assessment task *n.* standard test given to schoolchildren.
standard-bearer *n.* **1** soldier who carries a standard. **2** prominent leader in a cause.
standardize *v.* (also **-ise**) (**-zing** or **-sing**) cause to conform to a standard. □ **standardization** /-zeɪʃ(ə)n/ *n.*
standard lamp *n.* lamp on a tall upright with a base.
standard of living *n.* degree of material comfort of a person or group.
standard time *n.* uniform time for places in approximately the same longitude, established in a country or region by law or custom.
stand-by *n.* (*pl.* **-bys**) **1** (often *attrib.*) person or thing ready if needed in an emergency etc. **2** readiness for duty (*on stand-by*).
stand-in *n.* deputy or substitute.
standing —*n.* **1** esteem or repute, esp. high; status. **2** duration (*of long standing*). —*adj.* **1** that stands, upright. **2** established, permanent (*a standing rule, a standing army*). **3** (of a jump, start, etc.) performed with no run-up. **4** (of water) stagnant.
standing committee *n.* committee that is permanent during the existence of the appointing body.
standing joke *n.* object of permanent ridicule.
standing order *n.* instruction to a banker to make regular payments, or to a retailer for a regular supply of goods. **standing orders** *n.pl.* rules governing procedure in a parliament, council, etc.
standing ovation *n.* prolonged applause from an audience which has risen to its feet.
standing-room *n.* space to stand in.
stand-off *n.* *Rugby* half-back forming a link between the scrum-half and the three-quarters.
standoffish /stænd'ɒfɪʃ/ *adj.* cold or distant in manner.
standpipe *n.* vertical pipe extending from a water supply, esp. one connecting a temporary tap to the mains.
standpoint *n.* point of view.
standstill *n.* stoppage; inability to proceed.
stand-up *attrib. adj.* **1** (of a meal) eaten standing. **2** (of a fight) violent and thorough. **3** (of a collar) not turned down. **4**

(of a comedian) telling jokes to an audience.

stank *past of* STINK.

stanza /'stænzə/ *n.* basic metrical unit of a poem, typically of four to twelve rhymed lines. [Italian]

staphylococcus /ˌstæfɪlə'kɒkəs/ *n.* (*pl.* **-cocci** /-kaɪ/) bacterium sometimes forming pus. □ **staphylococcal** *adj.* [Greek *staphulē* bunch of grapes, *kokkos* berry]

staple[1] /'steɪp(ə)l/ —*n.* U-shaped metal bar or piece of wire with pointed ends for driving into and holding papers together, or holding an electrical wire in place, etc. —*v.* (**-ling**) fasten or provide with a staple. □ **stapler** *n.* [Old English]

staple[2] /'steɪp(ə)l/ —*n.* 1 principal or important article of commerce (*staples of British industry*). 2 chief element or main component. 3 fibre of cotton or wool etc. with regard to its quality (*cotton of fine staple*). —*attrib. adj.* 1 main or principal (*staple diet*). 2 important as a product or export. [French *estaple* market]

star /stɑː(r)/ —*n.* 1 celestial body appearing as a luminous point in the night sky. 2 large naturally luminous gaseous body such as the sun. 3 celestial body regarded as influencing fortunes etc. 4 thing like a star in shape or appearance. 5 decoration or mark of rank or excellence etc., usu. with radiating points. 6 a famous or brilliant person; principal performer (*star of the show*). b (*attrib.*) outstanding or present as principal performer(s). 2 (esp. as **starred** *adj.*) mark, set, or adorn with a star or stars. □ **stardom** *n.* [Old English]

starboard /'stɑːbəd, -bɔːd/ —*n.* right-hand side of a ship or aircraft looking forward. —*v.* (also *absol.*) turn (the helm) to starboard. [Old English, = *steer board*]

starch —*n.* 1 polysaccharide obtained chiefly from cereals and potatoes. 2 preparation of this for stiffening fabric. 3 stiffness of manner; formality. —*v.* stiffen (clothing) with starch. [Old English: related to STARK]

starchy *adj.* (**-ier, -iest**) 1 of, like, or containing starch. 2 prim, formal. □ **starchily** *adv.* **starchiness** *n.*

stardust *n.* 1 multitude of stars looking like dust. 2 romance, magic feeling.

stare /steə(r)/ —*v.* (**-ring**) 1 (usu. foll. by *at*) look fixedly, esp. in curiosity, surprise, horror, etc. 2 reduce (a person) to a specified condition by staring (*stared me into silence*). —*n.* staring gaze. □ **stare a person in the face** be evident or imminent. **stare a person out** stare at a

person until he or she looks away. [Old English]

starfish *n.* (*pl.* same or **-es**) echinoderm with five or more radiating arms.

star-gazer *n.* *colloq.* usu. *derog.* or *joc.* astronomer or astrologer.

stark —*adj.* 1 sharply evident (*in stark contrast*). 2 desolate, bare. 3 absolute (*stark madness*). —*adv.* completely, wholly (*stark naked*). □ **starkly** *adv.* **starkness** *n.* [Old English]

starkers /'stɑːkəz/ *predic. adj. slang* stark naked.

starlet /'stɑːlɪt/ *n.* promising young performer, esp. a film actress.

starlight *n.* light of the stars.

starling /'stɑːlɪŋ/ *n.* gregarious bird with blackish speckled lustrous plumage. [Old English]

starlit *adj.* 1 lit by stars. 2 with stars visible.

Star of David *n.* two interlaced equilateral triangles used as a Jewish and Israeli symbol.

starry *adj.* (**-ier, -iest**) 1 full of stars. 2 like a star.

starry-eyed *adj. colloq.* 1 enthusiastic but impractical. 2 euphoric.

Stars and Stripes *n.pl.* national flag of the US.

star-studded *adj.* covered with stars; featuring many famous performers.

START /stɑːt/ *abbr.* Strategic Arms Reduction Treaty (or /'ɑːks/.).

start —*v.* 1 begin. 2 set in motion or action (*started a fire*). 3 set oneself in motion or action. 4 begin a journey etc. 5 (often foll. by *up*) (cause to) begin operating. 6 a cause or enable (a person) to make a beginning (*started me in business*). b (foll. by *pres. part.*) cause (a person) to begin (*started me coughing*). 7 (often foll. by *up*) establish. 8 give a signal to (competitors) to start in a race. 9 (often foll. by *up, from,* etc.) jump in surprise, pain, etc. 10 spring out, up, etc. 11 conceive (a baby). 12 rouse (game etc.). 13 a (of timbers etc.) spring out. b cause (timbers etc.) to do this. —*n.* 1 beginning. 2 place from which a race etc. begins. 3 advantage given at the beginning of a race etc. 4 advantageous initial position in life, business, etc. 5 sudden movement of surprise, pain, etc. □ **for a start** *colloq.* as a beginning. **start off** begin; begin to move. **start out** begin a journey. **start up** arise; occur. [Old English]

starter *n.* 1 device for starting a vehicle engine etc. 2 first course of a meal. 3 person giving the signal for the start of a race. 4 horse or competitor starting in a race. □ **for starters** *colloq.* to start with.

starting-block n. shaped block for a runner's feet at the start of a race.

starting price n. odds ruling at the start of a horse-race.

startle /staːt(ə)l/ v. (-ling) shock or surprise. [Old English]

star turn n. main item in an entertainment etc.

starve v. (-ving) 1 (cause to) die of hunger or suffer from malnutrition. 2 colloq. feel very hungry (I'm starving). 3 a suffer from mental or spiritual want. b (foll. by for) feel a strong craving for. 4 (foll. by of) deprive of. 5 compel by starving (starved into surrender). □ **starvation** /-ˈveɪʃ(ə)n/ n. [Old English, = die]

starveling /ˈstaːvlɪŋ/ n. archaic starving person or animal.

Star Wars n.pl. colloq. strategic defence initiative.

stash colloq. —v. (often foll. by away) 1 conceal; put in a safe place. 2 hoard. —n. 1 hiding-place. 2 thing hidden. [origin unknown]

stasis /ˈsteɪsɪs/ n. (pl. **stases** /-siːz/) 1 inactivity; stagnation. 2 stoppage of circulation. [Greek]

state —n. 1 existing condition or position of a person or thing. 2 colloq. a excited or agitated mental condition (esp. in a state). b untidy condition. 3 (usu. **State**) a political community under one government. b this as part of a federal republic. 4 (usu. **State**) (attrib.) a of, for, or concerned with the State. b reserved or done on occasions of ceremony. 5 (usu. **State**) civil government. 6 pomp. 7 (**the States**) USA. —v. (-ting) 1 express in speech or writing. 2 fix, specify. 3 Mus. play (a theme etc.), esp. for the first time. □ **in state** with all due ceremony. **lie in state** be laid in a public place of honour before burial. [partly from ESTATE, partly from Latin STATUS]

stateless adj. having no nationality or citizenship.

stately adj. (-ier, -iest) dignified; imposing. □ **stateliness** n.

stately home n. large historic house, esp. one open to the public.

statement n. 1 stating or being stated; expression in words. 2 thing stated. 3 formal account of transactions in a bank account etc. 4 record of transactions in a bank account etc. 5 notification of the amount due to a tradesman etc.

state of emergency n. condition of danger or disaster in a country, with normal constitutional procedures suspended.

state of the art —n. current stage of esp. technological development. —attrib. adj. (usu. **state-of-the-art**) absolutely up-to-date (state-of-the-art weaponry).

stateroom n. 1 state apartment. 2 large private cabin in a passenger ship.

State school n. school largely managed and funded by the public authorities.

statesman n. (fem. **stateswoman**) distinguished and capable politician or diplomat. □ **statesmanlike** adj. **statesmanship** n.

static electricity n. electricity not flowing as a current.

static /ˈstætɪk/ —adj. 1 stationary; not acting or changing. 2 Physics concerned with bodies at rest or of forces in equilibrium. 2 = STATIC. —n. 1 static electricity. 2 atmospherics. □ **statically** adv. [Greek statikos from sta- stand]

statics n.pl. (usu. treated as sing.) 1 science of bodies at rest or of forces in equilibrium. 2 = STATIC.

station /ˈsteɪʃ(ə)n/ —n. 1 a regular stopping-place on a railway line. b buildings of this. c (in comb.) centre where vehicles of a specified type depart and arrive (coach station). 2 person or thing's allotted place or building etc. 3 centre for a particular service or activity. 4 establishment involved in broadcasting. 5 a military or naval base. b inhabitants of this. 6 position in life; rank, status. 7 Austral. & NZ large sheep or cattle farm. —v. 1 assign a station to. 2 put in position. [Latin statio from sto stat- stand]

stationary adj. 1 not moving. 2 not meant to be moved. 3 unchanging. [Latin: related to STATION]

stationer n. dealer in stationery.

stationery n. writing-materials, office supplies, etc.

stationmaster n. official in charge of a railway station.

Stationery Office n. the Government's publishing house.

station of the cross n. RC Ch. each of a series of images representing the events in Christ's Passion before which prayers are said.

station-wagon n. esp. US estate car.

statistic /stəˈtɪstɪk/ n. statistical fact or item. [German: related to STATE]

statistical adj. of statistics. □ **statistically** adv.

statistics n.pl. 1 (usu. treated as sing.) science of collecting and analysing significant numerical data. 2 such analysed data. □ **statistician** /ˌstætɪˈstɪʃ(ə)n/ n.

statuary /ˈstætʃʊərɪ/ —adj. of or for statues (statuary art). —n. (pl. -ies) 1 statues collectively. 2 making statues. 3 sculptor. [Latin: related to STATUE]

statue /ˈstætʃuː/ n. sculptured figure of a person or animal, esp. life-size or larger. [Latin *statua*]

statuesque /stætʃʊˈesk/ adj. like, or having the dignity or beauty of, a statue.

statuette /stætʃʊˈet/ n. small statue.

stature /ˈstætʃə(r)/ n. 1 height of a (esp. human) body. 2 calibre, esp. moral; eminence. [Latin *statura*]

status /ˈsteɪtəs/ n. 1 rank, social position, relative importance. 2 superior social etc. position. [Latin: related to STATURE]

status quo /ˌsteɪtəs ˈkwəʊ/ n. existing state of affairs. [Latin]

status symbol n. a possession etc. intended to indicate the owner's superiority.

statute /ˈstætʃuːt/ n. 1 written law passed by a legislative body. 2 rule of a corporation, founder, etc. intended to be permanent. [Latin *statuum* from *statuo* set up]

statute-book n. 1 book(s) containing the statute law. 2 body of a country's statutes.

statute law n. 1 (collect.) body of principles and rules of law laid down in statutes. 2 a statute.

statute mile see MILE 1.

statutory /ˈstætjʊtərɪ/ adj. required or enacted by statute. □ **statutorily** adv.

staunch /stɔːntʃ/ adj. 1 loyal. 2 (of a ship, joint, etc.) strong, watertight, airtight, etc. □ **staunchly** adv.

staunch² var. of STANCH.

stave – n. 1 each of the curved slats forming the sides of a cask, pail, etc. 2 = STAFF n. 3. 3 stanza or verse. – v. (-ving; past and past part. **stove** or **staved**) (usu. foll. by in) break a hole in, damage, crush by forcing inwards. □ **stave off** (past and past part. **staved**) avert or defer (danger etc.). [from STAFF]

stay¹ – v. 1 continue in the same place or condition; not depart or change. 2 (often foll. by at, in, with) reside temporarily. 3 (esp. in imper.) pause. 4 postpone (judgement etc.). 5 assuage (hunger etc.), esp. temporarily. – n. 1 act or period of staying. 2 suspension or postponement of a sentence, judgement, etc. 3 prop, support. 4 (in pl.) hist. (esp. boned) corset. □ **stay the course** endure to the end. **stay in** remain indoors. **stay the night** remain overnight. **stay put** colloq. remain where it is placed or where one is. **stay up** not go to bed (until late). [Anglo-French from Latin *sto* stand: sense 3 of n. from French, formed as STAY²]

stay² n. 1 Naut. rope or guy supporting a mast, flagstaff, etc. 2 supporting cable

on an aircraft etc. [Old English from Germanic]

stay-at-home adj. rarely going out. – n. such a person.

stayer n. person or animal with great endurance.

staying power n. endurance.

staysail /ˈsteɪseɪl, -s(ə)l/ n. sail extended on a stay.

STD abbr. subscriber trunk dialling.

stead /sted/ n. □ **in a person's (or thing's) stead** in a substitute; in a person's (or thing's) place. **stand a person in good stead** be advantageous or useful to him or her. [Old English, = place]

steadfast /ˈstedfɑːst/ adj. constant, firm, unwavering. □ **steadfastly** adv. **steadfastness** n. [Old English: related to STEAD]

steady /ˈstedɪ/ – adj. (-ier, -iest) 1 firmly fixed or supported; unwavering. 2 uniform and regular (steady pace, steady increase). 3 a constant. b persistent. 4 (of a person) serious and dependable. 5 regular, established (steady girlfriend). – v. (-ies, -ied) make or become steady. – adv. steadily. – n. (pl. -ies) colloq. regular boyfriend or girlfriend. □ **go steady** (often foll. by with) colloq. have as a regular boyfriend or girlfriend. **steady on!** be careful! □ **steadily** adv. **steadiness** n. [from STEAD]

steady state n. unvarying condition, esp. in a physical process.

steak /steɪk/ n. 1 thick slice of meat (esp. beef) or fish, usu. grilled or fried. 2 beef cut for stewing or braising. [Old Norse]

steak-house n. restaurant specializing in beefsteaks.

steal – v. (past **stole**; past part. **stolen**) 1 (also absol.) take (another's property) illegally or without right or permission, esp. in secret. 2 obtain surreptitiously, insidiously, or artfully (stole a kiss). 3 (foll. by in, out, away, up, etc.) move, silently or stealthily. – n. 1 US colloq. easy task or good bargain. 2 colloq. act of stealing or theft. □ **steal a march on** get an advantage over by surreptitious means. **steal the show** outshine other performers, esp. unexpectedly. **steal a person's thunder** take away the attention due to someone else by using his or her words, ideas, etc. [Old English]

stealth /stelθ/ n. secrecy, secret behaviour. [Old English: related to STEAL]

stealthy /ˈstelθɪ/ adj. (-ier, -iest) done or moving with stealth; furtive. □ **stealthily** adv. **stealthiness** n.

steam – n. 1 a gas into which water is changed by boiling. b condensed vapour formed from this. 2 a power obtained

from steam. □ **~v. 1 a** cook (food) in steam. **b** treat with steam. **2** give off steam. **3 a** move under steam power. **b** (foll. by *ahead, away,* etc.) *colloq.* proceed or travel fast or with vigour. **4** (usu. foll. by *up*) **a** cover or become covered with condensed steam. **b** (as **steamed up** *adj.*) *colloq.* angry or excited. [Old English]

steamboat *n.* steam-driven boat.

steam engine *n.* **1** engine which uses steam to generate power. **2** locomotive powered by this.

steamer *n.* **1** steamship. **2** vessel for steaming food in.

steam hammer *n.* forging-hammer powered by steam.

steam iron *n.* electric iron that emits steam.

steamroller *—n.* **1** heavy slow-moving vehicle with a roller, used to flatten new-made roads. **2** a crushing power or force. *—v.* crush or move forcibly or indiscriminately; force.

steamship *n.* steam-driven ship.

steam train *n.* train pulled by a steam engine.

steamy *adj.* (**-ier, -iest**) **1** like or full of steam. **2** *colloq.* erotic. □ **steamily** *adv.* **steaminess** *n.*

steatite /ˈstɪətaɪt/ *n.* impure form of talc, esp. soapstone. [Greek *stear steat-* tallow]

steed *n. archaic* or *poet.* horse. [Old English]

steel *—n.* **1** strong malleable alloy of iron and carbon, used esp. for making tools, weapons, etc. **2** strength, firmness (*nerves of steel*). **3** steel rod for sharpening knives. *—adj.* of or like steel. *—v.* (also *refl.*) harden or make resolute. [Old English]

steel band *n.* band playing chiefly calypso-style music on percussion instruments made from oil drums.

steel wool *n.* abrasive substance consisting of a mass of fine steel shavings.

steelworks *n.pl.* (usu. treated as *sing.*) factory producing steel. □ **steelworker** *n.*

steely *adj.* (**-ier, -iest**) **1** of or like steel. **2** severe; resolute. □ **steeliness** *n.*

steelyard *n.* balance with a graduated arm along which a weight is moved.

steep¹ *—adj.* **1** sloping sharply. **2** (of a rise or fall) rapid. **3** (*predic.*) *colloq.* **a** exorbitant; unreasonable. **b** exaggerated; incredible. *—n.* steep slope; precipice. □ **steepen** *v.* **steepish** *adj.* **steeply** *adv.* **steepness** *n.* [Old English]

steep² *—v.* soak or bathe in liquid. *—n.* **1** act of steeping. **2** liquid for steeping. **steep in 1** pervade or imbue with. **2**

make deeply acquainted with (a subject etc.). [Old English]

steeple /ˈstiːp(ə)l/ *n.* tall tower, esp. with a spire, above the roof of a church. [Old English: related to STEEP¹]

steeplechase *n.* **1** horse-race with ditches, hedges, etc., to jump. **2** cross-country foot-race. □ **steeplechasing** *n.*

steeplejack *n.* repairer of tall chimneys, steeples, etc.

steer¹ *v.* **1** (also *absol.*) guide (a vehicle, ship, etc.) with a wheel or rudder etc. **2** direct or guide (one's course, other people, a conversation, etc.) in a specified direction. □ **steer clear of** avoid. □ **steering** *n.* [Old English]

steer² *n.* = BULLOCK. [Old English]

steerage *n.* **1** act of steering. **2** *archaic* cheapest part of a ship's accommodation.

steering-column *n.* column on which a steering-wheel is mounted.

steering committee *n.* committee deciding the order of business, the course of operations, etc.

steering-wheel *n.* wheel by which a vehicle etc. is steered.

steersman *n.* person who steers a ship.

stegosaurus /ˌstegəˈsɔːrəs/ *n.* (*pl.* **-ruses**) plant-eating dinosaur with a double row of bony plates along the spine. [Greek *stegē* covering, *sauros* lizard]

stela /ˈstiːlə/ *n.* (*pl.* **stelae** /-liː/) (also **stele** /stiːl, ˈstiːli/) *Archaeol.* upright slab or pillar usu. as a gravestone. [Latin and Greek]

stellar /ˈstelə(r)/ *adj.* of a star or stars. [Latin *stella* star]

stem¹ *—n.* **1** main body or stalk of a plant. **2** stalk of a fruit, flower, or leaf. **3** stem-shaped part, as: **a** the slender part of a wineglass. **b** the tube of a tobacco-pipe. **c** a vertical stroke in a letter or musical note. **4** *Gram.* root or main part of a noun, verb, etc. to which inflections are added. **5** main upright timber at the bow of a ship (*from stem to stern*). *—v.* (**-mm-**) (foll. by *from*) spring or originate from. [Old English]

stem² *v.* (**-mm-**) check or stop. [Old Norse]

stench *n.* foul smell. [Old English: related to STINK]

stencil /ˈstensɪl/ *—n.* **1** (in full **stencil-plate**) thin sheet in which a pattern is cut, placed on a surface and printed or inked over etc. to reproduce the pattern. **2** pattern so produced. **3** waxed sheet etc. from which a stencil is made by a typewriter. *—v.* (**-ll-**; *US* **-l-**) **1** (often foll. by *on*) produce (a pattern) with a stencil. **2** mark (a surface) in this way. [French

estanceler sparkle, from Latin *scintilla* spark]

Sten gun *n.* [S and *T* (initials of its inventors' surnames) + *-en* after BREN]

stenographer /stɪˈnɒɡrəfə(r)/ *n.* esp. *US* shorthand typist. [Greek *stenos* narrow]

stentorian /stenˈtɔːrɪən/ *adj.* loud and powerful. [*Stentor*, name of a herald in Homer's *Iliad*]

step —*n.* **1 a** complete movement of one leg in walking or running. **b** distance so covered. **2** unit of movement in dancing. **3** measure taken, esp. one of several in a course of action. **4** surface of a stair, stepladder, etc.; tread. **5** short distance. **6** sound or mark made by a foot in walking or mark made by a foot in walking etc. **7** manner of walking etc. **8** degree in the scale of promotion or precedence etc. **9 a** stepping in unison or to music (esp. *in* or *out of step*). **b** state of conforming (*refuses to keep step with the team*). **10** (in *pl.*) (also *pair of steps*) = STEPLADDER. —*v.* (**-pp-**) **1** lift and set down one's foot or alternate feet in walking. **2** come or go in a specified direction by stepping. **3** make progress in a specified way (*stepped into a new job*). **4** (foll. by *off, out*) measure (distance) by stepping. **5** perform (a dance). □ **mind** (or **watch**) **one's step** be careful. **step by step** gradually; cautiously. **step down 1** resign. **step in 1** enter. **2** intervene, help, esp. *colloq.* accelerate; hurry up. **step out 1** be active socially. **2** take large steps. **step out of line** behave inappropriately or disobediently. **step up** increase, intensify. [Old English]

step- *comb. form* denoting a relationship resulting from a parent's later marriage. [Old English, = orphaned]

stepbrother *n.* son of one's step-parent by a previous partner.

stepchild *n.* one's husband's or wife's child by a previous partner.

stepdaughter *n.* female stepchild.

stepfather *n.* male step-parent.

stephanotis /stefəˈnəʊtɪs/ *n.* fragrant tropical climbing plant. [Greek]

stepladder *n.* short folding ladder with flat steps.

stepmother *n.* female step-parent.

step-parent *n.* mother's or father's spouse who is not one's own parent.

steppe *n.* level grassy unforested plain. [Russian]

stepping-stone *n.* **1** large stone in a stream etc. helping one to cross. **2** means of progress.

stepsister *n.* daughter of one's step-parent by a previous partner.

stepson *n.* male stepchild.

-ster *suffix* denoting a person engaged in or associated with a particular activity or quality (*brewster, gangster, young-ster*). [Old English]

stereo /ˈsterɪəʊ, ˈstɪə-/ —*n.* (*pl.* -s) **1 a** stereophonic record-player etc. **b** ste-reophonic sound reproduction (see STE-REOPHONIC). **2** = STEREOSCOPE. —*adj.* **1** = STEREOPHONIC. **2** = STEREOSCOPIC (see STEREOSCOPE). [abbreviation]

stereo- *comb. form* solid; having three dimensions. [Greek *stereos* solid]

stereophonic /ˌsterɪəˈfɒnɪk, ˌstɪə-/ *adj.* using two or more channels, giving the effect of naturally distributed sound.

stereoscope /ˈsterɪəskəʊp, ˈstɪə-/ *n.* de-vice for producing a three-dimensional effect by viewing two slightly different photographs together. □ **stereoscopic** /-ˈskɒpɪk/ *adj.*

stereotype /ˈsterɪətaɪp, ˈstɪə-/ —*n.* **1 a** person or thing seeming to conform to a widely accepted type. **b** such a type, idea, or attitude. **2** printing-plate cast from a mould of composed type. —*v.* (**-ping**) **1** (esp. as **stereotyped** *adj.*) cause to conform to a type; standardize. **2 a** print from a stereotype. **b** make a stereotype of. [French: related to STEREO-]

sterile /ˈsteraɪl/ *adj.* **1** unable to produce a crop, fruit, or young; barren. **2** unpro-ductive (*sterile discussion*). **3** free from living micro-organisms etc. □ **sterility** /stəˈrɪlɪtɪ/ *n.* [Latin]

sterilize /ˈsterɪlaɪz/ *v.* (also **-ise**) (**-zing**, **-sing**) **1** make sterile. **2** deprive of reproductive powers. □ **sterilization** /-ˈzeɪʃ(ə)n/ *n.*

sterling silver *n.* sterling of 92½/₂%

sterling *adj.* (of money) **1** of or in British money (*pound sterling*). **2** (of a coin or precious metal) genuine; of standard value or purity. **3** (of a person etc.) genuine, reliable. —*n.* British money. [Old English, = penny]

stern[1] *adj.* severe, grim, authoritarian. □ **sternly** *adv.* **sternness** *n.* [Old Eng-lish]

stern[2] *n.* rear part, esp. of a ship or boat. [Old Norse: related to STEER[1]]

sternum /ˈstɜːnəm/ *n.* (*pl.* -na or -nums) breastbone. [Greek *sternon* chest]

steroid /ˈstɪərɔɪd, ˈste-/ *n.* any of a group of organic compounds including many hormones, alkaloids, and vitamins. [from STEROL]

sterol /ˈsterɒl/ *n.* naturally occurring steroid alcohol. [from CHOLESTEROL, etc.]

stertorous /ˈstɜːtərəs/ *adj.* (of breathing etc.) laboured and noisy. [Latin *sterto* snore]

stet *v.* (-tt-) (usu. written on a proof-sheet etc.) ignore or cancel (the alteration); let the original stand. [Latin, = let it stand]

stethoscope /ˈsteθəskəʊp/ *n.* instrument used in listening to the heart, lungs, etc. [Greek *stēthos* breast]

stetson /ˈstets(ə)n/ *n.* slouch hat with a very wide brim and high crown. [*Stetson*, name of a hat-maker]

stevedore /ˈstiːvədɔː(r)/ *n.* person employed in loading and unloading ships. [Spanish *estivador*]

stew —*v.* 1 cook by long simmering in a closed vessel. 2 fret, be anxious. 3 *colloq.* swelter. 4 (of tea etc.) become bitter or strong from infusing too long. 5 (as **stewed** *adj.*) *colloq.* drunk. —*n.* 1 dish of stewed meat etc. 2 *colloq.* agitated or angry state. □ **stew in one's own juice** suffer the consequences of one's actions. [French *estuver*]

steward /ˈstjuːəd/ —*n.* 1 passengers' attendant on a ship, aircraft, or train. 2 official supervising a meeting, show, etc. 3 person responsible for supplies of food etc. for a college or club etc. 4 property manager. —*v.* act as a steward (of). [Old English]

stewardess /ˌstjuːəˈdɪs, ˈstjuːədɪs/ *n.* female steward, esp. on a ship or aircraft.

stick¹ *n.* 1 a short slender length of wood. b this as a support or weapon. 2 thin rod of wood etc. for a particular purpose (*cocktail stick*). 3 implement used to propel the ball in hockey or polo etc. 4 gear lever. 5 conductor's baton. 6 sticklike piece of celery, dynamite, etc. 7 (often prec. by *the*) punishment, esp. by beating. 8 *colloq.* adverse criticism. 9 *colloq.* piece of wood as part of a house or furniture. 10 *colloq.* person, esp. when dull or unsociable. [Old English]

stick² *v.* (*past* and *past part.* **stuck**) 1 (foll. by *in, into, through*) insert or thrust (a thing or its point). 2 stab. 3 (foll. by *in, into, on,* etc.) a fix or be fixed on a pointed thing. b fix or be fixed (as) by a pointed end. 4 fix or be fixed (as) by adhesive etc. 5 remain (in the mind). 6 lose or be deprived of movement or action through adhesion, jamming, etc. 7 *colloq.* a put in a specified position or place. b remain in a place. 8 *colloq.* (of an accusation etc.) be convincing or regarded as valid. 9 *colloq.* endure, tolerate. 10 (foll. by *at*) *colloq.* persevere with. □ **be stuck for** be at a loss for or in need of. **be stuck on** *colloq.* be infatu-

ated with. **be stuck with** *colloq.* be unable to get rid of. **get stuck in** (or **into** a thing) *slang* begin in earnest. **stick around** *colloq.* linger; remain. **stick at nothing** be absolutely ruthless. **stick by** (or **with**) stay loyal or close to. **stick in one's throat** be against one's principles. **stick it out** *colloq.* endure a burden etc. to the end. **stick one's neck out** be rashly bold. **stick out** (cause to) protrude. **stick out for** persist in demanding. **stick to 1** remain fixed on or to. 2 remain loyal to. 3 keep to (a subject etc.). **stick together** *colloq.* remain united or mutually loyal. **stick up 1** be or make erect or protruding upwards. 2 fasten to an upright surface. 3 *colloq.* rob or threaten with a gun. **stick up for** support or defend. [Old English]

sticker *n.* 1 adhesive label. 2 persistent person.

sticking-plaster *n.* adhesive plaster for wounds etc.

stick insect *n.* insect with a twiglike body.

stick-in-the-mud *n.* *colloq.* unprogressive or old-fashioned person.

stickleback /ˈstɪk(ə)lbæk/ *n.* small spiny-backed fish. [Old English. = thorn-back]

stickler *n.* (foll. by *for*) person who insists on something (*stickler for accuracy*). [obsolete *stickle* be umpire]

stick-up *n.* *colloq.* robbery using a gun.

sticky *adj.* (**-ier, -iest**) 1 tending or intended to stick or adhere. 2 glutinous, viscous. 3 humid. 4 *colloq.* difficult, awkward; unpleasant, painful (*sticky problem*). □ **stickily** *adv.* **stickiness** *n.* **sticky wicket** *n.* *colloq.* difficult circumstances.

stiff —*adj.* 1 rigid; inflexible. 2 hard to bend, move, or turn etc. 3 hard to cope with; needing strength or effort (*stiff climb*). 4 severe or strong (*stiff penalty*). 5 formal, constrained. 6 (of a muscle, person, etc.) aching owing to exertion, injury, etc. 7 (of esp. an alcoholic drink) strong. 8 (foll. by *with*) *colloq.* abounding in. —*adv.* *colloq.* utterly, extremely (*bored stiff; worried stiff*). —*n.* *slang* 1 corpse. 2 foolish or useless person. □ **stiffish** *adj.* **stiffly** *adv.* **stiffness** *n.* [Old English]

stiffen *v.* make or become stiff. □ **stiffening** *n.*

stiff-necked *adj.* obstinate; haughty.

stiff upper lip *n.* appearance of being calm in adversity.

stifle /ˈstaɪf(ə)l/ *v.* (**-ling**) 1 suppress. 2 feel or make unable to breathe easily; suffocate. □ **stiflingly** *adv.* & *adj.* [origin uncertain]

sense 3. **-mata** /-mata/. 'mɑːtə/) **1** shame, disgrace. **2** part of the pistil that receives the pollen in pollination. **3** (in *pl.*) marks like those on Christ's body after the Crucifixion, appearing on the bodies of certain saints etc. [Greek *stigma -mat-* brand, dot]

stigmatize /'stigmə.taiz/ *v.* (also **-ise**) (**-zing** or **-sing**) (often foll. by *as*) brand as unworthy or disgraceful. [Greek *stigmatizō*, related to STIGMA]

stile *n.* steps allowing people but not animals to climb over a fence or wall. [Old English]

stiletto /sti'letəu/ *n.* (*pl.* **-s**) **1** short dagger. **2** (in full **stiletto heel**) **a** long tapering heel of a shoe. **b** shoe with such a heel. **3** pointed instrument for making eyelets etc. [Italian diminutive: related to STILE]

still¹ -*adj.* **1** not or hardly moving. **2** with little or no sound; calm and tranquil. **3** (of a drink) not effervescing. -*n.* **1** photograph (as opposed to a motion picture), esp. a single shot from a cinema film. -*adv.* **1** without moving (*sit still*). **2** even now or at a particular time (*is he still here?*). **3** nevertheless. **4** (with greater emphasis etc.) even, yet, increasingly (*still greater efforts*). -*v.* make or become still; quieten. [Old English]

still² *n.* apparatus for distilling spirits etc. [obsolete *still* (v.) = DISTIL]

still-room *n.* **1** room for distilling. **2** housekeeper's storeroom or pantry.

stilt *n.* **1** either of a pair of poles with foot supports for walking at a distance above the ground. **2** each of a set of piles or posts supporting a building etc. [Low German or Dutch]

stilted *adj.* **1** (of literary style etc.) stiff and unnatural; bombastic. **2** standing on stilts.

Stilton /'stilt(ə)n/ *n. propr.* strong rich esp. blue-veined cheese. [*Stilton* in England]

stimulant /'stimjulənt/ -*adj.* stimulating, esp. bodily or mental activity. -*n.* stimulant substance or influence. [Latin: related to STIMULATE]

stimulate /'stimjuleit/ *v.* (**-ting**) **1** act as a stimulus to. **2** animate, excite, arouse. [Latin: □ **stimulation** /-'leiʃ(ə)n/ *n.* **stimulative** /-lətiv/ *adj.* **stimulator** *n.* [Latin: related to STIMULUS]

stimulus /'stimjuləs/ *n.* (*pl.* **-li** /-lai/) thing that rouses to activity. [Latin, = goad]

sting -*n.* **1** sharp wounding organ of an insect, snake, nettle, etc. **2 a** act of inflicting a wound with this. **b** the wound itself or the pain caused by it. **3** painful quality or effect. **4** pungency, vigour. **5** *slang* swindle. -*v.* (*past and past part.* **stung**) **1 a** wound or pierce with a sting. **b** be able to sting. **2** feel or give a tingling physical or sharp mental pain. **3** (foll. by *into*) incite, esp. painfully (*stung into replying*). **4** *slang* swindle, charge exorbitantly. □ **sting in the tail** unexpected final pain or difficulty. [Old English]

stinger *n.* stinging animal or thing, esp. a sharp blow.

stinging-nettle *n.* nettle with stinging hairs.

stingray *n.* broad flat fish with a poisonous spine at the base of its tail.

stingy /'stindʒi/ *adj.* (**-ier, -iest**) *colloq.* niggardly, mean. □ **stingily** *adv.* **stinginess** *n.*

stink -*v.* (*past* **stank** or **stunk**; *past part.* **stunk**) **1** emit a strong offensive smell. **2** (often foll. by *out*) fill (a place) with a stink. **3** (foll. by *out* etc.) drive (a person) out etc. by a stink. **4** *colloq.* be or seem very unpleasant. -*n.* **1** strong or offensive smell. **2** *colloq.* row or fuss. [Old English]

stink bomb *n.* device emitting a stink when opened.

stinker *n. slang* objectionable or difficult person or thing.

stinking -*adj.* **1** that stinks. **2** *slang* very objectionable. -*adv. slang* extremely (*stinking rich*).

stint -*v.* **1** supply (food or aid etc.) meanly or grudgingly. **2** (often *refl.*) supply (a person etc.) in this way. -*n.* **1** limitation of supply or effort (*without stint*). **2** allotted amount of work (*do one's stint*). **3** small sandpiper. [Old English]

stipend /'staipend/ *n.* salary, esp. of a clergyman. [Latin *stipendium*]

stipendiary /stai'pendiəri, sti-/ -*adj.* receiving a stipend. -*n.* (*pl.* **-ies**) person receiving a stipend. [Latin: related to STIPEND]

stipendiary magistrate *n.* paid professional magistrate.

stipple /'stip(ə)l/ -*v.* (**-ling**) **1** draw or paint or engrave etc. with dots instead of lines. **2** roughen the surface (of paint, cement, etc.). -*n.* **1** stippling. **2** effect of stippling. [Dutch]

stipulate /'stipjuleit/ *v.* (**-ting**) demand or specify as part of a bargain etc. □

stipulation /-'leɪʃ(ə)n/ n. [Latin *stipulari*]

stir¹ —v. (-rr-) 1 move a spoon etc. round and round in (a liquid etc.), esp. to mix ingredients. 2 a cause to move, esp. slightly. b be or begin to be in motion. 3 rise from sleep. 4 arouse, inspire, or excite (the emotions, a person, etc.). 5 *colloq.* cause trouble between people by gossiping etc. —n. 1 act of stirring. 2 commotion, excitement. □ **stir in** add (an ingredient) by stirring. **stir up** 1 mix thoroughly by stirring. 2 stimulate, excite. □ **stirrer** n. [Old English]

stir² n. *slang* prison. [origin unknown]

stir-fry —v. fry rapidly while stirring. —n. stir-fried dish.

stirrup /'strəp/ n. metal loop support- ing a horse-rider's foot. [Old English, = climbing-rope]

stirrup-cup n. cup of wine etc. offered to a departing traveller, orig. a rider.

stirrup-leather n. (also **stirrup-strap**) strap attaching a stirrup to a saddle.

stirrup-pump n. hand-operated water-pump with a foot-rest, used to ex- tinguish small fires.

stitch —n. 1 a (in sewing, knitting, or crocheting) single pass of a needle, or the resulting thread or loop etc. b par- ticular method of sewing etc. 2 least bit of clothing (*hadn't a stitch on*). 3 sharp pain in the side induced by running etc. —v. sew, make stitches (in). □ **in stitches** *colloq.* laughing uncontrol- lably. **stitch up** 1 join or mend by sew- ing. 2 *slang* trick, cheat, betray. [Old English; related to STICK²]

stitch in time n. timely remedy.

stoat n. mammal of the weasel family with brown fur turning mainly white in the winter. [origin unknown]

stock —n. 1 store of goods etc. ready for sale or distribution etc. 2 supply or quantity of anything for use. 3 equip- ment or raw material for manufacture or trade etc. (*rolling-stock*). 4 farm an- imals or equipment. 5 a capital of a business. b shares in this. 6 reputation or popularity (*his stock is rising*). 7 a money lent to a government at fixed interest. b right to receive such interest. 8 line of ancestry (*comes of Cornish stock*). 9 liquid basis for soup etc. made by stewing bones, vegetables, etc. 10 fragrant-flowered cruciferous cultiv- ated plant. 11 plant into which a graft is inserted. 12 main trunk of a tree etc. 13 (in *pl.*) *hist.* timber frame with holes for the feet in which offenders were locked as a public punishment. 14 base, sup- port, or handle for an implement or machine. 15 butt of a rifle etc. 16 (in *pl.*)

supports for a ship during building or repair. 17 band of cloth worn round the neck. —*attrib. adj.* 1 kept in stock and so regularly available. 2 hackneyed, con- ventional. —v. 1 have (goods) in stock. 2 provide (a shop or a farm etc.) with goods, livestock, etc. 3 fit (a gun etc.) with a stock. □ **in** (or **out of**) **stock** available (or not available) immediately for sale etc. **stock up** (often foll. by *with*) provide with or get stocks or supplies (of). **take stock** 1 make an inventory of one's stock. 2 (often foll. by *of*) review (a situation etc.). [Old English]

stockade /stɒˈkeɪd/ —n. line or enclos- ure of upright stakes. —v. (-ding) fortify with this. [Spanish *estacada*]

stockbreeder n. livestock farmer.

stockbroker n. = BROKER 2. □ **stock- broking** n.

stock-car n. specially strengthened car for use in racing with deliberate bump- ing.

Stock Exchange n. 1 place for dealing in stocks and shares. 2 dealers working there.

stockholder n. owner of stocks or shares.

stockinet /ˌstɒkɪˈnɛt/ n. (also **stock- inette**) elastic knitted fabric. [probably from *stocking-net*]

stocking n. 1 long knitted covering for the leg and foot, of nylon, wool, silk, etc. 2 differently-coloured lower leg of a horse etc. □ **in one's stocking** (or **stockinged**) **feet** without shoes. [from STOCK]

stocking-stitch n. alternate rows of plain and purl.

stock-in-trade n. 1 requisite(s) of a trade or profession. 2 characteristic or essential product; characteristic be- haviour, actions, etc.

stockist n. dealer in specified types of goods.

stockjobber n. = JOBBER 2.

stock market n. 1 = STOCK EXCHANGE. 2 transactions on this.

stockpile —n. accumulated stock of goods etc. held in reserve. —v. (-ling) accumulate a stockpile of.

stockpot n. pot for making soup stock.

stockroom n. room for storing goods.

stock-still *adj.* motionless.

stocktaking n. 1 making an inventory of stock. 2 review of one's position etc.

stocky *adj.* (-ier, -iest) short and sturdy. □ **stockily** *adv.* **stockiness** n.

stockyard n. enclosure for the sorting or temporary keeping of cattle.

stodge /stɒdʒ/ n. *colloq.* heavy fattening food. [imitative, after *stuff* and *podge*]

stodgy adj. (-ier, -iest) 1 (of food) heavy and glutinous. 2 dull and uninteresting. □ **stodgily** adv. **stodginess** n.

Stoic /ˈstəʊɪk/ n. 1 member of the ancient Greek school of philosophy which sought virtue as the greatest good and taught control of one's feelings and passions. 2 (stoic) stoical person. —adj. 1 of or like the Stoics. 2 (stoic) = STOICAL. [Greek *stoa* portico]

stoical adj. having or showing great self-control in adversity. □ **stoically** adv.

Stoicism /ˈstəʊɪsɪz(ə)m/ n. 1 philosophy of the Stoics. 2 (stoicism) stoical attitude.

stoke v. (-king) (often foll. by *up*) 1 feed and tend (a fire or furnace etc.). 2 *colloq.* fill oneself with food. [back-formation from STOKER]

stokehold n. compartment in a steamship containing its boilers and furnace.

stokehole n. space for stokers in front of a furnace.

stoker n. person who tends a furnace, esp. on a steamship. [Dutch]

stole[1] /stəʊl/ n. 1 woman's garment like a long wide scarf, worn over the shoulders. 2 strip of silk etc. worn similarly by a priest. [Greek *stolē* equipment, clothing]

stole[2] *past* of STEAL.

stolen *past part.* of STEAL.

stolid /ˈstɒlɪd/ adj. not easily excited or moved; impassive, unemotional. □ **stolidity** /-ˈlɪdɪtɪ/ n. **stolidly** adv. [Latin]

stoma /ˈstəʊmə/ n. (pl. -s or stomata) 1 minute pore in the epidermis of a leaf. 2 small mouthlike artificial orifice made in the stomach. [Greek *stoma* mouth]

stomach /ˈstʌmək/ n. —n. 1 internal organ in which digestion occurs. b any of several such organs in animals. 2 lower front of the body. 3 (usu. foll. by *for*) a appetite. b inclination. —v. 1 find palatable. 2 endure (usu. with *neg.: cannot stomach it*). [Greek *stoma* mouth]

stomach-ache n. pain in the belly or bowels.

stomacher n. *hist.* pointed bodice of a dress, often jewelled or embroidered. [probably French: related to prec.]

stomach-pump n. syringe for forcing liquid etc. into or out of the stomach.

stomach upset n. temporary digestive disorder.

stomp —v. tread or stamp heavily. —n. lively jazz dance with heavy stamping. [var. of STAMP]

stone —n. 1 a solid non-metallic mineral matter; rock. b small piece of this. 2 (often in *comb.*) piece of stone of a definite shape or for a particular purpose. 3 a thing resembling stone, e.g. the hard case of the kernel in some fruits. b (often in *pl.*) hard morbid concretion in the body. 4 (*pl.* same) unit of weight equal to 14 lb. 5 = PRECIOUS STONE. 6 (*attrib.*) made of stone. —v. (-ning) 1 pelt with stones. 2 remove the stones from (fruit). □ **cast** (or **throw**) **stones** speak ill of a person. **leave no stone unturned** try all possible means. **a stone's throw** a short distance. [Old English]

Stone Age n. prehistoric period when weapons and tools were made of stone.

stonechat n. small brown bird with black and white markings.

stone-cold adj. completely cold.

stone-cold sober *predic. adj.* completely sober.

stonecrop n. succulent rock-plant.

stoned adj. *slang* drunk or drugged.

stone-dead adj. completely dead.

stone-deaf adj. completely deaf.

stone-fruit n. fruit with flesh enclosing a stone.

stoneground adj. (of flour) ground with millstones.

stonemason n. person who cuts, prepares, and builds with stone.

stonewall v. 1 obstruct (a discussion or investigation) with evasive answers etc. 2 *Cricket* bat with excessive caution.

stoneware n. ceramic ware which is impermeable and partly vitrified but opaque.

stonewashed adj. (esp. of denim) washed with abrasives to give a worn or faded look.

stonework n. masonry.

stonker /ˈstɒŋkə(r)/ n. *slang* excellent person or thing. □ **stonking** adj. [20th c.: origin unknown]

stony adj. (-ier, -iest) 1 full of stones. 2 a hard, rigid. b unfeeling, uncompromising. □ **stonily** adv. **stoniness** n.

stony-broke adj. *slang* entirely without money.

stood *past* and *past part.* of STAND.

stooge *colloq.* —n. 1 butt or foil, esp. for a comedian. 2 assistant or subordinate, esp. for routine or unpleasant work. —v. (-ging) 1 (foll. by *for*) act as a stooge for. 2 (foll. by *about, around,* etc.) move about aimlessly. [origin unknown]

stook /stuːk, stʊk/ —n. group of sheaves of grain stood on end in a field. —v. arrange in stooks. [related to Low German *stūke*]

stool n. 1 single seat without a back or arms. 2 = FOOTSTOOL. 3 (usu. in *pl.*) = FAECES. [Old English]

stoolball n. team game with pairs of bases, batters scoring runs between two bases.

stool-pigeon n. 1 person acting as a decoy. 2 police informer.

stoop[1] — v. 1 lower the body, sometimes bending the knee; bend down. 2 stand or walk with the shoulders habitually bent forward. 3 (foll. by *to* + infin.) condescend. 4 (foll. by *to*) descend to (some conduct). — n. stooping posture. [Old English]

stoop[2] n. *US* porch, small veranda, or steps in front of a house. [Dutch *stoep*]

stop — v. (**-pp-**) 1 a put an end to the progress, motion, or operation of. b effectively hinder or prevent. c discontinue (*stop playing*). 2 come to an end (*supplies suddenly stopped*). 3 cease from motion, speaking, or action. 4 defeat. 5 *slang* receive (a blow etc.). 6 remain, stay for a short time. 7 (often foll. by *up*) block or close up (a hole, leak, etc.). 8 not permit or supply as usual (*stop their wages*). 9 (in full **stop payment of** or **on**) instruct a bank to withhold payment on (a cheque). 10 fill (a tooth). 11 press (a violin etc. string) to obtain the required pitch. — n. 1 stopping or being stopped. 2 designated stopping-place for a bus or train etc. 3 = FULL STOP. 4 device for stopping motion at a particular point. 5 change of pitch effected by stopping a string. 6 a (in an organ) row of pipes of one character. b knob etc. operating these. 7 *Optics & Photog.* = DIAPHRAGM 3a. 8 a effective diameter of a lens. b device for reducing this. 9 (of sound) = PLOSIVE. □ **pull out all the stops** make extreme effort. **put a stop to** cause to end. **stop at nothing** be ruthless. **stop off** (or **over**) break one's journey. [Old English]

stopcock n. externally operated valve regulating the flow through a pipe etc.

stopgap n. temporary substitute.

stop-go n. alternate stopping and restarting, esp. of the economy.

stopoff n. break in a journey.

stopover n. break in a journey, esp. overnight.

stoppage n. 1 interruption of work owing to a strike etc. 2 (in *pl.*) sum deducted from pay, for tax, national insurance, etc. 3 condition of being blocked or stopped.

stopper — n. plug for closing a bottle etc. — v. close with this.

stop press n. (often *attrib.*) late news inserted in a newspaper after printing has begun.

stopwatch n. watch that can be stopped and started, used to time races etc.

storage /ˈstɔːrɪdʒ/ n. 1 a storing of goods etc. b method of or space for storing. 2 cost of storing. 3 storing of data in a computer etc.

storage battery n. (also **storage cell**) battery (or cell) for storing electricity.

storage heater n. electric heater releasing heat stored outside peak hours.

store — n. 1 quantity of something kept available for use. 2 (in *pl.*) a articles gathered for a particular purpose. b supply of, or place for keeping, these. 3 a = DEPARTMENT STORE. b esp. *US* shop. c (often in *pl.*) shop selling basic necessities. 4 warehouse for keeping furniture etc. temporarily. 5 device in a computer for keeping retrievable data. — v. (often foll. by *up*, *away*) 1 put (furniture etc.) in a store. 2 stock or provide with something useful. 4 keep (data) for retrieval. □ **in store** 1 kept in readiness. 2 coming in the future. 3 (foll. by *for*) awaiting. **set store by** consider important. [French *estore(r)* from Latin *instauro* renew]

storehouse n. storage place.

storekeeper n. 1 storeman. 2 *US* shopkeeper.

storeman n. person in charge of a store of goods.

storeroom n. storage room.

storey /ˈstɔːrɪ/ n. (*pl.* **-s**) 1 = FLOOR n. 3. 2 thing forming a horizontal division. □ **-storeyed** *adj.* (in *comb.*). [Anglo-Latin: related to HISTORY, perhaps originally meaning a tier of painted windows]

storied /ˈstɔːrɪd/ *adj. literary* celebrated in or associated with stories or legends.

stork n. long-legged usu. white wading bird. [Old English]

storm — n. 1 violent atmospheric disturbance with strong winds and usu. thunder, rain, or snow. 2 violent political etc. disturbance. 3 (foll. by *of*) a violent shower of missiles etc. b outbreak of applause, hisses, etc. 4 a direct assault by troops on a fortified place. b capture by such an assault. — v. 1 attack or capture by storm. 2 (usu. foll. by *in*, *out*, etc.) move violently or angrily (*stormed out*). 3 (often foll. by *at*, *away*) talk violently, rage, bluster. □ **take by storm** 1 capture by direct assault. 2 rapidly captivate. [Old English]

storm centre n. 1 point to which the wind spirals inward in a cyclonic storm. 2 centre of controversy etc.

storm cloud n. 1 heavy rain-cloud. 2 threatening situation.

storm-door n. additional outer door.

storm in a teacup n. great excitement over a trivial matter.

storm petrel n. (also **stormy petrel**) 1 small black and white N. Atlantic petrel. 2 person causing unrest.

storm trooper n. member of the storm troops.

storm troops n.pl. 1 = SHOCK TROOPS. 2 hist. Nazi political militia.

stormy adj. (**-ier**, **-iest**) 1 of or affected by storms. 2 (of a wind etc.) violent. 3 full of angry feeling or outbursts (stormy meeting). □ **stormily** adv. **storminess** n.

storm petrel var. of STORM PETREL.

story /'stɔːrɪ/ n. (pl. **-ies**) 1 account of imaginary or past events; tale, anecdote. 2 history of a person or institution etc. 3 (in full **story-line**) narrative or plot of a novel, play, etc. 4 facts or experiences worthy of narration. 5 colloq. fib. [Anglo-French estorie from Latin: related to HISTORY]

storyteller n. 1 person who tells stories. 2 colloq. liar. □ **storytelling** n. & adj.

stoup /stuːp/ n. 1 basin for holy-water. 2 archaic flagon, beaker. [Old Norse]

stout —adj. 1 rather fat, corpulent, bulky. 2 thick or strong. 3 brave, resolute. —n. strong dark beer. □ **stoutly** adv. **stoutness** n. [Anglo-French from Germanic]

stout-hearted adj. courageous.

stove[1] n. closed apparatus burning fuel or using electricity for heating or cooking. [Low German or Dutch]

stove[2] past and past part. of STAVE v.

stove-pipe n. pipe carrying smoke and gases from a stove to a chimney.

stow /stəʊ/ v. pack (goods, cargo, etc.) tidily and compactly. □ **stow away** 1 place (a thing) out of the way 2 be a stowaway on a ship etc. [from BESTOW]

stowage n. 1 stowing. 2 place for this.

stowaway n. person who hides on a ship or aircraft etc. to travel free.

strabismus /strə'bɪzməs/ n. Med. squinting, squint. [Greek strabos squinting]

straddle /'stræd(ə)l/ v. (**-ling**) 1 a sit or stand across (a thing) with the legs spread. b be situated on both sides of. 2 part (one's legs) widely. [from STRIDE]

strafe /strɑːf, streɪf/ v. (**-fing**) bombard; attack with gunfire. [German, = punish]

straggle /'stræg(ə)l/ —v. (**-ling**) 1 lack compactness or tidiness. 2 be dispersed or sporadic. 3 trail behind in a race etc. —n. straggling or scattered group. □ **straggler** n. **straggly** adj. (**-ier**, **-iest**). [origin uncertain]

straight /streɪt/ —adj. 1 extending uniformly in the same direction; not bent or curved. 2 successive, uninterrupted (three straight wins). 3 ordered, level; tidy (put things straight). 4

honest, candid. 5 (of thinking etc.) logical. 6 (of theatre, music, etc.) serious, classical, not popular or comic. 7 a unmodified. b (of a drink) undiluted. 8 colloq. a (of a person etc.) conventional, respectable. b heterosexual. 9 direct, undeviating. —n. 1 straight part, esp. the concluding stretch of a racetrack. 2 straight condition. 3 sequence of five cards in poker. 4 colloq. conventional person; heterosexual. —adv. 1 in a straight line; direct. 2 in the right direction. 3 correctly. □ **go straight** (of a criminal) become honest. **straight away** immediately. **straight off** colloq. without hesitation. □ **straightish** adj. **straightness** n. [originally a past part. of STRETCH]

straightaway /streɪtə'weɪ/ adv. = straight away.

straighten /'streɪt(ə)n/ v. 1 (often foll. by out) make or become straight. 2 (foll. by up) stand or become erect after bending.

straight eye n. ability to detect deviation from the straight.

straight face n. intentionally expressionless face. □ **straight-faced** adj.

straight fight n. Polit. contest between two candidates only.

straight flush n. flush in numerical sequence.

straightforward /streɪt'fɔːwəd/ adj. 1 honest or frank. 2 (of a task etc.) simple.

straight man n. comedian's stooge.

strain[1] —v. 1 stretch tightly; make or become taut or tense. 2 injure by overuse or excessive demands. 3 exercise (oneself, one's senses, a thing, etc.) intensely. 4 strive intensely; press to extremes. 5 (foll. by to) tug, pull. 6 distort from the true intention or meaning. 7 a clear (a liquid of solid matter by passing it through a sieve etc. b (foll. by out) filter (solids) out from a liquid. —n. 1 act of straining. b force exerted in this. 2 injury caused by straining a muscle etc. 3 severe mental or physical demand or exertion (suffering from strain). 4 snatch of music or poetry. 5 tone or tendency in speech or writing (more in the same strain). [French estrei(g)n- from Latin stringo]

strain[2] n. 1 breed or stock of animals, plants, etc. 2 tendency; characteristic. [Old English, = begetting]

strained adj. 1 constrained, artificial. 2 (of a relationship) mutually distrustful or tense.

strainer n. device for straining liquids etc.

strait n. 1 (in sing. or pl.) narrow channel connecting two large bodies of

water. 2 (usu. in *pl.*) difficulty or distress. [French *estreit* from Latin *strictus* narrow]

straitened /'streit(ə)nd/ *adj.* of or marked by poverty.

strait-jacket —*n.* 1 strong garment with long sleeves for confining a violent prisoner etc. 2 restrictive measures. —*v.* (-t-) 1 restrain with a strait-jacket. 2 severely restrict.

strait-laced *adj.* puritanical.

strand[1] —*v.* 1 run aground. 2 (as **stranded** *adj.*) in difficulties, esp. without money or transport. —*n.* foreshore; beach. [Old English]

strand[2] *n.* 1 each of the twisted threads or wires making a rope or cable etc. 2 single thread or strip of fibre. 3 lock of hair. 4 element; component. [origin unknown]

strange /streindʒ/ *adj.* 1 unusual, peculiar, surprising, eccentric. 2 (often foll. by *to*) unfamiliar, foreign. 3 (foll. by *to*) unaccustomed. 4 not at ease. □ **strangely** *adv.* **strangeness** *n.* [French *estrange* from Latin *extraneus*]

stranger *n.* 1 person new to a particular place or company. 2 (often foll. by *to*) person one does not know. 3 (foll. by *to*) person unaccustomed to (*no stranger to controversy*).

strangle /'stræŋg(ə)l/ *v.* (**-ling**) 1 squeeze the windpipe or neck of, esp. so as to kill. 2 hamper, suppress. □ **strangler** *n.* [Latin *strangulo*]

stranglehold *n.* 1 throttling hold in wrestling. 2 deadly grip. 3 complete control.

strangulate /'stræŋgjʊleɪt/ *v.* (**-ting**) compress (a vein, intestine, etc.), preventing circulation. [Latin: related to STRANGLE]

strangulation /ˌstræŋgjʊˈleɪʃ(ə)n/ *n.* 1 strangling or being strangled. 2 strangulating.

strap —*n.* 1 strip of leather etc., often with a buckle, for holding things together etc. 2 narrow strip of fabric worn over the shoulders as part of a garment. 3 loop for grasping to steady oneself in a moving vehicle. 4 (**the strap**) punishment by beating with a leather strap. —*v.* (**-pp-**) 1 (often foll. by *down*, *up*, etc.) secure or bind with a strap. 2 beat with a strap. □ **strapless** *adj.* [dial. = STROP]

straphanger *n.* *slang* standing passenger in a bus, train, etc. □ **straphang** *v.*

strapping *adj.* large and sturdy.

strata *pl.* of STRATUM.

■ **Usage** It is incorrect to use *strata* as the singular noun instead of *stratum*.

stratagem /'strætədʒəm/ *n.* 1 cunning plan or scheme. 2 trickery. [Greek *stratēgos* a general]

strategic /strəˈtiːdʒɪk/ *adj.* 1 of or promoting strategy. 2 (of materials) essential in war. 3 (of bombing or weapons) done or for use as a longer-term military objective. □ **strategically** *adv.*

strategy /'strætɪdʒɪ/ *n.* (*pl.* **-ies**) 1 long-term plan or policy (*economic strategy*). 2 art of war. 3 art of moving troops, ships, aircraft, etc. into favourable positions. □ **strategist** *n.*

strathspey /stræθˈspeɪ/ *n.* 1 slow Scottish dance. 2 music for this. [*Strathspey*, valley of the river Spey]

stratify /'strætɪfaɪ/ *v.* (**-ies**, **-ied**) (esp. as **stratified** *adj.*) arrange in strata or grades etc. □ **stratification** /-fɪˈkeɪʃ(ə)n/ *n.* [French: related to STRATUM]

stratigraphy /strəˈtɪgrəfɪ/ *n.* *Geol.* & *Archaeol.* 1 relative position of strata. 2 the study of this. □ **stratigraphic** /ˌstrætɪˈgræfɪk/ *adj.* [from STRATUM]

stratosphere /'strætəˌsfɪə(r)/ *n.* layer of atmosphere above the troposphere, extending to about 50 km from the earth's surface. □ **stratospheric** /-ˈsferɪk/ *adj.* [from STRATUM]

stratum /'strɑːtəm/ *n.* (*pl.* **strata**) 1 layer or set of layers of any deposited substance, esp. of rock. 2 atmospheric layer. 3 social class. [Latin *sterno* strew]

straw *n.* 1 dry cut stalks of grain as fodder or material for bedding, packing, etc. 2 single stalk of straw. 3 thin tube for sucking drink through. 4 insignificant thing. 5 pale yellow colour. □ **clutch at straws** try any remedy in desperation. **straw in the wind** indication of future developments. [Old English]

strawberry /'strɔːbərɪ/ *n.* (*pl.* **-ies**) 1 pulpy red fruit with a seed-studded surface. 2 plant with runners and white flowers bearing this. [Old English: related to STRAW, for unknown reason]

strawberry mark *n.* reddish birthmark.

straw vote *n.* (also **straw poll**) unofficial ballot as a test of opinion.

stray —*v.* 1 wander from the right place or from one's companions; go astray. 2 deviate morally or mentally. —*n.* 1 strayed person, animal, or thing. —*adj.* 1 strayed, lost. 2 isolated, occasional. 3 *Physics* wasted or unwanted. [Anglo-French *strey*; related to ASTRAY]

streak —*n.* 1 long thin usu. irregular line or band, esp. of colour. 2 strain in a person's character. 3 spell or series (*winning streak*). —*v.* 1 mark with

streaks. 2 move very rapidly. 3 *colloq.* run naked in public. □ **streaker** *n.* [Old English, = pen-stroke]

streaky *adj.* (**-ier, -iest**) 1 full of streaks. 2 (of bacon) with streaks of fat.

stream —*n.* 1 flowing body of water, esp. a small river. 2 flow of a fluid or of a mass of people. 3 current or direction in which things are moving or tending. 4 group of school-children (schoolchildren) in streams. □ **on stream** in operation or production. [Old English]

streamer *n.* 1 long narrow strip of ribbon or paper. 2 long narrow flag. 3 banner headline.

streamline *v.* (**-ning**) 1 give (a vehicle etc.) the form which presents the least resistance to motion. 2 make simple or more efficient.

street *n.* 1 a public road in a city, town, or village. b this with the houses etc. in each side. 2 people who live or work in a particular street. □ **on the streets** living by prostitution. **streets ahead** (often foll. by *of*) *colloq.* much superior (to). **up** (or **right up**) **one's street** (or *colloq.* what one likes), knows about, etc. [Old English]

streetcar *n.* US tram.

street credibility *n.* (also **street cred**) *slang* familiarity with a fashionable urban subculture.

streetwalker *n.* prostitute seeking customers in the street.

streetwise *n.* knowing how to survive modern urban life.

strength *n.* 1 being strong; degree or manner of this. 2 a person or thing giving strength. 3 positive attribute. 3 number of people present or available; full number. □ **from strength to strength** with ever-increasing success. **in strength** in large numbers. **on the strength** of on the basis of. [Old English: related to STRONG]

strengthen /ˈstreŋθ(ə)n/ *v.* make or become stronger.

strenuous /ˈstrenjʊəs/ *adj.* 1 requiring or using great effort. 2 energetic. □ **strenuously** *adv.* [Latin]

streptococcus /ˌstreptəˈkɒkəs/ *n.* (*pl.* **-cocci** /-kaɪ/) bacterium of a type often causing infectious diseases. □ **streptococcal** *adj.* [Greek *streptos* twisted, *kokkos* berry]

streptomycin /ˌstreptəˈmaɪsɪn/ *n.* antibiotic effective against many diseaseproducing bacteria. [Greek *streptos* twisted, *mukēs* fungus]

streaks. 2 move very rapidly. 3 *colloq.* **stress** —*n.* 1 a pressure or tension. **b** quantity measuring this. 2 a physical or mental strain. **b** distress caused by this. 3 a emphasis. **b** emphasis on a syllable or word. —*v.* 1 emphasize. 2 subject to stress. □ **lay stress on** emphasize.

stressful *adj.* causing stress. [shortening of DISTRESS]

stretch —*v.* 1 draw, be drawn, or be able to be drawn out in length or size. 2 make or become taut. 3 place or lie at full length or spread out. 4 (also *absol.*) a extend (a limb etc.). **b** thrust out one's limbs and tighten one's muscles after being relaxed. 5 have a specified length or extension; extend. 6 strain or exert extremely; exaggerate (*stretch the truth*). —*n.* 1 continuous extent, expanse, or period. 2 stretching or being stretched. 3 (*attrib.*) elastic (*stretch fabric*). 4 *colloq.* period of imprisonment etc. 5 US straight side of a racetrack. □ **at a stretch** in one continuous period. **stretch one's legs** exercise oneself by walking. **stretch out 1** extend (a limb etc.). 2 last; prolong. **stretch a point** agree to something not normally allowed. □ **stretchy** *adj.* (**-ier, -iest**) [Old English]

stretcher *n.* 1 two poles with canvas etc. between, for carrying a person in a lying position. 2 brick etc. laid along the face of a wall.

strew /struː/ *v.* (*past part.* **strewn** or **strewed**) 1 scatter or spread about over a surface. 2 (usu. foll. by *with*) spread (a surface) with scattered things. [Old English: related to STRAW]

'strewth var. of 'STRUTH.

stria /ˈstraɪə/ *n.* (*pl.* **striae** /-iː/) slight ridge or furrow. [Latin]

striate —*adj.* /ˈstraɪət/ (also **striated** /-eɪtɪd/) marked with striae. —*v.* /straɪˈeɪt/ (**-ting**) mark with slight ridges. □ **striation** /straɪˈeɪʃ(ə)n/ *n.*

stricken /ˈstrɪkən/ *adj.* overcome with illness or misfortune etc. [archaic past part. of STRIKE]

strict *adj.* 1 precisely limited or defined; undeviating (*strict diet*). 2 requiring complete obedience or exact performance. □ **strictly speaking** applying words or rules in their strict sense. □ **strictly** *adv.* **strictness** *n.* [Latin *stringo strict-* draw tight]

stricture /ˈstrɪktʃə(r)/ *n.* (usu. in *pl.*; often foll. by *on, upon*) critical or censorious remark. [Latin: related to STRICT]

stride —*v.* (**-ding**; *past* **strode**; *past part.* **stridden** /ˈstrɪd(ə)n/) 1 walk with long firm steps. 2 cross with one step. 3 bestride. —*n.* 1 a single long step. **b** length of this. 2 gait as determined by

the length of stride. **3** (usu. in *pl.*) progress (*great strides*). **4** steady progress (*get into one's stride*). □ **take in one's stride** manage easily. [Old English]

strident /ˈstraɪd(ə)nt/ *adj.* loud and harsh. □ **stridency** *n.* **stridently** *adv.* [Latin *strido* creak]

strife *n.* conflict; struggle. [French *estryf*: related to STRIVE]

strike –*v.* (**-king;** *past* **struck;** *past part.* **struck** or *archaic* **stricken**) **1** deliver (a blow) or inflict a blow on; hit. **2** come or bring sharply into contact with (*ship struck a rock*). **3** propel or divert with a blow. **4** (cause to) penetrate (*struck terror into him*). **5** ignite (a match) or produce (sparks etc.) by friction. **6** make (a coin) by stamping. **7** produce (a musical note) by striking. **8 a** (also *absol.*) (of a clock) indicate (the time) with a chime etc. **b** (of time) be so indicated. **9 a** attack suddenly. **b** (of a disease) afflict. **10** cause to become suddenly (*struck dumb*). **11** reach or achieve (*strike a balance*). **12** agree on (a bargain). **13** assume (an attitude) suddenly and dramatically. **14** discover or find (oil etc.) by drilling etc. **15** occur to or appear to (*strikes me as silly*). **16** lower or take down (a flag or tent etc.). **17** take a specified direction. **19** (also *absol.*) secure a hook in the mouth of (a fish) by jerking the tackle. —*n.* **1** act of striking. **2 a** organized refusal to work until a grievance is remedied. **b** similar refusal to participate. **3** sudden find or success. **4** attack, esp. from the air. □ **on strike** taking part in an industrial etc. strike. **strike home 1** deal an effective blow. **2** have the intended effect. **strike off 1** remove with a stroke. **2** delete (a name etc.) from a list, esp. a professional register. **strike out 1** hit out. **2** act vigorously. **3** delete (an item or name etc.). **4** set off (*struck out eastwards*). **strike up 1** start (an acquaintance, conversation, etc.), esp. casually. **2** (also *absol.*) begin playing (a tune etc.). **struck on** *colloq.* infatuated with. [Old English, = go, stroke]

strikebreaker *n.* person working or employed in place of strikers.

strike pay *n.* allowance paid to strikers by their union.

striker *n.* **1** employee on strike. **2** *Football* attacking player positioned forward.

striking *adj.* impressive; attracting attention. □ **strikingly** *adv.*

Strine *n.* **1** comic transliteration of Australian pronunciation. **2** (esp. uneducated) Australian English. [= *Australian* in Strine]

string –*n.* **1** twine or narrow cord. **2** piece of this or of similar material used for tying or holding together, pulling, forming the head of a racket, etc. **3** length of catgut or wire etc. on a musical instrument, producing a note by vibration. **4 a** (in *pl.*) stringed instruments in an orchestra etc. **b** (*attrib.*) of stringed instruments (*string quartet*). **5** (in *pl.*) condition or complication (*no strings attached*). **6** set of things strung together; series or line. **7** tough side of a bean-pod etc. –*v.* (*past and past part.* **strung**) **1** fit (a racket, violin, archer's bow, etc.) with a string or strings, or (a violin etc. bow) with horsehairs etc. **2** tie with string. **3** thread on a string. **4** arrange in or as a string. **5** remove the strings from (a bean). □ **on a string** under one's control. **string along** *colloq.* **1** deceive. **2** (often foll. by *with*) keep company (with). **string out** extend; prolong. **string up 1** hang up on strings etc. **2** kill by hanging. **3** (usu. as **strung up** *adj.*) make tense. [Old English]

string-course *n.* raised horizontal band of bricks etc. on a building.

stringed *adj.* (of musical instruments) having strings.

stringent /ˈstrɪndʒ(ə)nt/ *adj.* (of rules etc.) strict, precise; leaving no loophole for discretion. □ **stringency** *n.* **stringently** *adv.* [Latin: related to STRICT]

stringer *n.* **1** longitudinal structural member in a framework, esp. of a ship or aircraft. **2** *colloq.* freelance newspaper correspondent.

string vest *n.* vest with large meshes.

stringy *adj.* (**-ier, -iest**) like string, fibrous. □ **stringiness** *n.*

strip[1] –*v.* (**-pp-**) **1** (often foll. by *of*) remove the clothes or covering from. **2** (often foll. by *off*) undress oneself. **3** (often foll. by *of*) deprive (a person) of property or titles. **4** leave bare. **5** (often foll. by *down*) remove the accessory fittings of or take apart (a machine etc.). **6** damage the thread of (a screw) or the teeth of (a gearwheel). **7** remove (paint) or remove paint from (a surface) with solvent. **8** (often foll. by *from*) pull (a covering etc.) off (*stripped the masks from their faces*). —*n.* **1** act of stripping. **2** *colloq.* distinctive outfit worn by a sports team. [Old English]

strip[2] *n.* long narrow piece. □ **tear a person off a strip** *colloq.* rebuke a person. [Low German *strippe* strap]

strip cartoon *n.* = COMIC STRIP.

strip club *n.* club at which striptease is performed.

stripe *n.* **1** long narrow band or strip differing in colour or texture from the

surface on either side of it. **2** Mil. chevron etc. denoting military rank. [perhaps from Low German or Dutch]

strip light n. tubular fluorescent lamp.

striped adj. marked with stripes.

stripling n. youth not yet fully grown. [from strap²]

stripper n. **1** person or thing that strips something. **2** device or solvent for removing paint etc. **3** striptease performer.

strip-search n. search involving the removal of all a person's clothes. —v. search in this way.

striptease /ˈstriptiːz/ n. entertainment in which the performer slowly and erotically undresses.

stripy adj. (-ier, -iest) striped.

strive v. (-ving; past **strove**; past part. **striven** /ˈstrivn/) **1** try hard (strive to succeed). **2** (often foll. by with, against) struggle. [French estriver]

strobe n. colloq. stroboscope. [abbreviation]

stroboscope /ˈstrəʊbəˌskəʊp/ n. **1** Physics instrument for determining speeds of rotation etc. by shining a bright light at intervals so that a rotating object appears stationary. **2** lamp made to flash intermittently, esp. for this purpose. □ **stroboscopic** /-ˈskɒpɪk/ adj. [Greek strobos whirling]

strode past of STRIDE.

stroke —n. **1** act of striking; blow, hit. **2** sudden disabling attack caused esp. by thrombosis; apoplexy. **3 a** action or movement, esp. as one of a series. **b** slightest action (stroke of work). **4** single complete motion of a wing, oar, etc. **5** (in rowing) the mode or action of moving the oar (row a fast stroke). **6** whole motion of a piston in either direction. **7** specified mode of swimming. **8** specially successful or skilful effort (a stroke of diplomacy). **9** mark made by a single movement of a pen, paintbrush, etc. **10** detail contributing to the general effect. **11** sound of a striking clock. **12** (in full **stroke oar**) oar or oarsman nearest the stern, setting the time of the stroke. **13** act or spell of stroking. —v. (-king) **1** pass one's hand gently along the surface of (a boat or crew), esp. to soothe. **2** act as the stroke of (a boat or crew). □ **at a stroke** by a single action. **on the stroke (of)** punctually (at). [Old English: related to STRIKE]

stroll /strəʊl/ —v. walk in a leisurely way. —n. short leisurely walk. [probably from German Strolch vagabond]

strolling players n.pl. hist. travelling actors etc.

strong —adj. (**stronger** /ˈstrɒŋgə(r)/; **strongest** /ˈstrɒŋgɪst/) **1** able to resist;

not easily damaged, overcome, or disturbed. **2** healthy. **3** capable of exerting great force or of doing much; muscular, powerful. **4** forceful in effect (strong wind). **5** firmly held (strong suspicion). **6** (of an argument etc.) convincing. **7** intense (strong light). **8** formidable (strong candidate). **9** (of a solution or drink etc.) not very diluted. **10** of a specified number (200 strong). **11** Gram. (of a verb) forming inflections by a change of vowel within the stem (e.g. swim, swam). —adv. strongly. □ **come on strong** colloq. behave aggressively. **going strong** colloq. continuing vigorously; in good health etc. □ **strongish** adj. [Old English]

strong-arm attrib. adj. using force (strong-arm tactics).

strongbox n. small strongly made chest for valuables.

strong language n. swearing.

strong-minded adj. determined.

strong point n. (also **strong suit**) thing at which one excels.

strongroom n. room, esp. in a bank, for keeping valuables safe from fire and theft.

strontium /ˈstrɒntɪəm/ n. soft silver-white metallic element. [Strontian in Scotland]

strontium-90 n. radioactive isotope of strontium found in nuclear fallout and concentrated in bones and teeth when ingested.

strop —n. device, esp. a strip of leather, for sharpening razors. —v. (-pp-) sharpen on a strop. [Low German or Dutch]

stroppy /ˈstrɒpɪ/ adj. (-ier -iest) colloq. bad-tempered; awkward to deal with. [origin uncertain]

strove past of STRIVE.

struck past and past part. of STRIKE.

structural /ˈstrʌktʃ(ə)r(ə)l/ adj. of a structure. □ **structurally** adv.

structuralism n. doctrine that structure rather than function is important. □ **structuralist** n. & adj.

structure /ˈstrʌktʃə(r)/ —n. **1 a** constructed unit, esp. a building. **b** way in which a building etc. is constructed. **2** framework (new wages structure). —v. (-ring) give structure to; organize. [Latin struo struct- build]

strudel /ˈstruːd(ə)l/ n. thin leaved pastry rolled round a filling and baked. [German]

struggle /ˈstrʌg(ə)l/ —v. (-ling) **1** violently try to get free of restraint. **2** (often foll. by for, or to + infin.) try hard under

difficulties (*struggled for power; struggled to win*). **3** (foll. by *with*, *against*) contend; fight. **4** (foll. by *along*, *up*, etc.) progress with difficulty. **5** (esp. as **struggling** *adj.*) have difficulty in gaining recognition or a living (*struggling artist*). —*n.* **1** act or spell of struggling. **2** hard or confused contest. [origin uncertain]

strum —*v.* (**-mm-**) **1** (often foll. by *on*; also *absol.*) play on (a guitar, piano, etc.), esp. carelessly or unskilfully. **2** play (a tune etc.) in this way. —*n.* sound or spell of strumming. [imitative: cf. THRUM[^1]]

strumpet /ˈstrʌmpɪt/ *n. archaic* or *rhet.* prostitute. [origin unknown]

strung *past* and *past part.* of STRING.

strut —*n.* **1** bar in a framework, designed to resist compression. **2** strutting gait. —*v.* (**-tt-**) **1** walk stiffly and pompously. **2** brace with struts. [Old English]

'struth /struːθ/ *int.* (also **'strewth**) *colloq.* exclamation of surprise. [*God's truth*]

strychnine /ˈstrɪkniːn/ *n.* highly poisonous alkaloid used in small doses as a stimulant. [Greek *strukhnos* nightshade]

Sts *abbr.* Saints.

stub —*n.* **1** remnant of a pencil or cigarette etc. **2** counterfoil of a cheque or receipt etc. **3** stump. —*v.* (**-bb-**) **1** strike (one's toe) against something. **2** (usu. foll. by *out*) extinguish (a cigarette) by pressure. [Old English]

stubble /ˈstʌb(ə)l/ *n.* **1** stalks of corn etc. left in the ground after the harvest. **2** short stiff hair or bristles. □ **stubbly** *adj.* [Latin *stupula*]

stubborn /ˈstʌbən/ *adj.* obstinate, inflexible. □ **stubbornly** *adv.* **stubbornness** *n.* [origin unknown]

stubby *adj.* (**-ier**, **-iest**) short and thick. —*n.* (*pl.* **-ies**) *Austral. colloq.* small squat bottle of beer. [from STUB]

stucco /ˈstʌkəʊ/ —*n.* (*pl.* **-es**) plaster or cement for coating walls or moulding into decorations. —*v.* (**-es**, **-ed**) coat with stucco. [Italian]

stuck *past* and *past part.* of STICK[^2].

stuck-up *adj.* conceited, snobbish. [STICK[^2]]

stud[^1] —*n.* **1** large-headed projecting nail, boss, or knob, esp. for ornament. **2** double button, esp. for use with two buttonholes in a shirt-front. —*v.* (**-dd-**) **1** set with or as with studs. **2** (as **studded** *adj.*) (foll. by *with*) thickly set or strewn with. [Old English]

stud[^2] *n.* **1 a** number of horses kept for breeding etc. **b** place where these are kept. **2** stallion. **3** *colloq.* young man, esp. one noted for sexual prowess. **4** (in full **stud poker**) form of poker with betting after the dealing of cards face up. □ **at**

stud (of a stallion) hired out for breeding. [Old English]

stud-book *n.* book containing the pedigrees of horses.

studding-sail /ˈstʌns(ə)l/ *n.* extra sail set in light winds. [Low German or Dutch]

student /ˈstjuːd(ə)nt/ *n.* **1** person who is studying, esp. at a place of higher or further education. **2** (*attrib.*) studying in order to become (*student nurse*). □ **studentship** *n.* [Latin: related to STUDY]

stud-farm *n.* place where horses are bred.

studio /ˈstjuːdɪəʊ/ *n.* (*pl.* **-s**) **1** workroom of a painter, photographer, etc. **2** place for making films, recordings, or broadcast programmes. [Italian]

studio couch *n.* couch convertible into a bed.

studio flat *n.* one-roomed flat.

studious /ˈstjuːdɪəs/ *adj.* **1** assiduous in study. **2** painstaking. □ **studiously** *adv.* [Latin: related to STUDY]

study /ˈstʌdɪ/ —*n.* (*pl.* **-ies**) **1** acquisition of knowledge, esp. from books. **2** (in *pl.*) pursuit of academic knowledge. **3** private room used for reading, writing, etc. **4** piece of work, esp. a drawing, done for practice or as an experiment. **5** portrayal in literature etc. of behaviour or character etc. **6** musical composition designed to develop a player's skill. **7** thing worth observing (*his face was a study*). **8** thing that is or deserves to be investigated. —*v.* (**-ies**, **-ied**) **1** make a study of; investigate (a subject) (*study law*). **2** (often foll. by *for*) apply oneself to study. **3** scrutinize closely (a visible object). **4** learn (one's role etc.). **5** take pains to achieve (a result) or pay regard to (a subject or principle etc.). **6** (as **studied** *adj.*) deliberate, affected (*studied politeness*). [Latin *studium*]

stuff —*n.* **1** material; fabric. **2** substance or things not needing to be specified (*lot of stuff on the news*). **3** particular knowledge or activity (*know one's stuff*). **4** woollen fabric. **5** trash, nonsense. **6** (*prec.* by *the*) *a colloq.* supply, esp. of drink or drugs. **b** *slang* money. —*v.* **1** pack (a receptacle) tightly (*stuff a cushion with feathers*). **2** (foll. by *in*, *into*) force or cram (a thing). **3** fill out the skin of (an animal etc.) with material to restore the original shape. **4** fill (food, esp. poultry) with a mixture, esp. before cooking. **5** (also *refl.*) fill with food; eat greedily. **6** push, esp. hastily or clumsily. **7** (usu. in *passive*) block up (the nose etc.). **8** *slang* (expressing contempt) dispose of (*you can stuff the job*). **9** *coarse slang offens.* have sexual intercourse with (a woman). □ **get**

stuffed *slang* exclamation of dismissal, contempt, etc. **stuff and nonsense** exclamation of incredulity or ridicule. [French *estoffe*]

stuffed shirt n. *colloq.* pompous person.

stuffing n. 1 padding for cushions etc. 2 mixture used to stuff food, esp. before cooking.

stuffy adj. (-ier, -iest) 1 (of a room etc.) lacking fresh air. 2 dull or uninterest-ing. 3 (of the nose etc.) stuffed up. 4 dull and conventional. □ **stuffily** adv. **stuffiness** n.

stultify /ˈstʌltɪfaɪ/ v. (-ies, -ied) make ineffective or useless, esp. by routine. □ **stultification** /-fɪˈkeɪʃ(ə)n/ n. [Latin *stultus* foolish]

stumble /ˈstʌmb(ə)l/ —v. (-ling) 1 invol-untarily lurch forward or almost fall. 2 stumbles. 3 speak haltingly. 4 (foll. by *on*, *upon*, *across*) find by chance. —n. act of stumbling. [related to STAMMER]

stumbling-block n. obstacle.

stump —n. 1 part of a cut or fallen tree still in the ground. 2 similar part (e.g. of a branch or limb) cut off or worn down. 3 *Cricket* each of the three uprights of a wicket. 4 (in pl.) *joc.* legs. —v. 1 (of a question etc.) be too hard for; baffle. 2 (as **stumped** adj.) at a loss, baffled. 3 *Cricket* put (a batsman) out by touching the stumps with the ball while he is out of the crease. 4 walk stiffly or noisily. 5 traverse (a district) making political speeches. □ **stump up** *colloq.* pay or produce (the money required). [Low German or Dutch]

stumpy adj. (-ier, -iest) short and thick. □ **stumpiness** n.

stun v. (-nn-) 1 knock senseless; stupefy. 2 bewilder, shock. [French: related to ASTONISH]

stung past and past part. of STING.

stunk past and past part. of STINK.

stunner n. *colloq.* stunning person or thing.

stunning adj. *colloq.* extremely attract-ive or impressive. □ **stunningly** adv.

stunt[1] v. retard the growth or develop-ment of. [obsolete *stunt* foolish, short]

stunt[2] n. 1 something unusual done for publicity. 2 trick or daring feat. [origin unknown]

stunt man n. man employed to perform dangerous stunts in place of an actor.

stupefy /ˈstjuːpɪfaɪ/ v. (-ies, -ied) 1 make stupid or insensible. 2 astonish, amaze. □ **stupefaction** /-ˈfæk(ʃ)(ə)n/ n. [French from Latin *stupeo* be amazed]

stupendous /stjuːˈpendəs/ adj. amaz-ing or prodigious, esp. in size. □ **stupen-dously** adv. [Latin: related to STUPEFY]

stupid /ˈstjuːpɪd/ adj. (**stupider**, **stupidest**) 1 unintelligent, foolish (a *stupid fellow*). 2 typical of stupid per-sons (*stupid mistake*). 3 uninteresting, boring. 4 in a stupor. □ **stupidity** /-ˈpɪdɪtɪ/ n. (pl. -ies). **stupidly** adv. [Latin: related to STUPENDOUS]

stupor /ˈstjuːpə(r)/ n. dazed, torpid, or helplessly amazed state. [Latin: related to STUPEFY]

sturdy /ˈstɜːdɪ/ adj. (-ier, -iest) 1 robust; strongly built. 2 vigorous (*sturdy resistance*). □ **sturdily** adv. **sturdi-ness** n. [French *estourdi*]

sturgeon /ˈstɜːdʒ(ə)n/ n. (pl. same or -s) large sharklike fish yielding caviare. [Anglo-French from Germanic]

stutter —v. 1 stammer, esp. by involun-tary repetition of the initial consonants of words. 2 (often foll. by *out*) utter (words) in this way. —n. act or habit of stuttering. [dial. *stut*]

sty[1] /staɪ/ n. (pl. **sties**) pigsty. [Old English]

sty[2] /staɪ/ n. (also **stye**) (pl. **sties** or **styes**) inflamed swelling on the edge of an eyelid. [Old English]

Stygian /ˈstɪdʒɪən/ adj. *literary* dark, gloomy, literally = of the Styx, a river of Hades in Greek mythology]

style /staɪl/ —n. 1 kind or sort, esp. in regard to appearance and form (*elegant style of house*). 2 manner of writing, speaking, or performing. 3 distinctive manner of a person, artistic school, or period. 4 correct way of designating a person or thing. 5 superior quality or manner (*do it in style*). 6 fashion in dress etc. 7 pointed tool for scratching or engraving. 8 *Bot.* narrow extension of the ovary supporting the stigma. —v. (-ling) 1 design or make etc. in a particu-lar (esp. fashionable) style. 2 designate in a specified way. [Latin *stilus*]

stylish adj. 1 fashionable; elegant. 2 superior. □ **stylishly** adv. **stylishness** n.

stylist /ˈstaɪlɪst/ n. 1 a designer of fashionable styles etc. b hairdresser. 2 stylish writer or performer.

stylistic /staɪˈlɪstɪk/ adj. of esp. literary style. □ **stylistically** adv.

stylized /ˈstaɪlaɪzd/ adj. (also **-ised**) painted, drawn, etc. in a conventional non-realistic style.

stylus /ˈstaɪləs/ n. (pl. **-luses** or **-li**) 1 sharp needle following a groove in a gramo-phone record and transmitting the recorded sound for reproduction. 2 pointed writing tool. [Latin: related to STYLE]

stymie /ˈstaɪmɪ/ (also **stimy**) —n. (pl. **-ies**) 1 *Golf* situation where an oppon-ent's ball lies between one's ball and the

hole. **2** difficult situation. —v. (-mies, -mied, -mying or -mieing) **1** obstruct; thwart. **2** *Golf* block with a stymie. [origin unknown]

styptic /'stɪptɪk/ —adj. checking bleeding. —n. styptic substance. [Greek *stuphō* contract]

styrene /'staɪəriːn/ n. liquid hydrocarbon easily polymerized and used in making plastics etc. [Greek *sturax* a resin]

suasion /'sweɪʒ(ə)n/ n. formal persuasion (*moral suasion*). [Latin *suadeo suas-* urge]

suave /swɑːv/ adj. smooth; polite; sophisticated. □ **suavely** adv. **suavity** /-vɪtɪ/ n. [Latin *suavis*]

sub colloq. —n. **1** submarine. **2** subscription. **3** substitute. **4** sub-editor. —v. (-bb-) **1** (usu. foll. by *for*) act as a substitute. **2** sub-edit. [abbreviation]

sub- prefix **1** at, to, or from a lower position (*subordinate; submerge; subtract*). **2** secondary or inferior position (*subclass; subtotal*). **3** nearly; more or less (*subarctic*). [Latin]

subaltern /'sʌbalt(ə)n/ n. officer below the rank of captain, esp. a second lieutenant. [Latin: related to ALTERNATE]

sub-aqua /sʌb'ækwə/ adj. of underwater swimming or diving.

subaquatic /sʌbə'kwætɪk/ adj. underwater.

subatomic /sʌbə'tɒmɪk/ adj. occurring in, or smaller than, an atom.

subcommittee n. committee formed from a main committee for a special purpose.

subconscious /sʌb'kɒnʃəs/ —adj. of the part of the mind which is not fully conscious but influences actions etc. —n. this part of the mind. □ **subconsciously** adv.

subcontinent /sʌb,kɒntɪnənt/ n. large land mass, smaller than a continent.

subcontract —v. /,sʌbkən'trækt/ **1** employ another contractor to do (work) as part of a larger project. **2** make or carry out a subcontract. —n. /sʌb'kɒntrækt/ secondary contract. □ **subcontractor** /'træktə(r)/ n.

subculture /'sʌb,kʌltʃə(r)/ n. distinct cultural group within a larger culture.

subcutaneous /,sʌbkjuː'teɪnɪəs/ adj. under the skin.

subdivide /,sʌbdɪ'vaɪd/ v. (-ding) divide again after a first division. □ **subdivision** /-,vɪʒ(ə)n/ n.

subdue /səb'djuː/ v. (-dues, -dued, -duing) **1** conquer, subjugate, or tame. **2** (as **subdued** adj.) softened; lacking in intensity; toned down. [Latin *subduco*]

sub-editor /sʌb'edɪtə(r)/ n. **1** assistant editor. **2** person who edits material for printing. □ **sub-edit** v. (-t-).

subfusc /'sʌbfʌsk/ —adj. formal dull dusky. —n. formal clothing at some universities. [Latin *fuscus* dark brown]

subgroup /'sʌbɡruːp/ n. subset of a group.

subheading /sʌb,hedɪŋ/ n. subordinate heading or title.

subhuman /sʌb'hjuːmən/ adj. (of behaviour, intelligence, etc.) less than human.

subject —n. /'sʌbdʒɪkt/ **1 a** matter, theme, etc. to be discussed, described, represented, etc. **b** (foll. by *for*) person, circumstance, etc., giving rise to a specified feeling, action, etc. (*subject for congratulation*). **2** field of study. **3** *Logic & Gram.* noun or its equivalent about which the verb agrees. **4** any person, except a monarch, living under a government. **5** *Philos.* **a** thinking or feeling entity; the conscious mind as opposed to anything external to it. **b** central substance of a thing as opposed to its attributes. **6** *Mus.* theme; leading phrase or motif. **7** person of specified tendencies (*a hysterical subject*). —adj. /'sʌbdʒɪkt/ **1** (foll. by *to*) conditional upon (*subject to your approval*). **2** (foll. by *to*) liable or exposed to (*subject to infection*). **3** (often foll. by *to*) owing obedience to a government etc.; in subjection. —adv. /'sʌbdʒɪkt/ (foll. by *to*) conditionally upon (*subject to your consent, I shall go*). —v. /səb'dʒekt/ (foll. by *to*) make liable; expose (*subjected us to hours of waiting*). [Latin *subjectus* placed under]

subjective /səb'dʒektɪv/ adj. **1** (of art, written history, an opinion, etc.) not impartial or literal; personal. **2** esp. *Philos.* of the individual consciousness or perception; imaginary, partial, or distorted. **3** *Gram.* of the subject. □ **subjectively** adv. **subjectivity** /,sʌbdʒek'tɪvɪtɪ/ n. [Latin: related to SUBJECT]

subjoin /sʌb'dʒɔɪn/ v. add (an illustration, anecdote, etc.) at the end. [Latin *subjungo* *-junct-*]

sub judice /sʌb 'dʒuːdɪsɪ/ adj. *Law* under judicial consideration and therefore prohibited from public discussion elsewhere. [Latin]

subjugate /'sʌbdʒʊɡeɪt/ v. (-ting) bring into subjection; vanquish. □ **subjugation** /-'ɡeɪʃ(ə)n/ n. **subjugator** n. [Latin *jugum* yoke]

subjunctive /səbˈdʒʌŋktɪv/ *Gram.* —*adj.* (of a mood) expressing what is imagined, wished, or possible (e.g. *if I were you; be that as it may*). —*n.* this mood or form. [Latin: related to SUBJOIN]

sublease —*n.* /ˈsʌbliːs/ lease granted by a tenant to a subtenant. —*v.* /sʌbˈliːs/ (-sing) lease to a subtenant.

sublet —*v.* /sʌbˈlet/ (-**tt**-; *past* and *past part.* -**let**) = SUBLEASE *v.* —*n.* /ˈsʌblet/ = SUBLEASE *n.* [SUB- + LET]

sub-lieutenant /sʌblɛfˈtɛnənt/ *n.* officer ranking next below lieutenant.

sublimate —*v.* /ˈsʌblɪmeɪt/ (-ting) 1 divert (esp. sexual energy) into socially more acceptable activity. 2 convert (a substance) from the solid state directly to vapour by heat, and usu. allow it to solidify again. 3 refine; purify; idealize. —*n.* /ˈsʌblɪmət/ sublimated substance. □ **sublimation** /-ˈmeɪʃ(ə)n/ *n.* [Latin: related to SUBLIME]

sublime /səˈblaɪm/ —*adj.* (**sublimer, sublimest**) 1 of the most exalted or noble kind; awe-inspiring. 2 arrogantly unruffled (*sublime indifference*). —*v.* 1 = SUBLIMATE *v.* 2. 2 purify or elevate by sublimation; make sublime. 3 become pure (as if) by sublimation. □ **sublimely** *adv.* **sublimity** /-ˈlɪmɪtɪ/ *n.* [Latin *sublimis*]

subliminal /sʌbˈlɪmɪn(ə)l/ *adj. Psychol.* (of a stimulus etc.) below the threshold of sensation or consciousness. □ **subliminally** *adv.* [Latin *limen -min-* threshold]

sub-machine-gun /ˌsʌbməˈʃiːngʌn/ *n.* hand-held lightweight machine-gun.

submarine /ˌsʌbməˈriːn, ˈsʌb-/ —*n.* vessel, esp. an armed warship, capable of operating under water. —*attrib. adj.* existing, occurring, done, or used under the sea. □ **submariner** /-ˈmærɪnə(r)/ *n.*

submerge /səbˈmɜːdʒ/ *v.* (-ging) 1 place, go, or dive under water. 2 inundate with work, problems, etc. □ **submergence** *n.* **submersion** /-ˈmɜːʃ(ə)n/ *n.* [Latin *mergo mers-* dip]

submersible /səbˈmɜːsɪb(ə)l/ —*adj.* submarine operating under water for short periods. —*adj.* capable of submerging.

submicroscopic /ˌsʌb.maɪkrəˈskɒpɪk/ *adj.* too small to be seen by an ordinary microscope.

submission /səbˈmɪʃ(ə)n/ *n.* 1 **a** submitting or being submitted. **b** thing submitted. 2 submissiveness. [Latin *submissio*: related to SUBMIT]

submissive /səbˈmɪsɪv/ *adj.* humble, obedient. □ **submissively** *adv.* **submissiveness** *n.*

submit /səbˈmɪt/ *v.* (-**tt**-) 1 (usu. foll. by *to*) **a** cease resistance; yield. **b** *refl.*

---

surrender (oneself) to the control of another etc. 2 present for consideration. 3 (usu. foll. by *to*) subject (a person or thing) to a process, treatment, etc. [Latin *mitto miss-* send]

subnormal /sʌbˈnɔːm(ə)l/ *adj.* below or less than normal, esp in intelligence.

suborder /ˈsʌbɔːdə(r)/ *n.* taxonomic category between an order and a family.

subordinate —*adj.* /səˈbɔːdɪnət/ (usu. foll. by *to*) of inferior importance or rank; secondary, subservient. —*n.* person working under another. —*v.* /səˈbɔːdɪneɪt/ (-ting) (usu. foll. by *to*) make or treat as subordinate. □ **subordination** /-ˈneɪʃ(ə)n/ *n.* [Latin: related to ORDAIN]

subordinate clause *n.* clause serving as an adjective, adverb, or noun in a main sentence.

suborn /səˈbɔːn/ *v.* induce by bribery etc. to commit perjury etc. [Latin *orno* equip]

sub-plot *n.* secondary plot in a play etc.

subpoena /səˈpiːnə/ —*n.* writ ordering a person to attend a lawcourt. —*v.* (*past* and *past part.* -**na'd** or -**na'ed**) serve a subpoena on. [Latin, = under penalty]

subscribe /səbˈskraɪb/ *v.* (-bing) (usu. foll. by *to, for*) **a** pay (a specified sum), regularly, for membership of an organization, receipt of a publication, etc. **b** contribute money to a fund, for a cause, etc. 2 (usu. foll. by *to*) agree with an opinion etc. (*I subscribe to that*). □ **subscribe to** arrange to receive (a periodical etc.) regularly [Latin *scribo script-* write]

subscriber *n.* 1 person who subscribes. 2 person hiring a telephone line.

subscriber trunk dialling *n.* automatic connection of trunk calls by dialling.

subscript /ˈsʌbskrɪpt/ —*adj.* written or printed below the line —*n.* subscript number etc.

subscription /səbˈskrɪpʃ(ə)n/ —*n.* 1 **a** act of subscribing. **b** money subscribed. 2 membership fee, esp. paid regularly. —*attrib. adj.* paid for mainly by advance sales of tickets (*subscription concert*).

subsection *n.* division of a section.

subsequent /ˈsʌbsɪkw(ə)nt/ *adj.* (usu. foll. by *to*) following, esp. as a consequence. □ **subsequently** *adv.* [Latin *sequor follow*]

---

subordinate related

subroutine *n. Computing* routine designed to perform a frequently used operation within a program.

sub rosa /sʌb ˈrəʊzə/ *adj. & adv.* in secrecy or confidence. [Latin, = under the rose]

subservient /səbˈsɜːvɪənt/ *adj.* 1 servile. 2 (usu. foll. by *to*) instrumental. 3

(usu. foll. by *to*) subordinate. □ **subservience** *n.* [Latin *subservio*]

subset *n.* set of which all the elements are contained in another set.

subside /səbˈsaɪd/ *v.* (**-ding**) **1** become tranquil; abate (*excitement subsided*). **2** (of water etc.) sink. **3** (of the ground cave in; sink. □ **subsidence** /ˈsaɪd(ə)ns, ˈsʌbsɪd(ə)ns/ *n.* [Latin *subsido*]

subsidiary /səbˈsɪdɪərɪ/ —*adj.* **1** supplementary; auxiliary. **2** (of a company) controlled by another. —*n.* (*pl.* **-ies**) subsidiary thing, person, or company. [Latin: related to SUBSIDY]

subsidize /ˈsʌbsɪdaɪz/ *v.* (also **-ise**) (**-zing** or **-sing**) **1** pay a subsidy to. **2** partially pay for by subsidy.

subsidy /ˈsʌbsɪdɪ/ *n.* (*pl.* **-ies**) **1** money granted esp. by the State to keep down the price of commodities etc. **2** any monetary grant. [Latin *subsidium* help]

subsist /səbˈsɪst/ *v.* **1** (often foll. by *on*) keep oneself alive; be kept alive. **2** remain in being; exist. [Latin *subsisto*]

subsistence /səbˈsɪst(ə)ns/ *n.* **1** state or instance of subsisting. **2 a** means of support; livelihood. **b** (often *attrib.*) minimal level of existence or income. □ **subsistence farming** *n.* farming which supports the farmer's household but produces no surplus.

subsoil /ˈsʌbsɔɪl/ *n.* soil immediately under the surface soil.

subsonic /sʌbˈsɒnɪk/ *adj.* of speeds less than that of sound.

substance /ˈsʌbst(ə)ns/ *n.* **1** particular kind of material having uniform properties. **2** reality; solidity. **3** content or essence as opposed to form etc. (*substance of his remarks*). **4** wealth and possessions (*woman of substance*). □ **in substance** generally; essentially. [Latin *substantia*]

substandard /sʌbˈstændəd/ *adj.* of less than the required or normal quality or size.

substantial /səbˈstænʃ(ə)l/ *adj.* **1 a** of real importance or value. **b** large in size or amount. **2** solid; sturdy. **3** commercially successful; wealthy. **4** essential; real: existing. **5** real existing. □ **substantially** *adv.* [Latin: related to SUBSTANCE]

substantiate /səbˈstænʃɪˌeɪt/ *v.* (**-ting**) prove the truth of (a charge, claim, etc.). □ **substantiation** /-ˈeɪʃ(ə)n/ *n.*

substantive /ˈsʌbstəntɪv/ —*adj.* /also səbˈstæntɪv/ **1** genuine, actual, real. **2** not slight; substantial. —*n.* *Gram.* = NOUN. □ **substantively** *adv.*

substitute /ˈsʌbstɪˌtjuːt/ —*n.* **1** (also *attrib.*) person or thing acting or used in place of another. **2** artificial alternative to a food etc. —*v.* (**-ting**) (often foll. by *for*) (cause to) act as a substitute. □

substitution /-ˈtjuːʃ(ə)n/ *n.* [Latin *substitutus*]

substratum /ˈsʌbˌstrɑːtəm/ *n.* (*pl.* **-ta**) underlying layer or substance.

substructure *n.* underlying or supporting structure.

subsume /səbˈsjuːm/ *v.* (**-ming**) (usu. foll. by *under*) include (an instance, idea, category, etc.) in a rule, class, etc. [Latin *sumo* take]

subtenant /ˈsʌbˌtɛnənt/ *n.* person renting a room etc. from its tenant. □ **subtenancy** *n.* (*pl.* **-ies**)

subtend /səbˈtɛnd/ *v.* (of a line) be opposite (an angle or arc). [Latin: related to TEND]

subterfuge /ˈsʌbtəˌfjuːdʒ/ *n.* **1** attempt to avoid blame or defeat esp. by lying or deceit. **2** statement etc. used for such a purpose. [Latin]

subterranean /ˌsʌbtəˈreɪnɪən/ *adj.* underground. [Latin *terra* land]

subtext *n.* underlying theme.

subtitle /ˈsʌbˌtaɪt(ə)l/ —*n.* **1** secondary or additional title of a book etc. **2** caption on a film etc., esp. translating dialogue. —*v.* (**-ling**) provide with a subtitle or subtitles.

subtle /ˈsʌt(ə)l/ *adj.* (**subtler**, **subtlest**) **1** elusive, mysterious; hard to grasp. **2** (of scent, colour, etc.) faint, delicate. **3 a** perceptive (*subtle intellect*). **b** ingenious (*subtle device*). □ **subtlety** *n.* (*pl.* **-ies**) **subtly** *adv.* [Latin *subtilis*]

subtotal *n.* total of one part of a group of figures to be added.

subtract /səbˈtrækt/ *v.* (often foll. by *from*) deduct (a number etc.) from another. □ **subtraction** /-ˈtrækʃ(ə)n/ *n.* [Latin *subtraho* draw away]

subtropics /sʌbˈtrɒpɪks/ *n.pl.* regions adjacent to the tropics. □ **subtropical** *adj.*

suburb /ˈsʌbɜːb/ *n.* outlying district of a city. [Latin *urbs* city]

suburban /səˈbɜːbən/ *adj.* **1** of or characteristic of suburbs. **2** *derog.* provincial in outlook. □ **suburbanite** *n.*

suburbia /səˈbɜːbɪə/ *n.* often *derog.* suburbs, their inhabitants, and their way of life.

subvention /səbˈvɛnʃ(ə)n/ *n.* subsidy. [Latin *subvenio* assist]

subversive /səbˈvɜːsɪv/ —*adj.* seeking to subvert (esp. a government). —*n.* subversive person. □ **subversion** *n.* **subversiveness** *n.* [medieval Latin *subversivus*: related to SUBVERT]

subvert /səbˈvɜːt/ *v.* overthrow or weaken (a government etc.). [Latin *verto vers-* turn]

subway /ˈsʌbweɪ/ n. **1** pedestrian tunnel beneath a road etc. **2** esp. US underground railway.

subzero /sʌbˈzɪərəʊ/ adj. (esp. of temperature) lower than zero.

suc- prefix assim. form of SUB- before c.

succeed /səkˈsiːd/ v. **1 a** (often foll. by in) have success. **b** be successful. **2** follow; come next after. **3** (often foll. by to) come into an inheritance, office, title, or property (succeeded to the throne). [Latin succedo -cess- come after]

success /səkˈses/ n. **1** accomplishment of an aim; favourable outcome. **2** attainment of wealth, fame, or position. **3** successful thing or person. [Latin: related to SUCCEED]

successful adj. having success; prosperous. □ **successfully** adv.

succession /səkˈseʃ(ə)n/ n. **1 a** process of following in order; succeeding. **b** series of things or people one after another. **2 a** right of succeeding to the throne, an office, inheritance, etc. **b** act or process of so succeeding. **c** those having such a right. □ **in succession** one after another, without another intervening. **in succession to** as the successor of.

successive /səkˈsesɪv/ adj. following one after another; consecutive. □ **successively** adv.

successor /səkˈsesə(r)/ n. (often foll. by to) person or thing that succeeds another.

succinct /səkˈsɪŋkt/ adj. brief, concise. □ **succinctly** adv. **succinctness** n. [Latin cingo cinct- gird]

succour /ˈsʌkə(r)/ (US **succor**) —n. aid, esp. in time of need. —v. give succour to. [Latin succurro run to help]

succubus /ˈsʌkjʊbəs/ n. (pl. **-bi** /-baɪ/) female demon formerly believed to have sexual intercourse with sleeping men. [Latin, = prostitute]

succulent /ˈsʌkjʊlənt/ —adj. **1** juicy; palatable. **2** Bot. (of a plant, its leaves, or stems) thick and fleshy. —n. Bot. succulent plant. □ **succulence** n. [Latin sucus juice]

succumb /səˈkʌm/ v. (usu. foll. by to) **1** surrender (succumbed to temptation). **2** die (from) (succumbed to his injuries). [Latin cumbo lie]

such —adj. **1** (often foll. by as) of the kind or degree indicated (such people; people such as these). **2** so great or extreme (not such a fool as that). **3** of a more than normal kind or degree (such awful food). —pron. such a person or persons; such a thing or things. □ **as such** as being what has been indicated or named; in itself (there is no theatre as such). **such as** for example. [Old English, = so like]

---

such-and-such —attrib. adj. of a particular kind but not needing to be specified. —n. such a person or thing.

suchlike colloq. —attrib. adj. of such a kind. —n. things, people, etc. of such a kind.

suck —v. **1** draw (a fluid) into the mouth by suction. **2** (also absol.) draw fluid from (a thing) in this way. **3** roll the tongue round (a sweet etc.). **4** make a sucking action or sound. **5** (usu. foll. by down, in) engulf or drown in a sucking movement. —n. act or period of sucking. □ **suck dry** exhaust the contents of by sucking. **suck in** **1** absorb. **2** involve (a person) esp. against his or her will. **suck up 1** (often foll. by to) colloq. behave obsequiously. **2** absorb. [Old English]

sucker /ˈsʌkə(r)/ n. **1 a** gullible person. **b** (foll. by for) person susceptible to. **2 a** rubber cup etc. adhering by suction. **3** shoot springing from a root or stem below ground. [suck]

suckle /ˈsʌk(ə)l/ v. (-ling) **1** feed (young) from the breast or udder. **2** feed by sucking the breast etc.

suckling n. unweaned child or animal.

sucrose /ˈsuːkrəʊz/ n. sugar from sugar cane, sugar beet, etc. [French sucre SUGAR]

suction /ˈsʌkʃ(ə)n/ n. **1** act of sucking. **2** a production of a partial vacuum by the removal of air etc. so that liquid etc. is forced in or adhesion is procured. **b** force so produced. [Latin sugo suct- suck]

Sudanese /ˌsuːdəˈniːz/ —adj. of Sudan. —n. (pl. same) **1** native, national, or inhabitant of Sudan. **2** person of Sudanese descent. [Sudan in NE Africa]

sudden /ˈsʌd(ə)n/ adj. done or occurring unexpectedly or abruptly. □ **all of a sudden** suddenly. □ **suddenly** adv. **suddenness** n. [Latin subitaneus]

sudden death n. colloq. decision in a tied game etc. dependent on one move, card, etc.

sudden infant death syndrome n. = COT-DEATH.

sudorific /ˌsuːdəˈrɪfɪk/ —adj. causing sweating. —n. sudorific drug. [Latin sudor sweat]

suds n.pl. froth of soap and water. □ **sudsy** adj. [Low German sudde or Dutch sudse marsh, bog]

sue /suː, sjuː/ v. (**sues, sued, suing**) **1** (also absol.) begin a law suit against. **2** (often foll. by to, for) make application to a lawcourt for redress. **3** (often foll. by to, for) make entreaty to a person for a favour. [Anglo-French suer from Latin sequor follow]

suede /sweɪd/ n. (often attrib.) **1** leather with the flesh side rubbed to a nap. **2** cloth imitating it. [French, = Sweden]

suet /ˈsuːɪt/ n. hard white fat on the kidneys or loins of oxen, sheep, etc. □ **suety** adj. [Anglo-French seu, from Latin sebum]

suf- prefix assim. form of sub- before f.

suffer /ˈsʌfə(r)/ v. **1** undergo pain, grief, damage, etc. **2** undergo, experience, or be subjected to (pain, loss, grief, defeat, change, etc.). **3** tolerate (does not suffer fools gladly). **4** (usu. foll. by to + infin.) archaic allow. □ **sufferer** n. [Latin suffero]

sufferance n. tacit consent. □ **on sufferance** tolerated but not encouraged. [Latin: related to SUFFER]

suffice /səˈfaɪs/ v. (-cing) **1** (often foll. by for, or to + infin.) be adequate. **2** satisfy. □ **suffice it to say** I shall say only this. [Latin sufficio]

sufficiency /səˈfɪʃənsɪ/ n. (pl. -ies) (often foll. by of) adequate amount. □

sufficient adj. sufficing, adequate. □ **sufficiently** adv.

suffix /ˈsʌfɪks/ —n. letter(s) added at the end of a word to form a derivative. —v. append, esp. as a suffix. [Latin figo fix- fasten]

suffocate /ˈsʌfəkeɪt/ v. (-ting) **1** choke or kill by stopping breathing, esp. by pressure, fumes, etc. **2** (often foll. by by, with) produce a choking or breathlessness in. **3** be or feel suffocated. □ **suffocating** adj. **suffocation** /-ˈkeɪʃ(ə)n/ n. [Latin suffoco from fauces throat]

suffragan /ˈsʌfrəgən/ n. **1** bishop assisting a diocesan bishop. **2** bishop in relation to his archbishop or metropolitan. [medieval Latin suffraganeus]

suffrage /ˈsʌfrɪdʒ/ n. right of voting in political elections. [Latin suffragium]

suffragette /ˌsʌfrəˈdʒet/ n. hist. woman seeking suffrage by organized protest.

suffuse /səˈfjuːz/ v. (-sing) (of colour, moisture, etc.) spread throughout from within. □ **suffusion** /-ˈfjuːʒ(ə)n/ n. [Latin suffundo pour over]

Sufi /ˈsuːfɪ/ n. (pl. -s) Muslim mystic. □ **Sufic** adj. **Sufism** n. [Arabic]

sug- prefix assim. form of sub- before g.

sugar /ˈʃʊgə(r)/ —n. **1** sweet crystalline substance esp. from sugar cane and sugar beet, used in cookery etc.; sucrose. **2** Chem. soluble usu. sweet crystalline carbohydrate, e.g. glucose. **3** esp. US colloq. darling (as a term of address). —v. sweeten or coat with sugar. [French sukere, from Arabic sukkar]

sugar beet n. beet yielding sugar.

sugar cane n. tropical grass yielding sugar.

sugar-daddy n. slang elderly man who lavishes gifts on a young woman.

sugar loaf n. conical moulded mass of sugar.

sugar soap n. alkaline compound for cleaning or removing paint.

sugary adj. **1** containing or like sugar. **2** excessively sweet or esp. sentimental. □ **sugariness** n.

suggest /səˈdʒest/ v. **1** (often foll. by that) propose (a theory, plan, etc.). **2 a** evoke (an idea etc.). **b** hint at. □ **suggest itself** (of an idea etc.) come into the mind. [Latin: related to SUGGEST]

suggestible adj. **1** easily influenced. **2** capable of being suggested. □ **suggestibility** /-ˈbɪlɪtɪ/ n.

suggestion /səˈdʒestʃ(ə)n/ n. **1** suggesting or being suggested. **2** theory, plan, etc., suggested. **3** slight trace, hint. **4** Psychol. insinuation of a belief etc. into the mind. [Latin: related to SUGGEST]

suggestive /səˈdʒestɪv/ adj. **1** (usu. foll. by of) hinting (at). **2** (of a remark, joke, etc.) indecent. □ **suggestively** adv.

suicidal /ˌsuːɪˈsaɪd(ə)l/ adj. **1** inclined to commit suicide. **2** of suicide. **3** self-destructive; rash. □ **suicidally** adv.

suicide /ˈsuːɪsaɪd/ n. **1 a** intentional killing of oneself. **b** person who commits suicide. **2** self-destructive action or course (political suicide). [Latin sui of oneself, -CIDE]

sui generis /ˌsuːaɪ ˈdʒenərɪs, ˌsuːɪ ˈgen-/ adj. of its own kind; unique. [Latin]

suit /suːt, sjuːt/ —n. **1** set of matching clothes, usu. a jacket and trousers or skirt. **2** (esp. in comb.) clothes for a special purpose (swimsuit). **3** any of the four sets (spades, hearts, diamonds, clubs) making up a pack of cards. **4** lawsuit. **5** a petition, esp. to a person in authority. **b** archaic courting a woman (paid suit to her). —v. **1** go well with (a person's appearance etc.). **2** (also absol.) meet the demands or requirements of; satisfy; agree with. **3** make fitting; accommodate; adapt. **4** (as suited adj.) appropriate. □ **suit oneself** do as one chooses. [Anglo-French siute]

suitable adj. (usu. foll. by to, for) well-fitted; appropriate. □ **suitability** /-ˈbɪlɪtɪ/ n. **suitably** adv.

suitcase n. case for carrying clothes etc., with a handle and a flat hinged lid.

suite /swiːt/ n. **1** set, esp. of rooms in a hotel etc. or a sofa and armchairs. **2** Mus. set of instrumental pieces performed as a unit. [French: related to SUIT]

suitor /ˈsuːtə(r), ˈsjuː-/ n. **1** man wooing a woman. **2** plaintiff or petitioner in a lawsuit. [Anglo-French from Latin]

sulfa US var. of SULPHA.

sulfate US var. of SULPHATE.

sulfide US var. of SULPHIDE.

sulfonamide US var. of SULPHONAMIDE.

sulfonamide US var. of SULPHON-AMIDE.

sulfur US var. of SULPHUR.

sulfuric US var. of SULPHURIC.

sulfurous US var. of SULPHUROUS.

sulk —v. be sulky. —n. (also in pl., prec. by *the*) period of sullen silence. [perhaps a back-formation from SULKY]

sulky adj. (**-ier, -iest**) sullen or silent, esp. from resentment or bad temper. □ **sulkily** adv. **sulkiness** n. [perhaps from obsolete *sulke* hard to dispose of]

sullen /'sʌlən/ adj. passively resentful, sulky, morose. □ **sullenly** adv. **sullenness** n. [Anglo-French *sol* sole³]

sully /'sʌli/ v. (**-ies, -ied**) disgrace or tarnish (a reputation etc.). [French *souiller*: related to SOIL²]

sulpha /'sʌlfə/ n. (US **sulfa**) any of various sulphonamides (often attrib.: *sulpha drug*). [abbreviation]

sulphate /'sʌlfeɪt/ n. (US **sulfate**) salt or ester of sulphuric acid. [Latin SULPHUR]

sulphide /'sʌlfaɪd/ n. (US **sulfide**) binary compound of sulphur.

sulphite /'sʌlfaɪt/ n. (US **sulfite**) salt or ester of sulphurous acid. [French: related to SULPHATE]

sulphonamide /sʌl'fɒnəmaɪd/ n. (US **sulfonamide**) any of a class of antibiotic drugs containing sulphur. [German *Sulfon* (related to SULPHUR), *amide* a derivative of AMMONIA]

sulphur /'sʌlfə(r)/ n. (US **sulfur**) 1 pale yellow non-metallic element burning with a blue flame and a suffocating smell. 2 pale greenish-yellow colour. [Anglo-French from Latin]

sulphur dioxide n. colourless pungent gas formed by burning sulphur in air and dissolving it in water.

sulphureous /sʌl'fjʊəriəs/ adj. (US **sulfureous**) of or like sulphur.

sulphuric /sʌl'fjʊərɪk/ adj. (US **sulfuric**) *Chem.* containing sulphur with a valency of six.

sulphuric acid n. dense oily highly corrosive acid.

sulphurous /'sʌlfərəs/ adj. (US **sulfurous**) 1 of or like sulphur. 2 *Chem.* containing sulphur with a valency of four.

sulphurous acid n. weak acid used as a reducing and bleaching acid.

sultan /'sʌlt(ə)n/ n. Muslim sovereign. □ **sultanate** n. [Arabic]

sultana /sʌl'tɑːnə/ n. 1 seedless raisin. 2 sultan's mother, wife, concubine, or daughter. [Italian]

sultry /'sʌltri/ adj. (**-ier, -iest**) 1 (of weather etc.) hot and close. 2 (of a person etc.) passionate, sensual. □ **sultrily** adv. **sultriness** n. [obsolete *sulter* (v.): related to SWELTER]

sum —n. 1 total resulting from addition. 2 amount of money (*a large sum*). 3 a arithmetical problem. b (esp. pl.) *colloq.* arithmetic work. —v. (**-mm-**) find the sum of. □ **in sum** in brief. **sum up** 1 (esp. of a judge) give a brief, summing-up. 2 form or express an opinion of (a person, situation, etc.). 3 summarize. [Latin *summa*]

sumac /'suːmæk, 'ʃuː-/ n. (also **sumach**) 1 shrub with reddish conical fruits used as a spice. 2 dried and ground leaves of this used in tanning and dyeing. [French from Arabic]

summary /'sʌməri/ —n. (pl. **-ies**) brief account. —adj. without details or formalities; brief. □ **summarily** adv. **summarize** /'sʌmə.raɪz/ v. (also **-ise**) (**-zing** or **-sing**) make or be a summary of. [Latin: related to SUM]

summation /sə'meɪʃ(ə)n/ n. 1 finding of a total. 2 a summing-up.

summer /'sʌmə(r)/ n. 1 (often attrib.) warmest season of the year. 2 (often foll. by of) mature stage of life etc. □ **summery** adj. [Old English]

summer-house n. light building in a garden etc. for sitting in in fine weather.

summer pudding n. pudding of soft fruit pressed in a bread case.

summer school n. course of summer lectures etc. held esp. at a university.

summer solstice n. solstice about 21 June.

summertime n. season or period of summer.

summer time n. period from March to October when clocks are advanced an hour.

summing-up n. 1 judge's review of evidence given to a jury. 2 recapitulation of the main points of an argument etc.

summit /'sʌmɪt/ n. 1 highest point, top. 2 highest degree of power, ambition, etc. 3 (in full **summit meeting, talks**, etc.) conference of heads of government. [Latin *summus* highest]

summon /'sʌmən/ v. 1 order to come or appear, esp. in a law-court. 2 (usu. foll. by *to* + infin.) call (upon) (*summoned her to assist*). 3 call together. 4 (often foll. by *up*) gather (courage, spirits, resources, etc.). [Latin *summoneo*]

summons —n. (pl. **summonses**) 1 authoritative call to attend or do something, esp. to appear in court. —v. esp. *Law* serve with a summons.

sumo /ˈsuːməʊ/ n. Japanese wrestling in which a wrestler is defeated by touching the ground with any part of the body except the soles of the feet or by moving outside the ring. [Japanese]

sump n. 1 casing holding the oil in an internal-combustion engine. 2 pit, well, hole, etc. in which superfluous liquid collects. [Low German or Dutch]

sumptuary /ˈsʌmptjʊəri/ adj. Law regulating (esp. private) expenditure. [Latin sumptus cost]

sumptuous /ˈsʌmptjʊəs/ adj. rich, lavish, costly. □ **sumptuously** adv. **sumptuousness** n. [Latin: related to SUMPTUARY]

Sun. abbr. Sunday.

sun n. 1 a the star round which the earth orbits and from which it receives light and warmth. b this light or warmth. 2 any star. —v. (-nn-) refl. bask in the sun. □ **under the sun** anywhere in the world. □ **sunless** adj. [Old English]

sunbathe v. (-thing) bask in the sun, esp. to tan the body. □ **sunbather** n.

sunbeam n. ray of sunlight.

sunbed n. 1 long lightweight, usu. folding, chair for sunbathing. 2 bed for lying on under a sun-lamp.

sunblock n. lotion protecting the skin from the sun.

sunburn n. inflammation and tanning of the skin from exposure to the sun. □ **sunburnt** adj. (also **sunburned**).

sundae /ˈsʌndeɪ/ n. ice-cream with fruit, nuts, syrup, etc. [perhaps from SUNDAY]

Sunday /ˈsʌndeɪ/ n. 1 first day of the week, a Christian holiday and day of worship. 2 colloq. newspaper published on Sundays. —adv. colloq. 1 on Sunday. 2 (**Sundays**) on Sundays; each Sunday. [Old English]

Sunday best n. joc. person's best clothes, esp. for Sunday use.

Sunday school n. religious class on Sundays for children.

sunder v. archaic or literary separate. [Old English: cf. ASUNDER]

sundew n. small insect-consuming bog-plant.

sundial n. instrument showing the time by the shadow of a pointer in sunlight.

sundown n. sunset.

sundry /ˈsʌndri/ —adj. various; several. —n. (pl. **-ies**) (in pl.) items or oddments not mentioned individually. [Old English: related to SUNDER]

sunfish n. (pl. same or **-es**) any of various almost spherical fish.

sunflower n. tall plant with large golden-rayed flowers.

sung past part. of SING.

sun-glasses n.pl. glasses tinted to protect the eyes from sunlight or glare.

sunk past and past part. of SINK.

sunken adj. 1 at a lower level; submerged. 2 (of the cheeks etc.) hollow, depressed. [past part. of SINK]

sun-lamp n. lamp giving ultraviolet rays for therapy, to tan, etc.

sunlight n. light from the sun.

sunlit adj. illuminated by sunlight.

sun lounge n. room with large windows to receive sunlight.

Sunni /ˈsʌni/ —n. (pl. same or **-s**) 1 one of the two main branches of Islam, accepting law based not only on the Koran, but on Muhammad's words and acts. 2 adherent of this branch. —adj. (also **Sunnite**) of or relating to Sunni. [Arabic Sunna = way, rule]

sunny adj. (-ier, -iest) 1 bright with or warmed by sunlight. 2 cheery, bright. □ **sunnily** adv. **sunniness** n.

sunrise n. 1 sun's rising. 2 time of this.

sun-roof n. panel in a car's roof that can be opened.

sunset n. 1 sun's setting. 2 time of this.

sunshade n. parasol; awning.

sunshine n. 1 a light of the sun. b area lit by the sun. 2 fine weather. 3 cheerfulness. 4 colloq. form of address.

sunspot n. dark patch on the sun's surface.

sunstroke n. acute prostration from excessive exposure to the sun.

suntan n. brownish skin colour caused by exposure to the sun. □ **suntanned** adj.

suntrap n. sunny, esp. sheltered, place.

sun-up n. esp. US sunrise.

sup¹ —v. (-pp-) 1 take by sips or spoonfuls. 2 esp. N.Engl. colloq. drink (alcohol). —n. sip of liquid. [Old English]

sup² v. (-pp-) archaic take supper. [French]

sup- prefix assim. form of SUB- before p.

super /ˈsuːpə(r)/ —adj. (also as int.) colloq. excellent; splendid. —n. colloq. 1 superintendent. 2 supernumerary. [shortening of words beginning super-]

super- comb. form forming nouns, adjectives, and verbs, meaning: 1 above, beyond, or over (superstructure; supernormal). 2 to an extreme degree (superabundant). 3 extra good or large of its kind (supertanker). 4 of a higher kind (superintendent). [Latin]

superabundant /ˌsuːpərəˈbʌnd(ə)nt/ adj. abounding beyond what is normal or right. □ **superabundance** n. [Latin: related to SUPER-, ABOUND]

superannuate /ˌsuːpərˈænjʊeɪt/ v. (-ting) 1 pension (a person) off. 2 dismiss or discard as too old. 3 (as **super-**

annuated *adj.* too old for work or use. [Latin *annus* year]

superannuation /ˌsuːpərˌanjuˈeɪʃ(ə)n/ *n.* 1 pension. 2 payment towards this.

superb /suːˈpɜːb/ *adj.* 1 colloq. excellent. 2 magnificent. □ **superbly** *adv.* [Latin *superbus* = proud]

supercargo /ˈsuːpəˌkɑːɡəʊ/ *n.* (*pl.* -es) officer in a merchant ship managing sales, etc. of cargo. [Spanish *sobrecargo*]

supercharge /ˈsuːpətʃɑːdʒ/ *v.t.* (-ging) 1 (usu. foll. by *with*) charge (the atmosphere etc.) with energy, emotion, etc. 2 use a supercharger on.

supercharger *n.* device supplying air or fuel to an internal-combustion engine at above atmospheric pressure to increase efficiency.

supercilious /ˌsuːpəˈsɪliəs/ *adj.* contemptuous; haughty. □ **superciliously** *adv.* **superciliousness** *n.* [Latin *supercilium* eyebrow]

supercomputer /ˈsuːpəkəmˌpjuːtə(r)/ *n.* powerful computer capable of dealing with complex mathematical problems.

superconductivity /ˌsuːpəˌkɒndʌk'tɪvɪti/ *n. Physics* property of zero electrical resistance in some substances at very low absolute temperatures. □ **superconducting** /-ˈkɒndʌktɪŋ/ *adj.* **superconductor** /-ˈkɒndʌktə(r)/ *n. Physics* substance having superconductivity.

superego /ˌsuːpərˈiːɡəʊ/ *n.* (*pl.* -s) *Psychol.* part of the mind that acts as a conscience and responds to social rules.

supererogation /ˌsuːpərˌerəˈɡeɪʃ(ə)n/ *n.* doing more than duty requires. [Latin *superogo* pay in addition]

superficial /ˌsuːpəˈfɪʃ(ə)l/ *adj.* 1 of or on the surface; lacking depth. 2 swift or cursory (*superficial examination*). 3 apparent but not real (*superficial resemblance*). 4 (esp. of a person) shallow. □ **superficiality** /-fɪʃiˈælɪti/ *n.* **superficially** *adv.* [Latin: related to FACE]

superfine /ˈsuːpəˌfaɪn/ *adj. Commerce* of extra quality. [Latin: related to FINE¹]

superfluity /ˌsuːpəˈfluːɪti/ *n.* (*pl.* -ies) 1 state of being superfluous. 2 superfluous amount or thing. [Latin *fluo* to flow]

superfluous /suːˈpɜːfluəs/ *adj.* more than is needed or wanted; useless. [Latin *fluo* to flow]

superglue /ˈsuːpəˌɡluː/ *n.* exceptionally strong glue.

supergrass /ˈsuːpəˌɡrɑːs/ *n. colloq.* police informer implicating many people.

superhuman /ˌsuːpəˈhjuːmən/ *adj.* exceeding normal human capability.

superimpose /ˌsuːpərɪmˈpəʊz/ *v.* (usu. foll. by *on*) lay (a thing) on something else. □ **superimposition** /-pəˈzɪʃ(ə)n/ *n.*

superintend /ˌsuːpərɪnˈtend/ *v.* supervise. direct. □ **superintendence** *n.*

superintendent /ˌsuːpərɪnˈtend(ə)nt/ *n.* 1 police officer above the rank of chief inspector. 2 a person who superintends. **b** director of an institution etc.

superior /suːˈpɪərɪə(r)/ —*adj.* 1 in a higher position; of higher rank. 2 a high-quality (*superior leather*). **b** supercilious (*had a superior air*). 3 (often foll. by *to*) better or greater in some respect. 4 written or printed above the line. —*n.* 1 person superior to another esp. in rank. 2 head of a monastery etc. (*Mother Superior*). □ **superiority** /-ˈɒrɪti/ *n.* [Latin comparative of *superus* above]

superlative /suːˈpɜːlətɪv/ —*adj.* 1 of the highest quality or degree; excellent. 2 *Gram.* (of an adjective or adverb) expressing the highest degree of a quality (e.g. *bravest, most fiercely*). —*n.* 1 *Gram.* superlative form of an adjective or adverb. 2 (in *pl.*) high praise, exaggerated language. [Latin: related to FACE]

superman /ˈsuːpəˌman/ *n.* (*pl.* -men) man of exceptional strength or ability. [French from Latin]

supermarket /ˈsuːpəˌmɑːkɪt/ *n.* large self-service store selling food, household goods, etc.

supernatural /ˌsuːpəˈnatʃ(ə)r(ə)l/ —*adj.* 1 not attributable to, or explicable by, the laws of nature; magical; mystical. —*n.* (prec. by *the*) supernatural forces, effects, etc. □ **supernaturally** *adv.*

supernova /ˌsuːpəˈnəʊvə/ *n.* (*pl.* -vae /-viː/ or -s) star increasing suddenly in brightness.

supernumerary /ˌsuːpəˈnjuːmərəri/ —*adj.* 1 in excess of the normal number; extra. 2 engaged for extra work. 3 (of an actor) appearing on stage but not speaking. —*n.* (*pl.* -ies) supernumerary person or thing. [Latin: related to NUMBER]

superphosphate /ˌsuːpəˈfɒsfeɪt/ *n.* fertilizer made from phosphate rock.

superpower /ˈsuːpəˌpaʊə(r)/ *n.* extremely powerful nation.

superscript /ˈsuːpəskrɪpt/ —*adj.* written or printed above. —*n.* superscript number or symbol. [Latin *scribo* write]

supersede /ˌsuːpəˈsiːd/ *v.* (-ding) 1 take the place of. 2 replace with another person or thing. □ **supersession** /-ˈseʃ(ə)n/ *n.* [Latin *supersedeo*]

supersonic /ˌsuːpəˈsɒnɪk/ *adj.* of or having a speed greater than that of sound. □ **supersonically** *adv.*

superstar /ˈsuːpəstɑː(r)/ n. extremely famous or renowned actor, musician, etc.

superstition /ˌsuːpəˈstɪʃ(ə)n/ n. 1 belief in the supernatural; irrational fear of the unknown. 2 practice, belief, or religion based on this. □ **superstitious** adj. **superstitiously** adv. [Latin]

superstore /ˈsuːpəstɔː(r)/ n. large supermarket.

superstructure /ˈsuːpəstrʌktʃə(r)/ n. structure built on top of another.

supertanker /ˈsuːpətæŋkə(r)/ n. very large tanker ship.

supertax /ˈsuːpətæks/ n. additional tax on incomes above a certain level.

supervene /ˌsuːpəˈviːn/ v. (-ning) formal occur as an interruption or change. □ **supervention** /-ˈvenʃ(ə)n/ n. [Latin supervenio]

supervise /ˈsuːpəvaɪz/ v. (-sing) superintend, oversee. □ **supervision** /-ˈvɪʒ(ə)n/ n. **supervisor** n. **supervisory** adj. [Latin supervideo -vis-]

superwoman /ˈsuːpəwʊmən/ n. colloq. woman of exceptional strength or ability.

supine /ˈsuːpaɪn/ adj. 1 lying face upwards. 2 inert, indolent. —n. Latin verbal noun used only in the accusative and ablative. [Latin]

supper n. 1 late evening snack. 2 evening meal, esp. light. [French souper]

supplant /səˈplɑːnt/ v. take the place of, esp. by underhand means. [Latin supplanto trip up]

supple /ˈsʌp(ə)l/ adj. (**suppler, supplest**) flexible, pliant. □ **suppleness** n. [Latin supplex]

supplement —n. /ˈsʌplɪmənt/ 1 thing or part added to improve or provide further information. 2 separate section, esp. a colour magazine, of a newspaper etc. —v. /ˈsʌplɪmənt, -ment/ provide a supplement for. □ **supplemental** /-ˈment(ə)l/ adj. **supplementary** /-ˈmentərɪ/ adj. **supplementation** /-ˈteʃ(ə)n/ n. [Latin suppleo supply]

suppliant /ˈsʌplɪənt/ —adj. supplicating. —n. supplicating person. [Latin: related to SUPPLICATE]

supplicate /ˈsʌplɪkeɪt/ v. (-ting) literary 1 petition humbly to (a person) or for (a thing). 2 (foll. by to, for) make a petition. □ **supplicant** adj. & n. **supplication** /-ˈkeɪʃ(ə)n/ n. **supplicatory** /-kətərɪ/ adj. [Latin supplico]

supply /səˈplaɪ/ —v. (-ies, -ied) 1 provide (a thing needed). 2 (often foll. by with) provide (a person etc. with a thing). 3 meet or make up for (a deficiency or need etc.). —n. (pl. -ies) 1 providing of what is needed. 2 stock, store, amount, etc., of something provided or obtainable. 3 (in pl.) provisions and equipment for an army, expedition, etc. 4 (often attrib.) schoolteacher etc. acting as a temporary substitute for another. □ **in short supply** scarce. **supply and demand** Econ. quantities available and required, as factors regulating price. □ **supplier** n. [Latin suppleo fill up]

supply-side attrib. adj. Econ. denoting a policy of low taxation etc. to encourage production and investment.

support /səˈpɔːt/ —v. 1 carry all or part of the weight of, keep from falling, sinking, or failing. 2 provide for (a family etc.). 3 strengthen, encourage. 4 bear out; tend to substantiate. 5 give help or approval to (a person, team, sport, etc.); further (a cause etc.). 6 speak in favour of (a resolution etc.). 7 (also absol.) take a secondary part to (a principal actor etc.); perform a secondary act to (the main act) at a pop concert etc. —n. 1 supporting or being supported. 2 person or thing that supports. 3 secondary act at a pop concert etc. □ **in support of** so as to support. [Latin porto carry]

supporter n. person or thing that supports a cause, team, etc.

supporting film n. (also **supporting picture** etc.) less important film in a cinema programme.

supportive /səˈpɔːtɪv/ adj. providing (esp. emotional) support or encouragement. □ **supportively** adv. **supportiveness** n.

suppose /səˈpəʊz/ v. (-sing) (often foll. by that) 1 assume; be inclined to think. 2 take as a possibility or hypothesis (suppose you are right; supposing you are right). 3 (in imper.) as a formula of proposal (suppose we try again). 4 (of a theory or result etc.) require as a condition (that supposes we're on time). 5 (in imper. or pres. part. forming a question) in the circumstances that; if (suppose he won't let you?). 6 (as **supposed**) presumed (his supposed brother). 7 (in passive; foll. by to + infin.) a be expected or required (was supposed to write to you). b (with neg.) ought not; not be allowed to (you are not supposed to go in there). □ **I suppose so** expression of hesitant agreement. [French: related to POSE]

supposedly /səˈpəʊzɪdlɪ/ adv. allegedly; as is generally believed.

supposition /ˌsʌpəˈzɪʃ(ə)n/ n. 1 thing supposed. 2 act of supposing.

supposititious /ˌsʌpəˈzɪʃəs/ adj. hypothetical.

suppository /sə'pɒzɪtərɪ/ n. (pl. -ies) medical preparation melting in the rectum or vagina. [Latin *suppositorius* placed underneath]

suppress /sə'pres/ v. 1 put an end to, esp. forcibly. 2 prevent (information, feelings, a reaction, etc.) from being seen, heard, or known. 3 a partly or wholly eliminate (electrical interference etc.). b equip (a device) to reduce the interference caused by it. □ **suppressible** adj. **suppression** n. **suppressor** n. [Latin related to PRESS[1]]

suppurate /'sʌpjʊreɪt/ v. (-ting) 1 form pus. 2 fester. □ **suppuration** /-'reɪʃ(ə)n/ n. [Latin: related to PUS]

supra- prefix above. [Latin]

supranational /su:prə'næʃən(ə)l/ adj. transcending national limits.

supremacy /su:'preməsɪ/ n. (pl. -ies) being supreme. 2 highest authority.

supreme /su:'pri:m/ adj. 1 highest in authority or rank. 2 greatest; most important. 3 (of a penalty or sacrifice etc.) involving death. □ **supremely** adv. [Latin]

Supreme Court n. highest judicial court in a State etc.

supremo /su:'pri:məʊ/ n. (pl. -s) person in overall charge. [Spanish, = SUPREME]

sur-[1] prefix = SUPER (surcharge; surrealism). [French]

sur-[2] prefix assim. form of SUB- before r.

surcease /sɜː'si:s/ literary -n. cessation. -v. (-sing) cease. [French *sursis* delayed, omitted]

surcharge -n. /'sɜːtʃɑːdʒ/ additional charge or payment. -v. /sɜː'tʃɑːdʒ, 'sɜːtʃɑːdʒ/ exact a surcharge from. [French: related to SUR-[1]]

surd Math -adj. (of a number) irrational. -n. surd number, esp. the root of an integer. [Latin, = deaf]

sure /ʃʊə(r), ʃɔː(r)/ -adj. 1 (often foll. by of or that) convinced. 2 having adequate reason for a belief or assertion. 3 (foll. by of) confident in anticipation or knowledge of. 4 reliable or unfailing. 5 (foll. by to + infin.) certain. 6 undoubtedly true or truthful. -adv. colloq. certainly. □ **be sure** (in imper. or infin.; foll. by that + clause or to + infin.) take care to; not fail to. **for sure** colloq. certainly. **make sure** make or become certain; ensure. **sure enough** colloq. in fact; certainly. **to be sure** admittedly; indeed, certainly. □ **sureness** n. [French from Latin *securus*]

sure-fire attrib. adj. colloq. certain to succeed.

sure-footed adj. never stumbling or making a mistake.

surely /'ʃʊəlɪ, 'ʃɔː-/ adv. 1 with certainty or safety (*slowly but surely*) 2 as an appeal to likelihood or reason (*surely that can't be right*).

surety /'ʃʊərətɪ, 'ʃɔː-/ n. (pl. -ies) 1 money given as a guarantee of performance etc. 2 (esp. in phr. **stand surety for**) person who takes responsibility for another's debt, obligation, etc. [French from Latin]

surf -n. foam of the sea breaking on the shore or reefs. -v. practise surfing. □ **surfer** n. [origin unknown]

surface /'sɜːfɪs/ -n. 1 a the outside of a thing. b area of this 2 any of the limits of a solid. 3 top of a liquid or of the ground etc. 4 outward or superficial aspect. 5 *Geom.* set of points with length and breadth but no thickness. 6 (attrib.) a of or on the surface. b superficial. -v. (-cing) 1 give the required surface to (a road, paper, etc.). 2 rise or bring to the surface. 3 become visible or known. 4 colloq. wake up; get up. □ **come to the surface** become perceptible. [French; related to SUR-[1]]

surface mail n. mail carried by land or sea.

surface tension n. tension of the surface-film of a liquid, tending to minimize its surface area.

surfboard n. long narrow board used in surfing.

surfeit /'sɜːfɪt/ -n. 1 an excess, esp. in eating or drinking. 2 resulting fullness. -v. (-t-) 1 overfeed. 2 (foll. by with) (cause to) be wearied through excess. [French related to SUR-, FEAT]

surfing n. sport of riding the surf on a board.

surge -n. 1 sudden rush. 2 heavy forward or upward motion. 3 sudden increase in price, activity, etc. 4 sudden increase in voltage of an electric current. 5 swell of the sea. -v. (-ging) 1 move suddenly and powerfully forwards. 2 (of an electric current etc.) increase suddenly. 3 (of the sea etc.) swell. [Latin *surgo* rise]

surgeon /'sɜːdʒ(ə)n/ n. 1 medical practitioner qualified in surgery. 2 naval or military medical officer.

surgery /'sɜːdʒərɪ/ n. (pl. -ies) 1 treatment of bodily injuries or disorders by incision or manipulation etc. as opposed to drugs. 2 place where or time when a doctor, dentist, etc., treats patients, or an MP, lawyer, etc., gives advice. [Latin *chirurgia*, from Greek *kheir* hand, *ergō* work]

surgical /'sɜːdʒɪk(ə)l/ adj. 1 of or by surgeons or surgery. 2 a used in surgery. b worn to correct a deformity etc. 3

(esp. of military action) swift and precise. □ **surgically** adv.

surgical spirit n. methylated spirit used for cleansing etc.

surly /ˈsɜːlɪ/ adj. (-ier, -iest) bad-tempered; unfriendly. □ **surliness** n. [obsolete sirly haughty: related to SIR]

surmise /səˈmaɪz/ —n. conjecture. —v. (-sing) (often foll. by that) infer doubtfully; guess; suppose. [Latin supermitto -miss- accuse]

surmount /səˈmaʊnt/ v. 1 overcome (a difficulty or obstacle). 2 (usu. in passive) cap or crown. □ **surmountable** adj. [French: related to SUR-¹]

surname /ˈsɜːneɪm/ n. family name, usu. inherited or acquired by marriage. [obsolete surnoun from Anglo-French: related to SUR-¹]

surpass /səˈpɑːs/ v. 1 be greater or better than, outdo. 2 (as **surpassing** adj.) pre-eminent. [French: related to SUR-¹]

surplice /ˈsɜːplɪs/ n. loose white vestment worn by clergy and choristers. [Anglo-French surplis]

surplus /ˈsɜːpləs/ —n. 1 amount left over. 2 excess of revenue over expenditure. —adj. exceeding what is needed or used. [Anglo-French]

surprise /səˈpraɪz/ —n. 1 unexpected or astonishing thing. 2 emotion caused by this. 3 catching or being caught unawares. 4 (attrib.) unexpected; made or done etc. without warning. —v. (-sing) 1 affect with surprise; turn out contrary to the expectations of. 2 (usu. in passive; foll. by at) shock, scandalize. 3 capture or attack by surprise. 4 come upon (a person) unawares. 5 (foll. by into) startle (a person) into an action etc. □ **take by surprise** affect with surprise, esp. by an unexpected encounter or statement. □ **surprising** adj. **surprisingly** adv. [French]

surreal /səˈrɪəl/ adj. unreal; dreamlike; bizarre. [back-formation from SURREALISM]

surrealism n. 20th-c. movement in art and literature, attempting to express the subconscious mind by dream imagery, bizarre juxtapositions, etc. □ **surrealist** n. & adj. **surrealistic** /-ˈlɪstɪk/ adj. **surrealistically** /-ˈlɪstɪkəlɪ/ adv. [French: related to SUR-¹, REAL¹]

surrender /səˈrendə(r)/ —v. 1 hand over; relinquish. 2 submit, esp. to an enemy. 3 refl. (foll. by to) yield to a habit, emotion, influence, etc. 4 give up rights under (a life-insurance policy) in return for a smaller sum received immediately. 5 abandon (hope etc.). —n. act of surrendering. □ **surrender to bail** duly appear in court after release on bail. [Anglo-French: related to SUR-¹]

surreptitious /ˌsʌrəpˈtɪʃəs/ adj. done by stealth; clandestine. □ **surreptitiously** adv. [Latin surripio seize secretly]

surrogate /ˈsʌrəgət/ n. 1 substitute. 2 deputy, esp. of a bishop in granting marriage licences. □ **surrogacy** n. [Latin rogo ask]

surrogate mother n. woman who bears a child on behalf of another woman, usu. by artificial insemination of her own egg by the other woman's partner.

surround /səˈraʊnd/ —v. come or be all round; encircle, enclose. —n. 1 border or edging, esp. an area of floor between the walls and carpet of a room. 2 surrounding area or substance. [Latin: related to SUR-¹, unda wave]

surroundings n.pl. objects or conditions around or affecting a person or thing; environment.

surtax /ˈsɜːtæks/ n. additional tax, esp. on high incomes. [French: related to SUR-¹]

surtitle /ˈsɜːtaɪt(ə)l/ n. explanatory caption projected on to a screen above the stage during an opera.

surveillance /sɜːˈveɪləns/ n. close observation undertaken by the police etc. [French: related to SUR-¹, veiller watch]

survey —v. /səˈveɪ/ 1 view or consider as a whole. 2 examine the condition of (a building etc.). 3 determine the boundaries, extent, ownership, etc. of (a district etc.). —n. /ˈsɜːveɪ/ 1 general view or consideration. 2 a act of surveying property. b statement etc. resulting from this. 3 investigation of public opinion etc. 4 map or plan made by surveying. [Latin: related to SUPER-, video see]

surveyor /səˈveɪə(r)/ n. person who surveys land and buildings, esp. for a living.

survival /səˈvaɪv(ə)l/ n. 1 surviving. 2 relic.

survive /səˈvaɪv/ v. (-ving) 1 continue to live or exist. 2 live or exist longer than. 3 remain alive after or continue to exist in spite of (a danger, accident, etc.). □ **survivor** n. [Anglo-French survivre from Latin supervivo]

sus var. of SUSS.

sus- prefix assim. form of SUB- before c, p, t.

susceptibility /səˌseptɪˈbɪlɪtɪ/ n. (pl. -ies) 1 being susceptible. 2 (in pl.) person's feelings.

susceptible /səˈseptɪb(ə)l/ adj. 1 impressionable, sensitive, emotional. 2 (predic.) a (foll. by to) liable or vulnerable to. b (foll. by of) allowing, admitting

sushi /ˈsuːʃi/ n. Japanese dish of balls of cold rice topped with raw fish etc. [Japanese]

suspect — v. /səˈspekt/ **1** be inclined to think. **2** have an impression of the existence or presence of. **3** (often foll. by *of*) mentally accuse. **4** doubt the genuineness or truth of. — *adj.* /ˈsʌspekt/ suspected person. — n. /ˈsʌspekt/ suspected person. subject to or deserving suspicion. [Latin *suspicio -spect-*]

suspend /səˈspend/ v. **1** hang up. **2** keep inoperative or undecided for a time. **3** debar temporarily from a function, office, etc. **4** (as **suspended** *adj.*) (of particles or a body in a fluid) floating between the top and bottom. [Latin *suspendo -pens-*]

suspended animation n. temporary deathlike condition.

suspended sentence n. judicial sentence left unenforced subject to good behaviour during a specified period.

suspender /səˈspendə(r)/ n. **1** attachment to hold up a stocking or sock by its top. **2** (in *pl.*) US braces.

suspender belt n. woman's undergarment with suspenders.

suspense /səˈspens/ n. state of anxious uncertainty or expectation. □ **suspenseful** *adj.* [French, = delay]

suspension /səˈspenʃ(ə)n/ n. **1** suspending or being suspended. **2** springs etc. supporting a vehicle on its axles. **3** substance consisting of particles suspended in a medium.

suspension bridge n. bridge with a roadway suspended from cables supported by towers.

suspicion /səˈspɪʃ(ə)n/ n. **1** unconfirmed belief; distrust. **2** suspecting or being suspected. **3** (foll. by *of*) slight trace of. □ **above suspicion** too obviously good etc. to be suspected. **under suspicion** suspected. [Latin: related to SUSPECT]

suspicious /səˈspɪʃəs/ *adj.* **1** prone to or feeling suspicion. **2** causing suspicion. □ **suspiciously** *adv.*

suss v. *slang* (also **sus**) (-ss-) (usu. foll. by *out*) **1** investigate. inspect. **2** work out, realize. □ **on suss** on suspicion (of having committed a crime). [abbreviation]

sustain /səˈsteɪn/ v. **1** support, bear the weight of, esp. for a long period. **2** encourage, support. **3** (of food) nourish. **4** endure, stand. **5** suffer (defeat or injury etc.). **6** (of a court etc.) uphold or decide in favour of (an objection etc.). **7** corroborate (a statement or charge). **8**

maintain (effort etc.). □ **sustainable** *adj.* [Latin *sustineo* keep up]

sustenance /ˈsʌstɪnəns/ n. **1** nourishment, food. **2** means of support. [Anglo-French: related to SUSTAIN]

suttee /sʌˈtiː, ˈsʌtiː/ n. esp. *hist.* **1** Hindu custom of a widow's suicide on her husband's funeral pyre. **2** widow undergoing this. [Sanskrit *satī* faithful wife]

suture /ˈsuːtʃə(r)/ n. **1** stitching of the edges of a wound or incision. **2** thread or wire used for this. — v. (**-ring**) stitch (a wound or incision). [Latin *suo sut- sew*]

suzerain /ˈsuːzəreɪn/ n. **1** *hist.* feudal overlord. **2** *archaic* sovereign or State partially controlling another State that is internally autonomous. □ **suzerainty** n. [French]

svelte /svelt/ *adj.* slender, lissom, graceful. [French from Italian]

SW *abbr.* **1** south-west. **2** south-western.

swab /swɒb/ — n. **1 a** absorbent pad used in surgery. **b** specimen of a secretion taken for examination. **2** mop etc. for cleaning or mopping up. — v. (**-bb-**) **1** clean with a swab. **2** (foll. by *up*) absorb (moisture) with a swab. **3** mop clean (a ship's deck). [Dutch]

swaddle /ˈswɒd(ə)l/ v. (**-ling**) wrap (esp. a baby) tightly. [from SWATHE]

swaddling-clothes n.pl. narrow bandages formerly used to wrap and restrain a baby.

swag n. **1** *slang* booty of burglars etc. **2** *Austral. & NZ* traveller's bundle. **3** festoon of flowers, foliage, drapery, etc. □

swagger — v. **1** walk or behave arrogantly. — n. swaggering gait or manner. [from SWAG]

swagger stick n. short cane carried by a military officer.

Swahili /swɑːˈhiːli/ n. (pl. same) **1** member of a Bantu people of Zanzibar and adjacent coasts. **2** their language. [Arabic]

swain n. **1** *archaic* country youth. **2** *poet.* young lover or suitor. [Old Norse, = lad]

swallow¹ /ˈswɒləʊ/ — v. **1** cause or allow (food etc.) to pass down the throat. **2** perform the muscular movement required to do this. **3** accept meekly or credulously. **4** repress (a feeling etc.) (*swallow one's pride*). **5** articulate (words etc.) indistinctly. **6** (often foll. by *up*) engulf or absorb, exhaust. — n. **1** act of swallowing. **2** amount swallowed. [Old English]

swallow² /ˈswɒləʊ/ n. migratory swift-flying bird with a forked tail. [Old English]

swallow-dive n. & v. dive with the arms outspread until close to the water

swallow-tail *n.* **1** deeply forked tail. **2** butterfly etc. with this.

swam *past of* SWIM.

swami /ˈswɑːmɪ/ *n.* (*pl.* -**s**) Hindu male religious teacher. [Hindi *swāmī*]

swamp /swɒmp/ —*n.* (area of) water-logged ground. —*v.* **1** overwhelm, flood, or soak with water. **2** overwhelm or make invisible etc. with an excess or large amount of something. □ **swampy** *adj.* (-**ier**, -**iest**). [origin uncertain]

swan /swɒn/ —*n.* large usu. white water-bird with a long flexible neck. —*v.* (-**nn**-) (usu. foll. by *about*, *off*, etc.) *colloq.* move or go aimlessly, casually, or with a superior air. [Old English]

swank *colloq.* —*n.* ostentation, swagger. —*v.* show off. □ **swanky** *adj* (-**ier**, -**iest**). [origin uncertain]

swansong *n.* person's last work or act before death or retirement etc.

swap /swɒp/ (also **swop**) —*v.* (-**pp**-) exchange or barter. —*n.* **1** act of swapping. **2** thing for swapping or swapped. [originally = 'hit', imitative]

SWAPO /ˈswɑːpəʊ/ *abbr.* (also **Swapo**) South West Africa People's Organization.

sward /swɔːd/ *n. literary* expanse of turf. [Old English, = skin]

swarf /swɔːf/ *n.* fine chips or filings of stone, metal, etc. [Old Norse]

swarm[1] /swɔːm/ —*n.* **1** cluster of bees leaving the hive with the queen to establish a new colony. **2** large cluster of insects, birds, or people. **3** (in *pl.*; foll. by *of*) great numbers. —*v.* **1** move in or form a swarm. **2** (foll. by *with*) (of a place) be overrun, crowded, or infested with. [Old English]

swarm[2] /swɔːm/ *v.* (foll. by *up*) climb (a rope or tree etc.) by clinging with the hands and knees etc. [origin unknown]

swarthy /ˈswɔːðɪ/ *adj.* (-**ier**, -**iest**) dark, dark-complexioned. [obsolete *swarty* from *swart* black, from Old English]

swashbuckler /ˈswɒʃˌbʌklə(r)/ *n.* swaggering adventurer. □ **swash-buckling** *adj.* & *n.* [*swash* strike noisily, BUCKLER]

swastika /ˈswɒstɪkə/ *n.* **1** ancient symbol formed by an equal-armed cross with each arm continued at a right angle. **2** this with clockwise continuations as the symbol of Nazi Germany. [Sanskrit]

swat /swɒt/ —*v.* (-**tt**-) crush (a fly etc.) with a sharp blow. **2** hit hard and abruptly. —*n.* swatting blow. [dial. var. of SQUAT]

swatch /swɒtʃ/ *n.* **1** sample, esp. of cloth. **2** collection of samples. [origin unknown]

swath /swɔːθ/ *n.* (also **swathe** /sweɪð/) (*pl.* -**s** /swɔːðs, swɔːðz, sweɪðz/) **1** ridge of cut grass or corn etc. **2** space left clear by a mower etc. **3** broad strip. [Old English]

swathe /sweɪð/ —*v.* (-**thing**) bind or wrap in bandages or garments etc. —*n.* bandage or wrapping. [Old English]

sway —*v.* **1** (cause to) lean or move unsteadily from side to side. **2** oscillate; waver. **3 a** control the motion or direction of **b** influence; rule over. —*n.* **1** rule, influence, or government (*hold sway*). **2** swaying motion. [origin uncertain]

swear /sweə(r)/ —*v.* (*past* **swore**; *past part.* **sworn**) **1 a** (often foll. by *to* + *infin.* or *that* + clause) state or promise solemnly or on oath. **b** (cause to) take (an oath) (*swore them to secrecy*). **2** *colloq.* insist (*swore he was fit*). **3** (often foll. by *at*) use profane or obscene language. **4** (foll. by *by*) **a** appeal to as a witness in taking an oath (*swear by Almighty God*). **b** *colloq.* have great confidence in (*swears by yoga*). **5** (foll. by *to*; usu. in *neg.*) say certainly (*could not swear to it*). □ spell of swearing. **swear blind** *colloq.* affirm emphatically. **swear in** induct into office etc. with an oath. **swear off** *colloq.* promise to abstain from (drink etc.). [Old English]

swear-word *n.* profane or indecent word.

sweat /swet/ —*n.* **1** moisture exuded through the pores, esp. from heat or nervousness. **2** state or period of sweating. **3** *colloq.* state of anxiety (*in a sweat*). **4** *colloq.* a drudgery, effort. **b** laborious task. **5** condensed moisture on a surface. —*v.* (*past* and *past part.* **sweated** or *US* **sweat**) **1** exude sweat. **2** be terrified or suffer. **3** (of a wall etc.) exhibit surface moisture. **4** (cause to) drudge or toil. **5** emit like sweat. **6** make (a horse, athlete, etc.) sweat by exercise. **7** (as **sweated** *adj.*) (of goods, labour, etc.) produced by or subjected to exploitation. □ **no sweat** *colloq.* no bother, no trouble. **sweat blood** *colloq.* **1** work strenuously. **2** be very anxious. **sweat it out** *colloq.* endure a difficult experience to the end. □ **sweaty** *adj.* (-**ier**, -**iest**). [Old English]

sweat-band *n.* band fitted inside a hat or worn round a wrist etc. to absorb sweat.

sweater *n.* jersey or pullover.

sweatshirt *n.* sleeved cotton sweater.

sweatshop *n.* factory where sweated labour is used.

Swede *n.* **1 a** native or national of Sweden. **b** person of Swedish descent. **2** (**swede**) large yellow-fleshed turnip

Swedish orig. from Sweden. [Low German or Dutch]

Swedish —adj. of Sweden, its people, or language. —n. language of Sweden.

sweep —v. (past and past part. swept) 1 clean or clear (a room or area etc.) (as) with a broom. 2 (often foll. by up) clean a room etc. in this way. 3 (often foll. by up) collect or remove (dirt etc.) by sweeping. 4 (foll. by aside, away, etc.) a (as) with a broom. b dismiss abruptly. 5 (foll. by along, down, etc.) carry or drive along with force. 6 (foll. by off, away, etc.) remove or clear forcefully. 7 traverse swiftly or lightly. 8 impart a sweeping motion to. 9 swiftly cover or affect. 10 a glide swiftly: speed along. b go majestically. 11 (of landscape etc.) be rolling or spacious. —n. 1 act or motion of sweeping. 2 curve in the road, sweeping line of a hill, etc. 3 range or scope. 4 = CHIMNEY-SWEEP. 5 sortie by aircraft. 6 colloq. = SWEEPSTAKE. □ make a clean sweep of 1 completely abolish or expel. 2 win all the prizes etc. in (a competition etc.). sweep away abolish swiftly. sweep the board 1 win all the money at stake. 2 win all possible prizes etc. sweep under the carpet see CARPET. [Old English]

sweeper n. 1 person who cleans by sweeping. 2 manual device for sweeping carpets etc. 3 Football defensive player positioned close to the goalkeeper.

sweeping —adj. 1 wide in range or effect (sweeping changes). 2 general, arbitrary (sweeping statement). —n. (in pl.) dirt etc. collected by sweeping.

sweepstake n. 1 form of gambling in which all stakes are pooled and paid to the winners. 2 race with betting of this kind. 3 prize(s) won in a sweepstake.

sweet —adj. 1 tasting of sugar. 2 smelling pleasant like roses or perfume etc.; fragrant. 3 (of sound etc.) melodious or harmonious. 4 fresh; not salt, sour, or bitter. 5 gratifying or attractive. 6 amiable, pleasant. 7 colloq. pretty, charming. 8 (foll. by on) colloq. fond of; in love with. —n. 1 small shaped piece of sweet substance, usu. made with sugar or chocolate. 2 sweet dish or course of a meal. □ sweetish adj. sweetly adv. [Old English]

sweet-and-sour attrib. adj. cooked in a sauce containing sugar and vinegar or lemon etc.

sweetbread n. pancreas or thymus of an animal, esp. as food.

sweet-brier n. wild rose with small fragrant leaves.

sweetcorn n. sweet-flavoured maize kernels.

sweeten v. 1 make or become sweet or sweeter. 2 make agreeable or less painful. □ sweetening n.

sweetener n. 1 substance used to sweeten food or drink. 2 colloq. bribe or inducement.

sweetheart n. 1 lover or darling. 2 term of endearment.

sweetie n. colloq. 1 = SWEET 1. 2 sweetheart.

sweetmeal n. sweetened wholemeal.

sweetmeat n. 1 = SWEET 1. 2 small fancy cake.

sweetness n. being sweet; fragrance. □ sweetness and light mildness and reason.

sweet pea n. climbing plant with fragrant flowers.

sweet pepper n. mild pepper.

sweet potato n. 1 tropical climbing plant with sweet tuberous roots used for food. 2 root of this.

sweetshop n. confectioner's shop.

sweet talk colloq. —n. flattery, blandishment. —v. (sweet-talk) flatter in order to persuade.

sweet tooth n. liking for sweet-tasting things.

sweet william n. cultivated plant with clusters of vivid fragrant flowers.

swell —v. (past part. swollen /'swəʊlən/ or swelled) 1 (cause to) grow bigger, louder, or more intense. 2 (often foll. by up) rise or raise up from the surrounding surface. 3 (foll. by out) bulge. 4 (of the heart etc.) feel full of joy, pride, relief, etc. 5 (foll. by with) be hardly able to restrain (pride etc.). —n. 1 act or state of swelling. 2 heaving of the sea with unbreaking waves. 3 a crescendo. b mechanism in an organ etc. for producing a crescendo or diminuendo. 4 colloq. dandy. 5 protuberance. —adj. colloq. esp. US fine, excellent. 2 smart, fashionable. □ have (or get) a swelled (or swollen) head be (or become) conceited. [Old English]

swelling n. abnormal bodily protuberance.

swelter —v. be uncomfortably hot. —n. sweltering condition. [Old English]

swept past and past part. of SWEEP.

swerve —v. (-ving) (cause to) change direction, esp. abruptly. —n. swerving movement. [Old English]

swift —adj. 1 quick, rapid. 2 prompt. —n. swift-flying migratory bird with long wings. □ swiftly adv. swiftness n. [Old English]

swig —v. (-gg-) colloq. drink in large draughts. —n. swallow of drink, esp. large. [origin unknown]

swill —v. 1 (often foll. by out) rinse or flush. 2 drink greedily. —n. 1 act of

swim rinsing. **2** mainly liquid refuse as pig food. [Old English]

swim —*v.* (**-mm-**; *past* **swam**; *past part.* **swum**) **1** propel the body through water with limbs, fins, or tail. **2** traverse (a stretch of water or distance) by swimming. **3** perform (a stroke) by swimming. **4** float on a liquid. **5** appear to undulate, reel, or whirl. **6** feel dizzy (*my head swam*). **7** (foll. by *in*, *with*) be flooded. —*n.* period or act of swimming. □ **in the swim** *colloq.* involved in or aware of what is going on. □ **swimmer** *n.* [Old English]

swimming-bath *n.* (also **swimming-pool**) artificial pool for swimming.

swimmingly *adv. colloq.* smoothly, without impediment.

swimsuit *n.* swimming-costume, esp. one-piece for women and girls.

swimwear *n.* clothing for swimming in.

swindle /ˈswind(ə)l/ —*v.* (**-ling**) (often foll. by *out of*) **1** cheat of money etc. **2** cheat a person (of money etc.) (*swindled £200 out of him*). —*n.* **1** act of swindling. **2** fraudulent person or thing. □ **swindler** *n.* [back-formation from *swindler* from German]

swine *n.* (*pl.* same) **1** *formal* or *US* pig. **2** *colloq.* (*pl.* same or **-s**) **a** a contemptible person. **b** unpleasant or difficult thing. □ **swinish** *adj.* [Old English]

swing —*v.* (*past* and *past part.* **swung**) **1 a** (cause to) move with a to-and-fro or curving motion, as of an object attached at one end and hanging free at the other; sway. **b** hang so as to be free to swing. **2** oscillate or revolve. **3** move by gripping something and leaping etc. (*swung from tree to tree*). **4** walk with a swing. **5** (foll. by *round*) move to face the opposite direction. **6** change one's opinion or mood. **7** (foll. by *at*) attempt to hit. **8** (also **swing it**) play (music) with a swing rhythm. **9** *colloq.* (of a party etc.) be lively etc. **10** have a decisive influence on (voting etc.). **11** *colloq.* achieve, manage. **12** *colloq.* be executed by hanging. —*n.* **1** act, motion, or extent of swinging or smooth gait, rhythm, or action. **3 a** seat slung by ropes etc. for swinging on or in. **b** period of swinging on this. **4 a** jazz or dance music with an easy flowing rhythm. **b** rhythmic feeling or drive of this. **5** discernible change, esp. in votes or points scored etc. □ **swings and roundabouts** situation affording equal gain and loss. □ **swinger** *n.* [Old English]

swing-boat *n.* boat-shaped swing at fairs.

swing-bridge *n.* bridge that can be swung aside to let ships pass.

swing-door *n.* self-closing door opening both ways.

swingeing /ˈswindʒɪŋ/ *adj.* **1** (of a blow) forcible. **2** huge or far-reaching (*swingeing economies*). [archaic *swinge* strike hard, from Old English]

swing-wing *n.* aircraft wing that can move from a right-angled to a swept-back position.

swipe *colloq.* —*v.* (**-ping**) **1** (often foll. by *at*) hit hard and recklessly. **2** steal. —*n.* reckless hard hit or attempted hit. [perhaps var. of SWEEP]

swirl —*v.* move, flow, or carry along with a whirling motion. —*n.* **1** swirling motion. **2** twist or curl. □ **swirly** *adj.*

swish —*v.* **1** swing (a thing) audibly through the air, grass, etc. **2** move with or make a swishing sound. —*n.* swishing action or sound. —*adj. colloq.* smart, fashionable. [imitative]

Swiss —*adj.* of Switzerland or its people. —*n.* (*pl.* same) **1** native or national of Switzerland. **2** person of Swiss descent. [French *Suisse*]

Swiss roll *n.* cylindrical sponge cake with a jam etc. filling.

switch —*n.* **1** device for completing and breaking an electric circuit. **2 a** transfer, change-over, or deviation. **b** exchange. **3** flexible shoot cut from a tree. **4** light tapering rod. **5** *US* railway points. —*v.* **1** (foll. by *on*, *off*) turn (an electrical device) on or off. **2** change or transfer. **3** exchange. **4** whip or flick with a switch. □ **switch off** *colloq.* cease to pay attention. [Low German]

switchback *n.* **1** ride at a fair etc., with extremely steep ascents and descents. **2** (often *attrib.*) such a railway or road.

switchboard *n.* apparatus for making connections between electric circuits, esp. in telephony.

switched-on *adj. colloq.* **1** up to date; aware of what is going on. **2** excited; under the influence of drugs.

swivel /ˈswɪv(ə)l/ —*n.* coupling between two parts enabling one to revolve without turning the other. —*v.* (**-ll-**; *US* **-l-**) turn on or as on a swivel. [Old English]

swivel chair *n.* chair with a revolving seat.

swizz *n.* (also **swiz**) *colloq.* **1** something unfair or disappointing. **2** swindle. [origin unknown]

swizzle /ˈswɪz(ə)l/ *n.* **1** *colloq.* frothy mixed alcoholic drink esp. of rum or gin and bitters. **2** *slang* = swizz. [origin unknown]

swizzle-stick *n.* stick used for frothing or flattening drinks.

swollen *past part.* of SWELL.

swoon *v. & n. literary* faint. [Old English]

swoop –v. 1 (often foll. by *down*) descend rapidly like a bird of prey. 2 (often foll. by *on*) make a sudden attack. –n. swooping movement or action. [Old English]

swop var. of SWAP.

sword /sɔːd/ n. 1 weapon with a long blade and hilt with a handguard. 2 (prec. by *the*) war. □ **military power**. □ **put to the sword** kill. [Old English]

sword dance *n.* dance with the brandishing of swords or with swords laid on the ground.

swordfish *n.* (*pl.* same or *-es*) large marine fish with swordlike upper jaw.

sword of Damocles /dæməkliːz/ n. an immediate danger. [from *Damokles*, who had a sword hung by a hair over him]

swordplay *n.* 1 fencing. 2 repartee; lively argument.

swordsman *n.* person of (usu. specified) skill with a sword. □ **swordsmanship** *n.*

swordstick *n.* hollow walking-stick containing a blade that can be used as a sword.

swore *past* of SWEAR.

sworn *past part.* of SWEAR. –*attrib. adj.* bound (as) by an oath (*sworn enemies*).

swot *colloq.* –v. (**-tt-**) 1 study hard. 2 (usu. foll. by *up, up on*) study (a subject) hard or hurriedly. –*n.* usu. *derog.* person who swots. [dial. var. of SWEAT]

swum *past part.* of SWIM.

swung *past* and *past part.* of SWING.

sybarite /ˈsɪbəraɪt/ *n.* self-indulgent or voluptuous person. □ **sybaritic** /-ˈrɪtɪk/ *adj.* [*Sybaris*, ancient city in S. Italy]

sycamore /ˈsɪkəmɔː(r)/ *n.* 1 large maple or its wood. 2 US plane-tree or its wood. [Greek *sukomoros*]

sycophant /ˈsɪkəfænt/ *n.* flatterer; toady. □ **sycophancy** *n.* **sycophantic** /-ˈfæntɪk/ *adj.* [Greek *sukophantēs*]

syl- *prefix* assim. form of SYN- before *l.*

syllabary /ˈsɪləbərɪ/ *n.* (*pl.* **-ies**) list of characters representing syllables. [related to SYLLABLE]

syllabic /sɪˈlæbɪk/ *adj.* of or in syllables. □ **syllabically** *adv.*

syllable /ˈsɪləb(ə)l/ *n.* 1 unit of pronunciation forming the whole or part of a word and usu. having one vowel sound often with consonant(s) before or after (e.g. *water* has two, *inferno* three). 2 the least amount of speech or writing. 3 character(s) representing a syllable. □ **in words of one syllable** plainly, bluntly. [Greek *sullabē*]

syllabub /ˈsɪləˌbʌb/ *n.* (also **sillabub**) dessert of flavoured, sweetened, and whipped cream or milk. [origin unknown]

syllabus /ˈsɪləbəs/ *n.* (*pl.* **-buses** or **-bi** /-ˌbaɪ/) programme or outline of a course of study, teaching, etc. [misreading of Greek *sittuba* label]

syllepsis /sɪˈlɛpsɪs/ *n.* (*pl.* **syllepses** /-siːz/) figure of speech in which a word is applied to two others in different senses (e.g. *caught the train and a cold*) or to two others of which it is grammatically suitable to one only (e.g. *neither you nor he knows*) (cf. ZEUGMA). [Greek: related to SYLLABLE]

syllogism /ˈsɪləˌdʒɪz(ə)m/ *n.* reasoning in which a conclusion is drawn from two given or assumed propositions. □ **syllogistic** /-ˈdʒɪstɪk/ *adj.* [Greek *logos* reason]

sylph /sɪlf/ *n.* 1 elemental spirit of the air. 2 slender graceful woman or girl. □ **sylphlike** *adj.* [Latin]

sylvan /ˈsɪlv(ə)n/ *adj.* (also **silvan**) 1 a of the woods. b having woods. 2 rural. [Latin *silva* a wood]

sylviculture var. of SILVICULTURE.

sym- *prefix* assim. form of SYN- before *b, m, p.*

symbiosis /ˌsɪmbaɪˈəʊsɪs, -bɪ-/ *n.* (*pl.* **-bioses** /-siːz/) 1 interaction between two different organisms living in close physical association, usu. to the advantage of both. 2 mutually advantageous association between persons. □ **symbiotic** /-ˈɒtɪk/ *adj.* [Greek, = living together]

symbol /ˈsɪmb(ə)l/ *n.* 1 thing regarded as typifying or representing something (*white is a symbol of purity*). 2 mark, sign, etc. representing an object, idea, function, or process; logo. □ **symbolic** /-ˈbɒlɪk/ *adj.* **symbolically** /-ˈbɒlɪkəlɪ/ *adv.* [Greek *sumbolon*]

symbolism /ˈsɪmbəˌlɪz(ə)m/ *n.* 1 use of symbols. b symbols collectively. 2 artistic and poetic movement or style using symbols to express ideas, emotions, etc. □ **symbolist** *n.*

symbolize *v.* (also **-ise**) (**-zing** or **-sing**) 1 be a symbol of. 2 represent by symbols. [French: related to SYMBOL]

symmetry /ˈsɪmɪtrɪ/ *n.* (*pl.* **-ies**) 1 a correct proportion of parts. b beauty resulting from this. 2 a structure allowing an object to be divided into parts of an equal shape and size. b possession of such a structure. 3 repetition of exactly similar parts facing each other or a centre. □ **symmetrical** /sɪˈmɛtrɪk(ə)l/ *adj.* **symmetrically** /-ˈmɛtrɪkəlɪ/ *adv.* [Greek *summetria*]

sympathetic /ˌsɪmpəˈθetɪk/ *adj.* **1** of or expressing sympathy. **2** pleasant, likeable. **3** (foll. by *to*) favouring (a proposal etc.). □ **sympathetically** *adv.*

sympathize /ˈsɪmpəθaɪz/ *v.* (also *-ise*) (*-zing* or *-sing*) (often foll. by *with*) **1** feel or express sympathy. **2** agree. □ **sympathizer** *n.*

sympathy /ˈsɪmpəθɪ/ *n.* (*pl.* *-ies*) **1 a** sharing of another's feelings. **b** capacity for this. **2 a** (often foll. by *with*) sharing or tendency to share (with a person etc.) in an emotion, sensation, or condition. **b** (in *sing.* or *pl.*) compassion or commiseration; condolences. **3** (often foll. by *for*) approval. **4** (in *sing.* or *pl.*; often foll. by *with* a person etc.) in opinion or desire. □ **in sympathy** (often foll. by *with*) having, showing, or resulting from sympathy. [Greek, = fellow-feeling]

symphony /ˈsɪmfənɪ/ *n.* (*pl.* *-ies*) **1** large-scale composition for full orchestra in several movements. **2** instrumental interlude in a large-scale vocal work. **3** = SYMPHONY ORCHESTRA. □ **symphonic** /-ˈfɒnɪk/ *adj.* [from SYN-, Greek *phōnē* sound]

symphony orchestra *n.* large orchestra suitable for playing symphonies etc.

symposium /sɪmˈpəʊzɪəm/ *n.* (*pl.* *-sia*) **1** conference, or collection of essays, on a particular subject. **2** philosophical or other friendly discussion. [Greek *sumpotēs* fellow-drinker]

symptom /ˈsɪmptəm/ *n.* **1** physical or mental sign of disease. **2** sign of the existence of something. □ **symptomatic** /-ˈmætɪk/ *adj.* [Greek *piptō* fall]

syn- *prefix* with, together, alike. [Greek *sun* with]

synagogue /ˈsɪnəgɒg/ *n.* **1** building for Jewish religious observance and instruction. **2** Jewish congregation. [Greek, = assembly]

synapse /ˈsaɪnæps, ˈsɪn-/ *n. Anat.* junction of two nerve-cells. [Greek *haptō* join]

sync /sɪŋk/ (also **synch**) *colloq.* —*v.* synchronize. —*n.* synchronization. □ **in** (or **out**) **of sync** (often foll. by *with*) according or agreeing well (or badly). [abbreviation]

synchromesh /ˈsɪŋkrəʊˌmeʃ/ *n.* (often *attrib.*) system of gear-changing, esp. in vehicles, in which the gearwheels revolve at the same speed during engagement. [abbreviation of *synchronized mesh*]

synchronic /sɪŋˈkrɒnɪk/ *adj.* concerned with a subject as it exists at one point in time. □ **synchronically** *adv.* [from SYN-, Greek *khronos* time]

synchronism /ˈsɪŋkrənɪz(ə)m/ *n.* **1** being or treating as synchronic or synchronous. **2** process of synchronizing sound and picture.

synchronize /ˈsɪŋkrənaɪz/ *v.* (also *-ise*) (*-zing* or *-sing*) **1** (often foll. by *with*) make or be synchronous (with). **2** make the sound and picture of (a film etc.) coincide. **3** cause (clocks etc.) to show the same time. □ **synchronization** /-ˈzeɪʃ(ə)n/ *n.*

■ **Usage** *Synchronize* should not be used in standard English to mean co-ordinate' or combine'.

synchronous /ˈsɪŋkrənəs/ *adj.* (often foll. by *with*) existing or occurring at the same time.

syncopate /ˈsɪŋkəˌpeɪt/ *v.* (*-ting*) **1** displace the beats or accents in (music). **2** shorten (a word) by dropping interior letters. □ **syncopation** /-ˈpeɪʃ(ə)n/ *n.* [Latin: related to SYNCOPE]

syncope /ˈsɪŋkəpɪ/ *n.* **1** *Gram.* syncopation. **2** fainting through a fall in blood pressure. [Greek *sunkopē* cutting off]

syncretize /ˈsɪŋkrɪˌtaɪz/ *v.* (also *-ise*) (*-zing* or *-sing*) attempt, esp. inconsistently, to unify or reconcile differing schools of thought. □ **syncretic** /-ˈkretɪk/ *adj.* **syncretism** *n.* [Greek]

syndic /ˈsɪndɪk/ *n.* any of various university or government officials. [Greek *sundikos* = advocate]

syndicalism /ˈsɪndɪkəˌlɪz(ə)m/ *n. hist.* movement for transferring industrial ownership and control to workers' unions. □ **syndicalist** *n.* [French: related to SYNDIC]

syndicate —*n.* /ˈsɪndɪkət/ **1** combination of individuals or businesses to promote a common interest. **2** agency supplying material simultaneously to a number of newspapers etc. **3** group of people who gamble, organize crime, etc. **4** committee of syndics. —*v.* /ˈsɪndɪˌkeɪt/ (*-ting*) **1** form into a syndicate. **2** publish (material) through a syndicate. □ **syndication** /-ˈkeɪʃ(ə)n/ *n.* [Latin: related to SYNDIC]

syndrome /ˈsɪndrəʊm/ *n.* **1** group of concurrent symptoms of a disease. **2** characteristic combination of opinions, emotions, behaviour, etc. [Greek *sun-dromē* running together]

synecdoche /sɪˈnekdəkɪ/ *n.* figure of speech in which a part is made to represent the whole or vice versa (e.g. *new faces at the club*; *England lost to India*). [Greek, = taking together]

synod /ˈsɪnəd/ *n.* Church council of delegated clergy and sometimes laity. [Greek, = meeting]

synonym /'sɪnənɪm/ n. word or phrase that means the same as another (e.g. *shut* and *close*). [Greek *onoma* name]

synonymous /sɪ'nɒnɪməs/ adj. (often foll. by *with*) 1 having the same meaning. 2 suggestive of, associated with (*his name is synonymous with terror*).

synopsis /sɪ'nɒpsɪs/ n. (pl. **synopses** /-siːz/) summary or outline. [Greek *opsis* view]

synoptic /sɪ'nɒptɪk/ adj. of or giving a synopsis. [related to SYNOPSIS]

Synoptic Gospels n.pl. Gospels of Matthew, Mark, and Luke.

synovia /saɪ'nəʊvɪə, sɪ-/ n. *Physiol.* viscous fluid lubricating joints etc. □ **synovial** adj. [medieval Latin]

syntax /'sɪntæks/ n. 1 grammatical arrangement of words. 2 rules or analysis of this. □ **syntactic** adj. **syntactically** /-'tæktɪkəlɪ/ adv. [Greek, = arrangement]

synth /sɪnθ/ n. *colloq.* = SYNTHESIZER.

synthesis /'sɪnθəsɪs/ n. (pl. **-theses** /-siːz/) 1 a combining of elements into a whole. b result of this. 2 *Chem.* artificial production of compounds from their constituents as distinct from extraction from plants etc. [Greek, = placing together]

synthesize /'sɪnθəsaɪz/ v. (also **-ise**) (-zing or -sing) make a synthesis of.

synthesizer n. electronic, usu. keyboard, instrument producing a wide variety of sounds.

synthetic /sɪn'θetɪk/ adj. 1 made by chemical synthesis, esp. to imitate a natural product. 2 affected, insincere. —n. synthetic substance. □ **synthetically** adv.

syphilis /'sɪfɪlɪs/ n. contagious venereal disease. □ **syphilitic** /-'lɪtɪk/ adj. [*Syphilus*, name of a character in a poem of 1530]

Syriac /'sɪrɪˌæk/ —n. language of ancient Syria, western Aramaic. —adj. of or in Syriac.

Syrian /'sɪrɪən/ —n. 1 native or national of Syria. 2 person of Syrian descent. —adj. of Syria.

syringa /sɪ'rɪŋgə/ n. 1 = MOCK ORANGE. 2 lilac or similar related plant. [related to SYRINGE]

syringe /sɪ'rɪndʒ, 'sɪr-/ —n. device for sucking in and ejecting liquid in a fine stream. —v. 1 (**-ging**) sluice or spray with a syringe. [Greek *surigx* pipe]

syrup /'sɪrəp/ n. (US **sirup**) 1 a sweet sauce of sugar dissolved in boiling water. b similar fluid as a drink, medicine, etc. 2 condensed sugar-cane juice; molasses, treacle. 3 excessive sweetness of manner or style. □ **syrupy** adj. [Arabic *sharāb*]

system /'sɪstəm/ n. 1 complex whole; set of connected things or parts; organized body of things. 2 a set of organs in the body with a common structure or function. b human or animal body as a whole. 3 method; scheme of action, procedure, or classification. 4 orderliness. 5 (prec. by *the*) prevailing political or social order, esp. regarded as oppressive. □ **get a thing out of one's system** *colloq.* get rid of a preoccupation or anxiety. [Greek *sustēma -mat-*]

systematic /ˌsɪstə'mætɪk/ adj. 1 methodical; according to a system. 2 regular; deliberate. □ **systematically** adv.

systematize /'sɪstəmətaɪz/ v. (also **-ise**) (-zing or -sing) make systematic. □ **systematization** /-ˌzeɪʒ(ə)n/ n.

systemic /sɪ'stemɪk/ adj. 1 *Physiol.* of the whole body. 2 (cf an insecticide etc.) entering the plant via the roots or shoots and freely transported within its tissues. □ **systemically** adv.

systems analysis n. analysis of a complex process etc. in order to improve its efficiency esp. by using a computer. □ **systems analyst** n.

T

T¹ /tiː/ n. (also **t**) (pl. **Ts** or **T's**) **1** twentieth letter of the alphabet. **2** T-shaped thing (esp. attrib.: T-joint). □ **to a T** exactly; to a nicety.

T² symb. tritium.

t. (also **t**) abbr. **1** ton(s). **2** tonne(s).

TA abbr. Territorial Army.

Ta symb. tantalum.

ta /taː/ int. colloq. thank you. [infantile form]

tab¹ —n. **1** small flap or strip of material attached for grasping, fastening, or hanging up, or for identification. **2** US colloq. bill (picked up the tab). **3** distinguishing mark on a staff officer's collar. —v. (**-bb-**) provide with a tab or tabs. □ **keep tabs** (or **a tab**) **on** colloq. **1** keep account of **2** have under observation or in check. [probably dial.]

tab² n. = TABULATOR 2. [abbreviation]

tabard /ˈtæbɑːd/ n. **1** herald's official coat emblazoned with royal arms. **2** woman's or girl's sleeveless jerkin. **3** hist. knight's short emblazoned garment worn over armour. [French]

tabasco /təˈbæskəʊ/ n. **1** pungent pepper. **2** (**Tabasco**) propr. sauce made from this. [Tabasco in Mexico]

tabby /ˈtæbɪ/ n. (pl. **-ies**) **1** grey or brownish cat with dark stripes. **2** a kind of watered silk. [French from Arabic]

tabernacle /ˈtæbə.næk(ə)l/ n. **1** hist. tent used as a sanctuary by the Israelites during the Exodus. **2** niche or receptacle, esp. for the Eucharistic elements. **3** Nonconformist meeting-house. [Latin: related to TAVERN]

tabla /ˈtæblə/ n. pair of small drums played with the hands, esp. in Indian music. [Arabic, = drum]

table /ˈteɪb(ə)l/ —n. **1** flat surface on a leg or legs, used for eating, working at, etc. (keeps a good table). **b** food provided in a household (keeps a good table). **b** group seated for dinner etc. **3 a** set of facts or figures in columns etc. (table of contents). **b** matter contained in this. **c** = MULTIPLICATION TABLE. —v. (**-ling**) **1** bring forward for discussion etc. at a meeting. **2** esp. US postpone consideration of (a matter). □ **at table** taking a meal at a table. **on the table** offered for discussion. **turn the tables** (often foll. by on) reverse circumstances to one's advantage (against). **2** very drunk. **2 under the table** colloq. **1** very drunk. **2** = under the counter (see COUNTER¹). [Latin tabula board]

tableau /ˈtæbləʊ/ n. (pl. **-x** /-əʊz/) **1** picturesque presentation. **2** group of silent motionless people representing a scene on stage. [French, = picture, diminutive of TABLE]

tablecloth n. cloth spread over a table, esp. for meals.

table d'hôte /ˌtɑːb(ə)l ˈdəʊt/ n. (often attrib.) meal from a set menu at a fixed price. [French, = host's table]

tableland n. elevated plateau.

table licence n. licence to serve alcoholic drinks with meals only.

table linen n. tablecloths, napkins, etc.

tablespoon n. **1** large spoon for serving food. **2** amount held by this. □ **tablespoonful** n. (pl. **-s**).

tablet /ˈtæblɪt/ n. **1** small solid dose of a medicine etc. **2** bar of soap etc. **3** flat slab of esp. stone, usu. inscribed. **4** US writing-pad. [Latin diminutive: related to TABLE]

table talk n. informal talk at table.

table tennis n. indoor ball game played with small bats on a table divided by a net.

tabletop n. surface of a table.

tableware n. dishes, plates, etc., for meals.

table wine n. wine of ordinary quality.

tabloid /ˈtæblɔɪd/ n. small-sized, often popular or sensational, newspaper. [from TABLET]

taboo /təˈbuː/ (also **tabu**) —n. (pl. **-s**) **1** ritual isolation of a person or thing as sacred or accursed. **2** prohibition imposed by social custom. —adj. avoided or prohibited, esp. by social custom (taboo words). —v. (**-oos**, **-ooed** or **-us**, **-ued**) **1** put under taboo. **2** exclude or prohibit, esp. socially. [Tongan]

tabor /ˈteɪbə(r)/ n. hist. small drum, esp. used to accompany a pipe. [French]

tabu var. of TABOO.

tabular /ˈtæbjʊlə(r)/ adj. of or arranged in tables or lists. [Latin: related to TABLE]

tabulate /ˈtæbjʊ.leɪt/ v. (**-ting**) arrange (figures or facts) in tabular form. □ **tabulation** /-ˈleɪʃ(ə)n/ n.

tabulator n. **1** person or thing that tabulates. **2** device on a typewriter etc. for advancing to a sequence of set positions in tabular work.

tacho /ˈtækəʊ/ n. (pl. **-s**) colloq. = TACHOMETER. [abbreviation]

tachograph /'tækə,grɑːf/ n. device in a vehicle recording speed and travel time. [Greek *takhos* speed]

tachometer /tə'kɒmɪtə(r)/ n. instrument measuring velocity or rate of rotation of a shaft (esp. in a vehicle).

tacit /'tæsɪt/ adj. understood or implied without being stated (*tacit consent*). □ **tacitly** adv. [Latin *taceo* be silent]

taciturn /'tæsɪtɜːn/ adj. saying little; uncommunicative. □ **taciturnity** n. [from TACIT]

tack¹ /tæk/ n. 1 small sharp broad-headed nail. 2 US drawing-pin. 3 long stitch for joining fabrics etc. lightly or temporarily. 4 (in sailing) direction, esp. taking advantage of a side wind (*starboard tack*). 5 course of action or policy (*change tack*). 6 sticky condition of varnish etc. —v. 1 (often foll. by *down* etc.) fasten with tacks. 2 stitch lightly together. 3 (foll. by *to, on, on to*) add or append. 4 **a** change a ship's course by turning its head to the wind. **b** make a series of such tacks. [probably related to French *tache* clasp, nail]

tack² n. colloq. saddle, bridle, etc., of a horse. [from TACKLE]

tack³ n. colloq. cheap or shoddy material; tat, kitsch. [back formation from TACKY²]

tackle /'tæk(ə)l/ —n. 1 equipment for a task or sport. 2 mechanism, esp. of ropes, pulley-blocks, hooks, etc., for lifting weights, managing sails, etc. 3 windlass with its ropes and broad-headed. 4 act of tackling in football etc. —v. (-ling) 1 try to deal with (a problem or difficulty). 2 grapple with (an opponent). 3 confront (a person) in discussion or argument. 4 intercept or stop (a player running with the ball). □ **tackler** n. [Low German]

tackle-block n. pulley over which a rope runs.

tacky¹ adj. (-ier, -iest) slightly sticky. □ **tackiness** n. [from TACK¹]

tacky² adj. (-ier, -iest) colloq 1 in poor taste, cheap. 2 tatty, shabby. □ **tackiness** n. [origin unknown]

taco /'tækəʊ/ n. (pl. -s) Mexican dish of meat etc. in a folded tortilla. [Mexican Spanish]

tact n. 1 skill in dealing with others, esp. in delicate situations. 2 intuitive perception of the right thing to do or say. [Latin *tango tact-* touch]

tactful adj. having or showing tact. □ **tactfully** adv.

tactic n. = TACTICS. [Greek from *tasso* arrange]

tactical adj. 1 of tactics (*tactical retreat*). 2 (of bombing etc.) done in direct support of military or naval operations.

3 adroitly planning or adroitly planned. □ **tactically** adv.

tactics n.pl. 1 also treated as *sing.* disposition of armed forces, esp. in warfare. 2 short-term procedure adopted in carrying out a scheme or achieving an end. □ **tactician** /tæk'tɪʃ(ə)n/ n.

tactile /'tæktaɪl/ adj. 1 of the sense of touch. 2 perceived by touch; tangible. □ **tactility** /'tɪltɪt/ n. [Latin: related to touch]

tactless adj. having or showing no tact. □ **tactlessly** adv

tadpole n. larva, esp. of a frog, toad, or newt. [related to TOAD, POLL]

taffeta /'tæfɪtə/ n. fine lustrous silk or silklike fabric. [French or medieval Latin from Persian]

taffrail /'tæfreɪl/ n. rail round a ship's stern. [Dutch *taffereel* panel]

Taffy /'tæfɪ/ n. (pl. -ies) colloq. often *offens.* Welshman. [a supposed pronunciation of *Davy* = *David*]

tag¹ —n. 1 label, esp. on an object to show its address, price, etc. 2 metal etc. point on a shoelace etc. 3 loop or flap for handling or hanging a thing. 4 loose or ragged end. 5 trite quotation or stock phrase. —v. (-gg-) 1 provide with a tag or tags. 2 (often foll. by *on, on to*) join or attach. □ **tag along** (often foll. by *with*) go along, accompany passively. [origin unknown]

tag² n. children's chasing game. —v. (-gg-) touch in a game of tag. [origin unknown]

tag end n. esp. *US* last remnant.

tagliatelle /,tæljə'telɪ/ n. narrow ribbon-shaped pasta. [Italian]

t'ai chi ch'uan /taɪ 'tʃiː tʃwɑːn/ n. (in full **t'ai chi**) Chinese martial art and system of callisthenics with slow controlled movements. [Chinese, = great ultimate boxing]

tail¹ —n. 1 hindmost part of an animal, esp. extending beyond the body. 2 **a** thing like a tail, esp. an extension at the rear. **b** rear of a procession etc. 3 rear part of an aeroplane, vehicle, or rocket. 4 luminous trail following a comet. 5 inferior, weaker, or last part of anything. 6 part of a shirt or coat below the waist at the back. 7 (in pl.) colloq. **a** tailcoat. **b** evening dress including this. 8 (in pl.) reverse of a coin as a choice when tossing. 9 colloq. person following another. —v. 1 remove the stalks of (fruit). 2 (often foll. by *after*) colloq. follow closely. □ **on a person's tail** following closely. **tail off** (or **away**) gradually decrease or diminish; end inconclusively. **with one's tail between one's legs** dejected, humiliated. [Old English]

tail² *Law* –*n.* limitation of ownership, esp. of an estate limited to a person and that person's heirs. –*adj.* so limited (*estate tail*). □ **in tail** under such a limitation. [French *tailler* cut: related to TALLY]

tailback *n.* long line of traffic caused by an obstruction.

tailboard *n.* hinged or removable flap at the rear of a lorry etc.

tailcoat *n.* man's coat with a long divided flap at the back, worn as part of formal dress.

tail-end *n.* hindmost, lowest, or last part.

tailgate *n.* **1** esp. *US* = TAILBOARD. **2** rear door of an estate car or hatchback.

tail-light *n.* (also **tail-lamp**) *US* rear light on a vehicle etc.

tailor /ˈteɪlə(r)/ –*n.* maker of clothes, esp. men's outer garments to measure. –*v.* **1** make (clothes) as a tailor. **2** make or adapt for a special purpose. **3** work as or be a tailor. [Anglo-French *taillour*: related to TAIL²]

tailored *adj.* **1** (of clothing) well or closely fitted. **2** = TAILOR-MADE.

tailor-made *adj.* **1** made to order by a tailor. **2** made or suited for a particular purpose.

tailpiece *n.* **1** rear appendage. **2** final part of a thing. **3** decoration in a blank space at the end of a chapter etc.

tailpipe *n.* the rear section of an exhaust-pipe.

tailplane *n.* horizontal aerofoil at the tail of an aircraft.

tailspin *n.* **1** spin by an aircraft with the tail spiralling. **2** state of chaos or panic.

tail wind *n.* wind blowing in the direction of travel.

taint –*n.* **1** spot or trace of decay, infection, corruption, etc. **2** corrupt condition or infection. –*v.* **1** affect with a taint; become tainted. **2** (foll. by *with*) affect slightly. [Latin: related to TINGE]

take –*v.* (-king; *past* **took** /tʊk/; *past part.* **taken**) **1** lay hold of, get into one's hands. **2** acquire, capture, earn, or win. **3** get by purchase, hire, or formal agreement (*take lodgings; took a taxi*). **4** (in a recipe) use. **5** regularly buy (a newspaper etc.) use. **6** obtain (*take a degree*). **7** occupy (*take a chair*). **8** make use of (*take the next turning on the left; take the bus*). **9** consume (food or medicine). **10 a** be affected by (*inoculation did not take*). **b** (of a plant, seed, etc.) begin to grow. **11** require or use up (*will only take a minute*). **12** carry or accompany (*take the book home; bus will take you*). **13** remove; steal (*someone has taken my pen*). **14** catch or be infected with (fire or fever etc.). **15**

a experience, seek, or be affected by (*take fright; take pleasure*). **b** exert (*took no notice*). **16** find out and note (*took his address; took her temperature*). **17** understand; assume (*I took you to mean yes*). **18** treat, deal with, or regard in a specified way (*took it badly; took the corner too fast*). **19** (foll. by *for*) regard as being (*do you take me for an idiot?*). **20 a** accept, receive (*take the offer; take a call; takes boarders*. **b** hold (*takes 3 pints*). **c** submit to; tolerate (*take a joke*). **21** wear (*takes size 10*). **22** choose or assume (*took a job; took the initiative*). **23** derive (*takes its name from the inventor*). **24** (foll. by *from*) subtract (*take 3 from 9*). **25** perform or effect (*take notes; take an oath; take a look*). **26** occupy or engage oneself in (*take a rest*). **27** conduct (*took prayers*). **28** teach, be taught, or be examined in (a subject). **29 a** make (a photograph). **b** photograph (a person etc.). **30** (in *imper.*) use as an example (*take Napoleon*). **31** *Gram.* have or require as part of a construction (*this verb takes an object*). **32** have sexual intercourse with (a woman). **33** (in *passive*; foll. by *by*, *with*) be attracted or charmed by. –*n.* **1** amount taken or caught at a time etc. **2** scene or film sequence photographed continuously at one time. □ **be taken ill** become ill, esp. suddenly. **have what it takes** *colloq.* have the necessary qualities for success. **take account of** see ACCOUNT. **take advantage of** see ADVANTAGE. **take after** resemble (a parent etc.). **take against** begin to dislike. **take aim** see AIM. **take apart 1** dismantle. **2** *colloq.* beat or defeat. **3** *colloq.* criticize severely. **take away 1** remove or carry elsewhere. **2** subtract. **3** buy (hot food etc.) for eating elsewhere. **take back 1** retract (a statement). **2** convey to an original position. **3** carry in thought to a past time. **4 a** return (goods) to a shop. **b** (of a shop) accept such goods. **5** accept (a person) back into one's affections, into employment, etc. **take the biscuit** (or **bun** or **cake**) *colloq.* be the most remarkable. **take down 1** write down (spoken words). **2** remove or dismantle. **3** lower (a garment worn below the waist). **take effect** see EFFECT. **take for granted** see GRANT. **take fright** see FRIGHT. **take heart** be encouraged. **take in 1** receive (a lodger etc.). **2** undertake (work) at home. **3** make (a garment etc.) smaller. **4** understand; observe (*did you take that in?*). **5** cheat. **6** include. **7** *colloq.* visit (a place) on the way to another (*took in Bath*). **8** absorb

into the body. **take in hand** 1 under-take; start doing or dealing with. 2 undertake to control or reform (a person). **take into account** see ACCOUNT. **take it** 1 (often foll. by *that*) assume. 2 *colloq.* endure in a specified way (*took it badly*). **take it easy** see EASY. **take it into one's head** see HEAD. **take it on one** (or *oneself*) (foll. by *to* + infin.) venture or presume. **take it or leave it** (esp. in *imper.*) accept it or not. **take it out of** 1 exhaust the strength of. 2 have revenge on. **take it out on** relieve one's frustration by treating aggressively. **take off** 1 a remove (clothing) from the body. b remove or lead away. c withdraw (transport, a show, etc.). 2 deduct. 3 depart, esp. hastily. 4 *colloq.* mimic humorously. 5 begin a jump. 6 become airborne. 7 (of a scheme, enterprise, etc.) become successful. 8 have (a period) away from work. **take oneself off** go away. **take on** 1 undertake (work etc.). 2 engage (an employee). 3 be willing to meet (an opponent at a game etc.). 4 acquire (new meaning etc.). 5 *colloq.* show strong emotion. **take out** 1 remove; extract. 2 escort on an outing or as a sexual partner. 3 get (a licence, summons, etc.) issued. 4 *US = take away*. 5 *slang* murder or destroy. **take a person out of himself** or **herself** make a person forget his or her worries. **take over** 1 succeed to the management or ownership of. 2 take control. **take up** 1 become interested or engaged in (a pursuit). 2 adopt as a protégé. 3 occupy (time or space). 4 begin (residence etc.). 5 resume after an interruption. 6 (often foll. by *on*) interrupt or question (a speaker) (on a point). 7 accept (an offer etc.). 8 shorten (a garment). 9 lift up. 10 absorb. 11 pursue (a matter etc.) further, esp. with those in authority. **take a person up on** accept (a person's offer etc.). **take up with** begin to associate with. [Old English from Old Norse]

take-away —*attrib. adj.* (of food) bought cooked for eating elsewhere. —*n.* 1 this food. 2 establishment selling this.
take-home pay *n.* employee's pay after the deduction of tax etc.
take-off *n.* 1 act of becoming airborne. 2 act of mimicking.
take-over *n.* 1 assumption of control (esp. of a business); buying-out.

taker *n.* person who takes a bet, accepts an offer, etc.
take-up *n.* acceptance of a thing offered.
taking —*adj.* attractive, captivating. —*n.* (in *pl.*) amount of money taken at a show, in a shop, etc.
talc *n.* 1 talcum powder. 2 magnesium silicate formed as soft flat plates, used as a lubricator etc. [Arabic from Persian *talk*]
talcum /'tælkəm/ *n.* 1 = TALC. 2 (in full **talcum powder**) powdered talc for toilet use, usu. perfumed. [medieval Latin: see TALC]

tale *n.* 1 (usu. fictitious) narrative or story. 2 allegation often malicious or in breach of confidence. [Old English]
talent /'tælənt/ *n.* 1 special aptitude or faculty (*talent for music*). 2 high mental ability. 3 a person or persons of talent. b *colloq.* attractive members of the opposite sex (*plenty of local talent*). 4 ancient esp. Greek weight and unit of currency. □ **talented** *adj.* [Greek *talanton*]
talent-scout *n.* (also **talent-spotter**) person seeking new talent, esp. in sport or entertainment.
talisman /'tælɪzmən/ *n.* (*pl.* -s) ring, stone, etc. thought to have magic powers, esp. to bring good luck. □ **talismanic** /-ˈmænɪk/ *adj.* [French and Spanish from Greek]

talk /tɔːk/ —*v.* 1 (often foll. by *to, with*) converse or communicate verbally. 2 have the power of speech. 3 (often foll. by *about*) a discuss; express; utter (*talked cricket; talking nonsense*). b (in *imper.*) *colloq.* as an emphatic statement (*talk about expense!*). 4 use (a language) in speech (*talking Spanish*). 5 (foll. by *at*) address pompously. 6 (usu. foll. by *into, out of*) bring into a specified condition etc. by talking (*talked himself hoarse; did you talk them into it?*). 7 betray secrets. 8 gossip (*people will talk*). 9 have influence (*money talks*). —*n.* 1 conversation, talking. 2 particular mode or style of speech (*baby-talk*). 3 informal address or lecture. 4 a rumour or gossip (*talk of a merger*). b its theme (*the talk was all babies*). 5 empty promises; boasting. 6 (often in *pl.*) discussions or negotiations. □ **now you're talking** *colloq.* I like what you say, suggest, etc. **talk back** reply defiantly. **talk down to** speak condescendingly to. **talk a person down 1** silence by loudness or persistence. 2 bring (a pilot or aircraft) to landing by radio instructions. **talk down** 1 discuss or mention. 2 (often foll. by verbal noun) express some intention of (*talked of moving to London*). **talk out block** (a

bill in Parliament) by prolonging discussion to the time of adjournment. **talk over** discuss at length. **talk a person over** (or **round**) gain agreement by talking. **talk shop** talk about one's occupation etc. **talk to** rebuke, scold. □ **talker** n. [from TALE or TELL]

talkative /'tɔːkətɪv/ adj. fond of or given to talking.

talkback n. (often attrib.) system of two-way communication by loudspeaker.

talkie n. colloq. (esp. early) film with a soundtrack.

talking —adj. 1 that talks, or is able to talk (talking parrot). 2 expressive (talking eyes). —n. in senses of TALK v. □ **talking book** n. recorded reading of a book, esp. for the blind.

talking-point n. topic for discussion.

talking-shop n. derog. arena or opportunity for empty talk.

talking-to n. colloq. reproof, reprimand.

tall /tɔːl/ —adj. 1 of more than average height 2 of a specified height (about six feet tall). 3 higher than the surrounding objects (tall building). —adv. as if tall; proudly (sit tall). □ **tallish** adj. **tallness** n. [Old English]

tallboy n. tall chest of drawers.

tall order n. unreasonable demand.

tallow /'tæləʊ/ n. hard (esp. animal) fat melted down to make candles, soap, etc. □ **tallowy** adj. [Low German]

tall ship n. sailing-ship with a high mast.

tall story n. colloq. extravagant story that is difficult to believe.

tally /'tælɪ/ —n. (pl. -ies) 1 reckoning of a debt or score. 2 total score or amount. 3 mark registering the number of objects delivered or received. 4 hist. a piece of notched wood for keeping account. b account kept thus. 5 identification ticket or label. 6 corresponding thing, counterpart, or duplicate. —v. (-ies, -ied) (often foll. by with) agree or correspond. [Latin talea rod]

tally-ho /ˌtælɪ'həʊ/ —int. huntsman's cry on sighting a fox. —n. (pl. -s) cry of this. —v. (-hoes, -hoed) 1 utter a cry of 'tally-ho'. 2 indicate (a fox) or urge (hounds) with this cry. [cf. French taïaut]

Talmud /'tælmʊd, -mʊd/ n. body of Jewish civil and ceremonial law and legend. □ **Talmudic** /-'mʊdɪk/ adj. **Talmudist** n. [Hebrew, = instruction]

talon /'tælən/ n. claw, esp. of a bird of prey. [Latin talus ankle]

talus /'teɪləs/ n. (pl. tali /-laɪ/) ankle-bone supporting the tibia. [Latin, = ankle]

tamarind /'tæmərɪnd/ n. 1 tropical evergreen tree. 2 fruit pulp from this used as food and in drinks. [Arabic, = Indian date]

tamarisk /'tæmərɪsk/ n. seashore shrub usu. with small pink or white flowers. [Latin]

tambour /'tæmbʊə(r)/ n. 1 drum. 2 circular frame holding fabric taut for embroidering. [French: related to TABOR]

tambourine /ˌtæmbə'riːn/ n. small shallow drum with jingling discs in its rim, shaken or banged as an accompaniment. [French, diminutive of TAMBOUR]

tame —adj. 1 (of an animal) domesticated; not wild or shy. 2 insipid; dull (tame entertainment). 3 (of a person) amenable. —v. (-ming) 1 make tame; domesticate. 2 subdue, curb. □ **tameable** adj. **tamely** adv. **tameness** n. **tamer** n. (also in comb.). [Old English]

Tamil /'tæmɪl/ —n. 1 member of a people of South India and Sri Lanka. 2 language of this people or language. —adj. of this people or language. [native name]

tam-o'-shanter /ˌtæmə'ʃæntə(r)/ n. floppy round beret, of Scottish origin. [hero of a poem by Burns]

tamp v. ram down hard or tightly. [tampion stopper for gun-muzzle, from French tampon]

tamper v. (foll. by with) 1 meddle with or change illicitly. 2 exert a secret or corrupt influence upon; bribe. [var. of TEMPER]

tampon /'tæmpɒn/ n. plug of soft material used esp. to absorb menstrual blood. [French: related to TAMP]

tam-tam /'tæmtæm/ n. large metal gong. [Hindi]

tan[1] —n. 1 = SUNTAN. 2 yellowish-brown colour. 3 bark, esp. of oak, used to tan hides. —adj. yellowish-brown. —v. (-nn-) 1 make or become brown by exposure to sunlight. 2 convert (raw hide) into leather. 3 slang beat, thrash. [medieval Latin tanno, perhaps from Celtic]

tan[2] abbr. tangent.

tandem /'tændəm/ —n. 1 bicycle with two or more seats one behind another. 2 group of two people etc. with one behind or following the other. 3 carriage driven tandem. —adv. with two or more horses harnessed one behind another (drive tandem). □ **in tandem** 1 one behind another. 2 alongside each other; together. [Latin, = at length]

tandoor /'tænduə(r)/ n. clay oven. [Hindustani]

tandoori /tænˈdʊərɪ/ n. food spiced and cooked over charcoal in a tandoor (often *attrib.*: *tandoori chicken*). [Hindustani]

tandoor n. a clay oven. [Hindustani]

tang n. **1** strong taste or smell. **2** characteristic quality. **3** projection on the blade of esp. a knife, by which it is held firm in the handle. [Old Norse *tange* point]

tangent /ˈtændʒ(ə)nt/ n. **1** (often *attrib.*) straight line, curve, or surface that meets a curve at a point, but does not intersect it. **2** ratio of two sides (other than the hypotenuse) opposite and adjacent to an acute angle in a right-angled triangle. □ **at a tangent** diverging from a previous course or from what is relevant or central (*go off at a tangent*). [Latin *tango tact- touch*]

tangential /tænˈdʒenʃ(ə)l/ adj. **1** of or along a tangent. **2** divergent. **3** peripheral. □ **tangentially** adv.

tangerine /ˌtændʒəˈriːn/ n. **1** small sweet thin-skinned citrus fruit like an orange; mandarin. **2** deep orange-yellow colour. [*Tangier* in Morocco]

tangible /ˈtændʒɪb(ə)l/ adj. **1** perceptible by touch. **2** definite; clearly intelligible; not elusive (*tangible proof*). □ **tangibility** /-ˈbɪlɪtɪ/ n. **tangibleness** n. **tangibly** adv. [Latin: related to TANGENT]

tangle /ˈtæŋg(ə)l/ —v. (**-ling**) **1** intertwine (threads or hairs etc.) or become entwined in a confused mass; entangle. **2** (foll. by *with*) *colloq.* become involved (esp. in conflict) with (*don't tangle with me*). **3** complicate (*tangled affair*). —n. **1** confused mass of intertwined threads etc. **2** confused state. [origin uncertain]

tangly adj. (**-ier**, **-iest**) tangled.

tango /ˈtæŋgəʊ/ —n. (pl. **-s**) **1** slow S. American ballroom dance. **2** music for this. —v. (**-goes**, **-goed**) dance the tango. [American Spanish]

tangy adj. (**-ier**, **-iest**) having a strong usu. acid tang.

tanh /θæn, tænʃ, tænˈeɪtʃ/ *abbr. hyperbolic tangent.*

tank —n. **1** large container, usu. for liquid or gas. **2** heavy armoured fighting vehicle moving on continuous tracks. —v. (usu. foll. by *up*) fill the tank of (a vehicle etc.) with fuel. □ **tankful** n. (pl. **-s**). [originally Indian. = pond, from Gujarati]

tankard /ˈtæŋkəd/ n. **1** tall beer mug with a handle. **2** contents of or amount held by this (*drank a tankard of ale*). [probably Dutch *tankaerd*]

tanked up *predic. adj. colloq.* drunk.

tank engine n. steam engine with integral fuel and water containers.

tanker n. ship, aircraft, or road vehicle for carrying liquids, esp. oil, in bulk.

tanner n. person who tans hides.

tannery n. (pl. **-ies**) place where hides are tanned.

tannic adj. of tan (sense 3).

tannic acid n. natural yellowish organic compound used as a mordant and astringent.

tannin /ˈtænɪn/ n. any of various organic compounds found in tree-barks and oak-galls, used in leather production. [French *tanin*: related to TAN[1]]

Tannoy /ˈtænɔɪ/ n. *propr.* type of public-address system. [origin uncertain]

tansy /ˈtænzɪ/ n. (pl. **-ies**) plant with yellow flowers and aromatic leaves. [Greek *athanasia* immortality]

tantalize /ˈtæntəlaɪz/ v. (also **-ise**) (**-zing** or **-sing**) **1** torment or tease by the sight or promise of the unobtainable. **2** raise and then dash the hopes of. □ **tantalization** /-ˈzeɪʃ(ə)n/ n. [*Tantalus*, mythical king punished in Hades with sight of water and fruit which drew back whenever he tried to reach them]

tantalum /ˈtæntələm/ n. rare hard white metallic element. □ **tantalic** adj. [related to TANTALIZE]

tantalus /ˈtæntələs/ n. stand in which spirit-decanters may be locked up but visible. [see TANTALIZE]

tantamount /ˈtæntəmaʊnt/ predic. adj. (foll. by *to*) equivalent to. [Italian *tanto montare* amount to so much]

tantra /ˈtæntrə/ n. any of a class of Hindu or Buddhist mystical or magical writings. [Sanskrit, = doctrine]

tantrum /ˈtæntrəm/ n. (esp. child's) outburst of bad temper or petulance. [origin unknown]

Taoiseach /ˈtiːʃəx/ n. prime minister of the Irish Republic. [Irish, = chief, leader]

Taoism /ˈtaʊɪz(ə)m, ˈtɑːəʊ-/ n. Chinese philosophy advocating humility and religious piety. □ **Taoist** n. [Chinese *dao* right way]

tap[1] —n. **1** device by which a flow of liquid or gas from a pipe or vessel can be controlled. **2** tapping of a telephone etc. —v. (**-pp-**) **1** provide (a cask) or let out (liquid) with a tap. **2** draw sap from (a tree) by cutting into it. **3** obtain information or supplies from. **4** extract or obtain; discover and exploit (*mineral wealth waiting to be tapped*; *tap skills of young people*). **5** connect a listening device to (a telephone etc.). □ **on tap 1** ready to be drawn off by tap. **2** *colloq.* freely available. [Old English]

tap[2] —v. (**-pp-**) **1** (foll. by *at, on*) strike a gentle but audible blow. **2** (often foll. by *against, on,* etc.) strike or cause (a thing) to strike lightly (*tapped me on the*

shoulder). **3** (often foll. by *out*) make by a tap or taps (*tapped out the rhythm*). **4** tap-dance. —*n.* **1 a** a light blow; rap. **b** sound of this. **2 a** a tap-dancing. **b** metal attachment on a tap-dancer's shoe. [imitative]

tapas /ˈtæpəs/ *n.pl.* (often *attrib.*) small savoury esp. Spanish dishes. [Spanish]

tap-dance —*n.* rhythmic dance performed with shoes with metal taps. —*v.* perform a tap-dance. □ **tap-dancer** *n.* **tap-dancing** *n.*

tape —*n.* **1** narrow strip of woven material for tying up, fastening, etc. **2** (in full **adhesive tape**) strip of adhesive plastic etc. for fastening, masking, insulating, etc. **3** a = MAGNETIC TAPE. **b** reel or cassette containing this. **c** tape recording. **5** = TAPE-MEASURE. —*v.* **1** (-*ping*) **1 a** fasten or join etc. with tape. **b** apply tape to. **2** (foll. by *off*) seal or mark off with tape. **3** record on magnetic tape. **4** measure with tape. □ **have** (or **get**) **a person** or **thing taped** *colloq.* understand (him, it, etc.) fully. [Old English]

tape deck *n.* machine for using audiotape (separate from the amplifier, speakers, etc.).

tape machine *n.* **1** machine for recording telegraph messages. **2** = TAPE RECORDER.

tape-measure *n.* strip of marked tape or flexible metal for measuring.

taper —*n.* **1** wick coated with wax etc. for conveying a flame. **2** slender candle. —*v.* (often foll. by *off*) **1** diminish or reduce in thickness towards one end. **2** make or become gradually less. [Old English]

tape recorder *n.* apparatus for recording and replaying sounds on magnetic tape. □ **tape-record** *v.* **tape recording** *n.*

tapestry /ˈtæpɪstrɪ/ *n.* (*pl.* -*ies*) **1 a** thick fabric in which coloured weft threads are woven to form pictures or designs. **b** (usu. wool) embroidery imitating this. **c** piece of this. **2** events or circumstances etc. seen as interwoven etc. (*life's rich tapestry*). □ **tapestried** *adj.* [*tapissery* from French *tapis* carpet]

tapeworm *n.* parasitic intestinal flatworm with a segmented body.

tapioca /ˌtæpɪˈəʊkə/ *n.* starchy substance in hard white grains, obtained from cassava and used for puddings etc. [Tupi-Guarani]

tapir /ˈteɪpə(r), -pɪə(r)/ *n.* nocturnal Central and S. American or Malaysian hoofed mammal with a short flexible snout. [Tupi]

tappet /ˈtæpɪt/ *n.* lever or projecting part in machinery giving intermittent motion. [from TAP²]

taproom *n.* room in a pub serving drinks on tap.

tap root *n.* tapering root growing vertically downwards.

tar¹ —*n.* **1** dark thick inflammable liquid distilled from wood or coal etc., used as a preservative of wood and iron, in making roads, as an antiseptic, etc. **2** similar substance formed in the combustion of tobacco etc. —*v.* (-rr-) cover with tar. □ **tar and feather** smear with tar and then cover with feathers as a punishment. **tarred with the same brush** having the same faults. [Old English]

tar² *n. colloq.* sailor. [from TARPAULIN]

taramasalata /ˌtærəməsəˈlɑːtə/ *n.* (also **taramosalata**) pâté made from roe with olive oil, seasoning, etc. [Greek *taramas* roe, *salata* SALAD]

tarantella /ˌtærənˈtelə/ *n.* **1** whirling S. Italian dance. **2** music for this. [Italian from *Taranto* in Italy]

tarantula /təˈræntjʊlə/ *n.* **1** large hairy tropical spider. **2** large black S. European spider. [medieval Latin: related to TARANTELLA]

tarboosh /tɑːˈbuːʃ/ *n.* cap like a fez. [Arabic from Persian]

tardy /ˈtɑːdɪ/ *adj.* (-ier, -iest) **1** slow to act, come, or happen. **2** delaying or delayed. □ **tardily** *adv.* **tardiness** *n.* [Latin *tardus* slow]

tare¹ *n.* **1** vetch, esp. as a cornfield weed or fodder. **2** (in *pl.*) *Bibl.* an injurious cornfield weed (Matt. 13:24-30). [origin unknown]

tare² *n.* **1** allowance made for the weight of packing or wrapping around goods. **2** weight of a vehicle without fuel or load. [Arabic *tarha*]

target /ˈtɑːgɪt/ —*n.* **1** mark fired or aimed at, esp. a round object marked with concentric circles. **2** person or thing aimed or fired at etc. (*an easy target*). **3** objective or result aimed at. **4** butt for criticism, abuse, etc. —*v.* (-t-) **1** identify or single out as a target. **2** aim or direct (*missiles targeted on major cities*). [French *targe* shield]

tariff /ˈtærɪf/ *n.* **1** table of fixed charges (*hotel tariff*). **2 a** duty on a particular class of goods. **b** list of duties or customs due. [Arabic, = notification]

tarlatan /ˈtɑːlət(ə)n/ *n.* thin stiff openweave muslin. [French; probably originally Indian]

Tarmac /ˈtɑːmæk/ —*n. propr.* **1** = TARMACADAM. **2** runway etc. made of this. —*v.* (**tarmac**) (-ck-) apply tarmacadam to. [abbreviation]

tarmacadam /ˌtɑːməˈkædəm/ n. stone or slag bound with bitumen, used in paving roads etc. [from TAR[1], MACADAM]

tarn n. small mountain lake. [Old Norse]

tarnish /ˈtɑːnɪʃ/ −v. 1 (cause to) lose lustre. 2 impair (one's reputation etc.). −n. 1 loss of lustre, esp. as a film on a metal's surface. 2 blemish, stain. [French ternir from terne dark]

taro /ˈtɑːrəʊ/ n. (pl. -s) tropical plant with tuberous roots used as food. [Polynesian]

tarot /ˈtærəʊ/ n. (often attrib.) 1 (in sing. or pl.) **a** a pack of mainly picture cards used in fortune-telling. **b** any game played with a similar pack of 78 cards. 2 any card from a tarot pack. [French]

tarpaulin /tɑːˈpɔːlɪn/ n. 1 heavy-duty cloth waterproofed esp. with tar. 2 sheet or covering of this. [from TAR[1], PALL[1]]

tarragon /ˈtærəgən/ n. bushy herb used in salads, stuffings, vinegar, etc. [medieval Latin from Greek]

tarry[1] /ˈtɑːrɪ/ adj. (-ier, -iest) of, like, or smeared with tar.

tarry[2] /ˈtærɪ/ v. (-ies, -ied) archaic linger, stay, wait. [origin unknown]

tarsal /ˈtɑːs(ə)l/ −adj. of the ankle-bones. −n. tarsal bone. [from TARSUS]

tarsus /ˈtɑːsəs/ n. (pl. **tarsi** /-saɪ/) 1 bones of the ankle and upper foot. 2 shank of a bird's leg. [Greek]

tart[1] n. 1 open pastry case containing jam etc. 2 pie with a fruit or other sweet filling. □ **tartlet** n. [French tarte]

tart[2] −n. 1 slang prostitute; promiscuous woman. 2 slang offens. girl or woman. −v. (foll. by up) colloq. (usu. refl.) smarten or dress up esp. gaudily. [probably abbreviation of SWEETHEART]

tart[3] adj. 1 sharp or acid in taste. 2 (of a remark etc.) cutting, bitter. □ **tartly** adv. **tartness** n. [Old English]

tartan /ˈtɑːt(ə)n/ n. 1 pattern of coloured stripes crossing at right angles, esp. denoting a Scottish Highland clan. 2 woollen cloth woven in this pattern (often attrib.: tartan scarf). [origin uncertain]

Tartar /ˈtɑːtə(r)/ −n. 1 **a** a member of a group of Central Asian peoples including the Mongols and Turks. **b** Turkic language of these peoples. 2 (**tartar**) harsh or formidable person. −adj. 1 of Tartars. 2 of Central Asia east of the Caspian Sea. [French or medieval Latin]

tartar /ˈtɑːtə(r)/ n. 1 hard deposit that forms on the teeth. 2 deposit that forms a hard crust in wine. [medieval Latin from Greek]

tartare /ˈtɑːˈtɑː(r)/ adj. (in phr. **sauce tartare**) = TARTAR SAUCE. [French]

tartaric /tɑːˈtærɪk/ adj. of or from tartar.

tartaric acid n. natural acid found esp. in unripe grapes, used in baking powders etc.

tartar sauce n. sauce of mayonnaise and chopped gherkins, capers, etc. [from TARTAR]

tartrazine /ˈtɑːtrəˌziːn/ n. brilliant yellow dye from tartaric acid, used to colour food etc.

tarty /ˈtɑːtɪ/ adj. colloq. (-ier, -iest) (esp. of a woman) vulgar, gaudy; promiscuous.

Tarzan /ˈtɑːz(ə)n/ n. colloq. agile muscular man. [name of a character in stories by E. R. Burroughs]

task /tɑːsk/ −n. piece of work to be done. −v. make great demands on (a person's powers etc.). □ **take to task** rebuke, scold. [medieval Latin tasca, probably = taxa TAX]

task force n. (also **task group**) armed force or other group organized for a specific operation or task.

taskmaster n. (fem. **taskmistress**) person who makes others work hard.

Tass n. official Russian news agency. [Russian]

tassel /ˈtæs(ə)l/ n. 1 tuft of loosely hanging threads or cords etc. as decoration. 2 tassel-like flower-head of some plants, esp. maize. □ **tasselled** adj. (US **tasseled**). [French tas(s)el clasp]

taste /teɪst/ −n. 1 **a** sensation caused in the mouth by contact with a soluble substance. **b** faculty of perceiving this (bitter to the taste). 2 small sample of food or drink. 3 slight experience (taste of success). 4 (often foll. by for) liking or predilection (expensive tastes). 5 aesthetic discernment in art, clothes, conduct, etc. (in poor taste). −v. (-ting) 1 sample the flavour of (food etc.) by taking it into the mouth. 2 (also absol.) perceive the flavour of (cannot taste with a cold). 3 (esp. with neg.) eat or drink a small portion of (had not tasted food for days). 4 experience (never tasted failure). 5 (often foll. by of) have a specified flavour (tastes of onions). □ **to one's taste** pleasing, suitable. [French from Romanic]

taste bud n. cell or nerve-ending on the surface of the tongue by which things are tasted.

tasteful adj. having, or done in, good taste. □ **tastefully** adv. **tastefulness** n.

tasteless adj. 1 lacking flavour. 2 having, or done in, bad taste. □ **tastelessly** adv. **tastelessness** n.

taster n. 1 person employed to test food or drink by tasting. 2 small sample.

tasting *n.* gathering at which food or drink is tasted and evaluated. □

tasty *adj.* (**-ier, -iest**) **1** pleasing in flavour; appetizing. **2** *colloq.* attractive. □ **tastily** *adv.* **tastiness** *n.*

tat¹ *n. colloq.* tatty things; rubbish; junk. [back-formation from TATTY]

tat² *v.* (**-tt-**) do, or make by, tatting. [origin unknown]

tat³ see TIT².

ta-ta /taˈtaː/ *int. colloq.* goodbye. [origin unknown]

tatter *n.* (usu. in *pl.*) rag; irregularly torn cloth or paper etc. □ **in tatters** *colloq.* **1** torn in many places. **2** destroyed, ruined. [Old Norse]

tattered *adj.* in tatters.

tatting /ˈtætɪŋ/ *n.* **1** a kind of handmade knotted lace used for trimming etc. **2** process of making this. [origin unknown]

tattle /ˈtæt(ə)l/ —*v.* (**-ling**) prattle, chatter, gossip. —*n.* gossip; idle talk. [Flemish *tatelen*, imitative]

tattoo¹ /taˈtuː, tæ-/ *n.* **1** evening drum or bugle signal recalling soldiers to quarters. **2** elaboration of this with music and marching as an entertainment. **3** rhythmic tapping or drumming. [earlier *tap-too* from Dutch *taptoe*, literally 'close the tap' (of the cask)]

tattoo² /taˈtuː, tæ-/ —*v.* (**-oos, -ooed**) **1** mark (skin) indelibly by puncturing it and inserting pigment. **2** make a (design) in this way. —*n.* such a design. □ **tattooer** *n.* **tattooist** *n.* [Polynesian]

tatty /ˈtætɪ/ *adj.* (**-ier, -iest**) *colloq.* **1** tattered; shabby. **2** inferior. **3** tawdry. □ **tattily** *adv.* **tattiness** *n.* [originally Scots, = shaggy, apparently related to TATTER]

tau /taʊ, tɔː/ *n.* nineteenth letter of the Greek alphabet (Τ, τ). [Greek]

taught *past* and *past part.* of TEACH.

taunt /tɔːnt/ —*n.* insult; provocation. —*v.* insult; provoke contemptuously. [French *tant pour tant* tit for tat, smart rejoinder]

taupe /təʊp/ *adj.* & *n.* grey tinged with esp. brown. [French, = MOLE¹]

Taurus /ˈtɔːrəs/ *n.* (*pl.* **-es**) **1** constellation and second sign of the zodiac (the Bull). **2** person born when the sun is in this sign. □ **Taurean** *adj.* & *n.* [Latin, = bull]

taut /tɔːt/ *adj.* **1** (of a rope etc.) tight; not slack. **2** (of nerves etc.) tense. **3** (of a ship etc.) in good condition. □ **tauten** *v.* **tautly** *adv.* **tautness** *n.* [perhaps = TOUGH]

tautology /tɔːˈtɒlədʒɪ/ *n.* (*pl.* **-ies**) repetition using different words, esp. as a fault of style (e.g. *arrived one after the other in succession*). □ **tautological**

/-təˈlɒdʒɪk(ə)l/ *adj.* **tautologous** /ˈtɔːtələgəs/ *adj.* [Greek *tauto* the same]

tavern /ˈtæv(ə)n/ *n. archaic* or *literary* inn, pub. [Latin *taberna*]

taverna /təˈvɜːnə/ *n.* Greek restaurant. [modern Greek: related to TAVERN]

tawdry /ˈtɔːdrɪ/ *adj.* (**-ier, -iest**) showy but worthless; gaudy. □ **tawdrily** *adv.* **tawdriness** *n.* [*tawdry lace* from *St Audrey's lace*]

tawny /ˈtɔːnɪ/ *adj.* (**-ier, -iest**) orange-brown or yellow-brown. [Anglo-French *tauné*: related to TAN¹]

tawny owl *n.* reddish-brown European owl.

tax —*n.* **1** money compulsorily levied by the State or local authorities on individuals, property, or businesses. **2** (usu. foll. by *on, upon*) strain, heavy demand, or burdensome obligation. —*v.* **1** impose a tax on. **2** deduct tax from (income etc.). **3** make heavy demands on (*taxes my patience*). **4** (often foll. by *with*) confront (a person) with a fault etc; call to account. □ **taxable** *adj.* [Latin *taxo* censure, compute]

taxa *pl.* of TAXON.

taxation /tækˈseɪʃ(ə)n/ *n.* imposition or payment of tax. [Latin: related to TAX]

tax avoidance *n.* minimizing payment of tax by financial manoeuvring.

tax-deductible *adj.* (of expenditure) legally deductible from income before tax assessment.

tax disc *n.* road tax receipt displayed on the windscreen of a vehicle.

tax evasion *n.* illegal non-payment or underpayment of tax.

tax-free *adj.* exempt from tax.

tax haven *n.* country etc. where taxes are low.

taxi /ˈtæksɪ/ —*n.* (*pl.* **-s**) (in full **taxi-cab**) car licensed to ply for hire and usu. fitted with a taximeter. —*v.* (**-xis, -xied, -xiing** or **-xying**) **1** (of an aircraft or pilot) drive on the ground before take-off or after landing. **2** go or convey in a taxi. [abbreviation of *taximeter cab*]

taxidermy /ˈtæksɪdɜːmɪ/ *n.* art of preparing, stuffing, and mounting the skins of animals. □ **taxidermist** *n.* [Greek *taxis* arrangement, *derma* skin]

taximeter /ˈtæksɪˌmiːtə(r)/ *n.* automatic fare-indicator fitted to a taxi. [French: related to TAXI]

tax rank *n.* (*US* **taxi stand**) place where taxis wait to be hired.

taxman *n. colloq.* inspector or collector of taxes.

taxon /ˈtæksɒn/ *n.* (*pl.* **taxa**) any taxonomic group. [back-formation from TAXONOMY]

taxonomy /tækˈsɒnəmɪ/ *n.* classification of living and extinct organisms. □

taxonomic /-sə'nɒmɪk/ *adj;* **taxonom-ical** /-sə'nɒmɪk(ə)l/ *adj;* **taxonom-ically** /-sə'nɒmɪkəlɪ/ *adv;* **taxonomist** *-nomia*

taxpayer *n.* person who pays taxes.

tax return *n.* declaration of income for taxation purposes.

tayberry /'teɪbərɪ/ *n.* (*pl.* -ies) hybrid fruit between the blackberry and rasp-berry. [River Tay in Scotland]

TB *abbr.* **1** tubercle bacillus. **2** tubercu-losis.

Tb *symb.* terbium.

t.b.a. *abbr.* to be announced.

T-bone /'ti:bəʊn/ *n.* T-shaped bone, esp. in steak from the thin end of a loin.

tbsp. *abbr.* tablespoonful.

Tc *symb.* technetium.

TCP *abbr. propr.* a disinfectant and germicide. [trichlorophenylmethyliodo-salicyl]

Te *symb.* tellurium.

te /ti:/ *n.* (also **ti**) seventh note of a major scale. [earlier *si:* French from Italian]

tea *n.* **1 a** (in full **tea plant**) Asian evergreen shrub or small tree. **b** its dried leaves. **2** drink made by infusing tea-leaves in boiling water. **3** infusion of other leaves etc. (*camomile tea; beef tea*). **4 a** light afternoon meal of tea, bread, cakes, etc. **b** = HIGH TEA. [prob-ably Dutch *tee* from Chinese]

tea bag *n.* small perforated bag of tea for infusion.

tea break *n.* pause in work etc. to drink tea.

tea caddy *n.* container for tea.

teacake *n.* light usu. toasted sweet bun eaten at tea.

teach *v.* (*past* and *past part.* **taught** /tɔːt/) **1 a** give systematic information, instruction, or training to (a person) or about (a subject or skill) (*taught me to swim*). **b** (*absol.*) practise this profes-sion. **c** communicate, instruct in (*suffering taught me patience*). **2** advoc-ate as a moral etc. principle (*taught forgiveness*). **3** (foll. by *to* + infin.) **a** instruct (a person) by example or punishment (*that will teach you not to disobey*). **b** *colloq.* discourage (a person) from (*that will teach you to laugh*). □ [Old English]

teachable *adj.* [Old English]

teacher *n.* person who teaches, esp. in a school.

teaching *n.* **1** profession of a teacher. **2** (often in *pl.*) what is taught: doctrine.

tea chest *n.* light metal-lined plywood box for transporting tea.

tea cloth *n.* = TEA TOWEL.

tea cosy *n.* cover to keep a teapot warm.

teacup *n.* **1** cup from which tea is drunk. **2** amount held by this. □ **teacupful** *n.*

tea dance *n.* afternoon tea with dan-cing.

teak *n.* **1** a hard durable timber. **2** large Indian or SE Asian deciduous tree yield-ing this. [Portuguese from Malayalam]

teal *n.* (*pl.* same) small freshwater duck. [origin unknown]

tea lady *n.* woman employed to make tea in offices etc.

tea-leaf *n.* **1** dried leaf of tea. **2** (esp. in *pl.*) these as dregs. **3** *rhyming sl.* thief.

team *n.* **1** set of players forming one side in a game. **2** two or more people working together. **3** set of draught an-imals. —*v.* **1** (usu. foll. by *up*) join in a team or in common action (*teamed up with them*). **2** (foll. by *with*) match or coordinate (clothes). [Old English]

team-mate *n.* fellow member of a team.

team spirit *n.* willingness to act for the communal good.

teamster *n.* **1** *US* lorry-driver. **2** driver of a team of animals.

teamwork *n.* combined action; co-operation.

tea-planter *n.* proprietor or cultivator of a tea plantation.

teapot *n.* pot with a handle, spout, and lid, for brewing and then pouring tea.

tear¹ /teə(r)/ —*v.* (*past* **tore**; *past part.* **torn**) **1** (often foll. by *up*) pull apart or to pieces with some force (*tore up the letter*). **2 a** make a hole or rent in this way; undergo this (*have torn my coat; curtain tore*). **b** make (a hole or rent). **3** (foll. by *away, off, at,* etc.) pull violently (*tore off the cover; tore down the notice*). **4** violently disrupt or divide (*torn by guilt*). **5** *colloq.* go hurriedly (*tore across the road*). —*n.* **1** hole etc. caused by tearing. **2** torn part of cloth etc. □ **be torn between** have difficulty in choos-ing between. **tear apart 1** search (a place) exhaustively. **2** criticize force-fully. **3** destroy; divide utterly. **tear to shreds** *colloq.* refute or criticize thor-oughly. **that's torn it** *colloq.* that has spoiled things etc. [Old English]

tear² /tɪə(r)/ *n.* **1** drop of clear salty liquid secreted by glands from the eye, and shed esp. in grief. **2** teardrop-like thing; drop. □ **in tears** crying. [Old English]

tearaway *n. colloq.* unruly young per-son.

tear-drop *n.* single tear.

tear-duct *n.* drain for carrying tears to or from the eye.

tearful *adj.* 1 crying or inclined to cry. 2 sad (*tearful event*). □ **tearfully** *adv.*

tear-gas *n.* gas causing severe irritation to the eyes.

tearing hurry *n. colloq.* great hurry.

tear-jerker *n. colloq.* sentimental story, film, etc.

tearoom *n.* small unlicensed café serving tea etc.

tea rose *n.* hybrid shrub with a tealike scent.

tease /tiːz/ –*v.* (**-sing**) (also *absol.*) 1 a make fun of playfully, unkindly, or annoyingly; irritate. b allure, esp. sexually, while withholding satisfaction. 2 pick (wool etc.) into separate fibres. 3 dress (cloth) esp. with teasels. –*n.* 1 *colloq.* person fond of teasing. 2 act of teasing (*only a tease*). □ **tease out** separate by disentangling. [Old English]

teasel /ˈtiːz(ə)l/ *n.* (also **teazel, teazle**) 1 plant with large prickly heads that are dried and used to raise the nap on woven cloth. 2 other device used for this purpose. □ **teaseler** *n.* [Old English: related to TEASE]

teaser *n.* 1 person who teases. 2 *colloq.* hard question or task.

teaset *n.* set of crockery for serving tea.

teashop *n.* = TEAROOM.

teaspoon *n.* 1 small spoon for stirring tea. 2 amount held by this. □ **teaspoonful** *n.* (*pl.* **-s**).

teat *n.* 1 mammary nipple, esp. of an animal. 2 rubber nipple for sucking from a bottle. [French from Germanic]

teatime *n.* time in the afternoon when tea is served.

tea towel *n.* towel for drying washed crockery etc.

tea trolley *n.* (*US* **tea wagon**) small trolley from which tea is served.

teazel (also **teazle**) var. of TEASEL.

TEC /tek/ *abbr.* Training and Enterprise Council.

tec *n. colloq.* detective. [abbreviation]

tech *n.* (also **tec**) *colloq.* technical college. [abbreviation]

technetium /tekˈniːʃ(ə)m/ *n.* artificially produced radioactive metallic element. [Greek *tekhnētos* artificial]

technic /ˈteknik/ *n.* 1 (usu. in *pl.*) a technology. b technical terms, details, methods, etc. 2 technique. [Greek *tekhnē* art]

technical *adj.* 1 of the mechanical arts and applied sciences (*technical college*). 2 of a particular subject or craft etc. 3 (of a book or discourse etc.) using technical language; specialized. 4 due to mechan-

ical failure (*technical hitch*). 5 strictly or legally interpreted (*lost on a technical point*). □ **technically** *adv.*

technicality /ˌteknɪˈkælɪtɪ/ *n.* (*pl.* **-ies**) 1 being technical. 2 technical expression. 3 technical point or detail (*acquitted on a technicality*).

technician /tekˈnɪʃ(ə)n/ *n.* 1 person doing practical or maintenance work in a laboratory etc. 2 person skilled in artistic etc. technique. 3 expert in practical science.

Technicolor /ˈteknɪˌkʌlə(r)/ *n.* (often *attrib.*) *propr.* process of colour cinematography. 2 (usu. **technicolor**) *colloq.* a vivid colour. b artificial brilliance.

technique /tekˈniːk/ *n.* 1 mechanical skill in art. 2 skilful manipulation of a situation, people, etc. 3 manner of artistic execution in music, painting, etc. [French: related to TECHNIC]

technocracy /tekˈnɒkrəsɪ/ *n.* (*pl.* **-ies**) 1 rule or control by technical experts. 2 instance or application of this. [Greek *tekhnē* art]

technocrat /ˈteknəˌkræt/ *n.* exponent or advocate of technocracy. □ **technocratic** /-ˈkrætɪk/ *adj.*

technology /tekˈnɒlədʒɪ/ *n.* (*pl.* **-ies**) 1 knowledge or use of the mechanical arts and applied sciences (*lacked the technology*). 2 these subjects collectively. □ **technological** /-nəˈlɒdʒɪk(ə)l/ *adj.* **technologically** /-nəˈlɒdʒɪkəlɪ/ *adv.* **technologist** *n.* [Greek *tekhnologia* systematic treatment, from *tekhnē* art]

tectonic /tekˈtɒnɪk/ *adj.* 1 of building or construction. 2 of the deformation and subsequent structural changes of the earth's crust (see PLATE TECTONICS). [Greek *tektōn* craftsman]

tectonics *n. pl.* (usu. treated as *sing.*) study of the earth's large-scale structural features (see PLATE TECTONICS).

Ted *n.* (also **ted**) *colloq.* Teddy boy. [abbreviation]

teddy bear /ˈtedɪ/ *n.* (also **Teddy**) (in full **teddy bear**) soft toy bear. [*Teddy*, pet form of *Theodore Roosevelt*]

Teddy boy /ˈtedɪ/ *n. colloq.* youth, esp. of the 1950s, wearing Edwardian-style clothes, hairstyle, etc. [*Teddy*, pet form of *Edward*]

tedious /ˈtiːdɪəs/ *adj.* tiresomely long; wearisome. □ **tediously** *adv.* **tediousness** *n.* [Latin: related to TEDIUM]

tedium /ˈtiːdɪəm/ *n.* tediousness. [Latin *taedium* from *taedet* it bores]

tee[1] *n.* = T. [phonetic spelling;

tee² /tiː/ —n. **1 a** a cleared space from which the golf ball is struck at the start of play for each hole. **b** small wooden or plastic support for a golf ball used then. **2** mark aimed at in bowls, quoits, curling, etc. —v. (**tees, teed**) (often foll. by *up*) place (a ball) on a golf tee. □ **tee off 1** play a ball from a tee. **2** *colloq.* begin. [origin unknown]

teem¹ /tiːm/ v. (often foll. by *with*) be full of or swarming with (*teeming with ideas*). [Old English, = give birth to]

teem² v. (often foll. by *down*) (of water etc.) flow copiously; pour (*teeming with rain*). [Old Norse]

teen *attrib. adj.* = TEENAGE. [abbreviation]

-teen *suffix* forming numerals from 13 to 19. [Old English]

teenage *attrib. adj.* of or characteristic of teenagers. □ **teenaged** *adj.*

teenager n. person from 13 to 19 years of age.

teens /tiːnz/ n.pl. years of one's age from 13 to 19 (*in his teens*).

teensy /ˈtiːnzi/ *adj.* (**-ier, -iest**) *colloq.* = TEENY.

teeny /ˈtiːni/ *adj.* (**-ier, -iest**) *colloq.* tiny. [var. of TINY]

teeny-bopper n. *colloq.* young teenager, usu. a girl, who follows the latest fashions.

teeny-weeny *adj.* (also **teensy-weensy**) very tiny.

teepee var. of TEPEE.

teeter v. totter; move unsteadily. [dial. *titter*]

teeth *pl.* of TOOTH.

teethe /tiːð/ v. (**-thing**) grow or cut teeth, esp. milk teeth.

teething-ring n. ring for an infant to bite on while teething.

teething troubles n.pl. initial difficulties in an enterprise etc.

teetotal /tiːˈtəʊt(ə)l/ *adj.* of or advocating total abstinence from alcohol. □ **teetotaller** n. [reduplication of TOTAL]

teetotalism n. **teetotaller** n.

teff n. an African cereal. [Amharic]

TEFL /ˈtef(ə)l/ *abbr.* teaching of English as a foreign language.

Teflon /ˈteflon/ n. *propr.* non-stick coating for kitchen utensils. [from *tetra-, fluor-, -on*]

te-hee var. of TEE-HEE.

Tel. *abbr.* (also **tel.**) telephone.

tele- *comb. form* **1** at or to a distance (*telekinesis, telescope*). **2**

(*telecast*). **3** by telephone (*telesales*).

tele-ad /ˈteliˌad/ n. advertisement telephoned to a newspaper etc.

telecast —n. television broadcast. —v. transmit by television. □ **telecaster** n.

telecommunication /ˌtelikəˌmjuːniˈkeɪʃ(ə)n/ n. **1** communication over a distance by cables using cable, fibre optics, satellites, radio etc. **2** (usu. in *pl.*) technology of this.

teleconference /ˌteliˌkonfərəns/ n. conference with participants linked by telephone etc. □ **teleconferencing** n.

telefax /ˈteliˌfaks/ n. = FAX. [abbreviation of *telefacsimile*]

telegram /ˈteliˌgram/ n. message sent by telegraph and delivered in printed form.

■ **Usage** Since 1931 *telegram* has not been in UK official use, except for international messages. See also *telemessage*.

telegraph /ˈteliˌgrɑːf/ —n. (often *attrib.*) device or system for transmitting messages or signals to a distance, esp. by making and breaking an electrical connection (*telegraph wire*). —v. **1** (often followed by *to*) send a message by telegraph to. **2** send or communicate by telegraph. **3** give advance indication of (*telegraphed his punch*). □ **telegraphist** /tɪˈlegrəfɪst/ n.

telegraphic /ˌteliˈgrafɪk/ *adj.* **1** of or by telegraphs or telegrams. **2** economically worded. □ **telegraphically** *adv.*

telegraphy /tɪˈlegrəfi/ n. communication by telegraph.

telekinesis /ˌtelikaɪˈniːsɪs/ n. supposed paranormal force moving objects at a distance. □ **telekinetic** /-ˈnetɪk/ *adj.* [Greek *kineō* move]

telemarketing /ˈteliˌmɑːkɪtɪŋ/ n. marketing of goods etc. by unsolicited telephone calls.

telemessage /ˈteliˌmesɪdʒ/ n. message sent by telephone or telex and delivered in printed form.

■ **Usage** *Telemessage* has been in UK official use since 1981 for inland messages, replacing *telegram*.

telemeter /ˈteliˌmiːtə(r)/ n. instrument for recording the readings of an instrument and transmitting them by radio. □ **telemetric** /-ˈmetrɪk/ *adj.* [Greek *metron* measure]

telemetry /tɪˈlemɪtri/ n. process of recording the readings of an instrument and transmitting them by radio.

---

teleology /ˌtiːlɪˈolədʒi, ˌtel-/ n. (*pl.* **-ies**) **1** explanation of phenomena by the purpose they serve. **2** *Theol.* doctrine of design and purpose in the material world. □ **teleological** /-əˈlodʒɪk(ə)l/ *adj.* [Greek *telos* end]

telepathy /tɪˈlepəθɪ/ *n.* supposed paranormal communication of thoughts. □ **telepathic** /ˌtelɪˈpæθɪk/ *adj.* **telepathically** /ˌtelɪˈpæθɪkəlɪ/ *adv.*

telephone /ˈtelɪˌfəʊn/ —*n.* **1** apparatus for transmitting sound (esp. speech) to a distance, esp. by using optical or electrical signals. **2** handset etc. used in this. **3** system of communication using a network of telephones. —*v.* (-ning) **1** speak to or send (a message) by telephone. **2** make a telephone call. □ **on the telephone** having or using a telephone. **over the telephone** using the telephone. □ **telephonic** /-ˈfɒnɪk/ *adj.* **telephonically** /-ˈfɒnɪkəlɪ/ *adv.*

telephone book *n.* = TELEPHONE DIRECTORY.

telephone booth *n.* (also **telephone kiosk, telephone box**) booth etc. with a telephone for public use.

telephone directory *n.* book listing telephone subscribers and numbers.

telephone number *n.* number used to call a particular telephone.

telephonist /tɪˈlefənɪst/ *n.* operator in a telephone exchange or at a switchboard.

telephony /tɪˈlefənɪ/ *n.* transmission of sound by telephone.

telephoto /ˌtelɪˈfəʊtəʊ/ *n.* (*pl.* **-s**) (in full **telephoto lens**) lens used in telephotography.

telephotography /ˌtelɪfəˈtɒɡrəfɪ/ *n.* photographing of distant objects with a system of lenses giving a large image. □ **telephotographic** /-fəʊtəˈɡræfɪk/ *adj.*

teleprinter /ˈtelɪˌprɪntə(r)/ *n.* device for transmitting, receiving, and printing telegraph messages.

teleprompter /ˈtelɪˌprɒmptə(r)/ *n.* device beside a television or cinema camera that slowly unrolls a speaker's script out of sight of the audience.

telesales /ˈtelɪˌseɪlz/ *n.pl.* selling by telephone.

telescope /ˈtelɪˌskəʊp/ —*n.* **1** optical instrument using lenses or mirrors to magnify distant objects. **2** = RADIO TELESCOPE. —*v.* (-ping) **1** press or drive (sections of a tube, colliding vehicles, etc.) together so that one slides into another. **2** close or be capable of closing in this way. **3** compress so as to occupy less space or time.

telescopic /ˌtelɪˈskɒpɪk/ *adj.* **1** of or made with a telescope (*telescopic observations*). **2** (esp. of a lens) able to focus on and magnify distant objects. **3** consisting of sections that telescope. □ **telescopically** *adv.*

telescopic sight *n.* telescope on a rifle etc. used for sighting.

teletext /ˈtelɪˌtekst/ *n.* computerized news and information service transmitted to the televisions of subscribers.

telethon /ˈtelɪˌθɒn/ *n.* exceptionally long television programme, esp. to raise money for charity. [from TELE-, MARATHON]

Teletype /ˈtelɪˌtaɪp/ *n. propr.* a kind of teleprinter.

televise /ˈtelɪˌvaɪz/ *v.* (-sing) broadcast on television.

television /ˈtelɪˌvɪʒ(ə)n, -ˈvɪʒ(ə)n/ *n.* **1** system for reproducing (on a screen visual images transmitted (usu. with sound) by radio signals or cable. **2** (in full **television set**) device with a screen for receiving these signals. **3** television broadcasting. □ **televisual** /-ˈvɪʒʊəl/ *adj.*

telex /ˈteleks/ (also **Telex**) —*n.* international system of telegraphy by teleprinters using the public telecommunications network. —*v.* send, or communicate with, by telex. [from TELEPRINTER, EXCHANGE]

tell *v.* (*past and past part.* **told** /təʊld/) **1** relate in speech or writing (*tell me a story*). **2** make known, express in words (*tell me your name*). **3** reveal or signify (to a person) (*your face tells me everything*). **4** utter (*tell lies*). **5 a** (often foll. by *of, about*) divulge information etc.; reveal a secret, the truth etc. (*told her about Venice; book tells you how to cook; promise you won't tell; time will tell*). **b** (foll. by *on*) *colloq.* inform against. **6** (foll. by *to* + infin.) direct; order (*tell them to wait*). **7** assure (*it's true, I tell you*). **8** decide, determine, distinguish (*tell one from the other*). **9** (often foll. by *on*) produce a noticeable effect or influence (*strain told on me; evidence tells against you*). **10** (often *absol.*) count (votes) at a meeting, election, etc. □ **tell apart** distinguish between (*could not tell them apart*). **tell off** *colloq.* scold. **tell tales** make known another person's faults etc. **tell the time** read the time from a clock or watch. **you're telling me** *colloq.* I agree wholeheartedly. [Old English: related to TALE]

teller *n.* **1** person working at the counter of a bank etc. **2** person who counts votes. **3** person who tells esp. stories (*teller of tales*).

telling *adj.* having a marked effect; striking; impressive. □ **tellingly** *adv.*

telling-off *n.* (*pl.* **tellings-off**) *colloq.* scolding.

tell-tale *n.* **1** person who reveals secrets about another. **2** (*attrib.*) that reveals or betrays (*tell-tale smile*). **3** automatic monitoring or registering device.

tellurium /te'ljʊǝriǝm/ n. rare lustrous silver-white element used in semiconductors. [Latin *tellus -ur-* earth]

telly /'teli/ n. (pl. -ies) colloq. 1 television. 2 television set. [abbreviation]

temerity /tɪ'merɪtɪ/ n. rashness; audacity. [Latin *temere* rashly]

temp colloq. –n. temporary employee, esp. a secretary. –v. work as a temp. [abbreviation]

temper –n. 1 mental disposition, mood (placid temper). 2 irritation or anger (fit of temper). 3 tendency to lose one's temper (have a temper). 4 composure, calmness (lose one's temper). 5 hardness or elasticity of metal. –v. 1 bring (metal or clay) to a proper hardness or consistency. 2 (foll. by with) moderate, mitigate (temper justice with mercy). □ in a bad (or out of) temper irritable, angry. in a good temper amicable, happy. [Latin *tempero mingle*]

tempera /'tempǝrǝ/ n. 1 method of painting using an emulsion, e.g. of pigment with egg-yolk and water, esp. on canvas. 2 this emulsion. [Italian]

temperament /'tempǝrǝmǝnt/ n. person's or animal's nature and character (nervous temperament). [Latin: related to TEMPER]

temperamental /tempǝrǝ'ment(ǝ)l/ adj. 1 of temperament. 2 a (of a person) unreliable, moody. b colloq. (of esp. a machine) unreliable, unpredictable. □ temperamentally adv.

temperance /'tempǝrǝns/ n. 1 moderation, esp. in eating and drinking. 2 (often attrib.) abstinence, esp. total, from alcohol (temperance hotel). [Latin: related to TEMPER]

temperate /'tempǝrǝt/ adj. 1 avoiding excess. 2 moderate. 3 (of a region or climate) mild. [Latin: related to TEMPER]

temperature /'temprɪtʃǝ(r)/ n. 1 measured or perceived degree of heat or cold of a thing, region, etc. 2 colloq. body temperature above the normal (have a temperature). 3 degree of excitement in a discussion etc. [Latin: related to TEMPER]

tempest /'tempɪst/ n. violent storm. [Latin *tempus* time]

tempestuous /tem'pestjʊǝs/ adj. stormy; turbulent. □ tempestuously adv.

tempi pl. of TEMPO.

template /'templɪt, -pleɪt/ n. piece of thin board or metal plate etc., used as a pattern in cutting or drilling etc. [originally *templet*, diminutive of *temple*, device in a loom to keep the cloth stretched]

temple¹ /'temp(ǝ)l/ n. building for the worship, or seen as the dwelling-place, of a god or gods etc. [Latin *templum*]

temple² /'temp(ǝ)l/ n. flat part of either side of the head between the forehead and the ear. [French from Latin]

tempo /'tempǝʊ/ n. (pl. -s or -pi /-piː/) 1 speed at which music is or should be played. 2 speed or pace. [Italian from Latin]

temporal /'tempǝr(ǝ)l/ adj. 1 worldly as opposed to spiritual; secular. 2 of time. 3 Gram. denoting time or tense (temporal conjunction). 4 of the temples of the head (temporal artery). [Latin *tempus -por- time*]

temporary /'tempǝrǝrɪ/ –adj. lasting or meant to last only for a limited time. –n. (pl. -ies) person employed temporarily. □ temporarily adv. temporariness n.

temporize /'tempǝraɪz/ v. (also -ise) (-zing or -sing) 1 avoid committing oneself so as to gain time; procrastinate. 2 comply temporarily; adopt a time-serving policy.

tempt v. 1 entice or incite (a person) to do what is wrong or forbidden (tempted him to steal it). 2 allure, attract. 3 risk provoking (fate etc.). □ be tempted to be strongly disposed to. □ tempter n. temptress n. [Latin *tempto, tento* try, test]

temptation /temp'teɪʃ(ǝ)n/ n. 1 tempting or being tempted, incitement, esp. to wrongdoing. 2 attractive thing or course of action. 3 archaic putting to the test.

tempting adj. attractive, inviting. □ temptingly adv.

tempura /tem'pʊǝrǝ/ n. Japanese dish of fish, shellfish, etc., fried in batter. [Japanese]

ten adj. & n. 1 one more than nine. 2 symbol for this (10, x, X). 3 size etc. denoted by ten. 4 ten o'clock. □ ten to one very probably. [Old English]

tenable /'tenǝb(ǝ)l/ adj. 1 maintainable or defensible against attack or objection (tenable position). 2 (foll. by for, by) (of an office etc.) that can be held for (a specified period) or by (a specified class of person). □ tenability /-'bɪlɪtɪ/ n.

tenacious /tɪ'neɪʃǝs/ adj. 1 (often foll. by of) keeping a firm hold. 2 persistent, resolute. 3 (of memory) retentive. □ tenaciously adv. tenacity /tɪ'næsɪtɪ/ n. [Latin *tenax -acis* from *teneo* hold]

tenancy /'tenǝnsɪ/ n. (pl. -ies) 1 status of or possession as a tenant. 2 duration of this.

tenant /'tenǝnt/ n. 1 person who rents land or property from a landlord. 2

(often foll. by *of*) occupant of a place. [French: related to TENABLE]

tenant farmer *n.* person who farms rented land.

tenantry *n.* tenants of an estate etc.

tench *n.* (*pl.* same) European freshwater fish of the carp family. [Latin *tinca*]

Ten Commandments *n.pl.* (prec. by *the*) rules of conduct given by God to Moses (Exod. 20:1–17).

tend[1] *v.* 1 (often foll. by *to*) be apt or inclined (*tends to lose his temper; tends to fat*). 2 be moving; hold a course (*tends in our direction*). [Latin *tendo tens-* or *tent-* stretch]

tend[2] *v.* take care of, look after (an invalid, sheep, a machine etc.). [from ATTEND]

tendency /ˈtendənsɪ/ *n.* (*pl.* -ies) (often foll. by *to, towards*) leaning or inclination. [medieval Latin: related to TEND[1]]

tendentious /tenˈdenʃəs/ *adj. derog.* calculated to promote a particular cause or viewpoint; biased; controversial. □ **tendentiously** *adv.* **tendentiousness** *n.*

tender[1] *adj.* (**tenderer**, **tenderest**) 1 easily cut or chewed, not tough (*tender steak*). 2 susceptible to pain or grief; vulnerable; compassionate (*tender heart*). 3 sensitive; delicate (*tender skin; tender reputation*). 4 loving; affectionate. 5 requiring tact (*tender subject*). 6 (of age) early, immature (*of tender years*). □ **tenderly** *adv.* **tenderness** *n.* [Latin *tener*]

tender[2] *v.* 1 offer, present (one's services, resignation, money as payment, etc.). 2 (often foll. by *for*) offer a tender. —*n.* offer, esp. in writing, to execute work or supply goods at a stated price. □ **put out to tender** seek competitive tenders for (work etc.). □ **tenderer** *n.* [French: related to TEND[1]]

tender[3] *n.* 1 person who looks after people or things. 2 supply ship attending a larger one etc. 3 truck coupled to a steam locomotive to carry fuel and water. [from TEND[2]]

tenderfoot *n.* (*pl.* -s or -feet) newcomer, novice.

tender-hearted /ˈtendəˈhɑːtɪd/ *adj.* easily moved; compassionate. □ **tender-heartedness** *n.*

tenderize /ˈtendəraɪz/ *v.* (also -ise) (-zing or -sing) make (esp. meat) tender by beating, hanging, marinading, etc. □ **tenderizer** *n.*

tenderloin *n.* 1 middle part of pork loin. 2 *US* undercut of sirloin.

tender mercies *n.pl. iron.* harsh treatment.

tender spot *n.* subject on which a person is touchy.

tendon /ˈtend(ə)n/ *n.* cord of strong connective tissue attaching a muscle to a bone etc. □ **tendinitis** /-ˈnaɪtɪs/ *n.* [Latin *tendo* stretch]

tendril /ˈtendrɪl/ *n.* slender leafless shoot by which some climbing plants cling. [probably from French *tendrillon*]

tenebrous /ˈtenɪbrəs/ *adj. literary* dark, gloomy. [Latin *tenebrosus*]

tenement /ˈtenɪmənt/ *n.* 1 room or flat within a house or block of flats. 2 (also **tenement-house** or **-block**) house or block so divided. [Latin *teneo* hold]

tenet /ˈtenɪt/ *n.* doctrine, principle. [Latin, = he holds]

tenfold *adj. & adv.* 1 ten times as much or as many. 2 consisting of ten parts.

ten-gallon hat *n.* cowboy's large broad-brimmed hat.

tenner *n. colloq.* ten-pound or ten-dollar note.

tennis /ˈtenɪs/ *n.* game in which two or four players strike a ball with rackets over a net stretched across a court. [probably French *tenez* take! (as a server's call)]

tennis elbow *n.* sprain caused by overuse of forearm muscles.

tenon /ˈtenən/ *n.* wooden projection made for insertion into a cavity, esp. a mortise, in another piece. [Latin: related to TENOR]

tenor /ˈtenə(r)/ *n.* 1 **a** male singing-voice between baritone and alto or countertenor. **b** singer with this voice. 2 (often *attrib.*) instrument with a similar range. 3 (usu. foll. by *of*) general meaning. 4 (usu. foll. by *of*) prevailing course, esp. of a person's life or habits. [Latin *teneo* hold]

tenosynovitis /ˌtenəʊˌsaɪnəˈvaɪtɪs/ *n.* injury of esp. a wrist tendon resulting from repetitive strain. [Greek *tenōn* tendon, SYNOVIA]

tenpin *n.* pin used in tenpin bowling.

tenpin bowling *n.* game in which ten pins or skittles are bowled at in an alley.

tense[1] —*adj.* 1 stretched tight, strained. 2 causing tenseness (*tense moment*). —*v.* (-sing) make or become tense. □ **tense up** become tense. □ **tensely** *adv.* **tenseness** *n.* [Latin *tensus*: related to TEND[1]]

tense[2] *n.* 1 form of a verb indicating the time (also the continuance or completeness) of the action etc. 2 set of such forms as a paradigm. [Latin *tempus* time]

tensile /ˈtensaɪl/ *adj.* 1 of tension. 2 capable of being stretched. □ **tensility** /-ˈsɪlɪtɪ/ *n.* [medieval Latin: related to TENSE[1]]

tensile strength

tensile strength *n.* resistance to breaking under tension.

tension /'tenʃ(ə)n/ —*n.* **1** stretching or being stretched. **2** mental strain or excitement. **3** strained (political, social, etc.) state or relationship. **4** stress produced by forces pulling apart. **5** degree of tightness of stitches in knitting, and machine sewing. **6** voltage (*high tension*; *low tension*). —*v.* (subject to) tension. □ **tensional** *adj.* [Latin: related to TEND]

tent *n.* **1** portable canvas etc. shelter or dwelling supported by poles and cords attached to pegs driven into the ground. **2** tentlike enclosure, e.g. supplying oxygen to a patient. [Latin: related to TEND']

tentacle /'tentək(ə)l/ *n.* **1** long slender flexible appendage of an (esp. invertebrate) animal, used for feeling, grasping, or moving. **2** channel for gathering information, exercising influence, etc. □ **tentacled** *adj.* [Latin: related to TEMPT']

tentative /'tentətɪv/ *adj.* **1** experimental. **2** hesitant, not definite (*tentative suggestion*). □ **tentatively** *adv.* **tentativeness** *n.* [medieval Latin: related to TEMPT']

tenter *n.* machine for stretching cloth to dry in shape. [medieval Latin *tentorium*: related to TEND']

tenterhook *n.* hook to which cloth is fastened on a tenter. □ **on tenterhooks** in a state of suspense or agitation due to uncertainty.

tenth *adj.* & *n.* **1** next after ninth. **2** any of ten equal parts of a thing. □ **tenthly** *adv.*

tent-stitch *n.* **1** series of parallel diagonal stitches. **2** such a stitch.

tenuous /'tenjʊəs/ *adj.* **1** slight, insubstantial (*tenuous connection*). **2** (of a property) **3** thin, slender, small. **4** rarefied. □ **tenuity** /tɪ'njuːɪtɪ/ *n.* **tenuously** *adv.* [Latin *tenuis*]

tenure /'tenjə(r)/ *n.* **1** condition or form of right or title, under which (esp. real) property is held. **2** (often foll. by *of*) **a** holding or possession of an office or property. **b** period of this. **3** guaranteed permanent employment, esp. as a teacher or lecturer. □ **tenured** *adj.* [Latin *teneo*]

tepee /'tiːpiː/ *n.* (also **teepee**) N. American Indian's conical tent. [Dakota]

tepid /'tepɪd/ *adj.* **1** lukewarm. **2** unenthusiastic. □ **tepidity** /tɪ'pɪdɪtɪ/ *n.* **tepidly** *adv.* [Latin]

tequila /tɪ'kiːlə/ *n.* Mexican liquor made from an agave. [*Tequila* in Mexico]

tera- *comb. form* denoting a factor of 10^{12}. [Greek *teras* monster]

terbium /'tɜːbɪəm/ *n.* silvery metallic element of the lanthanide series. [*Ytterby* in Sweden]

tercel /'tɜːs(ə)l/ *n.* (also **tiercel** /'tɪəs(ə)l/) male hawk (esp. a peregrine or goshawk. [Latin *tertius* third]

tercentenary /,tɜːsen'tiːnərɪ/ *n.* (*pl.* **-ies**) **1** three-hundredth anniversary. **2** celebration of this. [Latin *ter*, = three times]

teredo /tə'riːdəʊ/ *n.* (*pl.* **-s**) bivalve mollusc that bores into submerged timbers of ships etc. [Latin from Greek]

tergiversate /'tɜːdʒɪvəseɪt/ *v.* (**-ting**) **1** change one's party or principles; apostatize. **2** make conflicting or evasive statements. □ **tergiversation** *n.* **tergiversator** *n.* [Latin *tergum* back, *verto* turn]

term —*n.* **1** word for a definite concept, esp. specialized (*technical term*). **2** (in *pl.*) language used (*mode of expression* (*in no uncertain terms*). **3** (in *pl.*) relation, footing (*on good terms*). **4** (in *pl.*) **a** stipulations (*accepts your terms*). **b** charge or price (*reasonable terms*). **5 a** limited, usu. specified, period (*term of five years*; *in the short term*). **b** period of weeks during which instruction is given or during which a lawcourt holds sessions. **6** *Logic* word or words that may be the subject or predicate of a proposition. **7** *Math.* **a** each of the quantities in a ratio or series. **b** part of an algebraic expression. **8** completion of a normal length of pregnancy. —*v.* call, name (*was termed a bigot*). □ **bring to terms** cause to accept conditions. **come to terms** yield, give way. **come to terms with a** reconcile oneself to (a difficulty etc.). **b** in terms of in the language peculiar to; referring to. □ **termly** *adj.* & *adv.* [Latin TERMINUS]

termagant /'tɜːməgənt/ *n.* overbearing woman; virago. [French *Tervagan* from Italian]

terminate

terminable /'tɜːmɪnəb(ə)l/ *adj.* able to be terminated.

terminal /'tɜːmɪn(ə)l/ —*adj.* **1 a** (of a condition or disease) fatal. **b** (of a patient) dying. **2** of or forming a limit or terminus (*terminal station*). —*n.* **1** terminating thing; extremity. **2** terminus for trains or long-distance buses. **3** = AIR TERMINAL. **4** point of connection for closing an electric circuit **5** apparatus for the transmission of messages to and from a computer, communications system, etc. □ **terminally** *adv.* [Latin]

terminate /'tɜːmɪneɪt/ *v.* (**-ting**) **1** bring or come to an end. **2** (foll. by *in*) (of a word) end in (a specified letter etc.),

termination /ˌtɜːmɪˈneɪʃ(ə)n/ *n.* **1** terminating or being terminated. **2** induced abortion. **3** ending or result. **4** word's final syllable or letter.

termini *pl.* of TERMINUS.

terminology /ˌtɜːmɪˈnɒlədʒɪ/ *n.* (*pl.* -ies) **1** system of specialized terms. **2** science of the use of terms. □ **terminological** /-nəˈlɒdʒɪk(ə)l/ *adj.* [German: related to TERMINUS]

terminus /ˈtɜːmɪnəs/ *n.* (*pl.* -ni /-naɪ/ or -nuses) **1** station at the end of a railway or bus route. **2** point at the end of a pipeline etc. [Latin, = end, limit, boundary]

termite /ˈtɜːmaɪt/ *n.* small tropical antlike social insect destructive to timber. [Latin *termes -mitis*]

terms of reference *n.pl.* scope of an inquiry etc.; definition of this.

tern *n.* marine gull-like bird with a long forked tail. [Scandinavian]

ternary /ˈtɜːnərɪ/ *adj.* composed of three parts. [Latin *terni*, = three each]

terrace /ˈterəs/ —*n.* **1** flat area made on a slope for cultivation. **2** level paved area next to a house. **3** row of houses built in one block of uniform style. **4** tiered standing accommodation for spectators at a sports ground. —*v.* (-**cing**) form into or provide with a terrace or terraces. [Latin *terra* earth]

terrace house *n.* (also **terraced house**) house in a terrace.

terracotta /ˌterəˈkɒtə/ *n.* **1 a** unglazed usu. brownish-red earthenware. **b** statuette of this. **2** its colour. [Italian, = baked earth]

terra firma /ˌterə ˈfɜːmə/ *n.* dry land, firm ground. [Latin]

terrain /təˈreɪn/ *n.* tract of land, esp. in geographical or military contexts. [Latin: related to TERRENE]

terra incognita /ˌterə ɪnˈkɒgnɪtə, -ˈkɒgniːtə/ *n.* unexplored region. [Italian, = unknown land]

terrapin /ˈterəpɪn/ *n.* **1** N. American edible freshwater turtle. **2** (**Terrapin**) *propr.* type of prefabricated one-storey building. [Algonquian]

terrarium /təˈreərɪəm/ *n.* (*pl.* -s or -ria) **1** place for keeping small land animals. **2** sealed transparent globe etc. containing growing plants. [Latin *terra* earth, after *aquarium*]

terrazzo /teˈrætsəʊ/ *n.* (*pl.* -s) smooth flooring-material of stone chips set in concrete. [Italian, = terrace]

terrene /teˈriːn/ *adj.* **1** of the earth; worldly. **2** earthy. **3** terrestrial. [Latin *terrenus* from *terra* earth]

terrestrial /təˈrestrɪəl/ *adj.* **1** of or on the earth; earthly. **2** of or on dry land. [Latin *terrestris*: related to TERRENE]

terrible /ˈterɪb(ə)l/ *adj.* **1** *colloq.* very great or bad (*terrible bore*). **2** *colloq.* very incompetent (*terrible at maths*). **3** causing or likely to cause terror; dreadful, formidable. [Latin *terreo* frighten]

terribly *adv.* **1** *colloq.* very, extremely (*terribly nice*). **2** in a terrible manner.

terrier /ˈterɪə/ *n.* small dog of various breeds originally used for digging out foxes etc. [French *chien terrier* dog that chases to earth]

terrific /təˈrɪfɪk/ *adj.* **1** *colloq.* huge; intense (*terrific noise*). **b** excellent (*did a terrific job*). **2** causing terror. □ **terrifically** *adv.* [Latin: related to TERRIBLE]

terrify /ˈterɪfaɪ/ *v.* (-**ies**, -**ied**) fill with terror (*terrified of dogs*). □ **terrifying** *adj.* **terrifyingly** *adv.*

terrine /teˈriːn/ *n.* **1** pâté or similar food. **2** earthenware vessel, esp. for pâté.

territorial /ˌterɪˈtɔːrɪəl/ —*adj.* **1** of territory or a district (*territorial possessions*; *territorial right*). **2** tending to defend one's territory. —*n.* (**Territorial**) member of the Territorial Army. □ **territorially** *adv.* [Latin: related to TERRITORY]

Territorial Army *n.* local volunteer reserve force.

territorial waters *n.pl.* area of sea under the jurisdiction of a State, esp. within a stated distance of the shore.

territory /ˈterɪtərɪ/ *n.* (*pl.* -ies) **1** extent of the land under the jurisdiction of a ruler, State, etc. **2** (**Territory**) organized division of a country, esp. one not yet admitted to the full rights of a State. **3** sphere of action etc.; province. **4** commercial traveller's sales area. **5** animal's or human's defended space or area. **6** area defended by a team or player in a game. [Latin *terra* land]

terror /ˈterə/ *n.* **1** extreme fear. **2 a** terrifying person or thing. **b** *colloq.* formidable or troublesome person or thing, esp. a child. **3** organized intimidation; terrorism. [Latin *terreo* frighten]

terrorist *n.* (often *attrib.*) person using esp. organized violence against a government etc. □ **terrorism** *n.* [French: related to TERROR]

terrorize /ˈterəraɪz/ *v.* (also -**ise**) (-**zing** or -**sing**) **1** fill with terror. **2** use terrorism against. □ **terrorization** /-ˈzeɪʃ(ə)n/ *n.*

terror-stricken *adj.* (also **terror-struck**) affected with terror.

terry /ˈterɪ/ *n.* (often *attrib.*) looped pile fabric esp. for towels and nappies. [origin unknown]

terse *adj.* (**terser**, **tersest**) **1** brief, concise. **2** curt, abrupt. □ **tersely** *adv.* **terseness** *n.* [Latin *tergo ters-* wipe]

tertiary /ˈtɜːʃərɪ/ —*adj.* **1** third in order or rank etc. **2** (**Tertiary**) of the first period in the Cenozoic era. —*n.* (**Ter-tiary**) Tertiary period. [Latin *tertius* third]

tervalent /tɜːˈveɪlənt, ˈtɜːveɪlənt/ *adj.* having a valency of three. [from TERCEN-TENARY, VALENCE[1]]

Terylene /ˈterɪliːn/ *n. propr.* synthetic textile fibre of polyester. [from *tereph-thalic* acid, ETHYLENE]

TESL /ˈtes(ə)l/ *abbr.* teaching of English as a second language.

tesla /ˈteslə/ *n.* SI unit of magnetic induc-tion. [*Tesla*, name of a scientist]

TESSA /ˈtesə/ *abbr.* tax exempt special savings account.

tessellated /ˈtesə,leɪtɪd/ *adj.* **1** of or resembling a mosaic. **2** regularly chequered. [Latin *tessella* diminutive of TESSERA]

tessellation /,tesəˈleɪʃ(ə)n/ *n.* close arrangement of polygons, esp. in a repeated pattern.

tessera /ˈtesərə/ *n.* (*pl.* **tesserae** /-riː/) small square block used in mosaic. [Latin from Greek]

tessitura /,tesɪˈtʊərə/ *n.* range of a sing-ing voice or vocal part. [Italian, = TEX-TURE]

test[1] —*n.* **1** critical examination or trial of a person's or thing's qualities. **2** means, procedure, or standard for so doing. **3** minor examination, esp. in school (*spelling test*). **4** colloq. test match. —*v.* **1** put to the test. **2** try or tax severely. **3** examine by means of a re-agent. □ **put to the test** cause to undergo a test. **test out** put to a prac-tical test. □ **testable** *adj.* [Latin *tes-tu(m)* = *testa*: related to TEST[2]]

test[2] *n.* shell of some invertebrates. [Latin *testa* pot, tile, shell]

testa /ˈtestə/ *n.* (*pl.* **testae** /-tiː/) seed's protective outer covering. [Latin: related to TEST[2]]

testaceous /teˈsteɪʃəs/ *adj.* having a hard continuous shell.

testament /ˈtestəmənt/ *n.* **1** will (esp. in *last will and testament*). **2** (usu. foll. by *to*) evidence, proof (*is testament to his loyalty*). **3** *Bibl.* **a** covenant, dispensa-tion. **b** (**Testament**) division of the Bible (see OLD TESTAMENT, NEW TESTAMENT). [Latin *testamentum* will: related to TESTATE]

testamentary /,testəˈmentərɪ/ *adj.* of, by, or in a will.

testate /ˈtesteɪt/ —*adj.* having left a valid will at death. —*n.* testate person. □ **testacy** *n.* (*pl.* **-ies**). [Latin *testor* testify, from *testis* witness]

testator /teˈsteɪtə(r)/ *n.* (*fem.* **testatrix** /teˈsteɪtrɪks/) (esp. deceased) person who has made a will. [Latin: related to TESTATE]

test card *n.* still television picture out-side normal programme hours used for adjusting brightness, definition, etc.

test case *n. Law* case setting a preced-ent for other similar cases.

test drive *n.* drive taken to judge the performance of a vehicle. □ **test-drive** *v.*

tester[1] *n.* person or thing that tests. **2** sample of a cosmetic for trial in a shop.

tester[2] *n.* canopy, esp. over a four-poster bed. [medieval Latin *testrum* from Latin *testa* tile]

testes *pl.* of TESTIS.

test flight *n.* aircraft flight for evalu-ation purposes. □ **test-fly** *v.*

testicle /ˈtestɪk(ə)l/ *n.* male organ that produces spermatozoa etc., esp. one of a pair in the scrotum in man and most mammals. [Latin, diminutive of *testis* witness]

testify /ˈtestɪfaɪ/ *v.* (**-ies, -ied**) **1** (often foll. by *to*) (of a person or thing) bear witness; be evidence of (*testified to the facts*). **2** give evidence. **3** affirm or de-clare. [Latin *test.ficor* from *testis* wit-ness]

testimonial /,testɪˈməʊnɪəl/ *n.* **1** certi-ficate of character, conduct, or quali-fications. **2** gift presented to a person (esp. in public) as a mark of esteem etc. [French: related to TESTIMONY]

testimony /ˈtestɪmənɪ/ *n.* (*pl.* **-ies**) **1** witness's statement under oath etc. **2** declaration or statement of fact. **3** evid-ence, demonstration (*produce testi-mony*). [Latin *testimonium* from *testis*]

testis /ˈtestɪs/ *n.* (*pl.* **testes** /-tiːz/) *Anat. & Zool.* testicle. [Latin, = witness (cf. TESTICLE)]

test match *n.* international cricket or Rugby match, usu. in a series.

test paper *n.* **1** minor examination paper. **2** paper impregnated with a sub-stance changing colour under known conditions.

test pilot *n.* pilot who test-flies aircraft.

test-tube *n.* thin glass tube closed at one end, used for chemical tests etc.

test-tube baby *n. colloq.* baby con-ceived by *in vitro* fertilization.

testy *adj.* (**-ier, -ies**) irritable, touchy. □ **testily** *adv.* **testiness** *n.* [French *teste* head: related to TEST[2]]

tetanus /ˈtetənəs/ *n.* bacterial disease causing painful spasm of the voluntary muscles. [Greek *tetanos* stretch]

tetchy /ˈtetʃɪ/ *adj.* (**-ier, -iest**) peevish, irritable. □ **tetchily** *adv.* **tetchiness** *n.* [*teche* blemish, fault]

testosterone /teˈstɒstəˌrəʊn/ *n.* male sex hormone formed in the testicles. [from TESTIS, STEROL]

tête-à-tête /ˌtetaːˈtet/ —n. (often attrib.) private conversation between two persons. —adv. privately without a third person (dined tête-à-tête). [French, literally 'head-to-head']

tether /ˈteðə(r)/ —n. rope etc. confining a grazing animal. —v. tie with a tether. □ **at the end of one's tether** at the limit of one's patience, resources, etc. [Old Norse]

tetra- comb. form four. [Greek tettares four]

tetrad /ˈtetrad/ n. group of four. [Greek: related to TETRA-]

tetragon /ˈtetrəˌgon/ n. plane figure with four angles and sides. □ **tetragonal** /tɪˈtræɡən(ə)l/ adj. [Greek gōnos -angled]

tetrahedron /ˌtetrəˈhiːdrən/ n. (pl. **-dra** or **-s**) four-sided solid; triangular pyramid. □ **tetrahedral** adj. [Greek hedra base]

tetralogy /tɪˈtrælədʒɪ/ n. (pl. **-ies**) group of four related novels, plays, operas, etc.

tetrameter /tɪˈtræmɪtə(r)/ n. Prosody verse of four measures.

Teuton /ˈtjuːt(ə)n/ n. member of a Teutonic nation, esp. a German. [Latin Teutones, ancient tribe of N. Europe]

Teutonic /tjuːˈtɒnɪk/ adj. 1 of the Germanic peoples or languages. 2 German. [Latin: related to TEUTON]

text n. 1 main body of a book as distinct from notes etc. 2 original book or document, esp. as distinct from a paraphrase etc. 3 passage from Scripture, esp. as the subject of a sermon. 4 subject, theme. 5 (in pl.) books prescribed for study. 6 data in textual form, esp. as stored, processed, or displayed in a word processor etc. [Latin texo text- weave]

textbook —n. book for use in studying, esp. a standard account of a subject. —attrib. adj. 1 exemplary, accurate. 2 instructively typical.

text editor n. Computing system or program allowing the user to enter and edit text.

textile /ˈtekstaɪl/ —n. 1 (often in pl.) fabric, cloth, or fibrous material, esp. woven. 2 fibre, yarn. —adj. 1 of weaving or cloth (textile industry). 2 woven (textile fabrics). [Latin: related to TEXT]

text processing n. Computing manipulation of text, esp. transforming it from one format to another.

textual /ˈtekstʃʊəl/ adj. of, in, or concerning a text. □ **textually** adv.

texture /ˈtekstʃə(r)/ —n. 1 feel or appearance of a surface or substance. 2 arrangement of threads etc. in textile fabric. —v. (**-ring**) (usu. as **textured** adj.) 1 provide with a texture. 2 (of

vegetable protein) provide with a texture resembling meat. □ **textural** adj. [Latin: related to TEXT]

Th symb. thorium.

-th suffix (also **-eth**) forming ordinal and fractional numbers from four onwards. [Old English]

Thai /taɪ/ —n. (pl. same or **-s**) 1 a native or national of Thailand. b person of Thai descent. 2 language of Thailand. —adj. of Thailand. [Thai, = free]

thalidomide /θəˈlɪdəˌmaɪd/ n. sedative drug found in 1961 to cause foetal malformation when taken early in pregnancy. [from phthalimidoglutarimide]

thallium /ˈθælɪəm/ n. rare soft white metallic element. [Greek thallos green shoot]

than /ðæn, ðən/ conj. introducing a comparison (plays better than he did before; more bread than meat in these sausages; cost more than £100; you are older than I). [Old English, originally = THEN]

■ **Usage** With reference to the last example, it is also legitimate to say you are older than you, with than treated as a preposition, esp. in less formal contexts.

thane n. hist. 1 man who held land from an English king or other superior by military service. 2 man who held land from a Scottish king and ranked with an earl's son; chief of a clan. [Old English]

thank —v. 1 express gratitude to (thanked him for the present). 2 hold responsible (you can thank yourself for that). —n. (in pl.) 1 gratitude. 2 expression of gratitude. 3 (as a formula) thank you (thanks for your help). □ **thank goodness** (or **God** or **heavens** etc.) colloq. expression of relief etc. **thanks to** as the result of (thanks to my foresight; thanks to your obstinacy). **thank you** polite formula expressing gratitude. [Old English]

thankful adj. 1 grateful, pleased. 2 expressive of thanks.

thankfully adv. 1 in a thankful manner. 2 let us be thankful (that) (thankfully, it didn't rain).

■ **Usage** The use of thankfully in sense 2 is common, but is considered incorrect by some people.

thankless adj. 1 not expressing or feeling gratitude. 2 (of a task etc.) giving no pleasure or profit; unappreciated.

thanksgiving n. 1 expression of gratitude, esp. to God. 2 (**Thanksgiving** or **Thanksgiving Day**) fourth Thursday in November (a national holiday in the US).

that /ðæt/ —demons. pron. (pl. those /ðəʊz/) 1 person or thing indicated, named, or understood (I heard that; who is that in the garden?). 2 contrasted with this (this is much better than that). 3 (esp. in relative constructions) the one, the person, etc. (a table like that described above). 4 /ðət/ (pl. that) used instead of which or whom to introduce a defining clause (the book that you sent me; there is nothing here that matters). —demons. adj. (pl. those /ðəʊz/) designating the person or thing indicated, named, understood, etc. (cf. sense 1 of pron.). —adv. 1 to such a degree; so (have done that much). 2 colloq. very (not that good). —conj. /ðət/ introducing a subordinate clause indicating: 1 statement or hypothesis (they say that he is better). 2 purpose (we eat that we may live). 3 result (am so sleepy that I cannot work). □ all that very (not all that good). that is (or that is to say) a formula introducing or following an explanation of a preceding word or words. that's that colloq. there is nothing more to be said or done: they say he is ill. [Old English]

■ **Usage** In sense 4 of the pronoun, that usually specifies or identifies something referred to, whereas who or which need not: compare the book that you sent me is lost with the book, which I gave you, is lost. That is often omitted in senses 1 and 3 of the conjunction: they say he is ill.

thatch —n. 1 roof-covering of straw, reeds, etc. 2 colloq. hair of the head. —v. (also absol.) cover with thatch. □ **thatcher** n. [Old English]

thaw —v. 1 (often foll. by out) pass from a frozen into a liquid or unfrozen state. 2 (usu. prec. by it as subject) (of the weather) become warm enough to melt ice etc. 3 become warm enough to lose numbness etc. 4 become or make genial. —n. 1 thawing. 2 warmth of weather that thaws. [Old English]

the /before a vowel ðɪ; before a consonant ðə, when stressed ðiː/ —adj. (called the definite article) 1 denoting person(s) or -thing(s) already mentioned, under discussion, implied, or familiar (gave the man a wave). 2 describing as unique (the Thames). 3 a (foll. by defining adj.) which is, who are, etc. (Edward the Seventh). b (foll. by adj. used absol.) denoting a class described (from the sublime to the ridiculous). 4 best known or best entitled to the name (with the stressed: do you mean the Kipling?). 5 indicating a following defining clause or phrase (the book that you borrowed).

6 a indicating that: a singular noun represents a species etc. (the cat is a mammal). b used with a noun which figuratively represents an occupation etc. (went on the stage). c (foll. by the name of a unit) a, per (5p in the pound). —adv. (preceding comparatives in expressions of proportional variation) in or by that (or such a) degree; on that account (the more I see him the more I like him; the more the merrier; the more he has the more he wants). [Old English]

theatre /ˈθɪətə(r)/ n. (US **theater**) 1 building or outdoor area for dramatic performances 2 writing and production of plays. 3 room or hall for lectures etc. with seats in tiers 4 operating theatre. 5 a scene or field of action (the theatre of war). b (attrib.) designating weapons intermediate between tactical and strategic. [Greek theatron]

theatrical /θɪˈætrɪk(ə)l/ —adj. 1 of or for the theatre or acting. 2 (of a manner or performance etc.) calculated for effect; showy. —n. (in pl.) dramatic performances (amateur theatricals). □ **theatricality** /-ˈkælɪtɪ/ n. **theatrically** adv.

thee /ðiː/ pron. objective case of THOU. [Old English]

theft n. act of stealing. [Old English: related to THIEF]

their /ðeə(r)/ poss. pron. (attrib.) of or belonging to them. [Old Norse]

theirs /ðeəz/ poss. pron. the one or ones of or belonging to them (it is theirs; they are over here). □ of theirs of or belonging to them (a friend of theirs).

theism /ˈθiːɪz(ə)m/ n. belief in gods or a god, esp. a god supernaturally revealed to man. □ **theist** n. **theistic** /-ˈɪstɪk/ adj. [Greek theos god]

them /ðem/ —pron. 1 objective case of THEY. 2 colloq. they (it's them again). —demons. adj. [Old Norse]

theme n. 1 subject or topic of a talk, book, etc. 2 Mus. prominent melody in a composition. 3 US school exercise on a given subject. □ **thematic** /θɪˈmætɪk/ adj. **thematically** /θɪˈmætɪkəlɪ/ adv. [Greek thema -mat-]

theme park n. amusement park organized round a unifying idea.

theme song n. (also **theme tune**) 1 recurrent melody in a musical play or film. 2 signature tune.

themselves /ðəmˈselvz/ pron. 1 emphat. form of THEY or THEM. 2 refl. form of THEM. □ **be themselves** act in their normal, unconstrained manner. **by themselves** see by oneself.

then /ðen/ —adv. 1 at that time. 2 a next; after that. b and also. 3 a in that case (then you should have said so). b implying or imputing grudging or impatient concession

thence ... *(all right then, if you must).* **c** used parenthetically to resume a narrative etc. *(the policeman, then, knocked on the door).* —*attrib. adj.* such at the time in question *(the then King).* —*n.* that time *(until then).* □ **then and there** immediately and on the spot. [Old English]

thence /ðens/ *adv.* (also **from thence**) *archaic* or *literary* 1 from that place. 2 for that reason. [Old English]

thenceforth /ðensˈfɔːθ/ *adv.* (also **thenceforward** /-ˈfɔːwəd/) *archaic* or *literary* from that time onward.

theo- *comb. form* God or god(s). [Greek *theos* god]

theocracy /θɪˈɒkrəsɪ/ *n.* (*pl.* -ies) form of government by God or a god directly, or through a priestly order etc. □ **theocratic** /θɪəˈkrætɪk/ *adj.*

theodolite /θɪˈɒdəˌlaɪt/ *n.* surveying instrument for measuring horizontal and vertical angles with a rotating telescope. [origin unknown]

theologian /θɪəˈləʊdʒɪən, -dʒ(ə)n/ *n.* expert in theology. [French: related to THEOLOGY]

theology /θɪˈɒlədʒɪ/ *n.* (*pl.* -ies) the study or a system of theistic (esp. Christian) religion. □ **theological** /θɪəˈlɒdʒɪk(ə)l/ *adj.* **theologically** /θɪəˈlɒdʒɪkəlɪ/ *adv.* [Greek: related to THEO-]

theorem /ˈθɪərəm/ *n.* esp. *Math.* 1 general proposition that is not self-evident but is proved by reasoning. 2 rule in algebra etc., esp. one expressed by symbols or formulae. [Greek *theōreō* look at]

theoretical /θɪəˈretɪk(ə)l/ *adj.* 1 concerned with knowledge but not with its practical application. 2 based on theory rather than experience. □ **theoretically** *adv.*

theoretician /ˌθɪərɪˈtɪʃ(ə)n/ *n.* person concerned with the theoretical aspects of a subject.

theorist /ˈθɪərɪst/ *n.* holder or inventor of a theory.

theorize /ˈθɪəraɪz/ *v.* (also **-ise**) (-zing or -sing) evolve or indulge in theories.

theory /ˈθɪərɪ/ *n.* (*pl.* -ies) 1 supposition or system of ideas explaining something, esp. one based on general principles independent of the particular things to be explained *(atomic theory; theory of evolution).* 2 speculative (esp. fanciful) view *(one of my pet theories).* 3 abstract knowledge or speculative thought *(all very well in theory).* 4 exposition of the principles of a science etc. *(the theory of music).* 5 collection of propositions to illustrate the principles of a mathematical subject *(probability theory).* [Greek: related to THEOREM]

theosophy /θɪˈɒsəfɪ/ *n.* (*pl.* -ies) any of various philosophies professing to achieve knowledge of God by spiritual ecstasy, direct intuition, or special individual relations, esp. a modern movement following Hindu and Buddhist teachings and seeking universal brotherhood. □ **theosophical** /θɪəˈsɒfɪk(ə)l/ *adj.* **theosophist** *n.* [Greek *theosophos* wise concerning God]

therapeutic /ˌθerəˈpjuːtɪk/ *adj.* 1 of, for, or contributing to the cure of disease. 2 soothing, conducive to well-being. □ **therapeutically** *adv.* [Greek *therapeuō* wait on, cure]

therapeutics *n.pl.* (usu. treated as *sing.*) branch of medicine concerned with cures and remedies.

therapy /ˈθerəpɪ/ *n.* (*pl.* -ies) non-surgical treatment of disease or disability. □ **therapist** *n.* [Greek *therapeia* healing]

there /ðeə(r)/ —*adv.* 1 in, at, or to that place or position *(lived there for a year; goes there daily).* 2 at that point (in speech, performance, writing, etc.). 3 in that respect *(I agree with you there).* 4 used for emphasis in calling attention *(you there!).* 5 used to indicate the fact or existence of something *(there is a house on the corner).* —*n.* that place *(lives near there).* —*int.* 1 expressing confirmation, triumph, etc. *(there! what did I tell you?).* 2 used to soothe a child etc. *(there, there, never mind).* □ **then and there** = **then and there**. [Old English]

thereabouts *adv.* (also **thereabout**) 1 near that place. 2 near that number, quantity, etc.

thereafter *adv. formal* after that.

thereby *adv.* by that means, as a result of that. □ **thereby hangs a tale** much could be said about that.

therefore /ˈðeəfɔː(r)/ *adv.* for that reason; accordingly; consequently.

therein *adv. formal* 1 in that place. 2 in that respect.

thereof *adv. formal* of that or of it.

thereto *adv. formal* 1 to that or it. 2 in addition.

thereupon *adv.* 1 in consequence of that. 2 immediately after that.

therm *n.* unit of heat, esp. as the statutory unit of gas supplied, equivalent to 100,000 British thermal units (1.055 x 10^8 joules). [Greek *thermē* heat]

thermal /ˈθɜːm(ə)l/ —*adj.* 1 of, for, or producing heat. 2 promoting the retention of heat *(thermal underwear).* —*n.* rising current of warm air (used by gliders etc. to gain height). □ **thermally** *adv.* [French: related to THERM]

thermal unit *n.* unit for measuring heat.

thermionic /ˌθɜːmɪˈɒnɪk/ *adj.* of electrons emitted from a very hot substance. [from THERMO-]

thermionic valve *n.* device giving a flow of thermionic electrons in one direction, used esp. in the rectification of a current and in radio reception.

thermo- *comb. form* heat. [Greek]

thermocouple /ˈθɜːməʊˌkʌp(ə)l/ *n.* device for measuring temperatures by means of a pair of different metals in contact at a point and generating a thermoelectric voltage.

thermodynamics /ˌθɜːməʊdaɪˈnæmɪks/ *n.pl.* (usu. treated as *sing.*) the science of the relations between heat and other forms of energy. □ **thermodynamic** *adj.*

thermoelectric /ˌθɜːməʊɪˈlektrɪk/ *adj.* producing electricity by a difference of temperatures.

thermometer /θəˈmɒmɪtə(r)/ *n.* instrument for measuring temperature, esp. a graduated glass tube containing mercury or alcohol. [French: related to THERMO-, -METER]

thermonuclear /ˌθɜːməʊˈnjuːklɪə(r)/ *adj.* 1 relating to nuclear reactions that occur only at very high temperatures. 2 (of weapons) using thermonuclear reactions.

thermoplastic /ˌθɜːməʊˈplæstɪk/ *adj.* that becomes plastic on heating and hardens on cooling. —*n.* thermoplastic substance.

Thermos /ˈθɜːmɒs/ *n.* (in full **Thermos flask**) *propr.* vacuum flask. [Greek: related to THERMO-]

thermosetting /ˈθɜːməʊˌsetɪŋ/ *adj.* (of plastics) setting permanently when heated.

thermosphere /ˈθɜːməˌsfɪə(r)/ *n.* region of the atmosphere beyond the mesosphere.

thermostat /ˈθɜːməˌstæt/ *n.* device that automatically regulates or responds to temperature. □ **thermostatic** /ˌθɜːməˈstætɪk/ *adj.* **thermostatically** /ˌθɜːməˈstætɪkəlɪ/ *adv.*

thesaurus /θɪˈsɔːrəs/ *n.* (*pl.* **-ri** /-raɪ/ or **-ruses**) book that lists words in groups of synonyms and related concepts. [Greek: related to TREASURE]

these *pl.* of THIS.

thesis /ˈθiːsɪs/ *n.* (*pl.* **theses** /-siːz/) 1 proposition to be maintained or proved. 2 dissertation, esp. by a candidate for a higher degree. [Greek, = putting]

Thespian /ˈθespɪən/ *adj.* of drama. —*n.* actor or actress. [Greek *Thespis*, name of a Greek tragedian]

theta /ˈθiːtə/ *n.* eighth letter of the Greek alphabet (Θ, θ). [Greek]

they /ðeɪ/ *pron.* (*obj.* **them**; *poss.* **their, theirs**) 1 *pl.* of HE, SHE, IT. 2 people in general (*so they say*). 3 those in authority (*they have raised taxes*). [Old Norse]

they'd /ðeɪd/ *contr.* 1 they had. 2 they would.

they'll /ðeɪl/ *contr.* 1 they will. 2 they shall.

they're /ðeə(r)/ *contr.* they are.

they've /ðeɪv/ *contr.* they have.

thiamine /ˈθaɪəmɪn, -miːn/ *n.* (also **thiamin**) B vitamin found in unrefined cereals, beans, and liver, a deficiency of which causes beriberi. [Greek *theion* sulphur, *amin* from VITAMIN]

thick —*adj.* 1 of great or specified extent between opposite surfaces. 2 (of a line etc.) broad; not fine. 3 arranged closely; crowded together; dense. 4 (usu. foll. by *with*) densely covered or filled (*air thick with smoke*). 5 a firm in consistency; containing much solid matter. b made of thick material (*a thick coat*). 6 a muddy, cloudy; impenetrable by sight. b (of one's head) suffering from a hangover, headache, etc. 7 *colloq.* stupid. 8 a (of a voice) indistinct. b (of an accent) very marked. 9 *colloq.* intimate, very friendly. —*n.* thick part of anything. —*adv.* thickly (*snow was falling thick*). □ **a bit thick** *colloq.* unreasonable or intolerable. **in the thick of** at the busiest part of; through thick and thin under all conditions; in spite of all difficulties. □ **thickish** *adj.* **thickly** *adv.* [Old English]

thicken *v.* 1 make or become thick or thicker. 2 become more complicated (*plot thickens*). □ **thickener** *n.* **thickening** *n.*

thicket /ˈθɪkɪt/ *n.* tangle of shrubs or trees. [Old English: related to THICK]

thickhead *n. colloq.* stupid person. □ **thickheaded** *adj.*

thickness *n.* 1 being thick. 2 extent of this. 3 layer of material (*use three thicknesses*).

thickset *adj.* 1 heavily or solidly built. 2 set or growing close together.

thick-skinned *adj.* not sensitive to criticism.

thief *n.* (*pl.* **thieves** /θiːvz/) person who steals, esp. secretly. [Old English]

thieve *v.* (*-ving*) 1 be a thief. 2 steal (a thing). [Old English: related to THIEF]

thievery *n.* stealing.

thievish *adj.* given to stealing.

thigh /θaɪ/ *n.* part of the leg between the hip and the knee. [Old English]

thigh-bone *n.* = FEMUR.

thimble n. metal or plastic cap worn to protect the finger and push the needle in sewing. [Old English: related to THUMB]

thimbleful n. (pl. -s) small quantity, esp. of drink.

thin —adj. (**thinner**, **thinnest**) 1 having opposite surfaces close together; of small thickness or diameter. 2 (of a line) narrow or fine. 3 made of thin material (thin dress). 4 lean; not plump. 5 not dense or copious (thin hair). 6 of slight consistency. 7 weak; lacking an important ingredient (thin blood; a thin voice). 8 (of an excuse etc.) flimsy or transparent. —adv. thinly (cut the bread very thin). —v. (-nn-) 1 (often foll. by down) make or become thin or thinner. 2 (often foll. by out) make or become less dense or crowded or numerous. □ **have a thin time** colloq. have a wretched or uncomfortable time. **thin on top** balding. □ **thinly** adv. **thinness** n. **thinnish** adj. [Old English]

thine /ðaɪn/ poss. pron. archaic 1 (predic. or absol.) of or belonging to thee. 2 (attrib. before a vowel) = THY. [Old English]

thin end of the wedge see WEDGE.

thing n. 1 entity, idea, action, etc., that exists or may be thought about or perceived. 2 inanimate material object (take that thing away). 3 unspecified item (a few things to buy). 4 act, idea, or utterance (silly thing to do). 5 event (unfortunate thing to happen). 6 quality (patience is a useful thing). 7 person regarded with pity, contempt, or affection (poor thing!). 8 specimen or type (latest thing in hats). 9 colloq. one's special interest (not my thing). 10 colloq. something remarkable (there's a thing!). 11 (prec. by the) colloq. a what is proper or fashionable. b what is needed (just the thing). c what is to be considered (the thing is, shall we go or not?). d what is important. 12 (in pl.) personal belongings or clothing (where are my things?). 13 (in pl.) equipment (painting things). 14 (in pl.) affairs in general (not in the nature of things). 15 (in pl.) circumstances, conditions (things look good). 16 (in pl. with a following adjective) all that is so describable (poor things). □ **do one's own thing** colloq. pursue one's own interests or inclinations. **have a thing about** colloq. be obsessed or prejudiced about. **make a thing of** colloq. 1 regard as essential. 2 cause a fuss about. [Old English]

thingummy /ˈθɪŋəmɪ/ n. (pl. -ies) (also **thingumabob** /-ma,bɒb/, **thingumajig** /-ma,dʒɪg/) colloq. person or thing whose name one has forgotten or does not know.

think —v. (past and past part. **thought** /θɔːt/) 1 be of the opinion (think that they will come). 2 judge or consider (is thought to be a fraud). 3 exercise the mind (let me think for a moment). 4 (foll. by of or about) a consider; be or become aware of. b form or entertain the idea of; imagine. 5 have a half-formed intention (I think I'll stay). 6 form a conception of. 7 recognize the presence or existence of (thought no harm in it). —n. colloq. act of thinking (have a think). □ **think again** revise one's plans or opinions. **think aloud** utter one's thoughts as soon as they occur. **think better of** change one's mind about (an intention) after reconsideration. **think fit** see FIT[1]. **think little (or nothing) of** have a low opinion of. **think much (or a lot or highly) of** have a high opinion of. **think out** 1 consider carefully. 2 produce (an idea etc.) by thinking. **think over** reflect upon in order to reach a decision. **think through** reflect fully upon (a problem etc.). **think twice** use careful consideration, avoid hasty action, etc. **think up** colloq. devise. [Old English]

thinker n. 1 person who thinks, esp. in a specified way (an original thinker). 2 person with a skilled or powerful mind.

thinking —attrib. adj. intelligent, rational. —n. opinion or judgement.

think-tank n. colloq. body of experts providing advice and ideas on national or commercial problems.

thinner n. solvent for diluting paint etc.

thin-skinned adj. sensitive to criticism.

thiosulphate /ˌθaɪəʊˈsʌlfeɪt/ n. sulphate in which one oxygen atom is replaced by sulphur. [Greek theion sulphur]

third adj. & n. 1 next after second. 2 each of three equal parts of a thing. □ **thirdly** adv. [Old English: related to THREE]

third degree n. long and severe questioning, esp. by police to obtain information or a confession. —adj. (**third-degree**) denoting burns of the most severe kind, affecting lower layers of tissue.

third man n. fielder positioned near the boundary behind the slips.

third party —n. 1 another party besides the two principals. 2 bystander etc. —adj. (**third-party**) (of insurance) covering damage or injury suffered by a person other than the insured.

third person n. 1 = THIRD PARTY. 2 Gram. see PERSON.

third-rate adj. inferior; very poor.

third reading n. third presentation of a bill to a legislative assembly.

Third Reich n. Nazi regime, 1933-45.

Third World n. (usu. prec. by *the*) developing countries of Asia, Africa, and Latin America.

thirst —n. **1** need to drink; discomfort caused by this. **2** desire, craving. —v. (often foll. by *for* or *after*) feel thirst. **2** have a strong desire. [Old English]

thirsty *adj.* (**-ier, -iest**) **1** feeling thirst. **2** (of land, a season, etc.) dry or parched. **3** (often foll. by *for* or *after*) eager. **4** *colloq.* causing thirst (*thirsty work*). □ **thirstily** *adv.* **thirstiness** n. [Old English: related to THIRST]

thirteen /θɜː'tiːn/ *adj.* & n. **1** one more than twelve. **2** symbol for this (13, xiii, XIII). **3** size etc. denoted by thirteen. □ **thirteenth** *adj.* & n. [Old English: related to THREE]

thirty /'θɜːti/ *adj.* & n. (*pl.* **-ies**) **1** three times ten. **2** symbol for this (30, xxx, XXX). **3** (in *pl.*) numbers from 30 to 39, esp. the years of a century or of a person's life. □ **thirtieth** *adj.* & n. [Old English: related to THREE]

Thirty-nine Articles n.pl. points of doctrine assented to by those taking orders in the Church of England.

this /ðɪs/ —*demons. pron.* (*pl.* **these** /ðiːz/) **1** person or thing close at hand or indicated or already named or understood (*can you see this?, this is my cousin*). **2** (contrasted with *that*) the person or thing nearer to hand or more immediately in mind. —*demons. adj.* (*pl.* **these** /ðiːz/) **1** designating the person or thing close at hand etc. (cf. senses 1, 2 of *pron.*). **2** (of time) the present or current (*am busy all this week*). **3** *colloq.* (in narrative) designating a person or thing previously unmentioned (*then up came this policeman*). —*adv.* to the degree or extent indicated (*knew him when he was this high*). □ **this and that** *colloq.* various unspecified things. [Old English]

thistle /'θɪs(ə)l/ n. **1** prickly plant, usu. with globular heads of purple flowers. **2** this as the Scottish national emblem. [Old English]

thistledown n. light down containing thistle-seeds and blown about in the wind.

thistly *adj.* overgrown with thistles.

thither /'ðɪðə(r)/ *adv.* *archaic* or *formal* to or towards that place. [Old English]

tho' (also **tho**) var. of THOUGH.

thole n. (in full **thole-pin**) **1** pin in the gunwale of a boat as the fulcrum for an oar. **2** each of two such pins forming a rowlock. [Old English]

---

thong n. narrow strip of hide or leather. [Old English]

thorax /'θɔːræks/ n. (*pl.* **-races** /-rəˌsiːz/ or **-raxes**) *Anat.* & *Zool.* part of the trunk between the neck and the abdomen. □ **thoracic** /θɔː'ræsɪk/ *adj.* [Latin from Greek]

thorium /'θɔːrɪəm/ n. *Chem.* radioactive metallic element. [*Thor*, name of Scandinavian god of thunder]

thorn n. **1** sharp-pointed projection on a plant. **2** thorn-bearing shrub or tree. □ **thorn in one's flesh** (or **side**) constant nuisance. □ **thornless** *adj.* [Old English]

thorny *adj.* (**-ier, -iest**) **1** having many thorns. **2** problematic, causing disagreement. □ **thornily** *adv.* **thorniness** n. [Old English: related to THORN]

thorough /'θʌrə/ *adj.* **1** complete and unqualified; not superficial. **2** acting or done with great care and completeness. **3** absolute (*thorough nuisance*). □ **thoroughly** *adv.* **thoroughness** n. [related to THROUGH]

thoroughbred —*adj.* **1** of pure breed. **2** high-spirited. —n. thoroughbred animal, esp. a horse.

thoroughfare n. road or path open at both ends, esp. for traffic.

thoroughgoing *attrib. adj.* thorough; complete.

those *pl.* of THAT.

thou /ðaʊ/ n. (*pl.* same or **-s**) *colloq.* **1** thousand. **2** one thousandth. [abbreviation]

thou /ðaʊ/ *pron.* (*obj.* **thee** /ðiː/; *poss.* **thy** or **thine** /ðaɪn/; *pl.* **ye** or **you**) *archaic* second person singular pronoun. [Old English]

■ **Usage** *Thou* has now been replaced by *you* except in some formal, liturgical, dialect, and poetic uses.

though /ðəʊ/ (also **tho'**) —*conj.* **1** despite the fact that; in spite of being (*though it was early you left, though he annoyed, I agreed*). **2** (introducing a possibility) even if (*ask him though t.e may refuse*). **3** and yet; nevertheless. —*adv. colloq.* however; all the same. [Old Norse]

thought /θɔːt/ n. **1** process or power of thinking; faculty of reason. **2** way of thinking associated with a particular time, group, etc. **3** sober reflection or consideration. **4** idea or piece of reasoning produced by thinking. **5** (foll. by *of* + verbal noun or *to* + infin.) partly formed intention (*had no thought to go*). **6** (usu. in *pl.*) what one is thinking. **7** (prec. by *a*) somewhat (*a thought arrogant*). □ **in thought** meditating. [Old English: related to THINK]

thought² *past* and *past part.* of THINK.

thoughtful *adj.* **1** engaged in or given to meditation. **2** (of a book, writer, etc.) giving signs of serious thought. **3** (often foll. by *of*) (of a person or conduct) considerate. □ **thoughtfully** *adv.* **thoughtfulness** *n.*

thoughtless *adj.* **1** careless of consequences or of others' feelings. **2** due to lack of thought. □ **thoughtlessly** *adv.* **thoughtlessness** *n.*

thought-reader *n.* person supposedly able to perceive another's thoughts.

thousand /ˈθauz(ə)nd/ *adj. & n.* (*pl.* **thousands** or (in sense 1) **thousand**) (in *sing.* prec. by *a* or *one*) **1** ten hundred. **2** symbol for this (1,000, m, M). **3** (in *sing.* or *pl.*) *colloq.* large number. □ **thousandfold** *adj. & adv.* **thousandth** *adj. & n.* [Old English]

thrall /θrɔːl/ *n. literary* **1** (often foll. by *of, to*) slave (of a person, or of a power or influence). **2** slavery (*in thrall*). □ **thraldom** *n.* [Old English from Old Norse]

thrash –*v.* **1** beat or whip severely. **2** defeat thoroughly. **3** deliver repeated blows. **4** (foll. by *about, around*) move or fling (esp. the limbs) about violently. **5** = THRESH 1. –*n* **1** act of thrashing. **2** *slang* (esp. lavish) party. □ **thrash out** discuss to a conclusion. [Old English]

thread /θred/ –*n.* **1 a** spun-out cotton, silk, or glass etc.; yarn. **b** length of this. **2** thin cord of twisted yarns used esp. in sewing and weaving. **3** continuous aspect of a thing (*the thread of life*; *thread of his argument*). **4** spiral ridge of a screw. –*v.* **1** pass a thread through (a needle). **2** put (beads) on a thread. **3** insert (a strip of material, e.g. film or magnetic tape) into equipment. **4** make (one's way) carefully through a crowded place, over a difficult route, etc. [Old English: related to THROW]

threadbare *adj.* **1** (of cloth) with the nap worn away and the thread visible. **2** (of a person) wearing such clothes. **3** hackneyed.

threadworm *n.* parasitic threadlike worm.

threat /θret/ *n.* **1** declaration of an intention to punish or hurt if an order etc. is not obeyed. **2** indication of something undesirable coming (*threat of war*). **3** person or thing as a likely cause of harm etc. [Old English]

threaten *v.* **1** make a threat or threats against. **2** be a sign of (something undesirable). **3** (foll. by *to* + infin.) announce one's intention to do an undesirable thing. **4** (also *absol.*) warn of the infliction of (harm etc.). **5** (as

threatened *adj.*) (of a species etc.) likely to become extinct. [Old English]

three *adj. & n.* **1** a one more than two. **b** symbol for this (3, iii, III). **2** size etc. denoted by three. [Old English]

three-cornered *adj.* **1** triangular. **2** (of a contest etc.) between three parties.

three-decker *n.* **1** warship with three gun-decks. **2** thing with three levels or divisions.

three-dimensional *adj.* having or appearing to have length, breadth, and depth.

threefold *adj. & adv.* **1** three times as much or as many. **2** consisting of three parts.

three-legged race *n.* running-race between pairs, one member of each pair having the left leg tied to the right leg of the other.

three-line whip *n.* written notice to MPs from their leader insisting on attendance at a debate and voting a certain way.

threepence /ˈθrepəns, ˈθrʌp-/ *n.* sum of three pence.

threepenny /ˈθrepəni, ˈθrʌp-/ *attrib. adj.* costing three pence.

three-piece –*n.* three-piece suit or suite. –*attrib. adj.* (esp. of a suit or suite) consisting of three items.

three-ply –*adj.* of three strands or layers etc. –*n.* **1** three-ply wool. **2** three-ply wood.

three-point turn *n.* method of turning a vehicle round in a narrow space by moving forwards, backwards, and forwards again.

three-quarter *n.* (also **three-quarter back**) *Rugby* any of three or four players just behind the half-backs.

three-quarters *n.pl.* three parts out of four.

three Rs *n.pl.* (prec. by *the*) reading, writing, and arithmetic.

threescore *n. & adj. archaic* sixty.

threesome *n.* group of three persons.

three-way *adj.* involving three directions or participants.

threnody /ˈθrenədi/ *n.* (*pl.* -**ies**) song of lamentation or mourning. [Greek]

thresh *v.* **1** beat out or separate grain from (corn etc.). **2** = THRASH *v.* 4. □ **thresher** *n.* [Old English]

threshing-floor *n.* hard level floor for threshing esp. with flails.

threshold /ˈθreʃəʊld/ *n.* **1** strip of wood or stone forming the bottom of a doorway and crossed in entering a house etc. **2** point of entry or beginning. **3** limit below which a stimulus causes no reaction. [Old English: related to THRASH in the sense 'tread']

threw *past* of THROW.

thrice adv. archaic or literary **1** three times. **2** (esp. in comb.) highly (thrice-blessed). [related to THREE]

thrift n. **1** frugality; careful use of money etc. **2** the sea pink. [Old Norse: related to THRIVE]

thriftless adj. wasteful.

thrifty adj. (-ier, -iest) economical. □ **thriftiness** n.

thrill —n. **1** wave or nervous tremor of emotion or sensation (a thrill of joy). **2** throb, pulsation. —v. (-ling) **1** feel a thrill. **2** quiver or throb with or as with emotion. [Old English, = pierce: related to THROUGH]

thriller n. exciting or sensational story or play etc., esp. about crime or espionage.

thrips n. (pl. same) an insect harmful to plants. [Greek, = woodworm]

thrive v. (-ving; past **throve** or **thrived**; past part. **thriven** /'θrɪv(ə)n/ or **thrived**) **1** prosper, flourish. **2** grow rich. **3** (of a child, animal, or plant) grow vigorously. [Old Norse]

thro' var. of THROUGH.

throat n. **1 a** windpipe or gullet. **b** front part of the neck containing this. **2** literary narrow passage, entrance, or exit. □ **cut one's own throat** harm oneself or one's interests. **ram** (or **thrust**) **down a person's throat** force on a person's attention. [Old English]

throaty adj. (-ier, -iest) (of a voice) hoarsely resonant. □ **throatily** adv. **throatiness** n.

throb —v. (-bb-) **1** pulsate, esp. with more than the usual force or rapidity. **2** vibrate with a persistent rhythm or with emotion. —n. **1** throbbing. **2** (esp. violent) pulsation. [imitative]

throe n. (usu. in pl.) violent pang, esp. of childbirth or death. □ **in the throes of** struggling with the task of. [Old English, alteration of original throwe, perhaps by association with woe]

thrombosis /θrɒm'bəʊsɪs/ n. (pl. **-boses** /-siːz/) coagulation of the blood in a blood-vessel or organ. [Greek = curdling]

throne —n. **1** chair of State for a sovereign or bishop etc. **2** sovereign power. —v. (-ning; en-) (came to the throne). [Greek thronos]

throng —n. (often foll. by of) crowd, esp. of people. —v. **1** come in great numbers (crowds thronged to the stadium). **2** flock into or crowd round; fill with or as with a crowd. [Old English]

throstle /'θrɒs(ə)l/ n. song thrush. [Old English]

throttle /'θrɒt(ə)l/ —n. **1 a** valve controlling the flow of fuel or steam etc. in an engine. **b** (in full **throttle-lever**)

lever or pedal operating this valve. **2** throat, gullet, or windpipe. —v. (-ling) **1** choke or strangle. **2** prevent the utterance etc. of. **3** control (an engine or steam etc.) with a throttle. □ **throttle back** (or **down**) reduce the speed of (an engine or vehicle) by throttling. [perhaps from THROAT]

through /θruː/ (also **thro'**, US **thru**) —prep. **1 a** from end to end or side to side of. **b** going in one side and out the other of. **2** between or among (swarm through the waves). **3** from beginning to end of (read through the letter, went through many difficulties). **4** because of (lost it through carelessness). **5** US up to and including (Monday through Friday). —adv. **1** through a thing; from side to side, end to end, or beginning to end. **2** so as to be connected by telephone (will put you through). —attrib. adj. **1** (of a journey, route, etc.) done without a change of line or vehicle or with one ticket. **2** (of traffic) going through a place to its destination. **3** (of a road) open at both ends. □ **be through** colloq. **1** (often foll. by with) have finished. **2** (often foll. by with) cease to have dealings. **3** have no further prospects. **through and through** thoroughly, completely. [Old English]

throughout /θruː'aʊt/ —prep. right through; from end to and of. —adv. in every part or respect.

throughput n. amount of material put through a process, esp. in manufacturing or computing.

throve past of THRIVE.

throw /θrəʊ/ —v. (past **threw** /θruː/; past part. **thrown** /θrəʊn/) **1** propel with force through the air. **2** force violently into, or compel to be in, a specified position or state (thrown on the rocks; threw themselves down; thrown out of work). **3** turn or move (part of the body) quickly or suddenly (threw an arm out). **4** project or cast (light, a shadow, etc.). **5 a** bring to the ground in wrestling. **b** (of a horse) unseat (its rider). **6** colloq. disconcert (the question threw me). **7** (foll. by on, off, etc.) put (clothes etc.) hastily on or off. **8 a** cause to fall on a table etc. **b** obtain (a specified number) by throwing dice. **9** cause to pass or extend suddenly to another state or position (threw a bridge across the river). **10** operate (a switch or lever). **11** form on a potter's wheel. **12** have (a fit or tantrum etc.). **13** give (a party). —n. **1** act of throwing or being thrown. **2** distance a thing is or may be thrown. **3** (prec. by a) slang each; per item (sold at £10 a throw). □ **throw away 1** discard as

useless or unwanted. 2 waste or fail to make use of (an opportunity etc.). **throw back** 1 revert to ancestral character. 2 (usu. in *passive*; foll. by *on*) compel to rely on. **throw in** 1 interpose (a word or remark). 2 include at no extra cost. 3 throw (a football) from the edge of the pitch where it has gone out of play. **throw in the towel** (or **sponge**) admit defeat. **throw off** 1 discard; contrive to get rid of. 2 write or utter in an offhand manner. **throw oneself at** seek blatantly as a sexual partner. **throw oneself into** engage vigorously in. **throw oneself on** (or **upon**) rely completely on. **throw open** (often foll. by *to*) 1 cause to be suddenly or widely open. 2 make accessible. **throw out** 1 put out forcibly or suddenly. 2 discard as unwanted. 3 reject (a proposal). **throw over** desert, abandon. **throw together** 1 assemble hastily. 2 bring into casual contact. **throw up** 1 abandon. 2 resign from. 3 *colloq.* vomit. 4 erect hastily. 5 bring to notice. [Old English = twist]

throw-away *attrib. adj.* 1 meant to be thrown away after (one) use. 2 spoken in a deliberately casual way. 3 disposed to throwing things away (*throw-away society*).

throwback *n.* 1 reversion to ancestral character. 2 instance of this.

throw-in *n.* throwing in of a football during play.

thrown *past part.* of THROW.

thru *US var.* of THROUGH.

thrum[1] –*v.* (**-mm-**) 1 play (a stringed instrument) monotonously or unskilfully. 2 (often foll. by *on*) drum idly. –*n.* 1 such playing. 2 resulting sound. [imitative]

thrum[2] *n.* 1 unwoven end of a warp-thread, or the whole of such ends, left when the finished web is cut away. 2 any short loose thread. [Old English]

thrush[1] *n.* any of various songbirds, esp. the song thrush and mistle thrush. [Old English]

thrush[2] *n.* 1 fungous disease, esp. of children, affecting the mouth and throat. 2 similar disease of the vagina. [origin unknown]

thrust –*v.* (*past* and *past part.* **thrust**) 1 push with a sudden impulse or with force. 2 (foll. by *on*) impose acceptance of (a thing) forcibly; enforce acceptance of (a thing). 3 (foll. by *at, through*) pierce, stab; lunge suddenly. 4 make (one's way) forcibly. 5 (as **thrusting** *adj.*) aggressive, ambitious. –*n.* 1 sudden or forcible push or lunge. 2 propulsive force produced by a jet or rocket engine. 3 strong attempt to penetrate an enemy's line or territory. 4 remark aimed at a person. 5 stress between the parts of an arch etc. 6 (often foll. by *of*) chief theme or gist of remarks etc. [Old Norse]

thud –*n.* low dull sound as of a blow on a non-resonant surface. –*v.* (**-dd-**) make or fall with a thud. [probably Old English]

thug *n.* 1 violent ruffian. 2 (**Thug**) *hist.* member of a religious organization of robbers and assassins in India. □ **thuggery** *n.* **thuggish** *adj.* [Hindi]

thulium /ˈθjuːlɪəm/ *n.* metallic element of the lanthanide series. [Latin *Thule* region in the remote north]

thumb /θʌm/ –*n.* 1 short thick finger on the human hand, set apart from the other four. 2 part of a glove etc. for a thumb. –*v.* 1 wear or soil (pages etc.) with a thumb. 2 turn over pages with or as with a thumb (*thumbed through the directory*). 3 request or get (a lift) by signalling with a raised thumb. 4 use the thumb in a gesture. □ **thumb one's nose** (see SNOOK). **thumbs down** indication of rejection or disapproval. **thumbs up** indication of satisfaction or approval. **under a person's thumb** completely dominated by a person. [Old English]

thumb index *n.* set of lettered grooves cut down the side of a book for easy reference.

thumbnail *n.* 1 nail of a thumb. 2 (*attrib.*) concise (*thumbnail sketch*).

thumbprint *n.* impression of a thumb esp. for identification.

thumbscrew *n.* instrument of torture for crushing the thumbs.

thump –*v.* 1 beat or strike heavily, esp. with the fist. 2 throb strongly. 3 (foll. by *at, on,* etc.) knock loudly. –*n.* 1 heavy blow. 2 dull sound of this. [imitative]

thumping *adj. colloq.* (esp. as an intensifier) huge (*a thumping lie; a thumping great house*).

thunder /ˈθʌndə(r)/ –*n.* 1 loud noise caused by lightning and due to the expansion of rapidly heated air. 2 resounding loud deep noise (*thunders of applause*). 3 strong censure or denunciation. –*v.* 1 (prec. by *it* as subject) thunder sounds (*it is thundering; if it thunders*). 2 make or proceed with a noise like thunder. 3 utter (threats, compliments, etc.) loudly. 4 (foll. by *against* etc.) make violent threats etc. against. □ **steal a person's thunder** see STEAL. □ **thundery** *adj.* [Old English]

thunderbolt *n.* 1 flash of lightning with a simultaneous crash of thunder. 2 unexpected occurrence or announcement. 3 supposed bolt or shaft as a

destructive agent, esp. as an attribute of a god.

thunderclap n. 1 crash of thunder. 2 something startling or unexpected.

thundercloud n. cumulus cloud charged with electricity and producing thunder and lightning.

thunder-fly n. = THRIPS.

thundering adj. colloq. (esp. as an intensifier) huge (a thundering nuisance; a thundering great bruise).

thunderous adj. 1 like thunder. 2 very loud.

thunderstorm n. storm with thunder and lightning and usu. heavy rain or hail.

thunderstruck predic. adj. amazed.

Thur. abbr. (also **Thurs.**) Thursday.

thurible /ˈθjʊərɪb(ə)l/ n. censer. [Latin thus thur- incense]

Thursday /ˈθəːzdeɪ/ —n. day of the week following Wednesday. —adv. colloq. 1 on Thursday. 2 (**Thursdays**) on Thursdays: each Thursday. [Old English]

thus /ðʌs/ adv. formal 1 a in this way. b as indicated. 2 a accordingly. b as a result or inference. 3 to this extent; so (thus far; thus much). [Old English]

thwack —v. hit with a heavy blow. —n. heavy blow. [imitative]

thwart /θwɔːt/ —v. frustrate or foil (a person, plan, etc.). —n. rower's seat. [Old Norse, = across]

thy /ðaɪ/ poss. pron. (attrib.) (also **thine** predic. or before a vowel) archaic of or belonging to thee. [from THINE]

■ **Usage** Thy has now been replaced by your except in some formal, liturgical, dialect, and poetic uses.

thyme /taɪm/ n. any of several herbs with aromatic leaves. [Greek thumon]

thymol /ˈθaɪmɒl/ n. antiseptic obtained from oil of thyme.

thymus /ˈθaɪməs/ n. (pl. **thymi** /-maɪ/) lymphoid organ situated in the neck of vertebrates. [Greek]

thyroid /ˈθaɪrɔɪd/ n. (in full **thyroid gland**) 1 large ductless gland in the neck of vertebrates, secreting a hormone which regulates growth and development. 2 extract prepared from the thyroid gland of animals and used in treating goitre etc. [Greek thureos oblong shield]

thyroid cartilage n. large cartilage of the larynx, forming the Adam's apple.

thyself pron. archaic emphat. & refl. form of THOU; THEE.

Ti symb. titanium.

ti var. of TE.

tiara /tɪˈɑːrə/ n. 1 jewelled ornamental band worn on the front of a woman's

hair. 2 three-crowned diadem worn by a pope. □ **tiaraed** adj. [Latin from Greek]

tibia /ˈtɪbɪə/ n. (pl. **tibiae** /-bɪiː/) Anat. inner of two bones extending from the knee to the ankle. □ **tibial** adj. [Latin]

tic n. (in full **nervous tic**) occasional involuntary contraction of the muscles, esp. of the face. [French from Italian]

tick¹ —n. 1 slight recurring click, esp. that of a watch or clock. 2 colloq. moment. 3 mark (✓) to denote correctness, check items in a list, etc. —v. 1 (of a clock etc.) make ticks. 2 a mark with a tick. b (often foll. by off) mark (an item) with a tick in checking. □ **tick off** colloq. reprimand. **tick over** (of an engine etc.) idle. 2 (of a person, project, etc.) be functioning at a basic level. **what makes a person tick** colloq. person's motivation. [probably imitative]

tick² n. 1 parasitic arachnid on the skin of dogs, cattle, etc. 2 parasitic insect on sheep and birds etc. [Old English]

tick³ n. colloq. credit (buy goods on tick). [apparently an abbreviation of TICKET in on the ticket]

tick⁴ n. 1 cover of a mattress or pillow. 2 = TICKING. [Greek thēkē case]

ticker n. colloq. 1 heart. 2 watch. 3 US = TAPE MACHINE 1.

ticker-tape n. 1 paper strip from a tape machine. 2 this or similar material thrown from windows etc. to greet a celebrity.

ticket /ˈtɪkɪt/ —n. 1 written or printed piece of paper or card entitling the holder to enter a place, participate in an event, travel by public transport, etc. 2 notification of a traffic offence etc. (parking ticket). 3 certificate of discharge from the army. 4 certificate of qualification as a ship's master, pilot, etc. 5 price etc. label. 6 esp. US a list of candidates put forward by one group, esp. a political party. b principles of a party. 7 (prec. by the) colloq. what is correct or needed. —v. (**-t-**) attach a ticket to. [obsolete French étiquet]

ticking n. stout usu. striped material used to cover mattresses etc. [from TICK⁴]

tickle /ˈtɪk(ə)l/ —v. (**-ling**) 1 a touch or stroke (a person etc.) playfully or lightly so as to produce laughter and spasmodic movement. b produce this sensation. 2 excite agreeably: amuse. 3 catch (a trout etc.) by rubbing it so that it moves backwards into the hand. —n. 1 act of tickling. 2 tickling sensation. □ **tickled pink** (or **to death**) colloq. extremely amused or pleased. □ **tickly** adj. [probably frequentative of TICK¹]

ticklish adj. 1 sensitive to tickling. 2 (of a person) difficult to handle.

tick-tack n. a kind of manual semaphore used by racecourse bookmakers.

tick-tock n. ticking of a large clock etc.

tidal /ˈtaɪd(ə)l/ adj. relating to, like, or affected by tides. □ **tidally** adv.

tidal wave n. 1 exceptionally large ocean wave, one caused by an underwater earthquake. 2 widespread manifestation of feeling etc.

tidbit US var. of TITBIT.

tiddler n. colloq. 1 small fish, esp. a stickleback or minnow. 2 unusually small thing. [perhaps related to TIDDLY² and tittlebat, a childish form of stickleback]

tiddly¹ adj. (-ier, -iest) colloq. slightly drunk. [origin unknown]

tiddly² adj. (-ier, -iest) colloq. little. [origin unknown]

tiddly-wink /ˈtɪdlɪwɪŋk/ n. 1 counter flicked with another into a cup etc. 2 (in pl.) this game. [perhaps related to TIDDLY¹]

tide n. 1 a periodic rise and fall of the sea due to the attraction of the moon and sun. b water as affected by this. 2 time or season (usu. in comb.: Whitsuntide). 3 marked trend of opinion, fortune, or events. □ **tide** (-ding) over provide (a person) with what is needed during a difficult period. [Old English, = TIME]

tidemark n. 1 mark made by the tide at high water. 2 a line left round a bath by the dirty water. b colloq. line between washed and unwashed parts of a person's body.

tidetable n. table indicating the times of high and low tides.

tideway n. tidal part of a river.

tidings /ˈtaɪdɪŋz/ n. (as sing. or pl.) archaic or joc. news. [Old English, probably from Old Norse]

tidy —adj. (-ier, -iest) 1 neat, orderly. 2 (of a person) methodical 3 colloq. considerable (a tidy sum). —n. (pl. -ies) 1 receptacle for holding small objects etc. 2 esp. US cover for a chair-back etc. —v. (-ies, -ied) (also absol.; often foll. by up) put in good order; make (oneself, a room, etc.) tidy. □ **tidily** adv. **tidiness** n. [originally = timely etc., from TIDE]

tie /taɪ/ —v. (tying) 1 attach or fasten with string or cord etc. 2 a form (a string, ribbon, shoelace, necktie, etc.) into a knot or bow. b form (a knot or bow) in this way. 3 (often foll. by down) restrict (a person) in some way (is tied to his job). 4 (often foll. by with) achieve the same score or place as another competitor (tied with her for first place). 5 hold (rafters etc.) together by a tie. 6 Mus. unite (written notes) by a tie. —n. 1 cord or wire etc. used for fastening. 2 strip of material worn round the collar and tied in a knot at the front. 3 thing that unites or restricts persons (family ties). 4 draw, dead heat, or equality of score among competitors. 5 match between any pair from a group of competing players or teams. 6 (also **tie-beam** etc.) rod or beam holding parts of a structure together. 7 Mus. curved line above or below two notes of the same pitch indicating that they are to be played without a break between them. □ **tie in** (foll. by with) bring into or have a close association or agreement. the **up** 1 bind securely with cord etc. 2 invest or reserve (capital etc.) so that it is not immediately available for use. 3 (often foll. by with) = tie in. 4 (usu. in passive) fully occupy (a person). 5 bring to a satisfactory conclusion. [Old English]

tie-break n. (also **tie-breaker**) means of deciding a winner from competitors who have tied.

tied attrib. adj. 1 (of a house) occupied subject to the tenant's working for its owner. 2 (of a public house etc.) bound to supply the products of a particular brewery only.

tie-dye n. (also **tie and dye**) method of producing dyed patterns by tying string etc. to keep the dye away from parts of the fabric.

tie-in n. 1 connection or association. 2 joint promotion of related commodities etc. (e.g. a book and a film).

tie-pin n. ornamental pin for holding a tie in place.

tier n. row, rank, or unit of a structure, as one of several placed one above another (tiers of seats). □ **tiered** adj. [French tire from tirer draw, elongate]

tiercel var. of TERCEL.

tie-up n. connection, association.

tiff /tɪf/ n. slight or petty quarrel. [origin unknown]

tiffin /ˈtɪfɪn/ n. Ind. light meal, esp. lunch. [apparently from tiffing sipping]

tiger /ˈtaɪgə(r)/ n. 1 large Asian animal of the cat family, with a yellow-brown coat with black stripes. 2 fierce, energetic, or formidable person. [Greek tigris]

tiger-cat n. any moderate-sized feline resembling the tiger, e.g. the ocelot.

tiger lily n. tall garden lily with dark-spotted orange flowers.

tiger moth n. moth with richly spotted and streaked wings.

tight /taɪt/ —adj. 1 closely held, drawn, fastened, fitting, etc. (tight hold; tight skirt). 2 too closely fitting. 3 impermeable, impervious, esp. (in comb.) to a specified thing (watertight). 4 tense, stretched. 5 colloq. drunk. 6 colloq.

stingy. **7** (of money or materials) not easily obtainable. **8 a** (of precautions, a programme, etc.) presenting difficulties. **b** presenting difficulties (*tight situation*). **9** produced by or requiring great exertion or pressure (*tight squeeze*). —*adv.* tightly (*hold tight!*). □ **tightly** *adv.* **tightness** *n.* [Old Norse]

tight corner *n.* (also **tight place** or **spot**) difficult situation.

tighten *v.* make or become tighter.

tight-fisted *adj.* stingy.

tight-lipped *adj.* with or as with the lips compressed to restrain emotion or speech: determinedly reticent.

tightrope *n.* rope stretched tightly high above the ground, on which acrobats perform.

tights *n.pl.* **1** thin close-fitting wool or nylon etc. garment covering the legs, feet, and the lower part of the torso, worn by women and girls. **2** similar garment worn by a dancer, acrobat, etc.

tigress /'taigris/ *n.* female tiger.

tike var. of TYKE.

tilde /'tildə/ *n.* mark (~) put over a letter, e.g. over a Spanish *n* when pronounced *ny* (as in *señor*). [Latin: related to TITLE]

tile —*n.* **1** thin slab of concrete or baked clay etc. used for roofing or paving etc. **2** similar slab of glazed pottery, cork, linoleum, etc., for covering a wall, floor, etc. **3** thin flat piece used in a game (esp. in mah-jong). —*v.* (**-ling**) cover with tiles. □ **on the tiles** *colloq.* having a spree. □ **tiler** *n.* [Latin *tegula*]

tiling *n.* **1** process of fixing tiles. **2** area of tiles.

till¹ —*prep.* **1** up to or as late as (*wait till six o'clock*). **2** up to the time of (*faithful till death*). —*conj.* **1** up to the time when (*wait till I return*). **2** so long that (*laughed till I cried*). [Old Norse: related to TILL³]

till² *n.* drawer for money in a shop or bank etc., esp. with a device recording the amount of each purchase. [origin unknown]

till³ *v.* cultivate (land). □ **tiller** *n.* [Old English, = strive for]

tillage *n.* **1** preparation of land for growing crops. **2** tilled land.

tiller *n.* bar fitted to a boat's rudder to turn it in steering. [Anglo-French *telier* = weaver's beam]

tilt —*v.* **1** (cause to) assume a sloping position; heel over. **2** (foll. by *at*) strike, thrust, or run at, with a weapon. **3** (foll. by *with*) engage in a contest. —*n.* **1** tilting. **2** sloping position. **3** (of medieval

■ **Usage** In all senses, *till* can be replaced by *until* which is more formal in style.

knights etc.) charging with a lance against an opponent or at a mark. **4** attack, esp. with argument or satire (*have a tilt at*). □ **full tilt 1** at full speed. **2** with full force. **tilt at windmills** see WINDMILL. [Old English, = unsteady]

tilth *n.* **1** tillage, cultivation. **2** tilled soil. [Old English: related to TILL³]

timber *n.* **1** wood prepared for building, carpentry, etc. **2** piece of wood or beam, esp. as the rib of a vessel. **3** large standing trees. **4** (esp. as *int.*) warning cry that a tree is about to fall. [Old English, = building]

timbered *adj.* **1** made wholly or partly of timber. **2** (of country) wooded.

timberline *n.* line or level above which no trees grow.

timbre /'tambə(r), 'tæmbrə/ *n.* distinctive character of a musical sound or voice apart from its pitch and volume. [Greek: related to TYMPANUM]

timbrel /'timbrəl/ *n. archaic* tambourine. [French: related to TIMBRE]

time —*n.* **1** indefinite continued progress of existence, events, etc., in the past, present, and future, regarded as a whole. **2** progress of this as affecting persons or things. **3** portion of time belonging to particular events or circumstances (*the time of the Plague; prehistoric times*). **4** allotted or available portion of time (*had no time to eat*). **5** point of time, esp. in hours and minutes (*the time is 7.30*). **6** (prec. by *a*) indefinite period. **7** time or an amount of time as reckoned by a conventional standard (*eight o'clock New York time; the time allowed is one hour*). **8** occasion (*last time*). **9** moment etc. suitable for a purpose etc. (*the time to act*). **10** (in *pl.*) expressing multiplication (*five times six is thirty*). **11** lifetime (*will last my time*). **12** (in *sing.* or *pl.*) conditions of life or of a period (*hard times*). **13** *slang* prison sentence (*served his time*). **14** apprenticeship (*served his time*). **15** period of gestation. **16** date or expected date of childbirth or death. **17** measured time spent in work. **18 a** any of several rhythmic patterns of music. **b** duration of a note. —*v.* (**-ming**) **1** choose the time for. **2** do at a chosen or correct time. **3** arrange the time of. **4** ascertain the time taken by. □ **against time** with utmost speed, so as to finish by a specified time. **ahead of time** earlier than expected. **all the time 1** during the whole of the time referred to (often despite some contrary expectation etc.). **2** constantly. **at one time 1** in a known

but unspecified past period. **2** simultaneously. **at the same time 1** simultaneously. **2** nevertheless. **at times** intermittently. **for the time being** until some other arrangement is made. **half the time** *colloq.* as often as not. **have no time for 1** be unable or unwilling to spend time on. **2** dislike. **have a time of it** undergo trouble or difficulty. **in no time 1** very soon. **2** very quickly. **in time 1** not late, punctual. **2** eventually. **3** in accordance with a given rhythm. **keep time** move or sing etc. in time. **pass the time of day** *colloq.* exchange a greeting or casual remarks. **time after time 1** on many occasions. **2** in many instances. **time and** (or **time and time**) **again** on many occasions. **the time of one's life** period of exceptional enjoyment. **time out of mind** a longer time than anyone can remember. **time was** there was a time. [Old English]

time and a half *n.* one and a half times the normal rate of payment.

time-and-motion *adj.* (usu. *attrib.*) measuring the efficiency of industrial and other operations.

time bomb *n.* bomb designed to explode at a pre-set time.

time capsule *n.* box etc. containing objects typical of the present time, buried for future discovery.

time clock *n.* clock with a device for recording workers' hours of work.

time exposure *n.* exposure of photographic film for longer than the slowest normal shutter setting.

time-honoured *adj.* esteemed by tradition or through custom.

timekeeper *n.* **1** person who records time, esp. of workers or in a game. **2 a** watch or clock as regards accuracy (*a good timekeeper*). **b** person as regards punctuality. □ **timekeeping** *n.*

time-lag *n.* interval of time between a cause and effect.

timeless *adj.* not affected by the passage of time. □ **timelessly** *adv.* **timelessness** *n.*

time-limit *n.* limit of time within which a task must be done.

timely *adj.* (**-ier**, **-iest**) opportune; coming at the right time. □ **timeliness** *n.*

timepiece *n.* clock or watch.

timer *n.* person or device that measures or records time taken.

time-served *adj.* having completed a period of apprenticeship or training.

time-server *n.* *derog.* person who changes his or her view to suit the prevailing circumstances, fashion, etc. □ **time-serving** *adj.*

time-share *n.* share in a property under a time-sharing scheme.

time-sharing *n.* **1** use of a holiday home at contractually agreed different times by several joint owners. **2** operation of a computer system by several users for different operations at the same time.

time sheet *n.* sheet of paper for recording hours of work etc.

time-shift *–v.* move from one time to another, esp. record (a television programme) for later viewing. *–n.* movement from one time to another (*the continual time-shifts make the plot difficult to follow*).

time signal *n.* audible signal of the exact time of day.

time signature *n. Mus.* indication of tempo following a clef.

time switch *n.* switch acting automatically at a pre-set time.

timetable *–n.* list of times at which events are expected to take place, esp. the arrival and departure of transport or a sequence of lessons. *–v.* (**-ling**) include in or arrange to a timetable; schedule.

time zone *n.* range of longitudes where a common standard time is used.

timid *adj.* (**timider**, **timidest**) easily frightened; apprehensive. □ **timidity** /-'mɪdɪtɪ/ *n.* **timidly** *adv.* [Latin *timeo* fear]

timing *n.* **1** way an action or process is timed. **2** regulation of the opening and closing of valves in an internal-combustion engine.

timorous /'tɪmərəs/ *adj.* **1** timid. **2** frightened. □ **timorously** *adv.* [medieval Latin: related to TIMID]

timpani /'tɪmpənɪ/ *n.pl.* (also **tympani**) kettledrums. □ **timpanist** *n.* [Italian, pl. of *timpano* = TYMPANUM]

tin *–n.* **1** silvery-white metallic element, used esp. in alloys and in making tin plate. **2** container made of tin or tinned iron, esp. airtight for preserving food. **3** = TIN PLATE. *–v.* (**-nn-**) **1** seal (food) in a tin for preservation. **2** cover or coat with tin. [Old English]

tin can *n.* tin container, esp. an empty one.

tincture /'tɪŋktʃə(r)/ *–n.* (often foll. by *of*) **1** slight flavour or trace. **2** tinge (of a colour). **3** medicinal solution (of a drug) in alcohol (*tincture of quinine*). *–v.* (**-ring**) **1** colour slightly; tinge, flavour. **2** (often foll. by *with*) affect slightly (with a quality). [Latin: related to TINGE]

tinder *n.* dry substance that readily catches fire from a spark. □ **tindery** *adj.* [Old English]

tinder-box *n. hist.* box containing tinder, flint, and steel, formerly used for kindling fires.

tine n. prong, tooth, or point of a fork, comb, antler, etc. [Old English]

tin foil n. foil made of tin, aluminium, or tin alloy, used for wrapping food.

ting —n. tinkling sound as of a bell. —v. (cause to) emit this sound. [imitative]

tinge —v. (**-ging**) (often foll. by *with*; often in *passive*) 1 colour slightly. 2 affect slightly. —n. 1 tendency towards or trace of some colour. 2 slight admixture of a feeling or quality. [Latin *tingo* *tinct-* dye]

tingle /'tɪŋg(ə)l/ —v. (**-ling**) 1 feel a slight pricking, stinging, or throbbing sensation. 2 cause this (*the reply tingled in my ears*). —n. tingling sensation. □ **tingly** *adj*. [probably from TINKLE]

tin hat n. *colloq*. military steel helmet.

tinker —n. 1 itinerant mender of kettles and pans etc. 2 *Scot. & Ir.* Gypsy. 3 *colloq*. mischievous person or animal. 4 spell of tinkering. —v. 1 (foll. by *at, with*) work in an amateurish or desultory way. 2 work as a tinker. [origin unknown]

tinkle /'tɪŋk(ə)l/ —v. (**-ling**) (cause to) make a succession of short light ringing sounds. —n. 1 tinkling sound. 2 *colloq*. telephone call. □ **tinkly** *adj*. [imitative]

tinnitus /tɪ'naɪtəs/ n. *Med*. condition with ringing in the ears. [Latin *tinnio* *tinnit-* ring tinkle]

tinny *adj*. (**-ier, -iest**) 1 of or like tin. 2 flimsy, insubstantial. 3 (of sound) thin and metallic.

tin-opener n. tool for opening tins.

tin-pan alley n. world of composers and publishers of popular music.

tin plate n. sheet iron or sheet steel coated with tin.

tinpot *attrib. adj*. cheap, inferior.

tinsel /'tɪns(ə)l/ n. 1 glittering metallic strips, threads, etc., used as decoration. 2 superficial brilliance or splendour. 3 (*attrib*.) gaudy, flashy. □ **tinselled** *adj*. **tinselly** *adj*. [Latin *scintilla* spark]

tinsmith n. worker in tin and tin plate.

tinsnips n. clippers for cutting sheet metal.

tint —n. 1 variety of a colour, esp. made by adding white. 2 tendency towards or admixture of a different colour (*red with a blue tint*). 3 faint colour spread over a surface. —v. apply a tint to; colour. [*tinct*: related to TINGE]

tin-tack n. iron tack.

tintinnabulation /ˌtɪntɪˌnæbjʊ'leɪʃ(ə)n/ n. ringing or tinkling of bells. [Latin *tintinnabulum* bell]

tiny /'taɪnɪ/ *adj*. (**-ier, -iest**) very small or slight. □ **tinily** *adv*. **tininess** n. [origin unknown]

-tion see -ION.

tip¹ —n. 1 extremity or end, esp. of a small or tapering thing. 2 small piece or part attached to the end of a thing. 3 leaf-bud of tea. —v. (**-pp-**) provide with a tip. □ **on the tip of one's tongue** about to be said or remembered. **tip of the iceberg** small evident part of something much larger. [Old Norse]

tip² —v. (**-pp-**) 1 (often foll. by *over, up*) **a** lean or slant. **b** cause to do this. 2 (foll. by *into* etc.) **a** overturn or cause to overbalance. **b** discharge the contents of (a container etc.) in this way. —n. 1 **a** slight push or tilt. **b** light stroke. 2 place where material (esp. refuse) is tipped. □ **tip the scales** see SCALE². [origin uncertain]

tip³ —v. (**-pp-**) 1 make a small present of money to, esp. for a service given. 2 name as the likely winner of a race or contest etc. 3 strike or touch lightly. —n. 1 small money present, esp. for a service given. 2 piece of private or special information, esp. regarding betting or investment. 3 small or casual piece of advice. □ **tip off** give (a person) a hint or piece of special information or warning. **tip a person the wink** give a person private information. [origin uncertain]

tip-off n. hint or warning etc.

tipper n. (often *attrib*.) road haulage vehicle that tips at the back to discharge its load.

tippet /'tɪpɪt/ n. 1 long piece of fur etc. worn by a woman round the shoulders. 2 similar garment worn by judges, clergy etc. [probably from TIP¹]

tipple /'tɪp(ə)l/ —v. (**-ling**) 1 drink intoxicating liquor habitually. 2 drink (liquor) repeatedly in small amounts. —n. *colloq*. alcoholic drink. □ **tippler** n. [from TIP²]

tipstaff n. 1 sheriff's officer. 2 metal-tipped staff carried as a symbol of office. [from TIP¹]

tipster n. person who gives tips, esp. about betting at horse-races.

tipsy /'tɪpsɪ/ *adj*. (**-ier, -iest**) 1 slightly drunk. 2 caused by or showing intoxication (*a tipsy lurch*). □ **tipsily** *adv*. **tipsiness** n. [from TIP²]

tiptoe —n. the tips of the toes. —v. (**-toes, -toeing**) walk on tiptoe, or very stealthily. —*adv*. (also **on tiptoe**) with the heels off the ground.

tiptop *colloq*. —*adj*. highest in excellence. —*adv*. most excellently. —n. highest point of excellence.

tip-up *attrib. adj*. able to be tipped, e.g. of a theatre seat.

TIR *abbr*. international road transport. [French *transport international routier*]

tirade /taɪˈreɪd/ n. long vehement denunciation or declamation. [French from Italian]

tire[1] v. (-ring) 1 make or grow weary. 2 exhaust the patience or interest of; bore. 3 (in *passive*; foll. by *of*) have had enough of; be fed up with. [Old English]

tire[2] n. 1 band of metal placed round the rim of a wheel to strengthen it. 2 *US* var. of TYRE. [perhaps = archaic *tire* 'head-dress']

tired adj. 1 weary; ready for sleep. 2 (of an idea etc.) hackneyed. □ **tiredly** adv. **tiredness** n.

tireless adj. not tiring easily, energetic. □ **tirelessly** adv. **tirelessness** n.

tiresome adj. 1 wearisome, tedious. 2 *colloq.* annoying. □ **tiresomely** adv. **tiresomeness** n.

tiro /ˈtaɪərəʊ/ n. (also **tyro**) (pl. **-s**) beginner, novice. [Latin, = recruit]

'tis /tɪz/ archaic it is. [contraction]

tissue /ˈtɪʃuː, ˈtɪsjuː/ n. 1 any of the coherent collections of specialized cells of which animals or plants are made (*muscular tissue*). 2 = TISSUE-PAPER. 3 disposable piece of thin soft absorbent paper for wiping, drying, etc. 4 fine woven esp. gauzy fabric. 5 (foll. by *of*) connected series (*tissue of lies*). [French *tissu* woven cloth]

tissue-paper n. thin soft paper for wrapping etc.

tit[1] n. any of various small birds. [probably from Scandinavian]

tit[2] n. □ **tit for tat** blow for blow; retaliation. [= earlier *tip* in *tip for tap*: see TIP[2]]

tit[3] n. 1 *coarse slang* woman's breast. 2 *colloq.* nipple. [Old English]

titanic /taɪˈtænɪk/ adj. gigantic, colossal. □ **titanically** adv. [Greek: related to TITAN]

titanium /taɪˈteɪnɪəm, tɪ-/ n. grey metallic element. [Greek: related to TITAN]

titbit n. (*US* **tidbit**) 1 dainty morsel. 2 piquant item of news etc. [perhaps from dial. *tid* tender]

titchy adj. (**-ier**, **-iest**) *colloq.* very small. [*titch* small person, from *Tich*, name of a comedian]

tithe /taɪð/ —n. 1 one-tenth of the annual produce of land or labour, formerly taken as a tax for the Church. 2 tenth part. —v. (**-thing**) 1 subject to tithes. 2 pay tithes. [Old English, = tenth]

tithe barn n. barn built to hold tithes paid in kind.

Titian /ˈtɪʃ(ə)n/ adj. (of hair) bright auburn. [*Titian*, name of a painter]

titillate /ˈtɪtɪleɪt/ v. (**-ting**) 1 excite, esp. sexually. 2 tickle. □ **titillation** /-ˈleɪʃ(ə)n/ n. [Latin]

titivate /ˈtɪtɪveɪt/ v. (**-ting**) (often *refl.*) *colloq.* smarten up; put the finishing touches to. □ **titivation** /-ˈveɪʃ(ə)n/ n. [earlier *tidivate*, perhaps from TIDY after *cultivate*]

title /ˈtaɪt(ə)l/ n. 1 name of a book, work of art, etc. 2 heading of a chapter, document, etc. 3 **a** = TITLE-PAGE. **b** book, magazine, etc., in terms of its title (*brought out two new titles*). 4 (usu. in *pl.*) caption or credit in a film etc. 5 name indicating a person's status (e.g. *queen, professor*) or used as a form of address or reference (e.g. *Lord, Mr, Your Grace*). 6 championship in sport. 7 *Law* **a** right to ownership of property with or without possession. **b** (foll. by *to*) just or recognized claim. [Latin *titulus*]

title-deed n. legal instrument as evidence of a right.

title-holder n. person who holds a title, esp. a sporting champion.

title-page n. page at the beginning of a book giving the title, author, etc.

title role n. part in a play etc. that gives it its name (e.g. *Othello*).

titmouse n. (pl. **titmice**) small active tit. [Old English *tit* little, *māse* titmouse, as imitated to MOUSE]

titled adj. having a title of nobility or rank.

titrate /taɪˈtreɪt/ v. (**-ting**) *Chem.* ascertain the amount of a constituent in (a solution) by reaction with a known concentration of reagent. □ **titration** /-ˈtreɪʃ(ə)n/ n. [French *titre* title]

titter —v. laugh covertly; giggle. —n. covert laugh. [imitative]

tittle /ˈtɪt(ə)l/ n. 1 small written or printed stroke or dot. 2 particle; whit (*not one jot or tittle*). [Latin: related to TITLE]

tittle-tattle /ˈtɪt(ə)l,tæt(ə)l/ —n. petty gossip; chatter. —v. (**-ling**) gossip, chatter. [reduplication of TATTLE]

tittup /ˈtɪtəp/ —v. (**-p-** or **-pp-**) go about friskily or jerkily; bob up and down; canter. —n. such a gait or movement. [perhaps imitative]

titular /ˈtɪtjʊlə(r)/ adj. 1 of or relating to a title. 2 existing, or being, in name or title only (*titular ruler*). [French: related to TITLE]

tizzy /ˈtɪzɪ/ n. (pl. **-ies**) *colloq.* state of agitation (*in a tizzy*). [origin unknown]

T-junction n. road junction at which one road joins another at right angles without crossing it.

TI *symb.* thallium.

Tn *symb.* thallium.

TNT *abbr.* trinitrotoluene, a high explosive formed from toluene.

to /tə/, *before a vowel* /tu/, when stressed /tuː/. —*prep.* **1** introducing a noun expressing: **a** what is reached, approached, or touched (*fell to the ground; went to Paris; five minutes to six*). **b** what is aimed at (*throw it to me*). **c** as far as (*went on to the end*). **d** what is followed (*made to order*). **e** what is considered or affected (*am used to that; that is nothing to me*). **f** what is caused or produced (*turn to stone*). **g** what is compared (*nothing to what it once was; equal to the occasion*). **h** what is increased (*add it to mine*). **i** what is involved or composed as specified (*there is nothing to it*). **2** introducing the infinitive: **a** as a verbal noun (*to get there is the priority*). **b** expressing purpose, consequence, or cause (*we eat to live; left him to starve; I'm sorry to hear that*). **c** as a substitute for *to* + infinitive (*wanted to come but was unable to*). —*adv.* **1** in the normal or required position or condition (*come to; heave to*). **2** (of a door) in a nearly closed position. **to and fro 1** backwards and forwards. **2** repeatedly between the same points. [Old English]

toad *n.* **1** froglike amphibian breeding in water but living chiefly on land. **2** repulsive person. [Old English]

toadflax *n.* plant with yellow or purple flowers.

toad-in-the-hole *n.* sausages baked in batter.

toadstool *n.* fungus, usu. poisonous, with a round top and slender stalk.

toady —*n.* (*pl.* -**ies**) sycophant. —*v.* (foll. by *to*) (-**ies**, -**ied**) behave servilely to; fawn upon. □ **toadyism** *n.* [contraction of *toad-eater*]

toast —*n.* **1** sliced bread browned on both sides by radiant heat. **2** a person or thing in whose honour a company is requested to drink. **b** call to drink or an instance of drinking in this way. —*v.* **1** brown by radiant heat. **2** warm (one's feet, oneself, etc.) at a fire etc. **3** drink to the health or in honour of (a person or thing). [French *toster* roast]

toaster *n.* electrical device for making toast.

toasting-fork *n.* long-handled fork for making toast.

toastmaster *n.* (*fem.* **toastmistress**) person responsible for announcing toasts at a public occasion.

toast rack *n.* rack for holding slices of toast at table.

tobacco /tə'bækəʊ/ *n.* (*pl.* -**s**) **1** plant of American origin with narcotic leaves used for smoking, chewing, or snuff. **2** its leaves, esp. as prepared for smoking. [Spanish *tabaco*, of American Indian origin]

tobacconist /tə'bækənɪst/ *n.* dealer in tobacco, cigarettes, etc.

toboggan /tə'bɒgən/ —*n.* long light narrow sledge for sliding downhill over snow or ice. —*v.* ride on a toboggan. [Canadian French from Algonquian]

toby jug /'təʊbɪ/ *n.* jug or mug in the form of a stout man wearing a three-cornered hat [familiar form of the name *Tobias*]

tocsin /'tɒksɪn/ *n.* alarm bell or signal. [Provençal *tocasenh*]

tod *n.* *slang* □ **on one's tod** alone; on one's own. [rhyming slang *on one's Tod Sloan*]

today /tə'deɪ/ —*adv.* **1** on this present day. **2** nowadays. —*n.* **1** this present day. **2** modern times. [Old English]

toddle /'tɒd(ə)l/ —*v.* (-**ling**) **1** walk with short unsteady steps like a small child. **2** (usu. foll. by *off* or *along*) *colloq.* walk, stroll. —*n.* act of toddling.

toddler *n.* child who is just learning to walk.

toddy /'tɒdɪ/ *n.* (*pl.* -**ies**) drink of spirits with hot water and sugar etc. [Hindustani *tāṛī* palm]

to-do /tə'duː/ *n.* (*pl.* -**s**) commotion or fuss.

toe —*n.* **1** any of the five terminal projections of the foot. **2** corresponding part of an animal. **3** part of a shoe etc. that covers the toes. **4** lower end or tip of an implement etc. —*v.* (**toes**, **toed**, **toeing**) touch (a starting-line etc.) with the toes. □ **on one's toes** alert. **toe the line** conform, esp. under pressure. [Old English]

toecap *n.* (usu. strengthened) outer covering of the toe of a boot or shoe.

toe-hold *n.* **1** small foothold. **2** small beginning or advantage.

toenail *n.* nail of each toe.

toff *n.* *slang* upper-class person. [perhaps from *tuft*, = titled undergraduate]

toffee /'tɒfɪ/ *n.* **1** firm or hard sweetmade by boiling sugar, butter, etc. **2** this substance. □ **for toffee** *slang* (prec. by *can't* etc.) (denoting incompetence) at all (*they couldn't sing for toffee*). [origin unknown]

toccata /tə'kɑːtə/ *n.* musical composition for a keyboard instrument, designed to exhibit the performer's touch and technique. [Italian, = touched]

toffee-apple n. apple with a coating of toffee.

toffee-nosed adj. slang snobbish; superior.

tofu /'təufu/ n. curd of mashed soya beans. [Japanese]

tog[1] colloq. —n. (usu. in pl.) item of clothing. —v. (-**gg**-) (foll. by out, up) ultimately related to Latin toga]

tog[2] n. unit of thermal resistance used to express the insulating properties of clothes and quilts. [arbitrary, probably from tog[1]]

toga /'təugə/ n. hist. ancient Roman citizen's loose flowing outer garment. □ **togaed** adj. (also **toga'd**). [Latin]

together /tə'geðə(r)/ —adv. 1 in company or conjunction (walking together; were at school together). 2 simultaneously (both shouted together). 3 one with another (talking together). 4 into conjunction; so as to unite (tied them together; put two and two together). 5 into company or companionship. 6 uninterruptedly (he could talk for three hours together). —adj. colloq. well-organized; self-assured; emotionally stable. □ **together with** as well as. [Old English: related to TO, GATHER]

togetherness n. 1 being together. 2 feeling of comfort from this.

toggle /'tɒg(ə)l/ n. 1 fastener for a garment consisting of a crosspiece which passes through a hole or loop. 2 Computing switch action that is operated the same way but with opposite effect on successive occasions. [origin unknown]

toggle switch n. electric switch with a lever to be moved usu. up and down.

toil —v. 1 work laboriously or incessantly. 2 make slow painful progress. —n. intensive labour; drudgery. [Anglo-French toil(er) dispute]

toilet /'tɔɪlɪt/ n. 1 = LAVATORY. 2 process of washing oneself, dressing, etc. (at one's toilet). [French toilette diminutive of toile cloth]

toilet paper n. paper for cleaning oneself after excreting.

toilet roll n. roll of toilet paper.

toilette /twa:'let/ n. = TOILET 2. [French]

toilet-training n. training of a young child to use the lavatory. □ **toilet-train** v.

toilet soap n. soap for washing oneself.

toilet water n. dilute perfume used after washing.

toils /tɔɪlz/ n.pl. net, snare. [toil from French: related to TOILET]

toilsome /'tɔɪlsəm/ adj. involving toil.

toing and froing /ˌtu:ɪŋ and 'frəʊɪŋ/ n. constant movement to and fro; bustle; dispersed activity. [from TO, FRO]

Tokay /'tə'keɪ/ n. a sweet Hungarian wine. [Tokaj in Hungary]

token /'təʊkən/ n. 1 thing serving as a symbol, reminder, or mark (as a token of affection; in token of my esteem). 2 voucher. 3 thing equivalent to something else, esp. money. 4 (attrib.) a perfunctory (token effort). b conducted briefly to demonstrate strength of feeling (token strike). c chosen by tokenism to represent a group (token woman). □ **by this** (or **the same**) **token** 1 similarly. 2 moreover. [Old English]

tokenism n. 1 granting of minimum concessions, esp. to minority groups. 2 making of only a token effort.

told past and past part. of TELL[1].

tolerable /'tɒlərəb(ə)l/ adj. 1 endurable. 2 fairly good. □ **tolerably** adv. [Latin: related to TOLERATE]

tolerance /'tɒlərəns/ n. 1 willingness or ability to tolerate; forbearance. 2 allowable variation in any measurable property.

tolerant adj. 1 disposed to tolerate others or their acts or opinions. 2 (foll. by of) enduring or patient.

tolerate /'tɒlə,reɪt/ v. (-**ting**) 1 allow the existence or occurrence of without authoritative interference. 2 endure (suffering etc.). 3 find or treat as endurable. 4 be able to take or undergo (drugs, treatment, etc.) without adverse effects. [Latin tolero]

toleration /ˌtɒlə'reɪʃ(ə)n/ n. tolerating or being tolerated, esp. the allowing of religious differences without discrimination. [Latin: related to TOLERATE]

toll[1] /təʊl/ n. 1 charge to use a bridge, road, etc. 2 cost or damage caused by a disaster etc. □ **take its toll** be accompanied by loss, injury, etc.

toll[2] /təʊl/ —v. 1 a (of a bell) sound with slow uniform strokes. b ring (a bell) in this way. c (of a bell) announce or mark (a death etc.) in this way. 2 strike (the hour). —n. 1 tolling. 2 stroke of a bell. [now dial.] toll entice, pull, from an Old English root]

toll-bridge n. bridge at which a toll is charged.

toll-gate n. gate preventing passage until a toll is paid.

toll-road n. road maintained by the tolls collected on it.

toluene /'tɒljʊ,i:n/ n. colourless aromatic liquid hydrocarbon derivative of benzene, used in the manufacture of explosives etc. [Tolu in Colombia]

tom n. (in full **tom-cat**) male cat. [abbreviation of the name Thomas]

tomahawk /'tɒmǝhɔːk/ n. N. American Indian war-axe. [Renape]

tomato /tǝ'mɑːtǝʊ/ n. (pl. -es) **1** glossy red or yellow pulpy edible fruit. **2** plant bearing this. [ultimately from Mexican *tomatl*]

tomb /tuːm/ n. **1** burial-vault **2** grave. **3** sepulchral monument. [Greek *tumbos*]

tombola /tɒm'bǝʊlǝ/ n. lottery with tickets drawn from a drum for immediate prizes. [French or Italian]

tomboy n. boisterous girl who enjoys activities traditionally associated with boys. □ **tomboyish** adj. [from TOM]

tombstone n. memorial stone over a grave, usu. with an epitaph.

Tom, Dick, and Harry n. (also Tom, Dick, or Harry) (usu. prec. by any or every) person taken at random (any Tom, Dick, or Harry can walk in).

tome n. heavy book or volume. [Greek *temnō* cut]

tomfool n. foolish person.—attrib. adj. silly, foolish.

tomfoolery /tɒm'fuːlǝrɪ/ n. foolish behaviour.

Tommy /'tɒmɪ/ n. (pl. -ies) colloq. British private soldier. [Tommy Atkins, name used in specimens of completed official forms]

tommy-gun n. sub-machine-gun. [Thompson, name of its co-inventor]

tommy-rot n. slang nonsense. [from TOM]

tomography /tǝ'mɒgrǝfɪ/ n. method of radiography displaying details in a selected plane within the body. [Greek *tomē* a cutting]

tomorrow /tǝ'mɒrǝʊ/ —adv. **1** on the day after today. **2** at some future time. —n. **1** the day after today. **2** the near future. [from TO, MORROW]

tomtit n. tit, esp. a blue tit.

tom-tom /'tɒmtɒm/ n. **1** primitive drum beaten with the hands. **2** tall drum used in jazz bands etc. [Hindi *tamtam*, imitative]

ton /tʌn/ n. **1** (in full **long ton**) unit of weight equal to 2,240 lb (1016.05 kg). **2** (in full **short ton**) unit of weight equal to 2,000 lb (907.19 kg). **3** = METRIC TON. **4** (in full **displacement ton**) unit of measurement of a ship's weight or volume. **5** (usu. in pl.) colloq. large number or amount (tons of people). **6** slang a speed of 100 m.p.h. **b** £100. □ **weigh a ton** colloq. be very heavy. [originally the same word as TUN]

tonal /'tǝʊn(ǝ)l/ adj. of or relating to tone or tonality. □ **tonally** adv. [medieval Latin: related to TONE]

tonality /tǝ'nælɪtɪ/ n. (pl. -ies) **1** Mus. **a** relationship between the tones of a musical scale. **b** observance of the

tonic key as the basis of a composition. **2** colour scheme of a picture.

tone —n. **1** musical or vocal sound, esp. with reference to its pitch, quality, and strength. **2** (often in pl.) modulation of the voice expressing a particular feeling or mood (a cheerful tone). **3** manner of expression in writing or speaking. **4** Mus. **a** musical sound, esp. of a definite pitch and character. **b** interval of a major second, e.g. C–D. **5 a** general effect of colour or of light and shade in a picture. **b** tint or shade of a colour. **6** prevailing character of the morals and sentiments etc. in a group. **7** proper firmness of the body. **8** state of good or specified health. —v. (-ning) **1** give the desired tone to. **2** modify the tone of. **3** (often foll. by to) attune. **4** (foll. by with) (esp. of colour) be in harmony with. □ **tone down** make or become softer in tone. **tone up** make or become stronger in tone. □ **toneless** adj. **tonelessly** adv. **toner** n. [Greek tonos from teinō stretch]

tone-deaf adj. unable to perceive differences of musical pitch accurately.

tone poem n. orchestral composition with a descriptive or rhapsodic theme.

tongs n.pl. implement with two arms for grasping coal, sugar, etc. [Old English]

tongue /tʌŋ/ —n. **1** fleshy muscular organ in the mouth used in tasting, licking, and swallowing, and (in man) for speech. **2** tongue of an ox etc. as food. **3** faculty of or tendency in speech (a sharp tongue). **4** particular language (the German tongue). **5** thing like a tongue in shape or position, esp.: **a** a long low promontory. **b** a strip of leather etc. under the laces in a shoe. **c** the clapper of a bell. **d** the pin of a buckle. **e** a projecting strip on a board etc. fitting into the groove of another. —v. (-guing) use the tongue to articulate (notes) in playing a wind instrument. □ **find** (or **lose**) **one's tongue** be able (or unable) to express oneself after a shock etc. **hold one's tongue** see HOLD[1]. **with one's tongue in one's cheek** insincerely or ironically. [Old English]

tongue-and-groove —n. (often attrib.) planking etc. with a projecting strip down one side and a groove down the other. —v. **1** panel with tongue-and-groove. **2** (as **tongued and grooved** adj.) having a tongue-and-groove joint.

tongue-in-cheek —adj. ironic. —adv. insincerely or ironically.

tongue-tie n. speech impediment due to a malformation of the tongue.

tongue-tied adj. **1** too shy or embarrassed to speak. **2** having a tongue-tie.

tongue-twister n. sequence of words difficult to pronounce quickly and correctly.

tonic /'tonɪk/ —n. **1** invigorating medicine. **2** anything serving to invigorate. **3** = TONIC WATER. **4** Mus. keynote. —adj. invigorating. [Greek: related to TONE]

tonic sol-fa n. Mus. system of notation used esp. in teaching singing.

tonic water n. carbonated water flavoured with quinine.

tonight /tə'naɪt/ —adv. on the present or approaching evening or night. —n. the evening or night of the present day. [Old English]

tonnage /'tʌnɪdʒ/ n. **1** ship's internal cubic capacity or freight-carrying capacity. **2** charge per ton on freight or cargo. [related to TON]

tonne /tʌn/ n. = METRIC TON. [French: related to TON]

tonsil /'tɒns(ə)l/ n. either of two small organs, one on each side of the root of the tongue. [Latin]

tonsillectomy /,tɒnsɪ'lektəmɪ/ n. (pl. -ies) surgical removal of the tonsils.

tonsillitis /,tɒnsɪ'laɪtɪs/ n. inflammation of the tonsils.

tonsorial /tɒn'sɔːrɪəl/ adj. usu. joc. of a hairdresser or hairdressing. [Latin tondeo tons- shave]

tonsure /'tɒnʃə(r)/ —n. **1** shaving of the crown of the head or the entire head, esp. of a person entering the priesthood or a monastic order. **2** bare patch made in this way. —v. (-ring) give a tonsure to. [Latin: related to TONSORIAL]

ton-up attrib. adj. slang (of a motor cyclist) achieving a speed of 100 m.p.h., esp. habitually.

too adv. **1** to a greater extent than is desirable or permissible (too large). **2** colloq. very (not too sure). **3** in addition (I'm coming too). **4** moreover (food was bad, and expensive too). □ **none too** rather less than (feeling none too good). **too bad** see BAD. **too much** intolerable. **too much for 1** more than a match for. **2** beyond what is endurable by. **too right** see RIGHT. [stressed form of TO]

took past of TAKE.

tool —n. **1** implement used to carry out mechanical functions by hand or by machine. **2** thing used in an occupation or pursuit (tools of one's trade). **3** person merely used by another. **4** coarse slang penis. —v. **1** dress or shape on (leather). **3** (foll. by along, around, etc.) slang drive or ride, esp. in a casual or leisurely manner. [Old English]

toolmaker n. person who makes precision tools. □ **toolmaking** n.

tool-pusher n. worker directing the drilling on an oil rig.

toot —n. short sharp sound as made by a trumpet etc. —v. **1** sound (a trumpet etc.) with a short sharp sound. **2** give out such a sound. [probably imitative]

tooth n. (pl. teeth) **1** each of a set of hard bony enamel-coated structures in the jaws of most vertebrates, used for biting and chewing. **2** toothlike part or projection, e.g. the cog of a gearwheel, the point of a saw or comb, etc. **3** (often foll. by for) taste; appetite. **4** (in pl.) force, effectiveness. □ **armed to the teeth** completely and elaborately armed. **fight tooth and nail** fight very fiercely. **get one's teeth into** devote oneself seriously to. **in the teeth of 1** in spite of (opposition or difficulty etc.). **2** contrary to (instructions etc.). **3** directly against (the wind etc.). □ **toothed** adj. (also in comb.). **toothless** adj. [Old English]

toothache n. pain in a tooth or teeth.

toothbrush n. brush for cleaning the teeth.

tooth-comb n. = FINE-TOOTH COMB.

toothpaste n. paste for cleaning the teeth.

toothpick n. small sharp stick for removing food lodged between the teeth.

tooth powder n. powder for cleaning the teeth.

toothsome adj. (of food) delicious.

toothy adj. (-ier, -iest) having large, numerous, or prominent teeth.

tootle /'tuːt(ə)l/ v. (-ling) **1** toot gently or repeatedly. **2** (usu. foll. by along, around, etc.) colloq. move casually.

tootsy /'tutsɪ/ n. (pl. -ies) slang usu. joc. foot. [origin uncertain]

top[1] —n. **1** highest point or part. **2** a highest rank or place. **b** person occupying this. **c** upper end or head (top of the table). **3** upper surface or part of a thing. **4** stopper of a bottle, lid of a jar, etc. **5** garment for the upper part of the body. **6** utmost degree; height (at the top of his voice). **7** (in pl.) colloq. person or thing of the best quality. **8** (esp. in pl.) leaves etc. of a plant grown esp. for its root (turnip-tops). **9** Naut. platform round the head of the lower mast. **10** = TOP GEAR (climbed the hill in top). —attrib. adj. **1** highest in position. **2** highest in degree or importance. —v. (-pp-) **1** provide with a top, cap, etc. **2** be higher or better than; surpass; be at the top of (topped the list). **3** reach the top of (a hill etc.). **4** slang kill. **5** Golf hit (a ball) above the centre. □ **off the top of one's head** see HEAD. **on top** in a superior position; above. **on top of 1** fully in command of. **2** in close proximity to. **3** in addition to. **on top of**

the world colloq. exuberant. **over the top 1** over the parapet of a trench (and into battle). **2** beyond what is normally acceptable (*that joke was over the top*). **top off** (or **up**) put an end or the finishing touch to. **top up 1** complete (an amount or number). **2** fill up (a partly full container). **3** top up something for a person) (*may I top you up with sherry?*). □ **topmost** *adj.* [Old English]

top² *n.* toy spinning on a point when set in motion. [Old English]

topaz /ˈtəʊpæz/ *n.* transparent mineral, usu. yellow, used as a gem. [Greek *topazos*]

top brass *n. colloq.* highest-ranking officers.

topcoat *n.* **1** overcoat. **2** outer coat of paint etc.

top dog *n. colloq.* victor; master.

top drawer *n. colloq.* high social position or origin.

top-dress *v.* apply fertilizer on the top (of earth) instead of ploughing it in. □ **top-dressing** *n.*

tope *v.* (**-ping**) *archaic* or *literary* drink alcohol to excess, esp. habitually. □ **toper** *n.* [origin uncertain]

topee var. of TOPI.

top-flight *adj.* of the highest rank of achievement.

topgallant /topˈgælənt/ *n.* mast, sail, yard, or rigging immediately above the topmast and topsail.

top gear *n.* highest gear.

top hat *n.* tall silk hat.

top-heavy *adj.* disproportionately heavy at the top.

topi /ˈtəʊpi/ *n.* (also **topee**) (*pl.* **-s**) hat, esp. a sola topi. [Hindi. = hat]

topiary /ˈtəʊpɪərɪ/ *adj.* concerned with or formed by clipping shrubs, trees, etc. into ornamental shapes. —*n.* topiary art. [Greek *topos* place]

topic /ˈtɒpɪk/ *n.* subject of a discourse, conversation, or argument. [Greek *topos* place]

topical *adj.* dealing with the news, current affairs, etc. □ **topicality** /-ˈkælɪtɪ/ *n.* **topically** *adv.*

topknot *n.* knot, tuft, crest, or bow of ribbon, worn or growing on the head.

topless *adj.* **1** without a top. **2 a** (of clothes) having no upper part. **b** (of esp. a woman) bare-breasted. **c** (of a place) where women go topless; employing bare-breasted women.

top-level *adj.* of the highest level of importance, prestige, etc.

topmast *n.* mast next above the lower mast.

top-notch *adj. colloq.* first-rate.

topography /təˈpɒɡrəfɪ/ *n.* **1** detailed description, representation on a map, etc., of the features of a town, district, etc. **2** such features. □ **topographer** *n.* **topographical** /ˌtɒpəˈɡræfɪk(ə)l/ *adj.* [Greek *topos* place]

topology /təˈpɒlədʒɪ/ *n.* the study of geometrical properties unaffected by changes of shape or size. □ **topological** /ˌtɒpəˈlɒdʒɪk(ə)l/ *adj.* [Greek *topos* place]

topper *n. colloq.* = TOP HAT.

topping —*adj. archaic slang* excellent. —*n.* thing that tops another thing, esp. sauce on a dessert etc.

topple /ˈtɒp(ə)l/ *v.* (**-ling**) **1** (often foll. by *over*, *down*) (cause to) fall as if top-heavy. **2** overthrow. [from TOP¹]

topsail /ˈtɒpseɪl, -s(ə)l/ *n.* square sail next above the lowest; fore-and-aft sail on a gaff.

top secret *adj.* of the highest secrecy.

topside *n.* **1** outer side of a round of beef. **2** side of a ship above the water-line.

topsoil *n.* top layer of soil.

topspin *n.* spinning motion imparted to a ball in tennis etc. by hitting it forward and upward.

topsy-turvy /ˌtɒpsɪˈtɜːvɪ/ *adv. & adj.* **1** upside-down. **2** in utter confusion. [from TOP¹, obsolete *terve* overturn]

top-up *n.* addition; something that serves to top up.

toque /təʊk/ *n.* woman's small brimless hat. [French]

tor *n.* hill or rocky peak. [Old English]

torch *n.* **1** portable battery-powered electric lamp. **2** thing lit for illumination. **3** source of heat, illumination, or enlightenment. □ **carry a torch for** suffer from unrequited love for. [Latin: related to TORT¹]

torchlight *n.* light of a torch or torches. □ **torchlit** *adj.*

torch song *n.* popular song of unrequited love.

tore *past of* TEAR¹.

toreador /ˈtɒrɪədɔː(r)/ *n.* bullfighter, esp. on horseback. [Latin *taurus*]

torment —*n.* /ˈtɔːment/ **1** severe physical or mental suffering. **2** cause of this. —*v.* /tɔːˈment/ **1** subject to torment. **2** tease or worry excessively. □ **tormentor** /-ˈmentə(r)/ *n.* [Latin *tormentum*: related to TORT¹]

tormentil /ˈtɔːməntɪl/ *n.* low-growing plant with bright yellow flowers. [French from medieval Latin]

torn *past part. of* TEAR¹.

tornado /tɔːˈneɪdəʊ/ *n.* (*pl.* **-es**) violent storm of small extent with whirling winds. [Spanish *tronada* thunderstorm]

torpedo /tɔːˈpiːdəʊ/ —*n.* (*pl.* **-es**) **1** cigar-shaped self-propelled underwater missile that explodes on impact with a ship.

2 similar device dropped from an aircraft. —v. (**-es**, **-ed**) **1** destroy or attack with a torpedo. **2** destroy or damage (a policy, institution, plan, etc.). [Latin, = electric ray: related to TORPOR]

torpedo-boat n. small fast warship armed with torpedoes.

torpid /'tɔ:pɪd/ adj. **1** sluggish, inactive, apathetic. **2** numb. **3** (of a hibernating animal) dormant. □ **torpidity** /'pɪdɪtɪ/ n. [Latin: related to TORPOR]

torpor /'tɔ:pə(r)/ n. torpid condition. [Latin torpeo be sluggish]

torque /tɔ:k/ n. **1** Mech. twisting or rotating force, esp. in a machine. **2** hist. necklace of twisted metal, esp. of the ancient Gauls and Britons. [Latin: related to TORT]

torr /tɔ:(r)/ n. (pl. same) unit of pressure equal to 133.32 pascals ($^1/_{760}$ of one atmosphere). [Torricelli, name of a physicist]

torrent /'tɒrənt/ n. **1** rushing stream of liquid. **2** (in pl.) great downpour of rain. **3** (usu. foll. by of) violent or copious flow (torrent of abuse). □ **torrential** /tə'ren(ʃ)l/ adj. [French from Italian]

torrid /'tɒrɪd/ adj. **1 a** (of the weather) very hot and dry. **b** (of land etc.) parched by such weather. **2** passionate, intense. [Latin torreo tost- parch]

torrid zone n. the part of the earth between the Tropics of Cancer and Capricorn.

torsion /'tɔ:ʃ(ə)n/ n. twisting, esp. of one end of a body while the other is held fixed. □ **torsional** adj. [Latin: related to TORT]

torso /'tɔ:səʊ/ n. (pl. **-s**) **1** trunk of the human body. **2** statue of this. [Latin thyrsus rod]

tort n. Law breach of duty (other than under contract) leading to liability for damages. □ **tortious** /'tɔ:ʃəs/ adj. [Latin torqueo tort- twist]

tortilla /tɔ:'tiːjə/ n. thin flat orig. Mexican maize cake eaten hot. [Spanish diminutive of torta cake]

tortoise /'tɔ:təs/ n. slow-moving reptile with a horny domed shell. [medieval Latin tortuca]

tortoiseshell /'tɔ:təˌʃel/ n. **1** yellowish-brown mottled or clouded outer shell of some turtles. **2 a** = TORTOISE-SHELL CAT. **b** = TORTOISESHELL BUT-TERFLY. —adj. having the colouring or appearance of tortoiseshell.

tortoiseshell butterfly n. butterfly with wings mottled like tortoiseshell.

tortoiseshell cat n. domestic cat with markings resembling tortoiseshell.

tortuous /'tɔ:tʃʊəs/ adj. **1** full of twists and turns. **2** devious, circuitous. □

tortuously adv. [Latin: related to TORT]

■ **Usage** Tortuous should not be confused with torturous which means 'involving torture, excruciating'.

torture /'tɔ:tʃə(r)/ —n. **1** infliction of severe bodily pain, esp. as a punishment or means of persuasion. **2** severe physical or mental suffering. —v. (**-ring**) subject to torture. □ **torturer** n. **torturous** adj. [Latin tortura twisting: related to TORT]

Tory /'tɔ:rɪ/ —n. (pl. **-ies**) **1** colloq. = CONSERVATIVE n. **2**. **2** hist. member of the party that gave rise to the Conservative party (opp. WHIG). —adj. colloq. = CONSERVATIVE adj. **3**. □ **Toryism** n. [originally = Irish outlaw]

tosa /'tausa/ n. dog of a breed of mastiff, orig. kept for dog-fighting. [Japanese]

tosh n. colloq. rubbish, nonsense. [origin unknown]

toss —v. **1** throw up (a ball etc.), esp. with the hand. **2** roll about, throw, or be thrown, restlessly or from side to side. **3** (usu. foll. by to, away, aside, out, etc.) throw (a thing) lightly or carelessly. **4 a** throw (a coin) into the air to decide a choice etc. by the side on which it lands. **b** (also absol.; often foll. by for) settle a question or dispute with (a person) in this way. **5** (of a bull etc.) throw (a person etc.) up with the horns. **6** coat (food) with dressing etc. by shaking it. —n. **1** act of tossing (a coin, the head, etc.). **2** fall, esp. from a horse. □ **toss one's head** throw it back esp. in anger, impatience, etc. **toss off 1** drink off at a draught. **2** dispatch (work) rapidly or without effort. **3** coarse slang masturbate. **toss up** toss a coin. [origin unknown]

toss-up n. **1** doubtful matter. **2** tossing of a coin.

tot¹ n. **1** small child. **2** dram of liquor. [originally dial.]

tot² v. (**-tt-**) **1** (usu. foll. by up) add (figures etc.). **2** (foll. by up) (of items) mount up. □ **tot up to** amount to. [abbreviation of TOTAL or of Latin totum the whole]

total /'təʊt(ə)l/ —adj. **1** complete, comprising the whole (total number of votes). **2** absolute, unqualified (in total ignorance). —n. total number or amount. —v. (**-ll-**; US **-l-**) **1 a** amount in number to. **b** find the total of **2** (foll. by to, up to) amount to. [medieval Latin totus entire]

totalitarian /ˌtəʊtælɪ'teərɪən/ adj. of a one-party form of government requiring complete subservience to the State. □ **totalitarianism** n.

totality /təʊˈtælɪtɪ/ n. **1** complete amount. **2** time during which an eclipse is total.

totalizator /ˈtəʊtəlaɪˌzeɪtə(r)/ n. (also **totalisator**) **1** device showing the number and amount of bets staked on a race, to facilitate the division of the total among those backing the winner. **2** system of betting based on this.

totalize /ˈtəʊtəˌlaɪz/ v. (also **-ise**) (**-zing** or **-sing**) collect into a total; find the total of.

totally adv. completely.

tote¹ n. slang totalizator. [abbreviation]

tote² v. (**-ting**) esp. US colloq. carry, convey (toting a gun). [originally US, probably of dial. origin]

tote bag n. woman's large bag for shopping etc.

totem /ˈtəʊtəm/ n. **1** natural object, esp. an animal, adopted esp. by N. American Indians as an emblem of a clan or individual. **2** image of this. □ **totemic** /-ˈtemɪk/ adj. [Algonquian]

totem-pole n. pole on which totems are carved or hung.

t'other /ˈtʌðə(r)/ adj. & pron. dial. or joc. the other. [the other 'that other']

totter —v. **1** stand or walk unsteadily or feebly. **2 a** (of a building etc.) shake as if about to collapse. **b** (of a system etc.) be about to fall. —n. (of government etc.) shaky movement or gait. □ **tottery** adj. [Dutch]

totting-up n. **1** adding of separate items. **2** adding up of convictions for driving offences, possibly resulting in disqualification.

toucan /ˈtuːkən/ n. tropical American fruit-eating bird with an immense beak. [Tupi]

touch /tʌtʃ/ —v. **1** come into or be in physical contact with (a thing, each other, etc.). **2** (often foll. by with) bring the hand etc. into contact with. **3** bring (two things) into mutual contact. **4** rouse tender or painful feelings in. **5** (usu. with neg.) **a** disturb, harm, or affect. **b** have any dealings with. **c** consume, use (I don't touch alcohol). **7** concern. **8** a reach as far as, esp. momentarily. **b** (usu. with neg.) approach in excellence etc. (can't touch him for style). **9** modify (pity touched with fear). **10** (as **touched** adj.) colloq. slightly mad. **11** (usu. foll. by for) slang ask for and get money etc. from (a person) (touched him for £5). —n. **1** act of touching (felt a touch on my arm). **2** faculty of perception through physical contact, esp. with the fingers. **3 a** small amount; slight trace. **b** (prec. by a) slightly (a touch too salty). **4 a** manner of playing keys or strings. **b** response of

the keys or strings. **c** style of workmanship, writing, etc. **5** distinguishing manner or detail (a professional touch). **6** special skill (have lost my touch). **7** (esp. in pl.) light stroke with a pencil etc. **8** slang a act of getting money etc. from a person by asking. **b** = sort **touch**. **9** Football part of the field outside the side limits. □ **in touch** (often foll. by with) **1** in communication. **2** aware. **lose touch** (often foll. by with) **1** cease to be informed. **2** cease to be in contact. **out of touch** (often foll. by with) **1** not in correspondence. **2** not up to date. **3** lacking in awareness. **touch at** (of a ship) call at (a port etc.). **touch bottom 1** reach the bottom of water with one's feet. **2** be at the lowest or worst point. **touch down** (of an aircraft) make contact with the ground in landing. **touch off 1** explode by touching a match etc. **2** initiate (a process) suddenly. **touch on** (or **upon**) **1** refer to or mention briefly or casually. **2** verge on. **touch up 1** give finishing touches to or retouch. **2** slang sexually molest. **touch wood** touch something wooden to avert ill luck. [French tochier]

touch-and-go adj. critical, risky.

touchdown n. act of touching down by an aircraft.

touché /ˈtuːʃeɪ/ int. **1** acknowledgement of a justified accusation or retort. **2** acknowledgement of a hit by a fencing-opponent. [French, = touched]

touching —adj. moving; pathetic. —prep. literary concerning. □ **touchingly** adv.

touch-line n. (in various sports) either of the lines marking the side boundaries of the pitch.

touch-paper n. paper impregnated with nitre, for igniting etc.

touchstone n. **1** dark schist or jasper used for testing alloys by marking it with them. **2** criterion.

touch-type v. type without looking at the keys. □ **touch-typist** n.

touchwood n. readily inflammable wood etc., esp. when made soft by fungi.

touchy adj. (**-ier, -iest**) apt to take offence; over-sensitive. □ **touchily** adv. **touchiness** n.

tough /tʌf/ —adj. **1** hard to break, cut, tear, or chew. **2** able to endure hardship; hardy. **3** unyielding, stubborn, difficult (it was a tough job). **4** colloq. a acting sternly; hard (get tough with). **b** (of circumstances) luck, etc.; severe, hard. **5** colloq. criminal or violent. —n. tough person, esp. a ruffian. □ **toughen** v. **toughness** n. [Old English]

toupee /ˈtuːpeɪ/ n. hairpiece to cover a bald spot. [French]

tour /tʊə(r)/ —*n.* **1 a** a journey from place to place as a holiday; sightseeing excursion. **b** a walk round; inspection (*made a tour of the garden*). **2** spell of duty on military or diplomatic service. **3** series of performances, matches, etc., at different places. —*v.* **1** (usu. foll. by *through*) make a tour. **2** make a tour of (a country etc.). □ **on tour** (esp. of a team, theatre company, etc.) touring. [Latin: related to TURN]

tour de force /ˌtʊə də ˈfɔːs/ *n.* (*pl.* **tours de force**) outstanding feat or performance. [French]

tourer *n.* car or caravan for touring in.

tourism *n.* commercial organization and operation of holidays.

tourist *n.* **1** holiday-maker, esp. abroad (often *attrib.*: *tourist season*). **2** member of a touring sports team.

tourist class *n.* lowest class of passenger accommodation in a ship, aircraft, etc.

touristy *adj.* usu. *derog.* appealing to or visited by many tourists.

tourmaline /ˈtʊəməˌliːn/ *n.* mineral of various colours used as a gemstone. [French from Sinhalese]

tournament /ˈtʊənəmənt/ *n.* **1** large contest of many rounds (*chess tournament*). **2** display of military exercises etc. (*Royal Tournament*). **3** *hist.* pageant with jousting. [French: related to TOURNEY]

tournedos /ˈtʊənəˌdəʊ/ *n.* (*pl.* /-ˌdəʊz/) small round thick cut from a fillet of beef. [French]

tourney /ˈtʊənɪ/ —*n.* (*pl.* **-s**) tournament. —*v.* (**-eys, -eyed**) take part in a tournament. [French: related to TURN]

tourniquet /ˈtʊənɪˌkeɪ/ *n.* device for stopping the flow of blood through an artery by constriction. [French]

tour operator *n.* travel agent specializing in package holidays.

tousle /ˈtaʊz(ə)l/ *v.* (**-ling**) **1** make (esp. the hair) untidy. **2** handle roughly. [dial. *touse*]

tout —*v.* **1** (usu. foll. by *for*) solicit custom persistently; pester customers. **2** solicit the custom of (a person) or for (a thing), esp. sell (tickets) at a price higher than the official one. **3** spy out the movements and condition of racehorses in training. —*n.* person who touts, esp. tickets. [Old English, = peep]

tow¹ /təʊ/ —*v.* pull (a boat, vehicle, etc.) along by a rope etc. —*n.* towing or being towed. □ **have in** (or **on**) **tow 1** be towing. **2** be accompanied by and often in charge of (a person). **on tow** being towed. [Old English]

tow² *n.* coarse part of flax or hemp prepared for spinning. [Low German *touw*]

toward /təˈwɔːd/ *prep.* = TOWARDS.

towards /təˈwɔːdz/ *prep.* **1** in the direction of (*set out towards town*). **2** as regards; in relation to (*attitude towards death*). **3** as a contribution to; for (*put it towards her holiday*). **4** near (*towards the end of our journey*). [Old English] future: related to TO, -WARD]

tow-bar *n.* bar for towing esp. a caravan.

towel /ˈtaʊəl/ —*n.* absorbent cloth or paper etc. used for drying after washing. —*v.* (**-ll-**; *US* **-l-**) (often *refl.*) wipe or dry with a towel. [French *toail(l)e* from Germanic]

towelling *n.* thick soft absorbent cloth, used esp. for towels.

tower —*n.* **1** tall structure, often part of a church, castle, etc. **2** fortress etc. with a tower. **3** tall structure housing machinery etc. (*cooling tower*; *control tower*). —*v.* **1** (usu. foll. by *above*, *up*) reach or be high or above; be superior. **2** (as **towering** *adj.*) **a** high, lofty (*towering intellect*). **b** violent (*towering rage*). [Greek *turris*]

tower block *n.* tall building containing offices or flats.

tower of strength *n.* person who gives strong emotional support.

tow-headed *adj.* having very light or unkempt hair.

town *n.* **1 a** densely populated built-up defined area, between a city and a village in size. **b** densely populated area, esp. as opposed to the country. **2 a** London or the chief city or town in an area (*went up to town*). **b** central business area in a neighbourhood. □ **go to town** *colloq.* do something with great energy or enthusiasm. **on the town** *colloq.* enjoying night-life in a town. [Old English]

town clerk *n. US & hist.* official in charge of the records etc. of a town.

town crier *n.* = CRIER 2.

townee var. of TOWNIE.

town gas *n.* manufactured gas for domestic and commercial use.

town hall *n.* headquarters of local government, with public meeting rooms etc.

town house *n.* **1** town residence, esp. of a person with a house in the country. **2** terrace house. **3** house in a planned group in a town.

townie /ˈtaʊnɪ/ *n.* (also **townee** /-ˈniː/) *derog.* town inhabitant ignorant of country life.

town planning n. planning of the construction and growth of towns. □ **town planner** n.

townscape n. 1 visual appearance of a town or towns. 2 picture of a town.

townsfolk n. inhabitants of a town or towns.

township n. 1 S.Afr. urban area set aside for Black occupation. 2 US & Can. a division of a county, a district six miles square. 3 hist. small town or village forming part of a large parish. 4 Austral. & NZ small town.

townsman n. (fem. **townswoman**) inhabitant of a town.

townspeople n.pl. people of a town.

tow-path n. path by a river or canal, orig. used for towing a boat by horse.

toxaemia /tɒkˈsiːmɪə/ n. (US **toxemia**) 1 blood-poisoning. 2 increased blood pressure in pregnancy. [related to TOXIC, Greek haima blood]

toxic /ˈtɒksɪk/ adj. 1 poisonous. 2 of poison. □ **toxicity** /-ˈsɪstɪ/ n. [Greek toxikon poison for arrows]

toxicology /ˌtɒksɪˈkɒlədʒɪ/ n. the study of poisons. □ **toxicological** /-kəˈlɒdʒɪk(ə)l/ adj. **toxicologist** n.

toxin /ˈtɒksɪn/ n. poison produced by a living organism.

toxocara /ˌtɒksəˈkɑːrə/ n. parasitic worm in dogs and cats.

toxocariasis /ˌtɒksəkəˈraɪəsɪs/ n. disease resulting from infection by the toxocara.

toy —n. 1 plaything. 2 thing regarded as providing amusement. 3 (usu. attrib.) diminutive breed of dog etc. —v. (usu. foll. by with) 1 trifle, amuse oneself, flirt. 2 move a thing idly. [origin unknown]

toy boy n. colloq. woman's much younger boyfriend.

toyshop n. shop selling toys.

trace[1] —v. (**-cing**) 1 a observe or find vestiges or signs of by investigation. **b** (often foll. by along, through, to, etc.) follow or mark the track or position of. **c** (often foll. by back) follow to its origins. 2 copy (a drawing etc.) by drawing over its lines on superimposed translucent paper. 3 (often foll. by out) mark out, delineate, sketch, or write, (esp. laboriously). 4 make one's way along (a path etc.). —n. 1 a indication of something having existed; vestige. **b** very small quantity. 2 track or footprint. 3 track left by the moving pen of an instrument etc. □ **traceable** adj. [Latin traho draw]

trace[2] n. each of the two side-straps, chains, or ropes by which a horse draws a vehicle. □ **kick over the traces**

become insubordinate or reckless. [French trais, pl. of ˈtrai]

trace element n. chemical element required only in minute amounts by living organisms for normal growth.

tracer n. 1 bullet etc. that is visible in flight because of flames etc. emitted. 2 artificial radioactive isotope which can be followed through the body by the radiation it produces.

tracery n. (pl. -ies) 1 ornamental stone openwork, esp. in the upper part of a Gothic window. 2 fine decorative pattern.

trachea /trəˈkɪə/ n. (pl. **-cheae** /ˈkɪiː/) windpipe. [Latin from Greek]

tracheotomy /ˌtrækɪˈɒtəmɪ/ n. (pl. -ies) incision of the trachea to relieve an obstruction.

tracing n. 1 traced copy of a drawing etc. 2 act of tracing.

tracing-paper n. translucent paper for making tracings.

track —n. 1 a mark(s) left by a person, animal, vehicle, etc. **b** (in pl.) such marks, esp. footprints. 2 rough path, esp. one beaten by use. 3 continuous railway line. 4 a racecourse; circuit. **b** prepared course for runners etc. 5 a groove on a gramophone record. **b** section of a record, CD or magnetic tape containing one song etc. **c** lengthwise strip of magnetic tape containing a single sequence of signals. 6 line of travel (track of the comet). 7 band round the wheels of a tank etc. 8 line of thought or action. —v. 1 follow the track of. 2 trace (a course, development, etc. by vestiges. 3 (often foll by back, in, etc.) (of a film or television camera) move in relation to the subject being filmed. □ **in one's tracks** colloq. where one stands, instantly (stopped him in his tracks). **keep** (or **lose**) **track of** follow (or fail to follow) the course of. **make tracks** colloq. depart. **make tracks for** colloq. go in pursuit of or towards. **off the track** away from the subject. **track down** reach or capture by tracking.

tracker n. [French traci]

tracker dog n. police dog tracking by scent.

track events n.pl. running-races as opposed to jumping etc.

track record n. person's past performance.

track shoe n. runner's spiked shoe.

track suit n. loose warm suit worn for exercising etc.

tract[1] n. 1 stretch or extent of territory, esp. large. 2 bodily organ or system (digestive tract). [Latin traho tract- pull]

tract² n. pamphlet, esp. propagandist. [apparently Latin *tractatus* from *tracto* handle]

tractable adj. (of a person or material) easily handled; manageable. □ **tractability** /ˈbılıtı/ n. [Latin *tracto* handle]

traction /ˈtrak(ə)n/ n. **1** act of hauling or pulling a thing over a surface. **2** sustained therapeutic pulling on a limb etc. with pulleys, weights, etc. [French or medieval Latin: related to TRACT']

traction-engine n. steam or diesel engine for drawing heavy loads on roads, fields, etc.

tractor /ˈtraktə(r)/ n. **1** vehicle used for pulling farm machinery etc. **2** traction-engine. [related to TRACTION]

trad colloq. —n. traditional jazz. —adj. traditional. [abbreviation]

trade —n. **1 a** buying and selling. **b** this between nations etc. **c** business conducted for profit (esp. as distinct from a profession). **2** business of a specified nature or time (*Christmas trade; tourist trade*). **3** skilled craft practised professionally. **3** (usu. prec. by *the*) people engaged in a specific trade (*the trade will never agree*). **4** US transaction, esp. a swap. **5** (usu. in *pl.*) trade wind. —v. (**-ding**) **1** (often foll. by *in, with*) engage in trade; buy and sell. **2 a** exchange in commerce. **b** exchange (insults, blows, etc.). **c** US swap. **3** (usu. foll. by *with, for*) have a transaction with a person for a thing. □ **trade in** (often foll. by *for*) exchange (esp. a used car) in part payment for another. **trade off** exchange, esp. as a compromise. **take advantage of.** □ **tradable** adj. **tradeable** adj. [Low German, = track: related to TREAD]

trade-in n. thing given in part exchange for another.

trade mark n. **1** device or name secured by law or custom as representing a company, product, etc. **2** distinctive characteristic etc.

trade name n. **1** name by which a thing is called in a trade. **2** name given to a product. **3** name under which a business trades.

trade-off n. balance, compromise.

trade price n. price charged to the retailer.

trader n. **1** person engaged in trade. **2** merchant ship.

tradescantia /ˌtradɪˈskantɪə/ n. (usu. trailing) plant with large blue, white, or pink flowers. [*Tradescant*, name of a naturalist]

trade secret n. **1** secret device or technique used esp. in a trade. **2** joc. any secret.

tradesman n. (fem. **tradeswoman**) person engaged in trade, esp. a shopkeeper.

tradespeople n.pl. people engaged in trade.

Trades Union Congress n. official representative body of British trade unions.

trade union n. (also **trades union**) organized association of workers in a trade, profession, etc., formed to protect and further their rights and interests. □ **trade-unionism** n. **trade-unionist** n.

trade wind n. wind blowing continually towards the equator and deflected westward.

trading n. act of engaging in trade.

trading estate n. specially-designed industrial and commercial area.

trading post n. store etc. in a remote or unsettled region.

trading-stamp n. stamp given to customers by some shops and exchangeable in large numbers for goods or cash.

tradition /trəˈdɪʃ(ə)n/ n. **1 a** custom, opinion, or belief handed down to posterity. **b** this process of handing down. **2** artistic, literary, etc. principles based on experience and practice; any one of these. [Latin *trado -dit-* hand on, betray]

traditional adj. **1** of, based on, or obtained by tradition. **2** (of jazz) in the style of the early 20th c. □ **traditionally** adv.

traditionalism n. respect or support for tradition. □ **traditionalist** n. & adj.

traduce /trəˈdjuːs/ v. (**-cing**) speak ill of; misrepresent. □ **traducement** n. **traducer** n. [Latin, = disgrace]

traffic /ˈtrafɪk/ —n. **1** vehicles moving on a public highway or in the air or at sea. **2** (usu. foll. by *in*) trade, esp. illegal (*drugs traffic*). **3** coming and going of people or goods by road, rail, air, sea, etc. **4** dealings between people etc. (*had no traffic with them*). **5** messages etc. transmitted through a communications system; volume of this. —v. (**-ck-**) **1** (usu. foll. by *in*) deal in something, esp. illegally. **2** deal in; barter. □ **trafficker** n. [French from Italian]

traffic island n. raised area in a road to divide traffic streams and for pedestrians to use in crossing.

traffic jam n. traffic at a standstill because of roadworks, an accident, etc.

traffic-light n. (also **traffic-lights** n.pl.) signal controlling road traffic by coloured lights.

traffic warden n. official employed to help control road traffic and esp. parking.

tragedian /trəˈdʒiːdɪən/ n. **1** writer of tragedies. **2** (fem. **tragedienne** /-drɛn/)

actor in tragedy. [French: related to TRAGEDY]

tragedy /ˈtrædʒɪdɪ/ n. (pl. **-ies**) **1** serious play dealing with tragic events and ending unhappily, esp. with the downfall of the protagonist. **b** such plays as a genre. [Greek tragōidia]

tragic /ˈtrædʒɪk/ adj. **1** disastrous; greatly distressing; very sad. **2** of tragedy. □ **tragically** adv.

tragicomedy /trædʒɪˈkɒmɪdɪ/ n. (pl. **-ies**) play or situation with a mixture of comedy and tragedy. □ **tragicomic** adj.

trail –n. **1** track or scent left by a moving thing, person, etc. **2** beaten path, esp. through a wild region. **3** long line of people or things following behind something. **4** part dragging behind a thing or person. –v. **1** draw or be drawn along behind, esp. on the ground. **2** (often foll. by behind) walk or move wearily. **3** follow the trail of; pursue. **4** be losing in a contest (trailing by three points). **5** (usu. foll. by away, off) peter out; tail off. **6 a** (of a plant etc.) grow or hang over a wall, along the ground, etc. **b** hang loosely. **7** (often refl.) drag (oneself, one's limbs, etc.) along wearily etc. [French or Low German]

trail-blazer n. **1** person who marks a new track through wild country. **2** pioneer. □ **trail-blazing** n.

trailer n. **1** set of brief extracts from a film etc. used to advertise it in advance. **2** vehicle towed by another, esp. **a** the rear section of an articulated lorry. **b** an open cart. **c** a platform for transporting a boat etc. **d** US a caravan.

trailing edge n. rear edge of an aircraft's wing etc.

train –v. **1** (often foll. by to + infin.) teach (a person, animal, oneself, etc.) a specified skill, esp. by practice. **b** undergo this process (trained as a teacher). **2** bring or come to physical efficiency by exercise, diet, etc. **3** (often foll. by along, up) guide the growth of (a plant). **4** (usu. as **trained** adj.) make (the mind, etc.) discerning through practice etc. **5** (often foll. by on) point or aim (a gun, camera, etc.) at an object etc. –n. **1** series of railway carriages or trucks drawn by an engine. **2** thing dragged along behind or forming the back part of a dress, robe, etc. **3** succession or series of people, things, events, etc. (train of thought). **4** body of followers; retinue. □ **in train** properly arranged or directed. □ **trainee** /-ˈniː/ n. [Latin traho draw]

train-bearer n. person holding up the train of a robe etc.

trainer n. **1** person who trains horses, athletes, footballers, etc. **2** aircraft or simulator used to train pilots. **3** soft running shoe.

training n. process of teaching or learning a skill etc.

train-spotter n. person who collects locomotive numbers as a hobby. □ **train-spotting** n.

traipse colloq. –v. (**-sing**) tramp or trudge wearily. –n. tedious journey on foot. [origin unknown]

trait /treɪ, treɪt/ n. characteristic. [Latin tractus: related to TRACT[1]]

traitor /ˈtreɪtə(r)/ n. (fem. **traitress**) person who is treacherous or disloyal, esp. to his or her country. □ **traitorous** adj. [Latin traditor: related to TRADITION]

trajectory /trəˈdʒektərɪ/ n. (pl. **-ies**) path of an object moving under given forces. [Latin traicio -ject- throw across]

tram n. **1** (also **tramcar**) electrically-powered passenger road vehicle running on rails. **2** four-wheeled vehicle used in coalmines. [Low German and Dutch trame beam]

tramlines n.pl. **1** rails for a tramcar. **2** colloq. pair of long parallel lines at the sides of a tennis or badminton court.

trammel /ˈtræm(ə)l/ –n. **1** (usu. in pl.) impediment; hindrance (trammels of domesticity). **2** triple drag-net for fishing. –v. (**-ll-**; US **-l-**) hamper. [medieval Latin tremaculum]

tramp –v. **1 a** walk heavily and firmly. **b** go on foot, esp. a distance. **2 a** cross on foot, esp. wearily or reluctantly. **b** cover (a distance) in this way. **3** (often foll. by down) tread on; trample; stamp on. **4** live as a tramp. –n. **1** itinerant vagrant or beggar. **2** sound of a person, or esp. people, walking, marching, etc. **3** long walk. **4** slang derog. promiscuous woman. [Germanic]

trample /ˈtræmp(ə)l/ v. (**-ling**) **1** tread under foot. **2** press down or crush in this way. □ **trample on 1** tread heavily on. **2** treat roughly or with contempt. [from TRAMP]

trampoline /ˈtræmpəliːn/ –n. strong fabric sheet connected by springs to a horizontal frame, used for gymnastic jumping. –v. (**-ning**) use a trampoline. [Italian trampolino]

tramway n. rails for a tram.

trance /trɑːns/ n. **1 a** sleeplike state without response to stimuli. **b** hypnotic or cataleptic state. **2** such a state as entered into by a medium. **3** rapture, ecstasy. [Latin transeo pass over]

tranny /ˈtranɪ/ n. (pl. **-ies**, colloq. transistor radio. [abbreviation]

tranquil /ˈtræŋkwɪl/ *adj.* calm, serene, undisturbed. □ **tranquillity** /-ˈkwɪlɪtɪ/ *n.* **tranquilly** *adv.* [Latin]

tranquillize *v.* (*US* **tranquilize**, **-ise**) (**-zing** or **-sing**) make tranquil, esp. by a drug etc.

tranquillizer *n.* (*US* **tranquilizer**, **-iser**) drug used to diminish anxiety.

trans- *prefix* **1** across, beyond. **2** on or to the other side of. **3** through. [Latin]

transact /trænˈzækt/ *v.* perform or carry through (business). [Latin: related to ACT]

transaction /trænˈzækʃ(ə)n/ *n.* **1 a** piece of esp. commercial business done. **b** transacting of business etc. **2** (in *pl.*) published reports of discussions, papers read, etc., at the meetings of a learned society.

transalpine /trænzˈælpaɪn/ *adj.* on the north side of the Alps. [Latin]

transatlantic /ˌtrænzətˈlæntɪk/ *adj.* **1** beyond the Atlantic, esp.: **a** American. **b** *US* European. **2** crossing the Atlantic.

transceiver /trænˈsiːvə(r)/ *n.* combined radio transmitter and receiver.

transcend /trænˈsend/ *v.* **1** be beyond the range or grasp of (human experience, reason, belief, etc.). **2** excel; surpass. [Latin *scando* climb]

transcendent *adj.* **1** excelling, surpassing. **2** transcending human experience. **3** (esp. of God) existing apart from, not subject to the limitations of the material universe. □ **transcendence** *n.* **transcendency** *n.*

transcendental /ˌtrænsenˈdent(ə)l/ *adj.* **1** *Philos.* a priori, not based on experience; intuitively accepted; innate in the mind. **2 a** visionary, abstract. **b** vague, obscure. □ **transcendentally** *adv.*

transcendentalism *n.* transcendental philosophy. □ **transcendentalist** *n.*

Transcendental Meditation *n.* method of detaching oneself from problems, anxiety, etc., by silent meditation and repetition of a mantra.

transcontinental /ˌtrænzkɒntɪˈnent(ə)l/ *adj.* extending across a continent.

transcribe /trænˈskraɪb/ *v.* (**-bing**) **1** copy out. **2** write out (shorthand, notes, etc.) in full. **3** record for subsequent reproduction. **4** arrange (music) for a different instrument etc. □ **transcriber** *n.* **transcription** /-ˈskrɪpʃ(ə)n/ *n.* [Latin *transcribo -script-*]

transcript /ˈtrænskrɪpt/ *n.* written copy.

transducer /trænzˈdjuːsə(r)/ *n.* device for converting a non-electrical signal into an electrical one, e.g. pressure into voltage. [Latin: related to DUCT]

transept /ˈtrænsept/ *n.* **1** part of a cross-shaped church at right angles to the nave. **2** either arm of this. [Latin: related to SEPTUM]

transexual var. of TRANSSEXUAL.

transfer *—v.* /trænsˈfɜː(r)/ (**-rr-**) **1** (often foll. by *to*) **a** convey, remove, or hand over (a thing etc.). **b** make over the possession (of property, a ticket, rights, etc.) to a person. **2** change or move to another group, club, department, etc. **3** change from one station, route, etc., to another on a journey. **4** convey (a design) from one surface to another. **5** change (meaning) by extension or metaphor. *—n.* /ˈtrænsfɜː(r)/ **1** transferring or being transferred. **2** design etc. conveyed or to be conveyed from one surface to another. **3** football player etc. who is transferred. **4** document effecting conveyance of property, a right, etc. □ **transferable** /-ˈfɜːrəb(ə)l/ *adj.* [Latin *fero lat-* bear]

transference /ˈtrænsfərəns/ *n.* **1** transferring or being transferred. **2** *Psychol.* redirection of childhood emotions to a new object, esp. to a psychoanalyst.

transfiguration /ˌtrænsfɪgəˈreɪʃ(ə)n/ *n.* **1** change of form or appearance. **2 a** Christ's appearance in radiant glory to three of his disciples (Matt. 17:2, Mark 9:2–3). **b** (**Transfiguration**) festival of Christ's Transfiguration, 6 August.

transfigure /trænsˈfɪgə(r)/ *v.* (**-ring**) change in form or appearance, esp. so as to elevate or idealize. [Latin]

transfix /trænsˈfɪks/ *v.* **1** paralyse with horror or astonishment. **2** pierce with a sharp implement or weapon. [Latin: related to FIX]

transform /trænsˈfɔːm/ *v.* **1** make a thorough or dramatic change in the form, appearance, character, etc., of. **2** change the voltage etc. of (an alternating current). □ **transformation** /-ˈmeɪʃ(ə)n/ *n.* [Latin]

transformer *n.* apparatus for reducing or increasing the voltage of an alternating current.

transfuse /trænsˈfjuːz/ *v.* (**-sing**) **1 a** transfer (blood) from one person or animal to another. **b** inject (liquid) into a blood-vessel to replace lost fluid. **2** permeate. □ **transfusion** *n.* [Latin: related to FOUND[3]]

transgress /trænzˈgres/ *v.* (also *absol.*) go beyond the bounds or limits set by (a

commandment, law, etc.); sin. □ **transgression** n. **transgressor** n. [Latin *transgredior -gress-*]

transient /'trænzɪənt/ adj. of short duration; passing. □ **transience** n. [Latin: related to TRANSIRE]

transistor /træn'zɪstə(r)/ n. 1 semiconductor device with three connections, capable of amplification in addition to rectification. 2 (in full **transistor radio**) portable radio with transistors. [from TRANSFER, RESISTOR]

transistorize v. (also **-ise**) (**-zing** or **-sing**) equip with transistors (rather than valves).

transit /'trænzɪt/ n. 1 going, conveying, or being conveyed, esp. over a distance. 2 passage or route. 3 apparent passage of a celestial body across the meridian of a place, or across the sun or a planet. □ **in transit** while going or being conveyed. [Latin: related to TRANCE]

transit camp n. camp for the temporary accommodation of soldiers, refugees, etc.

transition /træn'zɪʃ(ə)n/ n. 1 passing or change from one place, state, condition, etc., to another. 2 *Art* change from one style to another, esp. *Archit.* from Norman to Early English. □ **transitional** adj. **transitionally** adv. [Latin: related to TRANSIRE]

transitive /'trænsɪtɪv/ adj. (of a verb) taking a direct object (whether expressed or implied), e.g. *saw* in *saw the donkey*, *saw that she was ill*. [Latin: related to TRANSIRE]

transitory /'trænsɪtərɪ/ adj. not permanent; brief, transient. □ **transitorily** adv. **transitoriness** n. [Latin: related to TRANSIRE]

translate /træn'sleɪt/ v. (**-ting**) 1 (also *absol.*) (often foll. by *into*) express the sense of (a word, text, etc.) in another language or in another, esp. simpler, form. 2 be translatable, bear translation (*does not translate well*). 3 interpret (*translated his silence as dissent*). 4 move or change, esp. from one person, place, or condition, to another. □ **translatable** adj. **translation** n. **translator** n. [Latin: related to TRANSFER]

transliterate /trænz'lɪtəreɪt/ v. (**-ting**) represent (a word etc.) in the closest corresponding letters of a different script. □ **transliteration** /-'reɪʃ(ə)n/ n. [Latin *littera* letter]

translucent /trænz'luːs(ə)nt/ adj. allowing light to pass through; semitransparent. □ **translucence** n. **translucency** n. [Latin *luceo* shine]

transmigrate /ˌtrænzmaɪ'greɪt/ v. (**-ting**) 1 (of the soul) pass into a different body. 2 migrate. □ **transmigration** n. [Latin]

transmission /trænz'mɪʃ(ə)n/ n. 1 transmitting or being transmitted. 2 broadcast programme. 3 mechanism transmitting power from the engine to the axle in a vehicle.

transmit /trænz'mɪt/ v. (**-tt-**) 1 a pass or hand on; transfer (*transmitted the message; how diseases are transmitted*). b communicate (ideas, emotions, etc.). 2 a allow (heat, light, electricity, etc.) to pass through. b be a medium for (ideas, emotions, etc.) (*his message transmits hope*). 3 broadcast (a radio or television programme). □ **transmissible** adj. **transmittable** adj.

transmitter n. 1 person or thing that transmits. 2 equipment used to transmit radio or other electronic signals. [Latin *mitto miss-* send]

transmogrify /trænz'mɒgrɪfaɪ/ v. (**-ies, -ied**) *joc.* transform, esp. in a magical or surprising manner. □ **transmogrification** /-fɪ'keɪʃ(ə)n/ n. [origin unknown]

transmute /trænz'mjuːt/ v. (**-ting**) 1 change the form, nature, or substance of. 2 *hist.* change (base metals) into gold. □ **transmutation** /-'teɪʃ(ə)n/ n. [Latin *muto* change]

transoceanic /ˌtrænzəʊʃɪ'ænɪk/ adj. 1 beyond the ocean. 2 crossing the ocean.

transom /'trænsəm/ n. 1 horizontal bar of wood or stone across a window or the top of a door. 2 *US* = TRANSOM WINDOW. [French *traversin*: related to TRAVERSE]

transom window n. window above a transom.

transparency /træns'pærənsɪ/ n. (pl. **-ies**) 1 being transparent. 2 picture, esp. a photograph, to be viewed by light passing through it. [medieval Latin: related to TRANSPARENT]

transparent /træns'pærənt/ adj. 1 allowing light to pass through so that bodies can be distinctly seen. 2 a (of a disguise, pretext, etc.) easily seen through. b (of a quality etc.) evident, obvious. 3 easily understood; frank. □ **transparently** adv. [Latin *pareo* appear]

transpire /træn'spaɪə(r)/ v. (**-ring**) 1 (usu. prec. by *it* as subject) (of a secret or fact) come to be known; turn out; prove to be the case (*it transpired that he knew nothing about it*). 2 occur; happen. 3 emit (vapour or moisture), or be emitted, through the skin, lungs, or leaves; perspire. □ **transpiration** /-spɪ'reɪʃ(ə)n/ n. [Latin *spiro* breathe]

of the Eucharistic elements wholly into the body and blood of Christ. [medieval Latin: related to TRANS, SUBSTANCE]

transuranic /ˌtrænsjʊəˈrænɪk/ adj. (of a chemical element) having a higher atomic number than uranium.

transverse /trænzˈvɜːs/ adj. situated, arranged, or acting in a crosswise direction. □ **transversely** adv. [Latin transverto -vers- turn across]

transvestite /trænzˈvestaɪt/ n. man deriving esp. sexual pleasure from dressing in women's clothes. □ **transvestism** n. [Latin vestio clothe]

trap –n. 1 device, often baited, for catching animals. 2 trick betraying a person into speech or an act. 3 arrangement to catch an unsuspecting person. 4 device for hurling an object, e.g. a clay pigeon, into the air to be shot at. 5 compartment from which a greyhound is released at the start of a race. 6 device that sends a ball into the air. 7 curve in a downpipe etc. that fills with liquid and forms a seal against the return of gases. 8 two-wheeled carriage (pony and trap). 9 = TRAPDOOR. 10 slang mouth (esp. shut one's trap). –v. (-pp-) 1 catch (an animal) in a trap. 2 catch or catch out (a person) by means of a trick etc. 3 stop and retain in or as in a trap. 4 provide (a place) with traps. [Old English]

trap² n. (in full **trap-rock**) darkcoloured igneous rock. [Swedish]

trapdoor n. door in a floor, ceiling, or roof.

trapeze /trəˈpiːz/ n. crossbar suspended by ropes as a swing for acrobatics etc. [Latin: related to TRAPEZIUM]

trapezium /trəˈpiːzɪəm/ n. (pl. -s or -zia) 1 quadrilateral with only one pair of sides parallel. 2 US = TRAPEZOID 1. [Greek trapezion]

trapezoid /ˈtræpɪˌzɔɪd/ n. 1 quadrilateral with no two sides parallel. 2 US = TRAPEZIUM 1. [Greek: related to TRAPEZIUM]

trapper n. person who traps wild animals, esp. for their fur.

trappings n.pl. 1 ornamental accessories. 2 harness of a horse, esp. when ornamental. [trap from French drap cloth]

Trappist –n. monk of an order vowed to silence. –adj. of this order. [La Trappe in Normandy]

trash –n. 1 esp. US worthless or waste stuff, rubbish. 2 worthless person or persons. –v. slang wreck, vandalize. □ **trashy** adj. (-ier, -iest). [origin unknown]

trash can n. US dustbin.

■ **Usage** The use of transpire in sense 2 is considered incorrect by some people.

transplant –v. /trænsˈplɑːnt/ 1 plant in another place (transplanted the daffodils). 2 transfer (living tissue or an organ) to another part of the body or to another body. –n. /ˈtrænsplɑːnt/ 1 a transplanting of an organ or tissue. b such an organ etc. 2 thing, esp. a plant, transplanted. □ **transplantation** /-ˈteɪʃ(ə)n/ n. [Latin]

transponder /trænˈspɒndə(r)/ n. device for receiving a radio signal and automatically transmitting a different signal. [from TRANSMIT, RESPOND]

transport –v. /trænsˈpɔːt/ 1 take or carry (a person, goods, etc.) to another place. 2 hist. deport (a criminal) to a penal colony. 3 (as **transported** adj.) (usu. foll. by with) affected with strong emotion. –n. /ˈtrænspɔːt/ 1 a system of conveying people, goods, etc., from place to place. b means of this (our transport has arrived). 2 ship, aircraft, etc. used to carry soldiers, stores, etc. 3 (esp. in pl.) vehement emotion (transports of joy). □ **transportable** /-ˈpɔːtəb(ə)l/ adj. [Latin porto carry]

transportation /ˌtrænspɔːˈteɪʃ(ə)n/ n. 1 conveying or being conveyed. 2 a system of conveying. b esp. US means of this. 3 hist. deportation of convicts.

transport café n. roadside café for (esp. commercial) drivers.

transporter n. vehicle used to transport other vehicles or heavy machinery etc. by road.

transporter bridge n. bridge carrying vehicles etc. across water on a suspended moving platform.

transpose /trænsˈpəʊz/ v. (-sing) 1 a cause (two or more things) to change places. b change the position of (a thing) in a series. 2 change the order or position (of words or a word) in a sentence. 3 put (music) into a different key. □ **transposition** /-pəˈzɪʃ(ə)n/ n. [French: related to POSE]

transputer /trænsˈpjuːtə(r)/ n. microprocessor with integral memory designed for parallel processing. [from TRANSISTOR, COMPUTER]

transsexual /trænˈsekʃʊəl/ (also **transsexual**) –adj. having the physical characteristics of one sex and an overwhelming psychological identification with the other. –n. 1 transsexual person. 2 person who has had a sex change. [from TRANS]

tranship /trænˈʃɪp/ v. (-pp-) transfer from one ship or form of transport to another. □ **transhipment** n.

transubstantiation /ˌtrænsəbˌstænʃɪˈeɪʃ(ə)n/ n. RC Ch. conversion

trattoria /ˌtrætəˈriːə/ n. Italian restaurant. [Italian]

trauma /ˈtrɔːmə/ n. (pl. **traumata** /-mətə/ or **-s**) **1** profound emotional shock. **2** physical injury. **3** physical shock syndrome following this. □ **traumatize** v. (also **-ise**) (**-zing** or **-sing**). [Greek, = wound]

traumatic /trɔːˈmætɪk/ adj. **1** of or causing trauma. **2** colloq. distressing (traumatic experience). □ **traumatically** adv. [Greek: related to TRAUMA]

travail /ˈtræveɪl/ literary —n. **1** painful effort. **2** pangs of childbirth. —v. make a painful effort, esp. in childbirth. [French travaillier]

travel /ˈtræv(ə)l/ —v. (**-ll-**; US **-l-**) **1** go from one place to another; make a journey, esp. a long one or abroad. **2 a** journey along or through (a country). **b** cover (a distance) in travelling. **3** colloq. withstand a long journey (wines that do not travel). **4** go from place to place as a salesman. **5** move or proceed as specified (light travels faster than sound). **6** colloq. move quickly. **7** pass, esp. in a deliberate manner, from point to point (her eye travelled over the scene). **8** (of a machine or part) move or operate in a specified way. —n. **1 a** travelling, esp. in foreign countries. **b** (often in pl.) spell of this. **2** range, rate, or mode of motion of a part in machinery. [originally = TRAVAIL]

travel agency n. agency that makes the necessary arrangements for travellers. □ **travel agent** n.

travelled adj. (US **traveled**) experienced in travelling (also in comb.: much-travelled).

traveller n. (US **traveler**) **1** person who travels or is travelling. **2** travelling salesman. **3** Gypsy.

traveller's cheque n. cheque for a fixed amount that may be cashed on signature abroad.

traveller's joy n. wild clematis.

traveller's tale n. incredible and probably untrue story.

travelling salesman n. = COMMERCIAL TRAVELLER.

travelogue /ˈtrævəlɒg/ n. film or illustrated lecture about travel. [from TRAVEL, after monologue]

travel-sick adj. suffering from nausea caused by motion in travelling.

traverse —v. /trəˈvɜːs/ (**-sing**) **1** travel or lie across (traversed the country); pit traversed by a beam). **2** consider or discuss the whole extent of (a subject). —n. /ˈtrævəs/ **1** sideways movement. **2** traversing. **3** thing that crosses another. □ **traversal** n. [French: related to TRANSVERSE]

travesty /ˈtrævɪstɪ/ —n. (pl. **-ies**) grotesque misrepresentation or imitation (travesty of justice). —v. (**-ies**, **-ied**) make or be a travesty of. [French travestir disguise, from Italian]

trawl —v. **1** fish with a trawl or seine. **2 a** catch by trawling. **b** (often foll. by through) search thoroughly (trawled her memory for their names). —n. **1** act of trawling. **2** (in full **trawl-net**) large wide-mouthed fishing-net dragged by a boat along the sea bottom. [probably Dutch traghel drag-net]

trawler n. boat used for trawling.

tray n. **1** flat board, usu. with a raised rim, for carrying dishes, etc. **2** shallow lidless box for papers or small articles, sometimes forming a drawer in a cabinet etc. [Old English]

treacherous /ˈtretʃərəs/ adj. **1** guilty of or involving treachery. **2** (of weather, ice, the memory, etc.) likely to fail or give way. □ **treacherously** adv. **treacherousness** n. [French from trichier cheat: related to TRICK]

treachery /ˈtretʃərɪ/ n. (pl. **-ies**) violation of faith or trust; betrayal.

treacle /ˈtriːk(ə)l/ n. **1** syrup produced in refining sugar. **2** molasses. □ **treacly** adj. [French from Latin theriaca antidote against a snake-bite, from thērion wild animal]

tread /tred/ —v. (past **trod**; past part. **trodden** or **trod**) **1** (often foll. by on) set down one's foot; walk, step. **2 a** walk on. **b** (often foll. by down) press or crush with the feet. **3** perform (steps etc.) by walking. **4** (often foll. by in, into) press down into the ground with the feet (trod dirt into the carpet). —n. **1** manner or sound of walking. **2** top surface of a step or stair. **3** thick moulded part of a vehicle tyre for gripping the road. **4 a** part of a wheel that touches the ground or rail. **b** part of a rail that the wheels touch. **5** part of the sole of a shoe that rests on the ground. □ **tread the boards** be an actor. **tread on air** feel elated. **tread on a person's toes** offend a person; encroach on a person's privileges etc. **tread water** maintain an upright position in water by moving the feet and hands. [Old English]

treadle /ˈtred(ə)l/ n. lever worked by the foot and imparting motion to a machine. [Old English: related to TREAD]

treadmill n. **1** device for producing motion by the weight of persons or animals stepping on steps attached to a revolving upright wheel. **2** similar device used for exercise. **3** monotonous routine work.

treadwheel n. = TREADMILL 1, 2.

treason /ˈtriːz(ə)n/ n. violation by a subject of allegiance to the sovereign or State. [Latin: related to TRADITION]

■ **Usage** The crime of *petty treason* was abolished in 1828. This is why *high treason*, originally distinguished from *petty treason*, now means the same as *treason*.

treasonable adj. involving or guilty of treason.

treasure /ˈtreʒə(r)/ —n. **1 a** precious metals or gems. **b** hoard of these. **c** accumulated wealth. **2** thing valued for its rarity, workmanship, associations, etc. (*art treasures*). **3** colloq. much loved or highly valued person. —v. (-**ring**) **1** value highly. **2** (often foll. by *up*) store up as valuable. [Greek *thēsauros*]

treasure hunt n. **1** search for treasure. **2** game in which players seek a hidden object from a series of clues.

treasurer n. person in charge of the funds of a society etc.

treasure trove n. treasure of unknown ownership found hidden.

treasury n. (pl. -**ies**) **1** place or building where treasure is stored. **2** funds or revenue of a State, institution, or society. **3** (**Treasury**) **a** department managing the public revenue of a country. **b** offices and officers of this.

Treasury bench n. front bench in the House of Commons occupied by Cabinet ministers etc.

treasury bill n. bill of exchange issued by the government to raise money for temporary needs.

treat —v. **1** act or behave towards or deal with (a person or thing) in a certain way (*treated me kindly; treat it as a joke*). **2** apply a process to (*treat it with acid*). **3** apply medical care or attention to. **4** present or deal with (a subject) in literature or art. **5** (often foll. by *to*) provide with food, drink, or entertainment at one's own expense (*treated us to dinner*). **6** (often foll. by *with*) negotiate terms (*with a person*). **7** (often foll. by *of*) give a spoken or written exposition. —n. **1** event or circumstance (esp. when unexpected or unusual) that gives great pleasure. **2** meal, entertainment, etc., designed to do this. **3** (prec. by *a*) extremely good or well (*they looked a treat; has come on a treat*). □ **treatable** adj. [Latin *tracto* handle]

treatise /ˈtriːtɪz/ n. a written work dealing formally and systematically with a subject. [Anglo-French: related to TREAT]

treatment n. **1** process or manner of behaving towards or dealing with a

person or thing. **2** medical care or attention. **3** manner of treating a subject in literature or art. **4** (prec. by *the*) colloq. the customary way of dealing with a person, situation, etc. (*got the full treatment*).

treaty /ˈtriːtɪ/ n. (pl. -**ies**) **1** formal agreement between States. **2** agreement between parties, esp. for the purchase of property. [Latin: related to TREAT]

treble /ˈtreb(ə)l/ —adj. **1 a** threefold. **b** triple. **c** three times as much or many (*treble the amount*). **2** high-pitched. —n. **1** treble quantity or thing. **2** hit on the narrow band between the two middle circles of a dartboard, scoring treble. **3 a** Mus. = SOPRANO (esp. a boy's voice or part, or an instrument). **b** high-pitched voice. **4** high-frequency output of a radio, record-player, etc. —v. (-**ling**) make or become three times as much or many; increase threefold; multiply by three. □ **trebly** adv. [Latin: related to TRIPLE]

treble chance n. method of competing in a football pool in which the chances of winning depend on the number of draws and home and away wins predicted by the competitors.

treble clef n. clef placing the G above middle C on the second lowest line of the staff.

tree —n. **1** perennial plant with a woody self-supporting main stem or trunk and usu. unbranched for some distance above the ground. **2** piece or frame of wood etc. for various purposes (*shoe-tree*). **3** = FAMILY TREE. —v. (**trees, treed**) force to take refuge in a tree. □ **grow on trees** (usu. with *neg.*) be plentiful. □ **treeless** adj. [Old English]

treecreeper n. small creeping bird feeding on insects in tree-bark.

tree-fern n. large fern with an upright trunklike stem.

tree line n. = TIMBERLINE.

tree ring n. ring in a cross-section of a tree, from one year's growth.

tree surgeon n. person who treats decayed trees in order to preserve them.

treetop n. topmost part of a tree.

trefoil /ˈtriːfɔɪl/ n. **1** leguminous plant with leaves of three leaflets, esp. clover. **2** three-lobed ornamentation, esp. in tracery windows. [Anglo-French: related to TRI-, FOIL²]

trek orig. S.Afr. —v. (-**kk-**) **1** travel or make one's way arduously. **2** esp. hist. migrate or journey with one's belongings by ox-wagon. —n. **1 a** long or arduous journey or walk (*quite a trek to the launderette*). **b** each stage of this. **2** organized migration of a body of people. □ **trekker** n. [Dutch, = draw]

trellis /ˈtrelɪs/ n. (in full **trellis-work**) lattice of light wooden or metal bars, esp. as a support for climbing plants. [French *treillis*]

trematode /ˈtrɛmətəʊd/ n. a kind of parasitic flatworm. [Greek *trēma* hole]

tremble /ˈtremb(ə)l/ —v. (-ling) 1 shake involuntarily from emotion, weakness, etc. 2 be in a state of extreme apprehension. 3 quiver (*leaves trembled in the breeze*). —n. trembling; quiver (*tremble in his voice*). [medieval Latin: related to TREMULOUS]

trembler n. automatic vibrator for making and breaking an electrical circuit.

trembly adj. (-ier, -iest) colloq. trembling.

tremendous /trɪˈmendəs/ adj. 1 colloq. remarkable, considerable, excellent. 2 awe-inspiring, overpowering. □ **tremendously** adv. [Latin *tremendus* to be trembled at: related to TREMOR]

tremolo /ˈtreməˌləʊ/ n. (pl. -s) trembling effect in music. [Italian: related to TREMULOUS]

tremor /ˈtremə(r)/ n. 1 shaking, quivering. 2 thrill (of fear, exultation, etc.). 3 (in full **earth tremor**) slight earthquake. [Latin *tremo* tremble]

tremulous /ˈtremjʊləs/ adj. trembling. □ **tremulously** adv. [Latin *tremulus*: related to TREMOR]

trench —n. 1 long narrow usu. deep ditch. 2 Mil. this dug by troops as a shelter from enemy fire. —v. 1 dig a trench or trenches in (the ground). 2 turn over the earth of (a field, garden, etc.) by digging a succession of ditches. [French *trenche*, -ier cut]

trenchant /ˈtrentʃ(ə)nt/ adj. (of style or language etc.) incisive, terse, vigorous. □ **trenchancy** n. **trenchantly** adv. [French: related to TRENCH]

trench coat n. 1 soldier's lined or padded waterproof coat. 2 loose belted raincoat.

trencher n. hist. wooden or earthenware platter for serving food. [Anglo-French: related to TRENCH]

trencherman n. person who eats well, or in a specified manner.

trench warfare n. war carried on from trenches.

trend —n. general direction and tendency (esp. of events, fashion, or opinion). —v. 1 bend or turn away in a specified direction. 2 have a general tendency. [Old English]

trend-setter n. person who leads the way in fashion etc.

trendy colloq.; often derog. —adj. (-ier, -iest) fashionable. —n. (pl. -ies) fashionable person. □ **trendily** adv. **trendiness** n.

trepan /trɪˈpæn/ —n. cylindrical saw formerly used by surgeons for removing part of the skull. —v. (-nn-) perforate (the skull) with a trepan. [Greek *trupanon* auger]

trepidation /ˌtrepɪˈdeɪʃ(ə)n/ n. fear, anxiety. [Latin *trepidus* flurried]

trespass /ˈtrespəs/ —v. 1 (usu. foll. by on, upon) make an unlawful or unauthorized intrusion (esp. on land or property). 2 (foll. by on) make unjustifiable claims on; encroach on (*trespass on your hospitality*). —n. 1 Law act of trespassing. 2 archaic sin, offence. □ **trespasser** n. [medieval Latin: related to TRANS-, PASS]

tress n. 1 long lock of human (esp. female) hair. 2 (in pl.) woman's or girl's head of hair. [French]

trestle /ˈtres(ə)l/ n. 1 supporting structure for a table etc., consisting of two frames fixed at an angle or hinged, or of a bar with two divergent pairs of legs. 2 (in full **trestle-table**) table of a board or boards on trestles etc. 3 (in full **trestle-work**) open braced framework to support a bridge etc. [Latin *transtrum* cross-beam]

trews /truːz/ n.pl. close-fitting usu. tartan trousers. [Irish and Gaelic: related to TROUSERS]

tri- comb. form three or three times. [Latin and Greek]

triad /ˈtraɪæd/ n. 1 group of three (esp. notes in a chord). 2 the number three. 3 (also **Triad**) Chinese secret society, usu. criminal. □ **triadic** /-ˈædɪk/ adj. [Latin from Greek]

trial /ˈtraɪəl/ n. 1 judicial examination and determination of issues between parties by a judge with or without a jury. 2 test (*will give you a trial*). 3 trying thing or person (*trials of old age*). 4 match held to select players for a team. 5 (often in pl.) contest involving performance by horses, dogs, motor cycles, etc. □ **on trial** 1 being tried in a court of law. 2 being tested; to be chosen or retained only if suitable. [Anglo-French: related to TRY]

trial and error n. repeated (usu. unsystematic) attempts continued until successful.

trial run n. preliminary operational test.

triangle /ˈtraɪæŋg(ə)l/ n. 1 plane figure with three sides and angles. 2 any three things not in a straight line, with

imaginary lines joining them. **3** implement of this shape. **4** musical instrument consisting of a steel rod bent into a triangle, struck with a small steel rod. **5** situation, esp. an emotional relationship, involving three people. □ **triangular** /'-æŋgjuːə(r)/ *adj.* [Latin: related to TRI-]

triangulate /traɪˈæŋgjuːleɪt/ *v.* (-**ting**) measure and map out (an area) by dividing it into triangles. □ **triangulation** /-ˈleɪʃ(ə)n/ *n.* [related to TRI-]

Triassic /traɪˈæsɪk/ *Geol.* –*adj.* of the earliest period of the Mesozoic era. —*n.* this period. [related to TRIAD]

triathlon /traɪˈæθlən/ *n.* athletic contest of three events for all competitors. [from TRI- after DECATHLON]

tribe *n.* **1** group of (esp. primitive) families or communities, linked by social, religious, or blood ties, and usu. having a common culture and dialect and a recognized leader. **2** any similar natural or political division. **3** usu. *derog.* set or number of persons, esp. of one profession etc. or family. □ **tribal** *adj.* **tribalism** *n.* [Latin *tribus*]

tribesman *n.* (*fem.* -**woman**) member of a tribe.

tribology /traɪˈbɒlədʒɪ/ *n.* the study of friction, wear, lubrication, and the design of bearings. [Greek *tribō* rub]

tribulation /ˌtrɪbjʊˈleɪʃ(ə)n/ *n.* great affliction. [Latin *tribulum* threshing sledge]

tribunal /traɪˈbjuːn(ə)l/ *n.* **1** board appointed to adjudicate in some matter. **2** court of justice. **3** seat or bench for a judge or judges. [Latin: related to TRIBUNE]

tribune /ˈtrɪbjuːn/ *n.* **1** popular leader or demagogue. **2** (in full **tribune of the people**) official in ancient Rome chosen by the people to protect their interests. [Latin *tribunus*: related to TRIBE]

tributary /ˈtrɪbjʊtərɪ/ –*n.* (*pl.* -**ies**) **1** river or stream flowing into a larger river or lake. **2** *hist.* person or State paying or subject to tribute. —*adj.* **1** (of a river etc.) that is a tributary. **2** *hist.* **a** paying tribute. **b** serving as tribute. [Latin: related to TRIBUTE]

tribute /ˈtrɪbjuːt/ *n.* **1** thing said or done or given as a mark of respect or affection etc. **2** (foll. by *to*) indication of (some praiseworthy quality) (*their success is a tribute to their perseverance*). **3** *hist.* **a** periodic payment by one State or ruler to another, esp. as a sign of dependence. **b** obligation to pay this. [Latin *tributum* neuter past part. of *tribuo -ut-* assign, originally divide between TRIBES]

trice *n.* □ **in a trice** in an instant. [*trice* haul up, from Low German and Dutch]

triceps /ˈtraɪsɛps/ *n.* muscle (esp. in the upper arm) with three points of attachment at one end. [Latin *caput* head]

triceratops /traɪˈsɛrə,tɒps/ *n.* dinosaur with three sharp horns on the forehead and a wavy-edged collar round the neck. [Greek, = three-horned face]

trichinosis /ˌtrɪkɪˈnəʊsɪs/ *n.* disease caused by hairlike worms usu. ingested in meat. [Greek *thrix trikh-* hair]

trichology /trɪˈkɒlədʒɪ/ *n.* the study of hair. □ **trichologist** *n.*

trichromatic /ˌtraɪkrəˈmætɪk/ *adj.* **1** having or using three colours. **2** (of vision) having the normal three colour-sensations, i.e. red, green, and purple.

trick –*n.* **1** action or scheme undertaken to deceive or outwit. **2** illusion (*trick of the light*). **3** special technique; knack. **4 a** feat of skill or dexterity. **b** unusual action (e.g. begging) learned by an animal. **5** foolish or discreditable act; practical joke (*a mean trick to play*). **6** idiosyncrasy (*has a trick of repeating himself*). **7 a** cards played in one round of a card-game. **b** point gained in this. **8** (*attrib.*) done to deceive or mystify (*trick photography; trick question*). –*v.* **1** deceive by a trick; outwit. **2** (often foll. by *out of*) swindle (*tricked out of his savings*). **3** (foll. by *into*) cause to do something by trickery (*tricked into marriage; tricked me into agreeing*). **4** foil, baffle; take by surprise. □ **do the trick** *colloq.* achieve the required result. **how's tricks?** *colloq.* how are you? **trick or treat** esp. *US* children's custom of calling at houses at Hallowe'en with the threat of pranks if they are not given a small gift. **trick out** (or **up**) dress or deck out. [French]

trickery *n.* deception, use of tricks.

trickle /ˈtrɪk(ə)l/ –*v.* (-**ling**) **1** (cause to) flow in drops or a small stream. **2** come or go slowly or gradually (*information trickles out*). –*n.* trickling flow. [probably imitative]

trickle charger *n.* electrical charger for batteries that works at a steady slow rate.

trickster *n.* deceiver, rogue.

tricksy *adj.* (-**ier**, -**iest**) full of tricks; playful.

tricky *adj.* (-**ier**, -**iest**) **1** requiring care and adroitness (*tricky job*). **2** crafty, deceitful. □ **trickily** *adv.* **trickiness** *n.*

tricolour /ˈtrɪkələ(r)/ *n.* (*US* **tricolor**) flag of three bands of different colours, esp. the French or Irish national flags. [French: related to TRI-]

tricot /ˈtriːkəʊ/ *n.* knitted fabric. [French]

tricycle /ˈtraɪsɪk(ə)l/ n. three-wheeled pedal-driven vehicle similar to a bicycle.

trident /ˈtraɪd(ə)nt/ n. three-pronged spear. [Latin *dens dent-* tooth]

Tridentine /trɪˈdentaɪn/ adj. of the Council of Trent, held at Trento in Italy 1545–63, esp. as the basis of Roman Catholic orthodoxy. [medieval Latin *Tridentum* Trento]

tried past and past part. of TRY.

triennial /traɪˈenɪəl/ adj. lasting, or recurring every, three years. [Latin *annus* year]

trier /ˈtraɪə(r)/ n. 1 person who perseveres. 2 tester, esp. of foodstuffs.

trifle /ˈtraɪf(ə)l/ —n. 1 thing of slight value or importance. 2 a small amount, esp. of money. b (prec. by *a*) somewhat (*a trifle annoyed*). 3 dessert of sponge cake with custard, jelly, fruit, cream, etc. —v. (-ling) 1 talk or act frivolously. 2 (foll. by *with*) treat or deal with frivolously; flirt heartlessly with. [originally *trufle* from French = *truf(f)e* deceit]

trifling adj. 1 unimportant, petty. 2 frivolous.

triforium /traɪˈfɔːrɪəm/ n. (pl. -ria) gallery or arcade above the arches of the nave, choir, and transepts of a church. [Anglo-Latin]

trig n. colloq. trigonometry. [abbreviation]

trigger —n. 1 movable device for releasing a spring or catch and so setting off a mechanism (esp. that of a gun). 2 event, occurrence, etc., that sets off a chain reaction. —v. (often foll. by *off*) set (an action or process) in motion; precipitate. □ **quick on the trigger** quick to respond. [*tricker* from Dutch *trekker* from *trekken* pull]

trigger-happy adj. apt to shoot on the slightest provocation.

trigger point n. reference point on high ground, used in triangulation.

trigonometry /ˌtrɪɡəˈnɒmɪtrɪ/ n. branch of mathematics dealing with the relations of the sides and angles of triangles and with the relevant functions of any angles. □ **trigonometric** /-nəˈmetrɪk/ adj. **trigonometrical** /-nəˈmetrɪk(ə)l/ adj. [Greek *trigōnon* triangle]

trilateral /traɪˈlætər(ə)l/ adj. 1 of, on, or with three sides. 2 involving three parties. [Latin: related to TRI-]

trilby /ˈtrɪlbɪ/ n. (pl. -ies) soft felt hat with a narrow brim and indented crown. [*Trilby*, name of a character in a novel by G. du Maurier]

trilingual /traɪˈlɪŋɡw(ə)l/ adj. 1 able to speak three languages. 2 spoken or written in three languages.

trill —n. 1 quavering sound, esp. a rapid alternation of sung or played notes. 2 bird's warbling. 3 pronunciation of *r* with vibration of the tongue. —v. 1 produce a trill. 2 warble (a song) or pronounce (*r* etc.) with a trill. [Italian]

trillion /ˈtrɪljən/ n. (pl. same) 1 a million million (10¹²). 2 (now less often) a million million million (10¹⁸). □ **trillionth** adj. & n. [French or Italian: related to TRI-, MILLION, after *billion*]

trilobite /ˈtraɪləbaɪt/ n. a kind of fossil marine arthropod. [from TRI-, Greek *lobos* lobe]

trilogy /ˈtrɪlədʒɪ/ n. (pl. -ies) group of three related novels, plays, operas, etc.

trim —v. (-mm-) 1 a make neat or of the required size or form, esp. by cutting away irregular or unwanted parts. b set in good order. 2 (foll. by *off*, *away*) cut off (unwanted parts). 3 ornament, decorate. 4 adjust the balance of (a ship or aircraft) by arranging its cargo etc. 5 arrange (sails) to suit the wind. 6 a associate oneself with currently prevailing views, esp. to advance oneself. b hold a middle course in politics or opinion. 7 colloq. a rebuke sharply. b thrash. c get the better of in a bargain etc. —n. 1 state of readiness or fitness (*in perfect trim*). 2 ornament or decorative material. 3 trimming of a person's hair. —adj. 1 neat or spruce. 2 in good order; well arranged or equipped. [Old English = make firm]

trimaran /ˈtraɪməræn/ n. vessel like a catamaran, with three hulls side by side. [from CATAMARAN]

trimeter /ˈtrɪmɪtə(r)/ n. Prosody line of verse of three measures. [Greek: see TRI-, -METER]

trimming n. 1 ornamentation or decoration, esp. for clothing. 2 (in pl.) colloq. usual accompaniments, esp. of the main course of a meal.

Trinitarian /ˌtrɪnɪˈteərɪən/ —n. believer in the Trinity. —adj. of this belief. □ **Trinitarianism** n.

trinitrotoluene /traɪˌnaɪtrəˈtɒljuːiːn/ n. (also **trinitrotoluol** /-ˈtɒljuɒl/) = TNT.

trinity /ˈtrɪnɪtɪ/ n. (pl. -ies) 1 state of being three. 2 group of three. 3 (the **Trinity** or **Holy Trinity**) Theol. the three persons of the Christian Godhead (Father, Son, and Holy Spirit). [Latin *trinitas* from *trinus* threefold]

Trinity Sunday n. Sunday next after Whit Sunday.

Trinity term n. university and law term beginning after Easter.

trinket /ˈtrɪŋkɪt/ n. trifling ornament, esp. a piece of jewellery. □ **trinketry** n. [origin unknown]

trio /ˈtriːəʊ/ n. (pl. -s) 1 group of three. 2 Mus. a composition for three performers. b the performers. [French and Italian from Latin]

trip —v. (-pp-) 1 a (often foll. by up) (cause to) stumble, esp. by catching the feet. b (foll. by up) (cause to) make a slip or blunder. 2 a move with quick light steps. b (of a rhythm etc.) run lightly. 3 make an excursion to a place. 4 a operate (a mechanism) suddenly by knocking aside a catch etc. b automatically cut out. 5 slang have a hallucinatory experience caused by a drug. —n. 1 journey or excursion, esp. for pleasure. 2 a stumble or blunder. b tripping or being tripped up. 3 nimble step. 4 slang drug-induced hallucinatory experience. 5 device for tripping a mechanism etc. [Dutch trippen skip, hop]

tripartite /traɪˈpɑːtaɪt/ adj. 1 consisting of three parts. 2 shared by or involving three parties. [Latin partior divide]

tripe n. 1 first or second stomach of a ruminant, as an ox, as food. 2 colloq. nonsense, rubbish. [French]

triple /ˈtrɪp(ə)l/ —adj. 1 consisting of three usu. equal parts or things; threefold. 2 involving three parties. 3 three times as much or many. —n. 1 threefold number or amount. 2 set of three. —v. (-ling) multiply by three. □ **triply** adv. [Latin triplus from Greek]

triple crown n. winning of all three of a group of sporting events, esp. in Rugby.

triple jump n. athletic contest comprising a hop, step, and jump.

triplet /ˈtrɪplɪt/ n. 1 each of three children or animals born at one birth. 2 set of three things, esp. three equal notes played in the time of two of the same value.

triplex /ˈtrɪpleks/ adj. triple, threefold.

triplicate —adj. /ˈtrɪplɪkət/ 1 existing in three examples or copies. 2 having three corresponding parts. 3 tripled. —n. /ˈtrɪplɪkət/ each of a set of three copies or corresponding parts. —v. /ˈtrɪplɪˌkeɪt/ (-ting) 1 make in three copies. 2 multiply by three. □ **in triplicate** in three copies. □ **triplication** /-ˈkeɪʃ(ə)n/ n. [Latin: related to TRIPLEX]

tripod /ˈtraɪpɒd/ n. 1 three-legged stand for a camera etc. 2 stool, table, or utensil resting on three feet or legs. [Greek, = three-footed]

tripos /ˈtraɪpɒs/ n. (at Cambridge University) honours examinations for primary degrees. [related to TRIPOD]

tripper n. person who goes on a pleasure trip.

triptych /ˈtrɪptɪk/ n. picture or relief carving on three panels, usu. hinged together at the sides. [after DIPTYCH]

trip-wire n. wire stretched close to the ground to trip up an intruder or to operate an alarm or other device when disturbed.

trireme /ˈtraɪriːm/ n. ancient Greek warship, with three files of oarsmen on each side. [Latin remus oar]

trisect /traɪˈsekt/ v. divide into three (usu. equal) parts. □ **trisection** n. [Latin seco sect- cut]

trite adj. (of a phrase, observation, etc.) hackneyed. □ **tritely** adv. **triteness** n. [Latin tero trit- rub]

tritium /ˈtrɪtɪəm/ n. radioactive isotope of hydrogen with a mass about three times that of ordinary hydrogen. [Greek tritos third]

triumph /ˈtraɪʌmf/ —n. 1 a state of victory or success (returned in triumph). b a great success or achievement. 2 supreme example (a triumph of engineering). 3 joy at success; exultation (triumph in her face). 4 processional entry of a victorious general into ancient Rome. —v. 1 (often foll. by over) gain a victory; be successful. 2 (of an ancient Roman general) ride in triumph. 3 (often foll. by over) exult. □ **triumphal** /-ˈʌmf(ə)l/ adj. [French from Latin]

■ **Usage** Triumphal, meaning 'of or used in celebrating a triumph' as in triumphal arch should not be confused with triumphant meaning 'victorious' or 'exultant'.

triumphalism /traɪˈʌmfəlɪz(ə)m/ n. excessive exultation over the victories of one's own party etc. □ **triumphalist** adj. & n.

triumphant /traɪˈʌmf(ə)nt/ adj. 1 victorious, successful. 2 exultant. □ **triumphantly** adv.

■ **Usage** See note at triumph.

triumvirate /traɪˈʌmvərət/ n. ruling group of three men, esp. in ancient Rome. [Latin tres three, vir man]

trivalent /traɪˈveɪlənt/ adj. Chem. having a valency of three. □ **trivalency** n.

trivet /ˈtrɪvɪt/ n. iron tripod or bracket for a pot or kettle to stand on. [apparently from Latin tripes three-footed]

trivia /ˈtrɪvɪə/ n.pl. trifles or trivialities.

trivial /ˈtrɪvɪəl/ adj. 1 of small value or importance; trifling. 2 (of a person etc.) concerned only with trivial things. □ **trivially** adv. [Latin trivialis commonplace, from trivium three-way street corner]

trivialize v. (also **-ise**) (**-zing** or **-sing**) make or treat as trivial; minimize. □

trivialization /ˌtrɪvɪəlaɪˈzeɪʃ(ə)n/ n.

trochee /ˈtrəʊkiː/ n. *Prosody* metrical foot consisting of one long followed by one short syllable (‒ ⌣). □ **trochaic** /trəˈkeɪɪk/ adj. [Greek, = running]

trod past and p.p. of TREAD.

trodden past part. of TREAD.

troika /ˈtrɔɪkə/ n. **1** a Russian vehicle with a team of three horses abreast. **b** this team. **2** group of three people, esp. as an administrative council. [Russian]

troglodyte /ˈtrɒɡlədaɪt/ n. cave-dweller. [Greek *trōglē* hole]

Trojan /ˈtrəʊdʒ(ə)n/ —adj. of ancient Troy in Asia Minor. —n. **1** native or inhabitant of Troy. **2** person who works, fights, etc. courageously. [Latin *Troia* Troy]

Trojan Horse n. **1** hollow wooden horse used by the Greeks to enter Troy. **2** person or device planted to bring about an enemy's downfall.

troll¹ n. (in Scandinavian folklore) fabulous being, esp. a giant or dwarf dwelling in a cave. [Old Norse]

troll² v. fish by drawing bait along in the water. [perhaps related to French *troller* to quest]

trolley /ˈtrɒlɪ/ n. (pl. **-s**) **1** table, stand, or basket on wheels or castors for serving food, transporting luggage etc., gathering purchases in a supermarket, etc. **2** low truck running on rails. **3** (in full **trolley-wheel**) wheel attached to a pole etc. used for collecting current from an overhead electric wire to drive a vehicle. [dial., perhaps from TROLL²]

trolley bus n. electric bus using a trolley-wheel.

trollop /ˈtrɒləp/ n. disreputable girl or woman. [perhaps related to archaic *trull* prostitute]

trombone /trɒmˈbəʊn/ n. brass wind instrument with a sliding tube. □ **trombonist** n. [French or Italian *tromba* TRUMPET]

trompe-l'œil /trɒ̃pˈlɜːɪ/ n. (often *attrib.*) painting etc. designed to give an illusion of reality. [French, literally 'deceives the eye']

-tron *suffix Physics* forming nouns denoting: **1** elementary particle (*positron*). **2** particle accelerator. [from ELECTRON]

troop —n. **1** assembled company, assemblage of people or animals. **2** (in *pl.*) soldiers, armed forces. **3** cavalry unit under a captain. **4** unit of artillery or armoured vehicles. **5** group of three or more Scout patrols. —v. (foll. by *in*, *out*, *off*, etc.) come together or move in large numbers. □ **troop the colour** transfer a

flag ceremonially at a public mounting of garrison guards. [French *troupe*]

trooper n. **1** private soldier in a cavalry or armoured unit. **2** *Austral. & US* mounted or State police officer. **3** cavalry horse. **4** troop-ship.

troop-ship n. ship used for transporting troops.

trope n. figurative use of a word. [Greek *tropos* turn]

trophy /ˈtrəʊfɪ/ n. (pl. **-ies**) **1** cup etc. as a prize in a contest. **2** memento or souvenir of success in hunting, war, etc. [Greek *tropaion*]

tropic /ˈtrɒpɪk/ —n. **1** parallel of latitude 23°27′ north (**tropic of Cancer**) or south (**tropic of Capricorn**) of the Equator. **2** each of two corresponding circles on the celestial sphere where the sun appears to turn when at its greatest declination. **3** (the **Tropics**) region between the tropics of Cancer and Capricorn. —adj. = TROPICAL. [Greek *tropē* turn]

tropical adj. of or typical of the Tropics.

troposphere /ˈtrɒpəsfɪə(r)/ n. lowest layer of atmosphere extending about 6–10 km upwards from the earth's surface. [Greek *tropos* turn]

Trot n. *colloq.* usu. *derog.* Trotskyite. [abbreviation]

trot —v. (**-tt-**) **1** (of a person) run at a moderate pace. **2** (of a horse) proceed at a steady pace faster than a walk, lifting each diagonal pair of legs alternately. **3** *colloq.* walk, go. **4** cause (a horse or person) to trot. **5** traverse (a distance) at a trot. —n. **1** action or exercise of trotting (*proceed at a trot*, *went for a trot*). **2** (the **trots**) *slang* diarrhoea. □ **on the trot** *colloq.* **1** continually busy (*kept me on the trot*). **2** in succession (*six days on the trot*). **trot out 1** *colloq.* introduce (an opinion etc.) tediously or repeatedly. **2** cause (a horse) to trot to show his paces. [Old English]

troth /trəʊθ/ n. *archaic* **1** faith, loyalty. **2** truth. □ **pledge** (or **plight**) **one's troth** pledge one's word, esp. in marriage or betrothal. [related to TRUTH]

Trotskyism /ˈtrɒtskɪɪz(ə)m/ n. political principles of — Trotsky, esp. as urging worldwide socialist revolution. □ **Trotskyist** n. **Trotskyite** n. *derog.*

trotter n. **1** (usu. in *pl.*) animal's foot as food. **2** horse bred or trained for trotting.

troubadour /ˈtruːbədɔː(r)/ n. **1** singer or poet. **2** French medieval lyric poet singing of courtly love. [Provençal *trobar* find, compose]

trouble /ˈtrʌb(ə)l/ —n. **1** difficulty or distress; vexation, affliction (*had trouble with my car*). **2 a** inconvenience; unpleasant exertion; bother. **b** cause of this

(she was no trouble). 3 perceived failing (the trouble with me is that I can't say no). 4 dysfunction (kidney trouble; engine trouble). 5 a disturbance (crowd trouble; don't want any trouble). b (in pl.) political or social unrest, public disturbances, esp. (the Troubles) in N. Ireland. —v. (-ling) 1 cause distress or anxiety to; disturb. 2 be disturbed or worried (don't trouble about it). 3 afflict; cause pain etc. to. 4 (often refl.) subject or be subjected to inconvenience or unpleasant exertion (sorry to trouble you; don't trouble yourself). □ ask (or look) for trouble colloq. invite trouble by one's actions, behaviour, etc.; be rash or indiscreet. in trouble 1 involved in a matter likely to bring censure or punishment. 2 colloq. pregnant while unmarried. [Latin: related to TURBID]

troublemaker n. person habitually causing trouble. □ troublemaking n.

troubleshooter n. 1 mediator in a dispute. 2 person who traces and corrects faults in machinery or in an organization etc. □ troubleshooting n.

troublesome adj. causing trouble, annoying.

trough /trof/ n. 1 long narrow open receptacle for water, animal feed, etc. 2 channel or hollow like this. 3 elongated region of low barometric pressure. [Old English]

trounce v. (-cing) 1 defeat heavily. 2 beat, thrash. 3 punish severely. [origin unknown]

troupe /tru:p/ n. company or band, esp. of artistes. [French, = TROOP]

trouper n. 1 member of a theatrical troupe. 2 staunch colleague.

trousers /'trauzəz/ n.pl. 1 two-legged outer garment reaching from the waist usu. to the ankles. 2 (trouser) (attrib.) designating part of this (trouser leg). □ wear the trousers (esp. of a wife) dominate in a marriage. □ trousered adj. [in pl. after drawers: Irish and Gaelic triubhas trews]

trouser suit n. woman's suit of trousers and jacket.

trousseau /'tru:səu/ n. (pl. -s or -x /-səuz/) bride's collection of clothes etc. [French: related to TRUSS]

trout n. (pl. same or -s) fish related to the salmon, valued as food. [Latin tructa]

trove n. = TREASURE TROVE. [Anglo-French trové from trover find]

trowel /'trauəl/ n. 1 small flat-bladed tool for spreading mortar etc. 2 scoop for lifting small plants or earth. [Latin trulla]

troy n. (in full troy weight) system of weights used for precious metals and gems, with a pound of 12 ounces or 5,760

grains; 1 oz troy = 31.1035 g. [probably Troyes in France]

truant /'tru:ənt/ —n. 1 child who stays away from school. 2 person who avoids work etc. —adj. shirking, idle, wandering. —v. (also play truant) be a truant. □ truancy n. (pl. -ies). [French, probably from Celtic]

truce /tru:s/ n. temporary agreement to cease hostilities. [originally trewes pl.: Old English, = covenant: related to TRUE]

truck[1] n. 1 lorry. 2 open railway wagon for freight. [perhaps from TRUCKLE]

truck[2] n. dealings. □ have no truck with avoid dealing with. [French troquer]

trucker n. esp. US long-distance lorry-driver.

truckle /'trʌk(ə)l/ —n. (in full truckle-bed) low bed on wheels, stored under a larger bed. —v. (-ling) submit obsequiously. (Latin trochlea pulley]

truculent /'trʌkjulənt/ adj. aggressively defiant. □ truculence n. truculently adv. (Latin trux truc- fierce]

trudge —v. (-ging) 1 go on foot, esp. laboriously. 2 traverse (a distance) in this way. —n. trudging walk. [origin unknown]

true /tru:/ —adj. (truer, truest) 1 in accordance with fact or reality (a true story). 2 genuine; rightly or strictly so called. 3 (often foll. by to) loyal, faithful 4 (foll. by to) accurately conforming to (a type or standard) (true to form). 5 correctly positioned or balanced; upright, level. 6 exact, accurate (a true copy). —adv. 1 archaic truly (tell me true). 2 accurately (aim true). 3 without variation (bred true). □ come true actually happen. out of true out of alignment. true to life accurately representing reality. [Old English]

true-blue —adj. extremely loyal or orthodox. —n. such a person, esp. a Conservative.

true-love n. sweetheart.

true north n. north according to the earth's axis, not magnetic north.

truffle /'trʌf(ə)l/ n. 1 edible richflavoured underground fungus. 2 sweet made of a chocolate mixture covered with cocoa etc. [probably Dutch from French]

trug n. shallow oblong garden-basket usu. of wood strips. [perhaps a dial. var. of TROUGH]

truism /'tru:ɪz(ə)m/ n. statement too hackneyed to be worth making, e.g. 'Nothing lasts for ever.'

truly /'tru:lɪ/ adv. 1 sincerely (am truly grateful). 2 really, indeed (truly, I do not know). 3 loyally (served them truly). 4

trump accurately (*is not truly depicted*). **5** properly (*well and truly*). [Old English: related to TRUE]

trump[1] —*n.* **1 a** playing-card of a suit temporarily ranking above the others. **b** (in *pl.*) this suit (*hearts are trumps*). **2** *colloq.* generous or loyal person (or with a trump). **2 colloq.** outdo. **c** come (or turn). **v. 1** defeat (a card or its player) with a trump. **trumps** *colloq.* **1** turn out better than expected. **2** be greatly successful or helpful. **trump up** fabricate or invent (an accusation etc.) (*trumped-up charge*). [corruption of TRIUMPH in the same (now obsolete) sense]

trump[2] *n. archaic* trumpet-blast. [French *trompe*]

trump card *n.* **1** card belonging to, or turned up to determine, a trump suit. **2** *colloq.* valuable resource, esp. kept in reserve.

trumpery /'trʌmpəri/ —*n.* (*pl.* -ies) **1** worthless finery. **2** worthless thing; rubbish. —*adj.* showy but worthless; trashy; shallow. [French *tromperie* deceit]

trumpet /'trʌmpɪt/ —*n.* **1** brass instrument with a flared bell and bright penetrating tone. **2** trumpet-shaped thing (*ear-trumpet*). **3** sound of or like a trumpet. —*v.* (-t-) **1 a** blow a trumpet. **b** (of an enraged elephant etc.) make a trumpet-like cry. **2** proclaim loudly. □ **trumpeter** *n.* [French diminutive: related to TRUMP[2]]

trumpet-call *n.* urgent summons to action.

truncate /trʌŋ'keɪt/ *v.* (-ting) cut the top or the end from; shorten. □ **truncation** /-'keɪʃ(ə)n/ *n.* [Latin: related to TRUNK]

truncheon /'trʌntʃ(ə)n/ *n.* short club carried by a police officer. [French *tronchon* stump: related to TRUNK]

trundle /'trʌnd(ə)l/ *v.* (-ling) roll or move, esp. heavily or noisily. [var. of obsolete or dial. *trendle*: related to TREND]

trunk *n.* **1** main stem of a tree. **2** body without the limbs and head. **3** large box with a hinged lid for luggage, storage, etc. **4** *US* boot of a car. **5** elephant's elongated prehensile nose. **6** (in *pl.*) men's close-fitting shorts worn for swimming etc. [Latin *truncus* cut short]

trunk call *n.* long-distance telephone call.

trunk line *n.* main line of a railway, telephone system, etc.

trunk road *n.* important main road.

truss —*n.* **1** framework supporting a roof, bridge, etc. **2** surgical appliance worn to support a hernia. **3** bundle of hay or straw. **4** compact terminal cluster of flowers or fruit. —*v.* **1** tie up (a fowl) for cooking. **2** (often foll. by *up*) tie (a person)

up with the arms to the sides. **3** support (a roof or bridge etc.) with a truss or trusses. [French]

trust —*n.* **1** firm belief in the reliability, truth, or strength etc. of a person or thing. **2** confident expectation. **3** responsibility (*position of great trust*). **4** commercial credit (*obtained goods on trust*). **5** *Law* arrangement whereby a person or group manages property on another's behalf. **b** property so held. **c** body of trustees. **6** association of companies for reducing competition etc. —*v.* **1** place trust in; believe in; rely on (a person or thing). **2** (foll. by *with*) allow (a person) to have or use (a thing) from confidence in its careful use (*trusted her with my car*). **3** (often foll. by *that*) have faith, confidence, or hope that a thing will take place (*I trust you will come*). **4** (foll. by *to*) consign (a thing) to (a person) with trust. **5** (foll. by *to*) place reliance on (*trust to luck*). □ **in trust** (of property) managed by one or more persons on behalf of another. **take on trust** accept (an assertion etc.) without evidence or investigation. [Old Norse]

trustee /trʌs'tiː/ *n.* person or member of a board managing property in trust with a legal obligation to administer it solely for the purposes specified. □ **trusteeship** *n.*

trustful *adj.* full of trust or confidence. □ **trustfully** *adv.*

trusting *adj.* having trust; trustful. □ **trustingly** *adv.*

trustworthy *adj.* deserving of trust; reliable. □ **trustworthiness** *n.*

trusty —*adj.* (-ier, -iest) *archaic* or *joc.* trustworthy (*a trusty steed*). —*n.* (*pl.* -ies) prisoner given special privileges for good behaviour.

truth /truːθ/ *n.* (*pl.* **truths** /truːðz, truːθs/) **1** quality or state of being true. **2** what is true. □ **in truth** *literary* truly, really. [Old English: related to TRUE]

truthful *adj.* **1** habitually speaking the truth. **2** (of a story etc.) true. □ **truthfully** *adv.* **truthfulness** *n.*

try /traɪ/ —*v.* (-ies, -ied) **1** make an effort with a view to success (often foll. by *to* + infin.; *colloq.* foll. by *and* + infin.; *tried to* be on time; *try and be early*). **2** make an effort to achieve (*tried my best*). **3** a test by use or experiment. **b** test the qualities of. **4** make severe demands on (*tries my patience*). **5** examine the effectiveness of for a purpose (*try cold water*, *have you tried kicking it?*). **6** ascertain the state of, or fasten (a door, window, etc.) by fastening of (a door, window, etc.). **7 a** investigate and decide (a case or issue) judicially. **b** (often foll. by *for*) subject (a

person) to trial (*tried for murder*). **8** (foll. by *for*) apply or compete for; seek to reach or attain (*try for a gold medal*). —*n.* (*pl.* **-ies**) **1** effort to accomplish something. **2** *Rugby* touching-down of the ball behind the opposing goal-line, scoring points and entitling the scoring side to a kick at the goal. □ **try one's hand** test how skilful one is, esp. at the first attempt. **try it on** *colloq.* try to get away with an unreasonable request etc. **try on** put on (clothes etc.) to see if they fit etc. **try out** test thoroughly, test for use. [originally = separate, distinguish, from French *trier* sift]

■ **Usage** Use of the verb *try* with *and* (see sense 1) is uncommon in negative contexts (except in the imperative, e.g. *don't try and get the better of me*) and in the past tense.

trying *adj.* annoying, vexatious; hard to endure.

try-on *n. colloq.* **1** act of trying it on or trying on (clothes etc.). **2** attempt to deceive.

try-out *n.* experimental test.

tryst /trɪst/ *n. archaic* meeting, esp. of lovers. [French]

tsar /zɑː(r)/ *n.* (also **czar**) (*fem.* **tsarina** /-ˈriːnə/) *hist.* title of the former emperors of Russia. □ **tsarist** *n.* (usu. *attrib.*). [Latin *Caesar*]

tsetse /ˈtsetsi, ˈtetsi/ *n.* African fly feeding on blood and transmitting esp. sleeping-sickness. [Tswana]

T-shirt /ˈtiːʃɜːt/ *n.* short-sleeved casual top having the form of a T when spread out.

tsp. *abbr.* (*pl.* **tsps.**) teaspoonful.

T-square /ˈtiːskweə(r)/ *n.* T-shaped instrument for drawing right angles.

tsunami /tsuːˈnɑːmɪ/ *n.* (*pl.* **-s**) long high sea wave caused by underwater earthquakes etc. [Japanese]

TT *abbr.* **1** Tourist Trophy. **2** tuberculin-tested. **3 a** teetotal. **b** teetotaller.

tub —*n.* **1** open flat-bottomed usu. round vessel. **2** tub-shaped (usu. plastic) carton. **3** *colloq.* bath. **4** *colloq.* clumsy slow boat. —*v.* (**-bb-**) plant, bathe, or wash in a tub. [probably Low German or Dutch]

tuba /ˈtjuːbə/ *n.* (*pl.* **-s**) low-pitched brass wind instrument. [Latin, = trumpet]

tubby /ˈtʌbɪ/ *adj.* (**-ier**, **-iest**) short and fat. □ **tubbiness** *n.*

tube —*n.* **1** long hollow cylinder. **2** soft metal or plastic cylinder sealed at one end and holding a semi-liquid substance (*tube of toothpaste*). **3** hollow cylindrical organ in the body. **4** (often prec. by *the*) *colloq.* London underground (*went by tube*). **5 a** cathode-ray tube, esp. in a television set. **b** (prec. by *the*) esp.

US colloq. television. **6** *US* thermionic valve. **7** = INNER TUBE. **8** *Austral. slang* can of beer. —*v.* (**-bing**) **1** equip with tubes. **2** enclose in a tube. [Latin]

tuber *n.* **1** thick rounded part of a stem or rhizome, usu. found underground and covered with modified buds, e.g. in a potato. **2** similar root of a dahlia etc. [Latin, = hump, swelling]

tubercle /ˈtjuːbək(ə)l/ *n.* small rounded swelling on the body or in an organ, esp. as characteristic of tuberculosis. □ **tuberculous** /-ˈbɜːkjʊləs/ *adj.* [Latin *tuberculum*, diminutive of TUBER]

tubercle bacillus *n.* bacterium causing tuberculosis.

tubercular /tjuːˈbɜːkjʊlə(r)/ *adj.* of or having tubercles or tuberculosis.

tuberculin /tjuːˈbɜːkjʊlɪn/ *n.* sterile liquid from cultures of tubercle bacillus, used in the diagnosis and treatment of tuberculosis.

tuberculin-tested *adj.* (of milk) from cows shown to be free of tuberculosis.

tuberculosis /tjuːˌbɜːkjʊˈləʊsɪs/ *n.* infectious bacterial disease marked by tubercles, esp. in the lungs.

tuberose /ˈtjuːbərəʊz/ *n.* plant with scented white funnel-like flowers.

tuberous /ˈtjuːbərəs/ *adj.* having tubers; of or like a tuber.

tubing *n.* length of tube or quantity of tubes.

tub-thumper *n. colloq.* ranting preacher or orator.

tubular /ˈtjuːbjʊlə(r)/ *adj.* **1** tube-shaped. **2** having or consisting of tubes. **3** (of furniture etc.) having a tubular framework.

tubular bells *n.pl.* orchestral instrument of vertically suspended brass tubes struck with a hammer.

tubule /ˈtjuːbjuːl/ *n.* small tube in a plant or animal body. [Latin *tubulus*, diminutive; related to TUBE]

TUC *abbr.* Trades Union Congress.

tuck —*v.* **1** (often foll. by *in*, *up*) **a** draw, fold, or turn the outer or end parts of (cloth or clothes etc.) close together so as to be held; push in the edge of (a thing) so as to confine it (*tucked his shirt into his trousers*). **b** push in the edges of bedclothes around (a person) (*came to tuck me in*). **2** draw together into a small space (*tucked its head under its wing*). **3** stow (a thing) away in a specified place or way (*tucked it in a corner*; *tucked it out of sight*). **4** make a stitched fold in (cloth etc.). —*n.* **1** flattened usu. stitched fold in cloth etc. **2** *colloq.* food, esp. cakes and sweets (also *attrib.*: *tuck box*). □ **tuck in** *colloq.* eat heartily. **tuck into** (or *away*) *colloq.* eat (food) heartily (*tucked into*

their dinner, could really tuck it away). [Low German or Dutch]

tucker —*n.* 1 *hist.* piece of lace or linen on or on a woman's bodice. 2 *Austral. & NZ slang* food. —*v.* (esp. in *pass-ive*, often foll. by *out*) *US & Austral. colloq.* tire.

tuck shop *n.* small shop selling sweets etc. to schoolchildren.

-tude *suffix* forming abstract nouns (*alti-tude, solitude*). [Latin *-tudo*]

Tudor /ˈtjuːdə(r)/ *adj.* 1 of the royal family of England 1485–1603 or this period. 2 of the architectural style of this period, esp. with half-timbering. [Owen *Tudor*, name of the grandfather of Henry VIII]

Tues. *abbr.* (also **Tue.**) Tuesday.

Tuesday /ˈtjuːzdeɪ/ —*n.* day of the week following Monday. —*adv. colloq.* 1 on Tuesday. 2 (**Tuesdays**) on Tuesdays. [Old English]

tufa /ˈtjuːfə/ *n.* 1 porous limestone rock formed round mineral springs. 2 = TUFF. [Italian: related to TUFF]

tuff *n.* rock formed from volcanic ash. [Latin *tofus*]

tuffet /ˈtʌfɪt/ *n.* 1 clump of grass; small mound. [var. of TUFT]

tuft *n.* bunch or collection of threads, grass, feathers, hair, etc., held or grow-ing together at the base. □ **tufted** *adj.* [probably French *tofe*]

tug —*v.* (**-gg-**) 1 (often foll. by *at*) pull hard or violently. 2 tow (a ship etc.) by a tug. —*n.* 1 hard, violent, or jerky pull. 2 sudden strong emotion. 3 small power-ful boat for towing ships. [related to TOW[1]]

tugboat *n.* = TUG *n.* 3.

tug of love *n. colloq.* dispute over the custody of a child.

tug of war *n.* 1 trial of strength between two sides pulling opposite ways on a rope. 2 decisive or severe contest.

tuition /tjuːˈɪʃ(ə)n/ *n.* 1 teaching, esp. if paid for. 2 fee for this. [Latin *tueor tuit-* look after]

tulip /ˈtjuːlɪp/ *n.* 1 bulbous spring-flowering plant with showy cup-shaped flowers. 2 its flower. [Turkish *tül(i)band* TURBAN (from its shape), from Persian]

tulip-tree *n.* tree producing tulip-like flowers.

tulle /tjuːl/ *n.* soft fine silk etc. net for veils and dresses. [*Tulle* in France]

tumble /ˈtʌmb(ə)l/ —*v.* (**-ling**) 1 (cause to) fall suddenly, clumsily, or headlong. 2 fall rapidly in amount etc. (*prices tum-bled*). 3 (often foll. by *about, around*) roll or toss to and fro. 4 move or rush in a headlong or blundering manner. 5 (often foll. by *to*) *colloq.* grasp the meaning behind an idea, circumstance, etc. (*he quickly tumbled to our plan*). 6 over-turn; fling or push roughly or carelessly. 7 perform acrobatic feats, esp. somer-saults. 8 rumple or disarrange. —*n.* 1 sudden or headlong fall. 2 somersault or other acrobatic feat. 3 untidy or confused state. [Low German *tummeln*]

tumbledown *adj.* falling or fallen into ruin; dilapidated.

tumble-drier *n.* (also **tumble-dryer**) machine for drying washing in a heated rotating drum. □ **tumble-dry** *v.*

tumbler *n.* 1 drinking-glass with no handle or foot. 2 acrobat. 3 part of a lock that holds the bolt until lifted by a key. 4 a kind of pigeon that turns over back-wards in flight.

tumbrel /ˈtʌmbr(ə)l/ *n.* (also **tumbril**) *hist.* open cart in which condemned persons were taken to the guillotine in the French Revolution. [French *tomber* fall]

tumescent /tjuːˈmes(ə)nt/ *adj.* swelling. □ **tumescence** *n.* [Latin: related to TU-MOUR]

tumid /ˈtjuːmɪd/ *adj.* 1 swollen, inflated. 2 (of style etc.) inflated, bombastic. □ **tumidity** /-ˈmɪdɪtɪ/ *n.* [Latin]

tummy /ˈtʌmɪ/ *n.* (*pl.* **-ies**) *colloq.* stomach. [a childish pronunciation]

tummy-button *n.* navel.

tumour /ˈtjuːmə(r)/ *n.* (*US* **tumor**) a swelling, esp. from an abnormal growth of tissue. □ **tumorous** *adj.* [Latin *tumeo* swell]

tumult /ˈtjuːmʌlt/ *n.* 1 uproar or din, esp. of a disorderly crowd. 2 angry demon-stration by a mob; riot. 3 conflict of emotions in the mind. [Latin: related to TUMOUR]

tumultuous /tjuːˈmʌltjʊəs/ *adj.* noisy; turbulent; violent.

tumulus /ˈtjuːmjʊləs/ *n.* (*pl.* **-li** /-laɪ/) ancient burial mound. [Latin: related to TUMOUR]

tun *n.* 1 large beer or wine cask. 2 brewer's fermenting-vat. [Old English]

tuna /ˈtjuːnə/ *n.* (*pl.* same or **-s**) 1 large edible marine fish. 2 (in full **tuna-fish**) its flesh as food. [American Spanish]

tundra /ˈtʌndrə/ *n.* vast level treeless Arctic region with underlying perma-frost. [Lappish]

tune —*n.* melody. —*v.* (**-ning**) 1 put (a musical instrument) in tune. 2 **a** adjust (a radio etc.) to the frequency of a signal. **b** (foll. by *in*) adjust a radio receiver to the required signal. 3 adjust (an engine etc.) to run efficiently. □ **in** or **out of** tune 1 having (or not having) the correct pitch or intonation (*sings in tune*). 2

tuneful (usu. foll. by *with*) harmonizing (or clashing) with one's company, surroundings, etc. ○ **to the tune of** *colloq.* to the considerable sum of. **tuned in** (often foll. by *to*) *colloq.* acquainted; in rapport; up to date. **tune up 1** bring one's instrument to the proper pitch. **2** bring to the most efficient condition. [var. of TONE]

tuneful *adj.* melodious, musical. □ **tunefully** *adv.*

tuneless *adj.* unmelodious, unmusical. □ **tunelessly** *adv.*

tuner *n.* **1** person who tunes musical instruments, esp. pianos. **2 a** part of a radio or television receiver for tuning. **b** radio receiver as a separate unit in a high-fi system. **3** electronic device for tuning a guitar etc.

tungsten /ˈtʌŋst(ə)n/ *n.* dense metallic element with a very high melting point. [Swedish, = heavy stone]

tunic /ˈtjuːnɪk/ *n.* **1** close-fitting short coat of police or military etc. uniform. **2** loose often sleeveless garment reaching to the knees. [Latin]

tuning-fork *n.* two-pronged steel fork giving a particular note when struck.

tunnel /ˈtʌn(ə)l/ —*n.* **1** underground passage dug through a hill or under a road, river, etc. esp. for a railway or road. **2** underground passage dug by an animal. —*v.* (-**ll-**; *US* -**l-**) **1** (foll. by *through*, *into*, etc.) make a tunnel through. **2** make (one's way) by tunnelling. [French diminutive of *tonne* TUN]

tunnel vision *n.* **1** vision which is poor or lost outside the centre of the normal field of vision. **2** *colloq.* inability to grasp a situation's wider implications.

tunny /ˈtʌnɪ/ *n.* (*pl.* same or -**ies**) = TUNA. [Greek *thunnos*]

tup —*n.* ram. —*v.* (-**pp-**) (of a ram) copulate with (a ewe). [origin unknown]

Tupi /ˈtuːpi/ —*n.* (*pl.* same or -**s**) **1** member of an American Indian people of the Amazon valley. **2** their language. —*adj.* of this people or language. [Tupi]

tuppence /ˈtʌpəns/ *n.* = TWOPENCE. [phonetic spelling]

tuppenny /ˈtʌpnɪ/ *adj.* = TWOPENNY. [phonetic spelling]

Tupperware /ˈtʌpəweə(r)/ *n. propr.* range of plastic containers for storing food. [*Tupper*, name of the manufacturer]

turban /ˈtɜːbən/ *n.* **1** man's headdress of fabric wound round a cap or the head, worn esp. by Muslims and Sikhs. **2** woman's hat resembling this. □ **turbaned** *adj.* [Persian: cf. TULIP]

turbid /ˈtɜːbɪd/ *adj.* **1** (of a liquid or colour) muddy, thick; not clear. **2** (of style etc.) confused, disordered. □ **turbidity** /-ˈbɪdɪtɪ/ *n.* [Latin *turba* crowd]

■ **Usage** *Turbid* is sometimes confused with *turgid* which means 'swollen, inflated; pompous'.

turbine /ˈtɜːbaɪn/ *n.* rotary motor driven by a flow of water, steam, gas, wind, etc. [Latin *turbo* -*in-* spinning-top, whirlwind]

turbo- /ˈtɜːbəʊ/ *n.* (*pl.* -**s**) = TURBO-CHARGER.

turbo- *comb. form* turbine.

turbocharger *n.* supercharger driven by a turbine powered by the engine's exhaust gases.

turbofan *n.* jet engine in which a turbine-driven fan provides additional thrust.

turbojet *n.* **1** jet engine in which the jet also operates a turbine-driven air-compressor. **2** aircraft powered by this.

turboprop *n.* **1** jet engine in which a turbine is used as in a turbojet and also to drive a propeller. **2** aircraft powered by this. [from PROP³]

turbot /ˈtɜːbət/ *n.* (*pl.* same or -**s**) large European flat-fish prized as food. [French from Swedish]

turbulent /ˈtɜːbjʊlənt/ *adj.* **1** disturbed; in commotion. **2** (of a flow of air etc.) varying irregularly. **3** restless; riotous. □ **turbulence** *n.* **turbulently** *adv.* [Latin *turba* crowd]

Turco- *comb. form* (also **Turko-**) Turkish; Turkish and. [medieval Latin: related to TURK]

turd *n. coarse slang* **1** lump of excrement. **2** contemptible person. [Old English]

tureen /tjʊˈriːn/ *n.* deep covered dish for soup. [from TERRINE]

turf —*n.* (*pl.* -**s** or **turves**) **1 a** layer of grass etc. with earth and matted roots as the surface of grassland. **b** piece of this cut from the ground. **2** slab of peat for fuel. **3** (prec. by *the*) **a** horse-racing courses. **b** general term for race-courses. —*v.* **1** cover (ground) with turf. **2** (foll. by *out*) *colloq.* expel or eject (a person or thing). □ **turfy** *adj.* [Old English]

turf accountant *n.* bookmaker.

turgescent /tɜːˈdʒes(ə)nt/ *adj.* becoming turgid. □ **turgescence** *n.* [Latin: related to TURGID]

turgid /ˈtɜːdʒɪd/ *adj.* **1** swollen, inflated. **2** (of language) pompous, bombastic. □ **turgidity** /-ˈdʒɪdɪtɪ/ *n.* [Latin *turgeo* swell]

■ **Usage** *Turgid* is sometimes confused with *turbid* which means 'muddy, not clear; confused'.

Turk *n.* **1 a** native or national of Turkey. **b** person of Turkish descent. **2** member

of a Central Asian people from whom the Ottomans derived, speaking a Turkic language. **3** *offens.* ferocious or wild person. [origin unknown]

turkey /'tɜːkɪ/ n. (pl. -s) **1** large orig. American bird bred for food. **2** its flesh as food. **3** US slang theatrical failure; flop. □ **talk turkey** US colloq. talk frankly; get down to business. [originally of the guinea-fowl, imported from Turkey]

turkeycock n. male turkey.

Turki /'tɜːkɪ/ adj. of a group of languages and peoples including Turkish. —n. this group. □ **Turkic** adj. related to Turki]

Turkish —adj. of Turkey, the Turks, or their language. —n. this language.

Turkish bath n. **1** hot-air or steam bath followed by washing, massage, etc. **2** (in sing. or pl.) building for this.

Turkish carpet n. wool carpet with a thick pile and traditional bold design.

Turkish coffee n. strong black coffee.

Turkish delight n. sweet of lumps of flavoured gelatine coated in powdered sugar.

Turkish towel n. towel made of cotton terry.

Turko- var. of TURCO-.

Turk's head n. turban-like ornamental knot.

turmeric /'tɜːmərɪk/ n. **1** E. Indian plant of the ginger family. **2** its powdered rhizome used as a spice in curry etc. or for yellow dye. [perhaps from French *terre mérite*]

turmoil /'tɜːmɔɪl/ n. **1** violent confusion; agitation. **2** din and bustle. [origin unknown]

turn /tɜːn/ —v. **1** move around a point or axis; give or receive a rotary motion (*turned the wheel; the wheel turns*). **2** change in position so that a different side, end, or part becomes outermost or uppermost etc.; invert or reverse (*it turned inside out; turned it upside down*). **3 a** give a new direction to (*turn your face this way*). **b** take a new direction (*turn left here*). **4** aim in a certain way (*turned the hose on them*). **5** (foll. by *into*) change in nature, form, or condition to (*turned into a frog; turned the book into a play*). **6** (foll. by *to*) a set about (*turned to doing the ironing*). **b** have recourse to (*turned to drink*). **c** go on to consider next (*let us now turn to your report*). **7** become (*turned nasty*). **8 a** about (*turned to me for help*). **b** (foll. by *against*) make or become hostile to. **9** (foll. by *on, upon*) become hostile to; attack (*suddenly turned on them*). **10** (of

milk) become sour **11** (of the stomach) be nauseated. **12** cause (milk) to become sour or (the stomach) to be nauseated. **13** (of the head) become giddy. **14** translate (*turn it into French*). **15** move to the other side of; go round (*turned the corner*). **16** pass the age or time of (*the has turned 40; it has turned 4 o'clock*). **17** (foll. by *on*) depend on; be determined by. **18** send or put; cause to go (*was turned loose; turned the water out into a basin*). **19** perform (a somersault etc.). **20** remake (esp. a sheet) putting the less worn outer side on the inside. **21** make (a profit). **22** divert (a bullet). **23** blunt (a knife etc.). **24** shape (an object) on a lathe. **25** give an (esp. elegant) form to (*turn a compliment*). **26** (of the tide) change direction. —n. — turning; rotary motion or tendency (*took a sudden turn to the left*). **3** point at which a turning or change occurs. **4** turning of a road. **5** change of direction of the tide. **6** change in the course of events (*a turn for the worse*). **7** tendency or disposition; facility of forming (*is of a mechanical turn of mind; has a neat turn of phrase*). **8** opportunity or obligation etc. that comes successively to each of several persons etc. (*my turn to pay*). **9** short walk or ride (*took a turn in the park*). **10** short performance, variety act. **11** service of a specified kind (*did me a good turn*). **12** purpose (*served my turn*). **13** colloq. momentary nervous shock (*gave me a turn*). **14** Mus. ornament consisting of the principal note with those above and below it. □ **at every turn** continually. **by turns** in rotation; alternately. **in turn** in succession. **in one's turn** when one's turn comes. **not know which way (or where) to turn** be at a loss, unsure how to act, etc. **out of turn 1** when it is not one's turn. **2** inappropriately (*did I speak out of turn?*). **take turns** (or **take it in turns**) act alternately. **to a turn** (esp. cooked) perfectly. **turn about** move so as to face in a new direction. **turn around** etc. **US** = *turn round*. **turn away 1** turn to face in another direction. **2** reject **3** send away. **turn back 1** begin or cause to retrace one's steps. **2** fold back. **turn down 1** reject (a proposal etc.). **2** reduce the volume or strength of (sound, heat, etc.) by turning a knob etc. **3** fold down. **turn one's hand to** see HAND. **turn a person's head** see HEAD. **turn in 1** hand in or return. **2** achieve or register (a performance, score, etc.). **3** colloq. go to bed for the night. **4** incline inwards. **5**

hand over (a suspect etc.) to the authorities. **6** *colloq.* abandon (a plan etc.). **turn off 1 a** stop the flow or operation of (water, electricity, etc.) by a tap, switch, etc. **b** operate (a tap, switch, etc.) to achieve this. **2** enter a side-road. **3** *colloq.* cause to lose interest. **turn on 1 a** start the flow or operation of (water, electricity, etc.) by means of a tap, switch, etc. **b** operate (a tap, switch, etc.) to achieve this. **2** *colloq.* excite; stimulate, esp. sexually. **turn on one's heel** see HEEL¹. **turn out 1** expel. **2** extinguish (an electric light etc.). **3** dress or equip (*well turned out*). **4** produce (goods etc.). **5** empty or clean out (a room etc.). **6** empty (a pocket). **7** *colloq.* assemble; attend a meeting etc. **8** (foll. by *to* + infin. or *that* + clause) prove to be the case; result (*turned out to be true; see how things turn out*). **turn over 1** reverse the position of (*turn over the page*). **2 a** cause (an engine) to run. **b** (of an engine) start running. **3** consider; ponder. **4** (foll. by *to*) **a** transfer the care or conduct of (a person or thing) to (a person) (*shall turn it all over to my deputy*). **b** = *turn* in 5. **5** do business to the gross value of (*turns over £5000 a week*). **turn over a new leaf** reform one's conduct. **turn round 1** turn so as to face in a new direction. **2 a** unload and reload (a ship etc.). **b** receive, process, and send out again; cause to progress through a system. **3** adopt new opinions or policy. **turn the tables** see TABLE. **turn tail** turn away; run away. **turn to** set about one's work. **turn turtle** see TURTLE. **turn up 1** increase the volume or strength of by turning a knob etc. **2** discover or reveal. **3** be found, esp. by chance. **4** happen or present itself; (of a person) arrive (*people turned up late*). **5** shorten (a garment) by raising its hem. **6** fold over or upwards. [Old English *tyrnan*, from Greek *tornos* lathe]

turn-about *n.* **1** turning about. **2** abrupt change of policy etc.

turn-buckle *n.* threaded device for tightly connecting parts of a metal rod or wire.

turncoat *n.* person who changes sides.

turner *n.* person who works with a lathe.

turnery *n.* **1** objects made on a lathe. **2** work with a lathe.

turning *n.* **1 a** road that branches from another. **b** place where this occurs. **2 a** use of a lathe. **b** (in *pl.*) chips or shavings from a lathe.

turning-circle *n.* smallest circle in which a vehicle can turn without reversing.

turning-point *n.* point at which a decisive change occurs.

turnip /ˈtɜːnɪp/ *n.* **1** plant with a globular root. **2** its root as a vegetable. □ **turnipy** *adj.* [dial. *neep* (Old English from Latin *napu*)]

turnip-top *n.* turnip leaves as a vegetable.

turnkey *n.* (*pl.* **-s**) *archaic* jailer.

turn-off *n.* **1** turning off a main road. **2** *colloq.* something that repels or causes a loss of interest.

turn-on *n. colloq.* person or thing that causes (esp. sexual) excitement.

turnout *n.* **1** number of people attending a meeting, voting at an election, etc. **2** set or display of equipment, clothes, etc.

turnover *n.* **1** act of turning over. **2** gross amount of money taken in a business. **3** rate at which goods are sold and replaced in a shop. **4** rate at which people enter and leave employment etc. **5** small pie made by folding pastry over a filling.

turnpike *n.* **1** *hist.* **a** toll-gate. **b** road on which a toll was charged. **2** *US* motorway on which a toll is charged.

turn-round *n.* **1 a** unloading and reloading between trips. **b** receiving, processing, and sending out again; progress through a system. **2** reversal of an opinion or tendency.

turnstile *n.* gate with revolving arms allowing people through singly.

turntable *n.* **1** circular revolving plate on which records are played. **2** circular revolving platform for turning a railway locomotive.

turn-up *n.* **1** turned-up end of a trouser leg. **2** *colloq.* unexpected happening.

turpentine /ˈtɜːpəntaɪn/ *n.* resin from any of various trees. [Latin *terebinthina*]

turpentine substitute *n.* = WHITE SPIRIT.

turpitude /ˈtɜːpɪtjuːd/ *n. formal* depravity, wickedness. [Latin *turpis* disgraceful]

turps *n. colloq.* oil of turpentine. [abbreviation]

turquoise /ˈtɜːkwɔɪz/ *–n.* **1** semiprecious stone, usu. opaque and greenish- or sky-blue. **2** greenish-blue colour. *–adj.* of this colour. [French, = Turkish]

turret /ˈtʌrɪt/ *n.* **1** small tower, esp. decorating a building. **2** low flat usu. revolving armoured tower for a gun and gunners in a ship, aircraft, fort, or tank. **3** rotating holder for tools in a lathe etc. □ **turreted** *adj.* [French diminutive: related to TOWER]

turtle /'tɜːt(ə)l/ n. **1** aquatic reptile with flippers and a horny shell. **2** its flesh, used for soup. □ **turn turtle** capsize. [alteration of earlier *tortue*: related to TORTOISE]

turtle-dove /'tɜːt(ə)l,dʌv/ n. wild dove noted for its soft cooing and affection for its mate. [Latin *turtur*]

turtle-neck n. high close-fitting neck on a knitted garment.

Tuscan /'tʌskən/ –n. **1** inhabitant of Tuscany. **2** form of Italian spoken in Tuscany: standard Italian. –adj. **1** of Tuscany or the Tuscans. **2** *Archit.* of the plainest of the classical orders. [Latin *Tuscanus*]

tusk n. long pointed tooth, esp. protruding from a closed mouth, as in the elephant, walrus, etc. □ **tusked** adj. [Old English]

tussle /'tʌs(ə)l/ –n. struggle, scuffle. –v. (-ling) engage in a tussle. [originally (-ling) *touse*: related to TOUSLE]

tussock /'tʌsək/ n. clump of grass etc. □ **tussocky** adj. [perhaps from dial. *tusk*, *tuft*]

tut var. of TUT-TUT.

tutelage /'tjuːtɪlɪdʒ/ n. **1** guardianship. **2** being under this. **3** tuition [Latin *tutela*: related to TUTOR]

tutelary /'tjuːtɪlərɪ/ adj. **1 a** serving as guardian. **b** of a guardian. **2** giving protection. [Latin: related to TUTELAGE]

tutor /'tjuːtə(r)/ –n. **1** private teacher. **2** university teacher supervising the studies or welfare of assigned undergraduates. –v. **1** act as tutor to **2** work as a tutor. □ **tutorship** n. [Latin *tueor tut-* watch]

tutorial /tjuː'tɔːrɪəl/ –adj. of a tutor or tuition. –n. period of undergraduate tuition individually or in a small group. [Latin *tutorius*: related to TUTOR]

tutti /'tuːtɪ/ *Mus.* –adj. & adv. with all voices or instruments together. –n. (pl. -s) such a passage. [Italian, pl. of *tutto* all]

tutti-frutti /,tuːtɪ'fruːtɪ/ n. (pl. -s) ice-cream containing small pieces of mixed glacé fruit. [Italian, = all fruits]

tut-tut /tʌt'tʌt/ (also **tut**) –int. expressing disapproval or impatience. –n. such an exclamation. –v. (-tt-) exclaim this. [imitative of a click of the tongue]

tutu /'tuːtuː/ n. ballet dancer's short skirt of stiffened frills. [French]

tu-whit, tu-whoo /tuˌwɪt tuˈwuː/ n. representation of the cry of an owl. [imitative]

-tux n. US colloq. = TUXEDO. [abbreviation]

tuxedo /tʌk'siːdəʊ/ n. (pl. -s or -es) US **1** dinner-jacket. **2** suit of clothes including this. [*Tuxedo* Park in US]

TV abbr. television.

TVEI abbr. Technical and Vocational Educational Initiative.

twaddle /'twɒd(ə)l/ n. silly writing or talk: nonsense. earlier *twattle*, alteration of TATTLE]

twain adj. & n. archaic two. [Old English, masculine form of two]

twang –n. **1** sound made by a plucked string or released bowstring. **2** nasal quality of a voice. –v. (cause to) emit this sound. □ **twangy** adj. [imitative]

'twas /twɒz/ archaic it was. [contraction]

twat /twɒt/ n. coarse slang **1** female genitals. **2** contemptible person. [origin unknown]

tweak –v. **1** pinch and twist sharply; jerk. **2** make fine adjustments to (a mechanism). –n. act of tweaking. [probably dial. *twick*, *twitch*]

twee adj. (**tweer**; **tweest**) affectedly dainty or quaint. [a childish pronunciation of SWEET]

tweed n. **1** rough-surfaced woollen cloth, usu. of mixed flecked colours. **2** (in pl.) clothes made of tweed. [alteration of *tweel* (Scots var. of TWILL)]

tweedy adj. (-ier, -iest) **1** of or dressed in tweed. **2** characteristic of country gentry; heartily informal.

'tween prep. archaic = BETWEEN. [abbreviation]

tweet –n. chirp of a small bird. –v. make this noise. [imitative]

tweeter n. loudspeaker for high frequencies.

tweezers /'twiːzəz/ n.pl. small pair of pincers for taking up small objects, plucking out hairs, etc. [originally *tweezes* pl. of obsolete *tweeze*, a case for small instruments]

twelfth adj. & n. **1** next after eleventh. **2** each of twelve equal parts of a thing. □ **Twelfth Nigh**: n. 5 Jan., eve of Epiphany.

twelve adj. & n. **1** one more than eleven. **2** symbol for this (12, xii, XII). **3** size etc. denoted by twelve. **4** twelve o'clock. **5** (the Twelve) the apostles. [Old English]

twelvefold adj. & adv. **1** twelve times as much or as many. **2** consisting of twelve parts.

twelvemonth n. archaic year.

twenty /'twentɪ/ adj. & n. (pl. -ies) **1** product of two and ten. **2** symbol for this (20, xx, XX). **3** (in pl.) numbers from 20 to 29, esp. the years of a century or of a person's life. □ **twentieth** adj. & n. [Old English]

twenty-twenty vision *n.* (also **20/20 vision**) 1 vision of normal acuity. 2 *colloq.* good eyesight.

'twere /twɛː(r)/ *archaic* it were. [contraction]

twerp *n.* (also **twirp**) *slang* stupid or objectionable person. [origin unknown]

twice *adv.* 1 two times; on two occasions. 2 in double degree or quantity (*twice as good*). [Old English: related to **TWO**]

twiddle /ˈtwɪd(ə)l/ —*v.* (**-ling**) twirl, adjust, or play randomly or idly. —*n.* act of twiddling. □ **twiddle one's thumbs** 1 make them rotate round each other. 2 have nothing to do. □ **twiddly** *adj.* [probably imitative]

twig[1] *n.* very small thin branch of a tree or shrub. □ **twiggy** *adj.* [Old English]

twig[2] *v.* (**-gg-**) *colloq.* understand; realize. [origin unknown]

twilight /ˈtwaɪlaɪt/ *n.* 1 light from the sky when the sun is below the horizon, esp. in the evening. 2 period of the faint light. 4 period of decline or destruction. [from **TWO**, **LIGHT**[1]]

twilight zone *n.* 1 decrepit urban area. 2 undefined or intermediate zone or area.

twilit /ˈtwaɪlɪt/ *adj.* dimly illuminated by twilight.

twill *n.* fabric so woven as to have a surface of diagonal parallel ridges. □ **twilled** *adj.* [Old English, = two-thread]

'twill *archaic* it will. [contraction]

twin —*n.* 1 each of a closely related or associated pair, esp. of children or animals born at a birth. 2 exact counterpart of a person or thing. 3 (**the Twins**) zodiacal sign or constellation Gemini. —*adj.* forming, or being one of, such a pair (*twin brothers*). —*v.* (**-nn-**) 1 a join intimately together. **b** (foll. by *with*) pair. 2 bear twins. 3 link (a town) with one in a different country, for friendship and cultural exchange. □ **twinning** *n.* [Old English: related to **TWO**]

twin bed *n.* each of a pair of single beds. □ **twin-bedded** *adj.*

twine —*n.* 1 strong coarse string of twisted strands of fibre. 2 coil, twist. —*v.* (**-ning**) 1 form (a string etc.) by twisting strands. 2 weave (a garland etc.). 3 (often foll. by *with*) garland (a brow etc.). 4 (often foll. by *round*, *about*) coil or wind. 5 *refl.* (of a plant) grow in this way. [Old English]

twin-engined *adj.* having two engines.

twinge /twɪndʒ/ *n.* sharp momentary local pain or pang. [Old English]

twinkle /ˈtwɪŋk(ə)l/ —*v.* (**-ling**) 1 (of a star or light etc.) shine with rapidly intermittent gleams. 2 (of the eyes) sparkle. 3 (of the feet) move lightly and rapidly. —*n.* 1 sparkle or gleam of the eyes. 2 twinkling light. 3 light rapid movement. □ **in a twinkle** (or **a twinkling** or **the twinkling of an eye**) in an instant. □ **twinkly** *adj.* [Old English]

twin set *n.* woman's matching cardigan and jumper.

twin town *n.* town twinned with another.

twirl —*v.* spin, swing, or twist quickly and lightly round. —*n.* 1 twirling motion. 2 flourish made with a pen. [origin uncertain]

twirp var. of **TWERP**.

twist —*v.* 1 **a** change the form of by rotating one end and not the other or the two ends in opposite directions. **b** undergo such a change. **c** wrench or pull out of shape with a twisting action (*twisted my ankle*). 2 **a** wind (strands etc.) about each other. **b** form (a rope etc.) in this way. 3 **a** give a spiral form to. **b** take a spiral form. 4 (foll. by *off*) break off by twisting. 5 misrepresent the meaning of (words). 6 **a** take a winding course. **b** make (one's way) in a winding manner. 7 *colloq.* cheat. 8 (as **twisted** *adj.*) *derog.* (of a person or mind) neurotic; perverted. 9 dance the twist. —*n.* 1 act of twisting. 2 twisted state. 3 thing formed by twisting. 4 point at which a thing twists or bends. 5 usu. *derog.* peculiar tendency of mind or character etc. 6 unexpected development of events, esp. in a story etc. 7 (prec. by *the*) popular 1960s dance with a twisting movement of the hips. □ **round the twist** *slang* crazy. **twist a person's arm** *colloq.* coerce, esp. using moral pressure. **twist round one's finger** easily persuade or dominate (a person). □ **twisty** *adj.* (**-ier**, **-iest**). [related to **TWIN**, **TWINE**]

twister *n. colloq.* swindler.

twit[1] *n. slang* foolish person. [originally dial.; perhaps from **TWIT**[2]]

twit[2] *v.* (**-tt-**) reproach or taunt, usu. good-humouredly. [Old English]

twitch —*v.* 1 (of features, muscles, etc.) move or contract spasmodically. 2 pull sharply at. —*n.* 1 sudden involuntary contraction or movement. 2 sudden pull or jerk. 3 *colloq.* state of nervousness. □ **twitchy** *adj.* (**-ier**, **-iest**) (in sense 3 of *n.*). [probably Old English]

twitcher *n. colloq.* bird-watcher seeking sightings of rare birds.

twitter —*v.* 1 (esp. of a bird) emit a succession of light tremulous sounds. 2 utter or express in this way. —*n.* 1 act of twittering. 2 *colloq.* tremulously excited state. □ **twittery** *adj.* [imitative]

'twixt prep. archaic = BETWIXT. [contraction]

two /tuː/ adj. & n. **1** one more than one. **2** symbol for this (2, ii, II). **3** size etc. denoted by two. a **two** o'clock. □ **in two** in or into two pieces. **put two and two together** infer from known facts. [Old English]

two-bit attrib. adj. US colloq. cheap, petty.

two-dimensional adj. **1** having or appearing to have length and breadth but no depth. **2** lacking substance; superficial.

two-edged adj. double-edged.

two-faced adj. insincere; deceitful.

twofold adj. & adv. **1** twice as much or as many. **2** consisting of two parts.

two-handed adj. **1** having, using, or requiring the use of two hands. **2** (of a card-game) for two players.

twopence /'tʌpəns/ n. **1** sum of two pence. **2** (esp. with neg.) colloq. thing of little value (don't care twopence).

twopenny /'tʌpənɪ/ attrib. adj. **1** costing two pence. **2** colloq. cheap, worthless.

twopenny-halfpenny /'tʌpnɪ'heɪpnɪ/ attrib. adj. cheap, insignificant.

two-piece —adj. (of a suit etc.) consisting of two matching items. —n. two-piece suit etc.

two-ply —adj. of two strands or layers etc. —n. **1** two-ply wool. **2** two-ply wood.

twosome n. two persons together.

two-step n. dance in march or polka time.

two-stroke —attrib. adj. (of an internal-combustion engine) having its power cycle completed in one up-and-down movement of the piston. —n. two-stroke engine.

two-time v. colloq. **1** be unfaithful to (a lover). **2** swindle. □ **two-timer** n.

two-tone adj. having two colours or sounds.

'twould /twʊd/ archaic it would. [contraction]

two-way adj. **1** involving two directions or participants. **2** (of a radio) capable of transmitting and receiving signals.

two-way mirror n. panel of glass that can be seen through from one side and is a mirror on the other.

-ty[1] suffix forming nouns denoting quality or condition (cruelty; plenty). [French from Latin -tas -tatis]

-ty[2] suffix denoting tens (ninety). [Old English -tig]

tycoon /taɪ'kuːn/ n. business magnate. [Japanese, = great lord]

tying pres. part. of TIE.

tyke /taɪk/ n. (also **tike**) **1** unpleasant or coarse man. **2** small child. [Old Norse]

tympani var. of TIMPANI.

tympanum /'tɪmpənəm/ n. (pl. **-s** or **-na**) **1** middle ear. **2** eardrum. **3** Archit. **a** vertical triangular space forming the centre of a pediment. **b** similar space over a door between the lintel and the arch. [Greek tumpanon drum]

Tynwald /'tɪnwəld/ n. parliament of the Isle of Man. [Old Norse, = assembly-field]

type /taɪp/ —n. **1** sort, class, or kind. **2** person, thing, or event exemplifying a class or group. **3** (in comb.) made of, resembling, or functioning as (cerami-type material; Cheddar-type cheese). **4** colloq. person, esp. of a specified character (a quiet type; not my type). **5** object, conception, or work of art, serving as a model for subsequent artists. **6** Printing **a** piece of metal etc. with a raised letter or character on its upper surface for printing. **b** kind or size of such pieces (printed in large type). □ set or supply of these (ran short of type). —v. (**-ping**) **1** write with a typewriter. **2** typecast. **3** esp. Biol. & Med. assign to a type; classify. [Greek tupos impression]

typecast v. (past and past part. **-cast**) assign (an actor or actress) repeatedly to the same type of role.

typeface n. Printing **1** inked surface of type. **2** set of characters in one design.

typescript n. typewritten document.

typesetter n. Printing **1** person who composes type. **2** composing-machine. □ **typesetting** n.

typewriter n. machine with keys for producing printlike characters one at a time on paper inserted round a roller.

typewritten adj. produced on a typewriter.

typhoid /'taɪfɔɪd/ n. (in full **typhoid fever**) infectious bacterial fever attacking the intestines.

typhoon /taɪ'fuːn/ n. violent hurricane in E. Asian seas. [Chinese, = great wind, and Arabic]

typhus /'taɪfəs/ n. infectious fever with a purple rash, headaches, and usu. delirium. [Greek, = stupor]

typical /'tɪpɪk(ə)l/ adj. **1** serving as a characteristic example; representative (a typical English pub). **2** (often foll. by of) characteristic of a particular person, thing, or type (typical of him to refuse). □ **typically** /-kəlɪ/ adv. [medieval Latin: related to TYPE]

typify /'tɪpɪfaɪ/ v. (**-ies, -ied**) **1** be typical of. **2** represent by or as a type or symbol. □ **typification** /-fɪ'keɪʃ(ə)n/ n. [Latin: related to TYPE]

typist /'taɪpɪst/ n. person who types, esp. for a living.

typo /ˈtaɪpəʊ/ n. (pl. -s) colloq. typographical error. [abbreviation]

typography /taɪˈpɒgrəfɪ/ n. 1 printing as an art. 2 style and appearance of printed matter. □ **typographer** n. **typographical** /-pəˈgræfɪk(ə)l/ adj. **typographically** /-pəˈgræfɪkəlɪ/ adv. [French: related to TYPE]

tyrannical /tɪˈrænɪk(ə)l/ adj. despotic; unjustly severe. □ **tyrannically** adv. [Greek: related to TYRANT]

tyrannize /ˈtɪrənaɪz/ v. (also **-ise**) (-zing or -sing) (often foll. by over) treat despotically or cruelly. [French: related to TYRANT]

tyrannosaurus /tɪ,rænəˈsɔːrəs/ n. (pl. -ruses) (also tyrannosaur) dinosaur with very short front legs and a long well-developed tail. [from TYRANT, after dinosaur]

tyranny /ˈtɪrənɪ/ n. (pl. -ies) 1 cruel and arbitrary use of authority. 2 a rule by a tyrant. b period of this. c State ruled by a tyrant. □ **tyrannous** adj. [Greek: related to TYRANT]

tyrant /ˈtaɪərənt/ n. 1 oppressive or cruel ruler. 2 person exercising power arbitrarily or cruelly. [Greek turannos]

tyre /ˈtaɪə(r)/ n. (US tire) rubber covering, usu. inflated, placed round a wheel to form a soft contact with the road. [var. of TIRE²]

Tyrian /ˈtɪrɪən/ —adj. of ancient Tyre in Phoenicia. —n. native or citizen of Tyre. [Latin Tyrus Tyre]

Tyrian purple see PURPLE n. 2.

tyro var. of TIRO.

tzatziki /tsætˈsiːkɪ/ n. Greek side dish of yoghurt with cucumber. [modern Greek]

U

U¹ /juː/ n. (also **u**) (pl. **Us** or **U's**) **1** twenty-first letter of the alphabet. **2** U-shaped object or curve.

U² /juː/ adj. colloq. upper class or supposedly upper class or suitable (of films classified as suitable for all).

U³ abbr. (also **U.**) universal (of films classified as suitable for all).

U⁴ symb. uranium.

UB40 abbr. **1** card issued to people claiming unemployment benefit. **2** colloq. unemployed person [unemployment benefit]

ubiquitous /juːˈbikwitəs/ adj. **1** (seemingly) present everywhere simultaneously. **2** often encountered. □ **ubiquity** n. [Latin ubique everywhere]

U-boat /ˈjuːbəʊt/ n. hist. German submarine. [German Unterse undersea]

UCCA /ˈʌkə/ abbr. Universities Central Council on Admissions.

u.c. abbr. upper case.

UDA abbr. Ulster Defence Association (a loyalist paramilitary organization).

UDI abbr. unilateral declaration of independence.

UDR abbr. Ulster Defence Regiment.

UEFA /juːˈeɪfə/ abbr. Union of European Football Associations.

UFO /ˈjuːfəʊ/ n. (also **ufo**) (pl. **-s**) unidentified flying object.

ugh /əx, ʌɡ/ int. **1** expressing disgust etc. **2** sound of a cough or grunt. [imitative]

Ugli /ˈʌɡli/ n. (pl. **-lis** or **-lies**) propr. mottled green and yellow hybrid of a grapefruit and a tangerine. [from UGLY]

ugly /ˈʌɡli/ adj. (**-lier, -liest**) **1** unpleasant to the eye, ear, or mind etc. (ugly scar; ugly snarl). **2** unpleasantly suggestive; discreditable (ugly rumours). **3** threatening, dangerous (an ugly look). **4** morally repulsive (ugly vices). □ **ugliness** n. [Old Norse]

ugly customer n. threatening or violent person.

ugly duckling n. person lacking early promise but blossoming later.

UHF abbr. ultrahigh frequency.

uh-huh /ˈʌhʌ/ int. colloq. yes; indeed. [imitative]

UHT abbr. ultra heat treated (esp. of milk, for long keeping).

UK abbr. United Kingdom.

Ukrainian /juːˈkreɪnɪən/ -n. **1** native or language of Ukraine. **2** person of Ukrainian descent. -adj. of Ukraine, its people, or language. [Ukraine in eastern Europe]

ukulele /ˌjuːkəˈleɪlɪ/ n. small four-stringed Hawaiian guitar. [Hawaiian]

ulcer n. **1** open sore on or in the body, often forming pus. **2** corrupting influence etc. □ **ulcerous** adj. [Latin ulcus-er-]

ulcerate /ˈʌlsəreɪt/ v. (**-ting**) form into or affect with an ulcer. □ **ulceration** n. [Latin]

-ule suffix forming diminutive nouns (globule). [Latin -ulus]

ullage /ˈʌlɪdʒ/ n. **1** amount by which a cask etc. falls short of being full. **2** loss by evaporation or leakage. [French from Latin]

ulna /ˈʌlnə/ n. (pl. **ulnae** /-niː/) **1** thinner and longer bone in the forearm, opposite to the thumb. **2** corresponding bone in an animal's foreleg or a bird's wing. □ **ulnar** adj. [Latin]

ulster n. long loose overcoat of rough cloth. [Ulster in Ireland]

Ulsterman n. (fem. **Ulsterwoman**) native of Ulster.

ult. abbr. ultimo.

ulterior /ʌlˈtɪərɪə(r)/ adj. not evident or admitted; hidden, secret (esp. ulterior motive). [Latin = further]

ultimate /ˈʌltɪmət/ -adj. **1** last or last possible, final. **2** fundamental, primary, basic (ultimate truths). -n. **1** (prec. by the) best achievable or imaginable. **2** final or fundamental fact or principle. □ **ultimately** adv. [Latin ultimus last]

ultimatum /ˌʌltɪˈmeɪtəm/ n. (pl. **-s**) final statement of terms, the rejection of which could cause hostility etc. [Latin]

ultimo /ˈʌltɪməʊ/ adj. Commerce of last month (the 28th ultimo). [Latin mense ultimo]

ultra /ˈʌltrə/ -adj. extreme esp. in religion or politics. -n. extremist. [see ULTRA-]

ultra- comb. form **1** extreme(ly), excessive(ly) (ultra-modern). **2** beyond, on the other side of [Latin ultra beyond]

ultra-high /ˌʌltrəˈhaɪ/ adj. (of a frequency) in the range 300 to 3000 megahertz.

ultramarine /ˌʌltrəməˈriːn/ -n. **1** brilliant blue pigment orig. from lapis

lazuli. **2** colour of this. –*adj.* of this colour. [Italian and medieval Latin, = beyond the sea, from where lapis lazuli was brought]

ultramicroscopic /ˌʌltrəˌmaɪkrə'skɒpɪk/ *adj.* too small to be seen by an ordinary optical microsˑᶜpe.

ultramontane /ˌʌltrə'mɒnteɪn/ –*adj.* **1** situated beyond the Alps. **2** advocating supreme papal authority. –*n.* **1** person living beyond the Alps. **2** advocate of supreme papal authority. [medieval Latin: related to MOUNTAIN]

ultrasonic /ˌʌltrə'sɒnɪk/ *adj.* of or using sound waves pitched above the range of human hearing. □ **ultrasonically** *adv.*

ultrasonics *n.pl.* (usu. treated as *sing.*) science of ultrasonic waves.

ultrasound /'ʌltrəˌsaʊnd/ *n.* ultrasonic waves.

ultraviolet /ˌʌltrə'vaɪələt/ *adj.* of or using radiation with a frequency just beyond the violet end of the visible spectrum.

ultra vires /ˌʌltrə 'vaɪəˌriːz/ *adv.* & *predic.adj.* beyond one's legal power or authority. [Latin]

ululate /'juːljʊˌleɪt/ *v.* (**-ting**) howl, wail. □ **ululation** /-'leɪʃ(ə)n/ *n.* [Latin]

um *int.* expressing hesitation or a pause in speech. [imitative]

umbel /'ʌmb(ə)l/ *n.* flower-cluster with stalks springing from a common centre and forming a flat or curved surface. □ **umbellate** *adj.* [Latin *umbella* sunshade]

umbelliferous /ˌʌmbɪ'lɪfərəs/ *adj.* (of a plant) bearing umbels, such as parsley and carrot.

umber /'ʌmbə(r)/ –*n.* **1** natural pigment like ochre but darker and browner. **2** colour of this. –*adj.* of this colour. [Latin *umbra* shadow]

umbilical /ʌm'bɪlɪk(ə)l/ *adj.* of the navel. [from UMBILICUS]

umbilical cord *n.* cordlike structure attaching a foetus to the placenta.

umbilicus /ʌm'bɪlɪkəs/ *n.* (*pl.* **-ci** /-ˌsaɪ/ or **-cuses**) navel. [Latin]

umbra /'ʌmbrə/ *n.* (*pl.* **-s** or **-brae** /-briː/) total shadow, esp. that cast on the earth by the moon during a solar eclipse. [Latin, = shadow]

umbrage /'ʌmbrɪdʒ/ *n.* offence taken (esp. *take umbrage at*). [Latin: related to UMBRA]

umbrella /ʌm'brelə/ *n.* **1** collapsible cloth canopy on a central stick, used against rain, strong sun, etc. **2** protection, patronage. **3** (often *attrib.*) coordinating agency (*umbrella organization*). [Italian diminutive: related to UMBRA]

umlaut /'ʊmlaʊt/ *n.* **1** mark (ˑˑ) used over a vowel, esp. in Germanic languages, to indicate a vowel change. **2** such a vowel change, e.g. German *Mann, Männer* /'menə(r)/, English *man, men*. [German]

umpire /'ʌmpaɪə(r)/ –*n.* person enforcing rules and settling disputes in esp. cricket or between disputants. –*v.* (**-ring**) (often foll. by *for*, *in*, etc.) act as umpire (in). [French *nonper* not equal: related to PEER¹]

umpteen /ʌmp'tiːn/ *colloq.* –*adj.* indefinitely many; a lot of. –*pron.* indefinitely many. □ **umpteenth** *adj.* [jocular formation on -TEEN]

UN *abbr.* United Nations.

un-¹ *prefix* **1** added to adjectives and participles and their derivative nouns and adverbs, meaning: **a** not (*unusable*). **b** reverse of (esp. with implied approval etc.) (*unselfish*; *unsociable*). **2** (less often) added to nouns, meaning 'a lack of', 'the reverse of' (*unrest*; *untruth*). [Old English]

■ **Usage** The number of words that can be formed with this prefix (and with un-²) is virtually unlimited, consequently only a selection can be given here.

un-² *prefix* added to verbs and (less often) nouns, forming verbs denoting: **1** reversal (*undress*; *unsettle*). **2** deprivation (*unmask*). **3** release from (*unburden*; *uncage*). **4** causing to be no longer (*unman*). [Old English]

■ **Usage** See note at un-¹.

un-³ *prefix Chem.* denoting 'one', combined with other numerical roots *nil* (= 0), *un* (= 1), *bi* (= 2), etc., to form the names of elements based on the atomic number, and terminated with *-ium*, e.g. *unnilquadium* = 104, *ununbium* = 112. [Latin *unus* one]

unabashed /ˌʌnə'baʃt/ *adj.* not abashed.

unabated /ˌʌnə'beɪtɪd/ *adj.* not abated; undiminished.

unable /ʌn'eɪb(ə)l/ *predic.adj.* (usu. foll. by *to* + infin.) not able.

unabridged /ˌʌnə'brɪdʒd/ *adj.* complete; not abridged.

unacademic /ˌʌnəkə'demɪk/ *adj.* (of a person, book, etc.) not academic.

unacceptable /ˌʌnək'septəb(ə)l/ *adj.* not acceptable. □ **unacceptably** *adv.*

unaccompanied /ˌʌnə'kʌmpənɪd/ *adj.* **1** not accompanied. **2** *Mus.* without accompaniment.

unaccomplished /ˌʌnə'kʌmplɪʃt/ *adj.* **1** uncompleted. **2** lacking accomplishments.

unaccountable /ˌʌnəˈkaʊntəb(ə)l/ *adj.* **1** without explanation; strange. **2** not answerable for one's actions. □ **unaccountably** *adv.*

unaccounted /ˌʌnəˈkaʊntɪd/ *adj.* (often foll. by *for*) unexplained; excluded.

unaccustomed /ˌʌnəˈkʌstəmd/ *adj.* **1** (usu. foll. by *to*) not accustomed. **2** unusual (*unaccustomed silence*).

unacknowledged /ˌʌnəkˈnɒlɪdʒd/ *adj.* not acknowledged.

unacquainted /ˌʌnəˈkweɪntɪd/ *adj.* (usu. foll. by *with*) not acquainted.

unadopted /ˌʌnəˈdɒptɪd/ *adj.* (of a road) not maintained by a local authority.

unadorned /ˌʌnəˈdɔːnd/ *adj.* plain.

unadulterated /ˌʌnəˈdʌltəˌreɪtɪd/ *adj.* **1** pure. **2** complete, utter.

unadventurous /ˌʌnədˈventʃərəs/ *adj.* not adventurous.

unadvised /ˌʌnədˈvaɪzd/ *adj.* **1** indiscreet; rash. **2** without advice. □ **unadvisedly** /-zɪdli/ *adv.*

unaffected /ˌʌnəˈfektɪd/ *adj.* **1** (usu. foll. by *by*) not affected. **2** free from affectation. □ **unaffectedly** *adv.*

unaffiliated /ˌʌnəˈfɪliˌeɪtɪd/ *adj.* not affiliated.

unafraid /ˌʌnəˈfreɪd/ *adj.* not afraid.

unaided /ʌnˈeɪdɪd/ *adj.* without help.

unalike /ˌʌnəˈlaɪk/ *adj.* not alike; different.

unalloyed /ˌʌnəˈlɔɪd/ *adj.* **1** complete; utter (*unalloyed joy*). **2** pure.

unalterable /ʌnˈɔːltərəb(ə)l/ *adj.* not alterable.

unaltered /ʌnˈɔːltəd/ *adj.* not altered; remaining the same.

unambiguous /ˌʌnæmˈbɪɡjʊəs/ *adj.* not ambiguous; clear or definite in meaning. □ **unambiguously** *adv.*

unambitious /ˌʌnæmˈbɪʃəs/ *adj.* not ambitious.

un-American /ˌʌnəˈmerɪkən/ *adj.* **1** uncharacteristic of Americans. **2** contrary to US interests, treasonable.

unamused /ˌʌnəˈmjuːzd/ *adj.* not amused.

unanimous /juːˈnænɪməs/ *adj.* **1** all in agreement (*committee was unanimous*). **2** (of an opinion, vote, etc.) by all without exception (*unanimous choice*). □ **unanimity** /-nəˈnɪmɪtɪ/ *n.* **unanimously** *adv.* [Latin *unus* one, *animus* mind]

unannounced /ˌʌnəˈnaʊnst/ *adj.* not announced; without warning (of arrival etc.).

unanswerable /ʌnˈɑːnsərəb(ə)l/ *adj.* **1** irrefutable (*unanswerable case*). **2** unable to be answered (*unanswerable question*).

unanswered /ʌnˈɑːnsəd/ *adj.* not answered.

unanticipated /ˌʌnænˈtɪsɪˌpeɪtɪd/ *adj.* not anticipated.

unappealing /ˌʌnəˈpiːlɪŋ/ *adj.* unattractive.

unappetizing /ʌˈæpɪˌtaɪzɪŋ/ *adj.* not appetizing.

unappreciated /ˌʌnəˈpriːʃɪˌeɪtɪd/ *adj.* not appreciated.

unappreciative /ˌʌnəˈpriːʃətɪv/ *adj.* not appreciative.

unapproachable /ˌʌnəˈprəʊtʃəb(ə)l/ *adj.* **1** inaccessible. **2** (of a person) unfriendly.

unarmed /ʌnˈɑːmd/ *adj.* not armed; without weapons.

unashamed /ˌʌnəˈʃeɪmd/ *adj.* **1** feeling no guilt. **2** blatant; bold. □ **unashamedly** /-mɪdlɪ/ *adv.*

unassailable /ˌʌnəˈseɪləb(ə)l/ *adj.* unable to be attacked; impregnable.

unassuming /ˌʌnəˈsjuːmɪŋ/ *adj.* not pretentious; modest.

unattached /ˌʌnəˈtætʃt/ *adj.* **1** not engaged, married, etc. **2** (often foll. by *to*) not attached, esp. to a particular organization etc.

unattainable /ˌʌnəˈteɪnəb(ə)l/ *adj.* not attainable.

unattended /ˌʌnəˈtendɪd/ *adj.* **1** (usu. foll. by *to*) not attended. **2** (of a person, vehicle, etc.) alone.

unattractive /ˌʌnəˈtræktɪv/ *adj.* not attractive. □ **unattractively** *adv.*

unattributable /ˌʌnəˈtrɪbjʊtəb(ə)l/ *adj.* (esp. of published information) not attributed to a source etc.

unauthorized /ʌnˈɔːθəraɪzd/ *adj.* (also **-ised**) not authorized.

unavailable /ˌʌnəˈveɪləb(ə)l/ *adj.* not available. □ **unavailability** /-ˈbɪlɪtɪ/ *n.*

unavailing /ˌʌnəˈveɪlɪŋ/ *adj.* achieving nothing. □ **unavailingly** *adv.*

unavoidable /ˌʌnəˈvɔɪdəb(ə)l/ *adj.* inevitable. □ **unavoidably** *adv.*

unaware /ˌʌnəˈweə(r)/ *—adj.* **1** (usu. foll. by *of* or *that*) not aware. **2** unperceptive. *—adv.* = UNAWARES. □ **unawareness** *n.*

unawares *adv.* **1** unexpectedly. **2** inadvertently.

unbalanced /ʌnˈbælənst/ *adj.* **1** emotionally unstable. **2** biased (*unbalanced report*).

unban /ʌnˈbæn/ *v.* (**-nn-**) remove prohibited status from; allow.

unbar /ʌnˈbɑː(r)/ *v.* (**-rr-**) **1** unlock, open. **2** remove a bar from (a gate etc.).

unbearable /ʌnˈbeərəb(ə)l/ *adj.* unendurable. □ **unbearably** *adv.*

unbeatable /ʌnˈbiːtəb(ə)l/ *adj.* not beatable; excelling.

unbeaten /ʌnˈbiːt(ə)n/ *adj.* **1** not beaten. **2** (of a record etc.) not surpassed.

unbecoming /ˌʌnbɪˈkʌmɪŋ/ *adj.* **1** unflattering (*unbecoming hat*). **2** (usu. foll.

by to, for) not fitting; indecorous. □ **unbecomingly** adv.

unbeknown /ˌʌnbɪˈnəʊn/ adj. (also **unbeknownst** /-ˈnəʊnst/) (foll. by to) without the knowledge of (unbeknown to us).

unbelief /ˌʌnbɪˈliːf/ n. lack of esp. religious belief. □ **unbeliever** n. **unbelieving** adj.

unbelievable /ˌʌnbɪˈliːvəb(ə)l/ adj. not believable; incredible. □ **unbelievably** adv.

unbend /ʌnˈbend/ v. (past and past part. **unbent**) 1 straighten. 2 relax; become affable.

unbending adj. 1 inflexible. 2 firm; austere.

unbiased /ʌnˈbaɪəst/ adj. (also **unbiassed**) impartial.

unbidden /ʌnˈbɪd(ə)n/ adj. not commanded or invited (arrived unbidden).

unbind /ʌnˈbaɪnd/ v. (past and past part. **unbound**) release; unfasten, untie.

unbleached /ʌnˈbliːtʃt/ adj. not bleached.

unblemished /ʌnˈblemɪʃt/ adj. not blemished.

unblinking /ʌnˈblɪŋkɪŋ/ adj. 1 not blinking. 2 steadfast; stolid.

unblock /ʌnˈblɒk/ v. remove an obstruction from.

unblushing /ʌnˈblʌʃɪŋ/ adj. 1 shameless. 2 frank.

unbolt /ʌnˈbəʊlt/ v. release the bolt of (a door etc.).

unborn /ʌnˈbɔːn/ adj. not yet, or never to be, born (unborn child; unborn hopes).

unbosom /ʌnˈbʊz(ə)m/ v. (often refl.) disclose (thoughts etc.); unburden oneself.

unbothered /ʌnˈbɒðəd/ predic. adj. not bothered; unconcerned.

unbound[1] /ʌnˈbaʊnd/ adj. 1 not bound. 2 unconstrained. 3 a (of a book) without a binding. b having paper covers.

unbound[2] past and past part. of UNBIND.

unbounded /ʌnˈbaʊndɪd/ adj. infinite (unbounded optimism).

unbreakable /ʌnˈbreɪkəb(ə)l/ adj. not breakable.

unbridgeable /ʌnˈbrɪdʒəb(ə)l/ adj. unable to be bridged.

unbridle /ʌnˈbraɪd(ə)l/ v. (-ling) remove a bridle, constraints, etc., from (a horse, one's tongue, etc.) (unbridled insolence).

unbuckle /ʌnˈbʌk(ə)l/ v. (-ling) release the buckle of (a strap, shoe, etc.).

unburden /ʌnˈbɜːd(ə)n/ v. (often refl.; often followed by to) relieve (oneself, one's conscience, etc.) by confession etc.

unbusinesslike /ʌnˈbɪznɪsˌlaɪk/ adj. not businesslike.

unbutton /ʌnˈbʌt(ə)n/ v. 1 unfasten the buttons of (a garment, person, etc.). 2 (absol.) colloq. relax.

uncalled-for /ʌnˈkɔːldfɔː(r)/ adj. (of a remark, action, etc.) rude, unnecessary.

uncanny /ʌnˈkænɪ/ adj. (-ier, -iest) seemingly supernatural; mysterious. □ **uncannily** adv. **uncanniness** n.

uncapped /ʌnˈkæpt/ adj. Sport (of a player) not yet awarded his cap or never having been selected to represent his country.

uncared-for /ʌnˈkeədfɔː(r)/ adj. disregarded; neglected.

uncaring /ʌnˈkeərɪŋ/ adj. neglectful, lacking compassion.

unceasing /ʌnˈsiːsɪŋ/ adj. not ceasing; continuous (unceasing effort).

uncensored /ʌnˈsensəd/ adj. not censored.

unceremonious /ˌʌnserɪˈməʊnɪəs/ adj. 1 abrupt; discourteous. 2 informal. □ **unceremoniously** adv.

uncertain /ʌnˈsɜːt(ə)n/ adj. 1 not certainly knowing or known (result is uncertain). 2 unreliable. 3 changeable, erratic (uncertain weather). □ **in no uncertain terms** clearly and forcefully. □ **uncertainly** adv. **uncertainty** n. (pl. **-ies**).

unchain /ʌnˈtʃeɪn/ v. remove the chain(s) from; release.

unchallengeable /ʌnˈtʃælɪndʒəb(ə)l/ adj. not challengeable; unassailable.

unchallenged /ʌnˈtʃælɪndʒd/ adj. not challenged.

unchangeable /ʌnˈtʃeɪndʒəb(ə)l/ adj. unable to be changed.

unchanged /ʌnˈtʃeɪndʒd/ adj. not changed; unaltered.

unchanging /ʌnˈtʃeɪndʒɪŋ/ adj. not changing; remaining the same.

unchaperoned /ʌnˈʃæpəˌrəʊnd/ adj. without a chaperone.

uncharacteristic /ˌʌnkærɪktəˈrɪstɪk/ adj. not characteristic. □ **uncharacter-istically** adv.

uncharitable /ʌnˈtʃærɪtəb(ə)l/ adj. censorious, severe in judgement. □ **uncharitably** adv.

uncharted /ʌnˈtʃɑːtɪd/ adj. not mapped or surveyed.

unchecked /ʌnˈtʃekt/ adj. 1 not checked. 2 unrestrained (unchecked violence).

unchivalrous /ʌnˈʃɪvəlrəs/ adj. not chivalrous. □ **unchivalrously** adv.

unchristian /ʌnˈkrɪstʃ(ə)n/ *adj.* contrary to Christian principles, esp. uncaring or selfish.

uncial /ˈʌnsɪəl/ *—adj.* of or written in majuscule letters similar to capitals, found in manuscripts of the 4th–8th c. *—n.* uncial letter, style, or MS. [Latin *uncia* inch]

uncircumcised /ʌnˈsɜːkəmsaɪzd/ *adj.* not circumcised.

uncivil /ʌnˈsɪvɪl/ *adj.* ill-mannered; impolite. □ **uncivilly** *adv.*

uncivilized /ʌnˈsɪvɪlaɪzd/ *adj.* (also **-ised**) 1 not civilized. 2 rough; uncultured.

unclaimed /ʌnˈkleɪmd/ *adj.* not claimed.

unclasp /ʌnˈklɑːsp/ *v.* 1 loosen the clasp(s) of. 2 release the grip of (a hand etc.).

unclassified /ʌnˈklæsɪfaɪd/ *adj.* 1 not classified. 2 (of State information) not secret.

uncle /ˈʌŋk(ə)l/ *n.* 1 a a brother of one's father or mother. b aunt's husband. 2 *colloq.* (form of address by a child to) parent's male friend. 3 *slang esp. hist.* pawnbroker. [Latin *avunculus*]

-uncle *suffix* forming nouns, usu. diminutives (*carbuncle*). [Latin *-unculus*]

unclean /ʌnˈkliːn/ *adj.* 1 not clean. 2 unchaste. 3 religiously impure, forbidden.

unclear /ʌnˈklɪə(r)/ *adj.* 1 not clear or easy to understand. 2 (of a person) uncertain (*I'm unclear as to what you mean*).

unclench /ʌnˈklentʃ/ *v.* 1 release (clenched hands etc.). 2 (of hands etc.) become relaxed or open.

Uncle Sam *n. colloq.* US government.

unclothe /ʌnˈkləʊð/ *v.* (**-thing**) 1 remove clothes, leaves, etc. from. 2 expose, reveal.

unclouded /ʌnˈklaʊdɪd/ *adj.* 1 clear; bright. 2 untroubled (*unclouded serenity*).

uncluttered /ʌnˈklʌtəd/ *adj.* not cluttered; austere, simple.

uncoil /ʌnˈkɔɪl/ *v.* unwind.

uncoloured /ʌnˈkʌləd/ *adj.* 1 having no colour. 2 not influenced; impartial.

uncombed /ʌnˈkəʊmd/ *adj.* (of hair or a person) not combed.

uncomfortable /ʌnˈkʌmftəb(ə)l/ *adj.* 1 not comfortable. 2 uneasy; disquieting (*uncomfortable silence*). □ **uncomfortably** *adv.*

uncommercial /ˌʌnkəˈmɜːʃ(ə)l/ *adj.* not commercial.

uncommitted /ˌʌnkəˈmɪtɪd/ *adj.* 1 not committed. 2 not politically attached.

uncommon /ʌnˈkɒmən/ *adj.* 1 unusual. 2 remarkably great etc. (*uncommon*

appetite). □ **uncommonly** *adv.* **uncommonness** *n.*

uncommunicative /ˌʌnkəˈmjuːnɪkətɪv/ *adj.* taciturn.

uncompetitive /ˌʌnkəmˈpetɪtɪv/ *adj.* not competitive.

uncomplaining /ˌʌnkəmˈpleɪnɪŋ/ *adj.* not complaining; resigned. □ **uncomplainingly** *adv.*

uncompleted /ˌʌnkəmˈpliːtɪd/ *adj.* not completed; incomplete.

uncomplicated /ʌnˈkɒmplɪkeɪtɪd/ *adj.* simple; straightforward.

uncomplimentary /ˌʌnkɒmplɪˈmentəri/ *adj.* insulting.

uncomprehending /ˌʌnkɒmprɪˈhendɪŋ/ *adj.* not comprehending. □ **uncomprehendingly** *adv.*

uncompromising /ʌnˈkɒmprəmaɪzɪŋ/ *adj.* stubborn; unyielding. □ **uncompromisingly** *adv.*

unconcealed /ˌʌnkənˈsiːld/ *adj.* not concealed; obvious.

unconcern /ˌʌnkənˈsɜːn/ *n.* calmness; indifference; apathy. □ **unconcerned** *adj.* **unconcernedly** /-nɪdli/ *adv.*

unconditional /ˌʌnkənˈdɪʃən(ə)l/ *adj.* not subject to conditions; complete (*unconditional surrender*). □ **unconditionally** *adv.*

unconditioned reflex *n.* instinctive response to a stimulus.

unconfined /ˌʌnkənˈfaɪnd/ *adj.* not confined; boundless.

unconfirmed /ˌʌnkənˈfɜːmd/ *adj.* not confirmed.

uncongenial /ˌʌnkənˈdʒiːnɪəl/ *adj.* not congenial.

unconnected /ˌʌnkəˈnektɪd/ *adj.* 1 not physically joined. 2 not connected or associated. 3 disconnected (*unconnected ideas*).

unconquerable /ʌnˈkɒŋkərəb(ə)l/ *adj.* not conquerable.

unconscionable /ʌnˈkɒnʃənəb(ə)l/ *adj.* 1 without or contrary to conscience. 2 excessive (*unconscionable waste*). □ **unconscionably** *adv.* [from UN-[1], CONSCIENCE]

unconscious /ʌnˈkɒnʃəs/ *—adj.* not conscious (*fell unconscious; unconscious prejudice*). *—n.* normally inaccessible part of the mind affecting the emotions etc. □ **unconsciously** *adv.* **unconsciousness** *n.*

unconsidered /ˌʌnkənˈsɪdəd/ *adj.* 1 not considered; disregarded. 2 not premeditated.

unconstitutional /ˌʌnkɒnstɪˈtjuːʃən(ə)l/ *adj.* in breach of a political constitution or procedural rules. □ **unconstitutionally** *adv.*

unconstrained /ˌʌnkənˈstreɪnd/ *adj.* not constrained or compelled.

uncontaminated /ˌʌnkənˈtæmɪneɪtɪd/ *adj.* not contaminated.

uncontested /ˌʌnkənˈtestɪd/ *adj.* not contested.

uncontrollable /ˌʌnkənˈtrəʊləb(ə)l/ *adj.* not controllable. □ **uncontrollably** *adv.*

uncontrolled /ˌʌnkənˈtrəʊld/ *adj.* not controlled; unrestrained.

uncontroversial /ˌʌnkɒntrəˈvɜːʃ(ə)l/ *adj.* not controversial.

unconventional /ˌʌnkənˈvenʃən(ə)l/ *adj.* unusual; unorthodox. □ **unconventionally** /-ʃəlɪ/ *adv.* **unconventionally** *adv.*

unconvinced /ˌʌnkənˈvɪnst/ *adj.* not convinced.

unconvincing /ˌʌnkənˈvɪnsɪŋ/ *adj.* not convincing. □ **unconvincingly** *adv.*

uncooked /ʌnˈkʊkt/ *adj.* not cooked; raw.

uncooperative /ˌʌnkəʊˈɒpərətɪv/ *adj.* not cooperative.

uncoordinated /ˌʌnkəʊˈɔːdɪneɪtɪd/ *adj.* **1** not coordinated. **2** clumsy.

uncork /ʌnˈkɔːk/ *v.* **1** draw the cork from (a bottle). **2** vent (feelings etc.).

uncorroborated /ˌʌnkəˈrɒbəˌreɪtɪd/ *adj.* (esp. of evidence etc.) not corroborated.

uncountable /ʌnˈkaʊntəb(ə)l/ *adj.* **1** inestimable, immense (*uncountable wealth*). **2** (of a noun) not used in the plural or with the indefinite article (e.g. *happiness, milk*).

uncouple /ʌnˈkʌp(ə)l/ *v.* (-**ling**) release from couplings or couples.

uncouth /ʌnˈkuːθ/ *adj.* uncultured, rough. [Old English, = unknown]

uncover /ʌnˈkʌvə(r)/ *v.* **1** remove a cover or covering from. **2** disclose (*uncovered the truth*).

uncritical /ʌnˈkrɪtɪk(ə)l/ *adj.* **1** not critical; complacently accepting. **2** not in accordance with the principles of criticism. □ **uncritically** *adv.*

uncross /ʌnˈkrɒs/ *v.* **1** remove from a crossed position. **2** (as **uncrossed** *adj.*) (of a cheque) not crossed

uncrown /ʌnˈkraʊn/ *v.* **1** deprive of a crown, a position, etc. **2** (as **uncrowned** *adj.*) **a** not crowned. **b** having the status but not the name of (*uncrowned king of boxing*).

unction /ˈʌŋkʃ(ə)n/ *n.* **1 a** anointing with oil etc. as a religious rite or medical treatment. **b** oil, ointment, etc. so used. **2 a** soothing words or thought. **b** excessive or insincere flattery. **3 a** emotional fervency. **b** pretence of this. [Latin *ungo unct- anoint*]

unctuous /ˈʌŋktʃʊəs/ *adj.* **1** unpleasantly flattering; oily. **2** greasy or soapy.

□ **unctuously** *adv.* related to UNCTION.]

uncultivated /ʌnˈkʌltɪveɪtɪd/ *adj.* not cultivated.

uncured /ʌnˈkjʊəd/ *adj.* **1** not cured. **2** (of pork etc.) not salted or smoked.

uncurl /ʌnˈkɜːl/ *v.* straighten out, untwist.

uncut /ʌnˈkʌt/ *adj.* **1** not cut. **2** (of a book) with the pages sealed or untrimmed. **3** (of a book, film, etc.) complete; uncensored. **4** (of esp. a diamond) not shaped. **5** (of fabric) with a looped pile.

undamaged /ʌnˈdæmɪdʒd/ *adj.* intact.

undated /ʌnˈdeɪtɪd/ *adj.* without a date.

undaunted /ʌnˈdɔːntɪd/ *adj.* not daunted.

undeceive /ˌʌndɪˈsiːv/ *v.* (often foll. by *of*) free (a person) from a misconception, deception, or error.

undecided /ˌʌndɪˈsaɪdɪd/ *adj.* **1** not settled. **2** irresolute.

undeclared /ˌʌndɪˈkleəd/ *adj.* not declared.

undefeated /ˌʌndɪˈfiːtɪd/ *adj.* not defeated.

undefended /ˌʌndɪˈfendɪd/ *adj.* not defended.

undefined /ˌʌndɪˈfaɪnd/ *adj.* not defined; vague, indefinite.

undemanding /ˌʌndɪˈmɑːndɪŋ/ *adj.* not demanding; easily pleased or satisfied (*undemanding reading*).

undemocratic /ˌʌndeməˈkrætɪk/ *adj.* not democratic.

undemonstrative /ˌʌndɪˈmɒnstrətɪv/ *adj.* not emotionally expressive; reserved.

undeniable /ˌʌndɪˈnaɪəb(ə)l/ *adj.* indisputable; certain. □ **undeniably** *adv.*

under –*prep.* **1 a** in or to a position lower than; below; beneath (*under the table*). **b** on the inside of (*vest under his shirt*). **2** inferior to; less than (*no-one under a major; is under 18; was under £20*). **3 a** subject to; controlled by (*under constraint; born under Saturn; prospered under him*). **b** undergoing (*is under repair*). **c** classified or subsumed in (*under two headings*). **4** at the foot of or sheltered by (*under the cliff*). **5** planted with (*a crop*). **6** powered by (*sail, steam, etc.*). –*adv.* **1** in or to a lower position or condition (*kept him under*). **2** *colloq.* in or into unconsciousness (*put him under*). –*adj.* lower (*under jaw*). **under arms** see ARM². **under one's belt** see BELT. **under one's breath** see BREATH. **under a cloud** see CLOUD. **under control** see CONTROL. **under the counter** see COUNTER. **under fire** see FIRE. **under a person's nose** see NOSE. **under the sun** anywhere in the world.

under way in motion; in progress.

under the weather see WEATHER. □ **undermost** adj. [Old English]

under- prefix in senses of UNDER: **1** below, beneath (*underground*). **2** lower; subordinate (*under-secretary*). **3** insufficiently, incompletely (*undercook*; *underdeveloped*).

underachieve /ˌʌndərəˈtʃiːv/ v. (-ving) do less well than might be expected (esp. academically). □ **underachiever** n.

underact /ˌʌndərˈakt/ v. Theatr. act with insufficient force.

under-age adj. (also **under age**) not old enough.

underarm —adj. & adv. Sport, esp. Cricket with the arm below shoulder-level. —attrib. adj. **1** under the arm (*underarm seam*). **2** in the armpit.

underbelly n. (pl. -ies) undersurface of an animal, vehicle, etc., esp. as vulnerable to attack.

underbid —v. /ˌʌndəˈbɪd/ (-dd-: past and past part. -bid) **1** make a lower bid than. **2** (also absol.) Bridge etc. bid less on (one's hand) than warranted. —n. /ˈʌndəbɪd/ such a bid.

undercarriage n. **1** wheeled retractable structure beneath an aircraft, used for landing etc. **2** supporting frame of a vehicle.

undercharge /ˌʌndəˈtʃɑːdʒ/ v. (-ging) **1** charge too little to (a person). **2** give too little charge to (a gun, electric battery, etc.).

underclothes n.pl. clothes worn under others, esp. next to the skin.

underclothing n. underclothes collectively.

undercoat n. **1 a** layer of paint under a topcoat. **b** paint for this. **2** animal's under layer of hair etc.

undercook /ˌʌndəˈkʊk/ v. cook insufficiently.

undercover /ˌʌndəˈkʌvə(r)/ adj. (usu. attrib.) **1** surreptitious. **2** spying incognito, esp. by infiltration (*undercover agent*).

undercroft n. crypt. [obsolete *croft* from Latin]

undercurrent n. **1** current below the surface. **2** underlying often contrary feeling, influence, etc. (*undercurrent of protest*).

undercut —v. /ˌʌndəˈkʌt/ (-tt-: past and past part. -cut) **1** sell or work at a lower price than. **2** strike (a ball) to make it rise high. **3** cut away the part below. **4** undermine. —n. /ˈʌndəkʌt/ underside of sirloin.

underdeveloped /ˌʌndədɪˈvɛləpt/ adj. **1** not fully developed; immature. **2** (of a country etc.) with unexploited potential. □ **underdevelopment** n.

underdog n. **1** oppressed person. **2** loser in a fight.

underdone /ˌʌndəˈdʌn/ adj. under-cooked.

underemployed /ˌʌndərɪmˈplɔɪd/ adj. not fully occupied. □ **underemployment** n.

underestimate —v. /ˌʌndərˈɛstɪmeɪt/ (-ting) form too low an estimate of. —n. /ˌʌndərˈɛstɪmət/ estimate that is too low. □ **underestimation** /-ˈmeɪʃ(ə)n/ n.

underexpose /ˌʌndərɪkˈspəʊz/ v. (-sing) expose (film) for too short a time etc. □ **underexposure** n.

underfed /ˌʌndəˈfɛd/ adj. malnourished.

underfelt n. felt laid under a carpet.

underfloor attrib. adj. beneath the floor (*underfloor heating*).

underfoot /ˌʌndəˈfʊt/ adv. (also **under foot**) **1** under one's feet. **2** on the ground.

underfunded adj. provided with insufficient money.

undergarment n. piece of underclothing.

undergo /ˌʌndəˈɡəʊ/ v. (3rd sing. pres. -goes; past -went; past part. -gone) be subjected to; suffer; endure.

undergraduate /ˌʌndəˈɡradʒuət/ n. person studying for a first degree.

underground —adv. /ˌʌndəˈɡraʊnd/ **1** beneath the ground. **2** in or into secrecy or hiding. —adj. /ˈʌndəɡraʊnd/ **1** situated underground. **2** secret, subversive. **3** unconventional (*underground literature*). —n. /ˈʌndəɡraʊnd/ **1** underground railway. **2** secret subversive group or activity.

undergrowth n. dense shrubs etc., esp. in a wood.

underhand adj. **1** deceitful; crafty; secret. **2** Sport, esp. Cricket underarm.

underlay —v. /ˌʌndəˈleɪ/ (past and past part. -laid) lay something under (a thing) to support or raise it. —n. /ˈʌndəleɪ/ thing so laid esp. under a carpet.

underlay[2] past of UNDERLIE.

underlie /ˌʌndəˈlaɪ/ v. (-lying; past -lay; past part. -lain) **1** (also absol.) lie under (a stratum etc.). **2** (also absol.) (esp. as **underlying** adj.) be the basis of (a doctrine, conduct, etc.). **3** exist beneath the superficial aspect of.

underline /ˌʌndəˈlaɪn/ v. (-lining) **1** draw a line under (a word etc.) to give emphasis, indicate italic type, etc. **2** emphasize, stress.

underling /ˈʌndəlɪŋ/ n. usu. derog. subordinate.

underlying pres. part. of UNDERLIE.

undermanned /ˌʌndəˈmand/ adj. having an insufficient crew or staff.

undermentioned /ˌʌndəˈmenʃ(ə)nd/ *adj.* mentioned later in a book etc.

undermine /ˌʌndəˈmaɪn/ *v.* (**-ning**) **1** injure (a person, reputation, health, etc.) secretly or insidiously. **2** wear away the base of (*banks were undermined*). **3** make an excavation under.

underneath /ˌʌndəˈniːθ/ —*prep.* **1** at or to a lower place than, below. **2** on the inside of. —*adv.* **1** at or to a lower place. **2** inside. —*n.* lower surface or part. —*adj.* lower. [Old English: related to NETHER]

undernourished /ˌʌndəˈnʌrɪʃt/ *adj.* insufficiently nourished. □ **undernourishment** *n.*

underpaid *past* and *past part.* of UNDERPAY.

underpants *n.pl.* undergarment, esp. men's, covering the genitals and buttocks.

underpart *n.* lower or subordinate part.

underpass *n.* **1** road etc. passing under another. **2** subway.

underpay /ˌʌndəˈpeɪ/ *v.* (*past* and *past part.* **-paid**) pay too little to (a person) or for (a thing). □ **underpayment** *n.*

underpin /ˌʌndəˈpɪn/ *v.* (**-nn-**) **1** support from below with masonry etc. **2** support, strengthen.

underplay /ˌʌndəˈpleɪ/ *v.* **1** make little of. **2** *Theatr.* underact.

underpopulated /ˌʌndəˈpɒpjʊleɪtɪd/ *adj.* having an insufficient or very small population.

underprice /ˌʌndəˈpraɪs/ *v.* (**-cing**) price lower than what is usual or appropriate.

underprivileged /ˌʌndəˈprɪvɪlɪdʒd/ *adj.* less privileged than others; having below average income, rights, etc.

underrate /ˌʌndəˈreɪt/ *v.* (**-ting**) have too low an opinion of.

underscore /ˌʌndəˈskɔː(r)/ *v.* (**-ring**) = UNDERLINE.

undersea *adj.* below the sea or its surface.

underseal —*v.* seal the underpart of (esp. a vehicle against rust etc.). —*n.* protective coating for this.

under-secretary /ˌʌndəˈsekrətərɪ/ *n.* (*pl.* **-ies**) subordinate official, esp. a junior minister or senior civil servant.

undersell /ˌʌndəˈsel/ *v.* (*past* and *past part.* **-sold**) sell at a lower price than (another seller).

undersexed /ˌʌndəˈsekst/ *adj.* having unusually weak sexual desires.

undershirt *n.* esp. *US* man's or boy's vest.

undershoot /ˌʌndəˈʃuːt/ *v.* (*past* and *past part.* **-shot**) land short of (a runway etc.).

undershot *adj.* **1** (of a water-wheel) turned by water flowing under it. **2** (of a lower jaw) projecting beyond the upper jaw.

underside *n.* lower or under side or surface.

undersigned /ˌʌndəˈsaɪnd/ *adj.* (usu. *absol.*) whose signature is appended (*we, the undersigned*).

undersized /ˌʌndəˈsaɪzd/ *adj.* smaller than average.

underskirt *n.* petticoat.

underslung /ˌʌndəˈslʌŋ/ *adj.* supported from above.

undersold *past* and *past part.* of UNDERSELL.

underspend /ˌʌndəˈspend/ *v.* (*past* and *past part.* **-spent**) (usu. *absol.*) spend less than (the expected amount), or too little.

understaffed /ˌʌndəˈstɑːft/ *adj.* having too few staff.

understand /ˌʌndəˈstænd/ *v.* (*past* and *past part.* **-stood**) **1** perceive the meaning of (words, a person, a language, a subject, etc.) (*understood you perfectly; cannot understand algebra*). **2** perceive the significance or cause of (*do not understand why he came*). **3** (often *absol.*) sympathize with, know how to deal with (*quite understand your difficulty; ask her, she understands*). **4** (often foll. by *that* or *absol.*) infer; take as implied (*am I to understand that you refuse?; he is old, I understand*). **5** supply (an implied missing word) mentally. □ **understand each other** or **1** know each other's views. **2** agree or collude. □ **understandable** *adj.* **understandably** *adv.* [Old English: related to STAND]

understanding —*n.* **1** ability to understand or think; intelligence. **2** individual's perception of a situation etc. **3** agreement, esp. informal (*had an understanding*). **4** sympathy; tolerance. —*adj.* **1** having understanding or insight. **2** sympathetic. □ **understandingly** *adv.*

understate /ˌʌndəˈsteɪt/ *v.* (**-ting**) **1** express mildly or in a restrained way. **2** represent as less than it actually is. □ **understatement** *n.*

understeer *n.* tendency of a vehicle not to turn sharply enough.

understood *past* and *past part.* of UNDERSTAND.

understudy esp. *Theatr.* —*n.* (*pl.* **-ies**) person ready to take on another's role etc. when required. —*v.* (**-ies, -ied**) **1** study (a role etc.) thus. **2** act as an understudy to.

undersubscribed /ˌʌndəsəbˈskraɪbd/ *adj.* without sufficient subscribers, participants, etc.

undersurface *n.* lower or under surface.

undertake /ˌʌndəˈteɪk/ *v.* (**-king**; *past* **-took**; *past part.* **-taken**) **1** agree to perform or be responsible for; engage in, enter upon (work, a responsibility, etc.). **2** (usu. foll. by *to* + infin.) promise. **3** guarantee (*undertake that he is innocent*).

undertaker /ˈʌndəˌteɪkə(r)/ *n.* professional funeral organizer.

undertaking /ˌʌndəˈteɪkɪŋ/ *n.* **1** work etc. undertaken, enterprise (*serious undertaking*). **2** promise. **3** /ˈʌn-/ professional funeral management.

underthings *n.pl.* underclothes.

undertone *n.* **1** subdued tone or colour. **2** underlying quality or feeling.

undertook *past of* UNDERTAKE.

undertow *n.* current below the surface of the sea contrary to the surface current.

underused /ˌʌndəˈjuːzd/ *adj.* not used to capacity.

undervalue /ˌʌndəˈvæljuː/ *v.* (**-ues**, **-ued**, **-uing**) **1** value insufficiently. **2** underestimate.

undervest *n.* vest.

underwater /ˌʌndəˈwɔːtə(r)/ *adj.* situated or done under water. —*adv.* under water.

underwear *n.* underclothes.

underweight —*adj.* /ˌʌndəˈweɪt/ below normal weight. —*n.* /ˈʌndəˌweɪt/ insufficient weight.

underwent *past of* UNDERGO.

underwhelm /ˌʌndəˈwelm/ *v. joc.* fail to impress. [alteration of OVERWHELM]

underworld *n.* **1** those who live by organized crime and vice. **2** mythical abode of the dead under the earth.

underwrite /ˌʌndəˈraɪt/ *v.* (**-ting**; *past* **-wrote**; *past part.* **-written**) **1 a** sign and accept liability under (an insurance policy, esp. on shipping etc.). **b** accept (liability) in this way. **2** undertake to finance or support. **3** engage to buy all the unsold stock in (a company etc.). □ **underwriter** /ˈʌn-/ *n.*

undescended /ˌʌndɪˈsendɪd/ *adj.* (of a testicle) not descending normally into the scrotum.

undeserved /ˌʌndɪˈzɜːvd/ *adj.* not deserved. □ **undeservedly** /-vɪdlɪ/ *adv.*

undeserving /ˌʌndɪˈzɜːvɪŋ/ *adj.* not deserving.

undesigned /ˌʌndɪˈzaɪnd/ *adj.* unintentional.

undesirable /ˌʌndɪˈzaɪərəb(ə)l/ —*adj.* objectionable, unpleasant. —*n.* undesirable person. □ **undesirability** /-ˈbɪlɪtɪ/ *n.*

undetectable /ˌʌndɪˈtektəb(ə)l/ *adj.* not detectable.

undetected /ˌʌndɪˈtektɪd/ *adj.* not detected.

undetermined /ˌʌndɪˈtɜːmɪnd/ *adj.* = UNDECIDED.

undeterred /ˌʌndɪˈtɜːd/ *adj.* not deterred.

undeveloped /ˌʌndɪˈveləpt/ *adj.* not developed.

undid *past of* UNDO.

undies /ˈʌndɪz/ *n.pl. colloq.* (esp. women's) underclothes. [abbreviation]

undifferentiated /ˌʌndɪfəˈrenʃɪˌeɪtɪd/ *adj.* not differentiated; amorphous.

undigested /ˌʌndɪˈdʒestɪd/ *adj.* **1** not digested. **2** (of facts etc.) not properly arranged or considered.

undignified /ʌnˈdɪgnɪˌfaɪd/ *adj.* lacking dignity.

undiluted /ˌʌndaɪˈljuːtɪd/ *adj.* **1** not diluted. **2** complete, utter.

undiminished /ˌʌndɪˈmɪnɪʃt/ *adj.* not diminished or lessened.

undine /ˈʌndiːn/ *n.* female water-spirit. [Latin *unda* wave]

undiplomatic /ˌʌndɪplɵˈmætɪk/ *adj.* tactless.

undisciplined /ʌnˈdɪsɪplɪnd/ *adj.* lacking discipline; not disciplined.

undisclosed /ˌʌndɪsˈkləʊzd/ *adj.* not revealed or made known.

undiscovered /ˌʌndɪsˈkʌvəd/ *adj.* not discovered.

undiscriminating /ˌʌndɪsˈkrɪmɪˌneɪtɪŋ/ *adj.* lacking good judgement.

undisguised /ˌʌndɪsˈɡaɪzd/ *adj.* not disguised; open.

undismayed /ˌʌndɪsˈmeɪd/ *adj.* not dismayed.

undisputed /ˌʌndɪˈspjuːtɪd/ *adj.* not disputed or called in question.

undistinguished /ˌʌndɪˈstɪŋɡwɪʃt/ *adj.* not distinguished; mediocre.

undisturbed /ˌʌndɪˈstɜːbd/ *adj.* not disturbed or interfered with.

undivided /ˌʌndɪˈvaɪdɪd/ *adj.* not divided or shared; whole, entire (*undivided attention*).

undo /ʌnˈduː/ *v.* (*3rd sing. present* **does**; *past* **did**; *past part.* **done**; *pres. part.* **-doing**) **1** unfasten (a coat, button, parcel, etc.), or the clothing of (a person). **2** annul, cancel (*cannot undo the past*). **3** ruin the prospects, reputation, or morals of.

undoing *n.* **1** ruin or cause of ruin. **2** reversing of an action etc. **3** opening or unfastening.

undone /ʌnˈdʌn/ *adj.* **1** not done. **2** not fastened. **3** *archaic* ruined.

undoubted /ʌnˈdautɪd/ *adj.* certain, not questioned. □ **undoubtedly** *adv.*

undreamed /ʌnˈdriːmd, ʌnˈdremt/ *adj.* (also **undreamt** /ʌnˈdremt/) (often foll. by *of*) not dreamed, thought, or imagined.

undress /ʌnˈdres/ —*v.* **1** take off one's clothes. **2** take the clothes off (a person). —*n.* **1** ordinary or casual dress, esp. as opposed to full dress or uniform. **2** naked or scantily clad state.

undressed /ʌnˈdrest/ *adj.* **1** not, or no longer, dressed. **2** (of food) without a dressing. **3** (of leather etc.) not treated.

undrinkable /ʌnˈdrɪŋkəb(ə)l/ *adj.* unfit for drinking.

undue /ʌnˈdjuː/ *adj.* excessive, disproportionate. □ **unduly** *adv.*

undulate /ˈʌndjʊˌleɪt/ *v.* (-ting) (cause to) have a wavy motion or look. □ **undulation** /-ˈleɪʃ(ə)n/ *n.* [Latin *unda* wave]

undying /ʌnˈdaɪɪŋ/ *adj.* immortal; never-ending (*undying love*).

unearned /ʌnˈɜːnd/ *adj.* not earned.

unearned income *n.* income from investments etc. rather than from working.

unearth /ʌnˈɜːθ/ *v.* discover by searching, digging, or rummaging.

unearthly /ʌnˈɜːθlɪ/ *adj.* **1** supernatural, mysterious. **2** *colloq.* absurdly early or inconvenient (*unearthly hour*). □ **unearthliness** *n.*

unease /ʌnˈiːz/ *n.* nervousness, anxiety.

uneasy /ʌnˈiːzɪ/ *adj.* (-ier, -iest) **1** nervous, anxious. **2** disturbing (*uneasy suspicion*). □ **uneasily** *adv.* **uneasiness** *n.*

uneatable /ʌnˈiːtəb(ə)l/ *adj.* not able to be eaten (cf. INEDIBLE).

uneaten /ʌnˈiːt(ə)n/ *adj.* left not eaten.

uneconomic /ˌʌnɪːkəˈnɒmɪk, ˌʌnek-/ *adj.* not economic; unprofitable.

uneconomical *adj.* not economical; wasteful.

unedifying /ʌnˈedɪˌfaɪɪŋ/ *adj.* distasteful, degrading.

unedited /ʌnˈedɪtɪd/ *adj.* not edited.

uneducated /ʌnˈedjʊˌkeɪtɪd/ *adj.* not educated.

unembarrassed /ˌʌnɪmˈbærəst/ *adj.* not embarrassed.

unemotional /ˌʌnɪˈməʊʃən(ə)l/ *adj.* not emotional; lacking emotion.

unemphatic /ˌʌnɪmˈfætɪk/ *adj.* not emphatic.

unemployable /ˌʌnɪmˈplɔɪəb(ə)l/ *adj.* unfit for paid employment. □ **unemployability** /-ˈbɪlɪtɪ/ *n.*

unemployed /ˌʌnɪmˈplɔɪd/ *adj.* **1** out of work. **2** not in use.

unemployment /ˌʌnɪmˈplɔɪmənt/ *n.* **1** being unemployed. **2** lack of employment in a country etc.

unemployment benefit *n.* State payment made to an unemployed person.

unencumbered /ˌʌnɪnˈkʌmbəd/ *adj.* **1** (of an estate) not having liabilities (e.g. a mortgage). **2** free; not burdened.

unending /ʌnˈendɪŋ/ *adj.* endless or seemingly endless.

unendurable /ˌʌnɪnˈdjʊərəb(ə)l/ *adj.* too bad to be borne.

unenlightened /ˌʌnɪnˈlaɪt(ə)nd/ *adj.* not enlightened.

unenterprising /ˌʌnˈentəˌpraɪzɪŋ/ *adj.* not enterprising.

unenthusiastic /ˌʌnɪnˌθjuːzɪˈæstɪk/ *adj.* not enthusiastic. □ **unenthusiastically** *adv.*

unenviable /ʌnˈenvɪəb(ə)l/ *adj.* not enviable.

unequal /ʌnˈiːkw(ə)l/ *adj.* **1** (often foll. by *to*) not equal. **2** of varying quality. **3** unfair (*unequal contest*). □ **unequally** *adv.*

unequalled *adj.* (*US* -aled) superior to all others.

unequivocal /ˌʌnɪˈkwɪvək(ə)l/ *adj.* not ambiguous, plain, unmistakable. □ **unequivocally** *adv.*

unerring /ʌnˈɜːrɪŋ/ *adj.* not erring; true, certain. □ **unerringly** *adv.*

UNESCO /juːˈneskəʊ/ *abbr.* (also **Unesco**) United Nations Educational, Scientific, and Cultural Organization.

unethical /ʌnˈeθɪk(ə)l/ *adj.* not ethical, esp. unscrupulous or unprofessional. □ **unethically** *adv.*

uneven /ʌnˈiːv(ə)n/ *adj.* **1** not level or smooth. **2** of variable quality etc. **3** (of a contest) unequal. □ **unevenly** *adv.* **unevenness** *n.*

uneventful /ˌʌnɪˈventfʊl/ *adj.* not eventful. □ **uneventfully** *adv.*

unexampled /ˌʌnɪɡˈzɑːmp(ə)ld/ *adj.* without precedent.

unexceptionable /ˌʌnɪkˈsepʃənəb(ə)l/ *adj.* entirely satisfactory.

■ **Usage** See note at *exceptionable*.

unexceptional /ˌʌnɪkˈsepʃən(ə)l/ *adj.* usual, normal, ordinary.

unexciting /ˌʌnɪkˈsaɪtɪŋ/ *adj.* not exciting; dull.

unexpected /ˌʌnɪkˈspektɪd/ *adj.* not expected; surprising. □ **unexpectedly** *adv.* **unexpectedness** *n.*

unexplained /ˌʌnɪkˈspleɪnd/ *adj.* not explained.

unexplored /ˌʌnɪkˈsplɔːd/ *adj.* not explored.

unexposed /ˌʌnɪkˈspəʊzd/ *adj.* not exposed.

unexpressed /ˌʌnɪkˈsprest/ *adj.* not expressed or made known (*unexpressed fears*).

unexpurgated /ʌnˈekspəgeɪtɪd/ *adj.* (esp. of a text etc.) complete.

unfading /ʌnˈfeɪdɪŋ/ *adj.* never fading.

unfailing /ʌnˈfeɪlɪŋ/ *adj.* not failing or dwindling; constant; reliable. □ **unfailingly** *adv.*

unfair /ʌnˈfeə(r)/ *adj.* not fair, just, or impartial. □ **unfairly** *adv.* **unfairness** *n.*

unfaithful /ʌnˈfeɪθful/ *adj.* 1 not faithful, esp. adulterous. 2 treacherous; disloyal. □ **unfaithfully** *adv.* **unfaithfulness** *n.*

unfamiliar /ˌʌnfəˈmɪljə(r)/ *adj.* not familiar. □ **unfamiliarity** /-lɪˈærɪtɪ/ *n.*

unfashionable /ʌnˈfæʃənəb(ə)l/ *adj.* not fashionable. □ **unfashionably** *adv.*

unfasten /ʌnˈfɑːs(ə)n/ *v.* 1 make or become loose. 2 open the fastening(s) of. 3 detach.

unfathomable /ʌnˈfæðəməb(ə)l/ *adj.* incapable of being fathomed.

unfavourable /ʌnˈfeɪvərəb(ə)l/ *adj.* (US **unfavorable**) not favourable; adverse, hostile. □ **unfavourably** *adv.*

unfeasible /ʌnˈfiːzɪb(ə)l/ *adj.* not feasible; impractical.

unfeeling /ʌnˈfiːlɪŋ/ *adj.* unsympathetic, harsh.

unfeigned /ʌnˈfeɪnd/ *adj.* genuine, sincere.

unfertilized /ʌnˈfɜːtɪlaɪzd/ *adj.* (also **-ised**) not fertilized.

unfetter /ʌnˈfetə(r)/ *v.* release from fetters.

unfilled /ʌnˈfɪld/ *adj.* not filled.

unfinished /ʌnˈfɪnɪʃt/ *adj.* not finished; incomplete.

unfit /ʌnˈfɪt/ *adj.* (often foll. by *for*, or *to* + infin.) not fit.

unfitted /ʌnˈfɪtɪd/ *adj.* 1 not fit. 2 not fitted or suited. 3 having no fittings.

unfitting /ʌnˈfɪtɪŋ/ *adj.* not suitable; unbecoming.

unfix /ʌnˈfɪks/ *v.* release, loosen, or detach.

unflagging /ʌnˈflægɪŋ/ *adj.* tireless, persistent.

unflappable /ʌnˈflæpəb(ə)l/ *adj. colloq.* imperturbable; calm. □ **unflappability** /-ˈbɪlɪtɪ/ *n.*

unflattering /ʌnˈflætərɪŋ/ *adj.* not flattering. □ **unflatteringly** *adv.*

unfledged /ʌnˈfledʒd/ *adj.* 1 (of a person) inexperienced. 2 (of a bird) not yet fledged.

unflinching /ʌnˈflɪntʃɪŋ/ *adj.* not flinching. □ **unflinchingly** *adv.*

unfold /ʌnˈfəʊld/ *v.* 1 open the fold or folds of, spread out. 2 reveal (thoughts etc.). 3 become opened out. 4 develop.

unforced /ʌnˈfɔːst/ *adj.* 1 easy, natural. 2 not compelled or constrained.

unforeseeable /ˌʌnfɔːˈsiːəb(ə)l/ *adj.* not foreseeable.

unforeseen /ˌʌnfɔːˈsiːn/ *adj.* not foreseen.

unforgettable /ˌʌnfəˈgetəb(ə)l/ *adj.* that cannot be forgotten; memorable, wonderful.

unforgivable /ˌʌnfəˈgɪvəb(ə)l/ *adj.* that cannot be forgiven.

unforgiving /ˌʌnfəˈgɪvɪŋ/ *adj.* not forgiving.

unformed /ʌnˈfɔːmd/ *adj.* 1 not formed; undeveloped. 2 shapeless.

unforthcoming /ˌʌnfɔːθˈkʌmɪŋ/ *adj.* not forthcoming.

unfortunate /ʌnˈfɔːtʃənət/ *adj.* 1 unlucky. 2 unhappy. 3 regrettable. —*n.* unfortunate person.

unfortunately *adv.* 1 (qualifying a sentence) it is unfortunate that. 2 in an unfortunate manner.

unfounded /ʌnˈfaʊndɪd/ *adj.* without foundation (*unfounded rumour*).

unfreeze /ʌnˈfriːz/ *v.* (-**zing**; *past* **unfroze**; *past part.* **unfrozen**) 1 (cause to) thaw. 2 derestrict (assets, credits, etc.).

unfrequented /ˌʌnfrɪˈkwentɪd/ *adj.* not frequented.

unfriendly /ʌnˈfrendlɪ/ *adj.* (-**ier**, -**iest**) not friendly; hostile.

unfrock /ʌnˈfrɒk/ *v.* = DEFROCK.

unfroze *past of* UNFREEZE.

unfrozen *past part. of* UNFREEZE.

unfulfilled /ˌʌnfʊlˈfɪld/ *adj.* not fulfilled.

unfunny /ʌnˈfʌnɪ/ *adj.* (-**ier**, -**iest**) failing to amuse.

unfurl /ʌnˈfɜːl/ *v.* 1 unroll, spread out (a sail, umbrella, etc.). 2 become unrolled.

unfurnished /ʌnˈfɜːnɪʃt/ *adj.* 1 (usu. foll. by *with*) not supplied. 2 without furniture.

ungainly /ʌnˈgeɪnlɪ/ *adj.* awkward, clumsy. □ **ungainliness** *n.* [obsolete *gain* straight, from Old Norse]

ungenerous /ʌnˈdʒenərəs/ *adj.* mean. □ **ungenerously** *adv.*

ungentlemanly /ʌnˈdʒentəlmənlɪ/ *adj.* not gentlemanly.

unget-at-able /ʌnɡetˈætəb(ə)l/ *adj. colloq.* inaccessible.

ungird /ʌnˈɡɜːd/ *v.* release the girdle, belt, etc. of.

ungodly /ʌnˈɡɒdlɪ/ *adj.* 1 impious, wicked. 2 *colloq.* outrageous (*ungodly hour*).

ungovernable /ʌnˈɡʌvənəb(ə)l/ *adj.* uncontrollable, violent.

ungraceful /ʌnˈɡreɪsful/ *adj.* lacking grace or elegance. □ **ungracefully** *adv.*

ungracious /ʌnˈgreɪʃəs/ *adj.* discourteous; grudging. □ **ungraciously** *adv.*

ungrammatical /ʌnɡrəˈmætɪk(ə)l/ *adj.* contrary to the rules of grammar. □ **ungrammatically** *adv.*

ungrateful /ʌnˈgreɪtful/ *adj.* not feeling or showing gratitude. □ **ungratefully** *adv.*

ungreen /ʌnˈgriːn/ *adj.* not concerned with the protection of the environment; harmful to the environment.

ungrudging /ʌnˈgrʌdʒɪŋ/ *adj.* not grudging.

unguarded /ʌnˈgɑːdɪd/ *adj.* 1 incautious, thoughtless (*unguarded remark*). 2 not guarded.

unguent /ˈʌŋɡwənt/ *n.* soft ointment or lubricant. [Latin *unguo* anoint]

ungulate /ˈʌŋɡjʊlət/ *—adj.* hoofed. *—n.* hoofed mammal. [Latin *ungula* hoof, claw]

unhallowed /ʌnˈhæləʊd/ *adj.* 1 not consecrated. 2 not sacred, wicked.

unhampered /ʌnˈhæmpəd/ *adj.* not hampered.

unhand /ʌnˈhænd/ *v. rhet.* or *joc.* take one's hands off (a person); release.

unhappy /ʌnˈhæpɪ/ *adj.* (-ier, -iest) 1 miserable. 2 unfortunate. 3 disastrous. □ **unhappily** *adv.* **unhappiness** *n.*

unharmed /ʌnˈhɑːmd/ *adj.* not harmed.

unharness /ʌnˈhɑːnɪs/ *v.* remove a harness from.

unhealthy /ʌnˈhelθɪ/ *adj.* (-ier, -iest) 1 in poor health. 2 a harmful to health. b unwholesome. c *slang* dangerous. □ **unhealthily** *adv.* **unhealthiness** *n.*

unheard /ʌnˈhɜːd/ *adj.* 1 not heard. 2 (usu. **unheard-of**) unprecedented.

unheeded /ʌnˈhiːdɪd/ *adj.* disregarded.

unhelpful /ʌnˈhelpful/ *adj.* not helpful. □ **unhelpfully** *adv.*

unhesitating /ʌnˈhezɪteɪtɪŋ/ *adj.* without hesitation. □ **unhesitatingly** *adv.*

unhindered /ʌnˈhɪndəd/ *adj.* not hindered.

unhinge /ʌnˈhɪndʒ/ *v.* (-ging) 1 take (a door etc.) off its hinges. 2 (esp. as **unhinged** *adj.*) make mad or crazy.

unhistorical /ʌnhɪˈstɒrɪk(ə)l/ *adj.* not historical.

unhitch /ʌnˈhɪtʃ/ *v.* 1 release from a hitched state. 2 unhook, unfasten.

unholy /ʌnˈhəʊlɪ/ *adj.* (-ier, -iest) 1 impious, wicked. 2 *colloq.* dreadful; outrageous (*unholy row*).

unhook /ʌnˈhʊk/ *v.* 1 remove from a hook or hooks. 2 unfasten the hook(s) of.

unhoped-for /ʌnˈhəʊptfɔː(r)/ *adj.* not hoped for or expected.

unhorse /ʌnˈhɔːs/ *v.* (-sing) throw (a rider) from a horse.

unhurried /ʌnˈhʌrɪd/ *adj.* not hurried.

unhurt /ʌnˈhɜːt/ *adj.* not hurt.

unhygienic /ʌnhaɪˈdʒiːnɪk/ *adj.* not hygienic.

uni /ˈjuːnɪ/ *n.* (*pl.* **-s**) esp. *Austral.* & *NZ colloq.* university. [abbreviation]

uni- *comb. form* one; having or consisting of one. [Latin *unus* one]

Uniat /ˈjuːnɪæt/ (also **Uniate** /-ət/) *—adj.* of the Church in E. Europe or the Near East, acknowledging papal supremacy but retaining its own liturgy etc. *—n.* member of such a Church. [Latin *unio* UNION]

unicameral /juːnɪˈkæmər(ə)l/ *adj.* having a single legislative chamber. [related to CHAMBER]

UNICEF /ˈjuːnɪsef/ *abbr.* United Nations Children's (orig. International Children's Emergency) Fund.

unicellular /juːnɪˈseljʊlə(r)/ *adj.* (of an organism etc.) consisting of a single cell.

unicorn /ˈjuːnɪkɔːn/ *n.* mythical horse with a single straight horn. [Latin *cornu* horn]

unicycle /ˈjuːnɪˌsaɪk(ə)l/ *n.* single-wheeled cycle, esp. as used by acrobats. □ **unicyclist** *n.*

unidentified /ʌnaɪˈdentɪfaɪd/ *adj.* not identified.

unification /juːnɪfɪˈkeɪʃ(ə)n/ *n.* unifying or being unified. □ **unificatory** *adj.*

Unification Church *n.* religious organization founded by Sun Myung Moon.

uniform /ˈjuːnɪfɔːm/ *—adj.* 1 unvarying (*uniform appearance*). 2 conforming to the same standard, rules, etc. 3 constant over a period (*uniform acceleration*). *—n.* distinctive clothing worn by soldiers, police, schoolchildren, etc. □ **uniformed** *adj.* **uniformity** /ˈfɔːmɪtɪ/ *n.* **uniformly** *adv.* [Latin: related to FORM]

unify /ˈjuːnɪfaɪ/ *v.* (-ies, -ied) make or become unified or uniform. [Latin: related to UNI-]

unilateral /juːnɪˈlætər(ə)l/ *adj.* done by or affecting only one person or party (*unilateral disarmament*). □ **unilaterally** *adv.*

unilateralism *n.* unilateral disarmament. □ **unilateralist** *n.* & *adj.*

unimaginable /ʌnɪˈmædʒɪnəb(ə)l/ *adj.* impossible to imagine.

unimaginative /ʌnɪˈmædʒɪnətɪv/ *adj.* lacking imagination; stolid, dull. □ **unimaginatively** *adv.*

unimpaired /ʌnɪmˈpeəd/ *adj.* not impaired.

unimpeachable /ʌnɪmˈpiːtʃəb(ə)l/ *adj.* beyond reproach or question. [Latin: related to IMPEACH]

unimpeded /ʌnɪmˈpiːdɪd/ *adj.* not impeded.

unimportant /ˌʌnɪmˈpɔːt(ə)nt/ *adj.* not important.

unimpressed /ˌʌnɪmˈprest/ *adj.* not impressed.

unimpressive /ˌʌnɪmˈpresɪv/ *adj.* not impressive.

uninformed /ˌʌnɪnˈfɔːmd/ *adj.* not informed; ignorant.

uninhabitable /ˌʌnɪnˈhæbɪtəb(ə)l/ *adj.* unfit for habitation.

uninhabited /ˌʌnɪnˈhæbɪtɪd/ *adj.* not inhabited.

uninhibited /ˌʌnɪnˈhɪbɪtɪd/ *adj.* not inhibited.

uninitiated /ˌʌnɪˈnɪʃɪeɪtɪd/ *adj.* not initiated, admitted, or instructed.

uninjured /ʌnˈɪndʒəd/ *adj.* not injured.

uninspired /ˌʌnɪnˈspaɪəd/ *adj.* not inspired; commonplace, pedestrian.

uninspiring /ˌʌnɪnˈspaɪərɪŋ/ *adj.* not inspiring.

unintelligent /ˌʌnɪnˈtelɪdʒ(ə)nt/ *adj.* not intelligent.

unintelligible /ˌʌnɪnˈtelɪdʒɪb(ə)l/ *adj.* not intelligible.

unintended /ˌʌnɪnˈtendɪd/ *adj.* not intended.

unintentional /ˌʌnɪnˈtenʃ(ə)n(ə)l/ *adj.* not intentional. □ **unintentionally** *adv.*

uninterested /ʌnˈɪntrəstɪd/ *adj.* not interested; indifferent.

uninteresting /ʌnˈɪntrəstɪŋ/ *adj.* not interesting.

uninterrupted /ˌʌnɪntəˈrʌptɪd/ *adj.* not interrupted.

uninvited /ˌʌnɪnˈvaɪtɪd/ *adj.* not invited.

uninviting /ˌʌnɪnˈvaɪtɪŋ/ *adj.* unattractive, repellent.

union /ˈjuːnjən/ *n.* **1** uniting or being united. **2** a whole formed from parts or members. **b** political unit so formed **3** = TRADE UNION. **4** marriage. **5** concord (*perfect union*). **6** (Union) a university social club and (at Oxbridge, Bristol, etc.) its buildings. **b** buildings of this. **7** *Math.* the totality of the members of two or more sets. **8** mixed fabric, e.g. cotton with linen or silk. [Latin *unio* one]

union-bashing *n.* colloq. media or government campaign against trade unions.

unionist *n.* **1 a** member of a trade union. **b** advocate of trade unions. **2** (usu. Unionist) member of a party advocating continued union between Great Britain and Northern Ireland. □ **unionism** *n.*

unionize *v.* (also **-ise**) (**-zing** or **-sing**) organize in or into a trade union. □ **unionization** /-ˈzeɪʃ(ə)n/ *n.*

Union Jack *n.* (also **Union flag**) national ensign of the United Kingdom.

unique /juːˈniːk/ *adj.* **1** being the only one of its kind; having no like, equal, or parallel. **2** remarkable (*unique opportunity*). □ **uniquely** *adv.* [Latin *unicus* from *unus* one]

■ **Usage** In sense 1, *unique* cannot be qualified by adverbs such as *absolutely*, *most*, and *quite*. The use of *unique* in sense 2 is regarded as incorrect by some people.

unisex /ˈjuːnɪˌseks/ *adj.* (of clothing, hairstyles, etc.) designed for both sexes.

unison /ˈjuːnɪs(ə)n/ *n.* **1** concord (*acted in perfect unison*). **2** coincidence in pitch of sounds or notes (*sung in unison*). [Latin *sonus* SOUND]

unit /ˈjuːnɪt/ *n.* **1 a** individual thing, person, or group, esp. for calculation. **b** smallest component of a complex whole. **2** quantity as a standard of measurement (*unit of heat. S₁ unit*). **3** smallest share in a unit trust. **4** part of a mechanism with a specified function. **5** fitted item of furniture, esp. as part of a set. **6** group of buildings, wards, etc., in a hospital. **8 a** single-digit number. **b** the number 'one'. [Latin *unus* one]

Unitarian /juːnɪˈteərɪən/ *n.* **1** person who believes that God is one, not of the Trinity. **2** member of a religious body so believing. — *adj.* of Unitarians. □ **Unitarianism** *n.* [Latin *unitas* UNITY]

unitary /ˈjuːnɪtərɪ/ *adj.* **1** of a unit or units. **2** marked by unity or uniformity. [from UNIT or UNITY]

unit cost *n.* cost of producing one item.

unite /juːˈnaɪt/ *v.* (**-ting**) **1** join together; combine esp. for a common purpose or action (*united in their struggle*). **2** join in marriage. **3** (cause to) form a physical or chemical whole (*oil will not unite with water*). [Latin *unio* -it- from *unus* one]

United Kingdom *n.* Great Britain and Northern Ireland.

United Nations *n.pl.* (es sing. or pl.) supranational peace-seeking organization.

United Reformed Church *n.* Church formed in 1972 from the English Presbyterian and Congregational Churches.

United States *n.* (in full **United States of America**) federal republic of 50 States, mostly in N. America and including Alaska and Hawaii.

unit price *n.* price charged for each unit of goods supplied.

unit trust *n.* company investing contributions from many persons in various securities and paying proportional dividends.

unity /ˈjuːnɪtɪ/ n. (pl. -ies) **1 a** oneness; being one; interconnected parts constituting a whole (*national unity*). **b** such a complex whole (*person regarded as a unity*). **2 a** being united; solidarity. **b** harmony (*lived together in unity*). **3** the number 'one'. [Latin *unus* one]

univalent /juːnɪˈveɪlənt/ adj. having a valency of one. [from UNI-, VALENCE?]

univalve /ˈjuːmɪˌvælv/ Zool. —adj. having one valve. —n. univalve mollusc.

universal /juːnɪˈvɜːs(ə)l/ —adj. of, belonging to, or done etc. by all; applicable to all cases. —n. term, characteristic, or concept of general application. □ **universality** /-ˈsælɪtɪ/ n. **universally** adv. [Latin: related to UNIVERSE]

universal coupling n. (also **universal joint**) coupling or joint which can transmit rotary power by a shaft at any angle.

universal time n. = GREENWICH MEAN TIME.

universe /ˈjuːnɪˌvɜːs/ n. **1** all existing things; Creation. **2** all mankind. **3** *Statistics & Logic* all the objects under consideration. [Latin *universus* combined into one]

university /juːnɪˈvɜːsɪtɪ/ n. (pl. -ies) **1** educational institution of advanced learning and research conferring degrees. **2** members of this. [Latin: related to UNIVERSE]

unjust /ʌnˈdʒʌst/ adj. not just, not fair. □ **unjustly** adv. **unjustness** n.

unjustifiable /ʌnˈdʒʌstɪˌfaɪəb(ə)l/ adj. not justifiable. □ **unjustifiably** adv.

unjustified /ʌnˈdʒʌstɪˌfaɪd/ adj. not justified.

unkempt /ʌnˈkempt/ adj. untidy, dishevelled. [= *uncombed*]

unkind /ʌnˈkaɪnd/ adj. not kind; harsh, cruel. □ **unkindly** adv. **unkindness** n.

unknot /ʌnˈnɒt/ v. (-tt-) release the knot(s) of, untie.

unknowable /ʌnˈnəʊəb(ə)l/ —adj. that cannot be known. —n. **1** unknowable thing. **2** (**the Unknowable**) the postulated absolute or ultimate reality.

unknowing /ʌnˈnəʊɪŋ/ adj. (often foll. by *of*) not knowing; ignorant, unconscious. □ **unknowingly** adv.

unknown /ʌnˈnəʊn/ —adj. (often foll. by *to*) not known, unfamiliar. —n. unknown thing, person, or quantity. □ **unknown to** without the knowledge of (*did it unknown to me*).

unknown quantity n. mysterious or obscure person or thing.

Unknown Soldier n. unidentified soldier etc. symbolizing a nation's dead in war.

Unknown Warrior n. = UNKNOWN SOLDIER.

unlabelled /ʌnˈleɪb(ə)ld/ adj. (US **unlabeled**) not labelled; without a label.

unlace /ʌnˈleɪs/ v. (-cing) **1** undo the lace(s) of. **2** unfasten or loosen in this way.

unladen /ʌnˈleɪd(ə)n/ adj. not laden.

unladen weight n. weight of a vehicle etc. when not loaded.

unladylike /ʌnˈleɪdɪˌlaɪk/ adj. not ladylike.

unlatch /ʌnˈlætʃ/ v. **1** release the latch of. **2** open in this way.

unlawful /ʌnˈlɔːfʊl/ adj. illegal, not permissible. □ **unlawfully** adv.

unleaded /ʌnˈledɪd/ adj. (of petrol etc.) without added lead.

unlearn /ʌnˈlɜːn/ v. (*past* and *past part.* unlearned or unlearnt) **1** forget deliberately. **2** rid oneself of (a habit, false information, etc.).

unlearned¹ /ʌnˈlɜːnɪd/ adj. not well educated; ignorant.

unlearned² /ʌnˈlɜːnd/ adj. (also **unlearnt** /ʌnˈlɜːnt/) not learnt.

unleash /ʌnˈliːʃ/ v. **1** release from a leash or restraint. **2** set free to engage in pursuit or attack.

unleavened /ʌnˈlev(ə)nd/ adj. not leavened; made without yeast etc.

unless /ʌnˈles/ conj. if not; except when (*shall go unless I hear from you*). [= *on less*]

unlettered /ʌnˈletəd/ adj. illiterate; not well educated.

unlicensed /ʌnˈlaɪs(ə)nst/ adj. not licensed, esp. to sell alcohol.

unlike /ʌnˈlaɪk/ —adj. **1** not like; different from. **2** uncharacteristic of (*greed is unlike her*). **3** dissimilar, different. —prep. differently from (*acts quite unlike anyone else*).

unlikely /ʌnˈlaɪklɪ/ adj. (-ier, -iest) **1** improbable (*unlikely tale*). **2** (foll. by *to* + infin.) not expected (*unlikely to die*). **3** unpromising (*unlikely candidate*). □ **unlikeliness** n.

unlike signs n.pl. Math. plus and minus.

unlimited /ʌnˈlɪmɪtɪd/ adj. unrestricted; enormous (*unlimited expanse*).

unlined¹ /ʌnˈlaɪnd/ adj. without lines or wrinkles.

unlined² /ʌnˈlaɪnd/ adj. without a lining.

unlisted /ʌnˈlɪstɪd/ adj. not in a published list, esp. of Stock Exchange prices or telephone numbers.

unlit /ʌnˈlɪt/ adj. not lit.

unload /ʌnˈləʊd/ v. **1** (also *absol.*) remove a load from (a vehicle etc.). **2** remove (a load) from a vehicle etc. **3** remove the ammunition from (a gun etc.). **4** colloq. get rid of.

unlock /ʌnˈlɒk/ v. **1 a** release the lock of (a door, box, etc.). **b** release or disclose by unlocking. **2** release thoughts, feelings, etc. from (one's mind etc.).

unlooked-for /ʌnˈlʊktfɔː(r)/ adj. unexpected.

unloose /ʌnˈluːs/ v. (also **unloosen**) unfasten, loose; set free.

unlovable /ʌnˈlʌvəb(ə)l/ adj. not lovable.

unloved /ʌnˈlʌvd/ adj. not loved.

unlovely /ʌnˈlʌvli/ adj. not attractive; unpleasant.

unloving /ʌnˈlʌvɪŋ/ adj. not loving.

unlucky /ʌnˈlʌki/ adj. (-ier, -iest) **1** not fortunate or successful. **2** wretched. **3** bringing bad luck. **4** ill-judged. □ **unluckily** adv.

unmade /ʌnˈmeɪd/ adj. (esp. of a bed) not made.

unmakeable /ʌnˈmeɪkəb(ə)l/ adj. too bad to be named or mentioned.

unmake /ʌnˈmeɪk/ v. (-king; past and past part. unmade) undo; destroy, depose, annul.

unman /ʌnˈmæn/ v. (-nn-) make weak, cowardly, etc.; cause to weep etc.

unmanageable /ʌnˈmænɪdʒəb(ə)l/ adj. not easily managed or controlled.

unmanly /ʌnˈmænli/ adj. not manly.

unmanned /ʌnˈmænd/ adj. **1** not manned. **2** overcome by emotion etc.

unmannerly /ʌnˈmænəli/ adj. ill-mannered. □ **unmannerliness** n.

unmarked /ʌnˈmɑːkt/ adj. **1** not marked. **2** not noticed.

unmarried /ʌnˈmærɪd/ adj. not married, single.

unmask /ʌnˈmɑːsk/ v. **1 a** remove the mask from. **b** expose the true character of. **2** remove one's mask.

unmatched /ʌnˈmætʃt/ adj. not matched or equalled.

unmentionable /ʌnˈmenʃ(ə)nəb(ə)l/ —adj. unsuitable for polite conversation. —n. (in pl.) joc. undergarments.

unmerciful /ʌnˈmɜːsɪfʊl/ adj. merciless. □ **unmercifully** adv.

unmerited /ʌnˈmerɪtɪd/ adj. not merited.

unmet /ʌnˈmet/ adj. (of a demand, goal, etc.) not achieved or fulfilled.

unmethodical /ˌʌnmɪˈθɒdɪk(ə)l/ adj. not methodical.

unmindful /ʌnˈmaɪndfʊl/ adj. (often foll. by of) not mindful.

unmissable /ʌnˈmɪsəb(ə)l/ adj. that cannot or should not be missed.

unmistakable /ˌʌnmɪˈsteɪkəb(ə)l/ adj. clear, obvious, plain. □ **unmistakably** adv.

unmitigated /ʌnˈmɪtɪɡeɪtɪd/ adj. not mitigated; absolute (unmitigated disaster).

unmixed /ʌnˈmɪkst/ adj. not mixed.

unmodified /ʌnˈmɒdɪfaɪd/ adj. not modified.

unmoral /ʌnˈmɒr(ə)l/ adj. not concerned with morality (cf. IMMORAL). □ **unmorality** /ˌʌnməˈrælɪtɪ/ n.

unmoved /ʌnˈmuːvd/ adj. **1** not moved. **2** constant in purpose. **3** unemotional.

unmusical /ʌnˈmjuːzɪk(ə)l/ adj. **1** discordant. **2** unskilled in or indifferent to music.

unnameable /ʌnˈneɪməb(ə)l/ adj. too bad to be named or mentioned.

unnamed /ʌnˈneɪmd/ adj. not named.

unnatural /ʌnˈnætʃ(ə)r(ə)l/ adj. **1** contrary to nature, not normal. **2** lacking natural feelings, esp. cruel or wicked. **3** artificial. **4** affected. □ **unnaturally** adv.

unnecessary /ʌnˈnesəsərɪ/ adj. **1** not necessary. **2** superfluous. □ **unnecessarily** adv.

unneeded /ʌnˈniːdɪd/ adj. not needed.

unnerve /ʌnˈnɜːv/ v. (-ving) deprive of confidence etc.

unnoticeable /ʌnˈnəʊtɪsəb(ə)l/ adj. not easily seen or noticed.

unnoticed /ʌnˈnəʊtɪst/ adj. not noticed.

unnumbered /ʌnˈnʌmbəd/ adj. **1** without a number. **2** not counted. **3** countless.

unobjectionable /ˌʌnəbˈdʒekʃən əb(ə)l/ adj. not objectionable; acceptable.

unobservant /ˌʌnəbˈzɜːv(ə)nt/ adj. not observant.

unobserved /ˌʌnəbˈzɜːvd/ adj. not observed.

unobtainable /ˌʌnəbˈteɪnəb(ə)l/ adj. that cannot be obtained.

unobtrusive /ˌʌnəbˈtruːsɪv/ adj. not making oneself or itself noticed. □ **unobtrusively** adv.

unoccupied /ʌnˈɒkjʊpaɪd/ adj. not occupied.

unofficial /ˌʌnəˈfɪʃ(ə)l/ adj. not officially authorized or confirmed. □ **unofficially** adv.

unofficial strike n. strike not ratified by the strikers' trade union.

unopened /ʌnˈəʊpənd/ adj. not opened.

unopposed /ˌʌnəˈpəʊzd/ adj. not opposed.

unorganized /ʌnˈɔːɡənaɪzd/ adj. (also **-ised**) not organized.

unoriginal /ˌʌnəˈrɪdʒɪn(ə)l/ adj. lacking originality; derivative.

unorthodox /ʌnˈɔːθədɒks/ adj. not orthodox.

unpack /ʌnˈpæk/ v. **1** (also absol.) open and empty (a package, luggage, etc.). **2** take (a thing) from a package etc.

unpaid /ʌnˈpeɪd/ adj. (of a debt or a person) not paid.

unpainted /ʌnˈpeɪntɪd/ *adj.* not painted.

unpaired /ʌnˈpeəd/ *adj.* **1** not being one of a pair. **2** not united or arranged in pairs.

unpalatable /ʌnˈpælətəb(ə)l/ *adj.* (of food, an idea, suggestion, etc.) disagreeable, distasteful.

unparalleled /ʌnˈpærəˌleɪld/ *adj.* unequalled.

unpardonable /ʌnˈpɑːdənəb(ə)l/ *adj.* that cannot be pardoned. □ **unpardonably** *adv.*

unparliamentary /ˌʌnpɑːləˈmentərɪ/ *adj.* contrary to proper parliamentary usage.

unparliamentary language *n.* oaths or abuse.

unpasteurized /ʌnˈpɑːstʃəˌraɪzd/ *adj.* (also **-ised**) not pasteurized.

unpatriotic /ˌʌnpætrɪˈɒtɪk/ *adj.* not patriotic.

unperson /ˈʌnpɜːs(ə)n/ *n.* person said not to exist, esp. by the State.

unperturbed /ˌʌnpəˈtɜːbd/ *adj.* not perturbed.

unpick /ʌnˈpɪk/ *v.* undo the sewing of (stitches, a garment, etc.).

unpin /ʌnˈpɪn/ *v.* (**-nn-**) unfasten or detach by removing or opening a pin or pins.

unplaced /ʌnˈpleɪst/ *adj.* not placed, esp. not one of the first three in a race etc.

unplanned /ʌnˈplænd/ *adj.* not planned.

unplayable /ʌnˈpleɪəb(ə)l/ *adj.* **1** *Sport* (of a ball) too fast etc. to be returned. **2** that cannot be played.

unpleasant /ʌnˈplez(ə)nt/ *adj.* not pleasant, disagreeable. □ **unpleasantly** *adv.* **unpleasantness** *n.*

unpleasing /ʌnˈpliːzɪŋ/ *adj.* not pleasing.

unplug /ʌnˈplʌɡ/ *v.* (**-gg-**) **1** disconnect (an electrical device) by removing its plug from the socket. **2** unstop.

unplumbed /ʌnˈplʌmd/ *adj.* **1** not plumbed. **2** not fully explored or understood.

unpointed /ʌnˈpɔɪntɪd/ *adj.* **1** having no point or points. **2** not punctuated. **3** (of brickwork etc.) not pointed.

unpolished /ʌnˈpɒlɪʃt/ *adj.* not polished or refined; rough.

unpolitical /ˌʌnpəˈlɪtɪk(ə)l/ *adj.* not concerned with politics.

unpopular /ʌnˈpɒpjʊlə(r)/ *adj.* not popular; disliked. □ **unpopularity** /-ˈlærɪtɪ/ *n.*

unpopulated /ʌnˈpɒpjʊleɪtɪd/ *adj.* not populated.

unpractical /ʌnˈpræktɪk(ə)l/ *adj.* **1** not practical. **2** (of a person) without practical skill.

unpractised /ʌnˈpræktɪst/ *adj.* (*US* **unpractised**) **1** not experienced or skilled. **2** not put into practice.

unprecedented /ʌnˈpresɪˌdentɪd/ *adj.* having no precedent; unparalleled. □ **unprecedentedly** *adv.*

unpredictable /ˌʌnprɪˈdɪktəb(ə)l/ *adj.* that cannot be predicted. □ **unpredictability** /-ˈbɪlɪtɪ/ *n.* **unpredictably** *adv.*

unprejudiced /ʌnˈpredʒʊdɪst/ *adj.* not prejudiced.

unpremeditated /ˌʌnprɪˈmedɪˌteɪtɪd/ *adj.* not deliberately planned, unintentional.

unprepared /ˌʌnprɪˈpeəd/ *adj.* not prepared; not ready.

unprepossessing /ˌʌnpriːpəˈzesɪŋ/ *adj.* unattractive.

unpretentious /ˌʌnprɪˈtenʃəs/ *adj.* simple, modest, unassuming.

unpriced /ʌnˈpraɪst/ *adj.* not having a price fixed, marked, or stated.

unprincipled /ʌnˈprɪnsɪp(ə)ld/ *adj.* lacking or not based on moral principles.

unprintable /ʌnˈprɪntəb(ə)l/ *adj.* too offensive or indecent to be printed.

unproductive /ˌʌnprəˈdʌktɪv/ *adj.* not productive.

unprofessional /ˌʌnprəˈfeʃən(ə)l/ *adj.* **1** contrary to professional standards. **2** unskilled, amateurish. □ **unprofessionally** *adv.*

unprofitable /ʌnˈprɒfɪtəb(ə)l/ *adj.* not profitable.

unprogressive /ˌʌnprəˈgresɪv/ *adj.* not progressive, old-fashioned.

unpromising /ʌnˈprɒmɪsɪŋ/ *adj.* not likely to turn out well.

unprompted /ʌnˈprɒmptɪd/ *adj.* spontaneous.

unpronounceable /ˌʌnprəˈnaʊnsəb(ə)l/ *adj.* that cannot be pronounced.

unpropitious /ˌʌnprəˈpɪʃəs/ *adj.* not propitious.

unprotected /ˌʌnprəˈtektɪd/ *adj.* not protected.

unprovable /ʌnˈpruːvəb(ə)l/ *adj.* that cannot be proved.

unproved /ʌnˈpruːvd/ *adj.* (also **unproven** /-v(ə)n/) not proved.

unprovoked /ˌʌnprəˈvəʊkt/ *adj.* without provocation.

unpublished /ʌnˈpʌblɪʃt/ *adj.* not published.

unpunctual /ʌnˈpʌŋktʃʊəl/ *adj.* not punctual.

unpunished /ʌnˈpʌnɪʃt/ *adj.* not punished.

unputdownable /ˌʌnpʊtˈdaʊnəb(ə)l/ adj. colloq. (of a book) compulsively readable.

unqualified /ʌnˈkwɒlɪfaɪd/ adj. 1 not legally or officially qualified. 2 complete (unqualified success). 3 not competent (unqualified to say).

unquenchable /ʌnˈkwentʃəb(ə)l/ adj. that cannot be quenched.

unquestionable /ʌnˈkwestʃ(ə)nəb(ə)l/ adj. that cannot be disputed or doubted. □ **unquestionably** adv.

unquestioned /ʌnˈkwestʃ(ə)nd/ adj. not disputed or doubted; definite, certain.

unquestioning /ʌnˈkwestʃənɪŋ/ adj. 1 asking no questions. 2 (of obedience etc.) absolute. □ **unquestioningly** adv.

unquiet /ʌnˈkwaɪət/ adj. 1 restless, agitated 2 anxious.

unquote /ʌnˈkwəʊt/ v. (as int.) verbal formula indicating closing quotation marks.

unravel /ʌnˈræv(ə)l/ v. (-ll-; US -l-) 1 make or become disentangled, unknitted, unknotted, etc. 2 probe and solve (a mystery etc.). 3 undo (esp. knitted fabric).

unread /ʌnˈred/ adj. 1 (of a book etc.) not read. 2 (of a person) not well-read.

unreadable /ʌnˈriːdəb(ə)l/ adj. too dull, bad, or difficult to read.

unready /ʌnˈredɪ/ adj. 1 not ready. 2 hesitant.

unreal /ʌnˈrɪəl/ adj. 1 not real. 2 imaginary. 3 sl. incredible. □ **unreality** /-ɪˈælɪtɪ/ n.

unrealistic /ˌʌnrɪəˈlɪstɪk/ adj. not realistic. □ **unrealistically** adv.

unrealizable /ʌnˈrɪəlaɪzəb(ə)l/ adj. (also **-isable**) that cannot be realized.

unrealized /ʌnˈrɪəlaɪzd/ adj. (also **-ised**) not realized.

unreason /ʌnˈriːz(ə)n/ n. madness; chaos; disorder.

unreasonable /ʌnˈriːzənəb(ə)l/ adj. 1 excessive (unreasonable demands). 2 not heeding reason. □ **unreasonably** adv.

unreasoning /ʌnˈriːzənɪŋ/ adj. not reasoning.

unrecognizable /ʌnˈrekəgˌnaɪzəb(ə)l/ adj. (also **-isable**) that cannot be recognized.

unrecognized /ʌnˈrekəgˌnaɪzd/ adj. (also **-ised**) not acknowledged.

unrecorded /ˌʌnrɪˈkɔːdɪd/ adj. not recorded.

unredeemed /ˌʌnrɪˈdiːmd/ adj. not redeemed.

unreel /ʌnˈriːl/ v. unwind from a reel.

unrefined /ˌʌnrɪˈfaɪnd/ adj. not refined.

unreflecting /ˌʌnrɪˈflektɪŋ/ adj. not thoughtful.

unreformed /ˌʌnrɪˈfɔːmd/ adj. not reformed.

unregenerate /ˌʌnrɪˈdʒenərət/ adj. obstinately wrong or bad.

unregistered /ʌnˈredʒɪstəd/ adj. not registered.

unregulated /ʌnˈregjʊleɪtɪd/ adj. not regulated.

unrehearsed /ˌʌnrɪˈhɜːst/ adj. not rehearsed.

unrelated /ˌʌnrɪˈleɪtɪd/ adj. not related.

unrelenting /ˌʌnrɪˈlentɪŋ/ adj. not abating, yielding, or relaxing; unmerciful. □ **unrelentingly** adv.

unreliable /ˌʌnrɪˈlaɪəb(ə)l/ adj. not reliable. □ **unreliability** /-ˈbɪlɪtɪ/ n.

unrelieved /ˌʌnrɪˈliːvd/ adj. monotonously uniform.

unremarkable /ˌʌnrɪˈmɑːkəb(ə)l/ adj. not remarkable; uninteresting, ordinary.

unremarked /ˌʌnrɪˈmɑːkt/ adj. not mentioned or remarked upon.

unremitting /ˌʌnrɪˈmɪtɪŋ/ adj. incessant. □ **unremittingly** adv.

unremunerative /ˌʌnrɪˈmjuːnərətɪv/ adj. not, or not very, profitable.

unrepeatable /ˌʌnrɪˈpiːtəb(ə)l/ adj. 1 that cannot be done, made, or said again. 2 too indecent to repeat.

unrepentant /ˌʌnrɪˈpent(ə)nt/ adj. not repentant, impenitent. □ **unrepentantly** adv.

unrepresentative /ˌʌnreprɪˈzentətɪv/ adj. not representative.

unrepresented /ˌʌnreprɪˈzentɪd/ adj. not represented.

unrequited /ˌʌnrɪˈkwaɪtɪd/ adj. (of love etc.) not returned.

unreserved /ˌʌnrɪˈzɜːvd/ adj. 1 not reserved. 2 total; without reservation. □ **unreservedly** /-ˈvɪdlɪ/ adv.

unresisting /ˌʌnrɪˈzɪstɪŋ/ adj. not resisting.

unresolved /ˌʌnrɪˈzɒlvd/ adj. 1 irresolute, undecided. 2 (of questions etc.) undetermined.

unresponsive /ˌʌnrɪˈspɒnsɪv/ adj. not responsive.

unrest /ʌnˈrest/ n. disturbed or dissatisfied state (industrial unrest).

unrestrained /ˌʌnrɪˈstreɪnd/ adj. not restrained.

unrestricted /ˌʌnrɪˈstrɪktɪd/ adj. not restricted.

unrewarded /ˌʌnrɪˈwɔːdɪd/ adj. not rewarded.

unrewarding /ˌʌnrɪˈwɔːdɪŋ/ adj. not rewarding or satisfying.

unrighteous /ʌnˈraɪtʃəs/ adj. wicked.

unripe /ʌnˈraɪp/ adj. not ripe.

unrivalled /ʌnˈraɪv(ə)ld/ adj. (US **unrivaled**) having no equal.

unroll /ʌnˈrəʊl/ v. **1** open out from a rolled-up state. **2** display or be displayed like this.

unromantic /ˌʌnrəʊˈmæntɪk/ adj. not romantic.

unruffled /ʌnˈrʌf(ə)ld/ adj. calm.

unruly /ʌnˈruːlɪ/ adj. (-ier, -iest) undisciplined, disorderly. □ **unruliness** n. [related to RULE]

unsaddle /ʌnˈsæd(ə)l/ v. (-ling) **1** remove the saddle from. **2** unhorse.

unsafe /ʌnˈseɪf/ adj. not safe.

unsaid /ʌnˈsed/ adj. not uttered or expressed (left it unsaid).

unsaleable /ʌnˈseɪləb(ə)l/ adj. not saleable.

unsalted /ʌnˈsɔːltɪd/ adj. not salted.

unsatisfactory /ˌʌnsætɪsˈfæktərɪ/ adj. poor, unacceptable.

unsatisfied /ʌnˈsætɪsˌfaɪd/ adj. not satisfied.

unsatisfying /ʌnˈsætɪsˌfaɪɪŋ/ adj. not satisfying.

unsaturated /ʌnˈsætʃəˌreɪtɪd/ adj. Chem. (of esp. a fat or oil) having double or triple bonds in its molecule and therefore capable of further reaction.

unsavoury /ʌnˈseɪvərɪ/ adj. (US **unsavory**) **1** disgusting, unpleasant. **2** morally offensive.

unsay /ʌnˈseɪ/ v. (past and past part. **unsaid**) retract (a statement).

unscalable /ʌnˈskeɪləb(ə)l/ adj. that cannot be scaled.

unscarred /ʌnˈskɑːd/ adj. not scarred or damaged.

unscathed /ʌnˈskeɪðd/ adj. without injury.

unscheduled /ʌnˈʃedjuːld/ adj. not scheduled.

unschooled /ʌnˈskuːld/ adj. uneducated, untrained.

unscientific /ˌʌnsaɪənˈtɪfɪk/ adj. not scientific in method etc. □ **unscientifically** adv.

unscramble /ʌnˈskræmb(ə)l/ v. (-ling) make plain, decode, interpret (a scrambled transmission etc.).

unscreened /ʌnˈskriːnd/ adj. **1 a** (esp. of coal) not passed through a screen or sieve. **b** not checked, esp. for security or medical problems. **2** not having a screen. **3** not shown on a screen.

unscrew /ʌnˈskruː/ v. **1** unfasten by removing a screw or screws. **2** loosen (a screw or screw-top).

unscripted /ʌnˈskrɪptɪd/ adj. (of a speech etc.) delivered impromptu.

unscrupulous /ʌnˈskruːpjʊləs/ adj. having no scruples, unprincipled. □ **unscrupulously** adv. **unscrupulousness** n.

unseal /ʌnˈsiːl/ v. break the seal of; open (a letter, receptacle, etc.).

unseasonable /ʌnˈsiːzənəb(ə)l/ adj. **1** not seasonable. **2** untimely, inopportune. □ **unseasonably** adv.

unseasonal /ʌnˈsiːzən(ə)l/ adj. not typical of, or appropriate to, the time or season. □ **unseasonally** adv.

unseat /ʌnˈsiːt/ v. **1** remove from (esp. a parliamentary) seat. **2** dislodge from a seat, esp. on horseback.

unseeded /ʌnˈsiːdɪd/ adj. Sport (of a player) not seeded.

unseeing /ʌnˈsiːɪŋ/ adj. **1** unobservant. **2** blind. □ **unseeingly** adv.

unseemly /ʌnˈsiːmlɪ/ adj. (-ier, -iest) **1** indecent. **2** unbecoming. □ **unseemliness** n.

unseen /ʌnˈsiːn/ — adj. **1** not seen. **2** invisible. **3** (of a translation) to be done without preparation. — n. unseen translation.

unselfconscious /ˌʌnselfˈkɒnʃəs/ adj. not self-conscious. □ **unselfconsciously** adv. **unselfconsciousness** n.

unselfish /ʌnˈselfɪʃ/ adj. concerned about others; sharing. □ **unselfishly** adv. **unselfishness** n.

unsentimental /ˌʌnsentɪˈment(ə)l/ adj. not sentimental.

unsettle /ʌnˈset(ə)l/ v. (-ling) **1** disturb; discompose. **2** derange.

unsettled /ʌnˈset(ə)ld/ adj. **1** restless, disturbed; unpredictable, changeable. **2** open to change or further discussion. **3** (of a bill etc.) unpaid.

unsex /ʌnˈseks/ v. deprive (a person, esp. a woman) of the qualities of her or his sex.

unshackle /ʌnˈʃæk(ə)l/ v. (-ling) **1** release from shackles. **2** set free.

unshakeable /ʌnˈʃeɪkəb(ə)l/ adj. firm; obstinate. □ **unshakeably** adv.

unshaken /ʌnˈʃeɪkən/ adj. not shaken.

unshaven /ʌnˈʃeɪv(ə)n/ adj. not shaved.

unsheathe /ʌnˈʃiːð/ v. (-thing) remove (a knife etc.) from a sheath.

unshockable /ʌnˈʃɒkəb(ə)l/ adj. unable to be shocked.

unshrinking /ʌnˈʃrɪŋkɪŋ/ adj. unhesitating, fearless.

unsighted /ʌnˈsaɪtɪd/ adj. **1** not sighted or seen. **2** prevented from seeing.

unsightly /ʌnˈsaɪtlɪ/ adj. ugly. □ **unsightliness** n.

unsigned /ʌnˈsaɪnd/ adj. not signed.

unsinkable /ʌnˈsɪŋkəb(ə)l/ adj. unable to be sunk.

unskilful /ʌnˈskɪlfʊl/ adj. (US **unskilful**) not skilful.

unskilled /ʌnˈskɪld/ adj. lacking, or (of work) not needing, special skill or training.

unsliced /ʌnˈslaɪst/ adj. (esp. of a loaf of bread) not sliced.

unsmiling /ʌnˈsmaɪlɪŋ/ adj. not smiling.

unsmoked /ʌnˈsməʊkt/ adj. not cured by smoking (unsmoked bacon).

unsociable /ʌnˈsəʊʃəb(ə)l/ adj. not sociable, disliking company.

■ **Usage** See note at *unsocial*.

unsocial /ʌnˈsəʊʃ(ə)l/ adj. 1 not social; not suitable for or seeking society. 2 outside the normal working day (un-social hours). 3 antisocial.

■ **Usage** *Unsocial* is sometimes con-fused with *unsociable*.

unsoiled /ʌnˈsɔɪld/ adj. not soiled or dirtied.

unsold /ʌnˈsəʊld/ adj. not sold.

unsolicited /ˌʌnsəˈlɪsɪtɪd/ adj. not asked for; voluntary.

unsolved /ʌnˈsɒlvd/ adj. not solved.

unsophisticated /ˌʌnsəˈfɪstɪkeɪtɪd/ adj. artless, simple, natural.

unsorted /ʌnˈsɔːtɪd/ adj. not sorted.

unsought /ʌnˈsɔːt/ adj. 1 not sought for. 2 without being requested.

unsound /ʌnˈsaʊnd/ adj. 1 unhealthy; not sound. 2 rotten, weak; unreliable. 3 ill-founded. □ **of unsound mind** insane.

unsoundness n.

unsparing /ʌnˈspeərɪŋ/ adj. 1 lavish. 2 merciless.

unsparingly adv.

unspeakable /ʌnˈspiːkəb(ə)l/ adj. 1 that cannot be expressed in words. 2 indescri-bably bad. □ **unspeakably** adv.

unspecific /ˌʌnspəˈsɪfɪk/ adj. not specific; general, inexact.

unspecified /ʌnˈspesɪfaɪd/ adj. not speci-fied.

unspectacular /ˌʌnspekˈtækjʊlər/ adj. not spectacular; dull.

unspoiled /ʌnˈspɔɪld/ adj. (also **unspoilt** /ʌnˈspɔɪlt/) not spoilt.

unspoken /ʌnˈspəʊkən/ adj. 1 not expressed in speech. 2 not uttered as speech.

unsporting /ʌnˈspɔːtɪŋ/ adj. not fair or generous.

unsportsmanlike /ʌnˈspɔːtsmanˌlaɪk/ adj. unsporting.

unstable /ʌnˈsteɪb(ə)l/ adj. (**unstabler**, **unstablest**) 1 not stable; likely to fall. 2 not stable emotionally. 3 changeable. □ **unstably** adv.

unstained /ʌnˈsteɪnd/ adj. not stained.

unstated /ʌnˈsteɪtɪd/ adj. not stated or declared.

unsteady /ʌnˈstedɪ/ adj. (**-ier**, **-iest**) 1 not steady or firm. 2 changeable 3 not uni-form or regular. □ **unsteadily** adv. **unsteadiness** n.

unstick /ʌnˈstɪk/ v. (past and past part. **unstuck**) separate (a thing stuck to another). □ **come unstuck** colloq. come to grief, fail.

unstinted /ʌnˈstɪntɪd/ adj. not stinted.

unstinting /ʌnˈstɪntɪŋ/ adj. lavish; limit-less. □ **unstintingly** adv.

unstitch /ʌnˈstɪtʃ/ v. undo the stitches of.

unstop /ʌnˈstɒp/ v. (**-pp-**) 1 unblock. 2 remove the stopper from.

unstoppable /ʌnˈstɒpəb(ə)l/ adj. that cannot be stopped or prevented.

unstrap /ʌnˈstræp/ v. (**-pp-**) undo the strap(s) of.

unstressed /ʌnˈstrest/ adj. not pro-nounced with stress.

unstring /ʌnˈstrɪŋ/ v. (past and past part. **unstrung** 1 remove or relax the string(s) of (a bow, harp, etc.) 2 remove (beads etc.) from a string. 3 (esp. as **unstrung** adj.) unnerve.

unstructured /ʌnˈstrʌktʃəd/ adj. 1 not structured. 2 informal.

unstuck past and past part. of UNSTICK.

unstudied /ʌnˈstʌdɪd/ adj. easy, natural, spontaneous.

unsubstantial /ˌʌnsəbˈstænʃ(ə)l/ adj. = INSUBSTANTIAL.

unsubstantiated /ˌʌnsəbˈstænʃɪˌertɪd/ adj. not substantiated.

unsubtle /ʌnˈsʌt(ə)l/ adj. not subtle; obvious; clumsy.

unsuccessful /ˌʌnsəkˈsesfʊl/ adj. not successful. □ **unsuccessfully** adv.

unsuitable /ʌnˈsuːtəb(ə)l/ adj. not suitable. □ **unsuitability** /ˈbɪlɪtɪ/ n. **unsuitably** adv.

unsuited /ʌnˈsuːtɪd/ adj. 1 (usu. foll. by for) not fit. 2 (usu. foll. by to) not adapted.

unsullied /ʌnˈsʌlɪd/ adj. not sullied.

unsung /ʌnˈsʌŋ/ adj. not celebrated, unrecognized (unsung heroes).

unsupervised /ʌnˈsuːpəvaɪzd/ adj. not supervised.

unsupported /ˌʌnsəˈpɔːtɪd/ adj. not sup-ported.

unsure /ʌnˈʃʊər/ adj. not sure.

unsurpassed /ˌʌnsəˈpɑːst/ adj. not sur-passed.

unsurprised /ˌʌnsəˈpraɪzd/ adj. not sur-prised.

unsurprising /ˌʌnsəˈpraɪzɪŋ/ adj. not surprising. □ **unsurprisingly** adv.

unsuspecting /ˌʌnsəˈspektɪŋ/ adj. not suspecting. □ **unsuspected** adj.

unsustainable /ˌʌnsəˈsteɪnəb(ə)l/ adj. that cannot be sustained.

unsweetened /ʌnˈswiːt(ə)nd/ adj. not sweetened.

unswept /ʌnˈswept/ adj. not swept.

unswerving /ʌnˈswɜːvɪŋ/ adj. steady, constant. □ **unswervingly** adv.

unsymmetrical /ˌʌnsɪˈmetrɪk(ə)l/ adj. not symmetrical.

unsympathetic /ˌʌnsɪmpəˈθetɪk/ adj. not sympathetic. □ **unsympathetically** adv.

unsystematic /ˌʌnsɪstəˈmætɪk/ *adj.* not systematic. □ **unsystematically** *adv.*

untainted /ʌnˈteɪntɪd/ *adj.* not tainted.

untalented /ʌnˈtæləntɪd/ *adj.* not talented.

untameable /ʌnˈteɪməb(ə)l/ *adj.* that cannot be tamed.

untamed /ʌnˈteɪmd/ *adj.* not tamed, wild.

untangle /ʌnˈtæŋg(ə)l/ *v.* (**-ling**) disentangle.

untapped /ʌnˈtæpt/ *adj.* not (yet) tapped or used (*untapped resources*).

untarnished /ʌnˈtɑːnɪʃt/ *adj.* not tarnished.

untaught /ʌnˈtɔːt/ *adj.* (of a person, knowledge, etc.) not taught.

untaxed /ʌnˈtækst/ *adj.* (of a person, commodity, etc.) not taxed.

unteachable /ʌnˈtiːtʃəb(ə)l/ *adj.* (of a person, subject, etc.) incapable of being taught.

untenable /ʌnˈtenəb(ə)l/ *adj.* (of a theory etc.) not tenable.

untested /ʌnˈtestɪd/ *adj.* not tested or proved.

untether /ʌnˈteðə(r)/ *v.* release (an animal) from a tether.

unthinkable /ʌnˈθɪŋkəb(ə)l/ *adj.* **1** unimaginable, inconceivable. **2** *colloq.* highly unlikely or undesirable. □ **unthinkably** *adv.*

unthinking /ʌnˈθɪŋkɪŋ/ *adj.* **1** thoughtless. **2** unintentional, inadvertent. □ **unthinkingly** *adv.*

unthread /ʌnˈθred/ *v.* take the thread out of (a needle etc.).

unthrone /ʌnˈθrəʊn/ *v.* (**-ning**) dethrone.

untidy /ʌnˈtaɪdɪ/ *adj.* (**-ier**, **-iest**) not neat or orderly. □ **untidily** *adv.* **untidiness** *n.*

untie /ʌnˈtaɪ/ *v.* (**untying**) **1** undo (a knot, package, etc.). **2** release from bonds or attachment.

until /ʌnˈtɪl/ *prep.* & *conj.* = TILL¹. [earlier *until*: *un* from Old Norse *und* as far as]

■ **Usage** *Until*, as opposed to *till*, is used esp. at the beginning of a sentence and in formal style, e.g. *until you told me, I had no idea*; *he resided there until his decease.*

untimely /ʌnˈtaɪmlɪ/ *adj.* **1** inopportune. **2** (of death) premature. □ **untimeliness** *n.*

untiring /ʌnˈtaɪərɪŋ/ *adj.* tireless. □ **untiringly** *adv.*

untitled /ʌnˈtaɪt(ə)ld/ *adj.* having no title.

unto /ˈʌntʊ/ *prep. archaic* = TO (in all uses except signalling the infinitive). [from UNTIL, with *to* replacing *til*]

untold /ʌnˈtəʊld/ *adj.* **1** not told. **2** immeasurable (*untold misery*).

untouchable /ʌnˈtʌtʃəb(ə)l/ *—adj.* that may not be touched. *—n.* member of a

hereditary Hindu group held to defile members of higher castes on contact. □ **untouchability** /-ˈbɪlɪtɪ/ *n.*

■ **Usage** The use of this term, and social restrictions accompanying it, were declared illegal under the Indian constitution in 1949.

untouched /ʌnˈtʌtʃt/ *adj.* **1** not touched. **2** not affected physically, emotionally, etc. **3** not discussed.

untoward /ˌʌntəˈwɔːd/ *adj.* **1** inconvenient, unlucky. **2** awkward. **3** perverse, refractory. **4** unseemly.

untraceable /ʌnˈtreɪsəb(ə)l/ *adj.* that cannot be traced.

untrained /ʌnˈtreɪnd/ *adj.* not trained.

untrammelled /ʌnˈtræm(ə)ld/ *adj.* not trammelled, unhampered.

untranslatable /ˌʌntrænsˈleɪtəb(ə)l/ *adj.* that cannot be translated satisfactorily.

untreated /ʌnˈtriːtɪd/ *adj.* not treated.

untried /ʌnˈtraɪd/ *adj.* **1** not tried or tested. **2** inexperienced.

untroubled /ʌnˈtrʌb(ə)ld/ *adj.* calm, tranquil.

untrue /ʌnˈtruː/ *adj.* **1** not true. **2** (often foll. by *to*) not faithful or loyal. **3** deviating from an accepted standard.

untrustworthy /ʌnˈtrʌstwɜːðɪ/ *adj.* not trustworthy. □ **untrustworthiness** *n.*

untruth /ʌnˈtruːθ/ *n.* **1** being untrue. **2** lie.

untruthful /ʌnˈtruːθfʊl/ *adj.* not truthful. □ **untruthfully** *adv.*

untuck /ʌnˈtʌk/ *v.* free (bedclothes etc.) from being tucked in or up.

unturned /ʌnˈtɜːnd/ *adj.* **1** not turned over, round, away, etc. **2** not shaped by turning.

untutored /ʌnˈtjuːtəd/ *adj.* uneducated, untaught.

untwine /ʌnˈtwaɪn/ *v.* (**-ning**) untwist, unwind.

untwist /ʌnˈtwɪst/ *v.* open from a twisted or spiralled state.

unusable /ʌnˈjuːzəb(ə)l/ *adj.* not usable.

unused *adj.* **1** /ʌnˈjuːzd/ **a** not in use. **b** never having been used. **2** /ʌnˈjuːst/ (foll. by *to*) not accustomed.

unusual /ʌnˈjuːʒʊəl/ *adj.* **1** not usual. **2** remarkable. □ **unusually** *adv.*

unutterable /ʌnˈʌtərəb(ə)l/ *adj.* inexpressible; beyond description. □ **unutterably** *adv.*

unvarnished /ʌnˈvɑːnɪʃt/ *adj.* **1** not varnished. **2** plain and straightforward (*the unvarnished truth*).

unvarying /ʌnˈveərɪɪŋ/ *adj.* not varying.

unveil /ʌnˈveɪl/ *v.* **1** uncover (a statue etc.) ceremonially. **2** reveal. **3** remove a veil from; remove one's veil.

unverified /ʌnˈverɪfaɪd/ *adj.* not verified.

unversed /ʌnˈvɜːst/ *adj.* (usu. foll. by *in*) not experienced or skilled.

unviable /ʌnˈvaɪəb(ə)l/ *adj.* not viable.

unvoiced /ʌnˈvɔɪst/ *adj.* 1 not spoken. 2 (of a consonant etc.) not voiced.

unwaged /ʌnˈweɪdʒd/ *adj.* not receiving a wage; unemployed.

unwanted /ʌnˈwɒntɪd/ *adj.* not wanted.

unwarrantable /ʌnˈwɒrəntəb(ə)l/ *adj.* unjustifiable. □ **unwarrantably** *adv.*

unwarranted /ʌnˈwɒrəntɪd/ *adj.* 1 unauthorized. 2 unjustified.

unwary /ʌnˈweərɪ/ *adj.* (often foll. by *of*) not cautious. □ **unwarily** *adv.* **unwariness** *n.*

unwashed /ʌnˈwɒʃt/ *adj.* not washed or clean. □ **the great unwashed** *colloq.* the rabble.

unwavering /ʌnˈweɪvərɪŋ/ *adj.* not wavering. □ **unwaveringly** *adv.*

unweaned /ʌnˈwiːnd/ *adj.* not yet weaned.

unwearying /ʌnˈweərɪɪŋ/ *adj.* persistent.

unwelcome /ʌnˈwelkəm/ *adj.* not welcome or acceptable.

unwell /ʌnˈwel/ *adj.* ill.

unwholesome /ʌnˈhəʊlsəm/ *adj.* 1 detrimental to physical or moral health. 2 unhealthy-looking.

unwieldy /ʌnˈwiːldɪ/ *adj.* (-ier, -iest) cumbersome or hard to manage, owing to size, shape, etc. □ **unwieldiness** *n.* [*wieldy* active, from WIELD]

unwilling /ʌnˈwɪlɪŋ/ *adj.* not willing or inclined; reluctant. □ **unwillingly** *adv.* **unwillingness** *n.*

unwind /ʌnˈwaɪnd/ *v.* (*past* and *past part.* **unwound**) 1 draw out or become drawn out after having been wound. 2 *colloq.* relax.

unwinking /ʌnˈwɪŋkɪŋ/ *adj.* 1 not winking. 2 vigilant.

unwise /ʌnˈwaɪz/ *adj.* foolish, imprudent. □ **unwisely** *adv.*

unwished /ʌnˈwɪʃt/ *adj.* (usu. foll. by *for*) not wished for.

unwitting /ʌnˈwɪtɪŋ/ *adj.* 1 not knowing or aware (*an unwitting offender*). 2 unintentional. □ **unwittingly** *adv.* [Old English: related to WIT]

unwonted /ʌnˈwəʊntɪd/ *adj.* not customary or usual.

unworkable /ʌnˈwɜːkəb(ə)l/ *adj.* not workable; impracticable.

unworkmanlike /ʌnˈwɜːkmən.laɪk/ *adj.* badly done or made.

unworldly /ʌnˈwɜːldlɪ/ *adj.* spiritual; naïve. □ **unworldliness** *n.*

unworn /ʌnˈwɔːn/ *adj.* not worn or impaired by wear.

unworried /ʌnˈwʌrɪd/ *adj.* not worried; calm.

unworthy /ʌnˈwɜːðɪ/ *adj.* (-ier, -iest) 1 (often foll. by *of*) not worthy of or befitting a person etc. 2 discreditable, unseemly. □ **unworthily** *adv.* **unworthiness** *n.*

unwound *past* and *past part.* of UNWIND.

unwrap /ʌnˈræp/ *v.* (-pp-) 1 remove the wrapping from. 2 open, unfold. 3 become unwrapped.

unwritten /ʌnˈrɪt(ə)n/ *adj.* 1 not written. 2 (of a law etc.) based on custom or judicial decision, not on statute.

unyielding /ʌnˈjiːldɪŋ/ *adj.* 1 not yielding. 2 firm, obstinate.

unzip /ʌnˈzɪp/ *v.* (-pp-) unfasten the zip of.

up –*adv.* 1 at, in, or towards a higher place or a place regarded as higher, e.g. the north, a capital or a university (*up in Scotland*; *went up to London*; *came up in 1989*). 2 to or in an erect or required position or condition (*stood it up*; *wound up the watch*), b in or into an active condition (*stirred up trouble*; *the hunt is up*). 3 in a stronger or leading position (*three goals up*; *am £10 up*; *is well up in class*). 4 to a specified place, person, or time (*a child came up to me*; *fine up till now*) 5 higher in price or value (*our costs are up*; *shares are up*). 6 a completely (*burn up*; *eat up*). b more loudly or clearly (*speak up*). 7 completed (*time is up*). 8 into a compact, accumulated, or secure state (*pack up*; *save up*; *tie up*). 9 out of bed, having risen (*are you up yet?*; *sun is up*). 10 happening, esp. unusually (*something is up*). 11 (usu. foll. by *before*) appearing for trial etc. (*up before the magistrate*). 12 (of a road etc.) being repaired. 13 (of a jockey) being in the saddle. –*prep.* 1 upwards and along, through, or into (*climbed up the ladder*; *went up the road*). 2 from the bottom to the top of. 3 at or in a higher part of (*is up the street*). b towards the source of (a river). –*adj.* 1 directed upwards (*up stroke*). 2 of travel towards a capital or centre (*the up train*). –*n.* 1 spell of good fortune. 2 (-pp-) 1 colloq. start, esp. abruptly, to speak or act (*upped and hit him*). 2 raise (*upped their prices*). □ **be all up with** hopeless for (a person), or the run of and up) *colloq.* steadily improving, **up against** 1 close to. 2 in or into contact with. 3 *colloq.* confronted with (a problem etc.), **up and about** (or **doing**) having risen from bed, active, **up and down** 1 to and fro (along). 2 *colloq.* in varying health or spirits, **up for** available for or standing for (office etc.) (*up

for sale). **up to 1** until. **2** below or equal to. **3** incumbent on (*it is up to you to say*). **4** capable of. **5** occupied or busy with. **up to date** see DATE. [Old English]

up- *prefix* in senses of *up*, added: **1** as an adverb to verbs and verbal derivations, = 'upwards' (*upcurved*; *update*). **2** as a preposition to nouns forming adverbs and adjectives (*up-country*; *uphill*; *up-stroke*). **3** as an adjective to nouns (*upland*; *up-stroke*).

up-and-coming *adj. colloq.* (of a person) promising; progressing.

up-and-over *adj.* (of a door) opening by being raised and pushed back into a horizontal position.

upbeat —*n.* unaccented beat in music. —*adj. colloq.* optimistic, cheerful.

upbraid /ʌpˈbreɪd/ *v.* (often foll. by *with, for*) chide, reproach. [Old English: related to BRAID = brandish]

upbringing *n.* rearing of a child. [obsolete *upbring* to rear]

up-country *adv. & adj.* inland.

upcurved /ˈʌpkɜːvd/ *adj.* curved upwards.

update —*v.* /ʌpˈdeɪt/ (-ting) bring up to date. —*n.* /ˈʌpdeɪt/ **1** updating. **2** updated information etc.

up-end /ʌpˈend/ *v.* set or rise up on end.

upfield *adv.* in or to a position nearer to the opponents' end of a field.

upfront /ʌpˈfrʌnt/ *colloq.* —*adv.* (usu. **up front**) **1** at the front; in front. **2** (of payments) in advance. —*adj.* **1** honest, frank, direct. **2** (of payments) made in advance.

upgrade *v.* /ʌpˈgreɪd/ (-ding) **1** raise in rank etc. **2** improve (equipment etc.).

upheaval /ʌpˈhiːv(ə)l/ *n.* violent or sudden change or disruption. [from *upheave*, = heave or lift up]

uphill —*adv.* /ʌpˈhɪl/ up a slope. —*adj.* /ˈʌphɪl/ **1** sloping up; ascending. **2** arduous.

uphold /ʌpˈhəʊld/ *v.* (*past* and *past part.* **upheld**) **1** confirm (a decision etc.). **2** support, maintain (a custom etc.). □ **upholder** *n.*

upholster /ʌpˈhəʊlstə(r)/ *v.* provide (furniture) with upholstery. [back formation from UPHOLSTERER]

upholsterer *n.* person who upholsters, esp. for a living. [obsolete *upholster* from UPHOLD in sense 'keep in repair']

upholstery *n.* **1** covering, padding, springs, etc. for furniture. **2** upholsterer's work.

upkeep *n.* **1** maintenance in good condition. **2** cost or means of this.

upland /ˈʌplənd/ *n.* (usu. in *pl.*) higher or inland parts of a country. —*adj.* of these parts.

uplift —*v.* /ʌpˈlɪft/ **1** raise. **2** (esp. as **uplifting** *adj.*) elevate morally or emotionally. —*n.* /ˈʌplɪft/ **1** *colloq.* elevating influence. **2** support for the bust etc.

up-market *adj. & adv.* of or directed at the upper end of the market; classy.

upmost var. of UPPERMOST.

upon /əˈpɒn/ *prep.* = ON. [from *up on*]

□ **Usage** *Upon* is sometimes more formal than *on*, but is standard in *once upon a time* and *upon my word*.

upper[1] —*attrib. adj.* **1** higher in place; situated above another part. **2** higher in rank etc. (*upper class*). —*n.* part of a boot or shoe above the sole. □ **on one's uppers** *colloq.* very short of money.

upper[2] *n. slang* amphetamine or other stimulant.

upper case *n.* capital letters.

upper crust *n. colloq.* (prec. by *the*) the aristocracy.

upper-cut —*n.* upwards blow delivered with the arm bent. —*v.* hit upwards with the arm bent.

upper hand *n.* (prec. by *the*) dominance, control.

Upper House *n.* higher house in a legislature, esp. the House of Lords.

uppermost —*adj.* (also **upmost**) **1** highest. **2** predominant. —*adv.* at or to the uppermost position.

uppish *adj. colloq.* uppity.

uppity /ˈʌpɪtɪ/ *adj. colloq.* self-assertive, arrogant.

upright —*adj.* **1** erect, vertical. **2** (of a piano) with vertical strings. **3** honourable or honest. —*n.* **1** upright post or rod, esp. as a structural support. **2** upright piano. [Old English]

uprising *n.* insurrection.

uproar *n.* tumult; violent disturbance. [Dutch, = commotion]

uproarious /ʌpˈrɔːrɪəs/ *adj.* **1** very noisy. **2** provoking loud laughter; very funny. □ **uproariously** *adv.*

uproot /ʌpˈruːt/ *v.* **1** pull (a plant etc.) up from the ground. **2** displace (a person). **3** eradicate.

uprush *n.* upward rush.

ups-a-daisy var. of UPSY-DAISY.

ups and downs *n.pl.* **1** rises and falls. **2** mixed fortune.

upset —*v.* /ʌpˈset/ (-tt-; *past* and *past part.* **upset**) **1** overturn. **2** disturb the composure or digestion of. **3** disrupt. —*n.* /ˈʌpset/ **1** emotional or physical disturbance. **2** surprising result. —*adj.* /ʌpˈset/ disturbed (*upset stomach*).

upshot *n.* outcome, conclusion.

upside down /ˌʌpsaɪd ˈdaʊn/ *adv. & adj.* **1** with the upper and lower parts reversed; inverted. **2** in or into total

upsilon /ʌpˈsaɪlən, ˈʌpsɪlon/ n. twentieth letter of the Greek alphabet (Υ, υ). [Greek, = slender U, from psilos slender, with ref. to its later coincidence in sound with Greek oi]

upstage /ʌpˈsteɪdʒ/ —adj. & adv. nearer the back of a theatre stage. —v. (-ging) 1 move upstage to make (another actor) face away from the audience. 2 divert attention from (a person) to oneself.

upstairs —adv. /ʌpˈsteəz/ to or on an upper floor. —attrib. adj. /ˈʌpsteəz/ situated upstairs. —n. /ʌpˈsteəz/ upper floor.

upstanding /ʌpˈstændɪŋ/ adj. 1 standing up. 2 strong and healthy. 3 honest.

upstart —n. newly successful, esp. arrogant, person. —adj. 1 that is an upstart. 2 of upstarts.

upstate US —n. provincial, esp. northern, part of a State. —attrib. adj. of this part. —adv. in or to this part.

upstream adv. & adj. in the direction contrary to the flow of a stream etc.

upstroke /ˈʌpstrəʊk/ n. upwards stroke.

upsurge n. upward surge.

upswept adj. (of hair) combed to the top of the head.

upswing n. upward movement or trend.

upsy-daisy /ˈʌpsɪˌdeɪzɪ/ int. (also ups-a-daisy) expressing encouragement to a child who is being lifted or has fallen. [earlier up-a-daisy]

uptake n. 1 colloq. understanding (esp. quick or slow on the uptake). 2 taking up (of an offer etc.).

upthrust n. 1 upward thrust. 2 upward displacement of part of the earth's crust.

uptight /ʌpˈtaɪt/ adj. colloq. 1 nervously tense or angry. 2 US rigidly conventional.

uptown US —attrib. adj. of the residential part of a town or city. —adv. in or into this part. —n. this part.

upturn —n. /ˈʌptɜːn/ upward trend; improvement. —v. /ʌpˈtɜːn/ turn up or upside down.

upward /ˈʌpwəd/ —adv. (also upwards) towards what is higher, more important, etc. —adj. moving or extending upwards. □ upwards of more than (upwards of forty).

upwardly adv. in an upward direction. □ upwardly mobile aspiring to advance socially or professionally.

upwind /ʌpˈwɪnd/ adj. & adv. in the direction from which the wind is blowing.

uranium /jʊˈreɪnɪəm/ n. radioactive grey dense metallic element, capable of

disorder. [from up as if down, perhaps = 'up as if down']

nuclear fission and used as a source of nuclear energy. [Uranus, name of a planet]

urban /ˈɜːbən/ adj. of, living in, or situated in a town or city. [Latin urbis city]

urbane /ɜːˈbeɪn/ adj. suave; elegant. □ **urbanity** /-ˈbænɪt/ n. [Latin: related to URBAN]

urban guerrilla n. terrorist operating in an urban area.

urbanize /ˈɜːbənaɪz/ v. (also -ise) (-zing or -sing) make urban, esp. by destroying the rural quality of (a district). □ **urbanization** /-ˈzeɪʃ(ə)n/ n.

urchin /ˈɜːtʃɪn/ n. 1 mischievous, esp. ragged, child. 2 = SEA URCHIN. [Latin ericius hedgehog]

Urdu /ˈʊədu, ˈɜː-/ n. language related to Hindi but with many Persian words, used esp. in Pakistan. [Hindustani]

-ure suffix forming: 1 nouns of action (seizure). 2 nouns of result (creature). 3 collective nouns (nature). [Latin -ura]

urea /ˈjʊərɪə/ n. soluble nitrogenous compound contained esp. in urine. [French urée from Greek ouron urine]

ureter /jʊˈriːtə(r)/ n. duct conveying urine from the kidney to the bladder. [Greek oureō urinate]

urethra /jʊˈriːθrə/ n (pl. -s) duct conveying urine from the bladder. [Greek: related to URETER]

urge —v. (-ging) 1 (often foll. by on) drive forcibly; hasten. 2 encourage or entreat earnestly or persistently. 3 (often foll. by on, upon) advocate (an action or argument etc.) emphatically (to a person). —n. 1 urging impulse or tendency. 2 strong desire. [Latin urgeo]

urgent adj. 1 requiring immediate action or attention. 2 importunate. □ **urgency** n. **urgently** adv. [French: related to URGE]

-uric /ˈjʊərɪk/ adj. of urine. [French urique related to URINE]

uric acid n. constituent of urine.

urinal /jʊəˈraɪn(ə)l/ n. place or receptacle for urination by men. [Latin: related to URINE]

urinary /ˈjʊərɪnərɪ/ adj. of or relating to urine.

urinate /ˈjʊərɪˌneɪt/ v. (-ting) discharge urine. □ **urination** /-ˈneɪʃ(ə)n/ n.

urine /ˈjʊərɪn/ n. waste fluid secreted by the kidneys and discharged from the bladder. [Latin urina]

urn n. 1 vase with a foot and usu. a rounded body, used esp. for the ashes of the dead. 2 large vessel with a tap, in which tea or coffee etc. is made or kept hot. [Latin urna]

urogenital /juərəʊˈdʒenɪt(ə)l/ *adj.* of the urinary and reproductive systems. [Greek *ouron* urine]

urology /juəˈrɒlədʒɪ/ *n.* the study of the urinary system. □ **urological** /-rəˈlɒdʒɪk(ə)l/ *adj.*

Ursa Major /ˌɜːsə/ *n.* = *Great Bear* (see BEAR²). [Latin]

Ursa Minor *n.* = *Little Bear* (see BEAR²). [Latin]

ursine /ˈɜːsaɪn/ *adj.* of or like a bear. [Latin *ursus* bear]

US *abbr.* United States.

us /əs, ʌs/ *pron.* **1** objective case of WE (*they saw us*). **2** *colloq.* = WE (*it's us again*). **3** *colloq.* = ME (*give us a kiss*). [Old English]

USA *abbr.* United States of America.

usable /ˈjuːzəb(ə)l/ *adj.* that can be used.

USAF *abbr.* United States Air Force.

usage /ˈjuːsɪdʒ/ *n.* **1** use, treatment (*damaged by rough usage*). **2** customary practice. esp. in the use of a language or as creating a precedent in law.

use —*v.* /juːz/ (**using**) **1** cause to act or serve for a purpose: bring into service. **2** treat in a specified manner (*used him shamefully*). **3** exploit for one's own ends. **4** /juːs/ did or had habitually (*I used to drink; it used not* (or *did not use*) *to rain so often*). **5** (as **used** *adj.*) second-hand. **6** (as **used** /juːst/ *predic. adj.*) (foll. by *to*) familiar by habit; accustomed (*used to hard work*). —*n.* /juːs/ **1** using or being used. **2** right or power of using (*lost the use of his legs*). **3** benefit, advantage (*a torch would be of use; it's no use talking*). **4** custom or usage (*established by long use*). □ **have no use for 1** not need. **2** dislike. **be contemptuous of. in use** being used. **make use of 1** use. **2** benefit from. **out of use** not being used. **use up 1** consume completely. **2** find a use for (leftovers etc.). [French *us*, *user*, ultimately from Latin *utor us-*]

useful *adj.* **1** that can be used to advantage; helpful; beneficial. **2** *colloq.* creditable, efficient (*useful footballer*). □ **make oneself useful** help. — **usefully** *adv.* **usefulness** *n.*

useless *adj.* **1** serving no purpose; unavailing. **2** *colloq.* feeble or ineffectual (*useless at swimming*). □ **uselessly** *adv.* **uselessness** *n.*

user *n.* person who uses a thing.

user-friendly *adj.* (of a computer etc.) easy to use.

usher —*n.* **1** person who shows people to their seats in a cinema, church, etc. **2** doorkeeper at a court etc. —*v.* **1** act as usher to. **2** (usu. foll. by *in*) announce, herald, or show in. [Latin *ostium door*]

usherette /ˌʌʃəˈret/ *n.* female usher, esp. in a cinema.

USSR *abbr. hist.* Union of Soviet Socialist Republics.

usual /ˈjuːʒʊəl/ *adj.* **1** customary, habitual (*the usual time*). **2** (*absol.*, prec. by *the*, *my*, etc.) *colloq.* person's usual drink etc. □ **as usual** as is (or was) usual. □ **usually** *adv.* [Latin: related to USE]

usurer /ˈjuːʒərə(r)/ *n.* person who practises usury.

usurp /jʊˈzɜːp/ *v.* seize (a throne or power etc.) wrongfully. □ **usurpation** /ˌjuːzəˈpeɪʃ(ə)n/ *n.* **usurper** *n.* [French from Latin]

usury /ˈjuːʒərɪ/ *n.* **1** lending of money at interest, esp. at an exorbitant or illegal rate. **2** interest at this rate. □ **usurious** /juːˈʒʊərɪəs/ *adj.* [Anglo-French or medieval Latin: related to USE]

utensil /juːˈtens(ə)l/ *n.* implement or vessel, esp. for kitchen use. [medieval Latin: related to USE]

uterine /ˈjuːtəraɪn/ *adj.* of the uterus.

uterus /ˈjuːtərəs/ *n.* (*pl.* **uteri** /-ˌraɪ/) womb. [Latin]

utilitarian /ˌjuːtɪlɪˈteərɪən/ —*adj.* **1** designed to be useful rather than attractive; severely practical. **2** of utilitarianism. —*n.* adherent of utilitarianism.

utilitarianism *n.* doctrine that actions are right if they are useful or benefit a majority.

utility /juːˈtɪlɪtɪ/ *n.* (*pl.* **-ies**) **1** usefulness. **2** useful thing. **3** = PUBLIC UTILITY. **4** (*attrib.*) basic and standardized (*utility furniture*). [Latin *utilis* useful: related to USE]

utility room *n.* room for domestic appliances, e.g. a washing-machine, boiler, etc.

utility vehicle *n.* vehicle serving various functions.

utilize /ˈjuːtɪlaɪz/ *v.* (also **-ise**) (**-zing** or **-sing**) use; turn to account. □ **utilization** /-ˈzeɪʃ(ə)n/ *n.* [Italian: related to UTILITY]

utmost /ˈʌtməʊst/ —*attrib. adj.* furthest, extreme, greatest. —*n.* utmost point or degree of anything. □ **do one's utmost** do all that one can. [Old English: = OUTMOST]

Utopia /juːˈtəʊpɪə/ *n.* imagined perfect place or state of things. □ **Utopian** *adj.* (also **utopian**). [title of a book by Thomas More, from Greek *ou* not, *topos* place]

utter¹ *attrib. adj.* complete, absolute. □ **utterly** *adv.* [Old English, comparative of OUT]

utter² *v.* **1** emit audibly. **2** express in words. **3** *Law* put (esp. forged money) into circulation. [Dutch]

utterance *n.* **1** act of uttering. **2** thing spoken. **3** power or manner of speaking.

uttermost *attrib. adj.* utmost.

U-turn /ˈjuːtɜːn/ *n.* **1** U-shaped turn of a vehicle so as to face in the opposite direction. **2** abrupt reversal of policy.

UV *abbr.* ultraviolet.

UVPC *abbr.* unplasticized polyvinyl chloride.

uvula /ˈjuːvjʊlə/ *n.* (*pl.* **uvulae** /-liː/) fleshy part of the soft palate hanging above the throat. □ **uvular** *adj.* [Latin diminutive of *uva* grape]

uxorial /ʌkˈsɔːrɪəl/ *adj.* of a wife. [Latin *uxor* wife]

uxorious /ʌkˈsɔːrɪəs/ *adj.* greatly or excessively fond of one's wife.

V

V¹ /viː/ n. (also v) (pl. **Vs** or **V's**) **1** twenty-second letter of the alphabet. **2** V-shaped thing. **3** (as a Roman numeral) 5.

V² abbr. volt(s).

V³ symb. vanadium.

v. abbr. **1** verse. **2** versus. **3** very. **4** vide.

vac n. colloq. **1** vacation. **2** vacuum cleaner. [abbreviation]

vacancy /ˈveɪkənsɪ/ n. (pl. **-ies**) **1** being vacant. **2** unoccupied job. **3** available room in a hotel etc.

vacant adj. **1** not filled or occupied. **2** not mentally active; showing no interest. □ **vacantly** adv. [Latin: related to VACATE]

vacant possession n. ownership of an unoccupied house etc.

vacate /vəˈkeɪt/ v. (**-ting**) leave vacant, cease to occupy (a house, post, etc.). [Latin vaco be empty]

vacation /vəˈkeɪʃ(ə)n/ —n. **1** fixed holiday period, esp. in universities and lawcourts. **2** US holiday. **3** vacating or being vacated. —v. US take a holiday. [Latin: related to VACATE]

vaccinate /ˈvæksɪˌneɪt/ v. (**-ting**) inoculate with a vaccine to immunize against a disease. □ **vaccination** /-ˈneɪʃ(ə)n/ n. **vaccinator** n.

vaccine /ˈvæksiːn/ n. preparation, orig. cowpox virus, used in vaccination. [Latin vacca cow]

vacillate /ˈvæsɪˌleɪt/ v. (**-ting**) be irresolute; fluctuate. □ **vacillation** /-ˈleɪʃ(ə)n/ n. **vacillator** n. [Latin]

vacuole /ˈvækjʊˌəʊl/ n. tiny space in an organ or cell, containing air, fluid, etc. [Latin vacuus empty]

vacuous /ˈvækjʊəs/ adj. **1** expressionless. **2** showing absence of thought or intelligence, inane. □ **vacuity** /vəˈkjuːɪtɪ/ n. **vacuously** adv. [Latin vacuus empty]

vacuum /ˈvækjʊəm/ —n. (pl. **-s** or **-cua**) **1** space entirely devoid of matter. **2** space or vessel from which all or some of the air has been pumped out. **3** absence of the normal or previous content, activities, etc. **4** (pl. **-s**) colloq. vacuum cleaner. —v. colloq. clean with a vacuum cleaner. [Latin vacuus empty]

vacuum brake n. brake worked by the exhaustion of air.

vacuum cleaner n. machine for removing dust etc. by suction. □ **vacuum-clean** v.

vacuum flask n. vessel with a double wall enclosing a vacuum, ensuring that the contents remain hot or cold.

vacuum-packed adj. sealed after the partial removal of air.

vacuum tube n. tube with a near-vacuum for the free passage of electric current.

vade-mecum /ˌvɑːdɪˈmeɪkəm/ n. handbook etc. used constantly. [Latin, = go with me]

vagabond /ˈvægəˌbɒnd/ —n. wanderer, esp. an idle one. —attrib. adj. wandering, roving. □ **vagabondage** n. [Latin vagor wander]

vagary /ˈveɪɡərɪ/ n. (pl. **-ies**) caprice, whim. [Latin vagor wander]

vagina /vəˈdʒaɪnə/ n. (pl. **-s** or **-nae** /-niː/) canal from the uterus to the vulva in female mammals. □ **vaginal** adj. [Latin, = sheath]

vagrant /ˈveɪɡrənt/ —n. wanderer, itinerant. —adj. wandering, roving. □ **vagrancy** n. [Anglo-French]

vague /veɪɡ/ adj. **1** uncertain or ill-defined. **2** (of a person or mind) imprecise; inexact in thought, expression, or understanding. □ **vaguely** adv. **vagueness** n. [Latin vagus wandering]

vain adj. **1** having too high an opinion of one's looks, abilities, etc. **2** empty, trivial (vain triumphs). **3** useless; futile (in the vain hope of finding it). □ **in vain 1** without success. **2** lightly or profanely (take his name in vain). □ **vainly** adv. [Latin vanus]

vainglory /veɪnˈɡlɔːrɪ/ n. boastfulness; extreme vanity. □ **vainglorious** adj. [French vaine gloire]

valance /ˈvæləns/ n. (also **valence**) short curtain round the frame or canopy of a bedstead, above a window, etc. [Anglo-French valer descend]

vale n. (archaic except in place-names) valley. [Latin vallis]

valediction /ˌvælɪˈdɪkʃ(ə)n/ n. formal **1** bidding farewell. **2** words used in this. □ **valedictory** adj. & n. (pl. **-ies**). [Latin vale farewell]

valence¹ /ˈveɪləns/ n. = VALENCY.

valence² var. of VALANCE.

valency /ˈveɪlənsɪ/ n. (pl. **-ies**) combining power of an atom measured by the number of hydrogen atoms it can displace or combine with. [Latin valentia power]

valentine /'vælən,tam/ n. 1 card sent, often anonymously, as a mark of love on St Valentine's Day (14 Feb.). 2 sweetheart chosen on this day. [Valentine, name of two saints]

valerian /və'lɪərɪən/ n. any of various flowering herbs, esp. used as a sedative. [French from medieval Latin]

valet /'vælɪt, -leɪ/ n. gentleman's personal servant. —v. (-t-) 1 work as ... (for). 2 clean or clean out (a car). [French va(s)let, related to VARLET, VASSAL]

valetudinarian /,vælɪtjuːdɪ'neərɪən/ n. person of poor health or who is unduly anxious about health. —adj. of a valetudinarian. □ **valetudinarianism** n. [Latin valetudo health]

valiant /'væljənt/ adj. brave. □ **valiantly** adv. [Latin valeo be strong]

valid /'vælɪd/ adj. 1 (of a reason, objection, etc.) sound, defensible. 2 a executed with the proper formalities; legally acceptable (valid contract; valid passport). b not yet expired. □ **validly** adv. □ **validity** /-'lɪd-/ n. [Latin validus strong; related to VALIANT]

validate /'vælɪdeɪt/ v. (-ting) make valid; ratify. □ **validation** /-'deɪʃ(ə)n/ n. [Latin validus]

valise /və'liːz/ n. US small portmanteau. [French from Italian]

Valium /'vælɪəm/ n. propr. drug diazepam used as a tranquillizer. [origin uncertain]

valley /'vælɪ/ n. (pl. -s) low area between hills, usu. with a stream or river flowing through it. [French: related to VALE]

valour /'vælə/ n. (US valor) courage, esp. in battle. □ **valorous** adj. [Latin valeo be strong]

valuable /'væljuəb(ə)l/ —adj. of great value, price, or worth. —n. (usu. in pl.) valuable thing. □ **valuably** adv.

valuation /,væljuː'eɪʃ(ə)n/ n. 1 estimation (esp. professional) of a thing's worth. 2 worth so estimated.

value /'væljuː/ —n. 1 worth, desirability, or utility, or the qualities on which these depend. 2 worth as estimated (set a high value on a thing). 3 amount for which a thing can be exchanged in the open market. 4 equivalent of a thing. 5 (in full value for money) something well worth the money spent. 6 effectiveness (news value). 7 (in pl.) one's principles, priorities, or standards. 8 Mus. duration of a note. 9 Math. amount denoted by an algebraic term. —v. (-ues, -ued, -uing) 1 estimate the value of, esp. professionally. 2 have a high or especial opinion of. □ **valueless** adj. **valuer** n. [French past part. of valoir be worth, from Latin valeo]

value added tax n. tax levied on the rise in value of services and goods at each stage of production.

value judgement n. subjective estimate of worth etc.

valve /vælv/ n. 1 device controlling flow through a pipe etc., esp. allowing movement in one direction only. 2 structure in an organ etc. allowing a flow of blood etc. in one direction only. 3 = THERMIONIC VALVE. 4 device to vary the effective length of the tube in a trumpet etc. 5 half-shell of an oyster, mussel, etc. □ **valved** adj. **valvular** /'vælvjʊlə/ adj. [Latin valva leaf of a folding door]

vamoose /və'muːs/ v. US slang depart hurriedly. [Spanish vamos let us go]

vamp[1] —n. 1 upper front part of a boot or shoe. —v. 1 (often foll. by up) repair or furbish. 2 (foll. by up) make by patching or from odds and ends. 3 improvise a musical accompaniment. [French avantpié front of the foot]

vamp[2] colloq. —n. woman who uses sexual attraction to exploit men. —v. allure and exploit (a man). [abbreviation of VAMPIRE]

vampire /'væmpaɪə(r)/ n. 1 supposed ghost or reanimated corpse sucking the blood of sleeping persons. 2 person who preys ruthlessly on others. 3 (in full vampire bat) tropical (esp. South American) bloodsucking bat. [French or German from Magyar]

van[1] n. 1 small covered goods vehicle. 2 railway carriage for luggage and for the guard. [abbreviation of CARAVAN]

van[2] n. vanguard, forefront. [abbreviation]

vanadium /və'neɪdɪəm/ n. hard grey metallic element used to strengthen steel. [Old Norse Vanadís name of the Scandinavian goddess Freyja]

vandal /'vænd(ə)l/ n. person who wilfully or maliciously damages property. □ **vandalism** n. [Vandals, name of a Germanic people that sacked Rome and destroyed works of art in the 5th c.: Latin from Germanic]

vandalize /'vændəlaɪz/ v. (also -ise) (-zing or -sing) wilfully or maliciously destroy or damage (esp. public property).

vane n. 1 weather-vane. 2 blade of a screw propeller or windmill etc. [dial. var. of obsolete fane banner]

vanguard /'vængɑːd/ n. 1 foremost part of an advancing army etc. 2 leaders of a movement etc. [French guant/garde from avant before: related to GUARD]

vanilla /və'nɪlə/ n. 1 a tropical fragrant climbing orchid. b (in full vanilla-pod) fruit of this. 2 extract from the vanilla-pod, or a synthetic substance, used as

vanish /ˈvænɪʃ/ v. 1 disappear. 2 cease to exist. [Latin: related to VAIN]

vanishing cream n. skin ointment that leaves no visible trace.

vanishing-point n. 1 point at which receding parallel lines appear to meet. 2 stage of complete disappearance.

vanity /ˈvænɪtɪ/ n. (pl. -ies) 1 conceit about one's appearance or attainments. 2 futility, unsubstantiality, unreal thing (the vanity of human achievement). 3 ostentatious display. [Latin: related to VAIN]

vanity bag n. (also **vanity case**) woman's make-up bag or case.

vanity unit n. wash-basin set into a unit with cupboards beneath.

vanquish /ˈvæŋkwɪʃ/ v. literary conquer, overcome. [Latin vinco]

vantage /ˈvɑːntɪdʒ/ n. 1 (also **vantage point**) place giving a good view. 2 Tennis = ADVANTAGE. [French: related to ADVANTAGE]

vapid /ˈvæpɪd/ adj. insipid; dull; flat. □ **vapidity** /vəˈpɪdɪtɪ/ n. [Latin vapidus]

vapor US var. of VAPOUR.

vaporize /ˈveɪpəˌraɪz/ v. (also -ise) (-zing or -sing) change into vapour. □ **vaporization** /-ˈzeɪʃ(ə)n/ n.

vapour /ˈveɪpə(r)/ n. (US vapor) 1 moisture or other substance diffused or suspended in air, e.g. mist, smoke. 2 gaseous form of a substance. 3 medicinal inhalant. □ **vaporous** adj. **vapoury** adj. [Latin vapor steam]

vapour trail n. trail of condensed water from an aircraft etc.

variable /ˈveərɪəb(ə)l/ —adj. 1 changeable, adaptable. 2 apt to vary; not constant. 3 Math. (of a quantity) indeterminate; able to assume different numerical values. —n. variable thing or quantity. □ **variability** /-ˈbɪlɪtɪ/ n. **variably** adv.

variance /ˈveərɪəns/ n. 1 (usu. prec. by at) difference of opinion; dispute (we were at variance). 2 discrepancy.

variant —adj. 1 differing in form or details from a standard (variant spelling). 2 having different forms (forty variant types). —n. variant form, spelling, type, etc.

variation /ˌveərɪˈeɪʃ(ə)n/ n. 1 varying. 2 departure from the normal kind, amount, etc. (prices are subject to variation). 3 extent of this. 4 variant thing. 5 Mus. theme in a changed or elaborated form.

varicoloured /ˈveərɪˌkʌləd/ adj. (US **varicolored**) 1 variegated in colour. 2 of various colours. [Latin varius VARIOUS]

varicose /ˈværɪˌkəʊs/ adj. (esp. of a vein etc.) permanently and abnormally dilated. [Latin varix varicose vein]

varied /ˈveərɪd/ adj. showing variety.

variegated /ˈveərɪˌɡeɪtɪd/ adj. 1 with irregular patches of different colours. 2 having leaves of two or more colours. □ **variegation** /-ˈɡeɪʃ(ə)n/ n. [Latin: related to VARIOUS]

variety /vəˈraɪətɪ/ n. (pl. -ies) 1 diversity; absence of uniformity; many-sidedness. 2 quantity or collection of different things (for a variety of reasons). 3 a class of things that differ from the rest in the same general class. b member of such a class. 4 (foll. by of) different form of a thing, quality, etc. 5 Biol. subdivision of a species. 6 series of dances, songs, comedy acts, etc. (variety show). [Latin: related to VARIOUS]

various /ˈveərɪəs/ adj. 1 different, diverse (from various reasons). 2 several (for various reasons). □ **variously** adv. [Latin varius]

■ **Usage** Various (unlike several) cannot be used with of as arrived late.

varlet /ˈvɑːlɪt/ n. archaic menial; rascal. [French: related to VALET]

varnish /ˈvɑːnɪʃ/ —n. 1 resinous solution used to give a hard shiny transparent coating (nail varnish). 2 similar preparation (nail varnish). 3 deceptive outward appearance or show. —v. 1 apply varnish to. 2 give a deceptively attractive appearance to. [French vernis, probably ultimately from Berenice in Cyrenaica]

varsity /ˈvɑːsɪtɪ/ n. (pl. -ies) colloq. (esp. with ref. to sports) university. [abbreviation]

vary /ˈveərɪ/ v. (-ies, -ied) 1 be or become different; be of different kinds; change. 2 make different; modify. [Latin vario: related to VARIOUS]

vas n. (pl. **vasa** /ˈveɪsə/) vessel or duct. [Latin, = vessel]

vascular /ˈvæskjʊlə(r)/ adj. of or containing vessels for conveying blood, sap, etc. [Latin vasculum diminutive of VAS]

vas deferens /væs ˈdefəˌrenz/ n. (pl. **vasa deferentia** /væsə ˌdefəˈrenʃɪə/) sperm duct of the testicle.

vase /vɑːz/ n. vessel used as an ornament or container for flowers. [Latin: related to VAS]

vasectomy /vəˈsektəmɪ/ n. (pl. -ies) removal of part of each vas deferens, esp. for sterilization.

Vaseline /ˈvæsɪˌliːn/ n. propr. type of petroleum jelly used as an ointment etc. [German Wasser water, Greek elaion oil]

vanilla flavouring. [Spanish diminutive of vaina pod]

vassal /'væs(ə)l/ n. **1** *hist.* feudal tenant of land. **2** humble dependant. □ **vassalage** n. [medieval Latin *vassallus*]

vast /vɑːst/ adj. immense, huge. □ **vastly** adv. **vastness** n. [Latin]

VAT /ˌviːeɪˈtiː, væt/ abbr. value added tax.

vat n. tank, esp. for holding liquids in brewing, distilling, food manufacture, dyeing, and tanning. [dial. var. of *fat*, from Old English]

Vatican /'vætɪkən/ n. palace or government of the Pope in Rome. [name of a hill in Rome]

vaudeville /'vɔːdəvɪl/ n. esp. *US* **1** variety entertainment. **2** light stage play with interspersed songs. □ **vaudevillian** /-'vɪliən/ adj. & n. [French]

vault /vɔːlt/ n. **1** arched roof. **2** vault-like covering (*vault of heaven*). **3** underground storage chamber or place of interment beneath a church or in a cemetery etc. **4** act of vaulting. —v. **1** leap, esp. using the hands or a pole. **2** spring over in this way. **3** (esp. as **vaulted** adj.) a make in the form of a vault. **b** provide with a vault or vaults. [Latin *volvo* roll]

vaulting n. arched work in a vaulted roof or ceiling.

vaulting-horse n. wooden box for vaulting over.

vaunt /vɔːnt/ v. & n. *literary* boast. [Latin: related to VAIN]

VC abbr. Victoria Cross.

VCR abbr. video cassette recorder.

VD abbr. venereal disease.

VDU abbr. visual display unit.

've abbr. (usu. after pronouns) have (*I've, they've*).

veal n. calf's flesh as food. [French from Latin *vitulus* calf]

vector /'vektə(r)/ n. **1** *Math. & Physics* quantity having direction as well as magnitude. **2** carrier of disease. [Latin *veho vect-* convey]

Veda /'veɪdə/ n. (in *sing.* or *pl.*) oldest Hindu scriptures. □ **Vedic** adj. [Sanskrit, = knowledge]

VE day n. 8 May, the day marking Victory in Europe (in 1945).

veer /vɪə(r)/ —v. **1** change direction, esp. (of the wind) clockwise. **2** change in course or opinion etc. —n. change of direction. [French *virer*]

veg /vedʒ/ n. *colloq.* vegetable(s). [abbreviation]

vegan /'viːgən/ —n. person who does not eat animals or animal products. —adj. using or containing no animal products. [shortening of VEGETARIAN]

vegeburger var. of VEGGIE BURGER.

vegetable /'vedʒtəb(ə)l/ —n. **1** plant, esp. a herbaceous plant used for food, e.g. a cabbage, potato, or bean. **2** *colloq. derog.* a offens. person who is severely mentally incapacitated, esp. through brain injury etc. **b** dull or inactive person. —adj. of, derived from, or relating to plant life or vegetables as food. [Latin: related to VEGETATE]

vegetable marrow see MARROW 1.

vegetal /'vedʒɪt(ə)l/ adj. of or like plants. [medieval Latin: related to VE-GETATE]

vegetarian /ˌvedʒɪ'teərɪən/ —n. person who does not eat meat or fish. —adj. excluding animal food, esp. meat (*vegetarian diet*). □ **vegetarianism** n. [from VEGETABLE]

vegetate /'vedʒɪteɪt/ v. (-ting) **1** live an uneventful or monotonous life. **2** grow as plants do. [Latin *vegeto* animate]

vegetation /ˌvedʒɪ'teɪʃ(ə)n/ n. plants collectively; plant life. [medieval Latin: related to VEGETATE]

vegetative /'vedʒɪtətɪv/ adj. **1** concerned with growth and development as distinct from sexual reproduction. **2** of vegetation. [French or medieval Latin: related to VEGETATE]

veggie /'vedʒɪ/ n. (also **vegie**) *colloq.* vegetarian. [abbreviation]

veggie burger n. (also **vegeburger**) flat cake like a hamburger but containing vegetables or soya protein instead of meat.

vehement /'viːəmənt/ adj. showing or caused by strong feeling; ardent (*vehement protest*). □ **vehemence** n. **vehemently** adv. [Latin]

vehicle /'viːɪk(ə)l/ n. **1** conveyance used on land or in space. **2** thing or person as a medium for expression or action. **3** liquid etc. as a medium for suspending pigments, drugs, etc. □ **vehicular** /vɪ'hɪkjʊlə(r)/ adj. [Latin *veho* carry]

veil /veɪl/ —n. **1** piece of usu. transparent fabric attached to a woman's hat etc., esp. to conceal or protect the face. **2** piece of linen etc. as part of a nun's headdress. **3** thing that hides or disguises (*a veil of silence*). —v. **1** cover with a veil. **2** (esp. as **veiled** adj.) partly conceal (*veiled threats*). □ **beyond the veil** in the unknown state of life after death. **draw a veil over** avoid discussing; hush up. **take the veil** become a nun. [Latin *velum*]

vein /veɪn/ n. **1** a any of the tubes conveying blood to the heart. **b** (in general use) any blood-vessel. **2** rib of an insect's wing or leaf. **3** streak of a different colour in wood, marble, cheese, etc. **4** fissure in rock filled with ore. **5** specified character or tendency; mood

(spoke in a sarcastic vein). □ **veined** adj. **veiny** adj. [-ier. -iest.] [Latin vena]

Velcro /'velkrəʊ/ n. propr. fastener consisting of two strips of fabric which cling when pressed together. [French velours croché hooked velvet]

veld /velt/ n. (also **veldt**) S.Afr. open country. [Afrikaans: related to FIELD]

veleta /vəˈliːtə/ n. ballroom dance in triple time. [Spanish, = weather-vane]

vellum /ˈveləm/ n. **1 a** fine parchment, orig. calfskin. **b** manuscript on this. **2** smooth writing-paper imitating vellum. [French vélin: related to VEAL]

velocity /vɪˈlɒsɪtɪ/ n. (pl. **-ies**) speed, esp. of inanimate things (*wind velocity; velocity of light*). [Latin velox swift]

velodrome /ˈveləˌdrəʊm/ n. place or building with a track for cycle-racing. [French vélo bicycle]

velour /vəˈlʊə(r)/ n. (also **velours** pronunc. same) plushlike fabric. [French velours]

velvet /ˈvelvɪt/ n. **1** soft fabric with a thick short pile on one side. **2** furry skin on a growing antler. —adj. of, like, or soft as velvet. □ **on velvet** in an advantageous or prosperous position. □ **velvety** adj. [Latin villus tuft, down]

velveteen /ˌvelvɪˈtiːn/ n. cotton fabric with a pile like velvet.

velvet glove n. outward gentleness, esp. cloaking firmness.

Ven. abbr. Venerable (as the title of an archdeacon).

venal /ˈviːn(ə)l/ adj. corrupt; able to be bribed; involving bribery. □ **venality** /-ˈnælɪtɪ/ n. **venally** adv. [Latin venum thing for sale]

■ **Usage** *Venal* is sometimes confused with *venial*, which means 'pardonable'. □

vend v. offer (small wares) for sale. □ **vendible** adj. [Latin vendo sell]

vendetta /venˈdetə/ n. **1** blood feud. **2** prolonged bitter quarrel. [Latin: related to VINDICTIVE]

vending-machine n. slot-machine selling small items.

vendor n. Law seller, esp. of property. [Anglo-French: related to VEND]

veneer /vɪˈnɪə(r)/ —n. **1** thin covering of fine wood etc. **2** (often foll. by of) deceptively pleasing appearance. —v. **1** apply a veneer to (wood etc.). **2** disguise. [German furnieren to furnish]

venerable /ˈvenərəb(ə)l/ adj. **1** entitled to deep respect on account of character, age, associations, etc (*venerable priest; venerable relics*). **2** title of an archdeacon in the Church of England. [Latin: related to VENERATE]

venerate /ˈvenəˌreɪt/ v. (**-ting**) respect deeply. □ **veneration** /-ˈreɪʃ(ə)n/ n. **venerator** n. [Latin veneror revere]

venereal /vɪˈnɪərɪəl/ adj. **1** of sexual desire or intercourse. **2** of venereal disease. [Latin venus veneris sexual love]

venereal disease n. disease contracted by sexual intercourse with an infected person or congenitally.

Venetian /vɪˈniːʃ(ə)n/ —n. native. citizen, or dialect of Venice. —adj. of Venice. [from French or medieval Latin Venetia Venice]

venetian blind n. window-blind of adjustable horizontal slats.

vengeance /ˈvendʒ(ə)ns/ n. punishment inflicted for wrong to oneself or one's cause. ■ **with a vengeance** to a high or excessive degree (*punctuality with a vengeance*). [French venger from Latin vindico avenge]

vengeful adj. vindictive; seeking vengeance. □ **vengefully** adv. [obsolete venge avenge: related to VENGEANCE]

venial /ˈviːnɪəl/ adj. (of a sin or fault) pardonable; not mortal. □ **veniality** /-ˈælɪtɪ/ n. **venially** adv. [Latin venia forgiveness]

■ **Usage** *Venial* is sometimes confused with *venal*, which means 'corrupt'.

venison /ˈvenɪs(ə)n/ n. deer's flesh as food. [Latin venatio hunting]

Venn diagram n. diagram using overlapping and intersecting circles etc. to show the relationships between mathematical sets. [*Venn*, name of a logician]

venom /ˈvenəm/ n. **1** poisonous fluid of esp. snakes. **2** malignity; virulence. □ **venomous** adj. **venomously** adv. [Latin venenum]

venous /ˈviːnəs/ adj. of, full of, or contained in veins. [Latin: related to VEIN]

vent¹ —n. **1** opening allowing the passage of air etc. **2** outlet; free expression (*gave vent to my anger*). **3** anus, esp. of a lower animal. —v. **1** make a vent in (a cask etc.). **2** give free expression to. □ **vent one's spleen on** scold or ill-treat without cause. [Latin ventus wind]

vent² n. slit in a garment, esp. in the lower edge of the back of a jacket. [French fente from Latin findo cleave]

ventilate /ˈventɪˌleɪt/ v. (**-ting**) **1** cause air to circulate freely in (a room etc.). **2** air (a question, grievance, etc.). **3** Med. **a** oxygenate (the blood). **b** admit or force air into (the lungs). □ **ventilation** /-ˈleɪʃ(ə)n/ n. [Latin ventilo blow, winnow: related to VENT¹]

ventilator n. **1** appliance or aperture for ventilating a room etc. **2** Med. = RESPIRATOR 2.

ventral /ˈventr(ə)l/ adj. of or on the abdomen. [venter abdomen, from Latin]

ventricle /ˈventrɪk(ə)l/ n. **1** cavity in the body. **2** hollow part of an organ, esp. the

brain or heart. □ **ventricular**
/-ˈtrɪkjʊlə(r)/ *adj.* [Latin *ventriculus*
diminutive of *venter* belly]

ventriloquism /venˈtrɪləkwɪz(ə)m/ *n.*
(also **ventriloquy**) skill of speaking
without moving the lips, esp. as entertainment with a dummy. □ **ventriloquist** *n.* [Latin *venter* belly, *loquor*
speak]

venture /ˈventʃə(r)/ —*v.* **1** risky undertaking. **2** commercial speculation. —*v.*
(-**ring**) **1** dare; not be afraid. **2** dare to go,
make, or put forward (*venture out; ven-
ture an opinion*). **3 a** expose to risk;
stake. **b** take risks. [from ADVENTURE]

Venture Scout *n.* senior Scout.

venturesome *adj.* **1** disposed to take
risks. **2** risky.

venue /ˈvenjuː/ *n.* place for a match,
meeting, concert, etc. [French, from
venir come]

Venus fly-trap /ˈviːnəs/ *n.* insectivorous plant. [Latin *Venus* goddess of love]

veracious /vəˈreɪʃəs/ *adj.* *formal* **1**
truthful by nature. **2** (of a statement
etc.) true. □ **veracity** /vəˈræsɪtɪ/ *n.*
[Latin *verax* from *verus* true]

veranda /vəˈrændə/ *n.* (usu. covered)
platform along the side of a house.
[Hindi from Portuguese *varanda*]

verb *n.* word used to indicate action, a
state, or an occurrence (e.g. *hear, be,
happen*). [Latin *verbum* word]

verbal —*adj.* **1** of words. **2** oral, not
written. **3** of a verb. **4** (of a translation)
literal. **5** talkative. —*n.* **1** *slang* verbal
statement to the police. **2** *slang* stream
of abuse. □ **verbally** *adv.* [Latin:
related to VERB]

■ **Usage** Some people reject sense 2 of
verbal as illogical, and prefer *oral*. However, *verbal* is the usual term in expressions such as *verbal communication*,
verbal contract, and *verbal evidence*.

verbalize *v.* (also -**ise**) (-**zing** or -**sing**)
put into words.

verbal noun *n.* noun derived from a
verb (e.g. *smoking* in *smoking is forbidden*); see -ING.

verbatim /vɜːˈbeɪtɪm/ *adv. & adj.* in
exactly the same words. [medieval
Latin: related to VERB]

verbena /vɜːˈbiːnə/ *n.* (*pl.* same) plant of
a genus of usu. annual or biennial
plants with clusters of fragrant flowers.
[Latin]

verbiage /ˈvɜːbɪɪdʒ/ *n. derog.* too many
words or unnecessarily difficult words.
[French: related to VERB]

verbose /vɜːˈbəʊs/ *adj.* using more
words than are needed. □ **verbosity**
/-ˈbɒsɪtɪ/ *n.* [Latin *verbosus* from *verbum*
word]

verdant /ˈvɜːd(ə)nt/ *adj.* **1** (of grass, a
field, etc.) green, lush. **2** (of a person)
unsophisticated, green. □ **verdancy** *n.*
[perhaps from French *verdeant* from
viridis green]

verdict /ˈvɜːdɪkt/ *n.* **1** decision of a jury
in a civil or criminal case. **2** decision;
judgement. [Anglo-French *verdit* from
ver true, *dit* saying]

verdigris /ˈvɜːdɪɡrɪ/ *n.* greenish-blue
substance that forms on copper or
brass. [French, = green of Greece]

verdure /ˈvɜːdjə(r)/ *n.* *literary* green
vegetation or its colour. [French *verd*
green]

verge¹ *n.* **1** edge or border. **2** brink (*on
the verge of tears*). **3** grass edging of a
road etc. [Latin *virga* rod]

verge² *v.* (-**ging**) **1** (foll. by *on*) border on.
2 incline downwards or in a specified
direction. [Latin *vergo* bend]

verger *n.* **1** church caretaker and attendant. **2** officer preceding a bishop
etc. with a staff. [Anglo-French: related
to VERGE¹]

verify /ˈverɪfaɪ/ *v.* (-**ies**, -**ied**) **1** establish
the truth, correctness or validity of by
examination etc. (*verified my figures*). **2**
(of an event etc.) bear out (a prediction
or promise). □ **verifiable** *adj.* **verifica-
tion** /-fɪˈkeɪʃ(ə)n/ *n.* [medieval Latin:
related to VERY]

verily /ˈverɪlɪ/ *adv. archaic* really, truly.
[from VERY]

verisimilitude /ˌverɪsɪmɪˈljuːd/ *n.*
appearance of being true or real. [Latin
verus true, *similis* like]

veritable /ˈverɪtəb(ə)l/ *adj.* real; rightly
so called (*a veritable feast*). □ **verit-
ably** *adv.* [French: related to VERITY]

verity /ˈverɪtɪ/ *n.* (*pl.* -**ies**) **1 a** fundamental truth. **2** *archaic* truth. [Latin
veritas truth]

vermicelli /ˌvɜːmɪˈtʃelɪ/ *n.* **1** pasta in
long slender threads. **2** shreds of chocolate as cake decoration etc. [Latin
vermis worm]

vermicide /ˈvɜːmɪsaɪd/ *n.* drug that
kills intestinal worms. [Latin *vermis*
worm]

vermiculite /vəˈmɪkjʊˌlaɪt/ *n.* a hydrous silicate mineral used esp. as a
moisture-holding medium for plant
growth. [Latin *vermiculatus* wormeaten, from *vermis* worm]

vermiform /ˈvɜːmɪfɔːm/ *adj.* worm-
shaped. [medieval Latin: related to VER-
MICIDE]

vermiform appendix *n.* small blind
tube extending from the caecum in man
and some other mammals.

vermilion /vəˈmɪljən/ —*n.* **1** cinnabar. **2
a** brilliant red pigment made esp. from
this. **b** colour of this. —*adj.* of this colour.

[Latin *vermiculus* diminutive of *vermis* worm]

vermin /'vɜːmɪn/ *n.* (usu. treated as *pl.*) **1** mammals and birds harmful to game, crops, etc., e.g. foxes and rats. **2** parasitic worms or insects. **3** vile people. □ **verminous** *adj.* [Latin *vermis* worm]

vermouth /'vɜːməθ/ *n.* wine flavoured with aromatic herbs. [German: related to WORMWOOD]

vernacular /və'nækjʊlə(r)/ *—n.* **1** language or dialect of a particular country. **2** language of a particular class or group. **3** homely speech. *—adj.* (of language) native; not foreign or formal. [Latin *vernaculus* native]

vernal /'vɜːn(ə)l/ *adj.* of or in spring. [Latin *ver* spring]

vernal equinox var. of SPRING EQUINOX.

vernier /'vɜːnɪə(r)/ *n.* small movable graduated scale for obtaining fractional parts of subdivisions on a fixed scale. [*Vernier*, name of a mathematician]

veronal /'verən(ə)l/ *n.* sedative drug. [German from *Verona* in Italy]

veronica /vɪ'rɒnɪkə/ *n.* speedwell. [medieval Latin, probably from St *Veronica*]

verruca /və'ruːkə/ *n.* (*pl.* **verrucae** /-siː/ or **-s**) wart or similar growth, esp. on the foot. [Latin]

versatile /'vɜːsətaɪl/ *adj.* **1** adapting easily to different subjects or occupations; skilled in many subjects or occupations. **2** having many uses. □ **versatility** /-'tɪlɪtɪ/ *n.* [Latin *verto* vers- turn]

verse *n.* **1** poetry. **2** stanza of a poem or song. **3** each of the short numbered divisions of the Bible. **4** poem. [Latin *versus*: related to VERSATILE]

versed /vɜːst/ *adj.* (foll. by *in*) experienced or skilled in. [Latin *versor* be engaged in]

versicle /'vɜːsɪk(ə)l/ *n.* each of a priest's short sentences in a liturgy, answered by the congregation. [Latin diminutive: related to VERSE]

versify /'vɜːsɪfaɪ/ *v.* (**-ies, -ied**) **1** turn into or express in verse. **2** compose verses. □ **versification** /-fɪ'keɪʃ(ə)n/ *n.* **versifier** *n.*

version /'vɜːʃ(ə)n/ *n.* **1** account of a matter from a particular point of view. **2** book etc. in a particular edition or translation (*Authorized Version*). **3** form or variant. [Latin *verto* vers- turn]

verso /'vɜːsəʊ/ *n.* (*pl.* **-s**) **1** left-hand page of an open book. **2** back of a printed leaf. [Latin *verso (folio)* on the turned (leaf)]

versus /'vɜːsəs/ *prep.* against (esp. in law and sport). [Latin: related to VERSE]

vertebra /'vɜːtɪbrə/ *n.* (*pl.* **-brae** /-briː/) each segment of a backbone. □ **vertebral** *adj.* [Latin *verto* turn]

vertebrate /'vɜːtɪbrət/ *—adj.* (of an animal) having a backbone. *—n.* vertebrate animal. [Latin *vertebratus* jointed: related to VERTEBRA]

vertex /'vɜːteks/ *n.* (*pl.* **-tices** /-tɪˌsiːz/ or **-texes**) **1** highest point; top, apex. **2 a** each angular point of a triangle, polygon, etc. **b** meeting-point of lines that form an angle. [Latin, = whirlpool, crown of a head, from *verto* turn]

vertical /'vɜːtɪk(ə)l/ *—adj.* **1** at right angles to a horizontal plane. **2** in a direction from top to bottom of a picture etc. **3** of or at the vertex. *—n.* vertical line or plane. □ **vertically** *adv.* [Latin: related to VERTEX]

vertical take-off *n.* take-off of an aircraft directly upwards.

vertiginous /vɜː'tɪdʒɪnəs/ *adj.* of or causing vertigo. [Latin: related to VERTIGO]

vertigo /'vɜːtɪˌgəʊ/ *n.* dizziness caused esp. by heights. [Latin, = whirling, from *verto* turn]

vervain /'vɜːveɪn/ *n.* any of several verbenas, esp. one with small blue, white, or purple flowers. [Latin: related to VERBENA]

verve *n.* enthusiasm, vigour, spirit. [French]

very /'verɪ/ *—adv.* **1** in a high degree (*did it very easily*). **2** in the fullest sense (foll. by *own* or superl. adj.: *do your very best; my very own room*). *—adj.* actual; truly such (*the very thing we need; his very words; the very same*). □ **not very 1** in a low degree. **2** far from being. **very good** (or **well**) formula of consent or approval. **very high frequency** (in radio) 30–300 megahertz. **Very Reverend** title of a dean. [Latin *verus* true]

Very light /'vɪərɪ/ *n.* flare projected from a pistol for signalling or illuminating part of a battlefield etc. [*Very*, name of its inventor]

vesicle /'vesɪk(ə)l/ *n.* small bladder, bubble, or blister. [Latin]

vespers *n.pl.* evensong. [Latin *vesper* evening]

vessel /'ves(ə)l/ *n.* **1** hollow receptacle, esp. for liquid. **2** ship or boat, esp. a large one. **3** duct or canal etc. holding or conveying blood or sap, etc., esp. = BLOOD-VESSEL. [Latin diminutive: related to VAS]

vest *—n.* **1** undergarment worn on the trunk. **2** *US & Austral.* waistcoat. *—v.* **1** (foll. by *with*) bestow (powers, authority, etc.) on. **2** (foll. by *in*) confer (property or power) on (a person) with

vestal virgin n. Rom. Antiq. virgin consecrated to Vesta and vowed to chastity. [Vesta, Roman goddess of the hearth and home]

vested interest n. 1 personal interest in a state of affairs, usu. with an expectation of gain. 2 Law interest (usu. in land or money held in trust) recognized as belonging to a person.

vestibule /'vestibju:l/ n. 1 hall or lobby of a building. 2 US enclosed space between railway-carriages. [Latin vestibulum]

vestige /'vestɪdʒ/ n. 1 trace; sign. 2 slight amount; particle. 3 atrophied part or organ of an animal or plant that was well developed in ancestors. □ **vestigial** /-'tɪdʒ(ə)l/ adj. [Latin vestigium footprint]

vestment /'vestmənt/ n. ceremonial garment, esp. a chasuble. [Latin: related to VEST]

vestry /'vestri/ n. (pl. -ies) church room or building for keeping vestments etc. in.

vet[1] —n. colloq. veterinary surgeon. —v. (-tt-) make a careful and critical examination of (a scheme, work, candidate, etc.). [abbreviation]

vet[2] n. US veteran. [abbreviation]

vetch n. plant of the pea family used largely for fodder. [Latin vicia]

veteran /'vetərən/ n. 1 (often attrib.) old soldier or long-serving member of any group (war veteran; veteran actor). 2 US ex-serviceman or servicewoman. [Latin vetus -er- old]

veteran car n. car made before 1916, or (strictly) before 1905.

veterinarian /ˌvetərɪ'neərɪən/ n. formal veterinary surgeon.

veterinary /'vetərɪnərɪ/ —adj. of or for the diseases and injuries of animals. —n. (pl. -ies) veterinary surgeon. [Latin veterinae cattle]

veterinary surgeon n. person qualified to treat animals.

veto /'vi:təu/ —n. (pl. -es) 1 right to reject a measure, resolution, etc. unilaterally. 2 rejection. prohibition. —v. (-oes, -oed) 1 reject (a measure etc.). 2 forbid, prohibit. [Latin, = I forbid]

vex v. 1 anger, irritate. 2 archaic grieve, afflict. [Latin vexo afflict]

vexation /vek'seɪʃ(ə)n/ n. 1 vexing or being vexed. 2 annoying or distressing thing.

vexatious /vek'seɪʃ(ə)s/ adj. 1 causing vexation. 2 Law (of litigation) lacking sufficient grounds and seeking only to annoy the defendant.

vexed adj. (of a question) much discussed; problematic.

v.g.c. abbr. very good condition.

VHF abbr. very high frequency.

via /'vaɪə/ prep. through (London to Rome via Paris; send it via your son). [Latin, ablative of via way]

viable /'vaɪəb(ə)l/ adj. 1 (of a plan etc.) feasible, esp. economically. 2 (esp. of a foetus) capable of developing and surviving independently. □ **viability** /-'bɪlɪtɪ/ n. [French vie life]

viaduct /'vaɪədʌkt/ n. long bridge, esp. a series of arches, carrying a road or railway across a valley or hollow. [Latin via way, after AQUEDUCT]

vial /'vaɪəl/ n. small (usu. cylindrical glass) vessel, esp. for holding medicines. [related to PHIAL]

viand /'vaɪənd/ n. formal (usu. in pl.) article of food. [Latin vivo live]

viaticum /vaɪ'ætɪkəm/ n. (pl. -ca) Eucharist given to a dying person. [Latin via road]

vibes n.pl. colloq. 1 vibrations, esp. feelings communicated. 2 = VIBRAPHONE. [abbreviation]

vibrant /'vaɪbrənt/ adj. 1 vibrating. 2 (often foll. by with) -th-illing, lively. 3 (of sound) resonant. 4 (of colours) bright and striking. □ **vibrancy** n. **vibrantly** adv. [Latin: related to VIBRATE]

vibraphone /'vaɪbrəfəun/ n. instrument like a xylophone but with motor-driven resonators under the metal bars giving a vibrato effect. [from VIBRATO]

vibrate /vaɪ'breɪt/ v. (-ting) 1 move rapidly to and fro. 2 (of a sound) throb, resonate. 3 (foll. by with) quiver, thrill. 4 swing to and fro. os oscillate. [Latin vibro shake]

vibration /vaɪ'breɪʃ(ə)n/ n. 1 vibrating. 2 (in pl.) a mental, esp. occult, influence. b atmosphere or feeling communicated. [Latin: related to VIBRATE]

vibrato /vɪ'brɑːtəu/ n. rapid slight variation in musical pitch producing a tremulous effect. [Italian: related to VIBRATE]

vibrator /vaɪ'breɪtə(r)/ n. device that vibrates, esp. an instrument for massage or sexual stimulation. □ **vibratory** adj.

viburnum /vaɪ'bɜːnəm/ n. a shrub, usu. with white flowers. [Latin, = wayfaring-tree]

vicar /'vɪkə(r)/ n. clergyman of a Church of England parish where he formerly received a stipend rather than tithes; cf. RECTOR 1. [Latin vicarius substitute: related to VICE[3]]

vicarage n. vicar's house.

vicarious /vɪ'keərɪəs/ adj. 1 experienced indirectly or second-hand. 2 acting or done for another. 3 deputed.

delegated. □ **vicariously** *adv.* [Latin: related to VICAR]

vice[1] *n.* **1** immoral conduct. **2** form of this (*the vice of gluttony*). **3** weakness; indulgence (*brandy is my one vice*). [Latin *vitium*]

vice[2] *n.* (*US* **vise**) clamp with two jaws holding an object so as to leave the hands free to work on it. [*vis* screw, from Latin *vitis* vine]

vice[3] /ˈvaɪsɪ/ *prep.* in the place of; succeeding. [Latin, ablative of (*vix*) *vicis* change]

vice- *comb. form* forming nouns meaning: **1** substitute, deputy (*vice-president*). **2** next in rank to (*vice-admiral*). [related to VICE[3]]

vice-chancellor /vaɪsˈtʃɑːnsələ(r)/ *n.* deputy chancellor (esp. administrator of a university).

vice-president /vaɪsˈprezɪd(ə)nt/ *n.* official ranking below and deputizing for a president. □ **vice-presidency** *n.* (*pl.* **-ies**). **vice-presidential** /-ˈdenʃ(ə)l/ *adj.*

viceregal /vaɪsˈriːg(ə)l/ *adj.* of a viceroy.

vicereine /ˈvaɪsreɪn/ *n.* **1** viceroy's wife. **2** woman viceroy. [French: related to VICEROY, *reine* queen]

viceroy /ˈvaɪsrɔɪ/ *n.* sovereign's deputy ruler in a colony, province, etc. [French: related to VICE[3], *roy* king]

vice squad *n.* police department concerned with prostitution etc.

vice versa /ˌvaɪsɪ ˈvɜːsə, vaɪs ˈvɜːsə/ *adv.* with the order of the terms changed; the other way round. [Latin, = the position being reversed]

vichyssoise /ˌviːʃiˈswɑːz/ *n.* (usu. chilled) creamy soup of leeks and potatoes. [French, = of Vichy]

Vichy water /ˈviːʃiː/ *n.* effervescent mineral water from Vichy in France.

vicinity /vɪˈsɪnɪtɪ/ *n.* (*pl.* **-ies**) **1** surrounding district. **2** (foll. by *to*) nearness. □ **in the vicinity** (often foll. by *of*) near (to). [Latin *vicinus* neighbour]

vicious /ˈvɪʃəs/ *adj.* **1** bad-tempered, spiteful (*vicious dog, remark*). **2** violent (*vicious attack*). **3** corrupt, depraved. **4** (of reasoning etc.) faulty, unsound. □ **viciously** *adv.* **viciousness** *n.* [Latin: related to VICE[1]]

vicious circle *n.* self-perpetuating, harmful sequence of cause and effect.

vicious spiral *n.* vicious circle, esp. as causing inflation.

vicissitude /vɪˈsɪsɪtjuːd/ *n.* *literary* change, esp. of fortune. [Latin: related to VICE[3]]

victim /ˈvɪktɪm/ *n.* **1** person or thing injured or destroyed (*road victim; victim of greed*). **2** prey; dupe (*fell victim to his charm*). **3** creature sacrificed to a deity or in a religious rite. [Latin]

victimize *v.* (also **-ise**) (**-zing** or **-sing**) **1** single out for punishment or discrimination. **2** make (a person etc.) a victim. □ **victimization** /-ˈzeɪʃ(ə)n/ *n.*

victor /ˈvɪktə(r)/ *n.* winner in a battle or contest. [Latin *vinco vict-* conquer]

Victoria Cross /vɪkˈtɔːrɪə/ *n.* highest decoration for conspicuous bravery in the armed services. [Queen *Victoria*]

Victorian *-adj.* **1** of the time of Queen Victoria. **2** prudish; strict. *-n.* person of this time.

Victoriana /vɪkˌtɔːrɪˈɑːnə/ *n.pl.* articles, esp. collectors' items, of the Victorian period.

Victoria sponge /vɪkˈtɔːrɪə/ *n.* sandwich sponge cake with a jam filling.

victorious /vɪkˈtɔːrɪəs/ *adj.* **1** conquering, triumphant. **2** marked by victory. □ **victoriously** *adv.* [Latin: related to VICTOR]

victory /ˈvɪktərɪ/ *n.* (*pl.* **-ies**) defeat of an enemy or opponent.

victual /ˈvɪt(ə)l/ *-n.* (usu. in *pl.*) food, provisions. *-v.* (**-ll-**; *US* **-l-**) **1** supply with victuals. **2** obtain stores. **3** eat victuals. [Latin *victus* food]

victualler /ˈvɪtlə(r)/ *n.* (*US* **victualer**) **1** person etc. who supplies victuals. **2** (in full **licensed victualler**) publican etc. licensed to sell alcohol.

vicuña /vɪˈkjuːnə/ *n.* **1** S. American mammal like a llama, with fine silky wool. **2 a** cloth from its wool. **b** imitation of this. [Spanish from Quechua]

vide /ˈviːdeɪ/ *v.* (in *imper.*) see, consult (a passage in a book etc.). [Latin *video* see]

videlicet /vɪˈdeɪlɪˌset/ *adv.* = viz. [Latin *video* see, *licet* allowed]

video /ˈvɪdɪəʊ/ *-adj.* **1** of the recording (or reproduction) of moving pictures on magnetic tape. **2** of the broadcasting of television pictures. *-n.* (*pl.* **-s**) **1** such recording or broadcasting. **2** *colloq.* = VIDEO RECORDER. **3** *colloq.* a film on videotape. *-v.* (**-oes, -oed**) record on videotape. [Latin, = I see]

video cassette *n.* cassette of videotape.

videodisc *n.* disc for recording moving pictures and sound.

video game *n.* computer game played on a television screen.

video nasty *n.* *colloq.* horrific or pornographic video film.

video recorder *n.* (also **video cassette recorder**) apparatus for recording and playing videotapes.

video shop *n.* shop hiring out or selling video films etc.

videotape —n. magnetic tape for recording moving pictures and sound. —v. (-ping) record on this.

videotape recorder n. = VIDEO RECORDER.

videotex /ˈvɪdɪəʊˌteks/ n. (also **videotext**) any electronic information system, esp. teletext or viewdata.

vie /vaɪ/ v. (**vies**, **vied**, **vying**) (often foll. by *with*) compete; strive for superiority. [probably French: related to ENVY]

Vietnamese /ˌvjetnəˈmiːz/ —adj. of Vietnam. —n. (pl. same) native or language of Vietnam.

view /vjuː/ —n. 1 range of vision (*came into view*). **2 a** what is seen; prospect, scene, etc. **b** picture etc. of this. **3 a** opinion. **b** manner of considering a thing (*took a long-term view*). **4** inspection by the eye or mind (*private view*). —v. 1 look at; inspect with the idea of purchasing; survey visually or mentally. **2** form a mental impression or opinion of; consider. **3** watch television. □ **have in view 1** have as one's object. **2** bear (a circumstance) in mind. **in view of** considering. **on view** being shown or exhibited. **with a view to 1** with the hope or intention of. [Latin *video* see]

viewdata n. news and information service from a computer source, connected to a television screen by a telephone link.

viewer n. 1 person who views, esp. television. **2** device for looking at transparencies etc.

viewfinder n. device on a camera showing the borders of the proposed photograph.

viewpoint n. point of view.

vigil /ˈvɪdʒɪl/ n. 1 keeping awake during the night etc., esp. to keep watch or pray. **2** eve of a festival or holy day. [Latin *vigilia*]

vigilance n. watchfulness, caution. □ **vigilant** adj. [Latin: related to VIGIL]

vigilante /ˌvɪdʒɪˈlæntɪ/ n. member of a self-appointed group maintaining order etc. [Spanish, = vigilant]

vignette /viːˈnjet/ n. 1 short description, character sketch. **2** book illustration not in a definite border. **3** photograph etc. with the background shaded off. [French, diminutive: related to VINE]

vigour /ˈvɪgə(r)/ n. (US **vigor**) 1 physical or mental strength or energy. **2** healthy growth. **3** forcefulness; trenchancy. animation. □ **vigorous** adj. **vigorously** adv. [French from Latin *vigeo* be lively]

Viking /ˈvaɪkɪŋ/ n. Scandinavian pirate and raider of the 8th–11th c. [Old Norse]

vile adj. 1 disgusting. **2** depraved. **3** colloq. abominable (*vile weather*). □

vilely adv. **vileness** n. [Latin *vilis* cheap, base]

vilify /ˈvɪlɪfaɪ/ v. (-ies, -ied) defame; malign. □ **vilification** /-fɪˈkeɪʃ(ə)n/ n. [Latin: related to VILE]

villa /ˈvɪlə/ n. 1 country house; mansion. **2** rented holiday home, esp. abroad. **3** (usu. as part of an address) detached or semi-detached house in a residential district. [Italian and Latin]

village /ˈvɪlɪdʒ/ n. 1 country settlement, larger than a hamlet and smaller than a town. **2** self-contained village-like community within a city etc. (*Greenwich Village; Olympic village*). □ **villager** n. [Latin: related to VILLA]

villain /ˈvɪlən/ n. 1 wicked person. **2** chief evil character in a play, story etc. **3** colloq. professional criminal. **4** colloq. rascal. [Latin: related to VILLA]

villainous adj. wicked.

villainy n. (pl. -ies) wicked behaviour or act. [French: related to VILLAIN]

villein /ˈvɪlɪn/ n. hist. feudal tenant entirely subject to a lord or attached to a manor. □ **villeinage** n. [var. of VILLAIN]

vim n. colloq. vigour. [perhaps from Latin, accusative of *vis* energy]

vinaigrette /ˌvɪnɪˈɡret/ n. 1 salad dressing of oil, wine vinegar, and seasoning. **2** small bottle for smelling-salts. [French, diminutive: related to VINEGAR]

vindicate /ˈvɪndɪˌkeɪt/ v. (-ting) 1 clear of blame or suspicion. **2** establish the existence, merits, or justice of (something disputed etc.). **3** justify by evidence or argument. □ **vindication** n. □ **vindicator** n. **vindicatory** adj. [Latin *vindico* claim]

vindictive /vɪnˈdɪktɪv/ adj. vengeful. □ **vindictively** adv. **vindictiveness** n. [Latin *vindicta* vengeance: related to VINDICATE]

vine n. 1 climbing or trailing plant with a woody stem, esp. bearing grapes. **2** stem of this. [Latin *vinea* vineyard]

vinegar /ˈvɪnɪɡə(r)/ n. sour liquid got from malt, wine, cider, etc., by fermentation and used as a condiment or for pickling. □ **vinegary** adj. [French, = sour wine: related to EAGER]

vineyard /ˈvɪnjəd/ n. plantation of grapevines, esp. for wine-making. [Latin]

vingt-et-un /ˌvæ̃teˈɜ̃/ n. = PONTOON[1]. [French, = twenty-one]

vino /ˈviːnəʊ/ n. slang wine, esp. of an inferior kind. [Italian = wine]

vinous /ˈvaɪnəs/ adj. 1 of, like, or due to wine. **2** addicted to wine. [Latin *vinum* wine]

vintage /ˈvɪntɪdʒ/ —n. 1 a season's produce of grapes. **b** wine from this. **2 a** gathering of grapes for wine-making. **b** season of this. **3** wine of high quality

from a particular year and district. 4 **a** year etc. when a thing was made etc. **b** thing made etc. in a particular year etc. —*adj.* 1 of high or peak quality. 2 of a past season. [Latin *vinum* wine]

vintage car *n.* car made 1917–1930.

vintner *n.* wine-merchant. [Anglo-Latin from French, ultimately from Latin *vinetum* vineyard, from *vinum* wine]

vinyl /'vaɪnɪl/ *n.* plastic made by polymerization, esp. polyvinyl chloride. [Latin *vinum* wine]

viol /'vaɪəl/ *n.* medieval stringed instrument of various sizes, like a violin but held vertically. [French from Provençal]

viola[1] /vɪ'əʊlə/ *n.* instrument larger than the violin and of lower pitch. [Italian and Spanish: related to VIOL]

viola[2] /'vaɪələ/ *n.* any plant of the genus including the pansy and violet, esp. a cultivated hybrid. [Latin, = violet]

viola da gamba /vɪˌəʊlə də 'gæmbə/ *n.* viol held between the player's legs. [Italian, = viol]

violate /'vaɪəleɪt/ *v.* (-ting) 1 disregard; break (an oath, treaty, law, etc.). 2 treat (a sanctuary etc.) profanely; disrespect. 3 disturb (a person's privacy etc.). 4 rape. □ **violable** *adj.* **violation** /-'leɪʃ(ə)n/ *n.* **violator** *n.* [Latin *violo*]

violence /'vaɪələns/ *n.* 1 being violent. 2 violent conduct or treatment. 3 unlawful use of force. □ **do violence to** act contrary to; outrage. [Latin: related to VIOLENT]

violent /'vaɪələnt/ *adj.* 1 involving or using great physical force (*violent person; violent storm*). 2 **a** intense, vehement (*violent pain; violent dislike*). **b** lurid (*violent colours*). 3 (of death) resulting from violence or poison. □ **violently** *adv.* [French from Latin]

violet /'vaɪələt/ *n.* 1 sweet-scented plant with usu. purple, blue, or white flowers. 2 bluish-purple colour at the end of the spectrum opposite red. 3 pigment or clothes or material of this colour. —*adj.* of this colour. [French diminutive of *viole* VIOLA[2]]

violin /ˌvaɪə'lɪn/ *n.* high-pitched stringed instrument played with a bow. □ **violinist** *n.* [Italian diminutive of VIOLA[1]]

violist /vɪ'əʊlɪst/ *n.* viol- or viola-player.
violoncello /ˌvaɪələn'tʃeləʊ/ *n.* (*pl.* **-s**) *formal* = CELLO. [Italian, diminutive of *violone* bass viol]

VIP *abbr.* very important person.

viper /'vaɪpə(r)/ *n.* 1 small venomous snake. 2 malignant or treacherous person. [Latin]

virago /vɪ'rɑːgəʊ/ *n.* (*pl.* **-s**) fierce or abusive woman. [Latin, = female warrior]

viral /'vaɪər(ə)l/ *adj.* of or caused by a virus.

virgin /'vɜːdʒɪn/ —*n.* 1 person who has never had sexual intercourse. 2 (**the Virgin**) Christ's mother Mary. 3 (**the Virgin**) sign or constellation Virgo. —*adj.* 1 not yet used etc. 2 virginal. [Latin *virgo virgin-*]

virginal —*adj.* of or befitting a virgin. —*n.* (usu. in *pl.*) *Mus.* legless spinet in a box. [Latin: related to VIRGIN]

virgin birth *n.* 1 (usu. preceded by *the*) doctrine of Christ's birth from a virgin mother. 2 parthenogenesis.

Virginia creeper /və'dʒɪnɪə/ *n.* ornamental vine. [*Virginia* in US]

virginity /və'dʒɪnɪtɪ/ *n.* state of being a virgin.

Virgo /'vɜːgəʊ/ *n.* (*pl.* **-s**) 1 constellation and sixth sign of the zodiac (the Virgin). 2 person born when the sun is in this sign. [Latin: related to VIRGIN]

virile /'vɪraɪl/ *adj.* 1 (of a man) vigorous or strong. 2 sexually potent. 3 of a man as distinct from a woman or child. □ **virility** /vɪ'rɪlɪtɪ/ *n.* [Latin *vir* man]

virology /vaɪ'rɒlədʒɪ/ *n.* the study of viruses. □ **virologist** *n.*

virtual /'vɜːtʃʊəl/ *adj.* being so in practice though not strictly or in name (*the virtual manager; a virtual promise*). [medieval Latin: related to VIRTUE]

virtually *adv.* in effect, nearly, almost.

virtual reality *n.* simulation of the real world by a computer.

virtue /'vɜːtʃuː/ *n.* 1 moral excellence; goodness. 2 particular form of this. 3 (esp. female) chastity. 4 good quality (*has the virtue of speed*). 5 efficacy (*no virtue in such drugs*). □ **by** (or **in**) **virtue of** on account of, because of. [Latin: related to VIRILE]

virtuoso /ˌvɜːtʃʊ'əʊsəʊ/ *n.* (*pl.* **-si** /-siː/ or **-s**) (often *attrib.*) highly skilled artist, esp. a musician (*virtuoso performance*). □ **virtuosic** /-'ɒsɪk/ *adj.* **virtuosity** /-'ɒsɪtɪ/ *n.* [Italian: related to VIRTUOUS]

virtuous /'vɜːtʃʊəs/ *adj.* 1 morally good. 2 *archaic* chaste. □ **virtuously** *adv.* [Latin: related to VIRTUE]

virulent /'vɪrʊlənt/ *adj.* 1 strongly poisonous. 2 (of a disease) violent. 3 bitterly hostile. □ **virulence** *n.* **virulently** *adv.* [Latin: related to VIRUS]

virus /'vaɪərəs/ *n.* 1 microscopic organism often causing diseases. 2 = COMPUTER VIRUS. [Latin, = poison]

visa /'viːzə/ *n.* endorsement on a passport etc., esp. allowing entrance to or exit from a country. [Latin, = seen]

visage /ˈvɪzɪdʒ/ n. *literary* face. [Latin *visus* sight]

vis-à-vis /ˌviːzɑːˈviː/ —*prep.* 1 in relation to. 2 in comparison with. —*adv.* opposite. [French, = face to face: related to VISAGE]

viscera /ˈvɪsərə/ *n.pl.* internal organs of the body. [Latin]

visceral *adj.* 1 of the viscera. 2 of feelings rather than reason.

viscid /ˈvɪsɪd/ *adj.* glutinous, sticky. [Latin: related to viscous]

viscose /ˈvɪskəʊs/ n. 1 cellulose in a highly viscous state, used for making rayon etc. 2 fabric made from this. [Latin: related to viscous]

viscount /ˈvaɪkaʊnt/ n. British nobleman ranking between an earl and a baron. □ **viscountcy** n. (*pl.* -**ies**). [Anglo-French: related to vice- COUNT²]

viscountess n. 1 viscount's wife or widow. 2 woman holding the rank of viscount.

viscous /ˈvɪskəs/ *adj.* 1 glutinous, sticky. 2 semifluid. 3 not flowing freely. □ **viscosity** /-ˈkɒstɪ/ n. (*pl.* -**ies**). [Latin *viscum* birdlime]

vise *US* var. of VICE².

visibility /ˌvɪzɪˈbɪlɪtɪ/ n. 1 being visible. 2 range or possibility of vision as determined by the light and weather.

visible /ˈvɪzɪb(ə)l/ *adj.* 1 able to be seen, perceived, or ascertained. 2 (of exports etc.) consisting of actual goods. □ **visibly** *adv.* [Latin: related to vision]

vision /ˈvɪʒ(ə)n/ n. 1 act or faculty of seeing, sight. 2 thing or person seen in a dream or trance. 3 mental picture (*visions of hot toast*). 4 imaginative insight. 5 statesmanlike foresight. 6 beautiful person etc. 7 television or cinema picture, esp. of specified quality (*poor vision*). [Latin *video vis-* see]

visionary —*adj.* 1 given to seeing visions or to fanciful theories. 2 having vision or foresight. 3 not real, imaginary. 4 not practicable. —n. (*pl.* -**ies**) visionary person.

visit /ˈvɪzɪt/ —v. (-**t**-) (also *absol.*) 1 go or come to see or inspect (a person, place, etc.). 2 stay temporarily with (a person) or at (a place). 3 (of a disease, calamity, etc.) attack. 4 a (foll. by *with*) punish (a person). b (often foll. by *upon*) inflict punishment (for a sin). —n. 1 a act of visiting. b temporary stay; esp. as a guest. 2 (foll. by *to*) occasion of going to a doctor etc. 3 formal or official call. [Latin: related to vision]

visitant /ˈvɪzɪt(ə)nt/ n. 1 visitor, esp. a ghost etc. 2 migratory bird resting temporarily in an area.

visitation /ˌvɪzɪˈteɪʃ(ə)n/ n. 1 official visit of inspection. 2 trouble etc. seen as

divine punishment. 3 (**Visitation**) a visit of the Virgin Mary to Elizabeth. b festival of this.

visor /ˈvaɪzə(r)/ n. (also **vizor**) 1 movable part of a helmet covering the face. 2 shield over the eyes, esp. one at the top of a vehicle windscreen. [Anglo-French *viser*: related to VISAGE]

vista /ˈvɪstə/ n. 1 long narrow view as between rows of trees. 2 mental view of a long series of events. [Italian]

visual /ˈvɪʒʊəl/ *adj.* of or used in seeing. □ **visually** *adv.* [Latin *visus* sight]

visual aid n. film etc. as a teaching aid.

visual display unit n. *Computing* device displaying data on a screen.

visualize v. (also -**ise**) (-**zing** or -**sing**) imagine visually. □ **visualization** /-ˈzeɪʃ(ə)n/ n.

vital /ˈvaɪt(ə)l/ —*adj.* 1 of or essential to organic life (*vital functions*). 2 essential, indispensable (*of vital importance*). 3 full of life or activity. 4 fatal (*vital error*). —n. (in *pl.*) the body's vital organs, e.g. the heart and brain. □ **vitally** *adv.* [Latin *vita* life]

vitality /vaɪˈtælɪtɪ/ n. 1 liveliness, animation. 2 ability to survive or endure. [Latin: related to VITAL]

vitalize v. (also -**ise**) (-**zing** or -**sing**) 1 endow with life. 2 make lively or vigorous. □ **vitalization** /-ˈzeɪʃ(ə)n/ n.

vital statistics *n.pl.* 1 *joc.* measurements of a woman's bust, waist, and hips. 2 the number of births, marriages, deaths, etc.

vitamin /ˈvɪtəmɪn/ n. any of various substances present in many foods and essential to health and growth (*vitamin A, B, C,* etc.). [Latin *vita* life, AMINE]

vitamin B complex n. any of a group of vitamins often found together in foods.

vitaminize /ˈvɪtəmɪˌnaɪz/ v. (also -**ise**) (-**zing** or -**sing**) add vitamins to.

vitiate /ˈvɪʃɪˌeɪt/ v. (-**ting**) 1 impair, debase. 2 make invalid or ineffectual. □ **vitiation** /-ˈeɪʃ(ə)n/ n. [Latin: related to VICE¹]

viticulture /ˈvɪtɪˌkʌltʃə(r)/ n. cultivation of grapes. [Latin *vitis* vine]

vitreous /ˈvɪtrɪəs/ *adj.* of or like glass. [Latin *vitrum* glass]

vitreous humour n. clear fluid in the eye between the lens and the retina.

vitrify /ˈvɪtrɪˌfaɪ/ v. (-**ies**, -**ied**) change into glass or a glasslike substance, esp. by heat. □ **vitrifaction** /-ˈfækʃ(ə)n/ n.

vitrification /ˌvɪtrɪfɪˈkeɪʃ(ə)n/ n. [French or medieval Latin: related to VITREOUS]

vitriol /ˈvɪtrɪəl/ n. 1 sulphuric acid or a sulphate. 2 caustic or hostile speech or criticism. [Latin *vitrum*]

vitriolic /ˌvɪtrɪˈɒlɪk/ adj. caustic, hostile.

viva[1] /ˈvaɪvə/ colloq. —n. (pl. -s) = VIVA VOCE. —v. (vivas, vivaed, vivaing) = VIVA-VOCE. [abbreviation]

viva[2] /ˈviːvə/ —int. long live. —n. cry of this as a salute etc. [Italian, = let live]

vivace /vɪˈvɑːtʃɪ/ adv. Mus. in a lively manner. [Latin: related to VIVACIOUS]

vivacious /vɪˈveɪʃəs/ adj. lively, animated. □ **vivacity** /vɪˈvæsɪtɪ/ n. [Latin *vivax* from *vivo* live]

vivarium /vaɪˈveərɪəm/ n. (pl. -ria or -s) 1 glass bowl etc. for keeping animals for scientific study. 2 enclosure for keeping animals in (nearly) their natural state. [Latin]

viva voce /ˌvaɪvə ˈvəʊtʃɪ/ —adj. oral. —adv. orally. —n. oral examination. —v. (viva-voce) (-voces, -voced, -vocing) examine orally. [medieval Latin, = with the living voice]

vivid /ˈvɪvɪd/ adj. 1 (of light or colour) strong, intense. 2 (of a memory, description, the imagination, etc.) clear, lively, graphic. □ **vividly** adv. **vividness** n. [Latin *vividus*]

vivify /ˈvɪvɪfaɪ/ v. (-ies, -ied) enliven, animate, give life to. [French from Latin]

viviparous /vɪˈvɪpərəs/ adj. Zool. bringing forth young alive. [Latin *vivus* alive, *pario* produce]

vivisection /ˌvɪvɪˈsekʃ(ə)n/ n. surgical experimentation on living animals for scientific research. □ **vivisectional** adj. **vivisectionist** n. & adj. **vivisector** /ˈvɪvɪˌsektə(r)/ n. [Latin *vivus* living, DISSECTION]

vixen /ˈvɪks(ə)n/ n. 1 female fox. 2 spiteful woman. [Old English: related to FOX]

viz. /vɪz, or by substitution ˈneɪmlɪ/ adv. namely; that is to say; in other words. [abbreviation of VIDELICET, z = medieval Latin symbol for abbreviation of *-et*]

vizier /vɪˈzɪə(r)/ n. hist. high official in some Muslim countries. [ultimately from Arabic]

vizor var. of VISOR.

V-neck n. (often attrib.) V-shaped neckline on a pullover etc.

vocable /ˈvəʊkəb(ə)l/ n. word not with reference to form not meaning. [Latin *voco* call]

vocabulary /vəˈkæbjʊlərɪ/ n. (pl. -ies) 1 words used by a particular language, book, branch of science, or author. 2 list of these, in alphabetical order with definitions or translations. 3 individual's stock of words (*limited vocabulary*). 4 set of artistic or stylistic forms or techniques. [medieval Latin: related to VOCABLE]

vocal /ˈvəʊk(ə)l/ —adj. 1 of or uttered by the voice. 2 outspoken (*very vocal about his rights*). —n. (in sing. or pl.) sung part or piece of music. □ **vocally** adv. [Latin: related to VOICE]

vocal cords n. voice-producing part of the larynx.

vocalist n. singer.

vocalize v. (also -ise) (-zing or -sing) 1 form (a sound) or utter (a word) with the voice. 2 articulate, express. □ **vocalization** /ˈzeɪʃ(ə)n/ n.

vocation /vəʊˈkeɪʃ(ə)n/ n. 1 a strong feeling of suitability for a particular career. b this regarded as a divine call to a career in the Church. 2 employment, trade, profession. □ **vocational** adj.

vocative /ˈvɒkətɪv/ Gram. —n. case of a noun used in addressing a person or thing. —adj. of or in this case.

vociferate /vəˈsɪfəˌreɪt/ v. (-ting) 1 utter noisily. 2 shout, bawl. □ **vociferation** /-ˈreɪʃ(ə)n/ n. **vociferator** n. [Latin: related to VOICE, *fero* bear]

vociferous /vəˈsɪfərəs/ adj. 1 noisy, clamorous. 2 insistently and forcibly outspoken. □ **vociferously** adv.

vodka /ˈvɒdkə/ n. alcoholic spirit distilled esp. in Russia from rye etc. [Russian]

vogue /vəʊg/ n. 1 (prec. by *the*) prevailing fashion. 2 (often attrib.) popular use (*had a great vogue*). □ **in vogue** in fashion. □ **voguish** adj. [French from Italian]

voice —n. 1 a sound formed in the larynx and uttered by the mouth, esp. by a person speaking, singing, etc. b power of this (*lost her voice*). 2 a use of the voice; spoken or written expression (*esp. give voice*). b opinion so expressed. c right to express an opinion. d medium for expression. 3 Gram. set of verbal forms showing whether a verb is active or passive. —v. 1 express. 2 (esp. as **voiced** adj.) utter with vibration of the vocal cords (e.g. *b*, *d*). □ **in good voice** singing or speaking well or easily. **with one voice** unanimously. [Latin *vox voc-*]

voice-box n. larynx.

voice in the wilderness n. unheeded advocate of reform.

voiceless adj. 1 dumb, speechless. 2 uttered without vibration of the vocal cords (e.g. *f*, *p*).

voice-over n. commentary in a film etc. by an unseen narrator.

void —adj. 1 empty, vacant. 2 (of a contract etc.) invalid, not legally binding (*null and void*). —n. empty space, vacuum. —v. 1 render void. 2 excrete, empty (the bowels etc.). □ **void of** lacking, free from. [French]

voile /vɔɪl/ n. fine semi-transparent fabric. [French, = VEIL]

vol. abbr. volume.

volatile /ˈvɒlətaɪl/ adj. 1 changeable in mood; fickle. 2 (of a substance etc.) unstable. 3 (of a political situation etc.) likely to erupt in violence. 4 *Chem.* evaporating rapidly. □ **volatility** /-ˈtɪlɪtɪ/ n. [Latin *volo* fly]

volatilize /vəˈlætɪlaɪz/ v. (also *-ise*) (-zing or *-sing*) turn into vapour. □ **volatilization** /-ˈzeɪʃ(ə)n/ n.

vol-au-vent /ˈvɒləʊˌvɒ̃/ n. small puff pastry case with a savoury filling. [French, literally 'flight in the wind']

volcanic /vɒlˈkænɪk/ adj. of, like, or from a volcano. □ **volcanically** adv.

volcano /vɒlˈkeɪnəʊ/ n. (pl. -es) 1 mountain or hill from which lava, steam, etc. escape through openings in the earth's crust. 2 volatile situation. [Latin *Volcanus* Vulcan, Roman god of fire]

vole n. small plant-eating rodent. [originally *vole-mouse* from Norwegian *voll* field]

volition /vəˈlɪʃ(ə)n/ n. act or power of willing. □ **of one's own volition** voluntarily. □ **volitional** adj. [Latin *volo* wish]

volley /ˈvɒlɪ/ —n. (pl. -s) 1 a simultaneous firing of a number of weapons. b bullets etc. so fired. 2 (usu. foll. by *of*) torrent (of abuse etc.). 3 playing of a ball in tennis, football, etc., before it touches the ground. —v. (-eys, -eyed) return or send by or in a volley. [French *volée* from Latin *volo* fly]

volleyball n. game for two teams of six hitting a large ball by hand over a high net.

volt /vəʊlt/ n. SI unit of electromotive force, the difference of potential that would carry one ampere of current against one ohm resistance. [*Volta*, name of a physicist]

voltage n. electromotive force expressed in volts.

volte-face /vɒltˈfɑːs/ n. sudden reversal of one's attitude or opinion. [French from Italian]

voltmeter n. instrument measuring electric potential in volts.

voluble /ˈvɒljʊb(ə)l/ adj. speaking or spoken fluently or at length. □ **volubility** /-ˈbɪlɪtɪ/ n. **volubly** adv. [Latin *volvo* roll]

volume /ˈvɒljuːm/ n. 1 single book forming part or all of a work. 2 a solid content, bulk. b space occupied by a gas or liquid. c (foll. by *of*) amount or quantity. 3 strength of sound, loudness. 4 (foll. by *of*) a moving mass of water etc. b (usu. in pl.) mass of smoke etc. [Latin *volumen*: related to VOLUBLE, ancient books being in roll form]

volumetric /ˌvɒljuːˈmetrɪk/ adj. of measurement by volume. □ **volumetrically** adv. [from VOLUME, METRIC]

voluminous /vəˈljuːmɪnəs/ adj. 1 (of drapery etc.) loose and ample. 2 (of writing etc.) great in length. [Latin: related to VOLUME]

voluntary /ˈvɒləntrɪ/ —adj. 1 acting, done, or given willingly; not compulsory; intentional. 2 (*voluntary work*) unpaid. 3 (of an institution) supported by voluntary charity. 4 (of a school) built by a charity but maintained by a local education authority. 5 brought about by voluntary action. 6 (of a movement, muscle, or limb) controlled by the will. —n. (pl. -ies) organ solo played before or after a church service. □ **voluntarily** adv. [Latin *voluntas* will]

voluntariness n. [Latin *voluntas* will]

volunteer /ˌvɒlənˈtɪə(r)/ —n. person who voluntarily undertakes a task or enters military etc. service. —v. 1 (often foll. by *to* + infin.) undertake or offer (one's services, a remark, etc.) voluntarily. 2 (often foll. by *for*) be a volunteer. [French: related to VOLUNTARY]

voluptuary /vəˈlʌptjʊərɪ/ n. (pl. -ies) person who seeks luxury and sensual pleasure. [Latin: related to VOLUPTUOUS]

voluptuous /vəˈlʌptjʊəs/ adj. 1 of, tending to, occupied with, or derived from, sensual or sensual pleasure. 2 (of a woman) curvaceous and sexually desirable. □ **voluptuously** adv. [Latin *voluptas* pleasure]

volute /vəˈljuːt/ n. spiral stonework scroll as an ornament of esp. Ionic capitals. [Latin *volvo* -ut- roll]

vomit /ˈvɒmɪt/ —v. (-t-) 1 eject (contents of the stomach) through the mouth; be sick. 2 (of a volcano, chimney, etc.) eject violently, belch forth. —n. matter vomited from the stomach. [Latin]

voodoo n. religious witch-craft as practised esp. in the W. Indies. —v. (-doos, -dooed) affect by voodoo; bewitch. [Dahomey]

voracious /vəˈreɪʃəs/ adj. 1 gluttonous, ravenous. 2 very eager (*voracious*

reader). □ **voraciously** adv. **voracity** /vɔˈræsɪtɪ/ n. [Latin vorax from voro devour]

vortex /ˈvɔːteks/ n. (pl. -texes or -tices /-tɪˌsiːz/) **1** whirlpool, whirlwind. **2** whirling motion or mass. **3** thing viewed as destructive or devouring (the vortex of society). □ **vortical** adj. [related to VERTEX]

vorticist /ˈvɔːtɪsɪst/ n. futuristic painter, writer, etc., of a school based on the so-called 'vortices' of modern civilization. □ **vorticism** n.

votary /ˈvəʊtərɪ/ n. (pl. -ies; fem. **votaress**) (usu. foll. by of) **1** person dedicated to the service of a god or cult. **2** devotee of a person, occupation, etc. [Latin: related to VOTE]

vote —n. **1** formal expression of choice or opinion by a ballot, show of hands, etc., in an election etc. **2** (usu. prec. by the) right to vote, esp. in a State election. **3** opinion expressed by a vote (vote of no confidence). **4** votes given by or for a particular group (the Welsh vote; the Labour vote). —v. (-ting) **1** (often foll. by for, against) give a vote. **2 a** enact or resolve by a majority of votes. **b** grant (a sum of money) by vote. **3** colloq. pronounce by that) suggest, urge. □ **vote down** defeat (a proposal etc.) in a vote. **vote in** elect by voting. **vote off** dismiss from (a committee etc.) by voting. **vote out** dismiss from office etc. by voting. **vote with one's feet** colloq. indicate an opinion by one's presence or absence. [Latin votum from voveo vot- vow]

voter n. person voting or with the right to vote at an election.

votive /ˈvəʊtɪv/ adj. offered or consecrated in fulfilment of a vow (votive offering). [Latin: related to VOTE]

vouch v. (foll. by for) answer for, be surety for (will vouch for the truth of this; can vouch for him). [French vo(u)cher summon, invoke]

voucher n. **1** document exchangeable for goods or services. **2** receipt. [from Anglo-French, or from VOUCH]

vouchsafe /vaʊtʃˈseɪf/ v. (-fing) formal **1** condescend to grant. **2** (foll. by to + infin.) condescend.

vow —n. solemn, esp. religious, promise (monastic vows; marriage vows). —v. **1** promise solemnly. **2** archaic declare solemnly. [French vou(er): related to VOTE]

vowel /ˈvaʊəl/ n. **1** speech-sound made with vibration of the vocal cords but without audible friction. **2** letter(s) representing this, as a, e, i, o, u, aw, ah. [Latin: related to VOCAL]

vox pop n. (often attrib.) colloq. popular opinion as represented by informal comments from the public. [abbreviation of VOX POPULI]

vox populi /ˌvɒks ˈpɒpjʊˌlaɪ/ n. public opinion, popular belief. [Latin, = the people's voice]

voyage /ˈvɔɪɪdʒ/ —n. journey, esp. a long one by sea or in space. —v. (-ging) make a voyage. □ **voyager** n. [Latin VIATICUM]

voyeur /vwaˈjɜː(r)/ n. **1** person who derives sexual pleasure from secretly observing others' sexual activity or organs. **2** (esp. covert) spectator. □ **voyeurism** n. **voyeuristic** /-ˈrɪstɪk/ adj. [French voir see]

VS. abbr. versus.

V-sign /ˈviːsaɪn/ n. **1** sign of the letter V made with the first two fingers pointing up and the back of the hand facing outwards, as a gesture of abuse etc. **2** similar sign made with the palm of the hand facing outwards, as a symbol of victory.

VSO abbr. Voluntary Service Overseas.

VSOP abbr. Very Special Old Pale (brandy).

VTO abbr. vertical take-off.

VTOL /ˈviːtɒl/ abbr. vertical take-off and landing.

VTR abbr. videotape recorder.

vulcanite /ˈvʌlkəˌnaɪt/ n. hard black vulcanized rubber. [related to VULCANIZE]

vulcanize /ˈvʌlkəˌnaɪz/ v. (also **-ise**) (-zing or -sing) treat (rubber etc.) with sulphur at a high temperature to strengthen it. □ **vulcanization** /-ˈzeɪʃ(ə)n/ n. [Vulcan: related to VOLCANO]

vulcanology /ˌvʌlkəˈnɒlədʒɪ/ n. the study of volcanoes. □ **vulcanological** /-nəˈlɒdʒɪk(ə)l/ adj. **vulcanologist** n.

vulgar /ˈvʌlɡə(r)/ adj. **1 a** coarse; indecent; tasteless. **b** of or characteristic of the common people. **2** common; prevalent (vulgar errors). □ **vulgarly** adv. [Latin vulgus common people]

vulgar fraction n. fraction expressed by numerator and denominator, not decimally.

vulgarian /vʌlˈɡeərɪən/ n. vulgar (esp. rich) person.

vulgarism n. vulgar word, expression, action, or habit.

vulgarity /vʌlˈɡærɪtɪ/ n. (pl. -ies) vulgar act, expression, or state.

vulgarize /ˈvʌlɡəˌraɪz/ v. (also **-ise**) (-zing or -sing) **1** make vulgar. **2** spoil by popularizing. □ **vulgarization** /-ˌzeɪʃ(ə)n/ n.

vulgar tongue n. (prec. by the) national or vernacular language.

Vulgate /'vʌlgeɪt/ *n.* 4th-c. Latin version of the Bible. [Latin: related to VULGAR]

vulnerable /'vʌlnərəb(ə)l/ *adj.* 1 easily wounded or harmed. 2 (foll. by *to*) exposed to damage, temptation, etc. □ **vulnerability** /-'bɪlɪtɪ/ *n.* **vulnerably** *adv.* [Latin *vulnus -er-* wound]

vulpine /'vʌlpaɪn/ *adj.* 1 of or like a fox. 2 crafty, cunning. [Latin *vulpes* fox]

vulture /'vʌltʃə(r)/ *n.* 1 large carrion-eating bird of prey reputed to gather with others in anticipation of a death. 2 rapacious person. [Anglo-French from Latin]

vulva /'vʌlvə/ *n.* (*pl.* -s) external female genitals. [Latin]

vv. *abbr.* 1 verses. 2 volumes.

vying *pres. part.* of VIE.

W

W¹ /ˈdʌb(ə)ljuː/ *n.* (also **w**) (*pl.* **Ws** or **W's**) twenty-third letter of the alphabet.

W² *abbr.* (also **W.**) **1** watt(s). **2** West; Western.

W³ *symb.* tungsten. [*wolframium*, Latinized name]

w. *abbr.* **1** wicket(s). **2** wide(s). **3** with.

W A *abbr.* Western Australia.

wacky *adj.* (**-ier**, **-iest**) *slang* crazy. [originally dial., = left-handed]

wad /wɒd/ *n.* **1** lump of soft material used esp. to keep things apart or in place or to block a hole. **2** bundle of banknotes or documents. —*v.* (**-dd-**) **1** stop up or keep in place with a wad. **2** line, stuff, or protect with wadding. [origin uncertain]

wadding *n.* soft fibrous material used in quilt-making etc., or to pack fragile articles.

waddle /ˈwɒd(ə)l/ —*v.* (**-ling**) walk with short steps and a swaying motion. —*n.* waddling gait. [from WADE]

wade —*v.* (**-ding**) **1** walk through water, mud, etc. esp. with difficulty. **2** (foll. by *through*) go through (a tedious task, book, etc.). **3** (foll. by *into*) *colloq.* attack (a person or task) vigorously. —*n.* spell of wading. □ **wade in** *colloq.* make a vigorous attack or intervention. [Old English]

wader *n.* **1** long-legged water-bird that wades. **2** (in *pl.*) high waterproof boots.

wadi /ˈwɒdɪ/ *n.* (*pl.* **-s**) rocky watercourse in N. Africa etc., dry except in the rainy season. [Arabic]

wafer *n.* **1** very thin light crisp sweet biscuit. **2** disc of unleavened bread used in the Eucharist. **3** disc of red paper stuck on a legal document instead of a seal. [Anglo-French *wafre* from Germanic]

wafer-thin *adj.* very thin.

waffle¹ /ˈwɒf(ə)l/ *colloq.* —*n.* verbose but aimless or ignorant talk or writing. —*v.* (**-ling**) indulge in waffle. [dial. = yelp]

waffle² /ˈwɒf(ə)l/ *n.* small crisp batter cake. [Dutch]

waffle-iron *n.* utensil, usu. of two shallow metal pans hinged together, for baking waffles.

waft /wɒft/ —*v.* convey or travel easily and smoothly as through air or over water. —*n.* (usu. foll. by *of*) whiff or scent. [originally 'convoy (ship etc.)' from Dutch or Low German *wachter* from *wachten* to guard]

wag¹ —*v.* (**-gg-**) shake or wave to and fro. —*n.* single wagging motion (*with a wag of his tail*). □ **tongues wag** there is talk. [Old English]

wag² *n.* facetious person. [Old English]

wage —*n.* (in *sing.* or *pl.*) fixed regular payment to an employee, esp. a manual worker. —*v.* (**-ging**) carry on (a war etc.). [Anglo-French from Germanic]

waged *adj.* in regular paid employment.

wage-earner *n.* person who works for wages.

wager *n. & v.* = BET. [Anglo-French: related to WAGE]

waggish *adj.* playful, facetious. □ **waggishness** *n.*

waggle /ˈwæg(ə)l/ *v.* (**-ling**) *colloq.* wag.

waggly *adj.* unsteady; waggling.

wagon /ˈwægən/ *n.* (also **waggon**) **1** four-wheeled vehicle for heavy loads. **2** railway vehicle, esp. an open truck. **3** tea trolley. □ **on the wagon** (or **water-wagon**) *slang* teetotal. [Dutch: related to WAIN]

wagoner *n.* (also **waggoner**) driver of a wagon.

wagon-load *n.* as much as a wagon can carry.

wagtail *n.* small bird with a long tail in frequent motion.

waif *n.* **1** homeless and helpless person, esp. an abandoned child. **2** ownerless object or animal. [Anglo-French, probably from Scandinavian]

waifs and strays *n.pl.* **1** homeless or neglected children. **2** odds and ends.

wail —*n.* **1** prolonged plaintive high-pitched cry of pain, grief, etc. **2** sound like this. —*v.* **1** utter a wail. **2** lament or complain persistently or bitterly. [Old Norse]

wain *n. archaic* wagon. [Old English]

wainscot /ˈweɪnskət/ *n.* boarding or wooden panelling on the lower part of a room-wall. [Low German *wagenschot* from *wagen* WAGON]

wainscoting *n.* **1** wainscot. **2** material for this.

waist *n.* **1 a** part of the human body below the ribs and above the hips; narrower middle part of the normal human figure. **b** circumference of this. **2** narrow middle of a violin, wasp, etc. **3 a** part of a garment encircling the waist. **b** *US* blouse, bodice. **4** part of a ship between the forecastle and the quarterdeck. □

waisted adj. (also in comb.). [Old English: related to WAX²]

waistband n. strip of cloth forming the waist of a garment.

waistcoat n. close-fitting waist-length garment without sleeves or collar, worn usu. over a shirt and under a jacket.

waist-deep adj. & adv. (also **waist-high**) up to the waist.

waistline n. outline or size of a person's body at the waist.

wait v. 1 a defer action or departure for a specified time, or until some event occurs (wait a minute; wait till I come). b be expectant. 2 await (an opportunity, one's turn, etc.). 3 defer (a meal etc.) until a person's arrival. 4 (usu. as **waiting** n.) park a vehicle for a short time. 5 act as a waiter or attendant. 6 (foll. by on, upon) a await the convenience of. b serve as an attendant to. c pay a respectful visit to. —n. 1 period of waiting. 2 (usu. foll. by for) watching for an enemy (lie in wait). 3 (in pl.) archaic street singers of Christmas carols. □ **wait and see** await the progress of events. **wait up** (often foll. by for) not go to bed until a person arrives or an event happens. **you wait!** used to imply a threat, warning, etc. [Germanic: related to WAKE¹]

waiter n. man who serves at table in a hotel or restaurant etc.

waiting game n. the delaying of action in order to have a greater effect later.

waiting-list n. list of people waiting for a thing not immediately available.

waiting-room n. room for people to wait in, esp. to see a doctor etc. or at a station.

waitress n. woman who serves at table etc.

waive v. (-ving) refrain from insisting on or using (a right, claim, opportunity, etc.). [Anglo-French weyver: related to WAIF]

waiver n. Law 1 waiving of a legal right etc. 2 document recording this.

wake¹ —v. (-king; past woke or waked; past part. woken or waked) 1 (often foll. by up) (cause to) cease to sleep. 2 (often foll. by up) (cause to) become alert or attentive. 3 archaic (except as **waking** adj. & n.) be awake (waking hours). 4 disturb with noise. 5 evoke (an echo). —n. 1 watch beside a corpse before burial; attendant lamentation and (less often) merrymaking. 2 (usu. in pl.) northern England. [Old English]

wake² n. 1 track left on the water's surface by a moving ship. 2 turbulent air left behind by a moving aircraft etc. □ **in the wake of** following, as a result of. [Low German from Old Norse]

wakeful adj. 1 unable to sleep. 2 (of a night etc.) sleepless. 3 vigilant. □ **wakefully** adv. **wakefulness** n.

waken v. make or become awake. [Old Norse]

wale n. 1 = WEAL². 2 ridge on corduroy etc. 3 Naut. a broad thick timber along a ship's side. [Old English]

walk /wɔːk/ —v. 1 a progress by lifting and setting down each foot in turn, never having both feet off the ground at once. b (of a quadruped) go with the slowest gait. 2 a travel or go on foot. b take exercise in this way. 3 traverse or tread the floor or surface of. 4 cause to walk with one (walk the dog). —n. 1 a act of walking, the ordinary human gait. b slowest gait of an animal. c person's manner of walking. 2 a distance which can be walked in a (usu. specified) time (ten minutes' walk from here). b excursion on foot. 3 place or track intended or suitable for walking. □ **walk all over** colloq. 1 defeat easily. 2 take advantage of. **walk away from** 1 easily outdistance. 2 refuse to become involved with. **walk away with** colloq. = **walk off with**. **walk into** colloq. 1 encounter through unwariness. 2 get (a job) easily. **walk off with** colloq. 1 steal. 2 win easily. **walk on air** feel elated. **walk out** 1 depart suddenly or angrily. 2 stop work in protest. **walk out on** desert, abandon. **walk the streets** be a prostitute. □ **walkable** adj. [Old English]

walkabout n. 1 informal stroll among a crowd by a visiting dignitary. 2 period of wandering in the bush by an Australian Aboriginal.

walker n. 1 person or animal that walks. 2 a framework in which a baby can walk unaided. b = WALKING FRAME.

walkie-talkie /ˌwɔːkɪˈtɔːkɪ/ n. two-way radio carried on the person.

walk-in adj. attrib. adj. (of a storage area) large enough to walk into.

walking frame n. tubular metal frame for disabled or old people to help them walk.

walking-stick n. stick carried for support when walking.

Walkman n. (pl. -s) propr. type of personal stereo.

walk of life n. occupation, profession.

walk-on n. 1 (in full **walk-on part**) non-speaking dramatic role. 2 player of this.

walk-out n. sudden angry departure, esp. as a protest or strike.

walk-over n. easy victory.

walkway n. passage or path (esp. raised) for walking along.

wall /wɔːl/ —n. 1 continuous vertical narrow structure of usu. brick or stone, esp. enclosing or dividing a space or supporting a roof. 2 thing like a wall, esp.: **a** a steep side of a mountain. **b** Anat. the outermost layer or enclosing membrane etc. of an organ etc. —v. 1 (esp. as **walled** adj.) surround with a wall. 2 **a** (usu. foll. by up, off) block (a space etc.) with a wall. **b** (foll. by up) enclose within a sealed space. □ **go to the wall** colloq. be defeated or pushed aside. **off the wall** US slang unorthodox. **up the wall** colloq. crazy or furious. **walls have ears** beware of eavesdroppers. □ **wall-less** adj. [Latin vallum rampart]

wallaby /ˈwɒləbɪ/ n. (pl. -ies) marsupial similar to but smaller than a kangaroo. [Aboriginal]

wallah /ˈwɒlə/ n. slang person concerned with or in charge of a usu. specified thing, business, etc. [Hindi]

wall bar n. one of a set of parallel bars attached to the wall of a gymnasium, on which exercises are performed.

wallet /ˈwɒlɪt/ n. small flat esp. leather case for holding banknotes etc. [Anglo-French]

wall-eye /ˈwɔːlaɪ/ n. 1 eye with a streaked or opaque white iris. 2 eye squinting outwards. □ **wall-eyed** adj. [Old Norse]

wallflower n. 1 fragrant spring garden plant. 2 colloq. woman sitting out a dance for lack of partners.

wall game n. form of football played at Eton.

Walloon /wɒˈluːn/ —n. 1 member of a people inhabiting S. and E. Belgium and neighbouring France. 2 French dialect spoken by this people. —adj. of or concerning the Walloons or their language. [medieval Latin Wallo -onis]

wallop /ˈwɒləp/ colloq. —v. (-p-) 1 thrash; beat. 2 (as **walloping** adj.) huge. —n. 1 heavy blow. 2 beer. [earlier senses 'gallop', 'boil', from French waloper from Germanic; cf. GALLOP]

wallow /ˈwɒləʊ/ —v. 1 (esp. of an animal) roll about in mud etc. 2 (usu. foll. by in) indulge in unrestrained pleasure, misery, etc. —n. 1 act of wallowing. 2 place used by buffalo etc. for wallowing. [Old English]

wallpaper —n. 1 paper for pasting on to interior walls as decoration. 2 usu. derog. trivial background noise, music, etc. —v. decorate with wallpaper.

wall-to-wall adj. 1 (of a carpet) fitted to cover a whole room etc. 2 colloq. ubiquitous (wall-to-wall pop music).

wally /ˈwɒlɪ/ n. (pl. -ies) slang foolish or inept person. [origin uncertain]

walnut /ˈwɔːlnʌt/ n. 1 tree with aromatic leaves and drooping catkins. 2 nut of this tree. 3 its timber. [Old English, = foreign nut]

walrus /ˈwɔːlrəs/ n. (pl. same or -es) large amphibious long-tusked arctic mammal. [Dutch]

walrus moustache n. long thick drooping moustache.

waltz /wɔːls/ —n. 1 ballroom dance in triple time performed by couples revolving with sliding steps. 2 music for this. —v. 1 dance a waltz. 2 (often foll. by in, out, round, etc.) colloq. move easily, lightly, casually, etc. □ **waltz off with** colloq. 1 steal. 2 win easily. [German Walzer from walzen revolve]

wampum /ˈwɒmpəm/ n. beads made from shells and strung together for use as money, decoration, etc. by N. American Indians. [Algonquian]

wan /wɒn/ adj. (**wanner**, **wannest**) pale; exhausted-looking. □ **wanly** adv. □ **wanness** n. [Old English, = dark]

wand /wɒnd/ n. 1 supposedly magic stick used by a fairy, magician, etc. 2 staff as a symbol of office. 3 colloq. conductor's baton. [Old Norse]

wander /ˈwɒndə(r)/ v. 1 (often foll. by in, off, etc.) go about from place to place aimlessly. 2 **a** wind about; meander. **b** stray from a path etc. 3 talk or think incoherently; be inattentive or delirious. □ **wanderer** n. [Old English: related to WEND]

wandering Jew n. person who never settles down.

wanderlust n. eagerness for travelling or wandering; restlessness. [German]

wane —v. (-ning) 1 (of the moon) decrease in apparent size. 2 decrease in power, vigour, importance, size, etc. —n. process of waning. □ **on the wane** waning; declining. [Old English]

wangle /ˈwæŋg(ə)l/ colloq. —v. (-ling) (often refl.) contrive to obtain (a favour etc.). —n. act of wangling. [origin unknown]

wank coarse slang —v. masturbate. —n. act of masturbating. [origin unknown]

Wankel engine /ˈwæŋk(ə)l/ n. internal-combustion engine with a continuously rotated and eccentrically pivoted shaft. [Wankel, name of an engineer]

wanker n. coarse slang contemptible or ineffectual person.

wannabe /ˈwɒnəbɪ/ n. slang 1 avid fan who tries to emulate the person he or she admires. 2 anybody who would like to be someone else. [corruption of want to be]

want /wɒnt/ —v. **1 a** (often foll. by to + infin.) desire; wish for possession of; need (wants a drink; wants it done immediately). **b** require to be attended to; need (garden wants weeding). **c** (foll. by to + infin.) colloq. ought; should (you want to be careful). **2** (usu. foll. by for) or lack; be deficient in (wants for nothing). **3** be without or fall short by. **4** (as **wanted** adj.) (of a suspected criminal etc.) sought by the police. —n. **1** (often foll. by of) lack, absence, or deficiency (could not go for want of time). **2** poverty; need. [Old Norse]

wanting adj. **1** lacking (in quality or quantity); not equal to requirements. **2** absent, not supplied.

wanton /ˈwɒnt(ə)n/ —adj. **1** licentious; sexually promiscuous. **2** capricious; arbitrary; motiveless (wanton destruction). **3** luxuriant; unrestrained (wanton profusion). —n. literary licentious person. □ **wantonly** adv. [from obsolete wantowen, = undisciplined]

wapiti /ˈwɒpɪtɪ/ n. (pl. -s) N. American deer. [a Cree word]

war /wɔː(r)/ —n. **1 a** armed hostilities between esp. nations; conflict. **b** specific instance or period of this. **c** suspension of international law etc. during this. **2** hostility or contention between people, groups, etc. **3** (often foll. by on) sustained campaign against crime, poverty, etc. —v. (-rr-) **1** (as **warring** adj.) rival; fighting. **2** make war. □ **at war** (often foll. by with) engaged in a war. **go to war** declare or begin a war. **have been in the wars** colloq. appear injured etc. [Anglo-French from Germanic]

warble /ˈwɔːb(ə)l/ —v. (-ling) **1** sing in a gentle trilling manner. **2** speak in a warbling manner. —n. warbled song or utterance. [French werbler]

warbler n. bird that warbles.

war crime n. crime violating the international laws of war. □ **war criminal** n.

war cry n. **1** phrase or name shouted to rally one's troops. **2** party slogan etc.

ward /wɔːd/ n. **1** separate part of a hospital or room for a particular group of patients. **2** administrative division of a constituency. **3 a** minor under the care of a guardian or court. **b** (in full **ward of court**) minor or mentally deficient person placed under the protection of a court. **4** (in pl.) the corresponding notches and projections in a key and a lock. **5** archaic guardian's control. □ **ward off 1** parry (a blow). **2** avert (danger etc.). [Old English]

-ward suffix (also **-wards**) added to nouns of place or destination and to adverbs (usu. -wards) of direction and forming: **1** adverbs (usu. -wards) meaning 'towards' (backwards homewards), **2** adjectives (usu. -ward) meaning 'turned or tending towards' (downward), and **3** (less commonly) nouns meaning 'the region towards or about' (look to the eastward). [Old English]

ward dance n. dance performed by primitive peoples etc. before a battle or to celebrate victory.

warden /ˈwɔːd(ə)n/ n. **1** (often in comb.) supervising official (traffic warden). **2** president or governor of a college, hospital, etc. [Anglo-French and French: related to GUARDIAN]

warder /ˈwɔːdə(r)/ n. (fem. **wardress**) prison officer. [French: related to GUARD]

wardrobe /ˈwɔːdrəʊb/ n. **1** large cupboard for storing clothes. **2** person's stock of clothes. **3** costume department of a theatre etc. [French]

wardrobe mistress n. (masc. **wardrobe master**) person in charge of a theatrical wardrobe.

wardroom n. mess in a warship for commissioned officers.

-wards var. of -WARD.

wardship n. tutelage.

ware n. **1** (esp. in comb.) things of a specified kind made usu. for sale (chinaware; hardware). **2** (usu. in pl.) articles for sale. **3** ceramics etc. of a specified kind (Delft ware). [Old English]

warehouse —n. **1** building in which goods are stored. **2** wholesale or large retail store. —v. /also -hauz/(-sing) store temporarily in a repository.

warfare n. waging war; campaigning.

war-game n. **1** military training exercise. **2** battle etc. conducted with toy soldiers.

warhead n. explosive head of a missile.

warhorse n. **1** hist. trooper's powerful horse. **2** colloq. veteran soldier, politician, etc.

warlike adj. **1** hostile. **2** soldierly. **3** military.

warlock /ˈwɔːlɒk/ n. archaic sorcerer. [Old English, = traitor]

warlord n. military commander or commander-in-chief.

warm /wɔːm/ —adj. **1** of or at a fairly high temperature. **2** (of clothes etc.) affording warmth. **3 a** sympathetic, friendly, loving. **b** hearty, enthusiastic. **4** colloq. dangerous, difficult, hostile. **5** colloq. **a** (in a game) close to guessing. **b** near to guessing. **6** (of a colour etc.) reddish or yellowish;

suggestive of warmth. **7** *Hunting* (of a scent) fresh and strong. —*v.* **1** make warm. **2 a** (often foll. by *up*) warm oneself. **b** (often foll. by *to*) become animated or sympathetic. —*n.* **1** act of warming. **2** warmth of the atmosphere etc. □ **warm up 1** make or become warm. **2** prepare for a performance etc. by practising. **3** reach a temperature for efficient working. **4** reheat (food). □ **warmly** *adv.* **warmth** *n.* [Old English]

warm-blooded *adj.* **1** having blood temperature well above that of the environment. **2** ardent.

war memorial *n.* monument to those killed in a war.

warm-hearted *adj.* kind, friendly. □ **warm-heartedness** *n.*

warming-pan *n. hist.* container for live coals with a flat body and a long handle, used for warming a bed.

warmonger *n.* person who promotes war. □ **warmongering** *n. & adj.*

warm-up *n.* period of preparatory exercise.

warm work *n.* **1** work etc. that makes one warm through exertion. **2** dangerous conflict etc.

warn /wɔːn/ *v.* **1** (also *absol.*) **a** (often foll. by *of* or *that*) inform of danger, unknown circumstances, etc. **b** (foll. by *to* + infin.) advise (a person) to take certain action. **c** (often foll. by *against*) inform (a person etc.) about a specific danger. **2** (usu. with *neg.*) admonish. □ **warn off** tell (a person) to keep away (from). [Old English]

warning *n.* **1** in senses of WARN. **2** thing that warns. [Old English]

war of nerves *n.* attempt to wear down an opponent psychologically.

warp /wɔːp/ —*v.* **1 a** make or become distorted, esp. through heat, damp, etc. **b** make or become perverted or strange (*warped sense of humour*). **2** haul (a ship) by a rope attached to a fixed point. —*n.* **1 a** warped state, esp. of timber. **b** perversion of the mind. **2** lengthwise threads in a loom. **3** rope used in warping a ship. [Old English]

warpaint *n.* **1** paint used to adorn the body before battle, esp. by N. American Indians. **2** *colloq.* make-up.

warpath *n.* □ **on the warpath 1** (of N. American Indians) going to war. **2** *colloq.* seeking a confrontation.

warrant /ˈwɒrənt/ —*n.* **1** thing that authorizes an action. **2 a** written authorization, money voucher, etc. **b** written authorization allowing police to search premises, arrest a suspect, etc. **3** certificate of service rank held by a warrant officer. —*v.* **1** serve as a warrant for; justify. **2** guarantee or attest to esp. the

genuineness of. □ **I** (or **I'll**) **warrant** I am certain, no doubt. [French *warant*, from Germanic]

warrant-officer *n.* officer ranking between commissioned officers and NCOs.

warranty *n.* (*pl.* -**ies**) **1** undertaking as to the ownership or quality of a thing sold etc., often accepting responsibility for defects or repairs over a specified period. **2** (usu. foll. by *for* + verbal noun) authority or justification. [Anglo-French *warantie*: related to WARRANT]

warren /ˈwɒrən/ *n.* **1** network of rabbit burrows. **2** densely populated or labyrinthine building or district. [Anglo-French *warenne* from Germanic]

warring see WAR *v.*

warrior /ˈwɒrɪə(r)/ *n.* **1** person experienced or distinguished in fighting. **2** fighting man, esp. of primitive peoples. **3** (*attrib.*) martial (*warrior nation*). [French *werreior*: related to WAR]

warship *n.* ship used in war.

wart /wɔːt/ *n.* **1** small hard round growth on the skin. **2** protuberance on the skin of an animal, surface of a plant, etc. □ **warts and all** *colloq.* with no attempt to conceal blemishes. □ **warty** *adj.* [Old English]

wart-hog *n.* African wild pig.

wartime *n.* period during which a war is being waged.

wary /ˈweərɪ/ *adj.* (-**ier**, -**iest**) **1** on one's guard; circumspect. **2** (foll. by *of*) cautious. **3** showing caution. □ **warily** *adv.* **wariness** *n.* [*ware* look out for, avoid]

was 1st & 3rd sing. past of BE.

wash /wɒʃ/ —*v.* **1** cleanse with liquid, esp. water. **2** (foll. by *out, off, away,* etc.) **a** remove (a stain) in this way. **b** (of a stain etc.) be removed by washing. **3** wash oneself or one's hands and face. **4** wash clothes, dishes, etc. **5** (of fabric or dye) bear washing without damage. **6** (of an argument etc.) stand scrutiny; be believed or acceptable. **7** (of a river, waters, etc.) touch. **8** (of liquid) carry along, in a specified direction (*was washed overboard; washed up on the shore*). **9** (foll. by *over, along,* etc.) sweep, move, or splash. **10** (foll. by *over*) occur all around without greatly affecting (a person). **11** sift (ore) by the action of water. **12** brush watery paint or ink over. **13** *poet.* moisten, water. —*n.* **1 a** washing or being washed. **b** (prec. by *the*) a laundry etc. (*sent them to the wash*). **2** clothes etc. for washing or just washed. **3** motion of agitated water or air, esp. from the passage of a ship etc. or aircraft. **4** kitchen slops given to pigs. **5 a** thin, weak, or inferior liquid food. **b** liquid food for animals. **6** liquid to spread over a surface to cleanse, heal, or

colour. **7** thin coating of water-colour. □ **come out in the wash** colloq. be resolved in the course of time. **wash one's dirty linen in public** let private quarrels or difficulties become generally known. **wash down 1** wash completely. **2** (usu. foll. by *with*) accompany or follow (food) with a drink. **wash one's hands of** renounce responsibility for. **wash out 1** clean the inside of by washing. **2** clean (a garment etc.) by brief washing. **3** colloq. rain off. **4** = sense 2 of *v.* **wash up 1** (also *absol.*) wash (dishes etc.) after use. **2** *US* wash one's face and hands. **3** carry on to a shore. □ **washable** adj. [Old English]

wash-basin n. plumbed-in basin for washing one's hands etc.

washboard n. **1** ribbed board on which clothes are scrubbed. **2** this as a percussion instrument.

washed out adj. (also **washed-out**) **1** faded; pale. **2** colloq. pale, exhausted.

washed up adj. (also **washed-up**) esp. *US slang* defeated, having failed.

washer n. **1** person or machine that washes. **2** flat ring inserted at a joint to tighten it and prevent leakage or under the head of a screw etc., or under a nut, to disperse its pressure.

washer-up n. (*pl.* **washers-up**) (also **washer-upper**) person who washes up dishes etc.

washerwoman n. laundress.

washing n. clothes etc. for washing or just washed.

washing-machine n. machine for washing clothes.

washing-powder n. soap powder or detergent for washing clothes.

washing-soda n. sodium carbonate, used dissolved in water for washing and cleaning.

washing-up n. **1** process of washing dishes etc. **2** used dishes etc. for washing.

wash-out n. colloq. complete failure, non-event.

washroom n. esp. *US* public toilet.

washstand n. piece of furniture to hold a basin, jug, soap, etc.

washy adj. (**-ier**, **-iest**) **1** too watery or weak. **2** lacking vigour or intensity. □ **washily** adv. **washiness** n.

wasn't /ˈwɒz(ə)nt/ contr. was not.

Wasp /wɒsp/ n. (also **WASP**) *US* usu. derog. middle-class American White Protestant. [White Anglo-Saxon Protestant]

wasp /wɒsp/ n. stinging insect with black and yellow stripes. [Old English]

waspish adj. irritable, snappish.

wasp-waist n. very slender waist.

related to WHOLE]

wassail /ˈwɒseɪl, ˈs(ə)l/ *archaic* —n. festive occasion; drinking-bout. —v. make merry. [Old Norse *ves heill* be in health]

wastage /ˈweɪstɪdʒ/ n. **1** amount wasted. **2** loss by use, wear, or leakage. **3** (also **natural wastage**) loss of employees other than by redundancy.

waste —v. (**-ting**) **1** use to no purpose or with inadequate result or extravagantly. **2** fail to use (*esp.* an opportunity). **3** (often foll. by *on*) **a** give (advice etc.) without effect. **b** (often in *passive*) fail to be appreciated or used properly (*she was wasted on him; feel wasted in this job*). **4** wear gradually away; wane. **5** devastate. —adj. **1** superfluous; no longer needed. **2** not inhabited or cultivated. **3** waste material. —n. **1** act of wasting. **2** waste material. **3** waste region. **4** being used up; diminution by wear. **5** = WASTE PIPE. □ **go** (or **run**) **to waste** be wasted. [Latin: related to VAST]

waste disposal unit n. device fitted to a sink etc. for disposing of household waste.

wasteful adj. **1** extravagant. **2** causing or showing waste. □ **wastefully** adv.

wasteland n. **1** unproductive or useless area of land. **2** place or time considered spiritually or intellectually barren.

waste paper n. used or valueless paper.

waste-paper basket n. receptacle for waste paper.

waste pipe n. pipe to carry off waste material.

waste product n. useless by-product of manufacture or of an organism.

waster n. **1** wasteful person. **2** colloq. wastrel.

wastrel /ˈweɪstr(ə)l/ n. good-for-nothing person.

watch /wɒtʃ/ —v. **1** keep the eyes fixed on. **2** keep under observation; follow observantly. **3** (often foll. by *for*) be in an alert state; be vigilant. **4** (foll. by *over*) look after; take care of. —n. **1** small portable timepiece for carrying on the wrist or in a pocket. **2** state of alert or constant observation or attention. **3** *Naut.* **a** usu. four-hour spell of duty. **b** (in full **starboard** or **port watch**) each of the halves into which a ship's crew is divided to take alternate watches. **4** *hist.* watchman or watchmen. □ **on the watch for** waiting for (an anticipated occurrence). **watch it** (or **oneself**) colloq. be careful. **watch for** waiting for. □ **watcher** n. [Old English: related to WAKE]

watchdog *n.* **1** dog guarding property etc. **2** person or body monitoring others' rights etc.

watchful *adj.* **1** accustomed to watching, alert. **2** on the watch. □ **watchfully** *adv.* **watchfulness** *n.*

watching brief *n.* brief of a barrister who follows a case for a client not directly concerned.

watchmaker *n.* person who makes and repairs watches and clocks.

watchman *n.* man employed to look after an empty building etc. at night.

watch-night service *n.* religious service held on the last night of the year.

watch-tower *n.* tower for keeping watch from.

watchword *n.* phrase summarizing a guiding principle.

water /ˈwɔːtə(r)/ — *n.* **1** colourless transparent liquid compound of oxygen and hydrogen. **2** liquid consisting chiefly of this and found in seas and rivers, in rain, and in secretions of organisms. **3** expanse of water; a sea, lake, river, etc. **4** (in *pl.*) part of a sea or river. **5** (often as **the waters**) mineral water at a spa etc. **6** state of a tide. **7** solution of a specified substance in water (*lavender-water*). **8** transparency and brilliance of a gem. **9** (*attrib.*) found in or near water. **b** of, for, or worked by water. **c** involving, using, or yielding water. **10** (usu. in *pl.*) amniotic fluid, released during labour. — *v.* **1** sprinkle or soak with water. **2** supply (a plant) with water. **3** give water to (an animal) **4** secrete water. **5** (as **watered** *adj.*) (of silk etc.) having irregular wavy glossy markings. **6** take in a supply of water. □ **by water** using a ship etc. for transport. **like water** in great quantity, profusely. **make one's mouth water** cause one's saliva to flow, stimulate one's appetite or anticipation. **of the first water** of the finest quality or extreme degree. **water down 1** dilute. **2** make less forceful or horrifying. **water under the bridge** past events accepted as irrevocable. [Old English]

Water-bearer var. of Water-carrier.

water-bed *n.* mattress filled with water.

water-biscuit *n.* thin crisp unsweetened biscuit.

water-buffalo *n.* common domestic Indian buffalo.

water bus *n.* boat carrying passengers on a regular run on a river, lake, etc.

water-cannon *n.* device using a jet of water to disperse a crowd etc.

Water-carrier *n.* (also Water-bearer) (prec. by *the*) zodiacal sign or constellation Aquarius.

water chestnut *n.* corm from a sedge, used in Chinese cookery.

water-clock *n.* clock measuring time by the flow of water.

water-closet *n.* lavatory that can be flushed.

water-colour *n.* (*US* water-color) **1** artists' paint made of pigment to be diluted with water and not oil. **2** picture painted with this. **3** art of painting with water-colours. □ **water-colourist** *n.*

water-cooled *adj.* cooled by the circulation of water.

watercourse *n.* **1** brook or stream. **2** bed of this.

watercress *n.* pungent cress growing in running water and used in salad.

water-diviner *n.* dowser.

waterfall *n.* stream flowing over a precipice or down a steep hillside.

waterfowl *n.* (usu. collect. as *pl.*) birds frequenting water.

waterfront *n.* part of a town adjoining a river etc.

water-glass *n.* solution of sodium or potassium silicate used esp. for preserving eggs.

water-hammer *n.* knocking noise in a water-pipe when a tap is suddenly turned off.

water-hole *n.* shallow depression in which water collects.

water-ice *n.* flavoured and frozen water and sugar etc.

watering-can *n.* portable container with a long spout, for watering plants.

watering-hole *n.* **1** = WATERING-PLACE 1. **2** *slang* bar.

watering-place *n.* **1** pool from which animals regularly drink. **2** spa or seaside resort.

water jump *n.* jump over water in a steeplechase etc.

water-level *n.* **1 a** surface of the water in a reservoir etc. **b** height of this. **2** level in a reservoir etc. **b** height of this. **2** level below which the ground is saturated with water. **3** level using water to determine the horizontal.

water lily *n.* aquatic plant with floating leaves and flowers.

water-line *n.* line along which the surface of water touches a ship's side.

waterlogged *adj.* saturated or filled with water.

Waterloo /ˌwɔːtəˈluː/ *n.* decisive defeat or contest. [*Waterloo* in Belgium, where Napoleon was defeated]

water main *n.* main pipe in a water-supply system.

waterman *n.* **1** boatman plying for hire. **2** oarsman as regards skill in keeping the boat balanced.

watermark —n. faint design in some paper identifying the maker etc. —v. mark with this.

water-meadow n. meadow periodically flooded by a stream.

water melon n. large dark-green melon with red pulp and watery juice.

water-mill n. mill worked by a water-wheel.

water-pistol n. toy pistol shooting a jet of water.

water polo n. game played by swimmers, with a ball like a football.

water-power n. mechanical force derived from the weight or motion of water.

waterproof –adj. impervious to water. —n. waterproof garment or material. —v. make waterproof.

water-rat n. = WATER-VOLE.

water-rate n. charge made for the use of the public water-supply.

watershed n. 1 line of separation between waters flowing to different rivers, basins, etc. 2 turning-point in affairs. [from *shed* ridge]

waterside n. edge of a sea, lake, or river.

water-ski —n. each of a pair of skis for skimming the surface of the water when towed by a motor boat. —v. travel on water-skis. □ **water-skier** n.

water-softener n. apparatus for softening hard water.

waterspout n. gyrating column of water and spray between sea and cloud.

water table n. = WATER-LEVEL 2.

watertight adj. 1 closely fastened or fitted so as to prevent the passage of water. 2 (of an argument etc.) unassailable.

water-tower n. tower with an elevated tank to give pressure for distributing water.

water-vole n. aquatic vole.

waterway n. navigable channel.

water-wheel n. wheel driven by water to work machinery, or to raise water.

water-wings n.pl. inflated floats fixed on the arms of a person learning to swim.

waterworks n. 1 establishment for managing a water-supply. 2 colloq. shedding of tears. 3 colloq. urinary system.

watery adj. 1 containing too much water. 2 too thin in consistency. 3 of or consisting of water. 4 vapid, uninteresting. 5 (of colour) pale. 6 (of the sun, moon, or sky) rainy-looking. 7 (of eyes) moist; tearful. □ **wateriness** n.

watt /wɒt/ n. SI unit of power; equivalent to one joule per second, corresponding to the rate of energy in an electric circuit where the potential difference is

one volt and the current one ampere. [*Watt*, name of an engineer]

wattage n. amount of electrical power expressed in watts.

watt-hour n. energy used when one watt is applied for one hour.

wattle¹ /wɒt(ə)l/ n. 1 structure of interlaced rods and golden flowers used as the national emblem. [Old English]

wattle² /wɒt(ə)l/ n. fleshy appendage on the head or throat of a turkey or other birds. [origin unknown]

wattle and daub n. network of rods and twigs plastered with clay or mud as a building material.

wave —v. (-ving) 1 a (often foll. by *to*) move a hand etc. to and fro in greeting or as a signal. b move (a hand etc.) in this way. 2 a show a sinuous or sweeping motion as of a flag, tree, corn, etc. in the wind. b impart a *waving* motion to. 3 direct (a person) by waving (*waved them away*; *waved them to follow*). 4 express (a greeting etc.) by waving. 5 give an undulating form to (hair etc.), 6 (of hair etc.) have such a form.—n. 1 ridge of water between two depressions. 2 long body of water curling into an arch and breaking on the shore. 3 thing compared to this, e.g. a body of persons in one of successive advancing groups. 4 gesture of waving. 5 a process of waving the hair. b undulating form produced by this. 6 temporary occurrence or increase of a condition or influence (*wave of enthusiasm*; *heat wave*). 7 Physics a disturbance of the particles of esp. a fluid medium for the propagation or direction of motion, heat, light, sound, etc. b single curve in this motion. 8 undulating line or outline. □ **make waves** colloq. cause trouble. **wave aside** dismiss as intrusive or irrelevant. **wave down** wave to (a vehicle or driver) to stop. [Old English]

waveband n. range of radio wavelengths between certain limits.

wave-form n. Physics curve showing the shape of a wave at a given time.

wavelength n. 1 distance between successive crests of a wave. 2 this as a distinctive feature of radio waves from a transmitter. 3 colloq. particular mode or range of thought.

wavelet n. small wave.

wave machine n. device at a swimming-pool producing waves.

waver v. 1 be or become unsteady; begin to give way. 2 be irresolute. 3 (of a light) flicker. [Old Norse: related to WAVE]

wavy *adj.* (-ier, -iest) having waves or alternate contrary curves. □ **waviness** *n.*

wax[1] —*n.* **1** sticky plastic yellowish substance secreted by bees as the material of honeycomb. **2** this bleached and purified, used for candles, modelling, etc. **3** any similar substance, e.g. the yellow substance secreted by the ear. —*v.* **1** cover or treat with wax. **2** remove unwanted hair from (legs etc.) using wax. □ **waxy** *adj.* (-ier, -iest) [Old English]

wax[2] *v.* **1** (of the moon) increase in apparent size. **2** become larger or stronger. **3** pass into a specified state or mood (*wax lyrical*). □ **wax and wane** undergo alternate increases and decreases. [Old English]

waxen *adj.* **1** smooth or pale like wax. **2** *archaic* made of wax.

waxwing *n.* any of various birds with tips like red sealing-wax to some wing-feathers.

waxwork *n.* **1** object, esp. a lifelike dummy, modelled in wax. **2** (in *pl.*) exhibition of wax dummies.

way —*n.* **1** road, track, path, etc., for passing along. **2** course or route for reaching a place (*asked the way to London; the way out*). **3** method or plan for attaining an object. **4** style, manner (*I like the way you dress*). **5** person's chosen or habitual course of action. **6** normal course of events (*that is always the way*). **7** travelling distance; length traversed or to be traversed. **8** unimpeded opportunity or space to advance (*make way*). **9** advance in some direction; impetus, progress (*under way*). **10** being engaged in movement from place to place; time spent in this (*on the way home*). **11** specified direction (*step this way*). **12** *colloq.* scope or range. **13** line of occupation or business. **14** specified condition or state (*is useful in some way*). **15** respect (*is useful in some ways*). **16** (in *pl.*) part into which a thing is divided (*split in three ways*). **17** (in *pl.*) structure of timber etc. down which a new ship is launched. —*adv. colloq.* far (*way off*). □ **by the way** incidentally. **by way of 1** as a form of. **2** passing through. **come one's way** become available to one. **get out of the way** stop obstructing a person. **go out of one's way** make a special effort. **in a way** to some extent. **in the (or one's) way** forming an obstruction. **lead the way** act as guide or leader. **look the other way** ignore what one should notice. **on the (or one's) way 1** in the course of a journey etc. **2** having progressed. **3** *colloq.* (of a child) conceived but not yet born. **on the way out** *colloq.* going out of fashion or favour. **out of the way 1** no longer an obstacle. **2** disposed of. **3** unusual. **4** (of a place) remote. [Old English]

way back *adv. colloq.* long ago.

waybill *n.* list of passengers or parcels on a vehicle.

wayfarer *n.* traveller, esp. on foot. □ **wayfaring** *n. & adj.*

waylay *v.* (*past* and *past part.* **waylaid**) **1** lie in wait for. **2** stop to talk to or rob.

way of life *n.* principles or habits governing all one's actions etc.

way-out *adj. colloq.* unusual; eccentric.

-ways *suffix* forming adjectives and adverbs of direction or manner (*sideways*).

ways and means *n.pl.* **1** methods of achieving something. **2** methods of raising government revenue.

wayside *n.* **1** side of a road. **2** land at the side of a road.

wayward *adj.* childishly self-willed; capricious. □ **waywardness** *n.* [from AWAY, -WARD]

Wb *abbr.* weber(s).

WC *abbr.* **1** water-closet. **2** West Central.

W/Cdr. *abbr.* wing commander.

we /wiː, wɪ/ *pron.* (*obj.* **us**; *poss.* **our**, **ours**) **1** *pl.* of I[2]. **2** used for or by a royal person in a proclamation etc. or by an editor etc. in a formal context. [Old English]

WEA *abbr.* Workers' Educational Association.

weak *adj.* **1** deficient in strength, power, vigour, resolution, or number. **2** unconvincing. **3** *Gram.* (of a verb) forming inflections by the addition of a suffix to the stem. □ **weakish** *adj.* [Old Norse]

weaken *v.* make or become weak or weaker.

weak-kneed *adj. colloq.* lacking resolution.

weakling *n.* feeble person or animal.

weakly —*adv.* in a weak manner. —*adj.* (-ier, -iest) sickly, not robust.

weak-minded *adj.* **1** mentally deficient. **2** lacking in resolution.

weak moment *n.* time when one is unusually compliant or susceptible.

weakness *n.* **1** being weak. **2** weak point. **3** (foll. by *for*) self-indulgent liking (*weakness for chocolate*).

weak point *n.* (also **weak spot**) **1** place where defences are assailable. **2** flaw in an argument or character or in resistance to temptation.

weal[1] —*n.* ridge raised on the flesh by a stroke of a rod or whip. —*v.* mark with a weal. [var. of WALE]

weal[2] *n. literary* welfare. [Old English]

wealth /welθ/ n. 1 riches. 2 being rich. 3 (foll. by *of*) abundance. [Old English]

wealthy adj. (-ier, -iest) having an abundance, esp. of money.

wean v. 1 accustom (an infant or other young mammal) to food other than (esp. its mother's) milk. 2 (often foll. by *from*, *away from*) disengage (from a habit etc.) by enforced discontinuance. [Old English]

weapon /ˈwepən/ n. 1 thing designed, used, or usable for inflicting bodily harm. 2 means for gaining the advantage in a conflict. [Old English]

weaponry n. weapons collectively.

wear /weə(r)/ -v. (*past* **wore**; *past part.* **worn**) 1 have on one's person as clothing or an ornament etc. 2 exhibit or present (a facial expression etc.) (*wore a frown*). 3 *colloq.* (usu. with *neg.*) toler-ate. 4 (often foll. by *away*, *down*) a injure the surface of, or partly obliterate or alter, by rubbing, stress, or use. b undergo such injury or change. 5 (foll. by *off*, *away*) rub or be rubbed off. 6 make (a hole etc.) by constant rubbing or dripping etc. 7 (often foll. by *out*) exhaust. 8 (foll. by *down*) overcome by persistence. 9 (foll. by *well* etc.) endure continued use or life. 10 (of time) pass, esp. tediously. 11 (of a ship) fly (a flag). -n. 1 wearing or being worn. 2 things worn; fashionable or suitable clothing (*sportswear*; *footwear*). 3 (in full **wear and tear**) damage from continuous use. □ **wear one's heart on one's sleeve** show one's feelings openly. **wear off** lose effectiveness or intensity. **wear out** 1 use or be used until useless. 2 tire or be tired out. **wear thin** (of patience, excuses, etc.) begin to fail. **wear the trousers** see TROUSERS. □ **wearer** n. [Old English]

wearisome /ˈwɪərɪsəm/ adj. tedious; tiring by monotony or length.

weary /ˈwɪərɪ/ -adj. (-ier, -iest) 1 very tired after exertion or endurance. 2 (foll. by *of*) no longer interested in, tired of. 3 tiring, tedious. -v. (-ies, -ied) make or grow weary. □ **wearily** adv. **weariness** n. [Old English]

weasel /ˈwiːz(ə)l/ n. small flesh-eating mammal related to the stoat and ferret. [Old English]

weasel word n. (usu. in pl.) word that is intentionally ambiguous or mislead-ing.

weather /ˈweðə(r)/ -n. 1 state of the atmosphere at a place and time as re-gards heat, cloudiness, dryness, sun-shine, wind, and rain etc. 2 (*attrib.*) *Naut.* windward. -v. 1 expose to or affect by atmospheric changes; season (wood). 2 be discoloured or worn in this way. 3 a come safely through (a storm). b survive (a difficult period etc.). 4 get to the windward of (a cape etc.). □ **keep a weather eye open** be watchful. **make heavy weather of** *colloq.* exaggerate the difficulty presented by. **under the weather** *colloq.* indisposed. [Old English]

weather-beaten adj. affected by ex-posure to the weather.

weatherboard n. 1 sloping board attached to the bottom of an outside door to keep out the rain etc. 2 each of a series of overlapping horizontal boards on a wall. □ **weatherboarding** n. (in sense 2 of n.).

weathercock n. 1 weather-vane in the form of a cock. 2 inconstant person.

weather forecast n. assessment of likely weather.

weatherman n. meteorologist, esp. one who broadcasts a weather forecast.

weatherproof adj. resistant to the effects of bad weather, esp. rain.

weather-vane n. 1 revolving pointer on a church spire etc. to show the direction of the wind. 2 inconstant per-son.

weave[1] -v. (-ving; *past* **wove**; *past part.* **woven** or **wove**) 1 a form (fabric) by interlacing long threads in two direc-tions. b form (thread) into fabric in this way. 2 make fabric in this way. 3 a (foll. by *into*) make (facts etc.) into a story or connected whole. b make (a story) in this way. -n. style of weaving. [Old English]

weave[2] v. (-ving) move repeatedly from side to side; take an intricate course to avoid obstructions. □ **get weaving** *slang* begin action; hurry. [Old Norse: related to WAVE]

weaver n. 1 person who weaves fabric. 2 (in full **weaver-bird**) tropical bird building elaborately woven nests.

web n. 1 a woven fabric. b amount woven in one piece. 2 complex series (*web of lies*). 3 cobweb; gossamer, or a similar product of a spinning creature. 4 membrane between the toes of a swim-ming animal or bird. 5 large roll of paper used in printing. 6 thin flat connecting part in machinery etc. □ **webbed** adj. [Old English]

webbing n. strong narrow closely-woven fabric used for belts etc.

weber /ˈveɪbə(r)/ n. the SI unit of mag-netic flux. [*Weber*, name of a physicist]

web-footed adj. having the toes con-nected by webs.

Wed. abbr. (also **Weds.**) Wednesday.

wed v. (-dd-; *past and past part.* **wedded** or **wed**) 1 usu. *formal or literary* marry. 2 unite. 3 (as **wedded** adj.) of or in

marriage (*wedded bliss*). **4** (as **wedded** *adj.*) (foll. by *to*) obstinately attached or devoted to (a pursuit etc.). [Old English, = pledge]

we'd /wiːd, wɪd/ *contr.* **1** we had. **2** we should; we would.

wedding /ˈwedɪŋ/ *n.* marriage ceremony. [Old English: related to WED]

wedding breakfast *n.* meal etc. between a wedding and departure for the honeymoon.

wedding cake *n.* rich iced cake served at a wedding reception.

wedding ring *n.* ring worn by a married person.

wedge —*n.* **1** piece of tapering wood or metal etc. driven between two objects or parts to secure or separate them. **2** anything resembling a wedge. **3** golf club with a wedge-shaped head. —*v.* (**-ging**) **1** secure or fasten with a wedge. **2** force open or apart with a wedge. **3** (foll. by *in, into*) pack or thrust (a thing or oneself) tightly in or into. □ **thin end of the wedge** *colloq.* thing of little importance in itself, but likely to lead to more serious developments. [Old English]

Wedgwood /ˈwedʒwʊd/ *n. propr.* **1** a kind of fine stoneware usu. with a white cameo design. **2** its characteristic blue colour. [*Wedgwood,* name of a potter]

wedlock /ˈwedlɒk/ *n.* the married state. □ **born in (or out of) wedlock** born of married (or unmarried) parents. [Old English, = marriage vow]

Wednesday /ˈwenzdeɪ/ —*n.* day of the week following Tuesday. —*adv. colloq.* **1** on Wednesdays. **2** (**Wednesdays**) on Wednesdays; each Wednesday. [Old English]

Weds. *abbr.* var. of WED.

wee¹ *adj.* (**weer** /ˈwiːə(r)/; **weest** /ˈwiːɪst/) **1** *esp. Scot.* little. **2** *colloq.* tiny. [Old English]

wee² *n. colloq.* = WEE-WEE.

weed —*n.* **1** wild plant growing where it is not wanted. **2** thin weak-looking person or horse. **3** (prec. by *the*) *slang* **a** marijuana. **b** tobacco. —*v.* **1 a** clear (an area) of weeds. **b** remove unwanted parts from. **2** (foll. by *out*) **a** sort out and remove (inferior or unwanted parts etc.). **b** rid of inferior parts, unwanted members, etc. **3** cut off or uproot weeds. [Old English]

weeds /wiːdz/ *n.pl.* (in full **widow's weeds**) *archaic* deep mourning worn by a widow. [Old English, = garment]

weedy *adj.* (**-ier, -iest**) **1** weak, feeble. **2** having many weeds.

weed-killer *n.* chemical used to destroy weeds.

week *n.* **1** period of seven days reckoned usu. from midnight on Saturday. **2** any period of seven days. **3** the six days between Sundays. **4 a** the five days Monday to Friday. **b** time spent working in this period (*35-hour week; three-day week*). [Old English]

weekday *n.* day other than Sunday or Saturday and Sunday.

weekend *n.* **1** Sunday and Saturday or part of Saturday. **2** this period extended slightly esp. for a holiday or visit etc.

weekender *n.* person who spends the weekend away from home; weekend visitor.

weekly —*adj.* done, produced, or occurring once a week. —*adv.* once a week. —*n.* (*pl.* **-ies**) weekly newspaper or periodical.

weeny /ˈwiːnɪ/ *adj.* (**-ier, -iest**) *colloq.* tiny. [from WEE¹]

weep —*v.* (*past and past part.* **wept**) **1** shed tears. **2** (often foll. by *for*) bewail, lament over. **3 a** be covered with or send forth drops. **b** come or send forth in drops; exude liquid. **4** (as **weeping** *adj.*) (of a tree) having drooping branches. —*n.* spell of weeping. [Old English]

weepie *n. colloq.* sentimental or emotional film, play, etc.

weepy *adj.* (**-ier, -iest**) *colloq.* inclined to weep; tearful.

weevil /ˈwiːvɪl/ *n.* destructive beetle feeding esp. on grain. [Low German]

wee-wee /ˈwiːwiː/ *colloq.* —*n.* **1** act of urinating. **2** urine. —*v.* (**-wees, -weed**) urinate. [origin unknown]

weft *n.* **1** threads woven across a warp to make fabric. **2** yarn for these. **3** thing woven. [Old English: related to WEAVE¹]

weigh /weɪ/ *v.* **1** find the weight of. **2** balance in the hands to guess or as if to guess the weight of. **3** (often foll. by *out*) take a definite weight of (a substance); measure out (a specified weight) (*weigh out the flour; weigh out 6 oz*). **4 a** estimate the relative value, importance, or desirability of. **b** (foll. by *with, against*) compare. **5** be equal to (a specified weight). **6** have (esp. a specified) importance; exert an influence. **7** (often foll. by *on*) be heavy or burdensome (to); be depressing (to). □ **weigh down 1** bring down by exerting weight. **2** be oppressive to. **weigh in** (of a boxer before a contest, or a jockey after a race) be weighed. **weigh in with** *colloq.* advance (an argument etc.) boldly. **weigh out** (of a jockey) be weighed before a race. **weigh up** *colloq.* form an estimate of. **weigh one's words** carefully choose the way one expresses something. [Old English, = carry]

weighbridge n. weighing-machine for vehicles.

weigh-in n. weighing of a boxer before a fight.

weight /wert/ n. 1 force experienced by a body as a result of the earth's gravitation. 2 heaviness of a body regarded as a property of it. 3 a quantitative expression of a body's weight. b scale of such weights (*troy weight*). 4 body of a known weight for use in weighing or weight training. 5 heavy body, esp. as used in a mechanism etc. 6 load or burden. 7 influence, importance. 8 *Athletics* = SHOT 7. □ v. 1 a attach a weight to. b hold down with a weight. 2 (foll. by *with*) impede or burden. □ throw one's weight about (or around) *colloq.* be unpleasantly self-assertive. worth one's weight in gold very useful or helpful. [Old English]

weighting n. extra allowance paid in special cases.

weightless adj. (of a body, esp. in an orbiting spacecraft etc.) not apparently acted on by gravity. □ **weightlessness** n.

weightlifting n. sport of lifting heavy weights. □ **weightlifter** n.

weight training n. physical training using weights.

weighty adj. (-ier, -iest) 1 heavy. 2 momentous. 3 (of utterances etc.) deserving consideration. 4 influential, authoritative. □ **weightily** adv. **weightiness** n.

weir /wɪə(r)/ n. dam across a river to raise the level of water upstream or regulate its flow. [Old English]

weird adj. 1 uncanny, supernatural. 2 *colloq.* queer, incomprehensible. □ **weirdly** adv. **weirdness** n. [Old English *wyrd* destiny]

weirdo /ˈwɪədəʊ/ n. (pl. -s) *colloq* odd or eccentric person.

Welch var. of WELSH.

welcome /ˈwelkəm/ —n. act of greeting or receiving gladly; kind or glad reception. —*int.* expressing such a greeting. —v. 1 (-ming) receive with a welcome. —adj. 1 that one receives with pleasure (*welcome guest, welcome news*). 2 (foll. by to, or to + infin.) cordially allowed or invited (*you are welcome to use my car*). □ **make welcome** receive hospitably. **you are welcome** there is no need for thanks. [Old English]

weld —v. 1 a hammer or press (pieces of iron or other metal usu. heated but not melted) into one piece. b join by fusion with an electric arc etc. c form by welding into some article. 2 fashion into an effectual or homogeneous whole. —n.

welded joint. □ **welder** n. [alteration of WELL², probably influenced by the form *welled*]

welfare /ˈwelfeə(r)/ n. 1 well-being, happiness; health and prosperity (of a person or community etc.). 2 (Welfare) a welfare centre or office. b financial support given by the State. [from WELL¹, FARE]

welfare state n. 1 system whereby the State undertakes to protect the health and well-being of its citizens by means of grants, pensions, etc. 2 country practising this system.

welfare work n. organized effort for the welfare of the poor, disabled, etc.

welkin n. *poet.* sky. [Old English, = cloud]

well¹ —adv. (better, best) 1 in a satisfactory way (*works well*). 2 with some distinction (*plays the piano well*). 3 in a kind way (*treated me well*). 4 thoroughly, carefully (*polish it well*). 5 with heartiness or approval (*speak well of*). 6 probably, reasonably (*you may well be right*). 7 to a considerable extent (*is well over forty*). —adj. (better, best) 1 (usu. *predic.*) in good health. 2 (*predic.*) a in a satisfactory state or position. b advisable (*it would be well to enquire*). —*int.* expressing surprise, resignation, etc. or used to introduce needless change or disturbance. □ **well alone** avoid needless change or disturbance. **well away** 1 having made completely satisfactory progress. 2 *colloq.* fast asleep or drunk. **well done!** expressing praise for something done. **well worth** certainly worth. [Old English]

well² —n. 1 shaft sunk into the ground to obtain water, oil, etc. 2 enclosed space like a well-shaft, e.g. in the middle of a building for stairs or a lift, or for light or ventilation. 3 (foll. by *of*) source. 4 (in *pl.*) spa. 5 = INK-WELL. 6 *archaic* water-spring. 7 railed space in a lawcourt. —v. (foll. by *out, up*) spring as from a fountain. [Old English]

we'll /wiːl, wɪl/ *contr.* we shall: we will.

well-adjusted adj. 1 mentally and emotionally stable. 2 in a good state of adjustment.

well-advised adj. (usu. foll. by *to* + infin.) prudent.

well-appointed adj. having all the necessary equipment.

well-attended adj. attended by a large number of people.

well-balanced adj. sane, sensible.

well-behaved adj. habitually behaving well.

well-being n. state of being contented, healthy, etc.

well-born adj. of noble family.

well-bred *adj.* having or showing good breeding or manners.

well-built *adj.* big, strong, and well-proportioned.

well-connected *adj.* associated, esp. by birth, with persons of good social position.

well-disposed *adj.* (often foll. by *towards*) friendly or sympathetic.

well-dressed *adj.* fashionably smart.

well-earned *adj.* fully deserved.

well-founded *adj.* (of suspicions etc.) based on good evidence.

well-groomed *adj.* with carefully tended hair, clothes, etc.

well-head *n.* source.

well-heeled *adj. colloq.* wealthy.

wellies /'weliz/ *n.pl. colloq.* wellingtons. [abbreviation]

well-informed *adj.* having much knowledge or information about a subject.

wellington /'welɪŋt(ə)n/ *n.* (in full **wellington boot**) waterproof boot usu. reaching the knee. [Duke of *Wellington*]

well-intentioned *adj.* having or showing good intentions.

well-judged *adj.* opportunely, skilfully, or discreetly done.

well-kept *adj.* kept in good order or condition.

well-known *adj.* known to many.

well-made *adj.* 1 strongly manufactured. 2 having a good build.

well-mannered *adj.* having good manners.

well-meaning *adj.* (also **well-meant**) well-intentioned (but ineffective).

wellnigh *adv.* almost (*wellnigh impossible*).

well off *adj.* (also **well-off**) 1 having plenty of money. 2 in a fortunate situation.

well-oiled *adj. colloq.* very drunk.

well-paid *adj.* 1 (of a job) that pays well. 2 (of a person) amply rewarded for a job.

well-preserved *adj.* 1 in good condition. 2 (of an old person) showing little sign of age.

well-read *adj.* knowledgeable through much reading.

well-received *adj.* welcomed; favourably received.

well-rounded *adj.* complete and symmetrical.

well-spoken *adj.* articulate or refined in speech.

well-spring *n.* = WELL-HEAD.

well-to-do *adj.* prosperous.

well-tried *adj.* often tested with good results.

well-trodden *adj.* much frequented.

well-wisher *n.* person who wishes one well.

well-worn *adj.* 1 much worn by use. 2 (of a phrase etc.) trite.

Welsh *adj.* of or relating to Wales or its people or language. —*n.* 1 the Celtic language of Wales. 2 the people of Wales. [Old English, ultimately from Latin *Volcae*, name of a Celtic people]

Welsh *v.* (also **welch**) 1 (of a loser of a bet, esp. a bookmaker) decamp without paying. 2 evade an obligation. 3 (foll. by *on*) **a** fail to carry out a promise to (a person). **b** fail to honour (an obligation). [origin unknown]

Welshman *n.* man who is Welsh by birth or descent.

Welsh rabbit *n.* (also, by folk etymology, **Welsh rarebit**) dish of melted cheese etc. on toast.

Welshwoman *n.* woman who is Welsh by birth or descent.

welt —*n.* 1 leather rim sewn round the edge of a shoe-upper for the sole to be attached to. 2 = WEAL¹. 3 ribbed or reinforced border of a garment. 4 heavy blow. —*v.* 1 provide with a welt. 2 raise weals on; thrash. [origin unknown]

welter¹ —*v.* 1 roll, wallow. 2 (foll. by *in*) lie prostrate or be soaked in. —*n.* 1 general confusion. 2 (foll. by *of*) disorderly mixture or contrast. [Low German or Dutch]

welter² *n.* heavy rider or boxer. [origin unknown]

welterweight *n.* 1 weight in certain sports intermediate between lightweight and middleweight, in the amateur boxing scale 63.5–67 kg. 2 sportsman of this weight.

wen *n.* benign tumour on the skin, esp. on the scalp. [Old English]

wench *n. joc.* girl or young woman. [abbreviation of *wenchel*, from Old English, = child]

wend *v.* □ **wend one's way** make one's way. [Old English, = turn]

Wendy house /'wendi/ *n.* children's small houselike tent or structure for playing in. [*Wendy*, name of a character in Barrie's *Peter Pan*]

went *past of* GO¹.

wept *past of* WEEP.

were 2nd sing. past, pl. past, and past subjunctive of BE.

we're /wɪə(r)/ *contr.* we are.

weren't /wɜːnt/ *contr.* were not.

werewolf /'weəwʊlf/ *n.* (pl. **-wolves**) mythical being who at times changes from a person to a wolf. [Old English]

Wesleyan /'wezlɪən/ —*adj.* of or relating to a Protestant denomination founded by John Wesley. —*n.* member of this denomination.

west —*n.* **1 a** a point of the horizon where the sun sets at the equinoxes. **b** compass point corresponding to this. **c** direction in which this lies. **2** (usu. the West) **a** European civilization. **b** States of western Europe and N. America. **c** western part of a country, town, etc. —*adj.* **1** towards, at, near, or facing the west. **2** from the west (*west wind*). —*adv.* **1** towards, at, or near the west. **2** (foll. by *of*) further west than. □ **go west** *slang* be killed or destroyed etc. to the west (often followed by *of*) in a westerly direction. [Old English]

westbound *adj.* travelling or leading westwards.

West Country *n.* south-western England.

West End *n.* main entertainment and shopping area of London.

westering *adj.* (of the sun) nearing the west.

westerly —*adj.* & *adv.* **1** in a western position or direction. **2** (of a wind) from the west. —*n.* (*pl.* -*ies*) such a wind.

western —*adj.* of or in the west. —*n.* film or novel about cowboys in western North America. □ **westernmost** *adj.*

westerner *n.* native or inhabitant of the west.

westernize *v.* (also -**ise**) (-**zing** or -**sing**) influence with, or convert to, the ideas and customs etc. of the West. □ **Westernization** *n.*

West Indian *n.* **1** native or national of the West Indies. **2** person of West Indian descent.

west-north-west *n.* point or direction midway between west and north-west.

West Side *n.* US western part of Manhattan.

west-south-west *n.* point or direction midway between west and south-west.

westward /'westwəd/ —*adj.* & *adv.* (also **westwards**) towards the west. —*n.* westward direction or region.

wet —*adj.* (**wetter, wettest**) **1** soaked or covered with water or other liquid. **2** (of the weather etc.) rainy. **3** (of paint etc.) not yet dried. **4** used with water (*wet shampoo*). **5** *colloq.* feeble, inept. —*v.* (-*tt-*; *past* and *past part.* **wet** or **wetted**) **1** make wet. **2** urinate in or on (*wet the bed*). **b** *refl.* urinate involuntarily. —*n.* **1** liquid that wets something. **2** rainy weather. **3** *colloq.* feeble or inept person. **4** *colloq.* Conservative with liberal tendencies. **5** *colloq.* drink. □ **wet behind the ears** *colloq.* immature, inexperienced. **wet through** (or **to the skin**) with one's clothes soaked. □ **wetly** *adv.* **wetness** *n.* [Old English]

wet blanket *n. colloq.* gloomy person hindering others' enjoyment.

wet dream *n.* erotic dream with the involuntary ejaculation of semen.

wether /'weðə(r)/ *n.* castrated ram. [Old English]

wetland *n.* (often in *pl.*) swamps and other damp areas of land.

wet-nurse —*n.* woman employed to suckle another's child. —*v.* **1** act as a wet-nurse to. **2** *colloq.* treat as if helpless.

wet suit *n.* rubber garment worn by skin-divers etc. to keep warm.

we've /wiːv/ *contr.* we have.

Wg. Cdr. *abbr.* wing commander.

whack *colloq.* —*v.* **1** strike or beat forcefully. **2** (as **whacked** *adj.*) tired out. —*n.* **1** sharp or resounding blow. **2** *slang* share. □ **have a whack at** *slang* attempt. [imitative]

whacking *colloq.* —*adj.* very large. —*adv.* very. □

whale —*n.* (*pl.* same or -**s**) very large marine mammal with a streamlined body and horizontal tail. —*v.* (-**ling**) hunt whales. □ **a whale of a** *colloq.* an exceedingly good or fine etc. [Old English]

whalebone *n.* elastic horny substance in the upper jaw of some whales.

whale-oil *n.* oil from the blubber of whales.

whaler *n.* whaling ship or seaman.

wham *int. colloq.* expressing forcible impact. [imitative]

wharf /wɔːf/ —*n.* (*pl.* **wharves** /wɔːvz/ or -**s**) quayside area to which a ship may be moored to load and unload. —*v.* **1** moor (a ship) at a wharf. **2** store (goods) on a wharf. [Old English]

wharfage *n.* **1** accommodation at a wharf. **2** fee for this.

what /wɒt/ —*interrog. adj.* **1** asking for a choice from an indefinite number or for a statement of amount, number, or kind (*what books have you read?*). **2** *colloq.* = WHICH *interrog. adj.* (*what book have you chosen?*). —*adj.* (usu. in an exclamation) how great or remarkable (*what luck!*). —*rel. adj.* the or any ... that (*will give you what help I can*). —*pron.* (corresponding to the functions of the *adj.*) **1** what thing or things? (*what is your name?; I don't know what you mean*). **2** (asking for a remark to be repeated) = WHAT *did you say?* **3** how much (*what you must have suffered*). **4** (as *rel. pron.*) that or those which; a or the or any thing which (*what followed was worse; tell me what you think*). —*adv.* to what extent (*what does it matter?*). □ **what about** what is the news or your opinion of. **what-d'you-call-it** *colloq.* substitute for a name not recalled. **what ever** what at all or in any way (*what*

ever do you mean?) (see also WHAT-EVER). **what** for *colloq.* **1** for what reason? **2** severe reprimand (esp. *give a person what for*). **what have you** (prec. by *or* or *and*) *colloq.* anything else similar. **what not** (prec. by *and*) other similar things. **what's-his** (or -*her* or -*its*) -**name** *colloq.* substitute for a name not recalled. **what's what** *colloq.* what is useful or important etc. **what with** *colloq.* because of (usu. several things). [Old English]

whatever /wɒt'evə(r)/ *adj.* & *pron.* **1** = WHAT (in relative uses) with the emphasis on indefiniteness (*lend me whatever you can; whatever money you have*). **2** though anything (*we are safe whatever happens*). **3** (with *neg.* or *interrog.*) at all; of any kind (*there is no doubt whatever*).

whatnot *n. colloq.* indefinite or trivial thing.

whatsoever /ˌwɒtsəʊ'evə(r)/ *adj.* & *pron.* = WHATEVER.

wheat *n.* **1** cereal plant bearing dense four-sided seed-spikes. **2** its grain, used in making flour etc. [Old English]

wheatear *n.* small migratory bird. [related to WHITE, ARSE]

wheaten *adj.* made of wheat.

wheat germ *n.* embryo of the wheat grain, extracted as a source of vitamins.

wheatmeal *n.* flour made from wheat with some of the bran and germ removed.

wheedle /'wiːd(ə)l/ *v.* (-**ling**) **1** coax by flattery or endearments. **2** (foll. by *out*) get (a thing) out of a person or cheat (a person) out of a thing by wheedling. [origin uncertain]

wheel —*n.* **1** circular frame or disc which revolves on an axle and is used for vehicular or other mechanical motion. **2** wheel-like thing. **3** motion as of a wheel, esp. the movement of a line of soldiers with one end as a pivot. **4** (in *pl.*) *slang* car. **5** = STEERING-WHEEL. —*v.* **1 a** turn on an axis or pivot. **b** swing round in line with one end as a pivot. **2 a** (often foll. by *about*, *round*) change direction or face another way. **b** cause to do this. **3** push or pull (a wheeled thing, or its load or occupant). **4** go in circles or curves. □ **at the wheel 1** driving a vehicle. **2** directing a ship. **3** in control. **on wheels** (or oiled wheels) smoothly. **wheel and deal** engage in political or commercial scheming. **wheels within wheels 1** intricate machinery. **2** *colloq.* indirect or secret agencies. □ **wheeled** *adj.* (also in *comb.*). [Old English]

wheelbarrow *n.* small handcart with one wheel and two shafts.

wheelbase *n.* distance between the axles of a vehicle.

wheelchair *n.* chair on wheels for an invalid or disabled person.

wheel-clamp *n.* = CLAMP[1] *n.* 2.

-**wheeler** *comb. form* vehicle with a specified number of wheels (*three-wheeler*).

wheeler-dealer *n.* person who wheels and deals.

wheel-house *n.* steersman's shelter.

wheelie *n. slang* stunt of riding a bicycle or motor cycle with the front wheel off the ground.

wheel-spin *n.* rotation of a vehicle's wheels without traction.

wheelwright *n.* person who makes or repairs wheels.

wheeze —*v.* (-**zing**) **1** breathe with an audible whistling sound. **2** utter with this sound. —*n.* **1** sound of wheezing. **2** *colloq.* clever scheme. □ **wheezy** *adj.* (-**ier**, -**iest**). **wheezily** *adv.* **wheeziness** *n.* [probably from Old Norse, = hiss]

whelk *n.* marine mollusc with a spiral shell. [Old English]

whelm *v. poet.* **1** engulf. **2** crush with weight. [Old English]

whelp —*n.* **1** young dog; puppy. **2** *archaic* cub. **3** ill-mannered child or youth. —*v.* (also *absol.*) give birth to (a whelp or whelps or (*derog.*) a child). [Old English]

when —*interrog. adv.* **1** at what time? **2** on what occasion? **3** how soon? —*rel. adv.* (prec. by *time* etc.) at or on which (*there are times when I could cry*). —*conj.* **1** at the or any time that; as soon as (*come when you like; come when ready*). **2** although (*why stand when you could sit?*). **3** after which; and then; but just then (*was nearly asleep when the bell rang*). —*pron.* what time? (*till when can you stay?; since when it has improved*). —*n.* time, occasion (*fixed the where and when*). [Old English]

whence *formal* —*interrog. adv.* from what place? —*conj.* **1** to the place from which (*return whence you came*). **2** (often prec. by *place* etc.). **3** and thence (*whence it follows that*). [Old English; related to WHEN]

■ **Usage** The use of *from whence* rather than simply *whence* (as in *the place from where they came*), though common, is generally considered incorrect.

whenever /wen'evə(r)/ *conj.* & *adv.* **1** at whatever time; on every occasion when. **2** every time that.

whensoever /ˌwensəʊ'evə(r)/ *conj.* & *adv. formal* = WHENEVER.

where /weə(r)/ *—interrog. adv.* **1** in or to what place or position? **2** in what respect? (*where does it concern us?*).*—rel. adv.* (prec. by *place* etc.), in or to which (*places where they meet*).*—conj.* **1** in or to the or any place, direction, or respect in which (*go where you like; tick where applicable*). **2** and there (*reached Crewe, where the car broke down*).*—pron.* what place? (*where do you come from?*).*—n.* place; scene of something (see WHEN *n.*). [Old English]

whereabouts *—interrog. adv.* /ˌweərəˈbaʊts/ approximately where? *—n.* /ˈweərəbaʊts/ (as *sing.* or *pl.*) person's or thing's location.

whereas /weərˈæz/ *conj.* **1** in contrast or comparison with the fact that. **2** (esp. in legal preambles) taking into consideration the fact that.

whereby /weəˈbaɪ/ *conj.* by what or which means.

wherefore *—adv.* for what reason? **2** for which reason.*—n.* see WHY. [from WHERE + FOR]

wherein /weərˈɪn/ *conj. formal* in what or which place or respect.

whereof /weərˈɒv/ *conj. formal* of what or which.

whereupon /ˌweərəˈpɒn/ *conj.* immediately after which.

wherever /weərˈevə(r)/ *—adv.* in or to whatever place. *—conj.* in every place that.

wherewithal /ˈweəwɪðɔːl/ *n. colloq.* money etc. needed for a purpose.

wherry /ˈwerɪ/ *n.* (*pl.* -ies) **1** light rowing-boat usu. for carrying passengers. **2** large light barge. [origin unknown]

whet *v.* (-tt-) **1** sharpen (a tool). **2** stimulate (the appetite or a desire etc.). [Old English]

whether /ˈweðə(r)/ *conj.* introducing the first or both of alternative possibilities (*I doubt whether it matters; I do not know whether they have arrived or not*). □ **whether or no** whether it is so or not. [Old English]

whetstone *n.* tapered stone used with water to sharpen tools.

whew /hwjuː/ *int.* expressing surprise, consternation, or relief. [imitative]

whey /weɪ/ *n.* watery liquid left when milk forms curds. [Old English]

which *—interrog. adj.* asking for choice from a definite set of alternatives (*which John do you mean?; say which book you prefer*).*—rel. adj.* being the one just referred to; and this or these (*ten years, during which time they admitted nothing*).*—interrog. pron.* **1** which person or persons? (*which of you is responsible?*). **2** which thing or things? (*say which you prefer*).*—rel. pron.* (poss.

---

whose, /huːz/) **1** which thing or things, usu. introducing a clause not essential for identification (*the house, which is empty, has been damaged*). **2** used in place of *that* after *in* or *on* (*there is the house in which I was born; that which you have just seen*). [Old English]

whichever /wɪtʃˈevə(r)/ *adj. & pron.* any which (*take whichever you like; whichever you have just seen*).

whiff *n.* **1** puff or breath of air, smoke, etc. **2** smell. **3** (foll. by *of*) trace of scandal etc. **4** small cigar. [imitative]

Whig *n. hist.* member of the British reforming and constitutional party succeeded in the 19th c. by the Liberal Party. □ **Whiggery** *n.* **Whiggish** *adj.* **Whiggism** *n.* [*whiggamer*, *-more*, nickname of 17th-c. Scots rebels]

while *—n.* period of time (*a long while ago; waited a while, all this while*). *—conj.* **1** during the time that; for as long as; at the same time as (*while I was away, the house was burgled; fell asleep while reading*). **2** in spite of the fact that; whereas (*while I want to believe it, I cannot*).*—v.* (-ling) (foll. by *away*) pass (time etc.) in a leisurely or interesting way.*—rel. adv.* by time etc.) during which (*the summer while I was abroad*). □ **between whiles** in the intervals, for a while for some time. **in a while** soon. **the while** in the meantime. **worth while** (or **worth one's while**) worth the time or effort spent. [Old English]

■ **Usage** *Worth while* ('two words') is used only predicatively, as in *thought it worth while to ring the police*, whereas *worthwhile* is used both predicatively and attributively.

whilst /waɪlst/ *adv. & conj.* while. [from WHILE]

whim *n.* **1** sudden fancy; caprice. **2** capriciousness. [origin unknown]

whimper *—v.* make feeble, querulous, or frightened sounds.*—n.* such a sound. [imitative]

whimsical /ˈwɪmzɪk(ə)l/ *adj.* capricious, fantastic. □ **whimsicality** /-ˈkælɪtɪ/ *n.* **whimsically** *adv.*

whimsy /ˈwɪmzɪ/ *n.* (*pl.* -ies) = WHIM.

whin *n.* (in *sing.* or *pl.*) gorse. [Scandinavian]

whinchat *n.* small songbird. [dialectal]

whine *—n.* **1** complaining long-drawn wail as of a dog. **2** similar shrill prolonged sound. **3** querulous tone or complaint.*—v.* (-ning) emit or utter a whine; complain. [Old English]

---

whinge /wɪndʒ/ v. (**-geing** or **-ging**) colloq. whine; grumble peevishly. [Old English]

whinny /ˈwɪni/ —n. (pl. **-ies**) gentle or joyful neigh. —v. (**-ies**, **-ied**) give a whinny. [imitative]

whip —n. 1 lash attached to a stick for urging on animals or punishing etc. 2 **a** member of a political party in Parliament appointed to control its discipline and tactics. **b** whips' written notice requesting or requiring attendance for voting at a division etc., variously underlined according to the degree of urgency (three-line whip). **c** (prec. by the) party discipline and instructions (asked for the Labour whip). 3 dessert made with whipped cream etc. 4 = WHIPPER-IN. —v. (**-pp-**) 1 beat or urge on with a whip. 2 beat (cream or eggs etc.) into a froth. 3 take or move suddenly, unexpectedly, or rapidly (whipped out a knife; whipped behind the door). 4 slang steal. 5 slang a excel. **b** defeat. 6 bind with spirally wound twine. 7 sew with overcast stitches. □ **whip in** bring (hounds) together. **whip on** urge into action. **whip up** excite or stir up. [Low German or Dutch]

whipcord n. tightly twisted cord.

whip hand n. 1 hand that holds the whip (in riding etc.). 2 (usu. prec. by the) advantage or control in a situation.

whiplash n. flexible end of a whip.

whiplash injury n. injury to the neck caused by a jerk of the head, esp. as in a motor accident.

whipper-in /ˌwɪpəˈrɪn/ n. (pl. **whippers-in**) huntsman's assistant who manages the hounds.

whippersnapper /ˈwɪpəˌsnæpə(r)/ n. 1 small child. 2 insignificant but presumptuous person.

whippet /ˈwɪpɪt/ n. crossbred dog of the greyhound type used for racing. [probably from obsolete whippet move briskly, from whip it]

whipping boy n. scapegoat.

whipping-top n. top kept spinning by blows of a lash.

whippoorwill /ˈwɪpʊəwɪl/ n. American nightjar. [imitative]

whip-round n. colloq. informal collection of money among a group of people.

whipstock n. handle of a whip.

whirl —v. 1 swing round and round; revolve rapidly. 2 (foll. by away) convey or go rapidly in a vehicle etc. 3 send or travel swiftly in an orbit or a curve. 4 (of the brain etc.) seem to spin round. —n. 1 whirling movement. 2 state of intense activity (the social whirl). 3 state of confusion (in a whirl). □ **give it a whirl**

colloq. attempt it. [Old Norse, and Low German or Dutch]

whirligig /ˈwɜːlɪɡɪɡ/ n. 1 spinning or whirling toy. 2 merry-go-round. 3 revolving motion.

whirlpool n. powerful circular eddy of water.

whirlwind n. 1 rapidly whirling mass or column of air. 2 (attrib.) very rapid.

whirr —n. continuous rapid buzz or soft clicking sound. —v. (**-rr-**) make this sound. [Scandinavian]

whisk —v. 1 (foll. by away, off) **a** brush with a sweeping movement. **b** take suddenly. 2 whip (cream, eggs, etc.). 3 convey or go (esp. out of sight) lightly or quickly. 4 wave or lightly brandish. —n. 1 whisking action or motion. 2 utensil for whisking eggs or cream etc. 3 bunch of grass, twigs, bristles, etc., for removing dust or flies. [Scandinavian]

whisker n. 1 (usu. in pl.) hair growing on a man's face, esp. on the cheek. 2 each of the bristles on the face of a cat etc. 3 colloq. small distance (within a whisker of). □ **whiskered** adj. **whiskery** adj. [from WHISK]

whisky /ˈwɪski/ n. (Ir. & US **whiskey**) (pl. **-ies** or **-eys**) spirit distilled esp. from malted grain, esp. barley or rye. [abbreviation of usquebaugh from Gaelic, = water of life]

whisper —v. 1 **a** speak very softly without vibration of the vocal cords. **b** talk or say in a barely audible tone or in a secret or confidential way. 2 rustle or murmur. —n. 1 whispering speech or sound. 2 thing whispered. □ **it is whispered** there is a rumour. [Old English]

whist n. card-game usu. for two pairs of players. [earlier whisk, perhaps from WHISK with ref. to whisking away the tricks; perhaps associated with whist! (= silence)]

whist drive n. social occasion with the playing of progressive whist.

whistle /ˈwɪs(ə)l/ —n. 1 clear shrill sound made by forcing breath through a small hole between nearly closed lips. 2 similar sound made by a bird, the wind, a missile, etc. 3 instrument used to produce such a sound. —v. (**-ling**) 1 emit a whistle. 2 **a** give a signal or express surprise or derision by whistling. **b** (often foll. by up) summon or give a signal to (a dog etc.) by whistling. 3 (also absol.) produce (a tune) by whistling. 4 (foll. by for) vainly seek or desire. [Old English]

whistle-stop n. 1 US small unimportant town on a railway. 2 politician's brief pause for an electioneering speech on tour.

Whit n. = WHITSUNTIDE. —attrib. adj. of Whitsuntide or Whit Sunday. [Old English, = white]

whit n. particle; least possible amount (not a whit better). [apparently = WIGHT]

white —adj. 1 resembling a surface reflecting sunlight without absorbing any of the visible rays; of the colour of milk or snow. 2 nearly this colour; pale, esp. in the face. 3 (White) a of the human group having light-coloured skin. b of or relating to White people. b of or relating to White people. 5 (of hair) having lost its colour (white mouse). 5 (of hair) having lost its colour. 6 (of coffee) with milk or cream. —n. 1 white colour or pigment. 2 a white clothes or material. b (in pl.) white garments as worn in cricket, tennis, etc. 3 a (in a game or sport) white piece, ball, etc. b player using these. 4 = EGG-WHITE. 5 whitish part of the eyeball round the iris. 6 (White) member of a light-skinned race. □ bleed white drain of wealth etc. □ whiteness n. whitish adj. [Old English]

white ant n. (pl. same) (usu. in pl.) termite.

whitebait n. small silvery-white young of herrings and sprats, esp. as food.

white cell n. leucocyte.

white-collar attrib. adj. (of a worker or work) non-manual; clerical, professional.

white corpuscle n. = WHITE CELL.

white elephant n. useless possession.

white feather n. symbol of cowardice.

white flag n. symbol of surrender.

White Friar n. Carmelite.

white goods n.pl. large domestic electrical equipment.

whitehead n. colloq. white or white-topped skin-pustule.

white heat n. 1 temperature at which metal emits white light. 2 state of intense passion or activity. □ white-hot adj.

white hope n. person expected to achieve much.

white horses n.pl. white-crested waves at sea.

white lead n. mixture of lead carbonate and hydrated lead oxide used as pigment.

white lie n. harmless or trivial untruth.

white light n. apparently colourless light, e.g. ordinary daylight.

white magic n. magic used for beneficent purposes.

white meat n. poultry, veal, rabbit, and pork.

whitener n.

white noise n. noise containing many frequencies with equal intensities.

white-out n. dense blizzard, esp. in polar regions.

White Paper n. Government report giving information.

white pepper n. pepper made by grinding a ripe or husked berry.

White Russian n. = BYELORUSSIAN.

white sauce n. sauce of flour, melted butter, and milk or cream.

white slave n. woman tricked or forced into prostitution.

white spirit n. light petroleum as a solvent.

white sugar n. purified sugar.

white tie n. man's white bow-tie as part of full evening dress.

whitewash —n. 1 solution of quicklime or whiting for whitening walls etc. 2 means employed to conceal mistakes or faults. —v. 1 cover with whitewash 2 attempt to clear the reputation of by concealing facts.

white wedding n. wedding at which the bride wears a formal white wedding dress.

white whale n. northern cetacean, white when adult.

whitewood n. pale wood, esp. prepared for staining etc.

whither /'wɪðə(r)/ archaic —adv. 1 to what place or state? 2 prec. by place etc.) to which (go whither you will). 2 —conj. 1 to the or any place to which (go whither you will). 2 and thither. [Old English]

whiting n. (pl. same) small white-fleshed fish used as food. [Dutch related to WHITE]

whiting n. ground chalk used in whitewashing etc.

whitlow /'wɪtləʊ/ n. inflammation near a fingernail or toenail, [originally white FLAW]

Whitsun /'wɪts(ə)n/ —n. = WHITSUN-TIDE. —adj. = WHIT. [Whitsun Day = Whit Sunday]

Whit Sunday n. seventh Sunday after Easter, commemorating Pentecost.

Whitsuntide n. weekend or week including Whit Sunday.

whittle /'wɪt(ə)l/ v. (-ling) 1 (often foll. by at) pare (wood etc.) with repeated slicing with a knife. 2 (often foll. by away, down) reduce by repeated subtractions. [dial. thwittle]

whiz (also whizz) —n. sound made by a body moving through the air at great speed. —v. (-zz-) move with or make a whiz. [imitative]

whiz-kid n. colloq. brilliant or highly successful young person.

WHO abbr. World Health Organization.

who /huː/ pron. (obj. whom /huːm/ or colloq. who; poss. whose /huːz/) 1 a what or which person or persons? (who

called?; *you know who it was*). **b** what sort of person or persons? (*who am I to object?*). **2** (a person) that (*anyone who wishes can come; the woman whom you met; the man who you saw*). **3** and or but he, they, etc. (*gave it to Tom, who sold it to Jim*). [Old English]

■ **Usage** In the last two examples of sense 2 *whom* is correct, but *who* is common in less formal contexts.

whoa /wəʊ/ *int.* used to stop or slow a horse etc. [var. of HO]

who'd /huːd/ *contr.* **1** who had. **2** who would.

whodunit /huːˈdʌnɪt/ *n.* (also **whodunnit**) *colloq.* detective story, play, or film. [= *who done it* (illiterate for *did it*)]

whoever /huːˈevə(r)/ *pron.* (*obj.* **whoever** or *formal* **whomever** /huːm-/; *poss.* **whosever** /huːz-/) **1** the or any person or persons who (*whoever comes is welcome*). **2** though anyone (*whoever else objects, I do not*).

whole /həʊl/ —*adj.* **1** uninjured, unbroken, intact, or undiminished. **2** not less than; all there is. **3** (of blood or milk etc.) with no part removed. —*n.* **1** thing complete in itself **2** all there is of a thing. **3** (foll. by *of*) all members etc. of (*the whole of London knows it*). □ **as a whole** as a unity; not as separate parts. **on the whole** taking everything relevant into account. **whole lot** see LOT. □ **wholeness** *n.* [Old English]

wholefood *n.* food which has not been unnecessarily processed or refined.

wholegrain *attrib. adj.* made with or containing whole grains (*wholegrain rice*).

wholehearted *adj.* **1** completely devoted. **2** done with all possible effort or sincerity. □ **wholeheartedly** *adv.*

wholemeal *n.* (usu. *attrib.*) meal or flour with none of the bran or germ removed.

whole number *n.* number without fractions; integer.

wholesale —*n.* selling of goods in large quantities to be retailed by others. —*adj.* & *adv.* **1** by wholesale. **2** on a large scale. —*v.* (-**ling**) sell wholesale. □ **wholesaler** *n.* [by *whole sale*]

wholesome *adj.* **1** promoting physical, mental, or moral health. **2** prudent (*wholesome respect*). [Old English: related to WHOLE]

wholewheat *n.* (usu. *attrib.*) wheat with none of the bran or germ removed

wholism var. of HOLISM.

wholly /ˈhəʊllɪ/ *adv.* **1** entirely; without limitation. **2** purely.

whom *objective case* of WHO.

whomever *objective case* of WHOEVER.

whomsoever *objective case* of WHO-SOEVER.

whoop /huːp, wuːp/ —*n.* **1** loud cry of or as of excitement etc. **2** long rasping indrawn breath in whooping cough. —*v.* utter a whoop. □ **whoop it up** *colloq.* **1** engage in revelry. **2** *US* make a stir. [imitative]

whoopee /wʊˈpiː/ *int.* expressing exuberant joy. □ **make whoopee** /ˈwʊpi/ *colloq.* **1** have fun, make merry. **2** make love. [imitative]

whooping cough /ˈhuːpɪŋ/ *n.* infectious bacterial disease, esp. of children, with a series of short violent coughs followed by a whoop.

whoops /wʊps/ *int. colloq.* expressing surprise or apology, esp. on losing balance or making an obvious mistake. [var. of OOPS]

whop *v.* (-**pp-**) *slang* **1** thrash. **2** defeat. [origin unknown]

whopper *n. slang* **1** something big of its kind. **2** great lie. [origin unknown]

whopping *adj. colloq.* (esp. as an intensifier) huge (*a whopping success; a whopping great lie*).

whore /hɔː(r)/ *n.* **1** prostitute. **2** *derog.* promiscuous woman. [Old English]

whore-house *n.* brothel.

whorl /wɜːl/ *n.* **1** ring of leaves etc. round a stem. **2** one turn of a spiral. [apparently var. of WHIRL]

whortleberry /ˈwɜːt(ə)l̩berɪ/ *n.* (*pl.* -**ies**) bilberry. [origin unknown]

whose /huːz/ —*interrog. pron.* of or belonging to which person (*whose is this book?*). —*interrog. adj.* of whom or which (*whose book is this?*). —*rel. pron.* of whom; of which (*the man, whose name was Tim; the house whose roof was damaged*).

whosever /huːˈsevə(r)/ *pron.* (*obj.* **whomsever**; *poss.* **whose-soever** /huːz-/) *archaic* = WHOEVER.

who's who *n.* **1** who or what each person is (*know who's who*). **2** list with facts about notable persons.

why /waɪ/ —*adv.* **1** for what reason or purpose (*why did you do it? I do not know why you came*). **2** (prec. by reason etc.) for which (*the reasons why I did it*). —*int.* expressing **1** surprised discovery or recognition (*why, it's you!*). **2** impatience (*why, of course I do!*). **3** reflection (*why, yes, I think so*). **4** objection (*why, what is wrong with it?*). □ **whys and wherefores** reasons; explanation. [Old English: related to WHAT]

WI *abbr.* **1** West Indies. **2** Women's Institute.

wick n. strip or thread feeding a flame with fuel. □ **get on a person's wick** *colloq.* annoy a person. [Old English]

wicked /ˈwikɪd/ adj. (-er, -est) 1 sinful, iniquitous, immoral. 2 spiteful. 3 playfully malicious. 4 *colloq.* very bad. 5 *slang* excellent. □ **wickedly** adv. **wickedness** n. [origin uncertain]

wicker n. plaited osiers etc. as material for baskets etc. [Scandinavian]

wickerwork n. 1 wicker. 2 things made of wicker.

wicket /ˈwikɪt/ n. 1 *Cricket* **a** three stumps with the bails in position defended by a batsman. **b** ground between two wickets. **c** state of this. **d** instance of a batsman being got out etc. 4 (in *bowler has taken four wickets*). 2 (in full **wicket-door** or **-gate**) small door or gate, esp. beside or in a larger one or closing the lower part only of a doorway. [Anglo-French *wiket* = French *guichet*]

wicket-keeper n. fieldsman stationed close behind a batsman's wicket.

widdershins /ˈwidəʃinz/ adv. (also **withershins** /ˈwiθ-/) esp. *Scot.* 1 in a direction contrary to the sun's course (considered unlucky). 2 anticlockwise. [German, = contrary]

wide —adj. 1 having sides far apart, broad, not narrow (*wide river, wide sleeve; wide angle*). 2 (following a measurement) in width (*a metre wide*). 3 **a** extending far (*wide range; wide experience*). **b** considerable (*wide margin*). 4 not restricted (*a wide public*). 5 **a** liberal; unprejudiced (*takes wide views*). **b** not specialized; general. 6 open to the full extent (*wide eyes*). 7 (foll. by *of*) not within a reasonable distance of, far from (*wide shot; wide of the target*). 8 (in comb.) extending over the whole of (*nationwide*). —adv. 1 widely. 2 to the full extent. 3 far from the target etc. (*shooting wide*). □ **wide ball** n. = WIDE BALL. **give a wide berth to** see BERTH. **wide open** 1 fully open. 2 exposed (to attack etc.). **the wide world** all the world, great as it is. [Old English]

wide awake adj. 1 fully awake. 2 *colloq.* wary, knowing.

wide ball n. *Cricket* ball judged to be beyond the batsman's reach, so scoring a run.

wide-eyed adj. surprised; naïve.

widely adv. 1 to a wide extent; far apart. 2 extensively. 3 by many people (*it is widely thought that*). 4 considerably; to a large degree (*holds a widely different view*).

widen v. make or become wider.

widespread adj. widely distributed.

widgeon /ˈwidʒ(ə)n/ n. (also **wigeon**) a kind of wild duck. [origin uncertain]

widow /ˈwidəʊ/ —n. 1 woman who has lost her husband by death and not married again. 2 woman whose husband is often away on a specified activity (*golf widow*). —v. 1 make into a widow or widower. 2 (as **widowed** adj.) bereft by the death of a spouse. □ **widowhood** n. [Old English]

widower n. man who has lost his wife by death and not married again.

widow's peak n. V-shaped growth of hair towards the centre of the forehead.

width n. 1 measurement from side to side. 2 large extent. 3 liberality of views etc. 4 strip of material of full width. □ **widthways** adv. [from WIDE]

wield v. hold and use; command, exert (a weapon, tool, power, etc.). [Old English]

Wiener schnitzel /ˈviːnə ˈʃnɪts(ə)l/ n. veal cutlet breaded, fried, and garnished. [German]

wife n. (pl. **wives**) 1 married woman, esp. in relation to her husband. 2 *archaic* woman. □ **wifely** adj. [Old English, = woman]

wig n. artificial head of hair. [abbreviation of PERIWIG]

wigeon var. of WIDGEON.

wigging n. *colloq.* reprimand. [origin uncertain]

wiggle /ˈwig(ə)l/ *colloq.* —v. (-ling) move from side to side etc. —n. act of wiggling. □ **wiggly** adj. (-ier, -iest). [Low German or Dutch *wiggelen*]

wight /waɪt/ n. *archaic* person. [Old English, = thing, creature]

wigwam /ˈwigwæm/ n. N. American Indian's hut or tent. [Ojibwa]

wild /waɪld/ —adj. 1 in its original natural state; not domesticated, cultivated or civilized (*wild cat; wild strawberry*). 2 unrestrained, disorderly, uncontrolled (*wild youth; wild hair*). 3 tempestuous (*wild night*). 4 intensely eager; frantic (*wild excitement; wild delight*). 5 (foll. by *about*) *colloq.* enthusiastically devoted to. 6 *colloq.* infuriated. 7 haphazard, ill-aimed, rash (*wild guess; wild venture*). 8 *colloq.* exciting, delightful. —adv. in a wild manner. —n. 1 wild tract of land. 2 desert. □ **in the wild** in an uncultivated state. **in the wilds** *colloq.* far from towns etc. **run wild** grow or stray unchecked or undisciplined. □ **wildly** adv. **wildness** n. [Old English]

wild card n. 1 card having any rank chosen by the player holding it. 2 *Computing* character that will match any character or combination of characters. 3 person or thing that can be used in several different ways.

wildcat —n. 1 hot-tempered or violent person. 2 exploratory oil well. —adj. (attrib.) 1 (of a strike) sudden and unofficial. 2 reckless; financially unsound.

wildebeest /ˈwɪldə.biːst/ n. (pl. same or -s) = GNU. [Afrikaans: related to WILD, BEAST]

wilderness /ˈwɪldənɪs/ n. 1 desert; uncultivated region or garden area. 2 (foll. by *of*) confused assemblage. [Old English: related to WILD, DEER]

wildfire n. *hist.* combustible liquid used in war. □ **spread like wildfire** spread with great speed.

wildfowl n. (pl. same) game-bird.

wild-goose chase n. foolish or hopeless quest.

wild hyacinth n. = BLUEBELL.

wildlife n. wild animals collectively.

Wild West n. western US before the establishment of law and order.

wile —n. (usu. in pl.) stratagem, trick. —v. (-ling) (foll. by *away*, *into*, etc.) lure. [perhaps from Scandinavian]

wilful /ˈwɪlfʊl/ adj. (US **willful**) 1 intentional, deliberate (*wilful murder*; *wilful neglect*). 2 obstinate. □ **wilfully** adv. [from WILL²]

will¹ v.aux. (3rd sing. present **will**; past **would** /wʊd/) 1 (strictly only in the 2nd and 3rd persons: see SHALL) expressing a future statement, command, etc. (*you will regret this*; *they will leave at once*). 2 expressing the speaker's intention (*I will return soon*). 3 wish or desire (*will you please open the window?*). 5 be able to (*the jar will hold a kilo*). 6 have a habit or tendency to (*accidents will happen*; *will sit there for hours*). 7 expressing probability or expectation (*that will be my wife*). [Old English]

will² —n. 1 faculty by which a person decides what to do. 2 strong desire or intention (*will to live*). 3 determination, will-power (*has a strong will*). 4 legal written directions for the disposal of one's property after death. 5 disposition towards others (*good will*). 6 *archaic* what one desires or ordains. —v. 1 try to cause by will-power (*willed her to win*). 2 intend; desire. 3 bequeath by a will. □ **at will** whenever one wishes. **with a will** energetically or resolutely. [Old English]

willful US var. of WILFUL.

willie var. of WILLY.

willies /ˈwɪlɪz/ n.pl. *colloq.* nervous discomfort (*gives me the willies*). [origin unknown]

willing adj. 1 ready to consent or undertake. 2 given or done etc. by a willing person. □ **willingly** adv. **willingness** n.

will-o'-the-wisp /ˌwɪləðəˈwɪsp/ n. 1 phosphorescent light seen on marshy ground. 2 elusive person. [= *William of the torch*]

willow /ˈwɪləʊ/ n. tree with pliant branches yielding osiers and timber for cricket-bats etc., usu. growing near water. [Old English]

willow-herb n. plant with leaves like a willow.

willow-pattern n. conventional Chinese design of blue on white porcelain etc.

willow-warbler n. small woodland bird with a tuneful song.

willowy adj. 1 lithe and slender. 2 having willows.

will-power n. control by deliberate purpose over impulse.

willy /ˈwɪlɪ/ n. (also **willie**) (pl. **-ies**) *colloq.* penis. [diminutive of *William*]

willy-nilly /ˌwɪlɪˈnɪlɪ/ adv. whether one likes it or not. [later spelling of *will I, nill I* I am willing, I am unwilling]

wilt —v. 1 wither, droop. 2 lose energy, flag. —n. plant-disease causing wilting. [originally dial.]

wily /ˈwaɪlɪ/ adj. (-**ier**, -**iest**) crafty, cunning. □ **wiliness** n.

wimp n. *colloq.* feeble or ineffectual person. □ **wimpish** adj. [origin uncertain]

wimple /ˈwɪmp(ə)l/ n. headdress also covering the neck and the sides of the face, worn by some nuns. [Old English]

win —v. (**-nn-**; past and past part. **won** /wʌn/) 1 secure as a result of a fight, contest, bet, effort, etc. 2 be the victor; be victorious in. —n. victory in a game etc. □ **win the day** be victorious in battle, argument, etc. **win over** persuade, gain the support of. **win one's spurs** *colloq.* gain distinction or fame. **win through** (or **out**) overcome obstacles. **you can't win** *colloq.* there is no way to succeed or to please. □ **winnable** adj. [Old English, = toil]

wince —n. start or involuntary shrinking movement of the face, showing pain or distress. —v. (-**cing**) give a wince. [Germanic: related to WINK]

wincey /ˈwɪnsɪ/ n. (pl. **-s**) lightweight fabric of wool and cotton or linen. [apparently an alteration of *woolsey* in LINSEY-WOOLSEY]

winceyette /ˌwɪnsɪˈɛt/ n. lightweight flannelette.

winch — *n.* 1 crank of a wheel or axle. 2 windlass. — *v.* lift with a winch. [Old English]

wind¹ — *n.* 1 air in natural motion, esp. a current of this. 2 a breath, esp. a needed in exercise or playing a wind instrument. b power of breathing easily. 3 empty talk. 4 gas generated in the bowels etc. 5 wind instruments of an orchestra etc. 6 scent carried by the wind. — *v.* 1 cause to be out of breath by exertion or a blow. 2 make (a baby) bring up wind after feeding. 3 detect the presence of by a scent. □ **get wind of** begin to suspect the existence of. **get (or have) the wind up** *colloq.* be alarmed or frightened. **in the wind** about to happen. **like the wind** swiftly. **put the wind up** *colloq.* alarm, frighten. **take the wind out of a person's sails** frustrate a person by anticipating an action or remark etc. □ **windless** *adj.* [Old English]

wind² /waɪnd/ — *v.* (*past* and *past part.* **wound**) 1 (often as **winding** *adj.*) go in a spiral, curved, or crooked course. 2 make (one's way) thus. 3 wrap closely, coil. 4 a provide with a coiled thread etc. b surround with or as with a coil 5 wind up (a clock etc.). — *n.* 1 bend or turn in a course. 2 single turn when winding. □ **wind down** 1 lower by winding. 2 unwind. 3 draw gradually to a close. **wind off** unwind. **wind up 1** coil the whole of. 2 tighten the coiling or coiled spring of. 3 *colloq.* a increase the intensity of (feelings etc.). b provoke (a person to anger etc.). 4 bring to a conclusion; end. 5 a arrange the affairs of and dissolve (a company). b cease business and go into liquidation. 6 *colloq.* arrive finally. [Old English]

windbag *n. colloq.* person who talks a lot but says little of any value.

wind-break *n.* thing serving to break the force of the wind.

windburn *n.* inflammation of the skin caused by exposure to the wind.

windcheater *n.* wind-resistant jacket.

wind-cone *n.* = WIND-SOCK.

wind-down *n. colloq.* gradual lessening of excitement or activity.

winder *n.* winding mechanism, esp. of a clock or watch.

windfall *n.* 1 fruit, esp. an apple, blown to the ground by the wind. 2 unexpected good fortune, esp. a legacy.

winding-sheet *n.* sheet in which a corpse is wrapped for burial.

wind instrument *n.* musical instrument sounded by an air-current, esp. the breath

wind-jammer *n.* merchant sailing-ship.

windlass /ˈwɪndləs/ *n.* machine with a horizontal axle for hauling or hoisting. [Old Norse, = winding-pole]

windmill *n.* 1 mill worked by the wind acting on its sails 2 toy consisting of a stick with curved vanes that revolve in a wind. □ **tilt at windmills** attack an imaginary enemy.

window /ˈwɪndəʊ/ *n.* 1 a opening in a wall etc., usu. with glass to admit light etc. b the glass itself. 2 space for display behind the window of a shop. 3 window-like opening. 4 opportunity to learn from observation. 5 transparent part in an envelope showing an address. 6 VDU display showing a particular part of the data. □ **windowless** *adj.* [Old Norse, = wind-eye]

window-box *n.* box placed outside a window for growing flowers.

window-dressing *n.* 1 art of arranging a display in a shop-window etc. 2 adroit presentation of facts etc. to give a deceptively favourable impression.

window-pane *n.* pane of glass in a window.

window-seat *n.* 1 seat below a window, esp. in an alcove. 2 seat next to a window in an aircraft, train, etc.

window-shop *v.* look at goods displayed in shop-windows, without buying anything.

window-sill *n.* sill below a window.

windpipe *n.* air-passage from the throat to the lungs.

windscreen *n.* screen of glass at the front of a motor vehicle.

windscreen wiper *n.* blade moving in an arc to keep a windscreen clear of rain etc.

windshield *n. US* = WINDSCREEN.

wind-sock *n.* canvas cylinder or cone on a mast to show the direction of the wind at an airfield etc.

windsurfing *n.* sport of riding on water on a sailboard. □ **windsurf** *v.* **windsurfer** *n.*

windswept *adj.* exposed to or swept back by the wind.

wind-tunnel *n.* tunnel-like device producing an air-stream past models of aircraft etc. for the study of aerodynamics.

wind-up — *n.* 1 conclusion; finish. 2 *colloq.* attempt to provoke. — *attrib. adj.* (of a mechanism) operating by being wound up.

windward /ˈwɪndwəd/ — *adj. & adv.* on the side from which the wind is blowing. — *n.* windward direction.

windy *adj.* (-**ier**, -**iest**) 1 stormy with or exposed to wind. 2 generating or characterized by flatulence. 3 *colloq.* wordy. 4

wine *colloq.* nervous, frightened. □ **windiness** *n.* [Old English: related to WIND²]

wine –*n.* **1** fermented grape juice as an alcoholic drink. **2** fermented drink resembling this made from other fruits etc. **3** dark-red colour of red wine. –*v.* (**-ning**) (foll. by *out*) extract with difficulty. (abbreviation of PERIWINKLE²)

winkle-picker *n. slang* long pointed shoe.

winner *n.* **1** person etc. that wins. **2** *colloq.* successful or highly promising idea etc.

winning –*adj.* **1** having or bringing victory. **2** attractive (*winning smile*). –*n.* (in *pl.*) money won. □ **winningly** *adv.*

winning-post *n.* post marking the end of a race.

winnow /ˈwɪnəʊ/ *v.* **1** blow (grain) free of chaff etc. by an air-current. **2** (foll. by *out*, *away*, *from*, etc.) get rid of (chaff etc.) from grain. **3** sift, examine (evidence etc.). [Old English: related to WIND²]

wino /ˈwaɪnəʊ/ *n.* (*pl.* **-s**) *slang* alcoholic.

winsome *adj.* attractive, engaging. □ **winsomely** *adv.* **winsomeness** *n.* [Old English, = joyous]

winter –*n.* **1** coldest and last season of the year. **2** (*attrib.*) characteristic of or fit for winter. –*v.* (usu. foll. by *at*, *in*) pass the winter. [Old English]

winter garden *n.* garden or conservatory of plants flourishing in winter.

wintergreen *n.* a kind of plant remaining green all winter.

winter jasmine *n.* jasmine with yellow flowers in winter.

winter solstice *n.* about 22 Dec.

winter sports *n.pl.* sports performed on snow or ice.

wintertime *n.* season or period of winter.

wintry *adj.* (**-ier**, **-iest**) **1** characteristic of winter. **2** lacking warmth; unfriendly. □ **wintriness** *n.*

winy *adj.* (**-ier**, **-iest**) wine-flavoured.

wine bar *n.* bar or small restaurant where wine is the main drink available.

winebibber *n.* tippler.

wine cellar *n.* **1** cellar for storing wine. **2** its contents.

wineglass *n.* glass for wine, usu. with a stem and foot.

wine list *n.* list of wines available in a restaurant etc.

winepress *n.* press in which grapes are squeezed in making wine.

wine vinegar *n.* vinegar made from wine as distinct from malt etc.

wine waiter *n.* waiter responsible for serving wine.

wing –*n.* **1** each of the limbs or organs by which a bird etc. is able to fly. **2** winglike structure supporting an aircraft. **3** part of a building etc. extended in a certain direction. **4 a** forward player at either end of a line in football, hockey, etc. **b** side part of a playing area. **5** (in *pl.*) sides of a theatre stage. **6** polarized section of a political party in terms of its views. **7** flank of a battle array. **8** the part of a vehicle over a wheel. **9** air-force unit of several squadrons or groups. –*v.* **1** travel or traverse on wings. **2** wound in a wing or an arm. **3** equip with wings. **4** enable to fly; send in flight. □ **on the wing** flying, in flight. **take under one's wing** treat as a protégé. **take wing** fly away. □ **winged** *adj.* **winglike** *adj.* [Old Norse]

wing-case *n.* horny cover of an insect's wing.

wing-chair *n.* chair with side-pieces at the top of a high back.

wing-collar *n.* man's high stiff collar with turned-down corners.

wing commander *n.* RAF officer next below group captain.

winger *n.* **1** (in football etc.) wing player. **2** (in *comb.*) member of a specified political wing.

wing-nut *n.* nut with projections for the fingers to turn it.

wing-span *n.* (also **wing-spread**) measurement right across the wings.

wink –*v.* **1** (often foll. by *at*) close and open one eye quickly, esp. as a signal. **2** close and open (one or both eyes) quickly. **3** (of a light etc.) twinkle; (of an indicator) flash on and off. –*n.* **1** act of winking. **2** *colloq.* short sleep. □ **in a**

wink very quickly. **wink at** purposely avoid seeing; pretend not to notice. □ **winker** *n.* (in sense 3 of *v.*). [Old English]

winkle –*n.* small edible sea snail. –*v.* (**-ling**) (foll. by *out*) extract with difficulty. (abbreviation of PERIWINKLE²)

wipe –*v.* (**-ping**) **1** clean or dry the surface of by rubbing. **2** rub (a cloth) over a surface. **3** spread (a liquid etc.) over a surface by rubbing. **4** (often foll. by *away*, *off*, etc.) **a** clear or remove by wiping. **b** erase or eliminate completely. –*n.* **1** act of wiping. **2** piece of specially treated material for wiping (*antiseptic wipes*). □ **wipe down** clean (a wall etc.) by wiping. **wipe the floor with** *colloq.* inflict a humiliating defeat on. **wipe off** annul (a debt etc.). **wipe out 1** destroy, annihilate, obliterate. **2** clean the inside of. **wipe up 1** dry (dishes etc.). **2** take up (a liquid etc.) by wiping. [Old English]

wiper *n.* = WINDSCREEN WIPER.

wire —n. **1 a** a metal drawn out into a thread or thin flexible rod. **b** piece of this. **c** (attrib.) made of wire. **2** length of wire for fencing or to carry an electric current etc. **3** collog. telegram. —v. (-ring) **1** provide, fasten, strengthen, etc., with wire. **2** (often foll. by *up*) install electrical circuits in (a building, equipment, etc.). **3** collog. telegraph. □ **get one's wires crossed** become confused and misunderstood. [Old English]

wire-haired adj. (esp. of a dog) with stiff or wiry hair.

wireless n. radio; radio receiving set.

wire netting n. netting of meshed wire.

wire-tapping n. tapping of telephone lines to eavesdrop.

wire wool n. mass of fine wire for scouring or rubbing down.

wireworm n. destructive larva of a kind of beetle.

wiring n. system or installation of wires providing electrical circuits.

wiry adj. (-ier, -iest) **1** sinewy, untiring. **2** like wire; tough, coarse. □ **wiriness** n.

wisdom /ˈwizdəm/ n. **1** experience and knowledge together with the power of applying them. **2** prudence; common sense. **3** wise sayings. [Old English]

wisdom tooth n. hindmost molar usu. cut at about 20 years of age.

wise¹ /waiz/ adj. **1** having, showing, or dictated by wisdom. **2** prudent, sensible. **3** having knowledge (often in *comb.*: *streetwise, worldly-wise*). **4** suggestive of wisdom. **5** US collog. alert, crafty. □ **be** (or **get**) **wise to** collog. be (or become) aware of. **none the wiser** knowing no more than before. **put wise** (often foll. by *to*) collog. inform (of). **wise up** esp. US collog. put or get wise. [Old English]

wise² /waiz/ n. archaic way, manner, or degree. □ **in no wise** not at all. [Old English]

-wise suffix forming adjectives and adverbs of manner (*clockwise; length-wise*) or respect (*moneywise*).

■ **Usage** More fanciful phrase-based combinations, such as *employment-wise* (= as regards employment) are restricted to informal contexts.

wiseacre /ˈwaizˌeikə(r)/ n. person who affects a wise manner. [Dutch *wijs-segghere* soothsayer]

wisecrack collog. —n. smart, pithy remark. —v. make a wisecrack.

wise guy n. collog. know-all.

wise man n. wizard, esp. one of the Magi.

wisent /ˈwiːz(ə)nt/ n. European bison. [German: cf. BISON]

wish —v. **1** (often foll. by *for*) have or express a desire or aspiration for (*wish for happiness*). **2** have as a desire or aspiration (*I wish I could sing*). **3** want or demand (*I wish to go; I wish you to do it*). **4** express one's hopes for (*wish you success*). **5** (foll. by *oz, upon*) collog. foist (a thing) on (a person). —n. **1 a** desire, request, or aspiration (*against my wishes*). **b** expression of this. **2** thing desired. □ **best** (or **good**) **wishes** hopes felt or expressed for another's happiness etc. [Old English]

wishbone n. fork ed bone between the neck and breast of a fowl often broken between two people, entitling the holder to make a wish.

wishful adj. (often foll. by *to* + infin.) desiring. □ **wishfully** adv.

wish-fulfilment n. tendency for subconscious desire to be satisfied in fantasy.

wishful thinking n. belief founded on wishes rather than facts.

wishing-well n. well into which coins are dropped and a wish is made.

wishy-washy /ˈwiʃiˌwɒʃi/ adj. collog. **1** feeble in quality or character. **2** weak, watery. [from WASH]

wisp n. **1** small bundle or twist of straw etc. **2** small separate quantity of smoke, hair, etc. **3** small thin person etc. □ **wispy** adj. (-ier, -iest). [origin uncertain]

wisteria /wiˈstiəriə/ n. (also **wistaria**) climbing plant with blue, purple, or white hanging flowers. [*Wistar*, name of an anatomist]

wistful adj. yearning, mournfully expectant or wishful. □ **wistfully** adv. **wistfulness** n. [apparently an assimilation of obsolete *wistly* 'intently' to *wishful*]

wit n. **1** (in *sing.* or *pl.*) intelligence; quick understanding. **2 a** unexpected combining or contrasting of ideas or expressions. **b** person possessing such power. □ **at one's wit's** (or **wits'**) **end** utterly at a loss or in despair. **have** (or **keep**) **one's wits about one** be alert. **live by one's wits** live by ingenious or crafty expedients, without a settled occupation. **out of one's wits** mad. **to wit** that is to say; namely. [Old English]

witch n. **1** sorceress, woman supposed to have dealings with the Devil or evil spirits. **2** old hag. **3** fascinating girl or woman. [Old English]

witch-doctor n. tribal magician of primitive people.

witchcraft n. **1** use of magic. **2** bewitching charm.

witchery n. = WITCHCRAFT.

witches' sabbath n. supposed midnight orgy of the Devil and witches.

witch-hazel *n.* (also **wych-hazel**) **1** American shrub with bark yielding an astringent lotion. **2** this lotion.

witch-hunt *n.* campaign against persons suspected of unpopular or unorthodox views, esp. Communists.

with /wɪð/ *prep.* expressing: **1** instrument or means used (*cut with a knife*). **2 a** association or company (*lives with his mother; works with Shell*). **b** parting of company (*dispense with*). **3** cause (*shiver with fear*). **4** possession (*man with dark hair; filled with water*). **5** circumstances (*sleep with the window open*). **6** manner (*handle with care*). **7** disagreement, antagonism (*incompatible with; quarrel with*). **8** disagreement (*sympathize with*). **9** understanding or regard (*be patient with them; how are things with you?*). **10** reference or regard (*be patient with them; how are things with you?*). □ **away** (or in or out etc.) **with** (as *int.*) take, send, or put (a person or thing) away (or in or out etc.). **with it** *colloq.* **1** up to date. **2** alert and comprehending. **with that** thereupon. [Old English]

withdraw /wɪðˈdrɔː/ *v.* (*past* **drew**; *past part.* **withdrawn**) **1** pull or take aside or back. **2** discontinue, cancel, retract. **3** remove; take away. **4** take (money) out of an account. **5** retire or move apart. **6** (as **withdrawn** *adj.*) abnormally shy and unsociable; mentally detached. [from WITH = away]

withdrawal *n.* **1** withdrawing or being withdrawn. **2** process of ceasing to take an addictive drug etc., often with an unpleasant reaction (*withdrawal symptoms*). **3** = COITUS INTERRUPTUS.

withe /wɪθ, wɪð, waɪð/ *n.* (also **withy** /ˈwɪðɪ/) (*pl.* **withes** or **withies**) tough flexible shoot, esp. of willow, used for binding, basketwork, etc. [Old English]

wither /ˈwɪðə(r)/ *v.* **1** (often foll. by *up*) make or become dry and shrivelled. **2** (often foll. by *away*) deprive of or lose vigour or freshness. **3** (esp. as **withering** *adj.*) blight with scorn etc. □ **witheringly** *adv.* [apparently var. of WEATHER]

withers /ˈwɪðəz/ *n.pl.* ridge between a horse's shoulder-blades. [obsolete *wither* against (the collar)]

withershins var. of WIDDERSHINS.

withhold /wɪðˈhəʊld/ *v.* (*past* and *past part.* **-held**) **1** hold back; restrain. **2** refuse to give, grant, or allow. [from WITH = away]

within /wɪˈðɪn/ —*adv.* **1** inside. **2** indoors. **3** in spirit (*pure within*). —*prep.* **1** inside. **2 a** not beyond or out of. **b** not transgressing or exceeding. **3** not further off than (*within three miles; within ten days*). □ **within one's grasp**

close enough to be obtained. **within reach** (or **sight**) **of** near enough to be reached or seen. [Old English: related to WITH, IN]

without /wɪˈðaʊt/ —*prep.* **1** not having or feeling or showing. **2** with freedom from. **3** in the absence of. **4** with neglect or avoidance of. **5** *archaic* outside. —*adv.* *archaic* or *literary* **1** outside. **2** out of doors. [Old English: related to WITH, OUT]

withstand /wɪðˈstænd/ *v.* (*past* and *past part.* **-stood**) oppose, hold out against. [Old English: related to WITH, STAND]

withy var. of WITHE.

witless *adj.* foolish, crazy. [Old English: related to WIT]

witness /ˈwɪtnɪs/ —*n.* **1** = EYEWITNESS. **2 a** person attesting sworn testimony. **b** person attesting another's signature to a document. **3** (foll. by *to, of*) person or thing whose existence etc. attests or proves something. **4** testimony, evidence, confirmation. —*v.* **1** be an eye-witness of. **2** be witness to the authenticity of (a signature etc.). **3** serve as evidence or an indication of. **4** (foll. by *against, for, to*) give or serve as evidence. □ **bear witness to** (or **of**) **1** attest the truth of. **2** state one's belief in. **call to witness** appeal to for confirmation etc. [Old English: related to WIT]

witness-box *n.* (*US* **witness-stand**) enclosure in a lawcourt from which witnesses give evidence.

witter /ˈwɪtə(r)/ *v.* (often foll. by *on*) *colloq.* chatter annoyingly or on trivial matters. [origin unknown]

witticism /ˈwɪtɪsɪz(ə)m/ *n.* witty remark. [from WITTY]

wittingly /ˈwɪtɪŋlɪ/ *adv.* aware of what one is doing; intentionally. [from WIT]

witty *adj.* (**-ier**, **-iest**) showing esp. verbal wit. □ **wittily** *adv.* **wittiness** *n.* [Old English: related to WIT]

wives *pl.* of WIFE.

wizard /ˈwɪzəd/ —*n.* **1** sorcerer; magician. **2** person of remarkable powers, genius. —*adj.* *slang* wonderful. □ **wizardry** *n.* [from WISE]

wizened /ˈwɪz(ə)nd/ *adj.* shrivelled-looking. [Old English]

WNW *abbr.* west-north-west.

WO *abbr.* Warrant-Officer.

woad *n.* **1** plant yielding a blue dye. **2** dye from this. [Old English]

wobble /ˈwɒb(ə)l/ —*v.* (**-ling**) **1** sway from side to side. **2** stand or go unsteadily; stagger. **3** waver, vacillate. —*n.* state or instance of wobbling. [cf. Low German *wabbeln*]

wobbly *adj.* (**-ier**, **-iest**) **1** tending to wobble. **2** wavy (*wobbly line*). **3** weak

after illness. **4** wavering, insecure (*the economy was wobbly*). □ **throw a wobbly** *slang* have a tantrum or fit of nerves.

wodge *n. colloq.* chunk, lump. [alteration of WEDGE]

woe /wəʊ/ *n.* **1** affliction, bitter grief. **2** (in *pl.*) calamities. □ **woe betide** see BETIDE. **woe is me** alas. [Old English]

woebegone /ˈwəʊbɪɡɒn/ *adj.* dismal-looking. [from WOE, *begone* = surrounded]

woeful *adj.* **1** sorrowful. **2** causing or feeling affliction. **3** very bad. □ **woefully** *adv.*

wog *n. slang offens.* foreigner, esp. a non-White one. [origin unknown]

woggle /ˈwɒɡ(ə)l/ *n.* leather etc. ring through which the ends of a Scout's neckerchief are passed at the neck. [origin unknown]

wok *n.* bowl-shaped frying-pan used in esp. Chinese cookery. [Chinese]

woke *past part.* of WAKE.

woken *past part.* of WAKE.

wold /wəʊld/ *n.* high open uncultivated land or moor. [Old English]

wolf /wʊlf/ —*n.* (*pl.* **wolves** /wʊlvz/) **1** wild animal related to the dog, usu. hunting in packs. **2** *slang* man who seduces women. —*v.* (often foll. by *down*) devour greedily. □ **cry wolf** raise false alarms. **keep the wolf from the door** avert starvation. □ **wolfish** *adj.* [Old English]

wolfhound *n.* dog of a kind used orig. to hunt wolves.

wolf in sheep's clothing *n.* hostile person who pretends friendship.

wolfram /ˈwʊlfrəm/ *n.* **1** tungsten. **2** tungsten ore. [German]

wolfsbane *n.* aconite.

wolf-whistle *n.* whistle made by a man to a sexually attractive woman.

wolverine /ˈwʊlvəriːn/ *n.* N. American animal of the weasel family. [related to WOLF]

wolves *pl.* of WOLF.

woman /ˈwʊmən/ *n.* (*pl.* **women** /ˈwɪmɪn/) **1** adult human female. **2** the female sex. **3** *colloq.* wife or girlfriend. **4** (prec. by *the*) feminine characteristics (*brought out the woman in him*). **5** (*attrib.*) female (*woman doctor*). **6** (in *comb.*) woman of a specified nationality, skill, etc. (*Englishwoman; horsewoman*). **7** *colloq.* charwoman. [Old English]

womanhood *n.* **1** female maturity. **2** womanly instinct. **3** womankind.

womanish *adj. derog.* effeminate, unmanly.

womanize *v.* (also **-ise**) (**-zing** or **-sing**) chase after women; philander. □ **womanizer** *n.* (also **womaniser**)

womankind *n.* (also **womenkind**) women in general.

womanly *adj.* having or showing qualities associated with women. □ **womanliness** *n.*

womb /wuːm/ *n.* organ of conception and gestation in a woman and other female mammals. [Old English]

wombat /ˈwɒmbæt/ *n.* burrowing plant-eating Australian marsupial. [Aboriginal]

women *pl.* of WOMAN.

womenfolk *n.* **1** women in general. **2** the women in a family.

women's lib *n. colloq.* supporter of women's liberation.

women's liberation *n.* (also **women's lib**) *colloq.* movement urging the liberation of women from domestic duties and subservient status.

women's rights *n.pl.* position of legal and social equality with men.

won *past and past part.* of WIN.

wonder /ˈwʌndə(r)/ —*n.* **1** emotion, esp. admiration, excited by what is unexpected, unfamiliar, or inexplicable. **2** strange or remarkable thing, specimen, event, etc. **3** (*attrib.*) having marvellous or amazing properties etc. (*wonder drug; wonder woman*). —*v.* **1** be filled with wonder or great surprise. **2** (foll. by *that*) be surprised to find. **3** desire or be curious to know (*I wonder what the time is*). □ **I shouldn't wonder** *colloq.* I think it likely. **no (or small) wonder** one cannot be surprised. **work (or do) wonders 1** do miracles. **2** be remarkably effective. [Old English]

wonderful *adj.* very remarkable or admirable. □ **wonderfully** *adv.* [Old English]

wonderland *n.* **1** fairyland. **2** land of surprises or marvels

wonderment *n.* surprise, awe.

wondrous /ˈwʌndrəs/ *poet.* —*adj.* wonderful. —*adv.* wonderfully (*wondrous kind*).

wonky /ˈwɒŋki/ *adj.* (**-ier, -iest**) *slang* **1** crooked, askew. **2** loose, unsteady. **3** unreliable. [fanciful]

wont /wəʊnt/ —*predic. adj. archaic* or *literary* (foll. by *to* - in fn.) accustomed. —*n. formal* or *joc.* what is customary. [Old English]

won't /wəʊnt/ *contr.* will not.

wonted /ˈwəʊntɪd/ *attrib. adj.* habitual, usual.

woo *v.* (**woos, wooed**) **1** court; seek the hand or love of. **2** try to win (fame,

fortune, etc.) **3** seek the favour or support of. **4** coax or importune. □ **wooer** *n.* [Old English]

wood /wʊd/ *n.* **1 a** a hard fibrous substance of the trunk or branches of a tree or shrub. **b** this for timber or fuel. **2** (in *sing.* or *pl.*) growing trees densely occupying a tract of land. **3** wooden cask for wine etc. **4** wooden-headed golf club. **5** = BOWL² *n.* 1. □ **not see the wood for the trees** fail to grasp the main issue from over-attention to details. **out of the wood** (or **woods**) out of danger or difficulty. [Old English]

wood anemone *n.* a wild springflowering anemone.

woodbine *n.* honeysuckle.

woodchuck *n.* N. American marmot. [American Indian name]

woodcock *n.* game-bird related to the snipe.

woodcraft *n.* **1** knowledge of woodland, esp. in camping etc. **2** skill in woodwork.

woodcut *n.* **1** relief cut on wood. **2** print made from this.

woodcutter *n.* person who cuts timber.

wooded *adj.* having woods or many trees.

wooden /ˈwʊd(ə)n/ *adj.* **1** made of wood. **2** like wood. **3 a** stiff, clumsy. **b** expressionless. □ **woodenly** *adv.* **woodenness** *n.*

woodland *n.* (often *attrib.*) wooded country, woods.

woodlouse *n.* (*pl.* **-lice**) small land crustacean with many legs.

woodman *n.* forester.

woodpecker *n.* bird that taps treetrunks in search of insects.

woodpigeon *n.* dove with white patches like a ring round its neck.

woodpile *n.* pile of wood, esp. for fuel.

wood pulp *n.* wood-fibre prepared for paper-making.

woodruff *n.* white-flowered plant with fragrant leaves.

woodshed *n.* shed where wood for fuel is stored. □ **something nasty in the woodshed** *colloq.* shocking thing kept secret.

woodwind *n.* **1** wind instruments that were (mostly) orig. made of wood, e.g. the flute, clarinet, oboe, and saxophone. **2** one such instrument.

woodwork *n.* **1** making of things in wood. **2** things made of wood. □ **crawl out of the woodwork** *colloq.* (of something distasteful) appear.

woodworm *n.* **1** wood-boring larva of a kind of beetle. **2** condition of wood affected by this.

woody *adj.* (**-ier, -iest**) **1** wooded. **2** like or of wood. □ **woodiness** *n.*

woodyard *n.* yard where wood is used or stored.

woody nightshade *n.* a kind of nightshade with poisonous red berries.

woof¹ /wʊf/ *—n.* gruff bark of a dog. *—v.* give a woof. [imitative]

woof² /wuːf/ *n.* = WEFT 1. [Old English: related to WEB]

woofer /ˈwuːfə(r)/ *n.* loudspeaker for low frequencies. [from WOOF¹]

wool /wʊl/ *n.* **1** fine soft wavy hair from the fleece of sheep etc. **2** woollen yarn or cloth or clothing. **3** wool-like substance (*steel wool*). □ **pull the wool over a person's eyes** deceive a person. [Old English]

wool-gathering *n.* absent-mindedness.

woollen (*US* **woolen**) *—adj.* made wholly or partly of wool. *—n.* **1** woollen fabric. **2** (in *pl.*) woollen garments. [Old English]

woolly *—adj.* (**-ier, -iest**) **1** bearing wool. **2** like wool. **3** woollen (*a woolly cardigan*). **4** (of a sound) indistinct. **5** (of thought) vague or confused. *—n.* (*pl.* **-ies**) *colloq.* woollen garment, esp. a pullover. □ **woolliness** *n.*

Woolsack *n.* **1** Lord Chancellor's woolstuffed seat in the House of Lords. **2** his position.

woozy *adj.* (**-ier, -iest**) *colloq.* **1** dizzy or unsteady. **2** slightly drunk. □ **woozily** *adv.* **wooziness** *n.* [origin unknown]

wop *n.* *slang offens.* Italian or other S. European. [origin uncertain]

Worcester sauce /ˈwʊstə/ *n.* a pungent sauce. [*Worcester* in England]

word /wɜːd/ *—n.* **1** meaningful element of speech, usu. shown with a space on either side of it when written or printed. **2** speech, as distinct from action. **3** one's promise or assurance. **4** (in *sing.* or *pl.*) thing said, remark, conversation. **5** (in *pl.*) text of a song or an actor's part. **6** (in *pl.*) angry talk (*have words*). **7** news, message (*send word*). **8** command (*gave the word to begin*). *—v.* put into words; select words to express. □ **in other words** expressing the same thing differently. **in so many words** in those very words; explicitly. **in a** (or **one**) **word** briefly. **my** (or **upon my**) **word** exclamation of surprise etc. **take a person at his or her word** interpret a person's words literally. **take a person's word for it** believe a person's statement without investigation etc. **the Word** (or **Word of God**) the Bible. **word for word** in exactly the same or (of translation) corresponding words. □ **wordless** *adj.* [Old English]

word-blindness *n.* = DYSLEXIA

word-game *n.* game involving the making or selection etc. of words.

wording n. form of words used.

word of mouth n. speech (only).

wordplay n. witty use of words, esp. punning.

word processor n. computer program, or device incorporating a computer, used for storing text entered from a keyboard, making corrections, and providing a printout. □ **word-process** v. **word processing** n.

wordy adj. (**-ier**, **-iest**) using or expressed in too many words. □ **wordily** adv. **wordiness** n.

wore past of WEAR.

work /wɜːk/ —n. 1 application of mental or physical effort to a purpose; use of energy. 2 task to be undertaken. 3 thing done or made by work; result of an action. 4 employment or occupation etc., esp. as a means of earning income, etc. 5 literary or musical composition. 6 actions or experiences of a specified kind (nice work!). 7 (in comb.) things made of a specified material or with specified tools etc. (ironwork; needlework). 8 (in pl.) operative part of a clock or machine. 9 Physics the exertion of force overcoming resistance or producing molecular change. 10 (in full the works) colloq. a all that is available or needed. b full, esp. harsh, treatment. 11 (in pl.) operations of building or repair (road works). 12 (in pl.; often treated as sing.) factory. 13 (usu. in pl.) Theol. meritorious act. 14 (usu. in pl. or in comb.) defensive structure (earthworks). —v. 1 do work; be engaged in bodily or mental activity. 2 be employed in certain work (works in industry). 3 make efforts (works for peace). 4 (foll. by in) be a craftsman in (a material). 5 operate or function, esp. effectively (how does this machine work?; your idea will not work). 6 operate, manage, control (cannot work the machine). 7 a put or keep in operation or at work; cause to toil (works the staff hard). b cultivate (land). 8 a bring about; produce as a result (worked miracles). b colloq. arrange (matters) (worked it so that we could go; can you work things for us?). 9 knead, hammer; bring to a desired shape or consistency. 10 do, or make by, needlework etc. 11 (cause to) make progress or penetrate, or make (one's way), gradually or with difficulty in a specified way (worked the peg into the hole; worked our way through the crowd). 12 (foll. by loose etc.) become (loose etc.) by gradual movement. 13 artificially excite (worked themselves into a rage). 14 a purchase with one's labour instead of money (work one's passage). b obtain by labour the money for (worked my way through university). 15 (foll. by on, upon) have influence. 16 be in motion or agitated; ferment. □ at work in action, engaged in work. get worked up become angry, excited, or tense. have one's work cut out be faced with a hard task. work in find a place for. work off get rid of by work or activity. work out 1 a solve (a sum) or find (an amount) by calculation. b solve, understand (a problem, person, etc.). 2 (foll. by at) be calculated. 3 give a definite result (this sum will not work out). 4 have a result (the plan worked out well). 5 provide for the details of (has worked out a scheme). 6 engage in physical exercise or training. work over 1 examine thoroughly. 2 colloq. treat with violence. work through arrive at an understanding of (a problem) etc. work to rule (as a protest) follow official working rules exactly in order to reduce output. work up 1 bring gradually to an efficient or (of a painting etc.) advanced state. 2 (foll. by to) advance gradually to a climax etc. 3 elaborate or excite by degrees. 4 mingle (ingredients). 5 earn (a subject) by study. work wonders see WONDER. [Old English]

workable adj. that can be worked, will work, or is worth working. □ **workability** /-'bɪlɪtɪ/ n.

workaday adj. ordinary, everyday, practical.

workaholic /wɜːkə'hɒlɪk/ n. colloq. person addicted to working.

work-basket n. basket for sewing materials.

workbench n. bench for manual work, esp. carpentry.

workbook n. student's book with exercises.

workbox n. box for tools, needlework, etc.

work camp n. camp at which community work is done, esp. by young volunteers.

workday n. day on which work is usually done.

worker n. 1 person who works, esp. for an employer. 2 neuter bee or ant. 3 person who works hard.

work experience n. scheme intended to give young people temporary experience of employment

workforce n. 1 workers engaged or available. 2 number of these.

workhouse n. hist. public institution for the poor of a parish.

working —attrib. adj. 1 a engaged in work (working mother; working man).

working capital *n.* capital actually used in a business.

working class *n.* social class employed, esp. in manual or industrial work, for wages. □ **working-class** *adj.*

working day *n.* 1 workday. 2 part of the day devoted to work.

working knowledge *n.* knowledge adequate to work with.

working lunch *n.* lunch at which business is conducted.

working order *n.* condition in which a machine works.

working party *n.* group of people appointed to study and advise on a particular problem.

workload *n.* amount of work to be done.

workman *n.* 1 man employed to do manual labour. 2 person with regard to skill in a job (*a good workman*).

workmanlike *adj.* competent, showing practised skill.

workmanship *n.* degree of skill in doing a task or of finish in the product made.

workmate *n.* person working alongside another.

work of art *n.* fine picture, poem, building, etc.

workout *n.* session of physical exercise or training.

workpiece *n.* thing worked on with a tool or machine.

workplace *n.* place at which a person works.

workroom *n.* room for working in.

worksheet *n.* 1 paper for recording work done or in progress. 2 paper listing questions or activities for students etc.

workshop *n.* 1 room or building in which goods are manufactured. 2 place or meeting for concerted discussion or activity (*dance workshop*).

work-shy *adj.* disinclined to work.

workstation *n.* 1 location of a stage in a manufacturing process. 2 computer terminal or the desk etc. where this is located.

work study *n.* assessment of methods of working so as to achieve maximum productivity.

work table *n.* table for working at.

worktop *n.* flat surface for working on, esp. in a kitchen.

b while so engaged (*all his working life, in working hours*). 2 functioning or able to function (*working model*). —*n.* 1 activity of work. 2 functioning. 3 mine or quarry. 4 (usu. in *pl.*) machinery, mechanism.

work-to-rule *n.* working to rule.

world /wɜːld/ *n.* 1 a the earth, or a planetary body like it. b its countries and people. 2 the universe, all that exists. 3 a the time, state, or scene of human existence. b (prec. by *the, this*) mortal life. 4 secular interests and affairs. 5 human affairs; active life. 6 average, respectable, or fashionable people or their customs or opinions. 7 all that concerns or all who belong to a specified class or sphere of activity (*the world of sport*). 8 (foll. by *of*) vast amount. 9 (*attrib.*) affecting many nations, of all nations (*world politics; world champion*). □ **bring** (or **come**) **into the world** give birth (or be born). **for all the world** (foll. by *like, as if*) precisely. **in the world** of all; at all (*what in the world is it?*). **man** (or **woman**) **of the world** person experienced and practical in human affairs. **out of this world** *colloq.* extremely good etc. **think the world of** have a very high regard for. [Old English]

world-beater *n.* person or thing surpassing all others.

world-class *adj.* of a quality or standard regarded as high throughout the world.

World Cup *n.* competition between football teams from various countries.

world-famous *adj.* known throughout the world.

worldly *adj.* (**-ier, -iest**) 1 of the affairs of the world, temporal, earthly (*worldly goods*). 2 experienced in life, sophisticated, practical. □ **worldliness** *n.*

worldly-wise *adj.* prudent or shrewd in one's dealings with the world.

world music *n.* pop music that incorporates local or ethnic elements (esp. from the developing world).

world war *n.* war involving many major nations.

world-weary *adj.* bored with human affairs. □ **world-weariness** *n.*

worldwide —*adj.* occurring in or known in all parts of the world. —*adv.* throughout the world.

worm /wɜːm/ —*n.* 1 any of various types of creeping invertebrate animals with long slender bodies and no limbs. 2 larva of an insect, esp. in fruit or wood. 3 (in *pl.*) intestinal parasites. 4 insignificant or contemptible person. 5 spiral part of a screw. —*v.* 1 (often *refl.*) move with a crawling motion. 2 *refl.* (foll. by *into*) insinuate oneself into favour etc. 3 (foll. by *out*) obtain (a secret etc.) by cunning persistence. 4 rid (a dog etc.) of worms. [Old English]

worm-cast n. convoluted mass of earth left on the surface by a burrowing earthworm.

wormeaten adj. 1 eaten into by worms; decayed. 2 old and dilapidated.

worm-hole n. hole left by the passage of a worm.

worm's-eye view n. view from below or from a humble position.

wormwood /'wɜːmwʊd/ n. 1 plant with a bitter aromatic taste. 2 bitter mortification; source of this. [Old English: cf. VERMOUTH]

wormy adj. (-ier, -iest) 1 full of worms. 2 wormeaten. □ **worminess** n.

worn /wɔːn/ past part. of WEAR. —adj. 1 damaged by use or wear. 2 looking tired and exhausted.

worrisome /'wʌrɪsəm/ adj. causing worry.

worry /'wʌrɪ/ —v. (-ies, -ied) 1 give way to anxiety. 2 harass, importune; be a trouble or anxiety to. 3 (of a dog etc.) shake or pull about with the teeth. 4 (as **worried** adj.) uneasy. —n. (pl. -ies) 1 thing that causes anxiety or disturbs tranquillity. 2 disturbed state of mind; anxiety. □ **worrier** n. [Old English, = strangle]

worry beads n.pl. string of beads manipulated with the fingers to occupy or calm oneself.

worse /wɜːs/ —adj. 1 more bad. 2 (predic.) in or into worse health or a worse condition (is getting worse). —adv. more badly; more ill. —n. 1 worse thing or things (you might do worse than accept). 2 (prec. by the) worse condition (a change for the worse). □ **none the worse** (often foll. by for) not adversely affected (by). **the worse for wear 1** damaged by use. **2** injured. **worse luck** unfortunately. **worse off** in a worse (esp. financial) position. [Old English]

worsen v. make or become worse.

worship /'wɜːʃɪp/ —n. 1 a homage or service to a deity. b acts, rites, or ceremonies of this. 2 adoration, devotion. 3 (**Worship**) (prec. by His, Her, Your) forms of description or address for a mayor, certain magistrates, etc. —v. (-pp-; US -p-) 1 adore as divine; honour with religious rites. 2 idolize or regard with adoration. 3 attend public worship. 4 be full of adoration. □ **worshipper** n. [Old English: related to WORTH, SHIP]

worshipful adj. (also **Worshipful**) archaic (esp. in old titles of companies or officers) honourable, distinguished.

worst /wɜːst/ —adj. most bad. —adv. most badly. —n. worst part or possibility (prepare for the worst). —v. get the better of; defeat. □ **at its** etc. **worst** in the worst state. **at worst (or the worst)** in the worst possible case. **do your worst** expression of defiance. **get the worst of it** be defeated. **if the worst comes to the worst** if the worst happening occurs. [Old English: related to WORSE]

worsted /'wʊstɪd/ n. 1 fine woollen yarn. 2 fabric made from this. [Worstead in Norfolk]

wort /wɜːt/ n. 1 archaic (except in names) plant (liverwort). 2 infusion of malt before it is fermented into beer. [Old English]

worth /wɜːθ/ —predic. adj. (used like a preposition) 1 of a value equivalent to (is worth £50; is worth very little). 2 such as to justify or repay (worth doing; not worth the trouble). 3 possessing or having property amounting to (is worth a million pounds). —n. 1 what a person or thing is worth; the (usu. high) merit of (of great worth). 2 equivalent of money in a commodity (ten pounds' worth of petrol). □ **for all one is worth** colloq. with one's utmost efforts. **for what it is worth** without a guarantee of its truth or value. **worth it** colloq. worth while. **worth one's salt** see SALT. **worth one's weight in gold** see WEIGHT. **worth while (or one's while)** see WHILE. [Old English]

worthless adj. without value or merit. □ **worthlessness** n.

worthwhile adj. that is worth the time, effort, or money spent.

■ **Usage** See note at while.

worthy /'wɜːðɪ/ —adj. (-ier, -iest) 1 deserving respect, estimable (lived a worthy life). 2 entitled to (esp. condescending) recognition (a worthy old couple). 3 a (foll. by of or to + infin.) deserving (worthy of a mention). b (foll. by of) adequate or suitable to the dignity etc. of (words worthy of the occasion). —n. (pl. -ies) 1 worthy person. 2 person of some distinction. □ **worthily** adv. **worthiness** n.

-worthy comb. form forming adjectives meaning: 1 deserving of (noteworthy). 2 suitable for (roadworthy).

would /wʊd/ past of WILL. v. aux. (3rd sing. **would**) used esp.: 1 in reported speech (the said he would be home by evening). 2 to express a condition (they would have been killed if they had gone). 3 to express habitual action (would wait every evening). 4 to express a question or polite request (would they like it?; would you come in, please?). 5 to express probability (she would be over fifty by now). 6 to express consent (they would not help).

would-be attrib. adj. desiring or aspiring to be.

wouldn't /ˈwʊd(ə)nt/ *contr.* would not.

wound[1] /wuːnd/ —*n.* **1** injury done to living tissue by a deep cut or heavy blow etc. **2** pain inflicted on one's feelings; injury to one's reputation. —*v.* inflict a wound on. [Old English]

wound[2] *past and past part.* of WIND[2].

wound up *adj.* excited; tense; angry.

wove *past* of WEAVE[1].

woven *past part.* of WEAVE[1].

wow[1] /waʊ/ —*int.* expressing astonishment or admiration. —*n. slang* sensational success. —*v. slang* impress greatly. [imitative]

wow[2] /waʊ/ *n.* slow pitch-fluctuation in sound-reproduction, perceptible in long notes. [imitative]

WP *abbr.* word processor.

w.p.m. *abbr.* words per minute.

WPC *abbr.* woman police constable.

WRAC *abbr.* Women's Royal Army Corps.

wrack *n.* **1** seaweed cast up or growing on the shore. **2** destruction. [Low German or Dutch *wrak:* cf. WRECK]

WRAF *abbr.* Women's Royal Air Force.

wraith *n.* **1** ghost. **2** spectral appearance of a living person supposed to portend that person's death. [origin unknown]

wrangle /ˈræŋg(ə)l/ —*n.* noisy argument or dispute. —*v.* (-ling) engage in a wrangle. [Low German or Dutch]

wrap —*v.* (-pp-) **1** (often foll. by *up*) envelop in folded or soft encircling material. **2** (foll. by *round, about*) arrange or draw (a pliant covering) round (a person). **3** (foll. by *round*) *slang* crash (a vehicle) into (a stationary object). —*n.* **1** shawl, scarf, etc. **2** esp. *US* wrapping material. □ **take the wraps off** disclose. **under wraps** in secrecy. **wrapped up** in engrossed or absorbed in. **wrap up** **1** *colloq.* finish off (a matter). **2** put on warm clothes (*wrap up well*). **3** (in *imper.*) *slang* be quiet. [origin unknown]

wraparound *adj.* (also **wrapround**) **1** (esp. of clothing) designed to wrap round. **2** curving or extending round at the edges.

wrap-over —*attrib. adj.* (of a garment) overlapping when worn. —*n.* such a garment.

wrapper *n.* **1** cover for a sweet, book, posted newspaper, etc. **2** loose enveloping robe or gown.

wrapping *n.* (esp. in *pl.*) material used to wrap; wraps, wrappers.

wrapping paper *n.* strong or decorative paper for wrapping parcels.

wrapround *var.* of WRAPAROUND.

wrasse /ræs/ *n.* bright-coloured marine fish. [Cornish *wrach*]

wrath /rɒθ/ *n. literary* extreme anger. [Old English: related to WROTH]

wrathful *adj. literary* extremely angry. □ **wrathfully** *adv.*

wreak *v.* **1** (usu. foll. by *upon*) give play to (vengeance or one's anger etc.). **2** cause (damage etc.) (*wreak havoc*). [Old English: = avenge]

wreath /riːθ/ *n.* (*pl.* -s /-riːðz/) **1** flowers or leaves fastened in a ring, esp. as an ornament for the head or for laying on a grave etc. **2** curl or ring of smoke, cloud, or soft fabric. [Old English: related to WRITHE]

wreathe /riːð/ *v.* (-thing) **1** encircle or cover as, with, or like a wreath. **2** (foll. by *round*) wind (one's arms etc.) round (a person etc.). **3** (of smoke etc.) move in wreaths.

wreck —*n.* **1** the sinking or running aground of a ship. **2** ship that has suffered a wreck. **3** greatly damaged building, thing, or person. **4** (foll. by *of*) wretched remnant. —*v.* **1** a seriously damage (a vehicle etc.). **b** ruin (hopes, a life, etc.). **2** cause the wreck (of a ship). [Anglo-French *wrec* from Germanic]

wreckage *n.* **1** wrecked material. **2** remnants of a wreck. **3** act of wrecking.

wrecker *n.* **1** person or thing that wrecks or destroys. **2** esp. *US* person employed in demolition or breaking up of damaged vehicles. **3** esp. *hist.* person on the shore who tries to bring about a shipwreck for plunder or profit.

Wren *n.* member of the Women's Royal Naval Service. [from the abbreviation WRNS]

wren *n.* small usu. brown short-winged songbird with an erect tail. [Old English]

wrench —*n.* **1** violent twist or oblique pull or tearing off. **2** tool like a spanner for gripping and turning nuts etc. **3** painful uprooting or parting. —*v.* **1** twist or pull violently round or sideways. **2** (often foll. by *off, away*, etc.) pull off with a wrench. [Old English]

wrest *v.* **1** wrench away from a person's grasp. **2** (foll. by *from*) obtain by effort or with difficulty. [Old English]

wrestle /ˈres(ə)l/ —*n.* **1** contest in which two opponents grapple and try to throw each other to the ground, esp. as an athletic sport. **2** hard struggle. —*v.* (-ling) **1** (often foll. by *with*) take part or fight in a wrestle. **2** a (foll. by *with, against*) struggle. **b** (foll. by *with*) do one's utmost to deal with (a task, difficulty, etc.). □ **wrestler** *n.* **wrestling** *n.* [Old English]

wretch *n.* **1** unfortunate or pitiable person. **2** (often as a playful term of

depreciation) reprehensible person. [Old English = outcast]

wretched /ˈretʃɪd/ adj. (**wretcheder**, **wretchedest**) **1** unhappy, miserable; unwell. **2** of bad quality; contemptible. **3** displeasing, hateful. □ **wretchedly** adv. **wretchedness** n.

wrick var. of RICK².

wriggle /ˈrɪg(ə)l/ —v. (**-ling**) **1** (of a worm etc.) twist or turn its body with short writhing movements. **2** make wriggling motions. **3** (foll. by *along, through*, etc.) go thus (*wriggled through the gap*). **4** be evasive. —n. act of wriggling. □ **wriggle out of** colloq. avoid on a pretext. □ **wriggly** adj. [Low German *wriggelen*]

wright /raɪt/ n. maker or builder (usu. in comb.: *playwright; shipwright*). [Old English: related to WORK]

wring —v. (past and past part. **wrung**) **1 a** squeeze tightly. **b** (often foll. by *out*) squeeze and twist, esp. to remove liquid. **2** break by twisting. **3** distress, torture. **4** extract by squeezing. **5** (foll. by *out, from*) obtain by pressure or importunity; extort. —n. act of wringing. □ **wring one's hands** clasp them as a gesture of distress. **wring the neck of** kill (a chicken etc.) by twisting its neck. [Old English]

wringer n. device for wringing water from washed clothes etc.

wringing adj. (in full **wringing wet**) so wet that water can be wrung out.

wrinkle /ˈrɪŋk(ə)l/ —n. **1** crease in the skin, esp. caused by age. **2** similar mark in another flexible surface. **3** colloq. useful tip or clever expedient. —v. (**-ling**) **1** make wrinkles in. **2** form wrinkles. [probably related to Old English *gewrinclod* sinuous]

wrinkly —adj. (**-ier, -iest**) having wrinkles. —n. slang offens. old or middle-aged person.

wrist n. **1** joint connecting the hand with the arm. **2** part of a garment covering this. [Old English]

wristlet n. band or ring to strengthen, guard, or adorn the wrist.

wrist-watch n. small watch worn on a strap etc. round the wrist.

writ¹ n. form of written command to act or not act in some way. [Old English: related to WRITE]

writ² archaic past part. of WRITE. □ **writ large** magnified or emphasized form.

write v. (**-ting**; past **wrote**; past part. **written**) **1** mark paper or some other surface with symbols, letters, or words. **2** form or mark (such symbols etc.). **3** fill or complete (a sheet, cheque, etc.) with writing. **5** transfer (data) into a computer store. **6** (esp. in passive) indicate (a quality or condition) by one's or its appearance (*guilt was written on his face*). **7** compose for written or printed reproduction or publication. **8** (usu. foll. by *to*) write and send a letter to (a person). **9** US write and send a letter to (a person). **10** convey (news etc.) by letter. **11** state in a book etc. **12** (foll. by *into, out of*) include or exclude (a character or episode) in, or from, a story by changing the text. □ **write down** record in writing. **write in** send a suggestion, query, etc., in writing to esp. a broadcasting station. **write off 1** (foll. by *for*) = *send away for* (see SEND). **2** cancel the record of (a bad debt etc.); acknowledge the loss of (an asset). **3** completely destroy (a vehicle etc.). **4** dismiss as insignificant. **write out** write in full or in finished form. **write up 1** write a full account of; bring (a diary etc.) up to date. **2** praise in writing. [Old English]

write-off n. thing written off, esp. a vehicle too badly damaged to be repaired.

writer n. **1** person who writes or has written something. **2** person who writes books, author.

writer's cramp n. muscular spasm due to excessive writing.

write-up n. written or published account, review.

writhe /raɪð/ v. (**-thing**) **1** twist or roll oneself about in or as in acute pain. **2** suffer mental torture or embarrassment (*writhed with shame*). [Old English]

writing n. **1** written words etc. **2** handwriting. **3** (usu. in pl.) author's works. □ **in writing** in written form. **the writing on the wall** ominously significant event etc.

writing-desk n. desk for writing at, esp. with compartments for papers etc.

writing-paper n. paper for writing (esp. letters) on.

written past part. of WRITE.

WRNS abbr. Women's Royal Naval Service.

wrong —adj. **1** mistaken, not true; in error. **2** unsuitable; less or least desirable (*the wrong road; a wrong decision*). **3** contrary to law or morality (*it is wrong to steal*). **4** amiss, out of order, in a bad or abnormal condition (*something wrong with my heart; has gone wrong*). —adv. (usually placed last) in a wrong manner or direction; with an incorrect result (*guessed wrong*). —n. **1** what is morally wrong, injustice. **2** unjust action (*suffer a wrong*). —v. **1** treat unjustly. **2** mistakenly attribute bad motives to. □

wrongdoer

do wrong sin. **do wrong to** malign or mistreat (a person). **get wrong 1** misunderstand (a person etc.). **2** obtain an incorrect answer to. **get** (or **get hold of**) **the wrong end of the stick** misunderstand completely. **go wrong 1** take the wrong path. **2** stop functioning properly. **3** depart from virtuous behaviour. **in the wrong** responsible for a quarrel, mistake, or offence. **on the wrong side of 1** out of favour with (a person). **2** somewhat more than (a stated age). **wrong side out** inside out. **wrong way round** in the opposite or reverse of the normal or desirable orientation or sequence etc. □ **wrongly** adv. **wrongness** n. [Old English]

wrongdoer n. person who behaves immorally or illegally. □ **wrongdoing** n.

wrong-foot v. colloq. **1** (in tennis, football, etc.) catch (an opponent) off balance. **2** disconcert; catch unprepared.

wrongful adj. unwarranted, unjustified (*wrongful arrest*). □ **wrongfully** adv.

wrong-headed adj. perverse and obstinate.

wrong side n. worse or undesired or unusable side of esp. fabric.

wrote past of WRITE.

wroth /rəʊθ/ predic. adj. archaic angry. [Old English]

wrought /rɔːt/ archaic past and past part. of WORK. —adj. (of metals) beaten out or shaped by hammering.

wrought iron n. tough malleable form of iron suitable for forging or rolling, not cast.

wrung past and past part. of WRING.

WRVS abbr. Women's Royal Voluntary Service.

wry /raɪ/ adj. (**wryer, wryest** or **wrier, wriest**) **1** distorted or turned to one side. **2** (of a face, smile, etc.) contorted in disgust, disappointment, or mockery. **3** (of humour) dry and mocking. □ **wryly** adv. **wryness** n. [Old English]

wryneck n. small woodpecker able to turn its head over its shoulder.

WSW abbr. west-south-west.

wt abbr. weight.

wych- comb. form in names of trees with pliant branches (*wych-alder, wychelm*). [Old English, = bending]

wych-hazel var. of WITCH-HAZEL.

Wykehamist /ˈwɪkəmɪst/ —adj. of Winchester College. —n. past or present member of Winchester College. [William of *Wykeham*, name of the founder]

WYSIWYG /ˈwɪzɪwɪg/ adj. (also **wysiwyg**) *Computing* denoting a form of text onscreen exactly corresponding to its printout. [acronym of *what you see is what you get*]

X

X¹ /eks/ *n.* (also **x**) (*pl.* **Xs** or **X's**) **1** twenty-fourth letter of the alphabet. **2** (as a Roman numeral) ten. **3** (usu. **x**) *Algebra* first unknown quantity. **4** unknown or unspecified number or person etc. **5** cross-shaped symbol used esp. to indicate position (*X marks the spot*) or incorrectness, or to symbolize a kiss or a vote, or as the signature of a person who cannot write.

X² *symb.* (of films) classified as suitable for adults only.

■ **Usage** This symbol was superseded in the UK in 1983 by *18*, but it is still used in the US.

X chromosome /ˈeks ˌkrəʊmə.səʊm/ *n.* (in humans and some other mammals) sex chromosome of which the number in female cells is twice that in male cells. [X as an arbitrary label]

Xe *symb.* xenon.

Xenon /ˈzenɒn, ˈziː-/ *n.* heavy inert gaseous element. [Greek, neuter of *xenos* strange]

xenophobia /ˌzenəˈfəʊbɪə/ *n.* hatred or fear of foreigners. □ **xenophobic** *adj.* [Greek *xenos* strange, stranger]

xerography /zɪəˈrɒgrəfɪ/ *n.* dry copying process in which powder adheres to areas remaining electrically charged after exposure of the surface to light from an image of the document to be copied. [Greek *xēros* dry]

Xerox /ˈzɪərɒks/ −*n. propr.* **1** machine for copying by xerography. **2** copy thus made. −*v.* (**xerox**) reproduce by this process.

xi /saɪ, ksaɪ/ *n.* fourteenth letter of the Greek alphabet (Ξ, ξ). [Greek]

-xion see *-ion*.

Xmas /ˈkrɪsməs, ˈeksməs/ *n. colloq.* = CHRISTMAS. [abbreviation, with X for the initial chi of Greek *Khristos* Christ]

X-ray /ˈeksreɪ/ −*n.* **1** (in *pl.*) electromagnetic radiation of short wavelength, able to pass through opaque bodies. **2** photograph made by X-rays, esp. showing the position of bones etc. by their greater absorption of the rays. −*v.* photograph, examine, or treat with X-rays. [X, originally with ref. to the unknown nature of the rays]

xylem /ˈzaɪləm/ *n. Bot.* woody tissue. [Greek]

xylophone /ˈzaɪləfəʊn/ *n.* musical instrument of graduated wooden or metal bars struck with small wooden hammers. □ **xylophonist** *n.* [Greek *xulon* wood]

Y

Y¹ /waɪ/ *n.* (also **y**) (*pl.* **Ys** or **Y's**) **1** twenty-fifth letter of the alphabet. **2** (usu. **y**) *Algebra* second unknown quantity. **3** Y-shaped thing.

Y² *symb.* yttrium.

-y¹ *suffix* forming adjectives: **1** from nouns and adjectives, meaning: **a** full of; having the quality of (*messy*). **b** addicted to (*boozy*). **2** from verbs, meaning 'inclined to', 'apt to' (*sticky*). [Old English]

-y² *suffix* (also **-ey**, **-ie**) forming diminutive nouns, pet names, etc. (*granny*; *Sally*; *nightie*). [originally *Scottish*]

-y³ *suffix* forming nouns denoting state, condition, or quality (*orthodoxy*). [Latin *-ia*, Greek *-eia*]

yacht /jɒt/ *n.* **1** light sailing-vessel. **2** larger usu. power-driven vessel for cruising. —*v.* race or cruise in a yacht. [Dutch *jaghtschip*, literally 'pursuit-ship']

yachtsman *n.* (*fem.* **yachtswoman**) person who sails yachts.

yack *slang* —*n.* trivial or unduly persistent conversation. —*v.* engage in this. [imitative]

yah /jɑː/ *int.* (also **yah boo**) expressing derision or defiance. [imitative]

yahoo /jɑːˈhuː/ *n.* bestial person. [name of a race of brutes in *Gulliver's Travels*]

Yahweh /ˈjɑːweɪ/ *n.* (also **Yahveh** /-veɪ/) = JEHOVAH.

yak *n.* long-haired Tibetan ox. [Tibetan]

Yale lock *n. propr.* type of lock with a revolving barrel, used for doors etc. [*Yale*, name of its inventor]

yam *n.* **1 a** tropical or subtropical climbing plant. **b** edible starchy tuber of this. **2** *US* sweet potato. [Portuguese or Spanish]

yammer /ˈjæmə(r)/ *colloq.* or *dial.* —*n.* **1** lament, wail, grumble. **2** voluble talk. —*v.* utter a yammer. [Old English]

yang *n.* (in Chinese philosophy) the active male principle of the universe (cf. YIN).

Yank *n. colloq.* often *derog.* American. [abbreviation of YANKEE]

yank *v.* & *n. colloq.* pull with a jerk. [origin unknown]

Yankee /ˈjæŋkɪ/ *n. colloq.* **1** often *derog.* = YANK. **2** *US* inhabitant of New England or of the northern States. [origin uncertain: perhaps from Dutch *Janke*, diminutive of *Jan John*, as a nickname]

yap —*v.* (-**pp**-) **1** bark shrilly or fussily. **2** *colloq.* talk noisily, foolishly, or complainingly. —*n.* sound of yapping. [imitative]

yappy *adj.* (**-ier**, **-iest**) (in sense 1 of *v.* [imitative]

yarborough /ˈjɑːbərə/ *n.* whist or bridge hand with no card above a 9. [Earl of *Yarborough*, said to have betted against it]

yard¹ *n.* **1** unit of linear measure (3 ft, 0.9144 metre). **2** this length of material. **3** square or cubic yard. **4** spar slung across a mast for a sail to hang from. **5** (in *pl.*; foll. by *of*) *colloq.* a great length. [Old English; = stick]

yard² *n.* **1** piece of enclosed ground, esp. attached to a building or used for a particular purpose. **2** *US & Austral.* garden of a house. [Old English; = enclosure]

yardage *n.* number of yards of material etc.

yard-arm *n.* either end of a ship's yard.

Yardie /ˈjɑːdɪ/ *n. slang* member of a Jamaican or W. Indian gang engaging in organized crime, esp. drug-trafficking. [Jamaican English; = house, home]

yardstick *n.* **1** standard of comparison. **2** measuring rod a yard long, usu. divided into inches etc.

yarmulke /ˈjɑːmʊlkə/ *n.* (also **yarmulka**) skullcap worn by Jewish men. [Yiddish]

yarn —*n.* **1** spun thread, esp. for knitting, weaving, etc. **2** *colloq.* story, traveller's tale, anecdote. —*v. colloq.* tell yarns. [Old English]

yarrow /ˈjærəʊ/ *n.* perennial plant, esp. milfoil. [Old English]

yashmak /ˈjæʃmæk/ *n.* veil concealing the face except the eyes, worn by some Muslim women. [Arabic]

yaw —*v.* (of a ship or aircraft etc.) fail to hold a straight course; go unsteadily. —*n.* yawing of a ship etc. from its course. [origin unknown]

yawl *n.* a kind of ship's boat or sailing- or fishing-boat. [Low German *jolle* or Dutch *jol*]

yawn —*v.* **1** open the mouth wide and inhale, esp. when sleepy or bored. **2** gape, be wide open. —*n.* **1** act of yawning. **2** *colloq.* boring idea, activity, etc. [Old English]

yaws /jɔːz/ *n.pl.* (usu. treated as *sing.*) contagious tropical skin-disease with large red swellings. [origin unknown]

Yb *symb.* ytterbium.

Y chromosome *n.* /ˈwaɪˌkrəʊməˌsəʊm/ (in humans and some other mammals) sex chromosome occurring only in male cells. [Y as an arbitrary label]

yd *abbr.* (*pl.* **yds**) yard (measure).

ye¹ /jiː/ *pron. archaic pl.* of THOU¹. (*ye gods¹*).

ye² /ðiː/ *adj. pseudo-archaic* = THE (*ye olde tea-shoppe*). [from the obsolete y-shaped letter for *th*]

yea /jeɪ/ *archaic* —*adv.* **1** yes. **2** indeed (*ready, yea eager*). —*n.* utterance of 'yea'; yes vote. [Old English]

yeah /jeə/ *adv. colloq.* yes. [a casual pronunciation of YES]

year /jɪə(r)/ *n.* **1** time occupied by the earth in one revolution round the sun, approx. 365¼ days. **2** = CALENDAR YEAR. **3** period of twelve months, starting at any point (*four years ago; tax year*). **4** (in *pl.*) age, time of life (*young for his years*). **5** (usu. in *pl.*) *colloq.* very long time. **6** group of students entering college etc. in the same academic year. [Old English]

yearbook *n.* annual publication dealing with events or aspects of the (usu.) preceding year.

yearling *n.* animal between one and two years old.

yearly —*adj.* **1** done, produced, or occurring once a year. **2** of or lasting a year. —*adv.* once a year.

yearn /jɜːn/ *v.* be filled with longing, compassion, or tenderness. □ **yearning** *n. & adj.* [Old English]

yeast /jiːst/ *n.* greyish-yellow fungous substance obtained esp. from fermenting malt liquors and used as a fermenting agent, to raise bread, etc. [Old English]

yeasty *adj.* (**-ier, -iest**) **1** of, like, or tasting of yeast; frothy. **2** in a ferment. **3** working like yeast. **4** (of talk etc.) light and superficial.

yell —*n.* loud sharp cry; shout. —*v.* cry, shout. [Old English]

yellow /ˈjeləʊ/ —*adj.* **1** of the colour of buttercups, lemons, egg-yolks, etc. **2** having a yellow skin or complexion. **3** *colloq.* cowardly. —*n.* **1** yellow colour or pigment. **2** yellow clothes or material. —*v.* turn yellow. □ **yellowish** *adj.* **yellowness** *n.* **yellowy** *adj.* [Old English: related to GOLD]

yellow-belly *n. colloq.* coward.

yellow card *n.* card shown by the referee to a football-player being cautioned.

yellow fever *n.* tropical virus disease with fever and jaundice.

yellow flag *n.* flag displayed by a ship in quarantine.

yellowhammer *n.* bunting of which the male has a yellow head, neck, and breast.

Yellow Pages *n.pl. propr.* telephone directory on yellow paper, listing and classifying business subscribers.

yellow pepper *n.* ripe yellow fruit of the capsicum plant.

yellow spot *n.* point of acutest vision in the retina.

yellow streak *n. colloq.* trait of cowardice.

yelp —*n.* sharp shrill cry as of a dog in pain or excitement —*v.* utter a yelp. [Old English]

yen¹ *n.* (*pl.* same) chief monetary unit of Japan. [Japanese from Chinese]

yen² *colloq.* —*n.* longing or yearning. —*v.* feel a longing. [Chinese]

yeoman /ˈjəʊmən/ *n.* **1** esp. *hist.* man holding and cultivating a small landed estate. **2** member of the yeomanry force. □ **yeomanly** *adj.* [from earlier *yoman*, *yeman*, etc., prob. = young man]

Yeoman of the Guard *n.* member of the sovereign's bodyguard.

yeomanry *n.* (*pl.* **-ies**) **1** body or class of yeomen. **2** *hist.* volunteer cavalry force raised from the yeoman class.

Yeoman Warder *n.* (correct term for) a "beefeater" at the Tower of London.

yep *adv. & n.* (also **yup**) *US colloq.* = YES.

yes —*adv.* **1** indicating that the answer to the question is affirmative, the statement etc. made is correct, the request or command will be complied with, or the person summoned or addressed is present. **2** (**yes?**) **a** indeed? is that so? **b** what do you want? —*n.* **1** utterance of the word *yes*. **2** affirmation or assent. **3** 'yes' vote. □ **say yes** grant a request, confirm a statement. [Old English; = *yea let it be*]

yes-man *n. colloq.* weakly acquiescent person.

yesterday /ˈjestədeɪ/ —*adv.* **1** on the day before today. **2** in the recent past. —*n.* **1** the day before today. **2** the recent past. [Old English]

yesteryear /ˈjestəjɪə(r)/ *n. archaic or rhet.* **1** last year. **2** the recent past. [Old English *yester-* as in *yesterday*, YEAR]

yet —*adv.* **1** as late as, or until, now or then (*there is yet time; your best work yet*). **2** (with *neg.* or *interrog.*) so soon as, or by, now or then (*is it not time yet; have you finished yet?*). **3** again; in addition (*more and yet more*). **4** in the remaining time available (*I will do it yet*). **5** (foll. by *compar.*) even (*a yet more difficult task*). **6** nevertheless; and or but in spite of that. —*conj.* but at the same time; but nevertheless. [Old English]

yeti /ˈjeti/ *n.* = ABOMINABLE SNOWMAN. [Tibetan]

yew *n.* 1 dark-leaved evergreen tree bearing berry-like cones. 2 its wood. [Old English]

Y-fronts /ˈwaɪfrʌnts/ *n. propr.* men's or boys' briefs with a Y-shaped seam at the front.

YHA *abbr.* Youth Hostels Association.

Yid *n. slang offens.* Jew. [back-formation from YIDDISH]

Yiddish /ˈjɪdɪʃ/ —*n.* language used by Jews in or from Europe, orig. a German dialect with words from Hebrew etc. —*adj.* of this language. [German *jüdisch* Jewish]

yield —*v.* 1 produce or return as a fruit, profit, or result. 2 give up; surrender; concede. 3 a (often foll. by *to*) surrender; submit; defer to. b (as **yielding** *adj.*) compliant; submissive; soft and pliable. 4 (foll. by *to*) give right of way to (other traffic). 5 (foll. by *to*) be inferior or confess inferiority to (*I yield to none in this matter*). —*n.* amount yielded or produced. [Old English, = pay]

yin *n.* (in Chinese philosophy) the passive female principle of the universe (cf. YANG).

yippee /jɪˈpiː/ *int.* expressing delight or excitement. [natural exclamation]

YMCA *abbr.* Young Men's Christian Association.

yob /jɒb/ *n. slang* lout, hooligan. □ **yobbish** *adj.* [back slang for BOY]

yobbo /ˈjɒbəʊ/ *n.* (pl. **-s**) *slang* = YOB.

yodel /ˈjəʊd(ə)l/ —*v.* (**-ll-**; *US* **-l-**) sing with melodious inarticulate sounds and frequent changes between falsetto and normal voice in the manner of Swiss mountain-dwellers. —*n.* yodelling cry. □ **yodeller** *n.* [German]

yoga /ˈjəʊgə/ *n.* 1 Hindu system of meditation and asceticism designed to effect reunion with the universal spirit. 2 system of physical exercises and breathing control used in yoga. [Sanskrit, = union]

yoghurt /ˈjɒgət/ *n.* (also **yogurt**) semisolid sourish food made from milk fermented by added bacteria. [Turkish]

yogi /ˈjəʊgi/ *n.* (pl. **-s**) devotee of yoga. [Hindustani: related to YOGA]

yoicks *int.* cry used by fox-hunters to urge on the hounds. [origin unknown]

yoke —*n.* 1 wooden crosspiece fastened over the necks of two oxen etc. and attached to the plough or wagon to be pulled. 2 (pl. same or **-s**) pair (of oxen etc.). 3 object like a yoke in form or function, e.g. a wooden shoulder-piece for carrying a pair of pails, the top section of a garment from which the rest hangs. 4 sway, dominion, or servitude. 5

bond of union, esp. of marriage. —*v.* (**-king**) 1 put a yoke on. 2 couple or unite (a pair). 3 (foll. by *to*) link (one thing) to (another). 4 match or work together. [Old English]

yokel /ˈjəʊk(ə)l/ *n.* rustic; country bumpkin. [perhaps dial.]

yolk /jəʊk/ *n.* yellow inner part of an egg. [Old English: related to YELLOW]

Yom Kippur /jɒm ˈkɪpə(r)/ *n.* most solemn religious fast day of the Jewish year, Day of Atonement. [Hebrew]

yon *adj. & adv. literary & dial.* yonder. [Old English]

yonder —*adv.* over there; at some distance in that direction; in the place indicated. —*adj.* situated yonder.

yonks *n.pl. slang* a long time (*yonks ago*). [origin unknown]

yoo-hoo /ˈjuːhuː/ *int.* used to attract a person's attention. [natural exclamation]

yore *n.* □ **of yore** a long time ago. [Old English, = long ago]

York *v.* Cricket bowl out with a yorker. [back-formation from YORKER]

yorker *n.* Cricket ball that pitches immediately under the bat. [probably with ref. to the practice of Yorkshire cricketers]

Yorkist /ˈjɔːkɪst/ —*n. hist.* follower of the House of York, esp. in the Wars of the Roses. —*adj.* of the House of York.

Yorkshire pudding /ˈjɔːkʃə/ *n.* baked batter eaten with roast beef.

Yorkshire terrier /ˈjɔːkʃə/ *n.* small long-haired blue and tan kind of terrier.

you /juː/ *pron.* (*obj.* **you**; *poss.* **your**, **yours**) 1 the person or persons addressed. 2 (as *int.* with a noun) in an exclamatory statement (*you fools!*). 3 (in general statements) one, a person, people (*you get used to it*). □ **you and yours** you and your family, property, etc. [Old English, originally objective case of YE]

you'd /juːd/ *contr.* 1 you had. 2 you would.

you'll /juːl/ *contr.* you will; you shall.

young /jʌŋ/ —*adj.* (**younger** /ˈjʌŋgə(r)/; **youngest** /ˈjʌŋgɪst/) 1 not far advanced in life, development, or existence; not yet old. 2 a immature, inexperienced. b youthful. 3 of or characteristic of youth (*young love*). 4 representing young people (*Young Farmers*). 5 a distinguishing a son from his father (*young George*). b as a familiar or condescending form of address (*listen, young lady*). 6 (**younger**) distinguishing one person from another of the same name (*the younger Pitt*). —*n.* (*collect.*) offspring, esp. of animals. □ **youngish** *adj.* [Old English]

young person

young person *n. Law* person aged between 14 and 17 years.

youngster *n.* child, young person.

your /jɔː(r)/ *poss. pron.* 1 of or belonging to you. 2 *colloq.* often *derog.* much talked of; well known (*your typical professor*). [Old English]

you're /jɔː(r)/ *contr.* you are.

yours /jɔːz/ *poss. pron.* 1 the one or ones belonging to you (*it is yours; yours are over there*). 2 your letter (*yours of the 10th*). 3 introducing a formula ending a letter (*yours ever; yours truly*). □ **of yours** of or belonging to you (*friend of yours*).

yourself /jɔːˈself/ *pron.* (*pl.* **yourselves**) 1 a *emphat. form* of you. b *refl. form* of you. 2 in your normal state of body or mind (*are quite yourself again*). □ **be yourself** see ONESELF.

youth /juːθ/ *n.* (*pl.* **-s** /juːðz/) 1 being young; period between childhood and adult age. 2 vigour, enthusiasm, inexperience, or other characteristic of this period. 3 young man. 4 (as *pl.*) young people collectively (*the youth of the country*). [Old English: related to YOUNG]

youth club *n.* place for young people's leisure activities.

youthful *adj.* young or still having the characteristics of youth. □ **youthfully** *adv.* **youthfulness** *n.*

youth hostel *n.* any of a chain of cheap lodgings for holiday-makers, esp. walkers and cyclists.

you've /juːv/ *contr.* you have.

yowl —*n.* loud wailing cry of or as of a cat or dog in distress. —*v.* utter a yowl. [imitative]

yo-yo /ˈjəʊjəʊ/ *n.* (*pl.* **yo-yos**) 1 toy consisting of a pair of discs with a deep groove between them in which string is attached and wound, and which can be made to fall and rise. 2 :thing that repeatedly falls and rises. [origin unknown]

Yt. *abbr.* 1 year(s. 2 younger. 3 your.

yrs. *abbr.* 1 years. 2 yours.

YTS *abbr.* Youth Training Scheme.

ytterbium /ɪˈtɜːbɪəm/ *n.* metallic element of the lanthanide series. [*Ytterby* in Sweden]

yttrium /ˈɪtrɪəm/ *n.* metallic element resembling the lanthanides. [related to YTTERBIUM]

yuan /juːˈɑːn/ *n.* (*pl.* same) chief monetary unit of China. [Chinese]

yucca /ˈjʌkə/ *n.* subtropical white-flowered plant with swordlike leaves, often grown as a house-plant. [Carib]

yuck /jʌk/ *int.* (also **yuk**) *slang* expression of strong distaste. [imitative]

yucky *adj.* (also **yukky**) (**-ier**, **-iest**) *slang* 1 messy, repellent. 2 sickly, sentimental.

Yugoslav /ˈjuːgəˌslɑːv/ (also **Jugoslav**) —*n.* 1 native or national of Yugoslavia. 2 person of Yugoslav descent. —*adj.* of Yugoslavia. □ **Yugoslavian** /-ˈslɑːvɪən/ *adj.* & *n.* [Serbo-Croat *jug* south: related to SLAV]

yuk var. of YUCK.

yukky var. of YUCKY.

yule *n.* (in full **yule-tide**) *archaic* the Christmas festival. [Old English]

yule-log *n.* 1 large log traditionally burnt on Christmas Eve. 2 log-shaped chocolate cake eaten at Christmas.

yummy /ˈjʌmɪ/ *adj.* (**-ier**, **-iest**) *colloq.* tasty, delicious. [from YUM-YUM]

yum-yum *int.* expressing pleasure from eating or the prospect of eating. [natural exclamation]

yup var. of YEP.

yuppie /ˈjʌpɪ/ *n.* (also **yuppy**) (*pl.* **-ies**) (often *attrib.*) *colloq.* usu. *derog.* young ambitious professional person working in a city. [from *young urban professional*]

YWCA *abbr.* Young Women's Christian Association.

Z

Z /zed/ n. (also **z**) (pl. **Zs** or **Z's**) **1** twenty-sixth letter of the alphabet. **2** (usu. **z**) *Algebra* third unknown quantity.

zabaglione /ˌzæbəˈljəʊnɪ/ n. Italian dessert of whipped and heated egg-yolks, sugar, and wine. [Italian]

zany /ˈzeɪnɪ/ adj. (**-ier**, **-iest**) comically idiotic; crazily ridiculous. [French or Italian]

zap slang —v. (**-pp-**) **1 a** kill or destroy; attack. **b** hit hard (*zapped the ball over the net*). **2** move quickly. **3** overwhelm emotionally. —int. expressing the sound or impact of a bullet, ray gun, etc., or any sudden event. [imitative]

zappy adj. (**-ier**, **-iest**) colloq. lively, energetic.

Zarathustrian var. of ZOROASTRIAN.

zeal n. earnestness or fervour; hearty persistent endeavour. [Greek *zēlos*]

zealot /ˈzelət/ n. extreme partisan; fanatic. □ **zealotry** n.

zealous /ˈzeləs/ adj. full of zeal; enthusiastic. □ **zealously** adv.

zebra /ˈzebrə, ˈziː-/ n. (pl. same or **-s**) black-and-white striped African animal of the family including the ass and horse. [Italian or Portuguese from Congolese]

zebra crossing n. striped street-crossing where pedestrians have precedence.

zebu /ˈziːbuː/ n. (pl. same or **-s**) humped ox of Asia and Africa. [French]

Zen n. letter Z. [Greek ZETA]

zee /ziː/ n. US letter Z. [var. of ZED]

Zeitgeist /ˈtsaɪtɡaɪst/ n. the spirit of the times. [German]

Zen n. form of Buddhism emphasizing meditation and intuition. [Japanese, = meditation]

Zend n. an interpretation of the Avesta. [Persian]

Zend-Avesta n. Zoroastrian sacred writings of the Avesta (or text) and Zend (or commentary).

zenith /ˈzenɪθ/ n. **1** point of the heavens directly above an observer. **2** highest point (of power or prosperity etc.). [Latin from Arabic]

zephyr /ˈzefə(r)/ n. literary mild gentle breeze. [Greek, = west wind]

Zeppelin /ˈzepəlɪn/ n. large dirigible German airship of the early 20th c. [Count F. von *Zeppelin*, name of an airman]

zero /ˈzɪərəʊ/ n. (pl. **-s**) **1** figure 0; nought; nil. **2** point on the scale of a thermometer etc. from which a positive or negative quantity is reckoned. **3** (*attrib.*) no, not any (*zero growth*). **4** (in full *zero-hour*) **a** hour at which a planned, esp. military, operation is timed to begin. **b** crucial moment. **5** lowest or earliest point (*down to zero; the year zero*). □ **zero in on** (*-oes, -oed*) **1** take aim at. **2** focus one's attention on. [Arabic: related to CIPHER]

zero option n. disarmament proposal for the total removal of certain types of weapons on both sides.

zero-rated adj. on which no VAT is charged.

zest n. **1** piquancy; stimulating flavour or quality. **2 a** keen enjoyment or interest. **b** (often foll. by *for*) relish. **c** gusto. **3** scraping of orange or lemon peel as flavouring. □ **zestful** adj. **zestfully** adv. [French]

zeta /ˈziːtə/ n. sixth letter of the Greek alphabet (Z, ζ). [Greek]

zeugma /ˈzjuːɡmə/ n. figure of speech using a verb or adjective with two nouns, to one of which it is strictly applicable while the other is not used appropriate to the other is not used (e.g. *with weeping eyes and* [sc. *grieving*] *hearts*) (cf. SYLLEPSIS). [Greek, = a yoking, from *zugon* yoke]

ziggurat /ˈzɪɡʊræt/ n. rectangular stepped tower in ancient Mesopotamia, surmounted by a temple. [Assyrian]

zigzag /ˈzɪɡzæɡ/ —adj. with abrupt alternate right and left turns (*zigzag line*). —n. zigzag line; thing having the form of a zigzag or having sharp turns. —adv. with a zigzag course. —v. (**-gg-**) move in a zigzag course. [French from German]

zilch n. esp. US slang nothing. [origin uncertain]

zillion /ˈzɪljən/ n. colloq. indefinite large number. [probably after *million*]

Zimmer frame n. propr. a kind of walking-frame. [*Zimmer*, name of the maker]

zinc n. greyish-white metallic element used as a component of brass and in galvanizing sheet iron. [German *Zink*]

zing colloq. —n. vigour, energy. —v. move swiftly, esp. with a high-pitched ringing sound. [imitative]

zinnia /'zɪnɪə/ n. garden plant with showy flowers. [Zinn, name of a physician and botanist]

Zion /'zaɪən/ n. **1** ancient Jerusalem; its holy hill. **b** the Christian Church. **3** the Kingdom of Heaven. [Hebrew ṣiyōn]

Zionism n. movement for the re-establishment and development of a Jewish nation in what is now Israel. □ **Zionist** n. & adj.

zip —n. **1** light fast sound. **2** energy, vigour. **3 a** (in full **zip-fastener**) fastening device of two flexible strips with interlocking projections, closed or opened by sliding a clip along them. **b** (attrib.) having a zip-fastener (zip bag). —v. (-**pp**-) **1** (often foll. by up) fasten with a zip-fastener. **2** move with zip or at high speed. [imitative]

Zip code n. US postcode. [zone improvement plan]

zipper n. esp. US = ZIP 3a.

zippy adj. (-**ier**, -**iest**) colloq. lively, speedy.

zircon /'zɜːkən/ n. zirconium silicate of which some translucent varieties are cut into gems. [German Zirkon]

zirconium /zə'kəʊnɪəm/ n. grey metallic element.

zit n. esp. US slang pimple. [origin unknown]

zither /'zɪðə(r)/ n. stringed instrument with a flat soundbox, placed horizontally and played with the fingers and a plectrum. [Latin: related to GUITAR]

zloty /'zlɒtɪ/ n. (pl. same or -s) chief monetary unit of Poland. [Polish]

Zn symb. zinc.

zodiac /'zəʊdɪˌæk/ n. **1** belt of the heavens including all apparent positions of the sun, moon, and planets as known to ancient astronomers, and divided into twelve equal parts (**signs of the zodiac**). **2** diagram of these signs. □ **zodiacal** /zə'daɪək(ə)l/ adj. [Greek zōion animal]

zombie /'zɒmbɪ/ n. **1** colloq. person who acts mechanically or lifelessly. **2** corpse said to have been revived by witchcraft. [West African]

zone —n. **1** area having particular features, properties, purpose, or use (danger zone; smokeless zone). **2** well-defined region of more or less beltlike form. **3** area between two concentric circles. **4** encircling band of colour etc. **5** archaic belt, girdle. —v. (-**ning**) **1** encircle as or with a zone. **2** arrange or distribute by zones. **3** assign as or to a particular area. □ **zonal** adj. [Greek zōnē girdle]

zonked /zɒŋkt/ adj. slang (often foll. by out) exhausted; intoxicated. [zonk hit]

zoo n. zoological garden. [abbreviation]

zoological /ˌzəʊə'lɒdʒɪk(ə)l, zu:ə-/ adj. of zoology.

zoological garden n. (also **zoological gardens** n.pl.) public garden or park with a collection of animals for exhibition and study.

zoology /zəʊ'blədʒɪ, zu:'bl-/ n. the study of animals. □ **zoologist** n. [Greek zōion animal]

■ **Usage** See note at zoology.

■ **Usage** The second pronunciation given for zoology, zoological, and zoologist, with the first syllable pronounced as in zoo, although extremely common, is considered incorrect by some people.

zoom —v. **1** move quickly, esp. with a buzzing sound. **2** cause an aeroplane to mount at high speed and a steep angle. **3** (often foll. by in or in on) (of a camera) change rapidly from a long shot to a close-up (of). **4** (of prices etc.) rise sharply. —n. **1** aeroplane's steep climb. **2** zooming camera shot. [imitative]

zoom lens n. lens allowing a camera to zoom by varying the focal length.

zoophyte /'zəʊəˌfaɪt/ n. plantlike animal, esp. a coral, sea anemone, or sponge. [Greek zōion animal, phuton plant]

Zoroastrian /ˌzɒrəʊ'æstrɪən/ (also **Zarathustrian** /ˌzærə'θʊstrɪən/) —adj. of Zoroaster (or Zarathustra) or the dualistic religious system taught by him. —n. follower of Zoroaster. □ **Zoroastrianism** n. [Zoroaster, Persian founder of the religion]

Zr symb. zirconium.

zucchini /zu'kiːnɪ/ n. (pl. -s) esp. US & Austral. courgette. [Italian, pl. of zucchino, diminutive of zucca gourd]

Zulu /'zuːluː/ —n. (pl. -s) **1** member of a S. African Bantu people. **2** their language. —adj. of this people or language. [native name]

zygote /'zaɪɡəʊt/ n. Biol. cell formed by the union of two gametes. [Greek zugó-tos yoked: related to ZEUGMA]

Better English Guide

The aim of this guide is to give a short description of accepted conventions in written standard English. It does not cover other forms and varieties of English.

A. PUNCTUATION MARKS

Punctuation is a complicated subject, and only the main principles can be discussed here. The explanations are based on practice in British English; usage in American English differs in some instances. The main headings are as follows:

1. General remarks
2. Capital letter
3. Full stop
4. Comma
5. Semicolon
6. Colon
7. Question mark
8. Exclamation mark
9. Apostrophe
10. Quotation marks
11. Brackets (Parentheses)
12. Dash
13. Hyphen

1. General remarks

The purpose of punctuation is to mark out strings of words into manageable groups and help clarify their meaning (or in some cases to prevent a wrong meaning being deduced). The marks most commonly used to divide a piece of prose or other writing are the full stop, the semicolon, and the comma, with the strength of the dividing or separating role diminishing from the full stop to the comma. The full stop therefore marks the main division into sentences; the semicolon joins sentences (as in this sentence); and the comma (which is the most flexible in use and causes most problems) separates smaller elements with the least loss of continuity. Brackets and dashes also serve as separators—often more strikingly than commas, as in this sentence.

2. Capital letter

2.1.1 This is used for the first letter of the word beginning a sentence in most cases:

He decided not to come. Later he changed his mind.

C

2.1.2 A sentence or clause playing a subordinate or parenthetic role within a larger one does not normally begin with a capital letter:

I have written several letters (there are many to be written) and hope to finish them tomorrow.

2.1.3 In the following, however, the sentence is a separate one and therefore does begin with a capital letter:

There is more than one possibility. (You have said this often before.) So we should think carefully before acting.

2.1.4 A capital letter also begins sentences that form quoted speech:

The assistant turned and replied, 'There are no more left.'

2.2 The use of capital letters for proper names, titles, etc. is discussed in section C of this appendix (p. 1087).

3. Full stop

3.1 This is used to mark the end of a sentence when it is a statement (that is, not a question or exclamation). In prose, sentences marked by full stops normally represent a discrete or distinct statement; more closely connected or complementary statements are joined by a semicolon (as here).

3.2.1 Full stops are used to mark abbreviations (*Weds.*, *Gen.*, *p.m.*). They are often omitted in abbreviations that are familiar or very common (*Dr*, *Mr*, *Mrs*, etc.), in abbreviations that consist entirely of capital letters (*BBC*, *GMT*, etc.), and in acronyms that are pronounced as a word rather than a sequence of letters (*Intelsat*, *Ernie*, etc.).

3.2.2 If the full stop following an abbreviation comes right at the end of a sentence, another full stop is not added:

They have a collection of many animals, including dogs, cats, tortoises, snakes, etc.

but note this example with two full stops:

They have a collection of many animals (dogs, cats, tortoises, snakes, etc.).

3.3 A sequence of three full stops is used to mark an ellipsis or omission in a sequence of words, especially when forming an incomplete quotation.

He left the room, banged the door, . . . and went out.

When the omission occurs at the end of a sentence, a fourth point is added as the full stop of the whole sentence:

The report said: 'There are many issues to be considered, of which the chief are money, time, and personnel. . . . Let us consider personnel first.'

3.4 A full stop is used as a decimal point (*10.5%*, *£1.65*), and to divide hours and minutes in giving time (*6.15 p.m.*), although a colon is usual in American use (*6.15 p.m.*).

4. Comma

4.1 Use of the comma is more difficult to describe than the use of other punctuation marks, and there is much variation in practice. Essentially, its role is to give detail to the structure of sentences, especially longer ones, and make their meaning clear. Too many commas can be distracting; too few can make a piece of writing difficult to read or, worse, difficult to understand.

4.2.1 The comma is widely used to separate the main clauses of a compound sentence when they are not sufficiently close in meaning or content to form a continuous unpunctuated sentence, and are not distinct enough to warrant a semicolon. A conjunction such as *and*, *but*, *yet*, etc., is normally used:

The road runs through a beautiful wooded valley, and the railway line follows it closely.

The bus was late, so we had to wait.

4.2.2 It is considered incorrect to join the clauses of a compound sentence without a conjunction. In the following sentence, the comma should either be replaced by a semicolon, or be retained and followed by *and*:

incorrect *I like swimming very much, I go to the pool every week.*

4.2.3 It is also considered incorrect to separate a subject from its verb with a comma:

incorrect *Those with the smallest incomes and no other means, should get most support.*

4.3.1 Commas are usually inserted between adjectives coming before a noun:

An enterprising, ambitious person.

A cold, damp, badly heated room.

4.3.2 But the comma is omitted when the last adjective has a closer relation to the noun than the others:

A distinguished foreign politician.

A little old lady.

4.4 An important role of the comma is to prevent ambiguity or (momentary) misunderstanding, especially after a verb used intransitively (without a noun as direct object) where it might otherwise be taken to be transitive (with a direct object):

With the police pursuing, the people shouted loudly.

Other examples follow:

He did not want to leave, from a feeling of loyalty.

In the valley below, the houses appeared very small.

However, much as I should like to I cannot agree.

(compare *However much I should like to I cannot agree.*)

4.5.1 Commas are used in pairs to separate elements in a sentence that are not part of the main statement:

I should like you all, ladies and gentlemen, to raise your glasses.

There is no sense, as far as I can see, in this suggestion.

It appears, however, that we were wrong.

4.5.2 The comma is also used to separate a relative clause from its antecedent when the clause is not serving an identifying function:

The book, which was on the table, was a present.

In the above sentence, the information in the *which* clause is incidental to the main statement; without the comma, it would form an essential part of it in identifying which book is being referred to (and could be replaced by *that*):

The book which/that was on the table was a present.

4.6.1 Commas are used to separate items in a list or sequence. Usage varies as to the inclusion of a comma before *and* and the last item; the practice in this dictionary is to include it:

The following will report at 9.30 sharp: Jones, Smith, Thompson, and Williams.

4.6.2 A final comma before *and*, when used regularly and consistently, has the advantage of clarifying the grouping at a composite name occurring at the end of a list:

We shall go to Smiths, Boots, Woolworths, and Marks and Spencer.

4.7 A comma is used in numbers of four or more figures, to separate each group of three consecutive figures starting from the right (e.g. 10,135,793).

5. Semicolon

5.1.1 The main role of the semicolon is to unite sentences that are closely associated or that complement or parallel each other in some way, as in the following:

In the north of the city there is a large industrial area with little private housing; further east is the university.

To err is human; to forgive, divine.

5.1.2 It is often used as a stronger division that is already divided by commas:

He came out of the house, which lay back from the road, and saw her at the end of the path; but instead of continuing towards her, he hid until she had gone.

5.2 It is also used in a similar way in lists of names or other items, to indicate a stronger division:

I should like to thank the managing director, Stephen Jones; my secretary, Mary Cartwright; and my assistant, Kenneth Sloane.

6. Colon

6.1 The main role of the colon is to separate main clauses when there is a step forward from the first to the second, especially from introduction to main point, from general statement to example, from cause to effect, and from premise to conclusion:

There is something I want to say: I should like you all to know how grateful I am to you.

It was not easy: to begin with I had to find the right house.

The weather was bad: so we decided to stay at home. (In this example, a comma could be used, but the emphasis on cause and effect would be much reduced.)

6.2 It also introduces a list of items. In this use a dash should not be added:

The following will be needed: a pen, pencil, rubber, piece of paper, and ruler.

6.3 It is used to introduce, more formally and emphatically than a comma would, speech or quoted material:

I told them last week: 'Do not in any circumstances open this door.'

7. Question mark

7.1.1 This is used in place of the full stop to show that the preceding sentence is a question:

Do you want another piece of cake?

He really is her husband?

7.1.2 It is not used when the question is implied by indirect speech:

I asked you whether you wanted another piece of cake.

7.2 It is used (often in brackets) to express doubt or uncertainty about a word or phrase immediately following or preceding it:

Julius Caesar, born (?) 100 BC.

They were then seen boarding a bus (to London?).

8. Exclamation mark

This is used after an exclamatory word, phrase, or sentence expressing any of the following:

8.1 Absurdity:
What an idea!

8.2 Command or warning:
Go to your room!
Be careful!

8.3 Contempt or disgust:
They are revolting!

8.4 Emotion or pain:
I hate you!
That really hurts!
Ouch!

8.5 Enthusiasm:
I'd love to come!

8.6 Wish or regret:
Let me come!
If only I could swim!

8.7 Wonder, admiration, or surprise:

What a good idea!

Aren't they beautiful!

9. Apostrophe

9.1.1 The main use is to indicate the possessive case, as in *John's book*, *the girl's mother*, etc. It comes before the *s* in singular and plural nouns not ending in *s*, as in *the boy's games* and *the women's games*. It comes after the *s* in plural nouns ending in *s*, as in *the boys' games*.

9.1.2 In singular nouns ending in *s* practice differs between (for example) *Charles'* and *Charles's*; in some cases the shorter form is preferable for reasons of sound, as in *Xerxes' fleet*.

9.1.3 It is also used to indicate a place or business, e.g. *the butcher's*. In this use it is often omitted in some names, e.g. *Smiths; Lloyds Bank*.

9.2 It is used to indicate a contraction, e.g. *he's, wouldn't, o'clock*.

9.3 It is sometimes used to form a plural of individual letters or numbers, although this use is diminishing. It is helpful in *cross your t's* but unnecessary in *MPs* and *1940s*.

9.4 For its use as a quotation mark, see section 10.

10. Quotation marks

10.1 The main use is to indicate direct speech and quotations. A single turned comma (') is normally used at the beginning, and a single apostrophe (') at the end of the quoted matter:

She said, 'I have something to ask you.'

10.2 The closing quotation mark should come after any punctuation mark which is part of the quoted matter, but before any mark which is not:

They were described as 'an unruly bunch'.

Did I hear you say 'go away'?

10.3 Punctuation dividing a sentence of quoted speech is put inside the quotation marks:

'Go away,' he said, 'and don't ever come back.'

10.4 Quotation marks are also used for cited words and phrases:

What does 'integrated circuit' mean?

10.5 A quotation within a quotation is put in double quotation marks:

'Have you any idea,' he said, 'what "integrated circuit" means?'

Many publications use single within double quotations:

"Have you any idea," he said, "what 'integrated circuit' means?"

11. Brackets

( ) [ ]

11.1 The types of brackets used in normal punctuation are round brackets ( ) and square brackets [ ].

The name 'parentheses' is also used, especially for round brackets.

11.2 The main use of round brackets is to enclose explanations and extra information or comment:

He is (as he always was) a rebel.

Zimbabwe (formerly Rhodesia).

They talked about Machtpolitik (power politics).

11.3 They are used to give references and citations:

Thomas Carlyle (1795–1881).

A discussion of integrated circuits (see p. 38).

11.4 They are used to enclose reference letters or figures, e.g. *(1)*, *(a)*.

11.5 They are used to enclose optional words:

There are many (apparent) difficulties.

(In this example, the difficulties may or may not be only apparent.)

11.6.1 Square brackets are used less often. The main use is to enclose extra information attributable to someone (normally an editor) other than the writer of the surrounding text:

The man walked in, and his sister [Sarah] greeted him.

11.6.2 They are used in some contexts to convey special kinds of information, especially when round brackets are used also for other purposes: for example, in this dictionary they are used to give the etymologies at the end of entries.

12. Dash

12.1 A single dash is used to indicate a pause, whether a hesitation in speech or to introduce an explanation or expansion of what comes before it:

'I think you should have—told me,' he replied.

12.2 A pair of dashes is used to indicate asides and parentheses, in the same way as commas, explained at 4.5.1 above but forming a more distinct break:

We then saw the reptiles—snakes, crocodiles, that sort of thing.

People in the north are more friendly—and helpful—than those in the south.

There is nothing to be gained—unless you want a more active social life—in moving to the city.

12.3 A single dash is sometimes used to indicate an omitted word, for example a coarse word in reported speech:

'— you all,' he said.

13. Hyphen

13.1 The hyphen has two main functions: to link words or elements of words into longer words and compounds, and to mark the division of a word at the end of a line in print or writing.

13.2.1 The use of the hyphen to connect words to form compound words is diminishing in English, especially when the elements are of one syllable, as in *birdsong*, *eardrum*, and *playgroup*, and also in some longer formations such as *figurehead* and *nationwide*. The hyphen is used more often in routine and occasional couplings, especially when reference to the sense of the separate elements is considered important or unavoidable, as in *ankle-bone*. It is often retained to avoid awkward collisions of letters, as in *fast-talk*.

13.2.2 The hyphen serves to connect words that have a syntactic link, as in *hard-covered books* and *French-speaking people*, where the reference is to books with hard covers and people who speak French, rather than hard books with covers and French people who can speak (which would be the sense conveyed if the hyphens were omitted). It is also used to avoid more extreme kinds of ambiguity, as in *twenty-odd people*.

13.2.3 A particularly important use of the hyphen is to link compounds and phrases used attributively, as in a *well-known man* (but

the man is well known), and *Christmas-tree lights* (but *the lights on the Christmas tree*).

13.2.4 It is also used to connect elements to form words in cases such as *re-enact* (where the collision of two *es* would be awkward), *reform* (= to form again, to distinguish it from *reform*), and some other prefixed words such as those in *anti-*, *non-*, *over-*, and *post-*. Usage varies in this regard, and much depends on how well established and clearly recognizable the resulting formation is. When the second element is a name, a hyphen is usual (as in *anti-Darwinian*).

13.2.5 It is used to indicate a common second element in all but the last of a list, e.g. *two-*, *three-*, or *fourfold*.

13.3 The hyphen used to divide a word at the end of a line is a different matter, because it is not a permanent feature of the spelling. It is more common in print, where the text has to be accurately spaced and the margin justified; in handwritten and typed or word-processed material it can be avoided altogether. In print, words need to be divided carefully and consistently, taking account of the appearance and structure of the word. Detailed guidance on word division may be found in the *Oxford Spelling Dictionary* (2nd edition, 1995).

B. SPELLING RULES

1. General remarks

British spelling was largely standardized by the middle of the 18th century, and American variants established by the early 19th century, but many spelling conventions were fixed by printers as early as 1500, and since various changes in pronunciation have occurred in the ensuing centuries, present-day pronunciation and spelling are often at variance. Also, the 'neutral' vowel sound of unstressed syllables gives no guidance as to spelling, which is usually determined by the origin of the word, and care must be taken with words containing unstressed syllables such as *de-*, *di-*, *en-*, *in-*, *-par-*, *-per-*. These notes cover a few of the more common difficulties: for other individual points of uncertainty, the main part of the dictionary should be consulted, e.g. for pairs of words distinguished by meaning, such as *affect/effect, amend/emend, complement/compliment, enquire/inquire, its/it's, loath/loathe, stationary/stationery*. The following words may be difficult to find in a dictionary if the spelling is not known: *diphtheria, dissect, eczema, fuchsia, guerrilla, minuscule, necessary, ophthalmic, pejorative, semantics*. Note that silent letters occur especially in the combinations *gn-, kn-, mn-, pn-, ps-, pt-, rh-*, and that words

encing in vowels other than *e* often have irregular inflections. (For a discussion of hyphenation see the section.)

2. *i* before e

2.1

For words pronounced with an 'ee' (/iː/) sound, the traditional rule '*i* before *e* except after *c*' is fairly reliable. The exceptions are (*a*) *seize* (and *seise*), (*b*) either and *neither* (if you pronounce them that way; also *heinous*, *inveigle*), (*c*) Latin words such as *prima facie* and *species*, and (*d*) words in which a stem ending in *-e* is followed by a suffix beginning with *-i*, e.g. *caffeine*, *casein*, *codeine*, *plebeian*, *protein*. Note that the syllable *-feit* is so spelt, e.g. in *counterfeit*, *forfeit*, *surfeit*, and that *mischief* is spelt like *chief*.

2.2

Words pronounced with an 'ay' (/eɪ/) or long 'i' (/aɪ/) sound generally have *-ei-*: e.g. *beige*, *heinous*, *reign*, *veil*, *eiderdown*, *height*, *kaleidoscope*. Words with other sounds follow no rules and must simply become familiar to the eye, e.g. *foreign* (related to *reign*), *friend*, *heifer*, *leisure*, *Madeira*, *sieve*, *sovereign* (like *foreign*), *their*, *view*, *weir*, *weird*.

3. Doubling consonants

3.1

When a suffix beginning with a vowel (such as *-able*, *-ed*, *-er*, *-ing*, or *-ish*) is added to a word ending in a consonant, the consonant is usually doubled if it is a single consonant preceded by a single vowel, and comes at the end of a stressed syllable. So *controllable*, *dropped*, *permitted*, *bigger*, *abetter*; *trekking*, *beginning*, *transferring*, *reddish*, *forgotten*, but *sweated*, *sweeter*; *appealing*, *greenish* (more than one vowel), *planting* (more than one consonant), *billeted*, *happened*, *preferable*, *profiting*, *rocketing* (not ending a stressed syllable). A secondary stress (not generally marked in this dictionary) is often sufficient to elicit a doubled consonant, e.g. *caravanned*, *confabbed*, *diagrammed*, *formatted*, *humbugged*, *programmed*, *zigzagged* and (in British use) *kidnapped*, *worshipped*, though note *invalided* and (in British use) *benefited*. Other variable or exceptional verbs include *canvas*, *coif*, *curvet*, *ricochet*, *target*, *tittup*, and *wainscot*. Verbs ending in a vowel followed by *-c* generally form inflections in *-cked*, *-cking*, e.g. *bivouac*, *mimic*, *picnic*.

3.2

Derivative verbs formed by the addition of prefixes follow the pattern of the root verb, as in *inputting*, *leapfrogging*, *outcropped*, *outfitting*: note that *benefit* is not derived from *fit*, and the forms *benefited* and *benefiting* are standard only in American English.

3.3

In British English, the letter *l* is doubled if it follows a single vowel, regardless of stress, e.g. *labelled*, *travelling*, *jeweller*, but *heeled*, *airmailed*, *coolish* (more than one vowel). In American Eng-

lish the double *l* occurs only if ending a stressed syllable, e.g. *labeled, traveling, jeweler* in American use, but *dispelled, gelled* in both British and American use (the double *l* may be retained in the present tense in American use, e.g. *appall, enthrall*). Exceptions retaining single *l*: *paralleled, devilish*; exceptions having double *l* (in British use): *woollen, woolly*; note variability of *cruel(l)er, cruel(l)est*.

3.4 The letter *s* is not usually doubled before the suffix *-es*, either in plural nouns, e.g. *focuses, gases, pluses, yeses*; or in the present tense of verbs, e.g. *focuses, gases, pluses, yeses*. However, verbal forms in *-s(s)ed, -s(s)ing* are variable, and doubling only after stressed syllables is often preferable, e.g. *gassing, nonplussed*, but *biased, focused, focusing*. Variants are common: e.g. see BUS. See also 'Forming plurals' below.

3.5 The consonants *h, w, x*, and *y* are never doubled: *hurrahed, guffawed, mower, boxing, stayed*. Silent consonants are also never doubled: *crocheting, précising*.

4. Dropping silent e

A final silent *e* is usually dropped when adding a suffix beginning with a vowel, e.g. *bluish, bravest, continuous, queued, refusal, writing*. Exceptions are noted below:

4.1 before *-ing* The *e* is retained in *dyeing, singeing, swingeing*, and (usually) *routeing*, to distinguish them from *dying, singing, swinging*, and *routing*. It is commonly retained in *ageing, bingeing, blueing, clueing, cueing, twingeing, whingeing*, and sometimes in *glu(e)ing, hing(e)ing, ru(e)ing, spong(e)ing, ting(e)ing*. It is also retained for words ending in *-ee, -oe, -ye*, e.g. *canoeing, eyeing, fleeing, hoeing, shoeing, tiptoeing*. Otherwise it is dropped: *charging, icing, lunging, staging*, etc.

4.2 words ending in *-ce* **or** *-ge* The *e* is retained to preserve the sound of the consonant, e.g. *advantageous, courageous, knowledgeable, noticeable, manageable, peaceable*.

4.3 before *-able* The dropping of *e* before *-able* is very unpredictable, and the first (or only) spelling given in the main part of the dictionary should be preferred. The endings *-ceable* and *-geable* are usual, and no letter is dropped in *agreeable, foreseeable*. The *e* is retained in *probeable* to distinguish it from *probable*. The *e* is more often dropped in American English.

4.4 before *-age* The *e* is usually dropped: *cleavage, dosage, wastage*. Exceptions: *acreage, metreage* (always), *mil(e)age* (optional). Note also that *linage* and *lineage* are different words.

A silent *e* is not usually dropped when adding a suffix beginning with a consonant, e.g. *useful, homeless, safely, movement, whiteness, life-like, awesome.* Exceptions: *argument, awful, duly, ninth, truly, wholly.* When such a suffix is added to words ending in *-dge*, American English tends to drop the *e*, e.g. *acknowledgment, fledging,* and this practice is sometimes seen in British English (notably in *judgment,* which is usual in legal contexts).

4.5 **before -y** The *e* is usually dropped: *bony, icy, grimy.* Exceptions: (a) after *u* (*gluey*); (b) after *g* (*cottagey, villagey,* but optional in *cagey, stagey*); (c) after *c* (usual in *dicey,* optional in *pricey* and *spacey,* occasionally seen in *pacy* and *spicy,* but otherwise dropped, e.g. *bouncy, chancy, fleecy, lacy,* etc.). The *e* is retained in *holey* to distinguish it from *holy,* and an extra *e* is added to separate two *ys,* e.g. *clayey.* It may be retained or added for clarity in more unusual words, e.g. *chocolatey, echoey.*

5. Forming plurals

5.1 Simple nouns Regular plurals are formed by adding *s,* or after *s, sh, ss, z, x, ch* (unless pronounced 'hard') by adding *es: books, boxes, pizzas, queues, arches, stomachs.* An apostrophe should not be used. Nouns ending in *-y* preceded by a consonant (or *-quy*) form plurals ending in *-ies,* e.g. *rubies, soliloquies,* but *boys, monkeys.* Exceptions: *laybys, stand-bys,* most names (e.g. *the Kennedys*). Nouns ending in *-f* or *-fe* (not *-ff, -ffe*) may form plurals in *-ves,* either always (e.g. *halves, leaves*) or optionally (e.g. *hooves, scarves*), or may always have regular plurals (e.g. *beliefs, chiefs*); these should be checked in the main part of the dictionary. Nouns ending in *-o* or *-i* are variable and should be checked in the main part of the dictionary; a number of long-established English words have only plurals in *-oes* (e.g. *heroes, potatoes, tomatoes*) but plurals in *-os* are common, and are usual among words which are less naturalized (e.g. *arpeggios*), or are formed by abbreviation (e.g. *kilos*), or have a vowel preceding the *-o* (e.g. *radios*). Nouns ending in *-ful* form regular plurals in *-fuls* (see Usage Note at CUPFUL). Only the letter *z* is regularly doubled in forming plurals: *fezzes, quizzes,* but *gases, yeses* (see 'Doubling consonants' above). Nouns ending in *-man* form plurals in *-men,* e.g. *chairmen, postmen, spokeswomen,* etc., but note *caymans, dragomans, talismans, Turcomans.* Other irregular plurals are noted in the main text of the dictionary.

5.2 Compound nouns Most compound nouns pluralize the last element: *break-ins, forget-me-nots, major generals, man-hours, ne'er-do-wells, round-ups, sergeant majors, vice-chancellors.* Exceptions include: (i) nouns followed by prepositional phrases, e.g. *Chancellors of the Exchequer, commanders-in-chief, daughters-in-law, ladies-in-*

waiting, men-of-war, rights of way; (ii) nouns denoting persons, followed by adverbs, e.g. *hangers-on, passers-by, runners-up*; (iii) nouns followed by adjectives, e.g. *battles royal, cousins german, heirs presumptive, notaries public, Governors-General* (though terms in common use, especially if hyphenated, may not follow this rule, e.g. *Secretary-Generals*); (iv) nouns denoting persons and containing *man* or *woman*, which pluralize both elements, e.g. *women doctors, menservants, gentlemen farmers*.

5.3 Foreign and classical plurals Words adopted into English generally form regular English plurals, but words not fully naturalized may form the plural as in the language of origin, e.g. *bureaux, cherubim, lire, virtuosi*. Many words of Greek and Latin origin retain classical plurals, though they may be used only in technical contexts, e.g. *formulae, indices, stadia*. In general, in forming classical plurals, *-us* becomes *-i* (occasionally *-era* or *-ora*); *-a* becomes *-ae; -um* and *-on* become *-a; -ex* and *-ix* become *-ices; -nx* becomes *-nges; -is* becomes *-es* or *-ides;* and *-os* becomes *-oi*. Note that many nouns regularly form only English plurals, e.g. *agendas, censuses, irises, octopuses, omnibuses, phoenixes, thermoses*. Care should be taken with words ending in *-a*, e.g. *addenda, bacteria, criteria, phenomena*, and *strata* are plural, but *nebula* and *vertebra* are singular.

6. Common suffixes

Several common suffixes occur in different forms, which may cause spelling difficulties: users of the dictionary should be careful to check if unsure of accepted usage. The most frequent sources of uncertainty are as follows:

6.1 -able/-ible The suffix *-ible* is found only in a number of long-established words taken directly from Latin or modelled on these. Modern formations on English roots use *-able* (see also 'Dropping silent *e*' above).

6.2 -ance/-ence (and -ant/-ent) These endings are largely dependent on the source of the word in Latin, and must be checked in the main part of the dictionary. Note especially *currant/current* and *dependant/dependent*.

6.3 -cede/-ceed The suffix *-ceed* occurs only in *exceed, proceed, succeed*; otherwise *concede, intercede, precede, recede*, etc. (note also *supersede*).

6.4 -ction/-xion The *-x-* is recommended in *complexion* and *crucifixion*, but not in other words in this dictionary.

6.5 -er/-or The ending -or is found mainly in words of classical or French origin, especially in the combinations -ator, -ctor, -essor. It is also retained in legal use where -er is more usual, e.g. divisor. See also Usage Note at ADVISER.

6.6 -er/-re American spelling often uses -er for -re in words such as centre, fibre, theatre, etc., but not in acre, cadre, lucre, massacre, mediocre, ogre, and wiseacre. Note also the usage indicated in the entries for meter and metre in the main part of the dictionary.

6.7 -ice/-ise In standard British use, licence and practise are nouns, license and practise are verbs; in American use, the -ise form is used for both noun and verb. Note also the distinction between prophesy and prophecy.

6.8 -ise/-ize/-yse The verbal ending -ize has been in general use since the 16th century; it is favoured in American English and in much British writing, and remains the current preferred style of Oxford University Press in academic and general books published in Britain. However, the alternative spelling -ise is now widespread in Britain, especially in the influence of French, and may be adopted provided that its use is consistent. A number of verbs always end in -ise in British use, notably advertise, chastise, despise, disguise, franchise, merchandise, surmise, and all verbs ending in -cise, -prise, -vise (including comprise, excise, prise (= open), supervise, surprise, televise, etc.), but -ize is always used in prize (= value), capsize, size. Spellings with -yze (analyze, paralyze) are acceptable only in American use.

6.9 -our/-or Most words ending in -our in British use are spelt with -or in American use. However, British spelling often uses -or (e.g. error, stupor, tremor), and the u is dropped before some suffixes (e.g. coloration, honorary, vaporize, but note colourist, honourable, savoury). It is advisable to check such spellings in the dictionary.

7. ae and oe

The use of the printed ligatures æ and œ is becoming rare, and there is a trend in favour of replacing ae and oe with simple e, especially in American and in scientific use. The main part of the dictionary should be checked for individual words.

C. CAPITALIZATION

The use of capital letters in punctuating sentences has been discussed above; their use to distinguish proper nouns or 'names' from ordinary words is subject to wide variation in practice. The standard

OUP style is outlined below, but the most important criterion is consistency within a single piece of writing.

1. Capital letters are used for the names of people and places (*John Smith, Paris, Oxford Street, New South Wales, the Black Sea, the Iron Duke*); the names of peoples and languages and derived words directly relating to them (*Englishman, Austrian, French, Swahili, Americanize*); the names of institutions and institutional groups (*the Crown, the Government, the British Museum, the House of Representatives, the Department of Trade*); the names of religious institutions and denominations and their adherents (*Judaism, Nonconformism, Methodist, Protestants*) and of societies and organizations (*the Royal Society*); the names of months and days (*Tuesday, March, Easter Day*); abstract qualities personified (*the face of Nature, O Death!*) or used as sobriquets (*a Blue* in university sport, *a Red* = communist); and names of other non-personal things (*the Flying Scotsman*).

Note that *the Baptist Church* is an institution, but *the Baptist church* is a building; a *Democrat* belongs to a political party, but a *democrat* simply supports democracy; *Northern Ireland* is a name with recognized status, but *northern England* is not.

2. A capital letter is used for words derived from a proper name, if the connection with the name is direct, or felt to be continuing (*Christian, Homeric, Marxism*), but not if it is more remote or conventional (*chauvinistic, quixotic, guillotine*).

3. A capital letter is used by convention in many names that are trade marks (*Elastoplast, Filofax, Hoover, Xerox*) or are otherwise associated with a particular manufacturer etc. (*Jaguar, Spitfire*). Some proprietary terms are now conventionally spelt with a lower case initial (*baby buggy, biro, cellophane, jeep*), and this is generally true of established verbs derived from proprietary terms (*to hoover, to xerox*).

4. Capital letters are used in titles of courtesy or rank, including compound titles (*His Royal Highness the Prince of Wales, President Carter, Sir John Smith, Lord Chief Justice, Lieutenant-Colonel, Vice-President, Your Grace, His Excellency*).

5. A capital letter is used for the personal pronoun *I* and for the interjection *O*.

6. A capital letter is used for the deity (*God, Father, Allah, Almighty*). However, the use of capitals in possessive determiners and possessive pronouns (*in His name*) is now generally considered old-fashioned.

7. Capital letters are used for the first and other important words in titles of books, newspapers, plays, films, television programmes, etc., and in headings and captions (*The Merchant of Venice, Pride and Prejudice, Book of Common Prayer, New Testament, Talmud, Guide to the Use of the Dictionary*).

8. Capital letters are used for historical events and periods (*the Dark Ages, Early Minoan, Perpendicular, the Renaissance, the First World War*); also for geological time divisions, but not for certain archaeological periods (*Devonian, Palaeozoic*, but *neolithic*).

9. Capital letters are frequently used in abbreviations, with or without full stops (*BBC, DoE, M.Litt.*).

10. A capital letter is used for a compass direction when abbreviated (*N, NNE, NE*) or when denoting a region (*unemployment in the North*).

11. A capital letter is frequently used to begin a line of English verse.

12. The use of a capital letter elsewhere than at the beginning of a word is seen in certain names (*MacDonald, O'Reilly*) and in some trade marks, and is conventional in some foreign languages.

D. ITALICIZATION

Italic type makes a word or phrase stand out from its context. It is used especially in the following ways:

1. For titles of books, plays, major musical works, works of art, long poems, periodical publications, and individual ships, trains, aircraft, etc.: *Jane Eyre, Henry V, The Magic Flute, Michelangelo's David, Paradise Lost*, the *Daily Telegraph*, the *Marie Celeste*, HMS *Dreadnought*.

The words *The* or *A* may or may not be part of a full title: the *Oxford Times, The Times, The Economist*, the *Messiah* by Handel, *A London Symphony*). Unless the exact title is to be cited, the article may be omitted if the work is well known or has already been cited: Darwin's *Origin of Species*.

Strictly, inflections are printed in roman: the *Marie Celeste*'s crew, a pile of *New Yorkers*.

2. For foreign words and phrases, when still perceived as foreign. When a foreign word becomes sufficiently naturalized, it is printed in roman. Headwords in this dictionary use italic or roman based on the current frequency of use in English. Words which would nor-

mally be printed in roman when other related words are being used, or when an English word exists with the same spelling, as with *pension* for a Continental boarding house.

3. For the Latin names of genera and species, e.g. *Malus*, *Homo sapiens*.

4. For distinguishing a word or phrase from the surrounding text, especially to emphasize it, or when mentioning a technical word for the first time. Italics may be used, for example, to distinguish stage directions in plays; in dictionaries, they typically distinguish markers for parts of speech, labels concerning register or restriction of use, and example sentences.

5. Italic type is *not* used for the following:

5.1 Titles of chapters in books, articles in periodicals, shorter poems, television and radio programmes; these may be referred to in quotation marks: an article on 'Oral Tradition' in the *Journal of Theology*, an episode of 'Neighbours', 'Sonnet VI' in *Selected Poems*.

5.2 The names of sacred texts or their subdivisions; quotation marks are not used: the Koran, Genesis, Epistle to the Romans.

5.3 Musical works identified by a description (Beethoven's Fifth Symphony).

5.4 Names of buildings or of types of vehicle (the Red Lion, the Colosseum, a Ford Cortina).

5.5 Most short abbreviations, including units of measurement (cf., e.g., ibid, i.e., km, op., pro tem, q.v.).

6. If a piece of text is already printed in italics, then the function of italicization is taken by roman type: She was reading *On the Use of* Verfremdungseffekt *in Brecht's Plays*.

E. REFERENCES TO PEOPLE

Names should normally be printed in the form by which the bearer is most commonly known, or is known to prefer: e.g. Arthur C. Clarke (not 'A. C. Clarke'), T. S. Eliot (not 'Thomas S. Eliot'), R. Vaughan Williams (not 'R. V. Williams'). Forenames should not be abbreviated (George not Geo., William not Wm.) unless reproducing a signature or manuscript or a commercial style.

Titles should have capital letters; they are frequently abbreviated for convenience. 'Mr' is applicable to any male; the use of 'Master' for

boys is old-fashioned. 'Mrs' usually designates a married woman who has adopted her husband's surname. Both 'Miss' and 'Ms' are used by unmarried women, and by married women (retaining their maiden name) who object to having attention drawn to their marital status. 'Dr' is appropriate for those holding university doctorates, and is also given as a courtesy title to medical doctors (but not surgeons); it should not be combined with any of the above titles, nor used together with the letters indicating the doctorate (e.g. D.Phil.). Married professional women often practise under their maiden names. 'Esq.' after a surname is used by professionals as an alternative to 'Mr' (no longer restricted to professionals and holders of a bachelor's degree). 'Reverend' is used for ministers of religion; it should not be used with a surname alone: e.g. the Rev. J. Brown (or the Rev. Mr Brown if the name or initial is unknown), but not 'the Reverend Brown'. The abbreviation 'Revd' is sometimes preferred.

Traditionally, a woman may adopt her husband's name on marriage, and the couple are then jointly called 'Mr and Mrs John Smith'. Strictly, the wife is correctly referred to as 'Mrs John Smith', and to give her own name ('Mrs Mary Smith') would at one time have indicated a divorcee. However, this distinction is now made only in the most formal circumstances. Divorced women may retain either their maiden or married names, with Mrs, Miss, or Ms according to preference, and 'Mrs Mary Smith' is generally acceptable as a form for married women. The maiden or unmarried name of a man or woman may be indicated by 'née'; e.g. Mary Seymour-Smith (née Seymour), John Seymour-Smith (né Smith).

A title should not be used in a signature, though it may be placed after it in brackets for information: e.g. Robin Smith (Miss), M.T. Brown (Mrs).

A person's former or alternative name or title is indicated only if necessary or to avoid confusion: Michael (now Sir Michael) Tippett, Laurence (later Lord) Olivier, Lord Home of the Hirsel (then Sir Alec Douglas-Home). (Further discussion of titles of rank and nobility is beyond the scope of this book.) The owner of an **adopted name** uses it for all purposes, and may have adopted it legally. Though a former name may be indicated, it should not be referred to as the person's 'real name': e.g. Woody Allen (born Allen Stuart Konigsberg), Mohammed Ali (formerly Cassius Clay).

A **pseudonym** is only used for a specific purpose, e.g. as a pen-name or stage name, though a person may be best known by it: e.g. George Eliot (pseudonym of Mary Ann, later Marian, Evans). It may appear in quotation marks: e.g. 'Lewis Carroll' (Charles L. Dodgson). A **nickname** supplements the owner's name and is often placed in quotation marks (Charlie 'Bird' Parker), though it may replace the original name altogether (Fats Waller). An **alias** is generally a false name assumed with intent to deceive.

F. OFFENSIVE LANGUAGE AND SEXISM

In general, terms should be avoided which convey an impression of over-generalization, describing people as though they were merely instances of a particular feature, or especially imposing on them a depreciatory stereotype. One should certainly avoid abbreviated colloquial forms referring to race (e.g. *Paki, Jap*); the term *race* is itself best avoided, except in strictly anthropological contexts, in favour of *nation, people, ethnic group, community*. Words referring to racial type or to physical or mental handicap which have been used as terms of abuse, or have been associated with discrimination, are frequently therefore avoided even in their original neutral senses. The use of adjectives rather than nouns in describing groups is usually preferable (e.g. *the Hispanic community* not *the Hispanics; disabled people* not *the disabled*).

See also Usage Notes at ESKIMO, MUHAMMADAN, NEGRESS, NEGRO, SCOTCH, UNTOUCHABLE, and at MONGOLISM and GAY.

The replacement of offensive or potentially offensive vocabulary with 'politically correct' euphemistic phrases, while often well-intentioned, can create confusion unless the replacements are familiar to the intended audience (e.g. 'learning difficulties': educational problems or mental handicap?), and frequently offers a target for ridicule.

There is a widespread tendency to replace terms for occupations or titles which are unnecessarily marked for gender (e.g. *flight attendant* for *stewardess*), and to substitute *-person* for *-man* in words such as *chairman, salesman,* and *spokesman*. Opinions vary very widely concerning the desirability of such substitutions. A balance needs to be struck between the desire to avoid sexist language and the common sense of one's audience; sensitivity to context is needed to determine the borderline between sensible accommodation and absurdity. The extending of this tendency to cover words with only tenuous etymological links with sex (e.g. *masterpiece, manhandle, manhole*) is not generally accepted, and extreme forms such as *herstory* for *history* have little place outside specifically feminist writing.

The English language lacks a third person singular pronoun or possessive adjective applying neutrally to both sexes. The older convention was to use *he, him, his* for both sexes (e.g. *Each member must pay his subscription*), but this is now often felt to exclude women and girls. Acceptable alternatives include (i) rephrasing in the plural (e.g. *All members must pay their subscriptions*); and (ii) using both pronouns or possessives (e.g. *Each member must pay his or her subscription*), though this is often cumbersome: *his/her* and *he/she* (or even *s/he*) are awkward to read aloud. The use of *they* and *their* in the singular (e.g. *Each member must pay their subscription*), but is still considered ungrammatical and should be avoided in formal speech and writing.